University Textbook Series

October, 1982

Especially Designed for Collateral Reading

HARRY W. JONES
Directing Editor
Professor of Law, Columbia University

ADMIRALTY, Second Edition (1975)
Grant Gilmore, Professor of Law, Yale University.
Charles L. Black, Jr., Professor of Law, Yale University.

ADMIRALTY AND FEDERALISM (1970)
David W. Robertson, Professor of Law, University of Texas.

AGENCY (1975)
W. Edward Sell, Dean of the School of Law, University of Pittsburgh.

BUSINESS ORGANIZATION AND FINANCE (1980)
William A. Klein, Professor of Law, University of California, Los Angeles.

CIVIL PROCEDURE, BASIC, Second Edition (1979)
Milton D. Green, Professor of Law Emeritus, University of California, Hastings College of the Law.

COMMERCIAL TRANSACTIONS, INTRODUCTION TO (1977)
Hon. Robert Braucher, Associate Justice, Supreme Judicial Court of Massachusetts.
Robert A. Riegert, Professor of Law, Cumberland School of Law.

CONFLICT OF LAWS, COMMENTARY ON THE, Second Edition (1980)
Russell J. Weintraub, Professor of Law, University of Texas.

CONSTITUTIONAL LAW, AMERICAN (A TREATISE ON) (1978) with 1979 Supplement
Laurence H. Tribe, Professor of Law, Harvard University.

CONTRACT LAW, THE CAPABILITY PROBLEM IN (1978)
Richard Danzig.

CORPORATIONS, Second Edition (1971)
Norman D. Lattin, Professor of Law, University of California, Hastings College of the Law.

CORPORATIONS IN PERSPECTIVE (1976)
Alfred F. Conard, Professor of Law, University of Michigan.

CRIMINAL LAW, Third Edition (1982)
Rollin M. Perkins, Professor of Law, University of California, Hastings College of the Law.
Ronald N. Boyce, Professor of Law, University of Utah College of Law.

i

CRIMINAL PROCEDURE (1980) with 1982 Supplement
Charles H. Whitebread, II, Professor of Law, University of Virginia.

ESTATES IN LAND & FUTURE INTERESTS, PREFACE TO (1966)
Thomas F. Bergin, Professor of Law, University of Virginia.
Paul G. Haskell, Professor of Law, University of North Carolina.

EVIDENCE: COMMON SENSE AND COMMON LAW (1947)
John M. Maguire, Professor of Law, Harvard University.

EVIDENCE, STUDENTS' TEXT ON THE LAW OF (1935)
The late John Henry Wigmore, Northwestern University.

JURISPRUDENCE: MEN AND IDEAS OF THE LAW (1953)
The late Edwin W. Patterson, Cardozo Professor of Jurisprudence, Columbia University.

LEGAL CAPITAL, Second Edition (1981)
Bayless Manning.

LEGAL RESEARCH ILLUSTRATED, Second Edition (1981) with 1982 Assignments Pamphlet
J. Myron Jacobstein, Professor of Law, Law Librarian, Stanford University.
Roy M. Mersky, Professor of Law, Director of Research, University of Texas.

LEGAL RESEARCH, FUNDAMENTALS OF, Second Edition (1981) with 1982 Assignments Pamphlet
J. Myron Jacobstein, Professor of Law, Law Librarian, Stanford University.
Roy M. Mersky, Professor of Law, Director of Research, University of Texas.

PROCEDURE, THE STRUCTURE OF (1979)
Robert M. Cover, Professor of Law, Yale University.
Owen M. Fiss, Professor of Law, Yale University.

THE PROFESSION OF LAW (1971)
L. Ray Patterson, Professor of Law, Emory University.
Elliott E. Cheatham, Professor of Law, Vanderbilt University.

PROPERTY, Second Edition (1975)
John E. Cribbet, Dean of the Law School, University of Illinois.

TAXATION, FEDERAL INCOME, Third Edition (1982)
Marvin A. Chirelstein, Professor of Law, Yale University.

TORTS, Second Edition (1980)
Clarence Morris, Professor of Law, University of Pennsylvania.
C. Robert Morris, Professor of Law, University of Minnesota.

TRUSTS, PREFACE TO THE LAW OF (1975)
Paul G. Haskell, Professor of Law, University of North Carolina.

WILLS AND TRUSTS, THE PLANNING AND DRAFTING OF, Second Edition (1979) with 1982 Supplement
Thomas L. Shaffer, Professor of Law, University of Notre Dame.

CRIMINAL LAW

By

ROLLIN M. PERKINS

Connell Professor of Law Emeritus, UCLA
Professor Emeritus, University of California,
Hastings College of the Law

and

RONALD N. BOYCE

Professor of Law, The University of Utah

THIRD EDITION

Mineola, New York
THE FOUNDATION PRESS, INC.
1982

Library of Congress Cataloging in Publication Data

Perkins, Rollin Morris, 1889–
  Criminal law.

  (University textbook series)
1. Criminal law—United States.   I. Boyce, Ronald N.
II. Title.   III. Series.
KF9219.P4   1982   345.73   82–15976
                            347.305

ISBN 0-88277-067-5

PREFACE TO THE THIRD EDITION

Because most states have recently adopted new penal codes, including important changes in the criminal law, this book requires much more in the way of new material than would ordinarily be expected in a third edition, but wide differences in these codes present a problem. A sweeping change in dealing with some matter may have been adopted in only a few codes, or it may have been adopted in many but not in all. It seems there is no part of the preexisting criminal law that is not still the law somewhere. Hence it is not feasible merely to substitute the new for the old. Changes found in a few, or in many, of the new codes must be given in addition rather than in substitution. Probably this is desirable in any event, because the old provides a helpful background for the new.

The Model Penal Code, completed since the first edition was published, represents the most outstanding contribution ever offered in the attempt to improve the criminal law. A multitude of references to its provisions will be found herein. Except when there was special reason for citing a preliminary draft, all citations to the Code are to the Proposed Official Draft of 1962.[1] For years the American Law Institute has been preparing "Model Penal Code and Commentaries", an important part of which is already in print. This gives, following each section, a consideration of why it was drafted in such form, a discussion of the problems involved, and the extent to which it has influenced the recently adopted new penal codes.

Complaint is sometimes voiced that lawyers, in discussing crime, are more interested in matters of definition than in the human values involved. But nothing could be more prejudicial to the human values than de-emphasis of definition. Under our penal philosophy no one can be convicted of crime without proof that he committed a specific offense that was clearly recognized as a crime when committed. If we substitute for this a plan under which judges and juries could convict one of crime based upon a whim or hunch that he ought to be punished, we would find that human values had been irreparably prejudiced. This, of course, does not require us to assume that nothing more is involved than definition of crime, detection thereof and punishment therefor. The full contribution of the behavioral sciences must be called upon if we are to succeed in a full-scale program of crime control. This will require a careful study of the causes of crime and potentially corrective measures, including a re-examination of family and social environments, the effectiveness of school programs and adult education, the need of increasing the size, quality and training of police forces, and above all the professional handling of those who have been

[1] All quotations from the Model Penal Code are authorized. Copyright 1962 by the American Law Institute. Reprinted with the permission of the American Law Institute.

v

found guilty of crime. The latter problem is all too frequently the target of a controversy between the "hawks" and the "doves," if these labels may be borrowed, and is waged on an emotional rather than an objective basis.

The chief contribution of the behavioral sciences will be in areas of discovery and correction of the causes of crime, the development of methods of dealing with certain instances of prohibited conduct other than by criminal prosecution,[2] and improvement of the processes that follow criminal conviction. But we shall not in the foreseeable future reach a point where no criminal prosecutions will be needed. And in the prosecution, insistence upon definition will be imperative in order to insure that criminal prosecution be based upon proof rather than whim or hunch. Hence in these pages reference to the behavioral sciences will be found chiefly in the footnotes rather than in the text itself.

A text should not attempt to substitute for a digest and hence the plan has been to use selective, rather than exhaustive citations. But because it is important to know whether the answers to specific problems have, or have not, been changed by the new codes, it was deemed important to have many very recent cases cited in the footnotes. It is necessary to acknowledge permission to reprint, in whole or in part, certain recently published articles.[3]

The material in the text which states material from the Model Penal Code is subject to Copyright 1962 by the American Law Institute.

ROLLIN M. PERKINS
RONALD N. BOYCE

September, 1982

2. "One of the [criminal justice] system's greatest needs is for the community to establish institutions and agencies to which policemen, prosecutors, and judges can refer various kinds of offenders, without being compelled to bring the full force of criminal sanctions to bear on them." The Challenge of Crime in a Free Society 14 (1967). This is the report of the President's Commission on Law Enforcement and the Administration of Justice and is available from the United States Government Printing Office, Washington, D.C.

3. Perkins, The Territorial Principle in Criminal Law. This was prepared for the VIII Congress of the International Academy of Comparative Law and published on pages 657-670 of Legal Thought in the United States of America Under Contemporary Pressures, for the American Association for the Comparative Study of Law, Inc., by Etablissements Emile Bruylant, Brussels, Belgium, 1970. By special arrangement it was published also in 22 Hastings L.J. 1155 (1971). Perkins, The Act of One Conspirator, 26 Hastings L.J. 337 (1974); Perkins, "Knowledge" as a Mens Rea Requirement, 29 Hastings L.J. 953 (1978); Perkins, Dealing With the Inconsistent Verdict, 15 Crim.L.Bull. 405 (1979); Perkins, Ignorance or Mistake of Law Revisited, 1980 Utah L.Rev. 473; Perkins, Impelled Perpetration Restated, 33 Hastings L.J. 403 (1981).

PREFACE TO THE SECOND EDITION

A new edition of this book was required for several reasons, including the need to correct omissions and to make revisions called for by legislation or decision. A few illustrations may be in order. The original assumption that piracy was of no more than historical interest was disproved by the epidemic of air piracies, and the theory that problems of nonsupport were covered adequately by the general discussion of negative acts failed to take notice of the numerous special problems involved. Hence the inclusion of these offenses was important. Examples of required revision include therapeutic abortion (by statute), and juvenile delinquency and contempt of court (by decision).

Much more pervasive, however, was a need for revision discovered by personal contact. For nearly twelve years the author has had an opportunity to work with students using the first edition, and these conferences have brought to light places where an exposition he had deemed adequate proved not to be so. Particular pains have been taken to reword these presentations in the light of questions and misunderstandings.

An additional acknowledgment is due to my wife, Florence Payne Perkins, who not only, as before, painstakingly read the manuscript, but for this edition did all the typing, cutting and pasting, as well as editing and proofreading. Without her help the work could not have been completed. It is also necessary to acknowledge permission to reproduce, in whole or in part, articles published in the Hastings Law Journal, University of Illinois Law Forum, Iowa Law Review, Minnesota Law Review and Virginia Law Review.[4]

ROLLIN M. PERKINS

February, 1969.

4. The Vagrancy Concept, 9 Hastings Law Journal 237 (1958); Some Weak Points in the Model Penal Code, 17 id. at 3 (1965); Collateral Estoppel in Criminal Cases, 1960 University of Illinois Law Forum 533; Alignment of Sanction with Culpable Conduct, 49 Iowa Law Review 325 (1964); An Analysis of Assault and Attempts to Assault, 47 Minnesota Law Review 71 (1962); The Corpus Delicti of Murder, 48 Virginia Law Review 173 (1962).

*

PREFACE TO THE FIRST EDITION

Within recent times, as pointed out herein, there has been a tremendous expansion of the area of human conduct regulated by the criminal law. In early days this law concerned itself only with conduct seriously antisocial in its character, and other agencies such as the church, the home, and even the neighborhood, were relied upon to regulate behavior in other respects. The present tendency is to place the entire burden upon the criminal law, and while this shift has been taking place, changes in the social and economic structure of the community have created many new conflicts and have added ingenious modes of infringing recognized rights. The result has been a constant increase in the public interest in this area of the law with which the legal profession itself has utterly failed to keep pace. That it is important for a lawyer to be well grounded in the field of criminal law even if he never tries a criminal case has been repeated and demonstrated, time and again down through the years, one of the recent illustrations involving a suit on a policy of insurance that indemnified against loss resulting from forgery. A warehouse receipt for grain had been issued although no grain had been received and the insured, who had suffered a loss in reliance upon this warehouse receipt, brought suit to recover on the policy. It was held quite properly, that since the warehouse receipt was genuinely signed by the warehouseman it was not a forgery despite the fraud perpetrated by issuing it without having the grain it purported to represent.[1] And had the plaintiff's lawyer been adequately trained in the criminal law the suit would not have been brought because he would have recognized instantly the basic distinction between a false document on the one hand and a genuine document containing a false statement on the other. Moreover, quite apart from duties in the courtroom—including the possibility of presiding as judge therein—the lawyer needs to be well grounded in the criminal law because he will be called upon for guidance by those who sincerely desire to obey the law but are bewildered by governmental programs of regulation. He will be looked to moreover, for leadership whenever any suggestion is made for improvement in the criminal law or its administration, and should be equipped to accept such responsibilities with confidence.

. . . . .

A desire to rekindle the interest in this tremendously important field has prompted the preparation of this volume. The historical

---

1. This case was not carried to an appellate court but the same point had been decided shortly before in a criminal case, Marteney v. United States, 216 F.2d 760 (10th Cir. 1954), and in an insurance case involving other documents (receipts and invoices). Pasadena Investment Co. v. Peerless Casualty Co., 132 Cal.App.2d 328, 282 P.2d 124 (1955).

To the original note it may be added that a purported but misrepresented agency indorsement is not a forgery. Gilbert v. United States, 370 U.S. 650, 82 S.Ct. 1399 (1962).

background has not been ignored because it is impossible to have a full understanding of the law of today without some appreciation of the roots from which it developed, but care has been taken not to permit the past to overshadow the present; and emphasis has been placed upon changes which have taken place whether with or without the aid of legislative enactment. The ceaseless process of change, moreover, must constantly be borne in mind because new applications of established doctrines will be made from time to time, and these will become a part of the established law and serve as guides for the solving of still other cases as they arise. An understanding of changes made, and to be made, requires an insight into the underlying philosophy of this area of the law; and hence, throughout these pages, an effort has been made to picture the criminal law in the light of the social interests sought to be protected by it.

It is impossible to give due acknowledgment to all the contributions to these pages, many of which have come through the years, from ordinary conversations with teachers, lawyers, judges, peace officers, probation officers, prison officials, criminologists and others. Certain specific references, however, are in order. Grateful acknowledgment is due to my wife who painstakingly read the manuscript, much of which was prepared in the form of several different drafts. And during part of the time when the manuscript was being prepared my office was directly across the hall from that of the greatest legal scholar of our time. As those doors were never closed there was hardly a day during that period when I was not in his office or he in mine. I may have failed to take full advantage thereof but I certainly had an opportunity to get Dean Roscoe Pound's ideas on a multitude of problems of criminal law as well as his ideas of effective presentation. It is also necessary to make grateful acknowledgment of permission generously granted to reproduce, in whole or in part, articles published in the following legal periodicals: Harvard Law Review, Yale Law Journal, University of Pennsylvania Law Review, Journal of Criminal Law, Criminology and Police Science, Boston University Law Review, University of Pittsburgh Law Review, Iowa Law Review, Vanderbilt Law Review and U.C.L.A. Law Review.[2]

Some books are cited so constantly in these pages that abbreviations have been employed such as Coke's Institutes (Co. Inst.), Hale, Pleas of the Crown (Hale P.C.), Hawkins, Pleas of the Crown (Hawk. P.C.), East, Pleas of the Crown (East P.C.) and Blackstone's

---

2. A Rational of Mens Rea, 52 Harv.L.Rev. 905 (1939); A Re-Examination of Malice Aforethought, 43 Yale L.Jour. 537 (1934); Ignorance and Mistake in Criminal Law, 88 U. of Pa.L.Rev. 35 (1939); Parties to Crime, 89 id. 581 (1941); The Civil Offense, 100 id. 832 (1952); The Law of Homicide, 36 J. of C.L. and Crim. 392 (1946); Partial Insanity, 25 id. 175 (1934); Non-Homicide Offenses Against the Person, 26 B.U.L.Rev. 119 (1946); Sampling the Evolution of Social Engineering, 17 U. of Pitt.L.Rev. 362 (1956); The Doctrine of Coercion, 19 Iowa L.Rev. 507 (1934); Negative Acts in Criminal Law, 22 id. 659 (1937); The Law of Arrest, 25 id. 201 (1940); The Tennessee Law of Arrest, 2 Vand.L.Rev. 509 (1949); Self-Defense Re-Examined, 1 U.C.L.A.L.Rev. 133 (1954); Criminal Attempt and Related Problems, 2 id. 319 (1955).

Commentaries (Bl.Comm). For the most part references in the form of *loc. cit. supra* and *op. cit. supra*, have been avoided since usually little is saved thereby, but when repeated references are made to the same book in the same section it has been deemed sufficient to give the author's name, the page, and the year of publication after several citations in full.

ROLLIN M. PERKINS

July, 1957

*

SUMMARY OF CONTENTS

*

TABLE OF CONTENTS

CHAPTER 3.   OFFENSES AGAINST HABITATION AND OCCUPANCY

CHAPTER 4. OFFENSES AGAINST PROPERTY

CHAPTER 5.   OTHER OFFENSES

CHAPTER 6. IMPUTABILITY

CHAPTER 7. RESPONSIBILITY: IN GENERAL

CHAPTER 8. RESPONSIBILITY: LIMITATIONS ON CRIMINAL CAPACITY

CHAPTER 9.   RESPONSIBILITY: MODIFYING CIRCUMSTANCES

CHAPTER 10. SPECIAL DEFENSES

*

CRIMINAL LAW

*

Chapter 1

INTRODUCTION

SECTION 1. SCOPE, PURPOSE, DEFINITION AND CLASSIFICATION

A. THE SCOPE OF CRIMINAL LAW

Often the term "criminal law" is used to include all that is involved in "the administration of criminal justice" in the broadest sense. As so employed it embraces three different fields, known to the lawyer as (1) the substantive criminal law, (2) criminal procedure,* and (3) special problems in the administration and enforcement of criminal justice.

The substantive criminal law defines murder, larceny, rape, burglary and all the other specific offenses. It deals also with general principles of liability to punishment and the limitations of such liability by special defenses, such as insanity or self-defense. Criminal Procedure is the formal machinery which has been established to enforce the substantive criminal law. Its broad outlines include (1) accusation of crime, (2) determination of guilt or innocence and (3) disposition of those convicted. Within these broad outlines are found many provisions which include among others, the complaint, warrant of arrest, arrest (with or without a warrant), preliminary examination, commitment (or release on bail or discharge at this point), complaint, indictment or information, arraignment, pleading, motions (such as for change of venue), trial, verdict, judgment and sentence, motion for new trial, appeal, execution of sentence, probation, parole and pardon; to which might be added, without exhausting the list, such terms as habeas corpus, coram nobis, and extradition.

Because the substantive criminal law and the formal machinery of criminal procedure do not include everything involved in the total scheme, a third category is added which, for lack of a better label, is called "special problems in the administration and enforcement of criminal justice." An illustration may be useful. An arrest has been made for burglary. One unfamiliar with the actual enforcement of justice might assume that a trial for burglary would probably follow; but there is considerable probability that no such trial will be held. For example, the one accused may plead guilty to the offense charged so that no trial is needed. Other possibilities may prevent the trial. The prosecuting attorney may dismiss the prosecution. In some jurisdictions the actual dismissal may be by the court on motion of the prose-

---

* "As related to criminal law and procedure, *substantive law* is that which declares what acts are crimes and describes the punishment therefor; whereas *procedural law* is that which provides or regu-
lates the stops (steps) by which one who violates a criminal statute is punished." State v. Hutchison, 228 Kan. 279, 615 P.2d 138, 145 (1980).

1

cuting attorney, but the court will seldom overrule the prosecutor's motion for dismissal and hence the actual result is much the same as where he himself can end the prosecution by a *nolle prosequi*. Some jurisdictions have adopted formal procedures for diverting persons charged with certain crimes from the usual criminal process and, if the person completes the conditions for diversion, no further action is taken.

A third possibility is that the case may be disposed of by a plea of guilty of some lesser offense—such as larceny. The jurisdiction may (but usually does not) have a statute which expressly authorizes a plea of a lesser offense under special circumstances including the consent of the court and of the prosecuting attorney. But in the particular case it may be found that although the arrest was for burglary, the only indictment or information was for some lesser offense, such as larceny. This is sometimes the result of the practice commonly called "plea bargaining." That is,—the prosecutor finds the defendant will plead guilty to larceny but will stand trial if the graver charge of burglary is insisted upon, and so he has the formal charge made for larceny in order to secure the plea of guilty and avoid the necessity of trial. In one case this may result from pure laziness. In another, the prosecutor's office may be so overburdened with cases that it would be impossible for him to avoid falling hopelessly behind with his work if he did not secure guilty pleas in most of his cases; and this case may have seemed to him less important than certain others which he intended to prosecute to the limit. In still another case the prosecutor may have been disappointed with the evidence available. He may have felt, with good reason, that if he insisted upon trial the result would be an acquittal, and have decided it was better to secure the conviction of the lesser offense (on a plea of guilty) than to risk having no conviction at all.[1] Even this does not exhaust the possibilities.

In one case of an arrest for burglary, for example, the prosecuting attorney found these to be the facts. The prisoner was a young man whose record was otherwise clear. His parents had died when he was a boy, leaving him entirely upon his own resources. At first he had been particularly successful, and had continued in school, earning his board and room by odd jobs during spare time. Then, with the onset of economic difficulties, he found this too difficult and gave up school to accept a full-time job. In this he showed every promise of advancement until his employer was forced into bankruptcy and the job disappeared. Passing hastily over the long and trying period during which he searched for a new job, at a time when jobs were not to be had, we come to the crucial evening. After walking untold miles during the day in the fruitless search for a job, this young man was turning his steps in the direction of the room from which he had not yet been ejected although the rent was long overdue. He had had nothing to eat during the day and very little to eat for many days. Passing a house located directly by the sidewalk, he looked into a lighted kitchen and saw a half-loaf of bread on

1. "Whatever might be the situation in an ideal world, the fact is that the guilty plea and often concomitant plea bargain are important components of this country's criminal justice system." Blackledge v. Allison, 431 U.S. 63, 71, 97 S.Ct. 1621, 1627 (1977). This was emphasized when the Court held it was not a violation of due process for the prosecutor to carry out his threat to bring a more serious charge if defendant refused to plead guilty to the original charge. Bordenkircher v. Hayes, 434 U.S. 357, 98 S.Ct. 663 (1978). It is the same, said the Court, as if the greater charge had been brought at the outset and the prosecutor had agreed to substitute a lesser charge if defendant would plead guilty to it.

a table near the window. No one seemed to be in sight and the sudden temptation was too much for him. He found the window unlatched, opened it, reached in and took the bread, which he hastily began to eat. He was mistaken, however, in his notion that no one was in sight. An officer saw what he did and took him into custody on a charge of burglary.

This misdeed constitutes burglary in the jurisdiction in which it occurred; and the law of that jurisdiction does not permit the judge to grant probation to one convicted of burglary. The prosecuting attorney was well aware of this law and was told the youth was ready to plead guilty to a charge of burglary. Yet he had never known a case in which probation seemed more clearly indicated. The young man's friends and acquaintances, including his former teachers and employers, were all positive that this misstep was a sudden yielding to temptation—which only by a technicality happened to be one of the gravest crimes—and that it would be gross injustice to send him to the penitentiary. Being convinced of this, the prosecuting attorney refused to word the charge in terms of burglary and drew the bill of indictment in terms of larceny from a building. This is a felony in the jurisdiction concerned, but it is not a felony which by statute is excluded from the benefit of probation. The defendant pleaded guilty to this charge, was placed on probation, and became a very substantial and respected citizen in the years that followed.

Nothing in the code of criminal procedure of that state mentions any such step as this. It is merely one of the multitude of *administrative devices* which play a leading role in the actual administration of criminal justice. Perhaps the fault in the situation described is with the substantive criminal law in being so worded as to include such a relatively slight misdeed within the scope of one of the gravest crimes. Perhaps the fault is with the formal criminal procedure in its attempt to determine in advance the exact peno-correctional treatment to be used for a certain offense. However that may be, we should be shocked by the gap between the letter of the law and the social need if this or some other extra-legal device had not been employed to save this young man from a long term in the penitentiary. Police are outraged (and rightly so) when they see released, with little or no actual incarceration, a dangerous felon they have arrested as a result of great effort and considerable risk; but the officers themselves were quite in favor of the procedure used in the case mentioned above.

The case might be thought to be one in which the prosecutor could wisely have refused to bring any formal charge at all. Circumstances not mentioned here seemed to make such a disposition unwise; but had this been done it also would have been an administrative device for achieving a result not mentioned in the code of criminal procedure of the state. Nothing new is involved in the resort to such administrative devices. They have come down through the ages, being changed from time to time to meet the social needs of the particular period.

Under the English common law all felonies were punishable by death, but there were very few felonies. Criminal homicide was a felony, as also were arson, rape, robbery, burglary, mayhem and larceny. This about completes the list of the common-law felonies, and if we recognize that in its origin larceny was concerned only with cattle-stealing, we realize that these would all be regarded as "hanging offenses" in a primitive community. In developing the rule that all felonies were punishable by death the judges merely reflected the general attitude of the community in which they lived.

For some reason Parliament added new felonies in surprising numbers. Blackstone tells us that in his day there were 160 different felonies on the statute books of England. And because the penalty for felony was death, each such statutory addition became a capital crime. For the most part these statutory felonies seem not to have merited the sentence of death, even as measured by the harsh attitude of the community in that early day. And the common-law judges were reluctant to pronounce the sentence of death on those convicted of these lesser statutory felonies. They did pronounce the dread sentence when they felt they must; but various devices were employed in the effort to avoid doing so. By far the best known of the devices used for this purpose was that known as "benefit of clergy."

"Benefit of clergy," in its origin, was the right of a clergyman not to be tried for felony in the King's Court. In ancient times, when the Church was at the peak point of its power, it preempted jurisdiction over felony charges against clergymen. It demanded that in any case in which a clergyman was charged with felony, the case be transferred to the Ecclesiastical Court for trial. The benefit was extreme because conviction of felony in the King's Court resulted in the sentence of death, whereas the Ecclesiastical Court did not make use of capital punishment. It pronounced no "judgment of blood." As the power of the King grew, the time came when he was no longer content that anyone should be tried for felony in other than the King's Court, and set about to have the change made. By this time the Church had lost something of its original strength of position, but it was still a power to be reckoned with, and the result was a compromise. This compromise was not achieved in a committee meeting some afternoon. It was hammered out over the years as part of the struggle between the Crown and the Church. In the end the net result was this: All charged with felony were to be tried in the King's Court, but if a clergyman was convicted the sentence of death could not be pronounced. "Benefit of clergy" was no longer concerned with the tribunal in which the trial would be held, but the ultimate result was the same. It was exemption from the sentence of death.

The judges seized upon this as a device by which the sentence of death could be avoided in certain cases. The "clergy" was not limited to ministers, but included a number of others, such as "readers," and the judges created a presumption that any man [2] who could read must be a member of the clergy and hence exempt from the sentence of death. Thus "benefit of clergy" was extended to any man who could read. In those early days very few could read, but the judges supplemented the presumption by the practice of regularly using the same passage of the Bible to test literacy. When this came to be realized, it was possible for the most illiterate defendant to be taught to hold the Bible in his hands, look at the page, and repeat the words from memory. If he stumbled a little in his "reading" this was overlooked, because the judge wanted him to pass the test. That is, this was true in the

2. In those days the clergy did not include women, other than nuns, so there was no possibility of a presumption that any woman who could read was a member of the clergy. Very few women were committing felonies at that time, and there was a presumption that if a man and his wife committed a felony together, she did so under the compulsion of her husband and hence was not guilty. This was to avoid the spectacle of a wife being executed for a crime, for which her husband received a much milder penalty.

ordinary case. If the defendant had been found guilty of a really heinous crime the judge did not want him to pass the test. So he "switched" passages. When the defendant was handed the Bible and directed to read from a certain page, but began repeating words from a different part of the book, it was obvious that he was unable to read, and the sentence of death was pronounced.

An early statute had substituted whipping for death for petit larceny. With this exception all felonies were still punishable by death according to the letter of the law; but by "benefit of clergy," with the presumption that any man who could read was a clergyman, administered in this benevolent fashion, the result was that those who committed really grievous crimes were executed while those convicted of lesser felonies were disposed of with milder penalties. And the administration of justice by this device seems to have been fairly satisfactory for a substantial period of time.

This procedure, however, had one unfortunate weakness. If one who committed the most brutal murder could actually read, he could pass the test no matter which passage of the Bible was selected for this purpose. And since he could pass the test, the judgment of death could not be pronounced. When Parliament became aware of this situation they would have none of it, and in the late 1400's legislation was enacted providing, in substance, that whoever was convicted of murder with malice aforethought must suffer death "without benefit of clergy." This did not mean, as some seem to have assumed, that the poor convict must be denied spiritual consolation in his final hour. It meant that one convicted of this offense must be sentenced to death, whether he could read or not, and even if he was an actual member of the clergy.

This was satisfactory because the judges at that time felt that a murderer should be executed. But after Parliament had removed murder from the protection of "benefit of clergy," this seemed to have been regarded by the members as such a desirable step that other similar statutes were enacted over the years, until most felonies were punishable by death "without benefit of clergy." In this way the use of this famous device was restricted almost to the point of elimination. Other devices were employed by the judges in the effort to restrict excessive executions, but our attention must be focused elsewhere.

The phrase "criminal law" is more commonly used to include only that part of the general field known as the substantive criminal law, as defined above. It is used in these pages with this limited meaning,—except in this introductory chapter.

B. THE PURPOSE OF CRIMINAL LAW

Punishment is sometimes spoken of as the purpose of the criminal law, but this is quite erroneous. The purpose of the criminal law is to define socially intolerable conduct, and to hold conduct within the limits which are reasonably acceptable from the social point of view.* If the criminal law was one hundred percent effec-

---

* Sauer v. United States, 241 F.2d 640, 648 (9th Cir. 1957). The "purpose of all law, and the criminal law in particular, is to conform conduct to the norms ex- pressed in that law, . . ." United States v. Granda, 565 F.2d 922, 926 (5th Cir. 1978).

tive there would be no punishment, because there would be no conduct which overstepped the boundaries it had established. An incidental but very important function of the criminal law is to teach the difference between right and wrong.

Within recent times there has been a tremendous expansion of the area of human conduct regulated by the criminal law. In early days this law concerned itself only with conduct seriously antisocial in its character. Other agencies such as the church and the home were relied upon to regulate conduct in other respects. The present tendency is to place the entire burden upon the criminal law, and while this shift has been taking place, changes in the social and economic structure of the community have created many new conflicts and have added ingenious modes of infringing recognized rights. Out of the combination have come countless regulations of trades, occupations, monopolies, banking and finance, sale of securities, foods, drugs, liquor, the use of automobiles and recreation activities and sporting events,—a legion of restrictions scattered throughout the statutes and frequently not in the criminal code itself. Many criminal restrictions are not contained in statutes, but are the result of administrative regulation or proclamation.

C. DEFINITION OF CRIME

The matter of definition is one of major importance in the whole field of criminal law. The reason is that our criminal philosophy does not permit a conviction for what was not clearly recognized as a crime at the time it was done. The result is that a statute which purports to provide for punishment, without making sufficiently precise just what is punishable thereunder, is held to be "void for vagueness." [3] A statute that is not sufficiently definite "to give a person of ordinary intelligence fair notice that his conduct is forbidden" violates standards of due process of law.[4] A statute on its face may be so ambiguous that its meaning is uncertain,[5] or its application may be beyond what reasonable persons would anticipate and not provide adequate notice as to its coverage.[6] In either case the statute is void. A statute may

---

3. For discussions of the void-for-vagueness problems see: Aigler, Legislation in Vague or General Terms, 21 Mich.L.Rev. 831 (1923); Collings, Unconstitutional Uncertainty—An Appraisal, 40 Cornell L.Q. 195 (1955); Freund, The Use of Indefinite Terms in Statutes, 30 Yale L.J. 437 (1921); Freund, The Supreme Court and Civil Liberties, 4 Vand.L.Rev. 533, 539–540 (1951); Scott, Constitutional Limitations on Substantive Criminal Law, 29 Rocky Mt.L.Rev. 275, 287–89 (1957); Note, The Void-for-Vagueness Doctrine in the Supreme Court, 109 U.Pa.L.Rev. 67 (1960); Note, Due Process Requirements of Definiteness in Statutes, 62 Harv.L.Rev. 77 (1948); Note, An Escape from Statutory Interpretation, 23 Ind.L.J. 272 (1948).

"No man shall be held criminally responsible for conduct which he could not reasonably understand to be proscribed." But "all that the statute need do is to provide fair notice to a person of ordina-

ry intelligence that his conduct is forbidden." Guzzardo v. Bengston, 643 F.2d 1300, 1304 (7th Cir. 1981).

"Statutes need not be drafted with such precision that citizens will never hazard their liberty upon an incorrect assessment of their conduct." State v. Mellinger, 52 Or.App. 21, 627 P.2d 897, 904 (1981).

4. United States v. Harriss, 347 U.S. 612, 617, 74 S.Ct. 808, 811 (1954).

5. Coates v. City of Cincinnati, 402 U.S. 611, 91 S.Ct. 1686 (1971). A statute disallowing "three or more persons to assemble . . . on any sidewalks . . . and conduct themselves in a manner annoying to persons passing by . . ." was held unconstitutional on its face.

6. Palmer v. City of Euclid, Ohio, 402 U.S. 544, 91 S.Ct. 1563 (1971); Bouie v. Columbia, 378 U.S. 347, 84 S.Ct. 1697 (1964).

also be infirm, even though the wording is clear and precise, if it intrudes into otherwise protected conduct. This is not a deficiency because of vagueness but rather the statute is overbroad.[7] A statute need not be unerringly precise.[8] The nature of the conduct regulated and persons against whom the statute is directed may be considered in determining whether a statute gives fair warning as to what is prohibited.[9] A statute that is unnecessarily obscure in meaning may trap the innocent, relegate on an ad hoc basis policy matters in the enforcement of the criminal law to policemen or juries,[10] and allow for selective enforcement.[11] The requirement of reasonable notice allows for an equal and evenhanded application of the criminal law and provides a barrier against expedient invocation of the criminal sanction.[12] These considerations have led to a holding that a statute punishing a person who "publicly treats contemptuously the flag of the United States" was void [13] because it failed "to draw reasonably clear lines between the kinds of non-ceremonial treatment that are criminal and those that are not." Equally void for vagueness was an ordinance providing that "no person shall loiter . . . in or upon any street, park or public place, or in any public building; . . ." with no definition of the word "loiter." [14] A portion of a harass-

---

7. Levshakoff v. State, 565 P.2d 504 (Alaska 1977); State ex rel. Purcell v. Superior Court, 111 Ariz. 582, 535 P.2d 1299 (1975). "While a statute may often be found both vague and overbroad at the same time, the two concepts are distinct. A statute is too vague when it fails to give fair notice of what it prohibits. It is overbroad when its language, given its normal meaning, is so broad that the sanctions may apply to conduct which the state is not entitled to regulate." 535 P.2d 1301.

8. United States v. Petrillo, 332 U.S. 1, 67 S.Ct. 1538 (1947). "The constitution does not require impossible standards of specificity in penal statutes. It requires only that the statute convey 'sufficiently definite warning as to the proscribed conduct when measured by common understanding and practices.' 332 U.S. p. 7." United States v. Woodard, 376 F.2d 136, 140 (7th Cir. 1967).

9. ". . . the law is full of instances where a man's fate depends on his estimating rightly . . ." Nash v. United States, 229 U.S. 373, 377, 33 S.Ct. 780 (1913). In writing criminal statutes "no more than a reasonable degree of certainty can be demanded. Nor is it unfair to require that one who deliberately goes perilously close to an area of proscribed conduct shall take the risk that he may cross the line." Boyce Motor Lines v. United States, 342 U.S. 337, 340, 72 S.Ct. 329, 331 (1952). Quoted by People v. Apodaca, 76 Cal.App.3d 479, 142 Cal.Rptr. 830, 835 (1977).

10. Grayned v. City of Rockford, 408 U.S. 104, 92 S.Ct. 2294 (1972).

11. Gottschalk v. State, 575 P.2d 289 (Alaska 1978).

12. If without the use of a true definition the statute is sufficiently precise so that one who would be law-abiding will understand what is necessary to comply with the law, and one who has been indicted or informed against for the offense will know exactly what kind of misconduct has been charged against him, the crime may be referred to, loosely, as having been "defined."

13. Smith v. Goguen, 415 U.S. 566, 94 S.Ct. 1242 (1974).

14. State v. Caez, 81 N.J.Super. 315, 195 A.2d 496 (1963).

The Idaho court held that while "prostitution" has a well-understood definition at common law, the legislative attempt to redefine it more expansively resulted in vagueness. State v. Lopez, 98 Idaho 581, 570 P.2d 259 (1977).

But the statute prohibiting the mailing of "firearms capable of being concealed on the person" is not void for vagueness, and a conviction based upon the mailing of a 22-inch long sawed-off shotgun is affirmed. The statute "intelligibly forbids a definite course of conduct: the mailing of concealable firearms. While doubts as to the applicability of the language in marginal fact situations may be conceived, we think that the statute gave respondent adequate warning that her mailing of a sawed-off shotgun of some 22 inches in length was a criminal offense." United States v. Powell, 423 U.S. 87, 93, 96 S.Ct. 316, 320 (1975).

ment statute which prohibited conduct that "alarms or seriously annoys" had been held unconstitutional.[15] However, a statute defining child abuse as "cruel and inhumane treatment" [16] has been held to be sufficiently specific to survive constitutional challenge because the terms have a commonly understood meaning.

Because of this it is important to start the study of criminal law with a clear understanding of exactly what constitutes a true definition, although it would be overemphasis to insist that nothing else could ever be recognized as sufficient for the designation of criminal conduct.[17]

A true definition is made up of three parts: (1) the term, (2) the genus and (3) the differentia. The term is the subject of the definition—the word or phrase to be defined; genus is a category of classification, a class or group ranking beneath a family and above a species; differentia is the attribute or characteristic by which one species of a genus is distinguished from every other. In other words a true definition must give (1) the word or phrase to be defined (the term), (2) the placement of this thing in a group of like things (the genus) and (3) the peculiarity which distinguishes it from other like things (the differentia).

One who undertakes to define, without having given careful thought to the true purpose of a definition, will often start in terms of "when" or "where" or "what." "Murder is when . . ." for example, or "murder is where . . .," although obviously neither time nor place represents any genus of which murder is a species. A small boy asked to define a screwdriver came up with this suggestion: "A screwdriver is what drives screws." This may convince us that he could recognize one on sight but it is quite unsatisfactory as a definition. It neither tells us what kind of thing a screwdriver is nor offers anything adequate in the way of differentia. It may call to mind the time when, not stopping for the proper implement, we impatiently

"A criminal statute must be sufficiently definite to give notice of the required conduct to one who would avoid its penalties, and to guide the judge in its application and the lawyer in defending one charged with its violation, but, . . . no more than a reasonable degree of certainty can be demanded. Nor is it unfair to require that one who deliberately goes perilously close to an area of proscribed conduct shall take the risk that he may cross the line." State v. Marley, 54 Hawaii 450, 460, 509 P.2d 1095, 1103 (1973).

15. State v. Sanderson, 33 Or.App. 173, 575 P.2d 1025 (1978).

16. Bowers v. State, 38 Md.App. 21, 379 A.2d 748 (1977). Contrast, State v. Hodges, 254 Or. 21, 457 P.2d 491 (1969) holding void a statute defining a delinquent child as one whose "behavior, condition or circumstance are such as to endanger his own welfare or welfare of others."

17. "The test is whether the language conveys sufficiently definite warning as to the proscribed conduct when measured by common understanding and practices." Anderson v. United States, 215 F.2d 84, 90 (6th Cir. 1954). Conduct "unbecoming an officer and gentlemen" and "to the prejudice of good order and discipline of the armed forces" under the general articles of the Uniform Code of Military Justice, 10 U.S.C.A. §§ 933 & 934 is not unconstitutionally vague. "And to maintain the discipline essential to perform its mission effectively, the military has developed what 'may not unfitly be called the customary military law' or 'general usage of the military service.'" Parker v. Levy, 417 U.S. 733, 744, 94 S. Ct. 2547, 2556 (1974); Secretary of Navy v. Avrech, 418 U.S. 676, 94 S.Ct. 3039 (1974).

A statute which prohibited conspiracy for the "perversion or obstruction of justice or the due administration of the laws" was not void for vagueness. The words have a well-settled meaning at common law. State v. Nielson, 19 Utah 2d 66, 426 P.2d 13 (1967).

pounded a screw into place with a hammer. Had he said: "A screwdriver is a tool for driving and withdrawing screws by turning them," we would have had a true definition.

Let us approach the definition of crime with this in mind. Blackstone offered this suggestion:

"A crime or misdemeanor is an act committed or omitted, in violation of a public law either forbidding or commanding it." [18] This was criticized by Bishop who offered this suggestion: "A crime is any wrong which the government deems injurious to the public at large, and punishes through a judicial proceeding in its own name." [19] Some courts misunderstood Bishop and thought he was giving merely an explanation of Blackstone's definition.[20] This resulted in one which sought to combine the two: "A crime is any act or omission prohibited by public law for the protection of the public, and made punishable by the state in a judicial proceeding in its own name." [21]

This corrects one fault in the definition suggested by Blackstone. It would be possible to have an act forbidden or commanded by public law without any provision for the punishment of a violation thereof (although this result could be avoided by a properly-worded general penalty clause). What cannot be punished does not come within our concept of "crime" and hence punishability is an essential element of the definition. But while correcting this defect it was thought not to give due emphasis to the fact that one may be of such tender years, or have a mind so completely disordered by mental disease, as to be entirely without criminal responsibility; and that special circumstances may be sufficient to constitute a recognized excuse for harmful conduct even in the absence of legal incapacity. What is done without criminal responsibility is not a *crime*, whether it is a case of legal incapacity or special circumstances of excuse. It is incorrect as a matter of juridical science to say that the crime is excused in such a case. What happened is excused and hence it was not a crime.

This consideration induced Burdick to offer this definition: "A crime is the voluntary commission or omission, by a person having criminal capacity, of any act, in violation of a public law either prohibiting or commanding it,

---

18. 4 Bl.Comm. *5.

19. 1 Bishop, New Criminal Law § 32 (8th ed. 1892).

20. E.g., after quoting Blackstone's definition it was said: "By this is meant, of course, those wrongs of which the law takes cognizance as injurious to the public, and punishes in what is called a criminal proceeding, prosecuted by the state in its own name, or in the name of the people or the sovereign. 1 Bishop on Cr.Law, § 32." In re Bergin, 31 Wis. 383, 386 (1872).

21. Clark and Marshall, Law of Crimes § 2.01, at p. 92 (7th ed. 1967). "A crime may be generally defined as the commission or omission of an act which the law forbids or commands under pain of a punishment to be imposed by the state by a proceeding in its own name." Miller, Criminal Law 16 (1934). "Crime is a violation or neglect of legal duty, of so much public importance that the law, either common or statute, provides punishment for it." May's Law of Crimes § 1 (Rev.Ed.1938). "A crime is an act or omission punishable as an offense against the state." 1 McClain, Criminal Law § 4 (1897). "A crime or public offense is an act committed or omitted in violation of a law forbidding or commanding it, and to which is annexed, upon conviction, either of the following punishments: . . ." West's Ann.Cal.Pen.Code § 15. (1970) So. Dak. Compiled Laws 1967, 22–1–3, § 40A–1–4 N.M. Statutes 1953.

and which is punishable by the offended government by a judicial proceeding in its own name." [22]

This labored addition to an already lengthy definition would not have been required had due attention been given to the first change of Blackstone's wording suggested by Bishop. According to Blackstone a crime is "an act committed or omitted" and so forth. The inaccuracy of this approach may be emphasized by illustration. Suppose a fatal traffic accident has resulted from the failure of a motorist to obey a stop sign on the highway. Suppose further that the failure to stop under the facts of the particular case was clearly a matter of criminal negligence. The motorist is guilty of manslaughter,[23] as will be pointed out in the following chapter. There is no manslaughter without loss of life, but the passing of the last spark of life is never the act of any other person, although it may be the result of such an act.[24] Blackstone's definition indicates that the motorist's crime in such a case is his failure to stop (act of omission), whereas in truth his crime is the harm (death of another) resulting from his criminally negligent failure to stop.

In many instances the act and the harm are identical.[25] If a building has been burglariously invaded the burglar's act of breaking into the dwelling of another, and so forth, is the harm which constitutes this offense. The unpermitted act of sexual intercourse is the harm involved in the crime of rape. Many other instances could be cited. This explains why the definition of crime has been worded so frequently in terms of "act or omission." But let attention be directed to situations in which the two are not identical. Suppose, for example, a flaming arrow is shot for the wrongful purpose of destroying the dwelling house of another. (1) The arrow lands on the roof and the building is burned. (2) The aim is good but a pigeon in flight collides with the arrow in mid-air. The pigeon is killed but the building unharmed. The difference is not in the act of the wrongdoer but in the consequences of the act. Extreme harm resulted in one case but not in the other. One was arson; the other was not. Or suppose a rock is thrown for the malicious purpose of putting out another's eye. The intended victim—(1) dodges successfully and experiences only the momentary apprehension of being hit; (2) succeeds in moving enough so that the rock strikes a glancing blow on the side of the head causing considerable pain but no lasting injury; (3) is unsuccessful in his attempt to dodge and loses the use of his eye; (4) is struck by the rock with fatal consequences. The crime committed is (1) assault, (2) battery, (3) mayhem, and (4) murder. Furthermore, in (3) or (4) whether the sight, or the life, is saved or lost may depend upon the promptness with

---

22. Burdick, The Law of Crime § 70 (1946).

23. This assumes that the deceased was someone other than the "motorist."

24. "The word 'act' is used in the Restatement of this Subject to denote an external manifestation of the actor's will and does not include any of its results even the most direct, immediate and intended." Restatement, Second, Torts § 2 (1965). See also Model Penal Code § 1.13. And even if a broader significance is given to the word it is necessary to distinguish the act, which is the cause

of death, from the result which is the loss of life. The wording of the text is not intended to imply that death is the act of the deceased. It is not an act of anybody. It may or may not be the result of an act.

25. The Model Penal Code § 1.04(1) appears to group act and harm under the term offense and provides: "An offense defined by this Code or by any other statute of this State, for which a sentence of [death or of] imprisonment is authorized, constitutes a crime."

which medical attention is received or the skill with which it is administered. It has been urged, at times, that the crime *should* depend entirely upon the wrongdoer's act or omission, and not upon the consequences, but this does not represent the common law or the trend of legislative enactment.

Since this is true the kind of thing crime is, its genus, must be found in the area of *harm*, but that word represents too large a category for this purpose. In the classification scale it will represent a *family* rather than a *genus*. It is necessary to identify crime with some particular kind of harm. A tornado or earthquake, for example, may cause tremendous harm which, however, is quite foreign to the concept being sought. Crime falls within that division of harm which results from human conduct,—social harm. With reference to this term, it may be mentioned that it is socially harmful not only to have a man murdered, a dwelling burglariously invaded, or property stolen, but also to have a conspiracy formed in the community, to have one member thereof challenge another to a duel, or offer to bribe an officer. In these latter instances, let it be emphasized, it is socially harmful to have such influences abroad in the community even if the criminal purpose of the conspiracy is not achieved, the challenge is refused, and the bribe rejected.

Basic to our theory of justice is the principle that there can be no punishment for harmful conduct unless it was so provided by some law in existence at the time. This has found expression in the doctrine: *Nulla poena sine lege*—no punishment without a law for it. This concept embodies the requirement of a reasonably specific definition of criminal wrong. This doctrine has not been recognized under all forms of government everywhere. The Nazis, for instance, by special decree substituted the doctrine that there should be no social harm without punishment.[26] Under such law the definition would be simply: A crime is any social harm. The present effort, however, is to define crime under our law—not under some other. And under our law he who has caused social harm is not punishable unless a punishment was provided therefor either by the common law [27] or by some statute in force at the time.

Many a small child, for example, has lost his or her life by climbing into an abandoned refrigerator and shutting the door, only to discover that it could not be opened from the inside. This has happened with such frequency that it is recognized as socially harmful to leave such an article where children have access to it without removing the door or taking some similar safety precaution. But such social harm did not constitute a crime until forbidden by statute. And since the constitutional prohibition of ex post facto

---

26. German Act of June 28, 1935: "Any person who commits an act which the law declares to be punishable or which is deserving of penalty according to the fundamental conceptions of a penal law and sound popular feeling, shall be punished. If there is no penal law directly covering an act it shall be punished under the law of which the fundamental conception applies most nearly to the said act." Quoted in Elliott & Wood, A Casebook on Criminal Law, 3d Ed. p. 12.

27. In some states common-law crimes are not punished as such, and there is no crime not included in the statutes. See State v. Bowling, 5 Ariz.App. 436, 427 P.2d 928 (1967). "No conduct constitutes an offense unless it is a crime or violation under this Code or another statute of this State." Model Penal Code § 1.05(1). "Common law crimes are abolished and no conduct is a crime unless made so by this Code, other applicable statute or ordinance," Utah Code Ann.1953, 76-1-105.

laws [28] not only forbids conviction for what was not recognized as a crime when done, but also the imposition of any punishment not provided for in advance, the differentia needed for our definition is clearly indicated. The genus—social harm—must be defined and made punishable by law.

Burdick thought, as mentioned above, that to define crime in terms of an "Act or omission prohibited by public law . . . and made punishable" and so forth, does not give sufficient recognition to the fact that no act or omission is a crime if by one lacking criminal capacity, or by another under circumstances sufficient to constitute a recognized excuse. Whether such criticism is or is not valid when directed at a definition worded in terms of an "act or omission," it has no application to one which speaks of "social harm." Homicide committed either by a two-year-old child or by an older person within the legal privilege of self-defense, for example, is not a crime. It is also not "social harm made punishable by law." Hence our definition is:

Crime is any social harm defined and made punishable by law.

The above definition should be understood as applying to the application of a sanction in a process that is primarily used for the prosecution and disposition of persons whose conduct resulting in social harm is classed as criminal. Although civil process may be punitive, civil violations are not true crimes although civil sanctions may assume many of the characteristics of criminal sanctions.[29] In the United States, a separate procedural process is usually employed in handling criminal matters, although some civil activity is processed through the use of criminal procedures.[30] Characterization of social harm as criminal may be made separate from the process used in dealing with a violator, however, the process employed frequently aids in deciding that a social harm is criminal or that before a given sanction may be imposed special processes for determining responsibility must be employed.[31] A defi-

28. "No . . . ex post facto law shall be passed." Art. I, § 9. "No State shall . . . pass any . . . ex post facto law. . . ." Art. I, § 10, paragraph 1.

29. Hart, The Aims of The Criminal Law, 23 Law and Contemp.Prob. 401, 402–406 (1958).

30. Bastardy proceedings in some jurisdictions apply criminal procedures although the action is civil. Utah Code Ann. 1953, 77–60–1, et seq. The cited section was repealed Laws of Utah 1980, Ch. 15 § 1. This reflects a trend to leave paternity proceedings to the field of civil litigation.

31. Brown v. Multnomah County District Court, 280 Or. 95, 570 P.2d 52 (1977) where driving under the influence of intoxicants was categorized as an infraction it was observed:

"Whether the legislature effectively carried out its purpose to 'decriminalize' the first offense of driving under the influence of intoxicants is a close question. . . ."

"It is beyond dispute that the legislature may define and enforce obligatory conduct by means other than the criminal law, as it does in taxation, or injunctive orders, or in creating private remedies, which may extend beyond compensatory damages. It may employ licenses—in effect, exemptions from a prohibition—conditioned upon prescribed qualifications and upon adherence to prescribed standards of conduct. It may take custody of persons in involuntary commitment or juvenile proceedings. Since the state has plenary power to devise its laws limited only by the state and federal constitutions, and cases there cited, it may decide to repeal criminal prohibitions, to define civil obligations enforceable by the state and its agencies, and to replace one with the other, so long as constitutional limits are observed. . . .

"There is no easy test for when the imposition of a sanction is a 'criminal prosecution' within the meaning of the constitutional guarantees. The starting point, of course, is the law under which the sanction is imposed. When the legislature has defined conduct as a criminal of-

nition of the term crime cannot practically be separated from the nature of proceedings used to determine criminal conduct.[32]

Crime has been given broader definition by some authorities analyzing human behavior. An expanded definition may be of value to the sociologist and behavioral scientist considering crime from an epidemiological perspective rather than the administration of the criminal law.[33] The definition of crime referred to above necessarily intends its application to the field of the criminal law and has inherent in it the restrictions necessarily involved in any definition of law.[34]

D. CLASSIFICATION OF CRIME

1. WITH REFERENCE TO THE GRADE OF THE OFFENSE

The common law divided crime into three major groups: (1) treason, (2) felony and (3) misdemeanor. Treason, in turn, was divided into (a) high treason and (b) petit treason.

High treason, in the words of Blackstone, is the term applied "when disloyalty so rears its crest as to attack even majesty itself." [35] In the ancient common law it consisted of killing the king, promoting revolt in the kingdom or in the armed forces, or counterfeiting the great seal.[36] A tendency to enlarge the scope of the offense by analogy led to such uncertainty that an act of Parliament was required to define it. This was the Statute of Treasons enacted in 1350.[37] It specified exactly what should constitute high treason including, among certain other wrongs, a manifested intent to kill the king, queen or prince, levying war against the king, adhering to his enemies, giving them aid and comfort.[38]

Petit treason, at common law, was based upon a grave breach of an inferior allegiance. It was a malicious homicide which involved a killing of husband by wife, master or mistress by servant, or prelate by clergyman.[39] In

fense, it is a criminal offense for constitutional purposes even if the same consequences could have been attached to the same conduct by civil or administrative proceedings. But it does not follow that a law can avoid this result simply by avoiding the term 'criminal' in defining the conduct to be penalized. Constitutional guarantees have more substance than that. . . .

"On reviewing these elements we conclude that, on balance, the code's offense of driving under the influence of intoxicants, and its enforcement and punishment, retain too many penal characteristics not to be a 'criminal prosecution' under article I, section 11 of the constitution. . . ."
United States v. Dixon, 347 U.S. 381, 74 S.Ct. 566 (1954).

32. Professor Glanville Williams referred to crime as "an act capable of being followed by criminal proceedings having a criminal outcome," Williams, The Definition of Crime, 8 Current L.Prob. 107, 125 (1955).

33. Gibbons, Society Crime and Criminal Careers, 35–41; Becker, The Outsiders, 1 Crime and Justice 21–25 (1971).

34. Radzinowicz, Ideology and Crime, pp. 101–104.

35. 4 Bl.Comm. *75.

36. 1 Hale P.C. *76–7.

37. 25 Edw. III, c. 2.

38. 1 Hale P.C. *91.

39. These were the harms specified as petit treason in the Statute of Treasons, 25 Edw. III, c. 2 (1350). This was but "an affirmance of the common law." 1 Hale P.C. *377. Certain other wrongs had been held to be petit treason prior to this Act, but they were probably enlargements of the ancient common law comparable to those found in the history of high treason.

England petit treason was abolished by statute in 1828.[40] The purpose of distinguishing this offense from murder was to apply a particularly brutal punishment,[41] and petit treason seems never to have been recognized in this country,—such a homicide being dealt with here as any other murder.

"Felony, in the general acceptation of our English law, comprises every species of crime which occasioned at common law the forfeiture of lands and goods." [42] If we are to insist upon the three-fold division of crime the statement should read "every species of crime other than treason" and so forth.[43] Under the English common law all felonies were punished by death except that the penalty for mayhem was mutilation.[44] Whipping was substituted for death as the penalty for petit larceny, but this was a change from the common law resulting from an early statute.[45] It should be added that the fiction of "benefit of clergy" was extended ultimately to the point where the death penalty was not applied to one convicted of felony unless by statute that offense had been declared to be without benefit of clergy. Hence, while it may be said in a general way that under the theory of the English common law a felon had "forfeited life and member and all that he had," [46] it is better to define felony, under that law, in terms of an offense punishable by forfeiture. The offenses which came within this definition under the common law of England were felonious homicide [47] (divided by statutes into murder and manslaughter), mayhem,[48] arson,[49] rape,[50] robbery,[51] burglary,[52] larceny,[53] prison breach (although an early statute took prison breach out of the felony class if the escape was by one in custody for a non-capital offense),[54] and rescue of a felon.[55] Sodomy is sometimes included in this list but this is an

---

40. 9 Geo. IV, c. 31, § 2.

41. "The punishment of petit treason in a man is, to be drawn and hanged, and in a woman to be drawn and burned; . . ." 4 Bl.Comm. *204. The "drawing" consisted of laying the malefactor on the ground and tying him to "a horse which dragged him along the rough road to the gibbet." 2 Pollock & Maitland 500 (2d ed. 1899).

42. 4 Bl.Comm. *94. By statute the forfeiture was limited sometimes to goods and chattels and did not include a freehold estate. This was true of petit larceny. 1 Hale P.C. *530.

43. Blackstone explained his statement as follows: "All treasons, therefore, strictly speaking, are felonies, though all felonies are not treason." 4 Bl.Comm. *95.

44. Id. at *94, *205. At an earlier day mutilation had been the usual punishment for felons. "Very slowly in the course of the thirteenth century the penalty of death took the place of mutilation as the punishment due for felons, and this without legislation. . . . Such changes could take place easily, because a main idea of the old law had been that by the gravest, the unemendable crimes a man 'forfeited life and member and all

that he had.'" 2 Pollock & Maitland, History of English Law 461–2 (2d ed. 1899).

45. Statute of Westminster I, c. 15 (1275).

46. 2 Pollock & Maitland, History of English Law 462 (2d ed. 1899).

47. 4 Bl.Comm. *177.

48. Id. at *205.

49. 3 Co.Inst. *66.

50. Id. at *60.

51. Id. at *68.

52. Id. at *63.

53. Id. at *107. Coke does not make the direct statement but his definition is in terms of a "felonious" taking.

54. 4 Bl.Comm. *130.

55. Id. at *131. One recognized authority adds wounding and false imprisonment to the list of common-law felonies. 2 Pollock & Maitland, History of English Law 470 (2d ed. 1899). But while there had been some tendency to add these to the felony group,—some early instances in which they had been punished as felonies—the development of the common law placed them definitely in

error if the statement refers to the English common law. Sodomy was originally punished only as an ecclesiastical offense although made a felony by a statute [56] old enough to be recognized as common law in this country.[57]

While the list of felonies as recognized by the English common law was very small, it was greatly enlarged by statute.[58] And although "the true criterion of felony is forfeiture," [59] insofar as the English common law was concerned, the enlargements by act of parliament in the early days tended to emphasize capital punishment as the chief characteristic of felony,[60] although a particular offender might void the extreme penalty by benefit of clergy unless the statute provided otherwise.

"Misdemeanor" was the label ultimately adopted to apply to all offenses other than treason or felony. The term included a wide variety of wrongs and misprisions. Many of the substantive legal principles and procedures applicable to felonies were not applied in the case of misdemeanors.[61] The difference in treatment between felonies and misdemeanors has carried over from common law to current practice, and today misdemeanors are often treated differently than felonies so far as the procedures employed in trying such cases as well as the consequences of a conviction. The traditional distinction between felonies and misdemeanors has been abolished in England.[62]

2. WITH REFERENCE TO MORAL TURPITUDE

Quite a different classification scheme divides offenses into two groups: (1) offenses mala in se, and (2) offenses mala prohibita.

"Acts *mala in se*," it has been said, "include, in addition to all felonies, all breaches of the public order, injuries to person and property, outrages upon public decency and morals, and breaches of official duty when done wilfully and corruptly. Acts *mala prohibita* include any matter forbidden or commanded by statute, but not otherwise wrong." [63]

the misdemeanor class. "The inferior offences or misdemeanors . . . are . . . wounding, false imprisonment, . . ." 4 Bl.Comm. *216.

56. Sodomy "(being in the times of popery only subject to ecclesiastical censures) was made felony without benefit of clergy by statute 25 Hen. VIII, c. 6, revived and confirmed by 5 Eliz. c. 17." 4 Bl.Comm. *216. See also 3 Co.Inst. *58, where it is said this offense is a felony "by authority of parliament."

57. 1533, revived and confirmed in 1562.

58. A study of Book IV of Blackstone's Commentaries will disclose the astonishing number of statutory felonies.

59. 4 Bl.Comm. *97.

The early English statute which substituted whipping for hanging as the penalty for petit larceny also limited the forfeiture to "all his goods." 3 Co.Inst. *109. But it was nevertheless a felony. 1 Bishop, New Criminal Law § 679 (8th ed. 1892). Hence the common law definition

of felony should be in terms of "forfeiture" rather than "forfeiture of lands and goods." 4 Bl.Comm. *97.

60. Id. at *97–8. E.g., every "such offence shall be judged felony, and the offender . . . suffer as in case of felony," although it was expressly provided that conviction should not result in corruption of blood or forfeiture of inheritance. Stat. of 31 Eliz. c. 4 (1589). Crimes punishable by mutilation were also considered felonies.

The identification of capital punishment with felonies was so strong that if a statute made a crime a felony it was implied that it would be punished by death. R v. Johnson, 3 M & S 539, 105 Eng.Rep. 712 (1815).

61. Harris's Criminal Law, 21st Ed. (Hooper) 11.

62. Criminal Law Act 1967 S. 1(1).

63. Commonwealth v. Adams, 114 Mass. 323, 324 (1873); Bartlett v. State, 569 P.2d 1235, 1238 (Wyo.1977).

Some have questioned the validity of this classification,[64] but the Supreme Court has referred to "the well-recognized distinction between *mala in se* and *mala prohibita*." [65] Those who question the distinction often do so because of a failure to understand exactly what is meant by an offense *malum prohibitum*. This invites the question: How can we tell whether an offense is *malum in se* or *malum prohibitum*?

The logical starting point is an example. Parking overtime in a restricted area is *malum prohibitum*. If the law limits parking in a certain area to one hour, this is not because of a belief that it would be inherently morally wrong for a car to be left there for a longer period. Perhaps too many motorists had difficulty finding a parking space there. It may have been estimated that most of those concerned would not need more than an hour so that it would best serve the interest of the greatest number by limiting all to that period. And so the law was enacted. Or it may have been decided that those who use the public street for parking should make a slight contribution to the public expense. So parking meters were installed and a law was passed limiting parking there to one hour and requiring a small payment for the privilege. In either case a penalty clause was added as a means of enforcement.

Whenever a law is enacted prohibiting certain conduct under the belief that such conduct is morally wrong, or requiring certain conduct for a comparable reason, the penalty clause provided for violation is for the purpose of punishing wrongdoing. And the offense is *malum in se*. But from early times [66] some laws have been enacted regulating certain conduct for reasons having nothing to do with morality; such as laws regulating the height of buildings in certain areas; requiring a railroad train to come to a complete stop before crossing another track; regulating the price of certain commodities; requiring a license for the privilege of driving a motor vehicle on the public ways; providing which car has the right of way in competing situations; or limiting the times during which certain animals or birds may be hunted. And each such regulatory enactment has a penalty clause. The penalty thus provided is not for the purpose of punishing wrongdoing, but is added solely for the reason that no one has ever yet suggested a reasonable method by which such a law can be enforced without resort to a penalty. And the resulting offense is *malum prohibitum*—a matter forbidden or commanded by statute, but not otherwise wrong.[67] In other words, the penalty clause of a regulatory statute, enacted for some purpose other than the enforcement of morality, is an offense *malum prohibitum*.

Two comments are in order. First, this distinction is limited to the misdemeanor group and has no application to treason or to felony. Second, an

---

64. The problem is discussed at length infra, ch. 7, sec. 5, The Civil Offense.

65. Shevlin Carpenter Co. v. Minnesota, 218 U.S. 57, 68, 30 S.Ct. 663, 666 (1910).

"A crime which is malum in se is defined as an act which is . . . 'naturally evil, such as murder, rape, arson, burglary and larceny,' . . . A crime which is malum prohibitum is one prohibited by statute . . . 'although no

moral turpitude or dereliction may attach,' . . ." State v. Hartzog, 26 Wn.App. 576, 615 P.2d 480, 489 (1980). See also, Wolfe, Mala in Se: A Disappearing Doctrine? 19 Criminology 131 (1981).

66. See the note by Chief Justice Fineux in Y.B. Mich., 11 Hen. VII, f. 11, pl. 35 (1495).

67. Commonwealth v. Adams, 114 Mass. 323, 324 (1873).

offense *malum prohibitum* does not represent *social harm* for which there would necessarily be wide societal condemnation. The conduct is defined as criminal and made punishable by law. It is forbidden or required "but not otherwise wrong." In other words, it represents a situation in which a regulation was deemed desirable as a matter of expediency or revenue, and a penalty imposed for purposes of enforcement.[68] It may be justifiably urged that it is not really a crime at all, but rather in the nature of a civil offense. In many instances this is true, and the criminal process merely provides a more convenient forum for managing certain defined wrongs. On the other hand, it may be urged that this will not hold true in the case of all offenses that would be subject to classification as *malum prohibitum*. With an increased sensitivity towards the need for social regulation in some areas of daily activity, aside from morality, matters *malum prohibitum* are properly viewed as "criminal" and carry as strong or stronger opprobrium than some offenses *malum in se*.[69]

The English common law, with certain statutory modifications, suggests a classification of offenses into three main groups, each of which has two sub-divisions:

I Treason

    A   High treason

    B   Petit treason

II Felony

    A   Not clergyable (without benefit of clergy)

    B   Clergyable

III Misdemeanor

    A   *Malum in se*

    B   *Malum prohibitum*

The first step in this classification scheme is illogical because the determinant for treason is the nature of the harm caused whereas that for felony or misdemeanor is the nature of the penalty to be imposed. For certain reasons it was very convenient in the early law to deal with treason as belonging to a class by itself, and it is still convenient so to speak when referring to the law of that period. For example, all guilty parties to treason were principals

---

68. In a case involving false certification of a notary it was stated:

"However, under modern statutes by virtue of the police power, many acts are now made unlawful because of the public welfare involved, which have no inherent evil in themselves or moral turpitude attached thereto. This type of statutory crimes is referred to as *malum prohibitum*, as contrasted with those referred to as *malum in se*, which involve evil and moral turpitude.

. . . . .

"We do not, however, have that issue here involved. The act charged here is purely *malum prohibitum* and not *malum in se*. There is no evil or moral turpitude involved in making a notary's certificate."

Noble v. State, 248 Ind. 101, 223 N.E.2d 755, 757–758 (1967).

69. An attorney convicted of willful failure to file an income tax return, an offense *malum prohibitum*, may on the basis of the conviction be subjected to disbarment proceedings. Iowa State Bar Assn. v. Bromwell, 221 N.W.2d 777 (Iowa 1974). Environmental concerns may cause conduct otherwise classed as *malum prohibitum* to be considered especially offensive and justify the imposition of strong sanctions where the conduct is willful. *Cf.* United States v. Hamel, 551 F.2d 107 (6th Cir. 1977).

whereas in cases of [other] felony some of them might be accessories. And anciently this was a difference of great importance. Even at that time, despite the separate place allotted in the classification scheme, it was recognized that treason was in truth but a species of felony.[70]

Traditionally, statutes in this country commonly divide crimes into two classes: (1) felony and (2) misdemeanor.[71] Recently in several jurisdictions an additional classification of crime for very minor offenses has been established.[72] The classification has been labeled "infraction," [73] "violation" [74] or petty offenses.[75]

The Model Penal Code [76] suggests a classification of *offenses* into four groups, three being crimes and the fourth not a crime:

I Felony

II Misdemeanor

III Petty misdemeanor

IV Violation

The types of offenses covered by these classifications are very minor, regulatory offenses. Such classifications, although included in the penal code, do not involve offenses that are true crimes and do not normally warrant moral condemnation.

Usually the determinant between misdemeanors and felonies, as was true at common law is the nature of the penalty that may be imposed, although the exact nature employed for this purpose is not uniform and nowhere has any resemblance to the common law in this regard, except that a capital offense is a felony. Probably murder is the only capital felony today.[77] Another classification used to distinguish between felonies and lesser offenses is based on penalty. Generally, this form of classification follows one of two patterns. It is based upon either: (1) the type of institution in which the

---

70. 3 Co.Inst. *15; 4 Bl.Comm. *95. In many respects the word "felony" was always understood to include treason. This is true, for example, in speaking of the difference between arrests for felony and arrests for misdemeanor. 3 Co.Inst. *489–90; 4 Bl.Comm. *292.

71. E.g., 18 U.S.C.A. § 1 (1969); V.T.C.A.Penal Code § 12.01 (1974).

72. Federal criminal law has long recognized petty offenses as a special category of misdemeanor. 18 U.S.C.A. § 1 (1969). "(3) Any misdemeanor, the penalty for which does not exceed imprisonment for a period of six months or a fine of not more than $500, or both, is a petty offense." This, by definition, is not a third category but a subdivision of misdemeanor. If a statute designates an offense a "misdemeanor" but provides a penalty, for violation thereof, not to exceed 5 years in prison—the crime is a fel-

ony despite the designation. Loos v. Hardwick, 224 F.2d 442 (5th Cir. 1955).

73. No.Dak.Cent.Code 12.1–32–01 (1971); Utah Code Ann. 1953, 76–3–105; West's Ann.Cal.Pen.Code § 16 (1970).

74. 55.10 McKinney's Consol. Laws of N.Y. (1975); Ore.Rev.Stat. 161.565 (1979); 13A–5–3 Code of Alabama 1975; 41–114 Ark.St.Ann. 1977. See also Model Penal Code 1.04(5).

75. 18–1–107, Colo.Rev.Stat., 1973; Hawaii Rev.Stat. Ch. 37, § 701–107 (1973).

76. Section 1.04.

77. In Coker v. Georgia, 433 U.S. 584, 97 S.Ct. 2861 (1977), the Supreme Court held the death penalty unconstitutional for the crime of rape of an adult woman. The decision suggests that only offenses involving the taking of human life justify a capital penalty.

offender may be incarcerated, or (2) the length of term which may be imposed. Typical examples are:

(a) "A felony is a crime which is punishable with death or by imprisonment in the state prison. Every other crime or public offense is a misdemeanor except those offenses that are classified as infractions." [78]

(b) "(1) Any offense punishable by death or for a term exceeding one year is a felony.

"(2) Any other offense is a misdemeanor." [79]

Needless to add treason is a felony under either definition.

The Model Penal Code [80] and the statutes of several jurisdictions [81] further divide felonies into degrees as well as provide for division of misdemeanors into classes.[82] These divisions provide for differing penalties for each degree or class of felony or misdemeanor. Under such penal codes the classification of offenses is by designation, such as: "Manslaughter is a Class C felony." "Criminally negligent homicide is a Class A misdemeanor." [83] In jurisdictions adopting this scheme wide variations in penalties may exist between degrees of felonies and classes of misdemeanors.

It is not uncommon for a statute dealing with a certain offense to specify that whoever violates its provisions is guilty of a felony, or is guilty of a misdemeanor.[84] The customary purpose of such a stipulation today (although it has not always been true) is to take advantage of a general penalty clause.

There are offenses under the statutes of some states that may be given a different classification. It is not uncommon, for example, to have a penalty-clause in some such form as "punishable by imprisonment in the county jail for not more than one year or in the state prison for not more than 10 years." [85] If the statute contained only one of these alternatives the first would make the offense a misdemeanor and the second would make it a felony. With both it would still be a felony if there was no qualification to the definition given above. The modern trend, however, is to provide a different answer by a qualifying clause such as: "When a crime is punishable, in the

---

78. West's Ann.Cal.Pen.Code § 17 (1970).

79. 18 U.S.C.A. §§ 1, 1(2) (1969).

80. § 6.01 The Code divides felonies into the three degrees.

The ABA Project on Standards for Criminal Justice, Standards Relating to Sentencing Alternatives and Procedures § 2.1(a) provides:

"All crimes should be classified for the purpose of sentencing into categories which reflect substantial differences in gravity. The categories should be very few in number. Each should specify the sentencing alternatives available for offenses which fall within it."

81. Ark.Stats. § 41–112 (1977); McKinney's Consol. Law of New York, § 55.05(1) (1975); Vernon's Tex.Code Ann. § 12.04 (1974).

82. Ark.Stats. § 41–113 (1977); McKinney's Consol. Law of New York § 55.05(2) (1975); Vernon's Tex.Code Ann. §§ 12.21–23 (1974).

83. Alabama Code, § 13A–6–4 (1979).

84. "Where an act is declared to be a public offense, crime or misdemeanor, but no other designation is given, such act shall be a simple misdemeanor." Iowa Code Ann. § 701.8 (1978).

85. West's Ann.Cal.Pen.Code § 489 (1970) (Grand Theft).

In California a public offense which may be either a felony or a misdemeanor is called a "Wobbler." People v. Municipal Court of City and County of San Francisco, 88 Cal.App.3d 206, 151 Cal.Rptr. 861 (1979).

discretion of the court, by imprisonment in the state prison or by fine or imprisonment in the county jail, it is a misdemeanor for all purposes under the following circumstances: After a judgment imposing a punishment other than imprisonment in the state prison." [86] Needless to say, for purposes of the original arrest, or any other purpose prior to judgment, the question whether the offense is felony or misdemeanor cannot depend upon the sentence that may be pronounced at a later time.[87] For such a purpose the probable cause determines the class of offense. But whether a defendant "has been convicted" of felony or misdemeanor depends upon the judgment rendered in such a case.

Since this permits a different classification for such an offense the label felony-misdemeanor [88] may be employed. Where this type of statutory change has been made the classification of crimes may be as follows:

I Felony

II Felony-misdemeanor

III Misdemeanor

Since the felony-misdemeanor designation is appropriate in some jurisdictions only, it is not employed in the pages after this section.

3. WITH REFERENCE TO PROCEDURE

For procedural purposes the field is often divided into (1) major crimes and (2) petty offenses.

Although no such division was known to the English common law, it was brought into existence by early statutes.[89] The common-law requirement of having the prosecution for every offense instituted by a grand-jury indictment (or its equivalent),[90] and conducted in the form of a trial by a petit jury, resulted in delay, expense and inconvenience, the inconvenience affecting jurors as well as defendants. It was not deemed necessary to use this cumber-

---

86. Id. at § 17(b)(1). "When the court grants probation to a defendant without imposition of sentence and at the time of granting probation, or on application of the defendant or probation officer thereafter, the court declares the offense to be a misdemeanor.

"When the prosecuting attorney files in a court having jurisdiction over misdemeanor offenses a complaint specifying that the offense is a misdemeanor, unless the defendant at the time of his arraignment or plea objects to the offense being made a misdemeanor, in which event the complaint shall be amended to charge the felony and the case shall proceed on the felony complaint.

"When, at or before the preliminary examination or prior to filing an order pursuant to Section 872, the magistrate determines that the offense is a misdemeanor, in which event the case shall proceed as if the defendant had been arraigned on a misdemeanor complaint.

"When a defendant is committed to the Youth Authority for a crime punishable, in the discretion of the court, by imprisonment in the state prison or by fine or imprisonment in the county jail, the offense shall, upon the discharge of the defendant from the Youth Authority, thereafter be deemed a misdemeanor for all purposes." See People v. Esparza, 253 Cal.App.2d 362, 61 Cal.Rptr. 167 (1967).

87. State v. Amey, 7 Ariz.App. 59, 436 P.2d 153 (1968). See In re Gutierrez, 82 Ariz. 21, 307 P.2d 914 (1957).

88. This is the term adopted by Witkin in his California Crimes § 40 (1963).

89. 4 Bl.Comm. *280.

90. The formal accusation might be by "*presentment* or *indictment*" by the grand jury, id. at *301, or by information, id. at *308–9. At common law the information was permitted in special cases only and was filed usually by the attorney general.

some machinery for the prosecution of "every minute offence," [91] and statutes were passed providing for summary proceedings in many such cases. This procedure was recognized by the colonists before the Revolution and became an accepted part of the common law in this country. Although the Supreme Court has held the right to trial by jury to be a fundamental right,[92] applicable to federal prosecutions as well as state, there is no federal constitutional right to trial by jury in petty offense cases.[93] Some states have broadly provided for jury trial in their constitutions or by statutes which are applied in petty offense cases.[94] In other instances, state courts have denied the right to a jury trial in petty offense cases.[95]

The dividing line might have been that previously mentioned between offenses *mala in se* and offenses *mala prohibita*. A Supreme Court opinion written half a century ago indicates a grouping in the direction of such a division. The prosecution was for receiving unstamped oleomargarine for sale. The law required that oleomargarine received for sale should be stamped to disclose its nature and imposed a fine of $50 for a violation. This was a clear case of something "commanded by statute but not otherwise wrong." It was without doubt a "petty offense," and equally without doubt it was an offense *malum prohibitum*. The defendant had been convicted in a trial without a jury and the question was whether this violated the third clause of section 2, Article III, of the Constitution, which provides that "the trial of all crimes, except in cases of impeachment, shall be by jury;" and the provision of the Sixth Amendment that "in all criminal prosecutions the accused shall enjoy the right to a speedy and public trial by an impartial jury. . . ." After referring to the fact that the original draft of Article III had spoken of "the trial of all criminal offenses," which was changed by unanimous vote to read "the trial of all crimes," the court said:

"If the language had remained 'criminal offenses', it might have been contended that it meant all offenses of a criminal nature, petty as well as serious, but when the change was made from 'criminal offenses' to 'crimes', and made in the light of the popular understanding of the meaning of the word 'crimes', . . . it is obvious that the intent was to exclude from the constitutional requirement of a jury the trial of petty criminal offenses. . . . In Callan v. Wilson, 127 U.S. 540, 8 S.Ct. 1301, reference was made to many decisions of state courts, holding that the trial of petty of-

---

91. Id. at *281.

92. Duncan v. Louisiana, 391 U.S. 145, 88 S.Ct. 1444 (1968). U.S. Const. art. III, § 2, cl. 3, "The Trial of all Crimes, except in Cases of Impeachment, shall be by Jury; . . ." U.S.Const. Amend. VI, "In all criminal prosecutions, the accused shall enjoy the right to a speedy and public trial, by an impartial jury . . ."

93. Cheff v. Schnackenberg, 384 U.S. 373, 86 S.Ct. 1523 (1966); Dyke v. Taylor Implement Manufacturing Co., 391 U.S. 216, 88 S.Ct. 1472 (1968). For the purposes of the right to jury trial a petty offense is one punishable by imprisonment for six months or less. Bloom v. Illinois, 391 U.S. 194, 88 S.Ct. 1477 (1968); Baldwin v. New York, 399 U.S. 66, 90 S.Ct. 1886 (1970); Frankfurter & Corcoran, Petty Federal Offenses and the Constitutional Guaranty of Trial by Jury, 39 Harv.L.Rev. 917 (1926).

94. Mills v. Municipal Court for San Diego Judicial District, 10 Cal.3d 288, 110 Cal.Rptr. 329, 515 P.2d 273 (1973); State v. Sklar, 317 A.2d 160 (Me.1974); State v. Jackson, 78 N.M. 29, 427 P.2d 46 (1967).

95. Goldman v. Kautz, 111 Ariz. 431, 531 P.2d 1138 (1975).

fenses was not within any constitutional provision requiring a jury in the trial of crimes. . . ."[96]

The Supreme Court has also stated that petty offenses carry "trivial penalties" and do not justify a jury trial.[97] Although there has been some suggestion that petty offenses might not be regarded as criminal, the Court later observed:

"Of necessity, the task of drawing a line 'requires attaching different consequences to events which, when they lie near the line, actually differ very little.' Duncan v. Louisiana, supra, at 161, 88 S.Ct. at 1453. One who is threatened with the possibility of imprisonment for six months may find little difference between the potential consequences that face him, and the consequences that faced appellant here. Indeed, the prospect of imprisonment for however short a time will seldom be viewed by the accused as a trivial or 'petty' matter and may well result in quite serious repercussions affecting his career and his reputation. Where the accused cannot possibly face more than six months' imprisonment, we have held that these disadvantages, onerous though they may be, may be outweighed by the benefits that result from speedy and inexpensive non-jury adjudications. We cannot, however, conclude that these administrative conveniences, in light of the practices that now exist in every one of the 50 States as well as in the federal courts, can similarly justify denying an accused the important right to trial by jury where the possible penalty exceeds six months' imprisonment."[98] It must be concluded that the Court regards petty offenses as criminal, but for historical and administrative purposes the same constitutional safeguards and other procedures extended to a defendant in other criminal cases are not deemed applicable to petty offenses.[99]

Despite the use of the phrase "petty criminal offenses" and this position expressed by the Supreme Court, we find here an apparent implication that a "petty offense" is not a "crime."[1] Much could be said for such a position but it is not the law at the present time. In the federal penal code, for example, it is provided that any misdemeanor "the penalty for which does not exceed imprisonment for a period of six months or a fine of not more than $500, or both, is a petty offense."[2] In Iowa, offenses are classified into felonies and misdemeanors,[3] but misdemeanors are classified into aggravated, serious, or simple misdemeanors.[4] Offenses of the latter class are pun-

---

96. Schick v. United States, 195 U.S. 65, 70, 24 S.Ct. 826, 827 (1904). The defendant had waived the jury but at the time of this case it was assumed that a jury could not be waived in a trial for a "crime." It was not until much later that the possibility of waiver in such a case was clearly recognized by the Supreme Court. Patton v. United States, 281 U.S. 276, 50 S.Ct. 253 (1930).

97. Cheff v. Schnackenberg, 384 U.S. 373, 399, 86 S.Ct. 1523, 1526 (1966).

98. Baldwin v. New York, 399 U.S. 66, 73, 90 S.Ct. 1886, 1890–91 (1970).

99. Grand jury indictment is not required and prosecution is often in a court of lesser jurisdiction. In the federal sys-

tem, prosecution may be had before a magistrate, 18 U.S.C.A. § 3401 (1979) and may proceed on complaint or citation, Rule 3, Federal Rules of Procedure, for the Trial of Minor Offenses Before United States Magistrates.

1. In New Jersey, prosecutions for drunken driving are not crimes. They are considered quasi criminal in nature. State v. Roth, 154 N.J.Super. 363, 381 A.2d 406 (1977).

2. 18 U.S.C.A. § 1(3) (1969).

3. Iowa Code Ann. §§ 701.7 and 701.8 (1978).

4. Id. § 701.8.

ishable by "imprisonment not to exceed thirty days, or a fine not to exceed one hundred dollars." [5]   This classification of offense includes fraudulent practices,[6] theft not exceeding fifty dollars,[7] and assault [8] (if without intent to inflict serious injury).[9]   In Pennsylvania, an offense category of summary offenses has been created [10] which encompasses some bad check offenses.[11] Thus, true crimes offenses *mala in se* are included within these classifications.

Under federal law, a United States magistrate may exercise jurisdiction over misdemeanor offenses when specially designated by the district court.[12] Cases prosecutable as misdemeanor offenses would include assault [13] and theft of less than one hundred dollars [14] and are triable under rules of procedure for misdemeanor offenses.[15]   The category of offenses known as infractions or violations also have some procedural distinctions over other classes of offenses.[16]   The right to counsel applicable in other criminal federal constitutional cases may not be applicable in the case of minor petty offenses.[17]

Hence under this classification scheme which, as suggested above, is important primarily for purposes of procedure, we have:

I Major crimes

   A Felony

   (B Felony-misdemeanor)

   C Misdemeanor

II Minor offenses

   A Misdemeanors

   B Infractions, and other summary and petty offenses

4.   WITH REFERENCE TO THE DEATH SENTENCE

A division which has received greatly enhanced attention in recent times is between capital and noncapital offenses.

According to the polls, in the opinion of the majority of the people in this country capital punishment should be retained, whereas a substantial minority are convinced that it should be abolished.   The dispute has been bitter, and has generated more heat than light.   Neither side has been able to con-

---

5. Id. § 903.1.

6. Id. § 714.13.

7. Id. § 714.2.

8. Id. § 708.1.

9. Id. § 708.2.

10. 18   Purdon's   Consol.Stat.Ann. § 106(c) (1973).

11. Id. § 4105.

12. 18 U.S.C.A. § 3401 (1979).

13. 18 U.S.C.A. § 113 (1969).

14. 18 U.S.C.A. § 641 (1976).

15. Rule of Procedure for the Trial of Misdemeanor Offenses Before United States Magistrates, 18 U.S.C.A. effective June 1, 1980.

16. The proposed codification and revision of the federal penal code classifies the offense of infraction as non-criminal. S. 1437 § 111, 95th Cong. 1st Sess.

17. Argersinger v. Hamlin, 407 U.S. 25, 92 S.Ct. 2006 (1972) extended the constitutional right to counsel under the Sixth and Fourteenth Amendments to all criminal prosecutions that actually result in imprisonment. An accused may waive his right to counsel in a criminal case and proceed to trial pro se, Faretta v. California, 422 U.S. 806, 95 S.Ct. 2525 (1975).

vince the other. In *Furman*,[18] for the first time, the Supreme Court was confronted with the claim that the punishment of death always, regardless of the enormity of the offense, or the procedure followed in imposing the sentence, is cruel and unusual punishment in violation of the Constitution. The Court disposed of that case without reaching this issue. Of the Justices, four indicated that capital punishment was not unconstitutional per se; two suggested the opposite conclusion; and three held that it was sufficient for the case at hand to hold that the statutes then before the Court, *as applied*, were invalid.

After *Furman*, because of similarities involved, it was widely assumed that the death sentence in most, if not all, the jurisdictions, was unconstitutional.[19] Several states, after the Supreme Court's decision in *Furman*, re-enacted their death penalty provisions to meet the objections voiced by some members of the Court in *Furman*. A majority of the states enacted new statutes in the effort to make provision for capital punishment which could survive a constitutional attack. Many of the new statutes provided the sentence of death for certain offenses other than murder, but the first test dealt only with this provision for murder. The statutes were of two types. One type provided that the penalty for murder should be either death or imprisonment for life, with a separate hearing after the establishment of guilt to determine which the sentence should be. In this hearing the jury (or judge) is to hear additional evidence in extenuation, mitigation or aggravation, and make the determination of punishment under the direction of carefully worded guidelines. In cases coming before the Court under this type of statute, the answer to the basic claim was that capital punishment is not per se unconstitutional, and that the specific statutes were valid.[20] The other type of statute, providing for the mandatory sentence of death for first-degree murder was held to be unconstitutional, with four justices dissenting.[21]

The answer to the basic question was overwhelming. The justices voted seven to two that capital punishment is not per se unconstitutional.[22] In reaching this result, they split three ways: four, three and two. Assuming a properly drawn statute on murder, four would uphold it even if the death sentence was mandatory; three would not do this, but would uphold the statute if it provided for either the death sentence or life imprisonment with appropriate guidelines to be used in making the determination; two would hold any provision for the death sentence unconstitutional. Based on these positions, a murder statute which is proper in other respects, if it provides

18. Furman v. Georgia, 408 U.S. 238, 92 S.Ct. 2726 (1972).

19. E.g., the Florida court held that the existing Florida death-penalty statutes were inconsistent with *Furman* and void. Donaldson v. Sack, 265 So.2d 499 (Fla.1972).

20. Gregg v. Georgia, 428 U.S. 153, 96 S.Ct. 2909, 2971 (1976); Proffitt v. Florida, 428 U.S. 242, 96 S.Ct. 2960 (1976); Jurek v. Texas, 428 U.S. 262, 96 S.Ct. 2950 (1976).

Ceja was convicted on two counts of first-degree murder and sentenced to death. As a result of the aggravation and mitigation hearing it was found as an aggravating circumstance that the murders were committed in an especially cruel, heinous or depraved manner, and no mitigating circumstance had been found. It was held that the death-penalty statute was valid and that the sentence was properly imposed. State v. Ceja, 115 Ariz. 413, 565 P.2d 1274 (1977).

21. Roberts v. Louisiana, 428 U.S. 325, 96 S.Ct. 3001 (1976); Woodson v. North Carolina, 428 U.S. 280, 96 S.Ct. 2978 (1976).

22. See cases n. 20.

for either death or imprisonment for life with proper guidelines, would be upheld. If the statute calls for a mandatory death sentence, it is unconstitutional.[23]

These cases, it should be emphasized, are neither for nor against capital punishment. While seven of the justices held that capital punishment is permissible under the Constitution, in a proper case, it was emphasized that whether is should or should not be authorized involves a policy judgment that should be exercised by the legislative branch of the government, not by the courts.

The first case to come before the Court under a new statute providing the death sentence for a crime other than murder, involved rape. In a Georgia case Coker was convicted of rape, and other offenses, and sentenced to death on the rape charge when the jury found two of the aggravating circumstances present for imposing such a sentence; that is, that the rape was committed (1) by a person with prior capital-felony convictions, and (2) in the course of committing another capital felony, armed robbery. The Georgia Supreme Court affirmed both the conviction and the sentence, but the judgment upholding the death sentence was reversed.[24] There was no opinion of the Court, but the line-up of the Justices indicates that the Court will hold that capital punishment is always, regardless of circumstances, a disproportionate penalty for the crime of rape. Powell, J., points out that not so much is involved in the case, and expresses the hope that the Court might uphold a statute providing the death penalty for rape if the jury found it was an outrageous rape,[25] resulting in serious and lasting harm to the victim.[26]

5. WITH REFERENCE TO INFAMY

Another dichotomy in crime classification is based upon the concept of infamy and divides the field into (1) Infamous crimes, and (2) Noninfamous crimes.

At common law an infamous crime rendered the person convicted thereof incompetent as a witness.[27] Untrustworthiness was originally the basic idea of infamy, and the disqualification was imposed to prevent the introduction

23. A statute providing a mandatory death sentence for the intentional murder of a peace officer who is performing his official duties, violates the Constitution by providing cruel and unusual punishment. Roberts v. Louisiana, 431 U.S. 633, 97 S.Ct. 1993 (1977).

No doubt the Court would uphold a first-degree-murder statute providing for either death or imprisonment for life, with appropriate guidelines for the determination, including the intentional killing of a peace officer who was performing his official duties as one circumstance of aggravation which might justify the death sentence. But to insure acceptance such a statute must avoid making the death sentence mandatory upon the finding of this circumstance.

24. Coker v. Georgia, 433 U.S. 584, 97 S.Ct. 2861 (1977).

Coker induced one writer to conclude that the Court has taken the position that as "a first principle of morality in law—society may not take the life of a defendant who has not taken the life of his victim." The Supreme Court, 1976 Term, 91 Harv.L.R. 70, 125 (1977). It should be added that the Court itself has not said so.

25. The Mississippi Supreme Court ruled the death penalty constitutional in the case of a rape of a child under 12. Upshaw v. State, 350 So.2d 1358 (Miss.1977).

26. See generally, Davis, The Death Penalty and The Current State of The Law, 14 Cr.L.Bull. 7 (1978); Goldberg, The Death Penalty for Rape, 5 Hast.C.L.Q. 1 (1978).

27. O'Connell v. Dow, 182 Mass. 541, 547, 66 N.E. 788, 790 (1903); People v.

of evidence thought not entitled to credence, rather than as an additional penalty. It was more likely to harm another than the one disqualified, because it developed side by side with the rule that a party to the suit or one interested in the outcome was not a competent witness in the case.[28] The starting point seems to have been the so-called *crimen falsi*,[29]—crime of falsifying. In the beginning, perhaps, one convicted of perjury was deemed too untrustworthy to be permitted to testify in any other case, and the idea grew until the term *"crimen falsi"* included any crime involving an element of deceit, fraud or corruption.[30]

" 'The term [crimen falsi] involves the element of falsehood, and includes everything which has a tendency to injuriously affect the administration of justice by the introduction of falsehood and fraud.' . . . It has been held to include, also, forgery, perjury, subornation of perjury, suppression of testimony by bribery or conspiracy to procure the absence of a witness, barratry, the fraudulent making or alteration of a writing to the prejudice of another man's right." [31]

The reason for distrusting a person found guilty of such an offense is obvious. A traitor is even less entitled to credence. The extension of the same disqualification to a felon seems to have its origin in the concept of increased penalty rather than that of untrustworthiness. In the words of Blackstone:

"When sentence of death, the most terrible and highest judgment in the laws of England, is pronounced, the immediate inseparable consequence from the common law is *attainder*. For when it is now clear beyond all dispute that the criminal is no longer fit to live upon the earth, but is to be exterminated as a monster and a bane to human society, the law sets a note of infamy upon him, puts him out of its protection, and takes no further care of him than barely to see him executed. He is then called attaint, *attinctus*, stained or blackened. He is no longer of any credit or reputation; he cannot be a witness in any court; he is no longer capable of performing the functions of another man; for, by an anticipation of his punishment, he is already dead in law." [32]

Parr, 4 N.Y.Cr. 545, 546 (1886); State v. Nolan, 15 R.I. 529, 530, 10 A. 481, 482 (1887); Cross on Evidence, 4th Ed., p. 145.

28. "All witness, of whatever religion or country, that have the use of their reason, are to be received and examined, except such as are *infamous*, or such as are *interested* in the event of the cause." 3 Bl.Comm. * 369. See also 2 Wigmore on Evidence §§ 520, 575 (3d ed. 1940).

29. Drazen v. New Haven Taxicab Co., 95 Conn. 500, 504, 111 A. 861, 862 (1920); Commonwealth v. Jones, 334 Pa. 321, 323, 5 A.2d 804, 805 (1939); Commonwealth v. Mueller, 153 Pa.Super. 524, 34 A.2d 321 (1943).

30. Ibid. "And from these decisions it may be deduced, that the 'crimen falsi' of the Common Law not only involves the charge of falsehood, but also is one which may injuriously affect the administration of justice, by the introduction of falsehood and fraud." 2 Wigmore on Evidence § 520 (3d ed. 1940).

31. Commonwealth v. Jones, 334 Pa. 321, 323, 5 A.2d 804, 805 (1939); "The specific contours of *crimen falsi* are uncertain. *Crimen falsi* describes crimes involving, or at least relating to, communicative, often verbal, dishonesty; we have said that they are 'crimes which touch the question of the honesty of the witness.' " Government of Virgin Islands v. Toto, 529 F.2d 278, 281 (3d Cir. 1976).

32. 4 Bl.Comm. * 380.

Three comments are in order. (1) At this point in the development of the common law the infamous crimes are treason, felony and the *crimen falsi*; [33] (2) we have in Blackstone's statement at least the basis for the suggestion that infamy depends upon the punishment inflicted, whereas originally it depended upon the nature of the crime committed; [34] and (3) we have the additional suggestion of the so-called "civil death." [35]

Testimonial disqualification because of infamous conviction has disappeared as a result of modern legislation[36] or court decision.[37] Such conviction may affect the credibility of the witness but today, it does not exclude the witness from the stand.[38] The ancient rule disqualifying a witness, however, has been replaced by the rule allowing the conviction of a witness for certain crimes to be used to attack the credibility of a witness.[39] Disqualifications

---

33. "At common law crimes which rendered the person doing them infamous were treason, felony and the *crimen falsi*, . . ." In re Westenberg, 167 Cal. 309, 319, 139 P. 674, 679 (1914). "Infamous crimes at common law were treason, felony, and the *crimen falsi*." Drazen v. New Haven Taxicab Co., 95 Conn. 500, 504, 111 A. 861, 862 (1920). And see Barker v. People, 4 Johns.Ch. 457, 460 (N.Y.1823); 2 Wigmore on Evidence § 520 (3d ed. 1940).

34. Blackstone's suggestion was not the first. Hale said persons who "have stood upon the pillory" were incompetent as witnesses, "for they are thereby infamous." 2 Hale P.C. * 277.

"The crime and not the punishment renders the offender infamous according to the common law." State v. Cram, 84 Me. 271, 273, 24 A. 853 (1892). See also Drazen v. New Haven Taxicab Co., 95 Conn. 500, 504, 111 A. 861, 862 (1920).

35. "*Civil death* is the state of a person who, though possessing natural life, has lost all his civil rights, and as to them, is considered as dead." Bouvier's Law Dictionary. "The statute of the 29th of *March*, 1799, enacted, that in all cases where any person should be duly convicted or attainted of any felony, *thereafter* to be committed, and adjudged to imprisonment for life, in the state prison, he should be deemed and taken to be civilly dead, to all intents and purposes, in the law." Platner v. Sherwood, 6 Johns.Ch. 118, 127–8 (1822). The concept seems to have had its origin in another field. "In one large department of law the fiction [civil death] is elegantly maintained. A monk or nun can not acquire or have any proprietary rights. When a man becomes 'professed in religion;' his heir at once inherits from him any land that he has, and, if he has made a will, it

takes effect at once as though he were naturally dead." 1 Pollock & Maitland, History of English Law 434 (2d ed. 1899).

36. The disqualification has generally been abolished by statute. 3 Weinstein and Berger, Weinstein's Evidence, p. 601–16 (1977); 2 Wigmore on Evidence § 519 (3d ed. 1940). And see People v. Parr, 4 N.Y.Cr. 545, 546 (1886).

37. The Supreme Court has ruled unconstitutional a statute which precluded a co-defendant from testifying on behalf of a defendant. Washington v. Texas, 388 U.S. 14, 87 S.Ct. 1920 (1967).

38. See People v. Parr, 4 N.Y.Cr. 545, 546 (1886); Rosen v. United States, 245 U.S. 467, 38 S.Ct. 148 (1918); State v. Bezemer, 169 Wash. 559, 571, 14 P.2d 460, 464–465 (1932); 2 Wigmore on Evidence § 519 (3d ed. 1940); Rule 601, Federal Rules of Evidence. For so many generations the witness *stood* in a special enclosure, provided for that purpose, that the phrase "witness stand" came to mean the place from which witnesses are to give their testimony. "Take the stand" means for the one so directed to go to such place.

39. "For the purpose of attacking the credibility of a witness, evidence that he has been convicted of a crime shall be admitted if elicited from him or established by public record during cross-examination but only if the crime (1) was punishable by death or imprisonment in excess of one year under the law under which he was convicted, and the court determines that the probative value of admitting this evidence outweighs its prejudicial effect to the defendant, or (2) involved dishonesty or false statement, regardless of the punishment." Rule 609, Federal Rules of Evidence, 28 U.S.C.A. (1975)

for conviction of crime would be constitutionally suspect.[40] Because of this transformation the phrase "infamous crime" would be of no more than historical interest now, in most jurisdictions, had it not been written into the Fifth Amendment and into certain state constitutional and statutory provisions. Where found in the modern written law its consequence is usually quite different from that of the common law. The Fifth Amendment, for example, reads:

"No person shall be held to answer for a capital, or otherwise infamous crime, unless on a presentment or indictment of a grand jury, except in cases arising in the land or naval forces, or in the militia, when in actual service in time of war or public danger; . . . ."

Some of the state provisions are similar to this; [41] others are perhaps echoes of the ancient rule that pronouncement of the sentence of death resulted instantly in "civil death." [42] "Civil death," it should be emphasized, was not a consequence of infamy, as such, at common law; but Blackstone, in referring to one under sentence of death as "already dead in law," had commented that "the law sets a note of infamy upon him." [43] This seems to suggest "civil death" as a consequence of infamy under such circumstances although not otherwise. The doctrine of "civil death" seems not have been accepted as a part of the common law in this country,[44] but statutes in several jurisdictions have provided that one serving a life sentence shall be deemed "civilly dead." [45] The trend today is to repeal or amend statutes that provided for civil death although some remain on the statute books.[46] Civil incapacitation statutes do not use the phrase "infamous crime" and hence raise no problem

40. Washington v. Texas, 388 U.S. 14, 87 S.Ct. 1920 (1967); A prohibition against sworn testimony by a defendant was held to violate the Fourteenth Amendment in Ferguson v. Georgia, 365 U.S. 570, 81 S.Ct. 756 (1961).

41. Smith-Hurd Ill.Ann.Stat.Const. art. 1 § 7 (1961), People ex rel. Akin v. Kipley, 171 Ill. 44, 73, 49 N.E. 229, 239 (1898); Me.Rev.Stat.Ann.Const. art. 1 § 7 (1964), State v. Cram, 84 Me. 271, 274, 24 A. 853, 854 (1892); R.I.Const.Amend. art. 40 § 1, State v. Nolan, 15 R.I. 529, 530, 10 A. 481, 482 (1887).

42. Blackstone emphasizes that it was not the verdict of the jury or the plea of guilty which made the prisoner "already dead in law." 4 Bl.Comm. *380. The reason is that between the verdict or plea and the sentence there is the allocution— the formal question put by the judge to the prisoner, asking him if he knows of any reason why sentence should not be pronounced. "Something may be offered in arrest of judgment; the indictment may be erroneous, which may render his guilt uncertain, and thereupon the present conviction may be quashed; he may obtain a pardon, or be allowed the benefit of clergy; . . . ." Id. at *381.

43. 4 Bl.Comm. *380.

44. In an early case Chancellor Kent said *obiter* that an early New York civil-death statute was declaratory of the common law. Troup v. Wood, 4 Johns.Ch. 228, 248 (1820). Two years later, after careful study of the matter, he expressly repudiated the statement. Platner v. Sherwood, 6 Johns.Ch. 118, 128–9 (1822).

45. Alaska Stats. 11.05.070, 11.05.080 (1962); Idaho Code § 18–310–311 (1978). § 11.05.080 of the Alaska Statutes provided:

"A person sentenced to imprisonment in the penitentiary for life is thereafter considered civilly dead."

The Statute codifies the English common law rule.

46. California's provisions on civil death were repealed and West's Ann.Cal.Pen.Code § 2600 (1970) now provides:

"A person sentenced to imprisonment in a state prison may, during any such period of confinement, be deprived of such rights, and only such rights, as is necessary in order to provide for the reasonable security of the institution in which he is confined and for the reasonable protection of the public."

as to its meaning; [47] but the term is found in certain constitutional or statutory provisions imposing some very limited disqualification, such as that no person convicted of an infamous crime "shall ever exercise the privileges of an elector in this State" [48] or "shall be eligible to a seat in the legislature." [49]

Had the three chief representatives of *crimen falsi*—perjury, subornation of perjury and forgery—remained misdemeanors as they were at common law, the nature of the offense committed would have been recognized clearly as at least one of the factors to be considered on the question of infamy. But all are quite generally felonies under modern statutes,[50] and the application of more severe penalties to these offenses may have given impetus to the suggestion that whether a crime is or is not infamous is determined solely by the punishment. The phraseology of the Fifth Amendment may also have had an influence in this direction. The key word there, in this regard, is not *"other"* but *"otherwise"*: "No person shall be held to answer for a capital, or otherwise infamous crime, unless on a presentment or indictment of a grand jury," and so forth. A possible implication is that just as punishability by death renders a crime infamous so also may certain other severe penalties.

Whatever the explanation, there has been unquestionably a trend in that direction. "The crime and not the punishment renders the offender infamous according to the common law," [51] but this is not the customary test used to interpret this phrase as it is found in the modern written law. In fact it has been stated flatly: "Whether a crime is infamous or not is not determined by the nature of the offense, but the punishment prescribed for such offense." [52]

In the determination of what is an "infamous crime," as the phrase is used in the Fifth Amendment, the federal courts were at first inclined to

---

47. For a discussion of the law of "civil death" see, The Collateral Consequences of a Criminal Conviction, 23 Vand.L.Rev. 929 (1970); Comment 29, So.Cal.L.Rev. 425 (1953); Rubin, Law of Criminal Correction, 2d Ed. ch. 17 § 3 (1973).

Civil disability statutes have recently come under constitutional attack. A local ordinance barring persons convicted of certain crimes from obtaining a chauffeur's license has been held to violate the equal protection guarantees of the XIVth Amendment. Miller v. Carter, 547 F.2d 1314 (7th Cir. 1977) aff'd by an equally divided court, 434 U.S. 356, 98 S.Ct. 786.

48. "No idiot, or insane person, or person convicted of any infamous crime, shall be entitled to the privileges of an elector." Constitution of Iowa, Art. II § 5.

Cf. Constitution of Indiana, Art. II § 8.

49. The ineligibility under the Arkansas Constitution is not restored by a subsequent pardon purporting to restore civil rights. Ridgeway v. Catlett, 238 Ark. 323, 379 S.W.2d 277 (1964).

50. E.g., 18 U.S.C.A. §§ 1621, 1622, 471 (1966); West's Ann.Cal.Pen.Code §§ 126, 127, 473 (1970).

The California forgery statute § 473 provides for an alternative period of imprisonment in the county jail for one year.

51. State v. Cram, 84 Me. 271, 273, 24 A. 853 (1892). This was unquestionably true of the *crimen falsi* which seems to have been the starting point of the infamous-crime concept. Drazen v. New Haven Taxicab Co., 95 Conn. 500, 504, 111 A. 861, 862 (1920). It may have been true also when treason was added to the list of infamous crimes. But when the whole field of felony was added also, the nature of the punishment became a second basis upon which infamy might be established.

See also Werdell v. Turzynski, 128 Ill.App.2d 139, 262 N.E.2d 833 (1969).

52. Briggs v. Board of Commissioners, 202 Okl. 684, 685, 217 P.2d 827 (1950).

consider the nature of the offense[53] but later tended to give consideration solely to the punishment provided therefor.[54]   And this is in line with the apparent trend.[55]   An extreme illustration of this trend is found in an Iowa case.[56]   The crime involved was forgery which was one of the chief representatives of *crimen falsi* and has been regarded as an offense infamous in its nature from earliest times.   This, however, was ignored by the court. "Any crime punishable by imprisonment in the penitentiary is an 'infamous crime,'" [57] said the court.   It then found that forgery was so punishable under the statutes, *for which reason* it was held to be infamous.

The determinant of infamy, it is often stated, is the potential penalty and not the punishment actually imposed.[58]   This, however, might well depend upon the purpose of the particular provision.   If, as in the Fifth Amendment, the restriction is that no one shall be required to stand trial for an infamous crime except upon a presentment or indictment by a grand jury,[59] the potential penalty is bound to control because the determination must be made in the early stages of the prosecution.   On the other hand, if the provision is that conviction of an infamous crime results in some special disqualification (and the crime is not infamous in its nature) there is no reason why the determinant should not be the punishment actually imposed.   This distinction, however, has not always been observed.   In one case for example, a policeman was held to have forfeited his office by conviction of an offense for which he could have been imprisoned in the penitentiary for two years although the penalty actually imposed was a fine of one hundred dollars.[60] Needless to say, if the purpose of the provision is to impose some disqualifi-

53.   United States v. Reilley, 20 F. 46 (C.C.Nev.1884).

54.   Ex parte Wilson, 114 U.S. 417, 5 S.Ct. 935 (1885); In re Claasen, 140 U.S. 200, 11 S.Ct. 735 (1891).

55.   See O'Connell v. Dow, 182 Mass. 541, 547, 66 N.E. 788, 790 (1903); State v. Cram, 84 Me. 271, 274, 24 A. 853 (1892); State ex rel. Anderson v. Fousek, 91 Mont. 448, 454, 8 P.2d 791, 793 (1932); People v. Parr, 4 N.Y.Cr. 545, 546 (1886); Briggs v. Board of Commissioners, 202 Okl. 684, 685, 217 P.2d 827 (1950); State v. Rezendes, 105 R.I. 483, 253 A.2d 233 (1969); State v. Payne, 6 Wash. 563, 570, 34 P. 317, 319 (1893); State v. Bezemer, 169 Wash. 559, 571, 14 P.2d 460, 464 (1932); Isaacs v. Board of Ballot Commissioners, 122 W.Va. 703, 705, 12 S.E.2d 510, 511 (1940).

56.   Blodgett v. Clarke, 177 Iowa 575, 159 N.W. 243 (1916).

57.   Id. at 578, 159 N.W. at 244.

58.   United States v. Moreland, 258 U.S. 433, 42 S.Ct. 368 (1922). "The question is whether the crime is one for which the statutes authorize the court to award an infamous punishment, not whether the punishment ultimately awarded is an infamous one." Ex parte Wilson, 114 U.S. 417, 426, 5 S.Ct. 935, 939 (1885).

59.   The Supreme Court has held an infamous crime for the purposes of the 5th Amendment right to grand jury indictment is one punishable by imprisonment in a penitentiary.   Green v. United States, 356 U.S. 165, 78 S.Ct. 632 (1958). Such an offense may be prosecuted by information if the defendant expressly waives the indictment, except that no waiver is permitted if the offense may be punished by death.   Federal Rules of Criminal Procedure, Rule 7(a), (b) 18 U.S.C.A. (1980).

60.   State ex rel. Anderson v. Fousek, 91 Mont. 448, 8 P.2d 791 (1932).

Anderson's conviction was in a federal case.   The court very properly held that the Montana statute was not limited to convictions in the Montana courts, but then unreasonably took the position that a conviction in some other court could result in forfeiture although a similar conviction in a Montana court would not. Forty years later *Anderson* was overruled, Melton v. Oleson, 165 Mont. 424, 530 P.2d 466 (1974).   The court determined that what was a felony for the purposes of Montana's voter disqualification law should be determined by Montana law which for such resolution looked to the sentence actually imposed.

cation as a result of conviction of an infamous crime, the actual sentence will control if the statute provides that the offense "shall be deemed a misdemeanor for all purposes after a judgment" imposing a sentence which would make the crime a misdemeanor if no higher penalty were permitted.[61]

The word "convicted" may require special attention in this regard. For example, the California Constitution at one time provided that " . . . no person convicted of any infamous crime, . . . shall ever exercise the privileges of an elector in this State . . . ."[62] Petitioner pleaded guilty to a felony. He was admitted to probation conditioned upon serving 90 days in jail. After serving this time in jail he withdrew his plea of guilty and entered a plea of not guilty, whereupon the cause was dismissed and the record expunged, as expressly authorized by statute.[63] The court held that he must be permitted to register as a voter because, while all felonies are infamous, he had not been "convicted" within the constitutional meaning of the word.[64] In another case, however, in which the order of probation included a pronouncement of judgment of conviction of felony and suspension of the execution of sentence, the defendant was held to be a convicted felon with the resulting disqualification.[65]

Whether it is potential penalty or actual sentence (depending upon the purpose of the particular provision) there has been a rather general agreement to the effect that if it is felony-punishment the offense is infamous.[66] Conversely, the trend seems clearly to be in the direction of holding that a

---

61. Cf. West's Ann.Cal.Pen.Code § 17(b)(1) (1970). However, even though an offense was characterized as a misdemeanor under California law, such offense could be classified as a felony for federal purposes by virtue of a controlling federal definition of felony, United States v. Houston, 547 F.2d 104 (9th Cir. 1977). A statute authorizing divorce if the spouse has been sentenced to an infamous punishment means the actual sentence and not the potential punishment. Hull v. Donze, 164 La. 199, 113 So. 816 (1927).

62. Art. II, § 1, Const. of California, Nov. 7, 1950 modified to exclude the provision on disqualification for conviction by infamous crime Nov. 7, 1972.

63. West's Ann.Cal.Pen.Code § 1203.-4 (1970).

64. Truchon v. Toomey, 116 Cal.App.2d 736, 254 P.2d 638 (1953). A petition for a hearing by the Supreme Court was denied. Id. at 116 Cal.App.2d 745, 254 P.2d 638.

A similar result was reached under a like provision at the time of the New York Constitution where a sentence on a felony offense was suspended without judgment. People v. Fabian, 192 N.Y. 443, 85 N.E. 672 (1908).

65. Stephens v. Toomey, 51 Cal.2d 864, 338 P.2d 182 (1959).

Conviction of a felony in federal court has been applied to a state provision denying the right to vote to one "convicted of a felonious or infamous crime" under New Mexico law when an appeal was pending. State ex rel. Chavez v. Evans, 79 N.M. 578, 446 P.2d 445 (1968). Person on probation for grand larceny has been "convicted" of infamous crime, Fonville v. McLaughlin, 270 A.2d 529 (Del. 1970).

66. See Thorm v. United States, 59 F.2d 419 (3d Cir. 1932); Truchon v. Toomey, 116 Cal.App. 736, 737, 254 P.2d 638, 639 (1953); Fonville v. McLaughlin, 270 A.2d 529 (Del. 1970); O'Connell v. Dow, 182 Mass. 541, 547, 66 N.E. 788, 790 (1903); State ex rel. Anderson v. Fousek, 91 Mont. 448, 454, 8 P.2d 791, 793 (1932); Briggs v. Board of Commissioners, 202 Okl. 684, 685, 217 P.2d 827 (1950); State v. Nolan, 15 R.I. 529, 531, 10 A. 481, 482 (1887); State v. Payne, 6 Wash. 563, 570, 34 P. 317, 319 (1893); State v. Bezemer, 169 Wash. 559, 571, 14 P.2d 460, 464 (1932). This conclusion is unavoidable if the premise is accepted that any felony-punishment is infamous. On the other hand, much may be said for the position that manslaughter is not an infamous crime. See State v. O'Shields, 163 S.C. 408, 413, 161 S.E. 692, 694 (1931).

misdemeanor is not an infamous crime unless it carries some unusual punishment of an infamous nature.[67]   Thus the Supreme Court has held that imprisonment at hard labor is an infamous punishment and makes the crime infamous even if it is a misdemeanor.[68]   So also, a crime is infamous if conviction results in a disqualification to hold office,[69] or to vote.[70]

Extreme emphasis upon punishment has tended to obscure, but has been unable to blot out completely, the original theory that the very nature of the offense itself may make it infamous.   As said by one court: "Crimes are infamous either by reason of their punishment or by reason of their nature." [71]   Unfortunately this problem also has been considered without reference to the purpose of the particular provision in which the phrase "infamous crime" is found.   If, as in the Fifth Amendment, the purpose is to provide certain safeguards for one prosecuted for an infamous crime, punishability may well be the sole determinant of infamy.   No one must be placed in jeopardy of such a punishment without the benefit of these safeguards, but they are not deemed necessary when only milder penalties are involved.   On the other hand, the nature of the offense cannot properly be disregarded if the purpose of the provision is to impose some special disqualification on one convicted of an "infamous crime."   In fact, for such a purpose the nature of the crime might well be held to be the sole determinant, and there is a trace of authority for such a position.

"But the fact that a crime is classified as a felony does not necessarily fix it as infamous.   A conviction of the crime of manslaughter does not disqualify one as a witness. . . .   On the other hand, a conviction of petit larceny is of the *crimen falsi*, rendering a witness incompetent to testify." [72]

---

67. Thorm v. United States, 59 F.2d 419 (3d Cir. 1932).   And see Falconi v. United States, 280 F. 766, 767 (6th Cir. 1922); State v. Payne, 6 Wash. 563, 570, 34 P. 317, 319 (1893).   Cf. Adams v. Elliott, 128 Fla. 79, 174 So. 731 (1937).

Where the punishment is imprisonment not to exceed a year [a misdemeanor—18 U.S.C.A. § 1] and not at hard labor, it is not infamous.   Wyman v. United States, 263 U.S. 14, 44 S.Ct. 10 (1923).

68. United States v. Moreland, 258 U.S. 433, 42 S.Ct. 368 (1922).   Hale had said that persons who had "stood upon the pillory" . . .   "are thereby infamous."   2 Hale P.C. * 277.

69. People ex rel. Akin v. Kipley, 171 Ill. 44, 73, 49 N.E. 229, 239 (1898); Baum v. State, 157 Ind. 282, 285, 61 N.E. 672, 673 (1901).   This was suggested in United States v. Waddell, 112 U.S. 76, 82, 5 S.Ct. 35, 38 (1884), and approved in Ex parte Wilson, 114 U.S. 417, 426, 5 S.Ct. 935, 939 (1885).   Cf. State ex rel. Stinger v. Kruger, 280 Mo. 293, 217 S.W. 310 (1919).

70. Perry v. Bingham, 265 Ky. 133, 95 S.W.2d 1099 (1936).   And see Baum v. State, 157 Ind. 282, 285, 61 N.E. 672, 673 (1901).

71. Matter of Application of Westenberg, 167 Cal. 309, 319, 139 P. 674, 679 (1914).   Quoted in Truchon v. Toomey, 116 Cal.App.2d 736, 737, 254 P.2d 638, 639 (1953).

72. State v. O'Shields, 163 S.C. 408, 413, 161 S.E. 692, 694 (1931).   And see State ex rel. Stinger v. Kruger, 280 Mo. 293, 306, 217 S.W. 310, 315 (1919).

The statute authorizing proof of former felony conviction to impeach a witness, uses the word "may" rather than "shall."   This leaves the court with discretion to exclude proof of prior felony convictions offered for impeachment. People v. Beagle, 6 Cal.3d 441, 99 Cal.Rptr. 313, 492 P.2d 1 (1972).   Reversal was ordered for failure to exclude evidence of prior convictions offered to impeach a defendant in People v. Antick, 15 Cal.3d 79, 123 Cal.Rptr. 475, 539 P.2d 43 (1975).

See also Rule 609(a)(1) Federal Rules of Evidence, 28 U.S.C.A.

Unquestionably sound as this position is, it had seemed about to disappear entirely, but recently there has been evidence of a partial swing toward the original significance of infamy. A former provision of the California Constitution contained a familiar provision that "no person convicted of any infamous crime . . . shall ever exercise the privileges of an elector in this State; . . ." [73] Acting under this provision the county registrar of voters refused to register O on the ground that he had been convicted of a violation of the federal Selective Service Act, which was a federal felony. In a suit to compel the registrar to register O as a voter the evidence was that O was a bona-fide conscientious objector who had pleaded guilty to the federal offense some 20 years before. The trial court upheld the refusal of the registrar and O appealed. In reversing the judgment the California Supreme Court took the position that the term "infamous crime" does not necessarily have the same meaning in all its applications. It recognized that for some purposes a felony is an infamous crime, but held that in regard to disfranchisement the term must be given a narrower meaning to make the California provision compatible with the requirements of the Fourteenth Amendment. It held in substance that the State has a proper interest in closing the voting privilege to persons convicted of crimes involving moral corruption and dishonesty, but not to persons convicted of felonies in which such an element is lacking. Hence the term "infamous crime" as used in this section of the California constitution must be limited to crimes involving moral corruption and dishonesty. As O's crime did not involve such an element he must be permitted to register as a voter. [74]

We shall probably see a tendency to return to the original meaning of "infamous crime" when the point in question is whether conviction results in some disadvantage in addition to the penalty specifically provided for the offense—such as forfeiture of office, or of the right to vote or hold office.

As punishments for various crimes unknown at common law are uncritically placed within a felony classification a construction of infamous crime along narrow lines or in accord with its original meaning is likely and appropriate where a conviction may result in serious loss of social or economic opportunity for an individual. [75]

6. WITH REFERENCE TO THE SOCIAL HARM CAUSED

Discussions of specific offenses usually make use of a classification based upon the type of social harm caused in each particular case. If it is personal harm the traditional label is "offense against the person" although this, in

---

73. Amended November 7, 1972 to remove the disqualification. Cal.Constitution Art. II § 1. A number of states have or have had similar provisions. 3 Crim.L.Bull. 404 (1967).

74. Otsuka v. Hite, 64 Cal.2d 596, 51 Cal.Rptr. 284, 414 P.2d 412 (1966). The constitutional determination in *Otsuka* was not fully accepted by the United States Supreme Court. It was later held in Richardson v. Ramirez, 418 U.S. 24, 94 S.Ct. 2655 (1974) that because of Amendment XIV § 2 disenfranchisement of convicted felons whose sentences had been served did not violate the equal protec-

tion clause of the United States Constitution.

Attacks on such a provision on the claim that it constitutes cruel and unusual punishment have been rejected on the ground that the disqualification is not a punishment but a nonpenal exercise of the power to regulate the franchise. Green v. Board of Elections of City of New York, 380 F.2d 445 (2d Cir. 1967). In this case *Otsuka* is cited and distinguished 2d at 452.

75. Cf. People v. Enlow, 135 Colo. 249, 310 P.2d 539 (1957).

reality, is but "shorthand" for "offense against the state in the form of harm to the person." [76] It is becoming increasingly common to add one or more penal clauses to statutes on many different subjects, but it is not feasible to include these in any ordinary discussion of specific offenses. If they were to be included it would be necessary to group most of them together under the label "other offenses," and probably it would be convenient to place all of them there. Ignoring them the classification based upon the type of social harm is usually in approximately this form:

I Offenses against the person.

II Offenses against the habitation.

III Offenses against property.

IV Offenses against morality and decency.

V Offenses against the public peace.

VI Offenses affecting the administration of governmental functions.

SECTION 2.   THE COMMON LAW

No discussion of the law of crimes can proceed far without reference to the "common law," as demonstrated by the preceding section. Hence it is important to have a clear understanding of this term. In one sense it is used to distinguish the science of jurisprudence prevailing in England and America from other great systems such as the Roman Law or the law of continental Europe ("civil law"). This is not, however, the usual signification of the phrase and it is not the meaning with which it is used in these pages. Other relatively rare uses might be mentioned, such as to denote that law which is common to the country as a whole in contradistinction to laws of purely local application, or to distinguish the law enforced by the state from the "canon law." As here used the "common law" has a meaning quite different from any of those suggested above.

Law has been said to be the sum total of the authoritative materials which guide and direct the judicial and administrative organs of the state in the performance of their official functions.[1]

Insofar as these materials are added to or changed at the present time it is chiefly by legislative enactment, although not entirely so as will be mentioned presently. The origin of these materials, however, in the early days of English life was by usage and custom. Needless to say a primitive people does not in the beginning enact an exhaustive and thoroughly integrated code of laws. By usage and custom certain rules come to be accepted both for settling ordinary disputes or controversies between man and man, and for dealing with those who commit misdeeds of a seriously antisocial nature.

---

76. And if it is a so-called "offense against property" the guilty party is prosecuted in the interest of the state and not in the interest of the individual whose property was involved. People v. Gilliam, 141 Cal.App.2d 824, 297 P.2d 468 (1956).

1. Dean Pound has pointed out that law is made up of three parts: (1) authoritative precepts (made up of rules, principles, conceptions and standards), (2) an authoritative technique, and (3) authoritative ideals. "There is a body of authoritative precepts, developed and applied by an authoritative technique in the light of authoritative traditional ideals." Pound, Justice According to Law 50 (1951).

"But the standards which guide prosecutors in the exercise of their discretion are as much a part of the law as the rules applied in court." Scott v. United States, 419 F.2d 264, 277 (D.C.Cir. 1969).

Hence there gradually develops a complicated set of rules, principles, concepts and standards which are enforced by the courts although they have never been adopted by any legislative enactment.

"As to general customs, or the common law, properly so called;" in the words of Blackstone, "this is that law, by which proceedings and determinations in the king's ordinary courts of justice are guided and directed. This, for the most part, settles the course in which lands descend by inheritance; the manner and form of acquiring and transferring property; the solemnities and obligation of contracts; the rules of expounding wills, deeds, and acts of parliament; the respective remedies of civil injuries; the several species of temporal offences, with the manner and degree of punishment; and an infinite number of minute particulars, which diffuse themselves as extensively as the ordinary distribution of common justice requires. . . . [A]ll these are doctrines that are not set down in any written statute or ordinance, but depend merely upon immemorial usage, that is, upon the common law, for their support." The authority of these doctrines, he tells us, "rests entirely upon general reception and usage; and the only method of proving, that this or that maxim is a rule of the common law, is by showing that it hath been always the custom to observe it." [2]

This, however pictures its beginning rather than its later stages. In its maturity the development of the common law is largely, if not wholly, the result of judicial decisions. Somehow, no one can say precisely how, certain principles came to be accepted as the law of the land. The judges held themselves bound to decide the cases which came before them according to those principles, and as new combinations of circumstances threw light on the way in which they operated, the principles were in such cases more and more fully developed and qualified.

In the course of time, the law developed in this manner was felt to be inadequate, or unsatisfactory for some other reason, and hence additions and changes were made by legislative enactment. And eventually these statutory additions or changes formed a large part of the total result. Legislation itself, however, became a new source of common-law growth. In cases applying the words of the statute to a multitude of widely varying factual situations, there came to be a body of authoritative material not found in the statutes themselves but only in the judicial decisions, and this also is regarded as a part of the common law. The concept of the common law, therefore, includes a wide span of activity encompassing several periods of growth and a variety of phases of legal development.

In brief, all of that part of the authoritative materials, used to guide and direct the judicial and administrative organs of the state in the performance of their official functions, which is not found in legislative enactment (or written constitution) is called the "common law" to distinguish it from the statutory law.

If, as is frequently the case, a statute merely restates some part of the common law, this is a matter of great importance because the words used in the statute may have a great body of common-law interpretation which does not appear in the enactment itself, but will be followed by the courts in deciding cases. All of this body of English law, except what was not properly applicable here because of different surroundings and conditions, was

2.   4 Bl.Comm. * 68.

brought to our shores by the colonists when they emigrated from England, and it became the starting point of our common law.[3] This included English statutes, as well as the English common law, although there are three views in regard to what statutes are included. (1) Dual basis. English statutes enacted prior to 1607, the "date of colonization" (other than those unsuited to conditions here), plus English statutes enacted after that date but prior to the Revolution which were generally accepted by the Colonies, became a part of our common law. (2) Single basis. Such English statutes as were enacted prior to the Revolution and had been generally recognized by the Colonies, and these only, became a part of our common law. (3) Specified by statute. A few states specified by legislation just what English statutes should be recognized here.[4]

This combined body of law is still common law in this country[5] except to the extent that it has been changed by statute or has been modified by the interpretations of our own courts. It is not the whole of our common law by any means. Courts are constantly required to pass upon new problems, partly due to changing social and economic conditions. They are required to declare what is the common law as applied to these new problems and in this way they make constant additions to the field. They are required also to interpret new statutes, and these interpretations (not being statutory themselves) become a part of the common law. Hence the common law is a constantly growing body of material. Actually each state is developing its own common law[6] and what is recognized as such in one state may not be recognized in another. When we speak as if there were one body of common law

3. "These statutes being passed before the emigration of our ancestors, being applicable to our situation, and in amendment of the law, constitute a part of our common law." Per Story, J., Patterson v. Winn, 5 Pet. 233, 241 (1831).

"The common law is all the statutory and case law background of England and the American colonies before the American Revolution." People v. Rehman, 253 Cal.App.2d 119, 150, 61 Cal.Rptr. 65, 85 (1967). This gives the general idea but requires qualification. A few provisions of the English law, such as those based upon feudalism, were never recognized in this country. On the other hand, the early English law, common and statutory, merely formed the starting point for the American common law. It has been developed by generations of judicial decision since the Revolution.

4. Utah Code Ann.1953, 68–3–1.

"The common law of England so far as it is not repugnant to, or in conflict with, the Constitution or laws of the United States, or the Constitution or laws of this state, and so far only as it is consistent with and adapted to the natural and physical conditions of this state and the necessities of the people hereof, is hereby adopted, and shall be the rule of decision in all courts of this state."

Some interesting discussions of this problem have been included in chapter four of Pound and Plucknett, Readings on the History and System of the Common Law (3d ed. 1927). As to Louisiana see note 12.

5. "The common law, except as modified by statute or unsuited to our local system or condition, is still in force in Arizona." Associated Students v. Arizona Board of Regents, 120 Ariz. 100, 584 P.2d 564, 567 (App.1978).

6. "Under the common law of Pennsylvania, . . ." Kenrich Corp. v. Miller, 377 F.2d 312, 314 (3d Cir. 1967). "The English common law, so far as it is reasonable in itself, suitable to the condition and business of our people, and consistent with the letter and spirit of our federal and state constitutions and statutes, has been and is followed by our courts, and may be said to constitute a part of the common law of Ohio." Bloom v. Richards, 2 Ohio St. 387, 390 (1853); State v. McElhinney, 88 Ohio App. 431, 433, 100 N.E.2d 273, 275 (1950). "Indeed, considering all these sources of unwritten and traditionary law, it is now more accurate, instead of the common law of England, which constitutes a part of it, to call it collectively the common law of Massachusetts." Per Chief Jus-

which applies to all the states we are in the area of comparative law rather than in that of specific law. But the general pattern tends to have so much more of similarity than of difference that we are accustomed to speak in terms of the common law of the country.

A question frequently asked is in regard to the appropriate tense to be used. Should the statement be: "The common law was . . ." or "the common law is . . ."? The answer depends upon the status of the rule or principle being considered. If the common law in point has been completely displaced or changed by modern statutes the past tense is appropriate, but otherwise the present tense should be used because the common law is still a living and growing body of jurisprudence.

Under the Constitution of the United States, as interpreted by the Supreme Court,[7] no misdeed is punishable by the federal courts merely because it was recognized as a common-law crime. This does not mean that there is no federal common law of crimes. Nothing is to be punished as a federal crime unless authority therefor can be found in some act of Congress,[8] but if Congress has declared some misdeed to be a crime and has provided a penalty therefor, the federal courts will resort to the common law in the interpretation and application of this statute. And if the statute makes use of the name of a common-law crime, without definition and without context indicating otherwise, the common-law definition will apply.[9]

The rule in some of the states is similar to the federal rule in this regard.[10] In other states the common-law crimes are punishable, as such, even

tice Shaw in Commonwealth v. Chapman, 54 Mass. 68, 69 (1847).

"The term common law, has reference not only to the ancient unwritten law of England, but also to that body of law created and preserved by the decisions of courts as distinguished from that created by the enactment of statutes by legislatures." Hogan v. State, 84 Nev. 372, 441 P.2d 620, 621 (1968).

"The common law of England has been by statute adopted as a rule of decision in this state. . . ." Goldsmith v. Cheney, 468 P.2d 813, 816 (Wyo.1970).

"The common law, followed in Oklahoma, refers not only to the ancient unwritten law of England, but also to that body of law created and preserved by decisions of courts. The common law is not static, but is a dynamic and growing thing and its rules arise from the application of reason to the changing conditions of society." McCormack v. Oklahoma Publishing Co., 613 P.2d 737, 740 (Okl.1980).

7. This was held in United States v. Hudson & Goodwin, 7 Cranch 32 (1812). A number of the justices were inclined to question the soundness of that decision, and when the problem came before them again four years later they were eager to have it argued. The Attorney General, however, declined to argue the case and

under these circumstances the court refused to overrule the earlier holding. United States v. Coolidge, 1 Wheat. 415 (1816). Hence the rule became established by default, so to speak.

8. United States v. Eaton, 144 U.S. 677, 12 S.Ct. 764 (1892); United States v. Berrigan, 482 F.2d 171 (3d Cir. 1973).

9. United States v. Turley, 352 U.S. 407, 77 S.Ct. 397 (1957); United States v. Dupree, 544 F.2d 1050 (9th Cir. 1976); Hite v. United States, 168 F.2d 973 (10th Cir. 1948); Boone v. United States, 235 F.2d 939 (4th Cir. 1956).

"Federal common law binds the states through the supremacy clause and is a law of first resort, subject to revisions by subsequent legislation." Jacobson v. Tahoe Regional Planning Agency, 558 F.2d 928, 937, note 14 (9th Cir. 1977).

"Although there are no common law offenses against the United States, it is a well established practice to give words their common law meanings where a federal criminal statute uses a common law term without defining it." United States v. Harold, 588 F.2d 1136, 1142 (5th Cir. 1979).

10. State v. Forsman, 260 N.W.2d 160 (Minn.1977); State v. Campbell, 217 Iowa

if not mentioned in the statutes.[11] The trend is away from the punishment of common law crimes not defined by statute.[12] The difference actually is very slight in practice. Most common-law offenses are included in the statutes of the several states (together with many additional crimes), but seldom if ever is the legislative explanation of such a crime so adequate as to enable the court to apply the statute without the aid of light thrown upon the offense by the common law. At times a statute merely specifies the penalty for an offense mentioned only by name, such as: "Any person who commits . . . voluntary manslaughter, shall be guilty of a felony. Voluntary manslaughter is punishable as a Class 5 felony." [13] Except as to the punishment, the court must rely as completely upon the common law of manslaughter as if no criminal statutes had ever been adopted in the state. Other statutes purport to define certain offenses, but many of these definitions are so general that they would be practically meaningless without elaborate common-law explanations of the words and phrases employed. For example:

"Murder defined. Murder is the unlawful killing of a human being or fetus with malice aforethought.

"Malice defined. Such malice may be express or implied. It is express when there is manifested a deliberate intention unlawfully to take away the life of a fellow-creature. It is implied, when no considerable provocation appears, or when the circumstances attending the killing show an abandoned and malignant heart." [14]

Centuries of judicial decisions give meaning to these words, which otherwise would be too uncertain to support a conviction.

In Louisiana, which started as a French settlement, the background was not the common law of England, but the "civil law." However, the common law of England was adopted as the basis of the criminal jurisprudence of that state by a statute passed in 1805.[15]

SECTION 3.   CRIMINAL JURISDICTION *

The word "jurisdiction" comes from *juris* (law) plus *dictio* (saying), the implication being an authoritative legal pronouncement. It may mean either

---

848, 251 N.W. 717 (1934); Mitchell v. State, 42 Ohio St. 383 (1884).

Common law crimes have not survived in this state, and unless certain conduct is singled out by a criminal statute it is not a crime no matter how reprehensible. State v. Bowling, 5 Ariz.App. 436, 427 P.2d 928 (1967).

11. State v. Egan, 287 So.2d 1 (Fla.1973); Pope v. State, 38 Md.App. 520, 382 A.2d 880 (1978).

12. Model Penal Code § 1.05(1) provides:

"No conduct constitutes an offense unless it is a crime or violation under this Code or another statute of this State."

§ 13A–1–4 Code of Alabama 1975; 18 Purdon's Consol.Stat.Ann. § 107 (1973); All crimes in Canada except contempt

have been codified, Criminal Code R.S.C. 1970 § 8(a).

13. Va.Code 1950, §§ 18.2–30, 18.2–35 (1975).

14. West's Ann.Cal.Pen.Code §§ 187, 188 (1970).

15. State v. Davis, 22 La.Ann. 77 (1870). The "statute of 1805, by which the Legislature of Louisiana adopted as the basis of the criminal jurisprudence the common law of England" is not affected by enactments of that kingdom subsequent to *that date.*

All crimes in Louisiana are statutory. State v. Heymann, 256 La. 18, 235 So.2d 78 (1970).

* By express permission the following was adapted from Perkins, The Territori-

(1) the power of a nation to declare what is the law, or (2) within the nation, the power of a particular court or agency to decide what the law is as applied to a particular case or situation. Jurisdiction is generally dealt with as a matter of procedure, which is beyond the scope of the present volume, but in the first sense, the power of a nation to declare what the law is, it is a matter of substantive law.

Using the term in the first sense, there are four [1] different theories of criminal jurisdiction, namely: (1) territorial, (2) Roman, (3) injured forum and (4) cosmopolitan. The territorial theory takes the position that criminal jurisdiction depends upon the place of perpetration. That is, a nation has the power to determine what the law is with reference to happenings within its own territory. It is a logical outgrowth of the conception of law enforcement as a means of keeping the peace. The perpetrator, rather than the place of perpetration, is the determinant under the Roman theory. A nation, in this view, has jurisdiction over its national wherever he may be, and can hold him accountable for his misdeed wherever committed. It is a logical outgrowth of the conception of law enforcement as a means of disciplining members of the tribe or clan. While sometimes referred to as the "personal" theory, the traditional label is "Roman" because this was the theory of the Roman law which held the Roman citizen accountable to it wherever he might be.

The injured forum theory places the emphasis upon the effect of the misdeed. A nation may take jurisdiction over any misdeed which has the effect of causing harm to it. Although the label was not used, this was the theory relied upon in *Hanks*,[2] which affirmed the conviction in Texas, of one who was not a Texan, for a forgery committed by him in Louisiana. Since the forged document purported to transfer title to Texas land, the court held that "(w)hen this forgery was committed in Louisiana, *eo instante* a crime was committed against, and injury done to, the State of Texas, because it affected title to lands within her sovereignty." [3] Whether or not the forged document ever reached Texas was considered so unimportant that it is not even mentioned in the opinion. As the court says the crime was committed when the false document was made.

The position of the cosmopolitan theory is that any nation has jurisdiction over any misdeed committed anywhere, by anyone. Needless to say no nation has ever assumed to exercise such jurisdiction to its full extent—or to any considerable extent. On the other hand, no nation ignores it entirely. While seldom mentioned by name, this theory is drawn upon to the extent

al Principle in Criminal Law, 22 Hastings L.J. 1155 (1971).

1. Some courts have listed five, designated as "territorial," "nationality," "protective," "universality" and "passive personality." Rivard v. United States, 375 F.2d 882, 885 (5th Cir. 1967); Rocha v. United States, 288 F.2d 545 (9th Cir. 1961); United States v. Rodriguez, 182 F.Supp. 479 (S.D.Cal.1960). In each case the classification was taken, directly or indirectly, from the Introductory Comment to a proposed Codification of International Law. See American Society of International Law, Jurisdiction With Respect to Crime (pt. 1), 29 Am.J.Int'l L., 443, 445 (Supp.1935). The so-called "passive personality" principle, based upon the nationality of the victim of the crime, was not included as a separate category in the Code itself. See id. at 579. It is unnecessary, being included within the "injured forum" category, designated therein as "protective."

2. Hanks v. State, 13 Tex.App. 289 (1882).

3. Id. at p. 309.

necessary to authorize any nation having actual control of a pirate, and evidence of his piracy, to convict him no matter who he may be, wherever his acts of piracy were committed, and without reference to who was harmed thereby.[4] It has been mentioned that it may be necessary to call upon the cosmopolitan theory to deal with certain other activities of so-called "international criminals" such as hijacking an airplane under such circumstances that the interests of more than one nation are involved.[5]

With one exception, these theories were never thought of as mutually exclusive. Rome did not hesitate to punish foreigners for crimes committed within its territory, and the same is true of nations whose law stems from the Roman. The exception was that the common law recognized only the territorial theory of criminal jurisdiction. The common-law judges did not hesitate to punish the pirate, wherever his piracy had been committed, but in doing so they were not applying the common law, but the law of nations.[6] And in deciding *Hanks*, it may be added, the court relied entirely upon a statute which expressly granted jurisdiction over the type of offense involved.

It would have been surprising if the common law had adopted any basis for criminal justice other than the territorial principle, because the beginning of our criminal justice in the troublous days of the dawn of civilization in the British Isles was concerned so exclusively with the keeping of the peace. This is evident from the old indictments which all concluded with some such phrase as "against the peace of the King." [7] And the territorial principle was in fact adopted by the English judges in those early days, was carried forward there and into this country, and became so firmly entrenched as to call forth the statement that "the general and almost universal rule is that the character of an act as lawful or unlawful must be determined wholly by the law of the country where the act is done." [8]

Not only did the common law regard the territorial theory of criminal jurisdiction as exclusive, but due to peculiarities in the common-law development of the theory,[9] it came to be accepted that each crime has a particular situs. In any case of difference, for example, homicide is committed, not at the place from which the killer started the fatal force, but where it impinged

---

4. "Pirates may, without doubt, be lawfully captured on the ocean by the public or private ships of every nation, for they are, in truth, the common enemies of all mankind, and, as such, are liable to the extreme rights of war." The Marianna Flora, 24 U.S. (11 Wheat.) 1, 40 (1826). Constitution of the United States, Art. I, § 8: 1. The Congress shall have power. . . . 10. To define and punish piracies and felonies committed on the high seas, and offenses against the law of nations.

5. Problems of Jurisdiction in The International Control and Repression of Terrorism, DeSchutter, International Terrorism and Political Crimes, Bassiouni, ed. 377, 383 (1975).

6. Bl.Comm. * 67, 69.

"Whoever, on the high seas, commits the crime of piracy as defined by the law of nations, and is afterwards brought into or found in the United States, shall be imprisoned for life." 18 U.S.C.A. § 1651.

7. "All offences are either against the King's peace, or his crown and dignity; and are so laid in every indictment." 1 Bl.Comm. * 268.

8. American Banana Co. v. United Fruit Co., 213 U.S. 347, 356, 29 S.Ct. 511, 512 (1909). "Every offender must be prosecuted for his offense in the place where the offense was committed." Levitt, Jurisdiction Over Crimes, 16 J.Crim.L. & P.S. 316, 324 (1925).

9. See 22 Hastings L.J. 1155, 1157–62 (1971).

upon the body of the victim.[10] Thus when one standing in North Carolina fired across the boundary line a shot which hit and killed the victim in Tennessee, this was not a North Carolina crime but a Tennessee crime, and a conviction in North Carolina had to be reversed.[11] To mention other examples, robbery is committed where the property is taken from the victim and not where he was first seized,[12] or where the property was subsequently taken.[13] Libel is committed at the place of publication,[14] and bigamy where the bigamous ceremony is performed.[15] Larceny was an exception. By resort to the so-called "continuing trespass" theory larceny was held to be committed not only in the county in which the goods were originally taken but also in any county into which the thief took the stolen property.[16]

Nothing inherent in the territorial principle of criminal jurisdiction requires the recognition of only one point where the actual perpetration of the crime has covered two or more, and modern legislation has tended to remove the restriction developed by the common law. The most common enactment for this purpose has been the so-called "in whole or in part" statute. The wording is in some such form as that punishability under the laws of the state shall include "all persons who commit, in whole or in part, any crime within this state."[17] Under such a provision it was held that a person who caused the death of another in Delaware, by mailing a box of poisoned candy from California, was properly triable for this murder in California.[18]

The wording of such a statute has been criticized as inaccurate. The argument is that as a matter of scientific jurisprudence, in the case mentioned, while the *homicide* was committed partly in California and partly in Delaware, the California *crime*—the violation of California law—was committed wholly in California.[19] This has not tended in the least to prevent carrying out the legislative intent,[20] as in the case mentioned, but at times has resulted in an additional legislative effort, such as the following:

> Whenever a person, with intent to commit a crime, does any act within this state in execution or part execution of such intent, which culminates in the commission of a crime, either within or without this state such person is punishable for such crime in this state in the same manner as if the same had been committed entirely within this state.[21]

10. It is committed "where the impingement happens." State v. Carter, 27 N.J.L. 499, 500 (1859).

11. State v. Hall, 114 N.C. 909, 19 S.E. 602 (1894).

12. Sweat v. State, 90 Ga. 315, 17 S.E. 273 (1892).

13. 2 Hale, P.C. * 163.

14. Commonwealth v. Blanding, 20 Mass. (3 Pick) 304 (1825).

15. 1 Hale P.C. * 692–93.

16. 4 Bl.Comm. * 305.

17. West's Ann.Cal.Pen.Code § 27.

18. People v. Botkin, 132 Cal. 231, 64 P. 286 (1901).

19. This argument seems not to have made its way into print, but when the American Law Institute's Code of Criminal Procedure was being drafted, it was this argument in the committee room which prevented the inclusion of an "in whole or in part" section in the proposed code. Such a provision received only casual mention in the commentaries. ALI Code of Criminal Procedure 693 (official draft with commentaries, 1931).

20. Cook, The Logical and Legal Bases of the Conflict of Laws, 33 Yale L.J. 457, 463 (1924).

21. West's Ann.Cal.Pen.Code § 778a. See 18 U.S.C.A. § 3237 which deals with offenses begun in one district and completed in another.

Either statute, it has been held, requires more than mere preparation. To constitute a local crime what was done within the state must constitute at least an attempt.[22]

Although the territorial theory was considered the exclusive basis of criminal jurisdiction by the common law, the judges did not hesitate to recognize the legislative power to establish jurisdiction on some other basis. Thus in *Hanks*,[23] mentioned above, the statute was drawing upon the injured forum theory because the forgery in Louisiana, while it harmed Texas by casting a possible cloud upon the title to Texas land, could not by any extension be brought under the territorial theory. And an English statute in the early 1800's [24] applied the Roman theory in a statute which provided for the punishment of any English subject for murder or manslaughter committed by him "whether within the King's Dominions or without."

Under our system of "dual sovereignty" each state, with certain limitations, has the powers of a nation. And this, for the most part at least, applies to criminal jurisdiction. It was assumed at one time that while the federal government could, by statute, exercise criminal jurisdiction on the Roman theory, the individual states could not.[25] The Supreme Court, however, did not recognize this limitation. Thus in *Skiriotes* the Court held it was within the power of Florida to punish specified acts by its citizens in the Gulf of Mexico outside any territorial limits, where there is no conflict with acts of Congress.[26]

In the so-called common-law countries, all criminal jurisdiction not based upon the territorial theory must have statutory authority, and the territorial theory has such a dominant position that no state may punish its citizen for what he does in the exclusive territorial jurisdiction of another state where what was done was lawful. California could not validly make it a crime for its citizens to "play the slot machines" in Las Vegas, Nevada, where this is lawful. Such a statute would violate the full faith and credit clause.[27]

The territorial theory of criminal jurisdiction extends to the ships of the nation which are its "floating territory" so to speak.[28] So far as the territorial theory per se is concerned, this jurisdiction is exclusive when the vessel is on the high seas[29] and concurrent when it is in a foreign port, in which case the local jurisdiction is dominant.[30] The established practice, however, is for the local jurisdiction to be exercised only in rather extreme cases.[31]

22. People v. Werblow, 241 N.Y. 55, 148 N.E. 786 (1925); People v. Utter, 24 Cal.App.3d 535, 101 Cal.Rptr. 214 (1972).

23. Hanks v. State, 13 Tex.App. 289 (1882).

24. 9 Geo. 4, ch. 31, sec. 7 (1828). The validity of the statute was upheld in Regina v. Azzopardi, 174 Eng.Rep. 776 (N.P.1843).

25. Restatement of Conflicts of Law sec. 63 (1934). See People v. Merrill, 2 Park.Cr.R. 590, 602 (N.Y.Super.Ct.1855).

26. Skiriotes v. Florida, 313 U.S. 69, 61 S.Ct. 924 (1941). See also Felton v. Hodges, 374 F.2d 337 (5th Cir. 1967).

27. "Full faith and credit shall be given in each State to the public Acts, Records, and Judicial Proceedings of every other State." U.S.Const. art. IV, sec. 1.

28. "Upon the high seas, every vessel, public or private, is, for jurisdictional purposes, a part of the territory of the nation of its owners." People v. Tyler, 7 Mich. 161, 209 (1859).

29. Ibid. See also United States v. Holmes, 18 U.S. (5 Wheat.) 412, 417 (1820).

30. Wildenhus's Case, 120 U.S. 1, 11, 7 S.Ct. 385, 387 (1887).

31. Id. at p. 12.

Novel situations developing in the "space age" have given rise to searching questions. One, which seems not to require extensive discussion is this: What would be the legal situation if in some future venture one of our astronauts should kill another in the spaceship, while far out in space? The answer is obvious. Just as a waterborne vessel on the high seas is part of the "floating territory" of the nation whose flag it flies[32] and the people thereon fully under its jurisdiction, so a spaceship, in space, is part of the "flying territory" of the nation from which it was launched, and the astronauts therein fully accountable under its laws.

The question which seems to have given rise to the greatest controversy is this: If in some future moonlanding venture one of our astronauts should kill another after the spaceship had landed and the men were walking about on the moon, would there be any law applicable to this homicide? For the answer to this question we need to turn to the common law of England. While this law did not adopt the Roman theory of criminal jurisdiction, it refused to accept any such concept as a legal vacuum. The judges would not admit the possibility of Englishmen being where there was no law. They were very specific.

> Where Englishmen establish themselves in an uninhabited or barbarous country, they carry with them not only the laws, but the sovereignty of their own State; and those who live amongst them and become members of their community become also partakers of and subject to the same laws.[33]

This, of course, is the basis of our common law in this country. When the English colonists came to these shores, finding no law here—or at least none that they recognized—they brought with them the English law. And this included not only the common law but also the English statutes in force at that time.[34] "The common law is all the statutory and case law background of England and the American colonies before the American Revolution." [35]

Hence with us, as in England, there is no such concept as a legal vacuum. If our people go to an uninhabited or barbarous place they carry with them not only the laws but the sovereignty of the United States. Our astronauts who land on the moon are as completely subject to the federal law as if they had landed upon ground under the special territorial jurisdiction of the United States.[36]

This does not mean that since our astronauts were first on the moon, the entire satellite is our territory, continuously subject to our law. The English colonists did not bring the law of England to this entire continent, but only to the part occupied by them and their followers and descendants. And if they had all given up and returned to England they would have taken the

---

32. People v. Tyler, 7 Mich. 161, 209 (1859).

33. Advocate-General of Bengal v. Ranee Surnomoye Dossee, 15 Eng.Rep. 811, 824 (P.C. 1863).

34. "These statutes being passed before the emigration of our ancestors, being applicable to our situation, and in amendment to the law, constitute a part of our common law." Patterson v. Winn, 30 U.S. (5 Pet.) 233, 241 (1831).

35. People v. Rehman, 253 Cal.App.2d 119, 150, 61 Cal.Rptr. 65, 85 (1967). As implied in the previous note, this is subject to a slight qualification. A few provisions of the English law, such as those based upon feudalism, were not appropriate to the conditions here and were not recognized in this country.

36. See 18 U.S.C.A. sec. 7(3).

English law back with them, leaving this continent as they had found it. If the decision to return had been made very promptly, but not before one Englishman had killed another on land here, the slayer would have been triable in England for that homicide.[37]

The answer to the question posed is that if, during some future venture, one of our astronauts should kill another after they had landed on the moon and were walking around thereon, he would be triable for that homicide in the federal district court of the district in which he landed on his return, or in any district in which he was found.[38] If only two had gone on that particular trip there might be no evidence to convict of either murder or manslaughter. Even so the slayer could not safely boast of what he had done.

This leaves one important question unanswered: If on some future moon-landing adventure American astronauts and Russian astronauts (for example) should happen to land at the same time, and approximately the same place, and moments later, while walking on the moon, a member of one group should kill a member of the other—what is to be said as to jurisdiction of this homicide if it is claimed to have been without justification or excuse?

The early judges did not give consideration to the problem arising out of the coincidental appearance of Englishmen and the nationals of another country at some barbarous or uninhabited place. They were clear that if the Englishmen were there first they took the laws and sovereignty of England with them and if others joined they were "partakers of, and subject to the same laws." This would mean that if Englishmen reached such a place already occupied by the others, the Englishmen would be subject to the laws of the other nation. We have, however, no firm basis for an answer to the problem arising out of simultaneous arrival.

Rather than leave it unanswered until the factual situation is actually presented, it would be wise to have the situation covered by appropriate federal legislation. The Act of Congress could be patterned somewhat after the suggestion found in a proposed new Federal Criminal Code. This provision is to the effect that federal jurisdiction is to be extended to include an offense if it "is committed by or against a national of the United States outside the jurisdiction of any nation." [39]

This would give the United States extraterritorial criminal jurisdiction by the exercise of the Roman theory (by a national of the United States) and by the injured forum theory (against such a national). The Power of Congress to extend criminal jurisdiction beyond the territorial in appropriate cases is well recognized,[40] but the suggested statute seems to be, in some respects too broad, and in others too narrow. The wording would seem to give the federal courts jurisdiction over cases that from the first have been dealt with exclusively as state cases. An ordinary murder on Market street in San Francisco, for example, is an offense "committed . . . outside the juris-

37. This would have been long before the English statute had applied the Roman theory of criminal jurisdiction to English subjects who commit homicide abroad. See note 24 supra.

38. 18 U.S.C.A. § 3238.

39. Study Draft of a New Federal Criminal Code sec. 208(h) (1970) prepared by the Nat'l Comm'n on Reform of Federal Criminal Laws established pursuant to Pub.L.No. 89–801 (Nov. 8, 1966).

40. United States v. Bowman, 260 U.S. 94, 43 S.Ct. 39 (1922); Rivard v. United States, 375 F.2d 882 (5th Cir. 1967); Rocha v. United States, 288 F.2d 545 (9th Cir. 1961).

diction of any nation," because California is not a nation.[41] On the other side, the wording is questionable because of the emphasis placed by many countries on the Roman theory of criminal jurisdiction. Because of the French statute on the subject [42] it is arguable that no place where a French citizen happens to be is "outside the jurisdiction of" France.

Despite possible arguments against these conclusions, it would seem wise to avoid controversy by wording such a statute in terms of extending the jurisdiction of the federal courts to include "an offense committed by or against a national of the United States outside the *territorial* jurisdiction of any *state* or nation."

41. Such a crime is within the United States but it is not "an offense within the jurisdiction of the United States" unless there is some federal aspect involved. That requirement would be satisfied if, for example, the victim was a federal marshal engaged in the performance of his official duties. 18 U.S.C.A. § 1114. Otherwise the case would be within the exclusive jurisdiction of the state court.

42. "Any French citizen who outside the territory of the Republic renders himself guilty of an act that qualifies as a felony punished by French law may be prosecuted and tried by French courts." French Code of Crim.Pro., art. 689 (G. Kock transl. 1964). The second paragraph makes a similar provision as to misdemeanors limited, for the most part, to acts punishable where committed.

Chapter 2

OFFENSES AGAINST THE PERSON

SECTION 1. THE LAW OF HOMICIDE

A. DEFINITION AND CLASSIFICATION

Homicide is the killing of a human being by another human being.[1]

The older authorities gave this definition: Homicide is the killing of a human being by a human being.[2] The difference between the two definitions above is that suicide is excluded by the first but included in the second. The problems of self-destruction are so different from those involved in the killing of another that it is desirable to use "suicide" and "homicide" as mutually exclusive terms. The trend is towards excluding suicide from the substantive criminal law and homicide is not a consideration in most suicides.

1. KILLING BY A HUMAN BEING

It is not homicide for a man to kill an animal or for an animal to kill a man.[3] An animal might be used as *a means* of committing homicide, as if one man on horseback should purposely run down another on foot with fatal consequences; but in such a case the law attributes the killing to the human rider and declares it to be homicide for this reason. In fact, whether a certain loss of life was brought about by a human being is a problem of fact rather than law except as a matter of causation. By an arbitrary rule in some jurisdictions, the law will not recognize a homicide unless the death has resulted within a year and a day from the time of the act which is alleged to have caused the death.[4] In other words death cannot be attributed to a blow or other harm which preceded it by more than a year and a day. In such a case the loss of life is attributed to natural causes rather than to the human act which occurred so long ago.

The year-and-a-day formula was adopted in ancient times[5] when it was assumed that a period of time would be figured by including the day on

1. Kinsey v. State, 49 Ariz. 201, 65 P.2d 1141 (1937). And see 22–16–1 South Dakota Compiled Laws 1967. "Homicide is the killing of one human being by another."

2. "Homicide properly so called, is either against a man's own life, or that of another." 1 Hawk.P.C. c. 27 (introductory paragraph).

3. If the killing "be done by an ox, a dog, or other thing, it is not properly termed homicide." Bracton, f. 120b.

4. Louisiana Rev.St. § 14.29 (1974); State v. Moore, 196 La. 617, 199 So. 661 (1940); Commonwealth v. Pinnick, 354 Mass. 13, 234 N.E.2d 756 (1968). An assault with a machete on April 21, 1966, resulting in the death of the victim on April 23, 1967, would not support a prosecution for murder, but would support a prosecution for assault with a dangerous weapon.

5. ". . . for if he die after that time, it cannot be discerned, as the law presumes, whether he died of the stroke

46

which the event happens which starts the running of the period and the additional day was added to insure inclusion of a whole year.[6] When it came to be recognized that, as a general rule, the day which starts the running is not itself counted in the period, the formula was retained with a qualifying explanation: "In order also to make the killing murder, it is requisite that the party die within a year and a day after the stroke received, or cause of death administered; in the computation of which the whole day upon which the hurt was done shall be reckoned the first." [7] This language has been copied in some of the statutes.[8] This rule was held to have been eliminated by judicial construction of the New York penal law,[9] and has been judicially abrogated in New Jersey.[10] The rule remains in full force in some states,[11] but the trend in most jurisdictions has been to repeal statutes embodying the rule or to leave the matter out of new codifications.[12] The year-and-a-day rule for homicide has been modified by a California statute worded "within three years and a day." [13] "The common law 'year and a day rule' does not conform to the present day medical realities, principles of equity or public policy. We reject it as an anachronism and declare that it is no longer part of the common law of this state." [14] The new rule was held applicable to the defendant and his conviction of murder upheld, although the death was 63 days and a year after the shooting.

or poison, etc. or a natural death." 3 Coke Inst. 52.

6. " 'Day' was here added merely to indicate that the 365th day after that of the injury must be included." Kenny, Outlines of Criminal Law 135 (19th ed. by Turner, 1966).

The "year-and-a-day" formula was common in the early law. For its use in other than the homicide cases see 1 Pollock and Maitland, History of English Law 648, 649 (2d ed. 1899), and 2 Id. 76, 102, 563.

7. 4 Bl.Comm. *197.

8. See West's Ann.Cal.Pen.Code § 194 (1970).

9. People v. Brengard, 265 N.Y. 100, 191 N.E. 850 (1934).

10. State v. Young, 148 N.J.Super. 405, 372 A.2d 1117 (1977); Commonwealth v. Lewis, ___ Mass. ___, 409 N.E.2d 771 (1980). The court observed the rule founded in common had been a part of the law of New Jersey, but that common principles would be rejected or modified when they no longer conform to present day views. On further review, a majority of the New Jersey Supreme Court favored abolishing the year and a day rule but no single majority prevailed as to the underlying basis or the effect. State v. Young, 77 N.J. 245, 390 A.2d 556 (1978).

The year and a day rule was said not to be a statute of limitations rather the crime of murder did not occur where the rule was followed. State v. Sandridge, 365 N.E.2d 898 (Ohio Com.Pl.1977).

11. State v. Brown, 21 Md.App. 91, 318 A.2d 257 (1974); Cole v. State, 512 S.W.2d 598 (Tenn.Cr.App.1974).

12. The Model Penal Code contains no such provision and states adopting new criminal codes based in part upon the Model Penal Code have no provisions as to the year and a day rule.

13. West's Ann.Cal.Pen.Code § 194, as amended in 1969.

14. State v. Young, 148 N.J.Super. 405, 372 A.2d 1117, 1119 (1977). The court said there is no evidence that defendant relied upon the "year and a day rule" and affirmed the conviction. The New Jersey Supreme Court reversed the conviction. State v. Young, 77 N.J. 245, 390 A.2d 556 (1978).

For a case adopting another new rule on a different matter, but reversing the conviction on the ground that it would be unconstitutional to apply the new rule to what had already been done, see, Commonwealth v. Klein, 372 Mass. 823, 363 N.E.2d 1313 (1977).

A. DEATH

From ancient times the end of cardiac and respiratory functions has been accepted as the end of life. One is dead when the heart-beat and breathing have stopped, once and for all.[15] Until recently this has been entirely adequate, but now that medical science is able to maintain cardiorespiratory systems in a dead body, it is not. It is very important for medical science to be able, by intricate machinery attached to the body, to cause the blood to circulate and respiration to continue after the body is dead. For example, the victim of fatal accident or murderous attack may be the potential donor of a vital organ needed to save the life of another, and the continual flow of blood, constantly revitalized by breath, is necessary to preserve the organ in proper condition for transplantation.[16] But because of this miraculous technique, it is essential to have another method of determining death.

In a murder trial [17] it was shown that the defendant, just "for kicks," hit a man on the head with a baseball bat. The victim was rushed to a hospital where a large portion of the front of his skull was removed to relieve pressure on his brain. He breathed with the aid of an artificial respirator. Two days later the respirator was momentarily disconnected, and he failed to breathe. Blood pressure and pulse were not observable, and an electroencephalogram and other tests showed a total lack of brain activity. He was placed back on the respirator and taken off again two days later with the same result. The respirator was reconnected then but was removed after a period of two more days.

It was claimed that the defendant could not properly be convicted of murder because if the respirator had not been removed the victim might have survived beyond the year-and-a-day period so that the death could not be attributed to the blow inflicted by the defendant. The court dismissed this odd argument by accepting the brain-death concept and holding that the deceased was already dead when the life-saving device was removed.

In another murder case[18] the defense made a more direct approach. It was claimed that defendant could not be convicted of murder because the doctors had caused the death of the victim by removing the life-saving device. In short, that the defendant was not guilty of murder because the deceased was not killed by the defendant but by the doctors. In rejecting this claim the court said:

> Because of increased interest in organ transplants, it was felt by some that a different definition of death was necessary. As a result, the National Conference of Commissioners on Uniform State Laws proposed the Uniform Brain Death Act that stated, "for legal and medical purposes an individual who has sustained irreversible cessation of all functioning of the brain including the brain stem is dead." The Uniform Law provides

---

15. "When the heart stopped beating and the lungs stopped breathing, the individual was dead according to physicians and according to law." In re Welfare of Bowman, 94 Wn.2d 407, 617 P.2d 731, 734 (1980).

16. See the reference to "the advent of successful organ transplantation capabilities which creates a demand for viable organs from recently deceased donors, ..." Ibid.

17. Commonwealth v. Golston, 373 Mass. 249, 366 N.E.2d 744 (1977).

18. State v. Fierro, 124 Ariz. 182, 603 P.2d 74 (1979).

that a determination of brain death must be made "in accordance with reasonable medical standards." [19]

The court added: "In the instant case expert testimony was received which showed that the victim had suffered irreversible 'brain death' before the life supports had been withdrawn." [20]

And in a civil case in which the point was involved the court said:

> We hold that it is for the law to define the standard of death, that the brain death standard of death should be adopted, and that it is for the medical profession to determine the applicable criteria—in accordance with accepted medical standards—for determining whether brain death is present.[21]

As indicated, a brain-death statute had been suggested some years ago and some states have enacted such legislation,[22] but that was not true in any of the states in which the cases above were decided. Those cases were all decided as a matter of common law. One court purported to distinguish between brain death and common-law death,[23] but as it was acting without the benefit of statute, the result it reached was common law. This is entirely proper because the common law is sufficiently vital to adapt to new situations. One of the cases repeated that: "The rules and principles on the common law . . . are broad and expansive enough to embrace all new cases as they arise." [24] This being a quotation from *Webster*, the famous Massachusetts case.[25] While perhaps in the nature of an over-statement, the message is clear. In dealing with an entirely different problem, the Michigan court gave this introduction to an important change: "Today we exercise our role in the development of the common law by. . . ." [26]

We now have the proposed Uniform Determination of Death Act, which is very simple and direct. "An individual who has sustained either (1) irreversible cessation of circulatory and respiratory functions or (2) irreversible cessation of all functions of the entire brain, including the brain stem, is dead. A determination of death must be made in accordance with accepted medical standards." [27]

Adoption of this uniform act by all the states would seem desirable, but is not indispensable as far as the law is concerned. Brain death has become part of the common law.

B. INFANTICIDE

The victim of the homicide—or alleged homicide—must also receive attention. The killing of an unborn child is not homicide according to the common law.[28] Statutes in a few states have provided punishment under the name of

---

19. Id., 603 P.2d at 77–78.

20. Ibid.

21. In re Welfare of Bowman, 94 Wn.2d 407, 617 P.2d 731, 732 (1980).

22. E.g. Iowa Criminal Code § 702.8 (1978).

23. State v. Fierro, 124 Ariz. 182, 603 P.2d 74, 78 (1979).

24. Commonwealth v. Golston, 373 Mass. 249, 366 N.E.2d 744, 749 (1977).

25. Commonwealth v. Webster, 59 Mass. (5 Cush.) 295, 322 (1850).

26. People v. Aaron, 409 Mich. 672, 299 N.W.2d 304, 321 (1980).

27. See Uniform Determination of Death Act, 12 Uniform Law Ann. (1981 Supp.) p. 187; In re Welfare of Bowman, 94 Wn.2d 407, 617 P.2d 731, 738 (1980).

28. 3 Co.Inst. *50; 1 Hale P.C. *433; 1 Hawk.P.C. c. 31, § 16; 1 East, P.C. *227; 4 Bl.Comm. *198. It seems to

manslaughter for the killing of an unborn quick child under certain circumstances,[29] but most states still follow the common-law rule that there is no homicide of any grade unless the deceased had been born alive.[30] Just what constitutes being "born alive" has presented something of a problem.[31] The early view was that to be born alive the infant must be fully expelled from the body of the mother and have established a separate circulation. It must live apart from the body and circulation of the mother, it must have achieved an independent and separate existence or circulation.[32] Some courts have required that the umbilical cord be severed.[33] This was quite generally modified, however, by the holding that it is sufficient if the child is alive after having been expelled from the mother's body even if the cord has not yet been cut.[34] A more advanced view, based upon practical considerations rather than the literal meaning of the phrase, is that after the actual start of the birth process by a viable child it is to be regarded as having been born alive for the purpose of the law of homicide.[35] This draws the line between stillborn and born alive, limiting the former to those instances in which the fetus is dead before birth starts. Where such is not the fact, under this view, the killing of a viable child shall have the same consequences whether it is during the birth process or after its completion. Whatever the rule, as to what shall be deemed to constitute live birth, the fact must be established by evidence and while the newer holding removes some of the difficulties it does not remove all.

have been otherwise in the ancient law. 1 Hawk.P.C. c. 31, § 16.

Even if a malicious attack on a pregnant woman caused an eight-month-old fetus to be born dead, this did not constitute murder. State v. Gyles, 313 So.2d 799 (La.1975).

"Homicide is not the killing of a 'person,' but is the killing of a 'human being,' R.S. 14:29, a phrase which has been restricted to those born alive throughout the United States in relation to the crime of murder. . . . We can only conclude that the indictment here, charging defendant with the murder of a 'fertilized implanted fetus in the womb' of its mother does not charge a crime." State v. Brown, 378 So.2d 916, 917–18, (La.1979).

29. For a New York statute to this effect enacted in 1869 see Evans v. People, 49 N.Y. 86 (1872). Oregon has made some abortions manslaughter, State v. Barrett, 249 Or. 226, 437 P.2d 821 (1968). And see, West's Fla.Stat.Ann. § 782.09 (1965), Mich.Comp.Laws Ann. § 28.554 (1968).

30. Cf. State v. Dickinson, 28 Ohio St.2d 65, 275 N.E.2d 599 (1971).

31. See Winfield, The Unborn Child, 8 Camb.L.J. 76, 79 (1944); Atkinson, Life, Birth and Live-Birth, 20 Law Quarterly Rev. 134, 146, 149 (1904); Proving Live Birth in Infanticide, 17 Wyo.L.J. 237 (1963); Meldman, Legal Concepts of Human Life: The Infanticide Doctrines, 52 Marquette L.Rev. 105 (1968).

32. A failure to show that an infant achieved separate and independent existence from its mother precluded murder conviction. White v. The State, 238 Ga. 224, 232 S.E.2d 57 (1977). See also, Rex v. Enoch, 172 Eng.Rep. 1089 (1833).

33. "It is usually said that the umbilical cord must have been severed. . . ." Morgan v. State, 148 Tenn. 417, 256 S.W. 433, 434 (1923).

34. II Bishop, New Criminal Law § 632 (8th ed. 1892); Kenny, Outlines of Criminal Law 134–35 (19th ed. by Turner, 1966). At times the presence or absence of air in the lungs of the newborn has been considered determinative, but this was found to be unsatisfactory since the infant might breathe in the process of being born, Rex v. Enoch, 5 C. & P. 539, 172 Eng.Rep. 1089 (1833), or "hold its breath" momentarily after birth was complete. Rex v. Brain, 6 C. & P. 349, 172 Eng.Rep. 1272 (1834).

35. People v. Chavez, 77 Cal.App.2d 621, 625–27, 176 P.2d 92, 94–95 (1947); Singleton v. State, 33 Ala.App. 536, 35 So.2d 375 (1948). And see Bennett v. State, 377 P.2d 634 (Wyo.1963).

It was held by a California court of appeals that a viable child in the womb is a human being and the subject of murder.[36] This was reversed by the supreme court of the state in *Keeler*,[37] which held that there is no murder without homicide, and no homicide without birth alive. *Keeler* has an interesting companion. The Court of Common Pleas of Ohio held that the Ohio vehicular-homicide statute applied to a seven-month-old fetus, capable of sustaining life outside the mother's body at the time of the automobile accident which caused it to be born dead.[38] The court relied upon the word "person" in the statute plus the fact that a viable fetus had been held to be a "person" in a civil action under the wrongful-death statute. This was unsound because the courts have often emphasized the different approach of the civil law and the criminal law with reference to the status of a fetus. For this reason the judgment of the lower court was reversed by a case which cited *Keeler* with approval.[39] *Keeler* created so much excitement that section 187 of the California Penal Code was amended to read: "Murder is the unlawful killing of a human being or a fetus, with malice aforethought . . . ." The word "fetus" in the statute has been interpreted to mean "a viable unborn child." [40]

In a later California case **D** was convicted of voluntary manslaughter of his wife and second-degree murder of the fetus she was carrying at the time. The conviction of second-degree murder of the fetus was by application of the felony-murder rule—the manslaughter of the wife being the felony. This was affirmed as to the conviction of manslaughter but reversed as to the second-degree murder conviction. The court talked at length in terms of the so-called doctrine of "transferred intent." What the court should have said is that since it was found that **D**'s act was without malice, because in the sudden heat of passion engendered by adequate provocation, the resulting unintentional killing of the fetus could not be murder. It was correctly pointed out that the California statute does not provide for the manslaughter of a fetus.[41]

The Model Penal Code, in the article on Criminal Homicide,[42] provides: (1) " 'human being' means a person who has been born and is alive; . . ."

New York in its revised penal code has redefined "homicide" to include the killing "of a person or an unborn child with which a female has been pregnant for more than twenty-four weeks . . . ." [43] But the overwhelm-

---

36. Keeler v. Superior Court, 80 Cal.Rptr. 865 (Cal.App.1969).

37. Keeler v. Superior Court, 2 Cal.3d 619, 89 Cal.Rptr. 481, 470 P.2d 617 (1970). The opinion states: "Opinion, Cal.App., 80 Cal.Rptr. 865 vacated." This means that the opinion of the lower court can be found only in the California Reporter. It is not an official opinion.

38. State v. Dickinson, 18 Ohio Misc. 151, 248 N.E.2d 458 (1969).

39. State v. Dickinson, 23 Ohio App.2d 259, 263 N.E.2d 253 (1970). The Utah Court reached the same conclusion in State v. Larsen, 578 P.2d 1280 (Utah 1978).

40. People v. Smith, 59 Cal.App.3d 751, 129 Cal.Rptr. 498 (1976).

41. People v. Carlson, 37 Cal.App.3d 349, 112 Cal.Rptr. 321 (1974).

42. Section 210.0(1).

43. Section 125.00. The Washington code sec. 9A.32.060 provides that a person is guilty of manslaughter in the first degree when: "He intentionally and unlawfully kills an unborn quick child by inflicting an injury upon the mother of such child." The Iowa Criminal Code sec. 707.7 provides: "Any person who intentionally terminates a human pregnancy after the end of the second trimester of the pregnancy where death of the fetus results commits feticide. Feticide is

ing majority of the newly-revised penal codes continue the position that there is no homicide except of one who has been born alive, either by express statement,[44] or by the use of wording that has been so interpreted from early days. "(W)e conclude that taking the life of a fetus is not murder under our current statute unless the fetus is born alive and subsequently expires as a result of the injuries inflicted." [45]

If a pregnant woman is injured by some act of another person and a child is born alive who dies of the injury inflicted before birth,[46] or who dies because that injury caused it to be born too soon, this is homicide.[47] But if such injury caused the child to be born dead it is not homicide (except, as mentioned, in a few states by reason of special enactments). The deed may be punishable, if committed under circumstances of culpability, but is given some other label such as "foeticide," "abortion" (where death is required by the statute, but the death of either the mother or the child is specified), or merely "felony." [48] The legal problems in this area have been complicated by the fact that abortion is the right of a woman up until at least viability, or when necessary for the preservation of her life.[49] If a fetus is legally aborted, can the physician[50] be prosecuted for an ensuing death of the fetus,[51] where the fetus was removed alive at the time of the abortion? Obviously not if the fetus is not capable of continued life apart from the mother and the abortion is otherwise lawful. If the fetus is capable of being continued,

a class C felony." (An exception is made for therapeutic abortion.)

44. Code of Alabama § 13A–6–1 (1975 as amended), " 'Person,' when referring to the victim of a criminal homicide, means a human being who has been born and was alive . . . ."

Oregon R.S. § 163.005 (1977), " 'Human being' means a person who has been born and was alive . . . ."

New Hampshire R.S.A. 630:1, IV (1974), "As used . . . 'another' does not include a fetus."

An unborn fetus, even if viable, is not a "person" in the law of homicide. People v. Guthrie, 97 Mich.App. 226, 293 N.W.2d 775 (1980).

45. People v. Greer, 79 Ill.2d 103, 37 Ill.Dec. 313, 319, 402 N.E.2d 203, 209 (1980).

46. 3 Co.Inst. *50; 1 Hawk.P.C. c. 31, § 16; 1 East P.C. *227–28; 4 Bl.Comm. *198; Morgan v. State, 148 Tenn. 417, 256 S.W. 433 (1923).

Fetuses which are the victims of a criminal blow or wound upon their mother, and are subsequently born alive, and thereafter die by reason of a chain of circumstances precipitated by such blow or wound, may be the victims of murder. State v. Anderson, 135 N.J.Super. 423, 343 A.2d 505 (1975).

47. Regina v. West, 2 Car. & K. 784, 175 Eng.Rep. 329 (1848); Kenny, Outlines of Criminal Law 135 (19th ed. by Turner, 1966).

48. "Whoever unlawfully kills an unborn child, or causes a miscarriage, abortion or premature expulsion of a fetus, by any assault or assault and battery wilfully committed upon a pregnant woman, knowing her condition, is guilty of a felony and shall be imprisoned . . ." Wyo.Stat.1957 § 6–71. See Goodman v. State, 573 P.2d 400 (Wyo.1977).

49. Roe v. Wade, 410 U.S. 113, 93 S.Ct. 705 (1973); Doe v. Bolton, 410 U.S. 179, 93 S.Ct. 739 (1973).

50. A person not authorized to practice medicine may be prosecuted for performing an abortion a physician may be lawfully allowed to perform. State v. Menillo, 171 Conn. 141, 368 A.2d 136 (1976).

51. A distinction should be drawn between measures that could be taken after removal of the fetus from the mother's womb that were reasonably available as distinct from heroic bio-medical environmental procedures. To constitute murder the neglect would normally have to be gross or reckless.

the failure to protect the aborted fetus[52] would be a homicide since the fetus would be an infant human being born alive.[53]

A very practical approach to this problem as a matter of social discipline is the enactment of a special statute making it a crime to conceal the birth of an infant. Most of the cases of killing before birth, or just after, are followed by concealment of the fact of birth, and could be prosecuted most successfully on that basis. "It has always been difficult to procure convictions in cases like these," said the Tennessee court speaking of murder or manslaughter prosecutions based upon alleged infanticide. "The necessary evidence is hard to obtain. In England there is a statute making it a crime to conceal the birth of an infant, and reference to the English cases will show that most of the convictions obtained are of concealment. . . ."[54] A few of the states in this country have legislation of this nature, such as statutes providing a penalty for concealing birth, concealing child's death, concealing the death of a bastard, concealing a child so that it cannot be told whether it was born dead or alive, or attempting to conceal the death of a child.[55]

C. ONE SERIOUSLY ILL OR WOUNDED

At the other extreme, since no homicide ever does more than to "hasten the inevitable event," it is homicide to shorten the life of one suffering from an incurable disease, or one already dying from a mortal injury.[56] For example, one who cuts off the head of a person who was alive when the blow first touched the body, has killed that person whether the victim had a reasonable life expectancy of many years, or could not have lived more than an hour because of some previous injury.[57]

On the other hand, two or more, though acting quite independently, may be the cause of a single homicide. Thus if **A** stabs **B** with a knife, and a few moments later **X**, acting quite independently, shoots **B**, whereupon **B** bleeds to death, with the blood gushing from both injuries, this is homicide by both **A** and **X**.[58] **B** has not been killed twice, but two men contributed to his death. Since **B** died from hemorrhage, each of the wounds shortened his life and the cause of each was a cause of his death. But if **X** had chopped off **B**'s head with an axe, **B** would have died instantly and no previous injury would have contributed to his death even if it had been so severe that it would have caused death if **B** had not been killed by the axe.[59]

---

52. Cf. No.Dak.Cent.Code 14–02.1–08 (1960) punishing the negligent cause of the death of a viable fetus born alive.

53. In Commonwealth v. Edelin, 371 Mass. 497, 359 N.E.2d 4 (1976), a manslaughter conviction for the death of a child during an abortion was reversed for insufficient evidence of wanton or reckless conduct. It was assumed the child would have to be born alive outside the mother. Three justices found insufficient evidence of live birth.

54. Morgan v. State, 148 Tenn. 417, 421, 256 S.W. 433, 434 (1923). Now in England such convictions are usually of a new statutory offense—infanticide. Infanticide Act 1938, § 1(1); Criminal Law Act 1967, § 12(5)(a); cf. Royal Commis-

sion on Capital Punishment (1949–1953) 57–59.

55. See NDCC (No.Dak.) § 14–02.1–10 (1960).

56. State v. BeBee, 113 Utah 398, 195 P.2d 746 (1958). A convict may be murdered during the night before the day set for his execution. Commonwealth v. Bowen, 13 Mass. 356 (1816).

57. People v. Ah Fat, 48 Cal. 61 (1874).

58. Henderson v. State, 11 Ala.App. 37, 65 So. 721 (1913); Pitts v. State, 53 Okl.Cr. 165, 8 P.2d 78 (1932).

59. An injury which would have been mortal is not the cause of death if some other injury intervened in such a manner

Shooting or otherwise damaging a corpse is not homicide even if done by one wholly unaware of the lifeless condition of the body.[60] However, the action may be otherwise punishable as another crime.[61]

D. THE PLACE AND TIME OF HOMICIDE

Since a fatal force may start far from the place at which it takes effect, and the victim be still elsewhere when death ensues, and since up to a year may elapse in the meantime, special problems are encountered in regard to the place and time of homicide.

The common-law judges deemed it important to determine the exact *situs* of every crime other than a continuing offense.[62] This was because by the common law "the offence must be inquired of and tried in the same county in which it was committed." [63] The first controversy of this nature in the homicide cases arose when the victim died in a county other than that in which the fatal force had been received. The conclusion was that such a murder was committed in the county in which the mortal blow had been given.[64] And the answer was the same in later cases in which the fatal force, started in one jurisdiction or venue, took effect in another. In other words the situs of homicide, at common law, is where the fatal force impinged upon the body of the victim.[65] Hence when **H** stood in North Carolina and shot across the state boundary, killing **B** who was in Tennessee, he could not be tried for this murder in North Carolina because the crime had been committed in Tennessee.[66] There is no sound reason why a state may not take jurisdiction of an offense committed by one who was within its boundaries at the time even if the point of completion of the crime was elsewhere, and such jurisdiction is commonly exercised today under the so-called "whole or part" statutes.[67] Thus California could prosecute for murder committed by sending poisoned candy by mail from that state to the victim in Delaware,[68] because there was

that the first was not a substantial factor in the loss of life. State v. Scates, 50 N.C. 420 (1858).

60. It is not homicide to throw into the sea a dead body supposed to be alive. United States v. Hewson, 26 Fed.Cas. 303, No. 15,360 (C.C.D.Mass.1844).

61. Abuse of A Corpse, Ark.Stats.1947, § 41–2920 (1977).

62. The typical continuing offense is the possession of "contraband." For example, the unauthorized possession of a counterfeit die for making United States coins is a federal offense. 18 U.S.C.A. § 487. This offense continues so long as the unauthorized possession is maintained and hence is committed wherever the die is taken. The judges included larceny within the scope of this exception on the theory that the offense continues until the unlawful possession is terminated.

63. 1 East P.C. 361.

64. Ibid., 1 Hale P.C. *426.

65. Restatement, Conflicts § 428, comment a (1934).

66. State v. Hall, 114 N.C. 909, 19 S.E. 602 (1894). Nor could he be extradited to Tennessee because he had not "fled" from that state. State v. Hall, 115 N.C. 811, 20 S.E. 729 (1894). Extradition in such a case is authorized under the Uniform Extradition Act which has been enacted in 44 states (including North Carolina).

Where Indians standing in Indian country, 18 U.S.C.A. § 1153, shot at police officers who were outside of Indian country, the crime of assault with intent to kill occurred outside of Indian country and subjected the Indians to the jurisdiction of the South Dakota courts, State v. Winckler, 260 N.W.2d 356 (S.D.1977).

67. See West's Ann.Cal.Pen.Code §§ 27, 778a (1970). And by another section if an offense is committed partly in one county and partly in another the venue is in either. § 781.

68. People v. Botkin, 132 Cal. 231, 64 P. 286 (1901).

express legislative authority therefor. This would have been impossible without the statute.

Had the courts approached the problem of time with the same narrow point of view employed in reference to place they would have felt it necessary to select some occurrence and say that at the moment of this occurrence, and then only, was the homicide committed. Had such an approach been used they would no doubt have said either that the homicide was committed at the moment the blow was struck, or other cause of death administered, even if the death did not follow until after the lapse of some days or months; or else they would have concluded that the murder was not committed until the moment the victim died.

Fortunately no such narrow view prevailed and the judges recognized frankly that the crime of murder, or manslaughter, starts when the cause of death is inflicted but is not completed until the resulting loss of life. And if it becomes necessary to pick one occurrence or the other for some special purpose the choice is dictated by the nature of the inquiry. If, for example, where capital punishment had not been authorized, a statute was enacted establishing the death penalty for murder, this could not be applied to any offense previously committed during the period when the death penalty was not in effect because of the ex-post-facto prohibition.[69] If, however, a murder was committed when a death penalty statute, later found to be constitutionally invalid, was in effect, if a death penalty statute is thereafter promulgated which meets constitutional requirements, a murderer prosecuted under the later statute could be punished by the imposition of the death penalty under the new statute without contravening the prohibition against ex-post-facto laws. The earlier statute is viewed as serving as an "operative fact" to warn the murderer of the penalty which the state would seek to impose on him were he convicted of first degree murder, and therefore complies with the ex-post-facto provision of the United States Constitution.[70] And if the statute was enacted after the fatal blow was struck but before the resulting death it would clearly violate the underlying principle to apply the new punishment to this case. Hence for this purpose the homicide is said to have been committed at the time of defendant's act.[71] On the other hand it would be unjust to convict one of being accessory after the fact to murder because of help given to the wrongdoer while the victim was still alive, since the helper might have refused to give any aid to a murderer. So for this purpose the murder dates from the death of the victim.[72] A Kentucky court reached a contrary conclusion based upon the particular language of a Kentucky statute requiring that the accessory merely have knowledge of a felony.[73] The

69. The term ex post facto laws "applies only to criminal laws; such laws as make acts, innocent when done, criminal, or, if criminal when done, aggravate the crime, or increase the punishment, or reduce the measure of proof. Every *ex post facto* law is necessarily retrospective; but the converse is not true." State v. Squires, 26 Iowa 340, 346 (1868).

70. Dobbert v. Florida, 432 U.S. 282, 97 S.Ct. 2290 (1977).

71. See People v. Gill, 6 Cal. 637 (1856). The factual situation was different but the same problem was presented.

72. State v. Williams, 229 N.C. 348, 49 S.E.2d 617 (1948).

Rudolph v. State, 40 Ala.App. 398, 114 So.2d 299 (1959). The Texas Court acknowledged the rule in Prine v. State, 509 S.W.2d 617 (Tex.Cr.App.1963) but found the defendant's silence after knowledge of the death to be an affirmative act supporting a prior statement before death and thereby sufficient to justify a conviction for being an accessory to murder.

73. Maddox v. Commonwealth, 349 S.W.2d 686 (Ky.1960).

defendant had knowledge that the victim had been shot, although not killed, which was enough to satisfy the statute. The court acknowledged that absent the statute the common-law rule was that knowledge of death was required before one could be convicted of being an accessory to homicide. In other words, a statute was not enacted *before the murder* unless it preceded the act of the defendant, and help was not given the wrongdoer *after the murder* unless it followed the death of the victim.

So far as the criminal law is concerned, homicide is divided into two classes—(1) innocent homicide, and (2) criminal homicide.

2. INNOCENT HOMICIDE

Innocent homicide, as a matter of criminal law, means homicide which does not involve criminal guilt.

Whether a killing classed as innocent homicide in criminal law might under some circumstances impose upon the slayer an obligation to pay damages in a civil action need not receive attention here. Innocent homicide is of two kinds, (1) justifiable and (2) excusable. Homicide is justifiable if it is either commanded or authorized by law. The two typical instances in which homicide is commanded by the state are (1) the killing of an enemy on the field of battle as an act of war and within the rules of war,[74] and (2) the execution of a sentence of death pronounced by a competent tribunal. In certain other instances a homicide may be duly authorized by law although not actually commanded by the state. The typical instances are killings which are necessary in (1) arresting a murderer or some felons or preventing their escape or recapturing them after escape; (2) lawful self-defense against an assault which places the slayer in imminent peril of death or great bodily harm; (3) actual resistance of an attempt to commit a violent felony, such as rape or robbery.

Homicide which is neither commanded nor authorized by law is excusable if committed under circumstances not involving criminal guilt. Common illustrations include: (1) Killing as the result of an unfortunate accident by one who was neither criminally negligent nor engaged in any unlawful act at the time, (2) death caused by a firearm discharged by a little child, (3) homicide by a raving maniac, (4) certain killings in self-defense. The self-defense cases offer a nice distinction between the proper use of the words "justifiable" and "excusable" as applied to homicides. Suppose one, himself free from fault, kills an assailant under the firm belief that this drastic act is necessary to save himself from death or great bodily harm. If the killing really is necessary to save him from such grievous harm at the hands of a murderous assailant, it is authorized by law and hence justifiable. On the other hand, if he was in no danger at all but was the victim of a practical joker with a rubber dagger, who played his part so effectively that the victim reasonably believed he was in imminent danger of being killed, the law does not authorize the killing but the homicide is excusable because of the reasonable mistake of fact. Or suppose a murderous attack upon an innocent victim sufficient to authorize him to kill his assailant but the shot fired for that purpose misses the assailant and kills a bystander. The law does not author-

---

74. A killing of the "enemy" in wartime may still be murder if not directed against a hostile force in combatant status or otherwise a part of accepted warfare. Cf. United States v. Calley, 22 USCMA 534, 48 CMR 19 (1973).

ize the slayer to kill the bystander; but if the fatal shot is fired without criminal negligence the homicide is excusable.[75]

3. CRIMINAL HOMICIDE

Criminal homicide is homicide without lawful justification or excuse. Just one offense under the ancient common law of England, it was divided into two crimes—(1) murder and (2) manslaughter—several centuries ago. Certain statutes played an important role in this division, but these are so old that murder and manslaughter are entirely creatures of the common law so far as this country is concerned. In some jurisdictions in this country an additional category of homicide, negligent homicide has been created. In many instances, the substance of this crime is the substance of manslaughter at common law.

B. MURDER

At common law and traditionally in the United States murder is homicide committed with malice aforethought.[76]

It was one of the few felonies under the common law of England and is a felony under modern statutes.

1. MALICE AFORETHOUGHT

The phrase "malice aforethought" is peculiarly confusing to the layman because each word has a different significance in legal usage than in ordinary conversation. Interestingly enough, while the law has gradually whittled away the original meaning of the second of these words, it apparently employs the term "malice" with very little variation from its ancient import, whereas the popular usage has undergone substantial change. One court has observed that malice, is a term of art. Contrary to the implication of the . . . charge, the term does not mean malice as used in ordinary speech.[77] There has been a trend away from the use of the term malice aforethought in recent legislative definitions of murder.[78]

A. AFORETHOUGHT

Undoubtedly the word "aforethought" was added to "malice" in the ancient cases to indicate a design thought out well in advance of the fatal act.

75. Pinder v. State, 27 Fla. 370, 8 So. 837 (1891).

See generally Kadish, Respect for Life and Regard for Rights in Criminal Law, 64 Cal.L.Rev. 871, 890–894 (1976).

76. People v. Yokum, 145 Cal.App.2d 245, 302 P.2d 406 (1956); Commonwealth v. Gricus, 317 Mass. 403, 58 N.E.2d 241 (1944). And see State v. Jacowitz, 128 Conn. 40, 20 A.2d 470 (1941); State v. Drosos, 253 Iowa 1152, 114 N.W.2d 526 (1962). If the statute on murder does not define it, the definition must be found in the common law. State v. Moore, 196 La. 617, 199 So. 661 (1941).

"At common law, murder was unlawful homicide done with 'malice afore-

thought.'" United States v. Wharton, 433 F.2d 451, 454 (8th Cir. 1970).

Under the revised statute malice is not an essential element of second-degree murder. People v. Gladney, 194 Colo. 68, 570 P.2d 231 (1977). Of the recently-adopted penal codes only those of Georgia, Iowa, Kansas and New Mexico include malice in the definition of murder.

77. People v. Goddard, 82 Mich.App. 424, 266 N.W.2d 832 (1978), error to a charge of malice in a murder case by equating it with wickedness.

78. Code of Ala. § 13A–6–2 (1975); V.T.C.A.Penal Code § 19.02 (1974).

But as case after case came before the courts for determination, involving killings under a great variety of circumstances, there came to be less and less emphasis upon the notion of a well-laid plan. And at the present day the only requirement in this regard is that it must not be an *after*thought.[79] "Killing with malice" is sufficient of itself to negative any possible notion of an afterthought, and apart from the historical background the word "afore-thought" would not be needed. However, the whole development of the mental requirement of the crime of murder has centered around the words "malice aforethought" and jurisdictions continuing the common-law standard of murder have retained the phrase to express the murder concept.[80]

The use of the word aforethought, however, must not be permitted to obscure the result. As a matter of law a killing may be with malice afore-thought although it is conceived and executed "on the spur of the mo-ment."[81] For example, if one should find himself alone with a political oppo-nent, and should suddenly slay the other with a heavy iron bar which happened to be at hand, the slayer would be guilty of murder even if no such thought had ever entered his mind before, and he carried out the idea as rapidly as thought can be translated into action.

B. MALICE

In ordinary conversation the word "malice" conveys some notion of ha-tred, grudge, ill-will, or spite, but no such limitation is incorporated in the legal concept of "malice aforethought."[82] Many murders are committed to satisfy a feeling of hatred or grudge, it is true, but this crime may be perpe-trated without the slightest trace of personal ill-will. Illustrations include the case of a mother who kills her illegitimate offspring to hide her own disgrace, feeling at the time no hatred toward it or any other person and even having the yearnings of a mother's love toward the innocent victim— "loving its life just less than her own reputation."[83] There may be added the case of the husband who killed his wife at her request, because his love was too great to permit the continuance of her suffering from a hopeless disease.[84] Even such extreme cases as these have been held to fill every requirement of malice aforethought,—but the possibility that acting under extreme compassion might constitute (not excuse but) mitigation seems not to have received adequate attention.

(A) Intent to Kill or to Inflict Great Bodily Injury

Every intentional killing is with malice aforethought unless un-der circumstances sufficient to constitute (1) justification, (2) ex-cuse, or (3) mitigation.

79. United States v. Wharton, 433 F.2d 451, 454 (8th Cir. 1970).

80. State v. Christener, 71 N.J. 55, 362 A.2d 1153 (1976).

81. State v. Heidelberg, 120 La. 300, 306, 45 So. 256, 258 (1907).

82. People v. Sedeno, 10 Cal.3d 703, 112 Cal.Rptr. 1, 518 P.2d 913 (1974); Peo-ple v. Lucas, 244 Ill. 603, 91 N.E. 659 (1910).

"The mental state constituting malice aforethought does not presuppose or re-quire any ill will or hatred of the particu-lar victim." People v. Cruz, 26 Cal.3d 233, 162 Cal.Rptr. 1, 5, 605 P.2d 830, 835 (1980).

83. Jones v. State, 29 Ga. 594, 607 (1860).

84. People v. Roberts, 211 Mich. 187, 178 N.W. 690 (1920).

Any intent to kill under other circumstances is malicious.[85] The more difficult aspect of the problem is that there may be malice aforethought without an actual intent to kill. The older authorities assumed the necessity of an intent to kill and then resorted to an "implied intent" of this nature when none in fact existed. But now the courts speak more factually and say frankly that murder may be committed under some circumstances without an intent to kill [86] (unless such intent is required by statute in the particular jurisdiction).

An intent to inflict great bodily injury is sufficient for malice afore-thought if there is no justification, excuse, or mitigation.[87] Thus if one should shoot at another's leg, intending to break his leg and keep him inactive for a few weeks, but not to kill him, this would be murder if the victim should die and there was no justification, excuse, or mitigation for the shooting. Mitigation most frequently arises under the so-called "rule of provocation"—to be considered in connection with manslaughter. Justification or excuse might arise in many ways. If, for example, a sheriff attempting to arrest a fleeing murderer finds it impossible to stop him by milder measures he may shoot. He would not be required to aim at a leg, but if he should do so with fatal consequences he would not be guilty of crime. (Nor would he under these facts if he had aimed at a vital point.) [88] The standard is whether he was lawfully justified in using deadly force, not how the ideal officer would behave.[89]

(B) Wanton and Wilful Disregard of Unreasonable Human Risk

Assuming the absence of justification, excuse, or mitigation, an act may involve such a wanton and wilful disregard of an unreasonable human risk as to constitute malice aforethought even if there is no actual intent to kill or injure.[90] For example, a man wants to destroy certain property by an explosion which he has no right to cause. He realizes there is great danger of killing someone by the kind of explosion he has in mind. He hopes no one will be killed but is determined to go on with his unlawful scheme notwithstanding this great risk. After taking such precautions as he can without abandonment of his plan he sets off the explosion; but despite his precautions a person is killed. This is homicide with malice aforethought and hence

85. Smithwick v. State, 199 Ga. 292, 34 S.E.2d 28 (1945); Government of Virgin Islands v. Lake, 362 F.2d 770 (3d Cir. 1966).

85. People v. Hartwell, 341 Ill. 155, 173 N.E. 112 (1930); Bessey v. State, 297 A.2d 373 (Me.1972); State v. Russell, 106 Utah 116, 145 P.2d 1003 (1944).

87. State v. Calabrese, 107 N.J.L. 115, 151 A. 781 (1930); Baldwin v. State, 538 S.W.2d 615 (Tex.Cr.App.1976). See also the controversial case of Director of Public Prosecutions v. Smith [1961] A.C. 290.

88. Petrie v. Cartwright, 114 Ky. 103, 70 S.W. 297 (1902).

89. See discussion in Hebah v. United States, 456 F.2d 696, 708–13 (Ct.Cl.1972).

90. Brewer v. State, 140 Tex.Cr. 9, 143 S.W.2d 599 (1940); Gautney v. State,

284 Ala. 82, 222 So.2d 175 (1969); Commonwealth v. Taylor, 461 Pa. 557, 337 A.2d 545 (1975).

When a defendant, with a wanton disregard for human life, does an act that involves a high degree of probability that it will result in death, "he acts with malice aforethought." People v. Cruz, 26 Cal.3d 233, 162 Cal.Rptr. 1, 5, 605 P.2d 830, 835 (1980).

"Malice may be established by evidence of conduct which is 'reckless and wanton, and a gross deviation from a reasonable standard of care, of such a nature that a jury is warranted in inferring that defendant was aware of a serious risk of death or serious bodily harm.'" United States v. Black Elk, 579 F.2d 49, 51 (9th Cir. 1978).

murder. The carrying of a bomb into a store, knowing it to be dangerous, where deaths result, is murder aside from any felonious intent of the actor.[91] In the early authorities an intent to kill was said to be "implied" from his act in such a case despite his obvious effort to avoid killing if possible. Now, as previously mentioned, this fiction is abandoned and it is frankly stated that such a reckless and wanton disregard of an obvious human risk is with malice aforethought even if there was no actual intent to kill or injure.[92]

On this basis one may be guilty of murder for death caused by shooting "regardless of consequences" into a house, or a room, or a train,[93] or an automobile, in which persons are known to be at the time. "If he did this," said one court in a case of this nature, "not with the design of killing anyone, but for his diversion merely, . . . he is guilty of murder."[94] In a very well-known case a man threw a heavy glass tumbler in the direction of his wife. The glass hit a lamp she was carrying and caused the oil therein to take fire and burn her, causing her death. This was held to be murder whether he intended the tumbler to hit his wife, or some other person, or whether, without any specific intent, he threw the glass with a general malicious recklessness, disregarding any and all consequences.[95] The standard has been codified in terms of activity which manifests "extreme indifference to the value of human life" and which creates a grave risk of death,"[96] or "where all the circumstances of the killing show an abandoned and malignant heart."[97]

In other words, the intent to do an act in wanton and wilful disregard of the obvious likelihood of causing death or great bodily injury is a malicious intent. The word "wanton" is the key word here. For reasons to be emphasized later a motorist who attempts to pass another car on a "blind curve" may be acting with such criminal negligence that if he causes the death of another in a resulting traffic accident he will be guilty of manslaughter. And such a motorist may be creating fully as great a human hazard as one who shoots into a house or train "just for kicks," who is guilty of murder if loss of life results. The difference is that in the act of the shooter there is an element of viciousness—an extreme indifference to the value of human life[98]—that is not found in the act of the motorist. And it is this viciousness which makes the act "wanton" as well as "wilful". Of course, if the facts are gross enough to show extreme indifference a resulting death could be murder rather than manslaughter.[99]

91. State v. Hokenson, 96 Idaho 283, 527 P.2d 487 (1974).

92. See, Darry v. People, 10 N.Y. 120, 138 (1854); People v. Farmer, 28 Ill.2d 521, 192 N.E.2d 916 (1963).

93. Banks v. State, 85 Tex.Cr. 165, 211 S.W. 217 (1919).

94. Brown v. Commonwealth, 13 Ky.L.Rep. 372, 373, 17 S.W. 220, 221 (1891).

95. Mayes v. People, 106 Ill. 306 (1883).

96. Colo.Rev.Stat.1973, 18–3–102(d).

97. Ga.Code § 26–1101(a) (1978).

98. One court referred to the "cruel and wicked indifference to human life." Jenkins v. State, 230 A.2d 262, 266 (Del.1967).

"In each such case where malice is found, there is an element of viciousness—an extreme indifference to the value of human life." People v. Love, 111 Cal.App.3d 98, 168 Cal.Rptr. 407, 411 (1980).

99. Hamilton v. Commonwealth, 560 S.W.2d 539 (Ky.1978).

(C) The "Felony-Murder Rule"

To give the background of the law of felony-murder the following, prepared years ago for the first edition is retained, although in some states at the present time it represents the law of yesterday rather than that of today.

Even without an intent to kill or injure, or an act done in wanton and wilful disregard of the obvious likelihood of causing such harm, homicide is murder if it falls within the scope of the felony-murder rule.[1] Traditionally, the robber who kills the one he is attempting to rob is guilty of murder whether he intended any personal harm or not.[2] If he holds up the victim at the point of a gun and the weapon goes off, causing death, it makes no difference that the discharge was quite accidental.[3] It is no element of mitigation that he was "shaking and nervous and pulled the trigger" unintentionally,[4] or that the weapon was seized and went off by accident during a struggle for its possession.[5] Train robbers who forced a brakeman to go with them to the express car to serve as a shield, were held guilty of his murder, although the death resulted from a shot fired in defense of the car, since they had feloniously exposed him to this risk.[6] One who commits arson may be found guilty of the murder of an inhabitant of the dwelling who lost his life in the fire although personal injury was neither intended nor expected.[7] Even if there was no person in the building when the fire was feloniously started the incendiary may be convicted of murder if a fireman lost his life in the effort to extinguish the blaze.[8] A rapist who causes the death of his victim by this felonious deed is guilty of murder.[9] This is true even if the death is quite unintentional and whether it resulted from violence used

1. As to the felony-murder rule see Hall, General Principles of Criminal Law 129 et seq. (2d ed. 1960); Moreland, Law of Homicide Ch. 6 (1952); Corcoran, Felony Murder in New York (1937); Crum, Causal Relations and the Felony Murder Rule, 1952 Wash.U.L.Q. 191; Ludwig, Foreseeable Death in Felony Murder, 18 Pitt.L.Rev. 51 (1956); Morris, The Felon's Responsibility for the Lethal Acts of Others, 105 U. of Pa.L.Rev. 50 (1956); Arent and MacDonald, The Felony Murder Doctrine and Its Application Under the New York Statutes, 20 Cornell L.Q. 288 (1935); Collings, Offenses of Violence Against the Person, 339 Annals 42, 44 (Jan. 1962); Ellegard, A Re-Examination of the Felony Murder Doctrine in New York, 10 St. John's L.Rev. 253 (1936); Note, The Felony Murder Doctrine Repudiated, 36 Ky.L.J. 106 (1947).

Note, The California Supreme Court Assaults The Felony-Murder Rule, 22 Stan.L.Rev. 1059 (1970).

2. Rogers v. State, 83 Nev. 376, 432 P.2d 331 (1967); State v. Jensen, 209 Or. 239, 296 P.2d 618 (1956); State v. Best, 44 Wyo. 383, 12 P.2d 1110 (1932).

3. Commonwealth v. McManus, 282 Pa. 25, 127 A. 316 (1925); Simpson v. Wainwright, 439 F.2d 948 (5th Cir. 1971).

4. McCutcheon v. State, 199 Ind. 247, 155 N.E. 544 (1927).

5. Commonwealth v. Lessner, 274 Pa. 108, 118 A. 24 (1922).

6. Keaton v. State, 41 Tex.Cr. 621, 57 S.W. 1125 (1900).

In the situation where a person is used as a shield and killed, the courts have upheld murder convictions on a general theory of implied malice aside from the felony murder rule, Wilson v. State, 188 Ark. 846, 68 S.W.2d 100 (1934); Pizano v. Superior Court of Tulare County, 21 Cal.3d 128, 145 Cal.Rptr. 524, 577 P.2d 659 (1978).

7. Reddick v. Commonwealth, 17 Ky.L.Rep. 1020, 33 S.W. 416 (1895); State v. Meadows, 330 Mo. 1020, 51 S.W.2d 1033 (1932); In re Anonymous, Juvenile Ct.No. 6358-4, 14 Ariz.App. 466, 484 P.2d 235 (1971).

8. State v. Glover, 330 Mo. 709, 50 S.W.2d 1049 (1932).

9. Commonwealth v. Hanlon, 8 Phila. 401 (Pa.1870); State v. Whitfield, 129 Wash. 134, 224 P. 559 (1924); People v. Goodridge, 70 Cal.2d 824, 76 Cal.Rptr. 421, 452 P.2d 637 (1969).

The repeal of a rape provision and enactment of a criminal sexual conduct law

by him during the act,[10] or from a disease communicated by him during the intercourse.[11] A burglar, moreover, is guilty of murder if homicide results from the perpetration of this offense.[12] In fact, statements have often indicated that homicide committed while perpetrating or attempting a felony is murder.[13]

While this is suggested by the name of the rule, and represents the law as it was during one period of its development, it is an overstatement of the rule as it stands today. An ancient writer spoke of death resulting from any unlawful act as murder. "If the act be unlawful," said Coke, writing in the early 1600's "it is murder."[14] Lord Hale, writing not long after, was unwilling to speak in such sweeping terms and gave illustrations of killings resulting from unlawful acts, some of which he said were murder and others manslaughter.[15] This was given more definite form by Foster, about a century and a half later, to this effect: An accidental homicide resulting from an unlawful act (with the qualification "if it be *malum in se*") is murder if the crime is of the grade of felony, but otherwise it is manslaughter.[16] This was the accepted view when Blackstone's Commentaries were published shortly before the Revolution, the statement therein being: "And if one intends to do another a felony, and undesignedly kills a man, this is also murder."[17] This position, however, was unacceptable to Judge Stephen who commented upon it about a century after Blackstone. "To take another very old illustration," said he in a famous case,[18] "it was said that if a man shot at a fowl with intent to steal it, and accidentally killed a man, he was to be accounted guilty of murder, because the act was done in the commission of a felony. I very much doubt, however, whether that is really the law, or whether the court for the Consideration of Crown Cases Reserved would hold it to be so."

Certain it is that the felony-murder rule in the sweeping form declared by Blackstone was modified by cases at a later time and does not represent the ultimate position of the English common law.[19] Under this view not every

did not preclude application of the felony murder rule to death during the commission of what would have been rape under the prior statute. People v. McDonald, 409 Mich. 110, 293 N.W.2d 588 (1980).

10. Buel v. People, 78 N.Y. 492 (1879); Director of Public Prosecutions v. Beard, [1920] A.C. 479.

11. Regina v. Greenwood, 7 Cox C.C. 404 (1857). As this was statutory rape the court permitted the jury to find the defendant guilty of manslaughter, but it is clear that the court would not have considered this less than murder had it been forcible rape.

12. People v. Green, 217 Cal. 176, 17 P.2d 730 (1932); State v. Ferrari, 112 Ariz. 324, 541 P.2d 921 (1975).

13. "In the perpetration of any felony." State v. Zimmer, 198 Kan. 479, 426 P.2d 267, 286 (1967). Perhaps the most common citation is a dictum in Rex v. Plummer, Kel. 109, 117 (1701): "So if two men have a design to steal a hen, and one shoots at the hen for that purpose, and a man be killed it is murder in both, because the design was felonious." See also Regina v. Horsey, 3 Fost. & F. 287, 288–89 (1862); State v. Cross, 72 Conn. 722, 729, 46 Atl. 148, 151 (1900); State v. Leeper, 70 Iowa 748, 30 N.W. 501 (1886); Smith v. State, 33 Me. 48, 55 (1851); State v. Hopkirk, 84 Mo. 278, 287 (1884); State v. Cooper, 13 N.J.L. 361, 370 (1833); Dolan v. People, 64 N.Y. 485 (1876).

14. 3 Co.Inst. *56. The first edition of this book seems not to have been published until 1648, but Coke died in 1634.

15. 1 Hale P.C. *465.

16. Foster C.C. *258.

17. 4 Bl.Comm. *200–201. And see 1 East P.C. *255.

18. Regina v. Serne, 16 Cox C.C. 311, 312–13 (1887).

19. The felony murder rule is no longer applied in England. Williams, Criminal Law 2d § 48; Homicide Act of 1957, 5 & 6 Eliz. II c. 11, Sec. 1.

death resulting from the perpetration or attempted perpetration of felony is murder, but such a homicide may constitute this crime without the same degree of human risk being involved as would otherwise be requisite. In a case of death resulting from a felonious act it is not necessary to show the doing of an act under such circumstances that there is obviously a wanton and wilful disregard of a plain and strong likelihood that death or great bodily injury may result. On the other hand, the element of human risk cannot be excluded entirely without at the same time eliminating the possibility of murder. Thus it was said in one case: [20] "If a man by the perpetration of a felonious act brings about the death of a fellow creature he is guilty of murder, unless when he committed the felonious act the chance of death resulting therefrom was so remote that no reasonable man would have taken it into consideration. In that case he is not guilty of murder, but only of manslaughter." This was further modified by reference to the use of "violent measures in the commission of a felony." [21] This suggests that the felony-murder rule in England came to be this: Homicide resulting from any felony committed in a dangerous way, is murder.[22]

In this country certain felonies have long been regarded as inherently dangerous. Those most frequently assigned to this category are arson, rape, robbery and burglary.[23] Common experience points to the presence of a substantial human risk from the mere perpetration of such wrongful acts. The intent to avoid personal harm formed in the mind of the transgressor at the time he embarks upon such a felony is no reasonable safeguard that death will not result before he has finished. And, it may be added, a study of the cases repeating the formula that homicide committed while perpetrating or attempting a felony is murder, will disclose that the other felony actually involved is one which may properly be classified as "dangerous", such as robbery,[24] common-law rape,[25] burglary,[26] arson,[27] criminal abortion,[28] may-

20. Regina v. Whitmarsh, 62 Just.P. 711 (1898). The quotation is from the syllabus. To the same general effect see Rex v. Lumley, 22 Cox C.C. 635 (1911).

21. "We think that the object and scope of this breach of the law is at least this, that he who uses violent measures in the commission of a felony involving personal violence does so at his own risk and is guilty of murder if those violent measures result, even inadvertently, in the death of the victim." Rex v. Jarmain, 2 All E.R. 613, 616 (1945).

22. Professor Kenny had been led "to formulate a restatement of the 'felony murder' rule as limited to 'such felonious acts as involve violence against an unwilling victim.'" Kenny, Outlines of Criminal Law 159, n. 2 (19th ed. by Turner, 1966).

§ 210.2 Model Penal Code defines murder without a specific felony-murder rule but provides:

"(1) . . . criminal homicide constitutes murder when:

. . .

(b) it is committed recklessly under circumstances manifesting extreme indifference to the value of human life. Such recklessness and indifference are presumed if the actor is engaged or is an accomplice in the commission of, or an attempt to commit, or flight after committing or attempting to commit robbery, rape or deviate sexual intercourse by force or threat of force, arson, burglary, kidnapping or felonious escape."

23. "The dangerous felonies commonly enumerated are arson, rape, robbery and burglary." Moreland, Law of Homicide 48 (1952).

24. Simpson v. Commonwealth, 293 Ky. 831, 170 S.W.2d 869 (1943); Commonwealth v. Madeiros, 255 Mass. 304, 151 N.E. 297 (1926); McDonald v. State, 54 Okl.Cr. 161, 15 P.2d 1092, 1094 (1932).

25. State v. Cross, 72 Conn. 722, 46 A. 148 (1900); State v. Whitfield, 129 Wash. 134, 224 P. 559 (1924). This has reference to common-law rape. See Regina v. Greenwood, 7 Cox C.C. 404 (1857).

26–28. See notes 26–28 on page 64.

hem,[29] train-wrecking,[30] kidnaping,[31] administering narcotics to a minor,[32] injecting heroin into the arm of a purchaser,[33] or child abuse.[34]

To test whether the so-called "felony-murder rule" in its unlimited form actually represents the law in this country, it is necessary to consider felonies of a non-dangerous character. Because such a felony will very rarely result in the death of a human being, few cases actually raise the question but it has not escaped attention entirely. The Kentucky court has given a striking illustration in a very famous case.[35] "Under our statute," said the court, "the removal of a cornerstone is punishable by a short term in the penitentiary, and is therefore a felony. If, in attempting this offense, death were to result to one conspirator by his fellow accidentally dropping the stone upon him, no Christian court would hesitate to apply this limitation." The "limitation" mentioned is that the homicide would be manslaughter rather than murder notwithstanding it resulted from the commission of a felony.

The leading American decision on this point is one handed down in Michigan.[36] The defendant sold liquor under circumstances amounting to a felony under the law of that day. The purchaser became drunk and died from exposure but the court refused to hold that the death resulting from this felony was murder. "Notwithstanding the fact that the statute has declared it to be a felony," reads the opinion, "it is an act not in itself directly and naturally dangerous to life." The California Supreme Court [37] has refused to apply the felony-murder rule to the offense of false imprisonment since when viewed as an abstract offense false imprisonment is not "inherently dangerous to human life."

In fact there has been a widespread tendency to abandon the early notion that death resulting from any felony is murder. In England until the felony-murder rule was abandoned by statute in 1957,[38] the rule came to be applied only to a felony perpetrated in a dangerous manner, as mentioned above. In this country a few states have retained the rule in its original form—death resulting from the perpetration or attempted perpetration of any felony is murder.[39] Elsewhere the rule has been limited, but not in a uniform manner. A few states have essentially the same position as had developed in Eng-

26. Conrad v. State, 75 Ohio St. 52, 78 N.E. 957 (1906); People v. Greenwall, 115 N.Y. 520, 22 N.E. 180 (1889).

27. State v. Glover, 330 Mo. 709, 50 S.W.2d 1049 (1932); State v. Cooper, 13 N.J.L. 361 (1833).

28. State v. Leeper, 70 Iowa 748, 30 N.W. 501 (1886); Smith v. State, 33 Me. 48 (1851).

29. People v. De La Roi, 36 Cal.App.2d 287, 97 P.2d 836 (1939).

30. Davis v. State, 51 Neb. 301, 70 N.W. 984 (1897).

31. State v. Zimmer, 198 Kan. 479, 426 P.2d 267 (1967).

32. People v. Poindexter, 51 Cal.2d 142, 330 P.2d 763 (1958).

33. State v. Forsman, 260 N.W.2d 160 (Minn.1977).

34. People v. Shockley, 79 Cal.App.3d 669, 145 Cal.Rptr. 200 (1978).

35. Powers v. Commonwealth, 110 Ky. 386, 416, 61 S.W. 935, 63 S.W. 776 (1901).

36. People v. Pavlic, 227 Mich. 562, 199 N.W. 373 (1924).

37. People v. Henderson, 19 Cal.3d 86, 137 Cal.Rptr. 1, 560 P.2d 1180 (1977).

38. Homicide Act of 1957, 5 & 6 Eliz. II, c. 11, sec. 1.

39. The "killing of a human being without any design to effect the death by a person engaged in the commission of any felony." Okl.Stat.Ann. sec. 701 (1961).

land—that death resulting from a felony perpetrated or attempted in a dangerous manner is murder.[40]

One limitation of the rule usually requires that the crime be a common-law felony.[41] Under the Model Penal Code malice is "presumed if the actor is engaged or is an accomplice in the commission of, or an attempt to commit, or flight after committing or attempting to commit robbery, rape or deviate sexual intercourse by force or threat of force, arson, burglary, kidnapping or felonious escape."[42] What seems to be the prevailing view is that the felony-murder rule is limited to felonies which are inherently dangerous.[43] As emphasized in one case,[44] a homicide resulting from the commission of an inherently-dangerous felony, other than those mentioned in the first-degree murder statute, constitutes at least murder in the second degree.[45] The in-

40. The felony-murder rule in Maine is limited to cases in which the felony was committed or attempted in a manner which presents a serious threat to human life or is likely to cause serious bodily harm. State v. Wallace, 333 A.2d 72 (Me.1975). The killing was felony-murder because the felony, theft of a motor vehicle, was committed in a manner that betokened a reckless disregard of life. State v. Chambers, 524 S.W.2d 826 (Mo.1975). A felony that is "inherently dangerous or committed under circumstances that are inherently dangerous." State v. Harrison, 90 N.M. 439, 564 P.2d 1321, 1324 (1977).

41. Death resulting from statutory rape is not murder because this is not a common-law felony. Commonwealth v. Exler, 243 Pa. 155, 89 A. 968 (1914).

42. Model Penal Code sec. 210.2(1)(b). The Model Penal Code, without good reason, avoids the use of the word "malice." This requires more words to express the idea, but the idea is the same; namely, that the mens rea needed for murder is presumed. As to the omission of the word "malice" see Perkins, Some Weak Points in the Model Penal Code, 17 Hastings L.J. 3, 11–12 (1965); State v. Hokenson, 96 Idaho 283, 527 P.2d 487 (1974).

43. People v. Phillips, 64 Cal.2d 574, 578, 51 Cal.Rptr. 225, 229, 414 P.2d 353, 357 (1966). "In our judgment, the California rule is supported by logic, reason, history and common sense." Jenkins v. State, 230 A.2d 262, 268 (Del.1967). In disapproving State v. Moffitt, 199 Kan. 514, 431 P.2d 879 (1967), the court said: "Accordingly, we hold that in determining whether a particular collateral felony is inherently dangerous to human life so as to justify a charge of felony murder under K.S.A. 21–3401, the elements of

the collateral felony should be viewed in the abstract, and the circumstances of commission should not be considered in making the determination." State v. Underwood, 228 Kan. 294, 615 P.2d 153, 162–63 (1980). Escape is not an inherently-dangerous felony. The fact that the escape in this case was by force and violence did not authorize an instruction on the felony-murder rule. People v. Sedeno, 10 Cal.3d 703, 112 Cal.Rptr. 1, 518 P.2d 913 (1974). "Evidence of intoxication alone does not necessitate the giving of instructions covering lesser degrees of homicide in a felony murder case when the underlying felony is aggravated robbery." State v. Rueckert, 221 Kan. 727, 561 P.2d 850, 856 (1977).

44. People v. Ford, 60 Cal.2d 772, 795, 36 Cal.Rptr. 620, 635, 388 P.2d 892, 907 (1964). Such a homicide might be shown to be a wilful, deliberate and premeditated murder, and hence in the first degree.

45. It was pointed out in another case that unlawful selling or administering narcotics to a minor is not only a felony by statute, but is a felony dangerous to human life so that death resulting therefrom constitutes murder in the second degree. People v. Poindexter, 51 Cal.2d 142, 330 P.2d 763 (1958).

"The distribution of heroin by direct injection into the body of another is a felony 'upon or affecting the person whose death was caused' thereby and punishable under the felony-murder rule, . . ." State v. Forsman, 260 N.W.2d 160, 162 (Minn.1977).

"The killing of one accidentally, contrary to the intention of the parties, while in the prosecution of some felonious act other than those specified . . . is murder of the second degree." Va.Code 1950, § 18.2–33.

herently-dangerous felony is well illustrated by *Henderson*.[46] Under the statute false imprisonment is a misdemeanor unless effectuated by "violence, menace, fraud or deceit," in which case it is a felony. Defendant, while falsely imprisoning Reinesto in an extremely dangerous manner, unintentionally shot and killed Mrs. Gilhooley. The judge instructed the jury on two theories of second-degree murder: (1) a killing resulting from an unlawful act involving a high degree of probability of death, and (2) felony-murder on the ground that it resulted from felony-false-imprisonment. The jury found defendant guilty of second-degree murder and conviction followed, but the conviction was reversed because of the error in instructing on felony-murder. It was inferred that if false imprisonment was a felony only if committed by violence or menace then felony-false-imprisonment would be an inherently-dangerous felony. But since it may also be committed by fraud or deceit, the felony is not inherently dangerous. Defendant's insistence that this case should be regarded as involving the felony of false imprisonment by violence or menace was rejected on the ground that there is just one offense of felony by false imprisonment—i.e., committed by violence, menace, fraud or deceit.

Courts have applied the requirement of an inherently-dangerous felony in two differing manners.[47] In the first the felony is examined in the abstract and the dangerousness determined from the nature of the crime.[48] In the second the nature of felony is examined along with the circumstances surrounding its commission to determine whether the felony is inherently dangerous.[49] In the later instance the issue is more significantly a jury question.

Michigan, it has been held, has neither a statutory felony-murder doctrine nor a common-law felony-murder doctrine. Malice is not in that state imputed to an act of killing from an intent to commit an underlying felony. Malice may be inferred from the nature of the underlying felony and the circumstances of its commission, but the question of malice in each case remains a question for jury determination.[50] And Colorado has held that under its statutes there is no felony-murder rule.[51]

46. People v. Henderson, 19 Cal.3d 86, 137 Cal.Rptr. 1, 560 P.2d 1180 (1977).

47. State v. Harrison, 90 N.M. 439, 564 P.2d 1321 (1977).

48. People v. Satchell, 6 Cal.3d 28, 98 Cal.Rptr. 33, 489 P.2d 1361 (1971).

49. State v. Thompson, 280 N.C. 202, 185 S.E.2d 666 (1972); State v. Schad, 24 Utah 2d 255, 470 P.2d 246 (1970).

The rule applies to a felony committed in a dangerous manner. State v. Nunn, 297 N.W.2d 752 (Minn.1980).

50. People v. Fountain, 71 Mich.App. 491, 248 N.W.2d 589 (1976).

The Michigan Supreme Court has confirmed the Appeals Court position and concluded that Michigan does not have a common-law felony murder rule where malice is based upon the commission of the underlying felony. "We conclude that Michigan has no statutory felony-murder rule which allows the mental element of murder to be satisfied by proof of the intention to commit the underlying felony. Today we exercise our role in the development of the common law by abrogating the common-law felony-murder rule. We hold that in order to convict a defendant of murder, as that term is defined by Michigan case law, it must be shown that he acted with intent to kill or to inflict great bodily harm or with wanton and willful disregard of the likelihood that the natural tendency of his behavior is to cause death or great bodily harm. We further hold that the issue of malice must always be submitted to the jury." People v. Aaron, 409 Mich. 672, 299 N.W.2d 304, 328–329 (1980).

51. Sawyer v. People, 173 Colo. 351, 478 P.2d 672 (1970).

Some of the new penal codes place limitations on vicarious liability in felony-murder cases. It may be by providing that it is "an affirmative defense . . . that the defendant did not commit the homicide act or in any way solicit, command, induce, procure, counsel, or aid in its commission." [52] More frequently there are additional provisions, such as;

> (b) Was not armed with a deadly weapon, or any instrument, article or substance readily capable of causing death or serious physical injury and of a sort not ordinarily carried in public by law-abiding persons; and

> (c) Had no reasonable ground to believe that any other participant was armed with such a weapon, instrument, article or substance; and

> (d) Had no reasonable ground to believe that any other participant intended to engage in conduct likely to result in death or serious injury.[53]

The "felony-murder rule" is often couched in some such form as "homicide committed while perpetrating or attempting" and so forth.[54] This suggests mere coincidence as sufficient for the result, but the actual requirement is causation.[55] This statement, however, must not be overinterpreted. It does not mean that the loss of life must have resulted from a step intentionally taken for the purpose of achieving the felony but only that the felony was a *sine qua non: but for* the felony the deceased would not have been killed.[56] Thus it is not necessary under most statutes to show that the kill-

---

52. E.g., Ark.Stats. § 41–1502 (1977).

53. E.g., Colorado, Connecticut, Maine, New York, North Dakota, Oregon and Washington.

54. The wording of an English author was "whilst committing or attempting to commit a felony." 9 Halsbury's Laws of England 437 (2d ed. 1933). The Kentucky court spoke of "during the commission" and so forth. Simpson v. Commonwealth, 293 Ky. 831, 170 S.W.2d 869 (1943).

55. It is necessary to show that "death ensued in consequence of the felony," Buel v. People, 78 N.Y. 492, 497 (1879); or that it was "consequent to the felony." Pliemling v. State, 46 Wis. 516, 521, 1 N.W. 278, 281 (1879).

"This means there must be a direct causal connection between the commission of a felony and the homicide." State v. Moffit, 199 Kan. 514, 431 P.2d 879, 894 (1967).

"Causation in the final analysis primarily deals with the actus reus of the crime." State v. Harrison, 90 N.M. 439, 564 P.2d 1321, 1324 (1977).

56. "The law of this state has never required proof of a strict causal relation between the felony and the homicide." People v. Chavez, 37 Cal.2d 656, 669, 234 P.2d 632, 640 (1951). But the court meant only that it was not necessary to show that the killing was "while commit-

ting" or "while engaged in" or "in pursuance of" the felony but only that it was part of the *res gestae* of the felonious conduct.

However, the fact that the wallet was taken from one who had been unlawfully and mortally wounded will not support a conviction of first-degree murder (robbery-murder) if there was no intent to rob before the fatal injury was inflicted. People v. Gonzales, 66 Cal.2d 482, 58 Cal.Rptr. 361, 426 P.2d 929 (1967).

Homicide in the perpetration or attempted perpetration of a felony, with no causal connection between the two, is quite unlikely. It would be difficult to find such a killing which would have happened even if no felony had been attempted. But a comparable situation developed under the companion misdemeanor-manslaughter rule. While an officer was violating the law by not arresting persons who were openly committing the crime of gambling in his presence, he shot and killed a woman. There was evidence indicating that the shooting was quite accidental but the judge submitted the case to the jury under instructions to the effect that defendant was guilty of involuntary manslaughter if the killing occurred while he was violating the law by not arresting the gamblers. A conviction of manslaughter was reversed. People v. Mulcahy, 318 Ill. 332, 149 N.E. 266 (1925). "To convict one of

ing was intended or even that the act resulting in death was intended. It may have been quite unexpected. If it is charged that homicide was committed during the perpetration of robbery the only intent required is the intent to commit robbery. If that intent is shown the resulting homicide is murder even if it was quite accidental.[57] If the victim of robbery attempts to disarm his assailant and is killed by an accidental discharge of the weapon during a struggle for its possession, the robber is guilty of murder.[58] Furthermore, if arson results in the death of a fireman who was trying to put out the fire, the arsonist is recognized as having caused this death and is guilty of murder under the felony-murder rule.[59] And even the accidental killing of an accomplice during the perpetration of arson is murder for the same reason.[60]

In one case a dwelling was broken into at night for the purpose of killing the dweller. This was burglary, but the resulting killing was held not to be felony-murder.[61] While not expressed in these words, the idea was that this was not homicide in the perpetration of burglary, but burglary in the perpetration of homicide. Thus if **D** broke into the dwelling with malice aforethought he is guilty of murder. But if **D** followed the other into the house in the sudden heat of passion engendered by adequate provocation he is guilty, not of murder but of manslaughter.

Emphasis upon causation rather than coincidence is important for quite a different reason. Under the prevailing view if the killing resulted from the perpetration of the design it falls within the rule even if the felony itself had been completed before the fatal blow was struck. It is homicide resulting from burglary, for example, although the burglar had abandoned his "loot," left the building empty-handed and was running to avoid arrest at the time of the killing.[62] Homicide is within the felony-murder rule if it is within the

manslaughter for killing a person while in the commission of an unlawful act," said the court, "the State must show more than a mere coincidence of time and place between the wrongful act and the death."

"Clearly a more exact definition of causation is required. We define it as follows: Causation must be physical; causation consists of those acts of defendant or his accomplice initiating and leading to the homicide without an independent force intervening, even though defendant's or his accomplice's acts are unintentional or accidental. Causation in the final analysis primarily deals with the *actus reus* of the crime." State v. Harrison, 90 N.M. 439, 564 P.2d 1321, 1323–24 (1977).

57. People v. Stamp, 2 Cal.App.3d 203, 82 Cal.Rptr. 598 (1970); State v. Jensen, 209 Or. 239, 296 P.2d 618 (1956).

58. People v. Perry, 14 Cal.2d 387, 94 P.2d 559 (1939). And see State v. Best, 44 Wyo. 383, 12 P.2d 1110 (1932); People v. Riser, 47 Cal.2d 566, 305 P.2d 1 (1956); Rex v. Jarmain, 31 Cr.App.R. 39, 2 All E.R. 613, 614 (1945).

59. State v. Glover, 330 Mo. 709, 50 S.W.2d 1049 (1932); Cf. In re Anonymous, 14 Ariz.App. 466, 484 P.2d 235 (1971).

60. Commonwealth v. Bolish, 391 Pa. 550, 138 A.2d 447 (1958); State v. Williams, 254 So.2d 548 (Fla.App.1971).

61. People v. Wilson, 1 Cal.3d 431, 82 Cal.Rptr. 494, 462 P.2d 22 (1969).

62. Conrad v. State, 75 Ohio St. 52, 78 N.E. 957 (1906).

It was killing in the perpetration of robbery although the robber had taken the money from his victim and was running away with it when the killing occurred. State v. McCarthy, 160 Or. 196, 83 P.2d 801 (1938). But while he was running away with the stolen money the robbery could be said not to have been completed.

Compare a case in which it was held that kidnaping after the perpetration of robbery was held to be kidnaping for the purpose of robbery if it was to effect the escape of the robber or remove the victim to another place where he might less easily sound an alarm. People v. Randazzo, 48 Cal.2d 484, 310 P.2d 413 (1957), certio-

"res gestae" of the initial felony.[63] "The res gestae embraces not only the actual facts of the transaction and the circumstances surrounding it, but the matters immediately antecedent to and having a direct causal connection with it, as well as acts immediately following it and so closely connected with it as to form in reality a part of the occurrence."[64] A killing occurring during the course of an escape from a robbery or felony is a part of the res gestae of the felony.[65] Where a robber returned to the premises of the robbery and killed one of the victims in order to avoid detection the killing is within the scope of the felony murder rule.[66]

A narrower interpretation is to be found in some of the cases, induced perhaps by a desire to limit the application of an unreasonably broad statute. Thus when the New York statute included within the category of first-degree murder the killing of a human being by a person engaged in the commission of any felony,[67] this was held not to include a homicide occurring after the completion of the felony.[68]

Another point must not be overlooked. It would be futile to recognize the sudden heat of passion, engendered by great provocation, as sufficiently mitigating to reduce a voluntary homicide to manslaughter, if in the next breath it was added that manslaughter is a dangerous felony and hence homicide resulting from such an attempt must be murder. The distinction between murder and manslaughter, felonies both, makes it necessary to qualify any rule as to homicide resulting from felony by limiting it to felonies other than felonious homicide itself,—or else to felonies other than manslaughter.[69] This has usually been taken for granted but at times has been forced upon the attention of the court. One view is that in order to bring the case within the "felony-murder rule" it is essential that the slayer was engaged in some *other felony*, so distinct "as not to be an ingredient of the homicide" itself.[70] Some courts have rejected this view[71] although, needless

---

rari denied 355 U.S. 865, 78 S.Ct. 98 (1957).

63. State v. Adams, 339 Mo. 926, 98 S.W.2d 632 (1936); People v. McCrary, 190 Colo. 538, 549 P.2d 1320 (1976).

It is "the established law of this state that flight from the scene of the crime may be considered as a part of the res gestae of the crime and a killing during flight may constitute felony murder." State v. Hearron, 228 Kan. 693, 619 P.2d 1157, 1159 (1980).

64. State v. Fouquette, 67 Nev. 505, 221 P.2d 404, 417 (1950).

65. State v. Harley, 543 S.W.2d 288 (Mo.App.1976).

66. People v. Johnson, 55 Ill.2d 62, 302 N.E.2d 20 (1973).

67. See People v. Wood, 8 N.Y.2d 48, 201 N.Y.S.2d 328, 167 N.E.2d 736 (1960). The New York Revised Penal Code of 1967 has a different provision, see infra.

68. People v. Walsh, 262 N.Y. 140, 186 N.E. 422 (1933); People v. Hüter, 184 N.Y. 237, 77 N.E. 6 (1906).

"We find no room for quarrel with appellant's assertion that larceny from the body of one killed, as an afterthought, would not constitute a capital felony . . . where the robbery and the killing are so closely connected in point of time, place and continuity of action as to constitute one continuous transaction, it is proper to consider both as a single transaction and the homicide as a part of the res gestae of the robbery. . . . The sequence of events is unimportant and the killing may precede, coincide with or follow the robbery and still be committed in its perpetration." Grigsby v. State, 260 Ark. 499, 542 S.W.2d 275 (1976).

69. This is generally the wording of Smith-Hurd Ill.Ann.Stat. Ch. 9 § 1 (1973).

70. People v. Wilson, 1 Cal.3d 431, 82 Cal.Rptr. 494, 462 P.2d 22 (1969); State v. Fisher, 120 Kan. 226, 230, 243 P. 291, 293 (1926); People v. Hüter, 184 N.Y. 237, 244, 77 N.E. 6, 8 (1906).

71. State v. Harris, 69 Wn.2d 928, 421 P.2d 662 (1966); State v. Thompson, 88 Wn.2d 13, 558 P.2d 202 (1976); cf. State

to say, it would have to make the exception mentioned above as to man-slaughter.[72]

Legislation in a particular jurisdiction may change this rule of the common law, the same as any other. If the statute changes the common law by adding the word "purposely" in the definition of murder, an unintentional killing will not qualify even if it results from a dangerous felony.[73] The statutes of some jurisdictions limit the specific types of felonies to which the felony-murder rule is applied and also require a specific mental state such as an intentional, purposeful or knowing killing either for felony murder or an enhanced degree of felony murder.[74] At the other extreme is a statute providing that a person is guilty of murder when "perpetrated by a person engaged in the commission of any felony." [75]

This provision seems to cover every case in which there is a legally recognizable causal connection between the felonious act and the death, however remote the element of human risk may have been.

Except where changed by statute the felony-murder rule in this country should be stated in this form:

Homicide is murder if the death results from the perpetration or attempted perpetration of an inherently dangerous felony.

The felony-murder rule is somewhat in disfavor at the present time. The courts apply it where the law requires,[76] but they do so grudgingly and tend to restrict its application where circumstances permit.[77] It was entirely logical, however, in the day of its inception, when all felonies were punishable with death.[78] Since the would-be felon was willing to risk his life it was relatively unimportant that he became guilty of a capital crime in a different manner than he intended. The primary purpose of the rule, it may be mentioned, was to deal with the case in which the homicide was caused in an attempted felony which failed. Conviction of felony resulted in total forfeiture, the loss of life and lands and goods,[79] so nothing would have been added by establishing guilt of a second felony. An attempt to commit a felony, however, was a mere misdemeanor at common law.[80] Hence to hold guilty of a capital crime one who made an unsuccessful attempt to commit burglary during which he had caused the loss of human life, however unintentionally and unexpectedly, put the wrongdoer in no worse position, in legal theory,

v. Goodseal, 220 Kan. 487, 553 P.2d 279 (1976).

"We agree that the defendant was properly charged with a felony-murder based upon the death caused while in the commission of an assault in the second degree." State v. Modica, 18 Wn.App. 467, 569 P.2d 1161, 1167 (1977).

72. Braxton v. State, 240 Ga. 10, 239 S.E.2d 339 (1977).

73. This was the wording of the Ohio Gen. Code § 2903.02 (1953).

74. West's Fla.Stat.Ann. § 782.04 (1976); N.H.Revised Stat.Ann. 630:1–a (1974); Utah Code Ann. 1953, 76–5–202.

75. E.g. Okl.St.Ann. § 701.7 (1958); See Wade v. State, 581 P.2d 914 (Okl.1978).

76. People v. Pulley, 225 Cal.App.2d 366, 37 Cal.Rptr. 376 (1964).

77. People v. Washington, 62 Cal.2d 777, 44 Cal.Rptr. 442, 402 P.2d 130 (1965).

78. "The judgment against a felon is, that he be hanged by the neck until he be dead: . . ." 3 Co.Inst. *47. Whipping had been substituted for hanging in case of petit larceny. Id. at *109. In the time of Foster "all felonies with the exception of petty larceny" were punished by death. Moreland, Law of Homicide 50 (1952).

79. 4 Bl.Comm. *95–98.

80. "An attempt at common law is a common law misdemeanour. . . ." Kenny, Outlines of Criminal Law 108 (19th ed. by Turner 1966).

than if he had succeeded in committing burglary without homicide. At the present time, with the removal of most felonies from the category of capital crimes, the reason for the rule has ceased to exist. One who, in the perpetration or attempted perpetration of arson, rape, robbery, burglary, or kidnaping, causes death purposely or with force used in wanton and wilful disregard of the plain likelihood of causing death or great bodily injury, may well be held to be guilty of murder in the first degree; but the statute might well be amended so that a *homicide* committed during such perpetration could be shown to have been so unexpected as to constitute no more than manslaughter. The Model Penal Code would move in this direction by substituting a rebuttable presumption for the unyielding felony-murder rule.[81]

The felony-murder rule was abolished in England by the Homicide Act of 1957.[82] It is to be noted, however, that two recent penal codes in this country, the Illinois Criminal Code of 1961, and the Revised Penal Law of New York of 1967, have both retained the felony-murder rule in limited form: One worded in terms of homicide committed by one who "is attempting or committing a forcible felony other than voluntary manslaughter;" [83] and the other of similar import but specifying the felonies, namely, robbery, burglary, kidnaping, arson, rape in the first degree, sodomy in the first degree, escape in the first degree or escape in the second degree.[84] A recent Wisconsin statute simply provides that where death occurs as a natural and probable consequence of the commission or attempt to commit a felony the actor is guilty of a class B felony.[85]

Confusion results from the assumption sometimes entertained that the felony-murder rule results in conviction of murder where the killing has been without malice.[86] Nothing could be farther from the common-law concept which is that one perpetrating or attempting to perpetrate a dangerous felony "possesses a malevolent state of mind which the law calls 'malice'; . . ." [87] In other words the intent to engage in such a felony *is malice aforethought*.[88]

---

81. Model Penal Code, Section 210.2(1)(b).

82. Section 1. For an analysis see Prevezer, The English Homicide Act, 57 Colum.L.Rev. 624 (1957).

83. S.H.A. (Ill.) § 9–1 (1973).

84. McKinney's Revised Penal Law (N.Y.) § 125.25.3 (1975).

Immediately after an armed robbery the car in which the robber was fleeing from pursuing officers struck another car, killing the occupants. This was held sufficient to support a conviction of felony-murder. People v. Tillman, 70 Ill.App.3d 922, 27 Ill.Dec. 204, 388 N.E.2d 1253 (1979).

85. Wis.Stat.Ann. 940.02(2) (1958).

86. For such an assumption see Recent Developments, 18 Stan.L.Rev. 690 (1966).

87. Bell, J., concurring in Commonwealth v. Thomas, 382 Pa. 639, 655, 117 A.2d 204, 211 (1955). *Thomas* was over-

ruled in Commonwealth v. Redline, 391 Pa. 486, 137 A.2d 472 (1958), but the overruling had nothing to do with this statement.

United States v. Branic, 495 F.2d 1066 (D.C.Cir.1974).

"If a murder is committed during the perpetration of a felony, the felonious conduct is held tantamount to the elements of deliberation and premeditation which are otherwise required for first degree murder." State v. Rueckert, 221 Kan. 727, 561 P.2d 850, 855 (1977). The felony was aggravated robbery.

88. "The felony-murder doctrine ascribes malice aforethought to the felon who kills in the perpetration of an inherently dangerous felony." People v. Washington, 62 Cal.2d 777, 780, 44 Cal.Rptr. 442, 445, 402 P.2d 130, 133 (1965). It "supplies the element of malice." Simpson v. Commonwealth, 293 Ky. 831, 170 S.W.2d 869 (1943). The law "implyeth a former malicious disposition

As mentioned above, the foregoing is intended to give only the background of the law of felony-murder. The field itself is left to be addressed infra under F. Degrees of Criminal Homicide.

(D) Resisting Lawful Arrest [89]

It was stated by the early writers that the killing of one who was making a lawful arrest was murder.[90] And it has frequently been stated that homicide resulting from resistance to lawful arrest, with knowledge of the facts, is murder. However, a study of the cases in which this statement appears will ordinarily disclose that the killing resulted from shooting or from the use of some other dangerous force, such as stabbing with a knife or striking with a heavy club. This suggests that in these cases there had been an intent to kill or to inflict great bodily injury, or at least an act done in wanton and wilful disregard of the obvious likelihood of doing so. In fact one author, searching for a case in which homicide while resisting arrest had been held to be murder although the facts would not have supported that conviction had no such resistance been involved, was forced to say: "This writer has not found such a case." [91] An accidental killing by resisting arrest in a manner neither intended nor likely to cause death or injury is quite improbable, but when such cases were presented the notion that an accident of this nature is necessarily murder was rejected on both sides of the Atlantic—in *Porter* [92] on the other side and *Weisengoff* [93] on this. Malice, it was said in the latter, "cannot be inferred from the mere effort to escape arrest." [94]

The statement that homicide resulting from resisting lawful arrest is necessarily murder may have been in accord with ancient theory but for generations its repetition has been merely *obiter* and there is no sound basis for its recognition today.[95]

in him. . . ." Lambard, Eirenarcha 241 (1619).

89. See Kean, Homicide in Resisting Arrest, 26 Ky.L.Q. 50 (1937); Moreland, The Use of Force in Effecting or Resisting Arrest, 33 Nebr.L.Rev. 408, 420–22 (1954).

90. Yong's Case, 4 Co.Rep. 40a (1586); 3 Co.Inst. *52; 1 Hale P.C. *457. Acts of resistance to arrest were considered "the strongest indications of malice." 1 East P.C. *295.

91. Dickey, Culpable Homicide in Resisting Arrest, 18 Cornell L.Q. 373, 376 (1933). He emphasized this by saying that "no case has been found where the decision had to rest on malice implied from the mere resistance to arrest." Id. at 388.

92. The Queen v. Porter, 12 Cox C.C. 444 (1873). One being arrested objected to being put in the vehicle which was to take him to jail. During the struggle his foot came in contact with the head of one of his arresters with fatal consequences. In a trial for murder the judge directed the jury to find the defendant guilty of murder if the kick was intentional, but to

find him guilty of manslaughter only if they should find that the kick was not intentional, but an accidental contact while the defendant was merely struggling to keep out of the vehicle. The verdict was "guilty of manslaughter."

93. State v. Weisengoff, 85 W.Va. 271, 101 S.E. 450 (1919). In this case the evidence might have supported a finding that the killing was murder because it resulted from an act done in wanton and wilful disregard of the obvious likelihood of causing death or great bodily injury, but the jury was not asked to make such a finding. The case was left to the jury on the theory that if the death resulted from resistance to lawful arrest it was murder. This was held to be reversible error.

94. Id., 101 S.E. at 456.

95. "The ancient doctrine that a murder conviction could be founded upon a death . . . occasioned by resistance to lawful arrest, . . . supported for centuries on dicta, is at last recognized as non-existent." Hall, The Substantive Law of Crimes—1887–1936, 50 Harv.L. Rev. 616, 642 (1937). And see Turner,

It may be introduced by statute, however. Thus the Arizona statute defining first-degree murder was amended by adding "which is committed in avoiding or preventing lawful arrest." Although the statute does not include the word "knowingly" it was held that the context in which this clause appears requires it to be interpreted as if it read that it is first-degree murder if "committed while *knowingly* avoiding or preventing a lawful arrest." [96]

THE MODEL PENAL CODE

The Model Penal Code does not mention killing while resisting arrest.

THE NEW PENAL CODES

One of the new penal codes provides that one is guilty of first-degree murder when: "He causes the death of another person in order to avoid or prevent the lawful arrest of any person, . . ." [97] It would seem that an unintentional killing, even if resulting from recklessness, could not be said to have been committed "in order to avoid or prevent arrest." The provision in one of the codes is in effect that what might otherwise be innocent homicide is manslaughter if caused by one resisting a lawful arrest. [98] This is only codification to the common law misdemeanor-manslaughter rule as applied to this situation.

2. "PERSON–ENDANGERING–STATE–OF–MIND"

Since murder cannot be adequately defined in terms of an intent to kill, without resort to the ancient fiction whereby such an intent was "implied" in certain cases in which it did not exist in fact, some other phrase must be used. And since malice aforethought is neither a self-explanatory phrase, as used in the law, nor one which designates any single and invariable frame of mind, it is probably wise to employ a phrase to which a meaning may be assigned quite arbitrarily. The phrase "person-endangering-state-of-mind" is suggested for this purpose with the assumption that it be arbitrarily understood to include every attitude of mind which includes (1) an intent to kill, or (2) an intent to inflict great bodily injury, or (3) an intent to do an act in wanton and wilful disregard of an unreasonable human risk (i.e. the wilful doing of a wanton act under such circumstances that there is obviously a plain and strong likelihood that death or great bodily injury may result), or (4) an intent to perpetrate a dangerous felony.

3. DEFINITION OF MALICE AFORETHOUGHT

The phrase "person-endangering-state-of-mind," if accepted for this purpose and with this explanation, tells only part of the story, for such a state of mind will not constitute malice aforethought if there are circumstances of justification, excuse or mitigation. It is the course of caution to call attention to the fact that malice aforethought is a matter of mind, however conve-

The Mental Element in Crimes at Common Law, 6 Camb.L.J. 31, 54 (1936); Moreland, Law of Homicide 58 (1952).

96. State v. Mincey, 115 Ariz. 472, 566 P.2d 273, 279 (1977).

97. 11 Del.Code § 636(a)(7) (1979). The result mentioned in the text is practically spelled out in the Maine code. 17A Me.Rev.Stat.Ann. § 201.2.D (1979).

98. Louisiana Rev.Stat.Ann. 14:31 (2)(b) (1974).

nient it may be to speak in terms of the absence of circumstances of justification, excuse or mitigation. It is a psychical fact just as homicide is a physical fact. It is the particular kind of mens rea or mind at fault required for the more serious of the two types of felonious homicide. Perhaps it would be more accurate to speak of it as a label placed upon a group of states of mind, any one of which is sufficient for murder. A person-endangering-state-of-mind is not malice aforethought if there are circumstances of justification, excuse or mitigation; but such a state of mind in the presence of these circumstances is a different psychical fact than it would be if they were wanting. An intent to kill, to give a very limited illustration, may be the same intent, in a certain sense, whether it is for self-preservation, or is formed in a sudden rage engendered by great provocation, or is part of a well-laid plan for financial gain; but the psychical fact in its totality is not the same in any two of these. Furthermore, the appraisal or evaluation of appearances is also a psychical fact. Hence an intent to kill for the purpose of self-defense under circumstances in which there is reasonable ground for believing this drastic step to be necessary, is psychically different from an intent to kill in self-defense with the same belief but when there is nothing to warrant such a belief. In fact no inquiry into justification, excuse or mitigation in a homicide case can be disassociated from the mental element involved in criminal guilt. Perhaps the most extreme test of this point is found in the act of carrying out a lawful sentence of death.

If a sheriff is carrying out such a sentence what difference does it make what his state of mind may be? The fallacy involved in this question lies in the fact that the mental element—the mind without fault—has been satisfied by the assumption that he is "carrying out" a lawful sentence of death. If a sheriff who had no knowledge of any sentence of death having been pronounced should take the life of his prisoner for some unlawful purpose of his own, it would be no answer to a murder charge that there existed, unknown to him, a mandate for him to execute that man on that very day. The extreme unlikelihood of the officer's being unaware of the existence of the sentence does not affect the legal view of the situation. The knowledge that he is carrying out a sentence of the court makes this altogether different as a psychical fact than if he acted in ignorance of this matter. A felon may be killed lawfully under certain circumstances other than the execution of a sentence of death, as for example where this is the only means of preventing him from murdering an innocent victim, or of stopping his flight from arrest after the murder is committed. And there is an interesting case in which the shooting of an actual felon, under circumstances sufficient to justify the act had the facts been known, was held not to constitute a justification in favor of one who did not know or have any reason to believe that the person was a felon.[99]

With this emphasis upon the fact that the focus is centered entirely upon the mental facts involved, although the mental picture cannot be portrayed adequately without reference to peculiarities in the factual situation in which the mind is called upon to function, the following definition is suggested:

99. Regina v. Dadson, 4 Cox C.C. 358 (1850). And see People v. Burt, 51 Mich. 199, 202, 16 N.W. 378, 379 (1833). "[H]e cannot be excused from his wilful malicious act by a showing of circumstances of which he was not aware." Collett v. Commonwealth, 296 Ky. 267, 273, 176 S.W.2d 893, 896 (1943). See infra chapter 7, section 8.

Malice aforethought is an unjustifiable, inexcusable and unmitigated person-endangering-state-of-mind.

In other words this phrase requires the presence of one, or more, of the four intents mentioned above and the absence of every sort of justification, excuse or mitigation. Even an intentional killing is no crime at all if done under circumstances constituting a legally-recognized justification or excuse. Such a homicide is not criminal and this field has been considered above under the heading of "innocent homicide." It is unnecessary to repeat here what was said in that connection. By definition a person-endangering-state-of-mind does not constitute malice aforethought if it is justifiable or excusable.

A man-endangering-state-of-mind may fall short of malice aforethought even in the absence of justification or excuse. This is because of the requirement that it must also be unmitigated. As a matter of juridical science, any circumstance of substantial mitigation should be sufficient to reduce to manslaughter a killing that would otherwise be murder. Suppose, for example, the defendant thought he was in imminent danger of death and must kill to save himself from being murdered, and that he did kill for that reason. Suppose, also, there was no actual danger to his life at the moment, and the facts fell a little short of reasonable grounds for a belief in such danger. His homicide is not excused; but if the circumstances came rather close to such as would constitute an excuse his guilt is of manslaughter rather than murder,[1] assuming the absence of any peculiar statute in the jurisdiction which might change the common law in this regard. For the same reason, a killing to prevent crime may fall short of justification or excuse and yet come close enough to be regarded as having been committed under circumstances of substantial mitigation, sufficient to reduce the homicide to manslaughter.[2] Some states have codified provisions reducing murder to manslaughter where the actor unreasonably believes his conduct is justified.[3] In the vast majority of cases, however, such mitigation has involved the so-called "rule of provocation."

4. THE PRESUMPTION OF MALICE

Coke spoke of "malice fore-thought, either expressed by the party, or implied by law. . . ."[4] The idea may have been suggested by Lambard who explained felony-murder as applied to the robber by saying that the law "implyeth a former malicious disposition in him rather to kill the man, than not to have his money from him."[5] Blackstone said that malice "may be either express or implied in law,"[6] and judges and writers have been speaking in

1. Pendergrast v. United States, 332 A.2d 919 (D.C.App.1975); People v. Vaughn, 26 Ill.App.3d 247, 324 N.E.2d 697 (1975); Bliss v. State, 117 Wis. 596, 94 N.W. 325 (1903).

2. Williams v. State, 127 Miss. 851, 90 So. 705 (1922).

"Our case law holds that as it relates to the crime of murder, the term "maliciously" imports and includes the term "willfully." Clinkingbeard v. State, 6 Kan.App.2d 716, 634 P.2d 159, 161 (1981) (Defendant's response "not on purpose" was a denial that the killing was malicious).

3. Smith-Hurd Ill.Ann.Stat. ch. 38 § 9–2 (1973).

4. 3 Co.Inst. *47.

5. Lambard, Eirenarcha 241 (1619).

6. 4 Bl.Comm. *198.

terms of "express malice" and "implied malice" ever since. These terms have found their way even into some of the penal codes.[7]

While not always used with the same import,[8] *"express malice"* is generally employed to indicate that type of malice aforethought represented by an intent to kill, whereas any state of mind sufficient for murder while lacking that specific intent is denominated "implied malice." [9] This distinction led to the notion of "constructive murder," which was based upon a misunderstanding of the malice-aforethought concept.[10]

The term "presumed malice" has been used at times in place of "implied malice," [11] the idea being that in those states of mind sufficient for murder the law conclusively presumes an intent to kill even if it does not exist in fact.[12] A so-called conclusive presumption is not a true presumption. To say the law conclusively presumes an intent which does not exist in fact is merely a cumbersome way of expressing the idea that no such intent is required by law. It is much better to abandon the "double-talk" and recognize frankly that there may be malice aforethought without an intent to kill— which has been the modern trend as mentioned earlier.

There is, however, a true presumption of malice aforethought.[13] It would be an unreasonable burden upon the prosecution to require it in every murder case to prove not only the killing of the deceased by the defendant, but also the non-existence of every conceivable set of circumstances which might be sufficient to constitute either innocent homicide or guilt of manslaughter only. Thus the prosecution is not required to prove in the first instance as a part of its case (in addition to the killing of the deceased by the defendant) that the defendant was not so insane as to be wanting in criminal capacity,[14] or that the killing was not by accident, or that it did not result from the privileged use of deadly force [15] or that it did not result from the sudden heat of passion engendered by adequate provocation, or other matters of this kind.[16] To require such proof would constitute an absurd waste of time,[17]

---

7. See e.g., Iowa Criminal Code Sec. 707.1 (1978).

8. For the various meanings of "express" and "implied" malice, see Perkins, A Re-Examination of Malice Aforethought, 43 Yale L.J. 537, 546–555 (1934).

9. Ibid. Cf. People v. Spinuzzi, 149 Colo. 391, 369 P.2d 427 (1962).

10. "It was evidently supposed . . . that the phrase, *malice-aforethought,* used in indictments for murder, necessarily imputed a charge of premeditated design to kill. To meet this averment, which in cases of constructive murder was not required to be proved, the law was said to *imply,* that is, to supply by *mere fiction,* the requisite degree of malice. There was, however, in truth not the slightest necessity for this fiction; the interpretation of the word malice, on which it was founded, being entirely erroneous." Darry v. People, 10 N.Y. 120, 138 (1854).

11. "Malice in law, or presumed malice, ..." Hale P.C. *451.

12. 3 Stephen, History of the Criminal Law of England 63 (1883).

13. "There is in truth but one kind of presumption; . . ." "Nevertheless, it must be kept in mind that the peculiar effect of a presumption 'of law' (that is, the real presumption) is merely to invoke a rule of law compelling the jury to reach the conclusion *in the absence of evidence to the contrary* . . ." 9 Wigmore, Evidence § 2491 (3d ed. 1940).

14. State v. Silverio, 79 N.J.L. 482, 488, 76 A. 1069, 1071 (1910); People v. DiPiazza, 24 N.Y.2d 342, 300 N.Y.S.2d 545, 248 N.E.2d 412 (1969).

15. Triplett v. Commonwealth, 245 Ky. 167, 53 S.W.2d 345 (1932); State v. Cooper, 273 N.C. 51, 159 S.E.2d 305 (1968).

16. Cerda v. State, 557 S.W.2d 954 (Tex.Cr.App.1977).

17. "Trials would be made even more unnecessarily long than they are if all possible defenses of this sort had to be

and would require proving in many instances the absence of a non-existent circumstance.[18] This difficulty is avoided by a rule of law in the form of a presumption.[19] It has sometimes been said that every homicide is presumed to be with malice aforethought and that it devolves upon the defendant to prove circumstances which will justify, excuse or mitigate the act. This, however, is quite generally recognized to be an overstatement of the position. If the evidence introduced by the state, while showing the killing of the deceased by the defendant, should at the same time establish some basis of justification or excuse, the defendant would be entitled to a directed verdict of acquittal without the introduction of evidence on his part.[20] Hence it is necessary to put the matter in this form: Every homicide is presumed to have been committed with malice aforethought "unless the evidence which proves the killing itself shows it to have been without malice." [21]

Since this is a presumption in the true sense it merely places upon the defendant the burden of going forward with the evidence.[22] It is rebuttable and may be overcome by evidence which throws a different light upon the situation [23] or indicates exculpating or mitigating circumstances.[24] If no

met in advance without waiting to see whether they are set up." Per Holmes, C. J., in Commonwealth v. Chance, 174 Mass. 245, 250, 54 N.E. 551, 554 (1899).

18. "For all homicide is presumed to be malicious until the contrary appeareth upon the evidence." 4 Bl.Comm. *201.

19. See, for example, the instruction of the judge in McDaniel v. State, 16 Miss. 401, 407 (1847). This was held to be "too broad and unrestricted."

20. The burden is always upon the state to rebut exculpatory evidence contained in its own case. State v. Copenbarger, 52 Idaho 441, 16 P.2d 383 (1932); State v. Gregory, 203 N.C. 528, 166 S.E. 387 (1932).

Some statutes authorize the judge to enter a "judgment of acquittal." See West's Ann.Cal.Pen.Code § 118.1 (1967 Amendment); Rule 29 Fed.R.Crim.P.

21. Murphy v. State, 37 Ala. 142, 144 (1861). "[W]hen the state has proved the commission of a homicide by a defendant, the presumption is that he is guilty of either murder in the first or second degree, unless the proof offered by the state itself tends to reduce the offense to manslaughter or show that the defendant was justifiable or excusable." Miranda v. State, 42 Ariz. 358, 26 P.2d 241, 243 (1933).

It is sometimes said, in substance, that in a murder trial, proof of defendant's commission of the homicide by evidence not tending to show any justification, excuse or mitigation, places upon him the burden of showing the existence of any such factor if he can. See e.g. State v.

Burris, 80 Idaho 395, 331 P.2d 265 (1958). This no doubt is traceable to Blackstone's statement that "we may take it for a general rule that all homicide is malicious, and of course amounts to murder, unless where *justified . . . excused . . . or alleviated* into manslaughter by being either the involuntary consequence of some act not strictly lawful, or (if voluntary) occasioned by some sudden and sufficiently violent provocation." 4 Bl.Comm. *201. But if we speak only of justification, excuse and mitigation we fail to include all Blackstone had in mind. If the evidence for the prosecution showed no more than homicide by criminal negligence, for example, there would be no presumption of malice.

Proof that D killed the deceased, it was said, does not establish a presumption of malice aforethought. State v. Gardner, 51 N.J. 444, 242 A.2d 1 (1968). This may have been true under the facts of the case, but the court was in error if it meant that in every murder trial the prosecution must take notice of every possible justification, excuse or mitigation that might ever be established in any murder trial, and come forward with independent evidence to prove that it did not exist in the present case.

22. 9 Wigmore, Evidence § 2491 (3d ed. 1940).

23. Mann v. State, 124 Ga. 760, 762, 53 S.E. 324, 325 (1906); State v. Cassim, 112 Va. 92, 97, 163 S.E. 769, 771 (1932).

24. See Stepp v. State, 170 Ark. 1061, 1067, 282 S.W. 684, 687 (1926).

such evidence is offered a conviction of murder is proper because of the "presumed malice." [25] Where the prosecution has the burden of proving a specific state of mind on the part of the defendant in order to establish culpable homicide, an instruction to the jury that "the law presumes a person intends the ordinary consequences of his voluntary acts" is constitutionally objectionable to the extent it may be taken by the jury as conclusive or as casting on the defendant the burden of proving to the contrary.[26]

5. THE BURDEN OF PROOF

In the past the term "burden of proof" has been used in two different senses.

(1) The burden of going forward with the evidence. The party having this burden must introduce some evidence if he wishes to get a certain issue into the case. If he introduces enough evidence to require consideration of this issue, this burden has been met.

(2) Burden of proof in the sense of carrying the risk of nonpersuasion. The one who has this burden stands to lose if his evidence fails to convince the jury—or the judge in a nonjury trial.

The present trend is to use the term "burden of proof" only with this second meaning—bearing the risk of nonpersuasion. That is the sense in which the concept is used herein.

It had been assumed by some that the burden was on the prosecution to prove beyond a reasonable doubt everything needed for a conviction. It turns out that, while this is very close to the actual procedure as it was for many years,[27] it is an overstatement of the legal requirement as it has been interpreted. Thus it has been held that the law may validly place upon the defendant the burden of proving some affirmative defenses. In fact, when Oregon law required an accused, claiming the insanity defense, to prove insanity beyond a reasonable doubt, this held to be constitutional. This was *Leland,*[28] which has recently been cited with approval.[29]

25. "Malice may be presumed from the proof of the homicide alone if the evidence adduced to establish the homicide shows neither mitigation nor justification or excuse." State v. Mendell, 111 Ariz. 51, 523 P.2d 79, 83 (1974).

Even so, the jury because of its "mercy dispensing power" may return a verdict of voluntary manslaughter. Commonwealth v. Whitfield, 474 Pa. 27, 376 A.2d 617, 620 (1977).

26. Sandstrom v. Montana, 442 U.S. 510, 99 S.Ct. 2450 (1979).

27. In 1895 it was held that if the insanity defense is fairly raised by defendant's evidence in a federal case, the prosecution must prove sanity beyond a reasonable doubt. Davis v. United States, 160 U.S. 469, 16 S.Ct. 353 (1895). "This ruling had wide impact on the practice in the federal courts with respect to the burden of proving various affirmative defenses, and the prosecution in a

majority of jurisdictions in this country sooner or later came to shoulder the burden of proving the sanity of the accused and of disproving the facts constituting other affirmative defenses, including provocation." Patterson v. New York, 432 U.S. 197, 202, 97 S.Ct. 2319, 2323 (1977). "The burden is upon the state to prove his guilt beyond a reasonable doubt; and if the evidence with respect to any defense, e.g., in this case alibi, is sufficient to raise a reasonable doubt as to defendant's guilt, he should be acquitted." State v. Wilson, 565 P.2d 66, 68 (Utah 1977). It was reversible error to place upon the defendant the burden of establishing self-defense. State v. McLaurin, 33 N.C.App. 589, 235 S.E.2d 871 (1977).

28. Leland v. Oregon, 343 U.S. 790, 72 S.Ct. 1002 (1952).

29. Patterson v. New York, 432 U.S. 197, 97 S.Ct. 2319 (1977).

The Supreme Court has held that the prosecution has the burden of proving beyond a reasonable doubt every element of the definition of the crime charged [30] and that any device to avoid this proof is unconstitutional. If, for example, the definition of murder, whether found in the statute or in interpretation, includes the element of unlawfulness, the prosecution will have the burden of proving that the killing was not in justifiable or excusable self-defense, if defendant's evidence in a murder trial fairly presents this issue, because if the killing was in such defense it was not unlawful. And it violated due process for the state to shift the burden of proof to the defendant by a presumption of unlawfulness from intentional killing with a deadly weapon.[31] And if murder has been defined in terms of a killing with malice aforethought, and it has been held that a killing in a sudden heat of passion engendered by adequate provocation is not with malice aforethought and hence is not murder but manslaughter, the state may not place upon defendant the burden of proving that the killing was in such heat of passion.[32] But if the murder statute makes no mention of malice aforethought, and the stated definition is satisfied if an act done with intent to kill a human being results in the death of a human being, the holding is quite different. If such a statute adds that it is an affirmative defense that such a killing was under the influence of extreme emotional disturbance for which there was a reasonable explanation or excuse, in which case the killing was not murder but manslaughter, the state may validly place upon defendant the burden of proving this affirmative defense by a preponderance of the evidence.[33]

The Court has stated that there are constitutional limits beyond which the state may not go in reallocating burdens of proof by labeling as affirmative defenses some of the elements of the crimes now defined in their statutes, without indicating what such limitations may be.[34] This invites an interesting question. How much can be eliminated from the definition of murder and still leave it a crime? One conclusion is obvious. The element of unlawfulness cannot be eliminated from murder without removing murder from the category of crime. However absurd it may seem, if murder is defined so that it may be justifiable or excusable, the inevitable result is that, under such a definition, murder is not a crime but only something that is criminal under some circumstances and not under others, just as homicide is not a crime although it may be under some circumstances and not under others. And if murder is so defined it becomes necessary to divide it into criminal murder and innocent murder, just as common-law homicide is divided into criminal homicide and innocent homicide. The next step is unavoidable. Under such a statute the *offense* charged is not murder but criminal murder, and what must be proved to secure a conviction are all the elements of criminal murder.

In discussing *Leland*, which held the state may validly require the defendant to prove insanity beyond a reasonable doubt, it was said that such a requirement "does not serve to negative any facts of the crime which the

30. The "Due Process Clause requires the prosecution to prove beyond reasonable doubt all of the elements included in the definition of the offense of which the defendant is charged." Id. at p. 204, 97 S.Ct. at p. 2327.

31. Hankerson v. North Carolina, 432 U.S. 233, 97 S.Ct. 2339 (1977).

32. Mullaney v. Wilbur, 421 U.S. 684, 95 S.Ct. 1881 (1975).

33. Patterson v. New York, 432 U.S. 197, 97 S.Ct. 2319 (1977).

34. "But there are obviously constitutional limits beyond which the States may not go in this regard." Id. at p. 210, 97 S.Ct. at p. 2327.

state is to prove to convict for murder. It constitutes a separate issue on which defendant is required to carry the burden of persuasion; . . ." [35] To test this it may be well to examine a different defense. The leading case on entrapment [36] shows a sharp split in regard to the theory of this defense. Five justices held that proof of entrapment establishes innocence of the offense charged, whereas the others took the position that when entrapment is established the crime has been proved but the government is denied a conviction because of the outrageous conduct of its own agent. This is in effect an estoppel doctrine—where the plaintiff's own agent has instigated the harm the judgment must be for the defendant. Since that case the innocence theory of entrapment has steadily lost ground and the prevailing view today is that proof of entrapment requires a judgment of acquittal because of the intolerable conduct of the public officer.

Under the "estoppel" theory of entrapment there is no constitutional objection to placing the burden of proof on defendant. This is obviously a situation in which this "does not serve to negative any facts of the crime which the state is to prove to convict for murder. It constitutes a separate issue on which defendant is required to carry the burden of persuasion." [37] What then of the insanity defense?

It seems to have been generally assumed that this defense entitles defendant to an acquittal on the ground that it establishes the lack of the mental element needed for conviction. It is arguable, however, that it entitles defendant to an acquittal, not because it establishes innocence, but because the state declines to convict one shown to have committed the crime while mentally disordered by disease or defect to such an extent as to be too abnormal to be recognized as "sane." This is clearly the theory of the Supreme Court which said that it "does not serve to negative any facts of the crime." On this theory there is no constitutional objection to placing the burden of proving insanity on defendant, since the prosecution retains the burden of proving every element of the crime, although an acquittal may be required by a showing unrelated thereto.

No similar explanation is possible for a defense such as justification or excuse. This has been referred to as an "affirmative defense" because it will not get into the case unless defendant introduces it. He has the burden of "going forward with the evidence" of such a defense. But the accepted view has been that if he introduces enough evidence to require consideration of this issue, the prosecution has the "burden of persuasion" and must prove beyond a reasonable doubt that the killing was not in justifiable self-defense,[38] if that is defendant's claim. And it would seem to be unconstitutional to place the burden of proof of this issue on defendant.

Whether murder is defined as at common law, or by other words of similar import, or so loosely as to include a killing under circumstances of justification or excuse, it is clear that there is no such crime as justifiable or excusable homicide. By definition, if the killing is justifiable or excusable it is not

---

35. Id. at p. 207, 97 S.Ct. at p. 2325.

36. Sorrells v. United States, 287 U.S. 435, 53 S.Ct. 210 (1932).

37. In explaining why entrapment is not governed by the general rule applicable to affirmative defenses, the court said the reason is because entrapment "is

not based on the defendant's innocence." People v. Moran, 1 Cal.3d 755, 83 Cal.Rptr. 411, 463 P.2d 763 (1970).

38. People v. Banks, 67 Cal.App.3d 379, 137 Cal.Rptr. 652 (1976); State v. Beyer, 258 N.W.2d 353, 356 (Iowa 1977).

criminal. Any homicide *offense*, however worded, must include the element of unlawfulness even if found only in the interpretation. This is one of the "facts of the crime which the state is to prove to convict." This means that the state has the burden of proving unlawfulness beyond a reasonable doubt.

The prosecution has the burden of proving beyond a reasonable doubt every element of the offense charged and any effort to shift this burden by a presumption or otherwise is unconstitutional. But if the defendant has an affirmative defense, which entitles him to a judgment on some ground other than innocence, it is not unconstitutional to require him to carry the burden of proof of this issue. And if a statute provides for offenses of different grades or degrees, it may be so worded as to place upon defendant the burden of proving he is entitled to be convicted of the lower grade or degree, rather than the higher.

THE MODEL PENAL CODE

Section 210.1 Criminal Homicide

(1) A person is guilty of criminal homicide if he purposely, knowingly, recklessly or negligently [39] causes the death of another human being.

(2) Criminal homicide is murder, manslaughter or negligent homicide.

This section is confusing and inconsistent. Elsewhere in the Code (Article 3) it is provided that a homicide which is committed purposely or knowingly may nevertheless be under circumstances of justification or excuse [40] and hence no crime at all. Hence if subsection (1) stood alone we would have the absurd result of criminal homicide that might be either criminal or innocent. But subsection (2) limits criminal homicide to murder, manslaughter and negligent homicide. This shows that subsection (1) does not really mean what it seems to say. It would have been much better if criminal homicide had been worded in terms of homicide committed without justification or excuse. But the interpretation will be the same. The Code further provides:

Section 210.2 Murder

(1) Except as provided in Section 210.3(1)(b) [voluntary manslaughter] criminal homicide constitutes murder when:

(a) it is committed purposely or knowingly; or . . ..

With the interpretation given to Section 210.1 this means "it is committed purposely or knowingly and without justification or excuse." Thus the word "murder" does not include any homicide which is not criminal.

---

39. The Code defines "negligently" in terms of criminal negligence. It "involves a gross deviation from the standard of care that a reasonable person would observe in the actor's position." Section 2.02(2)(d). This invites confusion because this is not what "negligently" means elsewhere in the law. It would be better to use "criminal negligence" where that is what is intended.

40. The Code speaks only in terms of "justification," but includes what has traditionally been spoken of as justification and excuse. The difference between the two has lost its original significance.

THE NEW PENAL CODES

Some of the new penal codes define "murder" in terms of "malice afore-thought" [41] or "maliciously." [42] This is the best plan because "malice" in relation to homicide has back of it centuries of interpretation, and it is easier to state the desired result in terms of this word than without it. And its use does not in any way interfere with making any changes in the traditional position which may be desired. Furthermore, substantially fewer words are needed to express various possibilities of killing "with malice" or "without malice" than are needed under statutes which require essentially the same mens rea, but without the use of the word "malice."

Some of the new codes follow the plan of the Model Penal Code by defin-ing "criminal homicide," and then defining "murder" in terms of "criminal homicide." [43] At times the confusion of the Model Penal Code is avoided by including "without justification or excuse" [44] or "unlawfully" [45] in the defini-tion of "criminal homicide." This is desirable, but a forced interpretation will reach the same result without such careful wording.

In any state which defines "murder" in terms of "malice" or "unlawful killing," [46] or which follows the plan of the Model Penal Code, the word "murder" does not include any killing which is not a crime, but that is not true under the wording of some of the other codes. If for example the stat-ute provides that a person is guilty of murder if he "purposely causes the death of another; or . . .," [47] or with some equivalent language,[48] with no exception or limitation stated or implied there, the only possible interpre-tation is that every such killing is murder. And when it is provided in a different part of the code that such a killing may be under circumstances of justification or excuse and hence no crime at all, the result is that in such a state "murder" may be either criminal or innocent. There is no such concept as "innocent murder" at common law and there should not be. It is hoped that amendments will be made where necessary to wipe this out.

C. MANSLAUGHTER

Manslaughter is unlawful homicide committed without malice aforethought.*

It was unknown to the English common law, having resulted from ancient statutes (see infra, F) designed to provide a penalty less than death for certain unlawful homicides. These statutes are

41. Ga.Code § 26–1101 (1978); Iowa Code Ann. § 690.1 (1978); New Mex.Stat. 1978 § 30–2–1.

42. Kan.Stat.Ann. § 21–3401 (1974).

43. Code of Ala., Tit. 13, § 13–6–1 (1975); Mont.Code Ann. § 45–5–101 (1981); Or.Rev.Stat. § 163.005, § 163.115 (1979); 18 P.S. § 2501 (Penn.1973); V.A.T.S.Penal Code § 19.01 (1974); Utah Code Ann. 1953, § 76–5–201.

44. Or.Rev.Stat. § 163.005 (1979).

45. Utah Code Ann. 1953, 76–5–201; Ill.Rev.Stat. 1971, ch. 38, § 9–1 (1973).

46. West's Fla.Stat.Ann. § 782.04 (1976).

47. N.H.Rev.Stat.Ann. 630:1 (1974).

48. Ark.Stats. § 41–1502 (1977); Colo.Rev.Stat. 1973, § 18–3–102(a); 11 Del.Code § 636(1) (1979); Hawaii Rev.Stat., Title 37, § 707–701(1) (1976).

* "To be 'unlawful,' a homicide must be neither justifiable nor excusable, . . ." In re Doe, ___ R.I. ___, 390 A.2d 920, 925 (1978).

part of our common law. Hence manslaughter is a noncapital felony under American common law and under modern statutes.

The early English judges tended to focus attention upon two points in the homicide cases. At one side careful attention was given to homicides to determine if they had been committed with malice aforethought. If this was found lacking they turned to the other extreme to see if there was any justification or excuse. All homicides which were neither with malice aforethought nor under circumstances of justification or excuse were dealt with as manslaughter.[49] Hence this was definitely a "catch-all" group, and confusion can be avoided best by thinking of the development of this crime in terms of this process of elimination.

Manslaughter is any homicide which is neither murder nor innocent homicide, and such a killing may be either intentional or unintentional.

1. CLASSIFICATION

Manslaughter is commonly referred to as being of two kinds,—(1) voluntary and (2) involuntary. This was purely a factual distinction at common law, the punishment being the same for both. Some statutes use the common-law plan in this regard, some follow the same plan except for the establishment of different penalties for the two types mentioned, and a few have an entirely different scheme of classification as will be pointed out under "degrees of criminal homicide."

An act causing death may have been intentional or unintentional. Moreover, an intended act may have unintended consequences. If death results from shooting, for example, the discharge itself may have been intentional or unintentional; and if the one holding the gun purposely pulled the trigger, the resulting loss of life may have been the very end he was seeking to achieve, or it may not have been contemplated by him at all,—to mention only the extreme possibilities. Hence in such a case it is essential to distinguish between an intentional shooting and an intentional killing. An intentional act, in the sense of pulling a trigger or driving an automobile, may cause involuntary manslaughter; but an intentional killing cannot fall within this category. The other side of the problem is not so simple. Many statements can be found to the effect that voluntary manslaughter requires an intentional killing;[50] but the tendency has been to give the phrase a meaning broad enough to cover any killing with a person-endangering-state-of-mind that is neither murder nor innocent homicide.[51] This latter usage has the advantage of simplicity because unlawful homicide with a person-endanger-

49. Johnson v. State, 70 Ga.App. 4, 27 S.E.2d 244 (1943). This has been codified at times. "Homicide, not excusable or justifiable, but perpetrated in a manner not constituting murder, is manslaughter." NDCC (No.Dak.) 12–27–15, since repealed, see currently NDCC 12.1–16–02 (1975).

50. People v. Forbes, 62 Cal.2d 847, 852, 44 Cal.Rptr. 753, 402 P.2d 825 (1965); Johnson v. State, 70 Ga.App. 4, 27 S.E.2d 244 (1943).

Involuntary manslaughter is distinguished from voluntary manslaughter by lack of an intent to kill. State v. Childers, 217 Kan. 410, 536 P.2d 1349 (1975).

51. Vires v. Commonwealth, 308 Ky. 707, 215 S.W.2d 837 (1948). Voluntary manslaughter does not require "the specific intent to kill." Barbeau v. United States, 13 Alaska 551, 193 F.2d 945, 947 (1952). Contra, "An accidental killing is not voluntary manslaughter." Searles v. State, 589 P.2d 386, 389 (Wyo.1979).

ing-state-of-mind is murder in the absence of mitigation, whereas unlawful homicide without such a state of mind is only manslaughter in any event.

A. VOLUNTARY MANSLAUGHTER

It is not the purpose of the law to unbridle human passions. On the contrary, one very important aim of the criminal law is to induce persons to keep their passions under proper control. At the same time the law does not ignore the weaknesses of human nature. Hence as a matter of common law an unlawful killing may even be intentional and yet of a lower grade than murder.[52]

This has been changed in some jurisdictions by a statutory definition of murder broad enough to include such homicides. This is true, for example, where the enactment provides in substance that the killing of a human being without authority of law, by any means or in any manner is murder when done with deliberate design to effect the death of person killed or any human being [53] (and also in certain instances when committed without such design). As such changes are the exception rather than the rule, and modern codes closely parallel the above-mentioned standard,[54] it is important to give careful consideration to the common law in this regard.[55]

The common statement with reference to the first type is this: An intentional homicide committed in a sudden rage of passion engendered by adequate provocation, and not the result of malice conceived before the provocation, is voluntary manslaughter. It is necessary to add that intentional homicide committed under other circumstances of mitigation may be voluntary manslaughter; but the consideration of those problems will be postponed for later attention because they are not involved in most of the actual cases.

(A) The Rule of Provocation

Not without interest is the starting point in the development of the so-called rule of provocation, which was merely a matter of evidence at a time when the word "aforethought" was assumed to have actual significance as used in the definition of murder. Thus Lambard, writing in 1581 [56] uses "malice aforethought" in the sense of real and substantial premeditation although he does not require direct and positive evidence thereof. Reflecting, perhaps, the current thinking of his day he resorts to an inference of fact— that an intentional killing without any apparent motive must have been due to a concealed motive. Hence he says that in case of such a killing without apparent provocation the law judges the fatal act "to have proceeded of former malice meditated within his owne minde, howsoever it bee kept secret from the sight of other men." [57] However, a killing in a sudden angry fist

---

52. Green v. State, 49 Ala.App. 163, 269 So.2d 179 (1972); State v. Jensen, 197 Kan. 427, 417 P.2d 273 (1966).

"Proof of extreme emotional disturbance does not negate the intentional element of murder but empowers the jury to find a reasonable explanation of his otherwise intentional conduct and convict him of the lesser crime of manslaughter in the first degree, . . ." State v. Davis, 44 Or.App. 549, 606 P.2d 671, 673 (1980).

53. Miss.Code Ann. 1942 § 97–3–19, § 97–3–55 (1973).

54. Code of Ala., Tit. 13A § 6–3(a)(2) (1975).

55. 3 Co.Inst. *55; 4 Bl.Comm. *191–92.

56. William Lambard, 1536–1601. His Eirenarcha was first published in 1581.

57. Lambard, Eirenarcha 239 (1619). He expresses the same idea in this form:

fight (anciently referred to as a "chance medley")[58] manifested its own explanation and gave no room for imputation of premeditation, hence the offense was manslaughter. "Some manslaughters be voluntary and not of malice aforethought, upon some sudden falling out."[59]

When it came to be recognized that the crime of murder required no actual premeditation a killing in a sudden rage inflamed by an angry fist fight was still held to be manslaughter, but a different explanation was needed.[60] Such circumstances, it was then said, are so mitigating that the slayer's state of mind cannot properly be characterized as "malicious."[61]

In order for a killing which would otherwise be murder to be reduced to manslaughter under the "rule of provocation" there are four requirements:

(1) There must have been adequate provocation.

(2) The killing must have been in the heat of passion.

(3) It must have been a sudden heat of passion—that is, the killing must have followed the provocation before there had been a reasonable opportunity for the passion to cool.

(4) There must have been a causal connection between the provocation, the passion, and the fatal act.[62]

(1) Adequate Provocation [63]

There must not only be provocation, but provocation of such a nature as to be recognized by law as adequate for this purpose.[64]

To emphasize this requirement some courts have spoken in other terms such as *great* provocation or *lawful* provocation. The latter form of expression is objectionable because the provocation is itself an *unlawful* act of another, since a lawful act, even if it involves physical violence, is not customa-

---

"So, many times the law doth (by the sequelle) judge of that malice which lurked before within the partie, and doth accordingly make imputation of it." Ibid.

58. The term is sometimes employed to refer to homicide in a casual affray but more properly indicates the affray itself. See 4 Bl.Comm. *184.

59. 3 Co.Inst. *55. "There is no difference between murder, and manslaughter; but that one is upon malice aforethought, and the other upon a sudden occasion: . . ." Ibid.

60. East did not clearly distinguish the new theory from the old, saying: "Herein is to be considered under what circumstances it may be presumed that the act done, though intentional of death or great bodily harm, was not the result of a cool deliberate judgment and previous malignity of heart, but imputable to human infirmity alone." 1 East P.C. 232 (1803).

61. Such a killing "is regarded as done through heat of blood or violence of anger, and not through malice, . . ." Commonwealth v. Webster, 59 Mass. (5 Cush.) *295, 308 (1850).

"There can be no such thing in law as a killing with malice, and also upon the *furor brevis* of passion; and provocation furnishes no extenuation, unless it produces passion. Malice excludes passion. Passion presupposes the absence of malice. In law they cannot co-exist." State v. Johnson, 23 N.C. 354, 362 (1840).

62. State v. Frederick, 20 Wn.App. 175, 579 P.2d 390, 394 (1978).

63. See Manslaughter and the Adequacy of the Provocation: The Reasonableness of the Reasonable Man, 106 U. of Pa.L.Rev. 1021 (1958); White, A Note on Provocation [1970] Crim.L.Rev. 446.

64. McHargue v. Commonwealth, 231 Ky. 82, 87, 21 S.W.2d 115, 117 (1929).

rily recognized by law as a mitigating circumstance.[65] The choice between the other two is merely a matter of convenience; the result is the same whether the requirement is worded in terms of "adequate provocation" or "great provocation." A provocation not "adequate" or "great" enough to reduce a voluntary killing to manslaughter may nevertheless be sufficient to bring it within the category of second degree murder rather than first [66] or to entitle it to consideration in the assessment of the punishment for murder if the law gives discretion in this regard; but such are not the problems under consideration here.

The problem of provocation in the homicide cases cannot be considered effectively without keeping constantly in mind the relation of the retaliatory act to the provocative one. The foundation principle is that where the former is not unreasonably excessive and out of proportion to the latter, the basis of mitigation is established (if the latter was not altogether inadequate); but where it is unreasonably excessive and out of proportion no mitigation will be recognized.[67] Thus a greater provocation will be required to reduce an intentional killing to manslaughter than would be sufficient for this purpose if the homicide was not actually intended, although under circumstances that would make it murder apart from the rule of provocation.[68] A killing however by one exercising a privilege of self-defense is no crime at all and must not be confused with a killing engendered by adequate provocation where self-defense is not a proper claim.[69]

The early view was that the adequacy of the provocation was a matter of law for the sole determination of the court.[70] This, however, is not feasible because provocation may be given under an infinite variety of circumstances. Hence it came to be recognized that the adequacy must be tested by a standard, it being the function of the court to explain the standard and the task of the jury to apply the standard to the facts of the particular case.[71] The

65. Holmes v. State, 88 Ala. 26, 7 So. 193 (1890).

66. State v. Robinson, 353 Mo. 934, 185 S.W.2d 636 (1945).

67. State v. Ellis, 101 N.C. 765, 7 S.E. 704 (1888).

68. State v. Hoyt, 13 Minn. 132 (1868).

69. State v. Ramey, 273 N.C. 325, 160 S.E.2d 56 (1968).

70. "There was no doubt that the prisoner was in a great fury, but the question of law is, was there a sufficient provocation to excite it? We are of opinion that there was not." Rex v. Carroll, 7 C. & P. 145, 146–47, 173 Eng.Rep. 64, 65 (1835). See also 1 Hawk.P.C. c. 31, § 36; 2 Bishop, Criminal Law § 713 (8th ed. (1892)).

71. "[B]ut herein circumstances of the fact must guide the jury." 1 Hale P.C. *453. And see Vick v. State, 116 Ga.App. 25, 156 S.E.2d 125 (1967).

"It is, doubtless, in one sense, the province of the court to define what, in law, will constitute a reasonable or adequate provocation, but not, I think, in ordinary cases, to determine whether the provocation proved in the particular case is sufficient or reasonable. This is essentially a question of fact, and to be decided with reference to the peculiar facts of each particular case. As a general rule, the court, after informing the jury to what extent the passions must be aroused, and reason obscured, to render the homicide manslaughter, should inform them that the provocation must be one, the tendency of which would be to produce such a degree of excitement and disturbance in the minds of ordinary men; and if they should find . . . that it did produce that effect in the particular instance, and that the homicide was the result of such provocation, it would give it the character of manslaughter." Maher v. People, 10 Mich. 212, 220–21 (1862).

If there was provocation it is for the jury to determine "whether it was such that they can attribute the act to the violence of passion naturally arising therefrom, and likely to be aroused thereby in

standard adopted here was the familiar one of a reasonable person under like circumstances.[72] Its use to test the adequacy of the provocation has been criticized at times on the argument that a reasonable person will not intentionally kill another under the circumstances in question.[73] This, however, assumes an over-statement of the position. To be adequate it is not necessary that the provocation would cause a reasonable person to commit intentional homicide but only that it would so inflame his passion as to tend to cause him for the moment to act from passion rather than reason,—that is, tend for the moment to deprive a reasonable person of self-control.[74] If a reasonable person would be strongly moved to kill, the fact that he would be able to control his temper sufficiently to avoid such an extreme measure, whereas **D** was unable to do so, does not mean that the circumstance is without the element of mitigation. If what we really meant was that **D** did no more than any ordinary reasonable person would have done we would be in the area of excuse rather than that of mitigation.

If an alleged provocation was so slight, or an actual provocation so great, as to leave no possible room for doubt as to the characterization, it is not necessary for the court to ask the jury to make the only finding of fact possible under the circumstances;[75] but in other than these extreme situations, and with the exceptions to be noted presently, the court should explain to the jurors that for a provocation to be adequate to reduce a voluntary homicide to manslaughter the law requires it to be of a nature calculated to inflame the passion of a reasonable person and tend to cause him to act for the moment from passion rather than reason. And he should instruct them that whether the provocation shown by the evidence was of such a nature is for them to determine under all the circumstances of the case. In other words

---

the breast of a reasonable man." Per Keating, J. in Regina v. Welsh, 11 Cox C.C. 336, 338 (1869).

72. "A provocation is deemed to be adequate, so as to reduce the offense from murder to manslaughter, whenever it is calculated to excite the passion beyond control. It must be of such a character as would, in the mind of an average just and reasonable man, stir resentment likely to cause violence . . ." State v. Porter, 357 Mo. 405, 208 S.W.2d 240, 243 (1948) (quoting from Wharton on Homicide). See also *Maher* and *Welsh* in the preceding note.

It was held not error to instruct the jury in terms of a provocation which would "irresistibly compel an ordinary reasonable person to commit the act charged." State v. Leggroan, 25 Utah 2d 32, 475 P.2d 57 (1970). N.B. This is an overstatement in defendant's favor. It is enough if the provocation is of a nature likely to cause the ordinary reasonable person to act for the moment from passion rather than reason.

An objective test is used. The "passion must be such a passion as would naturally be aroused in the mind of an ordi-

narily reasonable person under the given facts and circumstances, ..." State v. Marvin, 124 Ariz. 555, 606 P.2d 406, 410 (1980). The court is quoting from a California case.

73. See Williams, Provocation and the Reasonable Man, [1954] Crim.L.Rev. 740, 741–52.

74. See Michael and Wechsler, A Rationale of the Law of Homicide, 37 Colum.L.Rev. 1261, 1281–82 (1937). "To require, as the rule is sometimes stated, that the provocation be enough to make a reasonable man do as defendant did is patently absurd; the reasonable man quite plainly does not kill." Model Penal Code § 201.3, Comment (Tent. Draft No. 9, 1959).

See State v. Watkins, 147 Iowa 556, 126 N.W. 691 (1910); State v. Fisko, 58 Nev. 65, 70 P.2d 1113 (1937).

75. If there is no evidence to support the claim of adequate provocation the judge should instruct that it does not support a verdict of manslaughter, otherwise it is for the jury. Holmes v. Director of Public Prosecutions, [1946] 2 All Eng.R. 124.

the standard to be used is a matter of law and whether the provocation in a particular case measured up to that standard is a matter of fact.[76]

Special circumstances are not ignored even if they apply directly to the actor himself. Negligence, for example, is tested by the reasonable-person standard. But a blind person cannot be expected to exercise the care of one with normal vision and a cripple cannot use the same care as one who is not so disabled. Hence if such a question should arise it would be whether **D** had exercised the care to be expected of a reasonable blind person or a reasonable person crippled in a certain way—as the fact might be. The present problem is comparable. A fireman who has been without sleep and rest for thirty-six hours while vigorously fighting fires in an emergency cannot be expected to act with the same judgment and restraint as one who has been through no such ordeal. Hence if the question should arise it would be whether what had happened would have inflamed the passion of an exhausted person who had been without sleep and rest for thirty-six hours, and so forth.[77] However, the very fact that the standard is that of the ordinary reasonable person precludes consideration of the innate peculiarities of the individual actor. The fact that his intelligence is not high and his passion is easily aroused cannot be considered in this connection. So long as he is entitled to be at large in the community he must measure up to certain minimum standards for the public safety.

(a) Mutual Quarrel or Combat

A wordy altercation will not of itself be sufficient to mitigate to manslaughter a killing that is otherwise murder.[78] On the other hand a mutual encounter which goes beyond words to actual blows or to a manifestation of intent to use immediate and violent force may constitute adequate provocation; and in determining the ade-

76. "The function assigned to the jury with respect to the particular facts mentioned in s. 203(3) does not in any way differ from the function they have to decide all other questions of fact, whether these facts constitute elements of a crime or elements of an excuse or a justification for a crime charged. Indeed and in all of the cases, the valid exercise of the function of the jury is, according to the very words of the oath of office taken by them, to give a verdict according to evidence. They cannot go beyond the evidence and resort to speculation nor, of course, would it be proper for the trial Judge to invite them to do so. If, then, the record is denuded of any evidence potentially enabling a reasonable jury acting judicially to find a wrongful act or insult of the nature and effect set forth in s. 203(3)(a) and (b), it is then, as a matter of law, within the area exclusively reserved to the trial Judge to so decide and his duty to refrain from putting the defence of provocation to the jury." Parnerkar v. Regina, [1974] S.C.R. 449, 33 D.L.R.(3d) 683, 686–687 (S.C.C.).

77. "It would plainly be illogical not to recognize an unusually excitable or pugnacious temperament in the accused as a matter to be taken into account but yet to recognize for that purpose some unusual physical characteristic, be it impotence or another." Bedder v. Director of Public Prosecutions, 1954, 2 All Eng.R. 801, 803–04 [House of Lords]. But this position cannot be accepted. Clearly the taunts of impotence would not have the same effect on a potent man as on one who is impotent.

In a subsequent case the House of Lords held that a standard of provocation in a homicide committed by at 15-year old boy against his homosexual assailant was that of a reasonable 15-year old boy. DPP v. Camplin, [1978] 2 All E.R. 168.

The New Hampshire Code does require that the provocation for manslaughter be reasonable. N.H.Rev.Stat.Ann. 630:2 (1942).

78. State v. Lee, 36 Del. 11, 171 A. 195 (1933).

quacy of the provocation in such a case the entire quarrel, including the words, will be taken into consideration.[79]

Several cautions are needed in this regard. (1) If homicide results from force which was neither intended nor likely to cause death or great bodily injury, it will not be murder if no more than ordinary (non-deadly) fight or struggle was involved,[80] hence the problem of provocation does not become important in such a situation. (2) Attack and defense are not mutual. If one person attacks another who defends himself with no more force than he is privileged by law to use for his own protection, there is no problem of provocation. The assailant is acting without mitigation of any sort and the defender is fully justified or excused.[81] (3) If an unlawful attack is resisted by force obviously in excess of what is needed in self-defense, the case may or may not be within the rule of provocation. There is no mitigation in favor of the original assailant if he intended in the beginning to kill or to inflict great bodily injury;[82] whereas if the original assailant intended only a non-deadly scuffle the counter attack may constitute adequate provocation.[83] Whether the original assault was of a deadly nature or not, it may be sufficient to constitute adequate provocation so far as the victim of the original assault is concerned.

Suppose, for example, two persons were engaged in a tussle on a vacant lot and one caused the death of the other. If it was a friendly encounter—a mere test of strength without anger and without intent to cause serious harm, it was not unlawful. And if death resulted quite unexpectedly from such a struggle it is no crime at all, but excusable homicide. If the facts were the same except that the two were mutually engaged in an angry fight—but without intent to cause death or great bodily injury—and death should result quite unexpectedly to one, the other would be guilty of manslaughter.[84] This is not because of the rule of provocation but because the death resulted from an unlawful, although apparently not dangerous, battery. Such an accidental killing is not excused by the common law because it resulted from unlawful conduct characterized as *malum in se*.[85] This, it maybe added, is the law in most of our states today, although statutes in some states excuse an *accidental* killing in the heat of passion upon a sudden combat when no undue advantage is taken, and no dangerous weapon used.[86]

If the struggle mentioned was an encounter in which one had made an unlawful attack and the other was defending with merely such force as he

79. Regina v. Smith, 4 F. & F. 1066, 176 Eng.Rep. 910 (1886); Taylor v. Rex, [1947] S.C.R. 462, 89 C.C.C. 209.

80. Lanier v. State, 31 Ala.App. 242, 15 So.2d 278 (1943).

81. Allen v. United States, 157 U.S. 675, 15 S.Ct. 720 (1895).

82. Murphy v. State, 37 Ala. 142 (1861).

83. State v. Hill, 20 N.C. 629 (1839).

84. Kearns v. Commonwealth, 243 Ky. 745, 49 S.W.2d 1009 (1932).

85. Regina v. Caniff, 9 Car. & P. 359, 173 Eng.Rep. 868 (1840).

Under the common law death resulting from an unlawful act, *malum in se*, is not less than manslaughter. An intensive study resulted in the conclusion that no death resulting from battery is less than manslaughter "however improbable the fatal result, since the battery is an unlawful act." Model Penal Code 44 (Tent. Draft No. 9, 1959). Inflicting a beating is an unlawful act. Cf. State v. Holden, 85 N.M. 397, 512 P.2d 970, 973 (App.1973).

86. E.g., West's Ann.Cal.Pen.Code § 195 (1970).

was privileged by law to employ for his protection, and death should result quite unexpectedly from force neither intended nor likely to cause death or great bodily injury, the issue of crime would depend upon who survived. If the assailant caused the death of his victim he would be guilty of manslaughter,—death unexpectedly resulting from an *unlawful* battery which was not intended or likely to produce such a result. If the innocent defender unexpectedly caused the death of his assailant by force he was privileged to use in his own defense, it is excusable homicide.

If the killing was intentional, or resulted from the use of deadly force (force either intended or likely to cause death or great bodily injury) then it may become important to consider the question of provocation. If the two were engaged in a mutual fight of an angry and unlawful nature the killing is not excused but the blows inflicted upon the slayer in the encounter may be sufficient for adequate provocation.[87]

No killing is attributed to a sudden mutual combat if the intent to kill or to inflict great bodily harm was formed prior to the commencement of the encounter.[88] If one by words or acts provokes a difficulty for the purpose of killing the other, or of doing him great bodily injury, and does kill the other in carrying out his plan, he is guilty of murder.[89] Whatever blows he may receive from his adversary in such an encounter are ignored so far as mitigation is concerned because his deadly intent was formed before the blows were received.[90]

Another matter requires special attention. One who is not in any sense seeking an encounter, but has reason to fear an unlawful attack upon his life, does not forfeit his privilege of self-defense merely by arming himself in advance.[91] But one who has reason to expect an encounter into which he will enter as willingly as his adversary, and who secretly arms himself in order to have an unfair advantage over the other during their mutual combat, has given the matter entirely too much thought to be entitled to the rule of mitigation recognized in certain cases of killing in a *sudden* heat of passion.[92] This is not to be understood to exclude from mitigation every case in which an unarmed fighter is killed with a deadly weapon. Heat of passion suddenly engendered by actual blows received in mutual combat may be sufficient to reduce even such a homicide to manslaughter. The mere fact that when the quarrel began the slayer had a deadly weapon upon his person while the other was not so armed is not alone sufficient to preclude the possibility of mitigation, unless such a result is required by some unusual statute.[93] The question is whether or not the slayer entered the combat with the intention of using this dangerous instrument. Hence it is necessary to discriminate between the use of a deadly weapon procured beforehand for this

---

87. State v. Hill, 20 N.C. 629 (1839).

88. State v. Miller, 223 N.C. 184, 25 S.E.2d 623 (1943).

89. State v. Flory, 40 Wyo. 184, 201, 276 P. 458, 463 (1929).

90. Ballard v. Commonwealth, 156 Va. 980, 159 S.E. 222 (1931).

91. State v. Bristol, 53 Wyo. 304, 84 P.2d 757 (1938); State v. Evans, 124 Mo. 397, 28 S.W. 8 (1894).

A felon, prohibited from carrying a weapon, may claim the right of self-defense in using a weapon he could not legally possess. People v. King, 22 Cal.3d 12, 148 Cal.Rptr. 409, 582 P.2d 1000 (1978).

92. Ex parte Nettles, 58 Ala. 268 (1877).

93. Gourko v. United States, 153 U.S. 183, 14 S.Ct. 806 (1894). Cf. Caldwell v. State, 203 Ala. 412, 84 So. 272 (1919).

purpose, and the sudden angry use, in the heat of combat, of a weapon which the slayer merely happened to have available at the moment.[94]

The fact that both participants have an unlawful intent to kill will not be a mitigating circumstance for either if such intent was not formed and acted upon suddenly in the heat of combat. In "the case of a deliberate fight, such as a duel, the slayer and his second are murderers." [95] Even he who acted as second for the one vanquished in the duel has been held guilty of murder.[96] The absence of seconds or other requisites of the formal duel will not prevent the homicide from being murder. Nor is it important, on the other hand, that the duel was fairly conducted. If sufficient time elapsed "between the quarrel and the 'going out to fight' to enable blood to cool and passion to subside, the killing would be murder and not manslaughter." [97]

A mere challenge to a fist fight by an unarmed person is not sufficient to reduce an intentional killing to manslaughter. The same must be said of a threat to slap, made in the course of a verbal dispute, and the further step of removing the coat in preparation for fisticuffs. Even an actual physical contact during the course of a quarrel may be insufficient for this purpose. In one case, for example, the deceased pushed one of two persons with whom he was quarreling, whereupon they stabbed him to death with a knife. This homicide was held to be murder because the "provocation given by the deceased was but slight, and in the progress of the fight, the prisoners used an excess of violence, out of all proportion to the provocation." [98]

If the fight is really "mutual" in the sense that both enter into it willingly, as distinguished from the case in which one is clearly attacking and the other merely defending; if the intent to kill or to inflict great bodily injury is formed in the heat of the encounter, rather than in advance, and the slayer does not deliberately take unfair advantage of the other by secretly arming himself with a weapon to have ready "just in case"; and if the encounter reaches the proportion of actual physical contact, or dangerous threat of serious and immediate harm, sufficient to arouse the passions of a reasonable person, the law takes the position that in such mutual combat there is mutual provocation.[99] The combat is mutual if the intent to fight is mutual, and in such situations the question of which one actually strikes the first blow is not controlling.[1] In fact, if both intend to fight and are ready to do so it may be a "mutual combat" although one party did not actually strike any blow.[2]

---

94. State v. Barnwell, 80 N.C. 466 (1879).

95. State v. Rhodes, Houst.Cr. 476, 497 (Del.1877); Miss.Code Ann. § 97–3–23 (1973).

96. Regina v. Barronet, Dears. 51, 169 Eng.Rep. 663 (1852).

97. People v. Sanchez, 24 Cal. 17, 27 (1864).

98. State v. Gooch, 94 N.C. 987, 1014 (1886).

Where defendant asserts that he acted in the heat of passion, two variables must be weighed in relation to each other—the degree of provocation and the measures employed by the defendant in response to it. State v. Ross, 28 Utah 2d 279, 283, 501 P.2d 632, 635 (1972).

99. State v. Green, Houst.Cr. 217 (Del.1866).

1. Whitehead v. State, 9 Md.App. 7, 262 A.2d 316 (1970).

2. Roberts v. State, 189 Ga. 36, 44, 5 S.E.2d 340, 345 (1939).

(b) Battery

Not every technical battery is sufficient to constitute adequate provocation, but a hard blow inflicting considerable pain or injury will ordinarily be sufficient.

Knocking a person down with a heavy stick, or hitting him over the head with a revolver, are rather obvious instances of such force; but a weapon is not indispensable for this purpose. Thus even a blow with the fist may be sufficient to reduce an intentional killing to manslaughter, particularly if it is a blow in the face or a "staggering" blow.[3]

The need of considering all the circumstances of the particular case must not be overlooked. In one case, for example, a man killed his wife by inflicting five slashes with a razor after she had hit him over the head with a small poker about fifteen inches long. He claimed the blow caused a swelling but it left no mark visible later in the day. This killing was held to have been without adequate provocation,[4] although no one would doubt the possibility of a blow with a fifteen-inch poker being sufficient for mitigation if struck with great violence.

No amount of force which an individual was privileged by law to use will be recognized as adequate provocation, and hence the hard blow must have been unlawful to meet the present requirement.[5]

(c) Assault

If an assault results in a battery, the latter receives chief attention so far as provocation is concerned. There are homicide cases, however, in which the fatal force was used by the slayer because of an actual or apparent attempt to commit a battery upon him although it did not result in an actual application of force to his person. In these cases it is necessary to make a sharp distinction between defensive force and vindictive force. If the one assailed has killed his assailant within the legal privilege of self-defense he is guilty of no crime at all. That is not the present problem. For the moment we are concerned with a killing caused, not in self-defense, but in the heat of passion engendered by an attack that failed and after the immediate danger had passed. In one case, for example, deceased shot at the defendant and missed him. This so angered the defendant that he shot the other in the back while he was running away, thus causing his death. This was clearly not within the privilege of self-defense, but this provocation was held sufficient to reduce the grade of homicide to manslaughter.[6]

An unsuccessful attempt to commit a battery is seldom likely to arouse the same degree of passion in a reasonable person as will be engendered by the actual blow intended. Hence the fact that the assailant did not actually hit the defendant is one of the important circumstances in the particular case. Such an attack is less likely to be regarded as adequate provocation than one that succeeds. But just as not every actual blow will be sufficient for this purpose, so not every failure will leave it insufficient. The unsuccessful attack may be so vicious in extreme cases as to constitute adequate provocation. As said by one court: "A wilful or intentional killing of a

3. Stewart v. State, 78 Ala. 436 (1885); State v. Yarbrough, 8 N.C. 78 (1820).

4. Commonwealth v. Webb, 252 Pa. 187, 97 A. 189 (1916).

5. State v. Spaulding, 34 Minn. 361, 25 N.W. 793 (1885).

6. Beasley v. State, 64 Miss. 518, 8 So. 234 (1886).

human being may not be murder but voluntary manslaughter if it be provoked by . . . an attempt to commit a serious personal injury upon the slayer or by other equivalent circumstances calculated to excite sudden and uncontrollable passion." [7]

There is some authority for the position that an assault which does not result in an actual battery cannot constitute adequate provocation.[8] This should be rejected as an unnecessary carry-over from the early notion that the adequacy of the provocation is a matter of law to be determined by the court.

(d) Words

In certain areas the carry-over from the early law cannot be ignored.

Well established in the common law is the rule that provocative words are not recognized as adequate provocation to reduce a wilful killing to manslaughter, however abusive, aggravating, contemptuous, false, grievous, indecent, insulting, opprobrious, provoking, or scurrilous they may be.[9]

Actual cases afford extreme illustrations. In 1666 it was said: "If one calls another son of a whore and giveth him the lie, and upon those words the other kill him that gave the words, this notwithstanding those words is murder. . . ." [10] And modern cases involving equally vile epithets have reached the same conclusion.[11] Directing a racial remark or epithet does not compel a finding that such a reference is adequate provocation.[12]

There have been a few rare instances in which some court has questioned the soundness of this rule as to provocative words.[13] Even rarer instances of legislative modification may be found, such as the former Texas statute to the effect that "insulting words or conduct of the person killed toward a female relation of the party killing" were "adequate cause" to reduce a voluntary homicide to manslaughter.[14] There is also the more recent legislative action in that state repealing its general provision dealing with words or ges-

---

7. Swain v. State, 151 Ga. 375, 376–7, 107 S.E. 40, 41 (1921).

8. State v. Kizer, 360 Mo. 744, 230 S.W.2d 690 (1950). This seems to have developed from the rule that no insulting words are adequate in themselves. See State v. Starr, 38 Mo. 270, 277 (1866).

9. People v. Russell, 322 Ill. 295, 153 N.E. 389 (1926); State v. Nevares, 36 N.M. 41, 7 P.2d 933 (1932); Commonwealth v. Gelfi, 282 Pa. 434, 128 A. 77 (1925).

"We agree with the great weight of authority that words alone are not adequate provocation to justify reducing an intentional killing to manslaughter." State v. Doss, 116 Ariz. 156, 568 P.2d 1054, 1060 (1977). Accord, State v. Cook, 560 S.W.2d 299 (Mo.App.1977); State v. Watson, 287 N.C. 147, 214 S.E.2d 85 (1975).

"Words alone are not sufficient provocation to reduce a murder charge to vol-

untary manslaughter." State v. Montano, 95 N.M. 233, 620 P.2d 887, 890 (App.1980).

10. Huggett's Case, Kel. 59, 60, 84 Eng.Rep. 1082 (1666).

11. Harrison v. State, 18 Okl.Cr. 403, 408, 195 P. 511, 513 (1921); Barrett v. State, 98 Tex.Cr.R. 627, 267 S.W. 511 (1925). See also State v. Lucynski, 48 Wis.2d 232, 179 N.W.2d 889 (1970).

12. United States v. Alexander, 471 F.2d 923, 941 (D.C. Cir. 1972).

13. E.g., Commonwealth v. Hourigan, 89 Ky. 305, 313, 12 S.W. 550, 552 (1889); State v. Jarrott, 23 N.C. 76, 82 (1840). But cf. Sawyers v. Commonwealth, 18 Ky.L.Rep. 657, 38 S.W. 136 (1896); State v. McNeill, 92 N.C. 812 (1885).

14. Tex.Rev.Cr.Stat. § 1248 (1925). Repealed by Tex.Acts 1927, c. 274.

tures,—as judicially interpreted.[15] And the California court has held that the codification of this common-law rule in one statute, followed by its omission in a later one, manifests a legislative intent that it shall no longer be recognized there.[16] For the most part, however, it has been held with remarkable uniformity that even words generally regarded as "fighting words" in the community have no recognition as adequate provocation in the eyes of the law. Adequate provocation may sometimes be established by a combination of insulting words with some other circumstance which would not of itself be sufficient. For example, insulting words plus a blow too slight for provocation in itself may together constitute adequate provocation;[17] the same is true of insulting words plus an aggravated trespass to property;[18] and words accompanied by conduct indicating a present intention and ability to cause bodily harm.[19]

Insulting words, let it be added by way of caution, may be considered in determining the *degree of murder*,[20] or in assessing the punishment for murder if the law provides more than one possible penalty.[21]

Under the sound rule, recognized by most courts, informational words are placed upon a different footing than insulting words.[22] The sound theory is that it is the fact, or alleged fact, which really constitutes the adequate provocation, but the sudden disclosure of the fact may have the same effect as if it had just happened. Thus an intentional killing may be manslaughter only if the deceased had just told the slayer that he had raped the latter's wife or had committed adultery with her, or had ravished the latter's young daughter, or committed a serious battery upon his child.[23] To satisfy the requirement of *suddenness*, to be considered presently, it is necessary for mitigation in such a case that the slayer should not have long previously acquired the information from some other source.[24] On the other hand, if the slayer

15. Elsmore v. State, 132 Tex.Cr.R. 261, 104 S.W.2d 493 (1937).

16. People v. Valentine, 28 Cal.2d 121, 169 P.2d 1 (1946). But while provocative words may be so grievous as to be *mitigating* in a homicide case they cannot *justify* or *excuse* an assault likely to produce great bodily injury. People v. Mears, 142 Cal.App.2d 206, 298 P.2d 40 (1956).

17. Lamp v. State, 38 Ga.App. 36, 142 S.E. 202 (1928).

18. State v. Davis, 34 S.W.2d 133 (Mo. 1930).

19. Lang v. State, 6 Md.App. 128, 250 A.2d 276 (1969).

20. State v. Robinson, 353 Mo. 934, 185 S.W.2d 636 (1945).

21. Keirsey v. State, 131 Ark. 487, 199 S.W. 532 (1917).

22. Words "may be used, not as an expression of abuse, but as a means of conveying information of a fact, or what is alleged to be a fact." Holmes v. Director of Public Prosecutions [1946] 2 All Eng.R. 124, 127.

"While words of an insulting and scandalous nature are not sufficient cause of provocation, words conveying information of a fact which constitutes adequate provocation when that fact is observed would constitute sufficient provocation." Commonwealth v. Berry, 461 Pa. 233, 336 A.2d 262, 264 (1972).

23. State v. Flory, 40 Wyo. 184, 276 P. 458 (1929); Davis v. State, 161 Tenn. 23, 28 S.W.2d 993 (1930); State v. Grugin, 147 Mo. 39, 47 S.W. 1058 (1898); People v. Rice, 351 Ill. 604, 184 N.E. 894 (1933). Contra, under statute, Humphreys v. State, 175 Ga. 705, 165 S.E. 733 (1932).

The English court held that a wife's confession of adultery was not adequate provocation for her husband to kill her. Holmes v. Director of Public Prosecutions [1946] 2 All Eng.R. 124. But see State v. Flory, 40 Wyo. 184, 276 P. 458 (1929); Vick v. State, 116 Ga.App. 25, 156 S.E.2d 125 (1967).

24. Wife's confession of adultery five days before killing insufficient to constitute provocation. People v. Wax, 75 Ill.App.2d 163, 220 N.E.2d 600 (1966).

is told of such great harm which he had not heard of before, this may be sufficient for adequate provocation (according to most courts) even if the statement is untrue—provided it is made under circumstances calculated to cause it to be believed and it is actually believed by the slayer.[25] This is merely a particular application of the reasonable mistake of fact doctrine.

While the rule as to insulting words and provocation is firmly entrenched there is no sound reason for the application of an arbitrary rule of law in this regard. Legislation to authorize the submission of the issue of adequacy to the jury would seem to be desirable. This step has been taken in England [26] and is included in the recommendations of the Model Penal Code,[27] and presumably in the states whose new penal codes have followed the wording of the Code on this point.[28]

(e) Gestures

Insulting gestures alone are not adequate provocation.[29] Gestures indicating an intent to attack with deadly force may be adequate provocation in a mutual encounter,[30] and under other circumstances may completely justify or excuse a homicide under the self-defense privilege.[31]

(f) Trespass

If the force used is privileged under the circumstances, no problem of provocation is involved because no crime is committed even if death results. Hence discussions of trespass as constituting, or not constituting, adequate provocation presuppose a use of force beyond that authorized by law. A purely technical trespass, even in the dwelling house, will not be recognized as sufficient for this purpose; [32] but it is clearly recognized that a trespass in or upon the dwelling may be of a nature insufficient to authorize the use of deadly force, and yet sufficiently aggravating to constitute adequate provo-

Killing within an hour after being told that deceased had violated the chastity of D's 16-year-old daughter, and when D was obviously in great passion, was held not to warrant a verdict of second-degree murder. Toler v. State, 152 Tenn. 1, 260 S.W. 134 (1924).

In one case the court held that words may constitute adequate provocation—but made no distinction between insulting words and those conveying information. G, having heard that his young daughter had been ravished by H, went to H no doubt hoping to learn it was all a mistake. But to G's inquiry H made an insolent and defiant reply which amounted to an affirmation of guilt, whereupon G killed H. It was held that it should have been left to the jury to determine whether there was adequate provocation. State v. Grugin, 147 Mo. 39, 47 S.W. 1058 (1898).

25. State v. Yanz, 74 Conn. 177, 50 A. 37 (1901).

"Without doubt, the information provided to the appellant that his wife was engaged in adulterous conduct constituted, irrespective of its truth, adequate provocation." State v. Ramirez, 116 Ariz. 259, 569 P.2d 201, 213 (En Banc, 1977).

26. The English Homicide Act of 1957 authorizes the jury to take into consideration everything both done and said. 5 & 6 Eliz. 2, c. 11 Part I, 3.

27. See section 210.3(1)(b).

28. " . . . under the influence of extreme mental or emotional disturbance for which there is reasonable explanation or excuse." Ibid.

29. See Coleman v. State, 149 Ga. 186, 99 S.E. 627 (1919).

30. Hall v. State, 177 Ga. 794, 171 S.E. 274 (1933).

31. State v. Mason, 115 S.C. 214, 105 S.E. 286 (1920).

32. Carroll v. State, 23 Ala. 28 (1853).

cation.[33] It is often stated that no trespass will of itself amount to adequate provocation if it is not in or upon the dwelling house and does not involve any personal danger to the slayer.[34] The Georgia court spoke with commendable caution in referring to this as true "generally" and indicating the possibility of exceptions in cases of such trespasses more highly provoking in their nature than any yet involved in adjudicated cases.[35] And the Missouri court held that under the circumstances involved it was reversible error not to submit the question of adequacy to the jury.[36]

Statements ruling out trespass as adequate provocation if it is neither in or upon a dwelling, nor under circumstances endangering human life, are attributable in part to the early view that adequacy was purely a matter of law and in part to a failure to distinguish between trespass as a justification and trespass as a mitigating factor.[37] Some trespasses may be too slight as provocation to require submission to the jury, but where they are obviously not "slight" the question of adequacy should be dealt with as a matter of fact.

(g) Other Provocative Acts

In an early case an enraged husband, catching his wife in the act of adultery, instantly killed the paramour. This was held to be manslaughter, the court saying that "there could not be greater provocation than this." [38] And there are many statements to the effect that it is only manslaughter if, in the first transport of passion upon sight of the adultery the husband kills the paramour,[39] or the wife,[40] or both.[41] At one time the statutes of some jurisdictions went beyond the common law and provided that the husband's slaying of the adulterous paramour caught in the act is justified.[42] However

33.   State v. Adams, 78 Iowa 292, 43 N.W. 194 (1889); State v. Welch, 37 N.M. 549, 25 P.2d 211 (1933).

34.   Atterberry v. State, 261 So.2d 467 (Miss.1972).

35.   Hayes v. State, 58 Ga. 35, 47 (1877). Cf. State v. Reed, 154 Mo. 122, 55 S.W. 278 (1900).

36.   State v. Matthews, 148 Mo. 185, 49 S.W. 1085 (1899).

37.   In *Matthews* the court points out that the trial judge had failed to make this distinction.

38.   Manning's Case, T.Raym. 212, 83 Eng.Rep. 112 (1793).

39.   1 Hale P.C. *486; 1 East P.C. 234; 4 Bl.Comm. *191; Regina v. Kelly, 2 Car. & K. 814, 175 Eng.Rep. 342 (1848); Mays v. State, 88 Ga. 399, 14 S.E. 560 (1891); State v. Fox, 276 Mo. 378, 207 S.W. 779 (1918).

If the killing is of one committing violent rape upon the slayer's wife the homicide is justifiable. 1 Hale P.C. *486.

One court said it would be justifiable if done for the purpose of preventing, and was then and there necessary to prevent,

adultery with the slayer's wife. *Mays, supra.*

A conviction of murder was reversed because the evidence indicated that the killing was in the sudden heat of passion by defendant who found his wife and deceased in bed in deceased's motel bedroom. Gonzales v. State, 546 S.W.2d 617 (Tex.Cr.App.1977).

40.   Palmore v. State, 283 Ala. 501, 218 So.2d 830 (1969); Jones v. People, 23 Colo. 276, 283, 47 P. 275, 277 (1896). And see Vick v. State, 116 Ga. 25, 156 S.E.2d 125 (1967).

41.   Dabney v. State, 113 Ala. 38, 21 So. 211, 212 (1897).

A husband is not justified in taking the life of his adulterous wife or her lover to prevent adultery, but the facts of a particular case may support provocation and passion within the meaning of the voluntary manslaughter statute. Burger v. State, 238 Ga. 171, 231 S.E.2d 769 (1977).

42.   "Upon a prosecution for murder or manslaughter, in addition to other defenses which may be offered, it may be shown as a complete defense that the homicide resulted from the person's use

such conditions are generally held not to justify homicide although they may provide an adequate claim of provocation.

With reference to the husband's killing the paramour "caught in the act," in the absence of special statutory provision, the statements are frequently to the effect "that the law itself recognizes it as provocation sufficient to reduce the killing" to manslaughter,[43] or that such provocation is sufficient for this purpose "as matter of law." [44] "The law justifies a jury in calling it but manslaughter" was the conclusion of the Connecticut court.[45] "The circumstances must justify a reasonable belief of sexual contact and not just mere suspicion." [46]

Certain other outrageous acts *may* be found to constitute adequate provocation to reduce a voluntary homicide to manslaughter. In this list may be mentioned, without attempting to be exhaustive, seduction of the slayer's infant daughter,[47] rape of his close female relative,[48] murder or serious injury of his close relative,[49] or the act of sodomy with his young son.[50] It has been recognized that many factors, possibly not sufficient independently to constitute adequate provocation, may join together and be sufficient to raise an issue of provocation. It has been held where a defendant's wife rejected his advances towards reconciliation, denied affection for him, scorned him with racial epithets, stated she had intercourse "with everybody on the street," and threw a telephone and photographs at him, that the facts justified a proper instruction on provocation for common law manslaughter.[51] Further provocation may exist even where the defendant was the one who acted to bring about the provocation upon which he later must rely for a claim of manslaughter.[52] The unlawful arrest of the slayer should be add-

of deadly force upon another who was at the time of the homicide in the act of having sexual intercourse with the accused's wife. In order for this defense to be available to the accused, the accused and his wife must have been living together as husband and wife at the time of the homicide." Laws of N.M.1963, ch. 303, §§ 2–4 repealed by Laws of N.M.1973, ch. 241, § 6. Georgia apparently reached the same result as to a killing to prevent the commission or completion of adultery. Brown v. State, 228 Ga. 215, 184 S.E.2d 655 (1971). This position would not be sanctioned by current Georgia law. "In this day of no-fault, on-demand divorce when adultery is merely a misdemeanor, and when there is a debate ranging in the country about whether capital punishment even for the most heinous crimes is proper, any idea that a spouse is ever justified in taking the life of another—adulterous spouse or illicit lover— to prevent adultery is uncivilized. This is murder; and henceforth, nothing more appearing, an instruction on justifiable homicide may not be given. Such homicides will stand on the same footing as any other homicides. Our ruling should not, however, be read to mean that the peculiar facts of a given case may never

suggest 'passion' and 'provocation' within the meaning of the voluntary manslaughter statute." Burger v. State, 238 Ga. 171, 231 S.E.2d 769 (1977).

43. Dabney v. State, 113 Ala. 38, 21 So. 211, 212 (1897); State v. Ward, 286 N.C. 304, 210 S.E.2d 407 (1974).

44. Hooks v. State, 99 Ala. 166, 13 So. 767, 768 (1893).

45. State v. Yanz, 74 Conn. 177, 181, 50 A. 37, 39 (1901).

46. Tripp v. State, 36 Md.App. 459, 374 A.2d 384 (1977).

47. State v. Grugin, 147 Mo. 39, 47 S.W. 1058 (1898); Toler v. State, 152 Tenn. 1, 260 S.W. 134 (1924).

48. State v. Cooper, 112 La. 281, 36 So. 350 (1904); State v. Flory, 40 Wyo. 184, 276 P. 458 (1929).

49. People v. Rice, 351 Ill. 604, 184 N.E. 894 (1933).

50. Regina v. Fisher, 8 Car. & P. 182, 173 Eng.Rep. 452 (1837).

51. Moffa v. The Queen, 51 ALJR 403 (H.Ct.1977).

52. Edwards v. Reginan, [1972] 3 W.L.R. 893. The defendant killed the de-

ed,[53] although only under aggravating circumstances. The mere fact that the apprehension is beyond the actual authority of the law is not sufficient.[54] It should be pointed out that the modern trend is to provide by statute that one knowing he is being arrested by a peace officer should refrain from using force or any weapon in resisting such arrest[55] even if the arrest is unauthorized.[56]

Any effort to classify provocative acts into two groups—(1) "adequate" and (2) "inadequate"—would be to substitute the early view in place of the modern law. Except for the arbitrary rule of law that insulting words or gestures are not of themselves alone adequate, and perhaps a rule that "catching the paramour in the act" is adequate, the law furnishes only the standard and whether the facts of a particular case meet that standard is a question of fact. As pointed out previously an alleged provocation may be so slight, or an actual provocation so great, that it is not necessary to ask the jury to make the only finding of fact possible under the circumstances; but where this is not true, with the exception mentioned above, the question of adequacy should be determined by the jury.[57]

(2) Heat of Passion

To be within the rule of provocation the slayer must have killed the deceased in the heat of passion.[58] Passion does not necessarily mean rage or anger. It includes any "violent, intense, highly-wrought, or enthusiastic emotion."[59] Terror, for example, is one of the passions which may dethrone judgment and mitigate a killing to the level of voluntary manslaughter.[60] In speaking of the previous requirement it was mentioned that in determining whether or not there was adequate provocation an objective test is used: would what was done have inflamed the passions of the ordinary reasonable person? But the present requirement is measured by a subjective test; it depends upon the actual state of mind of the slayer at the moment of the fatal act. The question here is not what would have been the state of mind of someone else, but did the slayer kill in the actual heat of passion?[61] As

ceased after the deceased had attacked him. However, the defendant had sought to blackmail the deceased which led to the deceased's attack.

53. People v. White, 333 Ill. 512, 165 N.E. 168 (1929).

54. Galvin v. State, 46 Tenn. 283 (1869).

55. See West's Ann.Cal.Pen.Code § 834a (1970).

56. Where an arrest is unlawful, a police officer is not within the performance of his duty and therefore the assault is a simple battery. People v. Curtis, 70 Cal.2d 347, 74 Cal.Rptr. 713, 450 P.2d 33 (1969). One may properly resist where the officer is using excessive force regardless of the legality of the arrest. People v. Henderson, 58 Cal.App.3d 349, 129 Cal.Rptr. 844 (1976).

57. Maher v. People, 10 Mich. 212, 81 Am.Dec. 781 (1862).

58. "[P]rovocation furnishes no extenuation, unless it produces passion." State v. Johnson, 23 N.C. 354, 362 (1840).

59. People v. Borchers, 50 Cal.2d 321, 329, 325 P.2d 97, 102 (1958).

Heat of passion includes "an emotional state characterized by anger, rage, hatred, furious resentment or terror." State v. Lott, 207 Kan. 602, 485 P.2d 1314, 1317 (1971).

60. People v. Otwell, 61 Cal.Rptr. 427 (Cal.App.1967); Wood v. State, 486 P.2d 750 (Okl.Cr.1971).

61. Green v. State, 195 Ga. 759, 25 S.E.2d 502 (1943). "On the other hand, a killing upon provocation ordinarily calculated to excite the passion beyond control, would not make the killing voluntary manslaughter if the provocation did not, in fact, produce the sudden heat of passion, which is an essential ingredient of the offense." Cavanaugh v. Common-

frequently stated by the courts, neither adequate provocation without passion nor passion without adequate provocation will be sufficient to reduce voluntary homicide to manslaughter.[62] There can be no mitigation in the case of a cold-blooded killing.

To constitute the *heat of passion* included in this requirement it is not necessary for the passion to be so extreme that the slayer does not know what he is doing at the time; [63] but it must be so extreme that for the moment his action is being directed by passion rather than by reason.[64] Heat of passion, however, is not an element of the crime of manslaughter in the usual sense of that term, so that if death were caused which is a lesser degree of homicide or not homicide, the presence of passion would not make it manslaughter. Rather passion is a factor which when present with elements of murder may reduce the homicide to manslaughter.[65]

(3) Sudden—The Cooling Time

No matter how extreme the provocation, or how great the passion engendered thereby, there will be no mitigation sufficient to reduce voluntary homicide to manslaughter in the absence of another requirement. The killing must have been in a *sudden* heat of passion. That is, the fatal act must have followed the provocation before there had been a reasonable opportunity for the passion of the slayer to cool.[66]

This, like the adequacy of the provocation itself, is measured by an objective test. Whether or not there was a reasonable opportunity for the passion to cool, depends upon whether or not, under all the circumstances of the particular case, there has been such a lapse of time since the provocation was received that the mind of the ordinary reasonable person would have cooled sufficiently so that action once more would be directed by reason rather than by passion. If such time has elapsed before the fatal act the slayer does not have the benefit of the rule of provocation even if his own mind is still inflamed by passion at the time of the killing.[67] He is guilty of murder in such a case. The extent to which the passions have been aroused and the nature

wealth, 172 Ky. 799, 805, 190 S.W. 123, 127 (1916).

62. Vance v. State, 70 Ark. 272, 278, 68 S.W. 37, 40 (1902); State v. Johnson, 112 Ariz. 17, 536 P.2d 1035 (1975).

63. People v. Freel, 48 Cal. 436 (1874); Dye v. State, 127 Miss. 492, 90 So. 180 (1922).

State v. Gounagias, 88 Wash. 304, 153 P. 9 (1915).

64. Hannah v. Commonwealth, 153 Va. 863, 149 S.E. 419 (1929).

"However in order to determine whether the element of provocation has thus displaced the element of malice aforethought and effectuated such a reduction of the offense, it is settled that 'the fundamental of the inquiry is whether or not the defendant's reason was, at the time of his act, so disturbed or obscured by some passion—not necessarily fear and

never of course the passion for revenge—to such an extent as would render *ordinary men of average disposition* liable to act rashly or without due deliberation and reflection, and from this passion rather than from judgment.' " People v. Morse, 70 Cal.2d 711, 76 Cal.Rptr. 391, 405, 452 P.2d 607, 621 (1969).

65. Boissonneault v. State, 50 Wis.2d 662, 184 N.W.2d 846 (1971).

66. Sanders v. State, 26 Ga.App. 475, 106 S.E. 314 (1921); State v. Frederick, 20 Wn.App. 175, 579 P.2d 390 (1978).

67. State v. Robinson, 353 Mo. 934, 185 S.W.2d 636 (1945). The question is whether the interval was "sufficient to permit the passions to cool and to allow thought and reflection and reason to reassert itself." State v. Lee, 36 Del. 11, 19, 171 A. 195, 198 (1933).

of the act constituting the provocation are factors in determining whether there has been a sufficient cooling-off period.[68]

In one case it was held that where **D**, while helpless at the end of a drinking bout, was the victim of an act of sodomy by the deceased, and thereafter was continually taunted by words and gestures of those to whom deceased had detailed the story, until the cumulative reminders of the original outrage caused **D** to fly into a violent rage in which he rushed to deceased's home and killed him, no mitigation could be recognized in the absence of new acts of provocation by the deceased.[69] This seems to be quite unsound because deceased was the cause of the taunts by others who would not have known of the sodomy had they not been told by deceased after he had been urged by **D** to tell no one. It has been clearly recognized that one who controls his temper time after time, following repeated acts of provocation, may have his emotion so bottled-up that the final result is an emotional explosion, and that in such a case the "cooling time" begins to run not from earlier acts, but from "the last straw." [70]

It has been recognized, moreover, that passion may be suddenly revived by circumstances that bring the provocation vividly to mind,[71] —as where **D** had the first sight of the assailant who had viciously slapped **D**'s 8-year-old daughter.[72]

As was the position in regard to the adequacy of the provocation, so the early holding was that the cooling time was a matter of law for the court.[73] It was for the jury to determine what period of time had actually elapsed, but for the court to say whether or not such a period constituted "cooling time." [74] But when it was recognized that it was to be tested by a standard it became obvious that the law merely supplied the standard—a reasonable person under like circumstances—and whether that test was met in the particular case was a question of fact for the jury,[75] except that it need not be submitted to the jury if the period is so short, or so long, that the minds of reasonable men could not differ in the conclusion to be reached.[76]

---

68. "No yardstick of time can be used by the Court to measure a reasonable period of passion but it must vary as to the facts of every case." People v. Harris, 8 Ill.2d 431, 134 N.E.2d 315 (1956).

69. State v. Gounagias, 88 Wash. 304, 153 P. 9 (1915).

70. Where the killing results from an explosion of pent-up anger and emotion, built up by a series of provoking acts, the homicide is manslaughter. Baker v. People, 114 Colo. 50, 160 P.2d 983 (1945); Ferrin v. People, 164 Colo. 130, 433 P.2d 108 (1967). "It may fairly be concluded that the evidence . . . supports a finding that defendant killed in wild desperation induced by Dotty's long continued provocatory conduct." People v. Borchers, 50 Cal.2d 321, 329, 325 P.2d 97, 102 (1958).

71. State v. Flory, 40 Wyo. 184, 276 P. 458 (1929).

72. People v. Rice, 351 Ill. 604, 184 N.E. 894 (1933).

73. Regina v. Fisher, 8 Car. & P. 182, 173 Eng.Rep. 452 (1837).

74. Ibid.

75. State v. Gounagias, 88 Wash. 304, 153 P. 9 (1915); State v. Flory, 40 Wyo. 184, 276 P. 458 (1929).

76. "Viewing the facts in this case and considering the appellant's conduct from the provocation to the murder, we are of the opinion that reasonable men could not have differed in the conclusion that the appellant's blood had indeed cooled by the time he killed his wife. . . . We hold as a matter of law, the killing did not occur in the heat of passion." State v. Ramirez, 116 Ariz. 259, 569 P.2d 201 (En Banc 1977).

If the time between the provocation and the killing is a disputed factual issue, whether there was time for a "cooling

Requirement number two must not be forgotten in the consideration of number three. If the passion of the slayer actually had cooled at the time of the killing it was homicide with malice aforethought and hence murder, however short the time may have been, and however much might have been the continued passion of the ordinary reasonable person. In one case, for example, in which the killing took place within a very few moments of the provocation, there was evidence to show an attempted telephone call by the slayer in the interim. He was trying to reach the sheriff; and this incident, said the court, showed the most rational and reasonable state of mind, entirely inconsistent with the theory of overpowering excitement.[77] This particular individual had unusual control over his passions, but the law would not treat a cold-blooded killing as one committed in the sudden heat of passion. As said by another court in a leading case: "If in fact the defendant's passions did cool, which may be shown by circumstances, such as the transaction of other business in the meantime, rational conversation upon other subjects, evidence of preparation for the killing, etc., then the length of time intervening is immaterial." [78]

In certain other cases the killer has had less than the usual control over his passions and has been deprived of the benefit of the rule of provocation because the cooling time had passed although his passions were still inflamed.[79] There is no inconsistency between such cases because the second requirement is measured by a subjective test and the third by an objective test, and one accused of murder must satisfy both (as well as the first and the fourth), in order to prove that his crime is only manslaughter.[80]

There is no simple rule of thumb by which to measure the length of the cooling time in terms of so many hours or minutes. It varies according to the circumstances of each particular case.[81] The greater the provocation, the longer will be the cooling time.[82] It may also be affected by other factors. For example, if the provoker should flee immediately after the provoking act, and should be pursued for a considerable distance before being overtaken and killed, the very chase itself would tend to keep the passion inflamed—at least for a longer period than if no chase were involved.

It is the lapse of the cooling time which prevents the recognition of any mitigation where the fatal act resulted from a formal duel, and what was said in that regard under the head of "mutual quarrel or combat" might have been reserved for this subdivision.

off" must be submitted to the jury. People v. Cornelison, __ Colo.App. __, 616 P.2d 173 (1980).

In holding as a matter of law that defendant had had "sufficient time to cool off," the court said: "A 'reasonable person' would not have been so provoked by the statement that she would have considered homicide several hours later." LaLonde v. State, 614 P.2d 808, 811 (Alaska, 1980).

77. State v. Delbono, 306 Mo. 553, 268 S.W. 60 (1924).

78. In re Fraley, 3 Okl.Cr. 719, 722, 109 P. 295, 296–7 (1910).

See also Commonwealth v. Aiello, 180 Pa. 597, 36 A. 1079 (1897), in which in the interval between the provocation and the killing D had eaten dinner, and gone to a neighbor's house to listen to music.

79. People v. Sanchez, 24 Cal. 17 (1864); State v. Farris, 6 S.W.2d 903 (Mo.1928); Commonwealth v. Swaney, 445 Pa. 244, 284 A.2d 732 (1971).

80. See State v. McCants, 1 Spears 384, 388 (S.C.1843).

81. Maher v. People, 10 Mich. 212, 81 Am.Dec. 781 (1862).

82. State v. Connor, 252 S.W. 713 (Mo.1923).

(4) Causal Relation Between Provocation, Passion, and Fatal Act

In addition to the three requirements mentioned above it is necessary that they exist, not by coincidence, but by direct causal relation. The adequate provocation must have engendered the heat of passion, and the heat of passion must have been the cause of the act which resulted in death.[83] There is no mitigation, for example, if the intent to kill was formed before the provocation was received (unless such intent had been definitely abandoned by a change of mind) because in such a case the provocation, no matter how adequate, was not the cause of the fatal act.[84]

(a) Killing Innocent Third Person

Additional light may be thrown upon this subject by reference to an exceptional situation. If one who has received adequate provocation is so enraged that he intentionally vents his wrath upon an innocent bystander, causing his death, he will be guilty of murder;[85] but if his deadly force was directed at the provoker and hit the other by accident,[86] or if as a reasonable mistake of fact he thought the provocative act had been perpetrated by the deceased, he is guilty of manslaughter only, if he otherwise meets the requirements of the rule of provocation.[87] One court has allowed a claim of manslaughter to the killing of an innocent third person where the accused may have believed the innocent person was in fact a participant in the conduct giving rise to the provocation when in fact the innocent person was not so involved.[88]

(B) Mitigation Other Than Provocation

Since manslaughter is a "catch-all" concept, covering all homicides which are neither murder nor innocent, it logically includes some killings involving other types of mitigation, and such is the rule of the common law. For example, if one man kills another intentionally, under circumstances beyond the scope of innocent homicide, the facts may come so close to justification or excuse that the killing will be classed as voluntary manslaughter rather than murder. "It is not always necessary to show that the killing was done in the heat of passion, to reduce the crime to manslaughter;" said the Arkansas court, "for, where the killing was done because the slayer believes that

83. Rex v. Thomas, 7 Car. & P. 817, 173 Eng.Rep. 356 (1837).

84. State v. Johnson, 23 N.C. 354 (1840); State v. Spears, 76 Wyo. 140, 300 P.2d 551 (1956).

If a husband kills his wife immediately upon discovery of an act of adultery, but the killing is because of prior malice, hatred or wrong, and not in the heat of passion, the offense is murder. Farr v. State, 54 Ala.App. 80, 304 So.2d 898, 902 (1974).

85. Rex v. Simpson, 11 Cr.App.R. 218 (1915); State v. Vinso, 171 Mo. 576, 71 S.W. 1034 (1902).

D, who intentionally killed his infant son, was not entitled to an instruction on voluntary manslaughter based upon heat of passion resulting from a quarrel with his wife. "The weight of authority is against allowing transference of one's passion from the object of the passion to a related bystander." State v. Gutierrez, 88 N.M. 448, 541 P.2d 628 (1975).

86. Rex v. Brown, 1 Leach 148, 168 Eng.Rep. (1776); State v. Wynn, 278 N.C. 513, 180 S.E.2d 135 (1971).

87. Wheatley v. Commonwealth, 26 Ky.L.Rep. 436, 81 S.W. 687 (1904); White v. State, 44 Tex.Cr.R. 346, 72 S.W. 173 (1902).

88. R. v. Manchuk, [1938] 4 DLR 737, S.C.R. 18, SCC.

he is in great danger, but the facts do not warrant such a belief, it may be murder or manslaughter according to the circumstances, even though there be no passion." [89] To give another illustration, the intentional taking of human life to prevent crime may fall a little short of complete justification or excuse and still be without malice aforethought.[90] Here also is the possibility of change by statute,—a matter not to be ignored at any point in criminal law, particularly in the field of manslaughter.[91] For example, some legislative enactments have spoken of voluntary manslaughter in terms only of a killing in "a sudden heat of passion caused by a provocation" and so forth.[92] There is authority, however, for holding that such a statute is not exclusive, and that an intentional killing without provocation may be involuntary manslaughter on some nonstatutory basis, such as if it was by one suffering from diminished capacity by reason of mental illness or intoxication.[93]

The California court announced, as a rule of common law, that an honest but unreasonable belief in the need to defend, while not excusable, negates the element of malice so that a resulting homicide is manslaughter rather than murder. The announcement was made in a case holding that the failure of the judge to give such an instruction *sua sponte*, in the case at bench, was not reversible error, but adding that in all future cases such an instruction should be given *sua sponte* whenever called for by the evidence. The development of the rule is discussed at length in the opinion.[94]

THE MODEL PENAL CODE

In Article 3, dealing with general principles of justification, the Code is worded repeatedly in terms of what the actor "believes." It does not say "reasonably believes." In sections 3.03 through 3.08 justification is said to exist if "the actor believes" his action is required or authorized, or "the actor believes" that defensive force is immediately necessary, or that the actor may estimate the need for using protective force "under the circumstances as he believes them to be" and so forth. But in section 3.09 it is provided

---

89. Allison v. State, 74 Ark. 444, 453–4, 86 S.W. 409, 413 (1904).

The court emphasized that "recklessness or negligence may come about from holding the unreasonable belief that deadly force is justified." State v. Grant, 418 A.2d 154, 156 (Me.1980).

90. Williams v. State, 127 Miss. 851, 90 So. 705 (1921). Cf. Walker v. State, 188 Miss. 177, 189 So. 804 (1939).

"A person is guilty of voluntary manslaughter, if, in taking another's life, he believes that he is in danger of losing his own life or suffering great bodily harm but his belief is unreasonable." People v. Davis, 33 Ill.App.3d 105, 337 N.E.2d 256, 260 (1975).

If **D**, charged with murder, genuinely believed the circumstances to be such that killing would be justified, this will not excuse the killing if the belief was unreasonable; but even so, the killing may be voluntary manslaughter rather

than murder. People v. Vaughn, 26 Ill.App.3d 247, 324 N.E.2d 697 (1975). Accord, State v. Mendoza, 80 Wis.2d 122, 258 N.W.2d 260 (1977). But this very sound position has been rejected in Arizona. State v. Tuzon, 118 Ariz. 205, 575 P.2d 1231 (1978).

91. A Wisconsin statute defines manslaughter to include causing a death: "Unnecessarily, in the exercise of his privilege of self-defense or defense of others or the privilege to prevent or terminate the commission of felony." Wis.Stat.Ann. § 940.05 (1958).

92. Ariz.Rev.Stat. § 13–1103 (1978); West's Ann.Cal.Pen.Code § 192 (1970).

93. People v. Mosher, 1 Cal.3d 379, 385–86, 82 Cal.Rptr. 379, 382, 461 P.2d 659, 662 (1969); People v. Ray, 14 Cal.3d 20, 28, 120 Cal.Rptr. 377, 381, 533 P.2d 1017, 1021 (1975).

94. People v. Flannel, 25 Cal.3d 668, 160 Cal.Rptr. 84, 603 P.2d 1 (1979).

that the justification provided in the preceding sections is unavailable if the actor acquired such a belief recklessly or with criminal negligence [95] and the offense charged is one which requires no more than recklessness or criminal negligence, as the case may be, for culpability. What is meant is that his actual belief, even if the result of recklessness or criminal negligence, is a complete justification so far as the charge of murder is concerned, but is not a defense to a charge of manslaughter if he was reckless in having such a belief, and not a defense to a charge of negligent homicide if he was criminally negligent in having it.[96]

THE NEW PENAL CODES

Some of the new codes spell out such a result in detail, as by a statute providing: "A person who intentionally or knowingly kills an individual commits voluntary manslaughter if at the time of the killing he believes circumstances to be such that, if they existed, would justify the killing but his belief is unreasonable." [97] Or by a provision that a person commits negligent homicide if: "He intentionally or recklessly causes the death of another person in the good faith but unreasonable belief that one or more grounds for justification exist . . . ." [98]

B. INVOLUNTARY MANSLAUGHTER

Involuntary manslaughter is a "catch-all" concept. It includes all manslaughter not characterized as voluntary.

The trend of the case-law, where not hampered by statute, has been to include within "voluntary manslaughter" certain unintentional killings,—that is, it includes all homicides whether intentional or unintentional which are committed with a person-endangering-state-of-mind and are not justified or excused but are perpetrated under circumstances of recognized mitigation.[99] And since manslaughter itself is a "catch-all" concept, including as a matter

---

95. The Model Penal Code uses the word "negligently" but in Section 2.02(2)(d) it defines that word in terms of "a gross violation" of the reasonable-person standard, and that is criminal negligence.

96. Manslaughter and negligent homicide may be lesser included offenses in a prosecution for murder. In such a case the judge will charge the jury that if they find certain facts they must return a verdict of not guilty of the murder but may return a verdict of guilty of the lesser included offense. If the charge is negligent homicide, for example, the instruction will be that a belief resulting from criminal negligence is not a defense.

97. E.g., Pennsylvania. 18 Purdon's Penn.Statutes § 2503, § 2504 (1973). The Illinois statute, Smith-Hurd Ill.Ann.Stat. ch. 38, § 9–2 (1972), is to the same effect.

98. E.g., Alabama. Code of Ala., Tit. 13A, § 6–3, § 6–4 (1975). The Colorado

statute, Colo.Rev.Stat. 18–3–104, 18–3–105 (1973), is similar.

"Our legislature has provided that, although a good faith but unreasonable belief that justification exists is not exculpatory, it is nonetheless a mitigating factor in determining criminal culpability in a homicide case. . . . Here . . . the jury . . . should have been instructed on the lesser offense of criminally negligent homicide." People v. Duran, 40 Colo.App. 302, 577 P.2d 307, 310 (1978).

99. "We hold that in every future prosecution for murder wherein the evidence necessitates an instruction upon self-defense, the trial court shall also instruct upon voluntary or first degree manslaughter committed in the heat of passion as a lesser included offense . . . ." Morgan v. State, 536 P.2d 952 (Okl.Cr.1975). See also State v. Warner, 58 Hawaii 492, 573 P.2d 959 (1977).

of common law all homicide not amounting to murder on the one hand and not legally justifiable or excusable on the other, the general outline of involuntary manslaughter is very simple. Every unintentional killing of a human being is involuntary manslaughter if it is neither murder nor voluntary manslaughter nor within the scope of some recognized justification or excuse.[1]

Part of the boundary line of this "catch-all" concept having been dealt with in the consideration of malice aforethought and of voluntary manslaughter, it is necessary at this point to take up the factors which determine whether homicide is or is not excusable. Where loss of life has been neither intended nor the result of any other sort of person-endangering-state-of-mind, the killing will be excused if he who caused it was not engaged in any unlawful activity at the time and was free from negligence.[2] Homicide is excusable, so far as the common law of crimes is concerned, in some cases in which the slayer was not as fully free from fault as indicated by such a statement. This requires separate attention to killings resulting from (a) negligence, and (b) an unlawful act.

(A) Homicide by Criminal Negligence [3]

Negligence is any conduct, except conduct intentionally or wantonly disregardful of an interest of others, which falls below the standard established by law for the protection of others against unreasonable risk of harm.[4] The standard of conduct to which all except children and insane persons must conform to avoid being negligent is that of a reasonable person under like circumstances.[5] And whoever causes harm to another as a result of negligence thereby incurs liability,—but not necessarily criminal guilt.

The English authorities have long recognized the possibility of manslaughter being established upon a negligence basis.[6] And in the absence of some peculiarity in the statutory law,[7] this is uniformly recognized in the United States. On the other hand, also assuming the absence of unusual

---

1. To sustain a charge of involuntary manslaughter the state must prove an unintentional killing and that **D** was at the time of the killing either engaged in the commission of a misdemeanor or committing a lawful act in a wanton manner. State v. Betts, 214 Kan. 271, 519 P.2d 655 (1974).

2. Commonwealth v. Flax, 331 P. 145, 200 A.2d 632 (1938).

3. Criminal negligence is considered more in detail, infra, chapter 7, section 2. And see Moreland, A Rationale of Criminal Negligence (1944); Urowsky, Negligence and the General Problem of Criminal Responsibility, 81 Yale L.J. 949 (1972).

4. Restatement, Second, Torts § 282 (1965). The definition used here follows closely that used in the restatement. The word "wantonly" is substituted for "recklessly" because wantonness tends to make the act malicious within the usage of the criminal law, whereas reck-

lessness falls short of malice. See infra, c. 7, § 2(A).

5. Id. at § 283.

The Restatement excepts only children because mental disorder does not exempt from tort liability, but insane persons must be included within the exception here.

6. 4 Bl.Comm. *192.

7. The Ohio statute on manslaughter (at the time) provided for the punishment of unintentional homicide only if committed in the perpetration of an unlawful act. Under this statute it was held impossible to establish manslaughter upon the basis of culpable negligence. Johnson v. State, 66 Ohio St. 59, 63 N.E. 607 (1902). A more desirable result was reached in Indiana by holding that "unlawful act," as used in such a statute, includes reckless conduct. Minardo v. State, 204 Ind. 422, 183 N.E. 548 (1932).

statutory provisions,[8] it is possible to have negligence resulting in death without any crime being committed.

Starting with the premise that any homicide other than murder was manslaughter unless under circumstances of justification or excuse, the judges in the very early days seem to have been unwilling to accept an excuse if the loss of life resulted from any negligence whatever;[9] but long ago [10] they came to recognize "a marked distinction between simple and ordinary negligence, giving one a right of action for damages, and culpable negligence, rendering one guilty of a criminal offense." [11] Other modifiers have been applied to the word "negligence" in the effort to express the same idea, the choice frequently having been "gross" or "criminal," [12] with the tendency, rather appropriately, being to favor the latter.[13]

A special problem requires attention here as well as at certain other points in the criminal law. Is subjective fault required for criminal guilt or may such guilt be based upon objective fault? One who has caused the death of another by his negligence may have been aware of the risk created by his conduct or he may not have been so aware although he should have been—the ordinary reasonable person knowing what he knew would have been aware. If he was aware, his negligence was "advertent" and he is guilty of subjective fault; if unaware, his negligence was "inadvertent" and his fault objective.

8. See the discussion infra under "negligent homicide."

9. "Expressions will be found which indicate that to cause death by any lack of due care will amount to manslaughter, but as manners softened and the law became more humane a narrower criterion appeared." Andrews v. Director of Public Prosecutions, 26 Crim.App.R. 34 (1937).

10. "As to precedents, at least as early as 1664 the distinction is made between negligence so great as to be blameworthy and, therefore, deserving punishment and the slight degree of negligence that would not justify a criminal charge." People v. Angelo, 246 N.Y. 451, 455, 155 N.E. 394, 395 (1927).

11. State v. Baublits, 324 Mo. 1119, 1211, 27 S.W.2d 16, 21 (1930).

"To constitute involuntary manslaughter, the homicide must have resulted from the defendant's failure to exercise due caution and circumspection, which has been held to be the equivalent of 'criminal negligence' or 'culpable negligence.'" State v. Sorenson, 104 Ariz. 503, 507, 455 P.2d 981, 985 (1969).

More than ordinary negligence must be shown to support a conviction for negligent homicide. State v. Fateley, 18 Wn.App. 99, 566 P.2d 959 (1977).

It was reversible error for the court to omit the word "culpable" in its instruction on negligent manslaughter. Stork v. State, 559 P.2d 99 (Alaska 1977).

12. White v. State, 37 Ala.App. 424, 427, 69 So.2d 874, 876 (1954); People v. Penny, 44 Cal.2d 861, 879, 285 P.2d 926, 937 (1955); Hynum v. State, 222 Miss. 817, 818, 77 So.2d 313, 314 (1955); State v. Gooze, 14 N.J.Super. 277, 282, 81 A.2d 811, 814 (1951).

In upholding the conviction of the president of a fireworks manufacturer, based upon the death of three employees due to an explosion of fireworks, it was said: "An employer whose acts or omissions constitute a disregard for the probable harmful consequences and loss of life as to amount to wanton or reckless conduct is properly charged with manslaughter where a foreseeable death is caused thereby." Commonwealth v. Godin, 374 Mass. 120, 371 N.E.2d 438, 443 (1977).

13. There has been a tendency to use this term in the statutes. See West's Ann.Cal.Pen.Code § 20 (1970).

"Driving while intoxicated does not constitute criminal negligence per se in the crime of negligent homicide; it creates only presumptive evidence of criminal negligence." State v. Williams, 354 So.2d 152, 155 (La.1977).

Some have urged that awareness should be requisite for criminal negligence,[14] but this is not the position taken by the common law. Whether negligence is criminal or ordinary (slight) depends not upon the element of awareness but upon the degree of the negligence.[15] If harm has resulted from a failure to use the care which the ordinary reasonable person would have employed under the circumstances,[16] it has resulted from negligence; but it was not criminal negligence unless the conduct fell far short of measuring up to the standard. Whereas the civil law requires conformity to the standard there has been no criminal negligence without "a gross deviation from the standard of care that a reasonable person would observe in the actor's situation." [17] No doubt the element of awareness may be considered by the jury in determining whether there has been "a gross deviation from the standard," but it may be found to be gross without the element of awareness.[18] Thus a conviction of manslaughter was affirmed although the killing resulted from playing a joke with a firearm which was thought to be entirely harmless.[19] However, a mother who left her children unattended in a locked home was not criminally liable for their deaths resulting from fire. The act was declared to be the result of "misadventure." [20]

The practical effect of the requirement of criminal negligence in penal law is a caution to the jury not to convict of crime, where other elements of culpability are lacking, except where the conduct resulting in loss of life represents an extreme case of negligence. And, despite an unfortunate lack of

14. See Hall, Negligent Behavior Should Be Excluded from Penal Liability, 63 Colum.L.Rev. 632 (1963).

15. "Between criminal negligence, however, and actionable negligence, there is . . . a question of degree only." Nail v. State, 33 Okl.Cr. 100, 106, 242 P. 270, 272 (1925).

16. Brady, Punishment for Negligence: A Reply to Professor Hall, 22 Buff.L.Rev. 107 (1972).

Keedy would have used a standard of care which the particular actor rather than men in general can attain. Keedy, Ignorance and Mistake in Criminal Law, 22 Harv.L.Rev. 75, 84 (1908).

It seems clear, however, that unless an individual is abnormal in some discernible respect, this cannot be determined, as the German courts speedily discovered. Wechsler & Michael, A Rationale of the Law of Homicide, 37 Colum.L.Rev. 701, 754–55 n. 183 (1937).

17. This is the language used in the Model Penal Code to express the concept. § 2.02(2)(d).

18. For emphasis the courts often use such expressions as "knowledge, actual or imputed." People v. Penny, 44 Cal.2d 861, 880, 285 P.2d 926, 937 (1955). Or "knowledge of such facts as under the circumstances would disclose to a reasonable man, ..." People v. Eckert, 2

N.Y.2d 126, 130–31, 157 N.Y.S.2d 551, 133 N.E.2d 794, 797 (1955). "It is sufficient that the actor realizes, or should realize, ..." Beeman v. State, 232 Ind. 683, 692, 115 N.E.2d 919, 923 (1953).

19. State v. Hardie, 47 Iowa 647 (1878).

Deliberately pulling trigger of weapon not being certain of whether it was loaded while pointing gun at the deceased victim was enough to establish involuntary manslaughter. In re M, 70 Cal.2d 444, 75 Cal.Rptr. 1, 450 P.2d 296 (1969).

In drafting the Model Penal Code the Institute rejected the suggestion that criminal guilt be restricted to subjective fault. "Accordingly, we think that negligence, as here defined, [not involving awareness] cannot be wholly rejected as a ground of culpability which may suffice for purposes of penal law . . . ." Model Penal Code 127 (Tent. Draft No. 4, 1955). But homicide resulting from inadvertent criminal negligence would not be manslaughter but a lesser felony known as "negligent homicide." Model Penal Code § 210.4. See also Model Penal Code 52, 53 (Tent. Draft No. 9, 1959).

20. People v. Rodriguez, 186 Cal.App.2d 433, 8 Cal.Rptr. 863 (1961). Compare Delay v. Brainard, 182 Neb. 509, 156 N.W.2d 14 (1968).

uniformity in expressing the idea, there is a tendency to speak of the types of behavior amounting to criminal negligence in terms of "reckless conduct" or "recklessness." [21]

(B) Homicide by Unlawful Act (The Misdemeanor-Manslaughter Rule)

Companion to the felony-murder rule is the so-called misdemeanor-manslaughter rule, and just as the former requires explanation so also does the latter. In substance it is this: Homicide resulting from the perpetration or attempted perpetration of an unlawful act, less than a dangerous felony, is manslaughter if the unlawful act is malum in se.

If homicide by one engaged in an unlawful act were regarded as never excusable the law would be simpler than it is,—and more severe. The common law, despite statements suggesting such a simple and severe rule,[22] recognizes certain exceptions based upon (1) the nature of the unlawful act, and (2) the absence of causal connection between the unlawful act and the death. Each of these matters requires attention.

(1) Nature of the Unlawful Act

It has been common to define manslaughter in terms of "unlawful homicide" or "unlawful killing." This is entirely proper if sufficient emphasis is placed upon the conjunction of the two words. The homicide without malice aforethought which constitutes manslaughter is one in connection with which there is found not "unlawfulness" *and* "killing," but "unlawful killing." [23] The word "unlawful" is used in different senses, being broad enough at times to include what is "unpermitted but not necessarily forbidden." The phrase "unlawful act" is employed at times in a sense broad enough to include a deed wrongful only in the sense that it will support a civil action for damages. This usage has no place in the common law of manslaughter, although a few statutes have included a part of this field.[24] In fact, common-law references to homicide resulting from an unlawful act as being utterly beyond the realm of excuse, employ the phrase in a sense narrow enough to exclude a portion of the public-offense field. In one case, for example, a man drove his team of mules through a toll gate, urging them forward in an attempt to avoid the payment of the toll. The team became unmanageable

---

21. People v. Post, 39 Ill.2d 101, 223 N.E.2d 565 (1968); State v. Thomlinson, 209 Iowa 555, 228 N.W. 80 (1929); Commonwealth v. Farrell, 208 Pa.Super. 200, 222 A.2d 437 (1966); Goodman v. Commonwealth, 153 Va. 943, 151 S.E. 168 (1930); Albert v. Commonwealth, 181 Va. 894, 27 S.E.2d 177 (1943). The Model Penal Code would not use the word "recklessness" where the element of awareness is lacking, § 2.02(2)(c), but in the Restatement of Torts, reflecting existing judicial usage, no element of awareness is included in the definition of the term. Restatement, Second, Torts § 500 (1965) and see comment g to that section.

22. See the language in Jabich v. People, 58 Colo. 175, 179, 143 P. 1092, 1094 (1914); State v. Brown, 205 S.C. 514, 519, 32 S.E.2d 825, 827 (1945).

23. Blackstone defines manslaughter in terms of an unlawful killing. 4 Bl.Comm. *191. It is clear from his whole treatment of homicide that by "unlawful killing" he means a killing that is neither justifiable nor excusable. See id. *177–188.

24. ". . . by a person committing or attempting to commit a trespass, or other invasion of a private right, either of the person killed or another, not amounting to a crime." McKinney's (N.Y.) Pen.Law § 1052. This is not included in the Revised Penal Law of N.Y.

and ran over the keeper of the gate, thus causing his death. The driver was tried on the theory that he was guilty of manslaughter if the death was due to his unlawful attempt to pass through the gate without paying, whether the act was done in a careless manner or not. In reversing a conviction the court said: "The mere unlawfulness of the act does not in this class of cases, *per se* render the doer of it liable in criminal law for all the undesigned and improbable consequences of it" because the act itself was *malum prohibitum* only.[25]

To prevent an officer from consummating a levy upon his property, Packard induced the other to drink quantities of liquor, without compulsion of any sort, and after he became intoxicated, the officer was placed in a carriage and driven around for several hours, also without compulsion. Unexpectedly, the excessive drinking combined with the normal bumping around in the carriage to produce death. It was held that if what was done was "for the purpose of good fellowship, for making merry . . . this will not be a case of manslaughter," but if it was for the purpose of interfering with a public officer in the discharge of his official duty, obstruction of justice [26] —*malum in se*—manslaughter had been committed.[27]

Here we have the key to this compartment of the common law. While the boundary line has not yet been clearly marked it has been found necessary to distinguish between two types of public offenses. Sometimes the differentiation has been between "civil offenses," "public welfare offenses" or "public torts" on the one hand and "true crimes" on the other; but the traditional classification is between offenses *mala prohibita* and offenses *mala in se*. "Acts *mala in se*," it has been said, "include, in addition to all felonies, all breaches of public order, injuries to person or property, outrages upon public decency or good morals, and breaches of official duty, when done wilfully or corruptly. Acts *mala prohibita* include any matter forbidden or commanded by statute, but not otherwise wrong." [28] Death resulting from an offense *malum in se* is not excusable, but is manslaughter [29] (if not murder) in the absence of some special statutory excuse,[30] even if no substantial element of human risk seemed to be involved. For example, while accidental death resulting from a lawful boxing match is excusable [31] a loss of life will not be less than manslaughter if it occurred under circumstances otherwise the same but in a prize fight in a jurisdiction in which prize fight-

---

25. Estell v. State, 51 N.J.L. 182, 185, 17 A. 118, 119 (1889): Accord, State v. Strobel, 130 Mont. 442, 304 P.2d 606 (1956). And see State v. Massey, 271 N.C. 555, 157 S.E.2d 150 (1967).

26. See infra chapter 5, section 3, G.

27. Regina v. Packard, Car. & Mar. 236, 174 Eng.Rep. 487 (1841). The quotation is from pages 245 and 491.

Attempted suicide is malum in se and if it results in the death of another it is manslaughter. People v. Chrisholtz, 55 Misc.2d 309, 285 N.Y.S.2d 231 (1967).

28. Commonwealth v. Adams, 114 Mass. 323, 324 (1873).

"An act *malum in se* is defined as an act wrong in itself; an act involving ille-

gality from the very nature of the transaction." Grindstaff v. State, 214 Tenn. 58, 377 S.W.2d 921, 926 (1964).

29. State v. Kellison, 233 Iowa 1274, 11 N.W.2d 371 (1943); State v. Betts, 214 Kan. 271, 519 P.2d 655 (1974).

30. Killing is excused if "in the heat of passion, upon any sudden and sufficient provocation, or upon a sudden combat provided that no undue advantage is taken nor any dangerous weapon used, and that the killing is not done in a cruel and unusual manner." 21 Okl.St.Ann. § 731 (1958).

31. Regina v. Young, 10 Cox C.C. 371 (1866).

ing is unlawful.[32] The reason is that each blow in a forbidden prize fight is an assault and battery and death resulting from assault and battery (*malum in se*) is manslaughter,[33] if not murder. Furthermore, since an unlawful attempt to procure an abortion is *malum in se*, a death resulting from such an attempt will not be less than manslaughter no matter how much skill was employed.[34] Death resulting from an offense *malum prohibitum* is excusable if neither wilful nor the result of criminal negligence.[35] The violation of law is not ignored in such a case. It is one of the factors to be considered by the jury in determining whether or not defendant's conduct amounted to criminal negligence.[36] This distinction has not always been appreciated by the courts and the concept of unlawful act has been expressed at times to encompass an act which the defendant had no right to do.[37]

"Knowingly and intentionally to break a statute must . . . always be morally wrong"[38] and hence will supply the normal mens rea requirement for true crime, at least if the statute was intended for the protection and safety of person or property.[39] Because manslaughter requires this mens rea[40] whereas an ordinary traffic violation does not, it follows that death resulting from such a violation is not necessarily manslaughter.[41] As has been pointed out, however: "An intentional, wilful or wanton violation of a statute or ordinance, designed for the protection of human life or limb, which proximately results in injury or death, is culpable negligence."[42] If the con-

---

32. People v. Fitzsimmons, 34 N.Y.S. 1102 (1895).

33. Commonwealth v. Gricus, 317 Mass. 403, 58 N.E.2d 241 (1944). This is true even if the blow was neither intended nor likely to cause death. State v. Frazier, 339 Mo. 966, 98 S.W.2d 707 (1936); People v. Morgan, 275 Cal.App.2d 603, 79 Cal.Rptr. 911, 914 (1969).

34. Worthington v. State, 92 Md. 222, 48 A. 335 (1901).

35. State v. Horton, 139 N.C. 588, 51 S.E. 945 (1905).

Evidence that defendant had a fatal traffic accident while driving five miles over the speed limit does not establish involuntary manslaughter. Such deviation does not establish the culpability needed for manslaughter. Commonwealth v. Sisca, 245 Pa.Super. 125, 369 A.2d 325 (1976).

36. Minardo v. State, 204 Ind. 422, 183 N.E. 548 (1932).

The violation of a statute enacted for the safety of persons and property may be negligence *per se*. Kisling v. Thierman, 214 Iowa 911, 243 N.W. 552 (1932). But it is not criminal negligence *per se*. People v. Barnes, 182 Mich. 179, 148 N.W. 400 (1914).

37. "The crime of manslaughter charged here is the killing of another without malice while engaged in the doing of an unlawful act; that is something

which the defendant had no right to do." Littlejohn v. State, 59 Del. (9 Storey) 291, 219 A.2d 155 (1966).

38. The Queen v. Tolson, 23 Q.B.D. 168, 172 (1889). The statement was qualified by the possibility of exception "as, for instance, if a municipal regulation be broken to save life or to put out a fire." It is preferable to say that such an exception would be recognized legally as well as morally and hence such conduct does not "break" the statute.

39. Carrying a concealed weapon sufficient for misdemeanor manslaughter instruction. Johnson v. State, 506 P.2d 963 (Okl.Cr.1973).

40. The normal mens rea requirement for true crime. See infra chapter 7.

41. Cain v. State, 55 Ga.App. 376, 190 S.E. 371 (1937); Bartlett v. State, 569 P.2d 1235, 1241 (Wyo.1977).

42. State v. Cope, 204 N.C. 28, 31, 167 S.E. 456, 458 (1932).

If an individual knowingly takes a risk of the kind which the community condemns as plainly unjustifiable, then he is morally blameworthy and can properly be adjudged a criminal. . . . [I]f the actor knowingly goes counter to a valid legislative determination that the risk he is taking is excessive, even though he himself does not believe it to be, there is an independent basis for moral condemnation in this deliberate defiance of law.

sequences are fatal, manslaughter has been committed in such a case.[43] Such a violation, therefore, should be recognized as a true crime even if it did not result in death or injury, just as a violation of a penalty clause has been held to be *malum in se* rather than *malum prohibitum* if the statute itself requires a specific wrongful intent.[44]

(2) Causal Relation Between Unlawful Act and Death

At least since the time of Lord Hale,[45] the courts have been unwilling to ground manslaughter upon an act, otherwise inoffensive, merely because it was a violation of the penalty clause of some regulatory enactment. One writer [46] undertook to demonstrate that innocence in such a case is not because the act is *malum prohibitum* but because there is no causal relation between the act and the death. Since the causation problems are more difficult, it is not surprising that the courts have very generally grounded their decisions upon the inefficacy of an act *malum prohibitum* for this purpose since the conclusion was to be "not manslaughter" whether a causal relation between the act and the death could or could not be established.

As to causation, assume a fatal traffic accident by a motorist violating the law by driving without an operator's license. Is there any causal relation between the violation and the death?[47] If the accident was by a competent motorist a few days after he had inadvertently neglected to renew his license, there may be none. Suppose, however, the lack of license was because a driving test had demonstrated such incompetence that the applicant should not operate a motor vehicle on the highway. The failure of the test was not unlawful; the unlawfulness was in driving the car under the circumstances, and it was the driving which caused the accident. Because of the many variables involved in a traffic accident, moreover, the question whether it could have been avoided by a competent motorist will almost invariably result in pure speculation unless the obvious answer is "yes." The solution would seem to be, not to question the causal relation, but to emphasize that since the violation "was but *malum prohibitum*"—a civil offense—the inadvertent act of the first motorist is not sufficient for guilt of manslaughter; whereas the wilful violation of this provision established for the safety of life and limb is entirely adequate. It was criminally negligent for the second motorist to venture onto the highway at the wheel of a motor vehicle.[48] In fact, the inquiry in such a case is not whether the unlawful act caused the

Hart, The Aims of Criminal Law, 23 Law & Contemp.Prob. 401, 416 (1958).

In a motor vehicle case involving a violation of a traffic statute, it was stated that before the violation could be manslaughter it must "evince a marked disregard for the safety of others." State v. Lingman, 97 Utah 180, 198, 91 P.2d 457, 465 (1939).

43. State v. Phelps, 242 N.C. 540, 89 S.E.2d 132 (1955). Violation of a municipal ordinance resulting in death was held to be sufficient for conviction of manslaughter. State v. O'Mara, 105 Ohio St. 94, 136 N.E. 885 (1922). But this was overruled. Steele v. State, 121 Ohio St. 332, 168 N.E. 846 (1929).

44. United States v. Boyce Motor Lines, Inc., 188 F.2d 889, 891 (3d Cir. 1951), aff'd, Boyce Motor Lines, Inc. v. United States, 342 U.S. 337 (1952).

45. 1 Hale, Pleas of the Crown *475.

46. Wilner, Unintentional Homicide in the Commission of an Unlawful Act, 87 U.Pa.L.Rev. 811 (1939).

47. Commonwealth v. Williams, 133 Pa.Super. 104, 112, 1 A.2d 812, 816 (1938) (causal relation); Commonwealth v. Romig, 22 Pa.D. & C. 341, 342 (1934) (no causal relation).

48. It is not meant to imply that the element of causation may not be lacking in some of the *malum prohibitum* cases.

death but whether the homicide can be said "to be the causal result of the *unlawfulness* of the defendant's conduct." [49] This is but another way of asking whether the act was the kind of unlawful act that can qualify for the so-called misdemeanor-manslaughter rule.[50]

What has been said must not lead to the belief that no causal-relation problem is involved in this area. It has not been uncommon to speak of this branch of involuntary manslaughter as homicide committed by one "while committing an unlawful act," or "in the pursuit of an unlawful design." [51] To understand the true meaning of such a phrase it is necessary to do more than add by interpretation that it means unlawful in the sense of *malum in se*. For conviction of manslaughter in such a case the state must do more than establish mere coincidence between such an act and the fact of death. It must establish the "causal connection" between the violation and the loss of life.[52] An excellent illustration is provided by an Illinois case.[53] A policeman committed a breach of duty by failing to arrest certain gamblers and drunken persons. At the time he was violating his duty in this respect, he accidentally shot and killed a girl. He was convicted of manslaughter on the ground that he caused the death *while* committing an unlawful act. This was reversed because of the absence of any causal connection between the unlawful act and the death. His wilful breach of official duty was an offense *malum in se*; but it had no connection, other than coincidence, with the accidental homicide. A similar result was reached where the defendant violated a police regulation by carrying an unapproved weapon.[54]

Statutes defining manslaughter (in part) in terms of a killing "in the commission of an unlawful act" [55] or "any offense" [56] or a "misdemeanor" [57] ordinarily receive the same interpretation. Even under such legislation "the commission of a misdemeanor in no way connected with the death is not what is meant by the law." [58]

(3) Conclusion

Professor Robinson [59] (misled by cases in which the question was whether an act *malum prohibitum* was performed with such criminal negligence as to make resulting homicide manslaughter) concluded that the misdemeanor-manslaughter rule applies only where the unlawful act is one *"which is dangerous to the lives and safety of others."* [60] And this conclusion was supported by Professor Moreland on the unwarranted assumption that *malum in se* means a dangerous act.[61] Had these been suggestions for a change in

49. Wilner, Unintentional Homicide in the Commission of an Unlawful Act, 87 U.Pa.L.Rev. 811, 831 (1939).

50. The label is not entirely adequate because the result of the relaxation of the felony-murder rule is that in many jurisdictions homicide resulting from a nondangerous felony is manslaughter.

51. Smith v. State, 33 Me. 48, 55 (1851).

52. Kimmel v. State, 198 Ind. 444, 154 N.E. 16 (1926); State v. Nosis, 22 Ohio App.2d 16, 257 N.E.2d 414 (1969).

53. People v. Mulcahy, 318 Ill. 332, 149 N.E. 266 (1925).

54. Commonwealth v. Heard, 209 Pa.Super. 452, 228 A.2d 924 (1967).

55. Kan.Stat.Ann. 21 § 3404 (1974).

56. Iowa Code Ann. § 707.5-1 (1978).

57. Ohio Revised Code Ann. § 2903.84(B) (1975).

58. State v. Schaeffer, 96 Ohio St. 215, 243, 117 N.E. 220, 228 (1917).

59. Robinson, Manslaughter by Motorists, 22 Minn.L.Rev. 755 (1938).

60. Id. at 778.

61. "And . . . since the misdemeanor-manslaughter rule has broken down except where the misdemeanor is

the law, no fault could be found with them, but purporting to be statements of existing law, they cannot be supported.[62]

A moderate blow caused a slight laceration on the inside of the mouth which produced a hemorrhage lasting ten days and ending in death. This was manslaughter although defendant did not know the other was a hemophiliac and had no reason to believe any danger was involved.[63] An intensive study resulted in the conclusion that under the prevailing view no death resulting from battery is less than manslaughter.[64] And reference to the broader position that death resulting from any unlawful act *malum in se*, is manslaughter (if not murder) drew this conclusion: "Whatever may be said as to the *raison d'être* of the doctrine here under discussion, its existence as part of our law is almost universal in this country . . . ." [65]

To clarify confusion as to existing law: If homicide has resulted from an unlawful act not dangerous in itself the question is whether the unlawful act was *malum in se* or *malum prohibitum* (true crime or civil offense); if the homicide has resulted from an unlawful act *malum prohibitum* (civil offense) the question is whether or not it was performed in a criminally-negligent manner.[66]

dangerous in itself. . . . " Moreland, Law of Homicide 55 (1952). See id. at 188, 193–94.

62. Perhaps Professor Moreland, despite his categorical statement on page 55, supra note 79, was only urging that the law be changed. "It is concluded, then, that the misdemeanor-manslaughter rule, as well as the felony-murder doctrine, is fundamentally unsound and that it should be repudiated." Id. at 196.

63. State v. Frazier, 399 Mo. 966, 98 S.W.2d 707 (1936).

64. "It is an important feature of prevailing law that one who causes the death of another by simple battery is generally guilty of manslaughter or of involuntary manslaughter, where that is a separate statutory category, however improbable the fatal result, since the battery is an unlawful act." Model Penal Code 44 (Tent. Draft No. 9, 1959).

As 11.15.080 provided: "Every killing of a human being by the culpable negligence of another, when the killing is not murder in the first or second degree, or is not justifiable or excusable, is manslaughter, and is punishable accordingly." And the court held that this "comprehended within its ambit the misdemeanor-manslaughter rule . . . ." Valentine v. State, 617 P.2d 751, 753 (Alaska 1980).

65. Wilner, Unintentional Homicide in the Commission of an Unlawful Act, 87 U.Pa.L.Rev. 811, 817 (1939). It is "prevailing law that is very old." 36 ALI Proceedings 106 (1959).

An unintentional killing without malice is manslaughter if it occurs "while the defendant was *either* (a) committing some misdemeanor   *or* (b) performing some lawful (i.e., not criminal) act in a manner which, in turn, was either (i) unlawful or (ii) wanton." State v. Warren, 5 Kan.App.2d 754, 624 P.2d 476, 479 (1981).

"Because the evidence, even when construed most favorably to the appellant, shows at least an accidental homicide during the commission of a misdemeanor, it was not error for the trial court to refuse to instruct" on an offense less than first-degree manslaughter. Reynolds v. State, 617 P.2d 1357, 1360 (Okl.Cr.App. 1980).

Accidentally causing death by a pistol carried unlawfully is involuntary manslaughter under the misdemeanor-manslaughter rule. United States v. Walker, 380 A.2d 1388 (D.C.App.1977).

66. "In proving involuntary manslaughter in a case where the unlawful act can be classified as malum in se, such as driving while intoxicated, then there need be no further proof going to the requisite criminal intent—since the act is considered wrongful in and of itself. Where, however, the unlawful act is merely malum prohibitum—a matter forbidden by statute but not otherwise wrong—there must be a showing that the act was done in a criminally-negligent manner, and that the death comes about as a proximate cause [result] thereof." Bartlett v. State, 569 P.2d 1235, 1238 (Wyo.1977).

With reference to possible changes in the law: The misdemeanor-manslaughter rule may result in an unreasonably extreme extension of liability.[67] If one has unlawfully applied force to the person of another, he should be convicted of battery, but if death has resulted so unexpectedly that no reasonable person would have foreseen it, the homicide should be excused. Or at most the law should be changed to provide an increase in the penalty for battery in such a case, rather than conviction of manslaughter.[68] In fact, it would seem wise, by statute, to abolish the misdemeanor-manslaughter rule, as has been done by the 1957 English Homicide Act, [69] and as is recommended in the Model Penal Code.[70]

One case might be thought to suggest that in order to have manslaughter under the misdemeanor-manslaughter rule the misdemeanor must be inherently dangerous.[71] But the reference to "a misdemeanor which is inherently dangerous to human life" [72] came from a judge's instruction which had obviously been inadvertently adapted from a felony-murder instruction. An inherently-dangerous offense should be a felony rather than a misdemeanor; and any death resulting from an inherently-dangerous offense should be murder rather than manslaughter. Moreover the misdemeanor in the case was battery, which is not an inherently-dangerous offense. This particular battery was committed in a very dangerous way, but a slap in the face might be battery without involving the slightest danger to human life. And since the conviction of manslaughter was affirmed, it is clear that the misdemeanor-manslaughter rule does not require an inherently-dangerous misdemeanor. However the case may indicate that California is moving away from the common-law rule that death resulting from battery is not less than manslaughter "however improbable the fatal result, since battery is an unlawful act." [73]

---

67. It may result in additional liability based upon objective fault. Obstruction of justice, for example, does not require any special mental element and hence may result from inadvertent negligence if extreme enough to be characterized as "criminal." If so, and death resulted, it would be manslaughter under the rule even if the killing itself was not negligent.

68. This is suggested as a possibility because there is still considerable support for the position that the extent of the harm caused may increase the gravity of the crime. It is not intended to lend strength to that position.

69. 5 & 6 Eliz. 2, c. 11 (1957).

See also, Westling, Manslaughter by Unlawful Act: The "Constructive" Crime Which Serves No Constructive Purpose, 7 Sydney L.Rev. 211 (1974).

70. Model Penal Code § 210.3 (Proposed Official Draft 1962); see Model Penal Code 40–41 (Tent. Draft No. 9, 1959).

"Under the construction we have adopted today if a violation of the intentional pointing/unintentional discharge portion of the careless use statute is found, a misdemeanor-manslaughter conviction automatically results if the victim is killed." Keith v. State, 612 P.2d 977, 989–90 (Alaska 1980).

71. People v. Williams, 13 Cal.3d 559, 119 Cal.Rptr. 210, 531 P.2d 778 (1975).

72. The judge's instruction on involuntary manslaughter included this statement:

"A killing is unlawful within the meaning of this instruction if it occurred: (1) during the commission of a misdemeanor which is inherently dangerous to human life; or (2) . . . .."

73. See supra, note 16.

THE MODEL PENAL CODE

Section 210.3 Manslaughter

(1) Criminal homicide constitutes manslaughter when:

(a) it is committed recklessly; or

(b) a homicide which would otherwise be murder is committed under the influence of extreme mental or emotional disturbance for which there is reasonable explanation or excuse. The reasonableness of such explanation or excuse shall be determined from the viewpoint of a person in the actor's situation under the circumstances as he believes them to be.

This covers what constitutes manslaughter at common law except as follows: Subdivision (a), which is involuntary manslaughter without the use of the name,[74] differs from the common law in two respects. (1) It does not include the misdemeanor-manslaughter rule. And (2) since "recklessly" is defined in the Code[75] to mean advertent criminal negligence, inadvertent criminal negligence resulting in death is not included. Such a killing would be the lesser offense of negligent homicide under the Code.[76] Subdivision (2), voluntary manslaughter, does not include any mitigation sufficient to reduce to manslaughter what otherwise would be murder, except the so-called rule of provocation. This seems to be very unfortunate. An intentional homicide may fall a little short of justification or excuse, but come close enough so that the offense should be manslaughter rather than murder. And such mitigation in the form of "diminished capacity," resulting from mental disorder or intoxication, has been recognized in some of the cases.[77] The rule of provocation is worded differently than in the common law, but the interpretation will probably be much the same. The Code does not mention "sudden," but the case law has recognized the possibility of a long series of provocative acts resulting in an emotional explosion.[78] "Extreme mental or emotional disturbance," is the language of the Code, but "passion" has been interpreted to include any "violent, intense, high-wrought, or enthusiastic emotion."[79] The Code does not mention the "cooling time," but the explanation would not be "reasonable" if the mind of a reasonable person under like circumstances would no longer have been upset. The reasonableness of the explanation is determined under circumstances as the actor "believes them to be." This is subjective, and properly so. If he should not have had the belief because a reasonable person would not have done so, he was criminally negligent in having the belief. But criminal negligence is the mens rea needed for manslaughter, not for murder. And it should be em-

74. It should be kept in mind that there was only one offense of manslaughter at common law and that the early references to "voluntary manslaughter" and "involuntary manslaughter" were merely factual designations comparable to "murder by shooting" and "murder by stabbing." Judges will probably use these terms whether they are included in the statute or not.

75. Model Penal Code Section 2.02(2)(c).

76. Section 210.4 Negligent Homicide. Negligently is defined in the Code in terms of inadvertent criminal negligence. Section 2.02(2)(d).

77. State v. Green, 78 Utah 580, 6 P.2d 177 (1931).

78. E.g., People v. Borchers, 50 Cal.2d 321, 325 P.2d 97 (1958).

79. Ibid. And see People v. Logan, 175 Cal. 45, 49, 164 P. 1121, 1122 (1917). " 'Heat of passion' includes an emotional state of mind characterized by anger, rage, hatred, furious resentment, or terror." State v. Coop, 223 Kan. 302, 573 P.2d 1017 (1978). Syllabus by the court.

phasized that a major purpose of the Code's formula was to establish a standard to be applied in every such case, leaving it to the jury to determine as a matter of fact whether or not the standard had been met; and thus to do away with the arbitrary rule that insulting words alone can never be adequate provocation, together with any other remnant of the ancient notion that the adequacy of provocation was purely a matter of law.

THE NEW PENAL CODES

With reference to the new codes, some of them deal with this field in terms of "voluntary" or "involuntary manslaughter," [80] but many more do not make use of these terms, and some do not even mention "manslaughter." [81] These differences in wording do not affect the substantive law and probably will have little effect on the language of opinions dealing with the subject. Without copying exactly the Model Penal Code section on manslaughter, some of the new codes have been patterned after it,[82] sometimes with the use of "sudden heat of passion" and reference to the cooling time.[83] The wording in others is more in terms of the common law,[84] and sometimes merely leaves it to the case law.[85] The misdemeanor-manslaughter rule is expressly included in some, without use of the label,[86] and some include mitigation other than the rule of provocation.[87]

D. NEGLIGENT HOMICIDE

There is no common-law offense known as "negligent homicide." As a matter of the common law of crimes any killing below the grade of manslaughter is innocent homicide. Some of the new penal codes have a classification scheme which (omitting degrees or other variations) divides criminal homicide into murder, manslaughter and criminally negligent homicide—or simply negligent homicide. For the most part, however, this has been achieved by removing from manslaughter the offense of homicide by criminal negligence and using this to constitute the newly named offense.

---

80. Ga.Code § 26–1102, § 26–1103 (1978); Smith-Hurd Ill.Ann.Stat. ch. 38 § 9–2, § 9–3 (1972); Iowa Code Ann. § 707.4, § 707.5 (1978); Kan.Stat.Ann. 21–3403, 21–3404 (1974); N.Mex. 1953 Comp. Law § 40A–2–3; Ohio Rev. Code § 2903.03, § 2903.04 (1975); Purdon's Pa.Stat.Ann. § 2503, § 2504 (1973); V.A.T.S. Penal Code, § 19.04, § 19.05 (1974).

81. 17 Me.Rev.Stat.Ann. § 203 (1975); Va.Code 1950, § 18.2–35, § 18.2–36; Rev.Code Mont. 1947 § 94–2507.

82. Ark.Stats. § 41–1504 (1977); 11 Del.Code Ann. § 632 (1979); Hawaii Rev.Stat. § 707–702(h) (1976); Ky.Rev. Stat. 435.022 (1981); McKinney Consol. Laws of N.Y. Code Penal Code § 125.20 (1975); No.Dak.Cent.Code 12.1–16–02 (1975); Or.Rev.Stat. 163.118, 163.125 (1979); Utah Code Ann. 1953, 76–5–205.

83. Code of Ala., Tit. 13A, § 13A–6–3 (1975); Colo.Rev.Stat. '73, 18–3–104.

84. Ga.Code § 26–1102, § 26–1103 (1978); Iowa Code Ann. § 707.4, § 707.5 (1978); Kan.Stat.Ann. 21–3403, 21–3404 (1974); La.Stat.Ann.—Rev.Stat. 14:31 (Revised Statutes) (1974).

85. West's Fla.Stat.Ann. § 782.07 (1976).

86. Ga.Code § 26–1103(b) (1978); Burns' Ind.Ann.Stat. § 35–42–13 (1979); Iowa Code Ann. § 707.5 (1978); Kan. Stat.Ann. 21–3405 (1974); La.Stat.Ann.— Rev.Stat. 14:31 (Revised Statutes) (1974).

87. Smith-Hurd Ill.Ann.Stat. ch. 38 § 9–2, § 9–3 (1972); Purdon's Pa.Stat. Ann. § 2503, § 2504 (1973); Utah Code Ann. 1953, 76–5–205; Wis.Stat. § 940.05 (1965).

Thus, though there are a few exceptions, most states still have no homicide offense which would be below common-law manslaughter.

Numerous specific instances of negligent homicides may be found scattered through the various criminal codes, such as death caused by negligently operating a steamboat, railroad train, or automobile; overloading a steamboat; allowing a steam boiler to explode; using firearms; handling explosives; and allowing vicious animals to be at large with knowledge of their propensities. Others might be added such as the case of an intoxicated physician administering to a patient. For the most part these have been expressly declared to be manslaughter. They would have been held to be manslaughter either under the common law or under the more general provisions of the code if the careless conduct amounted to criminal negligence; and almost without exception these special provisions are so worded or interpreted as to include this requirement.

Statutory Changes. If none of the statutory provisions went beyond this, the subject could be handled by the addition of a sentence or two under the head of involuntary manslaughter. There are a few states, however, with legislative provisions for the punishment of certain homicides below the grade of manslaughter. This additional crime is generally known as "negligent homicide." Michigan, the leader in this field, enacted a negligent homicide statute in 1921, whereby a lesser penalty than that specified for manslaughter was provided for "any person who, by the operation of any vehicle at an immoderate rate of speed or in a careless, reckless, or negligent manner, but not wilfully or wantonly, shall cause the death of another." The enactment added: "The crime of negligent homicide shall be deemed to be included within every crime of manslaughter charged to have been committed in the operation of any vehicle, and in any case where a defendant is charged with manslaughter committed in the operation of any vehicle, if the jury shall find the defendant not guilty of the crime of manslaughter such jury may in its discretion render a verdict of guilty of negligent homicide." [88]

"By the enactment of this statute," said the court, "the Legislature obviously intended to create a lesser offense than involuntary manslaughter . . . where the negligent killing was caused by the operation of a vehicle. . . . Therefore this statute was intended to apply only to cases where the negligence is of a lesser degree than gross negligence." [89] In such a state one who has caused death on the highway by his negligent driving is guilty of manslaughter if his conduct amounted to criminal negligence, and guilty of this special statutory offense of negligent homicide if his conduct amounted to ordinary negligence. Needless to say, even in such a jurisdiction the death is innocent homicide if it results from driving not tainted by negligence in any degree.

Not in all jurisdictions having this additional crime can guilt of negligent homicide be established by mere proof of ordinary negligence. In most of them, in fact, more is required by the very language of the act itself.[90] Back of all such statutes seems to be the feeling of a need for a milder offense than manslaughter due to the reluctance of juries to convict of that offense

88. §§ 1 and 2 of Act 98 (1921). See Mich.Comp.Laws 1948, §§ 750.324–750.325.

89. People v. Campbell, 237 Mich. 424, 428–9, 212 N.W. 97, 99 (1927). The current California law is found in the manslaughter statute, West's Ann.Cal.Code § 192(3) (1970).

90. E.g., LSA–R.S. (La.), 14:32 (1974); Ore.Rev.St. 163.145 (1979).

in the fatal-traffic-accident cases.[91]   Hence for such a killing these statutes provide a lesser penalty than for manslaughter, sometimes declaring it to be a "misdemeanor."   A number of them seem to occupy concurrently a portion of the field of manslaughter merely to authorize the jury to apply the milder label and lesser penalty if they so desire in these fatal-traffic cases.   In Michigan, on the other hand, negligent homicide is an "included offense" in the ordinary sense, as previously explained.   In some states an offense of negligent homicide covering a vehicular homicide by negligence has been adopted as a part of the motor vehicle code rather than the penal code.[92]

THE NEW PENAL CODES

In 1942, in enacting the first of the recently revised penal codes, Louisiana carved out of the offense of manslaughter all of that part of the field grounded upon a negligence basis, and assigned this to the new statutory offense.   The result is a four-fold division of criminal homicide as follows:

(1) First-degree murder.

(2) Second-degree murder.

(3) Manslaughter.

(4) Negligent homicide (the killing of a human being by criminal negligence).[93]

Since then many penal codes have been revised.   Most of them have one or two homicide offenses in addition to murder and manslaughter, such as "reckless homicide," [94] "criminally negligent homicide," [95] "negligent homicide" [96] and "vehicular homicide." [97]   Except for "vehicular homicide" most of these statutory offenses are not limited to any particular form of killing.

"Reckless homicide" and "criminally negligent homicide" obviously require what would be called criminal negligence at common law, and some of the other criminal-homicide statutes are so worded as clearly to include this element.[98]   All of these have what would be manslaughter at common law, but under a different name and with a special penalty.   In some of the new codes all or part of the same field is included under the familiar heading of manslaughter.[99]   There may be a problem of interpretation under some of the other homicide statutes in the new codes.[1]   One has taken pains to make

---

91. Riesenfeld, Negligent Homicide, A Study in Statutory Interpretation, 25 Calif.L.Rev. 1, 7–8 (1936). And see State v. Wojahn, 204 Or. 84, 137–8, 282 P.2d 675, 701 (1955).

92. Utah Code Ann. 1953, 41–6–44.10; Wyo.Stat. 1977, 31–5–1115.

93. LSA–R.S.   (La.),   14:29–14:32 (1974).

94. E.g., Illinois, Indiana, Kentucky, and without using the name, Maine and Wisconsin.

95. E.g., Alabama, Colorado, Connecticut, Delaware, New York, Oregon, Texas and without using the name, Maine.

96. E.g., Arkansas, Hawaii, Louisiana, Montana, New Hampshire, North Dakota and Ohio.

97. E.g., Colorado, Florida, Kansas, Ohio, and without using the name, Connecticut, Indiana and Minnesota. "Automobile homicide" is the name used in Utah and Wisconsin.

98. E.g., Colorado, Florida, Kansas, Louisiana, Minnesota and Wisconsin.

99. E.g., New Mexico, Iowa, Pennsylvania and Washington.

1. E.g., Compare the following cases. State v. Anderson, 561 P.2d 1061 (Utah 1977); State v. Durrant, 561 P.2d 1056 (Utah 1977); State v. Wade, 572 P.2d 398 (Utah 1977).   The Utah Supreme Court reversed its position in State v. Chavez,

clear that it intends to punish the motorist who causes a fatal traffic accident by ordinary negligence, by using the term "simple negligence." [2] The necessary implication is that the term "negligent manner" used in another section [3] requires more than ordinary negligence. Some of the codes that define negligent homicide in terms of "negligently" causing the death, define the word elsewhere in the code in terms equivalent to criminal negligence [4] but that is not true of all.[5]

Statutes imposing criminal penalties for harm resulting from no more than ordinary (slight) negligence seem to have been ill-advised. If negligently-caused harm is to call for punishment it should be only in those cases in which there has been a gross deviation from the required standard of care. But within this area—criminal negligence—there should be a distinction based upon the presence or absence of the element of awareness. What seems to be the best suggestion in this regard is for legislation to provide that where homicide has been caused with no other element of culpability, the offense should be manslaughter if it resulted from advertent criminal negligence, and a lesser offense to be known as "negligent homicide" if it resulted from inadvertent criminal negligence. This is the provision of the Model Penal Code.[6]

E. SUICIDE

Suicide is the wilful and wrongful taking of one's own life.

It is convenient to consider suicide at this point and, at least in the light of the ancient law, it is not illogical to do so. The word "suicide" is broad enough, in its literal sense, to cover every case of self-killing. If limited to the self-killing of a human being, without other restriction, it would seem to include every instance in which such a one caused his own death within the accepted rules of causation. If the word were so used it might be common to divide suicide into three classes—justifiable, excusable, and culpable. If during a catastrophe, for example, two should find themselves in a situation in which both could not survive and one should deliberately abandon his position of momentary protection and plunge to destruction for the better safety

---

605 P.2d 1226 (Utah 1979), and required a show of criminal negligence for the negligence standard of the Utah automobile homicide statute. The Utah Legislature reacted by enacting a statute expressly stating the standard as "simple negligence." Utah Code Ann.1953, § 76-5-207 (1981 Supp.). Negligent homicide requires criminal negligence, but the term "negligent manner" used in the automobile homicide statute requires only ordinary negligence. The Wyoming court apparently frustrated at the Legislature's failure to act has ruled that the Wyoming negligent homicide statute governs over the manslaughter statute in vehicular homicide cases. Lopez v. State, 586 P.2d 157 (Wyo.1978).

2. E.g., Hawaii, sec. 707-704(2) (1976). This involves "a deviation from the standard of care that a law-abiding person would observe in the same situation."

3. Sec. 707-703.

4. E.g., New Hampshire, North Dakota and Ohio. See State v. Mattan, 207 Neb. 679, 300 N.W.2d 810 (1981).

5. E.g., In the Montana code "negligently" was defined in terms of "a want of such attention to the nature or probable consequences of the act or omission as a prudent man ordinarily bestows in acting in his own concerns." Now the term follows the Model Penal Code format, Mont.Code Ann. § 45-2-101(37) (1981).

6. Model Penal Code §§ 210.3(1)(a) and 210.4(1), with the interpretation of terms found in § 2.02(c) and (d). And see McKinney's (N.Y.) Revised Pen.Law § 125.10 (1975).

of the other, this heroic act of self-sacrifice should be classed as justifiable rather than as culpable or even merely excusable. Whereas, if one should cause his own death unintentionally, while doing nothing unlawful and without any culpable carelessness, his self-destruction would merely be excusable. Actually however, we do not refer to the one as "justifiable suicide" and the other as "excusable suicide," because Lord Hale used the word "suicide" as synonymous with *"felo de se"*[7] and such seems to have been the general usage ever since.[8]

1. AT COMMON LAW

"Felo de se," or felon of himself is freely spoken of by the early writers as self-murder.[9] Hence one who killed himself before he arrived at the age of discretion or while he was *non compos mentis*, was not a *felo de se*, or suicide.[10] Saving for a moment the consideration of the present law, it may be stated without hesitation that by the early common law suicide was a felony and was punished by ignominious burial and forfeiture of goods and chattels to the king. It was often spoken of as a voluntary act of intentional self-destruction, but was not actually limited to this alone. Thus if one by accident killed himself while attempting to murder another, or if a woman took poison with intent to procure a miscarriage, and died as a result, the wrongdoer in either case was *felo de se*.[11]

It has been ably argued that suicide was murder by the English common law.[12] But whether it is to be regarded as murder, or as a separate but similar offense, there is no dispute that suicide, as here explained, was a felony. Because of this fact an attempt to commit suicide was a misdemeanor.[13] One who encouraged another to commit suicide was guilty of felony as a principal if he was present at the act which caused the death, and as an accessory before the fact if he was not present when the fatal act was committed.[14] For this reason, if two mutually agreed to commit suicide together, and the means employed to produce death was effective only as to one, the survivor was guilty of the murder of the one who died.[15] Thus if two

---

7. 1 Hale P.C. *411.

8. Hepner v. Department of Labor and Industries, 141 Wash. 55, 59, 250 P. 461, 462 (1926). To establish "suicide" it must be shown not only that deceased took his own life but that he did so with "felonious intent." Southern Life & Health Insurance Co. v. Wynn, 29 Ala.App. 207, 194 So. 421 (1940).

D unlawfully shot at an officer coming to arrest him. The officer shot back and killed D. Since D had unlawfully caused his own death he had committed suicide. People v. Antick, 15 Cal.3d 79, 123 Cal.Rptr. 475, 539 P.2d 43 (1975).

9. "And first of the murder of a man's self, who is commonly called *felo de se*." 3 Co.Inst. *54. And see 4 Bl.Comm. *189.

10. Ibid.

11. 1 Hale P.C. *413; Rex v. Russell, 1 Moody C.C. 356 (1832).

12. Mikell, Is Suicide Murder? 3 Col.L.Rev. 379, 391 (1903). It was held, however, that an attempt to commit suicide, although a misdemeanor, was not an attempt to commit murder within the meaning of 24 and 25 Vict. c. 100. Regina v. Burgess, Leigh & Cave 258, 169 Eng.Rep. 1387 (1862).

13. Regina v. Doody, 6 Cox C.C. 463 (1854); Regina v. Burges, Leigh & Cave 258, 169 Eng.Rep. 1387 (1862).

14. Rex v. Russell, 1 Moody C.C. 356 (1832). When the mode of punishment changed, and there was no longer any penalty provided for the suicide, the accessory escaped punishment also by reason of the rule that an accessory could not be tried until after the principal had been tried and convicted. Ibid.; Regina v. Leddington, 9 Car. & P. 79, 173 Eng.Rep. 749 (1839).

15. Regina v. Allison, 8 Car. & P. 418, 173 Eng.Rep. 557 (1838).

persons encouraged each other to drown themselves, and both plunged into the water by their mutual agreement and encouragement, whereupon one was drowned while the other was saved, the survivor was guilty of the murder of the deceased.[16]

2. UNDER STATUTES

The present law on the subject of suicide has many points of conflict or uncertainty. Ignominious burial and forfeiture of goods are no longer used as penalties for crime and the present modes of punishment are not adapted to reach one already dead. The problem is emphasized by statutory definitions in terms of punishment. If, for example, the statutory definition of felony is "any crime punishable by death or imprisonment in the state prison," it seems not to include suicide.[17] One court has taken the position that "suicide is none the less criminal because no punishment can be inflicted," [18] and certain others have referred to it as criminal.[19] Elsewhere, on the other hand, the suicide has been held to be innocent of any crime,[20] and this conclusion seems unavoidable in those states which do not have common-law crimes and do not have any statute covering the case of suicide.[21]

Whether suicide is a crime or not is far from a purely academic problem. While present penalties are inapplicable to one who is dead, they can be used in the case of one who has tried to kill himself and failed, in the case of one who has unintentionally killed someone else while attempting self-destruction, or in the case of one who has encouraged another to kill himself or has actually assisted in the fatal act. As a matter of common law all of these misdeeds are offenses if suicide is a crime; but if suicide is not a crime it is arguable that no offense is involved in any of them except where actual assistance was given to the fatal act,—provided the killing of another during attempted suicide was not under such circumstances as to amount to malice aforethought or criminal negligence for reasons quite apart from suicidal effort. If, for example, a man should try to destroy himself with a bomb at a time and place where others were in obvious danger, and should kill someone else but not himself, he would clearly be guilty of manslaughter if not of murder. To put the matter in the most extreme form: One who has maliciously caused the death of another is not relieved from guilt of murder by the fact that he was trying to take his own life also.

To inquire further into these problems, what about the man who has attempted to take his own life without success and without causing harm to any other? It was a misdemeanor at common law, but is it under our modern codes? Under a statute providing that "all other offenses of an indictable nature at common law, and not provided for in this or some other act of the legislature, shall be misdemeanors, and be punished accordingly," it was

By statute in England the survivor of a suicide pact is guilty of manslaughter rather than murder. Homicide Act of 1957, 5 & 6 Eliz. II, c. II § 4; Suicide Act of 1961, 9 & 10 Eliz. II §§ 2 and 3 (schedule 2).

16. Rex v. Dyson, Russ. & Ry. 523, 168 Eng.Rep. 930 (1823).

17. See Commonwealth v. Mink, 123 Mass. 422, 429 (1877).

18. State v. Carney, 69 N.J.L. 478, 480, 55 A. 44, 45 (1903).

19. Suicide is "unlawful and criminal as *malum in se.*" Commonwealth v. Mink, 123 Mass. 422, 429 (1877).

20. Grace v. State, 44 Tex.Cr.R. 193, 69 S.W. 529 (1902).

21. See Blackburn v. State, 23 Ohio St. 146, 163 (1872).

held that an unsuccessful attempt to commit suicide was punishable in New Jersey.[22]   In Maine, on the other hand, where attempts are made crimes by the statutes only where the acts attempted are punishable, the attempt to commit suicide was held not to be an offense.[23]

The cases are also not in accord as to the effect of an accidental killing of another during an attempt to commit suicide. This has been held to be at least manslaughter, and perhaps murder, in Massachusetts,[24] manslaughter in New York,[25] murder in South Carolina [26] and no crime at all, without additional facts in Iowa.[27]

The decisions with reference to aiding and abetting in the suicide of another are equally divergent.

"Whatever may have been the law in England or whatever that law may be now with reference to suicides, and the punishment of persons connected with the suicide, by furnishing the means of other agencies, it does not obtain in Texas. So far as the law is concerned, the suicide is innocent; therefore the party who furnishes the means to the suicide must also be innocent of violating the law. We have no statute denouncing suicidal acts; nor does our law denounce a punishment against those who furnish a suicide with the means by which the suicide takes his own life." [28]

The Ohio court takes quite a different stand.

"If the prisoner furnished the poison to the deceased for the purpose and with the intent that she should with it commit suicide, and she accordingly took and used it for that purpose; or, if he did not furnish the poison, but was present at the taking thereof by the deceased, participating, by persuasion, force, threats, or otherwise, in the taking thereof, or the introduction of it into her stomach or body; then, in either of the cases supposed, he administered the poison to her, within the meaning of the statute." [29]

And Illinois has held that one who aids and abets a suicide is guilty of murder as a principal in the first degree.[30]

Actual assistance to the suicide may be carried too far for innocence in any jurisdiction. Texas has gone very far in holding that one who furnishes the means to the suicide is innocent, but even in that state it was held that one who furnished the poison to a suicide, knowing the intention of the other, and at the suicide's request placed the poison in his mouth, with fatal consequences, was guilty of murder.[31]

The whole approach of the law of suicide seems to have been unduly influenced by abstractions. Undoubtedly there is a social interest in the life of

22. State v. Carney, 69 N.J.L. 478, 55 A. 44 (1903).

23. May v. Pennell, 101 Me. 516, 64 A. 885 (1906).

24. Commonwealth v. Mink, 123 Mass. 422 (1877). Accord, People v. Chrisholtz, 55 Misc.2d 309, 285 N.Y.S.2d 231 (1967).

25. "Although suicide is not, as it was at common law, a crime, it is considered 'a grave public wrong.'" People v. Chrisholtz, 55 Misc.2d 309, 285 N.Y.S.2d 231 (Sup.1967).

26. State v. Levelle, 34 S.C. 120, 13 S.E. 319 (1890).

27. State v. Campbell, 217 Iowa 848, 251 N.W. 717 (1934).

28. Grace v. State, 44 Tex.Cr.R. 193, 194–5, 69 S.W. 529, 530 (1902).

29. Blackburn v. State, 23 Ohio St. 146, 163 (1872).

30. Burnett v. People, 204 Ill. 208, 68 N.E. 505 (1903).

31. Aven v. State, 102 Tex.Cr.R. 478, 277 S.W. 1080 (1925).

the individual. Without question one who wilfully takes his own life under circumstances to bring him within the *felo-de-se* label has caused social harm without justification or excuse. But when one is in the act of taking his own life there seems to be little advantage in having the law say to him: "You will be punished if you fail." [32] Almost invariably one who has made an unsuccessful attempt to kill himself is in serious need of medical attention,— which usually includes need of the psychiatrist as well as of the surgeon or general practitioner. What is done to him will not tend to deter others because those bent on self-destruction do not expect to be unsuccessful. It is doubtful whether anything is gained by treating such conduct as a crime. Several states have repealed former statutory provisions punishing attempted suicide. [33]

The method of dealing with one who has unintentionally killed another in the attempt to take his own life is possibly open to more question. Perhaps the best solution is to dispose of this on the same basis as other accidents and excuse the slayer if the circumstances did not involve such disregard for the safety of others as to constitute at least criminal negligence. Quite a different answer is required for the final point in the criminal law of suicide although even this can be clouded in doubt if approached from the viewpoint of theoretical abstractions. Thus, it is not a crime, generally speaking, to induce another to do what can be accomplished by him without criminal guilt, provided he has reached the age of discretion and is in his right mind at the time. This seems to suggest that wherever suicide itself is not a crime there can be no offense in inducing another to end his life. This position is assailable, even as an abstraction, because few generalizations of the breadth of the one mentioned are entirely free from exception. Moreover, this position assumes that the average suicide is sane at the time which, to state the matter mildly, is something to be established by proof rather than to be taken for granted by assumption.

On the other hand, if this point is approached as a problem of social discipline rather than as a theoretical abstraction, the solution is entirely free from doubt. This, let us hasten to add, has nothing in common with euthanasia, or "mercy killing," a problem entirely beyond the scope of the present chapter. If one (or any group) is ever to be authorized to act upon his own (or their own) determination that the time has come "to put another out of his misery" (which will require the aid of legislation since no such authority is recognized by common law, and as to which we studiously avoid any opinion here), [34] more adequate safeguards and more efficient methods will be required than can be found in the device of attempting to persuade the sufferer to take his own life. Actually, the "mercy killer" resorts to direct action, while the one who has induced another to kill himself has been prompt-

32. Larrimore, Suicide and the Law, 17 Harv.L.Rev. 331 (1904); Larrimore, Felo De Se, 47 Am.L.Rev. 210 (1913). See also Withers, Status of Suicide as a Crime, 19 Va.L.Reg. 641 (1914).

33. New York Laws, 1919, c. 414, repealed former sections 2302 and 2303 of the Penal Law. NDCC Title 12.1 repealed former provision 1943 § 12–3302. R.C.Wash. 9A.36.000, promoting suicide replaced R.C.Wash. 980.020.

34. It was held that a competent adult, whose condition was terminal, his situation wretched and his life continued only by artificial means, could refuse or discontinue medical treatment and such act could not be classed as attempted suicide. Satz v. Perlmutter, 362 So.2d 160 (Fla.App.1978).

ed by baser motives. The latter type of conduct is anti-social in the extreme and should be clearly branded as criminal. No statute should be required to bring this within the field of felonious homicide but a number of states have eliminated any possibility of doubt by legislation declaring that induced self-destruction is manslaughter [35] or an offense under some other name [36] on the part of the inducer.

THE MODEL PENAL CODE

The Model Penal Code does not deal with attempted suicide, as such, but it provides in Section 210.5 that one who purposely, by force, duress or deception, causes suicide is guilty of criminal homicide. And one who otherwise aids or solicits suicide is guilty of a lesser, independent offense which is only a misdemeanor if not so much as even attempted suicide results.

THE NEW PENAL CODES

With reference to causing or aiding suicide a few of the new codes are patterned rather closely after the Model Penal Code.[37] Some provide that one who intentionally causes or aids another to commit suicide is guilty of manslaughter.[38] An occasional code deals with causing or aiding suicide as an independent offense.[39]

F. DEGREES OF CRIMINAL HOMICIDE

Subdivisions of Criminal Homicide. It is often said that manslaughter is not a degree of the crime of murder, but a distinct offense.[40] This is beyond question since manslaughter is not murder; but it is commonly recognized as an "included crime." [41] While it is possible to find holdings to the effect that a charge of murder will not support a conviction of involuntary manslaughter,[42] the better view is that such a charge includes all grades of felonious homicide and will support a conviction of manslaughter whether voluntary or involuntary.[43] In other words, while manslaughter is not a de-

---

35. AS (Alaska) 11.15.050 (1962); Ariz.Rev.Stat. 13–1103A.3 (1974); West's F.S.A. (Fla.) § 782.08 (1976).

36. "Felony," maximum penalty 10 years or 1 year in the county jail. Miss.Code 1972, § 97–3–49; N.J.Stat.Ann. 2C:11–6 (1969).

37. Conn.Gen.Stat.Ann. §§ 53a–54a (1975); 11 Del.Code Ann. § 636 (1974); 17 Me.Rev.Stat.Ann. § 201 (1974); Purdon's Penn.Stat. § 2505 (1978); Burns' Ind.Ann.Stat. § 35–42–1–2 (1964).

38. Colo.Rev.Stat. '73, 18–3–104 (1973); Florida's section 782.07 doesn't mention suicide; Hawaii Rev.Stat. § 707–702(b) (1976); McKinney Consol.Laws of N.Y. Code Penal Code § 125.15 (1965); Or.Rev.Stat. 163.125 (1981).

39. Kan.Stat.Ann. 21–3406 (1974); N.H.Rev.Stat.Ann. 630:4 (1974).

40. See Folks v. State, 85 Fla. 238, 247, 95 So. 619, 621–22 (1923); State v. Trent, 122 Or. 444, 453, 252 P. 975, 977 (1927).

41. See State v. Johnson, 215 Iowa 483, 488, 245 N.W. 728, 731 (1932).

42. Commonwealth v. Mayberry, 290 Pa. 195, 138 A. 686 (1927).

43. People v. Long, 15 Cal.2d 590, 103 P.2d 969 (1940); State v. Baublits, 324 Mo. 1119, 27 S.W.2d 16 (1930); State v. Nortin, 170 Or. 296, 133 P.2d 252 (1943).

A conviction of second-degree murder was reversed because the judge, after giving an instruction on voluntary manslaughter and self-defense, refused to give an offered instruction on involuntary manslaughter, and the jury might have found that the killing occurred during a fight that started as an innocent, perhaps alcoholic, scuffle and ended with the unintentional death of the victim.

gree of murder, the two are really different degrees of felonious homicide,[44] in the broad sense, although the statutes do not make use of the word "degree" for this purpose. The Nebraska court has spoken of first and second degree murder and manslaughter as "degrees" of a single crime of criminal homicide; [45] and this has ample support in the historical development of the field.

What we now know as murder and manslaughter constituted just one offense under the common law of England.[46] Prior to ancient statutory changes any offense in this field was punishable by death and by forfeiture of lands and goods; and on the other hand it was within the scope of benefit of clergy whereby the life of the convict might be saved if he qualified.[47] A series of statutes, during the period from 1496 to 1547,[48] excluded from benefit of clergy certain of the more serious forms of felonious homicide, referring to them as murder committed with malice aforethought.[49] The wording of such legislation is quite significant. The killings which were to be punished by death without benefit of clergy were not referred to as *homicide* with malice aforethought, but as *murder* with malice aforethought. This suggests a concept of murder without malice aforethought, and in all probability the lawmakers at that time would have divided the crime of murder into two degrees, based upon this differentiation, had the idea occurred to them. Apparently they not only did not think of this but even overlooked the importance of giving any designation to that part of the field of felonious homicide which they left within benefit of clergy. At least they did not name it. The courts might have resorted to the technique used in speaking

State v. Rawls, 247 Or. 328, 429 P.2d 574 (1967).

An information charging murder includes voluntary manslaughter and involuntary manslaughter as lesser included offenses. People v. Morgan, 75 Cal. App.3d 32, 141 Cal.Rptr. 863 (1977). "[W]here the facts warrant it, a charge on voluntary manslaughter may indeed be given in a felony murder trial." Malone v. State, 238 Ga. 251, 232 S.E.2d 907, 908 (1977).

Under the Crimes Code "involuntary manslaughter is a lesser included offense of murder and thus is a permissible verdict when murder is charged." Commonwealth v. Gartner, 475 Pa. 512, 381 A.2d 114, 118 (1977).

Where the only defense in a murder trial was that the defendants did not kill the deceased, there was no error in refusing to instruct on either voluntary or involuntary manslaughter. State v. Burrow, 221 Kan. 745, 561 P.2d 864 (1977).

"Involuntary manslaughter is a form of homicide, and is a lesser degree of the offense of first-degree murder." State v. White, 225 Kan. 87, 587 P.2d 1259, 1268 (1978).

44. See Rhea v. Territory, 3 Okl.Cr. 230, 235, 105 P. 314, 316 (1909).

45. State v. Hutter, 145 Neb. 798, 804, 18 N.W.2d 203, 208 (1945). Although manslaughter and murder are technically different offenses, in substance they are different degrees of criminal homicide. Chisley v. State, 202 Md. 87, 95 A.2d 577 (1953).

"Under the Crimes Code, murder and voluntary manslaughter are both classifications of criminal homicide. 18 Pa.C.S.A. § 2501." Commonwealth v. Schaller, 493 Pa. 426, 426 A.2d 1090, 1095 (1980).

46. 3 Stephen, History of the Criminal Law of England 44 (1883).

47. Ibid. Nominally only members of the clergy were entitled to benefit of clergy; but the courts extended it to include every man who could read, on the fiction that if he could read he must be a member of the clergy.

48. 12 Hen. VII, c. 7 (1496); 4 Hen. VIII, c. 2 (1512); 23 Hen. VIII, c. 1, §§ 3, 4 (1531); 1 Edw. VI, c. 12, § 10 (1547).

49. The actual phrasing was (1) "wilful prepensed murders;" (2) "murder upon malice prepensed;" (3) "wilful murder of malice prepensed;" (4) "murder of malice prepensed." See the statutes cited in the preceding note.

of larceny and made use of the phrases "grand murder" and "petit murder" to distinguish the two grades of unlawful killing,—except for the obvious impropriety of referring to any grade of murder as "petit." [50] What they actually did was to reserve the word "murder" for homicide with malice aforethought and invent a new term, "manslaughter," for the other grade.

In some of the states in this country the statutes have made no further subdivision, making provision for the handling of specific cases by considerable latitude in the punishment provided for each of the two.[51] In Illinois, at one time, murder was punished by death, by imprisonment in the penitentiary for life, or by a term of not less than fourteen years; while the penalty for manslaughter was a term of from one to fourteen years.[52] Such a plan is probably wiser than any legislative effort to subdivide these offenses into degrees with less latitude in the punishment for each degree; but the tendency in this country has been in the direction of more subdivision. For the most part this extension has been moderate. Some of the states have provided two degrees of murder while leaving manslaughter without such division. Some of these, it must be added, have in effect created two degrees of manslaughter, without speaking in terms of degrees, by providing quite a different penalty for voluntary manslaughter than is specified for involuntary manslaughter.[53] In Pennsylvania, for example, voluntary manslaughter is punishable as a felony in the second degree, whereas, the penalty for involuntary manslaughter is a misdemeanor of the first degree.[54]

Other states have made this additional subdivision in form as well as in substance by providing for two degrees of murder and two classes of manslaughter, as is true in Iowa, Kansas and Tennessee.[55] Florida reaches a four-fold division by establishing three degrees of murder and leaving manslaughter undivided.[56] A few states have carried the process of division even farther. Wisconsin, prior to its adoption of the New Criminal Code of 1955, seemed to hold the "record" with three degrees of murder and four of manslaughter.[57] It may be added as a curiosity that New Mexico at one time had five degrees of murder.[58] The Maine statutes define the crimes of murder, felony murder and manslaughter.[59] Minnesota recognizes three degrees of murder and two degrees of manslaughter.[60] In Montana, homicide is de-

50. However, the phrase "petit treason" was used for the felonious homicide of master by servant, husband by wife, or prelate by clerk. 3 Co.Inst. *19–20.

51. Ga.Code 26–1101 (1978).

52. Ill.S.H.A. ch. 38, §§ 358–364. See now Ill.Crim.Code of 1961, as amended, §§ 9–1, 9–2, 9–3.

53. Burns, Ind.Ann.Stat. §§ 35–42–1–3 and 4 (1979).

54. 18 Purdon's Penn.Stat. §§ 2503, 2504 (1973).

55. Iowa Code Ann. §§ 701–705 (1978); K.S.A. 21–3401—3404 (1974); Tenn.Code Ann. §§ 39–2402, 2403, 2409, 2410 (1975).

56. West's F.S.A. (Fla.) §§ 782.04–782.07 (1975).

57. W.S.A. (Wis.) 340.02–340.27 (1979). For a discussion of the four degrees of manslaughter see State v. Scherr, 243 Wis. 65, 9 N.W.2d 117 (1943). There was an additional section on negligent homicide: § 340.271. The current code has two degrees of murder and six other sections dealing with criminal homicide, one of which uses the label "manslaughter." §§ 940.01–12.

58. N.M.Comp.Laws § 687 et seq. (1884). Currently New Mexico law provides for two degrees of murder and manslaughter and involuntary manslaughter, N.M. Stat. 1978, 30–2–3.

59. 17–A Me.Rev.Stat.Ann. §§ 201–203 (1976).

60. Minn.Stat.Ann. §§ 609.18–609.205 (1964).

fined as deliberate homicide, mitigated deliberate homicide and negligent homicide.[61]

1. MURDER

Under the common law a conviction of murder called for the sentence of death. Long ago this was recognized as too severe because of the widely-different circumstances under which murder can be committed, and the first ameliorative step was the Pennsylvania statute in 1794, which divided murder into two degrees with the death penalty for murder in the first degree and life-imprisonment for murder in the second degree. What has frequently been referred to as the "Pennsylvania pattern" is this: [62]

> **All murder which shall be perpetrated by means of poison, or by lying in wait, or by any other kind of wilful, deliberate and premeditated killing, or which shall be committed in the perpetration of, or attempt to perpetrate any arson, rape, robbery or burglary, shall be deemed murder of the first degree; and all other kinds of murder shall be deemed murder of the second degree.**

This general pattern has been followed in many of the states although slight changes have been made in a few of these. Some, for example, have added "torture" to "poison." [63] To the felony-murder clause of the statute some have added "mayhem" [64] and an occasional inclusion of some other felony may be found, such as kidnapping,[65] sodomy [66] or similar gross sexual imposition.[67] The Kansas statute adds the clause "in the perpetration or attempt to perpetrate any felony" [68] but the Kansas court has held under prior law where the term "or other felony" was used that under the rule of *ejusdem generis* [69] the phrase "or other felony" in this statute means a felony of

61. Mont. Code Ann., as amended, §§ 45–5–102—45–5–104 (1981).

62. This is the wording in the much-quoted Commonwealth v. Drum, 58 Pa. 9 (1868). The quotation in that case is from the statute of 1860 which differed from the original act of 1794 only in that the original "or premeditated" had been changed to "and premeditated," and the word "in" which appeared twice near the close had been changed to "of."

The present Pennsylvania statute has abandoned the above referenced classification and provides for three degrees of murder. First degree murder is an "intentional killing." Second degree murder is accomplished when death of the victim occurs "in the perpetration of a felony." Third degree murder includes all other murder. Intentional killing, however, is defined as killing "by means of poison, or by laying in wait, or any other kind of willful, deliberate and premeditated killing." Felony murder also includes "deviate sexual intercourse by force or threat" and kidnapping.   18 Purdon's Consol.Pa.Stat.Ann. § 2502 (1973).

The Alaska court required a killing to be purposely committed for a felony-murder to be of the first degree. Gray v. State, 463 P.2d 897 (Alaska, 1970). An intent to kill is a necessary element of first-degree murder in Ohio, even if the killing is in the perpetration of robbery. Palfy v. Cardwell, 448 F.2d 328 (6th Cir. 1971).

63. E.g., I.C. (Idaho) 1979 § 18–4003.

64. West's Ann.Cal.Pen.Code § 189 (1970).

65. E.g., I.C. (Idaho) 1979 § 18–4003.

66. Code of Ala. § 13A–6–2 (1975).

67. NDCC 1973 § 12.1–16–01.

68. Kan.Stat.Ann. 21–3401 (1974).

69. The rule of *ejusdem generis* is that where a statute has a designation of particular subjects or classes, followed by general words, the meaning of the general words will be restricted by the particular designation so as to include only subjects or classes of the same kind or nature as those specifically enumerated unless there is a clear manifestation of a contrary purpose.

the nature of those enumerated, namely a dangerous felony.[70] Virginia has added murder by imprisonment or starving.[71] Florida has added aircraft piracy, killing by bomb, and death from the unlawful distribution of opium.[72] A statutory provision sweeping into the category of first-degree murder all murder perpetrated "in the commission of or attempt to commit any felony" is not unknown.[73]

Frequently first degree murder is defined, in part, in terms of malice aforethought express or implied.[74] Florida has expressed the requirement in terms of a "premeditated" design to effect death.[75] Some types of implied malice aforethought are frequently specifically included.[76] In some of the codes, moreover, there are no degrees of murder,[77] but the division into degrees has been so general, and the pattern given in blackletter above has been so widely adopted, as to be entitled to special attention. Unlike voluntary manslaughter which depends upon mitigation, first-degree murder under this plan requires some circumstance of aggravation. Homicide is not murder of either degree, under its provisions, unless it amounts to common-law murder. If this is all it is second-degree murder. If it is common-law murder plus one or more of the aggravating circumstances mentioned it is murder of the first degree. In some jurisdictions the aggravating circumstances determine whether the murder is a capital crime.[78]

The form of the statute might seem to suggest four different kinds of first-degree murder, and this is the result of the interpretation in California where the court held that murder by "lying in wait" does not require a deliberate and premeditated plan to kill, but may be perpetrated by killing from ambush as a result of the intentional infliction of bodily injury under circumstances likely to cause death.[79] This would be quite proper if the phrase stood by itself, but the wording is: "All murder which shall be perpetrated by . . . lying in wait or any *other* kind of wilful, deliberate and premeditated killing, ..." This indicates that "lying in wait" is there employed as a specific illustration of "wilful, deliberate and premeditated" murder.[80]

70. State v. Moffit, 199 Kan. 514, 431 P.2d 879 (1967). Unlawful possession of a firearm is not a felony inherently dangerous to human life, overruling *State v. Moffit* on that issue. State v. Underwood, 228 Kan. 294, 615 P.2d 153 (1980). The felony must be inherently dangerous.

71. Va.Code 1975 § 18.2–32.

72. West's Fla.Stat.Ann. 1976, § 782.04.

73. E.g., N.M.Stat.Ann. 1978, § 30–2–1(3).

74. N.M.Stat. 1978 § 30–2–1. This is equated with a deliberate intention to take away life. State v. Noble, 90 N.M. 360, 563 P.2d 1153 (1977).

75. West's Fla.Stat.Ann. § 782.04 (1976).

76. The Delaware Code includes murder committed "In the course of and in furtherance of the commission or attempted commission of a felony or imme-

diate flight therefrom, he recklessly causes the death of another person." 11 Del.Code Ann. § 636 (1979). The Wisconsin statute does not use the phrase "express malice aforethought," but provides as follows: "Whoever causes the death of another human being with intent to kill that person or another . . . ." W.S.A. (Wis.) § 940.01 (1979).

77. See, e.g., Ill.S.H.A. Crim. Code § 9–1 (1974); McKinney's (N.Y.) Rev.Pen.Law § 125.25 (1975); Smith-Hurd Ill.Ann.Stat. Ch. 38 § 9–1 (1974).

78. Utah Code Ann. 1953, 76–5–202.

79. People v. Mason, 54 Cal.2d 164, 4 Cal.Rptr. 841, 351 P.2d 1025 (1960). See also People v. Harrison, 59 Cal.2d 622, 30 Cal.Rptr. 841, 381 P.2d 665 (1963).

80. Murder by "lying in wait" is one resulting from ambush for the purpose of killing. State v. Olds, 19 Or. 397, 24 p. 394 (1890); State v. Gause, 227 N.C. 26, 40 S.E.2d 463 (1946); Commonwealth v.

09-009-004-0116

Locator Code:

09-009-004-0116

Entered Date: 6/26/2013

Title: Criminal Law (University Textbook Series)

ISBN: 9780882770673

Entered By: Steven Siebold

This interpretation gives three categories of first-degree murder:

1. By specified means (by poison—perhaps by torture may be added).[81]

2. By lying in wait or any other kind of wilful, deliberate and premeditated killing.

3. By felony-murder restricted to certain specified felonies.

Such a statute, let it be emphasized, makes no attempt to define murder. "It has no application until a murder has been established." [82] If the homicide meets the requirements of murder in general, and is shown to have been committed in any of these ways, then the statute applies and makes the killing murder in the first degree.[83] If the death would not otherwise be murder at all this statute does not make it first degree murder, because it speaks of all "murder" so perpetrated—not all "homicide." [84] By such legislation "murder, as limited by the common law, has been divided into two classes" but the "boundaries between murder and manslaughter remain unchanged." [85] This is peculiarly important in cases of death by poison. Homicide, effected by means of poison, might be committed with malice aforethought or it might be committed without malice aforethought but under circumstances amounting to criminal negligence, or it might be committed without either malice aforethought or such want of care as to be denominated criminal negligence. In the latter event it would be no crime at all, but excusable homicide. If the killing by poison was without malice aforethought but under circumstances amounting to criminal negligence, it is manslaughter at common law and hence does not come within the terms of this statute at all—but remains manslaughter.[86] All homicide, however, which is committed with malice aforethought, and by means of poison, is murder in the first degree under this statute.[87] The same is true, moreover, if the killing is by some other means specified at this point of the particular statute,—such as "torture." [88]

It is to be noted that it is "murder" committed by one of the specified modes of aggravation that is made first-degree murder by this statute. Un-

Mondollo, 247 Pa. 526, 93 A. 612 (1915); Burgess v. Commonwealth, 4 Va. 483 (1825).

"The elements necessary to constitute lying in wait are watching, waiting and concealment from the person killed with the intention of inflicting bodily injury upon such person or killing such person." State v. Brooks, 103 Ariz. 472, 445 P.2d 831 (1968).

81. "Murder by means of torture . . . is murder committed with a wilful, deliberate and premeditated intent to inflict extreme and prolonged pain." People v. Steger, 16 Cal.3d 539, 128 Cal.Rptr. 161, 546 P.2d 665 (1976).

82. People v. Austin, 221 Mich. 635, 644, 192 N.W. 590, 593 (1923).

83. People v. Mattison, 4 Cal.3d 177, 93 Cal.Rptr. 185, 481 P.2d 193 (1971).

84. State v. Shock, 68 Mo. 552, 559 (1878).

85. State v. Johnson, 8 Iowa 525, 529 (1859). Statutes in some states have changed the boundaries between murder and manslaughter. See Davis v. State, 110 Tex.Cr.R. 605, 607–8, 10 S.W.2d 116, 117–8 (1928); State v. Cooley, 165 Wash. 638, 641–2, 5 P.2d 1005, 1007 (1931).

86. See State v. Phinney, 13 Idaho 307, 313, 89 P. 634, 635 (1907); People v. Austin, 221 Mich. 635, 644, 192 N.W. 590, 593 (1923).

87. State v. Bertoch, 112 Iowa 195, 83 N.W. 967 (1900).

Death resulting from a violation of Penal Code § 347 (mingling poison with food intended for human use) with no intent to kill, is murder in the second degree under the felony-murder rule. People v. Mattison, 4 Cal.3d 177, 93 Cal.Rptr. 185, 481 P.2d 193 (1971).

88. People v. Murphy, 1 Cal.2d 37, 32 P.2d 635 (1934).

der this provision no murder by poison, for example, can be less than in the first degree. It provides for no second-degree murder by poison. But if mental capacity, without being obliterated,[89] has been diminished by mental disease, or otherwise, to such an extent as to make it impossible to harbor the state of mind known as malice aforethought, an intentional killing by poison would not be murder in any degree, but voluntary manslaughter.[90] Diminished capacity, in this sense, seems to have had its first recognition in California.[91] It has been accepted elsewhere,[92] but not in all jurisdictions.[93]

"Lying in wait," as the phrase is used in the homicide cases, means "hiding in ambush or concealment." [94] It is not to be taken too literally. One may be "lying in wait" in this sense while standing erect. The words refer, not to the position of the body, but to the "purpose of taking the person attacked unawares" and necessarily imply "malice, premeditation, deliberation, and the wilful intent." [95] As previously suggested, this is merely a specific illustration of a "wilful," deliberate and premeditated murder, and it could be omitted from the statute without changing the substance of the provisions.

If murder is committed by means of poison, or while perpetrating or attempting to perpetrate any of the felonies named in the statute, it is first degree murder even in the absence of an actual intent to kill.[96] This actual intent is essential, however, to constitute a "wilful, deliberate and premeditated" murder.[97] Accordingly it has been held that one who unlawfully chokes another with intent to cause great injury but not to kill, is guilty of second-degree murder if death unintentionally results.[98] It is not essential,

89. The obliteration of mental capacity by mental disease would give rise to the defense of insanity and result in a verdict of not guilty. See infra, ch. 8, § 2.

90. People v. Mosher, 1 Cal.3d 379, 385–86, 82 Cal.Rptr. 379, 382, 461 P.2d 659, 662 (1969); People v. Ray, 14 Cal.3d 20, 28, 120 Cal.Rptr. 377, 381, 533 P.2d 1017, 1019 (1975).

91. People v. Conley, 64 Cal.2d 310, 318, 49 Cal.Rptr. 815, 411 P.2d 911 (1966).

92. Johnson v. State, 511 P.2d 118 (Alaska 1973); State v. Holden, 85 N.M. 397, 512 P.2d 970 (App. 1973).

93. It seems to have merit but is not a constitutional requirement. Hence Arizona's refusal to recognize it does not result in a violation of due process. Narten v. Eyman, 460 F.2d 184 (9th Cir. 1969).

94. State v. Tyler, 122 Iowa 125, 131, 97 N.W. 983, 985 (1904).

95. Ibid. The essentials are waiting, watching and concealment. People v. Merkouris, 46 Cal.2d 540, 297 P.2d 999 (1956).

96. People v. Lookadoo, 66 Cal.2d 307, 57 Cal.Rptr. 608, 425 P.2d 208 (1967); State v. Robinson, 126 Iowa 69, 101 N.W. 634 (1904); Burton v. United States, 80 U.S.App.D.C. 208, 151 F.2d 17, certiorari denied 326 U.S. 789, 66 S.Ct. 473 (1946); State v. Best, 44 Wyo. 383, 12 P.2d 1110 (1932).

97. See State v. Johnson, 211 Iowa 874, 879, 234 N.W. 263, 266 (1931).

If a defendant is charged with premeditated murder and felony-murder, the jury should be instructed on both, and may convict of either. Of course, a defendant may not be convicted of both on a single homicide. State v. Sullivan, 224 Kan. 110, 578 P.2d 1108 (1978).

"Malice aforethought is an element of murder, but malice aforethought *and* and premeditated homicide is murder in the first degree; intentional homicide *without* premeditation is, in the absence of legally cognizable provocation or mitigating circumstances, murder in the second degree." Hern v. State, ___ Nev. ___, 635 P.2d 278, 280 (1981).

98. Commonwealth v. Marshall, 287 Pa. 512, 135 A. 301 (1926).

however, for the intent to kill to be directed against the person whose life is actually destroyed.[99]

An additional requirement of this particular clause is that this intent be formed by a mind free from undue excitement. "Deliberation means that the act is done in a cool state of blood." [1] Insult by mere words, for example, is insufficient to reduce a killing from murder to manslaughter; but it may arouse the passion of the person insulted to such an extent that if he kills the speaker intentionally under the sudden excitement engendered by these words, the homicide will not be *deliberate* and hence not murder in the first degree.[2] Furthermore, while voluntary intoxication does not excuse crime, it is possible for one to be so excited by drink as to be incapable of *deliberate* action, and a homicide committed by one in such a condition is not a "wilful, deliberate and premeditated murder," [3] unless the intent to kill was formed before the mind was thus affected.

Even more is required by a proper interpretation of this clause of the statute, although this element has been overlooked at times. "Premeditation means 'thought of beforehand' for some length of time, however short." [4] One who has in mind how completely the element of time disappeared from the concept of malice aforethought need not be too surprised at the treatment sometimes accorded the word "premeditated." Those who first employed this word in this type of first-degree murder statute undoubtedly had in mind a malicious scheme thought out well in advance of the fatal act itself. And unless we are willing to ignore the plain meaning of words we are forced to recognize that a fatal act might be intentional and yet entirely too hasty to be deliberate and premeditated. The notion that a fully-formed intent is always deliberate and premeditated, no matter how short the time between the first thought of the matter and the execution of the plan, is preposterous. And yet some of the courts have taken just such a position.

---

99. Henderson v. State, 264 Ind. 334, 343 N.E.2d 776 (1976).

1. State v. Bowser, 214 N.C. 249, 253, 199 S.E. 31, 34 (1938). " 'Deliberate' means decided as a result of careful thought." State v. Marvin, 124 Ariz. 555, 606 P.2d 406, 408 (1980).

2. State v. Jackson, 344 Mo. 1055, 130 S.W.2d 595 (1939). In California, as a result of changes in the wording of the statutes, it has been held that provocative words may be sufficient to reduce a killing to manslaughter. But it was held to be necessary also to emphasize that such words, if insufficient for this purpose in the particular case, might be found to have had such an effect that the killing was not deliberate and premeditated. People v. Valentine, 28 Cal.2d 121, 169 P.2d 1 (1946).

3. Hopt v. People, 104 U.S. 631 (1881); United States v. Dye, 221 F.2d 763 (3d Cir. 1955); People v. Griggs, 17 Cal.2d 621, 110 P.2d 1031 (1941); People v. Crumble, 286 N.Y. 24, 35 N.E.2d 634 (1941); Goodman v. State, 573 P.2d 400 (Wyo. 1977).

Under the provisions of the deliberate homicide statute, the necessary requirements of mens rea and criminal intent are embodied in the use of new language in the terms of "purposely" and "knowingly" which have replaced "deliberately." State v. Sharbono, 175 Mont. 373, 563 P.2d 61 (1977).

And even voluntary intoxication may result in a mind temporarily incapable of harboring malice aforethought in jurisdictions in which the concept of "diminished capacity" is recognized, as explained above.

4. State v. Chavis, 231 N.C. 307, 311, 56 S.E.2d 678, 681 (1949). And see Chisley v. State, 202 Md. 87, 106, 95 A.2d 577, 586 (1953); People v. Hillman, 140 Cal.App.2d 902, 295 P.2d 939, 941 (1956); State v. Hammonds, 459 S.W.2d 365 (Mo. 1970).

" 'Premeditated' means resolved in the mind beforehand." State v. Marvin, 124 Ariz. 555, 606 P.2d 406, 408 (1980).

The leading case on this point is *Drum*,[5] in which the Pennsylvania court said: "Therefore, if an intention to kill exists, it is wilful; if this intention be accompanied by such circumstances as evidence a mind fully conscious of its purpose and design, it is deliberate; and if sufficient time be afforded to enable the mind fully to frame the design to kill, and to select the instrument, or frame the plan to carry this design into execution, it is premeditated. The law fixes upon no length of time as necessary to form the intention to kill, but leaves the existence of a fully formed intent as a fact to be determined by the jury, from all the facts and circumstances in the evidence." In line with this suggestion it has been said that one may be guilty of murder in the first degree although the intent to commit such homicide is "formed by the accused immediately before the act is actually committed,"[6] or "at the very moment the fatal shot was fired."[7]

The sound interpretation of such a statute is that a killing is deliberate and premeditated if, and only if, it results from real and substantial reflection.[8] It is not sufficient that the idea be fully formed and acted upon; it must be pondered over and weighed in the mind. The intent to kill must be turned over in the mind and given a "second thought."[9] It is true the law does not attempt to set a period of time for this requirement in terms of hours, or minutes or even seconds;[10] but premeditation takes "some appreci-

5.   Commonwealth v. Drum, 58 Pa. 9 (1868). The quotation is from p. 16.

6.   Wooten v. State, 104 Fla. 597, 599, 140 So. 474 (1932); State v. Bautista, 193 Neb. 476, 227 N.W.2d 835 (1975).

7.   State v. Hall, 54 Nev. 213, 239, 13 P.2d 624, 632 (1932). "Deliberation and premeditation may be instantaneous." Aldridge v. United States, 47 F.2d 407, 408 (D.C.Cir. 1931).

The period of time required for premeditation and deliberation in first-degree murder is only that which is necessary for one thought to follow another. Bradney v. People, 162 Colo. 236, 426 P.2d 765 (1967).

For a willful, deliberate and premeditated killing "it is not necessary that the intention to kill should exist for any particular length of time," but only that it came into existence at the time of the killing or any time previously. Baker v. Commonwealth, 218 Va. 193, 237 S.E.2d 88, 89 (1977).

8.   People v. Guadagnino, 233 N.Y. 344, 135 N.E. 594 (1922); State v. Clayton, 83 N.J.L. 673, 85 A. 173 (1912); State v. Arata, 56 Wash. 185, 105 P. 227 (1909). The words "wilful, deliberate and premeditated" require "considerably more reflection than the amount of thought necessary to form the intention." People v. Caldwell, 43 Cal.2d 864, 869, 279 P.2d 539, 542 (1955).

Premeditation requires "proof that the defendant 'could maturely and meaning-

fully reflect upon the gravity of his contemplated act.'" People v. Horn, 12 Cal.3d 290, 115 Cal.Rptr. 516, 524 P.2d 1300 (1974).

Use by the legislature of "wilful, deliberate and premeditated" in conjunction in the first-degree murder statute indicates its intent to require as an essential element substantially more reflection, understanding and comprehension of the character of the act than the mere amount of thought necessary to form the intention to kill. People v. Theriot, 252 Cal.App.2d 222, 60 Cal.Rptr. 279 (1967).

And see Hemphill v. United States, 402 F.2d 187, 189 (D.C.Cir. 1968).

9.   Instructions approved by the Supreme Court included the phrases: ". . . turning it over in the mind; giving it a second thought." Fisher v. United States, 328 U.S. 463, 469, 66 S.Ct. 1318, 1321 (1946).

There must have been time for reflection, for a "second look" between the formation of the homicidal intent and the fatal act. People v. Hoffmeister, 394 Mich. 155, 229 N.W.2d 305 (1975). Contra, premeditation and deliberation, sufficient for guilt of first-degree murder does not require a time lapse of more than an instant. Scott v. State, 92 Nev. 552, 554 P.2d 735 (1976).

10.   State v. Riggle, 76 Wyo. 1, 298 P.2d 349 (1956).

able time." [11]   It is not essential, however, for the deliberation and premeditation to take place *after* the intent is formed; such careful consideration may precede the intent. If one has pondered over the possibility of taking another's life and has reflected upon this matter cooly and fully before a decision is reached, he may truly be said to have killed "wilfully, deliberately and premeditatedly," although after his intent was fully formed he carried it into effect as rapidly as thought can be translated into action.[12]   But the same intent, suddenly formed without preliminary consideration, and executed with such speed, would result in action properly characterized as *hasty* and *impulsive* rather than *deliberate* and *premeditated*.[13]

In other words, if the killing is not by poison (or some other special means if specified by the particular statute, such as "torture"), and is not committed by one who is perpetrating or attempting to perpetrate one of the felonies enumerated in the statute, there are three basic requirements for murder in the first degree, in addition to the requirement that the homicide must be murder within the rules of the common law. The first of these is that the homicide be intentional; the second is that the intent to kill must be formed by a mind that is cool rather than one that is unreasonably inflamed or excited; and the third is that the thought of taking the victim's life must have been reflected upon for some appreciable length of time *before* it was carried into effect, although not necessarily *after* the fatal decision was made. Needless to add, deliberation, premeditation and malice may all be inferred from sufficiently probative facts and circumstances.[14]

11. State v. Zdanowicz, 69 N.J.L. 619, 627, 55 A. 473, 476 (1903).

"Appreciable time" is a meaningful way to express the idea to the jury. Austin v. United States, 127 U.S.App.D.C. 180, 382 F.2d 129 (1967).

"In order to show premeditation and deliberation, the State must prove that the defendant made a decision to kill prior to the act of killing . . . the record fails to support a finding of premeditation and deliberation." State v. Lacquey, 117 Ariz. 231, 571 P.2d 1027, 1030 (1977); Smith v. Commonwealth, 220 Va. 696, 261 S.E.2d 550 (1980).

12. People v. Russo, 133 Cal.App. 468, 24 P.2d 580 (1933).

13. People v. Deloney, 41 Cal.2d 832, 839, 264 P.2d 532, 536 (1953). "The deliberate killer is guilty of first degree murder; the impulsive killer is not." Jones v. United States, 175 F.2d 544, 549 (9th Cir. 1949).

"A mere unconsidered and rash impulse, even though it includes an intent to kill, is not a deliberate intention to kill. To constitute a deliberate killing, the slayer must weigh and consider the question of killing and his reasons for and against such a choice." State v. Garcia, 95 N.M. 260, 620 P.2d 1285, 1286 (1980).

14. People v. Cartwright, 147 Cal.App.2d 263, 305 P.2d 93 (1956).

"Malice may be inferred from the use of a deadly weapon in a dangerous and deadly manner if the facts and circumstances so allow." Smith v. State, 564 P.2d 1194, 1198 (Wyo. 1977).

In Sundstrom v. Montana, 442 U.S. 510, 99 S.Ct. 2450 (1979), the Supreme Court held that an instruction that the law "presumes that a person intends the ordinary consequences of his voluntary acts" was violative of due process of law since a jury might have concluded that the presumption was conclusive or as shifting the burden of proof on intent.

Some of the new penal codes are worded differently. Thus in Montana the offense of "deliberate homicide" is the counterpart of a deliberate and premeditated killing with malice aforethought. "Therefore . . . the burden of the State . . . was to prove Sunday by a *voluntary act* caused the death of a human being while having the mental state described as 'purposely' or 'knowingly.' " Those are the material elements of a deliberate homicide under the Montana Criminal Code of 1973. State v. Sunday, ___ Mont. ___, 609 P.2d 1188, 1197 (1980).

The remaining type of homicide made murder in the first degree by such a statute, is any murder committed in the perpetration of, or in the attempt to perpetrate, any arson, rape, robbery, or burglary (or perhaps one or more additional felonies). In discussing the general subject of malice afore-thought it was pointed out that homicide resulting from the commission of a dangerous felony, such as one of these, is murder at common law. This reference, however, suggests a matter entitled to attention. While homicide by poison might not be first-degree murder under the statute, because for example it was the result of an innocent accident; and while a wilful, deliberate and premeditated homicide might be justifiable, as the act of the officer in executing the sentence of death; any homicide resulting from one of these *felonies* is first-degree murder under the statute, because it is murder as a matter of the common law regardless of the attending circumstances.[15] Such is the proper interpretation of the typical first-degree murder statute. An Alaska statute states this result with precision:

"A person who . . . purposely, and either of deliberate and premeditated malice or by means of poison, or in perpetrating or attempting to perpetrate, rape, arson, robbery, or burglary *kills another*, is guilty of murder in the first degree . . ."[16]

The phrase "committed in the perpetration or attempt to perpetrate," as found in the common type of first degree murder statute, has not been narrowly construed. Although penetration completes the crime of rape, for example, and no more is required for conviction of this crime (where the other elements are present) it does not follow that the "commission" of rape ceases at the moment penetration is accomplished.[17] It is first degree murder if the offender killed the woman by blows of the fist struck either in reducing her to helplessness previous to raping her or, during or after the sexual act, in stilling her outcries as an incident of the rape and at the scene thereof,—"or substantially at the scene of the rape."[18] "If the killing followed the rape in point of time, that did not make the crimes independent of each other."[19]

---

15. One who has a pistol in his hand in furtherance of an attempt to rob, and who causes death by the discharge of the pistol, is guilty of murder in the first degree even though the discharge was not intended, but was the result of accident. People v. Lytton, 257 N.Y. 310, 178 N.E. 290 (1931). Accord in substance, State v. Jensen, 209 Or. 239, 296 P.2d 618 (1956).

A burglar is guilty of murder in the first degree if his confederate in the burglary shoots and kills a policeman during the perpetration of the crime. People v. Green, 217 Cal. 176, 17 P.2d 730 (1932).

Statutory rape is not "rape" as that word is used in the first-degree murder statute. Commonwealth v. Exler, 243 Pa. 155, 89 A. 968 (1914).

Malice is necessary for first-degree murder, but malice may be established by proof of an inherently dangerous felony. State v. Guebara, 220 Kan. 520, 553 P.2d 296 (1976).

16. Alaska St. 1962, 11.15.010.

17. Commonwealth v. Gricus, 317 Mass. 403, 58 N.E.2d 241 (1944).

18. ". . . it is inconsequential that the death of the victim preceded the sexual attack. The test . . . is whether the killing and the felony 'occurred as part of one continuous transaction in which rape was involved.'" Commonwealth v. Tarver, 369 Mass. 302, 345 N.E.2d 671, 679 (1975).

19. Commonwealth v. Osman, 284 Mass. 421, 425, 188 N.E. 226, 227 (1933).

Under Tennessee law, if the indictment charges murder in common-law form, without mention of felony-murder, it is nevertheless proper to admit evidence of the rape and robbery of the victim to prove premeditation and support conviction of first-degree murder. Blake v. Morford, 563 F.2d 248 (6th Cir. 1977).

"There is no requirement that the homicide occur while committing, or while engaged in the felony, or that the killing be part of the felony. It is suffi-

"When the homicide is within the res gestae of the initial crime, and is an emanation thereof, it is committed in the perpetration of that crime in the statutory sense. . . .

"The res gestae embraces not only the actual facts of the transaction and the circumstances surrounding it, but the matters immediately antecedent to and having a direct causal connection with it, as well as acts immediately following it and so closely connected with it as to form in reality a part of the occurrence." [20]

One problem has been in regard to the burglar who, frustrated in his intent to steal, leaves the building empty-handed and kills a moment later in the attempt to avoid being captured on fresh pursuit. The New York court held that in such a case the burglary had come to a complete end so that the killing was not in the perpetration of burglary.[21] This, however, was when the felony-murder clause of the statute mentioned no specific felonies but made killing in the perpetration of or attempt to perpetrate any felony, murder in the first degree.[22] With such a severe provision it is understandable why the court should tend to restrict its application narrowly. The prevailing view is that such a killing is within the res gestae of the burglary and hence is committed in the perpetration thereof.[23] Several states have enacted statutes that contain language expressly applying the felony-murder rule where the killing occurs during a flight from the commission of a felony.[24]

In every case in which the prosecution seeks to establish guilt of first-degree murder on the ground that it was committed in the perpetration of, or attempt to perpetrate, such a felony, the guilt of this other felony or attempted felony must be clearly shown. Thus if the charge is murder in the first degree on the ground that it was committed by defendant while he was perpetrating a robbery, this degree of murder is not established if it is shown that defendant was so intoxicated at the time that his intellect was prostrated to such an extent as to be incapable of forming an intent to steal. If he could not—and therefore did not—have an intent to steal, he was not guilty of committing or attempting to commit robbery and hence does not

cient that the homicide be related to the felony and have resulted as a natural and probable consequence thereof." People v. Taylor, 112 Cal.App.3d 348, 169 Cal.Rptr. 290, 295 (1980).

20. State v. Fouquette, 67 Nev. 505, 528–9, 221 P.2d 404, 416–7 (1950). A different offense may be mentioned for the purpose of analogy. Where a kidnaping takes place after the actual perpetration of robbery, this may constitute kidnaping for the purpose of robbery if it is to facilitate the escape of the robber or remove the victim to a place where he can less easily sound an alarm. People v. Randazzo, 132 Cal.App.2d 20, 281 P.2d 289 (1955).

21. People v. Hüter, 184 N.Y. 237, 77 N.E. 6 (1906).

22. McKinney's (N.Y.) Pen.Code § 1052. There is no such provision in the present N. Y. statute. See McKinney's N.Y.Rev.Pen.Law § 125.25 (1975).

23. Conrad v. State, 75 Ohio St. 52, 78 N.E. 957 (1906). It is in the perpetration of the crime during flight from the scene thereof, even after abandonment of the plan. Commonwealth v. Devlin, 335 Mass. 555, 141 N.E.2d 269 (1957). See McKinney's N.Y.Rev.Pen.Law, Art. 125 (1975).

Where the defendant fleeing in an automobile after a burglary caused the death of another the felony-murder rule was applicable. People v. Fuller, 86 Cal.App.3d 618, 150 Cal.Rptr. 515 (1978).

24. Code of Ala. Tit. 13A § 2005 (1975); Rev.Code Wash.Ann. § 9A.32.030 (1977).

come under this clause of the statute.[25] And if what would constitute robbery by an older person is not a crime but only an act of "juvenile delinquency" by reason of the youth of the offender, a homicide resulting from such an act has been held not to be committed during the perpetration of robbery.[26]

Wrongs which do not constitute murder at common law are sometimes included in the murder statutes, especially if a third degree of murder is added.[27] The more common plan, however, is to divide common-law murder into two degrees, and after setting forth in detail just what kinds of murder shall be of the first degree, to add that all other murder shall be of the second degree.[28] Under such statutes murder in the second degree is common-law murder without any of the aggravating circumstances which are sufficient to raise it to the first degree.[29]

A. FELONY-MURDER: COMMON LAW AND STATUTORY

As mentioned in giving the background of felony-murder, the rule was quite logical in the early days when every felony was a capital offense. If one undertook to commit robbery and was successful he was guilty of a capital offense. If he attempted robbery but failed, and in the effort caused death, even unintentionally, he was guilty of a capital offense. The application of the rule involved no great injustice because it left the wrongdoer in the same situation, so far as penalty is concerned, as if he had accomplished exactly what he set out to do without more.

At a later time, when most felonies carried milder penalties, there was obvious injustice in including every felony in the application of the rule. In England, before Parliament abolished the rule, the courts tended to apply it only to a felony attempted in a dangerous manner. In this country, although some states included every felony in the rule, the trend was in the direction of including only such felonies as are inherently dangerous. What seems to be the logical conclusion of the development of this age-old problem is found in a recent Michigan case of which the abbreviated name is *People v. Aaron*[30] although three different cases were involved, representing a diversity in the Courts of Appeals.

---

25. People v. Koerber, 244 N.Y. 147, 155 N.E. 79 (1926).

An intent to "burglarize the building" (to break into the building and steal) was all that is required concerning the accused's state of mind in order to convict him of first-degree murder under the felony-murder rule. State v. Henry, 114 Ariz. 494, 562 P.2d 374 (1977).

"Robbery," as used in the statute which provides that murder in the perpetration of robbery is in the first degree, requires a specific intent. An intoxication may be such as to negate the existence of the required specific intent. United States v. Lilly, 512 F.2d 1259 (9th Cir. 1975).

26. People v. Porter, 54 N.Y.S.2d 3 (1945); People v. Roper, 259 N.Y. 170, 181 N.E. 88 (1932).

27. E.g., Minn.St.Ann., 1964, 609.195.

28. E.g., West's Ann.Cal.Pen.Code § 189 (1970); W.Va.Code 1977 § 61–2–1.

29. See Commonwealth v. McLaughlin, 293 Pa. 218, 221, 142 A. 213, 215 (1928).

A specific intent to commit homicide is not an element of murder in the second degree. State v. Ramirez, 111 Ariz. 504, 533 P.2d 671 (1975). But while this was true of common-law murder, some statutes do require such an intent for second-degree murder. State v. Birrueta, 98 Idaho 631, 570 P.2d 868, 870 (1977).

Malice is a necessary element of murder in the second degree. State v. Kabinto, 106 Ariz. 575, 480 P.2d 1 (1971).

30. 409 Mich. 672, 299 N.W.2d 304 (1980).

This case is not the first to reach the result it announces, but the opinion of the court is so exhaustive, and the ultimate result is stated in such definite terms, that it may well be considered a benchmark. The opinion starts with the development of the rule in ancient days and follows it down to the present time, emphasizing the growing dissatisfaction with the application of the rule under modern conditions. It points out that at least three states have abolished the rule by statute.[31] It mentions efforts to narrow the application of the rule, such as cases requiring that the underlying offense be a common-law felony; [32] and notes cases holding that in every murder case the issue of malice aforethought must be submitted to the jury and that it may not be satisfied by proof of an intent to commit the underlying felony.[33] Such a decision, needless to say, results in an actual abrogation of the felony-murder rule.

The opinion then addresses the law in Michigan, showing that the state has not defined murder by statute, and that the court's definition is in terms of homicide with malice aforethought; so that: "The effect of the doctrine is to recognize the intent to commit the underlying felony, in itself, as a sufficient *mens rea* for murder." [34] It points out that the Michigan statute on felony-murder, like the original Pennsylvania enactment, gives no aid to the determination of what constitutes the offense, but merely serves to raise the grade of certain murders to first degree. Thus the court found itself free to deal with common-law felony-murder without any statutory handicap. And, recognizing frankly that felony-murder had long been the rule in Michigan, it held:

"Today we exercise our role in the development of the common law by abrogating the common-law felony-murder rule." [35]

In any state in which the statute on the point adopts the original pattern, the court is free to follow the Michigan lead if it so desires. Unfortunately, however, many of the new penal codes are not so worded. In many the wording is in some such terms as that a person commits the crime of murder if he . . . commits or attempts arson, and so forth, and in the furtherance of the crime or attempt he causes the death of any person. Such a statute makes the killing murder whether it would or would not be murder at common law, and hence would not be affected by a decision abrogating the common-law rule of felony-murder.

THE NEW PENAL CODES

The Model Penal Code provides that a person commits murder if a criminal homicide is committed purposely or knowingly.[36] This standard is semantic and substantively different than willful, deliberate, and premeditated killing, but in essence embodies a similar substantive concept.[37] The Model

31. Id. at 299 N.W.2d at pp. 314, 315. (Kentucky and Hawaii in specific terms and Ohio by requiring an intent to kill for murder).

32. Id. at 299 N.W.2d at p. 313. (Commonwealth v. Exler, 243 Pa. 155, 89 A. 968 (1914); State v. Burrell, 120 N.J.L. 277, 199 A. 18 (1938).).

33. Id. at 299 N.W.2d at p. 314. (State v. Galloway, 275 N.W.2d 736, 738 (Iowa 1979); State v. Millette, 112 N.H. 458, 462, 299 A.2d 150, 153 (1972).).

34. Id. at 299 N.W.2d at p. 321.

35. Id. at 299 N.W.2d at p. 321.

36. M.P.C. § 210.2(1)(a).

37. Farrow v. Smith, 541 P.2d 1107 (Utah 1975).

Penal Code also recognizes murder "committed recklessly under circumstances manifesting extreme indifference" to human life.[38] This provision is comparable to implied malice.

The effect of the Model Penal Code has been to cause some jurisdictions to modify their codes from the language of the common law and traditional definitions of murder.

One of the new codes does not use the term "murder," but employs a designation of "deliberate homicide" for what would be murder elsewhere.[39] Any change in the offense that might seem desirable could be made without changing the name and it seems unwise to abandon the term that has come down through the ages. If judges in those states studiously avoid the word "murder" it will be surprising. With these rare exceptions the new codes uniformly speak in terms of "murder" but the uniformity ends there. Some have no degrees of murder,[40] some have two degrees of murder.[41] Some three[42] and some use substitutes for degrees.[43] There are numerous differences in the wording of the new codes dealing with this offense, but for the most part these differences have to do with marginal situations rather than with the hard core of murder.

2. MANSLAUGHTER

Conjecture might lead to the belief that in the states in which manslaughter is divided into degrees the first degree will be assigned to voluntary manslaughter while involuntary manslaughter is declared to be in the second degree. This, however, is not the fact in all instances. Alaska defines manslaughter as the "unlawful killing" of a person other than murder[44] and in another statute also defines manslaughter as the killing of a human being by "culpable negligence."[45] The Alaska Court has held there is only one statutory crime of manslaughter although defined in two separate statutes.[46] Maryland divides manslaughter into a general offense and manslaughter by vehicle.[47] In Washington, manslaughter in the first degree is defined in terms of "recklessly" causing death or intentional and unlawful killing of a fetus. Second degree manslaughter is killing with "criminal negligence."[48]

38. M.P.C. § 210.2(1)(b).

39. Rev.Code Mont. 1974 § 94–5–102.

40. Code of Ala., Tit. 13A, § 134–6–2 (1975); Conn.Gen.Stat.Ann. § 53a–54a (1958); Ga.Code § 26–1101 (1953); Hawaii Rev.Stat. § 707–701 (1979); Ill.Rev. Stat. 1972, § 9–1; No.Dak.Cent.Code 12.1–15–04 (1960); Or.Rev.Stat. 163.005 (1979).

41. Colo.Rev.Stat. '63, 18–2–401 (1973); 11 Del.Code 636 (1979); Iowa Code Ann. § 707.2 (1978); Kan.Stat.Ann. 21–3401 (1974); La.Stat.Ann.—Rev.Stat. 14:29 (1974); N.Mex. 1978 Comp. Laws § 30–2–1; McKinney Consol. Laws of N.Y. Penal Code § 125.00 (1975); Utah Code Ann. 1953, 76–5–202, 76–5–203.

42. West's Fla.Stat.Ann. § 782.04 (1976); Minn.Stat.Ann. § 609.195, 1963; Title 18 Penn.Stat. § 250 (1973);

Wis.Stat. 1958, § 940.01; Rev.Code Wash.Ann. 9A.32.010, 9A.32.045, 9A.32.- 050 (1977); Ark.Stats. § 41–1501 (1977); N.H.Rev.Stat.Ann. 630:1, 630:1–a, 630:- 1–b (1974); Va.Code 1950, § 18.2–30, § 18.2–32.

43. Burns' Ind.Ann.Stat. § 35–42–1–1 (1979); Ky.Rev.Stat. 507.020 (1980); V.A.T.S. Penal Code, §§ 19.02, 19.03 (1974); Ohio Rev.Code §§ 2903.01, 2903.02 (1975).

44. Alaska Stat. 1962 § 11.15.040.

45. Alaska Stat. 1962 § 11.15.080.

46. Des Jardins v. State, 551 P.2d 181 (Alaska 1976).

47. 27 Md.Code Ann. §§ 387, 388.

48. Rev.Code of Wash. §§ 9A.32.060 and 9A.32.070 (1977).

Ohio divides manslaughter into voluntary and involuntary manslaughter [49] with voluntary being defined as "knowingly" causing death under extreme emotional distress brought on by serious provocation [50] and involuntary manslaughter as causing death during a felony or misdemeanor with the punishment being divided into degrees of felony.[51] It happens that in some of the states using degrees of manslaughter, the statutory definition of murder has been enlarged to include intentional killings amounting to voluntary manslaughter at common law.   And the actual division is by declaring certain aggravated types of manslaughter to be of the first degree and then either declaring all other manslaughter to be of the second degree, or specifying the lesser types and assigning them to the second or lower degrees.[52]   In New York, the division is on a different basis.   First degree manslaughter includes certain killings that were common law murder, i.e. causing death with the intent to cause serious physical injury.[53]   The rest of first degree manslaughter is similar to the common-law standard.   Second degree manslaughter is recklessly causing death or killing during an illegal abortion or causing suicide.[54]

The Model Penal Code has not defined manslaughter in degrees but provides for manslaughter committed "recklessly" or a "homicide which would otherwise be murder" when it is "committed under the influence of extreme mental or emotional disturbance . . ." [55]   The Code provides for a separate offense for negligent homicide.[56]   This pattern has been adopted in several states.[57]   The Colorado Court declared the distinction between reckless manslaughter and negligent homicide a distinction without a pragmatic difference and hence unconstitutional.[58]

3.   OTHER HOMICIDE OFFENSES

The Model Penal Code provides for the offense of negligent homicide [59] which is a lesser offense to manslaughter.   The standard for culpability is the standard of "negligently" [60] under the Code, which is comparable to the standard applied to the offense of involuntary manslaughter when committed by a lawful act done in an unlawful manner.

The statutory offenses of reckless homicide, criminally negligent homicide, negligent homicide and vehicular homicide, found in some of the new codes, were discussed elsewhere and need only be mentioned here.

---

49. Ohio Rev.Code § 7901.03 and 4 (1975).

50. Id. § 22901.03.

51. Ohio Rev.Code § 22901.04 (1975).

52. 21 Okl.St.Ann. § 711 et seq. (1958).

53. McKinney's N.Y. Penal Code § 125.20 (1975).

54. McKinney's N.Y. Penal Code § 125.15 (1975).

55. M.P.C. § 210.3.

56. M.P.C. § 210.4.

57. Code of Ala. 1975 13A–6–3 (1975); Ariz.Rev.Stat.1978 § 13–1102–3; 11 Del.Code Ann. § 631–2 (1979); Utah Code Ann. 1973, 76–5–205–6.

58. People v. Calvaresi, 188 Colo. 277, 534 P.2d 316 (1975); People v. Webb, 189 Colo. 400, 542 P.2d 77 (1975).

59. M.P.C. § 210.4.

60. Id. § 2.02(d).

G.   THE CORPUS DELICTI RULE [61]

The phrase "corpus delicti" does not mean dead body, but body of the crime,[62] and every offense has its corpus delicti.[63] Its practical importance, however, has been very largely limited to the homicide cases. It concerns the usability in a criminal case of a confession made by the defendant outside of court.

It has long been held that no involuntary confession may be introduced in evidence against a defendant in a criminal case. A confession is involuntary if it was impelled by any form of physical or psychological coercion or duress,[64] or if it was obtained under the influence of some promise or other inducement.[65] The traditional explanation for the exclusion of an involuntary confession was that it was inherently untrustworthy.[66]

Now, however, the Supreme Court has gone far with the exclusion of confessions that are both voluntary and trustworthy. The starting point was the so-called McNabb-Mallory rule.[67] This rule, developed on non-consti-

---

61. For a more complete treatment see Perkins, The Corpus Delicti of Murder, 48 Va.L.Rev. 173 (1962). Some of the material of this article is included herein with the express permission of the Virginia Law Review.

62. Hays v. State, 230 Ark. 731, 733, 324 S.W.2d 520, 522 (1959); Warmke v. Commonwealth, 297 Ky. 649, 651, 180 S.W.2d 872, 873 (1944).

63. "Proof of the corpus delicti of any crime requires evidence that the crime charged has been committed by someone." State v. Hamrick, 19 Wn.App. 417, 576 P.2d 912, 913 (1978). A charge of driving while under the influence of liquor, to which defendant had confessed, was discharged because there was no independent evidence of the corpus delicti.

"The corpus delicti of the crime of arson consists of two elements: (1) that the building in question was burned; and (2) that it burned as a result of the willful and criminal act of some person." State v. Nelson, 17 Wn.App. 66, 561 P.2d 1093, 1095 (1977); Accord, Hall v. State, 570 P.2d 955, 960 (Okl.Cr.1977).

To admit defendant's extrajudicial confession of larceny, there must be other evidence of the corpus delicti. This evidence must include a prima facie showing that the articles had been stolen by someone. State v. DePriest, 16 Wn.App. 824, 560 P.2d 1152 (1977).

Some offenses, such as tax evasion, have no "tangible *corpus delicti*." Identity of accused must be shown and the evidence must corroborate the guilt of the accused as well. Smith v. United

States, 348 U.S. 147, 154, 75 S.Ct. 194, 198 (1954).

64. It is not necessary to find anything comparable to the brutal beating shown in Brown v. Mississippi, 297 U.S. 278, 56 S.Ct. 461 (1936), or the 36 consecutive hours of questioning present in Ashcraft v. Tennessee, 322 U.S. 143, 64 S.Ct. 921 (1944). See, for example, Rogers v. Richmond, 365 U.S. 534, 81 S.Ct. 735 (1961).

A statement taken from a defendant in a hospital, while the defendant was in great pain from wounds, depressed to the point of coma, isolated from family and counsel, and encumbered by medical treatment was not voluntary and could not be used even for impeachment purposes. Mincey v. Arizona, 437 U.S. 385, 98 S.Ct. 2408 (1978).

65. Where a confession was obtained under the assurance that it would result in leniency from the judge, it was involuntary. Dorsciak v. Gladden, 246 Or. 233, 425 P.2d 177 (1967). So also was a confession which resulted when the police persuaded a "false friend" to pretend to be greatly jeopardized by defendant's failure to confess. Spano v. New York, 360 U.S. 315, 79 S.Ct. 1202 (1959).

Improper promise to release girlfriend rendered confession involuntary. Ferguson v. Boyd, 566 F.2d 873 (4th Cir. 1977).

66. 3 Wigmore, Evidence § 815 (3d ed. 1940).

67. McNabb v. United States, 318 U.S. 322, 63 S.Ct. 608 (1943); Mallory v. United States, 354 U.S. 449, 77 S.Ct. 1356 (1957).

tutional grounds, was based upon the Court's supervisory power over the lower federal courts and their officers. This rule was to the effect that no confession is admissible against the defendant in a federal case if it was obtained during illegal detention—that is, while the arrestee was held in violation of the statutory requirement that he be taken promptly before a committing magistrate.[68]

More recently the Court has gone far beyond this by developing constitutional grounds for the exclusion of voluntary confessions in both federal and state cases. The starting point was *Escobedo*.[69] The conduct of the police in this case was outrageous. For hours while the accused was being questioned in the station house, repeatedly demanding an opportunity to consult with his previously-retained counsel, and while his attorney in another part of the building was demanding to see his client, the officers prevented any such meeting until their lengthy interrogation had resulted in a confession. The Court might well have held such conduct to be so violative of fundamental fairness as to constitute a denial of due process under established principles, but the majority of the judges were interested in making new law. Starting with the premise that the right to counsel is such a fundamental right as to be implicit in the concept of due process, they held that this right attaches to one in custody on a criminal charge, so that to question him after denying his demand to have an opportunity to consult with his retained lawyer, and having failed to warn him of his "absolute constitutional right to remain silent," amounts to a denial of his right to counsel and hence a violation of due process. That, however, was only the beginning. In *Miranda*[70] the Court took the position that due process of law requires that before a suspect in custody[71] of the law is questioned by police officers he must be advised (1) that he has an absolute right to remain silent and say nothing, (2) that if he does talk

---

68. The rule has been supplanted by statute, 18 U.S.C.A. § 3501(c) which provides in part:

" . . . a confession made or given by a person who is a defendant therein, while such person was under arrest or other detention in the custody of any law-enforcement officer or law-enforcement agency, shall not be inadmissible solely because of delay in bringing such person before a magistrate or other officer empowered to commit persons charged with offenses against the laws of the United States or of the District of Columbia if such confession is found by the trial judge to have been made voluntarily and if the weight to be given the confession is left to the jury and if such confession was made or given by such person within six hours immediately following his arrest or other detention: *Provided,* That the time limitation contained in this subsection shall not apply in any case in which the delay in bringing such person before such magistrate or other officer beyond such six-hour period is found by the trial judge to be reasonable considering the means of transportation and the distance to be traveled to the nearest

available such magistrate or other officer."

The McNabb-Mallory concept has been followed in few states. Cf. Commonwealth v. Morton, 475 Pa. 374, 380 A.2d 769 (1977).

69. Escobedo v. Illinois, 378 U.S. 478, 84 S.Ct. 1758 (1964).

70. Miranda v. Arizona, 384 U.S. 436, 86 S.Ct. 1602 (1966).

71. "By custodial interrogation, we mean questioning initiated by law enforcement officials after a person has been taken into custody or otherwise deprived of his freedom of action in any significant way." Miranda v. Arizona, 384 U.S. 436, 444, 86 S.Ct. 1602 (1966).

Custody is a critical consideration as to whether the Miranda warning is required. If a defendant is not in custody although a suspect no warning is required. Oregon v. Mathiason, 429 U.S. 492, 97 S.Ct. 711 (1977). The mere fact that an investigation has focused on a person does not, of itself, mean that the interrogation of the suspect requires a preliminary warning if the suspect is otherwise not in custodial status. Beckwith

anything he says may be used in court against him, (3) that he has a right to counsel including the right to have counsel present during the interrogation, and (4) that if he is unable to employ counsel a lawyer will be appointed for him. From this it was held to follow that any "custodial interrogation" of a suspect who had not been given such a warning and voluntarily and intelligently waived such rights was a violation of the Due Process Clause, necessitating the exclusion from evidence against him of any resulting confession, admission or other statement, even one intended to be exculpatory. To forestall the upsetting of myriads of convictions which had resulted from trials in which such proscribed statements had been used against the defendants, the Court announced in *Johnson* [72] that the new rules are to be applied prospectively and do not affect trials held before the applicable decisions had been announced.[73] All of this is merely the "backdrop," so to speak, for what follows.

The corpus-delicti rule is that no criminal conviction can be based upon defendant's extrajudicial confession or admission, although otherwise admissible, unless there is other evidence tending to establish the corpus delicti.[74]

In the background is the shocking effect of the reappearance of a missing person, hale and sound, after his supposed murder has resulted in the execution of the alleged killer. Two such cases are mentioned by Hale,[75] one cited by Coke and the other within Hale's own knowledge. Neither of these involved a confession but this feature was added in what seems to be the most astounding case of its kind on record.[76] It is no doubt entitled to more than a mere citation here.

When one Harrison, who had been sent to collect certain rents failed to return, John Perry, a servant, was sent to look for him; and after John also failed to reappear when expected, a search was begun in earnest. The searchers first found John and later a hat, band and comb identified as belonging to Harrison, the hat and comb "being hackt and cut, and the band bloody." Although no trace of the body was found the appearance of the hat and band was accepted as proof that Harrison had been murdered, and John's peculiar behavior caused the finger of suspicion to point in his direction. He gave several utterly inconsistent statements of what had happened, starting with one which involved no guilt on his part and ending with the statement that in the perpetration of robbery his brother Richard had strangled Harrison while their mother stood by, and under circumstances which implicated John himself.

From start to finish Richard and their mother denied any guilt whatever, insisting that John's story was a complete fabrication; but from the moment John gave this version of what had happened (until he was on the scaffold) he firmly maintained that the killing had taken place exactly in that manner. A few years after the three Perrys had been executed for this "murder," Harrison reappeared with a weird tale of having been robbed, kidnaped and transported to Turkey where he had been held as a slave until he managed to

v. United States, 425 U.S. 341, 96 S.Ct. 1612 (1976).

72. Johnson v. New Jersey, 384 U.S. 719, 86 S.Ct. 1772 (1966).

73. *Escobedo*—June 22, 1964; *Miranda*—June 13, 1966.

74. State v. Anderson, 561 P.2d 1061 (Utah 1977).

75. 2 Hale P.C. *290.

76. Perrys' Case, 14 How.St.Tr. 1312 (1661).

escape. Many doubted that Harrison had ever been out of England, prefer-
ring to believe that his strange story was an effort to explain his mysterious
disappearance immediately after having received a substantial amount of
money belonging to another; but no one doubted that three persons had
been hanged for an uncommitted murder, under circumstances in which
there would have been no conviction without the unexplained confession of
one of them.

A companion case, so to speak, on this side of the Atlantic resulted in the
conviction of the Boorn brothers for the alleged murder of Russel Colvin.[77]
Many of the features were astonishingly similar to those of Perrys' Case,
including a full confession by Stephen Boorn. The end was not so tragic,
however, because Russel Colvin reappeared just in time to stop the execution.

These cases clearly refute the layman's assertion: "He would never have
confessed unless he was guilty." In fact Blackstone characterized confessions as the "weakest and most suspicious of all testimony." [78] This has
been echoed by some while quite the opposite position has been taken by
others. "Based on varying experiences," said Wharton,[79] "different courts
have described confessions in terms running all the way from the highest
and most satisfactory proof of guilt down the gamut of qualifying adjectives
to the weakest and most suspicious of all testimony." Wigmore attributed
the contradictory views to a failure to "distinguish the confession as evidence from the evidence of the confession," because "few have ever really
doubted that the first is in itself of the highest value, while the second is
always suspected." [80]

This conclusion is bolstered by the fact that only the extrajudicial confession is viewed with distrust; no evidence ranks higher than the confession in
open court. In the absence of some rare statute to the contrary nothing is
required in addition to a plea of guilty, or other judicial confession,[81] but the
almost universal rule in this country is that a conviction cannot be supported
by the uncorroborated out-of-court confession of the accused.[82] We do not
find complete uniformity in what is needed for this corroboration. A few
courts accept any other evidence which tends to indicate the trustworthiness
of the confession as sufficient for this purpose,[83] but the widely-accepted
view is that there must be independent evidence of the corpus delicti of the
crime charged.[84]

"It is clear that an analysis of every crime, with reference to this element
of it," in the words of Wigmore,[85] "reveals three component parts, *first*, the
occurrence of the specific kind of injury or loss (as, in homicide, a person

---

77. The Trial of Stephen and Jesse
Boorn, 6 Am.St.Tr. 73 (1819). The
strange facts are set forth in detail in
Borchard, Convicting the Innocent, 15–22
(1932).

78. 4 Bl.Comm. *357.

79. 2 Wharton, Criminal Evidence
§ 396 (12th ed. 1955).

80. 3 Wigmore, Evidence § 866, at
358 (3d ed. 1940).

81. "The rule requiring a confession
to be corroborated by proof of the

corpus delicti has no application to in-
frajudicial confessions." Manning v.
United States, 215 F.2d 945, 950 (10th
Cir.1954). And see 1 Underhill, Criminal
Evidence § 36 (6th Ed. 1973).

82. Warszower v. United States, 312
U.S. 342, 61 S.Ct. 603 (1941).

83. 7 Wigmore, Evidence § 2071, at
396 (3d ed. 1940).

84. Id. at 397.

85. Id. at § 2072, at 401.

deceased; in arson, a house burnt; in larceny, property missing); *secondly,* somebody's criminality (in contrast, e.g. to accident) as the source of the loss,—these two together involving the commission of the crime by *somebody*; and *thirdly,* the accused's *identity* as the doer of the crime." And while this analysis may not be entirely adequate so far as the crime of murder is concerned, it offers a useful starting point for consideration of the meaning properly assignable to the term "corpus delicti." The components for this crime, on this analysis, would be (1) that the alleged victim is actually dead; (2) that his death was caused by the criminal agency of some other person, and (3) that the defendant is that person. The noted author would have preferred to recognize the first of these alone as sufficient to constitute the corpus delicti of murder but recognized that most courts have insisted that the addition of the second is essential. The notion that all three should be required for this purpose he characterized as "absurd." [86]

1. NO BODY

At one time, Texas law [87] seemed literally to have incorporated the popular notion that there can be no conviction of any grade of homicide unless the dead body of the alleged deceased, or an identifiable portion thereof, has actually been found, but in the absence of some such unusual enactment there is no such requirement. Time and again courts have gone out of their way to emphasize that finding the dead body of the victim is not indispensable in a murder prosecution. Disposing of a piracy case in 1705, an English court said: "By the 'corpus delicti,' subject of the crime, is not meant that the subject of the crime must be so extant as to fall under the senses; but that the loss sustained is felt and known. As for example: in the crime of murder, though the body cannot be reached, yet the particular loss is known." [88] And in this country Mr. Justice Story felt so strongly on the point that although the case at bench was robbery on the high seas he said of the assumed necessity of finding the body in a murder case that a "more complete encouragement and protection for the worst offenses of this sort could not be invented, than a rule of this strictness. It would amount to a universal condonation of all murders committed on the high seas." [89]

While it would be an exaggeration to say there have been many convictions of murder or manslaughter in cases in which no trace of the body of the alleged victim was ever found, there have been a substantial number in addition to the four mentioned earlier in which the failure to find such a trace was emphasized as one of the most important facts of the case. One of these is *Hindmarsh* [90] where the defendant was seen to have thrown his

---

86. And see State v. Lung, 70 Wash.2d 365, 423 P.2d 72, 76 (1967), where it is said: "The corpus delicti in a homicide case requires (1) the fact of death and (2) a causal connection between the death and a criminal agency, but the corpus delicti does not require proof of a causal relation between the death and the accused."

"Even more to the point, . . . the identity of the perpetrator is not a part of the *corpus delicti,* . . ." People v. Ott, 84 Cal.App.3d 118, 148 Cal.Rptr. 479, 487 (1978).

87. See Puryear v. State, 28 Tex.Crim. 73, 11 S.W. 929 (1889); Batterbee v. State, 537 S.W.2d 12, 15 (Tex.Cr.App. 1976).

88. Captain Green's Trial, 14 How.St.Tr. 1199, 1246 (Scot.Adm. 1705).

89. United States v. Gilbert, 25 Fed.Cas. 1287, 1290 (1834).

90. The King v. Hindmarsh, 2 Leach 569, 168 Eng.Rep. 387 (1792).

captain (never seen again) from the vessel into the sea. Another was *Williams* [91] in which there was no eye-witness testimony but much in the way of circumstantial evidence. These of course must be labeled "old cases," [92] but to dispel any possible misunderstanding in this respect we may mention *Lettrich* in 1943,[93] *Warmke* in 1944,[94] *Cullen* in 1951,[95] *Onufrejczyk* in 1955,[96] *Scott* in 1959,[97] *Lung* in 1967,[98] and *Pyle* in 1975.[99]

It must be mentioned on the other hand that proof of the unexplained disappearance of the alleged victim is never sufficient in itself to establish the corpus delicti.[1] "It is . . . dangerous to *infer* the death of a person from . . . his sudden and unaccountable disappearance, even when followed by long continued absence . . . ." [2] In one case, for example, defendant was seen with her bastard child as late as six in the evening and arrived at her father's house two or three hours later without it. Lord Abinger, C. B., instructed the jury that she could not be called upon to account for the child or to say where it was unless there was other evidence to show it was actually dead.[3] The evidence introduced suggests very strongly that she had disposed of the child, but this she might have done as readily by finding someone to "adopt" it as by taking its life; and even if the former would have been a violation of law on her part it would have had no bearing on a prosecution for murder or manslaughter; in any event she was not bound to incriminate herself.

The finding of an unidentified body, it may be added, is no proof of the corpus delicti,[4] and the finding of the skull and bones of an unidentified female near the place where defendant's confession indicated he had hidden the body of a woman he said he murdered was not sufficient corroboration of his confession.[5] But finding the charred remains of the body of a man in a house destroyed by fire, plus the fact that the householder was not seen or heard from thereafter, was sufficient to establish the corpus delicti.[6]

---

91. United States v. Williams, 28 Fed.Cas. 636 (1858).

92. In this category we might add, with no attempt to exhaust the list, State v. Lamb, 28 Mo. 218 (1859); Campbell v. People, 159 Ill. 9, 42 N.E. 123 (1895).

93. Commonwealth v. Lettrich, 346 Pa. 497, 31 A.2d 155 (1943).

94. Warmke v. Commonwealth, 297 Ky. 649, 180 S.W.2d 872 (1944).

95. People v. Cullen, 37 Cal.2d 614, 234 P.2d 1 (1951).

96. Regina v. Onufrejczyk [1955] 1 All E.R. 247.

97. People v. Scott, 176 Cal.App.2d 458, 1 Cal.Rptr. 600 (1959), appeal dismissed 364 U.S. 471, 81 S.Ct. 245 (1960).

98. State v. Lung, 70 Wn.2d 365, 423 P.2d 72 (1967).

99. State v. Pyle, 216 Kan. 423, 532 P.2d 1309 (1975).

1. See People v. Kirby, 223 Mich. 440, 194 N.W. 142 (1923); 3 Underhill, Criminal Evidence § 630 (5th ed. 1956).

2. Edmonds v. State, 34 Ark. 720, 744 (1879). In this case, however, a skull was found and identified by the teeth.

3. Regina v. Hopkins, 8 Car. & P. 591, 173 Eng.Rep. 631 (1838).

4. See Follis v. State, 51 Tex.Crim. 186, 101 S.W.2d 242 (1907).

5. Parker v. State, 228 Ind. 1, 88 N.E.2d 556 (1949).

6. State v. Henderson, 186 Mo. 473, 85 S.W. 576 (1905). Compare Commonwealth v. Burns, 409 Pa. 619, 187 A.2d 552 (1963).

The remains of a human being were found. The teeth were unusual and the missing boy's father and dentist both said they appeared to be those of the boy. And with the remains was found a bracelet similar to the one regularly worn by the boy. This was held sufficient to establish the corpus delicti, for the preliminary purpose of the corpus delicti rule. People v. Cantrell, 8 Cal.3d 672, 105 Cal.Rptr. 792, 504 P.2d 1256 (1973).

2. THE BODY WITHOUT CORPUS DELICTI

Just as it is possible to prove the corpus delicti without finding any trace of the body of the alleged victim of murder, so on the other hand it is possible to have unmistakable evidence of the dead body without being able to prove the corpus delicti. As explained to the jury by Chief Justice Shaw in a very famous case: [7] "When the dead body of a person is found, whose life seems to have been destroyed by violence, three questions naturally arise. Did he destroy his own life? Was his death caused by accident? Or was it caused by violence inflicted on him by others?"

To authorize a *conviction* the corpus delicti must be established beyond a reasonable doubt, but much less will be sufficient to constitute such corroboration as to entitle the jury to consider defendant's extrajudicial confession.[8] Unless the dead body is actually found it will require convincing evidence to establish the fact of death, even for the preliminary purpose of "the corpus delicti rule," but the other element does not require anything like that degree of proof. In the words of a distinguished author: [9] "Thus in a homicide case it is sufficient if the proof of the corpus delicti *points to* an unlawful slaying despite the fact that it is consistent with an accident or suicide."

As a starting point, the corpus delicti is lacking if what we have found is the body of one whose death resulted from natural causes or was self-induced either by accident or suicide; hence the independent evidence needed to corroborate the extrajudicial confession must point in another direction.[10] The requirement, in the language of the Florida Court, is "evidence which tends to show that the deceased died, not as a result of natural or accidental causes, or by his own hand . . .." [11] What appears to be the most common phrase in this connection is "evidence tending to show" [12] the needed result, with certain variations such as "tending to establish" [13] or a "prima facie showing." [14] It is not sufficient if the evidence tends to point no more in one direction than in the other.

In a murder prosecution where the victim's bodies were destroyed beyond recognition, circumstantial evidence was enough to establish the corpus delicti. Smith v. State, 31 Md.App. 106, 355 A.2d 527 (1976).

7. Commonwealth v. Webster, 59 Mass. 295, 309 (1850).

8. If there is enough evidence to entitle the jury to consider the confession, any doubt otherwise existing might be removed by the confession itself.

9. 2 Wharton, Criminal Evidence, § 394 at 138–39 (12 ed. 1955). (Emphasis added).

"It has long been the law of this Commonwealth that the prosecution has no duty to affirmatively exclude the possibility of accident or suicide in order to establish the corpus delicti . . . [The] Commonwealth has met its burden of establishing a corpus delicti for the purpose of introducing appellant's extrajudicial statements when it has established that

the fire causing death resulted from human intervention even though the evidence is consistent with both accidental and criminal conduct. Commonwealth v. May, 451 Pa. 31, 301 A.2d 368, 370 (1973); People v. Towler, 31 Cal.3d 105, 181 Cal.Rptr. 391, 641 P.2d 1253 (1982).

10. See Jackson v. State, 210 Ga. 303, 309, 79 S.E.2d 812, 816 (1954); State v. Henderson, 182 Or. 147, 190, 184 P.2d 392, 411 (1947).

11. Jefferson v. State, 128 So.2d 132, 135 (Fla.1961).

12. Hall v. Superior Court in and for Sacramento County, 120 Cal.App.2d 844, 849, 262 P.2d 351, 353 (1953); State v. Tourville, 295 S.W.2d 1, 5 (Mo.1956).

13. Gantling v. State, 41 Fla. 587, 604, 26 So. 737, 742 (1899); McCormick, Evidence 230 (1954).

14. "A prima facie showing of the corpus delicti of the crime charged must be made before a defendant's extrajudi-

While most of the cases in which this problem arises involve an obviously unnatural death, corroboration would clearly be lacking if independent evidence failed to indicate anything other than death from natural causes.[15] When the dead body was found but the independent evidence was as consistent with death from natural causes as from poison, a conviction based upon defendant's extrajudicial confession that he poisoned the deceased was reversed.[16] And independent proof that the baby was born alive, that it died and the body was dumped into a privy was not sufficient to support the mother's confession that she killed it, when there were no marks on the body and no indication of death by suffocation.[17] Also medical evidence that a child breathed a few times after birth but death was due to lack of oxygen was held insufficient to show the child had been born alive and had separate existence from the mother.[18]

The same is true in the "accident" cases. It was necessary to reverse a conviction based upon defendant's confession of having ignited kerosene he had wilfully poured on deceased after knocking him out, since the independent evidence indicated no more than fatal burns received while trying to put out a fire in the house.[19] As explained in another case: "So far from the evidence in this record . . . it seems to us that all the surrounding circumstances indicate that she perished by the accidental burning of her dwelling house, and not . . . by any act of violence inflicted by any other person." [20] It was impossible to support a conviction based upon a confession that defendant had attacked a girl, knocked her unconscious and placed her on a railroad track where she was killed by a passing train, since her mangled body by the track with evidence that the train had caused her death was equally consistent with the theory that she had been killed by accident while walking on the track.[21]

With reference to the third possible category, it was found necessary to reverse a conviction based upon defendant's confession of having murdered deceased by hanging, plus the finding of the dead body dangling from the end of a rope attached to a limb, because the trial judge had excluded medical evidence to the effect that the death scene indicated suicide.[22]

cial statements, admissions or confessions may be received in evidence. To establish the corpus delicti . . . it was only necessary . . . to show a reasonable probability of the criminal act of another caused the death . . ." People v. Cantrell, 8 Cal.3d 672, 105 Cal.Rptr. 792, 504 P.2d 1256, 1260 (1973).

15. See Harris v. State, 28 Tex.Crim. 308, 12 S.W. 308 (1889); In re Flodstrom, 134 Cal.App.2d 871, 277 P.2d 101 (1954), appeal dismissed, 45 Cal.2d 307, 288 P.2d 859(1955).

"Corpus delicti means the body of the crime, and in homicide cases proof of the corpus delicti requires a showing (1) of a death and (2) that the death resulted from the criminal agency of another." Clouser v. Commonwealth, 504 S.W.2d 694, 695 (Ky. 1973).

16. Pitts v. State, 43 Miss. 472 (1870).

17. State v. Johnson, 95 Utah 572, 83 P.2d 1010 (1938).

18. Lane v. Commonwealth, 219 Va. 509, 248 S.E.2d 781 (1978).

19. Grimes v. State, 204 Ga. 854, 51 S.E.2d 797 (1949).

20. State v. Flanagan, 26 W.Va. 116, 134 (1885).

21. People v. Cuozzo, 292 N.Y. 85, 54 N.E.2d 20 (1944).

22. Commonwealth v. Puglise, 276 Pa. 235, 120 Atl. 401 (1923).

Simulated suicide is quite another matter. If a dead body is found under circumstances suggesting suicide, but a careful investigation proves suicide was impossible, the criminal agency of another is clearly indicated. Commonwealth v. Webster, 59 Mass. 295, 318 (1850).

3. HOMICIDE

To return to Wigmore's approach, it will in no way detract from the luster attaching to that distinguished name to point out that the analysis made by him over half a century ago, without special reference to the crime of murder, is not quite adequate so far as this particular offense is concerned. And if we start, as we must, with the premise that it is neither sufficient to prove the death of the alleged victim, nor necessary to connect the defendant with the loss of life, there still remain three possibilities as to what might be said to constitute the corpus delicti of murder: namely, proof that he was killed by (1) an act of some other person (homicide), (2) a criminal act of some other person (criminal homicide), or (3) an act of some other person with malice aforethought (murder).

Authorities can be found lending support to each of these positions. The majority of the statements in this regard point to criminal homicide as the corpus delicti of murder, expressed in some such terms as that there are "two components: death as a result and the criminal agency of another as the means . . . ."[23]; "the fact of death and the criminal agency of another causing the death . . . ."[24] or words of similar import.[25] On the other hand authorities may be found for the position that the corpus delicti of murder is nothing less than murder by some person,[26] or that it is merely the fact that a homicide was committed.[27] Perhaps these are differences of form rather than substance.

It is well established that homicide is presumed to have been committed with malice aforethought "unless the evidence which proves the killing itself shows it to have been done without malice."[28] This presumption will always be available for the preliminary purpose of corroborating a confession, since the mere finding of a dead body with evidence tending to indicate that the death was caused by some other person will never be sufficient to show that the killing was without malice aforethought. And a study of the cases points to the use of this presumption in aid of the corpus delicti rule, even though it has not been emphasized.[29]

23. Bruner v. People, 113 Colo. 194, 207, 156 P.2d 111, 117 (1945).

24. Ervin v. Leypoldt, 76 Nev. 297, 301, 352 P.2d 718, 720 (1960).

25. State v. Drew, 70 Wn.2d 793, 425 P.2d 349, 352 (1967); People v. Duncan, 51 Cal.2d 523, 528, 334 P.2d 858, 861 (1959); State v. Durham, 156 W.Va. 509, 195 S.E.2d 144 (1973).

26. "[T]he specific crime was committed by *someone*." Wahl v. State, 229 Ind. 521, 530, 98 N.E.2d 671, 675 (1951).

27. "[S]ome evidence tending to show the commission of a homicide." People v. Simonsen, 107 Cal. 345, 346, 40 Pac. 440 (1895). See also Jefferson v. State, 128 So.2d 132, 135–36 (Fla. 1961); People v. Lytton, 257 N.Y. 310, 314, 178 N.E. 290, 292 (1931).

28. Murphy v. State, 37 Ala. 142, 144 (1861); and see State v. Burris, 80 Idaho 395, 331 P.2d 265 (1958); Miranda v. State, 42 Ariz. 358, 364, 26 P.2d 241, 243 (1933); Gordon v. State, 478 S.W.2d 911 (Tenn.Cr.App. 1971).

29. "When a dead body is found floating in a stream with gun shot wounds in the head which experts testify were the cause of a death, an inescapable deduction arises of felonious homicide." Ford v. State, 184 Tenn. 443, 455, 201 S.W.2d 539, 544 (1945). Such evidence tends strongly to indicate that deceased did not kill herself, either by design or accident, but it does not in any way establish that she was not killed by accident by a shot fired by someone else, either while she was in the water or so situated that she fell into the water after being hit. Had the court used the word "presumption" in place of "inescapable deduction" no fault could be found with the statement.

References to accident are significant in this regard. If it is said that the independent evidence must point in some other direction than death from natural causes, suicide or accident, *whose* accident is meant? That of deceased himself—not the accident of some other person. The independent evidence is not sufficient to establish the corpus delicti if it does not tend to point to some conclusion other than that deceased caused his own death by accident while attempting to put out a fire,[30] walking on a railroad track,[31] falling into water where he drowned,[32] or running into some object which ruptured his liver.[33] But an accidental killing by some other person is quite another matter.

The independent evidence need not tend to exclude the possibility that the death of deceased was caused by the accident of some other person. This is demonstrated by the language of the cases. "Was his death caused by accident? Or was it caused by violence inflicted upon him by others?" [34] There "must be evidence from which it can reasonably be inferred that the external force or violence causing the death was applied by another and was not self-inflicted or the result of an accident." [35] "Suicide was out of the question. If he met death through accident, surely it was *not of his own causing.*" [36]

Thus the independent evidence has established the corpus delicti for the preliminary purpose of admitting a confession if the dead body has been found with a gun-shot wound as the cause of death, together with circumstances tending to indicate that the injury was not self-inflicted either by accident or design,[37] as where there are no powder burns,[38] the deceased was shot in the back,[39] he had not had possession of any weapon,[40] he had been killed by a bullet from a .22 caliber pistol whereas his own weapon was a .38,[41] or the fatal bullet came from defendant's gun which was found away from the victim and victim's statement that he'd "been shot." [42] Apart from the presumption, death resulting from a shot fired by another is as consistent with an accidental killing as with death resulting from a criminal act, but the possibility of such an accidental killing is not mentioned in discussions of this problem. For example, evidence that a mother caused the death of her tiny baby, by dropping it from a trestle into a flooded stream, is sufficient to permit the jury to consider her extrajudicial confession, even though the evidence apart from the confession indicated that the dropping was by

30. Grimes v. State, 204 Ga. 854, 51 S.E.2d 797 (1949).

31. People v. Cuozzo, 292 N.Y. 85, 54 N.E.2d 20 (1944).

32. Bell v. State, 177 Ark. 1034, 9 S.W.2d 238 (1928).

33. Hall v. Superior Court, 120 Cal.App.2d 844, 262 P.2d 351 (1953).

34. Commonwealth v. Webster, 59 Mass. 295, 309 (1850).

35. People v. Carmargo, 130 Cal.App.2d 543, 548, 279 P.2d 194, 196 (1955).

36. State v. Kindle, 71 Mont. 58, 65, 227 Pac. 65, 67–68 (1924). Emphasis added.

37. See State v. De Hart, 242 Wis. 562, 8 N.W.2d 360 (1943); Pearce v. State, 14 Ala.App. 120, 72 So. 213 (1916).

38. State v. Henderson, 182 Or. 147, 184 P.2d 392 (1947); State v. Kindle, 71 Mont. 58, 227 P. 65 (1924); Byrd v. State, 46 Ala.App. 278, 241 So.2d 120 (1970).

39. Vernon v. State, 239 Ala. 593, 196 So. 96 (1940). And see Note 103, U.Pa.L.Rev. 638, 644 (1955).

40. State v. Tourville, 295 S.W.2d 1 (Mo.1956).

41. Osborn v. State, 194 P.2d 176 (Okl.Cr.App.1948).

42. People v. Watts, 101 Ill.App.2d 36, 241 N.E.2d 463 (1968).

accident.[43] And if the body of a tiny baby is found with evidence showing that a blow on the head caused the death, the corpus delicti has been established.[44] While such evidence is as consistent with the conclusion of injury received from a fall as with any other, if the harm resulted from an accident it could not be attributed to the baby himself.

Differences of opinion may be found as to whether certain facts do or do not point in the direction of homicide, but extensive research has failed to reveal a single case in which independent evidence, admittedly indicating homicide, was not sufficient to corroborate defendant's confession.[45] There is no great objection to saying that the corpus delicti of murder is made up of two components, the death of one as a result and the criminal agency of another as the cause, with the understanding that all homicide is presumed to have resulted from criminal agency until and unless the evidence shows otherwise; but it would be much more realistic, and entirely in line with the result of the actual cases, to recognize frankly that the corpus delicti of murder is homicide.

Defendant appealed from a conviction of driving under the influence of intoxicants and inflicting bodily injury on another. His claim was that there was no independent evidence of the corpus delicti to support his admission that he was the driver of the car. But there was other evidence that a car driven on the highway overturned; that defendant was one of the occupants; that another occupant was severely injured; and that all three occupants were intoxicated. It was held that since this independent evidence established that the car was driven by an intoxicated driver, this established the corpus delicti and supported defendant's confession.[46]

Suppose in this case the injured occupant had been killed, and the offense charged had been manslaughter. If there was no independent evidence to indicate which occupant did or did not drive the car there would be no such evidence of the corpus delicti to support the confession. Proof of the corpus delicti, for the preliminary purpose of permitting the jury to consider the defendant's extrajudicial confession does not require identity of the one who caused the actus reus, but if the decedent caused his own death this was suicide rather than homicide, and without homicide there is no manslaughter—and no corpus delicti.[47]

---

43. Warmke v. Commonwealth, 297 Ky. 649, 180 S.W.2d 872 (1944). In this case the body was never found and the only proof of death was defendant's testimony in court that she had dropped it by accident into the flooded stream. Since it was never seen again and it "seems beyond the bounds of possibility that the baby survived this ordeal" the jury could find that it was in fact dead.

44. Stubbs v. State, 148 Miss. 764, 114 So. 827 (1927).

The Ohio Supreme Court held the corpus delicti insufficient for conviction where the only evidence of cause of death was a coroner's testimony that the injuries that produced the child's death could have been caused by a fall down stairs although it was unlikely. State v. Manago, 38 Ohio St.2d 223, 313 N.E.2d 10 (1974).

45. In a homicide case the corpus delicti is established by two facts. "That one person was killed and that another person killed him." State v. Phippen, 207 Kan. 224, 485 P.2d 336, 340 (1971).

46. State v. Knoefler, 563 P.2d 175 (Utah 1977). Identity of the assailant is not part of the corpus delicti of murder. Houck v. State, 563 P.2d 665 (Okl.Cr.App. 1977).

47. Allen v. State, 314 So.2d 154 (Fla.App. 1975).

SECTION 2.　ASSAULT AND BATTERY

Postponing definitions for a moment, the following familiar statements are offered merely for the purpose of introduction. An assault is an attempt or offer to commit a battery.[1] A battery is the successful accomplishment of that attempt.[2] A battery is a consummated assault.[3] A battery includes an assault.[4]

These statements show that when we speak of an *assault* we usually have in mind a *battery* which was attempted or threatened. The attempt may have failed or it may have succeeded. If it failed it constitutes an *assault* only. If it succeeded it is an assault and battery.[5] Hence a defendant may be convicted of assault although the evidence shows also a battery.[6] Under the same evidence two other forms of conviction are possible, as a matter of common law, namely—(2) battery, and (3) assault and battery. A conviction of assault and battery, it should be added, is in legal effect no more than a conviction of battery since the completed offense includes the attempt to commit it.[7] It is in truth an anomaly that the two words are coupled in this manner. One familiar only with other departments of the common law would expect to find a discussion of the law applicable to this type of social harm under the heading of "assault *or* battery."

It is not uncommon to detail the facts constituting a battery in speaking of an assault, but this seems quite unnecessary. We shall therefore turn our attention first to battery, so that we can substitute this word for a more detailed statement of the concept, when speaking of assault.

1. The statements are frequently not so concise as this. They often speak of the attempt or offer and then go on to describe a battery. See for example: State v. Hefner, 199 N.C. 778, 780, 155 S.E. 879, 880 (1930).

2. State v. Jones, 133 S.C. 167, 130 S.E. 747 (1925).

3. People v. Heise, 217 Cal. 671, 20 P.2d 317 (1933).

4. Hinkel v. Commonwealth, 137 Va. 791, 119 S.E. 53 (1923).

5. State v. Jones, 133 S.C. 167, 130 S.E. 747 (1925).

6. People v. Heise, 217 Cal. 671, 20 P.2d 317 (1933); United States v. Masel, 563 F.2d 322, 323–24 (7th Cir. 1977). By reason of an express provision of the Georgia Code, sec. 27–2508, it is reversible error to convict of assault if the evidence shows battery. Diamond v. State, 126 Ga.App. 580, 191 S.E.2d 492 (1972).

"A battery is a consummated assault." State v. Humphries, 21 Wn.App. 405, 586 P.2d 130, 133 (1978).

7. "Of course, 'simple assault' is included in the offense of battery. A conviction of the latter would subsume the assault. By definition one cannot commit battery without also committing a 'simple' assault which is nothing more than an attempted battery." People v. Fuller, 53 Cal.App.3d 417, 125 Cal.Rptr. 837, 839–840 (1975).

"Every battery includes an assault, but every assault does not include battery." State v. Thompson, 27 N.C.App. 576, 219 S.E.2d 566 (1975).

A battery is "an unlawful touching." A "touching may be unlawful because it was neither legally consented to nor otherwise privileged, and was either harmful or offensive." State v. Humphries, 21 Wn.App. 405, 586 P.2d 130, 133 (1978).

"A battery is any willful and unlawful use of force or violence upon the person of another." People v. Kaiser, 113 Cal.App.3d 754, 170 Cal.Rptr. 62, 69 (1980).

A. BATTERY

Battery is the unlawful application of force to the person of another.[8] It is a misdemeanor at common law,[9] and, for the most part, under modern statutes.

1. THE FORCE

It is sometimes spoken of as "the unlawful beating of another," [10] or the "use of physical violence by one person toward another." [11] Such expressions tend to be misleading. As a matter of law the slightest touching of another is a battery if it is unlawful.[12] As it has been said, "violence" and "force" are synonyms when used in this connection and include any application of force even though it entails no pain or bodily harm and leaves no mark.[13] As explained by one court a battery is "the actual infliction of corporal hurt on another (e.g., the least touching of another's person) willfully or in anger." [14] The "corporal hurt" in this case was the putting of a hand lightly on the shoulder. It was the touching of a woman by a man under

8. State v. Hefner, 199 N.C. 778, 780, 155 S.E. 879, 881 (1930).

A blow struck in privileged self-defense is lawful and hence is not a battery. State v. McMullen, 34 Or.App. 749, 579 P.2d 879 (1978).

9. "The inferior offences or misdemeanours that fall under this head are assaults, batteries, ..." 4 Bl.Comm. *216. And see 1 East P.C. 406–7 (1803).

10. 3 Bl.Comm. 120; Hunt v. People, 53 Ill.App. 111, 112 (1894).

The Illinois Criminal Code defines battery in terms of (1) causing bodily harm and (2) physical contact that is of insulting or provoking nature. Ill.Rev.Stats. ch. 38, par. 12–3(a) (1973). To establish that there has been bodily harm in a battery case, "there is no requirement that the evidence demonstrate a visible injury such as bruising, scratching or bleeding." People v. McEvoy, 33 Ill.App.3d 300, 337 N.E.2d 437, 439–40 (1975).

11. State v. Hamburg, 34 Del. 62, 143 A. 47 (1928).

12. State v. Brewer, 31 Del. 363, 114 A. 604 (1921); Smith v. State, 85 Ga.App. 215, 68 S.E.2d 719 (1952); Commonwealth v. McCan, 277 Mass. 199, 178 N.E. 633 (1931); Hinkel v. Commonwealth, 137 Va. 791, 119 S.E. 53 (1923).

"To constitute a criminal battery any willful and unlawful use of force or violence against the person of another is enough. It need not cause any bodily harm or even pain and it need not leave any mark." State v. Gordon, 120 Ariz. 172, 584 P.2d 1163, 1165 (1978).

13. People v. James, 9 Cal.App.2d 162, 48 P.2d 1011 (1935). It is a battery for a man to kiss a woman against her will, or to lay hands on her for this purpose. Moreland v. State, 125 Ark. 24, 188 S.W. 1 (1916). But it is not an assault (battery) for a man to kiss an intimate friend when he has good reason to believe this will be agreeable to her. Weaver v. State, 66 Tex.Cr. 366, 146 S.W. 927 (1912).

An unlawful touching is a battery; it is not necessary to prove that defendant intended more. United States v. Masel, 563 F.2d 322 (7th Cir. 1977).

The term "physical injury" in the assault statute is not synonymous with "bodily harm." It is synonymous with "physical force." State v. Bustamonte, 122 Ariz. 162, 593 P.2d 912 (1978).

14. Lynch v. Commonwealth, 131 Va. 762, 766, 109 S.E. 427, 428 (1921).

A battery "is an unlawful touching; a touching may be unlawful because it was neither consented to nor otherwise privileged, and was either harmful or offensive." State v. Garcia, 20 Wn.App. 401, 579 P.2d 1034, 1036 (1978).

This is changed in some of the new penal codes. Thus in a statute that uses the word "assault" to cover the entire field of assault and battery, it was said: "Petty batteries not producing injury do not constitute criminal assault." State v. Capwell, 52 Or.App. 43, 627 P.2d 905, 907, n. 3 (App. 1981).

But under a different statute it was held no defense to a charge of third degree assault that the repeated touching

circumstances causing great resentment as he had every reason to expect. Wilfully spitting on another is a battery.[15]

2. UNLAWFUL

Definitions of battery sometimes speak of the application of force to the person of another in an "angry, revengeful, rude, insolent, or hostile manner." [16] These are merely attempts to emphasize the requirement of unlawfulness. The same may be said of references to a touching "without consent." The lack of consent may be the very element which makes the touching unlawful in a particular case. In another situation, as will be mentioned presently, the application of force may be lawful although without consent, or unlawful even with consent.[17] If force against another is privileged, and the force is not excessive, there is no battery.[18] Hence it is preferable to define battery as "the unlawful application of force to the person of another" [19] and to consider these other elements on the issue of unlawfulness.

3. MEANS OF PERPETRATION

Force may be applied to the person of another in many ways, as by striking another with the fist or a stick or a stone,[20] by kicking or tripping, lassoing with a rope, cutting with a knife, or shooting. As has been said, a battery is an application of force to the person of another "by the aggressor himself, or by some substance which he puts in motion." [21] It may be committed by administering a poison or other deleterious substance,[22] by applying a caustic chemical,[23] or by communicating a disease.[24] It may be perpe-

of the other's head with fingers was intended only to be "insulting." State v. Johnson, 29 Wn.App. 307, 628 P.2d 479 (1981).

" 'Unlawful touching' must occur in the commission of the crime of assault and battery." Settle v. State, 619 P.2d 387, 389 (Wyo. 1980).

15. Regina v. Cotesworth, 6 Mod. 172, 87 Eng.Rep. 928 (1705). This was a case of spitting in the face and some of the statutes are so worded.

In a case charging an assault on a member of Congress, 18 U.S.C.A. § 351(e) the court observed, "It is ancient doctrine that intentional spitting upon another person is battery. No more severe injury need be intended." United States v. Masel, 563 F.2d 322, 324 (7th Cir. 1977).

Under the new penal code which incorporates battery in the section on assault, and provides: "A person commits assault by: . . . . Knowingly touching another person with intent to injure, insult or provoke such person," does not require a person-to-person contact. It was committed by throwing urine upon the other. State v. Mathews, 130 Ariz. 46, 633 P.2d 1039 (App. 1981).

16. State v. Foster, 156 La. 891, 895, 101 So. 255, 257 (1924).

17. "All attempts to do physical violence are unlawful unless permitted by law, and a person is not permitted by law to consent to an unlawful assault." State v. Roby, 194 Iowa 1032, 1035, 188 N.W. 709, 711 (1922).

18. Government of Virgin Islands v. Stull, 280 F.Supp. 460 (D.C. Virgin Islands 1968).

19. State v. Hefner, 199 N.C. 778, 780, 155 S.E. 879, 881 (1930). See also Commonwealth v. Gregory, 132 Pa.Super. 507, 1 A.2d 501 (1938).

20. State v. Foster, 156 La. 891, 101 So. 255 (1924).

21. State v. Hefner, supra n. 19. See also Commonwealth v. Remley, 257 Ky. 209, 77 S.W.2d 784 (1934); Woodward v. State, 164 Miss. 468, 474, 144 So. 895, 896 (1932); Lynch v. Commonwealth, 131 Va. 762, 109 S.E. 427 (1921).

22. State v. Monroe, 121 N.C. 677, 28 S.E. 547 (1897); Ariz.Rev.St. § 13–1205 (1978).

23. This obvious common-law result has been codified in some of the statutes. West's Ann.Cal.Pen.Code § 244 (1970).

24. See note 24 on page 154.

trated in even more indirect forms, as by exposing a helpless person to the inclemency of the weather,[25] or by threatening sudden violence and thereby causing another to jump from a window [26] or a moving vehicle or other place. A battery may be committed by directing a dog to attack a victim.[27] Force may be applied to the person of another without actually touching him, as by cutting his clothes while they are on his person.[28] A famous New York case involved these facts: one man stopped a sleigh being driven by another and, over the driver's protest, turned the horse and sleigh around and headed them the other way. Although there was no direct contact with the driver, this was held to be an application of force to his person and, as it was unlawful under the circumstances, it was a battery.[29] One who merely stands by watching a battery, or even approving it, is not guilty if this is all,—he is a mere bystander; but one who stands by for the known purpose of giving aid if necessary is a guilty party to the battery.[30]

4. EFFECT OF CONSENT

The application of force to the person of another is not unlawful,—and therefore not a battery—if the recipient consents to what is done, provided this consent (1) is not coerced or obtained by fraud, (2) is given by one legally capable of consenting to such a deed, and (3) does not relate to a matter as to which consent will not be recognized as a matter of law.

The violent tackle which wins applause on the football field would be a battery if practiced on an unwilling citizen on the street. This is because the player by entering the contest consents to such physical contact as is properly incident to the game. On the other hand, if one player should purposely strike another in the face with his fist, this would not only violate the rules of the game but could be made the basis for a criminal prosecution. The test is not necessarily whether the blow exceeds the conduct allowed by the rules of the game. Certain excesses and inconveniences are to be expected beyond the formal rules of the game. It may be ordinary and expected conduct for minor assaults to occur. However, intentional excesses beyond those to be reasonably contemplated in the sport are not justified.[31]

24. State v. Lankford, 29 Del. 594, 102 A. 63 (1917).

An English court acquitted under circumstances of allegedly transmitting a venereal disease. Regina v. Clarence, 22 QBD 23 (1888). See Lynch, Criminal Liability For Transmitting Disease, [1978] Crim.L.Rev. 612.

25. Pallis v. State, 123 Ala. 12, 26 So. 339 (1899). But it has been held that exposing a little child to the weather is not an assault if it is rescued before suffering any injury. Regina v. Renshaw, 2 Cox C.C. 285 (1847).

26. Regina v. Halliday, 61 L.T. (N.S.) 701 (1889).

27. J.A.T. v. State, 133 Ga.App. 922, 212 S.E.2d 879 (1975).

28. The Queen v. Day, 1 Cox C.C. 207 (1845).

29. People v. Moore, 50 Hun, 356, 3 N.Y.S. 159 (1888).

30. People v. Luna, 140 Cal.App.2d 662, 295 P.2d 457 (1956).

31. A player who dropped his stick and gloves in a hockey match, pursued an opponent, and beat him with his fists was properly convicted. Regina v. Watson, 26 CCC 2nd 150 (Prov.Ct.Ont. 1975).

See discussion Hichter, The Criminal Law and Violence in Sports, 19 Crim.L.Qtrly. 425 (1977). Note, 75 Mich.L.Rev. 148 (1976).

A. DURESS OR FRAUD

Submission under fear is not "consent" as the word is used in the law. If a man said, "I consent to be slapped," at the point of a pistol and in fear of instant death if he did not say so, this would be no real consent to the slapping and the blow would constitute a battery. It is equally clear that consent obtained by fraud has no standing in the law for this purpose because an application of force by consent so obtained is unlawful.[32]

B. UNDER THE AGE OF CONSENT

It constitutes a battery for a man to commit an act of indecent familiarity with the person of a woman without her consent,[33] and such an offense can be committed even upon one of the same sex. Thus, a man who hired a boy to ride with him as a guide, and put his arm around the boy and placed his hand over the other's private parts without the boy's consent, was guilty of assault and battery where he was motivated by lust and the act was offensive to the boy.[34] And if the act is committed upon one who is incapable of giving consent by reason of immaturity or feeble-mindedness, it is without consent so far as the law is concerned even if consented to in fact.[35] It is a battery, for example, for a man to take indecent liberties with a five-year-old girl, because she has no understanding of the nature of the act and is legally incapable of consenting thereto.[36] The sound view, although authority to the contrary can be found,[37] is that a girl under the "age of consent" is just as incapable of giving a legally-recognized consent to an indecent fondling of her person as she is of giving such consent to the act of intercourse itself, and hence her consent to such indecent liberties is no defense.[38] In several jurisdictions a special category of crime has been created prohibiting sexual conduct with children below a certain age and consent is no defense to such an offense.[39]

C. UNPERMITTED FORCE

Analogous to, although to be distinguished from, the incapacity of certain persons to consent to certain kinds of conduct, is the rule of law which does not recognize any consent to certain types of social harm. No person can validly consent to a breach of the peace or to a beating that may result in a serious injury.[40]

---

32. As to consent obtained by fraud see infra chapter 9, section 3.

33. Commonwealth v. Jaynes, 137 Pa.Super. 511, 10 A.2d 90 (1939); Breeding v. State, 146 Tex.Cr.R. 352, 175 S.W.2d 253 (1943); Smith v. State, 85 Ga.App. 215, 68 S.E.2d 719 (1952).

34. Levy v. State, 69 Ga.App. 265, 25 S.E.2d 153 (1943).

35. The consent of a feeble-minded woman to an assault upon her is no defense. State v. Marks, 178 N.C. 730, 101 S.E. 24 (1919).

Consent to injection of a drug is not consent to a battery during the victim's unconsciousness. Avery v. State, 15 Md.App. 520, 292 A.2d 728 (1972).

36. People v. James, 9 Cal.App.2d 162, 48 P.2d 1011 (1935). See also Beausoliel v. United States, 107 F.2d 292 (D.C.Cir.1939).

37. Regina v. Martin, 2 Moody 123, 169 Eng.Rep. 49 (1840).

38. Dunn v. State, 83 Ga.App. 682, 64 S.E.2d 478 (1951); People v. Gibson, 232 N.Y. 458, 134 N.E. 531 (1922). And see Colo.Rev.Stat., 1973, 118–3–408.

39. Ariz.Rev.Stat.Ann. 1978, 13–1204 (5); N.J.Stat.Ann. 1978, 2C:14–2.b.

40. Commonwealth v. Colberg, 119 Mass. 350 (1876).

". . . a person is not permitted by law to consent to unlawful assault."

On the other hand, force may cause inconvenience and pain, or even death, and yet be lawful in the absence of consent, if used under circumstances of legally-recognized justification or excuse, a matter to receive attention elsewhere.[41]

5. UNLAWFUL ACT

If the intentional doing of an unlawful act *malum in se* results in the death of another person the killing is either murder or manslaughter according to the common law, as mentioned in the discussion of homicide. In like manner, if such an act results in nonfatal harm to the person of another it constitutes a battery.[42] Thus hitting another with a shot fired unlawfully, in the sense of *malum in se*, is a battery although the injury was quite accidental;[43] and nonfatal harm caused by a gun is a battery even if pulling the trigger was unintentional if the weapon had been intentionally and unlawfully pointed at the person hit.[44] In another type of case a conviction of battery was reversed when the record disclosed no more than that a father while punishing his daughter had inadvertently hit a third person.[45] There was no claim of criminal negligence and since the punishment itself was warranted, and its administration moderate, the harmful contact was merely an unfortunate accident resulting from a lawful act,—which is not a crime.[46] Had the punishment of the child been unlawful the hitting of the third person would also have been a battery, however unintentional.[47]

6. CRIMINAL NEGLIGENCE

Statements can be found to the effect that a criminal battery requires an intentional application of force to the person of another.[48] This is an error

State v. Roby, 194 Iowa 1032, 1035, 188 N.W. 709, 711 (1922).

Consent is not defense to a sado-masochistic beating. People v. Samuels, 250 Cal.App.2d 501, 58 Cal.Rptr. 439 (1967).

41. See infra, chapter 10.

42. King v. State, 157 Tenn. 635, 11 S.W.2d 904 (1928). "The other exception is that a defendant is held answerable to a criminal prosecution for an assault and battery in cases where he intentionally does an illegal act from which another suffers personal violence, . . ." McGee v. State, 4 Ala.App. 54, 58, 58 So. 1008, 1009 (1912). And see State v. Lehman, 131 Minn. 427, 430, 155 N.W. 399, 400 (1915); Luther v. State, 177 Ind. 619, 624, 98 N.E. 640, 642 (1912). Such a battery has been omitted from some of the codes. E.g., Wis.St.1978, § 940.19.

43. In reversing a conviction of assault and battery because of erroneous instructions, the court made it clear that it would be battery to hit another with a shot fired unlawfully even if it was not done recklessly. Commonwealth v. Mann, 116 Mass. 58 (1874). "It is the general rule that a person who intention-

ally commits an unlawful act, and in doing so inflicts an unforeseen injury, is criminally liable for such injury. Discharging a firearm without justification to frighten another, although not intending to him him, is an assault and battery if the other be hit." State v. Lehman, 131 Minn. 427, 430, 155 N.W. 399, 400 (1915).

Suddenly throwing or swinging a glass striking the victim in a reckless manner justifies conviction. State in Interest of McElhaney, 579 P.2d 328 (Utah 1978).

44. Lane v. State, 65 Okl.Cr. 192, 84 P.2d 807 (1938).

45. Turner v. State, 35 Tex.Cr.R. 369, 33 S.W. 972 (1896).

46. "And if he was not in the commission of an unlawful act, the accidental blow to the wife was not a crime." Id. at 370, 33 S.W. at 973.

47. See ibid.

48. "Intent is a necessary element of assault and battery. . . ." Woodward v. State, 164 Miss. 468, 474, 144 So. 895, 896 (1932). See also the dictum in Commonwealth v. Gregory, 132 Pa.

(so far as the common law is concerned) [49] due to a failure to distinguish between criminal law and torts in the use of this word. "Battery" is the name given to a tort as well as the name given to a crime. As a tort it is a civil injury giving rise to an action for damages by the person harmed. As a crime it is social harm punished by the state. The same misdeed may be both,—and usually is. But the two are not identical although they have much in common. The name of the tort comes from the name of the common-law action originally used for the recovery of damages for wrongs of this nature. If one man harmed another, by an unlawful application of force to his person, the name of the common-law action was "trespass for battery" if the harm was intentionally inflicted,[50] and "trespass on the case" if it resulted from negligence. Hence,—in the law of torts—the word "battery" was used only where such harm was intentional, although liability also existed where it was negligent.

In criminal law, in the absence of statute,[51] there is no counterpart to the tort distinction between "trespass for battery" and "trespass on the case" and hence the word "battery" is applied to every punishable application of force to the person of another (unless this violation is merged in some felony such as murder, manslaughter, mayhem or rape). Such harm is not punishable if it resulted unintentionally from the doing of a lawful act without criminal negligence.[52] For battery, as for manslaughter, more is required than ordinary negligence sufficient to support a civil action.[53] But the rule is now well established that conviction of battery can be supported by harm to the person resulting from criminal negligence.[54] Thus if a person has been hurt

Super. 507, 512, 1 A.2d 501, 503 (1938), in which the court relies upon section 18 of the Restatement of Torts.

Restatement, Second, Torts § 18 now provides liability for battery if the actor "acts intending to cause harmful or offensive contact with the person of the other or a third person, or an imminent apprehension of such a contact . . ."

49. The statute reads: "Battery is the unlawful, intentional touching or application of force to the person of another, when done in a rude, insolent or angry manner." State v. Kraul, 90 N.M. 314, 563 P.2d 108 (App. 1977).

50. Restatement, Second, Torts § 13, comment a (1965).

51. An occasional statute applies the label "battery" only where there is an intent to cause bodily harm. Wis. Stats. § 940.19 (1978). Cf. id. §§ 940.20(1)–(3).

52. Turner v. State, 35 Tex.Cr.R. 369, 33 S.W. 972 (1896).

53. People v. Waxman, 232 App.Div. 90, 249 N.Y.S. 180 (1931). The rule is the same for battery and for manslaughter, "since manslaughter is simply a battery that causes death." Commonwealth v. Welansky, 316 Mass. 383, 406, 55 N.E.2d 902, 912 (1944). An unintentional injury

does not constitute a battery merely because a lack of due care was shown, since it would be necessary to show either recklessness or the commission of an unlawful act. Luther v. State, 177 Ind. 619, 98 N.E. 640 (1912).

54. State v. Hamburg, 34 Del. 62, 143 A. 47 (1928); Commonwealth v. McCan, 277 Mass. 199, 178 N.E. 633 (1931); West's Fla.Stats.Ann. § 784.05 (1976); Rev.Code Wash.Ann. 9A.08.010(1)(d) and 9A.36.020(1)(d) (1961); State v. Foster, 91 Wn. 466, 589 P.2d 789 (1979). If a physician causes bodily injury to his patient by criminal negligence he is guilty of battery. Banovitch v. Commonwealth, 196 Va. 210, 83 S.E.2d 369 (1954). A statute may apply a different label. For example: "Negligent injuring is the inflicting of any injury upon the person of another by criminal negligence." LSA–R.S. 14:-39 (1951).

For battery "nothing more is required than an intentional doing of an action which, by reason of its wanton or grossly negligent character, exposes another to personal injury, and causes such injury." Commonwealth v. Hawkins, 157 Mass. 551, 32 N.E. 862 (1893). Regina v. Venna, [1975] 3 All E.R. 788.

as a result of an accident caused by defendant's criminally negligent driving of a car, the defendant is guilty of battery.[55]

7. AGGRAVATED BATTERY

There was no crime known to the common law as "aggravated battery." If the harm to the person was sufficiently great it might constitute a felony,—such as murder, manslaughter, mayhem or rape. In such a case the battery (although technically present) became "merged" in the felony and was not punished as battery. In other cases the unlawful application of force to the person of another was just battery (or assault and battery),—a misdemeanor. Differences in circumstances were taken care of by the judges' common-law discretion in the punishment of misdemeanors.[56]

An occasional statute has created a special crime known as "aggravated battery." [57] This necessitates a second offense to provide a proper penalty for the unsuccessful attempt to commit such a battery.[58] Most of the states have handled this problem by providing special penalties for aggravated assaults. Since the assault is present whether the attempt succeeds or fails, such an offense will provide a special penalty for such misconduct in either event. This subject will be considered under the heading of "assault."

8. JUSTIFICATION OR EXCUSE

No *lawful* application of force to the person of another, however severe, is a battery. It would be a confusion of terms to speak of justification or excuse for a *battery*. If the application of force was justified or excused it was *not a battery*. Conversely, if what happened was a battery, there was no justification or excuse.

With reference to another problem: "No conduct or words, no matter how offensive or exasperating, are sufficient to justify a battery." [59]

---

55. Brimhall v. State, 31 Ariz. 522, 255 P. 165 (1927); Tift v. State, 17 Ga.App. 663, 88 S.E. 41 (1916); State v. Schutte, 87 N.J.L. 15, 93 A. 112 (1915); Commonwealth v. Gayton, 69 Pa.Super. 513 (1918). The courts sometimes resort to the fiction of imputing an intent from criminal negligence. Woodward v. State, 164 Miss. 468, 475, 144 So. 895 (1932); Davis v. Commonwealth, 150 Va. 611, 143 S.E. 641 (1928).

In *Woodward* it was said: "Of course mere negligence would not impute an intent. If negligence be relied on, then it must amount to reckless, willful, and wanton disregard of the rights of others, in which state of case the intent is imputed to the accused."

Cf. State v. Hamburg, 34 Del. 62, 143 A. 47 (1928). An inexperienced driver, who drove his car onto the sidewalk and

hit two persons, while he was attempting to dodge a child who suddenly ran into the street, was held not guilty of assault and battery. People v. Waxman, 232 App.Div. 90, 249 N.Y.S. 180 (1931).

56. Simpson v. State, 59 Ala. 1 (1877).

57. "Aggravated battery is a battery committed with a dangerous weapon." La.Rev.Stat. 14:34 (1974). And see Wis.St. 1958, § 940.19 (1977).

"On the facts of this case evidence of the purse snatching incident was admissible as part of the *res gestae* to prove the offenses charged," (aggravated battery against a law enforcement officer). State v. Ferris, 222 Kan. 515, 565 P.2d 275, 277 (1977).

58. La.Rev.Stat. 14:37 (1974).

59. People v. Martinez, 3 Cal.App.3d 886, 889, 83 Cal.Rptr. 914, 915 (1970).

B. ASSAULT [60]

An assault is (1) an attempt to commit a battery or (2) an intentional placing of another in apprehension of receiving an immediate battery. Furthermore (3) an assault is included in any actual battery.[61]

An assault is a misdemeanor at common law and under modern statutes except that many of the so-called aggravated assaults are statutory felonies.

1. DIFFERENT CONCEPTS OF ASSAULT

In the early law the word "assault" represented an entirely different concept in criminal law than it did in the law of torts. As an offense it was an attempt to commit a battery; as a basis for a civil action for damages it was an intentional act wrongfully placing another in apprehension of receiving an immediate battery.[62] The distinction has frequently passed unnoticed because a misdeed involving either usually involves both. If, with the intention of hitting X, D wrongfully threw a stone that X barely managed to dodge, then D would have been guilty of a criminal assault because he had attempted to commit a battery, and he would also have been liable in a civil action of trespass for assault because he had wrongfully placed X in apprehension of physical harm.

Some commentators have been so imbued with the tort theory of assault that they have had difficulty in realizing that in the early law a criminal assault was an attempt to commit a battery and that only. In the words of one notewriter, the "offense which the great majority of the courts are calling and punishing as a criminal assault is in effect an attempted battery, which is, and probably should be punished as, a distinct and separate criminal offense." [63] Research had disclosed to the writer what the courts were doing, but seemed to leave the impression that they were getting out of line. Current research has not located any case in the English reports that contains a common-law indictment charging "an attempt to commit a battery"; the indictment typically charged the defendant with an "assault." [64]

60. The following, in slightly different form, appeared as an article in 47 Minn.L.Rev. 71 (1962). It is reproduced here with the express permission of the Minnesota Law Review.

61. "It is an elementary legal concept that assault and battery are different acts. The assault is an offer to use force to injure another; a battery is the actual use of it on the other. . . . To constitute an assault, it is not necessary that any actual injury be inflicted." State v. Parker, 116 Ariz. 3, 567 P.2d 319, 322 (1977).

62. If we go back far enough we reach the time when the civil action for trespass for assault was "an action brought by the person aggrieved by the actor's attempt to commit a battery upon him." Restatement, Second, Torts § 24, comment c (1965).

63. Note, Is a Criminal Assault a Separate Substantive Crime or Is It an Attempted Battery?, 33 Ky.L.J. 189, 196 (1945).

64. But see 1 Bishop, Criminal Law § 764 (8th ed. 1892) ("there may be an indictable attempt to commit a battery"). The only case he cites in support of the statement is United States v. Lyles, 26 Fed.Cas. 1024 (No. 15646) (C.C.D.C.1834), which was an indictment for solicitation to commit a battery, which he says is a "form of attempt." He gives a cross reference to his own volume 2, § 62, which deals with assault. Hence, it is obvious he was not referring to an indictment

The fact that the original criminal assault was an attempt to commit a battery and nothing else is the reason behind the oft-quoted comment that an attempt to commit an assault is unknown to the law. In the words of the Georgia court, "as an assault is itself an attempt to commit a crime, an attempt to make an assault can only be an attempt to attempt to do it . . .. This is simply absurd."[65] Except for variations in wording, this has been the common explanation.[66] The same fact accounts for certain other statements such as that an assault in an inchoate battery;[67] that every battery includes an assault;[68] that battery is a consummated assault;[69] and that one "may obviously be assaulted, although in complete ignorance of the fact, and, therefore, entirely free from alarm."[70] It explains also why one who has committed a battery is frequently prosecuted for assault and battery.[71] This does not mean that two offenses are charged in separate counts of the accusatory pleading, but that one offense is charged in one count under the name of "assault and battery."[72] In substance, at least in the original us-

worded in terms of an attempt to commit a battery.

65. Wilson v. State, 53 Ga. 205, 206 (1874).

". . . we foresee serious pragmatic difficulties if attempted assault were judicially established as a punishable crime." In re M, 9 Cal.3d 517, 108 Cal.Rptr. 89, 510 P.2d 33, 36 (1973).

66. "As an assault is an attempt to commit a battery, there can be no attempt to commit an assault." 1 Wharton, Criminal Law and Procedure, § 72, at 154 (Anderson ed. 1957). "Thus embracery is an attempt to bribe a juror, an assault an attempt to commit a battery, and there can be no attempt to commit these offenses." 1 Burdick, Crime § 135, at 176 (1946). "There can be no such offense as an 'attempt to attempt' a crime. Since a simple assault is nothing more than an attempt to commit a battery, and aggravated assaults are nothing more than attempts to commit murder, rape, or robbery, an attempt to commit an assault, whether simple or aggravated is not a crime." Clark & Marshall, Crimes 246, (7th ed. 1967). *Accord,* 2 Bishop, Criminal Law § 62 (8th ed. 1892); Hochheimer, Crimes and Criminal Procedure § 266 (2d ed. 1904). LaFave & Scott, Criminal Law 610 (1972).

67. Luther v. State, 177 Ind. 619, 624, 98 N.E. 640, 641 (1912); People v. Lilley, 43 Mich. 521, 525, 5 N.W. 982, 985 (1880); Underhill, Criminal Evidence § 684 (5th ed. 1957).

68. Hall v. State, 309 P.2d 1096 (Okl.Cr.1957); 2 Bishop, Criminal Law § 33 (8th ed. 1892); 1 East, Pleas of the Crown 406 (1803); 1 Hawkins, Pleas of the Crown 263 (6th ed. 1788). This is not true of assault as a tort because appre-

hension on the part of the other is essential. See Prosser, Torts § 10, at 38 (4th ed. 1971).

69. Anderson v. Crawford, 265 F. 504 (8th Cir. 1920); People v. Heise, 217 Cal. 671, 673, 20 P.2d 317, 318 (1933); People v. Duchon, 165 Cal.App.2d 690, 332 P.2d 373 (1958); May v. Commonwealth, 285 S.W.2d 160 (Ky.1955); State v. Maier, 13 N.J. 235, 99 A.2d 21 (1953). See also Lawson v. State, 30 Ala. 14 (1857).

70. Chapman v. State, 78 Ala. 463, 465 (1885); *accord,* People v. Pape, 66 Cal. 366, 5 P. 621 (1885); People v. Lilley, 43 Mich. 521, 5 N.W. 982 (1880); State v. Cornwell, 97 N.H. 446, 91 A.2d 456 (1952); State v. Adamo, 9 N.J.Super. 7, 74 A.2d 341 (App.Div.1950); State v. Wilson, 218 Or. 575, 346 P.2d 115 (1959). This would not be recognized as an assault in the law of torts. Prosser, Torts § 10, at 39 (4th ed. 1971); Restatement, Second, Torts § 22 (1965).

An attempt to commit a battery is a criminal assault even if there was no apprehension on the part of the intended victim. State v. Wigley, 5 Wn.App. 465, 488 P.2d 766 (1971).

71. Hill v. State, 63 Ga. 578 (1879); Shaw v. State, 239 Ind. 248, 156 N.E.2d 381 (1959); Woodward v. State, 164 Miss. 468, 144 So. 895 (1932); State v. Monroe, 121 N.C. 677, 28 S.E. 547 (1897); Saunders v. State, 208 Tenn. 347, 345 S.W.2d 899 (1961). In one prosecution for assault and battery the evidence indicated "a rather severe beating." Clark v. State, 370 P.2d 46, 50 (Okl.Cr.1962).

72. See People v. Young, 12 A.D.2d 262, 263, 210 N.Y.S.2d 358, 360 (1961), where the court said that "assault and battery is an ancient crime cognizable at the common law."

age, it was a charge of a successful attempt to commit a battery. Not infrequently, however, the charge is merely an assault although the attack obviously resulted in a battery.[73] Often a criminal assault has been defined in terms of an attempt to commit a battery,[74] and the need for an intent to inflict such harm has been emphasized.[75] "The offer or attempt must be intentional," said the Mississippi court, "for if, notwithstanding appearances to the contrary, it can be collected that there is not a present purpose to do an injury, it is not an assault." [76]

2. THE CHANGING CONCEPT

The tort concept of assault seems to be substantially the same as it was in the early law,[77] but during the years two changes have tended to creep into the concept of criminal assault, both apparently making their appearance by inadvertence rather than by design. The two have moved in different directions, and while many jurisdictions have greatly enlarged the scope of criminal assault, a few have restricted its application.

A. CRIMINAL ASSAULT BASED UPON A TORT THEORY

While few jurisdictions have abandoned the original basis for establishing a criminal assault in the absence of statute,[78] there has been a tendency in

---

73. People v. Moore, 50 Hun, 356, 3 N.Y.S. 159 (Sup.Ct.1888); State v. Hemphill, 162 N.C. 632, 78 S.E. 167 (1913).

In Utah there is no statutory crime covering an act of battery, a battery must be prosecuted under the simple assault statute, Utah Code Ann. 1953, 76–5–102.

74. McKay v. State, 44 Tex. 43, 48 (1875); see Guarro v. United States, 237 F.2d 578, 580 (D.C.Cir.1956); Lane v. State, 85 Ala. 11, 14, 4 So. 730, 732 (1888); State v. Lasby, 174 A.2d 323, 324 (Del.Super.Ct.1961); State v. Rand, 156 Me. 81, 82, 161 A.2d 852, 853 (1960); Yantz v. Warden, 210 Md. 343, 351, 123 A.2d 601, 606 (1956).

75. Burke v. United States, 282 F.2d 763 (9th Cir.1960); State v. Crow, 23 N.C. 375 (1841); see People v. Carmen, 36 Cal.2d 768, 228 P.2d 281 (1951); Thomas v. State, 99 Ga. 38, 26 S.E. 748 (1896); State v. Crowl, 135 Mont. 98, 337 P.2d 367 (1959); People v. Lay, 254 App.Div. 372, 5 N.Y.S.2d 325 (1938); Johnson v. State, 43 Tex. 576 (1875); Riley v. State, 92 Tex.Cr. 237, 243 S.W. 467 (1922).

"One could not very well 'attempt' or try to 'commit' an injury on the person of another if he had no intent to cause any injury to such other person." People v. Coffey, 67 Cal.2d 204, 222, 430 P.2d 15, 27, 60 Cal.Rptr. 457, 469 (1967).

Apprehension by the one assaulted is not an element of second-degree assault.

State v. Stewart, 73 Wn.2d 701, 440 P.2d 815 (1968).

"By its statutes, Wyoming has limited criminal assault to attempted battery. This type of assault requires proof of specific intent to cause battery. Recklessness or negligence is not enough to prove that intent." Fuller v. State, 568 P.2d 900, 904 (Wyo.1977).

76. Smith v. State, 39 Miss. 521, 525 (1860); *accord*, State v. Sears, 86 Mo. 169, 174 (1885); cf. State v. Davis, 23 N.C. 125, 127 (1840).

77. Prosser, Torts § 10, at 37–40 (4th ed. 1971); Restatement, Second, Torts §§ 21, 22, 24 (1965). A Texas case held that a civil assault was determined by the definition of criminal assault. Texas Bus Lines v. Anderson, 233 S.W.2d 961 (Tex.Civ.App.1950), criticized in 30 Texas L.Rev. 120 (1951).

78. In Alaska, "neither fear nor apprehension are necessary elements in the crime of assault". Menard v. State, 578 P.2d 966, 971 (Alaska 1978).

Sometimes, however, an attempt to commit a battery, the original basis for criminal assault, seems to have been held not to constitute an assault. In one case a directed verdict of not guilty was affirmed because the intended victim did not see the weapon and knew nothing of the threat until afterwards. State v. Barry, 45 Mont. 598, 124 P. 775 (1912). In some cases the tort theory has been

many to add the tort theory as an additional ground. Where the tort theory has been added, a simple criminal assault "is made out from either an attempt to commit a battery or an unlawful act which places another in reasonable apprehension of receiving an immediate battery." [79] This position, it may be added, has now been taken by a majority of the jurisdictions. [80]

A notewriter considered this addition to be ground for complaint, [81] and there is something to be said for this position. In each jurisdiction where this was done without the aid of statute, the first case adopting the new theory resulted in a conviction for what had not been defined as a crime at the time the "assault" was committed. This did not violate the constitutional bar against ex post facto laws since that provision is directed to the legislative body, [82] but it clearly violated the underlying principle that no one should be punished for doing what had not been defined as a crime at the time it was done. [83] Had the change been made by legislative enactment, the courts would not have permitted it to have retroactive effect. The explanation for this apparent anomaly is that the change did not come about as a result of a conscious effort to enlarge the scope of a criminal offense, but as a consequence of the confusion caused by the use of the same word to represent two different concepts. [84] A threat of an immediate battery resulting in appre-

emphasized without holding that an attempt to commit a battery would not of itself constitute a criminal assault. Ladner v. United States, 358 U.S. 169, 79 S.Ct. 209 (1958); Commonwealth v. White, 110 Mass. 407 (1872). Some statutory definitions of criminal assault also have abandoned the original basis. Ill.Rev.Stat. ch. 38, § 12–1 (1973).

79. People v. Wood, 10 A.D.2d 231, 236, 199 N.Y.S.2d 342, 347 (1960).

"Apprehension of a person at whom a revolver is pointed may be inferred, unless he knows it to be unloaded. . . . The fact that an officer may have the courage and skill to disarm a person does not mean that he is devoid of apprehension when a gun is pointed at him." State v. Miller, 71 Wn.2d 143, 146, 426 P.2d 986, 988 (1967); People v. Gardner, 402 Mich. 460, 265 N.W.2d 1, 7 (1978); Ariz.Rev.Stat. § 13–1203.

Assault does not require an intent to harm. "The actor need only intend to communicate to the victim a threat to inflict bodily harm and have the apparent ability to do so, resulting in the immediate apprehension of bodily harm." In the Interest of Geisler, 4 Kan.App.2d 684, 610 P.2d 640, 644 (1980).

80. Model Penal Code § 201.10, comment (Tent. Draft No. 9, 1959).

"Simple assault 'is committed by either a willful attempt to inflict injury upon the person of another, or by a threat to inflict injury upon the person of another which, when coupled with an apparent

present ability, causes a reasonable apprehension of immediate bodily harm.' " United States v. Johnson, 637 F.2d 1224, 1242, n. 26 (9th Cir.1980).

81. Note, The Misuse of the Tort Definition of Assault in a Criminal Action, 11 Rocky Mt.L.Rev. 104 (1939).

82. "No . . . ex post facto Law shall be passed." U.S.Const. art. I, § 9. "No State shall . . . pass any . . . ex post facto Law . . .." U.S.Const. art. I, § 10. Forman v. Wolff, 590 F.2d 283 (9th Cir.1979).

83. For a scholarly discussion, see Hall, General Principles of Criminal Law 27–69 (2d ed.1960).

A judicial decision interpreting the law so as to hold one guilty for doing what had not been recognized as a crime when done, violates due process and a resulting conviction must be reversed. Bouie v. City of Columbia, 378 U.S. 347, 84 S.Ct. 1697 (1964).

In Ginzburg v. United States, 383 U.S. 463, 86 S.Ct. 942 (1966), the Court applied a new standard in determining obscenity and upheld the defendant's conviction where there was no prior application of such standard in similar cases.

84. See, e.g., State v. Hazen, 160 Kan. 733, 740, 165 P.2d 234, 239 (1946); People v. Wood, 10 A.D.2d 231, 236, 199 N.Y.S.2d 342, 347 (1960); State v. Allen, 245 N.C. 185, 189, 95 S.E.2d 526, 529 (1956); Dunbar v. State, 75 Okl.Cr. 275, 131 P.2d 116 (1942); State v. Sims, 3

hension, even when intended only as a bluff, is so likely to result in a breach of the peace that it should be a punishable offense;[85] hence there need be no regret that it is an offense in most jurisdictions even if we might wish that the enlargement of criminal assault had been made prospectively by legislative enactment rather than retroactively by "judicial legislation."

Where criminal assault has been given this dual scope, a definition in terms of "an attempt or offer" to commit a battery is assumed to represent both grounds. The word "offer," it is said, signifies a threat that places the other in reasonable apprehension of receiving an immediate battery.[86] It would be a mistake, however, to assume that the word carried any such significance when it first appeared in the definition of this offense. In one of its meanings, "offer" is a synonym of "attempt." Duplicity of expression was no stranger in the early law, and when the phrase was first used in this definition, it was as if it had been worded "an attempt or effort." This significance is manifest when the court says "the offer or attempt must be intentional" because if there, "is not a present purpose to do an injury, it is not an assault."[87] In fact, a real strain is placed upon the word "offer" when it is given the meaning of a mere pretense of impending harm, and the assumption that the word has this meaning when used in the definition of criminal assault is merely part of the explanation of how the tort theory was inadvertently added to the offense. Such connotation is employed only by those who seek to bring the two-fold aspect of criminal assault within its original definition, while writers,[88] courts,[89] and legislators[90] interested in emphasizing the point make use of a different form of expression, such as that an assault is either "an attempt to commit a battery, or the intentional placing of another in reasonable apprehension of receiving a battery."[91]

Strob. 137 (S.C.1848); State v. Wiley, 52 S.D. 110, 216 N.W. 866 (1927).

85. If "a person presents a pistol which has the appearance of being loaded, and puts the party into fear and alarm, that is what it is the object of the law to prevent." Regina v. St. George, 9 Car. & P. 483, 493, 173 Eng.Rep. 921, 926 (Cent.Crim.Ct.1840). See also Richels v. State, 33 Tenn. (1 Sneed) 606 (1854); Macon v. State, 295 So.2d 742 (Miss.1974); Hochheimer, Crimes and Criminal Procedure § 254 (2d ed. 1904); LaFave and Scott, Criminal Law, p. 612 (1972).

86. Thus, in holding an intent to strike unnecessary, the Kansas court held that an assault is committed by "a wilful offer with force or violence to do corporal injury to another . . . if the circumstances are such that the person threatened reasonably believes the injury will be done." State v. Hazen, 160 Kan. 733, 740, 165 P.2d 234, 239 (1946). The fact that the reference is not to an "apparent offer" but to a "wilful offer" is significant. See also Richels v. State, 33 Tenn. (1 Sneed) 606 (1854).

87. Smith v. State, 39 Miss. 521, 525 (1860); see Johnson v. State, 35 Ala. 363 (1860); State v. Blackwell, 9 Ala. 79 (1846); State v. Sears, 86 Mo. 169 (1885).

88. Model Penal Code § 201.10, comment (Tent. Draft No. 9, 1959); Perkins, Non-Homicide Offenses Against the Person, 26 B.U.L.Rev. 119, 132 (1946).

89. People v. Wood, 10 A.D.2d 231, 199 N.Y.S.2d 342 (1960).

90. La.Rev.Stat. § 14:36 (1978).

91. Ibid. See also Stephen, Digest of the Criminal Law 237 (9th ed. 1950):

"An assault is

"(a) an attempt unlawfully to apply the least actual force to the person of another directly or indirectly,

"(b) the act of using a gesture towards another giving him reasonable grounds to believe that the person using that gesture meant to apply such actual force to his person as aforesaid,

"(c) the act of depriving another of his liberty."

B. THE REQUIREMENT OF PRESENT ABILITY

The original concept of criminal assault developed at an earlier day than the doctrine of criminal attempt in general, and crystallized on a much narrower basis in the sense of a greater degree of proximity.[92] In the words of the Ohio Supreme Court:

"The distinction may be thus defined: An assault is an act done toward the commission of a battery; it must precede the battery, but it does so immediately. The next movement would, at least to all appearance, complete the battery . . . [A]n act constituting an attempt to commit a felony may be more remote . . . ."[93]

The emphasis here was upon the very strict interpretation of "proximity" in the law of assault. In making the same point, but with the emphasis upon the more liberal interpretation in the law of criminal attempt in general, it has been said: "This is a clear recognition of the principle that an attempt, or the overt act which is the initial stage thereof, does not require a physical act in the way of an assault or advance upon the person of the intended victim." [94] Therefore, since one may be guilty of an attempt to commit murder or rape, for example, without coming close enough to his intended victim to commit an assault,[95] it follows that the attempt is a lesser included offense in a prosecution for an aggravated assault of that nature.[96]

At times this difference in the requirement of proximity has found expression in statutes that provide for conviction of an attempt to commit murder where the attempt is by "any means not constituting the crime of assault with intent to murder," [97] or for conviction of an attempt to commit rape where the attempt was "not such as to bring it within the definition of an assault with intent to commit rape. . . ." [98] There has been some relaxation in the degree of proximity required,[99] but in the early days there was no

---

92. In State v. Davis, 23 N.C. 125, 127 (1840), an early North Carolina court said:

"It is difficult in practice, to draw the precise line which separates violence menaced, from violence begun to be executed—for until the execution of it is begun, there can be no assault. We think, however, that where an unequivocal purpose of violence is accompanied by any *act*, which, if not stopped—or diverted— will be followed by personal injury—the execution of the purpose is then begun— the battery is *attempted*."

93. Fox v. State, 34 Ohio St. 377, 380 (1878), quoted in part in State v. Green, 84 Ohio App. 298, 303, 82 N.E.2d 105, 107 (1948). See also State v. Hatzel, 159 Ohio St. 350, 112 N.E.2d 369 (1953).

94. State v. Mortensen, 95 Utah 541, 550, 83 P.2d 261, 265 (1938) (Hanson, J., dissenting). See also Valley v. State, 203 Tenn. 80, 309 S.W.2d 374 (1957).

95. People v. Welsh, 7 Cal.2d 209, 60 P.2d 124 (1936); Ramsey v. State, 204 Ind. 212, 183 N.E. 648 (1932).

96. People v. Rupp, 41 Cal.2d 371, 260 P.2d 1 (1953); People v. Miller, 17 Cal.Rptr. 535 (1961); State v. Staggs, 554 S.W.2d 620 (Tenn.1977). But see State v. Hewitt, 158 N.C. 627, 74 S.E. 356 (1912), in which the difference in the requirement of proximity was overlooked. See also 21 Minn.L.Rev. 213 (1937).

97. Mich.Stat.Ann. § 28.286 (1962).

98. Vernon's Ann.P.C. (Tex.) art. 1190, since repealed. During the force of this statute, the offense of attempt to rape was a distinct offense from assault with intent to rape, Diaz v. State, 491 S.W.2d 166 (Tex.Cr.App.1973). The current statutory format in Texas is to recognize only the crime of attempt to rape. V.T.C.A., Penal Code §§ 15.01 and 21.02.

99. Where D advanced upon X with a stick in a threatening manner, he was held guilty of assault even though he was stopped by Y before he was within striking distance of X. State v. Vannoy, 65 N.C. 532 (1871); *accord,* People v. Bird, 60 Cal. 7 (1881); People v. Hunter, 71 Cal.App. 315, 235 Pac. 67 (1925).

assault until assailant came within apparent reach of his intended victim.[1] This fact is helpful in understanding some of the early references to assault.

Apart from legal usage, "assault" means an attack, and that was its meaning when it first appeared in the law. The phrase "premeditated assault" is older than "malice aforethought," [2] and even the civil action of trespass for assault was originally based upon an attack.[3] Coke and Hale seem to have been too exclusively interested in felonies to bother with a definition of assault, although each used the term as meaning an attack.[4] Hawkins said that "an assault is an attempt, or offer, with force and violence, to do a corporal hurt to another; as by striking at him with, or without, a weapon; or presenting a gun at him, at such a distance to which the gun will carry . . .." [5] Blackstone's definition was "an attempt or offer to beat another." [6] East indicated that:

"[A]n assault is any attempt or offer with force and violence to do a corporal hurt to another, whether from malice or wantonness; as by striking at him, or even holding up one's fist at him in a threatening or insulting manner, or with such other circumstances as denote at the time an intention, coupled with a present ability of using actual violence against his person; as by pointing a weapon at him within the reach of it." [7]

Three comments are necessary. First, neither Hawkins nor Blackstone mentioned "present ability," and East did not include this phrase in his definition, but only used it by way of illustration. Second, East's reference to "present ability" was obviously meant to emphasize the requirement of proximity rather than any notion of actual present ability, for otherwise his illustration would have been in terms of "pointing a *loaded* weapon." Third, the inadvertent addition of the tort theory to the concept of criminal assault may have had its inception in the statement by East.[8] The statement that he was about to comment on "common assaults and batteries" for which there are "civil" remedies, which immediately preceded his definition of a criminal assault, indicates that he was thinking of assault as a crime and as a tort, with no appreciation of the difference between the two. That he was not thinking

1. Lane v. State, 85 Ala. 11, 4 So. 730 (1887); State v. Straub, 190 Iowa 800, 180 N.W. 869 (1921); People v. Lilley, 43 Mich. 521, 5 N.W. 982 (1880); Fox v. State, 34 Ohio St. 377 (1878).

2. 2 Pollock & Maitland, History of English Law 468 (2d ed. 1899). This meaning has tended to persist in the criminal law except where the tort theory has been added. E.g., Offences Against the Person Act, 1861, 24 & 25 Vict., c. 100, § 37 ("Whoever shall assault and strike or wound . . ."), 47 ("Whoever shall be convicted upon an indictment of any assault occasioning actual bodily harm . . .").

3. It was "an action brought by the person aggrieved by the actor's attempt to commit a battery upon him." Restatement, Second, Torts § 24, comment *c* (1965).

4. Coke, Institutes, pt. 3, at 54 (1648); 1 Hale, Pleas of the Crown 425 (1736).

5. 1 Hawkins, Pleas of the Crown 263 (Leach 6th ed. 1788).

6. 3 Blackstone, Commentaries *120. This is in the third book dealing with "private wrongs." In the fourth book dealing with "public wrongs" he says of assault: "I have nothing further to add to what has already been observed in the preceding book . . .." 4 id. at *216. There is no indication of awareness of any difference between assault as a crime and assault as a tort, but he seems to be thinking in terms of the former. Of assault he says: "This also is an inchoate violence . . . and therefore, though no actual suffering is proved, yet the party injured may have redress . . ." 3 id. at *120.

7. 1 East, Pleas of the Crown 406 (1803).

8. Ibid. Possibly the inadvertent addition should be attributed to Blackstone. See 3 Blackstone, Commentaries *120.

of assault exclusively in terms of the apprehension of the other party is shown by the words immediately following his definition of assault—"where the injury is actually inflicted, it amounts to a battery, (which includes an assault;) . . .."[9]

One English case that did not involve assault took the position that there could be no attempt to commit a crime if perpetration was impossible under the circumstances,[10] but this position was later repudiated in England[11] and has not been followed in this country.[12] Although there is no legally-recognized attempt to commit a crime unless the perpetration appeared to be possible to the one who is claimed to have made the attempt, actual present possibility is not required.[13] In this connection, the prevailing view quite soundly holds that apparent possibility is sufficient for an assault,[14] as where the offense was committed with an unloaded weapon.[15] It is true that most of the cases cited are from jurisdictions in which criminal assault has been enlarged by the addition of the tort theory, and obviously an unloaded weapon could cause reasonable apprehension in the mind of one who believed it was loaded.[16] It should be noted, however, that although where the dual basis is recognized there would be no inconsistency in holding apparent possibility sufficient for conviction on the tort theory while actual possibility is needed to establish an attempt to commit a battery, the cases rarely give any

---

9. 1 East, *op. cit.* supra note 7, at 406.

10. Regina v. Collins, 9 Cox Crim.Cas. 497 (Ct.Crim.App.1864) (no attempt to commit larceny by reaching into an empty pocket).

11. Regina v. Ring, 17 Cox Crim.Cas. 491 (Crown Cas.Res.1892).

12. State v. Wilson, 30 Conn. 500 (1862); Commonwealth v. Williams, 312 Mass. 553, 45 N.E.2d 740 (1942); Commonwealth v. McDonald, 59 Mass. (5 Pick.) 365 (1850); People v. Moran, 123 N.Y. 254, 25 N.E. 412 (1890).

13. Williams, Criminal Law 635 (2d ed. 1961).

"According to the weight of authority, an actual ability to commit a battery is not essential in simple criminal assault an apparent ability to do so being sufficient . . . ." Casey v. State, 491 S.W.2d 90, 93–94 (Tenn.Cr.App. 1972).

14. De Graff v. State, 34 Ala.App. 137, 37 So.2d 130 (1948); State v. Paxson, 29 Del. (6 Boyce) 249, 99 A. 46 (1916); State v. Hazen, 160 Kan. 733, 165 P.2d 234 (1946); State v. Adamo, 9 N.J.Super. 7, 74 A.2d 341 (App.Div.1950); State v. McIver, 231 N.C. 313, 56 S.E.2d 604 (1949); Fox v. State, 34 Ohio St. 377 (1878); State v. Linville, 127 Or. 565, 273 P. 338 (1928); State v. Wiley, 52 S.D. 110, 216 N.W. 866 (1927); State v. Deso, 110 Vt. 1, 1 A.2d 710 (1938); State v. Shaffer, 120 Wash. 345, 207 P. 229 (1922); Regina v. St. George, 9 Car. & P. 483, 493, 173 Eng.Rep. 921, 926 (Cent.Crim.Ct.1840).

In State v. Swails, 8 Ind. 524 (1857), it was held that there was no assault without both intent and present ability, but this was expressly repudiated in Kunkle v. State, 32 Ind. 220 (1869). Current Indiana statutes do not recognize the crime of assault as such. Cf. Burns Ind.Stat.Ann. Title 35 Art. 42 Chap. 1 (1979). An assault is apparently to be prosecuted as an attempted battery. 10 Ind.L.Rev. 1, 17 (1976).

15. Price v. United States, 156 F. 950 (9th Cir.1907); McNamara v. People, 24 Colo. 61, 48 P. 541 (1897); Crumbley v. State, 61 Ga. 582 (1878); State v. Shepard, 10 Iowa 126 (1859); State v. Coyle, 103 Kan. 750, 175 Pac. 971 (1918); Commonwealth v. White, 110 Mass. 407 (1872); Ford v. State, 71 Neb. 246, 98 N.W. 807 (1904); People v. Wood, 10 App.Div.2d 231, 199 N.Y.S.2d 342 (1960); People v. Morehouse, 6 N.Y.Supp. 763 (Sup.Ct.1889); State v. Atkinson, 141 N.C. 734, 53 S.E. 228 (1906); Clark v. State, 106 Pac. 803 (Okl.Cr.App.1910); State v. Smith, 21 Tenn. (2 Humph.) 457 (1842). At one time the Texas statute provided that "pointing an unloaded gun . . . cannot constitute an assault." Mackay v. State, 44 Tex. 43, 45 (1875). Under the present Texas statute an assault is intentionally or knowingly threatening another with imminent bodily injury, V.T.C.A., Penal Code § 22.01.

16. Casey v. State, 491 S.W.2d 90 (Tenn.Cr.App.1972).

such intimation.[17] The logical position is that one may be guilty of an assault by attempting to shoot another with a gun that one mistakenly believes to be loaded or by threatening with a gun that the other does not know is unloaded. The indications are that this position will be upheld.[18]

It is interesting to note that in most states the criminal law concept has been enlarged by the addition of the tort theory. Initially, much of the enlargement resulted from judicial decision, however, currently several states have such provisions in their codes [19] and the Model Penal Code accepts such a standard in defining assault.[20] But while several states have narrowed the concept of criminal assault by a statutory requirement of "present ability," [21] only a few jurisdictions achieved the same result by judicial interpretation.[22] Moreover, references to "such circumstances as denote at the time an intention, coupled with the present ability" [23] do not necessarily refer to actual present ability. Where criminal assault has been enlarged by the addition of the tort theory, this reference is to such circumstances as are sufficient to create a reasonable apprehension of receiving an immediate battery on the part of the other person.[24]

17. In reversing a conviction because of an instruction that would have authorized a verdict of guilty even if both parties knew the weapon was unloaded, the Tennessee court said that there must be circumstances "to satisfy a jury that there was an intent, coupled with an ability, to do harm, or that the other party had a right so to believe from the facts before him; otherwise, there is no danger of a breach of the peace." Richels v. State, 33 Tenn. (1 Sneed) 606, 609 (1954).

18. For example the Iowa court, in sustaining a conviction of assault with intent to do great bodily injury, said:

"[H]ow could defendant have intended to shoot the person assaulted unless the gun which he held in his hands was, in fact, or, as he believed, so loaded as that it could be fired? If he believed that it was loaded and intended to fire it at the person assaulted, he was guilty of an assault with intent to commit great bodily injury, although in fact and contrary to his belief it was not loaded."

State v. Mitchell, 139 Iowa 455, 459, 116 N.W. 808, 810 (1908).

19. Ariz.Rev.Stat. § 13–1203A.2 (1978); N.J.Stat.Ann. 2C:12–1(3) (1979); Purdon's Penn.Stat.Ann. Tit. 18 § 2701 (1973).

20. § 211.1(c).

21. West's Ann.Cal.Pen.Code § 240 (1970); Idaho Code § 18–901 (1972); Wyo.Stat.Ann. § 6–4–501 (1977). See Model Penal Code, § 201, app. H

(Tent.Draft No. 9, 1959). Under such a statute, it is error to instruct that apparent present ability is sufficient. Pratt v. State, 49 Ark. 179, 4 S.W. 785 (1887).

22. Flournoy v. State, 270 Ala. 448, 120 So.2d 124 (1960); Chapman v. State, 78 Ala. 463 (1885); Burton v. State, 8 Ala.App. 295, 62 So. 394 (1913); State v. Lasby, 174 A.2d 323 (Del.Super.Ct.1961); State v. Wilson, 218 Ore. 575, 346 P.2d 115 (1959); State v. Godfrey, 17 Ore. 300, 20 P. 625 (1889). The Maine court has said that a statute defining assault in the terms "whoever unlawfully attempts to strike, hit, touch . . . having an intention and existing ability . . . ." was a codification of common-law assault. State v. Rand, 156 Me. 81, 161 A.2d 852 (1960); State v. Mahoney, 122 Me. 483, 120 A. 543 (1923).

23. Guarro v. United States, 237 F.2d 578, 580 (D.C.Cir.1956).

24. *Compare*, Huffman v. State, 200 Tenn. 487, 292 S.W.2d 738 (1956), which includes such a reference, *with* State v. Smith, 21 Tenn. (2 Humph.) 457 (1841), which holds that a criminal assault may be committed with an unloaded gun.

The Kansas statute defines assault as an "intentional threat or attempt to do bodily harm to another coupled with apparent ability and resulting in immediate apprehension of bodily harm. No bodily contact is necessary." State v. Nelson, 224 Kan. 95, 577 P.2d 1178, 1181 (1978).

3.   ATTEMPT TO ASSAULT

From what has been said, it is apparent that reference may be made to an "attempt to assault" without logical absurdity.[25] There is nothing absurd in referring to an attempt to frighten, which would constitute, if successful, a criminal assault in most jurisdictions. Where an attempt to commit a battery with present ability is the only basis on which a criminal assault may be established, an "attempt to assault" would mean in substance an attempt to commit a battery without present ability. Even where a criminal assault still has its original meaning as an attempt to commit a battery, reference to an attempt to assault is not necessarily absurd. Because of the recognized difference between the requirement of proximity for an assault and for a general criminal attempt, an attempt to assault would indicate an effort to accomplish a battery that had proceeded beyond the stage of preparation, but had not come close enough to completion to constitute an assault. It is not surprising, therefore, that there is a tendency to break away from the ancient view that there is no such offense known to the law as an attempt to commit an assault.

A.   DEVELOPMENT OF THE CONCEPT OF AN
ATTEMPT TO ASSAULT

One of the earliest steps toward recognition of an attempt to commit an assault was in *O'Connell*,[26] a New York case. The charge was assault with a deadly weapon, and the prosecution was persuaded to accept a plea of guilty of an attempt to commit the offense. The defendant appealed from the conviction on the ground that the crime of which he had been convicted did not exist. In affirming the conviction, the court pointed out that to be guilty of an assault the defendant would have to be within reach of his intended victim, but he could be guilty of an attempt by arming himself and attempting to reach him.

Almost at the same time the Montana court, in *Herron*,[27] took the same position almost by default. The information was for "an attempt to commit an assault with a deadly weapon, with the intent to commit a violent injury." A verdict of acquittal was directed for lack of proof that the weapon was loaded. In holding this to have been erroneous, the court said: "This case is a prosecution for an attempt. The attempt is clear. The intent is expressly declared by defendant himself. The ability is proven, that is, if the gun was loaded." [28] The court held that the fact the gun was unloaded, if such was

---

25. "This view is in obvious recognition of the fact that all assaults are attempts, whereas all attempts are not necessarily assaults. A failure to grasp the somewhat elusive distinction between an assault and an attempt accounts for much of the confusion. Indeed, the distinction is largely semantic. To paraphrase the poet, assaults are sure to attempts allied, and thin partitions do their bounds divide." State v. Staggs, 554 S.W.2d 620, 623 (Tenn.1977).

26. People v. O'Connell, 60 Hun 109, 14 N.Y.S. 485 (Sup.Ct.1891). Loose statements can be found much earlier,

however. For example: "We hold, that if a slave, in the attempt, unjustifiably, to commit an assault, or assault and battery, on another slave, kill a white person by misadventure, he is guilty of involuntary manslaughter . . . ." Bob (a Slave) v. State, 29 Ala. 20, 25 (1856). This statement was made in a murder case in which Bob had unquestionably attempted to commit a battery upon another slave.

27. State v. Herron, 12 Mont. 230, 29 P. 819 (1892).

28. Id. at 234, 29 P. at 820.

the fact, is a matter of defense to be established by the defendant, and that the use of the weapon in this manner gives rise to a presumption that it is loaded. The fact that the information charged an attempt to assault rather than an assault was not discussed. A few years later, the same court said in affirming a directed verdict of not guilty: "We have not been called upon to consider whether this defendant might have been convicted of an attempt to commit an assault or of any other crime." [29]

The Alabama court was confronted with the problem more directly.[30] In a trial under an indictment charging an assault with intent to murder, it was shown that **D** threatened to kill **X**, and pulled from his pocket a pistol, which was immediately taken from him by a police officer. A request to charge the jury that **D** was not guilty unless he actually presented the pistol at **X** was refused, and this refusal was relied upon as error. In affirming the conviction, the appellate court held that the requested instruction was faulty because if the pistol had not been presented, **D** might have been convicted of an attempt to commit an assault.

Sometime later, in *Burton*,[31] the Alabama Court of Appeals made what seems to be the most helpful analysis of this type of case. **D** was indicted for assault with intent to rape, which was a statutory felony. The evidence showed that **D** accosted a fifteen-year-old girl at a remote spot and, as she fled screaming, ran after her for about a hundred yards, but then abandoned his pursuit without touching her. **D** was convicted of an "attempt to commit an assault with intent to rape." In affirming the conviction, the appellate court pointed out that: (1) an attempt to rape is a misdemeanor at common law and recognized as an offense under the law of the state; (2) an assault requires a present ability to do the threatened harm, but an attempt to commit rape requires only an apparent ability to do so; (3) if an attempt to rape falls short of an assault, it constitutes the misdemeanor of attempted rape; and (4) the verdict finding **D** guilty of an "attempt to commit an assault with intent to rape" can only mean that he was found guilty of "an attempt to commit rape." [32] And much more recently, in affirming a conviction worded in terms of an attempt to commit an assault with intent to rape, the same court repeated, quoting from *Burton*, " 'an attempt to commit an assault with intent to rape' . . . means an attempt to rape which has not proceeded far enough to amount to an assault." [33] In other words, if trial judges and jurors talk in terms of an attempt to commit an assault with intent to rape, this will be accepted as synonymous with an attempt to rape, which has always been recognized as a crime in Alabama.

The New Hampshire court, in refusing to quash an indictment, emphasized that the charging part of the pleading rather than the name used by the pleading determines the offense of which the defendant is accused.[34] The charge was that **D** attempted to make an aggravated assault upon a

29. State v. Barry, 45 Mont. 598, 604, 124 P. 775, 777 (1912).

30. White v. State, 107 Ala. 132, 18 So. 226 (1894).

31. Burton v. State, 8 Ala.App. 295, 62 So. 394 (1913).

32. Id. at 297, 62 So. at 395.

33. McQuirter v. State, 36 Ala.App. 707, 709, 63 So.2d 388, 390 (1953). See

also Morris v. State, 32 Ala.App. 278, 25 So.2d 54 (1946).

34. State v. Skillings, 98 N.H. 203, 97 A.2d 202 (1953). For reference to "an attempt to commit the crime of assault and battery," see Smith v. State, 79 Okl.Cr. 1, 27, 151 P.2d 74, 87 (1944).

woman by means of drugs capable of rendering her unconscious and inflicting serious physical injury upon her. **D** moved to quash the indictment upon the ground, *inter alia*, that since an assault may be no more than an attempt to commit a battery, an attempted assault is no more than an attempted attempt and, therefore, not a crime. In rejecting this contention, the court pointed out that according to the statute an assault *or battery* "of an aggravated nature" is a felony. Since the prosecution alleged not merely an "attempt to attempt" to commit a battery (an attempted assault), but an attempt to commit a battery of an aggravated nature, the indictment sufficiently alleged the attempt within the meaning of the statute punishing attempts.

The most significant case in point is *Wilson*,[35] which was decided by the Supreme Court of Oregon in 1959. **D** confronted and threatened his estranged wife in her place of employment, and then procured a shotgun from his car just outside to carry out his threat. He was unable to re-enter, however, because his wife secured herself safely behind locked doors. A prosecution for assault with a dangerous weapon resulted in a conviction of attempt to commit the offense charged. An appeal was taken primarily upon the ground that there is no such offense as that of which **D** had been convicted. In affirming the judgment of conviction, the Oregon court attempted to dispel forever the notion that there can be no attempt to assault. After discussing the problem *obiter* under a different definition of assault,[36] the court said, "we are of the opinion that criminal assault, even as defined by this court, should be regarded as a distinct crime rather than as an uncompleted battery." [37] This is quite unconvincing in view of the fact that the term, used in the Oregon statute without definition, was defined by the court as an attempt to commit a battery by one having present ability.[38] There was no intention of relying upon this point alone, as shown by this statement: "Assume that we are forced to deal with an attempt to attempt to commit a battery, is there any reason why we cannot and should not bring such conduct within the law of criminal attempt generally?" [39] The negative answer included the following:

"The mere fact that assault is viewed as preceding a battery should not preclude us from drawing a line on one side of which we require the present ability to inflict corporal injury, denominating this an assault, and on the other side conduct which falls short of a present ability, yet so advanced toward the assault that it is more than mere preparation and which we denominate an attempt." [40]

35. State v. Wilson, 218 Or. 575, 346 P.2d 115 (1959).

36. Id. at 582, 346 P.2d at 119.

37. Id. at 586, 346 P.2d at 120.

38. Ibid.

39. Id. at 585, 346 P.2d at 120.

40. Id. at 588, 346 P.2d at 121. The court added: "The contrary view is little more than a barren logical construction." Id. at 590, 346 P.2d at 122.

In California there is no such crime as an attempt to assault. In re M., 9 Cal.3d 517, 108 Cal.Rptr. 89, 510 P.2d 33 (1973). There is no such crime as attempted felonious assault. People v. Banks, 51 Mich.App. 685, 216 N.W.2d 461 (1974). There is no such crime as an attempt to commit an aggravated assault which is itself a particular type of attempt to commit a crime. Porter v. State, 124 Ga.App. 285, 183 S.E.2d 631 (1971).

B. BASES OF AN ATTEMPT TO ASSAULT

While the notion of an attempt to assault as a logical absurdity has been dispelled, steps taken to recognize it as a punishable offense have been, and probably should continue to be, very limited in scope. These steps have been based primarily on four theories.

(A) Attempts to Frighten

One judge has taken the position that "fright is such bodily harm that to shoot in the general direction of a person, with intent to 'bluff or scare' him, is an assault." [41] If this were true, then an unlawful attempt to place another in apprehension of receiving an immediate battery would, if successful, be an accomplished battery. But, while the unlawful creation of such apprehension is recognized as a criminal assault in most jurisdictions no case has been found in which it has been held to constitute a battery.

Wilson contains an elaborate dictum to the effect that an attempt to frighten would constitute the offense of attempt to assault in any jurisdiction where criminal assault may be established on the tort theory. [42] In Rhode Island, which is such a jurisdiction, the judge incorporated this idea in his instructions to the jury in a case in which the defendant unquestionably placed another in apprehension. [43] But this point was not raised on appeal because defense counsel admitted that an assault had been committed, claiming only that it was not an assault with a dangerous weapon.

Shooting in the direction of another, even without an attempt to hit him, is such a reckless and dangerous act that it should be made punishable even if it results neither in hitting anyone nor in placing anyone in apprehension of being hit. It would seem wiser, however, to take this step by legislation, such as that providing a penalty for improper use of weapons [44] or for endangering another by reckless conduct, [45] than by broadening the scope of criminal assault. [46] Criminal assault so broadly conceived would include any number of futile attempts to frighten or startle that are too insignificant to be added to the category of crime.

(B) Lack of Present Ability

Wilson held that an effort to commit a battery that goes beyond preparation but lacks the element of "present ability" is punishable as an attempt to assault. Because the statute in *Wilson* imposed a penalty without a definition of assault, the court was not confronted with a problem that would be involved in a state where criminal assault is defined by statute as an attempt

---

41. Edwards v. State, 4 Ga.App. 167, 171, 60 S.E. 1033, 1035 (1908) (Powell, J., concurring). When the case, which had been reversed for other reasons, came up again, Powell wrote the opinion and included the same statement. Edwards v. State, 4 Ga.App. 849, 850, 62 S.E. 565 (1908). He used somewhat similar language in a later case. Smallwood v. State, 9 Ga.App. 300, 70 S.E. 1124 (1911).

42. State v. Wilson, 218 Or. 575, 582, 346 P.2d 115, 119 (1959).

43. State v. Baker, 20 R.I. 275, 38 A. 653 (1897).

44. West's Ann.Cal.Pen.Code § 417 (1977).

45. The Model Penal Code § 211.2 provides for the offense of recklessly endangering another person and § 211.3 defines the offense of terroristic threats. Ill.Rev.Stat.1973, c. 38, § 12–5.

46. There is no such offense in Colorado as an attempt to commit an assault with a deadly weapon. Allen v. People, 175 Colo. 113, 485 P.2d 886 (1971). See also, Clark v. People, 176 Colo. 48, 488 P.2d 1097 (1971).

to commit a battery by one having present ability. Under the doctrine of manifested legislative intent, an omission from a penal provision evinces a legislative purpose not to punish the omitted act.[47] Therefore, if a statute defines criminal assault as an attempt to commit a battery by one having present ability and no offense known as an attempt to assault was recognized at the time the statute was adopted, then there would be a clear manifestation of legislative intent under this doctrine that an attempt to commit a battery without present ability should go unpunished. It would be wise to amend the statute by eliminating the requirement of present ability, but this should be done by the legislative body and not by "judicial amendment."

(C) Lack of Proximity

In *O'Connell* the New York court took the position that an effort to commit a battery that goes beyond preparation, but does not come close enough to completion to constitute an assault, is punishable as an attempt to commit an assault. If such misconduct is to be punished, it would seem more logical to charge an attempt to commit a battery rather than an attempt to commit an assault. In other words, two grades or degrees of attempt to commit a battery should be recognized—one coming very close to the intended victim and denominated an "assault," the other more remote and known only as an "attempt to commit a battery."

(1) The New Penal Codes

Some of the new penal codes include the whole field of assault and battery under the name of "assault." And some provide, inter alia, that one is guilty of "assault" if he "intentionally, knowingly or recklessly causes physical injury to another;" "physical injury" being defined as "impairment of physical condition or substantial pain." In one case, under such a statute, a victim warded off a blow with his arm. He reported that it hurt and was painful, but there was no indication of bruising, and he did not seek medical treatment or lose any work. It was held that this did not establish "substantial pain" and hence the assailant was not guilty of assault, but was guilty of "attempted assault." [48] At common law he would have been guilty of battery. Had he missed entirely, he would have been guilty of assault.

It should be added that not all of the new penal codes follow the Model Penal Code in requiring that battery (under the name of assault) include "impairment of physical condition or substantial pain." Some are worded in terms that include in addition to "pain or injury," physical contact that is "insulting or offensive." [49] It is most unusual, however, for a statute defining "assault" to fail to include an attempt to commit a battery, as that term

---

47. For example, if a statutory offense involves a transaction between two persons and provides a penalty for only one of them, the other may not be convicted as a conspirator, an inciter, or an abettor, since the omission evinces a legislative purpose to leave his participation unpunished. Gebardi v. United States, 287 U.S. 112 (1932); United States v. Farrar, 281 U.S. 624 (1930); Wilson v. State, 130 Ark. 204, 196 S.W. 921 (1917); State v. Teahan, 50 Conn. 92 (1882); People v. Levy, 283 App.Div. 383, 128 N.Y.S.2d 275 (1954).

48. State v. Capwell, 52 Or.App. 43, 627 P.2d 905 (1981). The court emphasized that under its statute: "Petty batteries not producing injury do not constitute criminal assault." Id. at 907, note 3.

49. E.g. Iowa Crim.Code § 708.1 (1978).

is defined in the statute. The more usual wording is in some such terms as "attempts to cause or."

(D) Aggravated Assault

Burton emphasized that an attempt to commit an assault with intent to rape is not the name of a crime, but is merely a description of the offense of attempted rape. The same is true of other "assaults with intent," such as assault with intent to murder or to rob. As an attempt to commit the designated felony is a lesser included offense, the conviction should be for the attempt where it, but not the assault, is established by the evidence.

Some aggravated assaults, such as assault with a dangerous weapon, include no lesser offense other than simple assault. In *Wilson* the court took the position that an assault, although defined as an attempt to commit a battery, was a separate substantive offense rather than an uncommitted battery. The court would have been much more convincing if, instead of speaking of simple assault, it had declared that since the statutory crime of assault with a dangerous weapon was unknown to the common law, it was a separate substantive offense and not a uncommitted battery. This would not have been entirely novel since it was intimated about a century ago by Bishop [50] and more recently by Thurman Arnold.[51]

Although the statutory definition of assault precludes the possibility of an attempt to commit an assault, the statutory definition of sexual assault on a child contains none of the "attempt language of the assault statute. . . . It follows that an attempt to commit sexual assault on a child is an offense under Colorado law.[52]

4. BATTERY INCLUDES ASSAULT

A problem related to attempt to assault arises out of the age-old assertion that every battery includes an assault.[53] This was a logical conclusion when a criminal assault was simply an attempt to commit a battery and a battery was assumed to be a personal harm perpetrated intentionally. A right to recover damages for negligent injury was recognized in the early days, but under common-law pleading the action was not trespass for battery but trespass on the case; [54] hence, the word "battery" was not used in tort law unless the harm was intentional. It has long been recognized, however, that a

---

50. "It would seem, therefore, not possible [that] there should be an indictable attempt to commit a simple assault. Yet perhaps there may be such to commit an aggravated or compound assault . . .." 2 Bishop, New Criminal Law § 62 (8th ed. 1892).

51. Arnold, Criminal Attempts—The Rise and Fall of an Abstraction, 40 Yale L.J. 53, 65 (1930).

52. People v. Martinez, 42 Colo.App. 257, 592 P.2d 1358, 1359 (1979). "When the definition of the major offense charged includes the attempt to commit that act, there can be no separate crime of attempt." Miles v. State, 374 So.2d 1167, 1168 (Fla.App. 1979).

53. See note 8 supra. "Simple assault is nothing more than an unlawful attempt to commit a violent injury on another . . . a battery cannot be committed without assaulting the victim. But an assault can occur without committing a battery." People v. McCaffrey, 118 Cal.App.2d 611, 258 P.2d 557, 562 (1953). See also State v. Mills, 19 Del. (3 Penne.) 508, 52 A. 266 (1902); State v. Grayson, 50 N.M. 147, 172 P.2d 1019 (1946); State v. Green, 84 Ohio App. 298, 82 N.E.2d 105 (1948); Wood v. Commonwealth, 149 Va. 401, 140 S.E. 114 (1927).

54. Restatement, Second, Torts, ch. 2 Topic 1 pp. 23–24 (1965).

criminal battery may be unintentional, as where personal injury results from criminal negligence [55] or from the perpetration of an unlawful act malum in se.[56]

This seems to suggest that a battery could be committed without an assault. This conclusion would be inescapable except for the well-known fact that terms used in criminal definitions are not always limited to their literal meanings. Suppose, for example, that **X** steals a pearl necklace and offers to sell it to **D** for only a fraction of its true value, telling **D** that he inherited it, but needs to raise money quickly; **D**, however, is convinced that **X** stole the necklace although he has no actual knowledge of how it was acquired. If **D** hands over the money and takes the necklace, he will be guilty of receiving stolen property.[57] Although the definition of this crime is in terms of a "person who buys or receives property which has been stolen . . . knowing the same to be so stolen," [58] the word "knowing" means "knowing or believing." [59]   In like manner, when the phrase "attempt to commit a battery" is employed in the definition of criminal assault, the legal signification is an "attempt to commit a battery or an actual battery." [60]   Even where the *statute* defines assault as an attempt to commit a battery, courts say that "a battery cannot be committed without assaulting the victim" [61] or that "when the assault culminates in a battery the offense is assault and battery . . . ." [62]

Such expressions as "a blow inflicted in the former manner would constitute an assault" [63] and "the assault alleged was a deliberate touching" of an unlawful nature [64] clearly indicate that actual battery is included within the definition of criminal assault since the courts are thinking of "assault" in terms of actual contact. Also significant is the tendency to prosecute for "assault" although a battery has clearly been committed.[65] Even more con-

---

55. Brimhall v. State, 31 Ariz. 522, 255 P. 165 (1927); Tift v. State, 17 Ga.App. 663, 88 S.E. 41 (1916); Banovitch v. Commonwealth, 196 Va. 210, 83 S.E.2d 369 (1954). For a scholarly discussion of battery based upon criminal negligence, see Hall, Assault and Battery by the Reckless Motorist, 31 J.Crim.L. & C. 133 (1940); Regina v. Venna [1975] 3 All E.R. 788.

56. McGee v. State, 4 Ala. 54, 58 So. 1008 (1912); King v. State, 157 Tenn. 635, 11 S.W.2d 904 (1928).

57. Lewis v. State, 81 Okl.Cr. 168, 172, 162 P.2d 201, 203 (1945); Reaves v. Commonwealth, 192 Va. 443, 451, 65 S.E.2d 559, 564 (1951).

58. West's Ann.Cal.Pen.Code § 496 (1970).

59. Meath v. State, 174 Wis. 80, 83, 182 N.W. 334, 335 (1921); People v. Holloway, 193 Colo. 450, 568 P.2d 29 (1977).

60. "Liability for *assault* has been imposed for reckless conduct causing injury, although ordinarily an assault (as distinguished from a battery) requires an intent to injure, or at least to alarm. But

these cases involve no more than interpreting the term 'assault' to include also a battery . . .." Hall, supra note 87, at 157. This has been spelled out in the Model Penal Code § 211.1 (Proposed Official Draft 1962):

"(1) *Simple Assault.* A person is guilty of an assault if he:

"(a) attempts to cause or purposely, knowingly or recklessly causes bodily injury to another; or

"(b) negligently causes bodily injury to another with a deadly weapon. . . ."

61. People v. McCaffrey, 118 Cal.App.2d 611, 618, 258 P.2d 557, 562 (1953); State v. Grayson, 50 N.M. 147, 172 P.2d 1019 (1946).

62. Hall v. State, 309 P.2d 1096, 1097 (Okl.Cr.App.1957) (syllabus by the court).

63. State v. Schutte, 87 N.J.L. 15, 18, 93 A. 112, 114 (Sup.Ct.1915).

64. Guarro v. United States, 237 F.2d 578, 579 (D.C.Cir.1956).

65. See, e.g., Medlin v. United States, 207 F.2d 33 (D.C.Cir.1953), cert. denied

vincing are the assault cases in which there was no actual attempt to commit a battery. Thus the crime of "assault and battery" has been committed if personal injury to another has resulted unintentionally, but through criminal negligence,[66] or where an injury has resulted unintentionally from an act malum in se.[67] In such prosecutions, it is not necessary for the accusatory pleading even to mention the word "battery" because proof of the battery will support a conviction of simple assault[68] or, if the facts warrant, of aggravated assault.[69] Many penal codes make no special provision for aggravated battery; it is unnecessary because battery includes assault, and the statutes providing penalties for aggravated assaults will cover such mis-

347 U.S. 905 (1954) (kicking another with shoes constitutes assault with a deadly weapon); Smith v. State, 105 Ala. 136, 17 So. 107 (1895) (seizing and holding another); Bonner v. State, 97 Ala. 47, 12 So. 408 (1893) (rolling a bale of cotton onto another); State v. Lankford, 29 Del. (6 Boyce) 594, 102 A. 63 (1917) (communication of a disease); Dyson v. United States, 97 A.2d 135 (D.C.Mun.App.1953) (unlawful touching); Allen v. People, 82 Ill. 610 (1876) (striking another over the head with a pistol); Carr v. State, 135 Ind. 1, 34 N.E. 533 (1893) (administration of poison); Rakes v. State, 227 Md. 172, 175 A.2d 579 (1961) (severe beating of a police officer); Commonwealth v. Cooley, 72 Mass. (6 Gray) 350 (1856) (excessive force in quelling an apparent fight); State v. Kinney, 34 Minn. 311, 25 N.W. 705 (1885) (putting a trespasser off a train in motion); State v. Kunkel, 244 S.W. 968 (Mo.Ct.App.1922) (hugging and kissing a woman against her will); State v. Norman, 237 N.C. 205, 74 S.E.2d 602 (1953) (choking); State v. Hedrick, 95 N.C. 624 (1886) (tripping another and causing him to fall); Hand v. State, 88 Tex.Cr. 422, 227 S.W. 194 (1921) (indecent familiarity with a woman); Skidmore v. State, 2 Tex.Cr. 20 (1877) (beating of a prisoner by a policeman).

One court has held that where there is proof of battery the conviction should be for battery. State v. Duran, 80 N.M. 406, 456 P.2d 880 (App.1969).

66. This arises most frequently from criminal negligence in the operation of an automobile. Wellons v. State, 77 Ga.App. 652, 48 S.E.2d 922 (1948); Tift v. State, 17 Ga.App. 663, 88 S.E. 41 (1916); Woodward v. State, 164 Miss. 468, 144 So. 895 (1932); State v. Schutte, 87 N.J.L. 15, 93 A. 112 (Sup.Ct.1915); State v. Suddreth, 184 N.C. 753, 114 S.E. 828 (1922). See also Fish v. Michigan, 62 F.2d 659

(6th Cir. 1933); Medley v. State, 156 Ala. 78, 47 So. 218 (1909) (criminal negligence in firing a gun); Hill v. State, 63 Ga. 578 (1879) (criminal negligence in throwing a stone).

67. See Commonwealth v. Smith, 312 Mass. 557, 45 N.E.2d 742 (1942) (an attempted suicide); Commonwealth v. Mann, 116 Mass. 58 (1874); State v. Lehman, 131 Minn. 427, 430, 155 N.W. 399, 400 (1915) (a shot fired with intent only to frighten another).

68. Commonwealth v. Hawkins, 157 Mass. 551, 32 N.E. 862 (1893); State v. Lehman, 131 Minn. 427, 155 N.W. 399 (1915); State v. Browers, 356 Mo. 1195, 205 S.W.2d 721 (1947); State v. McLean, 234 N.C. 283, 67 S.E.2d 75 (1951). See also Rex v. Chapin, 22 Cox Crim.Cas. 10 (Cent.Crim.Ct.1909), where in an effort to make voting papers illegible, a woman broke a bottle of some chemical over a ballot box and unintentionally splashed some of it on another's face with harmful results; this was held to constitute a common assault.

Some statutes have a separate offense of assault and battery. " 'Apparent ability' is a necessary element of the crime of assault. The same element is not a requirement of assault and battery. 'Unlawful touching' must occur in the commission of the crime of assault and battery." Settle v. State, 619 P.2d 387, 389 (Wyo.1980) (citation omitted).

69. People v. Henderson, 34 Cal.2d 340, 209 P.2d 785 (1949); People v. Weaver, 71 Cal.App.2d 685, 163 P.2d 456 (1945); Bailey v. State, 101 Ga.App. 81, 113 S.E.2d 172 (1960); State v. Patterson, 60 Idaho 67, 88 P.2d 493 (1939); People v. Benson, 321 Ill. 605, 152 N.E. 514 (1926); Lane v. State, 65 Okl.Cr. 192, 84 P.2d 807 (1938); State v. Cancelmo, 86 Or. 379, 168 P. 721 (1917).

deeds.[70] Thus it was not error to instruct in terms of "aggravated assault and battery" [71] in a trial for aggravated assault in which a battery was clearly established. The fact that a conviction of aggravated assault is warranted by proof of a corresponding aggravated battery has been so obvious as to induce courts to emphasize the lack of any requirement of actual injury or contact.[72]

Some courts have rationalized these cases in terms of a fiction—the law will presume an intent to injure from an injury caused by criminal negligence.[73] Others have spoken more frankly: "[A]ssault may be . . . done simply by operating the vehicle in such a reckless, heedless, and criminally negligent manner as to run him down without having any specific intent so to do." [74] As explained by one writer after exhaustive research, "there can be no *assault without physical injury*, unless there was an intention to inflict harm or at least to cause apprehension," [75] but no such intent is required for injurious assault. In the words of Mr. Justice Traynor, speaking for the California Supreme Court in regard to battery, "the assault, to adopt the statutory language, is 'necessarily included therein.' " [76]

Some, failing to understand the underlying history, have questioned whether a criminally negligent battery can be said to include an assault. The answer of the common law is that an assault is included.[77] Thus, where the tort theory of assault has been incor-

---

70. This has been spelled out in the Model Penal Code § 211.1 (Proposed Official Draft 1962):

"(2) *Aggravated Assault.* A person is guilty of aggravated assault if he:

"(a) Attempts to cause serious bodily injury to another, or causes such injury purposely, knowingly, or recklessly under circumstances manifesting extreme indifference to the value of human life; or

"(b) attempts to cause or purposely or knowingly causes bodily injury to another with a deadly weapon."

71. Gaston v. State, 11 Tex.Cr. 143 (1881).

72. People v. Rader, 24 Cal.App. 477, 141 P. 958 (1914); Lindsey v. State, 67 Fla. 111, 64 So. 501 (1914).

73. "The law has regard for personal safety and human life and if one with reckless indifference to results injures another it holds him to have intended the consequences of his act and treats him as if he had done an intentional wrong." Fish v. Michigan, 62 F.2d 659, 661 (6th Cir. 1933). *Accord,* Luther v. State, 177 Ind. 619, 98 N.E. 640 (1912); State v. Schutte, 87 N.J.L. 15, 19, 93 A. 112, 114 (Sup.Ct.1915). See also State v. Lankford, 29 Del. (6 Boyce) 594, 102 A. 63 (1917). Compare State v. Richardson, 179 Iowa 770, 785, 162 N.W. 28, 33 (1917), in which a conviction of assault

with intent to inflict great bodily injury, based upon criminal negligence was reversed, but the court said: "This does not exclude a conviction for assault and battery, or assault."

74. Bailey v. State, 101 Ga.App. 81, 84, 113 S.E.2d 172, 174 (1960).

75. Hall, supra note 95, at 137. An assault has not been committed (without actual contact) when there was neither an intent to commit a battery nor an intent to put the other in fear. State v. Storm, 124 Mont. 102, 220 P.2d 674 (1950); *accord,* Thomas v. State, 99 Ga. 38, 26 S.E. 748 (1896); State v. Chiarello, 69 N.J.Super. 479, 174 A.2d 506 (App.Div.1961).

76. People v. Greer, 30 Cal.2d 589, 597, 184 P.2d 512, 517 (1947), quoted with approval in Gomez v. Superior Court, 50 Cal.2d 640, 648, 328 P.2d 976, 981 (1958). The statute referred to is West's Ann.Cal.Pen.Code § 1023 (1970), which provides that "conviction, acquittal, or jeopardy is a bar to another prosecution for the offense charged . . . or for an offense necessarily included therein . . . ."

"Another established rule is that when an actual battery is committed it includes an assault." United States v. Jacobs, 632 F.2d 695, 697 (7th Cir.1980).

77. Commonwealth v. Hawkins, 157 Mass. 551, 32 N.E. 862 (1893); State v.

porated in the criminal law, a criminal assault may be committed in
any one of three different ways; namely by (1) attempting to commit a battery, (2) threatening to commit a battery, or (3) actually
committing a battery.

5. UNLOADED FIREARM

A firearm might be used as a club whether loaded or unloaded. If it is
used as a firearm, however, it is not *actually* capable of inflicting harm upon
the person by shooting if it is unloaded; but it is *apparently* capable of inflicting such harm if it is thought to be loaded. In jurisdictions giving full
scope to the modern rule of criminal assault it is possible to commit this
offense by pointing an unloaded weapon at another within normal range.[78]
This is not possible under a statute limiting criminal assault to an attempt to
commit a battery by one having present ability to do so.[79]

6. CONDITIONAL OFFER OF VIOLENCE

A gesture that might otherwise seem menacing is not an assault if accompanied by words explaining why no harm is to be inflicted. The classic example is the case of one who placed his hand on his sword and said: "If it
were not assize time, I would not take such language from you." [80] This is
not a condition offer of violence but an explanation for the lack of violence.

A conditional offer of violence without justification or excuse is sufficient
to constitute an assault.[81] It is no answer to a charge of assault in such a
case that the victim could avoid the threatened harm by complying with the
unlawful command, [82] nor that he did actually so avoid it.[83] Thus, it is an

---

Lehman, 131 Minn. 427, 155 N.W. 399
(1915); State v. Browers, 356 Mo. 1195,
205 S.W.2d 721 (1947); State v. McLean,
234 N.C. 283, 67 S.E.2d 75 (1951). See also Rex v. Chapin, 22 Cox Crim.Cas. 10
(1909). In an effort to make voting papers illegible, a woman broke a bottle of
some chemical over a ballot box and unintentionally splashed some of it on another's face with harmful results. This
criminally negligent battery was held to
constitute an assault.

"Assault is a lesser included offense of
a charge of battery." People v. Paul, 78
Cal.App.3d 32, 144 Cal.Rptr. 431, 439
(1978). "We note also that every battery
must include . . . an assault . . .."
United States v. Masel, 563 F.2d 322, 323
(7th Cir.1977). Proof of a battery will
support conviction of assault. United
States v. Dupree, 544 F.2d 1050 (9th
Cir.1976).

78. State v. Shepard, 10 Iowa 126
(1859); Commonwealth v. White, 110
Mass. 407 (1872); Macon v. State, 295
So.2d 742 (Miss.1974); State v. Brauner,
192 Neb. 602, 223 N.W.2d 152 (1974);
People v. Morehouse, 6 N.Y.S. 763 (1889);
State v. Wiley, 52 S.D. 110, 216 N.W. 866
(1927); State v. Deso, 110 Vt. 1, 1 A.2d

710 (1938); State v. Shaffer, 120 Wash.
345, 207 P. 229 (1922).

An unloaded firearm is a deadly weap-
on under the felony menacing statute.
People v. McPherson, ___ Colo. ___, 619
P.2d 38 (1980).

Since a starter's pistol has a plugged
barrel and cannot fire a projectile it is
neither a firearm nor a dangerous instrument. State v. Lawr, 263 N.W.3d 747
(Iowa 1978). But see Cox v. Commonwealth, 218 Va. 689, 240 S.E.2d 524
(1978).

79. People v. Sylva, 143 Cal. 62, 76 P.
814 (1904); Klein v. State, 9 Ind.App. 365,
36 N.E. 763 (1894).

80. Tuberville v. Savage, 1 Mod. 3, 86
Eng.Rep. 685 (1663). The more recent
counterpart is the case in which one
raised a whip in striking distance of another and said: "Were you not an old
man, I would knock you down." State v.
Crow, 23 N.C. 375 (1841).

81. State v. Morgan, 25 N.C. 186
(1842); People v. Thompson, 93
Cal.App.2d 780, 209 P.2d 819 (1949).

82. People v. Henry, 356 Ill. 141, 190
N.E. 361 (1934).

---

83. See note 83 on page 178.

assault to double the fist and run at another, saying, "If you say that again I will knock you down;" [84] to draw a pistol and point it at another with the threat, "If you do not pay me my money I will have your life;" [85] or to point a weapon in this manner and tell the other to take off his overalls and quit work or be shot.[86]

It should be noted that none of these three examples involves an attempt to commit a battery and hence none of them would seem sufficient to constitute an assault in a state limiting the offense to this basis alone.[87]

7. WORDS AND ACTS

"Threats are not sufficient; there must be proof of violence actually offered." [88] A threat of future violence is obviously insufficient for an assault, because it is neither an attempt to commit a battery nor an act of placing the other in apprehension of receiving an *immediate* battery.[89] It may be sufficient to place the intimidator under bond to keep the peace but not to convict him of the crime of assault. It has been said that no words in themselves can constitute an assault if unaccompanied by any menacing act or gesture.[90] This seems too broad. Suppose, for example, one standing back of another, should say: "I have you covered. If you move or turn I'll shoot you." This might cause more apprehension on the part of the other than if he saw a person pointing a pistol at him (because what is unseen often has added terror) although the speaker might be standing with his hands in his pockets. Two kinds of words are included here,—informational words and threatening words. And it would seem under these circumstances that the informational words might take the place of a threatening movement or gesture and complete the assault,—wherever wrongfully placing another in apprehension of receiving an immediate battery is sufficient for this offense.[91]

Statutes sometimes go entirely beyond the common law in this regard. The Model Penal Code [92] provides for a separate offense of terroristic threats

83. State v. Myerfield, 61 N.C. 108 (1867).

84. United States v. Myers, 27 Fed.Cas. 43, No. 15,845 (1806).

85. Keefe v. State, 19 Ark. 190 (1857).

86. People v. Connors, 253 Ill. 266, 97 N.E. 643 (1912).

87. A conditional offer of violence is not an attempt to commit a battery. Johnson v. State, 35 Ala. 363, 365 (1860); Wilson v. State, 53 Ga. 205 (1874); Cutler v. State, 59 Ind. 300 (1877); State v. Sears, 86 Mo. 169, 174 (1885). Contra, People v. McMakin, 8 Cal. 547 (1857); People v. McCoy, 25 Cal.2d 177, 153 P.2d 315 (1944); Pittman v. Superior Court, 256 Cal.App.2d 795, 64 Cal.Rptr. 473 (1967).

Pointing a pistol at another and saying "I will kill you now" constitutes an assault defined as an attempt to commit a battery. State v. Woods, 82 N.M. 449, 483 P.2d 504 (App.1971).

88. People v. Lilley, 43 Mich. 521, 525 (1880).

89. "Appellant's threats to extract vengeance in futuro were sufficient to establish the offense of terroristic threats." Commonwealth v. Ashford, 268 Pa.Super. 225, 407 A.2d 1328 (1979).

90. "Words in themselves no matter how threatening, unless accompanied by some act actually or apparently intended to carry the threat into execution, cannot put the other in immediate apprehension of immediate bodily contact and, therefore, cannot make the actor liable under the rule stated in section 21" (assault). Restatement, Torts, § 31, comment a (1934). This was later modified. See Restatement, Second, Torts, § 31, comment (1965).

91. Cf. People v. Rockwood, 358 Ill. 422, 193 N.E. 449 (1934); Commonwealth v. Delgado, 367 Mass. 432, 326 N.E.2d 716 (1975).

92. M.P.C. § 211.3.

as have some jurisdictions.[93] Communicating a threat[94] and provoking speeches or gestures[95] are punishable offenses under the Uniform Code of Military Justice. Sometimes a gross insult is made a statutory assault,[96] or wilfully threatening to physically injure the person or damage the property of another.[97]

Holding an axe and telling one standing three feet away (who had a right to interfere under the circumstances): "If you interfere I will cut you down with this axe," was held not to constitute a criminal assault in Indiana, because the statute in that state requires an attempt to commit a battery for this offense.[98] The result might have been different in a state in which either an attempt to commit a battery or an "offer" placing the other in reasonable apprehension of receiving an immediate battery is sufficient for an assault. As explained by one court: "if one in anger draw back his fist to strike, being within striking distance, it is an offer; but if he draw back and make a lick and miss, it is an attempt."[99]

The following have been held sufficient for conviction of assault: Riding after a person in such a manner as to compel him to take shelter to avoid being beaten;[1] stopping within striking distance of another, with the right hand clenched, the arm bent at the elbow but not drawn back, and saying, "I have a good mind to hit you;"[2] causing another to change his plans by brandishing a deadly weapon within range and with the threat of using it, although without leveling it;[3] drawing a pistol and ordering a person within ten steps to leave or be shot, although the weapon was neither cocked nor presented;[4] pointing a loaded weapon at the victim and stating that he ought to kill the victim and his family;[5] repeatedly accosting a young girl on the street with an improper solicitation until she was caused to flee in fright;[6] and standing in a state of indecent exposure close to a young girl and with intent to ravish her.[7] In a Michigan case a man induced a girl of ten to meet him in a secluded spot by promises of ice cream. There he asked her to have intercourse with him; and upon her refusal he first offered her money and then threatened to shoot her if she did not comply. He did not show either money or weapon. Upon her continued refusal he grabbed her younger brother roughly and threw him into the bushes; whereupon the girl ran away in fright. This was held sufficient to support a conviction of assault with intent to commit rape.[8]

93. Ark.Stat.Ann. § 41–1608 (1975); N.J.Stat.Ann. 2C:12–3 (1979); Utah Code Ann. 1973, 76–5–107.

94. United States v. Johnson, 21 USCMA 279, 45 CMR 53 (1972).

95. 10 U.S.C.A. § 917.

96. N.M.Stats.Ann. § 30–3–1C (1978).

97. N.C.Gen.Stat. § 14–277.1 (1981).

98. Cutler v. State, 59 Ind. 300 (1877).

99. State v. Milsaps, 82 N.C. 549 (1880).

1. Morton v. Shoppee, 3 Car. & P. 373, 172 Eng.Rep. 462 (1828).

2. State v. Hampton, 63 N.C. 13 (1868).

3. State v. Horne, 92 N.C. 805 (1885).

4. State v. Church, 63 N.C. 15 (1868).

5. State v. Seeley, 350 A.2d 569 (Me.1976).

6. State v. Williams, 186 N.C. 627, 120 S.E. 224 (1923).

7. Hays v. People, 1 Hill 351 (N.Y.1841).

8. People v. Carlson, 160 Mich. 426, 125 N.W. 361 (1910).

8. AGGRAVATED ASSAULT

The common law did not include any offense known as "aggravated assault." However, it did make provision for certain situations in this field, under other names. If, for example, the intended application of force to the person would have resulted in murder, mayhem, rape or robbery, if successful, and the scheme proceeded far enough to constitute an attempt the prosecution was for an attempt to commit the intended felony.[9] These were usually aggravated assaults although not prosecuted as such. An attempt to commit murder, for example, was prosecuted under that name and was a much more serious offense than an ordinary assault, although usually it included an assault; just as murder was prosecuted under that name and was a much more serious offense than an ordinary battery although it included a battery.

At the present time many states have made a different provision for the prosecution of such aggravated assaults, either in addition to the common-law method[10] or in lieu thereof. These are the so-called "assaults with intent." They differ somewhat from state to state. California, for example, provides special penalties for (1) assault with intent to commit murder, (2) assault with intent to commit rape, sodomy, mayhem, robbery or grand larceny, and (3) assault with intent to commit any other felony.[11]

A special problem is involved in aggravated assaults of this nature in jurisdictions in which actual present ability is required. The California statute defines an assault as "an unlawful attempt, coupled with a present ability, to commit a violent injury on the person of another."[12] This is a misdemeanor[13] but another section provides that "one who assaults another with intent to commit rape" is punishable by up to six years in prison.[14] It was held that the fact that **D** was so impotent as to be incapable of penetration did not prevent his conviction of assault with intent to rape. He had the present ability to commit an assault even if he lacked the ability to commit rape. And if he thought he had ability to accomplish sexual penetration he could intend to commit rape.[15]

---

9. Saunders v. State, 148 Miss. 685, 114 So. 747 (1927). As to attempt see infra, chapter 6, section 3.

10. People v. Henry, 356 Ill. 141, 190 N.E. 361 (1934); People v. Johnson, 407 Mich. 196, 284 N.W.2d 718 (1979).

Some of the new penal codes provide for degrees of assault. Thus it was held that a slight scratch was not sufficient to sustain a conviction for second-degree assault. State v. Rice, 48 Or.App. 115, 616 P.2d 538 (1980). The statute provides: "A person commits the crime of assault in the second degree if he: . . . Intentionally or knowingly causes physical injury to another by means of a deadly or dangerous weapon." **D** smashed a car window with a pickaxe, and the wife on the inside received a cut on the cheek so slight that she did not realize she had been cut until her daughter mentioned it.

11. West's Ann.Cal.Pen.Code (1977) §§ 217, 220 and 221.

It was not irrational for the legislature to impose a greater penalty for a threat to inflict serious bodily injury than for the actual infliction of bodily injury, because the latter may be slight. People v. Wimer, 197 Colo. 191, 591 P.2d 87 (1979).

12. West's Ann.Cal.Pen.Code § 240 (1970).

13. Id. at § 241 (1977).

14. Id. at § 220 (1978).

On a charge of assault with intent to commit rape, a finding that defendant only attempted rape requires an acquittal. People v. Duens, 64 Cal.App.3d 310, 134 Cal.Rptr. 341 (1976).

15. People v. Peckman, 249 Cal.App. 2d 941, 57 Cal.Rptr. 922 (1967).

Not all statutory aggravated assaults depend upon some specific intent. Other provisions sometimes found in the codes include assault with a deadly weapon,[16] assault with an caustic chemical,[17] assault by unlawfully administering intoxicating liquor, narcotic or drug,[18] assault upon a peace officer or fireman,[19] or other official,[20] or "assault with a deadly weapon or instrument or by any means of force likely to produce great bodily injury."[21] Such an assault, it has been held, is possible by means of the hands or feet, if so used as likely to cause great bodily injury.[22] Some jurisdictions make provision for aggravated assaults by the device of several "degrees" of assault.[23]

Many of the aggravated assaults are statutory felonies.[24]

Menacing. With reference to the new statutory offense the court said: "Menacing consists of intentionally attempting to place another person in fear of imminent serious physical injury. The victim's subjective state of mind is not a defined element of the crime." The court added that unsuccessful attempts to place another in fear are included within the statute.[25]

THE MODEL PENAL CODE

Article 211 would make significant changes in the law of assault and battery. Those who drafted the Code had some strange prejudice against the use of traditional terms and in the early drafts did not use either "assault" or "battery" but employed "bodily injury" as the name of the offense.[26] This caused such opposition that "assault" was substituted for "bodily injury" in the final draft. But whereas any unlawful application of force to the person of another is a battery at common law, and under most of the original statutes, it would not be punishable under the Code unless it causes "bodily

Whether one's hands and fists are used as dangerous weapons within the statute relating to assault and battery with intent to kill depends upon the facts and circumstances of the particular case. Pettigrew v. State, 430 P.2d 808 (Okl.Cr.1967).

"It is this Court's belief that this distinction based on the use of a weapon evidences a legislative intent that bare hands were not to be included as a dangerous weapon." People v. Van Diver, 80 Mich.App. 352, 263 N.W.2d 370, 372 (1978).

16. Ill.Rev.Stats. (1973), c. 38 § 12–2.

17. West's Ann.Cal.Pen.Code § 244 (1977).

18. Ariz.Rev.Stat. § 13–1205 (1978).

19. West's Ann.Cal.Pen.Code §§ 245, 245.1, 245.2, 245.4.

20. 18 U.S.C.A. §§ 111, 1114.

21. West's Ann.Cal.Pen.Code § 245 (1977).

The statutory offense of aggravated assault "does not require proof in fact of serious bodily injury as defined in the statute. It is only necessary to show (such an attack) that serious bodily injury was capable of being inflicted." State v. Klemann, ___ Mont. ___, 634 P.2d 632, 636 (1981).

22. People v. Kinman, 134 Cal.App.2d 419, 286 P.2d 28 (1955). See also Gonns v. United States, 231 F.2d 907 (10th Cir.1956); Sankadota v. State, 591 P.2d 324 (Okl.Cr.1979).

23. Code of Ala. Tit. 13A § 6–20–22 (1975); McKinney's N.Y.Rev.Pen.Law, §§ 120.00, 120.05, 120.10 (1967).

24. See McKinney's N.Y.Rev.Pen.Law §§ 120.05, 120.10. And see the Arizona, California and Iowa statutes cited in the notes supra.

"The difference between aggravated assault and the lesser included offense of misdemeanor assault is the intent of the defendant at the time the crime was committed." State v. Bouslaugh, 176 Mont. 78, 576 P.2d 261, 263 (1978).

25. State v. Lockwood, 43 Or.App. 639, 603 P.2d 1231, 1233 (1979).

26. M.P.C. Tentative drafts 9 and 11.

injury," which is defined in section 210.0(2) to mean physical pain, illness, or any impairment of the physical condition.

Subject to this limitation "assault" in the Code includes the prevailing common-law meaning of an attempt to commit a battery, a threat to commit a battery, or an actual battery, with additional modifications so far as punishability is concerned. A criminally negligent battery would be punishable only if it was the result of advertent negligence ("recklessly"), or was inflicted with a deadly weapon. And a threat to commit a battery would be punishable only if it was intended to put the other in fear of imminent "serious bodily injury," [27] which is defined in section 210.0(3) to mean an injury which "creates a substantial risk of death or causes serious permanent disfigurement, or protracted loss or impairment of the function of any bodily member or organ." But such a threat would be punishable whether it had any effect on the victim or not, which is not the common-law position.

"Aggravated Assault" under the Code includes only maliciously (worded differently) attempting to cause or causing "serious bodily injury" or an attempt to cause or causing "bodily injury" with a deadly weapon. Assault to murder, to rob, to rape and so forth, would be dealt with only as attempts to commit such offenses.

"Recklessly endangering another person" is also included in this Article. There was no such offense at common law but there have been various *ad hoc* statutes of this nature, the most common being reckless driving.

NEW PENAL CODES

A number of states that have recently recodified their penal laws along the lines of the Model Penal Code have adopted the format of defining offenses as assault, aggravated assault, reckless endangering and terroristic threats,[28] or adopting some of those offenses but not all.[29]

SECTION 3.   ABDUCTION

The social interest in the personal security of the individual member of the community goes far beyond the effort to safeguard his life and to protect him against an ordinary attack. Viewed in the most primitive light, the state must undertake to deal with various other types of personal harm in order to have any adequate check upon violent acts of private retaliation. It

---

27. In holding that the aggravated battery statute, which requires "great bodily harm," is not unconstitutionally vague, the court said: "*Bodily harm—* harm or injury to the body—is clear and unequivocal. *Great* distinguishes the bodily harm necessary in this offense from slight, trivial, minor or moderate harm, and as such it does not include mere bruises, which are likely to be sustained in simple battery. Whether the injury or harm is "great" is generally a question of fact for the jury." State v. Sanders, 223 Kan. 550, 575 P.2d 533, 535 (1978).

"The term 'extreme pain' is not so vague or overbroad as to render the first-

degree sexual assault statute unconstitutional." People v. Albo, 195 Colo. 102, 575 P.2d 427, 428–29 (1978).

The mere evidence that a woman was grabbed and pushed around does not show "serious bodily injury" and is insufficient to establish aggravated assault. Allen v. State, 559 S.W.2d 656 (Tex.Cr.App.1977).

28. Ariz.Rev.Stat.Ann.   § 13–1201– 1204 (1978); N.J.Stat.Ann. § 2C:12–1–3 (1979).

29. Kan.Stat.Ann. §§ 21–3408, 3410, 3419 (1964); Utah Code Ann. 1973, 76–5–102, 103, 107.

must do so, furthermore, if the organized group is to continue to strive for an ever higher level of cultural development, and "a more abundant life," intellectually and morally, as well as physically.

There was no such crime as abduction known to the English common law, but a statute,[1] passed a few years before Columbus discovered America, created a felony which is the forerunner of all the present statutes on abduction.

This early statute was designed primarily to protect young heiresses from designing fortune hunters, although its wording was not so limited. It provided in substance that if any person should take any woman ("maid, widow or wife") against her will, unlawfully, and such woman had substance in the form of lands or goods or was the heir apparent of her ancestor, such person should be guilty of felony. It was stated in an introduction to the statute that a woman, so taken, was often thereafter married to or defiled by the abductor, or to or by another with his consent, but this was not made an element of the original crime itself. This element, however, has been included in many of the modern statutes.[2] At the present time a large field has come to be referred to as "abduction." One jurisdiction may have only one or two provisions covering a small part of the total, another may have eight or ten sections with rather exhaustive coverage, while others occupy intermediate positions of varying degree. And whether the pertinent sections are few or several they may be grouped together, or may be separated in the code.

The statutes differ so widely that a general discussion can merely hint at the field covered. There is no factor common to all of the statutes on abduction other than that they are intended for certain types of personal protection. The closest approach to a broader common factor is that most of them forbid the taking (or enticing or detaining) of a *female person*, for some unlawful purpose directly associated with the fact that she is female rather than male. Some, however, require no more than the unlawful taking, and so forth, of a girl under a certain age from her parent or guardian for the purpose of depriving her parent or guardian of his lawful custody; and some make a similar provision with reference to such taking of "any child," and hence extend the protection to boys as well as to girls. Such a statute goes beyond the scope of "abduction" as it is ordinarily understood and carries over into the field of kidnaping. In fact it is properly included in the chapter on kidnaping [3] or as a clause of the kidnaping statute itself.[4] The word "abduction," meaning literally taking or drawing away, was employed by Black-

---

1. 3 Hen. VII, c. 2 (1487).

2. See for example, Ida.Code § 18–501 (1979).

3. "A person commits an offense if he knowingly takes or entices any child under the age of 18 from the custody of its parent, guardian or other lawful custodian when he has no privilege to do so, or he does so in violation of a court order . . . ." N.J.Stat.Ann. 2C:13–4 (1979) (In chapter on Kidnapping and Related Offenses). See also Ill.Rev.Stat. 1975, c. 38, § 10–1(b).

4. "Any person who forcibly or otherwise seizes and carries away any person from one place to another without his consent and without lawful justification or who takes, entices, or decoys away any child not his own and under the age of eighteen years, with intent to keep or conceal the child from his parent or guardian, commits second degree kidnaping . . . ." Colo.Rev.Stat. 1973, § 18–3–302.

stone in his definition of kidnaping,[5] and could logically have included that field as well.

The abductor may be either male or female under most of the provisions. Some of the statutes require an unlawful taking "by force, menace or duress;"[6] some speak only of unlawful taking and are interpreted to include fraudulent inducement and deception as well as force or threats;[7] some expressly speak of taking or "enticing;"[8] others add the element of unlawful detention or even knowingly harboring.[9]

If the statute speaks only of "taking,"[10] without mention of either enticement or threats, this means an *unlawful taking* and a taking under a fraudulently-induced consent is unlawful. Thus abduction was committed by one who induced the girl's father to permit the girl to be taken away by fraudulently representing that the purpose was to find a proper home for the girl.[11] And under such a statute a taking against the will of the parent is abduction even if the taker has an admirable religious and philanthropic motive.[12]

Some of the provisions prohibit the unlawful taking, and so forth, "of any woman;"[13] some limit the protection to an unmarried female, or to an unmarried female under a specified age;[14] a few add the element of chastity, although this element is of little present concern;[15] an occasional statute is directed at elopement with another's wife.[16]

The purpose for which the taking is prohibited may be to compel the woman to marry or to be defiled;[17] it may be for the purpose of prostitution;[18] or for prostitution or forced marriage;[19] or for prostitution or concubinage;[20] or for prostitution, concubinage or marriage; or for prostitution, concubinage or other immoral purpose;[21] or to engage in sexual activity.[22] It may be merely to deprive the parent, guardian or custodian of the lawful custody of the child.[23]

5.　4 Bl.Comm. *219.

6.　West's Ann.Cal.Pen.Code § 265, 1977; Ill.Rev.Stat. 1973, c. 38, § 10–1; Wis.Stat.Ann. § 940–32 (1958).

7.　AS 11.15.790 (1962). The question is not force, distance or time; but whether a chaste female was taken by force, fraud or persuasion beyond the control of her parents for prostitution or concubinage. Abbott v. Ledbetter, 1 Tenn.App. 458 (1925).

8.　Wyo.Stat.Ann. § 6–4–202 (1977).

9.　D.C.Code 1967, § 22–2704.

10.　Section 20 of the English Sexual Offenses Act of 1956 provides: "It is an offense for a person acting without lawful authority or excuse to take an unmarried girl under the age of sixteen out of the possession of her parent or guardian against his will."

11.　Regina v. Hopkins, Car. & M. 254, 174 Eng.Rep. 495 (1842).

12.　Regina v. Booth, 12 Cox C.C. 231 (1872).

13.　Ida.Code § 18–501 (1979).

14.　D.C.Code 1967, § 22–2704.

15.　F.S.A. (Fla.) § 795.02, repealed Laws 1972, c. 72–254 § 4. However, cf. So.Car.Code § 16–404 (1962). "Whoever shall so take away . . . and deflower any such maid or woman child . . ."

16.　The essential element of "abduction" or of "elopement" with another's wife, is subsequent adultery. State v. Ashe, 196 N.C. 387, 145 S.E. 784 (1928).

17.　West's Ann.Cal.Pen.Code § 265 (1977); Ida.Code § 18–501 (1979).

18.　D.C.Code 1967, § 22–2704.

19.　Ida.Code § 18–501 (1972).

20.　West's Ann.Cal.Pen.Code § 266 (1977).

21.　Wis.Stat.Ann. § 940.32. The words "other immoral purpose" in this statute mean purpose similar to illicit relationship or prostitution. State v. Duffy, 55 S.D. 110, 225 N.W. 61 (1929).

22.　Ohio Rev.Code § 290.01(4) (1953).

23.　Wyo.Stat. 1977 § 6–4–202; Ill.Rev.Stat. 1967, c. 38, § 10–1.

Needless to say, attention must be given to the wording of the particular statute under which the prosecution is instituted. If, for example, in referring to the prohibited purpose it mentions only "prostitution," it will not do to prove a single act of sexual intercourse, or even the relation of concubinage,[24] because these three terms are not identical. An intent that the girl shall have unlawful intercourse with one man only (either the taker himself or another) is not for the purpose of prostitution because that term implies promiscuous intercourse with more than one man.[25] An intent that she shall engage in a single act of sexual intercourse is usually held not sufficient even for the purpose of concubinage, since this term is usually interpreted to mean *habitual* sexual intercourse with one not a lawful spouse.[26]

The *intent* of the taking is the essence of abduction,[27] under most of the provisions.[28] If, for example, the statute says "taking for sexual intercourse" this must be shown to be the purpose of the taking.[29] It will not be necessary to prove that the intercourse actually took place, although if it did occur this fact is admissible on the question of intent.[30] Under some of the provisions the accomplishment of the intent is a circumstance of aggravation, and in one state, at one time, to take a woman against her will and by force, duress or menace, compel her to marry or be defiled was a capital crime.[31]

For abduction it is necessary that the female be taken beyond the control of her parent or guardian, but not that the deprivation of control be perma-

24. The confinement by a step-father of his step-daughter, against her will, in a room in his own house, and having sexual intercourse with her, do not constitute confinement for the purpose of prostitution. Bunfill v. People, 154 Ill. 640, 39 N.E. 565 (1895).

25. Nichols v. State, 127 Ind. 406, 409, 26 N.E. 839, 840 (1890). "[P]rostitution is . . . the practice of a female offering her body to an indiscriminate intercourse with men; the common lewdness of a female." Hence enticing an unmarried female to go to a nearby town and there having repeated intercourse with her, is not enticing her away "for the purpose of prostitution." State v. Stoyell, 54 Me. 24, 27 (1866). And see Ferguson v. Superior Court, 26 Cal.App. 554, 558, 147 P. 603, 605 (1915); Bayouth v. State, 294 P.2d 856, 859 (Okl.Cr.1956).

26. See State v. Richardson, 117 Mo. 586, 23 S.W. 769 (1893), in which the court approved an instruction which spoke only of an intent to have sexual intercourse with the girl.

Where a young woman living with her parents was enticed by a man to leave her home and meet him for a few hours, and have illicit intercourse with him, after which she returned to her house as usual, he was not guilty of having enticed her away for the purpose of concubinage. But where this practice contin-

ued for a period of nine months the offense is established. Slocum v. People, 90 Ill. 274 (1878). "When a man and a woman, not married, agree to cohabit with each other as though the marriage relation existed between them, without fixing any limit as to the duration of the relation, she becomes his concubine as soon as cohabitation begins." State v. Bussey, 58 Kan. 679, 691, 50 P. 891, 895 (1897).

27. State v. Carroll, 33 S.W.2d 900 (Mo.1930).

28. Some of the statutes punish the taking and compelling, and so forth. West's Ann.Cal.Pen.Code § 266b.

29. State v. Clough, 33 Del. 272, 134 A. 172 (1925).

30. People v. De Marcello, 31 N.Y.S.2d 608 (1941). If defendant enticed a girl from her home for the purpose of concubinage he is guilty of abduction even if the act was not completed and she was unaware of his intent. A sincere belief that he was carrying out religious principles does not make him less guilty because the religious liberty guaranteed by the constitution does not entitle one to violate the law of the land. People v. See, 258 Ill. 152, 101 N.E. 257 (1913).

31. Ark.Stats.Ann. § 2952 (1947).

nent. Thus one was guilty of abduction who persuaded a girl to leave her father's house and sleep with the wrongdoer for three nights despite the fact that he then sent her back home.[32] And a taking for only an hour or two was sufficient for guilt of abduction where during that short period the abductor married the girl[33] or had sexual intercourse with her.[34]

The crime of abduction is not for the protection of the child, as such, but for the maintenance of parental custody against all unlawful interruption. Hence it is no defense that the girl consented to being taken away,[35] or even that the taking was at her suggestion.[36]

The Model Penal Code does not include any section on abduction, under that name, but in the Article on "Kidnaping and Related Offenses" it has a section on "Interference with custody." This would make it an offense for one to take or entice "any child under the age of 18 from the custody of its parent, guardian or other lawful custodian, when he has no privilege to do so."[37] This seems to be the logical solution because much which has crept into the various sections on abduction belongs in the chapter on sexual offenses, whereas the importance of maintaining parental custody against unlawful interruption is not dependent upon the sex of the child.[38]

The original English statute on abduction did not involve conduct which would be kidnaping under the English common law, and this is true also of the American counterparts. But both it and most of them involved conduct which would constitute kidnaping under today's definition. It is safe to assume that if kidnaping had from the first had its present scope, there would have been no statutes on abduction. At present they are tending to disappear.

THE NEW PENAL CODES

Some of the new penal codes have a section on "child stealing," such as providing that a person is guilty of an offense "when, knowing that he or she has no authority to do so, forcibly or fraudulently takes, decoys, or entices away any child with intent to detain or conceal such child from its parents or guardian, or other persons or institutions having the lawful custody of such child, unless the person is a relative of such child, and the person's sole purpose is to assume custody of such child."[39]

SECTION 4.   ABORTION AND RELATED OFFENSES

There has been an unusual lack of precision in the use of words in this field. The word "abortion," in the dictionary sense, means no more than the expulsion of a fetus before it is capable of living. In this sense it is a synonym of "miscarriage." With respect to human beings, however, it has long

---

32. Regina v. Timmins, 8 Cox C.C. 401, 169 Eng.Rep. 1260 (1860).

33. Regina v. Baillie, 8 Cox C.C. 238 (1859).

34. Slocum v. People, 90 Ill. 274 (1878).

35. Regina v. Mankletow, Dears. C.C. 159, 169 Eng.Rep. 678 (1853). The girl, by prearrangement, left her father's house and met **D** at the appointed place.

36. Regina v. Robins, 1 Car. & K. 456, 174 Eng.Rep. 890 (1844). At the girl's suggestion **D** brought a ladder so the girl could get out of the house and elope with him.

37. Model Penal Code, Section 212.4.

38. See   Wis.Stat.Ann.   § 940.32(2) (1982).

39. E.g. Iowa Criminal Code § 710.5 (1978).

been used to refer to an intentionally-induced miscarriage as distinguished from one resulting naturally or by accident. There has been some tendency to use the word to mean a criminal miscarriage,[1] and there would be distinct advantages in assigning this meaning to it; but there are so many references to lawful abortion [2] or justification for abortion [3] that it is necessary to speak of "criminal abortion" [4] or the "crime of abortion" to emphasize the element of culpability.

One who produces a criminal abortion is spoken of as an "abortionist," [5] and the woman whose miscarriage was produced, as an "abortee." [6] A woman is "quick with child" or "pregnant with a quick child" after she has felt the child alive within her.[7] "Foeticide," which might be used with reference to any intentionally-induced miscarriage, at least after the fetus had quickened, is often used for a very special purpose to punish the unlawful killing of an unborn child or fetus caused by an assault and battery or other wrongful force directed against the mother." [8] The killing of a fetus has been classified as murder in some jurisdictions.[9] An "abortifacient" is a drug, article, or other thing designed or intended for producing an abortion except for sales to physicians.[10] Wisconsin prohibits display or advertising of any drug, etc. or device used or intended to be used to produce a miscarriage.[11]

A. ABORTION

Logically speaking, the crime of abortion is the wilful bringing about of the miscarriage of a woman without justification or excuse.[12] Some statutes punish, as a substantive offense, an attempt

1. Commonwealth v. Sierakowski, 154 Pa.Super. 321, 324, 35 A.2d 790 (1944). "Abortion is a crime. . . ." State v. Edwards, 9 N.J.Misc. 34, 36, 152 A. 452 (1930).

"The term 'abortion' by itself does not connote that the expulsion of the fetus is either the product of a criminal act or that it was induced by artificial means. At least, for the purposes of legal discussion, the terms 'abortion' and 'miscarriage' may be considered synonymous." People v. Nixon, 42 Mich.App. 332, 201 N.W.2d 635, 658 (1972).

2. Commonwealth v. Wheeler, 315 Mass. 394, 53 N.E.2d 4 (1944). "The statute does not declare every procurement of an abortion to be an offense. . . ." Moody v. State, 17 Ohio St. 111, 112 (1866). See also State v. Meek, 70 Mo. 355, 357 (1879).

3. McKinney's N.Y.Penal Code § 125.05.3 (1975); Ariz.Rev.Stat.Ann. § 13603; Ark.Stats.Ann. § 41–2551, 2254 (1977).

4. State v. Sturchio, 131 N.J.L. 256, 36 A.2d 301 (1944).

5. State v. Rudman, 126 Me. 177, 181, 136 A. 817, 820 (1927).

6. State v. Lisena, 21 N.J.Misc. 180, 184, 32 A.2d 513, 514 (1943).

7. State v. Forte, 222 N.C. 537, 23 S.E.2d 842 (1943). There has been an occasional attempt to make a distinction between these phrases. "A woman is 'quick with child' from the period of conception and the commencement of gestation, but is only 'pregnant with a quick child' when the child has quickened in the womb." Evans v. People, 49 N.Y. 86, 89 (1872). This, however, is neither the ancient nor the accepted usage. Blackstone, for instance, speaks of a woman "quick with child" just after reference to the stirring of the child in the womb. 1 Bl.Comm. *129.

8. Wyo.Stat.Ann. § 6–4–507 (1977).

9. West's Ann.Cal.Penal Code § 187 (1970).

10. Cf. La.Rev.Stat. § 14:88 (1974), punishing the distribution of abortifacients.

11. Wis.Stat.Ann. § 450.11 (1976). Display of such devices in the course of a free public lecture is protected by the First Amendment. Baird v. LaFollette, 72 Wis.2d 1, 239 N.W.2d 536 (1976).

12. Mississippi State Board of Health v. Johnson, 197 Miss. 417, 427, 19 So.2d 445, 448 (1944). This is the plan of the Model Penal Code § 230.3.

**to cause such an unlawful miscarriage.[13] The offense is frequently
defined in terms of the intent to produce a miscarriage.[14] In some
statutes an attempt itself is called abortion.[15]**

To support a conviction of either murder or manslaughter based upon alleged infanticide it was necessary, at common law, to prove that the child
was born alive. In the words of Sir Edward Coke: "If a woman be quick
with childe, and by a potion or otherwise killeth it in her wombe; or if a man
beat her, whereby the childe dieth in her body, and she is delivered of a dead
childe, this is a great misprision [misdemeanor],[16] and no murder; but if the
childe be borne alive, and dieth of the potion, battery or other cause, this is
murder." [17] In other words it was a common-law misdemeanor to administer
any drug or medicine or to perform an operation on a woman pregnant with
a quick child for the purpose of causing a miscarriage, and thereby causing
the child to be born dead,[18] unless such operation was necessary to save the
life of the woman. Such a misdeed seems not to have been a common-law
offense if the woman was not pregnant with a quick child and the administration or operation was with her consent,[19] although there is some authority
to the contrary.[20] If she did not consent, such an application of force to her
person was a battery upon her, for reasons pointed out in the consideration
of that offense.

Statutes, which differed widely, changed the common law of abortion in
various respects. The following discussion of those statutes, which appeared in previous editions, is repeated here because it gives the background
for the change which was made later, and will be discussed presently. While
the common law required an actual miscarriage for guilt of abortion, it is
necessary to keep in mind the common-law rule by which an attempt to commit any crime was itself punishable [21] although generally regarded as less
culpable than the completed offense. This cannot be relied upon under the
modern codes, without careful study of the particular jurisdiction, because
under many of them the position has been taken that no misdeed is punishable unless authority for such punishment can be found somewhere in the
code itself.[22]

13. Tenn.Code § 39–301(d) (1974);
Conn.Gen.Stat.Ann. § 53.29. This sec-
tion was declared unconstitutional on oth-
er grounds. Abele v. Markle, 342
F.Supp. 800 (D.C.Conn.1972) and 369
F.Supp. 807 (D.C.Conn.1973).

14. Ariz.Rev.Stat.Ann.   § 13–3603
(1978);   McKinney's   N.Y.Penal   Code
§ 125.05.2 (1975). In Iowa the offense is
classified as attempted feticide, Iowa
Code Ann. § 707.7 (1978).

15. New   Mex.Stat.Ann.   § 30–5–3
(1978).

16. Hale said it was "a very great
crime." 1 Hale P.C. *433.

17. 3 Co.Inst. *50.   And see 4
Bl.Comm. *198; State v. Prude, 76 Miss.
543, 24 So. 371 (1899).

18. Abrams v. Foshee, 3 Iowa 274
(1856); Mitchell v. Commonwealth, 78
Ky. 204 (1879); Commonwealth v.

Parker, 50 Mass. 263 (1845); State v.
Cooper, 22 N.J.L. 52 (1849); Williams,
Textbook of Criminal Law, pp. 252–253
(1978).

19. Ibid.

20. "The moment the womb is instinct
with embryo life, and gestation has begun, the crime may be perpetrated.
. . . There was therefore a crime at
common law sufficiently set forth and
charged in the indictment." Mills v.
Commonwealth, 13 Pa. 630, 633–4 (1850).
See also State v. Slagle, 83 N.C. 630, 632
(1880).

21. See infra, under chapter 6, section
3.

22. Some states have taken the position that what was punishable at common
law is still punishable unless otherwise
provided by statute. State v. Cawood, 2
Stew. 360 (Ala.1830). Others have taken

1. MISCARRIAGE

The tendency of modern legislation has been to emphasize the unauthorized operation or administration.[23] As pointed out before an offense created by such a statute is more properly called an attempt to procure an abortion than an "abortion," so far as the literal meaning of the word is concerned; but it is thought of as an unlawful act with a certain intent rather than as an attempt,—and this no doubt explains the tendency to apply the word "abortion" to the unlawful operation or administration itself.[24] Under such a statute the operation or administration, with the forbidden intent, is regarded as a completed offense,—not as merely part of something else. If a miscarriage results this may be important as a matter of evidence, but it adds nothing to the crime itself.[25] The most illuminating case on this point was decided on the matter of venue. Under Iowa law, as it existed at the time, an offense could be prosecuted in any county in which part of the crime occurred.[26] Thus, where an unlawful abortion was performed in Polk county and as a result the woman died in Black Hawk county, the abortionist was properly convicted of *murder* in the latter county because the death of the woman was an essential element of that crime.[27] In another case, however, in which the woman did not die, but suffered a miscarriage in a county other than the one in which the operation was performed, an indictment for "abortion" could not be prosecuted in the county in which the miscarriage took place because the operation had been performed in another county and the miscarriage was no part of the crime at all.[28]

Actual miscarriage is still essential under some of the statutes and where this is true it must be established the same as any other element of the crime and not by mere proof that *something* was expelled from the body which may or may not have been a fetus.[29] Under one rather unusual statutory provision, either miscarriage or death completed the crime of abortion.[30] The provision in some of states is that what would otherwise be the crime of abortion becomes manslaughter if it results in the death of the unborn

the position that: "No act . . . can be punished criminally, except in pursuance of a statute or ordinance lawfully enacted." Mitchell v. State, 42 Ohio St. 383, 385 (1884). In Iowa, for example, while not questioning that an attempt to commit suicide was punishable at common law, the court held that it was not an offense in Iowa because not included in the Code. State v. Campbell, 217 Iowa 848, 251 N.W. 717 (1933).

It should be added however that modern penal codes contain a general attempt section. See infra Chapter 6, Section 3.

23. Tenn.Code § 39–301(d) (1974). The Illinois abortion law defines abortion as ". . . the use of any instrument, medicine, drug or other substance, whatever, with the intent to procure a miscarriage of any woman, . . .," Ill. Ann.Stat. § 81–53 (1978).

24. La.Rev.Stat. § 14–87 (1974).

25. Hightower v. State, 62 Ariz. 351, 158 P.2d 156 (1945); State v. Lisena, 21 N.J.Misc. 180, 32 A.2d 513 (1943); State v. Sturchio, 131 N.J.L. 256, 36 A.2d 301 (1944).   Ariz.Rev.Stat.Ann. § 13–3603 (1978).

26. Iowa Code Ann. § 753.4 repealed Acts of 1972 (64 G.A.) ch. 1124 § 282. Now see, Iowa Code Ann. § 803.3 (1978).

27. State v. Sweeney, 203 Iowa 1305, 214 N.W. 735 (1927).

28. State v. Hollenbeck, 36 Iowa 112 (1872).

29. State v. Wilson, 116 Or. 615, 241 P. 843 (1925).

30. Hauk v. State, 148 Ind. 238, 46 N.E. 127, 47 N.E. 465 (1897); Swanson v. State, 222 Ind. 217, 52 N.E.2d 616 (1944).

child.[31] Such statutes tend somewhat to continue the common-law distinction between a "quick child" and a fetus that has not quickened.[32] According to the view of one court, a child has no distinct existence until advanced to that state of maturity designated by the term "quick with child," and until a woman has herself felt the child alive within her there is no "child" to be destroyed.[33] Another court held that "in the case of the death of such child" in its statute means the death of the fetus either before or after quickening.[34]

Manslaughter statutes of the type mentioned sometimes provide for this offense in event of the death either of the unborn child or the mother.[35] The death of the woman, it should be pointed out, resulting from an unlawful abortion committed upon her will be either murder or manslaughter under the general rules of homicide [36] unless some other provision is made by statute.[37] One modern statute subjects a person performing an abortion to homicide and manslaughter penalties for failing to preserve the life of a person born during an abortion.[38]

2. PREGNANCY

With reference to the matter of pregnancy the statutes tend to fall into three different patterns, although there are more than three variations in the actual wording. The first type speaks of "any woman." [39] Under such a provision it is not important whether she was pregnant or not so long as the wrongdoer thought she was and acted with the intention of producing a miscarriage.[40] The second type of statute makes use of some such phrase as "any pregnant woman," [41] or "any woman pregnant with child." [42] Under any such wording the pregnancy of the woman is an indispensable element of the crime.[43] On the other hand it is not essential for the abortionist to have positive knowledge of the woman's condition. If she really was preg-

---

31. State v. Willson, 116 Or. 615, 241 P. 843 (1925). One court held that such a statute does not apply to the mother herself. State v. Prude, 76 Miss. 543, 24 So. 871 (1899).

32. Miss.Code Ann. 1972 § 97–3–37.

33. State v. Forte, 222 N.C. 537, 23 S.E.2d 842 (1943).

34. State v. Atwood, 54 Or. 526, 102 P. 295, 104 P. 195 (1909).

35. Vernon's Ann.Mo.Stat. § 565.026 (1979).

36. People v. Clapp, 67 Cal.App.2d 197, 153 P.2d 758 (1944); State v. Crofford, 133 Iowa 478, 110 N.W. 921 (1907); Smith v. State, 33 Me. 48 (1851).

37. The statute may impose a severe penalty without use of the word manslaughter. D.C.Code 1973, § 22–201. ". . . if death of the mother results therefrom, the person procuring or producing or attempting to procure or produce the abortion or miscarriage shall be guilty of second degree murder."

38. Me.Rev.Stat.Ann. § 1594 (1978).

39. E.g. Conn.Gen.Stat.Ann. § 53–29 (1975); D.C.Code 1973, § 22–201.

40. People v. Gallardo, 41 Cal.2d 57, 257 P.2d 29 (1953); Urga v. State, 155 Fla. 86, 20 So.2d 685 (1945); Commonwealth v. Cheng, 310 Mass. 293, 37 N.E.2d 1010 (1941).

41. See for example Ala.Code 1975, § 13A–13–7; Ariz.Rev.Stat. § 3603 (1978).

42. Ga.Code § 26–1101 (1953). The current Georgia statute uses the phrase "any woman." Ga.Code § 1201 (1973). Some use other variations such as "any woman with child." Ark.Stats.Ann. § 41–2551 (1977). ". . . the pregnancy of a woman . . . ." Colo.Rev. Stats. § 18–6–092 (1973).

43. State v. Stewart, 52 Iowa 284, 3 N.W. 99 (1879); State v. Sturchio, 131 N.J.L. 256, 36 A.2d 301 (1944). After the Iowa case above the Iowa legislature amended the statute by striking out the word "pregnant." The current Iowa law provides for the crime of "feticide" for the "intentional termination of a human

nant, and he thought so, this part of the crime is complete even under such a statute.[44] It is possible to find statutes with the phrase "viable fetus", but these are usually provisions for something other than abortion, such as raising the offense to manslaughter or like offense if an aborted fetus born alive is destroyed.[45] Reference to this matter in the abortion statute itself (which is rare) is likely to be by way of negation, such as: "before or after the period of quickening . . ."[46]

A third type of statute is similar to those mentioned above, however the legislature has not been willing to leave anything to inference and has clearly expressed itself in a prohibition covering "the real or apparent pregnancy of a woman . . ."[47]

3. INTENT

The original concept of this offense was the unlawfully induced miscarriage, but the whole emphasis now is upon the unlawful operation or administration with intent to produce a miscarriage. The statutes tend to be very much alike in this respect, the common phrases being "with intent to procure the miscarriage,"[48] "with intent thereby to procure the miscarriage,"[49] "with intent to procure upon her a miscarriage or abortion,"[50] "with intent to produce an abortion,"[51] "with intent to produce a miscarriage or abortion,"[52] "with intent of procuring a premature delivery,"[53] or "with intent to cause a miscarriage . . ."[54] One state simply states the intent as "to induce an abortion."[55]

This specific intent is of the very essence of the crime,[56] and the fact that a brutal attack upon a pregnant woman has resulted in a miscarriage by her is not sufficient to constitute this offense if the assailant had no such purpose or intention in mind.[57]

---

pregnancy . . .," Iowa Code Ann. § 707.7 (1978).

44. People v. Browning, 132 Cal.App. 136, 22 P.2d 784 (1933).

45. Iowa Code Ann. § 707.9 (1978). See also Ark.Stats. § 41–2501 (1977).

46. Ark.Stat. § 41–2551 (1977). The phrase "either pregnant or quick with child" was interpreted to mean pregnant with a quick child. State v. Jordan, 227 N.C. 579, 42 S.E.2d 674 (1947). "In this section 'unborn child' means a human being from the time of conception until it is born alive." W.S.A. (Wis.) 940.04 (1957).

47. Colo.Rev.Stat. § 18–6–103 (1973).

48. See for example Smith-Hurd Ill.Ann.Stat. ch. 38 § 81–22(6) (1977).

49. Ariz.Rev.Stat.Ann. §§ 13–3603, 3604 (1978); West's Ann.Cal.Pen.Code § 274 (1977).

50. Conn.Gen.Stat.Ann. § 53–29 (1958).

51. Ark.Stats. § 41–2551 (1977).

52. Ga.Code § 26–1201 (1978).

53. La.Stat.Ann. § 14:87 (1974).

54. McKinney's N.Y.Penal Code § 125.05.

55. Code of Ala.Tit. 13 § 8–4 (1975).

56. Polly v. People, 107 Colo. 6, 108 P.2d 220 (1940); State v. Sturchio, 131 N.J.L. 256, 36 A.2d 301 (1944); State v. Robinson, 420 S.W.2d 272 (Mo.1967).

57. Slattery v. People, 76 Ill. 217 (1875); Limicy v. State, 148 Tex.Cr.R. 130, 185 S.W.2d 571 (1945).

4. MEANS

One of the simplest forms of statute on this subject is the following:

"Abortion is the performance of any of the following acts, with the intent of procuring premature delivery of the embryo or fetus:

(1) Administration of any drug, potion, or other substance to a female; or

(2) Use of any instrument or any other means whatsoever on a female." [58]

These two types of means are commonly included in the statutes with many variations in the wording.

The courts have emphasized that the word "instrument" as used in such a statute is not limited to surgical instruments,[59] but includes any means of applying external force to produce miscarriage.[60] The Alabama court pointed out that abortion may be induced by use of the hand,—this coming under the catch-all phrase "other means." [61]

One who arranged for an unlawful abortion with instruments to be performed by another was held guilty although not present when the operation was performed; [62] and the same result was reached in the case of a defendant who sent the medicine to produce an abortion and directed the woman, either in person or by letter, how to take it although not present when the medicine was delivered to or taken by her.[63]

Since the whole emphasis under most of the statutes is the doing of the prohibited act, with intent to produce a miscarriage, it is no defense that the means employed or substance used would not effect such a result so long as it was used with that intention.[64]

5. THE ABORTEE

Since the common-law crime of abortion included guilt of the woman herself if, being quick with child, she destroyed it "by a potion or otherwise," [65] and modern statutes are intended to enlarge the scope of that offense, it is clear that her solicitation or consent is no defense to an abortion performed upon her by another.[66] This can be found expressly stated in a statute,[67] but for the most part has seemed too obvious to warrant such inclusion. It would seem that the history back of such legislation would be sufficient to hold a woman guilty of such offense if she does the forbidden act herself or willingly submits thereto, without an express statement to this effect in the statute; but the trend of the cases has been the other way,—partly as a result of the construction of the exact wording of some of the laws and part-

---

58. La.Stat.Ann. § 14:87 (1974).

59. People v. Clapp, 67 Cal.App.2d 197, 153 P.2d 758 (1944); Polly v. People, 107 Colo. 6, 108 P.2d 220 (1940).

The finger is an "instrument" within the meaning of the abortion statute. Palmer v. People, 162 Colo. 92, 424 P.2d 766 (1967).

60. Wilson v. State, 36 Okl.Cr. 148, 252 P. 1106 (1927).

61. Dowdy v. State, 19 Ala.App. 503, 98 So. 365 (1923).

62. State v. Weiss, 130 N.J.L. 149, 31 A.2d 848 (1943), aff'd 131 N.J.L. 228, 35 A.2d 895 (1944).

63. Clayton v. State, 186 Ark. 713, 55 S.W.2d 88 (1932).

64. State v. Fitzgerald, 49 Iowa 260 (1878).

65. 3 Co.Inst. *50.

66. State v. Fitzgerald, 174 S.W.2d 211 (Mo.1943); State v. Edwards, 9 N.J.Misc. 34, 152 A. 452 (1930).

67. Ky.Rev.Stat. § 311.720 (1974).

ly in the effort to avoid the difficulties of evidence which would result from holding her to be an accomplice of the actual abortionist.[68] Despite this attitude on the part of the courts it has not been uncommon for the legislative body to provide a penalty for "any woman who shall do or suffer anything to be done" [69] for the forbidden purpose, or who for such purpose "solicits from any person any medicine, drug or substance whatever, and takes it, or who submits to an operation, or to the use of any means whatever." [70] Her offense has often been held to be a different crime than that committed by the other.[71]

6. JUSTIFICATION AND EXCUSE

What would otherwise be a criminal abortion is justified as a matter of common law if necessary to preserve the life of the woman. Even if not so necessary it is excused if done by one acting in the good-faith belief of such necessity, provided such belief is based upon reasonable grounds.[72] Statutes on the subject should be construed in the light of these common-law principles, and such justification or excuse should be recognized as applicable thereto even if not mentioned therein. The trend of authority is in that direction.[73] It is possible to find the suggestion that no excuse will be recognized if not incorporated in the statute itself,[74] but such a position is utterly indefensible. If a woman should hold up a pharmacist at the point of a pistol and require him to furnish her a drug which he knew she intended to use for the purpose of inducing a miscarriage, the druggist would not be guilty of crime even if the statute expressly forbade the "giving or providing" of any such drug and did not mention an exception in case of one forced to do so under threat of death.

Until recently it was common to speak of "therapeutic abortion." The literal meaning of the term is an abortion induced for medical reasons, but it was commonly understood to mean one for the purpose of saving the mother's life, since justifiable abortion was generally thus restricted in this country, England and Canada.[75] There was a growing belief that a substantial

68. Hatfield v. Gano, 15 Iowa 177 (1863); Simmons v. Victory Industrial Life Ins. Co. of La., 139 So. 68 (La.App.1932); Commonwealth v. Bricker, 74 Pa.Super. 234, 239 (1920).

69. Conn.Gen.Stat.Ann.   § 53–30 (1958).

70. Ariz.Rev.Stat. § 13–3604 (1978); West's Ann.Cal.Pen.Code § 275 (1977).

71. State v. Carey, 76 Conn. 342, 56 A. 632 (1904); People v. McGonegal, 136 N.Y. 62, 32 N.E. 616 (1892).

72. In a prosecution for abortion under a statute providing that the act was a crime "unless such miscarriage shall be necessary to save her life," the court held there was no guilt if the doctor in good faith believed it was necessary even if it were not so in fact. In other words the court added the common-law excuse to the statutory justification. State v. Dunklebarger, 206 Iowa 971, 221 N.W.

592 (1928). See also the cases in the following note.

73. In addition to the square holding in the preceding case see the dicta in the following: Beasley v. People, 89 Ill. 571, 577 (1878); Commonwealth v. Wheeler, 315 Mass. 394, 395, 53 N.E.2d 4, 5 (1944).

74. State v. Rudman, 126 Me. 177, 139 A. 817 (1927).

The Supreme Court's decision in Roe v. Wade, 410 U.S. 113, 93 S.Ct. 705 (1973), makes it clear that any limitation would be constitutionally invalid unless a statute incorporates a standard compatible with the exceptions recognized in that case.

75. "In the United States, England and Canada, the prevailing pattern is absolute prohibition, except for the purpose of saving the mother's *life*. Only half a dozen states go so far as to recognize preservation of *health* as an independent

relaxation of this restriction was desirable. Ethical and religious views were not overlooked but the motivating influence was the fact that unauthorized abortions were being performed in astounding numbers,[76] coupled with the belief that any abortion should be performed by a competent medical practitioner with hospital facilities rather than by a "quack" under unfavorable conditions.[77] The leading suggestions were that abortion should be authorized not only when necessary to save the life of the mother, but also when it is important to preserve (1) her health, including (2) mental health, and when it is necessary to prevent (3) gravely defective offspring or (4) offspring resulting from rape or incest. This is substantially the provision of the Model Penal Code, with the requirement that the abortion be performed only in a licensed hospital except in case of emergency, and only upon the certificate of two physicians explaining why they believe the abortion necessary.[78]

In 1967 two states, Colorado [79] and North Carolina,[80] following in general the pattern of the Model Penal Code, pioneered in this field, making the first significant changes in abortion legislation in this country.[81] In California the opinion was that a Therapeutic Abortion Act needs to be specific not only as to what shall be permitted, but also under what conditions; and that a penal code is not the place for detailing approved medical procedure. Hence the California Health and Safety Code was amended by including a Therapeutic Abortion Act, and the appropriate sections of the Penal Code were amended to provide exceptions as provided in the other Act.[82]

This was how the law stood up to the time in 1973 when *Roe*,[83] decided by the Supreme Court, made a drastic change in the law of abortion. In that case the Court concluded that the "right of privacy, . . . is broad enough to encompass a woman's decision whether or not to terminate her pregnancy." [84] It rejected, however, the argument that this right is absolute, holding it reasonable for a state to decide that at some point in time another interest, that of health of the mother or that of potential human life, becomes significantly involved. The conclusion was that the permissibility of state regulation must be viewed in three stages. During the first trimester the abortion decision must be left entirely to the woman and her physician

justification." Model Penal Code 146 (Tent.Draft No. 9, 1959).

76. "Estimates of the yearly number of abortions vary from 333,000 to 2,000,000, of which the proportion of illegal abortions has been put at anywhere from 30% to 70%." Id. at 147.

77. For an elaborate discussion of the problem see id. pp. 146–166, which includes liberal citations to the leading authorities. And for the discussion of the proposed section of the Model Penal Code at the annual meeting of the Institute see 36 ALI Proceedings 252–282 (1959) and 39 ALI Proceedings 188–191 (1962).

78. Model Penal Code, Section 230.3.

79. C.R.S.A. (Colo.) '67 Supp., §§ 40–2–50 to 52.

80. N.C.G.S. § 14–46 (Supp.1967).

81. Lader, Abortion 85–91 (1966). For a collection of all state laws on abortion at the time it was written, see the Appendix at the end of an interesting article by Sands, The Therapeutic Abortion Act: An Answer to the Opposition. 13 UCLA L.Rev. 285, 310–12 (1966).

82. Chapter 327 of the 1967 Regular Session, the amendment commencing with Section 25950 of the Health and Safety Code. For a discussion of this legislation see Note, The California Therapeutic Abortion Act: An Analysis. 19 Hastings L.J. 242 (1967).

83. Roe v. Wade, 410 U.S. 113, 93 S.Ct. 705 (1973). At the same time the Court decided Doe v. Bolton, 410 U.S. 179, 93 S.Ct. 739 (1973), in which it held, *inter alia*, that physician-appellants have standing to challenge the constitutionality of state abortion legislation.

84. 410 U.S. at 153, 93 S.Ct. at 727.

without interference by the state. After the first stage the state may, if it chooses, reasonably regulate the abortion procedure to preserve and protect maternal health. Subsequent to viability, a point intentionally left flexible for professional determination, the state may regulate an abortion to protect the life of the fetus and may even proscribe abortion except where necessary for the preservation of the life or health of the mother. The word "viable" was used to signify the point at which the fetus is "potentially able to live outside the mother's womb, albeit with artificial aid, . . ." a point "usually placed" at about seven months, but may occur earlier.[85]

After the earlier Missouri enactment had been held unconstitutional,[86] the state enacted a new statute intended "to reasonably regulate abortion in conformance with the decisions of the Supreme Court of the United States." The Act provided, *inter alia*, that during the first twelve weeks of pregnancy no abortion should be performed without the written consent of the woman, and that unless necessary to preserve the life of the woman no abortion should be performed without the written consent of the woman's husband, or if she was unmarried and under 18 years of age, without the written consent of one of her parents or person in *loco parentis*. The provision requiring written consent of the woman was held to be reasonable and valid; but the provisions requiring consent of the husband or parent were held to be unconstitutional, because the state may not delegate "a veto power which the state itself is absolutely and totally prohibited from exercising during the first trimester of pregnancy."[87]

The Supreme Court struck down a Pennsylvania statute[88] for being vague and unnecessarily intrusive into the physician's legitimate area of medical judgment in performing abortions "where it required the physician to use a statutorily prescribed technique when the fetus is viable."[89] The Court noted the judgment of viability was one for medical judgment and the state could not impose a standard of viability based on any one factor. The statute also did not provide for an adequate standard of mens rea to allow for legitimate medical judgment and the physician's duty to the patient.

The effect of the Supreme Court's decisions restricting the power to control abortions has been to raise doubt as to the constitutionality of abortion statutes in many states. Several other states have responded by enacting statutes in conformity with the Court's pronouncements.[90] The effect has also been to change the focus of the abortion problem from a criminal matter to a social policy question; and some states have removed their abortion provisions from the penal code.[91]

Abortions performed outside the doctor-patient relationship are not within the constitutional allowances of the Supreme Court's decisions and may still be prosecuted under the common-law standards.[92]

85. 410 U.S. at 160, 93 S.Ct. at 730.

86. Danforth v. Rodgers, 414 U.S. 1035, 94 S.Ct. 534 (1973).

87. Planned Parenthood of Central Missouri v. Danforth, 428 U.S. 52, 96 S.Ct. 2831 (1976). The statute made the same provisions for written consent for an abortion after 12 weeks of pregnancy, but such provisions were not before the Court.

88. Purdon's Penn.Stat.Ann.Tit. 35 § 6605(a) & 7 (1973).

89. Colautti v. Franklin, 439 U.S. 379, 99 S.Ct. 675 (1979).

90. Abortion Statutes After Danforth: An Examination, 15 J.Fam.L. 537 (1977).

91. No.Dak.Cent.Code 14–02.1 (1975).

92. A conviction has been upheld against a non-physician where the statute as applied to physicians was unconstitu-

The Utah abortion statute provides: "To enable the physician to exercise his best medical judgment, he shall: . . . (2) notify, if possible, the parents or guardian of the woman upon whom the abortion is to be performed, if she is a minor or the husband of the woman if she is married." A violation is punishable by imprisonment up to a year or a fine up to $1000. A 15-year-old girl in the first trimester of pregnancy desired an abortion and did not want her parents to know about it. When told by her physician that the abortion could not be performed without prior notice to her parents, she brought an action to have the statute declared unconstitutional. The court pointed out that this statute merely requires notice to the parents. They may be able to provide information which the physician can consider in forming his clinical judgment, but they have no veto power over the abortion. That decision is left entirely to the female and her physician. And since the state has a special interest in encouraging an unmarried pregnant minor to seek parental advice on such an important matter the statute was upheld.[93]

A city ordinance imposed a series of costly medical and building code regulations on abortion clinics in general and hence included those performing first-trimester abortions. It required each abortion service to be licensed and provided fine and imprisonment for a violation of any of its provisions. The medical testimony was to the effect that compliance with the requirements would require plaintiff to double or triple its fee, which would place it beyond the reach of many desiring an abortion. It was held that this ordinance burdened and denied the constitutional right of a woman to choose an abortion and was invalid.[94]

B. RESTRICTIONS ON ADVERTISING

Restriction on advertising covers many things and is referred to here only insofar as it relates to the present problem. Statutes forbidding the sale of abortifacients often forbid also the advertising thereof. In other jurisdictions the enactment may be directed against the advertising alone, such as the following:

"Every person who willfully writes, composes or publishes any notice or advertisement of any medicine or means for producing or facilitating a miscarriage or abortion, or who offers his services by any notice, advertisement, or otherwise, to assist in the accomplishment of any such purpose is guilty of a felony and shall be punished as provided in the Penal Code." [95]

In some states similar statutes provide for a misdemeanor penalty.[96] Idaho has provided an exception to the prohibition on advertising abortions for "licensed physicians of this state and those licensed or registered health care providers" acting under the supervision of a physician.[97]

tional. State v. Menillo, 171 Conn. 141, 368 A.2d 136 (1976).

93. H. L. v. Matheson, 604 P.2d 907 (Utah 1979). The decision of the Utah court was affirmed. H. L. v. Matheson, 450 U.S. 398, 101 S.Ct. 1164 (1981).

94. Mahoning Women's Center v. Hunter, 610 F.2d 456 (6th Cir. 1979).

Certain provisions of the Illinois abortion statute were held unconstitutional, including the 24-hour mandatory waiting period between consultation and operation, and the requirement that the woman be provided with a true copy of her pregnancy test by the physician who was to perform the operation. Charles v. Carey, 627 F.2d 772 (7th Cir. 1980).

95. West's Ann.Cal.Bus. & Prof.Code § 601 (1974).

96. Ariz.Rev.Stat. § 13–3605 (1978).

97. Idaho Code § 18–603 (1979).

The Supreme Court has cast doubt on the validity of broad prohibitions on advertising abortions by ruling that Virginia could not punish for an advertisement published in Virginia for lawful abortion services in New York.[98] The inference is clearly that a state may not totally prohibit advertisements of abortion services that are otherwise lawfully provided.

C. FEDERAL OFFENSES

Abortifacients have been grouped with a number of other things, such as obscene books and pictures or articles for any indecent or immoral use, and declared "nonmailable" by Act of Congress. Knowingly to deposit any such article for mailing or to take from the mails for the purpose of disposition is a federal felony.[99] It is also a federal felony to deposit such an article with an express company or other common carrier for interstate transportation,[1] or to import it into the United States from a foreign country.[2]

There is some indication that the federal courts will give such statutes a rather reasonable construction. A circuit court of appeals had occasion to interpret the former law forbidding deposit of contraceptives with a common carrier for interstate transportation. The statute described the forbidden cargo as any "article or thing designed, adapted or intended for the prevention of conception, or producing an abortion." It was held that proof of intention was essential to guilt and that sending articles having a legitimate medical and surgical use in the prevention of disease, and being shipped for that purpose, was not a violation.[3] The mailing of abortional literature and information on birth control is outside the prohibition of the statute.[4] General knowledge rather than specific intent is all that is required to support a conviction for mailing obscene material.[5]

SECTION 5.   RAPE AND CARNAL KNOWLEDGE OF A CHILD

Rape is unlawful sexual intercourse with a female person without her consent.[1] It is a common-law felony.[2]

98. Bigelow v. Virginia, 421 U.S. 809, 95 S.Ct. 2222 (1975).

99. 18 U.S.C.A. § 1461.

1. 18 U.S.C.A. § 1462.

2. Ibid.

3. Davis v. United States, 62 F.2d 473 (6th Cir. 1933).

In the present statute the reference to contraceptives was deleted. In Griswold v. Connecticut, 381 U.S. 479, 85 S.Ct. 1678 (1965), the Court struck down as unconstitutional a Connecticut statute making use of contraceptives or assisting or causing another to use such devices. The Court held such statute to be an invasion of the right of marital privacy.

A Massachusetts statute prohibiting selling, lending or giving away of a contraceptive was also ruled unconstitutional in Eisenstadt v. Baird, 405 U.S. 438, 92 S.Ct. 1029 (1972).

Recently, a New York anti-contraceptive statute restricting and prohibiting distribution of contraceptives was ruled unconstitutional. Carey v. Population Services International, 431 U.S. 678, 97 S.Ct. 2010 (1977). Valid anti-contraceptive legislation is virtually extinct.

4. Associated Students for University of California v. Attorney General, 368 F.Supp. 11 (D.C.Cal.1973).

5. United States v. Linetsky, 553 F.2d 192 (5th Cir. 1976).

§ 5

1. "Rape is the carnal knowledge of a female forcibly and against her will." People v. Cieslak, 319 Ill. 221, 149 N.E. 815 (1925); People v. Celmars, 332 Ill. 113, 163 N.E. 421 (1928). Rape is "unlawful carnal knowledge of a woman without her consent". Adams v. Commonwealth, 219 Ky. 711, 713, 294 S.W. 151, 152 (1927). Rape is forcible ravishment of a woman against her will, to which she makes the utmost possible re-

2. See note 2 on page 198.

Carnal knowledge of a child is unlawful sexual intercourse with a willing female child under the age of consent. It is a statutory crime, usually a felony.

Carnal knowledge of a child is frequently declared to be rape by statute and where this is true the offense is popularly known as "statutory rape" although not so designated in the statute.[3]

There was no rape according to the common law of England except where the unlawful intercourse was without the consent of the woman.[4] An ancient English statute declared that unlawful carnal knowledge of a woman child under the age of ten years was felony, without the limitation that it should be against her will. This permitted Coke to define rape as "unlawful and carnal knowledge and abuse of any woman above the age of ten years against her will, or of a woman child under the age of ten years with her will or against her will."[5] This statute is old enough to be a part of the common law of this country,[6] and it is arguable that our definition of rape as a common-law felony should be so worded. This, however, would require undue complexity of statement due to the fact that our statutes have made different provisions with regard to the age of consent, some of them raising it to as much as eighteen years,[7] "and as long as eleven years."[8] The trend in recent years has been to reduce the age of consent,[9] or to specially punish the offense where there is a substantial difference in age between the man

sistance. State v. Johnson, 316 Mo. 86, 289 S.W. 847 (1926). " 'Rape' consists in accomplishing the act of sexual intercourse by force and against the will of the female assaulted." Starr v. State, 205 Wis. 310, 311, 237 N.W. 96, 97 (1931). "Rape is the carnal knowledge of any woman above the age of consent against her will, and of a female child under the age of consent with or against her will: its essence is the felonious and violent penetration of the person of the female. . . ." Commonwealth v. McCan, 277 Mass. 199, 203, 178 N.E. 633, 634 (1931).

2. Originally, it was a capital offense. During one period the characteristic punishment was castration, often coupled with blinding. 2 Pollock & Maitland 490 (2d ed. 1899).

3. In Meloon v. Helgemoe, 564 F.2d 602 (1st Cir. 1977), it was held that a statutory-rape law violates the equal-protection clause by punishing males who have sex with underage females while not punishing females who have sex with underage males. The California court held that such a statute does not violate equal protection because an acceptable distinction is afforded by "the immutable physiological fact that it is the female exclusively who can become pregnant." Michael M. v. Superior Court of Sonoma County, 25 Cal.3d 608, 159 Cal.Rptr. 340, 601 P.2d 572 (1979). The court said that no state court has held such a statute in violation of equal protection, and that

Meloon, supra, is the only court that has taken such a position. The dissent did not question these statistics, but cited 31 states in which it has been provided by statute, in effect, that it is a crime for any person to have sex with any underage person other than the spouse.

The United States Supreme Court upheld the constitutionality of the California statute and affirmed the California court's position in Michael M. v. Superior Court of Sonoma County, 450 U.S. 464, 101 S.Ct. 1200 (1981).

4. 4 Bl.Comm. *210; 1 East P.C. 436 (1803).

5. 3 Co.Inst. *60.

6. Nider v. Commonwealth, 140 Ky. 684, 131 S.W. 1024 (1910).

7. See, for example, Idaho Code § 18–6101 (1977); West's Ann.Cal.Pen. Code § 261.5 (1970). The crime in California is called unlawful sexual intercourse. V.T.C.A.Penal Code § 21.09 (1975), "younger than seventeen years." As to age limit of fourteen see Hawaii Rev.Stat. (1972) § 707–731. Age twelve, see Ky.Rev.Stat. 510.040 (1974).

8. Ark.Stats. § 41–1803(c) (1975).

9. Indiana defines the offense as child molesting and sets the age at 12 for a Class B felony and 16 for a Class C felony. Burns' Ind.Ann.Stat. § 35–42–4–3 (1978).

and woman.[10]   And whether these enactments have included intercourse with a willing female under the age of consent in the general statute on rape, or have made separate provision for carnal knowledge of a child, they have merged the rule of the old English statute therein.[11]   Some of them provide for different penalties dependent upon the age of the girl, but they do so upon their own specification of age limits.[12]   If we are differentiating between "common-law rape" and "statutory rape" in one state, or between "rape" and "carnal knowledge of a child" in another, we do so as if common-law rape in this country were identical with common-law rape in England, and without reference to that early English enactment.

The point should not be labored one way or the other because it is a mere matter of terminology and does not affect the result.   Neither the statutes nor the instructions to the jury customarily make use of such terms as "common-law rape" or "statutory rape."   They speak more precisely with reference to the elements of the particular offense.   And if all intercourse with a girl under the age of consent has been incorporated into one statute with one penalty (or with different penalties dependent upon age alone) it is immaterial, so far as the outcome of a particular case is concerned, whether the unlawful intercourse was with or without the consent of the girl, if she was under the age specified.   Actually, the breadth of difference in statutory provisions is too wide to permit any simple generalization which will be applicable to every state.   One provision, for example, applies the "age of consent" to boys as well as to girls and includes within the offense of carnal knowledge of a child the act of a woman who has sexual intercourse with a boy below that age.[13]

Some idea of the legislative range may be obtained by examining three different statutes as they were worded a few years ago.

I

"Rape is the carnal knowledge of a female forcibly and against her will." [14]   It is a capital offense.[15]

"Every person convicted of carnally knowing or abusing unlawfully, any female person under the age of sixteen years . . . "   shall be punished by imprisonment for not less than one year nor more than twenty-one years.[16]

---

10.   N.J.Stat.Ann. 2C:14–2 (1978) "The victim is less than 13 years old and the actor is at least 4 years older than the victim."

11.   See the various rape statutes cited in this section.

12.   See, for example, Rev.Code Wash.Ann. 9.79.200–220 (1975).

13.   Iowa Criminal Law § 701.1 (1978). The fact that statutory rape does not apply to underage boys as well as to underage girls does not render it unconstitutional.   "On the other side of the situation a boy under age 16 cannot be pregnant and therefore is not in the same classification as is the girl of that age." State v. Housekeeper, 588 P.2d 139, 141 (Utah 1978).   Accord, In re W.E.P., 318

A.2d 286 (D.C.App.1974); Olson v. State, 95 Nev. 1, 588 P.2d 1018 (1979).   Contra, it violates the equal-protection clause. Meloon v. Helgemoe, 564 F.2d 602 (1st Cir. 1977).

14.   Ark.Stats.Ann. § 41–3401 (1964).

15.   Id. at § 41–3403.

In Coker v. Georgia, 433 U.S. 584, 97 S.Ct. 2861 (1977), the Supreme Court held that the death penalty was unconstitutional when imposed for the rape of an adult woman.   In Upshaw v. State, 350 So.2d 1358 (Miss.1977), the Court upheld the death penalty for the rape of a child under the age of twelve years.

16.   Id. at § 41–3406.

II

"Whoever ravishes and carnally knows any female who has attained her 14th birthday, by force and against her will, or unlawfully and carnally knows and abuses a female child who has not attained her 14th birthday, shall be punished by imprisonment for any term of years." [17]

"Whoever, having attained his 18th birthday, has carnal knowledge of the body of any female child who has attained her 14th birthday but has not attained her 16th birthday shall be punished by a fine of not more than $500 or by imprisonment for not more than two years. This section shall not apply to cases of rape as defined in section 3151." [18]

III

"Rape is the act of sexual intercourse accomplished with a female, not the wife of the perpetrator, under either of the following circumstances:

1st.   Where the female is under the age of sixteen years.

2nd.   Where the female is over the age of sixteen years and under the age of eighteen years, and of previous chaste and virtuous character.

3rd.   Where she is incapable through lunacy or any other unsoundness of mind, whether temporary or permanent, of giving legal consent.

4th.   Where she resists but her resistance is overcome by force and violence.

5th.   Where she is prevented from resistance by threats of immediate and great bodily harm, accompanied by apparent power of execution.

6th.   Where she is prevented from resisting by any intoxicating narcotic, or anesthetic agent, administered by or with the privy of the accused.

7th.   Where she is at the time unconscious of the nature of the act and this is known to the accused.

8th.   Where she submits under the belief that the person committing the act is her husband, and this belief is induced by artifice, pretense or concealment practiced by the accused, or by the accused in collusion with her husband with intent to induce such a belief. And in all cases of collusion between the accused and the husband of the female, both the husband and the accused shall be deemed guilty of rape.[19]

Most of the specifications of the third statute would constitute rape under the common-law interpretation of "without her consent" or "against her will," leaving the difference more of form than of substance.

---

17.   Me.Rev.Stat.Ann.Tit. 17, § 3151 (1964).

18.   Id. at Tit. 17, § 3152.

19.   21 Okl.Stat.Ann. § 1111 (1958).

A. SEXUAL INTERCOURSE

The ancient term for the act itself was "carnal knowledge" [20] and this is found in some of the recent cases [21] and statutes.[22] The phrase "sexual intercourse," more common today apart from legal literature, is also found in recent cases [23] and statutes.[24] Either term, when the reference is to rape, is sometimes coupled with the word "ravish." [25] And unlawful intercourse with a girl under the age of consent is often characterized as "carnal knowledge and abuse." [26]

Whatever form of words is used to express the idea, the really important question is to determine exactly what is needed for conviction in these cases. An occasional suggestion may be found to the effect that emission must be established.[27] If the theory back of this idea was pressed far enough it might reach the point of recognizing the effective use of a contraceptive as a complete defense to a prosecution for either rape or carnal knowledge of a child. It is safe to assume that no court would go this far. In fact, the premise itself is false. The sound rule which prevails very generally, if not uniformly today, is that emission is neither necessary [28] nor sufficient [29] to establish guilt in these cases. The essential element in this regard is sexual penetration.[30] Some statutes now describe the crime as unlawful sexual pen-

---

20. See 3 Co.Inst. *60; 4 Bl.Comm. *210.

21. People v. Selmars, 332 Ill. 113, 163 N.E. 421 (1928); Adams v. Commonwealth, 219 Ky. 711, 713, 294 S.W. 151, 152 (1927); State v. Whitener, 228 S.C. 244, 89 S.E.2d 701 (1955); Sanchez v. State, 567 P.2d 270, 275 (Wyo.1977).

22. Alaska Stats. 11.15.120 (1962); D.C.Code 1967, 22–2801; N.C.Gen.Stats. § 14–21 (1973).

23. State v. Lora, 213 Kan. 184, 515 P.2d 1086 (1973); Starr v. State, 205 Wis. 310, 311, 237 N.W. 96, 97 (1931).

24. La.Rev.Stat.Ann. 14:41 (1978); So.Dak.Compiled Laws 22–22–1 (1978); 21 Okl.St.Ann. § 1111 (1958); Wis.St. § 940.225 (1978).

25. "Ravish a woman", S.C.Code 1962, § 16–71. "The words 'rape' and 'ravish' are synonymous terms . . . of wide usage and plain English . . . ," State v. Moorer, 241 S.C. 487, 129 S.E.2d 330, 336 (1963); "Forcibly ravishing any female of the age of twelve years and upward . . . ," Miss.Code 1972, § 97–3–65.

26. ". . . whoever carnally knows and abuses a female child . . . ," D.C. Code 1967, § 22–2801. Arkansas had characterized several concepts associated with rape as carnal abuse. Ark.Stats.Ann. § 41–1804 (1975) (less

than 14 years if the actor is 18 years or older); 1805 (mentally defective or incapacitated); 1806 (less than 16 years if the actor is 20 years or older); N.C.Gen.Stat. § 14–21 (1977).

27. Hill's Case, 1 East P.C. 439 (1781); Rex v. Burrows, Russ. and Ry. 519, 168 Eng.Rep. 928 (1823); State v. Gray, 53 N.C. 170 (1860).

28. 1 Hale P.C. *628; 1 East P.C. 437 (1803); Rex v. Blomfield, 1 East P.C. 438 (1758); Rex v. Fleming, 1 East P.C. 440 (1799); Waller v. State, 40 Ala. 325 (1867); State v. Shields, 45 Conn. 256 (1877); Comstock v. State, 14 Neb. 205, 15 N.W. 355 (1883); State v. Brady, 104 W.Va. 523, 140 S.E. 546 (1927); State v. Williams, 111 Ariz. 175, 526 P.2d 714 (1974).

29. 3 Co.Inst. *60.

30. Ibid.; 1 Hale P.C. *628; Cochran v. State, 162 Tex.Cr.R. 253, 283 S.W.2d 947 (1955); Martinez v. People, 160 Colo. 534, 422 P.2d 44 (1966).

"Penetration is necessary, according to all authorities, to prove the crime of rape, and such fact must be proven beyond a reasonable doubt." State v. Machunsky, 129 Vt. 195, 274 A.2d 513, 515 (1971).

"Ohio's sexual-penetration statute does not encompass digital penetration." State v. Hooper, 57 Ohio St.2d 87, 386 N.E.2d 1348, 1350, 11 O.O.3d 250 (1979).

etration,[31] assault,[32] or abuse.[33] Without this there has been no more than an attempt [34] (or an assault with intent),[35] but the slightest penetration completes the crime.[36] It is sometimes referred to as "vulva penetration" [37] and in the case of a virgin it is not necessary that the hymen be ruptured.[38]

Just as a rogue bent on burglary has carried his plan far enough for conviction of this crime if he has broken open the dwelling and passed the line of the threshold without the completion of his nefarious scheme,[39] so the rapist has done enough to complete his guilt at the moment of sexual penetration even if his brutal lust was not gratified. A number of the statutes expressly provide that any penetration is sufficient for conviction,[40] and some specifically mention that emission is not required.[41] These are to be construed as codifications of the common law rather than modifications thereof.[42]

B. UNLAWFUL

A man cannot commit rape by having sex with his wife, even if he does so by force and against her will.[43] He is "legally incapable of raping his wife." [44] Lord Hale, reflecting the ancient view, offered this explanation: "But the husband cannot be guilty of rape committed by himself upon his lawful wife, for by their mutual matrimonial consent and contract the wife hath given up herself in this kind to her husband, which she cannot re-

31. "A person who subjects another to sexual penetration . . . is guilty of sexual assault." Nev.Rev.Stat. 200.366 (1977). Criminal sexual penetration, N.Mex.Stat.Ann.1978 § 30–9–11.

32. Neb.Rev.Stat. § 28–408.03 (1975); Wyo.Stat.1977, § 6–4–302.

33. Iowa Code Ann. § 709.1 etc. (1978).

34. 1 Hale P.C. *628.

35. Phillips v. State, 93 Fla. 112, 111 So. 515 (1927); State v. Bernhardt, 51 Idaho 134, 3 P.2d 537 (1931); Teagarden v. State, 33 Okl.Cr. 394, 244 P. 63 (1926).

36. Rex v. Ruffen, 1 East P.C. 438 (1777); Reed v. State, 175 Ark. 1170, 299 S.W. 757 (1927); State v. Oliver, 333 Mo. 1231, 64 S.W.2d 118 (1933); Vickers v. State, 105 Tex.Cr.R. 235, 288 S.W. 191 (1926); Rowland v. Commonwealth, 147 Va. 636, 136 S.E. 564 (1927); De Armond v. State, 285 P.2d 236 (Okl.Cr.1955); People v. Cole, 39 Ill.App.3d 559, 350 N.E.2d 543 (1976).

37. State v. Brady, 104 W.Va. 523, 140 S.E. 546 (1927).

38. Ibid.; Rex v. Ruffen, 1 East P.C. 438 (1777); Reed v. State, 175 Ark. 1170, 299 S.W. 757 (1927); McDonald v. State, 225 Ark. 38, 279 S.W.2d 44 (1955).

39. Rex v. Perkes, 1 Car. & P. 300, 171 Eng.Rep. 1204 (1824); Nash v. State, 20 Tex.App. 384 (1886).

40. See for example Ala.Code 1975, § 13A–6–60; Ark.Stats.Ann. § 41–1801 (1)(a) (1975); 21 Okl.Stats.Ann. § 1113 (1958); Rev.Code Wash.Ann. 9.79.-140(1)(b) (1975).

41. See for example La.Stat.Ann.Rev. Stat. 14:41 (1978); Tenn.Code Ann. § 39–3702(8) (1977).

42. See State v. Judd, 132 Iowa 296, 109 N.W. 892 (1906).

43. State v. Haines, 51 La.Ann. 731, 25 So. 372 (1899); State v. Clark, 218 Kan. 726, 728, 544 P.2d 1372, 1375 (1976).

The New Jersey Supreme Court has rejected the contention that the common law exempted a husband from the charge of rape where the parties were separated. State v. Smith, 85 N.J. 193, 426 A.2d 38 (1981).

It was held that under the new code "an actor does not commit first-through-fourth-degree criminal sexual conduct if the victim is his or her spouse unless the parties are living apart and one of them has filed for separate maintenance or divorce." People v. Kubasiac, 98 Mich.App. 529, 296 N.W.2d 298, 301 (1980).

44. State v. Bell, 90 N.M. 134, 560 P.2d 925, 931 (1977).

tract."[45] The notion that a wife is bound to submit to sex by her husband at all times and under all conditions was obsolete long ago, but that does not change the present problem. The real reason a husband cannot rape his wife is that an essential element of the crime is that the sex be unlawful,[46] and marital sex is not unlawful.[47] It is because the element of unlawfulness is lacking that sex between husband and wife is not statutory rape,[48] or carnal knowledge of a child,[49] even if the wife is below the "age of consent" set forth in the statute. On the other hand, adulterous sex with the consenting, underage wife of another is statutory rape,[50] because the act is unlawful.

In fact, any act of extra-marital sex is unlawful.[51] It is frequently not punishable as an offense, but since it is unlawful, any issue resulting therefrom is *illegitimate*.

A state may constitutionally enact a statute which makes it a crime for a husband to assault his wife sexually.[52] Without the aid of a statute, a husband who forces sex upon his unwilling wife is guilty of assault and battery. This is only a misdemeanor but various types of assault have been made statutory felonies. Forcible sex by a husband on his unwilling wife could be made a felony punishable as severely as rape; and in fact has been made so by a very few of the new penal codes. The marital sex is not unlawful; it is the violence with which it is perpetrated that is unlawful. Hence the appropriate label for such a statutory crime is "sexual assault," as worded in some of the codes.[53] Others use the label "rape"[54] for this offense, which is possible by statute although it is not necessary and seems undesirable. It is possible that in the first case tried under such a statute, the word "rape" may have had some influence in causing the jury to refuse to convict, under evidence which seemed to be adequate.[55]

Although at common law, the husband cannot *commit* rape by forcing sex upon his wife against her will, he can be *guilty* of rape upon his wife if he helps another man in doing so.[56] Thus a husband who at the point of a

---

45. 1 Hale P.C. *629.

46. Adams v. Commonwealth, 219 Ky. 711, 713, 294 S.W. 151, 152 (1927).

"We conclude, that under the statutes in effect at the time of the alleged offenses, the fact that the victim was the spouse of the defendant was no bar to a conviction of rape." Commonwealth v. Chretien, __ Mass. __, 417 N.E.2d 1203, 1205 (1981). The court emphasized that the word "unlawful" employed in the former rape statute had been omitted in the revision and that the effect was to abandon the common-law rule of spousal exclusion.

47. If "a person causes another to have 'unlawful' sexual intercourse, it follows that the person so caused is 'other than the spouse of' the accused." State v. Bell, 90 N.M. 134, 560 P.2d 925, 933 (1977).

"In light of these considerations, we conclude that the marital exception in section 18–3–409 [criminal sexual assault] is neither arbitrary nor irrational." Peo-

ple v. Brown, __ Colo. __, 632 P.2d 1025, 1029 (1981).

48. People v. Pizurra, 211 Mich. 71, 178 N.W. 235 (1920).

49. State v. Volpe, 113 Conn. 288, 155 A. 223 (1931).

50. People v. Courtney, 180 Cal. App.2d 61, 4 Cal.Rptr. 274 (1960).

51. "Unlawful" is sometimes used to mean criminal, but the broad sense of the word means only "unauthorized by law."

52. State v. Bateman, 25 Ariz.App. 1, 540 P.2d 732 (1975).

53. N.J.Stat.Ann. 2C:14–2 (1979); Iowa uses the term "sexual abuse," Iowa Code Ann. § 709.1 (1978).

54. Or.Rev.Stat. 163.375 (1981).

55. State v. Rideout, a celebrated Oregon case where a husband was prosecuted for rape of his wife. As the result was acquittal there was no appeal.

56. 1 Hale P.C. *629; Cody v. State, 361 P.2d 307 (Okl.Cr.1961).

gun compelled his wife to submit, and compelled another man to attempt sexual intercourse with her was held guilty of assault with intent to rape his own wife.[57] Another husband conspired with a rogue to secure grounds for divorce. While the husband was concealed close by with a witness the rogue solicited the former's wife to commit adultery with him. Upon the wife's obstinate refusal the rogue took her by force. Because of the husband's conspiracy and his act of standing by without coming to the aid of his wife he was held a guilty party to this unlawful intercourse without her consent, and hence guilty of rape.[58]

Intercourse with a former wife, after the bonds of matrimony have been severed by divorce, is rape if it is without her consent.[59]

Some of the statutes expressly exclude intercourse with the wife or spouse of the perpetrator,[60] others reach the same result by not mentioning the matter and thus adopting the common-law rule on this point.[61] The chief difference is that if the statute specifies intercourse with one not the wife of the perpetrator the indictment must allege that the victim was not the wife of the defendant,[62] which was not required at common law although proof that she was his wife constituted a defense as mentioned above.

The long rape statute quoted above adds a complicating factor. It specifies that the intercourse must be with a female "not the wife of the perpetrator" and then sets forth eight sets of circumstances constituting rape. As to one,—intercourse accomplished by fraudulently inducing the woman to believe it is with her husband—the statute says the husband is also guilty of rape if he acts in collusion with the perpetrator. This seems to suggest that the husband would not be guilty if he participated in any of the other circumstances set forth, such as helping to subdue his wife by force or threats while another had intercourse with her. Under the familiar rule of "inclusion and exclusion" in statutory construction the inclusion of the husband as a possible guilty party, in one of the eight items only, would seem to eliminate such a possibility from the other seven, but the court may be expected to avoid such an unsatisfactory result,—even if it is necessary to strain the normal rules of construction. This clause demonstrates the hazards of trying to include too many details in a statute.

---

57. State v. Dowell, 106 N.C. 722, 11 S.E. 525 (1890).

58. People v. Chapman, 62 Mich. 280, 28 N.W. 896 (1886).

59. State v. Parsons, 285 S.W. 412 (Mo.1926).

60. See for example, West's Ann.Cal.Pen.Code § 261 (1970); Burns' Stats.Ann. § 35–42–4–1 (1977); So.Dak. Compiled Laws 22–22–1 (1967); Rev.Code Wash.Ann. 9.79.17D (1975).

61. See for example, Ark.Stats.Ann. § 41–1803 (1975); Haw.Rev.Stat. § 707–730 (1974); Tenn.Code Ann. § 39–3701 (1978). Cf. id. at § 39–3707.

62. Hunley v. Commonwealth, 217 Ky. 675, 290 S.W. 511 (1927).

Although defendant might defend against a charge of rape by proof that the victim was his lawful wife, it is not necessary for the indictment to allege that she was not his wife. And unless he raises the point it is not necessary for the government to prove that she was not his wife. United States v. Lone Bear, 579 F.2d 522 (9th Cir. 1978). Under Montana law it is necessary to allege and prove that the victim was not defendant's wife. Ibid.

C. CHASTITY

Just as it is possible for a very wicked man to be murdered, so it is possible for a prostitute to be raped.[63]

There is no requirement of chastity on the part of the victim of this crime so far as the common law is concerned.[64] The analogy suggested leaves much to be desired. No matter how wicked a man may be he is still entitled to his life until deprived thereof by due process of law, and he has a keen and strong interest in preserving it. But to speak of sexual intercourse with a prostitute without her consent as an "outrage to her person and feelings" is in the nature of mockery.[65] Her unlawful career has not placed her beyond the protection of the law, it is true; but when her only grievance is that she was taken without being paid, the law of assault and battery would seem more appropriate than to include such an act within the scope of one of the grave felonies, which at least until recently was a capital crime in some states.[66]

The "rape shield law." At common law the character of the woman as to chastity or unchastity was held to be admissible in evidence[67] on the theory that it had probative value in determining whether she did or did not consent.[68] Defense counsel, in unrestrained zeal for an acquittal, took advantage of this to the point that it often seemed as if it was the victim of the rape, rather than the perpetrator, who was on trial.[69] The undue and unreasonable harassment of the prosecutrix produced two intolerable results: (1) Confused juries frequently returned verdicts of not guilty despite obvious evidence of guilt; and (2) many victims of rape preferred to suffer in silence rather than be subjected to such humiliation. Hence there has been a tendency to restrict the introduction of evidence concerning the previous sexual

---

63. People v. Gonzales, 96 Misc.2d 639, 409 N.Y.S.2d 497 (N.Y.City Crim.Ct.1978).

64. "But the law of England . . . holds it to be felony to force even a concubine or harlot." 4 Bl.Comm. *213. Previous chastity of the victim is not an essential element of rape. Patterson v. State, 224 Ala. 531, 141 So. 195 (1932); State v. Beltz, 225 Iowa 155, 279 N.W. 386 (1938). The bad reputation of the prosecutrix is no defense to a prosecution for assault to rape. Commonwealth v. Smith, 115 Pa.Super. 151, 175 A. 177 (1934).

65. "The essential guilt of rape consists in the outrage to the person and the feelings of the female." West's Ann.Cal.Pen.Code § 263 (1970). See also 21 Okl.St.Ann. § 1113 (1958).

66. In Coker v. Georgia, 433 U.S. 584, 97 S.Ct. 2861 (1977), the Supreme Court reversed the death sentence that had been pronounced in a rape case, holding it to be cruel and unusual punishment. The Justices could not agree upon an opinion, but the indication is that the Court will hold that capital punishment is always, regardless of circumstances, a disproportionate penalty for the crime of rape. However, see Upshaw v. State, 350 So.2d 1358 (Miss.1977).

67. 1 Wigmore, Evidence § 62 (3d ed.1940). And see Graves v. State, 161 Tex.Cr.R. 16, 274 S.W.2d 555 (1955).

68. "For it is certainly more probable that a woman who has done these things voluntarily in the past would be much more likely to consent, than one whose past reputation was without blemish, and whose personal conduct could not truthfully be assailed." People v. Johnson, 106 Cal. 289, 293, 39 P. 622, 623 (1895).

69. "We hold that the 1975 enactment of the South Dakota Legislature repealing and reenacting SDCL 22–22–1 was intended to modernize the rape statute to place the act in a proper perspective and to try the actor for the crime, not the victim." State v. Havens, 264 N.W.2d 918, 921 (S.D.1978). And see Berger, Man's Trial, Woman's Tribulation: Rape Cases in the Courtroom, 77 Colum.L.Rev. 1 (1977).

activity of the prosecutrix in a rape case. A typical "rape shield statute" [70] does not prevent the introduction of any relevant and otherwise admissible evidence, but requires that the relevancy of any evidence of the previous sexual conduct of the complaining witness must be determined in a pretrial hearing before the judge in camera. Such a statute has been held to be constitutional. When properly applied by the judge it does not deny the accused the right to confront and cross-examine witnesses, or to present witnesses on his own behalf. [71]

The New Mexico statute provides that evidence of the victim's past sexual conduct, opinion evidence thereof, or reputation for past sexual conduct, shall not be admitted in evidence unless, and only to the extent that the court finds, that evidence of the victim's past sexual conduct is material to the case and that its inflammatory or prejudicial nature does not outweigh its probative value. A defendant wishing to offer such evidence must file a written notice prior to trial, whereupon the court shall determine, in camera, whether such evidence is admissible. It was held that the claim of consent to the intercourse does not of itself make the victim's past sexual conduct material. There must be a showing of a reasonable basis for believing that such conduct is pertinent to the consent issue. [72] And further it was held, that in the absence of a showing of relevancy, no error was committed in precluding questions relating to the victim's vaginitis eleven months prior to the crime charged, and to the fact that the victim, a single woman, was fitted with an intrauterine device at the time in order to show past sexual conduct.

In one case, even without the aid of statute, the trial judge made a pretrial order "prohibiting the defense from making any reference at trial to any sexual activities which [the victim] may have had with men other than [the defendant], and from making any reference to the fact that she was wearing an intrauterine contraceptive device at the time of the alleged rape." It was held that under the facts of this case this order was not an abuse of discretion. [73]

---

70. Such a statute is quoted in Interest of Nichols, 2 Kan.App.2d 431, 580 P.2d 1370, 1372 (1978).

71. Ibid. State v. Williams, 224 Kan. 468, 580 P.2d 1341 (1978); People v. McKenna, 196 Colo. 367, 585 P.2d 275 (1978). The Kansas Rape Shield Statute is constitutional in that it merely establishes a procedure to determine the relevance of acts of prior sexual misconduct. State v. Blue, 225 Kan. 576, 592 P.2d 897 (1979).

72. State v. Herrera, 92 N.M. 7, 582 P.2d 384 (App.1978).

In a rape trial the statute which limits the admissibility of evidence of the victim's past sexual conduct includes not only consensual conduct but also evidence of past rape. State v. Montoya, 91 N.M. 752, 580 P.2d 973 (App.1978).

Under the evidence in this case it was held that no error was committed in excluding evidence offered to show that the victim had been sleeping with her boy friend and had been engaging in prostitution. State v. Romero, 94 N.M. 22, 606 P.2d 1116 (App.1980).

73. United States v. Kasto, 584 F.2d 268 (8th Cir. 1978). See also McLean v. United States, 377 A.2d 74, 78 (D.C. App.1977); People v. Thompson, 76 Mich. App. 705, 257 N.W.2d 268 (1977).

"In a rape case where the issue of consent is not raised, the substantive use of evidence of prior sexual promiscuity is obviously improper because it is irrelevant and serves only to inflame the minds of the jurors." State v. Johns, 615 P.2d 1260, 1263 (Utah 1980). See also State v. Workman, 47 Or.App. 1055, 615 P.2d 1140 (1980); Commonwealth v. Duncan, 279 Pa.Super. 395, 421 A.2d 257 (1980).

But where the issue was whether defendant or someone else was responsible for the pregnancy which the prosecutrix claimed was caused by the alleged rape by defendant, "we hold that the trial judge erred in not permitting appellant to cross-examine the prosecutrix or call witnesses on his behalf for the purpose of proving the prosecutrix's consensual sexual activity during the period in which conception might have occurred.[74]

The Federal Rules of Evidence [75] have also restricted the evidence that may be used to attack the credibility or character of a rape victim. Evidence of the victim's reputation or opinion as to past sexual behavior is generally inadmissible.[76]

It is to be noted, however, that there are constitutional limitations as to how far such a statute may go. The wording of a "rape shield statute" was to the effect that consensual sexual activity between the victim and anyone other than the defendant "shall not be admitted into evidence under this chapter." It was held that to uphold the constitutionality of the statute it must be interpreted to give the defendant "an opportunity to demonstrate that due process requires the admission of such evidence because the probative value in the context of that particular case outweighs its prejudicial effect on the prosecutrix." [77]

And since the prosecution had shown, as part of its case, that an examination of the alleged victim on the night of the alleged rape had shown the presence of live sperm in her vaginal tract, the "rape shield" statute will not prevent defendant from showing a previous act of sexual intercourse with another, if he can show that the presence of the live sperm could have been the result of that intercourse.[78]

More serious as a practical problem is the general rule that unchastity of the girl is no defense to a charge of having carnal knowledge of a female person under the age of consent.[79] It has been held that sexual intercourse with such a female is "statutory rape" even if she was an inmate of a house of prostitution.[80] It shocks the moral sense to see a normal and socially-minded boy convicted of felony for having been picked up on the street and led astray by a common prostitute who merely happened to be under the age mentioned in the statute,—particularly if she was actually older than he.[81]

A very salutary legislative trend is discoverable although it is by no means widespread and frequently covers only part of the need. Some statutes provide, for example, that unlawful sexual intercourse with a willing

74. Shockley v. State, 585 S.W.2d 645, 651 (Tenn.Cr.App.1978).

75. Federal Rules of Evidence, Rule 412, 28 U.S.C.A.

76. Ibid.

77. State v. Howard, ___ N.H. ___, 426 A.2d 457, 461 (1981).

78. People v. Martinez, ___ Colo. ___, 634 P.2d 26 (1981).

79. Alexander v. State, 202 Ind. 1, 170 N.E. 542 (1930); State v. Steele, 209 Iowa 550, 228 N.W. 75 (1929); Hunley v. Commonwealth, 217 Ky. 675, 290 S.W. 511 (1927); State v. Williams, 161 La. 851, 109 So. 515 (1926); State v. Mischiro, 165 La. 705, 115 So. 909 (1928); State v. Duncan, 82 Mont. 170, 266 P. 400 (1928); Willard v. State, 195 Wis. 170, 217 N.W. 651 (1928).

80. State v. Duncan, 82 Mont. 170, 266 P. 400 (1928); Montgomery v. State, 249 Ind. 98, 229 N.E.2d 466 (1967); Jones v. State, 249 Ind. 621, 232 N.E.2d 587 (1968).

81. That the accused was under his majority would be no defense to a prosecution for carnal knowledge of a female under the age of consent. Yates v. Commonwealth, 211 Ky. 629, 277 S.W. 995 (1925).

female fourteen years or older is a felony unless it is shown that the female was of bad moral repute and also a lewd female in which event the defendant may be found guilty of contributing to the delinquency of a minor or fornication.[82] Another type of statute provides punishment for sexual intercourse with a willing female over sixteen and under eighteen if she is "of previous chaste and virtuous character." [83] Another type recognizes the previous unchaste character of the female as a defense in the consent cases if she was over fourteen.[84] Without attempting to include every variation in this regard, mention may be made of a provision which goes very much farther, although it seems entirely sound and defensible. One statute provides in substance that any sexual intercourse with a girl under the age of twelve was a felony [85] and that unlawful sexual intercourse with a willing female over twelve and under eighteen years of age is a felony, except that no conviction can be had for such intercourse with a willing female over twelve if she was a "bawd, lewd or kept female;" and if she was not in that category, but was over fourteen at the time, her then reputation for want of chastity is admissible in behalf of the defendant.[86]

Where the statute provides a penalty for unlawful sexual intercourse with a willing female between certain ages provided she was of previous chaste and virtuous character, the chastity of the girl is an essential element of the offense and must be alleged and proved by the state; [87] it is reversible error for the judge to refuse to instruct the jury not to convict if they find the girl of such age and not of previous chaste character; [88] a conviction of "statutory rape" based upon intercourse with a willing, unchaste female of such age cannot stand; [89] and only the first act of sexual intercourse by a girl of such age will support a conviction if it was with her consent.[90] In one state [91] the carnal knowledge of a male under fourteen by a female over eighteen, where the male is not her husband, is punished as a misdemeanor.

An additional step is the occasional statutory provision with reference to the age of the offender in such cases, which will be mentioned in the consideration of "the perpetrator."

Under some of the provisions the subsequent marriage of the parties is a bar to prosecution.[92]

82. Va.Code 1950, § 18.2–65 (1975).

83. 21 Okl.St.Ann. § 1111 (1958).

84. V.T.C.A., Penal Code § 21.09 (1974).

85. Tenn.Code Ann. § 39.3706 (1971).

86. Id. at § 39–3706. Tennessee has since amended its statutes to remove the relevance of the actor's character. Thus the possible disparity mentioned in the text above can still occur in that a more sexually active and inciteful person can be the victim. See Tenn.Code Ann. §§ 39–3704, 39–3705 (1978).

87. Humphrey v. State, 34 Okl.Cr. 247, 246 P. 486 (1926).

88. Holman v. State, 104 Tex.Cr.R. 296, 283 S.W. 807 (1926).

89. Ellis v. State, 114 Tex.Cr.R. 197, 25 S.W.2d 347 (1930). And see Graves v. State, 161 Tex.Cr.R. 16, 274 S.W.2d 555 (1955).

90. Huckabee v. State, 115 Tex.Cr.R. 590, 27 S.W.2d 802 (1930); Searcy v. State, 116 Tex.Cr.R. 545, 33 S.W.2d 453 (1930). Even prior sexual intercourse with the defendant rendered the prosecutrix unchaste and within the application of this provision. Booker v. State, 116 Tex.Cr.R. 561, 28 S.W.2d 150 (1930).

91. Md.Code 1957 Art. 27 § 462A (1972).

92. See Va.Code 1960, § 18–2–66 (1975).

D. WITHOUT CONSENT

Rape and carnal knowledge of a child have so much in common that it would be unduly repetitious to consider each one separately with reference to each element of each offense. Hence they have been dealt with without such separation so far as concerns the intercourse itself, the unlawfulness of the intercourse, and (to some extent) the chastity of the victim. At one point, however, they cannot be discussed effectively without complete separation. That point has to do with the consent or lack of consent on the part of the female person alleged to have been raped or carnally known. Unlawful sexual intercourse with a girl under the age of consent is a crime whether she consents or not. If the statute has incorporated carnal knowledge of a child and rape into one offense, with one penalty,[93] it is immaterial whether she consented or not if she was unquestionably under the age specified.[94] Where the two types of misconduct are found in separate sections and with different penalties,[95] it is necessary to determine whether the act was with or without the consent of the girl (not to determine guilt or innocence but) to determine which of the two crimes was committed. On the other hand, if the intercourse was clearly without the consent of the victim, her age is unimportant[96] in the absence of some very unusual statutory provision.

Hence it must be emphasized that in the discussion of this topic,—without consent—we are referring to common-law rape as here defined, and without including carnal knowledge of a child under the age of consent, whatever that age may be in the particular jurisdiction. And as the word "rape" is used in this topic it is to be understood to mean "common-law rape," as so defined, and not to include the so-called "statutory rape."

"Against her will" was the phrase used in the ancient definition of rape,[97] and it is found in some of the recent cases[98] and statutes.[99] As used in this definition, however, the phrase was intended merely to raise the question: "Was the woman willing or unwilling?"[1] Hence "against the will" and

---

93. See for example Idaho Code § 18–6101 (1977). Rape is either sexual intercourse with a female under age 18, or the accomplishment of sexual intercourse through force, violence or threats. Age is the essential element of the former and force the essential element of the latter.

94. State v. Bailor, 104 Iowa 1, 73 N.W. 344 (1897); De Armond v. State, 285 P.2d 236 (Okl.Cr.1955); State v. Whitener, 228 S.C. 244, 89 S.E.2d 701 (1955).

95. See for example Ark.Stats.Ann. §§ 41–1803, 41–1804 (1975).

96. Page v. Commonwealth, 219 Ky. 151, 292 S.W. 741 (1927).

97. 3 Co.Inst. *60; 4 Bl.Comm. *210.

98. People v. Celmars, 332 Ill. 113, 163 N.E. 421 (1928); Starr v. State, 205 Wis. 310, 311, 237 N.W. 96, 97 (1931); Sanchez v. State, 567 P.2d 270, 275 (Wyo.1977).

99. Alaska Stats. 11.15.120 (1962); N.C.Gen.Stat. § 14–21 (1973); See also Iowa Code Ann. § 709.1 (1978) defining sexual abuse as ". . . done by force or against the will of the other."

1. Commonwealth v. Burke, 105 Mass. 376, 377 (1870). If she consents it is not rape unless she is under the age of consent.

If D believed, reasonably and in good faith, that the woman consented to go to his apartment and have sexual intercourse with him, he was not guilty of rape. People v. Mayberry, 15 Cal.3d 143, 125 Cal.Rptr. 745, 542 P.2d 1337 (1975).

If the woman freely consented to the penetration, but changed her mind during the intercourse, no rape was committed. State v. Way, 297 N.C. 293, 254 S.E.2d 760 (1979).

"In the absence of proof on the issue of consent, the State cannot obtain a conviction for second-degree sexual assault.

"without the consent" are equivalent terms in the law of rape.[2] Because of this fact the latter phrase is substituted in some of the recent cases[3] and statutes.[4] However the definition is worded in this regard it does not require an affirmative exercise of her will in opposition to the act if she is incapable of such an exercise of the will at the time; and on the other hand it is not necessary to have a verbally expressed consent in order to rule out this offense.

Several states simply use language that implies the act is without the consent of the victim by describing the offense as one committed by force or against resistance.[5]

1. FORCE

Blackstone defined rape as "carnal knowledge of a woman forcibly and against her will."[6] This reference to force was not found in the earlier definition given by Coke[7] and its use has tended to cause confusion rather than to clarify the law.[8] It led to a notion that "resistance to the uttermost" on the part of the woman is one of the elements of rape.[9] In the absence of intimidation, it was said by one court, "the female must resist to the utmost

---

The State must introduce evidence that there was no consent, and this evidence must be sufficient to convince the jury beyond a reasonable doubt. There is no presumption that all acts of sexual contact or intercourse are without consent unless shown to have been preceded by words or overt actions of consent." Gates v. State, 91 Wis.2d 512, 283 N.W.2d 474, 477 (1979). See also DPP v. Morgan, H.L. [1975] 2 All E.R. 347, 2 WLR 923; Regina v. Cogan, [1975] 3 WLR 316 (Crim.App.); Fletcher, Rethinking Criminal Law, pp. 698–707 (1978).

2. McDonald v. State, 225 Ark. 38, 279 S.W.2d 44, 46 (1955); Wilson v. State, 10 Terry 37, 109 A.2d 381 (1954); State v. Wheeler, 150 Me. 332, 110 A.2d 578, 579 (1954); State v. Flaherty, 128 Me. 141, 146 A. 7 (1929); State v. Catron, 317 Mo. 894, 899, 296 S.W. 141, 142 (1927).

3. Adams v. Commonwealth, 219 Ky. 711, 713, 294 S.W. 151, 152 (1927).

"The essential element in rape is the forcing of intercourse upon a woman 'without her consent' and 'against her will.' It is sometimes said that those terms mean essentially the same thing, but this is not true because such an act might occur in circumstances which would be 'without her consent' but which would not necessarily involve overcoming her will and her resistance, both of which must be proved." State v. Studham, 572 P.2d 700, 702 (Utah 1977). The Utah Court has confused the term against her will with the concept of overcoming will

and resistance which are not necessarily the same.

4. La.Stat.Ann.Crim.Code 14:41 (1978); Ariz.Rev.Stat. § 13–140 (1978); Utah Code Ann., 1953, 76–5–402 (1977).

5. Ark.Stats. § 41–1803 (1975); Rev.Code Wash.Ann. 979.170 (1975).

6. 4 Bl.Comm. *210.

7. 3 Co.Inst. *60.

8. Observe, for instance, the unnecessary and labored effort of a Georgia court in disposing of an attack upon a girl under the age of consent. The court says that the statute raises a presumption of non-consent and this supplies the force necessary to the commission of rape. Ollis v. State, 44 Ga.App. 793, 163 S.E. 309 (1932).

9. See a reference to this "obsolete" rule in Bulls v. State, 33 Okl.Cr. 64, 68–9, 241 P. 605, 606 (1926). "[T]he woman is not required to resist to the utmost of her physical strength, if she reasonably believes resistance would be useless and result in serious bodily injury to her. . . . The amount of resistance required necessarily depends on the circumstances, such as the relative physical condition of the parties and the degree of force manifested." Bradley v. Commonwealth, 196 Va. 1126, 1134, 86 S.E.2d 828, 833 (1955).

However, some jurisdictions retain the outdated requirement of resistance to the utmost. State v. Hamm, 577 S.W.2d 936 (Mo.App.1979).

of her ability, and such resistance must continue till the offense is complete." [10]

Obviously a man should not be convicted of this very grave felony where the woman merely put up a little resistance for the sake of "appearance," so to speak, taking care not to resist too much. The law goes beyond this. The absence of consent is necessary for this crime.[11] And even where the resistance is genuine and vigorous in the beginning, if the physical contact arouses the passion of the woman to the extent that she willingly yields herself to the sexual act before penetration has been accomplished,—or if she so yields before this time for any other reason—it is not rape.[12]

If force is declared to be an element of the crime it becomes necessary to resort to the fiction of "constructive force" to take care of those cases in which no force is needed beyond what is involved in the very act of intercourse itself.[13] A more sound analysis is to recognize that human nature will impel an unwilling woman to resist unlawful sexual intercourse with great effort if she is not disabled by any physical or mental incapacity at the moment, nor deterred by intimidation or deception. Hence the better view is that "force" is not truly speaking an element of the crime itself, but if great force was not needed to accomplish the act the necessary *lack of consent* has been *disproved* in other than exceptional situations.[14] The courts today frequently state the position that a woman's resistance need not be "more

10. Reidhead v. State, 31 Ariz. 70, 72, 250 P. 366, 367 (1926). "In order to prove the crime of rape the evidence must show that the act was committed by force, against the will of the female, and if she had the use of her faculties and physical powers the evidence must show such resistance as to demonstrate that the act was against her will." People v. Serrielle, 354 Ill. 182, 186, 188 N.E. 375, 377 (1933). To constitute rape the woman must resist in good faith and to the utmost of her physical ability so long as she has power to do so until the offense is consummated, but the degree of force necessary to overcome her resistance is relative, and where a woman was kidnaped by six strong men, who had forcible intercourse with her in turn, the fact that she did not exert the same degree of resistance (which had proved futile) after the first attack does not preclude a finding of guilt on the part of the others. Salerno v. State, 162 Neb. 99, 75 N.W.2d 362 (1956).

11. Adams v. Commonwealth, 219 Ky. 711, 294 S.W. 151 (1927). Resistance which is spasmodic and mostly by words is not sufficient to establish rape by force (first degree). Reid v. State, 290 P.2d 775 (Okl.Cr.1955).

12. Wade v. State, 37 Ga.App. 121, 138 S.E. 921 (1927). As the court said in

this case, "if, notwithstanding the use of such force, she finally consent to the sexual act and her will cease to operate against its operation, the offense is not rape." Id. at 122, 138 S.E. at 922.

D would be guilty of assault to rape if the woman's consent was after the assault but before penetration. Copeland v. State, 55 Ala.App. 99, 313 So.2d 219 (1975).

13. Force, actual or constructive, is an essential element of rape. Almon v. State, 21 Ala.App. 466, 109 So. 371 (1926).

If the prosecutrix submitted to sexual intercourse on the representation that her fiance who was in jail would be killed if she did not, there was rape by force. Fitzpatrick v. State, 93 Nev. 21, 558 P.2d 630 (1977). Lhost v. State, 85 Wis.2d 620, 271 N.W.2d 121, 126 (1978) ". . . consent or acquiescence does not arise from a victim's conduct that seeks to protect third parties such as sleeping children."

14. See for example State v. Catron, 317 Mo. 894, 899, 296 S.W. 141, 142 (1927); State v. Brewster, 208 Iowa 122, 222 N.W. 6 (1929); Bulls v. State, 33 Okl.Cr. 64, 68–9, 241 P. 605, 606 (1926). Compare State v. Lima, 624 P.2d 1374 (Hawaii 1981).

than her age, strength, the surrounding facts, and all attending circumstances" make reasonable.[15]

2. INTIMIDATION

If force were really an element of the crime of rape it should not be listed alone but with an alternate,—intimidation—just as robbery is defined as larceny from the person by force or intimidation.[16] Statutes which undertake to set forth in detail the different sets of circumstances under which unlawful sexual intercourse is rape commonly include both of these factors, among others, in some such form as this: "Where she resists but her resistance is overcome by force and violence. Where she is prevented from resisting by threats of immediate and great bodily harm accompanied by apparent power of execution."[17] A number of the statutes giving shorter definitions include the reference to force with no mention of intimidation or putting in fear,[18] while others mention both[19] or neither.[20] Some statutes refer to forcible compulsion,[21] or force or imminent threat of force.[22]

The differences, however, are matters of form rather than substance. A woman's consent to unlawful sexual intercourse, obtained by placing her in fear of great and immediate bodily harm, is so clearly no consent at all so far as the law is concerned that the act is unquestionably rape.[23]

3. INSENSIBILITY

One of the leading American cases on the law of rape involved unlawful sexual intercourse with a woman "so drunk as to be utterly senseless." She had given no consent prior to her insensibility, but counsel urged that it was not "against her will" because her will was quite inactive one way or the other, and the wording of the statute was "by force and against her will."

15. State v. Horne, 12 Utah 2d 162, 166, 364 P.2d 109 (1961); Schrum v. Commonwealth, 219 Va. 204, 246 S.E.2d 893 (1978).

16. People v. Kubish, 357 Ill. 531, 535–6, 192 N.E. 543, 545 (1934). The wording varies but the idea is constant. For example—"by means of force or fear," People v. Seaman, 101 Cal.App. 302, 304, 281 P. 660, 661 (1929).

17. 21 Okl.St.Ann. § 1111 (1958); West's Ann.Cal.Pen.Code § 261 (1970); and see Idaho Code § 18–6101 (1977); Rev.Code Mont. 1947 § 94–5–501; So.Dak.Comp.Laws (1967) § 22–22–1; Wyo.Stat.Ann.1977 § 6–4–302.

18. For example, "forcibly," Alaska Stats. 11.15.120 (1970); D.C.Code 1967 § 22–2801; "by force," Mass.Gen.Laws Ann. C265 § 22 (1974).

19. For example Colo.Rev.Stat.1973, 18–3–402 (1977).

20. R.I.Gen.Laws 1956, § 11–37–1; So.Carolina Code 1962 § 16–71. Although the South Carolina statute mentions "force" it is with reference to force before consent. The statute provides:

"Whosoever shall ravish a woman, married, maid or mother, when she did not consent, either before or after, or ravisheth a woman with force, although she consent after, shall be deemed guilty of rape."

21. Ark.Stats. § 41–1801 (1975); Rev.Code Wash.Ann. 9.79.140 (1975); W.Va.Code, 61–8B–3 (1976).

22. Burns' Ind.Ann.Stat. § 35–42–4–1 (1977).

23. State v. Schuster, 282 S.W.2d 553 (Mo.1955). A woman's consent to sexual intercourse is void if it is given in fear of personal violence. Deffenbaugh v. State, 32 Ariz. 212, 257 P. 27 (1927); Parrett v. State, 200 Ind. 7, 159 N.E. 755 (1928). And see the dictum to the effect that rape "by force" is accomplished by fraud or fear of serious personal injury. Pupero v. State, 190 Wis. 363, 208 N.W. 475 (1926).

Sex was without the consent of the victim where she yielded for fear of harm to her daughter. People v. LaSalle, 103 Cal.App.3d 139, 162 Cal.Rptr. 816 (1980).

The court pointed out that "against her will" means "without her consent," so far as the law of rape is concerned, and that unlawful intercourse "with a woman, without her consent, while she was, as he knew, wholly insensible so as to be incapable of consenting, and with such force as was necessary to accomplish the purpose was rape."[24] It is to be emphasized that this was not a case in which defendant had made the woman drunk but merely one in which he had taken advantage of her helpless condition. The court mentioned with approval the "established rule in England that unlawful and forcible connection with a woman in a state of unconsciousness at the time, whether that state has been produced by the act of the prisoner or not, is presumed to be without her consent, and is rape." "If it were otherwise," the court added, "any woman in a state of utter stupefaction, whether caused by drunkenness, sudden disease, the blow of a third person, or drugs which she had been persuaded to take even by the defendant himself, would be unprotected from personal dishonor. The law is not open to such a reproach." In another case it was held that unlawful intercourse with a woman who had fainted was rape.[25] However, the mere fact that a woman's inhibitions have been reduced or her judgment impaired or confused does not render an act of sexual intercourse punishable as rape.[26]

Several statutes have been enacted recognizing the concept of rape where the woman is unconscious as to the nature of the act.[27]

4. IDIOCY OR INSANITY [28]

It is well established in the common law of England that unlawful sexual intercourse with a woman so idiotic or insane as to be utterly incapable of giving or withholding consent is rape.[29] Such an act was regarded the same as such intercourse with an unconscious woman. This, however, had reference to an actual incapacity to give or withhold consent and not a "presumed" incapacity; and it was held that if she actually gave consent, though as a result of "animal instinct," this prevented the intercourse from being rape.[30] It is doubtful if the courts in this country would recognize an "animal-instinct" consent by a woman who was utterly inadequate mentally.[31] It has been held, for example, that unlawful sexual intercourse with an imbecile is rape although the woman offers no resistance.[32] If the common law of rape has not gone rather far in this direction in America it will be

---

24. Commonwealth v. Burke, 105 Mass. 376, 380–1 (1870).

25. Lancaster v. State, 168 Ga. 470, 148 S.E. 139 (1929).

26. Regina v. Lang, 62 Cr.App.Rep. 50 (1975).

27. "Where she is at the time unconscious of the nature of the act, and this is known to the accused." Idaho Code § 18–6101.5 (1977); 21 Okl.Stat.Ann. § 1111 (1958).

28. As to the meaning of idiocy and insanity see infra, Chapter 8, Section 2, B.

29. The Queen v. Ryan, 2 Cox C.C. 115 (1846); Regina v. Fletcher, 8 Cox C.C. 131 (1859).

30. See the Anonymous case referred to in Regina v. Fletcher in the preceding note, and observe the care taken to point out that there was no such consent in the Fletcher case. Id. at 134.

31. See, however, Crosswell v. People, 13 Mich. 427 (1865).

32. Smith v. State, 161 Ga. 421, 131 S.E. 163 (1925).

Although not involved in the decision, it was indicated that sexual intercourse with a 27-year old woman who was so mentally defective that she had the mind of a child of seven, would be statutory rape. United States v. Medley, 452 F.2d 1325 (D.C.Cir. 1971).

necessary in expressing the law in this field to add to rape and carnal knowledge of a child an additional statutory offense under some such name as "carnal knowledge of a female person of unsound mind," because some such enactment is common. Statutes undertaking to itemize the circumstances under which unlawful sexual intercourse is rape include some such provision as this: "Where she is incapable through lunacy or other unsoundness of mind, whether temporary or permanent, of giving legal consent." [33]   And even states that do not undertake to list all of the circumstances frequently have a special clause or statute to cover this situation.[34] Even under such a statute, however, the mere fact that the woman is somewhat deficient mentally will not be sufficient to make the act rape.[35]

5. FRAUD

The types of fraud perpetrated in order to obtain unlawful sexual intercourse in cases that have resulted in prosecutions for rape have tended to fall into two general categories each having two subdivisions.

A. PRETENDED MEDICAL TREATMENT

This type of fraud has usually involved a girl only slightly over the age of consent and definitely below the average mentality,—although not so completely inadequate as to be classified idiotic or insane. And a doctor, or pretended doctor, has had sexual intercourse with her under the fraudulent pretense of medical treatment.[36] It is to be gathered from the cases, although seldom so stated, that such a girl, as a result of embarrassment has sometimes shut her eyes against the sight of a man making an intimate examination of her person, and has not known what was really being done to her.[37]

33. West's Ann.Cal.Pen.Code § 261 (1970); 21 Okl.St.Ann. § 1111 (1958). See also Minn.St.Ann. § 609.342(e)(ii) (1975). Incapable of consent by reason of being . . . mentally incapacitated. Rev.Code Wash.Ann. 9.79.180 (1975).

34. See Md.Code 1957, Art. 27 § 462 (1975); La.Stat.Ann.Rev.Stat. 14:43 (1978); Miss.Code, 1972 § 97–3–65.

Such a statute does not require complete or absolute imbecility. State v. Haner, 186 Iowa 1259, 173 N.W. 225 (1919).

35. Williams v. State, 125 Tex.Cr.R. 447, 69 S.W.2d 418 (1934).

In upholding the rape conviction of a defendant for sexual relations with a mentally defective seventeen-year old girl, it was observed:

"As do all others, the mentally aberrant differ from one another in greater or lesser degree. Even mental retardation does not mean that an individual is incapable of consenting as a matter of law. The requisite degree of intelligence necessary to give consent may be found to exist in a person of very limited intellect. Crucial to a determination may be how such person actually functions in so-

ciety." People v. Easley, 42 N.Y.2d 50, 396 N.Y.S.2d 635, 364 N.E.2d 1328, 1331 (1977).

36. Regina v. Case, 4 Cox C.C. 220 (1850); Regina v. Flattery, 13 Cox C.C. 388 (1877). See Scutt, Fraud and Consent in Rape: Comprehension of The Nature and Character of The Act and Its Moral Implications, 18 Crim.L.Qtrly. 312 (1976).

"Where the actor engages in sexual penetration on the pretext of performing a medical examination or treatment for the purpose of achieving sexual penetration." Tenn.Code Ann. § 39–3705(A)(4) (1978).

37. In a case in which a doctor was convicted of rape for sexual penetration perpetrated upon a 44-year-old widow by surprise during a medical examination, the evidence disclosed something of this possibility. "Prosecutrix, because of embarrassment, closed her eyes, and covered them with her arm, and did not see what appellant was doing." He accomplished penetration before she realized what he was doing and she indicates she might not have realized then except for

It is well settled that if unlawful sexual intercourse was had with such a girl who thought she was being treated with medical or surgical instruments and had consented to nothing else, the man is guilty of rape.[38] It is not rape if the girl consents to the act of sexual intercourse although this consent was obtained by the fraudulent pretense that it was necessary as a medical treatment for a pretended serious disorder.[39] This is in line with the general view that consent obtained by fraud is recognized by law where there is no mistake as to what is actually being done.

However, a Canadian case upheld a conviction where the woman submitted to an act of sexual intercourse where she was aware of the nature of the act but was induced to submit under the false representation that it was proper medical treatment. The Court concluded the victim could have been unaware that the "nature and quality of the act" was carnal.[40] The Tennessee statute would seem to be broad enough to cover such a situation.[41]

A variation of the pretended medical treatment type of fraud is found in the case of a choirmaster who had sexual intercourse with a girl (over the age of consent) by pretending to test her breathing power with an instrument. As she had not consented to the act of sexual intercourse this was held to constitute rape.[42]

B. PRETENDED HUSBAND

A man may fraudulently pretend to be a woman's husband either by causing a married woman to be mistaken as to his identity or by deceiving an unmarried woman with a sham wedding. The former type of fraud has usually been perpetrated by a man getting into bed with a married woman in the dark and having intercourse with her while she assumed he was her husband. Several cases have held this not to be rape on the ground that the intercourse was with her consent.[43] The general rule is that if deception causes a misunderstanding as to the fact itself (fraud in the *factum*) there is no legally-recognized consent because what happened is not that for which consent was given; whereas consent induced by fraud is as effective as any other consent, so far as direct and immediate legal consequences are concerned, if the deception related not to the thing done but merely to some collateral matter (fraud in the inducement).[44] But it is quite unsound to hold that the woman is not deceived as to the very act done in the type of fraud

her marital experience. State v. Atkins, 292 S.W. 422, 423 (Mo.1926).

38. Regina v. Flattery, 13 Cox C.C. 388 (1877); Pomeroy v. State, 94 Ind. 96 (1883); Eberhart v. State, 134 Ind. 651, 34 N.E. 637 (1893); State v. Ely, 114 Wash. 185, 194 N.W. 988 (1921).

39. Don Moran v. People, 25 Mich. 356 (1872).

40. Rex v. Harms, [1944] 2 DLR (Sask. CA).

41. Tenn.Code Ann. § 39–3705(A)(4) (1978).

42. Rex v. Williams, 27 Cox C.C. 350 (1922).

43. Regina v. Barrow, 11 Cox C.C. 191 (1868); Lewis v. State, 30 Ala. 54 (1857); State v. Brooks, 76 N.C. 1 (1877). The Alabama court was reluctant to reach this result and recommended a change by statute, which was made at a later time. The English judges were inclined to question the soundness of Barrow. The Queen v. Flattery, 2 Q.B.D. 410, 413–4 (1877).

The English rule that intercourse obtained by this fraud was not rape was changed by the Criminal Law Amendment Act of 1885, § 4. This Act was repealed but the same provision was included in the Sexual Offenses Act of 1956.

44. See infra, chapter 9, section 3, B, 2. See People v. Harris, 93 Cal.App.3d 103, 155 Cal.Rptr. 472 (1979).

now under consideration. The act of marital intercourse and the act of adultery are as far apart as day and night and it is atrocious to suggest that willing submission by a wife to what is supposed by her in good faith, and on good grounds, to be lawful intercourse with her husband, is consent to an act of adultery with another. Hence other cases have refused to recognize any consent to such intercourse and have held the perpetrator guilty of rape.[45] These cases, said the Michigan court, "seem to us to stand upon the much better reasons, and to be more in accordance with the general rules of the criminal law." [46]

A related problem concerns the rogue who, in the dark, got into bed with a married woman who knew he was not her husband but submitted to sexual intercourse in the belief that he was her paramour with whom she had arranged a meretricious tryst. Although he had learned of the tryst, detained the paramour elsewhere with a false message and fraudulently imposed upon the woman, he had not committed rape. This was not fraud in the *factum*. There was nothing comparable to the difference between marital intercourse and adultery. The woman consented to the adulterous intercourse, having been induced to consent because deceived as to the person—fraud in the inducement. She would have no defense to a prosecution for adultery, where that is a punishable offense, nor to a charge of adultery in a divorce action, although the woman who submitted believing the man was her husband would have a complete answer to both. Misconduct such as that of the rogue is not included in the article on sexual offenses of the Model Penal Code although guilt by the impersonation of the husband is expressly stated.[47]

While no case seems to have involved the point it is conceivable that a woman, intending to get into bed with her husband, might get into bed with another man by mistake. Analogies suggest that it would be so fraudulent for him to take advantage of her mistake in silence (if aware of the mistake) that to do so would render him guilty of rape.[48]

In the absence of statute, sexual intercourse with a woman, procured by deceiving her with a "sham wedding," has been held not to be rape [49] on the theory that she knows she is having sexual intercourse with this very person and is deceived only as to a collateral matter. But while not so unquestionably fraud in the *factum* as the other type of case, it is arguable that a woman who consents to what would be entirely proper and chaste if the facts were as she believes them to be, has not agreed to an act of illicit intercourse; and hence this deception also goes, not merely to a collateral matter of inducement, but to the very fact itself.

45. Regina v. Dee, 15 Cox C.C. 579 (1884); State v. Shephard, 7 Conn. 54 (1828). And under statute: State v. Williams, 128 N.C. 573, 37 S.E. 952 (1901).

46. Crosswell v. People, 13 Mich. 427, 438 (1865).

47. "A male who has sexual intercourse with a female not his wife commits a felony of the third degree if:
. . .

    (c) he knows that . . . she submits because she falsely supposes that

he is her husband." Model Penal Code, Section 213.1(2). Gross Sexual Imposition.

48. As said in another connection, "silence may be deceitful means or artful practice." Crawford v. State, 117 Ga. 247, 250, 43 S.E. 762, 763 (1903).

49. State v. Murphy, 6 Ala. 765, 770 (1884).

C. STATUTES

It has not been uncommon to make some provision with reference to fraud in the statutes on rape although there has been no uniformity in this regard. One type of statute merely includes participation in the sexual act "because the victim erroneously believes the actor is the victim's spouse." [50] Another more common type is worded in this form: "Where she submits, under a belief that the person committing the act is her husband, and this belief is induced by any artifice, pretence or concealment practiced by the accused, with intent to induce such a belief." [51] Another punishes the act where "the actor pretends to be the victim's spouse and the victim reasonably believes the actor to be that spouse." [52] A fourth, simply defines rape as occurring when resistance is prevented by "force, threat of force or deception." [53] Texas provides for the offense of rape if the woman participates "because she erroneously believes that he is her husband." [54] This statute clearly covers the case of one who obtains sexual intercourse with another's wife by impersonating her husband and should be interpreted to cover the case of obtaining such intercourse with an unmarried woman by means of a sham wedding. Several of the statutes appear broad enough to cover the sham wedding as well as fraud in the fact of the participant. The more common provision noted above covers only a case of personating the woman's husband. The second covers both this and intercourse obtained by the device of "sham wedding," [55] unless an actual common-law marriage results from such a ceremony in the particular jurisdiction.[56] In one case a Canadian Court refused extradition where the alleged rape charged a sham marriage which was sufficient to make out rape under California law [57] noted above. The Court held that because the Canadian statute required the accused "personate" the victim's husband to constitute rape it did not cover a sham wedding, thus precluding extradition.[58] There has been a trend for whatever reason in recent statutes to omit such provisions.

"The essential elements of the common law crime of rape, from which the statutory offense of criminal sexual penetration was derived, were '(a) carnal knowledge or intercourse, (b) force, and (c) commission of the act without the consent or against the will of the victim.' " [59]

6. THE USE OF LIQUOR OR DRUGS

Another statutory provision, frequently encountered, includes within the definition of rape any unlawful sexual intercourse with a woman who is "prevented from resistance by any intoxicating, narcotic, or anaesthetic substance administered by or with the privity of the accused." [60] Unlawful sex-

50. Utah Code Ann., 1953, § 76–5–406(5) (1973); See also, Colo.Rev.Stat., 1973, 18–3–403(1)(d); Wyo.Stat.1972 § 6–4–303.

51. West's Ann.Cal.Pen.Code § 261 (1970); 21 Okl.St.Ann. § 1111 (1958); Ida.Code § 18–6101 (1977). See also La.Stat.Ann.Rev.Stat. 14:43 (1978).

52. Tenn.Code Ann. § 39–3703 (1978).

53. Ohio Rev.Code § 2907.02 (1975).

54. V.T.C.A., Penal Code § 21.02 (1975).

55. Lee v. State, 44 Tex.Cr.R. 354, 72 S.W. 1005 (1902).

56. Draughn v. State, 12 Okl.Cr. 479, 158 P. 890 (1916).

57. People v. McCoy, 58 Cal.App. 534, 208 P. 1016 (1922).

58. California v. Skinner, 2 WWR 209, 33 BCR 555 [1924].

59. State v. Keyonnie, 91 N.M. 146, 571 P.2d 413, 415 (1977).

60. Idaho Code § 18–6101 (1977); West's Ann.Cal.Pen.Code § 261 (1970).

ual intercourse by a man with a woman he has reduced to a state of insensibility by intoxicating liquors or drugs is rape;[61] but no special provision is needed for this purpose. Such intercourse with an unconscious woman, who had not consented to the act in advance, is rape no matter what caused the insensibility, as mentioned above.

The type of provision mentioned was no doubt intended to cover cases in which the intercourse was obtained without rendering the woman unconscious. Some of the statutes are very specific in this regard such as the following:

"Any person who has carnal knowledge of any female . . . by administering to her any substance or liquid which shall produce such stupor or such imbecility of mind or weakness of body as to prevent effectual resistance."[62]

Several current statutes are framed in terms that do not appear to require that the victim be unconscious. They apply the situation where the victim's ability to act is impaired.[63] One statute refers to "mental incapacity" which "prevents a person from understanding the nature and consequences of the act of sexual intercourse whether that condition is produced by illness, defect, the influence of a substance or from some other cause."[64]

The mere fact that alcohol or drugs have confused the victim's judgment or reduced inhibitions is not enough impairment to make the act rape.[65]

E. MISTAKE AS TO AGE

A man who has unlawful[66] sexual intercourse with a girl under the age of consent is guilty of carnal knowledge of a child (the so-called "statutory rape") although she consented and he mistakenly believed she was older than the limit thus established.[67] Under the prevailing view this is true no matter

See also Tenn.Code Ann. §§ 39–3701, 3705 (1978).

61. Regina v. Camplin, 1 Den.C.C. 89, 1 Cox C.C. 220 (1845); Melton v. State, 160 Tenn. 273, 23 S.W.2d 662 (1930); Quinn v. State, 153 Wis. 573, 142 N.W. 510 (1913).

62. Miss.Code, 19, § 97–3–65. And see Tenn.Code Ann. § 39–3702(4) (1978). For another provision more or less specific in this regard see Kan.Stat.Ann. § 21–3502 (1978).

63. ". . . impaired substantially the ability of the other person to appraise or control conduct by administering or employing drugs or intoxicants without the knowledge or against the will of the other person." Vt.Stat. 13 § 3252 (1977).

". . . any substance which substantially impairs the victim's power to appraise or control his conduct." Wyo.Stat., 1977 § 6–4–303.

See also Ark.Stats. § 41–1801 (1975); West's Fla.Stat.Ann. § 794.011 (1975).

64. Rev.Code Wash.Ann. 9.79.140(3) (1975).

65. Regina v. Lang, 62 Cr.App.Rep. 50 (1975).

66. Sexual intercourse between man and wife is not *unlawful* and hence not statutory rape even if the wife is under the "age of consent." State v. Volpe, 113 Conn. 288, 155 A. 223 (1931); People v. Pizurra, 211 Mich. 71, 178 N.W. 235 (1920).

67. People v. Ratz, 115 Cal. 132, 46 P. 915 (1896); Heath v. State, 173 Ind. 296, 90 N.E. 310 (1910); Commonwealth v. Murphy, 165 Mass. 66, 42 N.E. 504 (1896). Assault with intent to commit rape on a girl under the age of consent. State v. Newton, 44 Iowa 45 (1876).

Although the new statute, covering the same misconduct, does not use the word "rape" that appears in the repealed statute, there was no defect in the verdict finding defendant guilty of "statutory rape," since the record shows there could have been no uncertainty in the minds of

how reasonable the mistaken belief may have been,[68] as in cases in which both her appearance and her positive statement indicated she was older than the age specified in the statute,[69] or in which he had exercised considerable diligence in the effort to ascertain her age.[70] There is authority to the contrary, however, that a bona-fide and reasonable belief that the female is above the "age of consent" is an excuse.[71] One state has concluded that the statutory age of consent created only a rebuttable presumption.[72] Some states have provided for the defense by statute.[73] This problem can be considered to better advantage in connection with the general subject of ignorance or mistake of fact and hence will be reserved for later consideration.[74]

F. THE PERPETRATOR

According to the English common law a boy under the age of fourteen is incapable of committing rape,[75] or carnal knowledge of a child.[76] It may be possible for him to have unlawful sexual intercourse with a woman without her consent but because of his infancy the misdeed does not constitute rape. Some American courts have assumed that this rule resulted from the fact that boys in England seldom attain puberty before the age of fourteen,[77] but this is obviously unsound since it was recognized from early times that penetration without emission completes the crime of rape, where the other elements are present.[78] As to crimes in general it is only an infant under seven who lacks criminal capacity entirely under the common law, although there is a rebuttable presumption of incapacity on the part of one between the ages of seven and fourteen.[79] The special rule in regard to rape resulted from the unwillingness of the early judges to hang one so young for this type of misconduct.

The rule is sometimes expressed in terms of an irrebuttable presumption of incapacity [80] which, of course, means only that capacity to commit the crime is wanting as a matter of law. Evidence purporting to show capacity is inadmissible [81] but only because it is irrelevant. If it is clearly proved that the boy under fourteen had unlawful sexual intercourse, together with the

the court, the prosecutor or the defendant, of the crime of which he was convicted. Carver v. Martin, 664 F.2d 932 (4th Cir. 1981).

68. State v. Houx, 109 Mo. 654, 19 S.W. 35 (1892); Eggleston v. State, 4 Md.App. 124, 241 A.2d 433 (1968).

69. State v. Duncan, 82 Mont. 170, 266 P. 400 (1928). And see People v. Marks, 146 App.Div. 11, 12, 130 N.Y.S. 524, 525 (1st Dep't 1911).

70. Manning v. State, 43 Tex.Cr.R. 302, 65 S.W. 920 (1901).

71. People v. Hernandez, 61 Cal.2d 529, 39 Cal.Rptr. 361, 393 P.2d 673 (1964).

72. See State v. Watson, 264 N.W.2d 519 (S.D.1978).

73. Vernon's Ann.Mo.Stat. § 469.320 (1979); W.Va.Code, 61–8B–13 (1976); Wyo.Stat.1977, § 6–4–308.

74. See Chapter 7, Section 7.

75. 1 Hale P.C. *630; 4 Bl.Comm. *212; The King v. Groombridge, 7 Car. & P. 582, 173 Eng.Rep. 256 (1836).

76. Regina v. Waite [1892] 2 Q.B. 600.

77. See Gordon v. State, 93 Ga. 541, 21 S.E. 54 (1893); Williams v. State, 14 Ohio 222 (1846).

78. Lord Hale writing in the early 1600s said: "But the least penetration maketh it rape or buggery, yea although there be not emissio feminis." 1 Hale P.C. *628.

79. The Queen v. Smith, 1 Cox C.C. 260 (1845). And see infra Chapter 8, Section 1.

80. State v. Sam, 60 N.C. 293 (1864).

81. Regina v. Philips, 8 Car. & P. 736, 173 Eng.Rep. 695, 696 (1839).

other elements of the offense, it will not support a conviction under the English rule.[82]

In this country some of the courts followed the English rule that a boy under fourteen is incapable of committing rape.[83] Some courts took the position that there is a presumption of incapacity on the part of a boy under fourteen but that this is a prima-facie presumption which may be overcome by proof of capacity.[84] This seems to be entirely meaningless because there can be no conviction of rape without proof of penetration, and if the boy's capacity to commit rape means the capacity to accomplish penetration, this has been established in every case in which there is evidence sufficient to support a conviction apart from such a rule.[85]

The only meaningful choice is either to adopt the English rule or take the position that there is no presumption that a boy under fourteen is incapable of committing rape other than the general prima-facie presumption that one under fourteen is mentally incapable of distinguishing right from wrong, which is the position taken by the Louisiana court.[86]

Although some statutes have codified the rule of the English common law in this regard: "One under the age of fourteen at the time the offense was committed cannot be convicted of rape or assault with intent to commit rape." [87] Most states, however, have repealed such statutory provisions.[88] In certain other enactments there has been an attempt to put some meaning into a prima-facie presumption of incapacity. "No conviction of rape can be had against one who was under the age of fourteen years at the time of the act alleged, unless his physical ability to accomplish penetration is proved as an independent fact, and beyond reasonable doubt." [89]

Because of the privilege against self-incrimination the boy cannot be required to supply such proof, either in or out of court. This suggests difficulty in making the required proof, but it may be possible. Such a case arose under former § 262 of the California Penal Code, and it was held that vagi-

---

82. Regina v. White [1892] 2 Q.B. 600.

83. Preddy v. Commonwealth, 184 Va. 765, 36 So.2d 549 (1946); Foster v. Commonwealth, 96 Va. 306, 31 So. 503 (1898); State v. Sam, 60 N.C. 293 (1864). And see the inference in Waters v. State, 234 A.2d 147 (Md.App.1967).

84. Gordon v. State, 93 Ga. 541, 21 S.E. 54 (1893); Heilman v. Commonwealth, 84 Ky. 547, 1 S.W. 731 (1886).

85. See Wagoner v. State, 5 Lea (Tenn.) 352 (1880), in which the girl testified to penetration and the boy admitted it.

86. State v. Jones, 39 La.Ann. 935, 3 So. 57 (1887).

87. Vernon's Ann.P.C. (Tex.) art. 1188, now repealed.

"A male person of the age of 14 years and upwards . . ." Smith-Hurd Ill.Ann.Stat. ch. 38 § 11–1 (1978).

"We conclude that the Illinois forcible rape statute is to be construed as provid-

ing a defendant with the affirmative defense that he was under the age of fourteen when he committed the rape." In re Reed, 52 Ill.App.3d 143, 9 Ill.Dec. 849, 367 N.E.2d 283, 287 (1977).

88. Texas provides for general incapacity of persons under age 15 to commit crimes. V.T.C.A., § 8.07 (1975). California repealed its statute relating to the capacity of a defendant under age fourteen, West's Ann.Cal.Code § 262 repealed by Cal.Stats. 1978 C29 § 1; So.Dakota, SL 1975 ch. 169 § 8.

89. 21 Okl.St.Ann. § 1112 (1958); Idaho Code § 18–6102 (1972).

When a minor under the age of 14 is charged with rape, the prosecution must prove two kinds of capability; that is, the capacity for understanding the wrongfulness of the conduct, and the youthful offender's capacity to commit the act. Tony Lorenzo C. v. Fare, 71 Cal.App.3d 303, 139 Cal.Rptr. 429 (1977).

nal smears taken from the victim after the attack showing seminal fluid and sperm, plus evidence that the victim had not had sexual intercourse with anyone other than the minor, satisfied the requirement.[90] While emission is not an element of rape, this evidence proved penetration.

One of the salutary trends of statutory law in this field is in the direction of a substantial increase in the age of the boy required for conviction in the consent cases. Thus it may be provided that no one under sixteen shall be convicted because of sexual intercourse with a willing girl between twelve and sixteen; [91] or that no one under eighteen shall be convicted because of such intercourse with a willing girl between fourteen and eighteen.[92] Even higher ages are found in some of the statutes.[93] Some statutes provide that the actor is only guilty if there is an age difference of more than three or four years.[94] Such extensions of criminal immunity for this particular type of misconduct have no application to a case of unlawful sexual intercourse with a girl under the age specified but *without* her consent.[95]

Impotency has no significance in a rape case unless it is interpreted, for this purpose, to mean physical inability to accomplish sexual penetration. By definition, one who is impotent in this sense cannot commit rape.

THE MODEL PENAL CODE

Article 213 deals with Sexual Offenses. The first section (omitting those provisions dealing only with when rape is a first-degree felony and when it is second-degree) provides:

(1) Rape. A male who has sexual intercourse with a female not his wife is guilty of rape if:

(a) he compels her to submit by force or by threat of imminent death, serious bodily injury, extreme pain or kidnapping, to be inflicted on anyone; or

(b) he has substantially impaired her power to appraise or control her conduct by administering or employing without her knowledge drugs, intoxicants or other means for the purpose of preventing resistance; or

(c) the female is unconscious; or

(d) the female is less than 10 years old.

. . . .. Sexual intercourse includes intercourse per os or per anum, with some penetration however slight; emission is not required.

This covers familiar ground except for certain important changes. The definition of sexual intercourse is enlarged to include buggery, expanded to

---

90. In re Tony C., 21 Cal.3d 888, 148 Cal.Rptr. 366, 582 P.2d 957 (1978).

91. Ala.Code, 1975, Tit. 13A–6–62 (a)(1).

92. 21 Okl.St.Ann. § 1112 (1958).

93. For example: "If any person shall carnally know any female not his wife, between the ages of fourteen and sixteen years, such carnal knowledge shall be deemed a misdemeanor . . . provided, that this section shall not apply to male persons under the age of eighteen years." Md.Code, 1957, Art. 27 § 464.

94. "An actor who is at least four years older than the victim and who inflicts sexual penetration or sexual intrusion on a victim under the age of sixteen years is guilty of sexual assault in the fourth degree." Wyo.Stat., 1977, § 6–4–305.

95. McManus v. State, 50 Okl.Cr. 354, 297 P. 830 (1931).

cover per os as well as per anum. The marital exclusion is enlarged to include persons living as man and wife whether married or not (in § 213.6(2)). The coercive threat is enlarged to include "extreme pain or kidnapping, to be inflicted on anyone." The age of consent is reduced to 10 years retaining the common rule that ignorance or mistake as to the age is no defense (in § 213.6(1)). And it omits the act of fraudulently inducing the victim to submit under the belief that she is having marital intercourse.

Such fraudulently induced intercourse is included as a lesser offense in subsection (2) Gross Sexual Imposition. Section 213.2 covers Deviate Sexual Intercourse by Force or Intimidation. Section 213.3 covers Corruption of Minors and Seduction. This section includes a male who has sexual intercourse with a female not his wife, if she is less than 16 years old and at least 4 years younger than he. In this case it is a defense if he reasonably believed she was over 16 (in § 213.6(1)). The provision as to seduction applies to a female who is induced to participate by a promise to marry made without intention to perform. Section 213.5 covers Indecent Exposure.

NEW CODES

In recent years several states have abandoned the term rape and have adopted a reference to the offense as sexual assault [96] or sexual abuse.[97] It has been suggested that changing the name of the offense may reduce the stigma associated with term rape.[98] Some jurisdictions have lumped together forcible sodomy or other forcible sexual contact with the crime of rape into one statutory format.[99] In other code revisions an effort has been made to abolish the issue of consent and to focus only on the question of whether the sexual penetration was accomplished by force.[1] Michigan has abolished the traditional terminology of rape and provided for four categories of offense called "criminal sexual conduct".[2] However, a standard comparable to the resistance or non-consent standard of the common-law may still exist.[3] It is too early to tell whether the sexual offense reform efforts will have much practical effect.[4]

G. ASSAULT TO RAPE

As mentioned under "assault and battery" the common-law prosecution of one who had tried to rape a woman without success was in the form of an

96. Neb.Rev.Stat. 28–408.01 (1975); W.Va.Code § 61–8B–3 (1976); Wyo.Stats., 1977, § 6–4–301, etc.

97. Iowa Code Ann.Chap. 709 (1978).

98. In, Rape By Any Other Name, 20 Crim.Law Qtrly. 409 (1978) in discussing the proposal for changes in Canadian rape legislation it was observed:

"Not so long ago, newspapers when reporting rape incidents or trial used to refer to the victim as having being criminally assaulted. Presumably everyone knew what was meant and the only point of such senseless prudery was to avoid the shocking consequence of using a four letter word. The proposals in bill C–51 are not based on prudery but on a matter

perceived as being of fundamental principle. The result, however, may be equally senseless."

99. Colo.Rev.Stat., 1973, 18–3–402–4; New Mex.Stats.Ann., 1978 § 30–9–11.

1. Burns' Ind.Ann.Stat. 35–42–4–1 (1976); Mich.Stat.Ann. § 28.788(2) (1974).

2. Mich.Stat.Ann.Chap. LXXVI (1974).

3. See Note, 23 Wayne L.Rev. 203 (1976).

4. See generally, Ireland, Reform Rape Legislation: A New Standard of Sexual Responsibility, 49 Colo.L.Rev. 185 (1978); Recent Statutory Developments in the Definition of Forcible Rape, 61 Va.L.Rev. 1500 (1975).

indictment for an attempt to commit rape. Statutes not infrequently make a different provision either in addition to the common-law method, or in lieu thereof, in the form of an offense called "assault with intent to commit rape."[5] Michigan, reflecting the trend of sexual assault legislation, provides for the crime of "assault with intent to commit criminal sexual conduct involving sexual penetration."[6] Where such an offense is created by statute, an assault with intent to have carnal knowledge of a child,—or assault with intent to commit rape if the two have been incorporated into one offense— may be committed by indecently laying hands upon a female person under the age of consent for the purpose of having sexual intercourse with her.[7] It is not necessary to show that such acts were against her will,[8] or that the man expected to encounter any resistance.[9]

One additional point may be mentioned. If a man lays hands upon a woman over the age of consent with intent to have sexual intercourse with her without her consent, and exerts enough force to constitute an attempt to perpetrate this offense, he may be convicted of an assault with intent to commit rape although the woman ultimately gives her consent—whereupon he has intercourse with her which does not constitute rape.[10]

Under the English rule a boy of fourteen cannot commit an assault with intent to commit rape.[11] He may be convicted of assault, if the prima-facie presumption of mental incapacity is overcome, but since what he has in mind does not constitute rape under this rule, his assault is not with intent to commit rape. On the other hand, an older person who is physically unable to accomplish penetration might think it was possible, and hence could be guilty of an assault with intent to commit rape.[12]

The abandonment of the quest after the assault does not preclude conviction for assault with intent to rape.[13] However, if the defendant did not intend to overcome the victim's will by force or illegal means, there is no

---

5. See for example, West's Ann.Cal.Pen.Code § 220 (1978); Idaho Code § 18–907 (1972). For the difference between attempt to rape and assault with intent to rape see infra, chapter 6, section 3, B.

6. Mich.Stat.Ann. § 28.788(7) (1974).

7. Phillips v. State, 93 Fla. 112, 111 So. 515 (1927); State v. Garney, 45 Idaho 768, 265 P. 668 (1928).

"Assault with intent to rape is established by a use of and intent to use some physical force for the purpose of achieving sexual gratification but requires an intent to persist in such force even in face of and for the purpose of overcoming the victim's resistance." United States v. Huff, 442 F.2d 885, 890 (D.C.Cir. 1971).

One may be guilty of assault with intent to commit statutory rape. State v. Dippre, 121 Ariz. 596, 592 P.2d 1252 (1979).

8. Teagarden v. State, 33 Okl.Cr. 394, 244 P. 63 (1926).

9. State v. Carnagy, 106 Iowa 483, 76 N.W. 805 (1898).

10. State v. Cross, 12 Iowa 66 (1861); Copeland v. State, 55 Ala.App. 99, 313 So.2d 219 (1975).

11. Regina v. White [1892] 2 Q.B. 600.

12. State v. Ballamah, 28 N.M. 212, 210 P. 391 (1922); Waters v. State, 234 A.2d 147 (Md.App.1967). Or an attempt to commit rape which involves the same problem. Preddy v. Commonwealth, 184 Va. 765, 36 S.E.2d 549 (1946).

A statute prohibiting marriages between parents and children, ancestors and descendants of every degree, brothers and sisters of half as well as whole blood, and between uncles and nieces or aunts and nephews, does not include an uncle and a niece of half blood, who was the daughter of D's half-sister. People v. Baker, 69 Cal.2d 675, 69 Cal.Rptr. 595, 442 P.2d 675 (1968).

13. State v. Moshier, 19 N.C.App. 514, 199 S.E.2d 300 (1973); McBrayer v. State, 504 S.W.2d 445 (Tex.Cr.App.1974).

assault with intent to rape [14] and a rebuff followed by an abandonment of the pursuit will preclude conviction.

THE MODEL PENAL CODE

Section 213.4 provides that one is guilty of "sexual assault" if he subjects another not his spouse to any sexual contact if he knows that the contact is offensive to the other or, in effect, if it is under circumstances in which sexual intercourse would constitute rape or one of the lesser sexual offenses. Sexual contact is defined in terms of touching the sexual or other intimate parts of another for the purpose of arousing or gratifying the sexual desire of either.

SECTION 6.   FALSE IMPRISONMENT

False imprisonment, sometimes called false arrest, is the unlawful confinement of a person.[1] It results from any unlawful exercise or show of force by which a person is compelled to remain where he does not wish to remain or go where he does not wish to go.[2] It is a common-law misdemeanor.[3]

In the legal sense there may be "confinement of the person" not only by locking him in the public jail or in a private house, or in the stocks, but "even by forcibly detaining one in the public streets." [4] One is not "confined" merely because he is prevented from going in some one direction, or in several directions, so long as he may freely depart by some other known way; [5] but he may be confined either by being restrained by physical barriers or physical force, or by being subjected to threats of physical force, duress or an asserted authority to which he submits.[6] Confinement is not necessarily stationary. One might be locked in a moving ship or be "confined" by being forcibly removed from one place to another.[7]

Every intentional confinement, even detention in the public street, amounts to imprisonment [8] unless it is a very temporary confinement properly incident to the exercise of some privilege. The proper exercise of a privilege may involve a very temporary detention of the person of another without amounting to "imprisonment." Thus, if an officer who is privileged to stop a motorist on the highway to inspect his driver's license, requires a cer-

---

14. State v. Hamm, 577 S.W.2d 936 (Mo.App.1979).

1. People v. Agnew, 16 Cal.2d 665, 107 P.2d 601 (1940); People v. Zilbauer, 44 Cal.2d 43, 279 P.2d 534 (1955); McKinney v. State, 149 Tex.Cr.R. 46, 191 S.W.2d 27 (1945).

"False imprisonment can be defined as the detention of a person without his consent and without lawful authority." Cullison v. City of Peoria, 120 Ariz. 165, 584 P.2d 1156, 1160 (1978).

"An arrest or imprisonment is false if it is unlawful." "Unlawful imprisonment is the intentional confinement of another's person, unjustified under the circumstances." Kellogg v. State, 94 Wn.2d 851, 621 P.2d 133, 136, 137 (1980).

2. McKendree v. Christy, 29 Ill.App.2d 195, 199, 172 N.E.2d 380, 381–82 (1961).

3. 4 Bl.Comm. *216; 1 East P.C. 428 (1803).

4. Floyd v. State, 12 Ark. 43, 47 (1851).

5. Restatement, Second, Torts § 36, and comment d (1965).

6. Id. at § 38–41.

7. Id. at § 36, comment c; People v. Wheeler, 73 Cal. 252, 14 P. 796 (1887); McDaniel v. State, 145 Tex.Cr.R. 115, 166 S.W.2d 138 (1942).

8. Floyd v. State, 12 Ark. 43 (1851).

tain driver of a car to stop for this purpose, examines the license, finds it in order, and permits the driver to go on his way without unreasonable delay, there has been no "imprisonment." Exactly the same deed done officiously by one having no authority to do so would constitute false imprisonment,[9] but if the temporary confinement is not for the sake of confinement but is merely incidental to the proper exercise of a privilege, the word "imprisonment" is not used.

Any other wilful exercise of force, or threat of force, by which another is deprived of his liberty, or compelled to remain where he does not wish to remain, or to go where he does not wish to go is an imprisonment.[10] It is not necessary that there be any violence or laying on of hands.[11] There may be imprisonment without an assault,[12] because it might be accomplished by merely locking a door.[13] Mere words are sufficient to constitute imprisonment if they actually impose a restraint upon the person at whom they are directed.[14] For example, if an officer asserts his authority to arrest and orders the person to come with him, this is imprisonment if the order is obeyed even if the officer does not touch the other.[15] But the mere fact that a person considers himself under arrest is not sufficient for imprisonment if there has been neither any physical restraint, threat of force, nor assertion of authority.[16] The assertion of authority not followed by submission is equally ineffective. If an officer pronounces words of arrest and commands the other to come with him, without an actual touching, there is no imprisonment if the other immediately runs away.[17]

"To constitute the injury of false imprisonment there are two points requisite: (1) the detention of the person; and (2) the unlawfulness of such detention."[18] By the very definition of the phrase an imprisonment is not "false" unless it is unlawful.[19] Hence if the imprisonment itself is rightful,—whether by reason of public authority or domestic authority—and is imposed in a proper manner, it does not come under the head of "false imprisonment." A bona fide attempt to prevent a suicide, even if it involves

9. See Head v. State, 131 Tex.Cr.R. 96, 96 S.W.2d 981 (1936); Arnold v. State, 8 N.Y.S.2d 28, 30, 255 App.Div. 422, 425 (3d Dep't, 1938). A "momentary restraint on the liberty of the prosecutor would be only a false imprisonment, which it is now settled may be committed without an assault; though the opinion seemed once to have been entertained, that a false imprisonment included an assault." State v. Edge, 1 Strob. 91, 93 (S.C.1846).

10. People v. Agnew, 16 Cal.2d 655, 107 P.2d 601 (1940); People v. Zilbauer, 44 Cal.2d 43, 279 P.2d 534 (1955).

"False imprisonment is the unlawful violation of the personal liberty of another." People v. Gibbs, 12 Cal.App.3d 526, 90 Cal.Rptr. 866, 879 (1970).

11. People v. Scalisi, 324 Ill. 131, 154 N.E. 715 (1926).

12. State v. Edge, 1 Strob. 91 (S.C. 1846).

13. Restatement, Second, Torts § 38, comment a (1965).

One may be imprisoned by being locked in the trunk of an automobile. Woods v. State, 95 Nev. 29, 588 P.2d 1030 (1979).

14. Pike v. Hanson, 9 N.H. 491 (1838).

15. Gold v. Bissell, 1 Wend. 210 (N.Y.Sup.Ct.1828).

16. Commonwealth v. Brewer, 109 Pa.Super. 429, 167 A. 386, 389 (1933).

17. Russen v. Lucas, 1 Car. & P. 153, 171 Eng.Rep. 1141 (N.P.1824).

18. Commonwealth v. Brewer, 109 Pa.Super. 429, 436, 167 A. 386, 388 (1933).

19. Barber v. State, 13 Fla. 675 (1870); People v. Cohoon, 315 Ill.App. 259, 42 N.E.2d 969 (1942); Cargill v. State, 8 Tex.App. 431 (1880).

the detention of a person against his will, is not a crime.[20] The manner of enforcement is just as important as the basic authority itself in this regard. Thus the authority of a parent to impose reasonable restrictions upon the liberty of his minor child was no defense to a father who had kept a blind and helpless boy in a cold damp cellar under circumstances of extreme cruelty.[21]

Confinement is not unlawful if it is with the consent of the person confined,[22] provided the consent was freely and intelligently given by one not subjected to any coercion,[23] intimidation or deception, and not disqualified from giving consent by unsoundness of mind or tender years. Thus, a farmer who chained his wife to a bed while he went to town was held not guilty of false imprisonment where there was unmistakable evidence that she had requested him to do so, whatever the reason for this request may have been.[24]

Many of the false imprisonment cases involve alleged acts of misconduct by officers of the law, such as unlawful arrest or detention of a person without a warrant, when a warrant is needed, or with an illegal warrant, or a warrant illegally executed.[25] If, for example, an officer is acting under his authority to arrest without a warrant he must be certain that the alleged misconduct, for which the arrest is to be made, is an offense [26] and that the circumstances fall within the rule authorizing an arrest without a warrant.[27] In one case, to illustrate, an officer misunderstood his authority and in excess of his lawful privilege ordered a person to accompany him to a magistrate. The other obeyed. After they had proceeded about half a mile the officer "released" his prisoner and allowed him to go his own way, but although he had not actually touched the man, the officer was held liable in a civil action for false imprisonment.[28] In another case a deputy who transported a prisoner arrested without authority was held guilty of false imprisonment although he himself had not participated in the apprehension of the man.[29] Furthermore, undue detention after a lawful arrest will constitute false imprisonment,[30] as where a prisoner is detained an unreasonable length of time without being taken before a magistrate,[31] or is unlawfully refused an opportunity to be released on bail.[32] An officer is not guilty of false imprisonment, however, where there has been an unavoidable delay in provid-

20. State v. Hembd, 305 Minn. 120, 232 N.W.2d 872 (1975).

21. Fletcher v. People, 52 Ill. 395 (1869).

22. Floyd v. State, 12 Ark. 43 (1851); People v. Cohoon, 315 Ill.App. 259, 42 N.E.2d 969 (1942); State v. Lunsford, 81 N.C. 528 (1879).

23. A trip made under coercion is false imprisonment. McKinney v. State, 149 Tex.Cr.R. 46, 191 S.W.2d 27 (1945).

24. People v. Cohoon, 315 Ill.App. 259, 42 N.E.2d 969 (1942).

25. Reilly v. United States Fidelity & Guaranty Co., 15 F.2d 314 (9th Cir. 1926). And see Montgomery v. State, 145 Tex.Cr.R. 606, 170 S.W.2d 750 (1943).

26. State v. Hunter, 106 N.C. 796, 11 S.E. 366 (1890).

27. People v. Guertins, 224 Mich. 8, 194 N.W. 561 (1923); Gill v. State, 134 Tex.Cr.R. 363, 115 S.W.2d 923 (1938).

28. Gold v. Bissell, 1 Wend. 210 (N.Y.Sup.Ct.1828).

29. Roberts v. Commonwealth, 284 Ky. 365, 144 S.W.2d 811 (1940).

30. Anderson v. Beck, 64 Miss. 113, 8 So. 167 (1886). And see Kirk v. Garrett, 84 Md. 383, 407, 35 A. 1089, 1092 (1896).

31. Twilley v. Perkins, 77 Md. 252, 26 A. 286 (1893); Kangieser v. Zink, 134 Cal.App.2d 559, 285 P.2d 950 (1955).

32. Manning v. Mitchell, 73 Ga. 660 (1884).

ing an opportunity for release on bail,[33] nor where there has been a temporary detention for a lawful purpose.[34]

It is false imprisonment for an officer to arrest a person without color of justification,[35] as where the arrest is for drunkenness of one who is not intoxicated and not reasonably believed so to be.[36] And a deputy who makes an obviously unlawful arrest and detention cannot plead as a defense that he was ordered to do so by his superior.[37] A private person unlawfully imprisons another by wrongfully causing his arrest by an officer,[38] and this might be accomplished by an announcement in the presence of an officer that a "citizen's arrest" was being made, if this resulted in the detention of the other by an officer, even if the speaker did not actually touch the other or specifically direct the officer to detain him.[39] A citizen who makes an arrest without lawful authority or under pretended authority commits false imprisonment.[40] A bail bondsman who arrests a bonded principal for return to court, but without proper process, unlawfully imprisons the person arrested.[41]

Where a statute required an officer, in arresting a motorist for a violation of the speed laws, to detain him no longer than necessary to obtain the required information and to issue a citation for appearance at a future fixed date, it was false imprisonment for the officer to refuse to issue the citation and to require the motorist to accompany the officer at once to a justice of the peace.[42] It has also been held false imprisonment for an officer to put a man on a train without authority and detain him there until the train has started; [43] or for troops of one state to cross the boundary line into another state and there recapture a deserter.[44]

A mere error in judgment on the part of a magistrate in issuing a warrant of arrest which should not have been issued under the circumstances is not sufficient to make him guilty of false imprisonment.[45]

Any intentional confinement of another by a private person is false imprisonment, if not authorized by law, as where one improperly and forcibly removed another from public land; [46] unlawfully committed another to an

33. Cargill v. State, 8 Tex.App. 431 (1880).

34. Pine v. Okzewski, 112 N.J.L. 429, 170 A. 825 (1934).

35. People v. Sagehorn, 140 Cal.App. 2d 138, 294 P.2d 1062 (1956).

36. Kimbler v. Commonwealth, 269 S.W.2d 273 (Ky.1954).

37. Roberts v. Commonwealth, 284 Ky. 365, 144 S.W.2d 811 (1940).

38. Rogers v. Sears, Roebuck & Co., 48 Wn.2d 879, 297 P.2d 250 (1956).

39. People v. Agnew, 16 Cal.2d 665, 107 P.2d 601 (1940).

40. Finch v. Commonwealth, 419 S.W.2d 146 (Ky.1967).

41. Austin v. State, 541 S.W.2d 162 (Tex.Cr.App.1976).

42. Montgomery v. State, 145 Tex.Cr.R. 606, 170 S.W.2d 750 (1943).

Arrest of a diabetic in insular shock upon reasonable belief that he was intoxicated was lawful, but an action for false imprisonment lies for his continued detention after such time as the police should have known his true condition. Tufte v. City of Tacoma, 71 Wn.2d 866, 431 P.2d 183 (1967).

43. Bath v. Metcalf, 145 Mass. 274, 14 N.E. 133 (1887).

44. Commonwealth v. Blodgett, 53 Mass. 56 (1846).

45. Campbell v. State, 48 Ga. 353 (1873).

"At common law, good faith and probable cause were viable defenses against actions for false arrest and imprisonment." Greer v. Turner, 639 F.2d 229, 231 (5th Cir. 1981).

46. People v. Wheeler, 73 Cal. 252, 14 P. 796 (1887).

insane asylum;[47] stopped a carriage without authority and detained the driver against his will;[48] or wrongfully detained a passenger in an automobile by refusing to stop and by driving at such a speed that she dared not alight.[49]

For a storekeeper to pick a customer at random and detain him for questioning about a possible larceny as a routine check on shoplifting results in false imprisonment.[50]

On the other hand pranksters who decoyed a victim about a quarter of a mile on a fake search for a supposedly stolen horse were held not guilty of false imprisonment.[51]

False imprisonment was a misdemeanor at common law[52] and is an offense in many of the states today.[53] On the other hand it is omitted from some of the criminal codes[54] on the theory that if what was done did not constitute some other crime, such as assault, abduction or kidnaping, the civil remedy for damages, to be recovered by the person whose liberty was momentarily infringed, is sufficient.

Under some of the statutes false imprisonment is a crime if committed by a police officer, but only a civil offense if committed by any other.[55]

If the statute provides punishment for one who unlawfully imprisons another, with intent to cause the other to be secretly confined and imprisoned against his will, a conviction is not proper without proof of this intent to cause secret confinement.[56] Such a statute, however, is more properly classified under kidnaping than under false imprisonment.

It should be added that false imprisonment is a lesser included offense in the charge of kidnapping.[57]

The original Restatement of Torts took the position that there was no false imprisonment unless the victim was aware of the confinement at the

47. See People v. Camp, 139 N.Y. 87, 92, 34 N.E. 755, 756 (1893). See also State v. Halladay, 68 S.D. 547, 5 N.W.2d 42 (1942). This was a proceeding under a statute and it was held the statute was not violated in this case. But *unlawfully* committing a person to an insane asylum would be false imprisonment if done with mens rea.

48. See State v. Edge, 1 Strob. 91, 93 (S.C.1846).

49. McDaniel v. State, 145 Tex.Cr.R. 115, 166 S.W.2d 138 (1942). See also Smith v. State, 26 Tenn. 43 (1846), in which the keeper of a ferry detained another ten or fifteen minutes by refusing to release him and his horse and carryall on the claim the ferriage had not been paid.

Forcible detention of a person in his own home will constitute kidnaping. Tomsak v. People, 166 Colo. 226, 442 P.2d 825 (1968).

Wrongfully forcing one to change seats in a car and to remain in the car is

false imprisonment. People v. Zilbauer, 44 Cal.2d 43, 279 P.2d 534 (1955). But locking a person *out of* a particular room is not. Martin v. Lincoln Park West Corp., 219 F.2d 622 (7th Cir. 1955).

50. Clark v. Kroger Co., 382 F.2d 562 (7th Cir. 1967).

51. State v. Lunsford, 81 N.C. 528 (1879).

52. 4 Bl.Comm. *216, 218.

53. Most of the cases cited above were criminal cases.

54. See for example Miss.Code 1972 in which no provision is made for false imprisonment unless it amounts to kidnapping.

55. See People v. Hope, 257 N.Y. 147, 150, 177 N.E. 402, 403 (1931).

56. Holroyd v. State, 127 Fla. 152, 172 So. 700 (1937).

57. State v. Stirgus, 21 Wn.App. 627, 586 P.2d 532 (1978).

time.[58] Dean Prosser pointed out the unsoundness of this position [59] and it has since been changed by stating in substance that it is false imprisonment if the victim is aware of the confinement at the time "or is harmed thereby." [60] This is sound as a matter of civil liability, but since the purpose of the criminal law is not to compensate the victim for harm suffered by him but to punish the actor for his misconduct it would seem that false imprisonment as a criminal offense would not require that the victim either be conscious of the confinement at the time or be harmed thereby—just as one may be guilty of a criminal assault although the victim suffered no harm and was utterly unaware of any threatened danger at the time.[61]

THE MODEL PENAL CODE

Section 212.3 defines false imprisonment in terms of knowingly restraining another unlawfully so as to interfere substantially with his liberty. This standard has been followed in several states.[62]

SECTION 7.   KIDNAPING [1]

Kidnaping is aggravated false imprisonment.[2] At common law kidnaping was defined as the forcible abduction or stealing away of a man, woman or child from his own country and sending him into another.[3] It was a misdemeanor at common law but is a felony under modern statutes.

58. Restatement, Torts § 42 (1934).

59. Prosser, Law of Torts 42 (4th ed. 1971). And see Prosser, False Imprisonment: Consciousness of Confinement, 55 Colum.L.Rev. 847 (1955).

60. Restatement, Second, Torts § 42 (1965).

61. See supra chapter 2, section 2, B.

62. Vernon's Ann.Mo.Stat. § 565.130 (1979); N.J.Stat.Ann. 2C:13–3 (1978); Utah Code Ann., 1953, § 76–5–304.

1. This word appears with two different forms of spelling. Kidnaping (kidnaped, kidnaper): West's Ann.Cal.Pen.Code §§ 207–8 (1970). Kidnapping (kidnapped, kidnapper): Code of Ala. 1975 § 13A–6–40, Wyo.Stat. 1977 § 6–4–201. The form with a single "p" is to be preferred because it is a general rule of spelling that the accent determines whether or not to double the letter when the suffix is to be added to a word ending in a *single consonant* preceded by a *single vowel*. The final consonant is doubled if the word has only one syllable or has more than one with the accent on the last syllable. Wrap—wrapping, wrapped, wrapper; Equip—equipping, equipped, equipper. But the final consonant is *not* doubled if the word has more than one syllable and the accent is not on

the last. Develop—developing, developed, developer; offer—offering, offered, offerer; suffer—suffering, suffered, sufferer. Mawson, The Dictionary Companion, pp. 21–25 (1932).

2. East says that kidnaping is the "most aggravated species of false imprisonment." 1 East P.C. 429 (1803). And see Keith v. State, 120 Fla. 847, 163 So. 136 (1935); Vandiver v. State, 97 Okl. 217, 222, 261 P.2d 617, 623 (1953); Click v. State, 3 Tex. 282, 285 (1848). An unlawful arrest by a peace officer, resulting from a mistake as to his authority, does not constitute kidnaping. People v. Weiss, 276 N.Y. 384, 12 N.E.2d 514 (1938).

3. 4 Bl.Comm. *219. See also Collier v. Vaccaro, 51 F.2d 17 (4th Cir. 1931); Keith v. State, 120 Fla. 847, 163 So. 136 (1935); Commonwealth v. Cartusciello, 100 Pa.Super. 473 (1930); State v. Olsen, 76 Utah 181, 289 P. 92 (1930); Vandiver v. State, 97 Okl.Cr. 217, 222, 261 P.2d 617, 623 (1953). A federal officer, although lawfully arresting a man in Canada, was guilty of violating the Canadian law against kidnaping if he carried his prisoner forcibly into the United States. Vaccaro v. Collier, 51 F.2d 17 (4th Cir. 1931).

A consideration of kidnaping under modern statutes requires that attention be given to three different kinds or grades of the offense, namely (1) simple kidnaping, (2) aggravated kidnaping such as for ransom or where the victim is seriously injured, and (3) child stealing.

A. SIMPLE KIDNAPING

Kidnaping which is not in some aggravated form, such as holding for ransom or where the victim is injured, and does not fall within the type of misconduct known as child stealing, is commonly referred to as "simple kidnaping." [4]

1. ASPORTATION

Common-law kidnaping was unlawful confinement plus asportation—an extreme asportation in the form of transportation out of the country. This is no longer essential under modern statutes [5] but different provisions have been resorted to in the effort to modernize the crime. One plan has been to modify the asportation requirement, as by starting with a provision speaking in terms of carrying the victim "into another country, state or county" and later amending it by adding "or into another part of the same county." [6] Or it may be removal "from the place where he is found," [7] or abducting,[8] or "abducts or steals away," or "leads, takes or carries away," [9] or "from one place to another." [10] The forms of expression of asportation are varied. In some states the term "kidnap" is used [11] with other words of asportation. If the statute provides no substitute, such as the element of secrecy (to be mentioned presently) asportation, although in modified form, remains essential for the crime of kidnaping. Unlawful confinement without it is merely false imprisonment.

The California court, after first holding otherwise,[12] took the position that a movement which is merely incidental to another crime, such as robbery, and does not increase the risk of harm to the victim, is not kidnaping.[13] Thus compelling the victim to drive five blocks to facilitate the robbery was held not to be kidnaping.[14] The California rule, that movement merely incidental to the commission of some other crime, is insufficient to establish kid-

---

4. People v. O'Farrell, 161 Cal.App.2d 13, 21, 325 P.2d 102, 1007 (1958).

"Simple kidnapping is the intentional and forcible seizing and carrying of any person from one place to another without his consent." State v. Smith, 323 So.2d 797, 801 (La.1975).

5. ". . . the new statute is broader than common-law kidnapping in that it eliminates asportation as a necessary element of the crime . . ." State v. Fulcher, 34 N.C.App. 233, 237 S.E.2d 909, 913 (1977), affirmed 294 N.C. 503, 243 S.E.2d 338 (1978).

6. West's Ann.Cal.Pen.Code § 207 (1970). The amendment was added in 1905.

7. Vernon's Ann.Mo.Stat. § 565.110 (1979).

8. West's Fla.Stat.Ann. § 787.01 (1976).

9. Ga.Code § 26–303 (1977); Nev.Rev.Stat. 200.310 (1973).

10. Colo.Rev.Stat. 1973, 18–3–301–2; Burns' Ind.Ann.Stat. § 35–42–3–2 (1977).

11. Idaho Code § 18–4501 (1972); Miss.Code 1972 § 97–3–51–53.

12. People v. Chessman, 38 Cal.2d 166, 192, 238 P.2d 1001, 1017 (1951).

13. People v. Daniels, 71 Cal.2d 1119, 80 Cal.Rptr. 897, 459 P.2d 255 (1969), overruling *Chessman* in part.

14. People v. Timmons, 4 Cal.3d 411, 93 Cal.Rptr. 736, 482 P.2d 648 (1971).

naping, was expressly rejected by the Arizona court which emphasized that the essence of kidnaping is not the distance the victim is transported, but the unlawful compulsion against his will to go somewhere.[15] And where the victim was compelled to go to another room about six feet distant while the robber made his getaway, a conviction of both kidnaping for the purpose of robbery, and robbery, was proper since the carrying away movement was part of the robbery and these are distinct offenses.[16] Another court emphasized: "Neither resort to a tape measure or a stop watch" is necessary in determining whether kidnaping has been committed.[17]

Unlike kidnaping for ransom, simple kidnaping, under the provision mentioned, does not require a specific intent,[18] although proof of an innocent intent would be exculpating; as if a child or helpless person was moved from a position of danger to a place of safety.[19] The statute may provide, it may be added, that a specific intent to take the victim out of the state may be substituted for any actual asportation.[20]

2. SECRECY

Secrecy, though common in kidnaping, is neither necessary nor important under the type of statute mentioned above,[21] but some states adopted a different plan for modernizing this offense by substituting, for the original requirement of asportation, an intent to cause the victim to be secretly confined.[22] Under such a provision no movement of any kind is needed[23] but the proof must establish a purpose to cause such *secret* confinement.[24] As it was said, in such a jurisdiction one who seizes another unlawfully with intent merely to keep or detain him against his will is guilty of false imprisonment only; while one who seizes another unlawfully with intent to detain him secretly against his will is guilty of kidnaping.[25]

15. State v. Perry, 116 Ariz. 40, 567 P.2d 786 (App.1977).

16. State v. Rabon, 115 Ariz. 45, 563 P.2d 300 (App.1977).

17. State v. Fulcher, 294 N.C. 503, 243 S.E.2d 338, 351 (1978).

"In State v. Williams, 111 Ariz. 222, 224, 526 P.2d 1244, 1246 (1974), we indicated that the essence of the crime of kidnapping . . . is not the distance the victim is transported, but the unlawful compulsion to stay somewhere or go somewhere against the victim's will." State v. Pickett, 121 Ariz. 142, 589 P.2d 16, 20 (1978).

18. People v. Sheasbey, 82 Cal.App. 459, 465, 255 P. 836 (1927); People v. Fernandez, 127 Cal.App. 45, 48, 15 P.2d 172 (1932). Contra: Smith v. State, ___ Ind. ___, 386 N.E.2d 1193 (1979) based on a more specific wording in the statute.

19. See People v. Oliver, 55 Cal.2d 761, 12 Cal.Rptr. 865, 361 P.2d 593 (1961).

20. See e.g., West's Ann.Cal.Pen.Code § 207 (1970).

21. People v. Brazil, 53 Cal.App.2d 596, 128 P.2d 204 (1942).

22. Code of Ala. §§ 13A–6–40(2), 13A–6–43 (1975).

Tenn.Code Ann. § 39–2601 (1975). Actual asportation and secrecy are not essential elements, Brown v. State, 574 S.W.2d 57 (Tenn.Cr.App. 1978).

Asportation of the victim is not an element under Ill.Rev.Stat. ch. 38, sec. 10–1(a)(1), but secret confinement is the gist of kidnaping and must be proved beyond a reasonable doubt. People v. Mulcahey, 50 Ill.App.3d 421, 8 Ill.Dec. 627, 365 N.E.2d 1013 (1977).

23. Cowan v. State, 208 Tenn. 512, 347 S.W.2d 37 (1961).

24. People v. Camp, 139 N.Y. 87, 34 N.E. 755 (1893).

25. State v. Olsen, 76 Utah 181, 186, 289 P. 92, 94 (1930). See also Hackbarth v. State, 201 Wis. 3, 229 N.W. 83 (1930).

A band of robed and masked men seized an intoxicated person near a church and took him to the woods where they flogged him. It was held that this did not constitute kidnaping unless the confinement during the flogging was intended to be secret.[26] At the point of a gun a man was taken to a room and there was told to go to another city (within the same state) and not to come back or to write to his local friends. Under threat of being shot he agreed. One of the men put him on a train and rode with him part of the way. This was held to be kidnaping because it involved an unlawful imprisonment with intent to cause the victim to be confined secretly.[27]

A defendant, with two assistants, confined a boy at night and against his will, without authority of law, in the rear seat of an automobile, while they compelled his companion to drive the car as directed by them. Both of the boys were intimidated by threats and the show of a gun. This was held sufficient for kidnaping because the boy was seized unlawfully with intent to cause him to be confined secretly. The fact that the secret confinement was to be for only a limited time and as an incident to this other purpose did not save the false imprisonment from becoming kidnaping.[28]

On the other hand, a defendant who took a person to an insane asylum, in broad daylight and over public highways and railroads, and caused this person to be confined in the asylum unlawfully, well knowing her not to be insane, was held to be guilty of false imprisonment only, and not kidnaping, because no secrecy was involved.[29]

An additional caution is in order. The Courts have tended to construe the kidnaping statutes rather narrowly to avoid including the whole field of false imprisonment therein. One statute, until recently, read as follows: "Any person who shall, without lawful authority, forcibly or secretly confine or imprison another within this state against his will or shall forcibly carry or send another out of this state, or from place to place within this state against his will, and without lawful authority, or who shall, without such authority, forcibly seize, confine, inveigle, or kidnap another, with intent to cause such person to be secretly confined or imprisoned in this state against his will, or to be sent or carried out of this state against his will, or to be sold as a slave . . . ."[30]

It was held that the intent "to cause such person to be secretly confined . . . or carried out of this state," and so forth, qualifies each preceding clause of the section and that unlawful, forcible confinement or imprisonment of a person within the state was merely false imprisonment and not kidnaping if no intended secrecy was involved.[31]

One may be secretly confined, although he had originally selected the secluded spot for some purpose of his own, if he is compelled to remain there against his will. For example, two teenage couples had parked their car in

26. Doss v. State, 200 Ala. 30, 123 So. 231 (1929).

27. State v. Newman, 127 Minn. 445, 149 N.W. 945 (1914).

28. People v. Hope, 257 N.Y. 147, 177 N.E. 402 (1931). And see Pond v. State, 233 Ind. 585, 121 N.E.2d 640 (1954).

29. People v. Camp, 139 N.Y. 87, 34 N.E. 755 (1893).

30. Wis.Stats. 1953, § 340.54. See now Wis.Stats. 1958, § 940.31 (1958). Cf. Mass.Gen.Laws Ann. C265 § 26 (1971).

31. Smith v. State, 63 Wis. 433, 23 N.W. 879 (1885). Cited with approval in Doss v. State, 220 Ala. 30, 32, 123 So. 231, 232 (1929).

an isolated spot at night. **D** found them there and detained them for seven hours by threats with a pistol. His purpose was to have sexual intercourse with the girls, but their resistance was such that he finally gave up and left. It was held that he had forcibly and secretly confined them and was guilty of kidnaping.[32]

Total concealment is not required. A conviction was allowed where the victim was transported in public view in an automobile and removed from a heavily populated area to an isolated field.[33]

B. AGGRAVATED KIDNAPING

Kidnaping was a misdemeanor at common law, punished by fine, imprisonment and pillory.[34] Under modern statutes it is a felony,[35] and the special form of the offense known as "kidnaping for ransom" is regarded as one of the gravest crimes and has at times been made a capital offense.[36] Several codes have provided for a special offense of aggravated kidnaping providing for enhanced punishment where the victim is harmed or injured.[37]

Such statutes often are very specific, speaking in some such terms as confining, seizing or kidnaping "any individual by any means whatsoever with intent to hold or detain . . . such individual for ransom, reward or to commit extortion or to exact from relatives or friends of such person any money or valuable thing . . ." [38] In any event the word "ransom" as used in such a statute is employed in its ordinary sense as meaning the money, price or consideration paid or demanded for the release of the captured person.[39] One who detains another for the purpose of extorting money from him or from another person as the price of his release is guilty of kidnaping for ransom even if the victim is actually released without the payment having been made.[40] A wrongdoer is guilty of kidnaping for ransom, as a principal, if he participates in any of the three elements of the offense,—(1) the

32. Cowan v. State, 208 Tenn. 512, 347 S.W.2d 37 (1961).

33. State v. Weir, 506 S.W.2d 437 (Mo.1974).

34. 4 Bl.Comm. *218–19; State v. Holland, 120 La. 429, 45 So. 380 (1907).

35. See the statutes cited supra notes 6–11.

36. See Ala.Code 1959, Tit. 14, § 7, see now Ala.Code 1975, § 13A–6–43; West's Ann.Cal.Pen.Code § 209 (1951) amended to delete death penalty, see § 209 (1977); Burns' Ind.Crim.Code § 10–2903 (1956), see now § 35–42–3–2 (1977); Utah Code Ann., 1953, § 76–5–302 "Aggravated kidnaping is a capital felony unless the actor voluntarily releases the victim alive in a safe place before trial . . ." See also Rev.Code Mont. 1947, §§ 94–303, 304 (1974).

Indications are that the Supreme Court would hold that making kidnaping for ransom per se a capital offense would be cruel and unusual punishment. Compare Coker v. Georgia, 433 U.S. 584, 97 S.Ct. 2861 (1977).

37. McKinney's Consol.L.N.Y. Penal § 135.25 (1975); V.T.C.A., Penal Code § 20.04 (1974). See also Ala.Code 1975 § 13A–6–43(a)(4); Iowa Code Ann. § 710.2 (1978).

38. West's Ann.Cal.Pen.Code § 209 (1977). See also Idaho Code § 18–4502 (1978) "With intent to obtain ransom." Burns' Ind.Stat.Ann. § 35–42–3–2 (1978).

39. Keith v. State, 120 Fla. 847, 163 So. 136 (1935).

40. State v. Leuth, 128 Iowa 189, 103 N.W. 345 (1905). Kidnaping for the purpose of robbery is a separate and distinct offense from the robbery itself, and if the victim is forcibly carried away for this purpose and later robbed the offender is guilty of both offenses and may be convicted of both. People v. Cluchey, 142 Cal.App.2d 563, 298 P.2d 633 (1956).

unlawful seizure, (2) the secret confinement, or (3) the extortion of the ransom.[41] This includes one who acts as a go-between to collect the ransom for the actual abductors.[42] A fugitive from justice who forced a cab driver to drive an automobile in an attempted escape was held guilty of kidnaping with intent to obtain money or reward, on the ground that the benefit received from forcing the driver to assist him in this flight from justice was within the meaning of the word "reward." [43]

Some statutes have provided for aggravated kidnaping beyond the holding for ransom speaking, in substance, of kidnaping for ransom, extortion or robbery,[44] for the commission of a felony or to violate or abuse him sexually,[45] or to terrorize the victim [46] or where physical harm or injury has been inflicted.[47] The Model Penal Code would limit the crime of kidnaping to unlawful asportation *or* [48] secret confinement for any of the following purposes: (a) to hold for ransom or reward or as a shield or hostage; (b) to facilitate commission of any felony or flight thereafter; (c) to inflict bodily injury on or to terrorize the victim or another; or (d) to interfere with the performance of any governmental or political function.[49]

The Colorado statute provides that whoever commits first-degree kidnaping is guilty of a class 1 felony if the victim shall have suffered bodily injury. Although there was evidence of additional injury in this case, it was indicated that a kidnap victim who has been raped has suffered bodily injury.[50]

C. CHILD STEALING

Child stealing might be mentioned in the discussion of abduction, because it is sometimes considered a form of that offense.[51] On the other hand, it is often found in the chapter on kidnaping,[52] or even in the kidnaping section

41. People v. Petitti, 337 Ill. 625, 169 N.E. 749 (1929).

42. Ibid.

43. State v. Andre, 195 Wash. 221, 80 P.2d 553 (1938).

"The statute proscribes any kidnapping 'with the intent . . . to force the victim or any other person to make any concession or give up anything of value in order to secure a release,' and the phrase 'any concession' is sufficiently broad to encompass submission to a sexual assault." People v. Molina, 41 Colo.App. 128, 584 P.2d 634, 635 (1978).

44. West's Ann.Cal.Pen.Code § 209 (1977).

45. McKinney's Consol.L.N.Y.Penal § 135.25 (1973).

46. Hawaii Rev.Stat. §§ 707–720(e) (1972).

47. See Ala.Code, 1975, § 13A–6–43; Smith-Hurd Ill.Ann.Stat. ch. 38 § 10–2 (1978).

"There is no question but that rape involves serious physical and psychological consequences, perhaps greater than would be suffered as a result of a knife or gunshot wound. It would be contrary to the tenets of a civilized society to determine that rape is not harm. We therefore adopt the rule followed in California, that rape alone, without accompanying physical violence, constitutes harm to a kidnap victim." State v. Oakes, 373 A.2d 210, 215 (Del.1977).

48. Some of the statutes, particularly those dealing with kidnaping for ransom, are worded in terms of any person who "conceals, kidnaps or carries away." E.g. West's Ann.Cal.Pen.Code § 209 (1977); See also Alaska Stats. 11.15.260 (1970).

49. Model Penal Code, § 212.1.

As to a change in the New York statute see People v. Lombardi, 20 N.Y.2d 266, 229 N.E.2d 206 (1967).

50. Miller v. District Court in and for 19th Judicial District, 197 Colo. 485, 593 P.2d 1379 (1979).

51. State v. Miller, 322 Mo. 210, 14 S.W.2d 621 (1929).

52. Ariz.Rev.Stat.Ann. § 13–1302 (1978).

itself.[53] One rather logical solution is a chapter on abduction and kidnaping.[54] It cannot be omitted here because one of the common legislative patterns is to provide for three main categories of kidnaping: (1) (with considerable variations in the exact scope, and called herein) simple kidnaping, (2) kidnaping for ransom, and (3) child stealing.[55]

The "child-stealing" statutes commonly provide a penalty for any one who shall lead, take, entice or detain a child under a specified age with intent to keep or conceal it from its parent, guardian, or other person having lawful care or control thereof.[56]

Great variation is found in the age used for this purpose, such as any child under the age of 12,[57] or 14,[58] or 16,[59] or 18 or age of majority.[60] Kidnaping under such a statute, needless to say, may be accomplished by force, persuasion or enticement.[61] Many of these cases have involved a taking by one parent from another and only these require special attention because a taking by anyone else from a parent or other lawful custodian of the child with the intent to keep or conceal it from such person would clearly violate the statute in the absence of some special authority for the particular taking.

In the absence of any judicial decree granting the custody of the child to the mother, the father is not guilty of child stealing in taking their child from her against her will.[62] This is true even if the father had previously agreed that the mother should have the custody of the child,[63] or if a suit for divorce brought by the wife is pending, so long as no order has been made with reference to custody.[64] Obviously a father who has been awarded the custody of the child in a divorce decree cannot be guilty of kidnaping it from the mother.[65] In any of these cases, moreover, in which the father would not be guilty of this offense as a result of taking their child from the mother against her will, a third person who helps the father in doing so has a complete defense.[66]

53. Colo.Rev.Stat. 1973, 18–3–301.

54. Ala.Code, 1959, Tit. 14, ch. 1.

55. N.C.Gen.Stat. § 14–39 (1975).

56. See generally Burns' Ind.Ann.Stat. § 35–42–3–3 (1977); Ore.Rev.Stat. 163.245 (1971); Purdon's Consol.Penn.Stat.Ann. § 2904 (1973); Tenn.Code Ann. § 39–2602 (1975); Utah Code Ann., 1953, § 76–5–303; Wis.Stat.Ann. 940.32 (1958).

57. Wyo.Stat. 1977, § 6–4–202.

58. Burns' Ind.Ann.Stat. § 35–42–3–3 (1977); Can.Crim.Code § 250 (1978).

59. 13 V.S.A. (Vt.) § 2402 (1978); Tenn.Code Ann. § 34–2602 (1975).

60. N.J.Stat.Ann. § 2C:13–4 (1979). See also Wade v. State, 24 Ala.App. 176, 132 So. 71 (1931); People v. Edenburg, 88 Cal.App. 558, 263 P. 857 (1928).

61. State v. Trosla, 4 N.J.Misc. 678, 134 A. 290 (1926); Pond v. State, 233 Ind. 585, 121 N.E.2d 640 (1954).

62. Burns v. Commonwealth, 129 Pa. 138, 18 A. 756 (1889).

63. State v. Powe, 107 Miss. 770, 66 So. 207 (1914).

64. State v. Dewey, 155 Iowa 469, 136 N.W. 533 (1912).

65. In re Marceau, 32 Misc. 217, 65 N.Y.S. 717 (1900).

66. State v. Dewey, 155 Iowa 469, 136 N.W. 533 (1912).

"We are compelled by our reading of Oregon's statute to hold that a person who assists a parent entitled to custody in obtaining physical custody of a child cannot be guilty of kidnapping." State v. Edmiston, 43 Or.App. 13, 602 P.2d 282, 283 (1979).

There have been cases holding the agent guilty of kidnaping while exempting the parent at whose instance the taking occurred, on the ground that the danger to the child is less where the taking is by a parent likely to have the best interest of the child in mind; and that the parent from whose custody the child is taken will recognize the taker, if the other parent, thereby lessening the mental anguish and reducing the likelihood of

A father will be guilty of kidnaping under such a statute, however, if he takes the child from the mother without her consent, after the custody had been awarded to the mother by judicial decree; [67] and a mother will be guilty if she takes the child without the consent of the other after custody had been judicially awarded to the father, or even to a third person, such as a grandmother.[68] On the other hand, a father who took a daughter of eleven, who had been awarded to the custody of the mother in a divorce proceeding, and carried the girl out of the state to prevent her appearance as a witness in obedience to a subpoena, was held not guilty of kidnaping when it was shown that he had the consent of the mother to do so.[69] The fact that the act was very wrongful did not bring it within the scope of this offense.

The Model Penal Code includes this problem in Section 212.4. Interference with Custody.

D. CONSENT

There has been no kidnaping if the person who was confined or transported freely consented thereto,[70] without being under any physical or mental disability at the time, or being subjected to any coercion, threats or fraud. The consent of a child under the age specified in the statute on child stealing is no defense to a charge of that crime because the child is considered incapable of giving legal consent and the wrong is against the parent; [71] but the consent of the parent or other person having lawful custody of the child is a bar to conviction if there was no fraud or coercion.[72] It should be emphasized that kidnaping, like false imprisonment, is not defined in terms of confinement *without consent*, but *unlawful* confinement. And confinement under a fraudulently-induced consent is unlawful.[73] Thus a man was held guilty of kidnaping for having induced a woman to take passage on a steam-

---

breaches of the peace. State v. Brandenburg, 232 Mo. 531, 134 S.W. 529 (1911); Wilborn v. Superior Court of Humboldt County, 51 Cal.2d 828, 337 P.2d 65 (1959).

"We hold that where a person, while acting as an agent for a parent not entitled to custody, takes a child from one entitled to custody, the person can be convicted of both the substantive crime of kidnapping and conspiracy to kidnap." Crump v. State, 625 P.2d 857, 862 (Alaska 1981).

67. People v. Hyatt, 18 Cal.App.3d 618, 96 Cal.Rptr. 156 (1971); State v. Farrar, 41 N.H. 53 (1860).

68. State v. Crafton, 15 Ohio App.2d 160, 239 N.E.2d 571 (1968); In re Peck, 66 Kan. 693, 72 P. 265 (1903).

69. John v. State, 6 Wyo. 203, 44 P. 51 (1896).

70. Eberling v. State, 136 Ind. 117, 35 N.E. 1023 (1894).

The fact that the victim, who had been taken prisoner and carried away against his will, later with or without justifiable excuse, acquiesced in his detention and cooperated with his abductors, did not absolve them from guilt of kidnaping. United States v. Hall, 587 F.2d 177, 181 (5th Cir. 1979).

But when a hitchhiker who had voluntarily entered the car was restrained from leaving when the car turned off into a back road, he was being transported without his consent and the crime of second-degree kidnaping was committed. People v. Brown, ___ Colo.App. ___, 622 P.2d 109 (1980).

Although **F** willingly accompanied **R** at first, **R** was guilty of kidnaping when he later restrained **F** of his liberty and required **F** to accompany **R** further. State v. Racey, 225 Kan. 404, 590 P.2d 1064 (1979).

71. People v. Gillespie, 104 Cal.App. 765, 286 P. 502 (1930); State v. Metcalf, 129 Or. 577, 278 P. 974 (1929); State v. Randall, 187 Neb. 743, 193 N.W.2d 766 (1972).

72. State v. Musumeci, 116 N.H. 136, 355 A.2d 434 (1976); John v. State, 6 Wyo. 203, 44 P. 51 (1896).

73. See infra Chapter 9, section 3, B2.

er by the fraudulent pretense that he had secured employment for her as a governess in the family of a certain person, when in fact that person kept a house of prostitution and the woman was desired as an inmate.[74]

E. MISTAKE OF FACT

A mistake of fact is no excuse if the offense would be the same under either the actual facts or what the actor believes the facts to be.[75] Thus obviously it would be no defense that the kidnaper who intended to steal a rich man's son, took by mistake a playmate whose father was very poor. Moreover, a wrongdoer is not excused from responsibility for his intentional misconduct merely because he was mistaken as to the exact extent of his transgression, as mentioned in discussing carnal knowledge of a child. Hence one is guilty of child stealing if he has wrongfully enticed a girl away from her parents, and concealed her from them if she was actually under the age specified in the statute, even if he believed in good faith that she was over that age and had good reason for that belief.[76] Such a mistake is not an innocent mistake in any sense of the word. As said in a very famous case of this nature, "the prisoner knew that the girl was in the possession of her father, and   .   .   .   took her knowing that he trespassed on the father's rights, and he had no colour of excuse for so doing." [77]

The cases are not in agreement as to whether or not an excuse will be recognized in a case in which one parent has taken a child from the other, in ignorance of the fact that the custody of the child had been judicially awarded to the other,[78] but this should be recognized as a complete defense if the actor did not know or have reason to know of the judicial action.

Where a person takes custody of another in good faith under the belief he has a lawful right to detain or arrest the person, but is mistaken as to the legal authority, a defense of mistake of fact may be raised to a charge of kidnaping.[79]

F.   THE FEDERAL KIDNAPING ACT
(THE LINDBERGH LAW)

It is a federal felony wilfully to take a kidnaped person from one state to another if the captive is held "for ransom or reward or otherwise." The original statute provided that the punishment might be death unless the "kidnaped person has been released unharmed," but this provision was held to be unconstitutional.[80]

It is a violation of this law to transport an officer across the state line for the purpose of avoiding an arrest, because holding an officer to avoid being

---

74. People v. DeLeon, 109 N.Y. 226, 16 S.E. 46 (1888).

75. As to ignorance or mistake of fact in general see, infra, Chapter 9, section 1, B.

76. Smiley v. State, 34 Ga.App. 513, 130 S.E. 359 (1925).

77. Regina v. Prince, L.R. 2 C.C. 154, 170 (1875).

78. Excused: Hicks v. State, 158 Tenn. 204, 12 S.W.2d 385 (1928). Not excused: Commonwealth v. Bresnahan, 255 Mass. 144, 150 N.E. 882 (1926).

79. People v. Weiss, 276 N.Y. 384, 12 N.E.2d 514 (1938).

80. 18 U.S.C.A. § 1201; United States v. Jackson, 390 U.S. 570, 88 S.Ct. 1209 (1968).

arrested by him is holding for "ransom, reward or otherwise." [81] Thus, Congress has created an offense that is broader than the common law definition of kidnaping.[82] A conspiracy to violate this law [83] does not terminate with the release of the victim but continues until the ransom bills are exchanged for other money.[84] Hence one who knowingly aided the kidnapers by exchanging the ransom bills, seven months after the kidnaping, was guilty of such conspiracy.[85]

The statute also covers any kidnaping within the special maritime and territorial jurisdiction of the United States and includes aircraft hijacking.[86] Failure to release a kidnap victim within 24 hours of seizure creates a rebuttable presumption that the person was transported in interstate or foreign commerce. This allows federal investigative intervention in aid of local authorities.[87]

Another federal statute makes it a felony to bring into the United States, knowingly and wilfully, a person kidnaped in any foreign country, with intent to hold him in confinement or in involuntary servitude.[88] And a third provides a severe penalty for kidnaping during the robbery of a national bank.[89]

SECTION 8. OTHER OFFENSES AGAINST THE PERSON

A. MAYHEM

"Maim" is the modern equivalent of the old word "mayhem," [1] and some have long been inclined to abandon the earlier word entirely.[2] There is a special provision for one "who kidnaps or carries away any individual to commit robbery." See West's Ann.Cal.Pen.Code § 209 (1977). This covers the carrying of one away against his will for the purpose of robbery. People v. Thompson, 133 Cal.App.2d 4, 284 P.2d 39 (1955). It may even include a case where the enforced ride is after the robbery if the transportation is to effect the escape of the robber or to place the victim where he may less easily sound an alarm. People v. Randazzo, 132 Cal.App.2d 20, 281 P.2d 289 (1955).

81. Gooch v. United States, 297 U.S. 124, 56 S.Ct. 395 (1935). And see State v. Strauser, 75 S.D. 266, 63 N.W.2d 345 (1954).

82. United States v. Young, 512 F.2d 321 (4th Cir. 1975).

83. 18 U.S.C.A. § 1201(c).

84. Shannon v. United States, 76 F.2d 490 (10th Cir. 1935).

85. McDonald v. United States, 89 F.2d 128 (8th Cir. 1937).

86. 18 U.S.C.A. § 1201(a); United States v. Bendicks, 449 F.2d 313 (5th Cir. 1971).

87. Cf. United States v. Moore, 571 F.2d 76 (2d Cir. 1978) holding the presumption unconstitutional where applied by a court in aid of the prosecution's evidentiary burden.

88. 18 U.S.C.A. § 1584.

89. Whoever in committing robbery of a federal reserve bank or other bank organized under the laws of the United States, "forces any person to accompany him without the consent of such person" shall be punished by imprisonment for not less than ten years, or by death if the jury so directs. 18 U.S.C.A. § 2113(e) (1970). Some of the state statutes have a

Brief movements of a victim that are incidental to the commission of robbery and that do not substantially increase the risk of harm to the victim over that necessarily present in the robbery are insufficient for kidnaping, People v. Daniels, 71 Cal.2d 1119, 80 Cal.Rptr. 897, 459 P.2d 225 (1969). People v. Caudillio, 21 Cal.3d 562, 146 Cal.Rptr. 859, 580 P.2d 274 (1978).

1. State v. Thomas, 157 Kan. 526, 142 P.2d 692 (1943); State v. Kuchmak, 159 Ohio St. 363, 368, 112 N.E.2d 371, 374 (1953).

2. State v. Evans, 2 N.C. 281 (1796); Slattery v. State, 41 Tex. 619 (1874).

tendency, on the other hand, to retain "mayhem" for the offense and to use "maim" for the type of injury originally required for such a crime.[3] This usage has a distinct advantage because statutory enlargements have included another type of injury within the scope of this offense, and today mayhem (the offense) may involve something other than *maim* (the injury).

Mayhem, according to the English common law, is maliciously depriving another of the use of such of his members as may render him less able, in fighting, either to defend himself or to annoy his adversary.[4] It is a felony.

One of the accepted definitions of the word "maim," as a verb, is the infliction of just such an injury; and, as a noun, this type of injury.[5] And if we arbitrarily adopt this for purposes of criminal law we may restate the English common-law definition of the crime as follows: "Mayhem is maliciously maiming another." This shorter form will be particularly useful in speaking of the offense in its enlarged statutory form.

To cut off, or permanently[6] to cripple, a man's hand or finger, or to strike out his eye or foretooth, were all mayhems at common law, if done maliciously,[7] because any such harm rendered the person less efficient as a fighting man (for the king's army).[8] But an injury such as cutting off his ear or nose did not constitute mayhem, according to the English common law, because it did not result in permanent disablement, but merely disfigured the victim.[9] This was corrected by an early English statute. It seems that an assault was made upon Sir John Coventry on the street by persons who waylaid him and slit his nose in revenge for obnoxious words uttered by him in Parliament. This emphasized the weakness of the law of mayhem, and the so-called "Coventry Act" was passed. This provided the penalty of

---

3. For example: "[A] specific intent to maim was not a necessary element of the crime of mayhem, ..." Carpenter v. People, 31 Colo. 284, 289, 72 P. 1072, 1074 (1903). See also Terrell v. State, 86 Tenn. 523, 525, 8 S.W. 212 (1888).

4. 4 Bl.Comm. *205; State v. Martin, 32 N.M. 48, 52, 250 P. 842, 844 (1926); State v. Taylor, 105 W.Va. 298, 302, 142 S.E. 254, 255 (1928).

5. "Maim. To deprive of the use of a limb or member, so as to render a person in fighting less able either to defend himself or to annoy his adversary." Webster, New International Dictionary (1950).

6. "Forever disabled." 3 Bl.Comm. *121.

7. "But in order to found an indictment or appeal of mayhem the act must be done maliciously." 1 East P.C. 393 (1803).

8. 4 Bl.Comm. *205; State v. Kuchmak, 159 Ohio St. 363, 112 N.E.2d 371 (1953); State v. Benjamin, 102 Ohio App. 14, 132 N.E.2d 761 (1956).

"Mayhem in early common law was committable only by infliction of an injury which substantially reduced the victim's formidability in combat." Goodman v. Superior Court of Alameda County, 84 Cal.App.3d 621, 148 Cal.Rptr. 799, 800 (1978).

9. Ibid.; Coleman v. Commonwealth, 280 Ky. 410, 133 S.W.2d 555 (1939); State v. Kuchmak, 159 Ohio St. 363, 368, 112 N.E.2d 371, 374 (1953).

death for any one who should, with malice aforethought, "cut out or disable the tongue, put out an eye, slit the nose, cut off a nose or lip, or cut off or disable any limb or member of any subject; with the intention in so doing to maim or disfigure him." [10] This statute [11] did not displace the English common law of mayhem (malicious maiming) [12] but provided an increased penalty for *intentional* maiming and for the first time extended the crime to include disfigurement (if intentional). Hence a true definition of the crime according to the English law must be in some such form as this: *Mayhem is malicious maiming or maliciously and intentionally disfiguring another.* While some of our statutes employ the phrase "unlawfully and maliciously," [13] and others require a "malicious intent," [14] they do not differentiate between maiming and disfiguring in this regard.[15] In other words, one state includes within this offense both maiming and disfiguring if done "unlawfully and maliciously," [16] which will require a state of mind corresponding to that needed for common-law murder, and will include either an intent to maim or disfigure or an unlawful act done under such circumstances that there is a plain and strong likelihood of such a result (even if not actually intended).[17] Another state does not include either maiming or disfiguring *unless* done with a "malicious intent to maim or disfigure," which requires a specific intent to inflict such an injury,[18] although not necessarily the very maim or disfigurement actually perpetrated.[19] Even where such an intent is required

10. 1 East P.C. 394 (1803).

11. The statute was 22 and 23 Car. 2, c. 1 (1670).

12. See supra n. 7. East, in the very chapter in which he mentions the "Coventry Act," points out that the requirement for mayhem according to the English common law is that "the act be done maliciously."

13. "Every person who unlawfully and maliciously deprives a human being of a member of his body, or disables, disfigures or renders it useless, or cuts out or disables the tongue, puts out an eye, slits the nose, ear or lip, is guilty of mayhem." I.C. (Idaho) § 18–5001 (1972); West's Ann.Cal.Pen.Code § 203 (1970).

14. "A person who, with malicious intent to maim or disfigure: (1) cuts, bites or slits the nose, ear, or lip, cuts out or disables the tongue, puts out or destroys an eye, cuts off or disables a limb or any member of another person . . ." Alaska Stats. 11.15.140 (1970).

"Every person who unlawfully and intentionally . . ." Utah Code Ann., 1953, 76–5–105 (1973).

15. North Carolina provides for the crimes of malicious castration, malicious maiming, and malicious throwing of corrosive acid or alkali on a person. All require the mental element of malice aforethought, N.C.Gen.Stat. §§ 14–28, 14–30, 14–30.1 (1977).

16. Kennedy v. State, 223 Ark. 915, 270 S.W.2d 912 (1954); State v. Wilson, 188 N.C. 781, 125 S.E. 612 (1924); State v. Cody, 18 Or. 506, 23 P. 891, 24 P. 895 (1890); Key v. State, 71 Tex.Cr.R. 642, 161 S.W. 121 (1913). Sometimes the phrase "malice aforethought" is used in the statute. See n. 14 above. State v. Briley, 8 Porter 472 (Ala.1839); Kennedy v. State, 223 Ark. 915, 270 S.W.2d 912 (1954).

17. Under such a statute the crime of mayhem does not require a specific intent to injure, but malice only. People v. Crooms, 66 Cal.App. 491, 152 P.2d 533 (1944); Terrell v. State, 86 Tenn. 523, 8 S.W. 212 (1888); Davis v. State, 22 Tex.App. 45, 2 S.W. 630 (1886); Rankin v. State, 139 Tex.Cr.R. 247, 139 S.W.2d 811 (1940). And see Application of Ralls, 71 Nev. 276, 288 P.2d 450 (1955); State v. Atkins, 242 N.C. 294, 296, 87 S.E.2d 507, 509 (1955).

18. Hiller v. State, 116 Neb. 582, 218 N.W. 386 (1928); State v. Evans, 2 N.C. 281 (1796); Banovitch v. Commonwealth, 196 Va. 210, 83 S.E.2d 369 (1954); State v. Bloedow, 45 Wis. 279 (1878). Under such a statute the specific intent to maim and so forth must be alleged and proved. Tompkins v. Commonwealth, 177 Va. 858, 13 S.E.2d 409 (1941).

19. "Premeditated design to injure another" as an element of mayhem does not require a design to maim the person in the exact way or to the exact extent

it may be inferred from a deliberate act calculated to produce such a result in the absence of any circumstance inconsistent with such an inference.[20]

Although the statutes on this subject have many variations in the wording, other than with reference to the required state of mind, they are mostly differences in form rather than substance. A reasonably accurate outline of the picture can be presented in the following form:

Mayhem, under modern American statutes, is maliciously maiming or disfiguring another, except that in a number of states a specific intent to maim or disfigure is required.[21]

As to the maim itself, it may consist in the loss of an arm,[22] ear,[23] hand, finger,[24] leg, foot, toe,[25] eye,[26] front tooth,[27] or testicle,[28] to mention the obvious examples. Blackstone explains why castration is an injury weakening a man's fighting ability, in these words: "depriving him of those parts the loss of which in all animals abates their courage." [29]

The total destruction of the sight of an eye is sufficient for mayhem, even if the person is not deprived of the eyeball itself.[30] The loss of part of a finger, it may be added, is also sufficient, if it permanently cripples the finger.[31]

Disfigurement may be caused by severing or slitting the nose,[32] lip,[33] ear or tongue,[34] to mention the common examples. And as in the case of maim it

perpetrated. De Arman v. State, 33 Okl.Cr. 79, 242 P. 783 (1926).

20. Patterson v. State, 30 Ala.App. 135, 1 So.2d 759 (1941); State v. Hair, 37 Minn. 351, 34 N.W. 893 (1887); Banovitch v. Commonwealth, 196 Va. 210, 216, 83 S.E.2d 369, 373 (1954).

"It requires no specific intent to maim or disfigure, the necessary intent being inferable from the types of injuries resulting from certain intentional acts," Goodman v. Superior Court of Alameda County, 84 Cal.App.3d 621, 148 Cal.Rptr. 799 (1978).

21. "What, then, originated as the narrow common law offense of mayhem is generally today a statutory offense of considerably larger dimensions. The transition has been accompanied, if not induced, by a shift in emphasis from the military and combative effects of the injury to the preservation of the human body in normal functioning. The statutory counterparts of nonstatutory mayhem doubtless include all that the common law proscribed. But what is important now is not the victim's capacity for attack or defense, but the integrity of his person." United States v. Cook, 462 F.2d 301 (D.C.Cir. 1972).

22. Patterson v. State, 30 Ala.App. 135, 1 So.2d 759 (1941).

23. Commonwealth v. Michel, 367 Mass. 454, 327 N.E.2d 720 (1975).

24. Hemphill v. Commonwealth, 265 Ky. 194, 96 S.W.2d 586 (1936).

25. Davis v. State, 22 Tex.App. 45, 2 S.W. 630 (1886).

26. Williams v. State, 257 Ark. 8, 513 S.W.2d 793 (1974); Phillips v. State, 140 Tex.Cr.R. 84, 143 S.W.2d 591 (1940).

27. Osborn v. Union Pacific Railroad Co., 62 Idaho 243, 112 P.2d 1005 (1941); Keith v. State, 89 Tex.Cr.R. 264, 232 S.W. 321 (1921).

28. People v. Saylor, 319 Ill. 205, 149 N.E. 767 (1925); People v. Kopke, 376 Ill. 171, 33 N.E.2d 216 (1941).

29. 4 Bl.Comm. *205.

30. Phillips v. State, 140 Tex.Cr.R. 84, 143 S.W.2d 591 (1940).

". . . 'put out an eye' shall mean to so severely damage an eye that there is a partial or total loss of sight." Tenn.Code Ann. § 39–609 (1973).

31. Hemphill v. Commonwealth, 265 Ky. 194, 96 S.W.2d 586 (1936).

32. State v. Jones, 70 Iowa 505, 30 N.W. 750 (1886).

33. State v. Raulie, 40 N.M. 318, 59 P.2d 359 (1936).

34. The nose, lip, ear and tongue are commonly mentioned in the statutes. See for example West's Ann.Cal.Pen. Code § 203 (1970); Idaho Code § 18–5001 (1972); R.I.Gen.Laws 1969, § 11–29–1;

is not necessary for the entire member to be removed. The loss of a portion of a nose, for example, may be sufficient.[35]

For either maim or disfigurement the injury must be permanent in its nature.[36] It was not disfigurement, for example, where a lip was cut so as to require several stitches, but healed without leaving a permanent mark.[37] Whether an injury, permanent in its nature, would be held insufficient if corrected by one of the miracles of modern surgery, is perhaps still in doubt. The indication is that it would be sufficient for mayhem if permanent in its nature, despite such marvelous restoration.[38]

As mentioned earlier, every crime is an offense against the state, even if it happens to be classified as an "offense against the person" to distinguish it from other types of misdeed such as offenses against property or offenses against the habitation. Because of this fact, not even the consent of the person affected will serve as a defense to a criminal charge where the social harm is very great. And just as murder may be committed by complying with a person's request to take his life,[39] so mayhem may be committed with the consent of the person maimed or disfigured. Where accident, disease or other misfortune, has seemed to make amputation or other operation desirable for the welfare of the individual himself, he may consent thereto and this consent will be recognized by the law. But where, for no good reason, he consents to a maim that will seriously affect his usefulness to the community, this consent will be no defense to another who causes such mutilation. In one case, for example, a young, strong and lusty rogue had his left hand cut

Utah Code Ann. 1953, § 76–5–105 (1973); Wis.St. 1958, 940.21.

35. State v. Jones, 70 Iowa 505, 30 N.W. 750 (1886).

36. State v. Briley, 8 Porter 472 (Ala.1839); State v. Enkhouse, 40 Nev. 1, 160 P. 23 (1916); State v. Kuchmak, 159 Ohio St. 363, 112 N.E.2d 371 (1953); Lee v. Commonwealth, 135 Va. 572, 115 S.E. 671 (1923). Blackstone, speaking of maim, expressed the idea in these words: "This is a battery attended with this aggravating circumstance, that thereby the party is forever disabled." 3 Bl.Comm. *121.

See discussion Goodman v. Superior Court Alameda County, 84 Cal.App.3d 621, 148 Cal.Rptr. 799, 801 (1978); United States v. Cook, 462 F.2d 301 (D.C.Cir. 1972). Contra: Commonwealth v. Hogan, 7 Mass.App. 236, 387 N.E.2d 158 (1979) "Crippling" under Massachusetts statute on intent to maim may be temporary.

"Title 21 O.S. 1971, §§ 751 and 758, construed together, declare maiming to be the intentional injury to another whereby said injury or injuries permanently disfigure or disable, render lame or by any means seriously affect or di-

minish physical vigor by lessening or decreasing the victim's strength, activity or the like." State v. Bates, 628 P.2d 383, 384 (Okl.Cr.App. 1981).

37. State v. Raulie, 40 N.M. 318, 59 P.2d 359 (1936).

38. In a Texas case the court said hypothetically that if defendant had bit off such a portion of the victim's under lip as to deprive him of the lip, and the piece had been put back and made to grow "it would still be maiming under the law." Slattery v. State, 41 Tex. 619, 621 (1874). It was so held in Lamb v. Cree, 86 Nev. 179, 466 P.2d 660 (1970).

D bit off a portion of X's ear which was later replaced by an operation. D was convicted of mayhem and assault. On appeal the only issue considered, apart from procedure, resulted in a holding that the conviction of assault must be reversed because it was a lesser included offense. People v. De Angelis, 97 Cal.App.3d 837, 159 Cal.Rptr. 111 (1979).

39. A man who causes the death of his wife by poisoning is guilty of murder even if he did so at her request to put an end to her great suffering. People v. Roberts, 211 Mich. 187, 178 N.W. 690 (1920).

off by a companion, in order to get out of work and be more effective as a beggar. His consent to this maim was no defense.[40]

Mayhem was a common-law felony and the ancient punishment was mutilation,—the loss of the same member as suffered by the victim of the crime—except in the case of castration, for which the punishment was death.[41] It is punished as one of the grave felonies under most of the modern statutes.[42]

Where the statutory requirement for mayhem includes a specific intent to maim or disfigure, the same act cannot constitute both mayhem and an assault with intent to murder,[43] and assault with intent to maim is not included in a charge of assault with intent to kill.[44] On the other hand it was held that injuries resulting from one attack might be sufficient to support convictions on counts for (1) maiming and (2) disfiguring, under the statute.[45]

The Model Penal Code does not deal with mayhem as a separate offense. What would constitute mayhem under existing law would be included in a section called "Aggravated assault." [46]

B. DUELING

Dueling is prearranged fighting with deadly weapons, usually under certain agreed or prescribed rules.[47] The original so-called "code of honor" commonly established rules for the preliminary arrangements as well as for the fight itself. It is a misdemeanor at common law to fight a duel, even though no death result,[48] to challenge another to a duel,[49] intentionally to provoke such a challenge, or knowingly to be the bearer of such a challenge.[50]

40. Wright's Case, Co. Lit. 127a (1604). Accord, consent to the cutting off of fingers in order to collect insurance is not a defense to a charge of mayhem. State v. Bass, 255 N.C. 42, 120 S.E.2d 580 (1961).

Under the statute mayhem does not apply to a maim (biting off an ear) which occurred during a fight had by consent. Foster v. People, 1 Colo. 293 (1871); Carpenter v. People, 31 Colo. 284, 72 P. 1072 (1903). And see Henry v. State, 125 Ark. 237, 188 S.W. 539 (1916). Even without a statute it would seem that an injury inflicted in the sudden heat of passion engendered by mutual fighting would be under such provocation as not to be malicious—and hence not mayhem.

41. 1 Hawk.P.C. c. 44, § 3 (6th ed. 1788). Under some of the statutes the penalty for mayhem by castration is death. See Ga.Code Ann. c. 26–12 (1953).

42. See for example the statutes quoted above. In Georgia the offense of aggravated battery is descriptively the same as mayhem, and is punishable by imprisonment from one to twenty years. Ga.Code § 26–1305 (1976).

43. Swain v. State, 91 Ga.App. 561, 86 S.E.2d 642 (1955).

44. State v. Kuchmak, 159 Ohio St. 363, 112 N.E.2d 371 (1953).

45. State v. Benjamin, 102 Ohio App. 14, 132 N.E.2d 761 (1956).

46. Model Penal Code, section 211.1 (2).

47. ". . . . a duel is a combat with deadly weapons, fought according to the terms of a precedent agreement and under certain agreed or prescribed rules." Ward v. Commonwealth, 132 Ky. 636, 640, 116 S.W. 786, 787 (1909). "A duel is a combat or fight engaged in by two persons with deadly weapons by agreement or prearrangement." Griffin v. State, 100 Tex.Cr.R. 641, 643, 274 S.W. 611, 612 (1925).

48. 4 Bl.Comm. *145.

49. Id. at p. 150; Commonwealth v. Lambert, 36 Va. 603, 605 (1838).

50. Ibid. Not every absurd letter that mentions fighting is to be construed a challenge to a duel. Aulger v. People, 34 Ill. 486 (1864). An empty boast is not a challenge. Commonwealth v. Hart, 29

The social interest in the individual member of the community is too great to permit the settlement of private disputes and grudges by deadly combat.[51] Hence the law does not permit persons to consent to such an encounter, and no justification or excuse can be established upon the fact that such consent was given. Furthermore, as mentioned in the discussion of the "rule of provocation" under the offense of manslaughter, the deliberate prearrangement of the combat rules out whatever provocation there might have been in the beginning, and which might have been recognized as a mitigating circumstance had the conflict flared up in the heat of passion on the spur of the moment. Because of these facts one who kills another in a duel is guilty of murder.[52] And since the duel probably would not have been fought if no persons had been found willing to serve as seconds, the seconds are held to have aided and abetted in the killing and hence are also guilty of the murder.[53] This applies to the second for the deceased as well as to the second for the victor.[54] It has been suggested that the attending surgeon is also guilty.[55] If the duel does not result in death, the participants are guilty of an attempt to commit murder at common law, and, under many of the statutes, guilty of some aggravated assault, such as assault with intent to commit murder or assault with a deadly weapon.[56]

Even the agreement to fight a duel is a common-law misdemeanor, and if the agreement is made within the state it is punishable here even if the combat itself was fought beyond the borders.[57] So one who issued a challenge here for a duel to be fought in another state, is punishable here; [58] and one who agreed in this state to serve as a second in a duel is punishable here no matter where the duel was fought.[59]

Since a duel is a carefully prearranged combat, a sudden exchange of shots does not come within this category.[60] Hence a challenge to shoot now, issued in the sudden heat of passion, is not a challenge to fight a duel.[61] And because a duel is a fight "with deadly weapons," a challenge to a fair fight with fists is not a challenge to a duel.[62]

Statutes on dueling are common. They are variously worded but the matters frequently included are (1) killing in a duel (sometimes with special mention of a killing outside of the state resulting from an agreement made therein), (2) fighting a duel though no death ensue, (3) serving as second in a duel, (4) otherwise aiding or abetting (sometimes with specific mention of being present as surgeon), (5) challenging another to fight a duel, either in writing or orally, (6) accepting a challenge to fight a duel, (7) knowingly transmitting such a challenge, (8) agreeing to serve as second, aid or surgeon

Ky. 119 (1831). The mere fact that a letter challenging another to fight was unsealed is not proof that the carrier read it or knew it was a challenge. United States v. Shackelford, 27 Fed.Cas. 1037, No. 16,260 (1828).

51.   3 Co.Inst. *157.

52.   1 East P.C. 242 (1803).

53.   Ibid.

54.   Ibid.

55.   See the dictum in Cullen v. Commonwealth, 65 Va. 624, 636 (1873).

56.   See supra under "assault and battery."

57.   Harris v. State, 58 Ga. 332 (1877); State v. Farrier, 8 N.C. 487 (1821).

58.   State v. Farrier, 8 N.C. 487 (1821).

59.   Harris v. State, 58 Ga. 332 (1877).

60.   Griffin v. State, 100 Tex.Cr.R. 641, 274 S.W. 611 (1925).

61.   Ward v. Commonwealth, 132 Ky. 636, 116 S.W. 786 (1909).

62.   State v. Fritz, 133 N.C. 725, 45 S.E. 957 (1903).

at a duel, and (9) publishing a man as a coward for not accepting a challenge to fight a duel.[63]

Dueling is not included in the Model Penal Code which seems to be an unfortunate omission. No special provision is needed for killing in a duel, but we are not so far removed from violence as to render useless the penalties for challenging another to fight a duel, accepting such a challenge, knowingly transmitting such a challenge or publishing a man as a coward for refusing such a challenge.

C. ROBBERY

Robbery is larceny from the person by violence or intimidation.[64] It is both an offense against the person and an offense against property.[65] For discussion purposes it is commonly dealt with as an offense against property because it can be considered most advantageously in connection with the crime of larceny. The Model Penal Code classifies robbery as a crime against property and provides that a person is guilty of robbery if, in the course of committing theft, they (1) inflict serious bodily injury on another, or (2) threaten another with or purposely put the person in fear of immediate bodily injury, or (3) commit or threaten immediately to commit any felony of the first or second degree.[66] For that reason the mere mention of its name must suffice here, although as a matter of social harm its chief significance is that of an offense against the person.

D. LARCENY FROM THE PERSON

Larceny from the person is a statutory offense [67] similar to robbery except that there is no requirement of violence or intimidation.[68] What was just said about robbery could be repeated here except that harm to the person is less significant in this offense since the victim is usually unaware of it at the time.

---

63. See for example West's Ann.Cal. Pen.Code §§ 225–232 (1970); Mich.Stat. Ann. §§ 28.368–370 (1962); Miss.Code, 1972, 97–39–1–11; R.I.Gen.Laws 1956, 11–12–3–8 (1974).

64. Deal v. United States, 274 U.S. 277, 283 (1927); People v. Seaman, 101 Cal.App. 302, 304, 281 P. 660, 661 (1929); People v. Kubish, 357 Ill. 531, 535–6, 192 N.E. 543 (1934); Baygents v. State, 154 Miss. 36, 122 So. 187 (1929); Roberts v. State, 49 Okl.Cr. 181, 292 P. 1043 (1930).

"Since robbery is but larceny aggravated by the use of force or fear to accomplish the taking of property from the person or presence of the possessor, the felonious intent requisite to robbery is the same intent common to those offenses that, like larceny, are grouped in the Penal Code designation of 'theft.' "

People v. Butler, 65 Cal.2d 569, 55 Cal.Rptr. 511, 514, 421 P.2d 703, 706 (1967).

65. Parks v. State, 21 Ala.App. 177, 178, 106 So. 218 (1925).

66. M.P.C. § 222.1.

67. V.T.C.A., Penal Code § 31.03(4)(B) (1974). Under Texas law theft from a person is punishable as a felony of the third degree regardless of the value of the property taken.

68. "Larceny from the person is 'robbery' absent the element of force . . . Robbery is committed only when there is larceny from the person, with the additional element of violence or intimidation." People v. Chamblis, 395 Mich. 408, 236 N.W.2d 473, 481 (1975).

CHAPTER 3

OFFENSES AGAINST HABITATION AND OCCUPANCY

One of the well-recognized classes of crime at common law is that of offenses against the habitation, including two felonies known as burglary and arson. Modern statutes have extended the protection far beyond that of the habitation itself, but the coverage in general is so different from that of the traditional "offenses against property" that it gives a better emphasis to retain a separate classification. While legislative extensions have been such that no label will be entirely free from question, the social interest here protected may best be identified by referring to these crimes as "offenses against habitation and occupancy."

SECTION 1. BURGLARY

Burglary, a felony under the common law of England as well as under modern statutes, has traditionally been defined in some such terms as these:

Common-law burglary is the breaking and entering of the dwelling of another in the nighttime with intent to commit a felony.[1] There are six elements: (1) the breach, (2) the entry, (3) the dwelling, (4) "of another," (5) the nighttime and (6) burglarious intent.[2]

A. THE BREACH

The word "break" is used in a peculiar sense in the law of burglary. It does not require any damage to, or destruction of, the property,[3] while on the other hand more is necessary than the mere crossing of an imaginary line, which would constitute "breaking the close" in a civil action for trespass.[4]

Breaking in the law of burglary means making an opening of the building by trespass.[5] To enter through an *open* door or window is not a break-

---

1. 3 Co.Inst. *63; 1 Hale P.C. *549; 1 Hawk.P.C. c. 38, § 1 (6th ed. 1788); 4 Bl.Comm. *224; 2 East P.C. 484 (1803); State v. Ward, 147 La. 1083, 86 So. 552 (1920); State v. Mares, 61 N.M. 46, 294 P.2d 284, 287 (1956); Reagan v. State, 234 A.2d 278 (Md.App.1967).

2. 2 East P.C. 484 (1803).

3. It does not require "the actual fracturing of or injury to a material part of the building, . . ." Barrick v. State, 233 Ind. 333, 339, 119 N.E.2d 550, 553 (1954).

4. "There must in general be an actual breaking; not a mere legal *clausum fregit* (by leaping over invisible ideal boundaries, which may constitute a civil trespass,) . . . ." 4 Bl.Comm. *226.

5. "There must be a breach of the house made or procured by the felons; . . ." 1 Hale P.C. *485. ". . . by a trespasser . . . ." 3 Co.Inst. *64; 2 East P.C. 485. "Passing an imaginary line is a 'breaking of the close,' and will sustain an action of Trespass *quare clausum fregit*. In burglary more is required—there must be a breaking, removing, or putting aside of something material, which constitutes a part of the dwelling house, and is relied on as a security against intrusion." State v. Boon, 35 N.C. 244, 246 (1852). And see Barrick v. State, 233 Ind. 333, 339, 119 N.E.2d

246

ing.[6] No more is needed, however, than the opening of a door or window, even if not locked, or not even latched.[7] Pulling open a screen door held closed only by a spring is sufficient.[8] In fact, although some courts have held otherwise,[9] the mere unauthorized act of opening wider a door or window already partly open but insufficient for the entry, is generally held to be a *breaking*.[10]

The *breaking* is not limited to an outside door or window. If the outside door is open but the felonious design requires entrance into a part of the

550, 553 (1954); State v. Rosencrans, 24 Wn.2d 775, 779, 167 P.2d 170, 172 (1946).

"However, the breaking necessary to constitute the crime of burglary may be by any act of physical force, however slight, by which obstructions to entering are forcibly removed, . . ." Luker v. State, 552 P.2d 715, 718 (Okl.Cr.1976).

D and his wife had separated and were living apart in separate dwellings. D went to his wife's dwelling, knocked out the glass of the front door and entered. His conviction of aggravated burglary was affirmed. The court said that the husband had a possessory interest in the abode of his wife and hence would not commit trespass by an entry without violence, but did commit trespass by his violent entrance. State v. Winbush, 44 Ohio App.2d 256, 337 N.E.2d 639 (1975). Burglary requires trespass, and since a telephone booth is open to the public an unlawful entry is not possible. Macias v. People, 161 Colo. 233, 421 P.2d 116 (1966).

"This analysis demonstrates that criminal trespass . . . is an elementary part of the burglary definition involved in the present case." State v. Sangster, 299 N.W.2d 661, 664 (Iowa 1980).

6. 3 Co.Inst. *64; 1 Hale P.C. *552; Cox v. State, 81 Tex.Cr. 90, 194 S.W. 138 (1917); People v. Williams, 287 N.Y.S.2d 797 (1968); McLean v. State, 156 Ind.App. 437, 296 N.E.2d 924 (1973).

It was reversible error for the court to instruct the jury that going through a window that has its glass missing, with criminal intent, is a breaking and entering within the meaning of the burglary statute. People v. Wissler, 28 A.D. 918, 282 N.Y.S.2d 62 (1967). Accord, Rex v. Lewis, 2 Car. & P. 628, 172 Eng.Rep. 285 (1827).

7. 1 Hale P.C. *552; Rosenthal v. American Bonding Co., 143 App.Div. 362, 128 N.Y.S. 553 (1911).

"The breaking and entering necessary to constitute burglary may be by any act of physical force, however slight, by

which obstruction to entering is forcibly removed . . ." Finley v. State, 623 P.2d 1031, 1034 (Okl.Cr.1981).

8. State v. Gendusa, 193 La. 59, 190 So. 332 (1939). The requirement of "breaking" is obviously satisfied by such acts as breaking the glass out of a window, or removing the pane without breaking, or picking the lock *and opening* the door. 1 Hale P.C. *552. Or by "removing a window screen, . . . breaking a canvas shutter, . . . or opening a closed door." Barrick v. State, 233 Ind. 333, 339, 119 N.E.2d 550, 553 (1954). A breaking necessary to constitute burglary may be by any act of physical force, however slight, by which obstruction to entering is forcibly removed. Lumpkin v. State, 25 Okl.Cr. 108, 219 P. 157 (1923).

"It is not necessary that splinters fly to have a breaking. Opening a closed door, effecting an entrance thereby, is a breaking." United States v. Evans, 415 F.2d 340, 342 (5th Cir. 1969). Opening the trunk of a car, by breaking the cord which tied it shut because a TV prevented the cover from latching, was a breaking under the statute. Houchin v. State, 473 P.2d 925 (Okl.Cr.1970).

"The evidence for the state tends to show that defendant committed a breaking by removing the bathroom screen and entering the occupied dwelling of Barbara Smith in the nighttime." State v. Faircloth, 297 N.C. 388, 255 S.E.2d 366, 370 (1979).

9. Rose v. Commonwealth, 19 Ky.L.Rep. 272 (1897); Commonwealth v. Strupney, 105 Mass. 588 (1870).

10. State v. Sorenson, 157 Iowa 534, 138 N.W. 411 (1912); People v. White, 153 Mich. 617, 117 N.W. 161 (1908); State v. Rosencrans, 24 Wn.2d 775, 167 P.2d 170 (1946).

If a door is partly open, but insufficient for entrance, the further opening constitutes a breaking. Jones v. State, 537 P.2d 431 (Okl.Cr.1975).

building which is closed, the making of an opening into that part of the house is a breaking.[11] The opening of a gate in a wall which surrounds the house, however high the wall may be, is not enough,[12] although an occasional reference has confused breaking into the curtilage of a house with the ancient crime of breaking into a walled city.[13] Nor will the opening of a trunk, box or piece of furniture within the building meet the requirement.[14] Some part of the building itself must be opened. The opening of a cupboard door or drawer has been a useful testing point for the law in this regard. If the cupboard is an article of furniture within the building the opening of the door or drawer is not a breaking within the burglary meaning, but it is otherwise if the cupboard is a built-in part of the very building itself. The fact that an article of furniture is fastened to the wall, or the floor, will not necessarily make it a "part of the building." [15] This will depend upon the facts of the particular case.[16]

Although some statutes provide otherwise [17] there is no common-law burglary without a breaking; [18] but while the mere crossing of an imaginary line—or an actual threshold—will not meet the requirement, the law has recognized the possibility of a constructive breaking in some situations.[19] Under certain circumstances the opening of a door by the owner or his servant, having been occasioned by the criminal plan or scheme of the wrongdoer, "is as much imputable to him as if it had been actually done by his own hands," [20] and is deemed a constructive breaking. Thus in Le Mott's Case,[21] thieves came to the house with intent to rob the householder and finding the door locked they pretended they came to speak with him and thereupon a

---

11. 4 Bl.Comm. *226. Burglary may be committed by entering a room which is closed, although the outer doors of the house are open. Davidson v. State, 86 Tex.Cr.R. 243, 216 S.W. 624 (1919). Opening a window was a sufficient breaking to support a conviction of burglary, even if there was an outer shutter which was usually fastened but had not been closed on the particular occasion. Rex v. Haines, Russ. & Ry. 451, 168 Eng.Rep. 892 (1821).

12. Rex v. Davis, Russ. & Ry. 322, 168 Eng.Rep. 825 (1817); Rex v. Bennett, Russ. & Ry. 289, 168 Eng.Rep. 807 (1815).

13. 1 Hale P.C. *559, and see East's comment, 2 East P.C. 487–8 (1803). East's suggestion that climbing over a wall may be compared to climbing down a chimney seems also to be entirely without authority in the case-law.

14. 1 Hale P.C. *554; 2 East P.C. 488–9 (1803).

Securing electrical services without payment by breaking into an electrical meter does not constitute breaking and entering. State v. Scarmardo, 263 Ark. 396, 565 S.W.2d 414 (1978).

15. State v. Wilson, 1 N.J.L. 439 (1793).

16. A conviction of burglary was reversed because it was not shown whether the refrigerator which was broken into "was a mere fixture, or whether it was so constructed as to be a part of the building." Allen v. State, 28 Okl.Cr. 373, 376, 231 P. 96, 97 (1924).

17. E.g., West's Ann.Cal.Pen.Code § 459 (1978); Wis.St.1955, § 943.10 (1978); State v. Ocanas, 61 N.M. 484, 303 P.2d 390 (1956).

18. 1 Co.Inst. *64; 1 Hale P.C. *549; 4 Bl.Comm. *226. And see Faust v. State, 221 Miss. 668, 74 So.2d 817 (1954); People v. Swinson, 284 App.Div. 284, 131 N.Y.S.2d 467 (1954); Tice v. State, 283 P.2d 872 (Okl.Cr.App.1955); N.C.Gen.Stats. § 14–51 (1969), "as defined at the common law." The fact that D was seen going through an open window is not proof that he opened it. State v. Hart, 119 Vt. 54, 117 A.2d 387 (1955).

19. State v. Henry, 31 N.C. 463 (1849); Tice v. State, 283 P.2d 872 (Okl.Cr.1955); Clarke v. Commonwealth, 66 Va. 908 (1874).

20. 1 Hawk.P.C. c. 38, § 4 (6th ed. 1788).

21. J. Kelyng 42, 84 Eng.Rep. 1073 (1650).

maid servant opened the door and they went in and robbed him "and this being in the night time, this was adjudged burglary, and the persons hanged; for their intention being to rob, and getting the door opened by a false pretence this was *in fraudem legis*, and so they were guilty of burglary. . . ." This principle has been extended rather generally to cases in which entrance has been gained by means of some trick or artifice. Thus it is a constructive breaking "to knock at the door, and upon opening it to rush in with a felonious intent; or, under pretence of taking lodgings, to fall upon the landlord and rob him; or to procure a constable to gain admittance, in order to search for traitors, and then to bind the constable and rob the house;" [22] or to gain entrance by being concealed in a box.[23] Where admission to a motel room was gained by use of a fictitious driver's license and a forged check in order to commit theft from the room, a burglary conviction was upheld.[24] In order to bring the case within the rules of constructive breaking, where the opening of the door has been procured by some fraudulent device, the entry must be shown to have taken place rather promptly.[25] If, after there has been a reasonable opportunity for the door to be closed it is still left open, an entry will not be construed to have been through a constructive breaking.[26]

The rule of constructive breaking is not limited to cases in which entrance was obtained by trick or fraud, but has been extended to three other situations, at least.[27] The first of these is where "in consequence of violence commenced or threatened in order to obtain entrance, the owner, either from apprehension of the force, or with a view more effectually to repel it, opens the door, through which the robbers enter." [28] The second includes those cases in which a servant or other confederate within the house opens the door to admit a co-conspirator; [29] and to enter the building by coming down a chimney, although seldom possible under modern construction, was anciently

---

22. 4 Bl.Comm. *226. Accord, State v. Mordecai, 68 N.C. 207 (1873).

Although the statute does not require a breaking for burglary it does require an "unauthorized entry." "Where the consent to enter is obtained by fraud, deceit or pretense, the entry is trespassory" and hence unauthorized. State v. Ortiz, 92 N.M. 166, 584 P.2d 1306, 1308 (App.1978).

23. Nichols v. State, 68 Wis. 416, 32 N.W. 543 (1887).

24. State v. Pierce, 14 Utah 2d 177, 380 P.2d 725 (1963).

25. State v. Henry, 31 N.C. 463 (1849).

26. "There is no case, when the *entry* was not made *immediately* after the fastening was removed, or so soon thereafter, as not to allow a reasonable time for shutting the door and replacing the fastening." Id. at 468.

27. It has been said that there are three modes of constructive breaking—namely an unlawful entry effected (1) by threats, (2) by fraud, or (3) by conspiracy. Clarke v. Commonwealth, 66 Va. 908, 912–5 (1874). And see State v. Henry, 31 N.C. 463, 467 (1849).

28. 2 East P.C. 486 (1803). And see 1 Hale P.C. *553.

29. "Nay, if the servant conspires with a robber and lets him into the house by night, this is burglary in both; for the servant is doing an unlawful act, and the opportunity afforded him of doing it with greater ease rather aggravates than extenuates the guilt." 4 Bl.Comm. *227. See also 1 Hale, P.C. *553; 1 Hawk.P.C. c. 38, § 9; 2 East P.C. 486; Regina v. Johnson, Car. & M. 218, 174 Eng.Rep. 479 (1841); Cornwall's Case, 2 Strange 881, 93 Eng.Rep. 914 (1730).

held to be constructive breaking [30] "for that is as much closed as the nature of things will permit." [31]

Because *breaking*, as an element of common-law burglary, requires a breach of the building made by *trespass*, it cannot be established by the act of one who had authority to open that very door at that particular time.[32] Thus one who has been provided a key with the unrestricted right to enter at any time does not commit a *breaking* even if he uses it on one occasion to gain entrance for the purpose of larceny,[33] although it is otherwise if his right to enter is restricted to certain hours and he makes use of the key for his larcenous purpose at an unpermitted time.[34] And opening a door to enter a store during regular business hours is not a *breaking* even if done with intent to steal.[35] This not only gives proper recognition to the common-law concept of *breaking* (as an element of burglary) but reaches a very desirable result because one who enters a store for the purpose of shoplifting but without success, should not be subject to a penalty out of all proportion to that provided for the actual shoplifter.[36]

30. 1 Hale P.C. *552; 4 Bl.Comm. *226; 2 East P.C. 485; Walker v. State, 52 Ala. 376 (1875). And see State v. Thompson, 38 Wn.2d 774, 777, 232 P.2d 87, 89 (1951).

31. 4 Bl.Comm. *226. Although **D** got stuck in the chimney and was unable to get into any other part of the building he was guilty of burglary. Donohoo v. State, 36 Ala. 281 (1860); Olds v. State, 97 Ala. 81, 12 So. 409 (1893).

32. People v. Kelley, 253 App.Div. 430, 3 N.Y.S.2d 46 (1938). Burglary was not committed where an employee, pretending to co-operate with **D** but actually acting under the instructions of his employer, opened the door and let **D** in. Smith v. State, 362 P.2d 1071 (Alaska, 1961).

One element of burglary is that the entrance be trespassory. People v. Dias, 182 Colo. 369, 513 P.2d 444 (1973). Permission to enter when the dweller is present is not permission to enter when he is absent. Entry when he is absent is trespassory. State v. McKinney, 21 Or.App. 560, 535 P.2d 1392 (1975).

Although defendant's only authority to enter was to use the phone, it cannot be said that it was an unauthorized entry. People v. Peace, 88 Ill.App.3d 1090, 44 Ill.Dec. 365, 411 N.E.2d 334 (1980).

Under Arizona statutes neither a breaking nor an otherwise unlawful entry is an element of burglary. Hence even if defendant could have entered lawfully for another purpose, if he entered with intent to commit a felony he is guilty of burglary. State v. Van Dyke, 127 Ariz. 335, 621 P.2d 22 (1980).

33. Stowell v. People, 104 Colo. 255, 90 P.2d 520 (1939); State v. Starkweather, 89 Mont. 381, 297 P. 497 (1931); Davis v. Commonwealth, 132 Va. 521, 110 S.E. 356 (1922). Accord, Britton v. State, 140 Tex.Cr.R. 408, 145 S.W.2d 878 (1940); People v. Carstensen, 161 Colo. 249, 420 P.2d 820 (1966) People v. Rider, 411 Mich. 496, 307 N.W.2d 690 (1981).

Under Nevada's burglary statute "consent to entry was not a defense, so long as the defendant was shown to have made the entry with larcenous intent." Thomas v. State, 94 Nev. 605, 584 P.2d 674, 677 (1978).

34. State v. Corcoran, 82 Wash. 44, 143 P. 453 (1914); Davis v. Commonwealth, 132 Va. 521, 110 S.E. 356 (1922).

35. State v. Stephens, 150 La. 944, 91 So. 349 (1922); State v. Newbegin, 25 Me. 500 (1846). Contra, People v. Sine, 277 App.Div. 908, 98 N.Y.S.2d 588 (1950).

36. See State v. Stephens, 150 La. 944, 948, 91 So. 349, 350 (1922).

California has reached the harsh result of allowing conviction for burglary where the defendant entered a public store, as a customer, with the intent to commit theft, People v. Earl, 29 Cal.App.3d 894, 105 Cal.Rptr. 831 (1973). This resulted in application of the felony murder rule to death occurring during shoplifting. The result is because under West's Ann.Cal.Pen.Code § 459 (1978) a non-trespassory "entry" alone will suffice for burglary. See People v. Deptula, 58 Cal.2d 225, 23 Cal.Rptr. 366, 373 P.2d 430 (1962).

There is a trace of authority for the view that an exception is made in the case of a servant, and that whether or not his act constitutes a trespassory *breaking* within the rules of burglary may depend solely upon the secret intent in his mind at the time the door was opened.[37] This is quite unsound and results from a misunderstanding of the cases. It has been held, quite properly, that a servant may commit a *breaking* by opening a door into a part of the building which he has no authority to enter,[38] or into the house itself at an unpermitted time,[39] but the accepted view is that even a servant who has unrestricted authority to enter the very place at any time does not commit a *breaking* by doing so with a secret intent to commit larceny on this particular occasion.[40] It is true, as pointed out above, that a constructive breaking occurs, if a servant opens the door as a result of a conspiracy with an outsider, but this presents a different situation. In the first place a conspiracy requires a manifested intent and can never be based upon the secret intent in the mind of one person;[41] in the second place, under the law of conspiracy, the act of one in carrying out the common plan is the act of both (or of all),[42] and hence the opening of the door by the servant as a result of his conspiracy with an outsider is in legal theory an opening by the outsider who has no such authority whatever. It is not a breaking by either if the servant is only a *pseudo* conspirator and opens the door under instructions from his master to do so.[43]

An English statute in 1713[44] provided that one who entered without breaking should be guilty of burglary if he broke out of the place, provided all other elements of the crime were present. This statute seems not to have

---

37. State v. Howard, 64 S.C. 344, 42 S.E. 173 (1902). "The modern authorities have gone quite far, and we believe properly so, in holding that if a servant or a caretaker, or one having a bare charge (not possession) of premises, although fully authorized to enter for purposes within the scope of the employment or trust, actually enters for the purpose of carrying out a previously formed design to commit a felony, he will be guilty of burglary." Davis v. Commonwealth, 132 Va. 521, 523–4, 110 S.E. 356, 357 (1922). But the court cites only Clarke v. Commonwealth, 66 Va. 908 (1874) and State v. Corcoran, 82 Wash. 44, 143 P. 453 (1914). Clarke held there was no burglary because defendant had been given a key with unrestricted right to enter and the dictum relied upon is limited to conspiracy cases. Corcoran relied upon the fact that the key was used during unpermitted hours.

38. Hild v. State, 67 Ala. 39 (1880); Page v. State, 170 Tenn. 586, 98 S.W.2d 98 (1936); Rex v. Gray, 1 Strange 481, 93 Eng.Rep. 648 (1722).

39. Hawkins v. Commonwealth, 284 Ky. 33, 143 S.W.2d 853 (1940); Connor v. State, 85 Tex.Cr.R. 98, 210 S.W. 207 (1919); State v. Corcoran, 82 Wash. 44, 143 P. 453 (1914).

40. Stowell v. People, 104 Colo. 255, 90 P.2d 520 (1939). And see State v. Corcoran, 82 Wash. 44, 50, 143 P. 453, 455 (1914).

41. See infra, chapter 6, section 5.

42. Ibid.

43. Regina v. Johnson, Car. & M. 218, 174 Eng.Rep. 479 (1841); Allen v. State, 40 Ala. 334 (1867).

44. 12 Anne c. 7. There have been some suggestions that this statute merely removed a doubt and actually codified the common law on this point. See 2 Bishop, New Criminal Law § 99 (8th ed. 1892). Hale says it was not burglary, 1 Hale P.C. *554. But see the statement by Paxson, J., in Rolland v. Commonwealth, 82 Pa. 306, 324 (1876). Shooting through an open door and breaking the wall on the far side of the house was ruled not to be burglary. Resolution Anderson 114 (1584). It is believed that the notion of substituting a "breaking out" for a "breaking in," so far as common-law burglary is concerned, grew out of misinterpretations of statements dealing with breaking into an inner room. Thus East, describing an early case of burglary, finishes with the words, "and then unbolted the street door on the inside and went out." 1 East P.C. 488 (1803). But the burglary had been committed before

been recognized by the Colonies and has been held generally not to be a part of our common law.[45] A similar provision, however, has been provided by legislation in some states.[46] In a number of states, moreover, the requirement of a *breaking* has been eliminated by statute either for burglary in general,[47] or a lower degree of the crime or an associated statutory offense less than burglary.[48] Where breaking is not required there has been a tendency to hold that guilt may be established by proof that the proscribed intent was secretly entertained in the mind of the entrant although apart from this secret intent the entrance at that time and place would have been fully authorized.[49] The contrary view, even under such a statute, is not without support[50] and is much to be preferred as a practical result, whatever may be said as a matter of the soundness of statutory construction. Where necessary it would be wise to achieve this end by legislative amendment.

B. THE ENTRY

While a breaking, actual or constructive, is indispensable to common-law burglary, it is not sufficient unless there is also an en-

this happened because the intruder who entered through an open door, "afterwards broke open an inner door, and stole goods out of the room." Ibid. Breaking out could not have been sufficient for burglary under the early law because the requirement of a breach was to protect the security of the dwelling. Obviously, moreover, if the only breach was to get out of the building the *entry* could not have been "consequent upon the breaking." Regina v. Davis, 6 Cox C.C. 369 (1854).

45. Brown v. State, 55 Ala. 123 (1876); White v. State, 51 Ga. 285 (1874); Lockhart v. State, 3 Ga.App. 480, 60 S.E. 215 (1907); Casa v. State, 125 Tex.Cr.R. 186, 67 S.W.2d 288 (1934). Contra, State v. Ward, 43 Conn. 489 (1876). The court was inclined to the opinion that the statute of 12 Anne c. 7, was merely declaratory of the common law but held that if not it was a part of the common law here.

This is quite unsound because a breaking out is to get away and not to commit a felony.

46. E.g., N.C.Gen.Stat. § 14–53 (1969) ". . . shall be guilty of burglary." And see State v. Roadhs, 71 Wn.2d 705, 430 P.2d 586 (1967); Johnson v. The Queen, 34 C.C.C.2d 12 (Sup.Ct.Can.1977).

47. E.g., West's Ann.Cal.Pen.Code § 459 (1978). And see People ex rel. Patterson v. Barrow, 4 Ill.2d 52, 122 N.E.2d 179 (1954); People v. Swinson, 284 App.Div. 284, 286–7, 131 N.Y.S.2d 467, 470 (1954).

48. E.g., Mass.Gen.Laws Ann. C. 266 §§ 15, 17, 18 (1968).

49. "Under statutes providing that entry with intent to commit a felony is burglary, eliminating the common law requirement of breaking, it has been held that one could be convicted of burglary for entering a store with larcenous intent, although the entry was made during business hours and without force." Commonwealth v. Schultz, 168 Pa.Super. 435, 440, 79 A.2d 109, 111 (1951). Accord, People v. Brittain, 142 Cal. 8, 75 P. 314 (1904); State v. Bull, 47 Idaho 336, 276 P. 528 (1929); State v. Adams, 94 Nev. 503, 581 P.2d 868 (1978).

50. State v. Starkweather, 89 Mont. 381, 297 P. 497 (1931); Reagan v. State, 234 A.2d 278 (Md.1967).

Entering a building open to the public with intent to steal does not constitute burglary. Champlin v. State, 84 Wis.2d 621, 267 N.W.2d 295 (1978). Because such an entry cannot be trespassory. People v. Peery, 180 Colo. 161, 503 P.2d 350 (1972). At times the statute is specific, such as, the "place not being open to the public . . . ." Iowa Criminal Code § 713.1 (1978).

The Model Penal Code would reject the notion that burglary is committed when the premises are open to the public or the actor is licensed or privileged to enter. § 221.1(1). See the comment, Model Penal Code, 55 (Tent.Draft No. 11, 1960).

The statutory provision that "entry into a place during the time when it is open to the general public is with consent" does not apply to an unlighted basement even when the store above is open for business as usual. Leppek v. State, 636 P.2d 1117 (Wyo.1981).

try.[51] It is not necessary, however, for the trespasser to get entirely within the building. If any part of his person is within the house this is sufficient for an entry,[52] and has been applied even in very extreme situations. Thus if the wrongdoer puts his hand inside while he is raising a window this is sufficient;[53] and if, in pushing the pane out of a window, his finger was even momentarily within the room, there has been an entry.[54] There may even be an entry though no part of the person is at any time in the building.

Lord Hale uses the illustration of a man sending a child in through the window and points out that burglary may be committed by the man in this way even if the child is too young to be guilty of crime.[55] In the same way there might be an entry by sending in a trained monkey or other animal, or by the use of an inanimate instrument or tool. "So putting a hook to steal, or a pistol to kill, within the door or window, though the hand be not in, is an entry."[56] An interesting distinction, however, has been made between the entrance of some part of the body and the introduction of a tool or other instrument, with reference to the purpose with which it was put into the building. Where it is a part of the body itself, its insertion into the building is an entry, within the rules of burglary, whether the purpose was to complete the felonious design or merely to effect a breaking.[57] Thus if the mis-

---

51. 3 Co.Inst. *64. "[B]reaking without entering, or entering without breaking makes not burglary, . . ." 1 Hale P.C. *550. And see State v. Whitaker, 275 S.W.2d 316, 319 (Mo.1955); State v. Mares, 61 N.M. 46, 294 P.2d 284, 287 (1956); Tice v. State, 283 P.2d 872 (Okl.Cr.1955).

A fraudulently induced consent to enter leaves the entry unauthorized within the meaning of the burglary statute. State v. Lozier, 375 So.2d 1333 (La.1979).

52. Regina v. O'Brien, 4 Cox C.C. 400 (1850); People v. Failla, 64 Cal.2d 560, 51 Cal.Rptr. 103, 414 P.2d 39 (1966).

And the "burglary was complete as soon as Brownlee entered the victims' residences with the requisite criminal intent." People v. Brownlee, 74 Cal. App.3d 921, 141 Cal.Rptr. 685, 690 (1977).

"The crime of burglary is complete when entrance to a specific structure is gained with the requisite criminal intent." State v. Allen, 125 Ariz. 158, 608 P.2d 95, 96 (App.1980).

53. Ibid.

D was charged with a violation of 18 U.S.C.A. § 2113(a) which, in ¶ 2, makes it a felony to enter any federal or federally-insured bank, "with intent to commit in such bank . . . any larceny." The evidence showed that D drove up to the drive-up teller window of the bank and manipulated the drive-up teller mechanism. A coconspirator working inside as a teller sent up the money, whereupon D reached in, took out the money and drove off. D was convicted and appealed on the claim that the facts do not show any "entry" of the bank. It was held that there was an "entry" within the meaning of the statute. United States v. Phillips, 609 F.2d 1271 (8th Cir. 1979).

54. Rex v. Davis, Russ. & Ry. 499, 168 Eng.Rep. 499 (1823). And see Franco v. State, 42 Tex. 276 (1875). "Here it is undisputed that the defendant invaded the space between the outer storm window and the inner window. We hold under the circumstances that there was sufficient evidence of entry to the house to support the aggravated burglary conviction under Count 13." State v. Crease, 230 Kan. 541, 638 P.2d 939, 940 (1982).

55. 1 Hale P.C. *555–6. Needless to say one who aids a guilty confederate to enter may be convicted although there was no entry by the one himself. People v. McClure, 133 Cal.App.2d 631, 284 P.2d 887 (1955); State v. Peebles, 178 Mo. 475, 77 S.W. 518 (1903).

56. 2 East P.C. 490 (1803).

57. Regina v. O'Brien, 4 Cox C.C. 400 (1850). And see State v. Whitaker, 275 S.W.2d 316, 319 (Mo.1955).

Although it is otherwise as to the intrusion of an instrument, the "entry by part of the body is sufficient to support a burglary" whatever the purpose. People v. Palmer, 83 Ill.App.3d 732, 39 Ill.Dec. 262, 404 N.E.2d 853, 856 (1980).

creant should open a window too small to admit his body, and should insert his hand through this opening merely for the purpose of unlocking a door, through which he intends to gain entrance to the building, he has already made an "entry" even if he should get no farther.[58] But where a tool or other instrument is intruded, without any part of the person being within the house, it is an entry if the insertion was for the purpose of completing the felony [59] but not if it was merely to accomplish a breaking.[60] If the instrument is inserted in such a manner that it is calculated not only to make a breach but also to accomplish the completion of the felonious design, this constitutes both a breach and an entry.[61] Hence, if a shot is fired merely to break a lock, there would be no entry even if the bullet landed inside the building,[62] whereas if the weapon had been discharged for the purpose of killing an inmate of the house, the entrance of the ball into the dwelling would be sufficient for an entry as the word is used within the rules of burglary.[63]

The ancient style of lock and key, not entirely unknown even today, was such that when the key was inserted into the lock the tip went entirely through and extended out a fraction of an inch on the other side. And the special rule in regard to a tool or instrument was developed to insure that the mere insertion of the key would not be held sufficient to complete the burglary. This was unnecessary because it clearly would not constitute a breaking. There are many statements indicating that no more than the turning of a key is needed to constitute a breaking but this is obviously unsound. If a door is unlocked but not opened there has been no breaking. The rule was unnecessary for the purpose intended because of the requirement to be mentioned next—which may have developed later. But in any event the rule

---

58. Rex v. Perkes, 1 Car. & P. 300, 171 Eng.Rep. 1204 (1824); Rex v. Bailey, Russ. & Ry. 341, 168 Eng.Rep. 835 (1818).

59. 1 Hale P.C. *555. The forbidden entry may be accomplished by an intrusion into the building of any part of the body, "an arm, a hand, a finger or a foot, or in some instances, of an instrument, provided the instrument is inserted to effectuate the theft and not solely as a means of accomplishing the breaking into the building." State v. O'Leary, 31 N.J.Super. 411, 416, 107 A.2d 13, 15 (1954); State v. Liberty, 280 A.2d 805 (Me.1971).

60. "According to which, where thieves had bored a hole *through* the door with a center-bit, and part of the chips were found inside of the house, by which it was apparent that the end of the centre-bit had penetrated into the house; yet as the instrument had not been introduced for the purpose of taking the property or committing any other felony, the entry was ruled incomplete." 2 East P.C. 490–1 (1803). The special wording of a statute may require a different holding. Bailey v. State, 231 A.2d 469 (Del.1967).

To constitute a breaking the instrument must be inserted not merely for the purpose of breaking, but for the purpose of committing the contemplated felony. People v. Davis, 3 Ill.App.3d 738, 279 N.E.2d 179 (1972).

61. Where an auger was used to bore a hole through the floor to steal grain, and the grain was so situated that it ran out of the hole when the instrument was removed, this was at once a breaking and an entering. Walker v. State, 63 Ala. 49 (1879); State v. Crawford, 8 N.D. 539, 80 N.W. 193 (1899).

62. Boring a hole through the door, near the bolt to permit unlocking the door, is not an entry within the rules of burglary even if the point of the bit penetrates into the interior of the building. The King v. Hughes, 1 Leach 406, 168 Eng.Rep. 305 (1785).

63. 2 Hawk.P.C. c. 30, § 7 (6th ed. 1788); Holland v. State, 55 Tex.Cr.R. 27, 30, 115 S.W. 48, 50 (1908). Hale was doubtful on this point, 1 Hale P.C. *555, but there was no sound basis for the doubt. 2 East P.C. 490 (1803).

became firmly established that the insertion of a tool or instrument does not constitute an *entry*, within the law of burglary, if it is used merely to effect a breaking.

The common-law requirement was a "breaking into" the building.[64] A breach and an entry plus all other elements of the crime did not constitute burglary if these two were unrelated. If a wrongdoer, in the nighttime and with felonious intent, entered a dwelling other than his own through an open door, after which he broke an inner door, there was no burglary without some entry through this breach.[65] And there was no burglary if he opened a window without any entry there and then, while looking for something to stand on to help him climb in, found an open door through which he entered. As said in one case: "To constitute the crime, the entry must be consequent upon the breaking." [66]

The requirement of an entry has been retained very generally although it has been eliminated under a few statutes by use of the phrase "break or enter" [67] or by employment of the words "enter or remain." [68]

C. DWELLING

1. IN GENERAL

That every man's house is "his castle" is a concept that has been echoed down through the ages [69] and the social interest in the security of the "castle" [70] has its origin in antiquity; for just as an animal or a bird resents any intrusion into its place of abode, so no doubt did primitive man. The terms commonly used to indicate the place are "dwelling" or "dwelling house," but the "word 'dwelling' imports a human habitation," [71] and as a matter of common law, burglary is strictly an offense against the habitation.[72] Despite

64. 1 Hale P.C. *554. This fact is sometimes reflected in the wording of modern statutes. E.g., ". . . breaking and entering into." Tenn.Code Ann. §§ 39–901, 903 (1973).

65. Regina v. Davis, 6 Cox C.C. 369 (1854).

66. Ibid.

67. E.g., Ark.Stats. § 41–2003 (1975); N.C.Gen.Stat. § 14–54 (1969); State v. Vierk, 23 S.D. 166, 172, 120 N.W. 1098, 1101 (1909). And see People v. Swinson, 284 App.Div. 284, 286–7, 131 N.Y.S.2d 467, 470 (1954). The Louisiana court interpreted the phrase "break *or* enter" to mean "break *and* enter." State v. Stephens, 150 La. 944, 91 So. 349 (1922). The legislature later eliminated the requirement of breaking. See La.Stat.Ann. 14:60, 14:62 (1974).

The Arkansas court held that under its statute the crime of burglary (statutory) can be established, if the other elements are present, by either a breaking or an entering. Albright v. State, 253 Ark. 671, 488 S.W.2d 11 (1971).

68. Ky.Rev.Stat. 511.020 (1974); So.Dak.Compiled Law 22–32–1 (1976). "Enters or surreptitiously remains." 17–A Me.Rev.Stat.Ann. § 401 (1977).

E.g. Mont.Crim.Code of 1973, § 94–6–204. Under this statute wrongfully remaining in a store after closing hours constituted a trespass. State v. Watkins, 163 Mont. 491, 518 P.2d 259 (1974).

69. E.g., Semayne's Case, 5 Coke 91a, 77 Eng.Rep. 194 (1604); Carrier v. State, 227 Ind. 726, 731, 89 N.E.2d 74, 76 (1949).

70. "[E]very man by the law hath a special protection in reference to his house and dwelling." 1 Hale P.C. *547. "The dwelling-house of an individual hath peculiar sanctity in the estimation of the common law." Armour v. State, 22 Tenn. 379, 384 (1842).

71. Carrier v. State, 227 Ind. 726, 731, 89 S.E.2d 74, 76 (1949).

72. A church was the subject of burglary at common law because as Coke tells us it is the dwelling house of the Al-

the use of the term "mansion house" by the early writers [73] it is clear that a
man's actual place of abode does not fail to qualify merely because of its
poor or squalid condition, as in the case in which it consisted of a sheet
stretched over poles and fastened to boards nailed to posts for sides, being
closed at one end and having an old door at the other.[74] A regular place of
abode is a "dwelling house" for purposes of burglary, moreover, even if it is
on wheels and not restricted to a particular locality.[75] "A house trailer is
simply a mobile house. It is as much a dwelling as any house which is built
on a foundation and therefore not mobile." [76] Nor need it be elaborate or
expensive if on wheels, for the "sheep wagon" which is the actual place of
habitation of a sheep-herder, is his dwelling.[77]

    **To be a dwelling—or place of habitation—it must be used "as a
place to sleep in," [78] and the fact that the owner uses it for his
meals and all the purposes of his business is not enough.[79] Business buildings such as banks, stores, shops and factories are not, as
such, within the scope of common-law burglary although these and
other structures are protected by modern statutes either by an extension of the law of burglary,[80] or the creation of associated statutory offenses.[81] On the other hand the use of a building for business or other purposes does not prevent it from being a dwelling, as
in case of a store building which has sleeping apartments regularly
used by the proprietor or one in his employ.[82] On the other hand,
no building—store or otherwise—is converted into a dwelling by**

mighty. 3 Co.Inst. *64. And this was
recognized in a recent case. McGraw v.
Maryland, 234 Md. 273, 199 A.2d 229
(1964).

73. 3 Co.Inst. *64; 1 Hale P.C. *556;
4 Bl.Comm. *224.

74. Favro v. State, 39 Tex.Cr.R. 452,
46 S.W. 932 (1898).

75. Luce v. State, 128 Tex.Cr.R. 287,
81 S.W.2d 93 (1935). Under the Arizona
statute burglary of a "residential structure" is a distinct offense. Ariz.Rev.
Stat. § 13–1507 (1978).

"However, a dwelling house has been
defined as a place where a man lives with
his family. Thus, it is possible for a mobile home to be a dwelling house." (citations omitted) People v. Winhoven, 65
Mich.App. 522, 237 N.W.2d 540, 542
(1976).

76. Lower Merion Tp. v. Gallup, 158
Pa.Super. 572, 575, 46 A.2d 35, 36 (1946).
See West's Ann.Cal.Pen.Code § 459
(1978) specifically referencing "inhabited
camper."

A Winnebago mobile home in which
the family lived while on tour, was a
dwelling within the rules of burglary.
United States v. Lavender, 602 F.2d 639
(4th Cir. 1979).

77. State v. Ebel, 92 Mont. 413, 15
P.2d 233 (1932). Cf. People v. Burley, 26
Cal.App.2d 213, 79 P.2d 148 (1938). A
railroad car withdrawn from service and
used for the purpose of habitation is a
"dwelling house." Gibbs v. State, 8
Ga.App. 107, 68 S.E. 742 (1910).

78. Ex parte Vincent, 26 Ala. 145, 152
(1855).

79. Rex v. Martin, Russ. & Ry. 108,
168 Eng.Rep. 708 (1806). See also Rex v.
Harris, 2 Leach 701, 168 Eng.Rep. 451
(1795).

80. E.g., West's Ann.Cal.Pen.Code
§ 459 (1978).

81. E.g., Rev.Code Mont. 1947,
§ 94–6–203 (1974).

82. State v. Hudson, 78 N.M. 228, 430
P.2d 386 (1967); People v. Griffin, 77
Mich. 585, 43 N.W. 1061 (1889); Quinn v.
People, 71 N.Y. 561 (1878). It has been
held that this rule does not apply if the
person who sleeps in the building is employed as a watchman. State v. Potts, 75
N.C. 129 (1876). This is sound if it is a
temporary arrangement, Rex v. Davies, 2
Leach 876, 168 Eng.Rep. 537 (1800), but
not if the place becomes the *"regular
sleeping apartment"* of the employee.
State v. Outlaw, 72 N.C. 598 (1875).

reason of the fact that the owner or some employee may sleep there on rare occasions.[83]

There may be more than one dwelling under the same roof and this applies not only to apartment houses and similar structures but also to buildings of simpler types. Obviously each apartment in a tenement house is "the dwelling house of the particular occupant," [84] but even a single room in a private house [85] or a hotel [86] may be the dwelling of the occupant if it is actually the place where such person lives. The temporary occupancy of a room by a guest in a private home [87] or a transient in a hotel [88] is not sufficient for this purpose, but of course if the room does not become the separate dwelling of the occupant it remains a part of the dwelling of the host or innkeeper.[89] And for most purposes it is unimportant whether it is one or the other, except as a matter of procedure,—to charge properly whose dwelling was broken into.[90] In one respect, however, this point must be determined before it can be ascertained whether or not burglary has been committed because of the rule which limits this crime to violations of the habitation "of another," which will receive attention presently.

At one time, in speaking of this subject, there was a tendency to use "inhabited" to indicate that the building was a dwelling, and "occupied" to indicate the actual presence therein of the dweller, or his wife, servant or guest.[91] But statutory extensions of the area of protection to include buildings and structures other than dwellings have made it necessary to emphasize a socially-protected interest in the use of these places, and this can best be indicated as an interest in "occupancy." [92]

Whatever the terminology employed it should be emphasized that for common-law burglary it is necessary for the building to qualify as a "dwelling" although the actual presence of some person therein is not required.[93]

---

83. Marston v. State, 9 Md.App. 360, 264 A.2d 127 (1970); Scott v. State, 62 Miss. 781 (1885).

84. Mason v. People, 26 N.Y. 200 (1863).

85. People v. St. Clair, 38 Cal. 137 (1869). "Likewise a chamber or room, be it upper or lower, wherein any person doth inhabit or dwell, is *domus mansionalis,* in law." 3 Co.Inst. *65. And see 1 Hale P.C. *556.

86. "The indictment before us alleged the room in the Morrison Hotel entered by plaintiff in error was the room of Elizabeth Scharf. If she dwelt therein, as the language infers, it was her dwelling house, . . ." People v. Carr, 255 Ill. 203, 209, 99 N.E. 357, 359 (1912), Holt v. State, 46 Ala.App. 555, 246 So.2d 85 (1971).

A hospital room is a "dwelling." People v. Germany, 41 Colo.App. 304, 586 P.2d 1006 (1978).

87. 2 East P.C. 500 (1803).

88. 1 Hale P.C. *557; Rodgers v. People, 86 N.Y. 360 (1881); Robinson v. State, 364 So.2d 1131 (Miss.1978).

89. 1 Hale P.C. *557; 2 East P.C. 500 (1803).

90. Ibid. The room of a transient guest at a hotel should be laid as the dwelling house of the innkeeper, not of the guest, whether the innkeeper lives there or elsewhere. Rodgers v. People, 86 N.Y. 360 (1881).

91. E.g., People v. Loggins, 132 Cal.App.2d 736, 738, 282 P.2d 961, 963 (1955); State v. Bair, 112 W.Va. 655, 657, 166 S.E. 369, 370 (1932). The statement in the latter case was that "it remains a dwelling house, though temporarily unoccupied. . . ."

92. The Model Penal Code gives this definition:

"(1) 'Occupied structure' means any structure, vehicle or place adapted for overnight accommodation of persons, or for carrying on business therein, whether or not a person is actually present." Section 221.0.

93. 4 Bl.Comm. *225.

Such presence, however, may be a factor in determining the grade or degree of the offense under some of the statutes.[94] The phrase "inhabited dwelling," appearing in a statute, means only that it qualifies as a place of habitation and not that there is any person inside at the moment.[95] In other words it signifies no more than does the word "dwelling" at common law.

The mere fact that a house was built for the purpose of serving as a place of human habitation, and that it is entirely suitable therefor, will not be sufficient to qualify it as a dwelling so far as the law is concerned.[96] It is not such before the first dweller has moved in [97] nor after the last dweller has moved out with no intention of returning,[98] except that if an owner who has left with the intention of returning has rented the place in the meantime it might well be held that it is re-established as his dwelling after the tenant has left permanently even before the owner has actually moved back. But after a man has established a house as his dwelling it retains this character so long as he intends it to be his place of habitation even though he and his entire household are away, unless it is actually taken from him against his will. Blackstone speaking cautiously said that the character of the place is not changed by the absence of the dweller and his entire household "for a short season," [99] but the length of the absence seems to be significant only in connection with the matter of intention. One who leaves his house usually does so either intending to return or intending not to do so although his state of mind might be one of uncertainty in this regard. Despite the use of such terms as *"animo revertendi"* [1] or a "settled resolution of returning," [2] it would probably be held that a dwelling does not instantly lose its character as such because of a doubt in the mind of the dweller in this regard at the time of his departure, although a doubt and long-continued absence might be sufficient for this purpose. But it seems that no lapse of time, however

94. Harris v. State, 41 Okl.Cr. 121, 271 P. 957 (1928).

95. People v. Loggins, 132 Cal.App.2d 736, 282 P.2d 961 (1955).

"As used in this section 'inhabited' means currently being used for dwelling purposes, whether occupied or not." (West's Ann.Cal.Pen.Code § 459). People v. Moreland, 81 Cal.App.3d 11, 146 Cal.Rptr. 118, 123 (1978).

96. Johnson v. State, 188 So.2d 61 (Fla.1966); Rex v. Martin, Russ. & Ry. 108, 168 Eng.Rep. 708 (1806).

97. Woods v. State, 186 Miss. 463, 191 So. 283 (1939).

A renter who moved some of his belongings into the house and then left for California to pick up the rest of the family, was held to have established it as his dwelling although he had not spent a night in the building. State v. Matson, 3 Or.App. 518, 475 P.2d 436 (1970).

If the new tenant had moved into the apartment with the intention of living there, it became his dwelling. "The absence of any personal property from the apartment is not dispositive." Common-

wealth v. Kingsbury, 378 Mass. 751, 393 N.E.2d 391, 395 (1979).

98. Henderson v. State, 80 Fla. 491, 86 So. 439 (1920). And see State v. Meerchouse, 34 Mo. 344, 346 (1864); State v. Bair, 112 W.Va. 655, 656–7, 166 S.E. 369, 370 (1932).

A vacant apartment in which furniture was stored pending rental by a new tenant is a "storehouse" rather than a "dwelling." Poff v. State, 4 Md.App. 186, 241 A.2d 898 (1968).

A house which was unoccupied and up for sale was not a "dwelling" although the owner had resided there the preceding month. Tukes v. State, 346 So.2d 1056 (Fla.App.1977).

A house or apartment loses its character as a dwelling once the dweller leaves without intending to return. State v. Ferebee, 273 S.C. 403, 257 S.E.2d 154 (1979).

99. 4 Bl.Comm. *225.

1. Ibid.; State v. Bair, 112 W.Va. 655, 656–7, 166 S.E. 369, 370 (1932).

2. John Nutbrown's Case, Fost. 76, 77, 168 Eng.Rep. 38–9 (1750).

great, will alone be sufficient where there is throughout a fixed intention of returning,[3] although extremes have not been adequately tested by the cases.

Certain it is that the dweller and his entire household may be away for months, without depriving the house of its character as his dwelling.[4] It was ruled in the 1500's,[5] and often repeated since,[6] that a man may have two dwellings at the same time actually used during alternate periods and that burglary may be committed in the one not being used at the moment,—such as a winter home in the city and a summer cottage in the mountains.[7]

2. BUILDINGS WITHIN THE CURTILAGE

The dwelling concept at common law, so far as the law of burglary was concerned, "not only included the premises actually used as such, but also such out buildings as were within the curtilage or court yard surrounding the house," [8] and used in connection therewith. This included such buildings as the "barn, stable, cow-houses, dairy houses," [9] and more recently the garage.[10] In the early days of English life the dwelling was usually enclosed by a small fence or hedge, within which enclosure other buildings frequently were found, and all buildings within this small enclosure which were used in connection with the dwelling were regarded as a part thereof so that breaking and entering any such building was equivalent in law to breaking into the sleeping quarters themselves.[11] When fences and hedges became less frequent the notion of the curtilage seems to have been applied to such buildings, used in connection with the dwelling, as were close enough to be within a small enclosure if one were there.[12] A building on the opposite side of the

3. Although the owner had not lived in the building for a year and a half, during which time it had been used for storage, as he still regarded it as his home it had not lost its character as a "dwelling." Hamilton v. State, 354 So.2d 27 (Ala.App.1978).

4. Schwabacher v. People, 165 Ill. 618, 46 N.E. 809 (1897). It was over seven months in this case.

5. Resolution of Judges, Popham, 52, 79 Eng.Rep. 1169 (1593).

6. 1 Hale P.C. *556; 1 Hawk.P.C. c. 38, § 11 (6th ed. 1788); State v. Meerchouse, 34 Mo. 344, 346 (1864).

7. A summer cottage in the dead of winter, when all utilities were disconnected and the furniture was piled up in the middle of the rooms and covered, was a dwelling place within the meaning of the burglary statute. State v. Albert, 426 A.2d 1370 (Me.1981).

8. Armour v. State, 22 Tenn. 379, 385 (1842).

9. 3 Co.Inst. *64; 1 Hale P.C. *558; 2 East P.C. 492 (1803); Devoe v. Commonwealth, 44 Mass. 316, 325 (1841).

10. Harris v. State, 41 Okl.Cr. 121, 271 P. 957 (1928). In one case it was held that a garage used for the storage

of property was a "storehouse" rather than an outhouse of the dwelling, but this was a matter of statutory construction and defendant had been convicted of breaking into a storehouse. Bean v. Commonwealth, 229 Ky. 400, 17 S.W.2d 262 (1929); State v. Lara, 92 N.M. 274, 587 P.2d 52 (App.1978).

11. 3 Co.Inst. *64; 1 Hale P.C. *558.

12. Neither Coke nor Hale mentions the necessity of an actual enclosure. 3 Co.Inst. *64–5; 1 Hale P.C. *558–9. Breaking into a bake-house was held to be burglary although it was eight or nine yards from the dwelling house and not within a common enclosure. Castle's Case, 1 Leach 144, note (a), 168 Eng.Rep. 174, note (a). The fact that a picket fence extended from the dwelling to the bake-house was mentioned but not emphasized, and cannot have been regarded as a matter of importance.

The present English statute—the so-called Larceny Act of 1916, § 46(2)—does not include any building within the curtilage "unless there is a communication between such building and dwelling-house, either immediate or by means of a covered and enclosed passage leading from one to the other." And an occasional statute in this country has a correspond-

highway was not within the curtilage[13] because the encircling fence could not have crossed the king's highway. And the curtilage was never recognized as covering a large area. A wire fence around a quarter section, for example, would not make the entire piece within the curtilage of the dwelling. Lord Hale, in fact, suggests that to be within the curtilage the outhouse must be within "bow-shot" of the main building,[14] and Blackstone says that "no distant barn, warehouse, or the like are under the same privileges, nor looked upon as a man's castle of defence."[15]

There are some indications pointing to a requirement of the English law that an outhouse, to be regarded as part of the dwelling, must be either adjoining it or within a common fence.[16] However that may be, "the doctrine that a building not enclosed with the dwelling is not within the curtilage has no application here."[17]

An occasional holding that a building is not within the rule of the curtilage unless used for domestic purposes[18] is based upon a misunderstanding of the English cases. The reason for extending the protection of the law of burglary to other nearby buildings was because of the human risk involved,—the dweller or some member of his household might hear a prowler in such a building and go to investigate. This would be quite unlikely if the outbuilding had been rented to an outsider and was not used by any inhabitant of the dwelling. Hence the rule was that the outbuilding must be used in connection with the dwelling, or to use the ancient phrase it must be "parcel of the messuage"[19] in order to be within the rule of the curtilage. but this meant no more than that the building must be used by the dweller or some member of his household,[20] and many of the cases involved the breaking into a shop or store.[21]

---

ing provision. E.g., K.S.A. (Kan.) 21–519. But there was no such requirement at common law. See infra, notes 13 and 14.

13. Rex v. Westwood, Russ. & Ry. 495, 168 Eng.Rep. 915 (1822). "But here, to say nothing of the distance, there was a distinct separation from the house by a highway. . . ." Curkendall v. People, 36 Mich. 309, 310 (1877).

14. Hale suggests that the outhouse must be within a "bow-shot" of the main house. 1 Hale P.C. *559.

15. 4 Bl.Comm. *225.

16. This is stated in the much-quoted syllabus of an English case. The King v. Garland, 1 Leach 144, 168 Eng.Rep. 174 (1776). But the jury had failed to find that the outhouse was "parcel of the dwelling-house" and this would have ruled out burglary even if there had been a common enclosure. An English statute enacted after the Revolution and hence no part of our law required a "communication between such building and dwelling house, either immediate, or by means of a covered and enclosed passage lead-

ing from one to the other." 7 & 8 Geo.IV, c. 29, § 13 (1827).

17. State v. Bugg, 66 Kan. 668, 671, 72 P. 236, 237 (1903).

18. Armour v. State, 22 Tenn. 379 (1842). In another case it is said that a barn used solely for the storage of tobacco is not an "outhouse of the dwelling-house," but this building was from 90 to 200 yards from the dwelling proper. White v. Commonwealth, 87 Ky. 454, 9 S.W. 303 (1888).

19. 1 Hale P.C. *558; 2 East P.C. 492 (1803).

20. "If A. have a shop parcel of his mansion-house, and if it be broken open in the night &c. it is burglary, . . . for it is parcel thereof. But if A. lets the shop to B. for a year, and B. holds it, and works or trades in it, but lodgeth in his own house at night" it is otherwise "for it was severed by the lease . . . ." 1 Hale P.C. *557.

21. Ibid.; The King v. Gibson, 1 Leach 357, 168 Eng.Rep. 281 (1785); Rex v. Chalking, Russ. & Ry. 334, 168 Eng.Rep. 831 (1817).

It should be emphasized that it is not breaking into the curtilage which is important, but breaking into a building within the curtilage.[22] Modern statutes have provided penalties for breaking and entering buildings, other than dwellings,[23] with burglarious intent, and prosecutions for breaking into outbuildings are now usually brought under these statutes, so the rule of the curtilage plays a rather minor role in the law of burglary at the present time.[24]

D. "OF ANOTHER"

The law of burglary was designed to protect the dweller and hence the controlling question is occupancy rather than ownership.[25] The landlord can commit burglary by breaking into the house he has leased to another, if he does so at night and with intent to commit a felony,[26] but the dweller cannot commit burglary by breaking into his own dwelling no matter what the time or the purpose.[27] It must be remembered, however, that one who lives in

22. 1 Hawk.P.C. c. 39, § 17 (6th ed. 1788); 2 East P.C. 492 (1803).

Unauthorized entry into a fenced yard does not constitute simple burglary under the statute. State v. Alexander, 353 So.2d 716 (La.1977).

Contra under the Florida statute; breaking into the curtilage with intent to steal is burglary. Greer v. State, 354 So.2d 952 (Fla.App.1978).

23. E.g., Burns' Ind.Ann.Stat. § 35–43–2–1 (1977); N.J.Stat.Ann. 2C:18–2 (1979).

24. See Bean v. Commonwealth, 229 Ky. 400, 17 S.W.2d 262 (1929). But note N.C.Gen.Stats. § 14–51 (1953); State v. Mares, 61 N.M. 46, 294 P.2d 284 (1956).

A frame chicken house, having doors and a board roof, is an "other building" under the statute which punishes the breaking and entering of stores, warehouses or "other buildings." State v. Poole, 65 Kan. 713, 70 P. 637 (1902). But a small chicken coop which may be moved about from place to place is not such a "building." Bailey v. State, 26 Ohio Cir.Ct. 375 (aff'd in State v. Bailey, 69 Ohio St. 551, 70 N.E. 1130 (1903)). A portable box, 14 feet long, 6 feet wide and from 18 inches to 4 feet high, is not a house. Williamson v. State, 39 Tex.Cr.R. 60, 44 S.W. 1107 (1898).

The coin box of a telephone apparatus is not a "compartment" of a building within the burglary statute. Macias v. People, 161 Colo. 233, 421 P.2d 116 (1966).

A telephone booth has been held to be a "building" under a burglary statute, State v. Hogue, 15 Ariz.App. 434, 489

P.2d 281 (1971); People v. Nunez, 7 Cal.App.3d 655, 86 Cal.Rptr. 707 (1970).

Under the statute it was made burglary in the second degree to break and enter with intent to commit a crime, or, having committed a crime therein, to break out of "any building or part thereof, or a room or other structure wherein any property is kept for use, sale or deposit." It was held that while a fence is not a building,—where the fence was 6 to 7 feet high, with strands of barbed wire strung along the top making a barrier 9 to 10 feet high, erected mainly for the purpose of protecting property within its confines and was an integral part of a closed compound, it constituted a "structure" within the meaning of the statute. State v. Roadhs, 71 Wn.2d 705, 430 P.2d 586 (1967).

25. Smith v. People, 115 Ill. 17, 3 N.E. 733 (1885); State v. Lee, 95 Iowa 427, 64 N.W. 284 (1895); Rex v. Jarvis, 1 Moody 7, 168 Eng.Rep. 1163 (1824). "Burglary is an offense against possession or occupancy of a building, and the test for determining ownership of the premises for purposes of indictment is not title to the property broken and entered, but is occupancy or possession at the time the offense was committed unless the occupant is a mere servant." Nicholson v. State, 366 So.2d 1142, 1143 (Ala.App.1979).

26. "In burglary, the ownership may be laid in the occupant whose possession is rightful as against the burglar." Smith v. People, 115 Ill. 17, 20, 3 N.E. 733, 734 (1885).

27. Clarke v. Commonwealth, 66 Va. 908 (1874).

most of the house may have set apart one room, or set of rooms, as the exclusive dwelling of another; and if so it would be possible for him to commit burglary by breaking into that special part of the building.[28]

A plurality of dwellers in the same dwelling requires particular attention, because while a casual house guest or transient lodger is not recognized as a "dweller" in the house of his host or innkeeper,[29] there may be more than one dwelling under the same roof, as indicated above. But if two (or more) are recognized as dwellers in the same dwelling, neither one can commit common-law burglary therein.[30] Hence it might be more precise to designate the subject of burglary as a dwelling "other than one's own." This is an awkward phrase for use in a definition, and it seems unnecessary here because in the law of burglary the phrase "dwelling of another" has long been used to imply not only that someone else dwells there but also that the alleged burglar does not.[31] This implication was fostered by the artificial meaning assigned to another word in the same definition.

Under the accepted view, an opening made by one authorized to do so is not a *breaking* within the law of burglary as explained above. To unlock and open a door, for example, is not a *breaking* if done by one having a right to open that very door, at that time and in that manner, and this is so even if this particular opening was made with felonious intent. Because of this fact it would be possible to define burglary without specifying that the dwelling is "other than one's own" or "of another." In fact, statutes omitting any such reference[32] have made no change in the law of burglary,[33] since the requirement of a *breaking* precludes the burglary of one's own dwelling. This elimination is not made in the definition given here, for reasons of emphasis.

One problem invites special attention. If a house is habitually used as a place where persons sleep, it is properly to be regarded as a dwelling even if no one who lodges there has a sufficient interest therein to establish it as *his*

Defendant "cannot be guilty of burglarizing his own home, . . ." People v. Gauze, 15 Cal.3d 709, 125 Cal.Rptr. 773, 542 P.2d 1365 (1975).

28. Kelyng thought not if the landlord and tenant used the same outer door on the notion that such a tenant was a mere "lodger" and not a "dweller." J.Kel. 83–4, 84 Eng.Rep. 1093 (1708). "But otherwise it is," he added, "if a man sever some rooms from his house, and make another door to those rooms, and so divide the house, that divided part is the mansion-house of him who hires it; . . ." Id. at p. 85. Hale says a room in the house of *B* may be *domum mansionalum* of *A* without mention of a separate outside door. 1 Hale P.C. *556.

29. 1 Hale P.C. *557. A servant is not a "dweller." State v. Howard, 64 S.C. 344, 348, 42 S.E. 173, 175 (1902). If one casual house guest or transient lodger at a hotel wrongfully opens the door

of another, this is burglary if the other elements are present. 1 Hale P.C. *554. But the dwelling broken into in such a case is that of the host or innkeeper.

Under the Colorado statute it was held proper to allege that the burglary was committed against the transient guest who occupied the room at the time. Gallegos v. People, 150 Colo. 137, 370 P.2d 755 (1962).

30. Commonwealth v. Clarke, 66 Va. 908 (1874).

31. Although **D** shared the apartment with another, it was his home and he could not burglarize it. People v. Gauze, 15 Cal.3d 709, 125 Cal.Rptr. 773, 542 P.2d 1365 (1975).

32. E.g., Alaska Stats. 11.20.090 (1970).

33. No change in this regard has been suggested in Alaska for example.

dwelling.[34] Thus a hotel is a dwelling house even if all the inmates are transients, and the proprietor and his family and servants all sleep elsewhere. Obviously a corporation cannot make use of a building for its own sleeping quarters, but a building may be regarded as the dwelling of a corporation if it is owned by the company, and is a place where persons sleep under such circumstances that it does not become the dwelling of any individual.[35] Moreover, there seems to be no substantial difference in this regard between the case of a corporation which cannot sleep in the house, and an individual proprietor who in fact sleeps elsewhere.

Where a "building" or "structure" is all that is required for a burglary, corporate ownership or possession is sufficient to satisfy the requirement that the building be that of another.[36]

E. NIGHTTIME

Common-law burglary can be committed only in the night.[37] Furthermore both the breaking and the entering must be in the night [38] though it is not necessary for both to be during the same night.[39] The ancient rule seems to have been that from sunset until sunrise it was night for purposes of burglary,[40] but later it was regarded not to be night, even after sunset and before sunrise, if there was sufficient daylight to permit the countenance of a person to be discerned.[41] But "this does not extend to moonlight; for then many midnight burglaries would go unpunished." [42] For the same

34. 2 East P.C. 500–1 (1803).

35. Thus John Picket was convicted and executed for committing burglary "in the dwelling-house of the East-India company," 2 East P.C. 501 (1765). In this case the building was inhabited by servants of the company, but no reason appears why the same rule should not apply if it had been inhabited by their guests. In The King v. Peyton, 1 Leach 324, 168 Eng.Rep. 265 (1784), it was held improper to describe the building as the dwelling house of Bunbury as he was occupying the place as a servant of the king and the premises should have been said to be the dwelling house of the king. In Quinn v. People, 71 N.Y. 561 (1878), it was held proper to refer to the premises as the dwelling house of a partnership.

36. ". . . Since for present purposes ownership is any possession which is rightful as against those alleged to be burglars, we conceive that the sole corporate stockholder and operator of a corporate business, is as against burglars, the owner of the building used only for corporate business." Dorsey v. State, 324 So.2d 159, 160 (Fla.App.1975).

37. 1 Hale P.C. *549; 4 Bl.Comm. *224; 2 East P.C. 508 (1803); Bowser v. State, 136 Md. 342, 110 A. 854 (1920).

The requirement of nighttime was not found in the very early law. 3 Holdsworth, History of English Law 369 (5th ed. 1942). Where the breaking was through a thick brick wall into the vault of a bank, it was held sufficient if any technical entry was made during the night, even if the thief did not succeed in getting into the vault until after daylight. Commonwealth v. Glover, 111 Mass. 395 (1873).

38. 1 Hale P.C. *551; 2 East P.C. 508 (1803).

39. 1 Hale P.C. *551; 2 East P.C. 508 (1803); Rex v. Smith, Russ. & Ry. 417, 168 Eng.Rep. 874 (1820).

40. 1 Hale P.C. *550; 4 Bl.Comm. *224.

41. Ibid.

Nighttime under the Iowa statute is the same as at common law, "a period between sunset and sunrise during which there is not enough daylight to discern a man's face." State v. Billings, 242 N.W.2d 726 (Iowa 1976). The revised Iowa Criminal Code (1978) seems not to change this, but under the provisions of Chapter 713 "burglary," in either degree, is no longer a nocturnal crime.

42. 2 East P.C. 509 (1803).

reason it does not extend to artificial light.[43] **On the other hand even the densest fog or smog cannot turn midday into night in other than a figurative sense.**

Statutes have made two important changes in this regard,[44] the first having reference to the definition of night. Such statutory changes sometimes reenact the ancient rule of sunset to sunrise,[45] but more frequently establish a different rule such as thirty minutes after sunset until thirty minutes before sunrise,[46] one hour after sunset to one hour before sunrise,[47] or from nine in the evening until six in the morning.[48] The second type of statutory change is in the form of a penalty for misconduct which includes the general requirements of burglary except that the transgression did not occur during the night. Such provisions sometimes go to the statutory definition of burglary itself,[49] or are found in an inferior degree of burglary.[50] At other times they are in sections which create kindred offenses of a lower grade than burglary.[51]

The trend of recent codes in defining burglary [52] is to ignore any differentiation between daytime or nighttime.

F. BURGLARIOUS INTENT

Larceny is usually the purpose for which burglary is committed but it is not essential to guilt that the intruder succeed in carrying out the intent with which the dwelling was broken into,[53] **nor that it**

43. ". . . it is not sufficient that there was light enough caused by the moon, street-lights, or lights from buildings, aided by newly-fallen snow, to enable one to discern the features of another; there must be daylight enough left for that purpose." State v. Morris, 47 Conn. 179, 182 (1879). Cited with approval in State v. McKnight, 111 N.C. 690, 692, 16 S.E. 319, 320 (1892).

44. The common law governs in this regard in the absence of statutory change. Bowser v. State, 136 Md. 342, 110 A. 854 (1920).

45. 21 Okl.Stat.Ann. § 1440 (1958); West's Ann.Cal.Pen.Code § 463 (1970).

Under such a definition the court took judicial notice that on the date in question the official records indicated that sunrise occurred subsequent to the trespassory invasion. State v. Bishop, 90 Wn.2d 185, 580 P.2d 259 (En Banc, 1978).

46. Weathered v. State, 101 Tex.Cr.R. 520, 276 S.W. 436 (1925).

47. Gray v. State, 243 Wis. 57, 9 N.W.2d 68 (1943).

48. This was the period fixed in England. 6 & 7 Geo.V, c. 50, § 46. This was the so-called "Larceny Act," 1916, but it includes burglary. See § 25 et seq.

49. Ark.Stats.Ann. § 41–2002 (1975); Schwabacher v. People, 165 Ill. 618, 623, 46 N.E. 809, 811 (1897).

Where the evidence proved that the burglary was committed between 5:30 P.M. and the following 6:30 A.M., but at that time the sunset was at 7:29 P.M. and the sunrise at 5:21 A.M., it would not support a conviction of burglary in the first degree which requires perpetration in the nighttime. State v. Hunter, 102 Ariz. 472, 433 P.2d 22 (1967).

50. So.Dak.Compiled Laws 22–32–1 & 2 (1976); State v. Mares, 61 N.M. 46, 294 P.2d 284 (1956).

51. Okl.Stat.Ann. § 1438 (1958).

52. Ariz.Rev.Stat. Chap. 13–15 (1978); Iowa Code Ann. Chap. 7–13 (1978).

53. "Although it does not appear that any property was taken, actual stealing is not a requisite element of the crime. The crime was complete when the breaking and entering with intent to steal was effected." Matter of J. E. S., 585 P.2d 382, 484 (Okl.Cr.1978). Larceny is not included as a lesser-included offense in burglary. Hardin v. State, 458 S.W.2d 822 (Tex.Cr.App.1970). D may be convicted of both burglary and larceny committed in the same transaction. State v. Woolard, 3 Or.App. 291, 472 P.2d 837 (1970).

should be for the purpose of stealing.[54] With one exception, to be discussed presently, made necessary today by reason of a statutory change outside the field of burglary, there is no common-law burglary unless the intrusion is perpetrated with an intent to commit some felony.[55] Thus if a rogue breaks into the dwelling of another at night with intent to commit murder he is guilty of burglary even if he leaves without finding his intended victim and without having committed any felony in the house.[56] On the other hand he would not be guilty of burglary if he broke in for the purpose of trespass only even if he subsequently did commit some felony during his wrongful visit.[57]

For instance, in Dobbs' Case [58] the defendant, in the night, broke and entered a stable, within the curtilage of a dwelling, with intent to disable a race horse. The horse died, and Dobbs was subsequently convicted of the felony of maliciously killing the horse. But in the trial for burglary he was held not guilty, "for his intention was not to commit the felony, by killing and destroying the horse, but a trespass only to prevent his running; and therefore no burglary."

The intent may be to commit any felony, such as "a robbery, a murder, [or] a rape," [59] as well as the more common one of larceny. Moreover, it is

---

The value of property taken during burglary is immaterial. State v. Bundy, 181 Neb. 160, 147 N.W. 500 (1966).

Definitions of burglary often include the phrase "whether such intent be executed or not." E.g., 1 Hale P.C. *549. And see 3 Co.Inst. *63. Larceny actually committed in the house is not essential to guilt of burglary but if shown is merely evidence of the intent. Place v. State, 300 P.2d 666 (Okl.Cr.1956).

54. An intent to commit larceny is not specifically mentioned in the definition of burglary by Coke, Hale or Blackstone. 3 Co.Inst. *63; 1 Hale P.C. *484; 4 Bl.Comm. *223–4.

55. Ibid.; 1 Hawk.P.C. c. 38, § 18 (6th ed. 1788); Schwabacher v. People, 165 Ill. 618, 46 N.E. 809 (1897); State v. Mares, 61 N.M. 46, 294 P.2d 284, 287 (1956).

56. People v. Schwab, 136 Cal.App.2d 280, 288 P.2d 627 (1955). Accord, Ragland v. State, 71 Ark. 65, 70 S.W. 1039 (1902); Walker v. State, 44 Fla. 466, 32 So. 954 (1902); 1 Hale P.C. *561–2.

"The crime of burglary is complete upon entry, and the evidence of the completion of the intended crime is only evidence of intent; it is not a necessary element of burglary." Ziegler v. State, 610 P.2d 251, 254 (Okl.Cr.1980).

"Since burglary arises when the person makes entry with the requisite felonious intent, it is irrelevant that the felony was not subsequently committed." In re Anthony M., 116 Cal.App.3d 491, 172

Cal.Rptr. 153, 159 (1981); State v. Brooks, 631 P.2d 878 (Utah 1981).

57. 1 Hale P.C. *561; 2 East P.C. 509–10 (1803). Under some statutes it would be burglary if he committed a felony in the building and then broke out of the place. E.g., N.C.Gen.Stat. § 14–53 (1969).

Although the statute is worded in terms of "knowingly and without authority entering into or remaining within any building . . . with intent to commit a felony or theft therein," this refers to two different types of misconduct: (1) entering into with intent and (2) remaining within with intent. The second covers the case of one lawfully within the building who conceals himself until after closing time with intent. In the case of unauthorized entry the intent to commit felony of theft must exist at the time of entry. State v. Brown, 6 Kan.App.2d 556, 630 P.2d 731 (1981).

On the other hand, the Oregon statute, as interpreted, covers one who forms the burglarious intent after having made an unauthorized entry. State v. Papineau, 53 Or.App. 33, 630 P.2d 904 (1981).

58. 2 East P.C. 513 (1770).

59. 4 Bl.Comm. *227–8. In a much-cited English case the offense intended was rape. Rex v. Gray, 1 Strange 481, 93 Eng.Rep. 648 (1721).

The intent may be to commit any felony such as, in this case—murder. State

unimportant whether the particular offense intended was a felony at common law or became such only by virtue of a statute,[60] but an intent to commit a mere trespass, or even a misdemeanor [with the exception referred to above] will not satisfy the common-law definition.[61] Furthermore the intent must accompany both the breaking and the entry.[62] It may be added that while drunkenness is no excuse for crime, it may be shown that an intruder was too intoxicated to have any specific intent at the time, and if so he was not guilty of burglary.[63]

While the commission of a felony in the house, not contemplated at the time the building was broken into, is insufficient for burglary, the fact that such offense was committed is strong evidence that this was the purpose of the breach and entry,[64] and the intent may also be established by an attempt to commit a felony after the intrusion or even by preparations to do so.[65]

There is authority for the position that the indictment must be specific in charging the burglarious intent, and is demurrable if it merely alleges an intent to commit "a felony." [66] Some courts have taken the very common-sense position that an unexplained intrusion into the dwelling of another at night will support a jury's finding of an intent to steal.[67] And at times a

v. Castro, 92 N.M. 585, 592 P.2d 185 (App.1979).

60. 4 Bl.Comm. *228.

61. 1 Hale P.C. *561; 1 Hawk. c. 38, § 18 (6th ed. 1788); 2 East P.C. 509 (1803). In Commonwealth v. Newell, 7 Mass. 245 (1810), the indictment was for breaking and entering and so forth with intent to cut off one of the ears of an inmate. On demurrer, the indictment was held to be bad because while mayhem was a felony in the early common law, cutting off an ear was not mayhem; and while cutting off an ear was statutory mayhem in Massachusetts, it was not a felony in that state at the time.

62. 4 Bl.Comm. *227. Burglary cannot be committed unless the burglarious intent exists at the time of entry. People v. Hill, 67 Cal.2d 105, 60 Cal.Rptr. 234, 429 P.2d 586 (1967).

63. People v. Oakley, 251 Cal.App.2d 520, 59 Cal.Rptr. 478 (1967); Schwabacher v. People, 165 Ill. 618, 46 N.E. 809 (1897). And see People v. Henderson, 138 Cal.App.2d 505, 292 P.2d 267 (1956).

64. 2 East P.C. 510 (1803); State v. Dwyer, 33 Idaho 224, 191 P. 203 (1920); Commonwealth v. Hope, 39 Mass. 1, 5 (1839).

65. State v. Mecum, 95 Iowa 433, 64 N.W. 286 (1895). And see Walker v. State, 44 Fla. 466, 32 So. 954 (1902). Cf. People v. Henderson, 138 Cal.App.2d 505, 292 P.2d 267 (1956).

66. The crime must be specified, Gomez v. People, 162 Colo. 77, 424 P.2d

387 (1967); Martinez v. People, 163 Colo. 503, 431 P.2d 765 (1967).

In holding that an indictment for burglary must specify the particular crime intended, the Oregon court said: "We have been cited 14 jurisdictions with statutes comparable to the one here involved which have decided that the intended crime must be specified in the indictment." State v. Sanders, 280 Or. 685, 572 P.2d 1307, 1308 (1977). And see State v. Batson, 35 Or.App. 175, 580 P.2d 1066 (1978).

An indictment for burglary may lay the offense with several intents, as with intent to steal and intent to murder or rape. Such an indictment is not duplicitous. It is sufficient for the state to prove one of the alleged intents. If there is evidence of more than one intent the judge may submit the case to the jury on alternative theories. State v. Boyd, 287 N.C. 131, 214 S.E.2d 14 (1975).

67. People v. Shepardson, 251 Cal.App.2d 33, 58 Cal.Rptr. 809 (1967); Garrett v. State, 350 P.2d 983 (Okl.Cr.1960); State v. Hopkins, 11 Utah 2d 363, 359 P.2d 486 (1961); People v. Soto, 53 Cal. 415 (1879); Ex parte Seyfried, 74 Idaho 467, 264 P.2d 685 (1953).

"Evidence of an unauthorized and forcible entry is sufficient evidence from which the jury can find the requisite intent." State v. Calvery, 117 Ariz. 154, 571 P.2d 300, 303 (App.1977).

The specific intent in burglary may be presumed from an unlawful entry.

prima-facie presumption of burglarious intent, arising from such unexplained conduct, has been provided by statute.[68] Such a presumption is constitutionally valid,[69] and at least where there is such a presumption the indictment may allege the burglarious intent in general terms, without specifying the particular crime intended.[70]

"Under Michigan law, intent to commit larceny may be inferred from the totality of circumstances disclosed by the testimony. Such intent may be inferred from the nature, time, or place of the defendant's acts before and during the breaking and entering." [71]

A matter entitled to particular attention in regard to burglarious intent arises out of the fact that (as will be explained in the following chapter) any larceny was a felony under the common law of England, and the early English statute which substituted a milder penalty for death in case of petit (or petty) larceny did not reduce that offense to the grade of misdemeanor. Hence under our common law also any larceny is a felony although petit larceny has been made a misdemeanor by modern statutes. The common-law rule that any intent to steal, in the mind of one breaking into another's house, is a burglarious intent has been retained very generally in this country.[72] The common pattern is to define burglary in terms of an "intent to

Brinkman v. State, 95 Nev. 220, 592 P.2d 163 (1979). The jury may infer an intent to steal from evidence showing an unlawful entry. State v. Olson, 39 Or.App. 383, 592 P.2d 273 (1979).

"When one breaks and enters a building in the nighttime, without consent, an inference may be drawn that he did so to commit larceny." State v. Sisneros, 631 P.2d 856, 859 (Utah 1981).

68. State v. During, 71 Wn.2d 675, 430 P.2d 546 (1967); State v. Bishop, 90 Wn.2d 185, 580 P.2d 259 (En Banc, 1978).

Testimony that D entered the home of another without permission and that immediately thereafter money was missing from a jar in the kitchen, permitted conviction of second-degree burglary. Reed v. State, 580 P.2d 159 (Okl.Cr.App.1978).

69. Bayless v. United States, 381 F.2d 67 (9th Cir. 1967). And see Yee Hem v. United States, 268 U.S. 178, 45 S.Ct. 470 (1925); United States v. Gainey, 380 U.S. 63, 85 S.Ct. 754 (1965).

"The statutory presumption is not unconstitutional on its face as a matter of law. Given the proper timing, circumstances, or manner of entry, the presumed facts (i.e., intent to commit a crime in the dwelling) can flow beyond a reasonable doubt from the proven fact upon which it is made to depend (i.e., unlawfully entering the dwelling of another)." State v. Blight, 89 Wn.2d 38, 569 P.2d 1129, 1134 (1977).

Such a presumption "requires only that the defendant produce some evidence to dispute the presumed fact of criminal intent. The ultimate burden of persuasion remains with the prosecution and due process is not offended." Redeford v. State, 93 Nev. 649, 572 P.2d 219, 222 (1977). An instruction requiring such an inference is unconstitutional. Hollis v. State, 96 Nev. 207, 606 P.2d 534 (1980). Compare State v. Bowden, 93 Wis.2d 574, 288 N.W.2d 139 (1980).

70. Bayless v. United States, 381 F.2d 67 (9th Cir. 1967). The Washington statute had enlarged the burglarious intent to include an intent to commit a crime, and the allegation "with intent to commit some crime" was held to be sufficient.

Under the Oregon statute an indictment charging burglary in the second degree is required to contain a specific allegation as to the particular crime D intended to commit at the time of the unlawful entry. State v. Sanders, 280 Or. 685, 572 P.2d 1307 (1977).

71. Goldman v. Anderson, 625 F.2d 135, 137 (6th Cir. 1980).

72. The value of property actually stolen would not be controlling in any event, because there is no requirement that the intended crime be perpetrated, but one Arkansas case suggested that an intent to steal a specific chattel—and that only—would not be sufficient for burglary if the value was small. Sanders v. State, 198 Ark. 880, 131 S.W.2d 936 (1939). The statute now reads, "with the purpose of committing therein any of-

commit a felony or larceny," [73] or theft [74] or sometimes with a specific reference to "grand or petit larceny." [75]   At times the same result is reached by other means such as a statutory provision that any larceny committed in a building is a felony,[76] or by expressly stating that the petit-larceny section does not apply in a case of burglary.[77]

A few statutes have defined burglary in terms of an intent to commit "a crime," [78] or "crime against a person or property" [79] or "offense therein," [80] and on rare occasions some specific misdemeanor has been included such as "assault." [81]   Any such provision goes beyond the common law, but a statutory definition of burglary in terms of an "intent to commit a felony or larceny" merely makes use of more words to express the same state of mind as the common-law burglarious intent.[82]

In other words, a statute making no change from the ancient wording of the definition other than to say directly, or in substance, "an intent to commit a felony or petit larceny," adds nothing which was not included in the common-law offense and does not constitute what is hereinafter referred to as "statutory burglary." [83]

Modern statutes making petit larceny a misdemeanor require the definition of burglary to be re-worded in some such form as this:

Common-law burglary is the breaking and entering of the dwelling of another in the nighttime with intent to commit a felony or petit larceny.

G.   "THEREIN"

Some definitions of burglary, after listing the elements mentioned above, add with intent and so forth "therein." [84]   This wording emphasizes the nec-

fense punishable by imprisonment." Ark.Stats.Ann. § 41–2002 (1975).

Until recently, in Maryland, an intent to commit petit larceny was insufficient for burglary. McNeil v. State, 227 Md. 298, 176 A.2d 338 (1961). The statute was amended in 1965 to include an intent to steal goods of any value. See Md.Code art. 27, § 30 (1976).

A few statutes still define burglarious intent in terms of an "intent to commit a felony." Burns' Ind.Stat.Ann. 35–43–2–1 (1977). See infra, note 75.

73. With "intent to commit any felony, or any larceny therein." Mich.Stat. Ann. § 28.305 (1979).

74. Ga.Code § 26–1601 (1977); Kan. Stat.Ann. 21–3715 (1970).

75. With "intent to commit grand or petit larceny or any felony." West's Ann.Cal.Pen.Code § 459 (1978).

76. E.g., Mich.Stat.Ann. § 28.592 (1972).

77. E.g., N.C.G.S. § 14:72 (1977).

78. McKinney's (N.Y.) Rev.Pen.Law § 140.20 (1975).

79. Rev.Code Wash.Ann. 9A.52.020 (1977).

80. N.J.Stat.Ann. 2C:18–2 (1979).

81. Iowa Code Ann. § 7–3.1 (1978).

82. Hale, in fact, uses the phrase "intent to steal or commit a felony," in one place. 1 Hale P.C. *548. This was not necessary because petit larceny was a felony. Id. at *530. And Hale does not mention stealing or larceny in his definition of burglary. Id. at *549.

83. It may be statutory burglary under the statutes of a particular jurisdiction. For example, the Indiana statute on burglary proper is still worded in terms of an "intent to commit a felony." Burns' Ind.Stat.Ann. 35–43–2–1 (1977).

84. State v. Cook, 242 N.C. 700, 702, 89 S.E.2d 383, 385 (1955); Reagan v. State, 2 Md.App. 262, 234 A.2d 278 (1967) Coke adds the phrase "within the same." 3 Co.Inst. *63. Blackstone quotes Coke's definition without this phrase. 4 Bl.Comm. *223–4.

essary causal relation between the burglarious intent and the forced entrance, but seems to inject an unnecessary limitation. While it would not be burglary to break into another's dwelling at night merely to rest in preparation for a felony to be perpetrated elsewhere, it would be burglary, if the purpose was to use the building as a place of concealment from which to shoot an enemy as he passed by on the street,[85] although under well-recognized rules the situs of such a murder would be in the street at the point where the bullet hit the victim, and not the place inside the house from which the shot was fired.[86] Hence burglary was committed where it was necessary to break into the building to reach the property to be stolen, although such property was not actually within the building itself;[87] and also where the purpose was to commit a sexual offense in the seclusion available on the roof, which could be reached only by going through the house.[88]

The completion of the burglarious intent is not essential to guilt of burglary, as pointed out above, for a reason quite apparent in the light of the ancient law, since the common-law penalty for felony was forfeiture of lands and goods and life. If the burglar committed the intended felony the law had means of dealing with him to the fullest extent by reason of that offense alone, and the real purpose of the ancient law of burglary was to apply the same punishment to one who broke into another's dwelling at night with intent to commit a felony, even if he was caught (or frightened away) before his design was accomplished. And while the explanation must be modified at the present time[89] the trend has been to enlarge, rather than to narrow, the scope of what is in substance a criminal attempt, although not so labeled.

H. STATUTORY BURGLARY

There is reason to believe that certain invasions of the dwelling which fell short of burglary were punished as misdemeanors at common law although evidence is difficult to find because of the rule of English procedure which did not permit conviction of misdemeanor in a trial for felony,[90] and the fact that early writers on criminal law were interested chiefly in felony problems.[91] Certain it is that some of these invasions were made felonies by

85. Cf., Rolland v. Commonwealth, 85 Pa. 66 (1877). In this case it was held that breaking into an inner room as part of the felonious plan was sufficient though it was not the intent to commit the felony in that particular room.

86. State v. Hall, 114 N.C. 909, 19 S.E. 602 (1894).

87. People v. Wright, 206 Cal.App.2d 184, 23 Cal.Rptr. 734 (1962).

Where defendant entered one building to gain access to another in which to commit larceny, it was said:

"The evidence need not show that a larceny or other felony was in fact committed on the premises entered, but it is sufficient if the evidence shows that at the time of the entry the defendants had the intention to commit larceny or some other felony." State v. Syddall, 20 Utah 2d 73, 76, 433 P.2d 10 (1967).

88. People v. Shields, 70 Cal.App.2d 628, 161 P.2d 475 (1945).

If the statute defines burglary in terms of a crime committed "therein," burglary is not committed without this. Van Gorham v. State, 475 P.2d 187 (Okl.Cr.App.1970).

89. Under modern statutes the burglar who does not accomplish the felony he had in mind is punished more severely than if he had actually committed that felony without burglary, unless some very grave crime was intended such as murder or rape.

90. See infra, chapter 6, section 3, A, 2.

91. Hale speaks of "house-breaking . . . whether committed in the day or night to the intent to commit felony, . . . which in a vulgar and improper

statutes [92] early enough to have been recognized as common law in this country although they seem to have been overlooked by our courts. In any event the area of protected social interest represented by common-law burglary, being quite inadequate, has been greatly enlarged by legislation [93] and it is important to have a label to distinguish this enlargement from the common-law felony itself. The oldest term for this purpose,[94] still encountered at times,[95] is "housebreaking;" a more recent suggestion is "breaking and entering," [96] and peace officers sometimes speak of a "breakin."

Although any label selected for this purpose must have an arbitrarily-assigned meaning, in order to be fully effective, it is desirable to avoid any term that may tend to be misleading, and a serious objection to any of those mentioned above lies in the fact that an important part of the modern legislative extension has provided a penalty for misconduct resembling burglary but having no "breaking" as that term is defined in this regard; and needless to say this word when employed in this area will be understood in its common-law sense.[97] The label suggested here, while not entirely free from question, has the support of a very significant analogy; and just as "statutory rape" has traditionally been understood to mean conduct proscribed by statute kindred to, but not constituting, common-law rape, so "statutory burglary" is used here to signify the entire area of misconduct proscribed by statute which is kindred to, but does not constitute, common-law burglary.

The availability of mutually exclusive terms to distinguish the common-law felony from statutory additions thereto will be useful not only in theoretical discussions but also for very practical purposes. "It is . . . well settled," it was said in a recent case,[98] "that when a federal statute uses a term known to the common law to designate a common law offense and does not define that term, courts called upon to construe it should apply the common law meaning, . . ." Hence it was held that the word "burglary" as found in the federal Fugitive Felon Act meant only the common-law crime of that name and did not include other offenses given that name in a state statute, such as breaking into a store building by means of explosives.[99]

The federal statute has since been amended by substituting for the reference to certain felonies such as "burglary" the following: "A crime . . . which is a felony under the laws of the place from which the fugitive flees, or which, in the case of New Jersey, is a high misdemeanor under the laws of said State." [1] Hence this problem will not arise again under that statute, but it may arise under some other.[2] Other problems in the use of the word

acceptation is sometimes called burglary." 1 Hale P.C. *547–8.

92. Id. at *548–9.

93. For an elaborate discussion of the statutes see a note, 51 Col.L.Rev. 1009 (1951).

94. Hale hyphenated the term. 1 Hale P.C. *547.

95. D.C.Code, tit. 22, c. 18 (1951). Now titled "Burglary," D.C.Code Tit. 22C18 (1967).

96. See the catchwords in Mass. Gen.Laws Ann. C266 § 13–16A (1968).

97. State v. Hart, 119 Vt. 54, 117 A.2d 387 (1955).

98. United States v. Patton, 120 F.2d 73, 75 (3d Cir. 1941).

99. United States v. Brandenburg, 144 F.2d 656 (3d Cir. 1944).

1. 18 U.S.C.A. § 1073.

2. "Robbery," for example, as used in the Hobbs Act, proscribing the interference of interstate commerce by robbery, means common-law robbery. United States v. Nedley, 255 F.2d 350 (3d Cir. 1958). And see Le Masters v. United States, 378 F.2d 262 (9th Cir. 1967).

may be encountered, such as the Iowa case saying that the word "burglary" as used in the first-degree-murder statute does not include breaking into a building other than a dwelling.[3]

While there are many variations in the statutes on this subject, a reference to three different patterns may be helpful. Iowa, until its 1978 revision of criminal law, had a chapter on burglary, the first section of which came close to common-law burglary.[4] Following sections, without calling the offense "first-degree burglary" provided a much more severe penalty if the burglar was armed with a dangerous weapon or committed an actual assault within the building, or if he attempted to accomplish his criminal design by means of explosives, electricity or acetylene gas or other gas. The sections referring to the use of explosives, and so forth, did not require that the building broken into be a dwelling nor that the invasion be nocturnal, but these offenses were specifically named "burglary."

Other sections in the general chapter on burglary punished certain offenses which were not burglary proper, such as possession of burglar's tools with intent to commit burglary, and attempt to break and enter and so forth, with intent to commit a public offense. Other statutory offenses which were not common-law burglary provided, among other things, for a penalty just half as severe as that for "burglary without aggravation" for the following misdeeds:

1. Breaking and entering a dwelling in the daytime with intent to commit a public offense.

2. Entering such a house at night, without breaking, and with such intent.

3. Breaking and entering at any time and with such intent, "any office, shop, store, warehouse, railroad car, boat, or vessel, or any building in which any goods, merchandise, or valuable things are kept for use, sale or deposit."

4. Entering a bank with intent to rob.

The California Code combines common-law burglary and statutory burglary in one section[5] in these words:

"Every person who enters any house, room, apartment, tenement, shop, warehouse, store, mill, barn, stable, outhouse or other building, tent, vessel, railroad car, trailer coach as defined by the Vehicle Code, vehicle as defined

3. State v. Pinkerton, 201 Iowa 940, 943–4, 208 N.W. 351, 352 (1926).

4. I.C.A. (Iowa) § 708.1. The chief difference is in regard to burglarious intent which in this section includes an intent to commit any public offense. It *may* also include a "breaking out," where the other elements are present, but it does not use that term and may have been intended only to cover the breaking of an inner room.

The revised Iowa Criminal Code was published as a Supplement to the Code of Iowa, 1977, but it took effect on January 1, 1978. Its § 713.1 defines burglary in terms broad enough to include common-

law burglary and the familiar types of statutory burglary.

5. West's Ann.Cal.Pen.Code § 459 (1978).

All the doors of a car were securely locked and all the windows rolled up except one that was down five or six inches from the top. D reached through this opening and stole property from the seat of the car. It was held he could not be convicted of burglary of a vehicle because the partially open window prevented the car from being "locked." People v. Woods, 112 Cal.App.3d 226, 169 Cal.Rptr. 179 (1980).

by said code when the doors of such vehicle are locked, aircraft as defined by the Harbors and Navigation Code, mine or any underground portion thereof, with intent to commit grand or petit larceny or any felony is guilty of burglary."

The next section[6] is as follows:

"1. Every burglary of an inhabited dwelling-house or trailer coach as defined by the Vehicle Code, or the inhabited portion of any other building committed in the nighttime, is burglary of the first degree.

"2. All other kinds of burglary are of the second degree.

"3. This section shall not be construed to supersede or affect section four hundred sixty-four of the Penal Code."

Section 464 provides a special penalty for burglary perpetrated by means of explosives, electricity or gas—without calling it a "degree" of any kind.

The former Kansas plan made use of three degrees of burglary. Common-law burglary was first-degree burglary if there were certain elements of aggravation[7] and otherwise second-degree burglary.[8] The second degree also included certain other types of invasion, such as with burglarious intent, (1) breaking into a dwelling in the daytime,[9] (2) entering a dwelling at night,[10] or breaking into a shop, store, warehouse or other building, and so forth, at night.[11] Breaking into buildings other than dwellings in the daytime was third-degree burglary.[12]

From these examples it will be seen that the common types of statutory burglary involve unlawful invasions which would be common-law burglary except that they do not require one or more or any of the following: That the misconduct (1) occur during the nighttime, or (2) include a breaking, or (3) involve a dwelling or building within the curtilage,[13] or (4) an intended crime which constitutes a felony or petty larceny.[14]

---

6. Id. at § 460 (1978).

7. K.S.A. (Kan.) § 21–513. ". . . in which there shall be at the time some human being, . . ." plus aggravation in the manner of breaking.

8. Id. at § 21–515.

9. Id. at § 21–514.

10. Id. at § 21–516.

11. Id. at § 21–520.

12. Id. at § 21–521.

13. A building within the scope of statutory burglary is a "structure enclosing space within walls and roof." Pinkney v. United States, 380 F.2d 882, 885 (5th Cir. 1967).

Some types of statutory burglary include "structures" other than buildings, such as vehicles and vessels. And see State v. Roadhs, 71 Wn.2d 705, 430 P.2d 586 (1967).

A Salvation Army collection box, approximately six by four by four feet in size, and used to receive donated clothing, is a "structure" within the meaning of the statute and sufficient to support conviction of third-degree burglary. State v. Mann, 129 Ariz. 24, 628 P.2d 61 (App.1981).

14. To convict under the habitual criminal act, prior convictions of burglary in another jurisdiction may be shown if the misdeed would have constituted burglary if committed here. But the mere proof of a burglary conviction in Oklahoma, without more, is not sufficient because an intent to commit any misdemeanor is sufficient for the burglarious intent there while in California petit larceny is the only misdemeanor included in such category. People v. Stanphill, 166 Cal.App.2d 467, 333 P.2d 270 (1958).

THE MODEL PENAL CODE

In article 221 the Code deals with burglary and other criminal intrusion. It defines "occupied structure" in terms of any structure, vehicle or place adapted for human habitation or business use. And for night it adopts the definition that has become fairly common, "the period between thirty minutes past sunset and thirty minutes before sunrise." Burglary itself is defined in terms of the entrance of an occupied structure with intent to commit a crime *therein*,[15] except that it does not apply to premises that are open to the public at the time, or have been abandoned. The section is worded in terms of statutory burglary, but what would constitute common-law burglary (as also with certain other circumstances of aggravation) is made a felony of the second degree, which with few exceptions [16] is the most serious offense provided by the Code. The Code would not permit conviction of both burglary and the target offense unless the target offense is a felony of the first or second degree. The chief effect of this would be to prevent conviction of both burglary and larceny which is the offense most frequently in the burglar's mind.[17] It would not prevent conviction of both burglary and the target offense if the latter was murder, aggravated assault, kidnaping, rape, arson or robbery.[18]

I. CRIMINAL TRESPASS

Some statutes make it an offense, less than felony, for one to enter or remain unlawfully in or upon the premises of another, under certain circumstances without requiring the damage involved in malicious mischief,[19] or an intent to commit any other crime.[20] The Model Penal Code includes such a provision.[21]

SECTION 2. ARSON

Common-law arson is the malicious burning of the dwelling of another.[1]

15. The use of the word "therein" is unnecessarily, and it would seem unwisely, restrictive. See supra G. "Therein."

16. Under the Code there are very few felonies of the first degree. Murder is a felony of the first degree, § 210.2(2). Kidnaping is a felony of the first degree unless the victim is released alive in a safe place, in which case it is a felony of the second degree, § 212.1. Rape is a felony of the second degree unless aggravating circumstances put it in the first degree, § 213.1. Arson is a felony of the second degree, § 220.1(1). Robbery is a felony in the second degree unless put in the first degree by an attempt to kill or inflict serious bodily injury, § 222.1(2). Forgery in its most extreme form is a felony in the second degree, § 224.1(2).

17. Larceny (theft) of more than $500 worth of property is a felony of the third degree. Other larceny (theft) is either a

misdemeanor or a petty misdemeanor, § 223.1(2).

18. Aggravated assault is a felony of either the second or third degree, depending on the circumstances.

19. As to malicious mischief see, infra, chapter 4, section 7. See Smith-Hurd Ill.Ann.Stat. ch. 38 § 21–3 (1973); V.T.C.A., Penal Code § 30.05 (1974).

20. N.Mex.Stat.Ann. § 30–14–1 (1978); McKinney's N.Y.Rev.Pen.Code §§ 140.05–140.17 (1975).

Mass demonstrators, who refused to leave upon request were guilty of malicious trespass under the statute. State v. Quinnell, 277 Minn. 63, 151 N.W.2d 598 (1967).

21. Section 221.2.

1. 2 Bishop, New Criminal Law § 8 (9th ed. 1923). "It is an essential element of the common law crime of arson that the burning be done or caused mali-

It has been very common to include the word "wilful" or "voluntary" [2] in the definition and at times to add the phrase "by night or by day." [3] But the word "wilful" or "voluntary" as used (perhaps we should say misused) in this definition means no more than is included in the word "malicious," as will be explained, infra, in the discussion of malice, and hence may well be omitted. Common-law arson, unlike the rule in burglary, makes no distinction between day and night but may be committed at any time,[4] and hence the inclusion of a statement to this effect in the definition is not inaccurate. It is not needed, however, and is not used in the definitions of other crimes which may be perpetrated at any time, which is true of most. It may be added that although it is unimportant, so far as common-law arson is concerned, whether the burning was in the nighttime or during the day may be the determining factor in fixing the grade or degree of the crime under some of the modern statutes.[5]

From earliest days arson was recognized as a common-law felony and at one time the punishment was death by burning.[6] It is a felony under modern statutes, and although the death penalty may not be imposed for arson alone, if death results from an act of arson the crime of murder could result in the death penalty in extreme situations.[7] And without reference to the exact words which may be preferred for the definition it is necessary to give separate attention to what is meant by (1) malicious (2) burning of the (3) dwelling which must be the habitation (4) "of another."

A. MALICIOUS

Arson, in the common-law sense, usually results from a deliberate intent to burn the dwelling of another and without doubt this intent was at one time assumed to be an ingredient of the crime, which explains the use of the word "voluntary" or "wilful," as mentioned above, in many of the definitions. Either word, however, lost all meaning in this definition when it became established that by fiction an intent to burn might be recognized in law when it did not exist in fact. Thus Lord Coke, writing in the early 1600's said that the "law doth sometime imply, that the house was burnt maliciously and voluntarily," [8] giving as an illustration the instance of a fire spreading and causing damage beyond that actually intended. It is not common-law

---

ciously." State v. Long, 243 N.C. 393, 395, 90 S.E.2d 739, 741 (1956).

Knowingly and maliciously causing a fire or explosion which damages the dwelling of another is first-degree arson under the statute. State v. Lunstrum, 19 Wn.App. 597, 576 P.2d 453 (1978).

2. 3 Co.Inst. *66; 1 Hale P.C. *566; 1 Hawk.P.C. c. 39 (6th ed. 1788); 4 Bl.Comm. *220; 2 East P.C. 1015 (1803); State v. Heller, 2 N.J.Misc. 1023, 1024, 126 A. 298, 299 (1924).

3. 1 Hale P.C. *556; 1 Hawk.P.C. c. 39 (6th ed. 1788). Coke used the phrase "in the day or night."

4. 3 Co.Inst. *66; 1 Hale P.C. *566; 1 Hawk.P.C. c. 39 (6th ed. 1788).

5. E. g., Va.Code § 18.2–77 (1978).

6. 1 Hale P.C. *566; 4 Bl.Comm. *222.

7. Idaho Code § 18–4003 (1977); Nev.Rev.Stat. 200.030 (1977); Tenn.Code Ann. § 39–2402 (1977). Arson resulting in death was murder under the felony-murder rule of the common law, and is first-degree murder under many of the statutes, as explained, supra, in chapter 2, section B, 1, b(C).

8. 3 Co.Inst. *67.

At common law a specific intent to burn was not required for arson. A malicious burning was sufficient. And the statute is essentially the same. Since a specific intent is not required, evidence of diminished mental capacity is not a defense to arson. State v. Nelson, 17 Wn.App. 66, 561 P.2d 1093 (1977).

arson for a dweller to burn his own dwelling,[9] and this has given rise to the outstanding example of unintentional arson; for if such a fire obviously creates an unreasonable fire hazard for other nearby dwellings, and any of these is actually burned, common-law arson has been committed [10] even if the wrongdoer did not actually intend the consequence and may have hoped it would not happen. An intentional act creating an obvious fire hazard to the dwelling of another, done without justification, excuse or mitigation, might well be characterized as "wilful" (a word of many meanings),[11] and would certainly be malicious,[12] but as the law has developed it is a mistake to assume that the phrase "wilful and malicious," when found in the definition of common-law arson, adds some distinct requirement not included in the word "malicious" alone.[13]

"The malice which is a necessary element in the crime of arson need not . . . take the form of malevolence or ill will," [14] just as nothing of this nature is needed for malice in the law of homicide. Thus if a reward is offered to the person who first brings to the fire station the information of a house on fire, one who ignites a dwelling house for the sole purpose of claiming this reward is guilty of arson.[15] A prisoner who sets fire to the building in which he is confined, merely for the purpose of escape, is also guilty,[16] and this is true even if he intends only to burn a hole through which he may pass and does not intend that the building should be further damaged.[17] Further-

---

9. Ibid.

10. This was stated *obiter* in Proberts' Case, 2 East P.C. 1030 (1799), and confirmed by an express decision later the same year. Isaac's Case, 2 East P.C. 1031 (1799). "[T]he wilful and malicious setting fire to the house of another, the burning of which is only a misdemeanor, will become a capital felony, if a dwelling-house or barn with grain in it, be thereby burnt, where such burning is the probable consequence of the first illegal act." State v. Lauglin, 53 N.C. 354, 355 (1861).

11. See infra, chapter 7, section 4, D.

But note: "To be a wilful and malicious burning in the law of arson, the burning must simply be done voluntarily and without excuse or justification and without any bona fide claim of right. An animus against the property itself or its owner is not an element of common law arson. . . . 'Wilfully' means intentionally as distinguished from accidentally or involuntarily, i.e., the fire must be set knowingly and stubbornly with an unlawful purpose." Matter of Appeal in Pima County Juvenile Action No. J–37390–1, 116 Ariz. 519, 570 P.2d 206, 209 (App.1977).

12. Id. at section 4, B.

13. "To be a wilful and malicious burning in the law of arson, the burning must simply be done voluntarily and without excuse or justification and with-

out any bona fide claim of right." State v. Scott, 118 Ariz. 383, 576 P.2d 1383, 1385 (App.1978).

14. State v. Pisano, 107 Conn. 630, 632, 141 A. 660, 661 (1928). And see Crow v. State, 136 Tenn. 333, 339, 189 S.W. 687, 688 (1916). Motive, while often useful as evidence of defendant's guilt, is not an essential element of the crime. State v. Edmonds, 185 N.C. 721, 117 S.E. 23 (1923); State v. Dunn, 199 N.W.2d 104 (Iowa 1972).

15. Regina v. Regan, 4 Cox C.C. 335 (1850).

16. Luke v. State, 49 Ala. 30 (1873); Crow v. State, 136 Tenn. 333, 189 S.W. 687 (1916).

17. Lockett v. State, 63 Ala. 5 (1879). It was held otherwise in an early New York case under a statute providing the death penalty for aggravated arson. People v. Cotteral, 18 Johns. 115 (N.Y.1820). This rule was followed in State v. Mitchell, 27 N.C. 350 (1845); Delany v. State, 41 Tex. 601 (1874). This Texas case has since been overruled. Smith v. State, 23 Tex.App. 357, 5 S.W. 219 (1887); Rogers v. State, 102 Tex.Cr.R. 331, 277 S.W. 664 (1925). Such a burning would not suffice if the statute requires an intent to destroy the building, nor if there is a requirement that the house be "consumed or generally injured." Jenkins v. State, 53 Ga. 33 (1874).

more a landlord who had burned his tenant out of house and home could not successfully establish want of malice by showing that he had no ill will toward his lessee, but had burned the house to collect the insurance.[18]

Few types of harm of comparable gravity, on the other hand, are so likely to result from mischance or from negligence as the burning of a dwelling, and it has been emphasized repeatedly that no such burning constitutes common-law arson,[19] although under statutory additions to the field some negligent burnings of other property may be punished as a lesser offense, such as negligently burning prairie or timbered land.[20] Whenever criminal guilt is to be established on a negligence basis it should be understood, unless clearly directed otherwise by statute, to require the so-called criminal negligence,[21] but even that is insufficient for this purpose because "no negligence" will suffice for guilt of common-law arson.[22]

Moreover the mere fact that the burning resulted from an unlawful act will not make it arson,[23] and there is no felony-arson rule comparable to the felony-murder rule in homicide. The leading case on this point [24] involved an indictment for maliciously setting fire to a ship on the high seas in violation of a statute but the problem insofar as malice is concerned was the same as if it had been common-law arson. The defendant lighted a match to see, while attempting to steal rum from the hold of a ship, and the rum caught fire, starting a blaze which was communicated to the ship and destroyed it. A conviction was reversed because the judge had instructed the jury that defendant was guilty if the burning resulted from attempted larceny, which was held not to be the law. While holding that this instruction required a reversal the judges intimated that the evidence may have been sufficient to support a conviction had the jury been correctly advised as to the law. This was not on any theory of negligence but on the thought that the jury might have been satisfied that defendant's greed induced him to expose the ship deliberately to an obvious risk of destruction by fire, and if so "a malicious design to commit the injurious act with which he is charged might have been fairly *imputed* to him," although he did not actually "intend to set fire to the ship." [25] In another case the court indicated the mental element needed for arson by the phrase "reckless and indifferent whether the house was set fire to or not." [26] In brief, the state of mind which constitutes guilt of common-law arson, assuming the other elements of the crime are present and there are no circumstances of justification, excuse or mitigation,[27] is either an in-

---

18. Modern statutes sometimes declare that a burning to collect insurance is arson (see infra). But no such statute would be needed for the case stated in the text.

19. "For if it be done by mischance, or negligence, it is no felony, . . ." 3 Co.Inst. *67. Accord, 1 Hale P.C. *569; 1 Hawk.P.C. c. 39, § 5 (6th ed. 1788); 4 Bl.Comm. *222; 2 East P.C. 1019 (1803); Morris v. State, 124 Ala. 44, 47, 27 So. 336, 337 (1899). The presumption is that any fire is the result of accidental cause rather than criminal design. Hurst v. State, 88 Ga.App. 798, 78 S.E.2d 80 (1953).

20. Tenn.Code Ann. §§ 39–511, 512 (1975).

21. See infra, chapter 7, section 2.

22. 2 East P.C. 1019 (1803); Morris v. State, 124 Ala. 44, 47, 27 So. 336, 337 (1900).

23. 1 Hale P.C. *569.

24. Regina v. Faulkner, 13 Cox C.C. 550 (1877).

25. Per Fitzgerald, J., id. at p. 557. Emphasis added.

26. Regina v. Harris, 15 Cox C.C. 75, 77 (1882).

27. There is seldom any justification, excuse or mitigation involved in the burn-

tent to burn the dwelling of another, or an act done under such circumstances that there is obviously a plain and strong likelihood of such a burning.

Modern statutes on arson frequently make use of the phrase "wilfully and maliciously" [28] although some use "wantonly and wilfully" [29] or only "maliciously" [30] or employ both joined by the word "or." [31] In view of the history of the offense these should all be held to codify the state of mind required for common-law arson and there has seldom been any indication to the contrary.[32] In some instances enactments have made a definite change in the mental element required for arson as by substituting the word "intentional" [33] or "knowingly" [34] for the words commonly employed, or by using the customary words followed by the phrase "with intent to destroy it." [35] Neither of these, properly interpreted, would permit conviction on proof of a burning which meets the common-law requirement of malice although not actually intentional, and the second adds to the requirement of a malicious burning a specific intent which must be alleged in the indictment or information and established by proof.[36] There has been a tendency, it may be added, to eliminate the "intent to destroy" clause from statutes in which it once appeared.[37] One of the legislative extensions in this area is that of providing a penalty for burning property with intent to defraud the insurer, to be discussed presently, and such a provision, which is very common,[38] obviously requires the specific intent mentioned.

ing of another's dwelling but the exclusionary phrase seems to be required. Unless forbidden by statute, burning might be an acceptable mode of demolition in the case of an uninsured building so situated as not to endanger other property, and one entrusted with this task might make a mistake as to the building intended. And an act done in the sudden heat of passion engendered by such provocation that it would not be murder in a homicide case, should not be arson in a case of burning.

28. Alaska Stats. 11.20.10 (1970); West's Ann.Cal.Pen.Code § 448a (1978).

29. E.g., N.C.Gen.Stat. § 14–62 (1971).

30. E.g., D.C.Code, 1973 § 22–401; Va.Code § 18.2–77 (1978).

31. E.g., N.Mex.Stat.1978 § 30–17–5. "Wrongfully or maliciously" R.I.Gen. Laws 1956, § 11–4–2.

32. In State v. Willing, 129 Iowa 72, 105 N.W. 355 (1905), the court assumes that "wilful" and "malicious" have different meanings as used in an arson statute but the opinion is far from convincing. The conviction was reversed because the court felt the judge had misled the jury into believing that the burning was malicious if intentional—regardless of the circumstances. This is inaccurate as emphasized supra in note

26, but would be equally inaccurate as applied to the word "wilful" in an arson case. See also People v. George, 42 Cal.App.2d 568, 109 P.2d 404 (1941), in which the court says the burning must be both wilful and malicious, but is not using the words as they were employed in common-law arson.

The burning of personal property in the building under such circumstances that burning of the building was quite probable, and did in fact result, constitutes arson. Berry v. State, 499 P.2d 934 (Okl.Cr.1972).

33. LSA–R.S. (La.) §§ 14:51, 14:52 (1977); Wis.Stats.1958, § 943.02.

34. Colo.Rev.Stat.1973 § 18–4–102. "Knowingly or purposely," Rev.Code Mont.1947 § 94–6–102 (1974).

35. O'Brien v. State, 39 Ariz. 298, 6 P.2d 421 (1931); People v. Mooney, 127 Cal. 339, 59 P. 761 (1889).

36. Ibid.

37. Compare the cases in note 33 with the present statutes. Ariz.Rev.Stat. § 13–1703 (1978); West's Ann.Cal.Pen. Code § 447a (1978).

38. E.g., Alaska Stat. 11.20.070 (1970); D.C.Code, 1973 § 22–402; Kan.Stat.Ann. 21–3718(b) (1974); (La.) 14:53 (1974); Miss.Code 1972, § 97–17–11.

B. BURNING

Unless there is a burning there is no arson[39] but this must not
be construed to mean a total destruction of the building or even
any considerable damage thereto.[40]

If "any part of the house be burnt, the offender is guilty of felony, notwithstanding the fire afterwards be put out, or go out of itself." [41] The
slightest ignition of the building is sufficient, and hence the test is whether
"the fiber of the wood or other combustible material is charred, and thus
destroyed" by fire.[42] It is not necessary even that there should be a blaze,[43]
for "the charring of wood by fire is the burning of it." [44]

On the other hand a mere blackening by smoke or discoloration by heat
does not constitute a burning.[45] It is frequently said that there is no arson if
the building is merely "scorched," [46] but the use of this word is not to be
recommended because of the possible doubt as to its meaning. If the word
is used to imply a discoloration or even a shriveling from the heat, there is no
inaccuracy, but some might use it where there had been a charring of the
wood but no blaze.

Merely "putting fire into or towards a house, however maliciously, if either by accident or timely prevention the fire do not take, and no part be
burned, does not amount to arson at common law." [47] Nor will this offense
result from the burning of chattels in or about the building, if the fire is not

39. 3 Co.Inst. *66; 1 Hawk.P.C. c. 39
§ 4 (6th ed. 1788); 4 Bl.Comm. *222, 2
East P.C. 1020 (1803); Graham v. State,
40 Ala. 659 (1867); United States v. Carter, 522 F.2d 666 (D.C.Cir.1975).

40. 3 Co.Inst. *66; Mary v. State, 24
Ark. 44 (1862).

41. 1 Hawk.P.C. c. 39, § 4 (6th ed.
1788). And see 3 Co.Inst. *66; State v.
Morris, 98 N.J.L. 621, 625, 121 A. 290,
292 (1923).

42. State v. Spiegel, 111 Iowa 701,
705, 83 N.W. 722, 723 (1900). "Slightly
damaged." People v. Losinger, 331
Mich. 490, 502, 50 N.W.2d 137, 143 (1951).
See also Crow v. State, 136 Tenn. 333,
340, 189 S.W. 687, 689 (1916).

43. People v. Haggerty, 46 Cal. 354
(1873); State v. Rodgers, 168 N.C. 112,
83 S.E. 161 (1914).

44. Benbow v. State, 128 Ala. 1, 5, 29
So. 553, 555 (1901). Charring of threshold and lower board of the screen door
was sufficient to constitute a burning.
State v. Pisano, 107 Conn. 630, 141 A. 660
(1928). Accord, State v. Nielson, 25 Utah
2d 11, 474 P.2d 725 (1970).

45. Graham v. State, 40 Ala. 659, 664
(1867).

46. State v. Hall, 93 N.C. 571, 573
(1885). A lighted faggot was placed on
the floor of the kitchen. It was discov-

ered almost immediately and put into a
grate. The prosecuting witness testified:
"A part of the boards of the kitchen floor
was scorched black, but not burnt. The
faggot was nearly consumed, but no part
of the wood of the floor was consumed."
This was held insufficient to support an
indictment for arson. Regina v. Russell,
Car. & M. 541, 174 Eng.Rep. 626 (1842).
Setting of fire which scorched the wallpaper but did not burn through to the
wood of the house, is insufficient to constitute arson. Van Morey v. State, 112
Tex.Cr.R. 439, 17 S.W.2d 50 (1929).
There was some evidence in this case to
indicate that the wallpaper was on fire
but did not burn through to the wood.
But the reversal of the case was for refusal to instruct the jury that they should
acquit if they found that the house was
simply scorched or smoked.

47. 2 East P.C. 1020. And see Mary
v. State, 24 Ark. 44, 45 (1862); Cochrane
v. State, 6 Md. 400, 405 (1854). This
would, of course, constitute an attempt
to commit arson. See infra, chapter 6,
section 3. Many of the codes include specific references to attempt to commit arson. E. g., Mass.Gen.Laws Ann.C. 266,
§ 5A (1977); Md.Code, 1975, Art. 27,
§ 10 (1975); N.C.Gen.Stat. § 14–67
(1971).

communicated to any part of the structure itself.[48] Thus setting fire to paper in a drying loft is not arson if no part of the house itself is burned.[49]

Peculiarities in the origin of the fire may have an important bearing upon the question of whether it was the act of some individual or the result of natural causes. Furthermore, when it is known to have been caused by some person, anything unusual in the situation may throw light upon the inquiry as to whether it was an accident or was malicious within the rules discussed above. But when it is found in a particular case that the accused did maliciously burn the house of another, he is not excused from criminal responsibility because of indirectness or uniqueness of the method employed.[50] It is probably rather common in arson cases for the match to be applied to kindling or rubbish rather than directly to the frame of the building proper, but a stack or a shed or another building may be used for "kindling." [51] If matches are put in unginned cotton for the purpose of burning the gin house, and in the process of ginning, the matches ignite and start a fire which does in fact destroy the building, the defendant is just as guilty as if he had used the match in the ordinary way.[52] He would be equally guilty if he had caused the fire by focusing the sun's rays through a reading glass. For the same reason, arson may be committed by means of explosives, but a word of caution is necessary in this respect. Obviously there would be no common-law arson if the building was damaged by the explosion alone without any resulting fire, and if splinters are torn from the building and ignited by the explosion, the burning of these severed parts will not be sufficient for common-law arson, if no fire is communicated to the structure itself.[53]

Statutes which extend the crime of arson to include the burning of personal property,[54] change the result in those situations in which chattels were burned in a building without the fire being communicated to the house itself; the rule in the explosion cases is sometimes changed by such a provision as that the explosion of a house by means of gunpowder or other explosive matter comes within the meaning of arson; [55] and an occasional clause requires substantially more than the slightest possible burning; [56] but the most interesting problem in this connection results from the use of the phrase "set fire to." This phrase, as so used, dates back to the English statute of 1722.[57] It was there used in place of the word "burn," [58] and was employed as a syno-

48. Graham v. State, 40 Ala. 659 (1867); O'Daniel v. State, 188 Ind. 477, 123 N.E. 241 (1919).

49. The King v. Taylor, 1 Leach 49, 168 Eng.Rep. 127 (1759).

50. ". . . it is of no consequence by what means the fire is communicated to a house, if the burning is designed." Smith v. State, 23 Tex.App. 357, 362, 5 S.W. 219, 220 (1887). And see Combs v. Commonwealth, 93 Ky. 313, 20 S.W. 221 (1892); Regina v. Price, 9 Car. & P. 729, 173 Eng.Rep. 1029 (1841).

51. Rex v. Cooper, 5 Car. & P. 535, 172 Eng.Rep. 1087 (1833); People v. Hiltel, 131 Cal. 577, 63 P. 919 (1901); Grimes v. State, 63 Ala. 166 (1879).

52. Overstreet v. State, 46 Ala. 30 (1871).

53. State v. Landers, 39 Tex.Cr.R. 671, 47 S.W. 1008 (1898).

54. E.g., Ark.Stats.Ann. §§ 41–1901, 1902 (1975); Ga.Code Ann., § 26–1403 (1976).

55. V.T.C.A., Penal Code § 28.02 (1974). See also LSA–R.S. (La.) 14:51 (1977); Landers v. State, 39 Tex.Cr.R. 671, 47 S.W. 1008 (1898); Johnson v. State, 96 Tex.Cr.R. 216, 257 S.W. 551 (1923). Cf. Wis.Stats. § 943.02 (1978).

56. E.g., Ga.Code Ann. § 26–2202 (1953), now repealed. See Ga.Code Ann. Chap. 26–14 (1976).

57. 9 Geo. I c. 22.

58. Cf. the Malicious Damage Act of 1861. 24 and 25 Vict. c. 97, § 2.

nym.[59] This seems to be quite proper, for however logical it may be to view this phrase as the equivalent of "apply fire to," it is commonly used interchangeably with "set on fire." The expression "set fire to" has been held to be synonymous with "burn" in this country,[60] but there is also authority for the contrary view.[61] While the English enactment omitted the word "burn" and substituted "set fire to" in its place, some of our statutes make use of the clause, "any person who . . . sets fire to or burns . . . ."[62] There is more reason for suggesting a different meaning where both are employed than where only one is found, but the practice of saying the same thing twice is far from rare, and authority can be found for the position that even the use of both does not change the rule which requires some burning of the building itself.[63]

C. DWELLING

At common law arson, like burglary, was an offense against the habitation[64] and not against property, and except where otherwise provided by statute there can be no arson of a house in which there can be no burglary,[65] so that what was said concerning the "dwelling"[66] in the discussion of that felony is equally applicable here. A dwelling must be a place of residence although it remains such during the temporary absence of the dweller.[67] It is not sufficient that it was built for that purpose and quite suitable therefor, and burning a building is not common-law arson if it is before the first dweller has moved in[68] or after it has been vacated and the former dweller has no intention of returning.[69] On the other hand a structure built for use as a barn or a stable becomes a "dwelling" if it is usually occupied at night by a person lodging therein no matter "how rude and devoid of comforts" it may be.[70]

59. 2 East P.C. 1020 (1803); Regina v. Russell, Car. & M. 541, 174 Eng.Rep. 626 (1842).

60. Graham v. State, 40 Ala. 659 (1867); Benbow v. State, 128 Ala. 1, 29 So. 553 (1901); State v. Taylor, 45 Me. 322 (1858). An attempt statute reading "set fire, with intent to burn," must be distinguished. State v. Dennin, 32 Vt. 158 (1859).

61. Mary v. State, 24 Ark. 44 (1862); Howell v. Commonwealth, 46 Va. 664 (1848).

"The phrase 'sets fire to' in the First Degree Arson statute means something less than actual burning and therefore is not synonymous with the word 'burn.'" Lynch v. State, ___ Ind.App. ___, 370 N.E.2d 401, 403 (1978).

62. E.g., West's Ann.Cal.Pen.Code § 447a (1978); Miss.Code, 1972 § 97–17–1.

63. Graham v. State, 40 Ala. 659 (1867); Benbow v. State, 128 Ala. 1, 29 So. 553 (1900).

64. 4 Bl.Comm. *220; Simmons v. State, 234 Ind. 489, 129 N.E.2d 121 (1955); State v. Long, 243 N.C. 393, 90 S.E.2d 739 (1956).

65. The Queen v. Allison, 1 Cox C.C. 24, 25 (1843).

66. "The word 'dwelling-house' does not always have the same sense in all cases. It may mean one thing under an indictment for burglary or arson, another under a homestead law, another under pauper law, and another under a contract or devise." State v. Meservie, 121 Me. 564, 566, 118 A. 482, 483 (1922).

67. People v. Losinger, 331 Mich. 490, 50 N.W.2d 137 (1951).

68. State v. McGowan, 20 Conn. 245 (1850); State v. Wolfenberger, 20 Ind. 242 (1863).

69. State v. Warren, 33 Me. 30 (1851); State v. Clark, 52 N.C. 167 (1859); The Queen v. Allison, 1 Cox C.C. 24 (1843).

70. State v. Jones, 106 Mo. 302, 310, 17 S.W. 366, 368 (1891).

If the building is a dwelling it is not necessary for any person to be therein at the time of the burning, so far as arson is concerned,[71] but this is a factor which may determine the grade or degree of the offense under some of the statutes.[72] Arson resulting in the loss of human life is murder at common law under the felony-murder rule and is first-degree murder under most of the statutes which divide this crime into degrees.[73] It is specifically made capital under some statutes.[74]

In the law of arson, as in burglary, the term "dwelling" includes also any "barn, stable, cow-house, sheephouse, dairy house, millhouse, and the like, parcel of the mansion house:"[75] or to use the familiar expression, "within the curtilage."[76] The burning of such an outbuilding not "within the curtilage" or "parcel of the mansion house" is not common-law arson[77] with the possible exception of a barn containing corn or hay. It has been stated that "the common law . . . accounted it felony to burn a single barn in the field, if filled with hay or corn, though not parcel of the dwelling house,"[78] but this is open to substantial doubt.[79] Ancient statutes[80] or references antedating the common law[81] may be the basis for such a statement. Certain it is that English statutes went very far, including at one time the mere attempt to burn a stack of corn within the category of felony,[82] and after the repeal of that enactment it was made felony to burn maliciously in the nighttime "any ricks or stacks of corn, hay or grain, barns, or other houses or buildings, or kilns."[83]

71. People v. Losinger, 331 Mich. 490, 50 N.W.2d 137 (1951). "A dwelling house once inhabited, as such, and from which the occupant is but temporarily absent," is a building of which arson may be committed. State v. McGowan, 20 Conn. 245, 247 (1850).

72. E.g., Va.Code 1960, § 18.1–75.

73. See supra, chapter 2, section 1.

74. E.g., Code of Ala. § 13–A–6–2 (1978); Miss.Code, 1972, § 97–3–19(2)(c).

75. 3 Co.Inst. *67. And see 1 Hale P.C. *567; State v. Blumenthal, 133 Ark. 584, 585, 203 S.W. 36, 37 (1918).

76. Commonwealth v. Barney, 64 Mass. 480, 481 (1852); People v. Alpin, 86 Mich. 393, 394, 49 N.W. 148 (1891).

77. 3 Co.Inst. *67.

78. 4 Bl.Comm. *221. And see 2 East P.C. 1020 (1803).

79. Blackstone relies for his statement entirely upon Coke, 3 Co.Inst. *67, but that author does not say burning such a barn is common-law arson but only that it is "felony,"—which may have been the result of statute. It was said in another book that burning a barn full of corn was felony in 1220. Pollock & Maitland, History of English Law 492 (2d ed. 1899). The only reference is de Vere's case, 1 Selden Society, Select Pleas of the Crown 139, pl. 203 (1220).

This prosecution failed because of a variance between the pleading and the proof and hence no more was decided. It is mentioned that there was corn in the barn but this seems only a factual statement comparable to the reference to defendant's irritation at the failure to find the person he was seeking. It is *not* said that the barn was *not* parcel of the mansion and the references to the house and the barn tend strongly to suggest that it was.

80. Burning a barn containing corn was made felony without benefit of clergy by the statute of 23 Hen. VIII, c. 1, f. 3 (1531), and this may well have been the basis for Coke's statement made nearly a century later. 3 Co.Inst. *67. It was without doubt the basis for the statement in Barnham v. Nethersal, 4 Coke 20a, 76 Eng.Rep. 908 (1602).

81. Coke comments that "the ancient authors extended this felony . . . to stacks of corn, wayns or carts of cole, wood or other goods." 3 Co.Inst. *67. He does not accept this as a statement of common law but mentions that even an attempt to burn a stack of corn was made felony by a statute repealed before he wrote.

82. Ibid.

83. 22 & 23 Car. II, c. 7, § 2 (1670).

With us this is largely academic because English extensions beyond the "dwelling," meaning the mansion itself and outbuildings within the curtilage, seem not to have been accepted as common law here,[84] and our own statutes have covered the area very extensively. One plan has been to designate as "arson" the malicious burning of "any dwelling house, kitchen, shop, barn, stable or other outhouse that is parcel thereof, or belonging to or adjoining thereto,"[85] and to punish as a lesser offense the malicious burning of any building which is not a dwelling or parcel thereof,[86] adding as a still lesser offense such burning of "any barrack, cock, crib, rick or stack of hay, corn, wheat, oats, barley or other grain or vegetable product of any kind; or any field of standing hay or grain of any kind; or any pile of coal, wood or other fuel; or any streetcar, railway car, boat, automobile or other motor vehicle; or any personal property not herein specifically named."[87] The proscription may extend even further to include, for example, the wilful or *negligent* burning of prairie or timbered land, or an enclosed or cultivated field.[88] A second plan is to include much the same coverage in three or four degrees of arson.[89] Some statutes subordinate the common-law concept of arson and emphasize the element of human danger as by providing that it is "aggravated arson" if it involves "any structure, water craft, or movable, wherein it is foreseeable that human life may be endangered,"[90] and "simple arson" if such foreseeable hazard is lacking.[91]

Some years ago a Model Arson Law was proposed by the National Board of Fire Underwriters,[92] which was adopted, in whole or in part, by many states.[93] This provided for three degrees of arson depending upon the type of property burned. The first degree applied to the burning of dwellings, the second degree to the burning of other buildings and structures, while the third embraced the burning of other property of the value of $25 or more. A separate section, applicable to one's own property, covered any burning for the purpose of defrauding insurers.[94]

Any malicious destruction of, or damage to, the property of another which is not common-law arson constitutes a common-law misdemeanor known as malicious mischief,[95] and much that is found in the modern codes in chapters on arson might well have been included under the other heading. If a more severe penalty is desired for this type of damage it could be provided in a section entitled "malicious mischief by burning."[96] Actually many of the codes have considerable duplication in this regard, sometimes with strange results. In the California code under the chapter on arson the wilful

84. An occasional dictum has repeated Blackstone's statement as to the barn not within the curtilage. See Allen v. State, 10 Ohio St. 288, 300 (1859).

85. West's Ann.Cal.Pen.Code § 447a (1970).

86. Id. at § 448a.

87. Id. at § 449a.

88. Tenn.Code Ann. §§ 39–509–511 (1975).

89. Idaho Code §§ 18–801 to 18–804 (1972).

90. LSA–R.S. (La.) 14:51 (1977).

91. Id. at § 14–52 (1977).

92. For the Model Arson Law (quoted from Suggestions for Arson Investigators, National Board of Underwriters, 1956, pp. 45–46) see Model Penal Code 50–51 (Tent.Draft No. 11, 1960).

93. Idaho Code 18–801–3 (1972).

94. See Model Penal Code 35 (Tent.Draft No. 11, 1960).

95. See, supra, chapter 4, section 7.

96. See, e.g., West's Ann.Cal.Pen. Code §§ 600, 600.5. These sections were renumbered 449b and 449c respectively in 1966. See now 449b and 449c (1977).

and malicious burning of standing grain, and so forth, the property of another of the value of twenty-five dollars, is punishable by imprisonment in the state prison.[97] In the chapter on malicious mischief the same burning, but without reference to value, is punishable also by imprisonment in the state prison.[98]

D. "OF ANOTHER"

Common-law arson, like common-law burglary, is an offense which involves a disturbance of the "security of the dwelling house" [99] and hence the burning of one's own dwelling does not constitute this felony.[1] The statement frequently encountered is that it must be the "house of another," [2] but it is possession or occupancy [3] and not title [4] which determines whose house a building shall be said to be for such purposes. Hence if a rented building becomes the dwelling of the tenant, and his alone, it would be possible for the landlord to commit common-law arson by burning that house [5] but it would be impossible for the tenant to commit this offense by doing so,[6]— provided no other dwelling was harmed by the fire. And it does not constitute common-law arson for husband or wife to burn the house they both occupy as a place of habitation for the family, even if the title thereto is in the other spouse.[7] An English case extended this rule to cover a malicious act of a wife in burning her husband's dwelling after they had separated and she was living elsewhere, because of the ancient theory of "legal identity" of the two,[8] but this fiction serves no useful purpose in such a situation and the better rule reaches the contrary result where the two have parted and established separate dwellings.[9]

One who sets fire to his own dwelling for the purpose of burning the dwelling of another, or under such circumstances that there is obviously great danger of such a result, is guilty of common-law arson if the fire is

97. Id. at § 449a (1977).

98. Id. at § 600.5. This section was renumbered 449c, without other change, in 1966. See now id. 449c (1977).

99. State v. Haynes, 66 Me. 307 (1876). And see Simmons v. State, 234 Ind. 489, 129 N.E.2d 121 (1955).

1. 1 Hale P.C. *568; 2 East P.C. 1022 (1803); State v. Haynes, 66 Me. 307 (1876); Haas v. State, 103 Ohio St. 1, 132 N.E. 158 (1921).

2. 3 Co.Inst. *66; 1 Hale P.C. *566; 4 Bl.Comm. *220.

3. State v. Fish, 27 N.J.L. 323 (1859); Snyder v. People, 26 Mich. 106 (1872); The King v. Breeme, 1 Leach 220, 168 Eng.Rep. 213 (1780). It has been held that the offense is against the actual dweller even if his possession is wrongful. Rex v. Wallis, 1 Moody 344, 168 Eng.Rep. 1297 (1832).

4. People v. Handley, 93 Mich. 46, 52 N.W. 1032 (1892).

5. 4 Bl.Comm. *221; Harris' Case, Foster 113, 168 Eng.Rep. 56 (1753).

6. 1 Hale P.C. *568. The King v. Spalding, 1 Leach 218, 168 Eng.Rep. 211 (1780); Proberts' Case, 2 East P.C. 1030 (1799); State v. Fish, 27 N.J.L. 323 (1859). And see State v. Blumenthal, 133 Ark. 584, 585, 203 S.W. 36, 37 (1918).

Contra, Although the statute was worded in terms of setting fire to the building of another, the court held that where "a tenant sets fire to a unit which he occupies, he also damages the property interest of the owner in that building." People v. Brown, ___ Colo.App. ___, 622 P.2d 573, 576 (1980).

7. Snyder v. People, 26 Mich. 106 (1872). On the other hand a house is not the dwelling of a servant who lives there, and he may be guilty of common-law arson by burning it. Gowen's Case, 2 East P.C. 1027 (1786).

8. Rex v. Marsh, 1 Moody 182, 168 Eng.Rep. 1233 (1828).

9. Frazier v. State, 16 Ohio App. 8 (1922); Kopcyznski v. State, 137 Wis. 358, 118 N.W. 863 (1908).

actually communicated to the other house.[10] For this reason if a dweller in an apartment house burns the building he is guilty of arson and the building may properly be described as the dwelling of one of the other tenants.[11] And while it may be feasible in burglary to regard the separate apartments in a tenement house as if they were distinct buildings, this is not acceptable in the law of arson and the tenant who sets fire to his own rooms in such a house may be convicted of arson for burning the "dwelling" of one of the other tenants even if the fire was actually confined to the rooms occupied by the wrongdoer.[12] A tenant of a hotel was said to have only a right to occupy a room, which was not considered a sufficient interest apart from the owner, so that the owner could not be convicted of arson of the hotel under a statute requiring "property of another." [13]

The human hazard created by the conflagration of a dwelling is not limited to the dweller and his household because members of the fire department may be expected to come, friends and neighbors may attempt to be of assistance, and some of these may go onto or into the building to fight the blaze more advantageously, to save personal property or to search for those who may possibly have been trapped inside or overcome by smoke. In modern times legislators have regarded this human hazard as of such importance that the legislative trend has been in the direction of removing the requirement that the house burned be that of another. At times this result has been achieved by the simple expedient of omitting the phrase "of another" from the statutory definition of arson,[14] but the much more common plan has been the insertion of some such phrase as "the property of himself or of another." [15] One unfamiliar with the use of terms in this regard might suppose that the phrase mentioned has reference to title or ownership but such is not the fact, because in the common law of arson the word "property" was traditionally used to express possession or occupancy, as in Blackstone's explanation,—"for during the lease the house is the property of the tenant." [16] The purpose of such a clause is to change the rule of the common law and it has very properly been held to have accomplished this result and to have made it arson for one maliciously to burn his own dwelling.[17] Under statutes which have changed the rule of the common law in this regard the dweller may commit arson of his own dwelling whether he is a tenant in a building owned by another or is himself the owner and sole occupant thereof.[18] The claim that such a provision is an unconstitutional restriction of an owner's property rights was rejected on the ground that since the statute requires a malicious burning it would not be violated if one burned his own

---

10. 1 Hale P.C. *568; 4 Bl.Comm. *221; Isaac's Case, 2 East P.C. 1031 (1799). Hale and Blackstone mention the intent to burn the other's house but there is no such suggestion in Isaac's case which mentions only the "great danger" thereto.

11. Levy v. People, 80 N.Y. 327 (1880).

12. Ibid.

13. State v. Parrish, 205 Kan. 33, 468 P.2d 150 (1970).

14. E.g., Ariz.Rev.Stat. § 13–1703, 1704 (1978); McKinney's N.Y.Pen.Code § 150.00 (1975); State v. Hurd, 51 N.H.

176 (1871); State v. Dinagan, 79 N.H. 7, 104 A. 33 (1918).

15. E.g., West's Ann.Cal.Pen.Code § 447a (1978); N.J.Stat.Ann. 2C:17–1 (1979); Tenn.Code Ann. § 39–502 (1975); Va.Code 1950, § 18.2–77 (1975).

16. 4 Bl.Comm. *221.

17. Turner v. State, 155 Ark. 443, 244 S.W. 727 (1922). The same result was reached under a statute worded: "any dwelling house, whether it be his own or that of another." State v. Duelks, 97 N.J.L. 43, 116 A. 865 (1922).

18. State v. Katz, 7 N.J.Misc. 524, 146 A. 351 (1929).

property without harm or injury to any other person, or to the public, and without either an intent to cause such harm or injury, or under circumstances creating an obvious hazard thereof.[19] If one could burn his own dwelling without any such harm or injury caused, intended or hazarded it would probably have to be an uninsured cabin in a remote area.

Even where there is the rather common provision eliminating such a requirement from sections dealing with the burning of a dwelling or other building, those having to do with the burning of personal property ordinarily require that it be the "property of another" [20] unless it is with intent to defraud an insurer.[21] Since the burning of one's own personal property would not be malicious if no harm or injury to any other or to the public was caused, intended or hazarded, it is not necessary to restrict such a burning to the property "of another," and an occasional section omits such a requirement.[22]

E. HOUSEBURNING

Although it is not common-law arson for one to burn his own dwelling if no other is damaged by the fire, it is a common-law misdemeanor if the burning is intentional [23] and the house is situated in a city or town or is beyond those limits but "so near to other houses as to create danger to them." [24] Some of the early references mention an intent by the dweller to cause the burning of a neighbor's house by setting fire to his own,[25] because this had been averred in early indictments; [26] but it was not averred in later indictments,[27] and while a circumstance of aggravation it did not become an element of this common-law misdemeanor.[28] The social harm deemed sufficient for this purpose was the "great danger" when other dwellings were in close proximity,[29] and the "terror and affrightment of all liege subjects near the said house" when in a city or town.[30] For want of a better name this common-law misdemeanor is labeled "houseburning."

---

19. People v. George, 42 Cal.App.2d 568, 109 P.2d 404 (1941).

20. E.g., Colo.Rev.Stat.1973, 18–4–103; Smith-Hurd Ill.Ann.Stat. Ch. 38, § 20–1 (1977); Md.Code 1977, art. 28, § 8 (1977).

21. E.g., Colo.Rev.Stat., 1973, 18–4–104; Smith-Hurd Ill.Ann.Stat. Ch. 38, § 20–1 (1977).

22. E.g., Ark.Stats.Ann. § 41–503 (Off.1947). See now Ark.Stat.Ann. § 41–1902 (1975) using term "of another."

23. "Wilful" is the word used by Blackstone (4 Bl.Comm. *221) and while this is a word of many meanings (chapter VII, section 4(D)) he seems to have reference to an intentional burning.

24. The earliest case on the point involved a house in London. Rex v. Holmes, 2 East P.C. 1022 (1634). Black-stone speaks of "one's own house *in a town*." 4 Bl.Comm. *221. But East (from whom the quotation is taken) shows that either being in a town or in close proximity to other houses is sufficient.

25. 1 Hale P.C. *568; 1 Hawk.P.C. c. 39 § 3 (6th ed. 1788).

26. Rex v. Holmes, 2 East P.C. 1022 (1634); Rex v. Pedley, 2 East P.C. 1026 (1782).

27. Proberts' Case, 2 East P.C. 1030 (1799); Isaac's Case, 2 East P.C. 1031 (1799).

28. 2 East P.C. 1028 (1803).

29. Isaac's Case, 2 East P.C. 1031 (1799).

30. Proberts' Case, 2 East P.C. 1030 (1799).

F. ARSON WITH INTENT TO DEFRAUD

The actual collection of insurance as a result of a fire set for that purpose would probably have been held to constitute a common-law cheat prior to the statute on false pretenses and unquestionably constitutes that offense today.[31] But the burning of one's own dwelling for the purpose of collecting insurance did not constitute any common-law offense *for that reason* [32] although it would be "houseburning" if in town or in close proximity to other dwellings, and arson if other dwellings were actually burned as a result. Under modern statutes such burning is a felony, without the need of showing additional circumstances, either because the requirement that the dwelling be that of another has been eliminated,[33] or because of an express legislative provision therefor,[34] and some of the codes include both.[35] Statutory offenses also include the burning of other buildings [36] or of personal property [37] with intent to defraud the insurer.

If the prosecution is in the form of a general charge of maliciously burning a dwelling or other building not required by the statute to be that "of another," the particular purpose of the burning is not part of the required proof, but if it is under a special statute proscribing the burning of property to defraud an insurer the offense has a specific intent which must be alleged and proved.[38] This is not a particularly heavy burden because an intent to defraud the insurer "may be and generally is inferred from circumstances." [39] For this purpose it is not improper to consider the amount of insurance as compared to the value of the property,[40] and the fact that defendant believed his property was insured far in excess of its true value would offer strong support for such an inference,[41] but the offense may be committed even if the property is not overinsured and if defendant expects to compel the insurance company to pay others rather than himself.[42]

---

31. See infra, chapter 4, section 4.

32. 2 East P.C. 1028 (1803); The King v. Spalding, 1 Leach 218, 168 Eng.Rep. 211 (1780); Commonwealth v. Makely, 131 Mass. 421 (1881).

33. See supra, notes 11 and 12.

One burned a motor home in which he lived, and to which he held the title subject to a security interest held by another. In holding he could be convicted of arson it was "held that the statute manifested a legislative intent to criminally proscribe not only the common-law offense against habitation but also conduct directed against property rights as well:" People ex rel. VanMeveren District Court, ___ Colo. ___, 619 P.2d 494 (1980).

34. E.g., Ala.Code 1975, 13A-7-40 etc.; Va.Code 1950, § 18.2-77.

35. E.g., Alaska Stat. 11.20.010 (1970).

36. E.g., Alaska Stat. 11.20.070 (1970); Colo.Rev.Stat.1973, 18-4-104; Wyo.Stat.1977 § 6-7-105.

37. Id., Colo. at § 18-4-104; Iowa Code Ann. § 712.1 (1978); Id., Wyo. at § 6-7-105.

38. Mai v. People, 224 Ill. 414, 79 N.E. 633 (1906).

39. Commonwealth v. Cooper, 264 Mass. 368, 374, 162 N.E. 729, 731 (1928). And see People v. Vasalo, 120 Cal. 168, 52 P. 305 (1898); Commonwealth v. Asherowski, 196 Mass. 342, 82 N.E. 13 (1907).

40. State v. Gebhart, 70 W.Va. 232, 73 S.E. 964 (1912).

41. Commonwealth v. Cooper, 264 Mass. 368, 374, 162 N.E. 729, 731 (1928).

42. Commonwealth v. Alba, 271 Mass. 333, 171 N.E. 458 (1930).

If the statute proscribes the burning of "insured property" with intent to defraud the insurer, the fact that it was actually insured must be shown,[43] but under the more common provision which speaks in terms of burning the property with intent to defraud the insurer without designating it as "insured property," it is sufficient if the accused believed there was insurance and set the fire for the purpose of collecting on the supposed policy.[44] Furthermore, under such a provision, one may be guilty who has no interest in the property and no valid policy of insurance if he burns the place because he intends to collect on a policy which he assumes to be valid.[45] On the other hand there can be no conviction of one who was unaware of the existence of any insurance on the property.[46]

In one of the most interesting cases involving this offense there was uncertainty as to the exact origin of the fire but evidence to support the finding that defendant either started it on purpose or, after he had caused it by accident, purposely refrained from any attempt to extinguish it in order to collect the proceeds of the policy. The verdict of guilty by a jury which had been instructed that either finding would be sufficient for this purpose was held to support a conviction [47] although the court conceded that negligence on his part in failing to take steps or give an alarm in the emergency would not constitute guilt. The theory, of course, was that under the circumstances he had a legal duty to take reasonable measures to put out the fire, or have it extinguished, and that if he deliberately refrained from doing so in order to collect on the policy, the burning which he should have prevented was imputable to him and was with intent to defraud the insurer.[48]

G. STATUTORY ARSON

The term "statutory arson" is employed to designate the entire area of statutory proscription which is analogous to, but does not constitute, common-law arson. It is important to have mutually-exclusive labels here not only for the reasons mentioned in the preceding section, but because some of the state statutes provide a penalty for arson without defining the word and hence adopt the common-law definition.[49]

THE MODEL PENAL CODE

Article 220 deals with arson, criminal mischief and other property destruction. Section 220.1 covers, substantially, (1) common-law arson limited to a fire intentionally started, but including an intentionally caused explosion, (2) statutory arson "to collect insurance," which, however, does not apply to conduct not recklessly endangering any building or occupied structure

43. Meister v. People, 31 Mich. 99 (1875); People v. Butler, 62 App.Div. 508, 71 N.Y.S. 129 (1901).

44. McDonald v. People, 47 Ill. 533 (1868); State v. Steinkraus, 244 Mo. 152, 148 S.W. 877 (1912); Norville v. State, 144 Tenn. 278, 230 S.W. 966 (1921).

45. Brower v. State, 217 Miss. 425, 64 So.2d 576 (1953).

46. People v. Popoff, 289 N.Y. 344, 45 N.E.2d 904 (1942).

47. Commonwealth v. Cali, 247 Mass. 20, 141 N.E. 510 (1923).

48. See infra, chapter 6, section 4.

49. State v. Long, 243 N.C. 393, 90 S.E.2d 739 (1956).

Under the Maine Statute: "The concern, thus stated, is with the creation by arson of a risk of harm to human life in general rather than with the intent to cause harm by fire to a particular person." State v. Troiano, 421 A.2d 41 (Me.1980).

of another or placing any other in danger of death or bodily injury, and (3) intentionally starting a fire or causing an explosion which places another in danger of death or bodily injury, or places a building or occupied structure of another in danger of damage or destruction.

THE NEW PENAL CODES

Some of the new codes include within the sweep of a single short section on "arson," (1) common-law arson, (2) statutory arson, without requiring "an intent to defraud," and (3) certain attempts to commit arson.[50]

50. E.g. Iowa Criminal Code § 712.1
(1978).

Chapter 4

OFFENSES AGAINST PROPERTY

AN INTRODUCTION TO THE ACQUISITIVE OFFENSES

Law is never a mere abstraction. It is a very practical (however complicated) matter. It represents the sum total of the rules by which the game of life is played, so to speak (although law is much more than rules), but this is quite a different game in different lands and in different times. It is not surprising that different nations have some important differences in their laws, or that the laws of the same people undergo substantial changes during the centuries. It would be astounding if this were not the fact, for different moral standards and different social and economic conditions require different rules.

This preface is quite appropriate to the present topic because there is no department of the criminal law whose understanding requires more of an insight into the developmental background of existing rules than is needed here. It is not necessary for the present purpose to go back to the time when it was felt the public law would be doing all that could reasonably be expected of it in the direction of protecting moveable property, if only it could keep a proper check on "cattle lifting." We can view a later period in history when the public law undertook to protect individual interests in money, goods and chattels in general, and yet did so in a much more limited way than is attempted at the present time. In those days a person who deprived another of his property by force or by stealth was regarded by all as a very evil person, but he who got the better of another in a bargain by means of falsehood was more likely to be regarded by his neighbors as clever than as criminal; and if one appropriated to his own use some money or chattel that had been intrusted to him, this was felt to be merely the result of the owner's folly, unless the appropriation was by his servant. Hence in that early day punishment was provided for one who took and carried away the personal property of another by force or by stealth, with intent to deprive the other of it permanently, but in case of an advantage gained by ordinary cheating, or by the violation of a trust by one other than a servant, it was felt that the law made all the provision to be expected of it by providing a forum in which the private individuals could try their disputes, and a sheriff to enforce whatever decision the court should make.

If such a rule seems absurdly faulty, the explanation is that it would be so today, but was fairly adequate for the early period in which it was in force. The facts of life then were much simpler than they are today, so far as trade and commerce are concerned. Business transactions were relatively few and comparatively simple. Individuals had time to make their own investigations and usually did so, and it was not considered sound business or good common sense to rely on the mere oral statement of another. Cheating by false tokens, such as the use of false weights and measures, was a common-law misdemeanor because the use of ordinary precaution and prudence would not be an adequate protection against this type of fraud; but lesser forms of cheating were overlooked so far as the common law of crimes was concerned. Hence one who received pay for a bushel of some commodity, while intentionally delivering less than a bushel, was punishable at common law if he measured it in what purported to be a bushel measure, although actually smaller than that, but was not guilty if he measured it in a bushel measure which he did not fill—because the early notion was that the buyer should watch the measuring process for himself.

A civil remedy was provided for the victims of fraud, it is true; but this was not a powerful check on cheating. It is not much of a deterrent to a seller inclined to defraud his customers to say in effect: "You must not do that, because if you get caught in any instance you will have to make good the loss to that particular customer." The same may be said with reference to the unlawful conversion of property intrusted. The civil law gave a bailor a remedy against a bailee who wrongfully appropriated to his own use property intrusted to him; but one having such tendencies would be inclined to take a chance if the only penalty was that he must pay the value to the owner in any case in which wrongful appropriation could be proved against him.

The average member of the community is no longer inclined merely to smile when he hears of a bailee converting the property intrusted to him, or hears of a swindle perpetrated by an oral misrepresentation of facts. These misdeeds, once regarded as only mildly wrong, are now branded as definitely and gravely antisocial. The commercial life of the community is no longer simple; it is bewilderingly complex. Money and property must be frequently intrusted to one who is not the servant of the owner, and who is not well known to the owner. And countless transactions must be completed under such circumstances that one man must rely unhesitatingly upon the spoken word of another,—often, in fact, upon the implications of his mere silence. The original rules of the English common law of crimes are hopelessly inadequate for the protection of property at the present day, and they have been generously supplemented by legislation.

An additional problem in the developmental background of this part of the criminal law demands attention. Under the early law felonies were punishable by death, and larceny was a common-law felony. By early statute if the value of the property stolen did not exceed twelve pence the offense was punished by imprisonment or whipping; but whenever the value of the thing stolen exceeded twelve pence, the penalty was death. In the early days of this rule twelve pence represented about the price of a sheep, but money has greatly depreciated in value through the ages, and the rule was still in force when this sum was only a trifle (twelve pence is now about the equivalent of a dime). This practical lowering of the line between grand and petit larceny gave added influence to a tendency which would have been felt even without it: an increasing reluctance on the part of judges to order the execution of a thief. In ancient times human life had been valued rather lightly, but the development of civilization in England was accompanied by a rapid enlargement of the social interest in the life of the individual. Capital punishment seemed appropriate for heinous crimes such as murder and rape, and even (at that time) such as burglary and robbery, but execution for lesser felonies was out of line with the general moral sense of the times. The judges, confronted with a strict law which called for execution in felony cases (other than petit larceny), resorted to various devices to prevent excessive executions. One such device was to point out some peculiarity in the manner in which property had been appropriated in a particular case and to hold that such a misdeed did not constitute larceny.

This tendency resulted in many loop-holes in the enforcement of justice and from time to time statutes were enacted in the effort to fill these gaps. These statutes provided penalties (ordinarily less than death) for certain misdeeds that had been held not to constitute larceny. The result is a patchwork of offenses. The intricacies of this patchwork pattern are interesting as a matter of history but embarrassing as a matter of law-enforcement. The judge is forced to take notice of hair-splitting distinctions between various types of wrongful appropriation which are merely the result of historical accident, and contribute nothing to the social problem of protecting the property of individuals from predatory acts of others. The wrongful appropriation of another's money or chattels, with the wilful intent to deprive the other thereof permanently, should constitute just one offense, with sufficient latitude in the penalty to take care of differences in the circumstances of the wrongful confiscation. Instead of this, the field is usually divided into several offenses. The minimum is ordinarily three—larceny, embezzlement and false pretenses (not to include robbery which has an added element of personal violence or intimidation). In some jurisdictions a part of the field is incorporated in a fourth crime—such as malicious mischief and trespass. Miscarriage of justice has resulted in many a case because the prosecuting attorney made a wrong guess as to just what type of misappropriation would be shown when all the evidence was before the jury.

Considerable improvement has been made in a number of jurisdictions by a statute authorizing two or more of these offenses to be charged in different counts in the same indictment, with the provision that the jury may convict of whichever offense, charged in this manner, is established by the evidence. Some states have pointed to an even better solution, which is to abolish the separate offenses of larceny, embezzlement and false pretenses and classify the entire field as a new crime to be known by some other name, such as "theft."

After the above statement was prepared for the first edition a gigantic plan of consolidation was proposed by the Model Penal Code. This plan, which will be discussed in detail later, has been adopted in substance by about half-a-dozen of the new penal codes.[1] Most of them have rejected it, at least in its extreme form, but almost without exception they have been influenced by it, in greater or lesser degree. However, they differ among themselves so much in this area, that even after all states have recodified their penal law, there will probably be no part of the preexisting law which is not still in force here or there. Even apart from this it is important to have a clear understanding of the background in which larceny, embezzlement, false pretenses and the others were recognized and enforced as separate offenses.

1. Ark.Stats. 41–22–02 (1975); 17–A   Penal Code § 31.02 (1975); Utah Code
Me.Rev.Stat.Ann. 637:1 (1974); No.Dak.   Ann., 1953, 76–4–404.
Cent.Code § 12.1–23–01 (1976); V.T.C.A.

SECTION 1. LARCENY

Larceny is the trespassory taking and carrying away of the personal property of another with intent to steal the same.*

It was one of the few felonies under the common law of England.** Under modern American statutes it is either a felony or a misdemeanor depending upon the value of the property stolen.

Six concepts require attention. The subject of the crime must be (1) personal property (2) of another which must be (3) taken (4) by trespass and (5) carried away with (6) intent to steal.***

A. PERSONAL PROPERTY

1. PARTS SEVERED FROM REAL ESTATE

The severity of the ancient penalty for larceny was due no doubt to the frequency with which the crime was committed without leaving any clue by which the victim might hope to obtain redress. The chattel was taken away and never seen by the owner again. Real estate—in the sense of a portion of the surface of the earth measured by metes and bounds—did not require protection by such a drastic penalty. If possession of the land was unlawfully invaded this was a matter which could be inquired into by the courts; and the real estate would still be there after a decision had been rendered. It might be "taken" in the sense of "take possession," but it could not be carried away. Real estate in that sense was quite logically excluded from the realm of larceny, but the exclusion was not so limited. According to the common law if a piece was wrongfully severed from the real estate and carried away (without the owner's coming into possession of the piece after severance) this also was not larceny.[1] The rationalization was that since the owner had never had possession of it *as a chattel*, it was merely a trespass to real estate so far as he was concerned, and hence was not larceny.[2] Thus if a wrongdoer wilfully took another's apple and ate it without the consent of the owner, this was larceny if the owner had picked the apple from the tree and the wrongdoer had pilfered it from the owner's basket. It was larceny if the apple had been blown from the tree by the wind or had fallen from

---

* "Larceny, as defined in the common law, generally consists of the taking and carrying away of the personal property of another with the intent to deprive the owner of his property permanently, and to convert the property to the use of someone other than the owner." United States v. Waronek, 582 F.2d 1158, 1161 (7th Cir. 1978).

** Fletcher, The Metamorphosis of Larceny, 89 Harv.L.Rev. 469 (1976).

*** There being no statutory definition of larceny in Michigan, all the elements of common-law larceny are required. People v. Anderson, 7 Mich.App. 513, 152 N.W.2d 40 (1967).

1. State v. Jackson, 218 N.C. 373, 11 S.E.2d 149 (1940); State v. Collins, 188 S.C. 338, 119 S.E. 303 (1937).

2. Per Gibson J., Regina v. Foley, L.R. 26 Ir. 299 (1889).

Copper wire on a transmission pole is real property and not a subject of larceny. "While the cutting of the wires and their immediate asportation might have been trespass, we do not think it was larceny. Legislative action to make it larceny might be advisable, but we fail to find any such legislation." Parker v. State, 352 So.2d 1386, 1390 (Ala.App.1977). Contra: State v. Day, 293 A.2d 331 (Me.1972).

other natural causes, and the wrongdoer had picked it from the ground.[3] But it was not larceny if the wrongdoer had picked it from the tree. Nor was it larceny if the wrongdoer had shaken it from the tree even if it fell upon the ground, if he promptly picked it up and ate it—or carried it away.

A. SEVERANCE AND POSSESSION

In a case of this nature the first question asked by the common law is— did the wrongdoer sever the apple from the tree? If so his wrongful appropriation was not larceny unless he permitted the apple to come into the possession of the owner before his final act of appropriation. If that happened the final act of appropriation was larceny; but if the owner did not have possession at any time after severance it was not larceny. The owner might acquire possession of his apple without actually touching it. For example, if the wrongdoer went upon the land of another and shook his tree, thus shaking down a number of apples, after which he promptly picked up all his pockets would hold and departed, this was not larceny at common law because he had himself severed the apples from the real estate and by remaining there in control of the situation while he was picking up the fruit, he kept possession and thereby prevented the owner from acquiring possession of these chattels (which belonged to him and were on his land).[4] But when the wrongdoer went away and thereby relinquished his actual control of the situation, his wrongful possession of the apples still remaining on the ground came to an end; and since the law regards property as always in the possession of someone, these apples thereupon came into the possession of the owner. If the wrongdoer should later go back for more, his wrongful taking of additional apples would be larceny even if he had originally shaken from the tree all of the fruit taken on this second trip.[5] Had he intended to take all from the first, and with this in mind concealed the apples left behind, it seems his later removal of the fruit would not be common-law larceny since concealment is one means of retaining control—and hence possession. In such cases the courts sometimes give as the reason for the failure to convict of larceny that there was "one continuous act" by the wrongdoer. What they should emphasize is continuity of possession rather than a "single" act. Since the wrongdoer severed the piece from the land the piece was never in the possession of the owner *as a chattel* if the wrongdoer's possession was continuous.

3. An apple which has been severed from the tree is a chattel whether the severance was by man or by nature. On the other hand, a piece of a ledge of rock or ore which has been severed by nature and remains on the ground is as much real estate as other rocks or pebbles there. State v. Burt, 64 N.C. 619 (1870). It is a part of the land itself. An object which is neither a part of the land itself, nor attached thereto, is a chattel so far as the law of larceny is concerned even if it would be considered realty in a civil case by some rule of property law,—such as a key to a house. Hoskins v. Tarrence, 5 Blackf. 417 (Ind.1840). Cf. Jackson v. State, 11 Ohio St. 104 (1860).

4. Bell v. State, 63 Tenn. 426 (1874).

5. The Queen v. Foley, 26 L.R.Ir. 299 (1889); Stansbury v. Luttrell, 152 Md. 553, 137 A. 339 (1927).

"But if the thief severs them at *one* time, whereby the trespass is completed, and they are converted into personal chattels in the constructive possession of him on whose soil they are left or laid, and come again at *another* time, when they are so turned into personalty, and takes them away, it is larceny; and so it is if the owner or any one else has severed them." 4 Bl.Comm. *233. And see State v. Parker, 34 Ark. 158 (1879); State v. Prince, 42 La.Ann. 817, 8 So. 591 (1890); State v. Berryman, 8 Nev. 262 (1873).

Needless to say the apple has been used merely as a convenient illustration. The severance and appropriation of a portion of another's real estate is not common-law larceny, however wrongful, if the wrongdoer keeps possession from the moment of severance, no matter what the severed portion may be. It might be the tree itself. It might be rock, sand or clay. It might be coal or gold ore.[6] It might be posts or rails from a fence;[7] or it might be even a house. This is expressly made larceny in a few states by statute. And a few courts have abandoned the well-established common-law rule on this point and have held that the taking and carrying away of a part of the real estate is larceny.[8]

B. MODERN STATUTES

Such wrongful severance and appropriation is a crime under modern statutes unless there is some excuse (such as a bona-fide mistake as to the location of a boundary line). In a few of the states this is a statutory addition to the crime of larceny, but more frequently it is punished as some other offense, such as malicious mischief and trespass.

2. ANIMALS

Reluctance to extend the scope of a capital offense led to the differentiation of animals, and to the rule that it was not larceny to steal an animal of a base nature. Thus, it was common-law larceny to steal a horse, cow, pig or chicken; but not to steal a cat, monkey or fox. "Man's best friend," the dog, was held to be of a base nature so far as the law of larceny was concerned and hence dog-stealing was not larceny at common law.[9] Since there is no reason to suppose that English judges did not share the traditional Englishman's fondness for dogs, this result must no doubt be explained on entirely different grounds. Probably the question was raised when the death penalty for larceny was quite in disfavor but had not yet been abolished. This and similar problems with reference to other animals—originally held to be base or not base—are now merely of historical interest because modern statutes generally provide that the stealing of any animal that has been tamed or restrained is larceny (if it has value).

One other matter demands attention in this regard. A wild animal (or bird) in a state of nature does not belong to any person. A farmer does not own the wild mallard that happens at the moment to be winging its way over his land. Nor does he own the wild rabbit that merely happens to make its home on his farm. One who *lawfully* acquires possession of an unowned animal or bird, acquires title as well.[10] A moment ago it belonged to no one;

6. State v. Burt, 64 N.C. 619 (1870).

7. United States v. Wagner, 28 Fed.Cas.No. 16,630 (1806); State v. Graves, 74 N.C. 396 (1876). Contra, Junod v. State, 73 Neb. 208, 102 N.W. 462 (1905).

8. Stephens v. Commonwealth, 304 Ky. 38, 199 S.W.2d 719 (1947).

9. State v. Holder, 81 N.C. 527 (1879). And see Sentell v. New Orleans & C.R. Co., 166 U.S. 698, 701, 17 S.Ct. 693, 694 (1897).

But although a dog was not the subject of larceny at common law it is the subject of larceny under modern statutes. State v. Hernandez, 121 Ariz. 544, 592 P.2d 378 (App.1979).

10. "As a general rule, wild fish, birds and animals are owned by no one. Property rights in them are obtained by reducing them to possession." United States v. Long Cove Seafood, Inc., 582 F.2d 159, 163 (2d Cir. 1978).

now it belongs to the taker. Obviously such a taking is not larceny. At common law one, wrongfully hunting on the land of another as a trespasser, who wrongfully captured a wild animal there (by killing it or otherwise), acquired possession but not title. As between the two the landowner was entitled to the animal (wrongfully captured on his land), but as he had never had possession of it the wrongful act was not larceny.[11] Modern statutes sometimes assert state ownership of wild animals and birds that have not been tamed or restrained. This raises problems beyond the scope of the present undertaking, but ordinarily does not change the law so far as larceny is concerned. Also beyond the present effort are such problems as the implied consent to hunt based upon the customs and traditions of certain communities, and the extent to which a hunter is permitted to follow game in hot pursuit.

3. DOCUMENTS AND INSTRUMENTS

Another technique employed by the judges to narrow the scope of larceny while it still carried the penalty of death, was to hold that a document or instrument must be regarded, so far as the law of larceny is concerned, as being completely merged in whatever was represented by it. Thus a deed to land represented real estate and was not the subject of larceny for that reason.[12] A contract represented an intangible right which could not be stolen and hence the wrongful taking of the written evidence of a contract was held not to be larceny.[13] Even negotiable notes and bills were held to be outside the larceny field.[14] This also is of historical interest only, since under modern statutes all types of documents, instruments and other writings are the subject of larceny.[15]

4. INTANGIBLES

Under modern statutes it is larceny to steal a railroad *ticket*.[16] It is also an offense to defraud a common carrier by wrongfully securing a ride without paying for it. But it is not *larceny* to "steal a ride" on a train. The ride itself is not something which can be taken and carried away. Furthermore, it is not larceny to see a motion picture wrongfully without paying the required admission; to hear a communication over the telephone, intended only for another; or to sleep in a hotel bed without compensation. A deed of such nature may be an offense, as for example statutory wire-tapping, but it is not *larceny* (unless expressly made so by a statute). Natural gas is the subject of larceny because it can be taken and carried away, although it may not be so easily handled as some other things.[17] Electric current is generally the

11. Regina v. Townley, 12 Cox C.C. 59 (1871). But the trespasser had no title and could not pass title to a bona-fide purchaser. Blades v. Higgs, 11 H.L.Cas. 621, 11 Eng.Rep. 1474 (1865).

12. Rex v. Wody, Y.B.Mich. 49 Hy. VI, f. 14 Pl. 9, 10 (1470).

13. Regina v. Watts, 6 Cox C.C. 304 (1854).

14. State v. Dill, 75 N.C. 257 (1876).

By statute the value of a stolen check is its face value and the fact that payment has been stopped does not render it valueless. State v. Easton, 69 Wn.2d 965, 422 P.2d 7 (1966).

15. Tillery v. State, 44 Ala.App. 369, 209 So.2d 432 (1968); even a blank check, State v. Alden, 8 Or.App. 519, 495 P.2d 302 (1972).

16. Millner v. State, 83 Tenn. 179 (1885).

17. State v. Wellman, 34 Minn. 221, 25 N.W. 395 (1885).

It may be grand larceny as distinguished from being a theft of services.

subject of larceny (usually with the aid of legislation) although as a matter of physics it may be that what the taker acquires is not exactly what the other had before.[18] For practical purposes electric current may be said to be taken and carried away even if the actual phenomenon is not exactly that.

It has been held that the crime of larceny was not established where defendant used computer time and services.[19] Computer program documents have been held the subject of theft.[20] Some states have enacted specific statutes to cover computer frauds and thefts.[21]

5. VALUE

To be the subject of larceny the thing taken must be of some value, although it need not be worth as much as the smallest known coin. Larceny may be committed of an article which may be purchased at the rate of thirty for a penny, for example. Any value to the owner himself, is sufficient to satisfy this requirement,[22] but if an owner's lawn is covered with leaves which he is going to have raked off and hauled away to get rid of them, it would not be larceny to pick up one such leaf and carry it away.

6. MODERN STATUTES

Wrongs perpetrated by some means other than taking possession of a thing and removing it may be punished, but usually are not included in the crime of larceny. On the other hand, modern statutes have extended the law of larceny to include practically everything of value which can be actually taken and carried away, except that in many of the states the punishment for severing and appropriating a piece of another's real estate is under the name of some other offense—such as malicious mischief and trespass.

B. "OF ANOTHER"

1. IN GENERAL

Larceny is an offense against possession—in the sense that it (1) is committed only against one who has possession and (2) always results in dispossession.[23]

People v. Neiss, 92 Misc.2d 839, 401 N.Y.S.2d 422 (1978).

18. People v. Menagas, 367 Ill. 330, 11 N.E.2d 403 (1937); People v. McLaughlin, 93 Misc.2d 980, 402 N.Y.S.2d 137 (1978).

19. Lund v. Commonwealth, 217 Va. 688, 232 S.E.2d 745 (1977).

20. Hancock v. State, 402 S.W.2d 906 (Tex.Cr.App.1966).

21. Utah Code Ann., 1953, 76–6–702 (1979).

22. Commonwealth v. Cabot, 241 Mass. 131, 135 N.E. 465 (1922); Burick v. Boston El. Ry., 293 Mass. 431, 434, 200 N.E. 281, 282 (1936). Surreptitious procurement by telephone of confidential medical information was not a "thing of value" within theft statute, People v.

Home Insurance Co., 197 Colo. 260, 591 P.2d 1036 (1979).

The chief importance of the problem of value is in connection with grand larceny and for convenience the entire consideration is given there. See, infra, G.

The fact that property stolen may be of no value to the thief is unimportant. So long as it is of value to the owner, this requirement is satisfied. United States v. Alberico, 604 F.2d 1315 (10th Cir. 1979).

23. State v. Pulakis, 476 P.2d 474 (Alaska 1970).

It is this method of perpetration which distinguishes larceny from embezzlement and false pretenses. In the general sense all are offenses against property.

A consideration of this problem may well be prefaced by a brief statement of the various types of legal relation of person to things, and in regard to such a statement it must be frankly recognized that "possession" is a concept which tends to shift to some extent. What is said here is intended to have reference only to the law of larceny; for other purposes the use of terms might not be exactly the same.

Suppose **A** owns a horse. **B** wishes a horse to ride and as this horse is suitable for this purpose **A** rents the horse to **B** for a month for an agreed price. During the month **C** requests **B** to permit **C** to ride the horse for a few hours and **B** consents. **C** rides into a small village and desires to stop for a cigar. Finding no post to which to tie the horse, **C** asks **D** to hold the horse a moment while **C** purchases a cigar. **D** agrees and is now holding the horse. What is the legal interest of **A, B, C** and **D** so far as this horse is concerned? **A** is the owner; he has the title to the horse. **B** has the right to possession. As he has merely permitted **C** to take a ride he may terminate this privilege at any time if he is able to communicate with **C**, but for the time being **C** has possession of the horse. **D** who is merely holding the horse for **C** for a moment while **C** makes a purchase in a store nearby, has *custody* of the horse.

At common law a person, who upon demand was entitled to the immediate possession of a chattel, could maintain a civil action of trespass against any person who wrongfully harmed it. Hence in case of a bailment at will either the bailor or the bailee could maintain an action of trespass against one who wrongfully harmed the chattel. But only the possessor has a recognized interest in maintaining possession and only he can be dispossessed. As larceny involves the act of wrongful dispossession, the vital question is not who has title, or who has the right to possession, or who has custody,—but who has the legally-recognized possession. The lawful possessor of a chattel does not commit larceny by wrongful appropriation thereof. The original statute of embezzlement was enacted in England to provide a penalty for wilful wrongs of this nature. Hence, in the illustration given, if **C** after completing his purchase and receiving the horse from **D** should wrongfully ride away intending to keep the horse permanently for his own use, this misdeed would not be larceny but embezzlement. **D**, on the other hand, having mere custody and not possession, would be guilty of larceny if he should take away the horse intending to keep it.

Even the owner himself may commit larceny by stealing his own goods if they are in the possession of another and he takes them from the possessor wrongfully with intent to deprive him of a property interest therein.[24] An example of larceny committed by the owner is this: **O** delivers his watch to **J**, a jeweler, for certain repairs. **J** makes the necessary repairs, and has a lien on the watch for his proper charges for the work done. **O** goes to the

It is larceny to steal property from a dead body, because "the heirs or devisees become the rightful possessors of property until the estate has passed through probate or administration." People v. Walker, ___ Colo.App. ___, 615 P.2d 57, 59 (1980).

24. Henry v. State, 110 Ga. 750, 36 S.E. 55 (1900); People v. Long, 50 Mich. 249, 15 N.W. 105 (1883); State v. Parker, 104 Utah 23, 137 P.2d 626 (1943); State v. Stevenson, 161 Wash. 357, 296 P. 1052 (1931).

On the other hand, a guest in a motel does not have possession of the television set in the room rented to him; hence if he wrongfully appropriates it he commits larceny. State v. Lewis, 248 Or. 217, 433 P.2d 617 (1967).

jewelry store, and seeing his watch near at hand while **J** is engaged with another customer in a different part of the room, takes the watch and carries it away without the consent of **J**, with intent to thwart **J**'s claim for compensation. **O** is guilty of larceny of the watch. In other words the phrase "of another" in the definition of larceny has reference to possession rather than to title or ownership.

2. DISTINCTION BETWEEN POSSESSION AND CUSTODY

The distinction between possession and custody, insofar as the criminal law is concerned, was gradually developed by a long line of decided cases in which the incentive was first to narrow the scope of larceny while it carried the penalty of death, and later when this penalty no longer attached, to hedge so far as possible upon this "narrowing" process. The net result makes no contribution to the general scheme of social discipline; but so long as the distinction between larceny and embezzlement is retained, it requires attention.

In general it is important to distinguish between employees and others because an employee who has control of a chattel belonging to his employer usually has custody only, and not possession, whereas the control of a chattel by one who is not holding it as an employee is ordinarily possession.

A. ONE OTHER THAN AN EMPLOYEE

One who is holding property other than as an employee may have mere custody (and not possession) under exceptional circumstances. Thus a customer in a store who is handed a tie to examine momentarily, has custody only; a friend who holds a coat of one who wishes to demonstrate his ability to "walk on his hands" has mere custody of the coat; and a guest at the dinner table has mere custody of the tableware supplied by his host.[25] But in every bailment the bailee has possession of the chattel. Thus if a chattel is turned over to another (not an employee of the one) for repair, for use, for pledge, or for safekeeping, this will ordinarily be a bailment and possession will pass. A watch might be handed by the owner to a friend to be used only for a moment in timing a race, and to be kept right in the presence of the owner, and the friend would have custody only, but if it is lent to him only for a day, and quite gratuitously, he will have possession.[26]

Because larceny is an offense against possession, it is larceny for the customer in a store to run off with a tie handed to him merely to examine in the store (if he intends to keep it without paying for it).[27] But it is not larceny for a customer to keep an article he has been permitted to take home on approval (where his original receipt was without wrongful intent), even if he does not pay for it, because the delivery to him for the purpose of his taking it home constituted a transfer of possession to him.

---

25. 1 Hale P.C. *506; 4 Bl.Comm. *231.

26. A motel guest does not have possession of property in his rented room and can therefore be convicted of larceny of such property. State v. Lewis, 248 Or. 217, 433 P.2d 617 (1967).

27. Rex v. Chisser, T.Raym. 275, 83 Eng.Rep. 142 (1678).

B. AN EMPLOYEE

As previously mentioned, the control of an employee for his employer usually results in custody only. Whatever the employer gives to the employee to be used or kept for the employer is regarded as still in the possession of the employer and not in the possession of the employee—[28] unless the employee's control involves an unusual element of trust and confidence, in which case he has possession. Thus a bank teller is held to have possession of funds of the bank which have been intrusted to him for the purpose of transacting the business of the bank, but a hired hand has custody only of the hoe delivered to him by his employer to work in the employer's field, of the horse turned over to him by his employer to plow the employer's land or to be used in making a delivery of goods for the employer.[29]

The difference between the money intrusted to the bank teller and the hoe handed to the hired hand is rather obvious. The bank teller is expected to deal with the money honestly and efficiently but his employer expects these particular bills and coins to be transferred to various customers in the course of the day's business and has not the least notion who will actually receive them. The discretion of the teller in dealing with this money is so large that his control resembles that of an owner in many respects. The hired hand with the hoe, on the other hand, has no such discretion as this. It must not be assumed that the power to pass title is itself the controlling element, because the ordinary bailee has no such power but does have possession. The point is that although the employee usually has custody only and not possession, it was deemed necessary to regard him as having possession where the employer's property has been intrusted to him with such sweeping authority for control and disposition.

One explanation is that the hired hand is a servant whereas the bank teller is an agent; and that while a servant usually has custody only, an agent has possession.[30] In this connection, however, it is important to bear in mind that an agent is frequently not an "employee," and that an employee who is an agent may also serve to some extent as a servant. The bank teller, for example, would have possession of the bank's money intrusted to him in the normal way, but would have custody only of the bank's ledger.

---

28. 1 Hale P.C. *506.

A bank messenger who receives money to take from the bank to one of its branches has custody only and is guilty of larceny if he appropriates the money. United States v. Pruitt, 446 F.2d 513 (6th Cir. 1971); see also State v. Stahl, 93 N.M. 62, 596 P.2d 275 (App.1979).

29. If the servant converts money handed to him by the master to take out and send by mail, this is larceny because the servant had custody and not possession. Rex v. Paradice, 2 East P.C. 565 (1766).

One who has mere custody of property may commit larceny by appropriating it, whereas one to whom it has been entrusted as bailee or trustee commits embezzlement by conversion unless he had formed his wicked intent to convert before he received it. Then it is larceny. State v. Smitherman, 187 Kan. 264, 356 P.2d 675 (1960).

30. Morgan v. Commonwealth, 242 Ky. 713, 47 S.W.2d 543 (1932); Bismark v. State, 45 Tex.Cr. 54, 73 S.W. 965 (1903); Regina v. Goodbody, 8 C. & P. 665, 173 Eng.Rep. 664 (1838). Cf. Warren v. State, 223 Ind. 552, 62 N.E.2d 624 (1945).

C. AN EMPLOYEE—RECEIVING THING FROM THIRD PERSON

There is another important instance in which the employee has possession of his employer's goods—this one being based upon historical accident rather than upon an important difference in the nature of the employee's control. This is the case in which the money or chattel is in the possession of a third person who hands it to the employee for his employer. Such money or chattel is in the possession of the employee until it reaches the employer [31] or until it is placed in the employer's receptacle or place of deposit for the employer. Even when placed in the employer's receptacle it is still in the possession of the employee if he did not put it there for the employer but for some temporary purpose of his own while he remains there in actual control.[32]

So far as the law of larceny is concerned derivative possession is ignored when one whose property was converted had no possession other than that derived from the actual possession of the converter. For many purposes, for example, the actual possession of the employee may be held to result in constructive possession by the employer; but the employee who acquired his actual possession from a third person cannot be said to have *taken* the property *from* the employer. On rare occasions the language of the opinions is that the employer (in such a case) has no possession *other than that of the employee*.[33] Much more frequently the employer is said not to have possession if the question is whether the employee's conversion did or did not constitute larceny.

D. ILLUSTRATIONS OF CUSTODY AND POSSESSION

An owner takes his watch to a jeweler to be examined. The jeweler finds that only a slight adjustment is needed which can be made in the owner's presence while he waits. In this case the jeweler has custody only, and hence if he should wrongfully appropriate it, his offense would be larceny.

Under similar facts the jeweler finds it will take considerable time to repair the watch and advises the owner it will be necessary for him to leave the article there if he wishes the work done. The owner leaves the watch and goes away. In this case the jeweler has possession and hence if he should wrongfully appropriate it (after having received it with innocent intent), his offense would be not larceny but embezzlement. It may be added that if the owner left the watch with the jeweler, not for repair, but for some other purpose such as for safekeeping or to permit the jeweler to display it as an unusual timepiece, the jeweler would also have possession.

The watch case can be complicated by adding two employees. **O**, the owner of the watch in need of repair, calls in his employee, **A**, with directions

---

31. The King v. Bazeley, 2 Leach 835, 168 Eng.Rep. 517 (1799).

32. Regina v. Norval, 1 Cox C.C. 95 (1844); Regina v. Reed, 6 Cox C.C. 284 (1854); Commonwealth v. Ryan, 155 Mass. 523, 30 N.E. 364 (1892).

33. It "was not felony, inasmuch as the note was never in the possession of the bankers, distinct from the possession of the prisoner." The King v. Bazeley, 2 Leach 835, 849 note (a), 168 Eng.Rep. 517, 523 note (a) (1799). The conviction of larceny "was wrong, because as the masters never had possession of the change, except by the hands of the prisoner, he was only amenable under the statute 39 Geo. III C. 85" [embezzlement]. Rex v. Sullens, 1 Moody 129, 168 Eng.Rep. 1212 (1826).

that he deliver it to J, the jeweler. This is done and J turns the watch over to B, his employee, who makes the necessary adjustments. B then hands it back to J who notifies O that it is ready and O sends A for it. A receives the watch from J, takes it home and places it in O's jewel box where it is customarily kept when not being worn. Where was the possession during this series of events? It started with O and remained there while A was taking it to J, A having custody only at this time. When J accepted the watch he had possession and his possession continued while the repair work was being done by his employee, B, who had custody only. When J handed the watch to A the possession passed from J to A who had possession during the return trip. When A put the watch in O's jewel box (assuming he did so for O) the possession was now back again in O.

No wrongdoing occurred under these facts, but suppose there had been a wrongful appropriation somewhere along the line. An appropriation by J would not have been larceny, if he originally received the watch with innocent intent, because he had lawful possession. An appropriation by B would have been larceny because he at no time had possession, but custody only, prior to his wrongful taking. The position of A is not so simple. A conversion by him would have been larceny if it occurred during the trip from O to J, because at that time he had custody only, but not if it took place on the return trip because he then had possession. If the idea had not occurred to him until after he had placed the watch in the jewel box and he then went back and retook it, this would have been larceny because his possession had come to an end before the conversion. Any of these conversions which did not constitute larceny at common law would be punishable under statutes on embezzlement, to be considered later, but they were not punishable at common law.

E. EMPLOYEE AS BAILEE

When an employee receives, for his employer, property which has been handed over by a third person, the employee becomes a bailee of the article under broad definitions of bailment because for the moment possession is in the employee while title is in the employer. In certain situations the employee may become a bailee of property received *from his employer*, for the reason that in that particular transaction the chattel was delivered to him as a bailee rather than as an employee. Usually a chattel delivered by an employer to his employee is to be used or kept for the employer. This is the type of situation discussed earlier. Occasionally, however, an employer permits his employee to have a chattel to be used for the benefit of the employee, away from the presence and the premises of the employer. Suppose, for example, a farm hand wishes to visit his parents on a holiday but they live too far for him to make the journey on foot. His employer generously permits him to have a pickup truck for the day. Probably the lending of the pickup truck may be attributed as a matter of psychology to the employer-employee relation, but they are not turned over to be used for the employer. This is as much a case of lending these chattels as if the borrower was not in the employ of the lender. It is a bailment; the possession passes to the farm hand and the usual rules of bailment apply. If the employee received the truck under these circumstances with the honest intention of returning it, there would be no trespass in his acquisition of possession; and if he should later change his mind and appropriate the truck, this wrongful act would not be larceny but embezzlement. However, if he decided it was time to quit this employment anyway, and took the truck originally with the intent to keep it or to sell it, this would be a constructive trespass and the appropriation would be larceny.

3. CO-OWNERSHIP

In cases of co-ownership the original theory of the common law was that possession of one was possession by all and this led to the rule that one joint tenant or tenant in common cannot commit larceny from another.[34] Moreover, because the common law does not recognize a partnership as a legal entity but merely as an aggregate of the members it follows that in the absence of change by statute one partner cannot commit larceny of what is commonly referred to as "partnership property."[35] Modern legislation has tended to some extent to move in the direction of providing a penalty for the co-owner who wrongfully appropriates the property to which others are equally entitled,—although not necessarily under the label of "larceny."[36]

And "the trend of the law recognizing partnerships as separate legal entities and not merely as an aggregate of individuals" is sufficient to authorize embezzlement by a partner,[37] which would apply equally as to larceny.

C. TAKING

The word "taking" in the definition of larceny has reference to the taking of possession, but it is not necessary for the thief to take possession himself; he may commit larceny by causing possession to be taken by another. If, for example, one wrongfully "sells" another's bicycle to an innocent purchaser who rides away in the bona-fide belief that he has bought it from the true owner, the "seller" has committed larceny even if he did not touch the vehicle, as fully as if he had stolen it first and transported it from some distance before the "sale" was made[38] (although some courts have missed the point entirely in such a case).[39]

But there is no larceny unless there is a taking of possession either by the thief himself, or by someone else at the instigation of the thief. If a

---

34. 1 Hale P.C. *513. And because of the rule that a wife cannot commit larceny from her husband at common law it was held not to be larceny for a woman to appropriate money belonging to the members of an unincorporated society, one of the thirty or forty members being her husband. Rex v. Willis, 1 Moody 375, 168 Eng.Rep. 1309 (1833). As to appropriation by husband or wife see infra, D, 4.

"A co-owner of property cannot ordinarily be guilty of theft of that property." People v. Zimbelman, 194 Colo. 384, 572 P.2d 830, 832 (1977).

35. Application of Verona, 38 Wn.2d 833, 232 P.2d 923 (1951).

36. The Model Penal Code, under the broad provisions of "theft," which cover a great deal more than larceny, would provide criminal liability for the partner,

tenant-in-common, or joint-owner of property, whose misappropriation wrongfully infringed upon the property interest of the other party. Section 223.0(7). And see the comment in Tent.Draft No. 2, pp. 100–101 (1954).

37. People v. Pedersen, 86 Cal.App.3d 987, 150 Cal.Rptr. 577, 580 (1978).

38. Smith v. State, 11 Ga.App. 197, 74 S.E. 1093 (1912); State v. Hunt, 45 Iowa 673 (1877); Lane v. State, 41 Tex.Cr.R. 558, 55 S.W. 831 (1900).

39. State v. Laborde, 202 La. 59, 11 So.2d 404 (1942). The court points out that the innocent purchaser was not acting as an agent for the defendant, which is true. It overlooks the fact that defendant intentionally caused the chattel to be taken by trespass and carried away,—a result legally imputable to him.

wrongdoer wrongfully "sells" another's bicycle to an innocent purchaser who pays his money in the good-faith belief that he has bought the vehicle from the owner, no larceny is committed if the bicycle is not touched either by the "seller" or the buyer.[40] If the owner returns and claims his property before it is touched by the others, the "seller" has been guilty of receiving *money* under false pretenses, but he has not stolen the *bicycle*.

It should be added that under some of the new penal codes the "seller" could be convicted of theft of the bicycle because the requirement of the "classic taking and carrying away, . . . has not been continued in the criminal codes under which defendant was convicted." [41]

And if one, wrongfully intending to deprive another of money, jostles the other's arm so that money in his hand falls to the ground, the one is not guilty of larceny of the money if he does not find it, because in that case there is no taking of possession.[42] The harm to the owner may be just as great if he also does not find the money. He is deprived of his money as effectively as if it had been stolen. But the criminal law is a very technical field, and the fact that the owner was wrongfully caused to lose his money is not sufficient for larceny if no one else took possession thereof.

What was said in connection with the distinction between possession and custody is also important in this regard. One who has mere custody of a chattel in his hand may convert this custody into possession by dealing with the chattel in a manner inconsistent with his position as custodian. This will constitute a taking of possession and will be sufficient for larceny if the other requisites are present.

D. NECESSITY OF TRESPASS

The taking of possession, while indispensable, is not sufficient for larceny unless it is a *trespassory* taking.[43] A very common statement in the defini-

---

40. Hardeman v. State, 12 Tex.App. 207 (1882). Cf. Henderson v. State, 79 Ark. 333, 96 S.W. 359 (1906); Cummins v. Commonwealth, 5 Ky. 200 (1883).

41. State v. McCartney, 179 Mont. 49, 585 P.2d 1321, 1323 (1978).

42. Thompson v. State, 94 Ala. 535, 10 So. 520 (1891); Rex v. Farrell, 1 Leach 322, 168 Eng.Rep. 264 (1787).

"It must be a *taking*." 4 Bl.Comm. *230.

43. State v. Lewis, 248 Or. 217, 433 P.2d 617 (1967).

Regina v. Smith, 2 Den.C.C. 449, 169 Eng.Rep. 576 (1852). "There can be no larceny without a trespass, and there can be no trespass unless the property was in the possession of the one from whom it is charged to have been stolen." People v. Hoban, 240 Ill. 303, 307, 88 N.E. 806, 807 (1909); People v. Csontos, 275 Ill. 402, 407, 114 N.E. 123, 125 (1916).

Some analysts list the "trespassory taking" as a single element of the law of larceny. E.g., Clark & Marshall, Crimes

800 (7th ed. 1967). There can be no quarrel with this as a matter of logic—just as trespass is not dealt with as a separate element of burglary although there is no "breaking" without trespass. But while the trespass is so obvious in the ordinary case of burglary that it receives attention very rarely, there has been no problem that has received more attention in the field of common-law larceny. Hence it is convenient for emphasis to deal with it separately.

Blackstone gave a simpler definition saying that larceny is "the felonious taking and carrying away of the personal goods of another." 4 Bl.Comm. *230–31. Nothing was omitted in terms of the early law. Under the common law of England any larceny was a felony and it was the only offense against property which was a felony (except robbery which includes larceny). Hence "the felonious taking" meant a taking under such circumstances as to constitute a felony which required (1) a taking of possession

tions is that the taking must be "without the consent of the owner." If the taking is consented to by the one from whose possession the chattel is taken, there is no larceny if the consent was not procured by fraud or duress.[44] The fact that an owner leaves his chattel unguarded—even in a very careless manner—does not amount to consent that it be taken by another. Furthermore the element of conditional consent must be considered. If a store keeper places a box of matches on the counter to enable any customer who wishes to smoke to use a match to light his pipe, cigar or cigarette, this constitutes consent for the taking of a match for this purpose, but it does not authorize anyone to take and carry away the whole box of matches, and such a taking would be without consent and would be sufficient for larceny.[45]

It must be emphasized that a "trespassory taking" of a chattel has no reference to a trespass on or to real estate. Such a trespass is neither required, nor sufficient for larceny. An altogether different kind of trespass is involved here—the *trespass de bonis asportatis*, (trespass for goods carried away) to use the ancient label.[46] For this trespass it is necessary to find that someone other than the wrongdoer had possession of the money or chattel, and that this possession was brought to an end by a taking by the wrongdoer (or by another at his instigation), under such circumstances as to amount in law to trespass. In general it may be said that the taking of possession from another is always a trespass unless the other consents thereto, or there is some special authority for the taking,—as for example where a sheriff takes a chattel under a writ of attachment. It may be added that consent obtained by fraud, force or intimidation is the same as no consent so far as trespass is concerned (if fraud does not result in the acquisition of title).

1. CASES OF FRAUD

The cases of fraud have caused no little difficulty in this regard. The primitive law of larceny was concerned only with an actual *taking* by violence or *stealth*, and the original requirement of trespass was included in the offense for this reason. But in the course of time a fraudulent taking was held to constitute constructive trespass and hence was sufficient for larceny if the other elements were present. Tunnard's Case,[47] in 1729, seems to

(2) by trespass and (3) with intent to steal.

"A 'trespassory taking' means that there could be no larceny without a trespass, and there could be no trespass unless the property was in the possession of the person from whom it was charged to have been stolen." State v. Lopez, 94 N.M. 349, 610 P.2d 753, 755 (App. 1980).

The Idaho code is worded: "Larceny is the felonious stealing, taking, carrying, leading, or driving away the personal property of another." I.C. § 18–4601. The court correctly points out that the word "feloniously" does not mean that the crime is a felony, since it may be either a felony or a misdemeanor, depending on value. Sparrow v. State, 102 Idaho 60, 625 P.2d 414, 416 (1981).

"'Felonious taking' means a taking with intent to commit the crime of larceny." State v. Lopez, 94 N.M. 349, 610 P.2d 753, 755–56 (App. 1980).

44. "Appellant is correct that proof of the owner's or possessor's consent to the taking would render the taking nontrespassory, and there could be no larceny conviction." Randall v. State, 583 P. 2d 196, 198 (Alaska 1978).

45. Mitchum v. State, 45 Ala. 29 (1871).

46. "This type of 'trespassory taking' comes within the doctrine of *trespass de bonis asportatis* which means 'trespass for goods carried away.'" State v. Lopez, 94 N.M. 349, 610 P.2d 753, 755 (App. 1980).

47. 2 East P.C. 687 (1729).

have been the starting point for this new aspect of larceny. Tunnard borrowed a horse saying it was for a three-mile trip, but rode to London where he sold the horse. This was held to be larceny on the ground that "fraud supplied the place of force." [48] But it was a similar case, *Pear*,[49] fifty years later, that gave real impetus to this new development. Pear went to Finch's livery stable and hired a horse, saying he wanted to go to Sutton in a neighboring county and would return by eight o'clock. As he did not return, then or later, he was indicted for larceny. The evidence disclosed that he did not ride to Sutton but went to once to Smithfield Market where he sold the horse; and that he had given a false address. The judge directed the jury to determine what Pear's intent was at the time of hiring the horse. If his intent was to do as he said, and he was afterwards tempted to sell the horse, the jury was directed to return a verdict of not guilty. But if the jury found that the journey was a mere "pretence to get the horse into his possession" and he intended from the first to sell it, they should return a special verdict. The jury returned a special verdict, finding that Pear took the horse, and so forth, and that he did so with a fraudulent intention of selling it immediately. A special verdict is a verdict of guilty if the facts found constitute guilt of the offense charged; otherwise it is a verdict of not guilty. The court held this was a guilty verdict.

There were no official court reporters in England at that time. A case was reported, if at all, by some interested judge or lawyer. If it was of unusual interest it might be dealt with by more than one reporter, as was true of *Pear*, which was reported by both East and Leach. The holding of the court according to East was that Pear obtained possession of the horse when it was delivered to him; that because of his fraud he obtained possession by trespass;[50] and that since he rode away with *animus furandi* he was guilty of larceny.

Leach gave a different account which has resulted in confusion. The judges said that because of his fraud Pear did not acquire legal possession of the horse. Leach thought they meant that he did not acquire legally recognized possession, and hence indicated that Pear did not acquire possession until he sold the horse. What the judges meant, or at least what they should have meant, is that because of his fraud, Pear did not acquire *lawful* possession and therefore got possession by trespass. Possession is not like title which must be transferred. Possession can be taken with the will or against the will of the owner. Pear would have acquired possession if he had mounted the horse and gone away without the knowledge or consent of Finch. When Pear rode away with the horse he had hired he would have acquired possession whether he intended at the time (1) to sell it at the first opportunity (as the jury found); (2) to use it several days and then return it without paying for the extra use; or (3) to do exactly as he said he would do. But only under (3) would he have acquired lawful possession. Under either (1) or (2) he would have acquired unlawful possession which he obtained by trespass because of his fraud. Under (1) he was guilty of larceny at the time he rode away on the horse (which was the holding of the court according to

48. Id. at 688.

49. 2 East P.C. 688; 1 Leach 212; 168 Eng.Rep. 208 (1779).

50. The judges held that this was "such a taking as would have made the prisoner liable to an action of trespass at the suit of the owner, ..." 2 East P.C. 688.

East) although this might have been difficult to prove before he sold the horse or attempted to do so. Under (2) he would not have been guilty of larceny at that time because he then had no intent to steal; but as he had acquired the horse by trespass this element of the crime was established, and if he later changed his mind and decided to sell it, he would then have been guilty of larceny, as was held in a later case when this situation was presented to the court.[51]

It is true that cases can be found indicating that in a Pear-type case there is no larceny until there is some overt act of appropriation, such as a sale,[52] but they are clearly unsound. Thus the Pear-type borrower who drove the car into another state to sell it, was guilty of interstate transportation of a stolen car.[53] It is true that the car was actually sold in this case, but this was important only as a matter of evidence. If the car was not stolen until the sale, it would follow that interstate transportation would have been of a car that had not been stolen. It may be added that the thief who took and carried away property with intent to steal was guilty of larceny although he had changed his mind and abandoned the plan.[54] If it were true that in a Pear-type case the wrongdoer does not get possession until there is some overt act of appropriation such as a sale, it would follow that if, when Pear rode off on Finch's horse, he intended neither to return it nor to sell it, but to use it himself, he would not have been guilty of larceny. And if this continued with no change of plan, he could have used the horse till it died without ever acquiring possession. A conclusion which is utterly repugnant to the common-law concept of possession.

One who has actual control of property, which he intends to control in a general way for purposes of his own, has possession of it.[55] This is true whether he acquired it (1) with the normal consent of the owner; (2) with the fraudulently-induced consent of the owner; (3) without the consent of the owner; or (4) in any other way. It is necessary to accept East's account of the holding of the court in Pear. In fact, obtaining possession by fraud is a familiar common-law concept.[56]

In cases in which one, (not an employee) who received possession of a chattel *from the owner* thereafter wrongfully appropriated it contrary to the

---

51. State v. Coombs, 55 Me. 477 (1868). The court did not say Coombs did not originally acquire possession, but that the horses were not lawfully in his possession. "But if to such a taking there be subsequently superadded a felonious intent, that is an intent to deprive the owner of his property permanently . . . *the crime of larceny is complete.*" Emphasis added.

52. E.g., Blackburn v. Commonwealth, 28 Ky.L.R. 96, 89 S.W. 160 (1905).

53. Hand v. United States, 227 F.2d 794 (10th Cir. 1955). And see Stewart v. United States, 151 F.2d 386 (8th Cir. 1945); United States v. Turley, 352 U.S. 407, 77 S.Ct. 397 (1957).

54. Brennon v. Commonwealth, 169 Ky. 815, 185 S.W. 489 (1916). "A crime once committed may be pardoned, but it cannot be obliterated by repentence." State v. Hayes, 78 Mo. 307, 317-18 (1883).

55. Saying such a person has possession does not imply that no other would have. Lost property, for example, remains in the possession of the loser unless and until someone else takes possession. People v. Csontos, 275 Ill. 402, 407-08, 114 N.E. 123, 125 (1916).

56. The distinction is "that if a person, by fraud, induced another to part with the possession only . . . ." The Queen v. Killam, L.R. 1 C.C. 261 (1870). But "if possession of the property is obtained by fraud, . . ." State v. Harrison, 347 Mo. 1230, 1237, 152 S.W.2d 161, 165 (1941). Larceny "through obtaining possession by fraud . . . ." Wilkinson v. State, 215 Miss. 327, 60 So.2d 786 (1952).

consent of the owner, the time of the formation of the intent to appropriate is the determining factor. If the chattel was received with innocent intent and later appropriated as a result of a change of mind, the wrongful appropriation is not larceny (but embezzlement) because the misdeed was by one having lawful possession.[57] But if the intent to appropriate the chattel was formed before it was received, so that the owner was consenting to a temporary taking while the taker was intending to keep the chattel and was purposely misleading the other as to his intent, this is a trespassory taking and the fraudulent taker does not have lawful possession at any time.[58] This is the so-called "larceny by trick," sometimes enlarged to "larceny by trick and device." In some of these cases an elaborate scheme of fraud is employed,[59] but no more is needed for "larceny by trick" than the pretended taking for a temporary purpose by one whose real plan is to deprive the other of his property permanently.

A. Fraudulent Obtaining of Title

The foregoing might suggest the conclusion that consent obtained by fraud is the equivalent of no consent at all, at least so far as the law of larceny is concerned, but unfortunately the law is not so simple as this. The statement is correct insofar as *possession only* is obtained by consent induced by fraud, but if the fraud induces the owner to part with *title* as well as possession the fraudulent wrongdoer is not guilty of larceny.[60] The theory has been that while fraud in the acquisition of title will enable the defrauded party to reclaim his property (if he can reach it before it passes into the hands of a bona-fide purchaser for value and without notice), the title has nevertheless passed and is in the wrongdoer for the time being; and that one cannot be said to be a *trespasser* by taking and holding his own goods, delivered to him by the former owner, even if his title was fraudulently obtained.[61] The explanation does not sound convincing. Since larceny is an offense against possession, and can be committed by one holding the title, what difference does it make, so far as larceny is concerned, whether the wrongdoer by his fraud obtained possession only, or obtained both title and possession? The answer can be appreciated only in the light of the developmental background. The position with reference to possession obtained by fraud made its appearance relatively late in the common law of England. Before that time it had been held for generations that obtaining title by

---

57. Regina v. Thistle, 3 Cox C.C. 573 (1849); Synes [Sykes] v. State, 78 Fla. 167, 82 So. 778 (1919); Murray v. State, 93 Fla. 706, 112 So. 575 (1927); Stillwell v. State, 155 Ind. 552, 58 N.E. 709 (1900); Smith v. United States, 233 F.2d 744 (9th Cir. 1956).

The difference in cases of this nature is that in larceny the intent to appropriate must exist at the time the property is received whereas in embezzlement the wrongdoer has lawful possession before such intent is formed. Cunningham v. District Court, 432 P.2d 992 (Okl.Cr. 1967).

58. Fitch v. State, 135 Fla. 361, 366, 185 So. 435, 437–8 (1938). Ballard v. United States, 237 F.2d 582 (D.C.Cir. 1956).

59. The King v. Patch, 1 Leach 238, 168 Eng.Rep. 221 (1782).

60. Johnson v. State, 222 Ind. 473, 54 N.E.2d 273 (1943); Murchinson v. State, 30 Ala.App. 15, 199 So. 897 (1941).

61. The "title having passed, there is no one other than himself in whom an indictment for larceny can lay the ownership and possession of the thing taken." Murchinson v. State, 30 Ala.App. 15, 17, 199 So. 897, 899 (1941).

cheating was not larceny.[62]   In fact under the common law of England, obtaining title by cheating was no offense at all, unless with the aid of some false token such as a false weight or measure.   And even in such a case the offense was only a misdemeanor.   Hence when the courts took the position that possession obtained by fraud is by trespass, and hence larceny if the other elements of the offense are satisfied, this could be applied only where it would not conflict with established precedent.   It could be applied if the wrongdoer obtained possession only by his fraud, because there was no precedent to the contrary.   But a long line of decided cases made the application impossible if title as well as possession had been obtained by fraud.   Thus it came to be well recognized, where the other elements of the offense are present, that if the wrongdoer by fraud obtained possession only he is guilty of larceny, but if he obtained both possession and title he is not.[63]   This led to the enactment in England of a statute creating the offense of obtaining property by false pretenses.   That statute is old enough to be common law in this country, and was also copied very generally here.   Hence it came to be uniformly recognized that larceny and false pretenses are separate, and mutually exclusive, crimes.   The latter offense will be considered below in section 4.

2. LOST PROPERTY

A. POSSESSION OF LOST PROPERTY

An abandoned chattel (*res derelicta*) belongs to no one (*res nullius*).   By intentionally casting it aside the former owner has parted with both possession and title.[64]   Any comer may lawfully acquire title by taking possession of it.   Hence it is not the subject of larceny.   But a chattel that has been lost or a domestic animal that has strayed away does not thereby become abandoned.[65]   Even if a discouraged loser "abandons his search" this does not constitute an abandonment of the chattel.   Abandoned goods are those cast away by the owner with the intention of ceasing to have any interest therein.[66]

The ancient law also regarded a lost chattel as not the subject of larceny,[67] apparently on the notion that the loser had lost possession so that the taking by the finder could not constitute trespass, but this is no longer the legal view.[68]   Possession is a legal concept, and the modern common law regards every owned thing as being in the possession of someone.[69]   The per-

---

62. See infra section 4.

63. Even if the victim intended title to pass, if it could not pass under the circumstances, the offense is larceny.   English v. State, 80 Fla. 70, 85 So. 150 (1920).   And see Note, 9 Iowa L.Bull. 204, 209–10 (1924).

64. See Commonwealth v. Metcalfe, 184 Ky. 540, 543, 212 S.W. 434, 436 (1919).

"To constitute an abandonment there must be a clear voluntary act showing an intent to terminate ownership but not to vest title in another person."   Wright v. Hazen Investments, Inc., 53 Or.App. 700, 632 P.2d 1328, 1333 (1981).

65. Ibid.

66. "[W]ith the purpose to abandon it."   Ibid.; 2 Bl.Comm. *9.

67. 3 Co.Inst. *108.   As late as 1832 one judge questioned whether lost property was the subject of larceny.   Per Henderson, C.J. in State v. Roper, 14 N.C. 473 (1832).   Cf. Tyler v. People, 1 Ill. 227 (1829).

68. State v. Hayes, 98 Iowa 619, 67 N.W. 673 (1896).

69. See People v. Csontos, 275 Ill. 402, 407, 114 N.E. 123, 125 (1916).

son whose wallet has slipped from his pocket at some unknown spot on the street may assume that it is no longer in his possession, but this is not the fact if no one else has taken possession thereof. Since as a matter of law someone must have possession (so long as it continues to be "property") the losing owner is said to have "constructive possession" until someone else assumes the position of a possessor.[70] Hence today a lost chattel is the subject of larceny.[71]

The finder of lost property *takes possession* from the loser if he picks it up and takes it with him.[72] The finder may perhaps not touch it at all, or he may pick it up merely to examine it. If so he has only custody for the moment and if after his examination he puts its back where he found it, the *possession* of the loser remains undisturbed. But if the finder decides to take the lost chattel away with him and carries out this intent, the possession passes from the loser to the finder. This is a taking of possession from the loser and may be either *lawful or trespassory* depending upon all the facts of the particular case.[73]

B. "CLUE" TO OWNERSHIP

The first important inquiry in such case is whether there is a "clue" to ownership.[74] If the chattel has upon it the name or address of the owner this is a "clue," [75] but it may have a "clue" without this. If, under all the facts of the particular case the finder would have reason to believe the owner and his property could be brought together again, there is a "clue" to ownership;[76] but if the circumstances are such that the finder would have no ground to expect that the owner and his property could be reunited by any reasonable effort in that direction, there is no "clue."

70. "All personal property not abandoned is by construction of law regarded as in the possession of some person, and the law regards the possession of an article lost as being that of the legal owner who was previously in possession, until the article is taken into the actual possession of the finder." People v. Csontos, 275 Ill. 402, 407–8, 114 N.E. 123, 125 (1916).

71. State v. Courtsol, 89 Conn. 564, 94 A. 973 (1915); Commonwealth v. Titus, 116 Mass. 42 (1874); Reed v. State, 8 Tex.App. 40 (1880).

72. State v. Roper, 14 N.C. 473 (1832); Sessions v. State, 101 Tex.Cr.R. 40, 274 S.W. 580 (1925). And see Commonwealth v. Metcalfe, 184 Ky. 540, 543–4, 212 S.W. 434, 436 (1919).

73. Commonwealth v. Titus, 116 Mass. 42 (1874).

74. See State v. Posey, 88 S.C. 313, 316, 70 S.E. 612, 614 (1910); State v. Belt, 125 S.C. 473, 476, 119 S.E. 576, 577 (1923).

". . . the circumstances surrounding the finding must afford some reasonable clues for determining the identity of the rightful owner." State v. Campbell, 536 P.2d 105, 110 (Alaska 1975).

75. Stepp v. State, 31 Tex.Cr.R. 349, 20 S.W. 753 (1892) (name engraved on watch).

76. "A clue to ownership is the existence of such facts and circumstances at the time of the finding, as constitute reasonable grounds for believing, that the owner will be discovered. . . ." Commonwealth v. Metcalfe, 184 Ky. 540, 544, 212 S.W. 434, 436 (1919). An occasional suggestion may be found in some of the earlier cases to the effect that the finder of lost property who appropriates it to his own use is not guilty of larceny unless he knew the owner or there were identifying marks on the chattel itself. E.g., People v. Cogdell, 1 Hill 94 (N.Y.1869). This unsound view seems to have disappeared. See Commonwealth v. Titus, 116 Mass. 42 (1874); McAlister v. State, 206 Ark. 998, 178 S.W.2d 67 (1944); Rich v. State, 32 Ala.App. 156, 157, 22 So. 2d 617 (1945).

The nature of the property and the locality of the loss may be determining factors in this regard.[77] On a large range where thousands of horses belonging to many different owners are mingled together, an unbranded horse would be a chattel without a clue to ownership. On the other hand, an unbranded horse wandering loose on the streets of a city of two thousand population or in a rural district would have a clue to ownership because an honest person finding a horse under these circumstances would feel confident of his ability to locate the owner of the animal.[78] Value itself may be controlling in certain cases.[79] A dime found on the sidewalk on the corner of Forty Second Street and Broadway in New York City would be without a clue to ownership because no matter how honest the finder he would have no hope of determining the owner. A thousand dollar bill found at the very same place would be property with a clue to ownership. A multitude of persons lose small change every day and there is usually no possible way in which the loser could identify a small coin which he had lost on the street. On the other hand the loss of a thousand dollar bill is very rare and there will probably be no difficulty in finding the owner, and securing adequate proof of the loss, if such a bill comes into the hands of an honest person. Possibly even the number of the bill may have been recorded—but this is not indispensable.

The presence or absence of a "clue," let it be added, depends upon the facts at the time of the finding, and not upon subsequent developments. In peculiar situations it may be possible later to establish the ownership of property which had no "clue" to ownership when found; and in other equally unusual instances it may not be possible to locate the owner although there was a "clue" to ownership. Thus the finder of a dime on the street would have no reason to suppose the owner could ever be found or that there could be adequate proof of ownership even if the actual loser were at hand; and yet this particular coin may be an old one of such numismatic value that the owner may be able to establish his title beyond the possibility of doubt, and may take steps in this direction that will happen to come to the attention of the finder. No inconsistency is involved, therefore, in a statement which refers to a finder of a lost chattel with no "clue" to ownership, who subsequently learns to whom the lost article belongs.

c. "LOST" AND "MISLAID" PROPERTY

A distinction is drawn between lost property and mislaid property. An article is "mislaid" if it is intentionally put in a certain place for a temporary purpose and then inadvertently left there when the owner goes away. A typical case is the package left on the patron's table in a bank lobby by a depositor who put the package there for a moment while he wrote a check and then departed without remembering to take it with him. There is always a "clue" to the ownership of property which is obviously *mislaid* rather than *lost*, because of the strong probability that the owner will know where to return for his chattel when he realizes he has gone away without

---

77. Regina v. Thurborn, 1 Den.C.C. 387, 169 Eng.Rep. 293 (1849); Griggs v. State, 58 Ala. 425 (1877); State v. Holder, 188 N.C. 561, 125 S.E. 113 (1924).

78. Crockford v. State, 73 Neb. 1, 102 N.W. 70 (1905); State v. Epps, 223 N.C. 741, 28 S.E.2d 219 (1943).

79. Brooks v. State, 35 Ohio St. 46 (1878).

it.[80] Even if he does not recall the exact place where he left it, he will usually be able to locate it if it has not been disturbed.

D. LAWFUL OR TRESPASSORY TAKING OF LOST PROPERTY

The law of larceny approaches the problems of lost (or mislaid) and found chattels from the standpoint of the social interests involved. If an article has been lost under such circumstances that there is no reasonable likelihood of restoring it to the original owner, it is socially desirable for it to be used by someone else in order that it may not be lost to the community as well as to the loser himself. In such a case the finder has a better claim to the article than anyone else, other than the true owner. Hence (unless it is otherwise provided by statute) he may lawfully take the chattel and appropriate it for his own use if the owner remains unknown.[81] If an article has been lost under such circumstances that there is a "clue" to ownership, it is socially desirable for a finder to take charge of it for the purpose of restoring it to the owner, but socially undesirable for him to take it for the purpose of appropriating it to his own use and thereby depriving the known or ascertainable owner of his property. Therefore a finder who takes possession of lost property which has a "clue" to ownership, acquires lawful possession if his purpose is to restore it to the owner, but takes possession unlawfully and by trespass if his intent is to appropriate the thing to his own use.[82]

Since lost property is in the legal possession of the loser until someone else actually takes it into his own possession, it follows, that if a finder takes charge of a lost (or mislaid) article, he at that moment takes the possession from the owner. If this taking was unlawful he is guilty of larceny if his intent was to deprive the owner permanently of his property.[83] If this taking was lawful he is not guilty of larceny even if by a change of mind or a change of circumstances he should later be guilty of wrongfully appropriating the property of another.[84] The reason for the latter result is that this is misappropriation by one having lawful possession and hence lacking the element of a *trespassory* taking.[85]

Such an appropriation was not embezzlement under the early statutes on this subject, because they spoke of the unlawful appropriation by one to whom the property had been *intrusted* —and the loser had not *intrusted* the article to the finder. It would constitute embezzlement under a statute if sufficiently broad and liberally construed.[86]

80. State v. Courtsol, 89 Conn. 564, 94 A. 973 (1915).

81. McAlister v. State, 206 Ark. 998, 178 S.W.2d 67 (1944); State v. Dean, 49 Iowa 73 (1878). "If money is found under such circumstances that there is absolutely no clue to the ownership, and no reasonable expectation that the owner can be found, the finder has a legal right to appropriate it to his own use, and would not be guilty of larceny in doing so." State v. Posey, 88 S.C. 313, 316, 70 S.E. 612, 614 (1910); State v. Belt, 125 S.C. 473, 476, 119 S.E. 576, 577 (1923).

82. Regina v. Shea, 7 Cox C.C. 147 (1856). See Commonwealth v. Metcalfe, 184 Ky. 540, 543–4, 212 S.W. 434, 436

(1919); Commonwealth v. Titus, 116 Mass. 42, 44–5 (1874).

83. Crockford v. State, 73 Neb. 1, 102 N.W. 70 (1905).

84. People v. Betts, 367 Ill. 499, 11 N.E.2d 942 (1937); Regina v. Preston, 5 Cox C.C. 390 (1851).

85. See Commonwealth v. Metcalfe, 184 Ky. 540, 544, 212 S.W. 434, 436 (1919).

86. Not embezzlement—Commonwealth v. Hays, 80 Mass. 62 (1859). Embezzlement because the finder, taking charge for the owner, became a "self-imposed" bailee. Neal v. State, 55 Fla. 140, 46 So. 845 (1908).

E. ILLUSTRATIONS

(1) **L** loses an article which is found by **F** under such circumstances as to provide no "clue" to ownership. **F** picks it up and takes it with him intending to appropriate it to his own use. **F** is not guilty of larceny because his taking with such intent was lawful under these circumstances.[87] Should **F** later learn, quite unexpectedly, that this article belongs to **L**, it would be **F**'s duty to return it to **L** or permit **L** to retake it if still in **F**'s possession at that time, because the *title* is still in **L**. But if **F** should wrongfully remain silent (or even lie about the matter if asked whether he had found the thing) and continue to keep it when he should return it, he would still *not* be guilty of larceny, because his acquisition was without trespass.[88]

(2) **L** loses an article which is found by **F** under such circumstances that there *is* a "clue" to ownership. **F** picks it up not to restore to the owner but to appropriate to his own use. **F** is guilty of larceny.[89]

(3) If under facts similar to those just stated, **F** should pick up the article for the purpose of restoring it to the owner, he would not be guilty of larceny. His conduct would be commendable if he carries out that intent. If he should change his mind and later appropriate the article to his own use his conduct would be definitely antisocial, but he would not be guilty of larceny because his possession was lawfully acquired.[90]

He might run the risk of being convicted of larceny in the latter case because the jury might not believe he had changed his mind, but the judge would instruct the jury to find him not guilty of larceny if they found that his intent at the time of taking possession was to restore the chattel to its owner.[91]

F. STATUTORY PROVISIONS

Modern statutes specify just what the finder shall do with lost property taken into his possession. These statutes provide penalties for noncompliance with their requirements, but they do not ordinarily change the result so

---

87. McAlister v. State, 206 Ark. 998, 178 S.W.2d 67 (1944); Atkinson v. Birmingham, 44 R.I. 123, 16 A. 205 (1922).

88. See Reed v. State, 8 Tex.App. 40, 42 (1880).

89. Ibid.; State v. Courtsol, 89 Conn. 564, 94 A. 973 (1915); Commonwealth v. Metcalfe, 184 Ky. 540, 212 S.W. 434 (1919); Commonwealth v. Titus, 116 Mass. 42 (1874).

90. Starck v. State, 63 Ind. 285 (1878); State v. Belt, 125 S.C. 473, 119 S.E. 576 (1923); Worthington v. State, 53 Tex.Cr. R. 178, 109 S.W. 187 (1908); Milburne's Case, 1 Lewin 251, 168 Eng.Rep. 1030 (1829).

91. "On defendant's own testimony, he had obtained control over the checks for ten seconds. That length of time would be sufficient to enable defendant to learn the identity of the owner, whose name and address was on the face of each check. Moreover, defendant conceded that he suspected something was wrong with the checks. Again, on defendant's own testimony, his very act of deliberately throwing the checks into a litter basket on a public sidewalk is adequate evidence of an intent permanently to deprive the owner of the use or benefit of the property. There is no statutory requirement that this intent be for his own use or benefit. But, on defendant's own testimony, it is clear that control of the checks for ten seconds would make it impossible for defendant to have failed to take reasonable measures to restore the property to the owner, which is an essential element of the offense charged." People v. Hines, 12 Ill.App.3d 582, 299 N.E.2d 581, 584 (1973).

far as the law of *larceny* is concerned.[92] Sometimes a special statute is provided with reference to the appropriation of found property, such as the following:

"If any person come by finding to the possession of any personal property of which he knows the owner, and unlawfully appropriate the same or any part thereof to his own use, he is guilty of larceny, and shall be punished accordingly."

This statute has been interpreted in the light of the common law and the phrase "knows the owner" has been held to be satisfied if the finder actually knows the owner *or has reasonable means of knowing or ascertaining who he is.*[93]

An occasional statute makes it larceny for one to appropriate a found chattel with a "clue," without having taken reasonable steps to restore it to the owner.[94] This makes an important change and will include a finder who picked up such an article with intent to return it to the owner, but changed his mind and appropriated it before taking reasonable steps to do so.

3. DELIVERY BY MISTAKE

The general rule is that money or property delivered under a mistake of fact can be recovered if the recipient shared the mistake or fraudulently took advantage of it. Such a recipient has no right to keep what was not intended for him. His duty to return it is clear and his appropriation of it after learning of the mistake is wrongful. But such wrongful appropriation does not always have the same consequence so far as the criminal law is concerned.

In cases in which there has been delivery by mistake there may be an element of finding property that has been lost or mislaid. For example, after the delivery of a chest or bureau assumed to be just an empty piece of furniture, the recipient may find therein some article or money that got there by accident and unnoticed, or was concealed there and forgotten. On the other hand, it would be far-fetched even to suggest the presence of such an element in a case in which too much money has been handed over as the result of an error in counting, or in which the wrong thing is delivered as the result of mistaken identity of the article itself. Fortunately, it is not necessary to classify the cases on this basis. Even if the element of finding lost property is said to be present in a particular case of delivery by mistake, it is usually property with a "clue" to ownership, because the recipient ordinarily knows by whom it was delivered. The very exceptional case in which this fact is not known, and cannot reasonably be ascertained, will obviously fall outside the field of larceny, because there seems to be no way in which the thing can be restored to its owner, and the recipient is free from fault in using it for his own benefit. But the recipient is also not guilty of larceny in certain cases in which he is not free from fault.

92. Similarly, the statutory provision that the finder of lost goods shall be paid a named compensation when he makes restitution to the owner is not inconsistent with the statutory provision that he who unlawfully converts found property to his own use is guilty of larceny. Flood v. City National Bank, 218 Iowa 898, 253 N.W. 509 (1934).

93. State v. Hayes, 98 Iowa 619, 67 N.W. 673 (1896). Compare the statute quoted in Berry v. State, 4 Okl.Cr. 202, 111 P. 676 (1910).

94. West's Ann.Cal.Pen.Code § 485 (1970). This is the provision suggested in the Model Penal Code. Section 223.5.

A. THE TEST OF LAWFUL POSSESSION

The test used in these cases, while it is a hindrance rather than help so far as safeguarding the social interest in protecting property rights is concerned, is very logical in view of the requirement of trespass in the present law of larceny. It is this: If the recipient acquires lawful possession before he discovers the mistake, his appropriation to his own use is not larceny, however wrongful it may be;[95] if the discovery is made before he acquires lawful possession it is his duty to disclose the error, and taking by him without such disclosure is a *constructive trespass* and hence sufficient for larceny.[96] Two different types of cases should be distinguished—(1) ordinary cases, and (2) cases in which one thing is contained in another.

Myers received a social security check drawn in favor of another. Knowing he had no right to it, he participated in a scheme by which he demanded consideration to which he knew he was not entitled, as a condition of giving the check to the rightful owner. His conviction of theft and conspiracy to commit theft was affirmed.[97]

B. APPLICATION OF THE TEST

(A) Ordinary Cases

The ordinary cases of delivery by mistake include such typical examples as (1) handing over two bills for one, the two being stuck together and having the appearance of one; (2) handing over more money than intended as a result of an error in counting; (3) handing over one thing which is mistaken for another, as where a gold coin, delivered in the dark, is assumed to be a silver coin of the same general size. The actual cases have usually involved money but any of the types might involve something other than money. Two stamps, for example, might look like one; there might be an error in measuring a commodity such as wheat or corn; and one intending to give away a cheap watch might inadvertently hand over a very expensive timepiece in place of the one meant.

The test of the lawfulness or the unlawfulness of the taker's possession is relatively simple in such cases. If he sees the mistake before he takes what is offered him he is under a legal duty not to take what is not intended, and a taking by him is a constructive trespass;—and if it is with intent to appropriate the thing to his own use or benefit (as is almost invariably the fact if he takes with such knowledge) it is larceny.[98] If he does not discover the mistake until a later time and then wrongfully appropriates the thing, it is a case of wrongful appropriation by one in lawful possession and therefore

---

95. Robinson v. Goldfield Merger Mines Co., 46 Nev. 291, 206 P. 399, 213 P. 103 (1923); People v. Miller, 4 Utah 410, 11 P. 514 (1886); Cunningham v. District Court, 432 P.2d 992 (Okl.Cr.1967); State v. Smitherman, 187 Kan. 264, 356 P.2d 675 (1960); Moynes v. Cooper, 40 Cr.App. Rep. 20 (1956).

Knowledge of the mistake prior to the acquisition of possession would not be required for guilt of "theft" under the Model Penal Code. Section 223.5. And see Tentative Draft No. 2, pp. 82–87 (1954).

96. State v. Williamson, Houst.Cr. 155 (Del.1864).

97. People v. Myers, 43 Colo.App. 256, 609 P.2d 1104 (1980).

98. Thompson v. State, 55 S.W. 330 (Tex.Cr.1900); Hedge v. State, 89 Tex.Cr. R. 236, 229 S.W. 862 (1921).

not larceny.[99] So long as larceny and embezzlement are kept as separate offenses, such an appropriation should be punished as embezzlement,—or the so-called "larceny by bailee."[1] Whether or not it may be so punished in a particular jurisdiction depends upon the wording of the statutes in that state. It is not so included if the statute applies only to property intrusted.[2]

So far as the law of larceny is concerned one matter likely to cause confusion is at the moment of the transfer. If the one to whom delivery is made, while still in the presence of the other, counts what is handed to him or otherwise inspects it, before he expresses himself as satisfied, the transfer is regarded as incomplete during such counting or inspection. At that time this one has no more than custody, and hence if he discovers the mistake then and does not disclose it, his "taking" is held to be with knowledge thereof.

Another matter entitled to special attention is the distinction between two types of mistake. If a gold coin is handed over when a silver one is intended, or if a second, unseen bill is transferred when only one is meant, the mistake goes to the very identity of what is being delivered. This mistake does not prevent the passing of possession but it does prevent the passing of title. But if an owner knows exactly what he is handing over and intends that the other shall become the owner thereof, the title will pass despite some mistake as to what should be delivered. Suppose, for example, X takes $100 of his own money and hands it to D intending D to have title thereto, although he is laboring under a mistake and only $50 should be delivered. If this mistake was induced by false and fraudulent misrepresentations of fact by D, his wrongful appropriation of the entire amount would not be larceny be-

99. Bailey v. State, 58 Ala. 414 (1877); Jones v. State, 97 Ga. 430, 25 S.E. 319 (1895); Mitchell v. State, 78 Tex.Cr.R. 79, 180 S.W. 115 (1915); Regina v. Hehir, 18 Cox C.C. 267 (1895); Regina v. Jacobs, 12 Cox C.C. 151 (1872). In Regina v. Ashwell, 16 Cox C.C. 1 (1885), a conviction was allowed to stand because the judges were evenly divided. In the dark a gold sovereign had been handed to the defendant when a shilling had been intended. The judges who voted to uphold the conviction did so upon the theory that the defendant did not get possession of the coin until he later discovered it was gold. This is untenable. Because money or property delivered under mutual mistake of fact can be recovered, and the mistake of fact in such a case goes to the very identity of the thing handed over, it is proper to hold that title does not pass. Possession was delivered and as soon as the mistake was discovered it should have been redelivered. "When Leech handed the notes to Hehir he intended to give Hehir possession of the thing he handed." Regina v. Hehir, 18 Cox C.C. 267, 271 (1895). See Moynes v. Cooper, 40 Cr.App.Rep. 20 (1956). The wrongful withholding of property delivered by mis-

take, with knowledge of the mistake acquired subsequent to the receipt, may be punishable by statute under the name of larceny, but it is an offense distinct from common-law larceny. State v. Olds, 39 Wn.2d 258, 235 P.2d 165 (1951).

1. In an action for false imprisonment it was held that the fraudulent refusal to return the excess of an overpayment, which had been received innocently in the first place, would support conviction under a statute providing for the punishment of a bailee of money or property who should "fraudulently convert the same to his own use." Bergeron v. Peyton, 106 Wis. 377, 82 N.W. 291 (1900). A finder who took charge of lost money to return it to the owner, but later converted it to her own use, was held guilty of embezzlement on the theory that this was a "self-imposed" bailment. Neal v. State, 55 Fla. 140, 46 So. 845 (1908).

2. It was held that the excess of an overpayment, inadvertently made, was not delivered in bailment and would not support conviction of the crime of fraudulent conversion of money received as bailee. Fulcher v. State, 32 Tex.Cr.R. 621, 25 S.W. 625 (1894).

cause he acquired both title and possession by his fraud.[3] If **D** had nothing to do with causing the mistake made by **X**, but merely yielded to temptation when he saw an overpayment being tendered to him, his fraudulent taking advantage of **X**'s mistake cannot be common-law larceny for the same reason.[4] If he recognizes the mistake at the time it is made he has a duty to disclose it. His nondisclosure under these circumstances is fraudulent. But the delivery of $100 by the owner to **D**, with intent that **D** shall have title to that $100, will pass the title to **D**, if he accepts it, just as effectively as if he had induced the mistake by false and fraudulent misrepresentations. If **D** recognized the mistake at the time, and wrongfully failed to correct it, this fraudulent nondisclosure might well be recognized as the equivalent of an express misstatement. But this would result in finding that **D** had obtained the money by false pretenses rather than by larceny. Some courts have overlooked the basic distinction between these two different kinds of mistake—mistake in the *factum* and mistake in the inducement—[5] and have reached the result that the recipient who recognizes the mistake at the time, and fraudulently takes advantage of it, is guilty of larceny whichever type of mistake is made.[6] Perhaps the thought was that, since the penalty for false pretenses is now usually the same as that for larceny, it makes no real difference whether the offense is one or the other, but that is a matter for the legislature. It would be proper and desirable to wipe out the distinction between the two so far as criminal law is concerned and punish them as one and the same offense, but the distinction must still be recognized for other purposes. Suppose, for example, the delivery was of a mare. **D** is to have one of **X**'s mares for $200, the selection to be made by **D**. If **D** should go to **X** with a forged promissory note for $200, select one of the mares and fraud-

---

3. Regina v. Solomons, 17 Cox C.C. 93 (1890); The King v. Nicholson, 2 Leach 610, 168 Eng.Rep. 407 (1794).

Where a bank mistakenly put a large sum of money in the defendant's account, of which the defendant was aware, the withdrawal was theft, Regina v. Johnson, 42 CCC 2d 249 (Man.C.A.1978).

4. **D**, having a credit of $130 at the bank, went to draw out his deposit. The banker, mistaken as to the amount due, handed **D** $230, saying: "There are two hundred and thirty dollars." **D** counted it at the counter and then took it all away in silence. An indictment against **D** was in two counts, one of which was for larceny. **D** was found guilty after the judge had refused to instruct that such facts do not constitute larceny. It was so obvious to the court that this could not be larceny that in sustaining defendant's exceptions it devoted the entire opinion to the other count—embezzlement. Commonwealth v. Hays, 80 Mass. 62 (1859). An English case was similar except that the overpayment was made by a post-office clerk and some of the judges held that the clerk did not have power to pass title to the money to a person who had no right to it. Because three judges held this view and one

thought the defendant had taken the excess without delivery by the clerk, a conviction was upheld. The Queen v. Middleton, L.R. 2 C.C. 38 (1873). Bovill, C. J., says: "The case is very different where the goods are parted with by the owner himself, or by a person having authority to act for him, and where he or such agent intends to part with the property in the goods; for then, although the goods be obtained by fraud, or forgery, or false pretences, it is not a taking against the will of the owner, which is necessary in order to constitute larceny." Id. at 48.

5. Where the error was not caused by fraud we have to distinguish between these two kinds of mistake just as we distinguish between fraud in the *factum* and fraud in the inducement. When we speak of mistake in the inducement we do not mean that the inducement was by the other party. Because of his own mistake as to what should be done the owner was induced to hand over his property with intent that the title should pass,— and the title did pass. The mistake induced the intentional act.

6. Wolfstein v. People, 6 Hun 121 (N.Y.1875).

ulently induce **X** to deliver her to him in exchange for the false instrument, **D** would be guilty of two or three other crimes [7] but not of larceny.[8] **D** would have obtained title to the mare and could convey good title to a bona-fide purchaser for value and without notice,[9] which he could not do if he had obtained the mare by larceny.[10] Suppose under this same agreement **D** should go to **X** with no wrongful purpose in mind, and with $200 in his pocket with which to make payment. After he has made his choice **X**, laboring under a mistake on this point, says: "All right, you paid in full last week, so take her away." It would be fraudulent for **D** to take advantage of **X**'s mistake and lead the animal away without making payment. Should he do so **X** could repossess her if his effort was taken in time, but **X** could not recover her from a bona-fide purchaser, for value and without notice.

(B) One Thing Contained in Another

A case involving the handing over of one thing, having in it something else not known to be there, is quite properly spoken of as delivery by mistake although there is a question as to just what may properly be said to have been *delivered*. If the recipient knows of the mistake at the time of the original delivery and silently takes all with intent to appropriate the thing unintentionally passed over in this way, he is guilty of larceny for reasons already considered. As a matter of fact, he seldom does have this knowledge at such time, in this type of delivery by mistake; but he *may* be guilty of larceny notwithstanding this, because of the presence of an additional factor.

The test in this regard is whether or not the one thing intentionally handed over was regarded as a "container,"—meaning here not merely potentially capable of having contents but thought of as actually having contents at the moment. The reason is, that at least so far as the law of larceny is concerned, the following distinction is made: The delivery of a "container" (unless to a bailee who is not to open it) [11] is also a delivery of the contents, even if some unknown thing happens to be included, and hence the recipient receives lawful possession by the delivery (if he did not know of the mistake at the time); and if he wrongfully appropriates this thing when he later discovers it, the case is one of wrongful appropriation by one having *lawful* possession, and hence not larceny.[12] On the other hand, the delivery of something not intended as a "container" is not a delivery of the unknown contents, and hence the recipient does not acquire possession of such contents until his discovery thereof; and if he *then* intends to appropriate such

---

7. Uttering and false pretenses,—and forgery if he himself made the false instrument.

8. The Queen v. Prince, L.R. 1 C.C. 150 (1868).

9. 3 Williston on Sales § 650 (3d ed. 1948).

10. Id. at § 311.

11. See the anomalous "breaking bulk" doctrine, infra.

12. Cooper v. Commonwealth, 110 Ky. 123, 60 S.W. 938 (1901); Regina v. Flowers, 16 Cox C.C. 33 (1886); Regina v. Da-

vis alias Rush, 7 Cox C.C. 104 (1856); Rex v. Mucklow, 1 Moody 160, 168 Eng. Rep. 1225 (1827). Contra, State v. Ducker, 8 Or. 394 (1880). In this case the court confuses what is necessary to pass possession with what is necessary to pass title. The same confusion is found in the opinion in Rex v. Hudson, [1943] K.B. 458. In this case the decision is sound because the defendant received the "cheque" on two different occasions and had the *animus furandi* when he acquired possession the second time.

contents to his own use he commits a constructive trespass and is guilty of larceny.[13]

There is also the possibility of a limited container. Possession of such a container is also possession of normally expected contents but perhaps not of something quite different which obviously got there quite by accident.[14]

(C) Illustrations

If one incloses a letter in an envelope and sends or delivers it in person to the addressee, the envelope is obviously intended as a container. If he should have inadvertently let a ten-dollar bill slip into the envelope, this is merely a case of additional contents not known to be present in the container. The recipient of the letter would receive lawful possession of all of the contents of the envelope, by the delivery, if he did not know of the mistake at the time. Later when he opens the letter and discovers the bill which was not intended for him, it is his *legal duty to return it* to the other. If he should convert it to his own use he should be punished, but this misdeed is not common-law larceny because it was wrongful appropriation by one having lawful possession. Even if the envelope is regarded as a limited container, money would seem to be included among the normally expected contents,—at least under many circumstances.

If one sells his suit, and delivers it to the buyer, inadvertently leaving a ten-dollar bill in the pocket, the suit is obviously not intended as a "container" and the buyer would not receive possession of the unknown bill by this delivery of the suit. In legal theory (at least so far as the law of larceny is concerned) this bill is in the possession of the owner until the other finds it and takes control of it. This he may lawfully do for the purpose of returning it to the owner; but if he does so with intent to appropriate it to his own use, this is a constructive trespass and he is guilty of larceny.

If one sells and delivers a chest, having in it a ten-dollar bill not known to be there, the delivery of the chest will include a delivery of the bill if the chest is known to have other general contents which are intended to pass by the delivery; but it will not include a delivery of the bill if the chest is sold and handed over as a piece of furniture supposed to be empty. If the chest was a limited container—for books only, for example, a delivery of the chest might not pass possession of the bill.

Obviously these distinctions serve no useful purpose in the general scheme of social discipline, but they cannot be ignored in the present law of larceny. To disregard them, as some courts have, is nothing short of *ex post facto* judicial legislation.[15]

---

13. Robinson v. State, 11 Tex.App. 403 (1882); Merry v. Green, 7 M. & W. 623, 151 Eng.Rep. 916 (1841).

14. It was intimated that a clothes basket was a container for soiled clothes sent to be laundered but not for $2,000 in paper money that got into the basket by mistake. Neal v. State, 55 Fla. 140, 46 So. 845 (1908). In this case the court held that the conversion was not larceny because the laundress first took charge of the money with intent to return it to the owner. In another case it seems to have been taken for granted that a basket for clothes was not a container for small articles of jewelry. Calhoun v. State, 191 Miss. 82, 2 So.2d 802 (1941).

15. E.g., Rex v. Hudson, [1943] K.B. 458. A check received in the mail and obviously not intended for him was appropriated by **D**. The actual decision is correct because **D** returned the check for the addition of an initial and received it the second time with intent to steal, but the opinion leaves much to be desired. The court repeats the suggestion made

4. APPROPRIATION BY WIFE OR HUSBAND

As a matter of common law a wife cannot be guilty of the larceny of her husband's property, and a husband cannot be guilty of the larceny of property of his wife.[16] This rule had its origin in the ancient notion that husband and wife constituted a unity to such an extent that neither could be recognized as having possession separate from the possession of the other.[17] As the possession of either was possession by both, neither was legally capable of taking possession from the other. The rule is usually continued today on the theory that it is socially desirable to have such family matters settled in some manner other than by resort to the criminal courts. The rule is abrogated by the Married Women's Act as usually interpreted, and is greatly modified by the Model Penal Code.[18]

An additional point is to be noted. Although in general the common law regarded one who received property with the consent of the owner's wife as in the same position as if he had received it with the consent of the owner himself,[19] an exception was made in the case of the paramour who eloped with the owner's wife, receiving from her hands the husband's money or goods. Such a paramour was guilty of the larceny of the husband's property if he knew it to be such.[20] He was not guilty, let it be noted, of *receiving stolen property*, because the common law made no exception, even in such a case, to the rule that the wife cannot be guilty of larceny of her husband's property.[21]

5. APPROPRIATION BY BAILEE

Every bailment, as previously mentioned, results in lawful possession by the bailee except in the case in which he, at the very moment of the receipt,

---

by one of the judges in Ashwell (Regina v. Ashwell, 16 Q.B.D. 190 (1885)) that one who received a gold coin in the dark, thinking it was silver, did not take possession until he discovered his mistake. Suppose it was a watch made of white gold which he had been carrying for years under the belief that it was silver.

16. People v. Morton, 204 Misc. 1063, 127 N.Y.S.2d 246 (1954); 2 Bishop, New Criminal Law § 872 (8th ed. 1892). See Damm v. Lodge, 158 Ohio St. 107, 111–2, 107 N.E.2d 337, 340 (1952).

17. "[F]or the husband and wife are one person in law, . . ." 3 Co.Inst. *110; 1 Hale P.C. *513.

18. A wife may be guilty of larceny from her husband. State v. Koontz, 124 Kan. 216, 257 P. 944 (1927). A husband may be guilty of larceny from his wife. Hunt v. State, 72 Ark. 241, 79 S.W. 769 (1904); Beasley v. State, 138 Ind. 552, 38 N.E. 35 (1894); Fugate v. Commonwealth, 308 Ky. 815, 215 S.W.2d 1004 (1948). Contra, People v. Morton, 204 Misc. 1063, 127 N.Y.S.2d 246 (1954); State v. Phillips, 85 Ohio St. 317, 97 N.E. 976 (1912).

Under the present Virginia law a husband may be guilty of larceny of his wife's property. Stewart v. Commonwealth, 219 Va. 887, 252 S.E.2d 329 (1979).

The Model Penal Code provides: "It is no defense that theft was from the actor's spouse, except that misappropriation of household and personal effects, or other property normally accessible to both spouses, is theft only if it occurs after the parties have ceased living together." Section 223.1(4). See the earlier suggestion in Tent.Draft No. 2 pp. 102–107 (1954).

See also Williams, Textbook of Criminal Law 724 (1978).

"A spouse may be convicted of stealing the separate property of his or her spouse." People v. Green, 27 Cal.3d 1, 164 Cal.Rptr. 1, 31 (n. 37), 609 P.2d 468, 498 (n. 37) (1980).

19. State v. Banks, 48 Ind. 197 (1874).

20. People v. Swalm, 80 Cal. 46, 22 P. 67 (1889).

21. Regina v. Kenny, 13 Cox C.C. 397 (1877).

intends to appropriate the money or goods to his own use, or takes with some other wrongful purpose [22] (or from some one who has no power to pass lawful possession to him).[23] Apart from that exception, a conversion by him amounts to no more than wrongful appropriation by one having lawful possession, and hence not larceny,[24] unless we introduce the additional element of "breaking bulk." Even if the bailee's possession has become "wrongful" in the sense that he has retained the thing too long or has made an unauthorized use thereof, his appropriation is not larceny—according to the better view—because his wrongful conduct has not included any *trespass* either actual or constructive.[25]

A. BREAKING BULK

During the fifteenth century there was a practice in England that seems to have grown to alarming proportions. This was the practice of carriers opening boxes, parcels and other containers intrusted to them, purloining a portion of the contents, and delivering the rest as if it had been undisturbed. The carriers were liable to the owners, in a civil action, for every such conversion; but in many instances they were not sued because of the difficulty of proof or the expense of litigation. Thus the civil remedy proved entirely inadequate to control this peculiar social problem, and the first statute providing a criminal penalty for embezzlement was not enacted until several generations later.[26]

Confronted with this situation, the English judges extended the law of larceny in the effort to bring this peculiar social problem under control. Although the purpose was to check such conduct on the part of carriers, and the original case is known as "Carriers Case,"[27] the newly created doctrine was broad enough to apply to any bailee. This was in effect that the delivery to a bailee of a "bale" which was not to be opened by him, was not a delivery of the contents of the "bale." Hence this peculiar position was evolved. If such a bailee converted the entire thing—"bale" and all—it was not larceny. But if he broke open the "bale" and took out some or all of the contents he thereby committed a trespass and was guilty of larceny.[28]

22. 3 Co.Inst. *107. As emphasized by one court, one who has mere custody of property may commit larceny by appropriating it, whereas one to whom property has been entrusted as a bailee commits embezzlement by conversion unless he had formed the wicked intent to convert before he received it,—in which case it is larceny. State v. Smitherman, 187 Kan. 264, 356 P.2d 675 (1960). And see Cunningham v. District Court, 432 P.2d 992 (Okl.Cr.1967).

23. Regina v. Little, 10 Cox C.C. 559 (1867).

24. Regina v. Thristle, 3 Cox C.C. 573 (1849). "And this intent to steale must be when it cometh to his hands or possessions: for if he hath the possession of it once lawfully, though he hath *animum furandi* afterward, and carrieth it away, it is no larceny:" 3 Co.Inst. *107. The word "stolen," in the federal act forbid-

ding interstate transportation of a car known to have been stolen, includes embezzlement as well as larceny. United States v. Turley, 352 U.S. 407, 77 S.Ct. 397 (1957).

The conversion of property by one to whom it had been entrusted is not larceny but embezzlement. United States v. Waronek, 582 F.2d 1158 (7th Cir. 1978).

25. Rex v. Banks, Russ. & Ry. 441, 168 Eng.Rep. 887 (1821).

26. 39 Geo. III, c. 85 (1799). See Hall, Theft, Law and Society, c. One (2d ed. 1952).

27. Year Book, 13 Ed. IV, 9, pl. 5 (1473). See Fletcher, Rethinking Criminal Law, 66–70 (1978).

28. "For if a bale or pack of merchandize be delivered to carry to one to a certain place, and he goeth away with the whole pack, this is no felony: but if he

In the course of time the doctrine of "breaking bale" seems to have changed to one of "breaking bulk," which was even more peculiar. Under this notion if property such as wheat was delivered in bulk—even if not delivered in a container but transferred to the bailee's own container—it was not larceny if the bailee converted it all, but was larceny if he separated a portion from the mass and converted only that portion.[29]

B. MODERN STATUTES

Such absurd distinctions have almost entirely disappeared under the influence of modern statutes. These have many variations in the wording, of which the following, taken from the former Iowa code, is only one sample.

"If any carrier or other person to whom any money, goods, or other property which may be the subject of larceny has been delivered to be carried for hire, or if any other person entrusted with such property, embezzle or fraudulently convert to his own use any such money, goods, or other property, either in the mass as the same were delivered or otherwise, and before the same were delivered at the place or to the person where and to whom they were to be delivered, he is guilty of larceny." [30]

Another statute,[31] speaking even more generally provided that whoever embezzles money, goods, or property delivered to him "or any part thereof" shall be guilty of larceny.

Such statutes were intended to abolish not only the needless distinctions involved in the common-law doctrine of breaking bulk, but also to merge the offenses of larceny and embezzlement into one crime under the name of larceny. The first aim was accomplished, but the court held that the offense described in these sections is called "larceny" merely to adopt by incorporation the same penalty as was provided for larceny, and that it was nevertheless a distinct offense. Hence if the indictment was for larceny and the proof showed embezzlement by a carrier or other bailee there could be no conviction.[32] The indictment should charge (the court held) embezzlement, or perhaps "larceny by bailee." Additional legislation was needed to wipe out the distinction between the two crimes. This legislation was provided by § 714.1 of the new Iowa Criminal Code which took effect on January 1, 1978.

6. CONTINUING TRESPASS

The point, unavoidably stressed time and again, that the appropriation by one having lawful possession is not larceny, invites attention to cases in which possession was acquired by trespass but without an intent to steal at the time of the original acquisition. If it was acquired by trespass in the sense of a "trespassory taking," as previously defined, the subsequent ap-

open the pack, and take anything out *animo furandi*, this is larceny." 3 Co. Inst. *107. Cf. State v. Fairclough, 29 Conn. 47 (1860); Regina v. Poyser, 2 Den.C.C. 233, 169 Eng.Rep. 487 (1851).

29. Commonwealth v. Brown, 4 Mass. 580 (1808); Commonwealth v. James, 18 Mass. 375 (1823); Nichols v. People, 17

N.Y. 114 (1858); Rex v. Howell, 7 Car. & P. 325, 173 Eng.Rep. 145 (1836).

30. I.C.A. (Iowa) § 710.10.

31. Id. at § 710.4.

32. State v. Finnegan, 127 Iowa 286, 103 N.W. 155 (1905). Cf. Morgan v. Commonwealth, 242 Ky. 713, 47 S.W.2d 543 (1932).

propriation will be larceny even if the original taking was without intent to steal.[33]

One who takes the chattel of another wrongfully, for some temporary purpose and with intent to return it in a short time is not guilty of larceny by so doing because there is no intent to steal.[34] This was a trespassory taking, however, and if he should change his mind and keep the thing, or sell it, he would thereby render himself guilty of larceny.[35] One who takes another's chattel by mistake has also committed a trespass, however innocent he may be of any wrongful intent, unless he was receiving something delivered to him by the other. Hence a man who inadvertently walks off with another's hat, thinking it his own, is not guilty of larceny by so doing; but if he should keep it or sell it after discovery of the mistake he would thereby become guilty of larceny.[36]

Without repeating the consequence in each case it may be mentioned that there are various other ways in which property may be acquired by trespass without an intent to steal at the time of the original taking, such as: (1) property taken by one too drunk at the time to know what he is doing; or (2) property borrowed without intent to steal but with fraudulent deception as to the use to be made of it.[37]

The explanation given for the result in these cases is that the original trespassory taking is a "continuing trespass" so long as possession so acquired continues,[38] and that the larceny is complete if the intent to steal results in an appropriation of the thing during this "continuing trespass." [39] This is a fiction, and fictions are usually avoided in the criminal law. Because of this fact the doctrine of "continuing trespass" has been rejected in a few states.[40] General acceptance of the doctrine is due no doubt to a realization of the fact that it is merely a questionable explanation of a correct result. Wrongful appropriation of property lawfully possessed was held not to be larceny when it was a capital offense. This was too firmly established in

33. Weaver v. State, 77 Ala. 26 (1884); Commonwealth v. White, 65 Mass. 483 (1853). And see Meadows v. State, 36 Ala.App. 402, 403, 56 So.2d 789, 790 (1952).

"The general rule has long been stated to be that to constitute larceny the intent to steal must exist at the time of taking. . . . recognized as an exception to this rule [is] the principle that if the property is taken from the owner against his will, by a trespass or fraud, a subsequently formed intent to deprive the owner permanently of his property will constitute larceny." State v. Boisvert, 236 A.2d 419, 423 (Me.1967).

34. 4 Bl.Comm. *232.

35. 3 Co.Inst. *509.

36. The leading case on the point involved a lamb which was innocently taken in the first place but converted when the mistake was discovered. Regina v. Riley, 6 Cox C.C. 88, Dears. 149, 169 Eng.Rep. 674 (1853).

37. State v. Coombs, 55 Me. 477 (1868).

38. "The doctrine of the common law is, that . . . every moment's continuance of the trespass and felony amounts in legal consideration to a new caption and asportation." State v. Somerville, 21 Me. 14, 19 (1842).

39. On this principle, if goods stolen in one county or state are carried by the thief into another, he may be convicted of larceny in the latter. 1 Hale P.C. *507; Commonwealth v. Rand, 48 Mass. 475 (1844); State v. Ellis, 3 Conn. 185 (1819). "One who steals property elsewhere and brings it into Connecticut can be prosecuted here for the theft." State v. Pambiachi, 139 Conn. 543, 547, 95 A.2d 695, 697 (1953). And a thief may be convicted under a statute enacted after the original taking if his wrongful possession has continued. State v. Somerville, 21 Me. 14 (1842).

40. State v. Riggs, 8 Idaho 630, 70 P. 947 (1902).

the common law to be changed without statute, but it does not follow that the wrongful appropriation of property obtained by trespass *de bonis* is not larceny. The prevailing view is that this is larceny. It would have been better to have recognized frankly that the trespass and the intent to steal need not concur in point of time, but since the fiction of continuing trespass affects only the explanation and not the result it is unimportant.[41]

E. CARRYING AWAY

There is no larceny unless the personal goods of another which have been taken by trespass are "carried away," [42] but this technical requirement may be satisfied by a very slight movement. There must be "asportation," to use the word commonly found in the early cases, but the slightest start of the carrying-away movement constitutes asportation.[43] Thus a rogue who snatched a girl's earring was held to have committed larceny although the ring had been moved only a few inches until it caught in her hair and was jerked from his fingers.[44] And a similar result was reached in a case in which a watch chain, jerked from another's buttonhole, became entangled about a button on another part of the garment from which the thief was unable to dislodge it.[45] In each of these cases the article was for an instant of time in the hand of the thief and free from the person of the owner. Dur-

41. Had these cases been explained by the frank statement that the trespass and the intent to steal need not concur in point of time, the definition of larceny would be changed. It would be in some such form as this: Larceny is the trespassory taking and carrying away of the personal property of another with, *or followed by,* an intent to steal the same. But the doctrine and continuing trespass is too firmly established in the law of larceny to require such a change in the definition.

Needless to say there can be no continuing trespass if the chattel was taken without trespass. There is no doctrine of trespass *ab initio* in criminal law. If **D** took **X**'s gun as a privileged act of self-defense his subsequently-formed intent to deprive the owner permanently would not constitute larceny. State v. Boisvert, 236 A.2d 419 (Me.1967).

42. 4 Bl.Comm. *231; Davidson v. State, 351 So.2d 683 (Ala.App.1977); People v. Johnson, 136 Cal.App.2d 665, 289 P.2d 90 (1955).

Under the new Arizona statute "asportation is no longer an element of the crime of theft . . . ." State v. Curiel, 634 P.2d 988, 995 (Ariz.App.1981).

43. "To constitute larceny there must be a complete severance of the chattel from the possession of the person from whom it was taken, and an assumption of actual control by the taker: and if complete control is assumed and the goods

are actually carried away the least distance, it is enough, although the possession of the taker is immediately interrupted." Syllabus of the court in Blakley v. State, 49 Okl.Cr. 10, 292 P. 878 (1930). Quoted with approval in Winegar v. State, 92 Okl.Cr. 139, 141, 222 P.2d 170, 172 (1950); Hutchison v. State, 427 P.2d 112, 114 (Okl.Cr.1967).

"If **A** comes to the close of **B** and takes his horse with an intent to steal him, and before he gets out of the close is apprehended, this is a felonious taking and carrying way, and is larceny." 1 Hale P.C. *508.

Moving an air conditioner "four to six inches toward the door" was sufficient asportation for larceny. State v. Carswell, 296 N.C. 101, 249 S.E.2d 427 (1978).

Defendant, store customer, who removed shirts from a rack and placed them in a sack he was carrying with intent to permanently deprive is guilty of theft notwithstanding the goods were not removed from the store. People v. Contreras, 195 Colo. 80, 575 P.2d 433 (1978).

44. The King v. Lapier, 1 Leach 320, 168 Eng.Rep. 263 (1784). As the girl's ear had been pierced to hold the ring, and the ear was torn by the defendant's violence, this was robbery. But, as said by the court: "Robbery is only an aggravated species of larceny, ..."

45. Regina v. Simpson, Dears. 421, 169 Eng.Rep. 788 (1854).

ing that instant the thief had possession.[46] This—as well as the asportation—is essential to guilt. Had the earring been enmeshed in the hair while still on the ear, for example, so that while the rogue had it momentarily free from the ear, it was at all times attached to the owner's hair, no larceny would have been committed. In a very famous case a rascal walking by a store lifted an overcoat from a dummy and endeavored to walk away with it. He soon discovered that the overcoat was secured by a chain and he did not succeed in breaking the chain. This was held not to be larceny because the rascal did not at any time have possession of the garment.[47] He thought he did until he reached the end of the chain, but he was mistaken.

1. "CARRYING–AWAY" MOVEMENT

A movement does not amount to asportation unless it is a *carrying-away* movement.[48] If the article in question is a wheelbarrow which is upside down and is turned over merely to put it in a position to be wheeled away, the turning over motion is not asportation.[49] The movement which turns it over might start it on its journey away, and this would be sufficient for the "carrying away" however short the distance might be, but if the turning over movement is quite distinct from any carrying-away motion, and nothing of the latter nature has yet been started there has been no larceny so far. A few courts have overlooked this distinction. In one extreme case it was indicated that if a thief shot a standing cow, the mere falling of the animal to the ground was sufficient to complete the crime of larceny,[50] but this is quite unsound. The requirement of asportation may be eliminated entirely by statute, as has been done in Texas;[51] but so long as it is retained, the common-law concept of a carrying-away movement should be required.

The carrying-away movement may be complete although the chattel has not been removed from the real estate of the owner.[52] A shoplifter who

---

46. It "being in the possession of the prisoner for a moment, separate from the lady's person, was sufficient, although he could not retain it, but probably lost it again the same instant; . . ." The King v. Lapier, 1 Leach 320, 322, 168 Eng.Rep. 263, 264 (1784).

47. People v. Meyer, 75 Cal. 383, 17 P. 431 (1888).

48. D, intending to steal linen cloth, picked up the package and stood it on end for convenience in removing the cloth. This was held "not such a removal of the property as was necessary to constitute the offense of larceny." Cherry's Case, 1 Leach 236, note, 168 Eng.Rep. 221, note (1781). D shot a hog, turned it over on the ground and stabbed it to bleed it. This was held not to constitute asportation. Williams v. State, 63 Miss. 58 (1885). Smallwood v. Commonwealth, 438 S.W.2d 334 (Ky.1969).

49. A barrel of turpentine was turned from its head over on its side. This was held not sufficient asportation to constitute larceny. There had been a change

of position but no "removal." State v. Jones, 65 N.C. 395 (1871).

50. Driggers v. State, 96 Fla. 232, 118 So. 20 (1928). Contra, McKenzie v. State, 111 Miss. 780, 72 So. 198 (1916); State v. Alexander, 74 N.C. 232 (1876); State v. Eye, 415 S.W.2d 729 (Mo.1967).

51. V.T.C.A. Penal Code § 31.03 (1977); See Barnes v. State, 513 S.W.2d 850 (Tex.Cr.App.1974).

52. Hutchison v. State, 427 P.2d 112 (Okl.Cr.1967); People v. Hartman, 256 Cal.App.2d 547, 64 Cal.Rptr. 235 (1967). "To take an article feloniously is accomplished by simply laying hold of, grasping or seizing it animo furandi, with the hands or otherwise. And the very least removal of it from the place where found, by the thief, is an asportation or carrying away." Daugherty v. State, 154 Neb. 376, 381, 48 N.W.2d 76, 79 (1951).

Larceny was committed by removing clothing from its carton and concealing it in the body of the truck in which it was

wrongfully takes an article from the counter for the purpose of stealing it, for example, is guilty of larceny although arrested while still in the store.[53] (It may be wise for the detective to wait until the thief has left the store, before the arrest is made, because otherwise the thief will claim he intended to pay for it before leaving, and this claim may perhaps be believed by the jury; but this is a matter of evidence, and not the law of larceny.)

Khoury[54] was a case in which **K**, in a Fed Mart Store, removed a large boxed chandelier from the shelf and placed it on a shopping cart. Later he untaped the box, removed the chandelier and replaced it with over $900 worth of articles. He then retaped the box and wheeled the cart to the check stand. The cashier, noticing that the box had been retaped, stated that he would have to open the box and check the contents before he would allow **K** to pay the price marked and remove the box from the store. **K** then walked away, leaving the box with the cashier. He was arrested promptly after the box was opened. His conviction of grand larceny (under the statutory name of grand theft) was affirmed. One judge dissented, insisting that the facts established only an attempted grand larceny since the failure to get the articles past the cashier left the essential element of asportation without support. He cited *Thompson*,[55] in which **T** entered a Thrifty Drug Store, removed several records from the shelf and concealed them under his coat after which he went through the check stand without paying for them. He was arrested just ten feet from the check stand. In affirming he conviction in that case it was said: "The carrying of the records through the check stand constituted an asportation of the goods, as the act effectively removed them from the store's possession and control, even if only for a moment.[56]

In *Thompson*, when **T** had taken the records from the company's shelf, and concealed them under his coat with larcenous intent, it is arguable that the "taking and carrying away" had then occurred, so that he was guilty of larceny even before he reached the check stand. The situation in *Khoury* is different. The act of putting the articles in the company's box, with intent to take them to the check stand and the hope that the cashier would accept payment in the sum marked and, in legal effect, deliver the box to **K**, seems to have left possession for the time being in the store. The dissent has taken the better position.

---

being transported. United States v. Padilla, 374 F.2d 782 (2d Cir. 1967).

53. People v. Bradovich, 305 Mich. 329, 9 N.W.2d 560 (1943).

If a customer in a store wrongfully removed shirts from the rack and concealed them in a sack with intent permanently to deprive the owner thereof, he was guilty of theft although the goods were not removed from the premises. People v. Contreras, 195 Colo. 80, 575 P.2d 433 (1978). See also State v. Doherty, 29 Utah 2d 320, 509 P.3d 351 (1973); State v. White, 118 Ariz. 279, 576 P.2d 138 (App. 1978).

"If a shopper moves merchandise from one place to another within a store with the intention to steal it, there has been asportation and the shopper may be found guilty of larceny." Martin v. State, 371 So.2d 460, 461 (Ala.Cr.App. 1979).

54. People v. Khoury, 108 Cal.App.3d Supp. 1, 166 Cal.Rptr. 705 (1980).

55. People v. Thompson, 158 Cal.App. 2d 320, 322 P.2d 489 (1958).

56. 158 Cal.App. at p. 323, 322 P.2d at p. 490.

F. WITH INTENT TO STEAL

1. INNOCENT INTENT IS NOT INTENT TO STEAL

The taking of the personal goods of another by trespass and carrying them away is not larceny in the absence of an intent to steal. The physical part of the deed might be done quite inadvertently.[57] One might by mistake take another's hat from the rack and wear it away thinking it his own. However innocent his intent, this taking would involve a technical trespass and hence he has taken by trespass and carried away the personal property of another, but obviously he is not guilty of larceny. The error in such a case is one of mistaken identity of the chattel itself. In another case the taker might in good faith believe he had received permission from the owner to take the chattel, and such a taking would not be larceny.[58] Neither is it larceny if one takes away the chattel of another under a bona-fide claim of right, however mistaken he may be in this claim.[59] Even a mistake of property law itself which causes him to believe that he has the title and immediate right to possession of the chattel will leave his taking free from any taint of larceny.[60] Such a claim must be entertained in good faith. A mere *pretense* advanced in bad faith will not prevent conviction of larceny,[61] but so long as the claim is genuine and sincere there is no larceny, even if it is quite ill-grounded.

2. WRONGFUL INTENT MAY BE LESS THAN INTENT TO STEAL

So far the discussion of this sub-topic has been limited to instances in which the chattel was taken without any wrongful intent. It is possible to go beyond this and still fall short of the realm of larceny. One may take the chattel of another by trespass and with full knowledge of his trespass and still not be guilty of this crime. If, for example, it was a very hot day and one who had gone to his place of work without a hat wished to protect his bald head from the bright sun while he made a short walk, and for this purpose took another's hat with intent to return it, and did return it, after a brief time, this would not be larceny even if this use was not consented to by

---

57. Since larceny requires a specific intent a defendant who mistakenly treated a horse of similar description to one he owned as his, unaware that it belonged to another, could not be convicted of larceny. State v. Anderson, 102 Idaho 464, 631 P.2d 1223 (1981).

58. Mills v. United States, 228 F.2d 645 (D.C.Cir.1955).

59. Rex v. Knight, 2 East P.C. *510. There is no such thing as larceny by negligence. People v. Watson, 154 Misc. 667, 278 N.Y.S. 759 (1935), aff'd 245 App. Div. 838, 282 N.Y.S. 235 (1935); State v. Heyes, 44 Wn.2d 579, 269 P.2d 577 (1955); First National Bank & Trust v. State, 141 Ga.App. 471, 233 S.E.2d 861 (1977).

"Negligence is not a proper basis of liability for theft." ALI, Model Penal Code and Commentaries, Part II, v. 2, 228 (1980).

The effect of certain provisions in at least two of the new penal codes "is to create a category of negligent theft. The Model Code proceeds on the contrary view that theft has been and should be regarded as a crime of purposeful appropriation of the property interests of others." ALI, Model Penal Code and Commentaries, Part II, Vol. 2, page 152 (1980).

60. Scott v. State, 29 Ala.App. 110, 192 So. 288 (1939); State v. Sawyer, 95 Conn. 34, 110 A. 461 (1920); State v. Goldsberry, 160 Kan. 138, 160 P.2d 690.

61. Bridgeman v. State, 145 Ark. 554, 225 S.W. 1 (1920); State v. Carroll, 160 Mo. 368, 60 S.W. 1087 (1900).

the owner and the taker knew it would be very much against the other's wishes. The taking was an *intentional trespass*, but without intent to steal.

There is no larceny without an intent to steal, and an intent to steal requires more than an intent to use for a short time under circumstances which do not imperil the owner's substantial rights in the thing, however much the unpermitted use may be resented by him.[62] Needless to say, the intentionally unprivileged use of another's property is unlawful and antisocial, but it takes more than this to constitute the serious crime of larceny.[63]

3. INTENT TO DEPRIVE THE OTHER PERMANENTLY

The common statement is that the intent to steal—or *animus furandi*, to use the Latin substitute—requires an intent wrongfully to deprive the owner *permanently* of his property.[64] This conveys the idea in a general way but requires some explanation. Mention has been made of the possibility of larceny committed by the owner himself, by taking possession from another for the purpose of defeating a property right of the possessor.[65] Hence it must be understood that an intent to deprive a possessor of the benefit of a property right he has by reason of his possession may be sufficient for the intent to steal. The owner of goods shipped by railroad would be guilty of larceny if he should take possession of them without the consent of the railroad company and with intent to avoid paying the shipping charges,—this intent being an intent to steal within the legal meaning of the phrase. The word "permanently," as used here is not to be taken literally. Thus the trespassory taking of a bouquet of cut flowers from a florist with intent to return it the following week would be with intent to steal. This is expressed in the Model Penal Code by providing that "deprive" means "(a) to withhold property of

62. A wrongful taking with intent to use temporarily and then return the chattel, is not larceny. 1 Hale P.C. *509. Taking another's bicycle just for revenge, to cause the other anxiety, and to return it after a short time, is not larceny. People v. Brown, 105 Cal. 66, 38 P. 518 (1894).

63. If the taker is caught with the goods before he has an opportunity to carry out his intent to return them to the owner he runs the risk of being convicted of larceny because the jury may not believe that this was his intent. But he is entitled to an instruction to the effect that a wrongful taking with intent to use temporarily and then return is not larceny. People v. Brown, 105 Cal. 66, 38 P. 518 (1894).

64. "While the felonious intent of the party taking need not necessarily be an intention to convert the property to his own use, still it must in all cases be an intent to wholly and permanently deprive the owner thereof." Id. at 69, 38 P. at 519. Accord, People v. Johnson, 136 Cal. App.2d 665, 289 P.2d 90 (1955); State v. Wood, 6 Ariz.App. 80, 435 P.2d 857 (1968).

Although not necessary for the decision it was said in one case that larceny in the District of Columbia does not require "an intent to appropriate property permanently." Mitchell v. United States, 394 F.2d 767, 771 (D.C.Cir.1968). The customary statement of the requirement is not an intent to "appropriate" permanently but to "deprive" permanently.

The "intent to permanently deprive remains an element of the crime of theft as defined in RCW 9A.56.020(1)(a)." State v. Burnham, 19 Wn.App. 442, 576 P.2d 917, 918 (1978). Accord, Phipps v. State, 572 P.2d 588 (Okl.Cr.1977).

Although the statutory definition of larceny does not include an intent to deprive permanently, this must be included by interpretation. Government of Virgin Islands v. Williams, 424 F.2d 526 (3d Cir. 1970). And see, State v. Ross, 107 Ariz. 240, 485 P.2d 810 (1971).

65. And see Kirksey v. Fike, 29 Ala. 206, 209 (1856); People v. Long, 50 Mich. 249, 15 N.W. 105 (1883); State v. Parker, 104 Utah 23, 137 P.2d 626 (1943).

another permanently or for so extended a period as to appropriate a major portion of its economic value, or . . ." [66] In some of the new penal codes the word deprive is used in this sense without express statement.[67]

4. INTENTIONALLY CREATING SUBSTANTIAL RISK OF PERMANENT LOSS

It is also necessary to understand that there may be an intent to steal without a fixed purpose to deprive the owner of his property permanently. A wrongful use of a temporary nature is not sufficient for the intent to steal if it does not seriously imperil the owner's substantial rights in the property; but it is otherwise of a wrongful temporary use of a nature which intentionally creates an unreasonable risk of permanent loss to the owner.

An intent to take the property of another by trespass, use it for a temporary purpose and return it, is not an intent to steal.[68] An intent to take the property of another by trespass, use it for a temporary purpose and then abandon it, *may* be an intent to steal. An intent of the latter type is not an intent to steal if the intended abandonment is under such circumstances that the property will in all probability be restored to the owner; [69] but it is an intent to steal if the intended abandonment will create a considerable risk of permanent loss to the owner.[70] To take a horse from the owner's pasture on a farm, ride it a mile or two, and then turn it loose does not create any considerable risk of permanent loss to the owner; but such risk is created if a traveler, caught in an unexpected rain, takes an umbrella in one city and abandons it in another city some miles away. It should be emphasized, however, that there is no such concept known to the common law as larceny by negligence.[71] The negligent dealing with a chattel "borrowed" by trespass is not sufficient for larceny even if actual loss results. It is only the *intentional* dealing with the chattel in such a manner as to create an unreasonable risk of permanent loss that is held to constitute an *intent to steal*.

66. Section 223.0(1).

67. E.g. Iowa Criminal Code § 714.1 (1978). Under 18 U.S.C.A. § 661 defining larceny as intent to permanently deprive the owner of his property is not required. United States v. Maloney, 607 F.2d 222 (9th Cir. 1979).

68. Export Insurance Co. v. Royster, 177 Ark. 899, 8 S.W.2d 468 (1928); State v. South, 28 N.J.L. 28 (1859). "It is elementary that the taking of property temporarily and with the intention of returning it is not larceny." State v. Labbitt, 117 Mont. 26, 32, 156 P.2d 163, 165 (1945).

69. If a horse is taken wrongfully, driven a short distance and turned loose where it will in all likelihood return or be returned to its owner, it is not larceny. Rex v. Crump, 1 Car. & P. 658, 171 Eng. Rep. 1357 (1825); Dove v. State, 37 Ark. 261 (1881).

70. State v. Langis, 251 Or. 130, 444 P.2d 959 (1968). Thus if a horse is driven many miles and abandoned far from home it is larceny if the taking was by trespass. State v. Davis, 38 N.J.L. 176 (1875). A wrongful taking "with no intention of returning it, or having it returned, but intending to leave it a long distance away" is sufficient to support the finding of the jury "that a permanent deprivation of property was intended." State v. Ward, 19 Nev. 297, 305, 10 P. 133, 137 (1886). The reason is that this involves a "reckless exposure to loss." Id. at 303, 10 P. at 136. Accord, State v. Daniels, 584 P.2d 880 (Utah 1978); State v. Burnham, 19 Wn.App. 442, 576 P.2d 917 (1978).

71. Conviction of theft under the statute cannot be based upon "criminal negligence." People v. Andrews, ___ Colo. ___, 632 P.2d 1012 (1981).

5. INTENT TO PLEDGE

To take another's chattel by trespass for the purpose of raising money by pledging it may constitute larceny even if done with an intent to redeem the chattel and restore it to the owner.[72] This is because such a transaction may involve great risk of permanent loss to the owner. By the pledge the trespasser has placed it beyond his power to return the chattel to the owner without first repaying the creditor; and he may be unable to do this. The amount of the pledge, the financial circumstances of the pledgor and the length of time contemplated, are entitled to attention. If the amount of the loan is not large, the intent is to redeem promptly, and there is no reason to doubt the pledgor's ability to redeem, the jury may be warranted in finding the absence of any unreasonable risk of permanent loss by the owner.[73] But one who has wrongfully taken the chattel of another and pledged it, under circumstances which leave his ability to redeem it in doubt, or has pledged it for such an amount as to create a great temptation for him to leave it where it is, has done so with an intent to steal even if at the moment he thinks he will sometime redeem and return it.[74]

Retention of the pawnbroker's ticket may be very important as a matter of evidence. It will not disprove the intent to steal where an unreasonable risk of permanent loss was created, and it is not conclusive proof of an intent to return to the owner in any case. But it will be difficult to prove an intent to redeem and return if the ticket was not retained.

6. INTENT TO "SELL" TO OWNER

To take property by trespass for the purpose of "selling" it to the owner is larceny. For this result a similar explanation may be offered—without insisting that it is the only one. The classical case is the one where the trespasser took fat from the storehouse and put it in the owner's scales, pretending it belonged to another who was offering it for sale.[75] For all practical purposes a man has been permanently deprived of his property if he can get it back only by paying the full value thereof. But in the type of case suggested there is also a very considerable risk that he will not get back the property at all. If, for example, he should decide that his supply was ample and decline to pay the price, the trespasser would take away the property in order to conceal his own wrongdoing. In the case mentioned, some of the judges emphasized that a sale of property is a typical method of permanent

---

72. Union Trust Co. v. Oliver, 77 Misc. 652, 137 N.Y.S. 525 (1912), rev'd on other grounds 155 App.Div. 646, 140 N.Y.S. 681 (1913); Regina v. Phetheon, 9 Car. & P. 552, 173 Eng.Rep. 952 (1840). See the Model Penal Code, Tentative Draft No. 2, § 206.6(c) (1954).

73. State v. Wallin, 60 Mont. 332, 199 P. 285 (1921). As said in a case in which a horse was wrongfully taken and pledged for two dollars, this was not larceny if he did it "with the intention of redeeming it and restoring it to the owner and had a fair and reasonable expectation of doing so." Blackburn v. Commonwealth, 28 Ky. Law 96, 98, 89 S.W. 160, 161 (1905).

74. See the footnote to Regina v. Phetheon, 9 Car. & P. 552, 173 Eng.Rep. 952 (1840). For an interesting discussion of an intent to replace money, wrongfully used by a public officer, see State v. Baxter, 89 Ohio St. 269, 104 N.E. 331 (1914).

An attempt to redeem a gun that had been pawned, made a year later and after D had been charged with embezzlement, did not disprove an intent to convert. State v. Stamps, 203 Kan. 829, 457 P.2d 172 (1969).

75. Regina v. Hall, 3 Cox C.C. 245, 1 Den. 382, 169 Eng.Rep. 291 (1849).

appropriation, *for which reason* an intent to sell is an intent to steal, whoever the intended buyer may be.[76]

7. INTENT TO CLAIM REWARD

The trespassory taking of property for the purpose of pretending it was lost and found may also be mentioned in this connection. If such taking is for the purpose of returning the property to the owner in the *hope* of receiving a reward, it is not larceny.[77] If it is for the purpose of keeping it *unless* a reward is offered and paid it is larceny.[78] The reason is obvious. The first case involves no risk of permanent loss to the owner if the intent is carried out, whereas the second case does involve such a risk. In the second case the intent will result in a permanent loss to the owner if he fails to offer or give a reward for the return of the property.

8. INTENT TO PAY

Guilt of larceny is not precluded by a vague notion that at some future indefinite time payment will be made for property furtively taken.[79] In fact even a more definite intent to pay is not inconsistent with *animus furandi* if the property taken is not for sale. Suppose **D**, for example, wants a certain chattel belonging to **X** which is not for sale and which **X** has positively refused to sell, as **D** well knows. Since he is unable to buy the chattel, **D** takes it furtively, leaving in its place money or other property of equal value. This should be held to be larceny. The crime of larceny always involves the taking of a specific thing and not the taking of an abstraction such as value. Where, for example, a one-dollar bill was wrongfully substituted for a twenty-dollar bill, the larceny was held to be of the specific twenty-dollar bill and not of the abstract difference of nineteen dollars.[80] And **D**, in the hypothetical case, has taken by trespass and carried away the chattel of **X** with intent

---

76. The Utah Court held that a defendant could not be convicted of embezzlement from his employer by issuing short weight slips for meat scraps obtained from his employer's customers for which they were paid and then pocketing the cash from the additional scraps. The Court observed: "One could not sell that which he had already stolen." The Court indicated the proper charge would be larceny. State v. Taylor, 14 Utah 2d 107, 109, 378 P.2d 352, 354 (1963).

77. Micheaux v. State, 30 Tex.Cr.R. 660, 18 S.W. 550 (1892).

78. Commonwealth v. Mason, 105 Mass. 163 (1870); Commonwealth v. Tilley, 327 Mass. 540, 99 N.E.2d 749 (1951); Berry v. State, 31 Ohio St. 219 (1877); Dunn v. State, 34 Tex.Cr.R. 257, 30 S.W. 227 (1895). "Intent to pay for property does not preclude criminal liability for theft, except that a person who helps himself to property offered for sale or hire does not commit theft if he intends and is able to pay promptly." Model Penal Code, Tentative Draft No. 2, § 206.10(2) (1954).

Appropriating carts known to belong to certain markets and demanding a ransom for their return under a claimed "finders keepers law," constitutes theft. People v. Stay, 19 Cal.App.3d 166, 96 Cal. Rptr. 651 (1971).

79. An intent to repay at some indefinite future time does not negate an intent to appropriate. State v. Wilcox, 28 Utah 2d 71, 498 P.2d 357 (1972).

80. Walters v. State, 17 Tex.App. 226 (1884). A ten-dollar bill was handed over to pay for goods worth $1.90. The seller returned $3.10 in change and refused to give more, claiming only a five-dollar bill had been tendered. She was convicted of larceny of the difference, in a trial in which the point was not raised. But the appellate court said: "We think the larceny . . . consisted really in stealing the ten-dollar bill, and not simply that portion of the change to which the owner was entitled and which he failed to receive." Finkelstein v. State, 105 Ga. 617, 624, 31 S.E. 589, 591 (1898).

to deprive him of it permanently. Every element of larceny is present despite the fact that **X** was given something he did not want in place of the chattel he did want.

Quite a different problem is presented where property held for sale is taken with a fixed intent, and present ability, to make prompt payment. Since such an owner would rather have the price than the chattel the substitution would ordinarily be with his consent, and the taking would not be larceny for that reason. Thus in one case about thirty cents worth of property, which was held for sale, was taken on Saturday night. Early Monday morning the taker appeared with an explanation and an offer to pay. A conviction of larceny was reversed.[81] And in another case it was held that if a can of gasoline was taken in an emergency, with intent to return the can and a like amount of gasoline, there was no larceny.[82]

9. INTENT TO COLLECT A DEBT

An intent to collect a debt is not an intent to steal, particularly if it amounts to no more than an intent to receive legal tender in an amount legally and presently due [83] or bona fide believed to be due.[84] Suppose **X** owed **D** $10 and **D** went to **X**'s office to collect. There was no one in the office but on the desk **D** saw a ten-dollar bill which he took away leaving a note saying: "I took ten dollars to pay what you owe me and this is your receipt." While not recommended conduct this was obviously not larceny.[85] It should be emphasized that **D** would not be guilty of larceny even if he realized that the bill was not intended for him, and even if he had gone with the fear that **X** would put off payment to some future time. The intent to collect a debt is simply not the state of mind contemplated by the intent to steal. One is not wrongfully deprived of what he had a legal duty to pay. The receipt is important only as a matter of evidence. **D** would not be guilty of larceny if he took the bill in satisfaction of the debt, but might have difficulty convincing the jury of this in the absence of a receipt. If no money was available and **D** took property which **X** was displaying for sale for $10, this also should be held to be without an intent to steal; but it might be held to be larceny if **D** took property not for sale, even if the amount was reasonable.[86] An intent to take property not held for sale, without the consent of the owner, is something other than an intent merely to collect a debt. The owner is wrongfully deprived of property not held for sale if it is taken without authority and without his consent. And an intent to steal is not negated by insistence that it was taken to satisfy an unliquidated claim.[87]

81. Mason v. State, 32 Ark. 238 (1877).

82. State v. Savage, 37 Del. 509, 186 A. 738 (1936). "[I]f there was a bona fide intention to return the property or to pay for it" the animus furandi was lacking. Mullins v. Commonwealth, 285 Ky. 282, 286, 147 S.W.2d 704, 707 (1941).

83. Johnson v. State, 73 Ala. 523 (1883); State v. Sawyer, 95 Conn. 34, 110 A. 461 (1920); State v. Labbitt, 117 Mont. 26, 156 P.2d 163 (1945); Commonwealth v. Irvine, 125 Pa.Super. 606, 190 A. 171 (1937).

84. People v. Gallegos, 130 Colo. 232, 274 P.2d 608 (1954).

85. Hylton v. Phillips, 270 Or. 766, 529 P.2d 906 (1974); People v. Karasek, 63 Mich.App. 706, 234 N.W.2d 761 (1975).

86. Gettinger v. State, 13 Neb. 308, 14 N.W. 403 (1882).

87. State v. Lewis, 121 Ariz. 155, 589 P.2d 29 (App.1978). State v. Larsen, 23 Wn.App. 218, 596 P.2d 1089 (1979).

10. TAKING BY MISTAKE

If the wrong property is taken by mistake, or property is taken in the mistaken belief of authority or consent, it is not taken with an intent to steal. This is true so long as it is an honest mistake, even if it is unreasonable, and hence the result of negligence.[88]

11. RETURN OF PROPERTY

The return of property taken away by trespass may be the result of carrying out the intent with which it was taken, in which case there is no larceny;[89] but guilt of larceny cannot be wiped out by the return of stolen property.[90] A different problem is presented if the wrongdoer is unable to return property he had wrongfully taken away with intent to return. If there had been no change of this intent, the inability to return does not constitute larceny.[91] These situations may present some very difficult problems of proof, but the judge will have no difficulty in instructing the jury.

12. LUCRI CAUSA

"Lucri causa" literally means for the sake of gain. On rare occasions the suggestion has been made that no taking is with intent to steal unless the thief is motivated by some purpose of gain or advantage.[92] Even those advancing this suggestion have not insisted upon an intent to gain a *pecuniary* advantage. An intent to take away property and destroy it for the purpose of destroying evidence has been held to be sufficient even by those who have been inclined to insist upon *lucri causa* as essential to an intent to steal.[93] The generally accepted view does not include this element at all. It

88. The statute provided that for an act otherwise criminal, to be excusable because of a mistake of fact, it must be a mistake that "does not arise from a want of proper care on the part of the person acting." Even under this statute it was held that one who takes what he honestly believes to be his is not guilty of theft whether his belief did or did not result from want of due care. Green v. State, 153 Tex.Cr.R. 442, 221 S.W.2d 612 (1949). The case is sound because it is not a question of excuse—an element of the crime is lacking. "There is, of course, no question about the proposition: if the defendant took the property under an honest but mistaken belief that he was entitled to do so, that would negative his intent to steal; and he would not be guilty of theft; . . ." State v. Kazda, 545 P.2d 190, 192 (Utah 1976). Accord, Commonwealth v. Stebbins, 74 Mass. (8 Gray) 492 (1857); West v. State, 119 Neb. 633, 230 N.W. 504 (1930); People v. Rosen, 11 Cal.2d 147, 78 P.2d 727 (1938).

89. 1 Hale P.C. *509.

90. "And, contrary to defendant's contention, return of the property does not necessarily negate the existence of a wrongful intent." People v. American Health Care, Inc., 42 Colo.App. 209, 591 P.2d 1343, 1345 (1979).

91. People v. Brown, 105 Cal. 66, 38 P. 518 (1894).

92. Blackstone said: "This taking and carrying away must also be *felonious*; that is, done *animo furandi*: or, as the civil law expresses it, *lucri causa.*" 4 Bl.Comm. *232. Prior to this time there had been no requirement of a desire of gain by the thief but only an intent to deprive the owner. It is not clear whether Blackstone failed to recognize the difference between the common-law concept of *animus furandi* and the civil-law concept of *lucri causa*, or was intending to indicate that a difference existed. His statement had some tendency to introduce a new requirement into the law of larceny, an intent by the thief to gain some advantage for himself as well as to deprive the other of his property. This notion was repudiated in England and has had very little recognition in this country.

93. Rex v. Cabbage, Russ. & Ry. 292, 168 Eng.Rep. 809 (1815). Lord Ellenbor-

regards an intent to deprive the owner of his property permanently, or an intent to deal with another's property unlawfully in such a manner as to create an obviously unreasonable risk of permanent deprivation, as all that is required to constitute the *animus furandi*—or intent to steal.[94]

13. UNAUTHORIZED TAKING OF CHATTEL

A trespassory taking and carrying away of the personal property of another, however intentional the trespass, is not common-law larceny if it is done without the intent to steal, as explained above. Statutes have provided a penalty for certain instances of trespassory taking away without the intent to steal—usually without attaching the word "larceny," the most common example of which is the unauthorized use of an automobile. It is rather generally provided by statute that the taking of a motor vehicle without the consent of the owner is a crime. In a few states this is declared to be larceny (although there is no intent to steal), but it is more frequently made punishable without this label.[95]

The social problem back of this legislation is well known. When the automobile began to appear and was limited to the possession of a few of the more fortunate members of the community, many persons who ordinarily respected the property rights of others, yielded to the temptation to drive one of these new contrivances without the consent of the owner. This became so common that the term "joyrider" was coined to refer to the person who indulged in such unpermitted use of another's car. For the most part it was a relatively harmless type of trespass, although it was quite annoying if the "joyrider" had not returned when the owner came back for his automobile. The chief harm was due to the fact that the "joyrider" was frequently not a skillful driver, and sometimes unintentionally damaged the car while using it.

It was when "joyriding" was at its height that most of the legislative enactments providing a penalty therefor were passed and the mere preva-

ough held that the *lucri causa* was not essential to guilt of larceny. Some of the judges thought the *lucri causa* was necessary but held that the destruction of evidence was a benefit.

It is settled both at common law and under modern statutes that an intent to deprive the owner permanently is enough for larceny, even though the intent is to destroy the property. People v. Green, 27 Cal.3d 1, 164 Cal.Rptr. 1, 36, 609 P.2d 468, 503 (1980).

94. Williams v. State, 52 Ala. 411 (1875); People v. Juarez, 28 Cal. 380 (1865); Best v. State, 155 Ind. 46, 57 N.E. 534 (1900); Delk v. State, 64 Miss. 77, 1 So. 9 (1886); State v. Allen, 56 Utah 37, 189 P. 84 (1920). And see Roberts v. State, 181 Ind. 520, 521–2, 104 N.E. 970 (1913). "It was an advance on the old precedents when it was decided that the intent to deprive the owner of his property was sufficient." Holmes, The Common Law 73 (4th ed. 1946).

Wrongfully taking two dolphins from their tank and releasing them into the ocean constituted "theft." State v. LeVasseur, 613 P.2d 1328 (Hawaii 1980).

95. E.g., Colo.Rev.Stat., 1973, 18.4–409. Theft is defined, id. at 18.4–401. The word "theft" in an automobile insurance policy has reference to property taken by larceny and does not include the offense of "joyriding." Wheeler v. Phoenix Assurance Co., Ltd., 144 Me. 105, 65 A.2d 10 (1949).

10 U.S.C.A. § 921, p. 272, Uniform Code of Military Justice, provides:

"Any person . . . who wrongfully takes, obtains or withholds . . . with intent temporarily to deprive or defraud another person of the use and benefit of property or to appropriate it to his own use or the use of any person other than the owner, is guilty of wrongful appropriation."

lence of this type of wilful trespass is sufficient to explain the creation of this statutory crime. The severity of the punishment attached (the crime being a felony in many jurisdictions) [96] is attributable to two factors: First, the trespass occasionally resulted in great damage to the car, as previously mentioned; second, the prevalence of this kind of trespass made it very difficult to secure convictions in cases of outright larceny of motor vehicles, because the claim of an intent to return usually seemed plausible.

At the present time there is some tendency to reduce the grade of the offense and extend it to include the unauthorized temporary use of any vehicle. This statutory crime, whether called "larceny" or not, is in effect an "included offense." [97] It has all of the elements of larceny except the intent to steal, and is limited to a small portion of the general subject matter of larceny. It is impossible to predict the extent to which the unauthorized temporary use of property may be made criminal by future legislation. [98]

This element may be changed by statute. For example the Colorado statute, § 18–4–409(2)(a) provides: "A person commits aggravated motor vehicle theft if he knowingly obtains or exercises control over the motor vehicle of another without authorization . . . and:

96. E.g., Utah Code Ann. 1953, 41–1–112.

97. Joyriding is a lesser-included offense of theft of a motor vehicle. State v. Cornish, 568 P.2d 360 (Utah 1977); Grist v. State, 510 P.2d 964 (Okl.1973). Such an instruction should have been given where **D** took the car from the owner, used it for a frivolous venture and abandoned it. Spencer v. State, 501 S.W.2d 799 (Tenn.1973). Conviction of joyriding bars a subsequent prosecution for automobile theft based upon the same wrongful possession of the car. Brown v. Ohio, 432 U.S. 161, 97 S.Ct. 2221 (1977). "A violation of this section [joyriding] may be proved as a lesser included offense on an indictment or information charging theft." Iowa Criminal Code sec. 714.7 (1978). A federal case held that taking a car on one occasion may violate two laws and constitute (1) larceny and (2) joyriding, and authorize separate, though concurrent, sentences. United States v. Johnson, 433 F.2d 1160, 1163 (D.C.Cir. 1970). Contra, People v. Kehoe, 33 Cal. 2d 711, 204 P.2d 321 (1949).

"Defendants correctly observe that the temporary deprivation, or 'joy-riding' provision is a lesser offense included in the offense of theft of a motor vehicle." State v. Tucker, 618 P.2d 46, 50 (Utah 1980). Joyriding, under Ohio law, is a lesser included offense of automobile theft, and hence conviction of joyriding precludes a subsequent trial for theft based upon the same incident. Brown v. Ohio, 432 U.S. 161, 97 S.Ct. 2221 (1977).

Some joyriding statutes merely provide for the absence of an intent to deprive the owner of his vehicle permanently. But the Kansas statute on unlawful deprivation of property, which is not limited to motor vehicles, is worded in terms of an intent to deprive temporarily, but not with an intent to deprive permanently. Intent to deprive permanently and intent to deprive temporarily are mutually exclusive. Hence the one offense is not a lesser included offense of the other. State v. Burnett, 4 Kan.App.2d 412, 607 P.2d 88 (1980).

98. "It is declared a misdemeanor for any person or persons . . . to take from any hitching place or public highway, without the . . . owner's consent, his horse, mule, ass, or other beast of burden for the purpose of working or otherwise temporarily using it, and then returning it or abandoning it upon the highway." Tenn.Code Ann. § 39–4212 (1975).

The provision of the Model Penal Code is that it is a misdemeanor to operate another's automobile, airplane, motorcycle, motorboat, or other motor-propelled vehicle without the consent of the owner. Section 223.9.

In a trial for theft of a motor vehicle, in which defendant testified that he took it to use for a short time and then return it, the refusal to instruct on the lesser included offense of joyriding was reversible error. State v. Chestnut, 621 P.2d 1228 (Utah 1980).

"(a) Retains possession or control of the motor vehicle for more than seventy-two hours."

This statute is neither overbroad nor vague.[99]

14. RESTITUTION

If the crime has once been committed, it cannot be wiped out by a return of the property stolen, or restitution in any other form. "Ample authority exists that restitution does not nullify prior criminal activity and allow the guilty party to escape prosecution." [1]

G. GRAND LARCENY

The English law, as the result of an early statute,[2] classified this offense as either (1) grand larceny or (2) petit larceny (now frequently written petty larceny),[3] the former being a capital offense and the latter punishable by forfeiture of goods and whipping, but not death.[4] Both, as mentioned earlier, were felonies.[5] The offense was grand larceny if the value of the property stolen exceeded twelve pence and petit larceny if it did not. Modern statutes very generally retain this same classification (sometimes without using these labels) but with different penalties and different values set as the dividing line.

At one time $10 was not uncommon as the figure used for this purpose and that was continued in some states well into the present century.[6] More recently the commonest determinative value has been $50,[7] and it may be found as high as $200.[8] Statutes in a number of states provide that the larceny of certain things shall be grand larceny without reference to the value of the property stolen. These provisions are not uniform, but frequently include the larceny of motor vehicles and domestic animals.[9]

For many years the almost universal plan made grand larceny a felony and petit larceny a misdemeanor, although there were wide differences in

---

99. People v. Andrews, ___ Colo. ___, 632 P.2d 1012 (1981).

1. Glassey v. Ramada Inn, 5 Kan. App.2d 121, 612 P.2d 1261, 1264 (1980).

2. Statute of Westminster I, c. 15 (1275).

3. This is the spelling used in the Model Penal Code, Section 223.1(2)(b).

4. The penalty for petit larceny under the statute was that the one convicted should "forfeit all his goods, and suffer some corporal punishment, as whipping, etc." 3 Co.Inst. * 109. Bishop says, speaking of grand and petit larceny: "Both were felonies, but the latter was never visited with death." 1 Bishop, New Criminal Law § 679 (8th ed. 1892).

5. Ibid. The nature of grand larceny and petit larceny is the same; "they are both felony, . . ." 2 East P.C. 736 (1803).

6. See, e.g., Cowan v. State, 171 Ark. 1018, 287 S.W. 201 (1926).

7. Model Penal Code 108 (Tent. Draft No. 2, 1954).

8. West's Ann.Cal.Pen.Code § 487 (1970). The Model Penal Code adopts a three-step classification: A felony if the value exceeds $500, a misdemeanor if it does not exceed that amount but is over $50, and otherwise a petty (sic) misdemeanor. Section 223.1(2).

A.R.S. § 13–1802(C) (1978) provides the penalty for theft as follows: if the value of the property was more than $1,000 it is a class 3 felony; if the value was more than $100 but less than $1,000, it is a class 4 felony; and if the value of the property was $100 or less it is a class 1 misdemeanor unless it is taken from the person and so forth. State v. Arthur, 125 Ariz. 153, 608 P.2d 90 (App.1980).

9. Cal.Pen.Code, supra.

the determination of the grade.[10] This plan is continued, in substance, in some of the newly adopted penal codes, but not in others. Several of the new codes, in words or effect, divide larceny into degrees (in a consolidated offense under the name of "theft," which is addressed infra). While certain exceptions are based on special circumstances, the general grading is in terms of the value of the property stolen, as usual, but there are wide differences in the application. One extreme plan provides that the offense is of the—

First degree if the value is over $5,000, and is a class C felony.

Second degree if the value is over $500, but not over $5,000, and is a class D felony.

Third degree if the value is over $100, but not over $500, and is an aggravated misdemeanor.

Fourth degree if the value is over $50, but not over $100, and is a serious misdemeanor.

Fifth degree if the value is not over $50, and is a simple misdemeanor.[10a]

As mentioned earlier property to be the subject of larceny must have some value,[11] and it may be added that this means legally-recognized value. Thus it was held that even the $1250 winning ticket in an illegal lottery had no value which the law would recognize and hence was not the subject of larceny.[12] It was the lack of value and not the unlawfulness *per se* which ruled out larceny in this case because "contraband," in the form of narcotics or other property held illegally, is the subject of larceny since it has intrinsic value,[13] and larceny may be committed by stealing from the first thief the very property stolen by him.[14]

Legally-recognized value is not limited to a merchantable commodity. Thus the fact that payment had been stopped on a stolen check did not render it valueless.[15] Street value has been held to be a proper standard of value for stolen credit cards.[16] Value, in fact, except where it will not be recognized by law as in case of the so-called "illegal obligation," has little significance, if any, for this offense other than to distinguish grand larceny from petit larceny. "While a thing stolen must be of some value, it need not be an article having any special, appreciable, or market value." [17] Hence

---

10. Model Penal Code 108 (Tent. Draft No. 2, 1954).

10a. Iowa Criminal Code § 714.2 (1978).

11. The property "ought to have some worth." 1 Hawk.P.C. c. 33, sec. 22.

12. People v. Caridis, 29 Cal.App. 166, 154 P. 1061 (1915).

The surreptitious procurement of medical information was not "theft" because the information was not a "thing of value." People v. Home Insurance Co., 197 Colo. 260, 591 P.2d 1036 (1979).

13. People v. Otis, 235 N.Y. 421, 139 N.E. 562 (1923); People v. Odenwald, 104 Cal.App. 203, 285 P. 406 (1930). In Caridis, supra, the court recognized that

the lottery ticket would have some intrinsic value as a piece of paper, but defendant was not being prosecuted for the larceny of a piece of paper.

14. 1 Hale P.C. *507; 1 Hawk.P.C. c. 33, § 9; Conner v. State, 25 Ga. 515 (1858).

15. State v. Easton, 69 Wn.2d 965, 422 P.2d 7 (1967).

16. People v. Miller, 193 Colo. 415, 566 P.2d 1059 (1977).

17. Commonwealth v. Cabot (or Weston), 241 Mass. 131, 140, 135 N.E. 465, 468 (1922). As was said *obiter* in Caridis, supra, "some slight intrinsic value, however small, would have sufficed to make

even sentimental value to the owner is sufficient for petit larceny but grand larceny cannot be established on this basis. The burden is upon the state to prove that the value is sufficient for grand larceny, and the test is the fair market value at the time and place of the theft.[18] If the property has no fair market value then the replacement cost is admissible to aid in establishing the actual value.[19]

Whether goods stolen from a store have value sufficient for grand larceny is not dependent upon the cost to the store. **D** was tried for the larceny of a Winchester carbine which had cost the store $44.05 and was held for sale at a price of $69. The jury's verdict finding **D** guilty and fixing the value of the gun at $60 was held to support a conviction of grand larceny.[20] On the other hand, even the original cost to the store would not establish the value of two suits of clothes which were old stock that had been on the shelves over three years.[21]

Under the English common law an intangible right, since it could not be taken into possession and carried away, was not the subject of larceny. And it was held that paper or parchment became completely merged with any instrument or document written upon it. Thus a deed to land partook of the nature of real estate and was not the subject of larceny,[22] whereas a pawnbroker's ticket partook of the nature of a chattel and was the subject of larceny.[23] A contract represented an intangible right and hence the wrong-

---

the wrongful taking of it petit larceny." 29 Cal.App. at 169, 154 P. at 1062.

18. State v. Sorrell, 95 Ariz. 220, 388 P.2d 429 (1964); State v. Randle, 2 Ariz. App. 569, 410 P.2d 687 (1966).

"Market value," as this court recently stated, is "the price which a well-informed buyer would pay to a well-informed seller, where neither is obliged to enter into the transaction." State v. Coleman, 19 Wn.App. 549, 576 P.2d 925, 926 (1978).

"We stress 'money' value in order to make it clear that mere sentimental considerations cannot be attributed value when that term is used" to determine whether theft is felony or misdemeanor. State v. Robinson, 4 Kan.App.2d 428, 608 P.2d 1014, 1017 (1980).

"The criterion for value is market value of the property when stolen." State v. Blankinship, 127 Ariz.App. 507, 622 P.2d 66, 70 (1980).

"When the value of property alleged to have been taken must be determined, the market value at the time and in the locality of the theft shall be the test." State v. Kimbel, 620 P.2d 515, 518 (Utah 1980).

19. Ibid. "The wholesale and retail prices, established by experts if necessary, may fix the range within which the jury may find fair market value." State v. Marlin, 5 Ariz.App. 524, 428 P.2d 699, 703 (1967). Quoted from Sorrell, supra.

Where the property stolen was telephone cable which was unique and had no regular market value as such, the replacement cost to the company and not the "fair market value of the cable as junk," was determinative on the issue of grand or petty theft. People v. Renfro, 250 Cal.App.2d 921, 58 Cal.Rptr. 832 (1967).

State v. Jacquith, 272 N.W.2d 90 (S.D.1978). Although a credit card may have no market value in lawful channels, its "illegitimate" market value may be considered in prosecutions for felony-theft. Miller v. People, 193 Colo. 415, 566 P.2d 1059 (1977).

20. Lee v. People, 137 Colo. 465, 326 P.2d 660 (1958).

21. People v. Fognini, 374 Ill. 161, 28 N.E.2d 95 (1940). The "proof must show the fair, cash market value at the time and place of the theft." Id. at 165, 28 N.E.2d at 97.

If it is impossible to determine the value the conviction must be of petit larceny unless the value is clearly above that specified in the statute. The theft of a priceless art treasure is grand larceny even if witnesses are unable to express the value in a precise figure.

22. Rex v. Wody, Y.B.Mich. 49 Hy.VI, f. 14 pl. 9, 10 (1470).

23. Rex v. Morrison, 169 Eng.Rep. 1210.

ful taking of the written evidence of a contract was held not to be larceny.[24]
Even negotiable instruments were held to be outside the larceny field.[25] See
the dictum to the effect that it was larceny to steal a blank piece of parchment worth a shilling, but no offense to steal the parchment after a £10,000
obligation had been written on it.[26] By statute all kinds of instruments and
documents are the subject of larceny today, and a negotiable instrument is
taken at its face value so far as the law of larceny is concerned,[27] even if it is
a check on which payment has been stopped.[28] Even a stolen bank account
passbook is subject to a charge of criminal possession, the degree of the
crime being determined by the balance therein.[29] The federal statute making
the theft or embezzlement of government property a felony if the value is
over $100, and otherwise a misdemeanor, provides: "The word 'value' means
face, par, or market value, or cost price, either wholesale or retail, whichever
is greater." [30]

It is the actual value of the property stolen, and not the thief's belief, that
determines whether larceny is grand or petit.[31] And RCW 9A.56–020–030(1)
(a)(1977) requires for guilt of attempted first-degree theft that the thief attempted to steal property that had an actual value in excess of $1,500, but it
does not require that he had knowledge of that value.[32]

1. AGGREGATION

In affirming a conviction of the statutory offense of theft in the first
degree, in a case in which five separate acts during July were treated as one
offense in order to establish the necessary "value," the court mentioned "the
well-established common law rule that property stolen from the same owner
and from the same place by a series of acts constitutes one crime if each
taking is the result of a single continuing criminal impulse or intent pursuant
to a general larcenous scheme or plan."[33]

Reference to this as a well-established rule of the common law is perhaps
an overstatement, but there has at least been a trend in this direction. The
Model Penal Code would authorize the aggregation of "amounts involved in
thefts committed pursuant to one course of conduct, whether from the same
person or several persons" without specifying the same place.[34] And the

24. Regina v. Watts, 6 Cox C.C. 304 (1854).

25. State v. Dill, 75 N.C. 257 (1876).

26. Rex v. Morrison, 169 Eng.Rep. 1210.

27. E.g. West's Cal.Pen. Code § 492 (1970).

28. State v. Easton, 69 Wm.2d 965, 422 P.2d 7 (1966).

29. People v. Jenkins, 61 A.D.2d 705, 403 N.Y.S.2d 751 (1978).

30. 18 U.S.C.A. § 641. 18 U.S.C.A. § 2311, dealing with interstate transpor-
tation, sale or receipt of stolen property, provides: " 'Value' means the face, par, or market value, whichever is the great-est, ... "

31. Model Penal Code § 206.15, Com-ment 3 (Tent. Draft No. 2, 1954). N.B.

Under the Model Penal Code the defendant's belief of value would determine the
grade of the offense if the belief was not
recklessly entertained. If he stole what
he reasonably believed was costume jewelry his offense would be graded on that
basis even if what he actually took was a
genuine article of great value. Whereas
if his intent was to steal very expensive
jewelry he would be guilty of the highest
grade of theft, even if what he actually
took was a cheap imitation. ALI, Model
Penal Code and Commentaries, Part II, v.
2, 144–45 (1980).

32. State v. Delmarter, 94 Wn.2d 634, 618 P.2d 99 (1980).

33. State v. Barton, 28 Wn.App. 690, 626 P.2d 509, 512 (1981).

34. Section 223.1(2)(c).

Institute reports that this plan has been "followed by about half of the recent penal-code revisions and proposals," with no statutory-aggravation provision in the others, a few of which are worded in a manner that seems to exclude aggravation.[35]

The same section of the Model Penal Code does not mention "market value" but would authorize determination by the "highest value by any reasonable standard," which has been followed in only a very few of the new penal codes.[36]

H. COMPOUND LARCENY

1. GRAND LARCENY MAY NOT BE

Modern statutes frequently provide special penalties for certain types of compound larcenies. In some states larceny is divided into degrees and certain circumstances of aggravation place the larceny in a higher degree.[37] In others, separate offenses are created, such as larceny from a building in the nighttime, larceny from a building in the daytime, larceny from a building on fire or larceny from the person.[38] It is merely a matter of form whether compound larceny appears in the code as a higher degree of larceny or as a separate offense. In either case it is larceny plus some special element of aggravation, and a charge of the greater offense will include the lesser.

Grant larceny is not necessarily compound larceny but it is frequently provided in the statutes that compound larceny is grand larceny regardless of the value of the property stolen.[39]

As a matter of logic grand larceny might have been regarded as an aggravated form of larceny, but this was not the view. On the contrary, if the value of the property stolen did not exceed twelve pence this was regarded as a *mitigating* circumstance which entitled the thief to be spared from the extreme penalty (death). Even short of robbery, however, there were certain types of aggravated larceny. In the words of Blackstone, "Mixed or *compound* larceny is such as has all the properties of the former, but is accompanied with either one or both of the aggravations of a taking from one's *house* or *person*." [40]

2. LARCENY FROM A BUILDING

If a thief steals from the dwelling house of another, after having broken and entered the house in the nighttime for that purpose, he is guilty of two felonies,—burglary and larceny. The compound larceny which has come to be known as larceny from a building was not needed for that situation and was intended primarily for cases not including all of the elements of burgla-

35. ALI, Model Penal Code and Commentaries, Part II, vol. 2, page 144 (1980).

36. Id. at page 143.

37. Rev.Code Mont. 1947, § 74–6–302 (4)(1974); 21 Okl.St.Ann. §§ 1703–1708 (1958); Utah Code Ann., 1953, 76–6–412.

38. E.g., Idaho Code § 18–4604 (1979).

39. E.g., N.Mex.Stat. 1978, § 30–16–1.

"The defendant's culpability as to value is not an essential requisite of liability unless otherwise expressly provided." 17–A Me.Rev.Stat.Ann. § 352.5.F. (1976).

40. 4 Bl.Comm. *239.

ry, although the presence of those elements will not prevent guilt of this statutory crime.

At common law a burglar who breaks in to steal and is successful in his effort is not only guilty of both burglary and larceny but may be convicted and punished for both. Some statutes do not permit such "double punishment." [41]

A. THE PLACE

The earlier statutes merely provided a more severe penalty for larceny in a dwelling house than for simple larceny.[42] Modern statutes usually include more than this; some of them mention certain other buildings, while even more include any public or private building.[43] Not a few add certain places other than buildings, such as boats, vessels, motor vehicles and trailers.[44] Even with such provisions the offense is commonly known as "larceny from a building," although this label may not appear in the statute itself.

B. WHAT CONSTITUTES LARCENY FROM A BUILDING

Some of the statutes speak of larceny *from* a building and others refer to larceny *in* a building, but there is no difference in the meaning as interpreted by the courts. It is not essential to guilt that the thing stolen should have been carried out of the house by the thief, and on the other hand larceny committed inside a building does not always constitute this aggravated form of the offense. The issue is whether the property stolen was under the protection of the house. Property placed outside of a store to attract customers is not regarded as within the protection of the building.[45] The stealing of such property, therefore, is simple larceny only. If property is in the pocket of some person within the building, or under his personal care at the moment in some other way, it is not regarded as within the protection of the building.[46] The stealing of such property may be compound larceny, but it will be larceny from the person rather than larceny from a building.

On the other hand, goods do not need to be locked up or even contained in closed drawers in order to be within the protection of the building. Goods on open shelves, goods standing on the floor, goods arranged on tables or coun-

41. E.g., West's Ann.Cal.Pen.Code § 654 (1977). **D** who caused the death of his victim by throwing gasoline into the bedroom and igniting it could be convicted of both arson and murder, but under the statute he could be sentenced only for one. Neal v. People, 55 Cal.2d 11, 9 Cal.Rptr. 607, 357 P.2d 830 (1960). By analogy, if he committed theft by burglary he could be punished only for one— which should be burglary since it is the more serious. People v. Isenor, 17 Cal. App.3d 324, 94 Cal.Rptr. 746 (1971).

On the other hand some states make provision for the prosecution of burglary and larceny. See United States v. Manes, 420 F.Supp. 1013 (D.C.Or.1976); State v. Forteson, 8 Ariz.App. 468, 447 P.2d 560 (1968).

42. The original English statute provided that larceny in a house of property worth more than a shilling, should be without benefit of clergy. 2 East P.C. 623 (1803).

43. Idaho Code § 18–1401 (1979).

44. Ibid.

45. Middleton v. State, 53 Ga. 248 (1874); Martinez v. State, 41 Tex. 126 (1874).

46. "In order to constitute larceny in a dwelling-house or other building, the property stolen must indeed be under the protection of the house, and not under the eye or personal care of some one who happens to be in the house." Commonwealth v. Smith, 111 Mass. 429 (1873).

ters are normally treated as within the protection of the building.[47] One distinction, however, is to be noted. If a jewel or other valuable thing, normally kept out of open reach of customers, is placed on the counter under the eye of the storekeeper or clerk while it is being examined by a customer, this is regarded as under the personal protection of the storekeeper or clerk at the moment, rather than under the protection of the building; [48] whereas articles placed on the counter with the expectation that they will remain there all day, unless purchased, are under the protection of the building.

Larceny from the person is frequently punished more severely than larceny from a building,[49] but it is important to know whether a certain misdeed is one or the other.

Under the statute, a merchant is authorized to detain a person for a reasonable time for the purpose of investigating, if he has probable cause to believe the person is engaged in shoplifting.[50]

c. BUILDING OF ANOTHER

Statutes providing an added penalty for larceny *from* a building, or *in* a building, usually do not specify that it must be the building *of another*, but this has been the interpretation of the courts. The purpose of the statute was to protect the occupant from predatory acts of others rather than to protect others from the occupant. Hence this compound offense is not committed by one who commits larceny in his own house,—meaning "his" in the sense of occupancy rather than title.[51] On the other hand, unless the statute is unusually restrictive, its protection will extend to the property of one which is in the house of a second, except as against the occupant or occupants. If a third person steals it while it is under the protection of this house he is guilty of larceny from a building.[52]

Statutes in some of the states provide still more severe penalties if the larceny from a building is in the nighttime, or is from a building on fire.[53]

The stealing of "goods, wares or merchandise offered for sale by any store or other mercantile establishment" popularly known as "shoplifting" is sometimes punished as a separate offense under that name.[54]

3. LARCENY FROM THE PERSON

An early English statute provided a more severe penalty (by removing the possibility of benefit of clergy) for the offense of larceny from the per-

---

47. Commonwealth v. Nott, 135 Mass. 269 (1883).

48. Commonwealth v. Lester, 129 Mass. 101 (1880); State v. Patterson, 98 Mo. 283 (1889).

49. E.g., 21 Okl.Stat.Ann. §§ 1708, 1723–4 (1958).

50. People v. Buonauro, 113 Cal.App. 3d 688, 170 Cal.Rptr. 285 (1980).

51. For the same reason if the wife of the occupant steals in the building this is not larceny from a building. Commonwealth v. Hartnett, 69 Mass. 450 (1855).

52. Simmons v. State, 73 Ga. 609 (1884); Rex v. Taylor, Russ. & Ry. 418, 168 Eng.Rep. 875 (1820); Rex v. Gould, 1 Leach 217, 168 Eng.Rep. 211 (1780).

53. E.g., Mass.Gen.Laws Ann. C. 266, §§ 23, 24 (1968); Mich.Stat.Ann. § 28.590 (1972).

54. E.g., 11 Del.Code Ann. § 840 (1978); S.C. Code 1962, § 16.359.1.

"It was not the intent of the Legislature to have the larceny in a building statute applicable in shoplifting cases." People v. Carmichael, 86 Mich.App. 418, 272 N.W.2d 667, 668 (1978).

son of another, if committed without his knowledge.[55] The requirement that this offense be "without his knowledge" does not now appear in the English statute and is not commonly found in the modern statutes in this country.

Property is stolen "from the person," if it was under the protection of the person at the time. Property *attached* to the person is under the protection of the person even while he is asleep. And the word "attached" is not to be given a narrow construction in this regard. It will include property which is being held in the hand, or an earring affixed to the ear, or a chain around the neck, or anything in the pockets of clothing actually on the person's body at the moment. Moreover, property may be under the protection of the person although not actually "attached" to him.[56] Thus if a man carrying a heavy suitcase sets it down for a moment to rest, and remains right there to guard it, the suitcase remains under the protection of his person.[57] And if a jeweler removes several diamonds and places them on the counter for the inspection of a customer, under the jeweler's eye, the diamonds are under the protection of the person. On the other hand, one who is asleep is not actually protecting property merely because it is in his presence. Taking property belonging to a sleeping person, and in his presence at the time, is not larceny *from the person* unless the thing was attached to him, in the pocket of clothing being worn by him, or controlled by him at the time in some equivalent manner.[58]

In one case it was said that the statutory offense of larceny from the person was meant to apply to pickpocketing and hence requires an actual taking from the person, and is not committed by a taking from the immediate presence and actual control of the person.[59] This, however, has not been the general interpretion, as mentioned above. And it could not well be, because the statute made use of a phrase long used in connection with robbery,

55. 8 Eliz. c. 4, § 2 (1565). This applied only to grand larceny because petit larceny had not been a capital offense since the Statute of Westminster I, c. 15 (1275). Modern statutes ordinarily make no reference to the value of the property stolen but provide an added penalty for larceny from the person. E.g., N.J.Stat. Ann. 2C:20–26 (1979).

56. "The thing taken must be under the protection of the person, but it need not be attached thereto." 2 Bishop, New Criminal Law § 888 (8th ed. 1892.)

A woman sitting on a public bench with her purse by her side and her arm extended over it has the purse on her person. Prigmore v. State, 565 S.W.2d 897 (Tenn.Cr.App.1977).

"We conclude that the taking of the purse from the cart which the victim was pushing, and which was under her control and in her present possession, constitutes taking 'from the person of another' in violation of § 18–4–401(5), C.R.S. 1973."

People v. Evans, —— Colo.App. —— 612 P.2d 1153, 1156 (1980).

57. To grab the suitcase and run off with it without force or intimidation would be larceny from the person, just as it would be robbery to take it at the point of a pistol. It is robbery "if a thief comes in the presence of A. and with violence, and putting A. in fear, drives away his horse, cattle, or sheep." 1 Hale P.C. *533.

58. People v. McElroy, 116 Cal. 583, 48 P. 718 (1897).

59. Terral v. State, 84 Nev. 412, 422 P.2d 465 (1968).

Terral was approved and followed in Utah. The court emphasized that the robbery statute said from the person or in his presence, whereas the grand larceny statute said only from the person. State v. Lucero, 28 Utah 2d 61, 498 P.2d 350 (1972).

Accord: "In our view, larceny from the person requires an actual trespass to the person of the victim." State v. Crowe, 174 Conn. 129, 384 A.2d 340, 342 (1977).

and regularly understood to include property taken from one's presence and control. As said by Coke in the 1600's: "for that which is taken in his presence, is in law taken from his person."[60]

SECTION 2. ROBBERY

Robbery is larceny from the person by violence or intimidation. It is a felony both at common law and under modern statutes. Under some of the new penal codes robbery does not require an actual taking of property. If force or intimidation is used in the attempt to commit theft this is sufficient.*

A. LARCENY

One rather common definition is that robbery is "the felonious and forcible taking from the person of another any goods or money of any value, by violence or putting in fear."[1] Because all larceny was felony at common law, the word "felonious," used in connection with the taking of property means a taking with intent to steal.[2] The "taking" means a taking of possession in this definition, as in the definition of larceny. Thus if a would-be robber, by his violence, causes the other's money to fall to the ground, but fails to get possession of it, he is not guilty of robbery.[3] A taking of possession of another's goods by violence or putting in fear obviously involves a trespass and the element of asportation is necessarily included in the concept of "taking from the person." Since larceny is a trespassory taking and car-

---

60. 3 Co.Inst. *69.

"Furthermore, the authorities are in accord that it can be a taking from a person or in his presence even though the victim was not immediately present where the victim, by force or fear, had been removed from or prevented from approaching the place from which the asportation of the personalty occurred." State v. McDonald, 74 Wn.2d 141, 443 P. 2d 651, 653 (1968).

*** E.g. Iowa Criminal Code § 711.1 (1978). See also State v. Skaggs, 42 Or. App. 763, 601 P.2d 862 (1979).

"Both the statute and the instructions contain substantially the same basic elements as were required at common law. . . . 'Those elements are (1) a felonious taking, (2) accompanied by an asportation, of (3) personal property of value, (4) from the person of another or in his presence, (5) against his will, (6) by violence or by putting him in fear, (7) animo furandi (with intent to steal).' " McCarty v. State, 616 P.2d 782, 785 (Wyo.1980).

1. State v. Campbell, 41 Del. 342, 344–5, 22 A.2d 390, 391 (1941). Cf., People v. Gurdak, 357 Ill. 516, 521, 192 N.E. 554, 556 (1934); Application of Massie, 283 P.2d 573 (Okl.Cr.1955). And see People v. Gallegos, 130 Colo. 232, 274 P.2d 608 (1954).

2. Speaking of larceny, Blackstone says: "This taking and carrying away must also be *felonious;* that is, done *animo furandi:* . . ." 4 Bl.Comm. *232. It is otherwise if the statute defines robbery in terms of a "wrongful taking." Traxler v. State, 96 Okl.Cr. 231, 251 P.2d 815 (1952).

By omitting the word "felonious" from the robbery statute, the requirement of a specific intent was eliminated. Bell v. State, 354 So.2d 1266 (Fla.App.1978).

A specific intent permanently to deprive the owner of his property is still an element of the crime of robbery as defined by section 812.13, Florida statutes, 1975. Bell v. State, 394 So.2d 979 (Fla. 1981).

" 'Felonious taking' means a taking with intent to commit larceny." State v. Lopez, 94 N.M. 349, 610 P.2d 753, 755–56 (App.1980).

If there was no intent to deprive the owner of his property permanently, there was no robbery. People v. Thompson, 27 Cal.3d 303, 165 Cal.Rptr. 289, 611 P.2d 883 (1980).

3. 1 Hale P.C. *533; 1 Hawk.P.C. c. 34, § 3 (6th ed. by Leach, 1788). "[T]his is no taking, for the thief had never any possession thereof, . . ." 3 Co.Inst. *69.

rying away of the goods or money of another with intent to steal the same, it is simpler to define robbery in terms of larceny.

In the ancient law robbery and larceny were thought of as quite separate offenses. The primitive view was that the robber, who acted in the open, was not quite so low in the antisocial scale as the thief, who committed his depredation secretly.[4] It is to be noted in this connection that although the thief usually acts in secret, and although an open taking without force or intimidation tends to suggest a bona-fide belief in the right to do so, secrecy is not an element of the crime of larceny either at common law or under the statutes.[5] Despite the ancient view, the common law came to regard robbery "amongst the most heinous felonies."[6] It was deemed to be a more serious offense than larceny because of the added element of personal violence or intimidation.[7] In other words, although it carried a separate label, robbery was recognized as the extreme form of compound larceny.[8] Hence under an indictment for robbery the defendant may be convicted of larceny as a lesser included offense.[9]

Since robbery is larceny plus certain circumstances of aggravation, it would be possible, although quite unnecessary, to repeat here all that was said in the discussion of that offense. It has been held that it is not robbery to collect money that is legally and presently due, or bona fide believed to be due, by force or intimidation—even at pistol point.[10] This position is sound because as pointed out in the discussion of larceny, an intent to collect a debt is not an intent to steal.[11] But some courts reached the other conclusion,[12]

4. 1 Pollock & Maitland, History of English Law 493–4 (2d ed. 1899).

5. Speaking of larceny, Bishop says: "As a question of law, it is immaterial whether the force is secret or open, in the day or in the night; but these and other like circumstances are commonly important in evidence to the intent." 2 Bishop, New Criminal Law § 804 (8th ed. 1892).

6. 3 Co.Inst. *68.

7. "And is ranked in this place, for that it concerneth not only the goods, but the person of the owner." Ibid.

8. "Open and violent larceny from the *person*, or *robbery* . . . ." 4 Bl. Comm. *241.

"Robbery, as we have seen, is a compound larceny." 2 Bishop, New Criminal Law § 1158 (8th ed.1892). ". . . . robbery is but an aggravated form of larceny." People v. Gallegos, 130 Colo. 232, 235, 174 P.2d 608, 609 (1954).

9. People v. Nelson, 56 Cal. 77 (1880). Larceny is an essential element of robbery. Goldstine v. State, 230 Ind. 343, 103 N.E.2d 438 (1952).

"A comparison of the elements of these two crimes indicates that robbery cannot be committed without also committing theft. We conclude, therefore,

that theft is a lesser included offense of robbery." State v. Jackson, 121 Ariz. 277, 589 P.2d 1309, 1311 (1979).

10. Regina v. Hennings, 4 Fost. & F. 50, 176 Eng.Rep. 462 (1864); People v. Gallegos, 130 Colo. 232, 274 P.2d 608 (1954); State v. Hollyway, 41 Iowa 200 (1875)—approved although distinguished in State v. Kobylasz, 242 Iowa 1161, 1168, 47 N.W.2d 167, 171 (1951); Barton v. State, 88 Tex.Cr.R. 368, 227 S.W. 317 (1921). Many cases are cited in the Barton case, and in annotations, 13 A.L.R. 142 and 116 A.L.R. 997. And see People v. Butler, 65 Cal.2d 569, 55 Cal.Rptr. 511, 421 P.2d 703 (1967).

The court held that "the rule in Arizona is that a charge of robbery fails where the attempt is to collect a bona fide debt, since, to constitute that offense, there must be an animus furandi and this cannot exist if the person takes the property under a bona fide claim of right. However this rule does not apply where the amount claimed is unliquidated." State v. Bonser, 128 Ariz. 95, 623 P.2d 1251, 1252 (App.1981).

11. See supra under Intent To Collect a Debt, chapter 4, section 1, F, (9).

12. Edwards v. State, 49 Wis.2d 105, 181 N.W.2d 383 (1970); State v. Martin,

apparently assuming that, however illogical it may be, it is necessary to hold that such conduct is robbery because otherwise any creditor would be free to collect his claim by threat of violence. Obviously this is not the law. Collecting a debt in that manner would constitute statutory extortion (blackmail),[13] and would usually involve other offenses, particularly if a weapon is employed. In some of the new penal codes, it should be added, statutory extortion is included in the chapter on robbery,[14] and it has at times been labeled a lower degree of statutory robbery.[15] But whether it is viewed as a lower degree of statutory robbery, a lesser-included offense of robbery by intimidation, or a distinct offense, statutory extortion does not require an intent to steal.

It is robbery, it may be added, forcibly to extort money under pretense of a sale, even if some unwanted thing is handed over in exchange.[16] For the same reason it is robbery to require one, at gunpoint, to "sell" a chattel not held for sale even if payment is made at the time. Some early statements went to the extent of holding it robbery where a merchant is compelled by force to sell to one with whom he prefers not to deal, although the property is held for sale and he receives the full price,—but this seems not to be the law.[17]

15 Or.App. 498, 516 P.2d 753 (1973); State v. Ortiz, 124 N.J.Super. 189, 305 A.2d 800 (1973). And Texas overruled Barton (supra note 10a). Crawford v. State, 509 S.W.2d 582 (Tex.Cr.App.1974). No valid claim of right defense is recognized where there was no claim of title to the property taken. State v. Larsen, 23 Wn.App. 218, 596 P.2d 1089 (1979).

13. "It may be proper to say that although, in the absence of a felonious intent, it is not robbery to compel, by means of threats of personal violence and menaces, the payment of money against the will of the party menaced, it is nevertheless an offense under the statutes of Iowa." State v. Hollway, 41 Iowa 200, 203 (1875). Cf. People v. Fichtner, 281 App.Div. 159, 118 N.Y.S.2d 392 (1952).

Needless to add, if actual force was used it would constitute assault and battery, and the force might be such as to constitute a felonious assault. Guilt of extortion was established by proof that a debt was collected by informing the debtor, first indirectly and then directly, that if the debt was not paid, "she is going to have a broken head and be found floating in the river." United States v. Ochs, 595 F.2d 1247, 1261 (2d Cir.1979).

14. E.g., Iowa Criminal Code Chapter 711 (1978).

15. Under the former Kansas code common-law robbery was robbery in the first degree while statutory extortion was robbery in the second or third degree. Kan.R.S. § 21–527 through § 21–530.

16. 4 Bl.Comm. *243.

17. 1 Hawk.P.C. c. 34, § 7 (6th ed. by Leach, 1788); 4 Bl.Comm. *243.

By definition robbery requires larceny which includes an intent to steal. But the fact that D, who had taken X's wallet at gunpoint, dropped it in X's presence when it was found to be empty does not negate the *intent* to deprive X of his property permanently at the time of the taking, and leaves D guilty of robbery. People v. Hall, 253 Cal.App.2d 1051, 61 Cal.Rptr. 676 (1967). On the other hand it was not robbery when money was taken at gunpoint in the bona-fide, though mistaken, belief that it was being retaken from a thief who had just stolen it from the actor. Analytis v. People, 68 Colo. 74, 188 P. 1113 (1920). Whether it is robbery to retake at gunpoint money which has just been lost at cards depends upon the theory of the transaction. Where the holding was that property in the money did not pass, because of the illegality, the taking was held not to be robbery. Gant v. State, 115 Ga. 205, 41 S.E. 698 (1902); State v. Price, 38 Idaho 149, 219 P. 1049 (1923). The opposite conclusion was reached where the rule was that the law would leave the money where the parties themselves had placed it, despite the illegality. Baine v. State, 34 Tex.Cr. 448, 31 S.W. 368 (1895).

Since the special aggravation of robbery is the violence or threatened violence to the person, it is clear that the extent of the value of the property taken is unimportant. It may be of "any value."

B. FROM THE PERSON

Robbery is committed only where there is larceny *from the person*,[18] but as pointed out in the discussion of that form of compound larceny, this does not require that the thing stolen be taken from the hand of the owner, or from the pocket of clothing being worn at the time, or be attached to him in any literal sense. An important distinction is to be noted however. The owner may be very near to his property without having it under his personal protection at the moment, and a secret taking of such property is not larceny from the person.[19] A different problem is presented when a man's attention is directed to the need of safeguarding certain property which belongs to him and is so situated at the time that he could guard it if not prevented by violence or deterred by fear. Such property is regarded as being under his personal protection and the wrongful taking of it by violence or intimidation is robbery.[20]

To emphasize this point some of the statutes define robbery in terms of larceny from the person "or immediate presence" of another.[21] This adds nothing other than emphasis because, as pointed out by Coke, where deprivation is accomplished by violence or intimidation, "that which is taken in his presence, is in law taken from his person." [22] One of the illustrations of robbery, given by the early writers, is the wrongful driving off of another's horse or sheep while he, although present, is by violence or intimidation prevented from interfering.[23] And the modern decisions reach a similar result whether the statute has this additional phrase or not. Thus it was held to be robbery (1) where bandits gained entrance at gunpoint, bound and gagged the occupant, secured him in the bathroom while they ransacked the bedroom and left with personal property; [24] (2) where one armed with a revolver held menacingly took money from a cash register while the cashier stood helpless

4 Bl.Comm. *241. And as the owner would not part with it voluntarily it had some value to him and that is sufficient.

18. 3 Co.Inst. *68; 1 Hale P.C. *532; 4 Bl.Comm. *241.

19. People v. McElroy, 116 Cal. 583, 48 P. 718 (1897).

20. 3 Co.Inst. *69; 1 Hale P.C. *533.

"Under this statute, the requirement of a taking 'from the person assaulted' could be established by a taking of property that was in the victim's presence or under the victim's control." State v. Webber, 14 Or.App. 352, 513 P.2d 496 (1973).

21. "Robbery is the felonious taking of personal property in the possession of another, from his person or immediate presence, and against his will, accomplished by means of force or fear." West's Ann.Cal.Pen.Code § 211 (1970).

22. 3 Co.Inst. *69.

"The elements necessary to make out the offense of robbery are the taking must be felonious and forcible and from the person of the party robbed, either actual or constructive. It is actual when the taking is immediately from the person; and constructive when in the possession or in the presence of the party robbed." Morgan v. State, 220 Tenn. 247, 415 S.W.2d 879, 881 (1967).

23. Ibid.; 1 Hale P.C. *533; 1 Hawk. P.C. c. 34, § 5 (6th ed. by Leach, 1788).

24. State v. Campbell, 41 Del. 342, 22 A.2d 390 (1941).

D who telephoned a bank manager, threatening that a bomb would go off at his home unless money was delivered by throwing moneybag over the viaduct at a specified spot, whereupon the manager complied, was guilty of bank robbery, rather than extortion. Brinkley v. United States, 560 F.2d 871 (8th Cir.1977).

nearby;[25] and (3) where thugs struck and beat their victim after which they immediately took money from his clothing in a closet a few feet away.[26]

"A thing is in the presence of a person, in respect to robbery, which is so within his reach, inspection, observation or control, that he could, if not overcome with violence or prevented by fear, retain his possession of it." [27]

C. BY VIOLENCE OR INTIMIDATION

The ordinary pickpocket is guilty of larceny from the person, rather than robbery, because there is no violence or intimidation in perpetrating the theft.[28] The same is true of the thief who snatches money or a purse or other property from another's hand if no resistance is encountered.[29] But if the owner's grasp was sufficiently firm so that the original snatch was unsuccessful, and the thief did not gain possession until after a struggle, the offense is robbery.[30] It is also robbery if the original snatching was accom-

---

25. People v. Gurdak, 357 Ill. 516, 192 N.E. 554 (1934).

To threaten a storekeeper with a knife, force him to lie down on the floor, and then to take money from the cash register, constitutes robbery. People v. Day, 256 Cal.App.2d 83, 63 Cal.Rptr. 677 (1967).

Taking of a purse from a table while the victim was 10 to 12 feet away supported a finding that the purse was taken in the presence of the victim. Groce v. State, 250 Ind. 582, 236 N.E.2d 597 (1968).

26. Osborne v. State, 200 Ga. 763, 38 S.E.2d 558 (1946).

27. Commonwealth v. Homer, 235 Mass. 526, 533, 127 N.E. 517, 520 (1920).

"What emerges from these authorities is that where the victim has been intimidated or placed in fear by use or threat of force and the property is taken from an area sufficiently close and under his control that, but for the robber's intimidation or force he could have prevented the taking, the taking is from his 'presence' . . . and this conclusion is not defeated by an unawareness of the taking as it occurs." State v. Mosely, 102 Wis.2d 636, 307 N.W.2d 200, 208 (1981).

The court repeated that "an indictment or information charging a taking from the 'person' may be supported by proof of a taking from the 'presence,' since such proof does not constitute a fatal variance." Wilson v. State, 637 P.2d 900, 902 (Okl.Cr.App.1981).

28. Ramirez v. Territory, 9 Ariz. 177, 80 P. 391 (1905); State v. Parker, 262 Mo. 169, 170 S.W. 1121 (1914); State v. Sanchez, 78 N.M. 284, 430 P.2d 781 (1967).

29. Lear v. State, 39 Ariz. 313, 6 P.2d 426 (1931); People v. Church, 116 Cal. 300, 48 P. 125 (1897); Terry v. Surety Co., 164 Miss. 394, 145 So. 111 (1932). Contra, Jones v. Commonwealth, 112 Ky. 689, 66 S.W. 633 (1902); People v. Patton, 76 Ill.2d 45, 389 N.E.2d 1174 (1979).

"In Stewart's case it was ruled by Holt, C.J. that snatching a hat and wig from the head of a person walking in the street was no robbery, . . ." 1 East P.C. 702 (1803).

The statutory definition of robbery is sometimes extended to include (1) robbery by force, (2) robbery by intimidation, and (3) robbery by snatching. E.g., Code of Ga.Ann. § 26-1901 (1978).

In holding that purse-snatching constitutes robbery, the court recognized it was following "the minority or Kentucky rule on purse snatching." Commonwealth v. Brown, 2 Mass.App. 883, 318 N.E.2d 486 (1974).

Snatching a purse from the fingertips of the owner does not constitute robbery since no force or threat of force was used. People v. Patton, 76 Ill.2d 45, 27 Ill.Dec. 766, 389 N.E.2d 1174 (1979). Since the victim was not touched, nor placed in fear of bodily harm, snatching the wallet from her hand was not robbery, although there was a "brief tug of war over the wallet." Commonwealth v. Ostalaza, 267 Pa.Super. 451, 406 A.2d 1128, 1130 (1979).

30. Bauer v. State, 45 Ariz. 358, 43 P.2d 203 (1935).

"Of course if . . . a struggle ensues to overcome the active resistance of the victim to avoid the loss of his property the offense is robbery." People v.

panied by violence or intimidation.[31]   And the terms of a particular statute on robbery, as interpreted, may include any larceny from the person accomplished by an actual snatching from the hand.

Just as battery may be committed by the administration of poison,[32] so the force used to obtain property from a person against his will may be applied internally.   It was robbery, for example, to take money from a cash register, while the one in charge was helpless nearby, having been rendered unconscious by a drug administered for that purpose.[33]

Intimidation sufficient for guilt of robbery, if the felonious purpose is accomplished, "does not imply any great degree of terror or affright in the party robbed: it is enough that so much force or threatening by word or gesture be used as might create an apprehension of danger, or induce one to part with his property without or against his consent." [34]   One who places his money in another's hand for fear of consequences does not part with it voluntarily.[35]   Another matter is entitled to attention.   One may be intimidated into parting with his property without his consent by being required to submit to a fraudulent assertion of authority.   Robbery was committed, it was held, when rogues pretending to be police officers arrested a man, required him to accompany them, searched him and took his money from his pocket under a false pretense of authority.[36]

To emphasize the problem it has been pointed out that robbery may be accomplished in either of two ways: (a) by violence to the person, or (b) by putting him in fear of some immediate injury.[37]   The unlawful obtaining of property by threats of a different nature is ordinarily not robbery but a different offense, and the whole problem of such intimidation is discussed in detail under section 10, subsection B, "Statutory Extortion—Blackmail."

Blackstone, to emphasize that for robbery the larceny must be accomplished by violence or intimidation, said: "for if one privately steals sixpence from the person of another, and afterwards keeps it by putting him in fear, this is no robbery, for the fear is subsequent, ..." [38]   Occasionally this has been misapplied.   For example, during a chance meeting **D** suggested he might be interested in buying the gun **X** was carrying and asked permission

---

Patton, 60 Ill.App.3d 456, 17 Ill.Dec. 770, 376 N.E.2d 1099, 1101 (1978).

"If force is used to injure the victim or to overcome a struggle or resistance by the victim to the taking of his property, the crime is robbery, not theft." People v. Kennedy, 88 Ill.App.3d 365, 43 Ill.Dec. 520, 410 N.E.2d 520, 523 (1980) (the victim was pushed against a wall as her money bag was grabbed).

31.   State v. Clemons, 356 Mo. 514, 202 S.W.2d 75 (1947).

32.   State v. Monroe, 121 N.C. 677, 28 S.E. 547 (1897).

33.   State v. Snyder, 41 Nev. 453, 172 P. 364 (1918).

34.   4 Bl.Comm. *242. And see Application of Massie, 283 P.2d 573 (Okl.Cr. 1955). But see infra, chapter 9, section 3.

35.   State v. Stephens, 66 Ariz. 219, 183 P.2d 346 (1947).

36.   State v. Parsons, 44 Wash. 299, 87 P. 399 (1906).

37.   State v. Hawkins, 418 S.W.2d 921 (Mo.1967).

"Robbery is the felonious taking of personal property in the possession of another, from his person or immediate presence, and against his will, accomplished by means of force or fear." People v. Hall, 253 Cal.App.2d 1051, 1054, 61 Cal. Rptr. 676, 678 (1967).

38.   4 Bl.Comm. *242. The force or fear must be the moving cause inducing the victim to part with his property unwillingly.   State v. Sanchez, 78 N.M. 284, 430 P.2d 781 (1967).

to examine it, which was granted. Finding the gun loaded **D** then pointed it at **X** and told him to run for his life. As **X** backed away, **D** ran off with the weapon. A conviction of robbery was reversed on the theory that the resort to intimidation was after the acquisition of the gun.[39] This completely overlooks the distinction between possession and custody. When **D** received the gun to examine momentarily in the presence of **X**, **D** had custody only. Had he run off with the gun without violence or intimidation he would have been guilty of larceny because this would have been a trespassory taking and carrying away with all the elements of that offense.[40] And since he actually did this under a threat to kill he clearly committed robbery, as the same court had held earlier under an equivalent set of facts.[41] And a motorist whose tank had been filled with gas at his request, after which he held off the attendant at gunpoint, under threat to shoot while he drove away without making payment, was properly convicted of robbery.[42] Furthermore, if one snatches property from the hand of another and uses force or intimidation to prevent an immediate retaking by the other, this is all one transaction and constitutes robbery.[43] If the two transactions are essentially distinct,—if subsequent to the larceny the owner should come upon the thief and be prevented from retaking his property by force or violence, the thief would be guilty of larceny and assault, but not robbery. But if the violence or intimidation is part of the *res gestae* of the larceny the offense is generally held to be elevated to the category of robbery,[44] although there is still some authority for the earlier view that force or intimidation used to retain possession of property taken without it, is not sufficient.[45]

39. Thomas v. State, 91 Ala. 34, 9 So. 81 (1891).

40. Rex v. Chisser, T.Raym. 275, 83 Eng.Rep. 142 (1678).

41. James v. State, 53 Ala. 380 (1875).

42. People v. Phillips, 201 Cal.App.2d, 383, 19 Cal.Rptr. 839 (1962). Cf. Smith v. United States, 291 F.2d 220 (9th Cir. 1961).

43. People v. Reade, 197 Cal.App.2d 509, 17 Cal.Rptr. 328 (1961). The Model Penal Code in the section on robbery provides: "An act shall be deemed 'in the course of committing a theft' if it occurs in an attempt to commit theft or in flight after the attempt or commission." Section 222.1(1).

"Where one 'uses force or intimidation to prevent an immediate retaking . . . this is all one transaction and constitutes robbery.' " And it is immaterial whether the threat was intended to effectuate the robber's escape or to prevent the victim's retaking the money, "since the latter purpose was in fact served." Mangerich v. State, 93 Nev. 683, 572 P.2d 542, 543 (1977).

The use of force merely to remove a wallet from the victim's pocket is not "force" in the sense of robbery; but when immediately after the taking force and threats were used against the victim and his friends in order to retain the wallet, this did constitute robbery. State v. Miguel, 125 Ariz. 538, 611 P.2d 125 (App. 1980). The court emphasized that under the Arizona statute the force and threats may be applied to one other than the victim himself.

44. Where defendant assaulted the victim in order to commit rape, and the victim offered money to the defendant which he took but continued violence to effect his original purpose, it was held to be robbery because the defendant acquired the money by his original force. Rex v. Blackham, 2 East P.C. 711 (1787).

Under the Canadian Criminal Code it has been held that force used against a person justifies a conviction for robbery where thereafter the victim's property was taken but not necessarily because of the force previously employed. All that was required is that the force accompany the taking. Regina v. Downer, 40 CCC 2d 532 (Ont.App.1978).

45. "Under the rule which is firmly ingrained in this State, ... the force, violence or intimidation must precede or be contemporaneous with the taking of the property." State v. Samuel, 562 S.W.2d 733, 736 (Mo.App.1978).

D. COMPOUND OFFENSE

Since robbery "is a species of aggravated larceny" [46] a single taking of property will obviously not support a conviction of larceny as a separate offense in addition to the conviction of robbery.[47] The other ingredient of the combination requires equal attention. The act of violence relied upon for conviction of robbery will not support a separate conviction of assault, or assault with a deadly weapon.[48] On the other hand, if a robber who has taken money by violence thereafter slugs his victim, there are two separate acts of violence which will permit two convictions,—one for robbery and one for assault.[49]

Robbery violates the social interest in the safety and security of the person as well as the social interest in the protection of property rights. In fact, as a matter of abstract classification, it probably should be grouped with offenses against the person [50] rather than with offenses against property, but it is more expedient to include it at this point.

E. ROBBERY WITH AGGRAVATION

Statutes frequently make special provision for certain types of aggravated robbery such as armed robbery, bank robbery and train robbery, which obviously are not mutually exclusive, since either the second or the third might be armed robbery and usually is.

Armed robbery, the gravest offense of this nature and punishable under some of the statutes by life imprisonment,[51] is robbery "while armed with a dangerous weapon," [52] or perhaps limited to one who "uses or displays" a

46. United States v. Mann, 119 F.Supp. 406, 407 (D.C.D.C.1954).

47. "We agree with appellant, however, that the grand larceny charge against him for the items stolen from Miller's residence was a lesser included offense of the Miller robbery, precluding judgment and sentence on the larceny charge." McClendon v. State, 372 So.2d 1161, 1162 (Fla.App.1979). But in a robbery prosecution the defendant may be convicted of larceny as a lesser included offense if he is not found guilty of robbery. People v. Nelson, 56 Cal. 77 (1880).

48. People v. Logan, 41 Cal.2d 279, 260 P.2d 20 (1953).

"All of the elements of common assault are therefore included in the elements of the robbery charged and it is a lesser included offense of that charge which must be instructed upon if supported by evidence." State v. Lockett, 586 S.W.2d 90, 93 (Mo.App.1979).

49. Ex parte Chapman, 43 Cal.2d 385, 273 P.2d 817 (1954); Borrero v. United States, 332 A.2d 363 (D.C.App.1975).

50. The "gist of the offense is a crime against the person." United States v. Mann, 119 F.Supp. 406, 407 (D.C.D.C. 1954). Cf. People v. Carpenter, 315 Ill. 87, 89, 145 N.E. 664–5 (1924).

51. Ga.Code § 26–1902 (1976); Vernon's Ann.Mo.Stat. § 569.020 (1979).

52. La.Stat.Ann.Rev.Stat. 14:158; 17–A Me.Rev.Stat.Ann. § 651E (1978).

"The essential elements of robbery with firearms are: a wrongful taking of personal property in the possession of another from his person or presence against his will, by means of force or fear, and with the use of firearms." Harris v. State, 555 P.2d 76, 80 (Okl.Cr. 1976).

Armed robbery under the new code "is not satisfied by the defendant pretending to have a gun or even using a fake gun." State v. Laughter, 128 Ariz. 264, 625 P.2d 327, 330 (1981).

"We hold as a matter of law that a gun, whether loaded or unloaded, is a dangerous weapon when used in the commission of a robbery." State v. Parker, 139 Vt. 179, 423 A.2d 851, 853 (1980).

weapon during robbery,[53] or extended to one who causes physical injury to person, is armed with a deadly weapon or "threatens the immediate use of a dangerous instrument."[54]

Bank robbery is literally robbery committed in a bank. One who breaks into a bank to steal while the building is empty is guilty of statutory burglary, and one who commits secret larceny in a bank is guilty of larceny from a building, but neither may properly be said to have committed robbery of any kind.[55] A bank-robbery statute may include threatening or injuring any person with intent to steal from a bank.[56]

Train robbery, literally robbery committed in a train, may include not only that but also the unlawful stopping of a train for the purpose of robbery.[57]

SECTION 3. EMBEZZLEMENT

A. LEGISLATIVE HISTORY

Embezzlement is not a common-law crime. It is the result of legislative efforts to make provision for an unreasonable gap which appeared in the law of larceny as it developed.

Under the early English statute embezzlement was made a misdemeanor,[1] but under most modern American statutes it is either a felony or a misdemeanor depending upon the value of the property converted.

The word "imbezzle" was used in a statute in 1529.[2] This statute dealt with servants who, having been entrusted with money or property by their

---

53. McKinney's Consol. N.Y. Penal § 160.15.4.

54. McKinney's N.Y.Rev.Pen.Law § 160.15; See also Ky.Rev.Stat. 515.020(1)(c) (1974).

A full quart whiskey bottle is not a bludgeon, but when used to hit the victim over the head with such force as to shatter the bottle, it is a deadly weapon. Bowers v. People, ___ Colo. ___, 617 P.2d 560 (1980). A plastic bottle may be a deadly weapon when applied violently to the head of a four-and-a-half-week-old infant. State v. McGranahan, ___ R.I. ___, 415 A.2d 1298 (1980).

55. It was said in one case that the bank robbery statute is violated by an attempt to enter the bank to steal whether any person was therein or not. Williams v. United States, 301 F.2d 276 (7th Cir. 1962). But the statute involved is 18 U.S.C.A. § 2113 (1969), which is properly entitled "bank robbery and incidental crimes."

Under the federal bank robbery statute "a taking from the person or presence of another is an essential element of the crime." United States v. Alessandrello, 637 F.2d 131, 144 (3d Cir.1980).

56. Mass.Gen. Laws Ann.C. 265 § 21 (1968).

57. Mich.Stat.Ann. § 28.784 (1972).

1. There has been some misunderstanding due to the fact that the original English statute (see note 5) said one appropriating goods in violation of its provisions "shall be deemed to have feloniously stolen the same." But the penalty was transportation not to exceed fourteen years, whereas under the English law of the time, in the words of Blackstone, forfeiture was "an inseparable incident to felony." 4 Bl.Comm. *97. Hence the penalty would have needed to include at least forfeiture of goods (which the statute did not) to make the offense a felony. As Stephen said, referring to larceny and the new statutory offense, "the punishments for the two offences were different." 3 Stephen, History of the Criminal Law of England, 153 (1883). They were made the same later.

2. 21 Hen. VIII, c. 7 (1529). The statute had certain limitations, such as that it should not apply to an apprentice under the age of eighteen,—leaving such cases

masters, should leave the employment taking such money or property with them "to the intent to steal the same." This statute, however, did not create a new offense. As stated in the preamble it was merely to clarify a doubt as to the common law, and to do so such wrongful appropriation was declared to be larceny (felony). It was merely declaratory of the common law. As said years later, in holding that larceny was committed by a servant who stole goods delivered to him by his master, it is "like the case of a butler, who hath plate delivered to him; or a shepherd, who hath sheep delivered, and they steal any of them, that is felony at the common law." [3]

The statutes which created what has come to be known as the crime of "embezzlement" were enacted, not to clarify any doubt as to the common law, but to provide penalties for certain types of misconduct that had been held to be outside the scope of larceny. The first [4] of these statutes in England was in 1799 [5] and hence too late to be a part of our common law. This provided that "if any servant, clerk, or any person employed . . . by virtue of his employment receive or take into his possession any money, goods [etc.] for or in the name or on the account of his master . . . and shall fraudulently embezzle . . . the same, or any part thereof . . . [he] shall be deemed to have feloniously stolen the same . . . ."

"This enactment introduced much intricacy into the law. In the first place, though the statute expressly says that the offender shall be deemed to have stolen the property embezzled, it has been held that a person accused must be indicted for embezzlement and not for theft. This was, of course, necessary when the punishments for the two offences were different; . . . ." [6]

The legislative history of this new offense, known as embezzlement, may be briefly summarized so far as England is concerned. The first statute (mentioned above) in 1799 applied to servants or other employees who embezzled property of their masters which they had received from third persons. The additional steps, each dealing with the fraudulent appropriation of property, the possession of which was acquired without trespass, were:

"(2) Brokers, merchants, bankers, attorneys and other agents, misappropriating property intrusted to them, . . . 1812.

"(3) Factors fraudulently pledging goods intrusted to them for sale, . . . 1827.

"(4) Trustees under express trust fraudulently disposing of trust funds, . . . 1857.

"(5) Bailees stealing the goods bailed to them, . . . 1857." [7]

---

to the pre-existing law (i.e. subject to doubt).

3. Anonymous, J.Kel. 35, 84 Eng.Rep. 1070 (1664).

4. Earlier statutes had *enlarged the scope of larceny* in certain very limited areas: 15 Geo. II, c. 13, § 12 (1742, fraudulent appropriation by officer or servant of the Bank of England); 5 Geo. III, c. 25, § 17 (1765, fraudulent appropriation by deputy, clerk, agent or letter-

carrier of the Post Office). As these statutes merely enlarged the scope of larceny they did not contribute to the new offense of embezzlement.

5. 39 Geo. III, c. 85 (1799).

6. 3 Stephen, History of the Criminal Law of England 153 (1883). The penalty provided by the statute was transportation not to exceed fourteen years.

7. Id. at 159.

Thus the law remained until embezzlement was incorporated into the Larceny Act of 1861 [8] which in turn was superseded by the Larceny Act of 1916,[9] and the Theft Act of 1968.[10]

The legislative history of the offense in this country has been somewhat comparable to that in England, but a laborious statement of the various steps in the different states would not contribute to the present undertaking. Unfortunately here, as there, what was really one large gap in the law of larceny (although not the only one) [11] failed to receive recognition as such, and made its appearance piecemeal in the form of a number of small gaps. The large gap resulted from the firm position that there is no common-law larceny without trespass *de bonis.* Thus a servant who has received money or property for his master, from the hands of a third person, has possession rather than custody. For this reason a conversion by him is without trespass, and therefore not larceny, so an embezzlement statute was passed to cover such a case. And a bailee who converts the property bailed does so without trespass, if his original receipt was without fraudulent intent, so similar legislation was needed for such a misdeed. Frequently, however, the legislative attention was directed at some very limited type of bailee, such as a carrier for hire, and a statute was passed to cover that small part of the field leaving the rest for subsequent legislation which also might be step by step.[12]

Such statutes had one element in common in addition to the fact that they all applied to the fraudulent conversion of property which is accomplished without trespass. This was that the property had been *entrusted* to the converter either by or for the owner. The statutes are frequently worded in such terms [13] and the tendency has been to supply this element by interpretation where it is not expressed.[14]

Emphasis upon the violation of a trust in this statutory offense tended to focus attention upon another type of fraudulent conversion which did not come within the definition of common-law larceny. This was a conversion by one who had both title and possession which had been lawfully acquired and held in a fiduciary capacity. Fraudulent conversion of trust funds or property by a trustee is rather far removed from the scope of common-law larceny, but the separation is due to technicality and not to the general type of

---

8.   24 & 25 Vict. c. 96 (1861).

9.   6 & 7 Geo. V, c. 50 (1916).

10.   16 & 17 Eliz. II C.60 (1968).

11.   The other large gap resulted from the holding that no larceny was committed in the fraud cases if the wrongdoer obtained title as well as possession by his deceit. This led to the statutory offense known as "false pretenses."

12.   Evidences of such piecemeal enactment are still apparent. For example compare West's Ann.Cal.Pen.Code § 505 (1970) (embezzlement by carrier for hire) with id. § 507 (embezzlement by any bailee, and so forth, to whom property has been entrusted). "The Criminal Code creating and defining the crime of embezzlement is divided into numerous sec-

tions, each of which defines what acts of certain persons, classes of persons, or officials shall constitute a crime." People for the use of D. S. & T. Co. v. Birkett, 254 Ill.App. 96, 103 (1929).

13.   E.g., West's Ann.Cal.Pen.Code § 507 (1970).

14.   Statutes relating to embezzlement were intended to apply to certain situations in which property had been entrusted and "it may be said generally that they do not apply to cases where the element of a breach of trust or confidence in the fraudulent conversion of money or chattels is not shown to exist." Commonwealth v. Hays, 80 Mass. 62, 64 (1859).

wrongfulness involved. Suppose, for example, an agent fraudulently converts his principal's property. The wrongful character of the misdeed is the same whether the agent had possession only, and hence was a bailee, or had title as well as possession and hence occupied the position of a trustee. Hence the tendency has been to add sections making it embezzlement to convert funds or property held in trust by a trustee, agent, broker, factor, attorney, or other having a like position. They have not ordinarily included one holding under a constructive trust because he does not occupy a fiduciary relation.

B. DEFINITION

In some jurisdictions "embezzlement by public officers" is quite a different offense, as will be emphasized presently. Assuming this special offense is not to be included under the simple label "embezzlement," a definition may be suggested with the explanation that some particular jurisdiction may be found not to have occupied all of the field indicated, whereas there is now some tendency to go beyond the boundaries mentioned.

Embezzlement is the fraudulent conversion of personal property by a person to whom it was entrusted either by or for the owner.

C. INTERPRETATION

Since each statute on embezzlement was enacted to fill some gap in the law of larceny, the prevailing view has been that the statutory offense is not committed by an appropriation which would support a conviction of common-law larceny.[15] Although the English statute said that one who committed embezzlement, as defined, should be deemed to have stolen the property, the courts (as mentioned above) required the indictment to be for embezzlement and not for larceny. This was deemed necessary because the punishments were different.[16] In this country, if the statute said that the embezzler should be deemed guilty of larceny, without specifying the penalty, this was held to create a distinct offense, to be charged as such, and the reference to larceny was said to be merely for the purpose of applying the same penalty without the need of repeating it in detail.[17]

The result is, where not corrected by subsequent legislation, that the prosecution may fail notwithstanding clear proof of guilt, because the wrong offense was charged in the indictment or information. The tendency has

---

15. "There is a difference between the crimes of embezzlement and stealing. The crimes are inconsistent." United States v. Trevino, 491 F.2d 74, 75 (5th Cir.1974). In other word, proof of either would disprove the other.

Although a store clerk was in charge of the entire store, and was the only one in the store at the time, since the employer's money he wanted was in a locked box which he had to pry open since he had not been entrusted with the key, his offense was larceny and a conviction of embezzlement was reversed. State v. Stahl, 93 N.M. 62, 596 P.2d 275 (App. 1979).

16. 3 Stephen, History of the Criminal Law of England 153 (1883).

17. State v. Finnegan, 127 Iowa 286, 103 N.W. 155 (1905). And see State v. Cahill, 208 Or. 538, 293 P.2d 169, 178 (1956).

The difference between larceny, where it is perpetrated by fraud, and embezzlement, is that in larceny the intent to appropriate must exist at the time the property is taken whereas in embezzlement the wrongdoer has lawful possession before such intent is formed. Cunningham v. District Court, 432 P.2d 992 (Okl.Cr. 1967).

been to permit the statutory offense to be charged in terms of embezzlement, larceny by embezzlement,[18] larceny as bailee,[19] or some other designation which clearly distinguishes it from larceny. But, in the absence of express statutory authorization, the prevailing view is that an indictment for larceny will not support a conviction if the proof shows embezzlement [20] and there can be no conviction of what constitutes common-law larceny under a charge of embezzlement.[21]

The ordinary employee who receives the property from his employer has custody only and not possession. His fraudulent appropriation of the property so received is larceny,[22] hence he may properly be convicted if the charge is larceny [23] but not if it is embezzlement.[24] If, on the other hand, the employee had possession of the property converted, his crime was embezzlement and the conviction must be reversed if the charge was larceny.[25] The bailee who receives possession without wrongful intent does not commit trespass by a subsequent fraudulent conversion. His offense is embezzlement and his conviction under such a charge is proper.[26] But if his original intent was fraudulent his conversion is common-law larceny. He is properly convicted if tried under a charge of larceny [27] but the conviction must be reversed if the indictment was for embezzlement.[28]

There has been some tendency away from such strictness, even in the absence of statute.[29] And, in some states, statutes have been enacted to help the prosecuting officer who is handicapped by the fact that it is sometimes difficult to know in advance just what will be shown when the evidence is all in the record. One device has been to permit both offenses to be

18. State v. Cooper, 102 Iowa 146, 71 N.W. 197 (1897).

19. State v. McGuire, 107 Mont. 341, 88 P.2d 35 (1938). Or in some other distinctive form, see: Yost v. State, 149 Neb. 584, 31 N.W.2d 538 (1948).

20. Morgan v. Commonwealth 242 Ky. 713, 47 S.W.2d 543 (1932).

21. Commonwealth v. Berry, 99 Mass. 428 (1868); Jackson v. State, 211 Miss. 828, 52 So.2d 914 (1951).

22. State v. Ugland, 48 N.D. 841, 187 N.W. 237 (1922); Cunningham v. District Court, 432 P.2d 992 (Okl.Cr.1967).

23. Ibid.

24. Commonwealth v. Berry, 99 Mass. 428 (1868).

25. Morgan v. Commonwealth, 242 Ky. 713, 47 S.W.2d 543 (1932).

26. Smith v. United States, 233 F.2d 744 (9th Cir.1956); State v. Gould, 329 Mo. 828, 46 S.W.2d 886 (1932).

The following charge was held to be legally correct. "Embezzlement, ladies and gentlemen, means the wrongful or willful taking of property of someone else after the property has lawfully come within your possession or control." United States v. Williams, 642 F.2d 136, 140 (5th Cir. 1981). " 'Embezzlement' . . . encompasses the fraudulent appropriation of the property of another by one in lawful possession thereof." United States v. Andreen, 628 F.2d 1236, 1241 (9th Cir.1980).

27. Riley v. State, 64 Okl.Cr. 183, 70 P.2d 912 (1938); Bivens v. State, 6 Okl. Cr. 521, 120 P. 1033 (1912).

28. Phelps v. State, 25 Ariz. 495, 219 P. 589 (1923).

One who has mere custody of property may commit larceny by converting it, whereas one to whom property has been entrusted as bailee commits embezzlement by conversion unless he formed the wicked intent to convert before he received it. In that case it is larceny. State v. Smitherman, 187 Kan. 264, 356 P.2d 675 (1960). And see Poe v. People, 163 Colo. 20, 428 P.2d 77 (1967).

29. One who obtained money by cashing his employer's check with intent to use the money for himself, which he did, was held to be guilty of larceny. Skantze v. United States, 288 F.2d 416 (D.C.Cir.1961). Compare, Henry v. United States, 50 App.D.C. 366, 273 F. 330 (1921).

charged in separate counts in the indictment and (where so charged) to authorize conviction if either is established by the evidence. Another has been to authorize a conviction of either offense under an indictment charging larceny;—or more rarely to authorize a conviction of either under an indictment charging either.[30] A better solution, now rather widely adopted, has now been achieved in a number of the new penal codes by combining larceny, embezzlement and false pretenses (some have added others) into a single offense under the name of "theft." This was indicated earlier and will be considered under Section 5.

Much of the development of the law of embezzlement has taken the form of strict construction of a narrowly-worded statute followed by corrective legislation.[31] This makes an interesting study but contributes little to an understanding of the present law. As previously mentioned, the non-trespassory fraudulent conversion of property *entrusted*[32] has been fairly well covered in most jurisdictions. It is possible, however, for possession to be acquired lawfully without the element of trust, as where a finder of lost property takes possession of it for the purpose of returning it to the owner, or where an overpayment is inadvertently made and innocently received. Until recently the fraudulent conversion by such a possessor is still not covered by the criminal law.[33] On the other hand some of the statutes, as interpreted, have been held to cover at least part of this field. Thus in one case a finder who fraudulently appropriated a lost chattel after he had acquired lawful possession was held guilty of embezzlement because he became a "self-imposed" bailee.[34] One suggestion has been a statute to this effect:

Embezzlement is the fraudulent conversion by a bailee of money or goods held by him in bailment, or by a trustee of any funds or property held by him in trust. For the purpose of this statute a "bailment" denotes the possession of money or goods, rightful as between the parties to the bailment, by one not its owner;[35] and a "trustee" includes one holding the title to property in trust for another, whether commonly denominated "trustee," "agent," "broker," "factor," "attorney" or otherwise, if the property is held by him in a fiduciary relation.[36]

---

30. It "was enacted in 1857 that if upon a trial for embezzlement or theft the accused appeared to have committed either theft or embezzlement he should not be entitled to an acquittal. This was repealed and reenacted with some additions by 24 & 25 Vic. c. 96, § 72." 3 Stephen, History of the Criminal Law of England 153 (1883).

31. For example, the original English statute included the phrase "by virtue of his employment" which was later eliminated. Ibid. For a case in which the prosecution had been frustrated by this phrase see Rex v. Snowley, 4 Car. & P. 390, 172 Eng.Rep. 753 (1830).

32. "Underlying the crime of embezzlement is an intentional breach of trust." State v. Leeman, 119 Ariz. 459, 581 P.2d 693, 696 (1978).

33. It was held, for example, that the excess of an overpayment was not delivered in bailment and would not support a conviction of the crime of fraudulent conversion of property received as bailee. Fulcher v. State, 32 Tex.Cr.R. 621, 25 S.W. 625 (1894).

34. Neal v. State, 55 Fla. 140, 46 So. 845 (1908). This part of the field is sometimes covered by a special statute. E.g., West's Ann.Cal.Pen.Code § 485 (1970).

35. This is the definition given in the Restatement of Security § 1, comment f (1941), except that as the topic dealt with there is "pledges" the definition uses "chattel" rather than "money or goods."

36. See Amidon v. State, 565 P.2d 1248 (Alaska 1977) for distinction between embezzlement by a bailee and embezzlement by a trustee.

This eliminates the requirement of trust, or even of delivery. It would include within this statutory offense every case in which all the elements of larceny are present except that the possession was acquired without trespass. It would permit a definition in this form:

"Embezzlement is the fraudulent conversion of the personal property of another by one whose original acquisition did not involve a trespassory taking thereof." [37]

A bailee who offered to sell the bailed chattel, took the prospective purchaser to the truck in which it was being transported, where he exhibited the chattel in the effort to consummate the deal, was guilty of embezzlement although no sale was made and the chattel had not been moved. He had exercised dominion over it for the purpose of sale.[38]

D. THE ELEMENTS

Since the whole purpose of embezzlement is to proscribe certain conduct not involving trespass, it is obvious that three of the elements of larceny are not involved. They are (1) the taking (2) by trespass and (3) carrying away. For these there is substituted the requirement of fraudulent conversion.

1. FRAUDULENT

The element of embezzlement designated by "fraudulent" is the equivalent of the intent-to-steal element of larceny. It is possible that, if there had never been any doubt of the propriety of using "stolen" in this connection, the definition of embezzlement might have been in terms of "conversion with intent to steal." In a general way that is the usual plan of the new penal codes.[39] And cases involving problems related to the mental element of larceny are dealt with in the same way as in larceny cases. Thus retention by the creditor of funds belonging to the debtor, in payment of the debt, is not embezzlement,[40] unless made so by some unusual statute.[41] And in the absence of such a provision it is not embezzlement for an agent to

---

37. "[E]mbezzlement is '. . . the fraudulent appropriation of property by a person to whom such property has been entrusted, or into whose hands it has lawfully come.'" United States v. Pintar, 630 F.2d 1270, 1282, n. 15 (8th Cir.1980).

Under the new code the statute on theft includes embezzlement, but the distinction between larceny and embezzlement is retained. State v. Dorman, 30 Wn.App. 351, 633 P.2d 1340 (1981).

38. United States v. Faulkner, 638 F.2d 129 (9th Cir.1981).

39. Almost without exception the new codes do not provide for embezzlement as a separate offense, but include it in a consolidated offense with larceny and other crimes. The mental element is the same for all and may be in terms as an intent to deprive the owner. With "the intent to deprive the other thereof." Iowa Criminal Code § 714.1 (1978). The

mental element of theft under the statute is "with the purpose of depriving the owner thereof." Smith v. State, 264 Ark. 874, 575 S.W.2d 677 (1979).

Theft by exerting unauthorized control, Rev.Code Wash. 9A.56–010(7) (1977), includes what was embezzlement under prior law. State v. Dorman, 30 Wn.App. 351, 633 P.2d 1340 (1981).

40. Singer v. State, 195 Ark. 345, 112 S.W.2d 426 (1938); Lewis v. People, 99 Colo. 102, 60 P.2d 1089 (1936).

41. People v. Ranney, 123 Cal.App. 403, 11 P.2d 405 (1932); State v. Cochrane, 51 Idaho 521, 6 P.2d 489 (1931).

The federal statute on conversion by a United States Marshal, or other officer of the court, of money coming into his hands by virtue of his official relation, provides: "It shall not be a defense that the accused person had any interest in such moneys or fund," 18 U.S.C.A. § 645.

withhold money from his principal to pay a claim which he in good faith believes is due him even if it is not due in fact.[42] Such a withholding constitutes a conversion of his principal's money, but because of the good faith belief it is not fraudulent. And an agent who converts money belonging to his principal is not guilty of embezzlement if he honestly believes he is entitled to it as a commission.[43] But an intent to deal with the principal's property in such a way as to create a substantial risk of permanent loss, is fraudulent.[44]

2. CONVERSION

Conversion is the unique element of embezzlement,[45] and conversion of the property of another by one having lawful possession requires some affirmative act which is grossly antagonistic to the rights of the owner, or in violation of the express terms of a bailment.[46] The fact that the return of borrowed property is long overdue does not constitute conversion. In one case, for example, one who had borrowed a shotgun on his promise to return it the same day, had not returned it eight months later. He was held not guilty of embezzlement because there had been no demand for its return, or any evidence that he had sold, secreted or otherwise disposed of it. In other words there was no evidence, direct or circumstantial, to show that he had ceased to be a borrower and had become a converter.[47]

In the absence of a special statutory requirement of a formal demand,[48] no demand for the delivery of the property is needed if there is positive evidence of conversion. As said in one case: "A demand, followed by a refusal if the other essential facts exist, is evidence of embezzlement, and sometimes indispensable evidence of it, but it is the fraudulent and felonious conversion of the money or other property that constitutes the offense, and that may often be proved without a demand."[49] But unless the possessor has dealt with the property in some such way as to sell it, pledge it, give it away, secrete it, destroy it, consume it or otherwise dispose of it, an unsuccessful demand for the return of the property may be needed to establish a conversion. And even such an unsuccessful demand will not establish conversion if there is some adequate explanation, as where one entrusted with property had it taken from him at gun-point by robbers.[50] One may be able to "account for" what he is unable to deliver.

42. State v. Lanyon, 83 Conn. 449, 76 A. 1095 (1910); Brown v. State, 92 Fla. 538, 109 So. 438 (1926); State v. Hurley, 234 S.W. 820 (Mo.1921).

43. Lewis v. People, 99 Colo. 102, 60 P.2d 1089 (1936).

44. State v. Pratt, 114 Kan. 660, 220 P. 505 (1923).

45. Needless to say there is a conversion of the stolen property in every larceny, but conversion is not an element of that offense because it is only when the conversion takes the form of a taking by trespass and carrying away that common-law larceny is possible.

46. Restatement, Second, Torts §§ 223, 227, 228 (1965). If a diamond ring was pledged to secure a debt with the agreement that it would be kept under lock and key until redeemed, it would be a conversion for the pledgee to wear the ring. Restatement, Security § 22 (1941). But the wearing would not be embezzlement because it would not be fraudulent.

47. State v. Britt, 278 Mo. 510, 213 S.W. 425 (1919).

48. People, for the use of Dime Savings & Trust Co. v. Birkett, 254 Ill.App. 96, 103–4 (1929).

49. People v. Ward, 134 Cal. 301, 304, 66 P. 372, 373 (1901).

50. State v. McGuire, 107 Mont. 341, 88 P.2d 35 (1935).

In a general way it may be said that any unauthorized disposition of goods belonging to another, as if they were one's own, is a conversion thereof.[51] Statutes sometimes speak in terms of conversion "to one's own use" but this has not been narrowly construed. Thus embezzlement may be committed not only by depositing money of another in one's own bank account for use as such,[52] but also by wrongfully taking money from one transaction and transferring it to conceal a shortage in another,[53] or by the officer of a corporation mingling money of another with corporate funds.[54] And whenever there is a conversion, which is fraudulent, embezzlement has been committed if the other elements of the offense are present.

3. PROPERTY

As embezzlement was the result of a legislative effort to fill a gap in the law of larceny, the early statutes applied only to such property as was the subject of larceny. Thus at the time when a dog was regarded as a "base" animal and not the subject of larceny, the fraudulent conversion of another's dog would not have been embezzlement.[55] On the other hand, as in larceny, so in embezzlement, it is no defense that the property converted was held unlawfully,[56] or was acquired by unlawful means.[57] And it is embezzlement to convert property handed to a bailee for an unlawful purpose.[58] As in larceny, the property must have value, and the conversion of a void warrant was held not to be embezzlement because such a warrant has no value.[59] But any legally-recognized value will do here as in larceny, and value has little significance except to determine whether the offense is felony or misdemeanor.[60]

Broadening of the field of larceny to include tangible personal property in general has resulted in a corresponding broadening of the scope of embezzlement, and in recent times "property," as an element of embezzlement, has been enlarged to include much that cannot be taken by trespass and carried away. At times the general wording of an embezzlement statute has been held to include real estate.[61] And embezzlement statutes very generally in-

---

51. State v. Howard, 222 N.C. 291, 22 S.E.2d 917 (1942); State v. Bickford, 28 N.D. 36, 147 N.W. 407 (1914).

52. People v. Schnepp, 362 Ill. 495, 200 N.E. 338 (1936).

53. State v. Doolittle, 153 Kan. 608, 113 P.2d 94 (1941).

54. Milbrath v. State, 138 Wis. 354, 120 N.W. 252 (1909).

55. This was held under another statute intended to fill a gap in the law of larceny. Obtaining another's dog by false representations was held not to be false pretenses. Regina v. Robinson, Bell, C.C. 34, 169 Eng.Rep. 1156 (1859).

56. Commonwealth v. Smith, 129 Mass. 104 (1880).

57. State v. Patterson, 66 Kan. 447, 71 P. 860 (1903); McCue v. Smith, 124 Tex.Cr. 624, 65 S.W.2d 314 (1933). Failure of the corporation to have a permit authorizing the sale of bonds was no de-

fense to a charge of embezzling such bonds.

58. Commonwealth v. Cooper, 130 Mass. 285 (1880).

59. People v. Hayes, 365 Ill. 318, 6 N.E.2d 645 (1937). It was said *obiter* in one case that a telegraphic message was not the subject of embezzlement because it has no "intrinsic value." Primrose v. Western Union Telegraph Co., 154 U.S. 1, 14, 14 S.Ct. 1098, 1101 (1894). The suggestion that "intrinsic value" is essential is clearly unsound.

60. A jury verdict of guilty of embezzlement, although failing to find the value of the property, was not inadequate to support judgment and sentence. Hatheway v. State, 623 P.2d 741 (Wyo. 1981).

61. People v. Roland, 134 Cal.App. 675, 26 P.2d 517 (1933).

clude a trustee as one who may be guilty of the crime. A trustee has title to the property which he holds for the benefit of the beneficiary. This is important because while larceny is an offense against possession, embezzlement is an offense against title or ownership.[62]

A trust estate frequently includes real property, and may have intangible property, such as a bank account. While real property and the claim against the bank cannot be taken by trespass and carried away, they can be transferred.[63] And the trustee, having title, has the power to transfer it away so that the property will be lost to the beneficiary. The title of the trustee is a restricted title, held only for the purpose of the trust, and the beneficial ownership is in the one for whom the property is held. Hence a fraudulent conversion by the trustee is embezzlement.[64] Furthermore an agent may have power to transfer real estate belonging to his principal, or may have authority to draw checks upon his principal's bank account. Some courts have had difficulty in cases in which any such power or authority has been exercised on the ground that the wrongdoer did not have possession of the property converted.[65] This is the result of a mistake because embezzlement, being an offense against title, is not concerned with possession other than to find the absence of trespass, which would make the offense larceny.

While the courts have moved somewhat timidly in this area,[66] progress has been made.[67] The Model Penal Code, using "theft" to include embezzlement, provides: "A person is guilty of theft if he unlawfully transfers immovable property of another or any interest therein with purpose to benefit himself or another not entitled thereto."[68] And while this has seldom been copied verbatim in the new penal codes, it has influenced the drafting thereof. It should be held that if a trustee, or agent, or anyone in like position, in exercising a power or authority granted, conveys away property, personal or real, movable or immovable, and thereby deprives his beneficiary, or his principal or another, of his property, or any interest therein, thereby commits embezzlement if it is done fraudulently. Such an act is a fraudulent conversion of property, and the trend, aided by the wording of the new penal codes, is in this direction.

62. As so used anyone having a claim to the property which is superior to that of the one in possession has "title." Thus if the finder of lost property should hand it over for safekeeping while trying to locate the owner, the finder would have "title" as between himself and his bailee. And in the case of a trustee, the beneficiary has the beneficial ownership, and hence as between him and the trustee the beneficiary is the "owner."

63. It is only in some such case that the "title" can be taken from the "owner." The ordinary embezzler does not deprive the owner of title in the legal sense. He commits an offense against title because his misconduct tends to make the title worthless, as in cases in which the property has disappeared or ceased to exist.

64. Pilger v. State, 120 Neb. 584, 234 N.W. 403 (1931).

65. See Note, 88 A.L.R.2d 688 (1963).

66. State v. Tauscher, 227 Or. 1, 360 P.2d 764 (1961).

67. Simmons v. State, 165 Miss. 732, 141 So. 288 (1932); State v. Lockie, 43 Idaho 580, 253 P. 618 (1927); State v. Krug, 12 Wash. 288, 41 P. 126 (1895); State v. Peterson, 167 Minn. 216, 208 N.W. 761 (1926).

The assistant director of the city general services department who converted to his own use the services of trainees under a Comprehensive Employment and Training Act, was guilty of embezzlement of "property" that was the subject of a grant within the meaning of the statute. United States v. Coleman, 590 F.2d 228 (7th Cir. 1978).

68. Section 223.2(2).

4. OF ANOTHER

It is possible for the law to proscribe certain conduct in the way one deals with his own property, as in statutes on cruelty to animals,[69] but the purpose of embezzlement was to provide a penalty for certain misconduct in dealing with the property of another. As in larceny there has been a shift away from the original position in regard to co-ownership, and the prevailing view is that despite one's own part ownership he can be guilty of embezzlement by a fraudulent conversion of the property interest of the co-owner,[70] but there is no such thing as embezzlement by the sole owner. For example in the familiar phrase "borrow money" the word "borrow" is misused. This is a purchase of money by the promise to pay for it later, just as one may purchase a chattel on the promise to pay for it later. The fact that the price is fixed in terms of principal and interest is unimportant. That is what it costs to buy money. While spending money is a typical method of conversion, if it is the money of another, spending money by the so-called "borrower" is not conversion because he is spending his own money. And if he is unable to pay the so-called "lender" this is no different than any other situation in which a debtor is unable to pay his creditor.[71] Consider the baker who "borrows" 100 pounds of flour with the understanding that he is to use it in his business this week and "return" 100 pounds of like flour next week. This also is a purchase. Technically it is barter—the trade of goods for goods without use of money—but in the broad sense it is a purchase. The "borrower" could not commit embezzlement of this flour because it is his property. No one else has any property interest in it.

"On retrial, however, the jury should be carefully instructed that a mere purchase and sale of goods in the absence of earmarked or escrowed funds is not an intrustment within the meaning of the statute on embezzlement."[72]

E. EMBEZZLEMENT BY PUBLIC OFFICERS

The general statutes on embezzlement, as interpreted, ordinarily include all the elements of larceny other than the trespassory taking of possession. Hence they include the *animus furandi* or intent to deprive the other of his property. A mere unauthorized use by a bailee or wilful delay in returning the property will not of itself constitute this offense. There must be an intent to deprive the other of his property entirely. In fact, in statutes having the rather common provision, "whoever embezzles or fraudulently converts to his own use," the "or" clause is to be understood as explanatory rather than additional, because the word "embezzle" means to convert fraudulently to one's own use.

In addition to the general enactments on embezzlement, however, a number of states have sections in the chapter entitled "embezzlement" which provide a penalty for certain misconduct without a requirement that the wrongdoer shall "embezzle or fraudulently convert the property." One of

---

69. E.g. Iowa Criminal Code § 717.2 (1978). Compare "any domestic animal" in this section with "any animal of another" in the preceding section.

70. The language of most of the new penal codes would include such a conversion.

71. Commonwealth v. Stahl, 183 Pa. Super. 49, 127 A.2d 786 (1956).

72. Government of Virgin Islands v. Richards, 618 F.2d 242, 245–46 (3d Cir. 1980).

the most common of these, usually called "embezzlement by public officers," is broad enough to authorize the conviction of a public officer who has occasioned the loss of public money or property by keeping it in some place other than that required by law.[73] Many of the states have special statutes dealing with embezzlement by bank officers or employees, and some of these provide penalties for certain types of conduct resulting in the loss of funds or deposits even when there has been no actual intent to deprive the owner of his property.

Such offenses are quite in keeping with our general scheme of social discipline. It is quite proper, for example, to require a public officer having charge of large amounts of public funds, such as a state treasurer or a county treasurer, to keep such funds in a vault or safe provided for that purpose or in some bank legally designated as a depository of public funds. It is also proper to impose a penalty upon such an officer who occasions the loss of public funds by keeping them in some place other than that required by law, even if he did not intend or expect any such loss to result, or who endangers the funds by any unauthorized use thereof.[74] In one case, for example, the state superintendent of banks used public funds to redeem certain personal securities he had pledged. He sold the securities and replaced the "borrowed" money out of the proceeds. Although the replacement was before his use of the funds was known, he was held to have violated the statute.[75] If, as is quite possible, his intent was to replace the money promptly from the proceeds of securities redeemed, which were quite adequate for this purpose, his act although wrongful was without *animus furandi*. But the court emphasized that the purpose of the statute was to prevent public officers from using public funds in any manner or for any purpose not expressly authorized by law.

Such an offense is quite different from ordinary embezzlement. It is unfortunate that the statutes use this word in the sections dealing with this special offense,—and some do not do so.[76] This is not one of the "predatory offenses." It should have a separate classification and a milder penalty.[77]

Needless to add, the fact that one is a public officer does not exclude him from the field of ordinary embezzlement.[78] If he fraudulently appropriates

---

73. E.g., Miss. Code 1972, § 97–11–29. Under the statute referring to embezzlement of public funds, one who uses public funds in his possession or control in any manner or for any purpose not expressly authorized by law, is guilty. Tidd v. State, 42 Ohio App. 66, 181 N.E. 280 (1932). Intent to defraud is not an element of the crime of embezzlement by converting public funds. People v. Cahill, 208 Or. 538, 293 P.2d 169 (1956).

74. It is not necessary that there be a fraudulent appropriation of funds by public officers. Any unauthorized use is sufficient. Hutchman v. State, 61 Okl. Cr. 117, 66 P.2d 99 (1937).

75. State v. Baxter, 89 Ohio St. 269, 104 N.E. 331 (1914).

76. E.g., West's Ann.Cal.Pen.Code § 425 (1970).

77. Compare the section cited in the preceding note with § 424 of the same code. Some states seem to have overlooked the fact that such a section includes conduct much less antisocial in its nature than ordinary embezzlement, and have applied a severe penalty. Some states have set this class of crimes apart from the general law of theft and given them special treatment. E.g. Idaho Code §§ 18–5701—5704 (1972).

78. A public officer who embezzles public money may be prosecuted under the general statute on embezzlement. But he may be prosecuted under the special statute if he uses public funds in a manner forbidden by law, even if he has no fraudulent intent when he does so. People v. Dillon, 199 Cal. 1, 248 P. 230 (1926).

public money to his own use he should be punished as severely as any other embezzler, and perhaps should suffer an even greater penalty by reason of the peculiar nature of his trust. It is only when he has violated the statute without fraudulent appropriation that the milder penalty is indicated.

Any discussion of this subject should take notice of the fact that the phrase "embezzlement by public officers" does not have a uniform meaning throughout all the statutes. In fact there are three different possibilities. (1) It may be used as the name of a special offense intended to apply a penalty for the unauthorized use of public funds by a public officer even in the absence of a fraudulent appropriation by him. (2) It may indicate only one of the general embezzlement sections, being a carry-over from the days when the field was being covered piecemeal—applying first to one special class of persons and then another. (3) It may be a special embezzlement statute intended to apply an added penalty to the fraudulent conversion of funds by a public officer because of the special nature of the trust imposed upon him. Only the first of these, which is not embezzlement proper, is within the scope of this subsection.

Intentionally putting public money to a use not intended by the state is sufficient for conviction of embezzlement of public money.[79]

SECTION 4.   FALSE PRETENSES

The crime which is usually called "false pretenses" was unknown to the common law of England but was made a misdemeanor under a statute old enough to be common law in this country. Under modern American statutes it is usually either a felony or a misdemeanor depending upon the value of the property.

According to the theory of the English common law, as explained in the introduction to this chapter, the wrongful act of obtaining title to another's property by fraud was held not to constitute a crime but merely to give rise to a civil action. An exception was recognized in case of what came to be known as a common-law cheat. If a swindle was perpetrated by means of some false token, such as a false weight or measure, this was indictable as a misdemeanor.[1] But a swindle perpetrated without the use of such a token was not indictable even if it involved fraudulent misrepresentations of fact which were extreme and which deceived another into parting with the title to his chattel. An effort to explore the boundaries of the common-law cheat [2] would serve no useful purpose here because it has been swallowed entirely by the present law of false pretenses. It is mentioned only to explain why it was impossible to incorporate the common-law cheat and the corresponding nonindictable cheats into the common law of larceny. In the discussion of larceny [3] it was pointed out that, if the other elements of the offense are satisfied, a wrongdoer is guilty of larceny if by fraud he obtains possession only of his victim's property, but is not guilty of larceny if he obtains title as well as possession.[4] This strange legal position was explained as having been caused by the peculiar developmental background of the law, and hav-

79. People v. Skrbek, 42 Colo.App. 431, 599 P.2d 272 (1979).

1. 4 Bl.Comm. *157.

2. They are considered in detail in 2 Bishop, New Criminal Law c. X (8th ed. 1892).

3. Section 1, D, 1.

4. See also People v. Noblett, 244 N.Y. 355, 359–60, 155 N.E. 670, 671 (1927).

ing resulted in legislation intended to prevent any part of such misconduct from remaining beyond the reach of punishment.

The original English statute on this subject was enacted in 1757.[5] It seems to have been generally accepted in the Colonies and is to be regarded as a part of our common law,[6] although this is hardly more than of academic interest today because it has been superseded by statutes of our own. But while many of these statutes have gone beyond the English enactment, and some of them very much beyond it, our study should begin with that original Act because it gives us the main structure of the modern law of false pretenses. It provided that—

> **"All persons who knowingly and designedly, by false pretence or pretences, shall obtain from any person or persons, money, goods, wares or merchandizes, with intent to cheat or defraud any person or persons of the same . . . shall be . . . fined and imprisoned, or . . . be put in the pillory, or publickly whipped, or . . . transported . . . for the term of seven years . . .."**

In general, as well explained by Bishop,[7] "this offence is constituted whenever one to defraud another states to him as fact what he knows to be untrue, for the purpose of procuring from him some valuable thing within the terms of the statute; whereupon the other, believing the untruth and under the influence thereof, delivers or otherwise transfers the thing to the defrauder."

The statutes of the various states, while by no means uniform, have enough in common to suggest the following definition:

> **The crime of false pretenses is knowingly and designedly obtaining the property of another by means of untrue representations of fact with intent to defraud.**

A. THE SUBJECT OF FALSE PRETENSES

As the statute creating the crime of false pretenses was a legislative effort to fill a gap in the law of larceny it has generally been held to apply to the obtaining of only such property as is the subject of larceny, unless other property is expressly included by statute. Thus, at a time when dog-stealing was not larceny it was held not false pretenses to obtain another's dog by fraudulent representations.[8] The broadening of the field of larceny in this respect has enlarged the scope of false pretenses until now practically any chattel which has any value whatever may be the subject of either crime. Except where the false pretenses statute has itself been enlarged it applies only to "personal movable things."[9] Since there could be no common-law larceny of real estate, the obtaining of the title to land by fraudulent misrep-

---

5. 30 Geo. II, c. 24, § 1 (1757).

6. See, for example, State v. McMahon, 49 R.I. 107, 108, 140 A. 359, 360 (1928), which expressly states that this statute is common law in Rhode Island; and Durland v. United States, 161 U.S. 306, 312, 16 S.Ct. 508, 510 (1896), in which it is assumed to be common law in this country without express reference.

7. 2 Bishop, New Criminal Law § 414 (8th ed. 1892).

8. Regina v. Robinson, Bell, C.C. 34, 169 Eng.Rep. 1156 (1859).

9. State v. Miller, 192 Or. 188, 195, 233 P.2d 786, 790 (1951).

resentations does not constitute false pretenses [10] unless this has been added by an amendment to the statute,[11] which has been rather common.

"False pretenses" is a short title for "obtaining property by false pretenses," and hence this offense is not committed unless it results in the obtainment of "property." This includes real estate and intangible property if expressly included in the statute, as is not uncommon. It does not include the fraudulent obtaining of lodging,[12] for example, without something more. This might be held to be included under some general term, such as "any thing of value," and will certainly be included under the term "services" found in some of the new penal codes.[13] Such a term includes, among other services, accommodations in motels, hotels, restaurants or elsewhere, admissions to exhibitions or entertainments, computer services, and the supplying of equipment for use, sometimes so expressed in the statute.[14]

1. OTHER CHEATS

It has been very common to provide statutory penalties for various cheats *other than false pretenses proper*, such as (1) obtaining food, lodging or other accommodation at a hotel, inn, or boarding or eating house with intent to defraud; (2) the fraudulent suppression or destruction of a will; (3) conveyances with intent to defraud creditors; (4) the fraudulent use of false warehouse receipts or false bills of lading; (5) the fraudulent counterfeiting of another's mark, stamp or brand; (6) fraudulent advertisements; (7) false and fraudulent entries in corporation books; (8) removal of a mortgaged chattel from the state (or sometimes from the county) without the consent (usually required to be in writing) of the mortgagee; (9) unauthorized wearing of badge or garb of a secret society with intent to deceive; (10) circulation of false rumors as to stocks and bonds with intent to affect the market price; (11) the fraudulent sale of poppies, forget-me-nots, flags and other articles which are purportedly sold for patriotic purposes, but actually for personal profit; or (12) use of slugs in slot machines. This list is illustrative rather than exhaustive. While a particular state may not include them all, it will have a number of these (and perhaps others not mentioned here) in addition to the statute on false pretenses proper.[15] Part of such coverage may now be included in some of the new penal codes as false pretenses proper, as

10. People v. Cummings, 114 Cal. 437, 46 P. 284 (1896).

11. People v. Rabe, 202 Cal. 409, 261 P. 303 (1927).

12. Rex v. Bagley, 17 Cr.App. 162 (1923). And see State v. Miller, 192 Or. 188, 193, 233 P.2d 786, 789 (1951).

13. See for example the codes of Alabama, Arkansas, Connecticut, Georgia, Hawaii, Illinois, Kansas, Maine, New Hampshire, North Dakota, Pennsylvania, Texas, Utah and Washington.

14. E.g., Code of Alabama § 3210(2) (1975); Utah Code Ann. 1953 § 76–6–409.

15. The Idaho Code has a chapter entitled "False Pretenses, Cheats and Misrepresentations." Idaho Code chap. 31 (1979). The section on false pretenses is § 18–3101. The other sections in the chapter include many of the additional offenses mentioned in the text together with some others. The penalties differ from section to section.

The Montana Code contains a general theft provision which includes theft by deception, Rev.Code Mont. 1947, § 94–6–302. The same part of the Code also contains sections on other deceptive practices, §§ 94–6–307—308.1.

mentioned above; and part may be under some other designation, such as "fraudulent practices." [16]

In many states the false-pretenses section itself is expressly worded to include the act of designedly, by false pretense, and with intent to defraud, obtaining the signature of any person to any written instrument the false making of which would be punished as forgery.[17]

B. UNTRUE REPRESENTATION OF FACT

1. UNTRUE

The starting point in the search for guilt of false pretenses is a misrepresentation. The representation must have been untrue as a matter of fact.[18] A representation which corresponds to the actual fact is not untrue even if believed to be false.[19] Hence one who intends to perpetrate a swindle may be saved from guilt of this offense because of his own mistake of fact. He may purchase for a small sum what is supposed to be a *reproduction* of a fine painting and sell it at a high price by representing it to be the work of Grant Wood, for example. However fraudulent his intent he is not guilty of false pretenses if it should happen that this really is a genuine painting by that artist. Moreover if the representation, although false when made, becomes true before anything is obtained in reliance thereon, the crime is not committed.[20]

2. REPRESENTATION

As one purpose of this legislation is to extend the field of punishable frauds beyond the boundaries of the common-law cheat, it is clear that nothing in the nature of a false token is required for guilt.[21] The representation is not even required to be in writing;[22] a spoken lie is sufficient for convic-

---

16. As for example in the Iowa Criminal Code (1978). § 714.1 deals with theft, a consolidated offense including false pretenses. Subdivision 3 includes the deceptive obtainment of "the labor or services of another, . . ." § 714.8 deals with fraudulent practices, in ten subdivisions.

17. As to the form of the charge in such a case see Pettijohn v. State, 148 Neb. 336, 227 N.W. 380 (1947).

18. Drought v. State, 101 Ga. 544, 28 S.E. 1013 (1897); State v. Bratton, 56 Mont. 563, 186 P. 327 (1919); State v. Hale, 129 Mont. 449, 291 P.2d 229 (1955).

To constitute the crime of false pretenses there must be a "statement or pretense that some existing or past material fact is true when in fact it is false." Rowland v. Commonwealth, 487 S.W.2d 682 (Ky.1972).

19. Fox v. State, 102 Ark. 451, 145 S.W. 228 (1912); State v. Asher, 50 Ark. 427, 8 S.W. 177 (1887).

20. State v. Hendon, 170 La. 488, 128 So. 286 (1930).

21. Young v. The King, 3 Durn. & E. 98 (1879); Speer v. State, 50 Tex.Cr.R. 273, 97 S.W. 469 (1906). **D,** in presenting a bill, listed as one item $500 for the purchase of 4,000 feet of concrete tile pipe whereas only $400 had been paid, and received payment accordingly. This was held to be a false representation of fact. Dixon v. State, 152 Tex.Cr.R. 504, 215 S.W.2d 181 (1948).

22. Some states have enacted statutes providing for special standards of proof for false pretense cases:

"Upon a trial for having obtained, with an intent to cheat or defraud another designedly by any false pretense, the signature of any person to a written instrument, or from any person any money,

tion of false pretenses if the other elements of the crime are present. In fact the crime can be committed without an express statement either written or oral.[23] "Actions speak louder than words," and one who purported to sell a bushel of potatoes, collecting for that quantity while actually delivering less because of a short measure used in the sale, was guilty even before the statute. Any words, devices or conduct, employed with intent to deceive, and which do deceive, are sufficient to satisfy this requirement.[24] As pointed out by an English judge in an interesting case,[25] if a wrongdoer should pretend to be a college student by wearing clothing peculiar to the students of a particular college, and should obtain goods on credit because of the belief that he was a student, when in fact he was not, and should take them with intent to defraud the seller, he would be guilty of this offense even if he did not *say* he was a member of the college.[26]

A false personation, it may be added, is a representation and the crime of false pretenses may be committed in this manner even if the deception is accomplished entirely by means other than words. For false pretenses proper it is essential that property be obtained by this type of misrepresentation, the same as by any other.[27] In a leading case [28] Button, a very good runner,

---

personal property or valuable thing, the defendant shall not be convicted, if the false pretense was expressed in language, unaccompanied by a false token or writing, unless the pretense or some note or memorandum thereof is in writing, subscribed by or in the handwriting of the defendant, or unless the pretense is proved by the testimony of two witnesses, or that of one witness and corroborating circumstances; but this section shall not apply to a prosecution for falsely representing or personating another, and in such assumed character marrying, or receiving any money or property." Utah Code Ann., 1973, § 77–31–17.

23. People v. Carpenter, 141 Cal.App. 2d 884, 297 P.2d 498 (1956). "Where one intentionally creates a belief as to an existing fact which is false, and with intent to defraud another of his property, and does so, it cannot matter whether the erroneous belief was induced by words or acts, or both. The mischief may be done as effectually by one method as by another." Lee v. Commonwealth, 242 S.W. 2d 984, 986 (Ky.1951). "Verbal assertions or direct representation are not required to show a false pretense or representation. Such may be shown by the conduct and acts of the party." Dixon v. State, 152 Tex.Cr.R. 504, 505, 215 S.W.2d 181, 182 (1948).

During the open season D sold to X 2,000 muskrat hides which had been obtained earlier during the closed season and hence were contraband. A conviction of false pretenses was affirmed al-

though D made no statement as to when the animals were trapped. The court held that D's offer to sell included an implied representation that they were lawful furs which he had a right to sell. State v. Hastings, 77 N.D. 146, 41 N.W.2d 305 (1950).

24. "The false pretense may consist in any act, word, symbol, or token calculated and intended to deceive. It may be either express or implied from words or conduct." People v. Randono, 32 Cal. App.3d 164, 108 Cal.Rptr. 326, 332 (1973).

25. Rex v. Barnard, 7 Car. & P. 784 (1837).

26. The same result is reached in larceny cases. For example, D, when purchasing wheat, obtained 39 bushels more than he paid for by wrongfully manipulating the automatic scale used to deliver the grain into his truck. A conviction of larceny by fraud was upheld. Hagan v. State, 76 Okl.Cr. 127, 134 P.2d 1042 (1943).

27. It is sometimes found in a separate section in the code. See West's Ann. Cal.Pen.Code § 530 (1970).

Sheker was eager to locate a person who was a witness against him in a state prosecution. In this effort he pretended to be an agent of the Internal Revenue Service. He was convicted of impersonating a federal agent to obtain "a thing of value," in violation of 18 U.S.C.A. § 912. The conviction was affirmed on the ground that information can be a thing of value for the purposes of the

---

28. See note 28 on page 368.

entered a race under the name of Sims who was only a moderate performer, and by this deception was given a start of eleven yards in a 120-yard race. With this advantage Button won the race and claimed the prize which was worth ten guineas. The suspicion of the handicapper was aroused and the prize was withheld. Since Button obtained nothing by this deception the charge was attempting to obtain goods by false pretenses, and a conviction of this offense was upheld. It was pointed out that he would not have been guilty had his deception been only "for a lark" and with no intention of claiming the prize.

It should be emphasized that special provision may be made for certain types of false personation that do not come under the general section dealing with obtaining property by false pretenses. For example, a penalty may be provided for one who by false personation (1) marries or pretends to marry another; [29] (2) becomes bail or surety in any undertaking; (3) verifies, publishes, acknowledges, or proves a written instrument for the purpose of having it recorded; or (4) does any other act for the purpose of benefitting himself, or of a nature likely to subject the one impersonated to suit or prosecution.[30] Others might be mentioned such as obtaining telephone or telegraph service with intent to avoid payment therefor,[31] or impersonating a public officer.[32]

A representation may be made indirectly. A half-truth, for example, may convey an idea that is false. If it is deliberately stated for that purpose, and with intent to defraud, it is fraudulent.[33]

3. OF FACT

Because of the requirement that it be untrue, it is obviously not necessary that the representation *be* a fact, but it must be a representation *of* fact. It must purport to be a fact rather than something else. The boundaries may best be seen by observing what is not a representation *of fact*.

A. OPINION IS NOT

An expression of opinion or belief is not considered to be a representation of fact within the purport of the statute.[34] Hence conviction of this crime cannot be predicated upon the statement that certain real estate is "nicely

statute. United States v. Sheker, 618 F.2d 607 (9th Cir. 1980).

28. Regina v. Button, [1900] 2 Q.B. 597.

Where false impersonation at a driving test resulted in receipt of a certificate in the name of another person, which in turn enabled that other to obtain a driver's license, both were held guilty of false pretenses. Regina v. Potter [1958] All Eng.R. 51.

29. West's Ann.Cal.Pen.Code § 528 (1970).

30. Id. at § 529.

31. Idaho Code § 18–3114 (1972).

32. West's Ann.Cal.Pen.Code § 146a (1976); 18 U.S.C.A. § 912.

33. The following instruction was held to be correct. "A statement or representation may also be 'false' or 'fraudulent' when it constitutes a half-truth, or effectively conceals a material fact, with intent to defraud." United States v. Martino, 648 F.2d 367, 393 (5th Cir. 1981).

34. "The important antithesis is between 'knowledge' and 'opinion' not 'fact' and 'opinion,' since the existence of the opinion is itself a fact. But the form in which an assertion is made is not conclusive. Statements that things are 'good,' 'valuable,' 'large,' or 'strong,' necessarily involve an exercise of individual judgment, and even though made absolutely the hearer must know this; . . ." Restatement, Contracts § 474, comment c. (1932).

located" [35] or that a certain horse is a "beautiful animal." Nor will a statement that the seller *believes* certain property is worth a stated amount meet the requirement for guilt under this statute. Even if the opinion or belief expressed is not genuinely entertained, it is still not sufficient for conviction. Probably the chief difficulty in this regard is the lack of any satisfactory test or measurement. An employee in a noisy boiler factory might think a lot "nicely located" if near his place of employment, while another might have quite a different notion. And ten different people might have ten different notions as to the value of a certain piece of property. A statement that property has produced a certain income during the past year, or that the market review quoted a certain stock or bond as having closed at a certain figure the previous day, is a statement of fact, and will be sufficient to satisfy this part of the requirement.

"Dealer's puffing," so long as it remains in the realm of opinion or belief, will not support a conviction of false pretenses however extravagant the statements.[36] This is regarded as more or less meaningless chatter equivalent to the assertion that a motion picture is *stupendous*. But the phrase "dealer's puffing" will not excuse misrepresentations *of fact*.[37] And conceivably an expression of opinion by one who has or purports to have expert knowledge of the matter might be considered an assertion that such is in fact his expert opinion.[38]

B.   Prediction is Not

Only what exists now or has existed in the past is a *fact*, at least insofar as this term is used in the law. Hence any statement which refers solely to the future is not a representation of *fact*.[39] For a purchaser to secure a quantity of perishable goods at any excessively low figure because of his statement that the goods will probably be damaged unless disposed of at once "for it is going to turn very cold"—or very hot—is unethical if he does not really believe in his own prediction, but it is not considered to be a representation of *fact* within the purport of the statute, and will not sustain a conviction of false pretenses.

35. People v. Jacobs, 35 Mich. 36 (1876).

36. Regina v. Bryan, 7 Cox C.C. 312 (1857).

37. State v. Hefner, 84 N.C. 751 (1881). A landowner's statement of the value of his land is immaterial because it is merely an expression of opinion, but his statement of what he paid for the land is a statement of fact. Bates v. State, 124 Wis. 612, 103 N.W. 251 (1905).

38. "True, the law still recognizes that in bargaining parties will puff their wares in terms which neither side means seriously, and which either so takes at his peril (Vulcan Co. v. Simmons, 248 F. 853 [C.C.A. 2]); but it is no longer law that declarations of value can never be a fraud. Like other words they get their color from their setting, and mean one thing when exchanged among traders,

and another when uttered by a broker to his customer." United States v. Rowe, 56 F.2d 747, 749 (2d Cir. 1932). And see Restatement, Contracts § 474 (1932).

39. Whatley v. State, 249 Ala. 355, 31 So.2d 664 (1947). And see Dillingham v. State, 5 Ohio St. 280, 283 (1855). "The pretense must relate to past events. Any representation or assurance in relation to a future transaction may be a promise or covenant or warranty, but cannot amount to a statutory false pretense." Commonwealth v. Drew, 36 Mass. 179, 185 (1837).

A wilful misrepresentation as to the future, such as that the stock market would increase five-fold in a year, is admissible in evidence to show fraudulent intent. Kerby v. State, 233 Ark. 8, 342 S.W.2d 412 (1961).

To state that the thermometer has been steadily dropping for two hours is a representation of *fact*. It is also a representation of *fact* to say the radio broadcast has just announced a prediction of a sudden drop in the temperature, published by the weather bureau. What the weather bureau said the weather would be in the near future was a prediction, no matter how much scientific fact may have been back of it, but whether or not a certain prediction has been broadcast over the radio is a matter of fact—the broadcast statement is itself a matter of the past whether the prediction it included proves to be correct or not.

Guilt of false pretenses cannot be predicated upon a statement which spoke only of the future, but a prediction fortified by misrepresentations of fact may be sufficient. In such a case the prediction itself is disregarded and the representation of fact alone is relied upon.[40]

C. PROMISE IS NOT

The language of the English statute, quoted above, does not expressly mention or expressly exclude promissory fraud. It speaks in terms of "false pretence or pretences." The headnote added to one of the early cases [41] under the Act says it is no objection that the pretense consists in a representation as of some future transaction, but the case was not one dealing with a mere false promise. Defendants had said that a bet had been made. The bet was on the outcome of a future occurrence but the wager was stated to have been made in the past. Had there been such a wager as that claimed by the defendants they would have been very likely to win it and the victim of the fraud was induced to part with money in the expectation of sharing in this supposedly favorable wager. What seems to have been the first decision involving a false promise pure and simple was *Goodhall*.[42] A conviction of false pretenses was held to be wrong because a mere promise for future conduct "was not a pretence within the meaning of the statute." This conclusion, offered without elaborate explanation,[43] set the pattern that has been followed for the most part ever since. The leading case in this country is *Drew*,[44] although the facts were not limited to a false promise. But in speaking of what is to be considered "a false pretense, within the meaning of the statute," the court said:

"The pretence must relate to past events. Any representation or assurance in relation to a future transaction may be a promise or covenant or warranty, but cannot amount to a statutory false pretense." [45]

---

40. Regina v. Jennison, 9 Cox C.C. 158 (1862).

41. Young v. The King, 3 Durn. & E. 98 (1789).

42. Rex v. Goodhall, Russ. & Ry. 461, 168 Eng.Rep. 898 (1821).

43. See Pearce, Theft by False Promises, 101 U. of Pa.L.Rev. 967 (1953).

44. Commonwealth v. Drew, 36 Mass. 179 (1837).

45. Id. at p. 185.

The buyer's representation that he was getting a loan and would pay for the goods when he received the proceeds "pertained to the future and, even if false and fraudulent, cannot be the basis of a prosecution for cheating and swindling." Elliott v. State, 149 Ga.App. 579, 254 S.E.2d 900, 902 (1979).

A false representation of present intention to perform in the future is not enough to support a conviction of false pretenses because it does not relate to past or present existing fact. United States v. Fulcher, 626 F.2d 985 (D.C.Cir. 1980).

4. INTENT

Although a promise relates unquestionably and solely to the future, "the state of a man's mind is as much a fact as the state of his digestion." [46] Hence there is a distinction between a genuine promise subsequently broken and a *false* promise. A false promise is one made with no intention of performing it. An intent not to perform exists from the first, thus there is really a false representation of fact in a *false* promise. The promisor says, by clearest implication: "It is my present intent to keep this promise." If such is not his intent at the moment there is a misrepresentation of this fact.

The law does not hesitate to take notice of this in certain other regards. Thus a contractual promise made with the undisclosed intention of not performing it is recognized as fraud in a civil case. It will entitle the other party to rescind a contract entered into by him in reliance thereon.[47] A fraudulent misrepresentation of an intent to do or not to do a particular thing will subject the deceiver to tort liability in favor of one harmed by acting in justifiable reliance thereon.[48] Fraudulent promises may be the basis of conviction under the federal mail-fraud statute.[49] They may be relied upon even to establish guilt of common-law larceny. For example, one who secures the possession of a chattel of another by his promise to return it, is guilty of larceny if this was just a trick to gain possession and he intended not to return it, although he made no false statement other than the promise itself.[50]

Since the first enactment of a statute on the subject, however, a false promise has been held "by virtually unanimous authority" [51] not to be sufficient to support a conviction of false pretenses. The judges, in handing down these decisions over this long period of time, have not overlooked the presence of a factual representation of intent in connection with a promise. The insistence has been, not that a false promise could not be recognized as a false pretense for any purpose, but that it does not come within the scope of this phrase as it is used in this statute.

"In the construction of statutes like our own, this further proposition has come to be perfectly established—that the pretense or pretenses relied upon must relate to a past event, or an existing fact; and that any representation or *assurance* in relation to a future transaction, however false or fraudulent it may be, is not, within the meaning of the statute, a false pretense which lays the foundation for a criminal prosecution." [52]

46. Edington v. Fitzmaurice, L.R.Ch. Div. 459, 483 (1885); Restatement, Second, Torts, § 530, comment a (1977).

47. Restatement, Contracts §§ 472, 476 (1932).

48. Restatement, Second, Torts § 530 (1977).

49. Durland v. United States, 161 U.S. 306, 16 S.Ct. 508 (1896).

50. See Fitch v. State, 135 Fla. 361, 366, 185 So. 435, 437–8 (1938).

51. State v. Lamoreaux, 13 N.J.Super. 99, 103, 80 A.2d 213, 214 (1951).

A false promise is not sufficient to support a claim of false pretenses. Ross v. State, 244 Ark. 103, 424 S.W.2d 168 (1968); State v. Hamilton, 6 Kan.App. 646, 631 P.2d 1255, 1259 (1981).

52. Dillingham v. State, 5 Ohio St. 280, 283 (1855).

"This Court has held that the false representation upon which the offense is based must be a present or past fact" and does not include a false promise. State v. Ebner, 126 Ariz. 355, 616 P.2d 30, 35 (1980). This was based upon a transaction which occurred long before October 1, 1978. The result would be dif-

"A misstatement of the state of one's mind is a misstatement of fact upon which an action in fraud and deceit may be predicated (Roberts v. James, 83 N.J.L. 492 (E. & A. 1912)), but by virtually unanimous authority it is not a false pretense exposing one to criminal prosecution under 30 Geo. II, c. 24, and its American counterparts." [53]

In holding that unlawful use of the mails may be committed by posting a fraudulent scheme based upon false promises, the Supreme Court emphasized that the federal statute is not limited to such cases as would come within the definition of false pretenses.[54]   And in upholding a conviction of larceny of one who obtained possession only—not title—with the fraudulent intent at the time to convert what was received, the court intimated that there was not enough to have supported a conviction under the statute of false pretenses, if title had been obtained.[55]

One writer has suggested that interpreting the statute to exclude false promises crept into the decisions by inadvertence, so to speak.[56]   This may be true or it may be that the statute, as interpreted, was as great a step as the social order was prepared to take two hundred years ago.   After all, the change from the punishment of fraud perpetrated by the use of false tokens to the punishment of fraud perpetrated by naked deceit was considerable, even if the latter did not include a misrepresentation of one's own state of mind.   However that may be the original position which has been restated time and again in recent years.[57]   The first clear switch from this to the position that a false promise is sufficient to support a conviction of false pretenses (in recent times and without the aid of statute) seems to have been in California [58] although there was a Massachusetts dictum pointing in the

ferent under the revision of the criminal code that took effect on that date. Id. at page 37.

53.   State v. Lamoreaux, 13 N.J.Super. 99, 103, 80 A.2d 213, 214 (1951).

54.   Durland v. United States, 161 U.S. 306, 16 S.Ct. 508 (1896).

55.   Commonwealth v. Barry, 124 Mass. 325 (1878). "If . . . the offence is that of obtaining property by false pretences, provided the means by which they are acquired are such as, in law, are false pretences. If . . . the offence is larceny." Id. at p. 327.

The crime of larceny by trick does not require misrepresentation of a past or existing fact. And the statute requiring corroboration of false pretenses does not apply to larceny by trick. Lamascus v. State, 516 P.2d 279 (Okl.Cr. 1973).

56.   For a scholarly discussion of the entire problem see Pearce, Theft by False Promises, 101 U. of Pa.L.Rev. 967 (1953).

57.   Chaplin v. United States, 157 F.2d 697 (D.C.Cir.1946); James v. State, 218 Ark. 335, 236 S.W.2d 429 (1951); State v. Robington, 137 Conn. 140, 75 A.2d 394 (1950); State v. Pierson, 47 Del. 397, 91

A.2d 541 (1952); Suggs v. State, 69 Ga. App. 383, 25 S.E.2d 532 (1943); Pierce v. State, 226 Ind. 312, 79 N.E.2d 903 (1948); State v. Lamoreaux, 13 N.J.Super. 99, 80 A.2d 213 (1951); People v. Karp, 298 N.Y. 213, 81 N.E.2d 817 (1948); State v. Singleton, 85 Ohio App. 245, 87 N.E.2d 358 (1949); Hesbrook v. State, 149 Tex. Cr.R. 314, 194 S.W.2d 262 (1946); Ballaine v. District Court, 107 Utah 247, 153 P.2d 265 (1944). And see Frank v. State ex rel. Meiers, 244 Wis. 658, 660–1, 12 N.W.2d 923, 924 (1944). In the Ohio case the defendant was convicted but the court emphasizes that this was under a new statute. "Any representation or assurance in relation to a future transaction is not included" under the general statute on false pretenses. Id. at 256, 87 N.E.2d at 365.

58.   People v. Ashley, 42 Cal.2d 246, 267 P.2d 271 (1954); People v. Weitz, 42 Cal.2d 338, 267 P.2d 295 (1954). Rhode Island seems to have adopted this position from the first. State v. McMahon, 49 R.I. 107, 140 A. 359 (1928).

"We therefore hereby reject any previous position taken by this court that a promise to perform a future act, made with intent not to perform, is not suffi-

same direction.[59] A start has been made toward amending the statute of false pretenses to include promissory fraud within its scope,[60] which is entirely proper. Just as the social order of two hundred years ago had developed to the point where it was necessary to punish the swindler who operated without the aid of false tokens, so today it has developed to the further point where it is necessary to have adequate punishment for promissory fraud, but the change should be by legislative enactment. No court would permit such a statute to apply to a misdeed perpetrated before the act was passed, and for a court to convict a man by changing this interpretation which has been so firmly established for generations it is necessary to violate the principle upon which the *ex post facto* bar is grounded.

If the false promise is accompanied by misrepresentations of fact, conviction may be supported on the latter ground if the other elements of the crime are present.[61] If a man obtains money from a woman upon his promise to marry her, this in itself will not sustain a conviction of false pretenses even if he did not intend to keep the promise when made. But if he was a married man, and this fact was not known or communicated to the woman, he is guilty of false pretenses, if he intended to defraud her, because there was a representation of fact (express or implied) that he was a single man.[62]

THE MODEL PENAL CODE

The Model Penal Code in Section 223.3, Theft by Deception, expressly includes creating false impressions as to "intention or other state of mind."

THE NEW PENAL CODES

Some of the new penal codes have adopted the position of the Model Penal Code, on this point, either by copying its wording [63] or by providing that

cient to support a charge of cheating by false pretenses." State v. West, 252 N.W.2d 457, 461 (Iowa 1977). Accord, Balsamo v. Sheriff, Clark County, 93 Nev. 315, 565 P.2d 650 (1977).

Payment induced by a promise of something to occur in the future did not present a submissible issue of false pretenses. Bakri v. State, 261 Ark. 765, 551 S.W.2d 215 (1977). Accord, Ross v. State, 244 Ark. 103, 424 S.W.2d 168 (1968). "The California Court's departure from the great weight of authority on the point is of interest, but we do not find its reasoning persuasive."

59. "Further, the representations that the moneys contributed were to be invested in this fund were statements of fact as to the intention of those collecting for the fund." Commonwealth v. Green, 326 Mass. 344, 348, 94 N.E.2d 260, 264 (1950). Defendant had falsely represented that there was a fund to which wealthy investors had contributed. This was a misstatement of fact outside of de-

fendant's mind and the dictum was thrown in as an afterthought. The court cites Commonwealth v. Drew as authority for its position.

60. Reissue Neb.Rev.Stat. 1943 § 28–1207; Wis.Stat.Ann. 943.20 (1969). Ohio enacted a separate statute worded differently than the general statute on false pretenses, and held to include promissory fraud. State v. Singleton, 85 Ohio App. 245, 256, 87 N.E.2d 358, 365 (1949). It is also included in the Model Penal Code, Section 223.3.

61. State v. Neal, 350 Mo. 1002, 169 S.W.2d 686 (1943); Carter v. State, 150 Tex.Cr.R. 448, 203 S.W.2d 540 (1947); Frank v. State ex rel. Meiers, 244 Wis. 658, 12 N.W.2d 923 (1944).

62. Regina v. Jennison, 9 Cox C.C. 158 (1862).

63. E.g., Ky.Rev.Stat.Ann. § 434C.1–040 (1969); Me.Rev.Stat.Ann. 17A, § 354 (1964); N.H.Rev.Stat.Ann. § 637:4 (1974); 18 Pa.Const.Stat.Ann. § 3922 (1973).

deception in the theft statute includes a false promise, by name [64] or description.[65] Most of them have no such provision [66] and this leaves a problem of interpretation. Some courts may feel bound by the familiar holding that recodification leaves the preexisting law intact except where a change is manifested. And this may seem to be reinforced if the new code (as many do) follows the Model Penal Code to the extent of consolidating at least larceny, embezzlement and false pretenses into a single crime under the name of "theft," while not following its provision that theft by deception may be committed by creating a false impression as to "intention or other state of mind." It is to be hoped, however, that courts will recognize the need for providing a punishment for the fraudulent obtainment of property by a false promise, and if the new code uses new words in expressing the field (as most do), will find this sufficient for the purpose.

C. OBTAINED BY

1. TITLE OR OWNERSHIP

Unlike larceny which is an offense against possession (in the method of perpetration), false pretenses is an offense against ownership. The distinctive feature of false pretenses is the obtainment of ownership.

Note. In order for money to serve its intended purpose effectively, the rule has developed that in a transaction in which money is received as currency, in good faith, the recipient acquires a clear title thereto whether he receives the money from one who had (1) such title, (2) a defective title, or (3) no title at all. This means that, if necessary, the transaction itself creates a new title which is superior to any previous title. And in the case of a negotiable instrument, such as a negotiable check or bond, the rule is that a person who takes such an instrument as a "holder in due course" also acquires a clear title. This is mentioned to emphasize that the reference to differences in the following discussion assumes that the property involved was other than money or a negotiable instrument.

The victim of either larceny, embezzlement or false pretenses, suffers a total deprivation of the property if it has disappeared and he never succeeds in locating it. It is futile to talk of what rights, if any, he has to the property because it has, as to him, in effect, ceased to exist.

It is quite different if the victim learns where the property is. If the crime was common-law larceny he is entitled to reclaim the property, with the court's aid if necessary. This is true even if he finds it in the hands of an innocent person who paid full value for it in the belief he was buying from the owner. The reason is that while the thief could obtain possession of the property without the knowledge or consent of the owner, he could not obtain title by this method. The property still belongs to the victim. If the crime was false pretenses, on the other hand, the wrongdoer obtained the

---

64. E.g., Conn.Gen.Stat. § 53a–119(3) (1975); McKinney's N.Y.Penal Law Ann. § 155.05 (1975).

65. E.g., Ind.Code Ann. § 35–43–4–1 (Burns) (1979); Minn.Stat.Ann. § 609.-52(2)(b) (1964).

66. E.g., Alabama, Arkansas, Colorado, Delaware, Florida, Georgia, Hawaii, Illinois, Iowa, Kansas, Louisiana, Montana, North Dakota, Ohio, Oregon, Texas, Utah, Virginia and Washington.

title. It is a defective title because of his fraud, and the victim can reclaim his property if he finds it still in the hands of the wrongdoer. But if the property has been sold to a purchaser who paid for it in good faith, the title passed to him free from the original defect and he will prevail in any contest between him and the original owner with reference to this property.

If the crime was embezzlement the result is ordinarily the same in regard to the victim's rights, as if it had been larceny. The bailee had possession but he did not have title and had no power to pass title. But the law of embezzlement has been expanded, as we have seen, to include conversion by one who was holding title, as trustee, for another. The trustee has the power to convey the title, and if he does so wrongfully the result is the same as in false pretenses, so far as the victim's rights are concerned.

It must be emphasized that these differences are still in full effect even under such of the new penal codes as have joined larceny, embezzlement and false pretenses (and perhaps others) in a new offense under the name of "theft." Ownership and other rights of property are determined by property law and cannot be altered by changing the names of offenses. Hence with reference to the rights of the victim it will still be necessary to determine whether a particular "theft" was in the nature of larceny or embezzlement or false pretenses.

Where several different offenses have been combined in the statute on theft, and more than one of the offenses could be established by different findings under conflicting evidence, the jury must be instructed if more than one of these offenses is submitted, that for conviction they must unanimously agree upon which offense was committed.[*]

The purpose of legislation creating the crime of false pretenses must receive repeated attention if the offense is to be clearly understood. The common law of larceny was broad enough to cover a case in which possession alone was obtained by fraud with intent to deprive the owner of his property permanently. Hence the offense added by statute was not needed for such a situation. And although this point seems to have been overlooked in an occasional case, the generally accepted view is that the crime of false pretenses has not been committed unless the wrongdoer, by his fraudulent scheme, has obtained the title or ownership[67]—or whatever property interest the victim had in the chattel, if it was less than title. On the other hand, if the fraud induces the owner to part with both title and possession the offense is false pretenses and not larceny by trick or device.[68]

The point may be emphasized by reference to the much-cited case of *Pear*,[69] who obtained possession of a horse by pretending he was going to use it for a short trip, whereas he intended from the first to sell it. He was properly convicted of larceny; he could not have been convicted of false pretenses because by his fraud he obtained possession only and not title. Had

---

[*] Jackson v. State, 92 Wis.2d 1, 284 N.W.2d 685 (App.1979).

67. Courtney v. State, 174 Miss. 147, 164 So. 227 (1935). Where one by a false story obtained possession, but not title, of a car he was not guilty of false pretenses. If his intent was to sell the car for a commission, which the owner authorized him to do, it was neither false pretenses nor larceny by fraud. People v. Pillsbury, 59 Cal.App.2d 107, 138 P.2d 320 (1943); People v. Long, 409 Mich. 346, 294 N.W.2d 197 (1980).

68. Warren v. State, 95 Okl.Cr. 160, 241 P.2d 410 (1952).

69. 2 East P.C. 688; 1 Leach 212; 168 Eng.Rep. 208 (1779).

he obtained the horse with innocent intent and later sold it as a result of a change of mind, he would not have been guilty of either larceny or false pretenses. He would have been guilty of embezzlement except for the fact that this offense was created by a statute which had not been enacted at that time.[70]

Care is needed to avoid misunderstanding some of the statements with reference to this crime. One who is induced to part with money or goods as a result of fraudulent misrepresentations, usually starts with complete title and possession and passes to the defrauder either both or possession only. And references to the result, based upon whether the wrongdoer does or does not obtain "title," [71] are made in view of this normal situation. The use of the word "title" is correct in reference to this factual transaction but it is not to be understood that false pretenses can never be committed where title is not obtained. Obviously there could be no requirement that absolute title be obtained because the fraud itself makes the title of the wrongdoer voidable.[72] And if a swindler gets property on conditional sale he obtains a sufficient interest to support a conviction of false pretenses.[73] He has obtained the beneficial ownership despite the retention of "security title" by the vendor. Moreover there is no requirement that the one defrauded should have had the paramount title.[74] "Reference to the above statute discloses that it is not specified that the thing be obtained from the owner, but it is only required that it be obtained from 'any person, firm or corporation.'" [75] And in the words of another court: "'Actual ownership' of the money or goods by the person upon whom the cheat is practiced is not essential." [76]

A finder of lost property, for example, has a qualified and very limited "ownership" thereof. He has a claim superior to that of anyone other than the true owner and he is entitled to whatever reward may be payable to the finder. Hence if one other than the owner should obtain this property right by the fraudulent claim of being the loser he would be guilty of false pretenses.[77]

---

70. See, supra, section 3.

71. "[T]he gist of the crime of obtaining money or property by false pretenses is that the victim transferred the title to the property to the wrongdoer under the influence of the false pretenses. . . ." People v. Cravens, 79 Cal.App. 2d 658, 662, 180 P.2d 453, 456 (1947).

72. See Chappell v. State, 216 Ind. 666, 670–1, 25 N.E.2d 999, 1001 (1939).

73. Ibid.; Whitmore v. State, 238 Wis. 79, 298 N.W. 194 (1941).

In a situation where defendant obtained a motor vehicle without actual legal title the court observed:

"Michigan, however, does not emphasize the actual passage of title as determinative of the crime of false pretenses is defined as obtaining property with *intent* that title should pass." People v. Niver, 7 Mich.App. 652, 152 N.W.2d 714, 716 (1967).

74. State v. Hanks, 116 Mont. 399, 153 P.2d 220 (1944).

75. Moore v. State, 96 Okl.Cr. 118, 122, 250 P.2d 46, 51 (1952).

76. State v. Samaha, 92 N.J.L. 125, 126, 104 A. 305, 306 (1918). "The bank's possession of the money would support the conviction, whether it were legally authorized to do a banking business or not." Bond v. State, 129 Tenn. 75, 87, 165 S.W. 229, 232 (1914).

77. See the statement by Patteson, J., in The Queen v. Martin, 8 Ad. & E. 481, 488, 112 Eng.Rep. 921, 923 (1838), with reference to the pledgor who, by false representations, induces the pledgee to give up his security interest in the chattel. Had the pledgor taken the chattel without the consent of the pledgee the offense would have been larceny.

It is not essential to guilt of false pretenses that *possession* of the property be obtained *by fraud*. If the swindler has possession which he obtained without fraud he perpetrates this crime by obtaining the title (or other property interest) by fraudulent misrepresentations if all other elements of the offense are present.[78] But if the wrongdoer does not have possession, and does not succeed in getting possession away from the other, he does not commit this offense.[79] This is true even if the defrauded party suffers a loss on a resale of the property.[80]

"Under the common law, and under the accepted law of this State, a copartner in a business cannot be convicted for defrauding the partnership." [81] This is because of the common-law theory that a partnership is not a separate juristic entity but merely the sum total of the individual members.[82] It is the same concept which prevents the partner from being guilty of larceny or embezzlement of the "firm's" property.[83] Inducing a person to put money into a partnership in which he becomes a member does not constitute false pretenses, if the partnership is bona fide, even if false representations are employed for the purpose, because the incoming partner is still an owner of the money.[84] It is otherwise if "the partnership was used as an artifice or a part of a scheme to defraud and not as a going concern acting in good faith." [85] And the crime may be committed by inducing another to pay money to buy an interest in the firm if the money goes, not into the partnership, but into the pocket of the defrauder.[86]

If the other elements of the offense are present it is no defense that the title did not pass to the defrauder himself but, for example, to a corporation of which he was treasurer.[87] The distinction between false pretenses and larceny by fraud is often said to depend upon the intent of the one defrauded. The former offense is said to result if he intends to pass title as well as possession, but the offense is larceny if his intent is to pass possession only.[88] This statement is correct insofar as the facts of the ordinary

78. Allen v. State, 21 Ohio App. 403, 153 N.E. 218 (1926).

79. Parker v. Sawyer, 11 Neb. 309, 9 N.W. 33 (1881).

80. Commonwealth v. Randle, 119 Pa. Super. 213, 180 A. 720 (1935).

81. State v. Simmons, 209 S.C. 531, 536, 41 S.E.2d 217, 219 (1947).

82. People v. Bogert, 36 Cal. 245 (1868).

83. State v. Grumbles, 100 S.C. 328, 84 S.E. 783 (1914); Hall v. State, 103 Tex. Cr.R. 42, 279 S.W. 464 (1925).

84. People v. Cravens, 79 Cal.App.2d 658, 180 P.2d 453 (1947); State v. Smalley, 252 S.W. 443 (Mo.1923).

85. Id. at 663, 180 P.2d at 456; 252 S.W. at 445–6; People v. Jones, 36 Cal.2d 373, 242 P.2d 353 (1950).

86. People v. Cravens, 79 Cal.App.2d 658, 180 P.2d 453 (1947).

87. State v. Doudna, 226 Iowa 351, 284 N.W. 113 (1939); State v. Stratford, 55 Idaho 65, 37 P.2d 681 (1934); Commonwealth v. Langley, 169 Mass. 89, 47 N.E. 511 (1897).

88. See Commonwealth v. Barry, 124 Mass. 325, 327 (1878); People v. Miller, 169 N.Y. 339, 351–2, 62 N.E. 418, 422 (1902); Hagan v. State, 76 Okl.Cr. 127, 139–40, 134 P.2d 1042, 1050 (1943).

D was charged with obtaining money from Mrs. X by false pretenses. The evidence showed that D falsely represented to Mrs. X that he was an attorney at law, and she retained him to obtain a loan for her on certain real estate and pay the money to the Internal Revenue Service in payment of her federal income taxes. Further, that he obtained the loan on the real estate, but appropriated it instead of paying it to the Internal Revenue Service. It was held that if she did not intend D to have title to this money, but possession only, his offense was larceny rather than false pretenses. And a conviction of false pretenses was reversed because of the Judge's refusal to instruct

case are concerned because title will not pass unless the owner so intends. On the other hand an intent to pass title may be ineffective in an unusual case, as where one fraudulently uses the name of another in correspondence and thereby causes goods to be sent with intent to pass title to one who has not asked for them. In such a case the offense is larceny despite the victim's intent to pass title.[89]

2. VICTIM MUST BE DECEIVED

The property is not *obtained by* the untrue representation of fact if the real facts are known to the other. Hence it is essential to show that the owner was misled by the misrepresentation.[90] Some of the early cases held that the crime was not committed if the misrepresentation would not have deceived a person of ordinary prudence and intelligence,[91] but this is quite unsound. The social interest in safeguarding the individual against fraud includes the individual who is not well equipped to protect himself as well as one better endowed by nature.[92] Hence the accepted view today is that this requirement is satisfied if the misrepresentation was made with intent to deceive and did actually deceive, even though a more intelligent person would not have been misled by this type of fraud.[93]

D. KNOWINGLY AND DESIGNEDLY

The words "designedly and knowingly" appeared in the original English statute, were copied in early American statutes and repeated in many cases and discussions. "Designedly" means intentionally and in this offense

the jury properly on this point. Zarate v. People, 163 Colo. 205, 429 P.2d 309 (1967).

One who obtained possession, but not title, to money by a fraudulent scheme known as the "Jamaican Switch" was guilty of obtaining money by means of a scheme to defraud. This statute was not intended to codify the crime of false pretenses and does not require the obtainment of title. State v. Moses, 123 Ariz. 296, 599 P.2d 252 (App.1979).

89. English v. State, 80 Fla. 70, 85 So. 150 (1920). If the rule of the jurisdiction is that title does not pass to goods purchased by a check which is dishonored upon due presentment, the buyer is guilty of larceny if he obtained possession of the goods with fraudulent intent. Riley v. State, 64 Okl.Cr. 183, 78 P.2d 712 (1938).

90. "Textbook authorities are apparently in unison on the proposition that the completed crime of false pretense is not established unless it appears that the person alleged to have been defrauded believed the false representations to be true." Commonwealth v. Johnson, 312 Pa. 140, 143, 167 A. 344, 345 (1933). And see Ex parte Charles Franklin Stirrup, 155 Fla. 173, 175, 19 So.2d 712, 713

(1944); Rhodes v. State, 58 Okl.Cr. 1, 11, 49 P.2d 226, 231 (1935).

"One of the elements of larceny by false pretenses is the victim's reliance upon the accused's false representations." State v. Eppens, 30 Wn.App. 119, 633 P.2d 92, 98 (1981).

91. Commonwealth v. Norton, 93 Mass. 266 (1865).

92. Even "a man who is ineffably dull may not . . . be robbed with impunity." Bartlett v. State, 28 Ohio St. 669, 670 (1876).

93. People v. Gilliam, 141 Cal.App.2d 749, 297 P.2d 468 (1956); People v. Henninger, 20 Cal.App. 79, 128 P. 352 (1912); Clarke v. People, 64 Colo. 164, 171 P. 69 (1918); Ryan v. State, 104 Ga. 78, 30 S.E. 678 (1898); State v. Fooks, 65 Iowa 196, 21 N.W. 561 (1884); Palotta v. State, 184 Wis. 290, 199 N.W. 72 (1924); State ex rel. Hull v. Larson, 226 Wis. 585, 277 N.W. 101 (1938).

If the false representation was made with intent to defraud, and was relied upon, it is no defense that the victim was unusually credulous, State v. Zorich, 72 Wn.2d 31, 431 P.2d 584 (1967); or that the victim had the means at hand to discover the pretense, Burleson v. State, 449 S.W.2d 252 (Tex.Cr.App. 1969).

means an intent to defraud. "Knowingly" or "knowledge" has a broad sweep when used in connection with the element of a crime, and an untrue representation has been "knowingly" made if by one who knows it is untrue, believes it is untrue or is quite aware that he has not the slightest notion whether it is true or not.[94] On the other hand one could not knowingly obtain property by an untrue representation of fact if unaware of its falseness. The result is that the historic words add nothing and their omission does not change the meaning.[95] The definition might well be:

The crime of false pretenses is obtaining the property of another by means of untrue representations of fact with intent to defraud.

Some of the new penal codes are worded in such terms as by deception obtaining property of another "with intent to defraud him," [96] or "with intent to deprive the owner of his property." [97]

This so-called "knowledge" requirement will save from guilt of this offense if the misrepresentation was made in the honest belief of its truth.[98] Criminal negligence—sufficient for the mens-rea requirement of certain crimes—will not sustain a conviction of this offense.[99] Thus if one sells property which does not belong to him, he is not guilty of obtaining the purchase money by false pretenses if he honestly believes the property to be his. And this is true so long as this belief is genuine—even if he was negli-

---

94. "Whenever a representation is made that is in fact false, the mental attitude of the declarant with reference thereto must fall within one of four categories. First, he may know that the representation is false. Second, he may believe that the representation is false. Third, he may have neither any knowledge nor any belief whatsoever as to its truth or falsity. Fourth, he may believe the representation to be true. Each of the first three of these categories is distinguishable from the fourth in this— that in each of the first three the affirmative element of belief in the truth of the representation is absent. . . . Ethically there appears to be little difference when a man makes a false representation for the purpose of inducing another to act for his benefit between the quality of conduct of the man who knows or believes his representation is false and that of the man who has neither knowledge nor belief concerning it, but nevertheless makes the representation, neither knowing nor caring whether it be true or false." State v. Pickus, 63 S.D. 209, 230, 257 N.W. 284, 294 (1934).

False representations may be made by one who has no knowledge about the subject but who purposely conveys the impression that he does have knowledge and thereby deceives the other. State v. Paxton, 201 Kan. 353, 440 P.2d 650 (1968).

95. "[T]he representation . . . must have been made with knowledge of its falsity; . . ." Ex parte Charles Franklin Stirrup, 155 Fla. 173, 175, 19 So. 2d 712, 713 (1944). An information for false pretenses must charge that the accused knowingly and designedly made false and fraudulent representations, but the use of these words is not essential if the idea is clearly indicated. To say that the false and fraudulent representations were made with intent to deceive and defraud, and that money was obtained because of reliance thereon, sufficiently charges that the representations were "knowingly and designedly" made. State v. Freeman, 78 Ariz. 281, 279 P.2d 440 (1955).

96. E.g. Conn.Gen.Stat.Ann. § 53a–119(2) (1972).

97. E.g. Code of Ala. 13A, § 3201 (1975).

98. Ibid. An unqualified statement that a certain fact exists when in truth it does not exist, is not sufficient for conviction if the speaker honestly believes his statement is true. State v. Huckins, 212 Iowa 283, 234 N.W. 554 (1931).

99. It is not sufficient that defendant was "criminally careless." State v. McFarland, 180 N.C. 726, 729, 105 S.E. 179, 180 (1920).

gent in not knowing the facts,[1] and even if his erroneous belief was the result of a mistake of law.[2]

E. WITH INTENT TO DEFRAUD

1. WRONGFUL INTENT LESS THAN FRAUD

Even if an untrue representation of fact, wilfully made for the purpose of deceiving another and thereby inducing him to part with his money or goods, accomplishes this very result, there is no crime of false pretenses unless the deceit was practiced with intent to defraud.[3] Usually fraud is necessarily included in such a scheme but this is not always so. If, for example, such deception is practiced to induce a debtor to pay his debt, there is no fraud.[4] Such practice is far from commendable, but within the legal view an intent to induce another to perform his legal duty is not an intent to defraud. "It is not an indictable offense under the statute, for one to obtain by false statements payment of a debt already due, or personal property to the possession of which he is entitled, because no injury is done."[5]

2. REPRESENTATION BY SILENCE

The intent to defraud is lacking also in a case in which an untrue representation is designedly made with intent to deceive but without the intent to obtain the property which is obtained thereby, and *without* realization of the influence of the deceit.[6] On the other hand, since "silence may be deceitful means or artful practice,"[7] one who *knows* he is obtaining money or a chattel by his misrepresentation of fact and who *receives* it with intent to take a fraudulent advantage of the other, has obtained it by fraud whether his original statement was made for this purpose or not.[8] His silence at the moment, with full knowledge of what is happening, is the equivalent of a repeti-

---

1. Ibid.

2. And one who takes another's chattel by trespass, and carries it away with intent to keep it, is not guilty of larceny if he bona fide believes that it belongs to him and that he has the right to immediate possession, even if this is not true and his mistake is due to a misunderstanding of property law. Morningstar v. State, 55 Ala. 148 (1876); State v. Sawyer, 95 Conn. 34, 110 A. 461 (1920).

3. In reversing a conviction of "theft by deception" under the new penal code it was held that the instructions were "fatally defective" because they failed to tell the jury that to constitute the offense the obtainment must have been with "the conscious objective to withhold the property (the automobile) permanently." State v. Laine, 618 P.2d 33, 35 (Utah 1980).

4. State v. Williams, 68 W.Va. 86, 69 S.E. 474 (1910).

5. In re Cameron, 44 Kan. 64, 66 (1890). "A false representation, by which a man is cheated into his duty, is not within the statute." People v. Thomas, 3 Hill 169, 170 (N.Y.1842); Commonwealth v. McDuffy, 126 Mass. 467, 470 (1879).

6. Treadwell v. State, 99 Ga. 779, 27 S.E. 785 (1896).

7. Crawford v. State, 117 Ga. 247, 250, 43 S.E. 762, 763 (1903).

D, who received money from a gasoline service-station customer who believed D was the attendant, was guilty of stealing by deceit. State v. Watson, 562 S.W.2d 721 (Mo.App. 1978).

8. Clarke v. People, 64 Colo. 164, 171 P. 69 (1918).

"When one has knowingly and designedly by fraudulent representations defrauded another, the representations shall be treated as continuing so as to cover any money, property or services received as a result thereof." People v. Adams, 137 Cal.App.2d 660, 671, 290 P.2d 944, 950 (1955).

tion of the statement at the very moment of acquisition. This is true also of one who makes an untrue statement innocently, but learns of the mistake before the property is received and fraudulently fails to disclose the real facts known to him when the money or property is handed over.[9] There are other situations in which a party to a transaction has a legal duty to speak,[10] as where property subject to a recorded lien is sold to one who reasonably believes it to be free and clear of any encumbrance.[11] Nondisclosure by one under such a duty is a false representation.[12] In such cases the property of the other is knowingly and designedly *obtained* by means of untrue representations of fact and with intent to defraud.

Mere nondisclosure under other circumstances must be distinguished. However unethical it may be for one knowingly to take advantage of another's misunderstanding of facts, this is not sufficient for the crime of false pretenses unless the one has himself occasioned that misunderstanding, or because of some other unusual circumstance, is under a legal duty to disclose the facts.[13]

3. UNKNOWN RELATION BETWEEN DECEIT AND OBTAINMENT

An untrue representation of fact may be made with intent to deceive, for some purpose other than fraud,[14] and may result in the acquisition of property without the deceiver's being aware of the relation between the false statement and the subsequent transaction. Such cases almost invariably involve a substantial period of time between the two occasions,[15] because otherwise the deceiver would be fully aware of the connection between the two.

9. On the other hand the failure to correct an earlier misstatement is not fraudulent on the part of one who has forgotten that he ever made it. In one case, for example, an innocent misstatement was made in May and resulted in a transaction in September. Crawford v. State, 117 Ga. 247, 43 S.E. 762 (1903).

10. One who received a twenty-dollar gold piece from a child, who thought it was a dollar, had a legal duty to explain the mistake, if he accepted the coin, and it was fraudulent for him to keep the gold and give her only change for a dollar. Jones v. State, 97 Ga. 430, 25 S.E. 319 (1895).

11. Ballaine v. District Court, 107 Utah 247, 153 P.2d 265 (1944). But see note 97. Giving a lease for a year implies a representation that the lessor is in a position to deal with the property in this manner and for this length of time. See People v. Rocha, 130 Cal.App.2d 656, 660, 279 P.2d 836, 838 (1955).

12. Ibid. Montez v. People, 110 Colo. 208, 132 P.2d 970 (1943); Bright v. Sheriff, Washoe County, 90 Nev. 168, 521 P.2d 371 (1974).

13. "It must be borne in mind that mere silence and mere suppression of the truth, the mere withholding of knowledge upon which another may act, is not sufficient to constitute the crime of false pretenses." People v. Barker, 96 N.Y. 340, 348–9 (1884). Some courts have applied this rule to situations in which it would seem possible to find a legal duty to make the disclosure. Even the sale of mortgaged property without mention of the encumbrance has been held not to be false pretenses. McCorkle v. State, 170 Ark. 105, 278 S.W. 965 (1926); Stumpff v. People, 51 Colo. 202, 117 P. 134 (1911). As to a different type of nondisclosure see State v. Hastings, 77 N.D. 146, 41 N.W.2d 305 (1950).

14. It is error to instruct if a misrepresentation is made, with knowledge that it is false, the law will presume an intent to defraud. The fraudulent intent must be found as a fact. People v. Barker, 96 N.Y. 340 (1884).

15. Treadwell v. State, 99 Ga. 779, 27 S.E. 785 (1896).

An illustration may be helpful. A minor employee of a large corporation represents himself as a vice-president thereof, to one of his social acquaintances. His deceit is wilful, but is merely to feed his own vanity by being thought of as a man of considerable importance. Some months later the two have a business transaction in which the acquaintance delivers property on credit to the employee under the belief he is vice-president of the corporation, while the employee has forgotten that his misrepresentation was made to this person and hence is wholly unaware of any relation between the deceit and the acquisition of the property on credit. This is not the crime of false pretenses. The employee may have been negligent but he did not have an *intent to defraud*.

4. INTENT TO REPAY

A fraudulent scheme frequently involves the obtainment of money or goods on credit with the intent not to pay the creditor. In another connection it has been seen that for the crime of false pretenses, as generally interpreted, there must be something in addition to the false promise. It is now necessary to emphasize that an intent to repay will not necessarily prevent guilt of this crime.[16] A typical example is the case in which money is borrowed on worthless security falsely represented to be of adequate value; as where the security is a mortgage on property stated to be free from any other incumbrance but in reality subject to a prior mortgage of record which exceeds the value of the property.

One who is asked to lend money or to sell goods on credit has a right to determine for himself whether he chooses to be a secured creditor or an unsecured creditor, and if he chooses to be the former he has a right to know about the security. One who has extended credit in reliance upon a mortgage on real estate which is falsely represented to be a first mortgage when in fact it is subject to a prior recorded mortgage for more than the land is worth, or is a mortgage upon property which the mortgagor does not own, has been defrauded even if the debtor has an intent to pay the debt.[17] The lender intended to be a secured creditor but by reason of the false representation his position is for all practical purposes that of an unsecured creditor. There is an obvious and unreasonable *risk* of loss which has been forced upon him, without his knowledge or consent, by reason of the deceit. This risk which the creditor did not intend to assume was imposed upon him by the *intentional* act of the debtor, and this amounts to an intent to defraud.[18]

The illustration of a second mortgage on land already mortgaged beyond its value is for the sake of emphasis. The crime of false pretenses may be committed by one who intentionally makes false representations about the security he offers even without such an extreme factual situation. If by reason of the false representation of the debtor, the creditor has assumed a substantially greater risk than would have been his if the debtor's statements had been true, this requirement of the crime is satisfied even if the security is not entirely worthless, or even if it may turn out to be adequate.[19]

16. People v. Felsman, 257 Cal.App.2d 437, 64 Cal.Rptr. 870 (1967).

17. Odom v. State, 130 Miss. 643, 94 So. 233 (1922); State v. Mills, 96 Ariz. 377, 396 P.2d 5 (1964).

18. Ibid.; Moore v. State, 96 Okl.Cr. 118, 250 P.2d 46 (1952).

19. If a loan is obtained by use of collateral, which is fraudulently represented to be free from any encumbrance, it is no defense that part of it is free and clear

F. VICTIM ACTUALLY DEFRAUDED

A requirement that the intended victim be actually defrauded is usually included as one of the essential elements of this offense.[20] This is probably more in the nature of additional emphasis upon certain other requirements than a separate element. The deceit must actually deceive, as previously mentioned; and it must have some influence in inducing the victim to part with his property, although it is not required to be the *sole* inducement.[21] On the other hand, there is no requirement of actual pecuniary loss on the part of the intended victim.[22] If the false representation was with reference to the security given for money borrowed, or property purchased on credit, it is no defense to a charge of false pretenses that the debt has since been paid.[23] And the sound view, followed in most jurisdictions, is that this crime may be committed by obtaining a charitable donation by means of false representations.[24] The crime may be committed also by inducing a person to part with his property in return for something which is different from what he is induced to believe he is receiving even if what he gets has as much financial value as the thing he would have received if the representations had been true.[25] If, after a purchaser has selected a certain watch priced at

and that the value of that part is sufficient to protect the loan. People v. Talbott, 65 Cal.App.2d 654, 151 P.2d 317 (1944). See also Nelson v. United States, 227 F.2d 21 (D.C. Cir. 1955).

20. "The elements of the crime . . . are . . . (2) an actual fraud committed; . . ." People v. Rocha, 130 Cal.App.2d 636, 660, 279 P.2d 836, 838 (1955). "There must be actual fraud committed; . . ." Commonwealth v. Drew, 36 Mass. 179, 182 (1837).

21. "Inasmuch as deception is the essence of the crime, there must be a causal connection between the representation or statement made and the delivery of the property." Ex parte Charles Franklin Stirrup, 155 Fla. 173, 176, 19 So.2d 712, 713 (1944).

The victim must have relied upon the false representation although it need not have been the sole means of inducing the victim to part with his property. State v. Zorich, 71 Wn.2d 31, 431 P.2d 584 (1967).

22. State v. Sargent, 2 Wn.2d 190, 97 P.2d 692 (1940). "Financial loss is not a necessary element of the crime." People v. Talbott, 65 Cal.App.2d 654, 659, 151 P.2d 317, 320 (1944).

One who obtained a subscription to a magazine, by falsely stating that he was an orphan in need of securing subscriptions, thereby defrauded the other. People v. Conlon, 207 Cal.App.2d 86, 24 Cal. Rptr. 219 (1962).

23. Odom v. State, 130 Miss. 643, 94 So. 233 (1922); Moore v. State, 96 Okl.Cr.

118, 250 P.2d 46 (1952); Baskerville v. State, 23 Md.App. 439, 327 A.2d 918 (1974).

24. Commonwealth v. Whitcomb, 107 Mass. 486 (1871); Lanier v. State, 448 P.2d 587 (Alaska 1968).

25. If money was obtained upon a false and fraudulent draft it is no defense that there was a solvent indorser on the draft. State v. Decker, 36 Kan. 717, 14 P. 283 (1887). "When the wronged party gets what he bargained for no crime is committed." But if the seller of a real estate mortgage makes false and fraudulent representations as to the location of the land, its character, value and use, it is no defense that the maker of the note is financially responsible. State v. Talcott, 178 Minn. 564, 565, 227 N.W. 893, 894 (1929). The fact that property purchased is worth the consideration paid is no defense if the seller induced the purchaser to buy by false and fraudulent misrepresentations. People v. Pugh, 137 Cal.App.2d 226, 289 P.2d 826 (1955). D obtained property, giving his demand note and a chattel mortgage on a car as security. He represented that he owed on the car only one payment of $55, not then due, fraudulently concealing the fact that there was a prior chattel mortgage on the car for over $3000. The fact that his equity in this car was five times the value of the property received in this transaction was no defense to a charge of false pretenses. Nelson v. United States, 227 F.2d 21 (D.C.Cir. 1955). The car was damaged in a wreck. The securi-

$100, the seller should deceitfully wrap up an empty box and obtain the money by the delivery of this package, it would be the clearest case of false pretenses. It would also be false pretenses if the seller should deceitfully deliver a package containing a jeweled ring instead of the watch—even if the ring had the same value as the watch. A person who wishes to buy a watch is not to be tricked into parting with his money for something else which he does not want.

As the phrase is used in this branch of the law, a person is defrauded if, by intentionally false representations of fact, he has been induced to make a donation, or has been induced to pay money or deliver property upon receipt of something quite different from what he understood he was getting, or has been induced to lend money upon the strength of security which is not what it was represented to be. In this sense of the phrase, it is not inaccurate to say it is essential that the intended victim be defrauded; but it is doubtful if this statement makes any real contribution. It is rather an idea necessarily included in the statement that the crime of false pretenses is knowingly and designedly obtaining the property of another by means of untrue representations of fact with intent to defraud.

Restitution. Indicating a small step in a direction that has long been urged, the court in reversing a conviction because the verdict failed to determine the value of the property involved, quotes a Wyoming statute that requires, in addition to the penalty provided, that one convicted of false pretenses "shall be sentenced to restore the property so fraudulently obtained, if it can be done." [26]

G. CHEATING BY CHECK

A type of swindle entitled to separate attention is that which is perpetrated by the issuance of a check by one who has neither sufficient funds in the bank nor any arrangement for the payment. This does not include the use of a forged check.[27] A forged check is a false token and the fraudulent obtaining of money or goods by means of a forged check was punishable as a cheat at common law,[28] and unquestionably comes under the statute on false pretenses.[29] One's own check, however, even if issued with no reason to expect that it will be paid is not a false token but a mere "falsehood in writing" and hence not sufficient for a common-law cheat.[30] On the other hand, since a falsehood whether written, oral or by conduct is sufficient for guilt under the statute on false pretenses if it is a fraudulent representation of

ty still would have been adequate had the prior lien been only $55 as represented, but it was the original false pretense and not the subsequent accident which was important as to guilt.

26. Harris v. State, 635 P.2d 1165, 1168 (Wyo.1981).

27. Some of the special statutes on the subject, however, are broad enough to cover the use of a forged check. Loughridge v. State, 63 Okl.Cr. 33, 72 P.2d 513 (1937); In re Clemons, 168 Ohio St. 83, 151 N.E.2d 553 (1958).

28. 2 Bishop, New Criminal Law § 148 (8th ed. 1892).

29. Furey v. Hollowell, 203 Iowa 376, 212 N.W. 698 (1927); The Queen v. Prince, L.R. 1 C.C. 150 (1868).

30. Williams v. Territory, 13 Ariz. 27, 108 P. 243 (1910); 2 Bishop, New Criminal Law § 147 (8th ed. 1892). The courts have at times referred to a check, fraudulently issued without funds in the bank to meet it, as a "false token" under the statute on false pretenses. See People v. Donaldson, 70 Cal. 116, 118, 11 P. 681 (1886). But either a false token or a false pretense is sufficient under the statute and no more is needed than to say it is a false pretense.

fact, and the other elements of the crime are present, the question is whether the issuance of such a check is a fraudulent representation of fact. Does one who obtains money or property by means of a check, drawn by himself, thereby represent that he has funds in the bank sufficient to cover it, or some arrangement with the bank for its payment? An occasional court has come to the astounding conclusion that there is no such representation without an express statement to this effect.[31] Such a position is utterly unrealistic. One who parts with his money or goods in return for a check drawn by another, takes it for granted that the drawer has funds in the bank adequate to meet the check. As said by the Iowa court: "the weight of authority and reason is to the effect that the mere making of a check and delivering it to another to induce the other to deliver property or money to the maker is an assertion and pretense that the drawer has, at the time, money or credit in the bank on which the check is drawn. . . ."[32] In the first outstanding case [33] under the statute in this country it was held, under early banking practices, that for one to present a check, in the form of an overdraft, to his own bank was not a representation that the account was adequate but merely a request for a loan, but even there it was suggested *obiter* that it would be false pretenses to obtain money from another by knowingly issuing him a check without sufficient funds to cover it because in such a case there would be an implied assertion of sufficiency of the account.[34]

Various labels have been employed to indicate an unaltered check which has the genuine signature of the drawer but is drawn upon a bank in which he has neither sufficient funds nor any arrangement for its payment. Such an instrument has been referred to as a "bogus check,"[35] a "cold check"[36] or a "worthless check."[37] The layman is likely to refer to it as a "rubber check" because it "bounces." The term "false check" would be inappropriate because it indicates a forged check which is quite a different concept. "Bogus check" might indicate either and "cold check" sounds like slang, so the phrase "worthless check" is adopted herein for this purpose. It is perhaps not exactly descriptive because such a check may turn out to have some value later, but the term has been widely used for this purpose.[38]

---

31. Blackwell v. State, 41 Tex.Cr.R. 104, 51 S.W. 919 (1899). "The mere giving of a worthless check unaccompanied by any false statement is not an offense under this section." Commonwealth v. McCall, 186 Ky. 301, 305, 217 S.W. 109, 110 (1919).

A Michigan court has held that in order to obtain conviction under the false pretenses statute the passing of an insufficient funds check must be accompanied by an additional false representation. People v. LaRose, 87 Mich.App. 298, 274 N.W.2d 45 (1979).

32. State v. Foxton, 166 Iowa 181, 186, 147 N.W. 347, 349 (1914).

Obtaining goods by a check drawn on a closed account constitutes theft by deception. People v. Atterbury, 196 Colo. 509, 587 P.2d 281 (1978).

33. Commonwealth v. Drew, 36 Mass. 179 (1837).

34. Id. at p. 186.

35. Williams v. Territory, 13 Ariz. 27, 33, 108 P. 243, 245 (1910).

36. Commonwealth v. McCall, 186 Ky. 301, 217 S.W. 109 (1919).

37. Id. at p. 305, 217 S.W. at p. 110; 2 Williston on Sales § 346a (Rev. ed. 1948).

A statute on the subject is sometimes called "The Worthless Check Act." See State v. Morris, 190 Kan. 93, 372 P.2d 282 (1962); State v. Lee, 78 N.M. 421, 432 P.2d 265 (1967).

38. "To violate (the Worthless Check Act) one must issue the check in exchange for value, with the requisite intent and knowledge." State v. Libero, 91 N.M. 780, 581 P.2d 873, 875 (1978).

There is some authority for the position that common-law larceny is committed when goods are fraudulently obtained by a worthless check. The rationalization is as follows: A check given for goods is conditional payment only; if the check is duly presented to the drawee bank and dishonored the condition fails; if the condition fails the payment fails; as a "cash sale" was intended title does not pass if there is no payment; if title does not pass only possession is obtained and hence larceny is committed if it was a fraudulent scheme from the start. This is based upon a false premise in regard to the law of sales as pointed out by Williston.[39] It fails to distinguish between a voidable title and a complete lack of title. It has some following both in the law of sales [40] and in criminal law,[41] but is unsound and has not been widely adopted.

Most courts accepted the sound view that the fraudulent obtainment of money or goods by means of a worthless check is a violation of the statute on false pretenses, even without an express statement that the drawer has funds in the bank to meet it.[42] But because a few held otherwise, and the view that it constituted common-law larceny was generally rejected, statutes were needed in a few states to cope with the spread of this type of fraud.[43] And in the course of time the enactment of special statutes dealing with the fraudulent issuance of worthless checks became quite general. In some instances the special statute seems to have added nothing to the general law of false pretenses other than to require prosecution under the particular enactment.[44] Apparently a statute enacted to fill a need in one state was copied in another without realizing that it was unnecessary there. In other jurisdictions, on the other hand, a special statute was passed to provide penalties for the fraudulent issuance of worthless checks even when no money or property was obtained thereby.

Differences in the statutes permit little in the way of generalization. At times a fraudulent check clause is included in the false pretenses section itself,[45] but more frequently it is separate.[46] If the statute speaks only in terms of money, property or thing of value obtained by such a check it is not violated if nothing was obtained,[47] as for example where it is used to pay a

---

39. 2 Williston on Sales § 346a (Rev. ed. 1948).

40. Ibid.

41. Riley v. State, 64 Okl.Cr. 183, 78 P.2d 712 (1938).

42. People v. Donaldson, 70 Cal. 116, 11 P. 681 (1886); State v. Larsen, 76 Idaho 528, 286 P.2d 646 (1955); State v. Foxton, 166 Iowa 181, 147 N.W. 347 (1914); State v. Hammelsy, 52 Or. 156, 96 P. 865 (1908); Commonwealth v. Collins, 8 Phila. 609 (1871); State v. Augustine, 114 W.Va. 143, 171 S.E. 111 (1933); Rex v. Jackson, 3 Camp. 370, 170 Eng.Rep. 1414 (1813).

43. For example, the Georgia court indicated that the fraudulent obtainment of goods by a worthless check would not be false pretenses if there was no express false representation,—although this seems not to have been necessary for the disposition of the case. Williams v. State, 10 Ga.App. 395, 73 S.E. 424 (1911). Shortly thereafter a statute was enacted to cover such a case. Ga.Laws, 1914, p. 86. See the court's explanation in Berry v. State, 153 Ga. 169, 111 S.E. 669 (1922). Kentucky also needed such a statute. See Commonwealth v. McCall, 186 Ky. 301, 305, 217 S.W. 109, 110 (1919).

44. See, for example, State v. Marshall, 202 Iowa 954, 211 N.W. 252 (1926).

45. E.g., Idaho Code § 18–3106 (1979).

46. E.g., West's Ann.Cal.Pen.Code §§ 476a, 532 (1976).

47. Currlin v. State, 110 Tex.Cr.R. 18, 6 S.W.2d 767 (1928); Lochner v. State, 218 Wis. 472, 261 N.W. 227 (1935). Cf. Wis.Stats. § 943.41 (1955).

pre-existing debt,[48] or to pay an overdue note without taking up the note.[49] On the other hand, the statute may be so worded as to cover an area not included in the false pretenses statute. The Oregon court, for example, held that fraudulently obtaining a horse by means of a worthless check was the felony of obtaining property by false pretenses; whereas, had the horse been obtained on credit and later paid for with a worthless check this would have violated the statute against knowingly uttering a check without funds in the bank.[50] The Indiana Court has held that under its statutes also the fraudulent issuance of a worthless check for the purpose of obtaining property and the issuance of such a check to pay a past obligation are separate offenses.[51] And the California court has held that its special statute is violated if a worthless check is knowingly issued with intent to defraud even if nothing is obtained thereby, whereas false pretenses is committed if property is so obtained. Hence if such a check is issued with intent to defraud, and property is obtained by means thereof, both crimes have been committed.[52]

The Colorado court invalidated that state's worthless check statute on several grounds. The definition of insufficient funds was held void for vagueness, and the lack of any requirement of an intent to defraud together with a presumption of guilt was interpreted to be a collection measure authorizing imprisonment for debt.[53]

Disclosure by the drawer of a check that he does not have funds in the bank sufficient to cover it is ordinarily sufficient to purge the transaction of its criminal character and leave it essentially an extension of credit to the drawer,[54] but a request for delayed presentment is not always inconsistent with guilt.[55] Giving a post-dated check, with an agreement that it shall not be presented until the date it bears, does not violate the special check stat-

---

48. Berry v. State, 153 Ga. 169, 111 S.E. 669 (1922); Broadus v. State, 205 Miss. 147, 38 So.2d 692 (1948).

49. Douglas v. State, 80 Ga.App. 761, 57 S.E.2d 438 (1950).

50. State v. Cody, 116 Or. 509, 241 P. 983 (1925).

51. Tullis v. State, 230 Ind. 311, 103 N.E.2d 353 (1951); Rogers v. State, 220 Ind. 443, 44 N.E.2d 343 (1942).

The Kansas court emphasized that the purpose of the worthless check statute was to discourage overdrafts and resulting bad banking, to stop the practice of "checkkiting," and generally to avert the mischief to trade, commerce and banking which the circulation of worthless checks inflicts, adding: "Although the statute tends to suppress fraud committed by the worthless-check method, the evils referred to are all quite distinct from those consequent on fraud, and the statute is to be regarded as creating a new and distinct offense." State v. Avery, 111 Kan. 588, 591, 207 P. 838, 839 (1922). Quoted with approval in State v. Morris, 190 Kan. 93, 372 P.2d 282, 285 (1962). Hence

an intent to defraud is not required. In another state it was held that drawing a check on a bank in which the drawer has no funds is prima facie evidence of an intent to defraud. State v. Lee, 78 N.M. 421, 432 P.2d 265 (1967).

52. People v. Freedman, 111 Cal.App. 2d 611, 245 P.2d 45 (1952).

Under the California statute barring double punishment where two statutes are violated by a single act (West's Ann. Cal.Pen.Code § 654) (1976) **D** could be convicted of both offenses but could be punished only for one. See People v. Tideman, 57 Cal.2d 574, 21 Cal.Rptr. 207, 370 P.2d 1007 (1962).

53. People v. Vinnola, 177 Colo. 405, 494 P.2d 826 (1972).

54. State v. Ellis, 67 Ariz. 7, 189 P.2d 717 (1948); People v. Poyet, 15 Cal.App. 3d 717, 93 Cal.Rptr. 393 (1971); People v. Cundiff, 16 Ill.App.3d 267, 305 N.E.2d 735 (1973).

55. State v. Augustine, 114 W.Va. 143, 171 S.E. 111 (1933).

ute.[56] On the other hand, if a worthless check is fraudulently issued the criminality of the transaction is not purged by the fact that it was post-dated with the well-founded expectation that this fact would not be noticed by the payee.[57]

H. CHEATING BY CREDIT CARD

The newly-invented credit card, which in a very short time has come to play a tremendous role in the business world, presents new problems. One who, to obtain goods or other value, presents a forged or stolen credit card clearly represents thereby that this card is evidence of an arrangement by which the credit company has agreed to pay for the value received upon this use of the card. This is clearly a false representation because the company has made no such agreement. It is true the company will probably make the payment because the issuers of such cards have deemed it necessary to assume the risk of misuse in order to encourage the ready honoring of such cards. This has given rise to doubt as to whether such fraudulent use of a credit card constitutes the crime of false pretenses.[58] The thought apparently is that since the one who gives value on this use of the card will be paid by the credit company, he has not been defrauded. On the other hand, the company is not bound to pay for an unauthorized use of its card and for some reason might refuse to pay in a particular instance. Furthermore, in a typical case of false pretenses it would be no defense that the victim was covered by insurance. Ultimate loss is not an element of the crime.

Nevertheless, it is no doubt wise to have legislation which will clearly cover the misuse of credit cards. California passed such a statute in 1961 which was repealed and replaced by another in 1967.[59] The Model Penal Code includes a section on credit cards.[60]

The forgery of a credit card and knowingly offering a forged card as genuine would seem to be covered by the general offenses of forgery and uttering a forged instrument.[61] And the wrongful holder of a credit card issued to another who fraudulently signs that other's name to a sales slip, or a restaurant or bar slip, is guilty of forgery.[62]

---

56. Nedderman v. State, 198 Ind. 187, 152 N.E. 800 (1926). The statute may prohibit the issuance of a post-dated check upon an insufficient account. Application of Windle, 179 Kan. 239, 294 P. 2d 213 (1956).

57. Carter v. State, 150 Tex.Cr. 448, 203 S.W.2d 540 (1947). See also People v. Lane, 144 Cal.App.2d 87, 300 P.2d 321 (1956). See People v. Niver, 7 Mich.App. 652, 152 N.W.2d 714 (1967). As to a check issued with intent to stop payment thereon, see Whatley v. State, 249 Ala. 355, 31 So.2d 664 (1947); State v. Alick, 62 S.D. 220, 252 N.W. 644 (1934).

58. See for example under "Status of Section" Model Penal Code § 224.6 (Proposed Official Draft, 1962).

59. West's Ann.Cal.Pen.Code § 484a (as amended in 1961 and repealed in 1967). And §§ 484d through 484j (as amended in 1967). See People v. Churchill, 255 Cal.App.2d 488, 63 Cal.Rptr. 312 (1967). People v. Scott, 259 Cal.App. 2d 589, 66 Cal.Rptr. 432 (1968). The federal statute prohibiting interstate transportation of fraudulently obtained credit cards applies only to the cards themselves. It was not violated by a telephone call from Spokane to Reno by which credit card numbers were fraudulently obtained. United States v. Callihan, 666 F.2d 422 (9th Cir. 1982).

60. Section 224.6.

61. See infra, Section 8; State v. Gledhill, 67 N.J. 565, 342 A.2d 161 (1975).

62. State v. Vangen, 72 Wn.2d 548, 433 P.2d 691 (1967).

"The legislative decision to make credit card crimes punishable to a lesser degree than forgery is a rational one. . . .

Obtaining money from an automatic bank teller, by the fraudulent use of a bank card and personal identification code, constitutes obtaining money by deceit.[63]

In affirming conviction under the new deceptive practices act[64] enacted to replace the former statute on false pretenses, the court said:

Breaking the new statute down into its elements, we determine the State need prove only that:

(1) the defendant acted "purposely or knowingly" in

(2) making or directing another to make a false or deceptive statement

(3) addressed to the public or any person

(4) for the purpose of promoting or procuring the sale of property or services.

Gone are any requirements that the statements relate to past events or existing facts or that the injured party relied thereon in parting with money or property. . . . The legislative intent to expand the spectrum of criminal activities in the area of false pretenses is obvious.[65]

SECTION 5. THEFT

Common-law larceny and the crime of false pretenses have a basic difference which goes beyond the boundaries of criminal law. The wrongdoer who obtains the property by larceny does not obtain title, and unless what he steals is money, or an instrument or document in appropriate negotiable form, he has no power to convey title even to an innocent purchaser, for value, and without notice. Such a purchaser, however, is fully protected if he buys from one who obtained the chattel by false pretenses. In the first case the title remains throughout in the victim of the crime; in the second it was passed to the offender, being voidable in his hands but perfect when handed on to a bona-fide purchaser. And this distinction will remain even if the two offenses are completely merged. This, however, is not a sound reason for opposing such a merger. Under the more progressive embezzlement statutes an embezzler may have title to or only possession of the property he appropriates. Where such is the law the bona-fide purchaser from an embezzler may or may not get good title to the chattel. This is important in a civil action between the victim of the crime and the innocent purchaser of the property, but unimportant in a criminal prosecution of the embezzler.

In fact the distinctions between larceny, embezzlement and false pretenses serve no useful purpose in the criminal law but are useless handicaps from the standpoint of the administration of criminal justice. One solution has been to combine all three in one section of the code under the name of "larceny."[1] This has one disadvantage, however, because it frequently becomes necessary to add a modifier to make clear whether the reference is to

Even though the fraudulent use of a credit card may involve forgery, it need not in all cases, and the prosecutor has the discretion to charge forgery when the facts warrant such a charge." Mack v. State, 93 Wis.2d 287, 286 N.W.2d 563, 568, 570 (1980).

63. State v. Hamm, 569 S.W.2d 289 (Mo.App. 1978).

64. § 45–6–317 MCA (1973).

65. State v. Duncan, ___ Mont. ___, 593 P.2d 1026, 1030 (1979).

1. McKinney's Consol.L.N.Y. Penal § 155.05 (1975). This section "embraces

common-law larceny or to statutory larceny. To avoid this difficulty some states have employed another word to designate a statutory offense made up of a combination of larceny, embezzlement and false pretenses. And the word used for this purpose is "theft." [2] "Theft" is not the name of any common-law offense. At times it has been employed as a synonym of "larceny," but for the most part has been regarded as broader in its general scope.[3] Under such a statute it is not necessary for the indictment charging theft to specify whether the offense is larceny, embezzlement or false pretenses.[4] If **D** wrongfully appropriated **X**'s car, for example, it is immaterial, in a prosecution under such a statute, whether **D** embezzled the car or formed the wrongful intent before he received possession and hence committed larceny by trick.[5]

On the other hand, even determined efforts to merge these three offenses have not always been completely successful. California, for example, merged the three into one section under the name of "theft," [6] but in doing so the lawmakers seem to have overlooked another section [7] which provides for special proof for the conviction of false pretenses. If fraud was perpetrated without the use of a signed writing or false token, and the false pretense is not proved by the testimony of two witnesses, or one witness and corroborating evidence, there can be no conviction if the type of theft is that known as "false pretenses." [8] To achieve the desired merger this special section on proof should be either repealed or amended to include larceny as

every act which was larceny at common law, besides other offenses which were formerly indictable as false pretenses and embezzlement." People v. Katz, 209 N.Y. 311, 325, 103 N.E. 305, 309 (1913). See also N.Mex.Stat. 1978 § 30–16–1; 10 U.S.C.A. § 921, Uniform Code Military Justice.

2. Ariz.Rev.Stat. §§ 13–1801–1806 (1978); West's Ann.Cal.Pen.Code § 484 (1970); Wis.St. 1955, § 943.20 (1958). This is the word suggested in the Model Penal Code. See Art. 223.

"A conviction of theft by deception requires a determination by the jury that the defendant intentionally made a fraudulent misrepresentation." State v. Sorensen, 617 P.2d 333, 337 (Utah 1980).

The Arkansas statute on theft by deception was written to conform to the Model Penal Code and clearly includes properly obtained by a false promise. Hixson v. Housewright, 642 F.2d 242, 246 (8th Cir. 1981).

3. See, e. g., People v. Karp, 298 N.Y. 213, 216, 81 N.E.2d 817 (1948). The word "theft" is not a "technical word of art with a narrowly defined meaning but is, on the contrary, a word of general and broad connotation, intended to cover and covering any criminal appropriation of another's property to the use of the taker, particularly including theft by swindling, false pretenses, and any other

form of guile." Edwards v. Bromberg, 232 F.2d 107, 110 (5th Cir. 1956).

4. People v. Nor Woods, 37 Cal.2d 584, 233 P.2d 897 (1951).

The statute itself may include some such requirement. People v. Karp, 298 N.Y. 213, 81 N.E.2d 817 (1948).

"The Utah theft statute consolidates the offenses known under prior law as larceny, embezzlement, extortion, false pretenses, and receiving stolen property into a single offense entitled *theft*, and clearly evidences the legislative intent to eliminate the previously existing necessity of pleading and proving those separate and distinct offenses." State v. Taylor, 570 P.2d 697, 698 (Utah 1977).

5. People v. Corenevsky, 124 Cal.App. 2d 19, 267 P.2d 1048 (1954).

Guilt of theft under the new statute may be established by proof of any one or more of the methods enumerated in the statute. State v. Gilbert, 27 Or.App. 1, 555 P.2d 31, 33 (1976).

6. West's Ann.Cal.Pen.Code § 484 (1970).

7. Id. at § 1110. See also Utah Code Ann. 1953 § 77–31–17.

8. People v. Carter, 131 Cal.App. 177, 21 P.2d 129 (1933). And see People v. Reinschreiber, 141 Cal.App.2d 688, 297 P.2d 658 (1956); People v. Telsman, 257 Cal.App.2d 437, 64 Cal.Rptr. 870 (1968);

well as false pretenses. This was done in New York on another point. The former New York statute did not permit evidence that its statute on "larceny" was violated by fraud or false pretenses unless so alleged in the indictment or information. But it expressly provided that this was true whether the offense was common-law larceny or false pretenses.[9]

The merger of these three offenses is a constructive step which should be encouraged, but it should be borne in mind that combining them in a single section will not authorize punishment of what did not previously constitute guilt of any one. As said by the New York court:

"The new larceny law . . . was aimed at eliminating the subtle and confusing distinctions that had previously differentiated the various types of theft. It was not, however, designed to, and did not broaden the scope of the crime of larceny or designate as criminal that which was previously innocent.[10]

It should be emphasized that the New York law in this whole area has since been re-codified and now very definitely does cover types of misconduct not previously punishable.[11] This is true also of the sweeping provisions of the Model Penal Code from which the New York law was patterned to some extent.[12] Several states have adopted general theft statutes along the lines of the Model Penal Code thereby expanding the scope of their theft laws.

MODEL PENAL CODE

The most sweeping and complicated changes suggested by the Model Penal Code are those dealing with the acquisitive offenses. Space limitations permit only the barest introduction here.

Article 223. Theft and Related Offenses

Section 223.0 Definitions

In this article unless a different meaning plainly is required:

(1) "deprive" means: (a) to withhold property of another permanently or for so extended a period as to appropriate a major portion of its economic value, or with intent to restore only upon payment of reward or other

---

People v. Mason, 34 Cal.App.3d 281, 109 Cal.Rptr. 867 (1973).

9. McKinney's N.Y.Pen.Law, § 155.45 (1975).

10. People v. Karp, 298 N.Y. 213, 216, 81 N.E.2d 817 (1948). "However the elements of the several offenses have not thereby been changed." People v. Cravens, 79 Cal.App.2d 658, 662, 180 P.2d 453, 456 (1947). Accord, People v. Jones, 36 Cal.2d 373, 224 P.2d 353 (1950).

The crime of theft as defined in the new Oregon criminal code is designed "to eliminate technical distinction which has been the source of recurring problems relating to the charging and proof of the correct crime in a case falling somewhere within the general category of larceny-related offenses . . . ." Guilt of theft may be established by proof of any one of the methods enumerated in the statute. State v. Gilbert, 27 Or.App. 1, 555 P.2d 31, 33 (1976).

11. McKinney's N.Y.Rev.Pen.Law, tit. J (1975).

Theft under the Kansas statute, unlike common-law larceny, does not require asportation. State v. Knowles, 209 Kan. 676, 498 P.2d 40 (1972).

It may be added that the Kansas statute on unauthorized control over property includes real property. It was held to apply to an easement. State v. Greene, 5 Kan.App.2d 698, 623 P.2d 933 (1981).

12. Model Penal Code, art. 223.

compensation; or (b) to dispose of the property so as to make it unlikely that the owner will recover it. . . .

(6) "property" means any thing of value, including real estate, tangible and intangible personal property, contract rights, choses-in-action and other interests in or claims to wealth, admission or transportation tickets, captured or domestic animals, food and drink, electric or other power.

Section 223.1 Consolidation of Theft Offenses; . . .

(1) Consolidation of theft offenses. Conduct denominated theft in this Article constitutes a single offense embracing the offenses heretofore known as larceny, embezzlement, false pretense, extortion, blackmail, fraudulent conversion, receiving stolen property, and the like. . . .

Section 223.2 Theft by Unlawful Taking or Disposition

(Larceny, embezzlement and theft of immovable property. The latter includes a transfer of real estate or any interest therein.)

Section 223.3 Theft by Deception

(False pretenses, including a false promise.)

Section 223.4 Theft by Extortion

(Common-law extortion and blackmail.)

Section 223.5 Theft of Property Lost, Mislaid, or Delivered by Mistake

(To lost and mislaid property is added property delivered by mistake, so worded as to do away with all distinctions based upon mistake as to what is being delivered and mistake as to what should be delivered; or based upon the exact time the recipient discovered the mistake.)

Section 223.6 Receiving Stolen Property

(Knowing it has been stolen or believing it has probably been stolen.)

Section 223.7 Theft of Services

(Including the wrongful obtainment without payment of labor, professional service, telephone or other public service, accommodation in hotels, restaurants or elsewhere, admission to exhibitions, use of vehicles or other movable property.)

Section 223.8 Theft by Failure to Make Required Disposition of Funds Received

Section 223.9 Unauthorized Use of Automobile and Other Vehicles

(Includes the so-called joyriding without use of the word "theft.")

THE NEW CODES

A very few of the new codes show a preference for the old names such as "larceny," [13] but the great majority follow the Model Penal Code at least to the extent of using "theft" as the name of some or all of the acquisitive offenses. While the exact language of the Code has seldom been followed, most of the new codes have been more or less influenced by it. A few have a "consolidation clause." [14] Some have included a false promise as a false pretense, or "deception." [15] Several have added to lost or mislaid property, property delivered by mistake, so worded as to eliminate all distinctions based upon the type of mistake or time of its discovery by the recipient.[16] A few have enlarged the offense based upon the receipt of stolen property by adding the clause "or believing that it has probably been stolen," [17] or a clause, variously worded, to the effect that he should have believed it was stolen.[18] A slight majority have included "theft of services." [19] The influence of the Code, however, has not been sufficient to give the new codes anything approaching uniformity, so far as dealing with the acquisitive offenses is concerned.

In a case under a statute patterned somewhat after the Model Penal Code, an insurance company was charged with theft for having surreptitiously obtained confidential medical information concerning hospitalized claimants. It was pointed out for the defense that the information was obtained by transcribing what was read over the phone by reading from the confidential file, so that nothing was removed from the hospital; but the People insisted that in this way the confidentiality of personal medical information

13. Conn.Gen.Stat. § 53a–118 et seq. (1975); N.M.Stat.Ann. § 30–16–1 et seq. (1975); N.Y.Penal Law Art. 155 (McKinney) (1975); Va.Code § 18.2–95 et seq. (1950).

14. Ark.Stat.Ann. § 41–2202 (1977); Me.Rev.Stat. tit. 17–A, § 351 (1975); N.H.Rev.Stat.Ann. § 637:1 (1974); N.D. Cent.Code § 12.1–23–01 (1976); Or.Rev. Stat. § 164–025 (1977); Tex.Penal Code Ann. tit. 7, § 31.02 (Vernon) (1974); Utah Code Ann. § 76–6–403 (1953).

15. Conn.Gen.Stat. § 53a–119(3) (1975); Ga.Code Ann. § 26–1803 (1977); Ind.Code Ann. § 35–43–4–1(b)(6) (Burns) (1979); Ky.Rev.Stat.Ann. § 434C.1–040 (Baldwin) (1974); Me.Rev.Stat. tit. 17–A, § 354 (1975); Minn.Stat.Ann. § 609.52(3) (West) (1964); N.H.Rev.Stat.Ann. § 637:4 (1974); N.Y.Penal Law § 155.05(2)(d) (McKinney) (1975); Pa.Stat.Ann. tit. 18, § 3922 (Purdon) (1973); Wis.Stat.Ann. § 943.20(1)(d) (West) (1953).

16. Ala.Code tit. 13A, § 13A–8–6 (1977); Ark.Stat.Ann. § 41–2205 (1977); Conn.Gen.Stat. § 53a–119(4) (1975); Del. Code Ann. tit. 11, § 842 (1974); West's Fla.Stat.Ann. § 812.021(1)(f) (West) (1976); Haw.Rev.Stat. § 708–830(4) (1973); Ky.Rev.Stat.Ann. § 434C.1–050 (Burns) (1979); Me.Rev.Stat. tit. 17A,

§ 356 (1975); N.H.Rev.Stat.Ann. § 637:6 (1974); N.Y.Penal Law § 155.05(2)B(b) (McKinney) (1975); N.D.Cent.Code § 12.1–23–03 (1976); Or.Rev.Stat. § 164.- 065 (1977); Pa.Stat.Ann. tit. 18, § 3924 (Purdon) (1973); Utah Code Ann. 1953, § 76–6–407.

17. Conn.Gen.Stat. § 53a–119(8) (1975); Pa.Stat.Ann. tit. 18, § 3925 (Purdon) (1973).

18. West's Fla.Stat.Ann. § 812.031(1) (West) (1976); Ill.Ann.Stat. ch. 38, § 16–1(d) (Smith-Hurd) (1961); Iowa Code Ann. § 714.1(4) (West) (1979).

19. Ala.Code tit. 13A, § 13A–8–10 (1977); Ark.Stat.Ann. § 41–2204 (1977); Conn.Gen.Stat. § 53a–119(7) (1975); Ga. Code Ann. § 26–1807 (1977); Haw.Rev. Stat. § 708–830(5) (1973); Ill.Rev.Stat. ch. 38, § 16–3 (1961); Iowa Code Ann. § 714.1(3) (West) (1979); Kan.Stat. § 21–3701 (Supp.1975); Me.Rev.Stat. tit. 17–A, § 357 (1975); Mont.Rev.Codes Ann. § 94–6–34 (1973); N.H.Rev.Stat. Ann. § 637:8 (1974); N.D.Cent.Code § 12.1–23–03 (1976); Or.Rev.Stat. § 164.- 125 (1977); Pa.Stat.Ann. tit. 18, § 3926 (Purdon) (1973); Tex.Penal Code Ann. tit. 7, § 31.04 (Vernon) (1974); Utah Code Ann. § 76–6–409 (1953); Wash.Rev.Code Ann. § 9A.56.030(1)(a) (1977).

was obtained and that this is a "thing of value." This was rejected, however, and the prosecution dismissed, on the ground that even the sweeping provisions of such a statute did not include confidentiality.[20]

SECTION 6. RECEIVING (OR CONCEALING) STOLEN PROPERTY

At common law, and under early English statutes, one who received stolen property, knowing it was stolen, was punishable but not always under the same theory and usually not for felony.[1] Under most of the modern statutes such receiving has been made a substantive offense which some of them make a felony[2] while others provide that the offense is either a felony or a misdemeanor depending upon the value of the property.[3]

If no thief stole anything not desired for his own personal use, the problem of law enforcement would be greatly simplified. Any larceny is a violation of the social interest in the protection of property rights, it is true, but the "fence" stirs up countless larcenies which would otherwise not be committed, and tends to put this type of crime on an organized "business" basis. The "fence" is the popular name for the receiver of stolen property. Historically, receiving stolen property is a much lesser offense than larceny, but as a present social problem it should be ranked as a crime of graver degree. The receiver frequently induces misguided youths to steal and sometimes even teaches them the "tricks of the trade." He is "the one higher up." From the standpoint of social blameworthiness his fault is greater than that of the thief.[4] It is true that one who has never intentionally incited the commission of larceny may yield to the temptation to purchase at a small price property known to be stolen, but this very act tends to incite the thief to further depredation. Receiving stolen property is one of the crimes most difficult to prove to the satisfaction of the jury; but the extent of the social menace involved should not be underestimated.

In the ancient common law, at least in theory, any person who knew of a *felony* and did not bring the crime to the attention of the proper authorities, was guilty of a *misdemeanor* known as "misprision of felony."[5] And the original prosecutions for receiving stolen property were for this misdemeanor or for another common-law misdemeanor known as "compounding a felo-

---

20. People v. Home Insurance Co., 197 Colo. 260, 591 P.2d 1036 (1979).

1. Both misprision of felony (to the limited extent it was recognized—see infra Chapter 5, section 3, I) and compounding a felony were common-law misdemeanors. Under the English statute which punished the receiver as an accessory to larceny after the fact, he was a felon.

2. West's Fla.Stat.Ann. 812.031 (1976); Vernon's Ann.Mo.Stat. § 570.080 (1979); Miss.Code, 1972 § 97–17–69; West's Ann.Cal.Pen.Code § 496 (1977).

3. Colo.Rev.Stat. 1973, 18–4–410; Iowa Code Ann. §§ 714.1(4) and 714.2 (1978); Kan.Stat.Ann. 21–3701 (1978); V.T.C.A. Penal Code § 31.03 (1977).

In general the federal plan is to make the receiver guilty of felony or misdemeanor depending upon the value of the property. 18 U.S.C.A. §§ 659, 662. But it is a felony if the property was a motor vehicle, id. at § 2313, or mail matter, id. at § 1708.

It is a separate, distinct substantive offense. The punishment depends upon the value. Jackson v. State, 10 Md.App. 337, 270 A.2d 322 (1970).

4. See Hall, Theft, Law and Society, c. 5 (2d ed. 1952).

5. 1 Bishop, New Criminal Law § 699 (8th ed. 1892). As to the actual application of this theory see infra, chapter 5, section 3(I).

ny" (agreeing not to prosecute for a known felony, in return for some valuable consideration).[6] The receiver was not an accessory to the larceny after the fact, according to the common law, because he did not receive the felon, but only the goods. An English statute in 1691 [7] provided for the conviction of the guilty receiver as an accessory to the larceny after the fact; [8] but later statutes provided for his conviction either on this basis or under indictment for a separate substantive offense known as receiving stolen property.[9] The statutes in this country commonly provide for the punishment of such receiving as a separate substantive offense.

The traditional statutory pattern of the offense requires these elements:

1. The property must be "received."

2. It must have been stolen and must retain its character of stolen property at the time it is received.

3. It must be received with "knowledge," [and]

[4. With wrongful intent.] [10]

A. THE RECEIVING

The typical "fence" takes over the stolen property and pays the thief a price. He purports to "buy" the goods from the thief. This type of receiving, however, is not essential to guilt of this offense. It is sufficient, so far as this element of the crime is concerned, if the goods are left with the receiver for a temporary purpose, either with or without consideration.[11] In fact it is not necessary for the receiver to touch the goods with his own hands. If they are delivered into his control, this is sufficient.[12] Thus, possession may be taken for him by his servant or agent acting under his directions; [13] or he may direct the thief to deposit the goods at a certain place for

---

6. Ibid.

7. 3 Will. & M. c. 9, § 4.

8. Although petit larceny was a felony even after whipping was substituted for hanging as the penalty, there were no accessories. 2 East P.C. 743–4 (1803).

9. Id. at 745. And see 7 & 8 Geo. IV, c. 29, § 54 (1827).

10. "To sustain a conviction of receiving stolen property, the proof must show (1) that the property has, in fact, been stolen by a person other than the one charged with receiving it; (2) that the one charged with receiving it has actually received the property stolen or aided in concealing it; (3) that the receiver knew the property was stolen at the time he received it and (4) that he received the property for his own gain or to prevent the owner from possessing it." People v. Allen, 407 Ill. 596, 600, 96 N.E.2d 446, 448 (1950). And see Reade v. State, 155 Tex.Cr.R. 528, 530, 236 S.W.2d 798, 799 (1951).

"Implied in the language of the statute are the basic elements of the crime: (1) property belonging to another has been stolen; (2) the defendant received, retained or disposed of the stolen property; (3) at the time of receiving, retaining or disposing of the property the defendant knew or believed the property was stolen; and (4) the defendant acted purposely to deprive the owner of the possession of the property." State v. Murphy, 617 P.2d 399, 401 (Utah 1980).

11. Rex v. Richardson, 6 Car. & P. 335, 172 Eng.Rep. 1265 (1834).

12. Regina v. Smith, Dears. 494, 169 Eng.Rep. 818 (1855).

"The establishment of physical or actual possession of stolen property by the accused is not essential, but 'constructive' possession or control is sufficient." Eliason v. State, 511 P.2d 1066, 1073 (Alaska 1973).

13. Regina v. Miller, 6 Cox C.C. 353 (1854).

him and then lead an innocent "purchaser" to that place, or have the goods sent to him, and complete a "sale" without himself touching them.[14]

A husband may be guilty of receiving goods stolen by his wife if he had no part in the larceny itself,[15] but under the common law a wife could not be guilty of receiving from her husband.[16] This is similar to the rule that (except for certain offenses) a wife who committed a prohibited act in the presence of her husband was presumed to have acted under his coercion,[17] and would seem not properly applicable today when by modern conditions and statutory provisions a married woman has been "emancipated."[18]

There has been some confusion in regard to the receiving of stolen goods from one other than the thief, such as from a former "receiver." This is due to the historical background. When the receiver was punished, under the English statute, as an accessory to larceny after the fact, it was necessary that he receive from the thief himself because otherwise his act was too remote from the original felony.[19] And no doubt the same result was reached under the English common-law theory that the receiver was guilty of compounding a felony. But under modern statutes making this a separate substantive offense it makes no difference from whom the goods are received, if they are taken with knowledge of the fact that they are stolen, and the other elements of the offense are present.[20] It is not necessary that the receiver even know the name of the person from whom the goods were stolen.[21]

It is interesting that until quite recently an occasional statute still punished the receiver as an accessory to larceny after the fact[22] and that under such a provision receipt from the thief was required.[23]

B. CONCEALING

Concealment of stolen goods is evidence that may aid in establishing guilt of the theft, or the receiving, but under the common law and early statutes it had no other significance. In modern legislation, however, a clause expressly covering "aid in concealing" has been added to some of the statutes,[24] although not to others.[25]

14. Commonwealth v. Kuperstein, 207 Mass. 25, 92 N.E. 1008 (1910); Regina v. Smith, Dears. 494, 169 Eng.Rep. 818 (1855).

The receiver may agree to take the property from the place where the thief has concealed it. Regina v. Wade, 1 Car. & K. 739, 174 Eng.Rep. 1014 (1844).

It is sufficient if D and another received joint possession of the stolen property. People v. Lees, 257 Cal.App.2d 363, 64 Cal.Rptr. 888 (1967).

15. Regina v. M'Athey, Leigh & C. 250, 169 Eng.Rep. 1384 (1862).

16. Regina v. Brooks, Dearsly, C.C. 184, 169 Eng.Rep. 688 (1853); Regina v. Wardroper, Bell C.C. 249, 169 Eng.Rep. 1248 (1860).

17. Rex v. Hughes, 2 Lewin C.C. 229, 168 Eng.Rep. 1137 (1813); Commonwealth v. Adams, 186 Mass. 101, 71 N.E. 78 (1904).

18. State v. Renslow, 211 Iowa 642, 230 N.W. 316 (1930). And see People v. Statley, 91 Cal.App.2d Supp. 943, 206 P.2d 76 (1949).

19. State v. Ives, 35 N.C. (13 Iredell) 338 (1852).

20. Kirby v. United States, 174 U.S. 47, 19 S.Ct. 574 (1899); Anderson v. State, 38 Fla. 3, 20 So. 765 (1896); Ream v. State, 52 Neb. 727, 73 N.W. 227 (1847); Curran v. State, 12 Wyo. 553, 76 P. 577 (1904).

21. Wertheimer & Goldberg v. State, 201 Ind. 572, 169 N.E. 40 (1929).

22. Ga.Code, § 26–2620 (1953).

23. State v. Ives, 35 N.C. (13 Iredell) 338 (1852).

24. E.g., West's Fla.Stat.Ann. § 812.-031 (1976); La.Stat.Ann.Rev.Stat. 14:69 (1974).

25. E.g., Ga.Code § 16–1806 (1978); Kan.Stat.Ann. 21–3701 (1974); Miss.Code 1972, § 97–17–69.

An occasional statute has a clause expressly covering withholding from the owner property that had been innocently received.[26] This may be helpful as a matter of emphasis but is not necessary because such disposition would be held to be "aid in concealing." This phrase, in such a statute, does not require that the goods be secreted in a place of hiding.[27] Any act which assists the thief in his appropriation of the property,[28] or tends to prevent recovery by the owner,[29] is concealment.

To be guilty of receiving the wrongdoer must at least exercise control over the stolen goods, as mentioned above, but under statutes which include "aid in concealing" one may be convicted of this offense for rendering such assistance to the thief without either taking possession of the goods or exercising any control over them.[30] Another difference may be noted here. The perpetrator of the larceny cannot be guilty of receiving the goods he has stolen.[31] As put by one court, "a single act may not constitute both a larceny and a receiving of the stolen goods."[32] Although both are punishable they are separate crimes and a fatal variance results if one is charged and the proof shows the other.[33] On the other hand, since concealment may be subsequent to the acquisition, and quite distinct therefrom, the thief may be convicted of concealing the goods he has stolen, where this has been included in the statute,[34] although there is some authority that he may not.[35]

26. West's Ann.Cal.Pen.Code § 496 (1970).

27. Commonwealth v. Kuperstein, 207 Mass. 25, 92 N.E. 1008 (1910).

"Property need not be hidden in a vault or buried in the ground in order to be concealed . . . . All that is necessary is that its whereabouts be concealed from its rightful owner." Williams v. Superior Court, 81 Cal.App.3d 330, 146 Cal.Rptr. 311, 319 (1978).

It was proper to instruct that "concealing" "does not require an actual hiding or secreting of the property and includes anything done to prevent the owner's recovering it." Nipps v. State, 576 P.2d 310, 311 (Okl.Cr.1978).

28. People v. Reynolds, 2 Mich. 422 (1852).

29. Wertheimer & Goldberg v. State, 201 Ind. 572, 169 N.E. 40 (1929); Commonwealth v. Matheson, 328 Mass. 371, 103 N.E.2d 714 (1952).

30. State v. Golt and McDermott, 27 Del. 545, 90 A. 83 (1913).

31. Snider v. State, 119 Tex.Cr.R. 635, 44 S.W.2d 997 (1931).

A thief, acting alone, cannot be convicted of receiving the same property he has stolen. State v. Brooks, 348 So.2d 417 (Fla.App.1977). "Since a thief may not receive stolen property from himself, the appellant cannot be convicted of receiving stolen property where the evidence shows that she actually stole the proper-

ty." Davidson v. State, 360 So.2d 728, 731 (Ala.App.1978). But see State v. Watkins, 156 Mont. 456, 481 P.2d 689 (1971). Under a statute which prohibits "receiving, retaining or disposing of stolen property," the thief who sells the stolen property may be convicted of both the theft and the disposal. State v. Tapia, 89 N.M. 221, 549 P.2d 636 (App. 1976). See also United States v. Trzcinski, 553 F.2d 851 (3d Cir. 1976).

The thief cannot be guilty of receiving the property he stole. Guerin v. State, 396 So.2d 132 (Ala.App.1980) as corrected in 1981. Writ denied by Ala.Sup.Ct. April 10, 1981.

32. Weisberg v. United States, 49 App.D.C. 28, 258 F. 284, 286 (1919).

33. United States v. Fusco, 398 F.2d 32 (7th Cir. 1968). Coates v. State, 249 Ind. 357, 229 N.E.2d 640 (1967).

34. The thief could not be guilty of receiving stolen property, but he could be guilty of concealing stolen property. State v. Para, 120 Ariz. 26, 583 P.2d 1346 (App.1978). Accord, Hayes v. State, 581 P.2d 221 (Alaska, 1978). The federal Dyer Act, 18 U.S.C.A. § 2313, provides: "Whoever receives, conceals, stores, barters, sells or disposes of any motor vehicle . . . moving as, or which is a part of . . . interstate commerce . . . ." It was held that the fact that

35. See note 35 on page 398.

Either receiving or concealing must be in cooperation with the thief, or subsequent holder of the property, because stealing from a thief is larceny.[36]

Some of the new penal codes word this element of the crime in terms of one who "receives, retains or disposes of stolen property," [37] or "receives, retains or disposes of, or aids in the concealment of any stolen property." [38] The significance of such a provision will receive attention later.

C. STOLEN PROPERTY

Traditionally it has been an essential element of this offense that the goods should have been stolen.[39] In the absence of a special statute, one does not commit this crime by receiving what he thinks is stolen property if it is not such in fact.[40] This requires consideration of two problems: (1) what is stolen property to begin with and (2) when does property which has been stolen lose its character as stolen property?

1. WHAT IS STOLEN PROPERTY

Property acquired by larceny is clearly stolen property. This is true whether the crime was simple larceny or compound larceny, and whether the larceny was the sole offense or was perpetrated in connection with burglary.[41] It is also clear that property acquired by robbery is stolen property, whether robbery is viewed (according to the ancient notion) as essentially a different crime, or (according to the modern theory) as an aggravated form of larceny.[42]

It has been held in a few cases that a conviction of receiving stolen property cannot be supported by proof of the receipt of embezzled property. This result seems unavoidable if receiving stolen property and receiving embezzled property are listed as separate offenses in the statutes,[43] and particularly if the penalties are not the same.[44] It is unavoidable also if the statute on receiving is so specific in its wording as not to include the receipt of embezzled property.[45] In general, however, no such unfortunate distinction is required. Although embezzlement was held to be a separate offense, it

defendant was himself the thief did not prevent conviction under this act. United States v. West, 562 F.2d 375 (6th Cir. 1977).

35. People v. Kyllonen, 402 Mich. 135, 262 N.W.2d 2 (1978). This reversed a decision of the court of appeals which held that the thief could be convicted of "concealing."

36. 1 Hale P.C. *507.

37. E.g., Conn.Gen.Stat.Ann. § 53a–119(8) (1972).

38. E.g., West's Fla.Stat.Ann. § 812.-031 (1977).

39. State v. Hamilton, 172 S.C. 453, 174 S.E. 396 (1933); State v. Tindall, 213 S.C. 484, 50 S.E.2d 188 (1948); Bandy v. State, 575 S.W.2d 278 (Tenn.1979).

40. People v. Jaffe, 185 N.Y. 497, 78 N.E. 169 (1906); State v. Nguyen, 367 So. 2d 342 (La.1979).

A different type of statute, however, may make it an offense for one to receive property that he believes is stolen, even if in fact it is not stolen. People v. Adler, —— Colo. ——, 629 P.2d 569 (1981).

41. State v. Boyd, 195 Iowa 1091, 191 N.W. 84 (1922).

42. Marco v. State, 188 Ind. 540, 125 N.E. 34 (1919).

The statute providing a penalty for possession of stolen property does not apply to a vehicle used in violation of the joyriding statute. State v. Roberts, 16 Or.App. 397, 519 P.2d 380 (1974).

43. Gentry v. State, 223 Ind. 459, 61 N.E.2d 641 (1945); State v. George, 263 Mo. 686, 173 S.W. 1077 (1914).

44. Commonwealth v. Leonard, 140 Mass. 473, 4 N.E. 96 (1886).

45. Leal v. State, 12 Tex.App. 279 (1882).

was a legislative effort to fill certain gaps that had appeared in the common law of larceny. The original statute referred to embezzled property as having been "feloniously stolen," [46] and words in embezzlement statutes, relating this offense to larceny, have been common.[47] "Embezzlement is a species of larceny," [48] and there should be no hesitation in classifying property obtained by embezzlement as "stolen property," [49] unless a different result is required by some peculiarity of the statute in a particular jurisdiction.[50]

A similar problem may be encountered in regard to property obtained by false pretenses. If title was obtained, the property may be held not to be within the purview of a statute which speaks only of "stolen" property. On the other hand, the wording of a receiving statute may be clearly intended to cover property obtained by false pretenses, as well as that obtained by larceny or embezzlement.[51] If the jurisdiction has a separate statute dealing with the receiving of property obtained by false pretenses, the indictment or information for such an offense must be brought under this section.[52]

2. WHEN STOLEN PROPERTY LOSES ITS CHARACTER AS SUCH

The fact that property has been stolen does not remove it forever from the channels of legitimate commerce. Once it has been restored to the true owner it ceases to be stolen property. Because of this fact it has been held that if stolen property is once restored to the owner, or recovered on behalf of the owner, and is then turned back to the thief with instructions to make the intended disposition, it is too late for another to be guilty of receiving

---

46. 39 Geo. III, c. 85 (1799).

47. New Mex.Stat. 1978 Title 30 Prt. 16 is denominated larceny. § 30–16–8 defines embezzlement.

48. People v. Burr, 41 How.Pr. 293, 294 (N.Y.1871).

49. Shoop v. State, 209 Ark. 498, 190 S.W.2d 988 (1945); People v. Perini, 94 Cal. 573, 29 P. 1027 (1892).

"Wood was entrusted with the documents on a confidential basis. His expropriation of them for delivery to one with an interest adverse to his employer's constituted embezzlement." Williams v. Superior Court, 81 Cal.App.3d 330, 146 Cal. Rptr. 311, 319 (1978).

50. For example, taking across the state line a car obtained by embezzlement was held to violate the federal statute against interstate transportation of a motor vehicle "knowing the same to have been stolen." United States v. Turley, 352 U.S. 407, 77 S.Ct. 397 (1957).

Interstate transportation of property worth $5,000 or more, "knowing the same to have been stolen, converted or taken by fraud" is punishable by 18 U.S. C.A. § 2314. The word "converted" in this statute means appropriated dishonestly or illegally. United States v. Evans, 579 F.2d 360 (5th Cir. 1978).

51. Payne v. State, 435 P.2d 424 (Okl. Cr.1968).

The result is obvious where larceny, embezzlement and false pretenses have been consolidated in an offense called "theft" and the receiving statute speaks of property obtained by theft. E.g., West's Ann.Cal.Pen.Code § 496 (1977); V.T.C.A.Penal Code § 31.02 (1974).

Compare 18 U.S.C.A. § 641 (1976).

Property obtained by false pretenses is also included. See United States v. Frakes, 563 F.2d 803 (6th Cir. 1977).

52. Regina v. Wilson, 2 Moody 52, 169 Eng.Rep. 21 (1838); and see State v. Giangosso, 157 La. 360, 102 So. 429 (1924).

The word "stolen" as used in the National Stolen Property Act, 18 U.S.C.A. §§ 2314 and 2315, includes "all felonious takings . . . with intent to deprive the owner of the rights and benefits of ownership, regardless of whether or not the theft constitutes common-law larceny." United States v. McClintic, 570 F.2d 685, 688 (8th Cir. 1978).

stolen property, by receiving it from the thief.[53]   Such a receiver might think the property he was receiving was stolen, but it would not be so in fact.[54]

On the other hand stolen property may taint other property into which it is converted, thereby giving that also the character of stolen property. In one case a man who already had a wife pretended to marry another woman and fraudulently persuaded her to sell her property and give the proceeds to him, which she did in the form of a check. He converted the check into traveler's checks and then transported the traveler's checks from Houston, Texas, to New York. It was held that he had transported fraudulently obtained property in interstate commerce and hence was guilty of violating the National Stolen Property Act, 18 U.S.C.A. § 415 (now § 2314).[55] In another case a stolen check was converted into cash by an elaborate three or four-step maneuver. One who received part of this cash with knowledge of all the facts was held guilty of receiving stolen money.[56]

Although stolen property loses its character as such the moment it is recovered by an officer *for the owner*, this does not mean that such a change takes place whenever an officer touches the property. The fact that FBI agents took hold of stolen money long enough to count it and record the serial numbers, before a cooperating co-defendant delivered it to the receiver, did not prevent a conviction.[57] The court said: "To be sure, a government agent traveled with Beverly [the co-defendant], counted the money and recorded serial numbers, but these actions were performed as a form of observation and surveillance rather than as possession on behalf of the rightful owner."[58] And the fact that an undercover agent, at the direction of the thief, drove the truck carrying two stolen bulldozers, did not save the receiver from conviction of receiving stolen goods moving in interstate commerce.[59]

D. KNOWLEDGE

The common statement is that for guilt of this offense the property must be received with "knowledge" that it has been stolen.[60]

53. Regina v. Dolan, 6 Cox C.C. 449 (1855).

"Since the stipulated facts in this case conclusively establish that at the time of the alleged offense the watch, although previously stolen, had lost its stolen character through recovery by the owner's agent, the defendant cannot be held guilty for receiving the watch."   State v. Nguyen, 367 So.2d 342, 345 (La.1979).

In "accord with the common law rule, one cannot be convicted of receiving stolen goods when actual physical possession of the stolen goods has been recovered by the owner or his agent before delivery to the intended receiver."   United States v. Monasterski, 567 F.2d 677, 684 (6th Cir. 1977).

54. As to criminal attempt by such a receipt see infra, chapter 6, section 3.

55. United States v. Walker, 176 F.2d 564 (2d Cir. 1949). The statute is worded in terms of: "Whoever transports in interstate or foreign commerce any goods, wares, merchandise, securities or money, of the value of $5000 or more, knowing the same to have been stolen, converted or taken by fraud; . . ."

56. State v. Key, 118 Ariz. 196, 575 P.2d 826 (App. 1978).

57. United States v. Egger, 470 F.2d 1179 (9th Cir. 1972).

58. Id. at 1181.

59. United States v. Dove, 629 F.2d 325 (4th Cir. 1980).

60. See People v. Boyden, 116 Cal. App.2d 278, 287, 253 P.2d 773, 779 (1953). A verdict of "guilty of receiving stolen goods" is insufficient to support a conviction of receiving stolen goods knowing them to have been stolen. State v. Yow, 227 N.C. 585, 42 S.E.2d 661 (1947). "The inference arising from the recent posses-

This is satisfactory if a correct significance is given to the word "knowledge." Here, as so commonly in the criminal law, this word is used in a broad sense. If the property is in fact stolen, one who receives it does so with "knowledge" (as this word is used in this connection) if he either (1) knows it to be stolen, or (2) believes it to be stolen,[61] or (3) has his suspicions definitely aroused and refuses to investigate for fear he will discover that it is stolen.[62]

Negligence in not realizing that the property is stolen will not be sufficient for conviction.[63] The question is not whether the circumstances were such that they would have suggested this possibility to the ordinary reasonable person; but did they actually convey this suggestion to this very defendant?[64] If they did, and he wilfully "shut his eyes" for fear of what he would learn, he is held to have had "knowledge." If they did not, and he acted in the utmost good faith without the slightest notion the property was stolen, he took it without "knowledge" no matter how "dumb" he may have been.[65]

sion of stolen property has no application to the charge of receiving." Id. at 587, 42 S.E.2d at 662.

61. "While guilty knowledge of the larceny is an essential fact to be proved in a prosecution for receiving stolen goods, such knowledge need not be that actual and positive knowledge which is acquired from personal observation of the fact." People v. Boyden, 116 Cal. App.2d 278, 287–8, 253 P.2d 773, 779 (1953). "It is sufficiently shown if the circumstances proven are such as must have made or caused the recipient of stolen goods to believe they were stolen." Reaves v. Commonwealth, 192 Va. 443, 451, 65 S.E.2d 559, 564 (1951). "It is sufficient if the facts are such as to cause an actual belief that the property was stolen." Lewis v. State, 81 Okl.Cr. 168, 172, 162 P.2d 201, 203 (1945). "That guilty knowledge, or its equivalent, guilty belief is of the gist of this offense has been declared by many decisions, ..." Meath v. State, 174 Wis. 80, 83, 182 N.W. 334, 335 (1921).

The essential element of the offense is that the person, at the time of receiving the stolen goods, had knowledge that they had been stolen. If he did not have actual or positive knowledge, the question is whether from the circumstances he—not some other person—believed they had been stolen. State v. Alpert, 88 Vt. 191, 92 A.2d 32 (1914).

The "defendant knew or believed the property was stolen: . . . ." State v. Murphy, 617 P.2d 399, 401 (Utah 1980).

62. If defendant did not know that the goods were stolen or know facts sufficient to put him on inquiry he is not

guilty. William v. State, 106 Fla. 225, 143 So. 157 (1932); Arnivan v. State, 146 Tex.Cr.R. 382, 175 S.W.2d 598 (1943). "It was necessary for the State to show that appellant knew or knew of such facts as would put a man of ordinary intelligence and caution on inquiry that the money was embezzled." Monteresi v. State, 160 Fla. 489, 490, 35 So.2d 582 (1948). As said in another connection:

"Ethically there appears to be little difference . . . between the quality of conduct of the man who knows or believes his representation is false and that of the man who has neither knowledge nor belief concerning it, but nevertheless makes the representation, neither knowing nor caring whether it be true or false." State v. Pickus, 63 S.D. 209, 230, 257 N.W. 284, 294 (1934).

Gross inadequacy of price may also give rise to such an inference. See People v. Bycel, 133 Cal.App.2d 596, 599, 284 P.2d 927, 930 (1955).

63. Meath v. State, 174 Wis. 80, 182 N.W. 334 (1921).

64. The question is not what a prudent man, exercising ordinary care, would have believed or known under the circumstances, but what did defendant know or believe. State v. Ebbeler, 283 Mo. 57, 222 S.W. 396 (1920); State v. Beale, 299 A.2d 921 (Me.1973).

65. Schaffer v. United States, 221 F.2d 17 (5th Cir. 1955). "The infraction of this statute is not proved by negligence nor by failure to exercise as much intelligence as the ordinarily prudent man." Commonwealth v. Boris, 317 Mass. 309, 315, 58 N.E.2d 8, 12 (1944).

The unsuspecting receipt of goods under circumstances which would be sufficient to induce a prudent man, exercising ordinary care, to believe they were stolen, does not constitute "knowledge" of this fact even in the very broad sense in which the word is used in this connection,[66] although there is a trace of authority to the contrary.[67] It is reversible error to instruct that receipt of stolen goods under such circumstances is sufficient in itself to constitute guilt of this offense,[68] but such receipt may be sufficient to convince the jury that the recipient did in fact believe the goods were stolen, and will be sufficient to warrant an inference to this effect.[69]

It is possible for the mens-rea requirement of this offense to be changed by statute. This is a true crime and hence a provision would be invalid if it called for conviction of one who received stolen goods innocently, and without even so much as negligence on his part,[70] but there is no such objection to an enactment which provides for the conviction of one who receives stolen property "which he knows or has reason to believe has been stolen." [71] This enlarges the mens-rea requirement and authorizes conviction of one who has been criminally negligent in the receipt of stolen goods. Even under such a statute, however, it has been held that the receipt of goods, by one who has reasonable cause to believe they have been stolen, will not authorize conviction if they have not in fact been stolen.[72]

The Colorado statute which had provided punishment for receiving property with "knowledge" that it was stolen was amended to read: "A person commits theft by receiving when he receives . . . anything of value of another knowing or believing said thing has been stolen . . .." This was held to authorize conviction of one who received property, believing it was

---

66. State v. Ebbeler, 283 Mo. 57, 222 S.W. 396 (1920).

67. "The word 'knowing' only means, in the sense used in this statute, that, if a person has information from the facts and circumstances which should convince him that the property had been stolen or which would lead a reasonable man to believe that the property had been stolen, then in the legal sense he knew it." Francis v. State, 154 Miss. 176, 179, 122 So. 372, 373 (1929). The "clear weight of authority" is otherwise (citing cases). State v. Aschenbrenner, 171 Or. 664, 671, 138 P.2d 911, 914 (1943).

68. State v. Ebbeler, 283 Mo. 57, 222 S.W. 396 (1920); State v. Goldman, 65 N.J.L. 394, 47 A. 641 (1900); Pickering v. United States, 2 Okl.Cr. 197, 101 P. 123 (1909); State v. Beale, 299 A.2d 921 (Me. 1973).

69. State v. Gargare, 88 N.J.L. 389, 95 A. 625 (1915).

Sale of property at a disproportionately low price, or the alteration of property to prevent identification, may constitute suspicious circumstances which, coupled with the possession of recently stolen property may be sufficient to warrant an inference that it was received with knowledge of the larceny. People v. Malouf, 135 Cal.App.2d 697, 287 P.2d 834 (1955).

The statute may authorize conviction of one who receives recently stolen goods and is unable to show that he received them innocently. State v. Lisena, 129 N.J.L. 569, 30 A.2d 593 (1943).

70. The New York statute penalizing the receipt of stolen goods by a junkman without a requirement of knowledge or (prior to amendment) a requirement of diligent inquiry as to rights of the party selling or delivering such goods was invalid. People v. Estreich, 272 App.Div. 698, 75 N.Y.S.2d 267, aff'd 297 N.Y. 910, 79 N.E.2d 742 (1947).

71. Hutton v. State, 494 P.2d 1246 (Okl.Cr.1972); Holmes v. State, 568 P.2d 317 (Okl.Cr.1977). But see People v. Johnson, 193 Colo. 199, 564 P.2d 116 (1977), which held such a statute unconstitutional.

72. Farzley v. State, 231 Ala. 60, 163 So. 394 (1935).

Compare Model Penal Code § 223.-6(2).

stolen, although it never had been stolen.[73] The holding is quite logical. Had it been desired to hold the receiver who believed the property was stolen, only when it really was stolen, no change in the statute was needed.

It is possible also for the legislature to impose a duty of investigation on one who receives certain kinds of property under specified circumstances, and to provide for conviction if stolen property has been received without such required investigation to ascertain the right of the person who offered it for sale.[74] A pawnbroker, for example, was convicted under such a statute. Evidence that he purchased a stolen watch from a boy of 14 who brought it to the pawn shop, making no investigation beyond asking a few questions of the boy, was held sufficient to uphold the conviction.[75]

If the statute provides only for the conviction of one who receives stolen property, knowing it to be stolen, such "knowledge" at the time of the receipt is essential.[76] If the enactment includes concealment, as well as receipt, it has been held that the receiver is guilty if he conceals the property after receiving information of the larceny, although he had received it innocently in the first place.[77] And some of the statutes now provide for the conviction of one who withholds stolen property from the owner, knowing it to have been stolen.[78]

Those new penal codes in which this element of the crime is worded in terms of one who "receives, retains or disposes of stolen property," have made a very important addition. Such a statute not only forbids certain conduct, but what is forbidden necessarily requires other action. A duty is imposed upon the innocent recipient of stolen property who later learns of its true character. Since he is forbidden either to retain the property or to dispose of it, the result is that he is required to take positive steps to restore the property to the owner. Any good faith effort in this direction will save from criminal guilt, but nothing less will do.[79]

E. WITH WRONGFUL INTENT

"Whatever the law may be in that respect elsewhere," it was said by one court,[80] "intent is not, by our statute, a necessary fact to be averred or

73. People v. Holloway, 193 Colo. 450, 568 P.2d 29 (1977).

74. E.g., West's Ann.Cal.Pen.Code § 496a (1977).

75. People v. Seerman, 43 Cal.App. 506, 111 P.2d 457 (1941).

76. Walker v. State, 82 Okl.Cr. 352, 170 P.2d 261 (1946).

"There must be a *guilty* knowledge, . . . concurrent with the act." Arcia v. State, 26 Tex.App. 193, 205, 9 S.W. 685, 686 (1888).

77. Salcido v. State, 126 Tex.Cr.R. 281, 70 S.W.2d 706 (1934).

"One reason for including both receiving and concealing stolen property within the proscription of Penal Code section 496 is that it enables prosecution of one who innocently acquires property, but later learns that it is stolen and thereafter conceals it." Williams v. Superior Court, 81 Cal.App.3d 330, 146 Cal.Rptr. 311, 319 (1978).

78. "Every person who . . . knowing the same to be stolen . . . conceals, withholds or aids in concealing . . . or withholding any such property from the owner is punishable . . . ." West's Ann.Cal.Pen.Code § 496 (1977).

79. Where the defendant first learned from the police that furniture in his residence was stolen, defendant was guilty of receiving stolen property when he allowed his wife to consummate a sale of the furniture by making payments to the seller. State v. Thibeault, 390 A.2d 1095 (Me.1978).

80. State v. Smith, 88 Iowa 1, 3, 55 N.W. 16, 17 (1893).

proved in such a case." Probably this could be stated as the general rule in regard to receiving stolen property, but it must not be misinterpreted. A statutory definition of the offense may add some specific intent which the prosecution will be required to allege and affirmatively to prove—although such intent could be inferred from circumstances having proper probative significance if the jury should find them sufficient for this purpose.[81] But no such specific intent is found in the common-law definition. Stolen property might be received with knowledge of the larceny but with innocent intent, as if, for example, it was received to restore to the owner without accepting a reward.[82] Proof of such an intent would disprove the charge in any case.[83] On the other hand, the intent is not innocent if it is to preserve the property for the thief,[84] to keep it for the use of the recipient or for sale by him, or to gain any other advantage for him such as to claim a reward from the owner.[85] It is not incorrect to say that guilt of this offense requires a wrongful intent, but this is to be understood to mean no more than that an innocent intent is inconsistent with guilt.[86] It does not mean that there is some specific intent which is an additional element of the offense and which the prosecution is required to allege and affirmatively to prove.[87] Such an element, however, is incorporated in some of the statutory definitions by the inclusion of the words "with intent to deprive the true owner thereof," [88] "with intent to defraud the owner," [89] or "without the intention of restoring them to the

81. United States v. Lowenstein, 21 D.C. 515 (1893).

82. Aldrich v. People, 101 Ill. 16 (1881). "If the property was received or concealed with the purpose and intent of restoring it to the owner without reward, or with any other innocent intent, the mere knowledge that it was stolen property would not make the act criminal." Arcia v. State, 26 Tex.App. 193, 205, 9 S.W. 685, 686 (1888). And see State v. Hodges, 55 Md. 127, 137 (1880).

"We hold that the *innocent* intent of returning the property to the true owner is a defense to the charge of attempted receiving stolen property." People v. Osborne, 77 Cal.3d 472, 143 Cal.Rptr. 582, 585 (1978).

83. Aldrich v. People, 101 Ill. 16 (1881).

"If the intent is honest, of course the offense is not committed." State v. Alderman, 83 Conn. 597, 600, 78 A. 331, 332 (1910).

84. State v. Hodges, 55 Md. 127 (1880).

85. Baker v. State, 58 Ark. 513, 25 S.W. 603 (1894); State v. Golt and McDermott, 27 Del. 545, 90 A. 83 (1913). "To constitute the crime of receiving stolen property knowing the same to have been stolen, the act of receiving or concealing the same must be accompanied by a criminal intent of the accused to aid

the thief, or hope to obtain some gain or reward for restoring the stolen property to the owner, or in some way to derive a benefit or profit therefrom." Pickering v. United States, 2 Okl.Cr. 197, 101 P. 123 (1909). Syllabus by the court. And see State v. Alderman, 83 Conn. 597, 600, 78 A. 331, 332 (1910).

86. "Conceding that a person who receives such property, with a laudable intent, is not guilty of the commission of the crime, and a proviso to that effect has been incorporated in the act, it is not necessary for the pleader to negative the exception in the indictment. The fact might have been a defense, but it would be for the defendant to show that he came within the exception." People v. Weldon, 111 N.Y. 569, 574–5, 19 N.E. 279, 280 (1888).

87. State v. Smith, 88 Iowa 1, 55 N.W. 16 (1893); Steele v. State, 213 Miss. 739, 57 So.2d 574 (1952).

The crime of theft by controlling stolen property under A.R.S. § 13–1802A(5), does not require specific intent as an element. State v. Morse, 127 Ariz. 25, 617 P.2d 1141, 1147 (1980).

88. Baker v. State, 58 Ark. 213, 25 S.W. 603 (1894); Rice v. State, 50 Tenn. 215, 226 (1871).

89. Darrah v. State, 65 Neb. 201, 90 N.W. 1123 (1902).

owner." [90] Where such an intent is made an element of the offense the indictment or information must be worded accordingly.[91]

SECTION 7. MALICIOUS MISCHIEF

Malicious mischief is the malicious destruction of, or damage to, the property of another.

It was a misdemeanor under the English common law. Under modern statutes it is generally a misdemeanor, but under a few of them it may be a felony depending upon either the nature of the property or the value thereof.

Such phrases as "malicious mischief and trespass," "malicious injury," or "maliciously damaging the property of another," are merely additional labels used at times to indicate the same offense. It was a misdemeanor according to the common law of England,[1] although some confusion has resulted from Blackstone's statement that it was "only a trespass at common law." [2] Before the word "misdemeanor" became well established the old writers tended to use the word "trespass" to indicate an offense below the grade of felony.[3] And it was used at times by Blackstone for this purpose, as in the phrase "treason, felony, or trespass." [4] With this in mind there should be no misunderstanding if we do not isolate the clause but read the entire sentence: "And therefore any damage arising from this mischievous disposition, though only a trespass at common law, is now by a multitude of statutes made penal in the highest degree." [5] The reference is to a group of English statutes enacted to raise certain types of malicious mischief to the grade of felony, and to increase or make certain the penalty for other types, although leaving them in the misdemeanor category. Of this extensive legislative program Wharton had this to say:

90. Anderson v. State, 130 Ala. 126, 30 So. 375 (1900).

91. See the cases in the three preceding notes. If the indictment charges that the stolen goods were unlawfully, wilfully and feloniously received, it is not necessary to allege that they were received with the intention of permanently depriving the owner of the use thereof. Shuttles v. Commonwealth, 190 Ky. 176, 227 S.W. 154 (1921). Cf. State v. Elias, 74 Ariz. 374, 249 P.2d 941 (1952).

1. Malicious mischief was an offense at common law despite many English statutes. The statutes were merely to increase the penalties. Loomis v. Edgerton & Sykes, 19 Wend. 419 (N.Y.1838); State v. Briggs, 1 Aik. 226 (Vt.1826) and see the opinion of Powell, J. in State v. Council, 1 Tenn. 305 (1808). An early statute referred to the fact that the "Men of the Towns near will not indict such as be guilty" of overthrowing a hedge or dyke. 13 Edw. 1, c. 46 (1285). It was mentioned that such mischief was done at night when it could "not be known by Verdict of the Assize or Jury,

who did overthrow the Hedge or Dyke, ..." but the inference is that if done in the daytime it would have been known and there would have been an indictment. Coke says that defacing tombs, sepulchers and monuments was punishable at common law. 3 Co.Inst. *202. The context indicates that this is not due to some special rule but merely that they have not been taken out of the normal category.

2. 4 Bl.Comm. *243.

3. For example, in "a table of principal matters" to Hawkins Pleas of the Crown, there is no title "misdemeanor," but under "trespass" we find: "The word *trespass* is of a very general extent, and in a large sense not only comprehends all inferior offences which are properly and directly against the peace, but also all others which are only so by construction."

4. 4 Bl.Comm. *130.

5. Id. at *243. See State v. Watts, 48 Ark. 56, 58, 2 S.W. 342 (1886).

"Upward of eighteen hundred sections, it is estimated, of acts running from Henry VIII to George III, repealed or otherwise, were enacted for the special purpose of providing against malicious mischief; and as the statutory penalty was both more specific and more certain than that of the common law, the books, in this class of offenses, give but few examples of common-law indictments. But as the later English statutes are not in force in this country, malicious mischief, as a common-law offense, has here been the subject of frequent adjudication." [6]

Although malicious mischief is properly considered a common-law misdemeanor in this country [7] the field has been practically, if not entirely, preempted by legislation. The desire to provide different penalties for different types of mischief, making some felonies and others misdemeanors with varying grades of severity in each group, has often resulted in an elaborate set of sections.[8] Wherever this is true, or wherever the rule is that common-law offenses are not punished as such if not found in the code,[9] there is the risk that some part of the field may have been omitted from the category of crime in a particular jurisdiction unless a catch-all section is included, such as—

"Every person who maliciously injures or destroys any real or personal property not his own, in cases otherwise than such as are specified in this code, is guilty of vandalism." [10]

A. THE MISCHIEF

Except where limitations are found, due to the peculiarities of local statutes, malicious mischief done to any kind of property is a crime.[11] Penalties have been provided frequently for certain types of conduct related to, but falling short of malicious mischief, such as hunting on the land of another without his permission,[12] or entering a building or enclosed land after being forbidden to do so.[13] Such an offense, even if the section is found in the general chapter on the subject,[14] is not malicious mischief proper and cannot be relied upon to determine the requisites of that crime. The type of mischief required for guilt of this offense involves physical injuries to property

---

6. Wharton's Criminal Law § 1318 (12th ed. 1932).

7. Malicious mischief is an offense under American common law. State v. Watts, 48 Ark. 56 (1886); State v. Simpson, 9 N.C. 460 (1823). Maliciously wounding a colt is a misdemeanor at common law. The English statutes attaching severe penalties do not prove it was not a common-law offense but were enacted because the common-law penalties were too mild to prevent the harm, or were believed to be so. We cannot treat these statutes as common law. State v. Briggs, 1 Aik. 226 (Vt.1826).

8. E.g., West's Ann.Cal.Pen.Code §§ 594–625b (1970).

9. State v. Campbell, 217 Iowa 848, 251 N.W. 717 (1934). See Utah Code Ann., 1953, § 76–1–105 (1974).

10. West's Ann.Cal.Pen.Code § 594 (1977). When the English statutes were brought together in a single chapter a catch-all provision was included. 24 & 25 Vict. c. 97, §§ 51, 52 (1861). And see Pollet v. State, 115 Ga. 234, 41 S.E. 606 (1902).

11. Loomis v. Edgerton & Sykes, 19 Wend. 419 (N.Y.1838).

12. West's Ann.Cal.Pen. Code § 602 (k) (1978).

13. Ark.Stats. § 41–2056 (1977).

Intentionally dropping an empty bottle on the property of another, and leaving it there, came within the constitutional "core" of the littering statute. State v. Hood, 24 Wn.App. 155, 600 P.2d 636 (1979).

14. Idaho Code Title 18 Chap. 70 (1979).

"which impair utility or materially diminish value." [15]   It must be shown that the property "was either destroyed or suffered some material or substantial injury." [16]   The technical harm involved in trespassing on the land of another is not malicious mischief if no actual damage is done "however malicious the motive may be." [17]   The wilful removal of property,[18] or unpiling of cord wood,[19] or dumping of rubbish,[20] does not constitute malicious mischief if no damage resulted to the property, even if it caused inconvenience to the owner.   On the other hand, this offense may be committed by shooting a hole through the door of a house [21] or by denting the side of a car by a rock thrown at it.[22]   It should be emphasized that just as some statute may provide a penalty for certain conduct less than malicious mischief, so it is possible for an enactment to require damage of a specified nature, or even actual destruction of the property.[23]

B.   PROPERTY OF ANOTHER

Penalties have been provided for certain types of harm done to one's own property, such as burning insured property with intent to defraud the insurer,[24] or acts constituting cruelty to dumb animals.[25]   Such offenses are not malicious mischief proper, even if found in the general chapter on this subject,[26] and must be distinguished.[27]   For malicious mischief the damage must be done to the property of another.[28]   Hence its proper classification is with "offenses against property." [29]   Public property comes within the characteri-

---

15. State v. Watts, 48 Ark. 56, 59 (1886).

"A mere trespass to real property is not a crime at common law unless it amounts to a breach of the peace . . . .."   In re Appeal No. 631 (77), 282 Md. 223, 383 A.2d 684, 685 (1978).

16. Pollet v. State, 115 Ga. 234, 41 S.E. 606 (1902).

17. State v. McKee, 109 Ind. 497, 500, 10 N.E. 405, 406 (1886). If accompanied by an actual breach of the peace, it is a public offense. Henderson v. Commonwealth, 49 Va. 708 (1852).

18. State v. Cole, 90 Ind. 112 (1883).

19. Pollet v. State, 115 Ga. 234, 41 S.E. 606 (1902).

20. Patterson v. State, 41 Tex.Cr.R. 412, 55 S.W. 388 (1900). The disposal of refuse on the land of another without permission is sometimes a special statutory offense. Mass.Ann.Laws, c. 270, § 16 (1967). Maliciously dealing with the property of another in such a way as to cause inconvenience or expense might well be prohibited by statute. Cf. Model Penal Code, Tentative Draft No. 2, § 206.50(1)(b) (1954).

21. Funderburk v. State, 75 Miss. 20, 21 So. 658 (1897); State v. Dawson, 272 N.C. 535, 159 S.E.2d 1 (1968).

22. Gill v. State, 85 Ga.App. 584, 69 S.E.2d 804 (1952). Malicious mischief may be committed by polluting another's well. State v. Buckman, 8 N.H. 203 (1836).

23. See State v. Robinson, 20 N.C. 129, 131 (1838).

24. West's Ann.Cal.Pen.Code § 450a (1977).

25. Iowa Code § 717.2 (1978).

26. Id. at ch. 716.

27. State v. Avery, 44 N.H. 392 (1862).

28. Jackson v. State, 36 Ala.App. 466, 58 So.2d 901 (1952); People v. Ratcliff, 204 Ill.App. 595 (1917). ". . . injuries to the rights of another. . . ."   State v. Watts, 48 Ark. 56, 59 (1886). The statute which makes an injury to a house indictable does not apply to an injury by a lessee during the lease. State v. Whitener, 92 N.C. 798 (1885). In a prosecution for tearing down another's fence, it is no defense to show that title was in D if the other was in lawful possession. State v. Taylor, 172 N.C. 892, 90 S.E. 294 (1916).

29. State v. Avery, 44 N.H. 392, 395 (1862).

zation of "property of another," as the phrase is used in the definition of this offense, just as it does, for example, in the definition of larceny.

C. MALICE

By definition malicious mischief is not committed unless the damage was inflicted *maliciously*. "Malice is a state of mind," [30]—it is a special mental element required for the mens rea of this offense.[31] There has been no disagreement on this point but great confusion in the effort to explain just what state of mind meets this requirement. A frequent suggestion has been that the word "malice" is used here, not in its customary legal meaning, but in the sense of "actual ill-will or resentment toward its owner or possessor." [32] This is quite illogical and resulted from a faulty analysis of the legal meaning of the word "malice."

Consideration of this problem has frequently started with the premise that "malice," as it is generally used in the law, means intentional harm caused without lawful justification or excuse.[33] This premise is faulty on two counts: (1) malice does not require a specific intent to cause the harm done, whereas on the other hand, (2) harm may be caused intentionally, without justification or excuse, and still not be malicious. "Malice" has had its chief exposition in the homicide cases, and all the confusion at this point could have been avoided if due attention had been given to the results there reached. A homicide may be malicious without a specific intent to kill if it results from an act done in wanton and wilful disregard of a plain and strong likelihood that loss of life will result. On the other hand, an intentional homicide without justification or excuse is not malicious if committed under circumstances of recognized mitigation. And this application of "malice" to the homicide cases is in no sense an unusual treatment of the word as it is used in the law. In other words, the ordinary legal concept of malice requires two ingredients, one positive and the other negative. On the positive side "malice" requires an intent to cause the very harm that results or some harm of the same general nature, or an act done in wanton and wilful disregard of the plain and strong likelihood that some such harm will result. And on the negative side it requires the absence of any circumstance of justification, excuse or recognized mitigation. It will be illuminating to consider the malicious mischief cases in view of this concept.

In some of the cases referring to a supposed requirement of actual ill-will to the owner or a "spirit of wanton cruelty or wicked revenge," the trespass was too slight [34] for malicious mischief and the explanation should have been in terms of the absence of the required *mischief* rather than by any reference to malice. In one case, for example, the alleged harm was spitting on

---

30. Schtul v. People, 96 Colo. 217, 220, 40 P.2d 970 (1935).

31. Carstarphen v. State, 112 Ga. 230, 231-2, 37 S.E. 423, 424 (1900).

32. State v. Robinson, 20 N.C. 129, 131 (1838); State v. Wilcox, 11 Tenn. 278 (1832). "[M]alice towards the owner. . . ." State v. Churchill, 15 Idaho 645, 656, 98 P. 853, 857 (1909). "[M]alicious motive towards the owner of it. . . ." The King v. Pearce, 1 Leach 527, 168 Eng.Rep. 365 (1789).

33. See Commonwealth v. Williams, 110 Mass. 401, 403 (1872).

34. Commonwealth v. Waldon, 57 Mass. 558, 561 (1849). The harm may actually have been serious in this case, but the appellate court was considering only an instruction. The evidence was not before it. See State v. Johnson, 7 Wyo. 512, 54 P. 502 (1898).

the floor of a public hall.[35] At a later time this would have been punishable under another statute enacted for sanitary reasons.[36] And it would be possible for such an act to constitute malicious mischief, as for example, if an oriental rug was discolored by tobacco juice. But this was just a bare surface in an earlier day when spitting on the floor was commonplace if cuspidors were not provided,—and they had not been provided in this hall. The most extreme case in this regard involved driving a flock of sheep over land that was neither enclosed, cultivated nor improved in any way.[37] This was in the west in the days of the "open range" and the court doubted if even a civil trespass had been committed, although that issue was not involved. Obviously it did not constitute malicious mischief, but it is unfortunate that the court felt it necessary to suggest that this offense requires "a spirit of cruelty, hostility or revenge." [38]

In some of the cases the harm was serious enough but there was complete justification for what had been done, and by definition an act is not malicious if it is justified. Typical of this category are cases in which a landowner removed a well and pump from his own premises after due notice to former licensees that the license had been terminated; [39] a co-owner of an elevator broke a lock which had been wrongfully placed to bar the entrance to which he was entitled; [40] or a private nuisance was abated.[41]

The negligence cases also demand attention. Just as criminal negligence is not sufficient to place homicide in the category of murder, so it is not sufficient for guilt of any other offense having malice as an essential ingredient; [42] and in some of the cases in which there was substantial harm, without justification, there was no more than criminal negligence,—if so much. Defendants, in the best-known case of this nature,[43] found a wagon standing in the street and ran with it in sport. It got out of control and was damaged. The court said that malicious mischief involves "the wilful destruction of . . . property, from actual ill-will or resentment towards its owner or possessor," [44] but this was not necessary for the decision. It was held also, and quite properly, that malicious mischief was not committed by one who unintentionally broke a bridge by driving on it with a traction engine, without planking the bridge as required by law,[45] or by one who placed brush and stone on his own land to prevent erosion there, but did so with such negligence as to cause excessive erosion of the land of his neighbor.[46]

35. Commonwealth v. Williams, 110 Mass. 401 (1872).

36. Expectoration in public places. Mass.Ann.Laws, c. 270, § 14 (1968).

37. State v. Johnson, 7 Wyo. 512, 54 P. 502 (1898).

38. Id. at 516, 54 P. 503.

39. People v. Ratcliff, 204 Ill.App. 595 (1917).

40. Carstarphen v. State, 112 Ga. 230, 37 S.E. 423 (1900).

41. Permitting a scrub bull to run at large on a free range was a private nuisance and the owners of thoroughbred cattle who castrated the bull to protect their stock were not guilty of malicious mischief. The court mentioned the necessity of an intent to vex or annoy the owner but this was not necessary to the decision. Hummel v. State, 69 Okl.Cr. 38, 99 P.2d 913 (1940).

42. Jones v. People, 98 Colo. 190, 54 P.2d 686 (1936).

43. State v. Robinson, 20 N.C. 129 (1838).

44. Id. at 131.

45. Mayn v. People, 56 Colo. 170, 136 P. 1016 (1913).

46. Adams v. Commonwealth, 313 Ky. 654, 233 S.W.2d 285 (1950).

Probably the chief source of confusion in regard to the supposed require-ment of actual ill-will toward the owner of the property is found in cases involving unmistakable elements of mitigation, but overlooking the signifi-cance thereof. There has been a tendency in the malicious mischief cases to start with the false premise that any wilful act of a harmful nature is mali-cious if without justification or excuse,[47] and to assume that any qualifica-tion of this statement is peculiar to this offense. The best known of the English statutes on this subject, the so-called "Black Act," [48] provided the death penalty, without benefit of clergy, for anyone who should (among oth-er wrongs) "unlawfully and maliciously kill, maim or wound any cattle," and the word "cattle" in this statute was not limited to animals of the bovine family but included certain others, such as horses and pigs. But just as homicide committed in the sudden heat of passion engendered by adequate provocation is not malicious (and hence not murder), so the judges were not willing to sentence a man to death for killing or wounding an animal under similar circumstances. And it would have been astounding had they taken the position that no provocation can be regarded adequate for killing an animal unless it would be adequate also in a homicide case.

In a sudden burst of anger, for example, because a cow would not stand still, **D** ran a sharp stick into her body and was charged with a capital of-fense under the "Black Act." Confusion concerning the meaning of malice in malicious mischief might never have developed had the judge recognized this clearly as a case of mitigation under the "rule of provocation." Unfor-tunately, however, the judge groping for an explanation instructed the jury that for guilt it was "necessary to shew that the maiming of the animal was done from some malicious motive towards the owner of it, and not merely from an angry and passionate disposition towards the beast itself, ..." [49] That the underlying concept here is mitigation, based on the "rule of provo-cation," is more apparent from the language used in other cases, such as: "It is undoubtedly true that malicious mischief is not committed when the act alleged to be criminal . . . is merely done impulsively under the in-fluence of suddenly aroused passion," [50] or "it was prompted by the sudden resentment of an injury, which is calculated, in no slight degree, to awaken passion. . . ." [51]

Mitigation sufficient to negate the legal concept of malice, particularly in a crime such as malicious mischief, may be found apart from the "rule of provocation." A forest ranger, for example, acting in compliance with a reg-ulation promulgated by the Secretary of Agriculture, shot and killed a mare. It was held that the act done in bona-fide reliance upon supposed authority was not *malicious* even if the regulation itself was illegal.[52] In fact no act

47. The wilful doing of an unlawful act without excuse, which is ordinarily sufficient to establish criminal malice, is not alone sufficient under these stat-utes." State v. Johnson, 7 Wyo. 512, 516, 54 P. 502, 503 (1898). ". . . wrongful-ly and intentionally done—without just cause or excuse." Carstarphen v. State, 112 Ga. 230, 232, 37 S.E. 423, 424 (1900).

48. 9 Geo. I, c. 22 (1722).

49. The King v. Pearce, 1 Leach 527, 168 Eng.Rep. 365 (1789). For a similar

case, involving injury to a gelding, see The King v. Shepherd, 1 Leach 539, 168 Eng.Rep. 371 (1790).

50. State v. Martin, 141 N.C. 832, 839, 53 S.E. 874, 876 (1906).

51. State v. Landreth, 4 N.C. 331 (1816).

52. Fears v. State, 33 Ariz. 432, 265 P. 600 (1928).

done under a bona-fide claim of right should be held to be malicious.[53] Some of the cases have involved circumstances in which the claim of right was combined with suddenly aroused passion, as where a trespassing animal is shot for the protection of the landowner's property.[54] In one case, for example, **D** shot a hog that had been damaging his crops. The jury returned a verdict in these words: "We, the jury, find the accused guilty of the willful and unlawful killing of the hog, but not out of a spirit of mischief, revenge, or wanton cruelty." This was held to be a verdict of not guilty.[55] As said in another case: The question to be tried was, not whether he was *justified* in shooting the mule, but whether his motive in shooting was malicious." [56]

In considering offenses other than malicious mischief, intentional harm is held to be malicious in the absence of justification, excuse or recognized mitigation, without any requirement of actual spite or ill-will. Let attention now be directed to cases involving this problem. A "dry crusader," for example, broke plate glass doors and windows with an axe. On her trial for malicious mischief her defense was that she had no ill-will against the owner or design to destroy property just for the purpose of its destruction, but merely wanted to put out of business a place where liquor was being sold in violation of law. This was held not to constitute a valid defense.[57] In another case **D**, with a hypodermic syringe, injected a substance into the side of a mare which caused pronounced swelling. He had no ill-will toward the owner or the mare but did this because he was a veterinary surgeon and wanted to make money by pretending the mare was suffering from a new disease which he was competent to cure. It was held that the injury so inflicted was done maliciously.[58] And shooting a hole through the door of a house to murder or wound an innocent man who had sought refuge there, was held to be malicious mischief. The fact that there was no malice toward the owner of the house, nor any desire to injure the house, as such, was unimportant.[59] Enlightening are such expressions as: "Malice, either express *or implied*, is an essential ingredient of the offense of malicious mischief." [60] They disprove the existence of any requirement of actual ill-will or spite toward the owner.[61]

---

53. State v. Minor, 17 N.D. 454, 117 N.W. 528 (1908); Dye v. Commonwealth, 48 Va. 662 (1851).

One who closed an airway in a mine on orders from his employer, and in the bona-fide belief that the employer had a right to close it was not guilty of malicious mischief. Regina v. James, 8 Car. & P. 131, 173 Eng.Rep. 429 (1837).

And one who demolished a house in the bona-fide, though mistaken, belief that it was his property was not guilty. Regina v. Langford, Car. & M. 602, 174 Eng.Rep. 653 (1842).

54. State v. Churchill, 15 Idaho 645, 98 P. 853 (1909); State v. Sylvester, 112 Vt. 202, 22 A.2d 505 (1941).

55. Duncan v. State, 49 Miss. 331 (1873).

56. Wright v. State, 30 Ga. 325, 327 (1860).

57. State v. Boies, 68 Kan. 167, 74 P. 630 (1903).

58. Brown v. State, 26 Ohio St. 176 (1875).

59. Funderburk v. State, 75 Miss. 20, 21 So. 658 (1897).

60. Carstarphen v. State, 112 Ga. 230, 231–2, 37 S.E. 423, 424 (1900). Emphasis added.

61. Wilfully cutting a mare for no proper reason was indictable under the statute although there was no malice against the owner. Regina v. Tivey, 1 Car. & K. 704, 174 Eng.Rep. 999 (1844). If defendant was bent on mischief and wilfully destroyed the property in question it is wholly immaterial whether he knew who the owner was or not. State v. Waltz, 158 Iowa 191, 139 N.W. 458 (1913).

To constitute the offense "it is not necessary to prove actual ill-will or resentment towards the owner or possessor of the property; but if the act be done under circumstances which bespeak a mind prompt and disposed to the commission of mischief—or, in the language of the court, 'wantonly and recklessly,' it is sufficient." [62] A rum-runner, in one case, instructed his driver to crash through police cars if necessary. The driver, seeing two police cars, thought he might "skin through." The risk was obvious but he decided to go anyway and the cars were damaged. The employer was held guilty as accessory before the fact to malicious mischief.[63] This is the clearest case in which the property was not damaged to spite the owner, nor for the mere sake of damaging property. The driver did his best to get by without touching either car. It was a wanton and wilful disregard of an obvious likelihood of damaging property, without justification, excuse or mitigation, and hence was properly held to be malicious. But the court felt the necessity of giving lip-service to the supposed requirement of spite or ill-will. "Such a spirit of hostility and ill-will against the property and person of anyone, whoever he was, if he stood in the way, or barred the progress of Lavan, was wilful and malicious." [64] In another case D was driving a horse and buggy in a reckless manner from side to side of the road, endangering persons and property, and the shaft of his buggy penetrated the hip of another horse. A conviction of malicious mischief was affirmed, the court saying: "The result arose out of a spirit of general abandoned deviltry, which was tantamount to wilfulness as to all men and to all animals he might confront." [65] And a conviction of maliciously killing a mare was affirmed although there was no evidence of any ill-will toward the owner or the mare, or of any intent to injure the mare, since death resulted from a wanton and wilful act, without justification, excuse or mitigation.[66]

For a wanton and wilful act to qualify as the mens rea requirement of malicious mischief it is necessary that this state of mind be related to property damage. In *Faulkner* [67] the notion of a felony-malicious-mischief doctrine, comparable to the felony-murder doctrine was flatly rejected; and the oft-cited *Kelly* [68] emphasized that malice aforethought is not the mens-rea requirement of malicious mischief. The fact that a shot fired with intent to kill a man resulted in the death of a horse lacks the mens rea needed for malicious mischief as fully as it lacks the actus reus needed for murder. The same point was emphasized in the recent case which held that throwing at a person and hitting his car does not establish malicious mischief.[69]

Neither psychology nor law suggests that these states of mind must be mutually exclusive. A man might act with wanton and wilful disregard of the obvious likelihood of serious harm to both person and property. And an intent to kill or injure a person might be carried out in such a way as to create an obvious likelihood of causing property damage. If such an act should have this result, in the absence of justification, excuse or recognized

62. Mosely v. State, 28 Ga. 190, 192 (1859).

63. Commonwealth v. Hosman, 257 Mass. 379, 154 N.E. 76 (1926).

64. Id. at 385, 154 N.E. at 77.

65. Porter v. State, 83 Miss. 23, 26, 35 So. 218 (1903).

66. The Queen v. Welch, 1 Q.B.D. 23 (1875).

67. Regina v. Faulkner, 13 Cox C.C. 550 (1877).

68. Rex v. Kelly, 1 Craw. & D. 186 (1832).

69. People v. Washington, 18 N.Y.2d 366, 222 N.E.2d 378 (1966).

mitigation, the actor would be guilty of malicious mischief.[70] In a recent case, which expressly overruled earlier decisions, the court held that malice toward the owner of the property is not required for malicious mischief.[71]

In other words, the element of malice, as the special mental element of malicious mischief, requires either a specific intent to cause the destruction of, or substantial damage to, the property of another, or an act done in wanton and wilful disregard of the plain and strong likelihood of such harm, without any circumstances of justification, excuse or substantial mitigation. Stated in other words:

The mens-rea requirement of malicious mischief is a property-endangering state of mind, without justification, excuse or mitigation.

The Model Penal Code has a section called "Criminal Mischief." [72] This label is employed because the Code does not use the terms "malice" or "malicious." The change is unfortunate. Since the property of another may be damaged purposely, but under circumstances of justification, the result will be "justifiable criminal mischief"—which borders on absurdity. The provision of the Code goes beyond the common law and prevailing statutory law by including damage caused by criminal negligence "in the employment of fire, explosives, or other dangerous means" and certain situations not involving property damage.[73]

SECTION 8. FORGERY AND UTTERING A FORGED INSTRUMENT

If a person writes what purports to be a legal instrument and appends thereto the name of another person without any power or authority to do so, the other whose name is thus wrongfully used is not bound in any way by the provisions of this false writing.[1] Needless to say, however, there is a strong social interest in having the community entirely free from instruments that are not genuine. The very want of liability on the part of the one whose name is unlawfully used in this way means that ordinarily some other innocent person may lose the money or property he has parted with on the strength of the false writing, or may be harmed by it in some other way; and if false instruments tend to become at all common in a given community, this fact places a serious handicap upon the use of genuine paper, because of the uncertainty aroused.

---

70. See Regina v. Pembliton, 12 Cox C.C. 607 (1874). In this case the conviction was quashed but only because the special verdict finding that **D** "threw the stone at the people . . . intending to strike one or more of them with it, but not intending to break the window" was not sufficient to establish guilt. The act was at night and there was no evidence to show that **D** knew the window was there. The judges made it clear that **D** would be guilty if he was aware that breaking the window was a likely consequence of his act.

71. McDaris v. State, 505 P.2d 502 (Okl.Cr.1973).

72. Section 220.3.

73. "(b) purposely or recklessly tampers with tangible property of another so as to endanger person or property; or

(c) purposely or recklessly causes another to suffer pecuniary loss by deception or threat." Ibid.

1. This assumes the absence of any unusual circumstances which might constitute an estoppel. He might be defrauded, however, because he or his agent might pay the instrument without detecting the forgery, as suggested in State v. Cleveland, 6 Nev. 181 (1870).

A similar problem is involved in the fraudulent alteration of existing instruments. If one person makes a genuine note in the sum of one hundred dollars and another fraudulently "raises" it to twenty-one hundred dollars, the original maker (if himself free from fault) is not liable for this larger amount to any holder of the paper.[2] But it is socially desirable that there should be no such alterations for the reasons mentioned above. Hence the common law prohibited both the fraudulent creation and the fraudulent alteration of an instrument, and applied the label "forgery" to both.[3] Furthermore, the common law punished both the forgery and the guilty uttering of forged instruments. The recognition of two crimes in this connection was no doubt due originally to the desire to prevent one man from knowingly uttering what another had forged, as well as to prevent the original forgery itself. An important problem of law enforcement is also entitled to attention. One person is arrested, having in his possession one or more forged instruments obviously prepared by him; but there is no proof of his actually having uttered such an instrument (although perhaps good reason to believe he has probably issued several). Another person is arrested in the very act of passing a forged instrument. There is abundant proof of his knowledge that the writing was false, but no clear evidence that it was prepared by him or under his directions. It would unreasonably handicap the enforcement of justice if either set of facts was insufficient for conviction.

Forgery is the fraudulent making of a false writing having apparent legal significance.

Forgery and uttering were both misdemeanors at common law.[4] Under modern statutes they are almost universally made felonies.

Forgery often has been defined in some such form as this: "Forgery is the false making or material alteration, with intent to defraud, of any writing which, if genuine, might apparently be of legal efficacy or the foundation of a legal liability."[5] This definition is not adopted here for two reasons: (1) at one point the emphasis is faulty; (2) throughout it uses more words than are needed to express the meaning. One of the very significant aspects of forgery is that the immediate result is a false writing.[6] Hence the definition quoted is unsatisfactory because it speaks of the *false making* of a writing,

2. The rule of the common law was that the maker was discharged and was not liable to anyone for any amount. Davidson v. Cooper, 11 Mees. & W. 778, 152 Eng.Rep. 1018 (1843). Section 124 of the Negotiable Instruments Law changes the common law to the extent that a subsequent holder in due course of a negotiable instrument is permitted to enforce the paper according to its original tenor. Pickelsimer v. Chafin, 104 W.Va. 106, 139 S.E. 475 (1927). It is the same under the Uniform Commercial Code, Section 3–407.

3. Williams, Textbook of Criminal Law 860–865 (1978).

4. 2 Bishop, New Criminal Law §§ 523, 605 (8th ed. 1892); Kreuter v. United States, 201 F.2d 33, 36 (10th Cir.

1953); Hamilton v. State, 35 Ala.App. 570, 50 So.2d 449 (1951). "Forgery, or the *crimen falsi*, is an infamous offence." Brendin's Appeal, 92 Pa. 241, 246 (1879).

5. State v. Meeks, 245 Iowa 1231, 1237, 65 N.W.2d 76, 79 (1954). "Forgery is the fraudulent making or alteration of any writing to the prejudice of another's rights." Ratliff v. State, 175 Tenn. 172, 175, 133 S.W.2d 470, 471 (1939).

6. Kreuter v. United States, 201 F.2d 33, 36 (10th Cir. 1953); State v. Adcox, 171 Ark. 510, 513, 286 S.W. 880, 881 (1926). Forgery is "making a false instrument with intent to deceive." Commonwealth v. Ray, 69 Mass. 441, 446 (1855).

whereas the emphasis should be upon the making of a *false writing*.[7] Whatever is done with intent to defraud is done fraudulently, so these forms of expression are interchangeable. The definition suggested above makes no mention of material alteration, but this is not with any thought of excluding this possibility from the realm of forgery. The omission is because no such reference is needed, the idea being included in the definition given, and the additional statement would be repetitious. If a man takes a genuine instrument, and alters it materially with intent to defraud, he thereby makes the instrument false. He has just as effectively *made a false writing* as if he had started with blank paper.[8] In fact, any mention of material alteration in the definition of forgery is attributable to the faulty emphasis of some of the early writers. It would be incorrect to say that "forgery is the fraudulent making or materially altering of a false writing" and so forth, because what was altered was not a false writing. It was a genuine writing which was materially altered and thereby made a false writing. The definition must say something more, because the fraudulent making of a false writing is not forgery if what is made lacks even the appearance of legal significance. Any writing, which if genuine, might apparently be of legal efficacy or the foundation of a legal liability, has apparent legal significance. And since the two phrases have the same meaning the shorter is to be preferred for purposes of definition. To repeat: Forgery is the fraudulent making of a false writing having apparent legal significance.

The requisites of the offense are (1) a writing of such a nature that it is a possible subject of forgery, (2) which writing is false, and (3) was made false with intent to defraud.[9]

A. THE SUBJECT OF FORGERY

Here, as is very common in the law, the word "writing" is used in a broad sense. It is not limited to handwriting but includes also typewriting, printing, engraving and so forth.[10] With this explanation it may be said that the subject of forgery is any writing which has apparent legal significance.

---

7. "This is not merely a deed containing a false statement, but it is a false deed." Per Blackburn, J., in The Queen v. Ritson, L.R. 1 C.C. 200, 202 (1869). "The prosecution failed to distinguish between falsely making an instrument, and making a false instrument, ..." DeRose v. People, 64 Colo. 332, 334, 171 P. 359, 360 (1918).

"There is, of course, a valid and recognized distinction between the false making of a writing and the making of a false writing." United States v. Jones, 553 F.2d 351, 355 note 15 (4th Cir. 1977).

8. Rex v. Dawson, 1 Stra. 19, 93 Eng. Rep. 358 (1730). "If any part of a true instrument be altered, the indictment may lay it to be forgery of the whole instrument." 2 East P.C. 978 (1803). "Hence, an indictment for forging an order for nineteen dollars is supported by evidence that the order was originally made for nine dollars, and genuine, and

that it had been altered to nineteen dollars." Commonwealth v. Beamish, 81 Pa. 389, 391 (1876). A statute may require that the information charge the fraudulent alteration of the writing, and the particulars in which the instrument was altered. State v. Mitten, 36 Mont. 376, 92 P. 969 (1907).

9. "The essential elements of forgery to be charged and proved are: (1) A writing, in such form as to be apparently of some legal efficacy. (2) An evil intent of the sort deemed fraudulent in the mind of the defendant. (3) A false making of such writing." State v. Rosborough, 156 La.Ann. 1049, 1053, 101 So. 413, 414 (1924). And see People v. Fore, 384 Ill. 453, 455, 51 N.E.2d 548, 549 (1943).

10. Commonwealth v. Ray, 69 Mass. 441 (1855).

Restaurant and bar slips, or "checks," fraudulently signed with another's name,

Forgeries usually involve writings which purport to be negotiable instruments,[11] deeds,[12] mortgages, bills of lading, wills,[13] written contracts, bonds,[14] credit card sales slips,[15] or receipts.[16] They may, however, take quite a different form and have the appearance of an honorable discharge from the army,[17] a certified copy of a decree of divorce,[18] a diploma,[19] a certificate of marriage [20] or other certificate,[21] a judge's recommendation for a pardon,[22] a writ of attachment,[23] or a railroad ticket,[24]—to mention only a few of the possibilities.

For a writing to have legal significance it must have some value or purpose other than its own existence. Thus a negotiable instrument is a substitute for money, a deed to real estate passes title from one to another, a mortgage creates a security interest in land or chattels, a bill of lading acknowledges the receipt of certain goods and evidences a contract to carry and deliver the same (and does more if it is in negotiable form), a will disposes of the property of one who is dead, and a receipt acknowledges payment or some other form of satisfaction of an obligation.

Even a writing which does not have legal efficacy in such a sense may have legal significance because it may be the foundation of a legal liability. A university diploma is the formal evidence of graduation from one of the schools or colleges of the university. It does not purport to impose any obligation or liability upon the university, but it does purport to entitle the person named to whatever advantages such graduation may include. These advantages are more obvious if the college is a professional one but there are certain positions available only to the graduates of a college of liberal arts. The point of chief importance, however, is this: an officer of a university would subject himself to probable dismissal if he should wrongfully issue such a diploma to one known to him to be not a graduate. Such a wrongful act would be lawful grounds for the dismissal, hence a diploma may have

are within the purview of forgery. State v. Vangen, 72 Wn.2d 548, 433 P.2d 691 (1967).

Adding fictitious signatures to an election petition was forgery. People v. Brown, 101 Cal.App.2d 740, 226 P.2d 647 (1951).

It is no defense to forgery that is was written dimly in pencil on a small piece of paper. Baysinger v. State, 77 Ala. 63 (1884).

11. Duffin v. People, 107 Ill. 113 (1883); State v. Meeks, 245 Iowa 1231, 65 N.W.2d 76 (1954).

12. People v. Hall, 55 Cal.App.2d 343, 130 P.2d 733 (1942); State v. Shurtliff, 18 Me. 368 (1841). Trust deed, Bieber v. State, 8 Md.App. 522, 261 A.2d 202 (1970).

13. Coogan's Case, 2 East P.C. 948 (1787).

14. United States v. Calabro, 467 F.2d 973 (2d Cir. 1972).

15. People v. Gingles, 32 Cal.App.3d 1030, 108 Cal.Rptr. 744 (1973).

16. State v. Shelters, 51 Vt. 102 (1878); McDuffy v. State, 6 Md.App. 537, 252 A.2d 270 (1969).

17. Or a similar writing such as a certificate of a seaman's character upon his discharge. Regina v. Wilson, Dears. & B. 558, 169 Eng.Rep. 1119 (1858).

18. Ex parte Finley, 66 Cal. 262 (1884).

19. Regina v. Hodgson, Dears. & B. 3, 169 Eng.Rep. 891 (1856).

20. State v. Boasso, 38 La.Ann. 202 (1886).

21. The certificate of a justice of the peace authenticating the presentation and counting of gopher scalps for which a bounty had been offered is the subject of forgery. State v. Johnson, 26 Iowa 407 (1868).

22. State v. Rosborough, 156 La. 1049, 101 So. 413 (1924).

23. Commonwealth v. Mycall, 2 Mass. 136 (1806).

24. Commonwealth v. Ray, 69 Mass. 441 (1855).

legal consequences. Indirect consequences must be considered in other cases such as the making of a false letter of recommendation. The writer of a letter recommending another as an honest and reliable person entitled to a position of responsibility will be legally liable if he knows the other to be unreliable and the recipient of the letter incurs loss as a result of employing the person upon this recommendation. Hence forgery may be committed by fraudulently signing another's name to such a letter.[25] A mere letter of *introduction*, however, as distinguished from a letter of recommendation, is not the subject of forgery.[26] Except for such a letter all of the writings so far mentioned have *apparent legal significance*.

On the other hand, some writings exist for themselves alone. Suppose, for example, one should write the famous Gettysburg Address, simulating the handwriting and signature of Lincoln, and should sell it to an antique collector as the original manuscript. He would be guilty of obtaining money by false pretenses but would not be guilty of forgery, because the writing would not have even the appearance of legal efficacy or the foundation of a legal liability. It is not the writing itself but the oral or implied misstatement about the writing which would impose liability upon the writer if he obtained money or property by such deceit. For the same reason it is not *forgery* to copy a painting, even if the original signature is added with intent to defraud,[27] or for one manufacturer to imitate the wrapper of another.[28]

The requirement of apparent legal significance excludes a writing which would be *obviously* of no legal effect if genuine.[29] If in a particular jurisdiction a will has no legal effect unless attested by two witnesses, a false writing purporting to be a will, but having only one witness, will not support a conviction of forgery.[30] A writing, however, may have *apparent* legal significance although it would be void if genuine. This is true whenever the invalidity is not apparent from the face of the paper but can be ascertained only by reference to extrinsic evidence.[31] Thus a city warrant may be forged

---

25. Regina v. Moah, Dears. & B. 550, 169 Eng.Rep. 1116 (1858).

It was held that wrongfully signing another's name to a defamatory letter sent to an official in an effort to bar the immigration of the one defamed might be the basis for criminal libel but was not forgery. People v. Wong Sam, 117 Cal. 29, 48 P. 972 (1897). It is doubtful if this would be followed today.

26. A letter of introduction merely requesting courtesies with "a promise, of no legal obligation, to reciprocate them," is not the subject of forgery. "It is a mere letter of introduction, which, by no possibility, could subject the supposed writer to any pecuniary loss or legal liability." Waterman v. People, 67 Ill. 91, 93 (1873). A mere letter of introduction, merely inviting courtesies, while not the subject of common-law forgery, is a forgery under our statute. People v. Abeel, 182 N.Y. 415, 75 N.E. 307 (1905).

27. Regina v. Closs, Dears. & B. 460, 169 Eng.Rep. 1082 (1858).

28. Regina v. Smith, Dears. & B. 556, 169 Eng.Rep. 1122 (1858).

29. People v. Snyder, 274 App.Div. 371, 85 N.Y.S.2d 281 (1948).

Appeal dismissed 298 N.Y. 858, 84 N.E.2d 326 (1949). "An instrument void in law upon its face, is not the subject of forgery, because the genuine and counterfeit would be equally useless—imposing no duty, or conferring no right, . . ." State v. Smith, 16 Tenn. 150, 152 (1835). See annotation, Invalid Instrument as Subject of Forgery, 174 A.L.R 1300 (1948).

For the offense of forgery it is necessary that the instrument be such that if genuine it would be of some legal efficacy, real or apparent. Poe v. People, 163 Colo. 20, 428 P.2d 77 (1967).

30. Wall's Case, 2 East P.C. 953 (1800). There were two witnesses in this case but the law required three.

31. State v. Johnson, 26 Iowa 407 (1868).

although the city, having reached the constitutional limit of its borrowing power, could not issue a valid warrant; [32] and a check may be forged with the signature of only one of two trustees of an estate although the statute requires the signatures of both, if there are two.[33] In neither case is the defect apparent from the writing itself.

Imperfections not resulting in invalidity must be distinguished from those which render the writing void,[34] since it may be forged with an imperfection of the former type on its face. A note which has been "barred" by the statute of limitations, for example, is not void. Although a successful defense could be pleaded to any action brought upon it, the note has not been discharged. It still has such validity that if the money is handed by the maker to the holder the legal effect is not a gift but a payment.[35] Hence a note may be forged although dated more than the statutory period earlier than it is written.[36] And an order for the payment of money is the subject of forgery even without a required revenue stamp, because the stamp could be affixed later.[37]

Another imperfection has received attention. The fraudulent making of a false will is forgery although the man whose name is subscribed as testator is alive at the time.[38] This fact, of course, is not disclosed on the face of the writing, and furthermore, every genuine will is made during the life of the testator and it has validity as a legal instrument when made, although it does not take effect until his death and may never take effect because superseded by a later one.

B. MAKING A FALSE WRITING

1. THE FALSITY

For forgery it is not sufficient for the writing to tell a lie; the writing itself must BE A LIE.[39]

32. State v. Brett, 16 Mont. 360, 40 P. 873 (1895).

33. State v. Daems, 97 Mont. 486, 37 P.2d 322 (1934).

34. "It is also universally held that an instrument void on its face cannot be the subject of an indictment for forgery." Williams v. State, 333 So.2d 613 (Ala. 1976).

35. This might be very important if the maker was insolvent at the time or if the sum was large enough so that a gift would be taxable. Furthermore, if a debtor hands money to a creditor to whom he owes two accounts, without directing the application expressly or impliedly, the creditor can apply the payment to either. He could apply it to a claim unenforceable because of the statute of frauds if he had such a claim. Restatement, Contracts § 387, comment g (1932).

36. State v. Dunn, 23 Or. 562, 32 P. 621 (1893). The face of the writing does not tell the whole story in such a case because the running of the statute might have been "tolled" by some extrinsic event. But a written guaranty could be forged without stating the consideration in a jurisdiction in which this is required by the statute of frauds.

37. State v. Young, 47 N.H. 402 (1867).

38. Coogan's Case, 2 East P.C. 948 (1787).

39. "Where the 'falsity lies in the representation of facts, not in the genuineness of the execution,' it is not forgery." Gilbert v. United States, 370 U.S. 650, 658, 82 S.Ct. 1399, 1404 (1962).

"The writing or instrument must in itself be false, not genuine, a counterfeit, and not the true instrument it purports

It is an indispensable requirement of forgery that the writing be false.[40] It may have been false in its inception or may have been made so by subsequent tampering with what was originally genuine; but it must be a false writing. In this connection it is essential to distinguish between a false instrument and false statements in an instrument. No amount of misstatement of fact and no amount of fraud will make a false instrument out of what purports to be the very instrument which it is in fact and in law.[41]

If one fraudulently executes a deed to real estate with a covenant that it is free and clear of encumbrances, this is a *genuine* deed even if the grantor knows that the land is subject to a heavy mortgage. It is a genuine deed with a false covenant. This is a case of the false making of a writing with intent to defraud, but it will not support a conviction of forgery because for this purpose it would be necessary to show that the deed itself is false. Typical instances of writings which are falsely made with intent to defraud but are not forgery because they are genuine writings with false statements rather than false writings, are (1) a "padded" time roll issued by the one authorized to issue it,[42] (2) a warehouse receipt fraudulently issued by a warehouse which did not have the grain purportedly represented thereby,[43]

to be." State v. Young, 46 N.H. 266, 270 (1865).

Forgery is not committed by "the making of false statements in a genuine document." Reese v. State, 37 Md.App. 450, 378 A.2d 4, 8 (1977).

"In general, forgery is the false making, with intent to defraud, of a document which is not what it purports to be, as distinguished from a document which is genuine but nevertheless contains a term or representation known to be false." United States v. Price, 655 F.2d 958, 960 (9th Cir. 1981).

"Because the proof in this case showed only that the content of the Oregon title was false, and not that it was forged or falsely made, the conviction on Count II is reversed." United States v. Sparrow, 635 F.2d 794, 797 (10th Cir. 1980).

40. Winston v. Warden, 86 Nev. 33, 464 P.2d 30 (1970).

41. "This writing is what it purports to be: a true and genuine instrument, although it contains false statements. It is not a false paper, and the execution of such a document does not constitute forgery. The prosecution failed to distinguish between falsely making an instrument, and making a false instrument, . . . A false statement of fact in an instrument, which is itself genuine, by which another person is deceived and defrauded, is not forgery." De Rose v. People, 64 Colo. 332, 334, 171 P. 359, 360 (1918).

Alteration of a corporation's account payable documents, resulting in the issuance of checks payable to an improper payee, constitutes the crime of false pretenses, and not forgery. United States v. Jones, 553 F.2d 351 (4th Cir. 1977).

"Since she was both the actual and the ostensible drawer of the deeds in question, there was no forgery. Although the deeds may have contained false information, they were not falsely made." People v. Levitan, 49 N.Y.2d 87, 424 N.Y.S.2d 179, 182, 399 N.E.2d 1199, 1202 (1980).

"A misrepresentation of fact, so long as it does not purport to be the act of someone other than the maker, does not constitute forgery." State v. Mark, 94 Wn.2d 520, 618 P.2d 73, 74 (1980).

"Although entries recording fictitious transactions or inaccurately recording actual transactions are false within the meaning of 18 U.S.C. § 1005, an entry recording an actual transaction on a bank's books exactly as it occurred is not a false entry under that statute even though it is a part of a fraudulent or otherwise illegal scheme." United States v. Erickson, 601 F.2d 296, 303 (7th Cir. 1979).

42. De Rose v. People, 64 Colo. 332, 171 P. 359 (1918).

The making of a false or fictitious entry in the tax rolls of a county government does not constitute the crime of forgery either at common law or under the Maryland statute. State v. Reese, 283 Md. 86, 388 A.2d 122 (1978).

43. Marteney v. United States, 216 F.2d 760 (10th Cir. 1954). Accord, Pasadena Investment Co. v. Peerless

(3) a check wrongfully drawn on a bank in which the drawer has no funds, or insufficient funds,[44] or (4) a false entry made in one's own account book.[45]

Where an agent, who has a general power to sign for his principal, indorses his principal's name on a negotiable instrument in fraudulent abuse of his power, this is not forgery because the indorsement is fully effective.[46] An additional point is to be noted in cases in which one fraudulently purports to act as agent for another. If he has no power or authority to act in this capacity, the other will not be bound; but if the signature contains both names and shows that the signer was purporting to act as agent for the other, the writing is not a forgery.[47] Strictly speaking there is a false writing in such a case because it purports to be the instrument of the principal whereas it is not so in fact; but since any reliance will be upon the implied warrant of authority clearly manifested by the writing, rather than upon any deceptive appearance in the writing itself, it is felt not to come within the type of wrong which forgery is designed to punish. This is the theory back of the holding that signing a note in the name of a fictitious firm, purportedly made up of the writer and another person, is not forgery though done with intent to defraud.[48] The writing binds the man who wrote it and is false merely in the implied warrant of authority to bind the other.

The most common ways of making a false writing are (assuming the lack of power or authority for such purpose): (1) preparing a writing and subscribing the name of another thereto, (2) placing the name of another on the back of a genuine instrument so that it appears to be his indorsement thereof, or (3) making a material alteration of an instrument executed by another.

Casualty Co., 132 Cal.App.2d 328, 282 P. 2d 124 (1955).

44. State v. Adcox, 171 Ark. 510, 286 S.W. 880 (1926). This misconduct is punished under a "worthless check" statute which may be included in the general chapter on forgery (e.g., West's Ann.Cal. Pen.Code § 476a) but it is not forgery proper.

45. State v. Young, 46 N.H. 266 (1865). But a settlement of accounts between two, written in the ledger of one of them but signed by both, may be forged by the fraudulent alteration thereof by the owner of the book. Barnum v. State, 15 Ohio 717 (1846). A false entry in the book of account of the county treasurer is made forgery by statute. Vahlberg v. State, 96 Okl.Cr. 102, 249 P.2d 736 (1952).

46. Fitzgibbons Boiler Co. v. Employer's Liability Corp., 105 F.2d 893 (2d Cir. 1939). Where one, falsely representing that he had authority to sign another's name to a check, wrote that name on the check in the presence of the payee, this was held not to be forgery. Morgan v. State, 77 Ga.App. 164, 48 S.E.2d 115 (1948). This decision is questionable be-

cause the check itself was false and might defraud others who did not know of the oral statement.

The Utah court held a defendant guilty of forgery where he made a check with the purported maker's permission, where the maker had notified the bank of the loss of his checks, and both the defendant and the purported maker had the intent to defraud as a part of their scheme. The Utah forgery statute required only the making of the instrument with the intent to defraud. State v. Collins, 597 P.2d 1317 (Utah 1979).

47. Regina v. White, 1 Den. 208, 169 Eng.Rep. 214 (1847); Mallory v. State, 179 Tenn. 617, 168 S.W.2d 787 (1943); Selvidge v. United States, 290 F.2d 894 (10th Cir. 1961).

It would be forgery under the Illinois Criminal Code, Smith-Hurd Ill.Ann.Stat. 38, § 17–3(a)(1) (1977).

48. Commonwealth v. Baldwin, 77 Mass. 197 (1858). The use of a fictitious partnership name may be punishable under a special statute. Utah Code Ann., 1953, § 42–2–5, 10.

2. FICTITIOUS OR ASSUMED NAME

Other possibilities demand attention. Forgery may be committed by the use of a fictitious name. The use of an assumed name, whether it is a trade name, a stage name, or one assumed for some other purpose, is not forgery if the name is used as that of the very person who assumes it, and without a fraudulent design to gain some undue advantage by the use of this particular name.[49] But forgery is committed if one fraudulently employs a fictitious name which purports to represent someone other than himself,[50] or if he fraudulently assumes the name of a man entitled to credit for the purpose of gaining the advantage of the credit which such name can command but he himself cannot. Under some statutes the fraudulent use of a fictitious name is made a separate offense.[51]

3. USE OF ONE'S OWN NAME

Forgery may be committed even by one who makes use of his own name. The two typical examples of this are (1) false dating, and (2) using one's name as that of another. A writing may be innocently prepared with a date other than that of its issue, as where a renewal note is handed over before or after the maturity of the one it replaces, but is given a date as of that maturity merely to simplify the computation of interest.[52] Under some circumstances, on the other hand, an instrument will have quite a different effect if executed at one time than at another. And if one executes an instrument signed by himself but falsely dated as of a different time for the fraudulent purpose of defeating the rights of some other person, he is guilty of for-

49. "If a person give a note entirely as his own, his subscribing it by a fictitious name will not make it a forgery, the credit thus being given to himself without any regard to the name or without any relation to a third person." Regina v. Martin, 14 Cox C.C. 375 (1879). Walters v. State, 245 So.2d 907 (Fla.App. 1971).

Signing checks with a fictitious name which does not purport to be the name of anyone other than the signer is not forgery. State v. Cook, 93 N.M. 91, 596 P.2d 860 (App. 1979).

50. Jones v. United States, 234 F.2d 812 (4th Cir. 1956); Ex parte Finley, 66 Cal. 262, 264 (1884); State v. Meeks, 245 Iowa 1231, 65 N.W.2d 76 (1954). "So there may be a forgery by the use of a fictitious name, as well as by the use of a person's own name, if the intent exists to commit a fraud by deception as to the identity of the person who uses the name." Commonwealth v. Costello, 120 Mass. 358, 370–1 (1876). State v. Fick, 204 Kan. 422, 464 P.2d 271 (1970); United States v. Scott, 457 F.2d 848 (10th Cir. 1972).

When, with intent to defraud, Claxton Council Davis endorsed a check "Clayton Davis," he committed forgery. Davis v. McAllister, 631 F.2d 1256 (5th Cir. 1980).

51. One who signs a fictitious name to a check must be prosecuted under section 476 of the Penal Code and not for forgery, although it is intimated that a prosecution for forgery would have been proper had there not been a section expressly applying to such a case. People v. Elliott, 90 Cal. 586, 27 P. 433 (1891). See also In re Lamey, 85 Cal.App.2d 284, 193 P.2d 66 (1948). Under the statute, uttering a fictitious instrument is made a separate offense with a lesser penalty than for forgery proper. State v. Jensen, 103 Utah 478, 136 P.2d 949 (1943).

The signing of a fictitious name to a check by one who has opened a checking account in that fictitious name, and who represents the payee to be himself, is forgery. United States v. Metcalf, 388 F.2d 440 (4th Cir. 1968).

In Louisiana the use of a fictitious name is not forgery. State v. Mann, 250 La. 1086, 202 So. 259 (1967).

52. "The negotiability of an instrument is not affected by the fact that it is undated, antedated or postdated." Uniform Commercial Code § 3–114(1).

gery.[53] The second example is ordinarily involved in a case in which two persons have the same name. One without a checking account may commit forgery, if his name is the same as that of a depositor, by signing his name to a check and issuing it with the intention of having it accepted as the instrument of the other.[54]

When "a defendant signs his true name on a traveler's check which has never been issued and which he has no authority to sign, such conduct amounts to an alteration of the instrument within the meaning of the forgery statute." [55]

One plan included the authorized use of one's own signature. In carrying out a fraudulent scheme, **M** bought traveler's checks which he handed to **S** together with **M**'s driver's license. Using the license for identification, **S** signed the checks with **M**'s name and cashed them. Thereupon **M** reported the checks as stolen and received new checks from the issuer. As the act of **S** in signing **M**'s name was fraudulent it was forgery despite the authorization by the co-conspirator, and both **M** and **S** were convicted.[56]

4. OBTAINING GENUINE SIGNATURE OF ANOTHER

Another method of committing forgery is by procuring the genuine signature of another on an instrument which is to be used fraudulently as the instrument of a different person of the same name. The classic example is the case of a man who had his daughter sign a deed with him. The daughter did not understand what it was all about, but her name was the same as her mother's, and the deed was delivered as one having been signed by the man and his wife. This was forgery.[57]

5. SIGNATURE PROCURED BY FRAUD

Where fraud has been perpetrated on one who has signed a writing, two very different possibilities require attention. Suppose, for example, the signature is found at the bottom of a promissory note for one thousand dollars. It may be that false and fraudulent misrepresentations induced the signer to believe it was to his advantage to prepare and sign such a note, and he did so accordingly. This is *fraud in the inducement.* He knew exactly what he

---

53. Fraudulently antedating a deed, to make it apparently prior to a genuine deed of a later date, is a forgery, although it is executed by and between the parties named therein. The Queen v. Ritson, L.R. 1 C.C. 200 (1869). Opportunities for the actual perpetration of fraud by the false dating of a writing have been greatly reduced, but not eliminated, by modern recording acts.

54. Peoples Bank & Trust Co. v. Fidelity & Casualty Co., 231 N.C. 510, 57 S.E.2d 809 (1950). "The false writing, alleged to have been made, may purport to be the instrument of a person or firm existing, or of a fictitious person or firm. It may be even in the name of the prisoner, if it purports to be, and is desired to be received as the instrument of a third person having the same name." Com-

monwealth v. Baldwin, 77 Mass. 197, 198 (1858).

D, who had had his name changed by court order, committed forgery by fraudulently using his former name. Moore v. Commonwealth, 207 Va. 838, 153 S.E.2d 231 (1967).

"Where with intent to deceive, someone with the same name as the owner of the property executes an instrument as the owner thereof, he has committed forgery." People v. Levitan, 65 A.D.2d 502, 411 N.Y.S.2d 951 (1978).

55. Hill v. Sheriff, Clark County, 95 Nev. 438, 596 P.2d 234 (1979).

56. United States v. McGovern, 661 F.2d 27 (3d Cir. 1981).

57. State v. Farrell, 82 Iowa 553, 48 N.W. 940 (1891).

was signing and intended to sign that very note, although induced by fraud to have this intention. He has a defense against the fraudulent party and those who hold no stronger position, but his defense is lost if the paper is negotiated to a holder in due course.[58] But this is not a false writing; it is his genuine note whether he is able to avail himself of the defense or not. And since it is not a false writing, it is not forgery,[59] but it is squarely within a clause commonly found in the statute on false pretenses.[60]

On the other hand it may be that the signer was shown some quite different writing, such as a contract for agency. And after he decided to sign that contract a different paper was substituted by sleight-of-hand and his signature appeared at the foot of the note without his knowledge. This is *fraud in the factum*. He had no intention of signing the paper on which his signature appears. In legal theory it is not his note and he has a defense available against anyone in the absence of negligence,[61] unless the rule of the common law has been changed by statute.[62] If he was negligent in permitting his signature to be obtained on this note he will be liable to one having the rights of a holder in due course, the theory being not that it is really his note but that as against a holder in due course his negligence estops him from setting up the true situation. This is truly a false writing.[63]

There is no requirement that a forger must do the writing with his own hand; it is sufficient if he procures the false writing to be made.[64] And since by fraud in the *factum* the wrongdoer has procured the making of a false writing he has, in strict theory, committed forgery,—and such was the early view.[65] The tendency, however, has been to overlook the difference between the two types of fraud so far as forgery is concerned, although it is

58. Beachy v. Jones, 111 Kan. 254, 206 P. 895 (1922).

59. People v. Pfeiffer, 243 Ill. 200, 90 N.E. 680 (1910).

60. "Every person who knowingly and designedly by any false or fraudulent representation or pretense . . . obtains the signature of another to any instrument in writing whereby any liability is created . . . is punishable . . . ." Idaho Code § 18–3101 (1979).

61. C. I. T. Corporation v. Panac, 25 Cal.2d 547, 154 P.2d 710 (1944); United States v. Castillo, 120 F.Supp. 522 (D.C. N.M.1954).

62. The cases are not in accord as to whether a change was made by the Uniform Negotiable Instruments Law. See Beutel's Brannon, Negotiable Instruments Law pp. 758–762 (7th ed. 1948).

The Uniform Commercial Code does not follow the wording of the Negotiable Instruments Law and clearly re-establishes the original position in regard to *fraud in the factum*. Section 3–305(2) (c). And see the comment on page 277 of the Official Text (1957).

63. Where a signature to a promissory note is procured by fraudulently sub-

stituting it for a receipt, after the signer has just read the receipt, the note is a forgery. It is not the promissory note of the one whose signature was obtained in this manner and, in the absence of negligence on his part he is not liable to anyone thereon. Biddeford National Bank v. Hill, 102 Me. 346, 66 A. 721 (1907); Branz v. Stanley, 142 Me. 318, 51 A.2d 192 (1947).

64. "It is not necessary that the act should be done, in whole or in part, by the hand of the party charged. It is sufficient, if he cause or procure it to be done." State v. Shurtliff, 18 Me. 368, 371 (1841). Accord, Duncan v. State, 86 Tex.Cr.R. 191, 215 S.W. 853 (1919).

65. 2 Bishop, New Criminal Law § 589 (8th ed. 1892). Following an agreement for the sale of one acre of a farm the grantee prepared a deed which correctly described the area agreed upon. After the grantor read the deed the grantee substituted another which conveyed the grantor's entire farm and which the grantor signed supposing it was the paper he had read. This was held to be forgery. State v. Shurtliff, 18 Me. 368 (1841).

sharply distinguished elsewhere, and to hold that fraud of either type results, not in forgery, but in false pretenses.[66] This is reasonably acceptable since the moral turpitude is the same in both; it is simpler to treat them alike in the forgery cases; and there is no prejudice to the wrongdoer since the result tends to operate in his favor rather than otherwise. On the other hand a vigorous prosecutor could make out a strong case of forgery, if it is fraud in the *factum* and the jurisdiction has not taken a definite stand on the other side. A recent case took this position.[67]

This discussion of a signature procured by fraud concerns only instances in which the signature purports to be that of the person deceived. Where **A**, for the purpose of defrauding **B**, induced **B**'s daughter to sign **B**'s name to a promissory note by falsely representing that **B**, who was unable to write, had authorized the signature, it was a clear case of forgery.[68]

6. ALTERATION

The unauthorized alteration of a writing in any material way changes it from a genuine writing to one that is false. As previously mentioned, the reference to writings false from the inception, and others made false by alteration, is merely to emphasize factual possibilities because the legal result is the same,[69] unless changed by statute.[70]

66. **D** wrote a note for $141.26, payable to himself, and fraudulently read it to another as a note for $41.26, and procured him to sign it as maker. This was held not to be forgery. Commonwealth v. Sankey, 22 Pa. 390 (1853). Accord, Hill v. State, 9 Tenn. 76 (1824). An illiterate was persuaded to sign a deed under the false representation that it was a pension paper. It was held that this was not forgery but was expressly included under the statute on false pretenses. Johnson v. State, 87 Miss. 502, 39 So. 692 (1905). An illiterate signed a note with his "mark" after the defendant had fraudulently read it to him as a note for half the amount actually written. Defendant was held guilty of cheating and swindling but not of forgery. Wells v. State, 89 Ga. 788, 15 S.E. 679 (1892). If the figure on a writing is raised after the signer has read it, but before his signature is attached, this is not forgery even if the alteration was fraudulent and undetected by the signer [£9, raised to £12]. Regina v. Chadwick, 2 Mood. & R. 545, 174 Eng.Rep. 376 (1844). Accord, People v. Underhill, 142 N.Y. 38, 36 N.E. 1049 (1894). Procuring the signature to a deed by falsely reading it as an affidavit, to one who did not have his glasses and could not read without them, was not forgery but false pretenses. Austin v. State, 143 Tenn. 300, 228 S.W. 60 (1920). A signature obtained by fraud *in the factum* was spoken of as "forgery" in a civil case. United States v. Klatt, 135 F.2d 648, 650 (D.C.Cal.1955).

67. Buck v. Superior Court, 232 Cal. App.2d 153, 42 Cal.Rptr. 527 (1965). See also Commonwealth v. Zaleski, 3 Mass. App. 538, 336 N.E.2d 877 (1975).

68. Gregory v. State, 26 Ohio St. 510 (1875). It may be added that an instrument may be forged by preparing it and fraudulently adding the "mark" of one who cannot write. Rex v. Fitzgerald, 2 East P.C. 953 (1803).

69. Rex v. Dawson, 1 Stra. 19, 93 Eng.Rep. 358 (1730). And see Commonwealth v. Beamish, 81 Pa. 389, 391 (1876).

70. A statute may require that the information charge the fraudulent alteration of the writing, and the particulars in which the instrument was altered. State v. Mitten, 36 Mont. 376, 92 N.W. 969 (1907). If the instrument was made false in the beginning the one whose name was forged is not liable for any amount (in the absence of unusual circumstances amounting to estoppel or laches). This is also the common-law rule as to a forged alteration, but it is expressly provided by statute that if a negotiable instrument which has been altered gets into the hands of a holder in due course not a party to the alteration, he may enforce it according to its original tenor. Uniform Commercial Code § 3–407(3).

No change in the wording of a genuine writing will transform it into a false writing unless it amounts to a material alteration,—that is, unless there is a difference in legal meaning between the original wording and the changed form. Suppose, for example, a check is written in the sum of "fifty dollars" but with a blank in the space intended to represent the amount in figures. This is legally just as good a check as if the figures $50.00 were there, and the addition of these figures without consulting the drawer is not a material alteration. Moreover, if the drawer of this check had inadvertently written in the figures $5.00 it would not have been a material alteration for the holder to change the figures to $50.00. Whenever there is a discrepancy between the written words and the figures representing the sum payable on such an instrument, the words control, and hence to change the figures to agree with the words does not alter the legal meaning of the paper.[71] Such a case would not be forgery for the additional reason that there would be no intent to defraud, but the intent to defraud is not sufficient for forgery if no false writing results. In one case, for example, the holder of a check in which the sum was correctly represented in both words and figures, wrongfully raised the figures—but not the words—and tried to cash it for the higher amount. This was held not to constitute forgery because, despite the fraudulent intent, there was no change in the legal meaning of the check and hence no material alteration.[72] In another case the figures correctly represented the sum intended whereas the words were inadvertently written for ten times that amount. Fraudulently changing the figures to forestall any inquiry about discrepancy was held not to be forgery for the same reason.[73] If the amount of an instrument is expressed in figures only, any change in the figures is a material alteration and hence forgery if done with intent to defraud.[74] It may be added that the change of figures on a negotiable instrument, without changing the words, has such a tendency to mislead that legislation might well be enacted to declare a fraudulent change of this nature to be forgery.[75]

Probably the commonest type of fraudulent alteration is by "raising" the instrument so that it purports to represent a larger amount than the original.[76] The substitution of one name for another has also been rather common.[77] It may take any form by which the legal effect of the writing is changed, as by purporting to make a non-negotiable instrument negotiable,[78]

71. People v. Lewinger, 252 Ill. 332, 96 N.E. 837 (1911).

72. Wilson v. State, 85 Miss. 687, 38 So. 46 (1904). Accord, State v. Peterson, 192 So.2d 293 (Fla.1966).

73. People v. Lewinger, 252 Ill. 332, 96 N.E. 837 (1911).

74. Mitchell v. State, 64 Ga. 448 (1879); Lawless v. State, 114 Wis. 189, 89 N.W. 891 (1902).

75. It was held to be forgery in Commonwealth v. Hide, 94 Ky. 517, 23 S.W. 195 (1893). But this was an appeal by the Commonwealth after an acquittal and hence there was no adequate presentation to the appellate court. The court relied upon Mitchell in which the amount

had been expressed in figures only. Desirable as the result is, it is so squarely in conflict with the theory of the common law that the change should be by statute. But see White v. State, 83 Ark. 36, 102 S.W. 715 (1907).

76. State v. Wooderd, 20 Iowa 541 (1866); Commonwealth v. Boutwell, 129 Mass. 124 (1880); Lawless v. State, 114 Wis. 189, 89 N.W. 891 (1902); Rex v. Dawson, 1 Stra. 19, 93 Eng.Rep. 358 (1730) (£220 changed to £520).

77. People v. Hall, 55 Cal.App.2d 343, 130 P.2d 733 (1942); State v. Higgins, 60 Minn. 1, 61 N.W. 816 (1895).

78. State v. Stratton, 27 Iowa 420 (1869).

or by changing the date.[79] Even a slight change in the legal meaning will be material and hence an "alteration." Thus, forgery may be committed by a change of date although only one day is involved, if the alteration is with fraudulent intent.

A material alteration may be in the form of (1) an addition to the writing, (2) a substitution of something different in the place of what originally appeared,[80] or (3) the removal of part of the original. The removal may be by erasure[81] or in some other manner, such as by cutting off a qualifying clause appearing after the signature.[82]

7. FILLING BLANKS

Fraudulently defeating the intent of the signer of an instrument by the improper filling of a blank left by him is a forged alteration and is given separate attention merely for the sake of emphasis. Writing in a space intentionally left blank by the signer, for the purpose of subsequent completion, is physically different from changing what was there originally. And the difference in legal effect may be very great so far as civil liability is concerned. Suppose, for example, a note intended by the maker to be for one hundred dollars, reads twenty-one hundred dollars when it reaches the hands of a holder in due course. If it had been completed by the maker, and what he had written was later changed, without his fault or negligence, he is liable for no more than the original one hundred dollars,[83] and was not liable even for that amount prior to the change by statute.[84] If the maker had delivered the note with a blank as to the amount and instructions that it should be filled in not to exceed one hundred dollars, he is liable to the holder in due course for the full twenty-one hundred dollars.[85] Because of this difference there has been a tendency not to refer to the improper filling of a blank as an "alteration" in the civil law of negotiable instruments;[86] but as the result is a false instrument the present trend is in the direction of applying the label "alteration" in civil[87] as well as in criminal cases. Any unauthorized filling of a blank for a fraudulent purpose has consistently been held to constitute the crime of forgery.[88]

---

79. Barnum v. State, 15 Ohio 717 (1846).

80. State v. Floyd, 5 Strob. 58 (S.C. 1850).

81. Changing a special indorsement to a blank indorsement. Rex v. Birkett, Russ. & R. 251 (1813); Garner v. State, 73 Tenn. 21 (1880).

82. State v. Stratton, 27 Iowa 420 (1869).

Although the statute on "false alteration" used the word "maker," this word is not to be narrowly construed. One who endorses a note is the "maker" of the endorsement so that fraudulently changing the endorsement is within the statute. State v. Hamilton, 291 Or. 283, 634 P.2d 208 (1981) (The words "for deposit only" had been crossed out). But a forged endorsement does not make the

instrument false. Frazier v. Commonwealth, 613 S.W.2d 423 (Ky. 1981).

83. Uniform   Commercial   Code §§ 3–406, 3–407(3).

84. See the Commissioner's Note to section 124 of the Negotiable Instruments Law.

85. Uniform   Commercial   Code § 3–407(3).

86. The word "alteration" was not used, in reference to the unauthorized filling of a blank, in Negotiable Instruments Law § 14.

87. The later statute preserves the difference in the civil liability but applies the word "alteration" to both types of fraud.   Uniform   Commercial   Code § 3–407.

88. Clairborne v. State, 51 Ark. 88, 9 S.W. 851 (1888); State v. Daems, 97

8. FALSE DATING

The fraudulent change of the date of an instrument or document would be a material alteration, as mentioned above. And the use of a false date at the time of making, for the fraudulent purpose of gaining an advantage which the true date would not provide, is also the making of a false writing. Thus where certificates of deposit were "backdated" because of such circumstances that they would not be honored if correctly dated, it was held that they were "falsely made." [89]

C. INTENT TO DEFRAUD

Forgery is not established by the bare fact that one person has signed the name of another to a writing having apparent legal significance because the signing (1) may have been authorized, in which case the writing is not *false*,[90] or (2) though unauthorized may have been in the bona-fide belief in the existence of such authority, in which case, although the writing is actually false, it was prepared without an intent to defraud.[91] This intent is of the very essence of forgery[92] which is one of the leading representatives of the *crimen falsi*.[93]

Mont. 486, 37 P.2d 322 (1934); Meador v. State, 113 Tex.Cr.R. 357, 23 S.W.2d 382 (1930); Regina v. Wilson, 2 Car. & K. 527, 175 Eng.Rep. 219 (1848); People v. Pool, 185 Colo. 131, 522 P.2d 102 (1974); State v. Rovin, 21 Ariz.App. 260, 518 P.2d 579 (1974).

89. United States v. Mitchell, 588 F.2d 481 (5th Cir. 1979). The court suggests that it was the purpose of the federal statute to "broaden the statute beyond rigorous concepts of forgery . . . ." Whether that is true or not, it was not needed for this case. The statement shows a failure to distinguish between a false writing and a writing with a false statement. See Marteney v. United States, 216 F.2d 760 (10th Cir. 1954). The "backdated" certificates were not writings with false statements; they were false certificates.

90. Owen v. People, 118 Colo. 415, 195 P.2d 953 (1948). An interlineation of certain words in a lease, so as to make it conform to the understanding of the parties at the time of its execution, is not forgery. Pauli v. Commonwealth, 89 Pa. 432 (1879). But if one without authority cashes a check payable to another by indorsing the payee's name on it, an intent to defraud may be inferred. People v. Brown, 137 Cal.App.2d 138, 289 P.2d 880 (1955).

91. While the Kentucky statute requires written authority for an agent to sign his principal's name to a negotiable instrument a signature made in good

faith under oral authority is not forgery. Wiley v. Commonwealth, 229 Ky. 60, 16 S.W.2d 498 (1929). Cf. People v. Hall, 55 Cal.App.2d 343, 130 P.2d 733 (1942).

92. People v. Mitchell, 92 Cal. 590, 28 P. 597 (1891); Cohen v. People, 7 Colo. 274 (1883); State v. Baldwin, 69 Idaho 459, 208 P.2d 161 (1949); People v. Fore, 384 Ill. 453, 455, 51 N.E.2d 548, 549 (1943); Ratliff v. State, 175 Tenn. 172, 133 S.W.2d 470 (1939). The section which extends the rule of the common law, and includes a mere false letter of introduction as forgery in the third degree, does not require an intent to defraud. People v. Abeel, 182 N.Y. 415, 75 N.E. 307 (1905).

". . . the intent to defraud . . . is an essential element that must be proved." State v. Maxwell, 103 Ariz. 478, 445 P.2d 837, 838 (1968).

"Specific intent to defraud is an element of the offense of forgery." United States v. White, 611 F.2d 531, 538 (5th Cir. 1980).

"While the statute at issue does not in terms require proof of the fraudulent intent of the maker of the document, such proof was required for establishing the common-law crime of forgery." And the use of the verb "forge" is sufficient to imply the elements of common-law forgery. United States v. Bertrand, 596 F.2d 150, 151 (6th Cir. 1979).

---

93. See note 93 on page 428.

The original view seems to have been that forgery required "an intent to defraud a particular person or persons" [94] unless it involved the falsifying of a public record,[95] but usually now a general intent to defraud is sufficient.[96] Usually there are at least two potential victims in a forgery case: (1) the one whose name is forged and who may pay it without detecting the forgery although not legally bound, and (2) the person to whom the instrument is delivered.[97] And if the paper is in negotiable form even the forger himself has no way of knowing who may ultimately be harmed by it.

The actual accomplishment of fraud is not a necessary element of forgery,[98] and the intent itself does not require the contemplation of inflicting a monetary loss.[99] It is sufficient, for example, if the intent was to frustrate the administration of a statute, or to do something which would tend to impair a governmental function.[1] If a monetary loss is contemplated, it is not necessary that any advantage to the forger be anticipated,—the beneficiary may be some other.[2] An intent to use a false writing to gain some advantage is an intent to defraud even if the wrongdoer has an intent to make

---

Although the federal forgery statute does not explicitly include intent to defraud as an element, one "cannot be convicted of forgery unless he has 'an intent to defraud.'" United States v. Hester, 598 F.2d 247, 248 (D.C. Cir. 1979).

93. Commonwealth v. Jones, 334 Pa. 321, 323, 5 A.2d 804, 805 (1939).

94. 2 Bishop, New Criminal Law § 598 (8th ed. 1892).

95. Id. at § 596. "Formerly the indictment must either have alleged an intent to defraud a person named, or, as you say, have shown that that was unnecessary, on account of the public nature of the instrument forged. Now the particular person need not be named; . . . ." Regina v. Hodgson, 7 Cox C.C. 122, 124 (1856). In charging the forgery of a mortgage with intent to defraud the mortgagor it was held necessary to aver that there was such land as that described in the mortgage, and that the mortgagor had some interest in the same. People v. Wright, 9 Wend. 193 (N.Y.1832). As the statute required an intent to defraud "any person" it was held not to include an intent to defraud a corporation. Rex v. Harrison, 2 East P.C. 926 (1777). But this was corrected by a subsequent statute. Id. at 928.

96. State v. Christopherson, 36 Wis.2d 574, 153 N.W.2d 631 (1967); State v. Baldwin, 69 Idaho 459, 208 P.2d 161 (1949); State v. Cross, 101 N.C. 770, 7 S.E. 715 (1888); State v. Shelters, 51 Vt. 102, 105 (1878). While a general intent to defraud is sufficient an indictment which fails to charge such a general intent or a specific intent to defraud a particular person is fatally defective. Peo-

ple v. Fore, 384 Ill. 453, 51 N.E.2d 548 (1943).

97. State v. Cleveland, 6 Nev. 181 (1870).

98. People v. Morgan, 140 Cal.App.2d 796, 296 P.2d 75 (1956); Finley v. Commonwealth, 259 S.W.2d 32 (Ky.1953); State v. May, 93 Idaho 343, 461 P.2d 126 (1969).

The fact that a false signature is not sufficiently similar to the genuine to be likely to deceive officers of the bank does not prevent it from being forgery. Commonwealth v. Stephenson, 65 Mass. (11 Cush.) 481 (1853).

Misspelling the name signed is no defense. Baysinger v. State, 77 Ala. 63 (1884).

"Fraud, as distinguished from intent to defraud, has never been an essential element of forgery, and they are clearly distinct wrongs." Century Federal Savings, Etc. v. Roudebush, 618 F.2d 969, 971 (2d Cir. 1980).

"In a forgery prosecution, it is not required . . . that the defendant's fraudulent intent be carried out successfully." Jones v. State, 372 So.2d 892, 895 (Ala.App.1979).

99. Pina v. United States, 165 F.2d 890 (9th Cir. 1948).

1. Ibid. Utterance of a forged narcotics prescription tends directly to defraud the government in that it frustrates the administration of the narcotics law. French v. United States, 232 F.2d 736 (5th Cir. 1956).

2. State v. Cross, 101 N.C. 770, 7 S.E. 715 (1888). In this case a bank officer

reparation at some future time. Thus, it is no defense to a charge of forging a promissory note that the forger intended to take up the paper at maturity, or even that he has actually done so.[3] And an intent to use an instrument to which the signature of another is wrongfully attached is fraudulent even if that other actually owes the forger the amount of money represented and this is merely a device used to collect the debt.[4] These results are necessary because the social interest in the integrity of instruments is violated by the use of false writings, even under these circumstances. Furthermore, a false writing has such an obvious tendency to accomplish fraud that the jury is warranted in inferring such an intent from the mere creation of an instrument that is false, or the alteration which changes a genuine writing into a false one, unless some adequate explanation is offered; but preparing an unauthorized writing merely to exhibit as a specimen of skill and with no intention of letting it get into circulation, is not forgery.[5]

The fact that the one whose name was forged is willing to condone the offense and pay the obligation is no defense to forgery.[6]

D. UTTERING

Uttering a forged instrument is offering as genuine[7] an instrument known to be false, with intent to defraud.[8]

The instrument must be a writing which is of the kind that may be the subject of forgery[9] and it must be false.[10] It is unimportant whether the utterer is himself the forger or not.[11] It is not necessary that the instrument be actually passed or otherwise used.[12] The mere offer of a false writing as genuine is sufficient if the other

forged certain bonds and deposited them as assets of the bank.

3. Regina v. Geach, 9 Car. & P. 499, 173 Eng.Rep. 929 (1840); State v. May, 93 Idaho 343, 461 P.2d 126 (1969).

4. Clairborne v. State, 51 Ark. 88 (1888). A clerk given a blank check with directions to fill it in for the amount necessary to pay a certain bill and expenses, which came to something over £156, filled it in for £250. Instead of paying the bill and expenses he kept the entire amount claiming it was due him as salary. This was held to be forgery even if the clerk had a bona-fide claim for this sum. Regina v. Wilson, 2 Car. & K. 527, 175 Eng.Rep. 219 (1848).

D's act of forging her ex-husband's name to checks because he was behind in his alimony payments is not a defense to forgery. State v. Christopherson, 36 Wis.2d 574, 153 N.W.2d 631 (1967).

5. Rex v. Harris, 7 Car. & P. 428, 173 Eng.Rep. 189 (1836).

But while forgery requires an intent to defraud, the statute prohibiting the recording of a false instrument requires only that it be done knowingly. State v. Edgar, 124 Ariz. 472, 605 P.2d 450 (1979).

6. Finley v. Commonwealth, 259 S.W.2d 32 (Ky.1953); State v. Howland, 119 Mo. 421, 24 S.W. 1016 (1893).

7. Where checks were sold for 25% of their face value to one who knew they were forged, there was no uttering because they were not offered as genuine. United States v. Hyatt, 565 F.2d 229 (2d Cir. 1977).

8. Pollock v. People, 166 Colo. 340, 443 P.2d 738 (1968).

9. People v. Clark, 190 Misc. 725, 75 N.Y.S.2d 107 (1947), affirmed 274 App. Div. 953, 85 N.Y.S.2d 321 (1948), appeal dismissed 298 N.Y. 857, 84 N.E.2d 325 (1949).

10. State v. Singletary, 187 S.C. 19, 25, 196 S.E. 527, 529 (1938).

11. Ibid.; State v. Boasso, 38 La.Ann. 202 (1886). A forged paper may be uttered by means of an innocent agent. Girdley v. State, 161 Tenn. 177, 29 S.W.2d 255 (1929).

12. One may be guilty of uttering a forged instrument although he does not succeed in getting anything from the one to whom it is offered. State v. Meeks, 245 Iowa 1231, 65 N.W.2d 76 (1954); Finley v. Commonwealth, 259 S.W.2d 32 (Ky.

elements of the crime are present,[13] but having in possession with intent to offer (while some evidence of forgery) is not punishable as such[14] unless made so by statute.[15]

It may be offered in many ways, such as by offering it for sale, for use as security, or for the purpose of having it recorded.[16] It must be offered with "knowledge" of its falsity,[17] but the word "knowledge" has the same broad meaning here as mentioned in connection with receiving stolen property.[18] An intent to defraud is essential to uttering,[19] but this element is not different from the intent to defraud required for forgery.

The crime of forgery itself is complete as soon as the false instrument is made with intent to defraud, although it is never offered.[20] It is essential, however, that the fraudulent intent be present at the time of the writing. In one case, for example, the false writing seems to have been prepared merely to feed the vanity of the writer and with no thought of using it to defraud. Later he formed the intention of using it fraudulently but never actually produced it for that purpose. Hence he was not guilty of either forgery or ut-

---

1953); Scruggs v. State, 252 Ind. 249, 247 N.E.2d 213 (1969).

Presenting a forged check to a bank teller to be cashed constitutes forgery, not merely an attempt to commit forgery. State v. Linam, 90 N.M. 729, 568 P.2d 255 (App. 1977). N.B. at common law this would constitute uttering a forged check not attempted uttering.

13. Hill v. State, 266 P.2d 979 (Okl.Cr. 1954).

"The offering of the instrument with intent to defraud is in itself sufficient to constitute a passing or uttering." United States v. Jones, 648 F.2d 215, 217 (5th Cir. 1981).

14. Regina v. Hodgson, 7 Cox C.C. 122, Dears. & B. 3, 169 Eng.Rep. 891 (1856).

15. Having a forged instrument in possession with the intent fraudulently to pass it as genuine is an offense under the statute. Curtis v. State, 80 Ga.App. 244, 55 S.E.2d 758 (1949).

Iowa Code Ann. §§ 715.2(3) and 715.6 (1978) makes it an offense if one "possesses [an] instrument, knowing it to be false or knowing he or she has no right to use or possess it," with "intent to obtain fraudulently any thing of value . . . ."

16. Sending a forged deed to the clerk's office to be recorded, knowing it to be a forgery, was an uttering of a forged instrument. Thomas v. State, 144 Tex.Cr.R. 533, 164 S.W.2d 852 (1942).

17. People v. Mitchell, 92 Cal. 590, 28 P. 597 (1891). Guilty knowledge may be established by circumstantial evidence,

and flight by D when he saw the one to whom the check was offered go to the telephone is a strong circumstance indicating guilty knowledge. Smith v. State, 291 P.2d 378 (Okl.Cr.1955).

18. "This knowledge may come by two means, either of his own knowledge, or by the relation of another." 3 Co.Inst. *171. One is not guilty of uttering a forged deed if he had no "actual knowledge, information, or belief" that it was false. The fact that the genuine deed was duly recorded is not a substitute for "knowledge" that this one was spurious. Pearson v. State, 55 Ga. 659 (1876). In a trial for uttering a forged instrument it is reversible error to charge the jury that they may convict if they find the defendant uttered the instrument having reasonable ground to believe that it was forged. Carver v. People, 39 Mich. 786 (1878).

19. The three factors requisite to constitute uttering a forged instrument are: "(1) It must be uttered, or published as true or genuine. (2) It must be known by the party uttering or publishing it, as false, forged, or counterfeited. (3) It must be with intent to prejudice, damage, or defraud another person." State v. Singletary, 187 S.C. 19, 25, 196 S.E. 527, 529 (1938).

20. Rex v. Crocker, 2 Leach C.C. 987 (1805). "The fact of forgery was brought home to the prisoner, though the note was never published, it having been found in his possession at the time he was seized; and he was convicted." Elliott's Case, 2 East P.C. 951 (1777).

tering.[21] In another case, on the other hand, in which the false writing was subsequently passed to another, this was held to constitute guilt of uttering because the fraudulent intent existed at that time, although not at the time of the making.[22]

At common law forgery and uttering are two distinct offenses[23] but under some statutes they have been coupled together in the same section, under the name of "forgery." [24] The fact that the forger made use of the false instrument successfully, and hence could have been convicted of false pretenses, is no bar to his conviction of forgery.[25]

The Model Penal Code has a section on forgery which covers forgery, uttering and counterfeiting.[26] The Model Penal Code provides for forgery by conduct involving alteration, making, completing, executing, authenticating, issuing, transferring or uttering a writing.[27]

SECTION 9.   COUNTERFEITING

A. DEFINITION

Literally a *counterfeit* is an imitation intended to pass for an original.[1] Hence it is spurious or false, and *to counterfeit* is to make false. For this reason the verbs *counterfeit* and *forge* are often employed as synonyms[2] and the same is true to some extent of the corresponding nouns. No error is

---

21. Regina v. Hodgson, 7 Cox C.C. 122, Dears. & B. 3, 169 Eng.Rep. 891 (1856).

22. Ex parte Finley, 66 Cal. 262 (1884).

23. State v. Boasso, 38 La.Ann. 202 (1886).

Defendant can be convicted of both forgery and uttering a forged instrument, although committed at the same place and nearly the same time. Anderson v. State, 553 S.W.2d 85 (Tenn.Cr.App. 1977).

24. The statute makes no difference between the false making or counterfeiting an instrument with intent to defraud, and uttering such instrument with intent to defraud, knowing it to be a forgery. Everyone guilty of either is guilty of forgery. People v. Brown, 397 Ill. 92, 72 N.E.2d 859 (1947). Accord, People v. McGlade, 139 Cal. 66, 70, 72 P. 600, 601 (1903); State v. Baldwin, 69 Idaho 459, 208 P.2d 161 (1949). Although the statute declares that uttering is forgery it is a distinct offense. People v. Tower, 63 Hun 624, 17 N.Y.S. 395 (1892). One guilty of forging and uttering an instrument is guilty of but one offense,—forgery. State v. Singletary, 187 S.C. 19, 196 S.E. 527 (1938). Uttering a forged instrument for value with knowledge of its falsity is, by statute, forgery in the

second degree. Acuff v. State, 283 P.2d 856 (Okl.Cr.1955).

"In Arizona they have been so coupled but the distinction as separate offenses must still be observed since the elements of the offenses are not the same and the proof required may differ." State v. Reyes, 105 Ariz. 26, 458 P.2d 960 (1969).

25. State v. Grider, 74 Wyo. 88, 288 P.2d 766 (1955).

26. Section 224.1. Some of the present codes have chapters on Forgery and Counterfeiting, Alaska Stats. c. 25 (1970); Md.Code 1957, Art. 27, § 44 et seq.

27. Model Penal Code, Section 224.1.

1. A counterfeit coin is one made in imitation of a genuine coin. United States v. Hopkins, 26 F. 443 (D.C.N.C. 1885).

2. Every person who shall be convicted of having forged, counterfeited, or falsely altered any certificate or other public security . . ." Miss. Code, 1972 § 97–21–9. "Every person who shall forge or counterfeit any coin imitation or similitude of any gold or silver coin . . ." R.I. Gen.Laws 1956, § 11–17–7 (1970). Possession of a "false, forged, counterfeit, or altered note. . . ." Curtis v. State, 80 Ga.App. 244, 55 S.E.2d 758 (1949).

involved in this usage but it is important to distinguish between the words so far as possible when used as the labels of criminal offenses. In the most restricted sense—

Counterfeiting is the unlawful making of false money in the similitude of the genuine.

At one time under English statutes it was made treason. Under modern statutes it is a felony.

Had counterfeiting been limited to the making of false metallic coins the difference between this offense and forgery would have been clear, but with the advent of "paper money" it became less distinct.

Counterfeiting has usually been classified as an offense affecting the administration of governmental functions, which unquestionably it is, having been considered *crimen laesae majestatis* and punished as treason at one time in England.[3] On the other hand, since the customary use of false money is to buy property, exchange for genuine money, or some other purpose for which lawful property is commonly employed, it is also an offense against property.[4] The fact that this offense violates two different social interests, both under the protection of the criminal law, does not make it unique because this is true of certain other crimes such as extortion which violates the same two interests, or robbery which is at the same time an offense against the person and an offense against property. But the nature of the two interests violated by counterfeiting requires particular attention. The power to coin money is expressly granted to Congress,[5] and denied to the states,[6] by the terms of the Constitution. Hence, as an offense affecting the administration of governmental functions, counterfeiting is a federal crime; but as an offense against property, in the category with larceny, malicious mischief and so forth, it is also a state crime.[7] Congress, no doubt, could provide that jurisdiction in cases of counterfeiting money should be exclusively in the federal courts, but it has expressly refused to do so.[8] One case seemed to suggest that the actual making of false money is punishable in the federal courts whereas the passing of such money with intent to defraud is a state offense.[9] Such a position is not entirely illogical but it is

---

3. 3 Co.Inst. *2.

4. "However it must be owned that this method of reasoning is a little overstrained: counterfeiting or debasing the coin being usually practised rather for the sake of private and unlawful lucre than out of any disaffection for the sovereign. And therefore both this and its kindred species of treason, that of counterfeiting the seals of the crown or other royal signatures, seem better denominated by the later civilians a branch of the *crimen falsi* or forgery, . . ." 4 Bl. Comm. *88–9.

5. Art. I, sec. 8, par. 5.

6. Art. I, sec. 10, par. 1.

7. In re Dixon, 41 Cal.2d 756, 264 P.2d 513 (1953). "[I]n the case of counterfeiting the coin of the United States, the act may be an offence against the authority of a state as well as that of the

United States." United States v. Arjona, 120 U.S. 479, 487, 7 S.Ct. 628, 631, 632 (1887). Counterfeiting United States currency is punishable as forgery by the state. Cross v. State, 122 Ga.App. 208, 176 S.E.2d 517 (1970).

"While the federal government has primary jurisdiction for prosecuting charges relating to counterfeiting, it is also a state crime. The federal statutes do not wholly occupy the field and the states have concurrent jurisdiction to prosecute." United States v. Crawford, 657 F.2d 1041, 1046, n. 6 (9th Cir. 1981).

8. "Nothing in this title shall be held to take away or impair the jurisdiction of the courts of the several States under the laws thereof." 18 U.S.C.A. § 3231.

9. The two offenses of counterfeiting the coin and passing counterfeit money, are essentially different in their charac-

quite inadequate. There would be little incentive for the making of false money if it were not to be passed as genuine, so the passing with intent to defraud and even the knowing possession of such money with intent to defraud, are properly regarded as tending to affect the administration of a governmental function. On the other hand, without the making of false money there would be none to be fraudulently passed as genuine, and for this reason the making is itself in the nature of an offense against property. Hence penalties for counterfeiting and for passing counterfeit money are commonly found in the state statutes[10] as well as in the United States Code.[11] Under one very reasonable analysis the act which constitutes *counterfeiting*, under federal law, amounts to the state offense of *forgery*.[12]

Without question the administration of a *federal* governmental function may be affected adversely by *forgery* as distinguished from *counterfeiting*. Thus the forgery of the payee's name on the back of a genuine bond of the United States is a federal offense[13] although it would not come within any definition of counterfeiting. The same may be said of the fraudulent making of any false "deed, power of attorney, order, certificate, receipt, contract, or other writing, for the purpose of obtaining . . . from the United States or any officers or agents thereof, any sum of money; . . ."[14] And there can be no doubt of the power of Congress, whenever important for the protection of the administration of this federal governmental function, to provide penalties for misdeeds which would not come within the common-law definition of either forgery or counterfeiting,—such as photographing an obligation of the United States, "or any part thereof."[15]

ter. The former is an offense directly against the government, by which individuals may be affected; the latter is a private wrong, by which government may be remotely if it will in any degree be reached. Constitutional authority to provide punishment for the counterfeiting of securities and coin of the United States does not prevent a state from punishing the offense of circulating counterfeit coin of the United States. Fox v. Ohio, 46 U.S. 410 (1847).

10. Several states have forgery statutes that encompass counterfeiting. "Forgery is a crime . . . if the writing is or purports to be part of an issue of money, securities, postage or revenue stamps, or other instruments . . . is-sued by the government . . ." N.J. Stat.Ann. 2C:21–1b (1979). Iowa punishes the "use of a financial instrument with the intent to obtain fraudulently any thing of value . . ." Iowa Code Ann. § 715.6 (1978) and defines a financial instrument as a writing including ". . . money, coins, tokens . . ." Id. § 715.1; Burns' Ind.Ann.Stat. § 35–43–5–1 et seq. (1979). Other states have statutes that specifically treat counterfeiting as a separate offense.

Mass.Gen.Laws Ann. C. 267 §§ 17, 20, 21 (1968). Some have special provisions treating passing or possession of counterfeit bills or instruments. Tenn.Code Ann. §§ 39–1708, 1709 (1975).

11. 18 U.S.C.A. §§ 485, 486, 490.

12. These provisions are no longer in effect but illustrative of the position previously taken. "Every person who shall counterfeit, or cause or procure to be counterfeited, any gold or silver coin at the time current within this territory by law or usage, or in actual use or circulation within this territory, . . . shall on conviction, be adjudged guilty of forgery in the second degree." Kans.Ter. Stats. c. 50, § 7 (1855); ("this state") Kans.G.S. 21–607. Same in substance. McKinney's N.Y.Rev.Stats. part IV, c. 1, title 3, § 28 (1829).

13. Meadows v. United States, 11 F.2d 718 (9th Cir. 1926).

One who utters the instrument he forged can be convicted of both offenses. United States v. Jones, 648 F.2d 215 (5th Cir. 1981).

14. 18 U.S.C.A. § 495.

15. Id. at § 474 (par. 6).

Possession of a photographic negative of a ten dollar federal reserve note which was intended to be used in counterfeiting is a violation of 18 U.S.C.A. § 474 which

This entire area is covered in the United States Code in a chapter entitled "Counterfeiting and Forgery." [16] The words "forges" and "counterfeits" or "forged" and "counterfeited" are coupled together in section after section, whether the particular offense might be difficult to characterize or is clearly counterfeiting[17] or clearly forgery,[18] and in each case the penalty is set forth but the crime is not named. At the present time the word "counterfeit" is unquestionably applied to false money even if it is so-called "paper money." [19] And the sections of the Code which cover "paper money" speak in terms of an "obligation or other security of the United States." [20] Closely associated to such misconduct is the fraudulent making of false foreign coins "current in the United States," [21] or any false "bond, certificate, obligation, or other security of any foreign government," [22] or any false "bank note or bill issued by a bank or corporation of any foreign country, and intended by the law or usage of such foreign country to circulate as money." [23] And while, as mentioned, the Code does not apply the name "counterfeiting" to any specific section, it does say: "All counterfeits of any coins or obligations or other securities of the United States or of any foreign government, . . ." [24]

This seems to suggest a broader definition of counterfeiting. For the purpose of this definition, "money" will be used arbitrarily to include the United States coins, foreign gold and silver coins current in the United States, gold or silver bars stamped at the assay offices of the United States,[25] "paper money" including not only that issued by or under the authority of the United States, such as Federal Reserve notes, Treasury notes and silver certificates, but also any treasury note or bill, or bank bill and so forth, issued by or under the authority of a foreign country and intended by law or usage of such foreign country to circulate as money. With this meaning arbitrarily assigned to the word "money" the following definition is suggested:

> **Counterfeiting is the unlawful making, in the similitude of the genuine, of any false money, or of any false obligation or other security of the United States or of any foreign government.**
>
> **By express provision of the statute, it may be added, the term "obligation of the United States" includes "stamps . . . of whatever denomination, issued under any Act of Congress."[26]**

proscribes possession of "any plate, stone, or other thing" for such purpose. United States v. Dixon, 588 F.2d 90 (4th Cir. 1978).

16. Id. at c. 25.

17. Id. at § 485 (counterfeiting gold or silver coins), or § 490 (counterfeiting minor coins).

18. Id. at § 495 (forging deed, contract, and so forth to obtain money from the United States).

19. A defendant's contention that federal reserve notes are not lawful obligations of the United States was held incorrect and provided no defense to a counterfeiting charge. United States v. Grismore, 546 F.2d 844 (10th Cir. 1976);

United States v. Grismore, 564 F.2d 929 (10th Cir. 1977).

20. 18 U.S.C.A. §§ 8, 471, 472, 473.

21. Id. at § 485.

22. Id. at § 478.

23. Id. at § 482.

24. Id. at § 492.

25. Id. at § 485.

It is no defense to a charge of possessing counterfeit United States gold coins with intent to defraud, that gold coins are no longer legal tender in this country. United States v. Yeatts, 639 F.2d 1186 (5th Cir. 1981).

26. Id. at § 8. It includes also "canceled United States stamps." Ibid. In-

Counterfeiting frequently requires elaborate equipment in the form of such devices as dies, hubs, molds or other impressions for the making of false coins, or plates or stones for the printing of false paper money or securities. The unlawful making or possession of such counterfeiting paraphernalia is punishable under the statutes.[27] In fact this represents the highest display of the counterfeiter's skill, and at times the unlawful making of such paraphernalia is itself spoken of as "counterfeiting." [28]

B. FALSE MONEY OR SECURITY

To constitute the offense of counterfeiting it is essential that what is imitated be something which is recognized as the subject of counterfeiting. This problem has seldom arisen, but when the so-called "California five-dollar gold piece" was made without authority of Congress and contrary to the provisions of the Constitution, it was held that the false imitation thereof was not counterfeiting.[29]

Of more practical importance is the fact that one may make false money or a false security either by starting with raw materials or by starting with what is genuine and so altering it as to make it false or enable it to pass as something other than it is. For example, when gold coins were current one method of counterfeiting was to plate a silver coin with gold so that it might readily be mistaken for a gold coin of approximately the same size.[30] And a similar device has been to treat a copper cent in such a way as to give it a silver appearance and enable it to be passed as a dime.[31]

It is possible also to produce a false result by the improper union of parts of two originals. Thus a counterfeit stamp was made by joining together the uncanceled portions of two used stamps, thereby giving the appearance of one unused stamp.[32] And counterfeit Federal Reserve notes were made by splitting a $5 note and a $20 note and pasting one part of each to the other so that from one side they had the appearance of two $20 notes.[33] Connecting different parts of two or more genuine instruments with intent to defraud is now covered by a special section.[34]

A counterfeit is made in imitation of the genuine and hence there must be sufficient resemblance to be calculated to deceive a person exercising ordinary caution.[35] But persons habitually exercise less caution in receiving minor coins than in taking money of greater value. And the fact that a spurious

ternal revenue documentary stamps are obligations of the United States under the statute. Roberts v. Hunter, 140 F.2d 38 (10th Cir. 1943).

27. 18 U.S.C.A. §§ 474, 477, 481, 487, 488, 492.

28. For example, a section title (not a part of the section proper) speaks of "Counterfeit paraphernalia." Id. at § 492. Compare this to the court's reference to "Counterfeiting molds." Kaye v. United States, 177 F. 147, 150 (7th Cir. 1910).

29. Commonwealth v. Bond, 67 Mass. 564 (1854).

30. United States v. Russell, 22 F. 390 (C.C.Mass.1884).

31. Glass v. State, 45 Tex.Cr.R. 605, 78 S.W. 1068 (1904).

32. United States v. Pappas, 134 F.2d 922 (2d Cir. 1943).

33. Crouch v. United States, 298 F. 437 (6th Cir. 1924). And see Keese v. Zerbst, 88 F.2d 795 (10th Cir. 1937); Haynes v. State, 15 Ohio St. 455 (1864).

34. 18 U.S.C.A. § 484.

35. United States v. Hopkins, 26 F. 443 (D.C.N.C.1885).

"Counterfeit bills do not have to be perfect or even particularly good reproductions to be illegal as long as the jury finds that the bills" are calculated to deceive one dealing with a person supposed to be upright and honest. United

half-dollar was made of lead or pewter will not prevent it from being counterfeit.[36] A conviction of counterfeiting a sixpence was affirmed in England, although no impression had been stamped upon it, since care had been employed to give it the size, shape and appearance of a well-worn coin.[37] But a circular metal token bearing the words "good for amusement only" and "this token has no cash or trade value" did not bear any resemblance to a genuine United States coin and was not counterfeit money. Furthermore, the fact that it could be used to operate certain vending machines, music boxes, parking meters, and so forth, was not sufficient to make it counterfeit.[38]

C. RELATED OFFENSES

As previously mentioned, however, this federal governmental function may be affected adversely by certain misdeeds that fall short of common-law counterfeiting. This function is so affected if that which is not money is made or sold to be used in devices intended to be operated only by money. Hence a special statute provides a penalty for the manufacture or sale of any token, slug, disk or other device, with knowledge or reason to believe that it may be used to operate any automatic vending machine, coin-box, parking meter, or other contrivance designed to be operated by United States coins.[39] And as such use of a slug or token is also an offense against property, the fraudulent manufacture, sale or use of such a device is punished under a number of the state statutes.[40] In fact the wrongful act of obtaining property from a vending machine by the unauthorized use of a "slug" is sufficient to constitute common-law larceny.[41]

Conduct adversely affecting this federal governmental function, although no false or counterfeit money or security is made, is entitled to additional attention. D, for example, planned a swindle in which he told X that D could duplicate United States $5 bills by a chemical and rolling process. The plan was to induce X to furnish $2500 in new bills on the assurance that D could double the amount and they would divide the profit. To convince X that D could make a replica of a new bill by this process it was necessary to show X two $5 bills having the same serial numbers, check letters and face plate numbers. To be able to show such duplicates D changed the numeral 3 to 8 in the middle of the serial number of a genuine $5 bill and also made changes in the check letter and the face plate number. This was held to be a violation of the federal statute although it did not destroy or impair the validity of the bill, and although there was no intent to defraud the United States. This alteration was material to the fraudulent scheme and was made with intent to defraud.[42]

"The offense denounced . . . is the alteration of an obligation of the United States with intent to defraud. The alteration need not be one which

States v. Brunson, 657 F.2d 110, 114 (7th Cir. 1981).

36. Ibid.

37. Rex v. Welsh, 1 East P.C. 164 (1785).

38. United States v. Gellman, 44 F.Supp. 360 (D.C.Minn.1942).

39. 18 U.S.C.A. § 491.

40. In the chapter on forgery and fraudulent practices. Ark.Stats.

§ 41–2309 (1975). See also Tenn.Code Ann. §§ 39–1716, 1717, 1718, 1719, 1720 (1975).

41. Regina v. Hands, 16 Cox C.C. 188 (1887).

42. Foster v. United States, 76 F.2d 183 (10th Cir. 1935); Barbee v. United States, 392 F.2d 532 (5th Cir. 1968).

destroys or impairs the validity of the obligation." [43] So said the court and the statement is fully justified by the wording of the statute: "Whoever, with intent to defraud, falsely makes, forges, counterfeits, or alters any obligation or security of the United States, . . ." [44] The word "alters" would not have been needed if what was intended was such a material alteration as would make the obligation counterfeit. [45] And while the section is not free from redundancy the obvious intent is to insure broad coverage. To carry out this intent it was held that the statute was violated by fraudulently tinting a blue sixteen-cent special delivery stamp so as to color it green and thereby create a fictitious value above its true value[46] or, for a similar reason, by forging an overprint on a canceled stamp. [47]

D. INTENT

The common law makes a sharp distinction between the intent required for forgery and that required for counterfeiting. [48] An intent to defraud is required for forgery and hence this offense is not committed by the making of an unauthorized writing merely to exhibit as a specimen of skill and with no intention of having it used for any other purpose. [49] In counterfeiting, on the other hand, the only mental element required is an intent to make the false money. "So the purpose or intent with which counterfeit coins are made is of no concern. Simply, they must not be made." [50] And the man who plated silver coins with gold, so that they resembled gold coins of the same general size, was guilty of counterfeiting even if he had no actual intent to defraud. [51]

It is within the legislative power, however, to increase the mens rea requirement for any particular offense, and to some extent Congress has done so in this area. The intent to defraud is not included in the sections forbidding the making of false United States coins[52] or postage stamps. [53] Nor is it included in certain other provisions such as those forbidding the making of "any plate, stone, or other thing in the likeness of any plate designated for the printing" of an obligation or security of the United States, [54] or the mak-

---

43. Id. at 184.

44. 18 U.S.C.A. § 471.

45. Cf. United States v. Drumright, 534 F.2d 1383 (10th Cir. 1976).

46. Errington v. Hudspeth, 110 F.2d 384 (10th Cir. 1940).

47. United States v. Rabinowitz, 176 F.2d 732 (2d Cir. 1949).

D, who altered mint marks and dates on United States coins which were sold as rare collectors' items violated the statute prohibiting the fraudulent alteration of coins even if the alterations did not in any way affect the value of the coins as currency and were not intended to do so. Barnett v. United States, 384 F.2d 848 (5th Cir. 1967).

48. In Blackstone's definitions, for example, note that he does not use the word "fraudulent" in defining counterfeiting, but does use it in the definition of forgery. 4 Bl.Comm. *84, *247.

49. Rex v. Harris, 7 Car. & P. 428, 173 Eng.Rep. 189 (1836).

50. Kaye v. United States, 177 F. 147, 151 (7th Cir. 1910). Accord, Michener v. United States, 170 F.2d 973 (8th Cir. 1948).

A defendant's religious beliefs against the currency system are no defense. United States v. Grismore, 564 F.2d 929 (10th Cir. 1977).

51. United States v. Russell, 22 F. 390 (C.C.Mass.1884).

52. 18 U.S.C.A. §§ 485, 490.

53. Id. at § 501.

54. Id. at § 474.

Intent in causing reproduction to be made is not a factor to be considered. Wagner v. Simon, 412 F.Supp. 426 (D.C. Mo.1975) aff'd 534 F.2d 833 (8th Cir.).

ing of certain other counterfeiting paraphernalia.[55] On the other hand the section which forbids the making of any false obligation or security of the United States—including "paper money"—expressly requires an intent to defraud.[56]

The requirement of an intent to defraud is found in many of the provisions dealing with passing or uttering counterfeits or other false products forbidden by this chapter,[57] and also in provisions establishing penalties for knowingly having possession thereof.[58] For the most part this requirement, where it appears, is in terms of an "intent to defraud" without specification. Where detail is added it is in sweeping terms: "intent to defraud any body politic or corporate, or any person." [59] Even where the phrase is not so specific the courts have held that the intent to defraud anyone comes within the meaning of the statute;—it is not required that the intent be to defraud the United States.[60] Needless to say this intent may be inferred from circumstances having sufficient probative significance.[61]

E. KNOWLEDGE

The crime of counterfeiting is complete as soon as the false money is made and before even any attempt is made to pass it.[62] The uttering thereof is a separate offense.[63] The verb "utter" in this connection, as is true in the field of forgery, means no more than an offer to pass off the false as genuine.[64] And the federal statutes cover not only the passing or offering of counterfeits,[65] but even the wrongful possession there-

---

55. Id. at §§ 487, 488, 509.

56. Id. at § 471. This intent is not required, however, in the section forbidding the making of false obligations of the federal lending agencies. Id. at § 493.

57. Id. at §§ 472, 477, 479, 483, 485, 490. Section 473 speaks of an "intent that the same be passed, published, or used as true and genuine, . . ." It is not found in certain sections such as the section dealing with making, passing or uttering any false note, bond, and so forth, of a federal lending agency. Id. at § 493.

58. Id. at §§ 477, 480, 485. Unauthorized possession is prohibited in certain sections: Plates or stones for counterfeiting United States obligations or securities, § 474; plates or stones for counterfeiting foreign obligations or securities, § 481; counterfeit dies for coins, § 487; counterfeit dies for foreign coins, § 488. The intent to defraud clause at one time was found in section 487. Baender v. Barnett, 255 U.S. 224, 41 S.Ct. 271 (1921).

59. Id. at § 485.

60. United States v. Rabinowitz, 176 F.2d 732 (2d Cir. 1949); Errington v. Hudspeth, 110 F.2d 384 (10th Cir. 1940); Crouch v. United States, 298 F. 437 (6th Cir. 1924).

61. As for example, by secretly attempting to dispose of a roll of counterfeit bills. United States v. Kelley, 186 F.2d 598 (7th Cir. 1951).

62. 3 Co.Inst. *16; 1 East P.C. 165 (1803). Unlawfully procuring a plate to be made in likeness of a plate for printing an obligation or security of the United States by the Bureau of Printing and Engraving is a complete offense when the plate is procured to be made. An intent to use the plate unlawfully is not a necessary ingredient of the crime. Michener v. United States, 170 F.2d 973 (8th Cir. 1948).

63. 1 East P.C. 165 (1803). Cf. Curran v. Sanford, 145 F.2d 229 (5th Cir. 1944).

64. "It has been expressly adjudicated that the allegation of uttering and publishing is proved by evidence that the prisoner offered to pass the instrument to another person, declaring or asserting, directly or indirectly, by words or actions, that it was good." Walker v. State, 127 Ga. 48, 50, 56 S.E. 113 (1906); State v. Horner, 48 Mo. 520, 522 (1871). Quoted in substance: Curtis v. State, 80 Ga.App. 244, 246–7, 55 S.E.2d 758, 761 (1949).

65. "Whoever, with intent to defraud, passes, utters, publishes, or sells, or at-

of.[66] A distinction is to be noted, however, between making counterfeits on the one hand and uttering or possessing them on the other. As said in one case:

"There are many circumstances under which persons might come into possession of counterfeiting molds, either without knowledge of their character, or with such knowledge but without intent to use them fraudulently or unlawfully, as, for instance, the officers who took and held possession of the molds in question. Mere possession is inherently colorless; but the making of counterfeiting implements is inherently wrong, or at least was a proper matter for Congress to make wrong, as Congress unmistakably has done." [67]

Hence the sections which deal with uttering or possessing counterfeits frequently include some such phrase as "knowingly and with intent to defraud" [68] or "knowing the same to be false . . . with intent to defraud." [69] This makes "knowledge" an element of the crime,[70] but here as elsewhere when this word is used in the definition of a crime it is given a rather broad meaning. If the money is counterfeit it is not necessary that defendant should have witnessed the false making thereof. "Knowledge or belief of the counterfeit character of the money" is sufficient to satisfy this element of the crime.[71]

The mere fact that defendant passed or possessed counterfeit money is not sufficient to establish that he did so with knowledge of the fact.[72] Nor is knowledge shown by the fact that he used a counterfeit note to light a cigar, at a time when he was considerably under the influence of liquor.[73] But false statements as to the denomination of a bill used to make a certain payment, and an attempt to conceal relations with another who was known to have passed counterfeit bills at about the same time, are sufficient to support an inference of guilty knowledge.[74] And the same is true of a secret attempt to destroy a large roll of counterfeit bills.[75]

tempts to pass, utter, publish, or sell, ..." 18 U.S.C.A. § 472. Similar language is found in §§ 485, 493. Actually the word "utters" is sufficient and some of the sections are less verbose than the one quoted. §§ 479, 483, 486, 490, 494, 495, 500.

66. Id. at §§ 472, 474, 477, 480, 485, 487, 488, 489, 490, 491, 498, 501, 503, 506, 509.

"The defendant's possession of the counterfeit notes, while of extremely short duration, was sufficient to bring his conduct within the terms of the statute, for he 'had' and 'kept' in his possession the counterfeit notes from the time he received them until he turned them over . . . ." United States v. Johnson, 371 F.2d 800, 806 (3rd Cir. 1967).

67. Kaye v. United States, 177 F. 147, 150 (7th Cir. 1910).

68. E.g., 18 U.S.C.A. §§ 479, 480, 483, 485, 500.

69. E.g., § 485. Or "with intent to defraud . . . knowing the same to be so false, ..." § 483.

70. United States v. Litberg, 175 F.2d 20 (7th Cir. 1949).

"It is fundamental that the naked act of possessing and passing counterfeit money without knowledge that it is counterfeit does not establish the requisite knowledge essential to the crime of passing or the requisite intent to defraud." United States v. Bishop, 534 F.2d 214, 218 (10th Cir. 1976).

71. Marson v. United States, 203 F.2d 904, 906 (6th Cir. 1953).

72. United States v. Litberg, 175 F.2d 20 (7th Cir. 1949).

73. Ibid.

74. Marson v. United States, 207 F.2d 904 (6th Cir. 1953).

75. United States v. Kelley, 186 F.2d 598 (7th Cir. 1951).

Where knowledge is required it is not sufficient to show that defendant was negligent in not knowing.[76] The question is not what a prudent man, exercising ordinary care, would have known or believed under the circumstances, but what the defendant in fact did know or believe.[77] If circumstances suggested the possibility to him and he wilfully avoided inquiry for fear of what he would learn, he is held to have had "knowledge" of what would have been disclosed.[78] If they did not convey any such suggestion to him, and he acted in utmost good faith, he did so without "knowledge" no matter how "dumb" he may have been.[79]

In this connection it is important to note that one section in the federal chapter on "counterfeiting and forgery," and only one, makes use of the phrase "knowledge or reason to believe." [80] This is in the provision dealing with the manufacture or sale of slugs or tokens that may be used to operate vending machines or other devices designed to be operated by coins. And it is here expressly provided:

" 'Knowledge or reason to believe,' within the meaning of paragraph (b) of this section, may be shown by proof that any law-enforcement officer has, prior to the commission of the offense with which the defendant is charged, informed the defendant that tokens, slugs, disks, or other devices of the kind manufactured, sold, offered, or advertised for sale by him . . . are being used unlawfully or fraudulently to operate certain specified automatic merchandise vending machines, . . . or contrivances designed to receive or to be operated by lawful coins of the United States."

Some of the sections dealing with uttering or possessing counterfeits and so forth, make no reference to "knowing," "knowingly" or "with knowledge," but do require an "intent to defraud." [81] The requirement of "knowledge" is implicit in such a provision because one could not intend to defraud with counterfeit money without knowledge of the fact.[82] A few of the sections, however, make no reference either to "knowledge" or an "intent to defraud." [83] But even such a provision is not intended to punish one who has quite innocently passed or possessed the forbidden article. In the section, for example, dealing with counterfeiting dies, the provision is: "Whoever, without lawful authority, possesses any such die, hub, or mold, or any part thereof," shall be punished.[84] In rejecting the contention that this section is repugnant to the due process clause of the Fifth Amendment, the Supreme Court said: [85] "The statute is not intended to include and make criminal a possession which is not conscious and willing." That is, within the area of

76. Carver v. People, 39 Mich. 786 (1878); Meath v. State, 174 Wis. 80, 182 N.W. 334 (1921).

77. State v. Ebbeler, 283 Mo. 57, 222 S.W. 396 (1920).

78. Cf. State v. Pickus, 63 S.D. 209, 230, 257 N.W. 284, 294 (1934). "The jury have not found, either that the prisoner knew that these goods were Government stores, or that he wilfully shut his eyes to the fact." Per Willes, J., in Regina v. Sleep, 8 Cox C.C. 472, 480 (1861).

79. See Commonwealth v. Boris, 317 Mass. 309, 315, 58 N.E.2d 8, 12 (1944).

80. 18 U.S.C.A. § 491(b).

81. E.g., 18 U.S.C.A. §§ 472, 473, 477, 490.

82. "Knowledge or belief of the counterfeit character of the money is an essential element of the crime of passing counterfeit money; . . ." Marson v. United States, 203 F.2d 904, 906 (6th Cir. 1953). The counterfeits in this case were "paper money" which is covered by 18 U.S.C.A. § 471. This section mentions only "intent to defraud."

83. E.g., 18 U.S.C.A. §§ 486, 487.

84. Id. at § 487.

85. Baender v. Barnett, 255 U.S. 224, 225, 41 S.Ct. 271 (1921).

true crime a statute creating an offense includes the element of mens rea even if it is not expressly mentioned.[86]

There is an important difference, however, between an offense having a special mental element such as "knowledge" and one in which the mental element is only the so-called general mens rea. In the former "knowledge" is a positive factor which the prosecution is required to plead and prove; in the latter the prosecution has no such burden although the defendant may be entitled to an acquittal if he can establish that he acted under a reasonable mistake of fact.[87] No amount of negligence can be a substitute for "knowledge," [88] whereas an utterly unreasonable mistake of fact will not be recognized as an excuse in a prosecution for an offense which has no special mental element, but only the general mens rea.[89] The interpretation of the section in question may not go to that extent. Something more than the general mens rea may be read into this provision, despite the absence of any words expressive thereof, because of the court's statement that there is no guilt thereunder without a possession that is "conscious and willing." If this can be taken at its face value it means that unwitting possession of the forbidden article, or possession thereof without awareness of its nature is insufficient for guilt.[90] However this may be the court has left no doubt as to where the burden lies.

"Congress evidently intended that the unlawful possession of such dies should be sufficient to warrant a conviction, unless the accused could explain the possession to the satisfaction of the jury." [91]

86. Morissette v. United States, 342 U.S. 246, 72 S.Ct. 240 (1952); Regina v. Sleep, 8 Cox C.C. 472 (1861).

87. "There is also a third class in which, although from the omission from the statute of the words 'knowingly' or 'wilfully' it is not necessary to aver in the indictment that the offence charged was 'knowingly' or 'wilfully' committed, or to prove a guilty mind, and the commission of the act in itself *prima facie* imports an offence, yet the person charged may still discharge himself by proving to the satisfaction of the tribunal which tries him that in fact he had not a guilty mind." Per Edwards, J., in The King v. Ewart, 25 N.Z.L.R. 709, 731 (1905).

88. One is not guilty of uttering a forged instrument with knowledge of the forgery if he had no doubt of its genuineness, even if he was quite negligent in not discovering its falsity. Carver v. People, 39 Mich. 786 (1878); Wells v. Territory, 1 Okl.Cr. 469, 98 P. 483 (1908).

89. United States v. Thompson, 12 F. 245 (D.Or.1882); Dotson v. State, 62 Ala. 141 (1878); Hamilton v. State, 115 Tex. Cr.R. 96, 29 S.W.2d 777 (1930).

90. There is authority elsewhere for such an interpretation. An English statute provided a penalty for having possession of naval stores marked with the broad arrow. It was held that one having such stores was not guilty if he did not know that they were such stores, so marked. Regina v. Cohen, 8 Cox C.C. 41 (1858). Watson, B., said: "The word possession imports knowledge of what is possessed" (p. 42). Accord, State v. Labato, 7 N.J. 137, 150, 80 A.2d 617, 623 (1951).

91. Baender v. United States, 260 F. 832, 833 (1919), cert. den. 252 U.S. 586, 40 S.Ct. 396 (1920). "Lord Kenyon said, that it was clear, that in prosecutions under the statutes in question, it was sufficient for the Crown to prove the finding of the stores with the King's mark in the defendant's possession, to call him to account for that possession, and the manner of his coming by them; . . ." Rex v. Banks, 1 Esp. 144, 146–7, 170 Eng.Rep. 307, 307–8 (1794). This statute was amended later by adding the clause "knowing them to be so marked." 25 & 26 Vict. c. 24, § 7 (1862).

F. MULTIPLE OFFENSES

Counterfeiting and uttering counterfeit money are separate offenses whether committed by two wrongdoers or by one. In the early law the punishment was different [92] but the present trend is in the direction of providing the same penalty for each.[93] Legislation forbidding the unlawful possession of counterfeits has added a third offense. As carefully explained in one case.[94]

"The statute makes the possession of such a coin one offense, and the passing or uttering of it another. The two are not one continuous offense. They are separate and distinct, each complete within itself. . . . And the power of Congress to provide that each shall constitute a separate and distinct crime quite apart from the other is not open to doubt."

Counterfeiting, as an offense against property rather than an offense affecting the administration of governmental functions, is included in the Model Penal Code in the section on "Forgery." [95] Many other fraudulent and deceptive practices are included in the article which is called "Forgery and Fraudulent Practices." [96]

SECTION 10. EXTORTION

A. COMMON–LAW EXTORTION

Extortion, as a common-law misdemeanor,[1] is a species of official misconduct [2] closely akin to oppression.[3] As such it is usually classified as an offense affecting the administration of governmental functions, which unquestionably it is. As it always results in the unlawful obtainment of something of value, however, it is also an offense against property. And since the statutory additions under the name of "extortion" are mostly in the nature of

---

92. 1 East P.C. 165 (1803).

93. See e.g., 18 U.S.C.A. §§ 471, 472. But see §§ 485, 490.

94. Reger v. Hudspeth, 103 F.2d 825, 826 (10th Cir. 1939). In this case the court was talking about the same coin. In other cases the fact that there were two offenses is too clear for question. For example: An indictment in two counts charging that defendant passed a counterfeit silver half-dollar with intent to defraud, and that he possessed a counterfeit silver dollar with intent to defraud, charged separate offenses. Curran v. Sanford, 145 F.2d 229 (5th Cir. 1944). D was convicted of making a plaster of paris mold for the counterfeiting of half-dollar coins, and of unlawfully having such coins in his possession. It was held that these are two separate offenses. Power v. Squier, 130 F.2d 868 (9th Cir. 1942). See also United States v. Wilkerson, 469 F.2d 963 (5th Cir. 1972).

95. Section 224.1.

96. Article 224.

1. "The punishment is fine and imprisonment, and sometimes a forfeiture of the office." 4 Bl.Comm. *141.

2. Brackenridge v. State, 27 Tex.App. 513, 11 S.W. 630 (1889).

3. "Extortion technically is an official misdemeanor, while in its larger sense it signifies any oppression under color of right; in its strict sense it signifies the taking of money by any officer by color of his office where none is due or a part only is due." Kirby v. State, 57 N.J.L. 320, 321, 31 A. 213, 214 (1894); State v. Weleck, 10 N.J. 355, 371, 91 A.2d 751, 759 (1952).

"Extortion 'under color of official right' is the wrongful taking by a public officer of money or property not due him or his office, whether or not the taking was accomplished by force, threats or use of fear." United States v. Adcock, 558 F.2d 397, 403 (8th Cir. 1977).

offenses against property it is convenient to consider the entire problem at this point.

Common-law extortion is the corrupt collection of an unlawful fee by an officer under color of office, "with no proof of threat, force or duress required." [4]

At common law, and for the most part under modern statutes, it is a misdemeanor.

1. UNLAWFUL FEE

A fee collected under color of office is unlawful if—(1) the law does not authorize a fee for the purpose for which this fee is collected, or (2) a fee is authorized but only in an amount smaller than that collected,[5] or (3) a fee might be authorized but none was due at the time this fee was collected.[6] For this reason Blackstone defined extortion as "an abuse of public justice, which consists in any officer's unlawfully taking, by colour of his office, from any man, any money or thing of value that is not due to him, or more than is due, or before it is due."[7] Since a fee is unlawful under any one of the three circumstances the simpler wording is preferred for purposes of definition.

2. BY AN OFFICER

Although statutory extensions under the name of "extortion" ordinarily speak in terms of "whoever," [8] expressly or by implication, only an officer can perpetrate common-law extortion.[9] No officer, on the other hand, is excluded from the possibility of this offense unless this has resulted from the wording of a particular statute.[10]

4. United States v. Williams, 621 F.2d 123, 124 (5th Cir. 1980). "Extortion 'under color of official right' incorporates common law extortion, the taking of money by a public official not due him or his office for the performance or nonperformance of an official function." United States v. Rabbitt, 583 F.2d 1014, 1027 (8th Cir. 1978).

5. "[B]eyond that allowed by law." State v. Goodman, 9 N.J. 569, 584, 89 A.2d 243, 250 (1952).

6. Extortion may be committed by the exaction of a fee before it is due. Commonwealth v. Bagley, 28 Mass. 279 (1828); State v. Cooper, 120 Tenn. 549, 113 S.W. 1048 (1908). A constable arrested a woman on a "peace warrant" and collected payment of costs before the bond had been returned to the court. This was held to be extortion because no costs could lawfully be collected until the case had been passed upon by the judge. Levar v. State, 103 Ga. 42, 29 S.E. 467 (1897).

7. 4 Bl.Comm. *141. Extortion "is the taking by color of an office, money or other thing of value, that is not due, be-

fore it is due, or more than is due." Williams v. State, 34 Tenn. 160, 162 (1854); State v. Cooper, 120 Tenn. 549, 552, 113 S.W. 1048, 1049 (1908). Accord, State v. Weleck, 10 N.J. 355, 371, 91 A.2d 751, 759 (1952); Hanley v. State, 125 Wis. 396, 401, 104 N.W. 57, 59 (1905); Martin v. United States, 278 F. 913, 917 (2d Cir. 1922).

8. E.g., 18 U.S.C.A. §§ 873–877. Compare § 872 which reads: "Whoever, being an officer, or employee of the United States. . . ."

9. La Tour v. Stone, 139 Fla. 681, 190 So. 704 (1939). "It is thus apparent that the crime of extortion is committable only by an officer." Kirby v. State, 57 N.J.L. 320, 321, 31 A. 213, 214 (1894); State v. Weleck, 10 N.J. 355, 371, 91 A.2d 751, 759 (1952). See Harris's Criminal Law, 21st Ed. p. 168 (1968).

10. Under a statute reading: "If any officer authorized by law to charge fees" and so forth, it was held the offense could not be committed by an officer not authorized to charge fees. Ferkel v. People, 16 Ill.App. 310 (1885). A township policeman was held not to be an "officer

"In general it may be said that any officer, whether he be a federal, state, municipal, or a judicial officer . . . may be guilty of this offence." [11]

It should be mentioned, however, that a federal officer is probably amenable only to the federal statute[12] so far as extortion is concerned. There is a point of analogy between this and counterfeiting since each is an offense against property as well as an offense affecting the administration of a governmental function; but there is a great difference because this offense involves an officer whereas counterfeiting does not. It would open the door to state interference with federal business if a state should undertake to try an officer of the United States for anything done by him under color of his office.[13] It has been held, on the other hand, that an officer of one state, who goes into another and commits extortion there, may be convicted in the latter.[14]

Extortion may be committed by a de facto officer.[15] In one case it was held that the incumbent of an office under an unconstitutional statute is neither de jure nor de facto an officer and hence cannot be guilty of this offense,[16]—a result which seems to permit logic to override practical considerations. It would be better to give full scope to the following declaration:

"Any person who acts as an officer, and has assumed an officer's duties, cannot avoid liability by pleading the irregularity of his appointment." [17]

One who is not an officer, de jure or de facto, cannot commit common-law extortion unless he is acting in conspiracy with an officer. If an officer authorizes some other person to receive money under such circumstances that it would constitute extortion had the receiving been by the officer, and such money is received, it is extortion by both. But if a person without authority from an officer falsely represents himself as having such authority, and takes money under such circumstances that it would be extortion if the representations had been true, he is guilty of false pretenses but not of extor-

---

of this commonwealth" within the meaning of the statute. Although he was designated by statute as a deputy constable he was not clothed with the powers of a constable, but only those of a policeman. But he could be guilty of extortion as a common-law offense. Commonwealth v. Saulsbury, 152 Pa. 554, 25 A. 610 (1893).

11. Id. at 559–60, 25 A. at 611–12.

12. 18 U.S.C.A. § 872.

13. It was held, for example, that a state cannot apply its fraudulent banking statute to the officers of a national bank.

Easton v. State, 188 U.S. 220, 23 S.Ct. 288 (1903).

14. State v. Barts, 132 N.J.L. 74, 38 A.2d 838 (1944), aff'd 132 N.J.L. 420, 40 A.2d 639 (1944).

15. Commonwealth v. Saulsbury, 152 Pa. 554, 25 A. 610 (1893).

16. Kirby v. State, 57 N.J.L. 320, 31 A. 213 (1894).

17. Commonwealth v. Saulsbury, 152 Pa. 554, 560, 25 A. 610, 612 (1893); Commonwealth v. Lawton, 170 Pa.Super. 9, 14, 84 A.2d 384, 387 (1951).

tion,[18] unless a statute has enlarged the latter offense so as to include such misconduct.[19]

3. UNDER COLOR OF OFFICE

"The offence consists in the oppressive misuse of the exceptional power with which the law invests the incumbent of an office" [20] and hence is not committed unless the fee was collected under color of office.[21] Thus where a county solicitor was approached on behalf of a defendant and after repeated requests told him he could not advise him as solicitor because he was bound to prosecute, but for $20 would advise him as a lawyer, which he did (telling him to post bond and appeal) this was not extortion because it was not collected under color of office. It may have been official infidelity but it was no wrong to the one who paid him the money.[22] And an officer who solicits funds for charitable causes and keeps the money himself is not guilty of extortion, although this is a wrong to those who contribute, because this money also is not received under color of office.[23] The duties of an official's office are not necessarily limited to those expressly delineated by statute. Extortion can occur from activities associated with the office or by exploitation of the office.[24]

On the other hand, an officer who renders no service is guilty of extortion if he fraudulently represents that a service is necessary and charges for the

---

18. Drake v. State, 2 Okl.Cr. 643, 103 P. 878 (1909). An agent appointed by the Secretary of the Interior, with no tenure and no fixed salary and not named to any office created by Congress was held not to be an officer of the United States within the federal extortion statute. United States v. Schlierholz, 137 F. 616 (D.C. Ark.1905). The statute now reads: "Whoever, being an officer, or employee of the United States . . . ." 18 U.S. C.A. § 872. The proposed Federal Criminal Code § 1722 would continue to make the extortionist obtaining of property under color of official right a federal crime.

19. The federal statute covers at least part of the field that otherwise would be false pretenses. "Whoever, being an officer . . . or representing himself to be or assuming to act as such. . . ." 18 U.S.C.A. § 872.

20. Kirby v. State, 57 N.J.L. 320, 321, 31 A. 213, 214 (1894); State v. Weleck, 10 N.J. 355, 371, 91 A.2d 751, 759 (1952).

Quoting from an earlier case the court said: "Extortion under color of official right . . . need not involve force or threat. If a victim reasonably feels compelled to pay money to . . . (an official) because of that . . . [official's] wrongful use of his official position for the purpose of obtaining money, the requirements of the crime of extortion under color of official right are satisfied." United States v. Price, 617 F.2d 455, 458 (7th Cir. 1980).

21. Collier v. State, 55 Ala. 125 (1876); Hood v. State, 156 Ark. 92, 245 S.W. 176 (1922); La Tour v. Stone, 139 Fla. 681, 190 So. 704 (1939); State v. Pritchard, 107 N.C. 921, 12 S.E. 50 (1890).

"The Hobbs Act contains a definition of prohibited extortion as 'the obtaining of property of another, with his consent . . . under color of official right.'" United States v. French, 628 F.2d 1069, 1072 (8th Cir. 1980).

22. Collier v. State, 55 Ala. 125 (1876).

23. United States v. Sutter, 160 F.2d 754 (7th Cir. 1947).

24. Adler v. Sheriff, Clark County, 92 Nev. 641, 556 P.2d 549 (1976).

supposed service,[25] as for example if he wrongfully demands and receives money as a fee for discharging a void search warrant.[26]

4. FEE ACTUALLY RECEIVED

For common-law extortion the fee must actually be received,—a promise is not enough.[27] An early Massachusetts case[28] is sometimes cited as having held that the fee must be received in money and that receipt of a promissory note was not sufficient for guilt.[29] This, however, is inaccurate since the case was decided upon the ground of variance, the holding having been that proof of the receipt of a note would not support an indictment which charged the receipt of money. The court expressed a doubt whether the receipt of the note would be sufficient even under a proper indictment, but this doubt probably would have disappeared had this been the point at issue, as indicated by a decision a few years later.[30]

If the officer actually received money for performing the duties of his office, for which no such fee was due, it is no defense that he accepted it merely as a "tip or gratuity."[31] Some of the statutes, it may be added, have expressly enlarged the offense to include the wrongful exaction of a promise to pay an unlawful fee.[32]

5. CORRUPTLY

In the words of Bishop, "it is always held that extortion proceeds only from a corrupt mind."[33] That is, there is a special mental element which constitutes the mens-rea requirement of the crime, and this is corruption. Because of this fact extortion is not committed by the officer who innocently

25. Martin v. United States, 278 F. 913 (2d Cir. 1922). A county treasurer who exacts and receives from a taxpayer a fee as for a distress and sale of his goods for taxes, when they have actually not been made, is guilty of extortion. State v. Burton, 3 Ind. 93 (1851).

"This court has sustained convictions for extortion under color of official right even where the recipient had no legal control over the issuance of the desired permit." United States v. Rindone, 631 F.2d 491, 495 (7th Cir. 1980).

26. Hanley v. State, 125 Wis. 396, 104 N.W. 57 (1905).

27. La Tour v. Stone, 139 Fla. 681, 190 So. 704 (1939).

28. Commonwealth v. Conny, 2 Mass. 522 (1807).

29. May, Law of Crimes § 81 (4th ed. by Sears and Weihofen, 1938).

30. Acceptance of a note was held to be sufficient to sustain a charge of compounding a felony. Commonwealth v. Pease, 16 Mass. 91 (1891). This seems to dispel the earlier doubt which was based upon the idea that a note for an illegal

consideration is "void" and hence of no value.

31. Commonwealth v. Hopkins, 165 Pa.Super. 561, 69 A.2d 428 (1949).

32. E.g., West's Ann.Cal.Pen.Code § 70 (1970).

33. 2 Bishop, New Criminal Law § 396 (8th ed. 1892). Quoted with approval, Burns v. State, 123 Tex.Cr.R. 611, 613, 61 S.W.2d 512, 513 (1933). "The design on the part of the officer to collect fees to which he is not legally entitled, constitutes the corrupt intent which is the essence of the offense." Cleaveland v. State, 34 Ala. 254, 259 (1859). Extortion requires that the improper fees be received from corrupt motives. People v. Whaley, 6 Cowen 661 (N.Y.1827).

"In general, a public officer who corruptly seeks a payment in return for short-changing his duty to enforce the law has committed extortion. 'It matters not whether the public official induces payments to perform his duties or not to perform his duties.'" United States v. French, 628 F.2d 1069, 1074 (8th Cir. 1980).

receives an unlawful fee as a result of an honest mistake of fact or of law[34] although a few cases have held otherwise where the mistake is one of law.[35] If an officer should wrongfully exact a fee to which he knew he was not entitled he would not be heard to say he did not know a punishment was provided for that type of misconduct. That is a proper application of the maxim that ignorance of the law is no excuse. But it is quite unsound to start with a conclusive presumption of knowledge of the civil law in regard to the exact fee authorized in each particular situation, and by means of that presumption transform an honest and upright intent into one of assumed corruption. As said in one case in which a conviction of extortion was reversed:

"Whenever a special mental condition constitutes a part of the offence charged, and such condition depends on the question whether or not the culprit had certain knowledge with respect to matters of law, in every such case it has been declared that the subject of the existence of such knowledge is open to inquiry, as a fact to be found by the jury." [36]

The word "corruptly" has been omitted from some of the statutory definitions of the offense but "in such instances the old and the new law are to be construed together; and the former will not be considered to be abolished except so far as the design to produce such effect appears to be clear." [37] There is no indication, it may be added, of a legislative intent to change the substance of the offense. Under such a statute the burden may be on the officer to show affirmatively that he acted honestly and in good faith,[38] but a finding that he did so act should result in an acquittal.[39]

---

34. Cleaveland v. State, 34 Ala. 254 (1859); People v. Clark, 242 N.Y. 313, 151 N.E. 631 (1926); People v. Whaley, 6 Cowen 661 (N.Y.1827); State v. Pritchard, 107 N.C. 921, 12 S.E. 50 (1890); Lewis v. State, 124 Tex.Cr.R. 582, 64 S.W.2d 972 (1933); Haynes v. Hall, 37 Vt. 20 (1864).

35. Commonwealth v. Bagley, 28 Mass. 279 (1828); State v. Dickens, 2 N.C. 406 (1796). But compare State v. Pritchard in the preceding note.

36. Cutter v. State, 36 N.J.L. 125, 127 (1873).

37. Id. at p. 126.

38. Triplett v. Munter, 50 Cal. 644, 646 (1875). Where "corruptly" is included in the definition of the offense an indictment therefor is fatally defective if it does not allege that the unlawful fee was so received. Hood v. State, 156 Ark. 92, 245 S.W. 176 (1922). This requirement is removed by omitting this word from the definition or by appropriate simplification of the pleading by statute. See, e.g., the Institute's Code of Criminal Procedure § 164 (official draft, 1930). As to the

proof itself the difference if any will be slight. While there should be no conclusive presumption of the knowledge of the exact amount of each fee authorized by the civil law, there undoubtedly would be a true presumption (rebuttable) of such knowledge. Blumenthal v. United States, 88 F.2d 522, 530 (8th Cir. 1937).

39. Triplett v. Munter, 50 Cal. 644 (1875); Cutter v. State, 36 N.J.L. 125 (1873); Christian v. State, 123 Tex.Cr.R. 375, 59 S.W.2d 166 (1933). "The distinction between bribery and extortion seems to be that the former offense consists in offering a present or receiving one, the latter in demanding a fee or present by color of office." State v. Pritchard, 107 N.C. 921, 929, 12 S.E. 50, 52 (1890); Daniels v. United States, 17 F.2d 339, 342 (9th Cir. 1927). And see People v. Powell, 50 Cal.App. 436, 195 P. 456 (1920). For the distinction between extortion and false pretenses see Collier v. State, 55 Ala. 125, 128 (1876); Drake v. State, 2 Okl.Cr. 643, 103 P. 878 (1909); Chancellor v. State, 131 Tex.Cr.R. 617, 101 S.W.2d 570 (1937).

6.   (THREAT)

While statutory extortion (blackmail) requires a threat as an element of the offense, there is no such requirement in common-law extortion. In reference to the federal statute the court said: "we hold that a conviction under the Hobbs Act may be sustained upon a finding that property was unlawfully obtained under color of official right, absent a showing of 'actual or threatened force, violence, or fear . . . .' " [40]

B.   STATUTORY EXTORTION—BLACKMAIL

Statutory extortion is either (1) the extraction of money or other value by means of an unlawful threat, or (2) an unlawful threat made for that purpose.

It is commonly a felony. As it resulted from a legislative effort to plug a gap in the common law, it has been generally assumed that it and robbery are mutually exclusive. One theory is that it is a lesser-included offense of robbery by intimidation with the customary result which precludes conviction of both the inclusive offense and its lesser-included relative.

At one time sodomy was regarded as such an unspeakable crime that Blackstone literally refused to refer to it by name, speaking of it as "the infamous *crime against nature* . . . the very mention of which is a disgrace to human nature . . . a crime not fit to be named." [41] During that period a man was so terrified by a threat to accuse him of sodomy that he paid a sum of money to silence the threatener. There were circumstances of aggravation. The victim had been seized by the arm and threatened with mob violence which threat may have generated a well-grounded fear of personal danger. However that may be a conviction of robbery was upheld. [42] This lead was followed by two other convictions of robbery [43] based upon the same type of threat, but in which aggravating circumstances were less apparent although it seems that in each case the victim had been in fear of his life. [44] No such element was involved in the next case of this nature, [45] however, the victim having testified that he parted with his money for fear of losing his "character" but that he had no other fear. A conviction of rob-

---

40. United States v. Williams, 621 F.2d 123, 124 (5th Cir.1980). Note—the Hobbs Act includes, *inter alia*, both statutory extortion and common-law extortion. 18 U.S.C.A. § 1951(b) reads: "As used in this section—. . ..

"(2) The term 'extortion' means the obtaining of property from another, *with his consent, induced by wrongful use of actual or threatened force, violence, or fear,* or under color of official right." Emphasis added. With the words in italics it defines statutory extortion. The part without them is intended to codify common-law extortion. The interpretation will include the mens-rea requirement of "corruptly." "The government is merely required to prove that a public official obtained money to which he was not entitled and which he obtained only because of his official position." United States v. Hedman, 630 F.2d 1184, 1195 (7th Cir.1980).

41.   4 Bl.Comm. *215.

42.   Rex v. Jones, 1 Leach 164, 2 East P.C. 714 (1776).

43.   Harrold's Case, 2 East P.C. 715 (1778); Rex v. Donolly, 2 East P.C. 715 (1779).

44.   Harrold's Case was said to be similar to Rex v. Jones, ibid, and in Rex v. Donolly the jury found "that the prosecutor delivered his money through fear and under an apprehension that his life was in danger." Id. at 716.

45.   Hickman's Case, 2 East P.C. 728 (1783).

bery was held proper "for to most men the idea of losing their fame and reputation was equally if not more terrific than the dread of personal injury." [46] About the same time it was held robbery to coerce the payment of money under a threat that the victim's house would be destroyed by mob violence.[47]

Had robbery not carried the penalty of death, it might have had a substantial development along such lines, but one tradition of the common law is that a capital crime is narrowly limited in its scope, and this was no exception. "Robbery," it has been said, "may be committed by putting one in fear of injury to the person, to property or to character." [48] This is literally true but only in a very limited sense. Apparently the only exceptions to the requirement that the actual or threatened violence be to the person, so far as common-law robbery is concerned, are (1) the threat to destroy the dwelling house[49] and (2) the threat to accuse of sodomy.[50]

This left an important area to be covered by statute[51] and such legislation has been widespread although not uniform. The statutes of the various states have many differences in detail but tend to follow one of two general patterns. One emphasizes the extortion itself,—the actual obtainment of money or other thing of value (to which is often added a signature to a legal writing or other coerced act), with the addition of provisions for punishing threats made with intent to extort.[52] The fact that such statutes have reference to conduct not amounting to robbery or an attempt at robbery is frequently stated in so many words. The other general pattern punishes the extorsive threat whether anything was obtained thereby or not.[53] What con-

---

46. Id. at 728–9.

47. Rex v. Simons, 2 East P.C. 731 (1773); Brown's Case, 2 East P.C. 731 (1780); Regina v. Astley, 2 East P.C. 729 (1792).

48. Nelson v. State, 203 Ga. 330, 338, 46 S.E.2d 488, 494 (1948).

49. Bishop indicates that this exception is apparent rather than real because danger to the occupiers is involved. 2 Bishop, New Criminal Law § 1171 (8th Ed. 1892).

50. A threat of injury to character has never been deemed sufficient except a threat to accuse of "sodomitical practices." The King v. Knewland, 2 Leach 721, 730, 168 Eng.Rep. 461, 466 (1796). Obtaining money under a threat to accuse the other of sodomy is robbery whether the other is guilty or not. "This seems to be the only case in which a threat to prosecute, will supply the place of actual force." Long v. State, 12 Ga. 293, 319 (1852). Repeated in substance with Bishop's comment that there is clearly no foundation in principle for the exception. Montsdoca v. State, 84 Fla. 82, 87, 93 So. 157, 159 (1922). "The demonstrations or fear must be of a physical nature, with the single exception, that, if one parts with his goods through fear of

a threatened charge of sodomy, the taking is robbery." Houston v. Commonwealth, 87 Va. 257, 264, 12 S.E. 385, 387 (1890).

51. Threatening to start a prosecution against another is not indictable at common law. The King v. Southerton, 6 East 126, 102 Eng.Rep. 1235 (1805). Obtaining money or property by force or fear under circumstances not amounting to robbery might or might not involve an assault or battery, but did not constitute an independent common-law offense.

52. "Extortion is the obtaining of property from another, with his consent or the obtaining of an official act of a public officer, induced by a wrongful use of force or fear, . . ." West's Ann. Cal.Pen.Code § 518 (1970). Obtaining a signature by extortion. Id. at § 522. Sending threatening letter. Id. at § 523. Md.Code 1957, art. 27 § 563; Mass.Gen. Laws Ann. c. 265 § 25 (1968).

53. Ariz.Rev.Stat. § 13–1804 (1978); 21 Okl.Stat.Ann. §§ 1486, 1487 (1951).

"Fear of economic loss is sufficient to constitute extortion, . . . even if the interest threatened is only an anticipated one." United States v. Rabbitt, 583 F.2d 1014, 1027 (8th Cir. 1978).

stitutes an extorsive threat is sometimes stated in detail, such as (including in each category "any relative of his or member of his family"), any threat: "1. To do an unlawful injury to the person or property . . .; or, 2. To accuse . . . of any crime; or, 3. To expose or impute to him . . . any deformity or disgrace; or, 4. To expose any secret affecting him . . . .[54] It will be noted that the extorsive threat is punished under either type of statute. Under some of the enactments statutory extortion is included in robbery,[55] or an extorsive threat is deemed an attempt to rob.[56]

The cases holding that a threat to accuse of sodomy was equivalent to a threat of physical violence, so far as common-law robbery is concerned, consistently held that it was immaterial whether the victim was innocent or guilty of the crime threatened.[57] And in prosecutions for statutory extortion based upon a threat to accuse of crime, it is held to be immaterial whether the charge is false or true[58] with one exception recognized in some jurisdictions. Several cases have held that a threat to prosecute is not extortion if the one threatened is guilty of the offense charged and the threat is made in a bona-fide effort to collect a just claim based upon a civil liability resulting from such offense.[59] This exception is not recognized in all jurisdictions, however, and even such a threat may be held to be extortion.[60] As said in

"The crime of extortion is complete when a person makes the threat, intending to compel the victim to do something he would not have done." State v. Wheeler, 95 N.M. 378, 622 P.2d 283, 286 (App.1980).

54. E.g., West's Ann.Cal.Pen.Code § 519 (1970); Ariz.Rev.Stat. § 13–1804 (1978). Louisiana includes a threat against a member of his family "or other person dear to him" and adds as a fifth category a threat "to do any other harm." LSA–R.S. § 14–66 (1974).

The threat of a city electrical inspector to put an electrical contractor out of business unless he paid money that was not due, constituted extortion under color of official right. United States v. Glynn, 627 F.2d 39 (7th Cir. 1980).

55. "Every person who shall feloniously take the personal property of another, in his presence or from his person, which shall have been delivered or suffered to be taken through fear of some injury threatened to be inflicted at some different time to his person or property, or to the person of any member of his family or relative, which fear shall have been produced by threats of the person so receiving or taking such property, shall be guilty of robbery." Miss.Code 1972 § 97–3–77; See also Burns' Ind. Ann.Stat. § 35–42–5–1(2) (1978).

56. E.g., Miss.Code 1972 § 97–3–81: "Every person who shall knowingly send or deliver . . . any letter or writing . . . threatening therein to accuse any

person of a crime or to do any injury to the person or property of any one, with a view or intent to extort or gain money or property . . . shall be guilty of an attempt to rob. . . ."

57. Regina v. Richards, 11 Cox C.C. 43 (1868); Rex v. Gardner, 1 Car. & P. 479, 171 Eng.Rep. 1282 (1824).

58. People v. Choynski, 95 Cal. 640, 30 P. 791 (1892); Motsinger v. State, 123 Ind. 498, 24 N.E. 342 (1889); Eacock v. State, 169 Ind. 488, 82 N.E. 1039 (1907); State v. McKenzie, 182 Minn. 513, 235 N.W. 274 (1931); State v. Debolt, 104 Iowa 105, 73 N.W. 499 (1897).

It is the general rule that where the threat is to injure the reputation of another truth of the threatened disclosure is no defense. United States v. Von der Linden, 561 F.2d 1340 (9th Cir. 1977).

"No public policy is served by allowing accusations to be made, even against the guilty, for the sole purpose of extortion." People v. Hubble, 81 Ill.App.3d 560, 37 Ill.Dec. 189, 401 N.E.2d 1282, 1285 (1980).

59. State v. Hammond, 80 Ind. 80 (1881); Commonwealth v. Jones, 121 Mass. 57 (1876); State v. Ricks, 108 Miss. 7, 66 So. 281 (1914); State v. Barger, 111 Ohio St. 448, 145 N.E. 857 (1924).

60. Lindenbaum v. State Bar, 26 Cal. 2d 565, 160 P.2d 9 (1945); People v. Beggs, 178 Cal. 79, 172 P. 152 (1918); People v. Fichtner, 281 App.Div. 159, 118 N.Y.S.2d 392 (1952); In re Sherin, 27 S.D. 232, 130 N.W. 761 (1911).

one case: "The law does not contemplate the use of criminal process as a means of collecting a debt." [61]   And the Iowa court emphasized a similar problem when it pointed out that although the collection of a just debt at pistol-point does not amount to robbery it does constitute statutory extortion.[62]

"Black-mail" (black rent) was anciently used to indicate "rents reserved in work, grain or baser money" (i.e. baser than silver).[63]   It was also employed at one time to refer to "a tribute formerly exacted in the north of England and in Scotland by freebooting chiefs for protection from pillage." [64] Such practice was extortion, in the literal sense, and hence "blackmail" is frequently used to indicate statutory extortion or sometimes an extorsive threat.[65]   And the federal statute forbidding the sending of an extorsive threat by mail [66] has been referred to as the "blackmail statute." [67]   The "badger game" is a blackmailing trick, usually in the form of enticing a man into a compromising position with a woman whose real or pretended husband comes upon the scene and demands payment under threat of prosecution or exposure.[68]

The distinction between statutory extortion and robbery by intimidation is that in the former the victim consents to part with his money or property, although his consent is induced by the unlawful threat, whereas in robbery the intimidation is so extreme as to overcome the will of the victim and cause him to part with his money or property without consent.[69]   The Hobbs Act makes it a federal crime to obstruct, delay or effect commerce or the move-

---

61. People v. Beggs, 178 Cal. 79, 84, 172 P. 152, 154 (1918).

62. See State v. Hollyway, 41 Iowa 200, 203 (1875). The statute covers obtaining money by maliciously threatening. And while it is not false pretenses to induce one to pay a just debt by fraud it is extortion to compel one to pay a just debt by threatening to accuse the debtor of a crime. Commonwealth v. Coolidge, 128 Mass. 55 (1880).

"If the checks in this case were subject to collection as valid negotiable instruments, the threats of bodily harm would still bring the appellants within the ambit of the statute." People v. Rosenberg, 194 Colo. 423, 572 P.2d 1211, 1213 (1978).

63. 2 Bl.Comm. *42–3.

64. The American College Dictionary (1948).

65. See R.R.S. (Neb.) 1943, § 28–441; Trosper v. State, 128 Neb. 165, 258 N.W. 62 (1934).

It constitutes an extorsive threat if a transaction was entered into with an "understanding of the creditor and the debtor at the time . . . that delay in making repayment or failure to make repayment could result in the use of violence or other criminal means. . . ."

United States v. Dennis, 625 F.2d 782, 803 (8th Cir. 1980).

66. 18 U.S.C.A. §§ 875, 876 (1976).

67. United States v. Pignatelli, 125 F.2d 643, 646 (2d Cir. 1942).

"Subtle extortions are covered under the Hobbs Act, and the government satisfied its burden of proof if it showed circumstances surrounding the alleged extortionate conduct that rendered the victim's fear of threatened loss reasonable." United States v. Sander, 615 F.2d 215, 218 (5th Cir. 1980).

68. This is extortion but not an assault with intent to rob. Rippetoe v. People, 172 Ill. 173, 50 N.E. 166 (1898).

69. People v. Barondess, 61 Hun 571, 16 N.Y.S. 436 (1891), rev'd on other grounds 133 N.Y. 649, 31 N.E. 240 (1892). Compare statutes on the two crimes. E.g., "Extortion is the obtaining of property from another with his consent, . . . induced by a wrongful use of force or fear. . . ." West's Ann.Cal. Pen.Code § 518 (1970). "Robbery is the felonious taking of personal property in the possession of another from his person or immediate presence, and against his will accomplished by means of force or fear." Id. at § 211.

ment of any article or commodity in commerce "by robbery or extortion. . . ."[70]

The Model Penal Code incorporates part of extorsive extraction in its definition of robbery[71] and the rest (and more) in its section on Theft by Extortion.[72] These sections do not cover the extorsive threat as such, but it is covered by the general section on Criminal Attempt.[73]

Extortion, common law and statutory, will be found combined in one section in some of the new penal codes in some such form as this:

"A person commits extortion if the person does any of the following with the purpose of obtaining for oneself or another anything of value, tangible or intangible, including labor or services:

"1. Threatens to inflict physical injury on some person, or to commit any public offense.

"2. Threatens to accuse another of a public offense.

"3. Threatens to expose any person to hatred, contempt, or ridicule.

"4. Threatens to harm the credit or business or professional reputation of any person.

"5. Threatens to take or withhold action as a public officer or employee, or to cause some public official or employee to take or withhold action.

"6. Threatens to testify or provide information or to withhold testimony or information with respect to another's legal claim or defense.

"7. Threatens to wrongfully injure the property of another.

"It is a defense to a charge of extortion that the person making a threat other than a threat to commit a public offense, reasonably believed that he or she had a right to make such threats in order to recover property, or to receive compensation for property or services, or to recover a debt to which the person has a good faith claim.

"Extortion is a class D felony."[74]

Guilt of extortion was established by proof that a debt was collected by threatening the debtor that if the debt was not paid "she is going to have a broken head and be found floating in the river."[75]

---

70. 18 U.S.C.A. § 1951 (1970). Minimal effect on commerce is sufficient for a violation. United States v. Harding, 563 F.2d 299 (6th Cir. 1977).

71. "A person is guilty of robbery if, in the course of committing a theft, he: . . .

"(c) commits or threatens immediately to commit any felony of the first or second degree." Section 222.1.

72. Section 223.4.

73. Section 5.01.

74. Iowa Criminal Code § 711.4 (1978).

75. United States v. Ochs, 595 F.2d 1247, 1261 (2d Cir. 1979).

Chapter 5

OTHER OFFENSES

SECTION 1. OFFENSES AGAINST MORALITY AND DECENCY

The whole field of substantive criminal law constitutes a rather stern moral code. It is not exhaustive in this respect but represents the points at which conduct is deemed so offensive to the moral judgment of the community as to call for punishment.[1] This frequently leads to the question: Why are certain crimes spoken of as offenses against morality?

There is reason to believe that at a very early day the Church preempted jurisdiction over certain types of misconduct. It is known that the starting point of benefit of clergy was the Church's refusal to permit members of the clergy to be tried for crime in lay courts.[2] The time came when benefit of clergy could be claimed only after guilt had been established, by verdict or plea, but this was after a very substantial change in the relative power of Church and State. Much earlier the Church had said to the common-law judges, in effect: "If a charge of misconduct is brought against a clergyman, that is none of your business. That is our business; send him to us and we shall handle the matter." And for generations this is exactly what happened.

In like manner it is more than probable that at the peak of its power the Church made it known to the common-law judges that jurisdiction over certain types of misconduct belonged exclusively to the ecclesiastical court.[3] In any event the Church did take jurisdiction over those offenses and the common-law judges did not do so for many years—not in fact until they had been made punishable by acts of Parliament. Prior to that time they were no doubt referred to as "offenses only against morality."

At the present time many feel that part of this responsibility should be returned to the church. This is not to be understood too literally. The suggestion is not that an ecclesiastical court should be established in this country, (which the constitution would not permit) but only that in certain areas of so-called private morality where no threat to the public is involved, the responsibility should be placed upon the moral persuasion of the church and other influences in the community rather than upon the criminal law.[4]

---

1. "We proceed on the fundamental premise that moral responsibility and moral sanctions are the warp and woof of the law, . . ." Wion v. United States, 325 F.2d 420, 427 (10th Cir. 1963).

2. 4 Bl.Comm. *365–66.

3. "Some other crimes . . . were appropriated by the church and so escaped from lay justice. . . . But fornication, adultery, incest and bigamy were ecclesiastical offenses, and the lay courts had nothing to say about them, . . ." 2 Pollock & Maitland, History of English Law 543 (2d ed. 1899). This apparently started in the time of King Cnut and was well recognized by the middle of the twelfth century. Id. at 367.

4. See generally, Devlin, The Enforcement of Morals; Hart, Law, Liberty and Morality (1963); Packer, The Limits of

A. ADULTERY, FORNICATION AND ILLICIT COHABITATION

Adultery and *fornication* were punished by the Church as ecclesiastical offenses, but were not recognized as common-law crimes in England.[5] The English common law took notice of them for certain purposes, but did not give to the words exactly the same definitions as they received as ecclesiastical offenses.

1. DEFINITION BY CANON LAW

In the view of the canon law, adultery violated the marriage vow and hence this offense was committed if a married person—either man or woman—had sexual intercourse with one other than his or her spouse. Illicit intercourse was adultery if by a married person and fornication if by one not married. Hence if a married person had sexual intercourse with a single person this was adultery by the former and fornication by the latter, whether the married person was a man or a woman.

2. DEFINITION BY COMMON LAW

The common law, on the other hand, spoke of illicit intercourse as fornication unless it was calculated to adulterate the blood. If the female party to illicit intercourse was married this might tend to introduce spurious offspring into the home, but this could not result if the only married party was a man. Hence in the common-law view illicit intercourse was adultery by both if the woman was married [6] (whether the man was married or single) and was fornication by both if the woman was single (even if the man was married).[7]

3. STATUTORY CHANGES

In 1650, during the second year of the Commonwealth, adultery was made a capital crime in England; but this statute was repealed after the Restoration, and since then such misconduct there has been "left to the feeble coercion of the spiritual court according to the rules of canon law." [8] "In this country," therefore, "the offense is only punishable in the common-law courts when so provided by statute." [9] It was punished as a misdemeanor under many statutes, some of which provided that both parties to the illicit intercourse were guilty of adultery if either one was married to a third per-

The Criminal Sanction (1968); Dworkin, Lord Devlin and The Enforcement of Morals, 75 Yale L.J. 986 (1966).

5. 2 Pollock & Maitland, History of English Law 543 (2d ed. 1899).

6. Evans v. Murff, 135 F.Supp. 907 (C.D.Md.1955) Adultery is "criminal conversation with a man's wife." 3 Bl. Comm. *139.

7. Commonwealth v. Call, 38 Mass. (21 Pick.) 509 (1839).

8. 4 Bl.Comm. *64–65. Fornication was also capital upon the second conviction under the early statute. Ibid.

Although generally overlooked, statutes making adultery a capital offense were not unknown in the colonies here even before the English statute. See Commonwealth v. Call, 38 Mass. (21 Pick.) 509, 511 (1839).

9. United States v. Clapox, 35 F. 575, 578 (1888). There was a trace of authority contra, in "some of the colonies." Ibid.

son.[10]   If a statute provided for the punishment of adultery without a definition of the term, this gave rise to a difficulty as to the meaning of the word.
In England, (1) the common-law meaning of the word was sex with another's
wife, but this was not a common-law offense; (2) as the name of an offense
it referred to sex by a married person with one other than the spouse, but
that was recognized only in the ecclesiastical court.   If a statute defined the
offense it ordinarily adopted the latter meaning[11] unless it provided that both
were guilty if either was married to a third, as mentioned above.   If (although the section was called "adultery") the penalty was provided only for
those who "lasciviously associate, bed and cohabit together" [12] the offense
described was "illicit cohabitation" and proof of an isolated act of adulterous
intercourse was not sufficient.[13]

**Fornication was not a common-law crime but was made punish-
able by statute in a few states as a misdemeanor.[14]**

**Illicit cohabitation was living together either in adultery or in
fornication.   It was a misdemeanor under many statutes.**

A single act of illicit sex does not constitute "living together." [15]   On the
other hand parties may be living together although interrupted before the
second day.[16]   Even this was not a common-law offense unless so open and
notorious as to create a public scandal.   Illicit cohabitation was made a crime
by statute in many states.   Some statutes included the common-law requirement of notoriety, while others provided punishment for illicit cohabitation
even if committed quite secretly.[17]   Apart from illicit cohabitation, adultery
was made an offense in a little over half the states, and fornication in about
one third.[18]   Such statutes, where found, were so poorly enforced that the
principal influence seems to have been to breed disrespect for law while the
chief accomplishment was to provide an opportunity for blackmail.[19]

There seems to be a deep-seated and widely-held opinion to the effect that
this is an area which should be left to religious, educational and other social
influences.[20]   The most extreme position was found in Texas where (other

10.   E.g., Idaho Code § 18–6601 (1972).

11.   E.g., Colo.Rev.Stat. 1973, 18–6–
501; Utah Code Ann., 1953 § 76–7–103.

12.   N.C.Gen.Stat. § 14–184 (1969).

13.   Bodifield v. State, 86 Ala. 67, 5 So.
559 (1888).

14.   E.g., Idaho Code § 18–6603 (1972);
Wis.St.1955, § 944.15 (1978).

15.   Wright v. State, 5 Blackf. 358
(Ind. 1840).

16.   Hall v. State, 53 Ala. 463 (1875).

17.   The statutes differ widely.   E.g.,
(italics added): "If any man and woman,
not being married to each other, shall
lewdly and lasciviously, associate, bed
and cohabit . . ."   N.C.Gen.Stat. §
14–184 (1969).   "If any man and women
[sic], not being married to each other,
shall live and cohabit together as man
and wife, *or shall lewdly and notorious-*

ly associate together. . . ."   Idaho
Code § 18–6604 (1972).   When the California statute was worded in terms of
"living in a state of open and notorious
cohabitation and adultery" it was held
that proof of notoriety was as material
as proof of adultery.   People v. Gates, 46
Cal. 52 (1873).

18.   At the time of development of the
Model Penal Code a single act of adultery
was punishable in 30 states, four by fine
alone, and a single act of fornication was
punishable in 18 states, four by fine
alone.   Model Penal Code 204–205 (Tent.
Draft No. 4, 1955).   Since then there has
been a decline in the number of states
punishing adultery or fornication, Hale, 1
Crim.Just.Jnl. 65 (1976).

19.   Ibid.

20.   Ibid.

than to make it a ground for divorce)[21] the state ignored a single act of adultery[22] except to authorize the enraged husband to kill the paramour caught in the act, provided the execution was carried out promptly.[23]

Under the original plan the Model Penal Code was to have included a section on illicit cohabitation but none on adultery or fornication as such.[24] In the final draft all three were omitted.

This plan is followed in some of the new penal codes.[25]

B. BIGAMY

Bigamy is the purported marriage of another spouse by a married person. Included in bigamy under some statutes is cohabitation with a bigamous spouse, to cover such conduct by persons whose marriage ceremony was performed outside the state. And some statutes expressly include the purported marriage of one known to be married.

It was not a crime under the common law of England but was punished as an ecclesiastical offense.[26] It is a statutory offense today. Under early statutes it was regularly a felony, but is a misdemeanor under some of the new penal codes.

In discussions of this subject it is common to speak in terms of a married person marrying a second spouse, but the bigamous marriage is void as a matter of law.[27] It is a marriage ceremony, but only a purported marriage. Some statutes have been worded in terms of having a plurality of spouses at the same time,[28] but they do not mean what they say. Only the first ceremony resulted in a valid marriage.[29] The statute may be in some such form as this:

"If any person, being married, shall marry another person, the former husband or wife then living, or continues to cohabit with such second husband or wife in this state, such person shall be imprisoned in the penitentiary not less than two (2) years nor more than twenty-one (21) years."[30]

---

21. "Adultery is almost universally a ground for divorce, . . ." Id. at 208.

22. Where the term "habitual" was not defined the mere proof of four different occasions was held not to be sufficient. Hilton v. State, 41 Tex.Cr. 190, 53 S.W. 113 (1899). If there was any doubt that this represents firm state policy it was dissipated when a city ordinance seeking to make a single act of illicit intercourse punishable was held invalid because in conflict with the state statute. Brewer v. State, 113 Tex.Cr. 522, 24 S.W.2d 409 (1930).

23. The husband's instant killing of the paramour caught in the act was justifiable homicide. Vernon's Ann.Tex.P.C. art. 1220; now repealed. Almost all states have abandoned such a claim of justification.

24. Model Penal Code, section 207.1 (Tent. Draft No. 4, 1955). And see the comment beginning on page 204.

25. E.g., Iowa.

26. 2 Pollock & Maitland, History of English Law 543 (2d ed. 1899).

27. "This second marriage is merely void, and yet it maketh the offender a felon." 3 Co.Inst. *88. "Such second marriage, living the former husband or wife, is simply void, . . ." 4 Bl. Comm. *163.

28. "Polygamy or bigamy consists of knowingly having a plurality of husbands or wives at the same time." Code of Ga. Ann. § 26–5601 (1965), repealed. Currently see § 26–2007 (1978).

29. "It is the appearing to contract a second marriage, and the going through the ceremony which constitutes the crime of bigamy, otherwise it could never exist in the ordinary cases; . . ." Regina v. Brawn, 1 Car. & K. 144, 145, 175 Eng. Rep. 751, 752 (1843).

30. Tenn.Code Ann. § 39–701 (1975).

Where the definition is in terms of the second marriage some such clause as "continues to cohabit . . . in this state" is needed to authorize punishment for parties who come into the state and cohabit therein after having contracted a bigamous marriage beyond its boundaries.[31] Where the definition is in terms of the second marriage it is doubtful if even the "continues to cohabit" clause would cover the case of a man who marries two wives at the same time.[32]

All the statutes make provision for exceptions. Where the proscription is in terms of marriage by a person "having a former wife or husband living" it is necessary to add an exception to cover divorce and annulment. Another exception is added to cover cases of prolonged absence of the spouse, without evidence that the spouse was alive. In the great majority of jurisdictions it is a complete defense if the defendant did not actually know that the spouse was living.[33] The period specified ranges from two to seven years, with five being the most common.[34]

Apparently the authorized second marriage in such a case results in "an informal divorce" of the first spouse, if still alive, to avoid the impermissible result of plural spouses at the same time.[35]

Knowingly marrying a married person is expressly made a felony in a number of states,[36] and without such a provision would seem to be punishable under general principles of complicity.[37]

---

31. As explained by the Washington court, under its statute, bigamy may be committed by a person having a spouse, either marrying another spouse, in which case the gist of the offense is the second marriage which must occur within this state, or continuing to cohabit with a second spouse illegally married elsewhere in which case the continued cohabitation with the bigamous spouse in the state is the gist of the offense although the marriage was performed beyond its boundaries. State v. Lewis, 46 Wn.2d 438, 282 P.2d 297 (1955). In this case the information was held defective because it merely charged that defendant cohabited with the bigamous spouse within the state, whereas the statute says "continue to cohabit." A more desirable result was reached by the Iowa Court which held in effect that any cohabitation with the bigamous spouse in Iowa, after unlawful marriage elsewhere, was a continuing cohabitation since it started in the other state. State v. Nadal, 69 Iowa 478, 29 N.W. 451 (1886). A Mexican divorce is invalid if neither the husband nor the wife was domiciled in Mexico at any time and hence it was bigamy for the man to marry a second woman in New Jersey.

In re Ebert, 140 F.Supp. 596 (D.C.N.J. 1956).

32. The Model Penal Code has a special sub-section for this called "polygamy." Section 230.1(2). The reason being that the second marriage clause would not cover such a situation. Model Penal Code 226 (Tent. Draft No. 4, 1955). Such a marriage would be void and cohabitation with either spouse (or both) would be punishable as illicit cohabitation wherever that is included in the code.

33. Model Penal Code 223 (Tent. Draft No. 4, 1955).

34. In a few jurisdictions this defense is available only if the spouse is believed to be dead. And in some jurisdictions if the spouse has been "beyond the seas" or "outside the United States" for the period mentioned the second marriage is not bigamous even if the first spouse is known to be alive. Ibid.

35. Id. at 224.

36. E.g., West's Fla.Stat.Ann. § 826.-03 (1976); Miss.Code, 1972, 97–29–13; Ga.Code, § 26–2008 (1978).

37. See, infra, chapter 6, section 8.

Polygamy (many marriages) is employed at times as a synonym of bigamy[38] **and at other times to indicate the simultaneous marriage of two or more spouses.**[39]

Trigamy, literally three marriages, is often used for a special situation.

"Trigamy," [40] in the sense of the special problem of the third wife, stems from the premise that invalidity of the alleged prior marriage is a good defense to a charge of bigamy.[41] Thus in a bigamy prosecution a so-called common-law marriage can be relied upon to establish either the first or second marriage, if it is recognized in the jurisdiction as giving rise to the marital status,[42] but cannot be relied upon where it is not so recognized.[43]

A logical result is that a charge of bigamy may be defeated by showing that the alleged prior marriage, relied upon to support the charge, was itself void because of an even earlier marriage existing at the time—as was held about 1648 in Lady Madison's Case.[44] For example, D marries A, and afterward while A is alive marries B, and still later when A is dead but B alive, marries C. The marriage to C is not bigamy because the marriage to B was bigamous and void.[45]

Although this position seemed to hold firm for over three hundred years[46] the foundation is unsatisfactory. When we use the word "marriage" in speaking of bigamy we are obviously not limiting it to such contracts or ceremonies as result in a legally valid marital status. And since we give it a meaning broader than that in regard to the subsequent "marriage" there is no reason why it should not have the same meaning as to the former one.

Because of this a recent case has rejected the three-hundred-year-old position and held that a former marriage cannot be considered void for purposes of bigamy unless it has been "pronounced void, annulled or dissolved by the judgment of a competent court." [47] In reaching this result the court mentioned the statutory exception which has the wording quoted,[48] but did not emphasize the bigamy statute itself which is in terms of a "person having a husband or wife living who marries any other person." [49] The same result is reached by an occasional statute.[50]

---

38. E.g., Mass.Gen.Laws Ann. C. 272 § 15 (1969).

39. It is used in this sense by Coke, 3 Co.Inst. *88, and also in the Model Penal Code, Section 230.1(2).

40. Coke used the word although he merely equated it with bigamy. 3 Co.Inst. *88.

41. 1 Hale P.C. *693; Mulkey v. State, 26 Ala.App. 142, 154 So. 612 (1934); People v. Horton, 272 App.Div. 924, 71 N.Y.S.2d 57 (1947).

42. People v. Sokol, 226 Mich. 267, 197 N.W. 569 (1924).

43. Graves v. State, 134 Miss. 547, 99 So. 364 (1924). The alleged common-law marriage had been in Louisiana under whose law it was invalid.

44. 1 Hale P.C. *693.

45. Halbrook v. State, 34 Ark. 511 (1879).

46. Lady Madison's Case, supra, about 1648; Halbrook v. State, 34 Ark. 511 (1879); State v. Sherwood, 68 Vt. 414, 35 A. 352 (1896); Oxford v. State, 107 Tex.Cr. 23, 296 S.W. 535 (1927); People v. Horton, 272 App.Div. 924, 71 N.Y.S.2d 57 (1947); Wright v. State, 198 Md. 163, 81 A.2d 602 (1951).

47. State v. Crosby, 148 Mont. 307, 420 P.2d 431 (1966).

48. R.C.M. (Mont.) 1949, § 94–702.

49. Id. at § 94–701.

50. "Whoever, having entered into a contract of marriage with another person, whether such marriage is valid in law or not, . . ." 18 P.S. (Pa.) § 4503 (now repealed).

One of the major problems in bigamy cases, involving the marriage of a married person under the mistaken belief that the spouse is dead or divorced, is considered infra, under ignorance and mistake.[51]

The Model Penal Code has a section on Bigamy and Polygamy which is more specific than most of the existing statutes.[52] It expressly covers the marriage of more than one spouse at a time and knowingly marrying the spouse of another.

C. INCEST

Incest is either marriage, or sexual intercourse without marriage, between persons who are too closely related. It was not an offense under the common law of England but was punished as an ecclesiastical offense.[53]

Under modern statutes incest is usually a felony.

There is no uniformity as to what constitutes being "too closely related," or even where this is specified. One plan is by reference, such as:

"Persons who, being within the degrees of consanguinity within which marriages are by the laws of the State declared to be incestuous and void, intermarry with each other, or commit adultery or fornication with each other are punishable by imprisonment in the penitentiary not exceeding ten years." [54]

Sometimes the specification is in the incest section itself.[55] Most of the states restrict incest to blood relations, but a very substantial minority include some categories of non-blood relatives, the most common being father-in-law and daughter-in-law, mother-in-law and son-in-law, stepparent and stepchild, and in one state, Texas, stepbrother and stepsister by adoption.[56] Differences in the degrees of relationship specified in the different statutes cover a wide spectrum. The broadest coverage is found in Oklahoma.

"Marriages between ancestors and descendants of any degree, of a stepfather with a stepdaughter, stepmother with stepson, between uncles and nieces, aunts and nephews, except in cases where such relationship is only by marriage, between brothers and sisters of the half as well as the whole blood, and first cousins, are declared to be incestuous, illegal and void, and are expressly prohibited. . . ." [57]

The current Pennsylvania provision is similar to section 230.1 of the Model Penal Code, 18 Purdon's Penn.Stat. § 4301 (1973).

51. Chapter 9, Section I, C.

52. Section 230.1.

53. 2 Pollock & Maitland, History of English Law 543 (2d ed. 1899).

Incest was not a common-law crime but was punished only by the ecclesiastical court. Hence the incest statute is not a codification of a common-law crime and includes only what is expressly stated therein. People v. Baker, 69 Cal.2d 44, 69 Cal.Rptr. 595, 442 P.2d 675 (1968).

See Bailey and Blackburn, The Punishment of Incest Act 1908: A Case Study of Law Creation, [1979] Crim.L.R. 708.

54. 21 Okl.St.Ann. § 885 (1958).

55. 11 Del.C.Ann. § 771 (1975).

56. Model Penal Code 234–35 (Tent. Draft No. 4, 1955). V.A.T.S., Penal Code § 25.02(4) (1974).

57. 43 Okl.St.Ann. § 2 (1979). Marriages of first cousins in another state where this is lawful are recognized.

The California statute on incest does not apply to relationship by affinity but only to relationship by consanguinity. And it condemns sexual relations between persons related by half blood only when they are brothers and sisters.

The narrowest coverage is in Illinois whose statute covers only (1) father-daughter, (2) mother-son and (3) brother-sister.[58] Most common is the coverage of persons more closely related than first cousins and even first cousins are included in the incest laws of several states.[59]

For obvious reasons illegitimacy has no bearing upon the degree of consanguinity.[60] Hence when the brother was on trial for incest based upon intercourse with his sister it was no defense that both were illegitimate.[61] By express statutory provision or judicial interpretation the prevailing view is that consanguinity by half-blood is included at least as to brothers and sisters,[62] with a tendency to apply this also to the uncle-niece and aunt-nephew relation.[63] The fact that the intercourse was by force, or with one under the age of consent, and hence constituted rape by the male is no defense to him if prosecuted for incest,[64] although the female victim would not be guilty in such a case. In fact, if the same act results in both rape and incest the accused is guilty of both[65] and may be convicted and punished for both unless a special statute provides otherwise.[66]

Hence uncle and niece by half blood are not included. People v. Baker, 69 Cal.2d 44, 69 Cal.Rptr. 595, 442 P.2d 675 (1968).

58. Smith-Hurd Ill.Ann.Stat. ch. 38 §§ 11-10, 11 (1977).

59. Model Penal Code 234 (Tent. Draft No. 4, 1955).

60. People v. Lake, 110 N.Y. 61, 17 N.E. 146 (1888); State v. Laurence, 95 N.C. 659 (1886).

61. State v. Schaunhurst, 34 Iowa 547 (1872).

62. Model Penal Code 234 (Tent. Draft No. 4, 1955).

63. Sexual intercourse between a man and his half-sister's daughter was held to be incestuous under the statute. People v. Baker, 65 Cal.Rptr. 150 (Cal.App.1968). The California statute is worded in terms of "between brothers and sisters of the half as well as the whole blood, and between uncles and nieces or aunts and nephews, . . ." West's Ann.Cal.Civ. Code § 59 (1970), which is included by reference in West's Ann.Cal.Pen.Code § 285 (1970). The court felt bound to follow an earlier case which had reached this result but invited the defendant to take the case to the California Supreme Court.

The Supreme Court reversed holding the California statute prohibited sexual relations between persons related by half blood only when they are brothers and sisters, and did not prohibit relations between the defendant and a niece of half blood, who was the daughter of defendant's half sister. People v. Baker, 69 Cal.2d 44, 69 Cal.Rptr. 595, 442 P.2d 675 (1968). Niece-in-law is outside a statuto-ry prohibition covering nieces. State v. Moore, 158 Conn. 461, 262 A.2d 166 (1969).

64. State v. Hittson, 57 N.M. 100, 254 P.2d 1063 (1953). An early dictum *contra* is clearly unsound. State v. Ellis, 74 Mo. 385 (1881).

65. People v. Bowles, 178 Cal.App.2d 317, 2 Cal.Rptr. 896 (1960); Burdue v. Commonwealth, 144 Ky. 428, 138 S.W. 296 (1911). See also State v. Learned, 73 Kan. 328, 85 P. 293 (1906); Stewart v. State, 35 Tex.Cr. 174, 32 S.W. 766 (1895); Gunville v. United States, 386 F.2d 184 (8th Cir. 1967).

Double jeopardy is not involved because that involves the same offense, not the same act, and the two offenses are obviously different. An acquittal of one might, depending upon the evidence, bar a trial of the other on the ground of collateral estoppel. See Perkins, Collateral Estoppel in Criminal Cases, [1960] U. of Ill.Law Forum 553.

"The elements of the two offenses are such that each has its unique requirements for culpability, and in some instances, such as this case, the same conduct will violate both." Nelson v. State, 612 S.W.2d 605, 607 (Tex.Cr.App. 1981).

66. E.g., the California statute prohibits, not the conviction, but the double punishment. West's Ann.Cal.Pen.Code § 654 (1977). The difference is important. D was charged with abortion and with murder, both based upon the same illegal operation. When put upon trial for murder D tried to invoke the statutory bar because he had already pleaded guilty to the abortion. This was rejected on the

Where the statute expressly includes the stepparent-stepchild relation, proof of this relation and the forbidden conduct will support a conviction.[67] It has been held, however, that when a marriage has been terminated by death or divorce, the daughter of the man's former wife by another man is no longer his wife's daughter, and hence his intercourse with her is not incest.[68] This leads to a situation comparable to "trigamy." If D "married" a woman who was at the time the lawful wife of another man, D's "marriage" was void, the woman was not his wife and hence her daughter was not D's stepdaughter.[69] On the same reasoning the daughter of a woman whose marriage was incestuous would not be the stepdaughter of the other party to that void ceremony.

These situations, it should be emphasized, really have nothing in common with the social interest sought to be safeguarded by the crime of incest, and in this respect differ sharply from the problems involved in "trigamy."

Some statutes expressly require knowledge of the relationship.[70] Where this is not in the statute the accusatory pleading need not allege such knowledge[71] but this should not be interpreted to mean that one charged with this offense could not exculpate himself by showing that he did not know, or have reason to know, that the woman was related to him in any degree.[72]

The crime of incest can be committed in either of two ways: (1) by marriage and (2) by sexual intercourse. If reliance is upon the first it is unimportant that they were arrested when leaving the place where the ceremony was performed; if reliance is upon the second the fact that they were not married is no defense.[73] Some states have included deviate sexual acts as well as sexual intercourse within the prohibited conduct.[74]

The Model Penal Code started with a provision following for the most part the prevailing pattern by including, in substance, those related by blood, more closely than first cousins, but adding a third basis of guilt with the word "cohabits"[75] to avoid problems of proof where the parties are living together with the appearance of being married. In the proposed official draft they added "knowingly" and the "relationship of parent and child by

ground that the statute prohibits double punishment and not double conviction, and he had not been punished for the abortion. People v. Tideman, 57 Cal.2d 574, 21 Cal.Rptr. 207, 370 P.2d 1007 (1962).

67. Bauman v. State, 49 Ind. 544 (1875); Taylor v. State, 110 Ga. 150, 35 S.E. 161 (1910).

68. Johnson v. State, 20 Tex.App. 609 (1886); Landin v. State, 101 Tex.Cr. 373, 275 S.W. 1012 (1925).

The English court held that the prohibition continues after the termination of the marriage relation. Mounsen v. West, 1 Leon 88, 74 Eng.Rep. 82 (1588). And this has been adopted by statute in Massachusetts and Virginia.

69. Noble v. State, 22 Ohio St. 541 (1872).

70. Iowa Criminal Code, § 726.2 (1978).

71. People v. Koller, 142 Cal. 621, 76 P. 500 (1904); Bolen v. People, 184 Ill. 338, 56 N.E. 408 (1900).

72. In agreeing with a holding that an indictment need not allege D's knowledge of the prohibited relationship, the court added: "I must be allowed to doubt so much of the opinion as holds that knowledge of the relationship by the accused is not necessary." State v. Pennington, 41 W.Va. 599, 23 S.E. 918 (1896).

73. People v. MacDonald, 24 Cal.App. 2d 702, 76 P.2d 121 (1938).

74. V.T.C.A., Penal Code § 25.02 (1974).

75. Model Penal Code, section 207.3 (Tent. Draft No. 4, 1955).

adoption," but bracketed one clause to indicate doubt as to the inclusion of uncle, aunt, nephew and niece.[76]

D. SEDUCTION

There was no crime known as "seduction" under the common law of England.[77]

It is provided by statute in some states in this country that a male is guilty of seduction, if by means of a promise of marriage he induces a female of previously-chaste character to indulge in sexual intercourse with him; except that many of the statutes provide that a subsequent marriage of the parties is a bar to prosecution.[78] Under early statutes seduction was regularly a felony. It is not included in all the new penal codes, and where included is sometimes a misdemeanor.

There are differences in the wording of the statutes and to some extent in the interpretations.

1. THE SEDUCTION

As a matter of semantics it might perhaps be said that a woman could be seduced without being debauched, but as the word is used in this statutory offense there is no "seduction" without sexual intercourse.[79]

Under some statutes a promise of marriage is not required and any artful persuasion will meet the requirement.[80] Under such a provision it was held to be seduction by a married man who had promised a girl to give gifts to her, had represented that there was no harm in the act and that it would not harm or injure her.[81] At the other extreme, so to speak, are statutes worded in terms of more than a promise of marriage, such as "by persuasion and promises of marriage." [82] It has been held, however, that "to make love to a woman, woo her, make honorable proposals of marriage, have them accepted, and afterwards to undo her under a solemn repetition of the engagement vow, is to employ persuasion as well as the promise of marriage." [83] It is doubtful if such wording adds anything to the normal requirement because in no case would mere proof of sexual intercourse by an engaged couple be sufficient to convict the man of seduction.[84] The woman has not been seduced if she was the aggressor in the transaction or yielded for some reason other than the promise—there must be a causal connection between the

---

76. Section 230.2.

77. And it is not mentioned in recent editions of English texts. Kenney's Outlines of Criminal Law (19th ed. by Turner, 1966); Russell on Criminal Law (12th ed. by Turner, 1964).

78. For an exhaustive study of the statutes see Humble, Seduction as a Crime, 21 Colum.L.Rev. 144 (1921).

79. "The word 'seduction,' used in reference to man's conduct towards a female, ex vi termini implies sexual intercourse between them." State v. Bierce, 27 Conn. 319, 321 (1893). There must

have been "a fall from virtue." Carney v. State, 79 Ala. 14, 17 (1885).

80. Bracken v. State, 111 Ala. 68, 20 So. 636 (1896); State v. Hughes, 106 Iowa 125, 76 N.W. 520 (1898).

81. State v. Fitzgerald, 63 Iowa 268, 19 N.W. 202 (1884). Accord, State v. Hemm, 82 Iowa 609, 48 N.W. 971 (1891).

82. Ga.Code, § 26–2005 (1978). S.C. Code 1962 § 16–405 uses "deception and promises . . . ."

83. Wilson v. State, 58 Ga. 328 (1877).

84. State v. Preuss, 112 Minn. 108, 127 N.W. 438 (1910).

promise and the abandonment of virtue.[85] And where the offer of marriage had been flatly rejected prior to the intercourse there was obviously no reliance upon it.[86]

There is a diversity in the cases in which the promise was conditional, some holding this insufficient for conviction,[87] while others have reached the opposite conclusion.[88] But these were cases in which the woman had agreed to have intercourse with the man upon his promise to marry her if pregnancy should result and the courts holding this insufficient to support conviction may have been inclined to doubt the chastity of a woman who would enter into such a bargain.[89] That the promise was voidable has been held not to take it out of the scope of the statute,[90] and where all other elements of the offense are present it should be sufficient if the promise actually induced the submission.[91] A promise to marry may have been relied upon even if it had not been verbally accepted,[92] and there is no requirement that it must have been a false promise—made without intention of keeping it.[93]

2. THE VICTIM

A few of the statutes are worded in terms such as an unmarried woman or person of "previously chaste character. "[94] Most of them require the woman to be single,[95] and chastity is essential even if not mentioned in the statute.[96] There is no agreement, however, as to just what this means. Some courts have taken the position that any virgin is chaste[97] while others hold that if she engages in lascivious and indecent conduct and conversation she is unchaste.[98] One view is that a fallen woman who has fully reformed is chaste,[99] while another is that chastity before marriage means physical virginity[1]—a woman can be seduced only once.[2] There is nothing unchaste

---

85. Carney v. State, 79 Ala. 14 (1885); Parker v. State, 26 Ala.App. 61, 152 So. 610 (1934); Phillips v. State, 108 Ind. 406, 9 N.E. 345 (1884).

86. Walling v. Commonwealth, 211 Ky. 49, 276 S.W. 1071 (1925).

87. People v. Van Alstyne, 144 N.Y. 361, 39 N.E. 343 (1895); State v. Shatley, 201 N.C. 83, 159 S.E. 362 (1931).

88. State v. Hughes, 106 Iowa 125, 76 N.W. 520 (1898).

89. Such an arrangement "smacks too much of a corrupt and licentious bargain to fall within the statute." State v. Adams, 23 Or. 172, 35 P. 36 (1893).

90. Where, for example, the parties could not validly contract to marry without parental consent. Polk v. State, 40 Ark. 482 (1883).

91. State v. Sortviet, 100 Minn. 12, 110 N.W. 100 (1907).

92. State v. Eddy, 40 S.D. 390, 167 N.W. 392 (1918).

93. State v. Bierce, 27 Conn. 319 (1858); State v. Brandenburg, 118 Mo. 181, 23 S.W. 1080 (1893).

94. E.g., 21 Okl.Stat.Ann. § 1120 (1958). See also Mass.Gen.Laws Ann. c. 272 § 4 (1968).

95. Model Penal Code 260 (Tent. Draft No. 4, 1955). Because of the ease with which divorce is obtained this requirement is not recommended for the Code. Ibid.

96. Polk v. State, 40 Ark. 482 (1883).

97. People v. Kehoe, 123 Cal. 224, 55 P. 911 (1899).

98. Andre v. State, 5 Iowa 389 (1857).

99. Herbert v. State, 16 Ala.App. 213, 77 So. 83 (1917); Amburgey v. Commonwealth, 415 S.W.2d 103 (Ky.1967).

1. People v. Kehoe, 123 Cal. 224, 55 P. 911 (1899).

2. People v. Nelson, 153 N.Y. 90, 46 N.E. 1040 (1897).

about marital intercourse and hence, under either view, a widow[3] or divorcee[4] may be an unmarried female of previously-chaste character.

Some statutes put an age limit on the victim of seduction, as that she be under sixteen[5] or under eighteen[6] while others have no such provision.[7]

3. THE SEDUCER

There is no requirement that the seducer be single but the prevailing view is that it is a defense if the woman knew he was married,[8] except where the statute does not require a promise of marriage.[9] If she actually did not know, a claim that she "should have known" is not sufficient for exculpation.[10]

4. INTERMARRIAGE

Some statutes provide that intermarriage of the parties subsequent to the offense is a bar to prosecution therefor, but there are important differences as to the timing. Thus the resolution may be on marriage before indictment or information,[11] or subsequent thereto prior to judgment,[12] or even after sentence.[13] There is a diversity with reference to a bona-fide offer of marriage which is rejected.[14] Under one statute the marriage is only a conditional bar to the prosecution[15] and some statutes have no provision for the subsequent marriage of the parties.[16] One court, it may be added, considered breach of promise to be the actus reus of the offense—one who has obtained sexual intercourse by a promise to marry commits seduction by breaking that promise.[17]

3. State v. Eddy, 40 S.D. 390, 167 N.W. 392 (1918).

4. Amburgey v. Commonwealth, 415 S.W.2d 103 (Ky.1967).

5. E.g., S.C. Code, 1962 § 16–405.

6. E.g., R.I.Gen.Laws 1956 § 11–37–4.

7. E.g., Ga.Code § 2005 (1978).

8. Hinkle v. State, 157 Ind. 237, 61 N.E. 196 (1901); People v. Massaro, 288 N.Y. 211, 42 N.E.2d 491 (1942).

9. State v. Fitzgerald, 63 Iowa 268, 19 N.W. 202 (1884).

10. People v. Massaro, 288 N.Y. 211, 42 N.E.2d 491 (1942).

11. E.g., West's Ann.Cal.Code § 269 (1970).

12. 21 Okl.Stat.Ann. §§ 1121, 1122 (1958).

13. E.g., S.C.Code 1962 § 16–405.

14. See Annotation, 80 A.L.R. 833, 845.

15. 21 Okl.Stat.Ann. 1122 (1958). See Harp v. State, 158 Tenn. 510, 14 S.W.2d 720 (1928).

If the victim of rape marries the offender before trial she is incompetent, under the Iowa statute, to be a witness against him. State v. McKay, 122 Iowa 658, 98 N.W. 510 (1904).

16. "It is true, as stated, that society approves the act of defendant when he endeavors to make amends for the wrong done the injured female, by marrying her, and usually a good faith marriage between the parties to the wrong, prevents or terminates a prosecution; but the statute which defines the offense and declares the punishment therefor, makes no such provision. If the defendant has acted in good faith in marrying the girl, and honestly desires to perform the marital obligations resting upon him, and is prevented from doing so by the influence and interference of persons other than his wife, it may constitute a strong appeal to the prosecution to discontinue the same, or to the governor for the exercise of executive clemency, but as the law stands it furnishes no defense to the charge brought against the defendant. R.I.Gen.Laws 1956, 11–37–4.

"The judgment of the District Court will be affirmed." State v. Newcomer, 59 Kan. 668, 670, 54 P. 685, 686 (1898).

17. People v. Gould, 70 Mich. 240, 38 N.W. 232 (1888).

The Model Penal Code has a section which includes seduction.[18] It does not require that the female be unmarried or chaste but does require a false promise of marriage and makes no provision for subsequent intermarriage. The trend in several states has been to repeal statutes dealing with seduction apparently on the premise that the conduct is punishable under other provisions relating to sexual misconduct.[19]

E. SODOMY

Sodomy was not a crime under the common law of England but was an ecclesiastical offense only.[20] It was made a felony by an English statute[21] so early that it is a common-law felony in this country,[22] and statutes expressly making it a felony were widely adopted.

"Sodomy" is a generic term including both "bestiality" and "buggery."[23]

Bestiality is carnal copulation with beast by either man or woman.

Buggery is copulation per annum by a man either with another man or with a woman. If committed by a man with a young boy it is sometimes called "pederasty".

The scope of the crime has been enlarged to cover other acts of unnatural sexual intercourse.

The ancient city of Sodom, reputedly destroyed because of its unspeakable vices, is the source from which the word "sodomy" is derived.[24] The offense was regarded with such abhorrence in the early days that Blackstone literally refused to name it, referring to it only as "the infamous *crime against nature*." [25] This lead has frequently been followed in the statutes many of which have used some such designation in lieu of a name,[26] and it

18. Section 213.3. Corruption of Minors and Seduction.

19. Arkansas, Iowa, Missouri, Texas.

20. ". . . (being in the times of popery only subject to ecclesiastical censures) . . ." 4 Bl.Comm. *216. Hale deals with sodomy in his chapter *"Concerning the* new felonies *enacted in the times of . . ."* 1 Hale P.C. c. 63 and pp. *669–70. And Coke says it is an offense "by authority of parliament." 3 Co.Inst. *58.

21. 25 Hen. VIII, c. 6 (1533). Repealed by 1 Mary c. 1 (1553). Revived by 5 Eliz. I, c. 17 (1562).

22. Speaking of sodomy the court said: "As it is nevertheless a crime at common law in this state, . . ." Commonwealth v. Poindexter, 133 Ky. 720, 118 S.W. 943, 944 (1909). Accord, State v. Potts, 75 Ariz. 211, 254 P.2d 1023 (1953); Koontz v. People, 82 Colo. 589, 263 P. 19 (1927); People v. Dexter, 6 Mich.App. 247, 148 N.W.2d 915 (1967).

23. Coke used "buggery" and "sodomy" as synonyms. 3 Co.Inst. *58. The English statutes used "buggery" to cover the whole area, and that is true of the present English statute. Sexual Offenses Act, 1956, § 12(1). "Sodomy" has been preferred in this country. "Bestiality" is seldom used, and then only with the limited meaning given in the text. See however Ga.Code, § 26–2004 (1978).

Buggery is copulation per anum by a man either with another man or with a woman. If committed by a man with a young boy it is sometimes called "pederasty."

24. Commonwealth v. Poindexter, 133 Ky. 720, 118 S.W. 943, 944 (1909).

25. 4 Bl.Comm. *215.

26. Ariz.Rev.Stat. § 13–1411 (1978); Idaho Code § 18–6605 (1979); Tenn.Code Ann. § 39–707 (1975).

has been held that in an indictment the offense may be charged as "the abominable and detestable crime against nature." [27]

"There is almost complete accord among many text writers that at common law commission of the crime required penetration *per anum* and that penetration *per os* did not constitute the offense." [28]

This is the logical position since sodomy was not an offense under the common law of England and is an offense under American common law because of the early English statute which did not apply where the act is in the mouth.[29] It has not been uncommon, however, for this to be added to the offense, either by express provision of the statute[30] or by interpretation,[31] until "nearly all states punish fellatio (oral stimulus of the male sex organ [and] cunnilingus (oral stimulus of the female sex organ)" [32] in addition to anal intercourse and bestiality. Some states have gone even further,[33] including attempted sexual intercourse with a dead body,[34] or even masturbation when the one so induced is under twenty-one.[35] It held in England, it may be added, that the forbidden act by husband and wife is punishable as sodomy[36]—a problem which will receive attention later.

In England, for a short time, emission was thought to be necessary.[37] This, however, was after the Revolution and hence should have no recognition here since it was contrary to the early English view.[38] And while there is some authority for such a requirement here[39] the general holding is that

27. Phillips v. State, 248 Ind. 150, 222 N.E.2d 821 (1967).

In Stone v. Wainwright, 414 U.S. 21, 94 S.Ct. 190 (1973), the United States Supreme Court upheld the constitutionality of a Florida statute, couched in terms of an abominable crime against nature, against a claim of invalidity because of vagueness.

"Willett was convicted of three counts of an Infamous Crime Against Nature." Simpson v. State, 94 Nev. 760, 587 P.2d 1319 (1978).

28. State v. Morrison, 25 N.J.Super. 534, 96 A.2d 723 (1953). Accord, Koontz v. People, 82 Colo. 589, 263 P. 19 (1927) citing many cases; People v. Dexter, 6 Mich.App. 247, 148 N.W. 915 (1967).

29. Rex v. Jacobs, 1 Russ. & Ry. 331, 168 Eng.Rep. 830 (1817). For a discussion see Spence, The Law of Crime Against Nature, 32 N.C.L.Rev. 312 (1954).

30. E.g., Ark.Stats. § 41–1813 (1977); Colo.Rev.Stat. 1973, 18–3–401(6) contained in definition of "sexual penetration." And see State v. Putman, 78 N.M. 552, 434 P.2d 77 (App.1967).

31. State v. Altwater, 29 Idaho 107, 157 P. 256 (1916); Herring v. State, 119 Ga. 709, 46 S.E. 876 (1904); State v. Dietz, 135 Mont. 496, 343 P.2d 539 (1959); State v. Fenner, 166 N.C. 247, 80 S.E. 970

(1914); Berryman v. State, 283 P.2d 558 (Okl.Cr.1955); Blankenship v. State, 289 S.W.2d 240 (Tex.Cr.1956). And see State v. Phillips, 102 Ariz. 377, 430 P.2d 139 (1967); Hogan v. State, 84 Nev. 372, 441 P.2d 620 (1968).

32. Model Penal Code 279 (Tent. Draft No. 4, 1955).

33. The District of Columbia statute adds ". . . who shall be convicted of having carnal copulation in an opening of the body except sexual parts with another person. . . ." D.C. Code 1973 § 22–3502.

34. E.g., "Deviate sexual act" under a North Dakota statute includes sexual contact with an "animal, bird or dead person." No.Dak.Cent.Code 12–1–20–02 (1976).

35. Phillips v. State, 248 Ind. 150, 222 N.E.2d 821 (1967).

36. Regina v. Jellyman, 8 Car. & P. 604 (1838).

37. 1 East P.C. 480 (1803). This was by analogy from a case holding emission essential to guilt of rape. Hill's Case, 1 East P.C. 439 (1781). Cf. Rex v. Cozins, 6 C. & P. 351, 172 Eng.Rep. 1272 (1834).

38. 3 Co.Inst. *59; 1 Hale P.C. *669.

39. People v. Hodgkin, 94 Mich. 27, 53 N.W. 794 (1892). This was changed by statute. Mich.Comp.Laws 750.159 (1948).

the crime is completed by any penetration into forbidden parts.[40]   Some statutes expressly declare that emission is not essential, or that any penetration is sufficient.[41]

In the absence of some unusual statutory provision a conviction of sodomy cannot be sustained where the evidence fails to show penetration,[42] although of course it might be sufficient for an attempt to commit the offense,[43] or some other offense such as sexual assault,[44] or criminal sexual contact.[45]

If both parties are willing and capable of giving legally-recognizable consent, both are guilty; [46] but if the act is committed on a child only the older person is guilty and the child is not an accomplice.[47]   Under the English law a child under the age of fourteen was incapable of committing sodomy,[48] just as he was incapable of committing rape, and the reason was no doubt the same—unwillingness to hang one so young for this type of offense.[49]   In no case, it should be emphasized, is the consent of the other an essential element of the crime.[50]

Over the ages there has been a shift in the moral significance attaching to this offense which seemingly has no counterpart elsewhere.   Whereas the ancients regarded it with such abhorrence that they avoided even the mention of its name, and the mere threat to accuse one of sodomy was equated with a threat to kill or inflict great bodily injury, there is a wide-spread belief at the present time that homosexuality, or other deviate sexual practice by consenting adults in private, offers no threat to the general community, is practically impossible to control, and that to make it an offense accomplishes little other than to provide an opportunity for blackmail.[51]   Shortly before

40. State v. Massey, 58 N.M. 115, 266 P.2d 359 (1954).   Many cases are cited in this opinion.   Hopper v. State, 302 P.2d 162 (Okl.Cr.1956).

"Evidence that showed the victim's male organ penetrated beyond the lips of the defendant was a sufficient showing of penetration to complete the crime of sodomy."   State v. Lovelace, 227 Kan. 348, 607 P.2d 49, 53 (1980).

41. E.g., N.M.Stats.Ann. § 30–9–11 (1978); West's Ann.Cal.Pen.Code § 287 (1975).

42. Rozar v. State, 93 Ga.App. 207, 91 S.E.2d 131 (1956).

43. See, infra, Chapter 6, section 3.

44. E.g., Colo.Rev.Stat. 1973, 18–3–404.

45. N.M.Stats.Ann. § 30–9–12 (1978).

46. Strum v. State, 168 Ark. 1012, 272 S.W. 359 (1925); People v. Bond, 136 Cal. App.2d 572, 289 P.2d 44 (1955); Jones v. State, 17 Ga.App. 825, 88 S.C. 712 (1916); Miller v. State, 256 Ind. 296, 268 N.E.2d 299 (1971).

47. Mascolo v. Montesanto, 61 Conn. 50, 23 A. 714 (1891, twelve years old); State v. Panther, 230 Iowa 1115, 300

N.W. 291 (1941, ten years old); Means v. State, 125 Wis. 650, 104 N.W. 815 (1905, seven years old); State v. Shumate, 516 S.W.2d 297 (Mo.App.1974, eleven year old boy).

48. 3 Co.Inst. *59; 1 Hale P.C. *670. "It seems to be the law that a person under fourteen whether male or female, cannot be convicted as a principal in the first degree either as agent or patient." Smith & Hogan, Criminal Law 321 (1965).

49. See, supra, Chapter 2, section 6, F.

50. State v. Pfeiffer, 277 Mo. 202, 209 S.W. 925 (1918).   The statutory provision, that intoxication may be considered in determining the purpose, motive or intent with which an act was done, has no application to sodomy since no special mental element is there involved.   State v. Turner, 3 Utah 2d 285, 282 P.2d 1045 (1955).

51. Removing this type of conduct from the category of crime cannot guarantee the termination of blackmail in connection therewith but at least it would "withdraw the state from partnership in blackmail."   Note, 12 U. of Fla.L.Rev. 83, 88 (1959).   See also The Wolfenden Report, Report of the Committee on Ho-

the turn of the century an Illinois court could say: "The existence of such an offense is a disgrace to human nature." [52] But in 1961 the Illinois legislature removed sodomy from the category of crime in that state except to the extent that criminal sanctions are needed to protect (1) the individual against forcible acts, (2) the young and immature from sexual advances by older persons, and (3) the public from open and notorious conduct which flouts accepted standards of morality in the community.[53] This pattern has been followed in several other states.[54]

The Model Penal Code,[55] under the name of "deviate sexual intercourse," includes bestiality; and it includes buggery worded in terms of "sexual intercourse per os or per anum between human beings who are not husband and wife," provided it is committed under such circumstances that ordinary sex would be rape.

Suggestions for change must in most instances be presented to the legislative body since the constitutionality of sodomy statutes written along traditional lines has been upheld.[56]

C's wife charged that C had committed an act of sodomy with her. C pleaded guilty and was sentenced to a term of two to fourteen years. C filed a petition for a writ of habeas corpus in the federal court on the ground that the Indiana statute as applied to his case was unconstitutional. The district court dismissed the petition but this was reversed by the United States Court of Appeals. It was held that the state statute could not be constitutionally interpreted as making consensual physical relations between married persons a crime without a clear showing that the state had an interest in preventing such relations which outweighed the constitutional right to marital privacy.[57] The court relied upon a Supreme Court case which held that the right to marital privacy was violated by imposition of criminal sanctions for use of birth control devices by married couples.[58] This position has been accepted by some courts,[59] rejected by others[60] and has not as yet been resolved by the Supreme Court.[61] Where the acts between husband and wife

mosexual Offenses and Prostitution (1963).

52. Honselman v. People, 168 Ill. 172, 175, 48 N.E. 304, 305 (1897).

53. Illinois Crim.Code of 1961, art. 11. See Note, Deviate Sexual Behavior Under the New Illinois Criminal Code, 1965 U. of Wash.L.Q. 220.

A similar approach was taken under the English Sexual Offenses Act 1967, Walmsley, Indecency Between Males and The Sexual Offenses Act 1967 [1978] Crim.L.Rev. 400.

54. E.g., California, Iowa, New Jersey. See discussion 1 Crim.Just.Jnl. 99 (1976).

55. Article 213. And see Model Penal Code 276–291 (Tent. Draft No. 4, 1955).

56. State v. Rhinehart, 70 Wn.2d 649, 424 P.2d 906 (1967).

57. Coltner v. Henry, 394 F.2d 873 (7th Cir. 1968).

In another state case a man was convicted of fellatio upon complaint of his wife. Mahone v. State, 209 So.2d 435 (Ala.App.1968). In this case, however, while not divorced, D and his wife were living apart and the act was coerced at the point of a knife.

58. Griswold v. Connecticut, 381 U.S. 479, 85 S.Ct. 1678 (1965).

59. State v. Pilcher, 242 N.W.2d 348 (Iowa 1976); People v. Onofre, 51 N.Y.2d 476, 434 N.Y.S.2d 947, 415 N.E.2d 936 (1981).

60. State v. Bateman, 113 Ariz. 107, 547 P.2d 6 (1976); Pruett v. State, 463 S.W.2d 191 (Tex.Cr.App. 1970).

61. The Supreme Court has not passed on the specific issue, but in Doe v. Commonwealth's Attorney, 403 F.Supp. 1199 (E.D.Va.1975), aff'd 425 U.S. 901, 96 S.Ct. 1489 (1976) the Court summarily affirmed a conviction based on acts committed by consenting adults.

were not within the confines of marital privacy but involved acts with others as well as themselves the constitutional claim has been rejected.[62]

F. PROSTITUTION, OBSCENITY AND INDECENCY

The traditional definition of prostitution has been in some such form as "the practice of a female in offering her body to an indiscriminate intercourse with men for money or its equivalent."[63] Modern criminal law, however, has been forced to recognize the male prostitute,[64] particularly in regard to homosexual and other deviate sexual relations. This suggests the following definition:

Prostitution is commercialized sex, including deviate sex.

Being dealt with as an ecclesiastical offense,[65] prostitution was not itself a common-law crime, but there are several related common-law misdemeanors.

Bawdy house. A house to which persons commonly resorted for purposes of prostitution was known as a bawdy house (or a disorderly house, house of prostitution, or house of ill-fame) and the keeping of such a house was a nuisance at common law.[66] The owner of a house was guilty of a misdemeanor at common law if he leased it with knowledge that it was to be used for this purpose.[67]

Modern statutes generally enlarge upon this common-law basis. The following will give some idea of the field, although the statutes differ substantially in the different states:

"It shall be unlawful to engage in, or to knowingly aid or abet in, prostitution or assignation or to procure or solicit or to reside in, enter, or remain in any vehicle, trailer, conveyance, place, structure, or building for the purpose of prostitution or assignation, or to keep or set up a house of ill fame, brothel or bawdy house, or to receive or direct any person for purposes of prostitution or assignation into any vehicle, trailer, conveyance, place, structure or building, or to permit any person to remain for the purpose of prosti-

---

62. Lovisi v. Slayton, 539 F.2d 349 (4th Cir. 1976), cert. denied sub nom. Lovisi v. Zahradnick, 429 U.S. 977, 97 S.Ct. 485.

63. Ferguson v. Superior Court, 26 Cal.App. 554, 558, 147 P. 603, 605 (1915). The statute may include also the giving or receiving of the body for indiscriminate sexual intercourse without hire. Bayouth v. State, 294 P.2d 856 (Okl.Cr. 1956). And see Salt Lake City v. Allred, 19 Utah 2d 254, 430 P.2d 371 (1967).

"At common law, prostitution was generally understood to apply . . . only in connection with sexual intercourse for hire." State v. Lopez, 98 Idaho 581, 570 P.2d 259, 267 (1977).

64. Iowa Criminal Code § 725.1 Prostitution. A person who offers for sale his or her services as a partner in a sex act, or who purchases or offers to purchase such services, commits an aggravated misdemeanor.

65. It was an ecclesiastical offense because it was always either fornication or adultery, which were "left to the spiritual court." 4 Bl.Comm. *65.

66. 3 Co.Inst. *205; 4 Bl.Comm. *167. It is commonly included in the modern codes. State v. Weston, 235 Iowa 148, 15 N.W.2d 922 (1944).

"House of prostitution" is broadly interpreted. In this case apartments were used and the court noted that it had been held to apply to the forbidden use of a taxicab. People v. Hobson, 255 Cal.App. 2d 557, 63 Cal.Rptr. 320 (1967).

67. Cahn v. State, 110 Ala. 56, 20 So. 380 (1895); Kessler v. State, 119 Ga. 301, 46 S.E. 408 (1903); People v. Saunders, 29 Mich. 269 (1874). Renting with knowledge of such intended use is sometimes made a separate statutory offense. For the distinction between this separate offense and "keeping" see People v. Hoek, 169 Mich. 87, 134 N.W. 1031 (1912).

tution or assignation in any vehicle, trailer, conveyance, place, structure, or building, or to direct, take, or transport, or to offer or agree to take or transport, or to aid or assist in transporting or directing any person to any vehicle, conveyance, trailer, place, structure, or building, or to any other person with knowledge or having reasonable cause to believe that the purpose of such directing, taking or transporting is prostitution or assignation, or to lease or rent or contract to lease or rent any vehicle, trailer, conveyance, place, structure, or building, or part thereof, believing that it is intended to be used for any of the purposes herein prohibited, or to knowingly aid, abet, or participate in the doing of any of the acts herein prohibited." [68]

Other provisions deal with solicitation, keeping house of ill-fame, leasing house for prostitution, permitting minor females to be inmates, detention of females, enticing to house of ill-fame, and enticing female child for prostitution.

Pandering is the paid procurement of a female as an inmate of a house of prostitution. The procurer is often referred to as a "pimp." Many of the statutes include a provision for the punishment of pandering, and some of them include, under the same name, the paid procurement of a female for the purpose of illicit intercourse with another.[69]

Pandering it has been said, consists of either procuring a female for a place of prostitution, or procuring a place for a prostitute where she can ply her trade. Where either is done the pandering is complete even if no act of sexual intercourse has yet occurred.[70]

Prostitution is not itself a crime in England or Scotland, although certain activities of prostitutes and those who profit from prostitution are prohibited, such as soliciting in a public place, procuring, letting premises for the purpose of prostitution and so forth.[71] On the other hand, prostitution was, at least at one time, prohibited in all American jurisdictions.[72]

Despite some pressure to adopt the British view[73] the Model Penal Code includes a section on Prostitution and Related Offenses[74] which follows "the same basic policy of repressing commercialized sexual activity, as does present American law." [75] This section, which applies only to sexual activity

---

68. Tenn.Code Ann. § 39–3502 (1975).

Some statutes provide a penalty for enticing another to commit an act of lewdness. Baymouth v. State, 294 P.2d 856 (Okl.Cr.1956).

69. The existence of a common prostitute and receipt from her of part or all of her earnings by a man are essential elements of the crime of pandering or receiving earnings from a prostitute. State v. Goesser, 203 Or. 315, 280 P.2d 354 (1955). Solicitation of a customer for a prostitute, without receiving compensation or soliciting compensation from the prostitute, does not constitute pimping under West's Ann.Cal.Penal Code § 266h (1977). People v. Smith, 44 Cal.2d 77, 279 P.2d 33 (1955).

70. People v. Osuna, 251 Cal.App.2d 528, 59 Cal.Rptr. 559 (1967).

71. Model Penal Code 172 (Tent. Draft No. 9, 1959).

72. Id. at 169.

73. See 39 ALI Proceedings 220 (1962).

The English position is not without some restriction on prostitution activity by such legislation as the Sexual Offenses Act of 1956, S.32 and the Street Offenses Act of 1959 S.1. See Smith and Hogan, Criminal Law, 3rd Ed. (1973) pp. 352, 361.

74. Section 251.2.

75. Model Penal Code 174 (Tent. Draft No. 9, 1959). For a general discussion of the problem see id. at 169–182.

"for hire," includes homosexual and other deviate sexual behavior within the definition of prostitution. The penalty for the prostitute is relatively mild compared with the penalties for what it calls "promoting prostitution." This includes procuring, pandering, transporting and other activities auxiliary to prostitution.[76]

The *Mann Act*, or *White Slave Traffic Act*, is a federal statute which provides: "Whoever knowingly transports in interstate or foreign commerce . . . any woman or girl for the purpose of prostitution or debauchery, or for any other immoral purpose . . . . Shall be fined not more than $5,000 or imprisoned not more than five years or both." [77] Although this statute was designed as a check on commercialized prostitution, it was held that a violation does not require either promiscuity or compensation.[78] A polygamist who took his plural wives across the state line to live in a new home was convicted.[79] As said in another case, the statute covers a "noncommercial, isolated, single immoral transaction." [80] But the mere taking of a nude picture was held not to be an "immoral purpose" within the meaning of the statute.[81] The immoral purpose need not be the sole reason for the interstate transportation as long as it was a dominant or an efficient and compelling purpose.[82]

Obscenity is that which is offensive to chastity. *Indecency* is often used with the same meaning, but may also include anything which is outrageously disgusting. These were not the names of common-law crimes, but were words used in describing or identifying certain deeds which were.[83]

An obscene libel is a writing, book, picture or print of such an obscene nature as to shock the public sense of decency.[84] It is a misdemeanor at common law to publish such a libel. "To publish," in this sense, means to

76. Id. at 174.

This format and the substance of the Model Code provisions has been held not to violate constitutional provisions on privacy and equal protection. Hicks v. State, 373 A.2d 205 (Del. 1977).

77. 18 U.S.C.A. § 2421.

The proscribed purpose need not be the sole reason for the interstate trip. If it is one of the principal purposes that is sufficient. United States v. Jenkins, 442 F.2d 429 (5th Cir. 1971).

78. Caminetti v. United States, 242 U.S. 470, 37 S.Ct. 192 (1917). For interpretation see Mortensen v. United States, 322 U.S. 369, 64 S.Ct. 1037 (1944); Langford v. United States, 178 F.2d 48 (9th Cir. 1949); Gebardi v. United States, 287 U.S. 112, 53 S.Ct. 35 (1932).

79. Cleveland v. United States, 329 U.S. 14, 67 S.Ct. 13 (1946).

80. Brown v. United States, 237 F.2d 281 (8th Cir. 1956).

81. United States v. Mathison, 239 F.2d 358 (7th Cir. 1956).

82. United States v. Kotakes, 440 F.2d 342 (7th Cir. 1971).

83. Though prurient appeal is an element of "obscene," it is not an element of "indecent," which merely refers to nonconformance with accepted standards of morality. Hence an FCC order holding that language broadcast in the early afternoon on a radio program was indecent and thus prohibited by statute did not violate the First Amendment even if the broadcast was not obscene. F.C.C. v. Pacifica Foundation, 438 U.S. 726, 98 S.Ct. 3026 (1978).

84. "Dirty word description of the sweet and sublime, especially of the mystery of sex and procreation, is the ultimate of obscenity." Besig v. United States, 208 F.2d 142, 146 (9th Cir. 1953). In a statute penalizing the sale and advertisement of "obscene or indecent" books the quoted words are not unconstitutionally indefinite. People v. Alberts, 138 Cal.App.2d 909, 292 P.2d 90 (1955). One type of statutory offense is the possession of obscene pictures with intent to show them. State v. Silverman, 48 Wn. 2d 198, 292 P.2d 868 (1956).

sell, give or exhibit the matter, or in some other manner to expose it to the public view. State statutes quite generally provide a penalty for such "publication" or uttering, and sending such matter through the United States mail is a federal offense.[85]

The claim that the First Amendment protects the publication of obscenity was flatly rejected in *Roth*.[86] As said in *Ginsberg*:[87] "Obscenity is not within the area of protected speech or press." It was pointed out however that the constitutional protection greatly limits the application of statutes dealing with this subject. In *Memoirs*[88] it was said that for a book or other publication to be outside the protection of the First Amendment it must be "utterly without redeeming social interest," but this was later repudiated in *Miller*.[89] In this case it was held that a work may be subject to state regulation where, taken as a whole, it appeals to the prurient interest in sex; portrays in a patently offensive way, sexual conduct specifically defined by applicable state law; and taken as a whole, does not have serious literary, artistic, political or scientific value. And it is to be judged by "contemporary community standards" rather than by a national standard.[90]

The Illinois statute prohibited the sale of obscene matter and defined "obscene" as follows:

A thing is obscene if, considered as a whole, its predominate appeal is to prurient interest, that is, a shameful or morbid interest in nudity, sex or excretion, and if it goes substantially beyond customary limits of candor in description or representation of such matters.

W was convicted of violating this statute and appealed. In affirming the conviction the Supreme Court upheld the validity of the Illinois statute. It was held that the statute complied with the requirements of *Miller*, but the Court added that "even if this were not the case, appellant had ample guidance from the Illinois Supreme Court that his conduct did not conform to the Illinois law. Materials such as these, ... had been expressly held to violate the Illinois statute, ..."[91]

Two other cases decided during the same term are of interest. On appeal from a judgment of conviction of the sale of an obscene film, it was held that no First Amendment rights were violated by an instruction which permitted the jury to consider, in determining whether the film was obscene, whether the circumstances of sale and distribution indicated that the film was being

---

85. 18 U.S.C.A § 1461.

86. Roth v. United States, 354 U.S. 476, 77 S.Ct. 1304 (1957).

87. Ginsberg v. New York, 390 U.S. 629, 635, 88 S.Ct. 1274, 1278 (1968). Accord, United States v. Reidel, 402 U.S. 351, 91 S.Ct. 1410 (1971).

88. Memoirs v. Massachusetts, 383 U.S. 413, 86 S.Ct. 975 (1966).

89. Miller v. California, 413 U.S. 15, 93 S.Ct. 2607 (1973).

90. Ibid.

In a trial for possession of obscene matter with intent to distribute or exhibit, it was proper to reject an instruction that the standards for obscenity in the case were those of the "homosexual community." People v. Young, 77 Cal.App. 3d Supp. 10, 143 Cal.Rptr. 604 (1977).

"In regard to the interpretation of Section 76–10–1201(12), U.C.A. 1953 (Supp. 1975) (Distributing pornographic material) the trial court properly determined that the same did not require the application of a statewide standard. The wording of the statute clearly establishes a local standard as opposed to a statewide standard . . . .." State v. International Amusements, 565 P.2d 1112, 1113 (Utah 1977).

91. Ward v. Illinois, 431 U.S. 767, 97 S.Ct. 2085, 2088 (1977).

commercially exploited for the sake of its prurient appeal.[92] And it was held that Congress has the power to exclude from the mails materials that are judged to be obscene. The fact that the mailing was from one point to another in Iowa, and was not punishable under the Iowa statute, does prevent conviction under the Act of Congress.[93]

Obscene or indecent exhibitions of a nature to shock the public sense of decency are also public nuisances and indictable at common law. This label includes not only obscene and indecent theatrical performances or "side shows," but other disgusting practices such as letting a stallion to mares in the street or some other public place.[94]

Indecent exposure of the person to public view is also a common-law misdemeanor. Blackstone did not deal with it separately. "The last offense which I shall mention," he said, "more immediately against religion and morality, and cognizable by the temporal courts, is that of open and notorious *lewdness*; either by frequenting houses of ill fame, which is an indictable offense; or by some grossly scandalous and public indecency, for which the punishment is by fine and imprisonment." [95] In other words private indecency was exclusively under the jurisdiction of the ecclesiastical court but public indecency of an extreme nature was indictable. And, in the early view, indecent exposure of the person was merely one form of obscene exhibition. It is specifically made an offense under some of the statutes[96] and is included under more general clauses in others.

An accidental exposure of the private parts to public view is not an offense if it is without negligence, but the courts are not in accord as to the mens-rea requirement of this offense. Under one view a specific intent to expose is required[97] whereas a criminally negligent exposure is sufficient under the other.[98]

92. Splawn v. California, 431 U.S. 595, 97 S.Ct. 1987 (1977).

93. Smith v. United States, 431 U.S. 291, 97 S.Ct. 1756 (1977).

94. Crane v. State, 3 Ind. 193 (1851). See also, Hogue, Regulating Obscenity Through The Power to Define and Abate Nuisances, 14 Wake Forest L.Rev. 1 (1978).

95. 4 Bl.Comm. *64.

96. "It shall be unlawful for any person to expose or exhibit his sexual organs in any public place, or on the private premises of another, or so near thereto as to be seen from such private premises, in a vulgar and indecent manner. . . ." West's F.S.A. (Fla.) § 800.-03 (1976).

"The indecent exposure statute . . . finds its origins in the common law." State v. Gates, 118 Ariz. 357, 576 P.2d 1357, 1359 (1978).

"We find no difficulty in holding that the intentional exposure to public view of one's genitals is a lewd act within the proscription of the statute." State v. Bull, 61 Hawaii 62, 597 P.2d 10, 11 (1979).

Dancing nude in a beer bar was held to violate the statute. People v. Conway, 103 Cal.App.3d Supp. 7, 162 Cal.Rptr. 877 (1979).

The Public Sexual Indecency Act "gives clear notice that if one person engages in the activities described by the statute in the presence or view of others, that person will be in violation of the statute." State ex rel. Hamilton v. Superior Court, 128 Ariz. 184, 624 P.2d 862, 864 (1981).

97. Miller v. People, 5 Barb. 203 (N.Y. 1849); State v. Peery, 224 Minn. 346, 28 N.W.2d 851 (1947).

98. "Whatever his intention might be, the necessary tendency of his conduct was to outrage decency, and to corrupt the public morals." Rex v. Crunden, 2 Camp. 89, 90, 170 Eng.Rep. 1091 (1809).

Standing nude outside his home and moving his hand over his private parts in the presence of women and children supported a conviction of indecent exposure.

Obscene or profane language. Profane swearing was an ecclesiastical offense in England but not indictable unless it occurred in such places and under such conditions as to become an annoyance to the public, and hence a public nuisance.[99] Its use in public is made an offense under many of the statutes. Some of the statutes provide for the punishment of any vulgar, profane, or indecent language[1] while some have an additional requirement such as in a loud tone of voice, or in a public place which is likely to "provoke an immediate violent reaction." [2]

Disorderly Conduct. Some of the statutes on disorderly conduct include in this category, *inter alia,* one who "solicits anyone to engage in or who engages in lewd or dissolute conduct in any public place. . . ." [3] One who, in a public place, solicited another to go home with him to engage in oral copulation and sodomy was held to be guilty under this section. The fact that the solicitation was in a public place was held to be sufficient.[4]

Though prurient appeal is an element of "obscene," it is not an element of "indecent," which merely refers to nonconformance with accepted standards of morality. Hence an FCC order holding that language broadcast in the early afternoon on a radio program was indecent and thus prohibited by statute did not violate the First Amendment even if the broadcast was not obscene.[5]

The Model Penal Code has a section on "obscenity" [6] but it was drafted before the Supreme Court's formula was promulgated.

G. BLASPHEMY

Blasphemy is the malicious revilement of God and religion.

In England blasphemy was the malicious revilement of the Christian religion.[7]

It consisted in irreverently ridiculing or impugning the doctrines of the Christian faith. It was an offense against religion, but since "Christianity is part of the laws of England" [8] it was punishable in the temporal courts at

---

People v. Succop, 67 Cal.2d 785, 63 Cal. Rptr. 569, 433 P.2d 473 (1967).

99. Ex parte Delaney, 43 Cal. 478 (1872).

1. West's Fla.Stat.Ann. § 847.05.

2. West's Ann.Cal.Pen.Code § 415 (1976). Promoting or possessing any obscene material or performance. Conn. Gen.Stat.Ann. § 53a–194 (1969).

3. West's Ann.Cal.Pen. Code § 647 (1977).

The essential element of the offense under the statute governing disorderly conduct is intent or reckless disregard by defendant that his conduct will have specific consequence of causing actual or threatened physical inconvenience to, or alarm by, members of the public. State v. Nakasone, 1 Haw.App. 10, 612 P.2d 123 (1980).

4. People v. Dudley, 250 Cal.App.2d 955, 58 Cal.Rptr. 557 (1967).

5. Federal Communications Commission v. Pacifica Foundation, 438 U.S. 726, 98 S.Ct. 3026 (1978).

6. Section 251.4.

7. "[T]o reproach the Christian religion is to speak in subversion of the law." Taylor's Case, 1 Vent. 293, 86 Eng.Rep. 189 (1676). "In like manner, and for the same reason, any general attack on Christianity is the subject of criminal prosecution, because Christianity is the established religion of the country." Gathercole's Case, 2 Lewin 237, 254, 168 Eng.Rep. 1140, 1145 (1838). For a thorough and scholarly historical analysis of the offense of blasphemy, see Levy, Treason Against God (1981).

8. 4 Bl.Comm. *59.

common law.[9] If in written, printed or pictured form, and published, it was known as a blasphemous libel.[10] A writing is "published" in the legal sense, as mentioned above, if sold, distributed, exhibited or otherwise exposed to view.

It has been said that Christianity "is part of our common law" in this country.[11] It is not so in the sense of an established religion (forbidden by the First Amendment, and corresponding clauses in the state constitutions) "yet it is so in this qualified sense, that its divine origin and truth are admitted, and therefore it is not to be maliciously and openly reviled and blasphemed against, to the annoyance of believers or the injury of the public."[12] Blasphemy has been held to be a common-law crime in this country[13] because of its tendency to stir up breaches of the peace.[14] It is expressly made punishable by some of the statutes.[15]

In this country today it is most unlikely that a charge of blasphemy could withstand a constitutional challenge,[16] and it is to be noted that even in England prosecutions for this offense "have been extremely rare for over a hundred years."[17] Recently the House of Lords upheld a blasphemous libel prosecution holding the only mens rea required to sustain the conviction was the intent to publish a document determined to be blasphemous.[18]

9. Taylor's Case, 1 Vent. 293, 86 Eng. Rep. 189 (1676); Rex v. Woolston, 2 Strange 834, 93 Eng.Rep. 881 (1729); The King v. Waddington, 1 B. & C. 26, 107 Eng.Rep. 11 (1822).

In Scotland Thomas Aikenhead was executed for the blasphemy of denying the validity of the scriptures and contending among other things "that God, the World and Nature, are all one thing. . . ." Arnot, Celebrated Criminal Trials in Scotland 362, 366 (1812).

10. The King v. Waddington, 1 B. & C. 26, 107 Eng.Rep. 11 (1822).

11. Snavely v. Booth, 36 Del. 378, 388, 176 A. 649, 653 (1935); Updegraff v. Commonwealth, 11 Serg. & R. 394 (Pa. 1824); Commonwealth v. American Baseball Club of Philadelphia, 290 Pa. 136, 143, 138 A. 497, 499 (1927).

12. Vidal v. Girard's Executors, 43 U.S. 127, 198 (1844).

13. Commonwealth v. Kneeland, 37 Mass. 206 (1838); Updegraff v. Commonwealth, 11 Serg. & R. 394 (Pa. 1824). "It is because the common law gives expression to the changing customs and sentiments of the people that there have been brought within its scope such crimes as blasphemy, open obscenity, and kindred offenses against religion and morality, in short those acts which, being highly indecent, are *contra bonos mores.*" State v. Bradbury, 136 Me. 347, 349, 9 A.2d 657, 658 (1939). "The authorities show that blasphemy against God, and contumelious reproaches and profane ridicule of

Christ or the holy scriptures, (which are equally treated as blasphemy,) are offences punishable at common law, whether uttered by words or writings." People v. Ruggles, 8 Johns. 225, 227 (N.Y.1811). "The free, equal, and undisturbed enjoyment of religious opinion, whatever it may be, and free and decent discussions on any religious subject, is granted and secured; but to revile, with malicious and blasphemous contempt, the religion professed by almost the whole community is an abuse of that right." Id. at 228.

14. State v. Chandler, 2 Del. 553 (1837).

This is not the theory of the English law. "After all, an insult to a Jew's religion is not less likely to provoke a fight than to insult an Episcopalian's; . . . ." Bowman v. Secular Society, Ltd., [1917] A.C. 406, 460.

15. Okl.Stat.Ann. § 901–903 (1958); R.I.Gen.Laws 1956 11–11–6.

16. A New York statute prohibiting showing of sacrilegious film was held unconstitutional for vagueness but doubt was expressed as to whether such a prohibition short of obscenity could be sustained. Burstyn, Inc. v. Wilson, 343 U.S. 495, 72 S.Ct. 777 (1952).

17. Smith and Hogan, Criminal Law 524 (1965).

18. Regina v. Lemon, [1979] 2 WLR 281.

H. MISTREATMENT OF DEAD BODIES

At common law it was an offense to treat the dead human body indecently,[19] and it was indictable wantonly or illegally to disturb a dead human body after burial; to expose such body without proper burial; to sell it, for mere purposes of private gain, for dissection; or to disinter it,[20] unless so directed by the deceased in his lifetime, or by his relatives after his death, with consent of the public authorities and owners of the ground, where this is requisite.[21]

It is a misdemeanor to throw a dead body into a river, and this is true even if it is the body of a stillborn bastard.[22] Solemn burial at sea, on the other hand, has never been regarded as involving any element of indecency. Cremation is not an offense unless so done as to amount to a public nuisance,[23] or for the purpose of preventing a lawful inquest.[24] Any malicious mutilation of a corpse is indictable.[25]

In the absence of a statute providing otherwise, it was no offense for a father to bury the body of his infant child, properly clothed and enclosed in a rude wooden box, in a grave on his farm. Interment of the body of a child without a religious ceremony, and without notice to friends and relatives indicated a man lacking in parental instincts but did not violate the law. The court said:[26]

"The custom of the country, imposed upon appellant only the duty of decently burying his child. That is, it must be properly clothed when being taken to the place of burial, and then placed in the ground or tomb, so that it will not become offensive or injurious to the lives of others. He may not cast it into the street, or into a running stream or into a hole in the ground, or make any disposition of it that might be regarded as creating a nuisance, be offensive to the sense of decency, or be injurious to the health of the community."

19. "[A]ny disposal of a dead body which is contrary to common decency is an offense at common law." State v. Bradbury, 136 Me. 347, 351, 9 A.2d 657, 659 (1939).

20. Disinterring a body for the purpose of dissection is a misdemeanor. The King v. Lynn, 1 Leach 497, 168 Eng.Rep. 350 (1788). Or, for the purpose of sale. Rex v. Gilles, Russ. & Ry. 336, note, 168 Eng.Rep. 848, note (1820). It is a misdemeanor to remove a body from a grave without lawful authority. It is no excuse that the motive was laudable. Regina v. Sharpe, Dears. & Bell 160, 169 Eng.Rep. 959 (1857).

21. The text is substantially a quotation from People v. Baumgartner, 135 Cal. 72, 73, 66 P. 974, 975 (1901).

22. Kanavan's Case, 1 Me. 226 (1821). "If a dead body may be thrown into a river, it may be cast into a street:—if the body of a child—so, the body of an adult male or female. Good morals—decency—our best feelings—the law of the land—all forbid such proceedings." Id. at 227.

23. The Queen v. Price, 12 Q.B.D. 247 (1884). Cremation is not an offense but it is an offense if the body "was indecently burned, in such a manner that, when the facts should in the natural course of events become known, the feelings and natural sentiments of the public would be outraged." State v. Bradbury, 136 Me. 347, 351, 9 A.2d 657, 659 (1939).

24. The Queen v. Stephenson, 13 Q.B.D. 331 (1884).

25. The careful removal of two cemented gold crowns from the teeth of a dead body, with no impairment of the natural teeth and no change in the appearance of the face, was held not to be a mutilation of a dead body. People v. Bullington, 27 Cal.App.2d 396, 80 P.2d 1030 (1938).

26. Seaton v. Commonwealth, 149 Ky. 498, 149 S.W. 871 (1912). The quotation is from page 502, 149 S.W. 873.

D, apparently due to some strange religious belief, kept a body concealed for thirty days without burial. A conviction of the common-law offense of "indecent handling of a dead body" was affirmed.[27] The court said only four cases of conviction of this offense in this country had been found.

It has not been uncommon for statutes to provide for the distribution of unclaimed bodies for scientific study,[28] or to authorize a bequest for this purpose.[29]

The Model Penal Code has a section on "Abuse of Corpse." [30]

SECTION 2. OFFENSES AGAINST THE PUBLIC PEACE

A. BREACH OF THE PEACE

The beginning of our criminal justice, in the troublous days of the dawn of civilization on the British Isles, was concerned very largely with the problem of keeping the peace. Because of this fact all early indictments included some such phrase as "against the peace of the King;" [1] and until recent statutory provisions for simplification, indictments in this country were thought to be incomplete without some such conclusion as "against the peace and dignity of the state." [2] As a result of this history all indictable offenses are sometimes regarded as deeds which violate the public peace, and hence in a loose sense the term "breach of the peace" is regarded as a synonym for crime.[3] On the other hand there is a very obvious distinction in this regard between a secret act of embezzlement and the public tumult of a riot. The secret act of embezzlement does not disturb the public peace except in a purely theoretical sense. Our present concern is not with offenses which disturb the peace only theoretically, but with those crimes which are punished primarily because of their actual disturbance of the public tranquillity, or their tendency to cause such a disturbance. Needless to say, there is a social interest in preserving the peace and tranquillity of the community[4] and

27. State v. Hartzler, 78 N.M. 514, 433 P.2d 231 (1967).

28. E.g., Ala.Code 1975, Tit. 22, c. 19; I.C.A. (Iowa) c. 142 (1972); K.S.A. (Kan.) 65–901 (1972).

29. E.g., Ala.Code 1975, § 22–19–40, et seq.

30. Section 250.10.

1. Rawlins v. Ellis, 16 M. & W. 172, 173, 153 Eng.Rep. 1147, 1148 (1846). "All offences are either against the king's peace, or his crown and dignity; and are so laid in every indictment." 1 Bl. Comm. *268.

2. " 'Breach of the peace,' in view of the generally accepted definition, and of the constitutional provision that all indictments shall conclude 'against the peace and dignity of the state,' includes any violation of any law enacted to preserve peace and good order." Miles v. State, 30 Okl.Cr. 302, 307, 236 P. 57, 59 (1925).

3. The Constitution provides: "The Senators and Representatives . . . shall in all cases, except treason, felony and breach of the peace, be privileged from arrest during their attendance at the session of their respective Houses, and in going to and returning from the same; . . . ." Art. I, sec. 6, cl. 1. As so used "breach of the peace" includes any indictable offense. Williamson v. United States, 207 U.S. 425, 28 S.Ct. 163 (1908). For a similar interpretation of a state constitution see In re Emmett, 120 Cal.App. 349, 353, 7 P.2d 1096, 1098 (1932).

4. "The common law hath ever had a special care and regard for the conservation of the peace; for peace is the very end and foundation of civil society." 1 Bl.Comm. *349. "They attack directly that public order and sense of security, which is one of the first objects of the common law. . . ." State v. Huntly, 25 N.C. 418, 421 (1843).

the common law provided a penalty for any wilful deed which violates this interest without lawful justification or excuse.[5] If such a deed also violates some other social interest, such as the social interest in protecting the persons of individuals, the crime is commonly classified under some other appropriate heading. If such is not the fact, and the deed is punished primarily because of the violation of the social interest in the public peace and security, the offense may have some special name such as riot, affray, or disturbance of public assembly. If the deed is punished primarily because of the violation of this social interest, and there is no other special name for the particular offense, the phrase "breach of the peace," "disturbing the peace" or "disorderly conduct" is used as the name of the crime itself.[6] Stated in other words:

Any wilful deed committed without lawful justification or excuse, which unreasonably disturbed the public peace and tranquillity, or tended strongly to cause such a disturbance, was an offense at common law; and unless there was some special name for the misdeed, it was called a "breach of the peace." Some statutes follow this same plan; others employ some other label for each offense within this field and use "breach of the peace" only as part of the description of various misdeeds known by such other names.

5. An act which tends to a breach of the peace is indictable. The King v. Summers, 3 Salk. 194, 91 Eng.Rep. 772, 1 Lev. 139, 83 Eng.Rep. 337 (1664). "The breaking of windows in the night, while a family is in the house, is not a mere trespass upon property; but being calculated in its nature to frighten and disturb the people within the house, it may be considered as an indirect attack upon the persons of the family, and is clearly a breach of the peace." State v. Batchelder, 5 N.H. 549, 552–3 (1832).

"We hold that the statute as applied to this case requires only that one communicate with another by telephone or in writing 'in a coarse and offensive manner' with intent to alarm on the part of the sender. . . . The instant case is precisely the situation where the alternative of a 'coarse and offensive manner' is necessary to vindicate the rights of the recipient of spite messages and the State's interest in protecting citizens from such intrusion." Kramer v. State, 605 S.W.2d 861, 866 (Tex.Cr.App. 1980).

6. "Breach of the peace" is the phrase used in some of the statutes. E.g., West's Fla.Stat.Ann. § 877.03 (1976).

" 'The offense known as breach of the peace embraces a great variety of conduct destroying or menacing public order and tranquility. It includes not only violent acts but acts and words likely to produce violence in others.' Cantwell v.

State of Connecticut, 310 U.S. 296, 308, 60 S.Ct. 900 (1940)." United States v. Woodard, 376 F.2d 136, 141 (7th Ed. 1967).

The words "opprobrious words or abusive language, tending to cause a breach of the peace" have a definite meaning as to the conduct forbidden, measured by common understanding and practice, and are not unconstitutionally vague, indefinite or uncertain. "You son of a bitch, I'll choke you to death" are opprobrious and abusive. Wilson v. State, 223 Ga. 531, 156 S.E.2d 446 (1967).

The conduct of a "peeping Tom" is within the disorderly-conduct statute. District of Columbia v. Jordan, 232 A.2d 298 (D.C.Ct.App.1967).

"Disorderly conduct" tends to disturb the peace by an act of violence, or by any act likely to produce violence, or which by causing consternation and alarm, disturbs the peace and quiet of the community. State v. Doe, 92 N.M. 100, 583 P.2d 464 (1978), rev'd other grounds 92 N.M. 109, 583 P.2d 473 (App.1978). See In re Bushman, 1 Cal.3d 767, 83 Cal.Rptr. 375, 463 P.2d 727 (1970).

"State disorderly conduct statute is interpreted narrowly to apply to speech only in the form of fighting words and, as so interpreted, is constitutional." State v. Huffman, 228 Kan. 186, 612 P.2d 630 (1980).

B. FIGHTING

There is no common-law crime known by the name of "fighting," although there is seldom a fight without some crime being committed. If the word "fight" is used to include a friendly contest of strength, without anger or malice and with no intent to inflict any real physical injury, it may apply to situations in which no crime is committed, but whenever there is fighting in the sense that blows are struck in an angry or quarrelsome manner, or that force is used which is intended or likely to cause death or serious physical injury, there is a crime of some sort, unless the fighting is on the field of battle as an actual act of war. The crime may be due to the fact that the force used violates the social interest in the persons of individuals, or it may be that the fighting is a crime because it tends to disturb the peace and tranquillity of the community. Dueling belongs in the former group because it is ordinarily scheduled at a secluded place and does not alarm the community. For this reason it was discussed under the head of offenses against the persons of individuals. The concern here is with offenses which are punished primarily because of their tendency to disturb the peace and tranquillity of the community, and certain kinds of fighting have this effect. The fighting may amount to a riot, but as a riot does not necessarily involve fighting, it will receive attention under another head. Before that point is reached it is important to consider (a) affray and (b) prize fighting.

1. AFFRAY

At common law an affray is a mutual fight in a public place to the terror or alarm of the people.[7] It is a misdemeanor.

The word "affray" comes from the same source as the word "afraid," and the tendency to alarm the community is the very essence of this offense. A friendly scuffle or boxing match, properly conducted, is not a crime at all. A mutual fight conducted in a private place, which is waged in malice or which for any other reason exceeds the bounds of legal privilege, renders each participant guilty of assault and battery.[8] The same fight conducted in a public place to the disturbance of the public renders the contestants guilty of an affray. Definitions of affray frequently speak of the fighting of two or more persons, but this is unnecessary. One man cannot fight with himself. This form of expression has been used to emphasize that it does not require more than two to constitute an affray.

A. MUTUAL FIGHTING

The fighting must be mutual. If one person is unlawfully attacking another who is using privileged force in the effort to defend himself, the one is guilty of assault and battery while the other is entirely innocent of crime,—and there is no affray.[9] If, however, the person claiming to act in self-defense provoked the conflict by abusive or insulting language or conduct, intended or likely to produce such a result, his use of force is not within the

7. 4 Bl.Comm. *145.

8. Regina v. Lewis, 1 Car. & K. 414 (1844).

9. Bracewell v. State, 10 Ga.App. 830, 74 S.E. 440 (1912).

privilege of self-defense; hence the fighting is regarded as mutual and if the other elements are present it constitutes an affray.[10]

B. PUBLIC PLACE

The term "public place" in this sense includes any place open to public view and close enough to the public so that fighting there may tend to cause public alarm. Hence it is no defense to a charge of this offense to show that the fight occurred on a privately owned lot, if the lot was open to public view and close to a city street.[11] It is sometimes said that the public highway is not necessarily a public place in the sense that the term is used in defining this offense, but this is incorrect. A mutual fight at a secluded spot on a highway where the fighting could not be observed by others, is not an affray it is true, but for another reason. This is a public place, but under these circumstances the fight does not tend to alarm the public and this is one of the elements of this offense.[12] If the fight occurred in a private room, not exposed to view from the public street, it is not an affray even if there happened to be a third person present to see it.[13] If it took place in a public room, or on the public highway or other public place (including an open lot near a public street) and was seen by others, this is held to be *calculated* to alarm the public and hence to complete the offense, even without proof that those who saw it were *actually* terrified.[14]

C. STATUTORY PROVISIONS

Statutory definitions of affray are usually mere codifications of the common law, although a few of them include slight variations.[15] In some of the codes it is not listed as a separate offense but is punished under a general provision dealing with "breach of the peace," or disturbing the peace.[16] Some jurisdictions provide for a more specific offense such as "fighting" or "maliciously disturbing another person." [17]

An affray, if with intent to cause public alarm, or recklessly creating a risk thereof, would be punished as disorderly conduct under the Model Penal Code.[18]

2. PRIZE FIGHTING

Prize fighting is fighting for a reward or prize. It was not looked upon with favor by the common law as was a friendly boxing match or wrestling match. On the other hand it was not punishable by the common law unless it was fought in a public place, or for some other reason constituted a breach of the peace.

10. Hawkins v. State, 13 Ga. 322 (1853); State v. Fanning, 94 N.C. 940 (1886).

11. Carwile v. State, 35 Ala. 392 (1860).

12. State v. Warren, 37 Mo.App. 502 (1894).

13. A fight in a private field, at considerable distance from a highway, was not an affray although in the presence of a number of persons. The Queen v. Hunt, 1 Cox C.C. 177 (1845).

14. Carwile v. State, 35 Ala. 392 (1860); State v. Sumner, 5 Strobh. 53 (S.C. 1850).

15. 21 Okl.Stat.Ann. § 1321.8 (1958). Idaho provides for "challenging to fight or fighting. . . ." Idaho Code § 18–6409 (1979).

16. E.g., West's Fla.Stat.Ann. § 877.03 (1976).

17. West's Ann.Cal.Pen.Code § 415 (1976).

18. Section 250.2.

In some states prize fighting is prohibited unless licensed by public authority. One who causes the death of another in an *unlawful* prize fight is guilty of manslaughter.[19] The theory that prize fighting is socially harmful had its origin in the days when such a contest was conducted with bare fists and with wholly inadequate rules. The tendency at the present time is to regard it as socially harmful only when not properly regulated.

C. UNLAWFUL ASSEMBLY, ROUT AND RIOT

Unlawful assembly, rout and riot were misdemeanors at common law. It is convenient to speak of them as a group in terms of the common law before taking up the changes by modern statutes.

1. UNLAWFUL ASSEMBLY

An unlawful assembly is a meeting of three or more persons with a common plan in mind which, if carried out, will result in a riot.[20] In other words, it is such a meeting with intent to (a) commit a crime by open force, or (b) execute a common design, lawful or unlawful, in an unauthorized[21] manner likely to cause courageous persons to apprehend a breach of the peace.[22]

In the words of Baron Alderson:[23]

"I take it to be the law of the land that any meeting assembled under such circumstances as, according to the opinion of rational and firm men, are likely to produce danger to the tranquillity and peace of the neighborhood is an unlawful assembly . . . the alarm must not be merely such as would

19. People v. Fitzsimmons, 34 N.Y.S. 1102 (1895). All persons attending an unlawful prize fight are guilty of an offense. Rex v. Billingham, 2 Car. & P. 234, 172 Eng.Rep. 106 (1825).

20. 3 Co.Inst. *176. "[I]f they merely meet upon a purpose, which if executed, would make them rioters, and, having done nothing, they separate without carrying their purpose into effect, it is an unlawful assembly." Rex v. Birt, 5 Car. & P. 154, 172 Eng.Rep. 919 (1831). See also Rex v. Woolcock, 5 Car. & P. 516, 517, 172 Eng.Rep. 1078, 1079 (1833); Commonwealth v. Duitch, 165 Pa.Super. 187, 191, 67 A.2d 821, 822 (1949).

21. If the manner of execution is authorized, as in case of a *posse comitatus*, it is obviously not an unlawful assembly even if the situation is so serious as likely to cause public alarm. State v. Stalcup, 23 N.C. 30 (1840).

22. "An unlawful assembly is an assembly of three or more persons:—

(a) with intent to commit a crime by open force; or

(b) with intent to carry out any common purpose, lawful or unlawful, in

such a manner as to give firm and courageous persons in the neighborhood of such assembly reasonable grounds to apprehend a breach of the peace in consequence of it.

"Every unlawful assembly is a misdemeanor." Stephen, Digest of the Criminal Law 77 (8th ed. by Sturge, 1947).

". . . assembling with an intent to commit violence upon persons or property, to resist the execution of the laws, to disturb public order, or for the perpetration of acts inspiring public terror or alarm." People v. Judson, 11 Daly 1, 82 (N.Y.C.P.1849).

"California has no 'common law' crimes, yet the foregoing common law definitions, limitations and interpretation of the scope and nature of unlawful assembly are applicable and aid in interpretation of section 407 for that section is but a 'reaffirmation of the common law' crime of unlawful assembly." People v. Rodriguez, 116 Cal.App.3d 1, 171 Cal. Rptr. 832, 837 (1981).

23. In Regina v. Vincent, 9 Car. & P. 91, 109, 173 Eng.Rep. 754, 762 (1839).

frighten any foolish or timid person, but must be such as would alarm persons of reasonable firmness and courage."

At common law this offense cannot be committed by fewer than three persons, and it is not committed unless at least three come together at the same time.[24] They must have a common purpose to do one of the two things mentioned above, although it is not necessary that this purpose was the inducement of the assembly, because if three or more who gathered for some other purpose thereafter form such a design the meeting becomes an unlawful assembly.[25] It is not necessary that they carry out their unlawful plan,[26]—that would make them guilty of riot.[27] The mere presence of three or more persons together with this type of common purpose has such a tendency to result in a breach of the peace that the social interest in preserving the tranquillity of the community is violated by the very meeting itself.[28]

People have a right to gather at a proper place, in an orderly manner, for any lawful purpose, despite illegal threats made by others in the effort to prevent the meeting. And such a gathering does not become an unlawful assembly by reason of the fact that they may have cause to fear they will be violently attacked, and are so attacked.[29]

2. ROUT

A rout is the movement of unlawful assemblers on the way to carry out their common design.

24. 4 Bl.Comm. *116.

25. "For if persons who have assembled for a lawful purpose do afterwards associate themselves together to commit an unlawful act, such association will be considered an assembling together for that purpose." State v. Cole, 2 McCord 117, 123 (S.C.1822). See also State v. Johnson, 89 Iowa 594, 597, 57 N.W. 302, 303 (1894).

Those who assemble for a lawful purpose do not become guilty of unlawful assembly if the assembly becomes unlawful unless they participate in the unlawful act. Abbey v. City Court, 7 Ariz.App. 330, 439 P.2d 302 (1968).

"The statute provides a defense to one who participates in a lawful assembly which ultimately becomes unlawful, if he retires from the assembly when one of those assembled manifests an intent to engage in unlawful conduct." Faulk v. State, 608 S.W.2d 625, 631 (Tex.Cr.App. 1980).

26. "It ought to be known that if persons assemble to obstruct officers of the law, all persons so assembling are guilty of an unlawful assembly, whether a riot takes place or not, . . ." Per Fitzgerald, J., in The Queen v. McNaughten, 14 Cox C.C. 576, 578 (1881).

27. "The difference between a riot and an unlawful assembly is this: If the parties assemble in a tumultuous manner, and actually execute their purpose with violence, it is a riot; but if they merely meet upon a purpose, which, if executed, would make them rioters, and, having done nothing, they separate without carrying their purpose into effect, it is an unlawful assembly." Per Patterson, J., in Rex v. Birt, 5 Car. & P. 154, 172 Eng.Rep. 919 (1831). See also Rex v. Woolcock, 5 Car. & P. 516, 517, 172 Eng. Rep. 1078, 1079 (1833).

28. An indictment for unlawful assembly need not conclude "*in terrorem populi*." Rex v. Cox, 4 Car. & P. 538, 172 Eng.Rep. 815 (1831). Since an unlawful assembly may be verging on a riot it is the duty of officers to take immediate steps to disperse it. Regina v. Neale, 9 Car. & P. 431, 173 Eng.Rep. 899 (1839).

29. Beatty v. Gillbanks, 15 Cox C.C. 138 (1882).

In the context of the First Amendment a lawful gathering does not become unlawful because of the mere potential for violence from those objecting to the purposes of the gathering. Terminiello v. Chicago, 337 U.S. 11, 69 S.Ct. 894 (1949); Carroll v. President & Commissioners of Princess Anne, 393 U.S. 175, 89 S.Ct. 347 (1968).

The word "rout" comes from the same source as the word "route." It signifies that three or more who have gathered together in unlawful assembly are "on their way."[30] It is not necessary for guilt of this offense that the design be actually carried out, nor that the journey be made in a tumultuous manner.

3. RIOT

A riot is a tumultuous disturbance of the peace by three or more persons acting together (a) in the commission of a crime by open force, or (b) in the execution of some enterprise, lawful or unlawful, in such a violent, turbulent and unauthorized manner as to create likelihood of public terror and alarm.[31]

These are pyramiding offenses, so to speak, the lesser being included in the greater,[32] and at least three persons are necessary for each.[33] Assume there are three or more persons with a common design to commit a crime by open force or to carry out some enterprise, lawful or unlawful, in such a violent, turbulent and unauthorized manner as to cause courageous persons to apprehend a breach of the peace. When they come together for this purpose they are guilty of unlawful assembly. When they start on their way to carry out their common design they are guilty of *rout*. In the actual execution of their design they are guilty of *riot*. They cannot be convicted of

---

30. People v. Judson, 11 Daly 1, 83 (N.Y.C.P.1849). "A rout differs from a riot in that the persons do not actually execute their purpose, but only make some motion towards its execution; . . ." Commonwealth v. Duitch, 165 Pa.Super. 187, 190, 67 A.2d 821, 822 (1949).

31. Judge Stephen defines a riot as "an unlawful assembly which has actually begun to execute the purpose for which it assembled, by a breach of the peace, and to the terror of the public; . . ." Stephen, Digest of the Criminal Law 78 (8th ed. by Sturge, 1947). For his definition of unlawful assembly see *supra*, note 20. "A riot has been defined as a tumultuous disturbance of the peace by three or more persons assembled and acting with a common intent; either in executing a lawful private enterprise in a violent and turbulent manner, to the terror of the people, or as executing an unlawful enterprise in a violent and turbulent manner." State v. Abbadini, 38 Del. 322, 326, 192 A. 550, 551–2 (1937). "Bishop . . . says: A 'riot is such disorderly conduct in three or more assembled persons, actually accomplishing an object, as is calculated to terrify others.'" Salem Manufacturing Co. v. First American Tire Insurance Co., 111 F.2d 797, 803 (9th Cir. 1940). Several of the other common definitions are quoted in this case.

32. "There likewise seems to be no question but that the crime of unlawful assembly was an included offense of the crime of riot at common law." State v. Woolman, 84 Utah 23, 30, 33 P.2d 640, 643 (1934). "Riot, rout, and unlawful assembly are kindred offenses and the greater includes the less; . . ." Commonwealth v. Duitch, 165 Pa.Super. 187, 190, 67 A.2d 821, 822 (1949). An indictment for riot did not conclude *"in terrorem populi."* For want of this allegation it was held the defendants could not be convicted of a riot. But the defendants were convicted of an unlawful assembly, on this indictment. Rex v. Cox, 4 Car. & P. 538, 172 Eng.Rep. 815 (1831).

33. If three persons are indicted for riot with no averment or proof of any other participant, and one is acquitted, a conviction of the other two would be invalid. Cohen v. State, 173 Md. 216, 195 A. 532 (1937). "The offenses comprehended within this general definition constitute three kinds of offenses—an unlawful assembly, a rout, and a riot. The unlawful assembly is where the parties come together with the intent before stated; rout is where they move forward to the execution of their design, and riot takes place when they begin with force and violence to execute their design." People v. Judson, 11 Daly 1, 83 (N.Y.C.P. 1849).

three different offenses, since the "greater includes the less,"[34] but since all were common-law misdemeanors[35] there was no complete merger and conviction of unlawful assembly or rout was possible even if the evidence disclosed a riot.[36]

An occasional suggestion has intimated that one requisite of riot is that the original gathering of the wrongdoers must have been in the nature of an unlawful assembly,[37] but this is a mistake. No doubt every riot includes an unlawful assembly,[38] but it must be remembered that a gathering by accident or for an innocent purpose may suddenly be transformed into an unlawful assembly by a change of plan.[39] And if this riotous plan is executed the parties are guilty of a riot despite the propriety of the original meeting.[40] With whatever speed the plan was carried out, moreover, it must have been agreed upon before translated into action and hence, in theory at least, the riot was preceded by an unlawful assembly. The unlawful agreement, it may be added, need not have been expressed in words. A tacit understanding is sufficient and this may be inferred from what was actually done.[41] An important distinction is to be noted, however. If the meeting was an unlawful assembly from the beginning, and results in a riot, all of the assemblers are guilty of riot in the absence of a timely and duly manifested withdrawal. On the other hand, if a riotous plan is suddenly conceived and executed by part of those who have lawfully assembled, only those who participate therein, or lend it encouragement, are guilty.[42] A bystander, it may be added, who joins rioters in their forbidden conduct is as much guilty of riot as if he assembled with the others in advance.[43]

A sudden dissention among those who have gathered lawfully may proceed to violence without amounting to more than an affray,[44] but if the plan includes a tumultuous attack upon the persons or property of others it is riotous in its nature.[45] On the other hand an actual "assault or destruction of property may or may not be incident to the execution of a riot."[46] For example, a parade may be conducted in such a manner[47] or a charivari car-

---

34. Commonwealth v. Duitch, 165 Pa. Super. 187, 190, 67 A.2d 821, 822 (1949).

35. 4 Bl.Comm. *146–7. An English statute provided capital punishment under certain circumstances if the number was twelve or more. Ibid.

36. Rex v. Cox, 4 Car. & P. 538, 172 Eng.Rep. 815 (1831).

37. See State v. Woolman, 84 Utah 23, 35, 33 P.2d 640, 646 (1934). The court implies *obiter* that there was such a requirement at common law but holds otherwise under the Utah statute.

"The gist of the offense of riot at common law is the in terrorem populi effect of the assembly." Pan American World Airways, Inc. v. Aetna Casualty & Surety Co., 505 F.2d 989, 1021 (2d Cir. 1974).

38. See Commonwealth v. Duitch, 165 Pa.Super. 187, 190, 67 A.2d 821, 822 (1949); Whaley v. State, 496 S.W.2d 109 (Tex.Cr.App. 1973).

39. See State v. Cole, 2 McCord 117, 123 S.C. (1822).

40. State v. Abbadini, 38 Del. 322, 192 A. 550 (1937); Symonds v. State, 66 Okl. Cr. 49, 89 P.2d 974 (1939); Commonwealth v. Merrick, 65 Pa.Super. 482 (1917).

41. Ibid. (except Merrick).

42. Symonds v. State, 66 Okl.Cr. 49, 89 P.2d 974 (1939); State v. Woolman, 84 Utah 23, 33 P.2d 640 (1934).

43. State v. Abbadini, 38 Del. 322, 192 A. 550 (1937).

44. Commonwealth v. Duitch, 165 Pa. Super. 187, 67 A.2d 821 (1949).

45. Commonwealth v. Merrick, 65 Pa. Super. 482 (1917).

46. Cohen v. State, 173 Md. 216, 221, 195 A. 532, 534 (1937).

47. Commonwealth v. Frishman, 235 Mass. 449, 126 N.E. 838 (1920). In this case it seems an officer was stabbed but

ried to such an extent[48] as to constitute a riot. And a riot was committed by three men in front of another's house at night cursing and threatening him in loud voices, and repeatedly firing a gun, thereby frightening him and members of his family.[49]

4. MODERN STATUTES

The famous English statute,[50] commonly known as the "Riot Act," made it a felony, without benefit of clergy, for twelve or more rioters to continue together for one hour after the making by a magistrate of a proclamation to disperse. This Act, passed in 1714 was not generally accepted in the Colonies and is not a part of our common law. Under some of our statutes a riot may be a felony, and under some no more than two persons are required for riot, rout or unlawful assembly.[51] Rout has been omitted entirely from some of the codes.[52]

5. INCITING TO RIOT

Inciting to riot is the employment of words or other means intended and calculated to provoke a riot. Signs, actions and movements may be just as effective for this purpose as the use of inflammatory language.[53] It is a common-law misdemeanor [54] and if a riot results the inciter is guilty of the riot itself, even if not present when it occurs.[55] Congress has made it a federal crime to travel in interstate commerce to incite a riot.[56]

6. "READING THE RIOT ACT"

"Reading the riot act" is a slang expression used to indicate an official command for rioters to disperse. An order to disperse is not prerequisite to guilt of a common-law riot [57] but the English "Riot Act," as explained above, made it a capital offense for twelve or more rioters to continue together for an hour after the official proclamation by a magistrate. As explained by Judge Stephen:

" 'Our sovereign Lady the Queen chargeth and commandeth all persons being assembled immediately to disperse themselves and peaceably to depart to their habitations or to their lawful business, upon the pains contained in

the court held this was not necessary to establish the riot.

48. State v. Brown, 69 Ind. 95 (1879); Higgins v. Minaghan, 78 Wis. 602, 47 N.W. 941 (1891).

49. Lewis v. State, 2 Ga.App. 659, 58 S.E. 1070 (1907).

50. 1 Geo. I, stat. 2, c. 5 (1714).

51. State v. Woolman, 84 Utah 23, 33 P.2d 640 (1934); West's Ann.Cal.Pen. Code §§ 404, 406, 407 (1970).

The proposed Federal Criminal Code S. 1437 § 1834 would require ten or more persons as participants.

52. E.g., Iowa Code Ann. c. 723 (1978).

53. Commonwealth v. Albert, 169 Pa. Super. 318, 82 A.2d 695 (1951).

"To establish the charge of incitement to riot under K.S.A. 21–4105, the State must prove that the defendant as a member of a group of five or more persons by words or conduct urged others to engage in a riot under circumstances which induced a clear and present danger of injury to persons or property or a breach of the public peace." State v. Dargatz, 228 Kan. 322, 614 P.2d 430, 434 (1980).

54. Commonwealth v. Merrick, 65 Pa. Super. 482 (1917).

55. Regina v. Sharpe, 3 Cox C.C. 288 (1848).

56. 18 U.S.C.A. § 2101. The proposed Federal Criminal Code S. 1437 §§ 1831, 1832 provides for a similar offense.

57. Commonwealth v. Frishman, 235 Mass. 449, 126 N.E. 838 (1920).

the Act made in the first year of King George for preventing tumults and riotous assemblies. God save the Queen.' The making of this proclamation is commonly, but very inaccurately, called reading the Riot Act." [58]

Illegal conduct is not protected merely because it is in part initiated or carried out by language. When a clear and present danger of riot appears the power of the state to prevent or punish is obvious. [59]

The Model Penal Code has an article on "Riot, Disorderly Conduct, and Related Offenses," [60] which includes a subsection on "Failure of Disorderly Persons to Disperse Upon Official Order." [61]

D. DISTURBANCE OF PUBLIC ASSEMBLY

The disturbance of a public assembly by three or more persons might be so turbulent as to constitute a riot, but it may be punishable even if less violent or caused by a single disturber. "Under the common law," it was said by one court, [62] "it is a misdemeanor for a person at a public gathering, collected for a lawful purpose, to be guilty of conduct which will disturb such a gathering." A similar statement in another case by the same court was qualified by the word "wantonly." [63]

In England, because of the established church, meetings of dissenters were once deemed unlawful and hence might be disturbed legally until such a disturbance was made a crime by statute, but in this country there is no distinction as to creeds in this respect. [64] In fact, in the absence of statute, it is unimportant whether the meeting is for the purpose of religious worship or for some quite different purpose such as education or politics. Some of the statutes have specified certain types of assemblage, such as meetings for religious worship, [65] or for educational or literary purposes. And if the state has such an enactment and does not punish common-law crimes unless included in the code it will be necessary to show that the particular meeting comes within the legislative designation. Where not so restricted by statute or interpretation [66] the wilful [67] disturbance of any lawful gathering is

58. 1 Stephen, A History of the Criminal Law of England 203, note 1 (1883).

59. People v. Davis, 68 Cal.2d 481, 67 Cal.Rptr. 547, 439 P.2d 651 (1968).

The statute making incitement to riot a crime is constitutional. People v. Davis, 68 Cal.2d 481, 67 Cal.Rptr. 547, 439 P.2d 651 (1968).

60. Article 250.

61. Section 250.1(2).

62. Boswell v. Barnum and Bailey, 135 Tenn. 35, 39, 185 S.W. 692, 693 (1916).

63. State v. Watkins, 123 Tenn. 502, 504, 130 S.W. 839, 840 (1910).

64. State v. Jasper, 15 N.C. 323, 325–6 (1833).

65. Miss.Code Ann. 1972 § 97–35–17; Wyo.Stat.Ann. § 6–6–106 (1977).

66. Such a statute in Tennessee was held not to abrogate the common law offense of disturbing an assemblage other than specifically mentioned. State v. Watkins, 123 Tenn. 502, 130 S.W. 839 (1910).

67. An information for disturbing a religious meeting by loud talking and laughing was held fatally defective for want of an averment that it was done "wilfully." State v. Stroud, 99 Iowa 16, 68 N.W. 450 (1896). It was held that an intent to disturb was not a necessary element of the offense. If acts were wilfully done that had a tendency to disturb the meeting, and did so, this was sufficient. Culpepper v. State, 32 Ala.App. 276, 25 So.2d 56 (1946). On the other hand, the fact that the singing of a devout church member, who had no purpose to disturb the congregation but was conscientiously taking part in the religious services, was so peculiar as to excite mirth in some and indignation in others, did not constitute an offense. State v. Linklaw, 69 N.C. 214 (1873).

punishable as a misdemeanor.[68]   Many of the statutes expressly so provide.[69]

The Model Penal Code has a section on "Disturbing Meetings and Processions." [70]

E. DISORDERLY HOUSE

The keeping of one type of disorderly house—the bawdy house—is punished because it violates the social interest in maintaining proper standards of morality and decency. It was discussed in that connection. As included here a house may be disorderly for other reasons. Any house in which disorderly persons are permitted to congregate, and to disturb the tranquillity of the neighborhood by fighting, quarreling, swearing or any other type of disorder, is a disorderly house; and the keeping thereof is a misdemeanor at common law.[71]

F. FORCIBLE ENTRY AND DETAINER

To walk across another's land, or to enter his building, without privilege, is a trespass, but this in itself, while a civil wrong, is not a crime. However, if an entry upon real estate is accomplished by violence or intimidation, or if such methods are employed for detention after a peaceable entry, there is a crime according to English law, known as forcible entry and detainer.[72] This was a common-law offense in England, although supplemented by English statutes that are old enough to be common law in this country.[73]

The social interest in the peace and tranquillity of the community requires that no peaceful possession of real estate should be disturbed by such violent means.[74] Any disputes over the right of possession, which cannot be settled peaceably by the parties themselves must be submitted to the courts for their decision. Hence, it is no defense to a charge of this crime, that the defendant held the legal title to, and had the right of immediate possession of, the real estate in question.[75]

---

68. Commonwealth v. Hoxey, 16 Mass. 385 (1820); State v. Watkins, 123 Tenn. 502, 130 S.W. 839 (1910).

69. As to what constitutes the offense of disturbing a public meeting see 12 A.L.R. 650 (1921). See Carlson v. Tallahassee, 240 So.2d 866 (Fla.App.1970).

70. Section 250.8.

71. Bishop says it is better to limit the term "disorderly house" to this meaning. "In this sense, it is a violation of what in an earlier chapter is called the public order and tranquillity." 1 Bishop, New Criminal Law § 1106 (8th ed. 1892).

Maintaining a place for a "drunkard's convention" every weekend was a nuisance and was properly abated. Burgess v. Johnson, 223 Ga. 427, 156 S.E.2d 78 (1967). The persons were yelling and disturbing the peace and there was reckless driving nearby.

72. 4 Bl.Comm. *148.

73. State v. Morgan, 59 N.H. 322 (1879). "Forcible Entry and Detainer was a misdemeanor both at common law and under the early Statutes of England." Hearn v. Hearn, 39 Del. 427, 431, 1 A.2d 585, 587 (1937).

74. "Unquestionably the purpose of the law today remains as anciently to preserve the peace and prevent breaches of it; . . ." Commonwealth v. Kolenda, Luz.Leg.Reg. 45, 47 (Luz.Co.Pa. 1860).

75. 4 Bl.Comm. *148. "An indictment at common law lies for a forcible entry because it tends to disturb the peace; and in such indictment it is not necessary to allege, that the party trespassed upon had any estate in the land, but only that he was in quiet possession thereof." State v. Speirin, 1 Brev. 119, 123 (S.C.1802); State v. Jones, 14 S.C. 344 (1880). "It seems that at common law a man disseised of any lands, or tenements,

It has sometimes been said that there are two separate offenses—(1) forcible entry and (2) forcible detainer. This may be true under the peculiar wording of some particular statute, but in general it seems to be one offense which may be committed in two different ways.

Any unlawful act of forcible entry or detainer will usually involve some other crime, such as an assault.[76] For this reason some of the statutes do not include forcible entry and detainer as a separate offense, although in others it is expressly provided.[77]

The Model Penal Code has a section on "Criminal Trespass"[78] which makes it a petty misdemeanor for one, knowing he is not privileged to do so, to enter or remain in any place to which notice against trespass is given. Some states have passed special statutes prohibiting disrupting of institutions of higher learning or wrongfully remaining on the campus or facilities of such an institution.[79]

G.   LIBEL *

The word "libel" means literally "a little book" and is used in the designation of several offenses, namely (1) defamatory libel, (2) blasphemous libel, (3) obscene libel, and (4) seditious libel. Wherever the word is used without a modifying adjective, however, and apart from context definitely suggesting another meaning, it signifies a defamatory libel. It is employed here in the sense of defamatory libel, without the modifier, to conform to the customary usage.

Libel is the malicious publication of durable defamation.[80] It is a misdemeanor at common law,[81] and at least at one time was, in all the states except where it had been made a felony [82] which was not common.

(if he could not prevail by fair means,) might lawfully regain the possession thereof by force, unless he were put to the necessity of bringing his action, by having neglected to re-enter in due time: . . ." But to preserve the public peace it was necessary to change this by statute. Hawkins, P. C. c. 64 (6th ed. by Leach, 1788).

76. This is not always the case, however, since an actual terrorization of inhabitants is not necessary. It is sufficient for a forcible entry if doors or windows were broken to effect the entry. Commonwealth v. Kolenda, Luz.Leg.Reg. 45, 47 (Luz.Co.Pa.1860). It is not necessary that the owner should have made vocal protest to the entry. State v. Gibson, 226 N.C. 194, 37 S.E.2d 316 (1946).

77. Some of the codes omit it entirely. E.g., Iowa Code Annotated. Both the common law and the statutes on this subject were repealed. State v. Morgan, 59 N.H. 322 (1879).

78. Section 221.2. This is an offense against habitation and occupancy and is included in the article on Burglary and Other Criminal Intrusion (article 221).

79. West's Ann.Cal.Pen.Code § 626.8 (1970); Utah Code Ann., 1953 § 76–8–710.

* The elaborate discussion of libel which appeared in the earlier editions is no longer necessary or desirable.

80. A libel is any "printed or written defamation of a person, published maliciously and without justification." State v. Reade, 136 N.J.L. 432, 433, 56 A.2d 566 (1948). See also 4 Bl.Comm. *150; Cole v. Commonwealth, 222 Ky. 350, 358, 300 S.W. 907, 910 (1927); Commonwealth v. Clap, 4 Mass. 163, 168 (1808).

81. 4 Bl.Comm. *151; Beauharnais v. Illinois, 343 U.S. 250, 72 S.Ct. 725 (1952). Every American jurisdiction punished libel at the time of this case. The statutes are summarized in footnote 5 of Beauharnais.

82. A.R.S. (Ariz.) §§ 13–103, 13–351, repealed Laws of 1977 Chap. 142.

1. DEFAMATION

Defamation is that which "tends so to harm the reputation of another as to lower him in the estimation of the community or to deter third persons from associating or dealing with him." [83] It is involved in two related harms, libel and slander. A familiar statement is that libel is written whereas slander is oral. This covers the idea in a general way but tends to mislead because defamation may be published without the use of words and hence be neither written nor oral. Thus libel may be perpetrated by hanging a person in effigy [84] and slander, by sign or gesture.[85]

Libel might be written in the sand on the shore where it would soon be obliterated by the incoming tide. But the defamation is more or less enduring in libel but not in slander and this is the distinguishing feature between the two. Hence the definition should be in some such form as this: Libel is the malicious publication of durable defamation; slander is the malicious publication of transitory defamation. Libel is both a crime and a tort, but slander gives rise only to a civil action [86] unless it has been made punishable by statute.[87]

Publication, in the legal sense, is an act by which something is made known. Thus the "publication of a will" is merely the declaration by the one who prepared the document, made to the witnesses (usually in private) that it is his last will and testament. The publication of a libel might be in the form of a book, pamphlet or newspaper, but nothing of that nature is required. A letter sent to a single individual is sufficient.

The reason libel was recognized as a crime at common law was because of its tendency to stir up breaches of the peace; whereas its recognition as a tort was to provide compensation to one wrongfully harmed by defamation. And this led to some differences in the development of libel as a crime and as a tort. Thus in a civil action it was held that there was no libel if the defamatory matter was communicated only to the one defamed, because he could not be harmed if no one else knew about it.[88] But because of its tendency to stir up a breach of the peace, criminal libel could be committed by communicating the defamatory matter to anyone—either the one defamed or another.[89] There was also a difference based upon the truth of the matter published. In the belief that no one was entitled to a better reputation than warranted by the facts, it was held that truth of the matter stated was a complete defense to a civil action for libel,[90] but it was quite otherwise in a

---

83. Restatement, Second, Torts § 559 (1977).

84. "Sign or effigy." State v. Haffer, 94 Wash. 136, 141, 162 P. 45, 47 (1916).

85. Restatement, Second, Torts § 568, comment d (1977).

86. Restatement, Second, Torts § 568, historical note (1977). Libel is a crime. 3 Co.Inst. *174. Slander is not a crime. State v. Wakefield, 8 Mo.App. 11 (1879).

87. Some statutes provide for the punishment of certain types of slander such as orally imputing want of chastity to a woman, or accusing anyone of a felony or other offense involving moral turpi-

tude, or using insulting words while on enclosed lands of another to one lawfully on such lands. Kwass v. Kersey, 139 W.Va. 497, 81 S.E.2d 237 (1954). A few statutes punish slander without any such limitation. West's Ann.Cal.Pen.Code § 258 (1970); Wis.St.1958, § 942.01 (1978).

88. Restatement, Second, Torts § 577 (1977).

89. 4 Bl.Comm. *150.

90. 3 Bl.Comm. *125. "The truth of a defamatory statement of fact is a complete defense to an action for defamation." Restatement, Torts § 582 (1938). This has been modified by constitutional

prosecution for criminal libel. In fact in a criminal case the ancient notion was "the greater the truth, the greater the libel" based on the thought that one falsely libeled might get satisfaction by proving that the statement was not true; while the only hope for satisfaction by one truly libeled was to cause harm to the defamer. Hence truth was no defense in a prosecution for criminal libel.[91] In the course of time, however, there was an increasing recognition of the social interest in having the truth disclosed under certain circumstances, even if harmful; and at times this interest outweighed the interest in suppressing defamatory statements. Because of this fact it was held in an early New York case that there is no guilt of criminal libel if the defamatory statement is true *provided* it "was published with good motives and for justifiable ends."[92] And this came to be the prevailing view, frequently incorporated in the statutes,[93] although the requirement that the defamatory statement be false was not unknown.[94]

To constitute libel the defamatory matter must be published "maliciously," but this term in the legal sense requires no more than the intentional doing of a wrongful act. "The general rule is, that legal malice, which in law means a wrongful act done intentionally without just or lawful excuse, is sufficient to support a charge that the publication is libelous."[95]

An *excuse* would be recognized, so far as the criminal law is concerned, if the publication of defamation was unintentional, so long as it did not result from wanton recklessness, although such an occurrence is unlikely. And if published under duress—such as at pistol point under threat of death— it would be excused, although no such case has been found. Actually the excuse recognized in a libel case is ordinarily based upon a privilege.

It is provided in the Constitution[96] that for any speech or debate in either house of congress, the members "shall not be questioned in any other place."

or statutory enactment in a number of states. Ibid., special note. "Falsity is a *sine qua non* for the maintenance of state defamation . . . actions in the labor field." Hasbrouck v. Sheet Metal Workers Local 232, 586 F.2d 691, 694 (9th Cir. 1978).

91. De Libellis Famosis, 5 Co.Rep. 125a, 77 Eng.Rep. 250 (1605); 4 Bl. Comm. *150; Beauharnais v. Illinois, 343 U.S. 250, 72 S.Ct. 725 (1952).

92. Because of a doubt it was enacted in New York, in 1805, that the defendant in a prosecution for libel could defend on the ground of the truth of the statement made, provided it "was published with good motives and for justifiable ends." And because this was deemed a declaratory statute, a defendant who had previously been tried on a different theory was awarded a new trial. People v. Crosswell, 3 Johns.Cas. 337, 412, 413 (N.Y.1804).

93. E.g., West's Ann.Cal.Pen.Code § 251 (1970); Wis.St.1958, § 942.01 (1978). The law was changed in England to provide that truth should be a defense if it

was published for "the Public Benefit." 6 & 7 Vict. c. 96, § 6 (1843).

94. Under the criminal-libel statute the publication must be both false and scandalous and if there is no proof that it was false the defendant is entitled to a directed verdict. State v. Pierce, 140 Or. 1, 12 P.2d 320 (1932).

Truth is a complete defense to a charge of criminal libel in this state. State v. Kerekes, 225 Or. 352, 357 P.2d 413 (1960).

95. State v. Lambert, 188 La. 968, 974, 178 So. 508, 510 (1938). Accord, Commonwealth v. Snelling, 32 Mass. (15 Pick.) 337, 340 (1834).

96. Art. I, § 6, cl. 1.

This is a bar to a criminal charge that a Congressman received money from a private person for a speech made on the floor of Congress. United States v. Johnson, 337 F.2d 180 (4th Cir. 1964), aff'd 383 U.S. 169, 86 S.Ct. 749 (1966).

The Speech and Debate clause does not protect a member of Congress from prosecution for matters not involving legisla-

This privilege is absolute and complete and is not limited to conduct on the floor of the legislative hall, but extends to work of committees and sub-committees, either during session or recess of the main body.[97] Many of the states have similar provisions for members of their own legislatures, which seem to be mere declarations of the common law.[98]

Beyond the scope of the absolute privilege, circumstances may give rise to a strong social interest in having a person communicate what is in his mind without fear that some inadvertent mistake of fact will subject him to criminal prosecution or civil suit. Hence there is an area of qualified or conditional privilege.[99] It is socially desirable, for instance, that a prospective employer should be able to learn important facts about one who seeks to enter his employ, and a communication to him on this subject sent to him in confidence in response to his inquiry is protected by a qualified privilege.[1] This gives full protection to such a statement if it is made in good faith even if it is defamatory and inaccurate. Similarly, a confidential communication by a father to the custodian of his minor daughter, asking that the daughter not be allowed to visit a certain aunt, on the ground stated that the aunt had been guilty of adultery, was qualifiedly privileged and not libel, since he honestly believed the statement to be true though in fact it was not.[2] But a qualified privilege affords no protection to one who sends a falsely defamatory letter with knowledge of its falsity.[3]

There are indications that the word "defamation," as used in the common-law definition of libel, and as the word is defined at common law, is both vague and over-broad and hence fails to meet the constitutional requirement of fair notice of what the law demands. Although not essential to the decision, the Supreme Court made it a point to say that "since the English common law of criminal libel is inconsistent with the constitutional provisions, and since no Kentucky case has redefined the crime in understandable terms, and since the law must be made on a case by case basis, the elements of the crime are so indefinite and uncertain that it should not be enforced as a penal offense in Kentucky." [4] And a conviction of criminal libel in Alaska was reversed on the ground that the statute was unconstitutional.[5]

---

tive acts or motives. United States v. Brewster, 408 U.S. 501, 92 S.Ct. 2531 (1972) but precludes the introduction of evidence of a legislative act in proof of a criminal charge. United States v. Helstoski, 442 U.S. 477, 99 S.Ct. 2432 (1979).

97. Restatement, Second, Torts § 590, comment a (1977).

98. Id. at comment c.

99. "Privileged communications are either absolutely privileged or qualifiedly privileged." State v. Lambert, 188 La. 968, 975, 178 So. 508, 510 (1938). The Institute uses the phrase "conditional privileges." Restatement, Second, Torts c. 25, Topic 3 (1977).

1. See Restatement, Second, Torts § 595 and comment i (1977).

2. State v. Lambert, 188 La. 968, 178 So. 508 (1938).

3. And a publication by newspaper which would otherwise be protected by a qualified privilege will lose its protection if published with knowledge of its falsity or without reasonable grounds to believe in its truth. State v. Greenville Publishing Co., 179 N.C. 720, 102 S.E. 318 (1920). "Conditional privilege" does not protect one "knowing the defamatory matter to be false, or acting in reckless disregard as to its truth or falsity." Wright v. Haas, 586 P.2d 1093, 1097 (Okl.1978).

4. Ashton v. Kentucky, 384 U.S. 195, 86 S.Ct. 1407 (1966).

5. Gottschalk v. State, 575 P.2d 289 (Alaska 1978).

6. Omitted.

7. Omitted.

Most of the libel cases in modern times have been tort cases and there is substantial support for the view that this is an area properly left to control by civil sanctions. It is not included in the Model Penal Code.

H. CARRYING WEAPONS

Because of its tendency to stir up breaches of the peace, "terrifying the good people of the land" by *"riding or going armed* with dangerous or unusual weapons" was a common-law misdemeanor.[8] The statute of Northampton[9] provided a penalty for those who went armed to terrify the king's subjects but this was held to be merely declaratory of the common law.[10] The ancient law is somewhat obscure at the present time. Apparently the wearing of a sword in the customary manner by a person "of quality" was not deemed to be alarming, for this was not an offense, but the position of one of lower degree was less fortunate. This ancient misdemeanor has been held to be a common-law offense in this country,[11] but this is of little practical importance today because many states do not punish any uncodified common-law crime and most of them have statutory provisions on the subject of sufficient completeness to eliminate any unmentioned offense under the rule of inclusion and exclusion.

Unlike the theory of the ancient law, which regarded the display of arms in a manner calculated to cause alarm as the harm to be prevented, the modern basic statute on this subject has been directed against the carrying of *concealed* weapons. This offered an excellent opportunity to demonstrate the old saying that "a little learning is a dangerous thing," which is peculiarly applicable throughout the whole of the law. A few years ago a law student, after a careful study of the pertinent sections of the code, found that the statutes of his state did not forbid the carrying of a firearm unless the weapon was concealed. To demonstrate his learning he strapped on a pistol and started down the street with the weapon in an open holster for all to see. Before reaching the end of the first block he was arrested and taken to jail. When brought before the judge of the police court he proudly began to display his legal learning only to discover that he had been arrested for violating a *city ordinance* which prohibited the unlicensed carrying of any pistol, concealed or otherwise.

Statutes and ordinances on this subject vary so widely as to defy much in the nature of generalization. Probably the unauthorized carrying of a con-

8. 4 Bl.Comm. *149.

9. 2 Edw. III, c. 3 (1328).

10. "The Chief Justice said, that the meaning of 2 Edw. III c. 3, was to punish people who go armed to terrify the King's subjects. It is likewise a great offence at the *common law,* as if the King were not able or willing to protect his subjects; and therefore this act is but an affirmance of that law; . . .." Knight's Case, 3 Mod. 117, 118, 87 Eng. Rep. 75, 76 (1686).

11. State v. Huntley, 25 N.C. 418 (1843). And see Strickland v. State, 137 Ga. 1, 2, 72 S.E. 260, 261 (1911). This case gives an exhaustive study of the En-

glish and early American statutes. The Tennessee Court held that if the statute of 2 Edw. III, c. 3 was brought over by our ancestors as a part of our common law it was abrogated by the constitution of that state. Simpson v. State, 13 Tenn. 356 (1833). "An affray may be committed by 'going armed with unusual and dangerous weapons, to the terror of the people.'" State v. Griffin, 125 N.C. 692, 693, 34 S.E. 513 (1899). But while the ancient statute used the phrase "affray of the peace" the word "affray" as the name of an offense has been limited generally to a type of combat.

cealed weapon is punishable anywhere in the country, and some of the provisions do not go beyond this.[12] Some have a special clause with reference to carrying a pistol in a vehicle, concealed or otherwise;[13] some prohibit either the carrying of a concealed weapon or displaying or flourishing a deadly weapon in a threatening manner;[14] some are directed against either carrying a concealed weapon or going armed with a weapon with intent to use it unlawfully against any person;[15] some prohibit the act of going armed whether the weapon is concealed or not;[16] while others are directed against the very possession itself, such as the unlicensed possession of "any pistol, revolver or other firearm of a size which may be concealed upon the person," [17] or the possession or control of a machine gun by anyone "except law enforcement officers." [18] Differences are found also in regard to exceptions. Some of the statutes have provided an exception when the weapon is reasonably believed to be necessary in self-defense,[19] whereas others have not,[20] some have authorized the carrying of a weapon on one's own premises,[21] while others have not.[22] The Federal Firearms Act prohibits, among other things, the unlicensed transportation or shipment of any firearm or ammunition in interstate or foreign commerce, or the receipt of such unlicensed shipment.[23]

The Second Amendment reads: "A well-regulated militia, being necessary to the security of a free State, the right of the people to keep and bear arms, shall not be infringed." This, however, does not grant the right to bear arms; it means no more than that the right shall not be infringed by Con-

12. "In this connection it may be said that it is lawful to carry an unconcealed weapon for a lawful purpose." Eads v. State, 17 Wyo. 490, 505, 101 P. 946, 951 (1909).

13. § 724.4 provides:

A person who goes armed with a dangerous weapon concealed on or about his or her person, or who, within the limits of any city goes armed with a pistol or revolver, or any loaded firearm of any kind, whether concealed or not, or who knowingly carries or transports in a vehicle a pistol or revolver, commits an aggravated misdemeanor . . . Iowa Code Ann. § 724.4 (1978).

Under the Hawaii statute proscribing carrying concealed upon the person or "within any vehicle" it is not necessary that the weapon be concealed within the vehicle. The word "concealed" does not modify that clause. State v. Ogata, 58 Hawaii 514, 572 P.2d 1222 (1977).

14. People v. Boa, 143 Ill.App. 356 (1908).

15. State v. Lassley, 218 Kan. 752, 545 P.2d 379 (1976).

16. Kendall v. State, 118 Tenn. 156, 101 S.W. 189 (1906).

17. People v. Evergood, 74 N.Y.S.2d 12 (1947).

18. 18 U.S.C.A. § 922(b) provides:

It shall be unlawful for any licensed importer, licensed manufacturer, licensed dealer, or licensed collector to sell or deliver—

(4) to any person any destructive device, machinegun (as defined in section 5845 of the Internal Revenue Code of 1954), short-barreled shotgun, or short-barreled rifle, except as specifically authorized by the Secretary consistent with public safety and necessity.

19. Lewis v. State, 2 Tex.App. 26 (1877); State v. Workman, 35 W.Va. 367, 14 S.E. 9 (1891).

The use of a concealed firearm in defense of self or another in emergency situations is not punishable under a law forbidding a felon from possessing a firearm capable of being concealed. People v. King, 22 Cal.3d 12, 148 Cal.Rptr. 409, 582 P.2d 1000 (1978).

20. Heaton v. State, 130 Tenn. 163, 169 S.W. 750 (1914).

21. State v. Workman, 35 W.Va. 367, 14 S.E. 9 (1891).

22. Heaton v. State, 130 Tenn. 163, 169 S.W. 750 (1914); Pierce v. State, 42 Okl.Cr. 272, 275 P. 393 (1929). See Annotation, 73 A.L.R. 839 (1931).

23. 18 U.S.C.A. § 922 (1976).

gress and does not prevent regulation by the states.[24] Even as a limitation upon the power of Congress, the last half of the Amendment is not to be read out of context. The Supreme Court held, for instance, that a shotgun having a barrel less than 18 inches long has no reasonable relation to the preservation of a well-regulated militia and is not within the meaning of that provision.[25] Many of the state constitutions have clauses patterned more or less after the Second Amendment but for the most part these have been interpreted to permit the regulations mentioned above.[26]

I. VAGRANCY [27]

Vagrancy is a status resulting from misconduct and in the form of a socially harmful condition or mode of life which has been defined and made punishable by law. Until recently it was a misdemeanor, or group of misdemeanors, in most states.

In the early days in England the ordinary individual seldom, if ever, left his own community. For an adult to die in the same house in which he had been born was commonplace. If travel became necessary the traveler expected to be asked questions which he was ready and willing to answer. Hence the furtive stranger, who by idleness and unwillingness to offer any good reason for his presence, was quite reasonably suspected of being there for some improper reason. It is true such a person was usually obnoxious for some additional reason such as being a professional beggar, swindler or gambler, but the earliest use of the term "vagrant" or "vagabond" to indicate one whose mode of life was offensive to the community seems to have reference to one best described as a "tramp." [28]

He did not long remain the only vagrant, however. In those early days the adjective "worthless" was applied literally to mean without worldly goods. For one having adequate means for his support to idle away his time without engaging in any gainful activity was understandable, although it did not meet with wholehearted approval;[29] but such a mode of life by a "worth-

---

24. United States v. Cruikshank, 92 U.S. 542 (1875); Galvan v. Superior Court, 70 Cal.2d 851, 76 Cal.Rptr. 642, 452 P.2d 930 (1969).

25. United States v. Miller, 307 U.S. 174, 59 S.Ct. 816 (1938).

26. Junction City v. Lee, 216 Kan. 495, 532 P.2d 1292 (1975); State v. Buzzard, 4 Ark. 18 (1842); Strickland v. State, 137 Ga. 1, 72 S.E. 260 (1911); Pierce v. State, 42 Okl.Cr. 272, 275 P. 393 (1929). The State Constitution declared that, "The right of the people to keep and bear arms shall not be infringed," with a proviso that this should not prevent statutes against the carrying of concealed weapons. Under this provision a statute requiring a permit to carry a weapon openly was held invalid. State v. Kerner, 181 N.C. 574, 107 S.E. 222 (1921).

27. See Perkins, The Vagrancy Concept, 9 Hastings L.J. 237 (1958). With express permission the author has drawn freely upon the material used there.

See also Note, 59 Yale L.J. 1351 (1950); Foote, Vagrancy-type Law and its Administration, 104 U. of Pa.L.Rev. 603 (1956); Dubin and Robinson, The Vagrancy Concept Reconsidered, 37 N.Y.U.L. Rev. 102 (1962); Sherry, Vagrants, Rogues and Vagabonds—Old Concepts in Need of Revision, 48 Calif.L.Rev. 557 (1960).

28. "[T]he word vagrant in England . . . . is roughly equivalent to tramp . . . ." Lisle, Vagrancy Law; Its Faults and Their Remedies, 5 J.Crim.L. & C. 498 (1914). "A 'vagrant' is defined in Century Dictionary as 'One who strolls from place to place, one who has no settled habitation; an idle wanderer; an incorrigible rogue; a vagabond.'

"We know of no definition of a vagrant seriously at variance from those quoted." Ex parte Oates, 91 Tex.Cr. 79, 238 S.W. 930, 931 (1921).

29. "Idleness in any person whatsoever is also a high offence against the pub-

less person" was quite a different matter. His ability to get along without any "visible means of support" gave rise to the logical conclusion that he had sources of income which needed to be kept "invisible."

The earliest reference available to this category of vagrancy seems to be in 1349, when the Statute of Labourous [30] provided for the imprisonment of any able-bodied male, under sixty, without means of support, who refused to work. This was not, however, a criminal statute. It was comparable to a statute requiring a bond to keep the peace by one who has threatened harm to person or property.[31] The Statute authorized the "vagrant" to be taken up and imprisoned, unless he gave assurance that he would work, by posting a bond to that effect.[32] The primary purpose of the Statute was to require one without means to work for a living rather than to gain subsistence by begging, but another possibility may not have been overlooked. If such a one had difficulty in obtaining all he wanted by begging he might be tempted to try methods even more antisocial in nature,[33] hence the enforcement of this Statute may have had some tendency to prevent crime.

It was said by the Iowa court early in the present century: "Vagrancy is not punishable under the statute, which provides only for security against the commission of an offense." [34] This, however, represents practically the last stronghold of the ancient theory of vagrancy, because even then the statutes of most other states provided for fine or imprisonment or both.[35]

lic economy," said Blackstone (4 Bl. Comm. *169), but he was inadvertently picturing the law of an earlier day because it had been established before the commentaries were written that idleness *per se* was not a common-law offense. The Queen v. Branworth, 6 Mod. 240, 87 Eng.Rep. 989 (1704). In fact, Blackstone himself, in the rest of the paragraph following the sentence quoted above, shows that something more than idleness alone was needed for punishment.

"As a result of the historical conditions . . . the English law lost sight of the criminality of those who remained in their own parish, able to work but refusing to do so, and living on the county." Lisle, Vagrancy Law, Its Faults and Their Remedy, 5 J.Crim.L. & C. 498, 499–500 (1914).

30. 23 Edw. III (1349).

31. E.g., West's Ann.Cal.Pen.Code §§ 701–706 (1970); 22 Okl.Stat.Ann. 41–47 (1969); Ritchey v. Davis, 11 Iowa 124 (1860); Herz v. Hamilton, 198 Iowa 154, 197 N.W. 53 (1924).

32. 23 Edw. III (1349).

33. Daniel v. State, 110 Ga. 915, 36 S.E. 293 (1900).

34. State v. Dailey, 127 Iowa 652, 103 N.W. 1008 (1905).

"If it appear by the confession of such person, or by competent testimony that the person arrested is a vagrant, the magistrate may require an undertaking with sufficient surety, for good behaviour for the term of one year thereafter." I.C.A. (Iowa) (1950) § 746.8, now repealed. The bond for good behavior was sometimes authorized in lieu of conviction, in the discretion of the magistrate. E.g., Va.Code 1950, § 63–339, now repealed.

In discussing the South Carolina statute of an earlier day, it was pointed out that one convicted of vagrancy was required to give security for good behavior for twelve months and on failure thereof to be committed. State v. Maxey, 1 McMul. 501 (S.C.1837).

35. See the statutes of other jurisdictions cited infra. It is surprising that the ancient theory of vagrancy had any recognition in this country, because early English statutes had provided for the punishment of vagrancy as an offense. For example: An impotent beggar who wandered abroad and engaged in begging outside his "precinct" was to be whipped or placed in the stocks for three days and nights on bread and water. Impotent Poor Act, 22 Hen. 8, c. 12 (1530). Repealed by 14 Eliz. 1, c. 5 (1572). A more severe penalty was provided by the Vagabond Act, 14 Eliz. 1, c. 5 (1572). Repealed, 39 Eliz. 1, c. 4 (1597). And what is perhaps the best known of all the Vagabond Acts divided vagrants into three classes with different degrees of punish-

Insofar as the legal theory is concerned, the notion that vagrancy laws are not punitive in nature, is only an echo from an ancient position that no longer exists.

One of the familiar concepts of the early law was that of the "common vagrant," indicating a mode of life. Following this lead vagrancy statutes frequently provided punishment of such as a "common drunkard," [36] "common prostitute," [37] "common gambler," [38] or "professional fortune teller." [39] Other vagrancy statutes applied to "persons who go about begging," [40] "idle and disorderly persons," [41] "any person having no apparent means of support [who neglects] to apply himself to some honest calling," [42] or "all able-bodied persons without visible means of support who do not seek employment." [43] It should be mentioned that some vagrancy statutes were held to be unconstitutional because, as drawn, they were either (1) void for vagueness,[44] or (2) overbroad—covering both what may be proscribed and what may not.[45]

The gist of vagrancy is the condition or status [46] of being a vagrant, and not some specific act or omission.[47] This has sometimes led to the doubt as to whether it may properly be made a crime.[48] This doubt was removed by

ment. 17 Geo. 2, c. 5 (1744). Since this act, at least, there seems to have been no basis for considering vagrancy not to have been an offense in England.

36. Tatum v. State, 32 Ala.App. 128, 22 So.2d 350 (1945); Pollon v. State, 218 Wis. 466, 261 N.W. 224 (1935).

37. E.g., Miss.Code 1972, § 97–35–37.

The Massachusetts statute includes "common night walkers, both male and female." M.G.L.A. c. 272 § 53 (1973).

38. E.g., Miss.Code 1972, § 97–35–37.

"Professional gambler." Wis.St.1958, § 947.02 (1978). "Habitual gamesters." I.C.A. (Iowa) § 746.1 (1950) now repealed.

39. E.g., Wis.St.1958, § 947.02 (1978).

"All companies of gypsies, who, in whole or in part, maintain themselves by telling fortunes." Vernon's Ann.Tex. P.C. art. 607 now repealed.

40. F.S.A. (Fla.) § 856.02 now repealed.

41. Ibid.

42. Fonte v. State, 213 Tenn. 204, 373 S.W.2d 445 (1963).

43. E.g., La.Rev.Stats. § 14:107 (1974).

44. Palmer v. City of Euclid, Ohio, 402 U.S. 544, 91 S.Ct. 1563 (1971).

45. People v. Belcastro, 356 Ill. 144, 190 N.E. 301 (1934).

46. People v. Babb, 103 Cal.App.2d 326, 229 P.2d 843 (1951); People v. Banwer, 22 N.Y.S.2d 566, 569 (1940);

Titus v. State, 97 Tex.Cr. 444, 261 S.W. 1029 (1924); Cox v. State, 84 Tex.Cr. 49, 57, 205 S.W. 131, 134–5 (1918).

47. "Because vagrancy is a crime of being rather than of acting. . . ." Lacey, Vagrancy and Other Crimes of Personal Condition, 66 Harv.L.Rev. 1203, 1215 (1953). "The offence is being a vagrant." People v. Gray, 4 Park.Cr. 616, 617 (1860). "The offence of misconduct which is thus made punishable consists in being a person of the character and behavior described." Commonwealth v. Parker, 86 Mass. 313, 314 (1862). "The statute punishes being a certain kind of person, not doing a certain overt act." Commonwealth v. O'Brien, 179 Mass. 533, 534, 61 N.E. 213, 214 (1901). "The offence of which he is now accused consists in his having a character attached to him . . . namely the character of a common drunkard." State v. Flynn, 16 R.I. 10, 11, 11 A. 170, 171 (1887). People v. Allington, 103 Cal.App.2d 911, 919, 229 P.2d 495, 500 (1951).

"The crime 'consists not in proscribed action or inaction, but in the accused's having a certain personal condition or being a person of a specified character.' " State v. Perry, 249 Or. 76, 436 P.2d 252, 253–54 (1968).

48. People v. Cook, appellate department of the Superior Court of the County of Los Angeles in an unpublished opinion. Cited in People v. Babb, 103 Cal. App.2d 326, 328, 229 P.2d 843, 845 n. 1 (1951).

the Supreme Court. In referring to "the imposition of punishment on a status," it said: "Any thought that due process puts beyond the reach of the criminal law all individual associational relationships, unless accompanied by the commission of specific acts of criminality, is dispelled by familiar concepts of the law of conspiracy and complicity." [49] Conspiracy is constituted by an agreement, express or implied, but the conspiracy itself is not the agreement but the resulting unlawful combination which may endure for days, months or even years.[50]

The requirement of culpability will not permit punishment for a status which has come about without fault,[51] but this is not the usual situation of a vagrant. He has culpably made this condition his "habit of life." [52] And if the element of culpability is found, it is entirely proper to punish one who has the status of being (1) drunk in a public place,[53] (2) a member of a conspiracy, (3) the possessor of contraband,[54] (4) an alien crewman who unlawfully remains in the country after having entered under a conditional landing permit which has expired,[55] or (5) the parent of a child he is unlawfully failing to support.[56] Not all of these are vagrants, particularly the conspirator, but the point is that, assuming a statute properly drawn, and the element of culpability, there is no legal objection to the punishment of one who has a socially objectionable status.

It may be, however, that it would be more useful to substitute for most of the vagrancy laws statutes proscribing specified types of undesirable acts or omissions. This is the plan of the Model Penal Code and seems to be the present trend. But both the Model Penal Code and the new penal codes provide for the punishment of a parent who is unlawfully neglecting his legal duty to support a child.[57] This is obviously the imposition of punishment on a status, and has frequently been included among the vagrancy statutes.

49. Scales v. United States, 367 U.S. 203, 224, 225, 81 S.Ct. 1469, 1484 (1961).

50. United States v. Kissel, 218 U.S. 601, 608, 31 S.Ct. 124 (1910).

51. Conviction was improper if **D** was unaware of the intoxicating nature of the liquor or drug and did not voluntarily go into a public place after being aware of his condition. State v. Brown, 38 Kan. 390, 16 P. 259 (1888).

See also Robinson v. California, 370 U.S. 660, 82 S.Ct. 1417 (1962) holding unconstitutional a California statute making it a crime for a person to "be addicted to the use of narcotics. . . ."

52. Commonwealth v. O'Brien, 179 Mass. 533, 534, 61 N.E. 213, 214 (1901). The offense "not being a particular act, but a continued series of acts or habit of life . . . ." Stratton v. Commonwealth, 51 Mass. 217, 221 (1845).

53. The claim that a chronic alcoholic could not validly be convicted of public drunkenness was rejected by the Supreme Court. Powell v. Texas, 392 U.S. 514, 88 S.Ct. 2145 (1968). See infra Chapter 8, section 3, D.

54. United States v. Jewell, 532 F.2d 697 (9th Cir. 1976).

55. United States v. Cores, 356 U.S. 405, 78 S.Ct. 875 (1958).

56. Under the statute, a man who abandons his wife or children without just cause, leaving them without support or in danger of becoming a public charge, is to be punished as a vagrant. It was held that the failure of defendant to support his child without just cause was punishable. The fact that he has been prosecuted and punished for this offense will not bar a subsequent prosecution if he continues to leave the child without support. McRae v. State, 104 Miss. 861, 61 So. 977 (1913).

57. Model Penal Code, Section 230.5. Persistent Non-Support. It is doubtful that the phrase "persistently fails to provide support" will have much effect on the actual administration of the law, but it emphasizes the fact that this is a crime of status.

Section 250.5. Public Drunkenness; Drug Incapacitation.

SECTION 3.   OFFENSES AFFECTING SOVEREIGNTY OR THE ADMINISTRATION OF GOVERNMENTAL FUNCTIONS

Probably the original appearance of social interests was in this order: first, that of defending the group against harm threatened from without [war]; and second, defending the social organization as such against harm threatened from within.   The primitive form of the second social interest would provide a penalty for antisocial conduct in the form of treason.   As civilization developed, the socially organized group gradually expanded from the tribe or clan to the kingdom; and with the growth of government, one governmental function after another made its appearance.   Together with this growth there was a constant expansion of this second social interest, which enlarged to include the protection of each governmental function against wilful interference.   For example, as the system of courts and trials developed, there grew up the social interest in having only the truth told on the witness stand; as complicated governmental affairs required great numbers of public officials, there came a recognition of the social interest in having each officer act according to his best judgment, without having his official action influenced by compensation coming from some private source; and—to divert attention suddenly to a far side of the field—as the government undertook to administer the estates of bankrupt debtors, there appeared a social interest in having all the bankrupt's non-exempt property distributed among his creditors without wilful concealment on his part or fraudulent appropriation by others.

The common law tended in the direction of providing a punishment for every wilful interference with a recognized governmental function.   Statutory enlargements of this field are bewildering, and frequently include reckless interferences as well as those that are wilful.   In fact it is customary for each statute creating new governmental functions, or enlarging old ones, to include one or more penal sections.   The limitations of the present undertaking permit consideration of only a few of the well-recognized offenses in this field.

A.   TREASON

The frequent reference to *high* treason is a carry-over from an ancient division of the offense that has long since disappeared.   In the feudal stage of history the relation of lord to vassal was quite similar to the relation of king to subject.   The relation of husband to wife came to be regarded in the same category, as also did the relation of master to servant, and that of prelate to clergyman.   And just as it was *high* treason to kill the king, so a malicious homicide was *petit* treason if it involved a killing of (originally, lord by vassal,[1] and later) husband by wife, master or mistress by servant, or

---

Section 250.6.   Loitering or Prowling. This section was supposed to substitute a specific act for a status, but loitering (remaining) "in a place, at a time, or in a manner not usual for law-abiding individuals under circumstances that warrant alarm" seems to describe a condition or status rather than a specific act.

Iowa Criminal Code § 726.5.   Nonsupport.   "A person, who being able to do so, fails or refuses to provide for his or her child or ward, under the age of eighteen years commits nonsupport;" unless the child has left home without consent. "Nonsupport is a class D felony."

1.   1 Pollock & Maitland, History of English Law 300 (2d ed. 1899); 2 Id. at 504.

prelate by clergyman.[2] When the special brutality provided by the common law for the punishment of petit treason disappeared, this crime became merged with murder and only one crime of treason remained.[3]

In the earliest days to which references are obtainable it is found that the man who aided the enemies of his own tribe was executed. Probably the ancient procedure took the form of a religious rite rather than a criminal punishment,[4] but it is clearly the seed from which the crime of treason grew. High treason, in the words of Blackstone, is the term applied "when disloyalty so rears its crest as to attack even majesty itself." [5] In the ancient law it consisted of killing the king, promoting revolt in the kingdom or in the armed forces, or counterfeiting the great seal.[6] A tendency greatly to enlarge the scope of the offense by "construction" led to such uncertainty that an act of Parliament was required to limit and define it. This was the Statute of Treasons, enacted in 1350,[7] which specified exactly what should constitute high treason including, among certain other wrongs, a manifested [8] intent to kill the king, queen or prince, levying war against the king or adhering to his enemies.[9]

"No crime is greater than treason," [10] which threatens the very existence of the nation, and is the one offense whose definition is found in the Constitution itself.[11] Because of this fact "congress can neither extend nor restrict the crime; its power over the subject is limited to prescribing the punishment," [12] and hence as a federal offense no other definition is to be considered.

"Treason against the United States, shall consist only in levying war against them, or in adhering to their enemies, giving them aid and comfort."

1. BREACH OF ALLEGIANCE

Since treason was a common-law offense,[13] however, this constitutional definition is to be read in the light of the common law which regarded a

2. 1 Hale P.C. *377; 4 Bl.Comm. *203; State v. Bilansky, 3 Minn. 246, 3 Gil. 169, 174 (1859).

3. "The punishment of petit treason in a man is, to be drawn and hanged, and in a woman to be drawn and burned; . . ." 4 Bl.Comm. *204. The "drawing" consisted of laying the malefactor on the ground and tying him to "a horse which dragged him along the rough road to the gibbet." 2 Pollock & Maitland 500 (2d ed. 1899). As no such punishment was tolerated here the crime of petit treason was never recognized in this country. State v. Bilansky, supra. When the special penalty for petit treason disappeared this offense was merged with murder. 3 Stephen, History of the Criminal Law of England 35 (1883).

4. 2 Pollock & Maitland, History of English Law 503 (2d ed. 1899).

5. ". . . being equivalent to the *crimen laesae majestatis* of the Ro-

mans, as Glanvil denominates it also in our English law." 4 Bl.Comm. *75.

6. 1 Hale P.C. *76–7.

7. 25 Edw. III, c. 2.

8. The wording of the statute was: "When a man doth compass or imagine the death of our Lord the King, . . ." Blackstone comments: "But, as this compassing or imagining is an act of the mind, it cannot possibly fall under any judicial cognizance, unless it be demonstrated by some open or *overt* act." 4 Bl.Comm. *79.

9. 1 Hale P.C. *91.

10. Hanauer v. Doane, 79 U.S. 342, 347 (1870).

11. Art. III, § 3.

12. United States v. Greathouse, 4 Sawy. 457, 26 Fed.Cas. 18, No. 15,254 (1863).

13. 4 Bl.Comm. *74.

breach of allegiance as of the very essence of the crime.[14]   An American citizen owes allegiance to the United States wherever he may be[15] and this is true whether his citizenship was acquired by birth or naturalization.[16]   Furthermore, a resident alien owes a temporary allegiance to this government,[17] but a nonresident alien does not,[18] at least in the absence of unusual circumstances such as traveling under an American passport.[19]   In the absence of any such circumstance a nonresident alien does not commit treason by trading with the enemy.[20]   One of the recent treason cases involving the problem of allegiance is entitled to special attention.

K was a native-born citizen of the United States and also a national of Japan by reason of Japanese parentage and law.   While a minor, he took the oath of allegiance to the United States, went to Japan for a visit on an American passport, and was prevented from returning to this country by the outbreak of our war with Japan.   During the war he reached his majority in Japan, changed his registration from American to Japanese, showed sympathy with Japan and hostility to the United States, served as a civilian employee of a private corporation producing war materials for Japan, and brutally abused American prisoners of war who were forced to work there.   After Japan's surrender he registered as an American citizen, swore that he was an American citizen and had not done various acts amounting to expatriation, and returned here on an American passport.   His conviction of treason was affirmed on the ground that the evidence was sufficient to support the finding of the jury that he had not renounced or lost his American citizenship.[21]

2.   LEVYING WAR

A state of actual war may exist without any formal declaration thereof by either side; and this is true of both a civil war and a foreign war.[22]   Furthermore, war may be levied without a battle, although to support such a

---

14.   Ibid.   ". . . the ancient distinction between those who do and those who do not owe allegiance."

15.   Kawakita v. United States, 343 U.S. 717, 72 S.Ct. 950 (1952); Iva Ikuko Toguri D'Aquino v. United States, 192 F.2d 338, 359 (9th Cir. 1951).

16.   United States v. Fricke, 259 F. 673 (D.C.N.Y.1919).

17.   Carlisle v. United States, 83 U.S. 147 (1872).

18.   Young v. United States, 97 U.S. 39 (1877).

19.   An English case recognized such an exception.   A United States citizen of British descent who had spent most of his life within the "King's Dominions" applied for a British passport describing himself as a British subject by birth.   He was granted the passport and left the country.   Then during the war with Germany he broadcast propaganda on behalf of that country.   He was held guilty of treason against Great Britain and execut-

ed.   Joyce v. Director of Public Executions, 115 L.J. 146 (House of Lords, 1946).

"By the possession of that document he is enabled to obtain in a foreign country the protection extended to British subjects."   Id. at 151.

20.   Young v. United States, 97 U.S. 39 (1877).   The treason statute would not apply to a former American citizen who had actually become a naturalized citizen of the enemy country and was resident there.   Iva Ikuko Toguri D'Aquino v. United States, 192 F.2d 338 (9th Cir. 1951).

21.   Kawakita v. United States, 343 U.S. 717, 72 S.Ct. 950 (1952).   The text is almost a quotation from the syllabus.

22.   Prize Cases, 67 U.S. 635 (1862).

As applied to the Vietnam War see Massachusetts v. Laird, 451 F.2d 26 (1st Cir. 1971); Orlando v. Laird, 443 F.2d 1039 (2d Cir. 1971).

charge the intent to strike must be plainly proved.[23]　Thus the occupation of a fortress, in order to take it from the dominion of the government to which allegiance is owed, is treason even if no resistance is encountered in taking or holding the stronghold.[24]　As said in one case:[25]

"When a body, large or small, of armed men is mustered in military array for a treasonable purpose, every step which any one of them takes, by marching or otherwise, in part execution of this purpose, is an overt act of treason in levying war."

"To conspire to levy war," however, "and actually to levy war, are distinct offenses."[26]　An actual assemblage of persons for the purpose of effecting a treasonable design by force is essential to the levying of war, and a mere enlistment of men to serve against the government not followed by an actual muster of such persons, is not punishable as treason.[27]　Needless to add, if war actually is levied all parties to the conspiracy are traitors, however minute the part they play, or however remote from the scene of action they may be.[28]

The sudden outbreak of a mob, or an assemblage formed to prevent the execution of a law in one particular instance only, is not a levying of war such as to constitute treason, but such an effort to prevent the execution of any law of the United States in all cases, and thus completely to defeat an act of Congress, is treason.[29]　"The true criterion is the intention with which the people assembled.　When the intention is universal or general, as to affect some object of a general public nature, it will be treason, and cannot be considered, construed or reduced to a riot.　On the other hand, the commission of any member of felonies, riots, or misdemeanors cannot alter their nature so as to make them amount to treason," even if peace officers should be insulted or resisted.[30]

---

23. United States v. Burr, 25 Fed.Cas. 201, No. 14,694a (1807).

24. United States v. Greiner, 26 Fed. Cas. 36, No. 15,262 (1861).

25. Ibid.

26. Ex parte Bollman, 8 U.S. 75, 126 (1807).

27. Ibid.; United States v. Burr, 25 Fed.Cas. 2, No. 14,692a (1807); Charge to the Grand Jury, 30 Fed.Cas. 1015, No. 18,263 (1851).

28. Ex parte Bollman, 8 U.S. 75 (1807).

29. Charge to the Grand Jury, 30 Fed. Cas. 1015, No. 18,263 (1851). A conspiracy to use force to resist the execution of a federal law in particular instances only, for a personal or private as distinguished from a public or national purpose, is not treason, however great the violence or large the numbers.　United States v. Hanway, 2 Wall.Jr. 139, 26 Fed.Cas. 105, No. 15,299 (1851); United States v. Hoxie, 1 Paine 265, 26 Fed.Cas. 397, No.

15,407 (1808).　Opposing by force of arms an act of Congress with a view of defeating its efficacy and thus defying the authority of the government is levying war against the United States. Fries' Case, 3 Dall. 515, 9 Fed.Cas. 826, No. 5,126 (1799).

Armed resistance to the draft is levying war against the United States. Druecker v. Salomon, 21 Wis. 621 (1867). "To go with a large party in arms, marshaled and arrayed, to the houses of officers of the excise, and there commit acts of violence and devastation, with the avowed object of suppressing such offices, and compelling the resignation of the officers, for the purpose of nullifying an act of Congress, is treason, under the constitution and laws of the United States."　United States v. Vigol, 2 Dall. 346, 28 Fed.Cas. 376, No. 16,621 (1795). Accord, United States v. Mitchell, 2 Dall. 348, 26 Fed.Cas. 1277, No. 15,788 (1795).

30. Fries' Case, Whart.St.Tr. 610, 9 Fed.Cas. 924, No. 5,127 (1800).

3. "ADHERING TO THEIR ENEMIES, GIVING THEM AID AND COMFORT"

The wording of the Constitution might suggest three different types of treason but the Supreme Court has held that only two are involved. One is levying war against the United States and the other "consists of two elements: adherence to the enemy; and rendering him aid and comfort." [31] Adherence to the enemy is the mental element of the crime—"the disloyal state of mind," [32] while giving aid and comfort is the physical element.

Although an unassembled enlistment of men to serve against their government is not treason when there is no war, an enlistment in the service of the enemy in wartime was held to be clearly an act of treason.[33] At the present time, however, "enlistment to serve against the United States" is covered by a separate section of the Code[34] with a milder penalty than for treason proper,[35] and this seems to cover either type of wrongful enlistment although it might be interpreted to apply only to that which had been held to be less than treason.

Everyone owing allegiance to the United States who, with disloyal intent, gives aid and comfort to its enemy is guilty of treason,[36] and an effort made for this purpose will satisfy this requirement without proof that actual benefit resulted.[37] Aid and comfort may be given in various ways, such as buying a vessel and fitting it for service in aid of the enemy,[38] delivering prisoners and deserters to the enemy,[39] or selling critical materials with knowledge of the fact that the purchaser buys them to use in the manufacture of gunpowder for the enemy,[40] or otherwise to aid him in his prosecution of the war. And the courts have given short shrift to the claim that such a sale was not intended to aid the enemy but only to make a profit.

"He voluntarily aids the treason. He cannot be permitted to stand on the nice metaphysical distinction that, although he knows that the purchaser

---

31. Cramer v. United States, 325 U.S. 1, 29, 65 S.Ct. 918, 932 (1945).

32. Id. at 30.

33. Respublica v. Roberts, 1 Dall. 38 (O. & T.Phila.1778). "Enlisting, or procuring any person to be enlisted, in the service of the enemy, is clearly an act of treason." Respublica v. M'Carty, 2 Dall. 86, 87 (Pa.1781).

34. "Whoever enlists or is engaged within the United States or in any place subject to the jurisdiction thereof, with intent to serve in armed hostility against the United States, shall be fined $100 or imprisoned not more than three years or both." 18 U.S.C.A. § 2390. Recruiting for service against the United States is punishable by a fine of not more than $1000 or imprisonment not more than five years or both. Id. at § 2389.

35. Id. § 2381. The punishment may be death.

36. United States v. Fricke, 259 F. 673 (D.C.N.Y.1919).

37. Treason may be committed by giving aid and comfort to the enemy although the effort made for this purpose does not render actual assistance. United States v. Greathouse, 4 Sawy. 457, 26 Fed.Cas. 18, No. 15,254 (1863). "So, sending money, arms, ammunition, or other necessities to rebels, will prima facie make a man a traitor, though they should be intercepted." 1 East P.C. 72 (1803).

38. "The purchase of a vessel, and fitting her up for service with arms and ammunition, and the employment of men to manage it, in pursuance of a design to commit hostilities on the high seas, in aid of an existing rebellion against the United States, are overt acts of treason." United States v. Greathouse, 4 Sawy. 457, 26 Fed.Cas. 18, No. 15,254 (1863).

39. United States v. Hodges, 2 Wheeler, C.C. 477, 26 Fed.Cas. 332, No. 15,374 (1815).

40. Carlisle v. United States, 83 U.S. 147 (1872).

buys the goods for the purpose of aiding the rebellion, he does not sell them for that purpose. The consequences of his acts are too serious and enormous to admit of such a plea. He must be taken to intend the consequences of his own voluntary act." [41]

It was also treason, in the form of aid and comfort to the enemy, when an American citizen of Japanese ancestry broadcast from Japan, during the war with that country, to members of the American armed forces in the Pacific area with intent to destroy their confidence and undermine their morale. [42]

4. INTENT TO BETRAY

An intent to betray has been said to be "essential to the crime of treason" [43] and this is no doubt true if due significance be given to the concept of intention, which includes not only the purpose for which an act is done, but also the known consequences of an intentional act. [44] Thus the sale of critical materials with knowledge of the fact that they are to be used to help the enemy wage war against the seller's government is an intent to betray, although the motive may be avarice, as mentioned above. On the other hand, momentarily joining rebels while ignorant of their design is not treason, [45] and it has been indicated that help given to an enemy saboteur would not be treason, if it was aid given by father to son as an individual and not of a nature to further his hostile design. [46]

5. COMPULSION

No amount of compulsion, even the fear of immediate death, will excuse the intentional killing of an innocent countryman, [47] although it may be sufficient for the exculpation of other treasonable acts, such as joining enemy forces, [48] delivering prisoners and deserters to the enemy, [49] or giving aid and comfort in some other manner. [50] It has been said that nothing less than a well-grounded fear for life will be recognized for this purpose [51] and that joining the enemy to avoid death must be with the intent to escape at the earliest opportunity, [52] followed by appropriate action. [53]

41. Hanauer v. Doane, 79 U.S. 342, 347 (1870); Carlisle v. United States, 83 U.S. 147, 150–1 (1872); Sprott v. United States, 87 U.S. 459, 463–4 (1874). See also Regina v. Sullivan, 11 Cox C.C. 44, 45 (1868).

42. Iva Ikuko Toguri D'Aquino v. United States, 192 F.2d 338 (9th Cir. 1951).

43. Id. at 366. A treasonable intent is necessary for treason. Rex v. Steane, [1947] 1 All E.R. 813 (C.A.1947).

44. "The word 'intent' is used throughout the Restatement of this Subject to denote that the actor desires to cause the consequences of his act, or that he believes that the consequences are substantially certain to result from it." Restatement, Second, Torts § 8A (1965).

45. 1 East P.C. 70 (1803).

46. See Haupt v. United States, 330 U.S. 631, 641, 67 S.Ct. 874, 878, 879 (1947). In this case the conviction was affirmed, however, because the aid given the son was obviously of a nature to help him promote his destructive program.

47. Axtell's Case, Kelyng 13, 84 Eng. Rep. 1060 (1660). "Such compulsion or fear, however, is no excuse for any other sort of treason than that of joining with rebels or enemies" or giving them aid and comfort. 1 East P.C. 71, 72 (1803).

48. 1 East P.C. 71 (1803). Respublica v. M'Carty, 2 Dall. 86, 87 (Pa.1781).

49. United States v. Hodges, 2 Wheeler, C.C. 477, 26 Fed.Cas. 332, No. 15,374 (1815).

50. 1 East P.C. 72 (1803); United States v. Greiner, 26 Fed.Cas. 36, No. 15,262 (1861).

51. See cases in notes 45 and 46.

52. Respublica v. M'Carty, 2 Dall. 86, 87 (Pa.1781).

53. See note 53 on page 504.

"We think that the citizen owing allegiance to the United States must manifest a determination to resist commands and orders until such time as he is faced with the alternative of immediate injury or death. Were any other rule to be applied, traitors in the enemy country would by that fact alone be shielded from any requirement of resistance. The person claiming the defense of coercion and duress must be a person whose resistance has brought him to the last ditch." [54]

An English case held that if a British subject, trapped in Germany by the outbreak of war, broadcast for the enemy to save his wife and children from a concentration camp, he was not guilty.[55] It may well be that fear of having wife and children sent to such a camp was not less than fear of immediate loss of his own life.

6. THE "TWO–WITNESS RULE"

By express provision of the Constitution: "No person shall be convicted of treason unless on the testimony of two witnesses to the same overt act, or on confession in open court." [56] An "overt act" in the dictionary sense, is "a physical act, as distinguished from an act of the mind" [57] (a mere thought). The term is employed at different points in the law, and since the meaning is not always the same it must be considered in reference to each particular application.[58] Blackstone, recalling that a dream of assassinating Dionysius cost the subject his life on the theory that the dream proved he had contemplated such a deed while awake, says that for common-law treason "there must appear an open or *overt* act of a more full and explicit nature, to convict the traitor upon." [59] And with reference to the use of these words in the treason clause of the Constitution, the Supreme Court had this to say: "Overt acts are such acts as manifest a criminal intention and tend towards the accomplishment of the criminal object." [60] The very minimum function that an overt act must perform in a treason prosecution is that it show sufficient action by the accused, in its setting, to sustain a finding that the accused actually gave aid and comfort to the enemy." [61] The protection of the two-witness rule extends to all acts of the accused which are relied upon to draw incriminating inferences that treason was committed,[62] but one overt act properly proved and submitted will sustain a conviction if it is clear that the jury's finding of guilt was based upon that act.[63]

53. "It is incumbent, however, on the party setting up this defence to give satisfactory proof that the compulsion continued during all the time that he staid with the rebels . . . so that upon the whole he may fairly be presumed to have continued amongst them against his will, though not constantly under an actual force or fear of immediate death." 1 East P.C. 70 (1803).

54. Iva Ikuko Toguri D'Aquino v. United States, 192 F.2d 338, 359 (9th Cir. 1951).

55. Rex v. Steane, [1947] 1 All E.R. 813 (C.A.1947).

56. Art. IV, § 2, cl. 2.

57. Ballentine, Law Dictionary (1948).

58. See Cramer v. United States, 325 U.S. 1, 7, 65 S.Ct. 918, 921 (1945).

59. 4 Bl.Comm. *79.

60. Cramer v. United States, 325 U.S. 1, 7, 65 S.Ct. 918, 921 (1945). The Court was quoting Judge Learned Hand's quotation from Lord Reading.

61. Cramer v. United States, 325 U.S. 1, 34, 65 S.Ct. 918, 934 (1945); Iva Ikuko Toguri D'Aquino v. United States, 192 F.2d 338, 366 (9th Cir. 1951).

62. Cramer v. United States, 325 U.S. 1, 65 S.Ct. 918 (1945).

63. See Haupt v. United States, 330 U.S. 631, 641, note 1, 67 S.Ct. 874, 878, 879 (1947). Proof by the direct testimony of two witnesses that defendant gave

7. TREASON AGAINST A STATE

Many of the states have constitutional or statutory enactments for the punishment of treason, often copied closely from the national provision. Treason against the United States is not punishable by the state,[64] but what occurs within the boundaries of a particular state might be of such a nature as to constitute treason against it as well as against the federal government.[65] Treason against a state could be committed by open and armed resistance intended to frustrate completely some enactment of its legislature, or by a forcible attempt to overturn or usurp its government.[66]

In other words a given overt act might constitute (1) treason against the United States only, (2) treason against the United States and also against a particular state, or (3) treason only against a particular state. The first could be prosecuted only as a federal offense whereas either of the others could be prosecuted as a state offense during the "silence of Congress." It is within the power of Congress, however, to give to the federal courts exclusive jurisdiction over any conduct which constitutes treason against the United States, whether it does or does not constitute treason also against a state. This has been tested most thoroughly in cases of sedition and it is convenient to mention them here with reference to jurisdiction although that offense will receive separate attention. Thus it has been held that the Smith Act, 18 U.S.C.A. § 2385, which prohibits the knowing advocacy of the overthrow of the Government of the United States by force and violence supersedes the enforceability of a state sedition act which proscribes the same conduct,[67] and that in view of this Act of Congress advocacy of this nature cannot be prosecuted as a state offense even if it contemplates overthrow of the state government also and is charged only in that form in the indictment.[68] The courts took pains to emphasize, however, that they did not "wish to be understood as saying that there can never be any instance of any kind of sedition directed so exclusively against the State as to fall outside the sweep" of the Smith Act.[69]

shelter for a period of six days to an enemy agent who had entered the country for purposes of sabotage, helped him to buy an automobile and helped him to obtain employment in a plant manufacturing military equipment, all in aid of his known purpose of sabotage, was sufficient proof of overt acts to satisfy the constitutional requirements and authorize a conviction of treason. Haupt v. United States, 330 U.S. 631, 67 S.Ct. 874 (1947).

64. People v. Lynch, 11 Johns. 549 (N.Y.1814); Ex parte Quarrier, 2 W.Va. 569 (1866). "It being a crime against the United States, the indictment was dismissed as the offense was one against the United States, so that the State courts would not have jurisdiction of the crime." State v. Conti, 127 Misc. 244, 216 N.Y.S. 442 (1926).

65. The governor is authorized to call out the militia if necessary to suppress a mob in the state even if the mob may be committing treason against the United States. Druecker v. Salomon, 21 Wis. 621 (1867). Speaking on an analogous point the Court said: A "State may punish utterances endangering the foundations of organized government and threatening its overthrow by unlawful means. These imperil its own existence as a constitutional state." Gitlow v. New York, 268 U.S. 652, 666, 45 S.Ct. 625, 629, 630 (1925). But compare Pennsylvania v. Nelson, 350 U.S. 497, 76 S.Ct. 477 (1956).

66. See People v. Lynch, 11 Johns. 549, 553 (N.Y.1814).

67. Pennsylvania v. Nelson, 350 U.S. 497, 76 S.Ct. 477 (1956); Braden v. Commonwealth, 291 S.W.2d 843 (Ky.1956); Commonwealth v. Hood, 334 Mass. 76, 134 N.E.2d 12 (1956).

68. Commonwealth v. Gilbert, 334 Mass. 17, 134 N.E.2d 13 (1956).

69. Id. at 16. And see Braden at 844.

8. MISPRISION OF TREASON

**Misprision of treason is concealment and [or] nondisclosure of
the known treason of another.**

The federal statute [70] reads as follows:

"Whoever, owing allegiance to the United States and having knowledge
of the commission of any treason against them, *conceals and* does not, as
soon as may be, disclose and make known the same to the President or to
some judge of the United States, or to the governor or to some judge or
justice of a particular State, is guilty of misprision of treason and shall be
fined not more than $1,000 or imprisoned not more than seven years, or
both "

While this section seems not to have received judicial interpretation, the
similarly-worded section on misprision of felony [71] has been held to require
both concealment and failure to disclose.[72] "Under it some affirmative act
toward concealment of the felony is necessary. Mere silence after knowledge of the commission of the crime is not sufficient." [73]

Many of the state codes include misprision of treason which, whether expressly so provided or not, apply only to known treason against the state.
Some are worded similarly to the federal provision speaking in terms of concealment and nondisclosure.[74] Others refer only to concealment,[75] or only to
nondisclosure.[76]

Because cases in point are practically nonexistent, the leading case of
"misprision of treason" as a state offense (although it would not come under
the present definition) was a prosecution under the early Pennsylvania statute which included under this label anyone who should "maliciously and ad-
visedly endeavor to excite the people to resist the government of the commonwealth, or persuade them to return to a dependence upon the crown of
Great Britain; . . ." [77] It resulted in conviction.

9. RELATED OFFENSES

The federal statutes provide for a number of related offenses such as
inciting or assisting a rebellion or insurrection,[78] seditious conspiracy,[79] and
wilfully interfering with the operation of the armed forces in wartime.[80]
Best known of these is perhaps the so-called "Smith Act" which makes it a
crime knowingly or wilfully to advocate the violent overthrow or destruction

---

70. 18 U.S.C.A. § 2382 (1970). Emphasis added.

71. 18 U.S.C.A. § 4 (1969).

72. Neal v. United States, 102 F.2d
643 (8th Cir. 1939); Lancey v. United
States, 356 F.2d 407 (9th Cir. 1966); United States v. Johnson, 546 F.2d 1225 (5th
Cir. 1977).

73. United States v. Farrar, 38 F.2d
515, 517 (D.C.Mass.1930), aff'd 281 U.S.
624, 50 S.Ct. 425 (1930); Bratton v. United States, 73 F.2d 795, 798 (10th Cir.
1934).

74. E.g., N.R.S. (Nev.) § 196.030
(1957). "Conceals or withholds his

knowledge." Ill.Rev.Stats.1965, c. 38, §
30–2.

75. E.g., Mass.Code Ann. C. 264 § 3
(1968).

76. E.g., West's F.S.A. (Fla.) § 876.-
33.

77. Republica v. Weidle, 2 Dallas 88
(Pa.1781).

78. 18 U.S.C.A. § 2383 (1970).

79. Id. at § 2384.

80. Id. at § 2388. See also §§ 2389,
2390.

of the government of the United States, or of any government therein, or to organize any group for this purpose, or to become a member thereof with knowledge of its objective.[81] Those who would destroy the Constitution make the most exaggerated claims for protection under it but in the words of Mr. Justice Holmes: "The most stringent protection of free speech would not protect a man in falsely shouting fire in a theater and causing a panic." [82] There are also provisions for the punishment of espionage [83] and sabotage.[84] And while not directly in point it may be enlightening to add that Congress may constitutionally impose certain restrictions and deny certain benefits to any labor organization the officers of which fail to file the so-called "non-Communist" affidavits.[85]

There have been a multitude of state statutes in this general area, some of which have been too broad to be upheld. Thus a statute which provided for the punishment of "any person who displays a red flag . . . in any public place . . . as a sign, symbol or emblem of opposition to organized government . . ." was held to be unconstitutional because this might include "peaceful and orderly opposition to government by legal means and within constitutional limitations."[86] And a conviction of criminal syndicalism based upon advocacy of abolishing the "wage system," but without evidence that any violence or unlawful measure was advocated as a method of accomplishing that end, was reversed.[87] More carefully drawn enactments fared better. *Criminal anarchy* was defined by the New York statute as the doctrine that organized government should be overthrown by force and violence or other unlawful means, and the advocacy of such doctrine orally or in writing was made a felony. A conviction of this offense was af-

---

81. Id. at § 2385. A claim that this Act violates the First Amendment or other provisions of the Bill of Rights was rejected and a conviction affirmed. Dennis v. United States, 341 U.S. 494, 71 S.Ct. 857 (1951).

Advocacy of violent overthrow of the government is protected by the First Amendment if it does not urge that anything be done but only that it be believed. Yates v. United States, 354 U.S. 298, 77 S.Ct. 1064 (1957). But the "membership clause" of the Smith Act, interpreted to apply only to an "active" member of an organization and with knowledge of its intent to bring about the overthrow of the government as speedily as circumstances would permit, does not impute guilt to an individual merely on the basis of his associations in violation of the Fifth Amendment, nor infringe freedom of political expression and association in violation of the First Amendment. Scales v. United States, 367 U.S. 203, 81 S.Ct. 1469 (1961).

82. Schenck v. United States, 249 U.S. 47, 52, 39 S.Ct. 247, 249 (1919). And see United States v. Lebron, 222 F.2d 531 (2d Cir. 1955).

83. Espionage, or spying, has reference to the practice of "gathering, trans-mitting or losing" information respecting the national defense with intent or reason to believe that the information is to be used to the injury of the United States, or to the advantage of any foreign nation. 18 U.S.C.A. § 793.

84. Id. at c. 105. Sabotage has reference to the wilful destruction or injury of, or defective production of, war material or national-defense material, or harm to war premises or war utilities. Ibid.

85. American Communications Association v. Douds, 339 U.S. 382, 70 S.Ct. 674 (1950). In the words of Mr. Justice Jackson, concurring in part: "From information before its several Committees and from facts of general knowledge, Congress could rationally conclude that, behind its political party facade, the Communist Party is a conspiratorial and revolutionary junta, organized to reach ends and to use methods which are incompatible with our constitutional system." Id. at 424. And see United States v. Lebron, 222 F.2d 531 (2d Cir. 1955).

86. Stromberg v. California, 283 U.S. 359, 51 S.Ct. 532 (1931).

87. Fiske v. Kansas, 274 U.S. 380, 47 S.Ct. 655 (1927).

firmed.[88] In another case [89] the Supreme Court overruled a prior decision [90] and ruled unconstitutional an Ohio Criminal Syndicalism statute. The statute purported to punish mere advocacy and to proscribe assembly with others to advocate. The court held advocacy "of the use of force or of law violation except where such advocacy is directed to inciting or producing imminent lawless action and is likely to incite or produce such action" is protected.[91]

These decisions need to be examined in the light of the distinction between inciting to action as distinguished from teaching or advocating only what is to be believed. The latter is protected by the privilege of free speech.[92]

A. SEDITION

The word "sedition" has been misunderstood at times as illustrated by this faulty definition:

"The distinction between 'sedition' and 'treason' consists in this: that though the ultimate object of sedition is a violation of the public peace, or at least such a course of measures as evidently engenders it, yet it does not aim at direct and open violence against the laws or the subversion of the constitution." [93]

According to this suggestion the difference between the two lies in the objective but that is incorrect so far as the common law is concerned. While the objective of sedition may be less than is required for treason, it may be exactly the same and the difference between the offenses is that the former is committed by preliminary steps while some overt act directed towards execution is required for the latter.[94] Judge Stephen says that strictly speaking there is no such offense known to English law as "sedition," but that there are three misdemeanors of this nature. He defines seditious intention, in substance, as an intent to defame a member of the royal family or the government, or to incite the subjects to attempt to change the government "otherwise than by lawful means"—which of course might contemplate open rebellion although not so much would necessarily be involved. If such an intention is spoken orally it is (1) seditious speech, if it is communicated in written form it is the (2) publication of a seditious libel, and if two or more agree to promote such a plan it is (3) seditious conspiracy.[95] In other words, according to the common law of England, "sedition" (as a concept, if not the name of a specific offense) is a communication or an agreement which has as

---

88. Gitlow v. New York, 268 U.S. 652, 45 S.Ct. 625 (1925).

89. Brandenburg v. Ohio, 395 U.S. 444, 89 S.Ct. 1827 (1968).

90. Whitney v. California, 274 U.S. 357, 47 S.Ct. 641 (1927).

91. Brandenburg v. Ohio, 395 U.S. 444, 447, 89 S.Ct. 1827, 1829 (1969).

92. Yates v. United States, 354 U.S. 298, 77 S.Ct. 1064 (1957).

93. Black's Law Dictionary (4th Ed.), p. 1523, quoting Alison, Criminal Law.

94. "The only offense of this general character which is known to our law is attempts [sic] 'by word, deed or writing, to promote public disorder or to induce riot, rebellion or civil war, which acts are still considered seditions, and may by overt acts, be treason.' [Odgers on Libel and Slander, p. 419.]" State v. Shepherd, 177 Mo. 205, 222, 76 S.W. 79, 84 (1903).

95. Stephen, History of the Criminal Law of England 298-9 (1883). "It has been said very truly that there is no such offence as sedition itself, but it takes the form of seditious language either written or spoken, . . ." Regina v. Burns, 16 Cox C.C. 355 (1886).

its objective the stirring up of treason or certain lesser commotions, or the defamation of a member of the royal family or of the government.[96]

"During the administration of the elder Adams, a sedition law was enacted, making it an offense to libel the government, the Congress or the President of the United States, and four cases were prosecuted under it. But its constitutionality was always disputed by a large part of our citizens, and its impolicy was beyond question. It brought about the very conditions it was intended to repress, and was soon repealed." [97]

Except for that brief period, sedition in this country has always been thought of as involving something more than defamation. The present federal statutes on the subject are the ones on seditious conspiracy [98] and the so-called "Smith Act" [99] mentioned above, plus the statute on wartime sedition [1] which includes the circulation of false reports with intent to interfere with the success of our armed forces.

B. INSURRECTION, REVOLT AND MUTINY

An insurrection goes beyond sedition in that it is an actual and open arising against the government. A revolt goes beyond insurrection in aim, being an attempt actually to overthrow the government itself, whereas insurrection has as its objective some forcible change within the government. A large-scale revolt is called a rebellion and if it is successful it becomes a revolution.

Mutiny is organized resistance to authority within the armed forces.

Article 94 of the Uniform Code of Military Justice [2] couples mutiny with what it terms "sedition,"—using the latter word not in its common-law sense but with a defined meaning which covers both insurrection and revolt.

Article 94

(a) Any person subject to this code—(1) who with intent to usurp or override lawful military authority refuses, in concert with any other person or persons, to obey orders or otherwise do his duty or creates any violence or disturbance is guilty of mutiny;

(2) who with intent to cause the overthrow or destruction of lawful civil authority, creates in concert with any other person or persons revolt, violence, or other disturbance against such authority is guilty of sedition;

---

96. "For instance, in England, it was an offense, called sedition, to speak or write against the character and constitution of the government, or to seek to change it, by any means except those prescribed." State v. Shepherd, 177 Mo. 205, 219, 76 S.W. 79, 83 (1903). "Sedition is a crime against society, nearly allied to that of treason, and it frequently precedes treason by a short interval. . . . Sedition has been described as disloyalty in action, and the law considers as sedition all those practices which have for their object to excite discontent or dissatisfaction, to create public disturbance, or

to lead to civil war; to bring into hatred or contempt the Sovereign or the Government, the laws or constitution of the realm, and generally all endeavors to promote public disorder." Regina v. Sullivan, 11 Cox C.C. 44, 45 (1868).

97. State v. Shepherd, 177 Mo. 205, 221, 76 S.W. 79, 84 (1903).

98. 18 U.S.C.A. § 2384.

99. Id. at § 2385.

1. Id. at § 2388.

2. 10 U.S.C.A. § 894.

(3) who fails to do his utmost to prevent and suppress an offense of mutiny or sedition being committed in his presence, or fails to take all reasonable means to inform his superior or commanding officer of an offense of mutiny or sedition which he knows or has reason to believe is taking place, is guilty of a failure to suppress or report a mutiny or sedition.

(b) A person who is found guilty of attempted mutiny, mutiny, sedition, or failure to suppress or report a mutiny or sedition shall be punished by death or such other punishment as a court-martial may direct.

The Court of Military Appeals has construed the cited provision to embrace two forms of mutiny. First, if there exists the necessary intent to override military authority and concerted action it may be committed by a refusal to obey a lawful order. Second it may be accomplished by a person acting with similar intent alone or in concert with others by creating a violence or disturbance.[3]

B. PERJURY AND SUBORNATION

The social interest in the integrity of a sworn statement in a judicial proceeding was well recognized before such statements made elsewhere were either common or thought to be matters of much importance. Hence common-law perjury was limited to the false oath in a judicial proceeding.[4] The penalty was "antiently death; afterwards banishment, or cutting out the tongue; then forfeiture of goods; and now [in Blackstone's time] it is fine and imprisonment and never more to be capable of giving testimony."[5] It was one of the leading representatives of the so-called *crimen falsi*,[6] and the disqualification to serve as a witness was added rather to prevent the introduction of evidence thought not entitled to credence than as an additional penalty.[7] Thus in the maturity of the common law perjury was a misdemeanor although it carried the brand of infamy.

3. United States v. Woolbright, 12 USCMA 450, 31 CMR 36 (1961); United States v. Brown, 19 USCMA 591, 42 CMR 193 (1970).

4. 3 Co.Inst. *163; 4 Bl.Comm. *137.

"In other words, perjury is a corrupt, willful, false oath, taken in a judicial proceeding, in regard to a matter or thing material to a point involved in the proceeding." Stewart v. State, 25 Ala.App. 155, 142 So. 590, 591 (1932); State v. Heyes, 44 Wn.2d 579, 586–7, 269 P.2d 577, 582 (1954). And see Plummer v. State, 90 Ga.App. 773, 775, 84 S.E.2d 202, 204 (1954).

It has been said: "Blackstone to the contrary notwithstanding, the perjury of witnesses was not punishable at common law." Curtis, A Notion in Criminal Contempt, 41 Harv.L.Rev. 51, 59 (1927). This seems to be based upon a misunderstanding of a quotation from Stephen which is relied upon. 3 Stephen, History of the Criminal Law of England 241 (1883). But Stephen's reference is to the common law "in early times." Stephen mentions that a statute in 1487 (3 Hen. 7

c. 1) was considered by the Star Chamber to have "authorized them to punish perjury." Id. at 244. But this statute did not purport to create the offense, it took notice of it as an existing crime. Stephen adds: "The present law upon this subject . . . originated entirely as far as I can judge in decisions by the Court of Star Chamber." Id. at 245.

5. 4 Bl.Comm. *138, citing 3 Co.Inst. *163.

6. See Commonwealth v. Jones, 334 Pa. 321, 323, 5 A.2d 804, 805 (1939).

"Forgery constitutes dishonest conduct and reflects adversely on the perpetrator's veracity and integrity." People v. James, 88 Cal.App.3d 150, 151 Cal.Rptr. 354, 358 (1978).

7. It was more likely to harm another than the one disqualified because at the time of its origin a party to a suit, or one interested in the outcome, was not a competent witness in the case. 3 Bl.Comm. *369; 2 Wigmore on Evidence §§ 520, 575 (3d ed. 1940).

In time, sworn statements came to be required in many matters other than judicial proceedings and with the growing importance of this problem came recognition of the social interest in the integrity of such an oath. Hence the common law provided a penalty for wilful and corrupt false swearing of such a nature, although the name "perjury" was not employed.[8] As said by Lord Denman in such a case: "It is not, properly speaking, perjury because the same consequences do not attach. But it is a misdemeanour in falsely taking an oath which a party is required by Parliament to take before a magistrate."[9]

It was held to be a lesser included offense of which one could be convicted under an indictment for perjury.[10] Thus there were two offenses, both misdemeanors, known as (1) "perjury" and (2) "false swearing." At Common Law—

Perjury is a false oath in a judicial proceeding in regard to a material matter.[11] **A false oath is a wilful and corrupt sworn statement made without sincere belief in its truthfulness.**

False swearing is what would be perjury except that it is not in a judicial proceeding but in some other proceeding or matter in which an oath is required by law.[12]

In the various jurisdictions in this country the entire area has been covered by statutes which for the most part have made the crime a felony[13] **often with very severe punishment provided.**[14]

8. Rex v. De Beauvoir, 7 Car. & P. 17, 173 Eng.Rep. 8 (1835); The Queen v. Chapman, 1 Den.C.C. 432, 169 Eng.Rep. 314 (1849); The Queen v. Hodgkiss, L.R. 1 C.C. 212 (1869). And see State v. Coleman, 117 La. 973, 975, 42 So. 471, 472 (1906).

9. Rex v. De Beauvoir, 7 Car. & P. 17, 173 Eng.Rep. 8 (1835).

10. H was indicted for perjury for making a false affidavit under the Bills of Sale Act, and was found guilty. It was held that this was not strictly perjury and hence no sentence peculiar to perjury could be pronounced. But it was held that the conviction should be affirmed because his false swearing was a common-law misdemeanor since an affidavit is required for purposes of the statute. The Queen v. Hodgkiss, L.R. 1 C.C. 212 (1869).

11. "Perjury, by the common law, seemeth to be a wilful false oath, by one who being lawfully required to depose the truth in any proceeding in a course of justice, swears absolutely in a matter of some consequence to the point in question, whether he be believed or not." 1 Hawk.P.C. 318 (6th ed. by Leach, 1788). "Perjury is the wilful giving under oath, in a judicial proceeding or course of justice, of false testimony material to the is-

sue or point of inquiry." 2 Bishop, New Criminal Law § 1015 (8th ed. 1892).

12. "Although the term, false swearing, is used interchangeably with perjury, there is a definite distinction both at common law and under usual statutory schemes. The principal distinguishing factor is that perjury is committed only in a judicial proceeding whereas false swearing is not necessarily committed in a judicial proceeding but is rather the giving of false statement under oath." Nimmo v. State, 603 P.2d 386, 388 (Wyo. 1979).

A false oath in an affidavit given to obtain a marriage license will not support a charge of perjury because it is extrajudicial, but it will support a charge of false swearing which is a separate offense. Davidson v. State, 22 Tex.App. 372, 3 S.W. 662 (1886).

13. Where false swearing has been kept as a separate offense it is sometimes made a misdemeanor.

New Jersey punishes false swearing as a disorderly persons offense which is a minor violation. N.J.Stat.Ann. 2C:28–2, 2C:43–8 (1979).

14. E.g., for perjury committed in courts for penalty may be imprisonment for life. Mich.Stat.Ann. § 28.664 (1972).

There have been variations in the statutory plan. One plan has been to group all criminally false oaths into one offense known as "perjury;"[15] another has included distinctions which may take the form of different grades or degrees of perjury,[16] or may retain the common-law scheme of one offense known as "perjury" and another called "false swearing."[17] Under the latter plan, as at common law, false swearing is in the nature of a lesser included offense, convictable under a charge of perjury. Needless to say, since the greater includes the less, one corrupt oath will not support convictions of both.[18] Whatever plan is used there has been a tendency to enlarge the field of punishable sworn falsehood, as will be emphasized presently. And where precision is not required there is a tendency to use the word "perjury" throughout, despite the fact that some jurisdictions have a different label for a part thereof.

Perjury is to be distinguished from certain allied offenses such as obstructing public justice,[19] official misconduct,[20] and uttering a forgery (in the form of a false affidavit).[21] And it is worthy of note that in the early days witnesses before a legislative assembly or committee were not sworn, but gave their testimony under the penalty of being adjudged guilty of contempt, and punished accordingly, if they testified falsely.[22] On the other hand one may commit perjury in his own trial for a former alleged perjury.[23]

"We have stated the essential elements of the crime of perjury thus: . . . '(a) An oath to tell the truth must be taken by the accused, and (b) administered by legal authority, (c) in a judicial proceeding (or statutory affidavit). (d) The accused must have testified in such proceeding, and (e) his testimony must be material to the judicial proceeding. (f) The testimony as-

---

15. E.g., 18 U.S.C.A. § 1621; West's Ann.Cal.Pen.Code § 118 (1970). And see State v. Sailor, 240 N.C. 113, 114–5, 81 S.E.2d 191, 192 (1954); Tischler v. State, 206 Md. 386, 391, 111 A.2d 655, 658 (1955).

16. E.g., New York has three degrees of perjury. McKinney's N.Y.Pen.Law §§ 210.05 through 210.15 (1975). Michigan has two sections with different penalties but does not use the label "degree." Mich.Stat.Ann. §§ 28.664, 28.665 (1972).

17. E.g., N.J.Stat.Ann. 2C:28–1 and 2C:28–2 (1979). "The last act denounces false swearing. It must not be thought that false swearing is necessarily perjury. According to the common law false swearing is a substantive offense. In several of the states it is made an offense separate and distinct from perjury." State v. Coleman, 117 La. 973, 975, 42 So. 471, 472 (1906). And see United States v. Bailey, 34 U.S. 238, 253 (1835); Plummer v. State, 90 Ga.App. 773, 775–6, 84 S.E.2d 202, 204 (1954); State v. Engels, 32 N.J.Super. 1, 8, 107 A.2d 674, 677 (1954).

Under the statute false swearing is what would be perjury except that it is not in regard to a material issue. Hence

it is a lesser included offense of perjury. State v. Greenlaw, 50 Or.App. 97, 622 P.2d 325 (1981).

18. In like manner perjury, a felony by statute, is one means of obstructing justice, which is a misdemeanor, but the latter is merged in the former "so as to prevent the imposition of a separate penalty on the latter." A "conviction of either charge, but not of both, may be sustained." Commonwealth v. Russo, 177 Pa.Super. 470, 485, 111 A.2d 359, 366 (1955).

19. Ibid.

20. State v. Borrell, 18 N.J. 16, 112 A.2d 548 (1955).

21. Rex v. Obrian, 2 Stra. 1144, 93 Eng.Rep. 1090 (1740).

22. See ex parte McCarthy, 29 Cal. 395, 405 (1866).

For an annotation on "Perjury or false swearing as contempt" (meaning contempt of court) see 89 A.L.R.2d 1258 (1963).

23. United States v. Remington, 208 F.2d 567 (2d Cir. 1953), cert. denied 347 U.S. 913, 74 S.Ct. 476 (1954).

signed as perjury must be false, and (g) must be given wilfully, and corruptly, and with knowledge of its falsity (or given recklessly), and for the purpose of having it believed.' " [24]

1. THE OATH OR LEGALLY–RECOGNIZED EQUIVALENT

Perjury had its origin as a spiritual offense [25] and no *oath* was recognized by the English common law except one "calling Almighty God to witnesse, that his testimony is true." [26] Because of the religious convictions of great numbers of persons, however, it has been necessary to provide a substitute in the form of an *affirmation* which is a solemn declaration made under the penalties of perjury, by a person who conscientiously declines to take an oath.[27] And the form provided by statute is usually in some such wording as "solemnly swear (or affirm, as the case may be) . . . ." [28] Recently an additional substitute for an oath has made its appearance, this one being provided for the convenience of the declarant.[29] It is by virtue of legislation providing for certain signed statements (such as the declaration of an income tax return) to be made expressly "under the penalties of perjury." [30] The quoted words are a part of the signed declaration, and the statute provides the same penalties as for perjury if the signer does not believe the statement to be true and correct as to every material matter.[31]

Where precision is not required there is a tendency to employ the word "oath" to include a legally-recognized equivalent as well as an oath itself, and at times this has been expressly authorized by statute.[32]

2. LAWFULLY ADMINISTERED

The most recent substitute for an oath is not "administered" in any strict sense of the term. It is merely a declaration signed "under the penalties of

24. Commonwealth v. Russo, 177 Pa. Super. 470, 484, 111 A.2d 359, 365 (1955). And see United States v. Debrow, 346 U.S. 374, 376, 74 S.Ct. 113, 114, 115 (1953); Harrell v. United States, 220 F.2d 516 (5th Cir. 1955). Accord, Edwards v. State, 577 P.2d 1380 (Wyo.1978).

"Schramm gave his false statements to the police at the police station pursuant to a homicide investigation. An interrogation which is conducted solely at the hands of the police at a police station is simply not an official proceeding within the definition of the statute" on perjury. Schramm v. State, 374 So.2d 1043, 1045 (Fla.App.1979).

25. 3 Stephen, History of the Criminal Law of England 243 (1883). ". . . perjury itself being forbidden by the law of God, . . ." 3 Co.Inst. *163.

26. 3 Co.Inst. *165.

27. "Any person having conscientious scruples against taking an oath, may affirm with like effect." KSA (Kan.) § 54–103 (1976).

28. E.g., West's Ann.Cal.C.C.P. § 2094 (1970).

29. The congressional intent was merely to simplify the task of both the taxpayer and the Bureau of Internal Revenue by permitting a verified return to be substituted for a notarized return in certain situations. Cohen v. United States, 201 F.2d 386 (9th Cir. 1953), cert. denied 345 U.S. 951, 73 S.Ct. 864 (1953).

30. "But such a phrase demonstrates the intent of the legislature to have it serve as an oath or affirmation." Nimmo v. State, 603 P.2d 386, 389 (Wyo. 1979).

31. E.g., 26 U.S.C.A. § 7206 (1967).

"One who subscribes to a false statement under penalty of perjury pursuant to section 1746 may be charged with perjury under 18 U.S.C.A. § 1621, just as if the statement were made under oath." Dickinson v. Wainwright, 626 F.2d 1184, 1186 (5th Cir. 1980).

32. " 'Oath,' includes an affirmation, and every other mode authorized by law of attesting the truth of that which is stated." McKinney's N.Y.Pen.Law § 210.00 (1971).

perjury." Such a declaration, however, has no legal significance unless made under authority of an appropriate statute. If a signer should voluntarily write "under the penalties of perjury" over his signature, this would be just as meaningless as if a seller, just on his own initiative, should raise his right hand and "swear" that he had title to the goods he was purporting to sell.[33] And if this phrase appears in a printed form prepared by some commission, board or officer it is equally without legal effect unless its appearance is under statutory authority.[34]

Except for the very limited area of the declaration "under the penalties of perjury," there can be no conviction of this offense unless a lawful oath or affirmation had been duly administered to the defendant by one authorized to do so,[35] and there can be no such authority unless the particular oath or affirmation is one required or authorized by law.[36] Thus, at a time when a party could not lawfully be sworn as a witness he could not commit perjury if improperly so sworn;[37] if the law expressly excludes the oath of an applicant upon a certain point he cannot commit perjury as to that point;[38] if there is no authority for a sworn pleading, the unauthorized addition of an oath thereto will not support a charge of this offense;[39] and perjury cannot be predicated upon a false statement in an affidavit required by some board or officer if there is no law authorizing such an affidavit.[40] Furthermore, a conviction of perjury cannot be sustained if the oath was administered by an officer who acted (1) outside the jurisdiction of his state,[41] (2) before his term

---

33. A "false oath taken by one upon the making of a bargain, that the thing sold is his own, is not punishable as perjury." 1 Hawk. 320 (6th ed. by Leach, 1788). One court spoke of a "voluntary oath" as sufficient to support conviction but pointed out that the clerk had authority to administer it. Davidson v. State, 22 Tex.App. 372, 380, 3 S.W. 662, 664 (1886).

34. Cf. United States v. Maid, 116 F. 650 (D.C.Cal.1902).

A false statement in an affidavit which was not required by law will not support a conviction of perjury. The fact that it was required by the Commonwealth's Attorney is not sufficient. Mendez v. Commonwealth, 220 Va. 97, 255 S.E.2d 533 (1979).

35. See Stewart v. State, 25 Ala.App. 155, 269 P.2d 590, 591 (1932); Commonwealth v. Russo, 177 Pa.Super. 470, 484, 111 A.2d 359, 365 (1955); State v. Heyes, 44 Wn.2d 579, 586, 269 P.2d 577, 582 (1954). Whether the officer who administered the oath was duly authorized or not is a question of fact for the jury. Brooks v. United States, 240 F.2d 905 (5th Cir. 1957).

There can be no conviction of perjury if the oath was administered by one who had no authority to administer an oath. State v. Flamer, 54 Or.App. 17, 633 P.2d 860 (1981).

36. See United States v. Debrow, 346 U.S. 374, 376, 74 S.Ct. 113, 114, 115 (1953); Cooper v. United States, 233 F.2d 821, 823 (8th Cir. 1956); People v. White, 122 Cal.App.2d 551, 265 P.2d 115 (1954); State v. Gaige, 26 Mich. 30, 32 (1872).

37. State v. Hamilton, 7 Mo. 300 (1842).

38. State v. Helle, 2 Hill 290 (S.C. 1834).

39. "To constitute perjury, the oath or affirmation must be material, or be required by, or have some effect in law." Silver v. State, 17 Ohio 365, 368 (1848). Under the statute in effect at the time an affidavit of the truth of an answer in chancery had no legal effect unless the bill called for an answer on oath. Hence an answer on oath could not support a conviction of perjury unless the bill called for an answer on oath.

Where an inquiry under oath was not authorized, a false statement made under oath to a magistrate making inquiry as to a defendant's financial condition could not be the basis for a perjury charge. People v. Barajas, 273 Cal.App.2d 750, 78 Cal.Rptr. 647 (1969).

40. United States v. Maid, 116 F. 650 (D.C.Cal.1902).

41. Wyckoff v. Humphrey, 1 Johns. 498 (N.Y.1806).

of office began,[42] or (3) after his authority to act in this regard had come to an end.[43]

It may be added that a false affidavit made in support of a claim against the United States, sworn to before a justice of the peace of a state, would not have supported a conviction of perjury had it not been for an act of Congress expressly authorizing the administration of this oath by a state magistrate.[44] The federal law authorizes an oath to be taken before a notary public of a state upon a contested election of a member of the House of Representatives of the United States, but a state has no jurisdiction of a complaint of perjury alleged to be committed in testifying under this oath. This is a federal offense only.[45] On the other hand, it has been held that perjury committed in a state court, relative to an application for naturalization under the laws of the United States, is an offense against the state as well as against the Federal Government.[46]

If the oath or affirmation was authorized by law and was administered by a court, body or officer duly authorized to do so, a mere irregularity in form, such as the omission of the words, "So help me God," constitutes no defense to a prosecution for perjury.[47] If the defendant raised his hand and stated that the facts as set forth in a certificate were true, and added his signature, knowing that some of the asserted facts were untrue, he is guilty of perjury even if no such words as "oath," "swear" or "depose" were used.[48]

3.   FALSE OATH

A.   The Oath Itself

The word "oath" (apart from its use to indicate a profane expression) has two very different meanings: (1) a solemn appeal to God in attestation of the truth of a statement or the binding character of a promise; (2) a statement or promise made under the sanction of such an appeal. References to the necessity of an oath lawfully administered use the word in the first sense, whereas the common phrase "oath against an oath," [49] meaning the sworn testimony of one witness in opposition to the sworn testimony of another, makes use of the second. Some definitions of perjury employ the first mean-

---

42. State v. Phippen, 62 Iowa 54 (1883).

"A perjury prosecution may be predicated on false testimony made under an oath administered by a de facto officer." United States v. Allen, 409 F.Supp. 562, 565 (E.D.Va.1975).

43. State v. Cannon, 79 Mo. 343 (1883).

44. United States v. Bailey, 34 U.S. 238 (1835).

45. In re Loney, 134 U.S. 372, 10 S.Ct. 584 (1890). Needless to say, a state court does not have jurisdiction over perjury alleged to have been committed before a United States Commissioner who was investigating charges of federal crimes. Ross v. State, 55 Ga. 192 (1875).

46. State v. Whittemore, 50 N.H. 245 (1870); Rump v. Commonwealth, 30 Pa. 475 (1858). Contra, People v. Sweetman, 3 Parker Cr. 358 (N.Y.1857).

47. People v. Parent, 139 Cal. 600, 73 P. 423 (1903); State v. Anderson, 178 Kan. 322, 285 P.2d 1073 (1955).

48. People v. Brown, 125 Cal.App.2d 83, 269 P.2d 918 (1954).

Some statutes expressly provide that irregularities in the administering or taking of the oath do not constitute a defense. E.g., McKinney's N.Y.Rev.Pen. Code, § 210.30, 3. (1975). The Model Penal Code includes such a stipulation. Section 241.1(3).

49. See Weiler v. United States, 323 U.S. 606, 608, 65 S.Ct. 548, 549 (1945).

ing, such as "the wilful giving under oath . . . of false testimony," [50] and others the second, such as a "wilful, false oath." [51] While either is correct the second has the advantage of brevity and whichever is used in the definition it is essential to keep the two meanings of the word in mind in order to avoid confusion. Thus a promissory oath such as the president's oath of office, is not the type of oath referred to in the crime of perjury, in the absence of some very unusual statutory or constitutional provision. [52] One court was inclined to question this conclusion because it was thinking of the oath of a witness in the first sense rather than as a synonym of sworn testimony. [53]

B. THE FALSE-OATH CONCEPT

A false oath is the first requisite of perjury [54] but no error could be greater than the assumption that "false oath" means "untrue testimony." An innocent error by a witness who is testifying in good faith and to the best of his ability is not a "false oath" however great a mistake he may make, [55] whereas, if "a man swears that a thing is so or that he believes it to be so, when in truth, he does not believe it to be so, *the oath is false* though the fact really be as stated." [56] In the words of Coke, "falsehood in knowledge or minde . . . may be punished though the words be true." [57] This he illustrated by the case of witnesses who swore to the value of certain goods they had never seen or known about. And although their statements were correct, "yet because they knew it not, it was a false oath in them," and they

---

50. 2 Bishop, New Criminal Law § 1015 (8th ed. 1892).

51. 1 Hawk.P.C. *318 (6th ed. by Leach, 1788); Stewart v. State, 25 Ala. App. 155, 142 So. 590, 591 (1932); State v. Heyes, 44 Wn.2d 579, 586, 269 P.2d 577, 582 (1954).

52. "Also from what has been said it appears that the notion of perjury is confined to such public oaths only as affirm or deny some matter of fact, contrary to the knowledge of the party; and therefore, that it doth not extend to any promissory oaths whatsoever; . . . ." 1 Hawk.P.C. 320 (6th ed. by Leach, 1788). It is expressly provided in the Missouri constitution, however, that a violation of the oath of office by a legislator shall constitute perjury. Mo.Const. Art. III, § 15 (1945).

53. "In a strained sense, the oath of a witness sworn upon the trial of a case is promissory. He is sworn, not that he has told the truth, but that he will tell the truth." Norris v. State, 5 Ga.App. 586, 592, 63 S.E. 662, 665 (1909).

54. "To constitute perjury the oath must, of course, be false, . . ." State v. Cruikshank, 6 Blackf. 62 (Ind.1841). And see Stewart v. State, 25 Ala.App. 155, 269 P.2d 590, 591 (1932); State v. Sailor, 240 N.C. 113, 81 S.E.2d 191 (1954);

Commonwealth v. Russo, 177 Pa.Super. 470, 484, 111 A.2d 359, 365 (1955); State v. Heyes, 44 Wn.2d 579, 586, 269 P.2d 577, 582 (1954).

55. See Commonwealth v. Douglas, 46 Mass. 241, 245 (1842); United States v. Rose, 215 F.2d 615, 623 (3d Cir. 1954).

An untrue statement is not *false* if there is no intent to deceive. State v. Tedesco, 175 Conn. 279, 397 A.2d 1352 (1978).

"The term 'false' has generally been interpreted as connotating intentional untruth." Commonwealth v. Kraatz, 2 Mass.App. 196, 310 N.E.2d 368, 372 (1974); Nimmo v. State, 603 P.2d 386, 390 (Wyo.1979).

"A person who testified falsely but in good faith with the honest belief he is telling the truth is not guilty of perjury." State v. Barkwell, 585 S.W.2d 149, 154 (Mo.App.1979).

56. State v. Cruikshank, 6 Blackf. 62, 63 (Ind.1841). A sworn misstatement made with conscious indifference to whether it is true or false is deemed equivalent to an allegation known to be untrue. People v. Cook, 22 Cal.3d 67, 148 Cal.Rptr. 605, 583 P.2d 130 (1978).

57. 3 Co.Inst. *166.

were convicted.[58] "Nor does it matter that the statement is true," said the Kentucky court, "if the witness did not know it to be so." [59]

An important distinction is to be noted between this offense and false pretenses. Since an untrue representation of fact is essential for guilt of false pretenses, one who obtains property by a positive statement of fact without having any idea whether it is true or false, merely takes a chance. He is not guilty of that crime if his statement turns out to be true.[60] In perjury, on the other hand, since the requirement is not that the testimony be untrue but that the oath be false, the witness who testifies without any idea whether his statement is true or false, is not merely taking a chance. He is committing perjury whichever it may turn out to be.[61] It has been characterized as perjury even if the witness believed his statement to be true, if he realized that he had no knowledge one way or the other.[62] It is perhaps unnecessary to add that the phrase "false oath" is here used in a shorthand sense to include a "false affirmation," and also a "false declaration" under the most recent statutory addition to this field.

In *Bronston* [63] The Supreme Court held that one may not be convicted of perjury for an answer that is literally true, even if it is not responsive to the question and is calculated to mislead. In following that case it was held that a conviction of perjury could not be supported by proof that T had "handled the transmission" of certain checks when his only testimony in this regard was to the effect that he had not handled the "checks." [64] Quoting from *Bronston* it was said:

> If a witness evades, it is the lawyer's responsibility to recognize the evasion and to bring the witness back to the mark, to flush out the whole truth with the tools of adversary examination.

> It is no answer to say that here the jury found that the petitioner intended to mislead his examiner. A jury should not be permitted to engage in conjecture whether an unresponsive answer, true and complete on its face, was intended to mislead or divert the examiner; the state of mind of the witness is relevant only to the extent that it bears on whether "he does not believe [his answer] to be true."

> . . . [T]he perjury statute is not to be loosely construed, nor the statute invoked simply because a wily witness succeeds in derailing the questioner—so long as the witness speaks the literal truth. The burden is on the questioner to pin the witness down to the specific object of the questioner's inquiry. 409 U.S. 358–60, 93 S.Ct. 600–601 (citations omitted).[65]

58. Guerneis Case, 3 Co.Inst. *166 (1611).

59. Commonwealth v. Miles, 140 Ky. 577, 579, 131 S.W. 385, 386 (1910). Accord, United States v. Remington, 191 F.2d 246 (2d Cir. 1951); Miller v. State, 15 Fla. 577, 586 (1876); State v. Gage, 17 N.H. 373, 377 (1845); State v. Knox, 61 N.C. 312, 313 (1867).

60. Fox v. State, 102 Ark. 451, 145 S.W. 228 (1912).

61. See the cases in note 59.

62. See State v. Knox, 61 N.C. 312, 313 (1867). This is referred to sometimes as sworn testimony "given recklessly." See Commonwealth v. Russo, 177 Pa. Super. 470, 484, 111 A.2d 359, 365 (1955).

63. Bronston v. United States, 409 U.S. 352, 93 S.Ct. 595 (1973). "A statement literally true constitutes no offense, and similarly, a false answer, if immaterial, is also inoffensive." United States v. Dudley, 581 F.2d 1193, 1196 (5th Cir. 1978).

64. United States v. Tonelli, 577 F.2d 194 (3d Cir. 1978).

65. Id. at 198.

A witness who had never delivered timber to any place called Spane Mill was asked if he had ever delivered timber to Spane Mill, and answered that he had not. His conviction of perjury was reversed. The fact that the witness may have realized that the interrogator intended to ask about delivery to Spane Building, said the court, cannot make false an answer that was literally true. It is up to the interrogator to say what he means, and not for the court to speculate that the witness may have realized that the meaning intended was other than stated.[66]

C. WILFULLY AND CORRUPTLY FALSE

Wilfulness and corruption are inherent in the false-oath concept and it would be tautological to define perjury in terms of a "false oath wilfully and corruptly given." It is not improper to emphasize, however, that a false oath is one which is wilfully and corruptly false. A wrongful intent is an essential ingredient of the crime.[67] The "proper test of perjury is subjective, insofar as it is based upon the understanding of the witness himself regarding the words that he used, . . ."[68] Untrue testimony may be given by mistake or defect of memory without guilt of perjury or any other crime.[69] In this area the court will not hesitate to take notice of a mistake of law. Thus one who testified that no partnership existed between himself and another was held not to be guilty of perjury, although such a relation actually existed, because of his bona-fide belief that the dealings between the two did not as a matter of law create a partnership.[70] And a conviction of perjury was reversed in another case because the defendant was not permitted to explain his misstatement in the light of his erroneous understanding of the legal title to certain property and the extent of the exemption of the homestead law.[71]

Because of the requirement that the untrue testimony be wilfully and corruptly false,[72] a conviction of perjury cannot rest upon the mere fact that a witness testified differently on different occasions.[73] If on the first occasion he testified according to his honest belief he did not commit perjury however mistaken he may have been. If he discovered his mistake before he testified on the matter again he was bound to state the facts as he then knew them to be. It would have been perjury for him to have repeated his former statement under oath after learning of its inaccuracy. At common law, it may be added, a conviction of perjury could not be based upon two contradictory

---

66. State v. Olson, 92 Wn.2d 134, 594 P.2d 1337 (1979).

67. Beckanstin v. United States, 232 F.2d 1 (5th Cir. 1956). And see Costello v. Costello, 139 Conn. 690, 695, 96 A.2d 755, 757 (1953); People v. Frost, 204 Misc. 44, 120 N.Y.S.2d 911 (1953); United States v. Rose, 215 F.2d 615, 622 (3d Cir. 1954); Commonwealth v. Hawkins, 445 Pa. 279, 284 A.2d 730 (1971).

The word "corruptly" as applied to perjury means that the testimony was intentionally false. State v. Elder, 199 Kan. 607, 433 P.2d 462 (1967).

68. United States v. Lattimore, 127 F.Supp. 405 (D.C.D.C.1955).

69. Commonwealth v. Douglass, 46 Mass. 241, 245 (1842). And see United States v. Rose, 215 F.2d 615, 623 (3d Cir. 1954); Pitman v. State, 487 P.2d 716 (Okl. Cr.App.1971).

70. State v. McKinney, 42 Iowa 205 (1875). Compare a New Jersey case in which a conviction was reversed for improper instructions on what a "partner" is. State v. Engels, 32 N.J.Super. 1, 107 A.2d 674 (1954).

71. State v. Lazarus, 181 Iowa 625, 164 N.W. 1037 (1917).

72. See Stewart v. State, 25 Ala.App. 155, 142 So. 590, 591 (1932); State v. Heyes, 44 Wn.2d 579, 586, 269 P.2d 577, 582 (1954).

73. Henry v. Hamilton, 7 Blackf. 506 (Ind.1845).

sworn statements, even if one was obviously intentionally false, unless it could be established which one this was,[74]—a rule sometimes, and very wisely, changed by statute.[75] "Generally," it has been said,[76] "a belief as to the falsity of testimony may be inferred by the jury from proof of the falsity itself." And because of this fact prior testimony may be evidence that subsequent contradictory testimony proved to be untrue was knowingly false, but the burden is on the prosecution in this regard.[77]

A false oath is a sworn statement, whether accurate or not, given without sincere belief in its complete and undoubted accuracy. Any such oath is wilfully and corruptly false. An equivalent affirmation, or an equivalent declaration under special statutory authority therefor, is respectively a false affirmation or a false declaration. Except where precision is required as mentioned above, the term "false oath" is to be understood to cover all three.

4. MATERIALITY

"For if it be not material," said Coke, "then though it be false, yet it is no perjury," [78]—which was re-worded in a recent case in this form: "Where materiality is not shown, the indictment must fail." [79] In fact, in the absence of statutory change, the courts almost without exception list this as one of the essential elements of the crime.[80] Materiality need not concern the main point at issue,[81] the only requirement being that the testimony could have properly influenced the tribunal hearing the case.[82] An illustration may be

74. Conviction of perjury cannot be based upon two contradictory statements on oath alone, *"non constat,* which statement is the true one." Regina v. Hughes, 1 Car. & K. 519, 527, 174 Eng. Rep. 919, 923 (1844). Accord, State v. Sailor, 240 N.C. 113, 81 S.E.2d 191 (1954). Comment, 53 Mich.L.Rev. 1165 (1955).

75. E.g., N.J.Stat.Ann. 2C:28–2c (1979). See also 18 U.S.C.A. § 1623.

76. Young v. United States, 212 F.2d 236, 241, 94 U.S.App.D.C. 54 (1954), cert. denied 347 U.S. 1015, 74 S.Ct. 870 (1954).

"(A) belief as to the falsity of testimony may be inferred by the jury from proof of the falsity itself." United States v. Haldeman, 559 F.2d 31, 99 (note 189) (D.C.Cir. 1976).

77. State v. Sullivan, 33 N.J.Super. 138, 109 A.2d 430 (1954).

78. 3 Co.Inst. *167.

79. United States v. Laut, 17 F.D.R. 31 (D.C.N.Y.1955).

" 'Materiality' has traditionally been a necessary element in perjury, and it is a necessary element under ORS 162.065." State v. Greenlaw, 49 Or.App. 15, 618 P.2d 1291, 1292 (1980).

80. See United States v. Debrow, 346 U.S. 374, 376, 74 S.Ct. 113, 114, 115 (1953); United States v. Rose, 215 F.2d

617, 622 (3d Cir. 1954); State v. Swisher, 364 Mo. 157, 260 S.W.2d 6 (1953); State v. Sailor, 240 N.C. 113, 115, 81 S.E.2d 191, 192 (1954). Although the statute did not mention materiality it was held that Congress intended it should be an essential element. Meer v. United States, 235 F.2d 65 (10th Cir. 1956).

"Therefore, . . . this conviction must be reversed for lack of proof of materiality of the statements at issue." People v. Anderson, 57 Ill.App.3d 95, 14 Ill.Dec. 822, 825, 372 N.E.2d 1101, 1104 (1978). "Materiality is not required under the false swearing statute." State v. Devitt, 82 Wis.2d 262, 262 N.W.2d 73, 79 (1978). "The common-law crime of perjury, which requires materiality, has been modified in Alaska by AS 11.30.010(a)." State v. Nelson, 546 P.2d 592 (Alaska 1976).

81. Commonwealth v. Steward, 25 Leh.L.J. 464 (Leh.Co.Pa.1953).

82. Miles v. State, 268 P.2d 290 (Okl. Cr.1954).

False testimony as to his educational background, in holding himself out to be an expert witness, was material. State v. Elder, 199 Kan. 607, 433 P.2d 462 (1967). Testimony to support or attack the credibility of a witness is material. Ibid.

helpful. **W** executed a quit-claim deed in **M**'s office but it was not acknowledged there. This deed was later presented to **L**, at her home and she placed her acknowledgement thereon on **M**'s assurance that **W** had instructed him to present the deed to **L** for this purpose. In a civil action **M** testified that the deed was executed and notarized in his office. This was held to be perjury.[83] The question of materiality is one of law for the court and not one of fact for the jury.[84]

The grand jury has authority to investigate to determine whether a certain alleged offense was committed within its jurisdiction, and a false oath given in that investigation is not saved from taint of perjury by an ultimate conclusion that no indictment was warranted.[85] Although the witness could properly refuse to answer a question on the ground that the evidence called for is incompetent,[86] or self-incriminatory,[87] if he answers and does so falsely it is perjury. And an attorney is privileged not to disclose his client's confidential communications, unless the privilege is waived by the client, but he may not falsify to protect his client.[88] Furthermore, perjury may be committed by false evidence given in a trial under an indictment which is subsequently held to be invalid,[89] or in an affidavit which is not actually used.[90]

If it appears from the entire testimony of a witness who says "I think" or "I believe" that he means to give his best recollection of a fact observed by him, his testimony may be regarded as an affirmation of the fact and will support a conviction of perjury if it is wilfully false,[91] and the same is true of one who swears "to the best of his knowledge and belief" when in fact he

"Materiality is thus demonstrated if the question posed is such that a truthful answer could help the inquiry, or a false response hinder it, and these effects are weighed in terms of potentiality rather than probability." United States v. Berardi, 629 F.2d 723, 729 (2d Cir. 1980).

83. Miles v. State, 268 P.2d 290 (Okl. Cr.1954).

84. Ibid.; Dolan v. United States, 218 F.2d 454 (8th Cir. 1955).

"We have long held that in a prosecution for perjury the materiality of the alleged false statement is a question of law." United States v. Taylor, 574 F.2d 232, 235 (5th Cir. 1978). See also United States v. Thompson, 637 F.2d 267 (5th Cir. 1981).

85. United States v. Neff, 212 F.2d 297 (3d Cir. 1954).

"Testimony that is material to the grand jury investigation 'need not be material to the main issue and it need not be directed to the primary subject of the investigation.'" People v. Maestas, —— Colo. ——, 606 P.2d 849, 851 (1980).

86. Chamberlain v. People, 23 N.Y. 85 (1861); Barkley v. Commonwealth, 264 S.W.2d 297 (Ky.1954).

87. State v. Toscano, 13 N.J. 418, 100 A.2d 170 (1953).

The fact that an employee of the department of motor vehicles was compelled to make sworn statements before a deputy attorney general who was investigating alleged corruption among department personnel, in the sense that he thought his refusal would result in dismissal, did not give the employee a license to make untrue statements under oath. People v. Genser, 250 Cal.App.2d 351, 58 Cal.Rptr. 290 (1967).

88. Toscano, supra.

"The Supreme Court was unanimous in Mandujano (425 U.S. 564, 96 S.Ct. 1768) that the Fifth Amendment privilege provides no protection for the commission of perjury, at least where the false answers could not be said to have been procured by Government tactics or procedures so inherently unfair as to violate due process." United States v. Haldeman, 559 F.2d 31, 93 (D.C.Cir. 1976).

89. United States v. Remington, 208 F.2d 567 (2d Cir. 1953), cert. denied 347 U.S. 913, 74 S.Ct. 476 (1954).

90. State v. Dayton, 23 N.J.L. 49 (1850).

91. Shoulders v. United States, 218 F.2d 290 (8th Cir. 1955). People v. Sagehorn, 140 Cal.App.2d 138, 294 P.2d 1062 (1956). "[I]t has been held that a statement of belief or opinion known by

has no knowledge or information about the matter—even if his statement turns out to be in accord with the facts.[92] Moreover perjury may be predicated upon an affidavit despite the qualifying phrase "as affiant verily believes" if in fact he had no such belief and no probable grounds therefor.[93] It should be emphasized also that a witness who swears falsely and corruptly that he does not remember certain material facts, when in truth he does remember them, is guilty of perjury.[94] On the other hand it has been held, in conformity with the requirement of materiality, that an opinion expressed in regard to a matter not legally pertinent to the inquiry cannot be perjury.[95] At times the requirement of materiality has been removed by statute, particularly where different degrees or grades of perjury have been established.[96]

5. RETRACTION

While reasonably prompt retraction of a statement, before its falsity has been established otherwise, may tend to indicate inadvertence rather than corruption, the courts are divided on the question whether actual perjury can be purged by a reasonably prompt correction. One view is that if the witness recants in the same proceeding and corrects his testimony before its falsity has been established otherwise, there should be no conviction of perjury because it is socially desirable to keep the door open to this extent as an aid in the search for truth.[97] The Supreme Court rejected this position, saying:[98]

the witness to be false and deliberately and willfully made under oath, to mislead the court or jury, constitutes the offense of false swearing." State v. Engels, 32 N.J.Super. 1, 9, 107 A.2d 674, 678 (1954).

A witness cannot frustrate an inquiry with impunity simply by prefacing each sentence with the words "I believe." United States v. Ponticelli, 622 F.2d 985 (9th Cir. 1980).

92. Davis v. State, 7 Ga.App. 680, 67 S.E. 839 (1910). Cited with approval, Hicks v. State, 67 Ga.App. 485, 489, 21 S.E.2d 119, 122 (1942).

93. East Kentucky Rural Electric Coop. Corp. v. Phelps, 275 S.W.2d 592 (Ky. 1955). In holding an affidavit "to the best of my knowledge and belief" insufficient for the particular purpose, the court said: "I do not mean to infer that a petition and affidavit such as this, if false, may not be the basis of an indictment for false swearing." In re Rodgers, 35 N.J. Super. 185, 113 A.2d 535 (1955).

94. People v. Doody, 172 N.Y. 165, 64 N.E. 807 (1902).

"A witness who testified that he does not remember an event can be convicted of perjury if it can be proven beyond a reasonable doubt that he does, in fact, remember the event." Matter of Battaglia, 653 F.2d 419, 421 (9th Cir. 1981).

95. United States v. Margolis, 138 F.2d 1002 (3d Cir. 1943). Where a bank cashier, answering under oath in a liquidation proceeding expressed his judgment as to the value of certain assets of the bank, a charge of perjury could not be maintained without proof that he wilfully failed to exercise an honest judgment in his statements. In re Howell, 114 Cal. 250, 46 P. 159 (1896).

96. The statute enlarges the scope of perjury by eliminating the requirement of materiality. Beckley v. State, 443 P.2d 51 (Alaska, 1968). Under the Utah statute: "First degree perjury is perjury regarding material matters, while second degree perjury is regarding immaterial matters." State v. Dodge, 19 Utah 2d 44, 425 P.2d 781 (1967). And see N.Y. Pen.Code § 210.05 (1967).

97. People v. Ezaugi, 2 N.Y.2d 75, 141 N.E.2d 439, 141 N.E.2d 580 (1957); Commonwealth v. Irvine, 14 Pa.D. & C.2d 275 (1930).

98. United States v. Norris, 300 U.S. 564, 57 S.Ct. 535 (1937).

Accord, State v. Phillips, 157 Kan. 50, 259 P.2d 185 (1953).

See 51 Harv.L.Rev. 165 (1937); 64 A.L.R.2d 276 (1959).

Where **D** testified falsely in a grand jury proceeding, and later agreed to tell

"The argument overlooks the tendency of such a view to encourage false swearing in the belief that if the falsity be not discovered before the end of the hearing it will have its intended effect, but, if discovered, the witness may purge himself of crime by resuming his role as witness and substituting the truth for his previous falsehood. It ignores the fact that the oath administered to the witness calls on him freely to disclose the truth in the first instance and not to put the court and the parties to the disadvantage, hindrance, and delay of ultimately extracting the truth by cross-examination, by extraneous investigation or other collateral means."

Some codes expressly provide that such retraction shall be a defense,[99] and this is the position taken in the Model Penal Code.[1]

6. AFTER ACQUITTAL ON ANOTHER CHARGE

Where the defendant in a criminal prosecution has testified in his own behalf and thereby secured an acquittal, there is a diversity in the cases as to whether he may properly be prosecuted for perjury based upon the testimony so given. As perjury and the crime involved in the prior prosecution are obviously not the same offense there is clearly no former jeopardy, but the question is whether the issues that will be involved in the perjury trial have already been decided in the defendant's favor so that the prosecution should be barred by collateral estoppel.[2] Some courts have given an affirmative answer—the prosecution for perjury is barred,[3] but the prevailing view is otherwise,[4] sometimes with the emphasis that an acquittal is not a finding that all of defendant's testimony was true.[5] Perhaps the explanation should

the truth in the hope of escaping punishment, he was not acting under the type of coercion that the law condemns and was not entitled to have his subsequent statements to the FBI and the grand jury suppressed. United States v. Snyder, 428 F.2d 520 (9th Cir. 1970).

99. E.g., Ill.Crim.Code, § 32–2(c) (1972); McKinney's N.Y.Rev.Pen.Law, § 210.25 (1975).

18 U.S.C.A. § 1623(d) (1976) provides that recantation in the same proceeding is a defense to perjury if "the declaration has not substantially affected the proceeding, or it has not become manifest that such falsity has been or will be exposed." Hence retraction is no defense if made with awareness that the original testimony was known to be false. United States v. Scrimgeour, 636 F.2d 1019 (5th Cir. 1981).

1. 241.1(4).

2. See Perkins, Collateral Estoppel in Criminal Cases, 1960 U. of Ill.L.Forum 553.

3. Allen v. United States, 194 F. 664 (4th Cir. 1912); Wheatley v. United States, 286 F.2d 519 (10th Cir. 1961).

It was held that a perjury prosecution based on statements made by the defend-

ant at a previous trial was barred by a judgment of acquittal in the first case since the statements had necessarily been determined to be true. United States v. Hernandez, 572 F.2d 218 (9th Cir. 1978).

But note: "The acquittal of a defendant following a trial on criminal charges does not bar his subsequent conviction for perjury committed during the course of the trial. . . . Moreover, the burden is on the defendant to establish that the verdict in the prior trial necessarily determined in his favor the issue which he now contends should not be considered." United States v. Fayer, 573 F.2d 741, 745 (2d Cir. 1978).

4. People v. Niles, 300 Ill. 458, 133 N.E. 252 (1921); State v. Vandemark, 77 Conn. 201, 58 A. 715 (1904); State v. Carey, 159 Ind. 504, 65 N.E. 527 (1902).

The fact that **D** was acquitted of robbery will not bar a prosecution for perjury committed by him in that trial. State v. Noble, 2 Ariz.App. 532, 410 P.2d 489 (1966).

5. People v. Hardy, 64 Colo. 499, 174 P. 1117 (1918).

be that collateral estoppel is in the nature of an equitable doctrine and should not be used to defeat justice. In the words of the Kentucky court:[6]

"It is fundamental in the policy of the law that judicial proceedings and judgments shall be fair and free from fraud, and litigants and parties be encouraged, when sworn as witnesses, to tell the truth, and be punished if they do not. If, however, a party accused of crime could secure immunity from prosecution for false swearing or perjury by securing his acquittal through these means, the law would be offering a reward for false swearing by affording the person guilty of it protection instead of inflicting punishment."

Another approach is to apply the concept of collateral estoppel only where "issues of fact central to [the perjury] prosecution were necessarily determined in the former trial."[7] If it can be determined that a judgment of acquittal did not necessarily resolve the factual credibility of a defendant's testimony then there should be no bar to a prosecution for perjury of a defendant based on testimony given at a trial at which he was acquitted.[8]

7.   THE "TWO–WITNESS RULE"

Since equally honest witnesses may well have differing recollections of the same event we find a rule "rooted deep in the tradition that a conviction for perjury should not be obtained solely on the evidence of a single witness,"[9] or in other words that it should not rest entirely upon "an oath against an oath."[10] Hence the falsity of evidence relied upon for conviction of perjury must be established by the evidence of two independent witnesses or by that of one witness and corroborating circumstances.[11] The applica-

6. Teague v. Commonwealth, 172 Ky. 665, 189 S.W. 908, 910–11 (1916).

7. United States v. Haines, 485 F.2d 564, 565 (7th Cir. 1973). See also State v. Tate, 136 Ga.App. 181, 220 S.E.2d 741 (1975).

8. United States v. Dipp, 581 F.2d 1323 (9th Cir. 1978).

9. People v. Gleason, 285 App.Div. 278, 286, 136 N.Y.S.2d 220, 228 (1954).

10. Weiler v. United States, 323 U.S. 606, 608–9, 65 S.Ct. 548, 549, 550 (1945). More than this is needed "to turn the scales against the defendant's oath." State v. Sailor, 240 N.C. 113, 115, 81 S.E.2d 191, 192 (1954).

"The . . . two-witness rule . . . states that 'the uncorroborated oath of one witness is not enough to establish the falsity of the testimony of the accused . . . .' The policy behind this rule is that the conviction for perjury ought not to rest solely on one man's oath against that of another, . . . [It] may be satisfied by the direct testimony of one witness and sufficient corroborative evidence." United States v. Diggs, 560 F.2d 266, 269 (7th Cir. 1977).

"However, the 'two-witness' rule does not require testimony of two independent witnesses as to the falsity of the alleged perjurious statement. The testimony of a single witness as to falsity, if corroborated by other evidence, is sufficient." United States v. Haldeman, 559 F.2d 31, 97 (note 185) (D.C.Cir. 1976).

11. People v. Frost, 204 Misc. 44, 120 N.Y.S.2d 911 (1953); United States v. Neff, 212 F.2d 297, 306–7 (3d Cir. 1954); United States v. Knight, 126 F.Supp. 721 (D.C.Pa.1954). As to application of the rule see Arena v. United States, 226 F.2d 227 (9th Cir. 1955).

Testimony of two handwriting experts meets the requirement of the two-witness rule, but it was error for the judge not to explain the rule to the jury because if they disbelieved the testimony of either expert there was no basis for a perjury conviction. State v. Boratto, 154 N.J. Super. 386, 381 A.2d 794 (1977). Edwards v. State, 577 P.2d 1380 (Wyo.1978).

"It is well established that 'to authorize a conviction for perjury the falsity of the statement alleged to have been made by defendant must be established either by the testimony of two independent wit-

tion of this rule in state and federal courts has been said to be "well nigh universal." [12] It should, however, be limited to the situation for which it was designed, namely to prevent a conviction of perjury when there is no evidence other than the word of one witness against that of the defendant. It has no place in a case in which the falsity of defendant's testimony can be established by evidence of a different kind.[13] And while two sworn statements of the defendant, so conflicting that one is of necessity false, do not conclusively establish perjury, they should certainly obviate the need of any further evidence other than would be sufficient for conviction in a non-perjury criminal case.[14]

The Pennsylvania court has held that a statute has changed the two-witness rule insofar as perjury is concerned.[15]

8. SUBORNATION OF PERJURY

Subornation of perjury is the corrupt procurement of perjured testimony.[16]

In other words, it is intentionally causing perjury to be committed by another. Since, under the normal rule, one who with criminal intent procures the commission of a crime by another, is himself guilty of the crime committed,[17] the law student reasonably inquires why one who procures perjury is not guilty of perjury rather than something else. The answer seems to be found in the ancient belief that the guilt of the suborner was greater than

nesses, or by one witness and independent corroborating evidence which is inconsistent with the innocence of the accused.' " United States v. Forrest, 639 F.2d 1224, 1226 (5th Cir. 1981).

"The rule established in New Mexico is that evidence of one witness alone, not corroborated by any other evidence, is insufficient to warrant a conviction on a charge of perjury." State v. Naranjo, 94 N.M. 407, 611 P.2d 1101, 1114 (1980).

12. Weiler v. United States, 323 U.S. 606, 609, 65 S.Ct. 548, 549, 550 (1945); Hammer v. United States, 271 U.S. 620, 626, 46 S.Ct. 603, 604 (1926), citing many cases.

In federal cases 18 U.S.C.A. § 1623 (1976) eliminates the two-witness rule in cases of perjury committed before a court or grand jury. United States v. Dunn, 577 F.2d 119 (10th Cir. 1978) r'vd on other grounds 442 U.S. 100, 99 S.Ct. 2190 (1979).

13. The rule in perjury cases where one oath is to be placed against another, that there must be two witnesses to prove the charge or one witness and corroborating circumstances, has no application where the proof of the crime is necessarily based upon circumstantial evidence. People v. Doody, 172 N.Y. 165, 64 N.E. 807 (1902). Cited with approval,

People v. Smilen, 33 N.Y.S.2d 803, 805 (Sup.1942).

The falsity must be shown by the testimony of at least two witnesses or by the testimony of one witness corroborated by circumstances proved by independent testimony, except where indisputably established, as by documentary evidence. United States v. Thompson, 379 F.2d 625 (6th Cir. 1967).

If the falsity of the statement is established by the two-witness rule it is not necessary that D's knowledge of the falsity be established in that manner. La Placa v. United States, 354 F.2d 56 (1st Cir. 1965).

14. Commonwealth v. Russo, 177 Pa. Super. 470, 111 A.2d 359 (1955). The extra-judicial admission of the defendant is not sufficient for conviction without proper corroboration. Cuesta v. United States, 230 F.2d 704 (5th Cir. 1956).

15. Commonwealth v. Broughton, 257 Pa.Super. 369, 390 A.2d 1282 (1978).

16. State v. Sailor, 240 N.C. 113, 81 S.E.2d 191 (1954). *"Subornation* of perjury is the offence of procuring another to take such a false oath as constitutes perjury in the principal." 4 Bl.Comm. *137–8.

17. People v. Harper, 25 Cal.2d 862, 156 P.2d 249 (1945).

that of the perjurer himself.[18] In other words the suborner was originally thought of as committing a separate crime because it was a more serious offense than perjury,—although it was not a felony except in very ancient times.[19] Like perjury it carried the taint of infamy.[20] Under modern statutes the same penalty is usually provided for both offenses.[21]

To convict of subornation it is necessary to establish that perjury was actually committed by someone other than the defendant,[22] together with two additional facts: (1) that defendant induced the other to testify as he did, and (2) that defendant knew or believed this testimony would be a false oath on the part of the witness.[23] In other words, however untrue the sworn statement may have been—(1) if it was genuinely believed to be true by the witness there was no perjury, (2) if it was genuinely believed to be true by the defendant (with one qualification mentioned in the next paragraph) there was no corruption in his request [24] and (3) if the defendant did not believe that the witness knew the statement was false, the defendant was not knowingly procuring a false oath.[25] In the words of the Massachusetts court: "If he did not know or believe that the witness intended to commit the crime of perjury, he could not be guilty of the crime of suborning her." [26] Or as stated by another court, "the suborner must know or believe that the testimony of the witness about to be given will be false, and he must know or intend that the witness is to give the testimony corruptly or with knowledge or belief of its falsity." [27]

Without question testimony corruptly procured and corruptly given will support convictions of both subornation and perjury if the statements made under oath were believed to be false by both the procurer and the witness, although true in fact. It is equally clear that neither crime is committed if the witness knew that his statements were true although the procurer was

---

18. In this offense "plus peccat *author* [auctor] *quam actor*" (the author sins more than the actual perpetrator). 3 Co.Inst. *167. Coke states this as the "judgment of the parliament" which imposed a greater penalty upon the suborner than upon the perjurer, but in all likelihood the statute reflected the then prevailing view.

19. 4 Bl.Comm. *138.

20. Ibid.

21. E.g., 18 U.S.C.A. §§ 1621, 1622; West's Ann.Cal.Pen.Code § 127 (1970).

22. "It is elementary, of course, that a defendant is not guilty of subornation of perjury unless the perjury is, in fact, committed." United States v. Brumley, 560 F.2d 1268, 1278, n. 5 (5th Cir. 1977).

23. Boren v. United States, 144 F. 801, 802 (9th Cir. 1906); Commonwealth v. Douglass, 46 Mass. 241 (1842); State v. Sailor, 240 N.C. 113, 81 S.E.2d 191 (1954).

The elements of the crime of subornation of perjury consist of (1) corrupt agreement to testify falsely, (2) proof that perjury has in fact been committed,

(3) the statements of the perjurer were material, (4) evidence that such statements were wilfully made with knowledge as to the falsity thereof, and (5) knowledge of the procurer that the perjurer's statements were false. People v. Jones, 254 Cal.App.2d 200, 62 Cal.Rptr. 304 (1967).

24. To request a witness to testify to what is in fact false, and which the witness knows to be false will not result in subornation of perjury if the suborner did not know it to be false. Niehoff v. Sahagian, 149 Me. 396, 103 A.2d 211 (1954).

25. To constitute guilt of subornation of perjury it is not enough that both the accused and the witness knew the falsity of the statements sworn to, but the accused must have known that the witness knew the statements to be false. United States v. Evans, 19 F. 912 (D.C.Cal.1884).

26. Commonwealth v. Douglass, 46 Mass. 241, 244 (1842).

27. Boren v. United States, 144 F. 801, 802 (9th Cir. 1906).

convinced they were false. In theory, at least, both crimes would be committed if the witness thought his statements under oath were false, although the procurer knew them to be true,—if the procurer knew that the witness would not believe his statements while making them on the stand. In such case while the statements procured in evidence were true, the oath was false; and knowingly procuring a false oath is subornation of perjury.

The prevailing view seems to be that in a prosecution for subornation of perjury it is necessary to establish the falsity of the evidence by two independent witnesses or by one witness plus corroborating circumstances, but that this special requirement does not apply to proof of the procurement itself.[28]

9. ALLIED OFFENSES

The unsuccessful solicitation of another to swear falsely is punishable as attempted subornation of perjury,[29] provided the testimony would actually have been perjury had it been given.[30] Under some of the statutes punishing an endeavor to procure perjury it is not necessary to show that the one solicited knew that the testimony sought to be procured was false.[31] And it seems to have been a common-law offense to offer another money to swear to a particular thing whether true or false.[32] Furthermore, one method of committing the common-law misdemeanor known as obstruction of justice is by spiriting away a witness from a trial he should attend,[33] whether the witness consents thereto or not,[34] or by inducing or attempting to induce a witness to absent himself from a court where he is legally bound to appear.[35] In regard to this offense it is quite unimportant whether or not the witness would have any material evidence to give, because this fact cannot be known to the court until he appears, and the due course of the trial is handicapped by his absence.[36]

C. BRIBERY

A study of the law of bribery offers an excellent opportunity to chart the ever-expanding growth in the recognition of an important social interest. Such interest in preventing the disastrous effect of corrupting private influences upon official action had its early recognition on a very narrow base.

28. Hammer v. United States, 271 U.S. 620, 46 S.Ct. 603 (1926); Doan v. United States, 202 F.2d 674 (9th Cir. 1953); Catrino v. United States, 176 F.2d 884 (9th Cir. 1949); Commonwealth v. Douglass, 46 Mass. 241 (1842); State v. Ruskin, 117 Ohio St. 426, 159 N.E. 568 (1927); State v. Bixby, 27 Wis.2d 144, 177 P.2d 689 (1947). Contra, the special rule does not apply at all in a subornation case. State v. Richardson, 248 Mo. 563, 154 S.W. 735 (1912). Even the procurement cannot be established by the uncorroborated evidence of the alleged subornee. People v. Evans, 40 N.Y. 1 (1869).

29. State v. Johnson, 26 Del. 472, 84 A. 1040 (1912); Dodys v. State, 73 Ga. App. 483, 37 S.E.2d 173 (1946). And see 76–8–502(1) and 76–4–101, Utah Code Ann. 1953.

30. Nicholson v. State, 97 Ga. 672, 25 S.E. 360 (1895). One cannot be guilty of attempted subornation of perjury if the testimony solicited would not be perjury, if given, because of its immateriality. People v. Teal, 196 N.Y. 372, 89 N.E. 1086 (1909).

31. People v. Mosley, 338 Mich. 559, 61 N.W.2d 785 (1953).

32. See The Queen v. Darby, 7 Mod. 100, 101, 87 Eng.Rep. 1121, 1122 (1702).

33. State v. Early, 3 Del. 562 (1842).

34. State v. Sills, 85 Kan. 830, 118 P. 867 (1911).

35. State v. Ames, 64 Me. 386 (1875); United States v. Marionneaux, 514 F.2d 1244 (5th Cir. 1975).

36. State v. Early, 3 Del. 562 (1842).

The starting point in the law of bribery seems to have been when a judge, for doing his office or acting under color of his office, took a reward or fee from some person who had occasion to come before him,—and apparently guilt attached only to the judge himself and not to the bribe-giver.[37] So firmly fixed was the early notion that the offense was bribe-taking by one performing a judicial function, that Blackstone speaks of it as "an offence against public justice; which is when a judge, or other person concerned in the administration of justice, takes an undue reward to influence his behaviour in his office."[38] The English law, however, developed far beyond this narrow base, partly with the aid of legislation.[39] It came to include the bribe-giver as well as the bribe-taker[40] and to extend beyond the bribery of a judicial officer. The Earl of Middlesex, lord treasurer of England, was imprisoned, fined and deprived of office for exacting bribes.[41] And it was held to be bribery to pay a privy counsellor to procure an office,[42] to buy a vote for a particular candidate at a public election,[43] or to pay money to influence the testimony of a witness[44] or the verdict of a juror.[45] Even an offer to give a bribe was held punishable although apparently the theory was that this was attempted bribery rather than bribery itself.[46] As said by Lord Mansfield:[47] "Whatever it is a crime to take, it is a crime to give: they are reciprocal. And . . . the attempt is a crime: it is complete on the side who offers it." Since bribery was a common-law misdemeanor[48] the punishment could be the same for the attempt as for the completed offense and the distinction "was of little practical importance."[49]

Thus the common law as recognized in this country, came to look upon bribery as the giving of any valuable consideration or benefit to the holder of a public office, or to a person performing a public duty, or the acceptance thereof by such person, with the corrupt intention that he be influenced thereby in the discharge of his legal duty.[50] Stated in another way, a bribe

---

37. 3 Co.Inst. *145. The bribe-giver was punishable in Coke's day (id. at *147) but the form of his paragraph on bribery indicates that this was not always so.

38. 4 Bl.Comm. *139.

39. The early statutes are discussed in 1 Hawk.P.C. c. 67 (6th ed. by Leach, 1788). Compare The King v. Pitt, 1 W.Bl. 380, 383, 96 Eng.Rep. 214, 216 (1762).

40. Blackstone himself recognized this. 4 Bl.Comm. *140.

41. 3 Co.Inst. *148.

42. Rex v. Vaughan, 4 Burr. 2494, 98 Eng.Rep. 308 (1769).

43. The King v. Plympton, 2 Ld. Raym. 1377, 92 Eng.Rep. 397 (1737); The King v. Cripland, 11 Mod. 387, 88 Eng. Rep. 1105 (1724). And see Rex v. Vaughan, 4 Burr. 2494, 2500, 98 Eng. Rep. 308, 311 (1769).

44. Bushel v. Barrett, Ry. & M. 434, 171 Eng.Rep. 1074 (1826). This involved a conspiracy to bribe a witness which is not conclusive as to the bribery itself. But as infamy attached it is clear that the bribery of the witness was held to be a crime.

45. 4 Bl.Comm. *140. Bribery of a juror was called "embracery," which could be committed by persuasion and entreaty as well as by reward, but there is no question but that paying a juror to influence his vote was a misdemeanor by both the bribe-giver and the bribe-taker. Ibid.

46. The King v. Plympton, 2 Ld. Raym. 1377, 92 Eng.Rep. 397 (1737).

47. Rex v. Vaughan, 4 Burr. 2494, 2500, 98 Eng.Rep. 308, 311 (1769).

48. 3 Co.Inst. *145. Blackstone mentions that chief justice Thorpe was hanged for bribery in the 1300s, 4 Bl. Comm. *140, but it did not become established as a common-law felony. See 2 Pollock & Maitland, History of English Law 470 (2d ed. 1899).

49. People v. Peters, 265 Ill. 122, 128, 106 N.E. 513, 515 (1914).

50. See People v. Peters, 265 Ill. 122, 128, 106 N.E. 513, 515 (1914); People v. Swift, 59 Mich. 529, 543, 26 N.W. 694,

is something given for the purpose of improperly influencing official action, and either giving or accepting a bribe constitutes bribery. This suggests the following as a definition of the offense as recognized by the common law in this country:

> **Bribery is the corrupt payment or receipt of a private price for official action.**[51]

1. WHO MAY BE BRIBED

Except for those entirely without criminal capacity, anyone is a potential bribe-giver (briber), but only one within certain recognized categories can be a bribe-taker (bribee). It is within this area that the greatest growth is found in the law of bribery.

A. OFFICIAL BRIBERY

As mentioned above the English common law seemed to require originally that the bribee be a judge or at least a person performing a judicial function. This concept was expanded, partly by aid of legislation to include executive and legislative officers, and even one not an officer who was performing an official function. Thus Lord Mansfield was able to say in 1762 that bribery at public elections was always "punishable at common law." [52] Much difficulty would have been avoided in this country if emphasis had been placed upon public duty in the designation of potential bribees. All public officers, whether they be judicial, executive, legislative or administrative, have public duties to perform. Those who are not public officers may have public duties to perform on certain occasions, such as a juror, a witness, or a voter at an election of public officers or on public questions.[53] Any person having such a duty could be the recipient of a bribe according to the common law as it was received in this country,[54] but unfortunately parts of this field were excluded in many jurisdictions by unreasonably restrictive statutes. We are told, for example, that prior to 1905 the bribery statutes in Rhode Island "were apparently directed to offenses against public justice which involved only official acts of the judicial department" and subsequent legislation was required "to extend such crimes to include violations involving acts in the executive and legislative departments." [55] The California court was forced to hold that the statutory phrase *"officer of this state"* really meant officer *in* this state, in order to include a corrupt payment to a county or city officer

---

696 (1886); State v. Greer, 238 N.C. 325, 328, 77 S.E.2d 917, 919–20 (1953).

51. "Bribery is corruptly tendering or receiving a price for official action." 3 Wharton, Criminal Law § 2234 (12th ed. by Ruppenthal, 1932). "Bribery is the voluntary giving or receiving of anything of value in corrupt payment for an official act, done or to be done." 2 Bishop, New Criminal Law § 85 (8th ed. 1892). "The common thread that runs through common law and statutory formulations of the crime of bribery is the element of corruption, breach of trust, or violation of duty." United States v. Zacher, 586 F.

2d 912, 915 (2d Cir. 1978). "It is this element of corruption that distinguishes a bribe from a legitimate payment for services." Id. at 916.

52. The King v. Pitt, 1 W.Bl. 380, 383, 96 Eng.Rep. 214, 216 (1762).

53. "The function of a voter . . . is 'official' within the law of this offence." 2 Bishop, New Criminal Law § 86 (8th ed. 1892).

54. 3 Wharton, Criminal Law § 1380 (13th ed. 1957).

55. State v. Nadeau, 81 R.I. 505, 510, 105 A.2d 194, 196–7 (1954).

within the scope of bribery as there defined.[56] And the Georgia court found it necessary, for a similar reason, to hold that a deputy sheriff occupies an "office of government or of justice" within the meaning of its statute.[57] A sentence from a New York opinion is illuminating:

"A reference to the successive statutes on the subject of bribery . . . shows a constant tendency on the part of the legislature to extend the statutes against bribery to persons not embraced in previous laws." [58]

While a statute worded only in terms of a "public officer" would no doubt be interpreted to include his deputy, it would not cover a mere employee, but the tendency now is to speak in some such terms as "any public officer, agent, servant or employee." [59] The federal law, for example, reads "An officer or employee or person acting for or on behalf of the United States, or any department or agency or branch of government thereof, . . . in any official function." [60] This enabled the court to point out that if the examining physician of a draft board was not an officer of the United States, he was at least one called upon to act for the United States in an official function, and hence a potential bribee.[61] And the New York court was able to hold that the fact money was paid to a subordinate in the office did not prevent it from being bribery if an official function had been delegated to that employee.[62]

Although some jurisdictions do not yet have such complete coverage, the trend is in the direction of expanding the categories of potential bribees to include (1) any public officer, agent, servant or employee,[63] sometimes expressly stating that such a one is covered after election or appointment either before or after he has qualified or taken his post; [64] (2) electors, at times expressly including a bribe to refrain from voting; [65] (3) jurors, with inclusion of prospective jurors or jurors summoned on panel; [66] and (4) witnesses, including those about to be called as such.[67] Where not controlled by the restrictive language of some particular statute a de facto of-

---

56. Singh v. Superior Court, 44 Cal. App. 64, 185 P. 985 (1919); People v. Hallner, 43 Cal.2d 715, 277 P.2d 393 (1954).

57. Usry v. State, 90 Ga.App. 644, 83 S.E.2d 843 (1954).

58. People v. Jaehne, 103 N.Y. 182, 191, 8 N.E. 374, 377 (1886). And see People v. Swift, 59 Mich. 529, 543, 26 N.W. 694, 696 (1886).

For the position of the Model Penal Code see Article 240, Bribery and Corrupt Influence.

See also Perkins, Sampling the Evolution of Social Engineering, 17 U. of Pitt. L.Rev. 362 (1956). By express permission the author has drawn freely upon the material used there.

59. E.g., Mich.Stat.Ann. § 28.312 (1962).

60. 18 U.S.C.A. § 201.

61. Kemler v. United States, 133 F.2d 235 (1st Cir. 1943). And see Hurley v. United States, 192 F.2d 297, 299 (4th Cir. 1951).

62. People v. Salomon, 212 N.Y. 446, 106 N.E. 111 (1914).

63. E.g., Mich.Stat.Ann. § 28.312 (1962). And see Wilson v. United States, 230 F.2d 521 (4th Cir. 1956).

64. "Any person who is serving or has been elected . . ." Iowa Code Ann. § 722.1 (1979).

65. E.g., Id. at 722.8.

66. Calvaresi v. United States, 216 F.2d 891 (10th Cir. 1954). As to one mistakenly thought to be a juror, see State v. Porter, 125 Mont. 503, 242 P.2d 984 (1952).

67. E.g., Ala.Code § 13A–10–121 (1977); People v. Terry, 44 Cal.2d 371, 282 P.2d 19 (1955).

ficer may be bribed and he and the briber may both be convicted.[68]
Thus one who had been appointed to office, and was actually serving, could not defend on the ground that being a non-resident he was unqualified under the law.[69]

Because of the rule that the act of one conspirator, in carrying out the unlawful agreement, is imputed also to his co-conspirator, it follows, in a conspiracy case, that two (or more) may be convicted of accepting a bribe although only one of them is in the category of potential bribees.[70]

B. QUASI OFFICIAL BRIBERY

There is a social interest in keeping certain types of nonofficial action free from corrupting influences and this interest is beginning to receive recognition by statutory extensions of the crime of bribery into this area. Any such extension is actually outside the scope of offenses affecting the administration of governmental functions, but for obvious reasons it is convenient to consider all such problems at this place. The general rules and principles of bribery apply to all such additions to the field.

Certain types of action, while not actually official, have such close resemblance thereto that they may be included under the label of "quasi official action." Thus we find an increasing legislative tendency to enlarge the scope of criminal bribery by adding to the categories of potential bribees such persons as (1) officers [71] or employees [72] of public institutions; (2) officers or members of any legislative caucus, political convention, committee, or political gathering having for its purpose the nomination of candidates for public office; [73] or (3) representatives of a labor organization.[74]

C. OCCUPATIONAL BRIBERY

There is a social interest in the prevention of fraud, and fraud may be perpetrated by a corrupting influence which makes it to one's own advantage to violate his duty even quite apart from official or quasi official action.

---

68. It is no defense to the charge of accepting a bribe that the recipient was an officer *de facto* rather than *de jure*. State v. Duncan, 153 Ind. 318, 54 N.E. 1066 (1899); Ex parte Covell, 63 Okl.Cr. 256, 74 P.2d 626 (1937). And see People v. Jackson, 191 N.Y. 293, 300, 84 N.E. 65, 67 (1908); Wells v. State, 174 Tenn. 552, 556, 129 S.W.2d 203, 204 (1939); annotation, 115 A.L.R. 1263 (1938).

69. State v. Duncan, 153 Ind. 318, 54 N.E. 1066 (1899).

70. People v. Bompensiero, 142 Cal. App.2d 693, 299 P.2d 725 (1956). A Federal statute (18 U.S.C.A. § 281 repealed in part Pub.L. 87–849, 1962) punished employees of the United States who received outside compensation for any services rendered in any matter before a federal department or agency in which the United States is a party. Although **O** was not himself an employee his induce-

ment of an employee to accept compensation for such services by conspiring with him for that purpose is a violation of that law. Opper v. United States, 348 U.S. 84, 75 S.Ct. 158 (1954). See 18 U.S.C.A. § 203.

71. "More recent statutes apply to the officers of public institutions." People v. Swift, 59 Mich. 529, 543, 26 N.W. 694, 696 (1886). And see Mich.Stat.Ann. § 28.316 (1962).

72. E.g., see the statute forbidding a gift to an employee of the school for the blind by any person, firm or corporation having dealings with the institution. Ariz.Rev.Stat. § 15–818 (1978).

73. E.g., Ariz.Rev.Stat.Ann. § 13–2602 (1978).

74. E.g., McKinney's N.Y.Pen.Law §§ 180.10 through 180.30.

(A) Commercial Bribery [75]

One type of such fraud has been for a wholesaler, or his representative, by gift or promise to the agent or employee of a retailer, to induce such agent or employee to keep in mind the interest of the wholesaler rather than that of his own employer. "Bribery of purchasing agents," it has been said, "is incompatible with commercial honor. A bonus or commission, secretly given, is nothing short of a bribe to betray one's employer." [76] It is also frowned upon as a corrupt and unfair trade practice.[77] Hence there is a tendency in the direction of including such misconduct in the crime of bribery [78] and punishing it accordingly—although perhaps only as a misdemeanor.[79]

(B) Other Business or Professional Bribery

A gift or promise to an agent or employee by an outsider may be a corrupting influence apart from the so-called "commercial bribery," and some of the statutes are broad enough to cover much of this area. Thus the Michigan statute provides, in part:

"It shall be unlawful for any person to give, offer or promise to an agent, employee or servant of another . . . any commission, gift or gratuity whatever, or to do an act beneficial to such agent, employee or servant . . . with intent to influence the action of such agent . . . in relation to his principal's, employer's or master's business; or for an agent . . . to request or accept for himself or another any commission, gift or gratuity or promise . . . according to any agreement or understanding between him and any other person to the effect that he shall act in any particular manner in relation to his principal's, employer's or master's business . . . ." [80]

It has been said that the word "particular," as used in such a statute, has reference to a particular manner tending to serve the purpose of the donor rather than that of the employer; that the gratuity or promise was given and

---

75. "We hold that Congress intended 'bribery . . . in violation of the laws of the State in which committed' as used in the Travel Act to encompass conduct in violation of State commercial bribery statutes." Perrin v. United States, 444 U.S. 37, 100 S.Ct. 311, 318 (1979).

76. People v. Davis, 160 N.Y.S. 769, 777 (1915).

77. "The vice of conduct labeled 'commercial bribery,' as related to unfair trade practices, is the advantage which one competitor secures over his fellow competitors by his secret and corrupt dealing with employees or agents of prospective purchasers." American Distilling Co. v. Wisconsin Liquor Co., 104 F.2d 582 (7th Cir. 1939). Annotation 1 ALR 3rd 1350 (1965).

78. E.g., 27 U.S.C.A. § 205(c) (1979 Cum.Ann.Pkt.Pt.).

79. Though a misdemeanor it is one involving moral turpitude. In re Brown-

ing's Estate, 176 Misc. 308, 27 N.Y.S.2d 318 (1941).

80. Mich.Code Ann. § 28.320 (1962).

The Model Penal Code would make it a misdemeanor to solicit, accept or agree to accept any benefit as consideration for knowingly violating or agreeing to violate a duty of fidelity to which the actor is subject as (a) agent, partner or employee of another; (b) trustee, guardian, or other fiduciary; (c) lawyer, physician, accountant, appraiser, or other professional adviser or informant; (d) officer, director, manager or other participant in the direction of the affairs of an incorporated or unincorporated association; or (e) arbitrator or other purportedly disinterested adjudicator or referee. Conferring, offering or agreeing to confer such a benefit is also included. Model Penal Code § 224.8.

accepted to influence the conduct of the employee with respect to his employer's interest; [81] and that the purpose of the statute is the prevention of fraud on employers and principals through the use of such corrupting influences.[82] It has been pointed out that any "customs of trade" denounced by such a statute are "demoralizing to society," [83] and at times the evidence of any such custom has expressly been made inadmissible in the prosecution of such an offense.[84]

Congress has provided against bribery of foreign officials, parties or candidates by certain corporations subject to American law where the purpose is to assist the corporation in obtaining business.[85]

(C) Bribery in Sports

The field of sport, both professional and amateur, has so captivated the attention of the American people as to make inevitable a recognition of the social interest in preventing corrupting influences tending to affect the outcome of such events.[86]   A partial quotation from the former New York statute will give an idea of the trend in this direction.

"Whoever gives, promises or offers to any professional or amateur . . . player or referee or other official who participates or expects to participate in any professional or amateur game or sport or any jockey, driver, groom or any person participating or expecting to participate in any horse race, including owners of race tracks and their employees, stewards, trainers, judges, starters or special policemen, or to any manager, coach or trainer of any team or participant or prospective participant in any such game, contest or sport, any valuable thing with intent to influence him to lose or try to lose or cause to be lost or to limit his or his team's margin of victory, . . . is guilty of a felony, . . ." [87]

Another paragraph made a corresponding provision for the one on the receiving end of such a transaction.

81. People v. Graf, 261 App.Div. 188, 191–2, 24 N.Y.S.2d 683, 687 (1941).

82. June Fabrics, Inc. v. Teri Sue Fashions, Inc., 194 Misc. 267, 81 N.Y.S.2d 877 (1948).

83. People v. Davis, 160 N.Y.S. 769, 777 (1915).

84. E.g., Mich.Stat.Ann. § 28.320 (1962).

85. 15 U.S.C.A. §§ 78m, 78dd–1, 78dd–2, 78ff.

86. "Few will ever forget the most notorious commercial bribe in American history . . . (in which a gambler) bribed eight players of the Chicago White Sox to throw the first and second games of the 1919 World Series to the Cincinnati Reds." United States v. Perrin, 580 F.2d 730, 734 (5th Cir. 1978).

87. McKinney's N.Y.Pen.Law, § 382, as amended in 1952. The statute has since been divided into four sections to impose a heavier penalty on the briber

than on the bribee and to improve on the wording as a matter of legislative draftsmanship. It is not more helpful, however, in expressing the coverage. See now McKinney's N.Y.Pen.Law §§ 180.35–180.50 (1975).

See also West's Ann.Cal.Pen.Code, §§ 337b through 337e (1976); Mich.Stat.Ann. 28.319 (1962); State v. Dunivan, 77 Ariz. 42, 266 P.2d 1077 (1954) bribing a jockey; Glickfield v. State, 203 Md. 400, 101 A.2d 229 (1953) attempt to bribe a university football player.

Model Penal Code section 224.9. Rigging Publicly Exhibited Contest, includes non-sporting events and also includes any form of corrupt interference as by administering drugs to an athlete.

A beauty contest is not a "sports contest" for purposes of bribery. Davis v. Commonwealth, 564 S.W.2d 33 (Ky.App. 1976).

2. THE BRIBE

A bribe is a "price, reward, gift or favor bestowed or promised with a view to pervert judgment or corrupt the conduct of a person in a position of trust. . . ." [88] It is that which is employed as a corrupt device in the effort improperly to influence official action. "Official action," let it be understood, is used herein as a shorthand term to indicate official action in official bribery, quasi official action in quasi official bribery, commercial action in commercial bribery, and so forth. The bribe may be in the form of money, property, services or anything else of value. It need not be of pecuniary value,[89] "so long as it is of sufficient value in the eyes of the person bribed to influence his official conduct." [90]

It was held in an early Indiana case that a promissory note could not serve as a bribe because the note could not be enforced and hence was not value.[91] This notion that the requisite is a legally-approved value, rather than conduct-influencing value, is quite unsound. It would rule out every promise, since a promise made corruptly with intent to influence official action would be against public policy and hence unenforceable even if not criminal. But a promise to confer a benefit comes within the meaning of "value of any kind" as it is used in the law of bribery.[92] Much more sound was the decision that a promise to give illegal lottery tickets would constitute a bribe.[93]

If money or property is given or received for the improper purpose of influencing official action it is not kept out of the realm of bribery by a mere pretended purchase or sale. If, for example, property is sold for less than its true value it will be bribery if the real purpose, understood by both, is to enrich the purchaser for the purpose of influencing his official action.[94] The

88. Rowland v. State, 213 Ark. 780, 790, 213 S.W.2d 370, 376 (1948); Lowe v. Texas Liquor Control Board, 255 S.W.2d 252, 257 (Tex.Civ.App.1952).

"Indiana bribery is a continuing offense so that payments made as part of an arrangement to influence a public official in the discharge of his duties are violations of Indiana law regardless of whether the money is paid before or after the bargained-for acts are performed." United States v. Forszt, 655 F.2d 101, 104 (7th Cir. 1981). See also Shriver v. State, 632 P.2d 420, 428 (Okl. Cr.App.1981).

89. See People v. Hyde, 156 App.Div. 618, 624, 141 N.Y.S. 1089, 1093 (1913).

90. Scott v. State, 107 Ohio St. 475, 485, 141 N.E. 19, 22 (1923).

"Bribe receiving is committed when a public servant accepts or agrees to accept a benefit upon the understanding that his official actions will be influenced; it is the defendant's state of mind which is controlling. It is therefore of no moment that the white substance carried by the undercover was not a narcotic." Peo-

ple v. Holmes, 72 A.D.2d 1, 423 N.Y.S.2d 45, 48 (1979).

91. State v. Walls, 54 Ind. 561 (1876).

92. People v. Van de Carr, 87 App. Div. 386, 84 N.Y.S. 461 (1903). Cf. United States v. Wall, 225 F.2d 905 (7th Cir. 1955).

93. Zalla v. State, 61 So.2d 649 (Fla. 1952). There was a guarantee that the tickets would net the officers about $70 a week, but the guarantee could not have been enforced because it would have been part of the illegal transaction. An offer of official action in exchange for a woman's virtue is bribery. Scott v. State, 107 Ohio St. 475, 141 N.E. 19 (1923).

94. To sell a car at a discount of $600 off the list price to secure the vote of a city alderman was bribery. State v. Sawyer, 266 Wis. 494, 63 N.W.2d 749 (1954). And calling a transfer of money a "loan" will not take it out of the realm of bribery if the real purpose was to influence official action. Krogmann v. United States, 225 F.2d 220 (6th Cir. 1955).

same is true if property is "bought" for a sum in excess of its true value to enrich the seller for a like purpose.[95]

In no case, it may be added, is it essential for the corrupt agreement to be couched in express terms. An actual understanding is sufficient whether it is expressed or implied.[96]

3. SOLICITATION OR OFFER

The solicitation of a bribe on one side, or the offer to give a bribe on the other, is punishable at common law even if promptly rejected.[97]

The original theory was probably that such misconduct was punished as attempted bribery, rather than bribery itself, but this is not entirely clear[98] and it has been said flatly that such acts "are embraced by the common law crime of bribery."[99] This is of very little practical importance today because statutes so commonly control. At times the legislature has provided a comprehensive definition of a bribe in some such terms as "anything of value or advantage, present or prospective, asked, offered, given, accepted or promised with a corrupt intent to influence, unlawfully, the person to whom it is given, in his action, vote or opinion, in any public or official capacity."[1] A rather common pattern has been to express the two sides of the corrupt conduct in some such words as whoever (1) "offers, confers or agrees to confer,"[2] (2) "asks, receives or agrees to receive,"[3] or "solicits, accepts or agrees to accept."[4] Sometimes, on the other hand, bribery and attempted bribery have been kept separate with different penalties.[5] Occasionally part of the field has been excluded by the wording of a particular statute. Thus the California court held that a section providing for the conviction of an officer "who receives or agrees to receive any bribe" and so forth, does not cover the solicitation of a bribe because unless the offer to be bribed was accepted there was no agreement.[6]

To constitute bribery, as the offense is ordinarily recognized today, it is not essential that both parties have a corrupt intent. The guilty party may

---

95. An offer to a township trustee to sell the township certain property for $175 and to give him a receipt showing $194 purportedly paid therefor is an offer to bribe. State v. McDonald, 106 Ind. 233, 6 N.E. 607 (1885).

96. Commonwealth v. Dreier, 43 Luz. L.Reg. 195 (Luz.Co.Pa.1953).

Proof that D who was interested in gambling gave an officer (known to him only as an officer) $200 as a "Christmas gift in November" supported a charge of bribery. State v. Birns, 10 Ohio App. 103, 226 N.E.2d 149 (1967).

97. See Rex v. Vaughan, 4 Burr. 2494, 2500, 98 Eng.Rep. 308, 311 (1769); State v. Ivanhoe, 238 Mo.App. 200, 216, 177 S.W.2d 657, 667 (1944).

The Alabama bribery statute includes an offer to accept a bribe. Hence conviction does not require proof that the offer

was accepted. McDonald v. Headrick, 554 F.2d 253 (5th Cir. 1977).

98. See People v. Peters, 265 Ill. 122, 128, 106 N.E. 513, 515 (1914).

99. State v. Greer, 238 N.C. 325, 328, 77 S.E.2d 917, 919–20 (1953).

1. E.g., Ariz.Rev.Stat. § 1–215 (1974).

2. E.g., Ala.Code § 13A–10–61(a)(1) (1977).

3. E.g., Idaho Code § 18–1302 (1979).

4. Ala.Code § 13A–10–61(a)(2) (1977); Mont.Code Ann. § 45–7–101 (1979).

5. People v. Peters, 265 Ill. 122, 123, 106 N.E. 513, 515 (1914).

6. People v. Weitzell, 201 Cal. 116, 255 P. 792 (1927). Soliciting a bribe was later made an offense. West's Ann.Cal. Pen.Code § 653f (1976).

And see People v. Gliksman, 78 Cal. App.3d 343, 144 Cal.Rptr. 451 (1978).

be convicted if money corruptly solicited by an officer is paid only to provide evidence,[7] or if money corruptly offered to an officer is accepted for a like reason.[8] It is important to add, however, that the offense of offering a bribe is complete when the offer is made and it is not necessary to show an actual tender.[9]

4. THE PURPOSE OF THE BRIBE

The general purpose of the bribe, needless to say, is corruptly to influence official action,[10] but it is important to give attention to the specific purpose in particular instances. One very common type of bribery is the payment of "protection money" to an officer to induce him not to interfere with the criminal activities of the briber.[11] Only a few examples of obvious bribery need be added for the purpose of illustration, such as payment to an officer to induce him wrongfully to refrain from making an arrest,[12] to release an arrestee,[13] to postpone the service of process,[14] to remove records of traffic violations from the files of the court,[15] to permit horsemeat to be sold as beef,[16] or to permit private appropriation of public property.[17] And in the area of recent statutory additions to the field it was held bribery to offer a university football player the sum of $1000 to induce him so to play that his team would not win by more than twenty points.[18]

While possibly not quite so obvious, the corrupt purpose of the bribe may be to induce a member of a city council to cast his official vote in favor of a certain appropriation,[19] or the awarding of a construction contract,[20] or the granting of a specified license; [21] or to induce the city attorney to express his opinion in favor of the city's entering into a certain contract.[22]

7. People v. Lyons, 4 Ill.2d 396, 122 N.E.2d 809 (1954).

8. Wells v. State, 174 Tenn. 552, 129 S.W.2d 203 (1939).

9. Aaron v. State, 161 Tex.Cr.R. 156, 275 S.W.2d 693 (1955).

10. See Kemler v. United States, 133 F.2d 235, 238 (1st Cir. 1943); State v. Greer, 238 N.C. 325, 328, 77 S.E.2d 917, 920 (1953); United States v. Anderson, 509 F.2d 312 (D.C.Cir. 1974).

The Louisiana bribery statute is not restricted to acts in anticipation of specific official action. The practice of entertaining public officials in the hope that business expectations might be enhanced in the future could constitute a violation of this statute. United States v. L'Hoste, 609 F.2d 796 (5th Cir. 1980).

11. State v. Martin, 74 Ariz. 145, 245 P.2d 411 (1952); Usry v. State, 90 Ga. App. 644, 83 S.E.2d 843 (1954); Ford v. Commonwealth, 177 Va. 889, 15 S.E.2d 50 (1941); State v. Carr, 172 Conn. 458, 374 A.2d 1107 (1977).

12. People v. Longo, 119 Cal.App.2d 416, 259 P.2d 53 (1953).

13. Mays v. United States, 289 F. 486 (4th Cir. 1923).

14. People v. Salomon, 212 N.Y. 446, 106 N.E. 111 (1914).

15. People v. Nankervis, 330 Mich. 17, 46 N.W.2d 592 (1951).

16. People v. Siciliano, 4 Ill.2d 581, 123 N.E.2d 725 (1955).

17. Commonwealth v. Ricci, 177 Pa. Super. 556, 112 A.2d 656 (1955). It may be to obtain appointment to, or promotion in, public office. United States v. Wall, 225 F.2d 905 (7th Cir. 1955). The bribe may be in the form of an agreement by an officer that an action for trespass brought by the state shall be abandoned. State v. Emmanuel, 49 Wn.2d 109, 298 P.2d 510 (1956).

18. In terms of the gambling snydicates the margin of victory was not to exceed $20^1/_2$ points. Glickfield v. State, 203 Md. 400, 101 A.2d 229 (1953).

19. People v. Van de Carr, 87 App. Div. 386, 84 N.Y.S. 461 (1903).

20. State v. Brown, 364 Mo. 759, 267 S.W.2d 682 (1954).

21. Peccole v. McNamee, 70 Nev. 298, 267 P.2d 243 (1954).

22. People v. Salsbury, 134 Mich. 537, 96 N.W. 936 (1903).

For guilt of bribery it is obviously not necessary, that the act requested be one which the bribee has authority to do,[23] for it is frequently illegal as shown in some of the illustrations above. If he has the power or ability [24] or apparent ability [25] to comply with the request, no more is needed. And bribery is not precluded by the fact that the bribee is only one member of a board, council or other body, and hence will be unable to bring about the desired result if other members are obstinate.[26] The prevailing view is that bribery may be predicated upon an effort corruptly to influence the action of an officer or public employee provided the act requested is apparently within the ambit of the general scope of his duties or authority, but not if it is obviously unrelated thereto.[27]

5. THE INTENT

A corrupt intent is essential to guilt of bribery [28] but it is important to keep in mind just what constitutes corruption in this regard. On the part of

23. Hurley v. United States, 192 F.2d 297 (4th Cir. 1951); People v. Gordon, 120 Cal.Rptr. 840, 47 Cal.App.3d 465 (1975).

24. Ibid.

25. A coroner asked for and received $500 upon the agreement that his official action as coroner should be influenced thereby in a homicide he was investigating. The cause of death occurred in his borough but the death itself was elsewhere and under New York law he had no jurisdiction. But his conviction of bribery was affirmed. People v. Jackson, 191 N.Y. 293, 84 N.E. 65 (1908). Compare Goldsberry v. State, 92 Tex.Cr. R. 108, 242 S.W. 221 (1922). And a sheriff may be guilty of bribery for receiving money to refrain from arresting a woman or interfering with her operation of a house of prostitution although her place is outside the restricted area and not an offense under the statutes of the particular jurisdiction. State v. Martin, 74 Ariz. 145, 245 P.2d 411 (1952).

26. Raines v. State, 65 So.2d 558 (Fla. 1953).

27. State v. Nadeau, 81 R.I. 505, 105 A.2d 194 (1954); State v. Hibicke, 263 Wis. 213, 56 N.W.2d 818 (1953). And see annotation, 158 A.L.R. 323 (1945).

"The rule requiring that the matter in which the bribe is attempted be related to the officer's duty before it can be a crime, is a wise one. The possible perversion of justice is the touchstone and guide. And although it might be morally improper and may well involve some other crime to give or offer money to an officer to do an act totally unrelated to his job, it would not be bribery." State v. Hendricks, 66 Ariz. 235, 242, 186 P.2d 943, 948 (1947). Quoted with approval in State v. Bowling, 5 Ariz.App. 436, 427 P.2d 928, 935 (1967).

Bowling holds that it was not bribery for members of the legislature to accept money for obtaining a liquor license for the payor, since issuance of the license was exclusively in the discretion of the Superintendent of Liquor Licenses and Control, and there was no proof of any custom or usage for legislators to make fair and impartial—and hence "official"—recommendations to the Superintendent. The court added that there was an element of impropriety involved since the legislators did not disclose to the Superintendent that they were acting for a fee.

28. The crime of bribery requires "an evil or corrupt motive to be proved." State v. Alfonsi, 33 Wis.2d 469, 147 N.W.2d 550 (1967). This motive or intent may be established by circumstantial evidence. People v. Meacham, 256 Cal.App. 2d 735, 64 Cal.Rptr. 362 (1967). See also United States v. Glazer, 129 F.Supp. 285 (D.C.Del.1955); Zalla v. State, 61 So.2d 649, 651 (Fla.1952). Hence defendant is not guilty if he was too drunk at the time to entertain such an intent. White v. State, 103 Ala. 72, 16 So. 63 (1893). The Texas court said its statute "does not require allegation or proof that the acceptance of a bribe be with corrupt intent, . . ." Stoval v. State, 104 Tex.Cr.R. 210, 216, 283 S.W. 850, 853 (1925). "The requisite intent to sustain a conviction for bribery is that the official accept a thing of value 'corruptly.' However, under the unlawful gratuity subsection all that need be proven is that the official accepted, because of his position, a thing of value 'otherwise than as provided by law for the proper discharge of official du-

the briber this requires an intent to subject the official action of the recipient to the influence of personal gain or advantage rather than public welfare.[29] It does not require that the action sought to be induced should benefit the briber [30] or should actually be detrimental to the public. The social interest demands that official action should be free from improper motives of personal advantage,[31] and an intent to subject the action to such motives is a corrupt intent. If money is paid for such a purpose it is immaterial to the guilt of the briber whether the officer's official conduct was actually influenced or not.[32] On the part of the bribee, an intent to use the opportunity to perform a public duty as a means of acquiring an unlawful personal benefit or advantage, is a corrupt intent. Hence it is no defense to a charge of receiving a bribe that the recipient believed the action requested would be for the best interest of the public, or that he had determined upon that course of action before the bribe was offered.[33] An officer who has determined upon a certain course of public action might change his mind if free from corrupting influences. The social interest requires that there should be no such conflict.

6. NATURE OF THE OFFENSE

Bribery, which was in the misdemeanor category at common law, has very commonly been made a felony by statute.

Sections on the subject are frequently scattered throughout the code as they affect different types of officers or other persons having public duties to perform, not to mention the recent extensions into fields of nonofficial action. An unusual problem which requires attention here is this: If money has been corruptly paid and corruptly received, for the purpose of influencing official action, do we have one crime of which two are guilty, or two different crimes? No uniform answer is possible under existing statutes. Under some of the provisions bribery is one offense and references to (1) giving or offering a bribe, or (2) to receiving or soliciting a bribe, are merely factual statements in regard to the guilt of one party or the other. Under another plan "bribery" is employed as a generic term to cover two different offenses: (1) giving or offering a bribe, and (2) receiving or soliciting a bribe. A third plan uses the word "bribery" to indicate the offense of the briber and "receiving a bribe" for the other side of the transaction. Whichever plan is used bribery is not a joint offense in the sense that there must be guilt of at least two, or no guilt at all.[34] As pointed out above there may be guilt on either side alone.

ty.'" United States v. Evans, 572 F.2d 455, 481 (5th Cir. 1978). See also United States v. Fenster, 449 F.Supp. 435 (D.C. Mich.1978).

29. State v. Beattie, 129 Me. 229, 151 A. 427 (1930).

"It is clear . . . that the fraud involved in the bribery of a public official lies in the fact that the public official is not exercising his independent judgment in passing on official matters. United States v. Mandel, 591 F.2d 1347, 1362 (4th Cir. 1979).

30. Glover v. State, 109 Ind. 391, 10 N.E. 282 (1886).

31. The statute "prohibits agents from considering their own personal welfare, . . ." People v. Davis, 160 N.Y.S. 769, 775 (1915).

32. State v. Sawyer, 266 Wis. 494, 63 N.W.2d 749 (1954).

33. State v. Lyskoski, 47 Wn.2d 102, 287 P.2d 114 (1955). A legislator took money under his agreement to "work to kill" a certain bill on the floor of the senate. The fact that he himself was opposed to the bill was no defense to bribery. Sims v. State, 131 Ark. 185, 198 S.W. 883 (1917).

34. People v. Frye, 248 Mich. 678, 277 N.W. 748 (1929).

An additional problem is whether or not the briber and the bribee are accomplices, if both are guilty. This cannot be answered with confidence without an examination of the section on accomplices as well as of the bribery statutes.[35] Some years ago the California court said that by the rule of the common law, and in every state but one, the giver and the receiver of a bribe are accomplices,[36] but such is no longer the rule in that state by reason of an amendment to the accomplice statute.[37]

7. FAILURE TO REPORT OFFER OF BRIBERY

At least one state has created an additional offense in this area by making it a misdemeanor for the recipient thereof to fail to report an offer of bribery, making such a provision applicable to a "public officer, public employee or juror," [38] and also to any "person participating, officiating or connected with any professional or amateur athletic contest, sporting event or exhibition." [39]

8. ALLIED OFFENSES

Embracery is a common-law misdemeanor consisting of an attempt corruptly to influence a juror to one side of the case by promises, persuasions, entreaties, money and the like. The embracer was guilty whether he offered anything of value or not, and the juror was guilty if he accepted money.[40] Thus the bribery of a juror was embracery although the latter offense could be committed without enough to constitute the former.

Modern statutes sometimes make separate provisions, with different penalties, for (1) bribery of jurors [41] and (2) other acts of embracery,[42] the latter perhaps being included with various other misdeeds in a section on obstruction of justice.[43]

The dividing line between bribery and *extortion* is shadowy.[44] If one other than the officer corruptly takes the initiative and offers what he knows is not an authorized fee, it is bribery and not extortion. On the other hand, if

35. A person who receives a bribe is an accomplice of the person who accepts it. But if the offeree rejects the offer he is not an accomplice. People v. Hyde, 156 App.Div. 618, 141 N.Y.S. 1089 (1913). They are not accomplices because the offenses are distinct. State v. Emmanuel, 42 Wn.2d 799, 259 P.2d 845 (1953).

The payor of a bribe can be an aider and abettor to the payee. United States v. Kenner, 354 F.2d 780 (2d Cir. 1965).

36. People v. Coffee, 161 Cal. 433, 447, 119 P. 901, 907 (1911).

37. People v. David, 210 Cal. 540, 557, 293 P. 32, 39 (1930).

38. Smith-Hurd Ill.Ann.Stat. Ch. 38 § 33-2 (1977). This report to be made to the local prosecuting attorney.

39. Id. at § 29-3. This report to be made to the employer, promoter, a peace officer or the local prosecuting attorney.

40. 4 Bl.Comm. *140.

41. E.g., West's Ann.Cal.Pen.Code §§ 92, 93 (1976).

42. Id. at § 95.

43. E.g., 18 U.S.C.A. §§ 208, 1503, 1504.

44. See Richards v. State, 144 Fla. 177, 181-2, 197 So. 772, 774 (1940); United States v. Williams, 480 F.Supp. 1040 (E.D.La.1979).

"Bribery, of course, connotes a voluntary offer to obtain gain, whereas extortion connotes some form of coercion." United States v. Adcock, 558 F.2d 397, 404 (8th Cir. 1977).

"However, bribery and extortion need not be mutually exclusive." United States v. Rabbitt, 583 F.2d 1014, 1026 (8th Cir. 1978).

the officer corruptly makes an unlawful demand which is paid by one who does not realize it is not the fee authorized for the service rendered, it is extortion and not bribery. In theory it would seem possible for an officer to extort a bribe under such circumstances that he would be guilty of either offense whereas the outraged citizen would be excused.[45]

Bribery tends also to merge with *misconduct in office* (official misconduct). For example, in a case in which an officer was offered money to induce him to release a car that had been confiscated because of its use in a liquor violation, the court pointed out that had the officer corruptly accepted the money he would have been guilty of bribery, and had he released the car he would have been guilty of official misconduct.[46]

If a prosecuting attorney should accept money from another to induce the officer to prevent the finding of an indictment against that person this would be *compounding a crime* if the officer knew the other was guilty of an offense, but would be bribery whether he had such knowledge or not.[47]

Where several persons are involved it may be possible to secure convictions of *conspiracy* as well as of bribery.[48] And where payment was made to three councilmen to induce them to permit a private citizen to strip coal from city-owned property, this was held sufficient to support convictions of (1) giving a bribe, (2) accepting a bribe, (3) conspiracy, and (4) misconduct in office.[49]

It may be added in passing that the fact that an officer seems receptive to the offer of a bribe when he is merely attempting to procure evidence thereof, does not constitute the defense of entrapment.[50]

---

45. Although the statute makes it bribery to give money to a labor representative to influence his action for the union, a payment to a labor leader to prevent a ruinous strike which the leader was under no duty to call was not bribery but extortion. Hornstein v. Paramount Pictures, 37 N.Y.S.2d 404 (1942), aff'd 266 App.Div. 659, 41 N.Y.S.2d 210 (1943), appeal denied 266 App.Div. 828, 43 N.Y.S.2d 751 (1943).

In an extortion case it was said: "That such conduct may also constitute 'classic bribery' is not a relevant consideration." United States v. Price, 617 F.2d 455, 458 (7th Cir. 1980). Bribery and extortion are not mutually exclusive. United States v. Butler, 618 F.2d 411 (6th Cir. 1980).

"The fact that a public official may demand money to influence the performance of his official duties, and thus be guilty of bribery, does not mean that he may not also be guilty of the separate crime provided in Article 27 Section 562 (extortion), . . ." Carey v. State, 43 Md.App. 246, 405 A.2d 293, 301 (1979).

46. Wells v. State, 174 Tenn. 552, 129 S.W.2d 203 (1939). A city commissioner who was charged with bribery for allegedly asking a reward for casting his official vote in favor of an application for a gaming license was not entitled to have the prosecution dismissed on the claim that it should have been for misconduct in office. Peccole v. McNamee, 70 Nev. 298, 267 P.2d 243 (1954).

47. State v. Henning, 33 Ind. 189 (1870).

48. Calvaresi v. United States, 216 F.2d 891 (10th Cir. 1954); People v. Bennett, 132 Cal.App.2d 569, 282 P.2d 590 (1955); State v. Papalos, 150 Me. 370, 113 A.2d 624 (1955).

49. Commonwealth v. Ricci, 177 Pa. Super. 556, 112 A.2d 656 (1955).

50. People v. Finkelstein, 98 Cal.App. 2d 545, 220 P.2d 934 (1950).

As to entrapment see, infra, chapter 10, section 9.

D. MISCONDUCT IN OFFICE (OFFICIAL MISCONDUCT)

The prevention of outside influences tending toward corruption is not the only social interest in the official action of public officers. It is socially desirable, so far as reasonably possible, to insure that no public officer shall, in the exercise of the duties of his office or while acting under color of his office, (1) do any act which is wrongful in itself—malfeasance, (2) do any otherwise lawful act in a wrongful manner—misfeasance, or (3) omit to do any act which is required of him by the duties of his office—nonfeasance. And any corrupt violation by an officer in any of these three ways is a common-law misdemeanor[51] known by some such name as "misconduct in office" or "official misconduct."

It is possible, of course, for a public officer to misbehave in other ways. The corrupt receipt of a bribe by an officer, for example, is criminal misconduct of one *while in* office, but such a recipient is clearly not acting in the exercise of the duties of his office, nor is this wrongful act under color of his office, and bribery has always been recognized as a separate offense. In fact, if an officer corruptly receives a bribe and then corruptly does what he has been bribed to do, he is guilty of both bribery and misconduct in office.[52]

The common-law punishment for misconduct in office is by imprisonment or fine to which may be added removal from office and disqualification to hold office.[53] It is beyond the scope of the present undertaking to consider in which particular instances it is necessary to start (1) with impeachment, (2) with indictment or information, or (3) with some special removal procedure, but it may be pointed out that since removal from office is for the betterment of public service rather than for punishment, it may not be necessary to prove all that would be needed to convict of crime if no more is sought than removal from office, by reason of incompetence or neglect, under some special procedure established by statute for this purpose.[54] This point requires emphasis because care must be taken not to rely upon such a proceeding in the search for the elements of the crime known as misconduct in office.[55]

---

51. See State v. Seitz, 40 Del. 572, 14 A.2d 710 (1940); State v. Winne, 12 N.J. 152, 163, 96 A.2d 63, 68 (1953); Commonwealth v. Mecleary, 147 Pa.Super. 9, 21–2, 23 A.2d 224, 229 (1941).

52. State v. Jefferson, 90 N.J.L. 507, 101 A. 569 (1917); Wells v. State, 174 Tenn. 552, 129 S.W.2d 203 (1939). In the Tennessee case the officer accepted the proffered bribe only as evidence and at once arrested the briber. The court pointed out that had he accepted it corruptly he would have been guilty of bribery and had he done as wrongfully requested he would have been guilty of official misconduct.

53. 4 Bl.Comm. *121; State v. Bolitho, 103 N.J.L. 246, 261, 136 A. 164,

172 (1926); State v. Kruger, 280 Mo. 293, 217 S.W. 310 (1919).

54. As to removal see Coffey v. Superior Court, 147 Cal. 525, 82 P. 75 (1905); Ex parte Amos, 93 Fla. 5, 112 So. 289 (1927); State v. Henderson, 145 Iowa 657, 124 N.W. 767 (1910); Ford, Administrative Removal of Public Officers, 30 B.U.L.Rev. 521 (1950).

55. Burdick, for example, inadvertently relies upon a case involving only a special removal procedure, for his inaccurate conclusion that in the absence of statute no corruption or criminal intention is needed for misconduct in office. See 1 Burdick, The Law of Crime, § 272 and footnotes 36 and 37 (1946).

1. UNDER COLOR OF OFFICE

The mere coincidence that crime has been committed by one who happens to be a public officer is not sufficient to establish official misconduct. For this offense it is necessary not only that the offender be an officer, or one who presumes to act as an officer,[56] but the misconduct, if not actually in the exercise of the duties of his office, must be done under color of his office.[57] On the other hand the act of one who is an officer, which act is done because he is an officer or because of the opportunity afforded by that fact, is *under color of his office* despite his gesture of removing his badge plus his statement that he is not acting in the name of the law.[58]

2. CORRUPT INTENT

As indicated above, it may not be necessary to show corruption on the part of the officer if no more is sought than his removal from office because of incompetency or neglect under a special statutory proceeding provided for that purpose, and an officer who has levied on the wrong property quite inadvertently may be liable on his official bond,[59] but an honest mistake of an officer in the discharge of his duties cannot make him a criminal.[60] Even if his act was the result of ignorance it is not a crime [61] so long as it was done in good faith "no matter how erroneous." [62] The statement sometimes encountered that "neither willfulness, nor corruption need be alleged," [63] while definitely a minority view,[64] must not be misinterpreted even as such. It does not mean that the crime may be committed without any element of corruption but only that in some jurisdictions the prosecution has no affirmative burden of pleading and proof in this regard. Whether the prosecution does or does not have such a burden there should be no conviction of this offense

---

56. An officer *de facto* is punishable for misconduct in office the same as an officer *de jure*. State v. Goss, 69 Me. 22 (1878). See annotation, 64 A.L.R. 534 (1929). In Pennsylvania a municipal police officer is merely an employee and not a public officer and hence cannot be guilty of misconduct in office under the statutes of that state. Commonwealth v. Russo, 177 Pa.Super. 470, 111 A.2d 359 (1955).

The common-law crimes of misfeasance and malfeasance in office apply only to officers. An inspector of the Motor Vehicle Department was in public employ but was not an officer. Raduszewski v. Superior Court, 232 A.2d 95 (Del.1967).

57. As said in a case which was a proceeding for removal from office rather than a prosecution for crime, official misconduct (quoting Mechem) "must be such as affects his performance of his duties as an officer, and not such only as affects his character as a private individual." People v. Shawver, 30 Wyo. 366, 428, 222 P. 11, 31 (1923).

58. Catlette v. United States, 132 F.2d 902 (4th Cir. 1943).

59. Harris v. Hanson, 11 Me. 241 (1834).

60. See Commonwealth v. Wood, 116 Ky. 748, 750–1, 76 S.W. 842, 843 (1903); Robbins v. Commonwealth, 232 Ky. 115, 117, 22 S.W.2d 440, 441 (1929).

61. Ibid.

62. McNair's Petition, 324 Pa. 48, 55, 187 A. 498, 502 (1936).

63. State v. Winne, 12 N.J. 152, 176, 96 A.2d 63, 75 (1953).

64. People v. Ward, 85 Cal. 585, 24 P. 785 (1890); State v. Pinger, 57 Mo. 243 (1874); Jacobs v. Commonwealth, 29 Va. 709 (1830). "Corruption, in some form of words, must generally be averred; it is believed, always at common law" (Quoting Bishop). Commonwealth v. Wood, 116 Ky. 748, 750, 76 S.W. 842, 843 (1903). "The common-law offense, however, must be charged as having been wilfully or corruptly done or omitted." Ex parte Amos, 93 Fla. 5, 112 So. 289 (1927).

if the absence of any element of corruption has been clearly established,[65] unless the prosecution is under a statute substantially different from the common law in this respect. In the search for corruption, it is hardly necessary to add, there are many situations in which "actions speak louder than words." [66]

The word "corruption," as an element of misconduct in office, is used in the sense of depravity, perversion or taint.[67] An intent to defraud, for example, is a corrupt intent but such a state of mind is not essential to "corruption," [68] and the same may be said of an intent to "graft"—meaning to obtain an unlawful financial advantage.[69]

It is possible, of course, for legislation to go beyond the common law and to include within the area of punishability certain acts which were not previously criminal. If the statute provides that an intentional violation of its provisions constitutes guilt, no more is required,[70] but this is not truly an enlargement of the offense because it is *corrupt* for an officer purposely to violate the duties of his office. The statute, however, may provide for the punishment of a negligent failure of an officer to do as required,[71] and this does go beyond the common law because negligence is not corruption. A corrupt intent is clearly not required under a section providing for the punishment of neglect of duty if the word "corruptly" is not found therein but is added to another section on the same subject.[72] As has been pointed out, a statute might impose a penalty upon an officer who so conducts himself as to cause the finger of suspicion to be pointed at his official conduct,[73] and intoxication while in the performance of any official act or duty is punishable under some of the codes.[74] If the enactment is clear no problem is involved, but if not the courts will refuse to give a strained construction to a statute which will result in punishment of an officer for what is done without a corrupt motive.[75]

65. People v. Ward, 85 Cal. 585, 591–2, 24 P. 785, 787 (1890); Commonwealth v. Mecleary, 147 Pa.Super. 9, 23 A.2d 224 (1941); Jacobs v. Commonwealth, 29 Va. 709, 715 (1830); Rex v. Baylis, 3 Burr. 1318, 97 Eng.Rep. 851 (1762); Rex v. Young, 1 Burr. 447, 97 Eng.Rep. 447 (1758). "[W]ickedly abuses or fraudulently exceeds" his powers. State v. Glasgow, 1 N.C. 275 (1800). "[E]vil intent or corrupt motive." State v. Seitz, 40 Del. 572, 577, 14 A.2d 710, 712 (1940). "[B]ad faith." State v. Winne, 12 N.J. 152, 175, 96 A.2d 63, 74 (1953).

66. State v. Jefferson, 88 N.J.L. 447, 97 A. 162, 163 (1916).

67. Some "evil intent or motive." State v. Seitz, 40 Del. 572, 574, 14 A.2d 710, 711 (1940).

68. State v. Morse, 52 Iowa 509, 3 N.W. 498 (1879).

69. See Hizelberger v. State, 174 Md. 152, 164, 197 A. 605, 610 (1938); State v. Larson, 231 Wis. 207, 219, 286 N.W. 41, 43 (1939). The Wisconsin court spoke of "corrupt motives" as not essential to misconduct in office but was using the phrase in the sense of "graft."

70. State v. Millhaubt, 144 Kan. 574, 61 P.2d 1356 (1936).

71. Smith v. State, 71 Fla. 639, 71 So. 915 (1916); Kirkland v. State, 86 Fla. 130, 97 So. 510 (1923).

72. State v. Anderson, 196 N.C. 771, 147 S.E. 305 (1929).

73. See People v. Stoll, 242 N.Y. 453, 466, 152 N.E. 259, 263–4 (1926).

74. E.g., Miss.Code Ann. § 97–11–23 (1972).

75. People v. Stoll, 242 N.Y. 453, 152 N.E. 259 (1926).

3. MULTIPLICITY OF NAMES

Confusion has been injected into this area of the law by resort to a multiplicity of names or terms with varying degrees of generality or specificity. "Misconduct in office," for example, is used at times merely as a literal statement. In this sense it does not indicate a crime but merely one of the ingredients of a crime. And the phrase may have either one of two different meanings when employed to indicate a crime. This is because of the fact that some of the offenses of this nature have special names of their own, such as "extortion" or "oppression," whereas others do not. Thus the phrase may be used in a generic sense as in the statement: "Oppression is one type of misconduct in office." Or it may be used as the specific name of a crime in referring to an offense of this nature which has no name of its own, such as the case in which a prosecuting attorney corruptly procured the release of a prisoner by the improper approval of a bond.[76] When used to indicate a crime in either of the two senses mentioned—

Misconduct in office is corrupt behavior by an officer in the exercise of the duties of his office or while acting under color of his office.

While *misconduct in office* [77] is the term frequently employed many substitutes have been used for this phrase in all of the meanings suggested, and the definition could be re-worded by the substitution of any of the following: *official misconduct,*[78] *misbehavior in office,*[79] *malconduct in office,*[80] *malpractice in office,*[81] *misdemeanor in office* [82] and *corruption in office.*[83] No doubt others have found their way into the cases.

In addition to the terms used to represent the entire area will be found others intended to indicate certain parts thereof, and these partitioning phrases may be based either upon the nature of the misbehavior or upon the mode of misbehavior.

A. FRAUD IN OFFICE

Misconduct in office can be perpetrated without any element of fraud as when an officer corruptly abuses a prisoner in his custody.[84] On the other hand this offense is committed by any officer who, in the discharge of his

---

76. State v. Wedge, 24 Minn. 150 (1877). The phrase actually used in this case was one of the synonyms mentioned infra, "misbehavior in office." Id. at 151.

77. Coffey v. Superior Court, 147 Cal. 525, 529, 82 P. 75, 76 (1905); People v. Ward, 85 Cal. 585, 24 P. 785 (1890); State v. Leach, 60 Me. 58, 67 (1872); Duncan v. State, 282 Md. 385, 384 A.2d 456 (1978).

78. State v. Winne, 12 N.J. 152, 175, 96 A.2d 63, 75 (1953); State v. Bolitho, 103 N.J.L. 246, 261, 136 A. 164, 172 (1926); Craig v. State, 31 Tex.Cr.R. 29, 30, 19 S.W. 504 (1892).

79. State v. Wedge, 24 Minn. 150, 151 (1877); Jacobs v. Commonwealth, 29 Va. 709 (1830).

80. Ex parte Amos, 93 Fla. 5, 17, 112 So. 289, 294 (1927).

81. Ibid.

82. Commonwealth v. Mecleary, 147 Pa.Super. 9, 21-2, 23 A.2d 224, 229 (1941). This term could not be used properly as a mere ingredient of an offense.

83. State v. Douglass, 239 Mo. 674, 678, 144 S.W. 407 (1911). This also would indicate a crime although it might be used in either of the two meanings mentioned in the text.

84. Crews v. United States, 106 F.2d 746 (5th Cir. 1947). The same is true when an officer, knowing there had been no violation, corruptly arrested a man without a warrant. State v. Kruger, 280 Mo. 293, 217 S.W. 310 (1919).

office or under color thereof, commits any fraud or breach of trust affecting the public, whether such conduct would or would not be criminal if only a private person were involved.[85]   Thus an officer who fraudulently misappropriates public funds collected by him is guilty of this offense [86] if such misconduct is not covered by an embezzlement statute.[87]   Other instances of this offense are, for example, (1) the fraudulent issuance of a false witness pay certificate by a clerk of court,[88] (2) the corrupt non-disclosure of certain items due the public, such non-disclosure being by a public accountant who did not owe the items or handle the money,[89] and (3) the contract for public supplies on the condition that the profit should be divided between the purchasing officer and the supplier.[90]   In the last of these cases it is to be noted that it was fraudulent for the officer not to give the public the benefit of any reduction in profit the seller was willing to take, and also that since the officer shared the profits with the seller there was an incentive for the permission of excessive charges.

The phrase "fraud in office" is used to indicate this type of official misconduct.[91]

B.   MALFEASANCE IN OFFICE

As indicated above, misconduct may take any one of three different forms: (1) the doing of that which should not be done at all, (2) doing in an improper manner that which would otherwise be acceptable, and (3) failing to do that which should be done.   And the familiar labels used in the law are respectively, (1) malfeasance, (2) misfeasance and (3) nonfeasance.   Any one of the three could be perpetrated by any person, but when it is by an officer in the exercise of the duties of his office, or while acting under color of office, it becomes malfeasance in office—and so forth.[92]   And just as is true of the phrase "misconduct in office," as pointed out above, so "malfeasance in office," "misfeasance in office" or "nonfeasance in office" may be used in a particular instance to indicate (1) only an ingredient of the crime [93] or (2) the offense itself.[94]   Except where the contrary is clearly indicated by the context they are employed here to refer to the offense itself.

85. Stephen, Digest of the Criminal Law, art. 144 (8th ed. by Sturge, 1947).

86. State v. Douglass, 239 Mo. 674, 144 S.W. 407 (1911).

87. E.g., West's Ann.Cal.Pen.Code § 504 (1970).

88. Bracey v. State, 64 Miss. 17, 8 So. 163 (1886).

89. The King v. Bembridge, 3 Dougl. 327, 99 Eng.Rep. 679 (1783).

90. Rex v. Jones, 31 St.Tr. 251 (Eng. 1809).

91. Bracey v. State, 64 Miss. 17, 20, 8 So. 163, 164 (1886); State v. Douglass, 239 Mo. 674, 679, 144 S.W. 407, 408 (1911).

92. "The phrase 'misconduct in office' is broad enough to include any willful malfeasance, misfeasance, or nonfea-

sance in office."   Coffey v. Superior Court, 147 Cal. 525, 529, 82 P. 75, 76 (1905).

93. An officer who levied on the wrong property was guilty of malfeasance in office and was liable on his bond without a showing of corruption.   Harris v. Hanson, 11 Me. 241 (1834).

94. It is "malfeasance in office" for a coroner "wrongfully and corruptly" to hold an inquest which he knew he had no right under the law to hold.   Fuson v. Commonwealth, 241 Ky. 481, 483, 44 S.W.2d 578, 579 (1931).   The justice of the peace had no authority to remit fines but if he did so without a corrupt motive he is not guilty of malfeasance in office.   State v. Seitz, 40 Del. 572, 14 A.2d 710 (1940).

Typical instances of malfeasance in office are where, acting corruptly, a judge issued a warrant of arrest knowing there was no ground therefor,[95] a secretary of state issued a second land grant to the heirs of a soldier knowing he had previously issued the only grant to which they were entitled,[96] an officer removed and destroyed official records,[97] or substituted a false subpoena for the true one.[98]

C. MISFEASANCE IN OFFICE

The distinction between malfeasance in office and misfeasance in office is much less sharp in the actual cases than it is in legal theory, and since the reference is not to two different offenses,[99] but merely to two different modes of committing the offense, the courts have had little occasion to indulge in hairsplitting discussions of the problem. The distinction can be tested by assuming a county commissioner whose duties included the letting of contracts for public buildings and other work needed for county purposes, and who let a certain contract for the corrupt purpose of enriching a friend.[1] If the contract was one which should not have been let at all the misconduct was malfeasance in office, whereas if the work was needed in the public interest, but the commissioner dealt only with his friend instead of offering the project for competitive bidding, as required by law in the jurisdiction, it was a case of misfeasance in office. Since, however, nothing is involved other than the use of legal labels it is better to employ some such term as "misconduct in office" or "official misconduct"[2] than to labor the distinction between "malfeasance" and "misfeasance."

D. NONFEASANCE IN OFFICE

The distinction between nonfeasance in office and the other two modes of official misconduct is clear enough in legal theory. Each of the others requires an act of commission—positive action, whereas this one involves an act of omission—negative action. Questions may arise in certain cases, however, as where a contract is let under a statute requiring it to be given to the lowest responsible bidder. If the officer corruptly violates his duty in this regard should this be said to be "nonfeasance in office" because he failed to let the contract to the lowest responsible bidder or "misfeasance in office" because he improperly let it to one other than the lowest? Since the answer

95. Robbins v. Commonwealth, 232 Ky. 115, 22 S.W.2d 440 (1929).

96. State v. Glasgow, 1 N.C. 264 (1800).

97. People v. Peck, 138 N.Y. 386, 34 N.E. 347 (1893).

98. Baldwin v. State, 11 Ohio St. 681 (1860).

99. For example, "malfeasance, nonfeasance or misfeasance in office" is referred to as the "common-law offense." Ex parte Amos, 93 Fla. 5, 19–20, 112 So. 289, 294 (1927). In one case the language might be thought of as referring to different offenses but the court is merely following the wording of counsel while refuting counsel's contention that the offense shown by the evidence was not the offense charged. Fuson v. Commonwealth, 241 Ky. 481, 44 S.W.2d 578 (1931).

Probably the most careless statement to be found in the cases in this regard is the reference to "the *common law offenses* of malfeasance, misfeasance, nonfeasance, and misdemeanor in office." Commonwealth v. Mecleary, 147 Pa. Super. 9, 21–2, 23 A.2d 224, 229 (1941). One unfamiliar with the field might assume this had reference to three different felonies and one misdemeanor. As there was no common-law felony in this field no more need be said.

1. Commonwealth v. Steinberg, 240 Pa.Super. 139, 362 A.2d 379 (1976).

2. Ore.Rev.Stat. § 162.415 (1953).

would be utterly unimportant if given it is futile to labor the point [3] and references to "nonfeasance in office" should be only for the purpose of emphasizing that official misconduct may be committed in this manner, and the label should be applied only when unquestionably appropriate.[4]

Illustrations of nonfeasance in office include such cases as the wilful refusal of the officer upon whom the particular duty rests, to apprehend [5] or prosecute [6] a known offender, to execute criminal process entrusted to him,[7] or to deliver a copy of certain proceedings to one entitled thereto.[8] It would also be nonfeasance in office if an officer should refuse to take reasonable steps to prevent the lynching of a prisoner in his custody.[9]

Some of the statements used in discussions of nonfeasance in office require careful attention in order to avoid misunderstanding. Statements can be found, for example, which seem to indicate that when the duty is mandatory the omission itself is criminal, whereas when discretion is lodged in the officer it is necessary to show that the failure to act was corrupt.[10] Any such statement, let it be emphasized, is properly referable only to an intentional and deliberate forbearance by the officer.[11] Any intentional and deliberate refusal by an officer to do what is unconditionally required of him by the obligations of his office is *corrupt* as the word is used in this connection because he is not permitted to set up his own judgment in opposition to the positive requirement of the law.[12] Since this is corrupt misbehavior by an officer in the exercise of the duties of his office there is no reason to require more for conviction. On the other hand, when the officer has discretion in regard to a certain matter, his intentional and deliberate refusal to act indicates no more, on its face, than that this represents his judgment as to what will best serve the public interest. Even in such a case the officer will be guilty of misconduct in office if his forbearance results from corruption rather than from the exercise of official discretion,[13] but it will always be

---

3. In a case holding the officer indictable under such facts the court properly omitted any reference to nonfeasance or misfeasance. State v. Kern, 51 N.J.L. 259, 17 A. 114 (1889).

4. It is not "nonfeasance" where there is no clear duty to act. State v. Green, 376 A.2d 424 (Del.Super.1977).

5. State v. Winne, 12 N.J. 152, 96 A.2d 63 (1953).

6. Ibid.; Coffey v. Superior Court, 147 Cal. 525, 82 P. 75 (1905); State v. Jefferson, 90 N.J.L. 507, 101 A. 569 (1917).

7. State v. Berkshire, 2 Ind. 207 (1850); State v. Ferguson, 76 N.C. 197 (1877).

8. Wilson v. Commonwealth, 10 Serg. & R. 373 (Pa.1824). In this case the conviction was reversed because the fee had not been tendered to the officer and his refusal without such tender was not unlawful.

9. See Holliday v. Fields, 210 Ky. 179, 191, 275 S.W. 642, 647 (1925).

10. State v. Commissioners, 48 N.C. 399, 401 (1856); State v. Williams, 34 N.C. 172, 177 (1851); McNair's Petition, 324 Pa. 48, 55, 187 A. 498, 501(1936). The Pennsylvania court used the term "malfeasance in office" but had reference to the magistrate's failure to require bail.

11. The phrase "intentional and deliberate forbearance" is tautological because an unintentional omission is not a "forbearance," but emphasis is particularly important at this point.

12. State v. Ferguson, 76 N.C. 197 (1877). In affirming a conviction of the crime of corruptly endeavoring to obstruct the due administration of justice the court said: "The only intent involved in the crime is the intent to do the forbidden act. The defendant 'must have had knowledge of the facts though not necessarily the law, that made' his act criminal." Caldwell v. United States, 218 F.2d 370, 372 (D.C.Cir.1954).

13. Rex v. Williams, 3 Burr. 1317, 97 Eng.Rep. 851 (1762). This is sometimes

necessary to show something more than the intentional and deliberate forbearance to do a discretionary act.

Some confusion has resulted from use of the word "neglect" in discussions of that type of official misconduct spoken of as nonfeasance in office. This word is employed at times to mean a failure to perform and in this sense would include a negligent omission of duty by an officer, or perhaps an inadvertent omission without so much as negligence. As pointed out above however, even a negligent omission is insufficient for guilt of this offense except where it has been enlarged by statute.[14] The effort to express this view has resulted at times in some such phrase as "wilful negligence" when the idea intended to be conveyed was wilful forbearance.[15] And one court referred to "such gross negligence as to be the equivalent of fraud," when it had in mind fraud rather than any sort of negligence.[16] The word "neglect" itself has been used at times when deliberate forbearance was meant,[17] as in the statement that officers "are liable to indictment for any gross neglect of duty"[18] when the actual conduct referred to was the obstinate refusal to take required action,—or in any suggestion to the effect that wilful "neglect" of duty by an officer is criminal unless performance would be unreasonably dangerous under the circumstances.[19]

Confusion at this point has led to the occasional suggestion that the mental element required for the crime of misconduct in office is "wilfulness" if the act is one of omission and "corruption" if it is an act of commission.[20] "Wilfulness," as so used, is intended to mean deliberate forbearance, and to repeat a previous suggestion: what should be said is that the wilful refusal of an officer to perform a ministerial act[21] required by law constitutes cor-

expressly included in the statute. E.g., Wis.Stats.1955, § 946.12.

14. 10 U.S.C.A. § 892(3) provides for court-martial punishment of military personnel who are "derelict in the performance" of their duties. Negligence will suffice for a conviction.

15. State v. Berkshire, 2 Ind. 207, 208 (1850).

"As President of the Board of Education, Howell had an inherent duty under § 1211(2) not to profit personally from the services and property of the public agency. This was a duty clearly inherent in the nature of his office; and his knowing failure to perform such duty constitutes a violation of § 1211(2)." Howell v. State, 421 A.2d 892, 897 (Del.1980).

16. State v. Seitz, 40 Del. 572, 574, 14 A.2d 710, 711 (1940). The court emphasized that it was referring to conduct "accompanied by some evil intent or motive." Ibid.

"The crimes are, respectively, the wrongful doing of some official act, and the wrongful doing of an unofficial act. In both instances the act must be accompanied by some evil intent or motive, or with such gross negligence as to be

equivalent to fraud." Raduszewski v. Superior Court, 232 A.2d 95, 96 (Del. 1967).

17. " '[O]fficial misconduct' grows out of a willful or corrupt failure, refusal, or neglect of the officer to perform a duty enjoined on him by law, or out of some . . . .'' Craig v. State, 31 Tex.Cr.R. 29, 30, 19 S.W. 504 (1892).

18. State v. Woodbury, 35 N.H. 230, 232 (1857).

19. See State v. Wheatley, 192 Md. 44, 48, 63 A.2d 644, 646 (1949).

20. See State v. Winne, 12 N.J. 152, 175, 96 A.2d 63, 75 (1953). This is suggested also by any such juxtaposition as "willful or corrupt failure, refusal." See Craig v. State, 31 Tex.Cr.R. 29, 30, 19 S.W. 504 (1892).

21. "A ministerial duty, . . . is one in respect to which nothing is left to discretion . . . . A ministerial act is one which a person performs in a given state of facts in a prescribed manner, in obedience to the mandate of legal authority, without regard to or the exercise of his judgment upon the propriety of the act being done." State v. Staub, 61 Conn. 553, 568, 23 A. 924, 927 (1892).

ruption. A similar comment is appropriate to the statement in one case that "corruption has never been an element of nonfeasance." [22] The court went on to explain that the defendant was charged "with bad faith in his failure to perform the duties of his office," and the true explanation is not that corruption is unnecessary in such a case but that it is established by the bad faith. An officer charged with a duty which requires the exercise of discretion could be guilty of misconduct in office [23] but the state of mind required for guilt would be the same whether his misconduct took the form of omission or commission.

Where a special removal procedure has been provided, or the legislature has enlarged the scope of the offense, it may be sufficient to show that the officer's conduct has been negligent rather than corrupt, but this is not sufficient for guilt of the common-law crime of misconduct in office, or true codifications thereof. Discussions of the latter should avoid the word "negligence" (other than to emphasize its insufficiency), and "forbearance" is preferable to "neglect" when a wilful refusal to act is intended.

The law is not unreasonable in its demands. It neither requires the impossible nor any performance which would be "attended with greater danger than a man of ordinary firmness and activity may be expected to encounter." [24]

4. EXTORTION

If misconduct in office takes the form of the corrupt collection of an unlawful fee by an officer under color of office it is called extortion. [25] While this is an offense affecting the administration of governmental functions, it is also an offense against property and was considered in detail in Chapter IV.

5. OPPRESSION

Insofar as misconduct in office affects some particular individual the result may be either beneficial or harmful to him. Examples of the former, given above, include instances in which as a result of the officer's corruption the other has been unjustly enriched at public expense, or has been allowed to remain at large when he should be arrested. Official misconduct which is harmful to some individual is either extortion or oppression. Hence—

Oppression is any harm or disadvantage, other than extortion, corruptly caused to a person by an officer acting in the exercise of the duties of his office, or under color of office.

---

22. State v. Winne, 12 N.J. 152, 175, 96 A.2d 63, 75 (1953). The court added the astounding statement: "If it were, it would become identical with malfeasance." In the age-old discussions of malfeasance, misfeasance and nonfeasance this seems to be the first suggestion to the effect that the *differentia* is mental rather than modal.

23. Rex v. Williams, 3 Burr. 1317, 97 Eng.Rep. 851 (1762).

24. See State v. Wheatley, 192 Md. 44, 48, 63 A.2d 644, 646 (1949).

25. Bribery and extortion are mutually exclusive. People v. Feld, 262 App. Div. 909, 28 N.Y.S.2d 796, 797 (1941). However, see McKinney's N.Y. Penal §§ 135.70, 155.10, 180.30, 200.15 (1975) which eliminate mutual exclusivity of the two crimes.

"The essence of the crime of bribery is voluntariness while the essence of extortion is duress." United States v. Addonizio, 451 F.2d 49, 77 (3d Cir. 1971).

The classic illustration is that of officers who corruptly refused to issue licenses to those persons who had "voted the wrong way;" [26] and another well-known case involved a coroner who obstinately refused to hear part of the evidence and, after a verdict of accidental death, imprisoned, on a charge of murder, the one who had caused the unfortunate accident.[27]   Other examples include such cases as the officer who arrested a man without a warrant, knowing he had been guilty of no violation; [28] rudely detained another at pistol-point without pretense of lawful reason; [29] wilfully destroyed property without court order or other authority; [30] or cruelly beat an insane pauper.[31] As is true in other cases of misconduct in office there is no guilt of oppression unless the officer acted corruptly.[32]

6.   THE CIVIL RIGHTS ACT

Ordinarily an act of extortion or oppression is not a federal offense unless by a federal officer, or one presuming to act as such, under color of federal authority [33] but the United States Code expressly provides for the punishment of one who "under color of any law, statute, ordinance, regulation, or custom, wilfully subjects" another to the deprivation of "any rights, privileges, or immunities secured or protected by the Constitution or laws of the United States." [34]   Torture by a state officer for the purpose of procuring a confession has been held to be a violation of this federal law,[35] and an agreement under which persons were to be imprisoned under color of state law for the purpose of extorting money from them was held to be a conspiracy to violate that statute.[36]   One of the most extreme cases was that in which a town marshal, announcing that he would give his arrestee a 50-50 chance, compelled him to jump into deep water from which he did not emerge alive.   The officer by substituting his private "trial by ordeal" for a trial under the law was held to have deprived his prisoner of a constitutional right.[37]   Beating a defendant and directing a police dog to bite a defendant to extract a confession has justified a conviction [38] as have the acts of railroad policemen, having the authority of city police, who beat vagrants.[39] The Court has held that this statute requires "a specific intent to deprive a

---

26. Rex v. Williams, 3 Burr. 1317, 97 Eng.Rep. 851 (1762).

27. The King v. Scorey, 1 Leach 43, 168 Eng.Rep. 124 (1748).

28. State v. Kruger, 280 Mo. 293, 217 S.W. 310 (1919).

29. People v. Flynn, 58 Misc. 624, 111 N.Y.S. 1067 (1908).

30. United States v. Deaver, 14 F. 595 (D.C.N.C.1882).

31. State v. Hawkins, 77 N.C. 694 (1877).

32. State v. Ferguson, 67 N.C. 219 (1872); Rex v. Baylis, 3 Burr. 1318, 97 Eng.Rep. 851 (1762); Rex v. Young, 1 Burr. 447, 97 Eng.Rep. 447 (1758).

33. Extortion that delays or effects interstate commerce is punishable under the Hobbs Act, 18 U.S.C.A. § 1957 (1970).

34. 18 U.S.C.A. § 242 (1969).

35. United States v. Sutherland, 37 F.Supp. 344 (D.C.Ga.1940).   The fact that the officer's conduct may violate both state and federal laws does not bar federal prosecution.   United States v. Jones, 207 F.2d 785 (5th Cir. 1953).

36. Culp v. United States, 131 F.2d 93 (8th Cir. 1942).

37. Crews v. United States, 160 F.2d 746 (5th Cir. 1947).   Compare Catlette v. United States, 132 F.2d 902 (4th Cir. 1943).

38. Miller v. United States, 404 F.2d 611 (5th Cir. 1969).

39. United States v. Hoffman, 498 F.2d 879 (7th Cir. 1974) but see United States v. McClean, 528 F.2d 1250 (2nd Cir. 1976).

person of a federal right," [40] and an indictment is defective which fails to include this element.[41]

7.   REFUSAL TO SERVE

A wrongful refusal to undertake the duties of an office to which one had been duly elected or appointed was a common-law misdemeanor [42] which was incorporated in some of the early statutes in this country,[43] but will be found in few if any of the modern penal codes.

E.   EMBRACERY

Unless the case is to be tried by the judge alone, our system of justice entitles the parties to a trial by a fair and impartial jury, whether the proceeding be criminal or civil in its nature. Hence, any unlawful tampering with a jury is in direct conflict with a very important social interest, and any attempt to influence a juror corruptly by promises, threats, persuasions, entreaties, money, entertainments, or any other means except the production of evidence and argument in open court, was a misdemeanor known as embracery at common law.[44] It is unimportant whether the influence is in the direction of a verdict which others might think just or unjust, and it is not essential to guilt that the attempt should succeed.[45] It is deemed the task of the jury to make the determination upon evidence introduced and argument made in the duly authorized manner, entirely free from outside influences one way or the other.[46] The word "outside" must not be overemphasized because a juror may be guilty of common-law embracery by an effort to influence his fellow jurors by corrupt and unlawful methods.[47] The crime may be committed, needless to add, by either party to the case or by a stranger.[48] If the forbidden influence is exerted, the crime of embracery is complete

---

40. Screws v. United States, 325 U.S. 91, 103, 65 S.Ct. 1031, 1036 (1945).

41. An indictment is defective if it fails to charge that the acts were done "wilfully." The word "wilfully" in this statute means a specific intent to deprive a citizen of a federal right. Pullen v. United States, 164 F.2d 756 (5th Cir. 1947).

42. Stephen, Digest of the Criminal Law, art. 151 (8th ed. by Sturge, 1947). "It is an offence at common law to refuse to serve an office when duly elected." The King v. Bower, 1 B. & C. 585, 107 Eng.Rep. 215 (1823).

43. See The Guardians of the Poor v. Greene, 5 Binn. 554 (Pa.1813). It was held in this case that a clergyman, officiating as such, was not bound to accept secular service at common law and hence was not subject to the statutory penalty for not serving.

44. 1 Hawk P.C. c. 85, § 1; 4 Bl. Comm. *140; State v. Sales, 2 Nev. 268,

269–70 (1866). And see State v. Brown, 95 N.C. 685 (1886); Wiseman v. Commonwealth, 143 Va. 631, 635, 130 S.E. 249, 250 (1925).

45. "It is immaterial whether the juror is influenced by the attempt or not, the crime is complete when the attempt is made." Wiseman v. Commonwealth, 143 Va. 631, 636, 130 S.E. 249, 251 (1925).

46. "And the law so far abhors all corruption of this kind that it prohibits everything which has the least tendency to it, . . ." 1 Hawk P.C. c. 85, § 2.

47. "[I]t is as criminal in a juror, as in any other person, to endeavor to prevail with his companions to give a verdict to one side by any practices whatsoever, except only by arguments from the evidence which was produced, and exhortations from the general obligations of conscience to give a true verdict." Id. at § 4.

48. See State v. Sales, 2 Nev. 268, 269 (1866).

"whether the jurors on whom such attempt is made give any verdict or not, or whether the verdict given be true or false." [49]

To solicit a juror to vote for acquittal in a case on trial is a corrupt intent to obstruct the due administration of justice no matter what the purpose may be, even if "he personally knows an indicted person has a complete alibi." [50] Embracery may be committed by corruptly attempting to influence members of the grand jury.[51]

Private surveillance of jurors is contempt of court,[52] and an endeavor to ascertain the feelings or opinions of jurors while they are sitting in a case and prior to their verdict is a corrupt endeavor to obstruct or impede the due administration of justice.[53] "The only intent involved is the intent to do the forbidden act. "[54]

Embracery is an attempt, by corrupt and wrongful means, to influence a juror in regard to the verdict.[55]

Since this offense may be committed by threats, persuasions, entreaties or even by "instructing" the jury extrajudicially,[56] it is obvious that nothing in the nature of a bribe is required. If it takes the form of a bribe and is accepted, both the embracer (giver) and embracee (taker) are guilty of bribery.

At the present time embracery is tending to disappear as a separate offense.[57]

F. COUNTERFEITING

Savages, we are told, often used ornaments such as beads or shells as a medium of exchange, and such things are spoken of as the "money" of the savages. With the rise of civilization, however, money became a matter of outstanding importance and the regulation of its manufacture, use and value came to be recognized as a governmental function. With this development there grew up a strong social interest in the integrity of whatever had the appearance of money and counterfeiting came to be recognized as an offense. In its most restricted sense—

Counterfeiting is the unlawful making of false money in the similitude of the genuine.

49. 1 Hawk P.C. c. 85, § 1. The offense may be committed by exerting the forbidden influence upon those who have been selected for jury duty. Honey v. Goodman, 432 F.2d 333 (6th Cir. 1970).

50. Kong v. United States, 216 F.2d 665, 668 (9th Cir. 1954).

51. Jones v. State, 101 Ga.App. 851, 115 S.E.2d 576 (1960).

52. Private detectives kept the jurors under strict surveillance from early morning until late at night, whenever they were not actually within the courthouse. It was not shown that any operative actually approached any juror or that any juror actually knew he was being shadowed. A conviction of contempt of court was affirmed. Sinclair v. United States, 279 U.S. 749, 49 S.Ct. 471 (1929).

53. Caldwell v. United States, 218 F.2d 370 (D.C.Cir.1954).

54. Id. at 372.

55. E.g., Ga.Code Ann. § 2407 (1977); 27 Md.Code Ann. § 26 (1976).

"The offense of embracery is based on an attempt to influence improperly a juror. . . ." Hoston v. Silbert, 514 F.Supp. 1239 (D.C.D.C.1981).

56. See State v. Sales, 2 Nev. 268, 269 (1866).

57. See, infra, under G. Obstruction of Justice.

This crime is also an offense against property, and as it was considered in detail in Chapter IV this reference must suffice here.

G. OBSTRUCTION OF JUSTICE *

In the subsections above it was pointed out that (1) perjury was first recognized in judicial proceedings, (2) the original cases on bribery involved a judicial officer, and (3) embracery included any corrupt attempt to influence a juror to one side of the case, whether by bribery or otherwise. While there is an obvious social interest in keeping the stream of justice pure and unimpeded in all respects, this early piecemeal recognition is not surprising. The goal,—to proscribe every wilful act of corruption, intimidation or force which tends in any way to distort or impede the administration of law either civil or criminal—has been very largely attained, partly by aid of legislation. And any punishable misdeed of such a nature which is not recognized as a distinct crime, is usually called "obstruction of justice," or "obstructing justice,"—a common-law misdemeanor.[58] Perjury and bribery have been enlarged and firmly established as separate offenses. The word "embracery" on the other hand has tended to disappear. It is included in some of the codes [59] but the tendency has been to divide this common-law offense into two parts, placing that which is appropriate thereto in sections on bribery and the remainder in provisions dealing with obstruction of justice.[60]

18 U.S.C.A. § 1503 makes it a crime for: "Whoever corruptly . . . endeavors to influence, intimidate, or impede any . . . petit juror . . . in the discharge of his duty, . . ." This was held to apply to a prospective juror, although she was later discharged from the panel because of illness; the word "endeavors" was said to avoid any technicality attaching to "attempt;" and evidence that defendant talked with a prospective juror in the obvious hope of influencing her vote, if she was selected to serve, was held sufficient to support his conviction although he offered no bribe, made neither any threats nor promises, and did not tell the juror how to vote. He was corruptly endeavoring to influence a juror in the discharge of her duty.[61]

"The common law is sufficiently broad to punish as a misdemeanor, although there may be no exact precedent, any act which directly injures or tends to injure the public to such an extent as to require the state to interfere and punish the wrongdoer, as in the case of acts which injuriously

---

* "At common law it is an offense to do any act which prevents, obstructs, impedes, or hinders the administration of justice. The intentional failure of a responsible public official to report convictions of traffic violations so as to interrupt or prevent the mandated suspension of a motorist's drivers license is an obstruction of justice and punishable at common law." State v. Cogdell, 273 S.C. 563, 257 S.E.2d 748, 750 (1979).

58. Brown v. Commonwealth, 263 S.W.2d 238 (Ky.1954).

59. E.g., Ga.Code Ann., § 26–2407 (1977).

60. E.g., N.C.G.S. §§ 14–220, 14–226 (1980).

61. United States v. Jackson, 607 F.2d 1219 (8th Cir. 1979). An endeavor to influence a juror in the performance of his duty is an obstruction of justice. United States v. Ogle, 613 F.2d 233 (10th Cir. 1980).

"Approaching a juror through an intermediary is sufficient to constitute an attempt to influence a juror, . . . even though the endeavor failed . . . ." United States v. Forrest, 623 F.2d 1107, 1114 (5th Cir. 1980).

. . . obstruct, or pervert public justice, or the administration of government." [62]

It is an offense "which may take a variety of forms." [63] In addition to the corrupt attempt to influence a juror, [64] mentioned above, obstruction of justice may take the form of obstructing an officer in the performance of his official duties, [65] dissuading, preventing, or attempting to dissuade or prevent a witness from attending a trial or testifying therein, [66] suppression or destruction of evidence, [67] or even intimidation of a party to the proceeding, [68] not to mention other possibilities. Some of these require special attention.

1. RESISTING OR OBSTRUCTING AN OFFICER

One of the most common forms of obstruction of justice involves an interference with a public officer in the discharge of his official duty. [69] Resisting, delaying or obstructing one who is an officer does not constitute obstruction of justice unless the officer is at the time discharging or

62. Commonwealth v. Mochan, 177 Pa.Super. 454, 458, 110 A.2d 788, 790 (1955).

In an attempt to obtain probation for a friend, **D** approached **M**, a friend of the judge, and in discussing the possible probation asked **M** if he could "talk to the Judge, take him to lunch?" He was told this was out of the question, but later approached **M** again and told him he "should talk to Judge and take him out to lunch." Although **D** was told to "forget it" and no one approached the Judge, **D** was held properly convicted of obstructing justice. United States v. Fasolino, 586 F.2d 939 (2d Cir. 1978). The statute (U.S.C.A. § 1503) is worded in terms of "Whoever corruptly, . . . endeavors to influence, . . . any . . . officer . . . in the discharge of his duty, . . ."

63. Commonwealth v. Russo, 177 Pa. Super. 470, 484, 111 A.2d 359, 366 (1955).

64. An endeavor to ascertain the feelings or opinions of jurors while they are sitting in a case and prior to their verdict is a corrupt endeavor to obstruct or impede the due administration of justice. Caldwell v. United States, 218 F.2d 370 (D.C.Cir.1954). "In a criminal case, any private communication, contact, or tampering, directly or indirectly, with a juror during a trial about the matter pending before the jury is, for obvious reasons, deemed presumptively prejudicial, if not made in pursuance of known rules of the court and the instructions and directions of the court made during the trial, with full knowledge of the parties." Remmer v. United States, 347 U.S. 227, 229, 74 S.Ct. 450, 451 (1954).

65. Hall v. United States, 235 F.2d 248 (5th Cir. 1956). And see Speck v. State, 34 Ala.App. 325, 327, 41 So.2d 198, 199 (1949).

The statute prohibiting obstruction of justice may be violated by threatening an officer. Actual violence is not required. In re M.L.B., 110 Cal.App.3d 501, 168 Cal.Rptr. 57 (1980).

66. Kilpatrick v. State, 72 Ga.App. 669, 34 S.E.2d 719 (1945).

67. Commonwealth v. Russo, 177 Pa. Super. 470, 111 A.2d 359 (1955); State v. Nielsen, 19 Utah 2d 66, 426 P.2d 13 (1967).

68. "Any corrupt endeavor whatsoever, to 'influence, intimidate, or impede any party or witness, . . . commissioner, or any grand or petit juror,' etc., whether successful or not, is proscribed by the obstruction of justice statute." Catrino v. United States, 176 F.2d 884, 887 (9th Cir. 1949).

69. Not infrequently this is found in a separate section. E.g., 18 U.S.C.A. § 111 (1969); West's Ann.Cal.Pen.Code § 148 (1970).

S was convicted of violating 18 U.S. C.A. § 1510 (obstruction of criminal investigation). The evidence showed that S had threatened D who had been in communication with the FBI. It was held that a threat of retaliation for past communication with a criminal investigator, although reprehensible, does not violate § 1510. But since this threat was intended to interfere with future communication of additional information to the FBI, the conviction was affirmed. United States v. Segal, 649 F.2d 599 (8th Cir. 1981).

attempting to discharge some official duty,[70] but the mere fact that it happens during off-duty hours is unimportant if the officer is actually attempting to discharge an official duty at the time.[71]   Unlawfully to arrest a United States Attorney and take him to jail, when he was intending to go to his office, is wilfully to prevent him from performing his official duties,[72] and an attempt may be made improperly to intimidate, impede or obstruct the prosecuting attorney in regard to a criminal case, even before an information or indictment has been filed.[73]   Very often the interference is with a peace officer.

Under the common-law theory an officer undertaking an arrest which was in fact unlawful was neither discharging the duties of his office nor attempting to do so. This was not deemed to be an attempt by an officer to discharge the duties of his office,[74] and the intended arrestee was privileged to use reasonable force to prevent this unlawful deprivation of his liberty.[75] But the problems involved are so complicated that it is easy for either the officer or the arrestee to be mistaken in regard to the lawfulness of the arrest and it seems wise to require such issues to be decided in court rather than by force and the present trend, by statute, is to provide that there is no privilege to resist an arrest which the arrestee knows is being made by a peace officer, even if the arrest is unlawful.[76]

Where the officer has back of him the full authority of the law, it has always been clear that there is no privilege to interfere with him in any way.

A resister might be excused if he acted under reasonable mistake of fact,[77] but wilful resistance or opposition to such an effort, with knowledge

70. State v. Harvey, 242 N.C. 111, 86 S.E.2d 793 (1955).

The use of excessive force makes an arrest unlawful. An officer so conducting himself is not engaged in the performance of his official duties, and defending against him is not an obstruction of justice. People v. White, 101 Cal.App. 3d 161, 161 Cal.Rptr. 541 (1980). It is not "any crime." (p. 545).

71. State v. Kurtz, 78 Ariz. 215, 278 P.2d 406 (1954).

72. Hence an agreement to do so is a conspiracy. Finn v. United States, 219 F.2d 894 (9th Cir. 1955).

73. State v. Hartung, 239 Iowa 414, 30 N.W.2d 491 (1948).

74. Jackson v. Superior Court, 98 Cal. App. 189, 219 P.2d 879 (1950).

75. Galvin v. State, 46 Tenn. 283 (1869).

Penal Code, section 834a, making it an offense for one to resist an officer if he knows or in the exercise of reasonable care should know that he is being arrested by a peace officer, does not apply to one who is merely being detained for questioning because such detention is not an arrest. People v. Coffey, 67 Cal.2d 204, 430 P.2d 15, 60 Cal.Rptr. 457 (1967).

76. E.g., West's Ann.Cal.Pen.Code § 834a (1970). This is the position taken in the Model Penal Code, section 3.04(2)(a) (1).

Even in case of an unlawful arrest "a person is not justified in forcibly resisting an arrest unless and until he is faced with the illegal use by an officer of deadly force." State v. Hall, 36 Or.App. 133, 583 P.2d 587, 590 (1978).

"We hold that a private citizen may not use force to resist a search by an authorized police officer engaged in the performance of his duties whether or not the arrest is illegal." State v. Doe, 92 N.M. 100, 583 P.2d 464, 467 (1978).

Even where the right to resist an unlawful arrest has been abolished, an arrestee has the right of self-defense against a police officer who uses excessive force. State v. Kraul, 90 N.M. 314, 563 P.2d 108 (App.1977).

77. Starr v. United States, 153 U.S. 614, 14 S.Ct. 919 (1894); Mullis v. State, 196 Ga. 569, 27 S.E.2d 91 (1943). And see Hall v. United States, 235 F.2d 248, 249 (5th Cir. 1956). One who goes to the assistance of her father, who is being arrested, but without knowledge of the fact that the others are officers who are making an arrest, does not knowingly resist

of the facts, is punishable as a misdemeanor at common law.[78] Certain distinctions are to be noted. While it is the duty of the citizen to submit to lawful arrest, mere flight to avoid apprehension does not constitute resisting an officer because there is a distinction between avoidance and resistance or obstruction.[79] Jerking away from an officer is obstructing him but cursing him is not,[80] and if an arrestee while being taken to the police station struck the officer for the sole purpose of venting spleen upon him, this constituted an assault but not resistance to arrest.[81] On the other hand, any force wilfully employed to prevent the success of the officer's effort is an obstruction of justice whether by the one to be arrested or by another.[82]

Obstruction of justice may be committed by interference with an officer's discharge of duties other than that of making an arrest. It constitutes such an offense, for example, wilfully to drive away a car to prevent its search by officers who had lawfully taken it into custody,[83] or to threaten officers with a pistol in the effort to prevent the removal of the vehicle if that was the purpose for which they had taken possession.[84] The Pennsylvania statute authorizes a representative of the game commission, if in uniform and with badge displayed, to stop a vehicle at any time, without a warrant, and search for legally or illegally killed game. Such an officer stopped **R** and demanded that he open the rear compartment of the car, or deliver the key thereto. **R** refused to do either. This constituted wilful resistance to inspection in violation of the game law.[85] It is obviously an offense wilfully to obstruct an

an officer. The statute requires "knowingly." State v. Bandy, 164 Wash. 216, 2 P.2d 748 (1931).

One must have knowledge that the person obstructed is a peace officer, in order to be guilty of wilfully obstructing a peace officer. State v. Snodgrass, 117 Ariz. 107, 570 P.2d 1280 (App.1977).

78. See State v. Wright, 164 Tenn. 56, 58, 46 S.W.2d 59, 60 (1932).

79. Jones v. Commonwealth, 141 Va. 471, 126 S.E. 74 (1925). And see Anderson v. Commonwealth, 232 Ky. 159, 22 S.W.2d 599 (1929). But if, after an arrest has been made, the arrestee asks permission to enter his house for a temporary purpose and then locks the door and refuses to go with the officer, this constitutes an obstruction of justice. State v. Merrifield, 180 Kan. 267, 303 P. 2d 155 (1956).

80. McGeorge v. Commonealth, 237 Ky. 358, 35 S.W.2d 530 (1931).

81. State v. Thorne, 238 N.C. 392, 78 S.E.2d 140 (1953).

82. State v. Kurtz, 78 Ariz. 215, 278 P.2d 406 (1954); Granado v. State, 161 Tex.Cr.R. 128, 275 S.W.2d 680 (1955).

One being lawfully arrested who "goes limp" for the purpose of impeding and hindering the officer thereby commits the offense of resisting arrest. In re Bacon, 240 Cal.App.2d 34, 49 Cal.Rptr. 322

(1966). Contra: Regina v. Stortini, 42 CCC2d 214 (Ont.Prov.Ct.1978).

83. Brown v. Commonwealth, 263 S.W.2d 238 (Ky.1954). Particularly if the officer is placed in danger because partly in the car at the time. Carter v. United States, 231 F.2d 232 (5th Cir. 1956).

84. Hall v. United States, 222 F.2d 107 (4th Cir. 1955).

85. Commonwealth v. Rhone, 174 Pa. Super. 166, 100 A.2d 147 (1953). Officers inspecting trucks for overloading stopped several trucks and ordered the drivers to drive onto weighing scales. The drivers refused to do this, removed the ignition keys, locked the doors, and refused to deliver the keys to the officers. The court said this presented a case for the jury on the charge of resisting a public officer in the discharge of his duties, but it was error to charge the jury that the refusal to drive onto the scales constituted this offense. People v. Fidler, 280 App.Div. 698, 125 N.Y.S.2d 80 (1952).

The constitutionality of the search in *Rhone,* supra, may need to be re-examined in the light of Camara v. Municipal Court, 387 U.S. 523, 87 S.Ct. 1727 (1967) and See v. City of Seattle, 387 U.S. 541, 87 S.Ct. 1737 (1967). The fact that *Rhone* involved the search of a vehicle rather than an immobile place is probably sufficient to distinguish it. See Carroll

officer in his lawful effort to execute or serve any warrant, subpoena, writ or other process, and in this connection it is important to remember that an officer is authorized to execute a warrant regular and complete on its face and issued by a court or magistrate having jurisdiction over the matter, even if it was issued without proper grounds.[86]

While flight alone does not constitute an offense, as mentioned above, no actual force or violence is required. An officer may be obstructed in the discharge of his duty by one who merely blocks the way [87] or prevents the search of a bed by lying upon it.[88]

Statutes, of course, may either narrow or enlarge the scope of the crime. "In some jurisdictions either actual force, threats, or hostile demonstrations are essential to constitute the offense."[89] An attempt to frustrate an arrest, by falsely telling officers a wanted fugitive was not in a certain house, was held not to violate the federal law because of its use of the word "forcibly."[90] On the other hand the mere wilful report of a fictitious crime or other "false report" is made a misdemeanor under some statutes.[91] Legislation may also raise the grade of the offense to felony, perhaps depending upon the circumstances of its perpetration.[92]

Falsely reporting a crime is informing a law-enforcement officer that a specified crime has been reported, knowing that the information is false. This could well be under such circumstances as to constitute an obstruction of justice at common law, and has been specifically made an offense under some statutes.[93] One, while in possession of his car, telephoned to the police department to the effect that his car was missing and that he wanted to report it stolen. His conviction of falsely reporting a crime was affirmed.[94]

2. TAMPERING WITH WITNESSES

"The term, to obstruct justice, connotes an interference with the orderly administration of law."[95] Hence it includes any "coercion of witnesses" or wilful "interference with the obtaining of testimony."[96] To induce, or attempt to induce, a witness to absent himself from a court where he is legally

v. United States, 267 U.S. 132, 45 S.Ct. 280 (1925).

86.　Appling v. State, 95 Ark. 185, 128 S.W. 866 (1910).

87.　Ibid.

88.　Speck v. State, 34 Ala.App. 325, 41 So.2d 198 (1949).

89.　Id. at 327, 41 So.2d at 199.

90.　Long v. United States, 199 F.2d 717 (4th Cir. 1952).

91.　People v. Lay, 336 Mich. 77, 57 N.W.2d 453 (1953). A statement, written or oral, made upon the initiative of one who goes to the police department or a member thereof for the specific purpose of having some action taken with respect thereto, is a "report" within the meaning of the ordinance prohibiting false reports made with intent to mislead the police. People v. Minter, 135 Cal.App.2d 838, 287

P.2d 196 (1955). But one at the scene of an accident who merely answers questions addressed to him by investigating officers is not making a "report" in this sense. People v. Smith, 131 Cal.App.2d 889, 281 P.2d 103 (1955).

92.　Stuart v. State, 222 Ark. 102, 257 S.W.2d 372 (1953).

93.　Kan.Stat.Ann. § 21–3818 (1974).

94.　State v. Goodman, 3 Kan.App.2d 619, 599 P.2d 327 (1979).

95.　People v. Ormsby, 310 Mich. 291, 299, 17 N.W.2d 187, 190 (1945).

96.　Id. at 300, 17 N.W.2d at 191.

A mother who told her daughter not to testify, knowing her daughter was wanted as a witness, was guilty of witness tampering. State v. Danker, 599 P.2d 518 (Utah 1979).

bound to appear is a common-law offense,[97] generally codified in the statutes. It is also an offense to attempt in any other way to prevent him from attending, or from testifying, and it is not important whether the witness had been served with a subpoena or not so long as it was known that he was wanted as a witness.[98] If a witness has been spirited away, it is no defense that he consented thereto.[99] It is obstruction of justice to endeavor to intimidate a witness by attacking and beating him,[1] or by threatening a witness.[2] And while procuring untrue testimony is not subornation of perjury if the witness was induced to believe his statements were true, any corrupt endeavor to procure such testimony is an obstruction of justice.[3] By express provision of the federal code, it may be added, it is a felony to cross the state line with intent to avoid giving testimony in any criminal case punishable by imprisonment in the penitentiary.[4]

If the misconduct results in the absence of a witness it is quite unimportant whether or not he would have any material evidence to give, because this fact cannot be known until he is present and the due course of the trial is handicapped by his absence.[5]

The attempt to kill a chief prosecution witness while a case was on appeal after conviction has justified a subsequent conviction for obstruction of justice on the theory the person who testified retained his status as a prosecution witness pending retrial.[6]

97. State v. Ames, 64 Me. 386 (1875).

98. Kilpatrick v. State, 72 Ga.App. 669, 34 S.E.2d 719 (1945). "The terms of the statute, the evil it was enacted to prevent, and the protection it was intended to provide, leave no doubt that under its true interpretation each of those who are subpoenaed to come, of those who are called and accept the call to come without subpoenas, of those who are prompted to come by their interests, of those who expect to come, and of those who are selected and expected to come to testify in any case in any court of the United States, falls within the class described by the terms 'any witness, in any court of the United States,' in the section under consideration." Smith v. United States, 274 F. 351, 353 (8th Cir. 1921).

99. State v. Sills, 85 Kan. 830, 118 P. 867 (1911).

1. Smith v. United States, 274 F. 351 (8th Cir. 1921).

Endeavoring to have a government witness murdered constituted an obstruction of justice. 18 U.S.C.A. § 1503 does not require that the effort succeed. United States v. McCarty, 611 F.2d 220 (8th Cir. 1979).

2. Gesturing with one's fingers as if they were a gun and muttering "You're going to get" was sufficient to convict for obstruction of justice. In re Carr, 436 F.Supp. 493 (D.C.Ohio 1977).

3. Anderson v. United States, 215 F.2d 85 (6th Cir. 1954). The crime of obstructing justice was complete when defendant endeavored to induce a witness to commit perjury. Hence an acquittal on a count charging subordination of perjury based on the same general facts is not inconsistent with a verdict of guilty of the former offense. Catrino v. United States, 176 F.2d 884 (9th Cir. 1949).

4. 18 U.S.C.A. § 1073. See Durbin v. United States, 221 F.2d 520 (D.C.Cir. 1954).

5. State v. Early, 3 Del. 562 (1842).

One may be convicted of obstructing justice by unlawfully endeavoring to influence a witness under subpoena to appear before a grand jury although his effort was not successful. It is not necessary to have two witnesses to prove the falsity of the testimony which he endeavored to procure. United States v. Knohl, 379 F.2d 427 (2d Cir. 1967); People v. Broce, 76 Cal.App.3d 71, 142 Cal. Rptr. 628 (1977).

6. United States v. Chandler, 604 F.2d 972 (5th Cir. 1979).

3. DESTRUCTION OR SUPPRESSION OF EVIDENCE

It is also an obstruction of justice to stifle, suppress or destroy evidence knowing that it may be wanted in a judicial proceeding or is being sought by investigating officers,[7] or to remove records from the jurisdiction of the court, knowing they will be called for by the grand jury in its investigation.[8] In such a case the individual cannot turn himself into a court and make his own decision as to what records are admissible or inadmissible. He must be prepared to bring them to court and let the judge make this determination.[9]

The New York statute made it a misdemeanor to destroy evidence for the purpose of preventing it from being produced. **D**, knowing that police investigating a homicide wanted to see a certain rifle, threw the stock into the river, sawed the barrel in sections and buried the sections in the ground. The police recovered enough of the weapon to identify the rifle. A conviction of violating this statute was reversed because the evidence was not destroyed. The court pointed out that the weapon was rendered useless as a firearm but was not impaired as evidence, and that the statute made no reference to the concealment of evidence,[10] commonly found in corresponding enactments.[11]

Inducing a person to destroy certain records in his possession is not an obstruction of justice if such person has, at the time, no intention or expectation that they will be needed in any trial or other proceeding,[12] and there can be no contrivance to suppress evidence on the part of those who have no

---

7. United States v. Perlstein, 126 F.2d 799 (3d Cir. 1942); Commonwealth v. Russo, 177 Pa.Super. 470, 111 A.2d 359 (1955).

Where one intentionally deceives an officer by the use of verbal statements that impede or delay the discovery and apprehension of another suspected of perpetrating a crime, the one is guilty of harboring a fugitive within the meaning of the statute.   State v. Hough, 48 Ohio App.2d 304, 357 N.E.2d 412 (1976).

Evidence that the defendant provided a witness with a false story to give to the grand jury showed that he had the specific intent to impede the administration of justice for purposes of obstruction of justice under the Hobbs Act, 18 U.S.C.A. § 1951.   United States v. Gates, 616 F.2d 1103 (9th Cir. 1980).

To destroy corporate records with knowledge that the records are being sought by a grand jury investigating the company's activities is an obstruction of justice in violation of 18 U.S.C.A. § 1503. United States v. Faudman, 640 F.2d 20 (6th Cir. 1981).

During a routine search of a jail dormitory, an officer was examining some hand-rolled cigarettes and a substance that appeared to be marijuana. **F** grabbed it all and flushed it down the toilet. This was held to constitute an obstruction of justice. People v. Fields, 105 Cal.App.3d 341, 164 Cal.Rptr. 336 (1980).

8. Commonwealth v. Southern Express Co., 160 Ky. 1, 169 S.W. 517 (1914).

9. Ibid. Since preparing false evidence is a violation of section 134 of the Penal Code, one who forges a document and then has it introduced in evidence in the trial of a case is guilty of both forgery and obstruction of justice. People v. McKenna, 11 Cal.2d 327, 79 P.2d 1065 (1938).

10. People v. DeFelice, 282 App.Div. 514, 125 N.Y.S.2d 80 (1953).

The present statute includes concealment as well as destruction of evidence. McKinney's N.Y.Rev.Pen.Law, § 205.50 (1975).

11. E.g., West's Ann.Cal.Pen.Code § 1356 (1970).

12. Berra v. United States, 221 F.2d 590 (8th Cir. 1955).

knowledge of its existence.[13] It may be added that perjury of a witness may constitute obstruction of justice.[14]

H. ESCAPE AND KINDRED OFFENSES

Escape and the kindred offenses are clearly in the nature of obstructions of justice but they have been dealt with so commonly as distinct crimes that it seems wise to treat them as such. And before any effort to explore this field is attempted a clarification of terms is needed. The word "escape" is used in two different senses in regard to the factual occurrence indicated, and in two (or more) different senses in its use as the name of a crime. In the technical sense an "escape" is an unauthorized departure from legal custody; in a loose sense the word is used to indicate either such an unlawful departure or an avoidance of capture. And while the word is regularly used by the layman in the broader sense it usually is limited to the narrower meaning when used in the law,[15]—although this is not always so.[16] It is employed in this subsection exclusively in the technical sense. Thus if an officer approaches an offender for the purpose of making an arrest, which he is unable to do because the other eludes him by running away, there has been no "escape" as the term is used here. It is necessary, however, to bear in mind that "arrest" also is a technical term. If an officer having authority to make an arrest actually touches his arrestee, for the manifested purpose of apprehending him, the arrest is complete [17] "although he does not succeed in stopping or holding him even for an instant." [18] In such a case there is legal custody of the arrestee for an instant although the imprisonment is constructive [19] rather than effective. Hence there would be an escape if such an arrestee ran away after being touched by the officer with appropriate words of arrest and lawful authority for this purpose.[20]

The California Court has held that its statute on escape does not apply to one who has been lawfully arrested and is in the custody of an officer unless the arrestee has been "booked for, charged with or convicted of" a crime.[21] The court seemed to think this interpretation was required by the use of the word "prisoner" but that does not represent the common-law meaning of the word. In common-law terminology one is "in prison" if he is "in the custody of any person who had lawfully arrested him." [22]

---

13. Woollomes v. Heinze, 198 F.2d 577 (9th Cir. 1952).

14. United States v. Griffin, 589 F.2d 200 (5th Cir. 1979).

15. 2 Bishop, New Criminal Law § 1094 (8th ed. 1892).

16. "The term 'escape' is not to be taken in its technical sense, which would imply, as is argued, that the person was previously in custody of the officer, and had eluded his vigilance. It must be understood in its popular sense, which is, 'to flee from, to avoid, to get out of the way,' etc." Lewis v. State, 40 Tenn. 127, 147 (1859). And see Bircham v. Commonwealth, 238 S.W.2d 1008, 1016 (Ky. 1951).

17. 1 East P.C. *300, 330; Whithead v. Keyes, 85 Mass. 495 (1862); Restatement, Second, Torts § 112, comment a (1965).

18. State ex rel. Sadler v. District Court, 70 Mont. 378, 386, 225 P. 1000, 1002 (1924).

19. Ibid.

20. 1 East P.C. *330.

21. People v. Diaz, 22 Cal.3d 712, 150 Cal.Rptr. 471, 586 P.2d 952 (1978).

22. 2 Hawk. P.C., c. 18, § 1 (6th ed. 1788). And see 2 Co. Inst. *589; 1 Hale P.C. *609; State v. Reeves, 199 Neb. 725, 261 N.W.2d 110, 112 (1978).

The Model Penal Code would punish one who escaped from an arresting officer [23] but that is not true of all the new penal codes.[24]

Employment of the word "escape" to indicate more than one offense has its origin in the distant past. While no doubt minor offenses were punished even in very early times the ancient criminal law placed the emphasis almost entirely upon treason and felony. And since any such crime was punishable by forfeiture of life and lands and goods it is not surprising that when escape was first thought of as an offense it was not the prisoner who departed, but the custodian whose wilfulness or negligence made this possible, who was deemed to have incurred criminal guilt. And the name of the crime thus committed by the jailer was "escape." At a later time this was reflected in the words of Sir Matthew Hale:

"And these escapes are of three kinds, 1. By the person that hath the felon in his custody, and this is properly an escape; and 2. When the escape is caused by a stranger, and this ordinarily called a rescue of a felon. 3. By the party himself, which is of two kinds, *viz.* 1. Without any act of force, and this is a simple escape. 2. With an act of force, *viz.* by breach of prison." [25]

At the present day an inquiry as to who had "escaped" would regularly be answered by reference to the former prisoner and not to his jailer, and hence the word "escape" seems inappropriate as the name of the offense committed by the latter (if he was at fault). The archaic form is still encountered at times,[26] but the tendency is to speak of the officer's offense in some such terms as "suffering escape," "allowing escape," or "permitting escape." [27] The latter term will be employed for that purpose herein and hence the subdivision entitled "escape" will deal only with the one who departs from custody unlawfully,—the "escaper." [28]

1. ESCAPE

Speaking merely of the factual occurrence, but using the term in its technical sense, escape is unauthorized departure from lawful custody.[29] The

23. Section 242.6.

24. E.g., "A person convicted of a felony, or charged with the commission of a felony, who intentionally escapes from any detention facility or institution to which the person has been committed by reason of such conviction or charge, or from the custody of any public officer or employee to whom the person has been entrusted, commits a class D felony." Iowa Criminal Code § 719.4(1) (1978). Subsection 2 makes a similar provision for one convicted of or charged with a misdemeanor.

25. 1 Hale P.C. *590.

26. E.g., United States v. Davis, 167 F.2d 228, 229 (C.A.D.C.1947); State ex rel. Farrior v. Faulk, 102 Fla. 886, 890, 136 So. 601, 603 (1931).

27. E.g., 18 U.S.C.A. § 755 (1976); West's Ann.Cal.Pen. Code § 4533 (1970); Iowa Code Ann. § 719.5 (1979); Mass.

Ann.Laws Ch. 268 §§ 18–21 (1968); Md. Ann.Code Art. 27, § 139(c) (1957). And see Pentecost v. State, 107 Ala. 81, 82, 18 So. 146, 147 (1895).

28. The word "escapee" is employed at times by those who are not careful in the use of language. They probably think this word is comparable to "arrestee" or "employee." But the arrestee did not do the arresting and the employee did not do the employing. The employee does the work but that makes him a worker, not a workee.

29. See People v. Quijada, 53 Cal.App. 39, 41, 199 P. 854 (1921).

"18 U.S.C.A. § 751(a) (1976) required the prosecution to prove that (1) they had been in custody of the Attorney General, (2) as a result of a conviction, and (3) that they had escaped from custody . . . Although § 751(a) does not define the term 'escape,' courts and commentators

common law recognized two different offenses committed by escapers, depending upon whether freedom was gained with or without the use of force.[30] If accomplished by force it was called "breach of prison" [31] and was a graver offense than if no force was used, in which case it was a misdemeanor [32] and the name of the crime was "escape." Hence as the name of a common-law crime the word must be defined in some such form as this:

Escape is unauthorized departure of a prisoner from legal custody without the use of force.[33]

The distinction between these two offenses is still retained under some of the codes. More generally the two have been merged and where this is true the qualifying clause after the word "custody" is not needed in the definition. The theory is that one who has been deprived of his liberty by authority of law has the "duty to submit to such confinement until delivered by due course of the law, no matter whether he was committed to await a future trial, or as punishment after judgment of conviction, or for any other purpose authorized by law." [34]

A. Legal Custody

The departure of a prisoner who is unlawfully confined is not a crime [35] because there "can be no escape, in the sense of the law, unless there was lawful custody, . . ." [36] This requires consideration of the exact significance of this concept. Any imprisonment is legal custody so far as the common law is concerned if it is by authority of law and for some purpose of the law, whether it is on a criminal matter or in a civil case.[37] This is expressly codified in some of the modern statutes,[38] while in others the offense is expressly or impliedly limited to an escape from confinement upon a charge or

are in general agreement that it means absenting oneself from custody without permission." United States v. Bailey, 444 U.S. 394, 100 S.Ct. 624, 632–3 (1980).

"The crime of escape from legal custody is committed when the prisoner escapes from the custody of an arresting officer while being taken to the place of confinement." State v. Reeves, 199 Neb. 725, 261 N.W.2d 110, 112 (1978).

30. 1 Hale P.C. *590.

31. Ibid.; 4 Bl.Comm. *129–30.

32. 1 Hale P.C. *611; 2 Hawk.P.C. c. 18 § 9 (6th ed. 1788); Smith v. State, 145 Me. 313, 75 A.2d 538 (1950). Prison breach includes escape as a lesser-included offense. Brown v. State, 240 So.2d 615 (Miss.1970).

33. "At common law the crime of escape is committed by a prisoner when he voluntarily departs from lawful custody without breach of prison." United States v. Zimmerman, 71 F.Supp. 534, 537 (D.C. Pa.1947). And see People v. Quijada, 53 Cal.App. 39, 41, 199 P. 854 (1921); State v. Sutton, 170 Ind. 473, 476, 84 N.E. 824,

826 (1908); State v. Pace, 192 N.C. 780, 784, 136 S.E. 11, 12–3 (1926).

34. People v. Ah Teung, 92 Cal. 421, 425, 28 P. 577, 578 (1891).

35. People v. Clark, 69 Cal.App. 520, 231 P. 590 (1924); State v. Norris, 45 Del. 333, 337, 73 A.2d 790, 793 (1950); Saylor v. Commonwealth, 122 Ky. 776, 93 S.W. 48 (1906); State v. Davis, 199 Kan. 33, 427 P.2d 606 (1967).

36. People v. Ah Teung, 92 Cal. 421, 425, 28 P. 577, 578 (1891).

37. 2 Hawk.P.C. c. 18 § 1 (6th ed. 1788); Regina v. Allen, Car. & M. 295, 174 Eng.Rep. 513 (1841). There has been some confusion on this point because the *offense of the officer* who wilfully or negligently permitted his prisoner to depart unlawfully—anciently called an "escape"—applied only to an officer who had custody of a prisoner on a "criminal matter." 2 Hawk.P.C. c. 19 § 3 (6th ed. 1788).

38. Md.Code Ann. Art. 27 § 139 (1957).

conviction of crime.[39] Arrest on civil process is so narrowly restricted at the present time that this is not a problem of much consequence but a question of increasing importance arises in connection with juvenile delinquency. Under some of the more progressive types of legislation in this regard what would be a crime if by an older person is not a crime but a different type of misdeed if committed by a juvenile. Where this is true the tendency is to have the statute broad enough to provide for the punishment of a juvenile delinquent who escapes from legal custody.[40] Quite a different problem was presented to the California court which held that escape from a mental hospital is not a crime [41] unless the patient was there under court order in connection with some criminal case.[42] This problem has been specifically dealt with by statute in some states [43] making such custody subject to escape sanctions.

One who has been taken into the custody of the law by arrest or surrender remains in legal custody until he has been delivered by due course of the law or departs unlawfully. And unless there is some limitation due to a restrictive statute [44] he commits an escape if he wilfully departs without having been delivered by due course of the law even if he was not kept behind locked doors or in the immediate presence of a guard.[45] Thus a prisoner on a prison farm, who was permitted under the rules to move around within certain limits on the farm during the rest period, was guilty of an escape although at the time of his unlawful departure he was several hundred yards

39. "A person convicted of a felony, or charged with the commission of a felony" or "a person convicted or charged with a misdemeanor." Iowa Code Ann. 719.4 (1979).

40. E.g., McKinney's N.Y.Rev.Pen. Code, §§ 205.00, 205.10 (1975).

Although a youthful offender is not guilty of a "crime" he is guilty of an "offense" and the statute, as amended, covers the escape of such a person from the correctional institution to which he had been committed. People v. Chesley, 282 App.Div. 821, 123 N.Y.S.2d 42 (1953).

Although a juvenile delinquent is not detained for a crime the statute makes it a crime for him to escape from the Boys' Village to which he was committed. The legislative policy is that after such escape he shall be sent to a place of greater security. Baker v. State, 205 Md. 42, 106 A.2d 692 (1953).

"A juvenile has not committed a crime, including a felony, when he has committed an offense, 'an act designated as a crime *if committed by an adult.*' Since Frederick, a juvenile offender, could not be convicted of a felony he also could not be 'detained pursuant to a conviction of a felony,' an essential element of first-degree escape." In re Frederick, 93 Wn.2d 28, 604 P.2d 953, 954 (1980).

41. People v. Cavanaugh, 44 Cal.2d 252, 282 P.2d 53 (1955).

The California statute relating to escape is so worded that it does not apply to an arrestee until he has been booked preparatory to incarceration in a jail or other place of confinement. In re Culver, 69 Cal.2d 898, 73 Cal.Rptr. 393, 447 P.2d 633 (1968).

42. People v. Priegal, 126 Cal.App.2d 587, 272 P.2d 831 (1954). Compare United States v. Piscitello, 231 F.2d 443 (2d Cir. 1956).

43. Utah Code Ann. 1953, § 76–8–309.

44. Since the statute provides a penalty only for escape from jail or while in custody going to jail, an escape from a street commissioner by a prisoner who has been placed in the custody of such commissioner to work on the streets, is not punishable. State v. Owens, 268 Mo. 481, 187 S.W. 1189 (1916). Under the statute an escape from an officer is an offense only if some degree of force is used or it is a case of bribery. Brock v. Commonwealth, 242 S.W.2d 1007 (Ky. 1951).

45. People v. Hadley, 88 Cal.App.2d 734, 199 P.2d 382 (1948).

"And once the defendant has submitted to the control of the officer *and* the process of taking him to the police station or to a judge has commenced, his arrest is complete, and he is in 'custody,' for the purposes of the escape statute." State v. Rushing, 612 P.2d 103 (Hawaii 1980).

from any guard. He was within the constructive custody of the guards.[46] And an unauthorized departure from an "honor farm" is also an escape.[47] "Failure to return from furlough" [48] or community visits [49] is a departure from legal custody.

An escape is not justified or excused by reason of informality or irregularity in the process of commitment, arrest or information.[50] Imprisonment may be lawful within the meaning of "legal custody" although the prisoner would be entitled to be released by taking proper steps for this purpose; and if, in such a situation, he takes no such steps but wrongfully frees himself he is guilty of an escape.[51]

Escape "is a continuing offense and . . . an escapee can be held liable for a failure to return to custody as well as for his initial departure." [52] That is, even if conditions were such as to justify or excuse unpermitted departure from custody, the escaper has the duty to make himself available to

46. State v. Baker, 355 Mo. 1048, 199 S.W.2d 393 (1947). L was a prisoner in a prison camp and was permitted to attend a baseball game at a field an eighth of a mile from the kitchen where he worked, on land used for recreation of the inmates of the institution and belonging to the institution. He started toward the field but did not return to the camp. A conviction of escape was affirmed. Commonwealth v. LaRochelle, 264 Mass. 490, 162 N.E. 908 (1928).

"In this case, although appellant had been given permission to leave the halfway house for a limited period of time, he was still within the authority and custody of the District of Columbia Department of Corrections. As a result, his failure to return constituted an escape under D.C. Code 1973, § 22–2601." Days v. United States, 407 A.2d 702, 704 (D.C.App.1979).

47. People v. Wilson, 59 Cal.App.2d 610, 139 P.2d 673 (1943). The escape of a trusty while permitted to be at large was expressly covered by statute. Perry v. State, 80 Okl.Cr. 58, 157 P.2d 217 (1945). It would seem to be an unlawful departure from permitted limits even apart from the statute. Compare Saylor v. Commonwealth, 122 Ky. 776, 93 S.W. 48 (1906).

It was escape to fail to return to the institution after being allowed outside the walls for work. United States v. Wilke, 450 F.2d 877 (9th Cir. 1971).

48. State v. Holbrook, 318 A.2d 62 (Me.1974).

49. People v. Labrum, 25 Cal.App.3d 105, 101 Cal.Rptr. 602 (1972).

50. People v. McPheeley, 92 Cal.App. 2d 589, 207 P.2d 651 (1949); State v.

Palmer, 45 Del. 308, 72 A.2d 442 (1950); State v. Murray, 15 Me. 100 (1838).

Defendant was held in lawful custody at the time of his escape, though judgment and sentence were later voided. Phillips v. State, 622 P.2d 719 (Okl.Cr. App.1981).

51. People v. Hinze, 97 Cal.App.2d 1, 217 P.2d 35 (1950). The federal statute forbids the escape of anyone confined in a federal penal or correctional institution. The fact that such a prisoner's sentence is irregular or void does not permit him, before some court has so adjudged, to defy his guards and run away. Bayless v. United States, 141 F.2d 578 (9th Cir. 1944). One who has been duly convicted and imprisoned for violation of a statute is lawfully in custody and his escape from such custody is a crime. So long as the statute has not been held to be unconstitutional his remedy if he thinks it is invalid, is to test it by habeas corpus and not to resort to self help. Kelley v. Meyers, 124 Or. 322, 263 P. 903 (1928). Cf. Hofstetter v. Hollowell, 214 N.W. 698 (Iowa, 1927); Housh v. People, 75 Ill. 487 (1874).

Escape may be committed by one held under color of authority even if his imprisonment was unauthorized (the imprisonment was held to be authorized in this case). State v. Hart, 411 S.W.2d 143 (Mo.1967).

Proof of escape from the custody or confinement in which one is being held pending trial is admissible at the trial of the charge for which one is held. State v. Piche, 71 Wn.2d 583, 430 P.2d 522 (1967).

52. United States v. Bailey, 444 U.S. 394, 100 S.Ct. 624, 636 (1980).

the authorities as soon as he has reached a position where those intolerable conditions do not affect him.[53]

B.   THE PHYSICAL ACT

The physical act of the crime of escape is the departure of the prisoner which ordinarily is clear enough. A convict who refuses to work or is otherwise insubordinate or refractory may be punished by prison officials but cannot be convicted of an escape because there is no departure by him.[54] On the other hand a prisoner who goes beyond the prison walls unlawfully, with intent to keep going, is guilty of escape although immediately recaptured,[55] and a prisoner may be guilty of an escape from his cell although unable to get beyond the prison walls.[56] In other words the limits within which a prisoner may be required by law to remain, at a certain time, may be the walls of his cell, the walls of his prison, the boundaries of the prison farm,[57] the immediate presence of his guard on the street or elsewhere, the general area of a project on which he is working such as a road job,[58] or some other. Whatever the limits may be for him at the time a departure therefrom is the physical part of an escape.[59]

C.   INTENT

No state of mind is required for guilt of escape other than the intent to go beyond permitted limits,[60] and even this is not a positive factor of the crime which must be pleaded and proved by the prosecution.[61] Proof that the defendant was in legal custody and voluntarily departed therefrom without having been released by due course of law is sufficient for conviction in the absence of some satisfactory explanation.[62] An innocent mistake, how-

53. "We therefore hold that, where a criminal defendant is charged with escape and claims that he is entitled to an instruction on the theory of duress or necessity, he must proffer evidence of a bona fide effort to surrender or return to custody as soon as the claimed duress or necessity had lost its coercive force." Id. at 100 S.Ct. 637.

54. Carter v. State, 29 Tex.App. 5, 14 S.W. 350 (1890).

55. People v. Quijada, 53 Cal.App. 39, 199 P. 854 (1921).

56. State v. Cahill, 196 Iowa 486, 199 N.W. 191 (1923).

57. Since the prison farm is an integral part of the state prison, an escape from the farm is an escape from the prison. State v. Mead, 130 Conn. 106, 32 A.2d 273 (1943).

58. Saylor v. Commonwealth, 122 Ky. 776, 93 S.W. 48 (1906).

59. Perry v. State, 80 Okl.Cr. 58, 157 P.2d 217 (1945).

A prisoner having gone beyond the limits he was directed to go is guilty of escape. State v. Leckenby, 260 Iowa 973, 151 N.W.2d 567 (1967). See also People

v. Herrera, 255 Cal.App.2d 644, 63 Cal. Rptr. 96 (1967).

60. State v. Clark, 32 Nev. 145, 104 P. 593 (1909).

"Accordingly, we hold that the prosecution fulfills its burden . . . if it demonstrates that an escapee knew his actions would result in his leaving physical confinement without permission." United States v. Bailey, 444 U.S. 394, 100 S.Ct. 624, 633 (1980).

61. If there was no escape and the charge is attempted escape the intent is an element which must be alleged and proved, but it may be inferred from the acts done if they point clearly in this direction. Ibid.

62. Intent will be inferred from the unlawful departure. Wiggins v. State, 194 Ind. 118, 141 N.E. 56 (1923).

"Accordingly, we hold that the prosecution fulfills its burden under § 751(a) if it demonstrates that an escapee knew his actions would result in his leaving physical confinement without permission." United States v. Bailey, 444 U.S. 394, 100 S.Ct. 624, 633 (1980).

ever, may be sufficient for exculpation in such a case [63] as in most other situations. Should the prisoner and his jailer connive to bring about the unlawful release of the former, both are guilty of crime,[64] but if the prisoner is released by his jailer without such connivance, and departs in the innocent belief that he is authorized to do so, there is no criminal guilt on his part, however much the jailer may have exceeded his authority.[65] And a temporary departure is not a criminal escape if required as a safety measure in some emergency. Thus a prisoner is privileged to break out of a burning jail if this is necessary to save himself from death or serious harm, and is guilty of no offense if he makes himself available to his jailer when the emergency is past.[66] On the other hand the fact that a prisoner is innocent of the offense for which he was arrested is no excuse for his unpermitted departure from legal custody.[67]

D. Grade of the Offense

At common law the grade of the offense depended upon whether the escape was effected without the use of force, in which case it was a simple escape and a misdemeanor,[68] or was under circumstances amounting to a breach of prison,—a topic to be considered presently. Under many of the statutes this distinction has been abandoned [69] and the grade of the offense made to depend upon other circumstances such as the place from which the

---

63. "In order to constitute an escape, as well as other crime, a criminal intent is indispensable. The facts in this case clearly negative a criminal intent." Riley v. State, 16 Conn. 47, 52–3 (1843).

64. 1 Hale P.C. *590.

65. State v. Pace, 192 N.C. 780, 136 S.E. 11 (1926); Ex parte Eley, 9 Okl.Cr. 76, 130 P. 821 (1913). A prisoner who is told to leave by one in apparent authority does not commit an escape by departing. If he knew there was a mistake as to his identity, or if he had used any deception to obtain his release it would be otherwise, but the mere fact that he may have doubted the propriety of the officer's direction does not place him under a duty to instruct the officer as to what should be done. People v. Weiseman, 280 N.Y. 385, 21 N.E.2d 362 (1939).

66. 1 Hale P.C. *611. And see State v. Palmer, 45 Del. 308, 311, 72 A.2d 442, 444 (1950).

". . . in order to be entitled to an instruction on duress or necessity as a defense to the crime charged, an escapee must first offer evidence justifying his continued absence from custody as well as his initial departure and that an indispensible element of such an offer is testimony of a bona fide effort to surrender or return as soon as the claimed duress or necessity has lost its coercive force." United States v. Bailey, 444 U.S. 394, 100 S.Ct. 624, 635–636 (1980).

"Thus, while the Court recognizes the availability of the duress defense to the crime of escape, the Court also recognizes that duress exonerates only the departure from custody, and not the continued absence." "For this reason, an escape will not be excused by reason of duress if the escapee fails to submit to proper authorities immediately after attaining a position of safety." United States v. Michelson, 559 F.2d 567, 570 (9th Cir. 1977). See also People v. Lovercamp, 43 Cal.App.3d 823, 118 Cal.Rptr. 110 (1974); Annotation, 69 A.L.R.3d 678 (1976).

67. 2 Hawk.P.C. c. 18, § 5 (6th ed. 1788); State v. Bates, 23 Iowa 96 (1876).

"[T]he fact that one is serving a sentence which was unjustly imposed does not serve as justification for escape." State v. Bolden, 2 Kan.App.2d 470, 581 P.2d 1195, 1197 (1978).

Although the burglary indictment under which D had been arrested was later dismissed, this did not affect the validity of his conviction of escape. Rodriguez v. State, 457 S.W.2d 555 (Tex.App.1970).

68. 2 Hawk.P.C. c. 17, § 5 (6th ed. 1788).

69. Sometimes whether force was or was not used is a circumstance employed in connection with other circumstances. E.g., West's Ann.Cal.Pen.Code §§ 4530–4532 (1970); People v. Segura, 134 Cal.App.2d 532, 286 P.2d 471 (1955).

escape was made [70] or the type of offense for which the prisoner was in custody. A rather common provision is that the escape of a prisoner is a felony if he was in custody on a charge or conviction of felony, and a misdemeanor if he was in custody on a charge or conviction of misdemeanor.[71]

E. THE FUGITIVE-FELON ACT

A federal statute makes it a felony to flee across the state line for the purpose of avoiding prosecution or confinement for a state felony or attempted felony, or to avoid giving testimony in a state felony case.[72]

2. BREACH OF PRISON

While breach of prison, or prison breach, means breaking out of or away from prison, it is important to have clearly in mind the meaning of the word "prison." If an officer arrests an offender and takes him to jail the layman does not think of the offender as being "in prison" until he is safely behind locked doors, but no one hesitates to speak of him as a "prisoner" from the moment of apprehension. He is a prisoner because he is "in prison . . . whether he were actually in the walls of a prison, or only in the stocks, or in the custody of any person who had lawfully arrested him. . . ." [73] Hence the distinction between breach of prison and simple escape depends upon the manner in which the unlawful departure was accomplished and not upon the circumstances of the legal custody itself.[74] And the distinguishing factor which transforms what otherwise would be a simple escape into a breach of prison is the use of force.[75] This does not mean some act of extreme violence; the unlawful departure is breach of prison if it was "accomplished by the least imaginable force." [76] One who concealed himself in the prison yard until it was cleared and then scaled the wall did not use "force" as this word is used in the common-law rule of breach of prison,[77] but it was otherwise in the case of the escaping prisoner who knocked bricks down from the top of the wall, although they were loose bricks dislodged by accident.[78] Hence a prisoner, in the legal custody of an officer on the street, who takes advantage of the officer's inattention and runs away, is guilty of an escape; but if he resorts to the use of any force to liberate himself his crime is breach of prison.

Sometimes the penalty is provided only for an escape or attempt to escape "by force or fraud." See Ashley v. Delmore, 49 Wn.2d 1, 297 P.2d 958 (1956).

70. Iowa Code Ann. § 719.4 (1979).

71. Heath v. State, 50 Ga.App. 94, 177 S.E. 74 (1934); Ex parte Knapp, 73 Idaho 505, 254 P.2d 411 (1953); 18 U.S.C.A. § 751 (1976).

72. 18 U.S.C.A. § 1073 (1976). One who flees across a state boundary line to avoid confinement after conviction of robbery is guilty of a federal offense. He may be arrested by a state officer without a warrant—not for robbery but for the federal offense. Bircham v. Commonwealth, 238 S.W.2d 1008 (Ky.1951).

73. 2 Hawk.P.C. c. 18, § 1 (6th ed. 1788). And see 2 Co.Inst. *589; 1 Hale P.C. *609.

74. As mentioned in the discussion of "escape" the circumstances of the custody from which the escape was made have a bearing on the grade of the offense under some of the modern statutes.

75. 1 Hale P.C. *590; United States ex rel. Manzella v. Zimmerman, 71 F.Supp. 534, 537 (D.C.Pa.1947).

76. United States ex rel. Manzella v. Zimmerman, 71 F.Supp. 534, 537 (D.C.Pa. 1947).

77. State v. Hoffman, 30 Wn.2d 475, 191 P.2d 865 (1948).

78. Rex v. Haswell, Russ. & Ry. 458, 168 Eng.Rep. 896 (1821).

The original rule of the common law, that every breach of prison was a felony,[79] was modified in 1307 by the statute *de frangentibus prisonam*,[80] which provided that thereafter none should have judgment of life or member for this offense unless he had been in custody for some capital crime. Thereafter breach of prison was only a misdemeanor unless the escaper had been in custody for treason or felony.

Breach of prison is unauthorized departure of a prisoner from legal custody accomplished by the use of force.

As mentioned in the discussion of "escape" the trend of modern legislation has been to abandon the common-law distinction based upon the presence or absence of force and substitute other factors to determine the grade of the offense. If, on the other hand, the statute provides no penalty for an escape unless effected by "force or fraud" the word "force" as so used will be held to be the equivalent of the element needed to constitute breach of prison.[81]

3. RESCUE OR AIDING ESCAPE

Rescue is forcibly freeing another from legal custody.[82]

The word "knowingly" is sometimes added to the definition [83] but this is overemphasis because there is no special mental element which the prosecution is required to plead and prove unless it has been added by statute.[84] It is not an offense to rescue one from unlawful imprisonment [85] and rescue from lawful imprisonment might be excused because of reasonable mistake of fact. If the prisoner is in the custody of a known officer or is incarcerated in a public prison all are bound to take notice of this fact and if such custody is legal a belief to the contrary is not a reasonable mistake of fact.[86] It is otherwise if the prisoner was in legal custody of a private person. Satisfactory proof that he acted in the *reasonable belief* that the prisoner was being deprived of his liberty unlawfully by a private person will entitle the defendant to be acquitted of the charge of rescue,[87] but the burden of producing evidence on this point rests on the defendant.

At common law the rescue of a known traitor is treason, the rescue of a known felon is felony, and any other rescue is a misdemeanor.[88] It is unimportant so far as the ultimate conviction of the rescuer is concerned whether the one rescued had been convicted prior to the rescue or was then only in custody on a charge of treason or felony of which he was convicted later, but such conviction at one time or the other is necessary for treason or felony to be established against the rescuer at common law.[89] If such guilt on the

79. 1 Hale P.C. *607; 4 Bl.Comm. *130.

80. 1 Edw. II, st. 2.

81. State v. Hoffmann, 30 Wn.2d 475, 191 P.2d 865 (1948).

82. 1 Hawk.P.C. c. 21, para. 1 (6th ed. 1788); 2 Bishop, New Criminal Law § 1065 (8th ed. 1892). And see State v. Sutton, 170 Ind. 473, 476, 84 N.E. 824, 826 (1908).

83. 4 Bl.Comm. *131.

84. For a statute including the word "knowingly" in the definition of rescue

see Robinson v. State, 82 Ga. 535, 9 S.E. 528 (1889).

85. People v. Ah Teung, 92 Cal. 421, 28 P. 577 (1891).

86. 1 Hale P.C. *606; State v. Sutton, 170 Ind. 473, 84 N.E. 824 (1908).

87. Ibid.

88. 4 Bl.Comm. *131.

89. Ibid. Hawkins says this is true of felony but that the rescuer of a traitor could be convicted of treason although the prisoner himself was not convicted. He mentions that the rescuer in such a

part of the prisoner was never established, or if he was in custody for a misdemeanor only, or on a civil matter, the rescuer could be convicted of a misdemeanor.[90] Modern statutes usually make some different provision with reference to the grade of offense committed by a rescuer. Since treason is one form of felony at the present time the three-fold division is not needed, and one type of statute provides that the rescue of a prisoner by force or fraud is a felony if he was held upon a charge, commitment or conviction of felony, and otherwise is a misdemeanor.[91]

The common law makes no distinction between rescue and aiding a prisoner to escape.[92] If one in legal custody was liberated otherwise than by due course of the law, and if force used by a person who was neither the prisoner nor his jailer caused or aided this unlawful liberation, such person was guilty of rescue. On the other hand some of the statutes have provided for two separate offenses in this regard. Under such a legislative program there has been no rescue if the prisoner was trying to escape and was enabled to do so by help from another. In such a case the other had assisted the escape of the prisoner and was guilty of violating this section only. And there has been a rescue only where the unlawful deliverance was effected by the intervention of another and without the cooperation of the prisoner.[93]

There is no rescue unless the prisoner was actually liberated [94] but some of the statutes make it a crime to instigate or assist a prisoner in his effort to escape, whether successful or not,[95] or to convey an instrument into a place of confinement with intent to facilitate a prisoner's escape.[96] It has been held that the statute making it an offense to instigate or assist in the

case may be tried for a misdemeanor only "if the king please." 2 Hawk.P.C. c. 21 § 8 (6th ed. 1788).

90. Ibid. It is a misdemeanor at common law to aid a person to escape from custody although he was confined in a civil case and not on any criminal charge. Regina v. Allen, Car. & M. 295, 174 Eng. Rep. 513 (1841).

91. S.H.A.Ill. ch. 38, § 31–7 (1977). It is a misdemeanor unless the escape was of a person convicted of a felony.

The Model Penal Code would make it a felony if the detainee was held on a charge of felony or had been convicted of crime, and otherwise a misdemeanor. Section 242.6(2), (4). Under the California statute any rescue is a felony but the severity of the punishment depends upon whether the one rescued was or was not "in custody upon a conviction of a felony punishable with death." West's Ann.Cal. Pen.Code § 4550 (1977).

92. No such distinction is even mentioned by Hale, Hawkins or Blackstone.

"(Permitting or) Facilitating Escape. . . . Any person who knowingly causes or facilitates an escape commits an offense." Model Penal Code, section 242.6(2).

93. People v. Murphy, 130 Cal.App. 408, 20 P.2d 63 (1933); Robinson v. State, 82 Ga. 535, 9 S.E. 528 (1889).

94. Needless to say one guilty of an unsuccessful effort to liberate a prisoner from legal custody may be convicted of attempted rescue unless the code fails to make provision for such an attempt.

95. Day v. State, 86 Ga.App. 757, 72 S.E.2d 500 (1952). It has been pointed out that under such a statute one assisting another in his effort to liberate himself is guilty of assisting a prisoner and not guilty of a mere attempt. Perry v. State, 63 Ga. 402 (1879).

"A violation of the applicable statute occurs whenever aid is offered to an individual who is attempting, *or has completed*, an escape from official and lawful custody, prior to discharge by due process of law." State v. Tucker, 618 P.2d 46, 49 (Utah 1980).

96. The statute declared that it should be a crime (1) to convey an instrument into a place of confinement with intent to facilitate a prisoner's escape, (2) to aid a prisoner to escape or attempt to escape, or (3) to conceal or assist a prisoner after he has escaped. Intent is an element of the first only, hence an indictment for aiding a prisoner to escape need not al-

escape from a federal penitentiary applies to prison officials and to outsiders but is inapplicable to inmates.[97] The fact that the prisoner was innocent of the offense for which he was arrested is no defense to a charge of rescue or assisting an escape.[98]

4. PERMITTING ESCAPE

It is a crime for one wilfully or negligently to permit a prisoner to escape from his legal custody.[99] Originally the offense was called "voluntary escape" or "negligent escape," as the fact might be, but as mentioned above the present trend is to speak in terms of voluntarily or negligently "suffering," "allowing," or "permitting" escape. Judge Stephen's statement of the law, employing the archaic labels, was as follows:

"Everyone who knowingly, and with intent to save him from trial or execution, permits any person in his lawful custody to regain his liberty, otherwise than in due course of law, commits the offense of voluntary escape; and is guilty of high treason if the escaped prisoner was in his custody for and was guilty of high treason; becomes accessory after the fact to the felony of which the escaped prisoner was guilty, if he was in his custody for and was guilty of felony; and is guilty of a misdemeanor if the escaped prisoner was in his custody for and was guilty of a misdemeanor." [1]

"Everyone is guilty of the misdemeanor called negligent escape who, by the neglect of any duty, or by ignorance of law, permits a person in his lawful custody to regain his liberty otherwise than in due course of law.

"The person escaping is deemed to have regained his liberty as soon as he gets out of sight of the person from whom he escapes, and not before." [2]

This seems to be an accurate statement of the common law except for the qualification, which did not apply to the escaping prisoner himself,[3] that the jailer or other custodian was not criminally guilty of permitting escape unless the one who departed had been in his custody on "a criminal matter." [4] The reference to getting "out of sight" of the custodian, it should be emphasized, is a limitation which applies to this offense only. If one in legal custody wrongfully goes beyond permitted limits with intent to escape, but is recaptured without getting out of sight of his custodian, the latter has not permitted an escape but the prisoner himself is guilty of escape or prison

lege an intent. People v. Vraniak, 5 Ill. 2d 384, 125 N.E.2d 513 (1955).

97. Kahl v. United States, 204 F.2d 864 (10th Cir. 1953). But inmates may be guilty of a conspiracy to escape. Ibid.

98. State v. Bates, 23 Iowa 96 (1867).

99. 1 Hale P.C. *590; 4 Bl.Comm. *130. And see Martin v. State, 32 Ark. 124, 126 (1877); State ex rel. Farrior v. Faulk, 102 Fla. 886, 890, 136 So. 601, 603 (1931); State v. Pace, 192 N.C. 780, 784, 136 S.E. 11, 12–13 (1926).

1. Stephen, Digest of Criminal Law, art. 193 (8th ed. 1947).

2. Id. at art. 194. "The offense of negligent escape under the common law

has been thus defined: 'A negligent escape is when the party arrested or imprisoned doth escape against the will of him that arrested or imprisoned him, and is not freshly pursued and taken again, before he hath lost the sight of him.'" United States v. Davis, 167 F.2d 228, 229 (D.C.Cir.1947). And see State v. Wedin, 85 N.J.L. 399, 401, 89 A. 753, 754 (1914).

Any reference to "negligence" in these cases should be interpreted to require "criminal negligence." See, infra, chapter 7, section 2.

3. 2 Hawk.P.C. c. 18, § 1 (6th ed. 1788).

4. Id. at c. 19, § 3.

breach, as the fact may be.[5] The word "voluntarily" or "voluntary" used to designate the more serious of these two offenses has reference to a specific intent, as indicated by Stephen,—the intent to save the prisoner from trial or execution.[6] Thus a jailer who willingly lets his prisoner depart in the good-faith, though mistaken, belief that he has been lawfully discharged is not guilty of "voluntarily permitting him to escape" because there is no intent to save him from trial or punishment.[7] Where there has been an escape without any such corrupt intent the guilt or innocence of the custodian depends upon the presence or absence of negligence on his part. The mere fact of the escape raises a presumption of negligence on the part of the officer according to the common law,[8] which might be overcome by proof that due care had been used. What constitutes due care on the part of the jailer depends upon all the circumstances including the reason for the incarceration, since what would be reasonable in the case of one charged with a petty offense might be criminally negligent if the prisoner is being held on a charge of murder.[9] But if the escape was made possible because the jailer failed to make the intended use of bars, bolts and locks provided for security purposes, he is guilty of "that degree of carelessness which the law intends to punish." [10]

While the common law made use of two factors in determining the grade of this offense—(1) the crime of which the prisoner was guilty, if any, and (2) the custodian's state of mind—modern statutes sometimes employ only the latter.[11] One pattern is to provide that this offense is a misdemeanor unless the custodian "corruptly and wilfully" permitted the escape, in which case he is guilty of felony.[12]

5. REFUSING TO AID OFFICER

The sheriff, being the officer particularly charged by common law with keeping the peace and apprehending wrongdoers, was authorized whenever necessary for such purposes to "command all the people of his county to attend him; which is called the *posse comitatus*, or power of the county, . . ." [13] The power to require such assistance by all included the authority to call upon any individual for this purpose. In the course of time it was recognized that any peace officer is authorized to call upon private persons to aid him in making arrests or preventing crimes,[14] and this has been includ-

5. Stephen does not include this clause in the article dealing with the offense committed by the prisoner. Stephen, Digest of Criminal Law, art. 203 (8th ed. 1947).

6. See Meehan v. State, 46 N.J.L. 355, 358 (1884).

7. Meehan v. State, 46 N.J.L. 355 (1884).

8. See State v. Wedin, 85 N.J.L. 399, 402, 89 A. 753, 754 (1914).

9. Garver v. Territory, 5 Okl. 342, 49 P. 470 (1897).

10. Id. at 349, 49 P. at 473.

11. At times both factors are used, perhaps substituting "charge or convic-

tion" for the requirement of guilt of the prisoner. Iowa Code Ann. § 719.5 (1979). In light of the common law background the phrase "voluntarily permits" in the section will no doubt be held to mean with corrupt intent.

12. Under the Model Penal Code an officer who purposely permits an escape is guilty of a felony in the third degree. Section 242.6(4)(c). If he does so recklessly he is guilty of a misdemeanor. Ibid.

13. 1 Bl.Comm. *343.

14. 1 Wharton's Criminal Procedure § 52 (Torcia 12 Ed. 1974).

ed rather generally in the modern codes.[15] Persons acting under such a request are "not themselves officers, nor are they mere private persons, but their true legal position is that of a posse comitatus." [16] While the term is commonly used to signify a considerable group of persons called upon by an officer to aid him in the enforcement of the law, the legal position is not dependent upon the number and an officer may summon a posse of one.[17] A person called upon by an officer for assistance in making an arrest or preventing a crime is guilty of a misdemeanor if he improperly refuses.[18] He is not entitled to delay while he conducts an inquiry into the officer's authority in the particular case,[19] or to demand an inspection of the warrant if the officer is undertaking to arrest by virtue of such process.[20] He has no right to refuse to give the requested assistance merely because some danger is involved, but if the effort would be futile as well as dangerous his refusal may be excused in extreme circumstances.[21]

The theory of this offense is that the due administration of the law is handicapped by refusal to render assistance which an officer is authorized to require.

6. VIOLATION OF PROBATION OR PAROLE

The prison limits of a particular prisoner may be very narrow or rather broad and a wrongful departure from those limits, whatever they may be, is an escape at common law as pointed out above. On the other hand one who has been released on probation or parole, while not a "free man" in every sense of the term, is no longer "in prison" even in the broad sense of that phrase and hence cannot be guilty of a common-law escape. Some of the statutes, however, expressly provide that the wrongful departure of a parolee from the limits stipulated in his parole shall be "deemed" an escape and be punished as such.[22] A release on probation or parole is usually under certain conditions and restrictions in addition to territorial limitations. The normal penalty for the violation of probation or parole is that the order of conditional release will be revoked and the violator will be taken into custody to serve his sentence, or the remaining portion thereof, without the time during which he was at large being used to reduce his term.[23]

15. E.g., Downie v. Powers, 193 F.2d 760 (10th Cir. 1952).

16. Robinson v. State, 93 Ga. 77, 83, 18 S.E. 1018, 1019 (1893).

17. "A *posse* may be summoned under the form of 'deputizing' the person or persons composing it." Ibid.

18. 1 Bl.Comm. *343–4. The English common law required "every person above fifteen years old, and under the degree of a peer" to respond to such a request. The reference to a "peer" would have no application to the law here, and the provision might be in some such form as: "Every able bodied person above 18

years of age . . ." West's Ann.Cal. Pen.Code § 150 (1976).

19. See Firestone v. Rice, 71 Mich. 377, 380, 38 N.W. 885, 886 (1888).

20. McMahan v. Green, 34 Vt. 69 (1861).

21. Dougherty v. State, 106 Ala. 63, 17 So. 393 (1895).

22. By statute a parolee by leaving the territory, within which he is restricted by the terms of his parole, is guilty of escape. State v. Byrnes, 260 Iowa 765, 150 N.W.2d 280 (1967).

23. Idaho Code § 19.2603 (1979). See also 18 U.S.C.A. § 4201 et seq. (1976).

7. "JUMPING BAIL"

A prisoner who has been released on bail does not ordinarily have, as is sometimes supposed, a choice between returning for trial or other disposition on the one hand, and forfeiting his bail on the other. The normal rule is that one who has forfeited bail is subject to arrest,[24] and at times "jumping bail" as it is called is made a separate substantive offense.[25]

I. MISPRISION OF FELONY

Misprision of felony is nondisclosure and [or] concealment of the known felony of another.

It is sometimes said that misprision of felony also includes the criminal neglect to prevent a felony.

The word "misprision" has been employed with different meanings. While Blackstone thought of it as referring to a grave misdemeanor,[26] it seems to have been used earlier to indicate the entire field of crime below the grade of treason or felony [27] before the word "misdemeanor" became the generally accepted label for this purpose.[28] More recently it has been said: "Misprision is nothing more than a word used to describe a misdemeanor which does not possess a specific name." [29] It has been associated with two specific offenses, and only these, from the earliest times. They are misprision of treason and misprision of felony, which consist of the criminal default of one in regard to the crime of another. As the former was considered in the discussion of treason only the latter needs attention here.

In an early Michigan case, in which the only problem in connection with the use of force in aid of another had reference to a *privilege* in this regard, it was said: "It is held to be the duty of every man who sees a felony attempted by violence, to prevent it if possible, . . ." [30] This *dictum* has been repeated now and then, usually in a case in which the actual problem concerned privilege rather than duty, and sometimes with the added notion that a failure to take reasonable steps to prevent such a crime constitutes misprision of felony.[31] On rare occasion it has been added to the definition

---

24. E.g., West's Ann.Cal.Pen.Code § 1310 (1955).

25. A person admitted to bail who fails to appear as required and does not thereafter appear or surrender himself within 30 days is guilty of a felony if the charge was felony and of a misdemeanor if the charge was a misdemeanor. McKinney's N.Y.Pen.Law, §§ 215.56, 215.57 (1975). Giving "false bail" in a federal court is a felony. 18 U.S.C.A. § 1506 (1976).

26. "Misprisions . . . are . . . all such high offences as are under the degree of capital, but nearly bordering thereon: . . ." 4 Bl.Comm. *119.

27. Coke, for example, uses the phrase "great misprision" to indicate a grave misdemeanor. E.g., 3 Co.Inst. *149.

28. At one time the word "trespass" was used by some to indicate (among other things) an offense other than treason or felony. Hawkins, for example, says it "is a word of a very general extent, and in a large sense . . . comprehends all inferior offences. . . ." 2 Hawk.P.C., c. 8 § 38 (6th ed. 1788).

29. United States v. Perlstein, 126 F.2d 789, 798 (3d Cir. 1942).

30. Pond v. People, 8 Mich. 150, 177 (1860).

31. See Snell v. Derricott, 161 Ala. 259, 272, 49 So. 895, 900 (1909); Carpenter v. State, 62 Ark. 286, 308, 36 S.W. 900, 906 (1896). Bishop made such a statement. 1 Bishop, New Criminal Law § 717 (8th ed. 1892). He relied entirely upon a statement by Hale, 1 Hale P.C. *484, which was given in explaining why one is *privileged* to use force to prevent

of misprision of felony by wording it in terms of "criminal neglect either to prevent a felony from being committed, or to bring the defendant to justice after its commission, but without such previous concert with or subsequent assistance to the felon as would make the concealer an accessory before or after the fact." [32]   This, however, was in cases in which the issue was nondisclosure rather than prevention and the generally-accepted view is that a bystander is not bound to interfere in the effort to prevent a felony [33] unless he owes some special duty of protection to the intended victim.[34]   As Hawkins, J., said years ago:

"It is no criminal offence to stand by, a mere passive spectator of a crime, even of a murder.   Non-interference to prevent a crime is not itself a crime." [35]   And as said more recently: "According to the institutional writers it is a misdemeanour to forbear from preventing a felony, but this may safely be regarded as obsolete." [36]

On the other hand the early common law of England seems to have required the private citizen to play the role of informer as to any known felony.[37]   In theory at least, it was the duty of anyone having knowledge of a felony committed by another to disclose this information to some proper au-

the murder of an innocent victim. With reference to the supposed duty to prevent a felony Hale qualified his statement with a *"tamen quaere."* It is significant that Stephen says this offense was "concealment of either treason or felony without otherwise taking part in it." 2 Stephen, History of the Criminal Law of England 238 (1883). He makes no reference to the failure to prevent the crime.

32. State v. Flynn, 100 R.I. 520, 217 A.2d 432, 433 (1966); State v. Wilson, 80 Vt. 249, 67 A. 533 (1907).

33. " 'Every person may, upon such an occasion, interfere to prevent if he can, the perpetration of so high a crime; but he is not bound to do so at the peril, otherwise, of partaking of the guilt.' " State v. Powell, 168 N.C. 134, 140, 83 S.E. 310, 314 (1914). And see State v. Birchfield, 235 N.C. 410, 413, 70 S.E.2d 5, 7 (1952). The actual problem in such cases is usually whether or not the defendant was guilty of the felony being committed by another, but the judicial attitude is clear. "If the defendant 'did no act to aid, assist, or abet' the perpetration of the crime, he is guilty *of no violation of law* from the mere fact that he was present." People v. Woodward, 45 Cal. 293 (1873). Emphasis added. Even consent to the commission of a felony by another, if not expressed by any word or deed, does not make the one consenting guilty of any offense. State v. Douglass, 44 Kan. 618, 26 P. 476 (1890). The most we find in such opinions is that such conduct is "wrong morally." Moore v.

State, 4 Okl.Cr. 212, 216, 111 P. 822, 824 (1910); Anderson v. State, 66 Okl.Cr. 291, 298, 91 P.2d 794, 797 (1939). See also Pope v. State, 284 Md. 309, 396 A.2d 1054 (1979).

34. One may not stand idly by and permit another to drown one's infant children. Rex v. Russell [1933] Vict.L.R. 59 (1932).

35. The Queen v. Coney, 8 Q.B.D. 534, 557–58 (1882).

36. Williams, Criminal Law 422 (2d ed. 1961).

It was taken for granted that neither presence at the scene of the crime nor failure to take steps to prevent a crime, is sufficient for criminal guilt although the actual statement was that aiding and abetting are not established thereby. Pinell v. Superior Court, 232 Cal.App.2d 284, 42 Cal.Rptr. 676 (1965); People v. Adams, 259 Cal.App.2d 109, 66 Cal.Rptr. 161 (1968).

37. "It may be conceded that by the common law of England every man was bound, under pain of punishment, to make himself an informer as to any treason or felony that he witnessed, or that came to his knowledge. His failure to give information as to such a crime made him guilty of the misdemeanor called misprision of treason, or of felony, as the case might be, unless indeed he gave such countenance or aid as to make him a principal or an accessory before or after the fact." Commonwealth v. Lopes, 318 Mass. 453, 456, 61 N.E.2d 849, 850 (1945).

thority with reasonable diligence and it was the failure to discharge this duty which constituted the misdemeanor known as misprision of felony.[38]   Even this seems to have been largely theoretical.   It was employed without doubt in certain specific situations.   Thus before receiving stolen property was made a separate substantive offense it was punished, during one period of history, as a misprision of felony.[39]   The guilty receiver was convicted because of his failure to disclose a known felony.   It is obvious, however, that even the most half-hearted effort to punish the nondisclosure of all known felonies would have resulted in a large number of cases during the course of centuries, and the peculiar dearth of such material in the reports is quite significant.   In ancient times, when the hue and cry was at the peak point of its importance, the private person who was required to join the chase in the effort to track down the felon may have had also a well-recognized duty to disclose any known felony in order that the hue and cry might be started.[40] The theory of such a duty seemed to survive for a time as an explanation for the conviction in certain very limited situations rather than as a general basis for the establishment of criminal guilt.[41]   Judge Stephen stated that it was practically obsolete in England three-quarters of a century ago [42] and with rare exception it has not been recognized in this country.[43]   The reason for its failure to survive here was well expressed by Chief Justice Marshall many years ago:

"It may be the duty of a citizen to accuse every offender, and to proclaim every offence which comes to his knowledge, but the law which would punish him in every case for not performing this duty is too harsh for man." [44]

38. Misprision of felony is "concealment of felony . . . or not discovery [disclosure] of felony." 3 Co.Inst. *139; "the concealing of a felony which a man knows, but never consented to, for if he consented, he is either principal or accessory," 1 Hale P.C. *374; 4 Bl.Comm. *121; "a concealment of felony, or a procuring of the concealment thereof, whether it be a felony by the common law, or by statute." 1 Hawk.P.C. c. 59 § 2 (6th ed. 1788).

39. "Under the ancient common law, his offence was misprision of the felony, committed by knowing it and neglecting to prosecute the felon; . . . ." 1 Bishop, New Criminal Law § 699 (8th ed. 1892); 2 id. § 1137; and see Engster v. State, 11 Neb. 539, 542 (1881). By an English statute the receiver was punishable as accessory to larceny after the fact, and later receiving was made a separate substantive offense. See supra, c. IV, § 6.

40. In the days of the hue and cry it was misprision of felony for one who saw murder committed to fail to apprehend the felon if able to do so. 3 Co.Inst. *139; 1 Hale P.C. *439; 2 Hawk.P.C. c. 12 (6th ed. 1788).

In 1314 it was said that "it is the law of the land that such as be present when

such a felony as this (murder) is committed shall raise hue and cry and give aid towards arresting the felons."   And those who were present, and of age but did not report it, were fined half a mark apiece. Year Books of Edward II, 24 Selden Society, 152–53.

41. The fact that it was not a general basis for the establishment of criminal guilt, even in fairly early times, will be emphasized in the discussion of theftbote in the following subsection.

42. Many years ago Judge Stephen referred to the "practically obsolete offence of misprision." 2 Stephen, History of the Criminal Law of England 238 (1883). "Modern cases of prosecutions for misprision of felony in England have not been found, although there are instances of prosecutions for criminal obstruction of justice." Commonwealth v. Lopes, 318 Mass. 453, 457, 61 N.E.2d 849, 851 (1945).

43. Misprision of felony is not a common-law offense in Michigan and it is doubtful if the mere nondisclosure of a known felony was ever a common-law crime in England. People v. Lefkovitz, 294 Mich. 263, 293 N.W. 642 (1940).

44. Marbury v. Brooks, 20 U.S. 556, 575–76 (1882).

More recently it has been said: "The absence of a reported decision during the four hundred years since the offence first crept into a book is itself remarkable. It is equally remarkable that no book before *Chitty* contains a precedent of an indictment for misprision of felony. . . . We have it, indeed, on the authority of Lord Westbury, L. C., Stephen, J., and C. S. Greaves, that the offence had fallen into desuetude." [45]

It is now clear, however, that this is an overstatement so far as the common law in England is concerned. In upholding a conviction of this offense the court said recently, after a careful study: "In the light of this history it is plain that there is and always has been an offence of misprision of felony and that it is not obsolete." [46] It was held that the wrongful nondisclosure of a known felony constitutes the offense but indicated that it should be applied only in rather serious cases.[47]

There is also some authority for the view that misprision of felony is a common-law misdemeanor in this country.[48] It is interesting to note, however, that while many of the modern state codes include misprision of treason, this is not true of misprision of felony.[49] Michigan has a section called "misprision of treason" [50] but it applies only to those "who shall have knowledge of the commission of treason against this state." After inquiring whether there was any crime at common law if all the defendant did was to observe another's crime without actively concealing it or hindering law-enforcement officers it was concluded that "a negative answer would appear to be sounder." [51] And another court expressed it this way: "In modern criminal law mere nondisclosure of knowledge of crime by another is not misprision of felony nor any substantive crime," adding that the punishment of such mere nondisclosure would be "wholly unsuited to American law and procedure." [52]

45. Glazebrook, Misprision of Felony—Shadow or Phantom, 8 Am.J. of Legal Hist. 283, 299–300 (1964).

46. Sykes v. Director of Public Prosecutions [1961] 3 All Eng.L.Rep. 33, 40.

47. Ibid. "Here, therefore, there is reason for limiting the law against mere misprisions to the concealment of such crimes as are of an aggravated complexion." Williams, Criminal Law 423 (2d ed. 1961), quoting from the Criminal Law Commissioners).

The conviction in *Sykes* in the preceding note, was based on failure to disclose knowledge of the theft of 100 pistols, 4 submachine guns and 1960 rounds of ammunition.

48. State v. Flynn, 100 R.I. 520, 217 A.2d 432 (1966); State v. Wilson, 80 Vt. 249, 67 A. 533 (1907).

49. One author who had obviously been searching for authority (see note 35, infra) cites only Me.Rev.Stats.1954, c. 135, § 12. And that was not included in Me.Rev.Stats.Ann. (1964). A Louisiana case involved its statute on misprision of felony—then section 856. State v. Graham, 190 La. 669, 182 So. 711, 714 (1938).

But that was repealed in 1942. See LSA–R.S. (La.) vol. 1, p. 6.

"To conceal his knowledge of such an act (murder), and to remain passive and silent was, at common law, a misprision of felony, and which offence has been, in the passage cited from the crimes act, specialized and defined." State v. Hann, 40 N.J.Law 228, 229 (1878).

It is not included in the New Jersey Statutes Annotated of 1979 nor Ariz.Rev. Stat. of 1978.

50. Mich.Stat.Ann. § 28.812 (1972).

51. United States v. Worcester, 190 F.Supp. 548, 565 (D.C.Mass.1961).

52. People v. Lefkovitz, 294 Mich. 263, 293 N.W. 642, 643 (1940).

The South Carolina Supreme Court has held the offense of misprision of a felony known at common law was cognizable under the laws of that state and does not conflict with the privilege against self incrimination. "The General Assembly has neither enacted, modified nor repealed the common law offense of misprision of felony." State v. Carson, 274 S.C. 316, 262 S.E.2d 918, 920 (1980).

But while there seems to be no such offense as misprision of felony in most of the states, there is such a section in the United States Code, worded as follows:

"Whoever, having knowledge of the actual commission of a felony cognizable by a court of the United States, conceals and does not as soon as possible make known the same to some judge or other person in civil or military authority under the United States, shall be fined not more than $500 or imprisoned not more than three years, or both." [53]

Two comments are in order. (1) The penalty places this "misprision" in the category of felony rather than misdemeanor; [54] (2) the wording—"conceals and does not . . . make known"—as interpreted, is not violated by the mere nondisclosure of a known felony but only where there is some positive act such as suppression of the evidence of the crime. [55] "Under it some affirmative act toward concealment of the felony is necessary. Mere silence after knowledge of the commission of the crime is not sufficient." [56] The former National Prohibition Act, for example, made the unlawful sale of liquor a felony, but the buyer's failure to disclose the sale did not constitute misprision of felony under this section. [57] The same result has been reached under a statute which is similarly worded except that the two clauses are connected with the word "or" instead of "and." The word "or" as so used, it

Conviction of the offense of concealment of a fugitive cannot be supported by evidence which showed no more than that the defendant took no affirmative steps to come forward with information about the burglary. People v. Donelson, 45 Ill.App.3d 609, 4 Ill.Dec. 273, 359 N.E.2d 1225 (1977).

The Maryland Court of Appeals has held that the crime of misprision of felony is no longer available as an offense in that state it being incompatible with local circumstances and jurisprudence. Pope v. State, 284 Md. 309, 396 A.2d 1054 (1979).

53. 18 U.S.C.A. § 4 (1969).

54. "Any offense punishable by death or imprisonment for a term exceeding one year is a felony." Id. at § 1.

55. "In order to sustain a conviction for misprision of felony, it was necessary for the government to prove . . . (1) the principal has committed and completed the felony alleged, (2) the accused had full knowledge of the fact, (3) the accused failed to notify authorities, and (4) the accused took an affirmative step to conceal the crime." United States v. Hodges, 566 F.2d 674, 675 (9th Cir. 1977). See also Neal v. United States, 102 F.2d 643, 646–649 (8th Cir. 1939); Miller v. United States, 230 F.2d 486, 489 note 7 (5th Cir. 1956). This statute does not violate the self-incrimination privilege because it requires concealment in addition to nondisclosure. United States v. Dad-

dano, 432 F.2d 1119 (7th Cir. 1970), but see United States v. Jennings, 603 F.2d 650 (7th Cir. 1979).

"Misprision basically requires knowledge of the commission of a felony, and wilful concealment from the authorities by some affirmative act." United States v. Sampol, 636 F.2d 621, 653 (D.C.Cir. 1980).

56. "The Act of April 30, 1790, as amended (18 U.S.C.A. § 4) requires both concealment and failure to disclose. Under it some affirmative act toward the concealment of the felony is necessary. Mere silence after knowledge of the commission of the crime is not sufficient." United States v. Farrar, 38 F.2d 515, 517 (D.C.Mass.1930); Bratton v. United States, 73 F.2d 795, 798 (10th Cir. 1934).

Accord, and even if the element of concealment was present D cannot be convicted if disclosure by him might have tended to have caused him to be charged with complicity in the crime. United States v. King, 402 F.2d 694 (9th Cir. 1968).

57. United States v. Farrar, 38 F.2d 515 (D.C.Mass.1930). The "manifested intent of Congress" theory would no doubt have protected the buyer even under a different interpretation of the statute, but the court emphasized that mere nondisclosure of a known felony does not constitute misprision of felony as there defined. Id. at 517.

was held, must be interpreted "and" with the result that the mere nondisclosure of a known felony is not sufficient for guilt.[58]

Another point to be emphasized is that the word "knowledge" or "knowing" as used in the definition of misprision of felony has been interpreted to require actual knowledge and not mere information and belief.[59]

One author seemed to think misprision of felony should be revived,[60] but there is little support for this view. No such offense is included in the Model Penal Code.[61] The notion that misprision is needed, to prevent one who knows about another's felony from intentionally misleading investigating officers, is unfounded. If, when being questioned by officers who are investigating a felony, one who knows the facts intentionally misleads the officers by false statements and thereby "covers up" for the felon, he thereby makes himself an accessory to that felony after the fact.[62] If he impedes the investigation by falsely saying he does not know about it, or by refusing to talk, he should be held to be guilty of obstructing justice. There is a wide difference between a mere failure to hunt up an officer and tell about a felony, on the one hand, and a refusal to cooperate with an investigating officer, on the other.

J. COMPOUNDING CRIME

Compounding crime is the acceptance of anything of value under an unlawful agreement not to prosecute a known offender or to limit or handicap the prosecution of his case.*

The origin of this offense is the ancient crime of theftbote.[63] Larceny was a common-law felony because of the frequency with which the identity of the thief was unknown. In the rare case in which the thief was known, and evidence sufficient for conviction was available, nothing less would suffice, according to the ancient view, than the extreme penalty. The theory was no doubt unsound in the beginning, and it "backfired" in the course of time because the day came when judges as well as jurors were reluctant to have a man hanged for this offense, but for the moment our interest is in the ancient theory. When this theory prevailed in full force it was deemed a "heinous offence" [64] for the victim of larceny to compromise with the thief,— to bargain with him that if he would return the stolen goods, or make other amends, the victim would not cause the other to be prosecuted for the crime, or would "prosecute faintly," [65] to the end that no conviction would result.[66]

---

58. State v. Michaud, 150 Me. 479, 114 A.2d 352 (1955). A failure of military personnel to report a mutiny or sedition is punishable under Article 94 of the Uniform Code of Military Justice. 10 U.S.C.A. § 894.

59. State v. Michaud, 150 Me. 479, 114 A.2d 352 (1955). And see Brittin v. Chegary, 20 N.J.L. 625, 627–8 (1846).

60. Goldberg, Misprision of Felony: An Old Concept in New Context. 52 A.B.A.J. 148 (1966).

61. The Code would make it an offense to volunteer false information to a law enforcement officer. Section 242.-3(5). Or to aid the consummation of crime. Section 242(4).

62. See, infra, chapter 6, section 8, C. 4.

* "The elements of compounding may be described as (1) knowledge of the commission of the original crime; (2) an agreement not to report or prosecute that crime; and (3) the receipt of consideration." Hoines v. Barney's Club, Inc., 28 Cal.3d 603, 170 Cal.Rptr. 42, 46, 620 P.2d 628, 632 (1980).

63. 3 Co.Inst. *139.

64. 4 Bl.Comm. *363

65. 1 Hale P.C. *619.

66. "Of a nature somewhat similar to the two last is the offence of *theft bote*,

This perversion of justice was once deemed so extremely antisocial that the one making such an agreement was held guilty of felony, as accessory to larceny after the fact, but it was later treated as a separate substantive offense and punished as a misdemeanor,[67] unless the victim of the larceny went further and received the thief himself or otherwise gave him direct aid to enable him to avoid prosecution or punishment.[68]

It was the agreement not to prosecute or to "prosecute faintly" which made the victim of larceny guilty of theftbote, and if he received the goods back from the thief without any bargain with him this was "no offence"[69] "at all"[70] but was "lawful."[71] This shows how long ago the nondisclosure of a known felony ceased to be a general basis for the establishment of criminal guilt (if it ever was) and became merely a rationalization used to explain the conviction in very limited situations.

In the course of time theftbote came to be called "compounding of felony"[72] and the misdemeanor under this name was expanded to include an agreement for consideration not to prosecute for any felony.[73] Compounding a misdemeanor was not an offense under the common law of England, but such an agreement was unenforceable because contrary to public policy[74] and confusion has resulted at times from a failure to distinguish between "illegality" in this sense and punishability as a crime. A statute in 1576[75] made provision for the compromise of certain offenses with the consent of the court and provided a penalty for the *unlawful* settlement of any crime. As this statute has generally been recognized to be a part of our common law[76] compounding crime is here said to be the acceptance of anything of value under an agreement not to prosecute a known offender for any offense—treason, felony or misdemeanor[77]—unless the law of a particular jurisdiction is either narrower in its scope[78] or authorizes the compromise of certain offenses. The compromise of a misdemeanor "of very low grade"

which is where the party robbed not only knows the felon, but also takes his goods again, upon an agreement not to prosecute." 4 Bl.Comm. *133. The word "robbed" is used here loosely in the layman's sense as shown when the author refers back to it later under the name of "larceny." Id. at *363.

67. Id. at *134.

68. Such aid would make the aider an accessory to the larceny after the fact. 3 Co.Inst. *134. "If A hath his goods stolen by B, if A receives his goods again simply, without any contract to favor him in his prosecution, or to forbear prosecution, this is lawful; but if he receives them upon an agreement not to prosecute, or to prosecute faintly, this is *theft bote*, punishable by imprisonment and ransom, but yet it makes not A an accessory; but if he takes money to favor him, whereby he escapes, this makes him an accessory." [Quoted somewhat loosely but in substance, from 1 Hale, P.C. *619]. State v. Hodge, 142 N.C. 665, 668, 55 S.E. 626, 627 (1906).

69. 3 Co.Inst. *134.

70. 1 Hawk.P.C. c. 59, § 7 (6th ed. 1788).

71. 1 Hale P.C. *619.

72. 4 Bl.Comm. *134.

73. 1 Stephen, History of the Criminal Law of England 502 (1883).

74. Ibid.

75. 18 Eliz. I, c. 5.

76. 2 Wharton, Criminal Law § 1884 (12 ed. 1932). Bishop says it is not generally regarded as part of our common law although he admits there are no decisions directly in point. 1 Bishop, New Criminal Law § 712 (8th ed. 1892). His footnote mentions that Kilty regarded part of it as received in Maryland. Id. at n. 7. It seems clear that some parts of it have not been recognized in this country.

77. 1 Bishop, New Criminal Law § 709 (8th ed. 1892); State v. Carter, 69 N.H. 216, 39 A. 973 (1897).

78. The statute provides no penalty for compromising an offense unless it is a felony. State v. Guthrie, 150 Iowa 149, 129 N.W. 804 (1911).

has been said not to be a crime.[79] This has reference to the type of offense which is not a true crime but rather a "civil offense," [80] and is on the ground that the person harmed thereby is authorized to settle or condone it.[81] And it has been increasingly common for statutes to authorize the compromise of certain true crimes, usually in the misdemeanor category.[82] Hence compounding crime is likely to appear in the modern penal code in some such form as this:

> **"Every person who, having knowledge of the actual commission of a crime, takes money or property of another, or any gratuity or reward, or any engagement or promise thereof, upon any agreement or understanding to compound or conceal such crime, or to abstain from any prosecution thereof, or to withhold any evidence thereof, except in the cases provided for by law, in which crimes may be compromised by leave of court, is punishable as follows: . . ."** [83]

79. See State v. Carver, 69 N.H. 216, 218, 39 A. 973, 974 (1897); 1 Bishop, New Criminal Law § 711 (8th ed. 1892).

80. Offenses "having largely the nature of private injuries. . . ." A "crime in the nature of a civil tort. . . ." 1 Bishop § 711. See infra under "civil offense."

81. Holsey v. State, 4 Ga.App. 453, 61 S.E. 836 (1908). One important purpose of the statute, 18 Eliz. I, c. 5, was to try to insure for the crown the penalty to which it was entitled as a result of such an offense, but this part of the statute has not been recognized generally as common law in this country.

82. E.g., any misdemeanor for which the person injured by the act constituting the offense has a remedy by a civil action, except when it is committed: (1) by or upon an officer of justice while in the execution of his office; (2) riotously, or (3) with intent to commit a felony. West's Ann.Cal.Pen.Code § 1377 (1980). Under the statute all misdemeanors, such as obtaining money by false pretenses, in which there is a civil remedy available to the injured party, may be compromised and settled by the parties, with the concurrence of the court. The fact that the formalities of the statute are not strictly followed will not prevent the compromise when the aggrieved party receives satisfaction, appears before the magistrate

and the warrant is dismissed. Ornford v. Bond, 185 Va. 497, 39 S.E.2d 352 (1946). "It is well settled that an agreement in consideration of stifling or compounding a criminal prosecution or proceeding for a felony or a misdemeanor of a public nature is void. . . ." But the statute authorizes a compromise of the offense of obtaining property by false pretenses. Geier v. Shade, 109 Pa. 180 (1885). The only crime that may be compromised under the law of South Carolina is an offense for drawing and uttering a fraudulent check. George v. Leonard, 71 F.Supp. 665 (D.C.S.C.1947). The offense of disturbing the peace does not by its nature give rise to a civil remedy and is not compromisable under a misdemeanor compromise statute. State ex rel. Williams v. City Court of City of Tucson, 18 Ariz.App. 394, 502 P.2d 543 (1972). And see infra under "condonation by the injured party."

83. E.g., West's Ann.Cal.Pen.Code § 153 (1977).

"So far as research discloses the crime may be committed only by a person—including accomplices—receiving consideration pursuant to agreement to frustrate prosecution for criminal conduct." Hoines v. Barney's Club, Inc., 28 Cal.3d 603, 170 Cal.Rptr. 42, 46–47, 620 P.2d 628, 632–33 (1980).

Except where otherwise provided by statute [84] the elements of compounding are (1) a crime actually committed by one person,[85] (2) receipt of something of value by another,[86] (3) under an agreement not to prosecute for such crime or to limit or handicap such prosecution.[87] While one injured by a wrongful act may lawfully accept compensation for the harm he has received, if this is all, it becomes illegal if accompanied by a bargain that the other shall not be prosecuted.[88] And although consideration is essential to guilt it is not necessary that it accrue to the compounder.[89] In one case, for example, **A** stole $65 from **B**. **B**'s brother took a note from **A**'s father as consideration for a promise that **A** should not be prosecuted. This was held to be criminal compounding.[90] As indicated by this case a promissory note signed by, or on behalf of the first offender,[91] and it would seem any promise by or for him to confer a benefit, constitutes "value" as the word is used in the definition of this offense.

Knowledge by the compounder of the offense committed by the other has occasionally been listed as one of the elements of compounding [92] but this is open to serious question. In the ancient offense of theftbote the victim of the larceny who discovered where the stolen chattel was may have had good reason to believe the possessor was the thief but he seldom had "knowledge" in the strict sense of the word, and that is often true of the compounder of any offense. If compounding crime includes an element of "knowledge" it is in the loose sense in which this word is used in such offenses as receiving

84. The statute of 18 Eliz. I, c. 5, § 4, applies to a penalty incurred or pretended to have occurred. Rex v. Gotley, Russ. & Ry. 84, 168 Eng.Rep. 696 (1805). The part of the statute referring to an offense not actually committed seems not to have been accepted generally in this country, but see George v. Leonard, 71 F.Supp. 665, 667 (D.C.S.C.1947). A dictum often cited for the claim that there may be guilt of compounding although no other offense has been committed is in State v. Carter, 69 N.H. 216, 219, 39 A. 973, 975 (1897). But the statement is merely that it is not necessary that the one from whom the reward was received had committed an offense.

85. Hays v. State, 15 Ga.App. 386, 83 S.E. 502 (1914); State v. Hodge, 142 N.C. 665, 55 S.E. 626 (1906); Davidson v. State, 29 Okl.Cr. 46, 232 P. 120 (1925). "The reason of the thing accords better with the common law, for it cannot be held that the public is injured by the refusal of a private person to present or prosecute a charge of crime, if in fact no crime has been perpetrated." State v. Leeds, 68 N.J.L. 210, 211, 52 A. 288, 289 (1902).

86. A consideration is necessary. Hays v. State, 15 Ga.App. 386, 83 S.E. 502 (1914).

87. State v. Hodge, 142 N.C. 665, 55 S.E. 626 (1906). An agreement not to prosecute, or in some way to favor and protect the criminal, is an essential ingredient of the offense of compounding a crime. Brittin v. Chegary, 20 N.J.L. 625 (1846). "The reason that a private agreement, made in consideration of the suppression of a prosecution for crime, is illegal, is that it tends to benefit an individual at the expense of defeating the course of public justice." Partridge v. Hood, 120 Mass. 403, 405 (1876).

88. Shaw v. Reed, 30 Me. 105 (1849).

89. Hays v. State, 15 Ga.App. 386, 83 S.E. 502 (1914).

90. State v. Ruthven, 58 Iowa 121, 12 N.W. 235 (1882). The North Carolina court held it necessary to allege that the crime was committed by the person with whom the corrupt agreement was made. State v. Hodge, 142 N.C. 665, 55 S.E. 626 (1906). But the Iowa holding is preferable. It is no defense that the compounder acted for a superior to whom he gave the entire consideration received. State v. Ash, 33 Or. 86, 54 P. 184 (1898).

91. Accord, Commonwealth v. Pease, 16 Mass. 91 (1819).

92. E.g., 1 Burdick, Law of Crime § 298 (1946). His only citation is to a case which refers to the requirements of a specific statute.

stolen property and will include a belief which is correct even if based upon hearsay or inference. The very act of compounding is an indication of such a belief, which should be treated as conclusive if the offense by the other is clearly established, but even so it is doubtful if this is an element of the crime which the prosecution is required to plead and affirmatively to prove unless it has been added by statute.[93]

Criminal guilt is not established by the fact that the one particularly harmed by an offense has accepted compensation for his personal loss, plus the fact that the other has not been prosecuted for his crime, *if* there was no agreement or understanding that this should be the result.[94] The hope on the part of the offender that this compensation would stave off any prosecution, although fully realized, is not a substitute for an actual agreement or understanding to this effect. Thus accepting a note to make up a shortage resulting from embezzlement would not be compounding the offense if the note was offered in the mere hope that prosecution would not follow, but would be compounding if the note was accepted with an agreement or understanding that no prosecution would be instituted.[95]

Although the English rule is that a compounder may not be convicted if he has prosecuted the other to conviction prior to his own indictment[96] this seems quite unsound and the prevailing view in this country is that the offense is complete when the unlawful agreement is made and the compounder cannot purge himself of guilt by a violation of his criminal bargain.[97] The fact that the other party to the bargain has been tried and acquitted does not establish innocence on the part of the alleged compounder.[98] This may have resulted from the agreement to "prosecute faintly"[99] to use the ancient phrase.

It is a crime to demand and receive money on a threat that the other will be prosecuted if the money is not paid, even if the other has in fact committed no crime,[1] but this is statutory extortion and not compounding.[2] And if the public prosecutor took money to refrain from prosecuting known gamblers he was properly tried for misconduct in office and in this prosecution it is not necessary to prove the compounding of any specific offense.[3]

---

93. "Knowledge" is included in some of the statutory definitions. E.g., West's Ann.Cal.Pen.Code § 153 (1977); Fountain v. Bigham, 235 Pa. 35, 42, 84 A. 131, 134 (1912).

94. Harding v. Cooper, 1 Starkie 467, 171 Eng.Rep. 532 (1816); Flower v. Sadler, 10 Q.B.D. 572 (1882). "A person wronged by the criminal act of another may accept restitution for the civil wrong done to him, but he cannot lawfully agree not to prosecute the crime." In re Friedland, 59 N.J. 209, 280 A.2d 183, 188 (1971). An occasional statute withholds the penalty even if there has been such a promise, if the person who sustained the loss reasonably believed he was entitled to what he received. E.g., Wis.Stats. 1955, § 946.67 (1978).

95. Farmer's National Bank v. Tartar, 256 Ky. 70, 75 S.W.2d 758 (1934).

96. Rex v. Stone, 4 Car. & P. 379, 172 Eng.Rep. 749 (1830).

97. State v. Ash, 33 Or. 86, 54 P. 184 (1898); Campbell v. State, 42 Tex.Cr.R. 27, 57 S.W. 288 (1900).

98. People v. Buckland, 13 Wend. 593 (N.Y.1835).

99. 1 Hale P.C. *619.

1. Regina v. Best, 9 Car. & P. 367, 173 Eng.Rep. 871 (1840).

2. Wilson v. State, 306 P.2d 717 (Okl. Cr.1957).

3. State v. Jefferson, 88 N.J.L. 447, 97 A. 162 (1916).

While compounding was a misdemeanor at common law the compounding of a felony is itself a felony under many of the modern statutes.[4]

Under the Model Penal Code compounding would be a misdemeanor.[5] The most significant feature of this proposed section is that it would be an affirmative defense "that the pecuniary benefit did not exceed an amount which the actor believed to be due as restitution or indemnification for harm caused by the offense." The result would be to make a fair compromise lawful and to encourage the reduction of the trial load with dispositions of this nature. It was pointed out that in modern times the prosecution for compounding "is almost invariably against persons who, being merely witnesses of an offense with which they have no private concern as victim or otherwise, take money for a promise not to report or testify." [6]

K. MAINTENANCE, CHAMPERTY AND BARRATRY [7]

Three common-law misdemeanors, entitled to be mentioned in order to emphasize that they no longer exist in their ancient significance, are maintenance, champerty and barratry. In the original sense—

Maintenance is an officious intermeddling in a suit that in no way belongs to one, by maintaining or assisting either party, with money or otherwise, to prosecute or defend it.[8]

Champerty is a bargain by a volunteer with a claimant or a person against whom a claim has been asserted, that they will share the matter sued upon if they prevail at law, whereupon the volunteer (champertor) is to carry on, or defend, the suit at his own expense.[9]

Barratry—sometimes called common barratry—is the practice of exciting and stirring up suits either at law or otherwise.[10]

In other words maintenance was assistance in a suit or action in which the assistant had no interest of his own; champerty was maintenance plus an agreement to share the subject matter of the suit if successful; and barratry

---

4. E.g., West's Ann.Cal.Pen.Code § 153 (1977).

5. Section 242.5.

6. For a discussion of the problem of compounding, with many citations, see Model Penal Code 203–209 (Tent.Draft No. 9, 1959). The quotation in the text is from page 207.

7. The early spelling was "barretry." See 4 Bl.Comm. *134.

8. Ibid.

"Maintenance" is an officious intermeddling in a suit which in no way belongs to the intermeddler by maintaining or assisting either party to the action, with money or otherwise, to prosecute or defend it. In re Ratner, 194 Kan. 362, 399 P.2d 865 (1965).

9. Id. at *135. "Champerty is an agreement between the owner of a claim and a volunteer that the latter may take the claim and collect it, dividing the pro-

ceeds with the owner, if they prevail— the champertor to carry on the suit at his own expense. This doctrine is based upon the ground that no encouragement should be given to litigation by the introduction of a party to enforce those rights which the owners are not disposed to prosecute." Hamilton v. Gray, 67 Vt. 233, 235, 31 A. 315 (1894); Gibson v. Gillette, 34 Del. 331, 338, 152 A. 589, 593 (1929). And see Hannigan v. Italo Petroleum Corp., 36 Del. 442, 178 A. 589 (1935).

10. 4 Bl.Comm. *134. "Barratry is the offense of frequently exciting and stirring up quarrels and suits, either at law or otherwise." State v. Noell, 220 Mo.App. 883, 886, 295 S.W. 529, 530 (1927); Churchwell v. State, 195 Ga. 22, 26, 22 S.E.2d 824, 825 (1942); State v. Batson, 220 N.C. 411, 412, 17 S.E.2d 511, 512 (1941). There are slight variations in the wording.

was habitual maintenance,[11] —at least three instances being required.[12] These offenses were based upon a "mind your own business" philosophy once carried to such an absurd extent that it was criminal for one who knew the important facts, in regard to a case on trial, to testify therein if he had not been subpoenaed to do so.[13] Employing an attorney for another was a flagrant act of maintenance,[14] and it was suggested that one may have been punishable "for barely going along with him to enquire for a person learned in the law." [15]

"That such doctrine repugnant to every honest feeling of the human heart should soon be laid aside must be expected," [16] and how it ever found a place in the legal system can be understood only in the light of the peculiar background of ancient days.[17] If, at the present time, one owing money or other obligation should attempt to substitute someone else in his place as debtor without the consent of the creditor, he would learn very quickly that this cannot be done. If the creditor could not require performance by the original debtor no one would be willing to lend money or sell goods on credit. The reason for this is too obvious to warrant a labored explanation, but a point sometimes overlooked is that in the original theory of the common law the substitution of one creditor for another without the consent of the debtor was equally impossible. A fixed premise in the early law was that a debt or other chose in action was not assignable.

Following a suggestion found in Lampet's Case,[18] Blackstone gave the illegality of champerty as a main reason why a chose in action was not assignable at common law.[19] This is incorrect, however, as pointed out by Williston[20] and others,[21] and involves a confusion of cause and effect. Had the starting point been a clear recognition of champerty as inherently wrongful, the assignee of a chose in action—"the indubitably champertous assignee," [22] —would have had no more help from a court of equity than he had in a court of law. The result, however, was quite otherwise and the assignee's position was recognized and protected by courts of equity "from the earliest times." [23] The only theory which will explain the results reached in both law and equity emphasizes quite a different starting point. "The true reason for the non-assignability of choses in action in the English law, as well as in the

---

11. Radin, Maintenance by Champerty, 24 Calif.L.Rev. 48, 65 (1935).

12. 2 Bishop, New Criminal Law § 65 (8th ed. 1892); Churchwell v. State, 195 Ga. 22, 22 S.E.2d 824 (1942). There have been some suggestions to the effect that two instances were sufficient.

13. "[G]iving evidence officiously without being called upon to do it." 1 Hawk.P.C. c. 83, § 6 (6th ed. 1788). "[H]e must have had a subpoena, or suppress the truth." Master v. Miller, 4 T.R. 320, 340, 100 Eng.Rep. 1042, 1053 (1791).

14. 1 Hawk.P.C. c. 83, § 6 (6th ed. 1788).

15. Ibid.

16. Master v. Miller, 4 T.R. 320, 340, 100 Eng.Rep. 1042, 1053 (1791).

17. "The English common law and statutes against maintenance and champerty had their origin, if not their *necessity*, in a very different state of society from that which prevails at the present time, either in England or in this country." Hovey v. Thompson, 51 Me. 62, 64 (1863).

18. 10 Coke, 46a, 48a, 77 Eng.Rep. 994, 997 (1612).

19. 4 Bl.Comm. *135. See also Co. Litt. *214a, *266a.

20. 2 Williston, Law of Contracts § 405 (Rev. ed. 1938).

21. E.g., Radin, Maintenance by Champerty, 24 Calif.L.Rev. 48, 68 (1935).

22. Ibid.

23. Master v. Miller, 4 T.R. 320, 340, 100 Eng.Rep. 1042, 1053 (1791).

Roman law, seems to have been that the relation between the original obligor and obligee was regarded as a vital part of the obligation which could no more be changed than any other term of the obligation, the same reason that precludes acceptance of a revocable offer by anyone except the person to whom the offer is made." [24] Having taken this position the common-law judges would not be inclined to look with favor upon help given to a litigant on consideration that the helper should share the subject matter of the action if successful. They held this to be a punishable obstruction of justice because it tended to defeat the rule they had developed with such pains.

The crime of simple maintenance,—the punishability of help given to a litigant without bargaining for a share of the subject matter of the action, "may be said to be the last flaring up of feudalism." [25] One of the means by which powerful men aggrandized their estates was for a feudal magnate to increase his following by giving support "to his retainers in all their suits, without reference to their justification." This was the maintenance "against which the Star Chamber Act of 1487 and the Statute of Liveries of 1504 were specifically directed." [26] The law developed as mentioned above, to the point where any help, by money or otherwise, given to a litigant by one who had himself no interest in the action, was punishable.[27]

The idea back of barratry, or common barratry, was comparable to that back of modern statutes dealing with habitual criminals.

Feudalism and its problems passed into oblivion ages ago, as also did the general notion that a chose in action was nonassignable.[28] This left no foundation for the old offenses known as maintenance, champerty and barratry, and they were "laid aside" [29] in the distant past. Confusion has resulted, however, because in a particular jurisdiction we may find it necessary to say of any of them, what Judge Stephen said of one three-quarters of a century ago: "Although maintenance in the old sense of the word is a thing of the past, the name still survives in law books as the name of a crime, . . ." [30]

24. 2 Williston, Law of Contracts § 405 (Rev. ed. 1938).

25. Radin, Maintenance by Champerty, 24 Calif.L.Rev. 48, 65 (1935).

26. Id. at 64.

27. "At one time, not only he who laid out money to assist another in his cause, but he that by his friendship or interest saved him an expense which he would otherwise be put to, was held guilty of maintenance." Master v. Miller, 4 T.R. 320, 340, 100 Eng.Rep. 1042, 1053 (1791). Blackstone says one might lawfully maintain the suit of his near kinsman, servant or poor neighbor. 4 Bl.Comm. *135. This was said, however, when the law of maintenance had moved far from its original strictness.

28. When the common-law judges realized that the rights of the assignee of a chose in action would be protected by a court of equity they took a similar step, although in the guise of a fiction. They held that although the chose in action was not assignable, the assignment included a power of attorney under which the assignee could sue the debtor in the name of the assignor. The final step was the so-called "real party in interest" statute which in effect provided that the assignee should sue in his own name.

29. Master v. Miller, 4 T.R. 320, 340, 100 Eng.Rep. 1042, 1053 (1791). "As crimes they have become obsolete." Radin, Maintenance by Champerty, 24 Calif. L.Rev. 48, 67 (1935).

30. 3 Stephen, History of the Criminal Law of England 240 (1883). "Whoever is guilty of common barratry, maintenance or champerty, shall be fined not less than $50 nor more than $400." Del.Code Ann. Title 11, § 371. Maintenance and champerty are misdemeanors under the statute but are not there defined. Hannigan v. Italo Petroleum Corp., 36 Del. 442, 446–7, 178 A. 589, 591 (1935). "Indeed, the meaning of barratry, as applied to activities of attorneys at law, is greatly different today than existed in the early days of English jurisprudence." State v.

At the present time it is not unlawful for one, who has no interest of his own in the litigation, to give help by money or otherwise to either the plaintiff or the defendant, present or prospective, if the suit or the defense for which the help is given is just, or is reasonably believed to be so, and there is no impropriety in the manner in which, or the motive with which, the assistance is given.[31] As it is improper to stir up litigation known to be unfounded and unjust any wilful misconduct of this nature is punishable wherever a crime known as "maintenance" is found, if not limited otherwise by its terms and the practice of doing so (three or more instances) will constitute the offense of "barratry" which is much more frequently included in the modern codes.[32] It may be unreasonably vexatious, moreover, to incite certain litigation which is "just" in the sense that it will prevail if brought to trial. A demand note, for example, is suable without asking the maker for the money,[33] where the ancient rule remains unchanged. But while the maker has no defense to such a suit, and can only hold down expenses by promptly bringing the money into court, anyone who should urge the holder to bring the action without giving the maker an opportunity to pay without suit, is clearly prompted by improper motives.[34]

Misconduct under the name of "champerty" (and "maintenance" where this term is still employed) is much more likely to be encountered today as a defense to a civil action than as a criminal offense.[35] In either case with rare

Noell, 220 Mo.App. 883, 888, 295 S.W. 529, 531 (1927).

31. "The law of maintenance, as I understand it upon the modern construction, is confined to cases where a man improperly, and for the purpose of stirring up litigation and strife, encourages others either to bring actions, or to make defences which they have no right to make." Finden v. Parker, 11 Mees. & W. 675, 682, 152 Eng.Rep. 976, 979 (1843).

32. E.g., West's Ann.Cal.Pen.Code § 158 (1970); Ga.Code, § 26–2406 (1978); Idaho Code § 18–1001 (1979); 21 Okl.St. Ann. § 550 (1958); Va.Code 1975, § 18.2–451 et seq.

33. Uniform Commercial Code § 3–501 (Off.Text with commentaries, 1957). "Under this section as under the original act presentment for payment is not necessary to charge primary parties. . . ." Id. at p. 320. See also (Off.Text with commentaries, 1978 p. 307).

34. Some such point must have been in the background of a dictum to the effect that: "The exciting or stirring up of suits may be on grounds that are absolutely just and well founded; and yet . . . if any person makes a practice of stirring up suits or exciting quarrels between individuals he becomes guilty of a misdemeanor." Scott v. State, 53 Ga. App. 61, 65, 185 S.E. 131, 133 (1935). While this was undoubtedly true of the ancient law it is too broad a statement

under the Georgia statute, quoted in the opinion: "Any person who shall be found and adjudged a common barrator, vexing others with *unjust* and vexatious suits, shall be guilty of a misdemeanor, . . ." Id. at 64, 185 S.E. at 133. Emphasis added.

35. A glance at the digests will show that the cases are overwhelmingly on the civil side. A deed to land given by a former owner who never occupied the land and had not within a year received any rents or profits therefrom is champertous and void as against one in possession under color of title of a tax deed. Cox v. Montgomery, 282 P.2d 734 (Okl. 1955); Cox v. Kelley, 295 P.2d 1061 (Okl. 1956). The Kentucky statute providing that a conveyance of land of which another has adverse possession is void is highly penal, and where title to the minerals has been severed from title to the surface a conveyance of the minerals is not rendered champertous by reason of the fact that another has possession of the surface. Saulsberry v. Maddix, 125 F.2d 430 (6th Cir. 1942), cert. denied 317 U.S. 643, 63 S.Ct. 36 (1942).

Information of an outstanding title to land in adverse possession of another is good consideration for a promissory note, and the sale of such information is not "barratrous." Lucas v. Pico, 55 Cal. 126 (1880). The "common law doctrines of champerty and maintenance were never

exception [36] it will have a meaning quite different from the ancient concept. The ancient law was not directed against lawyers, in fact the "Statute of Westminster itself expressly exempts lawyers from its provisions as far as champerty is concerned." [37] Today, however, the statutes on maintenance and champerty, where found, are frequently directed against lawyers,[38] or at times against a very limited group including lawyers. Thus one type of "maintenance" statute provides a penalty for "any judge, justice of the peace, clerk of any court, sheriff, coroner, constable or attorney at law [who] shall encourage, excite and stir up any suit, quarrel or controversy between two or more persons, with intent to injure such person or persons. . . ." [39]

For a lawyer to take a case on a contingent fee is clearly champertous in its nature (under the ancient definition) and was long frowned upon for that reason. The result was harmful rather than beneficial because one with a just cause of action may be deterred from bringing it if he must pay a fixed attorney's fee, win or lose. For this reason the objection gradually disappeared and in general today the contingent fee is recognized as proper so long as it is fair and reasonable.[40] An early New York statute went so far as to make it an offense for a lawyer to buy a note, draft or chose in action except in payment for property sold or some comparable transaction.[41] It is a misdemeanor under a few of the modern statutes for a lawyer to *buy* any evidence of debt or thing in action "with intent to bring suit thereon." [42] But so far as the matter of retainer is concerned, while it is champertous for a lawyer to include as part of his agreement that he will bear the costs and expenses of suit, or some part thereof,[43] the prevailing view is that it is not champerty for an attorney to take a case on a contingent fee without this additional stipulation.[44] Some of the statutes make it a misdemeanor for a lawyer to buy legal work or to employ another to solicit business for him,[45] —sometimes called "ambulance chasing" because there have been occasions when it almost literally took this form, and it is improper for an attorney to agree with an investigator that the latter shall receive a share of the attorney's fees.[46]

adopted in this state." Cain v. Burns, 131 Cal.App.2d 439, 443, 280 P.2d 888, 890 (1955).

36. "Under the common law of Pennsylvania, an arrangement offends public policy against champerty and is illegal if it provides for the institution of litigation by and at the expense of a person who, but for that agreement, has no interest in it, with the understanding that his reward is to be a share of whatever proceeds the litigation may yield." Kenrich Corp. v. Miller, 377 F.2d 312, 314 (3d Cir. 1967). Hence the action brought by such a champertous plaintiff cannot be maintained.

37. Radin, Maintenance by Champerty, 24 Calif.L.Rev. 48, 65 (1935).

38. Id. at 68.

39. Rev.Stat.Neb. § 28–716 (1975).

40. Warvelle, Legal Ethics, 87–92 (2d ed. 1920). "A contract for contingent compensation is not illegal provided the

compensation specified is fair and reasonable." Gruskay v. Simenauskas, 107 Conn. 380, 386, 140 A. 724, 727 (1928). As to a contingent fee in a divorce case see Re Estate of Sylvester, 195 Iowa 1329, 192 N.W. 442 (1923); Welles v. Brown, 226 Mich. 657, 198 N.W. 180 (1924).

41. People v. Walbridge, 6 Cowen 512 (N.Y.1826).

42. Idaho Code § 18–1003 (1979); 21 Okl.St.A. § 554 (1958).

43. Rice v. Pigman, 94 Ohio App. 122, 114 N.E.2d 738 (1953).

44. Mock v. Higgins, 3 Ill.App.2d 281, 121 N.E.2d 865 (1954). And see Warvelle, Legal Ethics 89 (2d ed. 1920).

45. Ala.Code 1958, Tit. 46, § 53.

46. A contract between an attorney and an investigator that the latter shall receive one-third of the net attorney's fees is illegal, but it can be enforced

On the other side, an occasional statute provides a penalty for one who shall "make it a business to solicit employment for a lawyer," [47] and one who made a practice of going to persons injured in accidents, getting their "stories," shaping them up, talking to them about the possibility of recovering damages, and recommending a lawyer who would "co-operate" with him was held to have committed barratry.[48]

The one of these three names most frequently found in modern codes is "barratry," as mentioned above.[49] The Idaho provisions follow a rather common pattern, and attention to the wording and the arrangement will emphasize the vast change that has taken place. What purports to be the definitive section reads: "Common barratry is the practice of exciting groundless judicial proceedings." [50] The presence of the word "groundless" is sufficient to change the whole complexion of the crime, since there was no such requirement in the ancient law, but even more significant is the specific intent which is added by a subsequent section: "No person can be convicted of common barratry, except upon proof that he has excited actions or legal proceedings, in at least three instances, and with a corrupt or malicious intent to vex and annoy." [51] Under such a combination of statutes, using the word "practice" to indicate at least three instances, the definition is as follows:

Barratry is the practice of exciting groundless judicial proceedings with a corrupt or malicious intent to vex and annoy.[52]

"Since 1956 the seven southern states have been utilizing their amended barratry, champerty and maintenance laws as legal weapons to resist the efforts of such organizations as N.A.A.C.P. and C.O.R.E. in initiating civil rights suits." [53] The Supreme Court held that Virginia's maintenance and champerty laws, insofar as they prevented N.A.A.C.P. from seeking out prospective plaintiffs in desegregation cases, were invalid under the First and Fourteenth Amendments because they unduly inhibited protected freedoms of expression and association.[54] The Court later held that an injunction issued by a state court, prohibiting a labor union from advising injured members to obtain legal assistance before settling claims and recommending specific lawyers to handle such claims, infringed rights guaranteed by the same amendments.[55]

against the attorney because he only has violated the law. Cain v. Burns, 131 Cal. App.2d 439, 280 P.2d 888 (1955).

47. People v. Meola, 193 App.Div. 487, 184 N.Y.S. 353 (1920).

48. State v. Batson, 220 N.C. 411, 17 S.E.2d 511 (1941). The conviction in this case was for an attempt to commit barratry and it was this conviction which was affirmed. But the opinion makes it clear that had the conviction been for barratry it also would have been affirmed.

49. See note 26.

50. I.C. (Idaho) § 18–1001 (1979).

51. Id. at § 18–1002 (1978). Section 18–1001 (1979) provides that barratry is a misdemeanor.

52. "Barratry being a common law offense, and never having been the subject of legislation in North Carolina, and not being destructive nor repugnant to, nor inconsistent with, the form of government of the State, is in full force therein." State v. Batson, 220 N.C. 411, 413, 17 S.E.2d 511, 512 (1941). This, however, does not mean the offense in its ancient form. In fact this was said by the court in the extreme case mentioned in the text and cited in note 42.

53. Barratry—A Comparative Analysis of Recent Barratry Statutes. 14 DePaul L.Rev. 146, 147 (1964).

54. N. A. A. C. P. v. Button, 371 U.S. 415, 83 S.Ct. 328 (1963).

55. Brotherhood of Railroad Trainmen v. Virginia, 377 U.S. 1, 84 S.Ct. 1113 (1964). See also Mine Workers v. Illinois State Bar Association, 389 U.S. 217, 88

The Supreme Court has held that concerted anti-competitive activities of lawyers violate the federal antitrust acts.[56]   In keeping with the attitude that lawyers are not apart from other professions and businesses the Supreme Court has held that a blanket prohibition against attorneys advertising is a violation of the free speech clause of the First Amendment.[57]   False, deceptive, and misleading advertising could still be punished.[58]

L. CONTEMPT

1. CONTEMPT OF LEGISLATIVE BODIES

Punishment for contempt is very old, stemming from the ancient practice of avenging any insult to the king or his government with prompt retaliation.[59]   Because it was an important part of the king's government, "either house of Parliament could commit for contempt of itself." [60]   And in this country the power to commit for contempt extends to the Senate and House of Representatives of the United States and to the corresponding legislative bodies of the respective states.[61]   Such contempt includes any insult to the legislative body in the form of disrespectful or disorderly conduct in its presence and also any wilful obstruction of the performance of a legislative function.[62]   In the words of the Massachusetts court: "Even apart from any express constitutional provision . . .   any legislative body, in order to carry out the objects of its existence, must have the means of informing itself about subjects with which it may be called upon to deal, . . .   [and] has as an attribute of its legislative function power to summon witnesses and to compel them to attend and make disclosures of pertinent facts and documents," and to punish those who refuse to testify or to produce documents without lawful excuse.[63]   This applies whether the proceeding is before the house itself or by a duly constituted committee thereof,[64] except that the

S.Ct. 353 (1967); United Transportation Union v. State Bar of Michigan, 401 U.S. 576, 91 S.Ct. 1076 (1971).

56. Goldfarb v. Virginia State Bar, 421 U.S. 773, 95 S.Ct. 2004 (1975).

57. Bates v. State Bar of Arizona, 433 U.S. 350, 97 S.Ct. 2691 (1977).

58. Id. 433 U.S. at 383, 97 S.Ct. at 2708.

59. "From the most ancient times any insult to the king or his government was punishable as a contempt . . .   either by indictment or by mere attachment, . . ." Beale, Contempt of Court, Criminal and Civil, 21 Harv.L.Rev. 161–2 (1908).

60. Id. at 162; Murray's Case, 1 Wils. K.B. 299 (1751).

61. 2 Bishop, New Criminal Law § 247 (8th ed. 1892). Bishop mentioned that the jurisdiction of legislative bodies in this country is not the same as that of Parliament. This was emphasized by the Supreme Court. Marshall v. Gordon, 243 U.S. 521, 37 S.Ct. 448 (1916).

". . .   the Constitution imposes no general barriers to the legislative exercise of such power. . . .   There is nothing in the Constitution that would place greater restrictions on the States than on the Federal Government in this regard." Groppi v. Leslie, 404 U.S. 496, 499–500, 92 S.Ct. 582, 585 (1972).

62. The word "contempt" implies "a wilful disregard of the authority of a court of justice or legislative body, or disobedience to its lawful orders." Bridgewater v. Beaver Valley Traction Co., 27 Pa.Co. 328, 329 (1902).

63. Opinions of the Justices, 328 Mass. 655, 660, 102 N.E.2d 79, 85 (1951). "Punishment for contempt by summary conviction, either upon a rule to show cause, or by attachment in the first instance, was deemed at common law to be inherent in courts of justice and legislative assemblies." In re Barnes, 204 N.Y. 108, 113, 97 N.E. 508, 509 (1912).

64. In re Joint Legislative Committee, 285 N.Y. 1, 32 N.E.2d 769 (1941); State ex rel. Hamblen v. Yelle, 29 Wn.2d 68,

latter has no inherent power to punish for contempt.[65] The legislative body can require one who has refused to testify before a committee or a commission established by it to appear before the house to account for his behavior, and a wrongful refusal to testify there would constitute a contempt of the legislature, punishable by it.[66] On the other hand a committee may be empowered by the legislature not only to take testimony and compel the attendance of witnesses and the production of papers and documents, but also to punish for contempt,[67] and this power may extend to meetings of the committee during the interim between regular sessions of the legislative body.[68]

The investigative power of a legislative body, or a committee thereof, is limited to such investigations as are in fact auxiliary to and in aid of the legislative function "and does not extend to general investigations into private affairs of citizens." [69] And as the statute cannot deprive the witness of a constitutional privilege, such as that against self-incrimination, it follows that he cannot be punished for contempt because of his refusal to answer unless the question is pertinent to a proper legislative investigation *and* the circumstances do not entitle him to invoke the privilege.[70] On the other hand the field of potential legislation is of tremendous size and the legislative function is not to be handicapped by undue restrictions of the investigative power. The privilege against self-incrimination, moreover, does not entitle the witness to remain silent whenever he prefers not to speak, but is available only when the answer might have the proscribed effect. So strictly was this construed that one under examination in a federal proceeding was held not to be privileged to refuse to answer on account of probable incrimination under state law—an astounding decision which has since been overruled.[71]

Contempt of Congress or its committees has been made a misdemeanor by statute [72] and hence such misbehavior may now be dealt with the same as any other offense of corresponding grade.

185 P.2d 723 (1947); Sullivan v. Hill, 73 W.Va. 49, 79 S.E. 670 (1913). On the other hand a refusal to answer questions propounded by investigators for a congressional committee cannot be punished as a contempt of the committee. United States v. Brennan, 94 U.S.App.D.C. 184, 214 F.2d 268, 271 (1954), cert. denied 348 U.S. 830, 75 S.Ct. 53 (1954); United States v. Olson, 134 F.Supp. 481 (D.C. N.Y.1955).

65. Ex parte Youngblood, 94 Tex.Cr. R. 330, 251 S.W. 509 (1923).

66. McGrain v. Daugherty, 273 U.S. 135, 47 S.Ct. 319 (1926); Burnham v. Morrisey, 80 Mass. 226 (1859) and see Opinion of the Justices, 331 Mass. 764, 119 N.E.2d 385 (1954).

67. Sullivan v. Hill, 73 W.Va. 49, 79 S.E. 670 (1913). The power of a legislative committee to punish for contempt may be established without express words to that effect if it is to be fairly implied from the whole scope and purpose of the act creating the committee. People v. Learned, 5 Hun 626 (N.Y.1875).

68. State ex rel. Hamblen v. Yelle, 29 Wn.2d 68, 185 P.2d 723 (1947); Sullivan v. Hill, 73 W.Va. 49, 79 S.E. 670 (1913).

69. In re Ellis, 176 Misc. 887, 890, 28 N.Y.S.2d 988, 991 (1941).

For an annotation on the validity under the federal constitution of state contempt convictions of witnesses before a state legislative committee, see 6 L.Ed.2d 1357 (1961).

70. See Carlson v. United States, 209 F.2d 209, 212 (5th Cir. 1954).

71. The original decision was United States v. Murdock, 284 U.S. 141, 52 S.Ct. 63 (1931). This was expressly overruled in Murphy v. Waterfront Commission of New York, 378 U.S. 52, 84 S.Ct. 1594 (1964), in which it was held that the privilege protects either a state or a federal witness against incrimination under either state or federal law. See also Malloy v. Hogan, 378 U.S. 1, 84 S.Ct. 1489 (1964).

72. 11 Stat.L. 155 (1857), as amended by 52 Stat.L. 942 (1938), 2 U.S.C.A. §

2. CONTEMPT OF COURT

Although contempt of a legislative body or committee [73] has become a matter of substantial importance in recent years, it was long overshadowed by contempt of court,—a topic which cannot be exhausted here because a large part of it is clearly outside the area of criminal law.[74]

Under the common law of England courts had inherent power to punish for contempt [75] and this has been accepted as a part of our common law [76] at least so far as courts of record are concerned.[77] The Florida court refused to place any construction upon a statute purporting to confer power to punish for contempt for the reason that an acknowledgment of the power to grant "presupposes the authority to withdraw same." [78] Statutes dealing with contempt of court have been very generally upheld if they were wholly procedural in nature,[79] merely prescribed the punishments to be imposed,[80] or enlarged the field of punishable contempt [81] within constitutional limitations.[82] It has been emphasized, however, that the legislature may not, whether by procedural rules or the inadequacy of the penalty fixed, substantially impair or destroy the inherent power of the court to punish for contempt.[83]

192. See Carlson v. United States, 209 F.2d 209 (5th Cir. 1954).

73. As to the general power consult: Driver, Constitutional Limitations on the Power of Congress to Punish Contempts of its Investigating Committees, 38 Va.L. Rev. 887, 1011 (1952); Hervitz and Mulligan, The Legislative Investigating Committee, 33 Col.L.Rev. 1 (1933); Potts, Power of Legislative Bodies to Punish for Contempt, 74 U. of Pa.L.Rev. 691, 780 (1926); Landis, Constitutional Limitations on the Congressional Power of Investigation, 40 Harv.L.Rev. 153 (1926).

74. State ex rel. Nicomen B. Co. v. North Shore, etc., Co., 55 Wash. 1, 16, 107 P. 196, 198 (1910).

75. Douglas v. Adel, 269 N.Y. 144, 146, 199 N.E. 35, 36 (1935).

76. Austin v. City and County of Denver, 156 Colo. 180, 397 P.2d 743 (1964); Eilenbecker v. District Court, 134 U.S. 31, 36, 10 S.Ct. 424, 426 (1890); In re Shortridge, 99 Cal. 526, 34 P. 227 (1893); In re Hayes, 72 Fla. 558, 568, 73 So. 362, 365 (1916); State ex rel. Pulitzer Publishing Co. v. Coleman, 347 Mo. 1238, 1256, 152 S.W.2d 640, 646 (1941). "But independently of the statute we think that the power [to punish for contempt] is inherent in all courts." Middlebrook v. State, 43 Conn. 257, 268 (1876). Accord, Application of Stone, 77 Wyo. 1, 305 P.2d 777 (1957).

"There can be no question that courts have inherent power to enforce compliance with their lawful orders through civil contempt." Shillitani v. United States, 384 U.S. 364, 370, 86 S.Ct. 1531, 1535 (1966).

77. "The doctrine is generally asserted in these broad terms, and is believed to be sound; the narrower doctrine, about which there is no dispute, is that the power is inherent in all courts of record." 2 Bishop, New Criminal Law § 243 (8th ed. 1892). It was stated in the narrower form in Field v. Thornell, 106 Iowa 7, 75 N.W. 685 (1898).

Contempt of court is inherent in all courts. People v. Bloom, 35 Ill.2d 255, 220 N.E.2d 475 (1967).

78. State ex rel. Franks v. Clark, 46 So.2d 488, 489 (Fla.1950).

79. State ex rel. Rankin v. District Court, 58 Mont. 276, 191 P. 772 (1920); In re Coulter, 25 Wash. 526, 65 P. 759 (1901).

80. In re Garner, 179 Cal. 409, 177 P. 162 (1918); Ex parte Creasy, 243 Mo. 679, 148 S.W. 914 (1912).

81. Eilenbecker v. District Court, 134 U.S. 31, 10 S.Ct. 424 (1890).

82. United States v. Cunningham, 37 F.2d 349 (D.C.Neb.1929).

83. In re Garner, 179 Cal. 409, 177 P. 162 (1918); State ex rel. Rankin v. District Court, 58 Mont. 276, 191 P. 772 (1920). Cf. Dunham v. State, 6 Iowa 245, 247 (1858). The legislature lacks the power to declare that certain acts shall not constitute constructive contempt of

A. CLASSIFICATION

(A) Civil or Criminal

Contempt of court has been classified in two different ways: (a) depending upon the purpose of the proceeding into (1) civil contempt and (2) criminal contempt,[84] and (b) depending upon the factor of proximity or remoteness into (1) direct contempt and (2) constructive contempt,[85]—the latter also called at times indirect contempt or consequential contempt.[86]

Despite a faulty analysis which occasionally has caused doubt as to the validity of the first classification,[87] there is an important and clear-cut distinction between these two proceedings. Civil contempt is misconduct in the form of disobedience to an order or direction of the court by one party to a judicial proceeding to the prejudice of the other litigant. The harm is to the injured litigant and not to the public, and the "penalty" imposed, being purely coercive in purpose, can be avoided by compliance with the court's order.[88] If the judgment in the contempt proceeding is in the form of a "compensatory fine, payable to the complainant," [89] no special problem is involved, but the more usual judgment, that the contemnor be imprisoned until he obeys the order of the court, should not be entered until there has been an affirma-

court. In re San Francisco Chronicle, 1 Cal.2d 630, 36 P.2d 369 (1934).

The power of the court to punish for contempt is not derived from the legislature and cannot be made to depend upon legislative will. Austin v. City and County of Denver, 156 Colo. 180, 397 P.2d 743 (1964).

84. Juneau Spruce Corp. v. International L. & W. Union, 131 F.Supp. 866, 871 (D.C.Hawaii 1955); Wilson v. Prochnow, 359 Ill. 148, 194 N.E. 246 (1935). "In the Gompers Case this Court points out that it is not the fact of punishment but rather its character and purpose that makes the difference between the two kinds of contempts. For civil contempts, the punishment is remedial and for the benefit of the complainant, and a pardon cannot stop it." Ex parte Grossman, 267 U.S. 87, 111, 45 S.Ct. 332, 333, 334 (1925). Accord, MacNeil v. United States, 236 F.2d 149 (1st Cir. 1956).

85. Lapique v. Superior Court, 68 Cal. App. 407, 229 P. 1010 (1924); Ex parte Earman, 85 Fla. 297, 314, 95 So. 755, 760 (1923).

86. Snow v. Hawkes, 183 N.C. 365, 111 S.E. 621 (1922).

87. "Few legal distinctions are emptier" than the classification of contempts as "civil" and "criminal." Nelles, Summary Power to Punish for Contempt, 31 Col.L.Rev. 956, 960 (1931). Goldfarb, The Contempt Power, pp. 46–67 (1963).

88. United States v. Shine, 125 F.Supp. 734, 736 (D.C.N.Y.1954); State ex rel. Nicomen B. Co. v. North Shore, etc., Co., 55 Wash. 1, 16, 107 P. 196, 198 (1910). "In brief, a court, enforcing obedience to its orders by proceedings for contempt, is not executing the criminal laws of the land, but only securing to suitors the rights which it has adjudged them entitled to." In re Debs, 158 U.S. 564, 596, 15 S.Ct. 900, 911 (1895). "The power of a court to imprison a recalcitrant litigant under those circumstances is exercised to coerce obedience and not to punish him." State ex rel. Pulitzer Publishing Co. v. Coleman, 347 Mo. 1238, 1256, 152 S.W.2d 640, 646 (1941). "Quite otherwise is the action of the court where its injunction or other order or decree is violated by the person to whom it is addressed. In such case the violation is called to the attention of the court by the injured party, and if the violation is proved the wrongdoer is committed to prison to remain until he purges himself of his contempt by doing the right or undoing the wrong." Beale, Contempt of Court, Criminal and Civil, 21 Harv.L.Rev. 161, 169 (1908).

89. United States v. Shine, 125 F.Supp. 734, 736 (D.C.N.Y.1954). Such a judgment may not be authorized in a particular jurisdiction but is expressly provided in 18 U.S.C.A. § 402 (1966).

tive finding that it is within his power to comply,[90] unless this is obvious under the circumstances. It was held improper, for example, to continue the imprisonment of one who had been ordered to make alimony payments which he was unable to make through no fault of his own.[91] This part of the field is outlined only to point out that it has nothing in common with criminal law.

A criminal contempt, on the other hand, is an act which is disrespectful to the court, calculated to bring the court into disrepute, or of a nature which tends to obstruct the administration of justice.[92] And the purpose of convicting for such contempt is "vindication of the public interest by punishment of contemptuous conduct."[93] Much of the confusion in regard to this classification stems from a failure to recognize that certain misconduct may constitute both civil contempt and criminal contempt, although this point is well established.[94] In one case, for example, a judgment for contempt ordered that the contemnor be imprisoned for one day and also that he should be continued in prison after the expiration of the first day until he complied with the order of the court.[95] The first part of this judgment was punishment for criminal contempt and contained no provision whereby any part of it could be avoided. The second part was a coercive sentence for civil contempt and could have been avoided in full by prompt compliance with the court's order.

Whether "criminal contempt" really is or is not a crime is a question as to which there has been much dispute. "A prosecution for criminal contempt is not itself a criminal case," it has been said,[96] and in the words of another court, a criminal contempt is "in the nature of, but not, a crime."[97] On the other hand, it has been stated without qualification that it is a criminal offense.[98] Certainly the misconduct involved in criminal contempt is of the

90. A commitment to jail without such a finding was held to be punishment rather than coercion, and was void because it specified no definite time of imprisonment. State ex rel. Trezevant v. McLeod, 126 Fla. 229, 170 So. 735 (1936). It was improper for the trial court, after the close of the trial, to order a witness committed in coercive restraint for failure to answer questions propounded on cross examination. Yates v. United States, 227 F.2d 844 (9th Cir. 1955).

91. Politano v. Politano, 146 Misc. 792, 262 N.Y.S. 802 (1933).

Where the refusal to pay alimony or the like is not based on an inability to pay, the refusal may be punished by contempt and if imprisonment is given it does not constitute imprisonment for debt. Bott v. Bott, 22 Utah 2d 368, 453 P.2d 402 (1969).

92. Wilson v. Prochnow, 359 Ill. 148, 194 N.E. 246 (1935); Blanton v. State, 31 Okl.Cr. 419, 424, 239 P. 698, 700 (1925).

93. Lopiparo v. United States, 222 F.2d 897, 898 (8th Cir. 1955). "Criminal contempt is designed to protect the public interest in the effective functioning of the judicial system." Juneau Spruce

Corp. v. International L. & W. Union, 131 F.Supp. 866, 871 (D.C.Hawaii 1955).

"If the contemptuous act has been concluded and the only purpose for the sanction is to punish the offender and vindicate judicial authority, the contempt should be labeled a criminal contempt." State v. Stokes, 240 N.W.2d 867, 870 (N.D.1976).

94. State v. Spence, 6 Ariz.App. 107, 430 P.2d 453 (1967); Lopiparo v. United States, 222 F.2d 897 (8th Cir. 1955); United States v. Garden Homes, Inc., 144 F.Supp. 644 (D.C.N.H.1956); State ex rel. Nicomen B. Co. v. North Shore, etc., Co., 55 Wash. 1, 15, 107 P. 196, 198 (1910). "There is no essential dichotomy between 'civil' and 'criminal' contempt." Yates v. United States, 227 F.2d 844, 845 (9th Cir. 1955).

95. Smith v. Smith, 120 Cal.App.2d 474, 261 P.2d 567 (1953).

96. Osborne v. Owsley, 364 Mo. 544, 547, 264 S.W.2d 332, 333 (1954).

97. Flannagan v. Jepson, 177 Iowa 393, 397, 158 N.W. 641, 642 (1916).

98. State v. Cunningham, 33 W.Va. 607, 11 S.E. 76 (1890). A "specific crimi-

general character of obstruction of justice, and as such is *social harm which is defined and made punishable by law,*—which brings it squarely within the definition of crime. And all doubt on this point was removed by *Bloom,*[99] in which the Supreme Court said: "Criminal contempt is a crime in the ordinary sense; it is a violation of the law, a public wrong which is punishable by fine or imprisonment or both."

Since the time of the Court of Star Chamber, until quite recently, the typical proceeding for criminal contempt has been without benefit of trial by jury.[1] As late as 1958, in *Green,* the Supreme Court had held that the federal Constitution confers no right to a jury trial in a contempt case.[2] More recently it took the position that in a federal contempt case, where imprisonment for more than six months is involved, a jury trial may be demanded—not as a constitutional right but under the Court's supervisory power over federal courts.[3] And then in *Bloom,* just ten years after *Green,* the Court moved to an entirely new position. "Our deliberations have convinced us," the Court said,[4] "that serious contempts are so nearly like other serious crimes that they are subject to the jury trial provisions of the Constitution, now binding on the States, and that the traditional rule is constitutionally infirm insofar as it permits other than petty contempts to be tried without honoring a demand for a jury trial." The Court did not undertake to state precisely where the line falls between punishments that can be considered "petty" and those that cannot. But in *Bloom* it held that a sentence to 24 months imprisonment clearly brands the contempt as serious, whereas in

nal offense." Lapique v. Superior Court, 68 Cal.App. 407, 229 P. 1010 (1924).

99. Bloom v. Illinois, 391 U.S. 194, 201, 88 S.Ct. 1477, 1481 (1968). The Court added: "In the words of Mr. Justice Holmes: 'These contempts are infractions of the law, visited with punishment as such. If such acts are not criminal, we are in error as to the most fundamental characteristic of crimes as that word has been understood in English speech.' Gompers v. United States, 233 U.S. 604, 610, 34 S.Ct. 693, 58 L.Ed. 1115 (1914)." Ibid.

1. Curtis, A Notion in Criminal Contempt, 41 Harv.L.Rev. 51 (1927). "It has always been one of the attributes—one of the powers necessarily incident to a court of justice—that it should have this power of vindicating its dignity, of enforcing its orders, of protecting itself from insult, without the necessity of calling upon a jury to assist it in the exercise of this power." Eilenbecker v. District Court, 134 U.S. 31, 36, 10 S.Ct. 424, 426 (1890). Accord, State ex rel. Pulitzer Pub. Co. v. Coleman, 347 Mo. 1238, 152 S.W.2d 640 (1941).

The Supreme Court held that the federal constitution confers no right to a jury trial in a contempt case. Green v. United States, 356 U.S. 165, 78 S.Ct. 632 (1958).

It was stated that in a federal contempt case where imprisonment for more than six months is contemplated a jury trial may be demanded—not as a constitutional right but under the Court's supervisory power over federal courts. Cheff v. Schnackenberg, 384 U.S. 373, 86 S.Ct. 1523 (1966).

The Minnesota court held that as a matter of procedural fairness, if not a constitutional right, there should be a jury trial if demanded, on a charge of indirect or constructive criminal contempt. Peterson v. Peterson, 278 Minn. 275, 153 N.W.2d 825 (1967). The Illinois court reached the opposite conclusion. People v. Bloom, 35 Ill.2d 255, 220 N.E.2d 475 (1967).

2. Green v. United States, 356 U.S. 165, 78 S.Ct. 632 (1958).

3. Cheff v. Schnackenberg, 384 U.S. 373, 86 S.Ct. 1523 (1966). The Minnesota court held that as a matter of procedural fairness, if not a constitutional right, there should be a jury trial, if demanded, on a charge of indirect or constructive criminal attempt. Peterson v. Peterson, 278 Minn. 275, 153 N.W.2d 825 (1967).

4. Bloom v. Illinois, 391 U.S. 194, 198, 88 S.Ct. 1477, 1480 (1968).

Dyke,[5] decided at the same time, it held that a contempt for which the maximum sentence was ten days in jail and a $50 fine was petty. It was said *obiter* that "it is clear that a six-month sentence is short enough to be petty." [6] This was induced by the fact that a misdemeanor with such a maximum penalty is declared to be a "petty offense" in the United States Criminal Code.[7] Where criminal contempt charges arise from the same proceedings, if they are aggregated to where the penalty exceeds that for a petty offense the contemnor is entitled to a jury trial.[8]

Procedurally there may be some differences between a proceeding for criminal contempt and an ordinary criminal trial. No doubt a court which has no criminal jurisdiction, in any other respect, may have power to punish for criminal contempt.[9] The implication that a proceeding for contempt in a federal court does not require a grand-jury indictment [10] will need to be re-examined. Under the new position, if an infamous punishment (such as a penitentiary sentence) is involved it would seem such a prosecution could not proceed without an indictment unless the indictment had been waived. Now binding upon the states will be the position previously taken by the Court, that in federal prosecutions for contempt, except that committed in open court, the accused must be advised of the charges, have a reasonable opportunity to meet them by way of defense, with the assistance of counsel, and the right to call witnesses and to be convicted only if proved guilty beyond a reasonable doubt, in a public trial before an unbiased judge.[11] Where the trial judge is embroiled in the controversy he is assumed to be unable to maintain the calm detachment necessary to a fair adjudication.[12]

(B) Direct or Constructive

A direct contempt is one committed "in the immediate view and presence" of the court or of a judge at chambers [13] or "so near to the court or judge acting judicially as to interrupt or hinder judicial proceedings." [14] "An indirect or constructive contempt is an act

5. Dyke v. Taylor Implement Manufacturing Co., 391 U.S. 216, 88 S.Ct. 1472 (1968).

6. Id. at 220, 88 S.Ct. at 1475.

7. 18 U.S.C.A. § 1(3). In Cheff v. Schnackenberg, supra, the Court had taken the position that a contempt proceeding involving six-months' imprisonment was a petty offense which would not require a jury trial.

8. Codispoti v. Pennsylvania, 418 U.S. 506, 94 S.Ct. 2687 (1974).

9. 2 Bishop, New Criminal Law § 242 (8th ed. 1892). "Courts of chancery and probate courts have no criminal jurisdiction; and yet it will hardly be denied that they have the power to punish for contempt." Middlebrook v. State, 43 Conn. 257, 267 (1876).

"A criminal contempt action is a proceeding separate and independent of the action from which it arose." Skolnick v. State, ___ Ind.App. ___, 397 N.E.2d 986, 997 (1979).

10. Pendergast v. United States, 317 U.S. 412, 63 S.Ct. 268 (1943). And see People v. Rosenthal, 294 Ill.App. 274, 13 N.E.2d 814 (1938).

11. See Cooke v. United States, 267 U.S. 517, 537, 45 S.Ct. 390, 395 (1925); Gompers v. Bucks Stove and Range Co., 221 U.S. 418, 444, 31 S.Ct. 492, 499 (1911); In re Oliver, 333 U.S. 257, 63 S.Ct. 499 (1948); Offutt v. United States, 348 U.S. 11, 75 S.Ct. 11 (1954).

See Annotation, Contempt Proceedings As Violating Procedural Due Process—Supreme Court Cases, 39 L.Ed.2d 1031 (1974).

12. Mayberry v. Pennsylvania, 400 U.S. 455, 91 S.Ct. 499 (1971); Johnson v. Mississippi, 403 U.S. 212, 91 S.Ct. 1778 (1971); Taylor v. Hayes, 418 U.S. 488, 94 S.Ct. 2697 (1974).

13. Lapique v. Superior Court, 68 Cal. App. 407, 229 P. 1010 (1924).

14. Ex parte Earman, 85 Fla. 297, 314, 95 So. 755, 760 (1923).

done, not in the presence of the court or of a judge acting judicially, but at a distance under circumstances that reasonably tend to degrade the court or the judge as a judicial officer, or to obstruct, interrupt, prevent, or embarrass the administration of justice by the court or judge." [15]

If the contempt is committed "in the face of the court," to use Blackstone's phrase, the offender may be instantly apprehended and punished,[16] but if it takes place at a distance the familiar practice, where unchanged by statute, is for an affidavit or an information setting forth the facts to be presented to the court which then issues an order to show cause why the one complained of should not be punished.[17]

For the sake of illustration it may be mentioned that a direct criminal contempt may be committed in many different ways such as by an assault on the marshal in open court,[18] a vindictive and uncalled for remark addressed by counsel to the court after one of its rulings during the trial,[19] continued disobedience of counsel to the court's order to limit the opening statement and the cross-examination of a witness,[20] repeated and wilfully harassing tactics of counsel continued during the trial despite the court's admonition,[21]

". . . direct contempts are denoted as those contempts within the presence of the court, or so near the court as to interrupt its proceedings." In re Tarpley, 293 Ala. 137, 300 So.2d 409 (1974).

15. Ibid.

A "direct contempt" is one which occurs in the immediate presence of the court whereas an "indirect contempt" occurs outside the presence of the court. Jones v. Jones, 91 Idaho 578, 428 P.2d 497 (1967).

16. 4 Bl.Comm. *286.

17. Id. at *287. And see Lapique v. Superior Court, 68 Cal.App. 407, 229 P. 1010 (1924); In re Coulter, 25 Wash. 526, 65 P. 759 (1901). The Federal Rules of Criminal Procedure provide that a criminal contempt which was committed in the presence of the court, and actually seen or heard by the judge, may be punished summarily. Otherwise a criminal contempt "shall be prosecuted on notice." Rule 42 (1980). At times the procedure is for the court to issue an "attachment" under which the alleged contemnor is taken into custody and brought before the court where he is called upon to answer the charge that has been made against him.

18. Ex parte Terry, 128 U.S. 289, 9 S.Ct. 77 (1888).

19. An attorney's statement: "I'm getting out of this court if you can call it a court," constitutes contempt of court. A ten-day sentence was upheld. State v. Caffrey, 70 Wn.2d 120, 422 P.2d 307 (1966). And see MacInnis v. United States, 191 F.2d 157 (9th Cir. 1951), cert. denied 342 U.S. 953, 72 S.Ct. 628 (1952).

20. Hallinan v. United States, 182 F.2d 880 (9th Cir. 1950), cert. denied 341 U.S. 952, 71 S.Ct. 1010 (1951). Letters, motions and pleadings of a contemptuous nature, filed with the Supreme Court, constituted a direct contempt. Application of Stone, 77 Wyo. 1, 305 P.2d 777 (1957).

21. Sacher v. United States, 343 U.S. 1, 72 S.Ct. 451 (1952).

D's summary conviction for criminal contempt was upheld, where he had "bombarded" the trial judge with irrelevant, derogatory correspondence and exhibits allegedly relating to the domestic relations matter before the court, after he had been ordered not to do so. Such contempt is "in the presence of the court." McAllister v. McAllister, 95 N.J. Super. 426, 231 A.2d 394 (1967). During a fourteen-day criminal trial there were repeated clashes between defense counsel and the judge. At the close of the trial the petitioner was summarily found guilty of criminal contempt by the trial judge on the basis of a certificate filed under Rule 42(a). This was reversed on the ground that since the judge had become personally embroiled with counsel throughout the trial he should have invited the Chief Judge of the District Court to assign another judge to sit in the hearing of the charge against counsel. Offutt v. United States, 348 U.S. 11, 75 S.Ct. 11 (1954).

and taking a flashlight picture of the proceedings in violation of an express order of the court that no pictures be taken in the courtroom during that hearing.[22] Directing insulting or vile language to a witness is direct contempt.[23] And a constructive contempt is committed, for example, by violating the court's instruction to jurors not to separate or make contact with outsiders during the trial,[24] sounding out a juror to ascertain whether he can be corruptly influenced,[25] clandestinely removing a ward of the court from the custody of the appointed guardian,[26] wilfully destroying evidence to prevent its falling into the hands of officers searching for it under a valid warrant,[27] and wrongfully going to a court-appointed psychiatrist and attempting to sway his opinion in regard to the defendant in the case.[28] The determinant insofar as procedure is concerned is whether or not the contempt was committed under such circumstances that the judge has knowledge of all the facts and hence has no need to hear evidence. In one case, for example, an attorney was held in contempt for having wilfully and without excuse absented himself from the courtroom when his case came up for trial. The absence of the attorney from the courtroom was within the judge's own knowledge, but whether there was or was not any valid excuse therefor could not be known without extrinsic evidence. Hence the attorney could not properly be convicted without a hearing.[29]

The violation of an order of the court, whether it takes place in the courtroom or elsewhere, cannot properly be punished unless the order itself was

22. State v. Clifford, 97 Ohio App. 1, 118 N.E.2d 853 (1954).

23. Robinson v. State, 503 P.2d 582 (Okl.Cr.1972).

24. People v. Rosenthal, 294 Ill.App. 274, 13 N.E.2d 814 (1938).

25. "Approaching a juror to find out how he stands with reference to a case, or sounding out a juror to ascertain whether he can be corruptly influenced, or any attempt to influence the results of jury trials by improper means, or acts which have a tendency to enable a person to make certain the result of a litigated case involving a trial by jury, are justly regarded as acts tending to interfere with the due administration of justice, and are punishable as contempts." Baumgartner v. Joughin, 105 Fla. 335, 341-2, 141 So. 185, 188 (1932); State ex rel. Franks v. Clark, 46 So.2d 488, 489 (Fla.1950).

26. Wellesley's Case, 2 Russ. & M. 639, 39 Eng.Rep. 538 (1831). Or taking children out of the jurisdiction of the court in violation of a court order. Smith v. Smith, 120 Cal.App.2d 474, 261 P.2d 567 (1953), hearing denied by Supreme Court, Oct. 29, 1953.

27. Burch v. Zeuch, 200 Iowa 49, 202 N.W. 542 (1925). See note, 11 Iowa L.Rev. 85 (1925).

28. State ex rel. Huie v. Lewis, 80 So. 2d 685 (Fla.1955).

29. State v. Winthrop, 148 Wash. 526, 269 P. 793 (1928). Accord, Bowles v. United States, 44 F.2d 115 (4th Cir. 1930). An attorney is entitled to consideration of a claimed privilege not to disclose information which he honestly regards as confidential and should not stand in danger of imprisonment for contempt for asserting respectfully what he considers his lawful rights. Appeal of United States Securities and Exchange Commission, 226 F.2d 501 (5th Cir. 1955). "The privilege against compelled self-incrimination would be drained of its meaning if counsel, being lawfully present . . . could be penalized for advising his client in good faith to assert it . . . We conclude that an advocate is not subject to the penalty of contempt for advising his client, in good faith, to assert the Fifth Amendment privilege against self-incrimination in any proceeding embracing the power to compel testimony." Maness v. Meyers, 419 U.S. 449, 465–466, 468, 95 S.Ct. 584 (1975). A lawyer is not a court "officer" within the meaning of subsection (2) of 18 U.S.C.A. § 401, and hence cannot be punished summarily for conduct that does not come within either subsections (1) or (3). Cammer v. United States, 350 U.S. 399, 76 S.Ct. 456 (1956).

one the court had lawful authority to make.[30]　Thus a conviction for contempt was held to be improper where the alleged violation was the refusal of a mere spectator in the courtroom to answer questions the court had no authority to propound to him,[31] and where it was the newspaper publication of a true report of the testimony in a certain case which the court had ordered should not be published but under circumstances in which there was no valid reason for withholding publication.[32]

B.　SCANDALIZING THE COURT

One of the most widely-debated problems in the field of criminal contempt is in regard to published criticism of the court.[33]　This is associated with the so-called "trial by newspaper."　"Legal trials," it has been said, "are not like elections, to be won through the use of the meeting-hall, the radio, and the newspaper."[34]　And it has been inferred by the Supreme Court that a publication having a tendency to, and made for the purpose of, influencing the outcome of pending litigation would be punishable as contempt.[35]　Recent decisions from the Supreme Court have suggested that the press has wide allowance in reporting criminal trials[36] and commenting on judicial proceedings and although the contempt power may still be available to a court for use against the news media in order to insure a fair trial[37] the availability of other protective remedies[38] makes it unlikely the court would allow use of the contempt sanction except in the most extreme and deliberate attempts to prejudice the court proceedings[39] and it is very unlikely the court would allow a contempt sanction for simply criticizing a court in harsh and uncomplimentary terms.

The English courts have not hesitated to punish disrespectful comments made out of court even after the litigation has ended,[40] and the same has been true of the courts in Canada.[41]　A newspaper article, for example, pub-

---

30. If the court has power to make an order although a specific order may be legally erroneous a person violating the order can be held in contempt. "Persons who make private determinations of the law and refuse to obey an order generally risk criminal contempt even if the order is ultimately ruled incorrect." Maness v. Meyers, 419 U.S. 449, 458, 95 S.Ct. 584 (1975). See also Walker v. City of Birmingham, 388 U.S. 307, 87 S.Ct. 1824 (1967).

31. Ketcham v. Commonwealth, 204 Ky. 168, 263 S.W. 725 (1924).

A temporary restraining order which was constitutionally void on its face was issued in excess of jurisdiction, and a violation of such an order cannot produce a valid judgment for contempt. In re Berry, 68 Cal.2d 137, 65 Cal.Rptr. 273, 436 P.2d 273 (1968).

32. In re Shortridge, 99 Cal. 526, 34 P. 227 (1893).

For an annotation on a published article or broadcast as direct contempt see 69 A.L.R.2d 676 (1960).

33. See Goodhart, Newspapers and Contempt of Court in English Law, 48 Harv.L.Rev. 885 (1935); Comment, 24 Calif.L.Rev. 114 (1935).

34. Bridges v. California, 314 U.S. 252, 271, 62 S.Ct. 190, 197, 198 (1941).

35. Pennekamp v. Florida, 328 U.S. 331, 347, 66 S.Ct. 1029, 1037, 1038 (1946).

36. Nebraska Press Association v. Stuart, 427 U.S. 539, 96 S.Ct. 2791 (1976).

37. See Frankfurter in opinion on denying certiorari in Maryland v. Baltimore Radio Show, 338 U.S. 912, 70 S.Ct. 252 (1950).

38. See Sheppard v. Maxwell, 384 U.S. 333, 358–359, 86 S.Ct. 1507 (1966).

39. See Tribe, American Constitutional Law 623–631 (1978); Goldfarb, The Contempt Power, pp. 187–195 (1963). See also Salyer v. Commonwealth, 209 Va. 662, 166 S.E.2d 110 (1969).

40. Rex v. Editor of the New Statesman, 44 T.L.R. 301 (K.B.1928).

41. Re Duncan, 11 DLR 2d 616, [1958] S.C.R. 41; Regina v. Gash, 12 W.W.R.

lished after the conclusion of a homicide case referred to the jury as having murdered the defendant, and to the judge as having subjected him to torture. In holding both the author and the publisher guilty of contempt on the ground that such language was calculated to lower the dignity of the court and intimidate future juries, it was said:

"No wrong is committed by any one who criticizes the courts or a judge in good faith, but it is of vital importance to the public that the authority and dignity of the courts should be maintained and that when criticism is offered it should be legitimate. To refer to the jurors in this case as criminals and to describe the judge as causing exquisite torture is calculated to lower the dignity of the court and to destroy public confidence in the administration of justice, and a practice of this kind must be stopped immediately in the public interest." [42]

(A) The Federal Statute

The majority rule in this country has been that out-of-court criticism of litigation after its termination is not summarily punishable as contempt, regardless of its nature,[43] but this has faded into relative unimportance in recent times. The background is interesting although barely a hint can be included here.[44] The power of a judge to mete out summary punishment for what he considers an insult to himself (in his judicial capacity) has within it the possibilities of abuse, and it was greatly abused. "A succession of grievances against the exercise of arbitrary judicial power culminated in the proceedings of impeachment of James H. Peck, a judge of the Federal District Court for the District of Missouri." [45] This particular grievance was that a lawyer who had published a criticism of a judge's opinion, while an appeal therefrom was pending, was imprisoned and disbarred in a summary proceeding by the judge who had been criticised. The fact that Judge Peck was old and blind and that what he had done did not deviate much, if at all, from the familiar pattern of the time, saved him from conviction,[46] but the following day Congress instituted proceedings to define by statute all offenses punishable as contempts of the courts of the United States. The result was the Act of 1831 [47] limiting the power of the federal courts to inflict punishment for contempt. The present statute,[48] which differs from the original Act in phraseology but not in substance, is as follows:

"A court of the United States shall have power to punish by fine or imprisonment, at its discretion, such contempt of its authority, and none other, as—

"(1) Misbehavior of any person in its presence or so near thereto as to obstruct the administration of justice;

(N.S.) 349 (B.C.1954); Re Attorney-General of Canada and Alexander, 27 CCC 2d 387 (Sup.Ct. NW Terr. 1975); Re Quelkt, 32 CCC 2d 149 (Que.1976).

42. Id. at 358.

43. Storey v. People, 79 Ill. 45 (1875); State v. Dunham, 6 Iowa 245 (1858); State ex rel. Pulitzer Publishing Co. v. Coleman, 347 Mo. 1238, 152 S.W.2d 640 (1941); Kirkham v. Sweetring, 108 Utah 397, 160 P.2d 435 (1945). Contra, State v. Hildreth, 82 Vt. 382, 74 A. 71 (1909).

44. Consult Frankfurter and Landis, Power to Regulate Contempts, 37 Harv. L.Rev. 1010 (1924).

45. Id. at 1024.

46. Twenty-one of the forty-three senators pronounced him guilty. Id. at 1025.

47. 4 Stat. 487 (1831).

48. 18 U.S.C.A. § 401 (1966).

"(2) Misbehavior of any of its officers in their official transactions; [49]

"(3) Disobedience or resistance to its lawful writ, process, order, rule, decree or command."

As paraphrased, "the power of these courts in the punishments of contempts can only be exercised to insure order and decorum in their presence, to secure faithfulness on the part of their officers in their official transactions, and to enforce obedience to their lawful orders, judgments and processes." [50] When the constitutionality of this Act was challenged the Supreme Court, while expressing doubt whether its own power could be limited by statute since it "derives its existence and powers from the Constitution," [51] held that there "can be no question" of its applicability to the lower federal courts which were "created by act of Congress." [52] Problems of interpretation remained. In one case, for example, in an effort to terminate a suit for wrongful death, which the administrator had brought in a federal district court, strangers to the suit by resort to undue influence induced the administrator to file a final account and obtain his discharge as administrator, and to send letters to his attorney and to the judge asking dismissal of the suit. Though the misbehavior occurred more than a hundred miles from the court, the strangers were convicted of contempt on the ground that they were guilty of misbehavior so near the presence of the court as to obstruct the administration of justice within the meaning of the statute. This conviction was reversed on the ground that this was a criminal contempt and the words "so near" have a geographical rather than a causal connotation. [53]

(B) Constitutional Limitation

With this interpretation the statute prevents federal judges (except perhaps justices of the Supreme Court) from punishing those who make newspaper comments or similar out-of-court publications which are thought to be insulting, whether they refer to litigation which is past or pending. This act of Congress applies only to federal courts, and state cases continued to punish any publication concerning a pending cause which tended to reflect upon the court. [54] More recently, however, the Supreme Court has emphasized the existence of a constitutional limitation on the power to punish for contempt which in its own words applies to "all American courts, both state and federal, including this one." [55]

This is grounded upon the guarantee of freedom of speech and freedom of the press, expressly included as a limitation of federal power in the First Amendment and secured also against abridgment by a state in the more general wording of the Fourteenth. [56] So great and so important is the public interest in a public trial that out-of-court discussions and publications in re-

---

49. A lawyer is not a court "officer" within the meaning of this sub-section. Cammer v. United States, 350 U.S. 399, 76 S.Ct. 456 (1956).

50. Ex parte Robinson, 86 U.S. 505, 511 (1873).

51. Id. at 510.

52. Id. at 511.

53. Nye v. United States, 313 U.S. 33, 61 S.Ct. 810 (1941); In re Stewart, 571 F.2d 958 (5th Cir. 1978).

54. In re Hayes, 72 Fla. 558, 73 So. 362 (1916). Some states have rather narrow constitutional and statutory definitions of contempt. See, for example, Best v. Evans, 297 P.2d 379 (Okl.1956).

55. Bridges v. California, 314 U.S. 252, 260, 62 S.Ct. 190, 192 (1941).

56. Schneider v. State, 308 U.S. 147, 160, 60 S.Ct. 146, 150 (1939).

gard to such a proceeding are protected by the privilege even if they tend to cast discredit upon the court or the judge unless they are carried to such an extreme as to create a "clear and present danger" to the administration of justice.[57] Editorials and a cartoon which seemed to impugn the integrity of the court and tended to create distrust for the court were held not to constitute a contempt punishable by the state court, although one of the cases referred to was still pending, because: "We are not willing to say under the circumstances of this case that these editorials are a clear and present danger to the fair administration of justice in Florida."[58] And in another case, for the same reason, a conviction of newspapermen for contempt was held to violate the privilege of freedom of the press although the news articles unfairly reported events in a case and vehemently attacked the trial judge.[59] The law of contempt, it was said in this case, "is not made for the protection of judges who may be sensitive to the winds of public opinion. Judges are supposed to be men of fortitude, able to thrive in a hardy climate."[60] The court admitted that there had been "strong language, intemperate language, and, we assume, an unfair criticism," but added: "The vehemence of language used is not alone the measure of the power to punish for contempt. The fires which it kindles must constitute an imminent, not merely a likely threat to the administration of justice. The danger must not be remote or even probable; it must immediately peril."[61] In another case it was said:

"Courts must have power to protect the interests of prisoners and litigants before them from unseemly efforts to pervert judicial action. In the borderline instances where it is difficult to say upon which side the alleged offense falls, we think the specific freedom of public comment should weigh heavily against a possible tendency to influence pending cases. Freedom of discussion should be given the widest range compatible with the essential requirement of the fair and orderly administration of justice."[62]

C. SUMMARY PROCEEDING

This limitation, it should be noted, does not prevent a state court from punishing for a constructive criminal contempt if the contemnor is not protected by a constitutional privilege.[63] And it leaves untouched the punishability of direct contempt of court. As said by the Supreme Court:[64]

---

57. Craig v. Harney, 331 U.S. 367, 67 S.Ct. 1249 (1947); Pennekamp v. Florida, 328 U.S. 331, 66 S.Ct. 1029 (1946); Bridges v. California, 314 U.S. 252, 62 S.Ct. 190 (1941).

58. Pennekamp v. Florida, 328 U.S. 331, 348, 66 S.Ct. 1029, 1038 (1946).

59. Craig v. Harney, 331 U.S. 367, 67 S.Ct. 1249 (1947).

60. Id. at 376.

61. Ibid.

62. Pennekamp v. Florida, 328 U.S. 331, 347, 66 S.Ct. 1029, 1037, 1038 (1946).

The English rule has narrowed to some extent but publications which endanger the court process are still punishable. Atty.-Gen. v. Leveller Magazine Ltd. [1979] A.C. 440.

63. State ex rel. Huie v. Lewis, 80 So. 2d 685 (Fla.1955).

64. Sacher v. United States, 343 U.S. 1, 8, 72 S.Ct. 451, 454, 455 (1952). A witness at trial, who after a grant of immunity refuses to testify may be held summarily in contempt. United States v. Wilson, 421 U.S. 309, 95 S.Ct. 1802 (1975). Summary contempt proceedings are justified by the necessity of "vindication of the court's dignity and authority." If contempt action is postponed until after trial the need for a summary process does not exist. Taylor v. Hayes, 418 U.S. 488, 94 S.Ct. 2697 (1974).

"If the contempt be committed in the face of the court, the offender may be instantly apprehended and imprisoned, at the discretion of the judges, without any further proof or examination." Ex parte

"Summary punishment always, and rightly, is regarded with disfavor and, if imposed in passion or pettiness, brings discredit to a court as certainly as the conduct it penalizes. But the very practical reasons which have led every system of law to vest a contempt power in one who presides over judicial proceedings also are the reasons which account for it being made summary. . . . The rights and immunities of accused persons would be exposed to serious and obvious abuse if the trial bench did not possess and frequently exert power to curb prejudicial and excessive zeal of prosecutors. The interests of society in the preservation of courtroom control by the judges are no more to be frustrated through unchecked improprieties by defenders."

This position was reaffirmed in *Bloom* [65] in which the Court said: "Some special mention of contempts in the presence of the judge is warranted. Rule 42(a) of the Federal Rules of Criminal Procedure provides that '[a] criminal contempt may be punished summarily if the judge certifies that he saw or heard the conduct constituting the contempt and that it was committed in the actual presence of the court.' This rule reflects the common-law rule which is widely if not uniformly followed in the States. Although Rule 42(a) is based in part on the premise that it is not necessary specially to present the facts of a contempt which occurs in the very presence of the judge, it also rests on the need to maintain order and a deliberative atmosphere in the courtroom. The power of a judge to quell disturbance cannot attend upon the impaneling of a jury."

In other words, assuming a penalty which will leave the contempt in the category of a petty offense, there is no requirement of a trial by jury and if the contempt is in the presence of the judge there is no need for a trial by the judge since he already knows the facts.

D. THE GRAND JURY

The grand jury has no independent contempt authority. For example the refusal of a witness to answer a question before a grand jury, under a claim of privilege against self-incrimination, is not summarily punishable as contempt even if the question solicited needed information and the privilege is found to have been factually unavailable in his case.[66] The proper procedure in such a situation is to have the witness taken before a judge who shall be informed of the situation and shall pass upon the propriety of the question and the claim of self-incrimination. If the judge finds the claim of privilege well founded, or that the question is not pertinent to any matter pending before the grand jury, that ends it and the witness and the grand jury should be informed that the question need not be answered.[67] If the judge finds otherwise he should order the witness to return to the grand-jury room and answer the question. A refusal to comply with this order would constitute

Terry, 128 U.S. 289, 307, 9 S.Ct. 77, 80 (1888); Matsusow v. United States, 229 F.2d 335, 339 (5th Cir. 1956).

65. Bloom v. Illinois, 391 U.S. 194, 209–10, 88 S.Ct. 1477, 1486 (1968).

Evidence is unnecessary in a direct contempt since it was committed in the presence of the court. Badley v. City of Sheridan, 440 P.2d 516 (Wyo.1968).

66. Carlson v. United States, 209 F.2d 209 (1st Cir. 1954); Hooley v. United States, 209 F.2d 219 (1st Cir. 1954), cert. denied 347 U.S. 953, 74 S.Ct. 678 (1954).

67. Hobson v. District Court, 188 Iowa 1062, 177 N.W. 40 (1920).

contempt of court.[68]   If a wrongful refusal to testify before the grand jury
has been made a misdemeanor by statute, such refusal is punishable although the witness was not taken before the judge and directed by him to
answer.[69]   It would seem wise, however, to give the witness a right to have a
judge pass upon the propriety of the question and the claim of privilege before making his refusal to answer punishable.

What has been said has reference to a refusal to testify before the grand
jury and is based upon the informality of grand-jury proceedings.   It would
not apply to obvious misbehavior of another type.   For example, interrupting
the course of a grand-jury proceeding by a physical attack upon the foreman,
or tampering with a witness about to enter the grand-jury room, is misbehavior in the constructive presence of the court and punishable as a criminal
contempt, since the grand jury is an arm of the court.[70]

M. PIRACY

Piracy *jure gentium* (by the law of nations) is maritime brigandage.

It consists of brigandage committed on the sea or from the sea.

Recent statutes include aircraft or other vehicle seizure and interference under the term piracy.[71]

According to Blackstone: "The offence of piracy, by common law, consists in committing those acts of robbery and depredation upon the high seas
which, if committed upon land, would have amounted to felony there." [72]

At times this has been oversimplified by saying that piracy "is robbery
upon the sea".[73]   This might suggest that if one passenger on an ocean liner
should rob another while the vessel was in mid-ocean, he would thereby become a pirate; but this does not constitute piracy by the law of nations.[74]
When courts have undertaken to be precise they have spoken in some such
terms as these:

"A pirate is said to be one who roves the sea in an armed vessel, without
any commission from any sovereign state, on his own authority, and for the

68.   See Carlson v. United States, 209
F.2d 209, 214 (1st Cir. 1954).   As to the
limitation of the power to punish for contempt by a state judge sitting as a one-
man grand jury, see In re Murchison, 349
U.S. 133, 75 S.Ct. 623 (1955).   See 18 U.S.
C.A. § 1826(a).

69.   In re Bruns, 15 Cal.App.2d 1, 58
P.2d 1318 (1936).

70.   See Carlson v. United States, 209
F.2d 209, 213–4 (1st Cir. 1954).   Cf. Sav-
in, Petitioner, 131 U.S. 267, 9 S.Ct. 699
(1889).

71.   Ark.Stats. § 41–1705(2) (1977); 49
U.S.C.A. § 1472.

72.   4 Bl.Comm. *72.

73.   United States v. Smith, 18 U.S. (5
Wheat.) 153, 162 (1820).

74.   It was said in an early case that
any robbery on the high seas was piracy
under the statute.   United States v.
Jones, 26 F.Cas. 653 (No. 15,494, 1813).
The statute then read: "That if any person or persons shall commit upon the
high seas . . . murder or robbery
. . . every such offender shall be
deemed, taken and adjudged to be a pirate and felon, and being thereof convicted shall suffer death; . . ."   Act of
April 30, 1790, § 8.

By interpretation this was limited to
such offenses committed on an American
vessel.   United States v. Palmer, 16 U.S.
(3 Wheat.) 610 (1818).   This was clearly
statutory piracy only and in 1819 Congress enacted an additional statute substantially in its present form—"piracy as
defined by the law of nations."   This was
§ 5 of the act of 1819, and now 18 U.S.
C.A. § 1651.

purpose of seizing by force and appropriating to himself, without discrimination every vessel he may meet. For this reason pirates, according to the law of nations, have always been compared to robbers, the only difference being that the sea is the theater of the operations of the one and the land of the other." [75]

The same idea was expressed by referring to piracy as "the offense of depredating on the high seas without being authorized by any sovereign state, or with the commissions from different sovereigns at war with each other." [76] And it was implicit in the holding that a vessel loses her national character by assuming a piratical character, and that a piracy committed by a foreigner from on board such a vessel, upon any vessel whatever, is punishable under the act of Congress; [77] and in limiting guilt of piracy to those who actually participated therein, in case of a vessel which had not started out with a piratical design.[78]

The Constitution authorizes the Congress: "To define and punish piracies and felonies committed on the high seas, and offenses against the law of nations." [79] And the first section now implementing this provision is: "Whoever, on the high seas, commits the crime of piracy as defined by the law of nations, and is afterwards brought into or found in the United States, shall be imprisoned for life." [80] A challenge to the validity of this statute on the claim that it does not define the crime was rejected because "the crime of piracy, as defined by the law of nations" is sufficiently definite.[81] In another case the Court pointed out that pirates may lawfully be captured by the public or private ships of any nation, in peace or in war, for they are *"hostes humani generis"* (enemies of the human race).[82] In other words piracy, *jure gentium,* is a crime against every nation and the first nation to get its hands on the pirate may punish him.[83]

Courts pointed out, over a century ago, the difference between piracy by the law of nations and statutory piracy,[84] and Congress has provided a number of offenses in the latter category. They are: (1) murder or robbery by one citizen of another on the high seas under color of any commission from any foreign state; (2) a national of any foreign country taken on the sea making war on the United States contrary to the provisions of a treaty with

---

75. United States v. Baker, 24 F.Cas. 962, 965 (No. 14,501, 1861).

The court was repeating in substance what had been said earlier in Davidson v. Seal-Skins, 7 F.Cas. 192, 193–94 (No. 3,661, 1835).

76. The Ambrose Light, 25 F. 408, 412 (1885).

77. United States v. Furlong, 18 U.S. (5 Wheat.) 184 (1820).

78. United States v. Gilbert, 25 F.Cas. 1287 (No. 15,204, 1834).

79. Art. I, sec. 8, cl. 10.

80. 18 U.S.C.A. § 1651 (1966).

81. United States v. Smith, 18 U.S. (5 Wheat.) 153 (1820).

82. The Marianna Flora, 24 U.S. (11 Wheat.) 1 (1826).

83. "As it is an international crime it is within the jurisdiction of all maritime states wheresoever or by whomsoever committed." Dickinson, Is the Crime of Piracy Obsolete? 38 Harv.L.Rev. 334, 335 (1925).

84. The word "piracy" in the treaty does not mean piracy *jure gentium* but a crime made such by the municipal law of one of the parties to the treaty. Re Ternan, 9 Cox C.C. 522 (1864). "The legislative authority of a state may doubtless enlarge the definition of the crime of piracy, but the state must confine the operation of the new definition to its own citizens and to foreigners on its own vessels." Dole v. New England Mutual Marine Ins. Co., 2 Cliff. 394, 417 (1st Cir. 1864).

that country; (3) arming or serving on privateers; (4) assault by a seaman upon his commander; (5) felonious conversion or surrender of his vessel by an officer thereof; (6) corruption of seamen and confederating with pirates; (7) plunder of a distressed vessel; (8) attack to plunder a vessel; (9) unauthorized receipt of pirate property; and (10) robbery ashore by anyone engaged in any piratical cruise or enterprise.[85]

While the last provision may go beyond, it unquestionably includes conduct which would constitute piracy by the law of nations. If, for example, the crew of a pirate ship should land and plunder a village on the shore there, this would constitute an act of such piracy.[86]

As a matter of practical importance at the present time, none of the Acts of Congress mentioned above, whether dealing with piracy by the law of nations or statutory piracy, seem comparable to the most recent enactment in this area which reads as follows: "(1) Whoever commits or attempts to commit aircraft piracy, as herein defined, shall be punished; . . . (by death or not less than 20 years). (2) As used in this subsection, the term 'aircraft piracy' means any seizure or exercise of control, by force or violence or threat of force or violence 'or by any other form of intimidation, . . .' and with wrongful intent, of an aircraft within the special aircraft jurisdiction of the United States." [87]

It has been held that one may violate this statute without attacking or threatening the pilot. Thus a conviction was authorized by evidence that **D**, by interfering with the dual set of controls and turning off the ignition key, seriously interfered with the landing of the plane by the pilot.[88] It is also important to note that a private plane in the air is an "aircraft within the special aircraft jurisdiction of the United States" within the meaning of the statute.[89] It has been held under a prior statute of similar coverage that an offense was committed when **Ds**, at gunpoint, forced the pilot of a private plane to transport them from Florida to Cuba.[90]

---

85. These are found in 18 U.S.C.A. §§ 1652 through 1661.

86. If after the crew landed there was no crime on shore except that one member robbed one victim, this would be ordinary robbery and not an act of piracy. It would not be "depredation from the sea".

The elements of proof in aircraft piracy are "(1) Seizure or exercise of control of an aircraft; (2) by force, violence, or intimidation, or the threat thereof; (3) with wrongful intent; (4) while in the special aircraft jurisdiction of the United States." United States v. Dixon, 592 F.2d 329, 339–340 (6th Cir. 1979).

The federal statute on "aircraft piracy" is aimed at the acts commonly referred to in the press as the 'hijacking' of

aircraft." The hijacker may also be guilty of kidnaping. United States v. Dixon, 592 F.2d 329, 340 (6th Cir. 1979).

87. 49 U.S.C.A. § 1472(i) (1976).

Federal law applies to American and other aircraft while such aircraft are en route from an airport in the United States or are returning from a foreign country directly to an airport in the United States. Chumney v. Nixon, 615 F.2d 389 (6th Cir. 1980).

88. Mims v. United States, 332 F.2d 944 (10th Cir. 1964), cert. denied 379 U.S. 888, 85 S.Ct. 158 (1964).

89. 49 U.S.C.A. § 1301(38) (1978).

90. United States v. Healy, 376 U.S. 75, 84 S.Ct. 553 (1964).

Chapter 6

IMPUTABILITY

The word "impute" comes from im (in) and putare (reckon). It means to bring into the reckoning, to attribute or to ascribe. It is sometimes used to attribute vicariously,—to ascribe as derived from another. This is included properly within the general import of the term but it is not its primary meaning. It may be used in many senses. Thus we may impute (ascribe) intent, knowledge, guilt, and so forth. Here it is used in the basic sense of imputing (ascribing) the fact itself. Harm has been done. Did the defendant do it? Usually such an inquiry is purely factual. What really happened? At times, however, when all the facts are known we have to ask: Will the law impute (attribute or ascribe) what happened to the defendant? That is what is meant here by "imputability."

SECTION 1. THE NECESSITY OF AN ACT

A crime is any social harm defined and made punishable by law. This is the logical starting point of a study of the general principles of the criminal law. And this definition, or any other acceptable one, makes clear the necessity of an act for the existence of any crime. The intent with which a harmful act was done is a matter of special interest to the criminal law, but a wrongful intent which has no consequences in the external world,—which exists only in the secret recesses of the mind, is not.[1] Ordinarily such an intent would be known only to the person who entertained it, but if he freely admits that such a thought was once in his mind, no crime has been established. There has been no "social harm." Few are so upright as to be able to exclude any criminal thought from entering the mind under any and all circumstances. The average law-abiding citizen is not one who never has a criminal intent, but one who never permits such a thought to rule his conduct.

SECTION 2. WHAT CONSTITUTES AN ACT

Since an act is essential to the commission of a crime it is important to determine what constitutes an act.

A. THE DEGREE OF GENERALITY OF THE WORD

If death has resulted from a pistol shot, shall the *act* be said to be (1) killing, (2) impinging the bullet upon the body of the victim, (3) shooting, (4) pulling the trigger, or (5) crooking the finger?

Unfortunately this question does not permit a simple answer. The word "act," like the word "home," is one of ambiguous import, used in various senses of different degrees of generality.[1] A person who is asked what his home is by a resident of the same general neighborhood may reply by giving

1. "It is beyond contradiction that, regardless how heinous, no man can be convicted for having criminal intent alone. An *actus reus* is essential." State v. Otto, 102 Idaho 250, 629 P.2d 646, 647 (1981).

§ 2

1. Salmond, Jurisprudence, 381 (8th ed. 1930).

merely the street and number. In response to the same question asked by a Frenchman during a casual conversation in Spain, the same person may answer that the United States is his home. Under other circumstances he may give as his home the state of New York, New York City or the borough of Manhattan. These widely different forms of expression do not indicate any change in the place of his abode. They involve neither misstatement nor misunderstanding. The word has this much elasticity and the manner of its use will ordinarily indicate the degree of generality.

Holmes was inclined to limit the word "act" to the willed movement of the body itself, as the mere crooking of the finger in the case suggested.[2] Salmond tends to insist upon the inclusion of all factual occurrences occasioned by the exertion of the will (within the limits of legally-recognized causation), which requires the word "act" in such a case to express the killing, and nothing less.[3] Customary usage, either in juridical discussion or in ordinary conversation, lends some support to either view.

The present trend is in the direction of the position taken by Holmes rather than that by Salmond. For example, in the *Restatement of Torts* the word "act" is used "to denote an external manifestation of the actor's will and does not include any of its results even the most direct, immediate and intended." [4] Such a narrow meaning, however, is not entirely free from difficulty. In the case of an intentional killing by shooting, for example, to say the act is merely crooking the finger or pulling the trigger is clearly an oversimplification, because while the trigger is being pulled the weapon is being carefully aimed.[5] Aiming is as much an act as is the pulling of the trigger,[6]

---

2. "For instance, to crook the forefinger with a certain force is the same act whether the trigger of a pistol is next it or not. It is only the surrounding circumstances of a pistol loaded and cocked, and of a human being in such a relation to it as to be manifestly likely to be hit, that make the act a wrong." Holmes, The Common Law, 54 (1881).

3. "Every act is made up of three factors or constituent parts. These are (1) its *origin* in some mental or bodily activity or passivity of the doer, (2) its *circumstances*, and (3) its *consequences*. Let us suppose that in practicing with a rifle I shoot some person by accident. The material elements of my act are the following: its origin or primary state, namely a series of muscular contractions, by which the rifle is raised and the trigger pulled; secondly, the circumstances, the chief of which are the facts that the rifle is loaded and in working order, and that the person killed is in the line of fire; thirdly, the consequences, the chief of which are the fall of the trigger, the explosion of the powder, the discharge of the bullet, its passage through the body of the man killed, and his death." Salmond, op. cit. supra note 1, at 383. The traditional definition of crime uses the word "act" in this sense. "A crime or misdemeanor is

an act committed or omitted, in violation of a public law either forbidding or commanding it." 4 Bl.Comm. *5. Repeated (without the words "or misdemeanour") in Commonwealth v. Shields, 50 Pa. Super. 194, 202 (1912); Commonwealth v. Smith, 266 Pa. 511, 516, 109 A. 786, 788 (1920).

4. Restatement, Second, Torts § 2 (1965).

5. Something of the difficulty involved in the use of the word is disclosed in the comment to the section cited in the preceding note. It is said: "Thus, if the actor, having pointed a pistol at another, pulls the trigger, the act is the pulling of the trigger and not the impingement of the bullet upon the other's person. So too, if the actor intentionally strikes another, the act is only the movement of the actor's hand not the contact with the other's body immediately established thereby." Id. at Comment c. But it should have been said in the first instance—to follow the usage insisted upon by the Institute—that the act was the crooking of the finger which *caused* the movement of the trigger as its most direct and immediate result.

6. Ibid.

and it is very convenient to refer to the combination of the two as the act of shooting. On the other hand, to give to the word "act" such significance that the death of the victim, in a homicide case, would be a *part* of the act rather than a *result* of the act, would unduly complicate discussions in the field of causation.

The crooking of the finger, the pulling of the trigger, the shooting, the impinging of the bullet upon the body of the victim, and the killing, are concepts which will all be recognized no matter what meaning is given to the word "act" itself. If the "killing" is not an act, it is an act plus consequences so commonly visualized as a unity that it is proper as well as convenient to refer to it as such. The same may be said of "shooting." If the crooking of the finger is only part of an act and not "the act" itself (in a case of shooting), it is a part of sufficient importance to be entitled to special mention. And there need be no hesitation in the use of the phrase "pulling the trigger" whether this is understood to be (1) an act, (2) an act (of crooking the finger) plus a consequence, or (3) merely part of an act (of shooting or of killing).

Conceding the usability of all these terms whether each of them may properly be said to represent an *act* or not, and conceding the probability that the form of expression will ordinarily leave little room for misunderstanding even if the word "act" be given sufficient elasticity to apply to each in turn, it is necessary to choose whether or not to encourage such elasticity, and if not, whether to give preference to the narrow or the broad usage in respect to the occurrences which are to be included.

The choice must be based upon convenience rather than upon philology. And, for purposes of juridical discussion, convenience will best be served by encouraging the present trend toward the limitation of the word "act" "to denote an external manifestation of the actor's will" without the inclusion of the results which follow, leaving, however, sufficient latitude to permit the word to be used, as a sort of dialectic shorthand, to express certain common and complicated manifestations of the will, such as shooting and driving.

Recent codes and statutes have provided for the definition of an act in limited terms. The Model Penal Code defines act as "bodily movement whether voluntary or involuntary." [7] Proposed legislation to establish a federal criminal code defines act in terms of "bodily movement or activity" excluding unwilled movement. [8] Another jurisdiction has simply defined an act as "bodily movement." [9]

B. INTERNAL ACTS AND EXTERNAL ACTS

Is a thought an act? In one sense of the word an affirmative answer is required. A thought is the so-called "act of the mind" or "internal act." [10]

7. § 1.13(2).

8. § 111 S.1722 96th Congress, 1st Sess.

9. Ariz.Rev.Stat. § 13–105(1) (1978).

10. "In the second place, acts are either internal or external. The former are acts of the mind, while the latter are acts of the body. In each case the act may be either passive or negative, lying either in bodily activity or passivity, or in mental activity or passivity. To think is an internal act; to speak is an external act. . . . The term act is very commonly restricted to external acts, but this

If we start with the premise that thoughts will be matters of utter indifference to the law unless they are acts, it is necessary to include the former under the head of the latter. An act done with intent to defraud, for example, may have legal consequences quite different from those which attach to another act which is exactly the same except for the want of such an intention. But the suggested premise is faulty. Psychical facts may have very important legal consequences, at least insofar as they induce or accompany "external acts;" but this can be conceded and expressed without calling them "acts." As it is neither convenient nor common [11] to employ the word "act" to include the so-called "internal act," any such usage should be rejected. "Psychic facts and the psychic element in acts have been, and will continue to be, the object of juridical consideration, although . . . only when shown in action." [12]

C. VERBAL ACTS

Although "words" and "acts" are sometimes loosely used in a mutually exclusive sense to distinguish promise from fulfillment, an exertion of the will which is manifested in the form of speaking or writing is an act.[13]

Simple verbal expression may be sufficient to qualify as a punishable act such as in communicating a threat [14] or in making an harassing communication.[15] Congress has made it a crime to threaten to take the life of or inflict bodily harm on the President of the United States [16] even if the act is not in proximity to the President and there is no actual present intent to carry out the threat.[17] The First Amendment to the United States Constitution, however, places a limitation on the kind of verbal expression that may be criminally punished.[18]

is inconvenient for the reason already given in respect of the distinction between positive and negative acts." Salmond, op cit. supra note 1, at 831–832.

11. Salmond, who thinks it would be more convenient to give the word "act" a broader significance in this regard, admits that the common usage is otherwise. See note 7, supra.

12. Del Vecchio, Formal Bases of Law, 10 Modern Legal Philosophy Series 146 (1914).

13. "The beating of the heart is not a physical act, but the movement of the tongue which utters slanderous words is a physical act." Kocourek, An Introduction to the Science of Law, 268 (1930).

14. Model Penal Code § 211.3 Terroristic Threat provides:

"A person is guilty of a felony of the third degree if he threatens to commit any crime of violence with purpose to terrorize another or to cause evacuation of a building, place of assembly, or facility of public transportation, or otherwise to cause serious public inconvenience, or in reckless disregard of the risk of causing such terror or inconvenience."

15. Iowa Code Ann. 708.7 (1978).

16. 18 U.S.C.A. § 871(a) (1976).

17. United States v. Hall, 493 F.2d 904 (5th Cir. 1974). However, a true threat rather than political hyperbole is required. Watts v. United States, 394 U.S. 705, 89 S.Ct. 1399 (1969).

18. Use of mere offensive words, passively displayed, cannot be criminally punished as disturbing the peace. Cohen v. California, 403 U.S. 15, 91 S.Ct. 1780 (1970). A statute may not punish language in terms of simple insult or offensiveness but may punish fighting words or words very likely to lead to violence. Gooding v. Wilson, 405 U.S. 518, 92 S.Ct. 1103 (1972).

D. INTENTIONAL ACTS AND UNINTENTIONAL ACTS

An involuntary contraction of the muscles in the nature of a spasm is not an act.[19] Occurrences which take place independently of the will must be classed as "events" rather than "acts" [20] because volition is one of the constituents of positive action.[21] What then is meant by an unintentional act? The explanation must be made in terms of the degree of generality assigned to the word "act."

A homicide resulting from a pistol shot will serve for purposes of illustration. If the word "act" were used in the very broad sense of the "act of killing," the explanation would be simple enough. If the shot was fired at a target with no thought of fatal consequences, and the death resulted from an unexpected glance of the bullet, the act (the killing) would be classed as unintentional because of the inclusion of an element which was quite apart from the intention of the actor. But as the suggestion here made is that this extreme signification of the word "act" be definitely rejected, the explanation should be that the killing is an unintended consequence of an intentional act. This is true even if the word "act" be used (by way of dialectic shorthand) to express the shooting.

A fatal shot, however, does not necessarily involve an intent to shoot. If, for example, one is holding a gun supposed to be unloaded, and pulls the trigger expecting no more than a harmless snap of the hammer, but the gun is in fact loaded, and is discharged with fatal consequences, the shooting as well as the killing must be classed as unintentional. The one who caused the death in this manner may or may not be guilty of crime, depending upon all the circumstances,[22] but the present inquiry is limited to the act itself, and does not extend to the legal consequences thereof. And the act itself was unintentional if the word is used to express the shooting, but intentional if the word is used in the sense of crooking the finger or pulling the trigger.

But even the crooking of the finger may not have been intentional. One while intentionally pointing a pistol at another as a threat and with no thought of pulling the trigger might have a slight spasm which would cause the trigger to move and the weapon to be discharged. In such a case the crooking of the finger is not an act, but merely an event.[23] The pointing of the pistol, however, was an act, and this act has resulted in the death of a human being. The one who held the weapon may or may not be criminally responsible for the homicide, depending upon all the circumstances, and if so

---

19. "A spasm is not an act." Holmes, loc. cit. supra note 2.

State v. Taft, 143 W.Va. 365, 102 S.E.2d 152 (1958). However, where the reflexive or involuntary act can be anticipated because of a prior known condition, then placing oneself in a dangerous circumstance where the condition may cause a reflex that could injure another is an act. The act is in doing what is dangerous, such as driving with an active epileptic condition, which may result in injury or death. People v. Decina, 2 N.Y.2d 133, 157 N.Y.S.2d 558, 138 N.E.2d 799 (1956).

20. "By 'events' jurists mean those occurrences which take place independently of the will. By 'act' those which are subject to the control of the human will and so flow therefrom. Acts, then, are exertions of the will manifested in the external world." Pound, Readings on the History and System of the Common Law, 513 (3rd ed. 1927).

21. See John Stuart Mill, A System of Logic, 59 (1873).

22. See, for example, State v. Morrison, 104 Mo. 638, 16 S.W. 492 (1891); State v. Hardie, 47 Iowa 647 (1878).

23. See note 19, supra.

he may perhaps be guilty even of the crime of murder in the first degree,[24] but that again is quite apart from the present consideration. If the word "act" is used in the sense of shooting it was an unintentional act. If the word is used in the narrow sense, there was an unintentional shooting, resulting in an unintentional killing, both caused by the intentional act of pointing the weapon.

It is hardly necessary to elaborate further, as for example, by supposing the gun to be held in the hand in such a manner as to be unintentionally directed at another, whose death results from a discharge of the weapon which is also unintentional. Factual situations such as these will be expressed by speaking of one (not stated here in hypothetical form) as an intentional killing; of another, as an unintentional killing resulting from an intentional shooting; of a third, as an unintentional killing resulting from an unintentional shooting, and so forth. It may be added that in the field of negative action many unintentional acts will be found.

E. DEFINITION

Occurrences in general have been classified as (1) events and (2) acts.[25] An event has been spoken of as a movement of nature,[26] but is more accurately described as an occurrence which takes place independently of the will.[27] Thus not only is an earthquake, a flood, or the mere setting of the sun, an event; but so also is a spasm.

An act is an occurrence which is an exertion of the will manifested in the external world.[28]

24. Commonwealth v. Lessner, 274 Pa. 108, 118 A. 24 (1922): This was not a case in which the trigger was moved by a spasm. But an attempt by another to wrest the weapon from the hand of the robber caused the fatal discharge. Even this did not prevent his conviction of murder in the first degree.

25. "'Facts' . . . are either 'Events' or 'Acts.'" Holland, Jurisprudence, 107 (13th ed. 1924). This classification is based upon the broad signification of the word "act." For the narrow meaning of a three-fold classification is required—adding a word which will mean occurrences which are the consequences of acts.

26. Holland, loc. cit. supra note 17. Holland also includes under the head of "event" "the acts of another human being than the human being whose rights or duties are under consideration." Ibid. It is more precise, however, to express such an occurrence by the phrase "act of another."

27. "By 'events' jurists mean those occurrences which take place independently of the will." Pound, loc. cit. supra note 12. The word "event" is sometimes given sufficient scope to include positive acts as well as other occurrences. Some-

times the word is used, not to include all positive acts, but such acts on the part of a person other than the one whose rights and duties are under consideration. See note 18, supra.

28. "Acts are exertions of the will manifested in the external world." Pound, op. cit. supra note 12, at 453. "'Acts' . . . in the widest sense of the term, are movements of the will . . . An 'Act' may therefore be defined, for the purposes of the science, as 'a determination of the will, producing an effect in the sensible world.'" Holland, op. cit. supra note 17, at 108. "An act is the result of the exercise of the will." Duncan v. Landis, 106 F. 839, 848 (3d Cir. 1901). "The word 'act' is used throughout the Restatement of this Subject to denote an external manifestation of the actor's will and does not include any of its results even the most direct, immediate and intended." Restatement, Second, Torts, § 2 (1965).

Quoting from an earlier case it was said: "Where an act in itself may be susceptible of two interpretations, one innocent and the other criminal, then the intent with which the act is done becomes the critical element in determining its

If a person engages in conduct that would otherwise be criminal but does so without any exertion of will then there is no act. Thus, a person who acts under a hypnotic suggestion [29] or in a somnambulistic state [30] or a bodily movement not otherwise willed, such as in a state of automatism [31] does not commit an "act" that gives rise to criminal liability.

SECTION 3. ATTEMPT AND KINDRED PROBLEMS

A. ATTEMPT

1. IN GENERAL

A criminal attempt is a step towards a criminal offense with specific intent to commit that particular crime.[1]

An attempt to commit any indictable offense is punished as a misdemeanor according to the common law.[2] This is true whether the crime attempted was known to the common law or of statutory origin. Felony punishment is often provided by statute for attempts to commit certain of the more serious crimes, such as murder, rape or robbery. The modern penal codes often make specific provision for the punishment of attempts to commit certain offenses and cover the rest of the field with a general attempt clause, such as the following: "Whoever attempts to commit any offense prohibited by law, and does any act towards it but fails, or is intercepted or prevented in

character." State v. Brown, 4 Kan.App. 2d 729, 610 P.2d 655, 659 (1980).

29. M.P.C. § 2.01(c).

30. Ibid. § 2.01(b); Bradley v. State, 102 Tex.Cr.R. 41, 277 S.W. 147 (1925).

31. Bratty v. Attorney General for N. I., [1963] AC 386; People v. Grant, 46 Ill. App.3d 125, 4 Ill.Dec. 696, 360 N.E.2d 809 (1977), reversed on other grounds 71 Ill. 2d 551, 17 Ill.Dec. 814, 377 N.E.2d 4 (1978); People v. Newton, 8 Cal.App.3d 359, 87 Cal.Rptr. 394 (1970).

1. "A person commits an attempt when, with intent to commit a specific offense, he does any act which constitutes a substantial step toward the commission of that offense." Smith-Hurd Ill.Ann. Stat. Ch. 38 § 8–4 (1980). See also La. Stat.Ann.—Rev.Stat. 14:27 (1975).

An attempt to commit a crime contains only two elements, (1) a specific intent and (2) an overt act tending directly toward the accomplishing of the object. State v. Porter, 249 La. 784, 191 So.2d 498 (1966).

"A conviction for attempt requires proof of culpable intent and conduct constituting a substantial step toward commission of the crime that strongly cor-

roborates that intent." United States v. Snell, 627 F.2d 186, 187 (9th Cir. 1980).

2. Rex v. Scofield, Caldecott 397 (1784); Regina v. Martin, 9 Car. & P. 215, 173 Eng.Rep. 808 (1840).

"[A]n attempt to commit a misdemeanor is a misdemeanor, whether the offence is created by statute or was an offence at common law." Rex v. Roderick, 7 Car. & P. 795, 173 Eng.Rep. 347 (1837).

Statutes may make a different provision. Thus attempted possession of burglary tools is not a crime in Florida. State v. Thomas, 362 So.2d 1348 (Fla. 1978).

Because common-law offenses are not punishable as such in federal courts, an attempt to commit a federal offense is not itself a federal offense unless so provided in the statute. United States v. York, 578 F.2d 1036 (5th Cir. 1978).

". . . the common law misdemeanor of criminal attempt, notwithstanding its post-Revolutionary final crystallization, has always been recognized as part of the common law of Maryland." Gray v. State, 43 Md.App. 238, 403 A.2d 853, 855 (1979).

its execution, where no express provision is made by law for the punishment of such attempt, shall be punished, when the offense thus attempted is a felony, by imprisonment in the penitentiary not less than one, nor more than five years; in all other cases, by fine not exceeding $300, or by confinement in the county jail not exceeding six months." Another plan, found in several codes, is to provide that the penalty for an attempt shall not exceed one-half the maximum for the offense attempted,—with certain exceptions. The exceptions, for example, (1) may set a maximum term (such as twenty years) for attempting an offense that is, or may be, punishable by death or by imprisonment for life, and (2) provide for a maximum of one year in jail for attempting a crime punishable by imprisonment in a state prison for a term of less than five years.

"There is no general federal statute proscribing attempt, and it is therefore actionable only where, as in the present case, a specific criminal statute makes impermissible its attempted as well as its actual violation." [3]

2. ATTEMPT MAY BE SUCCESSFUL

Much of the discussion and many of the definitions point to failure as of the very essence of a criminal attempt,[4] but there is no factual background for such an approach. In the area of wrongdoing, as in the realm of law-abiding conduct, some attempts fail while many others are successful. Furthermore, nothing in the philosophy of juridical science requires that an attempt must fail in order to receive recognition. A successful attempt to commit a crime will not support two convictions and penalties,—one for the attempt and the other for the completed offense.[5] This is for the obvious reason that whatever is deemed the appropriate penalty for the total misconduct can be imposed upon conviction of the offense itself, but this does not require the unsound conclusion that proof of the completed offense disproves the attempt to commit it.[6] To insure against such a conclusion a number of

---

3. United States v. Manley, 632 F.2d 978, 987 (2d Cir. 1980).

4. Tender v. State, 2 Md.App. 692, 237 A.2d 65 (1968). "A failure to consummate the crime is as much an essential element of an attempt as the intent and the performance of an overt act towards its commission." People v. Lardner, 300 Ill. 264, 266, 133 N.E. 375, 376 (1921). Accord, Lewis v. People, 124 Colo. 62, 235 P.2d 348 (1951); Beddow v. State, 93 Nev. 619, 572 P.2d 526, 528 (1977).

5. "Unlike conspiracy, however, the prosecution may not obtain conviction for both the completed offense and the attempt as separate crimes if the attempt has in fact been completed." United States v. York, 578 F.2d 1036, 1040 (5th Cir. 1978).

One may be charged with a crime, and with an attempt to commit that crime, and both charges may be submitted to the jury if supported by evidence. But he may not be convicted of both. United States v. Rust, 650 F.2d 927 (8th Cir.

1981). It would not be necessary to charge the attempt if the statute authorized conviction of attempt to commit the offense charged.

6. The fact that the crime was committed does not prevent conviction of the attempt to commit it. Failure to consummate the crime of burglary is not an essential element of attempted burglary. State v. Gallegos, 193 Neb. 651, 228 N.W.2d 615 (1975). Failure to commit the crime is not an indispensable element of criminal attempt. A conviction of attempt may stand although the evidence established that the crime was consummated. Lightfoot v. State, 278 Md. 231, 360 A.2d 426 (1976). One court said "every completed crime necessarily involves an attempt to commit it." People v. Vanderbilt, 119 Cal. 461, 463, 249 P. 867, 868 (1926). The court obviously did not have in mind such crimes as involuntary manslaughter.

Provisions of the "Maine Criminal Code provide a consistent statutory pat-

the statutes expressly provide that a person may be convicted of an attempt to commit a crime although it appears on the trial that the crime attempted was perpetrated by the defendant.[7] It has been rather common to authorize conviction of an attempt to commit the crime charged in the indictment.[8] This type of statute does not expressly authorize conviction of an attempt where the proof shows success,—nor does it expressly exclude it. Such a provision does not require submission of the attempt issue where there is no evidence to warrant it. A defendant who has been convicted of the offense charged is not entitled to a reversal by reason of the judge's refusal to submit the attempt issue where there was no evidence of an attempt that failed.[9] The real test comes at another point. Suppose in such a trial the uncontradicted evidence shows beyond doubt that defendant attempted to commit the offense charged, but there is conflict in the testimony as to whether the attempt succeeded or failed. Some of the statements on the subject, if carried to their logical conclusion, would entitle the defendant to an instruction which would tell the jury in substance: (1) they must acquit the defendant of the completed offense unless satisfied beyond a reasonable doubt that the attempt was successful; (2) they must acquit the defendant of an attempt to commit the offense unless satisfied beyond a reasonable doubt that the attempt failed. In other words the position would be that defendant is entitled to a verdict of not guilty if there is doubt in regard to success or failure although no doubt that the attempt was made.[10] There is no proper basis for such a position, and probably no court would carry the unsound notion to such an absurd extreme.[11]

Where guilt is clear but there is doubt as to which of two grades or degrees the rule is not that defendant must be acquitted, but that conviction must be of the lower grade or degree. The same rule should apply in regard to an attempt to commit the offense charged.[12] The attempt is a lower

---

tern premised on the elimination of failure as an element of the crime of attempt." State v. Moores, 396 A.2d 1010, 1012 (Me.1979).

7. Many of the statutes define attempt in terms such as a "person who attempts to commit any crime, but fails, or is prevented or intercepted in the perpetration thereof, ..." E.g., West's Ann.Cal.Pen.Code § 664 (1978). Then, despite the inconsistency, it is frequently provided expressly that there may be conviction of the attempt although it was successful. Id. at § 663. See also Ariz. Rev.Stat. § 13–110 (1978); Colo.Rev.Stat. 1973, 18–2–101(1); Ga.Code § 26–1004 (1978); Idaho Code § 18–305 (1979); La. Rev.Stat. 14:27 (1974); Nev.Rev.Stat. 208.070 (1979); V.T.C.A.Penal Code § 15.01 (1974); Utah Code Ann.1953, 76–4–101.

At the other extreme some codes provide that there shall be no conviction of attempt when it appears that it was successful. E.g., 21 Okl.Stat.Ann. § 41 (1958); Miss.Code, 1972, § 97–1–9.

8. E.g., West's Ann.Cal.Pen.Code § 1159 (1970); C.G.S.A. (Conn.) § 54–60 (1975); Nev.Rev.Stat. 208.070 (1979); N.C.G.S. § 15–170 (1978); Wis.Stat.Ann. 939.66 (1958).

9. State v. Tennyson, 212 Minn. 158, 2 N.W.2d 833 (1942); People v. Gibbs, 12 Cal.App.3d 526, 90 Cal.Rptr. 866 (1970).

10. "Moreover, requiring the government to prove failure as an element of attempt would lead to the anomalous result that, if there were a reasonable doubt concerning whether or not a crime had been completed, a jury could find the defendant guilty neither of a completed offense nor of the attempt." United States v. York, 578 F.2d 1036, 1039 (5th Cir. 1978).

11. Such a statute has been held not to apply where it is doubtful whether the offense was or was not completed by defendant. In such a case conviction of the attempt is proper. Holley v. State, 175 Miss. 347, 166 So. 924 (1936).

12. The jury may convict of attempt although the evidence would warrant

grade or degree of the offense because it is a part of it. It is not something separate and distinct.

The opinions and text statements have so many references to the assumed requirement of failure as to invite inquiry in regard to the origin of this notion. Under the English common law the procedure for the trial of a misdemeanor was so different from that for the trial of a felony as to preclude a joinder of the two in the same indictment. And the rule developed that if the same act resulted in both a misdemeanor and a felony the former was merged in the latter. Isaac, for example, was indicted for houseburning, a misdemeanor. The charge was that he wilfully set fire to his own dwelling to defraud the insurer and thereby endangered other dwellings. But the proof showed not only that the fire set by him endangered other dwellings but that it actually destroyed several of them. This constituted arson, and the court held that the misdemeanor was merged in the felony and directed an acquittal on the houseburning charge.[13] For the same reason it was held in another case that proof of rape actually committed required acquittal of a charge of assault with intent to rape,[14] the latter being a misdemeanor under the law of England at that time.

Since an attempt to commit any indictable offense was punished as a misdemeanor at common law it followed that if an attempt to commit a felony was successful the attempt was merged in the felony and there could be no conviction of the misdemeanor.[15] This was not based upon any thought that the law of criminal attempt requires failure. It was merely an application of the general doctrine of merger. It would not apply to an attempt to commit a misdemeanor because one misdemeanor is not merged in another,[16] nor would it apply to an attempt to commit a felony if a statute had provided felony punishment for an attempt to commit that particular crime, because the doctrine of merger has no application where both are felonies.[17] But as much of the early development of the law of attempt was in connection with attempted felonies, and before statutes had increased the penalty for any attempt, there was considerable opportunity to overlook the fact that the failure to convict of an attempt which was shown to have been successful was due to the general doctrine of merger and not to any unusual requirement in the law of attempt.

Another influence was in operation at the same time. Strange as it may seem to us at this day, under the early English procedure the defendant in a felony trial was deprived of several important rights which would have been

conviction of the offense charged. Commonwealth v. Heisler, 10 Berks 102 (Berks Co., Pa.1917). "An acquittal of one charged with the attempt is an acquittal of the greater offense because the lesser offense is necessarily involved in the greater." State v. Harvey, 119 Or. 512, 515, 249 P. 172, 173 (1926).

"We hold that a defendant indicted and convicted for the crime of attempt to commit larceny is not entitled to a reversal of his conviction because the evidence at trial shows that his attempt was completed or amounted to perpetration of larceny." Richardson v. State, 390 So.2d 4, 6 (Ala.1980).

13. Isaac's Case, 2 East P.C. 1031 (1799).

14. Harmwood's Case, 1 East P.C. 411 (1787).

15. See Williams, Textbook of Criminal Law p. 384 (1978); Williams, Criminal Law, 2nd Ed. § 208 (1961).

16. People v. Mather, 4 Wend. 229, 265 (N.Y.1830).

17. Hamilton v. State, 36 Ind. 280 (1871); People v. Bristol, 23 Mich. 118 (1871).

available to him in a misdemeanor case.[18] Because of this fact a conviction of misdemeanor was not permitted under an indictment for felony.[19]

"The general rule at common law was, that when an indictment charged an offense which included within it another less offense or one of lower degree, the defendant though acquitted of the higher offense, might be convicted of the less.

"This rule however was subject to the qualification, that upon an indictment for a felony, the defendant could not be convicted of a misdemeanor." [20]

Hence, under the English common law, one being tried for felony could not be convicted of an attempt to commit the offense charged. This was not due to any peculiarity in the law of attempt, nor was it dependent in any way upon the proof in the particular case. It was merely an application of the general rule of procedure which did not permit conviction of a misdemeanor in a felony trial. But since the doctrine of merger and this application of a rule of procedure have tended to cause some confusion in regard to the law of attempt it may be well to give attention to the very beginning of the development of this law,—which was in regard to an attempt to commit a battery. While a special label was applied ("assault") it must be remembered that a criminal assault in the early common law was purely and simply an attempt to commit a battery. As a battery was a misdemeanor there was no occasion to apply the doctrine of merger. And proof that an attempt to commit a battery was successful has never been deemed a ground for acquittal in a trial for assault.[21]

Peculiarities in the criminal procedure in England in the early days may have given adequate support, at that time, for the rule that there could be no conviction of misdemeanor under an indictment for felony. However that may be, the procedure in this country does not do so,[22] and the prevailing view here is that such a conviction may be upheld.[23]

"So our common law has always permitted a conviction of the attempt, upon an indictment for rape." [24]

It has been rather common to give express authority by statute for the conviction of an attempt to commit the offense charged,[25] and even England has added such an enactment.[26] Under a provision of this nature it is unim-

---

18. Rex v. Westbeer, 1 Leach 12, 168 Eng.Rep. 108 (1739). And see Hanna v. People, 19 Mich. 316, 318–19 (1869).

19. Ibid.; Regina v. Eaton, 8 Car. & P. 417, 173 Eng.Rep. 556 (1838); Regina v. Woodhall, 12 Cox C.C. 240 (1872).

20. Hanna v. People, 19 Mich. 316, 318 (1869).

21. People v. Heise, 217 Cal. 671, 20 P.2d 317 (1933). And see State v. Deso, 110 Vt. 1, 6, 1 A.2d 710, 713 (1938).

In Utah there is no crime of battery and such an act must be prosecuted as a completed assault. Utah Code Ann.1953 §§ 76–5–102, 76–4–101(3)(a).

22. Hanna v. People, 19 Mich. 316 (1869).

23. Bryant v. State, 76 Ala. 33 (1884); Groves v. State, 76 Ga. 808 (1886); State v. Peters, 56 Iowa 263 (1881); State v. Vinsant, 49 Iowa 241 (1878); State v. O'Kane, 23 Kan. 244 (1880); People v. Arnold, 46 Mich. 268 (1881); Hill v. State, 75 Tenn. 685 (1881); Green v. State, 8 Tex.App. 71 (1880).

24. Rookey v. State, 70 Conn. 104, 112, 38 A. 911, 913 (1897).

25. See supra note 7.

Wisconsin's general attempt statute "does not operate to make failure an essential element of criminal attempt." Berry v. State, 90 Wis.2d 316, 280 N.W.2d 204, 209 (1979).

26. 14 & 15 Vict. c. 100, § 9 (1851).

portant that the offense charged may be a felony whereas the attempt is punished as a misdemeanor. It has a further advantage. It authorizes a conviction of the attempt although the attempt is not expressly within the averments of the indictment.[27]

Probably there was never any sound basis for the doctrine of merger of offenses,—if absolute merger is meant. The original English rule is ordinarily understood to have meant that if an act resulted in both a misdemeanor and a felony the former was so completely merged in the latter as to be unrecognizable for any legal purpose. Some indications point to this as an overstatement of the English rule,[28] even prior to the change by statute.[29] However that may be, the prevailing rule in this country is otherwise. Hence the tendency is to permit a conviction of the attempt even if the proof shows that it was successful.[30] As said by the Michigan court: [31]

"Defendant invokes the rule, operative in some jurisdictions by judicial holdings, and in others by statute, that there can be no conviction of an attempt to commit a felony if the evidence establishes consummation of the felony. This is the rule in Illinois. People v. Lardner, 300 Ill. 264 (133 N.E. 375). But the rule is not general, and does not prevail in this jurisdiction. If an information admits of conviction of an attempt to commit a felony, an accused may be found guilty of the attempt, though the evidence shows a completed offense [citing cases]. Such a verdict may be illogical, but the people cannot complain, and the defendant must accept it, even though less in measure than his just deserts; at least he cannot be heard to say that he has suffered injury."

Much will be gained by complete abandonment of any thought of failure as an element of a criminal attempt. Much will be gained by a clear recognition of the fact that a criminal attempt is not something separate and distinct, but merely a part of the offense attempted. It is punishable but this is

---

27. If the offense cannot be committed unintentionally, an indictment or information charging the offense would always include an attempt to commit it. This would be true of larceny, for example. But since murder may be committed without an actual intent to kill, the crime does not always result from an attempt to commit murder. Hence a charge of murder, in statutory short form, might not have any actual averment showing an attempt to commit murder. This will not bar conviction of the attempt under such statutes.

28. 2 Hawk.P.C. c. 47, § 6 (6th ed. 1788).

29. It is now provided that one on trial for misdemeanor may be convicted thereof although the evidence shows a felony, unless the judge in his discretion discharges the jury and directs a felony indictment. 14 & 15 Vict. c. 100, § 12 (1851).

30. "Therefore, every court, not otherwise bound by statute, that has considered the matter in recent years has re-

fused to require that a defendant be acquitted of an attempt because he was guilty of completing what he had set out to do." United States v. York, 578 F.2d 1036, 1039 (5th Cir. 1978).

It is sometimes provided by statute that proof of the completed offense does not bar conviction of the attempt. State v. Booke, 178 Mont. 225, 583 P.2d 405 (1978).

31. People v. Baxter, 245 Mich. 229, 232, 222 N.W. 149, 150 (1928); People v. Bradovich, 305 Mich. 329, 330–1, 9 N.W.2d 560, 561 (1943). "The reason for this last rule is that a defendant cannot complain where the determination of his case was more favorable to him than the evidence warranted." People v. Vanderbilt, 199 Cal. 461, 465, 249 P. 867, 868–9 (1926).

D can be convicted of the attempt to commit an offense even if the completed offense is proved. Greenwood v. United States, 225 A.2d 878 (D.C.Mun.App., 1967); State v. Fox, 159 N.W.2d 492 (Iowa 1968).

on the theory that it is such a large segment of the crime as to call for a penalty. Under the sound view an attempt to commit a crime is punishable whether the effort resulted in failure or success, although the charge and the conviction should normally be for the offense itself if evidence of consummation is clear.[32] But since the attempt is a part of the offense itself, and the whole of necessity includes every part, it follows that one successful attempt cannot possibly support two convictions,—one for the part (attempt) and the other for the whole (offense).

3. PREPARATION v. PERPETRATION

A distinction is made between measures taken by way of preparation for the commission of a crime and steps taken in the direction of its actual perpetration. As said by the California court: "Between preparation for the attempt and the attempt itself, there is a wide difference. The preparation consists in devising or arranging the means or measures necessary for the commission of the offense; the attempt is the direct movement toward the commission after the preparations are made." [33] The difference between the two may not be "wide" as a matter of fact. As one approaches the other we may find a difficult "twilight zone" rather than a sharp and clear dividing line. But it is wide as a matter of law.

So far as the common law is concerned there is no criminal attempt unless what was done went beyond the stage of preparation.[34] The "act must reach far enough toward the accomplishment of the desired result to amount to the commencement of the consummation;" [35] although it is not required to be the "last act" intended for the purpose.[36]

"[P]reparation alone is not enough, and some appreciable fragment of the crime must have been accomplished." [37] This requirement of the common law is not removed by a statutory provision that if "any person shall attempt to commit a crime, and in such attempt shall do any act towards the commission of such crime" and so forth, because preparation is not an act towards commission.[38]

32. "A person may be convicted of an attempt to commit a crime, although he actually committed the offense." State v. Garnick, 619 P.2d 1383, 1385 (Utah 1980).

33. People v. Murray, 14 Cal. 160 (1859). Repeated in substance, People v. Von Hecht, 133 Cal.App.2d 25, 38–9, 283 P.2d 764, 773 (1955); State v. Thomas, 438 S.W.2d 441 (Mo.1969).

34. Ibid.; United States v. Stephens, 8 Sawyer 116 (Cir.Ct.Dist. of Or., 1882); People v. Holbrook, 45 Cal.2d 228, 288 P.2d 1 (1955); State v. Bereman, 177 Kan. 141, 276 P.2d 364 (1954); Braham v. State, 571 P.2d 631 (Alaska 1977).

"It is a well-established principle that an attempt must consist of more than mere preparation and that there must be some overt act in furtherance of the offense charged." State v. Fish, ___ Mont. ___, 621 P.2d 1072, 1077 (1980).

35. Lee v. Commonwealth, 144 Va. 594, 599, 131 S.E. 212, 214 (1926); State v. Bereman, 177 Kan. 141, 142, 276 P.2d 364, 365 (1954); Bell v. State, 118 Ga. App. 291, 163 S.E.2d 323 (1968).

36. Ibid.; The King v. White, [1910] 2 K.B. 124; State v. Davis, 199 Kan. 33, 35, 427 P.2d 606, 609 (1967).

An attempt does not require the "last act." Cody v. State, 605 S.W.2d 271 (Tex.Cr.App.1980).

"The act need not be, as appellant herein asserts, actual commencement of the potentially death producing action." Moffett v. State, 96 Nev. 822, 618 P.2d 1223, 1224 (1980).

37. People v. Gallardo, 41 Cal.2d 57, 66, 257 P.2d 29, 35 (1953).

38. Groves v. State, 116 Ga. 516, 42 S.E. 755 (1902).

An illustration may be helpful. **D** has a grudge against **X** and decides to murder him. **D** considers possible methods of perpetration and settles upon shooting. With this in mind he steals a pistol and ammunition, and loads the pistol with some of the ammunition. He prepares a home-made shoulder holster so the weapon can be carried without being seen or causing telltale bulges in his clothing. He puts on the holster, with the pistol, so he will be used to it. He makes inquiries to determine just where **X** lives, where he works, when he quits work and how he goes home. He learns that **X** quits work at five in the afternoon, takes a certain bus at a nearby station, leaves the bus at its nearest stop to his home, which is about two blocks away, crosses the street to be on the same side as his home, and walks the remaining distance. He studies that side of this street and finds a thick clump of bushes by the side of the walk near **X**'s house. As it is mid-winter he knows it will be dark when **X** reaches that spot. He studies the street lights and finds that they will give enough light for his purpose without interfering with his concealment. He decides to hide there that night and shoot **X** as he goes by. But as it is noon when this decision is made, **D** goes home to wait until the proper time. He has been indiscreet in his inquiries and is arrested at his home on a charge of attempting to murder **X**. He is not guilty of such an attempt. All of these elaborate arrangements were matters of preparation.

Suppose, however, he was not arrested at that time. Towards evening **D** went to the neighborhood of **X**'s house. He knew about the time **X** would arrive on the bus and was near his intended place of ambush at that time. He saw the bus stop, directly under a bright light, and saw **X** as he left the bus and started to walk. **D** then concealed himself in the bushes. As **X** came in range **D** drew his pistol. He took aim to the best of his ability, waited until **X** was at the closest point, and then pulled the trigger. But his aim was faulty and **X** was not touched although the bullet went by within inches of his head. **D**'s guilt of an attempt to murder **X** under these facts is too clear for question.

The problem is to determine at what point his acts went beyond preparation and were in the nature of perpetration. The actual firing of the shot was not essential to the attempt.[39] There should be no doubt that **D** was guilty of the attempt when he took aim at his intended victim who was then in range,—or even when he drew the weapon. In fact the cases seem to make clear that **D** was guilty of attempt when he took his stand in the bushes. Although **X** was over a block away, and probably out of range of the pistol, this act was a step in the direction of perpetration.

In one case, for example, **D** offered to pay **A** $1000 for killing **X**. **D** procured a loaded gun and after dark, went with **A** to the intended place of ambush, where they had reason to expect **X** to appear shortly. As **D** was handing the weapon to **A**, **D** was arrested. A conviction of attempted murder was affirmed although it was not shown that **X** went by the place that night.[40] Two men planned to rob a payroll clerk of his payroll. They went to the bank where he was to receive the payroll and stationed themselves to waylay him, but were arrested just before the clerk appeared. This was held

---

39. State v. Mandel, 78 Ariz. 326, 278 P.2d 413 (1954); Lee v. Commonwealth, 144 Va. 594, 131 S.E. 212 (1926).

40. Stokes v. State, 92 Miss. 415, 46 So. 627 (1908).

to be an attempt to rob.[41] **D** placed a bomb in **X**'s yard in such a way that when **X** drove in he would break a string across the driveway and thereby cause the bomb to explode and kill **X**. **D** himself accidentally caused the bomb to explode. This was held to be an attempt to murder **X** although no one but **D** was there at the time of the explosion.[42] **D** and **A** agreed to place a home-made bomb on a streetcar track. **A** delivered dynamite cartridges to **D** who was to make the bomb. They agreed to meet at 4:30 the next morning at a place not far from where the bomb was to be set. **D** made the bomb and started with it for the meeting place shortly before the agreed time. Placing an obstruction on a track was a statutory offense and **D** was held to have attempted to commit that crime although arrested before reaching the meeting place.[43] "Before he left his house he was already fully prepared, and carried with him the instrument he was to use in effecting the crime he intended; nothing, in fact, remained for him to do but deposit it on the railway, at the time easily within his reach." [44] On the other hand when two men, who had agreed to rob a third, made inquiries about him, procured masks, and hired a taxi to look for him, this was held to be preparation only and not an attempt to rob.[45]

Each case, it should be emphasized, must be considered in the light of all the facts involved. In the case of attempting to place an obstruction on the streetcar track the court emphasized the nearness of **D** to the place of intended perpetration. Had the plan called for a journey of a hundred miles after the meeting place was reached, going to that place and even the journey itself would have been held to be part of the preparation. There is no rule of law which specifies what the distance must be, and in any approach to the borderline between preparation and the start of perpetration it would be futile to discuss distance apart from a consideration of the other facts of a particular case.

The time of intended perpetration is a factor to be considered, and may be controlling in certain situations. Suppose **D**, intending to burn down the dwelling house of **X**, has entered the building with combustible materials which he has so arranged that the lighting of a fuse will be followed in due time by a roaring fire. If **D** has no intention of lighting the fire now,—if he has merely "set the stage" so the fire can be started without loss of time when he returns on a future occasion—this is merely preparation. It is not an attempt to commit arson.[46] Had **D**, on the other hand, intended to light the fire at that time he would be guilty of attempted arson although arrested before he struck the match.[47] If such was his intention, in fact, he was

---

41. People v. Gormley, 222 App.Div. 256, 225 N.Y.S. 653 (1927).

42. Jambar v. State, 75 Wis. 664, 44 N.W. 963 (1890).

43. People v. Stites, 75 Cal. 570, 17 P. 693 (1888).

44. Id. at 576, 17 P. 696. The meeting place was actually farther from the track than **D**'s house but this was deemed unimportant since neither distance was great.

45. Groves v. State, 116 Ga. 516, 42 S.E. 755 (1902).

46. Commonwealth v. Peaslee, 177 Mass. 267, 59 N.E. 55 (1901).

47. Commonwealth v. Mehales, 284 Mass. 412, 188 N.E. 261 (1933). The court was aided by a statute in this case but makes clear that the facts were sufficient for a common-law attempt.

guilty of attempted arson when he entered the building,[48] or even before an actual entry was accomplished.[49]

To emphasize another point certain illustrations will be helpful although two of them repeat situations previously mentioned. **A**, intending to murder **X**, conceals a long dagger in his clothing and goes out to discover where **X** may be found. **A** is arrested on a charge of attempting to murder **X** before receiving a lead as to **X**'s whereabouts. **B** also intends to murder **X** but has a different plan. He has prepared some poisoned candy, knowing **X** is very fond of that kind, and intends to send it to **X**. **B** is arrested on a charge of attempted murder while the poisoned candy is still in his possession. **C** has placed combustibles in **X**'s dwelling house intending to return and set the fire at a later time. He is arrested on a charge of attempted arson while at his own home waiting for the appropriate moment. **D** intends to break into **X**'s house at midnight and steal certain valuable goods kept there. With this in mind he has procured an effective set of burglar's tools, but is arrested in his own home about noon on a charge of attempted burglary. **E** has obtained some counterfeit foreign treasury notes which he intends to pass as genuine. He received them late at night with no thought of using them until the following day. He is arrested that night on a charge of attempting to utter counterfeit foreign securities.

None of these persons is guilty of the attempt with which he is charged, so far as the common law is concerned, but this does not mean that he must go unpunished. Unless **A** has a special license, which is unlikely under the facts stated, he is no doubt guilty of violating the statute against carrying concealed weapons.[50] **B** may be guilty of violating a statute which forbids the mingling of poison with food with intent that it shall be taken by a human being.[51] **C** may be guilty of violating a statute forbidding the placing of combustible materials in or against a building with intent eventually to burn the building.[52] **D** is probably guilty of violating a statute prohibiting the possession of burglar's tools with intent to commit burglary.[53] And **E** is guilty of violating the federal statute against possessing counterfeit foreign securities with intent to defraud.[54] Occasionally such a statute may apply the label "attempt." [55]

48. State v. Dumas, 118 Minn. 77, 136 N.W. 311 (1912).

Going on the premises to dynamite the place is sufficient for an attempt to destroy it by dynamite. Bell v. State, 118 Ga.App. 291, 163 S.E.2d 323 (1968).

49. State v. Taylor, 47 Or. 455, 84 P. 82 (1906). In this case the one employed by **D** to burn the building was frightened away when about twenty feet distant. **D** was held guilty of the attempt. The sterilization of instruments to be used in an illegal operation, to be performed very promptly, is sufficient for an attempt. People v. Berger, 131 Cal.App.2d 127, 280 P.2d 136 (1955).

50. Iowa Code Ann. § 724.4 (1978). This is a very common statute and often makes the offense a felony. A number of statutes make it a felony to possess unlawfully certain kinds of weapon, such as a machine gun. West's Ann.Cal.Pen. Code § 12220 (1977).

51. Idaho Code § 18–5501 (1979). This statute, while not so common as the concealed weapon statute, is by no means rare. The penalty under the Idaho section is one to ten years.

52. Mass.Gen.Laws Ann. c. 266, § 5A (1978). State v. Olsen, 43 Wn.2d 726, 263 P.2d 824 (1953).

53. Mass.Gen.Laws Ann. c. 266, § 49 (1968). The penalty is limited to two and one-half years.

54. 18 U.S.C.A. § 480 (1976).

55. This is true of the Massachusetts statute cited in note 52. The same label is applied in the corresponding California statute. West's Ann.Cal.Pen.Code § 455 (1979).

Two points are entitled to emphasis: (1) These and similar types of conduct do not come within the common-law concept of criminal attempt and are not punishable in the absence of statute; (2) it is becoming increasingly common for legislative enactment to provide a penalty (often a severe one) for what the common law regarded as an unpunishable act of preparation. The Model Penal Code would include in criminal attempt much that is held to be preparation under present law.[56]

B and K had a "contract on P" by which K was to kill P and receive $600 from B. At B's request K visited P in the hospital to give P a fake message. The purpose of the visit was to bring K and P close together to allow K to gain P's trust and confidence and thus enable him to be in a position to carry out the "contract." After this K became alarmed by the activity of the Alaska State Troopers and decided for his own safety to double-cross B and cooperate with the Troopers. K pretended to have carried out the "contract" and received part of the agreed payment from B. B was convicted of attempted murder. The conviction was affirmed on the ground that K's act of going to visit P in the hospital, to gain his trust and confidence, went beyond preparation and constituted an attempt.[57] The decision was under a statute which did not follow the wording of the Model Penal Code but was obviously thought to have something in common with it.[58] There was a vigorous dissent based on the conclusion that B was guilty of criminal solicitation rather than attempted murder.[59]

The preparatory-perpetrating dichotomy is useful in discussing situations of a rather general nature, but the actual dividing line between the two is shadowy in the extreme.[60] There is reason to believe that in close cases the decision is based upon other considerations and that the label attached is that appropriate to the conclusion reached—after it is reached.

4. STEP TOWARDS A CRIMINAL OFFENSE

An act which does not go beyond the bounds of preparation is not a "step towards a criminal offense," as this phrase has been used in the law, and hence is not sufficient for a common-law attempt. On the other hand, an act may be in the nature of a perpetrating act rather than a preparatory one, and yet fail to be a step towards a criminal offense for another reason. If what D has in mind to do does not constitute a crime, nothing done in the effort to accomplish his purpose can be an attempt to commit a crime.

56. Section 5.01.

57. Braham v. State, 571 P.2d 631 (Alaska 1977).

58. The court says: "We conclude that Koelzer's visit with Peterson in the hospital, at Braham's direction, was the doing of a direct, unequivocal 'act toward the commission of the crime' of murder within the meaning of AS 11.05.020, ..." Id. at p. 683. This, while not a quotation from the Model Penal Code, is suggestive of the language of its section 5.01.

59. Id. at p. 649. The dissent seems to have the better position.

60. A recent decision is especially illustrative of the subjectivity of the distinction. An Illinois court overturned a jury finding of attempted rape where defendant entered the victim's home without authority, placed a knife at her throat, forced the victim to lie on the floor while defendant unzipped his pants and unbuckled his belt but then heard a noise and fled. The court concluded that although the acts manifested an intent to rape there was no "substantial step toward the commission of rape." People v. Clerk, 68 Ill.App.3d 1021, 25 Ill.Dec. 359, 364, 386 N.E.2d 630, 635 (1979).

"It is the well settled rule that there cannot be a conviction for an attempt to commit a crime unless the attempt, if completed, would have constituted a crime." [61] In other words, if **D** has accomplished everything he had in mind to do he is either guilty of a complete substantive offense or he is not guilty even of a criminal attempt.

A negotiable-instrument case offers a typical example. If such an instrument states the amount in both words and figures a fraudulent change in the figures without change of the words is not forgery. The reason is that when there is a discrepancy between the words and the figures, the words control, hence a change of the figures only does not change the purported amount and hence is an immaterial change. It follows that he who fraudulently made this change is not guilty of attempted forgery if that was the only change he intended to make,[62] because the definition of attempt requires that the completed act intended be a crime.

Down through the years has been echoed a statement to the effect that shooting at a post supposed to be a man does not constitute an attempt to commit murder. And while the statement has been perpetuated largely by dicta [63] and by text-writers,[64] it has become so firmly established in the framework of the common law that Holmes, in speaking of what does not constitute a criminal attempt, emphasized this by reference to the "classic instance of shooting at a post supposed to be a man."[65] The result is also implicit in our present procedure because a charge of attempted murder requires the same specificity as that of murder—it is as essential to specify the intended victim in an indictment for attempted murder as to specify the one actually killed in a murder indictment.[66]

---

61. State v. Weleck, 10 N.J. 355, 372, 91 A.2d 751, 760 (1952). If no criminal liability would attach upon completion the attempt is not a crime. State v. Stone, 83 N.J.L. 14, 84 A. 1063 (1912). "Steps . . . on the way to the doing of something, which is thereafter done, and which is no crime, cannot be regarded as attempts to commit a crime." Rex v. Percy Dalton, Ltd., 33 Cr.App.R. 102, 110 (1949).

". . . to be guilty of an attempt the end intended to be accomplished would have to constitute a crime if permitted to proceed to its ultimate end . . ." Martin v. People, 179 Colo. 237, 499 P.2d 606, 608 (1972).

62. Wilson v. State, 85 Miss. 687, 38 So. 46 (1905). This case receives additional attention infra, under "intent." See also supra, chapter 4, section 8, B, 6.

63. Baron Bramwell had spoken of striking at a block of wood supposed to be a man, with intent to murder. Regina v. McPherson, Dears. & B, 197, 201, 169 Eng.Rep. 975, 976 (1857).

64. E. g., "The most curious point on this subject is the question whether if a man . . . shoots at a figure which he falsely supposes to be a man with intent

to murder a man, . . . he has committed an attempt to murder. . . . By the existing law he has committed no offence at all. . . ." 2 Stephen, History of the Criminal Law, 225 (1883). Quoted with approval, 1 Burdick, Law of Crime 189 (1946).

65. Commonwealth v. Kennedy, 170 Mass. 18, 20, 48 N.E. 770 (1897).

Under the New York Revised Penal Code it is not a defense to a charge of attempted murder that the victim was already dead when the attempt was made. If it cannot be shown beyond a reasonable doubt that the victim was alive at the time, there can be no conviction of murder, but the defendant can be convicted of attempted murder if he thought the victim was alive when he shot him. People v. Dlugash, 41 N.Y.2d 725, 395 N.Y.S.2d 419, 363 N.E.2d 1155 (1977).

66. If the name of a murdered victim is unknown he could be identified by the familiar "John Doe whose true name is unknown." The same device could be used if D was seen to shoot at an intended victim who got away and whose name was unknown. But the reference would be to one particular human being. Our present pleading would not permit a

One who has shot at a post thinking it was a human being deserves to be punished severely, but this should not induce a court to punish for what was not clearly recognized as a crime when done. There should be no departure from *nullem crimen, nulla poena, sine lege* (there is no crime and no punishment without a law). The correction should be by statute.

It was said obiter: "If an assault should be made on a man dressed as a woman with intent to ravish, the assailant believing the person to be assaulted to be a woman, he could not be convicted of an attempt to ravish, . . ." [67] In fact, our present rules of pleading would not permit an indictment charging **D** with an "attempt to rape John Doe believing him to be a woman."

To suggest impossibility of achievement as the reason for holding that such acts do not constitute a criminal attempt would lead to confusion in other situations. The thought has been that no such act constitutes a step in the direction of the offense said to have been attempted.[68] Suppose we have more facts in the "shooting" case.

D decides to murder **X**. With this in mind **D** studies **X**'s habits, and finds that at exactly ten o'clock each evening when the weather is fair, **X** leaves his house and goes to a woods nearby where he spends thirty minutes or so "communing with nature." **D** decides to take advantage of this habit. One night when the moon is nearly full, **D** goes to this woods just before ten o'clock and conceals himself there. Just on the hour **X** leaves his house and approaches this place. As **X** enters the woods **D** draws his pistol, and when **X** is within range **D** prepares to take aim. Just then, however, a cloud covers the moon and, within the woods, it is too dark to see. As the cloud thins, light begins to filter through the foliage and **D** sees an object nearby which he mistakes for **X**. He has no doubt on this score because he had heard footsteps in that general direction a few moments earlier. At close range **D** takes aim and puts a bullet into this object—which turns out to be a tree stump of about the size and shape of a man. **X** himself was within easy range at the moment but in a different direction.

Did shooting at that stump constitute an attempt to murder **X**? The answer is that it is part of the evidence of such an attempt but that **D** was guilty of an attempt to murder **X** before the shot was fired and could properly be convicted of the attempt if arrested without having pulled the trigger.

From situations such as those mentioned an analogy has been drawn to cases of attempting to receive stolen property. One is not guilty of receiving stolen property if what he receives is not in that category, although believed to be so.[69] And it has been held that because of this fact his receipt of such

---

charge of an attempt to murder "what was supposed to be a human being but turned out to be a post."

67. People v. Gardner, 73 Hun 66, 70–1, 25 N.Y.S. 1072, 1075–76 (1893). This decision was reversed. People v. Gardner, 144 N.Y. 119, 38 N.E. 1003 (1894). But the reversal had no bearing on the dictum.

68. The reason given by Stephen to explain the instance of shooting at a figure falsely supposed to be a man is that

it "cannot be regarded as an attempt because the thing actually done was in no way connected with the purpose intended to be effected." 2 Stephen, History of Criminal Law 225 (1883).

69. People v. Rojas, 55 Cal.2d 252, 10 Cal.Rptr. 465, 358 P.2d 921 (1961). The House of Lords has recently reaffirmed this position in English law. Houghton v. Smith [1973] 3 All ER 1109 (H.L.), 58 Cr.App.R. 1988 (1973).

property cannot constitute an attempt to receive stolen property.[70]   Much could be said for this position if nothing was involved except the purchase of property under such circumstances that the buyer firmly, but mistakenly, believed it to be stolen.   More was involved, however, in these cases.   Property had in fact been stolen, the thief and **D** had made arrangements for **D** to receive it and **D** did receive it.   In the meantime the thief had been apprehended and the property recovered.   After it had thus lost its stolen character it was returned to the thief to carry out the original plan.   The courts overlooked everything except the very last step by which the property was actually handed over.   **D** had gone beyond preparation and moved in the direction of receiving stolen property before that last step and should have been convicted—as was held in another case.[71]

Reference to certain other situations may be helpful.   S, having stolen a large quantity of copper wire, concealed it in a certain park.   Finding **D** receptive, S offered to sell **D** the wire, and after some dickering a "deal" was reached.   S told **D** to obtain transportation and something to cover the wire, offering to go with him and show him the place of concealment.   **D** rented a horse and wagon, obtained a large canvas to conceal the wire, and started out with S to procure the "loot."   In the meantime officers had discovered the copper wire and taken it away so the "cupboard was bare" when **D** and S arrived at the place.   They searched diligently and were obviously disappointed in not finding the wire.   **D**'s conviction of an attempt to receive stolen property was affirmed.[72]   In the words of the court, "when he drove to the place where the goods had been concealed he committed the overt act that made the offense complete." [73]   Needless to add, had the officers returned the wire to the cache when they put the place under surveillance, and permitted **D** to take possession of it before arresting him, his going there to get it would have been no less an attempt.   This is quite in line with the holding that if **D**, intending to murder **X**, goes for that purpose to the place where he intends to find him, he is guilty of attempted murder even if **X** is not there.[74]

In one case of attempt to receive there had been no larceny whatever.   **D**, wanting to obtain from the telephone company certain property which was not for sale, approached an employee of the company in the effort to have it stolen.   The employee pretended to "go along" with the plan but reported it to his superiors who directed him to inform **D** that another employee would

---

70.   People v. Jaffe, 185 N.Y. 497, 78 N.E. 169 (1906); People v. Rollino, 37 Misc.2d 14, 233 N.Y.S.2d 580 (1962); Booth v. State, 398 P.2d 863 (Okl.App. 1964).

If he received the property believing it was stolen he could be convicted of an attempt to receive under a differently-worded statute.   People v. Holloway, 193 Colo. 450, 568 P.2d 29 (1977).   Compare, People v. Leichtweis, 59 A.D.2d 383, 399 N.Y.S.2d 439, 441–42 (1977).

71.   People v. Rojas, 55 Cal.2d 252, 10 Cal.Rptr. 465, 358 P.2d 921 (1961); State v. Carner, 25 Ariz.App. 156, 541 P.2d 947 (1975); People v. Darr, 193 Colo. 445, 568 P.2d 32 (1977).

If D believed the property was stolen he may be convicted of an attempt to receive stolen property even if it never was stolen.   State v. Sommers, 569 P.2d 1110 (Utah 1977).

One who receives property that had been stolen but recovered by or for the owner, may not be convicted of receiving stolen property, but may be convicted of the attempt.   Bandy v. State, 575 S.W.2d 278 (Tenn.1979).

72.   In re Magidson, 32 Cal.App. 566, 163 P. 689 (1917).

73.   Id. at 568, 163 P. at 690.

74.   Stokes v. State, 92 Miss. 415, 46 So. 627 (1908).

get in touch with him. **S**, a special agent of the company, was introduced to **D** and inquired what he had in mind, pretending to be an employee who was interested. **D** told **S** what he wanted and offered to pay $500 for the property, and was in no way deterred when told that what he had in mind was a felony. After several meetings to discuss the suggested larceny, it was agreed that at the next meeting the stolen property would be delivered to **D** for the stipulated $500. At that meeting **D** was handed a "dummy" package and promptly arrested when he accepted it and paid the agreed price.[75] It would have been quite unrealistic to have held that these vigorous steps in the effort to receive stolen property did not constitute an attempt to do so. The only question to be expected is whether the proper offense was charged in this case. After **D**'s earnest solicitation he would have been guilty of larceny had that offense resulted. The perpetrator of larceny cannot be convicted of receiving the very property he himself has stolen.[76] But one whose guilt at common law would have been that of an accessory before the fact is not subject to this incapacity.[77] **D** would have been guilty of receiving stolen property if it had in fact been stolen and the charge of attempting to receive was proper in this case.

In a comparable case **D**, after elaborate pains to procure heroin unlawfully, was given a package containing talcum powder instead of the expected contents. A conviction of an attempt to violate the narcotic act was upheld.[78]

Deeply intrenched in the common law is the principle that conviction of crime cannot be based upon intent alone [79] and there seems to be no reason to change this even by legislation. This raises the question of "inconsistent intents." At times one has two different intents which seem only one to him but are so inconsistent that only one is possible of achievement. Such a situation arises if **S** is discussing a sale with **B** under the impression that he is **C**.

---

75. People v. Meyers, 213 Cal.App.2d 518, 28 Cal.Rptr. 753 (1963). The statement that **D** was given a "dummy" package is not quite accurate. The package contained the very property **D** wanted to get except that it had not been stolen and was not intended for **D** to keep. It might as well have contained old newspapers so far as **D** was concerned because he was not permitted to keep it long enough to open it.

"The law is well settled that one who buys property believing it to be stolen is guilty of a criminal attempt to receive stolen property even though the property is not in fact stolen." Shadle v. City of Corona, 96 Cal.App.3d 173, 157 Cal.Rptr. 624, 628 (1979).

"He intended to buy stolen property and he tendered money in exchange for the property tendered to him. Under our statute and the modern decisional law, he has no defense that the property turned out not to be stolen." State v. Davidson, 20 Wn.App. 893, 584 P.2d 401, 404 (1978).

76. McGee v. State, 60 Okl.Cr. 436, 65 P.2d 207 (1937); Hair v. State, 294 P.2d 846 (Okl.Cr.1956); Coates v. State, 249 Ind. 357, 229 N.E.2d 640 (1967).

77. State v. Tindall, 213 S.C. 484, 50 S.E.2d 188 (1948). This is not changed by a statute which authorizes the accessory to be charged as a principal. State v. Boyd, 195 Iowa 1091, 191 N.W. 84 (1922).

78. People v. Siu, 126 Cal.App.2d 41, 271 P.2d 575 (1954).

The Florida Court assumed that one cannot be convicted of attempting to receive stolen property, at common law, without proof that it was stolen, but added: "Florida law now clearly authorizes such attempt convictions under Sections 812.019 and 777.04." Padgett v. State, 378 So.2d 118, 119 (Fla.App. 1980).

79. State v. Quick, 199 S.C. 256, 19 S.E.2d 101 (1942). "The mere intent to commit a crime is not a crime." State v. Rider, 90 Mo. 54, 1 S.W. 825 (1886). "But, as this . . . is an act of the mind, it cannot possibly fall under any judicial cognizance, unless it be demonstrated by some open or *overt* act." 4 Bl.Comm. 79.

S intends to deal with **B**, the man actually there. He also intends to deal with **C**, a man known to him to be a reputable merchant, but known only by reputation. In such a situation the law regards one intent as primary and the other as secondary and only the primary intent controls as to direct and immediate consequences. And in the situation mentioned the law regards the primary intent as that to deal with the man actually there in person rather than with the name of one who is not there. Hence if a sale is completed the title will pass to **B**.[80] If **B** was guilty of fraud, in pretending to be **C**, **S** may have the sale rescinded if he acts before title has passed to a bona-fide purchaser for value and without notice, but that is a collateral matter and not the direct result.

It has been said that if **D** takes his own umbrella, thinking it belongs to another and with intent to steal, this does not constitute an attempt to commit larceny.[81] Here also we find utterly inconsistent intents unrealized by the actor. He intends to take a particular umbrella (which actually belongs to him). He also has in mind the intent to steal the umbrella of another. His primary intent is to take the umbrella he actually seizes and hence there is nothing wrongful in what is actually done but only in his secondary, inconsistent intent. Hence in such a situation, if there is nothing in his conduct either preceding or following the taking, which manifests a criminal purpose he should not be held guilty of attempted larceny. To convict him merely because he admitted his mistaken notion at a later time would be to convict him on intent alone. But this does not mean that he should not be convicted of attempt to steal if his conduct at the time of the transaction clearly manifested a criminal purpose.

O was convicted of the attempted distribution of heroin. He had a substance which he said was heroin and offered to sell to one who happened to be an undercover agent. The agent said he would buy but would first have to test the substance. The test gave a positive result whereupon the agent promptly arrested **O**. Later a more careful test showed that the substance was not heroin but an uncontrolled substance. At the trial **O** testified that he knew the substance was not heroin and was merely intending to perpetrate a "rip off." The jury did not believe him and found him guilty under an instruction that he was guilty if he believed the substance was heroin. This was reversed because what **O** actually did, "the objective acts performed," do not establish guilt of the offense charged.[82] What he actually did, plus his statement that he was intending a "rip off," was sufficient to establish his guilt of attempted false pretenses, but he was not charged with that offense. In a later case which was much the same except that defendant's intent to sell cocaine was clearly established (he admitted it) a conviction of attempt was affirmed although the substance was not cocaine.[83]

80. Williston, Sales § 635 (Rev. ed. 1948).

81. Per Bramwell, B., in Regina v. Collins, 9 Cox C.C. 497, 498 (1864). The decision (that there can be no attempted larceny by reaching into an empty pocket) was later overruled. Regina v. Ring, 17 Cox C.C. 491 (1892). But the dictum was not questioned.

82. United States v. Oviedo, 525 F.2d 881 (5th Cir. 1976).

R was properly convicted of attempted sale of drugs even though the "drugs" sold proved not to be a controlled substance. People v. Reap, 68 A.D.2d 964, 414 N.Y.S.2d 775 (1979).

83. United States v. Hough, 561 F.2d 594 (5th Cir. 1977). **R** was properly convicted of attempted sale of drugs even though the "drugs" sold proved not to be a controlled substance. People v. Reap, 68 A.D.2d 964, 414 N.Y.S.2d 775 (1979).

Some jurisdictions have enacted special provisions creating the offense of delivering or possessing with intent to deliver any substance represented to be a controlled substance in order to cover instances where the seller or transferor delivers a non-controlled substance having no intent to deliver a controlled substance.[84]

M was convicted of an attempt to possess dangerous drugs. In affirming the conviction the court said:

"The defendant believed he had the ability to accomplish the crime of possession, and the fact that the pills were not dangerous drugs does not erase his attempt to possess. Mere intent alone does not amount to an 'attempt' . . . but intent plus conduct toward the commission of a crime may be an attempt." [85]

An additional point may be mentioned. If, without justification, excuse or mitigation, **D** shoots at **Y** with intent to kill, thinking **Y** is **X**, **D** is guilty of attempt to murder. But the attempt is to murder **Y** and not **X**.[86] The attempt is to murder the man who would have been murdered had the attempt been successful. This leads to an interesting possibility. If, with intent to murder **X**, **D** went to **X**'s back yard where he expected to find him he was guilty of attempt to murder **X** when **D** arrived there. If **X** was not there at the time but **D** saw **Y** there and shot, thinking it was **X**, that shot constituted an attempt to murder **Y**. Under these facts **D** seems to have attempted to murder both **X** and **Y**, but under other circumstances the shot at **Y** thinking **Y** was **X** would not constitute two attempts to murder.

5. IMPOSSIBILITY

No sane person ever really attempts to do what he knows is impossible. He may make futile gestures or motions with no thought of success, but any real attempt indicates a hope and hence a belief in the possibility of achievement even if the expectation thereof is slight. No one, it may be added, has lived long without having attempted, time and again, to do something which he learned later it was impossible for him to do. It would be quite unreasonable to take the view that any actual barrier to success, however much undetected at the moment, would prevent legal recognition of an attempt to commit a crime regardless of other circumstances. And the common law takes no such position [87] despite an occasional decision[88] or loose statement in an

21 U.S.C.A. § 846 punishes an attempt to commit an offense under the Federal Comprehensive Drug Abuse Prevention and Control Act of 1970.

84. Smith-Hurd Ill.Ann.Stat. 56½ § 1404 (1973). Under such a statute the offense is a separate substantive offense distinct from the sale or possession of a controlled substance. People v. Robinson, 7 Ill.App.3d 704, 288 N.E.2d 484 (1972).

85. State v. McElroy, 128 Ariz. 315, 625 P.2d 904, 906 (1981).

86. **D** "meant to murder the man at whom he shot." Per Parke, B., in Regina

v. Smith, Dears. 560, 169 Eng.Rep. 845 (1855).

87. State v. Mandel, 78 Ariz. 226, 278 P.2d 413 (1954); State v. Wilson, 30 Conn. 500 (1862); Commonwealth v. Williams, 312 Mass. 553, 45 N.E.2d 740 (1942); Commonwealth v. McDonald, 59 Mass. 365 (1850); People v. Jones, 46 Mich. 441 (1881); People v. Moran, 123 N.Y. 254, 25 N.E. 412 (1890); State v. Glover, 27 S.C. 602, 4 S.E. 564 (1887); State v. Wiley, 52 S.D. 110, 216 N.W. 866 (1927).

88. Regina v. Collins, 9 Cox C.C. 497 (1864). Overruled in Regina v. Ring, 17 Cox C.C. 491 (1892).

opinion.[89]   Recent statutory provisions in several jurisdictions have followed the Model Penal Code format [90] or used similar language providing that an attempt involves a "substantial step" "or any act" or the like towards the planned criminal end.[91]   The effect of these statutes is to lighten the standard necessary for an attempt over the common-law rule and some courts have expressed such a conclusion.[92]

One does not attempt to commit a crime which he knows he cannot perpetrate because there is no real intention to do what is known to be impossible.[93]   And it is generally assumed that an attempt will not be recognized if success was obviously impossible,—as if an effort is made to kill another by witchcraft.[94]

89. For example: "It is a legal solecism to say that a person can intend to do what he is physically impotent to do." State v. Sam, 60 N.C. 293, 294 (1864). The decision itself was sound. It held merely that if the act of sexual intercourse with a woman without her consent is not rape if the assailant is under fourteen years of age, it is also not an assault with intent to commit rape. In other words, an intent to do what is not rape is not an intent to commit rape. This does not support a generalization which suggests, for example, that one cannot intend to lift a certain rock if it is physically impossible for him to do so. "There was, therefore, a serious question whether a man could attempt to discharge a firearm which in fact could not possibly be discharged." The Queen v. Duckworth, [1892] 2 Q.B. 83, 86. The indictment was under a statute making it a felony to attempt to discharge a loaded firearm at another. And the holding was that the act charged was not committed unless the attempt was with a loaded firearm.

90. § 5.01.

91. Colorado   Rev.Stat.   1973, 18–2–101; 11 Del.Code Ann. § 531 (1979); West's Fla.Stat.Ann. § 777.04 (1976); Burns Ind.Stat.Ann. § 35–41–5–2 (1979); Kan.Stat. § 21–3301 (1974); ". . . tends to effect . . .," McKinney's Consol.Laws N.Y. Penal § 110.00 (1975).

92. Where the defendant was convicted of attempted receiving stolen property where the property was not stolen it was said:

"Corrective legislation usually takes a form similar to the Model Penal Code or the New York Penal Code's formulations of an attempt statute. These statutes define three elements of the offense of attempt: (1) culpability required to commit the completed offense; (2) intent to commit the offense; and (3) a substantial step toward completion of the offense." Darr v. People, 193 Colo. 445, 568 P.2d 32, 33–34 (1977).

"We agree with the trial judge that proof of the stolen character of the goods was not essential to proof of the offense of endeavoring to traffic in stolen property. Section 812.019 was enacted . . . as part of a broad revision of laws relating to theft and stolen property. . . . At common law one could not be convicted of attempting to receive stolen property absent proof that the property was stolen. Florida law now clearly authorizes such attempt convictions. . . ." Padgett v. State, 378 So.2d 118, 119 (Fla. App. 1980).

93. State v. Ballamah, 28 N.M. 212, 210 P. 391 (1922). In holding that there could be an assault with intent to kill although the gun was unloaded the court added obiter that this would not be true if the defendant knew it was unloaded. Mullen v. State, 45 Ala. 43 (1871).

94. "If a statute simply made it a felony to attempt to kill any human being, or to conspire to do so, an attempt by means of witchcraft, or a conspiracy to kill by means of charms and incantations, would not be an offence within such a statute. The poverty of language compels one to say 'an attempt to kill by means of witchcraft,' but such an attempt is really no attempt at all to kill. It is true the sin or wickedness may be as great as an attempt or conspiracy by competent means; but human laws are made, not to punish sin, but to prevent crime and mischief." Per Pollock, C. B., in The Attorney General v. Sillem, 2 H. & C. 431, 525–6, 159 Eng.Rep. 178, 221 (1863).

It can hardly be said, however, that such an assumption has been firmly established as a part of the common law. Probably it could seldom be established that one going through the motions of witchcraft was doing more than venting his wrath in the form of symbolic make-believe, with no actual expectation of fatal consequences. But if there was convincing evidence that he actually expected his actions to result in the death of his enemy there seems to be no reason why he should not be convicted of an attempt to murder him.

"Bishop says: 'Assuming the necessary intent to exist, the act must have some adaptation also to accomplish the particular thing intended. But the adaptation need be only apparent. . . . when the impediment is of a nature to be wholly unknown to the offender, who used appropriate means, the criminal attempt is committed.' " [95]

He "cannot protect himself from responsibility by showing that, by reason of some fact unknown to him at the time of his criminal attempt, it could not be fully carried into effect in that particular instance." [96]

Certain situations must be distinguished. If attempting to discharge a *loaded* gun at another is made a felony by statute, this offense is not established by proof of an effort to shoot a person with a gun that was not loaded.[97] This is not for any lack of the attempt but because the attempt was not made with a loaded gun. And if the statutory penalty is for attempting to discharge a loaded gun at another by drawing the trigger, a conviction of this offense is not authorized if the attempt was frustrated before any effort to draw the trigger,[98] although it may have gone far enough for an assault even without proof that the weapon was loaded.[99] An effort to shoot another with a shotgun, within shotgun range, is an assault whether the weapon was loaded or not,—but is not an assault "with a dangerous weapon" if it was unloaded.[1] If a statute punishes the administration of a noxious thing with intent to kill, the substance administered must be poisonous.[2] In a prosecution under a statute forbidding the attempt to procure the abortion of

---

95. Mullen v. State, 45 Ala. 43, 45 (1871). And see Kunkle v. State, 32 Ind. 220, 232 (1869).

96. Hamilton v. State, 36 Ind. 280, 286 (1871). Accord, People v. Cummings, 141 Cal.App.2d 193, 296 P.2d 610 (1956).

Defendant was properly convicted of attempting to purchase marijuana where he unknowingly received a bag of grass clippings. Police v. Jay [1974] 2 NZLR 204.

In R. v. Donnelly [1970] NZLR 980, 990 it was observed: "He who sets out to commit a crime may in the event fall short of complete commission of that crime for any one of a number of reasons . . . Fourth, he may suffer no such outside interference, but may fail to complete the commission of the crime through ineptitude, inefficiency or insufficient means. The jemmy which he has brought with him may not be strong enough to force the window open." This would not preclude conviction for attempt.

97. Rex v. Carr, Russ. & Ry. 377, 168 Eng.Rep. 854 (1819); Regina v. James, 1 Car. & K. 530, 174 Eng.Rep. 924 (1844); Regina v. Gamble, 10 Cox C.C. 545 (1867).

98. Regina v. Lewis, 9 Car. & P. 523, 173 Eng.Rep. 940 (1840); Regina v. St. George, 9 Car. & P. 483, 173 Eng.Rep. 921 (1840). St. George was overruled in The Queen v. Duckworth, [1892] 2 Q.B. 83, but this was because the evidence indicated that defendant had tried to pull the trigger. *Lewis*, in which defendant was disarmed before he had his weapon aimed, was approved.

99. In St. George, supra, Baron Parke said the defendant could be convicted of assault, even if the weapon was not loaded, although he could not be so convicted under that indictment.

1. State v. Wiley, 52 S.D. 110, 216 N.W. 866 (1927).

2. Rex v. Powles, 4 Car. & P. 571, 172 Eng.Rep. 830 (1831). And if it is harmful only in a large quantity a small amount

"any pregnant woman" there can be no conviction without proof of pregnancy.[3] This is not with any thought that the law must ignore an attempt whenever it is subsequently learned that success was impossible. It is because
there has been no violation of this particular statute unless the woman was
pregnant. Embracery is an attempt corruptly to influence a juror. Guilt of
this offense cannot be established by proof of threats and promises made to
one mistakenly thought to be a juror.[4] The reason is simply that an attempt
corruptly to influence one who is not a juror is not within the definition of
embracery.

Where the case is not controlled by limitations in the wording of a particular statute or the definition of a particular offense, the mere fact that the
effort is bound to fail for some reason unknown to the actor at the time,
does not prevent recognition of a criminal attempt. If, for example, the statute prohibits an attempt to procure the abortion of "any woman," guilt may
be established by proof of such an attempt upon a woman who was not pregnant,[5] if it is clear that the wrongdoer thought she was and acted with the
intention of producing a miscarriage. An attempt to commit murder by administration of a drug does not require that enough be used to endanger
life.[6] A man may be guilty of attempted rape although by reason of extreme age he has lost the ability to engage in the sexual relation [7] if he is not
aware of incapacity.[8] And one may be guilty of attempted larceny by reaching into an empty pocket [9] or an empty cash drawer.[10]

will not do. Regina v. Hennah, 13 Cox
C.C. 547 (1877). It is otherwise if the
statute says "any substance." State v.
Barrett, 197 Iowa 769, 198 N.W. 36
(1924).

3. State v. Stewart, 52 Iowa 284, 3
N.W. 99 (1879); State v. Sturchio, 131
N.J.L. 256, 36 A.2d 301 (1944). If a statute makes the use of tools, with intent to
procure a miscarriage, the substantive
offense, an attempt to make such use is
punishable as an attempt. People v. Berger, 131 Cal.App.2d 127, 280 P.2d 136
(1955).

4. State v. Porter, 125 Mont. 503, 242
P.2d 984 (1952). One who has been summoned as a juror is a juror for the purpose of this offense. People v. Connors,
70 Cal.App. 315, 233 P. 362 (1924);
Calvaresi v. United States, 216 F.2d 891
(10th Cir. 1954).

5. People v. Cummings, 141 Cal.App.
2d 193, 296 P.2d 610 (1956); Urga v.
State, 155 Fla. 86, 20 So.2d 685 (1944);
Commonwealth v. Aronson, 330 Mass.
453, 115 N.E.2d 362 (1953); Commonwealth v. Surles, 165 Mass. 59, 42 N.E.
502 (1895); People v. Axelsen, 223 N.Y.
650, 119 N.E. 708 (1918).

6. State v. Glover, 27 S.C. 602, 4 S.E.
564 (1887). The indictment in this case
was for assault with intent to kill. An

attempt to commit an offense and an as-
sault with intent to commit it are not
identical, as explained infra in the text.
But the difference is not at this point.
Accord with Glover, Rex v. Havard, 11
Cr.App.R. 2 (1914).

7. Hunt v. State, 114 Ark. 239, 169
S.W. 773 (1914); Territory v. Keyes, 5
Dak. 244, 38 N.W. 440 (1888); State v.
Bartlett, 127 Iowa 689, 104 N.W. 285
(1905). These also were charges of assault with intent. See the preceding
note.

8. State v. Ballamah, 28 N.M. 212, 210
P. 391 (1922); Waters v. State, 234 A.2d
147 (Md.App.1967); State v. Nicholson,
77 Wn.2d 415, 463 P.2d 633 (1969); Berg
v. State, 41 Wis.2d 729, 165 N.W.2d 189
(1969).

9. Commonwealth v. Williams, 312
Mass. 553, 45 N.E.2d 740 (1942).

10. Clark v. State, 86 Tenn. 511, 8
S.W. 145 (1888).

The fact that the television set purchased by defendant from an undercover
agent was not stolen property did not
preclude defendant from being convicted
of an attempt to receive stolen property.
State v. Sommers, 569 P.2d 1110 (Utah
1977).

The question may be asked: Why is reaching into an empty pocket not ruled out as an attempt to commit larceny on the theory that it is not a step in the direction of larceny? And it must be conceded that when this problem was first presented to the English court the holding was that it was not an attempt.[11] This decision, however, was later overruled,[12] and the courts in this country have consistently held that the wrongful act of reaching into another's pocket with intent to steal whatever may be found, is an attempt to commit larceny even if the pocket is empty.[13]

Illuminating is a type of case falling close to the field of false pretenses. D has made false representations to X for the fraudulent purpose of obtaining money and has actually received the money although X, being familiar with the facts, knew the statements were false. The crime of false pretenses has not been committed because X was not deceived, but X's knowledge was an impediment wholly unknown to D and hence D is guilty of an attempt to obtain money by false pretenses because he has taken a step in the direction of that offense with the intention of committing it.[14] This does not conflict with the rule stated above that one who has fully accomplished his purpose is either guilty of a complete offense or is not guilty of even an attempt to commit it, because an essential part of D's plan was to deceive X and that he failed to do. The handing over of the money was merely to strengthen the evidence and D would have been just as guilty of the attempt if X had refused to pay. D's being frustrated by X's knowledge in such a case would be no more significant than if an attempt to commit murder was frustrated by an unseen bullet-proof vest.

The assault cases have tended to cause some confusion in this regard because a number of the statutes define criminal assault in terms of an attempt to commit a battery "coupled with a present ability" [15] or the like.

---

11. Regina v. Collins, 9 Cox C.C. 497 (1865).

An attempt to commit larceny may be committed although the coin-box was in fact empty. Gargan v. State, 436 P.2d 968 (Alaska 1968).

12. Regina v. Ring, 17 Cox C.C. 491 (1892).

13. State v. Wilson, 30 Conn. 500 (1862); Commonwealth v. Williams, 312 Mass. 553, 45 N.E.2d 740 (1942); Commonwealth v. McDonald, 59 Mass. 365 (1850); People v. Jones, 46 Mich. 441, 9 N.W. 486 (1881); People v. Moran, 123 N.Y. 254, 25 N.E. 412 (1890); Rogers v. Commonwealth, 5 Serg. & R. 463 (Pa. 1820).

14. Commonwealth v. Johnson, 312 Pa. 140, 167 A. 344 (1933); Regina v. Hensler, 11 Cox C.C. 570 (1870); Rex v. Light, 11 Cr.App.R. 111 (1915). Accord, People v. Gardner, 144 N.Y. 119, 38 N.E. 1003 (1894). And see People v. Camodeca, 52 Cal.2d 142, 338 P.2d 903 (1959).

The defendant could not be found guilty of obtaining property by false pretenses if the victim knew his representation was false, but this is no defense to a charge of attempting to obtain property by false pretenses. State v. Greenberg, 154 N.J.Super. 564, 382 A.2d 58 (1977).

Mack was convicted of theft of lost property. The evidence showed that two boys went to his store and offered to sell him a diamond ring. They said they had found it in the park. Mack paid them $25 for the ring. The evidence also showed that the boys had not found the ring in the park, but one of them had taken it from his mother. Mack had made no effort to find the owner. It was held that he was not properly convicted of theft of lost property, since it was stolen rather than lost. But since he thought it was lost the conviction was remanded for resentencing for the crime of attempted theft of lost property. State v. Mack, 31 Or.App. 59, 569 P.2d 624 (1977).

15. E. g., West's Ann.Cal.Pen.Code § 240 (1970). Idaho Code § 18–901 (1979); Nev.Rev.Stat. 200.400 (1979).

Anything which makes the intended battery impossible under the circumstances, however much unsuspected by the actor, will prevent his effort from constituting an assault under such a statute. This is not because of the law of attempt but is due solely to the limitation in the enactment. In fact, the presence of such a clause is enlightening; it would not be needed if there could be no attempt without present ability. And an assault does not require present ability if there is no such limitation in the statute.[16] The point has been raised frequently in connection with an unloaded gun,—when used as a firearm and not as a club. If the statutory definition of criminal assault requires present ability, an attempt to shoot another with an unloaded weapon does not constitute this offense.[17] It is otherwise where this clause is omitted, or is defined in terms of a threat of force or attempting to put another in fear of injury.

"If he believed it was loaded and intended to fire it at the person assaulted, he was guilty of an assault with intent to commit great bodily injury, although in fact and contrary to his belief it was not loaded." [18]

It should be recognized that impossibility really has no bearing upon the question of attempt unless it is a case of legal impossibility. Legal impossibility has been distinguished from factual impossibility.[19] The position is that while factual impossibility of success does not prevent the attempt from being made, there can be no attempt in a case involving legal impossibility. What it boils down to is this: Attempting to do what is not a crime is not attempting to commit a crime.[20]

It is provided in the Model Penal Code: "A person is guilty of an attempt to commit a crime if, acting with the kind of culpability otherwise required for the commission of the crime, he: (a) purposely engages in conduct which would constitute the crime if the attendant circumstances were as he believes them to be; . . . ."[21]

16. State v. Wiley, 52 S.D. 110, 216 N.W. 866 (1927). The opinion gives a good discussion of the two types of statute.

17. People v. Sylva, 143 Cal. 62, 76 P. 814 (1904); Klein v. State, 9 Ind.App. 365, 36 N.E. 763 (1893); Nolen v. State, 45 Ala.App. 206, 228 So.2d 33 (1969).

18. State v. Mitchell, 139 Iowa 455, 459, 116 N.W. 808, 810 (1908). In a felony trial, in which the facts did not support the felony charged, Baron Parke was clear that defendant would be guilty of an assault if he tried to shoot the other, even if the weapon was not loaded,— although he could not be convicted of this assault in that trial. Regina v. St. George, 9 Car. & P. 483, 173 Eng.Rep. 921 (1840).

19. "In the instant case there was no legal impossibility of consummating the offense, only a factual impossibility— . . . ." Commonwealth v. Johnson, 312 Pa. 140, 147, 167 A. 344, 346 (1933).

20. "The statute does not impose criminal liability, however, in a related situation: where the defendant intended to do an act which he mistakenly believed to be a crime, but which has not been made criminal." State v. Davidson, 20 Wn.App. 893, 584 P.2d 401, 404 (1978).

"Factual impossibility refers to those situations in which a circumstance or condition, unknown to the defendant, renders physically impossible the consummation of his intended criminal conduct. Thus, the oft-cited example of the would-be thief who attempts to pick an empty pocket. . . .

"Legal impossibility refers to those situations in which the intended acts, even if successfully carried out, would not amount to a crime. Thus, attempt is not unlawful where success is not a crime, and this is true even though the defendant believes his scheme to be criminal." United States v. Frazier, 560 F.2d 884, 888 (8th Cir. 1977).

21. Section 5.01(1).

An attempt to kill a dead man is attempt under N.Y. Penal Law § 110.10 (McKinney 1975) which is similar to the

This would permit conviction of an attempt to commit a crime although its perpetration was legally impossible, which seems unsound. Something has to be said about legal impossibility because the phrase has resulted in extreme confusion. If it is said, for example, that it is legally impossible to receive stolen property if no property has been stolen, this may be supported, in a sense, but such an approach prevents any meaningful distinction between legal and factual impossibility, because it does not require an argument to show that it is factually impossible to receive stolen property if there is no such property to be received.[22]

Under the common law of England a boy under the age of fourteen years is incapable of perpetrating the crime of rape. In this country some states have adopted this rule and some have not.[23] In a state in which a thirteen-year-old boy is incapable of perpetrating rape this is obviously a legal impossibility because factual possibilities are the same in one state as in another. This offers the clue to the proper usage of the phrase "legal impossibility." It should be applied only in those cases in which the actor lacks the criminal capacity to commit the crime in question. Where the English rule prevails, since it is legally impossible for a boy under fourteen to commit rape, his attempt to have sexual intercourse with a woman against her will is not an attempt to commit rape.[24] His attempt is to do something which is not rape—namely battery.

Other situations may be mentioned. Under the common law a partner is legally incapable of committing larceny[25] or embezzlement[26] from his own firm, and hence his effort to appropriate such property does not (where the rule remains unchanged) constitute an attempt to commit such an offense. And if under the law of a particular jurisdiction a holdup by a juvenile does not constitute robbery, but an entirely different kind of misconduct known as "juvenile delinquency,"[27] such an effort by him (whether successful or otherwise) should not be held to be attempted robbery.

The wording of the Code would cause no difficulty in ordinary situations such as these because the attendant circumstances are exactly as the actor believes them to be—but it could happen otherwise. In the type of jurisdiction mentioned a juvenile, because of a mistaken notion as to the date of his

Model Penal Code if the actor believes the dead man is alive. People v. Dlugash, 41 N.Y.2d 725, 395 N.Y.S.2d 419, 363 N.E.2d 1155 (1977).

22. Use of non-pregnant investigator of conspiracy to commit abortion does not provide defense of legal impossibility. State v. Moretti, 97 N.J.Super. 418, 235 A.2d 266 (1967).

23. See supra, chapter 2, section 6F.

24. "So at common law a boy under 14 years of age cannot commit the crime of rape and thus cannot be convicted of attempted rape." Waters v. State, 2 Md. App. 216, 234 A.2d 147, 153 (1967).

25. Application of Verona, 38 Wn.2d 833, 232 P.2d 923 (1951). This has been changed in some states by statute which provides that a partner can commit larceny from his partnership. See State v.

Morales, 256 La. 940, 240 So.2d 714 (1970).

26. People v. Brody, 29 Cal.App.2d 6, 10, 83 P.2d 952 (1938).

It is impossible as a matter of law for one who is not an officer to commit misfeasance or malfeasance in office. Raduszewski v. Superior Court, 232 A.2d 95 (Del.1967). Hence one not an officer cannot perpetrate an attempt to commit misfeasance or malfeasance in office. Because of the wording of section 484, a partner can commit embezzlement from his partnership. The statute does not say "of another." People v. Sobiek, 30 Cal.App.3d 458, 106 Cal.Rptr. 519 (1973). See also State v. Siers, 197 Neb. 51, 248 N.W.2d 1 (1976).

27. People v. Roper, 259 N.Y. 170, 181 N.E. 88 (1932).

birth, might believe his age to be such that he was no longer within that favored category. Although a holdup by him would be robbery if the attendant circumstances were as he believes them to be, the legal impossibility should prevent it from being recognized as attempted robbery.[28] The Code should take the position that there is no criminal attempt if perpetration is legally impossible, with the explanation that, as used, the term applies only to situations in which the impossibility results from the criminal incapacity of the actor.

It is hardly necessary to add that no one has capacity to commit a non-existent crime. There can be no conviction of criminal attempt based upon D's erroneous notion that he was committing a crime.[29] This is a case of legal impossibility.

Furthermore, as will be emphasized infra, under "solicitation," if a statute forbids a deed which requires the cooperation of two, but provides a penalty for one only, this is a clear manifestation of the legislative intent that the other shall go unpunished. So far as that other is concerned, perpetration of such an offense is a legal impossibility.

The complexities of the concepts associated with legal and factual impossibility have led some jurisdictions to expressly by statute abandon the concept [30] and focus on the accused's state of mind as he believed the circumstances to be. This is the position taken by the Model Penal Code [31] and has found support in recent court decisions.[32] Under such an approach, in an

28. To take the position that the age of the actor is not one of the attendant circumstances would open up endless disputes as to what is included in the phrase.

29. There is no criminal liability where "the defendant intended to do an act which he mistakenly believed constituted a crime, . . ." State v. Davidson, 20 Wn.App. 893, 584 P.2d 401, 404 (1978).

"Thus, attempt is not unlawful where success is not a crime, and this is true even though the defendant believes his scheme to be criminal." United States v. Frazier, 560 F.2d 884, 888 (8th Cir. 1977).

30. "No defense to the offense of attempt shall arise: (b) Due to factual or legal impossibility if the offense could have been committed had the attendant circumstances been as the actor believed them to be." Utah Code Ann., 1953 § 76–4–101(3); McKinney's Consol. Laws New York Penal § 110.10 (1975); Rev. Code Wash.Ann. 9A.28020 (1977); Ala. Code § 13A–4–2 (1975).

31. 5.01. ". . . It should suffice, therefore, to indicate at this stage what we deem to be the major results of the draft. They are:

(a) to extend the criminality of attempts by sweeping aside the defense of impossibility (including the distinc-

tion between so-called factual and legal impossibility) and by drawing the line between attempt and non-criminal preparation further away from the final act; the crime becomes essentially one of criminal purpose implemented by an overt act strongly corroborative of such purpose, . . ."

. . .

"Of course, it is still necessary that the result desired or intended by the actor constitute a crime. If, according to his beliefs as to facts and legal relationships, the result desired or intended is not a crime, the actor will not be guilty of an attempt even though he firmly believes that his goal is criminal.

The basic premise here is that the actor's mind is the best proving ground of his dangerousness." Model Penal Code, Tentative Draft No. 10, p. 25, 31–32 (1960).

32. ". . . We hold that the district court correctly concluded that the defense of legal impossibility may not be invoked to bar a prosecution for attempt. . . ." State v. Bird, 285 N.W.2d 481 (Minn.1979).

"Our examination of these authorities convinces us that the application of the defense of impossibility is so fraught with intricacies and artificial distinctions that the defense has little value as an an-

exhaustively researched opinion, the Court of Military Appeals upheld the conviction of two servicemen for attempted rape where unknown to the defendants the victim at the time of the act was dead rather than merely drunk as the defendants had assumed.[33]

However forceful the argument for abandoning the impossibility concept the position has not been fully accepted by the courts or commentators and the impossibility doctrine remains viable in many jurisdictions.[34]

6. PROXIMITY

It is often said, with variations in the exact wording, that for a criminal attempt there "must be dangerous proximity to success." [35] Since the requirement previously discussed was not of actual possibility, but only of apparent possibility, the reference here is to apparent proximity. There can be no doubt of the need of apparent proximity, both as to time and space. The man setting combustibles in the house of another with the intention of burning it is guilty of an attempt if his plan is to set the blaze now, but not if he is to return on some future occasion to start the fire. And he who had prepared a bomb to set on the streetcar track, and had started with it to meet his confederate to carry out their unlawful plan, was guilty of an attempt because distances were short,—but would not have been guilty had it been necessary to travel many miles to reach the place of perpetration. This does not involve an additional requirement but is included within the preparation-perpetration concept. While the measures taken with criminal intent are obviously remote they remain under the label "preparation," and only when apparent proximity is reached has there been the beginning of "perpetration."

The subject is given separate attention here in the effort to clarify a point that has caused no end of confusion. The earliest development of the law of attempt, as previously mentioned, was the attempt to commit a battery,—

alytical method of reaching substantial justice." State v. Moretti, 52 N.J. 182, 244 A.2d 499, 503 (1968).

33. United States v. Thomas, 3 USCMA 278, 32 CMR 278 (1962).

"The lack of logic between some of the holdings, supra; the inherent difficulty in assigning a given set of facts to a proper classification; the criticism of existing positions in this area; and, most importantly, the denial of true and substantial justice by these artificial holdings have led, quite naturally, to proposals for reform in the civilian legal concepts of criminal attempts.

. . . .

After having given this entire question a great deal more than casual attention and study, we are forced to the conclusion that the law of attempts in military jurisprudence has tended toward the advanced and modern position, which position will be achieved for civilian jurisprudence if The American Law Institute is

completely successful in its advocacy of this portion of the Model Penal Code." Id. 285–286 CMR.

34. For an interesting comparison of the two approaches to the retention of a principle of impossibility see Gold, "To Dream An Impossible Dream:" A Problem In Criminal Attempts (And Conspiracy) Revisited, 21 Crim.L.Qtrly. 218 (1979) and Williams, Attempting The Impossible—A Reply, 22 Crim.L.Qtrly. 49 (1979).

35. Per Mr. Justice Holmes, dissenting, in Hyde v. United States, 225 U.S. 347, 388, 32 S.Ct. 793, 810 (1912).

"Each attempt case must be decided on its own unique facts, and the essential question which the intent answered is whether, given the intent to commit a specific offense, the defendant performed acts bringing him in dangerous proximity to success in carrying out his intent." People v. Brown, 75 Ill.App.3d 503, 31 Ill. Dec. 147, 149, 394 N.E.2d 63, 65 (1979).

assault. And in the development of the assault concept in those very early days the judges were thinking of proximity in terms of what was, or appeared to be, very close indeed. As one court explained the use of "attempt" in the assault cases: "if one in anger draw back his fist to strike, being within striking distance, it is an offer; but if he draw back and make a lick and miss, it is an attempt." [36] Where not prevented by limitations of statutory definition there has been a tendency to enlarge the scope of criminal assault by adding also the tort theory of an unlawful act which places another in reasonable apprehension of receiving an immediate battery.[37] But if attempted battery is relied upon to establish an assault, the requirement developed in the dawn of the common law has been carried down through the ages with little modification, as shown by the statement quoted. There must, apparently at least, have been "dangerous proximity to success." There is not sufficient proximity for an assault until he who intends to commit the battery has come at least apparently within reach of his intended victim if "reach" be given a reasonable interpretation [38] and be used to include the range of his weapon if he is armed. But one may be guilty of criminal attempt in other than the assault cases before his objective is even apparently within his reach. Thus one who was arrested while going up the steps to the house was held properly convicted of an attempt to break and enter.[39] And he who had set out with a bomb to place on the streetcar track nearby was held guilty of an attempt although he was still a substantial distance from the spot at which the bomb was to be set.[40]

No analogies should be drawn from assault cases to other cases of criminal attempt insofar as the degree of required proximity is concerned.[41] In fact, in referring to criminal attempt in other than the assault cases it is quite misleading to suggest a requirement of "dangerous proximity to success." The statement here should be only the general one—*non remota causa sed proxima spectatur* (not the remote cause but the one which is

---

36. State v. Milsaps, 82 N.C. 549, 550 (1880). "The distinction may be thus defined: An assault is an act done toward the commission of a battery; it must precede the battery, but it does so immediately. The next movement would, at least to all appearance, complete the battery. While an act constituting an attempt to commit a felony may be more remote, ..." Fox v. State, 34 Ohio St. 377, 380 (1878). "This is a clear recognition of the principle that an attempt, or the overt act which is the initial stage thereof, does not require a physical act in the way of an assault or advance upon the person of the intended victim." Hanson, J., dissenting in State v. Mortensen, 95 Utah 541, 550, 83 P.2d 261, 265 (1938).

37. Commonwealth v. Richards, 363 Mass. 299, 293 N.E.2d 854 (1973); State v. Wiley, 52 S.D. 110, 216 N.W. 866 (1927); State v. Deso, 110 Vt. 1, 1 A.2d 710 (1938); State v. Shaffer, 120 Wash. 345, 207 P. 299 (1922).

38. One pursuing another and striking with intent to hit him might be held

guilty of assault although it was obvious that the intended victim had managed to keep a few inches out of range. State v. Davis, 23 N.C. 125 (1840).

39. Commonwealth v. Clark, 10 Pa. Co.Ct. 444 (1860).

40. People v. Stites, 75 Cal. 570, 17 P. 693 (1888). The court says that the track at the time was "easily within his reach" (p. 576, 17 P. 696), but "reach" is used in a different sense. All that is meant is that he could reach it quickly. The spot he had in mind was obviously many steps away, because when he was interrupted "he had reached a point farther (by a distance equal to the width of his dwelling house) from the track than he was when he actually started out" (p. 578, 17 P. 697).

41. Assault with intent to commit sodomy requires a greater degree of proximity than an attempt to commit sodomy. State v. Still, 112 N.J.Super. 368, 271 A.2d 444 (1970).

proximate is regarded). In other than assault cases an act does not have to be very close to constitute an attempt but will not be considered in this category if it is obviously remote.

7. INTENT

The word "attempt" means to try; [42] it implies an effort to bring about a desired result. Hence an attempt to commit any crime requires a specific intent to commit that particular offense. [43] If other elements of an attempt are established "intent is the crucial question." [44] One does not attempt to commit a crime by negligently endangering the person or property of another however great the danger or extreme the negligence. [45] A few cases can be found in which the court has taken the position that a "reckless disregard of human life may be the equivalent of a specific intent to kill" [46] but this is

42. "One could not very well 'attempt' or try to 'commit' an injury on the person of another if he had no intent to cause any injury to such other person." People v. Coffey, 67 Cal.2d 204, 222, 430 P.2d 15, 27, 60 Cal.Rptr. 457, 469 (1967).

43. People v. Miller, 2 Cal.2d 527, 42 P.2d 308 (1935); People v. Goldstein, 146 Cal.App.2d 268, 303 P.2d 892 (1956); State v. Prince, 75 Utah 205, 284 P. 108 (1930); Merritt v. Commonwealth, 164 Va. 653, 180 S.E. 395 (1935); State v. Cass, 146 Wash. 585, 264 P. 7 (1928); Regina v. Donavan, 4 Cox C.C. 401 (1850); Rex v. Boyce, 1 Moody 29, 168 Eng.Rep. 1172 (1824); Allen v. People, 175 Colo. 113, 485 P.2d 886 (1971).

"Intent to do a particular act is a necessary element of attempt." State v. Norby, 20 Wn.App. 378, 579 P.2d 1358, 1360 (1978).

A charge that **D** attempted to commit theft means that he intended to commit theft and took a substantial step in that direction. State v. House, 37 Or.App. 131, 586 P.2d 388 (1978).

"Intent is an essential element of the crime of criminal attempt." State v. Faulkner, 61 Hawaii 177, 599 P.2d 285, 286 (1979).

"Hence an attempt to commit any crime requires an intent to commit that particular offense." State v. Wilson, 120 Ariz. 72, 584 P.2d 53, 55 (App. 1978).

The crime of attempt involves an intent to commit a substantive crime. Commonwealth v. Ware, 375 Mass. 118, 375 N.E.2d 1183 (1978).

44. Preddy v. Commonwealth, 184 Va. 765, 775, 36 S.E.2d 549, 553 (1946). The word "attempt" "necessarily includes intent." Scott v. People, 141 Ill. 195, 204, 30 N.E. 329, 330 (1892). "The essence of an attempt to commit a crime seems to

be an act done with the intent to commit the crime." De Krasner v. State, 54 Ga. App. 41, 43, 187 S.E. 402, 404 (1936).

45. Thacker v. Commonwealth, 134 Va. 767, 114 S.E. 504 (1922). Defendant, in the effort to "shoot the light out," shot through a tent knowing there were people inside. The bullet hit the head of the bed on which a woman and a baby were lying. It barely missed the heads of these two. As his intent was to put out the light and not to kill any person, a conviction of attempted murder was reversed. An intent to inflict grievous bodily harm is sufficient for murder but not for an attempt to commit murder. Rex v. Whybrow, 35 Cr.App.R. (1951).

"An instruction must make it clear that to convict for attempted murder nothing less than a criminal intent to kill must be shown." People v. Harris, 72 Ill.2d 16, 17 Ill.Dec. 838, 843, 377 N.E.2d 28, 33 (1978).

"We now hold that the State of Indiana has no statutory crime of attempted reckless homicide." Rhode v. State, ___ Ind. App. ___, 391 N.E.2d 666, 669 (1979).

See Enker, Mens Rea and Criminal Attempt, 1977 Am.B. Foundation Research J. 845.

"Although the recklessness or negligence may come about from holding the unreasonable belief that deadly force is justified (instead of the actual reckless firing of a gun, for example), an actor still cannot 'intend' to act recklessly or negligently." State v. Grant, 418 A.2d 154, 156 (Me. 1980).

46. Payne v. State, 74 Ga.App. 646, 652, 40 S.E.2d 759, 764 (1946). And see the following note.

Charlton v. Wainwright, 588 F.2d 162 (5th Cir. 1979); Garcia v. State, 541 S.W.2d 428 (Tex.Cr.App. 1976). The Su-

quite unsound.[47] It is grounded upon the notion that an act which would be sufficient for murder if death results should be attempted murder if life is not taken.

"The fallacy in this statement is that while a person may be guilty of murder though there was no actual intent to kill, he cannot be guilty of an attempt to commit murder unless he has a specific intent to kill." [48]

While there is no attempt to commit a crime without a specific intent to commit that very offense, it must be borne in mind that the law attaches its own labels to intents the same as it does to results. D intends to achieve a certain result under particular circumstances. If doing so would constitute a crime D is intending to commit a crime whether he would call it a crime or not. If doing so would not constitute a crime D is not intending to commit a crime even if he thinks his intended purpose falls within that category. An

preme Court of Canada held, under the special wording of a Canadian statute, that attempted murder did not require a specific intent. Lajoie v. The Queen, 33 DLR 3d 618, 622 (Can.Sup.Ct. 1973).

47. "The reason why a reckless Georgian driver is held guilty of assault with intent to murder, is because it is the only available statutory pigeonhole which is more severe in its consequences than reckless driving or assault and battery." Tulin, The Role of Penalties in Criminal Law, 37 Yale L.J. 1048, 1068–9 (1928). He points out that the same result is reached in Illinois and North Carolina for the same reason,—otherwise no adequate penalty is available where serious injury, less than death, has been caused by reckless driving. The absence of a law, needless to say, is no proper basis for conviction.

"Specific intent to kill is a necessary element of attempted murder. It must be proved, and it cannot be inferred from the commission of another dangerous crime." People v. Belton, 105 Cal.App.3d 376, 164 Cal.Rptr. 340, 342 (1980).

"We believe that reckless endangering in the second degree is a lesser included offense of attempted murder . . . ." State v. Feliciano, 62 Hawaii 637, 618 P.2d 306, 308 (1980).

48. Merritt v. Commonwealth, 164 Va. 653, 660, 180 S.E. 395, 398 (1935). Accord, Moore v. State, 18 Ala. 532, 534; State v. Taylor, 70 Vt. 1, 9, 39 A. 447, 450 (1896).

It is reversible error to give an instruction which might lead the jury to believe that if D's guilt would have been murder if death had resulted, he is guilty of an attempt to commit murder without a finding of an actual intent to kill. People v. Beverly, 63 Ill.App.3d 186, 19 Ill.Dec.

881, 379 N.E.2d 753 (1978); Ramos v. State, 95 Nev. 251, 592 P.2d 950 (1979).

There is no such crime as attempted homicide by reckless conduct. State v. Melvin, 49 Wis.2d 246, 181 N.W.2d 490 (1970); State v. Smith, 21 Or.App. 270, 534 P.2d 1180 (1975). An attempt to murder requires an intent to take human life, and this cannot be supplied by application of the felony-murder rule. People v. Wein, 69 Cal.App.3d 79, 137 Cal.Rptr. 814 (1977).

"However, if the actor believed that his conduct would cause the result forbidden by criminal law—in this case, death—and did 'all in his power to cause the result to occur' he could be convicted of attempted murder. . . . The belief on the part of an actor that certain results would follow his conduct is sufficient to show a specific intent for that result to occur." People v. Morano, 69 Ill. App.3d 580, 25 Ill.Dec. 940, 945, 387 N.E.2d 816, 821 (1979).

It was stated that "although the completed crime of arson is a crime that does not require a specific intent the crime of attempt under the statute requires a specific intent to commit the completed crime." State v. Miller, 123 Ariz. 491, 600 P.2d 1123, 1125 (App. 1979).

Acts that would have been sufficient to establish murder, if they had been fatal, are not sufficient to establish an assault with intent to commit murder. People v. Martinez, 105 Cal.App.3d 938, 165 Cal. Rptr. 11 (1980).

"Hence the trial court erred in instructing the jury that it need not find a specific intent to kill in order to convict of attempted murder." People v. Collie, 30 Cal.3d 43, 177 Cal.Rptr. 458, 469, 634 P.2d 534, 545 (1981).

intent to do what is not a crime is not an intent to commit a crime,—as mentioned in another connection. If, for example, the jurisdiction accepts the view that obtaining intercourse with a married woman by fraudulently impersonating her husband is not rape,[49] then intending to procure the intercourse by this means is not intending to commit rape.[50]

Furthermore, if doing what he has in mind would constitute a crime his intent is to commit that very offense even if he thinks it would be some other. **D**, for example, intends to kill **X** under the sudden heat of passion engendered by such provocation that if **X** is killed the homicide will be manslaughter. If **D** thinks he is intending to commit murder he is just as mistaken as he would be if he killed **X** and thought he had committed murder.[51] And if he thinks the law will excuse a killing in revenge for such an act by **X**, **D**'s design to kill is an intent to commit manslaughter notwithstanding.[52]

Needless to say, intent may be inferred from conduct where it is plainly indicated as a matter of logical probability.[53] The illegal use, upon a pregnant woman, of instruments capable of producing an abortion, in a manner calculated to have that result, will support an inference of an actual intent to procure an abortion, in the absence of any other reasonable explanation.[54] An intent to commit burglary may be inferred from the fact that defendant, equipped with burglar's tools and a flashlight, went to another's apartment at night, turned the knob of the door and tried to push it open, while having no lawful business there.[55] And shooting at another, within range, may be under such circumstances as to indicate quite plainly an intent to kill. But if

49. The Queen v. Barrow, L.R. 1 Cr. Cas.Res. 156 (1868).

50. State v. Brooks, 76 N.C. 1 (1877).

51. "Lord Kenyon, C. J., being of opinion that if death had ensued, it would only have been manslaughter, directed the jury to acquit the defendant upon the first count of the indictment, charging the assault to be with intent to murder." Mitton's Case, 1 East P.C. 411 (1788). And see State v. Crutcher, 231 Iowa 418, 1 N.W.2d 195 (1942).

52. There may be an attempt to commit voluntary manslaughter. State v. Norman, 580 P.2d 237 (Utah 1978). Accord, United States v. Jackson, 6 M.J. 261 (CMA 1979).

We "reject appellant's contention that commission of attempted voluntary manslaughter is a logical impossibility."

"An 'attempt' to commit involuntary manslaughter would require that the defendant intend to perpetrate an unintentional killing—a logical impossibility." People v. Van Broussard, 76 Cal.App.3d 193, 142 Cal.Rptr. 664, 666 (1977).

"An attempt to commit criminally negligent homicide thus requires proof that the defendant *intended* to perpetrate an *unintentional* killing—a logical impossibility. The words 'attempt' and 'negligence' are at war with one another; they

are internally inconsistent and cannot sensibly coexist." People v. Hernandez, ___ Colo.App. ___, 614 P.2d 900, 901 (1980).

53. "A person is guilty of attempted second-degree kidnapping if he knowingly engaged in conduct which is strongly corroborative of the firmness of his purpose to knowingly seize or carry another person from one place to another without his consent and without lawful justification." People v. Lahr, ___ Colo. ___, 615 P.2d 707, 708–09 (1980).

"In this circuit we have adopted a two tier test in reviewing convictions where criminal attempts were charged. The first tier inquiry relates to a determination as to whether sufficient proof exists to establish that the accused possessed the requisite criminal intent. Once intent has been established, the second tier inquiry concentrates on whether the accused's conduct may be viewed as sufficiently corroborative of his established criminal intent." United States v. Mowad, 641 F.2d 1067, 1073 (2d Cir. 1981).

54. Scott v. People, 141 Ill. 195, 30 N.E. 329 (1892).

55. State v. Cass, 146 Wash. 585, 264 P. 7 (1928); People v. Wong, 245 Cal.App. 2d 844, 54 Cal.Rptr. 273 (1966).

the required intent is actually lacking it cannot be supplied by any mere jingle of words,—such as that a person is presumed to intend the natural and probable consequences of his act. "The intent cannot be implied as a matter of law; it must be proved as a matter of fact, ..." [56] An instruction in a homicide case that the law presumes a person intends the ordinary consequences of his voluntary acts can be interpreted as conclusive or to require the defendant to bear the burden of proof to the contrary and therefore violates due process of law.[57]

In considering the requirement of an intent to commit the crime alleged to have been attempted due attention must be given to the possibility of a qualified intent, because a qualified intent is as effective as any other intent so far as this element of a criminal attempt is concerned. Suppose, for example, **D** sees an umbrella and realizing full well that it either may or may not be his, decides to take it and keep it as his own whichever the fact may be. This is a qualified intent to steal because he says to himself, in effect: "I realize this umbrella may not be mine and if it is not I intend permanently to deprive another of his property." If it is in fact not his he will be guilty of larceny if he takes it and carries it away with this state of mind, and guilty of attempted larceny if he attempts to do so.[58]

It is unnecessary to repeat what was said above in regard to "primary" and "secondary" intent. By reason of mistake of fact one may have two intents which seem identical to him but which are so inconsistent that one cannot be promoted to any degree by what is done to carry out the other. If what is actually done in such a situation fails to move in the direction of crime there is no criminal attempt. What is lacking there is the requirement that a criminal attempt be a step towards a criminal offense.

It is important to emphasize here that one, with mischief in his mind, may actually take a step in the direction of a criminal offense without attempting

---

56. Simpson v. State, 59 Ala. 1, 10 (1877).

57. Sandstrom v. Montana, 442 U.S. 510, 99 S.Ct. 2450 (1979).

58. See supra, chapter 6, section 3, A, (7). One writer reaches fantastic conclusions by overlooking entirely the qualified-intent concept. Smith, Two Problems in Criminal Attempts, 70 Harv.L. Rev. 422 (1957). Smith says that **D** in the umbrella case stated was "reckless" (id. at p. 431) which is certainly true in a sense because he runs the risk of committing larceny if he carries away the article and it turns out to belong to another; but he is guilty of larceny in such a case because he committed the trespass with *intent to steal*—despite the fact that it was a qualified intent. Likewise if **D**, not knowing or having any reason to know whether his first wife is alive or dead, decides to marry again notwithstanding, he has a qualified intent to commit bigamy because he says to himself in effect: "I realize that my first wife may be still alive and if so I intend to marry a second wife despite my status as a married man." Smith discusses these and similar cases on the assumption that *no intent* to commit the crime is involved therein, and then proceeds by analogy from this false premise until he reaches the astounding conclusion that **D** would be guilty of an attempt to drive negligently if he attempted to drive under such circumstances that actual driving would be negligent although utterly unaware of the circumstances that make it so (**D** should realize but does not). He admits that he has no authority for such a position and it is to be hoped there never will be such authority. Under no sound analysis can there be an attempt to drive negligently by one unaware of the circumstances that would make the driving negligent. On the other hand there could be an attempt to drive recklessly by one having full knowledge of the circumstances which would make such driving reckless. Williams, Criminal Law 619–20 (2d ed. 1961).

to commit that crime if his state of mind does not include an intent to commit it. A typical illustration is the well-known case of *Wilson*.[59] **D** had a draft for two dollars and a half which he intended to use to obtain a larger sum of money. With fraud in mind he inserted the figure "1" before the figure "2" so that the marginal figures read "12.50." The word "two" remained unchanged. In this form he made an unsuccessful attempt to negotiate the draft for twelve dollars and a half, whereupon he was indicted for forgery. He was held not guilty of forgery because the addition he had made did not constitute a material alteration. It is a familiar rule of construction that the words prevail in any case of discrepancy between the words and figures used to express the amount of a negotiable instrument.[60] Hence this draft would have called for only two dollars and a half even if it had been drawn originally in the form to which it was changed. A change which does not affect the legal meaning of the writing is not a "material" alteration,—without which there is no forgery when tampering with a genuine instrument is involved—unless the requirement of materiality has been removed by statute.

It was held also that **D** was not guilty of an attempt to commit forgery. "No purpose appears to change anything on the paper except the figures in the margin," [61] said the court. This did not constitute forgery as a matter of law, hence **D** did not intend to commit forgery whether he thought his intent fell within that category or was well acquainted with the legal rule. The physical act done by **D** would have been sufficient for an attempt to commit forgery if he had intended to change the words as well as the figures and had been interrupted before his plan was completely executed. In such a case he would have an intent to commit forgery and would have taken a step in that direction.[62] This would be sufficient for attempted forgery. But in *Wilson* the same physical act fell short of attempted forgery because it was committed without an intent to commit forgery. An intent to do what is not forgery is not an intent to commit forgery.

The law should be changed (by statute of course) to permit conviction in a case such as *Wilson*. The change, however, should be made in the law of forgery and not in the law of attempt. Holding that it is not forgery to change the figures on a negotiable instrument, if the amount is expressed also in words which are not changed, is entirely logical,—but quite unsatisfactory. The more-easily-read figures are so constantly relied upon in the rush of business today that any change in them is calculated to result in

59. Wilson v. State, 85 Miss. 687, 38 So. 46 (1905).

60. This rule was codified in section 17 of the Uniform Negotiable Instruments Law. That statute was not relied upon because it had not been enacted in Mississippi at the time of this case. The court reached the same result by saying that the marginal figures "are not part of the instrument." This unsound explanation of a clearly recognized result harks back to the early days when the marginal figures did not appear on the instrument as originally made but were added later for the convenience of the holder. The provision is found now in section 3–118(c) of the Uniform Commercial Code, 1978 Official Text.

61. Wilson v. State, 85 Miss. 687, 691, 38 So. 46, 47 (1905).

62. Although changing the words alone would change the meaning of the instrument, a discrepancy between the words and figures always tends to invite inquiry which is something the forger is eager to avoid. Hence a change of the figures is a part of the ordinary act of forgery.

harm.[63]   And the crime of forgery might well be enlarged to include any such change made with fraudulent intent.

B.   AGGRAVATED ASSAULT

The so-called "aggravated assaults" were not recognized as distinct offenses at common law.   Any criminal assault was a misdemeanor and circumstances of aggravation, if present, could be taken into consideration in fixing the penalty.   Statutory enactments have frequently created certain substantive offenses in the form of aggravated assaults although no uniform pattern has been established.   The aggravating circumstance relied upon for special punishment has usually been some grievous intent in the mind of the assailant,[64] or dangerous means of perpetration, although it might be something unusual in the circumstance of the offender such as an assault by one serving a life sentence, or some combination, such as assault with intent to rob while armed.   Where the dangerous means of perpetration has been the circumstance of aggravation it has frequently been assault with a "deadly weapon" or "dangerous weapon" or assault with a caustic chemical.   In this connection it may be noted that an attempt to shoot with an unloaded gun is not an assault with a "dangerous weapon;"[65] whereas shoes on the feet may constitute a "dangerous weapon" when used with the intention of inflicting

63.   In the midwest a few years ago a man entitled to two dollars received a check drawn in this form:

Pay to the order of John Doe. $200. Two . . . .   Dollars

This was cashed at another bank for two hundred dollars, cleared through the clearing house for two hundred dollars and accepted by the drawee bank for two hundred dollars.   Only when the drawer received her statement from the bank was the error discovered.

64.   "A person who acts in the 'heat of passion' cannot constitutionally be subjected to a greater penalty when he causes serious bodily injury than that which could have been imposed, had he caused the death of his victim. . . . Consequently,   where   a   defendant charged with first degree assault can establish that he acted in the 'heat of passion,' he cannot receive a greater penalty than he would have received had he been convicted of manslaughter."   People v. Grable, 43 Colo.App. 518, 611 P.2d 588, 590 (1980).

65.   State v. Wiley, 52 S.D. 110, 216 N.W. 866 (1927).   **D** made an assault with a pistol—not used as a club.   The gun at the time was apparently empty but **D** had a clip filled with live cartridges which could be inserted in the weapon instantly.   A conviction of assault with a deadly weapon was affirmed.   State v. Hanson, 20 Utah 2d 189, 436 P.2d 227 (1968).

Although recognizing that a majority of jurisdictions hold otherwise, it was held that "an unloaded revolver which is pointed in such a manner as to communicate to the person threatened an apparent ability to fire a shot and thus do bodily harm is a deadly weapon within the meaning expressed by the legislature in the assault statutes."   State v. Deutscher, 225 Kan. 265, 589 P.2d 620, 625 (1979).

A totally inoperable pistol cannot "constitute a 'dangerous weapon' so as to support a conviction of felonious assault."   People v. Stevens, 409 Mich. 564, 297 N.W.2d 120, 121 (1980).

serious injury.[66] An automobile may be a deadly or dangerous weapon when adapted to accomplishing an assault.[67]

The so-called "assaults with intent" require special attention in connection with the law of attempt. Assault with intent to murder, assault with intent to rob, assault with intent to rape, and assault with intent to inflict great bodily injury are found quite frequently in the codes. Others are not uncommon, and sometimes a section provides a special penalty for an assault to commit any felony not otherwise provided for by statute.

No more is needed here than a bare reference to what was said above in regard to proximity. Since an attempt to commit a battery is an assault, and since every murder includes a battery, logic suggests that every attempted murder includes an attempted battery and hence an assault. If this were true an attempt to commit murder and an assault with intent to commit murder would be merely different ways of expressing the same result.[68] Logical as this may seem, however, it fails to give a true picture of the common law because of peculiarities in the history of its development. The law of assault, crystallizing at a much earlier day than the law of criminal attempt in general, is much more literal in its requirement of "dangerous proximity to success" (actual or apparent) than is the law in regard to an attempt to commit an offense other than battery.[69]

Apart from this, the two are almost identical unless a statute defines assault in terms of "present ability." Such a statutory provision, as mentioned above, is interpreted to require an actual present ability rather than the common-law requirement of an apparent present ability, and will apply to an aggravated assault the same as to any other. Hence an assault with intent to commit a particular crime is, in general, the same as an attempt to commit that crime except for two additional requirements,—(1) a greater degree of proximity, and (2) actual present ability to commit a battery (the latter being limited chiefly to states in which this has been added by the statutory definition of assault). It follows that an assault with intent to commit a certain crime generally includes an attempt to commit that crime,[70] but an attempt

---

66. Medlin v. United States, 207 F.2d 33 (D.C.Cir. 1953); Berfield v. State, 458 P.2d 1008 (Alaska 1969); Orrill v. State, 509 P.2d 930 (Okl.Crim.App. 1973).

A handkerchief used to gag an old man in a way that could cause death or serious injury was a "dangerous instrument." People v. Ford, 60 A.D.2d 40, 400 N.Y.S.2d 35 (1977) rev'd on oth grds 46 N.Y.2d 434, 414 N.Y.S.2d 102, 386 N.E.2d 1070 (1979).

67. People v. Blacksmith, 66 Mich. App. 216, 238 N.W.2d 810 (1976); Harmon v. State, 260 Ark. 665, 543 S.W.2d 43 (1976). See Oberer, The Deadly Weapon Doctrine—Common Law Origin, 75 Harv. L.Rev. 1565 (1962).

68. "It is true an attempted murder and assault with a deadly weapon with intent to commit murder on the same victim at the same time are but two different ways of describing the same criminal

act." Mathews v. State, 82 Cal.App.3d 116, 145 Cal.Rptr. 443, 447 (1978).

69. "While an act constituting an attempt to commit a felony may be more remote" than is required to constitute an assault. Fox v. State, 34 Ohio St. 377, 380 (1878). And see State v. Hetzel, 159 Ohio St. 350, 112 N.E.2d 369 (1953).

"For inchoate, not fully consummated crime, society has long had available in its arsenal both the statutory offense of 'assault with intent to . . .' and the common-law offense of criminal attempt. Although these two offenses have a significant overlap, they are nonetheless distinct and each addresses certain pockets of inchoate criminal activity not covered by the other." Gray v. State, 43 Md.App. 238, 403 A.2d 853, 856 (1979).

70. Crockett v. State, 125 Tenn. 131, 140 S.W. 1058 (1911). "Certainly, every element of an attempt is comprised in an

to commit the crime does not include an assault with intent to commit it.[71] A verdict of guilty of attempted manslaughter, for example, will not support a conviction of assault with intent to commit manslaughter.[72] This difference has found its way into some of the statutes, such as the following: "Any person who shall attempt to commit the crime of murder by . . . any means not constituting an assault with intent to murder, . . ." [73]

Apart from the degree of proximity, and actual present ability where that has been added by statute, the problems of "assault with intent" are almost the same as those involved in criminal attempt. It must be added, moreover, that where actual present ability has been added this is in the statutory definition of assault. It applies to the ability to commit a battery, not to ability to commit the other offense intended. If an effort is made to commit murder by "shooting" with an empty gun, the lack of present ability goes to the battery as well as to the murder,[74] but this is not true in certain other types of offense. Suppose, for example, by reason of extreme age or some nervous disorder, a man has lost the ability to engage in the act of sexual intercourse although unaware of his weakness. He could intend to commit rape,[75] and his inability to copulate would not make it impossible for him to commit a battery. Hence he could be guilty of an assault with intent to commit rape even if the statute requires present ability for the assault.[76]

In this type of aggravated assault the intent with which it was alleged to have been committed is a "specific intent" which must be proved. Insofar as the problems here are identical with those involved in a criminal attempt they need not be repeated.[77] Some statutes dealing with aggravated assault

assault with intent to commit the offense of rape." Sekinoff v. United States, 283 F. 38, 41–2 (9th Cir. 1922). "Consequently, an assault with intent to commit a rape, is an *attempt*, by violence to commit a rape." Johnson v. State, 14 Ga. 55, 60 (1853). "An assault with intent to commit robbery is an attempt to rob. . . ." State v. Curtis, 149 Ohio St. 153, 155, 78 N.E.2d 46, 47 (1948).

An attempted rape and burglary with intent to commit rape are separate crimes. It has been held one could be guilty of burglary with intent to commit rape without being guilty of attempted rape. People v. Clerk, 68 Ill.App.3d 1021, 25 Ill.Dec. 359, 386 N.E.2d 630 (1979).

71. People v. Welsh, 7 Cal.2d 209, 60 P.2d 124 (1936); Ramsey v. State, 204 Ind. 212, 183 N.E. 648 (1932); State v. Hetzel, 159 Ohio St. 350, 112 N.E.2d 369 (1953). Thus "all assaults are attempts, whereas all attempts are not necessarily assaults." State v. Staggs, 554 S.W.2d 620, 623 (Tenn. 1977).

An attempt to rob is not necessarily an assault. And defendant who was charged only with attempt to rob could not be convicted of an assault with intent to rob. United States v. Smith, 553 F.2d 1239 (10th Cir. 1977).

72. Vogel v. State, 124 Fla. 409, 168 So. 539 (1936). An assault with intent to commit manslaughter is an assault with intent to kill under such circumstances that the killing would be manslaughter. State v. Crutcher, 231 Iowa 418, 1 N.W. 2d 195 (1942). See supra, Note 11.

73. Mich.Stat.Ann. 28.286 (1968). See also Mass.Gen.Laws Ann. c. 265 § 16 (1980).

74. People v. Sylva, 143 Cal. 62, 76 P. 814 (1904).

75. State v. Bartlett, 127 Iowa 689, 104 N.W. 285 (1905). Impotency is not a defense to a charge of assault with intent to commit rape, but evidence of known impotency is admissible on the question of intent. Territory v. Keyes, 5 Dak. 244, 38 N.W. 440 (1888); State v. Bellamah, 28 N.M. 212, 210 P. 391 (1922).

76. Hunt v. State, 114 Ark. 239, 169 S.W. 773 (1914). The statute defined assault as "an unlawful attempt, coupled with a present ability, to commit a violent injury on the person of another." The defendant in his futile effort to copulate actually had committed a battery upon the woman.

77. See Simpson v. State, 59 Ala. 1, 10 (1877); State v. Taylor, 70 Vt. 1, 9, 39 A. 447, 450 (1896).

include definitions of assault that do not require specific intent, to accomplish any result but require only a general act and in such cases a lesser state of mind such as recklessness will suffice.[78]   At one point, however, there is a problem which seems to be peculiar to this type of offense, and this is in regard to the conditional intent.   And here we may have an assault with intent which does not constitute an attempt.

No assault was committed by the one who raised his whip within striking distance and said: "Were you not an old man, I would knock you down."[79] He was neither attempting to commit a battery nor placing the other in apprehension of receiving a battery.   He was merely explaining why there was to be no battery.   This is not altogether true, however, in the case of a conditional threat.   If one within striking distance threatens to strike unless something is done or omitted, and the other does as commanded in order to avoid being struck, there has been apprehension.   It was the apprehension of being struck that induced compliance.

In this regard four possibilities must be distinguished.   One who makes such a threat may be (1) privileged to carry out his threat if disobeyed; (2) privileged to make the threat as a bluff but not to carry it out; (3) entitled to impose the condition but not to make such a threat; or (4) not entitled to impose the condition.   An officer seeking to apprehend a fleeing murderer is privileged to shoot him if the arrest cannot be effected otherwise.   He is privileged to carry out his threat: "Stop or I'll shoot."   In defense of land or chattels one is privileged to threaten to do more than he may lawfully do.[80] Thus one may be privileged to *threaten* to strike a trespasser with a stick although the circumstances are such that he would not be privileged to strike the blow.[81]   On the other hand one is not privileged to threaten with a deadly weapon merely to prevent or terminate an ordinary trespass.[82]

A privileged threat is not an assault of any kind.   On the other hand an unprivileged threat, made in a menacing manner, is an assault in the tort sense, if it places the other in apprehension of an immediate contact, even if there is an option to escape the contact by obedience to a command.[83]   And this is true whether the opportunity to avoid the contact is by doing something the threatener has no right to require,[84] or something he has a right to require in other ways but not by means of such a threat.[85]   An unprivileged threat, conditioned upon noncompliance, is not an attempt to commit a battery,[86] and hence is not a criminal assault in jurisdictions in which this of-

78.   State ex rel. McElhaney, 579 P.2d 328 (Utah 1978).

79.   State v. Crow, 23 N.C. 375 (1841).

80.   Restatement, Second, Torts § 81 (1965).

81.   Id. at Illus. 1 and 2.

82.   State v. Myerfield, 61 N.C. 108 (1867).

83.   Restatement, Second, Torts § 30 (1965).

84.   Id. at Illus. 2, 4.

"It is no defense that the intent to batter and do bodily harm is conditioned on some act of the victim where the accused cannot lawfully impose such a condition."

Gregory v. State, 628 P.2d 384, 386 (Okl. Cr.App. 1981).

85.   It is a civil assault to threaten a debtor with death, at gun point, unless he pays his debt.   Id. at Illus. 5.

86.   Such a threatener is not trying to commit a battery; he is trying to accomplish some other objective.   If he is bluffing he has no intent to commit a battery. If he is not bluffing he is postponing the first step in the direction of battery in the hope the battery will not be necessary.

Contra, the pointing of a loaded gun with a threat to shoot is sufficient to justify a finding of attempt.   State v. Mat-

fense can be established only on such a basis.[87] But it is a criminal assault where the definition of this offense includes either an attempted battery or the unlawful placing of another in apprehension of receiving an immediate battery.[88]

"If the condition be one which the party has a right to impose, the offer to strike unless the condition is complied with, is not an assault; . . . But if the condition be one which the party has no right to impose, the offer to strike is an assault, notwithstanding the condition, for no man can take advantage of his own wrong; as, if one raises a stick and says, 'pull off your hat'—or 'deliver up your money, or I will knock you down.' " [89]

The first sentence of this quotation was qualified by the decision itself. The actual holding was that a threat with a deadly weapon, although upon a condition the party has a right to impose, is an assault if employed to prevent an ordinary trespass. The defendant had a right to order the trespasser to desist,—but not at the point of a gun.

This discussion of assault in cases of conditional threat is merely to provide background for a consideration of the special problem. Obviously there can be no "assault with intent" if there is no assault at all, and it is important to keep the problem of the specific intent separate from the problem of the assault itself. The assault in these cases, it should be repeated, is based upon the apprehension of the other and not upon the intent of the threatener (other than the intent to cause the apprehension). The starting point is a conditional threat which, under the facts and the law of the jurisdiction, constitutes a criminal assault. The special problem is: If the conditional threat is to kill, under such circumstances that the homicide would be murder if the threat was executed, is this an assault with intent to commit murder?

The two leading cases on this point are *Hairston* [90] and *Connors*.[91] In the first of these cases the defendant, in an angry and profane manner and with pointed pistol, threatened to shoot another if he stopped the defendant's mules,—which stopping would have amounted to a trespass. The court said this constituted an assault but reversed a conviction of assault with intent to commit murder. The other case arose during a labor "war." Several goons pressed pistols against a workman and threatened to fill him full of holes unless he quit work. In this case an assault with intent to commit murder was affirmed. A superficial glance at these cases might suggest that whether the assault was with intent to commit murder depends upon whether the

thewson, 93 Idaho 769, 472 P.2d 638 (1970).

87. McKay v. State, 44 Tex. 43 (1875). The court relied upon the fact that the gun was unloaded and hence the defendant lacked the "present ability" required for assault by the Texas statute at that time. But this would seem to be merely additional support for a result that should have been reached without it. Later the Texas code was amended by enlarging criminal assault to include the wrongful placing of another in apprehension of an immediate battery. See Pearce v. State, 37 Tex.Cr.R. 643, 40 S.W. 806 (1897).

88. United States v. Myers, 1 D.C. 310 (1806); United States v. Richardson, 5 D.C. 348 (1837); State v. Church, 63 N.C. 15 (1868); State v. Rawles, 65 N.C. 334 (1871); State v. Martin, 85 N.C. 509 (1881); State v. Horne, 92 N.C. 805 (1885); Bloomer v. State, 35 Tenn. 66 (1855).

89. State v. Myerfield, 61 N.C. 108, 110 (1867).

90. Hairston v. State, 54 Miss. 689 (1877).

91. People v. Connors, 253 Ill. 266, 97 N.E. 643 (1912).

condition was one the threatener had a right to impose. In the one case defendant had a right to order the other not to interfere with his mules (although not at the point of a pistol). In the other there was no right to require the workman to quit work. This, however, is not an acceptable explanation. Whether an assault was or was not with intent to commit murder is dependent solely upon the state of mind of the assailant. If he intended to kill under circumstances which would have constituted murder it was an assault with intent to murder.[92] If he did not intend to kill it was not an assault with intent to murder.

These cases tend to establish the rule, which seems quite sound, that an assault with intent to murder does not require an unconditional intent to kill. An intent to kill, in the alternative, is nevertheless an intent to kill. And if the threat to kill if the mules were stopped was made with an intent to take life if disobeyed, there is no reason why it should not be held to be an assault with intent to commit murder. *Hairston* did not hold otherwise. It held only that the mere overstepping of bounds, in the manner in which an otherwise lawful order is given, is insufficient to support an inference of an actual intent to kill. And in *Connors* there was much more than the mere unlawfulness of the order to quit work. From all the circumstances there was enough to support the inference that defendants actually had homicide in mind. And the jury had been carefully instructed that they could not find defendants guilty as charged without finding a "specific intent to kill,"— although it was sufficient if such an intent was in the alternative.

A conditional intent is sufficient for an assault with intent to murder but logical probabilities cannot be ignored in the effort to establish such an intent. If the ordinary citizen accompanies an otherwise lawful order with a threat to kill, if disobeyed, the likelihood of a bluff is too great to permit an inference of an actual intent to kill, unless other facts are present to support it. But where a robber orders his victim to put up his hands or be killed, the probability is that he means what he says.

C. SOLICITATION (INCITEMENT)

The word "solicitation," in the sense of "criminal solicitation," is employed in the law as a general label to cover any use of words or other device by which a person is requested, urged, advised, counseled, tempted, commanded or otherwise enticed or incited to commit a crime.

One who successfully solicits another to commit a crime is guilty of the offense committed [93] unless some special defense is available to him. If a statute forbids a deed which requires the cooperation of two, but provides a penalty for one only, this is a clear manifestation of the legislative intent that the other shall go unpunished. Whether such a provision is wise or unwise is for the determination of the legislature, and hence the courts will not hold the other guilty on the theory that he solicited or otherwise aided

---

92. An intent to kill under such circumstances that the homicide would be murder is a different state of mind than an intent to kill under such circumstances that the homicide would be justifiable, or would amount only to manslaughter.

93. People v. Harper, 25 Cal.2d 862, 156 P.2d 249 (1945).

". . . solicitation of murder merges into the offense of being an accessory before the fact to the same murder." Lewis v. State, 285 Md. 705, 404 A.2d 1073, 1083 (1979).

and abetted the one. The normal rules of solicitation and abetment cannot be applied so as to defeat the obvious purpose of the statute. During National Prohibition, for example, the law forbade the sale of liquor but provided a penalty for the seller only.[94] Under such a statute the purchaser cannot be held to have aided and abetted the sale.[95] And if, to carry out the legislative intent, the solicitor would not have been guilty of the offense committed had the solicitation been successful, his ineffective effort is not punishable under the general rules of solicitation, even if the offense solicited is a felony.[96]

The view that one, who had unsuccessfully solicited another to commit a crime, might be punished by reason of the solicitation itself, was late in receiving recognition. It was held in the seventeenth century that it was punishable to agree to pay money for having a deed proved, in a trial, to be a forgery.[97] But this seems to have been thought of as attempted subornation of perjury.[98] It was said by counsel in 1769: "To solicit and counsel the committing of a crime, is criminal." [99] But the act charged was an offer to bribe and it was held punishable as an attempt to bribe. There were other indications of a developing rule [1] but the leading case—*Higgins*— [2] was not decided until 1801. To solicit a servant to steal his master's goods was there held to be a misdemeanor although no other act was done. Two points were emphasized by the court. Such an act was held to be indictable because it has a tendency to a breach of the peace. And since an attempt to commit a misdemeanor is itself a misdemeanor, the court added: "it would be extraordinary indeed if an attempt to incite to a felony were not also a misdemeanor." [3]

Since *Higgins* it has been the accepted view that to solicit another to commit any felony is punishable as a misdemeanor at common law,[4] in the ab-

---

94. United States v. Farrar, 281 U.S. 624, 50 S.Ct. 425 (1929); Norris v. United States, 34 F.2d 839 (3d Cir. 1929).

95. State v. Teahan, 50 Conn. 92 (1882). "In such situations, the participant who does not come within the scope of the penalty imposed cannot, through the medium of a charge of conspiracy to commit the crime, be held guilty, if he participated no further than was necessary to the accomplishment of the offense." State v. McLaughlin, 132 Conn. 325, 334, 44 A.2d 116, 121 (1945).

96. Lott v. United States, 205 F. 28 (1913). If a statute provides a penalty for a certain type of solicitation, guilt is not established without bringing the case squarely within the words and the purport of the enactment. Thus soliciting a customer for a prostitute without receiving compensation or soliciting compensation therefor does not violate California Penal Code § 266h. People v. Smith, 44 Cal.2d 77, 279 P.2d 33 (1955).

97. The King v. Johnson, 2 Show. 1, 89 Eng.Rep. 753 (1679).

98. "An endeavour . . . makes a man as guilty as the commission. . . ." Id. at 4, 89 Eng.Rep. at 756.

99. Rex v. Vaughan, 4 Burr. 2494, 2498, 98 Eng.Rep. 308, 310 (1769). "Holt, Chief Justice said . . . the indictment might perhaps be for the evil act of persuading." The Queen v. Daniel, 6 Mod. 99, 101, 87 Eng.Rep. 856, 857 (1704).

1. See, for example, The King v. Plympton, 2 Ld.Raym. 1377, 92 Eng.Rep. 397 (1737).

2. The King v. Higgins, 2 East 5, 102 Eng.Rep. 269.

3. Id. at 18, 102 Eng.Rep. at 275.

4. State v. Avery, 7 Conn. 266 (1828); State v. Schleifer, 99 Conn. 432, 121 A. 805 (1923); State v. Donovan, 28 Del. 40, 90 A. 220 (1914); Commonwealth v. Flagg, 135 Mass. 545 (1883); Commonwealth v. Randolph, 146 Pa. 83, 23 A. 388 (1892); State v. Bowers, 35 S.C. 262, 14 S.E. 488 (1891).

Solicitation of a felony is an indictable offense at common law. State v. Beckwith, 135 Me. 423, 198 A. 739 (1938).

sence of some special defense as mentioned above. It has been common to
add, with somewhat less assurance, that it is also indictable at common law
to solicit another to commit a serious misdemeanor which may tend to a
breach of the peace,[5]—and perhaps to solicit any indictable misdemeanor.[6]
Actually there has been no opportunity for an exhaustive judicial exploration
of this matter because of restrictive legislation. While it has been rather
common to include a general attempt clause in the penal codes, the tendency
has been to limit the punishability of solicitations to those involving a few
specified felonies.[7]

Within the area included in the particular jurisdiction, the solicitation itself is punished although promptly rejected by the other without any act being done by him.[8] If the one solicited acts upon the suggestion, and goes far
enough to incur criminal guilt, the solicitor is also guilty,—and this is true
whether the solicitation would or would not have been punished as such if it
had failed to induce such action. If the one solicited goes far enough to
incur guilt of an attempt to commit the crime, the solicitor is also guilty of
attempt.[9] If the one commits the crime the other is also guilty of that
crime [10] although at common law his guilt would be as an accessory before
the fact if it was a felony and he was not present at the time.[11] The solicita-

See also La.Stat.Ann.Rev.Stat. 14 § 28
(1974).

Solicitation to murder is indictable as a
common-law offense. State v. Foster,
379 A.2d 1219 (Me.1977).

5. State v. Boyd, 86 N.J.L. 75, 91 A.
586 (1914); Commonwealth v. Wiswesser,
134 Pa.Super.Ct. 488, 3 A.2d 983 (1939);
Rex v. Phillips, 6 East 464, 102 Eng.Rep.
1365 (1805). The solicitation of a misdemeanor is not indictable at common law
if it does not tend to a breach of the
peace or an obstruction of justice. Cox
v. People, 82 Ill. 191 (1876); Smith v.
Commonwealth, 54 Pa. 209 (1880); State
v. Blechman, 135 N.J.L. 99, 50 A.2d 152
(1946).

6. Kenny indicates that this is the law
in England. Kenny, Outlines of Criminal
Law 81 and note 1 (14th ed. 1933). An
early case had held that it was no offense
to solicit a servant to embezzle his master's goods unless they were in fact embezzled. The Queen v. Collingwood, 6
Mod. 288, 87 Eng.Rep. 1029 (1704).

7. Compare, for example, the following sections in West's Ann.Cal.Pen.Code
§ 664 (1978). "Every person who attempts to commit any crime. . . ." §
653f (1979). "Every person who solicits
another to offer or accept or join in the
offer or acceptance of a bribe, or to commit or join in the commission of robbery,
burglary, grand theft, receiving stolen
property, extortion, perjury, subornation
of perjury, forgery or kidnaping, arson
or assault with a deadly weapon or instrument . . ."

Under the present Iowa Criminal Code,
§ 705.1 (1978), the solicitation of any felony or aggravated misdemeanor is punishable.

8. People v. Burt, 45 Cal.2d 311, 288
P.2d 503 (1955); The King v. Higgins, 2
East 5, 102 Eng.Rep. 269 (1801); Commonwealth v. Flagg, 135 Mass. 545
(1883); State v. Hampton, 210 N.C. 283,
186 S.E. 251 (1936).

"The solicitation itself is a distinct offense, and is punishable irrespective of
the reaction of the person solicited; i.e.
the solicitor is guilty even though that
person immediately rejects the request or
proposal." Hutchins v. Municipal Court
of Santa Monica, 61 Cal.App.3d 77, 132
Cal.Rptr. 158, 165 (1976).

"Illinois law requires that to be guilty
of solicitation, a person must request or
encourage another to commit a crime
with intent that the crime be committed."
United States ex rel. Swimley v. Nesbitt,
608 F.2d 1130, 1131 (7th Cir. 1979). The
fact that the one solicited was an undercover agent was no defense.

9. State v. Jones, 83 N.C. 605 (1880);
Uhl v. Commonwealth, 47 Va. 706 (1849).

10. People v. Harper, 25 Cal.2d 862,
156 P.2d 249 (1945); State v. Johnson,
226 N.C. 671, 40 S.E.2d 113 (1946).

11. See Begley v. Commonwealth, 22
Ky.L.Rep. 1546, 1548, 60 S.W. 847, 849
(1901).

tion is so far merged in the resulting offense that the solicitor cannot be punished for both.[12] There is no sound reason why there should be any rule of absolute merger. If the evidence of an indictable solicitation is clear, for example, while there is a conflict as to whether the one solicited did or did not proceed far enough to have committed a criminal attempt, there should be no bar to a conviction for the solicitation.

Where a solicitation results in a criminal attempt by the other the solicitor is guilty of that attempt, as mentioned above. A further question is whether the solicitation itself is sufficient for guilt of a criminal attempt. This is a matter of vital importance in jurisdictions having a general attempt clause without any such sweeping provision in regard to solicitations. Among the authors Bishop alone takes the unqualified stand that a solicitation is an attempt.[13] The usual statement is to the effect that, although a few cases have held otherwise, a solicitation is not an attempt and if it is punishable the indictment or information must charge solicitation, and not attempt.[14] Without doubt this stand has been taken time and again in the cases [15] but it seems to represent an inadequate analysis of the problem.

If one requests another to burn the dwelling of a third next week, this is not an attempt because of the lack of proximity, if for no other reason.[16] A solicitation by mail is likely to involve a similar element of remoteness.[17] But if two persons are standing face to face, and one is reaching out his hand asking the other to give or to accept a bribe, this satisfies every requirement of attempted bribery, and it was so held in an early case [18] as well

12. "On retrial, if the defendant is again convicted of being an accessory before the fact to the murders of his wife and daughter, he may not also be convicted of solicitation." Lewis v. State, 285 Md. 705, 404 A.2d 1073, 1083 (1979).

One may not be convicted of both criminal mischief and solicitation of criminal mischief, based upon the same facts. State v. Mitchell, ___ Mont. ___, 625 P.2d 1155 (1981).

13. 1 Bishop, New Criminal Law §§ 767, 768 (8th ed. 1892). For a discussion of the views of Bishop and Wharton on this point, see Curran, Solicitation, A Substantive Crime, 17 Minn.L.Rev. 499 (1933).

14. It is generally held that solicitation does not constitute an attempt. Curran, Solicitation: A Substantive Crime, 17 Minn.L.Rev. 499, 509 N. 54 (1933). Williams, Textbook of Criminal Law, p. 386 (1978).

"The solicitation of another, assuming neither solicitor nor solicitee proximately acts toward the crime's commission cannot be held for an attempt." State v. Otto, 102 Idaho 250, 629 P.2d 646, 650 (1981).

15. State v. Donovan, 28 Del. 40, 90 A. 220 (1914); State v. Bowles, 70 Kan. 821, 79 P. 726 (1905); State v. Bereman,

177 Kan. 141, 276 P.2d 364 (1954); State v. Davis, 319 Mo. 1222, 6 S.W.2d 609 (1928); Stabler v. Commonwealth, 95 Pa. 318 (1880); State v. Awde, 154 Wash. 463, 282 P. 908 (1929); Rex v. Gordon, 79 CCC 315 (Sask.Ct.App. 1937).

16. There is also lack of proximity if the one solicited is urged to start now but the place to be burned is at a distance. Commonwealth v. Peaslee, 177 Mass. 267, 59 N.E. 55 (1901). The cases have tended to hold that solicitation to commit arson is not an attempt to commit arson even apart from a special factor as to time or space. State v. Hampton, 210 N.C. 283, 186 S.E. 251 (1936). Solicitation to commit arson plus furnishing oil and matches is not an attempt. McDade v. People, 29 Mich. 50 (1874); cited with approval in People v. Pippin, 316 Mich. 191, 194, 25 N.W.2d 164, 165 (1946). Contra, People v. Bush, 4 Hill 133 (N.Y.1843).

17. In upholding a conviction of attempted buggery based upon a more direct solicitation it was stated that two letters written by defendant would not have been sufficient. The King v. Barker, [1924] New Zealand 865, 868.

18. Rex v. Vaughan, 4 Burr. 2494, 98 Eng.Rep. 308 (1769).

as more recently.[19] Such decisions would no doubt be numerous were it not for the tendency to have a special statute dealing with the offer to give or receive a bribe.[20] It has been held also that if one solicits another to submit to the "unnatural act" this is sufficient for an attempt to commit buggery, if the two are together and prompt action is contemplated.[21]

In neither type of case, of the two just mentioned, does the solicitor expect to leave the perpetration entirely in the hands of the other. It is no part of his plan to withdraw from further participation if his persuasive effort is successful. He intends to take an active part until the crime is complete. And in general this seems essential if the solicitation is to be sufficient for a criminal attempt. Otherwise the attempt concept might be violated by finding an attempt to commit a crime without a specific intent to commit that offense. In a Missouri case,[22] for example, defendant solicited Dill to murder Lourie. Dill, a police officer posing as an ex-convict, merely pretended to agree in order to obtain evidence. The defendant himself did not intend to kill Lourie, or anyone else. Dill did not intend to kill Lourie, or anyone else. Defendant was convicted of attempted murder but this was reversed because neither solicitor nor solicitee had any intention of taking human life. "Of course, the defendant was guilty of soliciting another to commit a murder; a serious crime, but he was not charged with that, nor convicted of that offense." [23]

While in general the solicitor must plan to do more than solicit, if his solicitation is itself to be regarded as a criminal attempt,[24] this should not be required in an offense of such an unusual nature that the solicitation is the closest approach it is possible for him to make. If perjury, for example, is committed as a result of solicitation, the solicitor is guilty of subornation of perjury.[25] The statute of Elizabeth I punished the suborner more severely than the perjurer,[26] but the significant point for the moment is that one can never be guilty of subornation of perjury without the help of another, which takes a form other than joint action. Strictly speaking it is not a crime that is perpetrated,—it can only be procured. And solicitation, being the most direct and final step in the effort to procure this offense, has properly been

---

19. People v. Bloom, 133 N.Y.S. 708 (1912); Rudolph v. State, 128 Wis. 222, 107 N.W. 466 (1906); Contra, but due to legislative history in the state, State v. Bowles, 70 Kan. 821, 79 P. 726 (1905).

20. "A person is guilty of bribery . . . if he offers, confers or agrees to confer upon another, or solicits, accepts or agrees to accept from another . . . ." Idaho code, 18–1352 (1979).

See also N.H.Rev.Stat.Ann., 1974 640:2. "If any person shall bribe or attempt to bribe any executive officer . . . ." M.D.Code Ann., 1957 Art. 27 § 23.

21. The King v. Barker, [1924] New Zealand 865.

22. State v. Davis, 319 Mo. 1222, 6 S.W.2d 609 (1928). But cf. State v. Mandell, 78 Ariz. 226, 278 P.2d 413 (1954).

23. Id. at 1236, 6 S.W.2d at 616. See also the companion case. State v. Lourie, 12 S.W.2d 43 (Mo.1928).

24. "Generally . . . a person who merely counsels cannot be said to have attempted to commit the offense counselled for his intention is not to commit it but to have some other person do it and until that other person commits the offense or attempts to commit it the person who incites cannot, in the absence of some special provision, be guilty of the offense counselled or of an attempt to commit it." Rex v. Gordon, 79 CCC 315, 321 (Sask.Ct. of App. 1937).

It would be possible, of course, for a statute to declare that a solicitation shall be declared to be an attempt.

25. 4 Bl.Comm. *137.

26. 5 Eliz. c. 9. Id. at *138.

recognized as constituting an attempt.[27] It is not attempted perjury, it should be emphasized, but attempted subornation of perjury. Except where the offense said to have been attempted is one accomplished by procurement rather than by perpetration, such as subornation of perjury, the sound rule would seem to be this:

> **The solicitation of another to commit a crime is an attempt to commit that crime if, but only if, it takes the form of urging the other to join with the solicitor in perpetrating that offense,—not at some future time or distant place, but here and now, and the crime is such that it cannot be committed by one without the cooperation or submission of another, such as bribery [28] or buggery.[29] Where such cooperation or submission is an essential feature of the crime itself, the request for it now is a step in the direction of the offense.[30]**

An important distinction must be noted. A criminal solicitation is, in essence, asking a person to commit a crime. One who desires to accomplish a criminal purpose by the hand of another may plan to make use of either a guilty agent or an innocent agent. If, for example, the plan is to cause the death of a sick person by the administration of poison, it may be given to one who knows it is poison, or to one who believes it is a proper medicine and has no reason to think otherwise. In the first type of case the agent is asked to commit a crime because he will be guilty of crime if he complies. In the second type of case the agent is not asked to commit a crime because doing what is asked will not be a crime by the agent, but only by the asker. And, apart from the exceptional situations mentioned above, the result is as follows: The request in the first type of case is a criminal solicitation and is not a criminal attempt.[31] The request in the second type of case is not a criminal

---

27. State v. Johnson, 26 Del. 472, 84 A. 1040 (1912); Dodys v. State, 73 Ga. App. 483, 37 S.E.2d 173 (1946); The King v. Johnson, 2 Show. 1, 89 Eng.Rep. 753 (1679). It has been recognized at times in the statutes. For example, after a section dealing with subornation of perjury is found the following: "*Attempt to suborn perjury.* Every person who, without giving, offering or promising a bribe, shall incite or attempt to procure another to commit perjury, or to offer any false evidence, or to withhold true testimony, though no perjury be committed or false evidence offered or true testimony withheld, shall be guilty of a gross misdemeanor." Nev.Rev.Stat. 199.150 (1979). People v. Bloom, 133 N.Y.S. 708 (1912), must be distinguished. In that case **A** solicited **B** to procure **C** to commit perjury. This was too remote for an attempt.

28. See supra, notes 18, 19. A demand for the immediate payment of money, under such circumstances that the receipt would constitute extortion, is an attempt to extort. State v. Weleck, 10 N.J.2d 355, 90 A.2d 1 (1952).

29. See supra, note 21.

30. One court took the position that where cooperation is essential there can be no attempt until after an agreement has been reached. State v. Butler, 8 Wash. 194, 35 P. 1093 (1894). That involved a solicitation of adultery. The court confused the problem at hand with two others. (1) The rule that one asking to buy liquor is not guilty of attempting to violate a prohibition statute (which provided penalty only for the seller). (2) That an agreement of two to commit adultery is not punishable as a conspiracy. This was ruled out on the ground that a conspiracy must involve something more than is present whenever the crime is committed. But an attempt is not ruled out on any such basis.

31. State v. Lampe, 131 Minn. 65, 154 N.W. 737 (1915), conviction of attempted extortion reversed; State v. Davis, 319 Mo. 1222, 6 S.W.2d 609 (1928), conviction of attempted murder reversed; McDade v. People, 29 Mich. 50 (1874), conviction of attempted arson reversed. Contra, People v. Bush, 4 Hill 133 (N.Y. 1843).

"Although in some jurisdictions solicitations are tried as indictable attempts, either by virtue of judicial decisions fail-

solicitation [32] but is a criminal attempt—because it is the last guilty act contemplated and is expected to accomplish the unlawful result. A criminal attempt may be committed without the "last act," as pointed out earlier, but whenever the last guilty act contemplated has been done, with the expectation that it will result in the consummation of the crime, the plan has obviously moved beyond preparation and an attempt has been committed.

As pointed out by Williams,[33] one who is guilty of criminal attempt intended to commit the crime as a principal in the first degree whereas one guilty of solicitation intended to be in a secondary position—accessory before the fact or principal in the second degree. He gives this illustration: "Again, suppose that D unlawfully tells E to set fire to a haystack, and gives him a match to do it with. (1) If, as D knows, E (mistakenly) believes that it is D's stack and that the act is lawful, E is an innocent agent, and D is guilty of attempted arson; D, in instructing E, does the last thing he intends in order to effect his criminal purpose. (It would be the same if he only used words and did not give E a match.) (2) If, as D knows, E is to be a conscious party to the crime, D is guilty of incitement. He is not guilty of attempt, because he does not intend to commit the crime as principal in the first degree."

A special problem requires attention. Where an attempt to commit suicide is punishable [34] this is not an attempt to commit a crime but is a complete substantive offense, just as knowingly attempting to pass a forged instrument is not an attempt to commit a crime but the complete offense of uttering a forged instrument.[35] In such cases much greater proximity should be required than is needed for an ordinary criminal attempt.

Under the Model Penal Code the solicitation of any crime would be punishable [36] and it may be added that except where a felony of the first degree is involved the Code provides the same penalty for an attempt or a solicitation as for the complete offense.[37] Both of these positions seem to be extreme.[38] The argument that one who has attempted an offense is just as bad as one who completed it is subject to question. In many cases the actor's subconscious influence may have caused the attempt to fail. The fact that the Code makes an exception in cases of the gravest crimes is entitled to

ing to distinguish them, or by statutory provisions, the great weight of authority is otherwise. Analytically the two crimes are distinct." Sayre, Criminal Attempts, 41 Harv.L.Rev. 821, 859–60 (1928).

32. This may be changed by statute. Under a statute worded in terms of one who "facilitates the commission" of an offense, one may be convicted of solicitation although his criminal purpose was unknown to the solicitee. State v. Bush, ___ Mont. ___, 636 P.2d 849 (1981).

33. Williams, Criminal Law 616 (2d ed. 1961).

34. See supra, chapter 2, section I, E.

35. Ponds v. State ex rel. Eyman, 7 Ariz.App. 276, 438 P.2d 423 (1968). The statute includes both the fraudulent making and knowingly uttering in the section

called "forgery." And the court held that conviction of an "attempt to pass" was a conviction of forgery—not an attempt to commit forgery.

36. Section 5.02.

37. Section 5.05(1).

38. "The penalty for attempt is often fixed at one-half of that for the completed crime whereas the penalty for solicitation is usually less." Arnold, Criminal Attempts—The Rise and Fall of an Abstraction, 40 Yale L.J. 53, 76–77 (1930).

The Arizona Code punishes both attempt and solicitation, but provides a lesser penalty for solicitation of an offense than an attempt, Ariz.Rev.Stat. Ann. § 13–1001, 1002 (1978). Punishments are set on a scale based on the offense attempted or solicited.

attention. The same reason would seem applicable to lesser crimes. In the recently-adopted New York Code the policy applying the same penalty to an attempt as to a completed offense was rejected.[39]

D. ABANDONMENT

Much debate has centered around the question whether an attempt to commit a crime, or a criminal solicitation, is a "complete offense."[40] This debate seems to be merely a matter of words. An attempt to commit a crime is a "complete offense" in the sense that one having a piece of pie, representing twenty-five percent of the entire pastry, can be said to have a "complete quarter of a pie." So far as the common law is concerned an attempt to commit an indictable offense is "complete" in the sense that it is indictable and punishable. It is definitely not a "complete offense" within the meaning of the rule that an attempt to commit any indictable offense is itself indictable. If it were, we could have an attempt to commit an attempt to commit an offense, and so *ad infinitum*.[41] Rather than spending time seeking to maintain that a criminal attempt either is, or is not, a "complete offense" it is better to recognize frankly that it is complete in one sense and incomplete in another. It never exists in any form other than as part of a larger plan. It is always part of the ultimate harm intended, and the attempt is an "incomplete offense" in the sense that it is a part of it. On the other hand, if one intending murder, for example, has proceeded far enough to be convicted of attempted murder, that punishable part of his plan is complete.

The accepted view seems to have been that a criminal attempt is a "complete offense" in the sense that one who has carried a criminal effort to the point of punishability can no more wipe out his criminal guilt by an abandonment of his plan[42] than a thief can obliterate a larceny by restoration of the stolen chattel.[43] As said in one case,[44] "it is a rule, founded in reason and

---

39. McKinney's N.Y.Rev.Pen.Law § 110.05 (1979).

40. E. g., Skilton, The Mental Element in Criminal Attempt, 3 U. of Pitt.L. Rev. 181, note 1 (1937).

"An attempt in criminal law is an unfinished crime . . ." Johnson v. Commonwealth, 209 Va. 291, 163 S.E.2d 570, 573 (1968).

41. It was held that since an assault is an attempt to commit a battery there is no such offense as an attempt to commit an assault with intent to murder. White v. State, 22 Tex. 608, 609 (1858). On the other hand the Oregon court held that the statutory offense of assault with a dangerous weapon is something more than an uncompleted battery and upheld a conviction of an attempt to commit it. State v. Wilson, 218 Or. 575, 346 P.2d 115 (1959). Another Oregon case held an indictment charging an attempt to solicit was demurrable, on the ground that it was meaningless, although the phrase was used in the statute. State v. Underwood, 79 Or. 338, 155 P. 194 (1916). An

English case authorized conviction of an attempt to solicit. Regina v. Banks, 12 Cox C.C. 393 (1873). But no case has suggested the possibility of charging an attempt to attempt to murder. It may be mentioned that if a statute makes the use of tools with intent to produce a miscarriage the substantive offense, an attempt to make such use is punishable as an attempt. People v. Berger, 131 Cal.App.2d 127, 280 P.2d 136 (1955).

42. People v. Carter, 73 Cal.App. 495, 238 P. 1059 (1925); Bishop v. State, 86 Ga. 329, 12 S.E. 641 (1890); State v. McGilvery, 20 Wash. 240, 55 P. 115 (1898); Regina v. Taylor, 1 F. & F. 511, 175 Eng. Rep. 831 (1859); Stewart v. State, 85 Nev. 388, 455 P.2d 914 (1969).

43. Brennon v. Commonwealth, 169 Ky. 815, 185 S.W. 489 (1916). "Finally, we need hardly note that if defendant had the requisite intent at the time he took them, a subsequent return of the radios is no defense. However laudable re-

---

44. See note 44 on page 655.

supported by authority, that if a man resolves on a criminal enterprise and proceeds so far in it that his act amounts to an indictable attempt, it does not cease to be such though he voluntarily abandons the evil purpose." Wharton, at one time, suggested a different view,—that an attempt differs so far from the offense intended that there is in the former a *locus penitentiae*.[45]

Established beyond question is the view that guilt of a criminal attempt is not expunged by an abandonment due to some extrinsic cause such as the sight of police officers,[46] a discovery that the scene of the intended crime is under police surveillance[47] or that an attempt to commit larceny has been detected by the intended victim.[48] This was not questioned by Wharton, his statement being: "If an attempt be voluntarily and freely abandoned before the act is put in process of final execution, there being no outside cause prompting such abandonment, then this is a defense; . . ."[49] Four cases were cited for this conclusion, not one of which lends it the slightest support. One merely took the sound position that an abandonment of the felonious intent after the burglar has broken into the building does not preclude guilt of burglary.[50] Another was dealing with the problem of withdrawal by one conspirator so as to relieve him from responsibility for *subsequent* acts of

pentance may be, a later change of heart is no defense to a completed theft." State v. Burnham, 19 Wn.App. 442, 576 P.2d 917, 919 (1978). Robbery once committed cannot be wiped out by a subsequent return of the money. Lacy v. State, ___ Ind.App. ___, 375 N.E.2d 1133 (1978). In speaking of embezzlement it was said: "Restitution is only a defense when the defendant intended to return the property at the time it was taken." State v. Bretz, ___ Mont. ___, 605 P.2d 974, 999 (1979).

44. Glover v. Commonwealth, 86 Va. 382, 386, 10 S.E. 420, 421 (1889).

"Further, the fact that the defendant stopped short of actually having intercourse with the prosecutrix is of no consequence because the act of assault with intent to rape was completed at the moment defendant first laid hands on the victim with intent to rape." Colbert v. State, 567 P.2d 996 (Okl.Cr.App. 1977).

"Once a substantial step has been taken, and the crime of attempt is accomplished, the crime cannot be abandoned." State v. Workman, 90 Wn.2d 443, 584 P.2d 382, 386 (1978).

45. 1 Wharton, Criminal Law § 226 (12th ed. 1932). Later editions of Wharton take a different position. See 1 Wharton's Criminal Law and Procedure § 76 (Anderson ed. 1957). In dealing with a different problem, the statutory requirement of an overt act for conviction of conspiracy, the Supreme Court said: "The provision of the statute, that there

must be an act done to effect the object of the conspiracy, merely provides a *locus penitentiae*, so that before the act done either one or all of the parties may abandon their design, and thus avoid the penalty prescribed by the statute." United States v. Britton, 108 U.S. 199, 204–5, 2 S.Ct. 531, 534 (1883).

46. People v. Stites, 75 Cal. 570, 17 P. 693 (1888); People v. Walker, 33 Cal.2d 250, 201 P.2d 6 (1948); People v. Von Hecht, 133 Cal.App.2d 25, 283 P.2d 764 (1955).

Abandonment of an attempt as a result of the discovery of being watched, is not exculpating. People v. Davis, 70 Ill.App. 3d 454, 26 Ill.Dec. 886, 388 N.E.2d 887 (1979).

47. People v. Lombard, 131 Cal.App. 525, 21 P.2d 955 (1933); State v. Hansen, 290 Minn. 552, 188 N.W.2d 881 (1971).

48. People v. Gilmore, 25 Cal.App. 332, 143 P. 790 (1914).

"In proving a defense of renunciation, 'defendant must show by a preponderance of the evidence that his motive for desisting was due to a change of heart, and was not founded in fear of apprehension or because the actual commission of the crime posed unexpected difficulties.'" State v. Wasson, 45 Or.App. 169, 607 P.2d 792, 793 (1980).

49. 1 Wharton, Criminal Law § 226 (12th ed. 1932).

50. State v. McDaniel, 60 N.C. 245 (1864).

the others.[51] In the third, the court said that a voluntary abandonment "cannot purge the crime" but added that if the defendant, charged with attempted rape, did not take the woman by force although able to do so, this "should weigh much against" the allegation that he intended to have intercourse with her against her will.[52] The fourth case cited by Wharton tends to refute his position, the fact that the court was speaking of preparation rather than attempt having been overlooked by him. The dictum was:

"Anywhere between the conception of the intent and the overt act toward its commission, there is room for repentance; and the law in its beneficence extends the hand of forgiveness. But when the evil intent is supplemented by the requisite act toward its commission, the statutory offense is completed. 'A crime once committed may be pardoned, but it cannot be obliterated by repentance.' "[53]

Despite the utter lack of support in the cases cited, the position taken by Wharton has much to commend it. There are definite limitations, of course. Attempted murder cannot be purged after the victim has been wounded, no matter what may cause the plan to be abandoned. And probably the same is true after a shot has been fired with intent to kill. On the other hand, although a criminal plan has proceeded far enough to support a conviction of criminal attempt, it would be sound to recognize the possibility of a *locus penitentiae* so long as no substantial harm has been done and no act of actual danger committed. And there are indications that such a position has received legal recognition, such as this recent dictum:

"Abandonment is a defense if the attempt to commit a crime is freely and voluntarily abandoned before the act is put in process of final execution and *where there is no outside cause* prompting such abandonment . . . ."[54]

However this may turn out to be in regard to criminal attempt, or a corresponding problem relating to solicitation itself, it is clear that one who has solicited a crime can save himself from guilt of the ultimate offense by a timely and effective communication of his change of mind.[55] No amount of

---

51. State v. Allen, 47 Conn. 121 (1879).

52. Lewis v. State, 35 Ala. 380 (1860).

53. State v. Hayes, 78 Mo. 307, 317–8 (1883).

An attempt to murder that has proceeded far enough for conviction cannot be wiped out by abandonment. State v. Henry, 128 Ariz. 204, 624 P.2d 882 (App. 1981).

54. People v. Von Hecht, 133 Cal.App. 2d 25, 283 P.2d 764, 771 (1955). This had been preceded by other dicta to the same effect. See, People v. Walker, 33 Cal.2d 250, 259, 201 P.2d 6, 11 (1948); People v. Corkery, 134 Cal.App. 294, 297, 25 P.2d 257, 258 (1933).

The position has been accepted in a recent case in Michigan: "We are persuaded by the trend of modern authority and hold that voluntary abandonment is an affirmative defense to a prosecution for criminal attempt. The burden is on the defendant to establish by a preponderance of the evidence that he or she has voluntarily and completely abandoned his or her criminal purpose. Abandonment is not 'voluntary' when the defendant fails to complete the attempted crime because of unanticipated difficulties, unexpected resistance, or circumstances which increase the probability of detention or apprehension. Nor is the abandonment 'voluntary' when the defendant fails to consummate the attempted offense after deciding to postpone the criminal conduct until another time or to substitute another victim or another but similar objective." People v. Kimball, 109 Mich.App. 273, 311 N.W.2d 343 (1981).

55. State v. Peterson, 213 Minn. 56, 4 N.W.2d 826 (1942).

effort in an attempted countermand will have this effect, however, if it fails to reach the other in time.[56]

"By the specific terms of the statute, § 18–2–101(3), C.R.S. 1973, abandonment is an affirmative defense to an attempt crime. Consequently, even though, in a strict analytical sense, the crime of attempt is complete once the actor intentionally takes a substantial step towards the commission of the crime, nevertheless, the defense of abandonment is present if he thereafter voluntarily renunciates his criminal intent." [57]

Suppose **D** decided to satisfy a grudge against **X** by burning down **X**'s house. He knew **X** and his family were all away on vacation, with no one there at the moment, so the time was propitious. Being familiar with the house he decided that the open space under the rear porch was the place to start the fire. He procured paper, kindling, matches and a candle and set out for **X**'s house. On arrival there he saw no one, so he quickly went to the back porch and crept under. Having arranged the paper and kindling, he carefully set the candle in such a position that after it had burned down to a certain point the flame would come into contact with the paper, the burning paper would set fire to the kindling which in turn would set fire to the house, and burn it down—if all went as planned. Then he struck a match and lit the candle. His plan was to be far away at a cocktail lounge, when the fire started. But despite his caution he had been observed. The candle was put out before anything else had burned, and **D** was arrested before he had gone many blocks. Since the fire had not touched the building he was not guilty of arson, but was clearly guilty of attempted arson.

Just when did his effort reach the point of punishability? Suppose he was arrested after he struck the match but before he had succeeded in lighting the candle. Suppose he was just preparing to strike the match. Suppose he had just started to place the candle. Gathering the combustible materials and starting out for **X**'s house were merely acts of preparation, but under the modern view he passed beyond preparation and reached the point of punishability when he arrived at the porch—or even in close proximity thereto. (It should be noted that under a different assumption, if he went there merely to "set the stage" so there would be no delay when he returned to set the fire at a later time, this would not be a common-law attempt, although punishable under some statutes carrying the name "attempt.")

Assume the same plot with a different ending. After **D** had lit the candle and started away, he began having "second thoughts" about his plan. The

---

56. People v. Ortiz, 63 Cal.App. 662, 219 P. 1024 (1923).

57. People v. Johnson, 41 Colo.App. 220, 585 P.2d 306, 308 (1978).

The statute provides that one is not guilty of criminal attempt "if, under circumstances manifesting a voluntary and complete renunciation of his criminal intent, he avoids the commission of the crime attempted by abandoning his criminal effort . . . . (2) The defense of renunciation is an affirmative defense." State v. Lammers, 29 Or.App. 207, 562 P.2d 1223 (1977). It was held that this requires the defendant to show, by a preponderance of the evidence that his motive for desisting was due to a change of heart, and not founded in fear of apprehension or because the actual commission of the crime posed unsuspected difficulties. See also State v. Wasson, 45 Or. App. 169, 607 P.2d 792 (1980).

Under a comparable Minnesota statute it was noted: "This defense is made a part of the Minnesota Criminal Code because 'it is believed . . . to be desirable to encourage the voluntary good faith withdrawal from the commission of the crime." State v. Cox, 278 N.W.2d 62 (Minn.1979).

more he thought about it the less desirable it seemed. Then with a complete "change of heart" he hurried back, put out the candle, gathered the paper and kindling, and departed leaving the place just as it was before his first arrival. Would his truly voluntary abandonment have wiped out his guilt of attempted arson? At one time the answer was no. It should be yes, and hopefully the law has reached that point.

The Model Penal Code would provide an affirmative defense for either attempt [58] or solicitation [59] if there has been a timely, complete and voluntary renunciation of the criminal purpose. Some states have adopted this position by statute.[60]

SECTION 4.   NEGATIVE ACTS

Is it correct to speak of "acts of omission," or does the word "act" necessarily imply commission? Usage differs. The word is employed at times in a sense limited to positive acts, and is then opposed to forbearances and omissions; at other times it is given a meaning large enough to include negative acts as well as positive ones.[1] In a legislative enactment, for example, if the phrase act or omission [2] is found, the first word is being employed in the limited sense of act of commission; whereas if only the word "act" is used, it is construed ordinarily to include also forbearance or omission.[3] The choice between these two meanings must be made upon the ground of convenience rather than upon a scientific analysis of the conceptions involved. If the broad signification is adopted it will be necessary to say "act of commission" or "positive act" whenever the element of negative action is not to be included in the particular statement. If the narrow meaning is chosen some such phrase as "act of omission" is required whenever the possibility of negative action is not to be definitely excluded. Although, in the perpetration of offenses at least, positive acts are no doubt much more frequent than negative acts, the latter should be included much more frequently than excluded, when general statements are made in the field of criminal law. Hence, as a

---

58.   Section 5.01(4).

59.   Section 5.02(3).

60.   Code of Ala.1975 § 13A–4–2(c) (1975); Ky.Rev.Stat. 506.020 (1975); Utah Code Ann., 1953, § 76–2–307. S.1722, 96th Cong. 1st Sess. would provide: "It is an affirmative crime."

1.   "Of acts as so defined there are various species. In the first place, they are either positive or negative, either acts of commission or acts of omission. A wrongdoer either does that which he ought not to do, or leaves undone that which he ought to do. The term act is often used in a narrow sense to include merely positive acts, and is then opposed to omissions or forbearances instead of including them. This restriction, however, is inconvenient. Adopting the generic sense, we can easily distinguish the two species as positive and negative; but if we restrict the term to acts of commission, we leave ourselves without a name for the genus, and are compelled to re-

sort to an enumeration of the species." Salmond, Jurisprudence § 131 (10th ed. 1947).

2.   E. g., "A crime or public offense is an act committed or omitted in violation of a law forbidding or commanding it. . . ." West's Ann.Cal.Pen. Code § 15 (1970).

3.   See for example the Nevada statute providing for jurisdiction.

"Whenever a person, with intent to commit a crime, does any act within this state in execution or part execution of such intent, which culminates in the commission of a crime . . ." Nev.Rev. Stat. 171.020 (1979).

"Similar statutes have been construed to give a state, other than the one wherein the defendant resides, jurisdiction for non-support in a state where the omission occurs." State v. Shaw, 96 Idaho 897, 539 P.2d 250 (1975).

matter of convenience [4] in this field, the word "act" should be understood to include forbearances and omissions as well as positive acts, unless its meaning is limited by a modifier or by the context. In section 2, supra, the discussion was dealing with the field of positive action, and the definition of the word "act" was limited accordingly. A complete definition must be in some such form as this:

>   **An act is (1, positive) an occurrence which is an exertion of the will manifested in the external world, or (2, negative) a nonoccurrence which involves a breach of a legal duty to take positive action.**

A. FORBEARANCES AND OMISSIONS

Not every exertion of the will results in positive action. The result may be quite the reverse. One who stands his ground in the presence of great danger may remain motionless at the expense of greater exertion of the will than is involved in the hasty flight of another. But this important distinction is to be noted: whereas every exertion of the will resulting in positive action is an act, an exertion of the will resulting in inaction may or may not be an act. Furthermore, inaction may be an act even if it results, not from an exertion of the will, but from a failure of the will to exert itself.[5] In other words, inaction may (or may not) be an act whether it results from a determination not to act or from forgetfulness or inattention. A negative act which is consequent upon volition is a "forbearance;"[6] one which results, not from an exertion of the will, but from an absence of the will in the form of forgetfulness or inattention, is an "omission."[7] Stated differently:

>   **A "forbearance" is an intentional negative act; whereas, an "omission" is an unintentional negative act.[8] The latter word is not infrequently employed to serve the purpose of both,[9] but such usage is inconvenient and will not be adopted here.[10]**

B. IMPORTANCE OF DUTY TO TAKE POSITIVE ACTION

Doing nothing is not *acting* unless there is an obligation to do something. Furthermore, the nature of the inquiry is important in this connection, as

4. This is indicated, for example, by the following explanation (not limited to criminal law): "An omission is described as an act except when a distinction between them is expressly indicated." McLaughlin, Proximate Cause, 39 Harv.L. Rev. 149, 198 (1925). The traditional definition of crime speaks of "an act committed or omitted." 4 Bl.Comm. *5; Commonwealth v. Shields, 50 Pa.Super. 194, 202 (1912); Commonwealth v. Smith, 266 Pa. 511, 516, 109 A. 786, 788 (1920).

5. If death results from an omission of duty on the part of a switch-tender on a railroad, he may be convicted of manslaughter even if his will did not concur in the omission, but it was a matter of inattention, if the omission amounted to "criminal negligence." State v. O'Brien, 32 N.J.L. 169 (1867). State v. Benton, 38 Del. 1, 187 A. 609 (1936).

6. 1 Austin, Jurisprudence § 502 (Ed. by Campbell, 1875).

7. Ibid. One may be recognized as the cause of a death resulting from his nonperformance of duty, even if his will did not concur in the omission, but it was a matter of inattention. State v. O'Brien, 32 N.J.L. 169 (1867).

8. Salmond, op. cit. supra note 1.

9. Ibid.

10. Under the usage adopted in the text, there is a genus "negative act" divided into two species (1) "forbearance" and (2) "omission." If the word "omission" is used to express the genus it becomes necessary to add the word "intentional" or "unintentional" or both, to make the meaning clear in a particular instance.

well as the circumstances of the inaction. A person may commit an "act of discourtesy" by failing to acknowledge or speak to an acquaintance under certain circumstances. This is because the rules of polite society require acknowledgement in such a situation. Under the rules of baseball the failure of a batter to swing his bat at a properly pitched ball is as much a "strike" as if he had swung his bat and missed. But the failure of the batter to swing his bat at such a ball is not an "act of discourtesy," nor will the failure to acknowledge or speak have any consequences so far as the game of baseball is concerned. The juridical approach is along exactly the same line.

There is no negative act so far as the law is concerned unless there was a legal duty to take positive action.[11] The presence of a moral obligation is not sufficient for this purpose if there is no corresponding legal duty.[12]

Conversely, "a person failing to act when he has a legal duty to do so may be held criminally liable just as one who has acted improperly." [13]

General principles of morals and ethics form a part of the raw materials out of which law is made,[14] and a decided shift in the commonly-accepted view in the former field is almost invariably followed by a juridical change in the same direction. And yet the boundaries are not identical. Jeremy Bentham, for example, suggested long ago that there should be a legal duty to render assistance to one in need thereof if such aid could be given without unreasonable inconvenience;[15] but so far there is no general legal requirement that one must play the part of a Good Samaritan.[16]

11. Regina v. Shepherd, 9 Cox C.C. 123 (1862); United States v. Knowles, 26 Fed.Cas.800, No. 15,540 (N.D.Cal.1864); United States v. Van Schaik, 134 F. 592 (C.C.S.D.N.Y.1904); People v. Beardsley, 150 Mich. 206, 113 N.W. 1128 (1907); Anderson v. State, 27 Tex.Cr.R. 177, 11 S.W. 33 (1889). A bystander who could have prevented a murder, but did not, is not for that reason in the position of having caused the death. Connaughty v. State, 1 Wis. 159 (1853). See also 1 Hale P.C. *439. "The non-action of one who has no legal duty to act is nothing." Beale, The Proximate Consequences of an Act, 33 Harv.L.Rev. 633, 637 (1920). "It is the omission . . . of legal duties only which comes within the sphere of judicial cognizance." Union Pac. R.R. v. Cappier, 66 Kan. 649, 653, 72 P. 281, 282 (1903). A "legally required act." Johnston v. United States, 351 U.S. 215, 220, 76 S.Ct. 739, 742 (1956).

12. People v. Beardsley, 150 Mich. 206, 113 N.W. 1128 (1907).

13. United States v. FMC Corp., 572 F.2d 902, 906 (2d Cir. 1978).

14. "It would not be correct to say that every moral obligation involves a legal duty; but every legal duty is founded on a moral obligation. A legal common law duty is nothing else than the enforcing by law of that which is a moral obligation. . . . The prisoner was under a moral obligation to the deceased from which arose a legal duty towards her. . . ." Coleridge, C.J., in Regina v. Instan [1893] 1 Q.B. 450, 453–4. Another judge, referring to certain decisions, said: "These cases may be regarded as defining the legal sanctions which the law attaches to the moral duty of a parent to protect his children of tender years from physical harm." Mann, J., in Rex v. Russell, [1933] Vict.L.R. 59, 75 (1932).

15. "Every man is bound to assist those who have need of assistance, if he can do it without exposing himself to sensible inconvenience. This obligation is stronger, in proportion as the danger is the greater for the one, and the trouble of preserving him the less for the other . . .: the crime would be greater if he refrained from acting not simply from idleness, but from malice or some pecuniary interest." From a code proposed by Bentham, 1 Works of Jeremy Bentham 164 (1843).

16. "With purely moral obligations the law does not deal. For example, the priest and the Levite who passed by on the other side were not, it is supposed,

The so-called "Good Samaritan Statutes," enacted in many states, do not require aid to be given. They merely encourage doctors to stop and give aid to strangers in emergency situations by providing that no physician who *in good faith* renders such aid shall be liable in civil damages as a result of acts or omissions in rendering such aid. Some states have enacted statutes that require a person who is able to do so with no danger or peril to himself to come to the aid of another who is exposed to grave physical harm.[17]

The mere chance passer-by who happens to see a total stranger in danger of drowning will be regarded by the general community as under a moral duty to take steps to save the other if this can be done without unreasonable danger to himself, but the law imposes no duty upon him to go to the rescue.[18] "Suppose A," said Chief Justice Carpenter, "standing close by a railroad, sees a two-year-old babe on the track and a car approaching. He can easily rescue the child with entire safety to himself and the instincts of humanity require him to do so. If he does not, he may, perhaps, justly be styled a ruthless savage and a moral monster; but he is not liable in damages for the child's injury, or indictable under the statute for its death." [19]

The failure of the law to impose such a duty has probably been due to the difficulty of definition coupled with a rather pronounced mind-your-own-business philosophy. An infant starved to death in Chicago. Its parents did not supply it with the food necessary to sustain life. No one in the block fed it. No one in Chicago fed it. There were more than two hundred million people in the United States who did not feed it, not to mention the inhabitants of other lands. Obviously it would be absurd to say that everyone caused the death of the infant because nobody fed it. In the absence of unusual circumstances there will be no difficulty in finding a legally-recognized negative act here on the part of the father of the child.[20] But if neighbors who merely knew about the situation were held legally chargeable with the death, there might be no end of officious meddling in other homes because of a disagreement between parents and neighbors as to what children should eat.[21]

liable at law for the continued suffering of the man who fell among thieves, which they might and morally ought to have prevented or relieved." Buck v. Amory Manufacturing Co., 69 N.H. 257, 260, 44 A. 809, 810 (1898).

17. Vt.Stat.Ann. Tit. 12 § 519 (1971). See 25 Stan.L.Rev. 51 (1972).

18. Brakemen riding on an engine cannot be said to have caused the death of a child who was run over and killed because they were under no duty to be on the lookout for such hazards or to give notice—this was the duty of the engineer and fireman. Anderson v. State, 27 Tex. Cr.R. 177, 11 S.W. 33 (1889). A bystander cannot be said to have caused a murder even though it was committed in his presence and he made no effort to prevent it—if he did not in any way counsel, aid, assist or abet in the commission of the offense. 1 Hale, loc. cit. supra note 11; Foster, Crown Cases 350 (3d ed.

1809); Connaughty v. State, 1 Wis. 159 (1853).

19. Buck v. Amory Manufacturing Co., 69 N.H. 257, 260, 44 A. 809, 810 (1898).

20. Regina v. Conde, 10 Cox C.C. 547, (1867); State v. Staples, 126 Minn. 396, 148 N.W. 283 (1914).

21. "We are sensible that in some cases which we have put our rule may appear too lenient. But we do not think that it can be made more severe, without disturbing the whole order of society. It is true that the man who, having abundance of wealth, suffers a fellow creature to die of hunger at his feet, is a bad man,—a worse man, probably, than many of those for whom we have provided very severe punishment. But we are unable to see where, if we make such a man legally punishable, we can draw the line. If the rich man who refuses to save a beggar's life at the cost of a little copper

The gap between the legal position and the commonly accepted moral view is so wide in certain extreme situations of nonaction that the desirability of steps in the direction of bringing the former more nearly in line with the latter is clearly indicated; but the importance of having required positive action clearly defined and reasonably limited forces an important part of this field into the realm of legislation.[22] Even without the aid of statutes there has been a pronounced trend in the direction of bringing the legal position into line with the commonly-accepted moral view whenever the need is great and circumstances, other than mere chance, point out plainly the particular person who should take positive action and exactly what the action should be. Thus we find the courts recognizing negative action where there has been nonperformance of "a plain particular and personal duty," [23] or a "duty imposed by law directly or impliedly." [24] But so far there has been no change in the legal position that the need of one and the opportunity of another to be of assistance are not alone sufficient to give rise to a legal duty to take positive action.[25]

C. "DUTY IMPOSED BY LAW OR CONTRACT"

Certain duties of affirmative action are expressly imposed by statute. Under this head are to be found not only requirements such as the filing of an income tax return, but others of quite a different nature, such as the not-infrequent statutory obligation on the part of a motorist to give aid to one injured in an accident on the highway in which his car has been involved, even if he himself was not to blame for the accident.[26] In some situations the common law imposes certain duties by reason of the legal relation of the parties. Typical are the duty of the parent to provide food, shelter and protection for his child who is too young to supply his own wants,[27] and the duty of the husband to support his wife and to render special aid when she is in a

---

is a murderer, is the poor man just one degree above beggary also to be a murderer if he omits to invite the beggar to partake his hard earned rice? Again: if the rich man is a murderer for refusing to save the beggar's life at the cost of a little copper, is he also to be a murderer if he refuses to save the beggar's life at the cost of a thousand rupees? . . . .

"It is, indeed, most highly desirable that men should not merely abstain from doing harm to their neighbours, but should render active services to their neighbours. In general however the penal law must content itself with keeping men from doing positive harm and must leave to public opinion, and to the teachers of morality and religion, the office of furnishing men with motives for doing positive good." Macauly And Other Indian Law Commissioners, A Penal Code Prepared By The Indian Law Commissioners (1838 Indian Penal Code: Note M) pp. 103–106 (1938) quoted in Kadish, Criminal Law and Social Order Vol. II, p. 457–459 (1959).

22. Vt.Stat.Ann., Tit. 12 § 519 (1971).

23. State v. Barnes, 141 Tenn. 469, 472, 212 S.W. 100 (1919).

24. Anderson v. State, 27 Tex.Cr.R. 177, 11 S.W. 33 (1889).

25. Ibid.; see People v. Beardsley, 150 Mich. 206, 113 N.W. 1128 (1907). See Perkins, Negative Acts in Criminal Law, 22 Iowa L.R. 659, 667 (1937).

26. See, for example, I.C.A. (Iowa) § 321.263 (1971). Statutes and ordinances requiring fire-fighting apparatus for ships and buildings are common. In the Iroquois Theater fire case in Chicago the ordinance had been violated by using the theater without proper fire-fighting equipment. It was held that this omission was the proximate cause of the deaths resulting in the fire, and that the case should go to the jury on the question of negligence. People v. Davis, 1 Ill. Circ.Ct. 245 (1906).

27. Regina v. Senior, 19 Cox C.C. 219 (1898); State v. Staples, 126 Minn. 396, 148 N.W. 283 (1914); Commonwealth v. Breth, 44 Pa.Co.Ct. 56 (1915); Rex v. Russell, [1933] Vict.L.R. 59 (1932). As to the duty of the mother, see Lewis v.

helpless situation.[28]   Under some circumstances a factual situation may be sufficient to give rise to a legal duty to act for the benefit of another.   An excellent illustration of this type of obligation is found in the instance of one who undertakes to render to another aid which he is not legally bound to render.   While he could have done nothing, had he so chosen, the law does not permit him, without good reason, to abandon the undertaking at such a point that the other will suffer harm by reason of the partial performance.[29]   Furthermore a legal duty to act for the benefit of another may arise out of contract.

It may be questioned whether this really adds a distinct category.   It is arguable that every conviction of crime resulting from nonperformance of a contractual obligation can be based upon the ground of an undertaking improperly abandoned at a dangerous point.   Even the watchman, employed to close a gate or give a warning for the protection of the public at a point where the highway crosses a railroad, who fails to render the needed service because he does not appear at the time his contract calls for his first appearance, has by his contract deterred the employer from securing someone else for the position.   This, however, is rather an explanation of the reason for the imposition of criminal responsibility in cases of this nature, than a refutation of the view that negative action, with possible criminal consequences, may be predicated upon the nonperformance of a contract duty.

In the middle of the last century an English judge assumed that a person employed by a railroad as a crossing watchman was under no *legal* duty to those on the highway, to give them warning of approaching trains, unless his employer was required by law to keep a watchman at that place.[30]   Many years later the court said, in refusing to follow this suggestion, that "a man might incur criminal liability from a duty arising out of a contract," [31] and this is the accepted view at the present time.[32]   This idea is frequently ex-

State, 72 Ga. 164 (1883); Gibson v. Commonwealth, 106 Ky. 360, 50 S.W. 532 (1899).

28.   State v. Smith, 65 Me. 257 (1876); Territory v. Manton, 8 Mont. 95, 19 P. 387 (1888).

Several states now recognize the obligation extends to either parent or spouse.   E. g. Biddle v. Commonwealth, 206 Va. 14, 141 S.E.2d 710 (1965); People v. Burden, 72 Cal.App.3d 603, 140 Cal. Rptr. 282 (1977); Utah Code Ann., 1953, 76–7–201.

29.   Regina v. Nicholls, 13 Cox C.C. 75 (1874).

30.   Regina v. Smith, 11 Cox C.C. 210 (1869).   In this case the defendant had been employed as a watchman to warn persons when trains were about to cross a road.   In violation of his duties under his contract of employment he left his post and a user of the highway—supposing it was safe to proceed because he received no warning—was killed as he attempted to cross the track.   Counsel

contended that the prisoner owed no duty to the public because the statute did not require his employer to keep a watchman at that crossing.   This view was accepted by the trial judge.

31.   Rex v. Pittwood, 19 T.L.R. 37, 38 (1902).   This was also a crossing case and there was no evidence of any law requiring the employer to keep a watchman at this crossing.   Regina v. Smith, 11 Cox C.C. 210 (1869), was cited by counsel but not followed by the court.

32.   Rex v. Friend, Russ. & Ry. 20, 168 Eng.Rep. 662 (1802); Regina v. Marriott, 8 C. & P. 425, 173 Eng.Rep. 559 (1838); Regina v. Instan, [1893] 1 Q.B. 450, 17 Cox C.C. 602 (1893); State v. Benton, 38 Del. 1, 187 A. 609 (1936).   In the Benton case the court said: "The indictment charges a plain personal duty imposed upon the defendant by virtue of his employment, and an entire failure to perform that duty.   No more need be said." Id. at 18, 187 A. at 616.

pressed by use of the phrase "duty imposed by law or contract." [33] Unfortunately, the use of these words for this purpose is misleading. What constitutes a contract and what duties are imposed upon the contracting parties are matters of *law*. A contract to provide food and shelter for an infant of tender years, for example, results in a contractual obligation; but this contractual obligation includes a "legal duty"—one which is recognized by law and the breach of which is followed by legal consequences. Hence it seems preferable to say that the criminal law will recognize a negative act if—and only if—the one who has failed to take affirmative action was under a legal duty to do what was not done, with the explanation that such a legal duty may exist because of (1) an express provision of law, (2) a legal relation, (3) a factual situation or (4) a contract.[34]

D. REQUIRED PERFORMANCE

Apart from the statutory requirements of positive action, such as the filing of income tax returns (and these are myriad), the common [35] types of required performance which are important in the criminal law are (1) the duty to provide food, clothing and shelter, (2) the duty to provide medical care and attention, and (3) the duty to safeguard certain persons or the general public against special hazards. The types of required performance and the sources of the legal duty to perform are intertwined. Thus the parent of a child of tender years has the duty to provide the child with food, clothing and shelter,[36] also, in case of need, to provide him with medical care and attention,[37] and furthermore, to take reasonable steps, in cases of emergency, to safeguard him against special hazards, such as drowning.[38] On the other hand, the duty to supply food, clothing and shelter may arise out of a

---

33. See, for example, People v. Beardsley, 150 Mich. 206, 209, 113 N.W. 1128, 1129 (1907); State v. Barnes, 141 Tenn. 469, 472, 212 S.W. 100, 101 (1918).

34. Jones v. United States, 113 U.S. App.D.C. 352, 308 F.2d 307 (D.C.Cir. 1962).

The Model Penal Code § 2.01(3) states: "Liability for the commission of an offense may not be based on an omission unaccompanied by action unless: (a) the omission is expressly made sufficient by the law defining the offense; or (b) a duty to perform the omitted act is otherwise imposed by law."

35. These are by no means the only kinds of required performance. For example, if a master should see his servant taking coal from the street to the master's basement, which the servant in good faith thought belonged to the master, but which as the master well knew belonged to a neighbor, the master would be under a legal duty to speak in order that the other's property should not be taken and carried away. And it would seem that a forbearance to speak, by the master, in order that the neighbor's coal

should thus be taken by trespass and placed in the master's basement for his own furnace, followed by the actual appropriation of the property, would constitute larceny. Possibly such a duty could be brought under subdivision (3) of the text. A tavern keeper may be guilty of contributing to the delinquency of a 16 year old girl by allowing her to remain for hours in the tavern, dancing with various strange men and drinking enough beer to become drunk. State v. Sobelman, 199 Minn. 232, 271 N.W. 484 (1937). "[W]here the crime charged is a failure to do a legally required act, the place fixed for its performance fixes the situs of the crime." Johnston v. United States, 351 U.S. 215, 220, 76 S.Ct. 739, 742 (1956).

36. Regina v. Conde, 10 Cox C.C. 547 (1867); State v. Staples, 126 Minn. 396, 148 N.W. 283 (1914); Biddle v. Commonwealth, 206 Va. 14, 141 S.E.2d 710 (1965).

37. State v. Barnes, 141 Tenn. 469, 212 S.W. 100 (1919); Regina v. Moore, [1954] N.Z.L.R. 893.

38. Rex v. Russell, [1933] Vict.L.R. 59 (1932).

legal relation,[39] a factual situation,[40] or a contract,[41] or it may be imposed by express provisions of a statute.[42]

The legal relation of the parties has a very limited application as the source of such a duty. It probably does not extend beyond the examples already mentioned—the parent of a child of tender years and the spouse. A mother, for example, owes no legal duty to provide a midwife for her emancipated daughter who is about to give birth to a child.[43]

A factual situation may give rise to such a duty in many different ways. The owner of a car, who is actually in the vehicle at the time, has a duty to order more reasonable speed or care if his chauffeur is driving in obvious violation of the law,[44] and to forbid an intoxicated friend to drive the car while under the influence of liquor.[45] As previously mentioned, one who volunteers to play the part of a Good Samaritan has a legal duty to carry on rather than to abandon the undertaking at a point of danger. One, for example, who actually undertakes to care for a child of tender years, although not bound to do so either by reason of blood relationship or contract, must either continue such care or turn the infant over to proper authorities.[46]

The leading case of criminal responsibility based upon a negative act, where the duty to perform arose out of a factual situation is *Instan*.[47] A niece went to live with her aunt whose means supplied provisions for both. While they were so living together the aunt became too ill to care for herself, and during this period the niece took into the house food which was brought by the tradespeople and paid for by the aunt's money. There was no one else in the house. Friends and neighbors had no occasion to suppose anything was wrong because the niece had conversations with them without mentioning the helpless condition of the aunt. The failure of the niece, under these circumstances, to give her aunt anything to eat, to procure medical aid for her, or to notify anyone of her condition was held to be a clear violation of a *legal* duty. A niece has no common-law duty to look after her aunt merely by reason of the blood relationship, and the result would have been the same had consanguinity been entirely wanting. The factual relation of being common householders under their living arrangement imposed upon each certain legal duties which she could have avoided by living alone.

A man married a woman who had an illegitimate son. This boy, who was too young to look after his own needs, was taken into the household of this man and wife, and while living there his feet were severely frozen. As the man was not the boy's father and had not adopted him he could have shifted the responsibility by turning the child over to the public authorities for care and attention. But the court very properly held that he was under a legal duty to do *something*, in this emergency, and that his failure either to call in

---

39. See supra note 36.

40. Regina v. Instan, [1893] 1 Q.B. 450, 17 Cox C.C. 602 (1893).

41. Regina v. Marriott, 8 C. & P. 425, 173 Eng.Rep. 559 (1838).

42. The common-law duty to support a child may be codified, or even enlarged, by statute. See, for example, I.C.A. (Iowa) §§ 731.1, 731.7.

43. Regina v. Shepherd, 9 Cox C.C. 123 (1862).

44. Moreland v. State, 164 Ga. 467, 139 S.E. 77 (1927).

45. State v. Hopkins, 147 Wash. 198, 265 P. 481 (1928).

46. Regina v. Nicholls, 13 Cox C.C. 75 (1874); Jones v. United States, 113 U.S. App. D.C. 352, 308 F.2d 307 (D.C. Cir. 1962).

47. Regina v. Instan, [1893] 1 Q.B. 450, 17 Cox C.C. 602 (1893).

medical aid or to bring the matter to the attention of the proper authorities was a negative act on his part.[48] In another case a fifteen-year-old farm hand became so badly frost bitten that he was unable to care for himself, and the court had no difficulty in finding a legal duty imposed upon the employer to take some proper step for the protection of the lad.[49]

A situation arising from an accident may be such as to impose a legal duty upon him who caused it, even if he was free from fault in the beginning. One, for example, who accidentally sets fire to his house, creating a small blaze which he could easily extinguish without danger to himself, is guilty of burning with intent to defraud the insurer, if he forbears to put out the fire, or send in an alarm, for the purpose of having insured property destroyed.[50] *A fortiori* a danger created by a wrongful act may give rise to a legal duty requiring the wrongdoer to take steps to prevent further harm. An assailant whose battery has left another unconscious in the grass at night, with his head near the highway, where traffic conditions are such as to create an obvious danger, is the cause of death if he leaves the victim in that state and an automobile, whose driver does not see the helpless form, passes over it with fatal consequences.[51] The person who strikes and injures a dog may be responsible for cruelly treating the animal by failing to provide available veterinary care.[52]

Some contracts are entered into for the very purpose of protecting certain persons, such as contracts to provide food, clothing and shelter for one who is too young [53] or too old [54] to make proper provision for himself. Some con-

48. Stehr v. State, 92 Neb. 755, 139 N.W. 676 (1913).

49. The Queen v. Brown, 1 Terr.L. Rep. 475 (Can.1893).

50. Commonwealth v. Cali, 247 Mass. 20, 141 N.E. 510 (1923). A considerable development along this line seems probable. The driver of a horse and sleigh knocks unconscious a pedestrian, unintentionally and without negligence, on a little-traveled road in zero weather. Though the "hit and run" statute of the jurisdiction may speak only in terms of motor vehicles, there is reason to expect judicial recognition of a legal duty, on the part of the driver, to take reasonable steps for the welfare of the unfortunate victim of this accident. Other situations may be imagined, such as the hunter whose bullet happens by accident to cripple another in a remote spot, and who is aware of the harm thus caused and is able to be of assistance.

While VB was reaching for her glasses that had fallen to the floor of the car, she accidentally pressed the gas pedal hitting R who was walking in front of the car. She swerved around him and drove away leaving him in the roadway, where moments later he was hit and killed by another car. Her conviction of manslaughter was affirmed. "The crime was committed, not when appellant struck Rose, but when she abandoned him in a position of peril." Van Buskirk v. State, 611 P.2d 271, 273 (Okl.Cr.App. 1980).

51. People v. Fowler, 178 Cal. 657, 174 P. 892 (1918). While the result may be rationalized by saying that the death was caused by a foreseeable intervening cause, and hence was a proximate result of defendant's act, there can be no real doubt of the presence of a legal duty upon the part of the assailant to take steps to safeguard his victim against such a risk. A clear recognition of this duty would simplify some of the "causation" cases. See, for example, State v. Stephenson, 205 Ind. 141, 179 N.E. 633 (1932). See also Henderson v. Kibbe, 431 U.S. 145, 97 S.Ct. 1730 (1977). Special instruction on causation in causing death by abandoning robbery victim is unnecessary.

52. Commonwealth v. Putch, 18 Pa. D & C 680 (Alleg.Cty. 1932).

53. Rex v. Friend, Russ. & Ry. 20, 168 Eng.Rep. 662 (1802); Regina v. Bubb, 4 Cox C.C. 457 (1850); Jones v. United States, 113 U.S.App.D.C. 352, 308 F.2d 307 (D.C. Cir. 1962).

54. Regina v. Marriott, 8 C. & P. 425, 433, 173 Eng.Rep. 559, 563 (1838). The duty of an officer of the poor relief to render assistance in a proper case may

tracts are entered into for the purpose of protecting the general public against certain hazards, such as the employment of a railroad watchman whose duty is to signal [55] or to close a gate [56] when a train is approaching. Some contracts include similar duties together, perhaps, with many others, such as a railroad employee who is not engaged primarily for that purpose, but who has the duty when occasion arises to adjust a switch [57] or to send a train upon a proper track.[58] A brakeman, for example, may be employed chiefly for other purposes, and yet it may be clearly his duty, under the terms of his employment and the rules of the company, to go back and give warning to approaching trains whenever his own train makes an emergency stop at some place other than a station.[59] It may be the plain duty of the ground bailiff of a mine to cause the mine to be properly ventilated for the avoidance of explosions, whatever his other duties may be.[60] The one in charge of a ship on the high seas has, among many other responsibilities, the duty to take proper steps in the effort to rescue one who has fallen into the ocean.[61] And to speak further of this same officer, while it may be the duty of others to equip the vessel with life preservers and fire fighting apparatus, it is the duty of the master of the vessel to determine whether such provision has been properly made, and if not, to keep the ship in port until this defect has been corrected.[62] And one operating at the top of a shaft in which work is being done may have a duty to take certain precautions for the protection of the workmen below.[63]

On the other hand, one may have some connection with the circumstances which give rise to the need for help and yet have no legal duty to act in the matter. For example, employees of a railroad who are riding on an engine merely to get from one place of work to another may have no legal duty to be on the lookout for persons on the track, even if they happen to be riding on the front of a switch engine.[64] And where a construction job resulted in a fatal accident which might have been avoided by certain reasonable precautions in the general plan of the work, there was no act of omission *on the part of a section boss* who had no discretion as to the general plan, but was employed merely to carry out the work along lines arranged by the engineer and the managing superintendent.[65]

E. KNOWLEDGE OF CIRCUMSTANCES WHICH REQUIRE PERFORMANCE

In general one "cannot be said in any manner to neglect or refuse to perform a duty unless he has knowledge of the condition of things which

be mentioned in this connection. Regina v. Curtis, 15 Cox C.C. 746 (1885).

55. Regina v. Pargeter, 3 Cox C.C. 191 (1848); State v. Benton, 38 Del. 1, 187 A. 609 (1936).

56. Rex v. Pittwood, 19 T.L.R. 37 (1902).

57. State v. O'Brien, 32 N.J.L. 169 (1867).

58. State v. Irvine, 126 La. 434, 52 So. 567 (1910).

59. People v. Melius, 1 N.Y.Crim. 39 (1882).

60. Regina v. Haines, 2 C. & K. 368, 175 Eng.Rep. 152 (1847).

61. United States v. Knowles, 26 Fed. Cas. 800, No. 15,540 (N.D.Cal.1864).

62. United States v. Van Schaik, 134 F. 592 (2d Cir. 1904).

63. Regina v. Hughes, 7 Cox C.C. 301 (1857).

64. Anderson v. State, 27 Tex.Cr.R. 177, 11 S.W. 33 (1889).

65. Thomas v. People, 2 Colo.App. 513, 31 P. 349 (1892).

requires performance at his hands." [66]   This, however, is subject to one important qualification. If the legal duty of the person requires him not only to take positive action, but also to acquaint himself with certain facts in this connection, his forbearance or omission to do the latter will of itself constitute a negative act on his part.[67] For illustration, it is the duty of a father who sees his child of tender years in sudden peril to give aid if reasonably possible; [68] but the want of parental assistance would not be a negative act if the danger grew out of some sudden and unusual emergency which was unknown to the father. On the other hand, if a gate keeper whose duty it is to close a gate when a train is about to pass, fails to close the gate, his explanation that he was doing something else and did not see the train will not prevent this inaction from being an act of omission,[69] because failing to look when there is a legal duty to look is a negative act.[70] Statutes covering failure to stop at the scene of an accident require knowledge on the part of the actor that he has struck another vehicle. It has been held that where the element of personal injury is a factor the defendant must actually know of the injury or be possessed of knowledge which would lead to a reasonable anticipation that an injury occurred. In that latter instance the defendant must be alert to the inferences to be drawn from the circumstances of the accident.[71]

Except where the duty requires the person to acquaint himself with the facts it has been common to speak of (1) the duty to act and (2) knowledge of the circumstances which require performance. It would seem more accurate, as a matter of juridical science, to include knowledge (in such cases) as one of the circumstances which must exist in order to give rise to the duty. On this analysis three groupings may be suggested:

> **(1) Under some circumstances one may have no duty to act even though he has knowledge of another's need. (2) In some situations the law requires one to take positive action for the benefit of another if he is aware of the circumstances which require such action, but not otherwise. (3) The state of affairs may be such that the legal duty requires not only positive action for the welfare of another, but also alertness to determine when such action is needed.**

F. CAPACITY, MEANS AND ABILITY TO PERFORM

The possibility of doing what was not done is another matter which demands attention in this regard. The failure to perform the impossible is not an act. Two excellent reasons may be offered. In the first place any legal

---

66. Westrup v. Commonwealth, 123 Ky. 95, 101, 93 S.W. 646, 648 (1906); State v. Smith, 65 Me. 257, 266 (1876).

Failure to act may be punished as a felony only if **D** knew or reasonably should have known that there was a duty to act and a penalty imposed for a failure to discharge such duty, or was aware of circumstances which should have moved him to inquire. Lambert v. California, 355 U.S. 225, 78 S.Ct. 240 (1957).

67. State v. Irvine, 126 La. 434, 52 So. 567 (1910). In the words of the court, one is not "exculpated by his ignorance"

if "he was charged with the special duty of being informed." Id. at 446, 52 So. at 572. See Frankel, Criminal Omissions: A Legal Microcosm, 11 Wayne L.Rev. 367, 395 (1965).

68. Rex v. Russell, [1933] Vict.L.R. 59 (1932).

69. Rex v. Pittwood, 19 T.L.R. 37 (1902).

70. State v. Benton, 38 Del. 1, 187 A. 609 (1936).

71. State v. Porras, 125 Ariz. 490, 610 P.2d 1051 (App. 1980).

duty which exacts positive action will always fall short of requiring the impossible. In the second place the ability to do what was not done is inherent in the concept of negative action. A negative act does not require an actual exertion of the will, but there is no act unless the matter is "subject to the control of the will". [72] Hence one cannot properly be said to forbear or omit to do that which he has not the capacity, means or ability to accomplish.[73] The inaction of a father who sees his baby in sudden peril is not a negative act unless it was "in his power to interfere." [74] Nor is the failure of a parent to supply food to his little child an act of omission unless he "had the means to supply" it.[75] The element of time is frequently important in this connection. The owner of a car who is being driven by his chauffeur is not chargeable with an "omission" to instruct his servant to drive otherwise if a sudden and unexpected act of recklessness by an ordinarily careful driver has resulted in a wreck before there was an opportunity to speak.[76]

It must not be overlooked, however, that inability to do one thing may sometimes give rise to a legal duty to do something else. "If the parent," in the words of the Nebraska court, "has not the means for the child's nurture, his duty is to apply to the public authorities for relief; and failure to do so is itself culpable neglect wherever there are public authorities capable of affording such relief." [77] In this connection it is proper to point out that a change in the general social and economic conditions of life may give rise to duties not formerly recognized. The old cases, for example, indicate that a wife cannot be recognized as being the cause of the death of her young child who has died for want of proper food and nourishment unless it is shown that her husband supplied the necessary provisions and she omitted to give to the infant what was thus provided by the husband.[78] The law recognizes the duty of the wife to supply the provisions under certain conditions of home life and employment at the present time. And certainly the wife would be guilty of a negative act if she watched her child starve to death today without any effort either to supply its needs or to bring the matter to the attention of the public authorities, if such help was available.[79]

---

72. Salmond, op. cit. supra note 1. One who is unavoidably caught in a traffic jam does not violate an ordinance against stopping. Commonwealth v. Brooks, 99 Mass. 434 (1868).

73. Regina v. Hogan, 5 Cox C.C. 255 (1851). "To render criminal the neglect of parents and others, having charge of children or other dependents, there must be capacity, means and ability to provide support and care, or to prevent the threatened harm as well as the legal duty to provide and act. If there is not capacity, means and ability to perform the legal duty, the omission to perform it is not criminal." State v. Noakes, 70 Vt. 247, 262, 40 A. 249, 254 (1897).

74. Rex v. Russell, [1933] Vict.L.R. 59, 62 (1932). The court also said: ". . . in this possible view: that . . . the prisoner could have saved his wife and children if he had tried." Id. at 69. See also Territory v. Manton, 8 Mont. 95, 19 P. 387 (1888), in which the

ability of the defendant to aid his wife is emphasized.

75. Regina v. Conde, 10 Cox C.C. 547 (1867); Regina v. Hogan, 5 Cox C.C. 255 (1851).

76. People v. Scanlon, 132 App.Div. 528, 117 N.Y.S. 57 (1909).

77. Stehr v. State, 92 Neb. 755, 139 N.W. 676 (1913). See also Regina v. Mabbett, 5 Cox C.C. 339 (1851).

78. Rex v. Squire, 1 Russ.Cr. & M. 24 (1799); Rex v. Saunders, 7 C. & P. 276, 173 Eng.Rep. 122 (1836).

79. This was suggested in Regina v. Mabbett, 5 Cox C.C. 339 (1851).

A second degree murder conviction of a mother was upheld for the starvation death of an infant. State v. Nicholson, 585 P.2d 60 (Utah 1978).

Both parents convicted of manslaughter for failing to provide child adequate

G. EFFECT OF NONPERFORMANCE

A negative act may be the very basis of a criminal prosecution, or it may be merely a part of the evidence which is used to establish the offense charged.

In a prosecution for failure to file an income tax return,[80] the offense consists of the forbearance or omission itself. In a charge of manslaughter, on the other hand, the ultimate fact to be proved is that homicide was caused by the unlawful act of the defendant. It is possible to show that death was caused by a negative act, such as the failure to perform some act that the particular person was under a legal duty to perform, which duty was "connected with life, so that the ordinary consequence of neglecting it would be death."[81] But proof of such a negative act does not establish homicide unless it is shown that loss of life resulted from this nonperformance within the legally-recognized principles of causation.[82] "It was not enough to sustain the charge of manslaughter to show that the parent had neglected to use all reasonable means of saving the life of the child; it was necessary to show that what the parent neglected to do had the effect of shortening the child's life."[83] A mistress, for example, is not recognized by law as being the cause of the death of her servant who is alleged to have died by reason of the neglect of the mistress to supply her with necessary food and clothing, unless the servant was helpless and unable to take care of herself, or so under the dominion and restraint of her mistress as to be unable to withdraw herself from her control.[84] On the other hand, if one has failed to perform a legal duty connected with life, and death has resulted from this nonperformance within the legally-recognized principles of causation, such a one has caused this death, within the legal view, even if some other person was charged with the same duty and also failed to perform.[85] In other words, two or more may cause death by negative acts just as two or more may cause death by positive acts.[86]

One having a legal duty to take positive action for the protection of another, who maliciously refrains from performance for the very purpose of causing death, is guilty of murder if life is actually lost as a result of this malicious forbearance.[87] If the nonperformance is intentional and for the

medical care. State v. Williams, 4 Wn. App. 908, 484 P.2d 1167 (1971).

80. See, for example, 26 U.S.C.A. § 7203.

81. Regina v. Pocock, 5 Cox C.C. 172 (1851); Biddle v. Commonwealth, 206 Va. 14, 141 S.E.2d 710 (1965).

82. Regina v. Curtis, 15 Cox C.C. 746 (1885). See also United States v. Knowles, 26 Fed.Cas. 800, No. 15,540 (N.D.Cal.1864).

83. Regina v. Morby, 15 Cox C.C. 35, 38 (1882). And because of the want of such evidence the conviction was quashed. "It is not sufficient for you to believe that possibly he might have been saved. To find the defendant guilty, you must come to the conclusion that he would, beyond a reasonable doubt, have

been saved if proper efforts to save him had been seasonably made, and that his death was the consequence of the defendant's negligence in this respect." United States v. Knowles, 26 Fed.Cas.No.15,540, at 802 (N.D.Cal.1864).

84. Regina v. Smith, Leigh & Cave 607, 10 Cox C.C. 82 (1865).

85. Regina v. Haines, 2 C. & K. 368, 175 Eng.Rep. 152 (1847).

86. ". . . although a man cannot be killed twice, two persons, acting independently, may contribute to his death and each be guilty of a homicide." People v. Lewis, 124 Cal. 551, 559, 57 P. 470, 473 (1899).

87. On a murder trial the evidence showed that the defendant had undertaken to care and provide for a woman 73

purpose of causing death, but the determination not to act is suddenly formed in the heat of passion engendered by adequate provocation, a resulting homicide is voluntary manslaughter.[88] The third possibility, in a case of homicide resulting from a forbearance, is that while the nonperformance was intentional, it was without the intention or expectation of fatal consequences, and hence the crime is involuntary manslaughter because of criminal negligence.[89] Should homicide result from the *omission* of such a duty—an unintentional failure of performance due to forgetfulness or inattention—it would not amount to murder. It would be involuntary manslaughter if the omission amounted to criminal negligence,[90] but would be no crime at all if the neglect did not involve that degree of culpability.[91] In brief:

years of age and had taken her into his home for this purpose, and that she had died from want of proper food, warmth, medicine and other necessaries. The court instructed the jury that if they found the defendant guilty of neglect so wilful and gross as to satisfy them that the death was contemplated, they should find defendant guilty of murder; that if the death resulted from his negligence, but without being contemplated by him it was manslaughter, etc. Regina v. Marriott, 8 C. & P. 425, 173 Eng.Rep. 559 (1838).

In affirming a judgment of conviction of murder in the second degree, based upon the death of defendant's tiny baby, by starvation, the court said: "The omission of a duty is in law the equivalent of an act and when death results, the standard for determination of the degree of homicide is identical." People v. Burden, 72 Cal.App.3d 603, 140 Cal.Rptr. 282, 289 (1977). State v. Nicholson, 585 P.2d 60 (Utah 1978).

88. There seems to be no case in which such facts are involved, and such a situation is quite unlikely but not impossible. Suppose, for example, a man should climb into the tower where a watchman is stationed and should strike the watchman a violent blow in the face, breaking his nose and knocking out two teeth. The assailant at once leaves and gets into his car. The injured watchman sees a train approaching and the assailant driving toward the tracks, but in his rage and pain he purposely refrains from closing the gates, whereupon the assailant is killed on the crossing. Such a forbearance is not with malice aforethought if there has not been a reasonable time in which the passion should have cooled.

89. The owner of a car who is actually in the car at the time his chauffeur is driving in obvious violation of the law has a legal duty to order more reasonable speed or care. Moreland v. State, 164 Ga. 467, 139 S.E. 77 (1927). Should he intentionally keep silent because of being in a great hurry, he as well as the chauffeur could be criminally guilty of a homicide resulting from the improper driving, but the offense would be involuntary manslaughter if the driving did not amount to wanton and wilful recklessness. The owner might be guilty of the same offense because of a criminally negligent *omission* to speak, but a *forbearance* would not necessarily make him guilty of murder in such a case. Possibly a forbearance resulting in death might be held to be no crime at all, on the ground that while it constituted negligence, it fell short of criminal negligence, in a case such as the one above, i.e., where the facts in the particular instance indicated a relatively small deviation from the required standard.

90. State v. Benton, 38 Del. 1, 187 A. 609 (1936); State v. O'Brien, 32 N.J.L. 169 (1867). In the O'Brien case the court said: "The defendant in this case omitted his duty under such circumstances, as amounted to gross or culpable or criminal negligence." Id. at 172. See also the cases cited in note 87 supra.

91. Regina v. Nicholls, 13 Cox C.C. 75 (1874); State v. Tankersley, 172 N.C. 955, 90 S.E. 781 (1916). In the latter case the court said: ". . . even if he had not reduced his train to the speed required by the highest prudence, or even if he did fail to stop at within 120 feet, the distance he was able to see ahead, around the curve, this, while it might be considered an error of judgment, or even a negligent default on a civil issue, should not by any reasonable or just estimate of his conduct be imputed to him for a crime." Id. at 959, 90 S.E. at 782.

Homicide resulting from the forbearance to perform a duty connected with life may be (1) murder, (2) voluntary manslaughter, or (3) involuntary manslaughter; homicide resulting from the omission of such a duty may be (1) involuntary manslaughter, or (2) excusable homicide.

The position of the Model Penal Code on negative action follows the traditional approach.[92]

H. DESERTION AND NONSUPPORT

As mentioned above a negative act may result in a crime or a negative act may itself be a crime. Modern nonsupport legislation has created offenses in the second category and they have given rise to certain important problems. A man has a common-law duty to provide for his wife [93] and little child,[94] but a violation of this duty is not a common-law offense. The common law does not punish this violation of duty if no harm results,[95] but if the neglect is with mens rea and causes bodily harm this is a common-law crime which may be manslaughter or even murder if death ensues.[96]

Under modern legislation in this area, in addition to "non-support," other terms such as "desertion" or "abandonment" are encountered. Either of these two terms, taken literally, would refer to an affirmative act; and some of the statutory provisions mean just that.[97] But if under a different statute the offense consists of desertion or abandonment followed by a failure to support, or just the failure to support, it is a negative act which constitutes

---

92. Section 2.01.

93. DuPont v. DuPont, 32 Del.Ch. 56, 79 A.2d 680 (1951); Buss v. Buss, 252 Wis. 500, 32 N.W.2d 253 (1948); Williams v. Williams, 188 Va. 543, 50 S.E.2d 277 (1948).

94. See supra, note 27.

95. "Irrespectively of the intention to burthen the parish, it is quite clear that the mere act of deserting a child unable to take care of itself is not an indictable offence, unless it be followed by some injury to the health of the child." Per Parke, B., in Regina v. Hogan, 5 Cox C.C. 255 (1851).

"At common law, abandonment by or neglect of a husband to support his wife was not a criminal offence." Brooke v. State, 99 Fla. 1275, 128 So. 814, 817 (1930).

96. If death results from the wilful forbearance of a duty, the homicide is murder. Death ensuing from a negligent omission of a duty is manslaughter. Hence if the death of a child results from want of proper food and clothing, which have been wilfully withheld by the one whose duty it was to provide them, for the purpose of causing death, the homicide is murder. Lewis v. State, 72 Ga. 164 (1883). "But it has never been doubted that if death is the direct conse-

quence of the malicious omission of the performance of a duty (as of a mother to nourish her infant child) this is a case of murder." Regina v. Hughes, 7 Cox C.C. 301, 302 (1857). See also Rex v. Russell, [1933] Vict.L.R. 59 (1932); Pallis v. State, 123 Ala. 12, 26 So. 339 (1898); State v. Barnes, 141 Tenn. 469, 212 S.W. 100 (1919); Biddle v. Commonwealth, 206 Va. 14, 141 S.E.2d 710 (1965).

If the statute requires a parent to provide medical aid for his minor child in need thereof the parent cannot justify a failure to do so by his religious belief, and may be guilty of manslaughter if such failure results in the death of the child. People v. Arnold, 66 Cal.2d 438, 58 Cal.Rptr. 115, 426 P.2d 515 (1967).

97. "Abandonment of a child is the leaving of a child under the age sixteen (16) years, in a place where such child may suffer because of neglect, by the parent, guardian or other person to whom the care and custody of such child shall have been entrusted, when done with intent to abandon such child." Kan. Stat.Ann. § 21–3604 (1974).

"[A]s to the child there may be an abandonment constituting a crime without neglect to provide for it." State v. Stout, 139 Iowa 557, 117 N.W. 958 (1908).

the crime.[98] And it is with offenses of this nature that attention is needed here.

It is not necessary to repeat what was said above in regard to knowledge of circumstances which require performance, or capacity, means and ability to perform, since these considerations apply to nonsupport the same as to any negative act, except for one point of emphasis. One who, without fault, does not have the means to provide support is obviously not guilty of wilfully refusing to do so; [99] but this is not true of one whose lack of means was itself intentional. The capacity and opportunity to work combine to constitute an asset.[1] Some statutes expressly or impliedly cover this situation by providing "a person is guilty of a misdemeanor if he knowingly fails to provide support which he is legally obliged to provide and which he can provide. . . ." [2]

1. THE UNIFORM DESERTION AND NONSUPPORT ACT

The Model Penal Code Committee noted on one point:

"The criminal codes of all American jurisdictions prohibit desertion or non-support of minor children; all but three penalize also desertion or non-support of the wife." [3]

Several jurisdictions impose the support obligation on each spouse for the children and each other.[4]

At one time nearly half the states had adopted the Uniform Act, and while a few of the adopting states have made some changes in the wording, and other states have their own statutes on the subject, the key section of the Uniform Act will give a general idea of the coverage. It is as follows: [5]

"Any husband who shall, without just cause, desert or wilfully neglect or refuse to provide for the support and maintenance of his wife in destitute or necessitous circumstances; or any parent who shall, without lawful excuse, desert or wilfully neglect or refuse to provide for the support and maintenance of his or her child or children under the age of sixteen years in destitute or necessitous circumstances, shall be guilty of a crime and, on conviction thereof, shall be punished by fine not exceeding five hundred dollars, or imprisonment in the . . . not exceeding two years, or both, with or without hard labor, in the discretion of the court." Most states having the sub-

---

98. The actual leaving of the wife is not an element of the offense of wife desertion. The offense consists in the husband's refusal to provide for her. State v. Conway, 182 Iowa 1236, 166 N.W. 596 (1918).

99. Mobley v. State, 129 Tex.Cr. 379, 87 S.W.2d 740 (1935).

A father may defend a prosecution for child desertion by showing that he is physically or mentally unable to engage in any gainful occupation sufficient to earn support for his children.

Cox v. Commonwealth, 280 Ky. 94, 132 S.W.2d 739 (1939). State v. Nelson, 463 S.W.2d 614 (Mo.App. 1971).

1. Zitlow v. State, 213 Wis. 493, 252 N.W. 358 (1934).

2. N.H. Rev.Stat.Ann. 639:4 (1977).

3. Model Penal Code 189 (Tent.Draft No. 9, 1959). The quotation may be misleading in the reference to "minor children" since few of the statutes require support up to age 21. See infra, under "Child."

4. Louisiana criminal neglect of wife statute, La.RS 14:74A(1) is unconstitutional since sex is not a reliable basis for determining need. State v. Fuller, 377 So.2d 335 (La. 1979).

5. 10 Uniform Laws Annotated 1 (1922).

stance of the act have imposed the support obligation on the wife as well as the husband.[6] The Model Penal Code contains a similar provision.[7]

As is no doubt true of all such legislation, the chief purpose of the Uniform Act is to coerce performance of the duty rather than to punish for the violation,[8] although the possibility of punishment is essential to the plan. In line with the primary function a section is included under which an appropriate arrangement for providing the required support may be substituted for imposition of the penalty.[9]

2. DESTITUTE OR NECESSITOUS CIRCUMSTANCES

Sometimes wording of a desertion or nonsupport statute includes reference to the "destitute or necessitous circumstances" of the dependent.[10] The early statutes may have been intended merely to codify the common law and provide a penalty only where the failure to support caused actual harm in the form of suffering or distress due to inadequate food, clothing, shelter or medical attention,[11] but in any event such is not the present interpretation. Many codes no longer make reference to destitute or necessitous circumstances.

The duty of a husband or wife to support his or her dependent, as understood today, requires much more than that he or she be saved from starvation or dire need. The obligation is to furnish the dependent with such necessaries as are required for health and comfort, including suitable clothing, lodging, food and medical attendance—all determined in the light of the social position and circumstances of the particular persons involved.[12] A dependent may be in "destitute or necessitous circumstances" although every

---

6. West's Ann.Cal.Pen.Code § 270 et seq. (1976); Miss. Code 1972, 97–5–3; Nev.Rev.Stat. 201.020 (1979); 15 Vt.Stat. Ann. § 202 (1973).

The New Jersey statute is illustrative of the approach recently taken by legislatures:

"A person commits a crime of the fourth degree if he willfully fails to provide support which he can provide and which he knows he is legally obliged to provide to a spouse, child or other dependent." N.J. Stat. Ann. 2C:24–5 (1979).

7. Model Penal Code 230.5.

8. State v. Savastini, 14 N.J. 507, 103 A.2d 249 (1954).

"[I]mprisonment should be a last resort here, since it incapacitates the defendant from providing the very support which the community seeks to require and frustrates any broader effort to rehabilitate the family situation." Model Penal Code 188 (Tent. Draft No. 9, 1959).

9. Section 4.

10. The basic element of the crime is that the child be "then and there in destitute or necessitous" circumstances.

Ward v. State, 42 Ala.App. 529, 170 So.2d 500 (1964). Idaho Code § 18–401 (1979); Wis.Stat.Ann. 52.05 (1967).

11. "While it was, of course, his duty to furnish her with such necessaries, it was no crime for him not to do so if she was not actually in want of them even though he might have abandoned her within the meaning of the statute." People v. Selby, 26 Cal.App. 796, 802, 148 P. 807 (1915). But a later case held that the fact the wife was supported by others would not bar a conviction. People v. Martin, 100 Cal.App. 435, 280 P. 151 (1929).

If the child has received suitable clothes and support from the earnings of its mother, together with outside aid, it has not been deserted by its father. Cox v. Commonwealth, 200 Ky. 94, 132 S.W.2d 739 (1939).

12. State v. Moran, 99 Conn. 115, 121 A. 277 (1923).

See also, State v. Welden, 8 W.W.Harr. 158, 189 A. 586 (1937); Bruneel v. Bruneel, 14 N.J. 53, 100 A.2d 882 (1953).

need is adequately satisfied by charity, either public or private.[13] It has been said that the duty of a person to support is not dependent on the adequacy or inadequacy of the dependent's means. A husband may be guilty of nonsupport of his wife although she is being taken care of by her parents,[14] or by other friends or relatives. And it is no defense to a father that his child's grandfather or other friends and relatives are making the provision he has neglected.[15]

It has been said that the duty of a husband to support his wife is not dependent upon the adequacy or inadequacy of her means, or the fact that she is earning a living or capable of doing so,[16] but this cannot be accepted without qualification. It overlooks important changes that have taken place in modern times. For an extreme illustration take a childless couple, both employed, with the wife actually earning more than the husband. Obviously he cannot leave her in destitute or necessitous circumstances while she is making more than he is. If, under other circumstances, a wife with no training or experience is able to "get by" only by accepting distasteful employment, the husband might be held in default. Quite properly, however, it was held that a wife with an unencumbered estate worth $23,000 was not destitute.[17] The property and earning capacity of each spouse is taken into consideration, but if it is not sufficient to provide one with proper support the other spouse has a duty to do so.[18]

It is sometimes expressly provided in the statute that the duty to support is not relieved by the fact that "any other person, or organization, voluntarily or involuntarily furnishes such necessary food" and so forth.[19]

3. PARTIES LIVING APART

The husband or wife's duty to support his or her spouse is matched by the duty of each to live with his or her spouse in the home reasonably chosen by them. If without just cause one leaves that home and the other keeps the door open, figuratively, standing ready to provide support if and when the departed spouse returns, there is no obligation to support the spouse who

13. "Destitute condition means without money or property and dependent upon charity but is not removed because private or public charity intervenes." State v. Greer, 259 Iowa 367, 144 N.W.2d 322 (1966).

14. State v. Anderson, 209 Iowa 510, 228 N.W. 353 (1929).

15. Myrick v. State, 212 Miss. 702, 55 So.2d 426 (1951); Goodart v. State, 65 Okl.Cr. 472, 88 P.2d 911 (1939); Rhodes v. State, 76 Ga.App. 667, 47 S.E.2d 293 (1948).

It has been held that children are not destitute, as contemplated by the statute, if the mother in the discharge of her maternal duty, supports them. State v. Greer, 259 Iowa 367, 144 N.W.2d 322 (1966).

The fact that the child is being supported by its grandparents is no defense to the father charged with nonsupport.

Thompson v. Commonwealth, 461 S.W.2d 375 (Ky. 1970).

16. Bonanno v. Bonanno, 4 N.J. 268, 72 A.2d 318 (1950). See also Rowe v. Rowe, 256 Ala. 491, 55 So.2d 749 (1951). And see State v. Waller, 90 Kan. 829, 136 P. 215 (1913).

17. State v. Welden, 8 W.W.Harr. 158, 189 A. 586 (1937). Accord, State v. Wright, 200 Iowa 772, 205 N.W. 325 (1925). And see People v. Booth, 390 Ill. 330, 61 N.E.2d 370 (1945).

18. State v. Carroll, 150 W.Va. 765, 149 S.E.2d 309 (1966). Greggo v. Greggo, 41 Del.Ch. 289, 194 A.2d 58 (1963). And see *Bonanno*, supra note 6.

19. E.g., West's Ann.Cal.Pen.Code § 270 (1976). No such words appear in West's Ann.Cal.Pen.Code § 270a (1976). This may involve a special problem of statutory interpretation in California.

left the home in a place of isolation.[20] But if a spouse leaves and takes their children, the wrongful act could not be imputed to the children and the other spouse's duty to support the children would continue.[21]

It is only where a spouse desires the presence of the other in their home that the fact that a husband or wife may be living there can be made a condition precedent to the obligation of the other to provide support.[22] Hence, one cannot divest himself of his duty by driving the other spouse away either literally or by his gross misconduct.[23] The duty of a parent to support his children, it may be added, is imposed upon him by law and cannot be abrogated by an agreement with the other spouse.[24] Hence, no agreement between them is a defense to the other[25] unless it can be shown that the neglecting spouse had sufficient means to support the child and that his failure to support him was in bona-fide reliance upon the contract.[26] Even without children, if a husband and wife separate by mutual agreement and one becomes destitute the other has a duty to support and is guilty of non-support if aware of the condition of the other and able to provide support.[27] It may be added that a husband or wife may be guilty of failure to support the other spouse although he continues to live with such spouse.[28]

4. AFTER DIVORCE

A valid divorce terminates the marital relation and with it the duty of the husband to support his wife and vice versa except as to payments expressly included in the divorce decree, but it does not bring an end to the parent's duty to support a child,[29] even if custody was given to the other spouse without an order for its support.[30]

The prosecution of a divorced parent for failure to support his child is based upon that failure *per se*, and not upon a failure to perform the divorce decree[31] unless the statute makes it a crime for a parent wilfully to fail to make payments required by such an order.[32] But a parent cannot be deemed

---

20. Taylor v. State, 93 Tex.Cr. 317, 247 S.W. 513 (1923); State v. Chace, 124 Kan. 529, 261 P. 559 (1927); Columbo v. Columbo, 71 Cal.App.2d 577, 162 P.2d 995 (1945). And see Steffenson v. Steffenson, 259 Wis. 51, 47 N.W.2d 445 (1951).

21. Myrick v. Myrick, 212 Miss. 702, 55 So.2d 426 (1951); Amadeo v. Amadeo, 64 N.J.Super. 417, 166 A.2d 397 (1960).

22. Munger v. Munger, 21 N.J.Super. 49, 90 A.2d 539 (1952).

23. Turney v. Nooney, 21 N.J.Super. 522, 91 A.2d 418 (1952).

24. Kamp v. Morang, 277 Ala. 575, 173 So.2d 566 (1964).

25. Higgenbotham v. State, 20 Ala. App. 476, 103 So. 71 (1925).

26. State v. Prince, 42 Wn.2d 314, 254 P.2d 731 (1953).

27. Spencer v. State, 132 Wis. 509, 112 N.W. 462 (1907).

28. O'Brien v. State, 90 Tex.Cr. 276, 234 S.W. 668 (1921).

29. Freeman v. State, 103 Tex.Cr. 428, 280 S.W. 1069 (1926); State v. Rutledge, 122 Wash. 281, 210 P. 669 (1922).

30. Guyot v. State, 222 Ark. 275, 258 S.W.2d 569 (1953); Barrow v. State, 87 Ga.App. 572, 74 S.E.2d 467 (1953); Commonwealth ex rel. Prelec v. Prelec, 179 Pa.Super. 422, 115 A.2d 847 (1955).

Contra: Madison v. State, 163 Tenn. 198, 42 S.W.2d 209 (1931). This minority view was followed in California prior to statutory change in 1923, and in Washington prior to change in 1913.

31. Bohannon v. State, 271 P.2d 739 (Okl.Cr.1954); State v. Francis, 126 Or. 253, 269 P. 878 (1928).

32. Dimond v. State, 110 Neb. 519, 194 N.W. 725 (1923).

There is some authority for the position that the procedure should be for contempt for failure to abide by the decree. Boaze v. Commonwealth, 165 Va. 786, 183 S.E. 263 (1936). In any event a failure to comply with the support provisions

guilty of nonsupport while faithfully making the payments ordered by the divorce decree.[33]   If they are deemed inadequate the remedy is by modification of the decree and not by prosecution.[34]

If, under the particular statute, desertion or abandonment is the affirmative act of leaving the child as distinct from non-support this cannot be committed by the parent after a divorce in which custody was granted to the other parent.[35]

5. THE CHILD

Several problems are involved in the parental duty of child-support.

A. AGE

While the Uniform Act applies only to children under the age of sixteen, some of the statutes have a different provision such as any child "less than nineteen years of age" [36] for nonsupport or "less then eighteen years of age" for abandonment [37] or a "minor child." [38]

B. ILLEGITIMATE CHILD

Although the Uniform Desertion and Non-Support Act referred only to "child," [39] and some courts have held that there can be no prosecution thereunder if the child involved is not legitimate,[40] the position taken under most statutes today is to expressly recognize illegitimate children by such terms as "either a legitimate or illegitimate" child [41] or words of similar effect.[42] Some statutes define child as including legitimate or illegitimate children or have been so construed by the courts.[43]   The inclusion of illegitimate children within such statutes avoids constitutional problems and comports with the rights generally accorded such children.[44]

Another view is that no prosecution is warranted unless there has been a previous adjudication of paternity or a legal acknowledgment thereof,[45] while

of a divorce judgment is punishable by contempt. Lyon v. Superior Court, 68 Cal.2d 446, 67 Cal.Rptr. 265, 439 P.2d 1 (1968).

33. Manners v. State, 210 Ind. 648, 5 N.E.2d 300 (1936); State v. Galjour, 215 La. 553, 41 So.2d 215 (1949); Dimond v. State, 110 Neb. 519, 194 N.W. 725 (1923); State v. Holl, 25 Ohio App.2d 75, 266 N.E.2d 587 (1971).

34. State v. Miller, 111 Kan. 231, 206 P. 744 (1922); Martin v. State, 308 So.2d 925 (Miss.1975).

35. Hodges v. Commonwealth, 269 S.W.2d 280 (Ky.1954); Gomez v. State, 163 Tex.Cr. 99, 289 S.W.2d 269 (1956); State v. Sweet, 179 Minn. 32, 228 N.W. 337 (1929). Accord, People v. Dunston, 173 Mich. 368, 138 N.W. 1047 (1912).

36. E.g., Code of Ala. 1975, Tit. 13A–13–4.

37. Code of Ala. 1975, Tit. 13A–13–5.

38. E.g., Ariz.Rev.Stat. § 12–2458 (1978). "Child" means one under majority. Rhodes v. State, 76 Ga.App. 667, 47 S.E.2d 293 (1948).

39. 10 ULA.

40. Ex parte Cambetta, 169 Cal. 100, 145 P. 1005 (1902). This was prior to the amendment mentioned in the preceding note.

41. Nev.Rev.Stat. 201.020 (1979); Wis.Stat.Ann. 52.05 (1967).

42. In California the statute is applicable "whether the parents of such child are or were ever married or divorced." West's Ann.Cal.Pen.Code § 270 (1976).

43. State v. Rawlings, 38 Md.App. 479, 381 A.2d 708 (1978); Annotation 99 ALR 2d 746.

44. Gomez v. Perez, 409 U.S. 535, 93 S.Ct. 872 (1973).

45. Upton v. State, 255 Ala. 594, 52 So.2d 824 (1951); Kamp v. Morang, 277

other courts permit the prosecution of the putative father of an illegitimate child and allow paternity to be established in the prosecution itself.[46]

C. UNBORN CHILD

An unborn child is a child within the meaning of the statute and a father's wilful failure to furnish necessary food, clothing and shelter to such child is a misdemeanor. Though no penalty is imposed upon the father for the nonsupport of the unwed mother, *as such*, the unborn child can receive nourishment only from the mother and hence must suffer if the mother is not provided with the necessities of life.[47]

D. UNNATURAL CHILD

D is the "lawful father" of a child conceived through heterologous artificial insemination, pursuant to an agreement between **D** and his wife and born during their marriage. Hence his wilful failure to support the child, even after he and his wife have separated, is punishable under the statute.[48]

6. STATUTE OF LIMITATIONS

Where abandonment or desertion is dealt with as an affirmative act the statute of limitations begins to run immediately after **D** "walks out" and the prosecution is barred when the statutory time after that has elapsed; but nonsupport is a continuing offense [49] and it is unimportant when the nonsupport began if it was continued within the statutory period.[50]

7. ADDENDUM

Under the common law of nonsupport the primary duty was that of the father. The father had the duty to provide food, clothing and shelter for his child. If the father provided the food and the mother failed to make it available to the child, whether as a result of negligence or wilfulness, this was a negative act on her part. And if the father was dead, or otherwise unavailable, the duty to support the child fell upon the mother. Today in most jurisdictions the law of nonsupport is necessarily addressed in terms of the duty of the parent.

8. EX POST FACTO

Where the rule not permitting the prosecution of an illegitimate child has been changed this would not permit prosecution of desertion or abandonment, as an affirmative act, prior to the change, but prosecution for nonsup-

Ala. 575, 173 So.2d 566 (1964); State v. Rawlings, 38 Md.App. 479, 381 A.2d 708 (1978); State ex rel. Carrington v. Schutts, 217 Kan. 175, 535 P.2d 982 (1975).

46. Commonwealth ex rel. Riddle v. Anderson, 227 Pa.Super. 68, 323 A.2d 115 (1974).

47. People v. Saines, 134 Cal.App. 355, 25 P.2d 487 (1933). See West's Ann. Cal.Pen.Code § 270 (1976).

Contra, the father's duty extends only to a "child" and does not include an unborn fetus. Baby X v. Misiano, 373 Mass. 265, 366 N.E.2d 755 (1977).

48. People v. Sorensen, 68 Cal.2d 280, 66 Cal.Rptr. 7, 437 P.2d 495 (1968).

49. State v. Greenberg, 16 N.J. 568, 109 A.2d 669 (1954); Day v. State, 481 P.2d 807 (Okl.Cr.App.1971).

50. Goodart v. State, 65 Okl.Cr. 472, 88 P.2d 911 (1939).

port of such a child, born prior to the change, is permissible if the nonsupport continues after the statute takes effect.[51]

9. EXTRADITION

If **D** deserts his wife or child, leaving them in destitute or necessitous circumstances, and goes to another state he is a "fugitive" in the constitutional sense and may be extradited under the federal provisions.[52] If he sends his wife to another state under assurance that he will follow later and join her there, after which he does not join her but leaves her stranded and without support, he is not a "fugitive" because he has not fled from the state in which the crime was committed.[53]

In legal theory the situs of a negative act is where the performance of the duty would have occurred had there been no failure.[54] Hence the crime of nonsupport is committed in the state in which the wife is when the support is lacking.[55] Thus where **D** failed to support his wife in the state to which he had sent her he was guilty of nonsupport in that state and properly convicted when they obtained jurisdiction over him.[56] It was the same in a case in which the wife had left **D** and gone to the other state, since her leaving was justifiable because of ill-treatment by **D**.[57]

In the cases mentioned **D** might have avoided conviction had he obtained proper legal advice because he was not properly extraditable since he was not a "fugitive" from the state in which the crime was committed[58] and the cases were prior to the Uniform Extradition Act which has since been adopted in almost every state. This act does not required that one be a "fugitive" in the constitutional sense, but authorizes extradition of one who, from outside the demanding state, did an act "intentionally resulting in a crime" therein.[59] This would include intentionally withholding support from a dependent.

Under this act the husband would be extraditable in cases such as those mentioned, and it would be the same in regard to the nonsupport of a child where the duty to support is clear. In one case, however, the duty was not clear. **D**, a resident of New Hampshire, was indicted in Massachusetts for nonsupport of an illegitimate child which the mother claimed was begotten by **D** before she moved to Massachusetts from New Hampshire. **D** denied that he was the father of the child and paternity could not be established there because no proceedings had been instituted within the time required by New Hampshire law. Under Massachusetts law paternity could be estab-

---

51. People v. Stanley, 33 Cal.App. 624, 166 P. 596 (1917); Williams v. State, 213 Ga. 221, 98 S.E.2d 373 (1957).

52. Constitution Art. IV, sec. 2, par. 2; 18 U.S.C.A. § 3182.

53. Cf. State v. Hall, 115 N.C. 811, 20 S.E. 729 (1894).

54. As explained by one court, "one is answerable for his neglect in the place where others suffer in consequence." State v. Peabody, 25 R.I. 544, 545, 56 A. 1028, 1029 (1904).

55. In re Price, 168 Mich. 527, 529, 134 N.W. 721 (1912). The problem in this

case was venue. It was held that venue was in the county in which the wife resided.

56. State v. Jenkins, 189 Iowa 1233, 179 N.W. 541 (1920).

57. State v. Wellman, 102 Kan. 503, 170 P. 1052 (1918).

58. It seems that he was extradited in each case—but compare Hyatt v. People ex rel. Corkran, 188 U.S. 691, 23 S.Ct. 456 (1903).

59. The Uniform Extradition Act, § 6.

lished in the nonsupport prosecution. But there is no negative act without a legal duty to perform—no nonsupport without a legal duty to support—and Massachusetts could not reach across the boundary into New Hampshire and impose a duty upon a resident of that state. Hence although **D** had been arrested for extradition, his release was ordered under a writ of habeas corpus.[60]

All states have enacted legislation in the form of the Uniform Reciprocal Enforcement of Support Act whereby an obligee in one state can enforce duties of support owed by an obligor in another state.[61] The Act provides an alternative to criminal extradition proceedings for nonsupport under the Uniform Extradition Act [62] by empowering the governor of the initiating state to demand of the governor of the responding state the obligor who has failed to provide support and is charged with a crime in the initiating state.[63] Any demand by the initiating state need not show that the obligor has fled from that state or that at the time the crime was committed was in the initiating state.[64] Both the initiating and responding states must have adopted some version of the Act. It is not clear whether the obligor can be extradited if there has been no adjudication of paternity and the obligor contests that issue.[65]

. . .

The Model Penal Code has a section on nonsupport which follows the conventional position except for its emphasis upon *persistent* failure to support.[66]

SECTION 5. CONSPIRACY

A statement which is clearly in layman's language rather than with legal precision is to the effect that, "An agreement for a lawful purpose is a contract; an agreement for an unlawful purpose is a conspiracy." This conveys the idea in a very general way but is too broad to be of much help in the solution of specific problems. Probably no one would expect the contract

---

60. Hardy v. Betz, 105 N.H. 169, 195 A.2d 582 (1963).

61. 9A ULA 1980 Supp. pp. 37, 46; Clarkston v. Bridge, 273 Or. 68, 539 P.2d 1094 (1975).

62. "Since the enactment of the Uniform Reciprocal Enforcement of Support Act in this state, it is true there are now two distinct courses of action which a demanding state may take with respect to one who does not carry out his obligations of support to his family, namely (1) extradition on a charge of nonsupport, and (2) initiation of civil proceedings under the Uniform Reciprocal Enforcement of Support Act. However, either or both courses of action may be pursued, and the election lies wholly with the demanding state and the obligee." Conrad v. McClearn, 166 Colo. 568, 445 P.2d 222, 224 (1968).

63. Uniform Reciprocal Enforcement of Support Act § 5(1) (1968).

64. Id. § 5(2).

65. Nye v. District Court for County of Adams, 168 Colo. 272, 450 P.2d 669 (1969).

66. "A person commits a misdemeanor if he persistently fails to provide support which he can provide and which he knows he is legally obliged to provide to a spouse, child or other dependent." Model Penal Code, section 230.5.

The word "persistent" for the purpose of this offense probably contributes little other than add to the vagueness resulting from the extreme brevity of the provision. Compared with the Uniform Desertion and Nonsupport Act the Code section seems woefully inadequate.

For annotation and application of state statutes providing for reciprocal enforcement of duty to support dependents, see 42 A.L.R.2d 768 (1955).

technicalities of offer and acceptance to be carried over into the law of conspiracy, but a word of caution is needed to emphasize that, at least so far as criminal conspiracy is concerned, the word "unlawful" is not a true antonym of the word "lawful" as the two are used in the sentence quoted,[1] and the use of "contract" as an analogy is misleading.

Civil consequences, as well as liability to punishment, may result from a conspiracy [2] but it is possible, in theory at least, for a combination to have one effect without the other. Any consideration of "civil conspiracy" is beyond the scope of the present undertaking and whenever the word "conspiracy" is used below it is to be understood as the name of a crime—a "criminal conspiracy," which is a common-law misdemeanor [3] although under modern statutes it often may be either a misdemeanor or a felony depending upon the purpose of the confederation.[4]

A. DEFINITION

Whether a definition of conspiracy should be attempted has been doubted [5] because of the question whether it is possible to frame one in such a manner that it will include every wrong of this nature without including matters which do not belong therein. It would be helpful if a definition of a crime could be so formulated that it alone, without additional explanation, could accomplish such a perfect task of inclusion and exclusion, but there are few crimes if any for which such a simple solution is possible. The definition of a crime does not represent the end of the search but is merely a convenient starting point for the consideration of the problems involved. And such a starting point is useful here despite the need of extensive explanation and even some qualification. The familiar definition is in some such form as this: Conspiracy is a combination between two or more persons to accomplish a criminal or unlawful act, or to do a lawful act by criminal or unlawful means.[6] This covers the field about as well as the nature of the offense

1. "This contract is illegal in the sense of not being enforceable; it is not necessary that it should be such as to form the ground of criminal proceedings." Urmston v. Whitelegg Brothers, 63 L.T.Rep.N.S. 455 (1890).

2. Schaefer v. Berinstein, 140 Cal. App.2d 278, 295 P.2d 113 (1956); Cole v. Associated Construction Co., 141 Conn. 49, 103 A.2d 529 (1954).

3. Commonwealth v. Hunt, 45 Mass. 111, 121 (1842); State v. Buchanan, 5 Har. & J. 317, 352 (Md.1821); State v. McFeely, 25 N.J.Misc. 303, 52 A.2d 823 (1947); The King v. Journeymen-Taylors, 8 Mod. 10, 88 Eng.Rep. 9 (1791). "It is well settled that it is an offence of common-law origin." State v. Bacon, 27 R.I. 252, 256, 61 A. 653, 654 (1905). For the history of conspiracy in England consult 2 Stephen, History of the Criminal Law of England 227–9 (1883); 1 Russell on Crime, 12th Ed. pp. 200–203 (1964).

4. 18 U.S.C.A. § 371 (1966); West's Ann.Cal.Pen.Code § 182 (as amended in 1977). At one time in Georgia there was no crime of conspiracy but one could be found guilty of a crime caused by acts done pursuant to a conspiracy. Randall v. State, 73 Ga.App. 354, 36 S.E.2d 450 (1945). Georgia now has a general conspiracy statute. Code of Ga., Sec. 26–3201 (1978). For a consideration of the statutes on conspiracy see Note, 68 Harv.L.Rev. 1056 (1955).

5. "The comprehensiveness and indefiniteness of the offense of conspiracy has made an exact definition a very difficult one, as has often been stated." Commonwealth v. Donoghue, 250 Ky. 343, 347, 63 S.W.2d 3, 5 (1933). See also Smith v. People, 25 Ill. 17, 23 (1860); People v. Fisher, 14 Wend. 9 (N.Y.1835). It "almost defies definition." Per Mr. Justice Jackson concurring in Krulewitch v. United States, 336 U.S. 440, 446, 69 S.Ct. 716, 719, 720 (1949).

6. Commonwealth v. Donoghue, 250 Ky. 343, 347, 63 S.W.2d 3, 5 (1933); Pettibone v. United States, 148 U.S. 197, 203,

permits, but seems to be needlessly verbose. Since one person cannot combine with himself [7] the words "two or more persons" are not needed, and as whatever is criminal is unlawful the former does not require separate mention because it is included in the latter. Furthermore, since unlawfulness is equally objectionable whether it represents the end sought to be achieved, or the means to be employed to bring about that result, the separate mention of these adds nothing to the definition. While statutes require a change, as will be mentioned presently, the best definition of the common-law offense is as follows:

A conspiracy is a combination for an unlawful purpose.

B. THE COMBINATION

Holmes' famous reference to a conspiracy as a "partnership in criminal purposes" [8] was made rather to emphasize the significance of the *combination* than to offer a definition. The word "partnership" is frequently used in this connection,[9] and does not fail to carry the desired meaning; but rather than extend this term to include an unlawful alliance, the word "combination" is employed here.

That the gist of a conspiracy is the combination which is formed has been repeated time and again.[10] Holmes introduced the sentence quoted above with these words: "A conspiracy is constituted by an agreement, it is true, but it is the result of the agreement, rather than the agreement itself, just as a partnership, although constituted by a contract, is not the contract but is a result of it. The contract is instantaneous, the partnership may endure as one and the same partnership for years." [11] He had previously emphasized that a plot to bring about a continuous result is not a "cinematographic series of distinct conspiracies." [12] And because the resulting combination is

---

13 S.Ct. 542, 545 (1893); State v. Smith, 197 Tenn. 350, 354, 273 S.W.2d 143, 145–6 (1954); State v. McCullough, 244 N.C. 11, 92 S.E.2d 389, 391 (1956).

7. Some jurisdictions by special statute recognize a unilateral conspiracy. State v. Christopher, 305 Minn. 226, 232 N.W.2d 798 (1975); Garcia v. State, ___ Ind. ___, 394 N.E.2d 106 (1979). Burgman, Unilateral Conspiracy: Three Critical Perspectives, 29 DePaul L.Rev. 75 (1979).

8. United States v. Kissel, 218 U.S. 601, 608, 31 S.Ct. 124, 126 (1910). Frequently quoted—as in Orton v. United States, 221 F.2d 632, 633 (4th Cir. 1955); Scales v. United States, 227 F.2d 581, 587 (4th Cir. 1955).

9. "A conspiracy is a partnership in crime." Pinkerton v. United States, 328 U.S. 640, 644, 66 S.Ct. 1180, 1182 (1946). It is a "criminal partnership." People v. Lyon, 135 Cal.App.2d 558, 575, 288 P.2d 57, 68 (1955). It is a "community of criminal purpose." The King v. Brisac, 4 East 164, 171, 102 Eng.Rep. 792, 795 (1803). And see Orton v. United States,

221 F.2d 632, 633 (4th Cir. 1955); People v. Atley, 392 Mich. 298, 220 N.W.2d 465 (1974).

10. "A conspiracy is a combination or agreement to violate the law, ..." Miller v. United States, 382 F.2d 583, 586 (9th Cir. 1967). And see People v. Katzman, 258 Cal.App.2d 777, 66 Cal.Rptr. 319, 324 (1968).

See Bannon v. United States, 156 U.S. 464, 468, 15 S.Ct. 467, 469 (1895); United States v. Wootten, 29 F. 702, 703 (D.C. S.C.1887); People v. Klaw, 55 Misc. 72, 77, 106 N.Y.S. 341, 344 (1907); Wilson v. Commonwealth, 96 Pa. 56, 58 (1880); State v. Smith, 197 Tenn. 350, 355, 273 S.W.2d 143, 145 (1954).

"We have stated that the gist or gravamen of conspiracy is an *agreement* to effectuate a criminal act." United States v. Laughman, 618 F.2d 1067, 1074 (4th Cir. 1980).

11. United States v. Kissel, 218 U.S. 601, 608, 31 S.Ct. 124, 126 (1910).

12. Id. at 607. If one unlawful combination is brought to an end and is then

the gist of the conspiracy, it follows that those who, with knowledge of its existence, aid or assist in carrying out its criminal purposes thereby make themselves parties thereto and are equally guilty with the original conspirators; [13] and on the other hand, that one combination constitutes only one conspiracy even if it contemplates the commission of several offenses.[14] A plot, for example, to commit grand larceny and promptly flee from the scene in a car kept handy for that purpose constitutes only one conspiracy, although if executed it would include the statutory offense of "automobile banditry." [15] Needless to add, if the plot to commit several different offenses is carried out in full the conspirators may be convicted of each such offense, in addition to the conspiracy.[16]

Since the conspiracy is the combination resulting from the agreement, rather than the mere agreement itself, it follows that the verb "conspire," when used in the law, has reference to the formation of the combination. "To conspire" means "to combine" and not merely "to agree."

1. THE AGREEMENT

Although the conspiracy is the resulting combination rather than the agreement itself there must be a meeting of minds,[17]—a unity of design and purpose. It is not necessary, however, that any formal agreement be

followed by another the result is two conspiracies. United States v. Perlstein, 120 F.2d 276 (3d Cir. 1941).

13. Pattis v. United States, 17 F.2d 562 (9th Cir. 1927), cert. denied 274 U.S. 750, 47 S.Ct. 764 (1927). And see Orton v. United States, 221 F.2d 632, 633 (4th Cir. 1955); People v. Sears, 138 Cal.App. 2d 773, 292 P.2d 663 (1956). And see United States v. Sansone, 231 F.2d 887 (2d Cir. 1956); United States v. Smith, 600 F.2d 149 (8th Cir. 1979). See Note, 16 U.C.L.A. L.Rev. 155 (1968).

14. Braverman v. United States, 317 U.S. 49, 63 S.Ct. 99 (1942); People v. Nasworthy, 94 Cal.App.2d 85, 210 P.2d 83 (1949); United States v. Boyd, 595 F.2d 120 (3d Cir. 1978). A single criminal conspiracy has been recognized where the same conspiracy violated two separate conspiracy statutes. United States v. Mori, 444 F.2d 240 (5th Cir. 1971).

However, the Court has held that Congress intended to permit imposition of consecutive sentences for offenses of conspiracy to import marijuana and conspiracy to distribute marijuana even though such offenses arose from a single agreement or conspiracy having dual objectives. Albernaz v. United States, 450 U.S. 333, 101 S.Ct. 1137 (1981).

15. Steffler v. State, 230 Ind. 557, 104 N.E.2d 729 (1951).

16. Pinkerton v. United States, 328 U.S. 640, 66 S.Ct. 1180 (1946).

The Model Penal Code would not permit conviction of both the conspiracy and the target offense. Section 5.05(3).

17. "It is always 'predominantly mental in composition' because it consists primarily of a meeting of minds and an intent." Mr. Justice Jackson, concurring, in Krulewitch v. United States, 336 U.S. 440, 447–8, 69 S.Ct. 716, 720, 721 (1949). Indispensability of the agreement sometimes leads to the error of referring to it as the "gist of the crime." See Roll v. People, 132 Colo. 1, 284 P.2d 665 (1955); People v. Sears, 138 Cal.App.2d 773, 292 P.2d 663 (1956).

Elements of conspiracy are an agreement between two or more persons to commit a crime, entered into with specific intent to commit that crime, followed by some overt act in implementation. People v. Heredia, 257 Cal.App.2d 862, 65 Cal.Rptr. 402 (1968). Where there was no evidence of any communication between the two, conspiracy was not established. United States v. Bekowies, 432 F.2d 8 (9th Cir. 1970).

"The essence of the crime of conspiracy is an agreement to violate the law." United States v. Andrews, 585 F.2d 961, 964 (10th Cir. 1978).

For conspiracy "there must be an agreement. But such an agreement need be no more than a meeting of the minds and need not be written or oral." State v. Small, 229 Kan.App. 411, 625 P.2d 1, 3, (1981).

shown.[18] It is enough if the parties tacitly come to an understanding in regard to the unlawful purpose,[19] and this may be inferred from sufficiently significant circumstances,[20] although evidence which merely creates a suspicion will not be adequate.[21] In the words of the South Carolina court: [22]

"It is sufficient that the minds of the parties meet understandingly, so as to bring about an intelligent and deliberate agreement, to do the act and commit the offense charged, although such agreement be not manifested by any formal words."

Where more than two are involved the requirement of a meeting of minds does not mean that each conspirator must know the identity of all the others.[23]

2. END OR MEANS

In the words of Lord Denman: "An indictment for conspiracy ought to shew, either that it was for an unlawful purpose, or to effect a lawful purpose by unlawful means." [24] And while such a statement seems not to be needed in the definition, the fact that unlawfulness of either the end or the means is sufficient for conspiracy has been repeated time and again.[25] One form of expression is that a conspiracy is a combination "to do an unlawful act by any means . . . [or] any act by unlawful means." [26] The idea Lord Denman intended to convey was that the unlawfulness must be charged in the indictment, and that if the end itself is lawful the unlawful

"For an accused to be convicted of an unlawful conspiracy, there must be proof beyond a reasonable doubt that a conspiracy existed, that he had knowledge of it, and with this knowledge he voluntarily became a part of it." United States v. Bankston, 603 F.2d 528, 531 (5th Cir. 1979).

"Although an anticipated benefit may be evidence of an alleged coconspirator's mens rea, we agree with the Ninth Circuit that benefit, or a 'stake in the venture,' is not an element of § 371." United States v. Schoup, 608 F.2d 950, 957 (3d Cir. 1979). 18 U.S.C.A. § 371 (1969). Conspiracy to commit offense or to defraud United States.

"Stated another way, the 'act' of the crime of conspiracy is the agreement while the 'mens rea' of the crime is the intent to commit the offense which is the object of the conspiracy." People v. Coy, 119 Cal.App.3d 254, 173 Cal.Rptr. 889, 986–87 (1981).

18. People v. Campbell, 132 Cal.App. 2d 262, 281 P.2d 912 (1955); United States v. American Radiator & Standard Sanitary Corp., 433 F.2d 174 (3d Cir. 1970).

19. People v. Gem Hang, 131 Cal.App. 2d 69, 280 P.2d 28 (1955).

20. Delli Paoli v. United States, 352 U.S. 232, 77 S.Ct. 294 (1957); Steffler v. State, 230 Ind. 557, 104 N.E.2d 729 (1951); Piracci v. State, 207 Md. 499, 115 A.2d 262 (1955).

21. Robertson v. State, 231 Ind. 368, 108 N.E.2d 711 (1952).

22. State v. Cole, 107 S.C. 285, 288–9, 92 S.E. 624, 625 (1917).

23. People v. Goldstein, 136 Cal.App. 2d 778, 289 P.2d 581 (1955).

"In order to convict a defendant of conspiracy, it is not necessary to prove that he knew all of the conspirators or that he was aware of all details of the conspiracy. A showing that the defendant knowingly contributed efforts in furtherance of it is sufficient." United States v. Schmaltz, 562 F.2d 558, 560 (8th Cir. 1977).

24. The King v. Seward, 1 Ad. & E. 706, 713, 110 Eng.Rep. 1377, 1380 (1834).

25. See Jetton-Dekle Lumber Co. v. Mather, 53 Fla. 969, 974, 43 So. 590, 591 (1907); Commonwealth v. Hunt, 45 Mass. 111 (1842); Commonwealth v. Waterman, 122 Mass. 43 (1877); Lambert v. People, 9 Cow. 578, 606 (N.Y.1827); State v. Bacon, 27 R.I. 252, 256, 61 A. 653, 654 (1905); State v. Smith, 197 Tenn. 350, 354, 273 S.W.2d 143, 145–6 (1954).

26. Smith v. People, 25 Ill. 17, 23 (1860). And see People v. Klaw, 53 Misc. 72, 77, 106 N.Y.S. 341, 344 (1907).

means must be alleged. Where the end itself is unlawful the means need not be set forth,[27]—in fact guilt of such a conspiracy may be established even if the wrongdoers had not yet decided upon the means to be employed.[28] For example, it was not essential to conviction for conspiracy to obtain money from an insurance company by false pretenses, to prove that the details of the fake accident had been planned in advance.[29]

3. OVERT ACT

At common law guilt of conspiracy was incurred by the combination for a forbidden purpose, and no additional "overt act" was required for conviction,[30]—which is still the law where unchanged by statute.[31] This does not violate the basic precept that criminal guilt cannot rest upon intent alone because there could be no meeting of the minds resulting in the unlawful combination if the intent had not been manifested. And whether the manifestation of intent is by words or conduct it is an act and is sufficient to complete the crime.[32] On the other hand, while it is "elementary that a conspiracy to commit a crime may be punished even though the crime be not committed," [33] it has been provided by statute in such jurisdictions that there shall be no conviction for conspiracy unless there is proof of some "overt act" in furtherance of the unlawful plan.[34] Under some of the codes this additional requirement applies to certain conspiracies but not to all.[35]

27. The King v. Seward, 1 Ad. & E. 706, 110 Eng.Rep. 1377 (1834). As to setting forth the unlawful end see United States v. Apex Distributing Co., 148 F.Supp. 365 (D.C.R.I.1957).

28. The King v. Gill, 2 B. & Ald. 204, 106 Eng.Rep. 341 (1818). Where the ultimate objective of the agreement is unlawful it is a conspiracy despite the fact that the means to be used are in themselves lawful. Yates v. United States, 225 F.2d 146 (9th Cir. 1955).

29. People v. Goldstein, 136 Cal.App. 2d 778, 289 P.2d 581 (1955).

30. "It is true that the conspiracy, the unlawful combination, has been said to be the crime, and that at common law it was not necessary to aver or prove an overt act; . . ." Hyde v. United States, 225 U.S. 347, 359, 32 S.Ct. 793, 799 (1912). In an early case Wyndham said a conspiracy without an act done was not punishable, but the unlawful gathering was an act. The other judges said no act was needed. The King v. Sterling, 1 Lev. 125, 83 Eng.Rep. 331 (1663). Compare People v. Hines, 168 Misc. 453, 6 N.Y.S.2d 2 (1938).

31. Piracci v. State, 207 Md. 499, 115 A.2d 262 (1955); State v. Smith, 197 Tenn. 350, 273 S.W.2d 143 (1954).

"The overt act which constitutes the object of the conspiracy is no part of the crime of conspiracy; indeed, an overt act is not required, but the crime is complete

when the felonious agreement is reached." State v. Leyba, 93 N.M. 312, 600 P.2d 312, 313 (App. 1979).

32. "A conspiracy consists not merely in the intention of two or more, but in the agreement of two or more to do an unlawful act, or to do a lawful act by unlawful means, so long as such a design rests in intention only, it is not indictable. When two or more agree to carry it into effect, the very plot is an act in itself, and the act of each of the parties, promise against promise, *actum contra actum*, capable of being enforced, if lawful, punishable if for a criminal object or for the use of criminal means." Mulcahy v. The Queen, L.R. 3 H.L. 306, 317 (1868).

33. Frankfeld v. United States, 198 F.2d 679, 684 (4th Cir. 1952); United States v. Kellerman, 431 F.2d 319 (2nd Cir. 1971).

34. 18 U.S.C.A. § 371 (1969); West's Ann.Cal.Pen.Code § 184 (1970).

35. State v. Westbrook, 79 Ariz. 116, 118, 285 P.2d 161, 162 (1954).

The proposed Federal Criminal Code S. 1722, 96th Cong. 1st Sess. § 1002 would seem to require an overt act ". . . engages in any conduct with intent to effect . . ."

18 U.S.C.A. § 1117, conspiracy to murder, overt act required. 21 U.S.C.A. § 963, a conspiracy under the Comprehensive Drug Abuse Prevention and Control

Statutes with this additional requirement raise the question whether the "overt act" is a part of the offense itself or is merely a matter of evidence needed for conviction.[36] Both sides of the argument are found in *Hyde*[37] in which the Supreme Court held that the act was a part of the conspiracy while Holmes in his dissenting opinion urged the other view. This is not a matter of importance in the ordinary case because the same proof is needed under either theory, but it may be determinative if the special problem involved is one of venue,[38] jurisdiction[39] or the statute of limitations.[40]

It was held in one case that where an overt act is required for conviction more is needed than an act of preparation.[41] In substance the position taken was that nothing less than a criminal attempt will satisfy the requirement of the statute. On rehearing the court changed its view and held flatly that the overt act required for conviction of conspiracy need not amount to an attempt to commit the crime which is the object of the combination,[42] and this is unquestionably the sound view.[43] The function of the "overt act" is quite different in the two offenses. In the case of attempt the act must go beyond preparation because the attempt is deemed a punishable segment of the crime intended. But if the statute requires an "overt act" for conviction of conspiracy, whether such act is held to be a part of the conspiracy or only required evidence thereof, the purpose of the requirement is merely to afford "a *locus poenitentiae*, so that before the act done one or more of the parties

Act does not require an overt act. See United States v. Michel, 588 F.2d 986 (5th Cir. 1979).

36. The answer might depend upon the language of the particular enactment. Compare the statutes cited in n. 33 supra.

37. Hyde v. United States, 225 U.S. 347, 32 S.Ct. 793 (1912).

38. Though the conspiracy was formed in California and the conspirators on trial did not leave that state yet they may be tried in the federal court in the District of Columbia if an overt act was done there to effect the object of the conspiracy. Hyde v. United States, 225 U.S. 347, 32 S.Ct. 793 (1912). One act in the jurisdiction is sufficient for venue. Crosby v. United States, 231 F.2d 679 (5th Cir. 1956).

39. An overt act committed within the state gives it jurisdiction over a conspirator who was outside the state at the time, even if the conspiracy was formed outside the state. State v. Hicks, 233 N.C. 511, 64 S.E.2d 871 (1951). "[T]he gist of the offense is the conspiracy. . . . Hence, if the conspiracy was entered into within the limits of the United States and the jurisdiction of the court, the crime was then complete, and the subsequent overt act in pursuance thereof may have been done anywhere." Dealy v. United States, 152 U.S. 539, 547, 14 S.Ct. 680, 683 (1894). Cf. Bannon v. United States, 156 U.S. 464, 15 S.Ct. 467

(1895); Ramey v. United States, 230 F.2d 171 (5th Cir. 1956).

40. The indictment is subject to demurrer unless it alleges an overt act committed within the period of limitations. People v. Hines, 284 N.Y. 93, 29 N.E.2d 483 (1940). Cf. United States v. Cohen, 145 F.2d 82 (2d Cir. 1944). See Note, 29 N.Y.U.L.Rev. 1470 (1954).

41. People v. George, California District Court of Appeal, July 10, 1925, noted in 13 Calif.L.Rev. 491 (1925).

42. People v. George, 74 Cal.App. 440, 241 P. 97 (1925). "And this analysis disposes of the contention that a conspiracy to advocate, as distinguished from the advocacy itself, cannot be constitutionally restrained, because it comprises only the preparation. It is the existence of the conspiracy which creates the danger." Dennis v. United States, 341 U.S. 494, 511, 71 S.Ct. 857, 868 (1951). See also United States v. Waldin, 138 F.Supp. 791 (D.C.Pa.1956).

43. "Nothing in the language of the statute indicates an intention to require that that additional action be calculated or have a tendency to accomplish the object of the conspiracy." Collier v. United States, 255 F. 328, 329 (5th Cir. 1918).

We "conclude than an act which would support a conspiracy conviction would not necessarily be sufficient to support an attempt conviction." State v. Verive, 627 P.2d 721, 732 (Ariz.App.1981).

may abandon their design, and thus avoid the penalty prescribed by the statute." [44] Illustrative of acts sufficient to satisfy such a statute are (1) taking a position to observe the activities of the intended victim of a kidnaping planned for the future,[45] or (2) purchasing the necessary stamps to be used in a conspiracy to commit murder by poison sent through the mail.[46] A meeting to discuss plans was held not to be an act in addition to the agreement because it was a part of the agreement itself.[47]

A few of the new penal codes require that the overt act be a substantial step toward the crime, which may well be interpreted to mean that it must be sufficient to constitute an attempt.

Statutes adding such a requirement do not specify that each conspirator must do an "overt act," but as soon as any one of them has done an act in furtherance of the unlawful plan " 'all parties to such conspiracy' become liable." [48]

4. NO MERGER

Under the early procedure in England the prosecution for a felony was so different from a prosecution for a misdemeanor that the two could not be combined in a single trial. And since a conspiracy was a misdemeanor at common law an indictment for felony could not include a count for conspiracy to commit the offense. In fact the rule seems to have been that if a conspiracy resulted in the perpetration of a felony the former was completely merged in the latter and could not be prosecuted even under a separate indictment.[49] Since the doctrine of merger never applied to offenses of the same grade a conspiracy to commit a misdemeanor would never have been merged in the resulting misdemeanor,[50] nor would a conspiracy merge in a felony if, by statute, such a conspiracy had been raised to the grade of felony.

Unlike the case of a fatal blow struck with malice in which the battery is merged in the murder because it is an integral part of the homicide itself, a conspiracy, in most jurisdictions, is a distinct offense quite apart from the

---

44. Ibid.

"The requirement of an overt act before conspirators can be prosecuted and punished exists, . . . to provide a *locus poenitentiae* an opportunity for the conspirators to reconsider, terminate the agreement, and thereby avoid punishment." People v. Zamora, 18 Cal.3d 538, 134 Cal.Rptr. 784, 557 P.2d 75, 82 (1976).

Conspiracy may be established by proof of an omission to act which is in furtherance of the conspiracy. State v. Williams, ___ Mont. ___, 604 P.2d 1224 (1979).

45. People v. Stevens, 78 Cal.App. 395, 248 P. 696 (1926).

46. See People v. Corica, 55 Cal.App. 2d 130, 134, 130 P.2d 164, 167 (1942). The overt act need not itself be a crime. Poliafico v. United States, 237 F.2d 97 (6th Cir. 1956); People v. Katzman, 258

Cal.App.2d 777, 66 Cal.Rptr. 319, 324 (1968).

47. People v. Hines, 168 Misc. 453, 6 N.Y.S.2d 2 (1938).

48. Hyde v. United States, 225 U.S. 347, 359, 32 S.Ct. 793, 799 (1912); Poliafico v. United States, 237 F.2d 97 (6th Cir. 1956).

". . . it is not necessary that all or more than one of the conspirators participate in a particular overt act of the conspiracy." United States v. Robinson, 503 F.2d 208, 213 (7th Cir. 1974).

49. See People v. Tavormina, 257 N.Y. 84, 89–90, 177 N.E. 317, 318 (1931). The problem of merger in case of an attempt is discussed supra in chapter 6, section 3, A, 2.

50. State v. Murphy, 6 Ala. 765 (1844); People v. Mather, 4 Wend. 229, 265 (N.Y.1830).

contemplated crime.[51]   Because of this fact the notion that a conspiracy is
merged in the resulting offense is unsound and has been quite generally rejected in this country [52] even if the conspiracy is a misdemeanor and the substantive offense a felony.[53]   A conspiracy, for example, is not a lesser included offense of which the defendant might be convicted although it was not
mentioned in the indictment or information, and hence acquittal of the contemplated crime is no bar to conviction for the conspiracy to commit it.[54]
Illustrative cases of non-merger include those resulting in conviction of (1)
conspiracy to extort and attempted extortion,[55] (2) conspiracy to murder and
assault with intent to murder,[56] (3) conspiracy to escape and attempted escape,[57] (4) conspiracy to commit burglary and burglary,[58] (5) conspiracy to
rob, robbery and murder.[59]

Some of the new penal codes do not permit conviction of both the conspiracy and the target offense.[60]

51.   People v. Tavormina, 257 N.Y. 84,
177 N.E. 317 (1931).

"Conspiracy to commit an illegal act
and the commission of that act—the substantive offense—are separate and distinct offenses."   United States v. Chases,
558 F.2d 912, 914 (9th Cir. 1977). Conviction of both affirmed, see also 558 F.2d
1038.

52.   Johl v. United States, 370 F.2d
174 (9th Cir. 1966); Pinkerton v. United
States, 328 U.S. 640, 66 S.Ct. 1180 (1946);
Corcoran v. United States, 229 F.2d 295
(5th Cir. 1956); People v. Ormsby, 310
Mich. 291, 17 N.W.2d 187 (1945); People
v. Cadle, 202 Misc. 415, 114 N.Y.S.2d 451
(1952).

"The required proof of agreement is an
element not required to be proved for the
substantive counts . . . . The conspiracy does not merge, therefore, with the
substantive counts . . . ."   United
States v. Cantu, 557 F.2d 1173, 1177 (5th
Cir. 1977).

"Generally, a conviction of conspiracy
does not preclude the simultaneous conviction of the substantive crime contemplated by the conspiracy."   State v. Verive, 627 P.2d 721, 731 (Ariz.App.1981).

"Unlike the other preliminary offenses
of attempt and solicitation, conspiracy
does not merge into a conviction for the
substantive crime."   Lythgoe v. State,
626 P.2d 1082, 1083 (Alaska 1980).

53.   People v. Tavormina, 257 N.Y. 84,
177 N.E. 317 (1931).

"We agree that there is no longer any
justification for perpetuating in any form
the outmoded doctrine of merger of conspiracy with the consummated offense,

regardless to the classification of grade
of conspiracy and the substantive offense."   Bell v. Commonwealth, 220 Va.
87, 255 S.E.2d 498 (1979).

54.   State v. Westbrook, 79 Ariz. 116,
285 P.2d 161 (1954); People v. Robinson,
43 Cal.2d 132, 271 P.2d 865 (1954); Roll
v. People, 132 Colo. 1, 284 P.2d 665
(1955); Wilson v. Commonwealth, 96 Pa.
56 (1880).

This would seem to be the result under
the Model Penal Code, section 5.05(3), although conviction of the conspiracy
would not be permitted after *conviction*
of the target crime.   See 17A Me.Rev.
Stat. § 1155(3) (1976).

55.   People v. Fratiano, 132 Cal.App.2d
610, 282 P.2d 1002 (1955); People v. Rosenberg, 194 Colo. 423, 572 P.2d 1211
(1977).

56.   People v. Brown, 131 Cal.App.2d
643, 281 P.2d 319 (1955).

57.   People v. Havel, 134 Cal.App.2d
213, 285 P.2d 317 (1955); United States v.
Easom, 569 F.2d 457 (8th Cir. 1978).

58.   People v. Campbell, 132 Cal.App.
2d 262, 281 P.2d 912 (1955); Bell v. Commonwealth, supra n. 53.

59.   People v. Hoyt, 20 Cal.2d 306, 125
P.2d 29 (1942).   Conspiracy to commit
abortion and crime of abortion.   People
v. Escobedo, 138 Cal.App.2d 490, 292
P.2d 230 (1956).

One may be convicted of both first-degree murder and conspiracy to commit
first-degree murder.   People v. Steele,
193 Colo. 87, 563 P.2d 6 (1977).

60.   E.g., Utah Code Ann. 1953, §
76-4-32.

5. CRIMES REQUIRING CONCERTED ACTION—THE SO–CALLED "WHARTON RULE"

Conspiracies are made punishable because of the increased danger involved in group offenses.[61] The possibility of abandonment of an unlawful plan before execution is greatly reduced if it is a group plan rather than an individual plan, whereas the risk that attempted execution will succeed is enhanced, and the extent of the potential harm often increased. Hence the unlawful combination is socially harmful because of the added danger and is punished for this reason. Some unlawful combinations, however, do not have any element of *added* danger.

If the target offense requires concerted action and none participate other than the necessary parties there is no added danger because nothing is involved which will not be present whenever the offense is committed. In such a case there is no logical basis for conviction of other than the target offense, or an attempt, if the plan is carried that far, and a well-recognized exception to the general rule is that a combination "to commit an offense which can only be committed by the concerted action of two persons does not amount to conspiracy"[62] if only those two are involved.

"The crimes most frequently referred to as coming within the class designated are adultery, bigamy, incest, and dueling."[63] Other illustrations might be added such as receiving stolen goods,[64] a prohibited sale of "contraband,"[65] or bribery.[66] Needless to add, the exception in regard to offenses which require concerted action has reference to the target offense intended and not to the conspiracy itself.[67]

There is some authority for the view that a combination to commit an offense which requires the concerted action of two is not punishable as a conspiracy even if three or more are included.[68] This is quite unsound because the inclusion of more persons than are required for the concerted action brings in the element of *added danger* which is the very reason why any other conspiracy is punished. For this reason the prevailing view is other-

61. United States v. Feola, 420 U.S. 671, 95 S.Ct. 1255 (1975); People v. Comstock, 147 Cal.App.2d 287, 305 P.2d 228 (1956); Woods v. United States, 240 F.2d 37 (D.C.Cir.1957).

62. State v. Law, 189 Iowa 910, 911, 179 N.W. 145 (1920).

"But even if Martin and Creamer were buyer and seller, if sufficient evidence exists to prove a concert of action, a conspiracy will have been made out as a matter of law." United States v. Creamer, 555 F.2d 612, 615 (7th Cir. 1977). But the conspiracy referred to was not the agreement to sell by one to the other, but an agreement to distribute the heroin to others. Accord, State v. Langworthy, 92 Wn.2d 148, 594 P.2d 908 (1979). Accord, United States v. Nasser, 476 F.2d 1111 (7th Cir. 1973).

63. Ibid.

64. United States v. Zeuli, 137 F.2d 845 (2d Cir. 1943).

65. United States v. Katz, 271 U.S. 354, 355, 46 S.Ct. 513 (1926).

66. "[W]here concert is necessary to an offense, such as bribery, conspiracy to commit the substantive offense will not lie. . . ." Slade v. United States, 85 F.2d 786, 788 (10th Cir. 1936).

Wharton's Rule precluded prosecution of a police officer for conspiracy to obstruct justice on the basis of his agreement not to arrest another person in exchange for money. People v. Davis, 408 Mich. 255, 290 N.W.2d 366 (1980).

67. State ex rel. Durner v. Huegin, 110 Wis. 189, 85 N.W. 1046 (1901).

68. United States v. Sager, 49 F.2d 725 (2d Cir. 1931); People v. Wettengel, 98 Colo. 193, 58 P.2d 279 (1936).

wise [69] as expressed in the words of Mr. Justice Stone: "The conspiracy was also deemed criminal where it contemplated the cooperation of a greater number of parties than were necessary to the commission of the principal offense, . . . ".[70] Hence when three combine to violate the bookmaking statute they are guilty of conspiracy despite the fact that it requires two to make a bet.[71]

In a case where the defendants were charged with violation of a general conspiracy statute as well as conspiring to and violating a federal gambling statute [72] making it a crime for five or more persons to conduct a gambling business prohibited by state law the Supreme Court upheld all convictions.[73] The Court stated as to the so-called Wharton's Rule:

"Wharton's Rule applies only to offenses that *require* concerted criminal activity, a plurality of criminal agents. In such cases, a closer relationship exists between the conspiracy and the substantive offense because *both* require collective criminal activity. The substantive offense therefore presents some of the same threats that the law of conspiracy normally is thought to guard against, and it cannot automatically be assumed that the Legislature intended the conspiracy and the substantive offense to remain as discrete crimes upon consummation of the latter. Thus, absent legislative intent to the contrary, the Rule supports a presumption that the two merge when the substantive offense is proved. . . . More important, as the Rule is essentially an aid to the determination of legislative intent, it must defer to a discernible legislative judgment." [74]

On the other hand it has been suggested that any combination to commit a crime is punishable if the crime intended is not perpetrated, even if concerted action would have been necessary.[75] Because of the rule of non-merger this would lead to the possibility of an offender's purging himself of one offense by the commission of another, and the sound rule, where only two are included in the combination to commit such an offense is that they are

---

69. "[W]here it is impossible . . . to commit the substantive offense without cooperative action, the preliminary agreement between the same parties to commit the offense is not an indictable conspiracy. . . . But where a conspiracy contemplates the cooperation of a greater number of parties than are necessary to the commission of the offense, one who commits the principal offense may be convicted of that offense and also the conspiracy. See *Gebardi*, 287 U.S. at 122, n. 6, 53 S.Ct. 35; . . . ." Baker v. United States, 393 F.2d 604, 610 (9th Cir. 1968).

"The widely recognized rule of construction known as Wharton's Rule states that when a substantive offense necessarily requires the participation of two persons, and where no more than two persons are alleged to have been involved in the agreement to commit the offense, the charge of conspiracy will not lie. . . . If a third person does participate so as to enlarge the scope of the agreement, however, all three may be charged with conspiracy." State v. Langworthy, 92 Wn.2d 148, 594 P.2d 908, 910 (1979).

70. Note 6 to Gebardi v. United States, 287 U.S. 112, 122, 53 S.Ct. 35, 37, 38 (1932).

71. State v. Lennon, 3 N.J. 337, 70 A.2d 154 (1949). An agreement by two persons to bribe an officer is indictable even though a single person agreeing to bribe the officer would not be subject to such an indictment. United States v. Burke, 221 F. 1014, 1015 (D.C.N.Y.1915).

72. 18 U.S.C.A. § 1955 (1970).

73. Iannelli v. United States, 420 U.S. 770, 95 S.Ct. 1284 (1975).

74. Id. 420 U.S. 785–786.

75. 2 Wharton, Criminal Law § 1604 (12th ed. 1932). This is not repeated in the Anderson edition (1957).

not punishable for conspiracy even if the unlawful objective was never achieved.[76]

Recent developments require attention. Thus it was said in *Langworthy* : [77] The widely recognized rule of construction known as Wharton's Rule states that when a substantive offense necessarily requires the participation of two persons, and where no more than two persons are alleged to have been involved in the agreement Tent to commit the offense, the charge of conspiracy will not lie.

And the substance of this was repeated in *Cabus*,[78] with this addition: However, this case falls within the recognized "third party" exception to the rule which permits prosecution for conspiracy where, as here, the number of conspirators exceeds the essential participants in the contemplated crime.

While there is full agreement that the participation of persons, other than those legally necessary for the offense, may take the case out of the Rule, there is disagreement as to just what is needed for this purpose. If, for example, the charge is conspiracy to make an unlawful sale, and only two are involved, the charge will fail because there can be no sale without (1) a seller and (2) a buyer. If more than two were involved this may be because the seller (or the buyer) consisted of more than one person; or the addition may be because in the effort to disguise the unlawfulness of the transaction it was felt desirable to have a third person serve as a go-between.

One theory is that the exception to Wharton's Rule requires the addition of an unnecessary "party." Thus if two or more persons were making the sale (or the purchase) and no other was involved, there were just two parties, (1) the selling party, and (2) the buying party. No matter how many persons were involved, if no one was included in any capacity other than as a seller or a buyer, no exception to the Rule is found and conspiracy will not lie.[79] On the other hand, if a go-between had been added to the unlawful combination, conviction of conspiracy would be proper because in that case there would be (1) a selling party, (2) a buying party and (3) a third party (the go-between).[80]

76. Shannon v. Commonwealth, 14 Pa. 226 (1850).

The Model Penal Code would not permit conviction of both the conspiracy and the target offense. Hence it has no need for Wharton's Rule when the offense agreed upon has been committed. And those charged with drafting the Code were convinced that it would be proper to convict of conspiring to commit an offense requiring cooperative action, if the offense was not committed. See Model Penal Code § 5.03, Comment Tent. Draft No. 10, 1960; and id. at § 5.04, Comment.

77. State v. Langworthy, 92 Wn.2d 148, 594 P.2d 908, 910 (1979).

78. People v. Cabus, ___ Colo.App. ___, 626 P.2d 1159, 1160 (1981).

79. One of the best statements of this position is that of Judge Krentzman in United States v. Figueredo, 350 F.Supp. 1031 (M.D.Fla.1972). The appellate court did not agree with his stand and reversed his decision (490 F.2d 799) but did not bother to explain why. The one-paragraph *per curiam* of reversal barely mentions Wharton's Rule.

80. Thus all three were guilty of conspiracy to commit adultery when the combination included the two sex partners and a "matchmaker." State v. Clemenson, 123 Iowa 524, 99 N.W. 139 (1904). In *Langworthy* supra note 71a, the court said: "If a third person does participate *so as to enlarge the scope of the agreement*, all three may be charged with conspiracy." Emphasis added. And in *Cabus*, supra note 71b, the charge was conspiracy to dispense a dangerous drug, and the conspiracy included (1) the seller, (2) the buyer, and (3) at least one guilty agent.

The other theory is concerned only with the "number." If more persons were involved than were legally necessary to constitute the offense, the case is within the exception to Wharton's Rule.

The federal act prohibiting illegal gambling businesses [81] has been a battle-ground for the two competing theories. This statute requires, in addition to other elements, a gambling business in violation of state law, conducted by five or more persons. In *Greenberg* [82] thirteen defendants were charged with a conspiracy to violate this law. They claimed they were protected from conviction by Wharton's Rule. The prosecution insisted that since they were more than the number required by the statute, they were within the exception. The court agreed with the defendants and held the charge of conspiracy was not maintainable. It held, in substance, that the gambling business was one "party," and for a punishable conspiracy an additional "party" was required. Shortly thereafter the same problem was presented in *Becker* [83] in another circuit. The court in that case applied the "number" theory and held that since the statute requires only five persons, a charge of conspiracy to violate it, involving more than five, was within the exception to the Rule and maintainable.

The "party" theory is intriguing, and in fact has much to be said for it, but most of the cases have been disposed of by the "number" theory, frequently without recognizing that there is any other.

6. MANIFESTED LEGISLATIVE INTENT

A problem sometimes confused with the one just considered arises where conviction would violate the manifested legislative intent. If a statutory offense involves a transaction between two persons and provides a penalty only for engagement on one side, the party on the other side cannot be convicted as an inciter or abettor since his omission from the penal provision evinces a legislative purpose to leave his participation unpunished. [84] And he cannot be convicted of a conspiracy to engage in the prohibited transaction for exactly the same reason. [85] A similar problem may be involved where concerted action is not required for the offense. The Mann Act, [86] for example, forbids the transportation of any woman or girl in interstate commerce for prostitution, debauchery or other immoral purpose. The act applies a penalty to the one who transports but not to the one transported. Concert of action is not essential because the woman might be transported by force or

81. 18 U.S.C.A. § 1955 (1970).

82. United States v. Greenberg, 334 F.Supp. 1092 (N.D.Ohio 1971).

83. United States v. Becker, 461 F.2d 230 (2d Cir. 1972).

84. United States v. Farrar, 281 U.S. 624, 50 S.Ct. 425 (1930); Wilson v. State, 130 Ark. 204, 196 S.W. 921 (1917); State v. Teahan, 50 Conn. 92 (1882).

85. Norris v. United States, 34 F.2d 839 (3d Cir. 1929), rev'd on other grounds 281 U.S. 619, 50 S.Ct. 424 (1930).

The intent of the legislature manifested in the section creating the offense cannot be circumvented by a charge of conspiracy to commit that offense. Lythgoe v. State, 626 P.2d 1082 (Alaska 1980).

86. 18 U.S.C.A. § 2421 (1970).

The statute does not deny equal protection because it makes it unlawful to transport only females. United States v. Green, 554 F.2d 372 (9th Cir. 1977). The statute may be violated by either men or woman. United States v. Garrett, 521 F.2d 444 (8th Cir. 1975). The proposed Federal Criminal Code S. 1722, 96th Cong. 1st Sess. § 1843, would change the nature of the offense and apply sanctions regardless of sex. However, the exploited person would not be guilty of a federal offense.

intimidation. But since the woman will ordinarily be a voluntary party the failure of Congress to apply the penalty to her requires a holding that she cannot be punished for her mere voluntary participation by indicting her for conspiracy. And since she is not guilty of conspiracy neither is the transporter if no third person was involved.[87]

7. TWO OR MORE

The impossibility of one person forming a combination with himself is too obvious for discussion [88] but it should be emphasized that a conspiracy requires two *guilty* parties as shown by the case in the preceding paragraph. Because of this requirement, if one of two supposed confederates merely feigns acquiescence without criminal intent the other is not guilty of conspiracy since there is no second guilty party.[89] A purely technical result was the common-law rule that husband and wife, being considered one person for many purposes, could not be guilty of conspiracy if no third person was involved,[90] which may be still in force in some jurisdictions [91] but not in others.[92] A much more satisfactory result, reached by brushing aside technicality and concentrating upon the reason back of the law, is that two corporations cannot be guilty of conspiracy because of the activities of only one man, even if he is duly authorized to act as the agent of each.[93]

A procedural result of the two-or-more requirement is that if two are tried for a conspiracy in which no additional persons are implicated, a verdict finding one guilty and the other not guilty requires a judgment of acquittal

87. Gebardi v. United States, 287 U.S. 112, 53 S.Ct. 35 (1932). Where the statute on bribery in sports punished the bribery of participants and others but did not include the referee, the omission in the statute could not be cured by indicting the referee for conspiracy to violate the statute [the statute had been amended to include the referee but that was after the bribery alleged here]. People v. Levy, 283 App.Div. 383, 128 N.Y.S.2d 275 (1954).

The Model Penal Code would not require two *guilty* parties.

See Section 5.04.

88. "Two or more persons must participate to create the crime." United States v. Weinberg, 129 F.Supp. 514, 527 (D.C.Pa.1955).

"Of course at least two persons are required to constitute a conspiracy, but the identity of the other members of the conspiracy is not needed, inasmuch as one person can be convicted of conspiring with persons whose names are unknown." United States v. Indorato, 628 F.2d 711, 717–18 (1st Cir. 1980).

89. Delaney v. State, 164 Tenn. 432, 51 S.W.2d 485 (1932). State v. Mazur, 158 N.J.Super. 89, 385 A.2d 878 (1978).

There can be no conviction of conspiracy if defendant's "agreement" was with an undercover agent who merely feigned participation as part of his duties. Archbold v. State, ___ Ind.App. ___, 397 N.E.2d 1071 (1979). This position has been changed under the new Indiana Code Ann. § 35–41–5–2 (Burns 1979). See Garcia v. State, ___ Ind. ___, 394 N.E.2d 106 (1979).

This may be changed by statute and has been in New York. People v. Schwimmer, 66 A.D.2d 91, 411 N.Y.S.2d 922 (N.Y. 1978). Numerous other states have taken this position. Some thirty states appear to have adopted the Model Penal Code approach. Burgman, Unilateral Conspiracy: Three Critical Perspectives, 29 DePaul L.Rev. 75 (1979).

90. People v. Miller, 82 Cal. 107, 22 P. 934 (1889); People v. MacMullen, 134 Cal. App. 81, 24 P.2d 794 (1933).

91. See Dawson v. United States, 10 F.2d 106, 107 (9th Cir. 1926).

92. The tendency is to abandon the old rule and hold that husband and wife can be guilty of conspiracy even without the cooperation of anyone else. United States v. Dege, 364 U.S. 51, 80 S.Ct. 1589 (1960); People v. Pierce, 61 Cal.2d 879, 40 Cal.Rptr. 845, 395 P.2d 893 (1964).

93. United States v. Santa Rita Store Co., 16 N.M. 3, 113 P. 620 (1911).

of both,[94]—if no special immunity is involved. Impossibility of conviction is not the same as innocence and if the guilt of two is established one may be convicted although the other may be protected by diplomatic immunity or some other procedural bar.[95] The acquittal of one of three defendants on trial for conspiracy is of no avail to the two who were convicted,[96] and the acquittal of all but one on trial will not bar the conviction of that one if the indictment charged that one or more others were involved and this is established by the evidence.[97] The fact that one of two conspirators has not been arrested is no bar to the conviction of the other.[98]

Some of the new penal codes expressly provide that the acquittal of one conspirator shall not bar conviction of the other, and some do not require two guilty parties. Under the latter provision it is no defense, for example, that one party to the combination was an undercover officer who merely feigned acquiescence.[99]

94. Two charged with conspiracy were tried separately, the first being convicted and the second acquitted. It was held error to sentence the first. Sherman v. State, 113 Neb. 173, 202 N.W. 413 (1925). A conspirator who had entered a plea of guilty and appeared as a witness against his two confederates, was convicted although a nolle prosequi was entered as to the others after two trials failed to reach a verdict. United States v. Fox, 130 F.2d 56 (3d Cir. 1942). And see Note, 37 Ill.L.Rev. 370 (1943).

The dismissal of the charge against a co-conspirator (in consideration of her testimony) as distinguished from an acquittal, does not prevent D's conviction of conspiracy. State v. Goldman, 95 N.J. Super. 50, 229 A.2d 818 (1967).

The conviction of one, of only two alleged conspirators, must be reversed if the other alleged conspirator has since been tried and acquitted. People v. Brooks, 56 A.D.2d 634, 391 N.Y.S.2d 886 (N.Y.1977).

In affirming the traditional position that where only two are involved in an alleged conspiracy, the acquittal of one precludes conviction of the other, it was held that although the conspiracy statute in the new penal code is patterned after the Model Penal Code "we will not presume a change in a well-established principle of our law merely on the basis of Model Penal Code commentary, the import of which is in no way reflected in the statute adopted." Commonwealth v. Campbell, 257 Pa.Super. 160, 390 A.2d 761, 764 (1978).

95. Where two of three conspirators obtained immunity by testifying against the third, the conviction of the third will not be disturbed. Hurwitz v. State, 200 Md. 578, 92 A.2d 575 (1952).

96. Lazarov v. United States, 225 F.2d 319 (6th Cir. 1955).

It was error to give the jury only the choice of convicting all three charged with conspiracy or finding all innocent when it was possible that only two of the three were guilty. State v. Carroll, 51 N.J. 102, 237 A.2d 878 (1968).

97. Rosecrans v. United States, 378 F.2d 561 (5th Cir. 1967). Grove v. United States, 3 F.2d 965 (4th Cir. 1925); United States v. Weinberg, 129 F.Supp. 514 (D.C.Pa.1955); People v. Sagehorn, 140 Cal.App.2d 138, 294 P.2d 1062 (1956); United States v. Rivera-Diaz, 538 F.2d 461 (1st Cir. 1978).

P and Z were indicted for a conspiracy under an agreement that P and S were to bribe Z. S was not on trial and Z was acquitted while P was convicted. The conviction was affirmed. State v. Papalos, 150 Me. 370, 113 A.2d 624 (1955).

Granting of a nolle prosequi to an alleged co-conspirator does not preclude conviction of the remaining conspirator. United States v. Shipp, 359 F.2d 185 (6th Cir. 1966).

98. Commonwealth v. Stambaugh, 22 Pa.Super. 386 (1903); Commonwealth v. Salerno, 179 Pa.Super. 13, 116 A.2d 87 (1955).

99. While this is the rule of the common law, under the statute it is no defense that the one with whom defendant agreed was an undercover officer who had no intention of carrying out the unlawful plan. Garcia v. State, ___ Ind. ___, 394 N.E.2d 106 (1979); State v. St. Christopher, 305 Minn. 226, 232 N.W.2d 798 (1975).

The common-law rule has been changed in England by statute with the

C. UNLAWFUL

Use of the word "unlawful," though unavoidable, presents the greatest difficulty to be encountered in the law of conspiracy because a special meaning must be assigned to it, as here employed, to give validity to the definition offered. The use, in a definition, of a term which must be particularly defined for the purpose is something to be avoided if possible, but it cannot be avoided entirely in the criminal law without making definitions so unwieldy as to be useless. No workable definition of common-law burglary can be framed without the use of the word "breaking" (or some equivalent) although it is necessary to explain that the meaning of the term as so employed is quite unique. Other illustrations could be given such, for example, as either the term "carrying away," or the phrase "intent to steal" in the definition of larceny.

The logical starting point is that—apart from the exceptions mentioned above in certain cases involving "concerted action" or "manifested legislative intent"—any combination to commit a crime is punishable as a conspiracy.[1] As said by the Supreme Court: [2]

"For two or more to confederate and combine together to commit or cause to be committed a breach of the criminal laws, is an offense of the gravest character, sometimes quite outweighing, in injury to the public, the mere commission of the contemplated crime. It involves deliberate plotting to subvert the laws, educating and preparing the conspirators for further and habitual criminal practices. And it is characterized by secrecy, rendering it difficult of detection, requiring more time for its discovery, and adding to the importance of punishing it when discovered."

For this reason a more severe sentence for conspiracy than for the completed target offense does not preclude punishment on the conspiracy count.[3] An occasional case has held that a common-law conspiracy does not result from an agreement to commit an offense which is merely *malum prohibitum*,[4] but the prevailing view is clearly otherwise [5] although the courts have

---

Criminal Law Act, 1977 S. 5(8) and a co-conspirator may stand convicted even if the other conspirator has been acquitted "unless under all the circumstances of the case his conviction is inconsistent with the acquittal of the other person." See DPP v. Shannon, [1975] A.C. 717 (H.L.) plea of guilty may be maintained even though co-conspirator, separately tried, was acquitted.

The Supreme Court of Canada appears to accept a similar position, see Guimond v. The Queen, 44 CCC 2d 481 (SCC 1979).

If two conspirators are tried separately, the conviction of one is not affected by the subsequent acquittal of the other. "Gardner elected a separate trial where his guilt was established beyond a reasonable doubt; what happened in Lubow's subsequent trial is of no avail to Gardner." Gardner v. State, 286 Md. 520, 408 A.2d 1317, 1322 (1979).

1. State v. Martin, 229 Wis. 644, 282 N.W. 107 (1938). Additional exceptions

may be required in some jurisdictions because of statute.

The English court held that an agreement, made in England, to commit a crime abroad is not punishable as a conspiracy if the contemplated "crime" would not be indictable if committed in England. Board of Trade v. Owen, [1957] 1 All Eng.R. 411 (H.L.).

2. United States v. Rabinowich, 238 U.S. 78, 88, 35 S.Ct. 682, 684, 685 (1915); Pinkerton v. United States, 328 U.S. 640, 644, 66 S.Ct. 1180, 1182 (1946).

3. United States v. Stevenson (No. 2), 215 U.S. 200, 30 S.Ct. 37 (1909); Clune v. United States, 159 U.S. 590, 16 S.Ct. 125 (1895).

4. People v. Dorman, 415 Ill. 385, 114 N.E.2d 404 (1953).

5. State v. Martin, 229 Wis. 644, 282 N.W. 107 (1938); People v. Bucchierre, 57

found need for a special inquiry in the case of such a combination,[6] as will be mentioned presently. A federal statute, for example, makes it criminal to conspire "either to commit any offense against the United States, or to defraud the United States." [7] An indictment under this statute charged a conspiracy to counterfeit a patented tire gauge. Such counterfeiting was prohibited in the patent law which made the counterfeiter liable to a penalty recoverable in an action by an informer for the benefit of himself and the United States. A demurrer to the indictment was overruled on the ground that the indictment charged an "offense against the United States" within the meaning of the statute.[8]

As mentioned above, an appropriate definition of the common-law offense is—a conspiracy is a combination for an unlawful purpose. The use of the word "unlawful," though unavoidable in the common-law definition of conspiracy, presented a problem because that word is not limited to conduct punishable as a crime. The classic illustration of a punishable combination to do a non-criminal act was the combination to defraud another without the use of false tokens. Such a fraud, even by one alone, was made punishable by the statute of false pretenses. But before that statute was enacted it was held that a combination to perpetrate such a fraud was a criminal conspiracy.[9] More recently a combination for the purpose of cheating another by promissory fraud was held to be a criminal conspiracy although the jurisdiction had not then made promissory fraud sufficient for guilt of false pretenses.[10] In fact any combination for the purpose of cheating or defrauding another was a common-law conspiracy.[11] And apparently any conduct involving moral turpitude was "unlawful" within the conspiracy definition, even if it was not punishable in itself. Some of the statutes following the common-law pattern, as interpreted, were held to be void for vagueness,[12] but this is largely academic today because the new penal codes, almost without exception, have limited conspiracy to a combination for the purpose of committing a crime, which under an occasional provision must be a felony. Under such legisla-

Cal.App.2d 153, 163, 134 P.2d 505, 510 (1943).

6. Landen v. United States, 299 F. 75 (6th Cir. 1924); Commonwealth v. Benesch, 290 Mass. 125, 194 N.E. 905 (1935).

7. 18 U.S.C.A. § 371 (1966).

8. United States v. Winner, 28 F.2d 295 (D.C.Ill.1928).

In upholding a conviction of conspiracy based upon an agreement to have a prostitute transported from Missouri to Nevada, where prostitution is not unlawful, the court said: "the status of prostitution under Nevada law has no bearing on the legality of this agreement under the Mann Act." United States v. Pelton, 578 F.2d 701, 712 (8th Cir. 1978).

9. See State v. Loser, 132 Iowa 419, 423, 104 N.W. 337, 338 (1906); State v. Bacon, 27 R.I. 252, 61 A. 653 (1905).

10. People v. Campbell, 1 Cal.App.2d 109, 36 P.2d 198 (1934). This was long before California recognized promissory fraud as sufficient for guilt of false pretenses. The conviction in this case was reversed, but only for lack of proof.

11. The King v. Gill, 2 B. & Ald. 204, 106 Eng.Rep. 341 (1818). Fraud is probably the wrong most frequently mentioned in conspiracy statutes in addition to crime. The federal statute, for example, says, "either to commit any offense against the United States, or to defraud the United States, ..." 18 U.S.C.A. § 371.

12. Musser v. Utah, 333 U.S. 95, 68 S.Ct. 397 (1948); State v. Musser, 118 Utah 537, 223 P.2d 193 (1950); Lorenson v. Superior Court, 35 Cal.2d 49, 216 P.2d 859 (1950).

tion the definition should be: A conspiracy is a combination for the purpose of committing a crime (felony).

D. INTENT

Conspiracy is one of the crimes requiring a so-called "specific intent." [13] This phrase will receive further attention in the following chapter but two illustrations may be helpful. To take property of another by trespass and carry it away does not constitute larceny unless it is done with intent to steal, and to break and enter the dwelling house of another in the nighttime does not constitute common-law burglary unless done with intent to commit a felony or larceny. Each of these is referred to as a "specific intent" although an intent to commit any felony is much broader than an intent to steal. The "specific intent" required for conspiracy is much broader yet because it includes, subject to a qualification to be mentioned presently, an intent to bring about either as an end or a means anything that is a crime.

In other words the conspirator's intent is always two-fold—he intends (1) to combine with another or others, which in itself might be entirely innocent, and (2) thereby under the new codes, accomplish the commission of a crime, which is of the essence of conspiracy.[14]

E. KNOWLEDGE

The moral quality of an intent may be determined by knowledge, or lack of knowledge, of pertinent facts. One having no privilege to do so, for example, takes the chattel of another and carries it away with intent to appropriate it to his own use. If he knows the facts he has a very evil intent,—an intent to steal; if by reason of mistake of fact he bona fide believes the chattel to be his and that he has a right to its immediate possession his intent is innocent. Likewise one does not have the specific intent to bring about an unlawful result, and hence is not guilty of conspiracy, if he does not know or have reason to know the facts which make that result unlawful.[15] And since

---

13. People v. Horn, 12 Cal.3d 290, 115 Cal.Rptr. 516, 524 P.2d 1300 (1974). Harno, Intent in Criminal Conspiracy, 89 Univ. of Pa.L.Rev. 624 (1941); Note, 38 Harv.L.Rev. 96 (1924). As in other cases where intent is essential it may be inferred by the jury from sufficiently probative facts established by the evidence. McClanahan v. United States, 230 F.2d 919 (5th Cir. 1956).

14. Commonwealth v. Benesch, 290 Mass. 125, 194 N.E. 905 (1935). "The gist of the crime of conspiracy consists in a corrupt agreement between two or more individuals to do an unlawful act, unlawful either as a means or as an end." People v. Flack, 125 N.Y. 324, 332, 26 N.E. 267, 269 (1891). See also Elkin v. People, 28 N.Y. 177, 179 (1863). "[T]he conspirators must be held to have intended the necessary and direct consequences of their acts and cannot be heard to say the contrary. In other words by pur-

posely engaging in a conspiracy which necessarily and directly produces the result which the statute is designed to prevent, they are in legal contemplation, chargeable with intending that result." United States v. Patten, 226 U.S. 525, 543, 33 S.Ct. 141, 145 (1913).

15. Pettibone v. United States, 148 U.S. 197, 13 S.Ct. 542 (1893). The recipient of a stolen car, even if he has reason to believe it is stolen, cannot be convicted of conspiracy to violate the National Motor Vehicle Theft Act if he knows nothing about the interstate transportation of the car. Linde v. United States, 13 F.2d 59 (8th Cir. 1926).

In a prosecution for conspiracy to violate the Sherman Act for price fixing the United States Supreme Court held that the antitrust laws required mens rea but not a purposeful intent to violate the Sherman Act. The Court held that it was

two guilty parties are required there can be no conspiracy where such knowledge is limited to one.[16] Innocence because of lack of knowledge may be established even if what is not known is a matter of law if the "offense" contemplated by the combination is something not inherently wrong but merely prohibited by statute.[17] While a combination for the purpose of doing what is thus forbidden is wrongful if the law is known,[18] it is not wrongful otherwise. For example while the National Prohibition Act was in force certain wholesale druggists were convicted of a conspiracy to violate it, by selling liquor for non-beverage purposes but without a permit. Such sales were controlled by a regulation of the Internal Revenue Department and the trial judge charged that the defendants interpreted this regulation at their peril and were guilty of conspiracy even if they had been advised by counsel that their selling methods did not violate the regulation, and acted under a bona-fide belief that their plan was lawful. This conviction was reversed on the ground that there is no conspiracy without a "corrupt intent." [19] Needless to add the knowledge of such a law by only one is not sufficient for conspiracy [20] unless the statute has changed the rule of the common law and does not require two guilty parties.

A question arises in regard to the position of one who supplies goods or services with knowledge of the intended unlawful use thereof by the other. In *Falcone* [21] it was held that such knowledge is not sufficient for guilt of conspiracy. "It is not enough," said the court, "that he does not forego a normal lawful activity, of the fruits of which he knows that others will make an unlawful use; he must in some sense promote their venture himself, make it his own, have a stake in the outcome." [22] This, however, was a case in which yeast and cans were sold to distillers with knowledge that they were to be used to manufacture liquor without a license. Had a heinous crime been intended the court would no doubt have taken a different view. As it was said *obiter* in *Backun*,[23] "One who sells a gun to another knowing that he is buying it to commit a murder, would hardly escape conviction as an accessory to murder by showing that he received full price for the gun." And a conviction of manslaughter was affirmed because the seller had such knowledge that it was criminally negligent for him to sell it to one who used

sufficient to show that action was undertaken with the knowledge that its probable consequences would have the required anti-competitive effect. United States v. United States Gypsum Co., 438 U.S. 422, 98 S.Ct. 2864 (1978).

16. Morrison v. California, 288 U.S. 591, 53 S.Ct. 401 (1933); People v. Campbell, 1 Cal.App.2d 109, 36 P.2d 198 (1934); Le Maine v. Seals, 47 Wn.2d 259, 287 P.2d 305 (1955).

17. Commonwealth v. Benesch, 290 Mass. 125, 194 N.E. 905 (1935). And see Mitchell v. State, 248 Ala. 169, 27 So.2d 36 (1946).

18. People v. Bucchierre. 57 Cal.App. 2d 153, 134 P.2d 505 (1943). In upholding a conviction of conspiracy to violate the Employment Agency Act, on the ground that the guilty knowledge had

been established, the court said: "The association of persons with an honest intent is not conspiracy, and one of the tests on a conspiracy trial is, did the accused act in ignorance without criminal intent? In other words, did they honestly entertain a belief that they were not committing an unlawful act?" Id. at 163, 134 P.2d at 510.

19. Landen v. United States, 299 F. 75 (6th Cir. 1924).

20. Commonwealth v. Benesch, 290 Mass. 125, 194 N.E. 905 (1935).

21. United States v. Falcone, 109 F.2d 579 (2d Cir. 1940), affd. 311 U.S. 205, 61 S.Ct. 204 (1940).

22. Id. at 581.

23. Backun v. United States, 112 F.2d 635, 637 (4th Cir. 1940).

it to kill.[24] Conviction of conspiracy could not be based on criminal negligence, but where the unlawful use intended is known the guilty abettor would be also a conspirator as pointed out in *Falcone*. The "question is whether the seller of goods, in themselves innocent, becomes a conspirator with—or, what is in substance the same thing, an abettor of—the buyer because he knows that the buyer means to use the goods to commit a crime." [25] In a recent case [26] the court took the position that the answer is "no" if the known intended crime is only a misdemeanor but "yes" if it is a felony.

Differences in the role played by such knowledge have been recognized in the civil cases. One who sold a dress to a prostitute knowing she intended to use it in plying her "profession" could collect from the buyer; [27] and (in the absence of a statute to the contrary) a lease was not void merely because the lessor knew the lessee intended to use the place as a bawdy house.[28] But one who sold goods knowing they were to be used to aid the enemy had no enforceable action to collect the price.[29]

Recently a court had occasion to pass upon two aspects of this problem in dealing with proprietors of telephone-answering services who acted with knowledge that some of the customers were prostitutes. In *Lauria* [30] it was held that such knowledge is not alone sufficient to taint the proprietor with guilt of conspiracy, since the known offense is only a misdemeanor, but in *Ray* [31] it was pointed out that such guilt may be established by showing assistance to the prostitute beyond that given to customers in general. Guilt may be established also by proof that the seller or provider charged an inflated price because of his knowledge of the unlawful intended use,[32] or because of the absence of any lawful use. Thus the suppliers of horse-racing information by wire were guilty of conspiracy to promote bookmaking when it was shown that their wire-service information had no use other than to supply information needed by bookmakers to conduct illegal gambling services.[33]

Where the seller or provider of goods or services knows of the unlawful use to be made thereof by the other, this knowledge is in itself sufficient to

---

24. People v. Howk, 56 Cal.2d 687, 16 Cal.Rptr. 370, 365 P.2d 426 (1961).

25. United States v. Falcone, 109 F.2d 579, 581 (2d Cir. 1940).

26. People v. Lauria, 251 Cal.App.2d 471, 59 Cal.Rptr. 628 (1967).

27. Bowry v. Bennett, 1 Camp. 348, 170 Eng.Rep. 981 (1808).

28. Ashford v. Mace, 103 Ark. 114, 146 S.W. 474 (1912).

29. Hanauer v. Doane, 79 U.S. 342 (1870); Roquemore v. Alloway, 33 Tex. 461 (1870).

30. People v. Lauria, 251 Cal.App.2d 471, 59 Cal.Rptr. 628 (1967).

"Nor is mere approval or acquiescence in the object of an alleged conspiracy sufficient to render an individual a part of a conspiracy. There must be some element of affirmative cooperation or agreement to cooperate in the object of the conspira-

cy." United States v. Moss, 591 F.2d 428, 435 (8th Cir. 1979).

31. People v. Ray, 251 Cal.App.2d 459, 59 Cal.Rptr. 636 (1967).

One who sells goods knowing of the illegal use to which they are to be put, and fails to make required reports of his sales which would put a stop to the supply to this buyer, aids the unlawful venture and is guilty of conspiracy. United States v. Pecoraro, 115 F.2d 245 (2d Cir. 1940), cert. denied 312 U.S. 685, 61 S.Ct. 611 (1941).

32. Regina v. Thomas, [1957] 2 All E.R. 181, 342.

Landlord who allowed prostitute to use his premises and charged exorbitant rates was held to have become a part of the illicit scheme. Regina v. Calderwood, 68 Crim.App.Rep. 37 (1979).

33. People v. McLaughlin, 111 Cal. App.2d 781, 245 P.2d 1076 (1952).

establish his complicity therein,[34] if the offense intended is heinous, but more than knowledge is required for this purpose if the violation is of a minor nature. There is much to be said for the dictum in *Lauria* which is precise, making the distinction depend upon whether the intended offense is a felony or a misdemeanor.[35] In an English case,[36] it may be added, a supplier of oxygen-cutting equipment to one known to intend to use it to break into a bank was convicted as an accessory to the crime.

F.   ACT OR DECLARATION OF EACH *

A question which has received considerable attention recently is this: If one conspirator commits the crime which was the very objective of the wrongful combination, is the coconspirator guilty of that target offense, without having done more than join in the conspiracy?

In *Pinkerton*[37] the Supreme Court answered that question with an unqualified "yes."[38] Two brothers, Walter and Daniel, were charged with conspiracy to violate the Internal Revenue Code and with ten substantive violations. The evidence established the conspiracy and most of the substantive offenses charged, but there was no evidence that Daniel participated directly in these offenses, which were committed by Walter. Whether Daniel did more than merely join the conspiracy was not submitted to the jury, who were instructed that

> if you are satisfied from the evidence beyond a reasonable doubt that the two defendants were in an unlawful conspiracy . . . then you would have a right . . . to convict each of these defendants on all these substantive counts, provided the acts referred to in the substantive counts were acts in furtherance of the unlawful conspiracy or object of the unlawful conspiracy, which you have found from the evidence existed.[39]

34. In other words he will be guilty of a conspiracy to commit such offense, and guilty of the offense itself if it is committed by the other. Whether his guilt in such a case will be as accessory before the fact or as principal will depend upon the facts and the jurisdiction.

35. The early drafts of the Model Penal Code would have based complicity not only on a purpose of facilitating the commission of a crime but also on knowingly rendering substantial aid thereto. See Model Penal Code, Tent. Draft No. 1, Section 2.04(3)(b) (1953), and Tent. Draft No. 4, Section 2.06(3)(b) (1955). A convincing argument in favor of this position is found in the Comment in Draft No. 1 except that no distinction was made based upon the gravity of the intended crime. Because this distinction was not made, Judge Hand, thinking of his decision in *Falcone* in which the defendant had knowingly sold cans and yeast to illicit distillers, argued against this position. And he prevailed upon the annual meeting to eliminate any reference to knowingly rendering substantial aid to the commission of crime. See 1962 A.L.I. Proceedings 79. The ultimate position found in the Code is unfortunate.

36. Regina v. Bainbridge, 3 W.L.R. 656, C.C.A. 6 (1959).

* With express permission the following is adapted from Perkins, The Act of One Conspirator, 26 Hastings L.J. 337 (1974).

37. Pinkerton v. United States, 328 U.S. 640, 66 S.Ct. 1180 (1946).

38. The Court said: "A different case would arise if the substantive offense committed by one of the conspirators was *not in fact done in furtherance of the conspiracy*, did not fall within the scope of the unlawful project, or was merely a part of the ramifications of the plan which could not be reasonably foreseen as a necessary or natural consequence of the unlawful agreement." Id. at pp. 647–48.

39. Id. at pp. 645–46 n. 6.

In affirming Daniel's conviction of several of the substantive offenses, as well as of the conspiracy, the Court held that this instruction was correct. This ruling was reinforced a few years later when the Court stated

> In *Pinkerton* v. *United States* . . . a conspiracy and substantive offenses were charged. We held that a conspirator could be held guilty of the substantive offense even though he did no more than join the conspiracy, provided that the substantive offense was committed in furtherance of the conspiracy and as a part of it.[40]

Nothing new, it should be emphasized, was involved in *Pinkerton*. As early as 1827 Mr. Justice Story, speaking for the Court, said:

> So, in cases of conspiracy and riot, when once the conspiracy or combination is established, the act of one conspirator, in the prosecution of the enterprise, is considered the act of all, and is evidence against all. Each is deemed to consent to, or command, what is done by any other in furtherance of the common object.[41]

And the rule had been repeated by the Court down through the years.[42] It had also been announced long ago by other courts.

> It is also a familiar general rule that, when several parties conspire or combine together to commit any unlawful act, each is criminally responsible for the acts of his associates or confederates committed in furtherance or in prosecution of the common design for which they combine.[43]

At times the language has been very specific. Thus it was said that the coconspirator would be guilty of murder even if

> Harper went back alone and, faithful to the common design, delivered the fatal blows in the absence of Bolden. It is well settled that after a conspiracy to commit an unlawful act is established, every act of each member of the conspiracy in pursuance of their original plan is in contemplation of law the act of all of them.[44]

In other words: "It is hornbook law that a conspirator is criminally responsible for the acts of his co-conspirators which are committed in furtherance of

---

40. Nye & Nissen v. United States, 336 U.S. 613, 618, 69 S.Ct. 766, 769 (1949).

"The *Pinkerton* vicarious-liability rationale is based upon an agreement or common purpose shared by co-conspirators; they are partners in crime, and the act of one in furtherance of the unlawful plan is the act of all." United States v. Michel, 588 F.2d 986, 999 (5th Cir. 1979).

41. United States v. Gooding, 25 U.S. (12 Wheat.) 460, 469 (1827).

It was reversible error to fail to charge "that Allen's act which caused Brennan's death had to have been done in furtherance of the felony." Commonwealth v. Walters, 491 Pa. 85, 418 A.2d 312, 316 (1980). It is to be noted that some of the new penal codes have modified accomplice liability for felony-murder in some such way as by excluding one who did not in any way solicit, command, induce,

procure, counsel or aid in the commission of the homicide, was not armed and did not know any of the others was armed. E.g., Ark.Stat. 1947 § 41–1502 (1977).

42. See, e.g., Hyde v. United States, 225 U.S. 347, 359, 32 S.Ct. 793, 799 (1912); Logan v. United States, 144 U.S. 263, 308–09, 12 S.Ct. 617, 631 (1892).

43. Phillips v. State, 26 Tex.App. 228, 9 S.W. 557, 560 (1888). "Proof of conspiracy . . . may be introduced for the purpose of establishing the position of the members of the combination as accessories to the crime of murder." Spies v. People, 122 Ill. 1, 102, 12 N.E. 865, 915 (1887).

44. People v. Harper, 25 Cal.2d 862, 870, 156 P.2d 249, 254 (1945), quoted in part with approval in People v. Weiss, 50 Cal.2d 535, 563, 327 P.2d 527, 543–44 (1958).

the common design even though he was not present when the acts were committed." [45]   And this rule has been incorporated in some of the recently adopted criminal codes.[46]

However widespread this treatment of coconspirators may be, it is not universal. A different view was expressed by a Massachusetts court long ago:

> The fact of the conspiracy being proved against the prisoner, is to be weighed as evidence in the case having a tendency to prove that the prisoner aided, but is not *in itself* to be taken as a legal presumption of his having aided unless disproved by him. It is a question of evidence for the consideration of the jury.[47]

After this formulation had been repeated, in substance, in other cases,[48] it was recently spelled out in detail:

> If the defendant agreed with other persons to commit the crimes of robbery and assault and did nothing more, he is guilty of criminal conspiracy; but he was not charged with that crime. That alone does not make him an accessory before the fact or a principal to the substantive crime which was the objective of the conspiracy.[49]

This may have been the theory of those who drafted the Model Penal Code.[50]

Conspiracy and complicity are not identical; it is possible to have either without the other. The classic illustration of complicity without conspiracy is found in *Tally*.[51] **D**, and others, planned to murder **X**. **Y**, who knew of this plot, sent **X** a telegram to warn him of the plan so he might guard against it. **A**, who knew of both **D**'s murder plan and **Y**'s warning, sent a telegram which was intended to prevent the delivery of **Y**'s wire. And **A**'s telegram delayed **Y**'s warning so that it was not delivered in time, and **X** was murdered. **A**'s complicity in the murder is clear because he gave important aid to **D**, but there was no conspiracy because **D** was not even aware of the help he was receiving. The most obvious illustration of conspiracy without complicity in the target offense is found in the case of withdrawal. If one conspirator commits the target offense after having received timely and ef-

45. Commonwealth v. Burdell, 380 Pa. 43, 49, 110 A.2d 193, 196 (1955). See also State v. Alston, 17 N.C.App. 712, 714–15, 195 S.E.2d 314, 315 (1973).

46. See, e.g., Minn.Stats.Ann. sec. 609.05(1) (1963); Wis.Stats.Ann. sec. 939.05(2)(c) (1955).

47. Commonwealth v. Knapp, 26 Mass. (9 Pick.) 496, 518 (1830).

48. Commonwealth v. Stasiun, 349 Mass. 38, 47–48, 206 N.E.2d 672, 678–79 (1965); Commonwealth v. Bloomberg, 302 Mass. 349, 355–56, 19 N.E.2d 62, 66 (1939).

49. Commonwealth v. Perry, 357 Mass. 149, 152, 256 N.E.2d 745, 747 (1970).

50. The jury "should not be told that it (conspiracy) establishes complicity as a matter of law." Model Penal Code sec. 2.04(3), Comment at 23 (Tent. Draft No. 1, 1953).

51. State ex rel. Martin v. Tally, 102 Ala. 25, 15 So. 722 (1894). And see United States v. Valencia, 492 F.2d 1071, 1073–74 (9th Cir. 1974). "The cases are clear that one may cause another to commit a crime, 18 U.S.C. § 2(b), or aid and abet the commission of a crime, 18 U.S.C. § 2(a), without being a conspirator with the principal offender." United States v. Krogstad, 576 F.2d 22, 29 (3d Cir. 1978). "Conspiracy requires proof of agreement, aiding and abetting does not." United States v. Beck, 615 F.2d 441, 449 (7th Cir. 1980). See also People v. Malotte, 46 Cal.2d 59, 292 P.2d 517 (1956).

fective notice of withdrawal from his confederate, only the perpetrator is guilty of the substantive crime.[52]

Despite this possibility of separate existence, however, complicity and conspiracy normally go hand-in-hand.[53] And whether membership in the conspiracy should be sufficient for conviction of the offense committed in furtherance thereof, or whether something more should be required for this purpose, requires careful consideration.

It is well to keep in mind Holmes' insistence that a

> conspiracy is constituted by an agreement, it is true, but it is the result of the agreement, rather than the agreement itself, just as a partnership, although constituted by a contract, is not the contract, but a result of it. . . . A conspiracy is a partnership in criminal purposes.[54]

This conceptualization added color to the formulation of the idea, but the idea itself was not new. Hawkins, writing in the early 1700's, referred to conspiracies as "confederacies," [55] and the "confederacy" label has been repeated at times.[56] Another term frequently employed is "combination." [57]

The agreement, however, is indispensable to conspiracy.[58] There must be a "meeting of the minds," [59] or "joint assent of the minds." [60] This does not necessitate "the formalities of an agreement" [61] or any formal words.[62] Since "a conspiracy by its very nature is a clandestine offense, proof of the agreement must ordinarily rest upon inference drawn from competent circumstantial evidence.[63] It may be established by the conduct of the parties.[64]

So far as the common law is concerned, the crime of conspiracy is complete and punishable as soon as the unlawful combination is formed,[65] but many of the modern statutes require some overt act in furtherance of the plan.[66] One court held that the overt act needed for conviction of conspiracy under such an act must at least amount to an attempt to commit the target

---

52. State v. Peterson, 213 Minn. 56, 4 N.W.2d 826 (1942).

53. It "is in substance the same thing, ..." United States v. Falcone, 109 F.2d 579, 581 (2d Cir. 1940).

54. United States v. Kissel, 218 U.S. 601, 608, 31 S.Ct. 124, 126 (1910).

55. Hawkins, P.C. 348 (6th ed. by Leach, 1788).

56. Conspiracy is an unlawful "confederacy." Commonwealth v. Hunt, 45 Mass. (4 Metc.) 111, 118 (1842). See also Commonwealth v. Ward, 1 Mass. 473, 474 (1805).

57. United States v. Gooding, 25 U.S. (12 Wheat.) 460, 469 (1827); Miller v. United States, 382 F.2d 583, 586 (9th Cir. 1967).

58. Indispensability of the agreement sometimes leads to the error of referring to it as the "gist of the crime." See Roll v. People, 132 Colo. 1, 284 P.2d 665 (1955); United States v. Taylor, 562 F.2d 1345, 1352 (2d Cir. 1977).

59. Krulewitch v. United States, 336 U.S. 440, 447–48, 69 S.Ct. 716, 720 (1949).

60. State v. Phillips, 240 N.C. 516, 521, 82 S.E.2d 762, 766 (1954).

61. United States v. Varelli, 407 F.2d 735, 741 (7th Cir. 1969).

62. State v. Cole, 107 S.C. 285, 288–89, 92 S.E. 624, 625 (1917).

63. Miller v. United States, 382 F.2d 583, 586 (9th Cir. 1967); United States v. Edwards, 488 F.2d 1154, 1157 (5th Cir. 1974).

64. United States v. Kaczmarek, 490 F.2d 1031, 1035 (7th Cir. 1974); People v. Harper, 25 Cal.2d 862, 156 P.2d 249 (1945).

65. Piracci v. State, 207 Md. 499, 115 A.2d 262 (1955).

66. 18 U.S.C.A. §§ 371, 1511(a)(1) (1970); West's Ann.Cal.Pen.Code § 184 (1970).

offense,[67] but this view did not even survive a rehearing: the court reversed its position and held that any act in furtherance of the conspiratorial plan was sufficient.[68] In fact such overt act may be "of very small significance." [69]

The act of one conspirator alone is sufficient to satisfy the statutory requirement of an overt act.[70] This has some bearing upon the present question, as has the fact that the act of one conspirator alone will serve certain other purposes, such as to establish venue,[71] or mark the time from which the statute of limitations will run.[72]

Nearly a hundred years ago a court said that one who joins a conspiracy thereby becomes "a party to every act which had before been done by others . . . in furtherance of (the) common design." [73] Another court had earlier asserted that in such a situation "the acts of the others become his by adoption." [74] The same idea has been expressed time and again in other words.[75]

The imputation to a late joiner of the previously committed act of another conspirator is free from objection if the only purpose is to establish the statutorily required overt act.[76] The same is true where the reason for imputation is to show the "purpose, scope and existence" of the conspiracy,[77] to fix the starting point of the statute of limitations, or establish venue. But there can be no basis for imputing to one who joins an existing conspiracy any substantive offense previously committed by others in furtherance of its objectives,[78] although such a result is not unknown.[79] To convict on this basis would be to establish criminal guilt by ratification, which is not a crimi-

67. People v. George, 74 Cal.App. 440, 241 P. 97 (1925).

68. People v. George, 74 Cal.App. 440, 241 P. 97 (1925).

69. Wechsler, Jones & Korn, The Treatment of Inchoate Crimes in the Model Penal Code, 61 Colum.L.Rev. 957, 958 (1961).

70. United States v. Rabinowich, 238 U.S. 78, 86, 35 S.Ct. 682, 684 (1915); State v. Green, 116 Ariz. 587, 570 P.2d 755, 757 (1977).

71. Hyde v. United States, 225 U.S. 347, 32 S.Ct. 793 (1912). Landing an airplane in order to refuel and to make a telephone call to see that everything was in order was a sufficient overt act to establish venue for conspiracy. United States v. Barnard, 490 F.2d 907 (9th Cir. 1973).

72. United States v. Kissel, 218 U.S. 601, 31 S.Ct. 124 (1910).

73. Card v. State, 109 Ind. 415, 418, 9 N.E. 591, 593 (1886).

74. United States v. Johnson, 26 F. 682, 684 (5th Cir. 1885).

75. Lefco v. United States, 74 F.2d 66, 68–69 (3d Cir. 1934); Van Riper v. United States, 13 F.2d 961, 967 (2d Cir. 1926); McDonald v. United States, 89 F.2d 128 (8th Cir. 1937).

76. Commonwealth v. O'Brien, 140 Pa. 555, 560–61, 21 A. 385, 386 (1891).

77. United States v. Cohen, 489 F.2d 945, 949 (2d Cir. 1973); McDonald v. United States, 89 F.2d 128 (8th Cir. 1937).

78. "In the very nature of things, persons cannot retroactively conspire to commit a previously consummated crime." State v. Phillips, 240 N.C. 516, 522, 82 S.E.2d 762, 766 (1954). "Manifestly, a conspirator is not 'concerned' in the commission of a crime which was committed before he joined the conspiracy." People v. Weiss, 50 Cal.2d 535, 564, 327 P.2d 527, 544 (1958).

79. "But it is also a part of the law of joint crimes that, when a party joins an existing group already so engaged, he assumes responsibility for all that has been done theretofore." Van Riper v. United States, 13 F.2d 961, 967 (2d Cir. 1926). At least one defendant, Ackerson, seems to have been convicted of substantive offenses committed before he joined the conspiracy.

"When one knowingly joins a conspiracy in progress he is responsible for acts of the conspiracy occurring before or after his association with it." And apparently some members of the conspiracy were convicted of substantive offenses committed before they joined. United

nal-law doctrine.[80] "If she did join in the conspiracy," it was said in one case, "she is responsible for the substantive offenses *later* committed as a part of the conspiracy." [81]

Needless to say, neither the fact that certain prior acts of conspirators may properly be imputed to late joiners, nor the fact that prior substantive offenses may not be, is sufficient to resolve the question whether one who had joined in the beginning should be held guilty of such an offense by reason of his membership alone. And a very real problem in this area has arisen in recent years. This is where there is a large, complex and sprawling network of crime,[82] as illustrated by the "Hernandez Cases," in which a large-scale criminal syndicate, dealing with the smuggling and distribution of narcotics, included forty-nine known participants.[83] In another case sixty persons were included in an indictment which charged them with operating an illegal gambling business, and with conspiracy to do so.[84]

A large, complex organization engaged in unlawful activity does not fit neatly into the common law of conspiracy in all its applications, although it is definitely related thereto, there is a broad common goal, but those working toward that end often operate on different levels, so to speak.[85] This suggests the possibility that the specific objectives of those engaged in such a conspiracy may sometimes differ from one "level" to another. As asserted in one case, while a defendant's "participation as a salesman admittedly did not involve him in all aspects of the overall conspiracy (to import and dis-

States v. Michel, 588 F.2d 986, 1002 (5th Cir. 1979).

80. "If a man ratifies a thing done without his authority, this makes the act binding upon him, but his subsequent assent will not relate back and make that a crime (by him) which was not (such) an offense when the act was done." Cook v. Commonwealth, 141 Ky. 439, 440, 132 S.W. 1032 (1911).

81. Anderson v. Superior Court, 78 Cal.App.2d 22, 25, 177 P.2d 315, 317 (1947). Accord, State v. Garcia, 117 Ariz. 67, 570 P.2d 1080, 1082 (App.1977).

82. Model Penal Code sec. 5.03(1)–(3), Comment at p. 118 (Tent. Draft No. 10, 1960).

83. Because of the problems involved, the judge divided the forty-nine into three groups for trial. These cases came to be known as the "Hernandez Cases" because Robert and Helen Hernandez of Tijuana, Mexico, were in charge of the conspiracy. For details of the operation, and the many problems involved, see United States v. Baxter, 492 F.2d 150 (9th Cir. 1973); United States v. Murray, 492 F.2d 178 (9th Cir. 1973); United States v. Valdiva, 492 F.2d 199 (9th Cir. 1973); United States v. Mickens, 492 F.2d 211 (9th Cir. 1973).

84. United States v. Pacheto, 489 F.2d 554 (5th Cir. 1974).

85. Complex conspiracies have commonly been characterized as either "wheel" type or "chain" type. "There may be one person . . . round whom the rest resolve. The metaphor is of the center of the circle and the circumference. There may be a conspiracy of another kind, where the metaphor would be rather that of a chain . . . ." Rex v. Meyrick, 21 Crim.App. 94, 102 (1929). Actually the modern criminal syndicate is frequently structured like ordinary big business with different echelons of authority and responsibility.

Congress has addressed the problem of an extended criminal enterprise in the Racketeer Influenced and Corrupt Organizations Act, 18 U.S.C.A. §§ 1961–1968 (1978), see Atkinson, "Racketeer Influenced and Corrupt Organizations," 18 U.S.C.A. §§ 1961–1968: Broadest Of The Federal Criminal Statutes, 69 J.Crim.L. & C. (1978). See also, United States v. Whitehead, 618 F.2d 523 (4th Cir. 1980); United States v. McNary, 620 F.2d 621 (7th Cir. 1980). Enterprise under the RICO Act encompasses both legal and illegal enterprises. United States v. Turkette, 452 U.S. 576, 101 S.Ct. 2524 (1981).

tribute restricted drugs), it was sufficient to tie him to the conspiracy charged.[86]

This point is emphasized in a recent case [87] concerning a statewide scheme to stage fraudulent automobile accidents for the purpose of creating false personal-injury claims to be presented to insurance companies. The participants even coined their own terminology: there were "recruiters" who enlisted the "hitters," the "drivers," the "riders," and the "target" vehicles. The "hitter" would purposely drive his car against the "target" vehicle, containing the "driver" and the "riders." The planners determined that pregnant women would make desirable "riders" as they could claim pregnancy-related injuries that would be hard to disprove. The scheme also included doctors and lawyers. A doctor would facilitate spurious claims by creating a medical history for treatment of a nonexistent injury; a lawyer would present a claim to the appropriate insurance company. In the course of asserting and negotiating the fraudulent claims for settlement, use was made of the United States mails, and the matter thus became a federal case.

A thirteen-count indictment was lodged against twenty-one defendants, charging them all with conspiracy to violate the mail-fraud statute and alleging twelve substantive violations of the statute. Each count for a substantive offense named some, but not all, of those named in the conspiracy count, so that the list of defendants differed from count to count. After five counts had been dismissed for insufficient evidence, some defendants had entered pleas of guilty, and the trial judge had entered judgment of acquittal as to two persons, the case involving the remaining thirteen defendants was submitted to the jury, which returned a verdict of not guilty as to one, and guilty as to twelve. All those found guilty were convicted on the conspiracy count; five were convicted on that count only, while the other seven were found guilty also on from one to five substantive counts.[88]

In dealing with such a large and complex conspiracy it would no doubt have been unreasonable to hold every member guilty of every substantive offense committed by any member in furtherance of his part of the complicated plan. Special rules must be developed for dealing with organizations of this nature. One suggested response is the creation of a new crime, providing a very severe penalty for the leaders of large criminal syndicates.[89] Perhaps size, as such, may demand attention, at least in certain applications.[90] The possible multiplicity of criminal objectives in such an organization also requires special consideration; without doubt there may be situations in which those operating at a lower "level" must be dealt with in terms of objectives they are able to appreciate, rather than the goals of those higher up.[91]

86. United States v. Rizzo, 491 F.2d 215, 218 (2d Cir. 1974).

87. United States v. Perez, 489 F.2d 51 (5th Cir. 1973).

88. Id. at p. 89 (App. V).

89. Hearings on Reform of Federal Criminal Law Before the Subcomm. on Criminal Law and Procedure of the Senate Comm. on the Judiciary, 92d Cong., 1st Sess., pt. 1 at p. 225 (1971). See, Racketeer Influenced Corrupt Organiza-

tions Act, 18 U.S.C.A. §§ 1961–1968 (1978).

90. See United States v. Pacheto, 489 F.2d 554, 558–59 (5th Cir. 1974).

91. "The danger necessarily follows that the defendant 'might be found in the net of a conspiracy by reason of the relation of (his) acts to the acts of others, the significance of which (he) may not have appreciated.'" Note, The Conspiracy Dilemma: Prosecution of Group Crime or

The difficulties introduced by the large-scale criminal syndicate, however, must not be permitted to distort the law of simple conspiracy. The simplest conspiracy of all, and perhaps the most common, is the combination of two persons to commit one substantive offense. The mere inclusion of more than one offense in the plan, or the addition of more than two participants, should not in itself make the conspiracy complex.[92] And there is no basis for the assumption that most group crimes are perpetrated by large criminal organizations.[93]

If **A** said to **D** "I wish you would murder **X**," whereupon **D** hunted up **X** and killed him, **A** would be guilty of murder.[94] If **A** said to **D** "let us murder **X**," to which **D** agreed, and **D** promptly hunted up **X** and killed him, the only reasonable conclusion is that **A** is guilty of murder. One of the surest ways to encourage another to commit a crime is to enter into a conspiracy with him for the accomplishment of that very result.[95] In other words, the "application of traditional complicity rules alone will ordinarily be sufficient to hold each member of a small-scale conspiracy liable for acts committed in its furtherance."[96] And in a situation free from complications, Judge Hand dealt with complicity and conspiracy as "in substance the same thing."[97]

Thus, so far as the ordinary simple conspiracy is concerned, the question posed at the outset must be answered in the affirmative: the substantive offenses of one conspirator, in furtherance of the conspiracy, must be imputed to his coconspirator. *Pinkerton*[98] which dealt with just such a situation, is unquestionably sound. And the reason has never been stated better than in the opinion by Mr. Justice Douglas in that case:

> The criminal intent to do the act is established by the formation of the conspiracy. Each conspirator instigated the commission of the crime. The unlawful agreement contemplated precisely what was done. It was formed for that purpose. The act was done in execution of the enterprise. The rule which holds responsible one who counsels, procures, or commands another to commit a crime is founded on the same principle.[99]

Protection of Individual Defendants, 62 Harv.L.Rev. 276, 284 (1948).

92. "Whether the object of a single agreement is to commit one or many crimes, it is in either case that agreement which constitutes the conspiracy which the statute punishes. The one agreement cannot be taken to be several agreements and hence several conspiracies because it envisages the violation of several statutes rather than one." Braverman v. United States, 317 U.S. 49, 53, 63 S.Ct. 99, 101 (1942).

93. "It is an oversimplification to regard most group crimes as resulting from the machinations of large criminal organizations; . . ." Developments in the Law: Criminal Conspiracy, 72 Harv.L.Rev. 920, 999 (1959).

94. He who "procures a crime to be done, if it is done, is guilty of the crime . . . ." United States v. Gooding, 25 U.S. 12 (Wheat.) 460, 469 (1827). Accord, Alonzi v. People, 198 Colo. 160, 597 P.2d 550, 564 (1979).

95. For a reference to "the encouraging effect that knowledge of his allegiance has upon the other conspirators." See Model Penal Code sec. 5.03(7), Comment at p. 154 (Tent.Draft No. 10, 1960).

96. Developments in the Law: Criminal Conspiracy, 72 Harv.L.Rev. 920, 999 (1959).

97. United States v. Falcone, 109 F.2d 579, 581 (2d Cir. 1940).

98. Pinkerton v. United States, 328 U.S. 640, 66 S.Ct. 1180 (1946).

99. Id. at p. 647. "Basey, however, can be convicted of the substantive acts of her co-conspirators whether or not she directly participates in those acts." United States v. Basey, 613 F.2d 198, 202 (9th Cir. 1980).

In upholding a recent conviction of conspiracy it was said:

A party to a continuing conspiracy may be responsible for a substantive offense committed by a coconspirator in furtherance of the conspiracy even though that party does not participate in the substantive offense or have any knowledge of it.[1]

Emphasizing that the large-scale criminal syndicate is not included, and that the reference is only to the ordinary conspiracy, it may be emphasized in substance that when a conspiracy is formed each conspirator while a member thereof "is liable for every act and declaration of the conspirators, done or made in pursuance or furtherance of said conspiracy; . . ."[2] even if he was not present at the time,[3] or the other whose act or declaration is relied upon is not presently on trial.[4] If the purpose of the conspiracy is to commit a dangerous felony each member runs the risk of having the venture end in homicide, even if he has forbidden the others to make use of deadly force.[5] Hence each is guilty of murder if one of them commits homicide in the perpetration or attempted perpetration of an agreed-upon robbery[6] or burglary.[7] And where **D** and others, who had engaged in a burglary, were fleeing from

1. United States v. Rosado-Fernandez, 614 F.2d 50, 53 (5th Cir. 1980).

2. People v. Lyon, 135 Cal.App.2d 558, 575, 288 P.2d 57, 68 (1955). Accord, Delli Paoli v. United States, 352 U.S. 232, 77 S.Ct. 294 (1957); United States v. Battaglia, 394 F.2d 304 (7th Cir. 1968). "Conspiracy being established, the act of each pursuant thereto became the act of all." Dye v. State, 90 Ga.App. 736, 738, 84 S.E.2d 116, 117 (1954).

Acts and declarations of conspirators in furtherance of their purpose are admissible against all members of the conspiracy if the conspiracy itself is proven by evidence *aliunde*. People v. Batton, 9 Mich.App. 195, 156 N.W.2d 640 (1967).

When the substantive offense is committed by one conspirator in furtherance of the unlawful plan all members of the conspiracy are guilty of the substantive offense. United States v. Chambers, 382 F.2d 910 (6th Cir. 1967).

As to **D**'s liability for acts of co-conspirators done before **D** joined the conspiracy, see Baker v. United States, 21 F.2d 903 (4th Cir. 1927); Howle v. State, 15 Ala.App. 185, 72 So. 759 (1916). As to prior declarations see People v. Sherman, 127 Cal.App.2d 230, 273 P.2d 611 (1954); United States v. Reynolds, 511 F.2d 603 (5th Cir. 1975).

A conspirator is liable for acts of his co-conspirator in furtherance of the conspiracy even if he is unaware of the acts or the conspirators. United States v. Murray, 492 F.2d 178 (9th Cir. 1973).

3. Commonwealth v. Burdell, 380 Pa. 43, 49, 110 A.2d 193, 196 (1955).

He is bound by declarations of others made before he joined the conspiracy. United States v. Sansone, 231 F.2d 887 (2d Cir. 1956).

D can join a conspiracy at any time and may be found to have done so when, with knowledge of its existence, he has undertaken to further its design. Cave v. United States, 390 F.2d 58 (8th Cir. 1968). "Well settled is the principle that a party to a continuing conspiracy may be responsible for a substantive offense committed by a co-conspirator in furtherance of the conspiracy, even if that party does not participate in the substantive offense or have any knowledge of it." United States v. Michel, 588 F.2d 986, 999 (5th Cir. 1979).

4. Wellman v. United States, 227 F.2d 757 (6th Cir. 1955). An alleged conspirator cannot be held criminally responsible for the act of another if the only evidence purporting to indicate an agreement between them is evidence of the act and declarations of the latter. As conspirators are accomplices corroboration is needed. People v. Lyon, 135 Cal.App.2d 558, 288 P.2d 57 (1955). The statutory provision that defendant cannot be convicted of procuring an abortion on abortee's testimony unless corroborated by other evidence applies also to the crime of conspiracy to commit abortion. People v. MacEwing, 45 Cal.2d 218, 288 P.2d 257 (1955).

5. People v. Romero, 100 Cal.App.2d 352, 223 P.2d 511 (1950).

6. Ibid; People v. Raber, 168 Cal. 316, 143 P. 317 (1914).

7. See note 7 on page 709.

the scene in an automobile loaded with loot and shots were fired at pursuing police officers, the fact that **D** himself fired no shot was no defense to a charge of assault with a deadly weapon.[8] The act of one conspirator done in the effort to achieve the main object of the criminal plan will be imputed to the other even if it deviates from the agreed-upon method of perpetration,[9] as where stabbing or shooting is substituted for poison as the method of killing the intended victim.[10] But if one conspirator unexpectedly goes entirely outside the purpose of the combination to commit a crime he alone is guilty thereof.[11] If, for example, the conspiracy contemplates only an assault and battery and one confederate unexpectedly robs the victim, he alone is guilty of the robbery,[12] and the same is true if one conspirator goes out of his way to rob a watchman when only a secret larceny had been agreed upon.[13] As further explained by Mr. Justice Lush, "if two men concerted together to fight two other men with their fists, and one struck an unlucky blow causing death, both would be guilty of manslaughter. But if one used a knife, or other deadly weapon such as a piece of timber, without the knowledge or consent of the other, he only who struck with the weapon would be

State v. Jensen, 207 Or. 239, 296 P.2d 618 (1956).

A conspirator who participated in robbery with violence (including his own possession of brass knuckles) was guilty of first-degree murder by reason of the killing of the victim by his co-conspirator, using a knife, even if the first did not know of the knife. State v. Palfy, 11 Ohio App.2d 142, 229 N.E.2d 76 (1967).

After conspirators had agreed to "rob something" and split the proceeds, they cruised around looking for an appropriate target. They agreed to rob a certain store and one was sent to investigate. He found the store closed but in the alley he encountered a man whom he killed in an attempted robbery. It was held that this was within the scope of the conspiracy, which was to commit robbery, and that the co-conspirator was also guilty of robbery-murder. Commonwealth v. Tate, 485 Pa. 180, 401 A.2d 353 (1979).

Where the purpose of the conspiracy is to commit a dangerous felony, each member runs the risk of having the venture end in homicide, even if he has forbidden the others to make use of deadly force. Hence each is guilty of murder if one of them commits homicide in the perpetration of an agreed-upon robbery. McKinney v. Sheriff, Clark County, 93 Nev. 70, 560 P.2d 151 (1977). Note that this has been changed in some of the new penal codes.

"The abolition of the applicability to the felony-murder rule to co-felons who do not in fact cause the death would have constituted a startling departure from established Pennsylvania law . . . ."

The 1972 Code does not follow "the Model Penal Code to restrict felony-murder to the actual slayer. . . . As has been stated the cases are legion which provide that a participant in a robbery, such as appellant, 'acts with the kind of culpability' which is necessary to hold her responsible in a death caused by a co-defendant acting in furtherance of the conspiratorial scheme." Commonwealth v. Allen, 475 Pa. 165, 379 A.2d 1335, 1339–40 (1977).

7. Romero v. State, 101 Neb. 650, 164 N.W. 554 (1917). Arson. State v. Morran, 131 Mont. 17, 306 P.2d 679 (1957).

8. Shetsky v. State, 290 P.2d 158 (Okl. Cr.1955).

9. 2 Hawk.P.C. c. 29, § 20 (6th ed. 1788); McClanahan v. United States, 230 F.2d 919 (5th Cir. 1956).

10. 4 Bl.Comm. *37.

11. Ibid.

"A conspirator can be found guilty of a substantive offense based on the acts of a coconspirator done in furtherance of the conspiracy, unless the act 'did not fall within the scope of the unlawful project, or was merely a part of the ramifications of the plan which could not be reasonably foreseen as a necessary or natural consequence of the unlawful agreement.'" United States v. Moreno, 588 F.2d 490, 493 (5th Cir. 1979).

12. People v. Foley, 59 Mich. 553, 26 N.W. 699 (1886); Rex v. Hawkins, 3 C. & P. 392, 172 Eng.Rep. 470 (1828).

13. State v. Lucas, 55 Iowa 321, 7 N.W. 583 (1880).

responsible for the death resulting from the blow given by it." [14] The absence of knowledge is very important here because one who knows his confederate enters a fist fight carrying a deadly weapon will be held accountable for the consequences if that weapon is used in the encounter.[15]

The fact that one of the conspirators could not himself perpetrate the intended offense neither relieves him from guilt nor disables him from cooperating with another person who is able to do so.[16] For example a husband who conspires with another to have sexual intercourse with the former's wife against her will is guilty of rape if such intercourse is consummated.[17]

After the common enterprise has come to an end, whether by accomplishment or abandonment, no subsequent act or declaration of one former conspirator will be attributed to another.[18] Thus one conspirator who gave timely notice of withdrawal and directed that the plan be abandoned (although guilty of conspiracy) was not guilty of arson subsequently committed by the other.[19] It must be noted however that a conspiracy to commit a crime is not necessarily ended by the fact that enough has been done to incur guilt of that offense.[20] Thus a conspiracy to violate the National Motor Vehicle Theft Act is not terminated by the transportation of a stolen car in interstate commerce if the fruits of the plan are still to be claimed and divided,[21] and a conspiracy to commit larceny, robbery or burglary is not ended by accomplishment if the loot, although unlawfully obtained, is yet to be distributed.[22] Furthermore, one who has joined a combination for the purpose of committing a crime cannot shield himself from guilt thereof by a secret intent to abandon the plan. In fact no amount of effort in an attempted com-

---

14. Regina v. Caton, 12 Cox C.C. 624 (1874).

15. People v. Barrett, 261 Ill. 232, 103 N.E. 969 (1919).

16. United States v. Bayer, 26 Fed. Cas. 1046, No. 14,547 (1876); United States v. Wilson, 230 F.2d 521 (4th Cir. 1956); State v. Moretti, 52 N.J. 182, 244 A.2d 499 (1968).

The House of Lords has recently held that where the object of the conspiracy was impossible the offense of conspiracy is not punishable. The reasoning was based on the court's analogous position in the law of attempt. Regina v. Nock [1978] 3 WLR 57 (H.L.).

17. Bohanon v. State, 289 P.2d 400 (Okl.Cr.1955); Cody v. State, 361 P.2d 307 (Okl.Cr.1961); State v. Blackwell, 241 Or. 528, 407 P.2d 617 (1965); Annotation, 84 A.L.R.2d 1017 (1962). For other examples see infra, section 8, Parties to Crime. People v. Damen, 28 Ill.2d 464, 19 N.E.2d 25 (1963); Rozell v. State, 502 S.W.2d 16 (Tex.Cr.App.1973).

18. State v. Chernick, 280 S.W.2d 56 (Mo.1955).

"[A]n out-of-court declaration made after arrest may not be used at trial against one of the declarant's partners in crime." Wong Sun v. United States, 371 U.S. 471, 490, 83 S.Ct. 407, 418 (1963). Accord, Delli Paoli v. United States, 352 U.S. 232, 77 S.Ct. 294 (1957); Green v. United States, 386 F.2d 953 (1967).

After robbers had divided the "loot" the conspiracy had ended and the declaration of one was not admissible against the other. State v. Williams, 38 Or.App. 327, 590 P.2d 259 (1979).

19. State v. Peterson, 213 Minn. 56, 4 N.W.2d 826 (1942).

20. "Once a conspiracy is shown to exist, which in its nature is not ended merely by lapse of time, it continues to exist until consummated, abandoned or otherwise terminated by some affirmative act." United States v. Rucker, 586 F.2d 899, 906 (2d Cir. 1978).

21. Koury v. United States, 217 F.2d 387 (6th Cir. 1954).

22. Shetsky v. State, 290 P.2d 158 (Okl.Cr.1955).

munication of notice of withdrawal will be effective if it fails to reach the other conspirator, or conspirators, in time.[23]

G. CONTINUING OFFENSE

A conspiracy, since it is not the agreement itself but the resulting combination, always endures for some period of time although this may vary anywhere from a few seconds to many years. And the fact that it is a continuing offense has two important consequences in addition to those previously mentioned: (1) If the combination has continued after that time, the fact that it was originally formed prior to the statute which makes the purpose unlawful is no defense;[24] and (2) the statute of limitations begins to run not from the formation of the plot but from the termination thereof,[25] except that under the interpretation of some statutes requiring an overt act for conviction of conspiracy the statute will run from the time of the last provable overt act.[26]

H. FREEDOM OF SPEECH

The constitutional guarantee of freedom of speech is not to be frustrated by improper claims of conspiracy but that guarantee is not an unlimited license as shown in the discussion of such subjects as libel and contempt. And a conspiracy to destroy the government by force presents a "clear and present danger," justifying conviction of conspiracy despite the claim of freedom of speech,[27] but advocacy of forcible overthrow of the government is protected by the First Amendment if it does not urge that anything be done, but only that it be believed.[28] Pure speech and demonstrative acts having speech implications are not the same.[29] However, an agreement to violate the law must be clearly shown where the conduct involved is arguably also legitimate advocacy.[30]

The Model Penal Code would reject the age-old concept of conspiracy as a bilateral or multilateral relationship and substitute the somewhat astounding concept of a unilateral conspiracy.[31] The drafters of the Code were disturbed by the rule of the existing law that, where only two are involved, if one is innocent the other cannot be guilty. Hence if one lacks criminal capacity by reason of insanity[32] or infancy[33] or if one merely pretends to cooperate while having no intention of going through with the plan there is no conspiracy.

23. People v. Ortiz, 63 Cal.App. 662, 219 P. 1024 (1923).

24. Christianson v. United States, 226 F.2d 646 (8th Cir. 1955). A conspiracy is a continuing offense and if it continues after a statute increases the penalty the increased penalty may be imposed upon the conspirators. State v. Hayes, 127 Conn. 543, 18 A.2d 895 (1941).

25. United States v. Kissel, 218 U.S. 601, 31 S.Ct. 124 (1910).

26. People v. Hines, 284 N.Y. 93, 29 N.E.2d 483 (1940). And see Note, 29 N.Y.U.L.Rev. 1470 (1954).

27. Scales v. United States, 367 U.S. 203, 81 S.Ct. 1469 (1961).

28. Yates v. United States, 354 U.S. 298, 77 S.Ct. 1064 (1957); Street v. New York, 394 U.S. 576, 89 S.Ct. 1354 (1969).

29. Walker v. City of Birmingham, 388 U.S. 307, 87 S.Ct. 1824 (1967).

30. United States v. Spock, 416 F.2d 165 (1st Cir. 1969). See also, Church, Conspiracy Doctrine and Speech Offenses, 60 Cornell L.Rev. 569 (1975).

31. Model Penal Code 104 (Tent. Draft No. 10, 1960). And see Model Penal Code section 5.04.

32. As to mental disease or defect see infra, chapter 8, section 2.

33. As to immaturity see infra, chapter 8, section 1.

The guilty party to such an arrangement should not be entitled to an acquittal, it is true, but it would seem that instead of distorting the concept of conspiracy it would be wiser to provide that the guilty party to such an arrangement is guilty of an attempt to conspire,[34] with the additional provision that the penalty for such an attempt should be the same as that for the conspiracy itself.[35]

I. PROOF

The cases are full of statements such as these: "Once the existence of a conspiracy is established, even slight evidence connecting a defendant to the conspiracy may be sufficient proof of his involvement in the scheme."[36] "Once a conspiracy is shown, there need be only slight evidence to link a defendant with it."[37] "Only slight evidence is required to connect the individual defendants with the conspiracy once the evidence of a conspiracy has been proved."[38] To make sure that such statements would not be understood to mean that conspiracy offers an exception to the requirement that guilt be established beyond a reasonable doubt, one court took pains to say:

Accordingly, we think it appropriate here to restate the slight evidence rule correctly and as we are reasonably certain that our predecessors intended it: Once the existence of a conspiracy is established, evidence establishing beyond a reasonable doubt a connection of a defendant with the conspiracy, even though the *connection* is *slight*, is sufficient to convict him with knowing participation in the conspiracy. Thus, the word "slight" properly modifies "connection" and not "evidence."[39]

MODEL PENAL CODE

Four changes proposed by the Model Penal Code are entitled to particular attention. (1) "Unlawful act" which is not a crime; (2) exculpation by renunciation; (3) only one guilty party; and (4) only one conviction. As to the first, the common law recognizes that certain conduct, called an "unlawful act," may be sufficiently wrongful, although not itself punishable as a crime, so that an agreement to commit it is punishable as a conspiracy. The Code, however, limits conspiracy to an agreement "to commit a crime."[40] Renunciation. At common law a conspirator can save himself from guilt of the target offense by timely notice of his withdrawal to his confederate. If the confederate goes ahead and commits the target offense after having received timely notice of withdrawal, he alone is guilty of the target offense.[41]

34. While the sound view would preclude guilt of attempt in cases of "legal impossibility" the reason for the distinction between this and "factual impossibility" is restricted to cases in which the impossibility is due to the criminal incapacity of the *actor* and the term should be defined with this limitation.

35. While the position of the Code, in punishing all attempts the same as the offense attempted except for the gravest crimes seems extreme, equating the attempt with the conspiracy in the type of situation mentioned would seem entirely proper.

36. United States v. Schmaltz, 562 F.2d 558, 560 (8th Cir. 1977). And with a slight change of wording, United States v. Losing, 560 F.2d 906, 912 (8th Cir. 1977).

37. United States v. Oropeza, 564 F.2d 316, 321 (9th Cir. 1977).

38. United States v. Baldarrama, 566 F.2d 560, 566 (9th Cir. 1978).

39. United States v. Dunn, 564 F.2d 348, 357 (9th Cir. 1977).

40. Section 5.05(1).

41. State v. Peterson, 213 Minn. 56, 4 N.W.2d 826 (1942).

And if the law of the jurisdiction requires an overt act for conspiracy, one who has agreed to commit an offense may save himself from guilt of conspiracy by giving timely notice of withdrawal before there has been any such overt act.[42] But once the conspiracy is complete "no subsequent action can exonerate the conspirator of that crime." [43] The Code would provide otherwise. "It is an affirmative defense that the actor, after conspiring to commit a crime, thwarted the success of the conspiracy, under circumstances manifesting a complete and voluntary renunciation of his criminal purpose." [44] This might take the form of notice to the police in time to enable them to prevent the offense. A notice of withdrawal would not of itself be sufficient. But if the notice manifested a sufficient change of heart and caused the coconspirator not to commit the crime, this would seem sufficient to exculpate the one who gave the notice.[45]

Only one guilty party. One may be convicted of conspiracy at common law although no other person is available for trial, by reason of death or otherwise, and although no other person is subject to conviction by reason of some special bar to prosecution such as diplomatic immunity. But there is no common-law conspiracy if there is only one guilty person.[46] The purported agreement of an undercover agent, whose purpose is merely to obtain evidence will not support a conviction of conspiracy at common law.[47] It would be sufficient under the Code, however, which does not require more than one guilty person.[48]

42. United States v. Britton, 108 U.S. 199, 2 S.Ct. 531 (1883). A person who withdraws from a conspiracy may still be guilty of aiding and abetting the same conspiracy by subsequent conduct. May v. State, 97 Wis.2d 175, 293 N.W.2d 478 (1980).

43. Model Penal Code sec. 5.03, Comment (Tent. Draft No. 10 (1960)). "For an abandonment to be legally sufficient, it must occur before the commission of the crime becomes so imminent that avoidance is out of the question." Commonwealth v. Laurin, 269 Pa.Super. 368, 409 A.2d 1367 (1979).

44. Section 5.03(6).

45. The Supreme Court reversed a conviction under the anti-trust laws stating as to the defense of withdrawal from a conspiracy:

"The charge, fairly read, limited the jury's consideration to only two circumscribed and arguably impractical methods of demonstrating withdrawal from the conspiracy. Nothing that we have been able to find in the case law suggests, much less commands, that such confining blinders be placed on the jury's freedom to consider evidence regarding the continuing participation of alleged conspirators in the charged conspiracy. Affirmative acts inconsistent with the object of the conspiracy and communicated in a manner reasonably calculated to reach co-conspirators have generally been regarded as sufficient to establish withdrawal or abandonment."

United States v. United States Gypsum Co., 438 U.S. 422, 464, 98 S.Ct. 2864, 2887 (1978).

46. Gebardi v. United States, 287 U.S. 112, 53 S.Ct. 35 (1932); People v. Levy, 283 App.Div. 383, 128 N.Y.S.2d 275 (1954).

47. Delaney v. State, 164 Tenn. 432, 51 S.W.2d 485 (1932).

48. Section 5.04(1) provides that "it is immaterial to the liability of a person who . . . conspires with another person to commit a crime that: . . . the person . . . with whom he conspires is irresponsible or has an immunity to prosecution or conviction for the commission of the crime." See State v. St. Christopher, 305 Minn. 226, 232 N.W.2d 798 (1975); Saienni v. State, 346 A.2d 152 (Del.1975); Garcia v. State, ___ Ind. ___, 394 N.E.2d 106 (1979). Thus while an agreement with a six-year-old child to steal certain property would not be a common-law conspiracy because the child has no criminal responsibility, it would be a conspiracy under this section. And it should be noted that the "diplomatic immunity" of an ambassador, for example, is based upon international policy and protects him from prosecution however guilty he may be. See Farnsworth v.

Only one conviction. If a conspiracy results in the commission of the target offense, the common law permits conviction of both, and in federal cases it has been almost routine to charge both the conspiracy and the target offense whenever more than one defendant is involved. But this would not be permitted under the Code.[49] It would permit conviction of either but not both.

THE NEW PENAL CODES

Some of the new penal codes leave the law of conspiracy as it was, for the most part at least, either by making no provision except that the combination must include an intent to commit a crime,[50] or by having no general conspiracy statute.[51] One code is worded in terms of "whoever conspires with another to commit a crime" or "to cause a third person to be arrested or prosecuted on a criminal charge knowing the charge to be false . . . ."[52] A few limit conspiracy to a combination to commit a felony,[53] or something less than any offense.[54] But a substantial majority are worded in terms of a conspiracy to commit a crime,[55] or an offense.[56] It seems that no new code has included an "unlawful act" which is not itself punishable as a crime without naming it, such as the one for false arrest or prosecution. A few of the new codes provide for exculpation by renunciation.[57] One provides for withdrawal before there has been any overt act,[58] but this would be true wherever an overt act is required for conspiracy. A few have provided that guilt of conspiracy does not require more than one guilty party, either by following the provision of the Model Penal Code in substance,[59] or by doing so to the

Zerbst, 98 F.2d 541 (5th Cir. 1938). But the "immunity" of the undercover agent protects him because he is not guilty of crime.

49. Section 5.05(3).

50. E.g., New Mexico limits conspiracy to "combining . . . for the purpose of committing a felony," but makes no other provisions. N.M. Stat.Ann. § 30–28–2 (1978). Florida is the same except that the purpose mentioned is to commit "any offense." West's Fla.Stat. Ann. § 777.04(3) (1976).

51. E.g., Georgia.

52. E.g., Minn.Stat.Ann. § 609.175 (West 1975).

53. E.g., Ind.Code Ann. § 35–41–5–2 (Burns 1979); N.M.Stat.Ann. § 30–28–2 (1978); Ohio Rev.Code Ann. § 2923.01 (Page 1975); V.T.C.A. Penal Code § 15.02 (1974); Va.Code § 18.2–22 (1975).

54. E.g., Or.Rev.Stat. § 161.450 (1971).

55. E.g., Colo.Rev.Stat. § 18–2–201 (1973); Conn.Gen.Stat. § 53a–48 (1975); Del.Code Ann. tit. 11, § 521 (1974); Haw. Rev.Stat. § 705–520 (1976); Iowa Code Ann. § 706.1 (West 1979); Kan.Stat.Ann. § 21–3302 (1974); Ky.Rev.Stat.Ann. § 506–040 (Baldwin 1974); La.Rev.Stat.

Ann. § 14.26 (West 1974); Me.Rev.Stat. tit. 17A, § 151 (1975); N.H.Rev.Stat.Ann. § 629:3 (1974); N.Y. Penal Law § 105.00 et seq. (McKinney 1975); 18 Pa.Const. Stat.Ann. § 903 (Purdon 1973); Utah Code Ann., 1953 § 76–4–201 (1953); Wash.Rev.Code Ann. 28.040 (1977); Wis. Stat.Ann. § 939.31 (West 1958).

56. E.g., Ala.Code tit. 13A, § 4–3 (1975); Ark.Stat.Ann. § 41–707 (1977); West's Fla.Stat.Ann. § 777.04(3) (1976); Ill.Ann.Stat. ch. 38, § 8–2 (Smith-Hurd 1972); Mont.Rev.Codes Ann. § 45–4–102 (1981); N.D.Cent.Code § 12.1–06–04 (1971).

57. E.g., Ala.Code tit. 13A, § 4–3 (1975); Ark.Stat.Ann. § 41–707 (1977); Colo.Rev.Stat. § 18–2–201 (1973); Conn. Gen.Stat. § 53a–48 (1975); Ky.Rev.Stat. Ann. § 506–040 (Baldwin 1974); N.H. Rev.Stat.Ann. § 629:3 (1974); Ohio Rev. Code Ann. § 2923.01 (Page 1975); Or. Rev.Stat. § 161.450 (1971).

58. E.g., Kan.Stat.Ann. § 21–3302 (1974).

59. Ala.Code tit. 13A, § 4–3 (1975); Haw.Rev.Stat. § 705–520 (1976); Me. Rev.Stat. tit. 17A, § 151 (1975); N.H. Rev.Stat.Ann. § 629:3 (1974); N.Y. Penal Law § 105.00 et seq. (McKinney 1975);

extent of providing that the lack of criminal capacity by the other party is not a defense.[60] The overwhelming majority require an overt act for guilt of conspiracy.[61] At least two provide that where conspiracy has been followed by the target offense, this will not permit conviction and sentence for both,[62] while at least one expressly provides that "a conviction for one shall not bar a prosecution for the other." [63]

SECTION 6. AGENCY

One may incur criminal guilt by procuring the harm to be done by the hand of another whether that other is also culpable or acts as an innocent agent.[1] Criminal negligence, sufficient for guilt of certain crimes, such as manslaughter, may be established by proof that an employer entrusted a task to one known to be so incompetent to handle it that there was an obvious risk of the harm that was caused thereby.[2] An employer who knows or believes that his employee is about to do something within the scope of employment that will result in the commission of a crime has a legal duty to direct action which will not violate the law, and may be guilty of the resulting crime by his negative act in failing to perform this duty.[3] But the spe-

V.T.C.A. Penal Code § 15.02 (Vernon 1974). Under this provision one could be convicted of conspiracy although the other could not for whatever reason whether it is criminal incapacity (e.g. 5-year old child) he only pretended to agree (e.g., the undercover agent) or any other.

60. E.g., Ill.Ann.Stat. ch. 38, § 8–2 (Smith-Hurd 1972); Ind.Code Ann. § 35–41–5–2 (Burns 1979); Mont.Rev.Codes Ann. § 45–4–102 (1978); N.D. Cent.Code § 12.1–06–04 (1971). Under this provision one could be convicted although the other was a 5-year old child but not if he was an innocent undercover agent who was only seeking evidence.

61. E.g., Utah Code Ann., 1953, § 76–4–201.

62. E.g., Ohio Rev.Code Ann. § 2923.01 (Page 1975); Iowa Code Ann. § 706.1 (West 1979). Ohio permits only one conviction and Iowa permits only one sentence. The difference is very important. If only the double sentence is barred, conviction of both may be entered and if one conviction is reversed sentence may be entered on the other. But if only one conviction is permitted and that one is reversed no sentence can be pronounced.

63. La.Rev.Stat.Ann. § 14.26 (West 1974).

1. Las Vegas Merchant Plumbers Association v. United States, 201 F.2d 732 (9th Cir. 1954); Morgan v. United States, 149 F.2d 185 (5th Cir. 1945). One who had arranged to have stolen goods delivered to his agent was guilty of receiving

stolen goods when they were received by the agent. State v. Lisena, 129 N.J.L. 569, 30 A.2d 593 (1943), aff'd 131 N.J.L. 39, 34 A.2d 407 (1943). "One may be a principal who employs a person who cannot be punished for the commission of the offense." Cook v. State, 138 Tex.Cr. R. 109, 113, 134 S.W.2d 258, 260 (1939). In the terminology of parties to crime the guilty agent is a "principal" and the employer may be an accessory before the fact, but both are guilty. Commonwealth v. Mannos, 311 Mass. 94, 40 N.E.2d 291 (1942). And see infra, section 8, Parties to Crime.

One may be guilty of a crime by causing it to be committed by an innocent agent. United States v. Ruffin, 613 F.2d 408 (2nd Cir. 1979).

"A person is personally responsible for a crime committed by others if that person *intentionally* aids and abets the others in the commission of the crime." State v. McDaniel, 228 Kan. 172, 612 P.2d 1231, 1238 (1980).

2. Regina v. Lowe, 3 Car. & K. 123 (1850). And see The Queen v. Holbrook, 4 Q.B.D. 42, 50 (1878); Chisholm v. Doulton, 22 Q.B.D. 736, 743 (1889).

3. In this situation also the employee may be either guilty or innocent. A chauffeur had a fatal traffic accident as a result of his unlawful driving with criminal negligence. The employer, who was in the car at the time, observed the very improper driving and had ample opportunity to order the use of proper care but failed to do so, was also guilty of

cial problem raised by the "agency" cases is whether an employer who is himself entirely free from fault may be convicted of crime because of harm caused by his employee within the scope of employment, and so far as true crime is concerned the answer is that he may not.[4]

An employer may be civilly liable for harm caused by an employee within the scope of employment, under the doctrine of respondeat superior, even if the former had forbidden the latter to do what was done,[5] but this has no application to criminal law.[6]

In the words of the Minnesota Court: [7]

"Ordinarily the doctrine of *respondeat superior* has no application in criminal cases. Criminal liability, except for certain statutory offenses, and others not here material, is based upon personal guilt. Responsibility for the crimes of others rests upon causation. A defendant is held criminally liable for having counselled, procured, commanded, incited, authorized, or encouraged another to commit a particular crime. At the very time the rule of *respondeat superior* was being developed as a basis for vicarious civil liability it was rejected as a ground for similar criminal liability. . . ."

Thus a master who is himself free from fault is not criminally responsible for a death caused by his servant's negligence,[8] and where only the employee knows that representations made by him are false the employer is not guilty of false pretenses although money is received from another who is deceived thereby.[9] On the other hand, needless to say, it is no defense to one who has knowingly violated the law that he was not acting for his own benefit but only as agent for another.[10]

A different problem is involved in a prosecution for an offense which is not a true crime, as "where a statute commands that an act be done or omitted, which, in the absence of such statute, might have been done or omitted without culpability, ..." [11] Such an offense does not have the normal

---

manslaughter. Moreland v. State, 164 Ga. 467, 139 S.E. 77 (1927). Over an extended period of time employees took and carried away the property of another and appropriated it to the use of their employer. The employer, who knew about this and took advantage of it without protest was guilty of larceny although the employees innocently believed it to be his property. Regina v. Bleasdale, 2 Car. & K. 765, 175 Eng.Rep. 321 (1848).

4. Rex v. Huggins, 2 Ld.Raym. 1574, 92 Eng.Rep. 518 (1730); State v. Lamperelli, 141 Conn. 430, 106 A.2d 762 (1954).

5. Restatement, Second, Agency § 230 (1958).

6. United States v. Food and Grocery Bureau, 43 F.Supp. 966, 971 (S.D.Cal. 1942). Partly quoted. And see Lovelace v. State, 191 Miss. 62, 2 So.2d 796 (1941).

"My Lords, the principle respondeat superior finds no place in our criminal law." Lord Morris of Borth-Y-Gest in Vane v. Yiannopoullos [1964] 3 All E.R. 820, [1965] AC 486.

7. State v. Burns, 215 Minn. 182, 187, 9 N.W.2d 518, 520–1 (1943). The doctrine of the civil law by which a principal is bound by the acts of his agent, done within the scope of his authority, is not applicable to the criminal law except in cases in which the principal has aided, encouraged or connived at the perpetration of the crime or it is habitually done in the usual course of the business. State v. Pinto, 129 N.J.L. 255, 29 A.2d 180 (1942).

8. Chisholm v. Doulton, 22 Q.B.D. 736, 741 (1889).

9. State v. Burns, 215 Minn. 182, 9 N.W.2d 518 (1943).

10. Beacham v. State, 289 P.2d 397 (Okl.Cr.1955). One who acts as agent for an officer and at his request makes a purchase of narcotics with his money to get evidence against the seller is not guilty. Durham v. State, 162 Tex.Cr.R. 25, 280 S.W.2d 737 (1955); State v. Long, 206 Neb. 446, 293 N.W.2d 391 (1980).

11. Commonwealth v. Weiss, 139 Pa. 247, 251, 21 A. 10 (1891). "Now these

mens-rea requirement [12] (unless it has been added by some special wording of the particular statute) [13] and since one who is entirely without culpability, as for example being innocently unaware of the facts which bring his conduct within the proscribed area, can be found guilty thereof,[14] the courts have not hesitated to extend the doctrine of *respondeat superior* to such a situation.[15] And (comparable to civil liability) guilt of such an offense can be established by proof of the prohibited act by defendant's employee in the course of defendant's business and within the scope of the employment, even if it was contrary to his express instructions.[16] Illustrative is the case in which the employer was held guilty even if it was without his knowledge that oleomargarine was served in his restaurant in violation of the statute,[17]—but a detailed study of offenses having the possibility of vicarious liability,[18] because the normal mens-rea requirement is lacking, must be postponed.[19]

Nothing comparable was known to the common law except the public nuisance,[20] which was dealt with by the machinery established for the prosecution of crime, since no other was readily available, but was not regarded as a crime but in substance and effect "only a civil proceeding." [21] The theory is that the owner of an enterprise carried on for his profit by agents or servants is liable for a nuisance, either private or public, caused by their acts in carrying on the enterprise.[22]

Even an offense beyond the area of true crime may have the normal mens-rea requirement if this is added by the words of a particular statute,

prohibitory laws do not make the transgression a moral offence, or sin. . . ." 1 Bl.Comm. *58. And see infra, chapter 7, section 5, Strict Liability: The Civil Offense.

12. Kenny, Outlines of Criminal Law 44, 46–52 (19th ed.1966).

13. See, for example, 18 U.S.C.A. § 834 (transportation of explosives, etc.): "Whoever knowingly violates any such regulation. . . ."

14. Smith v. State, 223 Ala. 346, 136 So. 270 (1931); State v. Whitman, 52 S.D. 91, 216 N.W. 858 (1927).

15. Meigs v. State, 94 Fla. 809, 114 So. 448 (1927); Lunsford v. State, 72 Ga. App. 700, 34 S.E.2d 731 (1945); State v. Probasco, 62 Iowa 400, 17 N.W. 607 (1883); DeZarn v. Commonwealth, 195 Ky. 686, 243 S.W. 921 (1922); State v. Sobelman, 199 Minn. 232, 271 N.W. 484 (1937); Commonwealth v. Jackson, 146 Pa.Super. 328, 22 A.2d 299 (1941), aff'd 345 Pa. 456, 28 A.2d 894 (1942).

16. Groff v. State, 171 Ind. 547, 85 N.E. 769 (1908); State v. Brown, 73 Or. 325, 144 P. 444 (1914); State v. Schull, 66 S.D. 102, 279 N.W. 241 (1938); State v. James, 177 Tenn. 21, 145 S.W.2d 783 (1940); State v. Cray, 85 Vt. 99, 81 A. 450 (1911). Even in a prosecution for a civil offense an employer cannot be convicted because of the act of his employee unless this act is shown to be reasonably within the scope of employment. Scroggs v. State, 65 Okl.Cr. 293, 85 P.2d 764 (1938). Vane v. Yiannopoullos, [1965] AC 486 [H.L.].

17. Commonwealth v. Weiss, 139 Pa. 247, 21 A. 10 (1891).

18. For a scholarly study see Sayre, Criminal Responsibility for the Acts of Another, 43 Harv.L.Rev. 689 (1930).

19. See infra, chapter 7, section 5, Strict Liability: The Civil Offense.

20. The Queen v. Stephens, L.R. 1 Q.B. 702 (1866). The original English rule, according to some indications, held the proprietor of a newspaper criminally liable for libel on the basis of *respondeat superior*. Rex v. Walter, 3 Esp. 21 (1799). This was quite unsound and if it was ever the rule it was changed by statute. 6 & 7 Vict. c. 96 (1843). As to the doubt, see supra, chapter 5, section 2, G.

21. The prosecution for nuisance is not "strictly a criminal proceeding." Per Mellor, J., in The Queen v. Stephens, L.R. 1 Q.B. 702, 709 (1866). It is "in the nature of a civil proceeding." Id. at 708.

22. Ibid.; State v. James, 177 Tenn. 21, 145 S.W.2d 783 (1940).

and where this is true there can be no conviction on the basis of *respondeat superior*. Where for example the legislature has made negligence an ingredient of the offense the employer cannot be convicted if the only negligence is that of the employee.[23] A statute providing a penalty for a "smoke nuisance" may impose strict liability and if so the employer may be convicted because of a violation by the employee, but such a conviction is improper in a prosecution under a statute which provides a penalty for one who "shall so negligently use any such furnace as that the smoke arising therefrom shall not be effectively consumed." [24]

This brief reference to offenses outside the area of true crime must not be permitted to obscure the basic precept mentioned above which has found expression in these words:

> **"Criminal liability being essentially personal and individual has always depended upon proof of individual causation. Hence, the criminal law has never accepted the doctrine of respondeat superior, which is a form of liability without fault and outside of the ordinary principles of causation."** [25]

The Model Penal Code seems to make no changes in this area since its provision is that a person is legally accountable for the conduct of another when "he causes an innocent or irresponsible person to engage in such conduct" [26] or "solicits such other person to commit it." [27] *Respondeat superior* would not be recognized in the field of crime proper.[28]

SECTION 7. CORPORATION

"A corporation is not indictable, but the particular members are." This statement of Chief Justice Holt [1] represents the original position of the common law which held firm for many years. It was repeated in substance by Blackstone [2] and in judicial opinion in this country.[3] Now, however, it represents little more than an echo from a bygone day. The change from this position originated in the area where the proceeding is criminal in form but civil in substance,—the so-called "civil offense," [4] and the first step was unavoidable. To insure proper maintenance of roads and bridges a statutory fine was provided for those who, having the duty to make needed repairs thereof, failed to do so. If a corporation had such a duty which it neglected to perform no sound reason against its conviction was available, and it was but a short step from recognition of corporate guilt of a civil offense based upon nonfeasance to such guilt based upon affirmative misconduct. Since such an offense does not have the normal mens-rea requirement for criminal guilt, and conviction may be supported on the basis of *respondeat superior*,

---

23. Chisholm v. Doulton, 22 Q.B.D. 736 (1889).

24. Ibid.

25. Sayre, Criminal Responsibility for the Acts of Another, 43 Harv.L.Rev. 689, 723 (1930).

A New Hampshire statute imposing criminal liability on the parents of children for the improper operation of off-highway recreational vehicles violates due process of law. State v. Akers, 119 N.H. 161, 400 A.2d 38 (1979).

26. Section 2.06(2)(a).

27. Id. at (3)(a)(i).

28. Model Penal Code 18–20 (Tent. Draft No. 1, 1953).

1. Anonymous, 12 Mod. 559, 88 Eng. Rep. 1518 (K.B.1701).

2. 1 Bl.Comm. *476.

3. State v. Great Works Milling and Manufacturing Co., 20 Me. 41 (1841).

4. See infra, chapter 7, section 5, Strict Liability: The Civil Offense.

the possibility of convicting a corporation of a civil offense became firmly established.[5] For years it seemed the change from the original position would stop at this point and that a corporation would be held incapable of committing a true crime on the ground that it could not have mens rea. "[C]orporations are not properly indictable for crimes involving a criminal state of mind," said a writer [6] as late as 1914, and ten years later another writer pointed out that the numerous statements in regard to convicting a corporation were chiefly *dicta* except in the civil-offense field.[7] Gradually, however, the change moved over into the area of true crime.

Corporate criminal liability has been a very controversial subject. The fine paid by the corporation is ultimately borne by the shareholders most of whom, ordinarily, had nothing to do with the offense and were powerless to prevent it.[8] Moreover, the conviction of the corporation tends to divert attention away from the guilty individuals. So far as the law is concerned it would be quite proper to convict both the corporation and the particular individual or individuals responsible for the offense, but the conviction of the corporation often seems to be sufficient, either to the prosecutor or to the jury. At times a puzzled court has felt impelled to comment on this fact. "We cannot understand how the jury could have acquitted all of the individual defendants." [9] "How an intelligent jury could have acquitted any of the defendants we cannot conceive." [10]

There are, however, considerations on the other side. Apart from the civil-offense area, convictions of corporations have been very largely limited to the acquisitive offenses (theft, fraud, and so forth). And it is argued that corporate fines are often important to deprive the corporation of an unjust enrichment resulting from offenses committed by its officers or agents. Another argument is that "pressures" within the organization, often incapable of proof, may have induced the act of the particular agent who may be less at fault than undefinable others within the corporation. There is also the situation in which the guilty individual agent of the corporation is outside the jurisdiction.[11]

The basic question is whether a corporation can have mens rea, and since this has been answered in the affirmative, the secondary question concerns the person or persons, whose blameworthy state of mind shall be held to be the mind of the corporation. In a prosecution involving only a civil offense, it was said: "No distinctions are made in these cases between officers and agents, or between persons holding positions involving varying degrees of responsibility." [12] This is sound because *respondeat superior* applies to

5. United States v. Dotterweich, 320 U.S. 277, 64 S.Ct. 134 (1943); Overland Cotton Mill Co. v. People, 32 Colo. 263, 75 P. 924 (1904). Commonwealth v. United States Commercial Service, Inc., 179 Pa. Super. 395, 116 A.2d 745 (1955).

6. Canfield, Corporate Responsibility for Crime, 14 Col.L.Rev. 469, 480 (1914).

7. Francis, Criminal Responsibility of the Corporation, 18 Ill.L.Rev. 305 (1924).

8. "Punishment falls on the individual members alone. Such being the case, the punishment is awkward, unscientific and uncertain." Id. at 322.

9. United States v. General Motors Corp., 121 F.2d 376, 411 (7th Cir. 1941).

10. United States v. Austin-Bagley Corp., 31 F.2d 229, 233 (2d Cir. 1929).

11. See Model Penal Code 148–150 (Tent.Draft No. 4, 1955). And see Edgerton, Corporate Criminal Responsibility, 36 Yale L.J. 827 (1927); Flynn, Criminal Sanctions Under State and Federal Antitrust Laws, 45 Tex.L.Rev. 1301 (1967).

12. United States v. George F. Fish, Inc., 154 F.2d 798, 801 (2d Cir. 1946).

such a case and only two questions are involved: (1) Was the person whose act caused the violation in the employ of defendant corporation? If so, (2) was this act within the scope of his employment? Quite a different problem is added in any prosecution for a true crime because mens rea cannot be established by *respondeat superior*. The Supreme Court pointed the way in an analogous field by holding that a corporation may be held liable for punitive damages for harm caused by what was done with a wanton, malicious or oppressive intent "by its controlling officers," [13] but only for actual damages where such intent was entertained only by its employees.[14] It said: [15]

"No doubt a corporation, like a natural person, may be held liable in exemplary or punitive damages for the act of an agent within the scope of his employment, provided the criminal intent, necessary to warrant the imposition of such damages, is brought home to the corporation. . . . The president and general manager, or, in his absence, the vice-president in his place, actually wielding the whole executive power of the corporation, may well be treated as so far representing the corporation and identified with it, that any wanton, malicious or oppressive intent of his, in doing wrongful acts in behalf of the corporation to the injury of others, may be treated as the intent of the corporation itself. But the conductor of a train, or other subordinate agent or servant . . . occupies a very different position, and is no more identified with his principal, so as to affect the latter with his own unlawful and criminal intent, than any agent or servant standing in a corresponding relation to natural persons. . . ."

A corporation, while it may be guilty of larceny, cannot properly be convicted of such an offense unless the intent to steal is brought home to its controlling officer even if property was appropriated for the use of the company by an employee with such intent.[16] The president of a corporation is not himself criminally liable for the acts of his subordinate unless he authorized or consented to such acts,[17] but can be convicted on proper proof that he aided and abetted his subordinates in their criminal activities.[18] If a corporation and its president, who is also the general manager, are jointly indicted the jury may find the officer guilty though they fail to find the corporation guilty.[19]

If a truck driver has a fatal traffic accident as a result of his criminal negligence in driving the vehicle he is guilty of manslaughter. This will not of itself be sufficient to taint his employer with criminal guilt, but the employer might have sent out the driver with such instructions as to speed, or with a vehicle known to him to be so unsafe, that the employer also acted with criminal negligence. If so the employer also is guilty of manslaughter, if he is an individual, and the question arises: Could a corporate employer be

13.　Denver & Rio Grande Railway Co. v. Harris, 122 U.S. 597, 7 S.Ct. 1286 (1887).

14.　Lake Shore & Michigan Southern Railway Co. v. Prentice, 147 U.S. 101, 13 S.Ct. 261 (1893).

15.　Id. at 111, 114.

16.　People v. Canadian Fur Trappers Corp., 248 N.Y. 159, 161 N.E. 455 (1928);

State v. Adjustment Credit Bureau, 94 Idaho 156, 483 P.2d 687 (1971).

17.　State v. Carmean, 126 Iowa 291, 102 N.W. 97 (1905).

18.　Nye & Nissen v. United States, 336 U.S. 613, 69 S.Ct. 766 (1949).

19.　United States v. Dotterweich, 320 U.S. 277, 64 S.Ct. 134 (1943).

guilty of manslaughter in such a case? The New Jersey court said yes;[20] the New York court said no.[21] In the latter case, however, it was recognized that a corporation can be guilty of a true crime and the reversal of this conviction was based entirely upon the definition of the particular offense. The court pointed out that manslaughter requires homicide and that homicide is defined by its statute (as at common law) as the killing of one human being "by another." This was held, quite properly, to mean the killing of one human being by another human being. The court then concluded that a corporation cannot be guilty of manslaughter, overlooking entirely that the corporation can do nothing except by aid of human beings, and there never could be a case in which a corporation has killed a human being who was not killed by a human being,—such as the case posed of a killing by a servant employed to drive a truck. If it can be shown that life has been lost as a result of criminal negligence, and that both the driver and his employer were guilty of such negligence, there is no reason why both should not be convicted of manslaughter even if the employer is a corporation. Recently, an Indiana Court upheld a negligent homicide indictment against a motor vehicle manufacturer arising from the death of vehicle occupants allegedly due to reckless vehicle design and manufacture.[22]

The Model Penal Code [23] adopts a position which, for the most part, represents that toward which the cases have been tending. If the charge is a civil offense, called a "violation" in the Code, the corporation will be liable under the principle of *respondeat superior* for the act of any corporate agent on behalf of the corporation and in the scope of his employment. But if a true crime is charged *respondeat superior* will not apply and it will be necessary to establish mens rea by the corporation by showing that "the commission of the offense was authorized, requested, commanded, performed or recklessly tolerated by the board of directors or by a high managerial agent acting in behalf of the corporation within the scope of his office or employment." [24] It is added that a "high managerial agent" is one "having duties of such responsibility that his conduct may fairly be assumed to represent the policy of the company." [25] The present statutory extension of criminal liability to unincorporated associations, in certain situations, is recognized and implemented by the Code.[26] The Canadian Supreme Court has applied criminal culpability to a municipality on a strict liability theory.[27]

20. State v. Lehigh Valley Railway Co., 90 N.J.L. 372, 103 A. 685 (1917).

21. People v. Rochester Railway & Light Co., 195 N.Y. 102, 88 N.E. 22 (1909).

22. State v. Ford Motor Co., 47 L.W. 2515 (Ind.Super.1979). See also People v. Warner-Lambert Co., 69 A.D.2d 265, 417 N.Y.S.2d 997 (1979), indictment for negligent homicide in explosion at plant of chewing gum manufacturer.

23. Section 2.07.

24. Id. at (1)(c). The purpose of the phrase "in behalf of the corporation" "is to avoid the problem presented in Moore v. Bressler, Ltd. [1944] 2 A.E.R. 515, in which the corporation was held liable for criminal conduct committed by officers within the scope of their duties but for the purpose of concealing a fraud perpetrated by the same officers against the corporation." Model Penal Code 147 (Tent.Draft No. 4, 1955).

25. Id. at (4)(c). See Miller, Corporate Criminal Liability: A Principle Extended To Its Limits, 38 Fed.B.Jnl. 49 (1979).

26. Id. at (3).

27. "A municipality cannot slough off responsibility by contracting out the work." Regina v. City of Sault Ste-Marie, 85 DLR 3d 161, 185, 40 CCC 2d 353 (1978).

SECTION 8. PARTIES TO CRIME

A. TERMINOLOGY

In the field of felony the common law divided guilty parties into principals and accessories.[1] According to the ancient analysis only the actual perpetrator of the felonious deed was a principal. Other guilty parties were called "accessories," and to distinguish among these with reference to time and place they were divided into three classes: (1) accessories before the fact, (2) accessories at the fact,[2] and (3) accessories after the fact. At a relatively early time the party who was originally considered an accessory at the fact ceased to be classed in the accessorial group and was labeled a principal. To distinguish him from the actual perpetrator of the crime he was called a principal in the second degree.[3] Thereafter, in felony cases there were two kinds of principals, first degree and second degree, and two kinds of accessories, before the fact and after the fact.

As applied to homicide cases, the common law of parties was summarized in this form by the Supreme Court of North Carolina:

"The parties to a homicide are: (1) principals in the first degree, being those whose unlawful acts or omissions cause the death of the victim, without the intervention of any responsible agent; (2) principals in the second degree, being those who are actually or constructively present at the scene of the crime, aiding and abetting therein, but not directly causing the death; (3) accessories before the fact, being those who have conspired with the actual perpetrator to commit the homicide, or some other unlawful act that would naturally result in a homicide, or who have procured, instigated, encouraged, or advised him to commit it, but who were neither actually nor constructively present when it was committed; and (4) accessories after the fact, being those who, after the commission of the homicide, knowingly aid the escape of a party thereto."[4]

Since accessories are recognized only in felony cases, one who occupies a certain relation to a crime may be either an accessory or a principal depending upon whether the offense is a felony or not. In fact, as will be pointed out presently, one may occupy such a position that he is (1) a principal if the offense is treason, (2) an accessory after the fact if the offense is a felony, or (3) neither if the offense is a misdemeanor. To describe parties occupying various positions in relation to the crime, there should be appropriate words

1. "Etymologically the noun is primarily *accessary* and the adjective *accessory*; but present usage favors *accessory* for both." Webster's New Int. Dictionary (2d ed.1948).

2. 1 Hale P.C. *437; 2 Stephen, History of the Criminal Law of England 230 (1883); Matters of the Crown Happening at Salop, 1 Plo. 97, 99 n., 75 Eng.Rep. 152, 157 (1553); United States v. Hartwell, 26 Fed.Cas. 196, No. 15,318 (C.C. Mass.1869); State v. Scott, 80 Conn. 317, 323, 68 A. 258 (1907). At one time Colorado had a unique statute providing for "accessory during the fact." See C.R.S. (Colo.) 1964 § 40-1-12 since repealed. This is quite different from the ancient "accessory at the fact." Martinez v. People, 166 Colo. 524, 444 P.2d 641 (1968). And see, Vigil v. People, 174 Colo. 164, 482 P.2d 983 (1971).

3. Ibid.

4. State v. Powell, 168 N.C. 134, 138, 83 S.E. 310, 313 (1914).

which would be the same no matter what the crime may be. Both "principal" and "accessory" are unavailable for this purpose and hence other terms must be employed.

The starting point in a classification of parties in the field of criminal law is the distinction between innocent and culpable[5] parties. One who has caused, or has aided in causing, a socially harmful occurrence, or has interfered with the course of justice after such occurrence may, under certain circumstances, be excused by the law, for the part he has played. The most common excuse recognized by the law is the innocent mistake of fact, a mistake of fact based upon reasonable grounds, of such a nature that what was done would not have been socially harmful (or if so would have been privileged) had the facts been as they were bona fide believed to be. The classic example is the fatal act of a daughter in placing in her father's beverage a powder she believed to be a beneficial medicine, but which was in fact a deadly poison.[6] Excuses are also recognized where the socially-harmful occurrence is caused by one too young or too insane to have criminal capacity.[7] Other excuses might be mentioned, such as acts done under necessity[8] or compulsion, although they have rather limited application.[9] If the only person connected with a socially-harmful occurrence is an innocent party, or if there are several parties all within this group, no crime has been committed. On the other hand, if a culpable party makes use of an innocent agent in the perpetration of his criminal plan, it is the same, in the words of East, as if he had used "merely an instrument."[10]

Culpable parties are of four different kinds, who may be called respectively: (1) perpetrators, (2) abettors, (3) inciters, and (4) criminal protectors. A "perpetrator," as here used, is one who, with mens rea,[11] has caused a

5. The word "culpable" is used here rather than "guilty," because, although the two are nearly synonymous, it is believed the person who assists a misdemeanant to avoid arrest or conviction, may be classed as a "culpable" party, although such conduct does not render him *guilty* of the misdemeanor.

6. Memo. Kel.J. 53, 84 Eng.Rep. 1079 (1708).

7. See, e.g., Regina v. Tyler, 8 Car. & P. 616, 173 Eng.Rep. 643 (1838); Johnson v. State, 192 Ala. 70, 38 So. 182 (1905).

8. Necessity, as an excuse in the homicide cases, finds its chief recognition in the law of self-defense, and one cannot be convicted of abetting a homicide if the perpetrator was excused or justified in the killing. Harper v. State, 83 Miss. 402, 35 So. 572 (1904); Patton v. State, 62 Tex.Cr.R. 71, 136 S.W. 459 (1911). See also Hurd v. Commonwealth, 257 Ky. 315, 78 S.W.2d 9 (1935). Some jurisdictions and the Model Penal Code have recognized a form of defense of necessity based upon a concept of choice of a lesser evil. M.P.C. § 3.02.

9. The common law does not recognize any compulsion as sufficient to excuse the intentional killing of an innocent person. Brewer v. State, 72 Ark. 145, 78 S.W. 773 (1904). But one who is compelled under threat of death to go with wrongdoers, and who did not himself cause the loss of life, may have an excuse for a homicide caused by one of the group. See Rizzolo v. Commonwealth, 126 Pa. 54, 72, 17 A. 520, 521 (1889).

The House of Lords has recently ruled that the defense of compulsion or duress is available to a principal in the second degree to homicide although not necessarily to a principal in the first degree. Lynch v. D. P. P. [1975] 1 All E.R. 913 (H.L.). Accord Regina v. Paquette, 30 CCC 2d 417 (S.C.Can.1976).

10. 1 East P.C. *228. Where a crime is accomplished through the instrumentality of an innocent agent, the one who induced the act is a principal even though not present when the act was committed. Aldrich v. People, 224 Ill. 622, 627, 79 N.E. 964, 966 (1907).

11. That is, one who has acted with malice aforethought or with criminal negligence in a homicide case, with *animus furandi* in a larceny case, with intent to commit a felony in a burglary case or, in

socially-harmful occurrence either with his own hands, or by means of some tool or instrument or other non-human agency, or by means of an innocent agent. Nothing novel is involved in this suggestion, because the word has been employed with this meaning at least since the time of Blackstone.[12]

An "abettor," as here used, is one who is present, either actually or constructively, and who, with mens rea,[13] either assists the perpetrator in the commission of the crime, stands by with intent (known to the perpetrator)[14] to render aid if needed, or commands, counsels or otherwise encourages[15] the perpetrator to commit the crime. The limitation of the word "abettor" to one who was present at the time, either actually or constructively, is the preferred usage,[16] although the term has occasionally been employed to apply to a guilty party who was not present.[17] Rather than labor the point let it merely be said that this meaning is arbitrarily assigned to the word for the purpose of the present discussion. The term "aider and abettor" is more common and has been said to be necessary to express the idea,[18] although the very court making this suggestion has at other times used the word "abettor" alone.[19] The phrases "aid and abet" and "aider and abettor" seem unnecessarily verbose. To "aid" is to render assistance and hence one might

other words, with whatever kind of mind at fault is required in order that the particular socially-harmful occurrence may be classified as a crime.

12. 4 Bl.Comm. *34. See also Smith v. State, 37 Ark. 274, 276 (1881); In re Vann, 136 Fla. 113, 118, 186 So. 424, 426 (1939). One court has spoken of an offender who commits his offense by the aid of an innocent agent as "not the actual perpetrator." People v. Whitmer, 369 Ill. 317, 320, 16 N.E.2d 757, 759 (1938). But if emphasis is placed on the crime rather than the mere physical occurrence it seems proper to say that one who has contrived to bring about the prohibited result by the employment of innocent hands, has perpetrated his offense in this manner.

13. ". . . the word 'abet' includes the elements of knowledge of the wrongful purpose of the perpetrator and counsel and encouragement in the illegal act." Anderson v. Board of Medical Examiners, 117 Cal.App. 113, 114, 3 P.2d 344, 346 (1931); cf. State v. Ankrom, 86 W.Va. 570, 574, 103 S.E. 925, 927 (1920).

"To be guilty of the crime of 'aiding and abetting' one does not have to have an active stake in the outcome of the crime but merely participate therein." Wyatt v. United States, 388 F.2d 395, 400 (10th Cir. 1968). D's brother sold nontax-paid liquor and D helped the brother carry the liquor and place it in the purchaser's car.

To " 'abet' a person in the perpetration of a crime, one must aid or assist the perpetrator with the requisite mental state,

i.e., with knowledge of his wrongful purpose." People v. Ott, 84 Cal.App.3d 118, 148 Cal.Rptr. 479, 486 (1978).

14. State v. Tally, 102 Ala. 25, 15 So. 722 (1893).

The driver of a "getaway car" is equally chargeable as a principal with the one actually entering the bank in a prosecution for participating in the offense of entering a federally-insured savings and loan building with intent to commit larceny. Pinkney v. United States, 380 F.2d 882 (5th Cir. 1967).

15. "The plain meaning of 'abet' includes 'encourage.' " Hence one is himself guilty of the larceny which he encouraged another to commit. Alonzi v. People, 198 Colo. 160, 597 P.2d 560, 564 (1979).

16. "An abettor is one who is actually or constructively present at the commission of the deed and contributes to it by moral or physical force." Webster's New Inter. Dictionary (2d ed. 1950). See also 4 Bl.Comm. *34–36; Shelton v. Commonwealth, 261 Ky. 18, 24, 86 S.W.2d 1054, 1057 (1935); State v. Epps, 213 N.C. 709, 713, 197 S.E. 580, 583 (1938).

17. Robertson v. State, 23 Ala.App. 267, 125 So. 60 (1929); State v. Powell, 168 N.C. 134, 141, 83 S.E. 310, 313 (1914). Statutes have sometimes resorted to this usage. See, e.g., 21 Okl.St.Ann. § 172 (1958).

18. State v. Powell, 168 N.C. 134, 141, 83 S.E. 310, 314 (1914).

19. See State v. Baldwin, 193 N.C. 566, 567, 137 S.E. 590, 591 (1927).

innocently aid a perpetrator, without knowledge of his wrongful purpose.[20] The word "abet" includes either the element of aid, or that of commanding, counseling or encouraging the crime without actual assistance plus, in either case, the additional element of mens rea.[21] For this reason an instruction to convict the defendant if he aided *or* abetted any other person to commit the crime has been held reversible error.[22] In other words, one who is present (actually or constructively) may aid without abetting, where he acts innocently, or abet without aiding, as by merely encouraging the perpetrator. Furthermore, any aid given with mens rea is abetment; hence to add the word "aid" to the word "abet" is not necessary and is sometimes misleading.

An "inciter," as the word is here used, is one who, with mens rea, aids, counsels, commands, procures or encourages another to commit a crime, or, with mens rea, supplies him with the weapons, tools or information needed for his criminal purpose, the one not being present either actually or constructively at the moment of perpetration. The word has been so used at times by the courts.[23] If deemed necessary some such phrase as "absent inciter" might be employed. The need is for a term to express the position of a culpable party, not present either actually or constructively at the time of perpetration, whose guilt relates to the commission of the crime itself rather than to assistance rendered the offender afterwards. "Inciter" or even "absent inciter" will be more convenient than to refer to a misdemeanant as a "principal who would be an accessory before the fact if the crime had been a felony," or to refer to a felon under some of our statutes as a "principal who would have been an accessory before the fact at common law." [24]

There is also need of a term to designate a person who was in no way tainted with guilt of a crime when perpetrated but who, with full knowledge of the facts, thereafter conceals the offender or gives him some other assistance to save him from detection, arrest, trial or punishment. Under some of the statutes abolishing the distinction between the accessory before the fact and the principal, the word "accessory" has been employed for this purpose.[25] This may be the ultimate solution, but any general attempt to use the word in this sense at the present time will cause confusion. The same is true of the phrase "accessory after the fact," since the common law limited this to the felony cases. Since no other term seems to have been employed

---

20. Anderson v. Board of Medical Examiners, 117 Cal.App. 113, 3 P.2d 344, 346 (1931); People v. Etie, 119 Cal.App. 2d 23, 258 P.2d 1069 (1953).

21. Ibid.

"To be an 'aider,' a person must assist, support or supplement the efforts of another; to be an 'abettor,' a person must instigate, advise or encourage the commission of a crime and may in some circumstances include a person who is present at the commission of the crime without giving active assistance." Foster v. State, 11 Md.App. 40, 272 A.2d 810, 813 (1971).

22. People v. Dole, 122 Cal. 486, 55 P. 581 (1898); State v. Corcoran, 7 Idaho 220, 61 P. 1034 (1900); State v. Allen, 34 Mont. 403, 87 P. 177 (1906).

23. See, e.g., Griffith v. State, 90 Ala. 583, 588, 8 So. 812, 814 (1891); State v. Redden, 181 Neb. 423, 149 N.W.2d 98, 101 (1967).

24. "Instructions as to when accessories are principals reviewed, and held correct." (Syllabus). State v. Slycord, 210 Iowa 1209 (1930).

25. Drury v. Territory, 9 Okl. 398, 404, 60 P. 101, 103 (1900); Parrish v. State, 134 Tex.Cr.R. 187, 190, 114 S.W.2d 559, 560 (1938). See also Idaho Code § 18–205 (1979); Nev.Rev.Stat. 195.030 (1979); West's Ann.Cal.Pen.Code §§ 31, 32 (1970).

for this purpose, "criminal protector" is arbitrarily adopted for the present discussion.

Using the terms "perpetrator," "abettor," "inciter" and "criminal protector" with the meanings thus arbitrarily assigned, the common-law classification of principals and accessories may be expressed in this form:

(1) In treason, perpetrators, abettors, inciters and criminal protectors are all principals [26] "because of the heinousness of the crime",[27] and different degrees of principals are seldom even mentioned.

(2) In felony:

    (a) Perpetrators are principals in the first degree; [28]

    (b) Abettors are principals in the second degree; [29]

    (c) Inciters are accessories before the fact; [30] and

    (d) Criminal protectors are accessories after the fact.[31]

(3) In misdemeanors:

    (a) Perpetrators, abettors and inciters are all principals,[32] because the law "does not descend to distinguish the different shades of guilt in petty misdemeanors." [33]

    (b) Criminal protectors are not punishable as such.[34]

Stated in terms of the common law itself, those who would be accessories, either before or after the fact, in a felony case, are principals if the offense is treason; [35] whereas if the offense is only a misdemeanor, those who would be accessories before the fact, in a felony case, are principals,[36] while those who would be accessories after the fact are not regarded as parties to the misdemeanor, in any capacity.[37]

26. 4 Bl.Comm. *35. "It is to be known, that a fact which would make one *accessary* in *felony*, in treason . . . makes him a principal. . . . In treason all are principals; . . . ." Regina v. Tracy, 6 Mod. 30, 32, 87 Eng.Rep. 795, 796 (1703).

27. 4 Bl.Comm. *35.

28. "A principal in the first degree is he that is the actor or absolute perpetrator of the crime; . . ." 4 Bl.Comm. *34.

29. Neumann v. State, 116 Fla. 98, 156 So. 237 (1934); State v. Coleman, 126 Fla. 203, 170 So. 722 (1936); Shelton v. Commonwealth, 261 Ky. 18, 86 S.W.2d 1054 (1935).

30. 1 Hale P.C. *615; 4 Bl.Comm. *37; Griffith v. State, 90 Ala. 583, 8 So. 812 (1891); Neumann v. State, 116 Fla. 98, 156 So. 237 (1934); Shelton v. Commonwealth, 261 Ky. 18, 86 S.W.2d 1054 (1935).

31. 1 Hale P.C. *618; 4 Bl.Comm. *37–8; Skelly v. United States, 76 F.2d 483 (10th Cir. 1935), cert. denied 295 U.S.

757, 55 S.Ct. 914 (1935); Howard v. People, 97 Colo. 550, 51 P.2d 594 (1935).

32. 1 Hale P.C. *613; 4 Bl.Comm. *36; Regina v. Tracy, 6 Mod. 30, 32, 87 Eng. Rep. 795 (1703); Commonwealth v. Jaffas, 284 Mass. 417, 419, 188 N.E. 263, 264 (1933).

33. 4 Bl.Comm. *36.

34. 1 Hale P.C. *613; Sturgis v. State, 2 Okl.Cr. 362, 102 P. 57 (1909). Some statutes have provided a penalty for the criminal protector of a misdemeanant. 1 Hale P.C. *613.

35. 4 Bl.Comm. *35.

36. 1 Hale P.C. *613; 4 Bl.Comm. *36; Regina v. Tracy, 6 Mod. 30, 32, 87 Eng. Rep. 795 (1703); Cole v. State, 27 Ala. App. 90, 166 So. 58 (1936); Commonwealth v. Jaffas, 284 Mass. 417, 419, 188 N.E. 263, 264 (1934); State v. Garzio, 113 N.J.L. 349, 353, 175 A. 98, 100 (1934), aff'd 116 N.J.L. 189, 183 A. 166 (1936).

37. 1 Hale P.C. *613; Sturgis v. State, 2 Okl.Cr. 362, 102 P. 57 (1909). Under statute a penalty may be provided for the accessory after the fact to a misdemean-

There is some authority for using the word "accomplice" to include all principals and all accessories,[38] but the preferred usage is to include all principals and accessories before the fact, but to exclude accessories after the fact.[39] If this limitation is adopted, the word "accomplice" will embrace all perpetrators, abettors and inciters. It will also include criminal protectors if the offense is treason but will not do so if it is a felony or a misdemeanor.

B.   THE COMMON–LAW THEORY OF PARTIES

The concept of complicity had its development in the common law of parties particularly in felony cases because the early courts and writers were chiefly interested in offenses of that grade. Originally, as mentioned above, only the perpetrator of a felony was called a principal.[40] At that time there were three categories of accessories: (1) before the fact, (2) at the fact,[41] and (3) after the fact. Quite early the accessory at the fact ceased to be classed in the accessorial group and was recognized as a principal in the second degree.[42] Thereafter in felony cases there were two classes of principals— first degree and second degree, and two of accessories—before the fact and after the fact.[43]

In the very early days some seem to have had in mind the possibility of one felony with four guilty parties who were respectively (1) principal in the first degree, (2) principal in the second degree, (3) accessory before the fact and (4) accessory after the fact. They assumed that the accessory after the fact was guilty of the original felony. His assistance to the known felon was thought of as relating back to that crime and tainting him with guilt of that

or. United States v. Venturini, 1 F.Supp. 213 (D.C.Ala.1931).

38. Parrish v. State, 134 Tex.Cr.R. 187, 114 S.W.2d 559 (1938). And see State v. Powell, 168 N.C. 134, 141, 83 S.E. 310, 314 (1914).

39. Velasquez v. People, 162 Colo. 266, 425 P.2d 708 (1967). "The word [accomplice] includes in its meaning all persons who participate in the commission of a crime, whether they so participate as principals, aiders, and abettors, or accessories before the fact. . . . But . . . an accessory after the fact is not an accomplice. . . ." Levering v. Commonwealth, 132 Ky. 666, 677, 679, 117 S.W. 253, 257 (1909); accord, People v. Sweeney, 213 N.Y. 37, 46, 106 N.E. 913, 917 (1914). An accessory after the fact is not an accomplice of the principal and the principal may be convicted on the uncorroborated evidence of such a one. State v. Umble, 115 Mo. 452, 22 S.W. 378 (1893); People v. Chadwick, 7 Utah 134, 25 P. 737 (1891). Both aiders and abettors and accessories before the fact are generally described as "confederates." United States v. Moses, 220 F.2d 166 (3d Cir. 1955).

The accessory after the fact was not an accomplice of the principal offender.

Fajeriak v. State, 439 P.2d 783 (Alaska, 1968). State v. Murphy, 94 Idaho 849, 499 P.2d 548 (1972).

" 'Accomplice' is one who participates in a crime in such a way that he could be charged and tried for the same offense." State v. Comish, 560 P.2d 1134, 1136 (Utah 1977).

40. Anciently those who "were present aiding and assisting, were but in the nature of accessories . . . ." 1 Hale, P.C. *437.

41. Ibid. For a unique statute providing for an "accessory during the fact," see Colo.Rev.Stat.Ann. sec. 40–1–12 (1963) since repealed, discussed in Martinez v. People, 166 Colo. 524, 527, 444 P.2d 641, 643 (1968).

42. "But at this day, and long since, the law hath been taken otherwise, and namely, that all that are present, aiding and assisting, are equally principal with him that gave the stroke, . . . and tho they are called principals, in the second degree, yet they are principals . . . ." 1 Hale, P.C. *437.

43. "In case of felony there are principals and accessories, and accessories be of two sorts, either before the offense be committed, or after." 3 Co.Inst. *138.

very offense.[44] The law making the accessory after the fact to a felony guilty of felony is analogous to the rule of the English common law by which, if an officer voluntarily permitted his prisoner to escape, "this is felony in case the person be imprisoned for felony, and treason in case the person be imprisoned for treason." [45] But in case of either the accessory after the fact or the officer voluntarily permitting his prisoner to escape, the proper explanation is that he is guilty of *a* felony, not *the* original felony.

While the crime of the accessory after the fact made use of the name of the felony committed by the principal, such for example, as "guilty of murder as accessory after the fact," and at one time carried the same penalty, it was committed at a different time and was clearly a distinct offense. As said in an early case the accessory after the fact was not guilty of the original felony but had "a different species of guilt." [46] And this has frequently been emphasized.[47] Thus in California where "accessory" means accessory after the fact, since one who would have been an accessory before the fact has been made a principal by statute,[48] it was said: "It should be pointed out that one who is an accessory to a felony thereby commits a crime which is separate and distinct from the felony itself." [49]

The idea of guilt by relation back, or ratification, is not a criminal-law doctrine.[50] As has been said: "In the law of contracts a posterior recognition, in many cases, is equivalent to a precedent command; but it is not so in respect of crimes." [51] It may be helpful to mention other situations in which misconduct subsequent to a crime may be punished because of that crime, but clearly recognized as a separate offense. Perhaps misprision of felony should be mentioned in this connection. A "misprisor" is said to be one who knows of the commission of a felony and does not report it to the proper

---

44. Note Blackstone's use of the phrase "ex post facto." 4 Bl.Comm. *37. Not merely after the fact but "by an after fact." "In felony—not only the principal in the first or second degree is a felon, but so also are the accessories both before and after." 1 Bishop, New Criminal Law, sec. 605 (8th ed.1892).

45. 1 Hale, P.C. *590.

46. 4 Bl.Comm. *40. See also Hale, P.C. *625–26.

"Thus, the crime of accessory after the fact is a separate and distinct crime, standing on its own particular elements." State v. Truesdell, 620 P.2d 427, 428 (Okl. Cr.App.1980).

47. In Bollebbach v. United States, 326 U.S. 607, 611, 66 S.Ct. 402, 404 (1946), the Court clearly indicates that accessories after the fact are not guilty of the original felony. See also State v. Townsend, 201 Kan. 122, 439 P.2d 70 (1968); Box v. State, 241 So.2d 158 (Miss. 1970).

48. The legislature has abrogated the distinction between principals and accessories before the fact. People v. Ah Gee, 37 Cal.App. 1, 174 P. 371 (1918).

49. People v. Mitten, 37 Cal.App.3d 897, 883, 112 Cal.Rptr. 713, 715 (1974). The offense of robbery and the offense of being accessory after the fact to robbery are mutually exclusive. People v. Prado, 67 Cal.App.3d 267, 136 Cal.Rptr. 521 (1977).

There was no failure of the proof to conform to the charge in a statutory rape case where the information alleged that the defendant "did remove the clothing of the minor" and the proof showed that the minor removed her own clothes, since the "removal was accomplished through the instigation and acts of" defendant. Commonwealth v. Nabried, 264 Pa.Super. 419, 399 A.2d 1121, 1122, 1123 (1979).

50. "If a man ratifies a thing done without his authority, this makes the act binding upon him, but his subsequent assent will not relate back and make that a crime (by him) which was not (such) an offense when the act was done." Cook v. Commonwealth, 141 Ky. 439, 440, 132 S.W. 1032 (1911).

51. Morse v. State, 6 Conn. 9, 13 (1825).

authorities.[52] He was never regarded as a *party* to the original crime but anciently, in theory at least, misprision of felony was punished as a misdemeanor.[53] If this ever had more than very limited application it must have been in the very early days. At one time it was supposed to have become obsolete in England,[54] but it has recently been recognized there in extreme situations.[55] It never was accorded general recognition in this country.[56]

A "compounder" is one who knows of a crime by another and agrees, for some reward received or promised, not to prosecute.[57] There are indications of an ancient notion that the compounder of a felony was a *party* to the felony [58] but it came to be clearly recognized that his guilt was not that of the original felony but of a misdemeanor known as "compounding a felony."[59] Compounding a felony is generally a crime, either felony or misdemeanor,[60] and by some enactments the compounding of any offense is punishable unless a compromise is expressly authorized by law,[61] which is not uncommon as to certain misdemeanors.[62]

In the absence of some unusual statutory extension,[63] one must be more than a misprisor or a compounder to be recognized as a "criminal protector" as the term is here used. It is not enough that he merely keeps silent and fails to prosecute, either with or without a reward. To be a "criminal protector" he must, with guilty knowledge of the offense, "receive, relieve, comfort or assist" [64] the offender in order to hinder his "detection, apprehension, trial or punishment." [65]

Although the accessory after the fact was held to be guilty of a separate offense, the holding of the common law was that the principal in the first degree, the principal in the second degree and the accessory before the fact are all guilty of the same felony.[66] This merely gives recognition to the legal theory that one is considered to have done what he has caused to be

52. 1 Hale, P.C. *618.

53. Ibid.; 4 Bl.Comm. *121.

54. Glazebrook, Misprision of Felony—Shadow or Phantom, 8 Am.J. of Legal Hist. 283, 299–300 (1964).

55. See supra, ch. 5, sec. 3, I.

56. Ibid.

57. 4 Bl.Comm. *133–34.

58. 1 Hawk.P.C. ch. 59, sec. 6.

59. 4 Bl.Comm. *133–34.

60. E.g., West's Fla.Stat.Ann. § 843.14 (1976).

61. E.g. Id.

62. E.g., Utah Code Ann., 1953, 77–35–25(e).

63. E.g., Colo.Stats.Ann. sec. 40–1–12 (1964) now repealed.

64. 4 Bl.Comm. *37; Wren v. Commonwealth, 67 Va. (26 Grat.) 952, 955 (1875). Misprision of felony does not make the misprisor an accessory after the fact. State v. Doty, 57 Kan. 835, 48

P. 145 (1897); Hightower v. State, 78 Tex.Cr.R. 606, 182 S.W. 492 (1916). This is true even under a statute which punishes all persons who know of the commission of a felony and "conceal it" from the magistrate because "conceal" means more than mere nondisclosure. People v. Garnett, 129 Cal. 364, 61 P. 1114 (1900); State v. Brown, 197 Neb. 131, 247 N.W.2d 616 (1976).

65. Skelly v. United States, 76 F.2d 483, 487 (10th Cir. 1935), cert. denied 295 U.S. 757, 55 S.Ct. 914 (1935); United States v. Rux, 412 F.2d 331 (9th Cir. 1969).

66. "Accessories before the fact, principals in the second degree, and principals in the first degree in any felony, are each considered as having committed that felony." Stephen, A Digest of the Criminal Law, 21 (9th ed. by Sturge, 1950). The offense of felony as principal and as accessory before the fact "is in substance the same offense." 1 Hale P.C. *626; 2 Hale P.C. *244.

done.[67] As stated in the early law: One who has commanded or counseled a murder has committed no felony "until there has been a murder; but when the murder is committed he is guilty of it," [68] and as explained in detail by the Tennessee court:

> The offense is compounded of the connivance of the accessory and the actual killing by the principal felon, and the crime of the accessory, though inchoate in the act of counseling, hiring, or commanding, is not consummate until the deed is actually done. The law, in such a case, holds the accessory before the fact to be guilty of the murder itself, not as principal, it is true, but as accessory before the fact, for it is the doing of the deed, and not the counseling, hiring, or commanding that makes the crime complete; and it is for the murder that he is indicted, and not for the counseling and procuring.[69]

There were, however, important differences in procedure. As will be explained presently,[70] one charged as a principal could not be convicted by proof showing him to be an accessory; and one charged as an accessory could not be convicted by proof that he committed the offense as a principal. At a time when all felonies were punishable by death, and Parliament had added a multitude of offenses—some far short of heinous—to the felony group, this rule as to accessories was one of the devices developed by the judges to restrict excessive executions.[71] It was similar to the presumption, at a time when a clergyman could not be given the death sentence, that any man who could read must be a member of the clergy. But some did not understand what was back of the rule, and seemed to assume that since one charged as a principal could not be convicted by proof showing him to have been an accessory, and vice versa, this meant they were really different offenses. A different emphasis is observable even in the statement of the position. Hale would speak of "an accessory to murder before the fact," [72] whereas at the present time the statement may be in some such form as "an accessory before the fact to the crime of murder." [73] And some courts lost sight of the original concept entirely. Thus it has been said: "In murder, the felony of the accessory is not the act of a principal; and the felony of the principal is not the act of an accessory. In fact, they are different acts, done at different times and places: in law, they are different crimes." [74]

This was assumed by some to be a necessary result because, in every case of divergence, the accessory was tried in the county in which his act of

---

67. "It is a fundamental principal of law that he who procures a felony to be committed is himself a felony, though the criminal act done is by the intervention of a third person." Lee v. Tucker, 160 Fla. 962, 37 So.2d 582 (Fla.1948). In legal theory one has done what he has caused another to do. United States v. Ruffin, 613 F.2d 408 (2d Cir. 1979); Commonwealth v. Nabried, 264 Pa.Super. 419, 399 A.2d 1121 (1979).

68. 2 Pollock and Maitland, The History of English Law, 509 (2d ed.1899).

69. State v. Ayers, 67 Tenn. (8 Baxt.) 96, 100 (1874).

70. Infra, subsection D, 1, b.

71. Note that the judge-developed law of accessories applied only to felonies. There were no accessories to treason (all were principals) because the judges in that day were satisfied with the death penalty for treason; and there were no accessories in misdemeanor cases because there was no death sentence for a misdemeanor.

72. 1 Hale P.C. *435.

73. Feaster v. State, 175 Ark. 165, 166, 299 S.W. 737 (1927).

74. Commonwealth v. DiStasio, 297 Mass. 347, 357, 8 N.E.2d 923, 939 (1937); State v. Buzzell, 58 N.H. 257, 258 (1878).

accessoryship occurred, rather than in the county in which the felony was committed. But this was due to a statute and not to common-law theory. Before additional authority was granted by Parliament, grand jurors could inquire only into happenings in the county for which they were sworn, and not into any act done outside of that county. "And to so high a nicety was this matter antiently carried, that where a man was wounded in one county, and died in another, the offender was at common law indictable in neither, because no complete act of felony was done in any of them . . . ."[75] For the same reason, if the act of accessoryship occurred in one county and the target felony was committed in another, the ancient law did not permit indictment of the accessory, because in one county the grand jurors could know of the act on incitement but not that it had any felonious consequence; whereas the grand jurors of the other county could know of the felony but not the participation of the accessory.[76] It was to avoid this impasse that Parliament enacted a statute giving the county wherein the accessory had acted jurisdiction "as if the felony had been committed in the same county."[77] If there was any reason for placing venue in the county in which the incitement occurred, rather than in the other county, the reason is not known. Where the accessory before the fact is still recognized the trend is to place venue in the county in which the felony was committed.[78]

Another factor tending to cause confusion at this point is the possibility of convicting one person of murder and another of manslaughter, based upon the same killing.[79] This also was the result of legislation. In the English common law there was but one crime of felonious homicide (if petit treason is ignored). The division of this into murder and manslaughter resulted from early statutes intended to exclude the more heinous types of homicide from benefit of clergy.[80] In its origin this was merely a difference in penalty depending on the presence or absence of aggravating circumstances, and no doubt it would have been worded in terms of "degrees" of the crime if that concept had been in use at the time. For some purposes murder and manslaughter have come to be regarded as distinct offenses, but the common law never entirely lost sight of the notion that the crime is felonious homicide, of which murder and manslaughter are but different grades.[81] This is clearly the view taken with reference to the common law of parties.

75. 4 Bl.Comm. *303.

76. "If a man were accessory before or after in another county, at common law it was dispunishable . . . ." 1 Hale, P.C. *623.

77. But "now by the statute of 2 & 3 E. 6, cap. 24 the accessory is indictable in that county, where he was accessory, as if the felony had been committed in the same county . . . ." 1 Hale P.C. *623. The "accessory before the fact may be tried where the accessorial act took place and only there." Goldsmith v. Cheney, 468 P.2d 813, 816 (Wyo.1970).

78. See Mass.Gen.Laws Ann. ch. 274, sec. 3 (Supp.1974–75).

79. 1 Hale P.C. *438; 1 East P.C. 350 (1803). Several persons may be guilty of different degrees of the same homicide.

Red v. State, 39 Tex.Cr.R. 667, 47 S.W. 1003 (1898). One may abet in the heat of passion what another perpetrates with malice aforethought. State v. Phillips, 118 Iowa 660, 92 N.W. 876 (1902); Mickey v. Commonwealth, 72 Ky. (9 Bush.) 593 (1873). On the other hand one may with malice aforethought encourage another to kill which the other does in the sudden heat of passion. Parker v. Commonwealth, 180 Ky. 102, 201 S.W. 475 (1918). See also State v. McAllister, 366 So.2d 1340 (La.1978).

80. 12 Hen.VII, ch. 7 (1496); 4 Hen. VIII, ch. 2 (1512); 23 Hen.VIII, ch. 1 secs. 3, 4 (1531); 1 Edw.VI, ch. 12, sec. 10 (1547).

81. "Upon an indictment of murder, tho the party upon his trial be acquit of

The dispute as to whether the offense of the accessory before the fact is, or is not, the same as the offense of the principal led one court to conclude that the offense of the accessory to murder before the fact was something other than "murder" and hence not within a clause of the statute of limitations which excluded murder from its protection; [82] while another court ruling on the same point held that the accessory's offense was "murder" and so not protected by the general provisions of the statute.[83]

Under some of the modern statutes it may be necessary to speak of the accessory before the fact as guilty of a separate and "substantive" offense; but this is an undesirable fiction because his offense is separate and "substantive" only to the extent that certain procedural difficulties of the common law have been abrogated,[84] a result equally obtainable by more direct legislative language.[85]

Emphasis upon the theory of one offense with guilt attaching to several is quite appropriate because it is still part of the groundwork of our legal philosophy, so far as perpetrators, abettors and inciters are concerned, despite the fact that some of the statutes require lipservice to the notion of a separate substantive offense, in the effort to avoid certain procedural difficulties.[86] It explains how one may be guilty of a crime he could not perpetrate, by having caused or procured it as a result of his abetment or incite-

---

the murder, and convict of manslaughter, he shall receive judgment, as if the indictment had been of manslaughter, for the offense in substance is the same." 1 Hale P.C. *438. In a charge of first-degree murder, the crimes of second-degree murder, voluntary manslaughter and involuntary manslaughter are considered to be lesser grades of the crime charged. State v. Seelke, 221 Kan. 672, 561 P.2d 869 (1977).

82. The accessory's crime is not murder and hence prosecution is barred by the statute of limitations. State v. Patriarca, 71 R.I. 151, 43 A.2d 54 (1945).

83. The accessory's crime is murder and hence not barred by the statute. People v. Mather, 4 Wend. 229 (N.Y.S.Ct. 1830).

84. Karakutza v. State, 163 Wis. 293, 298, 156 N.W. 965, 967 (1916). Although the proof established that D, who was charged with robbery, aided and abetted another who committed the robbery, there was no fatal variance and the conviction of robbery was proper. McWilliams v. State, 87 Nev. 302, 486 P.2d 481 (1971). The federal statute does not make aiding and abetting a crime. It makes punishable as a principal one who aids and abets another in the commission of crime. And one indicted as a principal may be convicted on proof that he aided and abetted another in the commission

thereof. United States v. Megna, 450 F.2d 511 (5th Cir. 1971).

85. Compare M.G.L.A. ch. 74, sec. 3 (1959) with Iowa Code Ann. § 703.1 (1978) which reads:

"All persons concerned in the commission of a public offense, whether they directly commit the act constituting the offense or aid and abet its commission, shall be charged, tried and punished as principals. The guilt of a person who aids and abets the commission of a crime must be determined upon the facts which show the part he or she had in it, and does not depend upon the degree of another person's guilt."

86. "Every one is a party to an offense who either actually commits the offense or does some act which forms part of the offense, or assists in the actual commission of the offense, or of any act which forms part thereof, or directly or indirectly counsels or procures any person to commit the offense or do any act forming a part thereof." State v. Scott, 80 Conn. 317, 323, 68 A. 258, 260 (1907). As to statutes speaking of the accessory before the fact as guilty of a "substantive" offense, see West's F.S.A. (Fla.) § 776.02.

This has since been repealed. See West's Fla.Stat.Ann. § 777.03 (1976).

ment.[87] Thus while a woman cannot herself perpetrate rape she may be guilty of a rape resulting from her incitement [88] or her abetment; [89] and a man may be guilty of the rape of his own wife although he cannot himself perpetrate such rape.[90] On the same ground a woman may be guilty of assault to commit rape,[91] a single person may be guilty of bigamy,[92] one not related to any other party to the crime may be guilty of incest,[93] one who has given no mortgage may be guilty of unlawful disposal of mortgaged property,[94] and one who holds no federal office may be guilty of false return by a postmaster.[95] The possibility of guilt by one not in a position to do the prohibited deed has been recognized in connection with numerous other offenses, such as embezzlement by a fiduciary,[96] embezzlement by a public officer,[97] fraudulent withholding of funds by a tax collector,[98] misapplication of bank funds,[99] mother's concealment of the birth of a bastard child,[1] unlawful sale of its own securities by a corporation,[2] violation of election

87. Gibbs v. State, 37 Ariz. 273, 293 P. 976 (1930); State v. Nahoum, 172 La. 83, 133 So. 370 (1931).

A person who aids and abets another in violation of the Hobbs Act, 18 U.S.C.A. § 1951, can be convicted of the offense although he does not hold any office. United States v. Grande, 620 F.2d 1026 (4th Cir. 1980).

"A person incapable of committing a specified crime . . . who causes an innocent agent meeting the capacity requirements to engage in the proscribed conduct may be punished as a principal under 18 U.S.C. § 2." United States v. Ruffin, 613 F.2d 408, 409 (2d Cir. 1980).

88. People v. Haywood, 131 Cal.App. 2d 259, 280 P.2d 180 (1955); Rex v. Baltimore, 4 Burr. 2179, 98 Eng.Rep. 136 (1768).

89. Regina v. Ram, 17 Cox C.C. 609 (1893); State v. Burns, 82 Conn. 213, 72 A. 1083 (1909).

A female defendant who aided and abetted her male codefendant, by beating and holding down a female victim while the male had sexual intercourse with the victim, is guilty of rape. People v. Evans, 58 A.D.2d 919, 396 N.Y.S.2d 727 (1977).

90. People v. Chapman, 62 Mich. 280, 28 N.W. 896 (1886); People v. Meli, 193 N.Y.S. 365 (Sup.Ct.1922); State v. Dowell, 106 N.C. 722, 11 S.E. 525 (1890); Bohanon v. State, 289 P.2d 400 (Okl.Cr. 1955); Cody v. State, 361 P.2d 307 (Okl. Cr.1961); People v. Damen, 28 Ill.2d 464, 193 N.E.2d 25 (1963); Anno. 84 ALR2d 1017 (1962); See also Fletcher, Rethinking Criminal Law, pp. 664–667.

And a man who forces his wife to have sex with another man, is guilty of rape.

State v. Kennedy, 616 P.2d 594, 597 (Utah 1980).

91. State v. Jones, 83 N.C. 605 (1880).

92. Boggus v. State, 34 Ga. 275 (1866); State v. Warady, 78 N.J.L. 687, 75 A. 977 (1910). On this basis it has been held that an unmarried man who marries a married woman, knowing her to be married, may be convicted of bigamy even if there is no statute expressly covering such a case. Regina v. Brawn, 1 Car. & K. 144, 174 Eng.Rep. 751 (1843).

93. Cf. Whittaker v. Commonwealth, 95 Ky. 632, 633, 27 S.W. 83, 84 (1894).

94. State v. Elliott, 61 Kan. 518, 59 P. 1047 (1900).

95. United States v. Snyder, 14 F. 554 (C.C.Minn.1882). And see Opper v. United States, 348 U.S. 84, 75 S.Ct. 158 (1954). And one not a public official or employee may be guilty of an offense of acceptance of a bribe by a public official. Bompensiero v. Superior Court, 44 Cal.2d 178, 281 P.2d 250 (1955). One who is not capable of committing a certain crime, may be guilty of that crime by causing it to be committed by another. United States v. Ruffin, 613 F.2d 408 (2d Cir. 1979).

96. Gibbs v. State, 37 Ariz. 273, 293 P. 976 (1930).

97. State v. Rowe, 104 Iowa 323, 73 N.W. 833 (1898); Hutchman v. State, 61 Okl.Cr. 117, 66 P.2d 99 (1937).

98. Quillin v. State, 79 Tex.Cr.R. 497, 187 S.W. 199 (1916).

99. State v. Johnson, 50 S.D. 394, 210 N.W. 353 (1926).

1. State v. Sprague, 4 R.I. 257 (1856).

2. State v. Fraser, 105 Or. 589, 209 P. 467 (1922).

law,[3] and violation of traffic law by one other than the *driver* of a vehicle.[4] It is hardly necessary to add that two acting together may perpetrate a crime to which each contributes an essential part. Where, for example, one beats a victim with a stick while a confederate holds a gun on him to prevent resistance, both offenders may be convicted under a statute providing a special penalty for beating a person while possessing a deadly weapon to prevent him from defending himself.[5]

Three exceptions have been made to the general rule recognizing guilt by incitement or abetment: (1) where the very purpose of the crime is to protect one of the parties to the prohibited transaction, (2) where the purpose is other than this but the legislative body must have contemplated two parties and yet provided a penalty for only one, and (3) where a statute creating an offense limited in its application to persons who qualify in some particular manner, has its own incitement and abetment clause which is also limited in its scope.

(1) If the very purpose of the crime is to protect a type of person thought to be in need of special protection, one within this group is not guilty by reason of having incited or abetted the perpetration by another. Hence a girl under the age of consent cannot be convicted of "statutory rape," even upon proof that she enticed or procured a man to have carnal intercourse with her, because it "cannot be said that an Act . . . the whole object of which is to protect women against men, is to be construed so as to render a girl against whom an offence is committed equally liable with the man by whom the offence is committed." [6]   (2) If a statutory offense involves a transaction between two persons or groups of persons, and provides a penalty only for those engaging in one side of the transaction, those on the other side cannot be convicted as inciters or abettors since their omission from the penal provision evinces a legislative purpose to leave their participation unpunished.[7] Hence a purchaser of intoxicating liquor is not punishable under a statute which merely provides a penalty for the sale thereof.[8]   (3) A stat-

---

3. Bartlett v. State, 27 Ga.App. 7, 107 S.E. 347 (1921).

4. People v. Hoaglin, 262 Mich. 162, 247 N.W. 141 (1933). One charged with unlawful possession of three or more pieces of counterfeit coin (a felony) may be convicted on proof that such coins were in the possession of another with whom he was acting in guilty concert. Regina v. Rogers, 2 Mood. 85, 169 Eng. Rep. 34 (1839). One not an officer who incites or abets an officer to procure a bribe may be convicted of asking or receiving a bribe. Capshaw v. State, 69 Okl.Cr. 440, 104 P.2d 282 (1940).

5. Hardy v. State, 180 Miss. 336, 177 So. 911 (1938).

6. Regina v. Tyrell, 17 Cox C.C. 716, 719 (1893). Some modern statutes have broadened the offense to protect both girls and boys. E.g., § 76–5–401, 1953, Utah Code Ann. (1979 Supp.).

7. Holding that an unmarried person is not guilty of adultery by having sexual intercourse with a married person, even on the theory of aiding and abetting the other, because the manifested intent of the legislature was to apply the penalty only to the married person to such intercourse, the court adds: "Of course, an unmarried person might be guilty as a principal of this offense, under section 31 of the Penal Code, by aiding and assisting in its commission in some other way than by living in a state of illicit intercourse with a married person; . . . ." Ex parte Cooper, 162 Cal. 81, 85, 121 P. 318, 320 (1912).

8. United States v. Farrar, 281 U.S. 624, 50 S.Ct. 425 (1930); Wilson v. State, 130 Ark. 204, 196 S.W. 921 (1917); State v. Teahan, 50 Conn. 92 (1882); Wakeman v. Chambers, 69 Iowa 169, 28 N.W. 498 (1886); State v. Cullins, 53 Kan. 100, 36 P. 56 (1894). A contrary view was expressed in an early Tennessee case. State v. Bonner, 39 Tenn. 135 (1858). But this case was distinguished later in a

ute providing a penalty for certain misconduct by persons who qualify in some particular manner may limit guilt by incitement or abetment to those having the same qualifications by having a special incitement and abetment clause of its own limited in this manner.[9]

C. PRINCIPALS AND ACCESSORIES

Mention has been made of certain advantages to be derived from the use of terms other than "principal" and "accessory" to express the relation of a culpable party to the crime. Additional advantages are to be found as a result of the modern practice of dividing offenses into degrees. It is much less confusing, for example, to speak of a perpetrator of second degree murder, or an abettor of first degree murder, than it is to refer to a principal in the first degree to murder in the second degree, or a principal in the second degree to murder in the first degree.[10] With all of this, however, the suggested terms are merely offered as possible aids to a general consideration of the field and with no thought that the traditional terms can be abruptly abandoned. As will be mentioned presently, modern statutes have not completely removed from all jurisdictions the handicaps developed by the common-law distinction between principals and accessories, and these terms must be retained because of this fact alone. Even if the last trace of such handicaps had entirely disappeared it would still be necessary to speak of "principals" and "accessories" to explain how the present law differs from the old.

It is important to repeat that the common-law distinction between principals and accessories has no application to treason[11] or to misdemeanors,[12] and that this is just as true of offenses created by statute as of those originally recognized by the common law.[13] Nor are the parties to such offenses distinguished as principals in the first degree or in the second degree.[14] It is true that guilt of such crimes may be incurred by incitement or abetment[15] as well as by perpetration, but this has always been merely a matter of evidence and has never been permitted to develop stumbling blocks in the path of the enforcement of justice.[16] In these fields the position of the criminal protector has been equally free from procedural complications. He who aids

case recognizing the exception. Harney v. State, 76 Tenn. 113 (1881).

9. State v. Furth, 82 Wash. 665, 144 P. 907 (1914). This is not a well-considered opinion and it is doubtful if this statute has an abettor clause intended to exclude other abettors; but there is no doubt of the legislative power to include such a restriction by the use of a clause clearly manifesting such an intent.

10. "The indictment charged the defendant with the offense of murder in the first degree as principal in the second degree." McCall v. State, 120 Fla. 707, 708, 163 So. 38, 39 (1935).

11. 1 Hale P.C. *612–3; 4 Bl.Comm. *35–6.

12. Ibid.; Snead v. State, 62 Ga.App. 541, 8 S.E.2d 735 (1940); Kemp v. State, 61 Ga.App. 337, 339, 6 S.E.2d 196, 197–8

(1939); Stone v. State, 133 Tex.Cr.R. 527, 112 S.W.2d 465 (1938).

13. State v. Woodworth, 121 N.J.L. 78, 1 A.2d 254 (1938).

14. Dowdy v. State, 44 Ga.App. 569, 162 S.E. 155 (1932).

15. Commonwealth v. Bitler, 133 Pa. Super. 268, 281, 2 A.2d 493, 498, 499 (1938).

16. Collier v. State, 54 Ga.App. 346, 187 S.E. 843 (1936); State v. Cook, 149 Kan. 481, 87 P.2d 648 (1939). It is proper to charge one with aiding and abetting in the commission of a misdemeanor. People v. Hoaglin, 262 Mich. 162, 247 N.W. 141 (1933). But this is not necessary. Under an indictment charging the defendant with the commission of a misdemeanor his guilt may be established by showing that the offense was committed

a known traitor in the effort to save him from the legal consequences of his crime is guilty of treason as a principal; [17] while he who renders such aid to a misdemeanant does not by so doing become tainted with the guilt of that misdemeanor, and hence is not a party thereto.[18]

All of this was quite different in trials on charges of felony, including felonies created by statute [19] as well as others. The results of the common-law distinction between principals and accessories were of tremendous importance in the realm of procedure; but before speaking of these results it is necessary to consider the distinction itself. Confusion of terms must be carefully avoided. If one employs another to represent him in a legal transaction, the one is a principal and the other is his agent, but if one employs another to commit a felony for him, and the other carries out the unlawful commission with full knowledge of the facts, and in the absence of the first party, the employee (assuming criminal capacity on his part) is the principal and the employer is an accessory before the fact.[20]

1. PRINCIPAL IN THE FIRST DEGREE

The distinction between principals in the first and second degrees is a distinction without a difference [21] except in those rare instances in which some unusual statute has provided a different penalty for one of these than for the other.[22] A principal in the first degree is the immediate perpetrator of the crime while a principal in the second degree is one who did not commit the crime with his own hands but was present and abetting the principal.[23] It may be added, in the words of Mr. Justice Miller, that one may perpetrate a crime, not only with his own hands, but "through the agency of mechanical or chemical means, as by instruments, poison or powder, or by an animal, child, or other innocent agent" acting under his direction.[24]

There may be joint principals in the first degree, as where two or more cause the death of another by beating, stabbing, shooting or other means, in which both, or all, participate. If, however, one holds a victim while a second inflicts a fatal injury with a knife, only the stabber is a principal in the first degree, because the stabbing caused the death and the holding was merely aiding, thus rendering the holder guilty as a principal in the second degree.[25]

by his command or inducement. United States v. Gooding, 25 U.S. 460 (1827).

17. ". . . knowing receivers and comforters of traitors, are all principals." 1 Hale P.C. *613.

18. Ibid.

19. Ibid.; State v. Woodworth, 121 N.J.L. 78, 82–3, 1 A.2d 254, 258 (1938).

20. If "the person employed is guilty, he is the principal, and his employer but an accessory." Wixson v. State, 5 Park. Cr.R. 119, 129 (N.Y.1861).

21. State v. Whitt, 113 N.C. 716, 720, 18 S.E. 715, 716 (1893). Quoted.

22. State v. Woodworth, 121 N.J.L. 78, 83, 1 A.2d 254, 258 (1938). For an illustration of this very rare difference in

penalty see The King v. Sterne, 1 Leach, 473, 168 Eng.Rep. 338 (1787).

23. In re Vann, 136 Fla. 113, 118, 186 So. 424, 426 (1939). Quoted. See also 1 Hale P.C. *615; 4 Bl.Comm. *34.

"Principals in the first degree are those who commit the deed as perpetrating actors, . . ." Agresti v. State, 2 Md.App. 278, 234 A.2d 284 (1967).

24. Beausoliel v. United States, 71 App.D.C. 111, 107 F.2d 292, 297 (1939).

25. "And anciently, he that struck the stroke, whereof the party died was only the principal, and those, that were present, aiding, and assisting, were but in the nature of accessaries. . . ." 1 Hale P.C. *437. These assisters were the

It might be suggested that the principal in the second degree be limited to one whose abetment was in the form of counsel, command or encouragement, and that any principal giving physical aid be said to be of the first degree; but this is unacceptable because it would place in the latter category one who was unable to perpetrate the crime. It would be an obvious confusion of terms to speak of a woman as guilty of rape as a principal in the first degree, although she may be guilty of this crime as a principal in the second degree.[26]

If the crime is the result of two or more essential acts, all guilty parties, who perform any of these acts are joint principals in the first degree, as where one conspirator prints the blank forms to be used in forgery and another fills in the false signatures.[27] This is true, moreover, even if neither is present when the other is performing his part of the criminal plan.[28]

While speaking of presence it may be well to add that the actual perpetrator of a felony is always a principal in the first degree whether he was present at the moment of the culmination of his felonious scheme or not.[29] Perhaps it would be more in keeping with our mode of expression in other situations to say that the actual perpetrator *is* always present, either actually or constructively, at the moment of perpetration.[30] Whether we speak in terms of constructive presence in this connection or not, there is no question with reference to the guilt of the perpetrator, the one who, with mens rea, has caused the socially-harmful occurrence without the assistance of any guilty agent.[31] Typical instances of one who is guilty as a principal in the first degree, although he was not actually present in person at the moment of perpetration, include the perpetrator who left poison so that it was inadvertently taken by the victim while the former was not present;[32] the perpetrator who accomplished the same end by laying a bomb, trap or pitfall,[33] by setting a wild beast upon the other,[34] by shooting from a distance,[35] by sending poison to his victim by the hands of an innocent agent,[36] or by procuring

ancient accessories *at* the fact who later became principals in the second degree.

26. State v. Williams, 32 La.Ann. 335 (1880).

In affirming conviction of defendant as an aider and abettor of an unlawful sale, the court said, "an accused may be convicted as a causer even though not himself legally capable of personally committing the act forbidden by federal statute." United States v. Scannapieco, 611 F.2d 619, 620–21 (5th Cir. 1980).

27. Rex v. Bingley, Russ. & Ry. 446, 168 Eng.Rep. 890 (1821). See also Rex v. Kirkwood, 1 Mood. 304, 168 Eng.Rep. 1281 (1831).

28. Regina v. Kelly, 2 Car. & K. 379, 175 Eng.Rep. 157 (N.P.1847); Alexander v. United States, 95 F.2d 873 (8th Cir. 1938).

29. 1 Hale P.C. *435; 5 Bl.Comm. *35.

30. For example, in determining the issue of jurisdiction, a perpetrator is said to be constructively present at the point of perpetration. State v. Hall, 114 N.C. 909, 19 S.E. 602 (1894).

31. People v. Whitmer, 369 Ill. 317, 16 N.E.2d 757 (1938).

"Principals in the first degree are those who commit the deed as perpetrating actors, either by their own hand or by the hand of an innocent agent." Agresti v. State, 2 Md.App. 278, 234 A.2d 284, 285 (1968).

32. 1 Hale P.C. *435.

33. 4 Bl.Comm. *35. The use of the bomb for this purpose has developed since the time of Blackstone and hence it is not mentioned by him. State v. Rice, 188 Neb. 728, 199 N.W.2d 480 (1972).

34. 4 Bl.Comm. *35.

35. State v. Hall, 114 N.C. 909, 19 S.E. 602 (1894).

36. Regina v. Michael, 2 Mood. 121, 169 Eng.Rep. 48 (1840); Memo., J.Kel. 53, 84 Eng.Rep. 1079 (1708).

a child of tender years,[37] or a madman,[38] to commit the harmful deed. On the other hand, one who employs a *guilty* agent to commit a felony is not a principal in any degree, but is an accessory before the fact,[39] if the crime is committed during his absence. Thus one who procures a boy to steal for him while one is not around is a principal in the first degree if the boy carries away the property as an innocent agent,[40] but is an accessory before the fact if the boy does this act as a guilty party.[41]

2. PRINCIPAL IN THE SECOND DEGREE

Even as a matter of common law the distinction between principals in the first degree and those in the second degree is one of fact rather than of legal consequence. Their guilt is exactly the same [42] unless in a particular case some factor of mitigation or aggravation applies to one and not the other, and if this is true either principal may be guilty of a higher grade of the crime than the other.[43]

A principal in the second degree is one who is guilty of felony by reason of having aided, counseled, commanded or encouraged the commission thereof in his presence, either actual or constructive.[44]

He differs from the principal in the first degree in that he does not do the deed himself or with the aid of an innocent agent, but aids, commands, counsels or encourages a culpable party to perpetrate the felony,[45] and he differs from the accessory before the fact only in the requirement of presence. The

37. The Queen v. Manley, 1 Cox C.C. 104 (1844).

38. 1 Hawk.P.C. c. 1, § 7; 1 East P.C. 228 (1803). See also 4 Bl.Comm. *35; Regina v. Tyler, 8 Car. & P. 616, 173 Eng. Rep. 643 (1838); Johnson v. State, 142 Ala. 70, 38 So. 182 (1905); State v. Benton, 276 N.C. 641, 174 S.E.2d 793 (1970).

39. Wixson v. People, 5 Park.Cr.R. 119 (N.Y.1861).

40. People v. Walker, 361 Ill. 482, 198 N.E. 353 (1935); Asher v. State, 128 Tex. Cr.R. 388, 81 S.W.2d 681 (1935).

41. The Queen v. Manley, 1 Cox C.C. 104 (1844). See also Workman v. State, 216 Ind. 68, 23 N.E.2d 419 (1939).

42. In re Vann, 136 Fla. 113, 118, 186 So. 424, 426 (1939); Clift v. Commonwealth, 268 Ky. 573, 105 S.W.2d 557 (1937); State v. Holland, 211 N.C. 284, 189 S.E. 761 (1937); State v. Griggs, 184 S.C. 304, 192 S.E. 360 (1937). In very rare instances some unusual statute has provided for a different grade of guilt. See note 8 supra.

"It is well settled that even though a defendant is indicted solely for the commission of a substantive offense, he may be convicted as an aider and abettor even if not designated as such in the indictment." United States v. McCambridge, 551 F.2d 865, 871 (1st Cir. 1977).

"We hold that when a death results from the operation of a motor vehicle by an intoxicated person not the owner of that vehicle, the owner who is present in the vehicle and who with his knowledge and consent permits the intoxicated person to operate the vehicle is as guilty as the intoxicated driver." State v. Whitaker, 43 N.C.App. 600, 259 S.E.2d 316, 319 (1979).

Where one aided and abetted another in the commission of the crime it is not necessary to establish who played which role. State v. Baylor, 17 Wn.App. 616, 565 P.2d 99 (1977).

43. 1 Hale P.C. *438; Hawk.P.C. c. 29, § 7. And see Red v. State, 39 Tex.Cr. R. 667, 47 S.W. 1003 (1898).

44. Agresti v. State, 2 Md.App. 278, 234 A.2d 284 (1968).

45. 1 Hale P.C. *438; 4 Bl.Comm. *34; State ex rel. Dooley v. Coleman, 126 Fla. 203, 170 So. 722 (1936); Kinder v. Commonwealth, 262 Ky. 840, 91 S.W.2d 530 (1936); Walrath v. State, 8 Neb. 80 (1878); State v. Ray, 212 N.C. 725, 194 S.E. 482 (1938); Methvin v. State, 60 Okl. Cr. 1, 60 P.2d 1062 (1936); Pope v. State, 284 Md. 309, 396 A.2d 1054 (1979); State v. Gray, 44 N.C.App. 318, 260 S.E.2d 790 (1979).

principal in the second degree must be present at the perpetration of the felony, either actually or constructively,[46] whereas the accessory before the fact must be absent.[47] In other words, although neither presence nor absence is of itself a determinant of guilt,[48] yet if the mens rea is found to exist, the same aid, command, counsel, procurement or encouragement which will make a principal in the second degree of one who is present (actually or constructively) at the time a felony is committed, will make him an accessory before the fact if he is absent. One who is present, let it be added, may become a principal in the second degree, by guiltily rendering actual and immediate assistance to the perpetrator[49] which the accessory before the fact would be unable to contribute because of his absence.

Counsel, command or encouragement may be in the form of words or gestures.[50] Such a purpose "may be manifested by acts, words, signs, motions, or any conduct which unmistakably evinces a design to encourage, incite, or approve of the crime."[51] Promises or threats are very effective for this purpose,[52] but much less will meet the legal requirement, as where a bystander merely emboldened the perpetrator to kill the deceased.[53] Those

46. State v. Williams, 299 N.C. 652, 263 S.E.2d 774 (1980); State v. Ward, 284 Md. 189, 396 A.2d 1041 (1978); Duke v. State, 137 Fla. 513, 188 So. 124 (1939). It is possible to find suggestions to the effect that a conspirator need not be present to be a principal. See, e.g., Pinkard v. State, 30 Ga. 757, 759 (1860). But see Hale's statement that no man can be a principal in felony unless he be present, except in a case of leaving poison to be taken by the victim in his absence. 1 Hale P.C. *438, 439. See also Breaz v. State, 214 Ind. 31, 13 N.E.2d 952 (1938); Norton v. People, 8 Cow. 137 (N.Y.1828).

D was looking for X in order to kill him. Y who knew of D's plan sent a message to X to warn him. A intercepted this message to prevent the warning from reaching X who was shortly thereafter killed by D. State ex rel. Martin, Attorney General v. Tally, 102 Ala. 25, 15 So. 722 (1894). There may have been collusion in advance between D and A in this case, but we can conceive of such an occurrence in which there was no collusion between the two and D was quite unaware of the aid he received until afterward. If so, there would be no conspiracy, although the guilt of A would be clear. But it is very rare to find guilt of one who was not actually present at the time of perpetration except in cases of conspiracy.

A study of the cases resulting in conviction of accessory to felony before the fact indicates that only rarely was a conspiracy lacking.

47. Regina v. Brown, 14 Cox C.C. 144 (1878); Griffith v. State, 90 Ala. 583, 8

So. 812 (1891); Shelton v. Commonwealth, 261 Ky. 18, 24, 86 S.W.2d 1054, 1057 (1935).

48. Gillard v. State, 128 Tex.Cr.R. 514, 82 S.W.2d 678 (1935). Needless to say, presence, together with other facts may be very important as a matter of *evidence*. Furthermore, under the common-law requirement that one charged as a principal could not be convicted on proof that he was an accessory, and vice versa, the question of presence or absence might be a determinant of the question of guilt *as charged*.

49. Harmon v. State, 166 Ala. 28, 52 So. 348 (1910).

50. Kinder v. Commonwealth, 262 Ky. 840, 91 S.W.2d 530 (1936); Cordes v. State, 54 Tex.Cr.R. 204, 112 S.W. 943 (1908).

The words must be uttered as encouragement. A statement by a defendant to the primary actor who gouged out the victim's eyes that "a blind man can still talk." not for encouragement, but stated in disgust, is not sufficient to make defendant an aider and abettor to murder. Regina v. Curran, 38 CCC 2d 151 (Albt. 1977). Pope v. State, 284 Md. 309, 396 A.2d 1054 (1979).

51. State v. Wilson, 39 N.M. 284, 289, 46 P.2d 57, 60 (1935).

52. See State v. Scott, 80 Conn. 317, 323, 68 A. 258, 260 (1907).

53. People v. Blackwood, 35 Cal.App. 2d 728, 96 P.2d 982 (1939); Hurd v. Commonwealth, 257 Ky. 315, 78 S.W.2d 9 (1935); Cordes v. State, 54 Tex.Cr.R. 204,

present at an unlawful fist fight may encourage continued blows by shouts or gestures, and if so will be guilty of manslaughter if death should ensue.[54] A very illuminating case involved two drivers of different vehicles engaged in a race on a public highway, each thereby stimulating the other to drive at a criminally negligent pace, as a result of which a pedestrian was struck and killed by one of the vehicles. The driver of that vehicle was held guilty of manslaughter as a principal in the first degree and the other driver was held guilty of the same offense as a principal in the second degree.[55] One may also encourage a crime by merely standing by for the purpose of giving aid to the perpetrator if necessary, provided the latter is aware of this purpose.[56] Guilt or innocence of the abettor, let it be added, is not determined by the quantum of his advice or encouragement. If it is rendered to induce another to commit the crime and actually has this effect, no more is required.[57]

Actual aid may be rendered in many ways, typical examples being where a bystander, for the purpose of supplying the perpetrator with a deadly weapon for instant use, tosses him a bludgeon[58] or hands him a revolver[59] with which the victim is killed. He whose act contributes one of the elements of the crime itself is a principal in the first degree,[60] and hence the aid needed for guilt in the second degree is less than this. On the other hand, an act may have aided the actual result without involving guilt in any degree if it was an unwitting contribution. If felonious homicide is committed with a borrowed weapon the lender will not be guilty of either murder or manslaughter, although the killing follows very promptly after the lending, if he did not know or have reason to expect that any unlawful use was contemplated by the borrower.[61] And the fact that one strikes a person unlawfully

112 S.W. 943 (1908). This assumes an unlawful killing. A wife has a right to encourage her husband to exercise his lawful privilege of self-defense. See Hurd v. Commonwealth, supra, at p. 319, 78 S.W.2d at p. 11. Encouraging a companion to shoot the victim. People v. Hill, 53 Ill.App.3d 280, 11 Ill.Dec. 163, 368 N.E.2d 714 (1977).

54. Rex v. Murphy, 6 Car. & P. 103, 172 Eng.Rep. 1164 (1833); Rex v. Hargrave, 5 Car. & P. 170, 172 Eng.Rep. 925 (1831). These cases indicate that mere voluntary presence at an unlawful prize fight is sufficient for guilt of manslaughter if one of the combatants should be killed in the match, but this was rejected by a later case which required some encouragement to the fighters and held presence alone was insufficient for this. The Queen v. Coney, 8 Q.B.D. 534 (1882).

55. Regina v. Swindall and Osborne, 2 Car. & K. 230, 175 Eng.Rep. 95 (1846). Also, Jacobs v. State, 184 So.2d 711 (Fla. 1966).

A different result was reached in a case in which one of the drivers was killed. During a race on the highway one driver, attempting to pass the other in a no-passing zone, was killed by collision with an oncoming car. The other

driver was held not to be the proximate cause of this death so far as criminal law is concerned. Commonwealth v. Root, 403 Pa. 571, 170 A.2d 310 (1961).

56. ". . . known to the other. . . ." Skidmore v. State, 80 Neb. 698, 700, 115 N.W. 288, 289 (1908).

57. People v. Washburn, 285 Mich. 119, 280 N.W. 132 (1938); accord, Workman v. State, 216 Ind. 68, 21 N.E.2d 712 (1939).

"Evidence which fairly shows any form of affirmative participation that an accused in any way aided, abetted or encouraged another in the commission of a crime is sufficient to support conviction." State v. Rollie, 585 S.W.2d 78, 90 (Mo. App.1979).

58. Commonwealth v. Drew, 4 Mass. 391 (1808).

59. McCoy v. State, 50 Ga.App. 54, 176 S.E. 912 (1934); State v. Williams, 189 S.C. 19, 199 S.E. 906 (1938); Scales v. State, 289 So.2d 905 (Miss.1974).

60. Hardy v. State, 180 Miss. 336, 177 So. 911 (1938).

61. Anderson v. State, 66 Okl.Cr. 291, 91 P.2d 794 (1939); accord, Mowery v.

with his fist, after which another unexpectedly stabs the same victim fatally with a knife, will not constitute the first offender a guilty party to the murder if he had no knowledge of such an intent in the mind of the other and the two had no common purpose in the sense of a reciprocal criminal intent.[62]

In the words of Blackstone,[63] often quoted by the courts,[64] "presence need not always be an actual and immediate standing by, within sight or hearing of the fact; but there may be also a constructive presence, as when one commits a robbery or murder, and another keeps watch or guard at some convenient distance." A person is regarded as constructively present, within the rules relating to parties in criminal cases, whenever he is cooperating with the perpetrator and "is so situated as to be able to aid him, with a view known to the other, to insure success in the accomplishment of the common purpose." [65] The typical example of constructive presence is that of the "sentinel" stationed outside to watch, while his associates enter a building for the purpose of robbery or burglary.[66] Another illustration is found in the case of a "helper" who took his stand 150 yards away from the scene of the actual shooting, armed with a rifle which would be fatal at that distance, with intent to make use of it if the occasion should require.[67] The posting of a guard to give warning so that incriminating evidence might be disposed of before the arrival of officers has been a rather common device.[68] The most extreme application of the doctrine of "constructive presence" involved the holdup of a stagecoach. One of the conspirators stationed himself on a mountain-top, thirty or forty miles from the intended ambush, and signaled the approach of the vehicle by means of a controlled fire. Because he was so situated as to be of assistance at the moment, he was held to be a principal in the second degree.[69]

Presence, although indispensable to the position of the principal in the second degree, is not the only requirement.[70] In fact, presence at the scene

---

State, 132 Tex.Cr.R. 408, 105 S.W.2d 239 (1937).

"It is possible that one could aid and abet in the commission of an offense and still not be legally responsible for the conduct of one who committed the offense." Such as where there is no intent to promote or facilitate the offense. People v. Comer, 78 Ill.App.3d 914, 34 Ill. Dec. 257, 397 N.E.2d 929, 931 (1979).

62. Turner v. Commonwealth, 268 Ky. 311, 104 S.W.2d 1085 (1937).

63. 4 Bl.Comm. *34; cf. 1 Hale P.C. *439; Collins v. State, 88 Ga. 347, 14 S.E. 474 (1892); Walrath v. State, 8 Neb. 80 (1878).

64. Mulligan v. Commonwealth, 84 Ky. 229, 231-2, 1 S.W. 417, 418 (1886).

65. Skidmore v. State, 80 Neb. 698, 700, 115 N.W. 288, 289 (1908). See also Crow v. State, 190 Ark. 222, 79 S.W.2d 75 (1935). The driver of the "getaway" car, who remains outside in the car while others burglariously enter to steal, is as responsible and as culpable as those who enter. People v. Martin, 128 Cal.App.2d

361, 275 P.2d 635 (1954). Williams v. State, ___ Ind. ___, 395 N.E.2d 239 (1979).

66. State v. Berger, 121 Iowa 581, 96 N.W. 1094 (1903); Clark v. Commonwealth, 269 Ky. 833, 108 S.W.2d 1036 (1937).

"Of course it is elemental that one who keeps watch during the commission of the crime to facilitate the escape of the criminal is guilty as a principal." People v. Grant, 113 Cal.App.3d 457, 170 Cal. Rptr. 218, 228 (1980).

67. State v. Chastain, 104 N.C. 900, 10 S.E. 519 (1889).

68. State v. Weekley, 40 Wyo. 162, 275 P. 122 (1929).

69. State v. Hamilton and Laurie, 13 Nev. 386 (1878).

70. Gambrell v. Commonwealth, 282 Ky. 620, 139 S.W.2d 454 (1940); State v. Farr, 33 Iowa 553 (1871); State v. Odbur, 317 Mo. 372, 295 S.W. 734 (1927); Creasy v. Commonwealth, 166 Va. 721, 186 S.E. 63 (1936).

of an offense is not of itself sufficient to constitute any sort of criminal guilt.[71] Obviously a terrified onlooker is not to be punished for his mere misfortune in having been present at the commission of a felony.[72] The next point is not so obvious since the law might require a bystander to interfere in the effort to prevent a felony from being perpetrated in his presence, if he could do so without unreasonable danger to himself. However, this is not required under the present law[73] unless the bystander owes some special duty of protection to the intended victim.[74] In the words of the Supreme Court of North Carolina:

"Every person may, upon such an occasion, interfere to prevent, if he can, the perpetration of so high a crime; but he is not bound to do so at the peril, otherwise, of partaking of the guilt. It is necessary, in order to have that effect, that he should do or say something showing his consent to the felonious purpose and contributing to its execution, as an aider and abettor."[75]

Even the secret acquiescence or approval of the bystander is not sufficient to taint him with guilt of the crime.[76]

One may be guilty, as a principal in the second degree, of a felony committed by another in his presence although there has been no prearrangement or previous understanding between the two;[77] but unless he contributes actual aid it is necessary that his approval should be manifested by some word or act, in such a way that it operated on the mind of the perpetrator.[78] This is entirely logical. The bystander's approval of the felonious deed, or even his intent to offer physical assistance if necessary, cannot encourage the perpetrator in any manner if it is unknown to him, and hence it makes no contribution to the actual crime itself.[79] It is quite otherwise if the

---

71. Mere presence at the scene of a crime does not establish guilt. State v. Gomez, 102 Ariz. 432, 432 P.2d 444 (1967); State v. Salazar, 78 N.M. 329, 431 P.2d 62 (1967); State v. Irby, 423 S.W.2d 800 (Mo.1968).

Under the early common law one who was present at the commission of a felony was guilty of a misdemeanor if he did not "use means to apprehend the felon." 1 Hale P.C. *439. See id. at pp. *448–9, *593. But even this was presence plus the omission to take steps to apprehend a known felon, and it did not make him a party to the felony.

More than seeing the crime committed is necessary to make one an aider and abettor. State v. Starr, 24 Ohio App.2d 18, 263 N.E.2d 572 (1970).

72. Commonwealth v. Loomis, 267 Pa. 438, 444, 110 A. 257, 258, 259 (1920).

73. People v. Woodward, 45 Cal. 293 (1873); State v. Hildreth, 31 N.C. 440 (1849); Connaughty v. State, 1 Wis. 159 (1853). See State v. Birchfield, 235 N.C. 410, 413, 70 S.E.2d 5, 7 (1952). An occasional statute may impose a duty on the bystander to prevent the crime if he can.

This does not require him to endanger his own safety. Farrell v. People, 8 Colo. App. 524, 46 P. 841 (1896).

74. Rex v. Russell, [1933] Vict.L.R. 59 (1932); People v. Chapman, 62 Mich. 280, 28 N.W. 896 (1886).

75. State v. Powell, 168 N.C. 134, 140, 83 S.E. 310, 314 (1914).

76. State v. Douglass, 44 Kan. 618, 26 P. 476 (1891); True v. Commonwealth, 90 Ky. 651, 14 S.W. 684 (1890); State v. Odbur, 317 Mo. 372, 295 S.W. 734 (1927); Smith v. State, 66 Okl.Cr. 408, 92 P.2d 582 (1939); Anderson v. State, 66 Okl.Cr. 291, 91 P.2d 794 (1939). But one who stands by for the known purpose of giving aid if necessary is a guilty party. People v. Luna, 140 Cal.App.2d 662, 295 P.2d 457 (1956).

77. Harris v. State, 177 Ala. 17, 59 So. 205 (1912); State v. Lord, 42 N.M. 638, 84 P.2d 80 (1938); Espy v. State, 54 Wyo. 291, 92 P.2d 549 (1939).

78. Clem v. State, 33 Ind. 418 (1870).

79. Hicks v. United States, 150 U.S. 442, 14 S.Ct. 144 (1893).

bystander contributes actual physical aid to the accomplishment of the prohibited result. This will render him guilty (assuming mens rea on his part) even if the perpetrator is quite unaware of the assistance at the time.[80]

Aid or encouragement to another who is actually perpetrating a felony will not make the aider or encourager guilty of the crime if it is rendered without mens rea.[81] It is without mens rea if the giver does not know or have reason to know of the criminal intention of the other; [82] or if it is used as a mere pretension, for the purpose of having evidence sufficient to convict the real offender,[83] assuming this can be accomplished without irreparable harm. For guilt as principal in the second degree it is necessary that the acts or words of encouragement be employed with that intent,[84] unless the offense is one for which no more than criminal negligence is required.[85] In general it is the abettor's state of mind rather than the state of mind of the perpetrator which determines the abettor's guilt or innocence,[86] except that he is chargeable even with a specific intent if he gives his aid or encouragement knowing the other is acting with such an intent.[87] If the charge is first degree murder based upon an alleged deliberate and premeditated killing, the abettor is not guilty of this degree of the crime unless he either acted upon a premeditated design to cause the death of the deceased or knew that the perpetrator was acting with such an intent,[88] and the same may be said of assault with intent to kill.[89] A person who hands a loaded firearm to one of two engaged in a violent quarrel is guilty of assault with intent to murder if such an assault results from this abetment.[90] In this connection, it is to be borne in mind that "intention" includes not only the purpose in mind but also such results as are known to be substantially certain to follow.[91]

80. Way v. State, 155 Ala. 52, 46 So. 273 (1908); Commonwealth v. Kern, 1 Brewst. 350 (Pa.1867).

See supra, note 46.

81. "Thus with respect to the mental element, we hold that liability for the crime of another will attach only upon a showing that an individual had knowledge of the criminal enterprise and specifically intended, by his conduct, to aid, abet, assist, or participate in the criminal enterprise." Hensel v. State, 604 P.2d 222, 234 (Alaska 1979).

82. Mowery v. State, 132 Tex.Cr.R. 408, 105 S.W.2d 239 (1937); People v. Rigsby, 92 Mich.App. 95, 284 N.W.2d 499 (1979).

83. Price v. People, 109 Ill. 109 (1884); People v. Noelke, 29 Hun. 461 (N.Y.1883); Wright v. State, 7 Tex.App. 574 (1880).

84. Hicks v. United States, 150 U.S. 442, 14 S.Ct. 144 (1893).

85. Where the charge was manslaughter based upon death resulting from an unlawful race on the highway it seems the incitement of the one and the fatal act of the other were both criminally negligent rather than intentional. Regina v. Swindall and Osborne, 2 Car. & K. 230, 175 Eng.Rep. 95 (1846).

86. State v. Lord, 42 N.M. 638, 84 P.2d 80 (1938).

An "aider/abettor *may* have the same 'evil (criminal) intent' as the perpetrator, *or* he may aid and assist with simple knowledge or awareness of the wrongful purpose of the perpetrator." People v. Vernon, 89 Cal.App.3d 853, 152 Cal.Rptr. 765, 775 (1979).

87. Tanner v. State, 92 Ala. 1, 9 So. 613 (1891); Woolbright v. State, 124 Ark. 197, 187 S.W. 166 (1916).

88. Savage v. State, 18 Fla. 909 (1882); Leavine v. State, 109 Fla. 447, 147 So. 897 (1933).

89. State v. Hickam, 95 Mo. 322, 8 S.W. 252 (1888); State v. Taylor, 70 Vt. 1, 39 A. 447 (1898); Lisenby v. State, 260 Ark. 585, 543 S.W.2d 30 (1976).

90. Harmon v. State, 166 Ala. 28, 52 So. 348 (1910).

91. Restatement, Second, Torts § 8A (1965). This is the standard for the term "knowingly" under the Model Penal Code § 2.02(2)(b) (1962).

Counsel, command or encouragement to commit a crime may be counter-manded by the inciter or abettor so as to relieve him from criminal responsibility for subsequent acts of the perpetrator [92] if the countermand is duly communicated to the latter in time to enable him to govern his action thereby.[93] On the other hand, if the act of incitement or abetment has gone beyond mere words or gestures, an effective undoing of what has been done may be prerequisite to exculpation. For example, a man stepped up to a woman who was "cussing and fussing" with others, handed her his gun, and told her to "go ahead and kill them all." The man was held guilty as a principal in the second degree because of a homicide then and there committed by the woman, although he changed his mind after giving her the weapon and made an ineffective effort to disarm her.[94]

3. ACCESSORY BEFORE THE FACT

An accessory before the fact is one who is guilty of felony by reason of having aided, counseled, commanded or encouraged the commission thereof, without having been present either actually or constructively at the moment of perpetration.[95]

He is one who meets every requirement of a principal in the second degree except that of presence at the time. This makes it possible to include here by reference everything said above relative to such matters as (1) constructive presence, (2) what constitutes counsel, command or encouragement, as well as the need of communication to the perpetrator and the modes of such communication, (3) the requirement of mens rea, and (4) the possibility and limitations of countermand. Attention here may at once be directed to other matters.

The accessory before the fact is unable to render aid at the actual moment of perpetration, because anyone in such a position is held to be constructively present and therefore a principal. But he may render aid in advance, as by procuring for the perpetrator the weapon or other means by which the felony is to be committed.[96] The element of time requires special

92. 1 Hale P.C. *436, *617–8; Rex v. Richardson, 1 Leach 387, 168 Eng.Rep. 296 (1785); Harrison v. State, 269 Ind. 677, 382 N.E.2d 920 (1978).

93. Wilson v. United States, 5 Indian Ter. 610, 82 S.W. 924 (1904); People v. King, 30 Cal.App.2d 185, 85 P.2d 928 (1938).

"As is well settled, this burden of establishing withdrawal lies on the defendant and, in order for such a defense to prevail, a defendant must demonstrate some type of affirmative action which disavows or defeats the purpose of the conspiracy, either by 'making a clean breast to the authorities, or communication of the abandonment in a manner reasonably calculated to reach the co-conspirators.'" United States v. Dorn, 561 F.2d 1252, 1256 (7th Cir. 1977).

94. McCoy v. State, 50 Ga.App. 54, 176 S.E. 912 (1934).

95. 1 Hale P.C. *615; 4 Bl.Comm. *35; Wimpling v. State, 171 Md. 362, 189 A. 248 (1937); Commonwealth v. Bloomberg, 302 Mass. 349, 19 N.E.2d 62 (1939); State v. Farne, 190 S.C. 75, 1 S.E.2d 912 (1939). Presence, actual or constructive, is the determining factor in the distinction between principal in the second degree and accessory before the fact. Duke v. State, 137 Fla. 513, 188 So. 124 (1939). State v. Mower, 317 A.2d 807 (Me.1974).

96. 2 Co.Inst. *182; 1 Hale P.C. *616.

A conviction of felonious maiming, as accessory before the fact, was affirmed because the evidence had shown that **D**, a physician, had administered an anesthetic to deaden the fingers of an insured, knowing that the insured intended to have his fingers cut off to collect insurance money. State v. Bass, 255 N.C. 42, 120 S.E.2d 580 (1961).

mention here, but this is only to emphasize the want of any legally-established time limit within which the accessory's incitement may be recognized. It is no ground of immunity to him, for example, that his counsel and advice were given more than a year prior to the perpetration of the crime.[97] It is also possible for encouragement or persuasion to be recognized even where negotiations are conducted through an agent or representative.[98] And one may be guilty as accessory where the crime resulted from his incitement to engage in certain kinds of criminal activity although his instructions were general rather than special. Thus one who headed a conspiracy to commit robberies, equipped confederates with supplies and weapons, suggested prospective victims and shared in the spoils, is guilty of a robbery perpetrated by his associates even though he had not given them the name of this particular victim.[99]

One who incites the commission of a crime is guilty even if the perpetrator varies the method of perpetration, as where the counsel or command was to poison the victim and the perpetrator resorted to stabbing or shooting.[1] He is also guilty of all incidental consequences which might reasonably be expected to result from the intended wrong,[2] as where robbery, or attempted robbery results in the death of the victim.[3] But he is not guilty of a crime committed by the perpetrator which is entirely other than the one incited and not an incidental result thereof, as where the incitement was to commit arson and the perpetrator committed robbery.[4]

A. CRIMINAL FACILITATION

A special problem, dealt with here because factually the resulting crime is usually not in the presence of the one under consideration, arises when one conducting an ordinarily lawful business in the usual manner surmises that the other intends an unlawful use of the property or service being offered. Must such a one forego the profit of this transaction at the risk of being held

"The crime of accessory before the fact is a common law offense . . . the necessary elements are: (1) that the defendant counseled, procured, or commanded the principal to commit the offense; (2) that he was not present when the offense was committed; and (3) that the principal committed the crime." State v. Sauls, 29 N.C.App. 457, 224 S.E.2d 702, 704 (1976).

97. Workman v. State, 216 Ind. 68, 21 N.E.2d 712 (1939).

98. People v. Wright, 26 Cal.App.2d 197, 79 P.2d 102 (1938).

99. Breaz v. State, 214 Ind. 31, 13 N.E.2d 952 (1938).

The evidence would not support a finding that D was a principal, but would support a finding that he was an accessory before the fact. His conviction of conspiracy to commit robbery was affirmed and the case remanded so that he could be tried as accessory before the fact to armed robbery. State v. Wiggins, 16 N.C.App. 527, 192 S.E.2d 680 (1972).

1. 2 Hawk.P.C. c. 29, § 20; 4 Bl. Comm. *37.

"An instigator of a crime is an accessory before the fact even though unaware . . . of the precise method employed by the principal." McGhee v. Commonwealth, 221 Va. 422, 270 S.E.2d 729, 732 (1980).

2. 4 Bl.Comm. *37; People v. King, 30 Cal.App.2d 185, 85 P.2d 928 (1938); Workman v. State, 216 Ind. 68, 21 N.E.2d 712 (1939).

"An accessory is liable for the acts of a principal although he did not personally participate in them." Defendant guilty of accessory before the fact to second degree murder. Dozier v. State, 264 Ind. 329, 343 N.E.2d 783 (1976).

3. 2 Hawk.P.C. c. 29, § 18. Kidnapping resulting in the death of the victim. State v. Scott, 61 Ohio St.2d 155, 400 N.E.2d 375 (1980).

4. 4 Bl.Comm. *37. Simmons v. State, 594 S.W.2d 760 (Tex.Cr.App.1980).

a party to the crime if the surmise proves correct? The consideration will not be limited to accessories in the technical sense because the possibilities include treason and misdemeanor as well as felony, and may include a principal in the second degree in a felony case.

The solution of this problem is found, not in logical abstractions, but in the effort to make a proper adjustment between conflicting social interests. To whatever extent an affirmative answer is given, there will be some restraint on lawful business, because, at times, an illegal use will be erroneously expected. Furthermore, if an affirmative answer should be given without limitation a merchant might find it necessary to probe rather deeply into his customer's intentions, to safeguard himself against the possibility of conviction resulting from the jury's mistake. On the other side, of course, is the social interest in the prevention of crime. Hence the tendency has been to dispose of these cases as follows:

The gravity of the social harm resulting from the unlawful conduct is used to determine whether mere knowledge of the intended use will be sufficient to carry the taint of illegality.

As it was said *obiter* in *Backun:*[5] "One who sells a gun to another knowing that he is buying it to commit a murder, would hardly escape conviction as an accessory to murder by showing that he received full price for the gun." And a conviction of manslaughter was affirmed because the seller had such knowledge that it was criminally negligent for him to sell the gun to one who used it to kill.[6]

A seller who completes the sale of goods after correctly divining that the purchaser is buying them as an agent of an armed combination attempting to overthrow the government, thereby "voluntarily aids the treason."[7] Furthermore, "no man ought to furnish another with the means of transgressing the law, knowing that he intends to make that use of them"[8] to the extent of committing murder or other heinous crime. But the mere knowledge of one party to a transaction that the other intends later to make an unlawful use of the property or service involved, will not of itself be sufficient to taint that one with the offense subsequently committed if it is of a relatively minor nature.[9] This has been applied in such cases as the following, in which knowledge of the intent was held insufficient for guilt: sale of

---

5. Backun v. United States, 112 F.2d 635, 637 (4th Cir. 1940).

6. People v. Howk, 56 Cal.2d 687, 16 Cal.Rptr. 370, 365 P.2d 426 (1961).

Many of the cases are civil suits for the price of the thing sold or the service rendered, but as correctly stated *obiter* in an Indiana case, "where the act of selling is under such circumstances as would make the seller an accessory before the crime, he cannot recover from the buyer the purchase money of the thing so sold." Bickel v. Sheets, 24 Ind. 1, 6 (1865).

See also Steele v. Curle, 34 Ky. 381, 387 (1836).

7. Hanauer v. Doane, 79 U.S. 342, 347 (1870); cf. Tatum v. Kelly, 25 Ark. 209

(1868); Roquemore v. Alloway, 33 Tex. 461 (1870).

8. Lightfoot v. Tenant, 1 Bos. & Pul. 551, 556, 126 Eng.Rep. 1059, 1062 (1796).

"Mengal's mere giving of blood with the knowledge that it would be used for the unlawful purpose would be enough to convict him as an aider and abettor." United States v. Eberhardt, 417 F.2d 1009, 1013 (4th Cir. 1969). This blood with the addition of a large amount of animal blood was poured over documents in the Selective Service Files.

9. Partson v. United States, 20 F.2d 127 (8th Cir. 1927); Parsons Oil Co. v. Boyett, 44 Ark. 230 (1884).

liquor by an authorized dealer to a buyer who intended an unlawful resale; [10] sale of innocent ingredients to one who intended to use them in the unlawful manufacture of liquor; [11] sale of property purchased to be used for the purpose of gaming; [12] sale of a dress to a prostitute to be used in her "profession;" [13] the washing of clothes for a prostitute for a similar use; [14] work and labor done and materials furnished for a house to be used for gambling purposes; [15] transmittal of telegraph messages, innocent in themselves, to be used in maintaining a gaming house or installation of telephone apparatus and service in the regular manner in a place to be used as a gaming house.[16] It is otherwise, even as to such an offense, if the one charged as an inciter has not only had knowledge of the intended offense but has gone out of his way to promote it,[17] as by packing the goods sold in an unusual manner to conceal their identity.[18]

Where the seller or provider of goods or services knows of the unlawful use to be made thereof by the other, this knowledge is in itself sufficient to establish his complicity therein if the offense intended is heinous, but more than knowledge is required for this purpose if the violation is of a minor nature. There is much to be said for a dictum which would make the distinction depend upon whether the intended crime is a felony or a misdemeanor.[19]

Even offenders are not always accessories to separate offenses by other wrongdoers with whom they have dealt with knowledge of the unlawful intent.[20]

10. Hodgson v. Temple, 5 Taunt. 181, 128 Eng.Rep. 656 (1813); Graves v. Johnson, 179 Mass. 53, 58, 60 N.E. 383 (1901); Hill v. Spear, 50 N.H. 253 (1870); Kreiss v. Seligman, 8 Barb. 439 (N.Y.1850).

11. Jacobs v. Danciger, 328 Mo. 458, 41 S.W.2d 389 (1931).

12. Bickel v. Sheets, 24 Ind. 1 (1865).

13. Bowry v. Bennett, 1 Camp. 348, 170 Eng.Rep. 981 (1808).

14. Lloyd v. Johnson, 1 Bos. & Pul. 340, 126 Eng.Rep. 939 (1798).

15. Michael v. Bacon, 49 Mo. 474 (1872).

16. Commonwealth v. Western Union Telegraph Co., 112 Ky. 355, 67 S.W. 59 (1901); State ex rel. Dooley v. Coleman, 126 Fla. 203, 170 So. 722 (1936).

17. Danovitz v. United States, 281 U.S. 389, 50 S.Ct. 344 (1930); Zito v. United States, 64 F.2d 772 (7th Cir. 1933); O'Bryan v. Fitzpatrick, 48 Ark. 487 (1886). See also the statement of Lord Mansfield in Holman v. Johnson, 1 Cowp. 341, 345, 98 Eng.Rep. 1120, 1122 (1775). A druggist who sold croton oil and at the buyer's request dropped it into a piece of candy knowing it was to be used as a "joke" and not for medicinal purposes was guilty of battery on the innocent victim. State v. Monroe, 121 N.C. 677, 28 S.E. 547 (1897).

18. Biggs v. Lawrence, 3 T.R. 454, 100 Eng.Rep. 673 (1789); Clugas v. Penaluna, 4 T.R. 466, 100 Eng.Rep. 1122 (1791); Waymell v. Reed, 5 T.R. 599, 101 Eng.Rep. 335 (1794); Fisher v. Lord, 63 N.H. 514 (1885).

19. People v. Lauria, 251 Cal.App.2d 471, 59 Cal.Rptr. 628 (1967).

A supplier of oxygen-cutting equipment to one known to intend to use it to break into a bank was convicted as accessory to the crime. Regina v. Bainbridge, 3 W.L.R. 656, C.C.A. 6 (1959).

The problem here is similar to that involved in conspiracy cases. See supra, section 5, E. As pointed out in the footnote there the Model Penal Code, unsoundly, would not recognize any complicity based on knowledge alone. See Section 2.06.

For a discussion of the English cases see Williams, Criminal Law, p. 370 et seq. (2d ed.1961).

20. A defendant who sold counterfeit bills to a second party, who sold the same bills to a third person who was arrested while trying to pass them, all three having knowledge of the counterfeit nature of the bills, was not an accessory to the third person's possession, since the defendant's connection with the bills ended when he received his money from the second party, who might dispose of them as

The original draft of the Model Penal Code would have based complicity not only on a purpose of facilitating the commission of a crime but also on knowingly rendering substantial aid.[21] A convincing argument in favor of this conclusion is found in the comment to the first draft.[22] Unfortunately, however, the draft made no distinction in regard to the gravity of the offense involved, and would have applied to very minor offenses, which would be inappropriate. And when this section was being considered in the annual meeting of the Institute, with no suggestion of an amendment limiting its application to offenses of a grave nature, and with arguments which, in effect, showed how it would be undesirable as applied to very minor offenses, the section was voted down and hence eliminated from the official draft.[23]

The offense of knowing facilitation of a grave crime was developed by the common law and hence does not require a statute, but the Model Penal Code was intended as a complete code, and hence under it there would be no such offense. Certainly that was in the minds of the members who voted to eliminate such a section. If that is true then under the Code one could with impunity sell a firearm to a thug knowing it was to be used promptly to commit murder, so long as the seller could lawfully sell the weapon to an innocent buyer, and had no interest in this transaction other than the normal profit from the sale. And when reminded that such a murder had followed the sale in short order, the seller could answer that this was no concern of his. On the same premise a citizen, in time of war, could with impunity sell munitions to the enemy knowing they would be used to destroy our troops, so long as his only interest was in the profit made by the sale—but Code or no Code that would be treason under the Constitution.[24]

Some of the new codes have left no doubt on this point by a section to the effect that knowingly providing substantial assistance to a person in the commission of a felony is punishable as "criminal facilitation." [25]

4. ACCESSORY AFTER THE FACT

The accessory after the fact is one who, with knowledge of the other's guilt, renders assistance to a felon in the effort to hinder his detection, arrest, trial or punishment.[26] There are four requisites: (1) A felony must have been committed by another, and it must have been completed prior to the act of accessoryship,[27] although it

he chose. United States v. Peoni, 100 F.2d 401 (2d Cir. 1938).

21. See Model Penal Code, Tent.Draft No. 1, Section 2.04(3)(b) (1953), and Tent. Draft No. 4, Section 2.06(3)(b) (1955).

22. See note 21.

23. See 1962 A.L.I. Proceedings 79.

24. Constitution of the United States, Art. III, sec. 3, ¶ 2. "Treason against the United States, shall consist only in levying war against them, or in adhering to their enemies, *giving them aid* and comfort." Emphasis added.

25. E.g., N.Y.Pen.Law § 110.10.

26. 1 Hale P.C. *618; 4 Bl.Comm. *37; Whorley v. State, 45 Fla. 123, 33 So. 849 (1903); State v. Wells, 195 La. 754, 197

So. 419 (1940); Kuczensha v. State, 378 So.2d 1182 (Ala.App.1979).

27. 4 Bl.Comm. *38; State v. Tollett, 173 Tenn. 447, 121 S.W.2d 525 (1938). One who knowingly renders aid to help a murderer to escape, after the mortal blow is struck but before the deceased is dead (even if he dies shortly thereafter) cannot properly be convicted under an indictment charging him as accessory to murder after the fact. Harrell v. State, 39 Miss. 702 (1861); State v. Williams, 229 N.C. 348, 49 S.E.2d 617 (1948); Baker v. State, 184 Tenn. 503, 201 S.W.2d 667 (1947). It was suggested in Williams that defendant might be guilty as accessory after the fact to felonious assault.

is not necessary that a formal charge shall have been filed against the principal felon before this time; [28] **(2) the accessory must not himself be guilty of that felony as a principal;** [29] **(3) he must do some act to assist the felon personally in his effort to avoid the consequences of his crime;** [30] **and (4) this assistance must be rendered with guilty knowledge of the felony.** [31]

The ancient phrase used to describe the act of accessoryship after the fact is: "where a person knowing the felony to be committed by another, receives, relieves, comforts, or assists the felon," [32] but it was recognized even in the very early law that comfort or assistance which had no tendency to frustrate the due course of justice was not included. [33] The more accurate statement, in the absence of legislative enlargement of the field, [34] is: "An accessory after the fact is one who, knowing a felony to have been committed by another, receives, relieves, comforts or assists the felon in order to hinder the felon's apprehension, trial, or punishment." [35] One does not become an accessory after the fact merely by failing to arrest a known felon [36] or to disclose a known felony. [37] Even compounding a felony, although pun-

---

See Maddox v. Commonwealth, 349 S.W.2d 686 (1961).

28. State v. Jones, 91 Ark. 5, 120 S.W. 154 (1909); Howard v. People, 97 Colo. 550, 51 P.2d 594 (1935); Heyen v. State, 114 Neb. 783, 210 N.W. 165 (1926). But cf. People v. Garnett, 129 Cal. 364, 61 P. 1114 (1900) (under special statute).

29. Crosby v. State, 179 Miss. 149, 175 So. 180 (1937).

D was charged in two counts. (1) With armed robbery, and (2) as accessory (after the fact) to that robbery. Under instructions, which permitted it, he was convicted of both. This was reversed on the ground that the two are mutually exclusive. People v. Prado, 67 Cal.App.3d 267, 136 Cal.Rptr. 521 (1977).

30. 4 Bl.Comm. *37–8; Wren v. Commonwealth, 67 Va. 952, 956 (1875).

31. Ibid.; Jaso v. State, 131 Tex.Cr.R. 229, 97 S.W.2d 696 (1936).

In a prosecution for the offense of being an accessory after the fact to bank robbery all that was required to be proved was that defendant had actual knowledge of the commission of the offense and that he in some way assisted those who committed the robbery to hinder or prevent their apprehension, trial or punishment. Orlando v. United States, 377 F.2d 667 (9th Cir. 1967). Accord, Government of Virgin Islands v. Aquino, 378 F.2d 540 (3d Cir. 1967).

The New Jersey statute does not require that the accessory after the fact know that the one assisted had committed an enumerated crime. "We are of the opinion that N.J.S.A. 2A:85–2 re-

quires that the accessory need have only such notice as would reasonably alert one to the effect that another has committed a high misdemeanor." State v. Lynch, 79 N.J. 327, 399 A.2d 629, 634 (1979).

"The common law rule provided that a defendant was not guilty of being an accessory to a felony unless the government proved 'that the accused knew that *such* felony had been committed by the principal felon.'" United States v. Ferreboeuf, 632 F.2d 832, 836, n. 2 (9th Cir. 1980).

32. 1 Hale P.C. *618. See also 4 Bl. Comm. *37.

33. 1 Hale P.C. *620; Jones v. State, 137 Tex.Cr.R. 146, 128 S.W.2d 803 (1939).

34. As an example of such extension, see Howard v. People, 97 Colo. 550, 51 P.2d 594 (1935).

35. Skelly v. United States, 76 F.2d 483, 487 (10th Cir. 1935), cert. denied 295 U.S. 757, 55 S.Ct. 914 (1935). "Before one can be convicted as an accessory to a crime actually committed by another . . . [after the fact] it must be shown with reasonable certainty both that he knew such other had committed the crime, and also that in what the accused did he proposed, to some extent at least, to conceal the offender or give him aid in order that he might evade arrest or trial, or the execution of his sentence. . . ." Jaso v. State, 131 Tex.Cr.R. 229, 97 S.W.2d 696 (1936).

36. 1 Hale P.C. *618.

37. Levering v. Commonwealth, 132 Ky. 666, 117 S.W. 253 (1909). Some statutes provide that anyone who, after

ishable as such,[38] does not render the compounder guilty of that felony as accessory after the fact,[39] although the very ancient rule was otherwise.[40]

"As to the receiving, relieving or assisting, one known to be a felon, it may be said in general terms, that any assistance given to one known to be a felon in order to hinder his apprehension, trial or punishment, is sufficient to make a man an accessory after the fact; as that he concealed him in the house, or shut the door against the pursuers, until he should have an opportunity to escape; or took money from him to allow him to escape; or supplied him with money, a horse or other necessities, in order to enable him to escape; or that the principal was in prison, and the jailer was bribed to let him escape; or conveyed instruments to him to enable him to break prison and escape. This and such like assistance to one known to be a felon, would constitute a man accessory after the fact." [41]

One may be guilty as accessory after the fact by throwing suspicion away from the principal by swearing falsely at the coroner's inquest,[42] or by concealing the evidence in a homicide case by secreting the corpse.[43] One who performs a surgical operation upon a fugitive from justice for the purpose of obliterating his finger prints and altering his facial expression to enable him to evade arrest has been held guilty of conspiring to conceal him in violation of the federal statute,[44] and would seem to be an accessory after the fact in the absence of any special enactment.

"It is not necessary, however, for the principals to have come to a final resting place for the escape to have ended. The escape phase doctrine was developed to deal with those who are entangled in the consummation of the crime itself, such as getaway car drivers. In contrast, accessories after the

knowledge that a felony has been committed, conceals it from a magistrate, or harbors and protects the person who committed it, is an accessory after the fact. State v. Bowman, 92 Utah 540, 70 P.2d 458 (1937). The word "conceal" in such a statute implies some act or refusal to act by which it is intended to prevent or hinder the discovery of the crime; a mere failure to give information is not enough. United States v. Shapiro, 113 F.2d 891 (2d Cir. 1940); State v. Brown, 197 Neb. 131, 247 N.W.2d 616 (1976).

38. 4 Bl.Comm. *133-4.

39. Ibid. One can be convicted of misprision of a felony without being an accessory before or after the fact. State v. Carson, 274 S.C. 316, 262 S.E.2d 918 (1980).

"Thus, we interpret the statute's language to exclude the guilt of the named principal as an element necessary for the conviction of an accomplice." State v. Jansen, 120 N.H. 616, 419 A.2d 1108, 1110 (1980).

40. Ibid. See also I Hawk.P.C. c. 59, § 6.

41. Wren v. Commonwealth, 67 Va. 952, 956-7 (1875). Surreptitiously restoring to its original position the weapon used to commit the felony, or burning overalls used by the felon are facts admissible in evidence on such an issue. Crosby v. State, 179 Miss. 149, 175 So. 180 (1937).

42. Blakeley v. State, 24 Tex.Cr.R. 616, 7 S.W. 233 (1888). One who attempts to frustrate the prosecution of a murderer by telling those present not to tell what they know, is accessory after the fact. Fields v. State, 213 Ark. 899, 214 S.W.2d 230 (1948).

Making false statements to the police, in order to mislead them and direct attention away from the felon, makes the person accessory after the fact. Commonwealth v. Wood, 302 Mass. 265, 19 N.E.2d 320 (1939).

43. People v. Farmer, 196 N.Y. 65, 89 N.E. 462 (1909).

44. Piquett v. United States, 81 F.2d 75 (7th Cir. 1936), cert. denied 298 U.S. 664, 56 S.Ct. 749 (1936).

fact '[obstruct] justice by rendering assistance to hinder or prevent the arrest of the offender after he has committed the crime.' " [45]

One who is an accessory before the fact may also become an accessory to the same offense after the fact,[46] but this is not true of one who is guilty as a principal felon.[47] On the other hand, absence at the time of perpetration is not essential in the case of an accessory after the fact. For example, one who was present at the time a murder was committed, without abetting the felony in any way, but who thereafter, with guilty knowledge, assisted in concealing the evidence of the crime in order to protect the principal from prosecution, was guilty as an accessory after the fact.[48]

Under the common-law rule a wife cannot be accessory after the fact by reason of having concealed her husband or given him other assistance, knowing him to be a felon, but this does not apply to the husband who renders such assistance to his wife, nor to others such as parents or children.[49] The exception has been extended somewhat liberally by some of the modern statutes.[50]

D. PROCEDURAL PROBLEMS

1. UNDER THE COMMON LAW

The limitation of the principal-accessory distinction to felony cases offers a clue to its origin. There was no dissatisfaction with the common-law penalty for either treason or misdemeanor. The death penalty was thought to be quite appropriate for treason, and much milder penalties were provided for misdemeanor cases. On the other hand, there came to be great dissatisfaction with the rule applying the death penalty in all felony cases, particularly after the little group of common-law felonies had been greatly enlarged by statutory additions. This dissatisfaction led to the invention of various devices for the purpose of avoiding an excessive number of executions in felony cases, as, for example, benefit of clergy[51] and the doctrine of coercion.[52] Without doubt, the principal-accessory distinction was one of these devices, and because of this it is not surprising to find the development along lines

---

45. United States v. Balano, 618 F.2d 624, 631 (10th Cir. 1980).

46. Rex v. Blackson, 8 C. & P. 43, 173 Eng.Rep. 391 (1837).

47. "One who is a principal cannot be an accessory after the fact." People v. Chadwick, 7 Utah 134, 138, 25 P. 737, 738 (1891). If a murderer, and another with knowledge of the murder, dispose of the body, the murderer is an accomplice of the other. People v. Wallin, 32 Cal.2d 803, 197 P.2d 734 (1948).

Escape immediately following the taking of the money is a necessary phase of most violent bank robberies. Hence, even if defendant's first knowledge of the robbery came when the perpetrators ran out of the bank and into his car, he became an aider and abettor through his role as driver of the escape vehicle, and

is guilty as a principal rather than an accessory after the fact. United States v. Willis, 559 F.2d 443 (5th Cir. 1977).

48. White v. People, 81 Ill. 333 (1876).

49. "A feme covert cannot be an accessary for the receipt of her husband, for she ought not to discover him. But the husband may be an accessory for the receipt of his wife." 1 Hale P.C. *621. Except for the wife receiving her husband one may be accessory for receiving his "nearest relations." 4 Bl.Comm. *38-39.

50. E.g., M.G.L.A. c. 274, § 4 (1980).

51. 1 Stephen, History of the Criminal Law of England 461 (1883).

52. 2 Lewin C.C. 232n, 168 Eng.Rep. 1138, n.

which tended to prevent conviction despite clear evidence of guilt.[53] The technicalities tending to this result made their appearance in four different connections and may be grouped under the heads of (1) jurisdiction, (2) pleading, (3) trial and (4) degree of guilt.

A consideration of these problems of the principal-accessory distinction may well be prefaced by brief mention of felony cases which concern several guilty parties who are all principals. The difficulties held to be so insurmountable in cases involving accessories do not arise at all if the guilty parties are all principals, even if they are principals of different degrees. The problem of jurisdiction cannot arise in a form similar to that of the accessory cases. The common-law theory of criminal jurisdiction is that the place of trial depends upon the situs of the offense,[54] and since the principal in the second degree is always present, constructively if not actually, his abetment is in legal theory at the same place as the perpetration by the principal in the first degree. Hence, the court having jurisdiction over one principal will also have jurisdiction over the other.[55] It is not necessary for the pleading to disclose whether the defendant is a principal in one degree or the other.[56] A principal in the second degree may be charged in the indictment either as having committed the felony or as having been present aiding and abetting another in the commission thereof,[57] and if the indictment specifically charges one as the perpetrator and the other as the abettor, both may be convicted although the proof establishes that the one charged as abettor was in fact the perpetrator, while the other was present aiding and abetting him.[58] With reference to trial, the principal in the second degree may be tried and convicted prior to the trial of the principal in the first degree,[59] or

53. ". . . distinctions between accessories and principals rest solely in authority, being without foundation either in natural reason or the ordinary doctrine of law; for the general rule of law is that what one does through another's agency is to be regarded as done by himself." Carlisle v. State, 31 Tex.Cr.R. 537, 546, 21 S.W. 358, 359 (1893).

54. Connor v. State, 29 Fla. 455, 10 So. 891 (1892); Sweat v. State, 90 Ga. 315, 17 S.E. 273 (1893). Other systems may give primary importance to personal jurisdiction. See the French Code D'Instruction Criminelle, Art. 5. Statutes may provide criminal jurisdiction on this basis.

55. State v. Hamilton and Laurie, 13 Nev. 386 (1878).

56. Adkins v. State, 187 Ga. 519, 1 S.E.2d 420 (1939); Nelson v. State, 187 Ga. 576, 1 S.E.2d 641 (1939); Walrath v. State, 8 Neb. 80 (1878); State v. Ochoa, 41 N.M. 589, 72 P.2d 609 (1937).

57. Regina v. Crisham, C. & M. 189, 174 Eng.Rep. 466 (1841); Screws v. State, 188 Ga. 678, 4 S.E.2d 601 (1939); McKinney v. Commonwealth, 284 Ky. 16, 143 S.W.2d 745 (1940). It has been said this would not apply in the rare situation

in which a different penalty was provided for the two types of principal. State v. Woodworth, 121 N.J.L. 78, 83, 1 A.2d 254, 258 (1938). But the common-law rule is otherwise even in such a case. 1 East P.C. 348 (1803); The King v. Stearne, 1 Leach 473, 168 Eng.Rep. 338 (1787).

The fact that **D** was charged with bank robbery and convicted on proof that he aided and abetted the perpetrator in committing the crime did not violate any constitutional right. Levine v. United States, 430 F.2d 641 (7th Cir. 1970).

The statute governing aiding and abetting "does not define a crime but merely makes punishable as a principal one who aids or abets another in the commission of a substantive offense." United States v. Cowart, 595 F.2d 1023, 1030 (5th Cir. 1979).

58. 1 Hale P.C. *437–8; Mackalley's Case, 9 Coke 65b, 67b, 77 Eng.Rep. 828, 832 (1611); Neumann v. State, 116 Fla. 98, 105, 156 So. 237, 240 (1934); Reed v. Commonwealth, 125 Ky. 126, 134, 100 S.W. 856, 858 (1907).

59. 1 Hale P.C. *437; Regina v. Griffeth, 1 Pl. 97, 75 Eng.Rep. 152 (1553);

even after the latter has been tried and acquitted.[60] Furthermore, a principal in the second degree may be convicted of a higher degree of guilt than the principal in the first degree.[61] The former may be convicted of first-degree murder, for example, although the latter has been convicted of second-degree murder.[62] Similarly, the former may be convicted of murder although the latter has been convicted of manslaughter,[63] since an abettor may counsel with malice aforethought with the other perpetrates in the sudden heat of passion.[64] An abettor may be convicted of felony even though the perpetrator has been convicted of misdemeanor only.[65] Needless to say, the abettor may be convicted of a lower degree of crime than the perpetrator.[66]

None of these problems can be answered so simply if an accessory is involved. However, let us repeat that the involvement of an accessory requires a felony case because "in misdemeanors and in treason, all who take part in the crime are principals." [67]

A. JURISDICTION

As previously mentioned the common law adopted the territorial theory of criminal jurisdiction, by which the power to hear and determine a criminal case is dependent upon the situs of the offense. Thus if one standing in North Carolina shoots across the boundary line into the state of Tennessee and inflicts a fatal injury upon a person there, the common law does not authorize a conviction of this murder in North Carolina because, according to its view, the homicide is committed in Tennessee.[68] It is the same if a wrongdoer perpetrates a felony at a distance through the act of an innocent agent,[69] or if he incites a guilty party to commit treason or a misdemeanor in another jurisdiction.[70] In all such cases the offense may be tried and punished where the harm itself is done. But one who incites a guilty party to

see McCall v. State, 120 Fla. 707, 719, 163 So. 38, 43 (1935).

60. The King v. Taylor, 1 Leach C.L. 360, 168 Eng.Rep. 283 (1785); Rooney v. United States, 203 F. 928 (9th Cir. 1913); People v. Newberry, 20 Cal. 439 (1862); Christie v. Commonwealth, 193 Ky. 799, 237 S.W. 660 (1922); State v. Ross, 29 Mo. 32 (1859); State v. Martino, 27 N.M. 1, 192 P. 507 (1920); State v. Whitt, 113 N.C. 716, 18 S.E. 715 (1893); State v. Thompkins, 220 S.C. 523, 68 S.E.2d 465 (1951). Cf. State v. Haines, 51 La.Ann. 731, 25 So. 372 (1899). And see, Jeter v. State, 261 Md. 221, 274 A.2d 337 (1971).

61. Brown v. State, 28 Ga. 199 (1859); State v. Gray, 55 Kan. 135, 39 P. 1050 (1895); Red v. State, 39 Tex.Cr.R. 667, 47 S.W. 1003 (1898); State v. Tremblay, 4 Or.App. 512, 479 P.2d 507 (1971).

62. State v. Lee, 91 Iowa 499, 60 N.W. 119 (1894).

63. 1 Hale P.C. *438; Bruce v. State, 99 Ga. 50, 25 S.E. 760 (1896); Goins v. State, 46 Ohio St. 457, 21 N.E. 476 (1889); State v. McAllister, 366 So.2d 1340 (La. 1978).

64. 1 East P.C. 350 (1803).

65. Christie v. Commonwealth, 193 Ky. 799, 237 S.W. 660 (1922).

66. People v. Blackwood, 35 Cal.App. 2d 728, 96 P.2d 982 (1939).

67. Regina v. Clayton, 1 Car. & K. 128, 174 Eng.Rep. 743 (1843).

68. State v. Hall, 114 N.C. 909, 19 S.E. 602 (1894). The court suggested in this case that this want of jurisdiction to try such an offense in the state in which the offender stood at the time could be corrected by legislation. This is done in some jurisdictions by a statute authorizing the punishment of one who commits a crime "in whole or in part" within the state. See State v. Botkin, 132 Cal. 231, 64 P. 286 (1901).

69. Lindsey v. State, 38 Ohio St. 507 (1882).

70. Town of Barkhamsted v. Parsons, 3 Conn. 1 (1819); 1 Wharton, Criminal Law § 333 (12th ed. 1932).

perpetrate a felony in another jurisdiction is not punishable there, but only where his act of accessoryship occurred.[71] The same is true of an accessory after the fact who guiltily renders aid to the felon in another jurisdiction.[72]

"When a statute does not indicate where Congress considered the place of committing the crime to be, the site or *locus delicti* must be determined from the nature of the crime and the location of the acts or omissions constituting the offense."[73] And because of the statute authorizing trial in either district where more than one is involved,[74] it was held that failure to file a tax return is triable either "at the defendant's place of residence, or at the collection point where the return should have been filed."[75]

B. PLEADING

Under the common law standard a [the] case may be lost in advance either by carelessness in the pleading or by a mistaken notion as to whether the particular defendant was or was not present at the time the crime was committed. One charged with felony as a principal cannot be convicted if the evidence establishes accessorial guilt,[76] and one charged as an accessory cannot be convicted if the evidence shows him to have been a principal.[77] One may be charged as a principal and as an accessory in separate counts of the same indictment,[78] but the prosecution can be required to elect upon which count it will rely before the case is finally submitted to the jury.[79] How nicely this operates in favor of the accused is disclosed by the fact that while an acquittal of one charged as an accessory does not bar a subsequent trial upon an indictment charging him as principal,[80] he may be acquitted by

---

71. 1 Hale P.C. *623. It was the result of an early statute, early enough to be common law in this country although it was rejected in at least one state. State v. Ayers, 67 Tenn. 96 (1874).

"By decisions of this Nation's courts . . . it has been held, consistent with the common law rule, that absent a statute which provides otherwise an accessory before the fact may be tried where the accessorial act took place and only there." Goldsmith v. Cheney, 468 P.2d 813, 816 (Wyo.1970). Where the accessory before the fact is still recognized the statutory trend is to place venue in the county in which the felony was perpetrated. See Mass.Gen.Laws Ann. ch. 274, § 3 (Supp.1974–1975).

72. 1 Hale P.C. *623; Tully v. Commonwealth, 76 Ky. 142 (1877).

73. United States v. Clinton, 574 F.2d 464, 465 (9th Cir. 1978).

74. 18 U.S.C.A. § 3237 (1969).

75. United States v. Clinton, 574 F.2d 464, 465 (9th Cir. 1978).

A special venue provision allows a defendant in a tax case to elect to transfer venue to his place of residence. 18 U.S.C.A. § 3237.

76. Smith v. State, 37 Ark. 274 (1881); Shelton v. Commonwealth, 261 Ky. 18, 86 S.W.2d 1054 (1935); Skidmore v. State, 80 Neb. 698, 115 N.W. 288 (1908).

One indicted as a perpetrator cannot be convicted as an accessory after the fact. Box v. State, 241 So.2d 158 (Miss.1970).

The "offense of conspiracy and the offense of being an accessory before the fact are separate, distinct crimes, which do not merge into each other and neither of which is a lesser included offense of the other." State v. Looney, 294 N.C. 1, 240 S.E.2d 612, 618 (1978).

77. Agresti v. State, 2 Md.App. 278, 234 A.2d 284 (1967); Regina v. Brown, 14 Cox C.C. 144 (1878). One charged as accessory after the fact might be convicted although he was shown to be present at the time of the felony if he was not tainted with guilt until after the crime was complete. White v. People, 81 Ill. 333 (1876).

78. See Shelton v. Commonwealth, 261 Ky. 18, 24, 86 S.W.2d 1054, 1057 (1935).

79. Regina v. Brannon, 14 Cox C.C. 394 (1880).

80. 1 Hale P.C. *625; 4 Bl.Comm. *40.

both juries because of a doubt as to whether he was or was not present at the time.[81]

c. TRIAL

Where no change has been interposed by statute, an accessory, unless he waives his right in this regard,[82] cannot be tried before the principal.[83] The two may be joined in the same indictment and tried jointly,[84] unless the accessory is entitled to a severance,[85] but if they are tried together the jury must be instructed to inquire first into the guilt of the principal, and if they find him not guilty to acquit the accessory forthwith; but if they find the principal guilty then to consider whether or not the accessory is also guilty.[86] Needless to add, an acquittal of the principal bars a subsequent trial of the accessory.[87]

The results of this aspect of the principal-accessory concept are quite absurd. Anything which prevents conviction [88] of the principal makes impossible the conviction of the accessory.[89] Hence, if the principal is never apprehended,[90] or if before the moment of conviction he should die [91] or be pardoned,[92] the accessory must go free although his guilt may be well known

Acquittal of bank robbery as a principal does not bar a subsequent prosecution for being an accessory after the fact to such robbery. Orlando v. United States, 377 F.2d 667 (9th Cir. 1967); State v. Cox, 37 N.C.App. 356, 246 S.E.2d 152 (1978).

81. To warrant a conviction the prosecution must prove its case "beyond a reasonable doubt." 9 Wigmore, Evidence § 2497 (3d ed.1940).

82. If the accessory waives his right in this regard he may be tried before the principal, but if he is convicted it is necessary to respite judgment until the trial of the principal because the subsequent acquittal of the latter would annul this conviction. 1 Hale P.C. *623.

83. Ibid.; State v. Graham, 190 La. 669, 182 So. 711 (1938); see People v. Smith, 271 Mich. 553, 561, 260 N.W. 911, 914 (1935).

84. 1 Hale P.C. *623. And see State v. Duncan, 28 N.C. 98, 102 (1845).

85. Many statutes authorize any joint defendant in a felony indictment to require a separate trial. See, for example, Ala.Code § 15–14–20 (1975). Needless to say, under such authorization either the accessory or the *principal* could require a severance.

86. 1 Hale P.C. *624.

87. Bowen v. State, 25 Fla. 645, 6 So. 459 (1889); see State v. Hess, 233 Wis. 4, 288 N.W. 275 (1939).

88. Hale says that pardon of the principal after he "be only convict" and be-

fore attainder is a bar to the trial of the accessory. 1 Hale P.C. *625. Attainder resulted from the sentence of death which was included in the judgment of conviction of felony. In other words, it was not the establishment of guilt of the principal by plea or verdict which was the magical event in this regard, but the judgment of conviction which was entered thereon. It is in this sense, the correct one it is submitted, that the word "conviction" is used in the text. Under the ancient law outlawry in treason and felony amounted to attainder. 2 Hale P.C. *205. Hence the original statements were to the effect that "the accessory can not be brought to trial until the principal has been convicted or outlawed." 2 Pollock & Maitland, History of English Law 509 (2d ed.1898).

89. ". . . for if any thing obstruct judgment . . . the accessory is to be discharged." 1 Hale P.C. *625.

90. Anciently the fugitive felon could be reached by outlawry. See note 88 supra.

91. 1 Hale P.C. *625; Commonwealth v. Phillips, 16 Mass. 422, 425 (1820); State v. McDaniel, 41 Tex. 229 (1874).

92. 1 Hale P.C. *625. State v. Duncan, 28 N.C. 98, 102 (1845). "See in a writ of error in the Common Bench, that it was held by Thirning that in every case of felony, where a man is indicted as a principal and afterwards has a charter of pardon, or else he abjures the realm, the accessory, in that case, shall not be arraigned; for when the life of the princi-

and easy to prove. Furthermore, if both are convicted in due course, but the conviction of the principal is thereafter reversed, the conviction of the accessory cannot stand.[93]

A far-fetched corollary was that there could be no accessory to manslaughter before the fact.[94] The notion was that manslaughter is unlawful homicide in the heat of sudden passion and hence could not have been incited by one not present. If guilt of manslaughter is predicated upon some other basis, such as criminal negligence, this reasoning does not apply,[95] but even in the case of voluntary manslaughter the premise is not supported by fact. Under the rules of provocation and the cooling time it would easily be possible for one of two who have received great provocation from a third, to follow and kill the third, at the command or suggestion of the second, before the passion had had time to cool, although the fatal act was at such a distance from the inciter that it could not be said to be in his presence. The modern trend seems to be in the direction of recognizing an accessory before the fact even in the case of voluntary manslaughter.[96]

More logical was the rule in cases of suicide. Malicious self-destruction was recognized by the common law as "a peculiar species of felony." [97] By the ancient law punishment was provided in the form of ignominious burial and forfeiture of goods and chattels,[98] upon a determination of guilt by the coroner's jury.[99] Hence, one who had incited the self-destruction of another could be convicted as an accessory before the fact.[1] Later, when a change of the punitive system left no punishment available for the suicide, one who had counseled, commanded or otherwise encouraged such an act of self-destruction on the part of another, was held not subject to conviction if he was not present at the time, because he was accessory before the fact and the principal had not been convicted.[2] If such a one was present at the time he is convictable as a principal.[3] For example, where two, who have agreed to commit suicide, take poison for this purpose, each in the presence of the other, but only one dies, the survivor is guilty of murder.[4] Because suicide is

pal is pardoned by the law in whatever manner it may be, that felony is extinct in his person, and consequently he is acquitted and for the same reason the accessory is acquitted, etc. Query, if the principal resorts to his clergy." Anonymous, Stratham's Abr. (Klingelsmith's translation) 420, pl. 33. In some of our jurisdictions the power to pardon is restricted to "after conviction." See, e.g., Mo.Const., Art. IV, § 7 (1945).

93. Ray v. State, 13 Neb. 55, 13 N.W. 2 (1882). The party in this case was accessory after the fact.

94. 1 Hale P.C. *615–6; 4 Bl.Comm. *36; Bibithe's Case, 4 Coke 43b, 76 Eng. Rep. 991 (1597); see Jones v. State, 13 Tex. 168, 186 (1854).

95. State v. Braune, 363 Ill. 551, 2 N.E.2d 839 (1936); State v. McVay, 47 R.I. 292, 132 A. 436 (1926); see Wade v. State, 174 Tenn. 248, 251, 124 S.W.2d 710, 711, 712 (1939); People v. Gramag-

lia, 71 A.D.2d 441, 423 N.Y.S.2d 78 (1979).

96. Thomas v. State, 73 Fla. 115, 74 So. 1 (1917); Moore v. Lowe, 116 W.Va. 165, 180 S.E. 1 (1935); Charlton v. Wainwright, 588 F.2d 162 (5th Cir. 1979).

97. 4 Bl.Comm. *189.

98. Id. at 190; 3 Stephen, History of the Criminal Law of England 105 (1883).

99. 1 Hale P.C. *414–5. If the body could not be seen the inquisition was by the justices. Ibid.

1. Id. at 416; 4 Bl.Comm. *189.

2. Regina v. Leddington, 9 Car. & P. 79, 173 Eng.Rep. 749 (1839). And see Commonwealth v. Hicks, 118 Ky. 637, 641, 82 S.W. 265, 266 (1904).

3. Commonwealth v. Bowen, 13 Mass. 356 (1816); State v. Webb, 216 Mo. 378, 115 S.W. 998 (1909).

4. Regina v. Allison, 8 Car. & P. 418, 173 Eng.Rep. 557 (1838).

not punishable under modern penal systems it is held, in some jurisdictions, not to be a crime at all.[5] There is some authority for holding the abettor of suicide dispunishable where this view prevails,[6] although the better rule is otherwise.[7] Under some of the modern statutes abolishing the distinction between principals and accessories even the absent inciter of suicide has been held punishable.[8]

D. DEGREE OF GUILT

Under the original rule, "principals and accessories were felons, and were, as such, punishable with death."[9] However, this was modified at an early time to the extent of entitling accessories after the fact to benefit of clergy even in cases in which principals and accessories before the fact were excluded therefrom.[10] Ignoring this modification, the authorities tended toward such generalizations as "that accessories shall suffer the same punishment as their principals."[11] The law in this regard might easily have taken a different turn, because it was clearly recognized even in the time of Lord Hale that two who *jointly* kill a third may have different degrees of guilt, because one may act with malice aforethought and the other without.[12] And as previously mentioned an abettor may be convicted of either a higher[13] or a lower[14] degree of guilt than the perpetrator. With reference to the inciter, however, the rule came to be that "an accessory cannot be guilty of a higher crime than his principal."[15] The result of this rule combined with the manslaughter rule previously mentioned was, at one time, that if either the principal[16] or the accessory[17] before the fact was found guilty of manslaughter, no judgment of conviction could be entered against the accessory. This is largely a matter of history because the present trend is to recognize that one may be accessory to manslaughter before the fact.[18]

The rule that an accessory should not be convicted of a higher crime than his principal was based on the notion that the former should never suffer more punishment than the latter. This has been carried to such an extent

---

5. State v. Campbell, 217 Iowa 848, 251 N.W. 717 (1934).

6. Grace v. State, 44 Tex.Cr.R. 193, 69 S.W. 529 (1902).

7. People v. Roberts, 211 Mich. 187, 178 N.W. 690 (1920).

8. McMahan v. State, 168 Ala. 70, 53 So. 89 (1910); Commonwealth v. Hicks, 118 Ky. 637, 82 S.W. 265 (1904).

And see supra, chapter 2, section 1, E.

9. 2 Stephen, History of the Criminal Law of England 231 (1883).

10. Id. at 232; 4 Bl.Comm. *39.

11. 4 Bl.Comm. *39. And see People v. McArdle, 295 Ill.App. 149, 155, 14 N.E.2d 683, 685 (1938).

12. 1 Hale P.C. *438.

13. 4 Bl.Comm. *36; Bingham v. Commonwealth, 183 Ky. 688, 210 S.W. 459 (1919). The abettor was guilty of murder and the perpetrator of manslaughter.

14. Brown v. State, 28 Ga. 199 (1859); Speer v. State, 52 Ga.App. 209, 182 S.E. 824 (1935). The abettor was guilty of manslaughter and the perpetrator of murder.

15. 4 Bl.Comm. *36. Accord, Tomlin v. State, 155 Tex.Cr.R. 207, 233 S.W.2d 303 (1950).

In Maryland, which seems to be the only state in which the common-law of accessories remains unchanged, it was said: "The rule that an accessory before the fact may not be convicted of a higher crime than the principal has not been altered by statute or judicial decision in Maryland and is the law of this state at the present time." State v. Ward, 284 Md. 189, 396 A.2d 1041, 1049 (1978).

16. 1 Hale P.C. *437, *616.

17. State v. Robinson, 12 Wash. 349, 41 P. 51 (1895).

18. Moore v. Lowe, 116 W.Va. 165, 180 S.E. 1 (1935).

that if the principal is a corporation the penalty to be inflicted upon the accessory must be limited to a fine, since the corporation cannot be punished by imprisonment.[19]

Since the common-law distinction was between principals on the one hand and accessories on the other, the technical embarrassments to the prosecution which have just been mentioned apply to the accessory after the fact,[20] as well as to the accessory before, except that the possibility of an accessory to manslaughter after the fact seems to have been recognized from the first.[21] An additional difficulty, however, is involved in the prosecution of an accessory of the latter type. The origin of this technicality is the rule that one cannot be an accessory after the fact if his guilty conduct did not occur after the commission of the felony itself.[22] In ordinary circumstances, this rule works well enough, because one whose guilty aid was rendered before the completion of the felony is usually a principal in the second degree or an accessory before the fact, depending upon whether he was present or absent at the time. But the rule has been given an extreme application in certain situations such as the homicide cases. In these cases one who, with full knowledge of the facts, aided in the concealment or escape of a murderer after the mortal blow was struck but before the death of the victim, was held not to be an accessory to murder.[23] On the other hand, no indictment or other formal charge against the principal, at the time aid is given him, is required to constitute the aider an accessory after the fact. This result has been reached even under statutes which refer to the principal as the person "charged with or found guilty of the crime." [24] There is, however, authority for the opposite conclusion on this point.[25]

---

19. People v. Duncan, 363 Ill. 495, 2 N.E.2d 705 (1936); People v. McArdle, 295 Ill.App. 149, 14 N.E.2d 683 (1938).

20. Hale, for example, deals first with what constitutes accessoryship before the fact, then what constitutes accessoryship after the fact, and lastly the procedural problems involved. 1 Hale P.C. *612–626. The accessory after the fact is triable where his act of accessoryship took place rather than where the felony was committed. Id. at *623. One charged as a principal cannot be convicted as accessory after the fact. Reynolds v. People, 83 Ill. 479 (1876). But the acquittal of one charged as a principal is not a bar to a subsequent indictment against him as an accessory after the fact, and *vice versa.* Ibid. Such an accessory, unless he waives his rights in this regard cannot be tried until the principal is convicted. 1 Hale P.C. *623. And a conviction based upon such a waiver is annulled if the principal is subsequently acquitted. Ibid.

21. 1 Hale P.C. *616; State v. Burbage, 51 S.C. 284, 28 S.E. 937 (1898).

22. Gonzales v. State, 74 Tex.Cr.R. 458, 171 S.W. 1146 (1914); Roberts v. People, 103 Colo. 250, 87 P.2d 251 (1938).

23. Harrell v. State, 39 Miss. 702 (1861). Assault with intent to kill was a felony by statute and hence the aider was said to be accessory to that felony after the fact. But at common law he would not have been punishable at all because the assault, as such, even with this intent, was only a misdemeanor. Hence a verdict of not guilty was directed in the case of a defendant who helped a murderer to escape after the mortal blow but before the death of the victim. Commonwealth v. Costa, 2 D. & C. 612 (Pa.1922). Accord, State v. Williams, 229 N.C. 348, 49 S.E.2d 617 (1948); Baker v. State, 184 Tenn. 503, 201 S.W.2d 667 (1947). The rule that help given to the offender, after the fatal blow but prior to the death of the victim, cannot make one accessory to murder after the fact, although originating in technicality, has good ground for its support. There is no murder without death and one who might be willing to shield a lesser offender from the consequences of his crime might refuse to give any aid to a murderer.

24. State v. Jones, 91 Ark. 5, 120 S.W. 154 (1909).

25. People v. Garnett, 129 Cal. 364, 61 P. 1114 (1900).

2. STATUTORY CHANGES *

Since the reason for the principal-accessory distinction ceased to exist when most felonies were removed from the category of capital crimes, the distinction itself should be abrogated, and the legislative trend has long been in this direction.[26] Probably no jurisdiction retains the common law of accessories untouched by legislative change. However, statutes have been variously worded and have received different types of interpretation. It is grave error to assume that this common-law distinction with all its consequences has completely disappeared from the country as a whole.[27] For example, under variously worded statutes intended to improve the administration of justice by changes in this field we find in certain jurisdictions such conclusions as these: Under a statute expressly authorizing an accessory before the fact to be tried either in the county in which his act of accessoryship occurred or in the county in which the felony was perpetrated, the accessory is entitled to a directed verdict of acquittal if it is shown that all his acts of accessoryship were performed beyond the boundaries of the state.[28] A statute authorizing trial of the accessory "although the principal offender may not have been arrested and tried" does not permit the trial of the accessory before that of the principal if the principal is in custody and his case ready for trial.[29] A statute directing the accessory before the fact to be indicted and tried as a principal does not permit the trial of the accessory if the principal has been acquitted.[30] A statute authorizing trial of the accessory whether the principal has been convicted or not does not authorize the trial of the accessory if the principal has been tried and acquitted.[31] And a statute authorizing an accessory before the fact to be considered a principal and punished accordingly does not permit the inciter to be punished more severely than the perpetrator.[32] Again, where certain of the common-law technicalities have been removed by statute it is still impossible to convict one indicted as having committed the crime and proved to have incited it as an accessory

* "The first degree arson statute, W.Va.Code, 61–3–1, does not abolish the common law distinctions between principals in the first or second degree and accessories before the fact." State v. Jones, ___ W.Va. ___, 239 S.E.2d 763, 764 (1977).

26. See, e.g., Griffith v. State, 90 Ala. 583, 8 So. 812 (1891); State v. Burns, 82 Conn. 213, 72 A. 1083 (1909); State v. Bogue, 52 Kan. 79, 34 P. 410 (1893); Fleming v. State, 142 Miss. 872, 108 So. 143 (1926); In re Resler, 115 Neb. 335, 341, 212 N.W. 765, 768 (1927). Cf. Maupin v. United States, 232 F.2d 838 (10th Cir. 1956); State v. Shapiro, 29 R.I. 133, 69 A. 340 (1908); State v. Williams, 299 N.C. 652, 263 S.E.2d 774 (1980); Dusenbery v. Commonwealth, 220 Va. 770, 263 S.E.2d 392 (1980).

27. Maryland recognizes the distinction between principals and accessories before the fact, and follows the common-law distinction between presence and absence during the commission of the crime. Williamson v. State, 36 Md.App. 405, 374 A.2d 909 (1977) rev. other grds, 282 Md. 100, 382 A.2d 588 (1978).

28. State v. Sigh, 38 Del. 362, 192 A. 682 (1937); cf. State v. Tollett, 173 Tenn. 447, 121 S.W.2d 525 (1938).

29. Feaster v. State, 175 Ark. 165, 299 S.W. 737 (1927).

30. State v. Philip, 169 La. 468, 125 So. 451 (1929); State v. Ward, 284 Md. 189, 396 A.2d 1041 (1978).

31. People v. Wyherk, 347 Ill. 28, 178 N.E. 890 (1931); McCarty v. State, 44 Ind. 214 (1873); Pierce v. State, 130 Tenn. 24, 164 S.W. 851 (1914); State v. Austin, 31 N.C.App. 20, 228 S.E.2d 507 (1976).

32. People v. Duncan, 363 Ill. 495, 2 N.E.2d 705 (1936); People v. McArdle, 295 Ill.App. 149, 14 N.E.2d 683 (1938); cf. Neumann v. State, 116 Fla. 98, 156 So. 237 (1934).

before the fact; [33] or to convict one charged as a principal in the second degree and proved to be accessory before the fact,[34] or charged as accessory before the fact and proved to be a principal in the second degree.[35]

The statements in the preceding paragraph, let it be emphasized, represent merely the conclusions of a few courts under particular statutes. Some of them are quite unsound even as a matter of statutory construction, but no attempt will be made here to apportion the blame between the legislatures and the courts. By some of the statutes "the distinction between an accessory before the fact and a principal is abrogated," [36] and in such a jurisdiction it has been said: "No man can now be an accessory to a felony committed here 'he is a principal or nothing.' " [37] Some of the other enactments are worded quite differently.[38] It is proper to say that almost [39] everywhere the unavailability of the principal has ceased to be a bar to the conviction of the accessory before the fact.[40] Beyond this, generalizations are hazardous. A comparative study of the various enactments and the different interpretations of each type is quite beyond the scope of the present effort, but brief mention may be made of results achieved by well-worded statutes liberally interpreted.

It has been held, under legislative authority deemed sufficient for such changes, that the accessory may be tried and punished in the jurisdiction in which the felony was perpetrated, although he himself remained beyond its borders until afterwards; [41] that the indictment need not state whether the defendant was an accessory or a principal; [42] that the accessory may be pros-

33. Neumann v. State, 116 Fla. 98, 156 So. 237 (1934); State v. Ricker, 29 Me. 84 (1848); Edwards v. State, 174 Tenn. 532, 128 S.W.2d 629 (1939).

34. Shelton v. Commonwealth, 261 Ky. 18, 86 S.W.2d 1054 (1935).

35. Penny v. State, 140 Fla. 155, 191 So. 190 (1939).

36. E.g., 22 Okl.St.Ann. § 432 (1969); Bompensiero v. Superior Court, 44 Cal.2d 178, 281 P.2d 250 (1955); State v. Oldham, 92 Idaho 124, 438 P.2d 275 (1968); Rice v. State, 589 P.2d 419 (Alaska 1979).

37. State v. Burns, 82 Conn. 213, 218, 72 A. 1083, 1085 (1909); cf. State v. Gifford, 19 Wash. 464, 53 P. 709 (1898).

It was pointed out that "aiding and abetting is not a substantive crime, but merely a theory of liability." People v. Ott, 84 Cal.App.3d 118, 148 Cal.Rptr. 479, 487 (1978). "With the enactment of [18 U.S.C.A. § 2] . . . all participants in conduct violating a federal criminal statute are 'principals.' As such, they are punishable for their criminal conduct; the fate of other participants is irrelevant." Standefer v. United States, 447 U.S. 10, 100 S.Ct. 1999, 2006 (1980).

38. La.Stat.Ann.—Rev.Stat. 14:24 (1974); Mass.Ann. Law ch. 274 §§ 2, 3 (1980).

39. The word "almost" is required by the inference in State v. Sigh, 38 Del. 362, 192 A. 682 (1937).

40. In Florida it has been held that the accessory after the fact cannot be convicted prior to the conviction of the principal. Hysler v. State, 136 Fla. 563, 187 So. 261 (1939). Maryland follows the same rule. State v. Ward, 284 Md. 189, 396 A.2d 1041 (1978).

41. Carlisle v. State, 31 Tex.Cr.R. 537, 21 S.W. 358 (1893). The "antiquated rule" that one who, while out of the state, commits a felony within the state by the aid of a guilty agent, cannot be prosecuted for the crime where it was committed, is no part of Kansas jurisprudence. State v. Wolkow, 110 Kan. 722, 726, 205 P. 639, 642 (1922).

42. Hunter v. State, 47 Ariz. 244, 55 P.2d 310 (1936); Burns v. State, 197 Ark. 918, 125 S.W.2d 463 (1939); Miller v. People, 98 Colo. 249, 55 P.2d 320 (1936); Bowen v. State, 606 P.2d 589 (Okl.Cr. App.1980).

"The legislature did not make complicity a separate offense by merely codifying existing case law. We hold that under section 18–1–603, as before, one charged as a principal may be tried and convicted as a complicitor." People v. Pepper, 193 Colo. 505, 568 P.2d 446, 449 (1979).

ecuted although the principal has not been convicted,[43] or even after the principal has been acquitted;[44] and that the accessory may be convicted of either a higher [45] or a lower [46] grade of crime than the principal.

A consideration of the principles underlying the results sought by legislation in this field is entitled to special attention. "The reason of this rule is very plain," it was said at one time in support of the common-law position. "If there is no principal, there can be no accessory; and the law presumes no one guilty until conviction." [47] But, however "plain" this explanation may be, it lends no support to the conclusions reached. Had such support not been entirely wanting, the accessory concept would not have been excluded in cases of treason and misdemeanor.

Let a simple factual situation be assumed. Suppose there is abundant evidence to prove that A procured poison and handed it to B with instructions to B to administer it to C, that B did so with fatal results, and that A was prompted by a malicious purpose to cause the death of C. Let it further be supposed that there is substantial doubt whether B knew he was administering poison or had been led to believe it was a beneficial drug. Unless this doubt can be clarified it will be impossible to convict B of murder, but why should this doubt acquit the originator of this murderous scheme, as to whom there is no doubt? [48] "There can be no accessory without a guilty

43. Howard v. People, 97 Colo. 550, 51 P.2d 594 (1935); State v. Ricker, 29 Me. 84 (1848); Commonwealth v. Wiswesser, 124 Pa.Super. 251, 188 A. 604 (1936).

"Consequently, commencing with the date of our mandate in the instant case, the trials of accessories before or after the fact will not be precluded because the principals have not been sentenced or even have not been tried. Lewis v. State, 285 Md. 705, 404 A.2d 1073, 1079 (1979).

Defendant's husband was acquitted of grand larceny by check, and she was convicted as an aider and abettor on the same check. In affirming the conviction the court said: "while there must be evidence that a crime was committed there does not appear to be a necessity that the actual perpetrator be convicted in order to sustain a conviction for aiding and abetting." State v. Cleman, 18 Wn.App. 495, 568 P.2d 832, 835 (1977).

44. Rooney v. United States, 203 F. 928 (9th Cir. 1913); People v. Bearss, 10 Cal. 68 (1858); State v. Bogue, 52 Kan. 79, 34 P. 410 (1893); Commonwealth v. Long, 246 Ky. 809, 56 S.W.2d 524 (1933); People v. Smith, 271 Mich. 553, 260 N.W. 911 (1935).

"Read against its common-law background, the provision evinces a clear intent to permit the conviction of accessories to federal criminal offenses despite the prior acquittal of the actual perpetrator of the offense." Standefer v. United States, 447 U.S. 10, 100 S.Ct. 1999, 2005 (1980).

"An accessory may also 'be convicted notwithstanding the fact that the principal actor has not been tried or has been tried and acquitted.'" State v. Wilder, 25 Wn.App. 568, 608 P.2d 270, 274 (1980).

D's conviction for murder, premised on the existence of a conspiracy, can stand even though the person who allegedly perpetrated the homicide has been found not guilty. Commonwealth v. Jackson, 463 Pa. 301, 344 A.2d 842 (1975).

45. State v. Patterson, 52 Kan. 335, 34 P. 784 (1893); Fleming v. State, 142 Miss. 872, 108 So. 143 (1926).

46. Thomas v. State, 73 Fla. 115, 74 So. 1 (1917).

"Where the principal has been tried and convicted of a lower degree of a crime, an aider and abettor can be tried and convicted of a higher degree of a crime if the facts support such a conviction." State v. Wilder, 25 Wn.App. 568, 608 P.2d 270, 274 (1980). Or if the principal has been acquitted. Ibid.

47. Commonwealth v. Phillips, 16 Mass. 422, 425 (1820).

48. In explanation of the origin of the rule it has been said: "The modes by which guilt and innocence were proved were, or had lately been, sacral and supernatural processes which could not be allowed a chance of producing self-con-

principal" [49] it is true, but if **B** is a guilty party **A** is an accessory, and if **B** is an innocent party **A** is a principal in the first degree. Since the punishment is the same in either case, it is not indispensable, as a matter of criminal justice, that we should know which label is appropriate in this case.[50]

It has been said that even under modern statutes it is imperative for the state to prove the guilt of the principal as well as the instigation by the accessory.[51] Thus, it is said, one cannot be convicted for inciting or abetting a homicide where the person actually committing the act was justified in doing so,[52] as where one encourages another to use deadly force in self-defense.[53] With proper limitations this position may be accepted. If an innocent citizen is the subject of a murderous assault under such circumstances that he is privileged by law to defend himself by the use of deadly force, a bystander, who could not himself prevent the harm by milder measures, would incur no guilt by encouraging the one assailed to shoot in self-defense. But if there was no actual impending danger, although there appeared to be, the circumstances might well be such as to entitle the actual slayer to an excuse based upon a reasonable mistake of fact as to the necessity of using deadly force in self-defense,[54] whereas one who counseled him to take this extreme measure might be found to have made no mistake but to have spoken with the deliberate and malicious purpose of causing the death of one known to him to be acting in the capacity of a "practical" joker. If so, the instigator should be convicted of murder, as principal in the first degree if the common-law label must be retained.

If there is no evidence of defendant's guilt except on the theory that he caused a crime to be committed by another (whether by incitement or abetment), it will obviously be necessary for the prosecution to prove the crime was actually committed by another,[55] and this must be established with the same certainty as if the perpetrator himself were on trial.[56] Aside from outworn technicality, however, it is not necessary to have a judgment of conviction against the perpetrator to establish his actual guilt.[57] In fact if such a judgment is available and is introduced in evidence against the accessory it is not conclusive in his case but is only prima-facie evidence of the other's

tradictory results. What should we think of the God who suffered the principal to come clean from the ordeal after the accessory had blistered his hand?" 2 Pollock & Maitland, History of English Law 500 (2d ed. 1899).

49. People v. Walker, 361 Ill. 482, 488, 198 N.E. 353, 356 (1935).

50. Gambrel v. Commonwealth, 283 Ky. 816, 143 S.W.2d 514 (1940).

51. Miller v. People, 98 Colo. 249, 55 P.2d 320 (1936); Ogden v. State, 12 Wis. 532 (1860).

52. Harper v. State, 83 Miss. 402, 35 So. 572 (1904); Patton v. State, 62 Tex. Cr.R. 71, 136 S.W. 459 (1911).

53. Ibid.

54. Pinder v. State, 27 Fla. 370, 8 So. 837 (1891).

55. State v. Haines, 51 La.Ann. 731, 25 So. 372 (1899).

56. Aston v. State, 136 Tex.Cr.R. 12, 122 S.W.2d 1073 (1939).

57. "The principal in the first degree committed an act, which if he were an adult, would be a felony. Although the juvenile offender is not amenable to punishment as an adult, the defendant, a principal in the second degree, shall be punishable as if he were the principal in the first degree. The fact that the principal in the first degree cannot be punished for the felony he committed is immaterial." State v. Lamp, ___ W.Va. ___, 254 S.E.2d 697, 699–700 (1979). See also Standefer v. United States, 447 U.S. 10, 100 S.Ct. 1999 (1980).

guilt.[58] The accessory may contest this and introduce evidence to show the perpetrator really innocent despite his conviction.[59]

If criminal courts operated on a purely sporting theory of justice, and if there were added to this the assumption that the perpetrator always has greater moral guilt than the inciter, it might seem improper to convict the latter of a higher grade of crime than the former, or to punish the inciter after the perpetrator has been acquitted. But any such assumption is fallacious. While it is true, to take a test from the homicide cases, that one may incite in the heat of passion what another carries out in cold blood,[60] it is also true that one, acting with malicious premeditation, may instigate that which is perpetrated by another at once and in the heat of passion.[61] Furthermore, "different juries may reach different conclusions as to the guilt of the principal," [62] and through "failure of proof or caprice of the jury the principal may have been convicted of an offense of lower grade or even acquitted, but this alone does not determine the question of the guilt or innocence of the accessory of the crime charged. The actual guilt or innocence of the principal is the controlling fact, and, having determined that the principal is actually guilty of the crime charged, the accessory may be convicted and punished as a principal upon proof that he aided, abetted, and encouraged the commission of the crime." [63]

Suppose, for example, the trial of the actual slayer resulted in an acquittal because the jury was not satisfied with the evidence then available, but in following up leads from the evidence introduced in that trial the state has now the most convincing evidence that another man planned that homicide and hired the one first tried to do the deed. Certainly the interests of social discipline do not require that the "man higher up" should go free merely because his "tool" happened to be acquitted.[64]

---

58. Terry v. State, 149 Ark. 462, 233 S.W. 673 (1921); McCall v. State, 120 Fla. 707, 163 So. 38 (1935); Anderson v. State, 63 Ga. 675 (1879). A statute providing that a judgment of conviction of the thief "shall be conclusive evidence against said receiver, that the property of the United States thereon described had been embezzled, stolen, or purloined," was held unconstitutional. Kirby v. United States, 174 U.S. 47, 19 S.Ct. 574 (1899).

59. Commonwealth v. DiStasio, 298 Mass. 562, 11 N.E.2d 799 (1937); Aston v. State, 136 Tex.Cr.R. 12, 122 S.W.2d 1073 (1939). A confession by the principal does not prove his guilt in a prosecution against the accessory because it is only hearsay as to him. Ogden v. State, 12 Wis. 532 (1860). The husband of the victim was convicted of rape as principal in the second degree after the alleged principal in the first degree had been acquitted. The judgment was reversed and the husband discharged. State v. Haines, 51 La.Ann. 731, 25 So. 372 (1899). Cf. State v. Burbage, 51 S.C. 284, 28 S.E. 937 (1898).

60. State v. Smith, 100 Iowa 1, 69 N.W. 269 (1896); Moore v. Lowe, 116 W.Va. 165, 180 S.E. 1 (1935).

61. Bingham v. Commonwealth, 183 Ky. 688, 210 S.W. 459 (1919). The defendant was an abettor (present) in this case rather than an inciter, but the basic problem is the same.

62. Cummings v. Commonwealth, 221 Ky. 301, 313, 298 S.W. 943, 948 (1927); cf. Roberts v. People, 103 Colo. 250, 87 P.2d 251 (1938); Woody v. State, 10 Okl. Cr. 322, 136 P. 430 (1913).

The accessory who instigated the killing could be convicted of first-degree murder even if the principal's mental condition was so impaired that he could not form the specific intent necessary for that offense; or even if the principal was found not guilty by reason of insanity. People v. Steele, 193 Colo. 87, 563 P.2d 6 (1977).

63. Fleming v. State, 142 Miss. 872, 880–1, 108 So. 143, 145 (1926).

64. "We think a guilty accessory may be punished, even though the principal

The only sound basis for procedure in such cases is that the guilt of an inciter "must be determined upon the facts which show the part he had" [65] in the offense, and not upon the result of the trial of some other person. Needless to say, substantial rights, as distinguished from technicalities of purely historical significance, should be safeguarded.[66] But every effort should be made to avoid such positions as that miscarriage of justice in the trial of the perpetrator must of necessity cause justice to miscarry when the inciter is tried, or that a defendant must be acquitted if there is doubt as to which of two theories of the crime is the true one, if he would be equally guilty of the same offense under either,[67] just as we avoid any notion that the state is estopped to try and convict the real murderer merely because it has erroneously convicted the wrong man in a previous trial.[68]

One of the greatest social menaces of the present day is the one who would be termed an accessory before the fact by the common law but in lay language is referred to as the "brains" of a crime ring. He tends to put crime on a "business basis," he recruits members of the "profession," he provides the means by which crimes are perpetrated on an elaborate scale, and weapons so that death will result from any interference with his plans. The guilt of his terrified underlings, who carry out his commands because they dare not disobey, is certainly no greater than his. And it will not promote the general scheme of social discipline to handicap the prosecution of such an offender by unreasonable obstacles.

The position of the accessory after the fact has also been modified by statute in most jurisdictions. These enactments also are variously worded in the different states. The distinction between the principal and the accessory after the fact has been quite generally preserved,[69] but there has been a very definite trend in the direction of removing procedural technicalities from this branch of the law. Certain other important changes are to be found. The present state of the statutory law, however, requires these changes, and the details of the trend mentioned, to be spoken of as accomplishments in some states, rather than in more general terms.

Some of these enactments, for example, provide that the accessory after the fact may be tried in any court which shall have jurisdiction of the principal felon even if the act of accessoryship was committed outside of the state,[70] adding, sometimes, that if both events occur within the state, but in different counties, the accessory may be tried in either one.[71] Some authorize the trial, conviction and punishment of such an accessory even if the prin-

escape." State v. Bogue, 52 Kan. 79, 87, 34 P. 410, 412 (1893).

65. State v. Smith, 100 Iowa 1, 4, 69 N.W. 269 (1896).

66. People v. Singh, 11 Cal.App.2d 244, 53 P.2d 403 (1936); Warren v. Commonwealth, 222 Ky. 460, 1 S.W.2d 774 (1927).

67. The accused was properly convicted although it cannot be determined whether he fired the fatal shot himself or aided and abetted another in doing so. Gambrel v. Commonwealth, 283 Ky. 816, 143 S.W.2d 514 (1940).

68. State v. Couch, 341 Mo. 1239, 111 S.W.2d 147 (1937).

69. "These several distinctions have been abolished by statute in this Territory, *except as to accessories after the fact.*" Drury v. State, 9 Okl. 398, 403, 60 P. 101, 102 (1900). Italics added. See also the statutes cited in the following footnotes.

People v. Zierlion, 16 Ill.2d 217, 157 N.E.2d 72 (1959).

70. See e.g., N.C.G.S. § 14–7 (1969).

71. See e.g., Mass.Ann.Laws c. 274, § 5 (1980).

cipal is not amenable to justice,[72] or "whether his principal has or has not been convicted," [73] or has been prosecuted,[74] or is dead,[75] or has been acquitted.[76] On the other hand, the common-law requirement that the accessory after the fact must be charged as such in the indictment has commonly been retained.[77] Hence, one cannot be convicted as such accessory under an indictment charging him as principal, nor be convicted as principal if he is charged as an accessory after the fact. This seems to be more than a mere technicality, so far as an accessory of this type is concerned.

The social problem presented by the accessory after the fact is substantially different from that which arises in connection with the accessory before. The accessory after the fact has had no part in causing the felony itself, but has merely interfered with the due course of justice. This culpable interference is in itself a socially-harmful occurrence, and hence may properly be dealt with rather severely in the general scheme of social discipline. But the ancient notion that the accessory after the fact has become tainted with the principal felony, and has subjected himself to the same punishment as is provided for the felon he aided, is inconsistent with the theory that there is no doctrine of criminal guilt by ratification or "relation back," and seems out of line with the general view of the present day. In fact, as previously mentioned, the movement to moderate the penalty provided for such misconduct began at an early time in the form of according benefit of clergy to the accessory after the fact even in cases in which this privilege was denied to the principal or the accessory before. When benefit of clergy became obsolete,[78] the accessory after the fact was once more subject to the same punishment as the principal except where a different penalty had been provided by legislation. Modern statutes vary widely in this respect. At one time some statutes provided the same punishment for the accessory as the principal,[79] statutes now classify the offense of being an accessory differently than for the principal.[80] Under some statutes a different penalty is provided, such as "imprisonment for not more than seven years, or . . . a

72. Ga.Code Ann., § 26–802 (1977). ". . . though person claimed to have committed the crime has not been prosecuted or convicted. . . ." Rev.Code Wash. 9A.08.020 (1977).

73. E.g., 17 Me.Rev.Stat.Ann. § 57 (1980).

74. Ala.Code § 13A–2–25 (1975).

75. If the principal is dead this condition would be included under the more general provisions of a principal who "cannot be taken" or "is not amenable to justice." See note 45 supra.

76. At times this is expressly provided in the statute. See e.g., Ariz.Rev. Stat.Ann. § 13–304 (1978). It is sometimes held to be implied in some other phrase such as, "though the principals be not taken or tried." Commonwealth v. Long, 246 Ky. 809, 56 S.W.2d 524 (1933).

77. One charged as a principal cannot be convicted by proof that he was an accessory after the fact. People v. Zierlion, 16 Ill.2d 217, 157 N.E.2d 72 (1959); Peo-

ple v. Townsend, 201 Kan. 122, 439 P.2d 70 (1968). This results from the fact that the statutes preserve the distinction between the principal and the accessory after the fact and do not include any change in this part of the rule, while making modifications in other respects. See the statutes cited in the other footnotes to this paragraph.

78. It was abolished in England in 1827. 1 Stephen, History of Criminal Law of England 472 (1883). "In this country, although in some states recognized as a part of the common law, it has now universally been abolished either by express enactment or by implication." 3 Wharton Criminal Procedure § 1892 (10th ed. 1918).

79. See, e.g., Burns' Ann.Ind.Stats. § 9–103 (1956).

80. Iowa Code Ann. § 688.2 (1978) now refers to the offense of being an accessory as an "aggravated misdemeanor."

fine of not more than five hundred dollars, or by both." [81] There may be an even milder provision than this, as for example, that one convicted as accessory after the fact shall be fined not more than five hundred dollars or "confined in jail not more than one year." [82]

Some statutes, furthermore, have made a more realistic approach than did the ancient law, to the part of this problem affected by intimate relationship between the felon and one who conceals or otherwise aids him to protect him from the consequences of his crime. The common law was "so strict . . . that the nearest relations are not suffered to aid or receive one another" [83] in the effort to save a felon from trial and punishment; and were punishable as accessories after the fact if they did so. The only exception to this, made nominally at least on purely technical grounds,[84] was that a wife could not become an accessory after the fact by receiving and concealing or otherwise aiding her husband.[85] No such protection was accorded the husband who knowingly tried to save his wife from the consequences of her felony,[86] nor was it recognized in favor of the parent, child or brother of the principal felon.[87] In view of the moral timbre of our time, however, even if it be viewed as weakness, it is asking too much of a jury to expect a conviction of one who has merely opened his door or given some similar aid to a parent, child or other intimate relation.[88] Hence, a number of the statutes exclude from the field of accessoryship after the fact, any person "standing in the relation of husband or wife, parent or grandparent, child or grandchild, brother or sister, by consanguinity or affinity" to the principal felon,[89] with a qualification sometimes added, such as, where the accessory aids in an escape of a prisoner or removes an individual from the custody of a guard or other person exercising restraint over the individual aided.[90]

The ends of social discipline will be best served by abrogating entirely the distinction between the accessory before the fact and the principal, by removing procedural technicalities from the prosecution and conviction of the accessory after the fact, by providing milder penalties for such a party, and by excluding from this type of accessoryship those who are intimately related to the principal.

Complicity

Conspirators may carry out their unlawful plan by all co-operating as co-principals in the first degree. Where this is done no special problem is involved. If the target offense is a felony, and is committed without this type

81. E.g., Vt.Stat.Ann. Tit. 13 § 5 (1974).

82. W.Va.Code § 61-11-6 (1977).

83. 4 Bl.Comm. *38.

84. ". . . for she is presumed to act under his coercion. . . ." Id. at *39.

85. 1 Hale P.C. *621; cf. United States v. Oley, 21 F.Supp. 281 (E.D.N.Y. 1937).

86. 1 Hale P.C. *621.

87. 4 Bl.Comm. *38.

88. Even the court may be influenced by too harsh a rule. In one case a conviction of the felon's brother as accessory was reversed, although the guilt seems to have been clearly proved. Neal v. United States, 102 F.2d 643 (8th Cir. 1939).

89. E.g., West's F.S.A. (Fla.) § 777.03 (1976); Burns Ind. Code Ann. Tit. 35 § 44-3-2 (1979); Va.Code 1950, § 18.2-19. Some statutes have a similar provision without including the grandparent-grandchild relation. T.C.A. (Tenn.) § 39-112 (1975).

90. See, e.g., T.C.A. (Tenn.) § 39-112 (1975).

of cooperation, any conspirator who is not a principal in the first degree is guilty of the felony either as a principal in the second degree or as an accessory before the fact, where the common-law distinction between the two remains. Some students seem to think two separate problems are involved here, whereas it is all one. It is the conspiracy plus the resulting offense which makes the perpetrating conspirator guilty as principal in the first degree, the abetting conspirator guilty as principal in the second degree and the absent-inciting conspirator guilty as accessory before the fact. Exactly the same evidence which would convict **D** of conspiracy with **E**, if the offense charged is conspiracy, would convict **D** of murder (for example) if murder was perpetrated by **E** and **D** is charged with that murder as principal in the second degree or accessory before the fact.

The Model Penal Code is not worded in terms of principals or accessories. It takes the position that criminal liability is based upon behavior, and in addition to the actor's own behavior it covers cases in which his guilt of a substantive crime rests upon (1) the behavior of an innocent or irresponsible agent, (2) joint criminality or perpetration by an accomplice—a section called "Liability for Conduct of Another; Complicity."[91]

"Complicity" comes from the same source as "accomplice" and it goes outside the original meaning of the former to include guilt based upon induced conduct of an *innocent* person, but it may be useful to extend the meaning in order to have one term for the complete coverage.

The general effect of the section is to make all guilty participants in an offense principals, which has been the trend of modern legislation.[92]

Several jurisdictions have followed the format of the Model Penal Code and now provide that conduct which would have constituted being an accessory after the fact is punishable as "obstruction of justice" or the like.[93]

Aid and Abet

Although, as pointed out earlier, it would be better to use the word "abet" alone, and this is done at times,[94] the tendency is to employ the couplet "aid and abet," and to mean by it all parties guilty of the offense charged in any capacity other than as perpetrators. Thus it was pointed out that "aiding and abetting is not a substantive crime, but merely a theory of liability."[95] Another court emphasized that in addition to the statute, "the majority of the cases, and the Model Penal Code, all take the view that an aider and abettor should be treated like any other principal, and be required to 'stand

---

91. Section 2.06.

92. "That the indictment only accuses defendant of perpetrating a criminal act does not prevent his being found guilty as an aider and abetter." State v. Bunyea, 44 Or.App. 611, 606 P.2d 685, 687 (1980).

93. Ariz.Rev.Stat. § 13–2409 (1978); N.J.Stat.Ann. 2C:29–3 (1973); Utah Code Ann., 1953, § 76–8–306.

94. "Under the plain language of the statute, one who abets the commission of a criminal offense is legally accountable

for the violation of the substantive offense. The evidence at trial clearly supported the conclusion that the petitioner encouraged the substantive offense of theft in this case. Thus, the resolution of this issue turns on whether or not the definition of 'abets' encompasses 'encourages.' We hold that it does." Alonzi v. People, 198 Colo. 160, 597 P.2d 560 (1979).

95. People v. Ott, 84 Cal.App.3d 118, 148 Cal.Rptr. 479, 487 (1978).

on his own two feet.' " [96] "In the present case," said the federal court, "there was sufficient evidence to permit the jury to find that at least one defendant or co-defendant or conspirator participated in each of the alleged criminal acts, either as principal, an aider or abettor . . . ."[97] The Nevada court added that "it is clear that an individual can aid and abet a possessory crime." [98] In affirming a conviction of aiding and abetting an Internal Revenue Service agent in accepting unlawful compensation, after the agent had been tried and acquitted of the offense charged, the Court said:

> This history plainly rebuts petitioner's contention that § 2 was not intended to authorize conviction of an aider and abettor after the principal had been acquitted of the offense charged. With the enactment of that section, all participants in conduct violating a federal criminal statute are "principals." As such they are punishable for their criminal conduct; the fate of other participants is irrelevant.[99]

The Court added that nonmutual collateral estoppel is not appropriate for criminal cases, in which the juries may acquit regardless of what may be shown in the evidence, and such acquittals are final.

As put by the Wyoming court:

> Since this statute provides that an aider and abettor is to be "informed against, tried and convicted in the same manner as if he were a principal," no distinction is made between aider and abettor and principal; thus an aider and abettor is guilty of the principal crime. Proof of either participation is sufficient to convict a defendant as a principal and it is not necessary that the information refer to the aiding and abetting statute.[1]

"Under the evidence, Cueto was either a principal, or an aider and abettor who, in law, is deemed a principal . . . .. In short, the record amply supports a conviction regardless of whether the jury believed Cueto to be guilty as the principal or as an aider and abettor." [2] Quoting from an earlier case

---

96. United States v. Standefer, 610 F.2d 1076, 1098 (3d Cir. 1979).

97. United States v. Gleason, 616 F.2d 2, 20 (2d Cir. 1979). Charging criminal conduct without alleging that defendant acted as an aider and abettor did not preclude proof and conviction on such a theory. United States v. Cueto, 628 F.2d 1273 (10th Cir. 1980).

98. Roland v. State, 96 Nev. 300, 608 P.2d 500, 501 (1980). See also, United States v. Gallagher, 565 F.2d 981 (7th Cir. 1977).

99. Standefer v. United States, 447 U.S. 10, 100 S.Ct. 1999 (1980).

1. Hawkes v. State, 626 P.2d 1041, 1043 (Wyo.1981). "We do not agree . . . that aiding and abetting an armed robbery is a separate crime from committing an armed robbery . . . .." State v. C.J.S., ___ W.Va. ___, 263 S.E.2d 899 (1980). The statute governing aiding and abetting "does not define a crime but merely makes punishable one who aids or abets another in the commission of a sub-

stantive offense." United States v. Cowart, 595 F.2d 1023, 1030 (5th Cir. 1979). "A culpable aider and abettor need not perform the substantive offense, need not know its details, and need not even be present, so long as the offense committed by the principal was in furtherance of the common design." United States v. Sampol, 636 F.2d 621, 676 (D.C. Cir.1980). "By statute and case law this jurisdiction has long held that any person who counsels, aids or abets in the commission of any offense may be charged, tried and convicted in the same manner as if he were a principal." State v. Payton, 229 Kan. 106, 622 P.2d 651, 657 (1981). "It is our opinion that . . . one not in actual possession of a firearm may be charged with aiding and abetting one who does possess a firearm." People v. Wimbush, 94 Mich.App. 152, 288 N.W.2d 375, 376 (1979).

2. United States v. Cueto, 628 F.2d 1273, 1275 (10th Cir. 1980). "To show a violation of 18 U.S.C. § 2 it is not neces-

the court said that to " 'be an abettor the accused must have *instigated* or *advised* the commission of the crime *or been present for the purpose of assisting in its commission* . . ., shar(ing) the criminal intent with which the crime was committed.' " [3] "A person who acts with knowledge that the action will aid in criminal conduct can be held criminally responsible." [4] Words alone may be sufficient to make one liable as an abettor.[5]

The field of accessories after the fact is excluded entirely from this section and dealt with elsewhere as an obstruction of justice [6] which, of course, is where it always should have been.[7] Dealing with such participation on this basis permits enlargement of the coverage in two directions. (1) Justice may be obstructed although the one aided is not guilty of the offense charged against him. If **D** has been charged with murder, for example, justice has been impeded if **A** gave **D** the forbidden aid for the purpose of hindering his apprehension, even if it is established on the trial that **D**'s act of killing was in privileged self-defense. (2) The field is broadened substantially because the Code extends the provision to apply to misdemeanors as well as to felonies.

SECTION 9. CAUSATION

The first-act climax of a certain play was a murder scene, and night after night on the stage **A** would point a pistol at **B** and pull the trigger whereupon, after the flash and a loud report, **B** would clutch at his chest and sink gasping to the floor as the curtain dropped. **C**, an assistant manager of the play, thinking the action was beginning to lose its edge and that something was needed to liven it up a bit, decided a change of ammunition might serve the purpose and bought a box of cartridges with this in mind. These also were blanks but the construction made use of a substantial wad rather than the special material used in the stage ammunition which was completely disintegrated by the explosion. **C** had no intention of causing real harm but thought the sting of the paper wad might startle **B** into a little more effective action, and was quite unaware of a much more sinister plot. **D**, who knew all about **C**'s plan, had a box of cartridges made according to his specifications and these, although closely resembling the blanks purchased by **C**, were deadly ammunition. Surreptitiously **D** removed the box of blanks from the shelf in **C**'s room and put the other in its place. Shortly after that **C** decided the time for his plan had come, and after the pistol was prepared for the evening's performance he secretly made a substitution of cartridges. That night there was no make-believe but after the shot was fired by **A**, **B** lay dying on the floor. Who killed **B**?

sary to identify any principal at all, provided the proof shows that the underlying crime was committed by someone." United States v. Perry, 643 F.2d 38, 45 (2d Cir. 1981).

3. People v. Jones, 108 Cal.App.3d 9, 166 Cal.Rptr. 131, 133 (1980).

4. Record Revolution No. 6, Inc. v. City of Parma, 638 F.2d 916, 935 (6th Cir. 1980). The court cited United States v. United States Gypsum Co., 438 U.S. 422, 98 S.Ct. 2864 (1978).

5. United States v. Sacks, 620 F.2d 239 (10th Cir. 1980).

6. Section 242.3. Hindering Apprehension or Prosecution.

7. "[T]he crime imputable to this species of accessory (after the fact) is the hinderance of public justice, by assisting the felon to escape the vengeance of the law." 4 Bl.Comm. *38.

A. RESPONSIBILITY

It has been common to speak of causation in terms of responsibility,[1] but this invites confusion because in the criminal law the word "responsibility" is commonly used in the sense of "criminal responsibility," and hence carries with it the imputation of guilt. In the relatively rare cases in which the problem of causation demands special attention, the issue of responsibility is ordinarily present also, but this is not inevitable. If, for example, the state should offer a reward for the killing of Public Enemy Number One, the same kinds of causation problems which arise in connection with prosecutions for murder or manslaughter might also arise in connection with a claim for such a reward. If the claimant proved that he shot the Enemy and that the Enemy is now dead, his claim would not be established if there was no causal connection between the shooting and the death.[2] Because the law does not take notice of the entire field of factual causation,[3] and because the limitations are based upon matters of policy,[4] such problems might not all receive the same answers in the reward cases as they do receive in prosecutions, but for the most part the causation problems would be identical.

In some situations the act of one is regarded in law as also the act of another.[5] If this be assumed, and the word "act" be used to include also negative action,[6] it may be said that no one is criminally responsible except for a socially harmful result which was caused by his act.[7] But one is not criminally responsible for all the results of this nature that are caused by his acts. If, for example, one shoots another who dies immediately as a result of this shooting, the one has caused the death, and therefore has committed homicide; but whether he is or is not criminally *responsible* for the homicide

1. See, for example, Holland, Jurisprudence 117 (13th ed. 1924); Carpenter, Workable Rules for Determining Proximate Cause, 20 Cal.L.Rev. 471, 487; Hopkins v. United States, 4 App.D.C. 430, 439 (1894); Crews v. State, 44 Ga.App. 546, 162 S.E. 146 (1932); State v. Luster, 178 S.C. 199, 208, 182 S.E. 427 (1935).

2. The fact that a wounded person dies is not conclusive that death resulted from the wound. McCord v. State, 198 Tenn. 226, 278 S.W.2d 689 (1955).

3. "As the law of evidence excludes much that is evidential, the law of causation excludes much that is consequential." Henry W. Edgerton, Legal Cause, 72 U. of Pa.L.Rev. 343, 344 (1924). See also John S. Strahorn, Jr., Criminology and the Law of Guilt, 84 U. of Pa.L.Rev. 491, 505 (1936).

4. See, for example, Cardozo, The Paradoxes of Legal Science 83–4 (1928).

5. "All who are present concurring in a murder are principals therein, and the death, and the act which caused it, is, in law, the act of each and of all." State v. Luster, 178 S.C. 199, 206, 182 S.E. 427, 431 (1935). See also The Queen v. Salmon, 6 Q.B.D. 79, 83 (1880); Henderson v. State, 11 Ala.App. 37, 65 So. 721 (1914); People v. Rudecki, 309 Ill. 125, 140 N.E. 832 (1923). If a conspiracy to commit arson results in homicide, all conspirators, even those not present at the fire, are guilty of murder in the first degree. State v. Morran, 131 Mont. 17, 306 P.2d 679 (1957).

In legal theory one has done what he has caused another to do. Commonwealth v. Nabried, 264 Pa.Super. 419, 399 A.2d 1121 (1979). One may be guilty of a crime by causing it to be committed by an innocent agent. United States v. Ruffin, 613 F.2d 408 (2d Cir. 1979). "The plain meaning of 'abet' includes 'encourage.'" Hence one is himself guilty of the larceny which he encouraged another to commit. Alonzi v. People, 198 Colo. 160, 597 P.2d 560, 564 (1979).

6. For example, the omission to adjust a switch, which the one who fails to perform has a legal duty to adjust, resulting in a wreck in which fatal injuries are received, is homicide. State v. O'Brien, 32 N.J.L. 169 (1867).

7. Fine v. State, 193 Tenn. 422, 246 S.W.2d 70 (1952).

is dependent upon the absence or presence of legal justification or excuse for the shooting.[8] Hence it will be convenient to speak of causation in terms of imputability [9] rather than in terms of responsibility.[10] Although at times the want of criminal responsibility may be so obvious as to permit a case to be disposed of on that ground without inquiry into the problem of causation, the logical order of the inquiry in a homicide case, for example, is as follows: (1) Did the defendant cause the death of the deceased? If he did,—(2) is he criminally responsible for this homicide? If he is,—(3) what is the grade or degree of his guilt? A negative answer to either the first or the second question requires an acquittal.

B. ACTUAL CAUSATION

All antecedents which contribute to a given result are, as a matter of fact, the causes of that result.[11]

In homicide by shooting, for example, while the mind turns first to the man who pulled the trigger, it was obviously impossible for him to have committed that homicide (by shooting) without a loaded weapon. As he did not, in all probability, make the gun himself, it is necessary to consider others, such as those who made and sold the weapon, and even the inventor of that particular kind of firearm. Others perhaps were connected with the result because they made the shell or the bullet or the powder, or assembled the finished cartridge. The mind gets lost in the labyrinth of contributory factors long before the possibilities are exhausted. As only a portion of the factors which actually contribute to such a result will receive juridical consid-

---

8. "Homicide does not necessarily denote a crime." Patterson v. State, 181 Ga. 698, 705, 184 S.E. 309, 313 (1936). And see, Commonwealth v. Redline, 391 Pa. 486, 137 A.2d 472, 475 (1958).

"As a general proposition of law, all acts which, according to natural laws, would probably be and are proximately caused by an act performed by another person are considered the acts of the perpetrator of the original act. However if the resulting act or acts result in injury or damage, no legal responsibility attaches unless the original act was wrongful or negligent." Patterson v. State, 181 Ga. 698, 705, 184 S.E. 309, 313 (1936).

If one has an excuse for doing an act, he is not criminally liable for accidental consequences which are not attributable to his negligence. The Queen v. Bruce, 2 Cox C.C. 262 (1847).

9. ". . . the death is imputable to the wound." Powell v. State, 13 Tex.Cr. R. 244, 254 (1882).

10. If a socially-harmful result is caused unintentionally and without negligence and is charged to be a crime on the ground that it resulted from an unlawful act, the problems of causation and re-

sponsibility may be confused because the inquiry may be whether there is any causal relation between the *unlawfulness* of the act and the unintended result. See, for example, State v. McIvor, 31 Del. 123, 127, 111 A. 616, 617 (1920); Potter v. State, 162 Ind. 213, 70 N.E. 129 (1904); People v. Schwartz, 215 Mich. 197, 183 N.W. 723 (1921); State v. Horton, 139 N.C. 588, 51 S.E. 945 (1905); Jackson v. State, 101 Ohio St. 152, 127 N.E. 870 (1920).

11. "John Stuart Mill, in his work on logic [9th Eng.Ed. 378–383] says, in substance, that the cause of an event is the sum of all the antecedents, and that we have no right to single out one antecedent and call that the cause." Jeremiah Smith, Legal Cause in Actions of Tort, 25 Harv.L.Rev. 103, 104 (1911). "Causation is a fact. A cause is something regarded as a necessary antecedent; something without which the event would not have occurred. The term includes all things which have so far contributed to the result as to be essential to it." Prosser, Proximate Cause in California, 38 Calif.L. Rev. 369, 375 (1950).

eration, it is neither necessary nor useful to exhaust the philosophical possibilities of actual causation.[12]

1. SINE QUA NON

It has been common to examine problems of actual causation in terms of the *sine qua non,*—or the so-called "but for test" or "had not test." *Sine qua non* means literally "without which not." Without this, that would not be; [13] but for one thing, another would not have happened; [14] had not the defendant fired the shot the deceased would still be alive.[15]

2. ILLUSTRATIONS

Perhaps the most helpful illustration of the problem is homicide in which the deceased received two injuries from quite separate and independent sources. Passing over difficulties of proof, and numerous minor deviations, four major possibilities may be mentioned. (1) The death was due entirely to other causes and these injuries did not either singly or in combination shorten the life of the deceased. (2) One injury caused the death, whereas the other had nothing whatever to do with the loss of life,—as if one resulted in severing the head from the body while the other was a relatively harmless flesh wound in the arm. (3) Both wounds were rather serious, but whereas the deceased would have recovered from either one alone, the two in combination resulted in death. (4) Each injury was such that it alone would have been instantly fatal. In the first situation neither of the injuries stated was in fact a cause of the death, whereas in the second, one was such a cause and the other was not.[16] These, therefore, may be promptly eliminated. An examination of the third situation will disclose that each injury was a *causa sine qua non.* Since the deceased would have recovered from either wound alone, the test when applied to either one calls for the answer that *had not* that injury been inflicted the deceased would have survived. Therefore each of such injuries is in fact a cause of the death.[17]

---

12. "The question is not what philosophers or logicians will say is the cause. The question is what the courts will regard as the cause." Jeremiah Smith, Legal Cause in Actions of Tort, 25 Harv.L. Rev. 103, 104 (1911).

13. ". . . without which the result would not have occurred." State v. Des Champs, 126 S.C. 416, 420, 120 S.E. 491, 493 (1923). ". . . except for the unlawful act the injury and death would not have occurred." Warner v. State, 104 Ohio St. 38, 46, 135 N.E. 249, 251 (1922).

14. ". . . but for the wound death would not have ensued. . . ." Denman v. State, 15 Neb. 138, 141, 17 N.W. 347, 348 (1883).

15. ". . . if the wounds had not been, the man had not died. . . ." Rew's Case, J. Kelyng 26, 84 Eng.Rep. 1066 (1662). ". . . if the wound had not been given the party had not died." Clark v. Commonwealth, 90 Va. 360, 365,

18 S.E. 440, 442 (1893); Powell v. State, 13 Tex.Cr.R. 244, 254 (1882).

16. Although the deceased may have been mortally wounded by a pistol shot fired by another, at the time defendant killed him with a hatchet, defendant is none the less guilty of murder. People v. Ah Fat, 48 Cal. 61 (1874). A wound from a shotgun which would have produced death is not the cause of death if a shot from a pistol was the sole cause of death. Walker v. State, 116 Ga. 537, 42 S.E. 787 (1902). See also State v. Scates, 50 N.C. 420 (1858).

17. D cut X with a knife and A, acting quite independently shot X. X died from these injuries. The court held that D caused the death of X, if the knife wound contributed to the loss of life, even if the knife wound alone would not have been fatal. Henderson v. State, 11 Ala.App. 37, 65 So. 721 (1914). See also People v. Arzon, 92 Misc.2d 739, 401 N.Y.S.2d 156 (Sup.1978) where death was

The fourth situation, which seems clearer than the third as a matter of common sense, has been thought to present metaphysical difficulties. On the hypothesis that both injuries were inflicted at the same moment, and that each alone would have been instantly fatal, he who perpetrated either may suggest that his act is entirely unimportant because the deceased would have died exactly when he did had this act been omitted entirely.[18] On this ground it has been suggested that neither act is *in fact* a cause of the death in such a case,[19] but any doubt about factual causation here is the result of faulty analysis. Whenever *that* would not have happened *when and as* it did happen, had it not been for *this*, *this* is an actual cause of *that*. Suppose, for example, an unarmed man is so completely surrounded by enemies bent on his destruction, and armed with knives, that he has no possible chance to escape; but only one blow is struck because it is instantly fatal. It may be very true that without this blow he would have been killed at almost the same instant by some other knife; but no amount of repetition of such argument can conceal the fact that the actual cause of death was the blow struck. And the person who was killed by two bullets that hit him at the same time, each of which would have been instantly fatal, would not have died when *and as* he did die (by two bullets) had only one been fired. "One might have caused the result, but in fact both did so."[20] A proper analysis will show that no occurrence would have happened, *when and as* it did happen, had any contributing cause thereof been wanting. Consequently, if what happened would have happened exactly *when and as* it did happen regardless of what defendant did (or failed to do), he had nothing whatever to do with it and cannot be held criminally accountable for it, unless it was caused by the act of another imputable to him because of conspiracy or other incitement.

In the two-bullet case posed, if either shooter can claim correctly that his shot was not *in fact* a cause of the death, so may the other. The unavoidable conclusion would be that the deceased did not *in fact* die as a result of being shot—which is absurd.

The fact that something else *would have* caused the harmful result does not preclude recognition of what actually did cause it. Thus it may be established that death was caused by fire, despite proof that deceased had been the victim of an assault which would necessarily have been fatal.[21]

3. NEGATIVE ACTIONS

For the most part the problems of causation are the same whether the harm is alleged to have been caused by positive action or by negative action. No matter how clearly a legal duty to care for a child may have been violated, the forbearance or omission is not a cause of the child's death unless it "had the effect of shortening the child's life."[22] On the other hand, if nonperformance has resulted in death, one whose failure to perform the needful act constituted the violation of a legal duty, is a cause of the loss of life, even

caused by two fires only one of which the defendant started.

18. McLaughlin, Proximate Cause, 39 Harv.L.Rev. 149, 153 (1925).

19. Ibid.

20. Beale, The Proximate Consequences of an Act, 33 Harv.L.Rev. 633, 639 (1920).

21. People v. Gardner, 87 Cal.App.3d 476, 151 Cal.Rptr. 123 (1978).

22. Regina v. Morby, 15 Cox C.C. 35 (1882).

if a similar duty rested upon others who also failed to take action.[23]   If the
death would not have happened except for this non-performance the causal
relation is clear; if it would have happened just as it did even had the duty
been properly performed, the failure so to perform did not cause the loss of
life.[24]

C. PROXIMATE CAUSE

The discussion of causal relation up to this point has been limited to cause
as a matter of fact. No act will receive juridical consideration as a cause of
a given result unless it is in fact a cause thereof,[25] but it may be a cause as a
matter of fact without receiving legal recognition as such.[26]   If one chal-
lenges another to meet him in a secluded spot for an unlawful fistfight, and
while they are there for this purpose the other is killed by a stroke of lightning, the law does not recognize the challenger as the cause of death. Had
not the challenge been made the deceased would have been elsewhere at the
time and hence would not have been killed; but within the juridical view the
death in such a case is "by visitation of Providence and not from the act of
the party." [27]   The illustration could easily be made in more extreme form.
If the challenger happened to have been born out of wedlock it might be
mentioned that without the unlawful act of two other people he would not
have been born, and hence there would have been no challenge, no journey to
that secluded spot, and no death. Obviously the legal eye cannot, and should
not, see so far. This found expression in the maxim: *"In jure non remota
causa sed proxima spectatur"* (in law not the remote cause but the proximate cause is regarded). And for centuries judges, lawyers and writers
have used the phrase "proximate cause" to indicate a cause of which the law
will take notice.[28]   Among other terms used to convey the same meaning

23.   Regina v. Haines, 2 Car. & K. 368, 175 Eng.Rep. 152 (1847).

Although the beating of the child was by another, the mother who did not seek aid could be convicted of abuse to such minor child. State v. Fabritz, 276 Md. 416, 348 A.2d 275 (1975).

24.   Beale, The Proximate Conse-quences of an Act, 33 Harv.L.Rev. 633, 637 (1920).

25.   Fine v. State, 193 Tenn. 422, 246 S.W.2d 70 (1952). ". . . liability can-not be imputed to a man unless it is in some degree a result of his act." Beale, The Proximate Consequences of an Act, 33 Harv.L.Rev. 633, 637 (1920).

26.   "As the law of evidence excludes from consideration much that is eviden-tial, the law of causation excludes much that is consequential." Henry W. Edger-ton, Legal Cause, 72 U. of Pa.L.Rev. 343, 344 (1924). "To use the common lan-guage . . . the court will trace an act into its proximate but not into its remote consequences." Beale, The Proximate Consequences of an Act, 33 Harv.L.Rev. 633, 640 (1920). See also Cardozo, The Paradoxes of Legal Science 83–84 (1928);

Holland, Jurisprudence 153 (13th ed. 1924); John S. Strahorn, Jr., Criminology and the Law of Guilt, 84 U. of Pa.L.Rev. 491, 505 (1936).

27.   The quotation is from an opinion reversing a conviction of murder based upon a different set of facts, which pre-sent the same kind of problem. Defend-ant shot a girl, under circumstances which may have involved a deliberate in-tent to commit murder, and the jury found him guilty of this offense. But be-cause death resulted not from the wound, but from scarlet fever communicated to the girl by the physician who attended to the wound, the conviction was reversed. Bush v. Commonwealth, 74 Ky. 268, 271 (1880).

28.   See, for example, People v. Freudenberg, 121 Cal.App.2d 564, 582, 263 P.2d 875, 886 (1953); State v. Benton, 38 Del. 1, 16, 187 A. 609, 616 (1936); Wells v. State, 46 Ga.App. 412, 417, 167 S.E. 709, 711 (1933); Dunville v. State, 188 Ind. 373, 379, 123 N.E. 689, 690 (1919); State v. Newberg, 129 Or. 564, 575, 278 P. 568, 572 (1929); State v. Des Champs, 126 S.C. 416, 420, 120 S.E. 491,

may be mentioned "primary cause," [29] "efficient cause," [30] "efficient proximate cause," [31] "efficient adequate cause," [32] "legal cause" [33] and "jural cause." [34]

The American Law Institute has indicated its preference for the term "legal cause," [35] apparently on the notion that "proximate cause" indicates too much emphasis upon nearness in time or space.[36] The act of sending poisoned candy was recognized as the proximate cause of the death of the victim although the deadly sweets were sent across the continent on their terrible mission,[37] but the phrase was never intended to indicate nearness in time or space but only nearness in causal relation.[38]

The juridical import of the phrase is that cause and result are in such relation as to be within the legal view, and the term is merely a label placed upon the result. If so understood it is not calculated to mislead, and considerations of expediency and long usage suggest its retention. Within the field of juridical recognition we may speak of "proximate cause" and "proximate consequence" (or result), and beyond its boundaries the terms "remote cause" and "remote consequence" are available. If we speak of "legal cause" we may no doubt also employ the term "legal consequence," but it will not do to use the terms "illegal cause" and "illegal consequence" merely because there is causation in fact which is not recognized as a matter of law. In fact confusion is likely to result from an inquiry whether an unlawful act is a legal cause,[39] but the choice of a phrase is a mere matter of terminology which should not divert attention from the larger issues.

493 (1923); Franklin v. State, 41 Tex.Cr. R. 21, 27, 51 S.W. 951, 953 (1899); Taylor v. State, 193 Ark. 691, 694, 101 S.W.2d 956, 957 (1937); State v. Angelina, 73 W.Va. 146, 149, 80 S.E. 141, 142 (1913); State v. Osmus, 73 Wyo. 183, 197, 276 P.2d 469, 474 (1954); Parker v. United States, 406 A.2d 1275 (D.C.App.1979).

29. Thornton v. State, 107 Ga. 683, 688, 33 S.E. 673, 675 (1899); Clements v. State, 141 Ga. 667, 669, 81 S.E. 1117, 1118 (1914).

30. Commonwealth v. Fox, 73 Mass. 585, 586 (1856); Burnett v. State, 82 Tenn. 439, 446 (1884); Keller v. State, 155 Tenn. 633, 637, 299 S.W. 803, 805 (1927).

31. State v. Newberg, 129 Or. 564, 575, 278 P. 568, 572 (1929).

32. State v. Benton, 38 Del. 1, 17, 187 A. 609, 616 (1936).

33. Jeremiah Smith, Legal Cause in Actions of Tort, 25 Harv.L.Rev. 103 (1911); Edgerton, Legal Cause, 72 U. of Pa.L.Rev. 211, 343 (1924); Restatement, Torts §§ 279, 430, 431 (1934).

34. Wagner v. International Ry., 232 N.Y. 176, 181, 133 N.E. 437, 438 (1921); Cardozo, The Paradoxes of Legal Science

82 (1928). "Juridical Cause," McDaniel v. State, 76 Ala. 1, 7 (1884).

35. Restatement, Second, Torts § 9 (1965).

36. See Smith, Legal Cause in Actions of Tort, 25 Harv.L.Rev. 103, 106 (1911).

37. People v. Botkin, 132 Cal. 231, 64 P. 286 (1901).

38. "It must be clear that the proximity called for by the principle under discussion is proximity in causation; . . ." Beale, The Proximate Consequences of an Act, 33 Harv.L.Rev. 633, 643 (1920).

"In the present case the misdemeanor of the defendant must be regarded as too remote—not in time, to be sure, but as the cause." Hubbard v. Commonwealth, 304 Ky. 818, 202 S.W.2d 634, 637 (1947).

39. There is no actual inconsistency because "legal" is not synonymous with "lawful." Kokourek, An Introduction to the Science of Law 268 (1930). But it is confusing and furthermore it is useful to have a convenient term to use in contradistinction, such as "remote cause," whereas the use of "illegal cause" for this purpose would be confusing and misleading. McLaughlin, Proximate Cause, 39 Harv.L.Rev. 149, 150 n. 6 (1925).

1. LEGALLY–RECOGNIZED CAUSE

Whether the term used is "proximate cause," "legal cause," "jural cause," or some equivalent, the idea sought to be expressed is "legally-recognized cause," [40] which should be promptly tested by the question,—legally recognized for what purpose? The matters of policy which determine just where the limitations of juridical recognition shall be placed upon the broad field of actual cause, are grounded partly upon expediency [41] and partly upon notions of fairness and justice,[42] although even proximate cause must be distinguished from the concept of responsibility.[43] Since the boundary lines of proximate cause are governed by these considerations they may, and in fact do, vary according to the jural consequences of the particular kind of case involved.[44] The line of demarcation between causes which will be recognized as proximate and those which will be disregarded as remote "is really a flexible line." [45] "Legal causation reaches further" in some types of cases than it does in others.[46] It reaches further in tort actions based upon intentional harm than in those resulting from negligence,[47] and neither of the boundaries so established is necessarily controlling in other types of cases, such as actions for breach of contract,[48] those under Workmen's Compensation Acts,[49] or criminal prosecutions.[50]

40. "The question is what the courts will regard as the cause." Smith, Legal Cause in Actions of Tort, 25 Harv.L.Rev. 103, 104 (1911).

41. Beale, The Proximate Consequences of an Act, 33 Harv.L.Rev. 633, 640 (1920). "Justice involves practical considerations of which expedition of trials is one." McLaughlin, Proximate Cause, 39 Harv.L.Rev. 149, 155, n. 27 (1925).

42. "A legal cause is a justly-attachable cause; . . ." Edgerton, Legal Cause, 72 U. of Pa.L.Rev. 343, 348 (1924). Quoted with approval in Cardozo, The Paradoxes of Legal Science 86 (1928). "It would seem too clear for argument that considerations of fairness or justice have a bearing." McLaughlin, Proximate Cause, 39 Harv.L.Rev. 149, 155 (1925). "In the determination of proximate cause common sense is not to be eliminated." State v. Benton, 38 Del. 1, 16, 187 A. 609, 615 (1936).

43. The defendant fired two shots at the deceased, the first in privileged self-defense and the second after the need for self-defense had obviously passed. Whether the first shot or the second shot was the proximate cause of death, or whether both shots contributed in such a manner that each is a proximate cause, are matters to be determined by the law of proximate cause. If the first shot was the "sole cause" of death the slayer is not "responsible" for the killing for reasons which are quite apart from the principles of causation. Rogers v. State, 60 Ark. 76, 29 S.W. 894 (1894).

44. "Here is the key to the juridical treatment of the problems of causation. We pick out the cause which in our judgment ought to be treated as the dominant one with reference, not merely to the event itself, but to the jural consequences that ought to attach to the event." Cardozo, The Paradoxes of Legal Science 83 (1928).

45. 1 Street, Foundations of Legal Liability 111 (1906).

46. Jeremiah Smith, Legal Cause in Actions of Tort, 25 Harv.L.Rev. 223, 233 (1912).

47. Compare Restatement, Second, Torts, c. 16 (1965) with Restatement, Torts § 870 (1939).

48. "But cases laying down a restrictive rule of legal cause in actions for breach of contract are not necessarily authorities for a similar limitation of liability in actions of tort." Jeremiah Smith, Legal Cause in Actions of Tort, 25 Harv. L.Rev. 103, 126 (1911). "Thus the same event may have one jural cause when it is considered as giving rise to a cause of action upon a contract, and another when it is considered as giving rise to a cause of action for a tort." Cardozo, The Paradoxes of Legal Science 83–4 (1928).

49. An employee on a construction job who sought shelter in a barn during a heavy storm which interrupted the work, and was killed by a stroke of lightning

50. See note 50 on page 777.

Conceivably a different set of tests of proximate cause might be established for each particular crime. This has not been done, but since the degree of moral obliquity exhibited by the act, and the extent of the social menace involved, are factors to be considered,[51] the result will not necessarily be the same for all offenses. In particular, the legal eye reaches further in the examination of intentional crimes than in those in which this element is wanting, such as involuntary manslaughter.[52] Since either murder or manslaughter may be intentional or unintentional, it is not convenient to give this subject separate consideration in connection with the different types of criminal homicide, but it is important to limit the present inquiry very largely to criminal cases. Tort cases, for example, may be useful for very general purposes, but should be avoided when attention is directed to the boundary lines between proximate cause and remote cause as a problem of criminal law. Hence "proximate cause" or equivalent terms are used herein in the limited sense of cause which will receive juridical recognition in a criminal case,—except when broad generalizations are made, as in the following paragraph.

2. "TESTS" OR "CLUES" OF PROXIMATE CAUSE

The general subject of proximate cause has received the most exhaustive and painstaking consideration by legal writers,[53] much of the effort having been directed toward the discovery of some set of mechanical rules,—rules so simple and precise that by merely placing them beside any conceivable factual situation the difference between proximate and remote causes would at once be obvious. "But the question of causative relation is in reality one of fact and degree;" said Jeremiah Smith, over half a century ago, "and all attempts hitherto made at laying down universal tests of a more definite and more specific nature have resulted in propounding rules which are demonstrably erroneous."[54] And in the more recent expression of Mr. Justice Cardozo, any discussion of proximate cause is "mystifying and futile" so long as

while in the barn, was held to have suffered death from a risk which "arose out of employment" within the Workmen's Compensation Act. Buhrkuhl v. Odell Construction Co., 232 Mo.App. 967, 95 S.W.2d 843 (1936).

50. For example, if in a case similar to that in the preceding note the deceased had been taken into the barn for shelter after having been injured by the criminal negligence of another, the stroke of lightning would have been a superseding cause in a prosecution for manslaughter.

51. Legal causation may be broader in a case of felonious assault than in a case of non-felonious assault. Patterson v. State, 181 Ga. 698, 184 S.E. 309 (1936). And see 1 Street, Foundations of Legal Liability 111 (1906); Cardozo, The Paradoxes of Legal Science 84 (1928).

52. "It is generally agreed that results intended by an actor are proximate if they, in fact, take place." McLaughlin, Proximate Cause, 39 Harv.L.Rev. 149, 151 (1925).

53. See, for example, Green, Rationale of Proximate Cause (1927); 1 Street, Foundations of Legal Liability 110 et seq. (1906); Cardozo, The Paradoxes of Legal Science pp. 81 et seq. (1928); Jeremiah Smith, Legal Cause in Actions of Tort, 25 Harv.L.Rev. 103, 222, 303 (1911–12); Henry T. Terry, Proximate Consequences in the Law of Torts, 28 Harv.L.Rev. 10 (1914); Joseph H. Beale, The Proximate Consequences of an Act, 33 Harv.L.Rev. 633 (1920); Henry W. Edgerton, Legal Cause, 72 U. of Pa.L.Rev. 211, 343 (1924); James Angell McLaughlin, Proximate Cause, 39 Harv.L.Rev. 149 (1925); Charles E. Carpenter, Workable Rules for Determining Proximate Cause, 20 Calif.L.Rev. 229, 396, 471 (1932); Prosser, Proximate Cause in California, 38 Calif.L. Rev. 369 (1950); James and Perry, Legal Cause, 60 Yale L.Jour. 761 (1951). Many others are cited in the article by Prosser.

54. Legal Cause in Actions of Tort, 25 Harv.L.Rev. 303, 317 (1912).

effort is made "to give absolute validity to doctrines that must be conceived and stated in terms of relativity." [55] The guides propounded have value and significance, he points out, and yet they are in the last analysis "not tests, but clews." [56]

At one very narrow point, in the homicide cases, there is a purely mechanical test which has been handed down from ancient times. Under this test, no cause of death will receive juridical recognition as such, if it antedated the result by more than "a year and a day." [57] Unless the death occurs within this period after the wound or other harm complained of, the law conclusively presumes that the loss of life was due entirely to other causes and will not hear evidence to the contrary.[58]

The phrase "year and a day," in this test, means no more than a year. The accepted method of computing time today is by excluding the first day and including the last.[59] Thus a year from January first is the first day of the following January. In ancient times, however, there was a tendency to include both the first day and the last day so that a year from January first was thought of as the thirty-first of the following December,[60] and "the day was added that there might be a whole year." [61] The use of this peculiar phrase to mean just a year in the homicide cases has found expression in some of the statutes.[62] Other enactments have wisely dropped this ancient jingle.

Under some legislation, the requirement of this ancient rule has been held to be abrogated entirely; [63] although uncommon, there is growing support for this position.[64] Except where such change has been made there exists one simple mechanical rule of exclusion. It is, of course, not a final test of inclusion. If the death is found to have occurred within this period it is necessary to examine other "clues" to determine what shall be said to be the proximate cause.

55. Cardozo, The Paradoxes of Legal Science 85 (1928).

56. Ibid.

57. Fitz., Ab. Corone Pl. 163 (1330); 3 Co.Inst. *53; 1 Hale P.C. *426; 2 Ibid. *179; 2 Hawk.P.C. c. 25, sec. 77, 4 Bl. Comm. *197; 1 East P.C. 343–4; State v. Dailey, 191 Ind. 678, 134 N.E. 481 (1921); Hardin v. State, 4 Tex.Cr.R. 355 (1878). For an extensive list of citations for the rule that the death must occur within a year and a day, see a note in 20 A.L.R. 1006.

Some courts have concluded the year and a day rule should be abandoned. State v. Young, 148 N.J.Super. 405, 372 A.2d 1117 (1977), reversed 77 N.J. 245, 390 A.2d 556 (1978).

58. ". . . for if he die after that time, it cannot be discerned, as the law presumes, whether he died of the stroke or poyson, etc. or of a natural death;

. . ." 3 Co.Inst. *53. " . . . if death did not take place within a year and a day of the time of receiving the wound, the law draws the conclusion that it was not the cause of the death; and neither the Court nor Jury, can draw a contrary one." State v. Orrell, 12 N.C. 139, 141 (1826).

59. Aiken v. Appleby, Mor. 8 (Iowa, 1839).

60. "If the stroke or poyson, etc. be given the first day of January, the year shall end the last day of December:" 3 Co.Inst. *53.

61. Ibid.

62. Idaho Code § 18–4008 (1979).

63. See, for example, People v. Brengard, 265 N.Y. 100, 191 N.E. 850 (1934).

64. West's Ann.Pen.Code § 194 (1970). See State v. Young, 77 N.J. 245, 390 A.2d 556 (1978).

3. SUBSTANTIAL FACTOR

If every problem of proximate cause could be disposed of automatically by the application of some rule-of-thumb as simple as the year-and-a-day test of exclusion, much time and effort would be saved, but this saving would be at the expense of individual and social interests.[65] There are such infinite possibilities of variation in the field of actual cause, that solutions dependent upon purely mechanical rules would produce absurd results; whereas "in the determination of proximate cause common sense is not to be eliminated." [66] None of the other "tests" or "clues" in the field of proximate cause can be applied with the automatic precision of the year-and-a-day rule, but a guide which is helpful in reaching a socially-desirable result is not to be rejected or despised merely because it requires a certain amount of common sense in its application.

One such clue, which seems to prevail generally throughout the field of proximate cause, is that no cause will receive juridical recognition if the part it played was so infinitesimal or so theoretical that it cannot properly be regarded as a *substantial factor* in bringing about the particular result. This is merely a special application of the general maxim—*"de minimis non curat lex"* (the law is not concerned with trifles). An illustration may be useful. If a man bleeds to death from two wounds inflicted by different persons, acting quite independently, "both may properly be said to have contributed to his death." [67] If at the moment of death both injuries were substantially contributing thereto, the "law does not measure the effects of the several injuries in order to determine which is the more serious and which contributed in greater measure to bring about the death," but imputes the loss of life to both.[68] But suppose one wound severed the jugular vein whereas the other barely broke the skin on the hand, and as the life blood gushed from the victim's neck, one drop oozed from the bruise on his finger. No homicide "does more than to hasten the termination of life,"[69] and metaphysicians will conclude that the extra drop of lost blood hastened the end by the infinitesimal fraction of a second. But the law will apply the *substantial factor* test and for juridical purposes the death will be imputed only to the severe injury in such an extreme case as this. The facts may be changed by supposing the one injury to be a little less extreme and the other somewhat more appreciable than previously assumed. And by variations so gradual that each case seems indistinguishable from the last, the point will eventually be reached where the blood flowed with equal volume from each wound. Long before this point is reached the death will be imputed to both wounds

---

65. "A legal cause is a justly-attachable cause; (or) a legal consequence is a justly-attachable consequence; (or) a legal cause is a cause which stands in such a relation to its consequences that it is just to give legal effect to the relation: meaning by 'just,' not merely fair as between the parties, but socially advantageous, as serving the most important of the competing individual and social interests involved." Edgerton, Legal Cause, 72 U. of Pa.L.Rev. (211) 343, 348 (1924). Quoted with approval by Justice Benjamin N. Cardozo, The Paradoxes of Legal Science 86 (1928).

66. State v. Benton, 38 Del. 1, 16, 187 A. 609, 615 (1936).

67. People v. Lewis, 124 Cal. 551, 559, 57 P. 470, 473 (1899). See also Henderson v. State, 11 Ala.App. 37, 65 So. 721 (1914).

68. State v. Francis, 152 S.C. 17, 60, 149 S.E. 348, 364 (1928); State v Luster, 178 S.C. 199, 208, 182 S.E. 427, 431 (1935).

69. Wells v. State, 46 Ga.App. 412, 416, 167 S.E. 709, 711 (1932).

rather than merely to one, and whenever the nature of the injuries is such that the lesser of the two may have had some substantial effect "in hastening the death of the deceased" the question of whether it did so contribute is a question "for the determination of the jury." [70] Unavoidably the jurors must use common sense in applying the substantial factor "clue" to all the facts in evidence in the particular case.

The substantial factor test has been said to be useful only to determine the fact of causation.[71] Perhaps the statement should be that it serves to emphasize common sense and rule out purely theoretical abstractions. Rather than undertake a metaphysical argument in the effort to show that the drop of lost blood (or two dozen drops) did not hasten the death by even the most infinitesimal fraction of a second, it seems sufficient to say that in any event there was no hastening which will receive legal recognition. However it is expressed, the substantial factor test is one of exclusion only. What was not a substantial factor in causing harm was not a proximate cause thereof. What was a substantial factor may have been a proximate cause— or it may not.

4. "COME TO REST IN A POSITION OF APPARENT SAFETY"

Juridical consideration will not follow the consequences of an act beyond the point at which the "force" [72] which was thus set in motion has "come to rest in a position of apparent safety." [73] One, let us say, rolled a boulder down a mountain and this boulder killed a person in the valley below. If the boulder followed a relatively straight and unbroken course down the slope; or if a most strange and unusual bounce carried it over a certain shoulder of the mountain side and thus directed it to quite a different destination than would otherwise have been reached; or if at one point it paused momentarily in a precarious position before resuming its forward flight;—in any of these eventualities the act of starting the boulder down the mountain side is the proximate cause of the death. But suppose the forward motion had been definitely stopped. Several obstructions had perhaps tended to break the momentum and finally a tree checked it completely, where the stone was securely held; not even a substantial shove would have dislodged it, and there it remained week after week. As time passed, however, one limb of the tree was gradually bent by the weight of the stone, and six months after the original act, this limb had moved sufficiently to permit the boulder to start once more its downward course, with the resulting loss of life. In this case also the act of starting the boulder down the mountain side is *in fact* a cause of the death, but for juridical purposes it is a remote rather than a proximate cause of this result. The sequence of occurrences initiated by the act of starting the stone was effectively broken when it came to rest in a position of apparent safety.

70. State v. Luster, 178 S.C. 199, 207, 182 S.E. 427, 430, 431 (1935). And see, Thompson v. State, 220 Miss. 200, 70 So. 2d 341 (1954).

71. See Prosser on Torts 287 (3d ed. 1964).

72. In this connection "force" "is not used in a scientific sense. It is used in a popular sense." McLaughlin, Proximate Cause, 39 Harv.L.Rev. 149, 157 (1925).

73. Beale, The Proximate Consequences of an Act, 33 Harv.L.Rev. 633, 651 (1920); Edgerton, Legal Cause, 72 U. of Pa.L.Rev. 211, 239 (1924).

The principle underlying this guide is not limited to situations in which a force comes to rest in so literal a fashion as in the illustration given. For example, a man might cause the death of his wife by forcing her from the house in freezing weather. If she should die from the cold without being able to reach a place of safety he would unquestionably be the proximate cause of her death. But in one such case the wife's father lived not far away and she reached his house before suffering harm. It was then very late at night and although she would have been welcome there at any hour she did not like the thought of disturbing the household at that time and so she stretched out on the ground to wait for morning, but died from exposure during the night. As she had reached a place of apparent safety the original act of the husband was not the proximate cause of her death.[74]

The addition of the adjective, it may be mentioned, is merely to avoid captious objections. If the statement was in terms of a "force" which had come to rest in a position of "safety" there would be those who would insist that no such position had been reached if harm followed. The reference to "apparent safety" is merely to permit situations to be considered in terms of common sense rather than philosophical abstraction.[75]

5. SOLE CAUSE: SUPERSEDING CAUSE

As a matter of *fact* there are many causes of every result, but whenever a problem of this nature requires judicial determination, the point of approach is to see "which antecedent shall . . . be selected from an infinite series of antecedents as big with the event." [76] In other words, the effort is to determine which cause "ought to be treated as the dominant one with reference not merely to the event itself, but to the jural consequences that ought to attach to the event." [77] When this one dominant cause is found it is treated as the "sole cause" [78] for the purposes of the particular case, even if it might not be so treated in a different kind of cause of action. A "sole cause" which intervenes between defendant's act and the result in question is spoken of as a "superseding cause." [79]

74. State v. Preslar, 48 N.C. 421 (1856). The facts of the case were more complicated than the statement in the text but the same problem was presented. See also Hendrickson v. Commonwealth, 85 Ky. 281, 3 S.W. 166 (1887). It has been suggested that the explanation of these cases is the "contributory negligence" of the wife. See Carpenter, Rules for Determining Proximate Cause, 20 Cal.L.Rev. 471, 487 (1932). But this is unsound because contributory negligence of the person harmed is not a defense to a criminal prosecution.

75. "Probably Professor Beale's most helpful suggestion is that regarding apparent safety: . . ." Edgerton, Legal Cause, 72 U. of Pa.L.Rev. 211, 239 (1924).

This is merely another way of expressing the rule that for a "force" set in motion by D to be recognized as the proximate cause of harm that came later, "The force thus created must (a) have remained active. . . ." Commonwealth v. Almeida, 362 Pa. 596, 68 A.2d 595, 600 (1949).

76. Cardozo, The Paradoxes of Legal Science 82 (1928).

77. Id. at 83.

78. State v. Morphy, 33 Iowa 270, 276 (1871); Clark v. Commonwealth, 90 Va. 360, 365, 18 S.E. 440, 442 (1893).

79. "A superseding cause is an act of a third person or other force which by its intervention prevents the actor from being liable for harm to another which his antecedent negligence is a substantial factor in bringing about." Restatement, Second, Torts § 440 (1965). Sometimes the phrase "supervening cause" is used, as in the following case in which a certain fact was held not to be such. Embrey v. State, 94 Tex.Cr.R. 591, 592, 251 S.W. 1062, 1063 (1923).

The phrase "sole cause," meaning the only cause which will receive juridical recognition for the purposes of the particular case, is convenient to give emphasis to three points: (1) If defendant's act was the sole cause of the death or other socially-harmful occurrence, it is by definition a proximate cause thereof; (2) if something other than his act was the sole cause of the harm there need be no further inquiry so far as he is concerned; (3) it is not necessary that defendant's act should have been the sole cause of the harm,—which is merely another form of stating that a contributory cause is sufficient.

6. CONTRIBUTORY CAUSE

The search for *one dominant* cause may end with the discovery that more than one cause must receive juridical notice, and when this is true both (or all) of these are called "contributory causes." [80]

Mention has been made of death resulting from hemorrhage where two wounds had been inflicted. If at the time of death both wounds were substantially contributing to the loss of life,—"if the life current went out from both"—the act which inflicted either one is a proximate cause of the death,[81] and both "may properly be said to have contributed to his death." [82] This of course is merely illustrative; it is not essential to the existence of contributory causes that the death should result from loss of blood. If the deceased died from blows on the head inflicted by two persons who acted quite independently the acts of each are proximate causes if they "contributed" to the fatal result.[83] There may also be contributory causes of other socially-harmful consequences as, for example, a nuisance.[84]

If two (or more) are acting in concert to commit an unlawful act, such as murder, the act of each in furtherance of the criminal effort is for juridical purposes the act of both (or of all). Hence if two inflict injuries on a third in a concerted effort to commit murder, both are guilty of this crime if death results even if the wound inflicted by one did not contribute to the loss of life.[85] The present problem, therefore, is limited to injuries inflicted by persons who were acting, not in concert, but quite independently. Where this is true the two wounds might be inflicted at the same moment, but in the vast majority of instances one will precede the other. The element of time is not to be ignored in these cases, because this plus other elements may induce the conclusion that the act of one was not a *substantial factor* in bringing about

---

80. State v. Rounds, 104 Vt. 442, 453, 160 A. 249, 252 (1932). The form "contributing cause" is also used. State v. Wilson, 114 La. 398, 399, 38 So. 397, 398 (1905); Houston v. State, 220 Miss. 166, 169, 70 So.2d 338, 339 (1954).

81. Pitts v. State, 53 Okl.Cr. 165, 168, 8 P.2d 78, 79 (1932).

82. People v. Lewis, 124 Cal. 551, 559, 57 P. 470, 473 (1899).

"When the conduct of two or more persons contributes concurrently as proximate causes of death, the conduct of each person is a proximate cause regard-

less of the extent to which each contributes to the death." People v. Vernon, 89 Cal.App.3d 853, 152 Cal.Rptr. 765, 772 (1979).

83. Duque v. State, 56 Tex.Cr.R. 214, 216, 119 S.W. 687, 688 (1909).

84. People v. Gold Run Ditch and Mining Co., 66 Cal. 138, 4 P. 1152 (1884).

85. Henderson v. State, 11 Ala.App. 37, 65 So. 721 (1913). If two are engaged in the concerted effort to rob a third and one of the robbers kills the victim, both are guilty of murder. Commonwealth v. Shawell, 325 Pa. 497, 191 A. 17 (1937).

the harmful result.[86] In the absence of such a period as to bring into operation the year-and-a-day rule, however, no rule-of-thumb can be stated in this connection, and acts may be recognized as contributory even if they do not concur in point of time.[87] A wound which "materially promoted or hastened" death is a proximate cause thereof, "although the wound just previously inflicted on deceased by another assailant also could be said to have caused his death." [88] One, for example, who comes upon the scene after an officer has been shot and mortally wounded, may be a contributory cause of the death by firing an additional shot into the prostrate, but still living, form.[89] On the other hand, the act which inflicted the first injury may also be a proximate cause of the fatal result.[90] "The test . . . is whether, when death occurred, the first wound contributed to the event." [91]

It is important to repeat in this connection that the controlling question is not what *would have happened*, but what did actually happen.[92] If a certain act was a substantial factor in bringing about the loss of human life, it is not prevented from being a proximate cause of this result by proof of the fact that it alone would not have resulted in death,[93] nor by proof that another contributory cause would have been fatal even without the aid of this act.[94] If, for example, death results from the combined effects of a knife wound, and an injury inflicted by a shotgun in the hands of a different person who acted quite independently, the one who wielded the knife may be convicted of murder (if he struck with malice aforethought) even though the jury do not believe that the knife wound alone would have been fatal.[95] And if one mortally wounds another, after which a third, acting quite independently, inflicts a second injury upon the same victim, both assailants may be convicted of murder (if each acted with malice aforethought and the injury of each con-

---

86. Edgerton, Legal Cause, 72 U. of Pa.L.Rev. 343, 371 (1924).

Where defendants beat deceased and his body was found two days later, the defendant's claim that the time interval was a sufficient indication of an intervening cause was rejected. People v. Dillon, 28 Ill.App.3d 11, 327 N.E.2d 225 (1975).

87. Payne v. Commonwealth, 255 Ky. 533, 75 S.W.2d 14 (1934); Pitts v. State, 53 Okl.Cr. 165, 8 P.2d 78 (1932); State v. Weston, 155 Or. 556, 64 P.2d 536 (1937); State v. Luster, 178 S.C. 199, 182 S.E. 427 (1935).

88. Talley v. State, 174 Ala. 101, 105, 57 So. 445, 446–7 (1912).

89. State v. Weston, 155 Or. 556, 64 P.2d 536 (1937).

90. Henderson v. State, 11 Ala.App. 37, 65 So. 721 (1914); Payne v. Commonwealth, 255 Ky. 533, 75 S.W.2d 14 (1934); State v. Snider, 81 W.Va. 522, 94 S.E. 981 (1918).

Defendant was held to have caused the victim's death where defendant struck the victim with his car causing non-fatal injuries and left the scene of the accident and thereafter the victim, in a disabled condition, was run over by a second car. People v. Parra, 35 Ill.App.3d 240, 340 N.E.2d 636 (1975).

91. Pitts v. State, 53 Okl.Cr. 165, 168, 8 P.2d 78 (1932).

92. If the issue is responsibility, it may be important to consider what would have happened. If the defendant while driving his motorcycle, knocked down a girl who died as a result of the accident, there is no doubt of the causal relation between defendant's act and the death. But if the accident would have happened just the same, no matter how much care the defendant had used, the death cannot properly be attributed to criminal negligence or improper driving. Dunville v. State, 188 Ind. 373, 379, 123 N.E. 689 (1919).

93. Henderson v. State, 11 Ala.App. 37, 65 So. 721 (1914).

94. Duque v. State, 56 Tex.Cr.R. 214, 119 S.W. 687 (1909).

95. Henderson v. State, 11 Ala.App. 37, 65 So. 721 (1914).

tributed to the death) whether the second injury alone would or would not have been fatal.[96]

On the other hand, if defendant knocked down the deceased, whereupon a bystander kicked the fallen man with fatal consequences, the one is not the cause of the death if it resulted *solely* from the kick, which was not induced or anticipated by him, nor the result of any preconcert of action.[97] Nor is a blow the cause of death if the loss of life was due solely to arsenical poisoning.[98] Even a wound which *would have been* mortal is not juridically recognized as the cause of death, if some other cause intervened in such a manner that the first was not a substantial factor in the actual loss of life.[99] An extreme illustration would be a pistol shot inflicting an injury which *would have* resulted in death in two or three days, but which did not so result because of the act of a third person which severed the victim's head from his body. To adopt a dictum of the California court, the shooter was prevented from killing his victim as effectually "as he would have been if some obstacle had turned aside the bullet from its course and left Farrell unwounded."[1]

It is not improper to repeat, under the head of "contributory cause" that if a legal duty to take positive action for the safety of others rests upon two (or more) persons, both (or all) of whom fail to perform with the result that life is lost, the negative act of each is a proximate cause of the death.[2]

Either a sole cause which will at once disprove a charge of crime against a particular defendant, or a contributory cause which will not have this effect, may be found in the form of (1) an event,[3] (2) an act of a third person,[4] (3) an act of the deceased, or (4) another act of the defendant himself.

If the only acts which may have caused the social harm were committed by the accused himself, it is seldom important to inquire whether more than one of these acts can be brought under the label of proximate cause, but in rare cases it may be a controlling issue in the case. This situation arises where some of his acts were privileged or excused and some were not. The

96. Payne v. Commonwealth, 255 Ky. 533, 75 S.W.2d 14 (1934).

97. People v. Elder, 100 Mich. 515, 59 N.W. 237 (1894).

98. Lewis v. Commonwealth, 19 Ky.L. Rep. 1139, 42 S.W. 1127 (1897).

99. State v. Scates, 50 N.C. 420 (1858); State v. Wood, 53 Vt. 560 (1881); State v. Angelina, 73 W.Va. 146, 80 S.E. 141 (1913).

1. People v. Lewis, 124 Cal. 551, 554–5, 57 P. 470, 472 (1899).

2. Regina v. Haines, 2 Car. & K. 368, 175 Eng.Rep. 152 (1847); Commonwealth v. Howard, 265 Pa.Super. 535, 402 A.2d 674 (1979).

3. "If a wound causes a disease which produces death and there is no evidence of gross neglect or improper treatment, the death is imputable to the wound." Moore v. State, 126 Tex.Cr.R. 391, 395, 71 S.W.2d 531, 533 (1934). Event as sole cause. Bush v. Commonwealth, 78 Ky. 268 (1880); Quinn v. State, 106 Miss. 844, 64 So. 738 (1914). Event as contributory cause. Rex v. Cheeseman, 7 Car. & P. 455, 173 Eng.Rep. 202 (1836); Huckabee v. State, 159 Ala. 45, 48 So. 796 (1909); Wells v. State, 46 Ga.App. 412, 167 S.E. 709 (1933); Hopkins v. Commonwealth, 117 Ky. 941, 80 S.W. 156 (1904); State v. Wilson, 114 La. 398, 38 So. 397 (1905); Miller v. State, 263 Ind. 595, 335 N.E.2d 206 (1975).

4. Act of another as sole cause. Lewis v. Commonwealth, 19 Ky.L.Rep. 1139, 42 S.W. 1127 (1897); People v. Elder, 100 Mich. 515, 59 N.W. 237 (1894). Act of another as contributory cause. Henderson v. State, 11 Ala.App. 37, 65 So. 721 (1914); Payne v. Commonwealth, 255 Ky. 533, 75 S.W.2d 14 (1934); State v. Weston, 155 Or. 556, 64 P.2d 536 (1937); Duque v. State, 56 Tex.Cr.R. 214, 119 S.W. 687 (1909); State v. Snider, 81 W.Va. 522, 94 S.E. 981 (1918).

typical case is one in which defendant fired two shots at deceased, the first being in privileged self-defense and the second after the need for defensive action had so obviously passed that there was no justification or excuse for further shooting. If the second shot was the sole cause of death, or if it was a contributory cause thereof, the proof of self-defense has failed to exculpate the slayer; but if the first shot was the sole cause of the loss of life the claim of *criminal* homicide has been disproved.[5]

7. CONTRIBUTORY NEGLIGENCE

If an act of the deceased was a contributory cause of his death the problem is usually, though not necessarily, one of contributory negligence. Such negligence on the part of the deceased may be considered by the judge, together with all the other facts, in fixing the sentence in a particular case,[6] but it has no bearing upon either responsibility or imputability in the determination of guilt or innocence.[7] As said by the Alabama court: "The rule concerning contributory negligence is applicable in actions for damages for personal injuries and has no application in criminal cases."[8] Hence in a manslaughter prosecution the judge commits no error by his refusal to permit the jury to consider the contributory negligence of the deceased.[9] This is true, moreover, whether the contributory negligence preceded[10] or followed[11] the act of the person accused of criminal homicide.

One, for example, whose criminal negligence has caused a fire which resulted in the loss of life is the proximate cause of the death even if the deceased was negligent in his efforts to escape from the burning building;[12] a

5. Rogers v. State, 60 Ark. 76, 29 S.W. 894 (1894); Caughron v. State, 99 Ark. 462, 139 S.W. 315 (1911). ". . . but if the respondent's blows were partly justified and partly not justified, then he cannot be held responsible for homicide unless the unlawful blows contributed to the death." State v. Rounds, 104 Vt. 442, 456, 160 A. 249, 253 (1932).

6. Regina v. Longbottom, 3 Cox C.C. 439 (1849).

7. People v. Freudenberg, 121 Cal. App.2d 564, 263 P.2d 875 (1953); Cain v. State, 55 Ga.App. 376, 190 S.E. 371 (1937); People v. Barnes, 182 Mich. 179, 148 N.W. 400 (1914); Copeland v. State, 154 Tenn. 7, 285 S.W. 565 (1926).

Where defendant's wife thought defendant was going to commit suicide and was killed in an attempt to wrestle a gun from the defendant, it was held the wife's actions did not provide an exculpatory cause relieving the husband from responsibility. State v. Shanahan, 404 A.2d 975 (Me. 1979).

8. Broxton v. State, 27 Ala. 298, 300, 171 So. 390, 392 (1937).

"Contributory negligence of the victim is not a defense in a criminal prosecution." Wren v. State, 577 P.2d 235, 238 (Alaska 1978).

"We would first observe that . . . comparative negligence, like contributory negligence . . . is not a defense to a criminal charge." Overton v. State, 606 P.2d 586, 587 (Okl.Cr.App. 1979).

It "is well settled that contributory negligence of the victim is never a defense to a criminal prosecution, but it can be considered by the jury to show that the defendant was not negligent or that his acts did not constitute the proximate cause of the death." State v. Crace, 289 N.W.2d 54, 56 (Minn.1979).

9. Graives v. State, 127 Fla. 182, 172 So. 716 (1937). See also Stover v. State, 132 Tex.Cr.R. 356, 104 S.W.2d 48 (1937).

10. Cain v. State, 55 Ga.App. 376, 190 S.E. 371 (1937); Maxon v. State, 177 Wis. 319, 187 N.W. 753 (1922).

11. Rew's Case, J. Kelyng 26, 84 Eng. Rep. 1066 (1662); Regina v. Holland, 2 M. & Rob. 351, 174 Eng.Rep. 313 (1841); Bowles v. State, 58 Ala. 335 (1877); Payne v. Commonwealth, 20 Ky.L.Rep. 475, 46 S.W. 704 (1898); Embry v. Commonwealth, 236 Ky. 204, 32 S.W.2d 979 (1930); State v. Baker, 46 N.J. 267 (1854); Franklin v. State, 41 Tex.Cr.R. 21, 51 S.W. 951 (1899).

12. Embry v. Commonwealth, 236 Ky. 204, 32 S.W.2d 979 (1930).

driver whose criminal negligence on the highway has been a substantial factor in a fatal traffic accident is the proximate cause of this result even if decedent was equally negligent at the wheel of the other vehicle; [13] and one who inflicted a wound which resulted in death is the proximate cause thereof even if the victim's life might have been saved had he not left the hospital prematurely, [14] or neglected the injury. [15]

"It is enough to say," said the Iowa court, "that contributory negligence, if shown, is never a defense or excuse for crime, nor can it in any degree serve to purge an act otherwise constituting a public offense of its criminal character." [16]

Even the intentional cooperation of the person who has been harmed will not relegate to the field of remoteness an act of another which has been a substantial factor in producing the harm. And it will not excuse from criminal guilt if the law does not permit the act even with his consent, as in instances of the intentional taking of life, [17] or non-surgical mutilation. [18]

8. CONTRIBUTORY NEGLIGENCE OF THIRD PERSON

Although it amounts to no more than a specific application of the general principle mentioned under the head of contributory cause, it may be useful to add that one whose negligent act is a substantial factor in producing the death of a person is a proximate cause of the homicide, even though the contributory negligence of a third person aided in the fatal result. [19] Thus if a traffic accident results from negligence on the part of the drivers of two different cars, ending in the death of a *passenger* in one of the cars, the death may be imputed to both drivers. [20] And a railroad foreman whose negligence in removing rails, just as a train was due, caused a wreck in which lives were lost, was a proximate cause of the deaths even though the engineer was negligent in not keeping a more vigilant look-out. [21] In one case a defendant who had been convicted of manslaughter sought to have the conviction reversed because the deceased's mother had removed him from the hospital against the doctor's advice. The conviction was affirmed despite evidence that moving the patient, whose neck had been broken, hastened his

13. Maxon v. State, 177 Wis. 379, 187 N.W. 753 (1922).

14. See Pyles v. State, 78 So.2d 813, 815 (Ala.App.1954).

15. State v. Inger, 292 N.W.2d 119 (Iowa 1980).

16. State v. Moore, 129 Iowa 516, 519, 106 N.W. 16, 17 (1906). Repeated in substance in State v. Thomlinson, 209 Iowa 555, 556, 228 N.W. 80, 81 (1929).

"The victim's negligence is not a defense to criminal conduct." United States v. Kreimer, 609 F.2d 126, 132 (5th Cir. 1980).

17. Regina v. Allison, 8 Car. & P. 418, 173 Eng.Rep. 557 (1838). In a California case defendant inflicted an injury upon decedent which would have resulted in death in about an hour. Decedent then slashed his throat inflicting an injury from which he must have died in five

minutes. He actually bled to death from both. A conviction of manslaughter was affirmed. People v. Lewis, 124 Cal. 551, 57 P. 470 (1899).

18. Wright's case, Co.Litt. 127a (1604).

19. Regina v. Haines, 2 Car. & K. 368, 175 Eng.Rep. 152 (1847).

If defendant caused the death of others by criminal negligence he is guilty of involuntary manslaughter. The fact that others may have been equally negligent is not defense for him. State v. Dykes, 114 Ariz. 592, 562 P.2d 1090 (App. 1977); State v. Myers, 88 N.M. 16, 536 P.2d 280 (App.1975).

20. Schultz v. State, 89 Neb. 34, 130 N.W. 972 (1911); State v. Harris, 194 Neb. 74, 230 N.W.2d 203 (1975).

21. Regina v. Benge, 4 Fost. & F. 504, 176 Eng.Rep. 665 (1865).

death.[22] Insufficient or improper medical attention to the victim will not excuse an assailant's conduct.[23]

9. NEGLIGENCE OF OTHER AS SOLE CAUSE

It must not be assumed that negligence of the deceased or of another is to be entirely disregarded. Even though the defendant was criminally negligent in his conduct it is possible for negligence of the deceased or another to intervene between this conduct and the fatal result in such a manner as to constitute a superseding cause, completely eliminating the defendant from the field of proximate causation.[24] This is true only in situations in which the second act of negligence looms so large in comparison with the first, that the first is not to be regarded as a substantial factor in the final result. In one case, for example, the defendant by his criminal negligence had created a risk of explosion in a building. The deceased, after being fully warned of the danger and urgently requested to say out, went in and was killed. This death was held to be imputable solely to the negligence of the deceased and not at all to the negligent conduct of the defendant.[25] In another case, while the driver of a horse-drawn vehicle did not even have the reins in his hands, a child suddenly ran in front and was killed. Erle, J., charged the jury that if by the utmost care on his part the driver could not have prevented the accident, he must be acquitted.[26]

In like manner the negligence of a third person may intervene in such a way as to be the sole cause of resulting death within the legal view. For example, a starter was criminally negligent in starting a second train too soon after the first had departed and the second train crashed into the first, killing a passenger. But this homicide was imputed solely to the negligence of a flagman who got confused in his signals and held up the first train until it was struck by the second.[27]

10. DIRECT CAUSE

Juridical recognition is not limited to the direct cause of social harm. "One who inflicts an injury on another is deemed by law" to have caused homicide "if the injury contributes *mediately* or *immediately* to the death" of such person.[28] In fact, any reference to direct cause is largely for the sake of emphasis.

A cause which produces a result without the aid of any intervening cause is a direct cause.[29]

22. People v. Clark, 106 Cal.App.2d 271, 235 P.2d 56 (1951).

23. State v. Sauter, 120 Ariz. 222, 585 P.2d 242 (1978).

24. The Queen v. Dalloway, 2 Cox C.C. 273 (1847); Dunville v. State, 188 Ind. 373, 123 N.E. 689 (1919).

"Although contributory negligence is no defense to negligent homicide . . . evidence of contributory negligence may be material to whether defendant's negligence was a proximate cause of the death or whether the defendant was negligent at all." State v. Nerison, 28 Wn. App. 659, 625 P.2d 735, 737, n. 1 (1981).

25. Carbo v. State, 4 Ga.App. 583, 62 S.E. 140 (1908). See also Baylor v. United States, 407 A.2d 664 (D.C.App.1979).

26. Regina v. Dalloway, 2 Cox C.C. 273 (1847).

27. The Queen v. Ledger, 2 Fost. & F. 857, 175 Eng.Rep. 1319 (1862).

28. State v. Luster, 178 S.C. 199, 207–8, 182 S.E. 427, 431 (1935). See also State v. Wilson, 114 La. 398, 399, 38 So. 397, 398 (1905).

29. "A direct result is one which immediately and necessarily follows the act." Frey v. State, 97 Okl.Cr. 410, 413, 265 P.2d 502, 505 (1953).

If sequences follow one another in such a customary order that no other cause would commonly be thought of as intervening, the causal connection is spoken of as direct for juridical purposes even though many intervening causes might be recognized by a physicist.[30] If, for example, a person crooks his finger so as to cause the trigger of a firearm to move, whereupon numerous sequences are caused to follow one another, including among others the fall of the hammer, the spark, the sudden expansion as powder turns to gas, the violent expulsion of the bullet from the muzzle, the flight of the bullet governed by numerous laws of nature, the impingement of the bullet upon the body of another, and the loss of blood from the wound in such quantities that death follows very promptly,—the crooking of the finger is said to be a direct cause of death. Any inconsistency between this form of expression and the scientific view is unimportant in this regard, because the jural consequences are the same whether the original act caused the harm directly or with the aid of dependent intervening causes, unless the dependent intervening cause is the abnormal response of a human being or an animal. In the latter case the jural consequences *may* be different but where this is true the causation will not be spoken of as direct,—and is not commonly thought of as such.

With reference to that part of the field in which jural consequences are not dependent upon whether the causation is direct or is aided by dependent intervening forces, it is sufficient to say that there have been different analyses which have not affected the actual disposition of cases. Two decisions are illustrative. A man struck his wife in the face with his open hand, knocking her down, and as she fell her head came in contact with a chair and death resulted.[31] The driver of one vehicle ran into another, frightening the horses attached to the second vehicle and causing them to run away. The run-away horses overturned that carriage with fatal consequences to an occupant.[32] In each of these cases the act was very properly held to be a proximate cause of the death, but whereas in the second case there was said to be "direct causal connection between the collision and the death of the deceased," [33] the causation in the first case was spoken of as indirect.[34] Had the two explanations been reversed they would have been more in line with the usual forms of expression. There was nothing which would be recog-

---

"The burden was on the Commonwealth to prove beyond a reasonable doubt that the death of [the victim] was the direct result of the gunshot wound inflicted by [defendant]." Muse v. Commonwealth, 551 S.W.2d 564 (Ky.1977).

"He starts with a uniformly recognized definition: that proximate cause is the cause which through its natural and foreseeable consequence, unbroken by any sufficient intervening cause, produces the injury which would not have occurred but for that cause." State v. Hallett, 619 P.2d 335, 338 (Utah 1980).

30. "As indicated above any number of forces in the sense of physics may intervene between the defendant's act and the harm; but if each of these forces is brought into play, if each new source of

energy is tapped, by the disturbance or continuous series of disturbances started by defendant, the causation may still be direct." McLaughlin, Proximate Cause, 39 Harv.L.Rev. 149, 167 (1925).

31. Commonwealth v. McAfee, 108 Mass. 458 (1871).

32. Belk v. People, 125 Ill. 584, 17 N.E. 744 (1888).

33. Id. at 587, 17 N.E. at 745.

34. "If unlawful blows of the defendant caused the death, *either directly or by causing* the deceased to fall upon the floor by the force and effect thereof, and so death thereby ensued, then defendant is guilty of manslaughter." Commonwealth v. McAfee, 108 Mass. 458, 459–60 (1871). Italics added.

nized by law as an intervening cause of the death of the woman. The law of gravity played an important part in the fall, but it did not *intervene* because it was there all the time. It was "operating in defendant's presence . . . at the time of defendant's act." [35] The chair was *in the way*, perhaps, but it was not an intervening *cause* for the reason just mentioned. In the second case the running away of the horses was an intervening cause, but since it resulted from defendant's act it was dependent rather than independent, and did not "break the chain" of proximate cause.

The following cases are illustrative of the type of causation which is here spoken of as direct. One riding on a handcar stepped on the brake and jumped, just as the car was passing his boarding house. The application of the brake stopped the car so suddenly that all of the others were thrown off, one of them being instantly killed. The one who stepped on the brake was the proximate cause of the death.[36] A contractor having charge of the construction of a building was so culpably negligent in the use of inferior materials that the building fell and killed a person. The contractor was the proximate cause of this fatal result.[37] If a person sets fire to one building and the conflagration spreads in the normal manner to a second building nearby, the act of setting fire to the first building has been held to be the proximate cause of the burning of the second.[38] And the act of the master of a vessel in ordering aloft a seaman who was obviously too ill for such a task, was held to be the proximate cause of the seaman's falling to his death in the sea.[39]

A type of case in which the causation is very clearly direct, is that in which the victim of an assault has some disease or injury or other infirmity of such a nature that he suffers fatal consequences from injuries which would have been much less serious had he been in better physical condition.[40] If "a disease not caused by the blow" "supervened" between the blow and the death, the chain of proximate causation may be broken; [41] but if one "wounds another, and thereby hastens or accelerates his death by reason of some disease with which he is afflicted," the injury is the direct and proximate cause of death.[42] "It is the general rule that in a homicide case, if deceased was in feeble health and died from the combined effects of the injury and his disease, or if the injury accelerated the death from the disease, he

---

35. "An intervening force is a force which is neither operating in the defendant's presence nor at the place where defendant's act takes effect at the time of defendant's act, but comes into effective operation at or before the time of the damage." McLaughlin, Proximate Cause, 39 Harv.L.Rev. 149, 159–60 (1925).

36. White v. State, 84 Ala. 421, 4 So. 598 (1888).

37. People v. Buddenseick, 103 N.Y. 487, 9 N.E. 44 (1886).

38. Grimes v. State, 63 Ala. 166 (1879); Combes v. Commonwealth, 93 Ky. 313, 20 S.W. 221 (1892); Hennessee v. People, 21 How.Pr. 239 (N.Y.1861).

39. United States v. Freeman, 4 Mason 505 (1827).

40. See, for example, Beale's classification. The Proximate Consequences of an Act, 33 Harv.L.Rev. 633, 644–5 (1920).

41. Livingston v. Commonwealth, 55 Va. 592, 602 (1857).

42. Hopkins v. Commonwealth, 117 Ky. 941, 944, 80 S.W. 156 (1904); State v. Atkinson, 298 N.C. 673, 259 S.E.2d 858 (1979).

"The defendant must take his victim as he finds him, and it is no defense that the victim is suffering from physical infirmities." Hamrick v. People, __ Colo. __, 624 P.2d 1320, 1324 (1981).

who inflicted the injury" has directly caused the death, although the injury alone would not have been fatal.[43]

An aunt forced her niece to work for fourteen or fifteen hours a day and punished her severely whenever the required work was not completed. The niece died of consumption, the death having been hastened by the punishments.[44] A blow on the head with a beer glass resulted in death because the one assailed had an inflamed condition of the brain due to excessive use of alcohol.[45] An assault upon a boy proved fatal because he had heart disease.[46] A blow on the jaw which would otherwise have been relatively minor in its nature produced a fatal hemorrhage because the one assailed was a hemophiliac.[47] In each of these cases the act of the defendant was held to be the proximate cause of the death. The fact that the assailant did not know, or have reason to know, of the peculiar weakness of the other *in such a case* is unimportant as regards the problem of proximate cause,[48] although it may have a very important bearing upon the issue of responsibility.[49]

If it was a substantial factor thereof, an act which is a direct cause of a socially harmful occurrence is always a proximate cause of such result.[50]

11. INTERVENING CAUSE

An intervening cause is one which comes between an antecedent and a consequence.

If a strong wind is blowing at the time of an act, and cooperates with the act to produce a harmful result, the wind is not an intervening cause;[51] but

---

43. Rutledge v. State, 41 Ariz. 48, 52, 15 P.2d 255, 257 (1932).

44. Rex v. Cheeseman, 7 Car. & P. 455, 173 Eng.Rep. 203 (1836).

45. Griffin v. State, 40 Tex.Cr.R. 312, 50 S.W. 366 (1899).

46. State v. O'Brien, 81 Iowa 88, 46 N.W. 752 (1890).

47. State v. Frazier, 339 Mo. 966, 98 S.W.2d 707 (1937). See also Huckabee v. State, 159 Ala. 45, 48 So. 796 (1909).

The fact that the victim's death was hastened because of disease is not a defense. State v. Contreras, 107 Ariz. 68, 481 P.2d 861 (1971).

48. See Cheeseman, O'Brien, and Frazier in the preceding notes.

49. "In the present case therefore, if the evidence satisfies the jury that the prisoner, at the time he committed the assault and battery on the deceased, knew or had reasonable cause to believe that she was sick and suffering from disease, and was thereby put in such a weak and feeble condition that his attack would endanger her life, or inflict on her great bodily harm or hasten her death, it would justify the jury in finding implied malice, and convicting the prisoner of murder."

Commonwealth v. Fox, 73 Mass. 585, 588–89 (1856).

In Cheeseman, supra, the indictment was for murder, but a plea of guilty to manslaughter was accepted when it was shown that the aunt was unaware of the niece's illness and thought she had been shamming to avoid work.

50. "It is well settled, therefore, that a direct result of an active force is always proximate." Beale, The Proximate Consequences of an Act, 33 Harv.L.Rev. 633, 644 (1920).

In a case where murder was charged resulting from a robbery when the victim was left helpless in a roadway and was struck and killed by a vehicle it was held there was no violation of due process in prosecution of the robbers for the death of the victim where the trial judge failed to give an instruction to the jury other than that the defendants' conduct must have caused the victim's death. Henderson v. Kibbe, 431 U.S. 145, 97 S.Ct. 1730 (1977).

51. "Thus, when a fire is started in a then existing wind, the wind is not an intervening force, but a condition existing at the time of defendant's act." Mc-

if a sudden gust of wind sweeps up an article, which has previously been thrown upon the ground, and dashes it against a person with injurious consequences, this cause is an intervening one.[52]　An intervening cause is one "which is neither operating in defendant's presence, nor at the place where defendant's act takes effect at the time of defendant's act, but comes into effective operation at or before the time of the damage." [53]

An intervening cause may be either dependent or independent. It may have been produced by the first cause or it may merely happen to take effect upon a condition created by the first cause. If a shot fired at a dog so frightens the animal that it rushes blindly into the house, colliding with its master and knocking him down, the harmful activity of the dog cannot be said to be independent of the act of shooting because it was engendered by it.[54]　But if a negligent delay of transportation has left a person or property at a place which happens to be in the path of a stroke of lightning, a flood, or other so-called "act of God," the resulting harm is produced by an independent intervening cause.[55]　Such a cause may or may not be a superseding one, but it is unquestionably *independent*. The negligent act which placed the person or property at that place at the particular moment, is a *causa sine qua non*, because without it the harm would not have happened, but it did not cause the lightning or the flood. The shot which frightened the dog is the "cause of a cause" [56] which injured the master; the faulty transportation does not stand in this relation to the harm inflicted by the "act of God." The former is a proximate cause; the latter may be either proximate or remote.

An intervening event may be independent, let it be emphasized, without coming within the classification of an "act of God." Suppose while **X** was walking to his office, **D** hit him unlawfully and knocked him unconscious. A few moments later **X** recovered, suffering no more than a painful jaw. He then resumed his walk to the office but a block farther on a traffic accident dashed a car across the sidewalk, killing **X**. **D**'s act was in fact a cause of **X**'s death because "but for" his battery **X** would have been elsewhere at the time of the traffic accident. But **D**'s act did not cause the traffic accident— it would have happened just as and when it did even if no battery had been committed on **X**. The traffic accident was an *independent* intervening cause.

12.　DEPENDENT INTERVENING CAUSE

Intervening causes which are acts require separate consideration, but if no act is involved other than that of the person accused of crime nothing will be recognized as a superseding cause unless it can at least qualify as an "independent intervening cause." [57]

Laughlin, Proximate Cause, 39 Harv.L. Rev. 149, 160 (1925).

52.　Rex v. Gill, 1 Strange 190, 93 Eng.Rep. 466 (1719).

53.　McLaughlin, Proximate Cause, 39 Harv.L.Rev. 149, 159–60 (1925).

54.　Isham v. Dow's Estate, 70 Vt. 588, 41 A. 585 (1898).

55.　Morrison v. Davis, 20 Pa. 171 (1852).

56.　". . . if it is the cause of a cause, no more is required (quoting Bishop)." Bishop v. State, 73 Ark. 568, 571, 84 S.W. 707 (1905); Barnett v. State, 82 Tenn. 439, 443 (1884); State v. Rounds, 104 Vt. 442, 453, 160 A. 249, 252 (1932).

57.　State v. Pell, 140 Iowa 655, 665, 119 N.W. 154, 158 (1909).

"Where such intervening events are foreseeable and naturally result from a perpetrator's criminal conduct, the law

If the act of the accused was in fact a cause of a socially-harmful occurrence, and was a substantial factor thereof, it will be recognized as the proximate cause "unless another, not incident to it, but independent of it, is shown to have intervened between it and the result."[58]

An animal may be employed as a lethal weapon, as where a vicious beast is incited to attack a person,[59] or a venomous serpent is purposely dropped upon the intended victim. Should the animal or serpent perform as intended with resulting loss of life, the malicious act would be unquestionably the proximate cause of the death. Neither the malicious intent nor the viciousness of the animal is essential so far as causation is concerned. If criminally negligent driving results in a collision with a horsedrawn vehicle, which so frightens the horses that they run away and overturn the carriage with fatal consequences, the negligent driving is the proximate cause of the death.[60] Even inanimate forces may be said to intervene without doing so independently. Thus an act is within the field of proximate causation if it results in breaking a lighted lamp being carried by a person, whereupon oil is spattered upon the carrier and is ignited by the flame, burning him to death.[61]

No *independent* intervening cause is involved if the immediate cause of death is a latent condition activated by defendant's wrongful act. If, during the fright and excitement of a robbery the victim dies of a heart attack, the robber is the proximate cause of the death.[62] It is no defense that the death was wholly unintended and unexpected, or that the victim would not have died if he had been in better health.[63] The robber picked that particular victim, for whatever reason, and is in no position to insist that he was entitled to a victim in normal physical health. A robber takes his victim as he finds him. The decisive factor from the legal point of view is that victim would have been still alive if he had not been robbed. In fact this is a typical case of first-degree murder in the perpetration of robbery.[64]

A. INFECTION OR OTHER DISEASE

So far as the homicide cases are concerned, a dependent intervening cause has frequently appeared in the form of infection or other disease. We

considers the chain of causation unbroken and holds the perpetrator criminally responsible for the resulting harm." United States v. Guillette, 547 F.2d 743, 744 (2d Cir. 1976).

"A defendant's actions may still be a proximate cause of death regardless of the type of intervening act that occurred, but as 'common sense would suggest, the perimeters of legal cause are more closely drawn when the intervening cause was a matter of coincidence rather than response.' Hence an intervening cause that was a coincidence will be a superseding cause when it was unforeseeable. On the other hand, an intervening cause that was a response will be a superseding cause only where it was abnormal *and* unforeseeable." State v. Hall, 129 Ariz. 589, 633 P.2d 398, 403 (1981).

58. State v. Benton, 38 Del. 1, 17, 187 A. 609, 616 (1936).

59. 3 Co.Inst. *48. One who incites an insane person to kill another is himself the cause of the death. Regina v. Tyler, 8 Car. & P. 616, 173 Eng.Rep. 643 (1838). See also Johnson v. State, 142 Ala. 70, 38 So. 182 (1904).

60. Belk v. People, 125 Ill. 584, 17 N.E. 744 (1888). One who knowingly turns a vicious animal loose on the common is the cause of the death of a child who was killed by the animal. Regina v. Dant, 10 Cox C.C. 102 (1865).

61. Mayes v. People, 106 Ill. 306 (1883). See also Bliss v. State, 117 Wis. 596, 94 N.W. 325 (1903).

62. People v. Stamp, 2 Cal.App.3d 203, 82 Cal.Rptr. 598 (1970); State v. Edwards, 122 Ariz. 206, 594 P.2d 72 (1979).

63. Ibid.

64. Ibid.

are not here concerned with a disease already present and merely aggravated by the injury, nor even with a situation in which the germs of the disease were already latent in the victim's body at the time of the harm which is alleged to have caused the death.[65] The causation in such cases is direct. The present problem is limited to death from a disease of which the deceased was entirely free, even in latent form, prior to the act in question.[66]

"It is an ancient and well settled principle of the law of homicide, that, if a wound cause a disease which produces death, the death is imputable to the wound." [67] Thus if wounds cause lockjaw which results in death "the death was caused by said wounds." [68] Perhaps the most obvious example of this principle is the act which not only results in personal injury, but does so in such a manner that dirt and filth are carried into the wound, at the time of its infliction, whereupon blood poisoning develops from the foreign material thus injected.[69] The law of proximate cause, however, does not require proof that the source of infection or disease was actually introduced into the body by the very blow which inflicted the injury.[70] If defendant stabbed deceased with a knife, wounding him in the bowels, and "germs entered the incision made by the stab or wound, and peritonitis resulted from the entrance of said germs, from which disease the deceased died, the defendant in law would be" the proximate cause of the death.[71]

In each of the following cases the act of defendant was held to be the proximate cause of the death: Defendant inflicted a wound upon deceased with a knife, erysipelas resulted from the wound and caused death.[72] "De-

---

65. See, for example, Larson v. Boston Elevated Railroad Co., 212 Mass. 262, 98 N.E. 1048, (1912); Brown v. State, 145 Ga.App. 530, 244 S.E.2d 68 (1978); State v. Contraras, 107 Ariz. 68, 481 P.2d 861 (1971).

The fact that the victim's intoxication contributed to his death does not prevent a severe beating from being recognized as the cause of death. Drury v. Burr, 107 Ariz. 124, 483 P.2d 539 (1971).

Where a 70-year-old victim of a robbery had advanced heart disease, and died of a heart attack brought on by having been tied, beaten and robbed, the robber caused the death and may be convicted of murder. Wofford v. State, 584 P.2d 227 (Okl.Cr.App.1978).

66. The statement in the text is merely to emphasize differences in the factual situation. Obviously the causation would not be rendered remote by the presence of the disease, or the germs. If a beating aggravates pneumonia and thus hastens death, or *causes* pneumonia which causes death, it is the proximate cause of the death. Rutledge v. State, 41 Ariz. 48, 15 P.2d 255 (1932); Burnett v. State, 82 Tenn. 439 (1884). See also State v. Wilson, 114 La. 398, 38 So. 397 (1905).

67. Powell v. State, 13 Tex.Cr.R. 244, 254 (1882). See also 1 Hale P.C. *428;

Clements v. State, 141 Ga. 667, 81 S.E. 1117 (1914); Hall v. State, 199 Ind. 592, 159 N.E. 420 (1928); Moore v. State, 126 Tex.Cr.R. 391, 71 S.W.2d 531 (1934). "If one wilfully, unlawfully, and with malice aforethought strikes another on the head and face with a piece of wood, inflicting a wound which, though not necessarily mortal, is the primary cause of a disease which brings about the death of the wounded person, he is guilty of murder." Lochamy v. State, 152 Ga. 235, 109 S.E. 497 (1921).

68. State v. Harmon, 28 Del. 296, 92 A. 853 (1915).

69. People v. Townsend, 214 Mich. 267, 183 N.W. 177 (1921).

70. See, for example, Clements v. State, 141 Ga. 667, 81 S.E. 1117 (1914); Harrison v. State, 18 Okl.Cr. 403, 195 P. 511 (1921); Franklin v. State, 41 Tex.Cr. R. 21, 51 S.W. 951 (1899).

71. Bishop v. State, 73 Ark. 568, 569–70, 84 S.W. 707 (1905). Death attributable to peritonitis from a wound. State v. Hill, 124 Ariz. 491, 605 P.2d 893 (1980).

72. Denman v. State, 15 Neb. 138, 17 N.W. 347 (1883).

fendant . . . cut Young with a knife, inflicting a wound about three inches long upon the biceps muscle of his left arm. The wound became infected and Young suffered from lockjaw. Later galloping consumption developed, and Young died some thirty or forty days subsequent to the injury." [73] Defendant shot a pregnant woman; the wound caused a miscarriage; the miscarriage caused septic peritonitis, and the septic peritonitis caused the death of the woman on the third day after the shooting.[74] Defendant struck a violent blow upon the right breast of a pregnant woman, the blow produced premature labor and convulsions and resulted in her death in about fourteen hours.[75] Defendant inflicted blows upon deceased; the beating induced delirium; in his delirium the deceased fell out of bed, breaking some ribs; a chest infection set in, which entered the blood and resulted in death.[76]

The diverse methods of expressing factual situations in this and associated fields have already received attention. The physicist would probably find intervening causes in practically any case of homicide. Some jurists are inclined to speak of the causal relations mentioned in this section as "direct," [77] while others speak of the act in such cases as the "mediate cause" [78] of death, and recognize the presence of an "intervention" [79] or an "intervening cause," [80] which, however, is not an independent one. While the latter form of expression is probably more common in the criminal cases, the diversity of statement does not tend to any difference in the outcome, because:

A dependent intervening cause which is not an act is never a superseding cause.[81]

B. ACTS: IMPULSIVE AVOIDANCE OF DANGER

Factually any response of a human being to harm or threat of harm is a consequence of whatever produced such harm or threat, and insofar as the response is a normal one this actual causation is recognized by law. Hence an act resulting in harm or threat of harm is the proximate cause of further harm caused by such response thereto. On the other hand if a human being responds to

73. Commonwealth v. Kilburn, 236 Ky. 828, 34 S.W.2d 728 (1931). The statement of facts is quoted from 20 Ky.L. Jour. 93 (1931).

74. People v. Kane, 213 N.Y. 260, 107 N.E. 655 (1915).

75. People v. McKeon, 31 Hun 449 (N.Y.1884).

76. State v. Rounds, 104 Vt. 442, 160 A. 249 (1932). Another theory was that the ribs were broken by the blows of defendant. Defendant was the proximate cause of the death under either theory, but a conviction of manslaughter was reversed because part of defendant's blows were inflicted in privileged self-defense and there was no proper testimony as to just which blows caused the harm.

77. Belk v. People, 125 Ill. 584, 587, 17 N.E. 744, 745 (1888); Commonwealth v. Kennedy, 271 Pa.Super. 206, 412 A.2d 886 (1979).

78. "This is equivalent to saying, that if the wound was the mediate cause of death—that is, if but for the wound death would not have ensued, it is no defense that because of the wound fever or erysipelas set in and was the immediate cause of death." Denman v. State, 15 Neb. 138, 141, 17 N.W. 347, 348 (1883). See also State v. Luster, 178 S.C. 199, 208, 182 S.E. 427, 431 (1935).

79. People v. Kane, 213 N.Y. 260, 270, 107 N.E. 655, 657 (1915).

80. State v. Rounds, 104 Vt. 442, 453, 160 A. 249, 252 (1932).

81. It is believed that any case which might seem to require an exception to this statement could better be explained on the ground that the act of the defendant was not a substantial factor in the result.

such a situation in a manner that is clearly abnormal this is treated by law as the equivalent of an independent intervening force and may be, in fact usually is, superseding.

Perhaps the most typical instance of intervening cause in the form of an act, which is *dependent* upon a prior act, is the impulsive movement made in the effort to avoid sudden peril created by the prior act. In the words of Lord Coleridge: "If a man creates in another man's mind an immediate sense of danger which causes such person to try to escape, and in so doing he injures himself, the person who creates such a state of mind" is the proximate cause of the injuries which result.[82] If, in the effort to save himself from apparent death or great bodily injury, one grabs a firearm which has suddenly been pointed at him, and the force thus exerted by him causes a fatal discharge not intended by the pointer, the act of pointing the weapon has caused the death.[83] The pointer will not necessarily be criminally responsible for the death because his menacing act may have been justified or excused; [84] but there has been homicide which the law imputes to him, whether it is criminal or innocent. It is unquestionably criminal homicide if the weapon was pointed in the perpetration of robbery, however definitely the robber may have intended to use the weapon only as a bluff and not for the purpose of shooting.[85]

As said by an English court, if a person who is suddenly attacked should, from a reasonable apprehension of immediate violence, throw himself into a river in the effort to escape, and be drowned, the assailant would be the cause of the death within the legal view.[86] Outstanding cases in which the act which created sudden fear has been held to be the proximate cause of death, although the immediate cause was an impulsive act of the deceased (or another) in an effort to avoid the danger, include the following: W locked the door and made a violent assault upon his wife with a hand mirror, threatening to kill her; she was so terrorized that she jumped from an upstairs window in the effort to escape, and was killed by the fall.[87] T made a vicious assault upon his wife and she fell into a ditch and broke her neck trying to get away from him.[88] L saw some boys in a boat and shot into the river near them, intending not to hit them but merely to play a prank upon them. One of the boys became so frightened that he jumped out of the boat. This overturned the craft and two of the boys were drowned.[89] S, who had threatened to kill his wife, menaced her with a knife while they were in a rapidly moving automobile; in sudden fright, she opened the door and leaped from the car, being killed by the fall.[90] M drove a wagon in such a negligent

82. Regina v. Halliday, 61 Law T.R. 701, 702 (1889).

83. State v. Benham, 23 Iowa 154 (1867); People v. Olson, 60 Ill.App.3d 535, 18 Ill.Dec. 218, 377 N.E.2d 371 (1978).

84. Ibid. A conviction of manslaughter was reversed because the jury was not properly instructed on the law of self-defense.

85. ". . . and that the discharge was unintentionally caused while struggling with his victim, or with a third party who came to the latter's assistance, is immaterial." Conviction of murder in the first degree affirmed. Common-

wealth v. Lessner, 274 Pa. 108, 111, 118 A. 24, 25 (1922). See also State v. Best, 44 Wyo. 383, 12 P.2d 1110 (1932).

86. Regina v. Pitts, Car. & M. 284, 174 Eng.Rep. 509 (1842).

87. Whiteside v. State, 115 Tex.Cr.R. 274, 29 S.W.2d 399 (1930).

88. Thornton v. State, 107 Ga. 683, 33 S.E. 673 (1899).

89. Letner v. State, 156 Tenn. 68, 299 S.W. 1049 (1927).

90. Sanders v. Commonwealth, 244 Ky. 77, 50 S.W.2d 37 (1932).

manner as to endanger the life of deceased, who jumped, in fear, with fatal consequences.[91] **F**, driving a car while intoxicated, was guiding it in such an erratic manner that it zigzagged over the road in a terrifying way. A passenger grabbed the wheel and got her foot on top of his foot which was "on the gas." At a curve the car left the road and plunged against a pole killing one of the other passengers.[92]

V reached for a gun that the defendant was pointing at **V**'s wife, the gun discharged and **V** was killed.[93] Defendant shot at **H**'s vehicle which accelerated to get away and in the course struck and killed a pedestrian.[94]

(A) Reasonableness of the Apprehension

If a *felonious assault* engenders such terror as to cause an impulsive act of avoidance which results in loss of life, the attack is the proximate cause of the death "whether or not the act of avoidance was that of a reasonably prudent person under the circumstances."[95] It would be absurd to permit a murderous assailant to escape on the theory that the death resulted not from his act but from an imprudent defensive act of his victim in the sudden terror of the moment; and hence the juridical view of the causal relation is extended because of the moral obliquity of the defendant's action.

Where the intervening act is an impulsive movement in the effort to avoid impending danger, the law of proximate cause does not require that the harm which actually happened should have been foreseeable.[96] Frequently it is foreseeable. If a loaded weapon is pointed at another at close range it may be foreseeable that he may grab for it and perhaps cause a discharge in this way. It is foreseeable, perhaps, that one threatened with a knife may jump, even from a rapidly moving car. In other situations this element is clearly wanting. In one case, for example, defendant rode after deceased with intent to strike him with a small stick. The deceased drove his spurs into his horse with such vigor that the animal winced and threw him, whereby he was killed. The act of defendant was held to be the proximate cause of the death, without any labored effort to show that this was a foreseeable consequence.[97]

C.   ONE DEPRIVED OF HIS REASON

One who has been deprived of his reason has been robbed of his power to respond normally to whatever the situation may be, and hence the blow or other harm which produces this result is the proximate cause of further injury which the victim inflicts upon himself while out of his mind. Thus an assailant has committed homicide if his blows induced delirium and as a result of this delirium the victim fell out of bed,[98] or tore open his wound,[99]

---

91. Morris v. State, 35 Tex.Cr.R. 313, 33 S.W. 539 (1895).

92. People v. Freeman, 16 Cal.App.2d 101, 60 P.2d 333 (1936).

93. People v. Olson, 60 Ill.App.3d 535, 18 Ill.Dec. 218, 377 N.E.2d 371 (1978).

94. Wright v. State, 363 So.2d 617 (Fla.App.1978).

95. Patterson v. State, 181 Ga. 698, 707, 184 S.E. 309, 314 (1936).

96. Rex v. Hickman, 5 Car. & P. 151, 172 Eng.Rep. 917 (1831).

97. Ibid.

98. State v. Rounds, 104 Vt. 442, 160 A. 249 (1932).

99. Stanton's Case, 2 Rogers' N.Y. City H.Rec. 164 (1817). In this case defendant was acquitted, probably on the theory of self-defense. Gipe v. State, 165 Ind. 433, 75 N.E. 881 (1905). A conviction of murder was reversed on other

with fatal consequences; and homicide was imputable to a rapist whose peculiarly brutal act, followed by continued restraint, caused the victim to take
a fatal dose of poison while "distracted and mentally irresponsible"; [1] a conviction for murder was upheld where a robbery victim was left partially un-
dressed and helpless in a lane of traffic and was struck by a vehicle.[2]

D. Deliberate Avoidance of Harm

While an impulsive act which is merely the normal response to fear or
other emotional disturbance, or the undirected bodily movement of one who
has been deprived of his reason, will be imputed to him who has caused this
emotional disturbance or loss of mind, the scope of proximate cause goes far
beyond this. Even the deliberate act of the one threatened or endangered,
or that of another in his behalf, in the effort to avoid injury to person [3] or
damage to property,[4] will not be a superseding cause if it is merely the normal response of a human being to the stimulus of the situation created by
the wrongdoer.[5]

(A) Reasonableness of the Apprehension

Reasonableness of the apprehension and prudence of the act of avoidance
are entitled to attention [6] because if the act of avoidance is deliberate rather
than impulsive the chain of proximate causation will be broken if the fear of
danger was not well founded and the effort to avoid was made in an obviously imprudent manner.[7] This is particularly true if the act which created
the apprehension of danger resulted from criminal negligence rather than
from wilfulness.[8] If, for example, the criminal negligence of a captain resulted in a wreck of his ship, and several persons left the vessel and were
drowned, the negligence of the captain is not the proximate cause of the
deaths if the nature of the wreck was such that it was safe to remain on
board and very imprudent to take to the water, and all the passengers were
apprised of these facts.[9]

grounds, but the causal connection was
recognized.

1. Stephenson v. State, 205 Ind. 141,
179 N.E. 633 (1932); Commonwealth v.
Wright, 455 Pa. 480, 317 A.2d 271 (1974).

2. People v. Kibbe, 35 N.Y.2d 407, 362
N.Y.S.2d 848, 321 N.E.2d 773 (1974).

3. Keaton v. State, 41 Tex.Cr.R. 621,
57 S.W. 1125 (1900).

"For example, if a person acting on a
well grounded and reasonable fear of
death or bodily injury induced by accused's threats or actual assaults, dies in
an attempt to extricate himself from the
danger, the accused bears criminal liability for the death." United States v. Guillette, 547 F.2d 743, 749 (2d Cir. 1976).

4. State v. Glover, 330 Mo. 709, 50
S.W.2d 1049 (1932).

5. See Restatement, Second, Torts §
443 and comment (1965).

"It is enough that the act [of the other]
whether impulsive or deliberate, is the

child of the occasion." Wagner v. International Railway Co., 232 N.Y. 176, 181,
133 N.E. 437, 438 (1921).

6. ". . . acting upon reasonable
fear or apprehension. . . ." Sanders
v. Commonwealth, 244 Ky. 77, 82, 50
S.W.2d 37, 39 (1932).

7. See State v. Preslar, 48 N.C. 421,
428 (1856); Henderson v. Commonwealth,
85 Ky. 281, 3 S.W. 166 (1887).

8. Patterson v. State, 181 Ga. 698, 184
S.E. 309 (1936).

9. United States v. Warner, 4 McLean
463 (7th Cir. 1848). "On the other hand,
if these persons, under the pressure of
circumstances in which they were placed,
conducted with ordinary prudence and
discretion, then the allegation in the indictment, as to the means by which they
came to their death, is sustained." Id. at
476.

(B) Danger Invites Rescue

"Danger invites rescue. The cry of distress is the summons to relief. The law does not ignore these reactions of the mind in tracing conduct to its consequences. It recognizes them as normal." [10] Hence the act of one in the effort to avoid or minimize harm may be the proximate consequence of the act of another, which caused the danger or the harm, in situations quite beyond those mentioned above. Death in a fire of felonious origin offers an excellent illustration. If deceased was in the building at the time and was unable to get out after the fire was discovered the present problem is not involved,[11] because the causal relation between the act of setting fire to the building and the death is clearly unbroken in such a case.[12] At the other extreme, if the deceased was on the outside at the time, and had no proper reason to enter but took advantage of the opportunity thus afforded to rush into the flames for the purpose of ending his life, this utterly abnormal response to the situation is superseding and the incendiary act was not the proximate cause of his death.[13] The cases of special interest in connection with the present inquiry fall between these extremes.

Two boys were burned to death in a building which had been feloniously set on fire. They had either left the building or were on their way and had a clear opportunity to do so, but went back to save some property. Although the intervening act of each boy was the immediate cause of his death, such a consequence of the malicious burning was a normal human response and not a superseding cause. In affirming a conviction of murder the court pointed out that "the effort of a person to save property of value which is liable to destruction by fire is such a natural and ordinary course of conduct that it cannot be said to break the sequence of cause and effect." [14] It is also normal for a fireman to enter a burning building, in the line of his duty in attempting to extinguish a blaze, and if a fireman is killed under these circumstances in a fire of incendiary origin, the malicious act of setting fire to the building is the proximate cause of the death.[15] It is quite abnormal, however, for a fireman to enter a building after the fire is under control, if by reason of the contents there is an unusual risk of explosion of which he has been fully warned. And in a case not involving incendiarism it was held that the criminally *negligent* act of defendant was not the proximate cause of the

---

10. Wagner v. International Railway Co., 232 N.Y. 176, 180, 133 N.E. 437 (1921).

11. See, for example, People v. Goldvarg, 346 Ill. 398, 178 N.E. 892 (1931).

12. The one who committed the arson is guilty of murder in such a case even if "death ensues either contrary to or beside the original intention." Id. at 402, 178 N.W. at 894.

Pawloski v. State, 269 Ind. 350, 380 N.E.2d 1230 (1978). A defendant who started a house on fire cannot claim a lack of responsibility for the deaths of children in the house because adults failed to remove the children. People v. Nichols, 3 Cal.3d 150, 89 Cal.Rptr. 721, 474 P.2d 673 (1970).

13. Regina v. Horsey, 3 F. & F. 287, 176 Eng.Rep. 129 (1862).

14. State v. Leopold, 110 Conn. 55, 62, 147 A. 118, 121 (1929).

15. State v. Glover, 330 Mo. 709, 50 S.W.2d 1049 (1932). Conviction of first degree murder affirmed.

In an analogous case it was held that a traffic violator who speeded in the effort to avoid arrest was the proximate cause of the death of the officer who was killed while attempting to make the arrest. "Lang's conduct *directly* resulted in Officer Redding's death and was not a fortuitous or coincidental event unrelated to the direct result of his conduct." Commonwealth v. Lang, 285 Pa.Super. 34, 426 A.2d 691 (1981).

death of a fireman who "was *apprised* of the danger, and *unnecessarily* and over the protest of the defendant, exposed himself thereto." [16] A wife's death resulting from an attempt to wrest a gun from her husband to prevent his suicide was not an intervening cause so as to excuse the husband from responsibility for the wife's death.[17]

(C) Medical or Surgical Treatment

In the words of Lord Hale: "If a man give another a stroke, which it may be, is not of itself so mortal, but that with good care he may be cured, yet if he die of this wound within the year and day, it is homicide or murder, as the case is, and so it hath been always ruled." [18]

An injury from which the victim bleeds to death is the proximate cause of the decease even if the loss of blood might have been stopped had medical aid been promptly obtained.[19] Obviously the fact that a doctor was not at hand to render immediate aid cannot be regarded as a superseding cause; [20] but the result is not dependent upon unavailability. "The question is not what would have happened, but what did happen," [21] and there can be no break in the legally-recognized chain of causation by reason of a possibility of intervention which did not take place, because a "negative act" is never superseding.[22] Moreover, an injury is the proximate cause of resulting death although the deceased would have recovered had he been treated by the most approved surgical methods,[23] or by more skilful methods,[24] or "with

---

16. Carbo v. State, 4 Ga.App. 583, 62 S.E. 140, 141 (1908). Italics added. If arson results in the death of one accomplice the other is guilty of murder. "The attempt of an officer or person to put out the fire, or to rescue people or property therein, or the attempt of any person to escape from the burning building does not constitute in legal contemplation a superseding cause which is sufficient to relieve the arsonist from murder in the first degree. In reason, logic and principle we can see no valid distinction between those cases and a case where an accomplice is killed while setting fire to a house (or building) or attempting to escape therefrom, . . ." Commonwealth v. Bolish, 381 Pa. 500, 519, 113 A.2d 464, 474 (1955).

17. State v. Shanahan, 404 A.2d 975 (Me.1979).

18. 1 Hale P.C. *428.

19. Mason v. State, 94 Tex.Cr.R. 532, 251 S.W. 1065 (1923).

Defendant was held responsible for the death of a woman he stabbed when the woman refused a blood transfusion because of her religious belief. Regina v. Blaue, 1 W.L.R. 1411, 3 All ER 446 (C.A. 1975).

20. Embrey v. State, 94 Tex.Cr.R. 591, 592, 251 S.W. 1062 (1923).

21. Beale, The Proximate Consequences of an Act, 33 Harv.L.Rev. 633, 638 (1920).

22. See Restatement, Second, Torts, § 452 (1965). And see note 20, infra, under 16 Negative Acts.

An instruction that if defendant inflicted wounds upon decedent, that such wounds were not necessarily fatal, that if decedent died because of want of medical attention, and that no cause intervened, defendant would be guilty to the same extent as though decedent had died immediately, is correct. Rigsley v. State, 174 Ind. 284, 91 N.E. 925 (1910). See also People v. Townsend, 214 Mich. 267, 279, 183 N.W. 177, 181 (1921).

"The factual situation is in legal effect the same, whether the victim bleeds to death because surgical attention is not available, or because, although available, it is delayed by reason of the surgeon's gross neglect or incompetence." People v. McGee, 31 Cal.2d 229, 243, 187 P.2d 706, 715 (1947).

23. State v. Edgerton, 100 Iowa 63, 69 N.W. 280 (1896).

24. Downing v. State, 114 Ga. 30, 39 S.E. 927 (1901). In affirming a conviction of murder in the second degree the court held it was proper for the judge to exclude evidence tending to show that the deceased did not receive the proper

more prudent care," [25] or "with a different diet and better nursing," [26] or "with proper caution and attention." [27] The same is true even if the injured person did not take proper care of himself,[28] or neglected to obtain medical treatment,[29] or delayed too long in doing so,[30] or refused to submit to a surgical operation despite medical advice as to its necessity.[31] And if, because of the want of proper care and attention, the wound "turns to a gangrene, or a fever" [32] or results in septic poisoning [33] or lockjaw,[34] which is the immediate cause of death, there is still no superseding cause.

The ordinary administration of doctor or nurse in the effort to aid an injured person, it must be added, is the very normal response of a human being to the situation created by the injury inflicted and hence is not supersed-

treatment after his injury. ". . . where death follows an injury without other independent intervening cause calculated to produce the death of the injured person had he not been injured by the wrongful act of accused, proof of lack of proper treatment which might have saved or prolonged his life cannot be shown." State v. Pell, 140 Iowa 655, 665, 119 N.W. 154, 158 (1909).

See also State v. Tomassi, 137 Conn. 113, 75 A.2d 67 (1950); State v. Little, 57 Wash.2d 516, 358 P.2d 120 (1961).

25. "If the death be owing truly to the wound, it signifies not that the deceased would have recovered under more favorable circumstances, or with more prudent care; the death being the result of the wound, the party inflicting it must be held responsible for it." McAllister v. State, 17 Ala. 434, 439 (1850).

26. "Where death is caused by a dangerous wound, the person inflicting it is responsible for the consequences, though the deceased might have recovered with the exercise of more prudence and with a different diet and better nursing." Bailey v. State, 22 Ala.App. 185, 187, 113 So. 830, 831–2 (1927). "Where a person, by act or omission, does any thing that results in the death of a human being, he causes the death of that human being notwithstanding that death from that cause might have been prevented by resorting to proper means." Can.Crim. Code § 207 (Rev.Stat.1970).

27. State v. Baker, 46 N.C. 267 (1854).

28. Rew's Case, J. Kelyng 26, 84 Eng. Rep. 1066 (1662); Pyles v. State, 78 So.2d 813 (Ala.App.1954); State v. Johnson, 36 Del. 341, 175 A. 669 (1934); Hopkins v. United States, 4 App.D.C. 430 (1894); Commonwealth v. Hackett, 84 Mass. 136 (1861).

29. Hopkins v. United States, 4 App. D.C. 430 (1894).

30. Payne v. Commonwealth, 20 Ky. L.Rep. 475, 46 S.W. 704 (1898); State v. Hambright, 111 N.C. 707, 16 S.E. 411 (1892).

31. Regina v. Holland, 2 M. & Rob. 351, 174 Eng.Rep. 313 (1841); Franklin v. State, 41 Tex.Cr.R. 21, 51 S.W. 951 (1899). A conviction was affirmed although deceased may have hindered his recovery by walking seven or eight miles and by drinking whiskey. State v. Baker, 46 N.C. 267 (1854). ". . . the well established rule of the common law would seem to be, that if the wound was a dangerous wound, that is, calculated to endanger, or destroy life, and death ensued therefrom, it is sufficient proof of the offence of murder, or manslaughter; and that the person who inflicted it is responsible, though it may appear that the deceased might have recovered if he had taken proper care of himself, or submitted to a surgical operation, or that unskilful or improper treatment aggravated the wound and contributed to the death, or that death was immediately caused by a surgical operation rendered necessary by the condition of the wound." Commonwealth v. Hackett, 84 Mass. 136, 141 (1861). Quoted with approval in State v. Edgerton, 100 Iowa 64, 70, 69 N.W. 280, 283 (1896).

32. 1 Hale P.C. *428.

33. Harrison v. State, 18 Okl.Cr. 403, 195 P. 511 (1921).

34. Regina v. Holland, 2 M. & Rob. 351, 174 Eng.Rep. 313 (1841).

D was the proximate cause of death resulting from an operation to relieve a hematoma (swelling filled with extravasated blood) caused by a blow inflicted by D. People v. Paulson, 80 Ill.App. 44, 225 N.E.2d 424 (1967).

ing. And negligence, unfortunately, is entirely too frequent in human conduct to be considered "abnormal." [35] Hence even if the death of one who has been injured by another results, not from the want of medical or surgical treatment, but from treatment of this nature which is actually administered, the fatal consequence will be a proximate result of the injurious act, under ordinary circumstances.[36] "The true doctrine is," said the Alabama court, "that where the wound is in itself dangerous to life, mere erroneous treatment of it or of the wounded man suffering from it, will afford the defendant no protection against a charge of unlawful homicide." [37] The Iowa court said: "Lack of skill or bad judgment or mere *negligence* in any form on the part of the surgeon will not avail the slayer to protect him against the final consequences of his own act." [38] And it has repeatedly been held that "unskilful treatment," [39] "erroneous surgical or medical treatment," [40] "unskilful and improper treatment," [41] or "erroneous and unskilful" treatment [42] though the direct cause of death, will not prevent the injurious act from being recognized as the proximate cause of the fatal result.

(1) Character of the Injury

The character of the wound inflicted is one of the important factors and courts sometimes use terms such as "serious wound" [43] or "dangerous

35. People v. Freudenberg, 121 Cal. App.2d 564, 263 P.2d 875 (1953); State v. Inger, 292 N.W.2d 119 (Iowa 1980).

In reference to human conduct, in this connection, the word "normal" is used as the opposite of "abnormal or extraordinary" and not in the sense of "usual, customary, foreseeable or expected." Restatement, Second, Torts § 443, comment b (1965).

"If the wound is mortal or dangerous, the person who inflicted it cannot excuse his acts under the assertion of erroneous treatment." Pyles v. State, 78 So.2d 813, 815 (Ala.App.1954).

36. People v. Williams, 27 Cal.App. 297, 149 P. 768 (1915); Quillen v. State, 10 Terry 114, 110 A.2d 445 (1955); Nee Smith v. State, 92 Ga.App. 632, 89 S.E.2d 559 (1955); McCoy v. Commonwealth, 149 Ky. 447, 149 S.W. 903 (1912).

37. Daughdrill v. State, 113 Ala. 7, 34, 21 So. 378, 387 (1897); Thomas v. State, 139 Ala. 80, 86, 36 So. 734, 735 (1904); Johnson v. State, 64 Fla. 321, 323, 59 So. 894, 895 (1912). A conviction of murder in the first degree was affirmed in Daughdrill and Johnson. Such a conviction was reversed on other grounds in Thomas.

38. State v. Gabriella, 163 Iowa 297, 304, 144 N.W. 9, 12 (1913). Emphasis added. And see People v. Freudenberg, 121 Cal.App.2d 564, 263 P.2d 875 (1953).

"Where a person inflicts upon another a wound which is calculated to endanger or destroy life, it is not a defense to a charge of homicide that the alleged victim's death was contributed to or caused by the negligence of the attending physicians or" surgeons. State v. Rueckert, 221 Kan. 727, 561 P.2d 850, 859 (1977).

39. Bowles v. State, 58 Ala. 335, 337 (1877); McDaniel v. State, 76 Ala. 1, 7 (1884); Crews v. State, 44 Ga.App. 546, 552, 162 S.E. 146, 149 (1932).

40. People v. Kane, 213 N.Y. 260, 270, 107 N.E. 655, 657 (1915).

It was held that "medical malpractice will break the chain of causation and constitute a defense only if death is attributable *solely* to the medical malpractice and not induced at all by the original wound." State v. Hills, 124 Ariz. 491, 605 P.2d 893, 894 (1980).

41. Bishop v. State, 73 Ark. 568, 570, 84 S.W. 707 (1905); State v. Bantley, 44 Conn. 537, 540 (1877); Hall v. State, 199 Ind. 592, 608, 159 N.E. 420, 426 (1928); Commonwealth v. Hackett, 84 Mass. 136, 141 (1861).

42. Harrison v. State, 18 Okl.Cr. 403, 409, 195 P. 511, 513 (1921); Baker v. State, 48 Okl.Cr. 358, 372, 292 P. 82, 87 (1930).

43. Hall v. State, 199 Ind. 592, 608, 159 N.E. 420, 426 (1928). "Serious injury." Regina v. Davis, 15 Cox C.C. 174, 179 (1883).

wound" [44] in discussing the problem here under consideration, but it is not necessary that the wound should be a mortal one.[45] Probably no more is required than that the injury should be of sufficient gravity so that medical or surgical treatment may be regarded as normal.[46] For example, the fact that a lost drainage tube (resorted to by the surgeon as a matter of customary practice in such a case) found its way into decedent's spinal canal and caused his death, does not prevent the homicide from being imputed to him whose shot rendered the operation necessary.[47] And where a blow to the jaw (1) inflicted an injury (2) which caused resorting to a hospital (3) where competent medical men decided to perform an operation (4) which required the use of an anesthetic (5) under which the patient died, "the rule of law was that the death could be traced back to the man by whom the injury was done." [48] There was also no break in the chain of proximate cause where the immediate cause of death was the act of a surgeon in probing for a bullet,[49] or an overdose of morphine innocently administered as a medicine by a competent physician.[50]

If the wound is of such a relatively minor character that it is not of itself to be regarded as dangerous [51] or serious [52] and death is occasioned by "grossly erroneous treatment," the original act will not be regarded as the proximate cause of the loss of life.[53] In such a case "the death is solely attributable to the secondary agency, and not at all induced by the primary one," [54] within the limits of the juridical view. In other words grossly erro-

---

44. Pyles v. State, 262 Ala. 1, 78 So.2d 813, 815 (1954); Commonwealth v. Hackett, 84 Mass. 136, 141 (1861).

45. 1 Hale P.C. *428. ". . . the accused would not be relieved of the responsibility for the death of the deceased because of . . . unskilled treatment of a wound not necessarily mortal . . . ." Crews v. State, 44 Ga.App. 546, 162 S.E. 146, 149 (1932). See also McDaniel v. State, 76 Ala. 1 (1884); Clark v. Commonwealth, 90 Va. 360, 365, 18 S.E. 440, 442 (1893).

46. See Commonwealth v. Hackett, 84 Mass. 136, 142 (1861).

47. Commonwealth v. Eisenhower, 181 Pa. 470, 37 A. 521 (1897). See also Hamblin v. State, 81 Neb. 148, 115 N.W. 850 (1908).

48. Regina v. Davis, 15 Cox C.C. 174, 179 (1883). "For it would never do to have a serious injury by one man on another, and have the issue raised that death was due to want of skill on the part of the medical men." Id. at 179–180.

49. State v. Landgraf, 95 Mo. 97, 8 S.W. 237 (1888).

50. People v. Cook, 39 Mich. 236 (1878).

51. ". . . not a dangerous one, that is, one calculated or likely to endanger human life. . . ." State v. John-son, 36 Del. 341, 344, 175 A. 669, 670 (1934). "Neglect or mistreatment . . . will not excuse, except in cases where doubt exists as to the character of the wound." People v. Cook, 39 Mich. 236, 240 (1878).

52. The character of an injury depends upon the condition of the person injured as well as upon the nature and extent of the injury itself. For example, a very slight injury is *dangerous* if the person injured is a "bleeder." State v. Frazier, 339 Mo. 966, 98 S.W.2d 707 (1936).

53. Parsons v. State, 21 Ala. 300 (1852). A conviction of murder was reversed because the jury was not properly instructed upon this point. A similar conviction was reversed for the same reason in Tibbs v. Commonwealth, 138 Ky. 558, 128 S.W. 871 (1910).

54. People v. Kane, 213 N.Y. 260, 270, 107 N.E. 655, 657 (1915). This was dictum, as such statements usually are,—although the Parsons case and the Tibbs case in the preceding note are squarely in point. See also the instruction in State v. Johnson, 36 Del. 341, 175 A. 669 (1934). The courts have wisely refused to state the doctrine in the form of a rule-of-thumb which could be used to reach absurd results in extreme cases. The caution is frequently couched in the following quotation from Greenleaf: The death

neous treatment may loom so large in the particular case that the slight injury will not be deemed a substantial factor in causing the death.

(2) Wilfulness or Criminal Negligence

If a doctor should take advantage of an opportunity not to endeavor to cure an injured man but maliciously to take his life, this would be an *independent* intervening act and would be a superseding cause.[55] And even in the absence of actual malice, medical or surgical treatment which results in death may be a superseding cause, if it is administered in bad faith [56] or with criminal negligence.[57] An injury might be inflicted under such circumstances as to require "first-aid" as an emergency measure before competent medical aid was available. If so, such "first-aid" would not necessarily be a superseding cause even if it was the immediate cause of the death and (though in good faith) was quite erroneous from the standpoint of medical science. But harm resulting from the grossly erroneous treatment of a "quack" or an intoxicated physician will ordinarily not be imputed to one whose act resulted in the injury which received this extraordinary treatment.[58] Such treatment does not come within the category of the normal response of a human being to the situation created by defendant.

is attributable to the wound unless "the maltreatment of the wound, or the medicine administered to the patient, or his own misconduct, and not the wound itself, was the sole cause of his death; for if the wound had not been given the party had not died." State v. Morphy, 33 Iowa 270, 276 (1871); Powell v. State, 13 Tex.Cr.R. 244, 254 (1882); Taylor v. State, 139 Ark. 691, 101 S.W.2d 956 (1937); Clark v. Commonwealth, 90 Va. 360, 365, 18 S.E. 440, 442 (1893). Because of the Texas statute it is reversible error to fail to charge (if evidence calls for it) that "if the death of the deceased was brought about by improper treatment or gross neglect of the physicians, he would not be guilty of homicide." McMillan v. State, 58 Tex.Cr.R. 525, 126 S.W. 875 (1910).

A conviction for voluntary manslaughter was upheld despite malpractice of physician who did not discover a laceration of the deceased's aorta. "Medical malpractice will break the chain of causation and become the proximate cause of death only if it constitutes the sole cause of death." State v. Sauter, 120 Ariz. 222, 585 P.2d 242, 243 (1978).

See also Regina v. Smith, 43 Crim.App. 121 (Ct.Martial App.1959). Unavailability of sufficient medical personnel to adequately attend to a wound does not break the chain of causation.

55. "If the physician should seize the opportunity to experiment, or maliciously to harm the victim, the defendant's act would not cause the physician's." Beale,

The Proximate Consequences of An Act, 33 Harv.L.Rev. 633, 649 (1920).

56. "But, if the result is caused by the malpractice of the physician, the wound not being in itself mortal, and the physician not acting in concert with the defendant, then the defendant is not responsible; for the wound, though a condition of the killing, is not its juridical cause." McDaniel v. State, 76 Ala. 1, 7 (1884). Cases holding that medical or surgical treatment do not break the chain of proximate cause frequently emphasize the absence of any element of bad faith. See, for example, State v. Gabriella, 163 Iowa 297, 144 N.W. 9 (1913).

57. There was no allegation of "bad faith or criminal neglect." Commonwealth v. Hackett, 84 Mass. 136, 143 (1861). No evidence of "maltreatment." Hall v. State, 199 Ind. 592, 609, 159 N.E. 420, 426 (1928). And see People v. McGee, 31 Cal.2d 229, 240, 187 P.2d 706, 713 (1947).

58. Many of the cases include cautionary statements suggestive of such a conclusion. See, for example: If decedent took the "course of consulting competent medical men," etc. Regina v. Davis, 15 Cox C.C. 174, 179 (1883). "It was not claimed that these physicians were deficient in medical skill. . . . Here morphine was administered as a medicine by competent and skillful physicians." People v. Cook, 39 Mich. 236, 239 (1878). In Coffman v. Commonwealth, 73 Ky. 495 (1874), a conviction of manslaughter was reversed because the instruction of the

A premature removal of a life support system will not excuse a defendant from responsibility for the death if the defendant caused such severe trauma, by wrongful force, that placed a victim in the position where doctors are required to exercise judgment as to whether the victim is dead.[59]

(D) Attack Invites Defense

Just as danger invites rescue so attack invites defense, and insofar as the defense is the normal response of a human being to the situation it is not superseding. This is not limited to situations involving deadly force but is most likely to be apparent there. An early Massachusetts case [60] injected an element of confusion into the type of case in which deadly force employed in self-defense causes the death of an innocent bystander. A riotous mob made an assault upon an armory during which there was an exchange of shots and an innocent person was killed, but it was not shown whether the fatal shot was fired by the rioters or by the defending soldiers. The court reached the conclusion that the homicide could not be imputed to the rioters if the death resulted from shooting by the soldiers, basing its conclusion upon the ordinary rules of *parties to crime* and without an examination of the causation problem involved.[61] This lead was followed without question in several decisions,[62] but in a Texas case [63] the problem was presented in such extreme form as to require a re-examination of the principles involved. Train robbers had forced an innocent person to precede them as they made a felonious attack upon the mail car, and the human shield had been killed. This death was held imputable to the robbers whether the fatal shot was fired by them or by those who were defending the car. The fact that defendants forced deceased to act as a shield was emphasized. This is an important factor in the case but it did not cause the fatal shot. The felonious assault produced that result. And had the robbers seen a blind man unwittingly tapping his way toward the car, whereupon they had fallen in behind him as a protection for their felonious assault, the result should have been the same.

It sometimes happens, in the perpetration or attempted perpetration of a dangerous felony such as robbery, that death results from defensive force exerted by the intended victim or someone in his behalf. The first case to give adequate discussion of causation in such a situation is *Moyer*.[64] In this robbery case, during an exchange of shots, an employee of the intended victim was killed. There was sharp disagreement in the testimony. The evidence for the prosecution tended to show that the fatal shot was fired by one of the robbers, whereas that for the defense indicated that the deceased was accidentally killed by a defensive shot fired by his employer. The robbers were found guilty of murder in a trial in which the judge had instructed, in effect, that either version of the evidence would support such a verdict. In

jury did not contain any caution of this nature.

59. State v. Inger, 292 N.W.2d 119 (Iowa 1980).

60. Commonwealth v. Campbell, 89 Mass. 541 (1863).

61. "No person can be held guilty of homicide unless the act is either actually or constructively his, and it cannot be his act in either sense unless committed by his own hand or by some one acting in concert with him or in furtherance of a common object or purpose." Id. at 544.

62. Butler v. People, 125 Ill. 641, 18 N.E. 338 (1888); Commonwealth v. Moore, 121 Ky. 97, 88 S.W. 1085 (1905); State v. Oxendine, 187 N.C. 658, 122 S.E. 568 (1924).

63. Taylor v. State, 41 Tex.Cr.R. 564, 55 S.W. 961 (1900).

64. Commonwealth v. Moyer, 357 Pa. 181, 53 A.2d 736 (1947).

affirming the resulting conviction the Pennsylvania court emphasized that the murderous attack of the robbers made the return shot essential for the protection of person and property. The robbers were the cause of a cause. The famous *"Squib Case"* [65] was used as an analogy.

Causation was so obvious in this case that it would no doubt have been accepted and followed very generally had it not been for two countervailing influences: (1) The conviction was under the familiar clause providing that "all murder which shall be . . . committed in the perpetration of, or attempting to perpetrate any . . . robbery . . . shall be murder in the first degree." This was a capital offense and down through the ages judges have gone out of their way in the effort to limit the scope of a capital crime. (2) The felony-murder rule itself is sufficiently in disfavor to encourage effort to limit its application.

After following *Moyer*, more than once,[66] the Pennsylvania court was confronted with a new angle in *Redline*.[67] In this case a police officer shot and killed one of two robbers, the shot being fired to frustrate the robbery and arrest the robbers. The surviving robber was convicted of the murder of his accomplice, but this conviction was reversed. This case is different said the court. When an innocent person is accidentally killed by a defensive shot this is excusable homicide by the one who fired the shot; but when an officer kills a robber in a reasonable effort to frustrate the robbery or arrest the robbers, this is justifiable homicide. And the court added that no one can be convicted of murder based upon a justifiable homicide. The court admitted that this was a rather slim basis for distinguishing *Redline* from the earlier cases, but admitted frankly that it served the desirable end of restricting the application of the felony-murder rule. Some years later the Pennsylvania court recognized that it had taken an untenable position in *Redline*, and solved the difficulty by repudiating its original position.[68] Apparently the end result is that if someone is fatally shot during the perpetration or attempted perpetration of robbery in Pennsylvania, the robbers cannot be convicted of murder unless one of them fired the fatal shot.[69]

---

65. Scott v. Shepherd, 2 Wm. Blackstone 892, 96 Eng.Rep. 525 (1773). This case is discussed in the text, *infra*.

66. Commonwealth v. Almeida, 362 Pa. 596, 68 A.2d 595 (1949); Commonwealth v. Thomas, 382 Pa. 639, 117 A.2d 204 (1955).

In *Almeida* the court said: "A knave who feloniously and maliciously starts 'a chain reaction' of acts dangerous to human life must be held responsible for the natural fatal consequences of such acts." (68 A.2d at 614), having previously referred to holding the felon guilty "who engages in a robbery or burglary and thereby inevitably calls into action defensive forces against him, the activity of which forces the result in the death of a human being." (68 A.2d at 611–12). *Almeida* was quoted with approval. State v. Sunday, ___ Mont. ___, 609 P.2d 1188, 1195 (1980).

67. Commonwealth v. Redline, 391 Pa. 486, 137 A.2d 472 (1958).

68. Commonwealth ex rel. Smith v. Myers, 438 Pa. 218, 261 A.2d 550 (1970).

69. This is sometimes spelled out in a statute. For example the Colorado statute provides that one is guilty of first-degree murder if: "Acting alone or with one or more persons, he commits or attempts to commit arson, robbery, burglary, . . . and in the course of or furtherance of the crime . . . or of immediate flight therefrom, the death of a person, other than one of the participants, is caused by anyone; . . . ." It is an affirmative defense if the defendant did not cause the homicidal act or in any way solicit it, and was not himself armed and had no reason to believe any other participant was armed, and so forth. Colo.Rev.Stat.1974 § 18–3–102(b).

Before this last step had been taken in Pennsylvania, California was confronted with a case similar to *Redline*. This was *Washington*[70] in which two robbers had robbed the wrong man, who shot and killed one and seriously wounded the other who was trying to run away with the "loot." The surviving robber, having been convicted of first-degree murder by application of the felony-murder rule, urged on appeal that the position taken in *Redline* should be followed. The California court very properly refused to do that but did reverse the conviction upon an entirely different ground. It emphasized the wording of the statute and pointed out that the fatal shot fired by the victim was not to perpetrate or attempt to perpetrate robbery, but to thwart it. The felony-murder rule, it was held, cannot be applied to a killing which was not by one of the robbers in attempting to carry out the plan to rob, but by someone who was attempting to prevent it.

Chief Justice Traynor, who wrote the opinion of the court in this case, was too good a lawyer to overlook the problem of causation, and took pains to emphasize, *obiter*, that: "Defendants who initiate gun battles may also be found guilty of murder if their victims resist and kill." This is on ordinary principles of causation and malice aforethought, without any reference to felony-murder.

This case was thought at the time to have established a very simple rule of causation. If someone is killed by defensive fire during the perpetration of robbery, the question of proximate cause depends upon who fired first. The robbers can be held to be the proximate cause of the death if, but only if, they fired first. There is no question that in all such cases the robbers are in fact a cause of the death. *But for* the robbery the deceased would still be alive. Proximate cause, however, never includes the entire area of factual cause, and a particular limitation may require a policy judgment. A later case[71] seemed to reinforce that position. A killing by the victim of robbery or on his behalf may be imputed to the robbers if it was in response to a shooting by one of them, but not if it was merely to prevent the robbery.

A more recent case, *Taylor*,[72] shows that the test of proximate cause in such a situation is not so simple as had been supposed. Three men went to West's store with robbery in mind. One of them pointed a gun at West in an extremely menacing manner, threatening to blow his head off and "have an execution right here." This so alarmed Mrs. West that she opened fire on the robbers, thereby diverting their attention sufficiently to permit West to get his weapon with which he killed one of the robbers. One of the surviving robbers, being charged with the murder of his accomplice, sought a writ of prohibition to prevent the trial on the murder charge, on the claim that it could not be murder. The court refused to prohibit the trial on the murder charge saying: "However, depending upon the circumstances, a gun battle can be initiated by acts of provocation falling short of firing the first shot." What seems to be the position of the California court is that if, in the perpetration or attempted perpetration of robbery, a fatal shot was fired, not by one of the robbers but by the intended victim or on his behalf, felony-murder

70. People v. Washington, 62 Cal.2d 777, 44 Cal.Rptr. 442, 402 P.2d 130 (1965).

A killing in the attempt to prevent the felony cannot be held to be a killing "in furtherance" thereof. Weick v. State, 420 A.2d 159 (Del.1980).

71. People v. Gilbert, 63 Cal.2d 690, 47 Cal.Rptr. 909, 408 P.2d 365 (1965).

72. Taylor v. Superior Court, 3 Cal.3d 578, 91 Cal.Rptr. 275, 477 P.2d 131 (1970).

will not apply, and for the killing to be imputed to the robbers under the rules of proximate cause, the evidence must support a finding that the shot was fired to defend against apparent danger to life,—not merely to prevent the robbery.[73]

A complication to the problem was added by *Antick*.[74] So shortly after the commission of burglary by **A** and **B** that it was within the legal concept of "in the perpetration thereof," [75] they were momentarily separated. And while **A** was absent, an officer approached **B** to arrest him for that burglary. **B** opened fire with a shot that missed the officer, but the officer's return fire did not miss. It hit and killed **B**. On **A**'s trial for the murder of **B**, the judge instructed the jury (1) on the felony-murder rule, and (2) on the vicarious liability of one for the crime of his co-conspirator. This was held to be error. It could not be felony-murder, it was held on appeal, since the fatal shot was fired, not by one of the burglars, but by the police. And it was held that the vicarious-liability theory would also not apply. Since **B** initiated the gun battle, the return fire and its consequence are imputable to him, and by vicarious liability to his co-conspirator **A**. The result of this is that **B** is legally recognized as the cause of his own death; but this is suicide, not homicide, and there is no murder without homicide. **A** said the court, cannot be guilty of the murder of **B** on the basis of vicarious liability for the crime of his co-conspirator because **B** could not be guilty of the murder of himself.

This is a nice theory but not all courts may be willing to accept it. Some courts may approach the problem in some such manner as this. **B**'s death was not **B**'s act, but was the result of his act. **B**'s act was shooting at the officer. Under the circumstances the return shot is also imputable to him together with its consequence. Hence **B** is the cause of his own death, which is suicide. By vicarious liability **B**'s act of shooting is also imputable to **A**. And the return fire and its consequence is also imputable to **A**. Hence **A** also is recognized as the cause of **B**'s death. This is homicide,[76] and in the perpetration of burglary it is murder.[77]

Under the California approach the result of *Antick* was easy since **A** was not present at the time of the shooting—or at least was not shown to have

---

73. This was later emphasized in In re Joe R., 27 Cal.3d 496, 165 Cal.Rptr. 837, 612 P.2d 927 (1980).

74. People v. Antick, 15 Cal.3d 79, 123 Cal.Rptr. 475, 539 P.2d 43 (1975).

75. "Since the burglars were still being hotly pursued they are regarded as being engaged in the commission of the burglary at the time of their pursuit." Wiley v. Memphis Police Department, 548 F.2d 1247, 1253 (6th Cir. 1977).

76. No inconsistency is involved in holding that a single killing may be suicide as to one and homicide as to another. If **A** and **B** were acting quite independently and **A** inflicted an injury upon **B** with malice aforethought, shortly after **B** had injured himself with intent to take his own life, it might be found that the two injuries combined to cause the death. If so each was a contributing cause of

the death which is murder by **A** and suicide by **B**.

77. "A cause is concurrent if it was operative at the moment of death and acted with another cause to produce the death." People v. Abahai, 48 Cal.App.3d 628, 120 Cal.Rptr. 654 (1975). Jones v. States, 580 S.W.2d 329 (Tenn.Cr.App. 1978).

"Although the lethal shot was through the actions of a police officer attempting to apprehend the felons, the behavior of the officer was chargeable to [the defendants]. They were just as much the cause of [deceased's] death as if each had fired the fatal shot. Their acts themselves produced the intervening cause of [deceased's] death, and the result is not to be considered remote and was foreseeable." Jackson v. State, 286 Md. 430, 408 A.2d 711 (1979).

been present. Had he been shown to have been present the result would have been the same without some additional showing to establish that he participated in initiating the gun battle, so that his liability was personal rather than vicarious. Under this approach, if while three were committing robbery, one of the robbers shot at the victim who returned the fire and killed one of them, it would be necessary to determine which was which. If the robber killed was not the one who fired the shot the result is easy. Both survivors are guilty of murder—one by personal liability and the other by vicarious liability. On the other hand, if the robber killed was the one who fired the opening shot, without some additional showing, neither survivor could be convicted of murder. Under the other approach both survivors would be guilty of murder under either finding—a result many may find more acceptable.[78]

> **With the present desire to restrict the application of the felony-murder rule, it seems proper to hold that a statute worded in terms of a killing "in the perpetration or attempt to perpetrate" and so forth, does not apply to a killing caused by an effort to prevent the commission or consummation of a crime; but in offenses such as robbery or burglary, under ordinary principles of causation, it should be held that the felons have caused the death resulting from defensive fire, at least if the felons have threatened or endangered the lives of their victims, or others.[79]**

The California court was faced with still a different problem in a related case.[80] After robbers had forced their way into a building and robbed the inhabitants, they had reason to believe officers were approaching. One of them seized one of the victims, twisted his arm behind his back, and at gunpoint under threat of death, forced him to lead the way outside. A neighbor who knew the police had been called, and wanted to prevent the escape of the robbers before the officers arrived, was standing by with a gun on his porch. When the robbers with their "shield" emerged the neighbor opened fire without realizing he was seeing any but robbers. His shot killed the "shield." The robbers were informed against for robbery, conspiracy, burglary and murder. One of them sought a writ of prohibition to restrain the trial court from further proceeding on the murder count other than to dismiss it. He claimed that what had happened could not be murder because (1) the fatal shot was not fired by one of the robbers but against them, and (2) the robbers had not initiated the gun battle or in any way threatened the

---

78. Some believe the common law of complicity goes too far and should be changed to relieve a conspirator of vicarious liability in certain instances in which his co-conspirator has shot and killed the victim, or another, during the perpetration of the target crime,—such as where the one who did not fire the fatal shot did not know the other was armed and went into the venture with the assurance that there would be no violence. (Guilty of murder in a robbery case at common law, Miller v. State, 25 Wis. 384 (1870)). But this would have to do with the scope of vicarious liability, not its application.

79. In an attempted robbery the robber shot at the victim who returned the

fire. In the ensuing gun battle a third person was killed. "Whether the fatal act was done by the defendant, an accomplice, another victim, or a bystander is, under the facts here, not controlling. . . . The felony-murder conviction is affirmed." State v. Moore, 580 S.W.2d 747, 752–53 (Mo.1979). A robber, whose accomplice was killed by the victim in defending against the robbery, may not be convicted under the felony-murder doctrine. Jackson v. State, 92 N.M. 461, 589 P.2d 1052 (1979).

80. Pizano v. Superior Court of Tulare County, 21 Cal.3d 128, 145 Cal.Rptr. 524, 577 P.2d 659 (1978).

neighbor. The court refused to issue the writ. It was admitted that murder could not be established on the felony-murder basis and that the robbers had not initiated the gunplay; but held that malice could be established by the wanton act of forcing the "shield" into a position of obvious danger, since part of the purpose was to have him "absorb" any deadly force that might be encountered. The court further held that since murder could be established it could be found to be first-degree murder under the statute. Although the *killing* was not in the perpetration of robbery but in opposition to it, the *act* which made the killing murder—wantonly forcing the "shield" into a position of obvious danger—was in the perpetration of robbery, and hence constituted first-degree murder under the statute. The Chief Justice dissented from the holding that the murder could be found to be of the first degree. But there was no dissent from the holding that the "shield" theory presents an independent basis for the finding of malice and causation.

It is a normal human response for one threatened by harmful force, deadly or nondeadly, to take action in the effort to avoid the impending harm. Thus it is normal for one endangered by an explosive which has landed near him to throw the object away in order to avoid injury, and such an act is not superceding. Generations of lawyers have been familiar with the famous "squib" case. Shepherd threw a lighted squib into a crowded marketplace and it fell near Willis who, to protect himself, threw it away and it landed near Ryal who also threw it for his protection. It then fell upon Scott and exploded at that instant putting out one of his eyes. It was held that Shepherd had put out Scott's eye.[81] A recent case followed a similar pattern but with even more serious consequences. After defendant had released the trigger mechanism of a hand grenade and thrown it near a crowd, one member kicked it away from himself and it landed near another who was killed by the explosion. There was held to be no break in the line of causation and nothing which would preclude conviction of murder.[82]

13. INDEPENDENT INTERVENING CAUSE

An independent intervening cause is one which operates upon a condition produced by an antecedent but is in no sense a consequence thereof.

If a falling piece of cornice hits a man who had previously been knocked down and left unconscious on the sidewalk, the first blow is factually a cause of the second injury because without it the victim would not have been in the path of the falling object. But the blow which knocked the man down did not cause the piece of cornice to fall; it would have fallen just when and as it did had no battery been committed. An independent intervening cause may be superseding but is not so under all circumstances. It is not superseding if it merely cooperates with the antecedent cause so that both are contributory causes of the harmful result,[83] or if the consequence was intended just as it happened or if harm of the general kind which occurred was reasonably

---

81. Scott v. Shepherd, 2 Wm. Blackstone 892, 96 Eng.Rep. 525 (1773).

82. Madison v. State, 234 Ind. 517, 130 N.E.2d 35 (1955).

83. "If the deceased died of the combined effect of a wound inflicted with malice and of a disease disconnected from the wound, the accused is guilty. An intervening cause must be the efficient cause of death, or at least more than a contributing cause, before the accused is not guilty for such reason." Houston v. State, 220 Miss. 166, 169, 70 So.2d 338, 339 (1954).

foreseeable at the time of the act in question. Under other circumstances an independent intervening cause is superseding.

As was said in a Massachusetts case in which defendant was charged with having killed the deceased by a pistol shot,—if, while the victim was still alive, "another cause came in which, independently of the pistol wound, caused the death, so that the death resulted from that, and not from the pistol wound, then the jury cannot here find a verdict of homicide from the cause alleged in this indictment." [84] The same principle was expressed by the Virginia court which said that if there "supervened" between the blow and the death "a disease not caused by the blow, but coming by visitation of Providence," the blow is not the proximate cause of the death. [85] The most striking case of this nature arose in Kentucky and involved these facts: Defendant shot a girl who was treated by a physician just recovering from scarlet fever; the girl contracted this disease and died. The shooting was a *causa sine qua non* of the death, because but for this act the girl would not have been treated by this physician and hence would not have contracted the fever, but a conviction of murder was reversed on the ground that this was a superseding cause. [86]

A stroke of lightning, a flood, a tornado, or other violence of nature, which unexpectedly takes the life of one who merely happened to have been placed where the harm took effect, will be a superseding cause; and the blow or other act which merely chanced to leave him in the path of this unforeseen danger will be a remote cause of the loss of life rather than a proximate one. [87] However, if the victim is left in a place of foreseeable danger and death results the causal connection is established. [88]

A. INDEPENDENT INTERVENING ACT OR "EQUIVALENT"

If there are acts of two persons who have not acted in concert, and if the act of the second was not induced by the first and was not the normal response of a human being to the situation created by the first, the act of the

84. Commonwealth v. Costley, 118 Mass. 1, 26 (1875).

The court said that "a supervening cause is an independent intervening cause in which the defendant did not participate and which he could not foresee." Hamrick v. People, __ Colo. __, 624 P.2d 1320, 1324 (1981).

85. Livingston v. Commonwealth, 55 Va. 592, 602 (1857). See also Quinn v. State, 106 Miss. 844, 64 So. 738 (1914); Treadwell v. State, 16 Tex.Cr.R. 560 (1884).

86. Bush v. Commonwealth, 78 Ky. 268 (1880).

Where deceased was stabbed and in the process of healing but, because of an intolerance to a drug given to reduce infection which was administered after notice of the deceased's intolerance, death resulted, the Court found insufficient causation for homicide. Regina v. Jordan, 40 Crim.App. 152 (1956).

87. Cases as extreme as this seem not to result in prosecution, but an ancient case is illuminating. An indictment charged the defendants with throwing skins "into a man's yard, which was a public way, *per quod* another man's eye was beat out." But in view of the evidence that a sudden gust of wind picked up the skin and blew it "out of the way" and hence the harm occurred, the court felt that the injury was not imputable to the acts of defendants. Rex v. Gill, 1 Strange 190, 93 Eng.Rep. 466 (1719). The statement of facts in this case is very brief, but "the case of the hoy" (Amies v. Stevens, 1 Strange 127, 93 Eng.Rep. 428) relied upon, involved a "sudden gust of wind" which was of such a nature that it was referred to as an "act of God."

88. People v. Kibbe, 35 N.Y.2d 407, 362 N.Y.S.2d 848, 321 N.E.2d 773 (1974).

second will ordinarily not be imputed to the first.[89] If in the effort to avoid a man, for example, a woman jumps from a rapidly moving vehicle and is killed by the fall, it is necessary to inquire further. If he was attacking her with a knife and threatening to kill her the act of jumping (however unwise if tested by hindsight) was merely a normal human response to such sudden danger; but if his only effort was obviously to kiss her the act of jumping, under those circumstances, was such an extraordinary response that it is treated as the "equivalent" of an independent intervening cause.

In *Elder*[90] the defendant, during an altercation, had knocked down the deceased, whereupon a bystander stepped up and kicked the fallen man, causing his death. It was held that the defendant was not the proximate cause of this death if there was no preconcert of action between the two assailants and the defendant did not anticipate or induce the second blow. And in *Lewis*[91] the death of a wife was held not imputable to her husband who had knocked her down, if she died not from the blow but from arsenical poisoning administered by herself or by another. Probably the leading case in point is *Horsey*.[92] Defendant unlawfully set fire to a stack of straw and a person was burned to death; but there was doubt whether decedent had been there before the blaze was started or went in afterwards. As there seemed to be no normal reason why he should have gone into the flames the court ruled that there could be no conviction of homicide if the act of decedent "intervened between the death and the act of the prisoner."

Even an act which would otherwise have resulted fatally is not the proximate cause of death if another act intervenes to destroy the life before the first has an opportunity to do so,—as where the head is severed from the body of one who is yet alive but has been given a fatal dose of poison.[93] As said by the West Virginia court in reversing a conviction of murder: "if after a mortal blow or wound is inflicted by one person another independent responsible agent in no way connected in causal relation with the first, intervenes and wrongfully inflicts another injury, the proximate cause of the homicide, the latter and not the former is guilty of the murder."[94]

B. ACTS OF INSANE PERSON

An insane man might be used as an "instrument" of death, and obviously one will be legally recognized as the cause of homicide which he has pro-

89. "But if the wounded condition only afforded an opportunity for another unconnected person to kill, defendant would not be guilty of homicide, . . ." People v. Lewis, 124 Cal. 551, 555, 57 P. 470, 472 (1899). ". . . the wound, though a condition of the killing, is not its juridical cause." McDaniel v. State, 76 Ala. 1, 7 (1884). Obviously the act of the first will not be attributed to the second, if the two are acting quite independently. Wilson v. State, 24 S.W. 409 (Tex.Cr.1893).

90. People v. Elder, 100 Mich. 515, 59 N.W. 237 (1894).

91. Lewis v. Commonwealth, 19 Ky.L. Rep. 1139, 42 S.W. 1127 (1897).

92. Regina v. Horsey, 3 F. & F. 287, 176 Eng.Rep. 129 (1862).

93. Jackson v. Commonwealth, 100 Ky. 239, 38 N.W. 422, 1091 (1896). The issue in this case was not who killed the deceased but where did death occur, but it illustrates the point as to the actual cause of death.

94. State v. Angelina, 73 W.Va. 146, 149, 80 S.E. 141, 142 (1913). "It is true that if one man inflicts a mortal wound, of which the victim is languishing, and then a second kills the deceased by an independent act, the first cannot be said to have killed." State v. Hambright, 111 N.C. 707, 714, 16 S.E. 411 (1892). See also State v. Scates, 50 N.C. 420, 423-4 (1858); State v. Wood, 53 Vt. 560 (1881).

cured by such means.[95]   One who encouraged an insane person to resist the lawful authorities with deadly force was the proximate cause of a killing which resulted from such resistance;[96] and the death of an officer at the hands of an insane man he had taken into custody was imputable to defendant who had wrongfully interfered and released the lunatic's hand from the officer's grasp, thereby enabling him to strike the fatal blow.[97]   It seems however that the insanity was known to the one to whom the consequence was imputed in these cases and hence the element of foreseeability was involved.   It seems that an extraordinary response of a human being, even if insane, should be treated as the "equivalent" of an independent intervening cause except as to one who has himself caused the loss of mind.

14. FORESEEABILITY

It was said in the 1500's that "it is every man's business to foresee what wrong or mischief may happen from that which he does with an ill-intention."[98]   In that case poisoned food was passed on innocently by the intended victim to another who thereby became the actual victim of the defendant's malicious scheme.   There was quite obviously a foreseeable risk in such a case but the court did not, in its general discussion of the problem, separate the issues of causation and responsibility, or distinguish cases in which the defendant is held *because* the result was foreseeable from those in which the harm is imputable to him without reference to any problem of foreseeability. Similar confusion is involved in the oft-repeated clause "that every person is held to contemplate and to be responsible for the natural consequences of his own acts."[99]   The term "natural consequence," for example, is sometimes used to mean the absence of any intervening cause,[1] and at other times, to imply an intervening cause which is not superseding because foreseeable.[2]

95. 1 East P.C. 228 (1803).

96. Regina v. Tyler, 8 Car. & P. 616, 173 Eng.Rep. 643 (1838).

97. Johnson v. State, 142 Ala. 70, 38 So. 182 (1905).

98. Regina v. Saunders, 2 Plow, 473, 474, 75 Eng.Rep. 706, 708 (1575).

99. Sharp v. State, 51 Ark. 147, 150, 10 S.W. 228, 229 (1889); State v. Johnson, 36 Del. 341, 343, 175 A. 669, 670 (1934); Hall v. State, 199 Ind. 592, 608, 159 N.E. 420, 426 (1928); Bush v. Commonwealth, 78 Ky. 268, 271 (1880); Commonwealth v. Hackett, 84 Mass. 136, 142 (1861).

1. An assault resulted in death because the victim was suffering from heart disease.   A conviction of manslaughter was affirmed.   The court said that his failing health and death "were natural and probable results" of the assault and added: "Nor would ignorance on the part of the defendant of the diseased physical condition of Stocum excuse his acts."   State v. O'Brien, 81 Iowa 88, 93, 46 N.W. 752, 753 (1890).   In Bush v. Commonwealth, 78 Ky. 268 (1880), scarlet fever—an intervening cause not

foreseeable under the circumstances— "was not the natural consequence of the wound." (at p. 271).

2. Thus it has been said, in connection with the "natural consequences" clause that unskilful and improper treatment of the wound—a foreseeable intervening cause—"must in law be deemed to have been among those which were in contemplation of the guilty party, and for which he is to be held responsible."   Sharp v. State, 51 Ark. 147, 150, 10 S.W. 228, 229 (1888); Commonwealth v. Hackett, 84 Mass. 136, 142 (1861).   Sometimes it is used to mean a foreseeable direct consequence, as for example: "Every one must be presumed to intend the natural consequences of his acts.   If you throw a stone at a window it must be taken that you intend to break it, because it is a brittle substance."   Regina v. Kirkham, 8 Car. & P. 115, 117, 173 Eng.Rep. 422, 423 (1837).   "Of course, where one deliberately and intentionally fires a deadly weapon at a human being, into a crowd, or at a particular point where human beings are known to be, the law assumes that the actor intended to accomplish the

Sometimes a clause such as "natural and probable result," [3] or "reasonable, natural, and probable result" [4] is employed to emphasize the latter meaning.

What actually happened is that courts talked in terms of fiction before foreseeability was recognized as being non-essential in certain situations.[5] At the present time foreseeability is recognized as having no application to the issue of proximate cause in criminal cases except those in which the harm results from intervening causes.[6] In fact, it has no application even in such cases unless the intervening cause is "independent" or is a dependent intervening cause in the form of an abnormal response of a human being or an animal.[7] On the other hand, if defendant's act created merely a condition, and the actual harm resulted from an "independent" cause, or an abnormal response by man or animal, the issue of proximate cause is dependent upon whether or not such harm, or harm of the same general nature, was a foreseeable risk of the condition created by the defendant.[8]

The distinction between responsibility and causation will bear repeated emphasis. In a case in which it has no bearing upon the issue of proximate cause, foreseeability may be a determinant of the degree of guilt,[9] or even of the fact of guilt.[10] On the other hand, if defendant did not cause the death

natural result of his act, and if death results, the killing was intentional." State v. Hiatt, 187 Wash. 226, 233, 60 P.2d 71, 74 (1936).

3. Stephenson v. State, 205 Ind. 141, 159, 179 N.E. 633, 639 (1933).

4. Keaton v. State, 41 Tex.Cr.R. 621, 624, 57 S.W. 1125, 1129 (1900).

5. Intent experienced a similar development. "So there is occasional talk about 'constructive intent;' or about transposing or transferring the intent to the unintended result. These fictions should be discarded." Jeremiah Smith, Legal Cause in Actions of Tort, 25 Harv. L.Rev. 223, 231 (1912).

6. "In proximate cause, foreseeability has no application except where new causes intervene between the defendant's act and the consequence and the consequence results from the intervening cause and the question is whether this particular intervening cause or a cause of the genus from which the harm resulted was foreseeable as likely to occur." Carpenter, Workable Rules for Determining Proximate Cause, 20 Cal.L.Rev. 229, 240 (1932).

7. "Hence an intervening cause that was a coincidence will be a superseding cause when it was unforeseeable. . . . On the other hand, an intervening cause that was a response will be a superseding cause only where it was abnormal and unforeseeable." State v. Hall, 129 Ariz. 589, 633 P.2d 398, 403 (1981).

8. A government witness was killed by an explosion in his own home. De-

fendants claimed that the deceased had wired his home with dynamite to get at them because they were searching for him, and that he accidentally caused his own death. The judge instructed the jury that the defendants would be guilty of conspiracy resulting in death if the death of the deceased was "induced or brought about by some act of a conspiracy in furtherance of the purposes of the conspiracy." In affirming the resulting conviction the appellate court held that defendants "would still be considered in the chain of legal causation if the immediate cause of death—setting a bomb as a booby trap—was a foreseeable protective action to their criminal efforts to locate him and dissuade him from testifying." United States v. Guillette, 547 F.2d 743, 749–50 (2d Cir. 1976).

9. One who wrongfully hit another in the jaw, inflicting an injury from which the other bled to death, has caused the death within the rules of proximate causation, even if the injury would not have been fatal except for the fact that the victim was a "bleeder," and the flow of blood could not be stopped even from a relatively small wound. But in a particular case, whether the assailant's guilt is of murder or of manslaughter might depend upon his knowledge or ignorance of the peculiar condition of the decedent. For a case holding him guilty of manslaughter where he did not know of the condition, see State v. Frazier, 339 Mo. 966, 98 S.W.2d 707 (1936).

10. Suppose A is suffering from some malady which makes it probable that a

of decedent, within the rules of legally-recognized causation, he cannot be convicted of homicide even if he committed an assault and battery upon that person and is subject to conviction upon a charge of this lesser offense.[11]

A. TYPE OF CAUSAL RELATION

If a blow, which otherwise would have caused only a minor injury, results in death because the recipient was a "bleeder" or was suffering from heart disease or other ailment which rendered him incapable of surviving even this relatively slight force, the assailant's knowledge or ignorance of the victim's peculiar physical condition is immaterial *so far as the issue of causation is concerned*, because there was no intervening cause.[12] The assailant must take his victim as he in fact is. Furthermore if "a wound cause a disease which produces death, the death is imputable to the wound," [13] since the intervening cause was not an *independent* cause or an "equivalent" and hence causation is not limited by foreseeability. On the other hand if the wound results in medical treatment, during which the patient contracts scarlet fever from the physician who was just recovering from this ailment, this if not an independent intervening cause is an "equivalent" which will ordinarily relegate the wound to the position of remoteness, so far as resulting death is concerned.[14] This, however, is because the law does not impute a result to one who merely created a condition upon which an independent intervening force took effect with harmful results, unless this was a reasonably foreseeable hazard at the time of the act which created such a condition. And if the assailant knew the only available physician was just recovering from scarlet fever which was still in a communicable stage, and inflicted an injury in the hope the victim would contract the disease by reason of being attended by this doctor, there should be no difficulty in imputing this foreseeable result to the act which caused the injury.

B. CHARACTER OF INTERVENING ACT

If a harmful result was brought about by an intervening act the importance or unimportance of foreseeability is dependent upon the character of the intervening act. If the intervening cause was a normal human response to the situation the result may be imputed

blow on the back would prove fatal. **B** hits **A** on the back and **A** dies. If **B** knew of this condition and struck **A** hoping **A** would die, **B** is guilty of murder. If **B** did not know or have reason to know of this condition but struck **A** unlawfully, **B** is guilty of manslaughter. If **B** and **A** were old friends who were accustomed to greet one another with a resounding slap on the back, and **B** so greeted **A** in all friendliness and with no idea of the malady **A** had developed since last they met, **B** has caused **A**'s death, but it is excusable homicide.

11. See, for example, State v. Johnson, 36 Del. 341, 175 A. 669 (1934); Bush v. Commonwealth, 78 Ky. 268 (1880). In Reeves v. State, 131 Tex.Cr.R. 560, 101 S.W.2d 245 (1937), a conviction of murder was reversed because of doubt whether the death was caused by the injury inflicted by defendant or by an infection which came from quite an independent source.

12. State v. O'Brien, 81 Iowa 88, 46 N.W. 752 (1890); State v. Frazier, 339 Mo. 966, 98 S.W.2d 707 (1936). ". . . though the assailant did not know the enfeebled condition of the person assaulted." Cunningham v. People, 195 Ill. 550, 572, 63 N.E. 517, 525 (1902); State v. Atkinson, 298 N.C. 673, 259 S.E.2d 858 (1979).

13. Powell v. State, 13 Tex.Cr.R. 244, 254 (1882); People v. Baer, 35 Ill.App.3d 391, 342 N.E.2d 177 (1976); Muse v. Commonwealth, 551 S.W.2d 564 (Ky.1977).

14. Bush v. Commonwealth, 78 Ky. 268 (1880).

to the original act without the element of foreseeability, but an extraordinary response of a human being will be superseding if not reasonably foreseeable.

Thus the act of one who goes into a burning building is a normal response (and hence not a superseding cause) if it is for the purpose of rescuing valuable property,[15] or is the act of a fireman in line with his duty,[16] but is not normal (and hence is superseding) if it is for the purpose of committing suicide.[17] It is normal that medical or surgical treatment will be administered to one who has been injured, and that such treatment may not be the most skilful in its nature or may even be negligent;[18] but it is not normal for the injured person to be treated by a "quack," or by a physician or surgeon who is intoxicated, or by one who will cause injury as a result of malice or *criminal* negligence.[19] Hence medical or surgical treatment is not a superseding cause unless it falls within one of these abnormal categories, and even treatment of the latter type would be attributed to one who wilfully inflicted an injury with full knowledge that this very kind of treatment would be administered, since none other was available.

The cases indicate "a tendency not to look back of the last wrongdoer,"[20] but even this tendency fails to include a case in which the very consequence itself was foreseen. It has been held that one who knocks another down is not the proximate cause of death which resulted when a bystander took advantage of the helpless situation of the victim to administer a fatal kick,— with the qualification that the one did not anticipate such action.[21] And a druggist who dropped croton oil on a piece of candy at the request of a cus-

---

15. State v. Leopold, 110 Conn. 55, 147 A. 118 (1929).

16. State v. Glover, 330 Mo. 709, 50 S.W.2d 1049 (1932).

17. Regina v. Horsey, 3 F. & F. 287, 176 Eng.Rep. 129 (1862).

18. "A defendant causing a wound may be held responsible for the usual risks attendant thereon, which include those of medical treatment which frequently may not seem well advised or careful after the event." McLaughlin, Proximate Cause, 39 Harv.L.Rev. 149, 170 (1925). "Indeed it may be said that neglect of the wound or its unskilful and improper treatment, which were of themselves consequences of the criminal act, which might naturally follow in any case, must be deemed in law to have been among those which were in contemplation of the guilty party, and for which he is to be held responsible." Commonwealth v. Hackett, 84 Mass. 136, 142 (1861). State v. Sauter, 120 Ariz. 222, 585 P.2d 242 (1978). See also Annotation, 100 ALR 2d 769 (1965).

19. See Beale, The Proximate Consequences of an Act, 33 Harv.L.Rev. 633, 649 (1920). The absence of criminal negligence is frequently emphasized in cases holding medical or surgical treatment not

to be a superseding cause. Commonwealth v. Hackett, 84 Mass. 136, 143 (1861); People v. Cook, 39 Mich. 236 (1878). No evidence of "maltreatment." Hall v. State, 199 Ind. 592, 609, 159 N.E. 420, 426 (1928).

20. McLaughlin, Proximate Cause, 39 Harv.L.Rev. 149, 176 (1925).

21. People v. Elder, 100 Mich. 515, 59 N.W. 237 (1894).

"Accordingly, we hold that whenever a defendant's act would not have caused the death of another but for the intervention of an independent force, it must be determined whether the intervening force could have been reasonably foreseen. Only if it was unforeseeable does the (independent) intervening force become a superseding cause, relieving the defendant of the lethal consequences of his act." State v. Powers, 117 Ariz. 220, 571 P.2d 1016, 1021 (1977). The state's evidence indicated that defendant had pushed the victim into the path of an oncoming car which caused the death. That, of course was foreseeable. But if under other circumstances the pushing had left the victim in what turned out to be the path of an intervening force which had not been foreseeable, this would have been superseding.

tomer and with knowledge of the wrongful use to be made of it, was held guilty of assault and battery upon an innocent victim who was induced by the customer to eat the candy.[22]

C. NORMAL ROUTINE ACTS

Normal routine acts are clearly foreseeable and hence the intervention of such an act, although quite independent in its nature (not in any sense resulting from defendant's act), is not superseding. Men will walk, and automobiles and trains will be run; and if such a condition is created that these normal routine acts will produce harmful consequences, the result will be imputed to him who created the risk. A woman placed about five grains of strychnine in a glass of milk which she served her husband for breakfast. After partaking of some of the milk the husband attempted to get up from his chair, but was so weak or unsteady from the effect of the poison that he fell and was killed by striking his head upon an iron smoking stand, which was demolished by the fall. Although death resulted from his act of rising from his chair, the woman had created the condition which made this normal routine act hazardous and hence was the proximate cause of the death.[23] The same result was reached where a blow on the head rendered the victim so unsteady on his feet that he fell while attempting to leave the scene of the attack, and received a mortal injury as his head struck the cobblestones.[24] *Brown* [25] is a case in which the defendant was held to have caused the death of an engineer. He had placed an obstruction on the track, not for the purpose of causing a wreck, but to receive credit for giving notice of such an obstruction. Before he could give the intended notice, a fast through train he had not known about was wrecked and the engineer was killed. The normal routine act of operating the train was not a superseding cause. He was bound to take notice of the fact that trains would be run upon the track, and his ignorance in regard to this particular train, while perhaps having a bearing on responsibility,[26] had no bearing on imputability. In another case,[27] a defendant was held to be the proximate cause of the death of a victim he had knocked unconscious and left where he was likely to be killed, and was killed by an automobile which was driven in a normal and proper manner.[28]

22. State v. Monroe, 121 N.C. 677, 28 S.E. 547 (1897).

23. People v. Cobbler, 2 Cal.App.2d 375, 37 P.2d 869 (1934). There was some evidence indicating that death was due directly to the strychnine and other evidence that it was due to the brain injury resulting from the fall. A conviction of murder was affirmed on the ground that she had caused the death under either theory.

24. Cunningham v. People, 195 Ill. 550, 63 N.E. 517 (1902).

25. State v. Brown, Houst.Cr. 539 (Del.1878).

26. The indictment was for murder; the conviction was of manslaughter.

27. People v. Fowler, 178 Cal. 657, 174 P. 892 (1918). There was doubt

whether the death resulted from the blow by the defendant or from an automobile being driven in a proper manner. A conviction of murder was upheld on the ground that defendant was guilty under either theory.

D hit X and left her unconscious on a busy street where she was run over and killed by a car. A conviction of manslaughter was upheld on the ground that the jury could find this as a foreseeable result. Hamilton v. United States, 252 F.2d 862 (D.C.Cir.1958).

28. People v. Kibbe, 35 N.Y.2d 407, 362 N.Y.S.2d 848, 321 N.E.2d 773 (1974), affirmed Henderson v. Kibbe, 431 U.S. 145, 97 S.Ct. 1730 (1977).

Acts not as clearly "routine" as those mentioned may be readily foreseeable. An iron founder, employed to make a cannon to be used on a day of rejoicing, who made it so negligently that it burst and killed a bystander, was chargeable with his death within the rules of proximate cause.[29] And a man who gave a poisoned apple to his wife with intent to kill her was convicted of the murder of his three-year-old child to whom the woman had innocently handed the fruit, "for he was the original cause of the death."[30]

If poison is placed where it will be taken by the victim without suspecting the harmful quality of what he eats,[31] or a spring-gun is set so that the victim will cause the discharge unwittingly by his own movements,[32] the absence of superseding cause is obvious. Unlawfulness of the act which unintentionally discharges a spring-gun, it may be added, will not prevent the result from being imputed to him who set it,[33] although it may have a bearing upon the question whether he is guilty of any crime for having done so.[34]

D. APPRECIABLE PROBABILITY

Needless to say, consequences cannot be imputed on the basis of foreseeability alone. The one alleged to have been the proximate cause of a harmful result must be shown to have acted (positively or negatively) in such a manner that the risk of this result was at least created or enhanced by his act.[35] If such a risk was created or enhanced by such an act, and the only connection between the one accused and the result is that an independent intervening cause or an "equivalent" operated upon the condition of things created by the accused and thus produced the harm, the imputability of this result to the accused is dependent upon foreseeability. "Foreseeability" is not a "test" which can be applied without the use of common sense; it presents one of those problems in which "we must rely on the common sense of the common man as to common things."[36] It is employed in the sense of "appreciable probability."[37] It does not require such a degree of probability that the intervention was more likely to occur than not; and on the other hand it implies more than that someone might have imagined it as a theoretical possibility. It does not require that the defendant himself actually thought of it. For the purposes of proximate cause "an appreciable probability is one which a reasonable man in ordering his conduct in view of

29. Rex v. Carr, 8 Car. & P. 163, 173 Eng.Rep. 443 (1832).

30. Regina v. Saunders, 2 Plowd. 473, 474, 75 Eng.Rep. 706, 708 (1575).

31. Cassell v. Commonwealth, 284 Ky. 579, 59 S.W.2d 544 (1933).

32. Simpson v. State, 59 Ala. 1 (1877); State v. Green, 118 S.C. 279, 110 S.E. 145 (1921); State v. Barr, 11 Wash. 481, 39 P. 1080 (1895).

33. State v. Plumlee, 177 La. 687, 149 So. 425 (1933).

34. State v. Marfaudille, 48 Wash. 117, 92 P. 939 (1907). And see chapter 10, section 9.

35. Beale, The Proximate Consequences of an Act, 33 Harv.L.Rev. 633, 658 (1920).

36. Roscoe Pound, The Theory of Judicial Decision, 36 Harv.L.Rev. 940, 952 (1923). Dean Pound was speaking with reference to standards.

37. McLaughlin, Proximate Cause, 39 Harv.L.Rev. 149, 186 (1925).

From the evidence the jury might have found that D's reckless conduct left the victim in the street where she was run over and killed by a second car. Even so, D's reckless conduct was the cause of the death. The second car did not constitute a supervening cause but was an intermediate cause reasonably foreseeable by D. People v. Para, 35 Ill.App.3d 240, 340 N.E.2d 636 (1975).

his situation and his knowledge and means of knowledge, should, either consciously or unconsciously, take into account in connection with the other facts and probabilities then apparent." [38]

15. INTENDED CONSEQUENCES

It has been said that "any intended consequence of an act is proximate," [39] for the following reason: "It would plainly be absurd that a person should be allowed to act with an intention to produce a certain consequence, and then when that very consequence in fact follows his act, to escape liability for it on the plea that it was not proximate." [40] The famous case of *Michael* [41] may be mentioned in this connection. Catherine Michael, with intent to cause the death of the infant George Michael, procured poison which she handed to the child's nurse with the explanation that it was a proper medicine, and the instruction that a teaspoonful be given to the baby each night (a teaspoonful being a fatal dose). The nurse, thinking the child did not require the medicine, did not administer it, but placed it on a mantel. A few days later, while the nurse was absent, a boy found the bottle and innocently gave George Michael a dose of the poison which resulted in the infant's death. This was held to constitute murder on the part of Catherine. Additional facts may be mentioned. The nurse did not put the "medicine" aside to administer later, but had no intention of giving it to the child at any time; there is no evidence that anything had been written on the bottle to indicate either that it was supposed to be medicine or that it was intended for George Michael; the boy who innocently administered the poison was a lad of five. Hence there was an independent intervening cause of a highly improbable nature, but it was not superseding because the result was exactly what Catherine had intended. [42]

On the other hand the phrase "intended consequence" must not be given too broad a scope in this connection in a criminal case. The intended consequence in *Michael* was that the infant should receive a deadly dose of the poison. The "intended consequence rule" would no doubt apply if the consequence intended and the one which actually happened belong to the same genus even if they represent different species,—as if the victim was bound and left in a helpless condition with intent that he should be devoured by wild animals, and he was trampled to death by such animals. But if the "intended consequence" is said merely to be the death of the victim the rule would be in conflict with the leading case in point, which is *Bush*. [43] That is

---

38. Id. at 199.

The Model Penal Code § 2.03 formulates a causation standard that relates the required state of mind for the offense to the extent of causal responsibility. It embodies concepts of causation in fact and proximity. The latter standard is in substance a more specific classification of the appreciable probability concept. See also, Causation in The Model Penal Code, 78 Col.L.Rev. 1249 (1978).

39. Henry T. Terry, Proximate Consequences in the Law of Torts, 28 Harv.L. Rev. 10, 17 (1914); Henry W. Edgerton, Legal Cause, 72 U. of Pa.L.Rev. 343, 358 (1924).

40. Ibid.

41. Regina v. Michael, 9 Car. & P. 356, 2 Moody C.C. 120, 169 Eng.Rep. 48 (1840).

42. "The jury were directed that if the prisoner delivered to Sarah Stephens the laudanum, with intent that she should administer it to the child and thereby produce its death, the quantity so directed to be administered being sufficient to produce death," etc., it was murder. Ibid.

43. Bush v. Commonwealth, 78 Ky. 268 (1880).

the "scarlet fever case" in which the victim of shooting was not seriously injured by the bullet but died of fever which she contracted from the attending physician. The defendant intended her death [44] and the actual result was just that, but the manner in which the end was brought about was neither intended nor foreseeable, and was held to break the chain of legally-recognized causation. Hence the "intended consequence" in *Bush* must be limited (for the purposes of this rule) to the infliction of a mortal wound by shooting, or an injury which should result fatally by reasons of the risks which normally attend harm of this nature.

16. NEGATIVE ACTS

A negative act is not a superseding cause.[45]

It has seemed important to recognize the possibility of a negative act being superseding in a civil case,[46] but even there this applies only in very exceptional situations which seem to have no counterpart in criminal cases.[47]

One who has a legal duty to take action to prevent impending harm may incur liability by failing to take such action, but this failure does not prevent the original actor from being recognized as the proximate cause of the resulting harm. The negative act may be recognized as a contributory cause but not as a superseding cause. Suppose **D** stabbed **X**, inflicting an injury from which **X** bled to death. If **Y** had a legal duty to protect **X** and the circumstances were such that **Y** could have stopped the bleeding and thereby could have saved **X**'s life, but he did not do so, **Y** will be recognized as a contributory cause of **X**'s death. But the failure of **Y** to stop the flow of blood will not induce the court to conclude that the stabbing by **D** did not cause the fatal hemorrhage.[48] To quote an illustration used elsewhere:[49]

44. This may not have been actually true but it was one of the theories under the evidence and the jury returned a verdict of guilty of murder. Hence the court dealt with the case as if this were the fact.

45. "Where defendant by his positive act sets in operation forces, or by his omission of duty, fails to stop the operation of forces, and plaintiff is injured thereby, he cannot claim exemption from liability on the ground that the injury would not have happened if some other person had not failed to do his duty, and thereby stopped the operation of the cause for which he was responsible." Carpenter, Workable Rules for Determining Proximate Cause, 20 Cal.L.Rev. 471, 485 (1932). Even an unforeseeable omission is not a superseding cause. McLaughlin, Proximate Cause, 39 Harv.L. Rev. 149, 182 (1925).

46. "Third Person's Failure to Prevent Harm

"(1) Except as stated in Subsection (2), the failure of a third person to act to prevent harm to another threatened by the actor's negligent conduct is not a superseding cause of such harm.

"(2) Where, because of lapse of time or otherwise, the duty to prevent harm to another threatened by the actor's negligent conduct is found to have shifted from the actor to a third person, the failure of the third person to prevent such harm is a superseding cause." Restatement, Second, Torts § 452 (1965).

47. Under Subsection 2, "The shifted responsibility means in effect that the duty, or obligation, of the original actor in the matter has terminated, and has been replaced by that of the third person." Restatement, Second, Torts § 452, comment d (1965).

48. The foreman of a repair crew, as a result of criminal negligence in checking time tables, had the rails removed from a bridge shortly before a train was due. Under railroad regulations a flagman was sent back to warn any train that might approach but he failed to go back as far as his duty required. Even so the engineer could have seen the flag in time had he been properly alert. He did not see the flag in time and a fatal wreck resulted. Had either the flagman or the engineer done his duty the wreck would have been avoided. But the two

49. See note 49 on page 820.

"An automobile negligently driven by **A** strikes **B**, and leaves him on the highway, unconscious and slowly bleeding to death. **C**, a passing motorist, stops, looks over the situation, and decides to drive on without doing anything to aid **B**. **B** bleeds to death. *Regardless of whether* **C** *is under any duty to* **B** *to render such aid*, his failure to do so is not a superseding cause which will relieve **A** of liability for the death of **B**."

Nothing intervenes, in these cases, between the act of **D** (or **A**) and the resulting death, and the mere existence of an unperformed duty of intervention will not break the legally-recognized chain of causation.

Because of this principle, an injury which causes death as a matter of fact, is also a proximate cause thereof, notwithstanding the omission of some act, by doctors, nurses or others, which would have changed the natural course of events and saved the life. The same is true even if the failure to turn the tide in favor of life was due to neglect on the part of the person injured, or even to his positive refusal to submit to a surgical operation despite medical advice as to its necessity.[50]

Doing nothing, as pointed out earlier,[51] is just that—nothing—so far as the law is concerned, unless there is a legal obligation to take affirmative action. Students sometimes seem to assume that the existence of a duty to act will make nonperformance a positive act. It takes the duty to bring nonperformance into the category of an act; without the duty it would not be an act in the legal sense. With the duty to act the failure to perform becomes an act—but not doing is negative whether it is an inadvertent omission or a wilful forbearance.

In the application of this "test," the "substantial factor test" and the "position of apparent safety test" must not be ignored. Thus, in *Preslar*,[52] a wife who had been driven out of the house by her husband went to the home of her father. After reaching there she did not enter or make herself known for several hours, during which time she lay on the ground with inadequate protection from the cold, and later died from this exposure. The act of the husband was held not the proximate cause of this death. It is to be noted that death did not result from any blow or injury inflicted by the husband, but from exposure to the elements and that this exposure occurred after she had reached a place of refuge. If, for example, one man wrongfully deprived another of his dinner, and the other thereupon decided that if he could not have that food he would eat no other and starved to death with ample provisions available, the act of the one would not be juridically recognized as the cause of the death. The risk created by the deprivation of food on the one occasion came to rest in a position of apparent safety when other food was at hand before actual harm had been suffered, and hence the law will

intervening negative acts did not prevent the foreman from being guilty of manslaughter. Regina v. Benge, 4 F. & F. 504, 176 Eng.Rep. 665 (1865).

In this case it would seem that the risk created by the foreman might be held to have come to rest in a position of apparent safety after the flagman had been sent back in plenty of time. But this point seems not to have been raised.

49. Restatement, Second, Torts § 452, comment c, illus. 4 (1965). Emphasis added.

50. Regina v. Holland, 2 Moody & R. 351, 174 Eng.Rep. 313 (1841).

51. See supra, chapter 6, section 4, B.

52. State v. Preslar, 48 N.C. 421 (1856). See also Hendrickson v. Commonwealth, 85 Ky. 281, 3 S.W. 166 (1887).

follow it no farther.[53] And the risk created by *Preslar* in forcing his wife out of the house came to rest in a position of apparent safety when she reached the home of her father, which she might freely enter, before serious harm had resulted from exposure. But if an injury was inflicted from which the victim bled to death, it cannot be said that the risk created by the blow had come to rest in a position of apparent safety while the life blood was still flowing from the wound, even if the victim or others could have stopped it but did not.

17. KILLING BY WORDS

Words are acts [54] in the juridical sense and although it is quite unusual it is not impossible for homicide to be committed by this means. If, for example, words be used which are reasonably calculated to produce and do produce an act which is the immediate cause of death, it is homicide; as for example, if a blind man, a stranger, a child, or a person of unsound mind, be directed by words to a precipice or other dangerous place where he falls and is killed; or if one be directed to take any article of medicine, food, or drink, known to be poisonous and which does produce a fatal effect; in these and like cases the person so operating upon the mind or conduct of the decedent has committed homicide.[55] Words, moreover, may be used to kill in other ways, such as wilful and corrupt perjury in a capital case, which results in the execution of an innocent person.[56] There has been some reluctance in the matter of prosecuting wilful homicides so committed,[57] based apparently on the notion that witnesses might thereby be deterred from testifying in capital cases; [58] but an occasional statute has expressly provided that such a killing shall be murder on the part of the perjurer.[59]

53. See Beale, The Proximate Consequences of an Act, 33 Harv.L.Rev. 633, 640 (1920).

54. Kocourek, An Introduction to the Science of Law 268 (1930).

55. Vernon's Texas Penal Code art. 1206 (1961), now repealed, of which the text is largely a quotation, "contains nothing new. It only made a part of our statutory law what had long been recognized as a sound legal principle in the common law. . . ." Whiteside v. State, 115 Tex.Cr. 274, 279, 29 S.W.2d 399, 401 (1930). See Rev.Stat.Canada § 205(5) (1970).

56. "There was also, by the antient common law, one species of killing held to be murder which may be dubious at this day; as there hath not been an instance wherein it has been held to be murder for many ages past: I mean by bearing false witness against another, with an express premeditated design to take away his life, so as the innocent person be condemned and executed." 4 Bl. Comm. *196.

57. See, for example, The King v. McDaniel, 1 Leach 44, 168 Eng.Rep. 124 (1756).

"Notwithstanding anything in this section, a person does not commit homicide within the meaning of this act by reason only that he causes the death of a human being by procuring, by false evidence, the conviction and death of that human being by sentence of the law." Rev. Stat. of Canada, Can.Crim.Code, § 205(6) (1970).

58. 4 Bl.Comm. *196–7. See 1 East P.C. 333.

59. "Every person who, by wilful and corrupt perjury or subornation of perjury, shall procure the conviction and execution of any innocent person, shall be deemed and adjudged guilty of murder, . . ." N.R.S. (Nev.) 199.160 (1967). California provides that death, so caused, is a capital offense, without using the word "murder." West's Ann.Cal.Pen. Code, § 128. The omission of this word seems to have been due to an unfounded notion that such conduct could not properly be brought under the head of "murder."

18. FRIGHT OR OTHER "MENTAL FORCE"

If a person assaults another, causing both physical injury and great shock to the nervous system, which result in death, it is homicide although the shock to the nervous system contributes largely or even chiefly to the loss of life.[60] It is also homicide even if the assault fails to make direct contact with the body of the one assailed, if it puts him in such fear that he is killed as a result of his own impulsive act in the effort to avoid the threatened harm.[61] In fact "mental force," as it has been called,[62] will receive juridical recognition without question if it is accompanied by physical force, or results in physical contact.

Question has arisen, however, in cases in which harm has resulted from "mental force" without physical contact of any kind. The original notion was that courts could not take notice of the fact that death had been caused by fright,[63] for the reason that such a matter is impossible of proof, "and secret things belong to God." [64]

"Dr. Wharton rationalizes the rule thus: 'Death from nervous causes does not involve penal consequences.' This appears to me to substitute an arbitrary quasi-scientific rule for a bad rule founded on ignorance now dispelled. Suppose a man were intentionally killed by being kept awake till the nervous irritation of sleeplessness killed him; might not this be murder? Suppose a man kills a sick man, intentionally, by making a loud noise which wakes him when sleep gives him a chance of life; or suppose, knowing that a man has aneurism of the heart, his heir rushes into his room and roars in his ear, 'Your wife is dead!' intending to kill and killing him; why are not these acts murder? They are no more 'secret things belonging to God' than the operation of arsenic. As to the fear that by admitting that such acts are

---

60. A man knocked down his wife, inflicting a severe bruise, but no injury in itself fatal. Ten days later she died. The medical evidence showed that she was diseased, but might have lived for an indefinite period; and that the effect of the whole violence was to hasten her death, by a shock to the nervous system calculated to aggravate the disease. It was held that if this was so he was guilty of manslaughter, and the jury so found. Regina v. Murton, 3 Fost. & F. 492, 176 Eng.Rep. 221 (1862). "If his violence so excited the terror of the deceased that she died from the fright, and she would not have died except for the assault, then the prisoner's act was in law the cause of her death." Cox v. People, 80 N.Y. 500, 516 (1880). Commonwealth v. Tatro, 4 Mass.App. 295, 346 N.E.2d 724 (1976).

61. See supra.

The "consequences of defendant's act of binding Murdock and placing him in extreme fright and shock, which act was the proximate cause of Murdock's heart attack, are not excused, nor is the defendant's criminal liability lessened, by the preexisting heart condition of Mur-

dock which rendered him unable to withstand the situation which the defendant had thrust upon him." State v. Spates, 176 Conn. 227, 405 A.2d 656, 659 (1978).

62. 1 Bishop, New Criminal Law, § 562 (8th ed. 1892).

63. "If a man either upon working upon the fancy of another or possibly by harsh or unkind usage puts another into such passion of grief or fear, that the party either dies suddenly, or contracts some disease, whereof he dies, tho, as the circumstances of the case may be, this may be murder or manslaughter in the sight of God, yet *in foro humano* it cannot come under the judgment of felony, because no external act of violence was offered, whereof the common law can take notice, and secret things belong to God; . . ." 1 Hale P.C. * 429. ". . . working upon the fancy of another, or treating him harshly or unkindly, by which he dies of·fear or grief, is not such a killing as the law takes notice of." 1 East P.C. 225.

64. See the quotation from Hale in the preceding note.

murder, people might be rendered liable to prosecution for breaking the hearts of their fathers or wives by bad conduct, the answer is that such an event could never be proved. A long course of conduct, gradually 'breaking a man's heart,' could never be the 'direct or immediate' cause of death. If it was, and it was intended to have that effect, why should it not be murder?" [65]

To support this line of reasoning Sir James Stephen had the authority of *Towers*,[66] in which the defendant was charged with the killing of a baby. He had assaulted a girl who held in her arms a four-months-old infant which became so frightened at the assault that it went into convulsions and eventually died. As this was a matter susceptible of proof the jury was instructed to find the defendant guilty of manslaughter if they found that the assault on the girl was the cause of the baby's death. In a later case,[67] in which the language quoted was repeated in part, the court held that the law could take notice of a homicide caused by fright, where the fright had produced a rupture of an aneurism of the ascending aorta, and death had resulted.

It is sometimes said that no one is criminally responsible for the killing of another by any influence on the mind alone.[68] The obvious reply to such a statement is that where death results there always has been more than an influence on the "mind alone." It is a matter of common knowledge that fright, for instance, produces certain physical results, such as changes in the pulse rate and in the breathing. The convulsions of the infant and the ruptured aneurism in the other case are but extreme examples of *physical* consequences of fright. The influence may have been upon the mind in the first instance, in such cases, but it was certainly not upon the "mind alone."

In many instances it may be impossible to prove that death was caused by fright or grief or other "mental force." In other cases in which this proof is possible the person who has caused the fright or grief may not be criminally responsible for the fatal consequence. But leaving out of mind for the moment all matters of proof and responsibility, it seems correct to state in abstract form:

Death of a human being resulting from fright, grief or other "mental force" caused by another human being is homicide. In other words, to the extent to which science has torn away the veil of secrecy from this phenomenon, it will receive juridical recognition.[69]

19. THE FOUR "TESTS" or "CLUES"

The four "tests" or "clues" of proximate cause in a criminal case are (1) expediency, (2) isolation, (3) foreseeability and (4) intention.

65. Stephen, Digest of the Criminal Law, note 9 on page 217 (8th ed. 1947).

66. Regina v. Towers, 12 Cox C.C. 530 (1874).

67. In re Heigho, 18 Idaho 566, 110 P. 1029 (1910).

68. This is codified with modifications in the Canadian Criminal Code.

"A person commits culpable homicide when he causes the death of a human being . . . (c) by causing that human being, by threats or fear of violence or by deception, to do anything that causes his death, or (d) by wilfully frightening that human being, in the case of a child or sick person." Rev.Stat. of Canada, Can.Crim.Code § 205(5) (1970).

69. It can no longer be held that it is legally impossible for homicide to be committed in this manner. In re Heigho, 18 Idaho 566, 110 P. 1029 (1910).

Of these (1) and (2) are tests of exclusion while (3) and (4) are tests of inclusion—that is, either (3) or (4) may bring into the area of proximate cause what otherwise would be excluded by (2). Neither (3) nor (4) is needed for any other purpose.

The starting point is that except for the rule that under certain circumstances the act of one may be imputed by law to another, and the rule that the failure of a legally-required performance (negative act) is by law regarded for most purposes as the equivalent of a positive act, no one is held to be the proximate cause of harm, so far as criminal law is concerned, unless his act was in fact a cause thereof. If his act was in fact a cause of the harm it is also the proximate cause thereof unless excluded by (1) expediency or (2) isolation.

(1) **Expediency.** This is an application of *de minimus*. The law will not take notice of anything which was not a substantial factor in producing the harm. While blood gushed from a severed artery a few drops oozed from a slight bruise, and hemorrhage caused death. The bruise was not a substantial factor.

(2) **Isolation.** D's act may be isolated from subsequent harm either because—

(a) the risk created by him had come to rest in a position of apparent safety, or

(b) the direct cause of the harm was an independent intervening cause or an "equivalent" (an abnormal response by another person or an animal).

Harm which otherwise would be "remote" because of the second "test" may be found proximate because of either (3) or (4).

(3) **Probability.** An independent intervening cause, or "equivalent," will not make the harm remote if it was a realizable likelihood at the time of D's act.

(4) **Intention.** "An intended consequence is never remote" if it has reference to a sufficiently specific result. It is not sufficient that D intended X to die and X is dead (*Bush*), but is sufficient if poison that D started on its way to cause the death of X did cause the death of X (*Michael*).

With reference to intervening causes it may be added:

(a) A dependent intervening cause is not superseding. It is merely the normal operation of one physical force upon another (the first boulder dislodging the second) or the normal response of man or animal to the situation created by D's act (doctors, nurses or others try to aid an injured person or the victim returns the robber's "fire").

(b) A response of a person or an animal which is so far from normal as to be regarded extraordinary, even when viewed in retrospect, is dealt with in the same category as an independent intervening cause. This is done without any labored effort to insist that it is actually "independent." Thus if a young lady, with no provocation, speaks crossly to her lover and this so distresses him that he hangs himself, this is dealt with *as if* it were an independent intervening cause.

(c) An independent intervening cause, or an "equivalent," is superseding unless it comes within the scope of "tests" (3) or (4).

20. DEFINITION OF DEATH

What is regarded as the cause of death may sometimes depend upon the definition of the term. Thus one on trial for murder in Kansas defended on the claim that he was not the one who had killed the deceased. He insisted that the death was not caused by his act of shooting the victim in the head, but by the act of the doctor who removed the kidneys while the person was still alive. For generations death has been thought of as the permanent cessation of circulatory and respiratory functions. Often it has been reduced to this: The person is alive so long as the heart continues to beat, and dead when the heartbeat stops. Thus in a famous case [70] it was held that the spurting of blood for several inches when the head was severed from the body proved that the heart was beating at the time, and hence that death was caused by the decapitation of a living person. But the heart that has stopped may sometimes be caused to beat again; and by artificial means the heartbeat may be continued long after the brain has lost any possibility of functioning. This has caused many in the medical profession to think in terms of "brain death." The person is alive so long as brain-function is possible, but dead when the brain is dead. Evidence in the Kansas case showed that the deceased's kidneys had been removed, for transplantation, after he had suffered irretrievable brain damage. The court had no objection to the "brain death" theory, but held it was sufficient for the case at bench that the evidence warranted the jury in finding that defendant was at least a contributory cause of death.[71] A recent statutory definition is of interest.

"Death" means the condition determined by the following standard: A person will be considered dead if in the announced opinion of a physician, based on ordinary standards of medical practice, that person has experienced an irreversible cessation of spontaneous respiratory and circulatory functions. In the event that artificial means of support preclude a determination that these functions have ceased, a person will be considered dead if in the announced opinion of two physicians, based on ordinary standards of medical practice, that person has experienced an irreversible cessation of spontaneous brain functions. Death will have occurred at the time when the relevant functions ceased.[72]

Several states have adopted definitions of death encompassing brain death [73] or by couching the determination of death in the alternative of respiration and circulation cessation or brain death.[74]

70. Jackson v. Commonwealth, 100 Ky. 239, 38 S.W. 422, 1091 (1896).

71. State v. Shaffer, 223 Kan. 244, 574 P.2d 205 (1977).

72. Iowa Criminal Code sec. 702.8 (1978).

73. Alaska Stat. § 09.65.120 (1980); W.Va.Code § 16–19–1 (1980). See Frilous, Death, When Does It Occur? 27 Baylor L.Rev. 10 (1975); Capron & Kass, A Statutory Definition of The Standards for Determining Human Death: An Appraisal and a Proposal, 121 U.Penn.L. Rev. 87 (1972); Note, The Citadel for the Human Cadaver: The Harvard Brain Death Criteria Exhumed, 32 Univ.Fla.L. Rev. 275 (1980).

74. Kan.Stat. § 77–202 (1979); N.M. Stat.Ann. § 12–2–4.2 (1978); Va.Code 1950 § 54–325.7.

Chapter 7

RESPONSIBILITY: IN GENERAL

SECTION 1. MENS REA (THE MENTAL ELEMENT IN CRIME)

A. BASIS OF THE MENS REA CONCEPT

Deeply ingrained in human nature is the tendency to distinguish intended results from accidental happenings. This is the everyday experience of one on the street. One who has been greatly benefited by the act of another may be very much pleased in any event, but his feeling toward the other will not be the same if it was quite an accidental result as if it was the very purpose intended. And one who has been painfully injured by another's act will not have the same personal resentment if it was obviously an accidental injury as he will if the harm was inflicted upon him intentionally. "I didn't mean to" is an explanation accepted so frequently that it is often one of the early acquisitions of small children. In fact, in the words of Mr. Justice Holmes, "even a dog distinguishes between being stumbled over and being kicked." [1]

1. HARSH ATTITUDE OF ANCIENT LAW

Pure conjecture might thus lead to the conclusion that the ancient criminal law held a man answerable only for his intentional misdeeds, and that punishability for certain results of his actions which he did not intend came as a later development, but all the evidence points the other way. "Law in its earliest days tries to make men answer for all the ills of an obvious kind that their deeds bring upon their fellows." [2] The development was in the direction of recognizing first one and then another mitigation of this rule.

The harsh attitude of an ancient criminal law and the emergence and gradual development of the mens-rea concept have been detailed elsewhere [3] and need not be repeated here.

2. CRITICISM OF THE MENS REA DOCTRINE

Some years ago the mens-rea doctrine was criticized on the ground that the Latin phrase is "misleading." [4] If the words "mens rea" were to be regarded as self-explanatory they would be open to this objection, but they are to be considered merely as a convenient label which may be attached to any

---

1. Holmes, The Common Law 3 (1881).

2. 2 Pollock & Maitland, History of English Law 470 (2d ed. 1899).

3. Id. at 470–1, 479–80, 490–1, 499; Sayre, Mens Rea, 45 Harv.L.Rev. 974

(1932). See also Albert Levitt, The Origin of the Doctrine of Mens Rea, 17 Ill.L. Rev. 117 (1922).

4. See Stephen, J., in Regina v. Tolson, L.R. 23 Q.B.Div. 168, 185 (1889).

psychical fact sufficient for criminal guilt (in connection with socially-harmful conduct).[5] This includes a field too complex for any brief self-explanatory phrase, and since it is important to have some sort of dialectic shorthand to express the idea, this time-honored label will do as well as any.

More recently an attack has been made upon the basic concept itself. It has been asserted by one writer: "A crime is an act. It is *not* an act plus an intent. 'In jure actus non facit reum nisi mens sit rea' is no longer true. The modern maxim should be that most ancient one: Actus facit reum." [6] And another author has entitled an article: "The Obsolescence of Criminal Guilt." [7] But the notion that the mens-rea maxim is no longer true is based upon a misconception of the maxim itself. The present trend is very clearly not in the direction of removing the requirement of a mental element as one of the constituents of true crime (as distinguished from "public torts" or "civil offenses" [8]).

Unquestionably much has been *said* during the development of the mens-rea doctrine which is not acceptable today. When punishment was in the hands of the priests it took the form of an expiatory rite,[9] and traces of the "expiative theory" can be found in the language of some of the cases. The old notion seems to have been that punishment was necessary as a "just retribution" or requital of wickedness.[10] But since omniscience is required for divine justice, it is necessary to support social justice upon a utilitarian rather than upon a divine basis.[11] Furthermore, the mens-rea doctrine was developed before much of the modern knowledge of the human mind had been contributed by the sciences of psychology and psychiatry; and some of the implications of the early talk about "that free will which God has given to man" [12] do not give recognition to limitations now known to exist.[13]

In this connection, however, it is important to bear in mind that the results reached in decided cases are frequently better than the explanations offered in their support.[14] When the strict law called for punishments without reference to the state of mind of one whose act had resulted in harm, administrative techniques were developed in the effort to protect those who were not really at fault.[15] These techniques, adopted because of a general

---

5. Sayre, op. cit. supra, n. 3, at 1026.

6. Levitt, Extent and Function of the Doctrine of Mens Rea, 17 Ill.L.Rev. 578, 589 (1923).

7. Scanderett, 27 J.Crim.L. and Cr. 828 (1937).

8. See infra, section 5.

The Model Penal Code reflects the present trend of the law in most jurisdictions by providing:

"Except as provided . . . a person is not guilty of an offense unless he acted purposely, knowingly, recklessly or negligently, as the law may require, with respect to each material element of the offense." Section 2.02(1).

9. Alexander and Staub, The Criminal and Judge, and The Public 67–68 (1931).

10. Glueck, Principles of a Rational Penal Code, 41 Harv.L.Rev. 453, 456 (1928).

11. Woolsey's Political Science, § 107. Quoted in 1 Wharton Criminal Law sec. 13, note 5 (12th ed. 1932).

12. 4 Bl.Comm. * 27.

13. Glueck, Mental Disorder and the Criminal Law 95, note 1 (1925). Fingarette & Hasse, Mental Disabilities and Criminal Responsibility, 66–73 (1979).

14. Pound, The Theory of Judicial Decision, 36 Harv.L.Rev. 940, 951 (1923).

15. "On the patent rolls of Henry III pardons for those who have committed homicide by misadventure, in self-defence, or while of unsound mind, are common." Pollock & Maitland, op. cit. supra note 2 and 480. Henry III ascended to the throne in 1216.

feeling that the strict law was not properly fitted to the social need, resulted in a change in the criminal law itself, so that the "mind at fault" became an element of the crime. And this element, which has been strengthened by the trial and error process of many generations is not to be rejected merely because some of the explanations which have been offered to support it are unsatisfactory.[16]

As more is learned about human conduct in general, and about methods of regulating and controlling such conduct, many changes in the general administration of criminal justice may be expected.[17] There may be changes in the definitions of certain crimes. There may be different applications of the mens-rea doctrine in connection with certain defenses, such as the defense based upon insanity. There will probably be revolutionary changes in the treatment applied to those who have been convicted of crime. But so far as criminality itself is concerned the indications are that any change in regard to the psychical element involved will be in the direction of giving more heed to this part of the problem,—rather than less.[18]

In fact, one of the great contributions of the common law is the conception that there is no crime without a mind at fault.[19] In considering the specific offenses it was pointed out that the common law recognizes the possibility of criminal guilt on an objective basis in certain extreme situations. Suppose **D** unintentionally and, for him, most unexpectedly caused the death of **X**. If **D** was aware of such circumstances that he *should have* realized his conduct would create an unreasonable risk of death or serious injury, and in this he fell far short of measuring up to the reasonable-person standard, he is guilty of involuntary manslaughter at common law (under some of the new penal codes his guilt would be of a lesser, statutory offense usually named negligent homicide). This invites the question: Could **D** be said to have caused that death with a mind at fault? If **D**'s mind failed to recognize a grave risk which the ordinary mind would have recognized, the difference is obviously one of mind. It is a mental difference. And if as a result **D** is characterized as being in fault, it has to be a mind at fault. The fact that an objective test is used does not make the fault other than mental. We might not be willing to apply the label "wicked mind" but it is nevertheless a mind at fault. To repeat, one of the great contributions of the common law is the conception that there is no crime without a mind at fault—the reference being to true crime as distinguished from a civil offense (violation of the penalty clause of a regulatory statute).

---

16. If a *mala-in-se* statutory offense fails to include any words of mens rea, this element will be added by implication. United States v. Currier, 621 F.2d 7, 10 (1st Cir. 1980); State v. Minium, 26 Wn. App. 840, 615 P.2d 511, 512 (1980).

17. See, for example, Pound, Criminal Justice in America (1930); Glueck, Principles of a Rational Penal Code, 41 Harv.L. Rev. 453 (1928); Gausewitz, Considerations Basic to a New Penal Code, 11 Wis. L.Rev. 346 (1936); Harno, Rationale of a Criminal Code, 85 Univ. of Pa.L.Rev. 549 (1937).

18. Morissette v. United States, 342 U.S. 246, 72 S.Ct. 240 (1952).

Because trafficking in narcotic drugs is unquestionably conduct of moral turpitude, even if the statute with respect to manufacture and delivery of controlled substances failed to include the element of intent, it would be a necessary and implied element. State v. Smith, 17 Wn. App. 231, 562 P.2d 659 (1977).

19. Except in the enforcement of offenses *malum prohibitum* attention must be given to the "traditional requirement that criminal sanction be imposed only for blameworthy conduct that complies with the requirements of due process of law." Walker v. State, 356 So.2d 672 (Ala.1977).

The type of mind needed for criminal guilt is not the same for all offenses. It is obviously not the same for murder as for receiving stolen property, for example. The familiar statement that it differs from offense to offense might indicate a greater possible variety than actually exists, but conveys the idea in a general way. It is important to have a term to express the mental element needed for guilt of the offense under consideration, whatever the offense may be. And the common law, picking two words from the familiar maxim, adopted the term "mens rea." Thus the mens rea for murder at common law is malice aforethought. The same result could be achieved by speaking in terms of the mental element of crime—the mental element of murder is malice aforethought. And the modern trend seems to be in this direction; but the development of the conception has been in terms of mens rea.

A civil offense (violation of the penal section of a regulatory statute enacted for some purpose other than the punishment of wrongdoing) has no mens-rea requirement unless added by the words of an unusual statute, but it is quite otherwise as to a true crime. Every true crime requires a culpable state of mind—mens rea.[20] This is true of a common-law crime,[21] and a statute creating a true crime will be interpreted to include mens rea even if there are no mens-rea words in the enactment.[22] In the words of the Supreme Court: "We hold that mere omission from § 641 of any mention of intent will not be construed as eliminating that element from the crimes denounced."[23] And the same idea has been expressed in various ways. "Generally speaking, when an act is prohibited by statute only, the statute is construed in the light of the common law and the existence of a criminal intent is to be regarded as essential, although the terms of the statute do not require it."[24] The Kansas statute prohibiting the possession of burglary tools makes no mention of intent, but is interpreted to require an intent to use them to commit burglary.[25] "Where the purpose of a statute is the punishment of a crime . . . absolute liability will not be found to be the intent of the legislature. . . . Instead the statute will be read as incorporating a mental state requirement."[26] "Although the statute is silent regarding intent, this court has held that the 'taking' in the crime of robbery must be with the specific intent permanently to deprive the owner of his property."[27] "Though the statutory language of § 21.03 . . . does not prescribe a culpable mental state, it is clear that a culpable mental state is required."[28]

---

20. An "essential element of every orthodox crime is a wrongful or blameworthy mental state of some kind." In re Hayes, 69 Cal.Rptr. 310, 313, 442 P.2d 366, 369 (1968).

21. There are "no common law offenses in which mens rea is not required, . . ." Mueller, On Common Law Mens Rea, 42 Minn.L.Rev. 1043, 1101 (1955).

22. "Legislative silence on the element of intent in a criminal statute is generally not construed as an indication that no culpable mental state is required. . . . The required mental state may be implied from the statute." People v. Naranjo, ___ Colo. ___, 612 P.2d 1099, 1102 (1980).

23. Morissette v. United States, 342 U.S. 246, 263, 72 S.Ct. 240, 249 (1952).

24. State v. Shedoudy, 45 N.M. 516, 524, 118 P.2d 280, 285 (1941); State v. Lawson, 59 N.M. 482, 484, 286 P.2d 1076, 1077 (1955).

25. State v. Hart, 200 Kan. 153, 434 P.2d 999 (1967).

26. People v. Clark, 71 Ill.App.3d 381, 27 Ill.Dec. 680, 389 N.E.2d 911, 921 (1979).

27. Turner v. State, 96 Nev. 164, 605 P.2d 1140, 1141 (1980).

28. Banks v. State, 586 S.W.2d 518, 520 (Tex.Cr.App.1979). Accord, State v. Rushing, 62 Hawaii 102, 612 P.2d 103 (1980).

The Colorado riot statute does not mention any culpable mental state, but that did not prevent the court from finding one. "We conclude that the mental state 'knowingly' is implied by the statute and is required for the offense of engaging in a riot." [29]

3. ACTUS REUS

In the field of ethics, as in the teachings of the Church, guilt depends upon the state of mind alone. Accordingly, when the famous actor, Garrick, was said to have declared that he felt like a murderer whenever he acted Richard III, Dr. Johnson, as a moral philosopher, retorted: "Then he ought to be hanged whenever he acts it." But there is no criminal guilt without some socially-harmful result of the guilty mind. "For," explained Blackstone, "as no temporal tribunal can search the heart or fathom the intentions of the mind, otherwise than as they are demonstrated by outward actions, it therefore cannot punish for what it cannot know. For which reasons, in all temporal jurisdictions, an *overt* act, or some open evidence of an intended crime, is necessary . . . before the man is liable to punishment." [30] It might well be added that the difference between the average law-abiding citizen and the criminal is not that the former never has a momentary state of mind which could be labeled mens rea, but that he does not permit such a state of mind to rule his conduct; and it would not be feasible for the courts of men to apply punishment because of the bare mens rea even if it could be known.

To the basic principle that there is no criminal guilt unless the mens rea is manifested in the form of socially-harmful consequence, there *seem* to be some exceptions,—which are apparent only, and not real. If two or more combine to commit a crime they are punishable because of their conspiracy even if the wrongful purpose they have in mind is not accomplished. Furthermore, the conspiracy is complete as soon as the criminal combination is formed, and no overt act to effect the object is required for conviction, unless such a requirement has been added by statute. A second apparent exception is this: If one acting alone (or with others) undertakes to commit a certain crime and fails, but comes so near to success as to meet the requirements of a criminal attempt, he is punishable for this attempt. There is also a third apparent exception: If one solicits another to commit a felony (perhaps a serious misdemeanor should be added) the one is punishable at common law for his solicitation even if his proposal be promptly rejected.

These are not real exceptions to the requirement that mens rea alone is not a crime, because in legal theory a social interest, which is under the protection of a criminal sanction, is invaded by the mere combination to commit a crime, the mere attempt to commit a crime, or the mere solicitation to commit a felony.

If the phrase "social harm" is used to include every invasion of any social interest which has been placed under the protection of a criminal sanction (whether by common law or by statute), every crime may be said to involve, in addition to other requirements, (1) the happening of social harm and (2) the fact that the act of some person was the cause of this harm. And if all social harm which has *not* been placed under the protection of a criminal

---

29. People v. Bridges, —— Colo. ——, 620 P.2d 1, 3 (1980).

30. 4 Bl.Comm. * 21.

sanction is arbitrarily excluded, every remaining instance in which both of the factors mentioned above are present may be placed under the general label of *"actus reus,"* [31] "guilty act" or "deed of crime."

The phrase "deed of crime" as so used does not indicate the crime itself but merely one of the ingredients of crime; and this ingredient may be present without any crime at all, just as hydrogen is one of the ingredients of water but may be present without water. The words "deed of crime" are so suggestive of the crime itself, however, that perhaps the Latin phrase *"actus reus"* is less likely to cause confusion. The *actus reus* is essential to crime but is not sufficient for this purpose without the necessary mens rea, just as mens rea is essential to crime [32] but is insufficient without the necessary *actus reus.*

This is the great secret of criminal guilt, but even this fails to offer a complete explanation.

4. PHYSICAL AND MENTAL COMPONENTS OF CRIME

What has been said emphasizes the fact that there are two general components of every crime; [33] one is physical, the other is mental; one is the actus reus, the other is the mens rea. Although two or more offenses may have the same physical component as in the case of murder and manslaughter, the actus reus generally differs from crime to crime. The mental component does not have nearly so wide a variety, but is frequently different in one crime than in another, as mentioned above.

B. THE GENERAL MENS REA

The mental element of crime is sometimes considered as though there were one state of mind common to crime in general and sufficient for many offenses although some additional mental element is needed for certain crimes,[34] by indicating that mens rea may be adequately considered without reference to any specific offense. This is an overstatement, but it gives the idea in a general way.

A person may be so young that nothing in his mind will meet the juridical requirement of mens rea.[35] Furthermore, for mens rea the mental faculties must not be too greatly disturbed by mental disease, and under certain circumstances they must not have been misled by reasonable mistake of fact or have been constrained by certain types of compulsion. Without going fur-

---

31. This term has long been used for this purpose by Professor Kenny. See, for example, Kenny, Outlines of Criminal Law 45, 50, 75, 91, etc. (15th ed. 1936). Obviously it is not classical Latin, but neither is mens rea. It seems to be appropriate as "law Latin."

32. ". . . no crime is committed by the mere harboring of an evil intent not accompanied by an act, or omission to act, where there is a legal duty to act." In re LeRoy T., 285 Md. 508, 403 A.2d 1226, 1229 (1979). The word "crime" is used in the text to indicate "true crime,"—without the inclusion of the so-called civil offense. See infra, section 5.

33. "In law, the commission of a crime consists in the joint operation of an act and intent or criminal negligence." Brown v. State, 28 Ark. 126, 128 (1873). See also State v. Blue, 17 Utah 175, 180, 53 P. 978, 980 (1898). People v. Green, 27 Cal.3d 1, 164 Cal.Rptr. 1, 609 P.2d 468 (1980).

34. "[An] essential element of every orthodox crime is a wrongful or blameworthy mental state of some kind." In re Hayes, 69 Cal.Rptr. 310, 313, 442 P.2d 366, 369 (1968).

35. The Queen v. Smith, 1 Cox C.C. 260 (1845).

ther into detail it is sufficient to point out the need of excluding any factor sufficient in law to exculpate one who has done the particular deed in question. This is the negative component of mens rea. It is necessary to add an intent to do what constitutes the actus reus of that very crime, except that for certain offenses it is possible to substitute some other mental factor, such as criminal negligence for example, for the intent to do the actus reus.

In a prosecution for any particular crime the mens rea will be wanting unless the state of mind of the defendant at the time of the alleged offense was free from any factor which would be recognized as sufficient for exculpation in such a case, and included an intent to do what constitutes the actus reus of that very crime, or some other mental element, such as criminal negligence, recognized by law as a substitute therefor in an offense of that nature. This is the so-called general mens rea which is common to all true crime and sufficient for guilt of many offenses although some other mental element, such as an added specific intent or awareness of some special circumstance, is required for others.

If every such factor is excluded and there is present an intent to do the deed which constitutes the *actus reus* of a certain offense, there is present what may be said to be state-of-mind-X in the arbitrary use of this symbol. It will be necessary to add, however, that for certain crimes it will be possible to substitute some other mental factor, such, for example, as criminal negligence, for the actual intent to do the *actus reus*.

In brief, while state-of-mind-X has certain factors which remain constant, these have to do with the general outlines of the mental pattern rather than with the minute details. Nevertheless, these general outlines are entitled to attention. In a prosecution for any particular crime the mens rea will be wanting unless the state of mind of the defendant at the time of the alleged offense was free from every factor which would be recognized as sufficient for exculpation in such a case, and included an intent to do the deed which constitutes the *actus reus* of that very crime, or some other mental element (as for example criminal negligence) recognized by law as a substitute therefor in offenses of that nature. This is the so-called general mens rea which is common to all true crime and which is sufficient for guilt of many offenses although some additional mental element is required for others.[36]

C.   CRIMINAL INTENT

The phrase "criminal intent" is one that has been bandied about with various meanings not carefully distinguished. At times it has been used in the sense of the "intent to do wrong" (the *outline* of the mental pattern which is necessary for crime in general),—as, for example, in the phrase "the mental element commonly called criminal intent." [37] At times it has been used in

---

36. The statute required a motorist, involved in an accident resulting in injury, to stop and give aid to the injured person. And failure to stop and give aid was made punishable by imprisonment not to exceed a year. Although this is not codification of a common-law offense, the court will read into the statute the requirement that for guilt the motorist must have knowingly failed to comply. If he was not aware of the injury he is not guilty. Kimoktoak, 584 P.2d 25 (Alaska 1978).

37. State v. Smith, 71 Fla. 639, 642, 71 So. 915, 916 (1916).

D was charged with the unauthorized sale of government property and appeals claiming error because the information did not allege criminal intent.

In affirming a conviction the Court held that criminal intent is an essential

the sense of mens rea as the mental element requisite for guilt of the very offense charged, "a varying state of mind which is the contrary of an innocent state of mind, whatever may be pointed out by the nature of the crime as an innocent state of mind." [38] Often it is used to include criminal negligence as well as an actual intent to do the harmful deed,[39] although at other times such negligence is referred to as a substitute, so to speak, for criminal intent in connection with certain offenses.[40] Occasionally it is found in the sense of an intent to violate the law,—implying a knowledge of the law violated. On the other hand, as such knowledge is a factor not ordinarily required for conviction it has been pointed out that to establish ignorance of the law does not disprove criminal intent.[41] Thus it has been said (assuming the absence of any circumstance of exculpation) "whenever an act is criminal, the party doing the act is chargeable with criminal intent." [42]

Only by careful analysis can confusion be avoided. If, for example, it is said that criminal intent "may be inferred" as a matter of law from criminal negligence,[43] it is meant that in speaking of crimes in which criminal negligence is sufficient for the mens rea (such as involuntary manslaughter) the phrase "criminal intent" will be used although the harmful occurrence resulted from such negligence rather than from intention. This, of course, is not a frank statement of the actual mental element involved. A judge of the character of Holmes will state plainly that a man may sometimes be convicted of a very serious crime because his criminal negligence resulted in "consequences which he neither intended nor foresaw," [44] and add: "To say that he was presumed to have intended them, is merely to adopt another fiction, and

element of the offense but that the absence of an allegation of criminal intent was not prejudicial where the jury was instructed that the prosecution was required to prove that each sale was made by **D** with knowledge that the property belonged to the United States and had been stolen from the United States. Souza v. United States, 304 F.2d 274 (9th Cir. 1962).

"We previously have held that sexual assault offenses require general criminal intent or a means [sic] rea." Chavez v. State, 601 P.2d 166, 171 (Wyo.1979).

"A criminal intent is an essential element of every crime defined by the Kansas Criminal Code." State v. Brooks, 222 Kan. 432, 565 P.2d 241, 243 (1977).

38. 2 Wigmore on Evidence § 300 (3d ed. 1940).

39. See, for example, Bleiweiss v. State, 188 Ind. 184, 119 N.E. 375, 122 N.E. 577 (1918). An intent may be "inferred" from "a reckless disregard for the safety of others." Luther v. State, 177 Ind. 619, 625, 98 N.E. 640, 642 (1912).

40. ". . . such a degree of carelessness as, in contemplation of law, *supplied the place of* criminal intent." State v. Barnard, 88 N.C. 661, 665 (1883). Italics added.

41. State v. Armington, 25 Minn. 29 (1878). "Criminal intent" is an intent to do that which constitutes a violation of the law and does not necessarily involve an intent to violate the law. Hence ignorance of the illegal nature of the act does not preclude the possibility of a criminal intent. People v. Kuykendall, 134 Cal. App.2d 642, 285 P.2d 996 (1955). "If a man intentionally adopts certain conduct in certain circumstances known to him, and that conduct is forbidden by law under those circumstances, he intentionally breaks the law in the only sense in which the law ever considers intent." Crosby v. United States, 183 F.2d 373, 375 (10th Cir. 1950).

A statute making it an offense "knowingly" to possess, sell or offer to sell a cartridge capable of emitting tear gas does not require knowledge of the law forbidding it. His knowledge of the fact is sufficient. People v. Autterson, 261 Cal.App.2d 627, 68 Cal.Rptr. 113 (1968).

42. Weeks v. State, 24 Ala.App. 198, 199, 132 So. 870, 871 (1931).

43. Clark & Marshall, Crimes § 5.09 (7th ed. 1967).

44. Commonwealth v. Pierce, 138 Mass. 165, 178 (1884).

to disguise the truth." Another judge may resort to such language as: "There must be a criminal intent or negligence so gross as to imply it." [45]

It has been common to speak of crime as requiring the "joint operation of act and intent, or criminal negligence." [46] This suggests a helpful guide for the use of the phrase "criminal intent." Some other term such as mens rea or guilty mind should be employed for more general purposes, and "criminal intent" be restricted to those situations in which there is (1) an intent to do the *actus reus*, and (2) no circumstance of exculpation.

D. WHAT IS INTENT

Despite the loose and inaccurate use of the word in the phrase "criminal intent" the courts have not lost sight of the fact that "intent" comes from the same source as "intention," and in its strict sense has the same meaning. Hence we find them reiterating that intent means purpose [47] or design.[48] The effort to assign the true meaning has not been free from difficulty. "Intention then," says Markby,[49] "is the attitude of mind in which the doer of an act adverts to a consequence of the act and desires it to follow. But the doer of an act may advert to a consequence and not desire it: and therefore not intend it." At the other extreme, Austin says that a result is intended if it is contemplated as a probable consequence, whether it is desired or not.[50] Salmond requires the element of *desire* but gives this word a somewhat forced construction. He says that a man *desires* not only the end but also the means to the end and hence *desires*, although he may "*deeply regret*" the necessity for, the means.[51] If a robber finds it necessary to kill a man in order to rob him, and greatly regrets the necessity for the killing, but prefers to complete the robbery notwithstanding, he desires and hence intends the killing despite his regret.

So far as actual intention is concerned the position of Salmond comes closer to the juridical usage of the term than does either that of Markby or Austin. But Salmond adds a qualification which is not in accord with juridical usage. He says that consequences are not intended, if not desired, although they are "known to be certain, being the inevitable concomitants of the consequences which are desired, and for the sake of which the act is done." [52] This would mean that if X exploded a charge of dynamite for the purpose of wrecking a building, and realized at the time that a man was so close that he must die, the killing was unintentional, because it was neither

---

45. Fitzgerald v. State, 112 Ala. 34, 39, 20 So. 966, 967 (1895).

46. See, for example, Brown v. State, 28 Ark. 126, 128 (1873); Meadowcroft v. People, 163 Ill. 56, 69, 45 N.E. 991, 995 (1896); State v. Blue, 17 Utah 175, 180, 53 P. 978, 980 (1898); People v. Green, 27 Cal.3d 1, 164 Cal.Rptr. 1, 609 P.2d 468 (1980).

47. Harden v. State, 211 Ala. 656, 658, 101 So. 442, 444 (1924); Johnson v. State, 14 Ga. 55, 59 (1853); State v. Goldston, 103 N.C. 323, 325, 9 S.E. 580, 581 (1889). "The words 'intent' and 'purpose' express the same thought and idea." People v. Armentrout, 118 Cal.App.Supp. 761, 772, 1 P.2d 556, 562 (1931).

48. State v. Grant, 86 Iowa 216, 222, 53 N.W. 120, 121 (1892). "The resolve to commit an act constitutes the intent." People v. Kuhn, 232 Mich. 310, 312, 205 N.W. 188, 189 (1925). When intent is required for guilt it is error to instruct in terms of *intent or criminal negligence*. Schneider v. United States, 192 F.2d 498 (9th Cir. 1951).

49. Markby, Elements of Law § 220 (4th ed. 1889).

50. 1 Austin, Jurisprudence 424 (5th ed. 1885).

51. Salmond, Jurisprudence 380 (10th ed. 1947).

52. Ibid.

the end desired nor the means to the end, but merely a *known inevitable concomitant*. But the law does not regard such a killing as unintentional.[53]

So far as actual intention is concerned, more is required than an expectation that the consequence is likely to result from the act.[54] On the other hand it is not necessary that the consequence should be "desired" in the usual sense of that word, although this element may become important. If one acts "for the purpose of causing" a certain result, he intends that result whether it is likely to happen or not. As to consequences not included in his purpose he intends those, and only those, which he realizes are "substantially certain to be produced."[55] Stated in terms of a formula:

> **Intent includes those consequences which (a) represent the very purpose for which an act is done (regardless of likelihood of occurrence), or (b) are known to be substantially certain to result (regardless of desire).[56]**

The fact that an intent is conditional or qualified, while not without significance, does not exclude it from the "intent" category. It is a special type of intent rather than some other kind of state of mind.[57]

The Model Penal Code does not use "intent" or "intentionally" in dealing with culpability. It recognizes only four kinds of culpability, namely: (a) purposely, (b) knowingly, (c) recklessly and (d) negligently. The result is that where the traditional statement with reference to harm would be that: "it is committed intentionally," the wording of the Code is: "it is committed purposely or knowingly."[58] This plan has been followed in some of the new penal codes, while others continue the conventional terminology in this regard.

E.   CONSTRUCTIVE INTENT

Constructive intent is a fiction which permits lip service to the notion that intention is essential to criminality, while recognizing that unintended consequences of an act may sometimes be sufficient for guilt of some offenses. One court, for example, after stating that "intent . . . to apply the force . . . is . . . an essential element" of criminal battery, suggested that this intent may be "inferred" from "a reckless disregard for the safety of others," adding that "constructive intention to do an injury in such cases will

---

53. Cook, Act, Intention, and Motive in the Criminal Law, 26 Yale L.J. 645, 655–56 (1917).

The Israel Supreme Court, in the interpretation of intention, includes "knowledge that the harmful consequence will follow," provided this "knowledge" has "reached a high degree of probability." Bein, Knowledge Which Has Reached a High Degree of Probability, 2 Israel Law Review 18 (1967). See also Model Penal Code 2.02(2)(a) (1962).

54. Restatement, Second, Torts § 8A (1965).

55. Ibid.

56. This is in substance the position taken by the Institute. Ibid. What is meant by "substantially certain to result" is what the layman would speak of as something "bound to happen," and a lawyer would refer to as an "inevitable concomitant." Cook, op. cit. supra n. 40. The cautious wording, copied from the Institute, resulted from philosophical doubt whether anything can properly be said to be "bound to happen."

"Thus, under the criminal code, proof that the defendant acted 'purposely' is sufficient proof that he acted 'knowingly.'" State v. Sunday, __ Mont. __, 609 P.2d 1188, 1196 (1980).

57. People v. Connors, 253 Ill. 266, 97 N.E. 643 (1912).

58. E.g., Section 210.2(1)(a).

be imputed in the absence of an actual intent to harm . . . ." [59] Another indirect manner of expressing the result is to say that "the law *treats as intentional* all consequences due to that form of negligence which is distinguished as recklessness . . . ," [60] or that "the law infers guilty intention from reckless conduct." [61]

All such forms of expression should be supplanted by a frank recognition of the mental element which is sufficient for conviction in the particular case.

F. PRESUMED INTENT

It is frequently stated, with numerous variations as to the exact wording, that "everyone is presumed to intend the natural and probable consequences of his act." [62] The word "presumed" is the key to such a phrase although the formula is sometimes given without it, as that "a man is to be taken to intend what he does, or that which is the necessary and natural consequence of his own act." [63] A true presumption is a rule of evidence which calls for a certain result so far as the particular case is concerned unless the party adversely affected by the presumption comes forward with evidence to overcome it.[64] This is sometimes referred to as a "prima-facie presumption" to distinguish it from the so-called "conclusive presumption" which is a legal device in the form of a postulate used for the determination of a particular case whether it corresponds with the actual facts or not.[65] A third use is the so-called "presumption of fact" meaning "mere inferences of fact not affecting the accused with a duty to produce evidence." [66] Presumed intent has been used in all three of these senses.[67]

An intent which is conclusively presumed is one which does not exist in fact but only by legal fiction.[68] In other words it is a "constructive intent." [69] As this subject has already received attention, it is necessary to

---

59. Luther v. State, 177 Ind. 619, 625–7, 98 N.E. 640, 642 (1912).

60. Salmond, Jurisprudence 381 (10th ed. 1947). Emphasis added.

61. Pool v. State, 87 Ga. 526, 530, 13 S.E. 556, 557 (1891).

62. Dunlap v. United States, 70 F.2d 35, 37 (7th Cir. 1934); Curtis v. State, 118 Ala. 125, 131, 24 So. 111, 114 (1897); Rhine v. State, 184 Ark. 220, 224, 42 S.W.2d 8, 10 (1931); State v. Gilmore, 320 Ill. 233, 236, 150 N.E. 631, 633 (1926); Gipson v. State, 609 P.2d 1038 (Alaska 1980).

"It is black-letter law that a party is presumed to do that which he voluntarily or wilfully does in fact do and is also presumed to intend the natural, probable and usual consequences of his own acts." People v. Johnson, 104 Cal.App.3d 598, 164 Cal.Rptr. 69, 76 (1980).

The law presumes that a person intends the ordinary consequences of his voluntary act. State v. Cooper, 180 Mont. 68, 589 P.2d 133 (1979).

63. Harrison v. Commonwealth, 79 Va. 374, 377 (1884).

64. 9 Wigmore on Evidence § 2491 (3d ed. 1940).

65. Id. at § 2492.

66. Id. at § 2511a. See also State v. Gillett, 56 Iowa 459, 460, 9 N.W. 362, 363 (1881).

67. (1) State v. Selby, 73 Or. 378, 390, 144 P. 657, 660 (1914); (2) Bleiweiss v. State, 188 Ind. 184, 189, 122 N.E. 577, 577–8 (1919); State v. Webber, 179 Kan. 295, 293 P.2d 1014 (1956); (3) State v. Blacklock, 23 N.M. 251, 254, 167 P. 714, 715 (1917). Burglarious intent may be inferred from unlawful and forcible entry into the dwelling. People v. Stewart, 113 Cal.App.2d 687, 248 P.2d 768 (1952).

68. 9 Wigmore on Evidence § 2492 (3d ed. 1940).

69. ". . . constructive intention . . . in the absence of an actual intent." Luther v. State, 177 Ind. 619, 627, 98 N.E. 640, 642 (1912).

consider here only the question of true presumption or inference of fact. And despite some indications to the contrary [70] it seems fairly well established that the "presumed to intend" formula is not a true presumption, but (when used otherwise than "conclusive presumption") means merely an inference of fact.[71] This, however, is a problem of the law of evidence and has no bearing upon the substantive law of mens rea.[72] It may be useful in instructing juries to speak in terms of "presumed to intend," if care is taken to make clear exactly what is meant in the particular case [73] but this form of expression makes no important contribution to juridical science itself.[74]

G. VOLUNTARY ACT

It is sometimes said that no crime has been committed unless the harmful result was brought about by a "voluntary act." [75] Analysis of such a statement will disclose, however, that as so used the phrase "voluntary act" means no more than the mere word "act." [76] An act must be a willed movement [77] or the omission of a possible and legally-required performance. This is essential to the *actus reus* rather than to the mens rea. "A spasm is not an act." [78]

The use of this phrase as one of the requisites of crime owes its origin to early uncertainty as to the precise meaning of the word "act." A positive

---

70. See State v. Ockij, 165 Iowa 237, 240, 145 N.W. 486, 488 (1914); Combs v. State, 55 Tex.Cr.R. 332, 333, 116 S.W. 595, 596 (1909).

71. 9 Wigmore, Evidence § 2511a (3d ed. 1940). "The specific intent may, like any other fact, be shown by circumstances. Intent is a state of mind which can be evidenced only by the words or conduct of the person who is claimed to have entertained it. . . . Thus when a person without any provocation strikes another with a deadly weapon or throws a corrosive acid in his face and thereby maims or disfigures him, he is presumed to have intended to maim or disfigure because that was the natural and probable consequence of his act." Banovitch v. Commonwealth, 196 Va. 210, 216, 83 S.E.2d 369, 373 (1954).

72. Commonwealth v. Wiggins, 165 Ky. 73, 76, 176 S.W. 946, 947 (1915).

73. A jury instruction on presumed intent must be permissible in nature. An instruction given that "the law presumes that a person intends the ordinary consequences of his voluntary acts" was held to be susceptible to an interpretation by a jury that the presumption was mandatory and therefore was in conflict with the prosecution's constitutional burden of proof. Sandstrom v. Montana, 442 U.S. 510, 99 S.Ct. 2450 (1979).

74. Salmond, Jurisprudence 381–2 (10th ed. 1947).

The statutory presumption of intent to commit theft by failure to return rented property within 20 days after demand, is rebuttable. It places upon defendant the burden of introducing evidence sufficient, if believed, to support a finding of the nonexistence of such intent. If such evidence is introduced the burden is on the state to prove the criminal intent beyond a reasonable doubt. A statute which placed the burden of proving innocence on defendant would be unconstitutional. People v. Hedrick, 105 Cal.App. 3d 166, 164 Cal.Rptr. 169 (1980).

75. 2 Stephen, History of the Criminal Law of England 99 (1883). "But the rule applies only to unlawful acts which are voluntary and in that sense intentionally done." Smith v. State, 223 Ala. 346, 348, 136 So. 270, 271 (1931).

76. Stephen, for example, goes on to say: "Instances of involuntary actions are to be found not only in such motions as the beating of the heart and the heaving of the chest . . . coughing . . . the struggles of a person in a fit of epilepsy. . . ." Id. at 99–100.

77. "Acts are exertions of the will manifested in the external world." Pound, Readings on the History and System of the Common Law 513 (3d ed. 1927). See also Holland, Jurisprudence 108 (13th ed. 1924); Duncan v. Landis, 106 F. 839, 848 (3d Cir. 1901).

78. Holmes, The Common Law 54 (1881).

act (willed movement) always has a voluntary element and hence the phrase "voluntary act" is merely tautological as so applied. A negative act may be either a forbearance or an unintentional omission of a legally-required performance. The former is voluntary, the latter is not. If a watchman charged with the duty of lowering the gates at a crossing whenever a train is approaching fails to do so on a particular occasion, with fatal consequences to a motorist, the death is due to his (negative) act. But it would be absurd to speak of this act as "voluntary" if he was inattentive and did not know the train was approaching. As his legal duty required him to be attentive in this regard his want of knowledge of the need for immediate action will not excuse him, but it leaves his failure wholly unintentional. Hence the assertion that there is no crime without a "voluntary act" is redundant as to positive action and incorrect as to negative action.

Furthermore, such an assertion invites confusion in two directions—first because the modifier may be improperly extended to the legally-recognized consequences of the act, and second because it may raise a false issue as to the meaning of the word "voluntary." As to the first, assume the unintentional, but fatal, discharge of a weapon which had been pointed unlawfully at the deceased with no thought other than to intimidate him. The intentional pointing of the weapon was an act and the resulting death is imputable to the pointer. It is not improper to hold the slayer guilty of criminal homicide in certain cases of this nature,[79] but to speak of the "shooting" or the "killing" as voluntary or intentional is merely confusion of words. Without elaborating the second point it may be mentioned that the notion of a "voluntary act" as requisite to criminal guilt may result in the jury's being confused by argument of counsel to the effect that defendant's act was committed under the stress and strain of difficult circumstances and hence was not "voluntary."[80] If the harm was caused by a willed movement of the defendant it was caused by his "act" no matter how much "pressure" he may have been under at the moment. If this pressure was sufficient to negative the element of mens rea under the circumstances the law will excuse him.

H. SPECIAL MENTAL ELEMENT

The logical starting point in the search for the mental element required for conviction of any particular crime is the intent to do the deed which constitutes the actus reus of that offense. Frequently, however, the mens rea will be found to be something other than this. For various offenses, assuming the absence of any special circumstance of exculpation, such as extreme youth or insanity, the mens rea may consist of (a) this intent, (b) something distinctly less than this intent, (c) something distinctly more than this intent, or (d) something other than this intent which cannot be designated as distinctly either more or less than the intent itself.

For the crime of making a mold in the similitude of the genuine coins of the United States, the mental element essential to guilt is the intent to make

---

79. See McCutcheon v. State, 199 Ind. 247, 155 N.E. 544 (1927); Keith v. State, 612 P.2d 977 (Alaska 1980).

80. See M'Growther's Case, Fost.C.L. 13, 168 Eng.Rep. 8 (1746): "Though a man be violently assaulted, and has not other possible means of escaping death, but by killing an innocent person; this fear & force shall not acquit him of murder; for he ought rather to die himself, than escape by the murder of an innocent." 4 Bl.Comm. * 30.

the mold.[81]   It is not necessary for the prosecution to show that the mold was made for the purpose of counterfeiting United States money, or to be sold to another who might so use it; nor can the defendant excuse his deed by showing that no improper use was to be made of the mold.[82]   As such an object could not be produced by negligence, the element of criminal negligence is not involved.

Mens rea which is distinctly less than an intent to commit the *actus reus* is best exemplified by those offenses which may result from criminal negligence, such as involuntary manslaughter.   The *actus reus* of manslaughter is homicide, and if homicide results quite unintentionally, but from criminal negligence, it is manslaughter.[83]   This is true, moreover, even where the death is caused, not by positive action, but by the criminally negligent omission of a legal duty.[84]

Larceny is a typical example of a crime in which the mens rea is something distinctly more than an intent to do the *actus reus*.   An intentional trespassory taking and carrying away of the chattel of another is not larceny if it is only a temporary (though wrongful) "borrowing."

Mens rea which is other than an intent to commit the *actus reus* and yet something which cannot be designated as distinctly either more or less than this intent itself, finds an excellent illustration in the crime of murder.   The *actus reus* of murder is homicide, but the mental element of this offense (malice aforethought) is such that in one case an intentional killing may not be murder, whereas in another case an unintentional homicide may constitute this crime.   For example, a killing (though without legal justification or excuse) may be intentionally caused in the sudden heat of passion engendered by such provocation that the offense will be not murder but voluntary manslaughter,[85] while on the other hand the robber who kills the person he is attempting to rob is guilty of murder even if the killing was quite accidental.[86]

Any mental requirement for guilt of a particular offense which is in addition to an intent to commit the deed which constitutes the *actus reus* of that crime, or which is different from but not distinctly less than such an intent, may be spoken of as a "special mental element."   The term "specific intent" has sometimes been employed for this purpose,[87] but such usage is inaccurate and confusing.   Any specifically required actual intent other than to do the deed which constitutes the *actus reus* of the particular crime, is unquestionably a special mental element; but not every special mental element is a specific intent in the true sense of the word "intent."   Malice aforethought, for example, is a special mental element required for the crime of murder but it cannot properly be designated a "specific intent" since it may be present without a design to cause death, whereas an intentional killing may be either murder, manslaughter or innocent homicide.

81.   Kaye v. United States, 177 F. 147 (7th Cir. 1910).

82.   Ibid.

83.   Commonwealth v. Pierce, 138 Mass. 165 (1884).

84.   State v. O'Brien, 32 N.J.L. 169 (1867).

85.   State v. Hill, 20 N.C. 629 (1839).

86.   McCutcheon v. State, 199 Ind. 247, 155 N.E. 544 (1927); State v. Best, 44 Wyo. 383, 12 P.2d 1110 (1932); Davis v. State, 597 S.W.2d 358 (Tex.Cr.App. 1980).

87.   See Rucker v. State, 12 Ga.App. 632, 633, 77 S.E. 1129 (1913); Harrell v. State, 593 S.W.2d 664 (Tenn.Cr.App. 1980).

Typical examples of crimes involving a special mental element are (1) all offenses which require some specific intent (such as larceny, burglary, assault with intent to murder, using the mails with intent to defraud, criminal attempt), and any offense in which the requirement for guilt is that the *actus reus* be done (2) fraudulently (such as forgery, false pretenses), (3) maliciously, (murder, arson, malicious mischief, libel), (4) corruptly (such as perjury, common-law extortion), (5) wilfully where from the whole context this means something more than voluntarily (such as wilful trespass, wilful usurpation of office, wilful failure to file an income tax return), or (6) knowingly (such as uttering a forged instrument, receiving stolen property, knowingly transporting a stolen car in interstate commerce). Before turning to such problems, however, brief attention should be given to the peculiarities of the concept known as "criminal negligence."

SECTION 2. LACK OF DUE CARE

A. CRIMINAL NEGLIGENCE

Statements can be found to the effect that "negligence is a state of mind" [1] or on the other hand that it is "not a state of mind," [2] but the difference is largely in the use of terms. Thus if negligence is said to be a state of mind it is conceded that to have juridical consequences it must be *manifested*; [3] and if it is said not to be a state of mind this is to emphasize that "the state of mind, which is the cause, must be distinguished from the actual negligence, which is its effect." [4] The tendency is to use the word "negligence" as a synonym for "negligent conduct," [5] and this implies something done (or not done under circumstances involving a breach of duty to perform) [6] with some sort of blameworthy state of mind. The Model Penal Code standard of negligence is illustrative of negligence as a state of mind. [7]

Intentional harm falls into quite a different category, [8] and an act may be done with such a wanton and wilful disregard of a socially-harmful consequence, known to be likely to result, that the attitude of mind will be more socially blameworthy than is imported by the word "negligence." [9] Hence

1. Bigelow, Torts 19 (8th ed. 1907).

2. Terry, Negligence, 29 Harv.L.Rev. 40 (1915).

3. Bigelow, Torts 19 (8th ed. 1907).

4. Terry, Negligence, 29 Harv.L.Rev. 40, 41 (1915).

5. Ibid. ". . . negligence is any conduct, . . ." Restatement, Second, Torts § 282 (1965).

6. Juridical consequences do not follow the inaction of one who is under no legal duty to perform. Buck v. Amory Mfg. Co., 69 N.H. 257, 260, 44 A. 809, 811 (1898). It is otherwise where the inaction constitutes a breach of such a duty. State v. O'Brien, 32 N.J.L. 169 (1867).

7. "A person acts negligently with respect to a material element of an offense when he should be aware of a substantial and unjustifiable risk that the material element exists or will result from his conduct. The risk must be of such a nature and degree that the actor's failure to perceive it, considering the nature and purpose of his conduct and the circumstances known to him, involves a gross deviation from the standard of care that a reasonable person would observe in the actor's situation." M.P.C. § 2.02(2)(d).

8. "The definition of negligence given in this Section . . . excludes conduct which creates liability because of the actor's intention. . . ." Restatement, Second, Torts § 282, comment d (1965).

9. ". . . negligence is any conduct, except conduct recklessly disregardful of an interest of others. . . ." Id. at § 282. The word "recklessly" used at this point in the Restatement of Torts is not

attention must be directed to risks of such harm created by a state of mind other than either of these. Since some element of risk is involved in many kinds of useful conduct, socially-acceptable conduct cannot be limited to acts which involve no risk at all. To distinguish risks not socially acceptable from those regarded as fairly incident to our civilization, the former are spoken of as "unreasonable." [10] Even an unreasonable risk, however, may have been created without social fault, if the one who created the risk did not know or have reason to know of the existence of such risk under the circumstances. Hence a distinction is made between risks that are "realizable" [11] and those that are not. Conduct, therefore, may be said to fall below the line of social acceptability if it involves a realizable and unreasonable risk of social harm. With this preface the following definition may be offered:

> **Negligence is any conduct, except conduct intentionally or wantonly and wilfully disregardful of an interest of others, which falls below the standard established by law for the protection of others against unreasonable risk of harm.**[12]

The criminal-negligence concept has been clouded by semantic complication,—the use of the same words to express different ideas in different connections. This type of difficulty is encountered time and again in the law, such as the use of the word "assault" to express one meaning in the law of torts and something quite different in a criminal case, as explained in an earlier chapter. Any such shift of meaning tends to invite misunderstanding but is peculiarly confusing when it occurs without open recognition of the difference, which has all too frequently been true at this point.

As the law abandoned (for the most part) the theory of strict liability, and moved in the direction of liability grounded upon fault, the negligence concept made its appearance both in the field of torts and in the criminal law. In each the contrast was between the exercise of due care and caution [13] on the one hand and negligence (lack of due care and caution) on the other. This of course has reference to due care and caution under the circumstances, and the number of variables which may be found under different circumstances is so great that it would be futile to attempt to establish a rule for each possible combination.[14] The only possibility was to test such con-

---

employed here in the text, because in the criminal cases it is frequently adopted to signify criminal negligence rather than malice. See, for example, Dunville v. State, 188 Ind. 373, 123 N.E. 689 (1919); State v. Thomlinson, 209 Iowa 555, 228 N.W. 80 (1929); State v. Cope, 204 N.C. 28, 167 S.E. 456 (1933). "[T]he rule is that 'negligence and wilful and wanton conduct are so different in kind that words properly descriptive of one commonly exclude the other.'" Commonwealth v. Welansky, 316 Mass. 383, 400, 55 N.E.2d 902, 911 (1944); O'Leary v. State, 604 P.2d 1099 (Alaska 1979).

10. "Unreasonable risk" is the term used in the Restatement, Second, Torts § 282 (1965).

11. ". . . which the actor as a reasonable man should realize . . ." Id. at § 284.

12. This definition follows very closely that adopted by the Restatement, Second, Torts § 282. The Restatement does not include the word "intentionally" on the ground that the word "risk" excludes the idea of intentional harm, as explained in comment to § 282. The word "intentionally" is added in the text for emphasis, and whereas the Restatement uses the word "recklessly," the phrase "wantonly & wilfully" is substituted here for reasons explained in note 8. But see, infra, A, Recklessness.

13. Blackstone's phrase, frequently adopted, is "without due caution and circumspection." 4 Bl.Comm. * 192.

14. Pound, Introduction to the Philosophy of Law 119–20 (1922).

duct by a standard, and the standard formulated was that of a reasonable person under like circumstances.[15] The nature and significance of this standard is the clue to the whole situation. A standard is a legal device employed to enable the fact-finder to apply common sense to the complicated facts of a particular situation.[16] This standard was used in a tort case to enable the jury, by application of common sense to all the complicated facts of the situation, to determine whether the defendant had employed such care and caution that he should not be required to compensate one who had been unintentionally harmed or injured,—or had failed to exercise such care and caution and hence was subject to civil liability. And a standard expressed in the same words was used in a criminal case to enable the jury, by a similar application of common sense, to determine whether defendant had employed such a degree of care and caution that he should not be punished for unintended harmful consequences,—or had failed to exercise such care and caution and thereby incurred criminal guilt. Common sense compels the conclusion that there may be a grade or degree of fault sufficient to call for the payment of damages in a civil suit, but quite insufficient to authorize criminal punishment, and this is exactly the result reached by the common law.[17] The original position was once obscured because in the beginning a different "measuring stick" was employed in the two cases although the label was the same. The requirement was said to be "due care and caution" and the want thereof was "negligence," which was sufficient for a verdict against the defendant in either. But since the standard called "due care and caution" in a criminal case was much less exacting than that of the same name in a civil action, the failure thereof called "negligence" represented much more blameworthy conduct in the former than in the latter.

In the effort to express this distinction the courts, before a clearer explanation had been developed, referred to conduct as "culpable negligence" if it failed to measure up to the standard of care required for exculpation in a criminal case.[18] Although such use of the term has sometimes been thought to indicate that "culpable negligence" in a criminal case is the same as ordinary "negligence" in a civil case,[19] this is a great mistake because the inten-

---

15. Restatement, Second, Torts § 282 (1965).

16. "A standard is a measure of conduct prescribed by law from which one departs at his peril of answering for resulting damage or loss. Examples are the standard of due care not to subject others to unreasonable risk of injury; . . . There is a characteristic element of fairness or reasonableness in standards which makes them a point of contact between law and morals. This is a source of difficulty. As has been said, there is no precept defining what is reasonable and it would not be reasonable to formulate one. In the end reasonableness and what is fair have to be referred to conformity to the authoritative ideal." Pound, Justice According to Law 58–9 (1951).

17. "Culpable negligence in the law of crimes necessarily implies something

more than actionable negligence in the law of torts." State v. Phelps, 242 N.C. 540, 544, 89 S.E. 132, 135 (1955); Phillips v. State, 379 So.2d 318 (Miss.1980).

18. "To constitute involuntary manslaughter, the homicide must have resulted from appellant's failure to exercise due caution and circumspection, which is the equivalent of 'criminal negligence' or 'culpable negligence.'" State v. Stambaught, 121 Ariz. 226, 589 P.2d 469, 471 (App.1979).

19. See, for example, Clemens v. State, 176 Wis. 289, 303–4, 185 N.W. 209, 214–5 (1921). This interpretation of the manslaughter statute was so unsatisfactory that it was amended by substituting "gross negligence" for the original term "culpable negligence." See State v. Whatley, 210 Wis. 157, 245 N.W. 93 (1932).

tion was to emphasize the difference between them. This error has been avoided for the most part, fortunately, and it is significant that when the courts found a better method of expressing the distinction they employed it to express existing law and not to introduce any change therein.[20] At times, it may be added, the requirement of greater fault for criminal guilt then for civil liability has been expressed in terms reminiscent of "implied malice." Thus it has been suggested that crime requires "intention" and that intention may be "implied" from recklessness but not from lack of ordinary care.[21]

Under the newer, and better, form of explanation the "measuring stick" is the same in a criminal case as in the law of torts. It is the exercise of due care and caution as represented by the conduct of a reasonable person under like circumstances, and this in itself is intended to represent the same requirement whatever the case may be. But whereas the civil law requires conformity to this standard, a very substantial deviation is essential to criminal guilt.[22] "Notwithstanding language used commonly in earlier cases, and occasionally in later ones," said the Massachusetts court,[23] "it is now clear in this Commonwealth that at common law conduct does not become criminal until it passes the borders of negligence . . . and enters the domain of wanton or reckless conduct." And in reversing a conviction the North Carolina court had this to say: [24]

"It is settled law with us that 'a want of due care or a failure to observe the rule of a prudent man, which proximately produces an injury, will render one liable for damages in a civil action, while culpable negligence, under criminal law, is recklessness or carelessness, resulting in injury or death, as

20. "The terminology, not the law, is what has changed." Commonwealth v. Welansky, 316 Mass. 383, 400, n. 1, 55 N.E.2d 902, 911, n. 3 (1944). For an exhaustive study see Riesenfeld, Negligent Homicide: A Study in Statutory Interpretation, 25 Calif.L.Rev. 1 (1936).

21. See Radley v. State, 197 Ind. 200, 204, 150 N.E. 97, 98 (1926); Luther v. State, 177 Ind. 619, 98 N.E. 640 (1912).

22. Reed v. Madden, 87 F.2d 846 (8th Cir. 1937); White v. State, 37 Ala.App. 424, 69 So.2d 874 (1954); People v. Penny, 44 Cal.2d 861, 285 P.2d 926 (1955); Tongay v. State, 79 So.2d 673, 674 (Fla. 1955); State v. Wheeler, 70 Idaho 455, 220 P.2d 687 (1950); State v. Hamilton, 149 Me. 218, 100 A.2d 234 (1953); Sims v. State, 149 Miss. 171, 115 So. 217 (1928); Hynum v. State, 222 Miss. 817, 818, 77 So.2d 313, 314 (1955); State v. Studebaker, 334 Mo. 471, 66 S.W.2d 877 (1933); State v. Gooze, 14 N.J.Super. 277, 81 A.2d 811 (1951); People v. Angelo, 246 N.Y. 451, 159 N.E. 394 (1927); People v. Dawson, 206 Misc. 297, 133 N.Y.S.2d 423 (1954); State v. Phelps, 242 N.C. 540, 89 S.E.2d 132 (1955); Frey v. State, 97 Okl. Cr. 410, 265 P.2d 502 (1953); Common-

wealth v. Gill, 120 Pa.Super. 22, 182 A. 103 (1935); State v. Davis, 128 S.C. 265, 122 S.E. 770 (1924); Weaver v. State, 185 Tenn. 276, 278, 206 S.W.2d 293, 294 (1947); Bell v. Commonwealth, 170 Va. 597, 195 S.E. 675 (1938); Regina v. Spencer, 10 Cox C.C. 525 (1867); Andrews v. Director of Public Prosecutions, 26 Cr. App.R. 34 (H.L.1937). Contra, State v. Maxfield, 46 Wash.2d 822, 285 P.2d 887 (1955).

To establish criminal guilt on a negligence basis the Model Penal Code would require conduct which "involves a gross deviation from the standard of care that a reasonable person would observe in the actor's situation." Section 2.02(d).

23. Commonwealth v. Welansky, 316 Mass. 383, 400, 55 N.E.2d 902, 911 (1944). The words omitted from the quotation are "and gross negligence." Under the terminology employed by most of the courts in the criminal cases "gross negligence" and "reckless conduct" are equivalent terms.

24. State v. Becker, 241 N.C. 321, 328, 85 S.E.2d 327, 332 (1955).

imports a thoughtless disregard of consequences or a heedless indifference to the safety and rights of others.' "

The same point has been emphasized by other courts. "There is a marked distinction between simple or ordinary negligence, giving one a right of action for damages, and culpable negligence, rendering one guilty of a criminal offense." [25] "Culpable negligence is therefore something more than the slight negligence necessary to support a civil action for damages." [26] Other modifiers have been applied to the word "negligence" in the effort to express the same idea, the choice frequently having been either "gross" or "criminal." [27] The trend appears to be in the direction of employing the latter and this seems appropriate since the purpose is to indicate the type of negligence needed for criminal guilt.

The terms "gross negligence" and "degrees of negligence" were at one time misapplied in civil cases [28] and there has been a tendency to abandon both in that branch of jurisprudence.[29] In a criminal Court, on the contrary, the amount and degree of negligence are the determining question. There must be *mens rea*." [30] And as expressed by the Florida court,[31] the kind of negligence required to impose criminal guilt "must be of a higher degree than that required to establish simple negligence upon a mere civil issue." A different result may occasionally be required by statute. Thus under the former Michigan enactment [32] one whose operation of a motor vehicle had caused death, although not guilty of involuntary manslaughter because his conduct did not amount to criminal negligence, might be convicted of "negligent homicide" if his driving was such as to constitute ordinary negligence.[33]

For the most part, however, even as to offenses for which the mens-rea requirement can be established on a negligence basis there has been no change in the position that a greater degree of fault is required for conviction than is needed to establish tort liability, and this has found expression frequently in the statutes. Enactments may be found, for example, specify-

25. State v. Baublits, 324 Mo. 1199, 1211, 27 S.W.2d 16, 21 (1930). And see, State v. Ledford, 10 N.C.App. 315, 178 S.E.2d 235 (1971).

"While criminal responsibility may rest on acts of negligence, such negligence is generally of a higher degree than that required to establish civil liability." Graham v. State, 362 So.2d 924, 926 (Fla. 1978).

26. People v. Dawson, 206 Misc. 297, 301, 133 N.Y.S.2d 423, 427 (1954).

"Culpable negligence" as used in the manslaughter statute is sufficiently definite to create an ascertainable standard of conduct. State v. Kays, 492 S.W.2d 752 (Mo.1973).

27. White v. State, 37 Ala.App. 424, 427, 69 So.2d 874, 876 (1954); People v. Penny, 44 Cal.2d 861, 879, 285 P.2d 926, 937 (1955); State v. Wheeler, 70 Idaho 455, 460, 220 P.2d 687, 690 (1950); Hynum v. State, 222 Miss. 817, 818, 77 So.2d 313, 314 (1955); State v. Gooze, 14 N.J.Super. 277, 282, 81 A.2d 811, 814

(1951); United States v. Keith, 605 F.2d 462 (9th Cir. 1979).

28. Wilson v. Brett, 11 M. & W. 113, 115–6, 152 Eng.Rep. 737, 739 (1843).

29. Harper and James, Law of Torts, § 16.13 (1956).

30. Andrews v. Director of Public Prosecutions, 26 Cr.App.R. 34, 46 (H.L.1937). Accord, State v. Strobel, 130 Mont. 442, 304 P.2d 606 (1956).

31. Cannon v. State, 91 Fla. 214, 222, 107 So. 360, 363 (1926). And see People v. Angelo, 246 N.Y. 451, 454, 159 N.E. 394, 395 (1927); Weaver v. State, 185 Tenn. 276, 278, 206 S.W.2d 293, 294 (1947).

32. Mich.Comp.Laws § 750.324 (1948). For additional references see the discussion of negligent homicide in chapter 2.

33. People v. Orr, 243 Mich. 300, 220 N.W. 777 (1928); People v. McMurchy, 249 Mich. 147, 228 N.W. 723 (1930). See West's Ann.Cal.Pen.Code § 1923(b) (1970).

ing that a crime requires a "union or joint operation of act and intent, or criminal negligence," [34] or that criminal conduct includes "criminal negligence that produces criminal consequences," [35] or that accidental harm or injury shall not be deemed criminal if there was no evil intent, design, or "gross deviation from the standard of care that a reasonable person would observe in the actor's situation." [36]   At times such a provision may be included in a section dealing with a specific offense such as: "Every other killing of a human being, by the act, procurement or culpable negligence of another . . . shall be deemed manslaughter:" [37] "Negligent homicide is the killing of a human being by criminal negligence:" [38] "Negligent injuring is the inflicting of any injury upon the person of another by criminal negligence." [39]

Two cautions require particular attention.   One is in regard to certain other types of enactment such as that a killing by a lawful act, done "without due caution and circumspection" shall be manslaughter,[40] or that homicide is excusable when committed by accident and misfortune in doing a lawful act by lawful means "with usual and ordinary caution" and without any unlawful intent.[41]   Such terminology reflects the earlier usage by which such a phrase when used in a criminal case was understood to mean such care and caution as is required in order to avoid criminal responsibility for unintended harmful consequences, and should not be interpreted to authorize conviction of a crime where no more than ordinary negligence is involved.[42]

The second caution is of a comparable nature although not based upon the wording of a statute.   The negligence concept as applied in criminal law has had the most elaborate consideration in the homicide cases but the results found there are equally applicable elsewhere—a greater degree of fault is required for guilt of crime than is needed to establish civil liability.   This has been recognized as to battery [43] since the mens rea requirement for battery and for involuntary manslaughter is the same so far as negligence is concerned,[44] and it should have equal recognition elsewhere.   For example, if an excuse is claimed in a criminal case by reason of a mistake of fact, and the offense charged does not involve some special mental element, it is necessary to show that the mistake was "not superinduced by fault or negli-

---

34. West's Ann.Cal.Pen.Code § 20 (1970).

35. La.Rev.Stat.Ann. § 14:8 (1974).

36. Ark.Stat.Ann. § 41–203(4) (1977).

37. Vernon's Mo.Ann.Stat. § 565.005 (1979).

38. La.Rev.Stat.Ann. § 14:32 (1974).

39. Id. at 14:39.

40. West's Ann.Cal.Pen.Code, § 192 (1970).

41. West's Ann.Cal.Pen.Code § 195 (1970).

42. People v. Penny, 44 Cal.2d 861, 285 P.2d 926 (1955); People v. Angelo, 246 N.Y. 451, 159 N.E. 394 (1927). Homicide is not "in the commission of a lawful act without due caution and circumspection" unless it was the result of "criminal negligence." Carbo v. State, 4 Ga.App. 583, 62 S.E. 140 (1908). The statute must not be interpreted so as to punish one who is not culpable. People v. Stuart, 47 Cal.2d 167, 302 P.2d 5 (1956).

43. Bodily injury caused by "criminal negligence" is battery. Banovitch v. Commonwealth, 196 Va. 210, 83 S.E.2d 369 (1954). While one is not criminally liable for the results of ordinary negligence, if reckless conduct results in injury to another it constitutes a battery. Brimhall v. State, 31 Ariz. 522, 255 P. 165 (1927).

44. The rule is the same for both "since manslaughter is simply a battery that causes death." Commonwealth v. Welansky, 316 Mass. 383, 401, 55 N.E.2d 902, 912 (1944). Assault and battery may be committed by striking another with a car intentionally or recklessly. Tift v. State, 17 Ga.App. 663, 88 S.E. 41 (1916).

gence" [45] or that it did "not arise from a want of proper care." [46] Any such terminology is also reflective of the earlier forms of expression and should be understood in that light. A word such as "care" or "caution" as so used does not refer to what is needed to avoid tort liability, and the word "negligence" is to be understood to mean criminal negligence,—such negligence as is sufficient for guilt of crime.[47]

While it "is elementary that to support a conviction of crime, the accused must be guilty of negligence in a higher and grosser degree than is sufficient to support a judgment in a civil case," [48] some difficulty has been encountered in expressing this greater fault, and the trend has been in the direction of employing the word "reckless" for this purpose.[49] At times the suggestion has been that criminal negligence involves an "indifference" or "disregard" of consequences,[50] as for example: "Criminal negligence necessarily implies, not only knowledge of probable consequences which may result from the use of a given instrumentality, but also wilful or wanton disregard of the probable effects of such instrumentality upon others likely to be affected thereby." [51] But while such a state of mind would certainly qualify for this purpose it would hardly seem to be requisite. As explained by the English court,[52] "the accused may have appreciated the risk and intended to avoid it and yet shown such a high degree of negligence in the means adopted to avoid the risk as would justify a conviction." And certainly pains

---

45. Dotson v. State, 62 Ala. 141, 144 (1878).

"Reasonable ignorance is a defense but unreasonable ignorance is not." State v. Henderson, 296 So.2d 805, 807 (La.1974).

46. Stern v. State, 53 Ga. 229 (1874); Hamilton v. State, 115 Tex.Cr.R. 96, 29 S.W.2d 777 (1930).

47. "In defining crimes generally they are classified into those . . . and such offenses as the law attributes to culpable negligence." Rucker v. State, 12 Ga.App. 632, 633, 77 S.E. 1129 (1913).

The term negligence in the Utah Automobile Homicide statute was construed to require criminal negligence. State v. Chavez, 605 P.2d 1226 (Utah 1979).

The Utah Legislature reacted by passing a new statute making it specific that automobile homicide only required "simple negligence." Utah Code Ann. 1953 § 76–5–207 (1981 Supp.).

48. Weaver v. State, 185 Tenn. 276, 278, 206 S.W.2d 293, 294 (1947).

49. "Probably of all the epithets that can be applied 'reckless' most nearly covers the case." Andrews v. Director of Public Prosecutions, 26 Cr.App.R. 34, 47 (H.L.1937). And see Penny v. People, 44 Cal.2d 861, 879, 285 P.2d 926, 937 (1955); Tongay v. State, 79 So.2d 673, 674 (Fla. 1955); Hynum v. State, 222 Miss. 817, 818, 77 So.2d 313, 314 (1955); Radley v.

State, 197 Ind. 200, 204, 150 N.E. 97, 98 (1925); People v. Angelo, 246 N.Y. 451, 455, 159 N.E. 394, 395 (1927); Weaver v. State, 185 Tenn. 276, 279, 206 S.W.2d 293, 294 (1947); State v. Clark, 118 Utah 517, 527, 223 P.2d 184, 188 (1950).

"If death resulted from negligent conduct in doing a *lawful act* it is necessary in order to constitute manslaughter that the conduct be reckless, that is, be such as to evince disregard or indifference to consequences, under circumstances involving danger to life and safety to others, although no harm was intended." State v. Scott, 201 Kan. 134, 439 P.2d 78 (1968).

50. Tongay v. State, 79 So.2d 673, 674 (Fla. 1955); Thomas v. State, 91 Ga.App. 382, 384, 85 S.E.2d 644, 646 (1955); State v. Hamilton, 149 Me. 218, 239, 100 A.2d 234, 244 (1953); Hynum v. State, 222 Miss. 817, 818, 77 So.2d 313, 314 (1953); State v. Gooze, 14 N.J.Super. 277, 282, 81 A.2d 811, 814 (1951); People v. Dawson, 206 Misc. 297, 301, 133 N.Y.S.2d 423, 427 (1954).

51. Thomas v. State, 91 Ga.App. 382, 384, 85 S.E.2d 644, 645–6 (1955); Farr v. State, 591 S.W.2d 449 (Tenn.Cr.App. 1979).

52. Andrews v. Director of Public Prosecutions, 26 Cr.App.R. 34, 48 (H.L.1937).

should be taken not to define criminal negligence in terms of a wanton *and* wilful disregard of a harmful consequence known to be likely to result, because such a state of mind goes beyond negligence and comes under the head of malice.[53] Two persons, let it be assumed, are conducting themselves in a dangerous manner. One is a motorist who is not exceeding the speed limit but is traveling on an icy pavement, in heavy traffic, in a manner that involves extreme risk to others and to himself. He is fully aware of the hazard, hopes to avoid any harm, and intends to do all he can to prevent an accident,—other than to reduce his speed. The other is a hunter who shoots through a farm house with a high-power rifle. He is not trying to hit anyone because he has no idea in what part of the building the occupants may be, if anyone is actually there at the moment, but it is quite immaterial to him whether anyone is killed, injured, frightened, or not. The hunter is acting with a wanton and wilful disregard of an obvious human risk and hence has malice aforethought,[54] but this is not true of the motorist who is chargeable only with recklessness, although it may be that the danger involved in his conduct is no less, or even greater, than that caused by the hunter.

It is the viciousness of the hunter's wanton act which warrants a conviction of murder. It is, as said in another connection, "attended with such circumstances as carry with them the plain indications of a heart regardless of social duty, and fatally bent on mischief." [55]

An intoxicated motorist who drove on a public highway at night at 75 miles an hour, zigzagging from right to left and crossing over to the wrong side, was held to have been criminally negligent and guilty of manslaughter for death caused thereby; [56] but excessive speed alone is not necessarily more than ordinary negligence and a conviction of manslaughter was re-

---

53. The word "reckless" is not the equivalent of "wanton." Merrill v. Sheffield Co., 169 Ala. 242, 252, 53 So. 219, 222 (1910). "Our courts make a distinction between gross negligence and wanton and willful disregard of the rights and safety of others." State v. Gooze, 14 N.J.Super. 277, 283, 81 A.2d 811, 814 (1951). As to the meaning of wanton and wilful see id. at 282–3, 81 A.2d at 814. A "wicked and wanton disregard of the safety of others" goes beyond criminal negligence and constitutes malice aforethought. Commonwealth v. Aurick, 342 Pa. 282, 290, 19 A.2d 920, 924 (1941).

"When a defendant with wanton disregard for human life, does an act that involves a high degree of probability that it will result in death he acts with malice aforethought." People v. Cruz, 26 Cal.3d 233, 162 Cal.Rptr. 1, 5, 605 P.2d 830, 835 (1980).

The Model Penal Code § 2.02(2)(c) provides that conscious disregard coupled with a gross deviation from the proper standard of care is recklessness and not mere criminal negligence.

54. **D**, who shot through a moving freight train and killed a brakeman, was convicted of murder and the conviction was affirmed. Banks v. State, 85 Tex.Cr. R. 165, 211 S.W. 217 (1919). While **D** and **X** were playing "Russian poker," **D** placed against **X**'s side a revolver loaded with only one cartridge and pulled the trigger. Death resulted because the cartridge happened to be in the firing chamber, and a conviction of murder was affirmed. Commonwealth v. Malone, 354 Pa. 180, 47 A.2d 445 (1946).

"[W]here the fact has been attended with such circumstances, as carry in them the plain indications of a heart regardless of social duty, and fatally bent on mischief . . . malice is implied." Commonwealth v. Webster, 5 Cush. 295, 307 (Mass.1850).

Malice aforethought may be established either on a subjective standard or on an objective, reasonable man standard. Belton v. United States, 382 F.2d 150 (D.C. Cir. 1967). This, however, is unsound.

55. Commonwealth v. Webster, 59 Mass. (5 Cush.) 295, 307 (1850).

56. Hynum v. State, 222 Miss. 817, 77 So.2d 313 (1955).

versed in a case in which there was no additional showing.[57] It was more than ordinary negligence for a father to compel his reluctant five-year-old daughter to dive from a 33⅓-foot tower, and a conviction of manslaughter based on the fatal consequence was not disturbed;[58] but it was otherwise in a different case in which nothing of a "grossly negligent or improper manner" was shown.[59] One who drives a car with knowledge of the fact that he may at any time have an attack of vertigo during which he will be unable to control a moving car, and who has been cautioned not to drive alone, is guilty of manslaughter if such driving causes a fatal accident,[60] and of assault and battery if a non-fatal injury results;[61] but the fact that a smoker set fire to the mattress by accident while smoking in bed, and fled to the street without notifying other occupants of the building, does not disclose more than ordinary negligence and hence is insufficient for guilt of crime.[62] It has been held, quite properly it would seem, that while the violation of a statute or ordinance may be no more than ordinary negligence,[63] the intentional, wilful or wanton violation of a statute or ordinance designed for the protection of life or limb is criminal negligence.[64]

To express the added degree of fault required for criminal negligence the present trend is to word the requirement in some such terms as "a gross deviation from the standard of care that a reasonable person would observe in the actor's situation." Perhaps adding: "Gross deviation means a deviation that is considerably greater than lack of ordinary care." [65] As explained by one court: "A gross deviation under the statutory definition is analogous to gross negligence in the law of torts. Although somewhat nebulous in concept, gross negligence is generally considered to fall short of a reckless disregard for consequences and is said to differ from ordinary negligence only in degree, not in kind." [66]

See also People v. Farris, 82 Ill.App.3d 147, 37 Ill.Dec. 627, 402 N.E.2d 629 (1980).

57. Maxey v. State, 64 So.2d 677 (Fla. 1953); State v. Randol, 226 Kan. 347, 597 P.2d 672 (1979).

58. Tongay v. State, 79 So.2d 673 (Fla.1955).

59. White v. State, 37 Ala.App. 424, 69 So.2d 874 (1954).

One who continued to drive despite the fact that he was so drowsy that he should have known his driving was likely to result in some tragedy was guilty of manslaughter for a fatal accident that occurred after he apparently went to sleep. The Court says that such driving was *malum in se.* Grindstaff v. State, 214 Tenn. 58, 377 S.W.2d 921 (1964).

60. State v. Gooze, 14 N.J.Super. 277, 81 A.2d 811 (1951); People v. Decina, 2 N.Y.S.2d 133, 157 N.Y.S.2d 558, 138 N.E.2d 799 (1956).

61. Tift v. State, 17 Ga.App. 663, 88 S.E. 41 (1916).

62. People v. Hoffman, 162 Misc. 677, 294 N.Y.S. 444 (1937). In another case an indictment for manslaughter based upon a hunting accident was dismissed. People v. Dawson, 206 Misc. 297, 133 N.Y.S.2d 423 (1954).

63. State v. Cope, 204 N.C. 28, 167 S.E. 456 (1933).

64. Cain v. State, 55 Ga.App. 376, 190 S.E. 371 (1937); State v. Phelps, 242 N.C. 540, 89 S.E.2d 132 (1955).

65. M.C.A. § 45–2–101(31) (1981). The Montana statute defines negligent homicide in terms of homicide "committed negligently." But then defines "negligently" in terms of criminal negligence.

66. State v. Bier, ___ Mont. ___, 591 P.2d 1115, 1118 (1979). Culpable negligence requires substantially more than ordinary negligence but it does not require an actual subjective awareness of the risk being created. O'Leary v. State, 604 P.2d 1099 (Alaska 1979).

Unfortunately a few of the new penal codes authorize the establishment of guilt of some offenses on the basis of simple or ordinary negligence. It is also unfortunate that the Model Penal Code uses "negligence" to mean criminal negligence.

B. RECKLESSNESS

For the most part the common law overlooked the distinction between recklessness and criminal negligence. In fact the word "reckless" or "recklessly" was commonly used in expressing the concept of criminal negligence,[67] as mentioned in the preceding section. The wording of that section, prepared for previous editions, has been retained in order to give a picture of the common law as it was until quite recently; but the basic distinction between recklessness and criminal negligence is now receiving wide-spread recognition, aided by appropriate legislation, and is definitely a part of the law today. The following paragraph, also carried over from earlier editions, is repeated as throwing light upon the transition from the old to the new.

A problem entitled to far more attention than it has received in the decided cases is this: Does criminal negligence require subjective fault or is objective fault sufficient for this purpose? At the threshold, a semantic problem is encountered. Glanville Williams, an outstanding English scholar in the criminal-law field, distinguishes "advertent negligence" from "inadvertent negligence," depending upon whether the actor is or is not aware of the unreasonable risk he is creating, adding that the former is "commonly called recklessness."[68] Professor Hall, on the other hand, regards "recklessness" and "negligence" as mutually-exclusive terms, saying that "no degree of negligence, however great it may be deemed to be, can ever be recklessness."[69] Although the disagreement is limited to the meaning of "negligence" and both consider awareness of the unreasonable risk essential to "recklessness," judicial use of the term has usually not included such a requirement.[70] The American Law Institute employs "recklessness" and "neg-

---

67. For criminal negligence, there must be "knowledge, actual or imputed, that the act of the slayer tended to endanger life." People v. Penny, 44 Cal.2d 861, 880, 285 P.2d 926, 937 (1955); People v. Rodriguez, 186 Cal.App.2d 433, 440, 8 Cal.Rptr. 863, 867 (2d Dist. 1960). To constitute reckless or culpably negligent conduct it is necessary for the actor to have "knowledge of the highly dangerous nature of his actions or knowledge of such facts as under the circumstances would disclose to a reasonable man the dangerous character of his action. . . ." People v. Eckert, 2 N.Y.2d 126, 130–31, 138 N.E.2d 794, 797 (1955). For conviction of reckless homicide: "It is sufficient that the actor realizes, or should realize, that there is a strong probability that such harm will result." Beeman v. State, 232 Ind. 683, 692, 115 N.E.2d 919, 923 (1953). And see Commonwealth v. Welansky, 316 Mass. 383, 398–99, 55 N.E.2d 902, 910 (1944).

68. Williams, Criminal Law § 24, at 53 (2d ed. 1961). Compare Kenny, Outlines of Criminal Law ¶¶ 22–25 (19th ed. by Turner, 1966).

See also Gordon, Subjective and Objective Mens Rea, 17 Crim.L.Qtrly. 355, 372–381 (1975).

69. Hall, General Principles of Criminal Law 116 (2d ed. 1960). "The hard fact is that inadvertence is not awareness; on the contrary, where one is the other is not." Hall, The Scientific and Humane Study of Criminal Law, 42 B.U.L.Rev. 267, 270 (1962).

70. Defendant caused a fatal accident while playing a joke with a weapon he firmly believed to be entirely harmless. His conduct was said to be "grossly reckless." State v. Hardie, 47 Iowa 647, 649 (1878). This is in line with the prevailing use of the term. "It is sufficient that the actor realizes, or should realize, that there is a strong probability that such harm will result." Beeman v. State, 232

ligence" as mutually-exclusive terms, but while in the Model Penal Code it is recommended that "recklessness" be defined by statute in terms of one who "consciously disregards a substantial and unjustifiable risk," [71] in the Restatement of Torts, reflecting existing judicial usage, no element of awareness was included in the definition of that term.[72]

Today "recklessness" and "criminal negligence" represent different mens-rea concepts. This requires a different definition of negligence: Negligence is any conduct, except conduct intentionally or recklessly disregardful of an interest of others, which falls below the standard established by law for the protection of others against unreasonable risk of harm.

Recklessness and criminal negligence have one component in common. Each requires conduct which represents a gross failure to measure up to the reasonable-person standard of care. Assuming such conduct, if the actor was aware of the risk he was creating, and consciously disregarded that risk, however much he may have hoped that no harm would result, he was acting recklessly. If he was unaware of that risk, but under the circumstances he should have been aware of it, he was acting with criminal negligence. In the words of the Utah court: "The difference between the minimum required *mens rea* of recklessness for manslaughter and criminal negligence for negligent homicide is simply whether the defendant was *aware, but consciously disregarded* a substantial risk the result would happen, or was *unaware but ought to have been aware* of a substantial risk the result would happen." [73] The court emphasized that for criminal negligence the risk "must be of such a nature and degree that the failure to perceive it constitutes a gross deviation from the standard of care that an ordinary person would exercise in all the circumstances as viewed from the actor's standpoint." [74] Another code makes use of the same definitions of recklessness and criminal negligence to distinguish between first-degree manslaughter and second-degree manslaughter.[75] "Reckless endangerment," a statutory offense under some of

---

Ind. 683, 692, 115 N.E.2d 919, 923 (1953) (conviction under reckless homicide statute). See also Commonwealth v. Welansky, 316 Mass. 383, 55 N.E.2d 902 (1944); Rex v. Bonnyman, 28 Crim.App.R. 131 (1942); cf. Andrews v. Director of Public Prosecutions, [1937] A.C. 576, 583.

Professor Moreland regards "recklessness" as "the word best suited to describe the behavior required for the lower grade of criminal negligence. . . ." Moreland, Law of Homicide 34 (1952). And to indicate the added requirement of awareness, Professor Collings has used the phrase "subjective recklessness." Collings, Negligent Murder—Some Stateside Footnotes to Director of Public Prosecutions v. Smith, 49 Calif.L.Rev. 254, 293 (1961).

71. Model Penal Code § 2.02(2)(c).

Several states have adopted statutes patterned after the Model Penal Code provision. E.g. Ark.Stat.Ann. § 41-203

(1977); Colo.Rev.Stat. § 18-1-501 (1978); Or.Rev.Stat. § 161.085 (1979).

72. Restatement, Second, Torts § 500 (1965). "The difference between reckless misconduct and conduct involving only such a quantum of risk as is necessary to make it negligent is a difference in the degree of the risk, but this difference of degree is so marked as to amount substantially to a difference in kind." Id. at comment g.

73. State v. Howard, 597 P.2d 878, 881 (Utah 1979).

74. Id. at page 880.

"We conclude that the General Assembly intended to preserve the common law requirement of recklessness in its provisions for involuntary manslaughter." State v. Conner, 292 N.W.2d 682, 686 (Iowa 1980). And see State v. Inger, 292 N.W.2d 119 (Iowa 1980).

75. State v. Burley, 23 Wn.App. 881, 598 P.2d 428 (1979).

the new penal codes, is committed by recklessly creating a substantial risk of death or serious injury to another.[76]

As recklessness includes the very significant element of awareness, which is lacking in criminal negligence, it follows that these two are mutually exclusive. No matter how extreme criminal negligence may be it cannot be recklessness, as pointed out by Professor Hall. It may be noted, however, that an offense with the mens rea of criminal negligence is a lesser offense included in the charge of a crime having the same actus reus committed recklessly.[77]

So far the attempt to eliminate the concept of criminal guilt based upon objective fault has been rejected.[78] But the time may come when we shall insist that any true crime requires a mind subjectively at fault,—that criminal guilt depends upon what is actually in the mind of the actor and not upon what *should be* in his mind. If that time comes, homicide resulting from criminal negligence (so-called, although of course not including awareness) will be recognized as a non-criminal offense. As such it would be appropriate to deal with it by the imposition of a fine and, or, some other penalty such as suspension or revocation of a driver license—but *not by imprisonment*.

SECTION 3. SPECIFIC INTENT

A specific intent, when an element of the mens rea of a particular offense, is some intent other than to do the actus reus thereof which is specifically required for guilt.

Use of the phrases "criminal intent" and "general criminal intent" in the broad sense of punishable blameworthiness, has caused some confusion when actual intention was the idea to be expressed. At times the phrase "specific intent" has been employed for this purpose,[1] but actual intention

---

76. State v. O'Neal, 23 Wn.App. 899, 600 P.2d 570 (1979).

77. The court said "it is clear that negligent homicide is a lesser-included offense of manslaughter, the reckless causing of the death of another, . . ." State v. Parker, 128 Ariz. 107, 624 P.2d 304, 306 (App.1980). Affirmed except as to another point, State v. Parker, 128 Ariz. 97, 624 P.2d 294 (1981).

78. "Accordingly, we think that negligence, as here defined, [not involving awareness] cannot be wholly rejected as a ground of culpability, which may suffice for purposes of criminal law . . . ." Model Penal Code 127 (Tent. Draft No. 4, 1955). See Wechsler, On Culpability and Crime: The Treatment of Mens Rea in the Model Penal Code, Annals 24, 30 (Jan. 1962). Cf. Hall, Negligent Behavior Should Be Excluded from Penal Liability, 63 Colum.L.Rev. 632 (1963); Honig, Criminal Law Systematized, 54 J.Crim.L., C. & P.S. 273, 280–82 (1963).

"We recommend, therefore, that negligent homicide be made criminal." Model Penal Code 52, 53 (Tent.Draft No. 9, 1959).

1. "In defining crimes generally they are classified into those in which there is a specific intent to do a specific act, and such offenses as the law attributes to culpable negligence." Rucker v. State, 12 Ga.App. 632, 633, 77 S.E. 1129 (1913). See also People v. Clark, 242 N.Y. 313, 326, 151 N.E. 631, 635 (1926).

When, by definition, a crime consists of a designated act without reference to an intent to achieve a further consequence, the intent to do the proscribed act makes the crime a "general criminal intent offense;" when an intent to achieve some additional consequence is required by definition, it is a "specific intent" offense. People v. Love, 111 Cal.App.3d Supp. 1, 168 Cal.Rptr. 591 (1980).

can be expressed without the use of this phrase and it should be reserved for a more important meaning.

Some crimes require a specified intention in addition to the intentional doing of the *actus reus* itself,—an intent specifically required for guilt of the particular offense, as in larceny,[2] burglary,[3] assault with intent to commit murder,[4] using the mails with intent to defraud,[5] or criminal attempt.[6] The physical part of the crime of larceny, for example, is the trespassory taking and carrying away of the personal goods of another, but this may be done intentionally, deliberately, and with full knowledge of all the facts and complete understanding of the wrongfulness of the act, without constituting larceny.[7] If this wilful misuse of another's property is done with the intention of returning it (with no change of mind in this regard) the special mens-rea requirement of larceny is lacking. Such a wrongdoer is answerable in a civil suit, and may be guilty of some statutory offense such as operating a motor vehicle without the consent of the owner, but for guilt of common-law larceny he must not only intentionally take the other's property by trespass and carry it away,—he must do this with an additional design in mind known as the *animus furandi* or intent to steal.[8] Burglary, moreover, cannot be defined as "intentionally breaking and entering the dwelling of another in the nighttime," because this may be done without committing this felony. For common-law burglary there is required not only the intentional breaking and entering of the dwelling house of another in the nighttime, but also an additional purpose—which is to commit a felony (or petty larceny). This additional requirement is a "specific intent," an additional intent specifically required for guilt of the particular offense.[9]

Dobbs' Case [10] is one of the most illuminating on the problem of specific intent although this phrase was not used. One who nocturnally broke and entered the stable of another, "part of his dwellinghouse," with intent to cut

2. 1 Hale P.C. * 509; People v. Brown, 105 Cal. 66, 38 P. 518 (1894); People v. Johnson, 136 Cal.App.2d 749, 289 P.2d 90 (1955).

3. People v. Flores, 86 Cal.App. 235, 237, 260 P. 822 (1927); Simpson v. State, 81 Fla. 292, 87 So. 920 (1921).

4. Posey v. State, 22 Ga.App. 97, 95 S.E. 325 (1918); White v. State, 13 Tex. App. 259 (1882).

5. Hibbard v. United States, 172 F. 66, 96 C.C.A. 554 (7th Cir. 1909); United States v. Foshee, 569 F.2d 401 (5th Cir. 1978).

6. Merritt v. Commonwealth, 164 Va. 653, 180 S.E. 395 (1935).

7. People v. Brown, 105 Cal. 66, 38 P. 518 (1894).

8. Id. at 69, 38 P. at 519.

9. "We recognize, of course, that most crimes require a criminal intent in the doing of the act prohibited. Some require only a general intent to do an act, which is evil in itself. Examples are acts like murder, rape, kidnapping, which are said to be malum in se. In such circumstances, a person is presumed to intend the natural consequences of his act and the general criminal intent with which an act was done may be inferred from the words and conduct of the actor.

"There are other crimes which require a specific intent. In them the prosecution must prove the intent with which the act was done. For example, the elements of the crime of burglary are: (1) the act of entering a building, and (2) the specific intent to commit a 'felony, theft or assault' therein. The entering of a building is not inherently evil, and that act alone does not give rise to a presumption or an inference that the actor entered with the requisite intent to constitute burglary. In addition to the entry, the intent to commit a 'felony, theft or assault' therein must be proved, or circumstances shown from which the intent may reasonably be inferred." Peck v. Dunn, 574 P.2d 367, 369–370 (Utah 1978).

10. 2 East P.C. 513 (1770).

the sinews of a horse's foreleg to prevent his running in a particular race, was held not guilty of burglary although the horse died. Because the death of the horse was the result of an unlawful act done with wanton and wilful disregard of an obvious risk to the horse's life, Dobbs was guilty of the felony of maliciously killing the horse, but since he did not *intend* to kill the horse he was not guilty of burglary which required a specific intent to commit a felony.

As said by one court, "in burglary, where there must be an intent to commit a felony, and in larceny, where there must be an intent to deprive the owner of his property, the specific intent must appear, and although the breaking or taking of personal property be unlawful, amounting possibly to a trespass, the offense is not made out if the specific intent be wanting; as when one broke and entered intending to commit a simple assault and battery." [11]

The crime of assault with intent to murder has been a useful testing ground for this mental element. Murder may be committed without an actual intent to take life.[12] "But to constitute the offense of an assault with intent to murder there must be a specific intent to kill." [13] Hence it is error to instruct the jury that the same facts and circumstances which would make the offense murder, if death had ensued, will furnish sufficient evidence of intention to convict of assault with intent to murder.[14] An intent "to maim, rob, rape, or other than to kill" will not meet the requirement.[15] Even an assault with an actual intent to kill will be insufficient if the circumstances are such that resulting death would have been manslaughter rather than murder.[16]

11. People v. Comstock, 115 Mich. 305, 312, 73 N.W. 245, 248 (1897). See also Simpson v. State, 81 Fla. 292, 87 So. 920 (1921).

12. "Murder may be committed although a specific intent to kill the deceased does not exist in the mind of the slayer." Carter v. State, 28 Tex.App. 355, 360, 13 S.W. 147, 149 (1890).

13. Ibid. See also Posey v. State, 22 Ga.App. 97, 99, 95 S.E. 325, 327 (1918); State v. Richardson, 179 Iowa 770, 162 N.W. 28 (1917); State v. Taylor, 70 Vt. 1, 39 A. 447 (1898).

An assault with intent to commit murder requires an "intent to unlawfully kill a human being; and the mental state of malice aforethought." People v. Stevenson, 79 Cal.App.3d 976, 145 Cal.Rptr. 301, 307 (1978).

14. Moore v. State, 18 Ala. 532 (1851); Bonfanti v. State, 2 Minn. 123 (1858). The problem of attempted murder is the same in this regard. See supra, chapter 6, section 3, A, 7. It is possible to find authority the other way, as illustrated by the case in which a drunk driver was held properly convicted of this offense because his reckless driving resulted in a collision which injured a woman occupant

of another car. Chambliss v. State, 37 Ga.App. 124, 139 S.E. 80 (1927). This, however, is a typical example of judicial legislation. This case was followed in Easley v. State, 49 Ga.App. 275, 175 S.E. 23 (1934). But in the Easley case Broyles, C. J., filed a vigorous dissent, pointing out that the specific intent is not established in such a case.

15. White v. State, 13 Tex.App. 259, 263 (1882). See also Ogletree v. State, 28 Ala. 693 (1856); Coleman v. State, 373 So. 2d 1254 (Ala.App.1979).

16. Hankins v. State, 103 Ark. 28, 145 S.W. 524 (1912); Hall v. State, 9 Fla. 203 (1860); State v. Schaefer, 35 Mont. 217, 88 P. 792 (1907); State v. Butman, 42 N.H. 490 (1861). One being tried for assault with intent to commit murder may be convicted of assault with intent to commit manslaughter, the lesser being included in the greater. State v. Connor, 59 Iowa 357, 13 N.W. 327 (1882). There is no such offense as assault with intent to commit involuntary manslaughter. Stevens v. State, 91 Tenn. 726, 20 S.W. 423 (1892).

A person charged with first-degree assault who can establish that he acted in heat of passion is constitutionally pro-

Some of the other aggravated assaults are entitled to special mention. One cannot properly be convicted of assault with intent to commit rape without proof "of his intention to gratify his lustful desire against the consent of the female, notwithstanding resistance on her part." [17] An assault with intent to *persuade* the woman is not sufficient,[18] unless the woman is under the statutory age of consent.[19] It is reversible error in a trial for assault with intent to maim to instruct the jury to convict if they find the assault was with intent to maim *or to cause him bodily injury.*[20] And the fact that a truck driver disobeyed signals of his foreman and caused a serious injury to the latter by striking him with the truck does not establish guilt of assault with intent to do great bodily harm if there is no evidence that defendant "intended to have the truck strike him." [21]

Where a specific intent is an essential ingredient of the crime charged, it must be alleged and proved by the prosecution.[22] And in this regard it is imperative to make a careful analysis of the "presumed to intend" formula. "The doctrine of an intent in law, differing from the intent in fact, is not applicable" in such a case.[23] The intent with which a harmful act is done is usually not expressed in words, and the jury is permitted to draw such inferences of intent as are warranted under all the circumstances of the particular case,[24] but there is no presumption of law, either conclusive or disputable, that an act was done with any specific intent,[25] unless some statute provides for such presumption in the trial of a particular offense.[26]

tected against receiving a greater penalty than he could have received had he caused the death of the victim. People v. Montoya, 196 Colo. 111, 582 P.2d 673 (1978).

17. Jones v. State, 90 Ala. 628, 629, 8 So. 383, 384 (1890); State v. Silhan, 297 N.C. 660, 256 S.E.2d 702 (1979).

18. Barr v. People, 113 Ill. 471 (1885). See also State v. Kendall, 73 Iowa 255, 34 N.W. 843 (1887); Commonwealth v. Merrill, 80 Mass. 415, 416 (1860); State v. Hamm, 577 S.W.2d 936 (Mo.App.1979).

19. State v. Carnagy, 106 Iowa 483, 76 N.W. 805 (1898); State v. Penn, 45 N.C.App. 551, 263 S.E.2d 35 (1980).

20. State v. Meadows, 18 W.Va. 658 (1881). See also Rex v. Boyce, 1 Moody 29, 168 Eng.Rep. 1172 (1824); People v. Dahlberg, 225 Ill. 485, 80 N.E. 310 (1907).

21. People v. Smith, 217 Mich. 669, 674, 187 N.W. 304, 305 (1922).

22. Hibbard v. United States, 172 F. 66, 96 C.C.A. 554 (7th Cir. 1909); People v. Mize, 80 Cal. 41, 45, 22 P. 80, 81 (1889); People v. Anderson, 95 Cal.App. 225, 229, 272 P. 755, 756 (1928). Where a specific intent is required for guilt it is prejudicial error to instruct in terms of intent or criminal negligence. Schneider v. United States, 192 F.2d 498 (9th Cir. 1951).

Specific intent may, and ordinarily must, be proved by circumstantial evidence. State v. Oldham, 92 Idaho 124, 438 P.2d 275 (1968). It must be proved "as an independent fact." Sullateskee v. State, 428 P.2d 736 (Okl.Cr.1967). (Syllabus by the court.)

23. Chrisman v. State, 54 Ark. 283, 285, 15 S.W. 889, 890 (1891).

24. People v. Mize, 80 Cal. 41, 45, 22 P. 80, 81 (1889); People v. Markos, 146 Cal.App.2d 82, 303 P.2d 363 (1956); Banovitch v. Commonwealth, 196 Va. 210, 216, 83 S.E.2d 369, 373 (1954).

25. Simpson v. State, 81 Fla. 292, 296, 87 So. 920 (1921); People v. Sweeney, 55 Mich. 586, 589, 22 N.W. 50, 51, 52 (1885). The word "presumed" is sometimes used to mean inferred as a matter of fact from what was done. See Banovitch v. Commonwealth, 196 Va. 210, 216, 83 S.E.2d 369, 373 (1954).

The presumption of knowledge of the law cannot be used "to prove that the defendant voluntarily and intentionally violated a known legal duty." United States v. Davis, 583 F.2d 190, 193 (5th Cir. 1978).

26. Meadowcroft v. People, 163 Ill. 56, 45 N.E. 303 (1896); State v. Buck, 120 Mo. 479, 25 S.W. 573 (1894).

A. FRAUD

Fraud may make its appearance at different points in a criminal case, as for example when consent of the other person is urged as a defense but is found to have been induced by the defendant's fraudulent misrepresentations.[27] At the moment, however, it is important only insofar as it enters into the mens-rea requirement of certain offenses as is true whenever this element is included in the definition of a crime,—the typical illustrations being forgery and false pretenses. The word "fraudulent," when found in the definition of a crime, signifies "an intent to defraud" and whether the word or the phrase is employed in a particular instance is largely a matter of personal preference.[28] The point to be emphasized is that any crime which requires fraud for its perpetration is one which includes a specific intent whether or not the word "intent" is found in the definition.

An intent to deceive is not limited to an intent to cause financial loss but includes an intent to cause other types of harm. Thus a telegram falsely telling a man his son was dead supported conviction under a statute against causing a false message by telegram with intent to deceive, injure or defraud.[29]

SECTION 4. OTHER PARTICULAR STATES OF MIND

As mentioned above, if the mens-rea requirement of an offense is a state of mind other than an intent to do the *actus reus*, and not distinctly less than such intent (such as criminal negligence, for example), it may be referred to as a special mental element. Brief reference will be made to the more common states of mind within this category which do not belong properly under the specific-intent label.

A. CORRUPTION

The word "corruption" indicates impurity or debasement and when found in the criminal law it means depravity or gross impropriety.

An intent to defraud is a corrupt state of mind but the word is not needed in such cases because "fraud" is adequately expressive itself. On the other hand, a design to acquire any unlawful gain or advantage is corrupt and will ordinarily carry this label if fraud is not involved.[1] Thus it is corrupt for an

---

27. Consent induced by fraud may or may not constitute a defense to the charge of crime depending upon the nature of the offense and the type of fraud. See chapter 9, section 3.

28. Forgery, for example, is defined by use of the word "fraudulent" by one author. Miller, Criminal Law 404 (1934). Some authors prefer the phrase "an intent to defraud" in this definition. Clark & Marshall, Law of Crimes 951 (7th ed. 1967).

"To defraud means to deprive a person of property or interest, estate or right by fraud, deceit or artifice." State v.

Jarmin, 84 Nev. 187, 438 P.2d 250, 252 (1968).

Declarations made with reckless indifference for the truth may be viewed as fraudulent. United States v. Amrep Corp., 560 F.2d 539 (2d Cir. 1977).

29. People v. Tolstoy, 250 Cal.App.2d 22, 58 Cal.Rptr. 148 (1967).

1. See State v. Johnson, 77 Ohio St. 461, 467–8, 83 N.E. 702, 703–4 (1908).

"In this case, the word 'corruptly' means willfully, knowingly and with the specific intent to influence a juror to abrogate his or her legal duties as a petit

officer to accept a fee to which he knows he is not entitled by law,[2] or to accept private compensation offered for the purpose of influencing his official action. It is corrupt for an officer to accept such compensation, let it be emphasized, even if he does not intend that it shall influence his action. Thus a legislator who took money under his agreement to "work to kill" a certain bill on the floor of the senate was guilty of bribery although he was not in favor of it and had intended from the first to oppose it.[3] The fact that it may be possible at times to separate the intent itself from the element of depravity possibly associated therewith was emphasized from another point of view by the Michigan court:[4]

"If the position of the prosecutor was that he had been to trouble and expense in getting ready for trial, he would have had a right to demand as a condition to giving his consent that the county be reimbursed for what it had expended. The offer of money by respondent under these circumstances would have been for the purpose of influencing the action of the prosecuting attorney, and yet it would not have been a corrupt offer."

The Tennessee bribery statute provides punishment for an officer who "corruptly" accepts any gift, and so forth. It was properly held that the officer's act in pretending to go along with a scheme in order to get evidence of crime was not corrupt and hence not in violation of the law.[5]

B. MALICE

The malice concept is exceedingly useful despite its disparagement by those who have failed to understand it,[6] and despite some unfortunate statements made in the effort to explain it.[7] In the consideration of such offenses as murder, mayhem, arson, libel and malicious mischief, it was necessary to explore this concept in such detail that no more than a summary is warranted here.

juror." United States v. Jackson, 607 F.2d 1219, 1221 (8th Cir. 1979).

"In other words . . . an endeavor to influence a juror in the performance of his or her duty or to influence, obstruct or impede the due administration of justice is per se unlawful and is tantamount to doing the act corruptly." United States v. Ogle, 613 F.2d 233, 238 (10th Cir. 1980).

"The common thread that runs through common law and statutory formulations of the crime of bribery is the element of corruption, breach of trust or violation of duty. It is the element of corruption that distinguishes a bribe from a legitimate payment for services." United States v. Zacher, 586 F.2d 912, 916 (2d Cir. 1978). "The requisite intent to sustain a conviction of bribery is that the official accept a thing corruptly." United States v. Evans, 572 F.2d 455, 481 (5th Cir. 1978).

2. Ex parte Montgomery, 244 Ala. 91, 12 So.2d 314 (1943).

3. Sims v. State, 131 Ark. 185, 198 S.W. 883 (1917).

4. People v. Bilitzke, 174 Mich. 329, 333, 140 N.W. 590, 591 (1913); People v. Vinokurow, 322 Mich. 26, 32, 33 N.W.2d 647, 650 (1948).

5. Woodson v. State, 579 S.W.2d 893 (Tenn.Cr.App.1979). Note that no such word as "intentionally," "purposely" or "knowingly" would properly express the culpability intended here.

6. For a more elaborate study of the malice concept than is feasible here see— A Re-examination of Malice Aforethought, 43 Yale L.J. 537 (1934).

7. Confusion rather than clarification results from a statement that malice aforethought is "any evil design in general; the dictate of a wicked, depraved, and malignant heart; . . ." 4 Bl. Comm. * 198. The same may be said of the ancient effort to express the phrase: "a heart void of social duty, and fatally bent on mischief." Mayes v. People, 106 Ill. 306, 314 (1883).

Any mystery supposed to be associated with this concept will disappear completely if two points are constantly kept in mind: First, that in the absence of justification, excuse or recognized mitigation, it is malicious to intend to do what constitutes the *actus reus* of the crime in question; second, that a state of mind *may be* malicious even without an actual intent to bring about such a result. The first of these is the one more likely to be overlooked whereas the chief difficulty in connection with the second is in finding the proper words to express it.

Despite clear recognition of the non-necessity of any element of hatred, spite, grudge or ill-will,[8] it seems frequently to be assumed that malice, as a jural concept, must involve intent *plus* some matter of aggravation whereas, in truth, the requirement is fully satisfied by intent *minus* any matter of exculpation or mitigation. "Malice," it was stated in a homicide case, "may also be said to exist (in a legal sense) whenever there has been a wrongful or intentional killing of another without lawful excuse or mitigating circumstances." [9] The element of provocation has played such a minor role in some of the non-homicide offenses that in speaking of them the most common definition of malice is that it means "a wrongful act done intentionally without just cause or excuse." [10] On the other hand where this element does enter in we find that "one who, under such provocation, kills or injures an animal trespassing in his enclosure, cannot be said to have done so maliciously . . . ." [11]

Although employed for other purposes at times,[12] references to malice as being "implied," "inferred," or "presumed" frequently mean no more than that the mental element required for conviction and known to the law as "malice" requires no more than the intentional doing of the *actus reus* in the absence of any circumstance of exculpation or recognized mitigation.[13] And apart from peculiarities of expression it is recognized that an intent to cause the particular harm involved in the crime in question, without justification, excuse or mitigation, is sufficient to meet the mens-rea requirement of such

---

8. Commonwealth v. Buckley, 148 Mass. 27, 28, 18 N.E. 577 (1888).

9. State v. Williams, 185 N.C. 643, 666, 116 S.E. 570, 582 (1923). The word "wrongful" in the quotation is obviously not needed because any unexcused killing is wrongful.

"In a prosecution for murder, the term maliciously has been defined as willfully doing a wrongful act without just cause or excuse." State v. Dargatz, 228 Kan. 322, 614 P.2d 430, 438 (1980).

10. State v. Kinder, 184 Mo. 276, 296, 83 S.W. 964, 969 (1904); Alt v. State, 88 Neb. 259, 267, 129 N.W. 432, 436 (1911); State v. Murphy, 86 S.C. 268, 270, 68 S.E. 570 (1910); Keith v. State, 89 Tex.Cr.R. 264, 267, 232 S.W. 321, 323 (1921). And see Meraz v. Valencia, 28 N.M. 174, 178, 210 P. 225, 227 (1922); Sall v. State, 157 Neb. 688, 695, 61 N.W.2d 256, 261 (1953). The Nebraska case involved mayhem un-

der a statute which included the word "purposely."

"Malice is the deliberate intentional doing of a wrongful act without just cause or excuse." State v. Wraggs, 496 S.W.2d 38, 40 (Mo.App.1973).

11. Thomas v. State, 30 Ark. 433, 435 (1875). And see Mosely v. State, 28 Ga. 190, 192 (1859); State v. Martin, 141 N.C. 832, 839, 53 S.E. 874, 876 (1906).

12. The reference may be to the fact that often an unstated intent may "be inferred from acts committed." Stevens v. State, 42 Tex.Cr.R. 154, 173, 59 S.W. 545, 549 (1900). Or a true presumption may be intended. Miranda v. State, 42 Ariz. 358, 364, 26 P.2d 241, 243 (1933).

13. See, for example, Smith v. District of Columbia, 12 App.D.C. 33, 36 (1879); State v. Ward, 127 Minn. 510, 514, 150 N.W. 209, 211 (1914); State v. Davis, 88 S.C. 229, 238, 70 S.E. 811, 815 (1911).

offenses as murder,[14] mayhem,[15] libel,[16] malicious mischief,[17] or a statutory offense including the element of malice.[18]

Constant repetition of the fact that malice requires *no more* than an intent to do the *actus reus*, in the absence of any circumstance of exculpation or mitigation, must not obscure the fact that it does not actually require such an intent. In the absence of any circumstance of exculpation or mitigation an act may be done with such heedless disregard of a harmful result, foreseen as a likely possibility, that it differs little in the scale of moral blameworthiness from an actual intent to cause such harm. At times such a state of mind is said to be "the same as if defendant had deliberately intended the act committed," [19] which is quite inaccurate and misleading as an abstract assertion but is one way of expressing the fact that it is sufficient to meet the requirements of "malice." Another method is to suggest that while such an act is not done with an actual intent to cause the harm, it is "constructively with a malicious intention." [20] Thus one may be guilty of murder for death caused by shooting regardless of consequences into a house,[21] or a room,[22] or a train,[23] or an automobile,[24] in which others are known to be at the time. "If he did this," said one court in a case of this nature, "not with the design of killing anyone, but for his diversion merely, he is guilty of murder." [25] And one may be guilty of other offenses for which malice is required, such as arson [26] or malicious mischief,[27] for example, although he did not intend the resulting harm but acted under such circumstances that there was a plain and strong likelihood that it might happen.

The fact that malice does not require an actual intent to cause the *actus reus* has been well understood, but since it definitely requires something

14. 4 Bl.Comm. * 201; State v. Williams, 185 N.C. 643, 666, 116 S.E. 570, 582 (1923).

15. Worley v. State, 30 Tenn. 172 (1850); Terrell v. State, 86 Tenn. 523, 8 S.W. 212 (1888). In the Worley case a master had castrated his slave, not out of spite or ill-will, but to reform him.

16. State v. Mason, 26 Or. 273, 38 P. 130 (1894); Williams v. Hicks Printing Co., 159 Wis. 90, 150 N.W. 183 (1914). In the latter case it was said: ". . . perpetration of the act without lawful excuse—is sufficient." Id. at 101, 150 N.W. at 187.

17. State v. Boies, 68 Kan. 167, 74 P. 630 (1903).

18. Commonwealth v. Buckley, 148 Mass. 27, 18 N.E. 577 (1888).

19. Pool v. State, 87 Ga. 526, 530–1, 13 S.E. 556, 557 (1891).

20. Per Lush, J., in Regina v. Pembliton, 12 Cox C.C. 607, 611 (1874).

21. People v. Jernatowski, 238 N.W. 188, 144 N.E. 497 (1924); State v. Gill, 3 Or.App. 488, 474 P.2d 23 (1970).

22. State v. Capps, 134 N.C. 622, 46 S.E. 730 (1904).

Shooting at police station and killing a police officer standing outside. Ridyolph v. State, 545 S.W.2d 784 (Tex.Cr.App. 1977).

23. Banks v. State, 85 Tex.Cr.R. 165, 211 S.W. 217 (1919).

24. Davis v. State, 106 Tex.Cr.R. 300, 292 S.W. 220 (1927).

25. Brown v. Commonwealth, 13 Ky. Law Rep. 372, 373, 17 S.W. 220, 221 (1891).

26. Isaac's Case, 2 East P.C. 1031 (1799); State v. Lauglin, 53 N.C. 354 (1861).

27. Porter v. State, 83 Miss. 23, 35 So. 218 (1903); The Queen v. Welch, 1 Q.B.D. 23 (1875). "The jury might have found that he did intend actually to break the window or constructively to do so, as that he knew that the stone might probably break it when he threw it." Regina v. Pembliton, 12 Cox C.C. 607, 611 (1874). The same is true of mayhem, Kennedy v. State, 223 Ark. 915, 270 S.W.2d 912 (1954), unless the statute in the jurisdiction requires a specific intent. Banovitch v. Commonwealth, 196 Va. 210, 83 S.E.2d 369 (1954).

more than recklessness [28] there has been some difficulty in expressing just what is needed in this regard. To emphasize that malice requires a greater kind of social fault than is involved in the term "recklessness," and yet does not require an actual intent to cause the resulting harm, courts have resorted to such expressions as "absolute recklessness," [29] "a reckless indifference whether" the harm was caused or not,[30] a dangerous act "done so recklessly or wantonly as to evince depravity of mind and a disregard" of consequences,[31] or done with "knowledge of such circumstances that according to common experience there is a plain and strong likelihood that" a certain type of social harm will ensue.[32]

In other words the state of mind required for malice, when less than an actual intent to cause the *actus reus* of the crime in question includes a vicious or callous disregard of the likelihood of such harm resulting from what is being done; and it is this viciousness or callousness which distinguishes malice from recklessness.[33] The contrast used by way of illustration in the discussion of the latter topic was a hunter shooting through a dwelling house with a high-power rifle, neither knowing nor caring whether harm should result, and a motorist traveling too fast on an icy pavement with full awareness of the risk involved but hoping no harm would result and trying to avoid an accident by all means other than a reduction of speed. The hunter is acting with a "wanton and wilful" disregard of an obvious human risk and hence with malice aforethought; the motorist is driving recklessly.

Some seem to have been disturbed by the thought that malice, as a jural concept, changes its meaning from crime to crime, but this is no more true of malice that it is of intent. An intent to steal will not satisfy the mens-rea requirement of an attempt to murder, and for the same reason a state of mind which would constitute the element of malice needed for murder is not sufficient if the crime charged is malicious mischief.[34] In the discussion of homicide the phrase "person-endangering-state-of-mind" was given an arbitrarily-assigned meaning which included an intent to kill or inflict great bodily injury, and also an intent to do an act which was obviously likely to produce such a result. And if a corresponding meaning is arbitrarily assigned to the other phrases here employed it may be said—assuming in each instance the absence of any element of justification, excuse or recognized miti-

28. Jones v. People, 98 Colo. 190, 54 P.2d 686 (1936). Homicide resulting from criminal negligence, for example, is not murder but manslaughter because it is without malice.

29. Porter v. State, 83 Miss. 23, 26, 35 So. 218 (1903).

30. People v. Jernatowski, 238 N.Y. 188, 192, 144 N.E. 497, 498 (1924).

31. State v. Capps, 134 N.C. 622, 629, 46 S.E. 730, 732 (1904).

32. Per Holmes, C. J., in Commonwealth v. Chance, 174 Mass. 245, 252, 54 N.E. 551, 554 (1899).

33. "This killing was, therefore, murder, for malice in the sense of a wicked disposition is evidenced by the intentional doing of an uncalled-for act in callous disregard of its likely harmful effects on others." Commonwealth v. Malone, 354 Pa. 180, 188, 47 A.2d 445, 449 (1946). "Malice may be inferred from the wanton and reckless conduct of one who kills another from wicked disregard of the consequences of his acts. . . ." Commonwealth v. McLaughlin, 293 Pa. 218, 222, 142 A. 213, 215 (1928). While guilt of manslaughter requires more than "the slight negligence which will support a civil action for damages," it does not require "proof of acts or omissions exhibiting *reckless, wicked* and *wanton* disregard of the safety of others." This would constitute malice aforethought. Commonwealth v. Aurick, 342 Pa. 282, 289, 290, 19 A.2d 920, 923, 924 (1941); Fuentes v. State, 349 A.2d 1 (Del.1980).

34. Rex v. Kelly, 1 Craw. & D. 186 (Ireland, 1832).

gation—that what is needed for malice is (1) a person-endangering-state-of-mind for murder, (2) a property-endangering-state-of-mind for malicious mischief, (3) a dwelling-endangering-by-fire-state-of-mind for arson, (4) a defaming-state-of-mind for libel, and so forth.

In brief, malice in the legal sense imports (1) the absence of all elements of justification, excuse or recognized mitigation, and (2) the presence of either (a) an actual intent to cause the particular harm which is produced or harm of the same general nature, or (b) the wanton and wilful doing of an act with awareness of a plain and strong likelihood that such harm may result.

It is the course of caution to call attention to the fact that malice is a matter of mind however convenient it may be to speak in terms of the absence of circumstances of justification, excuse or mitigation. It is a psychical fact which represents the particular kind of mens rea or mind at fault required for guilt of certain offenses. For example, a person-endangering-state-of-mind is not malice aforethought if there are circumstances of justification, excuse or mitigation; but such a state of mind in the presence of such circumstances is a different psychical fact than it would be if they were wanting. An intent to kill, to give a very limited illustration, may be the same intent in a certain sense, whether it is (a) for self-preservation, (b) formed in a sudden rage engendered by great provocation, or (c) part of a well-laid plan for financial gain; but the psychical fact in its totality is not the same in any two of these. Furthermore the appraisal or evaluation of appearances is also a psychical fact. Hence an intent to kill for the purpose of self-defense under circumstances in which there is reasonable ground for believing this drastic step to be necessary, is psychically different from an intent to kill in self-defense when there is nothing to warrant such a belief. Obviously the state of mind of one having knowledge of important facts is different than it would be if these facts were unknown; and the killing of an actual felon under circumstances sufficient to justify the homicide, had the facts been known, was said not to constitute a justification or excuse in favor of one who did not know or have any reason to believe that the other was a felon.[35] And a shot that saves the life of the shooter is with malice aforethought if fired with no knowledge or thought of the pending danger.[36]

The Model Penal Code does not use "malice" because those who formulated the Code had a blind prejudice against the word. This is very regrettable because it represents a useful concept despite some unfortunate language employed at times in the effort to express it. Thus the recurring phrase "abandoned and malignant heart" seems more suggestive of cardiac tumor than a state of mind; and in the homicide cases there has been distortion by certain additions such as the felony-murder rule, which additions are quite foreign to the concept itself. Basically malice, as a legal concept, is made up of two components, one positive and the other negative. On the positive side malice requires an intent to cause particular harm (such as to take human life, if the crime is murder; to burn another's dwelling, if the crime is arson; to publish defamation of another, if the crime is libel), or an intent to act with wanton and wilful disregard of the obvious likelihood of causing such

35. People v. Burt, 51 Mich. 199, 202, 16 N.W. 378, 379 (1883).

36. Trogdon v. State, 133 Ind. 1, 32 N.E. 725 (1892). Accord, Josey v. United States, 77 App.D.C. 321, 135 F.2d 809 (1943). And see infra section 8.

harm. On the negative side it requires the absence of any circumstance of justification, excuse or recognized mitigation.[37]

We shall have some rather astounding concepts under the Code such as "justifiable murder" or—even more absurd—"justifiable criminal mischief." Because of the prejudice against the word it was felt necessary to avoid the customary label of malicious mischief. The Code provides that a person is guilty of criminal mischief if he "damages tangible property of another purposely . . . ." although elsewhere it is provided that such conduct is justifiable under certain circumstances such as under "the judgment of a competent court."[38] Had the offense been worded in terms of "malicious mischief," with an appropriate definition, any damage to the property of another under circumstances of justification or excuse would have been excluded.

C. KNOWLEDGE (SCIENTER)

It has been said that "the general rule at common law was that *scienter* was a necessary element . . . of every crime."[39] As so used the term is a synonym of mens rea and this usage makes it unsuitable for the present discussion although it has also been employed at times as a synonym of knowledge.

It is often said, in substance, that "when the statute is silent . . . concerning the knowledge of the defendant, the indictment need not allege . . . such knowledge."[40] Although literally true, such a statement in-

---

37. The following instruction was approved. "Maliciously means willfully doing a wrongful act without just cause or excuse. It requires the absence of any circumstance of justification, mitigation or excuse." State v. Cobb, 229 Kan. 522, 625 P.2d 1133, 1136 (1981).

38. Section 202.3 deals with "criminal mischief" and section 3.03 describes certain types of justifiable conduct. Another type of justification is provided in section 3.10.

The common law provides for justifiable homicide but has no such concept as justifiable murder—and there should be none. But the Code in attempting to define murder without use of the word malice would introduce such an objectionable concept. Section 201.1 provides: "(1) A person is guilty of criminal homicide if he purposely, knowingly, recklessly or negligently causes the death of another human being." Section 210.2 provides: "(1) Except as provided in Section 210.3(1)(b) [voluntary manslaughter], criminal homicide constitutes murder when:

(a) it is committed purposely or knowingly; . . . ."

It is to be noted that the only exception to the statement that the killing of another human being is murder if committed

purposely or knowingly is if it is committed under circumstances amounting to voluntary manslaughter. The mention of this exception emphasizes the lack of any other. Yet under Article 3 of the Code there are various situations in which the killing would be justifiable despite the fact that it was done purposely or knowingly—such as execution (3.03), self-defense (3.04) or law enforcement (3.07).

39. United States v. Balint, 258 U.S. 250, 251, 42 S.Ct. 301 (1922).

See Waterman v. State, 114 Ga. 262, 264, 40 S.E. 262, 264 (1901); Siegel, Cooper & Co. v. People, 85 Ill.App. 301, 303 (1899); Carver v. People, 39 Mich. 786, 787 (1878); State v. Pickus, 63 S.D. 209, 220, 257 N.W. 284, 289 (1934).

40. State v. Taylor, 130 W.Va. 74, 82, 42 S.E.2d 549, 555 (1947); United States v. Purvis, 580 F.2d 853 (5th Cir. 1978).

In the words of the Supreme Court: "If the offense is a statutory one, and intent or knowledge is not made an element of it, the indictment need not charge such knowledge or intent." United States v. Behrman, 258 U.S. 280, 288, 42 S.Ct. 303, 304 (1922). See State v. Masters, 106 W.Va. 46, 48–49, 144 S.E. 718 (1928); State v. Pennington, 41 W.Va. 599, 23 S.E. 918 (1896).

cludes a negative inference and has resulted in an unwarranted assumption—both false. The negative inference is that in charging a common-law crime it would be necessary to allege knowledge even if the definition makes no reference thereto; the unwarranted assumption has been that if knowledge need not be alleged it could be of no advantage to defendant to prove he did not know.

The relation of knowledge to guilt is a highly variable factor. At one extreme is found the type of offense for which knowledge of some particular matter is required for guilt by the very definition of the crime itself; as, uttering a forged instrument with knowledge of the forgery, receiving stolen property knowing it to have been stolen, knowingly and designedly obtaining the property of another by false pretenses, with intent to defraud, receipt of deposit by a banker knowing that his bank is insolvent, or transportation of a vehicle in interstate commerce, knowing it to have been stolen. At the other extreme is found the type (which should be restricted to the so-called civil offenses) [41] in connection with which the element of knowledge or lack of knowledge is so immaterial [42] that conviction may result although the defendant acted under such a mistake that, had the facts been as he reasonably supposed them to be, his conduct would have been acceptable in every respect.[43] Such "offenses" are within the category which does not include the normal mens rea, and are not true crimes. Between these two extremes are found offenses for guilt of which the matter of knowledge cannot be ignored although the definitions themselves contain no specific requirement thereof. This is because knowledge or lack of knowledge may be among the determining factors of some other attitude of mind, which is required, such as intent,[44] wilfulness,[45] malice,[46] recklessness,[47] or criminal negligence.[48]

41. See the following section.

42. Commonwealth v. Ober, 286 Mass. 25, 30, 189 N.E. 601, 603 (1934); State v. Whitman, 52 S.D. 91, 93, 216 N.W. 858, 859 (1927).

43. Thus a conviction of serving oleomargarine at a lunch counter was upheld although defendant was a waiter in charge of the counter who supposed the substance was butter. Welch v. State, 145 Wis. 86, 129 N.W. 656 (1911). See also the cases cited in the preceding note.

44. One is not guilty of removing property on which there was a lien with intent to defraud the lienholder if he had no knowledge of the lien. Jones v. State, 113 Ala. 95, 21 So. 229 (1897); Dolph v. State, 111 Miss. 668, 71 So. 911 (1916). The statute which provides for the punishment of every person who, with intent to defraud, utters any forged obligation of the United States, requires knowledge of the forgery even though the statute does not specifically mention "knowledge." United States v. Carll, 105 U.S. 611, (1881). "One cannot intend to steal property which he believes to be his own," even if he is careless in not knowing that it belongs to another. People v. Devine, 95 Cal. 227, 231, 30 P. 378, 379 (1892).

"In order to establish the statutory requirement of intent, the government's evidence must show that Staller had knowledge that the bills were counterfeit." United States v. Staller, 616 F.2d 1284, 1292 (5th Cir. 1980).

45. Spurr v. United States, 174 U.S. 728, 19 S.Ct. 812 (1899); Commonwealth v. Brady, 71 Mass. 78 (1855). "To establish a willful or wanton injury it is necessary to show that one with knowledge of existing conditions, and conscious from such knowledge that injury will likely or probably result from his conduct, and with reckless indifference to the consequences, consciously and intentionally does some wrongful act or omits to discharge some duty which produces the injurious result." Staub v. Public Service Ry., 97 N.J.L. 297, 300, 117 A. 48, 49–50 (1922); State v. Gooze, 14 N.J.Super. 277, 282–3, 81 A.2d 811, 814 (1951).

46. In a prosecution for malicious mischief for having cut down a tree on a neighbor's land, malice was disproved by showing that defendant did not know the tree was on the far side of the boundary

47–48. See notes 47–48 on page 863.

From the standpoint of the prosecution (leaving out of consideration those "offenses" which have no normal mens-rea requirement) knowledge may be a positive factor or the want of knowledge may be a negative factor. In some prosecutions the state must prove defendant's knowledge of some particular matter to make out even a prima-facie case of guilt.[49] "Such knowledge may be proven, like any other fact, by circumstantial evidence." [50] It "may be established from all the facts and circumstances of the case, although . . . denied by a defendant;" [51] but the "burden is on the State." [52] In other prosecutions the want of knowledge may be "peculiarly a matter of defence" [53]—the prosecution has no such burden as mentioned above, but this does not preclude the defendant from exculpating himself by showing that the lack of certain knowledge left his conduct blameless. Although in such a case "it is not necessary to aver in the indictment that the

line and that this fact was disclosed only by a subsequent survey. Wagstaff v. Schippel, 27 Kan. 450 (1882).

47. "A person acts recklessly with respect to a material element of an offense when he consciously disregards a substantial and unjustifiable risk . . . ." Model Penal Code § 2.02(2)(C).

48. Compare: Rineman v. State, 24 Ind. 80 (1865); Goetz v. State, 41 Ind. 162 (1872). Want of knowledge of a most important fact may be insufficient to negative criminal negligence in a particular case. Thus one who intentionally points a gun at another (without justification or excuse) and pulls the trigger, will be guilty of manslaughter if death results, even if he intended no harm and did not know the weapon was loaded. Rampton's Case, Kelyng 41, 84 Eng.Rep. 1073 (1664); State v. Hardy, 47 Iowa 647 (1878). But a fatal discharge resulting from the handling of a weapon not intentionally pointed at another will not necessarily amount to manslaughter. Fitzgerald v. State, 112 Ala. 34, 20 So. 966 (1895). In such a case, knowledge or lack of knowledge of the fact the gun was loaded might well be one of the factors to be considered on the question of criminal negligence.

49. Skarda v. State, 118 Ark. 176, 182, 175 S.W. 1190, 1192 (1915); Waterman v. State, 114 Ga. 262, 264, 40 S.E. 262, 263–4 (1901); Parker v. People, 97 Ill. 32, 38 (1880); People v. Tantenella, 212 Mich. 614, 619, 180 N.W. 474, 476 (1920). Where no change has been provided by statute, such knowledge must be alleged in the indictment. People v. Carmona, 80 Cal.App. 159, 164, 251 P. 315, 317, 318 (1926); Ham v. State, 118 Tex.Cr.R. 271, 40 S.W.2d 152 (1931).

"The requirement that the defendant act knowingly is an essential element of

first-degree assault." People v. Hardin, ___ Colo. ___, 607 P.2d 1291, 1294 (1980).

50. State v. Peeples, 71 Wash. 451, 453, 129 P. 108, 109 (1912). See also Meath v. State, 174 Wis. 80, 83, 182 N.W. 334, 335 (1921).

51. State v. Howard, 162 La. 719, 728, 111 So. 72, 75 (1927). Knowledge may be inferred by the jury from facts and circumstances which satisfy them of its existence. Katz v. United States, 281 F. 129 (6th Cir. 1922); Skarda v. State, 118 Ark. 719, 728, 175 S.W. 1190, 1192 (1915); Parker v. People, 97 Ill. 32, 38 (1880); People v. Tantenella, 212 Mich. 614, 621, 180 N.W. 474, 476 (1920). It is a matter of inference and not a true presumption. Blackett v. People, 98 Colo. 7, 17, 52 P.2d 389, 393 (1935); State v. Dunning, 130 Iowa 678, 681, 107 N.W. 927, 928 (1906); State v. Hatfield, 65 Wash. 550, 118 P. 735 (1911); State v. Peeples, 65 Wash. 673, 118 P. 906 (1911).

"Knowledge by the defendant of both the presence of the drug and its narcotic character is essential to establish unlawful transportation, sale, or possession of narcotics. . . . . Such knowledge may be shown by circumstantial evidence." Rideout v. Superior Court, 67 Cal.2d 474–75, 62 Cal.Rptr. 581, 583, 432 P.2d 197, 199 (1967).

The Model Penal Code provides a true presumption of knowledge by one who issues a "bad" check. Section 224.5.

52. State v. Sherman, 183 Iowa 42, 59–60, 166 N.W. 674, 680 (1918); McInerney v. Berman, 621 F.2d 20 (1st Cir. 1980).

53. Mergentheim v. State, 107 Ind. 567, 573, 8 N.E. 568, 571 (1886).

See also State v. Anklam, 43 Ariz. 362, 368, 31 P.2d 888, 890 (1934); State v. Cody, 111 N.C. 725, 16 S.E. 408 (1892).

offense was 'knowingly' or 'wilfully' committed, or to prove a guilty mind, and the commission of the act in itself prima facie imports an offence, yet the person charged may still discharge himself by proving to the satisfaction of the tribunal which tries him that in fact he had not a guilty mind." [54] Thus, innocence of the crime of malicious mischief could be established by showing that defendant did not know the tree he cut down was on his neighbor's land and that the fact of its being on the far side of the boundary was disclosed only by a subsequent survey.[55] An indictment for incest need not allege that defendant knew of the prohibited relationship between himself and the other,[56] but this should not be interpreted to mean that one charged with this offense for having married his niece could not exculpate himself by showing that he did not know or have reason to know that the woman was related to him in any degree.[57] And one charged with bigamy may defend by showing he had a bona-fide and well-grounded belief that his wife had divorced him although the state is not required to plead and prove that he knew the marriage relationship still existed.[58]

The explanation has been in such terms as, that if the offense charged has no special mental element, such as knowledge, the prosecution makes out a prima-facie case [59] by proof of the *actus reus* by defendant or that such proof raises a presumption [60] of guilt, thus placing upon the defendant

54. The King v. Ewart, 25 N.Z.L.R. 709 (1905); *accord*, State v. Hinkle, 129 W.Va. 393, 41 S.E.2d 107 (1946); State v. Sutter, 71 W.Va. 371, 76 S.E. 811 (1912).

Although guilty knowledge or intent to possess are not elements of the crime: "If the defendant can affirmatively establish his 'possession' was unwitting, then he had no possession for which the law will convict." State v. Cleppe, 96 Wn.2d 373, 635 P.2d 435, 439–40 (1981).

55. Wagstaff v. Schippel, 27 Kan. 450 (1882). It is not necessary for the accusatory pleading charging rescue to aver knowledge, although proof that defendant acted innocently, as by "giving a lift" to an escaping prisoner without knowing him to be such, would be exculpating. State v. Sutton, 170 Ind. 473, 83 N.E. 824 (1908).

56. People v. Koller, 142 Cal. 621, 76 P. 500 (1904). Compare a holding that although a defendant charged with rape as perpetrator could defend by proof of marriage to the alleged victim, it is not necessary to allege nonmarriage in the indictment. Commonwealth v. Fogerty, 74 Mass. 489 (1857). Under some statutes such an allegation would be required. See West's Ann.Cal.Pen.Code § 261 (1970).

57. In agreeing with a holding that an indictment need not allege defendant's knowledge of the prohibited relationship

the court added: "I must be allowed to doubt so much of that opinion as holds that knowledge of the relationship by the accused is not necessary." State v. Pennington, 41 W.Va. 599, 23 S.E. 918 (1896). See People v. Patterson, 102 Cal. 239, 242–43, 36 P. 436, 437 (1894) (dictum). Incest based upon illicit intercourse presents a different problem. State v. Dana, 59 Vt. 614, 622, 10 A. 727, 732 (1887).

58. People v. Vogel, 46 Cal.2d 798, 299 P.2d 850 (1956). Not all courts have made so sound an analysis of bigamy. United States v. Wisdom, 320 F.Supp. 286 (D.C.E.D.Tenn.1970), interpreting Illinois law. See infra Chapter 9, Section 1, C.

59. "[T]he commission of the act in itself *prima facie* imports an offence. . . ." The King v. Ewart, 25 N.Z.L.R. 709 (1905).

60. "*Mens rea* . . . will be presumed, until the defendant who is proven to have brought about the state of affairs, will have rebutted this presumption of his guilty mind." Mueller, Mens Rea and the Law Without It, 58 W.Va.L.Rev. 34, 63 (1955). "It is a fair presumption, then, in the absence of any evidence to the contrary, that there was present the guilty mind. . . ." Rex v. Wallendorf, So.Afr.L.R. [1920] App.Div. 383, 401, discussed in Blackwell, Mens Rea in Statutory Offenses II 77 S.A.L.J. 229 (1960).

the burden of introducing evidence to show that he in fact acted without mens rea.[61]

When knowledge is a positive factor, however,—when the crime is defined in such terms as "with knowledge" or "knowing"—the burden is upon the prosecution to prove the state of mind so indicated.[62]

The present discussion must be limited, for the most part, to knowledge as a positive factor, because to whatever extent it is not needed to make out a prima-facie case against the defendant, although his innocence can be established by proof of want of knowledge of some important fact, the problems can be handled to better advantage under the heading of "ignorance or mistake" dealt with in chapter nine, Section 1.

"Absolute knowledge can be had of very few things," [63] said the Massachusetts court, and the philosopher might add "if any." For most practical purposes "knowledge" "is not confined to what we have personally observed or to what we have evolved by our own cognitive faculties." [64] Even within the domain of the law itself the word is not always employed with exactly the same signification. Suppose a person has been told that a certain bill of exchange is a forgery and he believes the statement to be true. Does he have *knowledge* of this? Obviously not if the purpose of the inquiry is to determine whether he is qualified to take the witness stand and swear that the instrument is false; [65] but if he passes the bill as genuine he will be uttering a forged instrument with "knowledge" of the forgery if his belief is correct.[66] The need, therefore, is to search for the state of mind, or states of mind, which the courts have spoken of as "knowledge" for the purpose of a particular case.*

There is a trace of authority for the objective test of "knowledge" where this is required for guilt. That is, that one is regarded to have known what should have been known because a reasonable person in like circumstances would have known. Thus it has been said that

> the word "knowing" in its relation to receiving stolen goods means that, if a person has information from facts and circumstances which should convince him that property has been stolen, or which should lead a reasonable man to believe that property had been stolen, then in a legal sense he knew it.[67]

This is quite unsound. It may be within the legislative power to provide for the punishment of one who receives stolen property knowing it is stolen, or

61. Rex v. Banks, 1 Esp. 144, 170 Eng.Rep. 307 (1794); United States v. Mont, 306 F.2d 412, 416 (2d Cir. 1962). "In practice the essential burden is usually on the defense to come forward with some evidence which takes the accused out of the normal field of liability." Hughes, Criminal Omissions, 67 Yale L.J. 590, 606 (1958).

62. Mullaney v. Wilbur, 421 U.S. 684, 95 S.Ct. 1881 (1975).

63. Story v. Buffam, 90 Mass. 35, 38 (1864).

64. State v. Ransberger, 106 Mo. 135, 140, 17 S.W. 290, 292 (1891).

65. 2 Wigmore on Evidence § 657 (3d ed. 1940).

66. 1 Hale P.C. * 684–5. "This knowledge may come by two means, either of his own knowledge, or by the relation of another." 3 Co.Inst. * 171.

* By express permission the remainder of this subsection is adapted from Perkins, "Knowledge" As A Mens Rea Requirement, 29 Hastings L.J. 953 (1978).

67. Pettus v. State, 200 Miss. 397, 410, 27 So.2d 536, 540 (1946). The clear weight of authority is otherwise. See State v. Aschenbrenner, 171 Or. 664, 671, 138 P.2d 911, 914 (1943) (citing cases).

having reasonable cause to believe it is stolen,[68] but it is not proper to give this interpretation to a statute which speaks only in terms of "knowledge" or "knowing." [69] As said by Judge Learned Hand:

> The receivers of stolen goods almost never "know" that they have been stolen, in the sense that they could testify to it in a courtroom. The business could not be so conducted, for those who sell the goods—the "fences"—must keep up a more respectable front than is generally possible for the thieves. Nor are we to suppose that the thieves will ordinarily admit their theft to the receivers: that would much impair their bargaining power. For this reason, some decisions even go so far as to hold that it is enough, if a reasonable man in the receiver's position would have supposed that the goods were stolen. That we think is wrong; and the better law is otherwise, although of course, the fact that a reasonable man would have thought that they had been stolen, is some basis for finding that the accused actually did think so.[70]

This emphasizes both that "knowledge" or its equivalent as a mens-rea requirement must be determined by a subjective test and also that it does not require what is ordinarily meant by the word. Both points were emphasized also by the Massachusetts Supreme Court in reversing a conviction based on the objective test. It said:

> The infraction of this statute is not proved by negligence nor by failure to exercise as much intelligence as the ordinarily prudent man. The statute does not punish one too dull to realize that the goods which he bought honestly and in good faith had been stolen . . . . The knowledge or belief of the defendant must be personal to him and our statute furnishes no substitute or equivalent.[71]

In other words, it is not sufficient that one who receives stolen property does so under circumstances which should make him realize that it has been stolen, but if he receives it under the belief that it has been stolen, he has "knowledge" of this fact within the common-law interpretation.[72] The second point has been emphasized in various ways. "It is sufficient if the facts are such as to cause an actual belief that the property was stolen." [73] "That

---

68. E.g., Holmes v. State, 568 P.2d 317 (Okl.Cr.App.1977); Hutton v. State, 494 P.2d 1246 (Okl.Cr.App.1972). But see People v. Johnson, 193 Colo. 190, 564 P.2d 116 (1977) (such a statute unconstitutional). The legislature may validly define "knowledge" to include one who has information which would lead a reasonable person in the same situation to believe that the fact exists. State v. Van Antwerp, 22 Wn.App. 674, 591 P.2d 844 (1979), but see State v. Shipp, 93 Wn.2d 510, 610 P.2d 1322 (1980).

69. State v. Beale, 299 A.2d 921 (Me. 1973).

70. United States v. Werner, 160 F.2d 438, 441–42 (2d Cir. 1947) (footnotes omitted).

71. Commonwealth v. Boris, 317 Mass. 309, 315, 58 N.E.2d 8, 12 (1944).

Accord, Schaffer v. United States, 221 F.2d 17, 23 (5th Cir. 1955).

72. The question is what did the defendant know or believe. State v. Ebbeler, 283 Mo. 57, 222 S.W. 396 (1920).

73. Lewis v. State, 81 Okl.Cr. 168, 172, 162 P.2d 201, 203 (1945). See also Camp v. State, 66 Okl.Cr. 20, 23, 89 P.2d 378, 380 (1939). "[I]t is sufficient if the circumstances accompanying the transaction be such as to make the accused believe the goods had been stolen." People v. Rife, 382 Ill. 588, 596, 48 N.E.2d 367, 372 (1943). "Proof of actual or direct knowledge is not required, but facts and circumstances must be proved sufficient to create in the mind of the accused a belief that the goods were stolen." People v. Kohn, 290 Ill. 410, 418–19, 125 N.E. 293, 297 (1919). In a charge of receiving property stolen from interstate com-

guilty knowledge, or its equivalent, guilty belief, is of the gist of this offense, has been declared by many decisions . . . ." [74] And the same is true in case of other offenses having "knowledge" as the mens-rea requirement. Thus one "knowingly" obtained property by false pretenses if he knew or believed that his representation was false; [75] knowledge "or belief of the counterfeit character of the money is an essential element of the crime of passing counterfeit money . . ." [76] and belief of the forgery is sufficient for guilt of uttering a forged document.[77]

A recent Colorado case is of particular interest. A statute providing punishment for receiving property knowing it to be stolen was amended to read, "A person commits theft by receiving when he receives . . . anything of value of another knowing or believing . . . said thing had been stolen . . . ." This was held to authorize conviction of one who received property, believing it was stolen, although it never had been stolen.[78] The holding is quite logical. If it had been desired to punish the receiver who believed the property was stolen, only when it actually was stolen, no change in the statute was needed.

The holding that "knowledge," as a mens-rea concept, includes a guilty belief, does not exhaust its meaning. Circumstances sometimes cause a person to realize that what he plans to do may bring about a result which the law seeks to prevent. If he wilfully goes ahead with his plan, while deliberately refusing to find out about this, he is deemed at common law to have knowledge of what he would have known had he not made it a point not to know.[79] Such conduct has been designated in various ways, such as a "wilful shutting of the eyes," [80] "deliberate ignorance," [81] "studied ignorance," [82]

merce, it was held to be reversible error to charge that it was not necessary to prove that the defendant "actually knew" it was stolen property. United States v. Fields, 466 F.2d 119 (2d Cir. 1972). But this was to insist on the subjective test of knowledge rather than what is included within the term.

74. Meath v. State, 174 Wis. 80, 83, 182 N.W. 334, 335 (1921). The "question is whether from the circumstances *he*—not some other person—believed they had been stolen." State v. Alpert, 88 Vt. 191, 204, 92 A. 32, 37 (1914) (emphasis in original).

75. State v. Pickus, 63 S.D. 209, 230, 257 N.W. 284, 294 (1934).

76. Marson v. United States, 203 F.2d 904, 906 (6th Cir. 1953).

77. 1 Hale, Pleas of The Crown, * 684–85.

78. People v. Holloway, 193 Colo. 450, 568 P.2d 29 (1977).

79. The rule is that "if a party has his suspicion aroused but then deliberately omits to make further enquiries . . . he is deemed to have knowledge." G. Williams, Criminal Law: The General Part § 57, at 157 (2d ed. 1961). "Moreover, if a defendant did not learn what

the substance was because he deliberately chose not to learn so he could assert his ignorance if he was discovered with the substance in his possession, he is chargeable with knowledge." United States v. Moser, 509 F.2d 1089, 1092–93 (7th Cir. 1975).

80. "The jury have not found, either that the prisoner knew that the goods were Government stores, or that he wilfully shut his eyes to the fact." Regina v. Sleep, 8 Cox C.C. 472, 480 (1861). "We repeat also that lawyers cannot 'escape criminal liability on a plea of ignorance when they have shut their eyes to what was plainly to be seen.'" United States v. Frank, 494 F.2d 145, 152–53 (2d Cir. 1974) (quoting United States v. Benjamin, 328 F.2d 854, 863 (2d Cir. 1964)). "A banker receiving deposits of money cannot shut his eyes to his own financial status, and he is required to investigate conditions which are suggested by circumstances already known to him." State v. Drew, 110 Minn. 247, 250, 124 N.W. 1091, 1092 (1910). "He could not shut his eyes to information in his bank and falsely represent a fact with the intention to defraud and cheat . . . ."

81–82. See notes 81–82 on page 868.

"purposely abstaining from all inquiry as to the facts," [83] "avoidance of any endeavor to know," [84] "a conscious purpose to avoid learning the truth," [85] and "deliberately chose not to learn." [86] Whatever the particular form of expression, the intent is to make clear that, within the present context, the common law holds that one knew what he would have known if he had not deliberately avoided knowing.

State v. Linter, 141 Kan. 505, 509, 41 P.2d 1036, 1038–39 (1935). "If you find . . . either that the defendant knew that she was helping a cocaine transaction, or that she had a conscious purpose to avoid finding out the identity of the substance so as to close her eyes to the facts, you could find sufficient evidence to find her guilty . . ." was a proper instruction. United States v. Dozier, 522 F.2d 224, 226 (2d Cir. 1975). It "is recognized that one may not deliberately close his eyes to what otherwise would have been obvious to him." United States v. Squires, 440 F.2d 859, 864 (2d Cir. 1971). "The element of knowledge may be satisfied by proof that a defendant deliberately closed his eyes to what otherwise would have been obvious to him." United States v. Jacobs, 475 F.2d 270, 287 n. 37 (2d Cir. 1973). "We think . . . the Government can meet its burden by proving that a defendant deliberately closed his eyes to facts he had a duty to see . . . ." United States v. Benjamin, 328 F.2d 854, 862 (2d Cir. 1964). "No person can intentionally avoid knowledge by closing his eyes to facts which prompt him to investigate . . . ." United States v. Grizaffi, 471 F.2d 69, 75 (7th Cir. 1972), quoted in United States v. Joyce, 499 F.2d 9, 23 (7th Cir. 1974). "[T]he purpose in cases such as this was to prevent an individual . . . from circumventing criminal sanctions merely by deliberately closing his eyes to the obvious risk that he is engaging in unlawful conduct." United States v. Sarantos, 455 F.2d 877, 881 (2d Cir. 1972). "Construing 'knowingly' in a criminal statute to include wilful blindness to the existence of a fact is no radical concept in the law." United States v. Thomas, 484 F.2d 909, 913 (6th Cir. 1973).

81. United States v. Jewel, 532 F.2d 697, 702 (9th Cir. 1976).

"Such deliberate ignorance is the same as knowledge for purposes of conviction under § 841(a)(1). United States v. Meneses-Davila, 580 F.2d 888, 896 (5th Cir. 1978). (Possession of marijuana with intent to distribute.)

"In this situation, deliberate ignorance suffices for knowledge for purposes of conviction under § 841(a)(1)." United States v. Villalon, 605 F.2d 937, 939 (5th Cir. 1979).

"This Court has recognized that in cases where knowledge is an essential element, specific knowledge is not always necessary; rather, purposeful ignorance may suffice." United States v. Aulet, 618 F.2d 182, 190 (2d Cir. 1980).

82. "[T]hose who traffic in heroin will inevitably become aware that the product they deal in is smuggled, unless they practice a studied ignorance to which they are not entitled." Turner v. United States, 396 U.S. 398, 417, 90 S.Ct. 642, 653 (1970) (footnotes omitted). "Appellant concedes that 'studied ignorance' of a fact may, under decisions of the Supreme Court and of this court, constitute an awareness of so high a probability of the existence of the fact to justify the inference of knowledge of it." United States v. Joly, 493 F.2d 672, 675 (2d Cir. 1974) (quoted with approval in United States v. Dozier, 522 F.2d 224, 227 (2d Cir. 1975)).

83. State v. Rupp, 96 Kan. 446, 449, 151 P. 1111, 1112 (1915).

84. People v. Sugarman, 216 App.Div. 209, 215, 215 N.Y.S. 56, 63 (1926), aff'd 243 N.Y. 638, 154 N.E. 637 (1926).

85. United States v. Sarantos, 455 F.2d 877, 882 (2d Cir. 1972); United States v. Egenberg, 441 F.2d 441, 444 (2d Cir. 1971); United States v. Abrams, 427 F.2d 86, 91 (2d Cir. 1970).

86. United States v. Moser, 509 F.2d 1089, 1092–93 (7th Cir. 1975); United States v. Llanes, 374 F.2d 712, 716 (2d Cir. 1967) ("conscious purpose to avoid learning the source of the heroin.") "While negligence is not sufficient to charge a person with knowledge, one may not wilfully and intentionally remain ignorant of a fact, important and material to his conduct, and thereby escape punishment." Griego v. United States, 298 F.2d 845, 849 (10th Cir. 1962) (footnote omitted).

Deliberate avoidance of knowledge may also take another form. One having a silver candlestick he desires to sell, might realize that he does not have the slightest notion whether it is solid silver or merely a plated article. But desiring to obtain a very substantial sum for it, he takes pains not to find out, and desiring to forestall any investigation, he assures the purchaser that it is solid sterling silver. If it turns out to be a cheap plated article, he is held to have knowingly and designedly obtained money by false pretenses.[87] As said in a similar case:

> Ethically there appears to be little difference when a man makes a false representation for the purpose of inducing another to act for his benefit between the quality of conduct of the man who knows or believes his representation is false and that of the man who has neither knowledge nor belief concerning it, but nevertheless makes the representation, neither knowing nor caring whether it be true or false.[88]

In one case it was held that the "jury need only find that the defendant acted 'with reckless disregard of whether the statement . . . was true' or that appellant 'acted with a conscious purpose to avoid learning the truth.' " [89] No doubt the court was thinking of a situation comparable to our hypothetical seller of the silver candlestick,[90] but the word "reckless" added an element of inconsistency, at least to the extent of possibly leading the jury to believe that guilt could be established on a negligence basis, which is improper when "knowledge" is required. In place of "reckless" it would have been better if the court had used "wilful." In any event the court should make clear that it is referring to one who purposely purports to know what he realizes he does not know. That would be deliberate deception.[91] In a case which probably has the best-reasoned opinion on the point, the court reversed a conviction based on what was in substance a "reckless disregard" instruction.[92]

It is unfortunate that the word "knowledge" has been used to express this particular type of mens rea because it has an artificial meaning here at variance not only with its customary signification but also with its import

---

87. See Edwards, The Criminal Degrees of Knowledge, 17 Mod.L.Rev. 294 (1954).

88. State v. Pickus, 63 S.D. 209, 230, 257 N.W. 284, 294 (1934).

89. United States v. Egenberg, 441 F.2d 441, 444 (2d Cir. 1971). "These matters, with other evidence in the case, made a question for the jury whether defendant uttered such representations, knowing them to be false, or (which is tantamount to knowledge of falsity) recklessly and without information justifying a belief that they were true." People v. Cummings, 123 Cal. 269, 271–72, 55 P. 898, 899 (1899). Accord, Rand v. Commonwealth, 176 Ky. 343, 355, 195 S.W. 802, 808 (1917).

90. In a later case the court did not disapprove of the instruction in Egenberg, stating that the two clauses mean the same thing. It said it would have

been better if the connective had been "and" rather than "or." United States v. Sarantos, 455 F.2d 877, 882 (2d Cir. 1972).

91. If "he created the impression that he believed something to be true, when in fact he had no such belief on the subject, he has deceived . . . ." Model Penal Code § 206.2, comment (Tent.Draft No. 2, 1954).

92. State v. Pickus, 63 S.D. 209, 257 N.W. 284 (1934). The instruction was: "But making a statement that is in fact false recklessly without information to justify a belief in its truth is equivalent to making a statement knowing it to be false." Id. at 221, 257 N.W. at 289–90. The court said, "Just what the court may have meant or just what the jury may have understood by the word 'recklessly' in the instruction offers an almost unlimited field for speculation and conjecture." Id. at 228, 257 N.W. at 293.

when used elsewhere in the law,—as in determining whether a witness is qualified to testify with reference to a particular matter, as mentioned above. Further confusion is invited because, while extremely rare, it is possible to find "knowledge" with its usual meaning employed as a mens-rea requirement. Misprision of felony, it has been held, requires actual knowledge of the crime and not mere belief based upon hearsay,[93]—an interpretation due, it may be, to a desire to restrict the scope of this offense where it has not been permitted to pass into oblivion.[94] Apart from some such very rare exception, the meaning of "knowledge" as a mens-rea requirement may be summarized in outline form:

"Knowledge"
(1) **Guilty knowledge. Awareness of the fact as a result of personal observation.**
(2) **Guilty belief which is correct.**
(3) **Guilty avoidance of knowledge.**
   (a) **Guilty statement as of knowledge by one who is aware that he does not know,—which statement turns out to be contrary to the fact.**
   (b) **Guilty "shutting of the eyes" for fear of discovering the fact which an investigation would have disclosed.**

Want of "knowledge"
(4) **Bona-fide belief contrary to fact resulting from criminal negligence.**
(5) **Bona-fide belief contrary to fact but based upon reasonable grounds (or resulting from only slight negligence).**

The Model Penal Code would restrict very greatly any criminal liability based upon knowledge. It provides: [95]

"A person acts knowingly with respect to a material element of an offense when:

"(i) if the element involves the nature of his conduct or the attendant circumstances, he is aware that his conduct is of that nature or that such circumstances exist; and

"(ii) if the element involves a result of his conduct, he is aware that it is practically certain that his conduct will cause such a result."

It is further provided that: "When knowledge of the existence of a particular fact is an element of an offense, such knowledge is established if a person is aware of a high probability of its existence, unless he actually believes that it does not exist." [96]

---

93. State v. Michaud, 150 Me. 479, 114 A.2d 352 (1955). And see Brittin v. Chegary, 20 N.J.L. 625, 627–8 (1846).

94. See chapter 5, section 3, 1.

95. Section 2.02(2)(b).

96. Section 2.02(7).

The statute provided that a person commits second-degree murder by causing "the death of a person knowingly, but not after deliberation. . . . The statute also states that knowledge with respect to the result of one's conduct means awareness that the 'conduct is practically certain to cause the result.'" People v. Mingo, 196 Colo. 315, 584 P.2d 632, 633 (1978). "It is consistent with modern concepts of intent to define knowledge as an awareness of probable consequences." State v. Coleman, __ Mont. __, 605 P.2d 1000, 1055 (1979).

Needless to say this covers much less than "knowledge" as it has been interpreted as a mens-rea requirement in the common law. The Code compensates for this to some extent in dealing with receiving stolen property [97] by referring to the receipt of such property "knowing that it has been stolen, or believing that it has probably been stolen, . . ." This does not cover the case of the one who has no belief one way or the other, but has been put on notice that it may be stolen and "shuts his eyes" in order not to find out. Frequently the Code does not go as far even as this. It provides, for example, for guilt of one who "utters any writing which he knows to be forged" [98] without any reference to one who believes that it has been forged, or one who has been put on notice that it may be forged and "shuts his eyes" for fear of finding that it is so in fact. The Code would seem to leave unfortunate gaps in criminal liability in such matters as these.

"Wilful blindness," a term that has been used chiefly in England, recently made its appearance in a federal case, United States v. Jewell.[99] J was tried under an indictment which charged him in count one with knowingly or intentionally importing a controlled substance [1] and in count two with knowingly or intentionally possessing, with intent to distribute, a controlled substance.[2] It was undisputed that a package of 110 pounds of marijuana was contained in a secret compartment of the car J drove into the United States from Mexico. Other evidence included the following: while J and a companion were in Mexico a stranger, without identifying himself, offered to sell them marijuana and when they declined asked if they wanted to drive a car back to Los Angeles for $100. The companion "wanted no part of driving the vehicle" because "it didn't sound right to me." [3] J admitted that "he thought there was probably something wrong and something illegal in the vehicle, but he checked it over. He looked in the glove box and under the front seat and in the trunk, prior to driving it." When he looked into the trunk, he saw the secret compartment but did not investigate further. His explanation was: "He didn't find anything, and, therefore, he assumed that the people at the border wouldn't find anything either." [4] There was even evidence from which the jury could have concluded that J's purpose in going to Mexico was to drive back with a load of marijuana.[5] The judge instructed the jury that J's guilt would be established if the proof showed beyond a reasonable doubt that, if J was not actually aware of the presence of the marijuana, "his ignorance in that regard was solely and entirely a result of his having made a conscious purpose to disregard the nature of that which was in the vehicle, with a conscious purpose to avoid learning the truth." [6] The jury returned a verdict of guilty on both counts and judgment of conviction followed.

On J's appeal the court of appeals very properly upheld the conviction, but there was a very disturbing dissent. The dissent speaks of "the wilful blindness doctrine recognized primarily by English authorities." [7] This particular label has been primarily English, but the doctrine, which is well established in this country, is the same as that known by other labels, as shown

97. Section 223.6.

98. Section 224.1.

99. United States v. Jewell, 532 F.2d 697, 701 (9th Cir. 1976).

1. See 21 U.S.C.A. §§ 952(a), 960(a)(1).

2. See 21 U.S.C.A. § 841(a)(1).

3. 532 F.2d at 699, n. 2.

4. Id. (emphasis omitted).

5. Id. at n. 1.

6. Id. at 700.

7. Id. at 705.

above. One suggestion of the dissent is really fantastic. The dissent stated: "One problem with the wilful blindness doctrine is its bias towards visual means of acquiring knowledge." [8] "Wilful blindness" like its counterpart "wilfully shutting the eyes" has always been employed as a metaphor to indicate a deliberate effort to avoid knowing, by whatever method knowledge might be available. "Wilful blindness" has no more bias towards visual means of acquiring knowledge than does "deliberate ignorance," another term used to express the same idea. Another statement in the dissent is "that the English authorities seem to consider wilful blindness as a state of mind distinct from, but equally culpable, as 'actual' knowledge." [9] This is a misconception. Without doubt it was the fact that they were regarded as equally culpable which caused both to be included under the term "knowledge," but it is not true that they are regarded as distinct mens-rea concepts.

The dissent refers to the pertinent section of the Model Penal Code [10] which, as shown above, covers much less than "knowledge" as it has been interpreted as a mens-rea requirement in the common law and then deals with the Code provision as existing law—which of course it is not, except where it has been adopted by statute. The dissent also says: "It is not culpable to form 'a conscious purpose to avoid learning the truth' unless one is aware of facts indicating a high probability of that truth." [11] This will not stand examination. To support it, an illustration is given of a small boy who is handed a wrapped package by his mother in Mexico and who takes it into this country without the slightest notion that anything improper was contained. But suppose X went to D's store with a diamond necklace which he offered to sell. He said the necklace had been in the family for generations, but all female members of the family were now dead. He had no use for it and needed money. Assume that nothing about X's appearance or manner would give any reason to doubt his statement, but a jewelry store had been broken into a few nights before and several items stolen. The police had distributed a circular describing the stolen items, and one of these descriptions unquestionably represented the necklace offered by X. One of the circulars, moreover, had been delivered to D shortly after the larceny. Assume further that under all the circumstances D realized that there was a fifty percent chance that the necklace offered by X would be found described in the circular. But D did not want to risk what he might see if he looked. He had started to reach for the circular in his desk but changed his mind and bought the necklace without looking at the circular.

It is not true that D's conduct was not culpable because from what he knew there was an equal chance that the necklace might or might not be stolen. An honest person would have looked. And because of D's deliberate avoidance of looking at the circular, he is held to have known what he would have known if he had looked. He had the mens rea which has traditionally been included under the label "knowledge."

---

8. Id. The statement continues, "We may know facts from direct impressions of other senses or by deduction from circumstantial evidence, and such knowledge is nonetheless 'actual.' Moreover, visual sense impressions do not consistently provide complete certainty." Id. at 705–06 (footnote omitted).

9. Id. at 706.

10. Id. (referring to Model Penal Code § 2.02(7)).

11. Id. at 707.

It is not enough, it should be emphasized, that the police had handed **D** a circular unmistakenly identifying this necklace as stolen. Had he overlooked the circular, even under circumstances amounting to criminal negligence, that would not constitute "knowledge" even under the broad meaning assigned to the term as one type of mens rea. On the other hand assume, in a neighborhood bar, **D** had boasted of his "presence of mind" in refusing to look at the circular. He would not be entitled to an instruction that even under such facts he must be found not guilty.

Unfortunately, the dissenters in *Jewell* succeeded in imposing upon the majority their notion that there is no culpability in deliberately avoiding knowledge of the truth without awareness "of facts indicating a high probability of that truth." Thus the same court, in a later case, held that the government can meet the burden of proving knowledge that a prohibited substance was contained in the vehicle by proving "beyond a reasonable doubt that the defendant acted with a conscious purpose to avoid learning the truth of the contents of the vehicle." [12] The conviction was reversed, however, because the court held: "A deliberate avoidance of knowledge is culpable only when coupled with a subjective awareness of high probability," and the jury was not so instructed. [13]

Suppose two were employed to drive a car across the border. When one opened the trunk to put in his luggage, he noticed what appeared to be a secret compartment between the trunk and the back seat. He was about to pry into that compartment but desisted when the other said: "Don't do that. There's a fifty-fifty chance you might find it full of cocaine." Assume the circumstances known to them indicated no more than a fifty percent chance of finding any contraband in the compartment, although the drug was actually there. It would be absurd to suggest that they could drive that cocaine-loaded car into the country without culpability. It is not meant to suggest, moreover, that so much as a fifty percent probability would be required to make their conduct culpable. If circumstances known to them caused them to realize the *possibility* that the compartment might contain cocaine and the possibility was sufficient to cause them anxiously to avoid finding out for fear of finding its presence, this was culpable conduct. No honest person would *deliberately fail* to find out the truth *for fear of learning* that what he was thinking of doing would violate the law. No doubt the thought of unlawfulness might enter one's mind under circumstances which made it too utterly remote to be entitled to serious consideration. But this would not induce any fear of learning the truth.

Those who drafted the Model Penal Code apparently acted on the assumption that there never would be direct evidence of wilful avoidance of the truth. And if we are to permit such a finding without direct evidence, it should be limited to cases in which the person is aware of a high probability of unlawfulness. [14] The assumption, however, is quite unwarranted. The

12. United States v. Valle-Valdez, 554 F.2d 911, 914 (9th Cir. 1977).

13. Id.

14. The Supreme Court dealt with the issue of high probability in Barnes v. United States, 412 U.S. 837. 93 S.Ct. 2357 (1973). "The evidence established that petitioner possessed recently stolen Trea-sury checks payable to persons he did not know, and it provided no plausible explanation for such possession consistent with innocence. On the basis of this evidence alone common sense and experience tell us that petitioner must have known or been aware of the high probability that the checks were stolen

cases posed are hypothetical, but by no means out of the normal experience. The common law would permit the jury to take notice of the receiver's boast of his "presence of mind" in not looking at the circular. In the other case the fact may have been admitted by the parties, or there may have been witnesses to the fact that one would have opened the compartment had he not been warned by his partner that there was the risk of finding cocaine inside. And where there is direct evidence of a deliberate plan to avoid knowing the truth, the degree of probability is unimportant. The common law regards such a person as knowing what he would have known if he had not deliberately avoided knowing. And this should not be changed by statute.

The notion that it is not culpable to form "a conscious purpose to avoid learning the truth" unless one is aware of facts indicating a high probability of that truth results from a failure to distinguish culpability from proof. Whenever the need to investigate is recognized, culpability is established by a conscious effort to avoid learning the truth for fear of learning that contemplated action would be unlawful. But without awareness of facts indicating a high probability of unlawfulness, the need to investigate may be overlooked. And there is no conscious purpose to avoid learning the truth when the risk of unlawfulness has not been realized. In other words, without either other evidence or awareness of facts indicating a high probability of unlawfulness, there is no basis for an inference that the need to investigate had been recognized, and there could be no wilful avoidance without such recognition. Hence discussions in this area should place the emphasis on proof rather than culpability.[15]

The problem is comparable to the situation in which poison rather than unlawfulness is involved. If the need to investigate for poison in food is recognized, it is not a question of the degree of probability. If it is one's own food and he is not bent on suicide, he will make the investigation or he will not risk the eating. At the same time, in the absence of facts indicating a "high probability" of poison, some person might fail to recognize the need for an investigation. No doubt many have died as a result of having failed to realize the need to investigate for possible poison; but it is doubtful that many have died as a result of a wilful failure to make an indicated investigation for fear of finding the presence of poison in the food. Likewise if the risk is unlawfulness, some person may overlook the need to investigate if "high probability" is lacking. And there is no "wilful blindness" where the need to investigate is overlooked. But whenever the need is recognized, and the risk is assumed by wilfully failing to make an investigation for fear of discovering that contemplated action will bring about a result which the law seeks to prevent, the conduct is culpable. It is not the conduct of an honest person. Instead of the statement: "it is not culpable to form 'a conscious

. . . . Such evidence was clearly sufficient to enable the jury to find beyond a reasonable doubt that petitioner knew the checks were stolen." Id. at 845–46.

15. Thus a defendant's driving a car containing contraband into the country and the prosecution's proving beyond a reasonable doubt that the defendant acted with a conscious purpose to avoid learning the truth of the contents of the vehicle would establish his culpability. He would not have acted with a conscious purpose to avoid learning the truth about the contents of the vehicle unless he was afraid he would discover that driving the vehicle across the border would violate the law. No honest person avoids an investigation because of such a fear.

purpose to avoid learning the truth' unless one is aware of facts indicating a high probability of that truth," the statement should be: "the unintentional failure to realize the need of making an investigation is not culpable unless one is aware of facts indicating a high probability of unlawfulness in contemplated action."

Section 2.02(7) of the Model Penal Code should be amended in some form such as the following:

Whenever knowledge of the existence of a particular fact is an element of an offense, such knowledge is established if a person believes that it probably exists. And one is deemed to have knowledge of what he would have known if he had not deliberately avoided knowing. Deliberate avoidance of knowledge may be established by direct proof, or by proof that a person is aware of a high probability of the existence of the fact unless he actually believes that it does not exist.

As has been carefully stated: "One acts with knowledge of facts when the person has information which would put a reasonable person on inquiry as to such facts, but acts without making a reasonable inquiry." [16]

The Model Penal Code made an outstanding contribution to criminal law that has not been matched in modern times. The drafters did not claim perfection, however, and there should be no hesitation in taking notice of the few weak points to be found therein.[17] It is to be hoped that any state preparing to adopt a new penal code, if inclined to follow the Model Penal Code at this point, will do so with some such change as mentioned above and that states having already adopted new codes including this section will make some appropriate amendment. Never to be forgotten is the fact that one important function of the criminal law is to aid in teaching the difference between right and wrong.

D. WILFULNESS

The word "wilful" or "wilfully" when used in the definition of a crime, it has been said time and again, means only intentionally or purposely as distinguished from accidentally or negligently and does not require any actual impropriety; [18] while on the other hand it has been stated with equal repetition

16. Iowa Criminal Code § 715.3 (1978).

The statute defines knowledge (RCW 9A.08.010(b)): "A person knows or acts knowingly or with knowledge when: . . . (ii) he has information which would lead a reasonable man in the same situation to believe that facts exist which are facts described by a statute defining an offense." It was held that this equates knowledge with negligent ignorance and is unconstitutional. State v. Shipp, 93 Wn.2d 510, 610 P.2d 1322 (1980).

17. See Perkins, Some Weak Points in the Model Penal Code, 17 Hastings L.J. 3 (1965).

18. McBride v. United States, 225 F.2d 249 (5th Cir. 1955); In re Trombley, 31 Cal.2d 801, 807, 193 P.2d 734, 739 (1948); Ewell v. State, 207 Md. 288, 114 A.2d 66 (1955); Sall v. State, 157 Neb. 688, 696, 61 N.W.2d 256, 261 (1953); State v. Smith, 119 Tenn. 521, 525, 105 S.W. 68, 70 (1907).

The term "wilfully" in a statute means intentionally and designedly—not accidentally. State v. Stewart, 73 Wn.2d 701, 440 P.2d 815 (1968).

"The word 'willfully' when applied to the intent with which an act is done or omitted, implies simply a purpose or willingness to commit the act, or make the omission referred to. It does not require any intent to violate the law, or to injure another, or to acquire any advantage." Erickson v. Fisher, 170 Mont. 491, 554 P.2d 1336, 1337–38 (1976).

and insistence that the requirement added by such a word is not satisfied unless there is a bad purpose or evil intent.[19]   As emphasized by one case, what is needed for guilt is bad faith and not merely bad judgment.[20]   "We have recently pointed out that 'willful' is a word of many meanings, its construction often being influenced by its context," [21] commented the Supreme Court after having said in a previous case: [22]

"The word [willfully] often denotes an act which is intentional, or knowing, or voluntary, as distinguished from accidental.   But when used in a criminal statute it generally means an act done with a bad purpose; without justifiable excuse; stubbornly, obstinately, perversely.   The word is also employed to characterize a thing done without ground for believing it is lawful or conduct marked by a careless disregard whether or not one has the right so to act, . . ."

A clue to the solution of an important part of this problem is found in the suggestion that the meaning of such a word depends to a large extent upon whether or not the particular offense involves moral turpitude.[23]   A so-called "civil offense," as will be explained in the following section, does not have anything of the normal mens-rea requirement unless expressly added by the language of the statute creating it.   And since negligently or even accidentally doing what is thus proscribed would otherwise be included, the word "wilfully" will be added if the legislative intent is to exclude such happenings.   Hence when found in a statute creating a civil offense the word "wilful" means intentional as distinguished from inadvertent or negligent and does not imply anything in the nature of an evil intent or bad motive,[24] whereas such additional element is required when the word is found in a

"It is well-settled that to prove a violation of I.R.S. § 7205 (which proscribes 'willfully' supplying false information) the government is not required to show bad purpose or evil intent." United States v. Hinderman, 625 F.2d 994, 995 (10th Cir. 1980).

19.   United States v. Bishop, 412 U.S. 346, 93 S.Ct. 2008 (1973).   The Bishop decision has been restricted by United States v. Pomponio, 429 U.S. 10, 97 S.Ct. 22 (1976); Brown v. State, 137 Wis. 543, 549, 119 N.W. 338, 340 (1909).

"An act is done willfully if done voluntarily, with bad purpose either to disobey or disregard the law." United States v. Williams, 483 F.Supp. 453, 460 (E.D.N.Y. 1980).

"The act to be criminal must be willful, which means an act done with a fraudulent intent or a bad purpose or an evil motive." United States v. Andreen, 628 F.2d 1236, 1241 (9th Cir. 1980).

20.   State ex rel. Hopkins v. Wilson, 108 Kan. 641, 196 P. 758 (1921).

21.   Screws v. United States, 325 U.S. 91, 101, 65 S.Ct. 1031, 1035 (1945).

22.   United States v. Murdock, 290 U.S. 389, 394–5, 54 S.Ct. 223, 225 (1933). Citations are omitted.

23.   See Nabob Oil Co. v. United States, 190 F.2d 478, 480 (10th Cir. 1951). The statute defining the offense of wilfully and wrongfully placing another in a hospital for the insane by any method other than that prescribed by law does not create a civil offense because the words "willfully and wrongfully" imply an intent to injure, harass or wrong the person committed.   And where such action was taken in good faith for the benefit of the patient it did not violate the statute even if the prescribed form was not followed.   State v. Halladay, 68 S.D. 547, 5 N.W.2d 42 (1942).

24.   It is said that "wilful" implies an evil intent or motive in statutes dealing with felonies but merely intentional as distinguished from inadvertent in misdemeanor statutes.   But as the offense charged was the sale of beer over the ceiling price established by the Emergency Price Control Act, it is clear that the court had in mind the distinction between true crimes "involving moral turpitude" (p. 876) and civil offenses.   United States v. Perplies, 165 F.2d 874 (7th Cir. 1948).

common-law definition or in a statute dealing with a true crime.[25] A confusing tendency is added by the fact that while this additional element is found in such a true crime it may be expressed by some term other than the word "wilful." That is, if the mens-rea phrase of the statute employs "knowingly" and "maliciously" in addition to "willfully," only a limited meaning will be assigned to the last word;[26] and in speaking of a mayhem statute in which much more is required by other terms it is possible for the court to say: "The word 'willfully' or purposely means intentionally and not accidentally or involuntarily, . . ."[27]

Whatever the grade of the offense the presence of this word in the definition will carry with it the implication that for guilt the act must have been done willingly rather than under compulsion[28] and, if something is required to be done by the statute, the implication that a punishable omission must be by one having the ability and means to perform.[29]

Even when used in the definition of a crime involving moral turpitude the word "wilfully" does not mean awareness that a criminal penalty is being incurred.[30] One who intentionally does such an act has "a purpose to do wrong"[31] even if he mistakenly assumes no punishment has been provided therefor by law. For example, the presence of this word in a statute forbidding lewd and lascivious conduct with a child does not limit conviction to those offenders who have knowledge of the enactment.[32] Under other circumstances, however, the presence or absence of a bad purpose or evil intent may depend upon an understanding or misunderstanding of some other

25. Such as misconduct in office, for example. State ex rel. Hopkins v. Wilson, 108 Kan. 641, 196 P. 758 (1921).

In reversing a conviction it was said: "In the case at bar NRS 204.030 proscribes misapplication of public funds by a 'willful' omission to pay them over to the proper officer empowered to receive them. An element of this offense is a culpable mind." Robey v. State, 96 Nev. 459, 611 P.2d 209, 210 (1980).

26. State v. Smith, 119 Tenn. 521, 525, 105 S.W. 68, 70 (1907). And see McClanahan v. United States, 230 F.2d 919, 924 (5th Cir. 1956).

27. Sall v. State, 157 Neb. 688, 696, 61 N.W.2d 256, 261 (1953).

28. "Willful denotes a choice of the free will in either doing or not doing an act." People v. Fruci, 188 Misc. 384, 67 N.Y.S.2d 512, 514 (1947). "[I]t implies that the person knows what he is doing intends to do what he is doing and is a free agent." In re Trombley, 31 Cal.2d 801, 807, 193 P.2d 734, 739 (1948). Even without this word compulsion would be a defense in many cases. See infra, chapter 9 section 2.

It has been suggested also that an act is not wilful if it results, not from a preconceived design, but from a sudden impulse of anger excited unexpectedly. State v. Brigman, 94 N.C. 888, 889 (1886).

29. In re Trombley, 31 Cal.2d 801, 193 P.2d 734 (1948); Ewell v. State, 207 Md. 288, 114 A.2d 66 (1955). In each case a conviction was affirmed but only because defendant had such ability and means. The statement in the text is for emphasis only because not doing what is impossible is not recognized by law as an "act of omission." See supra, chapter 6, section 4.

30. Schmeller v. United States, 143 F.2d 544, 553 (6th Cir. 1944); Fields v. United States, 164 F.2d 97, 100 (D.C.Cir. 1947); Dennis v. United States, 84 U.S. App.D.C. 31, 171 F.2d 986, 990 (1948).

The statutory language "willfully misapplies" requires a showing that it was defendant's purpose "to bring about the conduct proscribed by the statute, and not that the defendant also intended that his conduct be violative of the law." United States v. Gregg, 612 F.2d 43, 51 (2d Cir. 1979).

31. Brown v. State, 137 Wis. 543, 549, 119 N.W. 338, 340 (1909).

32. State v. Johnson, 74 Idaho 269, 275, 261 P.2d 638, 641 (1953).

law.[33] Murdock, for example, refused to answer certain questions in a federal proceeding, on the ground that his answers might tend to incriminate him under state law, and was indicted under a statute providing a penalty for one who "willfully . . . refuses to answer any question pertinent to the question under inquiry, . . ." It was held that the fifth-amendment privilege did not extend to probable incrimination under state law and hence that Murdock was bound to answer,[34] but since the law on this point had not been definitely settled until after the original proceeding it was further held that his bona-fide claim of privilege, though resulting from a mistake of law, was not a wilful refusal to testify, and the conviction was reversed.[35]

An additional illustration may be taken from the federal revenue law which provides, among other things, the circumstances under which an income tax return must be filed, adding a statutory penalty for the failure thereof and making a wilful failure so to file a criminal offense. Suppose three persons failed to make required returns under these circumstances: **A** fully intended to file his return in time but became so preoccupied with other matters that he inadvertently forgot to do so; **B** carefully went over his books and by reason of some mistake concluded that no return was due by him, so he intentionally let the final day go by without filing a return because of a bona-fide belief that none was needed; while **C** intentionally failed to make a return although he knew one was due by him. All three have incurred the statutory penalty (which is not a crime) but only **C** is guilty of the crime of wilfully failing to file a return.[36] **B** intentionally omitted filing but without a bad purpose because of his bona-fide belief, but **C** intended the government to be deprived of taxes due under the law [37] which stamps his conduct as resulting from a bad purpose or evil intent and hence makes it "wilful" within the meaning of the statute.[38] As said in one case: [39]

"It is now settled that 'willfully', as used in this offense, means more than intentionally or voluntarily, and includes an evil motive or bad purpose, so that evidence of an actual *bona fide* misconception of the law, such as

---

33. "Ignorance of the law is no defense to crime, except that, where wilfulness is an element of the crime, ignorance of a duty imposed by law may negative wilfulness in failure to perform the duty." Yarborough v. United States, 230 F.2d 56, 61 (4th Cir. 1956).

The term willfully required that defendant have knowledge of the statutory reporting requirement when bringing monetary instruments in excess of $5,000 as to the United States. United States v. Granda, 565 F.2d 922 (5th Cir. 1978).

34. United States v. Murdock, 284 U.S. 141, 52 S.Ct. 63 (1931). This decision was expressly overruled in Murphy v. Waterfront Commission, 378 U.S. 52, 84 S.Ct. 1594 (1964).

35. United States v. Murdock, 290 U.S. 389, 54 S.Ct. 223 (1933).

36. Although the court did not find such lack of knowledge in this case it was pointed out that a failure to file in-

come tax returns, and returns of income taxes and social security taxes withheld from employees' wages, would not be "wilful" if defendant did not know it was his duty to file them. Yarborough v. United States, 230 F.2d 56 (4th Cir. 1956).

37. There are circumstances in which a return is required although no tax is due, but the government is entitled to have this information and the intentional withholding of it is inherently wrongful and hence "wilful."

38. For a careful statement of this problem see United States v. Murdock, 290 U.S. 389, 395–6, 54 S.Ct. 223, 225, 226 (1933).

39. Wardlaw v. United States, 203 F.2d 884, 885 (5th Cir. 1953). Needless to say "wilfulness", in the sense of a bad purpose or evil intent, may be inferred from sufficiently probative conduct. McKenna v. United States, 232 F.2d 431 (8th Cir. 1956).

would negative knowledge of the existence of the obligation, would, if believed by the jury, justify a verdict for the defendant."

Where the word "wilfully" requires a bad purpose or evil intent it is reversible error to instruct the jury that a person is presumed to intend the natural consequences of his act and hence if he intentionally did an act which had a harmful effect he intended that harm.[40]

E. WANTONNESS

Although the original meaning of "wanton" was undisciplined or not susceptible to control, it is now employed in several senses one of which is brutally insolent, merciless, or inhumane, as in the phrase "wanton cruelty," and this is the significance it carries when it is found in the criminal law. "It means that the act was done intentionally and without regard to consequences and under such circumstances as evince a wicked or mischievous intent." [41] Wanton misconduct "is something different from negligence however gross—different not merely in degree but in kind, and evincing a different state of mind," [42] so callously heedless of harmful consequences known to be likely to follow that "even though there be no actual intent, there is at least a willingness to inflict injury, a conscious indifference to the perpetration of the wrong." [43] While an intent to do an unlawful act in wanton disregard of the foreseen likelihood of harm [44] may differ little in the scale of moral blameworthiness from actual intent to cause such harm it is not the same state of mind and should not be confused therewith,[45] although it may be permissible to characterize it as *equivalent in spirit* to actual intent." [46]

Wanton differs from reckless both as to the actual state of mind and as to the degree of culpability. One who is acting recklessly is fully aware of the unreasonable risk he is creating, but may be trying and hoping to avoid any harm. One acting wantonly may be creating no greater risk of harm, but he is not trying to avoid it and is indifferent to whether harm results or

---

40. Ibid.

41. State v. Vinzant, 200 La. 301, 314, 7 So.2d 917, 922 (1942). And see State v. Brigman, 94 N.C. 888, 890 (1886); State v. Morgan, 98 N.C. 641, 643, 3 S.E. 927, 928 (1887).

42. Kasanovich v. George, 348 Pa. 199, 203, 34 A.2d 523, 525 (1943); Commonwealth v. Malinowski, 46 Berks 141, 143 (Berks Co. Pa.1953); Condor v. Hull Lift Trucks, Inc., ___ Ind.App. ___, 405 N.E.2d 538 (1980).

43. Ibid.

"Wanton conduct involves a realization of the imminence of danger to the person of another and a reckless disregard or complete indifference and unconcern for the probable consequences of such conduct." State v. Makin, 223 Kan. 743, 576 P.2d 666, 669 (1978).

44. "The essence of wanton or reckless conduct is intentional conduct, by way of either commission or omission where there is a duty to act, which in-

volves a high degree of likelihood that substantial harm will result to another." Commonwealth v. Welansky, 316 Mass. 383, 399, 55 N.E.2d 902, 910 (1944). The word "reckless' is usually employed in criminal law to indicate criminal negligence rather than wantonness, but the court uses it here in the tort sense and cites Restatement, Torts § 500 (1934). The court adds however that "wanton" contains a suggestion "of arrogance, or insolence or heartlessness that is lacking in the word 'reckless.'" Id. at 398, 55 N.E.2d at 910.

45. In such a case, for example, if the harm did not happen although the likelihood was great, the result would be quite different from what it would have been had the actor actually intended the harm to ensue.

46. Lancaster v. State, 83 Ga.App. 746, 756, 64 S.E.2d 902, 909 (1951). Emphasis added.

not. Wanton conduct has properly been characterized as "vicious" and rates extreme in the degree of culpability.[47] The two are not mutually exclusive. Wanton conduct is reckless plus, so to speak.

SECTION 5. THE CIVIL OFFENSE

It has been necessary to recognize that some offenses are not true crimes, of which parking overtime in a restricted zone is an extreme illustration.

In the absence of legislation a properly parked car could be left where it is for three hours as justifiably as for ten minutes. In the exercise of the police power, zones have been established in moderately congested areas in which parking is permitted, but for limited periods only, the length of the period depending upon the needs of the particular situation. If the limit established for a certain zone is thirty minutes this is not for the reason that it would be inherently wrong for a car to be left there for a longer period,— nothing but expediency is involved. Penalties are provided as a means of enforcement but no one considers the driver who has parked overtime a criminal. His violation differs from murder or theft by more than degree; it is a different kind of breach and is referred to as an offense *malum prohibitum* to distinguish it from a true crime which is *malum in se*.

The distinction between offenses *mala in se* and offenses *mala prohibita* was recognized at least as early as the fifteenth century.[1] It has been criticized repeatedly.[2] About a century and a half ago the distinction was said to be one "not founded upon any sound principle" and which had "long since been exploded." [3] The Supreme Court, however, has shown that it is just as firmly entrenched today [4] as it was in 1495. And after all these years it was necessary to say: "Neither this Court nor, so far as we are aware, any other has undertaken to delineate a precise line or set forth comprehensive criteria for distinguishing between" them.[5] This would call for little comment if it indicated no more than some areas of uncertainty along the actual boundary line, but the confusion goes far beyond that.

---

47. It is conduct "attended with such circumstances as carry with them the plain indications of a heart regardless of social duty, and fatally bent on mischief." Commonwealth v. Webster, 59 Mass. (5 Cush.) 295, 307 (1850).

1. See the note by Chief Justice Fineux in Y.B.Mich. 11 Hen. VII, f. 11, pl. 35 (1495).

2. The distinction between *malum in se* and *malum prohibitum* "is now exploded." 1 Wharton, Criminal Law § 157 n. 10 (12th ed. 1932). "The distinction is perhaps of no practical utility. . . ." 1 McClain, Criminal Law § 23 (1897). "But it is doubtful whether this distinction is now of any value. . . ." Archbold, Criminal Pleading, Evidence & Practice 888 (26th ed. 1922). It is "no longer adhered to." Note, 5 U. of Pitt.L.

Rev. 58, 59 (1938). The *"mala in se— mala prohibita* classification is neither a logically possible nor a valid one." Note, 24 Ind.L.J. 89, 97 (1948). But this has not been the view of the courts. For example: ". . . the well-recognized distinction between *mala in se* and *mala prohibita*." Shevlin-Carpenter Co. v. Minnesota, 218 U.S. 57, 68, 30 S.Ct. 663, 666 (1910).

3. Bensley v. Bignold, 5 B. & A. 335, 341, 106 Eng.Rep. 1214, 1216 (1822).

4. Morissette v. United States, 342 U.S. 246, 72 S.Ct. 240 (1952); United States v. Park, 421 U.S. 658, 95 S.Ct. 1903 (1975).

5. Id. Morissette v. United States, 342 U.S. at 260, 72 S.Ct. at 248.

It may be helpful at the outset to indicate some of the more important differences in the results reached. The starting point seems to have been in regard to royal dispensation. The king could grant a subject permission to do an act which otherwise would be an offense *malum prohibitum* but not one that would be *malum in se*.[6] The second difference made its appearance in the development of the law of homicide: "If the act be unlawful," said Coke speaking of an act causing death unintentionally, "it is murder."[7] Hale pointed out that such a killing might be manslaughter only, depending upon the nature of the offense, adding that it would be excusable homicide if the unlawful act "was but *malum prohibitum*."[8] This has been accepted[9] and extended to analogous situations. Thus if one is knocked down unintentionally, and without criminal negligence, the mere fact that the contact resulted from an act *malum prohibitum* will not make it a criminal battery.[10] The difference most frequently encountered involves a more general problem of mens rea. There is no offense *malum in se* without some form of mens rea,[11] but the normal mens-rea requirement is not a necessary ingredient of an offense *malum prohibitum*.[12] The typical case involves a mistake of fact. An act has been done under an innocent and nonnegligent[13] mistake of

---

6. Fineux's note, supra note 1.

7. 3 Co.Inst. *56.

8. 1 Hale, P.C. *475. Hale's phrase is "chance medley" but the context shows that he has reference to a killing by accident which does not involve criminal guilt.

9. People v. Stuart, 47 Cal.2d 167, 302 P.2d 5 (1956); Thomas v. State, 91 Ga. App. 382, 85 S.E.2d 644 (1955); State v. Horton, 139 N.C. 588, 51 S.E. 945 (1905). "Since it is *malum prohibitum*, not *malum in se*, for an unauthorized person to kill game in England contrary to the statutes, if, in unlawfully shooting at game, he accidentally kills a man, it is no more criminal in him than if he were authorized." 1 Bishop, Criminal Law § 332 (8th ed. 1892).

10. Commonwealth v. Adams, 114 Mass. 323 (1873).

11. "To prevent the punishment of the innocent, there has been ingrafted into our system of jurisprudence, as presumably in every other, the principle that the wrongful or criminal intent is the essence of crime, without which it cannot exist." State v. Blue, 17 Utah 175, 181, 53 P. 978, 980 (1898). "There can be no crime, large or small, without an evil mind." 1 Bishop, Criminal Law § 287 (8th ed. 1892). This requirement is included in a statutory crime even if not expressly mentioned. Leeman v. State, 35 Ark. 438 (1880); State v. Healy, 95 N.E.2d 244 (Ohio App.1950); Regina v. Tolson, 23 Q.B.D. 168 (1889); Regina v. Page, 8 Car. & P. 122, 173 Eng.Rep. 425 (1837). "[I]t is an essential ingredient in

a criminal offence that there should be some blameworthy condition of the mind, sometimes it is negligence, sometimes malice, sometimes guilty knowledge." Chisholm v. Doulton, 22 Q.B.D. 736, 741; State v. Minium, 26 Wn.App. 840, 615 P.2d 511 (1980).

12. State v. Waymire, 26 Wn.App. 669, 614 P.2d 214 (1980); Ohio R.R. v. Commonwealth, 119 Ky. 519, 84 S.W. 566 (1905). And see Sayre, Public Welfare Offenses, 33 Col.L.Rev. 55, 62 (1933).

The speed law creates an offense malum prohibitum which provides an inference of intent from the doing of the prohibited act. Where D exceeded the speed limit because the spring on the throttle broke and he was unable to stop until he put the car in neutral and was able to brake to a stop, the inference of intent is rebutted and D is not guilty. State v. Weller, 4 Conn.Cir. 267, 230 A.2d 242 (1967).

Hence, rather than say the civil offense has no mens rea it is better to say it does not have the normal mens-rea requirement.

13. A mistake of fact may be sufficient to establish innocence of the offense charged, even if it was due to negligence, in some cases. One does not commit larceny by carrying away the chattel of another in the mistaken belief that it is his own, no matter how great may have been the fault leading to this belief, if the belief itself is genuine. Regina v. Halford, 11 Cox C.C. 88 (1868); People v. Devine, 95 Cal. 227, 30 P. 378

fact of such a nature that what was done would have been not only lawful but entirely proper had the facts been as they were reasonably supposed to be. This is a complete defense to a prosecution for an offense *malum in se*.[14] It is no defense to a prosecution for an offense *malum prohibitum*[15] unless the wording of the particular statute has imposed a special mens-rea requirement,—as by providing a penalty for such an act only if "knowingly" committed.[16]

Another important difference between the two types of offense is in connection with respondeat superior. There can be no conviction of an offense *malum in se* upon this basis,[17] but it is quite otherwise if the prosecution is for an offense *malum prohibitum*.[18] In fact guilt of such an offense can be established by proof of the prohibited act by defendant's employee in the course of defendant's business and within the scope of the employment, even if it was contrary to his express instructions.[19] The degree of proof needed

(1892); Dean v. State, 41 Fla. 291, 26 So. 638 (1899). The use of the word "non-negligent" in the text was because of a desire to make the statement extreme.

14. Gordon v. State, 52 Ala. 308 (1875); Commonwealth v. Presby, 14 Gray 65 (Mass.1860); Commonwealth v. Power, 7 Metc. 596 (Mass.1844); State v. McDonald, 7 Mo.App. 510 (1879); State v. Fuentes, 91 N.M. 554, 577 P.2d 452 (App. 1978).

15. Smith v. State, 223 Ala. 346, 136 So. 270 (1931); People v. Johnson, 288 Ill. 442, 123 N.E. 543 (1919); McCutcheon v. People, 69 Ill. 601 (1873); Commonwealth v. Raymond, 97 Mass. 567 (1867); Commonwealth v. Farren, 91 Mass. 489 (1864); People v. Snowberger, 113 Mich. 86, 71 N.W. 497 (1897); Commonwealth v. Weiss, 139 Pa. 247, 21 A. 10 (1891); State v. Whitman, 52 S.D. 91, 216 N.W. 858 (1927); Welch v. State, 145 Wis. 86, 129 N.W. 656 (1911); State v. Hartfiel, 24 Wis. 60 (1869); Regina v. Woodrow, 15 M. & W. 404, 153 Eng.Rep. 907 (1846); People v. Dozier, 72 A.D.2d 478, 424 N.Y.S.2d 1010 (1980).

16. See 18 U.S.C.A. § 842(b) (1976) (distribution of explosive materials).

It is particularly significant when some such word as "knowingly" is used in one section of a statute and omitted from another. Commonwealth v. Raymond, 97 Mass. 567 (1867); People v. Snowberger, 113 Mich. 86, 71 N.W. 497 (1897). Or when such a word, originally in the statute, has been removed by amendment. State v. Dobry, 217 Iowa 858, 250 N.W. 702 (1934). One interesting suggestion is that what would otherwise be *malum prohibitum* becomes *malum in se* if the wording of the statute requires a wrongful intent for conviction. United States

v. Boyce Motor Lines, 188 F.2d 889, 891 (3d Cir. 1951), aff'd Boyce Motor Lines, Inc. v. United States, 342 U.S. 337, 72 S.Ct. 329 (1952).

17. The leading case is Rex v. Huggins, 2 Ld. Raym. 1574, 92 Eng.Rep. 518 (1730).

18. Meigs v. State, 94 Fla. 809, 114 So. 448 (1927); State v. Probasco, 62 Iowa 400, 17 N.W. 607 (1883); DeZarn v. Commonwealth, 195 Ky. 686, 243 S.W. 921 (1922); Commonwealth v. Sacks, 214 Mass. 72, 100 N.E. 1019 (1913); Commonwealth v. Warren, 160 Mass. 533, 36 N.E. 308 (1894); State v. Sobelman, 199 Minn. 232, 271 N.W. 484 (1937); Commonwealth v. Jackson, 146 Pa.Super. 328, 22 A.2d 299 (1941), aff'd 345 Pa. 456, 28 A.2d 894 (1942); Barnes v. Akroyd, L.R. 7 Q.B. 474 (1872). The opinions at times contain language suggestive of a requirement of a high degree of care on the part of the employer to avoid the forbidden act. This suggestion disappears when it is explained that he must avoid it at his peril. See People v. Roby, 52 Mich. 577, 18 N.W. 365 (1884). One of the best examples of a similar application to the general mens-rea problem is found in one of the most outstanding cases in the field. "[T]he policy of the law may, in order to stimulate proper care, require the punishment of the negligent person though he be ignorant of the noxious character of what he sells. . . . Its manifest purpose is to require every person dealing in drugs to ascertain at his peril. . . ." United States v. Balint, 258 U.S. 250, 252–4, 42 S.Ct. 301, 302, 303 (1922).

19. Groff v. State, 171 Ind. 547, 85 N.E. 769 (1908); State v. Brown, 73 Or. 325, 144 P. 444 (1914); State v. Schull, 66

for conviction also requires attention. Evidence beyond a reasonable doubt is required for conviction of an offense *malum in se* [20] whereas a preponderance of the evidence will support a conviction of an offense *malum prohibitum*,[21] except that if the offense is classified or punishable as a crime the offense must be established beyond a reasonable doubt.[22] Another difference is found in the conspiracy cases. If two or more agree to do an act which constitutes an offense *malum in se* they are guilty of conspiracy whether they do or do not know that the law provides for the punishment of such an act.[23] But if the agreement is to commit an act which is *malum prohibitum* they are not guilty of conspiracy if what is to be done would be proper except for the statute and they do not know, or have reason to know, that the act is prohibited by law.[24]

S.D. 102, 279 N.W. 241 (1938); State v. Cray, 85 Vt. 99, 81 A. 450 (1911); State v. Young, 294 N.W.2d 728 (Minn.1980).

20. Quinn v. State, 106 Miss. 844, 64 So. 738 (1914). "[I]n a strictly criminal prosecution the jury may not return a verdict against the defendant unless the evidence establishes his guilt beyond a reasonable doubt. . . ." United States v. Regan, 232 U.S. 37, 47–48, 34 S.Ct. 213, 216, 217 (1914).

21. United States v. Regan, 232 U.S. 37, 34 S.Ct. 213 (1914); Proctor v. People, 24 Ill.App. 599 (1887). Roberge v. Burnham, 124 Mass. 277 (1878); People v. Briggs, 114 N.Y. 56, 20 N.E. 820 (1889). "I think that the evidence which would support a civil action would be sufficient to support an indictment" [for nuisance]. Per Mellor, J., in The Queen v. Stephens, L.R. 1 Q.B. 702, 710 (1866). Some of the cases holding a preponderance of the evidence sufficient have emphasized that the prosecution was under a statute authorizing the penalty to be recovered in a civil proceeding. United States v. Regan, 232 U.S. 37, 48, 34 S.Ct. 213, 217 (1914); State v. Chicago, M. & St. P. Ry., 122 Iowa 22, 25–26, 96 N.W. 904, 905 (1903). But the reason such a statute does not violate constitutional safeguards is that the proceeding would have been civil in substance even if it had remained criminal in form. "It is quite true that this in point of form is a proceeding of a criminal nature, but in substance I think it is in the nature of a civil proceeding. . . ." Per Mellor, J. supra at 708. Cases can be found which speak of proof beyond a reasonable doubt in this field. E.g., Chaffee & Co. v. United States, 58 U.S. (18 Wall.) 516 (1873). But this is usually because the point was not considered. Hawloetz v. Kass, 25 F. 765 (1885). If the penalty is too extreme to be appropriate for an offense *malum prohibitum* the proceeding is criminal in substance as well as in form and proof beyond a reasonable doubt is required for conviction. United States v. Burdett, 34 U.S. (9 Pet.) 682 (1835).

See a note, Suit for a Statutory Penalty as a Civil or Criminal Prosecution, 27 L.R.A.,N.S., 739 (1910). Acquittal in a prosecution for wilful attempt to evade the payment of income tax does not bar a suit to recover a penalty for insufficient payment because of the difference in the quantum of proof. Helvering v. Mitchell, 303 U.S. 391, 58 S.Ct. 630 (1938).

In a suit to abate a public nuisance, the Constitution does not require proof beyond a reasonable doubt. Cooper v. Mitchell Brothers' Santa Ana Theater, ___ U.S. ___, 102 S.Ct. 172 (1981).

22. In re Winship, 397 U.S. 358, 90 S.Ct. 1068 (1970).

23. Since the premise is that the thing agreed to be done is wrong in itself the agreement is with mens rea whether the act is known to be punishable or not. In fact it is possible to have a conspiracy although the wrongful act agreed upon is not itself a punishable offense. Commonwealth v. Waterman, 122 Mass. 43 (1877). "Thus a conspiracy to cheat by false pretenses without false tokens, when a cheat by such pretenses by one person was not punishable, was held indictable. . . ." Id. at 57.

24. Landen v. United States, 290 F. 75 (6th Cir. 1924); Commonwealth v. Benesch, 290 Mass. 125, 194 N.E. 905 (1935). "Persons who agree to do an act innocent in itself, in good faith and without the use of criminal means, are not converted into conspirators because it turns out that the contemplated act was prohibited by statute." People v. Powell, 63 N.Y. 88, 92 (1875). "The agreement must have been entered into with an evil purpose, as distinguished from a purpose

One additional difference seems to be of sufficient importance to warrant inclusion here. If the offense is *malum in se* condonation by the injured party will not bar a public prosecution,[25] unless expressly authorized by statute.[26] An offense *malum prohibitum* will more frequently affect the public at large than some particular individual, but if it is of such a nature as to injure a particular person a prosecution therefor can be completely barred by his condonation.[27]

Three misconceptions are to be noted and avoided. The first stems from a misunderstanding of the terms themselves. As customarily used these phrases are mutually exclusive. An offense *malum prohibitum* is not a wrong which is prohibited, but something which is wrong *only* in the sense that it is against the law.[28] This is emphasized at times by such phrases as "*malum prohibitum* only"[29] or "but *malum prohibitum*,"[30] although it is understood without any such qualification. A failure to understand this us-

simply to do the act prohibited, in ignorance of the prohibition." People v. Flack, 125 N.Y. 324, 334, 26 N.E. 267, 270 (1891).

If, however, a corrupt motive is established it is not necessary to show that the conspirators had knowledge of the law even if it is merely *malum prohibitum*. Cruz v. United States, 106 F.2d 828 (10th Cir. 1939); People v. McLaughlin, 111 Cal.App.2d 781, 245 P.2d 1076 (1952); United States v. Reminga, 493 F.Supp. 1351 (W.D.Mich.1980).

25. State v. Dye, 148 Kan. 421, 83 P.2d 113 (1938); State v. Dejean, 159 La. 900, 106 So. 374 (1925); Cook v. Commonwealth, 178 Va. 251, 16 S.E. 635 (1941). A mother cannot condone the crime of arson committed when her son burned her barn. State v. Craig, 124 Kan. 340, 259 P. 802 (1927). Although larceny involves a taking without consent, the victim cannot purge the crime by a consent given after the larceny has been committed. State v. Thomas, 318 Mo. 605, 300 S.W. 823 (1927). A settlement which includes the compromise of a crime is void so far as it relates to the crime and constitutes no defense to a prosecution. See State v. Kiewel, 173 Minn. 473, 217 N.W. 598 (1928).

There are no constitutional objections to a change of this rule by statute because any such change would work to the advantage of the offender. And a number of such changes have been made. It is sometimes provided, for example, that no prosecution for adultery shall be brought except upon complaint of the injured spouse. Iowa Code Annotated § 702.1 (1970). Perhaps the most common provision for condonation is a statutory provision that intermarriage of the par-

ties shall bar a prosecution for seduction. West's Ann.Cal.Pen.Code § 269 (1970). Not infrequently there is statutory authority for the compromise of certain misdemeanors. West's Ann.Cal.Pen. Code § 1377 (1970). For an elaborate consideration of this field see Miller, The Compromise of Criminal Cases, 1 So.Calif.L.Rev. 1 (1927). While any such provision tends to work to the advantage of the offender, the legislators have had in mind the interests of the injured victim.

26. Utah Code Ann.1953 § 77–35–25(d).

27. Holsey v. State, 4 Ga.App. 453, 61 S.E. 836 (1908). "This ruling is to be taken, however, with the understanding that the principle is applicable only in that class of cases where the offense involves no crime against society or morals. . . ." Id. at 454–5. The court was referring to condonation without statutory authorization. See the preceding note.

28. "Acts *mala prohibita* include any matter forbidden or commanded by statute, but not otherwise wrong." Commonwealth v. Adams, 114 Mass. 323, 324 (1873). "But in relation to those laws which enjoin only *positive duties*, and forbid only such things as are not *mala in se*, but *mala prohibita* merely, without any intermixture of moral guilt, . . ." 1 Bl.Comm. *57.

29. Commonwealth v. Benesch, 290 Mass. 125, 135, 194 N.E. 905, 910 (1935).

30. 1 Hale, P.C. *475.

Sometimes a different emphasis is found. For example: "To sell it is not only *malum in see* [sic], but *malum prohibitum*." State v. Keever, 177 N.C. 114, 117, 97 S.E. 727, 728 (1919). The misprint is not found in the Southeastern.

age of the terms has led some to assume that all statutory additions to the common law of crimes are *mala prohibita*.[31]   One writer emphasized his confusion by speaking of embezzlement as *malum prohibitum*.[32]   This assumption is utterly without foundation.   An act may be *malum in se* although no punishment is provided by law.[33]   If this defect is corrected by appropriate legislation, what previously was *malum in se* does not cease to be so by reason of having been defined and made punishable by law.

The second misconception is much more broad in its nature.   It is the notion that the whole mens-rea concept of the criminal law is on the wane and may be expected to disappear entirely in the near future.[34]   This is due to the failure to distinguish between *malum in se* and *malum prohibitum*. In recent years there has been a tremendous increase in the latter type of offense.   And with this there has been a corresponding increase in the number of convictions without the need of establishing the normal mens-rea requirement.   But so far as offenses *malum in se* are concerned the mens-rea concept has lost none of its validity, as emphasized by *Morissette*,[35] and it is not likely to do so.[36]

The third misconception has resulted from a faulty analysis of the mistake-of-fact cases.   Many convictions of offenses *mala prohibita* have involved a mistake of fact which was not an excuse although it would have been recognized as such in a prosecution for an offense *malum in se*.   This has led some to jump to a faulty conclusion.   They have started with the generalization of a bona-fide and reasonable mistake of fact of such a nature that what was done would not constitute an offense if the facts were as supposed to be.   And they have assumed that whenever this is not recognized as a defense it must be on the basis of *malum prohibitum*.   On this assumption such an offense as statutory rape (carnal knowledge of a child) would be *malum prohibitum*.   This conclusion misses the point entirely.   In a prosecution for an offense *malum prohibitum*, if no special mens-rea element has been added by the words of the statute, the position in this regard is extreme.   A prohibited act done under an innocent and nonnegligent mistake of fact may not be excused even if the mistake was of such a nature that what was done would have been unpunishable *and entirely proper*, had the facts been as they were reasonably supposed to be.   The mistake as to the age of the girl in a statutory-rape case is not this kind of mistake.   The defendant's belief that the girl was over the age of consent may have been

31.   Levitt, Extent and Function of the Doctrine of Mens Rea, 17 Ill.L.Rev. 578, 587 (1923).   "The distinction between *mala in se* and *mala prohibita* is drawn on the basis of whether their origin is statutory."   Note 43 Harv.L.Rev. 117, n. 9 (1929).   A statutory offense if not *malum prohibitum* if a wrongful intent is required for conviction.   United States v. Boyce Motor Lines, 188 F.2d 889 (3d Cir. 1951), aff'd Boyce Motor Lines, Inc. v. United States, 342 U.S. 337, 72 S.Ct. 329 (1952).

32.   Levitt, supra note 29.   Embezzlement is *malum in se*.   State v. Prince, 52 N.M. 15, 189 P.2d 993 (1948).

33.   Regina v. Prince, L.R. 2 Cr.Cas. Res. 154 (1875).   And see State v. Audette, 81 Vt. 400, 403, 70 A. 833, 834 (1908).   These cases are discussed infra in the text.   Suicide or attempted suicide is not punished under the laws of Massachusetts, but any such act is unlawful and *malum in se*.   Commonwealth v. Mink, 123 Mass. 422 (1877).

34.   Levitt, supra note 31.

35.   342 U.S. 246, 72 S.Ct. 240 (1952). See also Smith v. California, 361 U.S. 147, 80 S.Ct. 215 (1959).

36.   Sayre, supra note 12.

genuinely entertained and based upon very reasonable grounds. But the conviction is upheld on the ground that what was done would not have been proper even if the facts had been as he reasonably supposed them to be.[37] It is not within the scope of this section to comment on the Kinsey Report,[38] but the theory of the courts in these cases has been that mistaking the age of the girl in a statutory-rape case is not an *innocent* mistake of fact. The mistake is not between an innocent act and a guilty one, but only in regard to the nature and extent of the wrong.[39]

The difference between the two types of offense seemed too obvious to Blackstone to require more than mention. One involved sin and the other did not. "The case is the same as to crimes and misdemeanors, that are forbidden by the superior laws, and are therefore styled *mala in se*, such as murder, theft, and perjury; which contract no additional turpitude from being declared unlawful by the inferior legislature . . . .. But with regard to things in themselves indifferent the case is entirely altered . . . .. Now these prohibitory laws do not make the transgression a moral offence, or sin: . . . .." [40] To some, on the other hand, it has seemed insoluble. "[W]e would hesitate to concur in the soundness of the view that the unlawful act . . . must be *malum in se*; for, outside of those things which are condemned as evil or wrong by the Holy Scriptures, the question of what would be evil or wrong in its nature depends on individual conception or environment." [41]

Let this problem be examined in the light of the important differences mentioned. An offense *malum prohibitum*, to repeat, (1) is within the royal power of dispensation; (2) is not an "unlawful act" in the sense that it alone is sufficient to make a resulting homicide manslaughter (or a lesser injury criminal battery); (3) does not have the normal mens-rea requirement (unless added by the words of the statute); (4) is within the application of respondeat superior; (5) requires only a preponderance of the evidence for conviction; is of such a nature that (6) an agreement to do such an act is not a conspiracy if it is not known to be against the law; and (7) condonation by the injured party is a complete bar to prosecution. These point irresistibly to just one conclusion:

An offense malum prohibitum is not a crime.[42]

---

37. The Iowa court, in distinguishing a case of this nature from the case of a man who has intercourse with a woman genuinely and reasonably believed by him to be his wife, said obiter of the latter: "In such a case there is no offense, for none was intended either in law or in morals." State v. Ruhl, 8 Iowa 447, 450 (1859).

38. Kinsey, Sexual Behavior in the Human Male (1948).

39. State v. Houx, 109 Mo. 654, 19 S.W. 35 (1891).

See also State v. Davis, 108 N.H. 158, 229 A.2d 842 (1967); Eggleston v. State, 4 Md.App. 124, 241 A.2d 433 (1968). Contra, People v. Hernandez, 61 Cal.2d 529, 39 Cal.Rptr. 361, 393 P.2d 673 (1964); State v. Guest, 583 P.2d 836 (Alaska 1978). See Annotation 8 A.L.R.3d 1100. This problem is discussed, infra, Section 7, Unlawful Act.

40. 1 Bl.Comm. *54, 55, 58.

41. Silver v. State, 13 Ga.App. 722, 725, 79 S.E. 919, 921 (1913).

42. See Model Criminal Code, Tentative Draft No. 2 pp. 8–9 (1954).

This was recognized by Blackstone and others,[43] and has even the beginnings of statutory recognition.[44] It is clearly indicated by the persistent search for an appropriate label, such as "public torts," [45] "public welfare offenses," [46] "prohibitory laws," [47] "prohibited acts," [48] "regulatory offenses," [49] "police regulations," [50] "administrative misdemeanors," [51] "quasi crimes," [52] or "civil offenses." [53] There is no magic in a label, of course, but the one last named is preferred here because of the implied emphasis. It divides the field into "crimes" ("criminal offenses") and "civil offenses." Those who have regarded the *malum in se—malum prohibitum* dichotomy as unsound in nature or insoluble in the human courts are unlikely so to regard division separating crimes from civil offenses. Some difficulties will be encountered at the boundary line, without doubt, but there is nothing unusual about this.

Before directing attention to that problem it is well to glance at the outline of the civil offense field. In a scholarly article Professor Sayre has shown the development of this field both in England and in the United States.[54] He finds eight general categories which he summarizes as follows.[55]

---

43. 1 Bl.Comm. *54, 55, 58. Gausewitz, Criminal Law—Reclassification of Certain Offenses as Civil Instead of Criminal, 12 Wis.L.Rev. 365 (1937). Statutory crimes without mens rea "go counter to the very common-law conception of a crime." Pound, The Law of the Land, 62 Am.L.Rev. 174, 182 (1928); 166 L.T. 208, 209 (1928). ". . . the enactments do not constitute the prohibited acts into crime. . . ." Regina v. Prince, L.R. 2 Cr.Cas.Res. 154, 163 (1875). ". . . that class of cases where the offense involves no crime against society or good morals. . . ." Holsey v. State, 4 Ga.App. 453, 61 S.E. 836, 845 (1908). ". . . our Constitution, in speaking of criminal prosecutions, does not refer to the enforcement of statutory penalties." Durham v. State, 117 Ind. 477, 481, 19 N.E. 327, 329 (1888). "An action to recover a forfeiture for violation of an ordinance is thus a civil proceeding. . . ." South Milwaukee v. Schantzen, 258 Wis. 41, 43, 44 N.W.2d 628, 629 (1950).

The Internal Revenue Code provides both criminal and civil penalties. Helvering v. Mitchell, 303 U.S. 391, 58 S.Ct. 630 (1938).

44. "Except that the acts defined as traffic infractions by the vehicle and traffic law heretofore or hereafter committed, are not crimes." McKinney's N.Y. Pen.Law § 2 (1909).

In the recent Revision we find: "As used in this title, the term offense does not include a traffic offense." McKinney's N.Y.Rev.Pen.Law § 55.00. See al-

so West's Ann.Cal.Pen.Code §§ 16, 19c and 19d, as amended in 1968.

45. Note, Public Torts, 35 Harv.L. Rev. 462 (1922).

46. Sayre, supra note 12.

47. 1 Bl.Comm. *58.

48. Regina v. Prince, L.R. 2 Cr.Cas. Res. 154, 163 (1875).

49. Morissette v. United States, 342 U.S. 246, 258, 72 S.Ct. 240, 247 (1952); Sayre, Criminal Responsibility for the Acts of Another, 43 Harv.L.Rev. 689, 720 (1930).

50. Hammond v. King, 137 Iowa 548, 552, 114 N.W. 1062, 1063 (1908).

51. Kirchheimer, Criminal Omissions, 55 Harv.L.Rev. 615, 636 (1942).

52. Stroud, Mens Rea 11 (1914); Fiorella v. Birmingham, 35 Ala.App. 384, 387, 48 So.2d 761, 764 (1950).

53. Gausewitz, supra note 43. It is called a "violation" in the Model Criminal Code. Section 1.04(5).

54. Sayre, Public Welfare Offenses, 33 Col.L.Rev. 55 (1933).

The violations of the narcotic laws have been deemed so serious that the tendency has been to treat them as true crimes. See Rideout v. Superior Court, 67 Cal.2d 474–75, 62 Cal.Rptr. 581, 583, 432 P.2d 197, 199 (1967).

55. Id. at 73. "Police Court convictions for violation of city ordinances are not convictions of crime." McClain v. United States, 224 F.2d 522, 524 (5th Cir. 1955).

"(1) Illegal sales of intoxicating liquor;

    (a) sales of prohibited beverage;

    (b) sales to minors;

    (c) sales to habitual drunkards;

    (d) sales to Indians or other prohibited persons;

    (e) sales by methods prohibited by law;

(2) Sales of impure or adulterated food or drugs;

    (a) sales of adulterated or impure milk;

    (b) sales of adulterated butter or oleomargarine;

(3) Sales of misbranded articles;

(4) Violations of anti-narcotic acts;

(5) Criminal nuisances;

    (a) annoyances or injuries to the public health, safety, repose, or comfort;

    (b) obstructions of highways;

(6) Violations of traffic regulations;

(7) Violations of motor-vehicle laws;

(8) Violations of general police regulations, passed for the safety, health, or well-being of the community."

Confusion was introduced into this problem during National Prohibition. The "crusaders" who engineered the enactment of statutes prohibiting the manufacture and sale of intoxicating liquor were bent on punishing conduct which they regarded immoral. The statutes were drawn and the penalties fixed from this point of view. The very word "prohibition" emphasizes that these were not mere penalty clauses added for the enforcement of statutes enacted for purposes other than to prevent wrongdoing. The violations of those laws were, and should have been uniformly recognized to be, *mala in se*. It was later decided that the enactment of those statutes had been a mistake and they were repealed; but prior to repeal they represented the manifested judgment of the public. And one is never permitted to substitute his individual judgment for the public judgment as to what is morally wrong. But ardent enforcers, realizing that it is much easier to convict of *malum prohibitum* than *malum in se*, tended to deal with them procedurally as the former, while applying penalties suitable only for the latter. The penalty frequently included imprisonment which is never appropriate for a civil offense.[56]

56. See Model Criminal Code, Tentative Draft No. 2, pp. 8–9 (1954). It has included imprisonment at times. The owner of a butcher shop was sentenced to ninety days in jail because of a short-weight sale by a clerk during the owner's absence despite undisputed evidence that the owner had not authorized such a sale or participated in any way. In re Marley, 29 Cal.2d 525, 175 P.2d 832 (1946). This was a habeas corpus proceeding. The court intimated that it might have refused to uphold the penalty imposed had the case come to it on appeal. The case is noted: 35 Calif.L.Rev. 583 (1947). The Oregon court intimated that its negligent homicide statute created a civil offense, although the penalty might be three years in the penitentiary. State v. Wojahn, 204 Or. 84, 282 P.2d 675 (1955). But to substitute ordinary negligence for criminal negligence as the mens-rea requirement of the offense does not remove it from the category of true crime.

If an ordinance is passed prohibiting the parking of cars in certain blocks of the public streets, restricting parking to one side of the street in certain other blocks, limiting parking to two hours in others, and to thirty minutes in still others; this is not with any thought of punishing wrongdoing. It has been decided that public convenience and the needs of traffic will be best served by such an arrangement. Or, to state it differently, that this will promote the general welfare. A penalty clause will be added for the reason that no other means of enforcement seems available. And the violation of this penalty clause is a typical offense *malum prohibitum*. Doing what was done was wrong only because it was made so by the enactment. On the other hand if a statute is passed prohibiting the obtaining of the property of another by promissory fraud, the very purpose of the enactment is to punish wrongdoing. The statute was passed because such conduct is deemed to be morally wrongful. And a violation thereof is *malum in se*. This distinction is clear enough, but there are complicating factors.

One such factor is the possibility of a statute embodying something of each of the two opposing positions. Thus a pure food and drug act may have some sections drawn to promote the public welfare for reasons unrelated to morality, and other sections intended to prevent wrongful conduct—such as a section prohibiting the unauthorized manufacture or sale of designated dangerous drugs. And a violation of this statute is *malum prohibitum* if the particular clause is of the former type, but *malum in se* if it is of the latter.

Another complicating factor requires particular attention. If an elaborate traffic statute includes a section requiring cars to stop before entering designated intersections, this is not in the belief that without such a statute it would be morally wrongful for a driver not to stop before entering such intersections. In the absence of a statute it would be proper for a driver to drive carefully into such an intersection, without stopping, when no cross-traffic was approaching from either direction. But many problems are involved, and it has been determined that the only safe arrangement is to require each car to be brought to a complete stop before entering such designated intersections. And it is morally wrong for one to substitute his personal judgment for the public judgment expressed in a statute designed for the protection of life and property. One who intentionally violates such a law is willing to risk a danger which the law seeks to prevent. And this is culpable conduct.[57] The result is that a violation of this particular clause of the statute is *malum in se*, a true crime, if intentional; but *malum prohibitum*, a civil offense, if inadvertent. This has been recognized in traffic cases,[58] and should be recognized in case of the violation of any provision of a regulatory law intended for the protection of life or property. If such a statute provides for a penalty in the form of either fine or imprisonment,

Judge Cardozo, in justifying convictions for certain *malum prohibitum* violations, whether intentional or not, emphasized that they were punishable only by a moderate fine; and indicated he would not sustain imprisonment for such violations. People ex rel. Price v. Sheffield Farms-Slawson-Decker Co., 225 N.Y. 25, 32–33, 121 N.E. 474, 476–77 (1918).

57. "An intentional, wilful or wanton violation of a statute or ordinance, designed for the protection of human life or limb, which proximately results in injury or death, is culpable negligence." State v. Cope, 204 N.C. 28, 31, 167 S.E. 456, 458 (1932).

58. Ibid.

only a fine should be imposed unless the infraction was shown to be intentional or reckless. An additional point should be noted. Assume a motorist has crossed the center line of the highway at a place where this is prohibited. The fact that he did so unintentionally and without negligence may be no defense to a charge of traffic violation; but it will be a complete defense to a charge of manslaughter if a fatal accident should result. This would be innocent homicide—homicide without the normal mens rea.[59] Obviously this does not mean that death resulting from an intentional violation of such a traffic law must be held to be innocent homicide.[60]

Another situation is entitled to attention. A statute forbids anyone to drive a motor vehicle upon the public highway without an operator's license and provides a penalty for doing so. D had a fatal accident while driving a car on the public highway without an operator's license. Is this fact sufficient for conviction of manslaughter without any evidence of negligence[61] in the operation of the vehicle at the time of the accident? One court said no.[62] "In the instant case, it is true that the death would not have occurred if appellant's automobile had not been on the highway . . . but appellant's violation of the Vehicle Code had no direct relationship to the cause of death . . . . It cannot be logically concluded that the death, 'happened in consequence of' such violation."[63] Another court said yes.[64] "The unlawful act was the driving of the automobile, not the failure to obtain a license."[65]

What about causation in such a case? Is there any direct causal connection between the unlawful act and the death? What was the unlawful act? It cannot be maintained that the only unlawful act involved was the failure to procure a license because this failure would have violated no law if there had been no driving. On the other hand driving a car on the public highway was not per se unlawful; it was unlawful only in the absence of a license. Both elements are involved. At the particular moment, however, D had no operator's license. Without that license his act of driving his car on the pub-

---

59. Finding that D had failed to yield the right of way in violation of the Vehicle Code but without a finding of wanton or reckless conduct is insufficient to sustain his conviction of involuntary manslaughter. Commonwealth v. Clowser, 212 Pa.Super. 208, 239 A.2d 870 (1968). Accord, State v. Weston, 273 N.C. 275, 159 S.E.2d 883 (1968). Compare, State v. Scott, 201 Kan. 134, 439 P.2d 78 (1968). See also, Thompson v. State, 108 Fla. 370, 146 So. 201 (1933); State v. Cope, 204 N.C. 28, 167 S.E. 456 (1933); Weaver v. State, 185 Tenn. 276, 206 S.W.2d 293 (1947). A fatal traffic accident by one violating a municipal ordinance was held sufficient for manslaughter. State v. O'Mara, 105 Ohio St. 94, 136 N.E. 885 (1922). But this was overruled. Steele v. State, 121 Ohio St. 332, 168 N.E. 846 (1929). The mere fact that D failed to stop for a stop sign and had a fatal traffic accident in the intersection is not sufficient to establish guilt of manslaughter. It is necessary to show that this act was the proximate cause of the death and

that D was culpably negligent. Frey v. State, 97 Okl.Cr. 410, 265 P.2d 502 (1953). Accord, Cain v. State, 55 Ga.App. 376, 190 S.E. 371 (1937); State v. Phelps, 242 N.C. 540, 89 S.E.2d 132 (1955).

60. State v. McLean, 234 N.C. 283, 67 S.E.2d 75 (1951).

It should be noted that under some of the new penal codes, if the death resulted from criminal negligence the offense would not be manslaughter, but a lesser statutory offense often called "negligent homicide."

61. Whether the element which might change the result if present would be negligence or criminal negligence need not be considered here. See chapter 2.

62. Commonwealth v. Williams, 133 Pa.Super. 104, 1 A.2d 812 (1938).

63. Id. at 112, 1 A.2d at 816.

64. Commonwealth v. Romig, 22 Pa. D. & C. 341 (1934).

65. Id. at 342.

lic highway was unlawful. That act of driving was the direct and immediate cause of death. The logic of the second case is unanswerable as a matter of causation. **D**'s act of driving that car on that occasion was in violation of law. **D**'s act of driving that car on that occasion was the direct and immediate cause of death. On the other hand, the court in the first case was not thinking about the causal connection between **D**'s *act* and the death. It was thinking in terms of the connection between the *unlawfulness* of **D**'s act and the death. This is just another way of saying that while **D** was violating the law his act was not such an "unlawful act" that a resulting death is manslaughter for this reason alone. Had the two courts been thinking, not in terms of causation, but in terms of the distinction between crimes and civil offenses they might have reached the same conclusion.

An additional question needs attention. Why was **D** without a license? The problem can be emphasized by giving two extreme answers. (1) **D** had been a licensed operator for years and had unwittingly permitted the day to go by without obtaining the required renewal. (2) **D** had been refused a license (or his license had been revoked) because a driving test had shown that it would be quite unsafe for him to drive a motor car on the public highway. In the latter case those who refused to grant the license (or who revoked it) might well urge that they foresaw that this was exactly the kind of tragedy which was to be expected if **D** drove a car on the public highway, and that this was why he had no license. The fact that the prosecution is unable to produce evidence of negligence in the actual operation of the vehicle at the time of the accident may be because **D** is the only surviving witness. Or it may be due to other difficulties in procuring evidence rather than to the fact that there was no negligence. There is not only a causal connection between **D**'s act (which was unlawful) and the death in such a case. There is also a causal connection between the unlawfulness of his act and the death, which would not be true if the reason for the lack of license was an inadvertent failure to renew promptly.

Stated in another way, there is nothing culpable in driving a car on the highway without a license if the lack is because what had been a valid license has expired as a result of inadvertence. The inadvertence will not save the driver from paying a fine if charged with this violation, but it should protect him against any sentence of imprisonment.[66] And if he should have the misfortune of causing a fatal traffic accident and is charged with any form of criminal homicide, it should be necessary in order to convict, to produce the same evidence of recklessness or criminal negligence that would have been required if the license had not expired, because this was homicide resulting from an offense *malum prohibitum*, or civil offense.[67] On the other hand, it is culpable for one to drive a car on the highway after having been denied a license because a driving test had shown that he could not operate a car with safety to others. His violation was an offense *malum in se*, a true crime. And if he should have a fatal accident it would not be inappropriate to convict him of criminal homicide even if he was the only surviving witness so that no evidence of recklessness or criminal negligence could be shown. This is a typical instance of a law enacted to promote the general welfare for purposes unrelated to issues of morality, but with a prime purpose of protecting life and property, so that a wilful violation becomes culpable.

66. See note 56 infra.

67. State v. Emmich, 39 Or.App. 769, 593 P.2d 1281 (1979).

The effort to determine whether a particular offense is *malum in se* or *malum prohibitum* should start with the basic premise that if the purpose of the law is to conform conduct to accepted moral standards the offense is *malum in se*, whereas if the law was enacted to regulate conduct for purposes unrelated to morality, with a penalty clause for enforcement, the offense is *malum prohibitum*. Certain guides are helpful. At common law the machinery of the criminal law (indictment) was used in the prosecution of a public nuisance, because no other was then available, but it was recognized as a civil offense [68] rather than a crime. Apart from the public nuisance all common-law public offenses were *malum in se*.[69] Hence if the law prohibits conduct which constitutes a common-law public offense, other than a public nuisance, the offense is *malum in se*. If the offense is popularly regarded as reprehensible, such as obtaining the property of another by promissory fraud, it is *malum in se*. If the obvious purpose of the lawmakers was to punish conduct which they considered morally wrongful, it is *malum in se* without reference to any individual's attempt to evaluate it. The legislative body is empowered to express the "voice" of the public. Any inquiry, moreover, has reference to the particular section of a multi-section statute rather than to what might be regarded as its all-over objective.

On the other hand, if the statute, meaning the very section violated, was enacted to promote the general welfare in ways unrelated to moral problems, a violation thereof is *malum prohibitum*.[70] With this important exception, if the regulation included the purpose of protecting life or property, an inadvertent violation is *malum prohibitum*, but a violation is *malum in se* if intentional or reckless.

Blackstone held the civil offense in very low esteem. It did not, in his view, place upon the individual any duty of compliance. He could obey the law and avoid the penalty or violate the law and pay the fine. Which election he made was a matter of indifference except to himself.[71] This is unsound. The theory that the individual is free to flout the law of the land—even such a law—is quite unacceptable. The driver who inadvertently leaves his car parked in a restricted zone beyond the permitted time has no legally-recognized excuse. But his conscience is clear. He is just as good a citizen as if this oversight had not occurred. This is not quite true of the driver who intentionally parks overtime, whether it is because he thinks he can retake his car before it is actually "tagged," or thinks if he gets a ticket he can have it "fixed" or that the officers will be too busy ever actually to enforce it. And the driver who intentionally and habitually parks his car overtime certainly cannot claim a rating of one hundred per cent in the scale of citizenship. If all drivers regularly made such a practice the enforcement of the parking law probably would break down entirely. The fact that it would be

68. The Queen v. Stephens, L.R. 1 Q.B. 702, 708 (1866). This case is discussed in the following subsection.

69. Mueller, On Common Law Mens Rea, 42 Minn.L.Rev. 1043, 1101 (1955).

70. "Such so-called statutory crimes are in reality an attempt to utilize the machinery of criminal administration as an enforcing arm for social regulations of a purely civil nature, with the punishment unrelated to questions of moral wrongdoing or guilt." Commonwealth v. Koczwara, 397 Pa. 575, 155 A.2d 825 (1959).

71. "But in these cases the alternative is offered to every man; 'either abstain from this, or submit to such a penalty:' and his conscience will be clear, whichever side of the alternative he thinks proper to embrace." 1 Bl.Comm. *58.

a matter of indifference how long the car remained there in the absence of statute does not leave it a matter of indifference after the regulatory enactment.

What has come to be one of the leading cases in the field is *Balint*.[72] The indictment charged a violation of the Narcotic Act. The question was whether the indictment was demurrable for want of an averment that defendants sold the inhibited drugs knowing them to be such. The obvious answer was no. Even on the premise that an innocent and nonnegligent mistake of fact would constitute an excuse, the prosecution was not required to plead and prove the absence of such a mistake. This would have been a matter to be shown in defense if it had been recognized as exculpatory in such a case. The court, however, insisted that such a mistake would not prevent conviction for this offense. And this has caused much confusion since the statute authorized a penitentiary sentence. Had the court added that the penalty must be limited to a fine if the sale resulted from an innocent and nonnegligent mistake of fact, we would be many years ahead in the development of this part of the law.

All of the above emphasizes the need to take a closer look at the familiar dichotomy.

Mala In Se: Mala Prohibita

Despite the apparent confusion in the cases and the texts, the distinction between offenses *mala in se* and offenses *mala prohibita* is basic, and the difference as clear as the difference between night and day. Reference to the comparison invites comment. When what had been day changed into night, this was in no way comparable to blowing out a candle or turning off an electric light. There was a twilight zone during which it might be difficult to say just when the transition actually took place. Hence to say the difference between two other concepts is as clear as the difference between night and day does not preclude the possibility of a "twilight zone" in which questions may arise. It does mean, however, that the difference is very real and substantial, and such that it is clearly distinguishable under most circumstances.

Offenses Mala In Se

In addressing offenses *mala in se* the threshold step is to repeat that all common-law offenses, other than public nuisance, are included. Obviously, however, it cannot be said that all offenses of statutory origin are *mala prohibita*. That would include embezzlement, for example, which as pointed out is clearly *malum in se*.[73] There is no common-law crime of embezzlement. It is entirely of statutory origin. It was created, not by one statute, but by a series of enactments, each for the purpose of providing punishment for conduct similar to larceny, and equally culpable, but omitted by technicalities in the development of the common law. Thus for a bailee to sell, as his own, a chattel that had been bailed to him, is as culpable as for another to steal it. But unless he had a wrongful intent at the time he originally re-

---

72. United States v. Balint, 258 U.S. 250, 42 S.Ct. 301 (1922).

73. State v. Prince, 52 N.M. 15, 189 P.2d 933 (1948).

ceived it, his misconduct is not common-law larceny.[74] And one of the statutes on embezzlement (although not the first)[75] was to correct this omission of the common law and provide a penalty for this grossly immoral conduct.

This provides the clue to statutory offenses *mala in se.* If the statute was for the purpose of providing punishment for culpable conduct, the resulting offense is *malum in se.*

Offenses *Mala Prohibita*

Not all offenses are of that nature, an extreme example being that of over-parking in a restricted zone, as previously mentioned. If parking in a certain area has been restricted to one hour this is not because it is deemed immoral to park there for a longer period. If some drivers park there extensively there may be others who are unable to find a parking space available when needed. Hence it has been determined that it will be for the best interest of the public in general to limit parking there, and the one-hour limit has been deemed most appropriate for that particular community. As is true of every other regulatory statute, it will have a penalty clause. This is not for the purpose of punishing evil-doers, but only because no other reasonable method of enforcing such an enactment has ever been devised. Parking overtime in a restricted zone is not conduct that is wrong in itself, it is wrong only because made so by statute.

This is the clue to offenses *mala prohibita.* If the statute involved was enacted, not for the purpose of prohibiting immoral conduct, but only to regulate some field of public welfare, for reasons unrelated to moral behavior, a violation is an offense *malum prohibitum.*

Complications

Having established the basic distinction—that a statute enacted for the punishment of evil-doers results in an offense *malum in se,* whereas a statute enacted to regulate some field of public welfare for reasons unrelated to moral behavior results in an offense *malum prohibitum*—it is necessary to recognize a complicating factor introduced by an occasional modern statute in this area that is not exclusively either one or the other. A food and drug act, for example, may have provisions intended to promote the public welfare for reasons unrelated to moral behavior, but also others, such as those prohibiting the unauthorized manufacture or sale of narcotics, intended for the punishment of wrongdoers. Even if it should have only one penalty clause, it is the same as two statutes so far as the present problem is concerned. Violations of the provisions intended to punish wrongdoers are offenses *mala in se,* whereas the other violations are offenses *mala prohibita.*

An additional problem requires special attention. Even if a regulatory statute does not prohibit any conduct that would be morally wrong, if it includes any provision intended for the safety of life or property, it presents a

---

74. See supra, ch. 4, § 3.

75. The first statute on embezzlement, 39 Geo. III, c. 85 (1799), made it an offense for an employee to appropriate his employer's property when the offense was not larceny because possession of the property was received from a third person. The provision as to bailees was not enacted until 1857. 3 Stephen, History of the Criminal Law of England 159 (1883).

comparable problem. This is because the intentional violation of a law intended for the safety of life or property is itself culpable conduct.[76] Hence if such a provision has been violated unintentionally, the violation is *malum prohibitum*; but if the violation was intentional it is *malum in se*. This distinction should have careful attention when it comes to pronouncement of the penalty. Imprisonment is appropriate only for punishment,[77] and hence should be applied only for convictions of offenses *mala in se*. If the penalty clause of a regulatory statute authorizes a penalty in the form of fine or imprisonment, this should be interpreted to permit no more than a fine unless the conviction was for violation of a clause of the statute intended to prohibit culpable conduct, or for the intentional violation of a provision intended for the safety of life or property. (Either fine or imprisonment or both would be appropriate for the punishment of offenses *mala in se* depending upon the crime and the circumstances).

Assume a statute enacted to promote the general public welfare, with no provision intended to punish because of culpable conduct, but with a provision requiring a motorist approaching a certain highway from the side to stop before entering. Without such a requirement it would not be wrong for a motorist to enter that highway cautiously, without stopping, at a time when no car was approaching on the highway near enough to be of any possible danger. But because of the circumstances, including the use of the highway and estimates of distance and speed, it has been determined that the only safe provision is to require every car to be brought to a complete stop before entering. If a motorist entered that highway without stopping, because he failed to notice the stop-sign and was unaware of the requirement to stop, his violation is an offense *malum prohibitum*. On the other hand, if he was fully aware of the requirement to stop, and entered without stopping because he decided it was safe to do so, his offense is *malum in se*. No one is permitted to substitute one's own judgment for the public determination of what is needed for the safety of others.

The problem becomes most acute when entering without stopping resulted in a fatal traffic accident. If the motorist had been unaware of the requirement to stop, a criminal prosecution against him should be on the claim of criminal negligence. And to convict him of manslaughter (or a lesser homicide offense under some of the new penal codes) it should be necessary to establish that under all the circumstances the driving was with criminal negligence and resulted in the fatal accident. If, however, the claim was that the motorist intentionally violated the statute, it should be necessary to establish only that he was aware of the requirement to stop, that he purposely entered the highway without stopping and that so doing caused the fatal accident. Some courts might instruct that intentional violation of this statute is criminal negligence. There is no objection to that, but under the com-

---

76. "An intentional, wilful or wanton violation of a statute or ordinance, designed for the protection of human life or limb, which proximately results in injury or death, is culpable negligence." State v. Cope, 204 N.C. 28, 31, 167 S.E. 456, 458 (1932). The mere fact that D failed to stop for a stop sign and had a fatal traffic accident in the intersection is not sufficient to establish guilt of manslaughter.

It is necessary to show that this act was the proximate cause of the death and that D was culpably negligent. Frey v. State, 97 Okl.Cr. 410, 265 P.2d 502 (1953). Accord, Cain v. State, 55 Ga.App. 376, 190 S.E. 371 (1937); State v. Phelps, 242 N.C. 540, 89 S.E.2d 132 (1955).

77. Model Penal Code, Tentative Draft No. 2, pp. 8–9 (1954).

mon law a killing as a result of the commission of an offense *malum in se* constitutes at least manslaughter, and no more need be established.

Conclusion

It may be well to repeat that the distinction between offenses *mala in se* and offenses *mala prohibita* is basic and the difference as clear as the difference between night and day. The familiar statement is to the effect that an offense *malum in se* is wrong in itself whereas an offense *malum prohibitum* is wrong only because prohibited. Although frequently misunderstood the statement is unquestionably true.

Since all common-law offenses (except public nuisance which is sui generis) are *mala in se*, search for the difference between them and offenses *mala prohibita* is restricted to a study of offenses of statutory origin. And the key to the difference is to be found in the reason for the imposition of penalty. Needless to say all legislation in this area is enacted in the effort to prevent specified conduct. As complete compliance seems unlikely a penalty for noncompliance is added, but not always for the same reason. If the violation was by conduct intolerably below the level of proper moral behavior, the penalty is for the purpose of punishment. If the violation was not of a nature to be morally culpable (e.g. parking overtime in a restricted zone) the penalty is merely for the purpose of enforcement. And the result is clear. If the penalty is for the purpose of punishment, the offense is *malum in se*; if it is merely for the purpose of enforcement, the offense is *malum prohibitum*.[78] Any doubt as to the purpose should be resolved by holding it to be merely for the purpose of enforcement, and the offense *malum prohibitum*.

A. STRICT LIABILITY

The development of the mens-rea doctrine left "no common law offenses in which mens rea is not required, notwithstanding an insignificant small number of badly reasoned cases to the contrary."[79] Public nuisance did survive as a strict-liability offense; but, as mentioned, this is not a true crime.[80] For some time the normal mens-rea requirement was applied to the civil offense, but later there was a resurgence of strict liability in this regard and public nuisance played such a prominent role in this development as to require particular attention.

78. "However, when the sanction is regulatory, rather than punitive, it does not support the characterization of the statute as criminal." State v. Rhoades, 54 Or.App. 254, 634 P.2d 806, 808 (1981).

79. Mueller, On Common Law Mens Rea, 42 Minn.L.Rev. 1043, 1101 (1955). As to libel, see id. at 1077. Bigamy was not a common-law crime being punished in the early days as an ecclesiastical offense. 4 Blackstone, Commentaries *163. When made a crime, there was much confusion as to the basis of enforcement. See, infra, chapter 9, section 1, C; Hall, Ignorance and Mistake in Criminal Law, 33 Ind.L.J. 1 30–34 (1957); Moore, Bigamy, A Crime Though Unwittingly Committed, 30 U.Cin.L.Rev. 35

(1961); Paton, Bigamy and Mens Rea, 17 Can.B.Rev. 94 (1939); Trowbridge, Criminal Intent and Bigamy, 7 Calif.L.Rev. 1 (1918). Part of the confusion resulted from statutory language itself. See, e.g., State v. Hendrickson, 67 Utah 15, 245 P. 375 (1926).

80. Kenny, Outlines of Criminal Law 46 (14th ed. 1933). In a recent edition public nuisance is regarded "too extensive for convenient inclusion." Kenny, Outlines of Criminal Law 424 (19th ed. by Turner, 1966).

"It . . . is in the nature of a civil proceeding." Per Mellor, J., in The Queen v. Stephens, L.R. 1 Q.B. 702, 708 (1866).

Reference to the corresponding tort will be useful. As was true of the early criminal law, the law of torts started with strict liability, and the change to liability based upon fault came later in the law of private nuisance than in most other fields. Today, however, an action for damages for an ordinary private nuisance will not result in a recovery if the harm was caused without either intention, recklessness, or negligence. On the other hand, in a suit in equity for an injunction, the chancellor is not interested in whether the alleged nuisance resulted from fault in the past but only in whether there is a condition which should not be permitted to continue in the future.[81]

The development of the public-nuisance concept was not in any sense the result of a desire to deal harshly with the offender. Quite the opposite—it was intended for his protection. If every member of the community who was annoyed by a public nuisance could maintain an action therefor, the result would be disastrous to the one who had caused it. Hence, the theory was that the King, acting for all the people, would maintain one action which, if it resulted in a judgment against the defendant, would call upon him to pay for the damage done, in the form of a fine, and to bring an end to the nuisance under an order of abatement. The necessary consequence was that no one could maintain a private action based upon a public nuisance. For the plaintiff to show that he is harmed more than others is not enough; to recover he must show that defendant is maintaining a private, as well as a public, nuisance in that it injures the plaintiff in a different manner than it affects the public in general.[82] This was of particular significance in the leading case of *Stephens*.[83]

Stephens was indicted for a public nuisance on the ground that waste materials from his slate quarry had been permitted to wash down into a river in such quantities as to impede navigation. The defense was that defendant, over eighty years of age, was unable personally to supervise the working of the quarry which was managed for him by his sons and that both defendant and his sons had given directions to the workmen which would have prevented what happened if obeyed: in other words, that the nuisance was brought about by employees in violation of express instructions as to the conduct of the work. The court, however, was not interested in how the condition came about but only in the future. Mr. Justice Mellor,[84] after pointing out that no private individual could maintain a private action on this public nuisance, con-

---

81. See Restatement, Second, Torts § 215 (1965), comment (b).

As to strict liability of one who carries on "an abnormally dangerous activity" see Restatement, Second, Torts §§ 519, 520 (1977).

82. Jardine v. City of Pasadena, 199 Cal. 64, 248 P. 225 (1926).

83. The Queen v. Stephens, L.R. 1 Q.B. 702 (1866).

84. Id. at 708–10. In another case, it was said: "As the object of the prosecution is to remove an injury to the public, with which the intent of the defendant has nothing to do, his intent is irrelevant." People v. Hess, 110 Misc. 76, 80,

179 N.Y.S. 734, 737 (Ct.Gen.Sess.1920) (quoting Wharton on Criminal Law).

In the following sentence, note the *non sequitur*. "The purpose of the statute is to prevent the recurrence of the nuisance, not to punish, although punishment must be prescribed in order to make the statute effective." People v. High Ground Dairy Co., 166 App.Div. 81, 82, 151 N.Y.S. 710, 711 (1915). If the nuisance had been caused without fault, an order of abatement would have been adequate. For a case in which the only purpose was abatement of the nuisance, see Attorney-General v. Tod Heatley, [1897] 1 Ch. 560 (1896).

tinued: "The prosecutor cannot proceed by action but must proceed by indictment. . . . [The] object of the indictment is not to punish the defendant, but really to prevent the nuisance from being continued. . . ." It is unfortunate he did not emphasize an additional point. Although a judgment against the defendant under an indictment for public nuisance ordinarily results in a sentence that he pay a fine and an order that he abate the nuisance, only the latter is appropriate in a case in which he is shown to have been without fault. Had this been emphasized, the case might not have served as the springboard for the resurgence of strict liability.[85]

One writer has come up with the phrase "partial absolute liability."[86] Without pausing to consider the propriety of attempting to qualify the absolute, let us hasten to recognize frankly that we have no offenses enforced on the basis of absolute liability. No doubt minor traffic violations would be high on the list claiming such a position, but it is submitted that if gangsters, fleeing from the scene of their robbery, should "commandeer" a car stopped for a red light and force the driver, under threat of death at pistol-point, to proceed without waiting for the signal to change and at a speed in excess of that permitted by law, this compulsion would be recognized as an excuse.[87] We have offenses enforced on the basis of strict liability—but not that strict.[88] The real problem for our present purpose, however, is the extent to which this strictness has been carried, and why.

---

85. "The new movement in England dates from the case of Regina v. Woodrow [15 M. & W. 404, 153 Eng.Rep. 907], decided in 1846 . . . . It was not, however, until after the decision, twenty years later, of Regina v. Stephens, . . . that the movement became consciously formulated in England." Sayre, The Present Signification of Mens Rea in the Criminal Law, in Harvard Legal Essays 399, 407 (1934).

86. Mueller, On Common Law Mens Rea, 42 Minn.L.Rev. 1043, 1068 (1958). Another writer referred to guilt based upon negligence as "a kind of absolute responsibility." Kelsen, General Theory of Law and State 67 (1945).

87. The bare command of the husband was held to excuse the wife for a minor traffic violation, as a survival of the ancient doctrine of marital coercion. People v. Statley, 91 Cal.App.2d Supp. 943, 206 P.2d 76 (1949). *Accord*, Commonwealth v. Daley, 148 Mass. 11, 18 N.E. 579 (1888) (illegal sale by wife in the presence of her husband).

If an officer learns that a "speeding" motorist is hurrying to a hospital in a case of an emergency properly calling for speed, the officer will assist the motorist in his effort. See also Goodwin v. State, 63 Tex.Cr. 140, 142, 138 S.W. 399, 400 (1911). The Kentucky court held that failure to supply a separate coach for colored passengers, as required by stat-

ute at that time, was excused where the failure was due to a landslide which delayed the coach that was to have been provided for that purpose, although it would have been possible to have had a spare coach in reserve. Chesapeake & Ohio Railroad Co. v. Commonwealth, 119 Ky. 519, 84 S.W. 566 (1905).

88. "Liability, then, we suggest, was never absolute." " 'Strict liability' seems to be a better term." Winfield, The Myth of Absolute Liability, 42 L.Q.Rev. 37, 46, 51 (1926). One writer thinks insanity should be no defense to a charge of traffic violation. Sayre, Public Welfare Offenses, 33 Colum.L.Rev. 55, 78 (1933). For a contrary view, see Mueller, How to Increase Traffic Fatalities: A Useful Guide for Modern Legislators and Traffic Courts, 60 Colum.L.Rev. 944, 958 (1960). "[P]resumably no court would convict a psychotic person . . . of any offense." Hall, General Principles of Criminal Law 342 (2d ed. 1960).

A conviction of a twelve-year-old girl for having made a prohibited sale of liquor was reversed because it was not shown that she had the necessary capacity. Commonwealth v. Mead, 92 Mass. 398 (1865). Professor Sayre thinks that the defense of infancy should not be available in such a case but even he would recognize the defense in case of a child under seven. Sayre, supra at 76.

Although the resurgence of strict liability has touched upon true crime as a result of an occasional misapplication,[89] this was not its purpose.[90] Two assumptions have been made, both seemingly correct: (1) The impressive group of governmental regulations, federal, state, and local, cannot be effectively enforced without the aid of penalties;[91] and (2) because of important differences between violations of these penalty-clauses on the one hand, and true crimes on the other, the former require greater strictness in their enforcement.

The historical development of this new enforcement technique has been detailed elsewhere,[92] and it must suffice here to say that it has taken place during a little more than the last hundred years[93] and in connection with the penalty-clauses of regulatory statutes in such fields as "(1) illegal sales of liquor; (2) sales of impure food or drugs; (3) sales of misbranded articles; (4) criminal nuisance; (5) traffic regulations; (6) motor vehicle laws, and (7) violations of general regulations, passed for the safety, health or well-being of the community."[94]

---

89. A leading case of obvious misapplication of the strict liability is Morissette v. United States, 187 F.2d 427 (6th Cir. 1951). The defendant was charged with having knowingly converted property of the United States. He admitted that he intentionally took the property but insisted that he honestly believed that the spent bomb casings had been abandoned by the government. Although this belief was quite reasonable under the circumstances, it was held not to be a defense. Fortunately, this decision was reversed by the Supreme Court, holding that such strict enforcement is not permissible in prosecutions of offenses *mala in se*. Morissette v. United States, 342 U.S. 246, 72 S.Ct. 240 (1952).

90. "This omission [of any words of mens rea in the statute] does not mean, of course, that § 751(a) defines a 'strict liability' crime for which punishment can be imposed without proof of any *mens rea* at all." United States v. Bailey, 444 U.S. 394, 406, n. 6, 100 S.Ct. 624, 632, n. 6 (1980). "We hold that mere omission from § 641 of any mention of intent will not be construed as eliminating that element from the crimes denounced." Morissette v. United States, 342 U.S. 246, 263, 72 S.Ct. 240 (1952). "Where the purpose of a statute is the punishment of a crime . . . absolute liability will not be found to be the intent of the legislature . . . . Instead the statute will be read as incorporating a mental state requirement." People v. Clark, 71 Ill. App.3d 381, 27 Ill.Dec. 680, 690, 389 N.E.2d 911, 921 (1979). "Although the statute is silent regarding intent, this court has held that the 'taking' in the crime of robbery must be with specific in-

tent permanently to deprive the owner of his property." Turner v. State, 96 Nev. 164, 605 P.2d 1140, 1141 (1980).

91. "The prosecution . . . is based on a now familiar type of legislation whereby penalties serve as effective means of regulation." United States v. Dotterweich, 320 U.S. 277, 280–81, 64 S.Ct. 134, 136 (1943); United States v. Park, 421 U.S. 658, 95 S.Ct. 1903 (1975).

92. Sayre, Public Welfare Offenses, 33 Colum.L.Rev. 55 (1933).

Wassertrom, Strict Liability in the Criminal Law, 12 Stan.L.Rev. 731 (1960).

93. "The pilot of the movement in this country appears to be a holding that a tavernkeeper could be convicted for selling liquor to an habitual drunkard even if he did not know the buyer to be such. Barnes v. State, 19 Conn. 398 (1849)." Morissette v. United States, 342 U.S. 246, 256, 72 S.Ct. 240, 246 (1952); see Howard, Strict Responsibility in the High Court of Australia, 76 L.Q.Rev. 547 (1960).

94. City of Toledo v. Kohlhofer, 96 Ohio App. 355, 361, 122 N.E.2d 20, 25 (1954). In partial elaboration of this field it was said: "Parking violations, parking meter violations, driving without proper lights, driving on the left side of the road, not displaying registration number, driving an automobile with a defaced number on the engine block, speeding, and overloading are some of the typical" offenses in this field. Mueller, How to Increase Traffic Fatalities: A Useful Guide for Modern Legislators and Traffic Courts, 60 Colum.L.Rev. 944, 959 (1960). Brett, J., added "statutes passed to pro-

The reasons for this development all seem grounded upon expediency. "The statute is drastic in its terms, but the Legislature was doubtless of the opinion that drastic measures are required to accomplish the purpose of enforcement of" such provisions.[95] Without such enforcement, "a wide door would be opened for evading the beneficial provisions of this legislation." [96] "It is needless to point out that, swamped with such appalling inundations of petty violations, the lower criminal courts would be physically unable to examine the subjective intent of each defendant, even were such determination desirable. As a matter of fact it is not, for the penalty in such cases is so slight that the courts can afford to disregard the individual in protecting the social interest." [97]

As will be pointed out in Chapter 9, no true crime results from an *actus reus* by one who acted under such a mistake of fact that what he did would have been neither an offense nor otherwise objectionable in any way had the facts been as he reasonably supposed them to be.[98] It is quite otherwise in case of a civil offense—in fact this is the chief point at which strict liability has developed in prosecutions of this nature.[99] Thus a reasonable mistake of fact has been held not a defense to a charge of forbidden possession,[1] sale,[2] or transportation[3] of intoxicating liquor; sale of intoxicating liquor to a minor,[4] or to an intoxicated person;[5] sale of oleomargarine,[6] of adulterated food or drugs,[7] or adulterated tobacco,[8] or unsound food;[9] sales from short

tect the revenue." Regina v. Prince, L.R. 2 Cr.Cas.Res. 154, 163 (1875).

95. State v. Lundgren, 124 Minn. 162, 168, 144 N.W. 752, 754 (1913).

96. Parker v. Adler, [1899] 1 Q.B. 20 (1898).

97. Sayre, Public Welfare Offenses, 33 Colum.L.Rev. 55, 69–70 (1933). Twenty years ago it was estimated that in cities of 25,000 or more, a combined total of about 6,500,000 traffic cases passed through their courts each year. Warren, Traffic Courts 29 (1942). Only a small per cent of those cases went to trial, but even a small per cent of that figure makes a staggering burden on the courts.

98. "Ignorance or mistake in fact, guarded by an honest purpose, will afford, at common law, a sufficient excuse for a supposed criminal act." Farrell v. State, 32 Ohio St. 456, 459 (1877). "For true crimes it is imperative that courts should not relax the classic requirement of the *mens rea* or guilty mind." Sayre, Public Welfare Offenses, 33 Colum.L. Rev. 55, 80 (1933). "Thus . . . mistake of fact is a defense if, because of the mistake, *mens rea* is lacking." Hall, Ignorance and Mistake in Criminal Law, 33 Ind.L.J. 1, 5 (1957). See 1 Hale, Pleas of the Crown *42.

99. The rule has developed that in all regulatory penal law mistake of fact is no defense. Mueller, Mens Rea and the Law Without It, 58 W.Va.L.Rev. 34

(1955). "On the other hand . . . ignorance of the fact or state of things contemplated by the statute will not excuse its violation." Welch v. State, 145 Wis. 86, 89, 129 N.W. 656, 657 (1911).

1. State v. Whitman, 52 S.D. 91, 216 N.W. 858 (1927).

2. Turnbow v. State, 153 Ga.App. 479, 265 S.E.2d 832 (1980); Troutner v. State, 17 Ariz. 506, 154 P. 1048 (1916); Commonwealth v. Boynton, 84 Mass. 160 (1861).

3. Commonwealth v. Hendrie, 97 Pa. Super. 328 (1929).

4. State v. Lundgren, 124 Minn. 162, 144 N.W. 752 (1913); State v. Cain, 9 W.Va. 559 (1876); State v. Hartfiel, 24 Wis. 60 (1869).

5. Cundy v. LeCocq, 13 Q.B.D. 207 (1884).

6. Commonwealth v. Weiss, 139 Pa. 247, 21 A. 10 (1891). Or serving it at a lunch counter. Welch v. State, 145 Wis. 86, 129 N.W. 656 (1911).

7. Groff v. State, 171 Ind. 547, 85 N.E. 769 (1909); Commonwealth v. Farren, 91 Mass. 489 (1864); People v. Snowberger, 113 Mich. 86, 71 N.W. 497 (1897); State v. Kelly, 54 Ohio St. 166, 43 N.E. 163 (1896); Parker v. Adler, [1899] 1 Q.B. 20 (1898).

8. Regina v. Woodrow, 15 M. & W. 404, 153 Eng.Rep. 907 (Ex.1846).

9. See note 9 on page 901.

weights or measures;[10] sales of misbranded articles;[11] admitting a minor to play in a pool-hall;[12] possession of an automobile with engine number altered;[13] operation of a motor vehicle without a rear light;[14] subscription to untrue statement with reference to securities;[15] solicitation of insurance on behalf of a company not authorized to do business within the state;[16] violation of parking regulations[17] or speed limits;[18] or environmental controls.[19]

In addition, many statements may be found to the effect that no mens rea is required for a civil offense,[20] the "act" (*actus reus*) alone being sufficient.[21] Although we may well doubt the implication that nothing will be recognized as an excuse for the *actus reus* of a civil offense because of possibilities such as the example of extreme compulsion mentioned earlier, yet we cannot doubt that many courts have taken the position that no mistake of fact can be recognized as such an excuse under any circumstances.

In upholding the conviction of a dealer for possessing adulterated tobacco, although he neither knew nor had any reason to suspect the adulteration, it was said that since he knew he was in possession of the tobacco "it is not necessary that he should know that the tobacco was adulterated . . . ."[22] A conviction of selling liquor to an intoxicated person was upheld although

9. Hobbs v. Winchester Corp., [1910] 2 K.B. 471.

10. Smith v. State, 223 Ala. 346, 136 So. 270 (1931); Commonwealth v. Sacks, 214 Mass. 72, 100 N.E. 1019 (1913).

11. United States v. Johnson, 221 U.S. 488, 31 S.Ct. 627 (1911).

12. State v. Furr, 101 W.Va. 178, 132 S.E. 504 (1926). Or to be admitted to a billiard room without the consent of his parent. Commonwealth v. Emmons, 98 Mass. 6 (1867).

13. People v. Johnson, 228 Ill. 442, 123 N.E. 543 (1919); State v. Dunn, 202 Iowa 1188, 211 N.W. 850 (1927); People v. Sequin, ___ Colo. ___, 609 P.2d 622 (1980).

14. Provincial Motor Cab Co. v. Dunning, [1909] 2 K.B. 599.

15. State v. Dobry, 217 Iowa 858, 250 N.W. 702 (1933).

16. McKnight v. State, 171 Tenn. 574, 106 S.W.2d 556 (1937).

17. Commonwealth v. Ober, 286 Mass. 25, 189 N.E. 601 (1934).

18. Goodwin v. State, 63 Tex.Cr. 140, 138 S.W. 399 (1911). A hitchhiker who drove the car on an errand at the request of the driver was convicted of using a motor vehicle without authority although he had no reason to doubt the driver's authority to use the car. Commonwealth v. Coleman, 252 Mass. 241, 147 N.E. 552 (1925).

19. Regina v. City of Sault Ste. Marie, 40 CCC 2d 353, 2 SCR 1299 (1978).

20. For example, Smith v. California, 361 U.S. 147, 150, 80 S.Ct. 215, 217 (1959) ("without any element of scienter"); Provincial Motor Cab Co. v. Dunning, [1909] 2 K.B. 599, 602 ("without a criminal intent or *mens rea*"); Pearks v. Gunston & Tee, Ltd. v. Ward, [1902] 2 K.B. 1, 11 ("whether he has any mens rea or not"); Parker v. Adler, [1899] 1 Q.B. 20, 25 (1898) ("*mens rea* is not necessary to constitute the offence"); Sayre, Public Welfare Offenses, 33 Colum.L.Rev. 55, 67 (1933) ("a special class of offense for which no *mens rea* was required").

21. Morissette v. United States, 342 U.S. 246, 256, 72 S.Ct. 240, 246 (1952) ("the guilty act alone makes out the crime"); In re Marley, 29 Cal.2d 525, 529, 175 P.2d 832, 835 (1946) ("the doing of the act constitutes the crime"); The Queen v. Tolson, 23 Q.B.D. 168, 173 (1889) ("The Acts are properly construed as imposing the penalty when the act is done, no matter how innocently."). In any such area one acts at his "peril." United States v. Balint, 258 U.S. 250, 254, 42 S.Ct. 301, 303 (1922); Groff v. State, 171 Ind. 547, 549, 85 N.E. 769, 770 (1908); Commonwealth v. Ober, 286 Mass. 25, 27, 189 N.E. 601, 602 (1934); State v. Furr, 101 W.Va. 178, 185, 132 S.E. 504, 507 (1926); The Queen v. Tolson, 23 Q.B.D. 168, 173 (1889).

22. Regina v. Woodrow, 15 M. & W. 404, 415, 153 Eng.Rep. 907, 912 (Ex. 1846).

In a trial for selling liquor to a minor, it was established that defendant had asked the six-foot-one-inch customer if he

the magistrate had ruled that it was "unnecessary to determine whether there had been on the part of the appellant or his servants a knowledge or means of knowledge of the drunkenness of the drunken person." [23]　A butcher was convicted of selling unsound meat although he and his assistants were unaware of the unsoundness and could not have discovered it by any examination which they could have been expected to make.[24]　An extreme case involved the sale of adulterated milk.[25]　By rail, the seller shipped pure milk which was adulterated in transit by some unknown person.　Starting with the premise that title did not pass until receipt by the consignee, the court held that the seller had committed the offense of selling adulterated milk although he "was entirely innocent morally, and had no means of protecting himself from the adulteration of this milk in the course of transit . . . ." [26]　None of these, however, can quite match the extremity of the case which held: "It is no defense to a prosecution for driving an overloaded truck in violation of the Vehicle Code that defendant had first obtained a weight certificate from a licensed weight-master which indicated that the truck was not overloaded." [27]

Fortunately, some courts have made a more realistic approach to problems of this nature.　In one case, for example, a truck driver whose cargo contained undersized fish was held not guilty of violating the statute if he had no knowledge that the cargo consisted of undersized fish and the cargo was so packed that it would have been unreasonable and impracticable to require him to inspect it.[28]　And in reversing a conviction in another case, it was said: "We are convinced that the ordinance making it unlawful 'to frequent, enter, be in, or be found in, any place where narcotics, narcotic drugs or their derivatives are unlawfully used, kept or disposed of,' and giving a person found in such place no opportunity to explain his presence unless he can show some authorization, goes far beyond what is reasonably necessary to achieve its legitimate purpose and constitutes an abuse of the police power of the city." [29]

---

was of age and received an affirmative answer.　The jury was instructed that ignorance or mistake of fact was no excuse.　In affirming the conviction, it was held that since the statute contained no such word as "wilfully" or "knowingly" the sale of liquor to a minor is an offense, the court adding, "where a statute commands that an act be done or omitted, which, in the absence of such statute, might have been done or omitted, without culpability, ignorance of the fact or state of things contemplated by the statute, will not excuse its violation." State v. Hartfiel, 24 Wis. 60, 61 (1869).

23. Cundy v. LeCocq, 13 Q.B.D. 207 (1884).

24. Hobbs v. Winchester Corp., [1910] 2 K.B. 471.

25. Parker v. Adler, [1899] 1 Q.B. 20 (1898).

26. Id. at 25.

27. Commonwealth v. Olshefski, 64 Pa. D. & C. 343 (Montour County Ct. 1948).

This is comparable to the case in which the vendor's precaution of having a sample of feeding meal analyzed did not protect him when it was shown that the product did not measure up to what was certified in the analyst's report.　Laird v. Dobell, [1906] 1 K.B. 131 (1905).

28. State v. William, 94 Ohio App. 249, 115 N.E.2d 36 (1952); *accord*, Maher v. Musson, 52 C.L.R. 100, 105 (Austl. 1934).　The recent trend in the interpretation of federal criminal statutes has been to imply a mens-rea requirement rather than a lack thereof.　Taussig v. McNamara, 219 F.Supp. 757 (D.C.1963).

29. City of Seattle v. Ross, 54 Wn.2d 655, 344 P.2d 216 (1959); State v. Millington, 377 So.2d 685 (Fla.1979).

Another case is enlightening. Charged with violating the statute by serving oleomargarine at a lunch counter without giving notice that it was not butter, defendant proved that he had requisitioned butter and received what he believed was butter because of its great resemblance thereto. His claim that there should be no conviction without at least objective fault on his part was not rejected, but the conviction was affirmed because he had not established a lack of opportunity to learn the truth of the matter.[30]

The conviction of a railroad on a charge of obstructing a crossing, the delay having resulted from the wrongful pulling of the emergency switch by a stranger,[31] seems to have been an imposition of liability without either mens rea or *actus reus*. Much more sound was the refusal to uphold a conviction where the charge was violation of an ordinance against stopping vehicles in the street and the evidence was that the defendant's progress was blocked by stalled traffic.[32] And approval should be given to the dictum exonerating the owner whose car was abandoned beside a fire hydrant by the thief who had stolen it.[33]

The object of strict enforcement of the civil offense has been said to be "to impose a high standard of care." [34] And this seems indicated by some references such as, starting with the assumption that some hardship is unavoidable, "Congress has preferred to place it upon those who have at least the opportunity of informing themselves . . . rather than to throw the hazard on the innocent public who are wholly helpless." [35] And it was said *obiter* in an outstanding case: [36] "The accused, if he does not will the violation, usually is in a position to prevent it with no more care than society might reasonably expect and no more exertion that it might reasonably exact from one who has assumed the responsibilities."

Too often, however, only lip-service is given to the importance of care. Thus, the dictum just quoted went on to the conclusion that "the guilty act alone makes out the crime." Compare a statement that the "public interest in the purity of its food is so great as to warrant the imposition of the highest standard of care on distributors," with its conclusion that "ignorance of the character of the food is irrelevant." [37]

30. Welch v. State, 145 Wis. 86, 129 N.W. 656 (1911).

31. Commonwealth v. New York Central & Hudson River Railroad Co., 202 Mass. 394, 88 N.E. 764 (1909).

32. Commonwealth v. Brooks, 99 Mass. 434 (1868).

33. People v. Forbath, 5 Cal.App.2d 767, 772, 42 P.2d 108, 110 (1935).

An ordinance may impose prima-facie liability on the owner of a car when the identity of the driver cannot be established. City of Columbus v. Webster, 170 Ohio St. 327, 164 N.E.2d 734 (1960). The registered owner of a car may relieve himself of liability by showing who actually parked his car illegally. People ex rel. Hunter v. Department of Sanitation, 193 Misc. 233, 86 N.Y.S.2d 437 (Magis.Ct.1948). Compare City of Chicago v. Crane, 319 Ill.App. 623, 49 N.E.2d 802 (1943) (owner guilty no matter who parked car). Due process is violated by a parking ordinance holding the owner liable for an illegally parked car without the owner's consent. Seattle v. Stone, 67 Wn.2d 886, 410 P.2d 583 (1966).

34. Howard, Strict Responsibility in the High Court of Australia, 76 L.Q.Rev. 547 (1960).

35. United States v. Dotterweich, 320 U.S. 277, 285, 64 S.Ct. 134, 138 (1943).

36. Morissette v. United States, 342 U.S. 246, 256, 72 S.Ct. 240, 246 (1952).

37. Smith v. California, 361 U.S. 147, 152, 80 S.Ct. 215, 218 (1959). The two quotes are joined by, "in fact an absolute standard which will not hear the distributor's plea as to the amount of care he has used."

Although a civil offense has no *normal* mens-rea requirement—that is, does not need that degree of blameworthiness essential for true crime—this should not be interpreted in the sense of liability without fault. It should be understood to mean that civil offense has its own peculiar mens rea [38] which requires, not culpability, but at least a mind that is not too young and not too greatly affected by mental disorder or compulsion,[39] plus a degree of fault in that the *actus reus* could have been avoided by some method which it is not against good conscience to require under all the circumstances.[40]

The penalty clause of a regulatory enactment may add a special mental element by the use of a word such as "knowingly" and thereby place upon the prosecution the burden of pleading and proving this special requirement. In the absence of any such words in the statute, the prosecution is not required to allege mens rea,[41] but this should not be interpreted to mean that no form of mens rea is material.[42]

In speaking of a true crime, it was said: "It is a fair presumption, then, in the absence of any evidence to the contrary, that there was present the guilty mind which is necessary to constitute the offence, and the onus would therefore be upon them to show that they had acted innocently." [43] So far as true crime is concerned, this so-called "onus" should be no more than a burden of going forward with the evidence [44] although not always so limit-

---

38. "Indeed, there is no such thing as a 'strict liability' offense except in terms of a partial rather than a complete discarding of *mens rea* . . . ." Packer, Mens Rea and the Supreme Court, The Supreme Court Review 107, 140 (Kurland ed. 1962).

Perhaps some other label should be chosen for the state of mind referred to in the text, but the phrase "mens rea" is no longer restricted to the "vicious will." 4 Blackstone, Commentaries *21. "In some cases it denotes mere inattention." The Queen v. Tolson, 23 Q.B.D. 168, 185 (1889). "For instance, in the case of manslaughter by negligence it may mean forgetting to notice a signal." Ibid.

The use of "mens rea" to refer to a state of mind other than that needed for ordinary criminal guilt is not new. "In other words, negligence is not the kind of *mens rea* that characterizes the ordinary run of crimes." Williams, Criminal Law § 36, at 103 (2d ed. 1961).

39. See notes 67 & 68, supra.

40. United States v. Park, 421 U.S. 658, 95 S.Ct. 1903 (1975). Professor Hall's suggestion is "a separate code of 'civil offenses' requiring negligence and tried by administrative tribunals or civil courts." Hall, General Principles of Criminal Law 359 (2d ed. 1960).

"On the other hand, it is also a legal commonplace that where a statute com-

mands that an act be done or omitted which in the absence of such statute might be done or omitted without culpability, ignorance of the fact or state of things contemplated by the statute will not excuse its violation." But the court did not rule out the possibility of exculpation by affirmative proof of the impossibility of finding out the fact. Welch v. State, 145 Wis. 86, 89, 129 N.W. 656, 657 (1911).

41. State v. Hinkle, 129 W.Va. 393, 41 S.E.2d 107 (1946); State v. Sutter, 71 W.Va. 371, 76 S.E. 811 (1912).

42. Congress has not specified the mens rea for a violation of the Sherman Antitrust Act, 15 U.S.C.A. § 1. However, in United States v. United States Gypsum Co., 438 U.S. 422, 444, 98 S.Ct. 2864, 2877 (1978), the Court imposed a standard requiring a defendant act "with knowledge of [the] probable consequences."

43. Rex v. Wallendorf, So.Afr.L.R. [1920] App.Div. 383, 401, quoted in Blackwell, Mens Rea in Statutory Offences III, 77 S.A.L.J. 308, 311 (1960).

44. Perkins, A Re-Examination of Malice Aforethought, 43 Yale L.J. 537, 550–51 (1934). And see People v. Gazulis, 212 N.Y.S.2d 910 (Poughkeepsie City Ct.1961); Model Penal Code § 1.12 (Proposed Final Draft 1962).

ed.[45] If the penalty clause of a regulatory statute has no such words as "knowingly" or "wilfully," it is clear that whatever mens-rea requirement may be involved will be presumed from the mere fact of bringing about the state of affairs sought to be prevented,[46] and in the prosecution of the civil offense, it may not be unreasonable for this presumption to throw upon defendant the risk of nonpersuasion.[47] However, an irrebuttable presumption of guilt should not be tolerated.[48]

Because the civil offense involves no element of culpability, there can be no objection to the enforcement thereof on the basis of objective fault—the defendant did not use that degree of care required by law, or he *should have known* that his conduct would produce the result prohibited by the statute. And because of the nature of the regulatory enactments to which these penalty-clauses are attached, it is not unreasonable to require a very high degree of care in some of the fields thus regulated. To insist upon knowledge of what could not possibly be known—or what could not be known by any degree of care which could in good conscience be demanded—is altogether another matter. To require a man to pay a fine in the absence of any fault, either subjective or objective, is not necessary or desirable in the enforcement of these regulatory measures.[49] The concept of a civil offense as consisting of the act alone without reference to the actor's state of mind or the actor's ability to comply should be abandoned.[50]

45. "Some courts have held, however, that the defendant has the burden of proving that he was mistaken." Keedy, Ignorance and Mistake in the Criminal Law, 22 Harv.L.Rev. 75, 86 (1908). See 2 Underhill, Criminal Evidence § 452 (5th ed. 1956). If defendant claims lack of guilt because of ignorance or mistake, it is proposed that he must prove this by a preponderance of the evidence. Model Penal Code § 2.04(4).

46. Mueller, Mens Rea and the Law Without It, 58 W.Va.L.Rev. 34, 63 (1955).

In a case in which some of the language indicated absolute liability, the opinion concluded with a statement that the evidence offered by the prosecution made out "a prima facie case which was not met by evidence offered by the defendant." Commonwealth v. Ober, 286 Mass. 25, 32, 189 N.E. 601, 604 (1934).

47. "These are not mere 'bare' or 'naked' presumptions of the type which vanish when the defendant goes forward with the evidence; they actually throw a burden of proof on him to *satisfy* the jury that he had no *mens rea*." Nord, The Mental Element in Crime, 37 U.Det.L.J. 671, 684 (1960).

48. City of Seattle v. Ross, 54 Wn.2d 655, 660, 344 P.2d 216, 219 (1959). Cf. Mullaney v. Wilbur, 421 U.S. 684, 95 S.Ct. 1881 (1975).

49. Opinions differ in regard to the deterrent effect of absolute liability. "The surest method of securing conformity to a rule of conduct is to impose liability for every violation of the rule whether intentional, reckless, negligent, or in the exercise of reasonable care." Glassman, Why Don't We Teach Criminal Law?, 15 J.Legal Ed. 37, 42 (1962). See Wasserstrom, Strict Liability in Criminal Law, 12 Stan.L.Rev. 731, 736 (1960); Model Penal Code 126–27 (Tent.Draft No. 4, 1955). "While liability imposed regardless of fault fails to have any deterrent effect upon either the offender or the community at large," Mueller, Mens Rea and the Law Without It, 58 W.Va.L. Rev. 34, 63 (1955), it "cannot operate as a deterrent." Wechsler, A Thoughtful Code of Substantive Law, 45 J.Crim.L., C. & P.S. 524, 528 (1955). "[T]o punish conduct without reference to the actor's state of mind is both inefficacious and unjust." Packer, Mens Rea and the Supreme Court, The Supreme Court Review 107, 109 (Kurland ed. 1962).

50. "Nothing is to be gained by convicting **D** if he proves that he took reasonable care, or, if this is to be desired, all possible care." Howard, Strict Responsibility in the High Court of Australia, 76 L.Q.Rev. 547–48 (1960).

Two comments may be added: (1) Administrative agencies have been able to operate without resorting to a liability-without-fault basis;[51] and (2) where such a basis has been adopted this has been largely, if not entirely, the result of judicial interpretation—seldom, if ever, is this expressly provided in the regulatory statute itself.[52]

Years ago, a court thinking it was bound to enforce a civil offense on the basis of liability without fault, went out of its way to say that if defendant was entirely innocent he should not have been prosecuted,[53] and today the trend seems to be in the direction of requiring conviction to be supported by at least objective fault.[54] Thus, a conviction of permitting an unlicensed driver to drive the owner's car was reversed because the owner did not know or have any reason to know that the other had no license.[55] And conviction of violating the city ordinance by driving through a flashing red light without stopping was held to be unsupportable in the face of an express finding that the driver was unable to stop because of brake failure, having experienced no prior brake trouble and having no knowledge of the defective condition of the brake.[56]

---

51. A study of the actual enforcement of the Wisconsin food and drug statutes, and the fish and game statutes, led to the conclusion that there is no actual attempt to enforce them on a liability-without-fault basis. Comment, 1956 Wis.L.Rev. 626. And in speaking of the enforcement by the Department of Agriculture, it was said: "Standard operating procedure calls for the issuance of a warning notice by the field inspector immediately upon discovery of an inadvertent offensive condition or action." Only if the warning is disregarded is prosecution instituted. Id. at 653.

"The public interest, with which administrative agencies are charged, includes an interest in procedures fair to those whom they affect." Benjamin, A Lawyer's View of the Administrative Program—The American Bar Association Program, 26 Law & Contemp.Prob. 203, 204 (1961).

52. Professor Remington, referring to a Wisconsin study said: "There is no statute which expressly provides for liability without fault." Remington, Liability Without Fault Criminal Statutes, 1956 Wis.L.Rev. 625.

53. Parker v. Adler [1899] 1 Q.B. 20 (1898).

54. "Now courts show more and more reluctance in applying absolute criminal liability. . . ." Mueller, Criminal Law and Administration, 34 N.Y.U.L.Rev. 83, 88; 1958 Ann.Survey of Am.L. 111, 116 (1959); see Force, Criminal Law and Procedure, 35 N.Y.U.L.Rev. 1430 (1960).

A Canadian study suggests that strict liability ought to be eliminated or severely restricted. Paulus, Strict Liability: Its Place in Public Welfare Offenses, 20 Crim.L.Qtrly. 445 (1978).

In a food and drug prosecution the Supreme Court held the prosecution had the responsibility to prove that a corporate official "was not without the power or capacity to affect the conditions which founded the charges in the information." United States v. Park, 421 U.S. 658, 676, 95 S.Ct. 1903, 1913 (1975).

55. People v. Irving, 24 Misc.2d 37, 203 N.Y.S.2d 531 (Sup.Ct.1960).

A statute making it an offense for the owner of a vehicle to permit an intoxicated person to operate the vehicle requires the owner know or should have known of the intoxicated condition. State v. Wetmore, 121 N.J.Super. 90, 296 A.2d 92 (1972).

56. State v. Kremer, 262 Minn. 190, 114 N.W.2d 88 (1962); cf. Proudman v. Dayman, 67 C.L.R. 536 (Austl.1941); Hill v. Baxter, [1958] 1 All E.R. 193. Knowledge of the narcotic character of the thing possessed is an essential element of the offense of possession of marijuana. Language in several lower-court cases to the contrary was disapproved. People v. Winston, 46 Cal.2d 151, 293 P.2d 40 (1956).

The guilty intent is the intent to carry the weapon concealed and does not depend upon the intent to use it. Pueblo v. Sanders, 151 Colo. 216, 376 P.2d 996 (1962). The court did not suggest that the non-negligent ignorance of the presence of the weapon would not be a defense.

An important difference in procedure is to be noted. In a criminal trial the prosecution has the burden of proof as to every element of the offense charged. A presumption may serve the purpose of evidence as to some point unless the defendant raises the issue. But if defendant produces evidence to raise the issue, the prosecution has the burden of satisfying the trier of fact that this element was also present. On the other hand, in the trial of a civil offense the only burden on the prosecution is to prove the actus reus. If the prosecution proves that the defendant did what the statute says should not be done, or failed to do what the statute says should be done, that is sufficient for conviction—if the evidence stops there. But, as pointed out, this does not preclude the possibility of exoneration. The defendant should not be found guilty if he is able to prove that he did not know, and could not be expected to know, the forbidden nature of the contents of a package he was carrying, for example; or that he could not stop because of a sudden brake failure that he could not possibly have foreseen; or that he was forced to act under compulsion that he could not be expected to resist; or other evidence to show that he should not, in good conscience, be held accountable.[57] In such proof in a civil-offense case, however, it is not sufficient for defendant to raise the issue—he has the burden of convincing the trier of fact.

B. DUE PROCESS OF LAW

"It is within the power of the legislature to declare an act criminal, irrespective of the intent of the doer of the act."[58] Although this and other sweeping statements[59] might indicate otherwise, the Supreme Court has emphasized that "there is precedent in this Court that this power is not without limitations."[60] This was said in a case in which a bookseller had been con-

D exceeded the speed limit momentarily because the spring on the throttle broke and he was unable to stop until he put the car in neutral. He was held not guilty of the traffic violation. State v. Weller, 4 Conn.Cir. 267, 230 A.2d 242 (1967).

A speed of 67 miles an hour in a 50-mile zone was excused when it was necessary in an emergency to avoid a traffic accident. People v. Cataldo, 65 Misc.2d 286, 316 N.Y.S.2d 873 (1970).

Unfortunately some courts reach absurd results by failing to recognize the modern trend. D was charged with driving 65 miles an hour in a 55-mile zone. It was held that the fact that his speedometer was defective and registered 10 miles below the actual speed, plus the fact that D did not know the speedometer was defective and had no reason to know, was no defense. People v. Caddy, 189 Colo. 353, 540 P.2d 1089 (1975).

57. The Canadian Supreme Court has recognized three categories of regulatory offenses. First those with a traditional mens rea evidenced by the statutory use of words like "intend" or "knowledge." Second, an offense of strict liability where the offense is subject to the defendant showing some excuse or inability to comply. Third, absolute liability where the prosecution need only show the act. Regina v. City of Sault Ste. Marie, 40 CCC 2d 353, [1978] 2 SCR 1299; Regina v. Chapin, 45 CCC 2d 333, [1979] SCR 121.

58. State v. Winger, 41 Wn.2d 229, 233, 248 P.2d 555, 557 (1952).

59. "There is wide latitude in the lawmakers to declare an offense and to exclude elements of knowledge and diligence from its definition." Lambert v. California, 355 U.S. 225, 228, 78 S.Ct. 240, 242 (1957). "Intent is only an element of a crime if it is made so by statute. Many crimes may be committed without the ordinary prerequisite of criminal intent." City of Columbus v. Webster, 170 Ohio St. 327, 328, 164 N.E.2d 734, 736 (1960); see United States v. Balint, 258 U.S. 250, 252–54, 42 S.Ct. 301, 302–03 (1922); The Queen v. Tolson, 23 Q.B.D. 168, 172 (1889); Jackson, Absolute Prohibition in Statutory Offences, 6 Camb.L.J. 83, 88 (1938).

60. Smith v. California, 361 U.S. 147, 150, 80 S.Ct. 215, 217 (1959). "The Su-

victed of violating an ordinance construed by the state court as making him liable for the mere possession in his store of a book later determined to be obscene—even if he did not know or have reason to know the contents of the book. As thus construed, the ordinance was held to violate the freedom of the press which is protected by the due process clause of the fourteenth amendment, since such strict liability would tend to cause booksellers to use such care that their shelves might be depleted. And the quotation above was expressly not limited to cases where freedom of expression is involved.

A statute would be clearly invalid, it has been pointed out, stating the obvious for the purpose of emphasis, if it prohibited the defense from introducing evidence to establish an alibi.[61] It is unconstitutional to make it impossible for defense to prove to the jury that defendant is not guilty by reason of insanity.[62] Also, although it is permissible to aid the prosecution by a prima-facie presumption if there is a proper relation between it and the foundation thereof,[63] it is a violation of due process to provide for the establishment of any essential element of guilt by an irrebuttable presumption.[64] As said by the Supreme Court: "A statute creating a presumption that is arbitrary or that operates to deny a fair opportunity to repel it violates the due process clause of the Fourteenth Amendment. . . . Mere legislative fiat may not take the place of fact in determination of issues involving life, liberty or property. . . . 'it is not within the province of a legislature to declare an individual guilty or presumptively guilty of a crime.' "[65] It may be added that while a presumption may place upon the defendant the burden of

preme Court of the United States has had occasion only recently to impose due process limitations upon the actions of a state legislature in making unknowing conduct criminal." Commonwealth v. Kempisty, 191 Pa.Super. 602, 604–05, 159 A.2d 541, 542 (1960); Commonwealth v. Koczwara, 397 Pa. 575, 586, 155 A.2d 825, 830 (1959).

61. Laylin & Tuttle, Due Process and Punishment, 20 Mich.L.Rev. 614, 632 (1922).

62. "Whatever may be the power in the Legislature . . . we are of the opinion that such power cannot be exercised to the extent of preventing one accused of crime from invoking the defense of his insanity at the time of committing the act charged and offering evidence thereof before the jury." State v. Strasburg, 60 Wash. 106, 121, 110 P. 1020, 1024 (1910). See State v. White, 60 Wn. 2d 551, 374 P.2d 942, 965 (1962). "[W]here the offense itself is triable, under the Constitution, by jury, the accused has the constitutional right to have his defense of insanity tried by jury." State v. Lange, 168 La. 958, 966, 123 So. 639, 642 (1929). Cf. Goldstein & Katz, Abolish the "Insanity Defense"—Why Not?, 72 Yale L.J. 853 (1963).

63. A disputable presumption may be made to supply evidence which it is diffi-

cult for the prosecution to produce if there is a proper relation between what was proved and the resulting prima-facie presumption. Adams v. New York, 192 U.S. 585, 24 S.Ct. 372 (1904). This presumption should do no more than place upon the defendant the burden of going forward with the evidence. See note 63 supra.

64. "By the same token, if an irrebuttable presumption of guilt is created by city ordinance, any deprivation of life, liberty, or property by virtue of such ordinance is a deprivation without due process of law." City of Seattle v. Ross, 54 Wn.2d 655, 660, 344 P.2d 216, 219 (1959). Accord, State v. Birdsell, 235 La. 396, 104 So.2d 148 (1958); Hankerson v. North Carolina, 432 U.S. 233, 97 S.Ct. 2339 (1977).

65. Manley v. Georgia, 279 U.S. 1, 6, 49 S.Ct. 215, 217 (1929). In rejecting the argument that the counterfeiting statute penalized innocent persons the Court said: "The statute is not intended to include and make criminal a possession which is not conscious and willing. While its words are general, they are to be taken in a reasonable sense and not in one which works manifest injustice or infringes constitutional safeguards." Baender v. Barnett, 255 U.S. 224, 225–26, 41 S.Ct. 271 (1921).

introducing enough evidence to present an issue to be decided, no presumption may validly place upon the defendant the burden of establishing the lack of any *element* of the offense charged.[66]

The requirement of due process, frequently overlooked in such cases, has been held repeatedly to be violated by a provision for conviction based upon liability without fault. Where the possession of intoxicating liquor with intent to sell was prohibited while the possession thereof for personal use was lawful, a statute making the possession of such liquor conclusive evidence of "unlawful keeping, storing and selling" was held to be unconstitutional and void.[67] An ordinance making it unlawful to be in any place where narcotics are used or kept unlawfully and giving a person found in such a place no opportunity to explain his presence unless he could show some "authorization," was held to violate due process of law.[68] A statute on receiving stolen property which provided for the conviction of a junk dealer who received certain kinds of property, in fact stolen, without a diligent inquiry in the effort to ascertain the seller's right to dispose thereof, was upheld.[69] But when the statute was amended by striking out the diligent-inquiry clause, so that a junk dealer who received such property could be convicted despite utmost diligence and good faith, it was held the enactment no longer measured up to constitutional requirements and could not support a conviction.[70] A similar disposition was made of an embezzlement statute which would authorize the conviction of one who appropriated another's property while innocently believing it to be his own.[71] And in *Morissette*,[72] the Supreme Court went out of its way to emphasize that a larceny-type statute must not be so interpreted as to eliminate the normal mens-rea requirement even if express words for this purpose are lacking. One interesting case involved a statute which purported to punish the printing of a device for a policy or numbers game with no requirement that the printer be aware of the intended use.

66. Mullaney v. Wilbur, 421 U.S. 684, 95 S.Ct. 1881 (1975); Sandstrom v. Montana, 442 U.S. 510, 99 S.Ct. 2450 (1979).

67. State v. Sixo, 77 W.Va. 243, 87 S.E. 267 (1915).

68. City of Seattle v. Ross, 54 Wn.2d 655, 344 P.2d 216 (1959).

Other courts have given a narrow construction to such statutes in order to sustain them against constitutional challenge. State v. Sawyer, 346 So.2d 1071 (Fla.App.1977); State v. Smith, 31 Or. App. 749, 571 P.2d 542 (1977).

69. People v. Rosenthal, 197 N.Y. 394, 90 N.E. 991 (1910). A statute is unconstitutional if it includes unquestionably legitimate sales in the proscribed criminal conduct. People v. Bunis, 9 N.Y.2d 1, 172 N.E.2d 273 (1961).

Statutes in several jurisdictions now require pawnbrokers and second hand dealers to obtain specific information before accepting property and provide for a presumption of receiving stolen property

in the absence of compliance. E.g. Utah Code Ann. 1953, § 76–6–408.

70. People v. Estreich, 272 App.Div. 698, 75 N.Y.S.2d 267, aff'd 297 N.Y. 910, 79 N.E.2d 742 (1947).

71. State v. Prince, 52 N.M. 15, 189 P.2d 993 (1948). One judge dissented, but only because he did not believe the statute, properly interpreted, would reach this prohibited result.

72. Morissette v. United States, 342 U.S. 246, 72 S.Ct. 240 (1952). The statute in this case, 18 U.S.C.A. § 641, did not lack appropriate mens rea words. It provided for the conviction of "whoever embezzles, steals, purloins or knowingly converts . . . ." property of the United States. And the indictment charged that Morissette "did unlawfully, wilfully and knowingly steal and convert" such property. But, the Court took advantage of the opportunity to correct false notions that had developed after the decision of United States v. Balint, 258 U.S. 250, 42 S.Ct. 301 (1922).

This was held to be a violation of due process since the product was entirely inoffensive apart from the secret intent of the customer.[73]

The time has come to recognize that there has been a violation of due process whenever there has been any deprivation of liberty or property resulting from a conviction based upon liability without fault.[74] This suggests one of the very disturbing aspects of the Model Penal Code which is its suggested introduction of absolute liability into the criminal law:

"Section 2.05. . . .   (1) The requirements of culpability prescribed by Sections 2.01 and 2.02 do not apply to:

. . .

(b) offenses defined by statutes other than the Code, insofar as a legislative purpose to impose absolute liability for such offenses or with respect to any material element thereof plainly appears."[75]

Under this provision and an appropriately-worded drug act, a pharmacist who should hand a narcotic to one not entitled to receive it could be convicted though he acted unwillingly under fear of death at pistol-point. We have no such liability at present and should not have. If it be argued that the section quoted is subject to qualification by other sections which provide an excuse in cases of compulsion, insanity, or infancy, the answer is that if the liability is qualified it is *not absolute* and should have no such label. If the provision is held actually to mean absolute liability, it should, and no doubt would, be held unconstitutional if adopted, but we should not ask the legislature to adopt what the court should hold to be invalid. In addition, the resurgence of strict liability has passed its peak, and the trend is to require that guilt even of a civil offense must be based upon some degree of fault even if it is only the failure to exercise an extremely high degree of care.[76] Proposed legislation should promote this very wholesome trend rather than frustrate it.

---

73. State v. Lisbon Sales Book Co., 182 N.E.2d 641 (Ohio C.P.1961).

A second-degree arson statute, so worded as to authorize punishment for innocent conduct, was held to be unconstitutional. State v. Paquet, 61 Wn.2d 789, 279 P.2d 188 (1963); State v. Spino, 61 Wn.2d 246, 377 P.2d 868 (1963).

74. In State v. Hudson County News Co., 35 N.J. 284, 173 A.2d 20 (1961), dealing with an obscenity statute, "the court construed the words 'without just cause' as incorporating the *mens rea* requirement, and thus saved the statute from unconstitutionality." Mueller & Pieski, Criminal Law Administration, 1961 Ann. Survey Am.L. 107, 110, n. 26 (1962). And see the reference to "the moral proposition that any absolute criminal liability is immoral—and in that sense inconsonant with due process . . . ." Mueller, On Common Law Mens Rea, 42 Minn.L.Rev. 1043, 1101 (1958).

75. The omitted sub-section reads: "(a) offenses which constitute violations, unless the requirement involved is included in the definition of the offense or the Court determines that its application is consistent with effective enforcement of the law defining the offense; or . . . ."

See also id. §§ 2.05(2)(a), 2.05(2)(b), 2.07(2).

The fact that the code permits the imposition of absolute liability is regarded by one writer as a major achievement. Packer, The Model Penal Code and Beyond, 63 Colum.L.Rev. 594, 595–96 (1963). But Professor Packer could have made his point as effectively by referring to "strict liability." See supra, notes 10 and 58.

76. The standard to be applied is "not the conduct of a prudent man in general, but the conduct of a conscientious man of his profession or licensed activities." Honig, Criminal Law Systematized, 54 J.Crim.L., C. & P.S. 273, 283 (1963).

SECTION 6.   VICARIOUS LIABILITY

In 1730, a prison warden and his deputy were indicted for the murder of a prisoner. The jury returned a special verdict finding that the deputy had maliciously confined the prisoner in such an insanitary cell that death resulted. This was held to be a verdict of guilty so far as the deputy was concerned; but since there was no finding that the warden commanded, directed, or consented to this unwholesome confinement, or knew anything of the circumstances, it was held to be a verdict of not guilty as to him. "Though he was warden . . . yet he is not to answer criminally for the offences of his under-officer." [1] And from that day to this, the courts have refused to convict of true crime on the basis of *respondeat superior*.[2]

There are many instances in which the employer is criminally responsible for the misdeed of his employee. This is true whenever it can be shown to have been done "(1) by authorization, procurement, incitation or moral encouragement, or (2) by knowledge plus acquiescence." [3] If the employer is present when the employee is doing his work in such a manner as unreasonably to endanger the lives of others, the former has a duty, if opportunity permits, to direct the latter to use more care; [4] and a criminally-negligent failure to speak in such a situation is sufficient to establish the employer's guilt of manslaughter if death results.[5] And if the work involved requires special skill to avoid danger to others, the employment of an obviously incompetent person may per se constitute such criminal negligence that resulting death will be manslaughter.[6] Moreover, the circumstances may be such as to require a very high degree of supervision of the work of employees with criminal responsibility resulting from an inexcusable failure in this regard.[7] On this basis, the publisher of a newspaper may be guilty of a libel appearing in its pages without his knowledge.[8] Criminal guilt, however, does not attach to him if there has been no lack of due care on his part.[9] The employer, it should be added, may be criminally liable for the act of his employee even if the latter is entirely innocent, as where the former knows, and the latter does not, that the act will result in wrongfully depriving a third person of his property.[10]

---

1. Rex v. Huggins, 2 Ld.Raym. 1574, 92 Eng.Rep. 518 (K.B.1730).

2. "The principal is never criminally answerable for the act of his deputy; they must each answer for their own acts, and stand or fall by their own behaviour." Paley, Principal and Agent 195–96 (1st ed. 1812). "Hence, the criminal law has never accepted the doctrine of *respondeat superior* . . . ." Sayre, Criminal Responsibility for the Acts of Another, 43 Harv.L.Rev. 689, 723 (1930). A city ordinance making parents criminally liable for the illegal conduct of their children was declared unconstitutional. Doe v. City of Trenton, 143 N.J. Super. 128, 362 A.2d 1200 (1976). But see State v. Wedin, 85 N.J.L. 399, 402, 89 A. 753, 754 (Sup.Ct.1914) (sheriff liable for act of deputy in negligently permitting prisoner to escape).

3. Sayre, op.cit. supra note 2, at 702.

4. Moreland v. State, 164 Ga. 467, 139 S.E. 77 (1927).

5. Ibid.

6. Regina v. Lowe, 3 Car. & K. 123, 175 Eng.Rep. 489 (Q.B.1850).

7. The circumstances may show "criminal neglect to exercise proper care and supervision over the subordinates in his employ." Commonwealth v. Morgan, 107 Mass. 199, 204 (1871).

8. Ibid.

9. Regina v. Holbrook, 13 Cox Crim. Cas. 650 (1877).

10. Regina v. Bleasdale, 2 Car. & K. 765, 175 Eng.Rep. 321 (Ex.1848).

One may be guilty of a crime by causing it to be committed by an innocent

The act of an employee in the course of his employment is, in law, the act of his employer: *qui facit per alium facit per se.*[11] Stated in other terms, the act (*actus reus*) of the employee is imputable to the employer—but the state of mind necessary for criminal guilt cannot be so imputed.[12] This is the reason why guilt of true crime cannot be established on the basis of *respondeat superior.*[13]

Generally accepted, however, is the view holding the employer vicariously liable for a civil offense committed by his employee in the course of his employment.[14] As said, speaking of the penalty clauses of regulatory statutes, "it is quite common under their provisions for a man to be held criminally responsible for acts of his servant which he has not authorized, and indeed which he has forbidden, provided that the servant when committing the offence was acting within the general scope of his employment."[15] Thus, it was no defense to a charge of selling liquor to a minor, in violation of the statute, that the sale was made by defendant's barkeeper without defendant's knowledge or consent and contrary to his general instructions.[16]

agent. United States v. Ruffin, 613 F.2d 408 (2d Cir. 1979). In legal theory one has done what he has caused another to do. Commonwealth v. Nabried, 264 Pa. Super. 419, 399 A.2d 1121 (1979).

11. Originally, this referred only to an act which had been commanded or procured. In time, it came to include also the act of an employee in the "course of business" and "scope of employment." Sayre, Criminal Responsibility for Acts of Another, 43 Harv.L.Rev. 689, 690–93 (1930).

12. "Liability for all true crimes . . . must be based exclusively upon personal causation." Commonwealth v. Koczwara, 397 Pa. 575, 585, 155 A.2d 825, 830 (1959), cert. denied, 363 U.S. 848, 80 S.Ct. 1624 (1959).

13. Sayre wrote of the "error of basing upon the *mens rea* requirement the inapplicability of the doctrine of *respondeat superior* to all serious crimes." He suggested that if criminality may be based upon the physical activity of his servant "why may it not equally be based upon the accompanying mental activity of his servant?" He pointed out that corporations may be convicted of crimes "requiring not only *mens rea*, but specific intent as well." But he failed to distinguish between the mens rea or specific intent of the controlling officers of the corporation, on the one hand, and the mental state of a mere servant or agent of the company, on the other. Sayre, op.cit. supra note 183, at 721–22. Compare supra, chapter 6, section 7.

14. Writing over thirty years ago, Sayre cited an imposing array of cases refusing to enforce such liability without proof of authorization or knowledge. Sayre, op.cit. supra note 183, at 715, n. 100. Even at that time, not one was a recent case and the trend has been the other way. Compare the following cases from the same jurisdictions in his note. Groff v. State, 171 Ind. 547, 85 N.E. 769 (1909); Commonwealth v. Sacks, 214 Mass. 72, 100 N.E. 1019 (1913); Commonwealth v. Koczwara, 397 Pa. 575, 155 A.2d 825 (1959), cert. denied 363 U.S. 848, 80 S.Ct. 1624 (1959).

A partnership can be guilty of "knowingly and willfully" violating regulations for the safe transportation in interstate commerce of explosive and other dangerous articles. United States v. A & P Trucking Co., 358 U.S. 121, 79 S.Ct. 203 (1958). "As in the case of corporations, the conviction of the entity can lead only to a fine levied on the firm's assets." Id. at 127.

15. Kenny, Outlines of Criminal Law 53 (19th ed. by Turner, 1966).

"We note that similar 'public welfare' statutes, making defendants liable for the acts of their employee-agents, with or without the defendant's knowledge or intent, have long been recognized and upheld in Michigan." People v. Najy Jaboro, Wonder Super Foods, 76 Mich. App. 8, 12, 255 N.W.2d 355, 356 (1977). See also State v. Young, 294 N.W.2d 728 (Minn.1980).

16. State v. Lundgren, 124 Minn. 162, 144 N.W. 752 (1913).

At times, this vicarious liability has been called for expressly by the penalty clause itself as by providing that a prohibited sale by an employee shall "be deemed the act of the employer as well," [17] or that "every person who by himself or his employee or agent" does the proscribed act "is guilty of a misdemeanor." [18] Courts, however, have not hesitated to make the application in civil-offense cases even when the statute was silent on the point. [19]

In most of the cases in which a defendant has been held vicariously liable for a civil offense, the employee was undoubtedly negligent, if not more blameworthy, [20] as where the violation was permitting a minor to play in a pool hall, [21] selling liquor to a minor, [22] selling adulterated food, [23] selling by false weight, [24] or distributing free samples of medicine to children. [25] There have been instances of such liability where neither the defendant nor his employee knew the fact which constituted the violation or could have discovered it by any method which could have been required of him, [26] but such a position is neither necessary nor reasonable and should be rejected as previously mentioned. Some fault should be required for conviction even if it is no more than failure to exercise a rather high degree of care. [27] Although the tendency has been to explain this vicarious liability on the ground that "the act constitutes the crime," [28] the proper explanation should be that since the liability is civil rather than criminal the fault of the employee, as well as his act (*actus reus*), may be imputed to the employer. [29]

Although there have been instances in which imprisonment has been imposed on the basis of vicarious liability, [30] any such disposition is manifestly

17. Id. at 167, 144 N.W. at 754.

18. In re Marley, 29 Cal.2d 525, 526, 175 P.2d 832, 833 (1946). Commonwealth v. Sacks, 214 Mass. 72, 100 N.E. 1019 (1913) ("Whoever, by himself or by his servant or agent").

19. Vicarious liability was enforced although the statutory prohibition was in terms—"for any person" and so forth. Groff v. State, 171 Ind. 547, 85 N.E. 769 (1909). In another case, the statute was in terms of "a person, firm or corporation." State v. Cray, 85 Vt. 99, 100, 81 A. 450, 451 (1911).

20. In one case, for example, the court pointed out that defendant had been permitted to introduce evidence tending to show that the short-weight sale by his employee during his absence had been by accident or mistake, but that the jury had found against him on this point. In re Marley, 29 Cal.2d 525, 175 P.2d 832 (1946).

21. State v. Furr, 101 W.Va. 178, 132 S.E. 504 (1926).

22. State v. Lundgren, 124 Minn. 162, 144 N.W. 752 (1913); Commonwealth v. Koczwara, 397 Pa. 575, 155 A.2d 825 (1959), cert. denied 363 U.S. 848, 80 S.Ct. 1624 (1959).

23. Groff v. State, 171 Ind. 547, 85 N.E. 769 (1909).

24. In re Marley, 29 Cal.2d 525, 175 P.2d 832 (1946); Commonwealth v. Sacks, 214 Mass. 72, 100 N.E. 1019 (1913).

25. State v. Cray, 85 Vt. 99, 81 A. 450 (1911).

26. Hobbs v. Winchester Corp., [1910] 2 K.B. 471. And see Cundy v. LeCocq, 13 Q.B.D. 207 (1884).

27. Hall, General Principles of Criminal Law 359 (2d ed. 1960).

28. In re Marley, 29 Cal.2d 525, 529, 175 P.2d 832, 835 (1946); State v. Weisberg, 74 Ohio App. 91, 95, 55 N.E.2d 870, 872 (1943).

29. Linnett v. Commissioner of Metropolitan Police, [1946] 1 K.B. 290. This explanation, although not entirely satisfactory, is preferable to holding that conviction does not require any degree of fault on the part of either employer or employee.

30. In re Marley, 29 Cal.2d 525, 175 P.2d 832 (1946). This case, it should be emphasized, involved a collateral attack upon the judgment by a proceeding in habeas corpus and the only issue before the court was the constitutionality of the statute under which defendant had been convicted. It cannot be assumed that the court would have upheld the judgment of imprisonment if the point had been raised directly by an appeal.

unsound.[31] For example, in a trial for a violation of the liquor-license law based upon selling beer to minors, the evidence disclosed sales by employees of defendant during his absence and without his knowledge or consent. He was convicted and sentenced to three months in jail and fine of 500 dollars. The court upheld the conviction and the fine but declared the sentence of imprisonment to be invalid on the ground that to imprison a man on the basis of vicarious liability is a violation of due process.[32]

SECTION 7. "UNLAWFUL ACT"

"It is a general rule," said the Minnesota court[1] echoing in substance a comment made many generations earlier by Lord Hale,[2] "that a person who intentionally commits an unlawful act, and in doing so inflicts an unforeseen injury, is criminally liable for such injury." The more recent statement was made in discussing a case of battery, and the other in connection with the law of homicide, and while such a generalization finds firm support in the common law so far as these specific areas are concerned, it has certain limitations.

If the offense charged requires some special mental element which was absent, the crime has not been committed. This is just as true where the lack of the necessary element resulted from a guilty mistake as from an innocent one—reasonable or unreasonable. Thus, one is not guilty of "knowingly" transporting in interstate commerce a man unlawfully abducted, if mistaken as to the boundary line and unaware of crossing it.[3] Also, one does not "wilfully" resist an officer if unaware of the fact that the other is an officer.[4] If, however, the offense charged does not have any special mental element which was lacking, a guilty mistake of fact has consequences quite different than those resulting from a mistake which was innocent and reasonable.

It was held when the point first arose that one making an unlawful attack upon a person, who was in fact a foreign minister, was guilty of the federal crime of assaulting a foreign minister although unaware of the official char-

---

31. Conviction, if it "carries with it a jail sentence, must be based upon personal causation." Commonwealth v. Koczwara, 397 Pa. 575, 155 A.2d 825, 830 (1959), cert. denied 363 U.S. 848, 80 S.Ct. 1624 (1959). "Where the offense . . . is punishable by imprisonment . . . it seems clear that the doctrine of *respondeat superior* must be repudiated. . . ." Sayre, Criminal Responsibility for the Acts of Another, 43 Harv.L.Rev. 689, 717 (1930).

32. Commonwealth v. Koczwara, supra note 31.

1. State v. Lehman, 131 Minn. 427, 430, 155 N.W. 399, 400 (1915).

2. "[T]he act itself being unlawful, he is criminally guilty of the consequence, that follows:" 1 Hale P.C. *30.

Killing is not excusable under Miss. Code Ann. sec. 2219 where the killing was done in the course of an unlawful act. Powell v. State, 279 So.2d 161 (Miss. 1973).

3. Wheatley v. United States, 159 F.2d 599 (4th Cir.1946). One who did not know the other was an officer seeking to levy an execution was not guilty of "knowingly" obstructing an officer in the execution of his office. State v. Murphy, 66 A. 335 (Del.Gen.Sess. 1907).

Another statute was differently worded. "The language of the statute [kidnapping], however, does not require that the offender know that he is crossing state lines. So long as he 'willfully transports' his victim and, in doing so, travels in interstate commerce, he need not do so knowingly." United States v. Bankston, 603 F.2d 528, 533 (5th Cir. 1979).

4. State v. Winter, 24 Idaho 749, 135 P. 739 (1913); State v. Gasser, 223 Kan. 24, 574 P.2d 146 (1977).

acter of the victim.[5] This position was followed in later cases,[6] and a similar position was taken in certain prosecutions for violations of interstate commerce. One may be guilty of the federal offense of receiving a stolen motor vehicle moving in interstate commerce if he knows it is stolen although entirely unaware of the interstate transportation.[7] It is no defense that he thought he was committing only a state crime.[8] As recently said *obiter*: "It would be no defense to robbing an insured bank that the robbers thought it was not insured, and had selected it for that reason, hoping thereby to avoid entanglement with federal law." [9] And he may violate the federal law by altering the numbers on a car knowing it had been stolen without knowing anything about its movement in interstate commerce.[10] It may be added that an unlawful attack upon a federal officer is a federal offense even if the assailant did not know he was a federal officer.[11]

5. United States v. Liddle, 26 Fed. Cas. 936 (No. 15,598) (C.C.D.Pa.1808).

6. United States v. Benner, 24 Fed. Cas. 1084 (No. 14,568) (C.C.E.D.Pa.1830); United States v. Ortega, 27 Fed.Cas. 359 (No. 15,971) (C.C.E.D.Pa.1825). But it was held that an attack upon the house of a foreign minister, without knowing it to be such, was not a violation of the law of nations. United States v. Hand, 26 Fed.Cas. 103 (No. 15,297) (C.C.D.Pa. 1810).

The present statute on assaulting a foreign minister includes "in violation of the law of nations," 18 U.S.C.A. § 112.

7. Knowledge of interstate transportation is not essential to guilt under the Dyer Act. If D knew the car was stolen and it in fact moved in interstate commerce he is guilty. Odom v. United States, 377 F.2d 853 (5th Cir.1967). And see Whitehorn v. United States, 380 F.2d 909 (8th Cir.1967).

"Though the plain language of section 2314 requires knowledge that the goods were stolen, it imposes 'no requirement . . . that the accused know, foresee, or intend that instrumentalities of interstate commerce will be used.'" United States v. Franklin, 586 F.2d 560, 565 (5th Cir.1978). Accord, United States v. Eisenberg, 596 F.2d 522 (2d Cir.1979); United States v. Luman, 624 F.2d 152 (10th Cir.1980). But if the statute makes it an offense to have possession of property knowing it to have been stolen from a bank, that must be established. United States v. Kaplan, 586 F.2d 980 (2d Cir. 1978).

Proof that D knew the money he stole belonged to the United States is not necessary in order to prove a violation of the statute making it an offense to rob another of any kind of personal property belonging to the United States. United States v. Roundtree, 527 F.2d 16 (8th Cir. 1975.).

8. Katz v. United States, 281 F. 129 (6th Cir.1922). *Accord,* Pilgrim v. United States, 266 F.2d 486 (5th Cir.1959); Brubaker v. United States, 183 F.2d 894 (6th Cir.1950); United States v. Tannuzzo, 174 F.2d 177 (2d Cir.1949), cert. denied 338 U.S. 815, 70 S.Ct. 38 (1949), reh. denied 338 U.S. 896, 70 S.Ct. 233 (1949); Loftus v. United States, 46 F.2d 841 (7th Cir. 1931); Wolf v. United States, 36 F.2d 450 (7th Cir.1929).

Because of one statute making petit larceny a misdemeanor, and another statute making the larceny of any property belonging to the District of Columbia a felony, it was held that the legislative intent must have been to impose guilt of the latter offense only on a thief who knew he was taking such property. Mitchell v. United States, 394 F.2d 767 (D.C.Cir.1968).

9. Lubin v. United States, 313 F.2d 419, 422 (9th Cir.1963).

One who entered a bank with intent to steal was guilty of violating 18 U.S.C.A. § 2113(a) even if he did not know the building was a bank. United States v. Schaar, 437 F.2d 886 (7th Cir.1971).

Knowledge that the stolen property belonged to the government is not required for guilt of larceny of government property. United States v. Speir, 564 F.2d 934 (10th Cir.1977).

10. Donaldson v. United States, 82 F.2d 680 (7th Cir.1936).

11. United States v. Wallace, 368 F.2d 537 (4th Cir.1966); McEwen v. United States, 390 F.2d 47 (9th Cir.1968); Burke v. United States, 400 F.2d 866 (5th Cir. 1968); United States v. Ganter, 436 F.2d 364 (7th Cir.1970); United States v. Linn, 438 F.2d 456 (10th Cir.1971); United

A mistake of fact relating only to the degree of the crime or gravity of the offense will not shield a deliberate offender from the full consequences of the wrong actually committed.[12] Thus, no case has been found in which defendant's belief rather than actual value was used to determine whether his larceny was grand or petty.[13] Bramwell seems to have been quite sound in his intimation that an intruder's mistaken belief that night had just come to an end would not save him from conviction of common-law burglary.[14] One unlawfully engaged in the "numbers racket" was deliberately violating the law, and hence his employment of a minor in that activity made him guilty of the graver offense of contributing to the delinquency of a minor despite his mistake as to the youth's age.[15]

Care must be taken to distinguish cases in which the conduct would have been quite proper under the supposed facts. Thus, one whose resistance would have been privileged had no officer been involved and who was unaware of the official character of an officer in plain clothes was not guilty of resisting the police.[16] This offense has been committed, however, if what was done would have constituted an assault and battery even had the other been a private person, as supposed.[17]

States v. Nerone, 563 F.2d 836 (7th Cir. 1977). See also United States v. Feola, 420 U.S. 671, 95 S.Ct. 1255 (1975).

"All the statute requires is an intent to assault, not an intent to assault a federal officer." United States v. Hanson, 618 F.2d 1261, 1265 (8th Cir.1980) (quoting from United States v. Feola, 420 U.S. 671, 684, 95 S.Ct. 1255, 1264 (1975)).

But one cannot be guilty of wilfully obstructing a peace officer without knowing that he is a peace officer. State v. Snodgrass, 117 Ariz. 107, 570 P.2d 1280 (App.1977).

12. "He . . . cannot set up a legal defence by merely proving that he thought he was committing a different kind of wrong from that which in fact he was committing." Regina v. Prince, L.R. 2 Cr.Cas.Res. 154, 179 (1875). "It is a familiar rule that, if one intentionally commits a crime, he is responsible criminally for the consequences of his act, if the offense proves to be different from that which he intended." Commonwealth v. Murphy, 165 Mass. 66, 70, 42 N.E. 504, 505 (1896). "In such a case a person who deliberately breaks the law must take the risk of his offence turning out to be of a more serious nature than he had intended." Rex v. Wallendorf, So.Afr.L.R. [1920] App.Div. 383, 397.

13. "Under existing law the amount actually stolen determines whether an offense is grand or petty theft." Model Penal Code 110 (Tent. Draft No. 2, 1954).

The fact that defendant thought his crime was only a misdemeanor will not

prevent his conviction of a felony. State v. Forshee, 588 P.2d 181 (Utah 1978).

14. Regina v. Prince, L.R. 2 Cr.Cas. Res. 154, 156 (1875). This was questioned by one writer. Smith, The Guilty Mind in the Criminal Law, 76 L.Q.Rev. 78 (1960). But he seems to be advancing a theory rather than stating existing law. The culpability (mens rea) required for common-law burglary is not an intent to operate in the nighttime but an intent to commit a felony.

15. State v. Davis, 95 Ohio App. 23, 117 N.E.2d 55 (1953), appeal dismissed 160 Ohio St. 205, 115 N.E.2d 5 (1953).

16. Mongouma v. Rex, an unreported case mentioned with approval in Rex v. Wallendorf, So.Afr.L.R. [1920] App.Div. 383, 398–99.

In a prosecution for assaulting a federal officer (18 U.S.C.A. § 111) it was said: "While knowledge of the officer's status is not an essential element of the offense, lack of knowledge may be relevant and material to the defense of either self defense or defense of others." United States v. Nerone, 563 F.2d 836, 850 (7th Cir.1977).

17. Regina v. Forbes, 10 Cox Crim. Cas. 362 (1865); Rex v. Wallendorf, So. Afr.L.R. [1920] App.Div. 383. Mens rea was said to be present in the latter case because "whether or not the accused were aware of the fact that Mooney was a constable, they were guilty of committing an assault upon him." Id. at 397.

"A man was held liable for assaulting a police officer in the execution of his du-

Conduct may be sufficiently wrongful to supply the general mens rea even if no punishment has been provided therefor,[18] and a mistake which would merely leave the supposed deed in such a category is not exculpating.[19] Thus, it was wrongful for a man to abandon his wife without just cause, and although this alone would not have been punishable, he was guilty of the crime of abandoning a pregnant wife—since this was the fact although unsuspected by him.[20] The more familiar applications of the rule are found in prosecutions for statutory rape (carnal knowledge of a child), abduction, and adultery. A man who has illicit sexual intercourse with a girl under the age of consent is guilty of statutory rape although she consented and he mistakenly believed she was older than the limit thus established.[21] This is true no matter how reasonable his mistaken belief may have been,[22] as in cases in which both her appearance and her positive statement indicated she was older than the statutory age [23] or in which he had exercised considerable pains in the effort to ascertain her age.[24]

For the most part there has been little change in the age-old rule that **D**'s ignorance of the female's age and his lack of intention to have intercourse with an underage female is not a defense to statutory rape; [25] but recently the California court has held that a bona-fide and reasonable mistake as to the age should be recognized as a defense.[26] While admitting it was departing from what had been the uniform holding both within and without the state, the court insisted that "the courts have uniformly failed to satisfactorily explain the nature of the criminal intent" of one acting under such a mistake. This is astounding in view of the fact that the courts, down through the ages, have explained that one intending to have illicit sexual intercourse has mens rea because he is purposely engaging in a wrongful act. Great reliance was placed upon *Vogel* [27] which held a reasonable and bona-fide be-

ty, though he did not know he was a police officer. Why? Because the act was wrong in itself." Regina v. Prince, L.R. 2 Crim.Cas.Res. 154, 176 (1875) (Bramwell, B.). And see, supra, note 10.

18. Commonwealth v. Mink, 123 Mass. 422 (1877).

19. People v. Ratz, 115 Cal. 132, 46 P. 915 (1896); Smiley v. State, 34 Ga.App. 513, 130 S.E. 359 (1925); Heath v. State, 173 Ind. 296, 90 N.E. 310 (1910).

20. White v. State, 44 Ohio App. 331, 185 N.E. 64 (1933).

21. People v. Ratz, 115 Cal. 132, 46 P. 915 (1896); Heath v. State, 173 Ind. 296, 90 N.E. 310 (1910); Commonwealth v. Murphy, 165 Mass. 66, 42 N.E. 504 (1896).

22. Ibid.; State v. Houx, 109 Mo. 654, 19 S.W. 35 (1892).

23. See People v. Marks, 146 App.Div. 11, 12, 130 N.Y.S. 524, 525 (1911).

24. Manning v. State, 43 Tex.Cr. 302, 65 S.W. 920 (1901).

25. State v. Davis, 108 N.H. 158, 229 A.2d 842 (1967); Eggleston v. State, 4 Md.App. 124, 241 A.2d 433 (1968); State v. Fulks, 83 S.D. 433, 160 N.W.2d 418 (1968).

" 'The Supreme Court has never held that an honest mistake as to the age of the prosecutrix is a constitutional defense to statutory rape.' The plaintiff intended to have intercourse with this child and the burden was on him to determine her age or act at his peril." Goodrow v. Perrin, 119 N.H. 483, 403 A.2d 864 (1979).

The fact that no defense based upon reasonable belief as to the victim's age is recognized in a charge of statutory rape, is not unconstitutional. Commonwealth v. Robinson, 264 Pa.Super. 345, 399 A.2d 1084 (1979).

26. People v. Hernandez, 61 Cal.2d 529, 39 Cal.Rptr. 361, 393 P.2d 673 (1964).

Alaska followed *Hernandez* in State v. Guest, 583 P.2d 836 (Alaska 1978). The court seems to indicate that while one acting under a reasonable mistake may not be convicted of statutory rape, he may be convicted of contributing to the delinquency of a minor, although the wording of the decision is confusing.

27. People v. Vogel, 46 Cal.2d 798, 299 P.2d 850 (1956).

lief that a prior marriage had been terminated was a defense to a charge of bigamy. The analogy is faulty because one contracting a marriage under such a belief would have no thought of wrongdoing.[28]

In the background, no doubt, is the growing belief that private sexual relations between consenting adults should, for the most part, be removed from the control of the criminal law.[29] "This area of private morals is the distinctive concern of spiritual authorities." [30] The present problem does not involve adult females but there is obvious dissatisfaction with legislation which has raised the "age of consent" from 10 to 18.[31] Another California statute makes it an offense to take a female under the age of 18 from her parent, without his consent "for the purpose of prostitution." [32] It is unlikely the court would consider such a taking for this purpose without mens rea merely because of a mistake as to age. One who has illicit intercourse with a married person is guilty of adultery (where this is an offense) even if he has no idea that the other is married.[33] Violation of the abduction statute by taking a girl under a certain age from the possession of her parent or guardian without his consent for the purpose of prostitution or concubinage, will support a conviction notwithstanding a reasonable mistake as to the age of the girl.[34] And if a statute prohibits harboring a prostitute under a certain age, a mistake on this point is not exculpating.[35]

Although suggested at times that the result in such cases is because these are offenses which do not have the normal mens-rea requirement,[36] this is quite unsound and would lead to very unsatisfactory results in certain cases such as those involving an *innocent* mistake of fact. The latter problem has arisen most frequently in the adultery cases. If the intercourse is obviously illicit, the mistaken belief in the unmarried status of the paramour is not an *innocent* mistake. "In such a case there is a measure of wrong in the act as the defendant understands it and his ignorance of the fact that makes it a greater wrong will not relieve him from the legal penalty." [37] On the other hand, despite some indication to the contrary,[38] it is clearly established that if the intercourse follows a marriage ceremony entered into in good faith, with no thought or reason to believe that the other party is al-

---

28. For a criticism of *Hernandez* see a Note, 16 Hastings L.J. 270 (1964).

29. See Model Penal Code 276–281 (Tent.Draft No. 4, 1955).

30. Id. at 277–78.

31. The 1889 amendment increased the age from 10 to 14. Cal.Stat.1889, c. 191. It was raised to 16 in 1897. Cal. Stat.1897, c. 139, and to 18 in 1913. Cal. Stat.1913, c. 122.

32. West's Ann.Cal.Pen.Code § 267 (1970).

33. State v. Anderson, 140 Iowa 445, 118 N.W. 772 (1908); Commonwealth v. Elwell, 43 Mass. 190 (1840).

34. People v. Dolan, 96 Cal. 315, 31 P. 107 (1892); Smiley v. State, 34 Ga.App. 513, 130 S.E. 359 (1925); State v. Ruhl, 8 Iowa 447 (1859); State v. Johnson, 115 Mo. 480, 22 S.W. 463 (1893).

35. Brown v. State, 23 Del. 159, 74 A. 836 (1909).

36. See, e.g., State v. Winger, 41 Wn. 2d 229, 233, 248 P.2d 555, 557 (1952); May, Law of Crimes 62, n. 117 (4th ed. 1938).

37. State v. Audette, 81 Vt. 400, 403, 70 A. 833, 834 (1908) (dictum). As said *obiter* in another case, "the act of abduction of which the prisoner was guilty, being a morally wrong act, afforded abundant proof of his criminal mind." The Queen v. Tolson, 23 Q.B.D. 168, 194 (1889).

38. The case commonly cited for this contrary position is Commonwealth v. Thompson, 93 Mass. 23 (1865). There was no reasonable ground for the mistaken belief in this case.

ready married, it does not constitute the crime of adultery [39] if it does not occur after the mistake has been discovered.[40] As said *obiter* in a reference to intercourse resulting from a mistake as to the identity of the person: "In such a case there is no offense for none was intended, either in law or in morals." [41]

Probably the most-cited case dealing with offenses against an underage girl is *Prince*,[42] in which the defendant was charged with unlawfully taking a girl under sixteen out of the possession of the father against his will. Although he had done that, the girl, actually fourteen, appeared to be much older and had told defendant she was eighteen. The jury found that he acted upon a bona-fide belief that she was eighteen and that the belief was reasonable. In holding this not to be a defense, the judges left no doubt as to their position. Denman, J., said: [43] "He . . . cannot set up a defence by merely proving that he thought he was committing a different kind of a wrong from that which in fact he was committing." Blackburn, J., pointed out: [44]

"No question arises . . . as to how far an honest though mistaken belief that such circumstances as would justify the taking existed, might form an excuse; for as the case is reserved we must take it as proved that the prisoner knew that the girl was in the possession of her father, and that he took her knowing that he trespassed on the father's rights, and had no colour of excuse for so doing."

Bramwell, B., emphasized: [45] "This opinion gives full scope to the doctrine of mens rea. If the taker believed he had the father's consent, though wrongly, he would have no mens rea . . . .."

This and similar crimes are not strict-liability offenses in the sense that an innocent and reasonable mistake would not be exculpating. They merely take the customary position that intentional misconduct may be so wrongful that the actor runs the risk of committing an unintended crime. As has been said: "His intent to violate the law of morality and the good order of society, though with the consent of the girl, and though in a case when he supposes he shall escape punishment, satisfied the demands of the law, and he must take the consequences." [46]

In the words of Professor Sayre: [47] "Crimes such as . . . carnal knowledge, seduction and the like, where the offense depends upon the girl's being below a designated age . . . do require a *mens rea*," although a reasonable mistake of fact as to her age is no defense.

39. Banks v. State, 96 Ala. 78, 11 So. 404 (1892); Vaughan v. State, 83 Ala. 55, 3 So. 530 (1888); State v. Cutshall, 109 N.C. 764, 14 S.E. 107 (1891); State v. Audette, 81 Vt. 400, 70 A. 833 (1908).

40. Hildreth v. State, 19 Tex.Cr. 195 (1885).

41. State v. Ruhl, 8 Iowa 447, 450 (1859).

42. L.R. 2 C.C. 154 (1875).

43. Id. at 179.

44. Id. at 170. Cockburn, C.J., Mellor, Lush, Quain, Lenman, Archibald, Field, and Lindley, J.J., and Pollock, B., concurred in this opinion.

45. Id. at 175. Kelly, C.B., Cleasby, Pollock, and Amphlett, BB., and Grove, Quain, and Denman, JJ., concurred in this opinion. Brett, J., thought the conviction wrong.

46. Brown v. State, 23 Del. 159, 171, 74 A. 836, 840 (1909); State v. Houx, 109 Mo. 654, 661, 19 S.W. 35, 37 (1892).

47. Sayre, Public Welfare Offenses, 33 Colum.L.Rev. 55, 73–74 (1933).

Turning attention from what "is" to what "should be," opinion seems to be almost unanimous that the present law of statutory rape is in urgent need of change. This insistence, it should be noted, did not result in abandonment of the rule in regard to mistake as to the girl's age, but only a modification thereof in the case of the English statute,[48] the recent Illinois Code,[49] and the proposed Model Penal Code.[50] The plan of the Illinois Code under which a reasonable mistake as to the girl's age results in a very material reduction in the grade of the offense and the penalty to be imposed has much to be said in its favor.

In the development of the mens-rea concept, the language was in terms of the guilty mind, but the emphasis was upon the innocent mind. One who had caused harm should not be convicted of crime unless he had a guilty mind (*"nisi mens sit rea"*), but the theory was that the mind was either innocent or guilty and hence the real question was whether it was innocent. One who was intending to commit crime did not have an innocent mind and hence had the necessary mens rea for another unintended offense unless it required some special mental element. The same was true of one whose intent was quite wrongful even if no punishment had been provided by law for the particular wrong he had in mind. The result—that a guilty mistake of fact is not exculpating—does not base guilt upon objective fault, but the application has permitted the penalties to get entirely out of line with the degree of subjective fault involved. Perhaps the time has come to jettison the age-old concept of risk-assumption by intentional wrongdoing, but such a step should not be lightly taken. It seems to have been left out of the Model Penal Code.[51]

---

48. The English Sexual Offences Act, 4 & 5 Eliz. 2, c. 69, pt. 1, § 6(3) (1956), provides: "A man is not guilty of an offence under this section because he has unlawful sexual intercourse with a girl under the age of sixteen, if he is under the age of twenty-four and has not previously been charged with a similar offence, and he believes her to be of the age of sixteen or over and has reasonable cause for the belief."

49. Reasonable mistake as to the age of the child is a defense to indecent liberties with a child (including sexual intercourse) the offense being punishable as a class I felony. S.H.A.Ill. ch. 38, § 11–4 (1979). It is not a defense to contributing to the sexual delinquency of a child (including sexual intercourse), the penalty being not to exceed a fine of $1000 or imprisonment not to exceed one year. S.H.A.Ill. ch. 38, § 11–5 (1979).

50. "(1) *Mistake as to age.* Whenever in this Article the criminality of conduct depends on a child's being below the age of 10, it is no defense that the actor did not know the child's age, or reasonably believed the child to be over 10. When criminality depends on the child's being below a critical age other than 10, it is a defense for the actor to prove by a preponderance of the evidence that he reasonably believed the child to be above the critical age." Model Penal Code § 213.6(1).

See Collings, Offenses of Violence Against the Person, 339 Annals 41, 52 (Jan. 1962). In Utah when the child is under age fourteen the statute is drastic providing a possible penalty of life imprisonment. Utah Code Ann. 1953, §§ 76–5–402, 406.

The recent Minnesota Code provision seems to leave the common-law rule unchanged. See M.S.A. (Minn.) § 609.02, subd. 9(6) (1964). See also 4 W.S.A. (Wis.) 939.43(2), 944.10 (1980).

Montana, by statute, has made a reasonable belief that the girl is not under the age of consent, a defense to statutory rape, but requires the defendant to prove such reasonable belief by a preponderance of the evidence. This provision is valid. State v. Smith, 176 Mont. 159, 576 P.2d 1110 (1978).

51. See Section 2.03(3).

SECTION 8.　"TRANSFERRED INTENT"

A tort concept, which serves a useful purpose in that field [1] but has no proper place in criminal law, is the so-called "doctrine of the transfer of the intent to the unintended act." [2] In the field of crime this concept has the vice of being a misleading half-truth, often given as an improper reason for a correct result, but incapable of strict application. It has found expression occasionally in some such form as that "whenever a man intending one wrong does another he is punishable" unless some specific intent is required for the offense,[3] the reason offered being that "the thing done, having proceeded from a corrupt mind, is to be viewed the same whether the corruption was of one particular form or another." [4]

This inaccurate conclusion stems from an imperfect analysis of certain offenses. Burglary, for example, is the nocturnal breaking into the dwelling of another with intent to commit a felony.[5] In other words an intent to commit some other crime (usually although not necessarily larceny) is the very psychical element essential for the mens rea in a burglary case. There are some offenses, moreover, for which an intent to commit some other crime, while not essential to the mens rea, may be sufficient for this purpose. Murder offers an excellent example. Certain crimes such as arson, rape, robbery and burglary, have been found to involve such an unreasonable element of human risk, even if the wrongdoer had no such thought in mind at the start, that one perpetrating or attempting such an offense is held to have a state of mind which also falls under the label of "malice aforethought" so that if homicide is caused thereby it is murder, however unintended the killing may be.[6] Manslaughter, also must be mentioned in this connection because, as pointed out in the section on homicide, death resulting from a true crime will be manslaughter if the "unlawful act" was not sufficient to make it murder,[7]—although this well-entrenched position has very little reason to support it. Thus an intent to commit any true crime (*malum in se*) is held to be a state of mind sufficient for the mens rea either for murder or manslaughter (one or the other) if homicide results. This however is due to the peculiarities of the law of homicide and not to any general concept of "transferred intent." Such an intent would also furnish the mens rea needed for battery, if a non-fatal personal injury should result, which is based entirely upon the law of battery.

---

1. If defendant shoots at **A** and hits **B** instead, the "intent is said to be 'transferred' to the victim—which is obviously only a fiction, or a legal conclusion, to accomplish the desired result of liability." Prosser, Law of Torts 32 (4th ed. 1971).

2. 1 Bishop, New Criminal Law § 335 (9th ed. 1923).

3. Id. at § 327.

4. Ibid.

5. 3 Co.Inst. *63; 1 Hale P.C. *549; 4 Bl.Comm. *224; State v. Ward, 147 La. 1083, 86 So. 552 (1920). Under statute the mental element is often enlarged, such as an intent to commit any public offense.

6. State v. Meadows, 330 Mo. 1020, 51 S.W.2d 1033 (1932); State v. Whitfield, 129 Wash. 134, 224 P. 559 (1924); State v. Bell, 205 N.C. 225, 171 S.E. 50 (1933); People v. Green, 217 Cal. 176, 17 P.2d 730 (1933); State v. Jordan, 126 Ariz. 283, 614 P.2d 825 (1980).

7. For example, see The Queen v. Porter, 12 Cox C.C. 444 (1873); State v. Weisengoff, 85 W.Va. 271, 101 S.E. 450 (1919). Killing resulting from an unlawful act in the nature of *malum prohibitum* is excusable homicide if there was no negligence. State v. Horton, 139 N.C. 588, 51 S.E. 945 (1905); Keith v. State, 612 P.2d 977 (Alaska 1980).

To test the soundness of the transferred-intent doctrine it is necessary to consider offenses other than burglary (which always requires an intent to commit some other crime) or felonious homicide or battery (for which the mens-rea requirement may be supplied by an intent to commit some other true crime). A man who has in his pocket a weapon which he has no authority to carry is not guilty of the crime of carrying a concealed weapon if it was secretly put there by another and he himself is wholly unaware of its presence.[8] If while having this weapon upon his person under these circumstances he should marry a second wife, thinking the first alive although she was in fact dead, the intent to commit bigamy could not be coupled with the unintentional carrying of the concealed weapon so as to establish guilt of either offense. If he borrowed the coat containing the unknown weapon for the sole purpose of wearing it during the supposedly bigamous wedding ceremony there would be a causal connection between the bigamous intent and the carrying of the concealed weapon, but the two would still not match together in such a manner as to constitute guilt of either.

A. SAME MENTAL PATTERN

It was stated by Lord Hale,[9] and repeated in substance by Blackstone,[10] that "if A by malice aforethought strikes at B and missing him strikes C whereof he dies, tho he never bore any malice to C yet it is murder, and the law transfers the malice to the party slain." Unquestionably the slayer is guilty of murder in such a case,[11] and if any resort is to be made to the notion of transferred intent it should be limited to this general type of situation. The general mental pattern is the same whether the malicious endeavor was to kill B or to kill C.[12] If the word "malicious" is omitted the statement might not be true. An intent to kill B might represent a very different mental pattern than an intent to kill C. For example, B might at the time have been making a murderous assault upon A under such circumstances that A was privileged to kill B in the lawful defense of A's life. If such was the fact an intent by A to kill B in his own defense would not be a guilty state of mind; it would not involve mens rea. If at the same time C was obviously not offering any harm to A, an intent by A to kill C would amount to malice aforethought. If, under those circumstances, A should shoot at B in the proper and prudent exercise of his privilege of self-defense, and should happen unexpectedly, by a glance of the bullet, to cause the death of C, A would be free from criminal guilt.[13] This seems to lend support to the theo-

8. State v. Williams, 184 Iowa 1070, 169 N.W. 371 (1918); Miles v. State, 52 Tex.Cr.R. 561, 108 S.W. 378 (1908).

9. 1 Hale P.C. *466.

10. 4 Bl.Comm. *201.

11. People v. Weeks, 104 Cal.App. 708, 286 P. 514 (1930); Durham v. State, 177 Ga. 744, 171 S.E. 265 (1933); State v. Ochoa, 61 N.M. 225, 297 P.2d 1053 (1956).

"In any prosecution for criminal homicide, evidence that the actor caused the death of a person other than the intended victim shall not constitute a defense for any purpose to criminal homicide." § 76–5–204, 1953, Utah Code Ann.

12. Commonwealth v. DeMatteo, 328 Pa. 359, 361, 195 A. 873 (1938).

One court, after repeating the transferred-intent formula, summed up the situation by quoting from an earlier case: "In other words, the crime is exactly what it would have been if the person against whom the intent to kill was directed had been in fact killed." People v. Siplinger, 252 Cal.App.2d 817, 825, 60 Cal.Rptr. 914, 920 (1967).

13. Pinder v. State, 27 Fla. 370, 8 So. 837 (1891).

ry of "transferred intent." The intent to kill **B** did not constitute mens rea (because of the privilege of self-defense) and this innocent intent *seems* to be transferred to the unintended victim and makes the killing of **C** innocent homicide.

The hypothetical situation, however, supposes not only the privilege to direct deadly force against **B** in the defense of **A**'s life, but also the proper and prudent exercise of this privilege. If, on the other hand, he exercised this privilege so imprudently and improperly as to constitute a criminally-negligent disregard of the life of the innocent bystander, **C**, the killing of **C** would be manslaughter.[14] Hence, in such a case it is clearly inaccurate to say that the intent is transferred to the unintended result.

In general it may be said that if one intends injury to the person of another under circumstances in which such a mental pattern constitutes mens rea, and in the effort to accomplish this end he inflicts harm upon a person other than the one intended, he is guilty of the same kind of crime as if his aim had been more accurate.[15] The same is true of offenses which do not involve injury to the person. Thus if **A** starts a fire for the malicious purpose of burning the house of **B**, which destroys the house of **C** instead, **A** is guilty of arson.[16] While the "transferred intent" theory does not reach erroneous conclusions if sharply limited to cases of this type, it is unnecessary even here. The true explanation is this: In every such case both components of the crime are present. The psychical element consists of a certain general mental pattern which is not varied by the particular person or piece of property which may be actually harmed (unless there is a privilege that applies to one and not the other). And where the intent is directed at one whereas another is accidentally hit we have at most only a "so-called" transfer of intent.[17]

B. DIFFERENT MENTAL PATTERN

Where the state of mind which prompted the action does not constitute the particular mens rea required by law for the offense charged, the courts have not hesitated to repudiate the notion of transferred intent. In *Faulkner*,[18] the defendant went into the hold of a ship to steal some rum. After boring a hole in the cask he held a lighted match in his hand to see where to put a spile in the hole out of which the rum was running, and the rum caught

---

14. Henwood v. People, 54 Colo. 188, 129 P. 1010 (1913); People v. Mathews, 91 Cal.App.3d 1018, 154 Cal.Rptr. 628 (1979).

15. The word "aim" is used in the text because the infliction of harm upon one other than the intended victim usually results from shooting, throwing, stabbing or striking. Such a result might happen—with like legal effect—from some other type of harm, such as poisoning. 1 Hale P.C. *466.

16. 1 Hale P.C. *569.

17. "In the case of People, on Complaint of Starvis v. Rogers, 170 Misc. 609, 10 N.Y.S.2d 722, a wife threw a missile at her husband but unfortunately struck the complainant. This is an example of the so-called 'constructive' or 'transferred' intent mentioned in the textbooks and resulted in the conviction of the wife, Judge Fasso commenting (170 Misc. at page 610, 10 N.Y.S.2d at page 723): 'An assault, however, may be committed despite the absence of an intent to injure a particular individual. Under the provisions of our Penal Law, a person commits an assault when he wilfully and wrongfully assaults another. There is no requirement that there exist a specific intent to do injury to the person assaulted.'" People v. Fruci, 188 Misc. 384, 386, 67 N.Y.S.2d 512, 514 (1947).

18. Regina v. Faulkner, 13 Cox C.C. 550 (Ireland, 1877).

fire with the result that the ship was destroyed. Defendant was charged with the felony of maliciously setting fire to a ship on the high seas, and the case was tried on the theory that if the fire resulted from the perpetration of another felony (larceny), guilt is established by this fact alone, and a conviction resulted. The reviewing court indicated that this offense might be committed by an act done in wanton and wilful disregard of an obvious fire hazard, without a specific intent to burn the ship,—but quashed the conviction because the case had not been left to the jury on this basis, but was submitted on the transferred-intent theory. In *Pembliton*,[19] the prisoner threw a stone for the malicious purpose of hitting a person, but missed the person and broke a window. He was indicted for malicious injury to property and convicted, but this conviction also was quashed. It was indicated that this offense also might be committed by an act done with wanton and wilful disregard for this property hazard, without an actual intent to break the window, but the throwing was done at night and the jury made no finding upon this point.[20] In another case it was held that the killing of a horse by a shot fired with intent to kill a person is not sufficient of itself to support a conviction of maliciously killing a horse.[21]

C. "WITH INTENT TO KILL (OR INJURE) HIM"

Murder is homicide committed with malice aforethought. It is possible to express the same idea in other words but it would add an element never required by common law, and almost never by statute,[22] to say: Murder is homicide committed with malice aforethought against the deceased. If, without justification, excuse or mitigation, **D** with intent to kill **A** fires a shot which misses **A** but unexpectedly causes the death of **B**, **D** is guilty of murder. To speak of transferring the malice from **A** to **B** is merely to offer an unsound explanation (carried over from the law of torts) to support a very sound conclusion. The proper explanation is that **D** is guilty of murder in such a case because all elements of the offense are present, with mention if it seems necessary of the fact that as a crime the wrong was committed against the state. An intent to commit homicide without justification, excuse or mitigation, is malice aforethought; **D** had such an intent and therefore had malice aforethought; an act done by **D** with this malice aforethought

---

19. Regina v. Pembliton, 12 Cox C.C. 607 (1874).

20. The jury found that he threw the stone "intending to hit one or more of them with it, but not intending to break the window." Whether his throwing was with reckless disregard of an obvious hazard of windowbreaking was not submitted to the jury. Id. at 608.

21. Rex v. Kelly, 1 Craw. & D. 186 (Ireland, 1832).

22. "The malice aforethought necessary to commit murder need not be directed at the one actually killed." State v. Alford, 260 Iowa 939, 151 N.W.2d 573, 574 (1967).

The Tennessee court held that for murder to be in the first degree under the "wilful, deliberate, malicious and premeditated" clause of the first-degree statute it was necessary that the slayer have an intent to kill the very person slain. Bratton v. State, 29 Tenn. 103 (1849). The statute was amended later so that a killing with intent to commit first-degree murder, which results in the killing of the one intended, or another, is first-degree murder. Sullivan v. State, 173 Tenn. 475, 121 S.W.2d 535 (1938).

"There is no requirement that the knowing conduct essential to extreme indifference murder and second degree murder be directed against the person actually killed." People v. Marcy, __ Colo. __, 628 P.2d 69, 79 (1981).

caused the death of another—and hence **D** has committed homicide with malice aforethought, which is murder by definition.

If, without justification, excuse or mitigation **D** with intent to kill **A** fires a shot which misses **A** but unexpectedly inflicts a non-fatal injury upon **B**, **D** is guilty of an attempt to commit murder,—but the attempt was to murder **A** whom **D** was trying to kill and not **B** who was hit quite accidentally. And so far as the criminal law is concerned there is no transfer of this intent from one to the other so as to make **D** guilty of an attempt to murder **B**.[23] Hence an indictment or information charging an attempt to murder **B**, or (under statute) an assault with intent to murder **B**, will not support a conviction if the evidence shows that the injury to **B** was accidental and the only intent was to murder **A**.[24]

The problem was discussed in some detail in *Martin*[25] in which defendant (with others) was charged with felonious assault "with intent to maim Lloyd DeCasnett." As two cars passed on the street at night an electric light bulb filled with sulphuric acid was thrown by defendant, or an accomplice, from one vehicle at the other, striking the left front door near an open window, splattering the acid over the car and the upholstery inside. An intent to maim could clearly be inferred from such conduct, and the trial resulted in a conviction; but the difficulty, as brought out by the evidence, was that De-Casnett was riding in the rear seat on the far side and there was nothing to show that anyone in defendant's car could see that any person was riding there as the two cars passed at night. Why DeCasnett was named as the intended victim, rather than the driver or the other passenger who was on the near side of the back seat, was not disclosed; and the court indicated the conviction would have been upheld had the driver been named whether defendant was able to identify him—or even see him at all in the dark—because it was obvious someone was driving the car whether he could be seen or not. But the court emphasized that the law does not transfer the intent from the intended victim to someone else who was not intended, and reversed the conviction for want of any evidence to show that defendant knew DeCasnett was in the car or that there was any person riding on the far side of the rear seat.

The fault in *Martin*, as in similar cases, was in the preparation of the information in such form that it named the wrong person as the intended victim,—a defect as serious as naming someone other than the deceased in a charge of murder. For the most part any difficulty of this nature can be avoided by the exercise of due care on the part of the prosecuting attorney, after complete rejection of the false notion of "transferred intent" as a criminal-law concept, but in a few instances the fault has been in the legislative enactment itself. A former Kentucky statute, for example, provided that "if any person shall willfully and maliciously shoot at and wound another with

---

23. "On the other hand, the intent will not be imputed in the sense of being transferred or transposed from the person aimed at and missed to a person . . . mistakenly hit." State v. Martin, 342 Mo. 1089, 1094, 119 S.W.2d 298, 301 (1938).

24. Lacefield v. State, 34 Ark. 275 (1879); Jones v. State, 159 Ark. 215, 251 S.W. 690 (1923); Commonwealth v. Mor-

gan, 74 Ky. 601 (1876); State v. Mulhall, 199 Mo. 202, 97 S.W. 583 (1906); State v. Williamson, 203 Mo. 591, 102 S.W. 519 (1907); State v. Shanley, 20 S.D. 18, 104 N.W. 522 (1905); People v. Robinson, 6 Utah 101 (1889); Rex v. Holt, 7 Car. & P. 518, 173 Eng.Rep. 229 (1836).

25. State v. Martin, 342 Mo. 1089, 119 S.W.2d 298 (1938).

an intention *to kill him*," [26] he should be guilty of felony. This defect could not be cured by the prosecuting attorney because there could be no felony conviction under this statute in the type of case under consideration here.[27] As said by the court: "If he willfully and maliciously shoots at one with an intention to kill him and wounds another, he does not violate the statute." [28]

There is no need for a statute to limit its application by specificity of this nature and the tendency today is to omit any such restricting terms. This permits the court to say that "the statute does not require that the intent must be to kill the person actually shot; it merely requires that there must be an intent to kill." [29]

In case of an attack made upon the wrong person as a result of mistaken identity, needless to say, the law will recognize that the assailant "meant to murder the man at whom he shot" [30] although he had in mind the name of another man who was not there.[31]

The particularities of legal theory in this regard are for the guidance of the judge, who should not permit "transferred intent" to be introduced in a case in which it would produce a legally unacceptable result. But if in a trial the evidence for the prosecution indicates the presence of the mens rea as well as the actus reus of the offense charge, although the force took effect upon an unintended victim, it would not be misleading to the jury, and might perhaps be helpful, to give an instruction in terms of "transferred intent." [32]

SECTION 9. MOTIVE

"Although sometimes confused, motive and intent are not synonymous terms." [1] Motive has been said to be "that something in the mind, or that condition of the mind, which incites to the action," [2] or the "moving power which impels to action," [3] "induces action," [4] or "gives birth to a purpose." [5] The difference between intent and motive may be emphasized by illustration. If one person caused the death of another by a pistol shot, his intent may have been any one of a number, such as (a) to kill the deceased, (b) to frighten the deceased by shooting near him without hitting him, (c) to intimidate the deceased by pointing the weapon at him without shooting (the trigger having been pulled by accident), (d) to shoot at a target (perhaps without

---

26. See Commonwealth v. Morgan, 74 Ky. 601, 602 (1876). Emphasis added.

27. Ibid.

28. Hall v. Commonwealth, 17 Ky.L. Rep. 1365, 1366 (1896).

29. State v. Thomas, 127 La. 576, 580, 53 So. 868, 870 (1910).

Accord, State v. Alford, 260 Iowa 939, 151 N.W.2d 573 (1967).

30. Per Parke, B., in Regina v. Smith, Dears. 559, 169 Eng.Rep. 845 (1855).

See also Sashington v. State, 56 Ala. App. 698, 325 So.2d 205 (1975).

31. State v. Wansong, 271 Mo. 50, 195 S.W. 999 (1917).

32. State v. Clinton, 25 Wn.App. 400, 606 P.2d 1240 (1980). For a case in which the "transferred intent" instruc-

tion was held to be improper see, People v. Williams, 102 Cal.App.3d 1018, 162 Cal.Rptr. 748 (1980).

1. People v. Kuhn, 232 Mich. 310, 312, 205 N.W. 188, 189 (1925). "Intent, in its legal sense, is quite distinct from motive." Baker v. State, 120 Wis. 135, 145, 97 N.W. 566, 570 (1903).

2. State v. Johnson, 139 La. 829, 830, 72 So. 370, 371 (1916).

3. People ex rel. Hegeman v. Corrigan, 195 N.Y. 1, 12, 87 N.E. 792, 796 (1909).

4. State v. Santino, 186 S.W. 976, 977 (Mo.1916).

5. People v. Kuhn, 232 Mich. 310, 312, 205 N.W. 188, 189 (1925).

realizing that any other person was present), or (e) to test the "trigger-pull" of a gun supposed to be unloaded. If in the particular case the intent was to kill the deceased, the *motive* of the shooter may also have been one (or more) of a number of possible motives such as (a) hatred, (b) revenge, (c) jealousy, (d) avarice, (e) fear or even (f) love (as where a loved one is slain to end the suffering from an incurable disease).

Some writers have advanced the notion that when an act is committed with more than one object in view, only the most immediate intent is called "intent" and any "ulterior intent is called the motive of the act." [6] Stroud, for example, would say that if a burglar breaks and enters the dwelling of another in the nighttime with intent to steal, his mental attitude in regard to the contemplated larceny is not (at the time of breaking into the building) an *intent* but a *motive*.[7] This, however, is quite at variance with juridical usage of these terms, and the burglar's design to steal is so far from being no intent at all that it is called a "specific intent." [8] The search for the distinction must go much deeper than this. If in the supposed case the burglar's purpose was to steal food which he wished to eat, his intent to eat would also be an *intent* although one more step removed from his immediate intent at the time of the breaking, but his emotional urge to satisfy his appetite would be, not an *intent*, but a *motive*. This urge might come from the immediate pangs of hunger or from the recollection of such pangs on previous occasions. The burglarious act of another may be prompted by the urge for the feeling of power which money may give, or by any other impulse which may prompt a man to desire that which he does not have.

An emotional urge, unless counteracted by other impulses, "leads the mind to desire" [9] a particular result. This desire in turn may—or may not— prompt an intent to bring about that end. If the mental activity continues until such an intent is developed (all of which might occur with lightning speed) the desire is coupled with the intention and may in a sense be a part thereof. Nevertheless it is important to distinguish between the basic urge itself and the intent which resulted in the mind of the particular person, but which might not have been generated in the mind of another. When, for example, it is said that a legatee, who was aware of a large bequest in his favor, had a motive for killing his deceased testator, it is not meant that this fact is sufficient to establish an intent to kill. No more is meant than that this fact was sufficient to generate a primitive urge in that direction, although it might be completely checked by more social impulses.

"It may be stated as a general rule," said Wharton,[10] "that the proof of motive for the commission of the offense charged does not show guilt, and that a want of proof of such motive does not establish the innocence of the accused." It is said frequently that "motive is not an essential element of

6. Hitchler, Motive as an Essential Element of Crime, 35 Dick.L.Rev. 105, 108 (1931).

7. Stroud, Mens Rea 113 (1914).

8. People v. Comstock, 115 Mich. 305, 312, 73 N.W. 245, 248 (1897). See also Simpson v. State, 81 Fla. 292, 296, 87 So. 920, 921 (1921).

9. Williams v. State, 113 Neb. 606, 610, 204 N.W. 64, 66 (1925); Baker v. State, 120 Wis. 135, 145–6, 97 N.W. 566, 570 (1903).

10. Wharton, Criminal Law § 156 (12th ed.1932). This, in substance, has been quoted frequently. See, for example, Van Dyke v. Commonwealth, 196 Va. 1039, 1046, 86 S.E.2d 848, 852 (1955); State v. Janasky, 258 Wis. 182, 183, 45 N.W.2d 78, 79 (1950).

crime," [11] and at times in even more positive form such as : "Motive is never an essential element of a crime." [12]   Such sweeping generalizations must be tested, not by frequency of repetition, but by a search of the cases to see if factual situations may arise in which motive may have a determining influence upon the issue of guilt or innocence.   And since cases disclosing such situations may be found, the statement should appear in some modified form such as: "Proof of motive is never necessary to support a conclusion of guilt *otherwise sufficiently established*." [13]

The motive with which an actus reus was committed is always relevant [14] and material.[15]   The presence or absence of a motive on the part of the defendant which might tend to the commission of such a deed may always be considered by the jury on the question of whether he did commit it.[16]   But whenever it is clearly established that he committed it, with whatever state of mind is required for the mens rea of the particular offense, all the requisites of criminal guilt are present, even if no possible motive for the deed can be shown.[17]   In fact, in such a case, even proof of a good motive will not save the defendant from conviction.[18]

It is no answer to a prosecution for violation of a law requiring vaccination for smallpox that defendant was actuated by the urge for good health, and sincerely believed it was more healthful not to be vaccinated; [19] one who intentionally sends obscene matter through the mail is guilty of violating the federal statute even if his act is induced by the highest motives; [20] bigamy is committed by one who intentionally takes two wives even if his doing so is

11.   People v. Zammuto, 280 Ill. 225, 227, 117 N.E. 454, 455 (1917); Wright v. Commonwealth, 221 Ky. 226, 228, 298 S.W. 673, 674 (1927); State v. Koch, 321 Mo. 352, 356, 10 S.W.2d 928, 930 (1928). The same idea is expressed in somewhat different words in State v. Tapia, 41 N.M. 616, 617, 72 P.2d 1087, 1088 (1937); State v. Hansen, 195 Or. 169, 195, 244 P.2d 990, 1001 (1952).

12.   People ex rel. Hegeman v. Corrigan, 195 N.Y. 1, 12, 87 N.E. 792, 796 (1909).   "It is never necessary to show a bad motive before convicting a man of crime."   Wright v. Commonwealth, 221 Ky. 226, 228, 298 S.W. 673, 674 (1927). One court went almost to the other extreme, saying: "However, motive is a convenient thing but not always a necessary one."   Whitaker v. State, 160 Tex. Cr.R. 271, 280, 268 S.W.2d 172, 177 (1954).

13.   State v. Guilfoyle, 109 Conn. 124, 140, 145 A. 761, 767 (1929).   Italics added.   See also State v. Close, 106 N.J.L. 322, 331, 148 A. 764, 768 (1930).

14.   People v. Kuhn, 232 Mich. 310, 312, 205 N.W. 188, 189 (1925); State v. Hansen, 195 Or. 169, 195, 244 P.2d 990, 1001 (1952).

15.   State v. McHamilton, 128 La. 498, 54 So. 971 (1911).

16.   State v. Guilfoyle, 109 Conn. 124, 145 A. 761 (1929); People v. Doody, 343 Ill. 194, 208, 175 N.E. 436, 443 (1931); Van Dyke v. Commonwealth, 196 Va. 1039, 1046, 86 S.E.2d 848, 852 (1952).

17.   Wright v. Commonwealth, 221 Ky. 226, 298 S.W. 673 (1927).   "There can be no escape from punishment for crime when all the elements of it are proved, whether the evidence be positive or circumstantial, simply because the motive lies hidden in the heart of the only one who knows it."   Commonwealth v. Danz, 211 Pa. 507, 517, 60 A. 1070, 1073 (1905).

18.   Walls v. State, 7 Blackf. 572 (Ind. 1845); People ex rel. Hegeman v. Corrigan, 195 N.Y. 1, 87 N.E. 792 (1909).   If shots are fired with intent to kill, and without justification or excuse, the motive for the shooting is wholly immaterial.   "The courts frequently point out that not even the highest motive, outside the well-recognized legal justifications, is a defense to purposed killing."   Hence it also would be no defense to an indictment for an assault with intent to kill. Lebron v. United States 229 F.2d 16, 20 (D.C.Cir.1955).

19.   Commonwealth v. Pear, 183 Mass. 242, 66 N.E. 719 (1903).

20.   Knowles v. United States, 170 F. 409 (8th Cir.1909).

impelled by sincere religious convictions that this should be done; [21] and one who drowns his small children because he loves them and is prompted by the urge to prevent their suffering in poverty, [22] or who administers a fatal dose of poison to his wife, at her request, because of the impulse to end her agony from an incurable disease, [23] is guilty of murder.

All this, however, is on the assumption that the mens rea as well as the *actus reus* has been clearly established in the particular case, and the vital problem is whether proof of motive may ever be a determinant of guilt or innocence. An affirmative answer is indicated in several situations but some of these seem to require a different explanation, as is true when the suggestion is found in connection with offenses requiring a special state of mind expressed by the word "corrupt" or "corruptly." In some opinions may be found statements indicating the necessity of an "improper motive" for a corrupt state of mind [24] but the word "motive" seems to be misused at this point. While perjury, for example, requires wilful and corrupt false swearing, [25] it must be borne in mind that an intent to testify under oath to what is known to be untrue is a corrupt intent regardless of the motive. [26] If a witness was prompted by the impulse to see justice done, and was firmly convinced that his lie was necessary to overcome the lies of others and thus lead the jury to the correct conclusion, his false oath would still be perjury. It is hardly necessary to mention what the result would be if it should become established that a witness should say under oath what he thinks would do the most good rather than what he sincerely believes to be the truth.

In one case defendant claimed he was forced to testify falsely by threats of personal violence. In rejecting this defense it was said:

> The purpose of the perjury statute with respect to a judicial proceeding is to keep the process of justice free from the contamination of false testimony. . . . Without truthful testimony, the court system cannot function. For that reason, a court cannot accept the threats as a compulsion to lie under oath and a court will use all its force to protect the one threatened. [27]

Criminal libel presents quite a different problem. It is not necessary for the prosecution to establish a bad motive to make out a prima-facie case of guilt of this offense; [28] but if defendant seeks to justify his publication the motive which prompted it may become an important issue in the case. [29] At common law the truth of the statement published was no defense to a prose-

21. Reynolds v. United States, 98 U.S. 145 (1878); Davis v. Beason, 133 U.S. 333, 10 S.Ct. 299 (1890).

22. People v. Kirby, 2 Park.Cr.R. 28 (N.Y.1823).

23. People v. Roberts, 211 Mich. 187, 178 N.W. 690 (1920).

24. State v. Boyd, 196 Mo. 52, 72, 94 S.W. 536, 542 (1906).

25. Rex v. Smith, 2 Shower K.B. 165, 89 Eng.Rep. 864 (1681).

26. People ex rel. Hegeman v. Corrigan, 195 N.Y. 1, 12, 87 N.E. 792, 796 (1909).

27. Edwards v. State, 577 P.2d 1380, 1384 (Wyo.1978).

28. People v. Talbot, 196 Mich. 520, 162 N.W. 1017 (1917).

29. State v. Pape, 90 Conn. 98, 107, 96 A. 313, 316 (1916); People v. Fuller, 238 Ill. 116, 133, 87 N.E. 336, 341 (1909); State v. Hoskins, 109 Iowa 656, 657, 80 N.W. 1063 (1899); Commonwealth v. Snelling, 32 Mass. 337, 342 (1834); State v. Tolley, 23 N.D. 284, 294, 136 N.W. 784, 787 (1912); Thomas v. State, 34 Okl.Cr. 63, 66, 244 P. 1116, 1117 (1926); State v. Herman, 219 Wis. 267, 278, 262 N.W. 718, 723 (1935).

cution for criminal libel;[30] in fact the early view was that "the greater the truth the worse the libel." [31]   But by a very common provision in this country justification is established if "the matter charged as libelous was true, and was published with good motives and for justifiable ends." [32]   Furthermore, even when a communication is privileged (unless the privilege is absolute) the protection is lost if a libelous statement is published with an improper motive.[33]   In such a case "motive is a potent factor as to the guilt of one sought to be charged with criminal libel . . . and, therefore, malice must be alleged." [34]   Furthermore, as so used, the word "malice" does not have the usual meaning in law, but is employed "in the popular conception of the term, that is, a desire or disposition to injure another founded upon spite or ill will." [35]

In a prosecution for the publication of an obscene libel motive might also play a determining role under extreme circumstances.   A standard work on surgery, properly sold to and used by members and students of the medical profession, might be of such a nature that it would be a punishable offense to divert it from its proper purpose and exhibit it indiscriminately to others for the sole purpose of lustful excitement.[36]

Motive may also be a determinant of guilt or innocence in an unusual case of homicide.   Suppose a grave felony is about to be committed under such circumstances that the killing of the offender to prevent the crime would be justified by law, and at that very moment he is shot and killed.   If the slayer was prompted by the impulse to promote the social security by preventing the felony he is guilty of no offense; if he had no such impulse but merely acted upon the urge to satisfy an old grudge by killing a personal enemy, he is guilty of murder.[37]   The intent is the same in either case,—to kill the per-

30.   4 Bl.Comm. *150.

31.   Thomas v. State, 34 Okl.Cr. 63, 67, 244 P. 1116, 1117 (1926).

32.   Utah Const.Art. I § 15 (1896); Wyo.Const.Art. I § 20 (1890).

33.   McLean v. Altringer, 114 Cal.App. 363, 300 P. 79 (1931); Browning v. Commonwealth, 116 Ky. 282, 76 S.W. 19 (1903); Haase v. State, 53 N.J.L. 34, 40, 20 A. 751, 753 (1890).

34.   State ex rel. Arnold v. Chase, 94 Fla. 1071, 1076, 114 So. 856, 858 (1927).

35.   McLean v. Altringer, 114 Cal.App. 363, 365, 300 P. 79, 80 (1931).   "A lie is never privileged; it always has malice coiled up in it."   Commonwealth v. Foley, 282 Pa. 277, 281, 141 A. 50, 51 (1928).

36.   Extracts from standard medical books, which would be proper enough for use of members and students of the medical profession, are obscene and indecent when printed in pamphlet form for general distribution to persons of all classes, including girls and boys.   United States v. Chesman, 19 F. 497 (C.C.Mo.1881).

Compare Redrup v. New York, 386 U.S. 767, 87 S.Ct. 1414 (1967) with Ginsberg v. United States, 383 U.S. 463, 86

S.Ct. 942 (1966).   And see People v. Marler, 199 Cal.App.2d 889, 18 Cal.Rptr. 923 (1962).

37.   Laws v. State, 26 Tex.Cr.R. 643 (1888).   See also Garcia v. State, 91 Tex. Cr.R. 9, 11, 237 S.W. 279, 281 (1922). "And where the life of an actual felon is taken by one who does not know or believe his guilt, such slaying is murder." People v. Burt, 51 Mich. 199, 202, 16 N.W. 378, 379 (1883).   An officer shot and wounded a person who was at the moment a fleeing felon who could not otherwise be stopped; but as the officer did not know, or believe, or have any reason to believe he was a fleeing felon a conviction of shooting with intent to do grievous bodily harm was affirmed.   The Queen v. Dadson, 2 Den. 35, 169 Eng. Rep. 407 (1850).   "[H]e cannot be excused from his wilful malicious act by a showing of circumstances of which he was unaware."   Collett v. Commonwealth, 296 Ky. 267, 273, 176 S.W.2d 893, 896 (1943).   Accord, Josey v. United States, 77 App.D.C. 321, 135 F.2d 809 (1943).   See also Restatement, Second, Torts § 63, comment f, and illustration 2 (1965).

son; the difference between innocence and guilt lies in the motive which prompted this intent. While it is true that to convict in such a case it would probably be necessary to prove that the slayer was wholly unaware of the felony contemplated by the deceased, there could be no doubt of his guilt if he was unaware of this fact.[38] Needless to say he would not be convicted because of this ignorance *per se*, but because this ignorance disproves any claim he might make to a proper motive for his deed.[39]

In such situation some insist that if the actor is aware of the circumstances, his shot is fired with intent to prevent the atrocious felony, and if not aware it is with intent to "get even;" so we are dealing with intent rather than with motive. The important consideration is to recognize that the thought which motivated the intent to kill may make the difference between guilt and innocence, whatever label is applied.[40]

An English author would prefer another conclusion because he undertakes to define *actus reus* not merely as the physical element of crime but as this element plus an additional requirement.[41] According to his position the *actus reus* of murder, for example, is not homicide but the killing of a man who ought not to be killed,—with the unavoidable though astounding conclusion that there are some not entitled to live who may be killed with malice aforethought without the commission of crime. Since malice, by definition, requires the absence of justification or excuse this theory would require adoption of the unacceptable notion that intentional homicide may be innocent although without anything in the nature of excuse or justification. While he admits that with his definition "the term *actus reus* is somewhat misleading" in some of its applications [42] he concludes that the case-law is wrong because it does violence to his theory. Actually he cites only *Dadson*, but others are also in conflict with his position such as *Trogden, Laws, Collett, Garcia and Burt*.[43] In his support he cites only a dictum from a case in which the actual holding was that it was not illegal for a British ship to sail into a port previously captured by the British, although it had been an enemy port during part of the voyage.[44] The illustration of a shot fired with malice aforethought causing the death of one who could have been killed intentionally, without malice, had the facts been known, was not a proper analogy for

---

38. Trogdon v. State, 133 Ind. 1, 8, 32 N.E. 725, 727 (1892).

39. Compare Golden v. State, 25 Ga. 527 (1858).

40. "However, knowledge is a mental state that is closely related to that constituting a motive or purpose and we believe that knowledge is fairly embraced within the concepts of motive and purpose as used in AS 11.70.030." Kimoktoak v. State, 584 P.2d 25, 34 (Alaska, 1978).

41. Williams, Criminal Law § 12 (2d ed. 1961). His statement that *actus reus* is the "whole situation forbidden by law with the exception of the mental element (but including so much of the mental element as is contained in the definition of an act)" is free from objection because there can be no homicide, criminal or innocent, without an act—either of commis-

sion or omission. But he adds more than this to his notion of *actus reus*, as explained in the text herein.

42. Id. at p. 22.

43. See supra notes 36, 37. Williams' position has been quoted with approval by another English writer. Smith, Two Problems in Criminal Attempts, 70 Harv. L.Rev. 422, 445–6 (1957). Smith also seems to be unfamiliar with any of the cases in point other than Dadson.

44. The "Abby," 5 C.Rob. 251, 254, 165 Eng.Rep. 765, 766–7 (1804). The proceeding was one to condemn the vessel as a ship taken in trade with a colony of the enemy. The voyage started before war was declared and the colony was not reached until after its capture by the British. In the meantime there may have been a lack of due diligence to alter the voyage.

the case at hand which leaves it without much force even as dictum. The proper analogy for the court to have drawn would have been from a case in which one, having set out to commit murder, fired a shot into the body of his intended victim, supposed to be alive but already dead from some other cause. That, of course, would not be murder because while the shot was fired with malice aforethought (mens rea) there was no resulting homicide (*actus reus*). It is to be hoped there will be no departure from the juridical view that the *actus reus* of murder is homicide and that homicide committed with malice aforethought is murder.

Only in exceptional instances does motive become a determinant of guilt or innocence, and it should be emphasized in conclusion that just as a good motive is not sufficient for exculpation when both the mens rea and the *actus reus* are clearly established, so a bad motive is not sufficient for guilt if either is lacking. For example, when sentence of death is duly pronounced by a court of competent jurisdiction, the person designated by law for this purpose has both the privilege and the duty to execute this sentence,[45] and it can be of no legal significance whether he does so regretfully, joyfully or indifferently. The only legally-recognized motive for his act is the urge to carry out the mandate imposed upon him, whatever emotional impulses he may actually experience at the moment. And when a murderous attack is made under such circumstances that the innocent victim is privileged to use deadly force to save his own life the dominant motive is self-preservation and the legal eye will see no other.[46]

SECTION 10. CONCURRENCE OF MENS REA AND ACTUS REUS

The mens rea and the actus reus must concur to constitute a true crime.[1]

The effort to express this requirement has frequently taken some such form as: "An evil intention and an unlawful action must concur in order to constitute a crime," [2] or "In law, the commission of a crime consists in the joint operation of an act and intent or criminal negligence." [3] The doctrine of trespass *ab initio*, no longer entrenched in the law of torts,[4] has no application in criminal jurisprudence.[5] One, for example, who has acquired lawful possession of the property of another does not commit common-law larce-

45. The verb "execute" (*ex + sequi*) means to carry out and hence what is executed is literally the *sentence* in a capital case the same as in a noncapital case. References to the *prisoner* as being executed in the former were originally in the nature of slang although fully accepted now as a result of long usage.

46. This is what the court meant by its rather lurid statement in Golden v. State, 25 Ga. 527, 532 (1858).

1. "Under section 20, the defendant's wrongful intent and his physical act must concur in the sense that the act must be motivated by the intent." People v. Green, 27 Cal.3d 1, 164 Cal.Rptr. 1, 33, 609 P.2d 468, 500 (1980).

2. Commonwealth v. Mixer, 207 Mass. 141, 142, 93 N.E. 249 (1910).

"To constitute a crime there must be unity of act and intent. In every crime or public offense there must exist a union or joint operation of act and intent, or criminal negligence." West's Ann. Cal.Pen.Code § 20 (1970).

3. Brown v. State, 28 Ark. 126, 128 (1873). See also State v. Blue, 17 Utah 175, 180, 53 P. 978, 980 (1898).

4. Restatement, Second, Torts § 214(2), comment f, and § 278(2), comment c (1965).

5. Milton v. State, 40 Fla. 253, 24 So. 60 (1898); State v. Moore, 12 N.H. 42 (1841).

ny by a subsequently-formed intent to steal,[6] and he who breaks into the dwelling house of another at night, but without burglarious intent, is not guilty of burglary even if he actually commits a felony while therein.[7] The doctrine of continuing trespass is altogether different because *trespass de bonis asportatis* is deemed to continue, for purposes of the law of larceny, so long as the trespasser keeps possession of the property so obtained.[8] This, however, requires an original trespass, and never (so far as criminal law is concerned) undertakes to make a trespass out of what was not such at the time by any theory of "relation back." Also excluded entirely from the criminal-law field is the familiar maxim *omnis ratihabitio retrotrahitur et mandato priori equiparator* (every ratification relates back and is equivalent to a prior command) and one, for example, cannot commit crime by ratifying an unauthorized act previously done by his servant.[9]

One error to be avoided is the false notion that "concurrence," as here used, means no more than mere coincidence, because the actual requirement is that the two elements of crime must be "brought together" in the sense of a causal relation between the mens rea and the *actus reus*. Stated in other words the *actus reus* must be attributable to the mens rea, and if this relation is clearly shown it is unimportant that the two were not present at the same time, whereas coexistence is not sufficient if the causal relation is lacking. The law will recognize homicide, for example, although a long period of time elapsed between the blow and the death, if it was within the established "year and a day," but the killing will be murder if, and only if, the loss of life *resulted from* a state of mind meeting the requirements of malice aforethought. If the blow was struck with malice aforethought the resulting death is murder despite the fact that the assailant subsequently changed his mind and was hoping very sincerely, before the end came, that his victim would survive; whereas, if the blow was struck in privileged self-defense it is innocent homicide although the defender later decided to kill his former assailant in cold blood and was searching for him, unsuccessfully with this thought in mind at the very moment of death.

For example, a defendant who caused the death of another by reckless driving was guilty of criminal homicide despite the fact that he did everything he could to avoid the accident after it was too late;[10] one who stabbed a sheep with intent to steal it was guilty of killing a sheep with intent to steal although he did not succeed in taking the animal away and had no

---

6. The finder of lost property may lawfully take possession for the purpose of returning it to the owner, and if he does so his subsequent conversion is not larceny. Ransom v. State, 22 Conn. 153 (1852); People v. Bates, 367 Ill. 499, 11 N.E.2d 942 (1937).

7. 2 East P.C. 509 (1803); Dobbs' Case, 2 East P.C. 513 (1770). The intent at the time of entry controls but it may be inferred from sufficiently indicative circumstances. State v. Johnson, 77 Idaho 1, 287 P.2d 425 (1955), cert. denied 350 U.S. 1007, 76 S.Ct. 649 (1956).

8. State v. Coombs, 55 Me. 477 (1867). And see Meadows v. State, 36 Ala.App. 402, 403, 56 So.2d 789, 790 (1952).

9. Morse v. State, 6 Conn. 9 (1825). One who "ratifies" the act of another who had received stolen property on one's behalf is guilty of receiving—but not on the theory of *ratification*. If there was no authority for the receipt of such property it was not "received" by the principal until he had knowledge of the facts and decided to take unlawful advantage thereof. See, supra, chapter 4, section 6, D.

10. State v. Stentz, 33 Wash. 444, 74 P. 588 (1903).

thought of larceny in mind at the time of its death two days later;[11] and a prisoner who had joined a conspiracy to escape by means of deadly force, if necessary, was guilty of the murder of a guard who was killed in the attempt although this particular conspirator had abandoned the effort and returned to his cell before the killing occurred—without giving the others notice by word or act of his change of intent.[12] On the other hand, if X made a murderous assault upon D under such circumstances that D was forced to kill X to save his own life, D is guilty of no crime although he had armed himself and set out to murder X,—if D had changed his mind and abandoned his purpose entirely before finding where X was or making any communication to him.[13]

In one of the best-known cases in this field the defendant, who attempted to kill a girl in Ohio and thought he had done so, then took her to Kentucky where he cut off her head to prevent identification, firmly believing her to be dead at the time. As he was mistaken in this regard, however, it was this act which caused her death and he was prosecuted for this murder in Kentucky. This could not be murder, it was argued for the defense, because defendant who thought he was merely cutting the head from a corpse was not acting with malice aforethought. A conviction of murder was upheld, however, on the ground that defendant had set out to murder the girl and had caused her death in the perpetration of his plan.[14]

The problem of negative action must not be ignored in this regard because a positive act without mens rea may be followed later by a negative act with mens rea and the latter may be sufficient for criminal guilt although the former was not. Thus the owner of an insured building who accidentally causes a fire that destroys it is not, for this reason, guilty of burning it with intent to defraud the insurer even if quite pleased with the result; but if he sees the blaze while quite small and realizes he could easily put it out without danger to himself, but purposely refrains from doing so in order to collect the insurance, he is guilty.[15] Under such circumstances he was under a legal duty to put out the fire and his forbearance is the legally-recognized cause of all harm his performance would have prevented. And a law making it unlawful to possess a certain article may apply to such an article lawfully acquired prior to the statute because the penalty is imposed "for continuing to possess [it] after the enactment of the law."[16] One having possession of such an article has a legal duty to dispose of it prior to the effective date of the statute and guilt is based upon the omission to do what the law requires.

---

11. Regina v. Sutton, 2 Moody 29, 169 Eng.Rep. 12 (1838).

12. State v. Allen, 47 Conn. 121 (1879).

13. State v. Rider, 90 Mo. 54, 1 S.W. 825 (1886).

14. Jackson v. Commonwealth, 100 Ky. 239, 38 S.W. 422 (1896). And see 33 Harv.L.Rev. 611 (1920). A companion case is In re Palani Goudan, 26 Madras L.T. 68 (India, 1919). D struck his wife with a plowshare rendering her unconscious. It was not shown that the blow was likely to cause death or that D had intended to cause death, but under the belief that she was dead D hung her to a beam to give the appearance of suicide. In fact it was the hanging and not the blow that caused death. The court said this would be manslaughter by English Law, but was not murder or culpable homicide under the Penal Code of India, in which every offense is defined "both as to what must be done and with what intention it must be done, ..." Id. at 75.

15. Commonwealth v. Cali, 247 Mass. 20, 141 N.E. 510, (1923).

16. Samuels v. McCurdy, 267 U.S. 188, 193, 45 S.Ct. 264, 265 (1925).

This of course assumes "a willing and conscious possession" [17] because while "unwitting possession" is a legally-recognized concept it is not included within the proper interpretation of such a statute.[18]

Because of the requirement of causal relation between mens rea and *actus reus*, an *actus reus* which is not a crime when done cannot become a crime because of something happening thereafter which was not in contemplation of the actor when done. Thus a statute was invalid which purported to make it a federal offense for one to obtain property on credit by false pretenses and to become bankrupt within three months thereafter.[19] The statute could have validly provided a punishment for the act of obtaining property on credit by false pretenses *in contemplation of bankruptcy*, or of filing a *voluntary* petition in bankruptcy within three months after having obtained property in such a manner; but the enactment was not so written.

17. Baender v. Barnett, 255 U.S. 224, 225, 41 S.Ct. 271 (1921).

18. Ibid.; State v. Labato, 7 N.J. 137, 80 A.2d 617 (1951).

If a firearm was put in **D**'s car without his knowledge he may not be convicted of the unlawful possession thereof unless he was aware of its presence for a sufficient period to have been able to terminate his possession. State v. Flaherty, 400 A.2d 363 (Me. 1979).

19. United States v. Fox, 95 U.S. 670 (1877).

Chapter 8

RESPONSIBILITY: LIMITATIONS ON CRIMINAL CAPACITY

SECTION 1. IMMATURITY (INFANCY)

Every civilized society must recognize criminal incapacity based upon extreme immaturity, because no matter what harm is caused by one of very tender years the situation must be dealt with by some means other than the machinery established for the administration of criminal justice. Although this is too clear to admit of any possibility of doubt there are differences of opinion as to just what should be considered such immaturity as to preclude criminal guilt.

A. THE COMMON LAW

While failing to develop techniques comparable to those found in modern juvenile court or youth-correction authority acts, the common law made a very reasonable approach to this problem by taking notice of two ages in order to give due recognition to individual differences. According to the common law a child under the age of seven has no criminal capacity;[1] one who has reached the age of fourteen has the same criminal capacity as an adult,[2] that is, he is fully accountable for his violations of law unless incapacity is established on some other basis such as insanity; while between the ages of seven and fourteen there is a rebuttable presumption of criminal incapacity[3] and conviction of crime is permitted only upon clear proof of such precocity as to establish a real appreciation of the wrong done.[4] This presumption is extremely strong at the age of seven and diminishes gradually until it disappears entirely at the age of fourteen,[5] such references being to physical age and not to some so-called "mental age."[6]

1. "At common law, children under seven were considered incapable of possessing criminal intent." Application of Gault, 387 U.S. 1, 16, 87 S.Ct. 1428, 1438 (1967).

2. 1 Hale P.C. *25–28; 4 Bl.Comm. *22–4; The Queen v. Smith, 1 Cox C.C. 260 (1845); Clay v. State, 143 Fla. 204, 208, 196 So. 462, 463 (1940); Triplet v. State, 169 Miss. 306, 152 So. 881 (1934).

3. Ibid.

4. 4 Bl.Comm. *24; The Queen v. Smith 1 Cox C.C. 260 (1845).

Homicide by a boy of 10 was held not to be murder on the ground that one of

his age was not shown to have the mens rea needed for murder. State In re S.H., 61 N.J. 108, 293 A.2d 181 (1972).

5. State v. George, 20 Del. 57, 58, 54 A. 745, 746 (1902); Clay v. State, 143 Fla. 204, 208, 196 So. 462, 463 (1940); Miles v. State, 99 Miss. 165, 167, 54 So. 946 (1911); Little v. State, 261 Ark. 859, 554 S.W.2d 312 (1977).

6. State v. Jackson, 346 Mo. 474, 142 S.W.2d 45 (1940). See Woodbridge, Physical and Mental Infancy in the Criminal Law, 87 U. of Pa.L.Rev. 426, 438–454 (1939).

It may mentioned as a matter of curiosity that a year-old baby was once indicted for nuisance in New York,[7] and an English two-year-old was once charged with vagrancy,[8] although in each instance such liability was promptly and emphatically denied; in a Georgia case the court had occasion to comment *obiter* that "a person three and one-half years old is not accountable for any act he commits;"[9] and in the early thirteenth century a seven-year-old boy was actually tried for murder with the result that: "The death penalty is pardoned for the king's sake, and therefore Thomas is quit therein."[10] Turning to the grimmer side the English records show the execution of a thirteen-year-old girl who had killed her mistress,[11] a ten-year-old boy who slew a companion,[12] and a child of eight who maliciously burned some barns;[13] and our records disclose the execution of two boys of twelve for murder,[14] and the conviction of one of eleven for the same kind of offense although in this case a new trial was granted because of an erroneous ruling as to the competency of a witness.[15] It may be added that a 13-year old boy was recently convicted of second-degree murder.[16]

The English common law did not permit a minor, even if over the age of fourteen, to be convicted of certain misdemeanors, but these were offenses in the category of nonfeasance such as "not repairing a bridge, or a highway" and the reason was that "not having the command of his fortune till twenty-one, he wants the capacity to do those things which the law requires."[17] This immunity had no application to ordinary misdemeanors such as assault and battery,[18] and the true explanation is that the failure to convict is based, not upon criminal incapacity in the strict sense, but upon the fact that since legally-required performance always falls short of the impossible or the unreasonable, the *actus reus* itself, which here is negative action,[19] is missing in such a case. Certain other instances may be mentioned such as the case involving the prosecution of a minor just under twenty-one for a violation of the bankruptcy act. The refusal to permit a conviction in this case was upon the ground that his obligations, none of them for necessaries, were all voidable by him and hence he was not truly within the proscription of the statute.[20] This would be true, it should be noted, regardless of the penalty provided for a violation of the bankruptcy law and it came to be recognized that the common-law rules as to criminal incapacity based up-

---

7. People v. Townsend, 3 Hill 479 (N.Y.Sup.Ct.1842). It should be added that the indictment named 27 defendants one of whom turned out to be a baby.

8. Rex v. Inhabitantes de King's Langley, 1 Strange 631, 93 Eng.Rep. 744 (1725).

9. Russell v. Corley, 212 Ga. 121, 91 S.E.2d 24, 25 (1956).

10. Wooldale's Case (the boy's name was Thomas) Eyre of York (1218–19), 56 Selden Society, 415 Pl. 1134 (1937).

11. 1 Hale P.C. *26. Execution was by burning because killing her mistress was petit treason. In the nineteenth century a boy just "a few days short of fourteen" was convicted of murder and transported for life. Rex v. Wild, 1 Moody 452, 168 Eng.Rep. 1341 (1835).

12. 4 Bl.Comm. *23. A co-defendant of nine was also convicted and sentenced to death, ibid., but this sentence was later respited. 1 Hale P.C. *27, note c. (ed. by Emlyn, 1800).

13. 4 Bl.Comm. *23–4.

14. Godfrey v. State, 31 Ala. 323 (1858); State v. Guild, 10 N.J.L. 163 (1828).

15. State v. Aaron, 4 N.J.L. 263 (1818).

16. Poole v. State, ___ Nev. ___, 625 P.2d 1163 (1981).

17. 4 Bl.Comm. *22.

18. Ibid.

19. See supra, chapter 6, section 4.

20. The Queen v. Wilson, 5 Q.B.D. 28 (1879).

on immaturity were the same in misdemeanors as in felony cases. [21] The common-law concept of infancy was a person who had not yet reached majority,[22] and while criminal incapacity did not extend over the full period of nonage it was limited entirely therein and was commonly spoken of as the defense of "infancy." [23]

As customarily expressed there is a presumption of criminal incapacity on the part of an infant below the age of fourteen, which is conclusive prior to the age of seven and rebuttable thereafter.[24] In other words, while it is otherwise in the case of one under the age of seven, the common law recognizes the possibility of criminal guilt by a person between the ages of seven and fourteen if the individual is shown to have sufficient maturity as a matter of fact despite the lack of years. The burden of proof in such a case is on the prosecution,[25] and different phrases have been employed to indicate what is needed for this purpose, such as "discretion to judge between good and evil," [26] capacity "to appreciate the wrong," [27] "a guilty knowledge of wrongdoing," [28] "appreciate the wrongfulness of their conduct," [29] or "competent to know the nature and consequences of his conduct and to appreciate that it was wrong." [30] The prosecution, in brief, cannot obtain the conviction of such a person without showing that he had such maturity in fact as to have a guilty knowledge that he was doing wrong.[31] Conduct of the defendant such as concealing himself or the evidence of his misdeed may be such under all the circumstances as to authorize a finding of such maturity.[32] Such a finding was warranted, for example, in the case of a boy who, having caused the death of a playmate, at once tried to silence another boy by a promise that he "would give him five dollars, would treat him every time he had money, and would let no one in the hollow hit him if he would not tell." [33] Incidents which, with other facts, have had a bearing in producing a similar result include the reporting of a hatchet-slaying as the work of Indians,[34] and in a

---

21. State v. Goin, 28 Tenn. 175 (1848). *A fortiori* they apply to offenses *mala prohibita.* Commonwealth v. Mead, 92 Mass. 398, 399 (1865).

22. 4 Bl.Comm. *22. At common law majority is reached on the day *preceding* the twenty-first anniversary of birth. Wells v. Wells, 6 Ind. 447 (1855).

23. Ibid; 1 Hale P.C. *16.

24. See State v. George, 20 Del. 57, 58, 54 A. 745, 746 (1902); Miles v. State, 99 Miss. 165, 167, 54 So. 946 (1911).

25. Miles v. State, 99 Miss. 165, 167, 54 So. 946 (1911).

26. 1 Hale P.C. *26. Or to "discern between good and evil." 4 Bl.Comm. *23.

27. State v. Goodsell, 138 Iowa 504, 506, 116 N.W. 605, 606 (1908).

28. Heilman v. Commonwealth, 84 Ky. 457, 459, 1 S.W. 731, 732 (1886).

29. In re Gladys R., 1 Cal.3d 855, 83 Cal.Rptr. 671, 464 P.2d 127 (1970).

30. Can.Crim.Code § 13 (1970).

31. Rex v. Owen, 4 Car. & P. 236, 172 Eng.Rep. 685 (1830). The jury must be satisfied that defendant "had arrived at that maturity of the intellect which was a necessary condition of the crime charged." Regina v. Vamplew, 3 F. & F. 520, 176 Eng.Rep. 234 (1862).

32. 4 Bl.Comm *23.

33. State v. Milholland, 89 Iowa 5, 7 56 N.W. 403, 404 (1893).

34. Godfrey v. State, 31 Ala. 323 (1858).

In upholding the murder conviction of a 13-year-old boy the court said: "Poole hid the murder weapon, as well as other pieces of evidence. He fabricated stories in attempting to establish an alibi. He claimed the shooting had been accidental; and he testified that he knew killing people was wrong. There was ample evidence that Poole knew the wrongfulness of his act." Poole v. State, ___ Nev. ___, 625 P.2d 1163, 1165 (1981).

different type of homicide an anxious inquiry whether the presence of poison in a dead body could be detected.[35]

Immaturity not sufficient for exculpation may have a bearing on the grade or degree of guilt as in the case of a thirteen-year-old girl who was convicted of manslaughter under circumstances that undoubtedly would have been held to be murder on the part of an adult.[36]

By a special rule of the English common law, followed in some of our states but not in others, no boy under fourteen can be convicted of rape. This strange immunity, based upon a conclusive presumption of physical immaturity rather than of mental immaturity, was outlined in the discussion of that offense and no more than this reminder is needed here.

Insofar as the common law of criminal capacity or incapacity is concerned the age of the defendant at the time of the alleged offense, and not that at the time of the indictment or the trial, will control.[37] The jury is not permitted to make an estimate of age based upon its observation of the defendant but whenever this is a material matter there must be evidence upon which the jury can base a finding.[38]

B.　STATUTES

The common law relating to this matter has sometimes been codified as follows:

"No person shall be convicted of an offence in respect of an act or omission on his part while he was under the age of seven years.

"No person shall be convicted of an offence in respect of an act or omission on his part while he was seven years of age or more, but under the age of fourteen years, unless he was competent to know the nature and consequences of his conduct and to appreciate that it was wrong." [39]

On the other hand there has been a tendency to raise the age below which there is complete criminal incapacity, which for example has by statute been set at eight in England,[40] ten in Louisiana,[41] fourteen in New Jersey,[42] fifteen in Texas,[43] and sixteen in New York.[44] And the net result under some of the juvenile delinquency statutes or corresponding enactments, to be considered presently, is to raise it even higher. Some of the codes make no mention of any age under which there is complete criminal incapacity, provid-

---

35. Regina v. Vamplew, 3 F. & F. 520, 176 Eng.Rep. 234 (1862).

36. Ibid. In a prosecution for murder the judge gave an instruction on manslaughter which would not have been called for in the case of an adult defendant and the verdict was guilty of manslaughter.

37. This is unavoidable just as capacity to enter into a binding obligation depends upon age at the time of the contract and not at the time of trial, but whether a case is to be handled as a criminal case or under special proceedings provided for juveniles is controlled by statute and in some states depends upon age at the time of the proceeding. See

Peterson v. State, 156 Tex.Cr.R. 105, 235 S.W.2d 138 (1950).

38. People v. Grizzle, 381 Ill. 278, 44 N.E.2d 917 (1942).

39. Can.Crim.Code §§ 12, 13 (1970).

40. 23 Geo. V c. 12, § 50 (1933).

41. La.Rev.Stat.Ann. § 14:13 (1974).

42. N.J.Stat.Ann. 2C:4-11 (1978).

43. V.T.C.A., Penal Code § 8.07 (1974).

44. McKinney's N.Y.Pen. Code § 30.00 (1979). Special provisions apply in murder cases imposing criminal responsibility at a younger age.

ing merely that children under fourteen are not capable of committing crime "in the absence of clear proof that at the time of committing the act charged against them, they knew its wrongfulness." [45]   Such a provision recognizes the existence of a presumption, although the word is not used, and the logical interpretation would seem to be that this is the common-law presumption, which is conclusive below the age of seven, extremely strong at that age, of gradually diminishing strength until the age of fourteen is reached when it disappears entirely.   Whether this is or is not the proper interpretation seems to be an academic question.   The presumption of incapacity is conclusive only as to one *under* the age of seven, [46] and hence in the absence of legislative change it has always been possible, in legal theory, to rebut the presumption of incapacity of a seven-year-old child,—but it seems never to have been done.   Where the age under which criminal incapacity is conclusively presumed has been raised by statute, without other change in this regard, there is still a rebuttable presumption of incapacity between that age and fourteen[47]—unless the new age is fourteen or more.

What amounts to a limitation of criminal capacity has been established in some states by a statutory provision that no one shall be deprived of life by reason of any act done before attaining a certain age such as fifteen[48] or eighteen.[49]

C. JUVENILE DELINQUENCY

"Juvenile delinquency," when employed as a technical term rather than merely a descriptive phrase, is entirely a legislative product and hence might appropriately be considered under the sub-section above, but is given a separate heading for the sake of emphasis.

Our first juvenile court act was passed in Illinois in 1899,[50] and now comparable enactments will be found in all the states, but there are so many differences, some of them quite basic, that only a very general introduction can be attempted here.   The philosophy underlying this legislation is that wayward youth is in need of protection and rehabilitation.   The theory is not

45. E.g., West's Ann.Cal.Pen.Code § 26 (1970).

46. Blackstone forgot a year, saying: "Under seven years of age, indeed, an infant cannot be guilty . . . but at eight years old he may be . . . ." 4 Bl.Comm. *23.

47. Clemmons v. State, 66 Ga.App. 16, 16 S.E.2d 883 (1941).

48. E.g., V.T.C.A., Penal Code § 8.07 (1974).

49. E.g., West's Ann.Cal.Pen.Code § 190.1 (1970).

50. Ill.Laws 1899, p. 131 et seq.; 2 Abbott, The Child and the State 330 (1938).   Part II of Volume II of Abbott, entitled The State and the Child Offender, gives an extensive treatment of this subject.   See also Glueck, One Thousand Juvenile Delinquents (1934); Glueck, Unraveling Juvenile Delinquency (1950); Ludwig, Youth and the Law (1955).

And see Goddard, Responsibility of Children in the Juvenile Court, 3 J.C.L. and Crim. 365 (1912); Adler, Work of Juvenile Courts, 7 J. of Comp.Leg. (3d ser.) 217 (1925); Criswell and Adams, A Juvenile Court Manual for Florida, 10 Fla.L.J. 281 (1936); Kean, History of the Criminal Liability of Children, 53 L.Q.Rev. 364 (1937); MacPherson, The Juvenile Court in Connecticut, 11 Conn.B.J. 231 (1937); Ludwig, Responsibility for Young Offenders, 29 Neb.L.Rev. 521 (1950); Levy, Criminal Liability for the Punishment of Children, 43 J.C.L. and Crim. 719 (1953); Williams, Criminal Responsibility of Children, 1954 Crim.L.Rev. 493; Ludwig, Considerations Basic to Reform of Juvenile Offender Laws, 29 St. John's L.Rev. 226 (1955); Hellum, Juvenile Justice: The Second Revolution, 25 Crime and Delinq. 299 (1979); Klempner and Parker, Juvenile Delinquency and Juvenile Justice 25–29 (1981).

that a defendant is on trial charged with a crime for which he will be punished if found guilty, but that a proceeding is being conducted by a chancellor, so to speak, representing the state's paternalistic solicitude for its ward, seeking to determine whether he has in fact deviated from the path of acceptable conduct, and if so what care, protection, training and guidance are needed to develop him into an upright and useful citizen.[51] At times no more has been done than the establishment of an alternative procedure, leaving to the discretion of the judges which cases falling within its terms are to be dealt with by it and which handled as criminal prosecutions in the ordinary court;[52] some of the statutes require that appropriate cases must receive the attention of the juvenile court although making it possible for some to be transferred to the criminal court for ultimate disposition by it;[53] while other enactments take such cases, with perhaps some exceptions, entirely out of the jurisdiction of the ordinary court and require disposition by this special procedure.[54] One important goal of this type of legislation is "to hide youthful errors from the full gaze of the public and bury them in the graveyard of the forgotten past; "[55] hence it is not uncommon to provide for the exclusion of the general public from such hearings,[56] or to insist that a finding against the child therein shall not be deemed a conviction of crime[57] and that the fact of such a finding or evidence in the hearing shall not be available as evidence elsewhere.[58] Some statutes are less inclusive. Thus the Oregon court held that the statutory provision to the effect that no order of a juvenile court or any evidence in such a proceeding shall be used against "such child" does not preclude the use of such evidence against a mature offender.[59] The court reasoned that the purpose of the statute was to protect a child from the stigma of his wrongdoing in his effort to rehabilitate himself; but if after reaching maturity he has demonstrated a lack of rehabilitation there is no reason to preclude the use of the evidence of the juvenile proceeding for the purpose of fixing his sentence. Quite similar is the Pennsylvania statute which bars the use of a juvenile court record as evidence in a criminal case to determine guilt or innocence, but does not bar its use for the determination of sentence.[60] In explanation of another statute it was said that the juvenile

---

51. Wissenburg v. Bradley, 209 Iowa 813, 816, 229 N.W. 205, 207 (1930). And see People v. Hopkins, 205 Misc. 666, 670, 129 N.Y.S.2d 851, 854 (1954); State ex rel. Pukalis v. Superior Court, 14 Wn.2d 507, 128 P.2d 649 (1942).

"The spirit that animated the juvenile court movement was fed in part by a humanitarian compassion for offenders who were children. That willingness to understand and treat people who threaten public safety and security should be nurtured, not turned aside as hopeless sentimentality, both because it is civilized and because social protection itself demands constant search for alternatives to the crude and limited expedient of condemnation and punishment." McKeiver v. Pennsylvania, 403 U.S. 528, 546 n. 6, 91 S.Ct. 1976, 1986 n. 6 (1971).

52. State v. Doyal, 59 N.M. 454, 286 P.2d 306 (1955); Lingo v. Hann, 161 Neb. 67, 71 N.W.2d 716 (1955); Tilton v. Commonwealth, 196 Va. 774, 85 S.E.2d 368 (1955).

53. E.g., West's Fla.Stats.Ann. § 39.02 (1974); Marks v. State, 69 Okl.Cr. 330, 102 P.2d 955 (1940).

54. People v. Hopkins, 205 Misc. 666, 129 N.Y.S.2d 851 (1954); State v. Musser, 110 Utah 534, 175 P.2d 724 (1946).

55. State v. Guerrero, 58 Ariz. 421, 430, 120 P.2d 798, 802 (1942). And see People v. Smallwood, 306 Mich. 49, 10 N.W.2d 303 (1943).

56. Mich.Stat. Ann. § 27.3178 (598.17) (1980).

57. Ibid., § 27.3178 (598.1).

58. Ibid.; People v. Smallwood, 306 Mich. 49, 10 N.W.2d 303 (1943).

59. Mitchell v. Gladden, 229 Or. 192, 366 P.2d 907 (1961).

60. Commonwealth ex rel. Hendrickson v. Myers, 393 Pa. 224, 144 A.2d 367

court record was not used as "evidence" when included in a pre-sentence report to the court.[61]

The definitive section of the federal Juvenile Delinquency Act [62] is worded as follows: "For the purposes of this chapter, a 'juvenile' is a person who has not attained his eighteenth birthday, . . . and 'juvenile delinquency' is the violation of a law of the United States committed by a person prior to his eighteenth birthday which would have been a crime if committed by an adult." In the state statutes there is no uniformity as to the age *under* which a person is to be deemed a juvenile, the common provisions being sixteen,[63] seventeen,[64] or eighteen,[65] with an occasional variation but the juvenile court is seldom given exclusive jurisdiction of those in the higher age brackets.[66]

Prior to the 1974 amendment the wording of the federal statute was that " 'juvenile delinquency' is the violation of a law of the United States committed by a juvenile and not punishable by death or life imprisonment." The new wording of the definitive section seems to suggest that a juvenile could not be tried for crime as an adult in the federal district court, no matter what he had done. But the following section provides that under certain circumstances a juvenile can be tried as an adult for a felony "punishable by a maximum penalty of ten years imprisonment or more, life imprisonment or death, . . ." and committed after his sixteenth birthday.[67]

The former federal provision which excluded those juveniles who commit acts which if committed by adults would be offenses punishable by death or life imprisonment, has its counterpart in many of the state enactments,[68] but

(1958); United States ex rel. Jackson v. Myers, 374 F.2d 707 (3d Cir. 1967). Accord, People v. Terry, 61 Cal.2d 137, 390 P.2d 381 (1964); People v. Reeves, 64 Cal. 2d 766, 51 Cal.Rptr. 691, 415 P.2d 35, note 3 (1966); State v. Manning, 149 Mont. 517, 429 P.2d 625 (1967); State v. McClendon, 611 P.2d 728 (Utah 1980).

61. State v. Ferro, 101 Ariz. 118, 416 P.2d 551 (1966); State v. McClendon, 611 P.2d 728 (Utah 1980).

62. 18 U.S.C.A. § 5031 (1974).

63. McKinney's Consol. L. N.Y. Penal § 30.00 (1978).

64. West's F.S.A. (Fla.) § 39.01 (1974).

65. 18 U.S.C.A. § 5031 (1974); Ariz. Rev.Stat. § 8–201 (1980); Iowa Code Ann. § 232.1 (1978).

66. If the juvenile court does not have exclusive jurisdiction at all there is no problem in this regard. See Code of Ala. § 15–19–1 (1977). In some states the juvenile court may have exclusive jurisdiction over younger children but not those in higher age brackets. See Whitfield v. State, 236 Ala. 312, 182 So. 42 (1938); Commonwealth ex rel. Young v. Johnston, 180 Pa.Super. 631, 121 A.2d 601 (1956). The court upheld the death penalty for a fifteen-year-old boy who committed rape under heinous and aggravated circumstances. Mickens v. Commonwealth, 178 Va. 273, 16 S.E.2d 641 (1941). And a life sentence was affirmed in case of a fifteen-year-old boy who committed lewd and lascivious acts on a girl of thirteen in a brutal manner. State v. Iverson, 77 Idaho 103, 289 P.2d 603 (1955).

67. 18 U.S.C.A. § 5032 (1974).

68. E.g., 10 Del.C.Ann. § 921 (1975). See also West's F.S.A. (Fla.) §§ 39.02 and 39.09 (1974); I.C.A. (Iowa) § 232.44 (1978); W.Va.Code Ann. § 49–5–10 (1980). Sometimes a different type of exclusion is found such as any offense other than murder. Commonwealth ex rel. Young v. Johnston, 180 Pa.Super. 631, 121 A.2d 601 (1956).

"When a petition alleges that a juvenile has committed an act which would be murder or a Class A, B or C crime if committed by an adult, the court shall, upon request of the prosecuting attorney, continue the case for further investigation and for a bindover hearing to determine whether the jurisdiction of the juvenile court over the juvenile should be

in "approximately half the states the jurisdiction of the juvenile court over children under sixteen is exclusive, even where the offense would constitute murder if committed by an adult." [69] Where exclusive jurisdiction has not been conferred upon the juvenile court the change is merely one of procedure, however advantageous the result may be in individual cases, because what otherwise would be a crime is still a crime although it may (or may not) be disposed of in quite a different manner than a criminal prosecution; but where the juvenile court does have exclusive jurisdiction, and full recognition is accorded to this fact, there has been a change in the substantive law itself, since such a transgression is not a crime at all but a different kind of a misdeed known as "juvenile delinquency," [70] and hence there has been a change in the capacity to commit crime. Stated in terms of the common law the age under which a person is *conclusively presumed* to be incapable of committing crime has been raised from seven to sixteen (or whatever the statute may provide) and this, according to the particular enactment, may be as to all crimes or as to all other than those so grave as to be punished by death or life imprisonment.

One of the leading cases to emphasize this change in the substantive law of crimes was *Roper* [71] in which a fifteen-year-old boy was convicted of first-degree murder. Since first-degree murder was punishable by death or imprisonment for life under the New York statute, and such an offense was not within the juvenile-court act of that state[72] such a conviction was entirely possible but the homicide had been committed during an attempted hold-up and the instructions permitted the jury to convict on the felony-murder basis. As robbery was not so punishable as to be excluded from the juvenile-court act it was held that what would constitute the felony of robbery by an adult

waived." 15 Me.Rev.Stat.Ann. § 3101–4 (1978).

Under the statute the juvenile court has no jurisdiction over one charged with murder. One who was 13 at the time of the act must be prosecuted in the district court the same as anyone else charged with murder. Poole v. State, ___ Nev. ___, 625 P.2d 1163 (1981).

69. State v. Monahan, 15 N.J. 34, 104 A.2d 34, 42; 104 A.2d 21, 25 (1954).

70. "A person less than sixteen years old is not criminally responsible for conduct.

"In any prosecution for an offense, lack of criminal responsibility by reason of infancy, . . . is a defense." McKinney's N.Y.Rev.Pen.Law § 30.00 (1975).

Under the Children's Code a child under the age of 16 cannot be held criminally responsible for actions which, if committed by an adult, would constitute a felony. Such misconduct is not a crime. People ex rel. Terrill v. District Court, 164 Colo. 437, 435 P.2d 763 (1967).

The Model Penal Code does not deal with juvenile delinquency, as such, but does raise the age of criminal incapacity to less than 16. It gives the juvenile court exclusive jurisdiction over misconduct by one under 16, and discretionary jurisdiction of offenders who are 16 or 17. Section 4.10.

71. People v. Roper, 259 N.Y. 170, 181 N.E. 88 (1932).

72. The New York law at the time of that case did not include as juvenile delinquency any act, which if committed by an adult would be punishable by death or life imprisonment. In 1948 an amendment to the New York statutes enlarged the phrase "juvenile delinquency" to include an act which would be capital on the part of an older person except that it does not include an act punishable by death or life imprisonment if committed by a child of fifteen. Such an offender may be tried as an adult unless there is an order transferring his case to the children's court. McKinney's N.Y.Pen.Law §§ 486, 2186. As the defendant in *Roper* was fifteen the result would have been the same, but the court's discussion of criminal capacity would have been different.

is not a crime of any kind when committed by a juvenile, but an entirely different kind of misdeed known as "juvenile delinquency" and hence this killing was not committed during the perpetration or attempted perpetration of a felony. The conclusion is entirely logical because, while a crime is any social harm defined and made punishable by law, and *robbery* is unquestionably such social harm, a *hold-up* by one under sixteen is not *punishable* under such legislation but *must be* handled on an entirely different basis, and hence is not a crime and therefore not a felony.

The controlling age under juvenile court legislation is that at the time of the misconduct under some of the statutes,[73] and at the time of prosecution under others,[74] and where the latter is true it has been held that the state may wait until the offender has reached the age which permits him to be prosecuted as an adult.[75] Which time is selected for this purpose is entirely a matter of legislative discretion so long as only procedure is involved but a statute would be invalid if it purported to make the capacity to commit crime dependent not on the act of the wrongdoer but upon the whim of the prosecuting attorney.[76]

With all the good that has resulted from juvenile court legislation there are those who have become disturbed by the thought that juvenile misbehavior has flourished under this type of procedure and insofar as acts of violence and brutality by teenagers are concerned has climbed to an all-time high. No one familiar with the problem would wish to abolish this method of dealing with misguided children but there seem to be an increasing number who question the wisdom of giving the juvenile court exclusive jurisdiction over these cases,—at least so far as acts of violence and brutality are involved. In one four-to-three decision both sides of the problem are discussed in opinions covering thirty-five pages, the high points being: 1. "Centuries of history indicate that the pathway lies not in unrelenting and vengeful punishment, but in persistently seeking and uprooting the causes of juvenile delinquency and in widening and strengthening the reformative process through socially enlightened movements."[77] 2. "I cannot comprehend the reasoning that suggests that marauding gangs of little hoodlums armed with guns, knives, switch knives or other lethal weapons are to be considered as a matter of law incapable of committing murder."[78]

One author[79] of wide experience and extensive investigation in this area, who favors the juvenile court program in general but believes certain changes are needed, has this word of caution:

73. United States v. Fotto, 103 F.Supp. 430 (D.C.N.Y.1952); State v. Jones, 220 Tenn. 477, 418 S.W.2d 769 (1966); State v. Musser, 110 Utah 534, 175 P.2d 724 (1946).

74. Peterson v. State, 156 Tex.Cr.R. 105, 235 S.W.2d 138 (1950); State ex rel Koopman v. County Court, 38 Wis.2d 492, 157 N.W.2d 623 (1968).

75. Ibid.

76. Such a statute would violate the *ex post facto* clause because the mere election of the prosecuting attorney to wait for the child to grow older would purport to make that a crime which was not a crime when done.

77. State v. Monahan, 15 N.J. 34, 45, 104 A.2d 21, 27 (1954).

78. Id., at 61–2, 104 A.2d at 36.

79. Professor Frederick J. Ludwig, of the law faculty at St. John's University, served as special counsel in the district attorney's office in New York County, as a Captain in the Police Department of New York City and as legal consultant to the Youth Counsel Bureau of New York City. His book Youth and the Law published in 1955 is an outstanding contribu-

"Certainly, one consequence of abolishing punitive treatment for young offenders is to deprive the criminal law of its efficacy as an instrument of moral education. . . . Making treatment of all criminal behavior of young offenders, regardless of its seriousness or triviality, depend solely upon the individual need of the offender for rehabilitation may well lead our impressionable young community to conclude that fracturing someone's skull is no more immoral than fracturing his bedroom window." [80]

"At least one purpose of the penal law is to express a formal social condemnation of forbidden conduct, ..." [81]

Recent developments require a reappraisal of both the theory and the practice of juvenile delinquency proceedings.[82] Such legislation was based upon high motives and noble ideals. The misbehaving child was to be treated, not as a criminal, but as an unfortunate in need of help and guidance. Hence the inquiry was to be, not whether he was "guilty" or "innocent," but to determine what caused him to be as he was, and what could be done in his interest and in the interest of society to rehabilitate him. There was to be no thought of crime and punishment but only of solicitation for the welfare of the child. And since the whole program was to be "clinical" rather than punitive, the rigidities and technicalities of criminal procedure were to be discarded.

"These results were to be achieved, without coming to conceptual and constitutional grief, by insisting that the proceedings were not adversary, but that the State was proceeding as *parens patriae*." [83]

tion. See also Alexander, You Are Just as Dead if Killed by a Juvenile Delinquent as by an Adult Criminal. 8 National Sheriff 7 (1956).

80. Ludwig, Considerations Basic to Reform of Juvenile Offender Laws, 29 St. John's L.Rev. 226, 234 (1955), repeated in Ludwig, Youth and the Law 311 (1955). By the same author see also Control of the Sex Criminal, 25 St. John's L.Rev. 203 (1951); Delinquent Parents and the Criminal Law, 5 Vand.L.Rev. 719 (1952); Rationale of Responsibility for Young Offenders, 29 Neb.L.Rev. 521 (1950).

In New York the Youthful Offender Law, applicable to youths over sixteen and under nineteen, "presents a compromise between the completely separate juvenile court system of handling child offenders and the traditional penal rigor of one for adults." It does not apply to one charged with an offense punishable by death or life imprisonment. Ludwig, Youth and the Law 77–8 (1955). The youthful offender proceedings are unlike juvenile proceedings in the children's court. People v. Shannon, 1 A.D.2d 226, 149 N.Y.S.2d 550 (1956). See also American Law Institute, Youth in Crime (1940); Ibid., Youth Correction Authority Act (1940); Hall, The Youth Correction Authority Act, 28 A.B.A.J. 317 (1942).

81. Sauer v. United States, 241 F.2d 640, 649 (9th Cir. 1957).

82. See, for example, Gardner, The Kent Case and the Juvenile Court: A Challenge to Lawyers, 52 A.B.A.J. 923 (1966); Lehman, A Juvenile's Right to Counsel in a Delinquency Hearing, 17 Juvenile Court Judges Journal 53 (1966); Paulsen, Juvenile Courts, Family Courts, and the Poor Man, 54 Calif.L.Rev. 694 (1966); Paulsen, Kent v. United States: The Constitutional Context of Juvenile Cases, 1966 Sup.Ct.Rev. 167; Ketcham, The Legal Renaissance in the Juvenile Court, 60 N.W.U.L.Rev. 585 (1965); Allen, The Borderland of Criminal Justice 19–23 (1964); Skoler and Tenney, Attorney Representation in Juvenile Court, 4 J.Fam.Law 77 (1964); Riederer, The Role of Counsel in the Juvenile Court, 2 J.Fam.Law 16 (1962). See also Note, Rights and Rehabilitation in Juvenile Courts, 67 Col.L.Rev. 281 (1967); Note, Juvenile Delinquents: The Police, State Courts, and Individualized Justice, 79 Harv.L.Rev. 775 (1966).

83. Application of Gault, 387 U.S. 1, 16, 87 S.Ct. 1428, 1437 (1967).

The heart and conscience of the erring youth were to be touched by the parental advice and admonition of a parental judge who, if necessary, would call upon the guidance and help of wise and benevolent institutions. It is a great misfortune that this program was not carried out, uniformly, along the high level which had been intended. No doubt many a juvenile court judge has done exactly that. But there are nearly 3000 of such judges in the country, about half of whom are not college graduates and only a few of whom devote much of their time to juvenile matters.[84] A report in 1964 showed only 213 full-time juvenile judges and that the great majority of the others devoted less than one-quarter of their time to such work.[85] In view of this it is not surprising that a program which was designed to substitute individual skill and wisdom for procedural safeguards has resulted in much injustice to the children it was intended to protect. As said by the Supreme Court: "There is evidence . . . that there may be grounds for concern that the child receives the worst of both worlds: that he gets neither the protections accorded to adults nor the solicitous care and regenerative treatment postulated for children." [86]

This statement appeared in *Kent* in which a juvenile had been convicted of a very serious crime in the District of Columbia. The law of the District is not patterned after the New York plan under which what would be a crime by an older person is not a crime at all by a juvenile. In the District, as in many states, what would be a crime by an older person is also a crime by a juvenile although the fact that it is a crime may be overlooked and the case handled in the juvenile court. The juvenile judge, however, has discretion to send the case to the District Court for criminal prosecution if he determines that it is not a proper one for the juvenile process. Since the law left this to his discretion the juvenile judge thought, as apparently many such judges have thought, that the only necessity was for him to make up his mind as to the disposition and act accordingly. He overlooked the fact that discretion in such context means sound judicial discretion and not mere arbitrary whim. In any event he completely frustrated the attempt of the juvenile and his counsel to have a hearing on this matter and forthwith sent the case to the other court where a felony conviction resulted. In reversing this conviction the court said, "there is no place in our system of law for reaching a result of such tremendous consequences without ceremony—without hearing, without effective assistance of counsel, without a statement of reasons." [87]

---

84. National Council of Juvenile Court Judges 1 (1964).

85. Ibid. See also The Challenge of Crime in a Free Society 80 (1967). This is the Report of the President's Commission on Law Enforcement and the Administration of Justice.

In recent years there has been some significant improvement in the qualifications of juvenile judges, Smith, Profile of Juvenile Court Judges in the United States, 25 Juvenile Justice 27 (1974); Rubin, Juvenile Justice p. 264 (1979).

86. Kent v. United States, 383 U.S. 541, 546, 86 S.Ct. 1045, 1050 n. (1966).

87. Id., at 554, 86 S.Ct. at 1053.

After *Kent* was decided the District of Columbia Act was amended to read: "The term 'child' means an individual who is under 18 years of age, except that the term 'child' does not include an individual who is 16 years of age or older and—

"(A) charged by the United States attorney with (1) murder, forcible rape, burglary in the first degree, robbery while armed" (or certain other offenses).

B, who was 16, was charged as an adult under this amended statute. His claim that this statute deprived him of due process was rejected, and his petition for a writ of certiorari was denied.

Whether the youth was to have a juvenile court hearing or be prosecuted for felony in the criminal court was, as the Court said, a matter of "tremendous consequences" and the Court had no occasion to consider the conduct of a juvenile court hearing as such. But the Court let it be known that it would welcome an opportunity to give specific attention to this problem and soon had such a case—*Gault.*[88] A 15-year-old boy was charged as a juvenile delinquent for having made a lewd telephone call to a woman. Had he been over 18 the maximum punishment would have been a fine of $5 to $50, or imprisonment in jail for not more than two months. But as a juvenile delinquent he was committed to custody for a maximum of six years. The Supreme Court was not asked to pass upon the validity of a longer term for "juvenile rehabilitation" than for criminal punishment but only upon the alleged violation of procedural safeguards. It emphasized that it was concerned only with proceedings to determine whether a minor is delinquent *and* which may result in commitment to a state institution.

In this case the recipient of the alleged lewd telephone call did not appear as a witness. She merely reported the call to an officer by phone. The boy admitted having made the call, or at least to having participated in it, but he had not been advised of his privilege against self-incrimination or of his right to counsel. In addition neither the boy nor his parents had been given advance notice of the specific charge that was to be made against him.

The Supreme Court held that the due process clause of the Fourteenth Amendment requires that a juvenile delinquency hearing measure up to the essentials of due process and fair treatment. And at least in any hearing in which the youth's freedom and his parents' right to his custody are at stake—

1. They must have timely notice, in advance of the hearing, of the specific issues they must meet.

2. The child and his parents must be notified of the child's right to be represented by counsel retained by them, or if they are unable to afford counsel, that counsel will be appointed to represent the child.

3. They have the right to confrontation and cross-examination of the witnesses against the child. In other words, without a valid confession there can be no commitment to a state institution in the absence of sworn testimony subjected to the opportunity for cross-examination.

4. The court has a duty to advise the child of his privilege against self-incrimination, and his right to counsel, and may not consider any confession or admission if such advice had not been given.

The requirement of these procedural safeguards, the Court took pains to emphasize, does not in any way repudiate the basic theory of juvenile legislation. It is quite proper to regard a juvenile hearing as something altogether different from a criminal trial, and the adjudicated juvenile delinquent as something quite apart from a convicted criminal. The emphasis upon reha-

Bland v. United States, 412 U.S. 909, 93 S.Ct. 2294 (1973).

88. Application of Gault, 387 U.S. 1, 87 S.Ct. 1428 (1967).

The Juvenile Court may not detain a juvenile in custody prior to a hearing un-

der any automatic rule, but must consider specific facts urged in support of his release. In re M., 3 Cal.3d 16, 89 Cal. Rptr. 33, 473 P.2d 737 (1970).

bilitation remains intact. The holding "will not compel the States to abandon any of the substantial benefits of the juvenile process." [89] Even the methods of avoiding undue publicity of the trial and treatment of juveniles may be retained in line with the law's policy "to hide youthful errors from the full gaze of the public and bury them in the graveyard of the forgotten past." [90]

Whether the juvenile in a juvenile hearing is entitled to a public trial and-or a jury trial were not issues in this case. Mr. Justice Black, in a concurring opinion, indicated his answer would be "yes". The Supreme Court has, however, held that trial by jury is not constitutionally required in a juvenile proceeding.[91] A sound solution would be to hold that the juvenile is entitled to a public trial by jury if he demands it, but also is entitled to a trial in chambers, without a jury and with the public excluded if that is his preference. In *Gault* the court repeated what it had said in *Kent*: "We do not mean . . . to indicate that the hearing to be held must conform with all the requirements of a criminal trial . . . [92]

However it was held that a statute providing that juvenile court records should not be admissible in any other court, could not validly prevent a defendant in a criminal case from getting evidence needed for his defense. D was on trial for burglary and the chief witness against him had been adjudicated a juvenile delinquent, based on a burglary charge, and placed on probation. Defense counsel wanted to bring this out on cross-examination to show possible bias of the witness. Refusal to permit this was held to be reversible error. Effective cross-examination for bias of an adverse witness is too vital a constitutional right to be cut off in this way.[93] The Court recognized the state's policy interest in protecting the confidentiality of a juvenile offender's record; but held it must be enforced by some method that does not defeat such an important constitutional right. One possibility might be to prohibit the prosecuting attorney from putting a juvenile offender on the witness stand in a case such as this.

In discussions of the juvenile process, particularly in attempting to justify the denial of safeguards that would be essential in a prosecution for crime, it has been common to insist (1) it is not an "adversary proceeding" and (2) that it is not a criminal trial. Clearly we must now abandon any notion that a juvenile hearing is not an "adversary proceeding." We may continue to insist that it is not a criminal trial, and should do so with emphasis. But the fact that the attributes of a criminal trial do not attach, as such, does not mean all rights are excluded. In any juvenile hearing in which the youth's freedom and his parents' right to his custody are at stake, due process requires recognition of certain rights, including—(1) due notice, (2) assistance of counsel, (3) confrontation and (4) advice of the privilege against self-in-

---

89. Id. at 21, 87 S.Ct. at 1440.

90. Id. at 24, 87 S.Ct. at 1442. This is a familiar quotation.

The court added in the following paragraph: "In any event, there is no reason why, consistently with due process, a State cannot continue, if it deems appropriate, to provide and to improve provision for the confidentiality of records of police contacts and court action relating to juveniles."

91. McKeiver v. Pennsylvania, 403 U.S. 528, 91 S.Ct. 1976 (1971).

92. The constitution does not require a jury trial in a state juvenile court proceeding. McKeiver v. Pennsylvania, 403 U.S. 528, 91 S.Ct. 1976 (1971).

93. Davis v. Alaska, 415 U.S. 308, 94 S.Ct. 1105 (1974).

crimination, the right to counsel, and the requirement of proof beyond a reasonable doubt.[94]

D. YOUTH CORRECTION AUTHORITY

A step beyond juvenile court legislation, possibly presaging even further modifications of traditional criminal procedure and penal treatment, is in the form of modified handling of young offenders, sometimes including young adults, who have been convicted of crime—which means, or includes, conviction in other than the juvenile court. The theory is "that corrective treatment of young persons, with segregation when necessary, is a more effective preventive of repeated crime than any mere punishment could be." [95]

The Federal Youth Corrections Act [96] is an example of such legislation. As defined in this Act,[97] " 'Youth offender' means a person under the age of twenty-two years at the time of conviction; 'Committed youth offender' is one committed for treatment hereunder to the custody of the Attorney General pursuant to . . . this chapter. 'Treatment' means corrective and preventive guidance and training designed to protect the public by correcting the antisocial tendencies of youth offenders; . . ."

C, who had been convicted of a federal misdemeanor, was sentenced under this Act.[98] As the maximum sentence provided for his offense was one year, C objected to his sentence to the custody of the Attorney General with its four-to-six-year provision. He claimed that it imposed cruel and unusual punishment in violation of the Eighth Amendment and also that it violated due process of law guaranteed by the Fifth. The court rejected both claims and upheld the constitutionality of the Act.

This enactment, the court said, provides "not heavier penalties and punishment than are imposed upon adult offenders, but the opportunity to escape from the physical and psychological shocks and traumas attendant upon serving an ordinary penal sentence while obtaining the benefits of corrective treatment, looking to rehabilitation and social redemption and restoration." [99]

---

94. The requirement of proof beyond a reasonable doubt at the adjudicatory stage of a juvenile delinquency proceeding is constitutionally required as a matter of due process of law. In re Winship, 397 U.S. 358, 90 S.Ct. 1068 (1970).

95. Criminal Justice—Youth, Proposed Final Draft No. 1 (Youth Correction Authority Act) 15 (1940). See also the companion draft, prepared by the American Law Institute, Criminal Justice—Youth, Proposed Final Draft No. 2 (Youth Court Act) (1940). See also Model Penal Code 24–31 (Tent.Draft No. 7, 1957); and section 6.05 of the Proposed Official Draft.

An adjudicatory hearing in the juvenile court to determine whether the juvenile committed the acts charged and hence should be declared a "ward of the court," constitutes exposure to jeopardy, and precludes subsequent prosecution for the same course of conduct on which the adjudication was based. But a "fitness hearing" to determine whether the juvenile is a fit subject for juvenile court proceedings does not involve jeopardy. In such a proceeding the juvenile was found to be unfit, and was certified for criminal proceedings. The subsequent trial for murder did not involve double jeopardy. In re Hurlic, 20 Cal.3d 317, 142 Cal.Rptr. 443, 572 P.2d 57 (1977).

Legislation extending the maximum date for discharge of juveniles held by the Youth Authority could not constitutionally be applied to persons committed to the Youth Authority's custody prior to the enactment of such legislation. The clause purporting to do so is ex post facto. In re Dewing, 19 Cal.3d 54, 136 Cal.Rptr. 708, 560 P.2d 375 (1977).

96. 18 U.S.C.A. c. 402 (1976).

97. Id. at § 5006 (1976).

98. Cunningham v. United States, 256 F.2d 467 (5th Cir. 1958).

99. Id. at 472.

While agreeing with the majority that the Act is constitutional, one judge[1] dissented on the ground that it was improper to apply it in this case after permitting C to waive counsel and plead guilty without informing him that he might be sentenced under it for a much longer term than that otherwise provided. Failure to explain this difference was held, where prejudicial, sufficient to entitle the defendant to withdraw his plea of guilty.[2]

The Supreme court has held that sentencing of a youth offender should be in accordance with the act unless the court makes an express finding that the offender would not benefit from treatment under the act.[3]

While there may be justification for a longer period of rehabilitative treatment than is provided as the normal penalty for a given offense, such permissible disparity is not unlimited. Some of the provisions may need to be examined from this point of view. And the holdings in *Kent* and *Gault* suggest the possibility of additional unsolved problems in this newer program. Undoubtedly, however, it is a step in the right direction.

SECTION 2. MENTAL DISEASE OR DEFECT (INSANITY)

A. THE EARLY LAW

The starting point from an historical point of view is the ancient position which did not regard mental disorder, or insanity, as having any bearing upon the matter of criminal guilt. Principles of criminal liability dating prior to the Norman Conquest persisted into the thirteenth century and "a man who has killed another by misadventure, though he may deserve a pardon, is guilty of a crime; and the same rule applies . . . to a lunatic . . .."[1] By the time of Henry III (1216–1272) it was not uncommon for the king to grant a pardon as a special act of grace for one who had committed homicide while of unsound mind,[2] and in the reign of Edward I (1272–1307) although there was no change in the theory of guilt as a strict matter of law, such a homicide was regarded as pardonable to the extent that it entitled the defendant to a special verdict saying he committed the crime while mad and this practically insured the issuance of a pardon, which in time came to be granted as a matter of course.[3] During the reign of Edward II (1307–1327) insanity was beginning to be recognized as a defense to crime, and life was spared although chattels were still forfeited, while in the time of Edward III (1327–1377) absolute "madness" became a complete defense to a criminal charge.[4]

1. Reeves, Circuit Judge.

2. Pilkington v. United States, 315 F.2d 204 (4th Cir. 1963).

And see Eller v. United States, 327 F.2d 639 (9th Cir. 1964); Freeman v. United States, 350 F.2d 940 (9th Cir. 1965); United States v. Stimpson, 549 F.2d 1286 (9th Cir. 1977).

3. Dorszynski v. United States, 418 U.S. 424, 94 S.Ct. 3042 (1974).

§ 2

1. 3 Holdsworth, History of English Law 371 (5th ed. 1942).

2. Pollock & Maitland, History of English Law 480 (2d ed. 1899).

3. 2 Stephen, History of the Criminal Law of England 151 (1883); 1 Wharton & Stille, Medical Jurisprudence c. 26 (5th ed. 1905).

4. Glueck, Mental Disorder and the Criminal Law 125 (1925). Sayre, Mens Rea, 45 Harv.L.Rev. 974, 995–6 (1932). And see 3 Holdsworth, 372, n. 9 (5th ed. 1942).

Prior to the time when pardons were issued as a matter of course in such cases the kind and degree of unsoundness of mind needed for the purpose could not be determined as a matter of law "for all depended upon the king's 'grace.'"[5] Bracton who was Chief Justiciary in the middle of the thirteenth century had given the following definition: "A madman (furiosus) is one who does not know what he is doing, who lacks in mind and reason and is not far removed from the brutes."[6] And when the law began to take notice of insanity as a legal defense to a criminal charge it was on the theory that one who was insane had *no mind* and hence could not have mens rea. Thus in 1548 it was said: "So if a man *non sanae memoriae* kills another . . . he has not broken the law, because he had no memory or understanding . . . and therefore . . . there is no fault in him . . . ."[7] In 1603 Sir Edward Coke quoted Bracton's definition of an insane man with approval,[8] and in 1628 he classified *non compos mentis* (other than that resulting from drunkenness which he said did not excuse) into (1) the born idiot, (2) [the madman] he that by sickness, grief, or accident "wholly loseth his memorie and understanding," and (3) the lunatic, who has lucid intervals but is *non compos mentis* during those periods when "he hath not understanding."[9] This places the idiot and the madman in the same category, so far as criminal incapacity is concerned, and years before Fitzherbert had defined an idiot as "such a person who cannot account or number twenty pence, nor can tell who was his father or mother, nor how old he is &c. so as it may appear that he hath no understanding of reason what shall be for his profit, or what for his loss. But if he have such understanding that he know and understand his letters and do read by teaching or information of another man, then it seemeth he is not a sot nor natural idiot."[10] In 1668 a married woman being delivered of a child unattended, after having lost sleep for many nights, killed her infant during a temporary frenzy, and the charge to the jury in her trial for murder was "that if it did appear, that she had any use of her reason when she did it, they were to find her guilty."[11] And in 1724 Judge Tracy instructed the jury: "If a man be deprived of his reason and consequently of his intention he cannot be guilty;" with the explanation that "it is not every kind of frantic humour . . . that points him out to be such a madman as is to be exempted from punishment: it must be a man that is totally deprived of his understanding and memory, and doth not know what he is doing, no more than an infant, than a brute, or a wild beast, such a one is never the object of punishment; . . . ."[12]

In those early days, it should be noted, the possibility of mental disorder of a lesser nature was clearly recognized, but only disorder that totally deprived the person of his understanding and memory, at least for the time being, and therefore precluded the possibility of mens rea, was sufficient to destroy the capacity to commit crime.[13]

5. 2 Pollock & Maitland, 484 (2d ed. 1899).

6. Quoted in Beverley's Case, 4 Coke 123b, 124b, 76 Eng.Rep. 1118, 1121 (1603).

7. Reniger v. Fogossa, 1 Plow. 1, 19, 75 Eng.Rep. 1, 31 (1550).

8. Beverley's Case, 4 Coke 123b, 124b, 76 Eng.Rep. 1118, 1121 (1603).

9. 2 Co.Litt. 247a (Rev. ed. 1823).

10. Fitzherbert, New Natura Brevium, f. 233b. (9th ed. 1793).

11. Anonymous, 1 Hale P.C. 36 (1668). The verdict was not guilty.

12. Rex v. Arnold, 16 Howell State Trials 695, 764–5 (Eng.1724). See also Vol. 1 The Psychological Foundation of Criminal Justice 47 (1978).

13. Hale, it is true, had mentioned the possibility of quite a different result with

B. TERMINOLOGY

When the presumption of criminal incapacity disappears at the age of fourteen (or other if provided by statute) it is replaced by another and from that time on the person is presumed to be capable of committing crime. This new presumption is not conclusive and may be overcome by a proper showing of incapacity no matter what the age may be. The word "insanity" is commonly used in discussions of this problem although some other term would seem to be preferable such as "mental disease or defect,"—which may be shortened to "mental disorder" in general discussions if this is clearly understood to include disease of the mind, congenital lack, and damage resulting from traumatic injury, but to exclude excitement or stupefaction resulting from liquor or drugs. Apart from its uses in the law "insanity" is usually employed to indicate mental disorder resulting from deterioration or damage as distinguished from congenital deficiency. Criminal incapacity may result as readily from one as from the other, but while the early authorities spoke of the "idiot" and the "madman," as pointed out above, the more recent tendency in the law has been to include both under the "insanity" label.[14]

Another objection to the word "insanity" is the unwarranted assumption that it refers to a very definite mental condition, seldom put into words but apparent in many discussions of the problem. The common law is very precise in the meaning attached to the word "infancy," which covers the period from the instant a person is born until the first moment of the day preceding the twenty-first anniversary of his birth.[15] Thus one who was born on September 23, 1828, became of full age on September 22, 1849.[16] Both the year and the day are subject to legislative change. For example, under the former Oklahoma statute males became of age at twenty-one and females at eighteen, but the time in each instance arrived on the anniversary of the birth and not on the day before.[17] But whether a particular jurisdiction is operating under the common-law definition or one which has been changed by statute, no uncertainty is involved. No such precise meaning is attached to the word "insanity," and neither "sanity" nor "soundness of mind," it should be added, are to be regarded as synonyms of mental perfection. If they were so used it might be difficult to find the individual who could measure up to the requirement, just as if "soundness of body" meant physical perfection the rank and file of the human race would not be included.[18] In common usage we speak of soundness of either mind or body, not in the

the suggestion that criminal incapacity by reason of insanity means less understanding than a normal child of fourteen. 1 Hale P.C. *30. This was an afterthought thrown in after he had stated the then accepted view, and was not supported by any authority. This view has not been accepted because there is no proper basis of comparison between the disordered mind of an adult and the normal mind of a child. State v. Schilling, 95 N.J.L. 145, 112 A. 400 (1920).

14. "Deficiency of intellect is a species of insanity. . . ." State v. Schilling, 95 N.J.L. 145, 148, 112 A. 400, 402 (1920).

"We are of the opinion that for purposes of criminal responsibility, there is no legal difference between insanity and lunacy." State v. Billhymer, 114 Ariz. 390, 561 P.2d 311, 313 (1977). See also In re Ramon M., 22 Cal.3d 419, 149 Cal. Rptr. 387, 584 P.2d 524 (1978).

15. Wells v. Wells, 6 Ind. 447 (1855).

16. Ibid.

17. Bynum v. Moore, 101 Okl. 128, 223 P. 687 (1923).

18. "So when we are told that no one is perfect, that perfection in anatomy,

absolute sense of perfection, but in the relative sense of being reasonably sound, which, however, is only part of the picture. Using soundness of mind in this sense, the deviations from this condition are found to be of various kinds and degrees. If, for example, the word "idiot" is used to describe one born with practically no mind at all, such a gap is left between this condition and mental soundness that the word "imbecile" has been employed to indicate one with more mind than an idiot although quite deficient mentally. An early classification of "moron" was added to designate a person who was mentally defective. The Binet classification developed a hierarchy of I.Q. classifications.[19] However, the moron terminology is no longer in use and the current relevant I.Q. classification range is as follows:

69 and below = mentally defective; 70–79 = borderline defective; 80–89 = low average; 90–109 = average; 110–119 = high average.[20]

This terminology has limited application in reference to the legal standard of mental responsibility. The classifications are primarily useful for evidentiary purposes.

No corresponding legal vocabulary has been developed for use when speaking of mental disorder resulting from disease or damage, and the tendency is to speak only of the "sane" and the "insane;"[21] but whether the deficiency is congenital or acquired the possible shades of difference between theoretical mental perfection and theoretical total absence of mind are not two or five or a dozen—but infinity.[22] At what point in this imperceptible shading from one extreme to the other does the dividing line between sanity and insanity appear? As ably said in a case involving testamentary capacity:

"There is no difficulty in the case of a raving madman or of a drivelling idiot, in saying that he is not a person capable of disposing of his property. But between such an extreme case and that of a man of perfectly sound and vigorous understanding, there is every shade of intellect, every degree of mental capacity. There is no possibility of mistaking midnight for noon; but at what precise moment twilight becomes darkness is hard to determine."[23]

It is just as difficult, of course, to point out the exact boundary line between mental soundness and mental disorder, as that between sanity and insanity, but no unwarranted assumption of precise meaning is attached to the phrase "mental disorder."

physiology, and mentality does not exist, this is true." Meagher, Crime and Insanity, 16 J.C. & Crim. 360, 367 (1925).

19. Guttmacher & Weihofen, Psychiatry and Law 178 (1952). The subdivision of the moron is added.

"While it is true that defendant introduced evidence to the effect that she was retarded having an I.Q. of 58, that standing alone did not establish a viable defense of unsound mind and insanity." West v. State, 617 P.2d 1362, 1366 (Okl. Cr. 1980).

20. Terman & Merrill, Stanford-Binet Intelligence Scale, 3rd Revision 17–19.

21. See, e.g., Stout v. State, 142 Tex. Cr.R. 537, 155 S.W.2d 374 (1941).

22. "In taking up the question of insanity, then, we have found it to shade by almost imperceptible degrees into so called normality. Just as infancy emerges slowly into maturity and as there is an unbroken gradation from idiocy to genius, so there is no place where a sharp line of division can be drawn between the so-called normal and the mentally sick." Woodard, Psychological Aspects of the Question of Moral Responsibility, 21 J.C. & Crim. 267, 278 (1930).

23. Boyse v. Rossborough, 6 H.L.Cas. 2, 45, 10 Eng.Rep. 1192, 1210 (1857).

A third objection to the word "insanity" is that it may convey quite a different meaning in one case than it does in another. Mental disorder may become important at five different points in connection with a criminal case: (1) at the time of the *actus reus*, because the person may then have been without criminal capacity and if so is entitled to an acquittal; (2) at the time of arraignment, because if he is incapable of understanding the charge against him he should not be permitted to plead until his reason is restored; (3) at the time of trial, which should be postponed if he is then unable to understand the charge against him and possible defenses thereto, whatever his mental condition may have been at an earlier time;[24] (4) at the time of allocution, for he must not be required to answer whether he knows of any reason why judgment should not be pronounced against him if he is incapable of understanding the question; (5) at the time of execution, at least in a capital case, for if he had his reason he might be able to allege something in stay of execution.[25] The defendant's mental condition at some time other than the commission of the *actus reus* has no bearing upon the question of his criminal capacity, except as it may tend to indicate what the condition

---

24. "The test for competency to stand trial is whether the defendant 'has sufficient present ability to consult with his lawyer with a reasonable degree of rational understanding—and whether he has a rational as well as factual understanding of the proceedings against him.'" United States v. Hayes, 589 F.2d 811, 822 (5th Cir. 1979).

"RCW 10.77.010(6) defines incompetency as follows: 'Incompetency' means a person lacks the capacity to understand the nature of the proceedings against him or to assist in his own defense as a result of mental disease or defect." State v. Crenshaw, 27 Wn.App. 326, 617 P.2d 1041, 1044 (1980).

The fact that defendant was competent to stand trial only with the aid of insulin, does not mean that he was not competent to stand trial. United States v. Hayes, 589 F.2d 811 (5th Cir. 1979).

"Insanity at the time of the *alleged offense* is a complete defense to the criminal charge. . . . Hence, incompetency (to stand trial) merely abates the action and is procedural in effect, while insanity is substantive and renders the defendant not guilty." People v. Gillings, 39 Colo.App. 387, 568 P.2d 92, 97 (1977).

25. 4 Bl.Comm. *24–5; Guttmacher & Weihofen, Psychiatry and the Law 433–4 (1952); Forthoffer v. Swope, 103 F.2d 707, 709 (9th Cir. 1939). The text states the common-law position; as to whether it would violate the due-process clause to provide for the execution of insane convicts by statute see Guttmacher & Weihofen at 435. "But granting that insani-

ty arising after sentence of death cannot affect the question of guilt or innocence, does it not offend our moral sense to execute a person who is too ill mentally to understand what is happening to him and why?" Ibid. See opinion Marshall, J., Gilmore v. Utah, 429 U.S. 1012, 97 S.Ct. 436 (1976). The Supreme Court has held that it does not violate the Fourteenth Amendment to vest discretionary power in the Governor, aided by physicians, to determine whether the convict should be executed or committed to an insane asylum. Solesbee v. Balkcom, 339 U.S. 9, 70 S.Ct. 457 (1950).

One who has been *convicted* while he was incompetent to stand trial has been deprived of due process. United States v. Knohl, 379 F.2d 427 (2d Cir. 1967). See also Pate v. Robinson, 383 U.S. 375, 378, 86 S.Ct. 836 (1966).

"[L]egal standards for competence to stand trial and act as a witness are not the same as the legal standards of capacity to form the requisite *mens rea* in the commission of the crime." United States v. Westerhausen, 283 F.2d 844, 852 (7th Cir. 1960). Accord, People v. Pennington, 66 Cal.2d 508, 58 Cal.Rptr. 374, 426 P.2d 942 (1967).

D is unfit to stand trial if he has a condition of mental illness or retardation which prevents him from comprehending his position and from consulting intelligently with counsel in the preparation of his defense. State v. Caralluzzo, 49 N.J. 152, 228 A.2d 693 (1967). Accord, State v. Bradley, 102 Ariz. 482, 433 P.2d 273 (1967).

was when the deed was done, and if arraignment, trial or allocution is postponed because of his mental condition he will be transferred to a hospital and returned when and if restored to his reason, to see if proceedings can be carried forward to judgment of conviction.[26] Moreover, if execution is postponed because of mental derangement, it is to be carried out when and if that condition is corrected.

Quite apart from a criminal case, it may be added, one who is mentally disordered to such an extent as to be a menace to himself, or to others, may be committed to a proper hospital so long as such confinement is needed for security reasons,[27] and one of unsound mind is incapable of making a valid contract or of executing a valid will, to mention the two best-known instances in which the problem is involved without reference to the general security. In regard to commitment of the "insane," it may be added parenthetically, whether under penal code provisions or ordinary psychopathic procedure, the discharge from the hospital does not abridge the state's right to place the person on trial for a crime committed prior to such commitment;[28] and if the commitment is by a federal court on the ground that one under indictment for a federal offense is incompetent to stand trial, and if released would probably endanger the officers, property or other interests of the United States, he may be continued in custody to await trial when restored to his reason even if his condition makes this a very unlikely occurrence, and the federal court would have no jurisdiction to commit him apart from the federal indictment.[29]

---

26. One so committed is not entitled to his freedom on a writ of habeas corpus because if his reason is restored he must be returned to the court for further proceedings there. Miller v. Spring Grove State Hospital, 198 Md. 659, 80 A.2d 898 (1951).

Under the statute, one who has been found *not guilty by reason of insanity* may be confined in the state hospital for the criminally insane until he has fully recovered his sanity. People v. Mallory, 254 Cal.App.2d 151, 61 Cal.Rptr. 825 (1967).

A special verdict, after finding **D** not guilty by reason of insanity, found him not a safe person to be at large. It was held that the statute authorizing this special verdict was valid. State v. Kolocotronis, 73 Wn.2d 92, 436 P.2d 774 (1968).

In some states, acquittal by reason of insanity is followed by mandatory commitment to a mental hospital. Goldstein, The Insanity Defense 143 (1967). The author adds that in most other states the acquitted defendant may be committed for a limited period if this is determined to be desirable because of his condition.

A defendant found incompetent to stand trial and not likely to regain competence cannot be continued to be confined unless civilly committed. Jackson v. Indiana, 406 U.S. 715, 92 S.Ct. 1845

(1972). See Altman v. Hofferber, 28 Cal. 3d 161, 167 Cal.Rptr. 854, 616 P.2d 836 (1980).

27. See Weihofen and Overholser, Commitment of the Mentally Ill, 24 Tex. L.Rev. 307 (1946).

The mere finding that **D** was an imbecile was not sufficient to authorize his commitment. The judge should have permitted proof to show whether or not he was a hazard to himself or to others. State v. Caralluzzo, 49 N.J. 152, 228 A.2d 693 (1967).

The purpose of a statute providing for the commitment of those who are dangerous because of mental derangement is to insure hospitalization and makes no change in the law of criminal capacity. State v. Johnson, 233 Wis. 668, 290 N.W. 159 (1940).

28. People v. Cowan, 38 Cal.App. 144, 100 P.2d 1079 (1940).

29. Greenwood v. United States, 350 U.S. 366, 76 S.Ct. 410 (1956). The commitment was under 18 U.S.C.A. §§ 4244–4248, and was held to be valid under the Necessary and Proper clause of the Constitution, Art. I, § 8 cl. 18.

"Specifically, we hold that principles of equal protection require (subject to the availability of either an extended commitment . . . or a civil commitment

At a time when the law took notice of mental disorder only in the most extreme instances of the "raving madman" or the "driveling idiot" it was not remarkable that the mind was looked upon as either "on" or "off," so to speak. However brilliant or dim the mental light might be it was given recognition, and only when it disappeared entirely was incapacity present. A sane person had a mind while an insane person had no mind,—such was the ancient theory; and a man with no mind could not execute a will, make a contract, commit a crime, stand trial for crime or do anything else for which competence was required.

The increasing tendency of recent times to take notice of less extreme deviations from the normal mind has been accompanied by a corresponding tendency to examine alleged unsoundness in the light of the particular problem involved, and the question ceases to be whether the individual had *some* mind or *no* mind and comes to be whether he had *mind enough* for the particular purpose,—or conversely, was his mind impaired to such an extent and in such a way as to result in some particular incapacity? [30] In the words of an eminent neurologist, "a man might need commitment for a depression, yet this of itself would not show that he was unable to make a valid will." [31] The Ohio court declared that a person "who is a fit subject for confinement in an insane asylum does not necessarily have immunity from punishment for crime." [32] The Florida court said: [33]

"The degree of insanity with which the accused may have been afflicted when the alleged offense was committed and which would work an acquittal is of a higher or greater degree of dementia than that degree of dementia which would incapacitate a person to plead or to rationally conduct a defense on a murder charge."

And the Supreme Court has pointed out that one might not be "insane" in the sense of being incapable of standing trial and yet be "insane" to the

. . .) that persons committed to a state institution following acquittal of a criminal offense on the ground of their insanity cannot be retained in institutional confinement beyond the maximum term of punishment for the underlying offense of which, but for their insanity, they would have been convicted." In re Moye, 22 Cal.3d 457, 149 Cal.Rptr. 487, 491, 584 P.2d 1097, 1103 (1978).

30. "[T]here is a distinction between civil and criminal cases in the application of the rules of law, in relation to insanity." Commonwealth v. Farkin, 2 Pars. Eq.Cas. 439, 441 (Pa.1844).

"[A]n accused may have a mental disorder or deficiency and in some cases still be mentally competent to be held legally responsible for his crime." Mims v. United States, 375 F.2d 135, 142 (5th Cir. 1967).

31. Meagher, Crime and Insanity, 16 J.C. & Crim. 360, 373 (1925).

A condition "that would make one a 'mentally ill person' for purposes of hospitalization does not necessarily relieve one of criminal responsibility . . . ." State v. Weller, 285 Or. 457, 591 P.2d 732, 734 (1979).

32. State ex rel. Davey v. Owen, 133 Ohio St. 96, 104, 12 N.E.2d 144, 148 (1937). "Fitness for commitment to a mental hospital is quite different from the mental disorder that . . . justifies a verdict of 'not guilty by reason of insanity.'" Overholser, Psychiatry and the Law, 38 Mental Hygiene 243, 244 (1954).

33. Deeb v. State, 118 Fla. 88, 93, 158 So. 880, 882 (1935). In determining whether accused is "insane" at the time of the trial inquiry should be made to determine whether he has sufficient mental capacity to recall events so that he can furnish counsel with facts needed to be presented in his defense. State ex rel. Davey v. Owen, 133 Ohio St. 96, 12 N.E. 144 (1937). And see Freeman v. People, 4 Denio, 9, 24–5 (N.Y.1847); United States ex rel. Roberts v. Yeager, 402 F.2d 918 (3d Cir. 1968).

extent that it would be a denial of due process to force him to trial without the benefit of counsel.[34]

The result has been an unfortunate tendency to use the word "insanity" to indicate that kind and degree of mental disorder which results in criminal incapacity if guilt or innocence is the issue; which results in incapacity to stand trial if that is the problem; in testamentary incapacity in a will case, and so forth. In other words whether a given person is or is not "insane" depends, as so used, not only upon the condition of his mind but also upon the particular nature of the problem at stake.

At other times, however, the word "insanity" is employed as the equivalent of mental disorder or unsoundness of mind, with no particular legal consequence being implicit in the term itself. Thus the question comes to be, not whether the mental condition is such as to justify the label "insanity," but whether there is present that "kind and degree of insanity" which is sufficient to establish criminal incapacity or testamentary incapacity or committability or whatever the particular problem may be.

This usage is to to be preferred, and finds a direct counterpart in the infancy cases. We speak of criminal incapacity by reason of infancy; but not every infant lacks the capacity to commit crime. A boy of eighteen is an infant at common law, but is presumed to be capable of committing crime. If he is not so capable it is for some reason other than infancy. In other words *infancy may be such* as to negative criminal capacity—or it *may not*.

In like manner "insanity" may be of such kind and degree as to destroy criminal capacity or it may be insufficient for this purpose, as in the statement: "The kind and degree of insanity available as a defense to crime has many times been defined by the decisions of this court." [35] This was recognized at an early day[36] and has been repeated time and again when the problem has been brought directly to the attention of the court.[37] In the medical profession, moreover, it has been said, "amongst the insanities are to be

34. Massey v. Moore, 348 U.S. 105, 75 S.Ct. 145 (1954).

Since then the Court has held it to be a denial of due process to force any indigent defendant to trial without benefit of counsel in a felony case. Gideon v. Wainwright, 372 U.S. 335, 83 S.Ct. 792 (1963). Later the Court extended this right to counsel to any case in which liberty is at stake. Argersinger v. Hamlin, 407 U.S. 25, 92 S.Ct. 2006 (1972). And then explained that this does not extend to a case in which imprisonment was authorized but not imposed. Scott v. Illinois, 440 U.S. 367, 99 S.Ct. 1158 (1979).

35. People v. Gilberg, 197 Cal. 306, 313, 240 P. 1000, 1003 (1925).

36. Judge Tracy referred to "such a madman as is to be exempted from punishment." Rex v. Arnold, 16 Howell St. Tr. 695, 763 (1724).

37. "Whilst such a person could not be regarded as sane, yet he would be criminally responsible for his acts unless . . . ." State v. Stickley, 41 Iowa 232, 240 (1875). "If he was insane at the time to the extent . . . ." State v. Strasburg, 60 Wash. 106, 119, 110 P. 1020, 1024 (1910). "It has been announced by learned doctors, that if a man has the least taint of insanity entering into his mental structure, it discharges him from all responsibility to the laws. To this monstrous error may be traced both the fecundity in homicides, which has dishonoured this country, and the immunity that has attended them." Commonwealth v. Mosler, 4 Pa. 264, 266–7 (1846). See also, Regina v. Layton, 4 Cox C.C. 149 (1849); United States v. Faulkner, 35 F. 730, 731 (1888); Hornish v. People, 142 Ill. 620, 32 N.E. 677 (1892); Hoover v. State, 161 Ind. 348, 68 N.E. 591 (1903); State v. Buck, 205 Iowa 1028, 219 N.W. 17 (1928).

found derangements of slight degree and importance." [38]   As explained by one of the leading authorities on this subject:[39]

" 'Insanity' . . . has no technical meaning either in law or in medicine, and it is used by courts and legislators indiscriminately to convey either of two meanings: (1) any type or degree of mental defect or disease, or (2) such a degree of mental defect or disease as to entail legal conse- quences (i.e. . . . . to avoid a contract or relieve from responsibility for crime)."

The word "responsibility" also requires attention. One who lacks crimi- nal capacity is not criminally responsible. He who possesses criminal capaci- ty may be criminally responsible, or he may not, depending upon other facts. For example, if a man who has criminal capacity should kill another under circumstances such as to constitute a legal excuse or justification, he would *not be criminally responsible* for the homicide.

"Responsibility" is often used in the sense of potential criminal responsi- bility,—that is, to imply that criminal guilt would attach to misbehavior of sufficiently serious character. The use of "responsibility" in this sense tends to be misleading and to divert attention from the exact problem in- volved; hence "criminal capacity" is much to be preferred. Whether a given individual is *a responsible person* means one thing to a banker and some- thing quite different to a chaperon, neither of which meanings corresponds to the capacity to commit crime. The psychiatrist seems to use the phrase in a sense that differs from any of these. This fact induced a doctor, when talking about answerability to the criminal law, to make the following state- ment: "The whole question of responsibility has been considered too exclu- sively from the standpoint of the law . . . ."[40] On the question of crimi- nal capacity or criminal responsibility the law will not ignore psychology or psychiatry or any other branch of learning which may throw light upon the subject, but the ultimate determination is distinctly a legal one.[41] Whether a given individual has criminal capacity, and if so whether he is criminally re- sponsible for a particular offense with which he is charged, are questions of fact for the jury, under the court's instructions as to what these phrases mean as a matter of law.

C. M'NAGHTEN

Over a hundred years ago one Daniel M'Naghten shot and killed a man, and on his trial for murder the medical evidence showed he was laboring under an insane delusion and in a seriously disordered mental condition. The jury returned a verdict of not guilty under an instruction telling them to convict if the defendant "was in a sound state of mind" at the time, but to acquit if he "had not the use of his understanding, so as to know he was

---

38. Dr. Morton Prince (discussion of committee report) 2 J.C. & Crim. 538, 540 (1911). "The lawyers refer to 'insanity'. This is a legal term only, and one that is not used by the psychiatrist; the latter prefers to speak of mental disorder, mental illness, or of psychosis and neuro- sis." Overholser, Psychiatry and the Law, 38 Mental Hygiene, 243, 244 (1954). See also Overholser, The Psychiatrist and the Law 61 (1953).

39. Weihofen, Insanity as a Defense in Criminal Law 11–12 (1933); Weihofen, Mental Disorder as a Criminal Defense 5 (1954).

40. White, Insanity and the Criminal Law 96 (1923).

41. See United States v. Brawner, 471 F.2d 969 (D.C.Cir. 1972).

doing a wrong or wicked act." [42] The case was so clear on the facts that it would have been quickly forgotten had it not been for a peculiar aftermath; but because the shot had been intended for Sir Robert Peel there was great public excitement, and the House of Lords, after extended debate, put certain questions to the judges. The answers of the judges, given in the House of Lords, were printed together with this case in the published report, although actually no part thereof, and ever since that time "M'Naghten's Case" has been understood to refer to the answers of the judges and not to the actual trial. The substance of these answers, except as to matters of procedure, is adequately disclosed in two excerpts. Speaking generally of the problem the answer was:

"[T]o establish a defense on the ground of insanity, it must be clearly proved that, at the time of the committing of the act, the party accused was labouring under such a defect of reason, from disease of the mind, as not to know the nature and quality of the act he was doing; or, if he did know it, that he did not know he was doing what was wrong." [43]

And in answer to the question concerning an insane delusion they said: "To which question the answer must of course depend upon the nature of the delusion: but, making the same assumption as we did before, namely, that he labours under such partial delusion only, and is not in other respects insane, we think he must be considered in the same situation as to responsibility as if the facts with respect to which the delusion exists were real. For example, if under the influence of his delusion he supposes another man to be in the act of attempting to take away his life, and he kills that man, as he supposes in self-defence, he would be exempt from punishment. If his delusion was that the deceased had inflicted a serious injury to his character and fortune, and he killed him in revenge for such supposed injury, he would be liable to punishment." [44]

Four points stand out and should be understood whenever reference to M'Naghten is made other than in regard to procedure.

(1) **It applies only in case of "a defect of reason, from disease of the mind" and without this the following do not apply except that "disease" as so used will be interpreted to include congenital defect or traumatic injury.**

(2) **If, because of this "defect of reason," the defendant did not know what he was doing he is not guilty of crime.**

(3) **Even if the defendant knew what he was doing he is not guilty of crime if, because of this "defect of reason," he did not know he was doing wrong.**

42. M'Naghten's Case, 10 Clark & F. 200, 8 Eng.Rep. 718 (1843).

43. Id. at 210, 8 Eng.Rep. at 722.

"If the defendant have capacity and reason sufficient to enable him to distinguish right from wrong as to the particular act in question, and has knowledge and consciousness that the act he is doing is wrong and will deserve punishment, he is, in the eye of the law, of sound mind and memory, and should be held responsible for his acts." Criswell v. State, 84 Nev. 459, 443 P.2d 552, 554 (1968). Accord, State v. Coltharp, 199 Kan. 598, 433 P.2d 418 (1967); McKinney v. State, 566 P.2d 653 (Alaska 1977).

44. Id. at 211 and 723.

(4) If the defendant acted under an insane delusion, and was not otherwise insane,[45] his accountability to the criminal law is the same as if the facts were as they seemed to him to be.

D. THE RIGHT–WRONG TEST

Except for the reference to insane delusions, which had been forced into the debate in Parliament because the occasion was a case in which the defendant suffered from severe delusions of persecution, *M'Naghten* merely crystallized the law as it had been developing for generations. In the old days of the so-called "wild beast test," when criminal incapacity because of mental disorder required a total deprivation of mind and memory, the explanation was that such a person could not commit a crime because if he "could not distinguish between good and evil, and did not know what he did" there was no "wicked will and intention" [46] (no mens rea). And since this was the *reason* why such a person was incapable of committing crime it was only logical to take the position that one also lacked criminal capacity if he did not know what he was doing, or was unable to distinguish between right and wrong in regard thereto, even if his mental derangement fell a little short of a total deprivation of mind and memory.

The phrase found in *M'Naghten* is inability "to know the nature and quality of the act he was doing" and this has been repeated in substance time and again.[47] Instead of "nature and quality" of the act the reference is sometimes to the "nature and consequences," [48] "nature, character and consequences," [49] or "character and quality"[50] of the act; and occasionally a fancy label is employed as by referring to the "comprehension and consequence" rule.[51] In substance these all have reference to whether the defendant really knew what he was doing,[52] and this is true whether we have in mind an extreme situation such as Stephen's illustration of a man who

---

45. The judges, it should be emphasized, did not say whether such a condition could or could not exist. They answered reluctantly because the questions were hypothetical and there was no opportunity for argument by counsel. This assumption was made because otherwise an answer to the specific question asked would have been impossible. It has been said that "no such person exists." Guttmacher & Weihofen 418 (1952). See Weihofen, Mental Disorder as a Criminal Defense 109 (1954). It must be remembered, however, that the word "insanity" is one of different meanings, and that the judges had reference to a man who had delusions but was not insane in the sense of being incapable of distinguishing right from wrong.

46. Rex v. Arnold, 16 Howell St.Tr. 695, 764 (1724).

See Platt and Diamond, The Origins of the "Right and Wrong" Test of Criminal Responsibility and Its Subsequent Development in the United States: An Historical Survey, Vol. 1 The Psychological Foundation of Criminal Justice, 51, 56–59 (1978).

47. State v. Marcias, 60 Ariz. 93, 131 P.2d 810 (1942); People v. Ashland, 20 Cal.App. 168, 181, 128 P. 798, 804 (1912); People v. Walter, 1 Idaho 386, 390 (1871); State v. Upton, 60 N.M. 205, 290 P.2d 440 (1955).

48. Hoover v. State, 161 Ind. 384, 393, 68 N.E. 591, 593 (1903); McCune v. State, 156 Tex.Cr.R. 207, 211, 240 S.W.2d 305, 308 (1951).

49. Regina v. Townley, 3 Fost. & F. 839, 847, 176 Eng.Rep. 384, 387 (1863).

50. People v. Pico, 62 Cal. 50, 54 (1882).

51. State v. Buck, 205 Iowa 1028, 1039, 219 N.W. 17, 21 (1928).

52. His mind was "so impaired and unsound that he did not have sufficient reason to know what he was doing, ..." Newsome v. Commonwealth, 287 Ky. 649, 654, 154 S.W.2d 737, 740 (1941).

thought his homicidal act was "breaking a jar," [53] or an inquiry whether there was an understanding of the "real nature and true character of the act as a crime, and not . . . the mere act itself."[54]

Criminal incapacity, according to *M'Naghten*, is not limited to one whose mental disorder prevented him from knowing what he was doing because of the additional clause—"or, if he did know it, that he did not know he was doing what was wrong." Two centuries earlier, when offered merely as an explanation for the criminal incapacity of one totally without mind or memory, the reference had been to inability to "distinguish between good and evil," [55] or to "discern the difference between moral good and evil;" [56] and almost at the same time as *M'Naghten* a judge in this country mentioned inability to "discriminate between moral good and evil." [57] A recent reference to the "lack of mental ability to distinguish between right and wrong" [58] indicates the present trend as to the mode of expression in this regard.[59]

Mental disorder resulting in inability to distinguish between right and wrong as to any and every act would constitute complete incapacity to commit crime, but so long as it resulted in inability to make this distinction "in respect to the very act with which he is charged" it prevented the possibility of that particular crime, as emphasized by *M'Naghten* [60] and other cases.[61]

The question is sometimes raised whether "wrong" in this "test" means morally wrong or legally wrong. This is usually quite immaterial, because "by far the vast majority of cases in which insanity is pleaded as a defense to criminal prosecutions involve acts which are universally regarded as morally wicked as well as illegal. . . ." [62] The defendant is not entitled to an acquittal merely because he did not know the act was illegal, since "the law is administered upon the principle that every one must be taken conclusively to know it;" [63] hence, if the accused "was conscious that the act was one which he ought not to do, and if that act was at the same time contrary to the law of the land, he is punishable, . . ." [64]

53. Stephen, Digest of the Criminal Law art. 6, illustration (1) (8th ed. 1947).

54. Brown v. Commonwealth, 78 Pa. 122, 128 (1875).

55. Rex v. Arnold, 16 Howell St.Tr. 695, 764 (1724).

56. Per Yorke, Solicitor General, in his argument in Rex v. Ferris, 19 Howell St.Tr. 885, 948 (1760).

57. Commonwealth v. Farkin, 2 Pars. Eq.Cas. 439, 441 (Pa.1844).

58. State v. Van Vlack, 57 Idaho 316, 366, 65 P.2d 736, 759 (1937).

59. Lee v. United States, 91 F.2d 326 (5th Cir. 1937); Newsome v. Commonwealth, 287 Ky. 649, 154 S.W.2d 737 (1941); Fisher v. State, 140 Neb. 216, 299 N.W. 501 (1941); Whisenhunt v. State, 279 P.2d 366 (Okl.Cr.1954).

Some early American court cases had also made reference to a "good from evil" standard. Platt and Diamond, The Origins of the "Right and Wrong" Test of Criminal Responsibility and Its Subse-

quent Development in the United States: An Historical Survey, Vol. I The Foundations of Criminal Justice 51, 72 (1978).

60. 10 Clark & F. at 210, 8 Eng.Rep. at 723.

61. Fisher v. State, 140 Neb. 216, 299 N.W. 501 (1941); Whisenhunt v. State, 279 P.2d 366 (Okl.Cr.1954).

D, charged with arson and assault with a deadly weapon, was found not guilty by reason of insanity on the arson charge, but guilty of assault with a deadly weapon. State v. Doyle, 117 Ariz. 349, 572 P.2d 1187 (1977). Because an instruction had placed upon D the burden, not merely of raising the issue of insanity, but of proving it, the conviction was reversed. But the court found no other fault.

62. Glueck, Mental Disorder and the Criminal Law 184 (1925).

63. M'Naghten's Case, 10 Clark & F. 200, 210, 8 Eng.Rep. 718, 723 (1843).

64. Ibid.

The wording of the right-wrong test sometimes suggests two distinct components both of which are needed for exculpation: (1) inability to know what he was doing, and (2) inability to distinguish between right and wrong with reference thereto.[65] This cannot be correct because a man who does not know what he is doing is in no position to distinguish between right and wrong in reference to the happening which he does not understand, although he might know what he is doing without being able to distinguish between right and wrong as to such an act. Hence the statement of criminal incapacity on this basis properly uses the word "or" to connect these two,[66] and it has been held reversible error to substitute "and." [67]

In brief the one indispensable fact needed to establish criminal incapacity under the right-wrong test is inability to distinguish right from wrong because of mental disorder and the modern trend is to express it substantially in these terms[68] which accounts for the name. This is quite logical but has proved to be very unfortunate because emphasis upon ability to distinguish right from wrong has tended to divert the attention of the medical expert along lines of philosophical imponderables[69] when he should be concentrating upon the understanding or lack of understanding of the defendant. A person who is doing a very wrongful act and knows what he is doing, in the

"We believe that the proper interpretation of *M'Naghten* is that an individual is unable to tell right from wrong with reference to the particular act charged, if, at the time of the commission of the offense, he is unable to tell that his act is one which he 'ought not to do.' . . . If the accused knew his act was wrong—either legally or morally—then he cannot be excused for his crime by the insanity defense." State v. Crenshaw, 27 Wn. App. 326, 617 P.2d 1041, 1048–49 (1980).

65. See People v. Ashland, 20 Cal. App. 168, 181, 128 P. 798, 804 (1912); Leache v. State, 22 Tex.App. 279, 311 (1886).

66. "The test . . . is whether he knew the nature and quality of his action or whether he could distinguish right from wrong at the time of the commission of the offense." State v. Steelman, 120 Ariz. 301, 585 P.2d 1213, 1225 (1978).

67. Knights v. State, 58 Neb. 225, 78 N.W. 508 (1899); Accord, State v. Moeller, 433 P.2d 136 (Hawaii, 1967). Needless to say it would be proper to use "and" in speaking of criminal capacity—the defendant must have been able to know what he was doing *and* to distinguish between right and wrong with reference thereto to be guilty of crime. Whisenhunt v. State, 279 P.2d 366 (Okl. Cr.1954).

68. "[T]he general rule, throughout the United States, as regards criminal responsibility, is an individual's ability to distinguish between right and wrong." Arridy v. People, 103 Colo. 29, 35–6, 82 P.2d 757, 760 (1938). And see Lee v. United States, 91 F.2d 326, 330 (5th Cir. 1937); State v. Van Vlack, 57 Idaho 316, 366, 65 P.2d 736, 759 (1937); Fisher v. State, 140 Neb. 216, 218, 299 N.W. 501, 502 (1941); McGann v. State, 175 Miss. 320, 323, 167 So. 53, 54 (1936); State v. Roy, 40 N.M. 397, 403, 60 P.2d 646, 650 (1936); Kobyluk v. State, 94 Okl.Cr. 73, 79, 231 P.2d 388, 394 (1951); Commonwealth v. Lockard, 325 Pa. 56, 60, 188 A. 755, 757 (1937); State v. Henke, 196 Wash. 185, 189, 82 P.2d 544, 547 (1938). The basic test is "the ability to distinguish right from wrong at the time of the commission of the alleged crime." State v. Coey, 82 Ariz. 133, 309 P.2d 260, 262 (1957).

69. "To force a psychiatrist to talk in terms of the ability to distinguish between right and wrong and of legal responsibility is—let us admit it openly and frankly—to force him to violate the Hippocratic Oath, even to violate the oath he takes as a witness to tell the truth and nothing but the truth, to force him to perjure himself for the sake of justice." Guttmacher & Weihofen 406 (1952) (quoting from an address by Dr. Gregory Zilboorg). See also Hall, Principles of Criminal Law 497–504 (1947); Glueck, Mental Disorder and the Criminal Law 220–231 (1925).

But a religious belief that it is one's duty to kill an unfaithful spouse is not a defense. State v. Crenshaw, 27 Wn.App. 326, 617 P.2d 1041 (1980).

sense of having a full appreciation of the nature and quality of his act, almost invariably has the *ability* to distinguish between right and wrong with reference thereto,[70] whether he *chooses* to make the distinction or not; and it is only the inability to do so which constitutes criminal incapacity under the right-wrong test.

Under very unusual circumstances, however, mental disorder might render it impossible for one who knows what he is doing to distinguish between right and wrong with reference thereto, as in Cardozo's dictum with reference to one acting under an insane delusion that the deed had been commanded by God.[71] For this reason the judges when formulating the rule in *M'Naghten* were unwilling to ground incapacity solely upon inability to know the nature and quality of the act being done and added the clause with reference to knowing that it was wrong. But the emphasis was upon the person's inability to know what he was doing, which otherwise would not have been mentioned at all since logic does not require it; and had some other label been devised such as "cognition" test, and attention been concentrated upon the ability to know what was being done (in other than exceptional cases), much difficulty would have been avoided although it would not have been universally acceptable.[72]

No one familiar with the problem, it is assumed, would consider criminal capacity present if mental disorder made it impossible to distinguish right from wrong, although several of our jurisdictions do not accept this as the sole test and a few would object to wording it in the form of a rule because of the negative inference involved.[73] In several states, however, the right-wrong test was made the sole determinant of criminal incapacity based upon mental disorder.[74]

The essence of M'Naghten is that for mental disease or defect to incapacitate it must be of such a degree as to leave the person irrational,—that is, no rational person lacks criminal capacity by reason of insanity.

70. "[A]ny number of the obviously and unquestionably mentally ill and insane have a keen perception of right and wrong; . . ." McCarthy & Maeder, Insanity and the Law 136 (1928).

71. See People v. Schmidt, 216 N.Y. 324, 340, 110 N.E. 945, 949 (1915). The Tennessee court held this would not be exculpating. McElroy v. State, 146 Tenn. 442, 242 S.W. 883 (1922). But such a view is utterly unrealistic; a man could not possibly know that what he thought was commanded by God was wrong.

72. "Only those persons 'who have lost contact with reality so completely that they are beyond any of the influences of the criminal law' may benefit from the insanity defense." State v. Crenshaw, 27 Wn.App. 326, 617 P.2d 1041, 1048 (1980).

73. Model Penal Code 161 (tent.dr. 4, 1955).

74. Arizona, Florida, Georgia, Iowa, Kansas, Louisiana, Minnesota, Nevada, Pennsylvania, South Carolina, Washington. Canada see Can.Crim.Code S.16 (1972). For recent decisions following the M'Naghten "rule," see State v. Sisk, 112 Ariz. 484, 543 P.2d 1113 (1975); State v. Sandstrom, 225 Kan. 717, 595 P.2d 324 (1979); State v. Luna, 93 N.M. 773, 606 P.2d 183 (1980); Clark v. State, 95 Nev. 24, 588 P.2d 1027 (1979); Matter of M.E., 584 P.2d 1340 (Okl.Cr.App. 1978); Commonwealth v. Beatty, 281 Pa.Super. 85, 421 A.2d 1159 (1980); State v. Goolsby, 275 S.C. 110, 268 S.E.2d 31 (1980); State v. Ferrick, 81 Wn.2d 942, 506 P.2d 860 (1973). Canada see Cooper v. Queen, 51 CCC 2d 129 (SC Can. 1980); Regina v. Barnier, 51 CCC 2d 193 (SC Can. 1980).

E. DELUSION

A delusion—always the product of mental disorder—is a false belief in something that would be incredible to people of the same class, age, education, and race, as the person who expresses it; such belief being persisted in, despite proof to the contrary.[75]

This was called "monomania" in the earlier medical books,[76] reflecting the theory since discarded by science, that such a disorder affected only one compartment of the mind, without affecting the mind as a whole.[77] It is apparently what Hale had in mind in that subdivision of partial insanity which he referred to as partial "in respect to things" as distinguished from "partial in respect of degrees."[78] Delusions of grandeur and delusions of persecution seem to be the most common, leading the persons so affected into exaggerated beliefs that they are great personages, such as Napoleon, or that they are the victims of sinister plots against their persons or their property.[79]

The eloquence of Lord Erskine in Hadfield's Case (1800)[80] is the foundation for so much that has since appeared in the law on this subject as to be entitled to more than passing attention. Erskine, it must be borne in mind, was not making an impartial pronouncement from the bench; he was an advocate making an impassioned plea in the effort to save the life of a client charged with high treason, and he called upon all his resources to the accomplishment of that end. The attorney general [Sir John Mitford, afterwards Lord Redesdale] had referred to the passages of Coke and Hale, which required for incapacity to commit crime because of insanity, "an absolute madness, and a total deprivation of memory."[81] This did not suit Erskine at all, for his client was obviously not in such a prostrated mental condition as this. He therefore began by questioning whether the ancient authorities had really meant what they said when they used such expressions. "If a *total deprivation of memory* was intended by these great lawyers to be taken in the *literal* sense of the words:" said Erskine, "then no such madness ever existed in the world. It is *idiocy* alone which places a man in this helpless condition," which, he explained, exists "where, from an *original* mal-organization, there is the human frame alone, without the human capacity; . . ."[82]

A moment later, apparently forgetting in his eloquence, his statement that "no such madness ever existed," he pictured this very condition in striking language. "It is true, indeed, that in some, perhaps in many cases, the human mind is stormed in its citadel, and laid prostrate under the stroke of frenzy; . . . There indeed all the ideas are overwhelmed—for reason is not merely disturbed, *but driven wholly from her seat.*"[83] In the midst of this sentence the contradiction seems to have occurred to him, and he interpolated the suggestion that "these cases are not only extremely rare, but never can become the subjects of judicial difficulty. There can be but one

75. Quoted from Glueck, Mental Disorder and the Criminal Law 183 (1925). The author is quoting from Clouston, Unsoundness of Mind 185 (1911).

76. Id. at 365, n. 5

77. Id., at 158.

78. 1 Hale P.C. *30.

79. Glueck 300 (1925).

80. 27 Howell St.Tr. 1281 (1800).

81. Id. at 1287.

82. Id. at 1312.

83. Id. at 1313.

judgment concerning them." He then continued in his illuminatingly pictur-esque style:

"In other cases, reason is not driven from her seat, but distraction sits down upon it along with her, holds her, trembling upon it, and frightens her from her propriety. Such patients are victims to delusions of the most alarming description, which so overpower the faculties, and usurp so firmly the place of realities, as not to be dislodged and shaken by the organs of perception and sense." Then after elaborating upon delusions of a less "frightful character," which interfere with the reasoning of the persons so afflicted because of creating false "premises from which they reason," he made another reference to the type of madness which he had undertaken to say did not exist: "Delusion, therefore, where there is no frenzy or raving madness, is the true character of insanity; . . . ."

Three points are noteworthy in Erskine's argument, which it should be repeated because the point has been overlooked so frequently, was not a ju-dicial decision but an advocate's plea: (1) While delusion seems to have been what Hale referred to in his reference to partial insanity "in respect to things" it was Erskine who definitely forced it into the picture as one of the factors to be considered with reference to criminal capacity. (2) He suggest-ed it as the "true character of insanity" "where there is no frenzy or raving madness." This was an accident, says Professor Glueck, due to the fact "that Erskine had happened to have seen in his experience only such mental-ly diseased patients as paranoiacs, for example, whose symptoms were large-ly and characteristically delusional." [84] (3) He pointed to delusions as creat-ing false "premises from which they reason," thus suggesting the "mistake of fact" theory of the legal importance of delusion which was to receive judi-cial recognition shortly thereafter.

Erskine's eloquence was sufficient to secure the acquittal of Hadfield, but his doctrine of delusion did not at once gain a secure footing in the law. Thus in Bellingham's Case, a few years later,[85] the court is once more talk-ing of a man "deprived of all power of reasoning" and "destitute of all power of judgment." [86] But in 1843 the delusional aspect of insanity received rec-ognition in *M'Naghten*, the key paragraph dealing with this part of the prob-lem having been quoted above. The substance of this pronouncement was that if one "not in other respects insane" labors under such a delusion, his accountability to the law is the same as if the imaginary facts were real; and if, for example, "under the influence of his delusion he supposes another man to be in the act of attempting to take away his life, and he kills that man, as he supposes, in self-defence, he would be exempt from punishment." One not suffering from an insane delusion would not be excused for such a killing unless the mistake was a reasonable one under the circumstances, but the delusion will take the place of reasonable grounds for the belief in the mistake of fact cases.

It has also been held, quite soundly it would seem, that a delusion may take the place of "adequate provocation" and thereby reduce to manslaugh-ter a homicide which would otherwise be murder, if the killing resulted from rage or passion engendered by delusional belief of great harm done by the

---

84. Glueck 147 (1925).

85. Cited in Collinson on Lunacy, Ad-denda 636 (1812).

86. Id. at 671.

person slain.[87] It is commonly said that to make out a case of voluntary manslaughter rather than murder there must be both the fact of great provocation and the sudden rage or passion resulting therefrom, and that "if there be provocation without passion, or passion without a sufficient cause of provocation" the killing will be murder.[88] But this generalization should be considered in the light of the other doctrine that in such a case one laboring under a mistake of fact, based upon reasonable grounds, will be treated as if the facts were as they reasonably seemed to him to be, together with the supplement that a delusional belief will take the place of a reasonable belief in the mistake-of-fact cases.

So far, attention has been given to only one part of the "mistake of fact" rule announced by the judges in *M'Naghten*,—namely that an insane delusion will excuse an act if facts such as are supposed to exist by the disordered mind would constitute an excuse if really present. The other part of this rule, that an insane delusion of any other sort does not exempt from punishment, must be read in the light of the assumption upon which it is based: "that he labours under such partial delusion only, and is not in other respects insane." This assumption seems to be grounded upon an "erroneous conception of the human mind," [89] by which a mere symptom[90] of the disease is mistaken for the disease itself. Stephen presents the matter in this form:

"How would it be if medical witnesses were to say (as Dr. Griesinger says, and as the witnesses in M'Naghten's case said in substance) that a delusion of the kind suggested never, or hardly ever, stands alone, but is in all cases the result of a disease of the brain, which interferes more or less with every function of the mind, which falsifies all the emotions, alters in an unaccountable way the natural weight of motives of conduct, weakens the will, and sometimes, without giving the patient false impressions of external facts, so enfeebles every part of his mind, that he sees and feels, and acts with regard to real things as a sane man does with regard to what he supposes himself to see in a dream?" [91]

The delusion rule as stated in *M'Naghten* has been severely criticized, one frequently-repeated statement being this: "If he dare fail to reason, on the supposed facts embodied in the delusion, as perfectly as a sane man could do

---

87. Davis v. State, 161 Tenn. 23, 28 S.W.2d 993 (1930). This assumes, of course, that the mind was not so disordered as to lack criminal capacity, for in that case the result should be an acquittal.

88. Commonwealth v. Paese, 220 Pa. 371, 373, 69 A. 891, 892 (1908).

89. Glueck 158 (1925). And see Guttmacher & Weihofen 417–8 (1952). "The truth probably is as Dr. Mercier, a distinguished psychiatrist and psychologist, says: 'There is not, and never has been, a person who labors under partial delusion only and is not in other respects insane.' " Per Doctor Morton Prince, quoted by Keedy, 2 J.C.L. & Crim. 539 (1911), and by Weihofen, Insanity as a Defense in Criminal Law, 77 (1933).

Quoted in part by Weihofen, Mental Disorder as a Criminal Defense 109 (1954). While the assumption seems to be incorrect it probably is not. The word "insane" is used in different senses as explained in subsection (B) above. No doubt what the judges meant is that if a man, who is not insane within the right-wrong rule, has a delusion he will be treated as if the imaginary facts were real.

90. "Delusion is a symptom of different varieties of mental disease and should be considered in connection with the general symptomatology." Keedy, Insanity and Criminal Responsibility, 30 Harv.L.Rev. 535, 559 (1917).

91. 2 Stephen, History of the Criminal Law of England 157 (1883).

on a like state of realities, he receives no mercy at the hands of the law." [92]
This is based upon a complete misunderstanding of the position taken by the
judges in that famous "case." They were called upon to answer questions
including specific references to delusion, and what they obviously meant was
that if a man has a delusion, without being insane within the meaning of the
right-wrong rule previously announced by them, his accountability to the law
would be the same as if the imaginary facts were real.

It has been held very properly that a defendant who acted under an insane delusion *may not* have been guilty even if the imaginary facts were not
of such a nature as to excuse a sane man in committing such a deed,[93] because the delusion may have so far corrupted the defendant's mental
processes that he had become incapacitated from distinguishing right from
wrong with respect to the act committed,[94] and hence was without criminal
guilt for that reason.[95]

The delusion test is not required as a matter of logic because whenever
disease has forced into the mind imaginary facts, which cannot be dislodged
and which if real would justify or excuse what is done, the owner of this
disordered mind is in no position to discriminate between right and wrong
with reference thereto.[96] On the other hand the delusion rule when properly
understood and applied can never work to the disadvantage of the defendant,
and should be stated in some such form as this:

**(1) A delusion will excuse the commission of a prohibited act
(or will diminish the degree of guilt) if actual facts such as are fan-
cied by the deluded mind would justify or excuse the act (or diminish the degree of guilt).**

**(2) A mental disease, even if the chief symptom is a delusion,
may have so impaired the mental processes as to destroy criminal
capacity without regard to the nature of the resulting mistake of
fact. In this event the delusion does not itself constitute a defense
but is part of the evidence which may establish a defense on some
other basis.[97]**

---

92. Parsons v. State, 81 Ala. 577, 595, 2 So. 854, 866 (1887); State v. Keerl, 29 Mont. 508, 516, 75 P. 362, 364 (1903); Kraus v. State, 108 Neb. 331, 341, 187 N.W. 895, 899 (1922). "It is, in effect, saying to the jury, the prisoner was mad when he committed the act, but he did not use sufficient reason in his madness." State v. Jones, 50 N.H. 369, 387–8 (1871). And see Ray, Medical Jurisprudence 49 (5th ed. 1871).

93. Parsons v. State, 81 Ala. 577, 2 So. 854 (1887); Woodall v. State, 149 Ark. 33, 231 S.W. 186 (1921); Ryan v. People, 60 Colo. 425, 153 P. 756 (1915).

94. Kraus v. State, 108 Neb. 331, 336, 187 N.W. 895, 897 (1922).

95. Ibid.; Ryan v. People, 60 Colo. 425, 153 P. 756 (1915).

96. The defense of delusional insanity can be presented under the M'Naghten rule because the delusion may have af-fected the defendant's ability to distinguish right from wrong or his knowledge of the nature and quality of his act. State v. Nicholson, 1 Wn.App. 853, 466 P.2d 181 (1970).

97. "A person who is so diseased in mind at the time of the act as to be incapable of distinguishing right from wrong with respect to it, or being able to so distinguish, has suffered such an impairment of mind by disease as to destroy the will power and render him incapable of choosing the right and refraining from doing the wrong, is not accountable. And this is true howsoever such insanity may be manifested, by insane delusions of whatever nature, by irresistible impulse, or otherwise." Ryan v. People, 60 Colo. 425, 433, 153 P. 756, 759 (1915). "[N]or can it be asserted that, medically, the presence of delusion is always a symptom that the mental disease has

(3) If the imaginary facts resulting from delusion are of such a nature that they would not constitute a defense if real it is reversible error to instruct the jury in terms of the M'Naghten delusion rule since such an instruction could serve no useful purpose in such a case and would tend only to confuse the jury.[98]

F. IRRESISTIBLE IMPULSE

At the threshold of this inquiry is encountered one of the imponderables with which the human mind has been baffled throughout the ages. The religion which teaches fatalism—that everything one is to do has been determined before his birth beyond any possibility of change—is as far apart as the poles from the doctrine of personal responsibility found in other religions. Whether or not one has any power to direct the course of his life has been approached from other points of view and has given us the "determinists" and the "free-willists" in the field of philosophy and the "behaviorists" and the "mentalists" in the science of psychology. Is one "a shipwrecked sailor on a rudderless vessel, at the mercy of whatever wind may blow," or is he the "captain of his soul?"

If one is merely a "conscious automaton," an interested observer of his conduct but with no power to choose what he shall do, there is no real mind at fault and it is unfortunate that some have to be punished; but it is futile to argue the administration of criminal justice on this premise, for if it is sound neither judges, jurors nor officers can do other than cause the punishments which are imposed. Either conscious striving plays a part in human affairs or it does not; if it does the criminal law rests upon a workable basis,[99] if it does not it is illusory to assume that anything can be done about the matter.

Without going into metaphysical considerations, "The law, following common sense and common morality, assumes a certain degree of purposive capacity possessed by the normal mind."[1] The powerful influences exercised by one's hereditary make-up and by his developmental and environmental background are not ignored, but the law takes the position "that most men, in most of the relations of life, can act purposefully and can inhibit antisocial, illegal tendencies."[2] It regards the criminal law and its enforcement as an important part of the environment, with a distinct tendency to cause most people to act in a socially-acceptable manner.

progressed to such a serious stage as materially to interfere with the patient's ordinary mental capacities." Glueck 175–6 (1925).

98. Ryan v. People, 60 Colo. 425, 153 P. 756 (1915); Kraus v. State, 108 Neb. 331, 187 N.W. 895 (1922).

99. "The writer is aware of the fact that the nineteenth century over-emphasized 'the Will' in its legal writings, and held a 'wicked' or 'depraved' will as the punishable entity; however, with the advent of the criminological studies of the later nineteenth century, with the development of the biological and social sciences and the tracing of abnormal conduct to psychological and social causes, the view of 'Will' as an entity presiding over the mind and dictating its conduct has gradually given way to an interpretation of it as the organized integrated capacity for purposive activity, in spite of the fact that the polemical *terminology* has often remained unaltered." Glueck 95, note 1 (1925).

1. Id. at 99.

"As punishments are therefore only inflicted for the abuse of that free will which God has given to man . . .," 4 Bl.Comm. *27.

2. Ibid.

A subsequent generation may evolve a wiser method for maintaining the social security and discipline but until such time the criminal law will be used for this purpose.[3] And while it is so used, it will be enforced upon the assumption that most persons can more or less choose between various possible lines of action; and that when they fail to achieve the legally-acceptable minimum of required conduct, they are subject to conviction of crime unless there is something so *extraordinary* about them as to remove them entirely from the ordinary run of people. As has been seen one may be so young or so insane as to put him in this special category of those who are beyond the reach of criminal justice.

In those jurisdictions, therefore, in which irresistible impulse is recognized as a defense to a criminal charge, this is not grounded upon some metaphysical abstraction that "men cannot help what they do," [4] but upon proof that the particular defendant is suffering from mental disorder of such an extreme nature that his conduct has practically nothing in common with that of the ordinary person. The "heat of passion and feeling produced by motives of anger, hatred or revenge, is not insanity. The law holds the doer of the act under such conditions, responsible for the crime; because a large share of homicides committed are occasioned by just such motives as these".[5] As stated by another court, one who is sane "will not be excused from a crime he has committed while his reason is temporarily dethroned not by disease, but by anger, jealousy or other passion; nor will he be excused because he has become so morally depraved 'that his conscience ceases to control his actions.' " [6]

The phrases "moral insanity" and "emotional insanity" are not to be recommended because they tend to invite confusion. Some courts have used these terms to mean unsoundness of mind of such a nature as to result in a marked disturbance of the affective volitional modes of mental life, which if sufficiently extreme may lead to the "insane irresistible impulse." [7] The same phrases have been used by other courts to refer to situations in which "reason is temporarily dethroned *not by disease*, but by anger, jealousy or other passion." [8] As explained by one court, that convenient form of insanity "which enables a person who does not choose to bridle his passion, to

3.   "Law does but a part of this whole task of social control; and the criminal law does but a part of that portion which belongs to the law." Pound, Criminal Justice in America 4 (1924). Among the non-legal agencies of social control Dean Pound lists the household, religious and fraternal organizations, "social clubs, professional and trade organizations and the like." (p. 5).

4.   "The law adopts the theory of the responsibility of man, notwithstanding the controlling supervision of Providence." People v. McDonnell, 80 Cal. 285, 295, 22 P. 190, 193 (1889).

5.   People v. Foy, 138 N.Y. 664, 667, 34 N.E. 396, 397 (1893).

6.   Bell v. State, 120 Ark. 530, 555, 180 S.W. 186, 196 (1915). Quoted with approval in Woodall v. State, 149 Ark. 33,

37, 231 S.W. 186, 187–8 (1921). See also State v. Stickley, 41 Iowa 232 (1875); Spencer v. State, 69 Md. 28, 13 A. 809 (1888). And see McCarty v. Commonwealth, 114 Ky. 620, 626, 71 S.W. 656, 657 (1903).

" . . . impulsive behavior, irresistible impulse or accused's inability to control his actions is immaterial to prove insanity unless predicated upon the presence of a disease of the mind." State v. Hartley, 90 N.M. 488, 565 P.2d 658, 661 (1977).

7.   Boswell v. State, 63 Ala. 307, 321 (1879); Commonwealth v. Mosler, 4 Pa. 264, 267, 6 Pa.L.J. 90, 94 (1846).

8.   Bell v. State, 120 Ark. 530, 555, 180 S.W. 186, 196 (1915); Woodall v. State, 149 Ark. 33, 37, 231 S.W. 186, 188 (1921). Italics added.

allow it to get and keep the upper hand just long enough to enable him to commit an act of violence, and then subside," does not relieve from criminal responsibility.[9]

When the phrases "moral insanity" or "emotional insanity" are employed in such a sense there is no disagreement as to the presence of criminal capacity, but with reference to the so-called insane irresistible impulse there is a sharp difference in the actual result in different jurisdictions. There are sometimes said to be three different views in the law with reference to the insane irresistible impulse: (1) that it is not a defense to a criminal charge; (2) that it constitutes a defense if it is of such a nature as to destroy the capacity to distinguish between right and wrong, but not otherwise; (3) that even one who knows the nature and character of the act he is doing and that it is wrong, is not accountable to the criminal law if he acts under such duress of mental disease as to be incapable of choosing between right and wrong. However, there seems to be no real difference of position such as appears between (1) and (2) but only a difference in statement. If the insane irresistible impulse (or the disease which causes this impulse) has obliterated the ability to distinguish between right and wrong as to the act done there would be no criminal capacity with reference to that act under the theory of any jurisdiction. But (1) and (3) present a substantial difference in legal theory.

Before delving into this difference, a word with reference to the meaning of the term "irresistible impulse" may serve a useful purpose. For example, reference is found to "a woman who was afflicted by an 'irresistible impulse' to slay her child, an act which she *avoided doing* only by separating herself from the child." [10] There is also this interesting statement in one of the cases: "The law says to men who are afflicted with irresistible impulses: 'If you can not resist an impulse in any other way, we will hang a rope in front of your eyes and perhaps that will help.' " [11] As so used the term seems to have reference to a "possibly resistible but abnormally compelling urge." [12] This gives rise to the inquiry: Does "irresistible impulse" mean one that could not be resisted under any circumstances, or one that cannot be resisted under the particular circumstances? If there is medical evidence in a larceny case to the effect that the defendant took the property as the result of an irresistible impulse, would it be fair to ask the expert: "Could the impulse to take the property have been resisted if there had been a policeman in uniform standing nearby?" [13] If that is not a fair question, then certainly the court was correct in saying: "But if an influence be so powerful as to be

---

9. People v. Finley, 38 Mich. 482, 484 (1878).

10. Waite, Irresistible Impulse and Criminal Liability. 23 Mich.L.Rev. 443, 446 (1925).

11. Rex v. Creighton, 14 Can.Crim. Cas. 349, 350 (1908).

12. Waite, op. cit. supra note 10, at 454.

13. Whether such question may refer to the defendant or must be in hypothetical form is apart from the present problem.

". . . the accused's ability to adhere to the right in the face of the prospect of immediate detection and apprehension is not the legally controlling consideration in determining whether he is mentally responsible . . . it cannot be made the subject of a governing instruction or used to limit the testimony of expert witnesses." United States v. Jensen, 14 USCMA 353, 358, 34 CMR 133 (1964).

Policeman at the elbow is not a proper test for the irresistible impulse standard of insanity. State v. Sharp, 604 S.W.2d 886 (Tenn.Cr.App. 1980).

termed irresistible, so much the more reason is there why we should not withdraw any of the safeguards tending to counteract it." [14] In other words some courts have refused to recognize irresistible impulse as a defense to a criminal charge because not convinced that these impulsive urges cannot be inhibited.[15]

Care must be taken not to read an unintended meaning into words taken out of context. Sergeant Hawkins says for example: "The guilt of offending against any law whatsoever, necessarily supposing a wilful disobedience, can never justly be imputed to those who are either incapable of understanding it, or of conforming themselves to it." [16] But when placed in context we find this author dealing with infants and lunatics under the head of those "incapable of understanding" and with persons acting under coercion and duress under the head of those incapable of "conforming themselves to it." [17] And a judge's reference to criminal capacity, in a case in which mental disorder was urged as a defense, as "a state of mind in which at the time of the deed, he was free to forbear or to do the act," [18] may be found on further reading to mean no more than that one who cannot understand what he is doing has no such choice. What seems to be the earliest clear-cut recognition of irresistible impulse as a possible ground of defense on the part of one who knew what he was doing and understood that it was wrong, is found in an instruction given by Chief Justice Gibson to a Pennsylvania jury in 1846. He said:

"But there is a *moral* or *homicidal* insanity, consisting of an irresistible inclination to kill, or to commit some other particular offence. There may be an unseen ligament pressing on the mind, drawing it to consequences which it sees but cannot avoid, and placing it under a coercion, which, while its results are clearly perceived, is incapable of resistance." [19]

A few years later the matter was put in this language by Chief Justice Dillon, of Iowa:

"But, if, from the observation and concurrent testimony of medical men who make the study of insanity a specialty, it shall be definitely established to be true, that there is an unsound condition of the mind,—that is, a diseased condition of the mind, in which, though a person abstractly knows that

---

14. Regina v. Haynes, 1 Fost. & F. 666, 667, 175 Eng.Rep. 898 (1859).

15. Ibid.; Rex v. Creighton, 14 Can. Crim.Cas. 349 (1908).

16. 1 Hawk.P.C. 1 (6th ed. 1788).

17. Id. at 1–5. See also 1 Hale P.C. *14; 4 Bl.Comm. *20–21.

18. State v. Thompson, Wright, 617, 622 (Ohio, 1834). For other statements having something of the "ring" of the irresistible impulse doctrine but found on careful study not to go beyond M'Naghten, see Regina v. Oxford, 9 Car. & P. 525, 547, 173 Eng.Rep. 941, 950 (1840); Clark v. State, 12 Ohio 483, 495 (1843); Commonwealth v. Rogers, 48 Mass. 500, 501–2 (1844). In Rogers the court made use of the phrase "irresistible and uncontrollable impulse," saying an

act so committed is "not the act of a voluntary agent, but the involuntary act of the body, without the concurrence of a mind directing it;" but he went on to explain: "A man is not excused from responsibility, if he has capacity and reason sufficient to enable him to distinguish right from wrong, as to the particular act he is then doing; a knowledge and consciousness that the act he is doing is wrong and criminal will subject him to punishment." This does not go beyond M'Naghten as pointed out by Dean Pound in discussing a committee report. 2 J.C.L. & Crim. 544 (1911). And see Keedy, Insanity and Criminal Responsibility, 30 Harv.L.Rev. 724, 725–30 (1917).

19. Commonwealth v. Mosler, 4 Pa. 264, 267, 6 Pa.L.J. 90, 94 (1846).

a given act is wrong, he is yet, by an *insane impulse*, that is, an impulse proceeding from a diseased intellect, irresistibly driven to commit it,—the law must modify its ancient doctrines and recognize the truth, and give to this condition, when it is satisfactorily shown to exist, its exculpatory effect." [20]

The insane irresistible impulse test, let it be emphasized, has never been viewed as a substitute for *M'Naghten* but only as an additional defense in cases of mental disorder.[21]   It was seized upon by the judges with considerable enthusiasm when the idea was relatively new to the profession;[22] and was accepted at one time in nearly half the states.[23]   On the other hand some of these jurisdictions have rejected this defense after more mature deliberation, as was true in both Pennsylvania[24] and Iowa.[25]   Needless to say an *insane* irresistible impulse is never of itself incriminating and if mental disease has so far dethroned reason as to leave no ability to understand what is being done there is no criminal capacity,—[26] but that does not go beyond *M'Naghten*.

Courts that have refused to recognize an insane irresistible impulse (by one able to know what he is doing and to understand its wrongfulness) as a defense in a criminal case, other than those refusing to accept the view that such an impulse is really uncontrollable, have based their stand on the ground that this refusal is necessary for the proper administration of justice. In fact Judge Gibson, after his oft-quoted metaphor of the "unseen ligament pressing on the mind" threw out this word of caution:

"The doctrine which acknowledges this mania is dangerous in its relations, and can be recognized only in the clearest cases. . . .   If juries were to allow it as a general motive, operating in cases of this character, its recognition would destroy social order as well as personal safety."

Statements such as the following are not uncommon: " . . .   the difficulty would be great, if not insuperable, of establishing by satisfactory proof whether an impulse was or was not uncontrolable." [27]   "The legal view does not deny the possibility of affective insanity, but holds it unsafe to make it a legal defense." [28]   "It will be a sad day for this state, when uncontrollable impulse shall dictate 'a rule of action' to our courts." [29]   "The vagueness and

20. State v. Filter, 25 Iowa 67, 82–3 (1868).

21. Smith v. United States, 36 F.2d 548, 549–550 (D.C. Cir. 1929); Sauer v. United States, 241 F.2d 640, 642 (9th Cir. 1957).

22. The leading case in support of this defense is Parsons v. State, 81 Ala. 577, 2 So. 854, 60 Am.Rep. 193 (1887). See also Ryan v. People, 60 Colo. 425, 153 P. 756 (1915); State v. Windsor, 5 Del. 512 (1851); Stevens v. State, 31 Ind. 485 (1869); Scott v. Commonwealth, 61 Ky. 227 (1863); Miller v. Commonwealth, 236 Ky. 448, 33 S.W.2d 590 (1930).

23. See Glueck 267–73 (1925); Goldstein, The Insanity Defense 67 (1967).

24. Commonwealth v. Schroeder, 302 Pa. 1, 10, 152 A. 835, 837 (1930).

25. State v. Buck, 204 Iowa 1028, 219 N.W. 17 (1928).

26. Ibid. Irresistible impulse is not recognized unless the mental disease is of such a high degree as to overwhelm reason, judgment and conscience. Johnson v. State, 223 Miss. 56, 76 So.2d 841 (1955), cert. denied 349 U.S. 946, 75 S.Ct. 874 (1955); Thompson v. State, 159 Neb. 685, 68 N.W.2d 267 (1955).

27. State v. Bundy, 24 S.C. 439, 445 (1885).

28. United States v. Young, 25 F. 710, 712 (D.C.N.C.1885).

29. State v. Pagels, 92 Mo. 300, 317, 4 S.W. 931, 937 (1887).

uncertainty of the inquiry which would be opened, . . . may well cause courts to pause before assenting to it." [30] Irresistible impulse is "too incapable of a practical solution, to afford a safe basis of legal adjudication." [31] "It may serve as a metaphysical or psychological problem, to interest and amuse the speculative philosopher, but it must be discarded by the jurist and the lawgiver in the practical affairs of life." [32]

It has been rather the fashion, however, for writers to take the opposite view[33] which has quite generally had the support of medical men;—but as an eminent neurologist has said, "some psychiatrists ridicule the legal idea of insanity, i.e. not having understanding. The emotions and the unconscious life are important, but in law are rather indefinite standards with which to measure responsibility." [34] From a similar source we have this suggestion: "When offered as a defense for crime, the allegation of a morbid and irresistible impulse must always be regarded with suspicion and release from responsibility on such grounds under present conditions . . . can rarely be justified." [35] "It can be stated definitely and flatly that compulsions are always unimportant and harmless acts. A patient . . . may have to avoid stepping on the cracks of a pavement, he may have to leave the elevator on the twelfth floor and walk up to the thirteenth, but he never has to commit a truly compulsive criminal act . . . . The medico-legal theory of irresistible impulse is advocated only by laymen and by psychiatrists who are scientifically not sufficiently oriented. It lends an air of scientific literalness and accuracy to a purely legal definition without any foundation in the facts of life or science." [36]

Irresistible impulse as a defense to a charge of crime was rejected in England,[37] in Canada,[38] and in a majority of our jurisdictions. In 1955 the American Law Institute found it had been added to the right-wrong test in

---

30. Flanagan v. People, 52 N.Y. 467, 470 (1873).

31. Cunningham v. State, 56 Miss. 269, 279 (1879).

32. Ibid. One acting under an irresistible impulse may still form an intent to kill. Hence irresistible impulse is no defense to a charge of voluntary manslaughter. People v. Jennings, 66 Cal. App.3d 743, 136 Cal.Rptr. 249 (1977).

33. See, for example, 2 Stephen, History of the Criminal Law of England 168 (1883); 1 Bishop, New Criminal Law § 383b (8th ed. 1892); 1 Wharton, Criminal Law § 62 (12th ed. 1932); Glueck 232 et seq. (1925); Weihofen, Insanity as a Defense in Criminal Law 44 et seq. (1933); and see under the discussion of Durham in the next subsection. On the other side see Waite, Irresistible Impulse and Criminal Liability, 23 Mich.L.Rev. 443 (1925); Hall, Principles of Criminal Law 505 et seq. (1947).

34. Meagher, Crime and Insanity, 16 J.C.L. & Crim. 360, 374 (1925).

35. Singer and Krohn, Insanity and Law 162 (1924).

36. Wertham, The Show of Violence 13–14 (1949). And see Hall, In Defense of the McNaghten Rules, 42 A.B.A.J. 917, 918–9 (1956).

37. Regina v. Barton, 3 Cox C.C. 275 (1848); Rex v. Kopsch, 19 Cr.App.R. 50 (1925); Rex v. Flavelle, 19 Cr.App.R. 141 (1926). Atty.-Gen. for South Australia v. Brown, [1960] A.C. 432, 1 All E.R. 734 (P.C.). It was proposed to be accepted in England in the bill of 1878, but rejected in the Draft Code of 1879. It was recommended by the Atkin Committee in 1923, supported by the British Medical Association but was blocked by influential opposition. The Royal Commission on Capital Punishment in 1953 recommended that the M'Naghten rules be abrogated "and the jury left to decide simply whether the accused ought to be held irresponsible for insanity." Williams, Criminal Law § 99 (1953). And see § 163 of the second edition (1961).

38. Can.Crim.Code § 16 (1970). See Regina v. Wolfson, 51 D.L.R.2d 428, 46 C.R. 8 (Albta. 1965).

fourteen states, the federal jurisdiction and the army plus one state having a delusional-impulse test.[39]

A recent trend in this general area has been to avoid the phrase "irresistible impulse" [40] on the ground that while such a condition exists "in the irrational acts of confused epileptics, paretics, and schizophrenics" (who lack criminal capacity under the right-wrong rule), the true problem concerns mentally-disordered persons who "are subject to abnormal urges which they have little power to control," and hence "some other term such as 'inability to adhere to the right' would be preferable . . . to express the idea." [41] Objection to the older phrase has been raised also on the thought that it implies "excitement or impulsive action" [42] which are not necessarily involved in lack of control.

One writer, emphasizing that the whole problem deals with the actor's control or lack of control over his conduct, urges that the familiar phrase should be abandoned and the rule stated in terms of "control." [43] Since, however, as he points out, the courts which use the "irresistible impulse" test do not limit it to sudden, unplanned action, the need for a change of label seems not to be urgent.

The proposal of the British Medical Association was the adoption of a formula on the following lines:

"To establish a defence on the ground of disease of the mind, the party accused must prove that, at the time of the committing of the act, he was labouring, as a result of disease of the mind, under

(1) a defect of reason such that he did not know (a) the nature and quality of the act he was doing; or (if he did know this) (b) that he was doing what was wrong; or

(2) a disorder of emotion such that, while appreciating the nature and quality of the act, and that it was wrong, he did not possess sufficient power to prevent himself from committing it." [44]

And the majority of the Royal Commission on Capital Punishment concluded that this was the best addition to M'Naghten that can be devised.[45]

---

39. Model Penal Code 161 (Tent.Draft No. 4, 1955). The states were Alabama, Arkansas, Colorado, Connecticut, Delaware, Indiana, Kentucky, Massachusetts, Michigan, New Mexico, Utah, Vermont, Virginia and Wyoming. Georgia has a delusional-impulse test. Many of these states no longer apply the rule but have adopted the ALI standard.

Irresistible impulse was not recognized as a defense in California. People v. Noah, 5 Cal.3d 469, 96 Cal.Rptr. 441, 487 P.2d 1009 (1971). That is, it was not equated with insanity and is not a complete defense. It could be introduced to show diminished capacity. People v. Cantrell, 8 Cal.3d 672, 105 Cal.Rptr. 792, 504 P.2d 1256 (1973). California has now adopted the "Substantial Capacity" standard, see infra note 72 (under H).

Irresistible impulse is not a defense to crime. State v. Billhymer, 114 Ariz. 390, 561 P.2d 311 (1977).

40. One author insists that "irresistible impulse" and "uncontrollable impulse" should be distinguished. Smoot, Law of Insanity 51 (1929).

41. Guttmacher & Weihofen 410, 411 (1952).

42. State v. White, 58 N.M. 324, 329, 270 P.2d 727, 730 (1954).

43. Goldstein, The Insanity Defense, c. Five, The Misnamed "Irresistible Impulse" Rule (1967).

44. Royal Commission on Capital Punishment, 1949–53 Report 93 (1953).

45. Id. at 116.

In this country one of the states following the so-called "irresistible impulse" rule undertook to clarify the law applicable there by declaring: "The jury must be satisfied that, at the time of committing the act, the accused as a result of disease of the mind . . . (a) did not know the nature and quality of the act or (b) did not know that it was wrong or (c) was incapable of preventing himself from doing it." [46] And the proposal of the Model Penal Code with reference to this part of the problem is a statute reading: "A person is not responsible for criminal conduct if at the time of such conduct as a result of mental disease or defect he lacks substantial capacity . . . to conform his conduct to the requirements of law." [47]

The first reaction of the legal profession to the irresistible impulse defense, when it was introduced to the law many years ago, was inclined to be favorable. Then a change set in and for many years the prevailing view was strongly against its recognition. Present indications are that the tide is changing again. There seems to be a growing belief to the effect that ignoring the possibility of such a defense fails to give full recognition to the fundamental concept of mens rea. [48]

G. DURHAM—THE "PRODUCT" RULE

In *Durham*, [49] decided in 1954, the District of Columbia court concluded that the proper solution is to discard all tests of insanity and have the jury determine (1) whether the defendant was sane or insane at the time of the alleged crime, and if he was insane (2) whether the harmful act was the product of his insanity. "The rule . . . is simply that an accused is not criminally responsible if his unlawful act was the product of mental disease or mental defect." [50] Although this, as the court admits, [51] did not present anything new other than the mere form of statement, but was essentially the same as the position taken by the New Hampshire court [52] nearly a century earlier,—a position it may be added which had been studied and rejected in every other state with one possible exception— [53] it called forth a flood of literature [54] such as might be expected from a decision of utmost novelty.

---

46. State v. White, 58 N.M. 324, 330, 270 P.2d 727, 731 (1954).

47. Section 4.01.

48. This court has modified the M'Naghten rule by adding that the accused is insane if as a result of disease of the mind he "was incapable of preventing himself from committing" the crime. But proof of such incapacity is of no avail unless it is the result of disease of the mind. State v. Hartley, 90 N.M. 488, 565 P.2d 658 (1977).

49. Durham v. United States, 94 U.S. App.D.C. 228, 214 F.2d 862 (1954). And see ibid., 237 F.2d 760 (D.C.Cir. 1956). After further consideration of the problem the court seems to have taken the position that the right-wrong test and the irresistible impulse test have not been displaced but are merely supplemented by the "product" test and that it is proper for the jury to be instructed as to all three. Douglas v. United States, 239

F.2d 52 (D.C.Cir. 1956). And see United States v. Fielding, 148 F.Supp. 46, 51 (D.C.D.C. 1957).

50. Id. at 874–5.

51. Id. at 874.

52. State v. Pike, 49 N.H. 399 (1870); State v. Jones, 50 N.H. 369 (1871).

53. Prior to Durham the New Hampshire solution had never been adopted elsewhere except perhaps in Montana. Weihofen, The Flowering of New Hampshire, 22 U. of Chi.L.Rev. 356, 362–3 (1955).

54. A symposium with articles by doctors Roche, Guttmacher, Zilboorg and Wertham, and by lawyers de Grazia, Weihofen, Wechsler, Hill and Katz. Insanity and the Criminal Law—a Critique of Durham v. United States, 22 U. of Chi.L.Rev. 317 (1955). See also Clements, Criminal Insanity: A Criticism of the New York Rule, 20 Albany L.Rev. 155 (1956);

For the most part the reaction of the commentators was favorable, much of it enthusiastic,[55] but other notes were sounded by some. In the words of Dr. Fredric Wertham, a noted psychiatrist: "As a legal test this new definition is insufficient: it gives undemocratic leeway to the partisan and/or bureaucratic expert, and, on account of its wording, lends itself to grave abuse. It does not guide the jury as to the degree of mental disease, a term which includes both psychosis and neurosis." [56] The conclusion of Judge Learned Hand, whose judgment always carries great weight in the legal profession, was that the position taken in *Durham* "did not seem to me to give us any guidance that perceptibly would help." [57] And lay comment included reference to the fact that in the District of Columbia convictions had been reversed in "case after case in which insanity was pleaded as a defense;" expressed fear that "thousands of defendants will be able to avoid prison if courts across the nation follow" this precedent, and that "not all those acquitted as insane will be committed to mental hospitals," mentioning the names of defendants "now free, neither in jail nor in a hospital." [58]

Hardly was the ink dry on *Durham* when Judge Brosman[59] pointed out its inherent weakness which is that it provides no criteria for the guidance of the jury but hands the case to them for a verdict to be returned on the basis of intuition or conjecture rather than law. Judge Bazelon, who wrote the opinion in *Durham*, seems to have thought he was giving help to the jury by insistence upon "causal connection between such mental abnormality and the act," [60] but "the *Durham* rule that mental disease or defect exonerates if the

Sobeloff, Insanity and the Criminal Law: From McNaghten to Durham and Beyond, 41 A.B.A.J. 793 (1955); Morris, Taft and Angus, Criminal Responsibility and Insanity: The Significance of Durham v. United States for Australian Courts, 3 Annual L.Rev. 309 (1955); Douglas, The Durham Rule: A Meeting Ground for Lawyers and Psychiatrists, 41 Iowa L.Rev. 485 (1956); Bennett, The Insanity Defense, A Perplexing Problem of Criminal Justice, 16 La.L.Rev. 484 (1956); Thornton, Military Law, 31 N.Y. U.L.Rev. 148, 155–7 (1956); Hall, Psychiatry and Criminal Responsibility, 65 Yale L.J. 761 (1956); Hall, In Defense of the McNaghten Rules, 42 A.B.A.J. 917 (1956). See also, among other notes and comments on Durham: 4 Buffalo L.Rev. 318 (1955); 54 Col.L.Rev. 1153 (1954); 40 Cornell L.Q. 135 (1954); 43 Geo.L.J. 58 (1954); 68 Harv.L.Rev. 364 (1954); 30 Ind.L.J. 194 (1955); 10 Rutgers L.Rev. 425 (1955); 9 Sw.L.J. 110 (1955); 33 Tex. L.Rev. 482 (1955); 29 Tul.L.Rev. 376 (1955); 40 W.Va.L.Rev. 799 (1954).

55. It was "warmly supported by psychiatrists." Model Penal Code 159 (Tent. Draft No. 4, 1955).

56. Wertham, Psychoauthoritarianism and the Law, 22 U. of Chi.L.Rev. 336, 337 (1955). An Australian psychiatrist concluded that "it is unlikely to make easier

the presentation in courts of law of psychiatric testimony in a form that will have meaning both for the legally qualified practitioner and for the psychiatrist." Angus, Criminal Responsibility and Insanity: The Significance of Durham v. United States for Australian Courts, 3 Annual L.Rev. 327, 333 (1955).

See Washington v. United States, 390 F.2d 444 (D.C. Cir. 1967).

57. Judge Hand found it inconvenient to contribute an article on the case but permitted a quotation from his letter. See 22 U. of Chi.L.Rev. at 319 (1955).

One writer referred to Durham as having established a "non-rule." Goldstein, The Insanity Defense 84 (1967).

58. United States News and World Report 62 (Feb. 11, 1955). But see Report No. 112 of the Senate Committee on the District of Columbia, 1967, which found no objection to the working of the rule as modified by later cases.

59. United States v. Smith, 5 U.S. C.M.A. 314, 17 C.M.R. 3 (1954).

60. Durham v. United States, 94 U.S. App.D.C. 228, 241, 242, 214 F.2d 862, 875 (1954). Judge Bazelon refers to inability to distinguish right from wrong as a "symptom" of mental disease but this could hardly be accepted by psychiatrists

unlawful act was its 'product' sets forth a concept of causation but affords no guide in determining the degree of causation that is to be required. . . . And . . . it may well be queried whether it is really an improvement on *M'Naghten* simply to 'pass the buck' to the jury." [61]

Durham received some slight support from lawmakers[62] but not from the courts.[63] And it was rejected by those drafting the Model Penal Code after the most careful consideration.[64] It seems to have had little more effect in this century than did the same position taken eighty-four years earlier by the New Hampshire Court.

The court that decided *Durham* did not like the way this approach was working and attempted to modify the testimony being given.[65] Later it said that "psychiatrists should not speak directly in terms of 'product' or even 'result' or 'cause.' " [66] After struggling with *Durham* for 18 years the court overruled it in favor of the substantial capacity standard of the Model Penal Code.[67] The court observed that the District of Columbia courts had struggled with the "product" or causation element of the *Durham* rule. Once

who frequently question the ability of scientists to make such a determination. See, for example, a quotation from an address by Dr. Gregory Zilboorg, Guttmacher & Weihofen, 406–7 (1952).

The court later found it necessary to modify its position to some extent. See McDonald v. United States, 312 F.2d 847, 851 (D.C.Cir. 1962); Washington v. United States, 390 F.2d 444 (D.C.Cir. 1967). In the latter case it said: "A judgment of acquittal by reason of insanity is appropriate only when a jury verdict of guilty would clearly violate the law or the facts." Id. at 446. See Acheson, McDonald v. United States: The Durham Rule Redefined, 51 Geo.L.J. 580 (1963).

Where evidence to the effect that D was suffering from a mental disease or defect and that the crime was the product thereof, was disputed by other evidence to the contrary, it was not error for the judge to refuse to direct a judgment of acquittal. Hence a conviction of second-degree murder was affirmed on appeal. Stewart v. United States, 394 F.2d 778 (D.C.Cir. 1968).

61. Thornton, Military Law, 31 N.Y. U.L.Rev. 148, 156–7 (1956). "But the emphasis of the Durham test is on the question of causation; and here too the jury can do no more than speculate." Hall, Psychiatry and Criminal Responsibility, 65 Yale L.J. 761, 779–80 (1956).

62. Maine adopted the position of *Durham* by statute. 15 M.R.S.A. (Me.) § 102 (1965). State v. Armstrong, 344 A.2d 42, 51–52 (Me. 1975); State v. Wallace, 333 A.2d 72, 75–76 (Me. 1975). Maine has now rejected *Durham* and adopted the substantial capacity standard.

In the Virgin Islands 14 V.I.C. § 14(4) (1964) provides: "All persons are capable of committing crimes or offenses except: . . . persons who are mentally ill and committed the act charged against them in consequence of such mental illness." This seems to state the "product rule" of *Durham*, but the court has held that this statute is not at odds with the *Currens* rule which is that acquittal should result if at the time of the alleged conduct, the defendant, as a result of mental disease or defect, lacked substantial capacity to conform his conduct to the requirements of the law. Government of Virgin Islands v. Fredericks, 578 F.2d 927 (3d Cir. 1978).

63. In the first six years, *Durham* was rejected by five federal courts and the courts of twenty-two states. Krash, The Durham Rule and Judicial Administration of the Insanity Defense in the District of Columbia, 70 Yale L.J. 905, 906 n. 8 (1961). It still seems not to have been adopted by any other court.

64. "The draft rejects the formulation warmly supported by psychiatrists and recently adopted by the Court of Appeals for the District of Columbia in Durham v. United States, . . ." Model Penal Code 159 (Tent.Draft No. 4, 1955).

65. McDonald v. United States, 114 U.S.App.D.C. 120, 312 F.2d 847 (1962).

66. Washington v. United States, 129 U.S.App.D.C. 29, 41, 390 F.2d 444, 455–56 (1967).

67. United States v. Brawner, 153 U.S.App.D.C. 1, 471 F.2d 969 (1972).

mental disease, in the legal sense, had been established, causation became the ultimate issue. Expert testimony often represented "nothing more than the witness's own conclusion about the defendant's criminal responsibility." [68]

H. THE "SUBSTANTIAL CAPACITY" STANDARD

The solution proposed in the Model Penal Code is as follows: [69]

"(1) A person is not responsible for criminal conduct if at the time of such conduct as a result of mental disease or defect he lacks substantial capacity either to appreciate the criminality [wrongfulness] of his conduct or to conform his conduct to the requirements of law.

"(2) As used in this Article, the terms 'mental disease or defect' do not include an abnormality manifested only by repeated criminal or otherwise antisocial conduct."

This, it should be emphasized, proposes to test criminal capacity in such cases by a standard rather than by any rule. A legal rule is a device for attaching a clear-cut legal consequence to a clear-cut state of facts.[70] For example: A writing which meets all other requirements but does not have words of negotiability is not a negotiable instrument. A legal standard, on the other hand, does not generalize by eliminating the features of particular cases or particularize by including them, but offers a guide to enable fact finders to apply common sense to various situations in which the facts will ordinarily differ from case to case,[71] such as the standard of a reasonable person under like circumstances used to test due care in driving on the highway.

The Code seems to be adapting the reasonable person standard to this situation. The application is different because the problem is different. *Any* reasonable person would have substantial capacity to appreciate the wrongfulness of the harmful act in question and to conform his conduct to the requirements of law (not, of course, that every reasonable person would so conform, but only that he would have the capacity). Hence if **D**, by reason of mental disease or defect, was so far from normal that he did not have that substantial capacity, he was lacking in reason and should not be held criminally accountable for his conduct.

Unlike *Durham*, the formula of the Model Code has experienced a friendly reception by courts and legislative bodies.[72] The Massachusetts court,

---

68. Id. n. 67, 471 F.2d at 979.

69. Section 4.01.

70. "A rule is a precept attaching a definite detailed legal consequence to a definite detailed state of facts." Pound, Justice According to Law 56 (1951).

71. Pound, Criminal Justice in America 30–1 (1945).

72. In substituting the Model Code formula for the M'Naghten wording which had been followed for over a hundred years it was said: "Adhering to the fundamental concepts of free will and criminal responsibility, the American Law Institute test restates M'Naghten in

language consonant with the current legal and psychological thought . . . . It has won widespread acceptance, having been adopted by every federal circuit except for the first circuit and by fifteen states." People v. Drew, 22 Cal.3d 333, 149 Cal.Rptr. 275, 281, 583 P.2d 1318, 1324 (1978). The court cited:

Alaska: Schade v. State, 512 P.2d 907, (Alaska, 1973). Connecticut: Conn.Gen.Stats., § 53a–13. Idaho: State v. White, supra, 93 Idaho 153, 456 P.2d 797 (1969). Illinois: Ill.Rev. Stats., ch. 38, § 6–2. Indiana: Hill v. State, 252 Ind. 601, 251 N.E.2d 429

which has long applied M'Naghten supplemented by the irresistible impulse test, concluded that the Code's position was in effect a codification of its own, although it decided the wording of the Code was preferable.[73]

The Rhode Island Supreme Court has adopted an interesting variation on the Model Penal Code test. That court has stated the test to be:

"A person is not responsible for criminal conduct, if at the time of such conduct, as a result of mental disease or defect, his capacity either to appreciate the wrongfulness of his conduct or to conform his conduct to the requirements of the law is so substantially impaired that he cannot justly be held responsible.

"The terms 'mental disease or defect' do not include an abnormality manifested only by repeated criminal or otherwise antisocial conduct."[74]

The test is similar to that proposed by the British Royal Commission on Capital Punishment in 1953.[75] The court believed it was appropriate to leave the responsibility issue, to some extent, to the jury's sense of community justice.

THE NEW PENAL CODES

Some of the new penal codes have adopted the substantial capacity standard of the Model Penal Code by copying the essential wording,[76] and some by using equivalent language.[77] On the other hand some have adopted M'Naghten[78] or M'Naghten plus irresistible impulse.[79]

(1969). Kentucky: Terry v. Commonwealth, 371 S.W.2d 862 (Ky. 1963). Maryland: Md.Code, art. 59, § 25. Massachusetts: Commonwealth v. McHoul, 352 Mass. 544, 226 N.E.2d 556 (1967). Missouri: Rev.Stats.Mo., § 552.030(3)(1). Montana: Mont.Rev. Codes, § 95–501. Ohio: State v. Statton, 18 Ohio St.2d 13, 247 N.E.2d 293 (1969). Oregon: ORS 161.295(1). Texas: V.T.C.A., Penal Code § 8.01. Vermont: Vt.Stats., tit. 13, § 4801. Wisconsin: State v. Shoffner, 31 Wis.2d 412, 143 N.W.2d 458 (1966).

See also United States v. Frederick, 3 M.J. 230 (C.M.A. 1977).

In rejecting an effort to have the court adopt the Model Penal Code provision as to insanity, it was held that the M'Naghten rule is the proper test for insanity. State v. Noble, 113 Ariz. 99, 546 P.2d 1130 (1976). "The test long utilized in Kansas for such determination is the M'Naghten rule." Application of Jones, 228 Kan. 90, 612 P.2d 1211 (1980). "The M'Naghten rule has long been the test for criminal responsibility in the State of Nevada, . . ." Clark v. State, 95 Nev. 24, 588 P.2d 1027, 1029 (1979). Reaffirmed, Poole v. State, ___ Nev. ___, 625 P.2d 1163 (1981). The "M'Naghten Rule is the present and exclusive test to deter-

mine the question of insanity." Richardson v. State, 569 P.2d 1018, 1019–20 (Okl. Cr.App. 1977). It was pointed out "that the legislature has codified the M'Naghten rule in RCW 9A.12.010, . . ." State v. Crenshaw, 27 Wn.App. 326, 617 P.2d 1041, 1047 n. 1 (1980).

73. An instruction defining "lack of substantial capacity" as "capacity which has been impaired to such a degree that only an extremely limited amount remains" gave proper guidance to the jury. State v. Nuetzel, 606 P.2d 920, 930, 931 (Hawaii 1980).

74. State v. Johnson, ___ R.I. ___, 399 A.2d 469, 476 (1979).

75. The Royal Commission proposed a test that a person would not be responsible for his unlawful act if at the time of the act "the accused was suffering from a disease of the mind to such a degree that he ought not to be held responsible."

76. E.g., Alabama, Connecticut, Hawaii, Illinois, Kentucky, Maine, Oregon and Utah.

77. E.g., Arkansas and Delaware.

78. E.g., Iowa, Louisiana, Minnesota, New York and Washington.

79. E.g., Colorado, Georgia and Texas.

I. DIMINISHED CAPACITY

For obvious reasons the legal conception of criminal capacity can neither be limited to those of high intellectual endowments nor restricted to those of average mental powers. A few may be recognized as so far from normal as to be entirely beyond the reach of criminal justice but this device for social control must be potentially applicable to the "mine run" of the population, so to speak, and therefore must be capable of reaching most of those below the median line as well as all above it. Hence criminal incapacity is not established by a mere showing of weakness of intellect, a low order of intellect, susceptibility to suggestion,[80] or a sub-normal mentality.[81] Neither is it sufficient to show that defendant is more ignorant and more stupid than common people[82] or is an illiterate, ignorant and passionate person,[83] or (without additional showing) is suffering from "shell shock."[84] Furthermore one may have criminal capacity although of an irritable temper and excitable disposition[85] or despite being deaf and dumb;[86] and needless to say a harmful act is punishable although committed by an incorrigible offender.[87]

80. People v. Hurley, 8 Cal. 390 (1857); State v. Palmer, 161 Mo. 152, 61 S.W. 651 (1901); Powell v. State, 37 Tex. 348 (1872); Commonwealth v. Szachewicz, 303 Pa. 410, 154 A. 483 (1931).

81. "A sub-normal mentality is not a defense to a charge of crime unless the accused is by reason thereof unable to distinguish between right and wrong with respect to the particular act in question." People v. Marquis, 344 Ill. 261, 267, 176 N.E. 314, 316 (1931). Accord, Daniels v. State, 186 Ark. 255, 53 S.W.2d 231 (1932).

82. United States v. Cornell, 25 Fed. Cas.No. 14,868 (1820).

83. Fitzpatrick v. Commonwealth, 81 Ky. 357 (1883). Accord, Tuggle v. State, 73 Okl.Cr. 208, 119 P.2d 857 (1941).

84. "Shell-shock" does not constitute such insanity as to bar criminal responsibility if there is sufficient reasoning capacity to distinguish between right and wrong as to the particular act and knowledge and consciousness that it is wrong and criminal, and will be subject to punishment. People v. Gilberg, 197 Cal. 306, 240 P. 1000 (1925).

But see E. Burke, Vietnam Stress A Winner in Drug Case, Nat'l L.J., Oct. 6, 1980 at 4 col. 1; E. Burke, The 'Bombshell' Defense: Vietnam Stress Disorder Wins Acquittals, Lower Sentences for Veterans, Nat'l L.J., May 12, 1980 at 1 col. 1.

85. Willis v. People, 32 N.Y. 715 (1865). One who loses control of his mind as a result of passion is not excused whether the passion is of an amorous nature or the result of hate, prejudice or vengeance. Korsak v. State, 202 Ark. 921, 154 S.W.2d 348 (1941). It is no defense that defendant became so depraved that his conscience ceased to influence his conduct. State v. Moore, 42 N.M. 135, 76 P.2d 19 (1938).

86. Regina v. Whitfield, 3 Car. & K. 121, 175 Eng.Rep. 488 (1850). In ancient times there was no known method of communicating ideas to one who was *born* deaf, blind and dumb. Hence the early law presumed such a person to be an idiot. 1 Bl.Comm. *304. But since it is now known that such an unfortunate is not by reason of this fact alone "wanting all those senses which furnish the human mind with ideas" (ibid.), this presumption no longer prevails. See State v. Howard, 118 Mo. 127, 143, 24 S.W. 41, 45 (1893). Thus the test of the contractual capacity of such persons "is placed upon its proper ground—their mental capacity." Barnett v. Barnett, 54 N.C. 221, 222 (1854).

87. "(2) As used in this Article, the terms 'mental disease or defect' do not include abnormality manifested only by repeated criminal or otherwise antisocial conduct." Model Penal Code § 4.01. It has been argued that such a person should not be punished because he cannot be deterred but it is necessary to consider the protection of the community and the effect upon others.

Hale divided the subject of mental disorder into (1) partial insanity and (2) total insanity,[88] the latter being characterized by him as "total alienation of the mind," thus picturing the "total deprivation of memory and understanding" concept anciently read into the word "insanity" itself. Partial insanity he said may be (1) "in respect to things" or (2) "in respect of degrees," saying in reference to the first: "some persons, that have a competent use of reason in respect of some subjects, are yet under a particular *dementia* in respect of some particular discourses, subjects or applications . . .."

This suggests the idea of "monomania." If we think of a house divided into rooms, walled apart with soundproof partitions, permitting one room to be in the wildest confusion while order prevails in the rest of the building, we have the basis for a very fair analogy to the primitive notion of what might take place in the human mind. From the standpoint of science, however, this is quite an obsolete theory. The mind is not composed of independent compartments. It is not a group of units, but is itself a unit, the parts of which are so interrelated and interdependent that unsoundness at any point disturbs the soundness of the whole.[89] Hence, if we are to speak without contradiction it is necessary to abandon Hale's subdivision of partial insanity "in respect to things."

Partial insanity "in respect of degrees" is an outgrowth of the ancient notion that insanity referred to one totally deprived of his understanding and memory. Starting with this point of view any recognition of mental disorders of a lesser kind or degree suggested the idea of "partial insanity." If the matter were so simple as to permit a classification of minds as (1) sane, (2) partially insane, and (3) totally insane, representing well-defined groups to which legal consequences might be assigned, without further inquiry, it would be highly desirable for this to be done. The actual complexities, however, are such that an oversimplification of this nature would tend to confusion rather than to clarity. It is highly unlikely that one "totally insane" in the original sense would offer any legal problem at the present time. His case will take care of itself.[90] If only one legal problem were involved, the phrase "partial insanity" might be assigned to mental disorder which is less than total deprivation of memory and understanding but still requires a legal consequence other than when no insanity is present. But many different problems may be involved, as previously mentioned, and disorder which incapacitates for one purpose may not do so for another. Hence the search is not for a label such as "insanity" or "partial insanity," but for mental disease or defect of such a kind and degree as to negative criminal capacity, testamentary capacity, capacity to stand trial or whatever the particular problem may be.

88. 1 Hale P.C. *30.

89. "So long as we bear in mind that mental life consists primarily of a striving (conation) of certain innate tendencies (instincts), elaborated into sentiments (and complexes), toward more or less consciously conceived goals; that the higher mental processes involved in intention cannot be divorced from the conative-emotional modes of mental life and the sentiments built about them; so long, in brief, as we bear in mind the *unity of mind*, we will run little danger of becoming confused. . . ." Glueck, Mental Disorder and the Criminal Law 119 (1925), with a footnote reference to McDougall, Body and Mind c. XXI (5th ed.).

90. "But these cases are not only extremely rare, but can never become the object of judicial difficulty. There can be but one judgment concerning them." From Erskine's famous argument in Hadfield's Case, 27 Howell St.Tr. 1281, 1313 (1800).

"Partial insanity in respect of degrees," therefore, does not involve the element of contradiction inherent in the reference to "partial insanity in respect to things;" but it seems to make no contribution. One who is "partially insane" may or may not have criminal capacity, depending upon the nature and extent of his mental disorder,[91] but this can be said as effectively without the use of the adverb. Furthermore, we are never upon a secure footing in this field until we recognize that, as the word is commonly used at the present time, it is possible for an insane person to be guilty of crime—that it is only insanity of a certain kind or degree which precludes criminal guilt.[92]

Whether anything may be considered advantageously under the head of "partial responsibility" remains to be considered. As one may commit homicide unlawfully, but under a sudden heat of passion engendered by such provocation that the offense will be manslaughter rather than murder because of the law's recognition of the "frailty of the human frame," [93] it is clear that partial responsibility is not unknown to the law. The present inquiry, however, is whether there may be a partial lack of criminal responsibility due to a partial lack of criminal capacity,—or in other words, does the criminal law take notice of diminished or partial criminal capacity?

From one point of view an affirmative answer is required because, without going beyond the right-wrong test, the inquiry is not necessarily inability to distinguish right from wrong in general, but such inability "in respect to the very act with which he is charged." Thus in legal theory at least one who has done two quite different prohibited acts at the same time, while laboring under mental disease or defect of a certain nature, might be found to have had criminal capacity with reference to one and not as to the other. This, however, is not the point at which such an inquiry is ordinarily directed. Whether the phrase is partial responsibility, or as seems preferable, diminished or partial capacity, the problem usually is whether or not mental disease or defect insufficient to require an acquittal may call for conviction of some lesser grade or degree of crime than would otherwise be the case. "Can evidence of some degree of mental unsoundness reduce to murder in the second degree or manslaughter a crime which had the defendant been perfectly sound mentally, would have been first degree murder?" [94] If the

91. State v. Hockett, 70 Iowa 442, 30 N.W. 742 (1886); Commonwealth v. Rogers, 48 Mass. 500 (1844); State v. Harrison, 36 W.Va. 729, 15 S.E. 982 (1892).

". . . the law does not recognize every degree of feeble-mindedness as a defense to a criminal charge . . .." State v. Schilling, 95 N.J.L. 145, 148, 112 A. 400, 402 (1920).

92. "The kind and degree of insanity available as a defense to crime has many times been defined by the decisions of this court." People v. Gilberg, 197 Cal. 306, 313, 240 P. 1000, 1003 (1925). "Whilst such a person could not be regarded as sane, yet he would be criminally responsible for his acts, unless . . . .." State v. Stickley, 41 Iowa 232, 240 (1875). "If he was insane at the time to the extent . . . .." State v. Stras-

burg, 60 Wash. 106, 119, 110 P. 1020, 1024 (1910). "Much of the criticism directed from the medical side is based upon a misapprehension . . . .. When once it is appreciated that the question is a *legal* question, and that the law is that a person of unsound mind *may* be criminally responsible, the criticism based upon a supposed clash between the legal and medical conceptions of insanity disappears." Report of Lord Atkin's committee published in 1923. Quoted in Meredith, Insanity as a Criminal Defence, 112.

93. State v. Hill, 20 N.C. 629, 635 (1839).

94. Glueck, Mental Disorder and the Criminal Law, 199–200 (1925). "To conceive that an individual is either absolutely responsible or absolutely irresponsible

trial is for first degree murder in California, for example, may it be possible for such mental disorder to be shown as to support a conviction of some sort, but not of murder in the first degree, on the ground that defendant's mind at the time was incapable of a *deliberate* and *premeditated design* to effect the death of the person killed?[95]

The courts are not agreed as to how these questions should be answered. Some have rejected the notion that there may be mental disorder of such a nature as to diminish the degree of guilt without establishing innocence,[96] announcing flatly that insanity must be either a complete defense or none at all.[97] They have mentioned specifically that there is no grade of insanity sufficient to acquit of murder but not of manslaughter,[98] or to negative de-

is to fly in the face of perfectly patent facts that are in everybody's individual experience and is only comparable to such beliefs of the Middle Ages that a person is possessed of a devil or is not possessed of a devil, and therefore is or is not a free moral agent." White, Insanity and the Criminal Law 89 (1923); H. Fingarette & A. Hasse, Mental Disabilities and Criminal Responsibilities, 117–119 (1979).

95. The California statute provides other grounds for first-degree murder, but this may be the one relied upon in a particular case. See West's Ann.Cal.Pen. Code § 189 (1970).

96. Commonwealth v. Cooper, 219 Mass. 1, 106 N.E. 545 (1914); United States v. Fisher, 328 U.S. 463, 66 S.Ct. 1318 (1946). Weihofen found several states in this category. Weihofen, Mental Disorder as a Criminal Defense 185 (1954).

In a murder trial it is not error to refuse to give an instruction on the theory of "diminished responsibility" whereby the verdict would be reduced from second-degree murder to manslaughter. Stewart v. United States, 394 F.2d 778 (D.C.Cir.1968).

The Model Penal Code has this provision: "Evidence that the defendant suffered from a mental disease or defect is admissible whenever it is relevant to prove that the defendant did or did not have a state of mind which is an element of the offense." Section 4.02(1).

The concept of diminished capacity seems to have merit but it is not a constitutional requirement. Thus, Arizona's use of the M'Naghten rule without the qualification of diminished capacity does not involve a deprivation of due process. Narten v. Eyman, 460 F.2d 184 (9th Cir. 1972).

"We hold, . . . that until established by the General Assembly as a pro-

vision collateral to the Statutes governing insanity and extreme emotional distress, the doctrine of diminished responsibility may not be invoked in this State." Bates v. State, 386 A.2d 1139, 1134–44 (Del.1978).

The judge instructed the jury "that a person with a mind capable of knowing right from wrong must be regarded as capable of entertaining intent and of deliberating and premeditating." The Nevada court, which does not recognize diminished capacity, held this was not error. It was emphasized that the instruction did not tell the jury that such a person had intent, deliberation and premeditation, but only that he was capable of it. Ogden v. State, 96 Nev. 258, 607 P.2d 576, 578 (1980).

97. Commonwealth v. Wireback, 190 Pa. 138, 42 A. 542 (1899). "We have no degrees of insanity in the criminal law, and a person is entitled to be acquitted by reason of his insanity if he does not know the right or wrong of the act he is charged with; if he has sufficient mind to know and appreciate the fact that the act is wrong, he is held responsible for the act he commits, and the law is or should be measured out to each individual alike." Kirby v. State, 68 Tex.Cr.R. 63, 74, 150 S.W. 455, 460 (1912). ". . . we have but two classes of people, the 'sane' and the 'insane.' Actual insanity, however partial it may be, is, consequently, with us a defence, and not a mitigating circumstance, in a prosecution for a crime." Sage v. State, 91 Ind. 141, 145 (1883); Commonwealth v. Ahearn, 421 Pa. 311, 218 A.2d 561 (1966).

98. United States v. Lee, 4 Mackey 489 (D.C.1885); Witty v. State, 75 Tex.Cr. R. 440, 171 S.W. 229 (1914); State v. DiPaolo, 34 N.J. 279, 294, 168 A.2d 401, 409, cert. denied 368 U.S. 880, 82 S.Ct. 130 (1961).

liberation and premeditation and reduce a murder from first degree to second.[99] Other courts have reached the opposite conclusion, recognizing the possibility of unsoundness of mind of such a character as to negative guilt of a certain grade or degree without establishing innocence. These tribunals find no legal inconsistency in the notion that mental disorder may be such as to disprove guilt of murder without requiring an acquittal of manslaughter,[1] or may be such as to negative the element of wilfulness, deliberation and premeditation needed to establish a certain charge of murder in the first degree without disproving the malice aforethought which is sufficient to convict of murder in the second degree.[2]

Logic seems to favor the second view.[3] Just as intoxication, while not an excuse for crime, may disprove the presence of some particular state of mind and hence show "that the less and not the greater offense was in fact committed," [4] it would seem possible for mental disorder to be of such a nature as to produce the same result. The problem may be approached from another angle, once more limiting the attention to the right-wrong test of insanity. Since the question is not ability to distinguish right from wrong in general "but in respect to the very act," there would be no legal inconsistency in the notion that a man suffering from mental disorder of a certain nature could make this distinction with reference to killing a man but not with reference

---

99. Fisher v. United States, 328 U.S. 463, 66 S.Ct. 1318 (1946).

1. Fisher v. People, 23 Ill. 283, 295 (1860); People v. Henderson, 60 Cal.2d 482, 35 Cal.Rptr. 77, 386 P.2d 677 (1963).

Diminished capacity is relevant in a murder prosecution not only on the issues of deliberation and premeditation but also on the issue of malice aforethought, whether caused by intoxication, trauma or disease. People v. Hoxie, 252 Cal.App.2d 901, 61 Cal.Rptr. 37 (1967).

A person who kills intentionally may be incapable of harboring malice aforethought because of diminished capacity, and in such a case his killing is voluntary manslaughter. People v. Cruz, 26 Cal.3d 233, 162 Cal.Rptr. 1, 605 P.2d 830, 834 (1980).

The defense of diminished capacity is not available if the crime does not require any specific intent or other special mental element. Mill v. State, 585 P.2d 546 (Alaska, 1978). It does not apply for example to the offense of assault with a dangerous weapon.

"We hold that to prove a section 95–503 defense (diminished-capacity defense), a defendant must prove by a preponderance of the evidence that he lacked the ability, due to mental disease or defect, to form that criminal mental state which is defined by statute as an element of the crime with which he is charged." State v. McKenzie, ___ Mont. ___, 608 P.2d 428, 454 (1980).

"A defendant then, due to mental disease or defect precluding him from forming the intent to commit criminal homicide, might be found guilty of the lesser included offense of aggravated assault." State v. McKenzie, ___ Mont. ___, 608 P.2d 428, 453 (1980).

The Colorado court has held that evidence of diminished capacity due to a chemical brain disorder is relevant to a defendant's ability to form the intent to kill. People v. Gallegos, ___ Colo. ___, 628 P.2d 999 (1981).

2. People v. Bassett, 69 Cal.2d 122, 70 Cal.Rptr. 193, 443 P.2d 777 (1968); Becksted v. People, 133 Colo. 72, 292 P.2d 189 (1956); State v. Anselmo, 46 Utah 137, 148 P. 1071 (1915). Weihofen found at least ten states in this category. Weihofen, Mental Disorder as a Criminal Defense 183–84 (1954).

3. See Keedy, Insanity and Criminal Responsibility, 30 Harv.L.Rev. 535, 552–4 (1917); Glueck, Mental Disorder and the Criminal Law, 199 et seq. (1925). And see Note, Mental or Emotional Disturbance as Diminishing Responsibility for Crime, 22 A.L.R.3d 1228 (1968).

Because of the evidence in this arson case it was reversible error for the judge to refuse to instruct on the defense of diminished intent. State v. Stockett, 28 Or. App. 35, 558 P.2d 1241 (1977).

4. State v. Johnson, 40 Conn. 136, 144 (1873).

to burning a building. If so he would have criminal capacity to commit murder, but not to commit arson, and it would seem to follow that if he were charged with first degree murder on the ground that he committed homicide while perpetrating arson, the circumstances might be such as to establish only murder in the second degree on the ground that his burning would not amount to arson.[5]

After all—if the state of mind requisite for guilt of the offense charged was missing, whether because of mental disease or defect or for any other reason, the crime has not been committed. "Mental capacity to commit a crime is a material part of total guilt for there can be no crime without mens rea." [6]

J. GUILTY BUT MENTALLY ILL

WHY IS INSANITY A DEFENSE?

The word "insanity" is frequently used in the criminal law to mean mental disease or defect of such a nature and degree as to meet the legal requirements for acquittal of the offense charged in the jurisdiction. Using the word in this sense it may be pointed out that an important question, which is frequently overlooked, is this: Why is insanity a defense to a charge of crime?

Under the prevailing view insanity is a defense because it negatives an element of the offense charged. "Mental capacity to commit a crime is a material part of the total guilt for there can be no crime without mens rea." [7] "According to the M'Naghten rule, those who do not understand the nature and quality of their actions or do not know that what they do is wrong, are incapable of forming criminal intent." [8] "The sanity of the accused is always an element of the crime charged." [9] "(I)diots, lunatics, and insane persons are not of sound mind, cannot entertain general criminal intent, and therefore cannot commit criminal acts." [10] "The burden of proof in a criminal prosecution as to all essential elements of the crime, including the sanity of the defendant, of course, rests upon the prosecution . . . ." [11]

---

5. Cf. People v. Roper, 259 N.Y. 170, 181 N.E. 88 (1932).

6. State v. Daniels, 106 Ariz. 497, 478 P.2d 522, 527 (1970). See Lewin, "Psychiatric Evidence in Criminal Cases for Purposes Other Than the Defense of Insanity," 26 Syracuse L.Rev. 1051 (1975); Arehella, "The Diminished Capacity and Diminished Responsibility Defenses: Two Children of a Doomed Marriage", 77 Colum.L.Rev. 327 (1977).

7. State v. Daniels, 106 Ariz. 497, 478 P.2d 522, 527 (1970). "However, the burden ultimately rests with the State to prove the defendant sane at the time of the alleged offense to the exclusion of every reasonable doubt." Mayes v. State, __ Ind.App. __, 417 N.E.2d 1147, 1153 (1981).

8. State v. Steelman, 120 Ariz. 301, 585 P.2d 1213, 1225 (1978).

9. United States v. Hall, 583 F.2d 1288, 1293 (5th Cir. 1978).

10. In re Ramon M., 22 Cal.3d 419, 149 Cal.Rptr. 387, 390, 584 P.2d 524, 527 (1978).

11. United States v. Carr, 550 F.2d 1058, 1059 (6th Cir. 1977).

Statements worded in terms of sanity as, or as not, an element of the crime are in the nature of semantic shorthand. If the statement is that sanity is an element of the crime, the court has in mind that insanity negates the possibility of mens rea, so that unless defendant was sane he could not have the mental element required for guilt. If the statement is that sanity is not an element of the crime, the

Some courts, on the other hand, consider that proof of insanity does not disprove any element of the offense charged, but establishes an excuse which entitles defendant to an acquittal. "In this state, sanity is not considered an element of the offense . . . ." [12] It "is not an element of the crime; rather it involves the separate issue of capacity, . . ." [13] This is the position of the Supreme Court. It has held that the Due Process Clause requires the prosecution to prove beyond a reasonable doubt all the elements of the offense charged.[14] This was reinforced later. The Court conceded that in a proper situation a presumption may require a defendant to introduce enough evidence to make some certain element of the crime an issue in the case, if he makes such a claim. Without such evidence this element is established by the presumption; with such evidence the presumption is overcome, and the prosecution has the burden of establishing this element by proof beyond a reasonable doubt—the same as any other element. But, it was *held*, it is unconstitutional for the presumption to go further and place upon the defendant the burden of proving the nonexistence of this element.[15] This makes clear the position of the Court on the nature of the insanity defense when it holds that the state may validly place the burden of proving insanity on the defendant,[16] because proof of insanity "does not serve to negative any facts of the crime which the state is to prove to convict of murder. It constitutes a separate issue on which the defendant is required to carry the burden of persuasion." [17]

It may be added that the diminished capacity concept, recognized in a number of jurisdictions, is that a mental disease or defect, although insufficient to establish a complete defense, may make a person incapable of entertaining the *mental element* required for guilt of some particular crime.[18]

The scope of the present undertaking does not permit consideration of procedural problems unless they become important in discussions of the substantive law. Were space available detailed attention would be given to the presumption of sanity[19] and the rules with reference to overcoming it,[20] to

court has in mind that insanity does not negate mens rea, but constitutes an excuse for what was done.

12. Clark v. State, 95 Nev. 24, 588 P.2d 1027, 1030 (1979).

13. Andrews v. State, 265 Ark. 390, 578 S.W.2d 585, 591 (1979).

14. Mullaney v. Wilbur, 421 U.S. 684, 95 S.Ct. 1881 (1975). And see Patterson v. New York, 432 U.S. 197, 211, 97 S.Ct. 2319, 2327 (1977).

15. Sandstrom v. United States, 442 U.S. 510, 99 S.Ct. 2450 (1979).

16. Leland v. Oregon, 343 U.S. 960, 72 S.Ct. 1002 (1952).

17. Patterson v. New York, 432 U.S. 197, 207, 97 S.Ct. 2319, 2325 (1977). Although not constitutionally required, the rule in federal courts is that the defendant does not have the burden of proving insanity. The prosecution must establish sanity by proof beyond a reasonable

doubt. Davis v. United States, 160 U.S. 469, 16 S.Ct. 353 (1895).

18. State v. McKenzie, 177 Mont. 280, 581 P.2d 1205 (1978). But the court added: "We hold that, to prove a section 95–502 defense, a defendant must prove by a preponderance of the evidence that he lacked the ability, due to mental disease or defect, to form that criminal mental state which is defined by statute as an element of the crime with which he is charged." Id. at 329, 581 P.2d 1233. But, as pointed out in the text, since this is dealing with an element of the offense charged, the Supreme Court holds that it violates the Due Process Clause to impose the burden of proof on the defendant.

19. Davis v. United States, 160 U.S. 469, 486, 16 S.Ct. 353, 357 (1895).

20. What seems to be the sound rule, although found in a minority of jurisdictions, is that the defendant has the bur-

the procedural provisions being proposed in the Model Penal Code,[21] to the so-called "bifurcated trial" authorized in some jurisdictions which provides for a separate trial of this issue if a plea of not guilty by reason of insanity is offered,[22] and to the law of Massachusetts. The Massachusetts law provides "that when a court doubts whether a defendant in a criminal case is competent to stand trial or is criminally responsible by reason of mental illness or mental defect it may at any stage of the proceedings order an examination by one or more qualified physicians." [23] This causes a careful study

den of producing evidence tending to show insanity, but if on all the proof the jury have a reasonable doubt of defendant's sanity at the time of the act, he is entitled to an acquittal. In most jurisdictions defendant has not only the burden of going forward, but also the risk of nonpersuasion, and must establish his insanity (dependent upon the jurisdiction) (1) by a preponderance of the evidence, (2) to the satisfaction of the jury, or (3) beyond a reasonable doubt. Weihofen, Insanity as a Defense in Criminal Law 172–200 (1933). And see Weihofen, Mental Disorder as a Criminal Defense 212–272 (1954).

A state statute requiring **D** to prove insanity beyond a reasonable doubt was held not to violate due process. Leland v. Oregon, 343 U.S. 790, 72 S.Ct. 1002 (1952). In Patterson v. New York, 432 U.S. 197, 97 S.Ct. 2319 (1977), the Supreme Court held that requiring the defendant to bear the burden of proving the affirmative defense of insanity did not violate due process of law.

The state may rely upon the presumption of sanity if the point is not raised by **D**. Cox v. Page, 431 P.2d 954 (Okl.Cr. 1967).

An early draft of the Model Penal Code included an alternative provision requiring the defendant to establish the defense of mental disease or defect by "a preponderance of the evidence." Model Penal Code, § 4.03(1) (Tent. Draft No. 4, 1955). This was eliminated by a vote of the Institute at the May 1955 meeting.

The accused is presumed sane until the contrary is shown. Insanity is an affirmative defense and **D** has the burden of proving insanity by a preponderance of the evidence. Criswell v. State, 84 Nev. 459, 443 P.2d 552 (1968).

21. Sections 4.02–4.09.

22. If defendant pleads not guilty and also not guilty by reason of insanity he is tried first upon the not guilty plea and in that trial he is conclusively presumed to have been sane at the time of the alleged crime. If found guilty on that trial he is

then tried again by the same or another jury to determine whether or not he was insane. West's Ann.Cal.Pen.Code § 1026 (1980). Under such procedure it was said that evidence tending to show incapacity to commit the crime because of insanity would be inadmissible in the first trial, but that on such trial it would be error to exclude evidence of mental disorder tending to disprove (1) malice aforethought in a murder trial, (2) deliberation and premeditation in a first-degree murder trial, or (3) the specific intent to steal or to commit felony in a trial for burglary. People v. Wells, 33 Cal.2d 330, 202 P.2d 53 (1949). And see Leich v. People, 131 Colo. 353, 281 P.2d 806 (1955).

In a burglary trial psychiatrists were prepared to testify that by reason of mental disease **W** had a delusion that the apartment he entered was his. It was pointed out that if this was true he did not enter with intent to commit theft and hence was not guilty of burglary. And it was held reversible error to exclude this evidence from the guilt phase of the trial, although it would establish innocence because of insanity. The court indicated that the bifurcated trial in insanity cases was not working as expected and suggested that the legislature reconsider the wisdom of such procedure. People v. Wetmore, 22 Cal.3d 318, 149 Cal.Rptr. 265, 583 P.2d 1308 (1978).

It was held that the Wyoming statute which provides for a bifurcated trial if defendant pleads both not guilty and not guilty by reason of insanity, violates the State and Federal Constitutions and was applied in violation of due process. Sanchez v. State, 567 P.2d 270 (Wyo. 1977).

See Louisell and Hazard, Insanity as a Defense, The Bifurcated Trial, 49 Calif.L. Rev. 805 (1961).

23. Mass.Ann.Laws, ch. 123 § 15 (1972). This section authorizes court ordered examinations to determine both competency to stand trial and criminal responsibility. Blaisdell v. Commonwealth, 372 Mass. 753, 364 N.E.2d 191 (1977).

of the defendant by competent medical personnel, under favorable circumstances, producing an unbiased report available to both sides and to the court, and seems to have resulted in a satisfactory disposition of most of such cases without the need of a jury trial.[24]

Although these interesting procedural matters must be by-passed here there are others requiring attention, including particularly legislative efforts to change the trial by taking the insanity issue away from the jury. The early "no mind" theory of the insanity defense, it may be mentioned by way of preface, had the merit of being definitely clear-cut. There was little difficulty in putting the matter to the jury on that basis, and when Judge Tracy instructed the jury in 1724 [25] that "to be such a madman as is to be exempted from punishment, it must be a man that is totally deprived of his understanding and memory, and doth not know what he is doing, no more than . . . a wild beast," he was using the "wild beast" merely as an illustration to drive home the point that a defendant had criminal capacity unless he was entirely bereft of his reason. And without doubt the jury were able to grasp this point and apply it to the case. Every step in the relaxation of this rigid law has been accompanied by a corresponding difficulty in finding words to convey the idea to the jury, and an additional difficulty on the part of the jury in applying the law to the facts of the case. Difficulties such as these, within reasonable limits, must be tolerated in order to permit the law to grow and develop as civilization progresses, but they cannot be ignored.

The classical school proceeded upon the theory that each offense should carry the exact amount of punishment which it "merited." This led to the dividing of crimes into degrees and otherwise in order that circumstances of mitigation or aggravation should all be provided for in advance. This notion is largely giving way in favor of the view that there should be substantial opportunity to individualize the treatment in order to make provision for factors other than the nature of the offense and the circumstances of its commission,[26] but this seems largely to have been overlooked insofar as mental disease or defect is concerned.

The needless assumption that unsoundness of mind at the time of the transgression is a matter to be considered only at the point of determining guilt or innocence, has caused the attempt to inject into the trial refinements with which the jury is utterly unable to cope. Realization of the fact that jurors were being asked to solve problems quite beyond the capabilities of the ordinary layman led to attempts to change the procedure by taking the insanity issue entirely away from the jury, but this impinged upon the substantive criminal law. Defendant's right to have his guilt or innocence decided by a jury necessarily included the right to have every determinant of cul-

24. Overholser, The Psychiatrist and the Law 120–5 (1953).

25. Rex v. Arnold, 16 Howell St.Tr. 697, 764–5 (1724).

26. The jurisdictions have recently moved away from individualized sentencing and treatment by enacting various forms of determinate sentencing statutes which equalize the penalties among categories of offenders regardless of the individual characteristics of the crime or the offender. Determinate Sentencing, National Institute of Law Enforcement and Criminal Justice, et al. (1978). This movement has been validly criticized in the literature by experienced members of the legal profession and scholars. Forear, Criminals and Victims (1980); A. Von Hirsch, Doing Justice (1976); Morris, The Future of Imprisonment (1974); Crump, Determinate Sentencing: The Promises and Perils of Sentence Guidelines, 68 Ky.L.J. 1 (1979).

pability disposed of in that manner, and this required a change in the law of criminal capacity in order to accomplish the result intended. Had these attempts succeeded, although this may have been overlooked by legislators, it would have carried us back not merely to the time of the "wild beast" test, but to the much earlier time when even the driveling idiot and the raving madman had criminal capacity and could be convicted the same as one whose reason was unimpaired. The fact that much wiser provisions were to be made for dealing with one so convicted than had anciently been found, could not change the underlying legal theory. The first enactment of this nature, passed in Washington in 1909, provided: [27]

"It shall be no defense to a person charged with the commission of a crime, that at the time of its commission, he was unable by reason of insanity, idiocy or imbecility, to comprehend the nature and quality of the act committed, or to understand that it was wrong; or that he was afflicted with a morbid propensity to commit prohibited acts, nor shall any testimony or other proof thereof be admitted in evidence."

This was held unconstitutional because it prevented the defendant from establishing his innocence by disproving the possibility of "criminal intent" (mens rea) at the time of the crime.[28] A Mississippi statute declaring that "the insanity of the defendant at the time of the commission of the crime shall not be a defense against indictments for murder," met a similar fate,[29] as did also a Louisiana enactment which provided in substance for a "bifurcated" trial in which the jury might pass upon other matters, but the defendant's sanity or insanity was withdrawn from them and left for the determination of a lunacy commission.[30]

One all-too-common difficulty is illustrated by Yankulov [31] in which one recently found not guilty by reason of insanity was released on habeas corpus although admittedly there had been no change in his mental condition. The court took the position, not expressed in words, that the jury's mistake in returning such a verdict in one case would not authorize the court in depriving one of sound mind of his liberty on the pretense that he was incompetent. In England, at one time, such a verdict resulted in commit-

---

27. Wash.Laws of 1909, p. 892.

28. State v. Strasburg, 60 Wash. 106, 110 P. 1020 (1910).

29. Sinclair v. State, 161 Miss. 142, 132 So. 581 (1931).

30. State v. Lange, 168 La. 958, 123 So. 639 (1929).

One court has seen the basic problem involved but with no appreciation of the solution. It said: "The ideal solution, perhaps, would be to exclude the question of criminal responsibility from the trial, leaving to penologists the answers to the question of criminal responsibility, with leave to record the court's commitment as criminal or civil depending upon the answer to that question and to the question of the kind and duration of the custodial care and treatment he receives." United States v. Chandler, 393 F.2d 920, 928 (4th Cir. 1968).

One piece of legislation to revise the Federal Penal Code, H.R. 6046, 93d Congress, 1st Session (1973) § 502, provided as to insanity, "It is a defense to a prosecution under any federal statute that the defendant, as a result of mental disease or defect, lacked the state of mind required as an element of the offense charged. Mental disease or defect does not otherwise constitute a defense." See also Goldstein and Katz, Abolish the Insanity Defense—Why Not?, 72 Yale L.J. 583 (1963); Wales, An Analysis of the Proposal to "Abolish" the Insanity Defense in S 1: Squeezing a Lemon, 124 Pa. L.Rev. 687 (1976).

31. Yankulov v. Bushong, 80 Ohio App. 497, 77 N.E.2d 88 (1945). See also In re Remus, 119 Ohio St. 166, 162 N.E. 740 (1928).

ment to a hospital during the king's (queen's) pleasure and it so seldom pleased the monarch to do anything about the matter that the normal result was hospitalization for life, for which reason such a plea was used only as a last resort.[32] In Massachusetts a former law was quite similar, such a verdict resulting in a commitment to a hospital for life with power reserved to the governor to grant a release when satisfied after an investigation by the department of mental diseases that such discharge will not cause danger to others.[33] Such a statute today would be held to violate constitutional provisions in this country unless there were some review of the commitment. Massachusetts law currently provides for a limited commitment, mental examination and evaluation and a periodic review.[34]

"The commitment is not in the nature of a penalty for a crime because the accused has been acquitted of the crime." And under "the rules applicable to *habeas corpus* a person committed to a hospital as insane is entitled to be released from restraint upon establishing the fact that he is sane." [35] A former Michigan statute [36] very similar to that in Massachusetts was upheld, but only because it was interpreted not to preclude the availability of habeas corpus whereby there might be a subsequent judicial determination concerning sanity.[37] In Jackson v. Indiana,[38] the Supreme Court held that where a person was ruled mentally unfit to stand trial and committed for life he could not be subjected to a more stringent release standard than a person civilly committed. Some courts have by analogy applied this standard in cases where the defendant was found not guilty by reason of insanity.[39]

The form of verdict in England under the Criminal Lunatics Act of 1800 was "not guilty on the ground of insanity," but when such a verdict was rendered in the case of one who had shot at Queen Victoria, she questioned it because of having seen him fire the pistol. Since then, until recently, the formula in England was "guilty of the act or omission charged against him,

---

32. Kenny, Outlines of Criminal Law 60–1 (13th ed. 1933). See now id. at 95–96 (19th ed. 1966).

33. M.G.L.A. c. 123 § 101, now repealed.

Such a statute was held unconstitutional in Underwood v. People, 32 Mich. 1 (1875). The Mississippi case is the same in substance. Sinclair v. State, 161 Miss. 142, 132 So. 581 (1931). The conviction here was to the effect that defendant was guilty but insane at the time of the act;—but this was under a statute which did not permit the jury to acquit on the ground of insanity.

34. Mass.Ann.Laws ch. 123 §§ 15–17 (1972).

35. Yankulov v. Bushong, 80 Ohio App. 497, 504, 77 N.E.2d 88, 92 (1945).

36. Mich.Comp.Laws § 766.15c (1948).

37. People v. Dubina, 304 Mich. 363, 8 N.W.2d 99 (1943), cert. denied 319 U.S. 766, 63 S.Ct. 1331 (1943). An earlier statute had been held invalid because it was interpreted to exclude any subsequent judicial determination concerning sanity. Underwood v. People, 32 Mich. 1 (1875). Mich.Stat.Ann. § 14.800 (1050) (1976) has replaced the former Michigan law. The new statute provides for an elaborate procedural requirement for commitment.

38. 406 U.S. 715, 92 S.Ct. 1845 (1972).

39. People v. McQuillan, 392 Mich. 511, 221 N.W.2d 569 (1974).

"Specifically we hold that principles of equal protection require [subject to extended or civil commitment] that persons committed to a state institution following acquittal of a criminal offense on the ground of their insanity cannot be retained in institutional confinement beyond the maximum term of punishment for the underlying offense of which, but for their insanity, they would have been convicted." In re Moye, 22 Cal.3d 457, 149 Cal.Rptr. 491, 497, 584 P.2d 1097, 1103 (1978). See also Weiner, Not Guilty by Reason of Insanity: A Sane Approach, 56 Chi-Kent L.Rev. 1057 (1980).

but insane at the time." Frequently the verdict was spoken of as if it were "guilty but insane" but this was quite misleading since it was one of acquittal.[40]

This suggests the possibility of a true verdict of "guilty but insane," which strangely enough seems never to have been given a fair trial.[41] To avoid constitutional difficulties a statute authorizing such a verdict would need to permit an acquittal on the ground of insanity if mental disease or defect at the time of the harmful act was so extreme as to preclude criminal capacity. The suggestion is that in a case in which evidence of mental disease or defect at the time of the act has been introduced, the jury be authorized to bring in any one of four verdicts (apart from the possibility of lesser included offenses): (1) guilty as charged, (2) guilty but insane, (3) not guilty by reason of insanity, or (4) not guilty. The authorization of (1) and (4) would enable the jury to bring in an appropriate verdict if satisfied that defendant was not suffering from mental disorder at the time of the alleged crime. The verdict of "guilty but insane" would be proper if the jury found that defendant was suffering from mental disease or defect at the time but nevertheless committed the prohibited act with the requisite mens rea. "Not guilty by reason of insanity" would be the appropriate verdict if the jury found the mental disease or defect so extreme that defendant lacked criminal capacity at the time of the act, which he in fact committed.

Where resulting from a judgment based upon a verdict of "guilty but insane" the commitment would not be because of insanity but because of conviction, and the one so convicted would not be in a position to embarrass hospital authorities by repeated writs of habeas corpus. The sentence under such a judgment might well be for life, if the offense in general permitted so severe a penalty, but the treatment should not be that provided for ordinary offenders. The one so convicted should be sent where he could be examined by competent medical authorities and his treatment should be determined by them and might be entirely therapeutic rather than penal in its nature except to the extent that compulsory therapeutic treatment might seem to him to be punitive. The possibility of such a verdict would not force the jury to acquit one who is obviously guilty, but who should not suffer the penalty normally

---

40. Williams, Criminal Law § 90 (1953).

Under the Act of 1964 the special verdict is now "that the accused is not guilty, by reason of insanity." Kenny, Outlines of Criminal Law 95 (19th ed. by Turner, 1966).

41. The following committees met in joint session in the Mayflower Hotel, Washington, D.C., May 11, 1934: American Psychiatric Association—Dr. William A. White, Washington, D.C., Dr. V. C. Branham, Albany, New York, Dr. Winfred Overholser, Boston, Massachusetts, Dr. C. P. Oberndorf, New York City; American Medical Association—Dr. William C. Woodward, Chicago, Illinois, Dr. Winfred Overholser, Boston, Massachusetts; New York Academy of Medicine—Dr. Israel Strauss, New York City, Dr. Dudley D. Schoenfeld, New York City;

American Bar Association, Criminal Law Section—Mr. Louis S. Cohane, Detroit, Michigan, Mr. Rollin M. Perkins, Iowa City, Iowa.

At this meeting it was unanimously agreed that it is desirable to keep within rather narrow limits the kind and degree of mental disorder which will entitle the defendant in a criminal case to an acquittal, and to readjust the machinery after the point of conviction to the end that mental disorder which is not sufficient for an acquittal may result in treatment other than that provided for persons who are not mentally disordered.

The statement after the word "agreed" was incorporated in a resolution adopted by the American Bar Association at its annual meeting in Los Angeles in 1935. 60 A.B.A.Rep. 109 (1935).

provided for such an offense.[42] It would not force the state either to *punish* the insane or to refuse to defend itself against one inflicted with mental disorder by giving him a "hunting license to commit further crimes without punishment." [43] It would permit every contribution of science in the field of mental disorder to be employed in the treatment of such inmates and might provide a laboratory in aid of scientific development along these lines. It would not require confinement in cases in which release seemed clearly to be indicated in the judgment of the medical authorities in charge,—except for a possible stipulated minimum term.

While the word "insane" has been used for convenience in this discussion it might be wise to avoid it in the verdict, which might be in some such form as this: We find the defendant guilty but that he was suffering from mental disease or defect at the time of the crime.

The misplaced chromosome has begun to have a place in the newspapers, but not yet in the law.[44]

The defense of insanity should not be confused with a claim of automatism. The later defense is not based upon a disease or defect of the mind, but is available where the action of the defendant is not the product of his will due to some external influence such as a blow or the like.[45]

The foregoing, prepared for the first edition in 1957 and adequate for the second edition in 1969, now requires important modification. What seems to be the pioneer move in the direction indicated is a Michigan statute enacted in 1975.[46]

---

42. "When the M'Naghten rule indicated 'guilty' and common sense indicated 'guilty but insane,' the common sense of juries and judges usually prevailed." Douglas, The Durham Rule: A Meeting Ground for Lawyers and Psychiatrists, 41 Iowa L.Rev. 485, 489 (1956).

43. "In that event the murderer may go completely free with, in addition, what amounts to a hunting license to commit further crimes without punishment." Wertham, The Show of Violence 250 (1949). The proposal in the text does not eliminate the possibility of a verdict of "not guilty because of insanity" because of constitutional limitations, but if such a verdict is restricted to extreme cases of insanity it will not present a serious problem. In fact if duly restricted it would seldom be rendered because cases in which it would be appropriate are usually disposed of without trial.

See the section on The Sexual Psychopath Laws, Weihofen, Mental Disorder as a Criminal Defense 195 (1954).

44. Evidence did not establish that possession of an extra Y chromosome resulted in mental disease which constitutes insanity under M'Naghten, People v. Tanner, 13 Cal.App.3d 596, 91 Cal. Rptr. 656 (1970). Similar results were reached in People v. Yukl, 83 Misc. 364, 372 N.Y.S.2d 313 (1975); Millard v. State, 8 Md.App. 419, 261 A.2d 227 (1970).

See Burke, The "XYY Syndrome:" Genetics, Behavior and the Law, 46 Denver L.J. 261 (1969); Fox, XYY Chromosomes and Crime, 2 Aust. and N.Z.J. Crim. 5 (1969), Note, XYY Syndrome and the Judicial System, 6 N.C. Central L.J. 66 (1974).

45. See Bratty v. Attorney-General of N.J. [1963] A.C. 386; People v. Grant, 71 Ill.2d 551, 17 Ill.Dec. 814, 377 N.E.2d 4 (1978). The Canadian courts appear to have drawn a sharp distinction between the defense of insanity and the claim of automatism. Regina v. Leod, 52 CCC 2d 193 (B.C.Ct.App. 1980); Regina v. Revelle, 48 CCC 2d 267 (Ont.Ct.App. 1979); Regina v. Sproule, 26 CCC 2d 93 (Ont.Ct.App. 1975).

46. 1975 P.A. 180, sec. 36; M.C.L.A. sec. 768.36; M.S.A. sec. 28.1059 (1978).

If the defendant asserts a defense of insanity in compliance with section 20a, the defendant may be found "guilty but mentally ill" if, after trial, the trier of fact finds all of the following beyond a reasonable doubt:

(a) That the defendant is guilty of an offense.

(b) That the defendant was mentally ill at the time of the commission of that offense.

(c) That the defendant was not legally insane at the time of the commission of that offense.

In an arson trial after the effective date of this statute the defendant was found "guilty of arson but mentally ill." The trial judge held that the statute was invalid, set aside the verdict of guilty but mentally ill, and ordered a new trial. She did this not as a result of finding any basic fault in the statute itself, but on the conclusion that under existing conditions it was impossible to carry out the post-sentence treatment contemplated by the statute. On appeal the order granting a new trial was reversed. The Court of Appeals, holding that the statute was constitutional and valid, remanded the case to the trial court for the imposition of sentence.[47]

This decision is fortunate. It may require considerable experimentation to develop an adequate program of post-sentence treatment under a conviction of "guilty but mentally ill," but the plan is sound and should be encouraged. The term used for the new verdict is quite appropriate, and is recommended:

GUILTY BUT MENTALLY ILL

K. AUTOMATISM

"Sleepwalking" is a word that has been around for many years. It was recognized long ago that sometimes some person may walk around, with eyes open, and do other things in a seemingly meaningful manner, while actually unconscious. The word "somnambulism" was often used to express the phenomenon, but the more recent label is "automatism," although this term includes situations too extreme to be considered "sleepwalking."[48] The explanation is that such a person is acting automatically rather than voluntarily.

If one in such a condition should do what is prohibited by law, it should ordinarily be held that he is not guilty of crime for the same reason that harm resulting from a spasm is not criminal. It has been pointed out that "unconsciousness is not a complete defense under all circumstances."[49] Thus in California "unconsciousness produced by voluntary intoxication does not render a defendant incapable of committing a crime."[50] In Colorado one who precipitated a fracas during which he was hit on the head and rendered unconscious cannot maintain that he has no criminal responsibility for what

47. People v. McLeod, 77 Mich.App. 327, 258 N.W.2d 214 (1977). The statute has also been upheld against a claim of denial of equal protection of the laws. People v. Darwall, 82 Mich.App. 652, 267 N.W.2d 472 (1978).

48. "Sleepwalking is not the same as the 'automatism' of the patient in an at-tack of psychomotor epilepsy." Fulcher v. State, 633 P.2d 142, 161 (Wyo.1981).

49. Id. at page 145, n. 5. The three following cases in the text are taken from that footnote.

50. People v. Cox, 67 Cal.App.2d 166, 153 P.2d 362 (1944).

he did next.[51] And in Oklahoma a motorist who had a fatal traffic accident during a "blackout" was guilty of manslaughter if he was driving with full knowledge that he was subject to frequent "blackouts." [52]

In the absence of some special circumstance, however, automatism has been held to be a defense to harm committed while in that condition,[53] although there have not been a multitude of cases involving the problem.

The chief controversy seems to have been whether automatism is a form of "insanity." As pointed out above the word "insanity" has no accepted definition and the real question is whether automatism is a form of mental disease or defect. "Automatism," it was said in one case,[54] "may be caused by an abnormal condition of mind capable of being designated a mental illness or deficiency. Automatism may also be manifest in a person with a perfectly healthy mind." And in another case it was said: "The defenses of insanity and unconsciousness are not the same in nature, for unconsciousness at the time of the alleged criminal act need not be the result of a disease or defect of the mind." [55] The court went on to explain that the importance of the difference is that "a defendant found not guilty by reason of unconsciousness, as distinct from insanity, is not subject to commitment to a hospital for the mentally ill."

This does not sound convincing in view of the fact that defendant has caused death or serious injury in some of the cases in which the defense of automatism was recognized. Certainly it would be important to determine whether the peculiarity is such that the person is likely to cause similar harm in the future. In a Kentucky case in which there was evidence that defendant was a "somnambulist" and committed the acts charged while unconscious, the court said: "We fail to see how these facts would constitute any defense other than that embraced in a plea of insanity." [56]

In a recent case [57] the only question to be decided by the Supreme Court of Wyoming was whether the trial judge had committed error in refusing to instruct on automatism on the ground there was no evidence to warrant it. The justices were unanimous in affirming the conviction, but the trial judge had permitted the defense to introduce evidence in the effort to establish automatism although defendant had refused to enter a plea of "not guilty by reason of mental illness or deficiency," [58] and the justices were narrowly divided on whether such procedure was valid. The majority would require such a plea for the introduction of evidence of automatism if such was not due to any unusual circumstance, but in this case the claim was that condition resulted from a blow on the head that produced no lasting injury. And

51. Watkins v. People, 158 Colo. 485, 408 P.2d 425 (1965).

52. Carter v. State, 376 P.2d 351 (Okl. Cr.App. 1962).

53. Fain v. Commonwealth, 78 Ky. 183 (1879); People v. Freeman, 61 Cal. App.2d 110, 142 P.2d 435 (1943); State v. Mercer, 275 N.C. 108, 165 S.E.2d 328 (1969); Regina v. Charlson, 1 All E.R. (1955).

54. Fulcher v. State, 633 P.2d 142, 145 (Wyo.1981).

55. State v. Cahill, 287 N.C. 266, 215 S.E.2d 348, 360 (1975).

56. Tibbs v. Commonwealth, 138 Ky. 558, 567, 128 S.W. 871, 874 (1910).

57. Fulcher v. State, 633 P.2d 142 (Wyo.1981). The various opinions in this case take up 26 pages of the Pacific Reporter and cite most of the important cases.

58. Actually the defendant originally entered such a plea but later withdrew it and insisted on going to trial on the sole plea of not guilty.

they indicated that if automatism was so induced it was not "mental illness or deficiency" but merely a temporary condition of a "perfectly healthy mind." [59] The minority insisted that if the blow caused automatism it follows that the mind, while in that condition, was in a state of "mental illness or deficiency," so that the special plea was required for the introduction of evidence tending to establish automatism.

If one acts with such violence as to cause death,[60] or hits a ten-year-old with a mallet and throws him out the window, [61] and is able to accomplish all of such harm while unconscious, the ultimate conclusion is bound to be that such behavior manifests mental disease or defect, and should be dealt with on that basis. In fact there is reason to question that ordinary sleepwalking is not a case of mental deficiency "under current advanced medical knowledge." [62]

SECTION 3. DRUNKENNESS (INTOXICATION)

Logic would restrict the present consideration to matters dealing with limitations of criminal capacity, but it is convenient to have an overall picture of criminal-law problems arising out of overindulgence in liquor or drugs and such a picture will throw useful light upon the part particularly pertinent to this chapter. Hence, brief attention will be given to drunkenness as an offense and as an aggravation of some other offense, as well as to the question whether it may constitute a defense to a charge of crime.

A. AS AN OFFENSE

1. IN GENERAL

Drunkenness was not of itself an offense under the common law of England but this must be considered together with the fact that it was punishable in the ecclesiastical courts[1] and this raises the possibility that had this sanction been lacking the common law itself might have provided a penalty. If drunkenness was carried to the point of constituting a public nuisance it was punishable as such by the common law; [2] a breach of the peace caused by drunken misbehavior was punishable as readily as if caused by a sober person; and if an officer imbibed to such an extent as to be unable to discharge his duty with decency, decorum and discretion he was guilty of misconduct in office.[3] Drunkenness itself was made an offense in England by statute in 1606.[4]

---

59. See the text at note 54.

60. As in *Fain* supra note 53.

61. As in *Charlson* supra note 53.

62. Per Raper, J., supra note 57, at page 161.

1. 2 Stephen, History of the Criminal Law of England 410 (1883). The statute making it an offense is discussed by Hawkins and Blackstone under the head of offenses against religion. 1 Hawk. P.C. c. 6, § 5 (6th ed. 1788); 4 Bl.Comm. *64. But after this statute it was questioned whether the Spiritual Court could meddle with the punishment of drunkenness or whether this was merely temporal. Cucko v. Starre, Cro.Car. 285, 79 Eng.Rep. 850 (1632).

2. 2 Wharton, Criminal Law § 1720 (12th ed. 1932). And see Moser v. Fulk, 237 N.C. 302, 306, 74 S.E.2d 729, 731 (1953).

3. Commonwealth v. Alexander, 14 Va. 522 (1808). Accord, Pennsylvania v. Keffer, Addison 290 (Pa.1796).

4. 4 Jac. 1, c. 5 (1606).

This statute is old enough to be common law in this country and, although there are decisions to the contrary,[5] there is substantial authority to the effect that public drunkenness[6] is a common-law offense here.[7] As said by the Michigan court quoting from a Kansas case: "Voluntary drunkenness in a public place was always a misdemeanor at common law; and it was always wrong morally and legally. It is malum in se."[8] It is punished because of its evil example and it is not necessary to establish additional facts sufficient to constitute a breach of the peace or a nuisance.[9]

It has been very common by statute,[10] or ordinance,[11] to provide a penalty for public drunkenness and the dual possibility must not be overlooked. For example, no such penalty is provided in the California Penal Code, and the state does not punish merely on the basis of a common-law offense,[12] but one who is drunk in a public place may land in jail because of having violated a city ordinance.[13] Some enactments have specified certain places such as a public road, street, alley, hotel, railroad car, railroad depot, and so forth, but such specification has been of little importance because of the addition of "other public place."[14] "A public place does not mean a place devoted solely

---

5. "No authority has been found for maintaining such an indictment at common law unless it becomes a public nuisance and is so charged in the indictment." State v. Locker, 50 N.J.L. 512, 513, 14 A. 749, 750 (1888). Accord, State v. Munger, 43 Wyo. 404, 4 P.2d 1094 (1931).

6. The English statute did not speak of "public drunkenness" or being drunk in a "public place" (which has been common in corresponding statutes here) but seems to have been assumed to have had this meaning. It was repealed in 1828. See Williams, Criminal Law § 110, note 1 (1953).

Any person found intoxicated shall be fined not more than twenty dollars or imprisoned not more than thirty days. Conn.Gen.Stat.Ann. § 53a–184 (1975); Ark.Stats. § 48–943 (1976).

7. State v. Gardner, 174 Iowa 748, 749, 156 N.W. 747, 751 (1916); State v. Brown, 38 Kan. 390, 397, 16 P. 259, 262 (1888); State v. Budge, 126 Me. 223, 228, 137 A. 244, 247 (1927); People v. Townsend, 214 Mich. 267, 273, 183 N.W. 177, 179 (1921); Tipton v. State, 10 Tenn. 542 (1831); Inman v. State, 195 Tenn. 303, 259 S.W.2d 531 (1953); Cates v. State, 198 Tenn. 270, 279 S.W.2d 262 (1955).

8. People v. Townsend, 214 Mich. 267, 273, 183 N.W. 177, 179 (1921). The quotation is from Brown. See also Gardner and Budge.

"The provisions of G.S. 14–447 to the effect that no person may be *prosecuted* solely for being intoxicated in a public place make it abundantly clear that no person may be *arrested* solely for being intoxicated in a public place. Those who are intoxicated but not disruptive may be *assisted* but not arrested." State v. Cooke, 49 N.C.App. 384, 271 S.E.2d 561, 565 (1980).

9. Inman v. State, 195 Tenn. 303, 259 S.W.2d 531 (1953).

10. State v. Moriarty, 74 Ind. 103 (1881); Thompson v. State, 153 Miss. 593, 121 So. 275 (1929); State v. Stevens, 36 N.H. 59, 62–3 (1858); State v. Myrick, 203 N.C. 8, 164 S.E. 328 (1932); January v. State, 66 Tex.Cr.R. 302, 146 S.W. 555 (1912); Rickett v. Hayes, 251 Ark. 395, 473 S.W.2d 446 (1971).

11. Johnston v. Brewer, 40 Cal.App. 2d 583, 105 P.2d 365 (1940); State v. McNinch, 87 N.C. 567 (1882).

12. West's Ann.Cal.Pen.Code § 6 (1970).

13. Johnston v. Brewer, 40 Cal.App. 2d 583, 105 P.2d 365 (1940).

The California statute provides a penalty for one who is drunk in a public place "in such a condition that he is unable to exercise care for his own safety or the safety of others" and so forth. West's Ann.Cal.Pen.Code § 647(f) (1970). And see People v. Murrietta, 251 Cal.App.2d 1002, 60 Cal.Rptr. 56 (1967); People v. Superior Court for Monterey County, 29 Cal.App.3d 397, 105 Cal.Rptr. 695 (1972).

14. See, for example, the statutes referred to in State v. Stevens, 36 N.H. 59 (1858); State v. Myrick, 203 N.C. 8, 164 S.E. 328 (1932).

to the uses of the public, but it means a place which is in point of fact public, as distinguished from private, a place that is visited by many persons and usually accessible to the neighboring public." [15] This includes not only the public roads and streets,[16] but various other places such as a schoolhouse being used at the moment as a place of public worship,[17] a combination beer tavern and restaurant,[18] a hotel including the porches and verandas thereof,[19] and police headquarters.[20] It does not include drunkenness in a private dwelling [21] but an occasional statute has gone beyond drunkenness in a public place and has expressly included drunkenness at, or within the curtilage of, the private residence of another.[22] In a prosecution for public drunkenness, whether as a common-law offense or under the usual type of enactment, it is not necessary to show that the intoxication was manifested by indecent or offensive conduct or that it was sufficiently habitual to constitute a public nuisance,[23] but under a few statutes some additional showing is required such as that the drunken condition be manifested by "boisterous or indecent conduct, or loud or profane discourse." [24] Under such a provision drunkenness in a public place without such manifestation is not punishable,[25] and if the statute makes it an offense to be "drunk and disorderly in any public place" guilt is not incurred without both elements.[26]

A word of caution is important in this regard. A common drunkard was guilty of a nuisance at common law[27] the same as a common scold or a common brawler.[28] The word "common" in this sense imports frequency[29] and the terms "common drunkard" and "habitual drunkard" have been used as synonyms.[30] A nuisance was punished on the ground of being an annoyance

15. People v. Soule, 142 N.Y.S. 876, 880 (County Ct.1913).

16. State v. Moriarty, 74 Ind. 103 (1881); Thompson v. State, 153 Miss. 593, 121 So. 275 (1929). See Annotation, "Location of Offense as 'Public' Within Requirement of Enactments Against Drunkenness", 8 A.L.R.3d 930 (1966).

17. January v. State, 66 Tex.Cr.R. 302, 146 S.W. 555 (1912).

18. Ginter v. Commonwealth, 262 S.W.2d 178 (Ky.1953).

19. People v. Soule, 142 N.Y.S. 876, 880 (County Ct.1913).

20. People v. Lane, 32 N.Y.S.2d 61 (City Ct.1942).

21. Commonwealth v. Vincent, 282 Ky. 95, 137 S.W.2d 1081 (1940). Nor does it include drunkenness in a meadow some distance from a highway. Mayes v. State, 80 Okl.Cr. 52, 156 P.2d 822 (1945).

22. Mullis v. State, 196 Ga. 569, 27 S.E.2d 91 (1943).

23. Tipton v. State, 10 Tenn. 542 (1831); Inman v. State, 195 Tenn. 303, 259 S.W.2d 531 (1953).

24. Ala.Code § 13A–11–10 (1980). The requirements for conviction under the statute are that the accused be intoxicated, in a public place, to the degree that he endangers himself or others, or engages in boisterous and offensive conduct which annoys others.

25. Mullis v. State, 196 Ga. 569, 27 S.E.2d 91 (1943). Whether defendant's conduct was such as to offend public decency is a question of fact for the jury. Sullivan v. State, 17 Ga.App. 122, 86 S.E. 287 (1915). But it was held that mere staggering was not enough, and that the answer "Hell no" when asked if he was drunk was not profane. Thompson v. State, 34 Ala.App. 608, 42 So.2d 640 (1949).

26. State v. Myrick, 203 N.C. 8, 164 S.E. 328 (1932).

27. 2 Wharton, Criminal Law § 1720 (12th ed. 1932).

28. Id. at §§ 1715, 1716.

29. Commonwealth v. McNamee, 112 Mass. 285, 286 (1873). It was held that proof of drunkenness on five to seven occasions during three or four months would sustain a conviction when there was no evidence of the condition at other times.

30. Tatum v. State, 32 Ala.App. 128, 22 So.2d 350 (1945).

to the public and an essential element of the offense of being a common drunkard was that the overindulgence be open and notorious.[31] On the other hand the modern counterpart of the early concept of common drunkenness as a nuisance is the familiar statutory provision declaring an habitual drunkard to be a vagrant,[32] and one may be punished for vagrancy because of intoxication with habitual frequency even in his own home.[33] And while drinking by an officer while on duty does not constitute misconduct in office as a matter of common law so long as it does not prevent him from faithfully, honestly and correctly discharging all his official duties,[34] such drinking may be forbidden by statute or ordinance.[35]

Statutes have created certain special offenses in this area such as being drunk when in possession of a loaded firearm,[36] or being drunk on a passenger vessel and refusing to leave when requested,[37] but the most familiar provisions are those that provide a penalty for the operation or actual physical control of a motor vehicle on the highway while intoxicated[38] or while under the influence of intoxicating liquor or narcotic drugs.[39] The two are not the same; [40] one who is intoxicated is "under the influence" but it is possible to be "under the influence" without being intoxicated.[41] One who has imbibed to such an extent as to lose that clearness of intellect and control he would ordinarily have, and thereby appreciably lessen his ability to handle his car in traffic, is "under the influence" as the phrase is used in such a statute.[42]

A former California statute providing for the punishment of a "common drunkard" was held unconstitutional for uncertainty. In re Newbern, 53 Cal.2d 786, 3 Cal.Rptr. 364, 350 P.2d 116 (1960).

31. State v. Waller, 7 N.C. 229 (1819); Moser v. Fulk, 237 N.C. 302, 306, 74 S.E.2d 729, 731 (1953).

32. Such a statute was declared unconstitutional in, In re Newbern, 53 Cal. 2d 786, 3 Cal.Rptr. 364, 350 P.2d 116 (1960). Most states have repealed such enactments.

33. Pollon v. State, 218 Wis. 466, 261 N.W. 224 (1935). The same is true of the less-familiar enactment making it a misdemeanor to be drunk habitually in the presence of a child in one's care, custody or control. West's Ann.Cal.Pen.Code § 273g (1970).

34. Commonwealth v. Williams, 79 Ky. 42 (1880).

35. A different type of provision is a statute providing for the punishment of an officer who is intoxicated while in the performance of any official duty. E.g., Section 105.250 RSMo 1949, V.A.M.S. (Repealed Jan. 1, 1979).

36. Licensing Act, 35 & 36 Vict. c. 94, § 12 (1872).

37. Merchants Shipping Act, 57 & 58 Vict. c. 60, § 287 (1894).

38. McKinney's N.Y.Veh. and Traf.L. § 1192(1) and (3) (1971).

39. McKinney's N.Y.Veh. and Traf.L. § 1192(4) (1971).

"Driving" a vehicle and "operating" a vehicle are not identical. The former has reference to a moving violation while this in not required in the other. McDuell v. State, 231 A.2d 265 (Del.1967).

40. State v. Budge, 126 Me. 223, 228, 137 A. 244, 247 (1922); Cashion v. Hartnett, 234 App.Div. 332, 255 N.Y.S. 169 (1932).

See a comment, analysis of the drunken driving statutes in the United States, 8 Vand.L.Rev. 888 (1955).

41. State v. Hanson, 73 N.W.2d 135 (N.D.1955).

If **D** was steering a car while intoxicated he is guilty of drunken driving although the car was being pushed. Walker v. State, 241 Ark. 396, 408 S.W.2d 474 (1966).

42. Ibid.; People v. Dingle, 56 Cal. App. 445, 205 P. 705 (1922); People v. Coppock, 206 Misc. 89, 133 N.Y.S.2d 174 (1954). One judge, while indicating that not quite so much was required by law, quoted this ancient jingle:

Not drunk is he who from the floor
    Can rise again or drink once more:
But drunk is he who prostrate lies
    And cannot either drink or rise!

State v. Myrick, 203 N.C. 8, 9, 164 S.E. 328, 329 (1932).

These statutes have given rise to many interesting problems of proof but these are beyond the scope of the present undertaking.[43]

An occasional statute has made it a misdemeanor to operate a train, navigate a vessel,[44] or avigate an airplane,[45] while in an intoxicated condition.[46]

2. INVOLUNTARY INTOXICATION (INNOCENT INTOXICATION)

Since public drunkenness and other offenses in this area are true crimes it has been held very properly that involuntariness of the intoxication may negative the mens rea and thereby establish innocence.[47] The leading case is *Brown*[48] in which the evidence indicated that defendant was unaware of the intoxicating character of what he drank and it was held reversible error to instruct that such ignorance was no excuse in a prosecution for public drunkenness. In *Koch*[49] a conviction of operating a motor vehicle while in an intoxicated condition was reversed because the evidence disclosed that the intoxication had resulted from luminol which defendant had taken on a doctor's prescription for medical purposes; and it was added *obiter* in *Brown* that one made drunk by force or fraud and carried into a public place would also be free from guilt.

An important qualification is to be noted. If one should become intoxicated as a result of an innocent mistake, force or fraud, but after becoming drunk was still sufficiently in possession of his faculties to know what he was doing, and to understand the character of his acts, and with such knowledge and understanding should voluntarily go into a public place or drive a motor vehicle on a public highway, the involuntariness of the intoxication would not excuse him because the prohibited act itself was done voluntarily.[50] Conversely, one who has overindulged in drink voluntarily, but in his own home or some other place which does not constitute a violation of law,

---

43. See, for example, Ladd & Gibson, Medico-Legal Aspects of the Blood Test to Determine Intoxication, 24 Iowa L.Rev. 191 (1939); Shupe, Validity of New York Statute Setting Out Motorists' Implied Consent to Chemical Test for Intoxication, 51 Mich.L.Rev. 1195 (1953); Breath Tests for Alcohol, 1 J.For.Med. 249 (1954); Shrader, Chemical Tests to Determine Degree of Intoxication, 15 Ala.L.Rev. 396 (1954); Chemical Tests for Intoxication in Tennessee, 23 Tenn.L. Rev. 178 (1954); Fisher, Gundry, Krantz, Solter, Symposium on Compulsory Use of Chemical Tests for Alcoholic Intoxication, 14 Md.L.Rev. 111 (1954); Chemical Tests for Drunken Driving, 29 Conn.B.J. 147 (1955); Survey and Background of State Statutes Concerning Chemical Tests for Intoxication, 46 J.C.L. & Crim. 73 (1955); Weinstein, Statute Compelling Submission to a Chemical Test for Intoxication, 45 J.C.L. & Crim. 541 (1955); Spelman, Results of Blood Alcohol Testing Program in a Rural State, 2 J.For.Med. 175 (1955); Muelberger, Medicolegal Aspects of Alcohol Intoxication, 35 Mich.S.B.J. 36

(1956); Mason & Dubowski, Breath-Alcohol Analysis: Uses, Methods and Some Forensic Problems—Review and Opinion, 21 J.For.Sci. 33 (1976); Fitzgerald and Hume, The Single Chemical Test for Intoxication: A Challenge to Admissibility, 66 Mass.L.Rev. 23 (1981).

44. Utah Code Ann. 1953, § 73–18–12.

45. Va.Code § 5.1–13 (1979).

46. Recently there have been some interesting developments in regard to public drunkenness but these will be postponed until the end of the Section.

47. State v. Brown, 38 Kan. 390, 16 P. 259 (1888); People v. Koch, 250 App.Div. 623, 294 N.Y.S. 987 (1937); Pennsylvania v. Keffer, Addison 290 (Pa.1796).

48. Brown, supra, approved in State v. Eastman, 60 Kan. 557, 559, 57 P. 109, 110 (1899).

49. People v. Koch, 250 App.Div. 623, 294 N.Y.S. 987 (1937).

50. This was added by way of *dictum* in Brown, supra, at 397, 16 P. at 262.

and while in that condition is taken to a public place against his will by police officers, is not guilty of public drunkenness, for while the drunkenness was voluntary, being in a public place in that condition was not.[51]

B. AS AN AGGRAVATION OF OTHER OFFENSE

Both Coke and Blackstone took the position that drunkenness at the time of the commission of a crime was a matter of aggravation,[52] but if this was intended as a statement of law, rather than an expression of opinion, it is incorrect. So far as the common law is concerned a crime committed by a drunken man is not aggravated thereby in the sense of being made a worse crime,[53] and a homicide, for example, which would be manslaughter by a sober man is not murder because the slayer is drunk.[54] An occasional statute has provided such an element of aggravation as, for example, the enactment providing that one who drives a motor vehicle while under the influence of intoxicating liquor and while doing so does any act forbidden by law, or neglects any duty imposed by law, and thereby causes bodily injury to another is guilty of a felony,[55] whereas had the same thing happened while he was sober it might have been a misdemeanor. More common are enactments which make intoxication a matter of aggravation in the sense of making an act punishable which otherwise would not be an offense. In this category may be mentioned a statute which makes the prescribing or administering by any person of drugs or medicine while intoxicated which endangers the life of a person a misdemeanor,[56] and is guilty of manslaughter if the result is fatal;[57] and the federal act which provides that if a master, seaman, or other person employed on a vessel, by reason of drunkenness does any act tending to the immediate loss or destruction of the vessel, or tending to endanger life or limb of any person on the vessel, he is guilty of a misdemeanor.[58]

---

51. Brown v. State, 38 Ala.App. 312; 82 So.2d 806 (1955); People v. Lane, 32 N.Y.S.2d 61 (City Ct. 1942). However, where it could be anticipated that a person might be lawfully removed to a public place a prosecution for public intoxication has been upheld. O'Sullivan v. Fisher, [1954] SASR 33 (So.Audt.)

52. "A drunkard says Sir Edward Coke, who is *voluntarius daemon*, hath no privilege thereby; but what hurt or ill soever he doth, his drunkenness doth aggravate it." 4 Bl.Comm. *26. Blackstone also cites the Greek enactment "that he who committed a crime when drunk should receive double punishment." Ibid.

53. State v. Neuman, 157 La. 564, 102 So. 671 (1925).

54. McIntyre v. People, 38 Ill. 514 (1865); State v. Donovan, 61 Iowa 369, 16 N.W. 206 (1883).

55. West's Ann.Cal.Veh.Code § 23101 (effective July 1, 1982); State v. Twitchell, 8 Utah 2d 314, 333 P.2d 1075 (1959). The English Inebriates Act provided that if one found guilty of crime was found to be an habitual drunkard he might, in addition to any other sentence, be detained in a state inebriate reformatory not to exceed three years. 61 & 62 Vict. c. 60 (1898).

56. Wyo.Stat.Ann. 6–4–604 (1977).

57. Id. at § 605 (1977).

58. 18 U.S.C.A. § 2196 (1970).

C. AS A DEFENSE IN A CRIMINAL CASE

1. INVOLUNTARY INTOXICATION (INNOCENT INTOXICATION)

Since the refusal to place intoxication and insanity on the same basis (insofar as criminal incapacity is concerned) is due to the fact that the former is usually a "voluntarily contracted madness," [59] it follows that they should be dealt with alike when the intoxication is involuntary, and such is the law,[60]— "this puts him into the same condition, in reference to crimes, as any other phrenzy, and equally excuseth him." [61] Whether intoxication results from alcohol or from drugs[62] is immaterial, so far as the general rules are concerned, in regard to either voluntary or involuntary intoxication, but one of the most significant determinations to be made is just when the latter label is properly to be applied.

A. THE MEANING OF INVOLUNTARY INTOXICATION

Voluntary intoxication is not limited to those instances in which drunkenness was definitely desired or intended[63] but includes all instances of culpable intoxication. It may be voluntary although the drinking was induced by the example or persuasion of another,[64] and the mere fact that the liquor or drug was supplied by someone else does not tend in any way to show that the intoxication was involuntary.[65] Drunkenness will be presumed to be voluntary unless some special circumstance is established to remove it from that category.

59. 4 Bl.Comm. *25.

60. Pearson's Case, 2 Lewin 144, 168 Eng.Rep. 1108 (1835); People v. Robinson, 2 Park.Cr.R. 235, 304 (N.Y.1855); Burrows v. State, 38 Ariz. 99, 297 P. 1029 (1931); Strickland v. State, 137 Ga. 115, 72 S.E. 922 (1911). One judge, in a case in which insanity was claimed as a defense, told the jury: "If the defendant had a mental disease . . .; he is innocent—as innocent as if the act had been produced by involuntary intoxication." State v. Jones, 50 N.H. 369, 373 (1871).

See Model Penal Code, Section 2.08(4). Hanks v. State, 542 S.W.2d 413 (Tex.Cr. App. 1976). See also 11 Del.Code Ann. § 423 (1979).

"Escape as defined in RCW 9.31.010 is a general intent crime, thus, temporary insanity caused by involuntary intoxication is a complete defense." State v. Gilcrist, 25 Wn.App. 327, 606 P.2d 716, 717 (1980).

61. 1 Hale P.C. *32.

62. People v. Baker, 42 Cal.2d 550, 268 P.2d 705 (1954); People v. Koch, 250 App.Div. 623, 294 N.Y.S. 987 (1937).

63. Pennsylvania v. Keffer, Addison 290 (Pa.1796).

Involuntary intoxication means that the intoxicant was forcibly, unwittingly or unknowingly ingested. And the reference to force "means physical compulsion by another, trickery, deception or other type of *external* force." State v. Palacio, 221 Kan. 394, 559 P.2d 804, 806 (1977).

"Mere addiction is not sufficient to render the injection of heroin involuntary or unknowing." Tacorante v. People, ___ Colo. ___, 624 P.2d 1324, 1327 (1981).

64. Burrows v. State, 38 Ariz. 99, 297 P. 1029 (1931); Borland v. State, 158 Ark. 37, 249 S.W. 591 (1923); McCook v. State, 91 Ga. 740, 17 S.E. 1091 (1893).

65. State v. Sopher, 70 Iowa 494, 30 N.W. 917 (1886). See Annotation, When Intoxication Deemed Involuntary so as to Constitute a Defense to Criminal Charge, 73 A.L.R.3d 195 (1976).

(A) Intoxication by Mistake

Involuntary intoxication includes all instances in which, as a result of a genuine mistake as to the nature or character of the liquor or drug, the drunkenness has resulted from taking something not known to be capable of producing such a result. Down through the ages, with different forms of wording, has been echoed the rule that intoxication is not voluntary if brought about by the fraud, artifice or stratagem of another.[66] The leading cases are *Alie*[67] and *Penman*.[68] In *Alie* a schemer with robbery in mind made secret use of "knock-out drops" to aid in his nefarious plan, while in *Penman* cocaine tablets were handed over by a friend with the statement that they were "breath perfumers,"—apparently as some sort of joke. In each case the innocent victim committed homicide, the evidence indicating that he had done so while completely out of his mind as a result of the drug unwittingly taken, and in each it was held that the slayer was innocent of crime if this was the fact.

What prevents the intoxication from being voluntary in these cases of fraud is not the trickery of the other person but the innocent mistake of fact by the one made drunk, and an actual ignorance of the intoxicating character of the liquor or drug has the same effect whether the mistake is induced by the artifice of another or not.[69]

(B) Intoxication Under Duress

Obviously the intoxication is not voluntary if the one who drank was forced to do so against his will.[70] The cases dealing with this subject have spoken in terms of "coercion" and "duress," [71] and this has induced one author[72] to conclude that the rule is (although he thinks it should not be) that "a person would need to be bound hand and foot and the liquor literally poured down his throat, or . . . would have to be threatened with immediate serious injury before" the resulting intoxication would be held to be involuntary. This, however, overlooks the fact that the ancient harsh rule in regard to duress has been modified very greatly in modern times.[73] Inquiry as to whether intoxication was voluntary or involuntary becomes particularly important when serious harm or injury has resulted therefrom, but the claim of duress in these cases is not that such coercion was employed that defend-

---

66. 1 Hale P.C. *32; Pearson's Case, 2 Lewin 144, 168 Eng.Rep. 1108 (1835); People v. Robinson, 2 Park.Cr.R. 235, 304 (N.Y.1855); Bartholomew v. People, 104 Ill. 601, 606 (1882); Choate v. State, 19 Okl.Cr. 169, 197 P. 1060 (1921); Johnson v. Commonwealth, 135 Va. 524, 534, 115 S.E. 673, 676 (1923).

67. State v. Alie, 82 W.Va. 601, 96 S.E. 1011 (1918).

68. People v. Penman, 271 Ill. 82, 110 N.E. 894 (1915).

69. State v. Brown, 38 Kan. 390 (1888).

Instruction on involuntary intoxication is warranted where defendant believed drug was aspirin. People v. Carlo, 46 A.D.2d 764, 361 N.Y.S.2d 168 (1974).

The fact that the drunkenness was by one quite unfamiliar with intoxicating liquor is entitled to consideration. People v. Tidwell, 3 Cal.3d 82, 89 Cal.Rptr. 58, 473 P.2d 762 (1970).

70. Burrows v. State, 38 Ariz. 99, 297 P. 1029 (1931); Borland v. State, 158 Ark. 37, 45, 249 S.W. 591, 594 (1923).

71. Ibid.; Burrows at 116, 297 P. at 1035.

72. Hall, Principles of Criminal Law 540 (2d ed. 1960).

73. As to the early harsh rule and the relaxation thereof see 5 Williston, Contracts §§ 1601 et seq. (rev.ed. 1937). See also Model Penal Code Tent. Draft No. 10 (1960) § 2.09 comment.

ant chose to do the *actus reus* of a crime rather than endure the harm that was being inflicted upon, or threatened to, him but only that he was caused to drink, unwillingly. No more coercion should be required in such a case than for general purposes such as the making of a contract and "the correct rule is that any unlawful threats which do in fact overcome the will of the person threatened, and induce him to do an act which he would not otherwise have done, and which he was not bound to do, constitute duress." [74]

The leading case on intoxication under duress is *Burrows*[75] which involved homicide committed by an 18-year-old boy. The evidence indicated that while the boy and a man were driving across the desert the man, who had been drinking heavily, asked the boy also to have a drink which he refused because he had never tasted liquor and did not wish to do so. Thereupon the man became abusive and insisted with great vehemence that the boy should drink and the latter, fearing he might be put out of the car and left penniless on the desert, did drink several bottles of beer, and later after further vehement insistence some whiskey, as a result of which he went completely out of his head and killed the man without knowing what he was doing. To be left penniless on the desert—by the side of a paved and well-traveled highway—is far from a desperate plight but the significant fact is that the court held it was for the jury to determine whether, under these facts, the defendant had been compelled "to drink against his will and consent." [76] The defense had claimed that the intoxication was involuntary if the boy had been induced by "any means" to drink what otherwise he would not have taken. This claim was rejected, and properly so, because it would include a mere request or even a casual suggestion, but the jury were to determine whether the boy had in fact been compelled to drink against his will although the only evidence tending to establish compulsion was conduct of the man causing the boy to fear he might be compelled to get out of the car on the desert.

(C) Intoxication from Medicine

To be dealt with in the same manner as a case of insanity Lord Hale listed also intoxication of a person resulting from the "unskillfulness of his physician," [77] a statement which has had frequent repetition.[78] Such intoxication is involuntary, because the patient is entitled to assume that an intoxicating dose would not be prescribed,[79] but lack of skill by the doctor is not indispensable to this result. If, for example, an ordinarily proper dose

74. Williston at § 1605. "Duress may be exercised by . . . (e) any other wrongful acts that compel a person to manifest apparent consent to a transaction without his volition. . . ." Restatement, Contracts § 493 (1932).

75. Burrows v. State, 38 Ariz. 99, 297 P. 1029 (1931).

76. It is true that the jury returned a verdict of guilty but the only evidence of the man's insistence was the boy's own story which the jurors may not have believed. Since the conviction had to be reversed because of errors unrelated to this problem, the significant part of the case for the present purpose is that in the new trial also the jury were to decide whether the defendant's story (if believed by them) showed that he had been compelled to drink against his will.

77. 1 Hale, P.C. *32.

78. People v. Robinson, 2 Park.Cr.R. 235, 304 (N.Y.1855); Johnson v. Commonwealth, 135 Va. 524, 534, 115 S.E. 673, 676 (1923).

79. "A patient is not bound to presume that a physician's prescription may produce a dangerous frenzy." Perkins v. United States, 228 F. 408, 415 (4th Cir. 1915).

should unexpectedly produce intoxication because of some unusual weakness or susceptibility, unsuspected by either patient or doctor, the condition would be involuntary without the need of any forced attempt to find fault on the part of the latter.[80] In fact, if the intoxication was caused by taking more than the prescribed amount it is involuntary if the overdose was taken inadvertently.[81]

(D) Other Nonculpable Intoxication

It has been assumed at times that any intoxication is voluntary if the intoxicating character of the liquor or drug was understood and known to be present and it was not taken under duress or medical advice,[82] but such a position is utterly unrealistic. "Lord Bacon said," quoted the Kansas court, "if a drunken man commit a felony, he shall not be excused, because the imperfection came by his own default." [83] This assumes culpability in regard to the intoxication and the label "voluntary" should never be added where there is no element of substantial fault. One who has become drunk as a result of reckless overindulgence cannot claim the condition is involuntary merely because he misjudged his capacity, but there are many instances in which intoxication has resulted neither from intent nor from recklessness, although the character of the liquor or drug was known and it was not taken under duress or medical advice. Where one drank liquor insufficient in itself to make him drunk, and then received a blow on the head which caused the liquor taken to produce intoxication, it was held to be involuntary.[84] The result is the same if one by reason of sickness or want of sleep is reduced to such a condition that a small quantity of stimulant which would ordinarily have no such effect causes intoxication; [85] and if one has a dormant tendency to excitement so that intoxication is likely to produce an extraordinary degree of mental derangement, and drinks without knowing of this peculiar weakness he will "not be held responsible for such extraordinary effects." [86]

---

80. Burnett v. Commonwealth, 284 S.W.2d 654 (Ky.1955). "The last kind of involuntary intoxication recognized in case law arises when defendant is unexpectedly intoxicated due to the ingestion of a medically prescribed drug. Several courts have declared that such intoxication constitutes a valid defense to criminal liability if the prescribed drug is taken pursuant to medical advice and without defendant's knowledge of its potentially intoxicating effects." City of Minneapolis v. Altimus, 306 Minn. 462, 238 N.W.2d 851, 856–857 (1976).

81. People v. Koch, 250 App.Div. 623, 294 N.Y.S. 987 (1937). Cf. Perkins v. United States, 228 F. 408 (4th Cir. 1915).

82. See Perryman v. State, 12 Okl.Cr. 500, 502, 159 P. 937 (1916).

83. State v. Yarborough, 39 Kan. 581, 597 (1888).

84. Leggett v. State, 21 Tex.App. 382, 17 S.W. 159 (1886).

Involuntary intoxication instruction was proper where defendant, who had consumed some liquor, was repeatedly sprayed with an animal repellant before he shot the victim. Peterson v. State, 586 P.2d 144 (Wyo. 1978).

85. Regina v. Mary R. (1887), cited in Kerr, Inebriety 395 (2d ed.), and in 1 Wharton & Stille, Medical Jurisprudence § 243, note 17 (5th ed. 1905).

86. Roberts v. People, 19 Mich. 401, 422 (1870). "But . . . where there is an infirmity and the drinking is for relief of pain occasioned by that infirmity, rather than for voluntary intoxication, he is entitled to an instruction combining the two." Teeters v. Commonwealth, 310 Ky. 546, 549–50, 221 S.W.2d 85, 87 (1949). See Banay, Pathological Reactions to Alcohol, 4 Quar. J. Study on Alcohol 580 (1968).

But one who was fully aware, while drinking, of his unusual psychotic reaction to alcohol, was just as voluntarily drunk as if the reaction had not been unusual. Pauling v. State, ___ S.C. ___, 275 S.E.2d 881 (1981).

One who is aware of a peculiar susceptibility may be found to be reckless in even slight indulgence, but both argument and authority, says Wharton, lead to the conclusion that if by temporary debility or disease a man is maddened by a quantity of wine which on former occasions he wisely and soberly took as a tonic, the intoxication is involuntary.[87]

B. THE EFFECT OF INVOLUNTARY (INNOCENT) INTOXICATION

The fact that one is in a state of involuntary intoxication does not necessarily establish criminal incapacity on his part;[88] it establishes only that his derangement is without culpability and hence is to be dealt with the same as if it were the result of mental disease or defect.[89] He does not have criminal capacity if his mind is so deranged for the moment that he is unable "to know what he is doing and that it is wrong,"[90] and if the particular jurisdiction goes beyond the right-wrong rule in dealing with insanity it should do likewise in cases of involuntary intoxication.[91]

2. VOLUNTARY INTOXICATION (CULPABLE INTOXICATION)

A. IN GENERAL

It is often said that voluntary drunkenness is no excuse for crime.[92] This statement conveys the general idea and is too common to be ignored, but it should be explained that as a matter of scientific jurisprudence it makes no

---

87. 2 Wharton's Criminal Law § 110 (14th ed. 1979).

Under the Model Penal Code "pathological" intoxication would be equated with insanity as a defense. Section 2.08(4).

" '[P]athological intoxication' means intoxication grossly excessive in degree, to which the actor does not know he is susceptible." Id. at (5)(c).

Where the defendant is aware of his reduced tolerance for alcohol and drinks anyway the intoxication is not involuntary. Kane v. United States, 399 F.2d 730 (9th Cir. 1968).

88. See Commonwealth v. Gilbert, 165 Mass. 45, 57, 42 N.E. 336, 337 (1895). Cf. State v. Brown, 38 Kan. 390, 397, 16 P. 259, 262 (1888).

89. People v. Penman, 271 Ill. 82, 110 N.E. 894 (1915); Choate v. State, 19 Okl. Cr. 169, 197 P. 1060 (1921); Hanks v. State, 542 S.W.2d 413 (Tex.Cr.App.1976); United States v. Jewett, 438 F.2d 495 (8th Cir. 1971).

90. State v. Alie, 82 W.Va. 601, 608, 96 S.E. 1011, 1014 (1918).

"Since involuntary intoxication acts to excuse the criminality of the act, it must rise to the level of insanity, which in this jurisdiction is determined by the M'Naghten test." State v. Mriglot, 88 Wn.2d 573, 564 P.2d 784 (1977).

"Unconsciousness due to involuntary intoxication is recognized as a complete defense to a criminal charge." People v. Cruz, 83 Cal.App.3d 308, 147 Cal.Rptr. 740, 754 (1978).

91. State v. Pike, 49 N.H. 399 (1870).

The Model Penal Code applies the "substantial capacity" standard. Section 2.08(4).

92. Pearson's Case, 2 Lewin 144, 168 Eng.Rep. 1108 (1835); Regina v. Gamlen, 1 Fost. & F. 90, 175 Eng.Rep. 639 (1858); People v. Burkhart, 211 Cal. 726, 297 P. 11 (1931); Perry v. State, 116 Tex.Cr.R. 226, 229, 33 S.W.2d 1072, 1073 (1930).

"Intoxication is no defense to any crime, . . ." Morse v. State, 438 P.2d 309, 310 (Okl.Cr.1968).

"Even the most permissive society recognizes that voluntary intoxication will not be tolerated as an excuse or justification for anti-social behavior. . . . The cases are legion in this jurisdiction reaffirming the principle that voluntary intoxication neither exonerates nor excuses criminal conduct. Commonwealth v. Bridge, 495 Pa. 568, 435 A.2d 151, 153 (1981).

contribution because, while voluntary drunkenness is no excuse for crime, neither is anything else.[93] Harm may be excused but not crime. If life has been taken under circumstances amounting to legally-recognized excuse a careful analysis will disclose that the *homicide is excused* and therefore is *not a crime*. Excusable homicide is an important legal concept but it is confusion of terms to speak of either excusable murder or excusable manslaughter. Without attempting to banish the customary statement it will aid in explaining the present problem to point out a more accurate form of expressing the idea, which is: Voluntary drunkenness is no excuse for an *actus reus*. Suppose for example **D** has killed **X** without justification and the only explanation **D** has to offer is that he was voluntarily drunk at the time and did not know what he was doing. Voluntary drunkenness is no excuse for homicide (the *actus reus* for either murder or manslaughter), hence we find homicide committed without justification or excuse which cannot be less than manslaughter at common law.[94] Suppose on the other hand **D** has been arrested for larceny, having been found walking off with **X**'s glass which he had no privilege or authority to carry away. Suppose again the only explanation he has to offer is that he was voluntarily drunk at the time and did not know what he was doing, the evidence indicating that he staggered away from the bar where he had been overindulging and walked out into the street still clutching the glass from which he had been drinking, but too befuddled by liquor to know he was holding anything in his hand,—and when the glass was taken from him by the apprehending officer **D** stared at it blankly with no idea where it came from. The *actus reus* of larceny is the trespassory taking and carrying away of the personal property of another. **D** has done this and his voluntary intoxication is no excuse, but the facts stated fail to establish larceny.[95] Nothing has been excused, but one essential element of

Voluntary intoxication is not a defense to a charge of assault on a federal officer. United States v. Hanson, 618 F.2d 1261 (8th Cir. 1980).

"Mental irresponsibility induced by voluntary intoxication does not raise the defense of insanity." State v. Berge, 25 Wn. App. 433, 607 P.2d 1247, 1250 (1980).

93. Entrapment may be thought to be an exception because even if all elements of the offense are present the defendant is not convicted because of the improper conduct of the officer. See chapter 10, section 7. But the true explanation is that the state is estopped rather than that the defendant is excused.

94. Kriehl v. Commonwealth, 68 Ky. 363 (1869); Choate v. State, 19 Okl.Cr. 169, 197 P. 1060 (1921). It cannot be less than manslaughter under existing law but the statement is not intended to mean that the law could not be otherwise. Perhaps the law should be changed so as to recognize even voluntary intoxication as an excuse for an *actus reus* under certain circumstances.

The rule that voluntary intoxication may be taken into consideration to show

that a particular state of mind did not exist applies to first-degree murder but not to second-degree murder or voluntary manslaughter. United States v. Lopez, 575 F.2d 681 (9th Cir. 1978).

Voluntary intoxication is not a defense to voluntary manslaughter. Commonwealth v. Bridge, 495 Pa. 568, 435 A.2d 151 (1981).

95. Johnson v. State, 32 Ala.App. 217, 24 So.2d 228 (1945); Gower v. State, 298 P.2d 461 (Okl.Cr.1956).

An essential element of robbery in the first degree is the intent. Hence defendant is not guilty if he was so intoxicated at the time as to be unable to form the necessary intent, even if the intoxication was voluntary. Mishler v. Commonwealth, 556 S.W.2d 676 (Ky.1977).

"Voluntary intoxication or drunkenness is not in itself a defense to a charge of crime. But the fact, if it is a fact, that the defendant may have been intoxicated at the time of the commission of the offense may negative the existence of a state of mind that is an essential element of the offense." In a prosecution for entering a bank with intent to rob, in which

larceny, the intent to steal, is completely missing. If he was unaware of having the glass in his hand he is equally innocent of larceny, it should be emphasized, whether he was so drunk he did not know what he was doing and was hence incapable of formulating any intent to control his conduct or was merely *absent-minded* in regard to the glass because his mind was distracted for the moment either by a lesser degree of intoxication or from some cause having nothing to do with intoxication, such as sudden excitement in the street.

B. MENS REA

One so insane as to be incapable of committing crime while sober will not be held to acquire criminal capacity by becoming drunk,[96] while on the other hand one having criminal capacity when unexcited by liquor or drug, still has criminal capacity (to some extent at least) after he has deprived himself of this ability by voluntary intoxication.[97]

Evidence of voluntary intoxication is admissible for the purpose of showing that defendant was physically incapable of committing the crime at the time, and hence could not have been the perpetrator,[98] and also to establish that although he committed the *actus reus* he did so without the special mens rea required for the offense charged, if it has such a requirement.[99] Such a condition, if properly limited to culpable intoxication, will supply the mens rea requirement if no more than criminal negligence is needed for the offense charged,[1] but it cannot take the place of a required specific intent or

there was evidence of intoxication, it was error to refuse such an instruction. United States v. Scott, 529 F.2d 338, 339 (D.C.Cir. 1975).

"Burglary . . . requires that entry be the specific intent to commit a felony or theft. . . . Intoxication may be shown to negate this specific intent." State v. Ruiz, 94 N.M. 771, 617 P.2d 160, 162 (App. 1980).

96. Bailey v. State, 26 Ind. 422 (1866).

97. Choice v. State, 31 Ga. 424 (1860); Thomas v. State, 105 Ga.App. 754, 125 S.E.2d 679 (1962).

98. Jenkins v. State, 93 Ga. 1, 18 S.E. 992 (1893).

99. People v. Freedman, 4 Ill.2d 414, 123 N.E.2d 317 (1954); Long v. Commonwealth, 262 S.W.2d 809 (Ky.1953); State v. Newman, 157 La. 564, 102 So. 671 (1925); People v. Guillett, 342 Mich. 1, 69 N.W.2d 140 (1955).

1. See People v. Townsend, 214 Mich. 267, 273, 183 N.W. 177, 179 (1921).

"Voluntary intoxication is not a defense to a general intent crime, although it may be used to demonstrate the inability to form a particular state of mind necessary for a specific intent crime . . . . Specific intent is not an element of aggravated robbery." State v. Rueckert, 221 Kan. 727, 561 P.2d 850, 856 (1977).

In a prosecution for a specific intent crime, intoxication although voluntary, which precludes formation of the necessary intention may be established as a defense. But conviction of "robbery" of a federally-insured bank does not require proof of a specific intent, and the defense of voluntary intoxication was not available. United States v. Lemon, 550 F.2d 467 (9th Cir. 1977). The statute is 18 U.S.C.A. § 2113(a). Bank robbery and incidental crimes. The first paragraph does not mention intent, although intent is specified in several other paragraphs of the statute.

Voluntary intoxication is not a defense to rape which is a general intent crime. Leary v. Queen, 33 CCC 2d 473 (SCC 1977). Intoxication is no defense to indecent assault, a general intent crime. Swietlinski v. Queen, 55 CCC 2d 481 (SCC 1980).

"The rule in Missouri is that 'voluntary intoxication is not a defense to a criminal charge and . . . the rule does not even allow a jury to consider such intoxication on the issue of specific intent.' State v. Richardson, 495 S.W.2d 435, 440

other special state of mind which is actually missing.[2] For this reason a careful statement of the law should be in some such form as this:

> **No act committed by a person while in a state of voluntary intoxication, shall be deemed less criminal by reason of his having been in such condition. But whenever the actual existence of any particular purpose, motive or intent is a necessary element to constitute a particular species or degree of crime, the jury may take into consideration the fact that the accused was intoxicated at the time, in determining the purpose, motive or intent with which he committed the act.[3]**

One who drinks to nerve himself for the commission of a crime already decided upon is guilty of that crime, if the purpose is carried out, regardless of the mens rea requirement of the particular offense or the extent of the intoxication.[4] Carrying out the preconceived design speaks for itself so far as intent is concerned, and the perpetration is properly held to have been deliberate and premeditated (if needed for the degree of the offense charged)

(Mo. banc 1973) . . .. We must follow the rule in Richardson." State v. Hegwood, 558 S.W.2d 378, 381 (Mo.App. 1977).

2. "Voluntary intoxication is not a defense to a general intent crime, although it may be used to demonstrate an inability to form a particular state of mind necessary for a specific intent crime." State v. McDaniel, 228 Kan. 172, 612 P.2d 1231, 1237 (1980).

3. Carey v. State, 91 Idaho 706, 429 P.2d 836 (1967).

See People v. Burkhart, 211 Cal. 726, 297 P. 11 (1931); Aszman v. State, 123 Ind. 347, 24 N.E. 123 (1890); O'Grady v. State, 36 Neb. 320, 321-2, 54 N.W. 556 (1893); Pigman v. State, 14 Ohio 555, 556 (1846); State v. Turner, 3 Utah 2d 285, 282 P.2d 1045 (1955).

If voluntary intoxication was such that D was incapable of premeditation and deliberation the homicide was not first-degree murder, and if he was so intoxicated at the time as to be incapable of harboring malice aforethought the killing was not murder but manslaughter. State v. Brooks, 150 Mont. 399, 436 P.2d 91 (1967). Accord, People v. Castillo, 65 Cal.Rptr. 202 (Cal.App.1968).

If the crime charged requires some particular mental state, such as knowledge, even voluntary intoxication cannot be ignored. Kimoktoak v. State, 584 P.2d 25 (Alaska 1978).

"While voluntary drunkenness does not constitute a criminal defense per se, it may prove a mental incapacity to form

a specific intent." United States v. Zink, 612 F.2d 511, 515 (10th Cir. 1980).

Under the new Code of Criminal Justice purpose or knowledge has been made an element of many offenses. In a prosecution for any such offense, voluntary intoxication is a defense if so extreme as to negative the required mental element. State v. Stasio, 78 N.J. 467, 396 A.2d 1129 (1979). The court cast doubt on the appropriateness of such a broad standard.

4. One who drinks to "nerve" himself to commit a crime already decided upon, and who thereupon does commit the crime, is not in a position to maintain that he was too drunk at the time to entertain the intent which he executed. State v. Butner, 66 Nev. 127, 206 P.2d 253 (1949). And see People v. Bartz, 342 Ill. 56, 67, 173 N.E. 779, 783 (1930); Harris v. Commonwealth, 183 Ky. 542, 547, 209 S.W. 509, 511 (1919); State v. Robinson, 20 W.Va. 713, 741 (1882).

"The principle here invoked, however, is not without exception. It does not apply where the intention to commit the crime precedes the act as, for example, in the instance of an accused who, meaning and intending to commit a criminal act requiring specific intent fortifies himself by drink for the event." State v. Reposa, 99 R.I. 147, 206 A.2d 213, 216 (1965).

There was evidence that defendant drank in order to quiet his fears before going out to pass counterfeit money. United States v. Zink, 612 F.2d 511 (10th Cir. 1980).

even if the offender was too drunk to deliberate at the time of the act,[5] because it resulted from prior deliberation and premeditation, and the requirement of "concurrence" is not one of coincidence but of causation.[6] No amount of argument can obscure the fact that in the legal view homicide resulting from a deliberate and premeditated intent to kill is a deliberate and premeditated killing.

Quite otherwise is the situation when one in a state of voluntary intoxication commits the *actus reus* of some crime which he had no thought of committing while sober. If too drunk at the time to know what he is doing, and therefore incapable of forming any intent, his trespassory carrying away of a chattel is not larceny because there is no intent to steal,[7] his awkward wrenching of property from the hands of another is not robbery for the same reason,[8] and his fumbling into another's building is not burglary because the breaking and entering are without burglarious intent.[9] For a like reason one too drunk to be capable of forming any intent (and who had no such intent while sober) cannot commit (1) felony-murder based upon homicide committed in alleged perpetration of robbery,[10] (2) an attempt to commit suicide[11] or (3) a statutory offense requiring a specific intent.[12]

No amount of voluntary intoxication precludes the possibility of committing assault and battery,[13] because culpable negligence is sufficient for guilt of this offense,[14] and the same is true of an assault with a deadly weapon where the culpable placing of another in apprehension of an immediate bat-

---

5. State v. Butner, 66 Nev. 127, 206 P.2d 253 (1949); State v. Hammonds, 216 N.C. 67, 3 S.E.2d 439 (1939). And see State v. Robinson, 20 W.Va. 713, 741 (1882); Harris v. Commonwealth, 183 Ky. 542, 547, 209 S.W. 509, 511 (1919); Garner v. State, 28 Fla. 113, 9 So. 835 (1891).

6. See chapter 7, section 9.

7. Johnson v. State, 32 Ala.App. 217, 24 So.2d 228 (1945); Wood v. State, 34 Ark. 341 (1879); Brennen v. State, 169 Ky. 815, 185 S.W. 489 (1916); People v. Walker, 38 Mich. 156 (1878); State v. Koerner, 8 N.D. 292 (1899); Jamison v. State, 53 Okl.Cr. 59, 7 P.2d 171 (1932); Gower v. State, 298 P.2d 461 (Okl.Cr. 1956). And if sudden deprivation of the drug drives a dope-addict into such a frenzy that he does not know what he is doing he is not guilty of larceny. Rogers v. State, 33 Ind. 543 (1870).

"We emphasize that we do not question that intoxication, even though quite voluntary, may negate the existence of the specific intent required for conviction of many crimes." United States v. Shuckahosee, 609 F.2d 1351, 1356 (10th Cir. 1979).

8. Keeton v. Commonwealth, 92 Ky. 522, 18 S.W. 359 (1892); Snipes v. State, 261 Ind. 581, 307 N.E.2d 470 (1974).

9. Schwabacher v. People, 165 Ill. 618, 46 N.E. 809 (1897); State v. Bell, 29 Iowa 316 (1870); State v. Phillips, 80 W.Va. 748, 93 S.E. 828 (1917).

10. People v. Koerber, 244 N.Y. 147, 155 N.E. 79 (1926); Commonwealth v. Graves, 461 Pa. 118, 334 A.2d 661 (1975).

11. Regina v. Doody, 6 Cox C.C. 463 (1854).

12. People v. Freedman, 4 Ill.2d 414, 123 N.E.2d 317 (1954); People v. Pasquino, 65 A.D.2d 629, 409 N.Y.S.2d 518 (1978) (bribery).

13. Englehardt v. State, 88 Ala. 100, 7 So. 154 (1890); Commonwealth v. Malone, 114 Mass. 295 (1873); State v. Murphy, 128 Vt. 288, 262 A.2d 456 (1970).

Since the crime of gross sexual misconduct does not require any specific intent, voluntary intoxication is not a defense. State v. Keaten, 390 A.2d 1043 (Me.1978).

"Voluntary intoxication, therefore, cannot negate the element of recklessness." State v. Watkins, 126 Ariz. 293, 614 P.2d 835, 843, n.5 (1980). This is said to follow from the wording of the statute. At common law it would seem that while voluntary intoxication cannot negate criminal negligence, it can negate recklessness which requires awareness of the risk.

14. See chapter 2, section 2, A, 6.

tery is sufficient to constitute a criminal assault,[15] but this is not true of an assault with intent to wound or to murder[16] or to commit rape.[17]   One too drunk to know the essential fact, it may be added, cannot commit a crime which requires such knowledge for guilt unless he knew before he placed himself in this condition.[18]

(A) Homicide Cases

The problem of voluntary intoxication tends to become complicated in the homicide cases and to avoid repetition it is to be understood that any element of preconceived intent to kill or injure is assumed to be lacking in the following discussion.   The starting point, free from substantial dispute, is that a mind may be so confused by intoxication as to be incapable of deliberation and premeditation, and hence one in this condition even if the drunkenness is voluntary is incapable of a deliberate and premeditated killing.[19]   At the other extreme, and equally well established by the cases, is the rule that no amount of voluntary intoxication can entirely excuse a homicide and thereby entitle the slayer to an acquittal.[20]   At the same time no homicide which would be only manslaughter by a sober man can be held to be murder merely because of the slayer's intoxication,[21] a point entitled to particular attention if provocation is involved.

As explained above[22] the "rule of provocation," whereby homicide which otherwise would be murder is held to be voluntary manslaughter, requires a killing in a sudden heat of passion (the actual state of the slayer's mind) engendered by adequate provocation (measured by an objective test—the ordinary reasonable person).   Whatever would be sufficient for this purpose in

15. State v. Johnson, 207 La. 161, 20 So.2d 741 (1944).

Assault with a deadly weapon is a general intent crime and intoxication is no defense. People v. Rocha, 3 Cal.3d 893, 92 Cal.Rptr. 172, 479 P.2d 372 (1971).

16. Crosby v. People, 137 Ill. 325, 27 N.E. 49 (1891); State v. Pasnan, 118 Iowa 501, 92 N.W. 682 (1902); Cline v. State, 43 Ohio St. 332 (1885); People v. Phillips, 37 Mich.App.2d 242, 194 N.W.2d 501 (1971).

17. People v. Guillett, 342 Mich. 1, 69 N.W.2d 140 (1955).

18. O'Grady v. State, 36 Neb. 320, 54 N.W. 556 (1893); Pigman v. State, 14 Ohio St. 555 (1846). In these cases convictions of uttering forged checks or counterfeit money were reversed. The syllabus of another case says that the offense of passing a false and worthless check was neither mitigated nor excused by the voluntary intoxication of the defendant. State v. Zumwalt, 129 Mont. 529, 291 P.2d 257 (1955). But while the defendant had been drinking the evidence disclosed that he dickered extensively with the clerk before making the purchase for which the check was given, and hence knew what he was doing.

19. State v. Johnson, 40 Conn. 136 (1873); Johnson v. Commonwealth, 135 Va. 524, 115 S.E. 673 (1923). "The recognized doctrine is that the state of intoxication of the accused may be invoked to negative . . . deliberate intent, in the absence of evidence, aliunde, to prove premeditation." State v. Trivas, 32 La. Ann. 1086, 1089 (1880); State v. Hogan, 117 La. 863, 873, 42 So. 352, 355 (1906); State v. Newman, 157 La. 564, 566, 102 So. 671, 672 (1925); Goodman v. State, 573 P.2d 400 (Wyo.1977).

In reducing the offense from first to second-degree murder the court said, "the judge omitted to instruct the jury about the bearing of intoxication on the question of deliberate premeditation." Commonwealth v. King, 374 Mass. 501, 373 N.E.2d 208, 212 (1978).

20. Kriehl v. Commonwealth, 68 Ky. 363 (1869); Choate v. State, 19 Okl.Cr. 169, 197 P. 1060 (1921); State v. Contreras, 107 Ariz. 68, 481 P.2d 861 (1971).

21. McIntyre v. People, 38 Ill. 514 (1865).

22. Chapter 2, section 1, C, 1, (A).

the case of a sober person is equally adequate provocation for one who is drunk,[23] and conversely nothing otherwise inadequate will be held to be sufficient provocation merely because the killer happened to be voluntarily intoxicated at the time.[24] The standard by which the adequacy of provocation for this purpose is measured "is the same for all men whether drunk or sober." [25] If the provocation itself is adequate, however, even voluntary drunkenness may be taken into consideration in determining the actual state of the slayer's mind at the time,—that is, whether the killing was in the heat of passion or in cold blood.[26] And even where the provocation was inadequate to reduce an intentional killing to manslaughter, "drunkenness may be taken into consideration to explain the probability of a party's intention in the case of violence committed on sudden provocation." [27] It may be considered, for example, to determine whether a shooting was intentional or resulted from the reckless handling of a firearm.[28]

The problem is much the same in certain cases in which the defendant's claim is that the killing was in self-defense. If one, who was in no imminent danger of death or bodily injury at the time he killed another, claims an excuse on the ground of self-defense he must establish (1) that there were reasonable grounds to induce him to believe he was in such danger, and (2) that he actually did so believe.[29] The voluntary intoxication of the defender has nothing whatever to do with the reasonableness of the grounds for a belief of imminent peril,[30] but if such grounds actually existed the jury may "take into consideration, among other circumstances, the fact of the prisoner['s] being drunk at the time, in order to determine whether he acted under a *bona fide* apprehension" of such an attack.[31] One who has an exaggerated belief of danger because of his voluntary intoxication and kills under a supposed need of such action in self-defense is guilty, not of murder, but of manslaughter, because his unfounded belief presents a case of culpable negligence rather than of malice aforethought.[32] It may be added that under some of the new penal codes the offense would be of a lower grade, under some such name as negligent homicide.

23. McIntyre, note 20. And see Bishop v. United States, 71 App.D.C. 132, 107 F.2d 297, 302–3 (1939).

24. Garner v. State, 28 Fla. 113, 9 So. 835 (1891); Jones v. State, 29 Ga. 594 (1860); Commonwealth v. Hawkins, 69 Mass. 463 (1855); Keenan v. Commonwealth, 44 Pa. 55 (1862); Pirtle v. State, 28 Tenn. 663 (1849).

25. Bishop v. United States, 71 App. D.C. 132, 107 F.2d 297, 303 (1939).

26. See People v. Rogers, 18 N.Y. 9, 25 (1858); State v. McCants, 1 Spears 384, 394 (S.C.1843); Rex v. Thomas, 7 Car. & P. 817, 820, 173 Eng.Rep. 356, 358 (1837); Regina v. Olbey, 30 N.R. 152, 50 CCC 2d 257 (SCC 1979).

If voluntary intoxication resulted in diminished capacity, the resulting homicide would be voluntary manslaughter. People v. Tidwell, 3 Cal.3d 82, 89 Cal.Rptr.

58, 473 P.2d 762 (1970). If it resulted in unconsciousness the guilt would be involuntary manslaughter.

27. Pearson's Case, 2 Lewin 144, 145, 168 Eng.Rep. 1108 (1835).

28. See Long v. Commonwealth, 262 S.W.2d 809 (Ky.1953).

29. Grubbs v. Commonwealth, 240 Ky. 473, 42 S.W.2d 702 (1931).

30. Springfield v. State, 96 Ala. 81, 11 So. 250 (1892).

31. Marshall's Case, 1 Lewin 76, 168 Eng.Rep. 965 (1830). See also Regina v. Gamlen, 1 Fost. & F. 90, 175 Eng.Rep. 639 (1858).

32. United States v. King, 34 F. 302, 313 (C.C.N.Y.1888); People v. Ray, 14 Cal.3d 20, 120 Cal.Rptr. 377, 533 P.2d 1017 (1975).

The subject of malice has presented more than a little perplexity in this field. Bishop's statement that "the intention to drink may fully supply the place of malice aforethought," [33] has been repeated at times,[34] but is clearly unsound and cannot be accepted. The explanation offered by Bishop, actually quite different and fully supported by the cases, is that "the mere fact of drunkenness will not reduce to manslaughter a homicide which would otherwise be murder." [35] Needless to say there is a wide difference between asserting that voluntary intoxication will not reduce to manslaughter a homicide which would otherwise be murder, and on the other hand that it may make murder out of what would not otherwise be so. One rather careful statement is as follows:

"And when we admit evidence of intoxication to rebut a guilty knowledge requiring nice discrimination and judgment, to rebut a charge of deliberation and premeditation, and to show that the accused did not at the time intend to do the act which he did do, we think we have gone far enough; and, that looking to the practical administration of the criminal law, a due regard to the public safety requires that the mere question of malice should be determined by the other circumstances of the case, aside from the fact of intoxication, as in other cases." [36]

"A drunken malice is as dangerous," said the same court,[37] "and may be quite as wicked, as a sober malice," and hence intentional homicide by one voluntarily drunk is murder in the absence of recognized justification, excuse or mitigation.[38] On the other hand intoxication, even if voluntary, may be of such a character and to such a degree as to show that the mind was incapable of malice at the time.[39] To repeat an extreme illustration, used long ago, a mother in a drunken stupor who should unintentionally smother her infant

33. 1 Bishop, New Criminal Law § 401 (8th ed. 1892).

34. High v. State, 197 Ark. 681, 684, 120 S.W.2d 24, 25–6 (1938).

35. Ibid.

36. Nichols v. State, 8 Ohio St. 435, 439 (1858). See also D.P.P. v. Beard [1920] AC 479; D.P.P. v. Majewski, [1977] AC 443. In cases refusing to go beyond manslaughter the courts may be adopting a pragmatic solution to a problem that ought not be handled by pure principles of logic. ". . . it is quite impossible to deal with this matter (the intoxication defense) logically." Regina v. Howell, 2 ALL E.R. 807, 808 (1974). See Williams, Textbook of Criminal Law p. 423–437 (1978).

37. Id. at 438.

38. Warner v. State, 56 N.J.L. 686, 29 A. 505 (1894). "Where the requisite proof is adduced to show a wicked intentional murder, he (the respondent) is not permitted to show a voluntary and temporary intoxication in extenuation of his crime." State v. Stacy, 104 Vt. 379, 407,

160 A. 257, 269 (1932). "A man who can voluntarily shoot is capable of malice, unless he can plead some infirmity besides drunkenness." Marshall v. State, 59 Ga. 154, 156 (1877).

39. Pash v. Commonwealth, 146 Ky. 390, 142 S.W. 700 (1912); Smith v. State, 4 Neb. 277 (1876); Tubby v. State, 15 Okl.Cr. 496, 178 P. 491 (1919); Choate v. State, 19 Okl.Cr. 169, 197 P. 1060 (1921). "The recognized doctrine is that the state of intoxication of the accused may be invoked to negative malice. . . ." State v. Trivas, 32 La.Ann. 1086, 1089 (1880); State v. Hogan, 117 La. 863, 873, 42 So. 352, 355 (1906); State v. Newman, 157 La. 564, 566, 102 So. 671, 672 (1925).

Intoxication may be a defense to a murder charge in the killing of a woman, but not to the general intent crime of feticide. Goodman v. State, 573 P.2d 400 (Wyo.1977). In Regina v. Caldwell, [1981] Crim.L.Rev. 392 (H.L.) it was held that intoxication could be a defense to intentional arson but not reckless arson.

in her embrace by overlying it in bed would not be held to have caused the death by malice aforethought and therefore would not be guilty of murder.[40]

(B) Degree of Intoxication

The words "drunk" and "intoxicated" as customarily used do not necessarily signify complete mental prostration, and hence the mere fact that an alleged burglar was drunk at the time does not negative the possibility of his having broken in with burglarious intent.[41] To accomplish this purpose the intoxication must be shown to have been of such a character as "to create a state of mental confusion, excluding the possibility of a specific intent . . . ."[42] One voluntarily intoxicated to such an extent has diminished criminal capacity because (in the absence of preconceived design) he is temporarily incapable of committing any crime which requires (1) a specific intent, (2) knowledge of some pertinent fact, or (3) any other special mental element. One whose mind is confused by liquor or drug in a slightly less degree might be capable of forming an intent to kill but unable to do so with deliberation, and even mild intoxication might result in an inadvertent act such as heedlessly carrying away the glass when leaving the bar. All such matters demand attention because the *actus reus* without the required mens rea is not a crime.

C. CRITICISM OF ACCEPTED VIEW

"If a man is punished for doing something when drunk that he would not have done when sober," it has been asked, "is he not in plain truth punished for getting drunk?"[43] And although Markby answered this question in the affirmative[44] such a position will not stand up under analysis. If a man is punished for a homicide committed by him when drunk, which he would not have committed when sober, he is not punished *because of* his intoxication but *despite* it, just as one punished for killing in a sudden heat of passion engendered by adequate provocation is punished, not because of, but despite his heat of passion. In the latter case, we are at once reminded, the heat of passion so engendered is regarded as a mitigating circumstance because "of forbearance for the weakness of human nature."[45] One who is voluntarily drunk cannot claim to have been provoked by his own intoxication, because nothing could be less adequate in point of law, but provocation is not the only possible basis for mitigation. He who, while unduly excited by liquor, has committed a prohibited deed he would never have thought of doing while sober, is not in the same scale of moral culpability, even if the intoxication was voluntary, as another who has done the same thing without such excitement, or who made the decision first and drank to nerve himself for the per-

40. People v. Robinson, 2 Park.Cr.R. 235, 302 (N.Y.1855).

41. People v. Henderson, 138 Cal.App. 2d 505, 292 P.2d 267 (1956). Accord, Baker v. State, 24 Ala.App. 215, 132 So. 708 (1931); State v. Estrada, 86 N.M. 286, 523 P.2d 21 (1974); State v. Austad, 166 Mont. 425, 533 P.2d 1069 (1975).

42. State v. Trivas, 32 La.Ann. 1086, 1089 (1880); State v. Hogan, 117 La. 863, 873, 42 So. 352, 355 (1906); State v. New-man, 157 La. 564, 566, 102 So. 671, 672 (1925). The quotation did not refer to burglary but the problem is the same. See also Yarber v. State, 224 Ind. 616, 179 N.E.2d 882 (1962).

43. Williams, Criminal Law 373 (1953).

44. Ibid.

45. People v. Freel, 48 Cal. 436, 437 (1874).

petration.[46] This has been recognized at one very important point in certain prosecutions for first-degree murder (where reliance is upon deliberation and premeditation) as pointed out above, but perhaps it should receive much more recognition. It may be logical to say that a voluntarily drunk person is capable of committing an assault with intent to murder so long as he has enough mind left to be capable of forming such an intent, even if too befuddled to appreciate the moral qualities of the act,[47] but due consideration "for the weakness of human nature" might find some other solution. Any step in this direction may require the aid of legislation but the matter is entitled to very thoughtful study.

Some courts have now taken just such a step without the aid of legislation under the concept of diminished capacity. Thus in one case [48] in which there was evidence of diminished capacity by reason of intoxication, and no evidence that the intoxication was involuntary, the judge had instructed the jury that they could not find defendant guilty of murder in either degree if, by reason of diminished capacity due to intoxication he did not harbor malice aforethought. But the conviction of murder was reversed because the judge did not go further and instruct the jury that it could convict defendant of *voluntary manslaughter* if it found that defendant had intentionally taken life but in doing so lacked malice because of intoxication. The California court, because of "human frailty," recognizes diminished capacity caused by intoxication as a mitigating circumstance even if the intoxication was voluntary, comparable to the "rule of provocation" which applies even if the provoking circumstance was mutual fisticuffs.[49]

3. DELIRIUM TREMENS

An otherwise normal mind temporarily unbalanced by intoxication is not "what is termed an unsound mind," [50] and no amount of excitement or stupor which is the direct result of liquor or drugs is recognized as insanity, in the true sense, or will be dealt with in the same category unless it is involuntary. On the other hand long-continued overindulgence in liquor or drugs may result in an actual disease of the mind and when this occurs it affects criminal capacity "in the same way as insanity which has been produced by any other cause." [51] Unfortunately the term *delirium tremens* has been used at times

46. "There is nothing the law so abhors as the cool, deliberate, and settled purpose to do mischief." O'Grady v. State, 36 Neb. 320, 323, 54 N.W. 556, 557 (1893); Pigman v. State, 14 Ohio St. 555, 556 (1846).

47. Roberts v. People, 19 Mich. 401, 418–9 (1870). Voluntary drunkenness which excites a fearful rage does not disprove an assault with intent to do grievous bodily harm unless the defendant was so drunk he did not know what he was doing and merely happened to hit the other while striking wildly about. Regina v. Stopford, 11 Cox C.C. 643 (1870). See also State v. Guiden, 46 Wis. 2d 328, 174 N.W.2d 488 (1970); State v. Turley, 113 R.I. 104, 318 A.2d 455 (1974).

48. People v. Castillo, 70 Cal.2d 264, 74 Cal.Rptr. 385, 449 P.2d 449 (1969).

49. People v. Conley, 64 Cal.2d 310, 49 Cal.Rptr. 815, 411 P.2d 911 (1966).

50. Rennie's Case, 1 Lewin 76, 168 Eng.Rep. 965 (1825).

51. People v. Griggs, 17 Cal.2d 621, 625, 110 P.2d 1031, 1034 (1941). Accord, 1 Hale P.C. *32; United States v. Drew, 25 Fed.Cas. 913, No. 14,993 (C.C.Mass. 1828); Beasley v. State, 50 Ala. 149 (1873). And see Public Prosecutor v. Beard, [1920] A.C. 479, 500 (1920); People v. Guillett, 342 Mich. 1, 6, 69 N.W.2d 140, 142–3 (1955).

"The majority of courts have drawn a distinction between (1) the mental effect of intoxication, which is the immediate result of a particular alcoholic bout; and (2) an alcoholic psychosis, such as delirium tremens, resulting from long contin-

loosely to indicate a mere "fit of drunken frenzy" although technically it designates a mental disease sometimes called *mania a potu*.[52] Care must be taken to distinguish between the two because the first is a case of drunkenness[53] and the second one of mental disease.[54] Logic alone might have indicated a different answer because more fault is involved in long-continued overindulgence than in a single debauch, but as it developed the "law takes no notice of the cause of insanity." [55]

4. MODEL PENAL CODE

For the most part the Model Penal Code follows the general pattern of existing law as to intoxication.[56] It substitutes "self-induced intoxication" for "voluntary intoxication," which is probably an improvement since the old labels were never satisfactory; but it would seem even better to speak of "culpable intoxication" and "innocent intoxication" since these are the concepts actually intended. It agrees with the prevailing position by providing that any intoxication will disprove a criminal charge if it was such as to negative a special mental element essential to conviction. And it is in line with existing law by equating non-self-induced intoxication with insanity insofar as a defense to crime is concerned; but since this means applying the "substantial capacity standard" in determining criminal capacity, there is an important difference in the application.

D. RECENT DEVELOPMENTS[57]

The fact that alcoholism (*dipsomania*) is a disease, not to be cured by frequent periods of incarceration for public drunkenness or disorderly conduct, has not received due attention in the enforcement of justice. The right of the social group to protect itself against such persons is free from dispute but a mere multiplicity of arrests without therapeutic treatment is not the solution. Recently there have been important steps in the direction of a new development. One of the first of these was *Robinson*,[58] in which the defendant was charged under a former California statute which made it a misdemeanor to "use . . . or be addicted to the use of narcotics, . . ." The

ued habits of excessive drinking." O'Leary v. State, 604 P.2d 1099, 1102 (Alaska 1979).

52. Cheadle v. State, 11 Okl.Cr. 566, 571, 149 P. 919, 922 (1915).

Current medical nomenclature would characterize the pathology attendant to the extreme and prolonged use of alcohol in terms of, "alcohol withdrawal delirium, alcohol hallucinosis," and alcohol related "dementia." Diagnostic and Statistical Manual of Mental Disorders, 3rd ed. pp. 134–137 (1980).

53. Nestlerode v. United States, 74 App.D.C. 276, 122 F.2d 56 (1941).

54. See State v. Riley, 100 Mo. 493, 499, 13 S.W. 1063, 1064 (1890); People v. Rogers, 18 N.Y. 9, 17 (1853).

55. Director of Public Prosecutions v. Beard, [1920] A.C. 479, 500 (1920). It was suggested *obiter* that the result

might be otherwise if insanity resulted from a drinking spree entered into by one who had reason to believe from experience that this would be the consequence. Roberts v. People, 19 Mich. 401, 422 (1870).

56. Section 2.08.

57. See, for example, Mullan and Sangiuliano, Alcoholism: Group Psychotherapy and Rehabilitation (1966); Block, Alcoholism—Its Facets and Phases (1965); Jellinek, The Disease Concept of Alcoholism (1960); Siragusa, The Trail of the Poppy (1966); Masters and Houston, The Varieties of Psychedelic Experience (1966); O'Donnell and Ball, Narcotic Addiction (1966); Wilner and Kassbaum, Narcotics (1965).

58. Robinson v. California, 370 U.S. 660, 82 S.Ct. 1417 (1962).

jury had been instructed that a guilty verdict would be authorized if they found either that defendant had used a narcotic in a specific instance or that he had the "status or condition" of a narcotics addict; and a verdict of guilty was returned by the jury. The validity of the addiction clause of the statute had been questioned on the ground that addiction is an illness which can be innocently contracted,[59] and a conviction based upon this verdict was challenged on the theory that to punish for the "status or condition" of an addict was cruel and unusual punishment in violation of the Due Process clause of the Fourteenth Amendment.

An earlier statute providing punishment for the unlawful possession of contraband had been challenged on the theory that possession may be "unwitting" and hence not culpable, but it was saved by interpretation. The Court held that the statute must be construed to mean "a willing and conscious possession" and therefore culpable.[60] No such interpretation was available in this case because of the judge's instruction, and the Supreme Court held that the statute, so interpreted, was in violation of the constitution.[61]

While this was the actual holding, because only this was involved, the Court made clear that it would not permit the punishment of narcotic addiction, as such, even if culpably contracted.[62] The Court compared such addiction to the status of having a common cold although a much better analogy would be the one suffering from delirium tremens, who is dealt with the same as one suffering from any other mental disease or defect. In sum, the Court takes the position that narcotic addiction is an illness and that illness cannot be punished as such. The validity of protective measures by way of compulsory civil commitment for rehabilitation was conceded.

There has been increasing sentiment in favor of a change of procedure when police find, in a public place, an intoxicated person who is actually unoffending and merely helpless. Rather than to arrest him for crime it would seem preferable to take him into protective custody and deliver him to a rehabilitation center. The pilot case in this area is *Easter*,[63] and back of the case is a statute of the District of Columbia providing in part:

"The purpose of this chapter is . . . to substitute for jail sentences for drunkenness medical and other scientific methods of treatment which will benefit the individual involved and more fully protect the public." [64] It was held that the full text of the statute of which this is a part precludes "attaching criminality in this jurisdiction to intoxication in public of a chronic alcoholic." [65] A concurring opinion by three justices was to emphasize that the statute does not address itself "to some revised standards for determining criminal responsibility as to yet other crimes than public drunkenness." [66]

One United States Court of Appeals went far beyond *Easter*. The North Carolina statute providing punishment for any person found drunk in a pub-

---

59. See 2 Witkin, California Crimes § 711 (1963).

60. Baender v. Barnett, 255 U.S. 224, 41 S.Ct. 271 (1921).

61. Robinson, supra, note 2.

62. Id. 667, 82 S.Ct. at 1420. As to civil commitment for narcotic addiction see Narcotic Control Commission v.

James, 22 N.Y.2d 545, 393 N.Y.S.2d 531, 240 N.E.2d 29 (1968).

63. Easter v. District of Columbia, 361 F.2d 50 (D.C.Cir. 1966).

64. D.C.Code 1961, § 24–501.

65. *Easter*, at 52.

66. Id. at 61.

lic place was held to constitute cruel and unusual punishment as applied to a chronic alcoholic.[67] The court approved defendant's syllogism: "Driver's chronic alcoholism is a disease which has destroyed the power of his will to resist alcohol; his appearance in public in that condition is not his volition, but a compulsion symptomatic of the disease; and to stigmatize him as a criminal for this act is a cruel and unusual punishment." [68]

Later the Supreme Court had occasion to consider this problem in *Powell*.[69] A chronic alcoholic had been convicted of public drunkenness under a state statute on the ground that chronic alcoholism was not a defense to the offense charged. The Court affirmed this conviction because they were "unable to conclude, on the state of this record or on the current state of medical knowledge, that chronic alcoholics in general, and Leroy Powell in particular, suffer from such an irresistible compulsion to drink and to get drunk in public that they are utterly unable to control their performance of either or both of these acts and thus cannot be deterred at all from public intoxication." [70]

While the actual decision in *Powell* was based upon the failure to show that the accused was utterly incapable of being drunk in a public place (White, J., based his concurrence expressly on this ground), most of the Justices were apparently prepared to hold that conviction for what cannot be resisted is permissible under the constitution. The four dissenting Justices would have recognized the defense in this case; but they would distinguish between an alcoholic who gets drunk, and one who commits a crime such as robbery or assault while drunk, because such "offenses require independent acts or conduct and do not typically flow from and are not part of the syndrome of the disease of chronic alcoholism." [71] They were unwilling to make

---

67. Driver v. Hinnant, 356 F.2d 761 (4th Cir. 1966).

68. Id. at 763.

69. Powell v. Texas, 392 U.S. 514, 88 S.Ct. 2145 (1968).

70. Id. at 535, 88 S.Ct. at 2155. Four Justices would have reversed the conviction.

The position taken in *Driver* was rejected in California.

In re Spinks, 253 Cal.App. 748, 61 Cal. Rptr. 743 (1967).

"An alcoholic may at different times be in varying degrees of intoxication, and may at times be sober. As a defense to an accusation of crime (in the absence of insanity or mental irresponsibility), the issue is not whether or not the perpetrator is an alcoholic, but whether or not the person is intoxicated to the extent of being unable to form the intent which is an element of the crime charged." State v. Shelton, 71 Wn.2d 838, 431 P.2d 201, 204 (1967). The jury had found defendant guilty of assault in the first degree.

The fact that D was a chronic alcoholic is no defense to a charge of driving while under the influence of liquor. Shelburne v. State, 446 P.2d 56 (Okl.Cr.1968).

A statute punishing being drunk in a public place is valid even as to an alcoholic. He is punished, not for being an alcoholic, but for his behavior of being drunk in a public place. Seattle v. Hill, 72 Wn. 2d 786, 435 P.2d 692 (1967). See Murtagh, Arrests for Public Intoxication, 35 Fordham L.Rev. 1 (1966); Note, The Criminal Responsibility of Chronic Drunks, 52 Cornell L.Q. 470 (1967). Lovall and Stub, The Revolving Door, 59 V. of Crim.L.C. and P.S. 525 (1968).

Heroin addiction alone does not require an involuntary intoxication instruction even if the addiction diminishes a person's capacity to refrain from using heroin. Tacorante v. People, ___ Colo. ___, 624 P.2d 1324 (1981).

"If the defendant has the ability to resist the initial drink, the condition is within his control. Particularly when person has reason to know that his behavior while intoxicated often approaches criminality, we do not wish to remove whatever deterrent effect the criminal law has on such behavior." United States v. Shuckahosee, 609 F.2d 1351, 1355 (10th Cir. 1979).

71. 392 U.S. at 559, 88 S.Ct. at 2167, note 2.

the defense of "irresistible impulse" a constitutional requirement. Four of the other Justices were unwilling to take a position which might lead to the adoption of any of the various insanity tests as such a requirement.

The decision in *Powell* would not seem to affect *Easter* since that case relied primarily upon a statute of the District of Columbia. But it is otherwise as to *Driver*. The Fourth Circuit will have to find more than was shown in that case to upset another state conviction of being drunk in a public place. Where there is no alcoholic psychosis a defendant cannot claim his drinking was involuntary merely because he is a "chronic alcoholic." [72]

Some state legislatures have followed the lead of the *Easter* case and have provided for detoxification programs for the treatment and rehabilitation of alcoholics. The process is civil rather than criminal. [73]

SECTION 4. COERCION OF WIFE BY HUSBAND (THE "DOCTRINE OF COERCION")

Although as an abstract statement any action or restraint imposed upon one by another may be spoken of as coercion, there has been a tendency in the criminal law to employ the word "compulsion" for the general field and to reserve the word "coercion" to indicate the exercise of such influence (actual or presumed) over a married woman by her husband. And since the latter is not merely a specific instance of the former, but is something which differs from it in kind so far as common-law consequences are concerned, there are important reasons for retaining this difference in the meaning to be assigned to these terms.

As will be pointed out in the following chapter one may be excused for a prohibited act he has been compelled to perpetrate against his will,—subject to certain important restrictions and limitations, but compulsion in general is a modifying circumstance rather than a limitation of criminal capacity. On the other hand the "doctrine of coercion" as it was developed by the common law, resulted in a definite, though very narrow, diminution of the criminal capacity of a married woman. [1]

For the most part, a married woman is answerable to the criminal law as fully as is a man or a *feme sole* for prohibited acts which she commits voluntarily and of her own free will. [2] Furthermore, the mere fact of the marital relation does not raise any presumption of the husband's control, [3] but the books are full of statements to the effect that if the husband has in fact coerced the act, the wife is excused, except for certain offenses, [4] and that

72. O'Leary v. State, 604 P.2d 1099 (Alaska 1979).

73. E.g., Mont.Code Ann. 53–24–101 et seq. (1979). See Note, Alcohol Abuse and The Law, 94 Harv.L.Rev. 1660 (1981).

1. ". . . the disability of the wife by virtue of marriage." Morton v. State, 141 Tenn. 357, 360, 209 S.W. 644, 645 (1919). ". . . incapable of committing an offence." Commonwealth v. Burk, 77 Mass. 437, 438 (1858).

2. 1 Hawk.P.C. c. 1, § 11 (6th ed. 1788); Regina v. Cohen, 11 Cox C.C. 99

(1868); Regina v. John, 13 Cox C.C. 100 (1875); Pennybaker v. State, 2 Blackf. 484 (Ind.1831); State v. Nelson, 29 Me. 329, 337 (1849); Commonwealth v. Murphy, 68 Mass. 510 (1854); People v. Wright, 38 Mich. 744 (1878); Emmons v. State, 291 P.2d 838 (Okl.Cr.1955); State v. Funk, 490 S.W.2d 354 (Mo.App.1973).

3. Brown v. Attorney-General, [1898] App.Cas. 234, 237 (1897).

4. Sarah Connolly's Case, 2 Lewin C.C. 229, 168 Eng.Rep. 1137 (1829); Burk, supra, n. 1. Where a married woman is engaged by her husband in his

such coercion will be presumed, in the absence of evidence to the contrary, if the husband was present when the act was committed.[5]

The so-called "doctrine of coercion" has been attributed to the "legal identity of husband and wife;"[6] to the "duty of obedience to her husband;"[7] to the original status of the wife as only "the servant of the husband,"[8] or a "marionette, moved at will by the husband;"[9] to the power of the husband to chastise the wife;[10] to the "matrimonial subjection of the wife to her husband;"[11] to the "power and authority which her husband has over her;"[12] and even to a "relic of a belief in the ignorance and pusillanimity of women which is not, and perhaps never was, well founded."[13] The relation of some of these notions to certain offenses is obvious enough. Thus the common-law theory that husband and wife are one makes it impossible for them to be guilty of conspiracy[14] unless some other person is also involved,[15] or the original rule has been changed.[16] The power and authority which the common law gave the husband over the wife is such that she is not "deemed accessory to a felony for receiving her husband, who has been guilty of it,"[17] al-

store in the sale of obscene cards, her sale will be presumed to be under his coercion. State v. Martini, 80 N.J.L. 685, 78 A. 12 (1910).

5. Rex v. Hughes, 2 Lewin C.C. 229, 168 Eng.Rep. 1137 (1813); Rex v. Price, 8 Car. & P. 19, 173 Eng.Rep. 381 (1837); Commonwealth v. Adams, 186 Mass. 101, 71 N.E. 78 (1904); State v. Henderson, 356 Mo. 1072, 204 S.W.2d 774 (1947); Matter of Gault, 546 P.2d 639 (Okl.Cr. 1976).

6. Morton v. State, 141 Tenn. 357, 360, 209 S.W. 644 (1919). See also Schuler v. Henry, 42 Colo. 367, 369, 94 P. 360 (1908). "The legal theory is, that marriage makes the husband and wife one person, and that person is the husband, that there may be an indissoluble union of interest between the parties." State v. Burlingham, 15 Me. 104, 106 (1838).

7. Haning v. United States, 59 F.2d 942, 943 (8th Cir. 1932); State v. Murray, 316 Mo. 31, 39, 292 S.W. 434, 438 (1926).

8. Rex v. Saunders, 7 Car. & P. 277, 279, 173 Eng.Rep. 122, 123 (1836).

9. Smith v. Meyers, 54 Neb. 1, 7, 74 N.W. 277, 278 (1898).

10. Ibid.

11. State v. Nelson, 29 Me. 329, 337 (1849).

12. 1 Hawk.P.C. c. 1, § 9 (6th ed. 1788).

13. United States v. De Quilfeldt, 5 F. 276, 278 (C.C.Tenn.1881).

14. Dawson v. United States, 10 F.2d 106 (9th Cir. 1926); People v. Miller, 82 Cal. 107, 22 P. 934 (1889).

15. State v. Clark, 14 Del. 536, 540 (1891).

16. This has been abandoned "in all our legislation in respect to the marital relation." Dalton v. People, 68 Colo. 44, 48, 189 P. 37, 38 (1920). Accord, People v. Martin, 4 Ill.2d 105, 122 N.E.2d 245 (1954).

The cases in note 14 have since been overruled. United States v. Dege, 364 U.S. 51, 80 S.Ct. 1589 (1960); People v. Pierce, 61 Cal.2d 879, 40 Cal.Rptr. 845, 395 P.2d 893 (1964).

"Some authorities also speak of the natural state of a wife's submissiveness to her husband and conclude that because of such natural state, the wife, lacking a will of her own, could not possibly formulate the necessary criminal intent to be guilty of conspiracy with her husband. There is no reason to perpetuate the fiction that husband and wife are one person with one will in the eyes of the law. They are not. They are separate individuals. Each has a distinct personality and a will which is not destroyed by any process of spousal fusion. Each acts separately and should be separately responsible for their conduct. We have so recognized in other areas of the law. Women should not lose their identity—or their responsibility—when they become wives. The status of wife or husband should not relieve any person of one's obligation to obey the law." Commonwealth v. Lawson et ux., 454 Pa. 23, 309 A.2d 391, 396 (1973).

17. 1 Hawk.P.C. c. 1, § 10. See also Regina v. Good, 1 Car. & K. 185, 174 Eng.Rep. 768 (1842); Regina v. M'Clarens, 3 Cox C.C. 425 (1849). This

though the husband would be guilty for receiving her under similar circumstances except where the rule has been changed by statute.[18]   For the same reason she could not be convicted of receiving stolen property from her husband.[19]   By reason of the legal identity of the two, "a wife cannot be convicted for stealing her husband's goods;"[20] and if the two were living together certain duties with reference to the household were by law imposed upon the husband rather than upon the wife so that she could not be convicted upon mere proof of nonperformance.[21]   But without suggesting that any of the reasons mentioned has failed to have an influence upon the doctrine of coercion, it may safely be asserted that they do not, singly or collectively, give the true background.   Hence a further investigation is warranted.

In ancient times the lay courts did not have criminal jurisdiction over the clergy in felony cases.[22]   The member of this favored group who found himself charged with a crime in the lay court had only to assert his *benefit of clergy* and establish his claim thereto.   He was thereupon turned over to the ecclesiastical court,[23] in which the procedure was such that he rarely failed to clear himself.[24]   At the outset, the "only persons who could claim the privilege were ordained clerks, monks, and nuns;"[25] and the clerk was required to prove he was ordained by the production of the bishop's letters of ordination.[26]   By the statute *pro clero* of 1350[27] the privilege was extended to secular as well as religious clerks, that is, to persons such as door-keepers, readers or exorcists, who merely assisted the clergy in the services of the church.[28]   With the increasing prestige of the common-law courts, the day came when this transfer at the time of indictment was no longer permitted, and the privilege could be claimed only by one who had confessed the felony or had been convicted by verdict.[29]   Then by pleading his clergy he could avoid the capital part of the punishment, although his goods were forfeited to the crown.[30]   Even so it was a privilege of outstanding advantage in view of the multitude of offenses punishable by death,[31] and because of this fact was seized upon as a means of alleviating to some extent the harsh over-severity of the penal system of the time.   This was accomplished by an extension of the privilege to every man who could read "whether he had the

did not apply to treason. Regina v. Good, supra.

18.   1 Hawk.P.C. c. 1, § 10. See supra, chapter 6, section 8, C, 4.

19.   Regina v. Brooks, 6 Cox C.C. 148 (1853). And see Regina v. Wardroper, 8 Cox C.C. 284 (1860). "The desire to shield her husband from detection is hardly a fault in a wife." Per Parke, B., in Brooks, supra, at 149.

20.   Regina v. Glassie & Cooney, 7 Cox C.C. 1 (1854).

21.   Rex v. Saunders, 7 Car. & P. 277, 279, 173 Eng.Rep. 122, 123 (1836); West v. State, 74 Ga.App. 453, 40 S.E.2d 156 (1946).

22.   3 Holdsworth, History of English Law 294 (5th ed. 1942); 1 Stephen, History of Criminal Law of England 459 (1883).

23.   3 Holdsworth 294 (5th ed. 1942).

24.   Ibid. 296.

25.   1 Pollock & Maitland, History of English Law 445 (2d ed. 1899); 3 Holdsworth 296 (5th ed. 1942).

26.   3 Holdsworth 296 (5th ed. 1942).

27.   25 Edw. III st. 3, c. 4.

28.   1 Stephen 461 (1883); 3 Holdsworth 297 (5th ed. 1942).

29.   2 Hale P.C. *378.

30.   3 Holdsworth 298–9 (5th ed. 1942).

31.   During the thirteenth century the penalty of death came to be established as the punishment due for felons. 2 Pollock & Maitland 461 (2d ed. 1899). And while the common-law felonies were few many were added by statute. Something of the picture may be seen in the statement of Blackstone that there were in his day one hundred and sixty "felonies without benefit of clergy." 4 Bl.Comm. *18.

clerical dress and tonsure or not." [32]   It was not, however, made available to women (except professed nuns) "because they were incapable of being ordained." [33]

This suggested an amazing possibility. If a man and his wife were convicted of a felony they had committed together, and in which he had been perhaps the leading spirit, the husband (if able to read) would be punished with a mere brand upon the brawn of the thumb and imprisonment not to exceed a year,[34] while nothing less than the sentence of death would be available for the wife. The most obvious escape from such an absurd result seemed to lie in the direction of not convicting the woman in such a case; and the rationalization of this procedure took the form of a presumption that a woman who had taken part in a felony in the presence of her husband, had acted under his coercion and hence was to be regarded as not criminally responsible for the deed.[35]

In resorting to this device to avoid the execution of the wife for an offense which her husband could expiate with a much milder penalty, the court did not venture far from the beaten path. It merely made use of an ancient principle which was slightly modified to meet the requirements of the situation. The notion that a wife might be excused for a criminal act committed by her at the command of her husband is so venerable that Blackstone credits it with being a thousand years old at the time he wrote.[36] This would place its origin somewhere in the eighth century. And in 1353, which was about the time when benefit of clergy was extended to include any man who could read,[37] we find it stated that the "command of a husband, without other coercion" is sufficient to excuse the wife from criminal guilt.[38]

The modifications of this rule to fit it into the benefit-of-clergy scheme are too obvious to escape attention. The end in view was to avoid the odious result of executing the wife and releasing the husband with a slight punish-

---

32. 1 Stephen 461 (1883). The statement that the privilege was extended to every man who could read is subject to an exception "which may almost be called grotesque." This exception was that "bigamus" was excluded from clergy. " 'Bigamus' was not a bigamist in our sense of the word, but a man who 'hath married two wives or one widow.' " This exception was repealed by statute. 1 Edw. VI, c. 12, sec. 16 (1547). Ibid.

33. Ibid.; 3 Holdsworth 296 (5th ed. 1942).

34. 1 Stephen 462 (1883). The provision for branding was added by statute in 1487 (4 Hen. VII, c. 13) and that for imprisonment not to exceed one year in 1576 (18 Eliz. c. 7, §§ 2, 3). The statement in the text refers only to the corporal part of the punishment; the benefit of clergy did not prevent the forfeiture of goods to the crown. 3 Holdsworth, 298–9 (5th ed. 1942).

35. 1 Hale P.C. *45. "It is said, that the reason why a wife was excused in burglary, larceny, etc., was, that she could not tell what property the husband might claim in the goods. (10 Mod. 63, 355). But the better reason seems to be, that, by the ancient law, the husband had the benefit of clergy if he could read, but in no case could women have that benefit; it would, therefore, have been an odious proceeding to have executed the wife, and to have dismissed the husband with a slight punishment. To avoid this, it was thought better that she should, in all cases, be acquitted,—but this reason did not apply to misdemeanors." 2 Lewin C.C. 232 note, 168 Eng.Rep. 1138, note.

36. 4 Bl.Comm. *28.

37. It was just three years before this time that the statute *pro clero* had extended the privilege to include secular as well as religious clerks. 25 Edw. III, st. 3, c. 4 (1350). The general extension of the privilege was not long after. As to an exception, see supra, n. 32.

38. Anonymous, Lib.Ass., 27, f. 137, pl. 40 (1353).

ment for the same offense. This suggests that husband and wife should not both be convicted of the same felony; and with the exceptions to be mentioned later, such was the form the development took in its early stages.[39] Thus Lord Hale says, "the wife cannot be guilty, if the husband is guilty of the same larciny or burglary." [40] And Blackstone says, that except for crimes to which this defense is not available, if the wife commits the act "by the coercion of her husband; *or even in his company*, which the law construes a coercion; she is not guilty of any crime. . . ." [41] The explanation is given in full by the former writer, who is using larceny and burglary merely as illustrations. After pointing out that according to the original theory the wife could be guilty, where she and her husband commit such crimes together, "unless the actual coercion of the husband appear," he goes on to explain that the practice later came to be "that if the husband and wife commit burglary and larciny together, the wife shall be acquitted, and the husband only convicted . . . because otherwise for the same felony the husband may be saved by the benefit of his clergy, and the wife hanged, . . ." [42] "But," adds East, "if the husband be acquitted, and it appear that the felony were by her own voluntary act, (by which must be understood that the husband, if present, had no knowledge of or participation in the fact,) she may . . . be convicted." [43]

The exceptions are next entitled to attention. The excuse of coercion by the husband was not available to the wife in cases of treason,[44] murder,[45] or misdemeanor.[46] Treason was not within benefit of clergy even at common law,[47] and murder was excluded from this privilege by the ancient statutes which created the distinction between murder and manslaughter;[48] hence both husband and wife would be executed if convicted of these crimes. Misdemeanors were not capitally punished and consequently the penalty could be the same for both in such cases. In the course of time most felonies were excluded from the benefit of clergy by statute,[49] and the reason which shaped the development of the doctrine of coercion might have added these to the exceptions. The actual trend, however, was the other way; and gradually this excuse was extended into the field of misdemeanors except as to offenses such as keeping a brothel which are assumed to be "generally conducted by the intrigues of the female sex." [50]

In 1692 the benefit of clergy was extended to women by statute.[51] Since that time there has been no reason for the rule that a man and his wife

39. Upon a joint charge of felony against husband and wife, the wife cannot properly be convicted if the husband is. Rex v. Archer, 1 Moody 143, 168 Eng.Rep. 1218 (1826).

40. 1 Hale P.C. *46.

41. 4 Bl.Comm. *28. Italics added.

42. 1 Hale P.C. *45.

43. 2 East P.C. 559 (1803).

44. 1 Hale P.C. *45.

45. Ibid. ". . . but as to murder, if husband and wife doth join in it, they are both equally guilty . . ." Anonymous, J. Kelyng, 31, 84 Eng.Rep. 1068 (1664).

46. Hale speaks of the excuse in felony cases only. 1 Hale P.C. *44–48. See also 2 Lewin C.C. 232 note, 168 Eng.Rep. 1138, note.

47. 2 Hale P.C. *c. xlv.

48. A series of statutes, during the period from 1496 to 1547, excluded murder from benefit of clergy. 12 Hen. VII, c. 7 (1496); 4 Hen. VIII, c. 2 (1512); 23 Hen. VIII, c. 1, §§ 3, 4 (1531); 1 Edw. VI, c. 12, § 10 (1547).

49. 4 Bl.Comm. *18.

50. 4 Bl.Comm. *29. See also 1 Hawk.P.C. c. 1, § 12.

51. 4 Wm. and Mary c. 9. "21 James I, c. 6 had allowed women the privilege in

cannot both be convicted of the same felony, and that notion was gradually transformed into a prima-facie presumption of coercion.[52] What was perhaps entitled to be spoken of as the majority view, was that except[53] in cases of treason,[54] murder,[55] and offenses "conducted by the intrigues of the female sex" such as keeping a house of ill fame,[56] there was a prima-facie[57] presumption that a wife was coerced by her husband, and was therefore entitled to an acquittal, if she committed a prohibited act jointly with him,[58] or while he was present.[59] The presumption was said to arise whenever the husband was near enough at the time "for her to be under his immediate control or influence; "[60] and it was suggested that it was available, not only in defense of the wife, but also in favor of the prosecution when it is attempting to convict the husband.[61] The wife was guilty if she committed a crime voluntarily and not under coercion even if it was in the presence of her husband or perpetrated jointly by the two;[62] and the presumption of coercion was overcome by proof that it was the wife who suggested the deed,[63] or by such conduct as indicates complete willingness on her part.[64]

the case of the larceny of goods under 10 s. in value." 3 Holdsworth 300, note 6.

52. Mosely v. State, 19 Ala.App. 335, 97 So. 247 (1923); Caldwell v. State, 193 Ind. 237, 244, 137 N.E. 179, 181 (1922); Tomasello v. State, 91 Ind.App. 670, 173 N.E. 235 (1930); Commonwealth v. Daley, 148 Mass. 11, 18 N.E. 579 (1888); Commonwealth v. Helfman, 258 Mass. 410, 416, 155 N.E. 448, 450 (1927); State v. Asper, 35 N.M. 203, 292 P. 225 (1930); State v. McMillan, 144 S.C. 121, 142 S.E. 236 (1928); State v. Minor, 171 S.C. 120, 171 S.E. 737 (1933); Brown v. Commonwealth, 135 Va. 480, 115 S.E. 542 (1923); State v. Buchanan, 111 W.Va. 142, 160 S.E. 920 (1931).

53. In addition to the exceptions stated in the text the offense of robbery has been suggested. State v. Buchanan, 111 W.Va. 142, 143, 160 S.E. 920, 921 (1931). This was also included by Hawkins, 1 Hawk.P.C. c. 1, § 12. But see Regina v. Torpey, 12 Cox C.C. 45 (1871); Regina v. Dykes, 15 Cox C.C. 771 (1885). The Massachusetts court has said, quite properly it would seem, that there is no presumption of coercion if the wife commits perjury in the presence of her husband, because she has the protection of the court. Commonwealth v. Moore, 162 Mass. 441, 38 N.E. 1120 (1894).

54. Caldwell, Tomasello, and Buchanan, supra n. 52.

55. In addition to the cases in the preceding note see Bibb v. State, 94 Ala. 31, 10 So. 506 (1892); Martin v. Commonwealth, 143 Va. 479, 129 S.E. 348 (1925).

56. Dawson v. United States, 10 F.2d 106 (9th Cir. 1926); State v. Grossman, 95 N.J.L. 497, 499, 112 A. 892 (1921);

Haffner v. State, 176 Wis. 471, 477, 187 N.W. 173 (1922).

57. See supra n. 52.

58. State v. Buchanan, 111 W.Va. 142, 143, 160 S.E. 920, 921 (1931).

59. Haning v. United States, 59 F.2d 942 (8th Cir. 1932); Ferguson v. State, 29 Okl.Cr. 238, 239, 233 P. 497 (1925); Davis v. State, 53 Okl.Cr. 85, 7 P.2d 911 (1932).

60. Commonwealth v. Daley, 148 Mass. 11, 13, 18 N.E. 759 (1888).

61. State v. Boyle, 13 R.I. 537 (1882). ". . . it was presumed that she did so under constraint by him, and she was therefore excused, and he was presumably guilty." Morton v. State, 141 Tenn. 357, 359, 209 S.W. 644, 645 (1919).

62. People v. Wright, 38 Mich. 744 (1878); Emmons v. State, 291 P.2d 838 (Okl.Cr.1955).

63. People v. Ryland, 97 N.Y. 126 (1884).

64. Emmons v. State, 291 P.2d 838 (Okl.Cr.1955). Where the wife throttled the victim and told him to keep still while the husband and another rifled his pockets there was sufficient evidence to warrant the jury in finding that she acted voluntarily. Wright, supra n. 62. A woman committed mayhem in the presence of her husband, but she by her own evidence exonerated him from any participation in the offense. It was held that the prima-facie evidence of coercion was fully rebutted. State v. Ma Foo (Baker), 110 Mo. 7, 19 S.W. 222 (1892); Goodwin v. State, 506 P.2d 571 (Okl.Cr.1973); State v. Funk, 490 S.W.2d 354 (Mo.App. 1973).

The common law concept is of doubtful application in today's world,[65] the trend against it is so obvious and so persistent as to forecast its disappearance. Some courts have said that it is only a "slight" presumption which may be overcome by "slight evidence," [66] or by "very slight circumstances;"[67] some have questioned "the advisability of maintaining the rule in modern times," [68] or have pointed out that it "has been abrogated by statute in some states, and might well be in all; " [69] some have expressed doubt as to whether it is still in existence.[70] In other jurisdictions the trend against it has proceeded beyond the stage of doubt. About a century ago the Arkansas statute was held to have eliminated this presumption; [71] and many states now hold that it has been abrogated.[72]

The law relating to this subject has been overshadowed by the *presumption* of coercion, but the exculpatory effect of actual coercion by the husband is not removed by the abrogation of the presumption, whether by statute[73] or otherwise. And since the wife is excused for a prohibited act (other than one of those excluded from the rule) done by her under actual coercion by her husband, whether the presumption remains in greatly modified form,[74] or has disappeared entirely,[75] it is important to inquire what is

65. See United States v. Dege, 364 U.S. 51, 80 S.Ct. 1589 (1960).

66. Brown v. Commonwealth, 135 Va. 480, 485, 115 S.E. 542, 543 (1923).

67. State v. Cleaves, 59 Me. 298, 302 (1871). See also State v. Stoner, 189 Iowa 1304, 179 N.W. 867 (1920). Compare the peculiar statement of the Alabama court, to the effect that this "presumption" may be overcome by "the total lack of any evidence showing or tending to show that such coercion existed." Mosely, supra n. 52.

68. State v. Buchanan, 111 W.Va. 142, 144, 160 S.E. 920, 921 (1931). And see State v. Seahorn, 166 N.C. 373, 377, 81 S.E. 687, 688 (1914); Buchanan, supra n. 52; Farrell v. Turner, 25 Utah 2d 351, 482 P.2d 117 (1971). Pace, Marital Coercion-Anachronism or Modernism, [1979] Crim.L.Rev. 82.

69. United States v. De Quilfeldt, 5 F. 276, 278 (C.C.Tenn.1881). It "presents a pressing necessity for legislative consideration and action." Mosely v. State, 19 Ala.App. 335, 338, 97 So. 247, 250 (1923).

70. Haning v. United States, 59 F.2d 942, 943 (8th Cir. 1932); Smith v. Meyers, 54 Neb. 1, 7, 74 N.W. 277, 278 (1898).

71. Edwards v. State, 27 Ark. 493, 499 (1872).

72. Dalton v. People, 68 Colo. 44, 47–8, 189 P. 37, 38 (1920); Bell v. State, 92 Ga. 49, 51, 18 S.E. 186, 187 (1893);

People v. Martin, 4 Ill.2d 105, 122 N.E.2d 245 (1954); State v. Renslow, 211 Iowa 642, 230 N.W. 316 (1930); State v. Hendricks, 32 Kan. 559, 4 P. 1050 (1884); King v. City of Owensboro, 187 Ky. 21, 24–5, 218 S.W. 297, 298, 299 (1920); Wampler v. Norton, 134 Va. 606, 113 S.E. 733 (1922). "It is clear that the common-law fiction of unity of husband and wife has no place in modern criminal law." Kivette v. United States, 230 F.2d 749 (5th Cir. 1956). "It is not a defense, to a married woman charged with crime, that the alleged criminal act was committed by her in the presence of her husband." McKinney's N.Y.Pen.Law § 1092 (1909). This was omitted from the Revision of 1967, no doubt on the theory that it is unnecessary. "The independence of women in political, social, and economic matters renders the doctrine of coercion outdated and inapplicable to modern society." Commonwealth v. Santiago, 462 Pa. 216, 340 A.2d 440, 445 (1975).

73. "In the prosecution . . . no presumption shall be indulged that a married woman committing an offense does so under coercion because she commits it in the presence of her husband." Mich.Comp.Laws 1968, § 780.401.

74. See Commonwealth v. Jones, 1 D. & C.2d 269, 272–5 (Pa.1954).

75. Common law presumption judicially abolished. People v. Statley, 91 Cal. App.2d Supp. 943, 206 P.2d 76 (1949).

needed for the purpose. And the starting point is that the requirement is substantially less than that needed for ordinary compulsion.[76]

The ordinary rule (not involving the marital relation) is that the mere existence of an order or command constitutes no excuse for the intentional doing of a prohibited act.[77] "Neither a son nor a servant are [sic] excused the commission of any crime whether capital or not capital, by the command or coercion of the father or master."[78] The common statement is that one cannot shield himself from criminal responsibility for the intentional killing of an innocent person, even to save his own life,[79] but under the majority rule except for murder and perhaps certain related offenses such as mayhem and assault with intent to murder, compulsion may constitute an excuse for a harmful act,[80] provided it is "present, imminent and impending, and of such a nature as to induce a well-grounded apprehension of death or serious bodily harm if the act is not done."[81] On the other hand the "command of a husband, without other coercion" was anciently held sufficient to excuse the wife.[82]

It has been said that "the bare command of her husband" is not sufficient for coercion today,[83] and this may be true if understood to mean the command of a husband who is remote from the scene when the prohibited act is committed;[84] but his command plus his presence is sufficient.[85] Where the presumption of coercion still exists,[86] it is "slight and may be rebutted by slight circumstances," but the proof needed is that she was acting freely and not under any subjection of her husband.[87] The mere fact that she was not

76. Kelso v. State, 96 Okl.Cr. 367, 255 P.2d 284 (1953).

77. Thomas v. State, 134 Ala. 126, 33 So. 130 (1902); United States v. Calley, 22 USCMA 534, 48 CMR 19 (1973).

78. 1 Hawk.P.C. c. 1, § 14 (6th ed. 1788); 4 Bl.Comm. *28.

79. State v. Weston, 109 Or. 19, 34–5, 219 P. 180, 185 (1923); State v. Nargashian, 26 R.I. 299, 302, 58 A. 953, 954, 955 (1904); Leach v. State, 99 Tenn. 584, 585, 42 S.W. 195, 197 (1897). "[H]e ought rather to die himself than escape by the murder of an innocent." 4 Bl.Comm. *30.

80. ". . . the law will excuse a person when acting under coercion or compulsion for committing most, if not all, crimes, except taking the life of an innocent person." Nall v. Commonwealth, 208 Ky. 700, 702, 271 S.W. 1059, 1060 (1925).

81. Ibid.; Moore v. State, 23 Ala.App. 432, 433, 127 So. 796, 797 (1930); People v. Merhige, 212 Mich. 601, 610–11, 180 N.W. 418, 422 (1920); State v. Jones, 119 Ariz. 555, 582 P.2d 645 (App.1978); State v. Taylor, 22 Wn.App. 308, 589 P.2d 1250 (1979).

82. Anonymous, Lib.Ass. f. 137, pl. 40 (1353).

83. State v. Patton, 347 Mo. 303, 308, 147 S.W.2d 467, 469 (1941).

84. Cf. Commonwealth v. Davis, 148 Mass. 11, 13, 18 N.E. 759 (1888). The actual problem in this case was presumption of coercion. Farrell v. Turner, 25 Utah 2d 351, 482 P.2d 117 (1971); Gray v. State, 527 P.2d 338 (Okl.Cr.1974).

85. People v. Statley, 91 Cal.App.2d Supp. 943, 206 P.2d 76 (1949). The question is whether the wife acted freely and not under any subjection of her husband. Powell v. State, 88 Okl.Cr. 404, 203 P.2d 892 (1949). And see the instruction approved in State v. Carpenter, 67 Idaho 277, 176 P.2d 919 (1947). It is sufficient if the husband gave "express orders" and was near enough to exercise control at the time. State v. Fertig, 98 Iowa 139, 67 N.W. 87 (1896).

86. O'Donnell v. State, 73 Okl.Cr. 1, 7, 117 P.2d 139, 141 (1941).

87. Powell v. State, 88 Okl.Cr. 404, 203 P.2d 892 (1949). The rule does not apply if there is "nothing to show that what [she] was doing was at the command or persuasion of the husband." Gentry v. State, 158 Tex.Cr.R. 112, 113, 253 S.W.2d 862 (1953).

acting in immediate fear of life or limb would not overcome the presumption, or disprove actual coercion.

Complete rejection of coercion as a separate concept would leave a married woman without any excuse on this basis except such compulsion as would be sufficient for any other person, and such a position is not entirely unknown.[88] However, it is quite unusual although an occasional statute has provided that coercion of a woman by her husband shall call for a substantial reduction in the punishment rather than exculpation.[89]

At common law the defense of coercion was not available in prosecutions for certain offenses, and most states that had statutes recognizing the common-law presumption or some variation thereof have repealed their statutes[90] thereby leaving the question of a defense due to coercion by a spouse to the general statutory provision dealing with the defense of coercion.

A presumption of coercion based upon the mere presence of the husband would be quite out of place in the modern world[91] if it had not been reduced to such a slight presumption—so readily rebuttable—as to be of very little practical importance. The presumption itself might well disappear entirely, but recognition of the exculpatory effect of the husband's actual coercion is quite a different matter. With appropriate exceptions this should be retained so long as the general rule of compulsion is applied with unreasonably harsh limitations,[92] and whenever made appropriate by the evidence the instructions should direct the jury to determine whether the wife committed the prohibited act of her own free will and accord or did so unwillingly under the influence of her husband. Under the latter finding the guilt should be held to be exclusively his. As said in one case:[93]

"Granting that the original actual reasons for the rule are no longer valid, the rule would not have survived so long had it not appealed to some new reason, which we are convinced is human experience of the wife's tendency to follow her husband's bidding. . . . The rule is based upon human experience and therefore its continuing validity is not affected by any change in a wife's property or personal rights. While a married woman may not be her husband's chattel . . . we have not yet reached the point where we decry the nobility, dignity or grace of a wife's deference to her husband's wishes. Chivalry alone would call for this explanation of a married woman's participation in her husband's crime."

Without questioning the sentiment of the quotation it is necessary to repeat that both the ancient rule of coercion of a wife and the presumption of such coercion have virtually disappeared. And they should disappear when

88. Johnson v. State, 152 Tenn. 184, 187, 274 S.W. 12, 13 (1925); Evans v. State, 188 Tenn. 637, 221 S.W.2d 952 (1949); Wis.Stats. § 939.46 (1955).

89. Vernon's Ann.Tex.P.C. art. 32, repealed 1974. No special defense for a wife or spouse is currently recognized in Texas, see V.T.C.A. Penal Code § 8.05(e).

90. E.g., Arkansas, Arizona, California, Colorado, Georgia, Oklahoma, Utah.

91. "This statute has been on the books since the 19th Century. It is difficult to make a married man believe it has

any valid basis for its existence." Farrell v. Turner, 25 Utah 2d 351, 482 P.2d 117 (1971). Current Utah law expressly rejects such a presumption. Utah Code Ann., 1953, § 76–2–302(3) (1973).

92. See infra, chapter 9, section 2.

93. Commonwealth v. Jones, 1 D. & C.2d 269, 274–75 (Pa.Dist. and Co. 1954). Nominally the words were used with reference to the presumption but the court was obviously thinking of the coercion itself.

the general rule of compulsion is established on a reasonable basis. No doubt the ultimate position everywhere will be that a wife wishing to establish a defense on this basis will need to satisfy the requirements of the general rule of compulsion. Even so, the fact that the compulsion was being exerted by the victim's husband would not be a factor which would have to be ignored.

THE MODEL PENAL CODE

Those drafting the Model Penal Code concluded that there should be no special rule, or presumption, in regard to the coercion of a wife by her husband and included an express statement to this effect.[94] It was deemed that under the present state of the law this could not be handled adequately by mere omission.[95]

THE NEW PENAL CODES

It is safe to assume that under a number of the New Penal Codes a woman will have no excuse based upon the coercion of her husband unless his conduct was sufficient to constitute compulsion under the general provision on that subject, although this result is reached by the omission of any special rule in her favor.[96]

94. Section 2.09(3).

95. See pages 10 and 11 of Tent.Draft No. 10 (1960).

96. E.g. Iowa Code § 704.10 (1978).

Chapter 9

RESPONSIBILITY: MODIFYING CIRCUMSTANCES

SECTION 1. IGNORANCE OR MISTAKE

Ignorance of law is no excuse, but mistake of fact is sufficient for exculpation if what was done would have been lawful had the facts been as they were reasonably supposed to be. This, like any other statement which seeks to compress a large field of law into the confines of a single sentence, is entirely too broad for certain specific situations. It indicates the result of the ordinary case, but its scope and limitations can be understood only in the light of important exceptions which have been recognized. A study of these problems may well be prefaced by brief reference to two words repeatedly encountered in this field.

It has been said that the words "ignorance" and "mistake" "do not import the same significance and should not be confounded. Ignorance implies a total want of knowledge in reference to the subject matter. Mistake admits a knowledge, but implies a wrong conclusion." [1] For the most part, however, this distinction has not been recognized. [2] Some courts have brushed it aside as "a refinement too subtle to be applied to the every-day business of life," [3] or one which "rests on no solid foundation." [4] Most of them have merely ignored it.

Frequently these words have appeared in the phrases "ignorance of law" [5] and "mistake of fact." [6] At times the word "ignorance" [7] or the word "mistake" [8] has been applied alone to both types of error, whereas elsewhere both words are coupled together in referring to each type. [9] Whatever phra-

1. Hulton v. Edgerton, 6 S.C. 485, 489 (1875).

2. The most scholarly attempt to emphasize the distinction between the words "ignorance" and "mistake" is that by Professor Keedy in his article Ignorance and Mistake in the Criminal Law, 22 Harv.L.Rev. 75 (1908). This distinction is not here insisted upon because the courts seem disinclined to recognize the approach from that angle. But the difference between certain types of misunderstanding, which Professor Keedy insisted upon, cannot be ignored.

3. Schlesinger v. United States, 1 Ct. Cl. 16, 25 (1863).

4. Champlin v. Laytin, 18 Wend. 407, 416 (N.Y.1837).

5. Blumenthal v. United States, 88 F.2d 522, 530 (8th Cir. 1937); Weeks v. State, 24 Ala.App. 198, 199, 132 So. 870, 871 (1931).

6. Stern v. State, 53 Ga. 229, 230 (1874); Chapman v. State, 77 Tex.Cr.R. 591, 595, 179 S.W. 570, 572 (1915); Regina v. Tolson, 23 Q.B.D. 168, 190 (1889). Both frequently appear in the same sentence. See People v. Cohn, 358 Ill. 326, 331, 193 N.E. 150, 153 (1934); Hunter v. State, 158 Tenn. 63, 73, 12 S.W.2d 361, 363 (1928).

7. Reynolds v. United States, 98 U.S. 145, 167 (1878).

8. Hamilton v. State, 115 Tex.Cr.R. 96, 97, 29 S.W.2d 777, 778 (1930).

9. "His mistake or ignorance, if any, was one of law, and not of fact." State v. Armington, 25 Minn. 29, 38 (1878). ". . . ignorance or mistake, as to these facts, *honest and real* . . . absolves from criminal responsibility." Dotson v. State, 62 Ala. 141, 144 (1878).

seology is employed it is necessary to explore to some depths the exact nature and effect of the misunderstanding in a particular case. The field of possible error is too great for any one simple solvent. It is important to inquire whether the ignorance or mistake was of law or of fact, but it is also necessary to carry the investigation far beyond this point.

A. IGNORANCE OR MISTAKE OF LAW*

1. THE MAXIM

The maxim that has come down through the ages, with various slight changes in the wording, is to the effect that "ignorance of a law is not a defense to a charge of its violation." [10] For obvious reasons, what shall constitute a crime must be determined by the state and not by each individual for himself. The distinction between moral and immoral conduct, for purposes of social discipline, must of necessity be objective.[11] The criminal law represents certain moral precepts which would be undermined if ignorance or mistake of its law were recognized as a defense.[12] If the finder of lost property appropriates it under such circumstances that his conduct constitutes larceny according to law,[13] it would not do to permit him to defend on the claim that "finders keepers" represents his moral judgment of such a situation.[14] There are a few extreme situations, to be discussed presently, in which a defense may be based upon a mistake of law as to the very offense charged, but they are very few and do not apply to the finder of lost property.

"Public necessity" has also been said to support the maxim. "The welfare of society and the safety of the state" have been felt to require it in order to administer justice among men.[15] "If a person accused of crime,"

---

* By express permission the following has been adapted from Perkins, Ignorance or Mistake of Law Revisited, 1980 Utah Law Review 973.

10. Hale v. Morgan, 22 Cal.3d 388, 396, 584 P.2d 512, 517, 149 Cal.Rptr. 375, 380 (1978). "Mistake of law is no defense to the underlying crime or the conspiracy charge." United States v. Jones, 642 F.2d 909, 914 (5th Cir. 1981).

11. "At least one purpose of the penal law is to express a formal social condemnation of forbidden conduct . . . ." Sauer v. United States, 241 F.2d 640, 648 (9th Cir. 1957). See Cohen, Moral Aspects of the Criminal Law, 49 Yale L.J. 987, 1017 (1940).

12. J. Hall, General Principles of Criminal Law 383 (2d ed. 1960); see Hall, Ignorance and Mistake in Criminal Law, 33 Ind. L.J. 1, 42 (1957).

13. State v. Courtsol, 89 Conn. 564, 94 A. 973 (1915); Commonwealth v. Metcalfe, 184 Ky. 540, 212 S.W. 434 (1919); Commonwealth v. Titus, 116 Mass. 42 (1874).

14. "The law cannot accept the actor's moral judgment as a defense, as an excuse." 36 ALI Proceedings 214 (1959). Cf. Gaetano v. United States, 406 A.2d 1291, 1294 (D.C.App.1979) ("The 'bona fide belief' defense was not meant to, and does not, exonerate individuals who believe they have a right, or even a duty, to violate the law in order to effect a moral, social, or political purpose, regardless of the genuineness of the belief or the popularity of the purpose").

"In other words, it is commonly conceded that exercise of a moral judgment based upon individual standards does not carry with it legal justification or immunity from punishment for breach of the law." United States v. Hanson, 618 F.2d 1261, 1264 (8th Cir. 1980) (quoting from an earlier case).

15. People v. O'Brien, 96 Cal. 171, 176, 31 P. 45, 47 (1892). See also State v. O'Neil, 147 Iowa 513, 519, 126 N.W. 454, 456 (1910).

said the California court, "could shield himself behind the defense that he was ignorant of the law which he violated, immunity from punishment would in most cases result. . . . The plea would be universally made, and would lead to interminable questions, incapable of solution." [16] Without doubt, the claim of such a defense would be very common if it were available. And in the ordinary case it would present an issue of which the only direct evidence would be defendant's assertion that he was mistaken as to the law. The jurors are not bound to believe what defendant (or any other witness) says. But he would frequently be able to create at least a reasonable doubt in their minds, and no more would be needed to secure an acquittal.

The counterpart of the maxim is that "[e]very person is presumed to know the law." [17] This does not mean that the probabilities are sufficient to raise an inference that everyone knows the law. That would be absurd.[18] Nor does it refer to a procedural device that may be overcome by evidence to the contrary.[19] The explanation is that the law sometimes uses the word "presumption" to mean "conclusive presumption," as in the common-law rule that all prior parties are presumed to have delivered a negotiable instrument that has reached the hands of a holder in due course.[20] This is neither an inference nor a rule of procedure that may be overcome by evidence to the contrary. It is a postulate used for the determination of such a case regardless of the actual facts.[21] A case involving such an instrument will be decided as if the instrument had been delivered by all prior parties whether it had actually been so delivered or not. Illuminating is the fact that the Uniform Commercial Code now reaches the same result by a direct statement that does not mention "presumed." [22]

This is the explanation of the statement that "everyone is presumed to know the law." The meaning is sometimes expressed in such terms as that every person is "bound to know or ascertain the law" [23] or "must know what the law is, and he acts at his own peril." [24] It is a postulate used in the determination of a case regardless of the actual facts. What it means is that, except for the rare exceptions referred to, a *criminal case* will be decided as if the defendant had full knowledge of the *pertinent criminal law* without any consideration of the actual facts in this regard.[25]

---

16. People v. O'Brien, 96 Cal. 171, 176, 31 P. 45, 47 (1892).

17. Weeks v. State, 24 Ala.App. 198, 199, 132 So. 870, 871 (1931). See also 4 W. Blackstone, Commentaries *27; 1 M. Hale, The History of the Pleas of the Crown *42.

18. Mr. Justice Maule questioned the propriety of stating the rule in terms of a presumption. Martindale v. Falkner, 135 Eng.Rep. 1124, 1129–30 (1846).

19. This is the so-called "prima facie presumption." See 9 J. Wigmore, Evidence § 2491 (3d ed. 1940).

20. F. Beutel, Brannan's Negotiable Instruments Law § 16 (7th ed. 1948).

21. "It is not so much a presumption of fact as a fact, as it is a conclusion or presumption of the law . . . ." Jellico Coal Mining Co. v. Commonwealth, 96 Ky. 373, 375, 29 S.W. 26 (1895). "[E]veryone is conclusively presumed to know the law . . . ." State v. Woods, 107 Vt. 354, 356, 179 A. 1, 2 (1935).

22. U.C.C. § 3–305 & Comment 3 (1958 official text).

23. State v. Goodenow, 65 Me. 30, 33 (1876). See State v. O'Neil, 147 Iowa 513, 519, 126 N.W. 454, 456 (1910) (every person "is bound to obey the law"). See also 1 M. Hale, supra note 8, at *42.

24. Needham v. State, 55 Okl.Cr. 430, 434, 32 P.2d 92, 93 (1934).

25. "He must be presumed to have known the provisions of s. 7, whether he was actually acquainted with its terms or not." Bank of New South Wales v. Piper, [1897] A.C. 383, 390.

2. MISTAKE OF NONPENAL LAW

While the criminal law represents a moral code, the nonpenal law does not. Assume a gratuitous promise to make a gift of specified property on a named day in the future. It is important to have a rule of law to govern such a situation, because when the day arrives we need to know who owns the property. The rule is that the property does not pass as a result of this gratuitous promise. It still belongs to the promisor; but the rule could be otherwise so far as moral values are concerned. No moral precept points to the result reached. With this in mind, suppose **X** gratuitously promised to give his horse to **D**. **X** said: "I need the horse the rest of the week, but I retire on Friday, so on Saturday he is yours." But during the week there was a change of plan and **X** did not retire. He would need the horse and decided to keep it, but did not bother to tell **D**. On Saturday **D** eagerly hurried to **X**'s place to get the horse. **X** was not there. In fact no one was there, but the horse was tied to a post in the yard. In the firm belief that the animal was his, and that he had the right to the immediate possession, **D** took him home with intent to keep him. He was charged with larceny.

Of course, if **D** is conclusively presumed to know the pertinent rule of property law he is guilty, and this was the ancient view.[26] But the reasons upon which the maxim is grounded do not call for such a presumption. Recognition of **D**'s mistake of this rule of property law will not undermine any precept of the criminal law. It will not "open the door" for the insertion of this defense in every criminal case. Hence it is not surprising that at an early day it was recognized that an intent to take a chattel that the taker bona fide believes is his property which is being wrongfully held by another is not *animus furandi*, however erroneous the belief may be.[27] Hence one who takes and carries away the chattel of another under such a bona-fide belief is not guilty of larceny even if his error was due to a mistake of some nonpenal law.[28] And in time it came to be accepted as a general rule that if the offense charged requires any specific intent, a mistake of nonpenal law that negatives that intent leaves the defendant innocent.[29]

A. Special Mental Elements

Reasons for expanding the rule are so obvious that the change might have taken place all at once. Actually the development was piecemeal, but it came to be firmly established that defendant is not guilty if the offense charged requires any special mental element, such as that the prohibited act be committed knowingly, fraudulently, corruptly, maliciously or wilfully, and

26. The ancient notion that ignorance of the law is no defense was a stern and inflexible rule of law without any exception. See Hoover v. State, 59 Ala. 57, 60 (1877) (ignorance of the validity of a statute prohibiting miscegenation no defense to a charge of living together in a state of fornication).

27. Morningstar v. State, 55 Ala. 148 (1876); Brown v. State, 28 Ark. 126 (1873); 2 E. East, Pleas of the Crown *510 (describing the 1782 case of Rex v. Knight).

28. State v. Sawyer, 95 Conn. 34, 110 A. 461 (1920); People v. Schultz, 71 Mich. 315, 38 N.W. 868 (1888).

"There is, of course, no question about the proposition: if the defendant took the property under an honest but mistaken belief that he was entitled to do so, that would negative his intent to steal; and he would not be guilty of theft." State v. Kazda, 545 P.2d 190, 192 (Utah 1976).

29. See, e.g., United States v. One Buick Coach Automobile, 34 F.2d 318 (N.D.Ind.1929).

this element of the crime was lacking because of some mistake of nonpenal law.

1. *Knowingly*—It was very properly held, for example, that one who cast his ballot in good faith, and upon advice of competent counsel, was not guilty of the statutory offense of voting "knowing himself not to be a qualified voter" even though the advice was erroneous.[30] An officer who receives a fee to which he is not entitled, while acting under the bona-fide belief that the fee is legally due, is not guilty under a statute that provides a penalty for an officer who shall "knowingly" receive a fee to which he is not entitled.[31] And it is error to instruct that ignorance of the law is no defense to a charge of wilfully and knowingly attempting to evade the payment of income taxes.[32]

2. *Fraudulently*—It is obvious that conduct was not fraudulent if done under a mistake of nonpenal law of such a nature that what was done would have been entirely proper had the nonpenal law been as assumed; but a special problem is entitled to attention. It is no offense to trick another into performing his legal duty.[33] Suppose **D** congratulated **X**. **X** inquired why and was told: "Haven't you heard? It was just over the radio. Your rich uncle just died and left you a large amount of money." Feeling very happy over his apparent good fortune, **X** paid **D** a debt that **X** had persistently postponed paying although it was long overdue. Then **X** learned that his uncle was very much alive and had made no will. **D**'s statement was a deliberate falsehood. "It is not an indictable offense under the statute, for one to obtain by false statements payment of a debt already due, or of personal property to [the possession of which he is entitled], because no injury is done."[34] Assume a change in the factual situation, **X** actually owed nothing to **D** but **D**, because of a mistake as to some nonpenal law, genuinely believed that **X** owed the sum claimed. And **X** was so elated by his apparent good fortune that he handed over the sum demanded, although convinced that he did not owe it. **D** is bound to return the money. On the other hand, **D** is not guilty of crime. His conduct, although not praiseworthy, was not fraudulent because he sought to have done only what he sincerely believed was due.[35]

3. *Corruptly*—One who testified that no partnership existed between himself and another, was held not guilty of perjury although such a legal

---

30. Commonwealth v. Bradford, 50 Mass. 268 (1845).

31. Cleaveland v. State, 34 Ala. 254, 259 (1859).

32. Hargrove v. United States, 67 F.2d 820 (5th Cir. 1933).

The maxim "ignorance of the law is no defense" has no application to a charge of an offense in which knowledge of some other law is a material element. United States v. Squires, 440 F.2d 859 (2d Cir. 1971).

33. State v. Williams, 68 W.Va. 86, 69 S.E. 474 (1910).

34. In re Cameron, 44 Kan. 64, 66, 24 P. 90, 91 (1890). See Commonwealth v. McDuffy, 126 Mass. 467, 470 (1879) (false representations to obtain payment of a debt not the offense of obtaining property by false pretenses); People v. Thomas, 3 Hill 169, 170 (N.Y.Sup.Ct. 1842) ("A false representation, by which a man may be cheated into his duty, is not within the statute").

"But where no independent crime has been committed, it surely should not be the case that the actor is subject to a charge of theft for resorting to deceit to obtain what he believes to be the return of his own property." ALI, Model Penal Code and Commentaries, Part II, vol. 2, pages 153–54 (1980).

35. Rand v. Commonwealth, 176 Ky. 343, 352, 195 S.W. 802, 808 (1917).

relation actually existed, if he gave his testimony in good-faith reliance upon advice of counsel that the dealings between the two did not create a partnership.[36] His testimony, although inaccurate, was not given corruptly, which is required for perjury.[37] Conviction of perjury was reversed in another case because defendant was not permitted to explain his misstatement in the light of his misunderstanding of the legal title to certain property and the extent of the homestead law.[38]

4. *Maliciously*—A bona-fide belief in the lawfulness of what was done, although due to a misunderstanding of some nonpenal law, was held to be a defense to a prosecution for maliciously setting fire to a furze,[39] maliciously removing rails from a fence,[40] maliciously tearing down a fence,[41] and maliciously removing crops from the field of another.[42] While a mistake of law will not excuse a homicide, the possibility of its being sufficient under some circumstances to negate the existence of malice aforethought should be recognized. The common law tended to overlook such a defense, but sometimes the jury reached the proper result by applying common sense to the situation.[43] Some of the new penal codes reach the proper result without the use of "malice." [44]

5. *Wilfully*—At times the word "wilfully" in a statute may mean no more than a willingness to do the particular deed,[45] but in certain connections it has been held to mean "not merely 'voluntarily,' but with a bad purpose." [46] One who cuts timber from the land of another without proper authority, is liable in a civil action for damages even if he thinks the land is his own; [47] but if a statute provides a penalty for one who wilfully commits such a trespass, he is not guilty of this offense.[48] One who without protest

36. State v. McKinney, 42 Iowa 205 (1875).

37. The King v. Smith, 2 Shower K.B. 165, 89 Eng.Rep. 864 (1681).

38. State v. Lazarus, 181 Iowa 625, 164 N.W. 1037 (1917).

39. Regina v. Twose, 14 Cox's Crim.L. Cas. 327 (1879).

40. Goforth v. State, 27 Tenn. 37 (1847).

41. Palmer v. State, 45 Ind. 388 (1873).

42. State v. Luther, 8 R.I. 151 (1865). The statute in this case did not use the word "maliciously" or any other word of like import, but the court held that it must be implied.

43. In People v. Cook, 39 Mich. 236 (1878), the court did not suggest that a bona-fide belief, resulting from a mistake of law as to the right to use deadly force to prevent crime or to defend property, might negate malice aforethought. However, although the charge was murder, the jury found defendant guilty of manslaughter.

44. See, e.g., Ill.Ann.Stat. ch. 38, § 9–2(b) (Smith-Hurd Supp. 1979):

A person who intentionally or knowingly kills an individual commits voluntary manslaughter if at the time of the killing he believes the circumstances to be such that, if they existed, would justify or exonerate the killing under the principles stated in Article 7 of this Code, but his belief is unreasonable.

Such a mistake would more likely be a mistake of fact, but the result would be the same if it was a mistake of nonpenal law.

45. Finn v. United States, 219 F.2d 894, 900 (9th Cir. 1955); People v. O'Brien, 96 Cal. 171, 176, 31 P. 45, 47 (1892); Commonwealth v. Robinson, 305 Pa. 302, 308, 157 A. 689, 692 (1931); United States v. Hinderman, 625 F.2d 994, 995–96 (10th Cir. 1980).

46. Felton v. United States, 96 U.S. 699, 702 (1877). And see Hentzner v. State, 613 P.2d 821, 826 (Alaska 1980).

47. State v. Shevlin-Carpenter Co., 102 Minn. 470, 113 N.W. 634 (1907), aff'd on rehearing, 114 N.W. 738 (1908).

48. Hateley v. State, 118 Ga. 79, 44 S.E. 852 (1903). The Minnesota case in the preceding note held that if the trespasser acted under a bona-fide claim of right, he is not liable for punitive dam-

crossed the land of another by a certain path for fifteen years, and continued such practice by tearing down part of a fence after the owner attempted to close that way, was not guilty of wilful trespass under the statute if he in good faith believed his long use gave him a right to cross there, even if the law of the state required a longer period of use for this purpose.[49] And one who exercised the functions of an office to which he had not been duly elected, but under the bona-fide and reasonable belief that he had been lawfully elected, was not guilty of wilful usurpation of office.[50]

One point is to be emphasized in all such cases. For example, the officer who received a fee to which he was not entitled could defend on the ground that because of a mistake as to the fee schedule he thought he was entitled to that fee, but not on the ground that he did not know it was an offense to collect an unauthorized fee. One charged with perjury for having testified that he was not in partnership with another, although a partnership actually existed, could defend on the ground that by reason of a mistake of commercial law he genuinely believed there was no such legal relation, but not on the ground that the facts were so unusual that he thought a false statement would be more likely to result in a correct decision of the case than an attempt to explain the real facts. One who had made a hole in another's fence could defend on the ground that by reason of a mistake of real-estate law he thought his unopposed use of a path for fifteen years had created an easement in his favor so that the fence was wrongfully blocking his passage, but not on the ground that he believed that the wrongful tearing down of another's fence was not a crime. And one charged with larceny could defend on the ground that by a mistake of property law he believed the chattel was his and that he had the right of immediate possession, but not on the ground that he believed it was no offense to appropriate lost property even if it had an obvious clue to ownership.[51]

The latter case has given rise to certain questions. Since larceny requires a specific intent to steal, and the finder thought he had a right to appropriate the property, does not this mean that he had no intent to steal and so is not guilty of larceny? One answer is that he intended to appropriate the property, which would necessarily result in the owner being permanently deprived, and this is an intent to steal. A better answer is that knowledge of the law of larceny is conclusively presumed. Another question is: Is not the mistake in this case a mistake of property law rather than a mistake of the law of larceny? The answer is that the law of lost property was developed exclusively in the larceny cases. The result reached was not that it is necessary to have a rule one way or the other, or that logic favors this result rather than another. The result was reached on the conclusion that to appropriate property which another has lost, if the circumstances are such that the owner and his property can readily be brought together again, is so

ages as a wilful trespasser, even if his mistake was one of law. 102 Minn. 470, 113 N.W. at 637–38.

49. State v. Hause, 71 N.C. 518 (1874). See also Wiggins v. State, 119 Ga. 216, 46 S.E. 86 (1903).

50. People v. Bates, 29 N.Y.S. 894 (Sup. 1894).

51. See, e.g., Commonwealth v. Doane, 55 Mass. 5 (1848) (customary practice among ship's officers of appropriating loose cargo without consent not a defense to larceny). Cf. Lewis v. People, 99 Colo. 102, 118, 60 P.2d 1089, 1097 (1936) (crime of embezzlement requires criminal intent and defendant's mistake "as to right in the thing taken" may negative the required intent). See generally Note, Mistake of Law in Texas Criminal Cases, 15 Tex.L.Rev. 287 (1937).

morally wrong as to call for punishment. And the law of lost property is frequently codified in the penal codes. It has also been asked: Why should the law impose upon the finder of lost property a duty which may sometimes be burdensome? The answer is that the law imposes no duty upon the finder. If the finder of lost property does not want to bother with it, he is free to leave it where he finds it. If he takes charge of it and carries it away, he thereby imposes upon himself the duty to take reasonable steps to return it to the owner, or to enable the owner to recover it.

Another point entitled to special emphasis is that if defendant has been acquitted because his mistake of some nonpenal law negated a special mental element of the crime charged, this is not in any sense based on the theory that what has been done is excused. The acquittal is due to the fact that the offense has not been committed. An offense has not been committed if any essential element of guilt is missing, whether what is lacking is a mental element or the actus reus itself. The distinction is significant because if mistake is claimed as an excuse it will be necessary to show that the mistake was reasonable, whereas if a mistake resulted in an element of the crime being absent, it is immaterial whether the mistake was reasonable or unreasonable.[52] One who carries away the chattel of another in the honest belief that it is his, is not guilty of larceny, even if the ground for his belief is "weak;"[53] and one who appropriates money which he had collected for another is not guilty of embezzlement "however mistaken . . . or ill-founded his claim of right might in fact be, if he honestly entertained such a belief."[54] The jury is not bound to accept defendant's statement that he believed he had a lawful right to do as he did,[55] and the absence of reasonable grounds for the alleged belief may be considered by them in determining whether he "honestly believed"[56] he had such a right or was merely resorting to a "pretext."[57]

In some of the offenses cited earlier, defendant had relied upon the advice of counsel. This is important as a matter of evidence. It would be difficult to offer more convincing evidence that the mistake had actually been made. But that is its only importance. If because of a mistake of nonpenal law an element of the crime is missing, defendant is not guilty whether he relied upon advice of counsel, undertook to interpret the statute himself, or was even more careless in forming his belief. If an element of the crime

---

52. If the property is "openly taken under an honest, although groundless, claim of right," it is not larceny. Territory v. Dowdy, 14 Ariz. 145, 147, 124 P. 894, 895 (1912).

53. Morningstar v. State, 55 Ala. 148, 149 (1876). See also State v. Abbey, 13 Ariz.App. 55, 474 P.2d 62, 64 (1970) ("[T]he taking of property under a contractual claim of right, in good faith, however ill-advised, is not larceny"); People v. R. V., 606 P.2d 1311 (Colo.App. 1979) (one who took and carried away the property of another, believing it had been abandoned, is not guilty of theft whether his belief was reasonable or unreasonable); State v. Cude, 14 Utah 2d 287, 383

P.2d 399 (1963) (owner of car who removed his automobile from garage without paying bill not guilty of larceny if he thought he had a right to take his own car).

54. Eatman v. State, 48 Fla. 21, 29, 37 So. 576, 579 (1904).

55. Commonwealth v. Brisbois, 281 Mass. 125, 183 N.E. 168 (1932).

56. Morningstar v. State, 55 Ala. 148, 149 (1876).

57. Id. A dishonest pretense of ignorance or mistake of law will never be recognized. State v. Carroll, 160 Mo. 368, 60 S.W. 1087, 1088 (1901).

charged is absent, the reason why it is lacking has no bearing on the result. The defendant is not guilty.

B. MENS REA

Some offenses have no special mental element, but so far as true crimes are concerned "there are no common law offenses in which mens rea is not required, notwithstanding an insignificantly small number of badly reasoned cases to the contrary." [58] And a statute creating a true crime will be interpreted as having a requirement of mens rea even if there are no mens rea words in the enactment.[59] Hence if the offense charged requires no special mental element, but by reason of mistake of some nonpenal law the defendant lacked the mens rea needed for guilt, the obvious conclusion is that he is not guilty; [60] but this has often been overlooked by the courts.[61] An important distinction is to be noted here which may have contributed to the oversight. The general mens rea may be established by criminal negligence. So for a mistake of nonpenal law to negate the mens rea of the offense charged (if no special mental element is required), it is necessary that the mistake be reasonable—meaning one not resulting from criminal negligence.[62]

In sum, a mistake of nonpenal law may be such as to negate any special mental element required for guilt of the offense charged, whether the mistake is reasonable or unreasonable, but if the offense charged requires no special mental element, but only the general mens rea, this element can be negated by a mistake that is reasonable but not by one that is unreasonable.

---

58. Mueller, On Common Law Mens Rea, 42 Minn.L.Rev. 1043, 1101 (1958). "The jury was charged as though the crime were a regulatory offence [sic] instead of a true crime requiring mens rea." United States v. Rybicki, 403 F.2d 599, 601 (6th Cir. 1968) (quoting appellant's brief with approval).

59. E.g., Morisette v. United States, 342 U.S. 246, 263 (1952) ("We hold that mere omission from § 641 of any mention of intent will not be construed as eliminating that element from the crimes denounced"); People v. Clark, 71 Ill.App. 3d 381, 389 N.E.2d 911, 921 (1979) ("Where the purpose of a statute is the punishment of a crime . . . absolute liability will not be found to be the intent of the legislature. . . . Instead the statute will be read as incorporating a mental state requirement"); Turner v. State, 605 P.2d 1140, 1141 (Nev. 1980) ("Although the statute is silent regarding intent, this court has held that the 'taking' in the crime of robbery must be with the specific intent permanently to deprive the owner of his property"); Cutter v. State, 36 N.J.L. 125 (1873) (corrupt intent required for conviction of taking fees to which official not entitled; Banks v. State, 586 S.W.2d 518, 520 (Tex.Crim. App. 1979) ("Though the statutory language of § 21.03 . . . does not pre-

scribe a culpable mental state, it is clear that a culpable mental state *is* required . . ."). Accord, State v. Rushing, 62 Hawaii 102, 612 P.2d 103 (1980). "Legislative silence on the element of intent in a criminal statute is generally not construed as an indication that no culpable mental state is required. . . . This required mental state may be implied from the statute." People v. Naranjo, ___ Colo. ___, 612 P.2d 1099, 1102 (1980).

60. See, e.g., Long v. State, 44 Del. 262, 65 A.2d 489 (1949).

61. A misconception of the marriage law may induce a bona-fide belief of singleness based upon the assumption that a former marriage was invalid. Some courts will not even recognize such a mistake of law as a defense in a bigamy case. E.g., People v. Hartmen, 130 Cal. 487, 62 P. 823 (1900) (expressly overruled in People v. Vogel, 46 Cal.2d 798, 299 P.2d 850, 855 (1956); State v. Hughes, 58 Iowa 165, 11 N.W. 706 (1882); State v. Zibchfeld, 23 Nev. 304, 46 P. 802 (1896).

62. See Long v. State, 44 Del. 262, 65 A.2d 489 (1949). The court emphasized that defendant's mistake of law was very reasonable because of his effort to determine the validity of a divorce. Id. at 497–98.

3.   CIVIL OFFENSES

Civil offenses—violations of regulatory statutes enacted for public convenience, revenue, or any reason other than to punish wrongdoing—do not represent a moral code. No moral precepts would be undermined by permitting ignorance or mistake of such a law to be shown. But if this were done, as said in another connection, "a wide door would be opened for evading the beneficial provisions of this legislation."[63] While it is an overstatement to say that civil offenses are enforced on the basis of absolute liability,[64] the enforcement is so strict that not even a reasonable mistake of fact is available as a defense.[65] *A fortiori* (with the rare exceptions previously referred to) no defense can be established on the ground of ignorance or mistake of the offense charged. Knowledge of such regulatory laws is conclusively presumed.

4.   MISTAKE AS TO NATURE OF OFFENSE

The Model Penal Code has a provision dealing with a situation in which, as a result of mistake of *fact or law*, defendant would have been guilty of a different offense, had he been correct, than he was guilty of in fact.[66] The effect of this provision would be to limit the punishment to what would have been appropriate for the offense of which he would have been guilty had the situation been as he supposed.

The Model Penal Code provision does not pretend to be a statement of existing law. It is intended to introduce a significant change in the law, a change which is not entirely free from controversy. Deeply entrenched in the common law is the concept of risk-assumption by intentional wrongdoing. Conduct with intent to commit one crime may result in guilt of another crime if the latter does not require some special mental element that is lacking. An early federal statute applied a special penalty to the crime of assaulting a foreign minister. And one who made an assault upon a person who was in fact a foreign minister was held guilty of this crime although quite unaware of the official character of his victim.[67] Under the present code it is a federal felony to assault (among others) a federal peace officer while he is engaged in the performance of his official duties.[68] If force has been applied to such an officer who was not reasonably known to be such, the result is as follows. If the force would have been privileged had the other not been a federal officer the mistake is a defense.[69] In that case there would have

---

63. Parker v. Alder, [1899] 1 Q.B. 20, 25 (1898).

64. For example, a truckdriver whose cargo contained undersized fish was held not guilty of violating a statute prohibiting undersized fish since he had no knowledge that the cargo contained such fish, and it was so packed that it would have been unreasonable and impracticable to require him to inspect it. State v. Williams, 94 Ohio App. 249, 115 N.E.2d 36 (1952).

65. State v. Hartfiel, 24 Wis. 60 (1869); Cundy v. LeCocq, 13 Q.B.D. 207 (1884).

66. Model Penal Code § 2.04(2) (Proposed Official Draft, 1962).

67. United States v. Benner, 24 F.Cas. 1084, 1087 (C.C.E.D. Pa. 1830); United States v. Ortega, 27 F.Cas. 359, 362 (C.C. E.D. Pa. 1825); United States v. Liddle, 26 F.Cas. 936, 938 (C.C.D. Pa. 1808).

68. 18 U.S.C. §§ 111, 1114 (1976).

69. The court's meaning is similar in United States v. Rybicki, 403 F.2d 599 (6th Cir. 1968), in which the charge was a violation of I.R.C. § 7212(a) on the claim that defendant obstructed two officers of the IRS who were engaged in the performance of their duties. The officers

been no intentional wrongdoing. But if the attack would have been an assault upon any person, the assailant is guilty of this federal felony.[70] Such an assailant was intentionally engaged in wrongdoing and ran the risk of committing a much more serious offense than he intended. As was said in reference to another federal offense: "It would be no defense to a charge of robbing an insured state bank that the robbers thought it was not insured, and had selected it for that reason, hoping thereby to avoid entanglement with federal law." [71]

It is because of risk-assumption by intentional wrongdoing that the common law holds it is no defense to statutory rape that the man thought the girl was above the "age of consent," [72] even if it was a reasonable mistake.[73] The reasoning was that the man was engaged in intentional wrongdoing, because fornication is immoral,[74] and hence ran the risk of committing an unintended offense. It is noteworthy that, despite the provision mentioned above, the Model Penal Code continues the rule that mistake as to age is no defense to sex with an underage girl, although the age for this purpose is lowered to 10.[75] It should be added that the common-law rule as to mistake of age in a statutory-rape situation has been abandoned in a number of states, in rare instances by judicial decision,[76] but more frequently by legislation.[77] But comparable situations remain. Violation of the abduction statute by taking a girl under a specified age from the possession of her parent or guardian for the purpose of prostitution will support a conviction despite a reasonable mistake as to her age.[78] And if a statute prohibits harboring a

---

were seizing a truck from defendant's driveway in satisfaction of a tax debt, and defendant threatened them with a gun. It was held error to refuse to charge that guilt required defendant to know that the men were IRS officers, since the force would have been privileged if they had not been such. And the Supreme Court has pointed out that on a trial for obstructing an officer it must be shown that the accused was aware of the officer's identity. Pettibone v. United States, 148 U.S. 197, 204–07 (1893).

70. Burke v. United States, 400 F.2d 866 (5th Cir. 1968); McEwen v. United States, 390 F.2d 47 (9th Cir. 1968); United States v. Wallace, 368 F.2d 537 (4th Cir. 1966).

A senate bill pending in Congress, S. 1723, is intended to revise the federal criminal law. Section 2314 of this bill, if enacted as written, would make a change at this point. For the corresponding federal felony, this section would require that the assailant know the victim is a federal law-enforcing officer, if this is the fact. S. 1723, 96th Cong., 1st Sess. § 2314 (1979). But it is interesting that the bill does not require similar knowledge if the victim is in certain other categories, such as a member of Congress or a federally protected foreign individual. Compare id. § 2311 with id. § 2314.

71. Lubin v. United States, 313 F.2d 419, 422 (9th Cir. 1963).

72. See People v. Ratz, 115 Cal. 132, 46 P. 915 (1896); Heath v. State, 173 Ind. 296, 90 N.E. 310 (1910).

73. State v. Houx, 109 Mo. 654, 19 S.W. 35 (1892); State v. Fulks, 83 S.D. 433, 160 N.W.2d 418 (1968).

74. Anciently, fornication was punished by the Church. 2 F. Pollock & F. Maitland, The History of English Law 542 (1895).

75. Model Penal Code § 213.6(1) (Proposed Official Draft, 1962).

76. E.g., People v. Hernandez, 61 Cal. 2d 529, 39 Cal.Rptr. 361, 393 P.2d 673 (1964).

77. E.g., Mont.Rev.Codes Ann. § 45–5–506(1) (1979) (a reasonable belief that the girl is not under the age of consent is a defense to statutory rape). See also State v. Smith, 176 Mont. 159, 576 P.2d 1110 (1978).

78. People v. Dolan, 96 Cal. 315, 31 P. 107 (1892); Smiley v. State, 34 Ga.App. 513, 130 S.E. 359 (1925); State v. Ruhl, 8 Iowa 447 (1859); State v. Johnson, 115 Mo. 480, 22 S.W. 463 (1893).

prostitute under a certain age, a mistake on this point is not exculpating.[79] Another mistake-of-age case may be mentioned. One unlawfully engaged in the "numbers racket" was intentionally violating the law, hence his employment of a minor in that activity made him guilty of the graver offense of contributing to the delinquency of a minor despite his mistake as to the youth's age.[80]

A mistake relating only to the degree of the crime or the gravity of the offense will not shield a deliberate offender from the full consequences of the offense actually committed.[81] Thus it is the actual value of the property, and not the thief's belief, that determines whether larceny is grand or petty.[82] Should the law be changed to use the thief's belief for the determination, the number of convictions of the graver crime would be drastically reduced. Almost never would the prosecution have any direct evidence of what was in the defendant's mind in this regard. The jurors may draw inferences from probative circumstances, but in this situation it would be all too easy, in many cases, to leave them harboring a reasonable doubt. It should be mentioned that the Model Penal Code would permit grading of the offense on the basis of defendant's belief of the value, if there was no recklessness in entertaining that belief.[83] This would work both ways. Thus a thief who stole what he believed was a very valuable piece of jewelry could be convicted of the highest grade of theft even if what he stole was actually a cheap imitation.

5. AUTHORIZED RELIANCE

Almost at the start, it was mentioned that there are a few special circumstances in which a defense may be established on the ground of ignorance or mistake of the very offense violated. These are cases of authorized reliance. They are cases in which the defendant is able to say to the state, in effect, that he relied upon what the state had told him.

A. RELIANCE ON STATUTE OR JUDICIAL DECISION

1. *New Offense*—The state, by statute or decision, has declared what its law is. If a new offense has been created, and there has been delay in the publication thereof, ignorance or mistake of that law is available as a defense to a charge based upon what was done before knowledge of the new law had been made reasonably available to the public.[84] The actor was au-

79. Brown v. State, 23 Del. 159, 74 A. 836 (1909).

80. State v. Davis, 95 Ohio App. 23, 117 N.E.2d 55, *appeal dismissed* 160 Ohio St. 205, 115 N.E.2d 5 (1953).

81. "[H]e cannot set up a legal defence by merely proving that he thought he was committing a different kind of wrong from that which in fact he was committing." Regina v. Prince, L.R., 2 Cr.Cas.Res. 154, 179 (1875). "It is a familiar rule that, if one intentionally commits a crime, he is responsible criminally for the consequences of his act, if the offense proves to be different from that which he intended." Commonwealth v. Murphy, 165 Mass. 66, 70, 42 N.E. 504,

505 (1896). "In such a case a person who deliberately breaks the law must take the risk of his offence turning out to be of a more serious nature than he had intended." Rex v. Wallendorf, So.Afr.L.R. (1920) App.Div. 383, 397.

82. "Under existing law the amount actually stolen determines whether an offense is grand or petty theft." Model Penal Code § 206.15, Comment 3 (Tent. Draft No. 2, 1954).

83. ALI, Model Penal Code with Commentaries, Part II, Art. 223, comment c (1980).

84. An early case held that one is bound to know the new law whether or

thorized to rely upon the law which had been previously declared until the change had been duly published.[85]   Delay of publication is extremely unlikely if the new offense is a true crime, but the defense should be available whenever the situation exists.

2. *Statute Declared Unconstitutional*—If a statute has been judicially, and finally, declared unconstitutional, the legal result is that it never was the law.[86]   The court has no power to repeal legislation.   If the legislative branch has exceeded its authority, and included in its statutes one that it had no power to enact, the court may so declare.   The result of such a decision is not only that this statute *is* not valid, but of necessity that it *never was*. But by enactment of the statute the state had declared that it was part of its law.[87]   And ignorance or mistake of law is a valid defense to a charge based upon what was done while the statute was on the books, and before it had been declared unconstitutional, if what was done would have been no offense had the statute been valid.[88]

3. *Case Overruled*—If a court that has held a statute unconstitutional later changes its mind, overrules the earlier case, and holds the statute valid, the legal result is that the statute has at all times been in full force.   The court has no power to enact legislation.   But when the state's court held the statute unconstitutional, the state declared that this statute was no part of its law.   And ignorance or mistake of law is a defense to any charge based upon what was done in the interim, if what was done would have been no offense if the statute had been invalid.[89]

Comparable problems are encountered whenever a decision interpreting a statute,[90] or the common law,[91] is later overruled by a case holding that the law is other than originally declared.   The public was authorized to rely upon

not it has been officially published. State v. Click, 2 Ala. 26 (1841).   That is clearly unsound and does not represent the modern view.   See Model Penal Code § 2.04, Comment (Tent. Draft No. 4, 1955).   And if a statute worded in terms of "entry upon the lands of another . . . after notice" is interpreted to include also "remaining on the premises of another after receiving notice to leave," this broadened scope of the statute may be applied in the future, but not to anything done prior to this case.   Bouie v. City of Columbia, 378 U.S. 347, 355, 361 (1964).   "Furthermore, when a statute creates a new offense it must be sufficiently explicit to inform those who are subject to it what conduct on their part will render them liable to its penalties." Cardarella v. City of Overland Park, 228 Kan. 698, 620 P.2d 1122, 1128 (1980).

85. This would be codified by Model Penal Code § 2.04(3)(a) (Proposed Official Draft, 1962).

86. "There exists a rule of statutory construction that a statute declared unconstitutional is considered void *ab initio* and has no effect."   State v. Coleman, 605 P.2d 1000, 1013 (Mont. 1979).

"When a statute is adjudged to be unconstitutional, it is as if it had never been." 1 I. Cooley, Constitutional Limitations 382 (8th ed. 1927).

87. To require the citizen to determine for himself, at his peril, to what extent, if at all, the Legislature has overstepped the boundaries defined by the Constitution in passing this mass of statutes, would be to place upon him an intolerable burden, one which it would be absolutely impossible for him to bear—a duty infinitely beyond his ability to perform.

Lang v. Mayor of Bayonne, 74 N.J.L. 455, 460, 68 A. 90, 92 (1907).

88. Brent v. State, 43 Ala. 297 (1869); State v. Godwin, 123 N.C. 697, 31 S.E. 221 (1898); Claybrook v. State, 164 Tenn. 440, 51 S.W.2d 499 (1932).

89. State v. O'Neil, 147 Iowa 513, 126 N.W. 454 (1910).

90. E.g., State v. Longino, 109 Miss. 125, 67 So. 902 (1915).

91. E.g., Stinnett v. Commonwealth, 55 F.2d 644 (4th Cir. 1932).

the law as stated in the first case until it had been overruled. And conduct in the interim, which would have been no offense if the original position had prevailed, may be effectively defended on the ground of ignorance or mistake of law.

The right to rely upon a judicial declaration of the law is free from question if the decision is by the highest court in the jurisdiction.[92] The Supreme Court of Iowa has held that reliance on the decision of an inferior court is no defense to a violation of law.[93] The court said no case had been cited to it in which the decision of an inferior court had been recognized as a defense, but there had been such cases.[94] The citizen should not be expected to know more about law than a court of record, and there has been no doubt about this since the Supreme Court, in refusing to take the position that reliance could not be had upon opinions of lesser courts during its own silence, said that "unless we are to hold that parties may not reasonably rely upon any legal pronouncement emanating from sources other than this Court, we cannot regard as blameworthy those parties who conform their conduct to the prevailing statutory or constitutional norm." [95]

Recently the Kansas Supreme Court said that

a person's belief that his conduct does not constitute a crime because of reliance on a court decision is a defense only when he has relied on a decision of the Supreme Court of Kansas or of a United States appellate court later overruled. Such belief is not a defense when reliance is based on decisions of the various district, county and other lower courts of the state.[96]

But this was based upon the wording of an ill-advised statute. The sound view is that a mistaken belief as to the law based upon a decision of a court

92. State v. O'Neil, 147 Iowa 513, 126 N.W. 454 (1910).

93. State v. Striggles, 202 Iowa 1318, 210 N.W. 137 (1926). The case is very interesting. S was charged with keeping a gambling house on the claim that he permitted a gambling machine to be operated in his restaurant. It was a vending machine. The customer inserted a nickel in the slot and secured a five-cent package of mints. It was the same kind of package of mints that was bought for five cents wherever such product was sold. But this machine was so programmed that an occasional customer also received two or three "chips" worth five cents in trade. It was an advertising gimmick in effort to induce people to buy there. Since the customer would never lose, the municipal court had held that the machine was not a gambling device. For reasons that have never seemed persuasive, the Iowa Supreme Court subsequently held that it *was* a gambling device and refused to allow S to use the municipal court's decision as a defense. In *Striggles*, the court mentioned that it

previously had held that the machine was a gambling device in State v. Ellis, 200 Iowa 1228, 206 N.W. 105 (1925). This might suggest that the municipal court had overlooked a contrary decision by a higher court. But a study of the records will disclose that *Ellis* was decided December 15, 1925, and that S had been indicted several months before that decision. In other words, S relied upon a decision of a court of record at a time when there was no contrary decision by a higher court. It may be added that S had been shown a certified copy of that decision before he permitted the machine to be installed in his restaurant.

94. See State v. Chicago, Milwaukee & St. Paul Railway Co., 130 Minn. 144, 153 N.W. 320 (1915); Coal & Coke Railway Co. v. Conley, 67 W.Va. 129, 67 S.E. 613 (1910).

95. United States v. Peltier, 422 U.S. 531, 542, 95 S.Ct. 2313, 2320 (1975).

96. State v. V.F.W. Post No. 3722, 215 Kan. 693, 527 P.2d 1020, 1025 (1974).

of record, prior to a contrary determination by a higher court, will be recognized as an excuse.[97]

B. RELIANCE ON ADVICE

1. *Official Advice*—Some official bodies or public officers have functions that include a duty, or at least an authority, to advise the public in regard to certain areas of the law. This situation has produced an occasional case so astounding as to be almost unbelievable. Thus a truckdriver was held guilty of violating the law by driving an overloaded truck, although before the trip he had had the vehicle weighed by a licensed weighmaster who had given him a weigh slip that gave the weight of the load at a figure well within lawful limits.[98] The court pointed out that this was not a true crime but an offense *malum prohibitum* and assumed that nothing could be a defense. In this case it might have been appropriate for the state to punish its own agent for negligence in weighing the load, but it was outrageous to punish the citizen who had acted in reliance upon the declaration of the state's agent.[99]

Needless to say, the fact that one is an officer does not necessarily mean that he is authorized to speak for the state as to the meaning of its laws. A court clerk is in no position to give authoritative advice as to the law of concealed weapons;[1] and a city mayor is not authorized to speak for the state as to the effect of the election law.[2] But registration officers or election judges are obviously authorized to advise members of the public in regard to the election law. And one who made a full disclosure of the facts to such officers and was advised by them that he had a lawful right to vote, was not guilty of unlawful registration as a voter, or illegal voting, although the advice he received was erroneous.[3] And if the offense charged is the violation of a law that forbids the doing of certain things without securing a permit from a specified commission or department, the bona-fide reliance upon advice given by that very commission or department to the effect that contemplated action falls without the scope of the statute and hence requires no permit, is a complete defense to a charge of such violation.[4]

2. *Advice of Counsel*—A lawyer is an officer of the court and is licensed to advise clients as to the meaning and effect of the law. But he is not empowered to speak for the state.[5] This illogical position is no doubt an

---

97. United States v. Mancuso, 139 F.2d 90 (3d Cir. 1943); State ex rel. Williams v. Whitman, 116 Fla. 196, 156 So. 705 (1934).

98. Commonwealth v. Olshefski, 64 Pa.D. & C. 343 (1948).

99. Cf. People v. Donovan, 53 Misc.2d 687, 279 N.Y.S.2d 404 (1967) (prosecution estopped from convicting one for doing what he had been officially told to do).

1. State v. Simmons, 143 N.C. 613, 56 S.E. 701 (1907).

2. Jones v. State, 32 Tex.Cr. 533, 25 S.W. 124 (1894) (city officer's assurance that it was all right to open a saloon after the polls closed on election day not a defense to a charge of operating a saloon

on election day). See also State v. Striggles, 202 Iowa 1818, 210 N.W. 137 (1926) (letters from mayor and county attorney, and decision of municipal court, that machine not a "gambling device" not a defense to charge of operating a gambling device).

3. State v. White, 237 Mo. 208, 140 S.W. 896 (1911); State v. Pearson, 97 N.C. 434, 1 S.E. 914 (1887). Cf. United States v. Mancuso, 139 F.2d 90 (3d Cir. 1943) (obedience to an invalidly issued injunction held to be a defense).

4. People v. Ferguson, 134 Cal.App. 41, 24 P.2d 965, 970 (1933).

5. Weston v. Commonwealth, 111 Pa. 251, 2 A. 191 (1886).

inadvertent carry-over from the time, which prevailed for generations, when a lawyer practiced his profession without any license from the state. It was appropriate at that time, but now that the lawyer is licensed by the state to practice law, including the right to advise clients as to the meaning of the law—which license is granted only after the state has purportedly determined that the applicant is qualified and fit to receive it—it would be more appropriate to hold that this is authorization to give advice upon which the client is entitled to rely. The notion that to do so would encourage lawyers to be ignorant of the law in order to be "sought after" [6] is quite unconvincing. If a lawyer should cause the law to be violated by erroneous advice he would be subject to disciplinary action (which might include disbarment in an extreme case) if there was evidence of wilfulness or gross negligence on his part. But the position that reliance on advice of counsel is not a defense is firmly established.[7] It has even been held that a defense of ignorance or mistake of the law violated cannot be based upon advice of the prosecuting attorney.[8] This may be necessary for his protection.[9] If he had authority to advise the general public on the criminal law this might take an unreasonable amount of his time.

6. CONCLUSION

The conclusion is that ignorance or mistake of any non-offense law will be recognized as a defense if it negates the mens rea of the offense charged, but that knowledge of the offense charged is conclusively presumed except as to situations coming within the scope of authorized reliance as it has been interpreted.[10]

6. "If ignorance of counsel would excuse violations of the criminal law, the more ignorant counsel could manage to be, the more valuable, and sought for, in many cases, would be his advice." State v. Downs, 116 N.C. 1064, 1066, 21 S.E. 689 (1895).

7. See, e.g., People v. McCalla, 63 Cal. App. 783, 220 P. 436 (1923), appeal dismissed, 267 U.S. 585 (1924) (reliance on attorney's advice that a document was not a "security" not a defense to "knowingly" selling securities without a permit); State v. Huff, 89 Me. 521, 36 A. 1000 (1897) (reliance on advice of counsel and fish commissioner not a defense to a strict liability offense of illegal fishing); State v. Western Union Tel. Co., 12 N.J. 468, 97 A.2d 480, appeal dismissed, 346 U.S. 869 (1953) (company staff opinion that state law did not prohibit the transmission of betting messages not a defense to operating a disorderly house); Needham v. State, 55 Okl.Cr. 430, 32 P.2d 92 (1934) (advice of counsel including county attorney that defendant might operate his sanitarium so long as he employed a regular licensed physician to operate it not a defense to practicing medicine without a license); Hunter v. State, 158 Tenn. 63, 12 S.W.2d 361 (1928)

(advice of counsel that state salary law unconstitutional not a defense to general-intent crime of embezzlement by a public officer). See People v. Vineberg, 125 Cal.App.3d 127, 177 Cal.Rptr. 819 (1981) (Advice of counsel no defense to a general intent crime but may be a defense in the case of a specific intent crime if there is good faith belief).

8. State v. Striggles, 202 Iowa 1318, 210 N.W. 137 (1926); Hopkins v. State, 193 Md. 489, 69 A.2d 456 (1950), appeal dismissed, 339 U.S. 940 (1950).

9. For a contrary view, see Hall & Seligman, Mistake of Law and Mens Rea, 8 U.Chi.L.Rev. 641, 679 (1941).

10. The general provision of the Model Penal Code would seem to go beyond this. Model Penal Code § 2.04(1) (Proposed Official Draft, 1962). But when it deals specifically with defenses based upon ignorance or mistake of the offense charged, it includes only what is covered by authorized reliance. Id. § 2.04(3).

"It is hornbook law that a mistake of law is no defense to a criminal charge, unless that mistake of law is made in reliance upon a statement from an authoritative source." People v. Carmichael, 164

B. IGNORANCE OR MISTAKE OF FACT

1. IN GENERAL

Ignorance or mistake of fact is very often an excuse for what would otherwise be a crime. A street car conductor, for example, who forcibly ejects a passenger from the car under the honest and reasonable (though mistaken) belief that his fare has not been paid, is liable to the passenger in a civil action but not guilty of criminal assault and battery.[11] Other examples of mistakes of fact sufficient to disprove a charge of assault and battery, include such cases as that of the railroad employee who forcibly removed from the platform one who was there as a passenger but was believed to be there for an unlawful purpose;[12] the police officer who arrested a person for being intoxicated on a public street, mistakenly believing him to be drunk;[13] and the householder who wounded a member of a crowd thought to be making a felonious assault upon the dwelling at night, although the shots by members of the crowd were fired, not at the house, but only in the spirit of frolic.[14] In addition there are numerous cases recognizing mistake of fact as an excuse in prosecutions for other offenses.[15]

"Ignorantia facti excusat,"[16] however, is obviously too sweeping even for a general statement of law, because it is clear (to mention only one point for the moment) that if a certain deed would constitute exactly the same crime under either of two factual situations, it will be no excuse that one was mistaken for the other.[17] Hence some modification is needed, such as that "in some cases *ignorantia facti* doth excuse,"[18] or "an honest mistake of

---

Cal.Rptr. 872, 889 (Cal.App.1980). (The claimed mistake was in regard to the offense charged).

"In the absence of legislative history to the contrary, Congress' use of the word 'knowingly' in a criminal statute aimed at regulating dangerous objects does not in itself abrogate the ancient maxim that ignorance of the law is no excuse." United States v. Currier, 621 F.2d 7, 10 (1st Cir. 1980). "It is generally acknowledged that ignorance, or lack of knowledge, of the law which forbids the conduct with which one is charged is no defense." State v. Morse, 127 Ariz. 25, 617 P.2d 1141, 1147 (1980).

11. State v. McDonald, 7 Mo.App. 510 (1879).

12. Commonwealth v. Power, 48 Mass. 596 (1844).

13. Commonwealth v. Presby, 80 Mass. 65 (1860).

14. State v. Nash, 88 N.C. 618 (1883).

15. *Carrying concealed weapons*: Miles v. State, 52 Tex.Cr.R. 561, 108 S.W. 378 (1908). See also State v. Williams, 184 Iowa 1070, 169 N.W. 371 (1918).

Embezzlement: State v. Smith, 47 La. Ann. 432, 16 So. 938 (1895); Commonwealth v. Wilson, 266 Pa. 236, 109 A. 913 (1920). *Forgery*: Scott v. State, 91 Miss. 156, 44 So. 803 (1907); Crossland v. State, 111 Tex.Cr.R. 357, 12 S.W.2d 1036 (1929); Rex v. Forbes, 7 C. & P. 224, 173 Eng.Rep. 99 (1835). *Harboring a slave*: Birney v. State, 8 Ohio 230 (1837). *Illegal voting*: Gordon v. State, 52 Ala. 308 (1875). *Larceny*: Bird v. State, 48 Fla. 3, 37 So. 525 (1904); State v. Barrackmore, 47 Iowa 684 (1878). *Malicious trespass*: Wagstaff v. Schippel, 27 Kan. 450 (1882). *Murder*: Regina v. Rose, 15 Cox C.C. 540 (1884). *Unwholesome provisions*: State v. Snyder, 44 Mo.App. 429 (1891). *Uttering a forged instrument*: United States v. Carll, 105 U.S. 611 (1881). *Nonwilful intoxication*: State v. Brown, 38 Kan. 390, 16 P. 259 (1888).

16. Farrell v. State, 32 Ohio St. 456, 459 (1877).

17. The Queen v. Lynch, 1 Cox C.C. 361 (1846); State v. Griego, 61 N.M. 42, 294 P.2d 282 (1956).

18. 1 Hale P.C. *42.

fact will generally shield one from a criminal prosecution." [19]   To be more specific:

> **It may be stated as a general rule (subject, however, to exceptions in certain cases [20]) that mistake of fact will disprove a criminal charge if the mistaken belief is (a) honestly entertained, (b) based upon reasonable grounds and (c) of such a nature that the conduct would have been lawful and proper had the facts been as they were reasonably supposed to be.[21]**

2.   HONEST AND REASONABLE BELIEF

The term "honest belief," and equivalent phrases,[22] are sometimes used to express two different ideas: (1) that the belief must have been sincere and (2) that what was done would have been proper had the facts been as they were mistakenly supposed to be.[23]   It will be more convenient, however, to deal with these matters separately, and the second will be reserved for subsequent attention.   As to the first no more need be said than that the possibility of excuse based upon mistake of fact never has any application "where there is no honest belief . . . but . . . a dishonest pretense is resorted to in the endeavor to escape punishment." [24]   The mistaken belief must always be "honest and real" rather than "feigned;" [25] sincere rather than a mere "pretext." [26]

While there is no exception to the requirement that the mistaken belief of the factual situation must be genuine, the question whether it must be based upon reasonable grounds is not so simple.   Undoubtedly the second requirement is frequently present, as indicated by the repeated occurrence of such phrases as "reasonable grounds," [27] "well-grounded," [28] "reasonable ground for believing," [29] "due care to ascertain," [30] "might reasonably have been expected to induce such a belief in a man of ordinary firmness and intelli-

---

19.   People v. Cohn, 358 Ill. 326, 331, 193 N.E. 150, 153 (1934).

20.   In certain cases the statement requires too much, in certain other cases it is inadequate.   See infra.

21.   See Regina v. Tolson, 23 Q.B.D. 168, 190 (1889); Marmont v. State, 48 Ind. 21, 31 (1874).

22.   Such as "bona fide belief". Mulreed v. State, 107 Ind. 62, 66, 7 N.E. 884, 887 (1886).

23.   "Ignorance or mistake in fact, guarded by an honest purpose, will afford, at common law, a sufficient excuse for a supposed criminal act." Farrell v. State, 32 Ohio St. 456, 459 (1877).

24.   State v. Carroll, 160 Mo. 368, 371, 60 S.W. 1087, 1088 (1901).

25.   Dotson v. State, 62 Ala. 141, 144 (1878).

26.   Barton v. State, 88 Tex.Cr.R. 368, 370, 227 S.W. 317, 318 (1921).

27.   Hale v. Commonwealth, 165 Va. 808, 813, 183 S.E. 180, 182 (1936); State v. Henderson, 296 So.2d 805 (La.1974).

28.   State v. Rhone, 223 Iowa 1221, 1233, 275 N.W. 109, 116 (1937).

29.   Shorter v. People, 2 N.Y. 191, 197 (1849); State v. Nash, 88 N.C. 618, 621 (1883).   ". . . reasonable ground to believe. . . ." Marmont v. State, 48 Ind. 21, 31 (1874). ". . . honest and reasonable belief." United States v. Short, 4 USCMA 437, 16 CMR 11 (1954); People v. Wong, 35 Cal.App.3d 812, 111 Cal.Rptr. 314 (1973).

30.   Mulreed v. State, 107 Ind. 62, 66, 7 N.E. 884, 887 (1886). ". . . proper care to ascertain. . . ." Welch v. State, 46 Tex.Cr.R. 528, 530, 81 S.W. 50, 51 (1904).   "He is bound to exercise reasonable diligence to ascertain the facts. . . ." Gordon v. State, 52 Ala. 308, 310 (1875).

gence," [31] "not superinduced by fault or negligence," [32] or "it must also be such a mistake as does not arise from a want of proper care." [33]

If no specific intent or other special mental element is required for guilt of the offense charged, a mistake of fact will not be recognized as an excuse unless it was based upon reasonable grounds; [34] but even an unreasonable mistake, if entertained in good faith, is inconsistent with guilt if it negates some special element required for guilt of the offense such as intent or knowledge. [35]

One, for example, who kills another because of a mistaken belief that his own life is in imminent peril at the hands of the other, is not excused if there is no reasonable ground for this belief. [36] If a specific intent or other special mental element is required for guilt of the offense charged, the possibility of excuse due to a mistake of fact not based on reasonable grounds is obvious. The ultimate question in any prosecution is whether or not all the essential elements of guilt are established. If any such element is found to be wanting, guilt has not been substantiated; and hence if proof of a mistake of fact, even without the support of reasonable grounds, negatives the existence of such an element, it also disproves the charge itself.

This problem is essentially the same as that involved where the existence of such an element is negatived by proof of a mistake of law. The distinction is not always clear-cut. An erroneous belief of ownership and right to immediate possession of a chattel, for example, may be due to misapprehension of property law or to mistaken identity of the thing itself. In another case misunderstanding of law and fact may combine. But since the result is the same if it is sought to disprove the existence of some required specific intent or other special mental element, it is not essential for the mistake to be classified as belonging to one type or the other. Because of the requirement of a specific intent to steal there is no such thing as larceny by negligence. [37] One does not commit this offense by carrying away the chattel of another in the mistaken belief that it is his own, no matter how great may have been the fault leading to this belief, if the belief itself is genuine. [38]

---

31. State v. Cook, 78 S.C. 253, 264, 59 S.E. 862, 866 (1907).

32. Dotson v. State, 62 Ala. 141, 144 (1878); State v. Dizon, 47 Hawaii 444, 390 P.2d 759 (1964).

33. Hamilton v. State, 115 Tex.Cr.R. 96, 97, 29 S.W.2d 777, 778 (1930). And see Stern v. State, 53 Ga. 229, 231 (1874).

34. United States v. Thompson, 12 F. 245 (D.C.Or.1882); Gordon v. State, 52 Ala. 308 (1875); Dotson v. State, 62 Ala. 141 (1878); Stern v. State, 53 Ga. 229 (1874); Goetz v. State, 41 Ind. 162 (1872); Mulreed v. State, 107 Ind. 62, 7 N.E. 884 (1886); State v. Thornhill, 188 La. 762, 178 So. 343 (1938); Hamilton v. State, 115 Tex.Cr.R. 96, 29 S.W.2d 777 (1930); United States v. Short, 4 USCMA 437, 16 CMR 11 (1954); Albert v. Lavin, [1981] Crim.L.Rev. 238 (High Ct.1980).

One dealing with products or activities having a dangerous or deleterious effect,

"or engaging in such activities may be required to ascertain at his peril whether his actions violate the law." McQuoid v. Smith, 556 F.2d 595, 598 (1st Cir. 1977).

35. People v. Navarro, 99 Cal.App.3d Supp. 1, 160 Cal.Rptr. 692 (1979).

36. Hill v. State, 194 Ala. 11, 69 So. 941 (1915); People v. Williams, 32 Cal. 280 (1867); State v. Towne, 180 Iowa 339, 160 N.W. 10 (1916); State v. Allen, 111 La. 154, 35 So. 495 (1903); Loy v. State, 26 Wyo. 381, 185 P. 796 (1919).

37. People v. Watson, 154 Misc. 667, 278 N.Y.S. 759 (1935), aff'd 245 App.Div. 838, 282 N.Y.S. 235 (2d Dept.).

38. Regina v. Halford, 11 Cox C.C. 88 (1868); People v. Devine, 95 Cal. 227, 30 P. 378 (1892); Dean v. State, 41 Fla. 291, 26 So. 638 (1899); People v. Shaunding, 268 Mich. 218, 255 N.W. 770 (1934); Stanley v. State, 61 Okl.Cr. 382, 69 P.2d 398 (1937).

And a conversion of property intrusted is not embezzlement if it was due to a mistake giving rise to a bona-fide belief of authority to appropriate, whether the "belief was well founded or not." [39]

A mental element required for guilt of the particular offense, other than a specific intent in the true sense of the word, may be negatived by a bona-fide belief resulting from an ill-grounded mistake of fact. Thus an untrue statement under oath is not wilfully and corruptly false and hence not perjury if genuinely believed to be true, however great the carelessness which induced the belief.[40] Because of the similarity of this problem to that previously discussed in connection with ignorance or mistake of law, it is not necessary to give further attention to it other than to speak of the most obvious type of case in which a special mental element, other than specific intent, may be disproved by evidence of mistake of fact, whether based upon reasonable grounds or not. This is where the prosecution is for an offense the very definition of which requires knowledge of some particular matter actually unknown to the defendant.

In this connection it is important to bear in mind that the word "knowledge," as used at this point in the law, includes not only actual knowledge, but also guilty belief which corresponds to the fact,[41] and even "guilty avoidance of knowledge," as where the fact would have been known had not the person wilfully "shut his eyes" in order to avoid knowing.[42] It does not include, however, a bona-fide belief contrary to fact, even if not based upon reasonable grounds.[43]

If defendant in good faith believed that the property he took had been abandoned by the owner, he was not guilty of larceny even if his belief was unreasonable under the circumstances. People v. Navarro, 99 Cal.App.3d Supp. 1, 160 Cal. Rptr. 692 (1979).

39. Lewis v. People, 99 Colo. 102, 117, 60 P.2d 1089, 1096 (1936). See also People v. Parker, 355 Ill. 258, 189 N.E. 352 (1934); Commonwealth v. Wilson, 266 Pa. 236, 109 A. 913 (1920). In Parker the court speaks of "reasonable grounds," but this seems to have been an inadvertent use of the familiar phrase because the holding is that guilt is disproved by a bona-fide belief of the right to appropriate certain funds "even if the claim of the defendant was ill-founded or without merit." In Wilson the court reverses a conviction for failure to instruct properly upon the question of mistake of fact. There is no suggestion of the need for "reasonable grounds."

"There is, of course, no question about the proposition: if the defendant took the property under an honest but mistaken belief that he was entitled to do so, that would negative his intent to steal; and he would not be guilty of theft. . . ." State v. Kazda, 545 P.2d 190, 192 (Utah 1976).

40. United States v. Shellmire, 27 Fed.Cas. 1051, No. 16,271 (C.C.Pa.1831); Commonwealth v. Brady, 71 Mass. 78 (1855).

41. Regina v. White, 1 F. & F. 665, 175 Eng.Rep. 898 (1859); State v. Friend, 210 Iowa 980, 987, 230 N.W. 425, 429 (1930); Meath v. State, 174 Wis. 80, 83, 182 N.W. 334, 335 (1921).

42. State v. Lintner, 141 Kan. 505, 41 P.2d 1036 (1935); People v. Sugarman, 216 App.Div. 209, 216, 215 N.Y.S. 56, 63 (1st Dept.1926), aff'd 243 N.Y. 638, 154 N.E. 637. "The jury have not found, either that the prisoner knew that these goods were Government stores, or that he wilfully shut his eyes to the fact." Regina v. Sleep, 8 Cox C.C. 472, 480 (1861); United States v. Jewell, 532 F.2d 697 (9th Cir. 1976); United States v. Restrepo-Granda, 575 F.2d 524 (5th Cir. 1978).

43. United States v. Shellmire, 27 Fed.Cas. 1051, No. 16,271 (C.C.Pa.1831); State v. Dunning, 130 Iowa 678, 107 N.W. 927 (1906); Commonwealth v. Wilson, 266 Pa. 236, 109 A. 913 (1920); State v. Pickus, 63 S.D. 209, 257 N.W. 284 (1934).

One, for example, is not guilty of uttering a forged instrument with knowledge of the forgery if he actually had no doubt of its genuineness, even if he was quite negligent in not discovering its falsity.[44] A charge of receiving stolen goods knowing the same to have been stolen is not established by proof of the receipt of the goods under circumstances which should have induced a belief of this fact if the defendant actually had no such belief.[45] If the statute on fraudulent banking requires receipt of a deposit by a banker *knowing* his bank to be insolvent at the time, "mere negligence is not enough." [46] In a prosecution for obtaining property by false pretenses it is reversible error to give an instruction which will permit the jury to find the defendant guilty if he was quite careless in making the untrue statement— because he might in good faith believe the statement to be true despite his fault in not having a correct understanding of the facts.[47] One who sends non-mailable matter through the mail without suspecting the presence of the forbidden contents is not guilty of knowingly depositing such matter in the mails even if he was negligent in not knowing.[48] As said by the California court in reversing a conviction of procuring false evidence in the form of an affidavit from one who was to defendant's knowledge incapable of making an affidavit,"facts which would ordinarily suggest the inquiry are not sufficient. The jury must believe that they did in fact suggest the inquiry to the defendant." [49]

The English House of Lords has applied the concept to the crime of rape. It has held a mistaken belief that the woman was consenting would not be unreasonable if genuine. The mistake may negative the mens rea required for recklessness.[50] This position is in accord with the Model Penal Code position on mistake and has been accepted by courts in this country.[51]

3.   OFFENSES NOT REQUIRING NORMAL MENS REA

In the discussion of Strict Liability [52] it was pointed out that courts at one time tended to hold that no mistake of fact would be recognized as a defense to a prosecution for a civil offense, unless the statute expressly included some special mental element. This was unnecessary and unreasonable and the modern trend is away from such an extreme position.[53] In the civil-offense area it is proper to require a very high degree of care and to impose upon **D** the burden of convincing the factfinder that there was no failure of this requirement. But he should not be held accountable for what he could

---

44. Carver v. People, 39 Mich. 786 (1878); Wells v. Territory, 1 Okl.Cr. 469, 98 P. 483 (1908).

45. State v. Alpert, 88 Vt. 191, 92 A. 32 (1914); Meath v. State, 174 Wis. 80, 182 N.W. 334 (1921); State v. Beale, 299 A.2d 921 (Me.1973).

46. State v. Dunning, 130 Iowa 678, 682, 107 N.W. 927, 928 (1906). Accord, State v. Tomblin, 57 Kan. 841, 48 P. 144 (1897); State v. Drew, 110 Minn. 247, 124 N.W. 1091 (1910). Contra, McClure v. People, 27 Colo. 358, 61 P. 612 (1900).

47. State v. Pickus, 63 S.D. 209, 257 N.W. 284 (1934).

48. Konda v. United States, 166 F. 91 (7th Cir. 1908).

49. See People v. Brown, 74 Cal. 306, 310, 16 P. 1, 3 (1887).

50. Regina v. Morgan [1976] AC 182. See discussion Williams, Textbook of Criminal Law p. 100 (1978).

51. See Model Penal Code § 2.04.

52. Chapter 7, section 5, A.

53. Ibid.

not possibly have known—or could not have known by any means which he could in good conscience have been required to employ.[54]

4.　MISTAKE ONLY AS TO EXTENT OF WRONG

In the discussion of Unlawful Act [55] it was pointed out that while the judges, in the development of the mens-rea doctrine, spoke in terms of the guilty mind (*nisi mens sit rea*), they regarded the mind as either innocent or guilty and hence were actually looking to see whether the mind was or was not innocent.　One who was intending to commit a crime did not have an innocent mind.　Hence he was acting with mens rea and if he committed the *actus reus* of some unintended crime he was guilty of that crime unless it required a specific intent or some other special mental element.　As he was acting with mens rea it was unimportant that the mistake he made was based upon reasonable grounds.　The courts also held that the mind was not innocent if the actor was intending to commit a very wrongful act, even if no punishment was provided for that act, and hence he was acting with mens rea and might be guilty of an unintended crime.　This doctrine of risk-assumption by intentional wrongdoing has been followed through the ages. As said in the earlier discussion: Perhaps the time has come to jettison this age-old concept, but such a step should not be lightly taken.

The general mens rea of the common law can be established by either criminal negligence or the intent to commit an unlawful act.　The Model Penal Code does not deal with the general mens rea but provides that criminal negligence is the special mental element of any crime for which it is sufficient for guilt.[56]　The result is that a genuine mistake of fact may be a defense to any crime for which more than criminal negligence is needed for guilt, even if the mistake is unreasonable, but a defense to a crime that needs no more than criminal negligence, only if the mistake of fact was not the result of criminal negligence.[57]　This does not depart from what the holding should be under existing law.　Adoption of the Code would make a substantial change in the law, however, by abrogating the concept of risk-assumption by intentional wrongdoing—which may, or may not, be desirable.

Ignorance or mistake of fact may be summarized by emphasizing that if it negates the mental element of the offense charged, the crime has not been committed.

If the offense charged requires a specific intent, or any other special mental element, this may be negated by pertinent ignorance or mistake of fact whether the error is reasonable or unreasonable.

If the offense charged requires no special mental element, but only the general mens rea, this requirement may be established by criminal negli-

54.　United States v. Park, 421 U.S. 658, 95 S.Ct. 1903 (1975).

55.　Chapter 7, section 7.

56.　Except as to "violations" (civil offenses) "a person is not guilty of an offense unless he acted purposely, knowingly, recklessly or negligently, as the law may require, with respect to each material element of the offense."　Section 2.02(1).　"Negligently" is defined in

terms of criminal negligence.　Id. at subsection (2)(d).

57.　Section 2.04(1).　"Ignorance or mistake as to a matter of fact . . . is a defense if: (a) the ignorance or mistake negatives the purpose, knowledge, belief, recklessness or negligence required to establish a material element of the offense; . . . "

gence. Hence ignorance or mistake of fact may negate this element if reasonable, but not if it was the result of criminal negligence.

The ordinary civil offense has neither any special mental element nor the general mens rea, hence there is nothing for ignorance or mistake to negate. (It has been held, properly although not uniformly, that a violation will be excused if the situation was so extreme that the accused not only was unaware of the relevant facts, but the circumstances were such that it was practically impossible for him to have known).

C. BIGAMY

Problems of ignorance and mistake have presented unusual difficulties in connection with the crime of bigamy, and on some of the points involved the present state of the authorities is far from satisfactory. Difficulty is encountered even in the choice of words to be used in discussing the matter because a marriage ceremony in due form will not create the marital relation if either party has another spouse at the time. Such a ceremony is not in the true legal sense a marriage, nor is either party the lawful husband or wife of the other. Yet it is common to speak of a "bigamous marriage" and to define bigamy as the offense of "having a plurality of wives or husbands at the same time." [58]

Quite obviously one charged with bigamy will not be excused because of ignorance of the statute prohibiting a second marriage by one who has a lawful spouse living at the time,[59] or because of a mistaken belief as to the impropriety and invalidity of such an enactment.[60] The claim of ignorance or mistake of law in a bigamy case, however, almost invariably arises from some other angle. That is, the mistake was not as to the law of bigamy but as to some other law. And here is found, perhaps, the most striking illustration of the strange delay of the courts in recognizing that a reasonable mistake of a nonpenal law may leave the crime charged unsupported by mens rea, even if the crime does not require any special mental element. Despite "frequent statements in judicial opinions and elsewhere that the offense of bigamy does not require 'mens rea' " [61] the law is clearly otherwise.[62] It does not require any specific intent or other special mental element but does require the general mens rea which will be absent if there was such a reasonable mistake of nonpenal law as to leave the conduct blameless. Many cases, however, have been decided on the false premise that no mistake of law can be recognized as a defense if the crime charged does not require a specific intent or some other special mental element. In some of the following cases the mistake may not have been reasonable but that was not the ground on which the decision was based. A misconception of the marriage law may induce a bona-fide belief of singleness based upon the assumption of invalidity of a former marriage. Not even such a mistake of law was recognized as an excuse in a bigamy case.[63] One who contracted a common-

58. See, e.g., May's Criminal Law § 138 (4th ed. 1938); Ga.Code Ann. § 26–2007 (1978).

59. Eldridge v. State, 126 Ala. 63, 28 So. 580 (1900).

60. Reynolds v. United States, 98 U.S. 145 (1878); Long v. State, 192 Ind. 524, 137 N.E. 49 (1922).

61. Model Penal Code 222 (Tent. Draft No. 4 (1955).

62. Ibid.; Edwards, "Mens Rea" and Bigamy, 2 Current Legal Problems 47 (1949).

63. State v. Hughes, 58 Iowa 165, 11 N.W. 706 (1882); State v. Zichfeld, 23 Nev. 304, 46 P. 802 (1896).

law marriage, where valid, was held to have committed bigamy by marrying another spouse while the first relation continued, despite his belief that the first relation did not constitute a marriage because not solemnized by the customary ceremony performed by clergyman or magistrate.[64] And even reliance upon the advice of counsel that a former marriage with a cousin was void was held in one case not to be an excuse for a second marriage with another.[65]

A mistaken belief of singleness by a married person may be due to the erroneous notion that the marriage tie has been dissolved by divorce, and this type of mistake may be either one of fact or one of law. If such a claim is made by one who knows just what steps were taken to obtain a divorce his mistake is one of law, if such steps were not sufficient to constitute a legal dissolution of the bonds of matrimony, and did not save him from conviction of bigamy.[66] On the other hand, if reliance is placed upon incorrect information to the effect that a divorce has been obtained by the spouse, the mistake is one of fact. In a bigamy case it is clear that the state is not required to allege and prove knowledge of the lack of divorce.[67] The burden is on the defendant to establish his bona-fide belief that his marriage had been dissolved by divorce,[68] and reasonable grounds to support such belief.[69] If his second marriage was contracted by him while entertaining a bona-fide and reasonable belief of this nature, resulting from mistake of fact, he is entitled to an acquittal[70] unless something in the statute requires a different result. Some courts have held that innocence may be established by a proper showing of this nature[71] while others have reached the opposite conclusion.[72] Some of the cases can be distinguished by differences in the wording of the various statutes[73] but more frequently there has been a disagreement as to

64. State v. Zichfeld, 23 Nev. 304, 46 P. 802 (1896).

65. Staley v. State, 89 Neb. 701, 131 N.W. 1028 (1911).

66. State v. Armington, 25 Minn. 29 (1878); State v. DeMeo, 20 N.J. 1, 118 A.2d 1 (1955); cf. State v. Stank, 9 Ohio Dec. 8 (1883).

67. People v. Priestley, 17 Cal.App. 171, 118 P. 965 (1911).

By way of analogy: At common law it is a complete defense to a charge of rape that defendant is the lawful husband of the "victim;" but the state does not have the affirmative duty to allege and prove that this is not the fact. Rogers v. State, 267 Ind. 654, 373 N.E.2d 125 (1978).

68. State v. Cain, 106 La. 708, 31 So. 300 (1902).

69. Ibid.; Lesueur v. State, 176 Ind. 448, 95 N.E. 239 (1911). A mere rumor of death is insufficient basis for such belief. White v. State, 157 Tenn. 446, 9 S.W.2d 702 (1928).

70. People v. Vogel, 46 Cal.2d 798, 299 P.2d 850 (1956). Bigamy has been regarded as extremely anti-social and has been severely punished. Hence the nor-

mal mens rea requirement will be present unless excluded by the language of the statute. Ibid.; The Queen v. Tolson, 23 Q.B.D. 168 (1889); Regina v. Gould, [1968] 1 All E.R. 849; Thomas v. The King, (1937 Aust.) 59 CLR 279.

71. People v. Vogel, 46 Cal.2d 798, 299 P.2d 850 (1956); Robinson v. State, 6 Ga.App. 696, 65 S.E. 792 (1909); Squire v. State, 46 Ind. 459 (1874); Lesueur v. State, 176 Ind. 448, 95 N.E. 239 (1911); State v. Sparacino, 164 La. 704, 114 So. 601 (1927); Baker v. State, 86 Neb. 775, 126 N.W. 300 (1910); State v. Stank, 9 Ohio Dec. 8 (1883); Chapman v. State, 77 Tex.Cr.R. 591, 179 S.W. 570 (1915); Adams v. State, 110 Tex.Cr.R. 20, 7 S.W.2d 528 (1928); and see Alexander v. United States, 136 F.2d 783, 784 (D.C.Cir.1943).

72. Russell v. State, 66 Ark. 185, 49 S.W. 821 (1899); Ellison v. State, 100 Fla. 736, 129 So. 887 (1930); People v. Spoor, 235 Ill. 230, 85 N.E. 207 (1908); State v. Trainer, 232 Mo. 240, 134 S.W. 528 (1911); State v. Hendrickson, 67 Utah 15, 245 P. 375 (1926).

73. For example, compare Robinson v. State, 6 Ga.App. 696, 65 S.E. 792 (1909)

construction. This can be considered to best advantage in connection with the problem which follows.

Still another type of mistake may lead to a married person's believing he is single. This is the erroneous belief that his spouse is dead, and is purely a mistake of fact. The general problem is similar to the mistake of fact that a divorce has been granted. Like such a mistake it will not excuse if not based upon reasonable grounds,[74] but a bona-fide and well-grounded belief that the other spouse is dead should entitle the defendant to an acquittal in a bigamy case unless the language of the statute precludes this defense.[75] Some interpretations have admitted this defense [76] and others have not.[77]

Since it is within the power of the legislature in enacting the statute to include either more or less than the normal mens-rea requirement, it is necessary to consider each case in the light of the words used in that jurisdiction. Limitations of space permit only a very general comment on this subject here. The statutes differ from the extreme of stipulating "knowingly" as a special mental element of the offense [78] to provisions which go rather far in the other direction.[79] For the most part they provide two exceptions which are, in substance, (1) statutory presumption of death and (2) dissolution of the bonds of matrimony by judicial decree. The issue is whether the inclusion of these two exceptions impliedly excludes others not mentioned. The solution requires a careful examination of the purposes of these clauses.

Where one has left his home and not been heard from afterwards, an inference of death might arise in a relatively short time under some circumstances, whereas many years of absence and lack of information would fail to support such an inference if it was an obvious case of desertion by one who wished never to see his deserted spouse again. It would be so unwise to leave this matter unregulated that the statutes very generally provide for a statutory presumption of death or defense in the event of absence for a certain period (varying from two[80] to seven[81] years) during which the absent one is not known to be alive by the other spouse.[82] It is peculiarly important also for a bigamy statute to take a position on the matter of divorce because the state might (1) prohibit a divorcee from marrying any other person during the life of the original spouse, (2) distinguish between the innocent party and the guilty party in the divorce proceeding with reference to the right to

with State v. Trainer, 232 Mo. 240, 134 S.W. 528 (1910).

74. Dotson v. State, 62 Ala. 141 (1878). Mere reliance upon a rumor is not sufficient. Gillum v. State, 141 Tex. Cr.R. 162, 147 S.W.2d 778 (1941).

75. See a comparison of the bigamy statute and the adultery statute in State v. Audette, 81 Vt. 400, 70 A. 833 (1908).

76. The Queen v. Tolson, 23 Q.B.D. 168 (1889); Dotson v. State, 62 Ala. 141 (1878); Welch v. State, 46 Tex.Cr.R. 528, 81 S.W. 50 (1904).

77. Rand v. State, 129 Ala. 119, 29 So. 844 (1900); Cornett v. Commonwealth, 134 Ky. 613, 121 S.W. 424 (1909); Commonwealth v. Hayden, 163 Mass. 453, 40 N.E. 846 (1895); State v. Ackerly, 79 Vt. 69, 64 A. 450 (1906).

78. Ga.Code Ann. § 26–2007 (1978). See also id. § 26–2008. Compare Robinson v. State, 6 Ga.App. 693, 65 S.E. 792 (1909) with Parnell v. State, 126 Ga. 103, 54 S.E. 804 (1906).

79. Kan.Stat.Ann. § 21–3601 (1974).

80. Purdon's Consol. Pa.Stat.Ann. § 4301 (1973). The statute requires that the actor not know the prior spouse to be alive.

81. Mass.Gen.L.Ann. 272 § 15 (1980).

82. West's Ann.Cal.Pen.Code § 282 (1970); West's F.S.A. (Fla.) § 826.02 (1979).

remarry, or (3) permit either party to remarry after the divorce has become effective. Hence a clause on this subject is commonly included.[83]

In other words, these are two exceptions which have nothing to do with ordinary crimes but are peculiarly important to bigamy. Because of this fact it is quite out of line with sound principles of statutory construction to hold that the inclusion of these special and unusual defenses results in an implied exclusion of all general defenses, such as, for example, compulsion, insanity or mistake of fact.[84] Moreover, had the cases which originally tested the issue been "shotgun marriages" enforced under the threat of immediate death, and marriages of insane persons, there would probably be no support for the view that bigamy is an offense with no requirement of mens rea. In fact, there seems to be no case, and probably will be none, excluding the possibility of such defenses in a prosecution for bigamy. The much narrower issue presented by the decided cases is (1) whether the statutory mention of absence and want of information for a certain period excludes bona-fide belief of death based upon other reasonable grounds and (2) whether the reference to (actual) divorce excludes a reasonable mistake of fact that a divorce has been granted.

The most careful analysis is to be found in *Tolson* [85] which is the leading case for the view that the defenses mentioned in the statute do not exclude others of a more general nature. It is there pointed out that other evidence may indicate death much more convincingly than mere absence and want of information, and that it would be absurd to punish a wife for acting in bona-fide reliance upon evidence strong enough to collect a policy of insurance or to probate a will—as where her second marriage is after she had watched the burial of a body, disfigured beyond recognition by an explosion, but confidently believed by her and by others in the community to be that of her first husband.[86]

What has come to be regarded as the leading case for the opposite view is *Mash*,[87] in which the actual decision of guilt was unavoidable because the only basis for the belief of the husband's death was absence and want of information for substantially *less* than the statutory period. Language in this opinion quite beyond the needs of the decision has been relied upon by those courts which have regarded the inclusion of these special defenses as excluding any defense based upon the bona-fide and reasonable belief of divorce or of death (unless supported by absence for the statutory period). The same court, it should be added, may interpret the statute as excluding one of these defenses but not the other.[88]

83. See the statutes cited supra note 79. The statute may also mention annulment and perhaps add a special clause on annulment because of nonage, thus making three clauses on the subject of judicial decree. Ark.Stats.Ann., § 41–2402(2)(c) (1977) (Off.1947).

84. See People v. Vogel, 46 Cal.2d 798, 299 P.2d 850 (1956).

85. The Queen v. Tolson, 23 Q.B.D. 168 (1899).

86. Id. at 191.

87. Commonwealth v. Mash, 84 Mass. 472 (1844).

88. See, for example, The King v. Wheat, [1921] 2 K.B. 119, which refused to recognize a bona-fide and reasonable belief of divorce as a defense and distinguished The Queen v. Tolson, in which the belief was of death. There is more reason for this distinction if the legislature in attempting to correct the situation gives as an additional excuse "good reason to believe such husband or wife to be dead" and fails to make similar provision for belief of divorce. In Wheat, it should be added, the court seems to be speaking of a mistake of law rather than a mistake of fact.

The wish to insure against the harsh interpretation reached by some courts has no doubt been responsible for the inclusion of certain special provisions in the bigamy statutes, such as the word "knowingly," [89] or an additional exception where the belief that the husband or wife is dead is based upon good grounds other than mere absence and want of information.[90] The latter amendment takes care of one difficulty but tends to add strength to the argument against recognizing reasonable belief of divorce as an excuse.[91] The unsound view that a bona-fide belief based upon reasonable grounds is not a defense in a bigamy case has some recognition in this country[92] but as said *obiter* in a recent case there is much to be said for the other position [93] and fortunately the trend is in that direction.[94] It is quite significant that the recent wars have produced many Enoch Ardens[95] which seem to have resulted in few prosecutions for bigamy,—if any.

If one having a lawful spouse married again under the bona-fide and *reasonable* belief that he was single we have the *actus reus* of bigamy but not the mens rea, and the only acceptable answer is that the crime was not committed.

SECTION 2.   IMPELLED PERPETRATION

A. OVERMASTERING PHYSICAL FORCE (VIS ABSOLUTA)

A choice between two evils, however desperate the situation, must not be confused with no choice at all. One finding himself faced by the former may sometimes wish it were the latter but the basic distinction remains. As pointed out by Holmes an attempt to treat leaving the ship under stress of perils of the sea as not distinguishable from being torn bodily away from it by the tempest "is one of the oldest fallacies of the law. The difference between the two is the difference between an act and no act. The distinction is well settled in the parallel instance of duress by threats, as distinguished from overmastering physical force applied to a man's body and imparting to it a motion sought to be attributed to him." [1]

Typical illustrations are: (1) At gunpoint, and under threat of instant death, A orders B to thrust a knife through the heart of a sleeping victim which B does to save his own life; and (2) as A, C and D are standing near the edge of a precipice, A suddenly shoves C against D, causing D to fall to his death. In both cases A has committed homicide but the present problem does not concern him, and as we turn our attention to the others we find that B also has committed homicide, but C has not.[2] The difference is between compulsion of the will (*vis compulsiva*) which results in an act though not of

---

89. Ga.Code Ann., § 26–2007 (1978).

90. 11 Del.C.Ann. § 1001 (1979); Iowa Code Ann. § 726.1 (1978); Mich.Comp. Laws 1968, § 750.439.

91. White v. State, 157 Tenn. 446, 9 S.W.2d 702 (1928).

92. Alexander v. United States, 136 F.2d 783, 784 (D.C.Cir. 1943).

93. State v. DeMeo, 20 N.J. 1, 14, 118 A.2d 1, 8 (1955).

94. Ibid.; People v. Vogel, 46 Cal.2d 798, 299 P.2d 850 (1956). See also the court's statement in Alexander v. United States, 136 F.2d 783, 784 (C.A.D.C.1943), and the statutes cited supra, in notes 79 and 80.

95. Tennyson's classic involving such a situation was entitled "Enoch Arden."

1. The Eliza Lines, 199 U.S. 119, 130, 26 S.Ct. 8, 10 (1905).

2. 1 Hale P.C. *434.

free volition, and physical compulsion (*vis absoluta*) in which the unavoidable movement is no act at all.[3]

The distinction is emphasized for the purpose of exclusion because whenever a man's body is used as the means of causing harm by overmastering physical force, whether by another person or by the elements, it is not a case of impelled perpetration since so far as he is concerned there is no perpetration at all. As the word "compulsion" is used in the rest of this section it is to be understood to mean compulsion of the will and not actual physical compulsion.

B. THE "INEXCUSABLE CHOICE" *

From first to last the common law has held firm to the proposition that one may not choose between oneself and another, who may live and who must die, by intentionally killing an obviously innocent and unoffending[4] person in order to preserve one's life. Such a killing is criminal homicide.[5] It has been argued at times that an excuse should be recognized on the ground that when one is threatened with instant death unless a terrible deed is done, if one's own conscience will not prevent the deed, no threat of what the law may do at some distant, future time can have any deterring influence.[6] The statement is true, of course, but the argument misses the point. The criminal law is a moral code and if an excuse were recognized in such a case this would declare that such an intentional killing is morally acceptable. The consistent holding of the common-law judges that such a killing is not excused has been to emphasize that it is so morally wrong as to call for punishment.[7] As explained by Blackstone, "he ought rather to die himself than to escape by the murder of an innocent."[8] Hale had pointed out that while one, even facing death, has no excuse for killing an innocent victim, the killing of the threatener may be excused.[9]

---

3. Holland, Jurisprudence 108–9 (12th ed. 1916).

* By express permission the following is adapted from Perkins, Impelled Perpetration Restated, 33 Hastings L.J. 403 (1981).

4. One would be justified in using deadly force if it reasonably seemed necessary to save his life from a raving maniac, even if the latter would be "innocent" of crime because of his mental disorder. The word "unoffending" has customarily been added to provide for this situation although perhaps another such as "harmless" might have been more appropriate. The use of the phrase "innocent and unoffending" for this purpose dates back at least to the time of Lord Coleridge. The Queen v. Dudley and Stephens, 14 Q.B.D. 273, 286, 15 Cox C.C. 624, 636 (1884).

5. 1 Hale P.C. *51; 4 Bl.Comm. *30; Brewer v. State, 72 Ark. 145, 78 S.W. 773 (1904). "(C)oercion is not a defense to murder." United States v. Buchanan,

529 F.2d 1148, 1153 (7th Cir. 1976). "The defense, where available, justifies any crime short of homicide." State v. Greene, 5 Kan.App.2d 698, 623 P.2d 933, 936 (1981).

6. Williams, Criminal Law: The General Part § 246 (2d ed. 1961).

7. See Arp v. State, 97 Ala. 5, 12, 12 So. 301, 303–4 (1892). "Knowledge of the wrong of killing an innocent person even to preserve one's own life can be inculcated by the dramatic instruction of the criminal courts." Hall, Principles of Criminal Law 418 (1947). "At least one purpose of the penal law is to express a formal social condemnation of forbidden conduct, ..." Sauer v. United States, 241 F.2d 640, 648 (9th Cir. 1957).

8. 4 Bl.Comm. *30.

9. 1 Hale P.C. *51. And see Leach v. State, 99 Tenn. 584, 595, 42 S.W. 195, 197 (1897). The word "may" is used in the text to avoid an overstatement. See infra, chapter 10, section 4.

As stated by one court: [10] "The authorities seem to be conclusive that, at common law, no man can excuse himself, under the plea of necessity or compulsion, for taking the life of an innocent person." This has been repeated, in substance, time and again,[11] sometimes in spectacular situations. *Holmes*,[12] for example, was a famous American case that arose out of a situation in which a ship struck an iceberg and sank in midocean. Before the vessel went down boats were lowered, carrying the passengers and members of the crew. These boats were soon separated. One was so overloaded the people were barely able to move in their crowded positions, and the next day a squall developed, threatening to send the overcrowded craft (not a modern lifeboat) to the bottom. In this emergency the officer in charge gave the order to jettison a portion of the human freight. Holmes was one of the two sailors who carried out the mandate to eliminate every third man, by seizing fourteen men and throwing them overboard. The boat thus lightened managed to ride the waves until a rescue ship arrived on the following day. The officer and most of the crew disappeared shortly after landing, but Holmes went on to Philadelphia, where he was arrested for murder on the high seas, a crime under federal law. Although it was conceded that the boat would not have survived the storm if the load had not been lightened, no excuse was recognized.

In *Dudley*,[13] an equally famous English case, two men were indicted for wilful murder, and on the trial the jury returned a special verdict stating, in effect, that the prisoners and another sailor, able-bodied English seamen and the deceased a boy of about seventeen, the crew of an English yacht, were cast away in a storm on the high seas 1600 miles from land and were compelled to put into an open boat. That the food they took with them was all consumed in twelve days, and having been without food for eight days and without water for six days, the prisoners killed the boy. That the boy when killed was lying on the bottom of the boat, quite helpless and weak, unable to make any resistance, but did not assent to being killed. That the sailors fed upon the body and blood of the boy for four days, when they were picked up by a passing vessel. That at the time of the killing there appeared to the prisoners every possibility that unless they fed upon the boy, or one of themselves, they would die of starvation. That there was no appreciable chance of saving life except by killing someone for the others to eat. That there was no greater necessity for killing the boy than any of the others. The court held that this special verdict showed no justification or excuse for the killing and was a verdict of guilty of wilful murder.

While the common law never excuses one who makes a choice between oneself and an obviously innocent person, by intentionally killing the latter, certain situations require attention, and may be presented in hypothetical

10. Arp v. State, 97 Ala. 5, 12, 12 So. 301, 303 (1893).

11. R. I. Recreation Center v. Aetna Casualty & Surety Co., 177 F.2d 603, 605 (1st Cir. 1949); People v. Martin, 13 Cal. App. 96, 102, 108 P. 1034, 1036 (1910); State v. Clay, 220 Iowa 1191, 1203, 264 N.W. 77, 83 (1935); State v. St. Clair, 262 S.W.2d 25 (Mo.1953); State v. Weston, 109 Or. 19, 219 P. 180 (1923); State v. Nargashian, 26 R.I. 299, 58 A. 953 (1904);

State v. Lee, 78 N.M. 421, 432 P.2d 265 (1967); State v. Taylor, 22 Wn.App. 308, 589 P.2d 1250 (1979); Esquibel v. State, 91 N.M. 498, 576 P.2d 1129 (1978).

12. United States v. Holmes, 26 Fed. Cas. 360, No. 15,383 (C.C.Pa.1842).

13. The Queen v. Dudley & Stephens, 14 Q.B.D. 273, 286, 15 Cox C.C. 624, 636 (1884).

form. A man and a boy, total strangers, were paid passengers in a small horse-drawn vehicle in which they were being driven around the countryside. At a remote spot they were suddenly attacked by ferocious beasts. The driver did his best to elude them but it was obvious that the horse could not pull the vehicle rapidly enough to do so. At practically the last moment the man threw the boy to the beasts. They stopped to devour the boy, and this enabled the others to reach a place of safety. The man insisted that if it had not been for his foresight in throwing out the boy, he and the boy and the driver would all three have been destroyed so that, unfortunate as it was, it was the best act under the circumstances. A choice resulting in saving two at the expense of one, all else being equal, would be morally right in a proper case, but the man had a choice. He could have achieved the result of sacrificing one for the safety of two by heroically jumping out and facing the animals himself. He intentionally chose to kill the boy to save his own life and has no excuse at common law.

Band C were climbing a mountain, being roped together for mutual protection. As they were inching along a narrow ledge, B slipped off so suddenly that he dragged C over with him. C managed to get a firm grip as he went over the ledge and found himself hanging there, with B dangling at the end of the rope some feet below. C could hold on momentarily with one hand but could not pull up B with the other, and B had been knocked unconscious by the fall, and was unable to help. C held on grimly until it was obvious that very shortly his grip would slip and both be plunged to death. Just before that was about to happen, C cut the rope and let B drop to his death. Without the weight of B to overcome, C was then able to pull himself up to safety. This was not a case in which C made a choice between C and B. B was doomed. There was nothing C could do to save B. The choice here was between C and B on the one hand and C on the other. C may have violated the mountaineer's code but the law should recognize that his act was excusable.[14] It would have been morally wrong for C to have sacrificed his own life merely because there was no way to save B.

A ship sank in midocean, going down so suddenly and unexpectedly that it carried almost everything with it. After it disappeared there was nothing on the water there except X, Y and one life preserver. The weather was so rough that the only hope of survival was to have the preserver firmly fastened. (1) X reached the preserver first and had it firmly fastened when Y arrived. Y could not survive without the preserver and so he took it. He was sufficiently powerful and skillful to be able to take the preserver without inflicting any physical injury upon X, but without it X drowned. Or (2) Y reached the preserver first and swam away with it and X drowned because he had no life preserver. In (1) Y killed X. He chose to sacrifice an obviously innocent person and has no excuse even though it was necessary to save his own life. In (2) Y did not kill X. He did not take the preserver from X because X never had it. X drowned for want of a preserver but this cannot be attributed to Y.

In the *Holmes* trial the evidence indicated that the captain, who was in another boat and not even in sight when some were thrown overboard, had

14. C killed B. By cutting the rope he advanced the death of B by at least a few seconds, and this constitutes homicide. But this was not the "inexcusable choice," because that assumes the other would not have been lost otherwise, and that was utterly lacking.

given instructions that lots should be cast if such an emergency was reached. And the court indicated that this is "the fairest mode, and, in some sort, as an appeal to God, for the selection of the victim." Such a suggestion was disapproved *obiter* in *Dudley*,[15] but it seems to have much to commend it. If an actual case is presented in which the fatal selection is shown to have been fairly made by lot, it is to be expected that the procedure will be approved.

A few of the new penal codes do not include the "inexcusable choice," [16] but they are very few. For the most part today, as at common law, one is not excused for the intentional killing of an obviously innocent person, even if it was necessary to save oneself from death. But the holding that a killing in such an extremity is necessarily murder has not been adequately considered. While moral considerations require the rejection of any claim of excuse, they do not require that the mitigation of the circumstances be overlooked. A killing in such an extremity is far removed from cold-blooded murder, and should be held to be manslaughter. Although such a claim has been expressly rejected,[17] the result has been reached indirectly at times. In *Holmes* the grand jury refused to indict for murder. The indictment was for manslaughter and the conviction resulted in six-months imprisonment. In *Dudley* the conviction was for wilful murder but the sentence of death was commuted to imprisonment for six months. And some of the new penal codes expressly provide that such a killing is manslaughter.[18]

A suggestion occasionally encountered is that duress cannot be recognized as an excuse for felony-murder even if the defendant did not do the killing and joined the others in their wrongdoing only to save his life.[19] This is unacceptable. There is no such concept as excusable felony, because if what is done is excused it is not a felony. A prohibited act done under excusable duress is not a crime,[20] so far as the unwilling actor is concerned. If D, for example, is compelled under threat of death to provide a getaway car for robbers, he is not guilty of robbery.[21] And if one of the guilty parties

---

15. The Queen v. Dudley & Stephens, L.R. 14 Q.B.D. 273, 285 (1883). For an interesting commentary on this case, see Mallin, In Warm Blood: Some Historical and Procedural Aspects of Regina v. Dudley and Stephens, 34 U.Chi.L.Rev. 387 (1967).

16. E.g. Conn. Gen.Stat. 53a–14 (1975), McKinney's Consol.L. N.Y. Pen.L. § 40.00 (1975).

One statute that did not include the "inexcusable choice" was amended to correct this omission. "The Criminal Law Study Committee's Notes on the enactment of Code Ann. § 26–906 explain the addition to the former law, Code Ann. §§ 26–401, 402, removing the defense of coercion to a charge of murder, as adopting the common law approach that one should die himself before killing an innocent person." Thomas v. State, 246 Ga. 484, 272 S.E.2d 68, 70 (1980).

17. State v. Nargashian, 26 R.I. 299, 58 A. 953 (1904). "Thus coercion can only act to reduce a *reckless* killing to man-

slaughter. It has no application to an intentional killing, ..." State v. Rhymes, 129 Ariz. 56, 628 P.2d 939, 942 (1981).

18. E.g. Minn. Stat.Ann. 1963 § 609.20; Wis.Stat.Ann. 939.46 (1958). Mont. Code Ann. § 45–2–212 (1981). In DPP v. Lynch, (1975), AC 653, 1 All E.R. 913 (1975), it was held that duress could be pled as a defense to murder by a principal in the second degree. See also Paquette v. The Queen, 30 CCC 2d 417 (SCC 1976).

19. People v. Petro, 13 Cal.App.2d 245, 56 P.2d 984 (1936); State v. Moretti, 66 Wash. 537, 120 P. 102 (1912). In neither case was duress established by the evidence.

20. Harris v. State, 91 Tex.Cr.R. 446, 241 S.W. 175 (1922); White v. State, 150 Tex.Cr.R. 546, 203 S.W.2d 222 (1947).

21. People v. Merhige, 212 Mich. 601, 180 N.W. 418 (1920); State v. St. Clair, 262 S.W.2d 25 (Mo.1953).

causes death in the perpetration of the offense all the robbers are guilty of felony-murder [22] (except where this has been changed by statute),[23] but **D**, who is not a robber is not guilty of homicide in the perpetration of robbery.[24] He cannot be a perpetrator of a robbery of which he is innocent. This is not comparable in any way to the claim of one, who willingly joined in the robbery, that he was compelled during the perpetration to do something against his will. Such a claim will be rejected because the situation was the result of extreme culpability.[25]

C. THE RULE OF DURESS [26]

While the common law recognizes no excuse for the intentional killing of an innocent person, even if necessary to save oneself from instant death, this is an *exception* to the rule of duress, which is that the doing of a prohibited act is not a crime if reasonably believed to be necessary to save the actor from imminent death or great bodily injury.[27] This excuse is recognized not only in prosecutions for such offenses as reckless driving,[28] malicious mischief,[29] larceny, embezzlement,[30] receiving stolen goods,[31] or es-

22. "As has been stated the cases are legion which provide that a participant in a robbery, such as appellant, 'acts with the kind of culpability' which is necessary to hold her responsible in a death caused by a co-defendant acting in the furtherance of the conspiratorial scheme." Commonwealth v. Allen, 475 Pa. 165, 379 A.2d 1335, 1340 (1977). Accord, McKinney v. Sheriff, Clark County, 93 Nev. 70, 560 P.2d 151 (1977). A willing driver of the getaway car would be liable for the robbery. State v. Case, ___ Mont. ___, 621 P.2d 1066, 1069 (1980).

23. Some of the new penal codes provide an affirmative defense to a charge of felony-murder where the killing was by an accomplice, and the defendant did not in any way solicit, command, induce, procure, counsel or aid in its commission. E.g. Ark.Stats. § 41–1501(2) (1977).

24. Cf. People v. Roper, 259 N.Y. 170, 181 N.E. 88 (1932).

25. "Such compulsion must have arisen without the negligence or fault of the person who insists upon it as a defense." People v. Merhige, 212 Mich. 601, 611, 180 N.W. 418, 422 (1920). Accord, Ross v. State, 169 Ind. 388, 82 N.E. 781 (1907). One conspirator is frequently in fear of the other "to a certain extent." Regina v. Tyler, 8 Car. & P. 616, 620, 173 Eng. Rep. 643, 645 (1838).

As said in another connection: "The defense is not available where the compelling circumstances have been brought about by the accused . . . ." State v. Diana, 24 Wn.App. 908, 604 P.2d 1312, 1316 (1979). "Such a defense is not available to one who willfully or wantonly placed himself in a situation in which it was probable that he would have been subjected to compulsion or threat." State v. Rider, 229 Kan. 394, 625 P.2d 425, 437 (1981).

26. The defendant must raise the issue of duress, but if he does this it is error to instruct that he has the burden of proving duress. Whenever the issue is raised the government must prove him guilty. It was noted however, that while this is the federal rule, it is not a constitutional requirement. United States v. Calfon, 607 F.2d 29 (2d Cir. 1979).

27. "It appears to be established, however, that although coercion or necessity will never excuse taking the life of an innocent person, it will excuse lesser crimes." R. I. Recreation Center, Inc. v. Aetna Casualty & Surety Co., 177 F.2d 603, 605 (1st Cir. 1949); State v. Taylor, 22 Wn.App. 308, 589 P.2d 1250 (1979). See discussion DPP v. Lynch, [1975] AC 653, [1975] 1 All E.R. 913.

"We hold that duress is a defense available in New Mexico except when the crime charged is a homicide or a crime requiring an intent to kill." Esquibel v. State, 91 N.M. 498, 576 P.2d 1129, 1132 (1978).

28. Browning v. State, 31 Ala.App. 137, 13 So.2d 54 (1943).

29. Rex v. Crutchley, 5 Car. & P. 133, 172 Eng.Rep. 909 (1831).

30. State v. McGuire, 107 Mont. 341, 88 P.2d 35 (1938).

31. Attorney-General v. Whelan [1934] Ir.Rep. 518 (1933).

cape;[32] but also for such grave felonies as burglary,[33] robbery,[34] kidnaping or arson.[35] Even one who joins the enemy forces in time of war is not guilty of treason if he does so in reasonable fear of death or great bodily injury, and escapes at the first reasonable opportunity,[36] without having engaged in homicidal conduct.[37]

In a prosecution for arson and homicide, the court held that defense of duress would lie for arson, but not homicide. State v. Taylor, 22 Wn.App. 308, 589 P.2d 1250 (1979).

D. NATURE OF THE COMPULSION

It has been said that no fear of loss or destruction of property, however well grounded, will be recognized as sufficient compulsion to excuse in a criminal case,[38] not even a threat "to burn his house and destroy all his cattle and stock of corn and to lay waste all that belongs to him." [39] This was formulated in a treason case, which would be expected to be very strict, but it is implicit in the frequent statement that for duress to be recognized in a criminal case it must be such as to induce a well-grounded apprehension of imminent death or great bodily injury.[40] Clearly no excuse is available to one who had an obviously safe avenue of escape before committing the prohibited act.[41]

32. It was held that in view of the evidence that there had been an attempt to kill defendant, and he had received a note threatening him on the night of the escape, he was entitled to an instruction on duress. People v. Strock, 42 Colo.App. 404, 600 P.2d 91 (1979), rev'd on other grds, —— Colo. ——, 623 P.2d 42 (1981). The Supreme Court emphasized that "where a criminal defendant is charged with escape and claims that he is entitled to an instruction on the theory of duress or necessity, he must proffer evidence of a bona fide effort to surrender or return to custody as soon as the claimed duress or necessity had lost its coercive force." United States v. Bailey, 444 U.S. 394, 100 S.Ct. 624, 637 (1980).

33. Nall v. Commonwealth, 208 Ky. 700, 271 S.W. 1059 (1925).

34. See note 21.

35. Ross v. State, 169 Ind. 388, 82 N.E. 781 (1907). In this case compulsion was not established but the court did not question that a reasonable fear of immediate death would have excused the burning of the dwelling.

36. State v. Nargashian, 26 R.I. 299, 302, 58 A. 953, 954 (1904).

37. Axtell's Case, Kelyng 13, 84 Eng. Rep. 1060 (1660).

38. United States v. Vigol, 2 U.S. 346, 347 (1795); Respublica v. M'Carty, 2 U.S. 86 (1781); United States v. Greiner, 26 Fed.Cas. 36, 39, No. 15,262 (1861); Gordon's Case, 1 East P.C. 71 (1746).

39. MacGrowther's Case, 18 Howell St.Tr. 391, 393–4 (1746).

40. Moore v. State, 23 Ala.App. 432, 433, 127 So. 796, 797 (1929), cert. denied 221 Ala. 50, 127 So. 797 (1930); State v. Lee, 78 N.M. 421, 432 P.2d 265 (1967); People v. Colone, 56 Ill.App.3d 1018, 14 Ill.Dec. 592, 372 N.E.2d 871 (1978); United States v. Gordon, 526 F.2d 406 (9th Cir. 1975).

"Duress was said to excuse criminal conduct where the actor was under an unlawful threat of imminent death or serious bodily injury, which threat caused the actor to engage in conduct violating the literal terms of the criminal law." United States v. Bailey, 444 U.S. 394, 400, 100 S.Ct. 624, 634 (1980).

United States v. Haskell, 26 Fed.Cas. 207, No. 15,321 (1823); McCoy v. State, 78 Ga. 490, 496, 3 S.E. 768, 769 (1887); Ross v. State, 169 Ind. 388, 82 N.E. 781 (1907); State v. St. Clair, 262 S.W.2d 25, 27 (Mo.1953); United States v. Nickels, 502 F.2d 1173 (7th Cir. 1974).

41. Arp v. State, 97 Ala. 5, 12 So. 301 (1892); People v. Villegas, 29 Cal.App.2d 658, 85 P.2d 480 (1938). And see R. I. Recreation Center v. Aetna Casualty & Surety Co., 177 F.2d 603, 605 (1st Cir. 1949); United States v. Bailey, 444 U.S. 394, 100 S.Ct. 624, 637 (1980).

It is important to note that the civil law anciently insisted upon the same harsh requirement. One who sought to avoid obligation on a contract needed to show that it had been signed in fear of imminent death or great bodily injury; but this has been greatly modified in modern times.[42] It is now sufficient to show coercion that would be sufficient to induce a reasonable person to do what was done. It has been stated that what may be legally sufficient as compulsion in a civil case may not necessarily be sufficient for an excuse in a criminal prosecution.[43] True, but it would be more appropriate to suggest that what would be sufficient to excuse petty larceny may not be sufficient to excuse armed robbery. The need to measure the degree of compulsion in terms of the gravity of the offense was long overlooked.[44] Where the problem has been squarely presented, however, there has been a tendency to hold that a threat of less than death or great bodily injury may be recognized as an excuse in some prosecutions.[45] Thus in a case in which the prosecution was for a relatively minor offense it was held the jury should have been instructed that defendant had a defense if he had been compelled to act under "such violence or threats . . . as are calculated to operate on a person of ordinary firmness and inspire a just fear of great injury to person, *reputation or property* . . .." [46]

The cases have spoken of harm threatened to the actor himself,[47] but that was the harm ordinarily threatened or claimed. The possibility of recognizing the defense where the threat was to a close relative has been indicated.[48] Actually such a threat may be more coercive than a threat to the actor. A man might be willing to chance that a threat to kill was only a bluff, if directed to himself, but not if it was a threat to kill his wife or child. It is

42. 5 Williston, Contracts §§ 1601, 1605 (Rev.ed. 1937).

43. McCoy v. State, 78 Ga. 490, 497, 3 S.E. 768, 769 (1887); Ross v. State, 169 Ind. 388, 390–1, 82 N.E. 781, 782 (1907).

44. "The authorities already cited demonstrate, however, that the courts have not carefully graduated the injury which must be threatened to the enormity of the crime for which it is invoked as an excuse." Hitchler, Duress as a Defense in Criminal Cases, 4 Va.L.Rev. 519, 555 (1917).

45. Perryman v. State, 63 Ga.App. 819, 12 S.E.2d 388 (1940). In this case a boy submitted to an act of sodomy under a threat that the other would "slap him down" but there was no suggestion of a fear of death or great bodily injury.

"The court instructed the jury that to find the defendant acted under duress they must find that 'the compulsion must be present and immediate and of such a nature as to induce a well-founded fear of impending death or serious bodily injury.' The standard imposed by the Trial Term is a more stringent one than required by statute and is based on the old penal law § 859." People v. Pryor, 70 A.D.2d 805, 417 N.Y.S.2d 490, 492 (1979).

46. Commonwealth v. Reffitt, 149 Ky. 300, 303–4, 148 S.W. 48, 50 (1912) (emphasis added). The prosecution was for violation of a statute against selling pooled tobacco.

"Henceforth, duress shall be a defense to a crime other than murder if the defendant engaged in conduct because he was coerced to do so by the use of, or threat to use, unlawful force against his person or person of another, which a person of reasonable firmness in his situation would have been unable to resist." State v. Toscano, 74 N.J. 421, 378 A.2d 755, 765 (1977).

47. An occasional statute is so worded. E.g. Ga.Code Ann. § 26–906 (1978). See People v. Jones, 105 Cal.App. 3d 1, 164 Cal.Rptr. 124, 134–35 (1980).

48. Magruder, concurring in R. I. Recreation Center v. Aetna Casualty & Surety Co., 177 F.2d 603, 606–07 (1st Cir. 1949). An occasional statute adds "or another." E.g. Wis.Stat.Ann. § 939.46 (1958). The Kansas statute is less general, but includes "spouse, parent, child, brother or sister." Kan.Stat.Ann. § 21–3209 (1974).

necessary, however to go far beyond this. If the only choice is between the loss of human life and the loss of property, a decision in favor of life is morally required.[49] Assume a case in which a bank-robber was holding a woman with a knife against her throat, threatening to kill her unless the teller filled a bag with money and handed it over. And the teller reasonably believing that the woman would be killed unless he obeyed, filled the bag with the bank's money and handed it over. Add, for good measure, that the teller had never seen the woman before. It is almost beyond belief that such a case would be taken to court, but it may be safely assumed that if such a case is presented to the court today, a prosecution for embezzlement will be defeated on the ground that the teller acted under duress.[50]

E. COMMAND OR ORDER

Under the English "rule of coercion" the bare command of the husband was a complete defense to the wife, with a few exceptions such as treason or murder.[51] This rule, which was the product of peculiarities of English procedure,[52] has no proper place in the law today, has been tending to disappear and many states now hold that it has been completely abrogated.[53]

A military command is ordinarily a complete defense to the soldier who executes it. Military discipline does not permit the subordinate to conduct a collateral inquiry as to the lawfulness of an order received, and hence he is fully protected even if the order was unlawful if it was of a kind that might under any circumstances be lawful and he does not know that it is not.[54] But an order to a sentry to kill anyone using opprobrious words, being obviously unlawful and void, would not justify or excuse such a killing.[55] And an order to a soldier to assist his superior in the perpetration of rape is not a

---

49. "The law deems the lives of all persons far more valuable than any property." United States v. Ashton, 24 Fed. Cas. 873, No. 14,470 (C.C.Mass.1834).

50. Compare People v. Lawson, 65 Mich.App. 562, 237 N.W.2d 559 (1976) (L entered S's store, grabbed a woman from behind, held a gun to her head and said to S, "give me your money or she will get it." S took some money from the cash register and placed it in a brown bag which was delivered to L. L's conviction of armed robbery was affirmed. The court said that L's action had placed S in fear.

51. Blackstone says that, except for crimes to which the defense is not available, if the wife commits the act "by the coercion of her husband; or even in his company, which the law construes a coercion; she is not guilty of any crime . . . ." 4 Bl.Comm. *28. And it was stated earlier that the "command of a husband, without other coercion" is sufficient to excuse the wife from criminal guilt. Anonymous, Lib.Ass. 27, f. 137, pl. 40 (1335).

52. The explanation was "that if the husband and wife commit burglary and

larceny together, the wife shall be acquitted, and husband only convicted . . . because otherwise for the same felony the husband may be saved by the benefit of his clergy, and the wife hanged, ..." 1 Hale P.C. *45.

53. Dalton v. People, 68 Colo. 44, 47–8, 189 P. 37, 38 (1920); Bell v. State, 92 Ga. 49, 51, 18 S.E. 186, 187 (1893); Wampler v. Corporation of Norton, 134 Va. 606, 113 S.E. 733 (1922). The Model Penal Code has an express statement to this effect. Section 2.09(3). And see pp. 10 and 11 of Tent.Draft No. 10 (1960).

54. Riggs v. State, 43 Tenn. 85 (1866).

"It is an affirmative defense to a penal charge that the defendant, in engaging in the conduct and causing the result which he did not know to be unlawful, did no more than execute an order of his superior in the armed services." Haw.Rev. Stats. (1976 Replacement Ed.) § 702–232.

55. United States v. Bevans, 24 Fed. Cas. 1183, No. 14,589 (C.C.Mass.1816), reversed on other grounds 16 U.S. 336 (1818); United States v. Calley, 22 USCMA 534, 48 CMR 19 (1973).

military command.[56]　A peace officer's request to his deputy is no defense for making an obviously illegal arrest;[57] and the orders of a foreign government to its subject give him no immunity in regard to a prohibited act committed by him here if there is no mistake of fact.[58]　Even the command of a parent has been held no excuse for a child who commits a prohibited act if the facts are known and no compulsion was employed.[59]　Although if the child is under fourteen the fact that the deed was in obedience to the parents command may be taken into consideration by the jury in determining whether or not the child had criminal capacity.[60]

Under circumstances involving a mistake of fact, one who has carried out a command or order may be free from guilt although the criminal law was violated.　If, for example, the command was not obviously wrongful and was carried out in ignorance of the criminal purpose intended, the innocent agent is not guilty of crime.　This may happen in different ways, such as where an employer commits larceny by directing an employee to take another's property and place it in the employer's house or store.　The employee is not guilty if he carries out the instruction in the innocent belief that it is his employer's chattel.

If no problem such as those mentioned above is involved, the customary statement is that the mere existence of an order or command by an employer constitutes no excuse for the intentional perpetration of a prohibited act,[61] even if it is by an employee whose job depends upon obeying his employer's orders.[62]　This will be recognized at once as an echo of the ancient view that nothing less than a well-grounded fear of imminent death or great bodily injury can be recognized as duress.　As the modern trend is clearly in the direction of modifying this strict position by conceding that less may be sufficient for duress in some criminal cases, the employer's command should be reassessed in this light.　It is not necessary to punish the employee on the theory that otherwise the crime must go unpunished, because the employer who gave the order is clearly guilty.[63]　And the fact that he had caused the

---

56. State v. Roy, 233 N.C. 558, 64 S.E.2d 840 (1951).

57. Roberts v. Commonwealth, 284 Ky. 365, 144 S.W.2d 811 (1940).

58. Giugni v. United States, 127 F.2d 786 (1st Cir. 1942).

59. Cagle v. State, 87 Ala. 38, 6 So. 300 (1889); People v. Richmond, 29 Cal. 414 (1866); Carlisle v. State, 37 Tex.Cr.R. 108, 38 S.W. 991 (1897).

60. Commonwealth v. Mead, 92 Mass. 398 (1865).

61. 1 Hawk.P.C. c. 1, § 14 (6th ed. 1788); Thomas v. State, 134 Ala. 126, 132, 33 So. 130, 132 (1902); Hately v. State, 15 Ga. 346, 348 (1854); City of New York v. Flynn, 140 Misc. 497, 498–9, 250 N.Y.S. 488, 490 (1931).

"Loyalty to a superior does not provide a license for crime." United States v. Decker, 304 F.2d 702, 705 (6th Cir. 1962). Restatement, Second, Agency § 359A (1957).

"The fact that a person is acting as an employee of another constitutes no defense in a criminal prosecution where the individual charged intentionally violated the law." People v. McCauley, 192 Colo. 545, 548, 561 P.2d 335, 337 (1977).

62. Moore v. State, 23 Ala.App. 432, 127 So. 796 (1930), cert. denied 221 Ala. 50, 127 So. 797. "An employee is not immune from punishment for his participation in criminal conspiracy upon any such idea as that his employment required him to engage therein." Susnjar v. United States, 27 F.2d 223, 224 (6th Cir. 1928).

63. "[A] person who causes an innocent party to commit an act which, if done with the requisite intent, would constitute an offense may be found guilty as a principal even though he personally did not commit the act." United States v. Gleason, 616 F.2d 2, 20 (2d Cir. 1979). In legal theory one has done what he has caused another to do. Commonwealth v.

crime to be committed by his employee might be included in the scales against him if there is discretion as to the punishment. Where the employee's job is at stake the coercive force of the employer's command may be very great and there are certainly possible cases where the excuse should be recognized. It may be noted that whether the job was actually at stake or not, the impelling force would be the same if the employee believed it was.

F. FUTURE HARM

Although it has been repeated time and again that no threat of future harm is sufficient to constitute duress,[64] when an extreme case was presented the court did not hesitate to recognize that a threat of future harm may be under such circumstances as to meet the requirement.[65] And it would be utterly unrealistic to insist that no threat of future harm could ever be sufficient to excuse a prohibited act, no matter how grave the threat or small the offense.

The time has come to reject the notion that there is any really impelling influence that could never be duress in any criminal case. It should be emphasized, in this connection, that the wording of the rule had to be in extreme form in order to be recognized as a valid rule of law. But the formulation of a rule of law does not exhaust the possibilities.

G. THE DURESS STANDARD

Except in the very few states that have changed the second part of the statement by statute,[66] the age-old rule of duress—that the doing of a prohibited act is not a crime if reasonably believed to be necessary to save from death or great bodily injury, together with the equally ancient exception in the form of the "inexcusable choice," are as firm today as ever except for the realization that they cover only part of the field. The rule and its exception give the answers whenever they apply. In the areas in which they do not apply two conclusions emerge: (1) The possibility of excuse in some of these situations must be recognized, and (2) in this area the facts will differ from case to case.

If unlawful physical injury is threatened, it may be of a nature that would be very painful without remotely suggesting death or great bodily injury. It is equally possible that such threatened harm may be very moderate. And the prohibited act committed to avoid the threatened harm may be in the nature of a grave felony without involving death or great bodily inju-

---

Nabried, 264 Pa.Super. 419, 399 A.2d 1121 (1979).

64. People v. Martin, 13 Cal.App. 96, 108 P. 1034 (1910); State v. Clay, 220 Iowa 1191, 1203, 264 N.W. 77, 83 (1935); State v. St. Clair, 262 S.W.2d 25 (Mo. 1953); State v. Jones, 2 Kan.App.2d 220, 577 P.2d 357 (1978); United States v. Agard, 605 F.2d 665 (2d Cir. 1979). But compare Perryman v. State, 63 Ga.App. 819, 12 S.E.2d 388 (1940).

65. Perryman v. State, 63 Ga.App. 819, 12 S.E.2d 388 (1940). In this case there was a threat of present harm, but it was not a deadly threat and the threat

of constant repetition made it particularly coercive. A prisoner was threatened by a guard.

Duress was held to be an available defense to a perjury even though immediate harm could not be effected in the courtroom where the threats were otherwise real. Regina v. Hudson, [1971] 2 All E.R. 244, 56 Crim.App. 1.

66. E.g. Conn.Gen.Stat.Ann. § 53A–14 (1974); N.Y.Pen.Law § 40.00 (1975). These statutes make no exception to the defense based upon a threat which a person of reasonable firmness would have been unable to resist.

ry; or it may be in the nature of a very minor misdemeanor. Moreover either the harm threatened or the act done to avoid that harm might be somewhere between the extremes mentioned with an almost limitless possibility in the degrees of variation. An attempt to match each degree of one with every possible degree of the other would be frustrating. If the harm threatened (or caused) was the loss or destruction of property, the value might vary from a few cents to millions of dollars. Perhaps no other form of harm will be able to match this spread, but there will always be the possibility of more or less. An attempt to regulate this field with rules and exceptions would be futile and should not be attempted. This can be dealt with only by a standard,[67] and the appropriate standard is the conduct of a reasonable person in like circumstances.

In sum, whenever the compulsion was less than a threat of death or great bodily injury, and the threatened harm was avoided without the killing of an innocent person, it is necessary to weigh one against the other. If under all the circumstances a reasonable person would have been impelled to avoid such threatened harm by doing what was done by the defendant, the defense should be recognized—otherwise it should not.[68] It is for the judge to instruct that this is the law, and for the jury to decide, as a matter of fact, whether or not the standard has been met.

H. NECESSITY (DURESS OF CIRCUMSTANCES) [69]

If, not due to the compulsion of another but as a result of natural forces, one is faced with a situation in which he must either suffer detriment or commit an act that violates the letter of the law, it is spoken of as a case of necessity.[70] The "inexcusable choice" applies as firmly here as in the law of

67. A standard is a legal device employed to enable the fact-finder to apply common sense to the complicated facts of a particular situation. Pound, Justice According to Law 58–9 (1951). It is sometimes complained that a standard is not certain. But if it was certain it would not be a standard but a rule, which is a device for attaching a clear-cut consequence to a clear-cut state of facts. Id. at page 56. Thus it is a rule of common law that there is no homicide (a clear-cut consequence) unless death followed the harm within a year and a day (a clear-cut set of facts). A standard is employed where rules are not practicable. The best-known example is the care a reasonable person would employ in like circumstances to distinguish between care and negligence.

68. Although the Model Penal Code covers only part of the field of duress, it is worded in terms of an affirmative defense when the compulsion is such that "a person of reasonable firmness in his situation would have been unable to resist." Section 2.09(1).

69. "Generally, necessity is available as a defense when the physical forces of nature or the pressure of circumstances cause the accused to take unlawful action to avoid a harm which social policy deems greater than the harm resulting from a violation of the law." State v. Diana, 24 Wn.App. 908, 604 P.2d 1312, 1316 (1979). See also United States v. Cassidy, 616 F.2d 101, 102 (4th Cir. 1979).

70. One of the earliest references is found in Pollard's argument for the defendant to the effect that "a man may break the words of the law, and yet not break the law itself," as where the words are broken "through necessity." Reniger v. Fogossa, 1 Plowd. 1, 18, 75 Eng.Rep. 1, 29 (1550). He includes a biblical reference to the excuse for eating sacred bread, normally forbidden, because it was "through necessity of hunger." Matthew c. 12, v. 3, 4. Stephen refers to "compulsion by necessity." History of Criminal Law 105 (1883). United States v. Micklus, 581 F.2d 612, 615 (7th Cir. 1978).

"To summarize, medical necessity exists if the court finds that (1) the defendant necessarily believed his use of marijuana was necessary to minimize the effects of multiple sclerosis; (2) the bene-

duress. One may not intentionally kill an innocent person even if this is necessary to save one's own life.[71]   In fact the best-known cases in the field, *Holmes*[72] and *Dudley*,[73] were both cases of "necessity."   On the other side, if circumstances have generated a well-grounded belief that, without a prompt act of avoidance, death or great bodily injury will result, the doing of any prohibited act necessary for safety will be excused if it does not involve the "inexcusable choice."

The biblical reference to the jettison of the cargo of a vessel to save the lives of those on board,[74] unquestionably excusable if reasonably seemed necessary for the purpose, has its counterpart in modern cases.   What would otherwise constitute attempted revolt on the high seas may be excused if the sailors returned to port in violation of the captain's orders because the vessel was unseaworthy and they were in danger of imminent death from the elements.[75]   And if the master of a vessel takes refuge in a certain port during a violent storm for the safety of all on board, he has not violated the embargo although the wording of the law forbids that vessel to enter that port.[76]

Moreover, although the courts had been unduly tardy in taking such a position in cases of duress, they did not hesitate to recognize that something less than utter extremity would be sufficient to constitute an excuse in some cases of "necessity."   Thus a father is not guilty of the offense of withdrawing a child from school without first obtaining permission of the school board, if the absence is necessary because of the illness of the child.[77]   One unavoidably caught in a traffic jam is not guilty of violating the law against stopping at that place.[78]   And a carrier has not violated the statute that requires a specified coach if the failure to provide that coach on a particular occasion was due to an unavoidable accident that ordinary prudence could not have guarded against.[79]   These are not situations, it should be noted, in which no choice was possible.   The driver elected to stop rather than to proceed until the vehicle was brought to a stop by actual contact with the one ahead; and the carrier could have avoided sending the train without the specified coach, by sending no train at all.   In another case it may be added, the court reversed a conviction of killing a deer in violation of the game law because it was shown this killing was necessary to prevent substantial dam-

---

fits derived from its use are greater than the harm sought to be prevented by the controlled substance law; and (3) no drug is as effective in minimizing the effects of the disease." State v. Diana, 24 Wn. App. 908, 604 P.2d 1312, 1317 (1979).

71.   See notes 72 and 73.

72.   United States v. Holmes, 26 Fed. Cas. 360 No. 15,383 (C.C.Pa.1842).

73.   The Queen v. Dudley and Stephens, L.R. 14 Q.B.D. 273, 15 Cox C.C. 624 (1843).

74.   Jonah c. I, v. 5.

75.   United States v. Ashton, 24 Fed. Cas. 873, No. 14,470 (C.C.Mass.1834).

76.   The William Gray, 29 Fed.Cas. 1300, No. 17,694 (C.C.N.Y.1810).

77.   State v. Jackson, 71 N.H. 552, 53 A. 1021 (1902).

An illegal abortion charge may be subject to the defense of necessity under proper circumstances.   Regina v. Mogentaler, 64 D.L.R. (3d) 718, 27 CCC 2d 81 (1976).

78.   Commonwealth v. Brooks, 99 Mass. 434 (1868); Regina v. Kennedy, 7 CCC 2d 42 (Nov.Scotia Cty.Ct. 1972).

79.   Chesapeake & Ohio Railway Co. v. Commonwealth, 119 Ky. 519, 84 S.W. 566 (1905).

age to defendant's property.[80] And an emergency may excuse what would otherwise be a violation of the speed law.[81]

The problem that has caused the most discussion [82] and the least litigation, is that of taking food. Lord Bacon said that "if a man steals viands to satisfy a present hunger, this is no felony nor larceny." [83] This was denied by Hale, Blackstone and East.[84] These writers, however, were not directing their attention to the true problem as evidenced by such explanations as that "by the laws of this kingdom sufficient provision is made for the supply of such necessities for the poor . . .," [85] and "it is impossible that the most needy stranger should ever be reduced to the necessity of thieving to support nature." [86]

Without doubt the so-called "economic necessity" is no defense to a criminal charge,[87] but this phrase, as it has been used, falls far short of an actual need to satisfy hunger; and obviously the law cannot excuse one merely because a "false sense of shame" [88] has induced him to steal rather than make application to the proper authorities.[89] Such thievery, however, is prompted not by necessity but only by convenience.

If a mountaineer, being trapped in a remote spot by a sudden blizzard, and finding a cabin whose unknown owner was away, should break in, and being "imprisoned" for several days by the continuance of the storm, should eat some of the food in the cabin to satisfy his hunger, this would be excused because of "necessity." [90] Here there would be no alternative; and the fact that he would not actually have died of starvation would not prevent recognition of the excuse.

I. CHOICE OF EVILS

One entirely without fault, and in no danger of injury or harm to himself, may come to such a situation that what is being done is bound to cause injury or harm to some other innocent person. This is the typical unavoidable accident without implication of criminal guilt. Under somewhat similar circumstances one may be in a situation in which what is being done is bound to cause harm to some other innocent person, but there is a choice as to which of two is to suffer. If it will be the same type of harm in either event this is

80. State v. Ward, 170 Iowa 185, 152 N.W. 501 (1915). Accord, Cross v. State, 370 P.2d 371 (Wyo.1962).

81. A speed of 67 miles an hour in a 50-mile zone was excused when it was shown to have been necessary to avoid an accident in an emergency. People v. Cataldo, 65 Misc.2d 286, 316 N.Y.S.2d 873 (1970). Military necessity is a defense to a charge of violation of the state speed law. State v. Burton, 41 R.I. 303, 103 A. 962 (1918).

82. It "has occasioned great speculation among the writers. . . ." 4 Bl. Comm. *31.

83. Bacon: Maxims, reg. 5.

84. 1 Hale P.C. *53–4; 4 Bl.Comm. *31–2; 2 East P.C. 698–9 (1803).

85. 1 Hale P.C. *54.

86. 4 Bl.Comm. *32.

87. State v. Moe, 174 Wash. 303, 24 P.2d 638 (1933); United States v. Ramzy, 446 F.2d 1184 (5th Cir. 1971), cert. denied 404 U.S. 992, 92 S.Ct. 537; Harris v. State, 486 S.W.2d 573 (Tex.Cr.App. 1972).

88. 2 East P.C. 699 (1803).

89. The defense of necessity is not available if the threatened harm could reasonably have been avoided by some means other than those taken. United States v. Cassidy, 616 F.2d 101 (4th Cir. 1979).

90. Model Penal Code Section 3.02, Comment (Tent. Draft No. 8) (1958).

the practical equivalent of no choice at all. It is necessary to search further for a true problem of choice of evils.

Suppose a motorist, carefully observing all traffic rules, driving with due care and in all respects free from fault, was suddenly confronted with a terrible situation. Three small children, oblivious to all else in the excitement of play, dashed into the street in front of the car and so close that there was no possibility of avoiding all. Had nothing been done to minimize the harm all three would have been killed. But (1) the driver swerved quickly to the left, thus avoiding two but killing one. Or (2) the sudden swerve was to the right, thus avoiding one but killing two. Either should be recognized as an unavoidable accident, without implication of criminal guilt, because it was all so sudden there was no opportunity for a deliberate choice. The driver made a split-second decision in the effort to minimize unavoidable harm. In (1) he accomplished the best possible result under the circumstances. In (2) he did not. But human nature being what it is, we should not require that an effort to be helpful in a sudden emergency should always achieve the best possible result. It is necessary to explore still further to reach a true choice-of-evils problem.

Assume an emergency, either in traffic or elsewhere, in which the problem is similar to the one above except that there was time to evaluate the situation and make a deliberate choice. In that case an act that was bound to kill one, but necessary to avoid killing the other two, would have been morally right and without any suggestion of criminal guilt; whereas an act that was bound to kill two, but necessary to avoid killing one would have been so morally wrong as to call for punishment. Although the actor may have thought that the loss of the one saved would have been a greater harm than the death of the other two, the law regards all alike for such a purpose as in the formula one-person, one-vote.

The same would be true, it may be added, even if the facts were different and the actor was himself one of the three in danger. The "inexcusable choice" has been premised on the basis of one against one. More than two have at times been involved, but under such circumstances that the actual choice was one against one.[91] Thus in the hypothetical case in which the man threw the boy to the pursuing beasts, he could have achieved the result of sacrificing one to save two by jumping out and facing the animals himself. And in *Dudley*, in which the sailors killed the boy in order that they might live, each sailor could have saved three at the expense of one by offering that he himself should be the one to die. Each made a one-against-one decision.

If the stage was set differently, if it was a certain two against a certain one, with no possibility of realignment, the only morally acceptable choice

---

91. This is not mentioned in the cases but is actually involved as shown infra in the text. Assume the pilot of a large ship, with hundreds on board, is faced with a sudden emergency in which he must either swerve suddenly to the right or wreck the vessel with great loss of life. But to make this turn he will run down a man in a rowboat, which will no doubt mean his death. Obviously the pilot must do what is necessary to save his ship in such a situation, and he will do this without criminal guilt. He will intentionally kill the rower and thereby save his own life, but that is a small part of the whole picture. He will not make a choice between himself and the man in the boat; he will make a choice between hundreds of lives and one life—and the choice he makes is morally required. The large number is not required for the result, but is given for emphasis.

would be that in favor of the two. And this would be true whether the actor making the choice was the one or half of the two.

This assumes everything else was equal, which will not always be the fact. It was mentioned in *Holmes* that according to the tradition of the sea sailors should sacrifice themselves for the safety of passengers, except that a "sufficient number of seamen to navigate the boat must be preserved." And there might be inequality for other reasons such as fault on one side, the extreme situation being attempted murder. One who is free from fault is privileged to use deadly force if this reasonably seems necessary to save an innocent victim from being murdered.[92] The scales in such a case are used, not to weigh numbers, but to weigh innocence against murder. The killing of two or more would-be murderers is justifiable if reasonably necessary to save the life of one innocent victim.

Assuming everything is equal, certain other conclusions may be mentioned. If the choice is between the destruction of life and the destruction of property, a decision in favor of life is morally right, while a decision in favor of property is so morally wrong as to call for punishment.[93] If the only threat to person is of a minor nature a decision in favor of preventing great property loss would be morally acceptable. Thus a sudden and violent shove of an innocent person would be excusable if necessary to prevent loss or destruction of very valuable property.

The choice of evils is not a substitute for the reasonable-person standard. It is used only in exceptional situations. It is employed in any case in which only persons other than the actor were endangered. And except for the rule of duress, with its age-old exception, it is employed whenever human life is at stake. In the ordinary case, however, the issue is whether the duress or necessity was such that a reasonable person, under like circumstances would have been impelled to do what was done by the defendant.[94]

The Model Penal Code has a reasonable-person standard for duress, worded in terms of a "person of reasonable firmness." [95] This wording seems appropriate although it does not change the meaning, because a reasonable person would be reasonably firm. The section, however, does not provide for the "inexcusable choice," which is unwise and has not generally been accepted. Quite properly it includes a threat of "unlawful force against his person or that of another." This adopts the trend towards which the modern law has been developing in two respects. It does not limit duress to (1) a threat of deadly force, or (2) a threat of violence against the actor himself. But the section ignores the full scope towards which the mod-

92. The common law authorizes the use of deadly force if reasonably necessary to prevent a forcible felony. 4 Bl. Comm. *180; Storey v. State, 71 Ala. 329, 330 (1882); State v. Nyland, 47 Wn.2d 240, 287 P.2d 345 (1955). This is incorporated in some of the new penal codes. E.g., deadly force may be used if reasonably believed necessary to prevent "the commission of a forcible felony." Ill. Rev.Stat. c. 38, § 7–1 (1972). A few have some restriction, such as a belief that the other "is using or about to use deadly force." E.g. N.Y.Pel.Law. § 30.10 (1975). Needless to say this would not affect the position stated in the text. See generally Kadish, Respect for Life and Regard for Rights in the Criminal Law, 64 Cal.L.Rev. 871 (1976).

93. "The law deems the lives of all persons far more valuable than any property." United States v. Ashton, 24 Fed. Cas. 873, No. 14,470 (C.C.Mass.1834).

94. The wording of the Model Penal Code is "would have been unable to resist." Section 2.09(1). This however does not apply in the Choice of Evils Section 3.02.

95. Section 2.09(1).

ern law has been developing by failing to include duress in any form other than personal violence or the threat thereof. This is very unfortunate. It would have been much better if the section had been named "duress and necessity," with every type of substantially impelling influence included, and with the provision that except for the intentional or reckless killing of an innocent person, the actor has a defense if a person of reasonable firmness in like circumstances would have been impelled to do what actually was done.

Some may have assumed that adequate provision was made for all omitted from the section on duress, by the provision that when conduct of the actor would otherwise be justifiable under the choice-of-evils section,[96] he has a defense. This section provides that conduct believed to be necessary to avoid harm or evil to the actor, or another, is justified if the harm avoided is greater than the harm sought to be prevented by the law. And it seems to have been assumed that many, perhaps most, of the problems of impelled perpetration would be governed by this section. But this presents a real difficulty.

In regard to the loss of life of innocent persons the court would recognize that in the legal view the greater the number, the greater the harm. And it would be easy to establish as a rule of law that the harm avoided by saving some is greater than the harm resulting from the death actually caused if, but only if, more were saved than were killed. And if the choice was between the loss of life and the loss of property, the law regards the loss of life a greater harm than the loss of any property,[97] so the rule of law in such a case is obvious. But for the most part no such rule is available.

Suppose for example an employee is ordered by his employer to perform a task that will necessarily involve an unlawful application of force to an innocent person, although without any risk of death or serious bodily injury; and the employee knows he will be fired if he does not obey. There is no possibility of a rule of law to the effect that loss of job is a greater harm than such a battery, because a job may be only temporary, or otherwise relatively unimportant, whereas even such a battery may be serious and very painful. Nor could it be established as a rule of law that the loss of a job is not greater harm than such a battery, because a job may be very important and a battery very moderate. The case likely to get into court will not be at either extreme, but somewhere near the middle, so to speak. And since this is not a situation in which rules are feasible, it is necessary to establish a standard. A possible standard would be to submit the case to the jury with an instruction that defendant has a defense if a reasonable person, so situated, would have believed that the harm avoided was greater than the harm caused.[98] But the Code section on choice of evils is concerned with actuality rather than with belief,[99] possibly due to a doubt whether the ordinary rea-

---

96. Model Penal Code, Section 3.02. Justification Generally: Choice of Evils.

97. See note 94.

98. Some of the recent penal codes have such a provision. For example, Ill. Stat. c. 38, § 7–13 (1972), is worded in terms of a defendant who reasonably believed his conduct was necessary to avoid greater harm than it caused.

99. Section 3.02 is worded in terms of conduct "which the actor believes to be necessary to avoid harm or evil to himself or to another," but is justifiable if "the harm sought to be avoided by such conduct is greater than that sought to be prevented by the law defining the defense charged." There is no reference to a "person of reasonable firmness," that is found in the section on duress (§ 2.09).

sonable person has any belief as to the relative degree of harmfulness of unrelated harms.

The interpretation of the Oregon choice-of-evils statute is that the defense is available if "it was reasonable for the defendant to believe that the need to avoid the injury was greater than the need to avoid the injury the [other statute] seeks to prevent." [1] As the only legal test of reasonableness, for such a purpose, is in terms of a reasonable person, the court's statement is equivalent to saying that the defense is available if "a reasonable person would have believed that the harm avoided was greater than the harm caused." This provides a standard that enables cases to be decided on an acceptable basis. The determinant is in terms of belief and not actuality. It is not whether the harm avoided was in fact greater than the harm caused, but whether the defendant reasonably believed it to be so. If it were necessary to bring in extrinsic evidence to determine the actual degree of the unrelated harms, the result might be in some case, although human life was in no way involved, that defendant would be convicted for doing what any ordinary person would have done under the circumstances—and that is not acceptable.

Possibly the result reached under the Oregon statute will frequently be the same as would follow from the other. Belief as to the relativity of degree of competing harms may tend to influence action. But the change makes no useful contribution. It leaves the law as before to the extent that the result is to be determined by a standard, which is good, except that the standard employed seems less satisfactory than the one replaced. The simplest and best way to present such a problem to the jury is one which, in effect, invites consideration of what each juror would have done under the circumstances.

The only purpose of a statute on choice of evils is to provide for a situation in which it is proper for the law to dictate the choice that must be made,

---

The Alaska Court held the defense of "necessity" was not available in a trespass case as part of an anti-abortion demonstration at a medical clinic. The court observed:

"The defense of necessity requires a showing of three essential elements:

(1) The act charged must have been done to prevent a significant evil; (2) there must have been no adequate alternative; (3) the harm caused must not have been disproportionate to the harm avoided.

It is available if the accused reasonably believed at the time of acting that the first and second elements were present, even if that belief was mistaken; but the accused's belief will not suffice for the third element. An objective determination must be made as to whether the defendant's value judgment was correct, given the facts as he reasonably perceived them."

Cleveland v. Municipality of Anchorage, 631 P.2d 1073, 1078 (Alaska 1981).

1. State v. Burney, 49 Or.App. 529, 619 P.2d 1336, 1339 (1980). In this case defendant was held to have a defense to a charge of being an ex-convict in possession of a firearm if he took possession to defend himself against a threat of great bodily harm and was arrested before he had a reasonable opportunity to divest himself of the weapon in a manner that would not create a public peril. It is to be noted that without the statute he would be held to have a defense under the common-law rule of duress. E.g., use of a concealable fire-arm in defense of self or others in an emergency situation does not violate the statute making it an offense for a felon or addict to have in his possession a firearm capable of being concealed on his person. People v. King, 22 Cal.3d 12, 148 Cal.Rptr. 409, 582 P.2d 1000 (1978).

for the reason that no other would be morally acceptable. Sometimes this is emphasized in the statute itself. In holding it proper to exclude evidence of a claimed choice-of-evils defense, because no proper foundation therefor had been laid, the court underlined a sentence of the Colorado statute.

> When evidence relating to the defense of justification under this section is offered by the defendant, before it is submitted for the consideration of the jury, the court shall first rule as a matter of law whether the claimed facts and circumstances would, if established, constitute a justification.[2]

Defendant was found guilty after the jury had been duly instructed on the law of duress, including the familiar standard.[3]

Some may assume that the "inexcusable choice" is taken care of by the section of the Model Penal Code on choice of evils.[4] As mentioned this section provides in substance that an actor who has done an act that violates the letter of the law has a defense if what he avoided would have caused a greater harm than was caused by his act. This would be no defense to an actor who has made the "inexcusable choice," because what he avoided (loss of his own life) would never in the legal view be greater than the harm he caused by killing an innocent person. But the fact that the actor would have no defense under this section does not in any way rule out his "affirmative defense" under the duress section.[5]

J. CONCLUSION

What has been said emphasizes that the age-old rules of duress and necessity, with their equally ancient exception, are as sound today as ever but occupy only a part of the potential field; that an effort to formulate rules and exceptions for the rest of the field would be futile so resort to a standard is necessary, the desirable standard being in terms of what a reasonable person would do in such a situation; and that a statute on choice of evils is appropriate only in extreme situations in which only one choice is morally acceptable.

Legislation in this field might well consist of two statutes in substantially the following form.

Duress and Necessity. Except for the intentional or reckless taking of human life, one who did not culpably cause, or enter into, the critical situation and is not otherwise at fault, has a defense if he acted under such compulsion, from whatever source, that a person of reasonable firmness in such a situation would have been unable to resist doing what was done.

Choice of Evils. In a criminal prosecution it shall be a defense if it can be established as a matter of law that the actor's conduct, in the only way that seemed reasonably possible under the circumstances, avoided greater harm than it caused.

2. People v. Strock, ___ Colo. ___, 623 P.2d 42, 44 (1981).

3. "A person may not be convicted of an offense, other than a class 1 felony, based upon conduct in which he engaged because of the use or threatened use of unlawful force upon him or upon another person, which force or threatened use thereof a reasonable person in his situation would have been unable to resist." Id. at 623 P.2d 45.

4. Section 3.02.

5. Section 2.09.

The first relies upon the reasonable-person standard for all situations not within the exception. The other allows the reasonable-person standard to determine whether the conduct, as such, is acceptable but relies entirely upon the law to determine whether one harm was, or was not, greater than the other. For example, if the conduct in question avoided the loss of two or more lives by causing the death of one, this is clearly a case in which the harm avoided was greater than the harm caused. But the proposed section would not provide an excuse for the hypothetical man who threw the boy to the beasts because that was not the only way to accomplish the result that seemed reasonably possible under the circumstances. His choice that the boy must be the one to die is not acceptable.

With most actual cases tested by whether or not a reasonable person would have been able to resist doing what was done, it will inevitably happen now and then that some person is excused (found not guilty) although his conduct actually caused greater harm than it avoided. This, of course, does not meet the test of strict morality, but is unavoidable and need cause no concern. The criminal law was never intended to be a complete moral code.[6] Only when conduct falls far below proper moral behavior, is punishment deemed appropriate.[7] And if extreme situations are dealt with by rules of law, leaving only lesser problems to be tested by the standard, conduct no worse than that of the ordinary reasonable person may at times fall short of the full measure of strict morality, but not very far short—not far enough to merit punishment.

The criminal law does not hesitate to dictate that no one may choose between oneself and another, who may live and who must die, by intentionally killing an obviously innocent person, and that no one may intentionally sacrifice human life for the protection of property; but in general it is not primarily concerned with the relativity of different harms. Its chief concern in this regard is that, except for certain extreme situations, no one should be punished for doing what any reasonable person would have done.[8]

Some states have made impelled perpetration a statutory crime in itself. Thus the Oregon statute provides:[9]

> (1) A person commits the crime of Coercion when he compels or induces another person to engage in conduct from which he has a right to abstain, or to abstain from engaging in conduct in which he has a legal

6. "The criminal law cannot be simply a code or right behavior. It must be, rather, a specification of behavior so far below common standards that it identifies the actor as a dangerous and reprehensible person, who does not respond to the normal restraints of education, morality and custom." ALI, Model Penal Code and Commentaries, Part II, vol. 3, p. 483 (1980).

7. Reference is made to "the settled principle that penal sanctions should be reserved for that which virtually the entire community is willing to condemn." Id. at p. 489.

8. It is not intended to suggest that a reasonable person would intentionally kill an obviously innocent person in order to save his own life, but only that the law does not leave this for the determination of either the individual or the jury.

9. Or.Rev.Stat. § 163.275 (1979). The statute also covers threats of: causing physical injury to some person; causing property damage; criminal activity; accusation of a crime or instigation of criminal charges; exposing a secret; subjecting a person to hatred, contempt, or ridicule; causing a strike or boycott; testifying or withholding testimony with respect to a legal claim of defense; use or abuse of a position as a public servant; or inflicting other harm.

right to engage, by means of instilling in him a fear that, if the demand is not complied with, the actor or another will: . . . . (e) Expose a secret or publicize an asserted fact, whether true or false, tending to subject some person to hatred, contempt or ridicule; . . . .

Under this statute it was held that a man who had compelled a woman to submit to deviate sex by a threat to expose a damaging secret, could properly be charged in count one with sodomy and in count two with coercion.[10] This statute is to be distinguished from statutory extortion (blackmail),[11] under which it is the extorsive threat that constitutes the offense, whereas under the Oregon statute it is the resulting impelled perpetration that constitutes the offense of "coercion." The same kinds of threat can be included whichever statute is adopted, but the Oregon statute has the advantage of covering both results, since the extorsive threat can be punished as attempted "coercion."

Brainwashing

Recently, some defendants have raised a variation on the duress and necessity defenses by claiming that they should not be held responsible for their criminal acts because they were compelled by brainwashing.[12] The courts have generally rejected this contention.[13] Under traditional concepts of duress and necessity a true brainwashing situation would not be available as a defense since the actor is "converted" to the commission of the crime and is acting with the requisite mens rea and actus reus. However, under some situations, depending on the nature of circumstances and the brainwashing technique used, the Model Penal Code section on duress[14] would provide a basis for a defense.

SECTION 3.   CONSENT OF OTHER PARTY

The problem of consent in criminal law requires particular attention to two different matters: (1) What is the legal effect of consent or nonconsent? (2) What will be regarded as consent within the legal meaning of the term?

A.   LEGAL EFFECT OF CONSENT

In studying the legal effect of consent or nonconsent it is important to recognize three different categories of crime.

(1) In certain offenses the *absence* of consent of the person harmed is an essential ingredient of the crime by the very words of the definition. Thus in common-law rape the phrase "without her consent" (or the equivalent "against her will") is found in the definition itself. The finding of consent on

---

10. State v. Robertson, 54 Or.App. 630, 635 P.2d 1057 (1981). There was a dissent in this case, but only on the belief that the statute as worded is unconstitutionally vague. This, which was the chief claim on appeal, was vigorously rejected by the majority.

11. See supra ch. 4, sec. 10B. As pointed out there, in one type of extortion statute the impelled perpetration is proscribed, which is entirely logical.

12. Lunde & Wilson, Brainwashing as a Defense to Criminal Liability: Patty Hearst Revisited, Crim.L.Bull. 341 (1977); Delgado, Ascription of Criminal States of Mind: Toward a Defense Theory for the Coercively Persuaded ("brainwashed") Defendant, 63 Minn.L.Rev. 1 (1979).

13. Id. Lunde & Wilson.

14. Section 2.09.

the part of the person alleged to have been harmed disproves the commission of such a crime.

(2) At the other extreme will be found those offenses which are as readily possible with the consent of the person harmed as without it, such as "statutory rape" (carnal knowledge of a child) or murder. Furthermore, despite some authority to the contrary,[1] touching a girl under the age of consent with intent to have sexual intercourse with her is an assault with intent to commit rape,[2] or an attempt to commit rape,[3] although no force or violence is intended and she is entirely willing. And the sound view is that such a girl is just as incapable of giving a legally-recognized permission to an indecent fondling of her person as she is of giving such license to the act of intercourse itself, and hence her consent to such liberties is no defense.[4] A girl under the age of consent is frequently said to be incapable of giving consent to such misdeeds, by which is meant that her consent is incapable of giving a legally-recognized permission.

(3) Between these two extremes is a third category in which consent or nonconsent will determine whether the conduct was lawful or unlawful within certain limits,—but not beyond. The typical example is battery. What is called a "fond embrace" when gladly accepted by a sweetheart is called "assault and battery" when forced upon another without her consent; and the act of one who grabs another by the ankles and causes him to fall violently to the ground may result in a substantial jail sentence under some circumstances, but receive thunderous applause if it stops a ball carrier on the gridiron. The difference is because one who engages in a game such as football consents to such physical contact as is normally and properly to be expected in playing the game.[5]

There are limits, however, to the extent to which the law will recognize a privilege based upon such consent.[6] Just as there can be no legally-valid permission to be killed, so the law will not recognize a license unnecessarily to be maimed.[7] One may permit an amputation made necessary by accident or disease, but he who struck off the hand of a "lustie rogue" to enable him

1. State v. Pickett, 11 Nev. 255 (1876).

2. People v. Babcock, 160 Cal. 537, 117 P. 549 (1911); Commonwealth v. Murphy, 165 Mass. 66, 42 N.E. 504 (1895); Fannin v. State, 65 Okl.Cr. 444, 88 P.2d 671 (1939); Steptoe v. State, 134 Tex.Cr.R. 320, 115 S.W.2d 916 (1938); Allison v. United States, 133 U.S.App.D.C. 159, 409 F.2d 445 (1969).

3. Alford v. State, 132 Fla. 624, 181 So. 839 (1938); Rainey v. Commonwealth, 169 Va. 892, 193 S.E. 501 (1937); Regina v. Martin, 9 Car. & P. 213, 169 Eng.Rep. 49 (1840).

4. People v. Gibson, 232 N.Y. 458, 134 N.E. 531 (1922); Carter v. State, 121 Tex. Cr.R. 493, 51 S.W.2d 316 (1932); State v. Landino, 38 Or.App. 447, 590 P.2d 737 (1979).

5. See Comment, The Consent Defense: Sports Violence, and the Criminal Law, 13 Am.Crim.L.Rev. 235 (1975).

6. It was no defense to a charge of manslaughter, based on a homicide resulting from an overdose of heroin that the victim, already "loaded," importuned D to administer the injection. People v. Cruciana, 36 N.Y.2d 304, 367 N.Y.S.2d 758, 327 N.E.2d 803 (1975).

"Consent is not an element of the crime against nature nor is the crime less of a crime if committed with a consenting person." Slaughterback v. State, 594 P.2d 780, 781–82 (Okl.Cr.App.1979). But see State v. Foust, 588 P.2d 170 (Utah 1978) requiring corroboration of the testimony of a consenting incest victim.

7. People v. Lenti, 44 Misc.2d 118, 253 N.Y.S.2d 9 (1964).

to beg more effectively was guilty of mayhem despite the other's request.[8] A wrongdoer may give effective consent to moderate chastisement and he who inflicts such permitted punishment is not guilty of assault and battery although he would be guilty without consent,[9] and persons may lawfully engage in a friendly boxing match as a test of skill; but if two engage in an angry fist fight, by mutual consent, exchanging blows intended or likely to cause great bodily injury, both are guilty of assault and battery.[10] And the fact that a masochist consented to a severe beating by a sadist was not a defense to a charge of aggravated assault.[11] A victim could not legally consent to an aggravated assault by providing the defendant with a gun and telling defendant to shoot the victim.[12]

Because of the peculiar nature of the third category it requires particular attention but the other two are sharply divided so far as the present problem is concerned. In a prosecution for any offense falling within the second category it is futile to talk of consent because this will not be exculpating even if clearly established, whereas if the crime falls within the first category the prosecution must negative consent to make out even a prima-facie case. This invites inquiry as to just what will be regarded as consent within the legal meaning of the term and it is clear to begin with that conditional or limited consent is no consent at all beyond the terms of the condition or the boundaries indicated. If, for example, one places an article in the hands of another for inspection with the understanding that the other will promptly either return it or pay for it, there is no consent for him to run off with it without payment;[13] and the proprietor of a store who placed a large box of matches on the counter, for the convenience of customers in lighting pipes and cigars in the store, did not consent that the whole box of matches should be carried away.[14] Consent to one thing, moreover, is not consent to a different or additional thing. The girl who willingly ate a fig did not consent to eat a deleterious drug added without her knowledge,[15] nor would her consent

---

8. Wright's Case, Co. Litt. 127A (1604).

9. State v. Beck, 19 S.C.L. (1 Hill) 363 (1833).

10. State v. Newland, 27 Kan. 764 (1882); Commonwealth v. Collberg, 119 Mass. 350 (1876); The King v. Donovan [1934] K.B. 498.

11. People v. Samuels, 58 Cal.Rptr. 439, 250 Cal.App.2d 501 (1967).

In a prosecution for atrocious assault a battery where the defendant and his wife had an understanding that if she drank alcohol he would physically punish her the court refused to recognize consent as a defense. The court concluded "that as a matter of law, no one has the right to beat another even though that person may ask for it. Assault and battery cannot be consented to by a victim, for the state makes it unlawful and is not a party to any such agreement between the victim and the perpetrator." State v. Brown, 143 N.J.Super. 571, 364 A.2d 27,

31 (1976) aff'd 154 N.J.Super. 511, 381 A.2d 1231 (App.Div.).

12. State v. Fransua, 85 N.M. 173, 510 P.2d 106 (App.1973).

13. Rex v. Chisser, T. Raym. 275, 83 Eng.Rep. 142 (1678). See also, Wells v. State, 613 P.2d 201 (Wyo.1980).

Consent that customers wishing to buy articles might remove them from the shelf, did not apply to one who removed an article with intent to keep it without paying for it. Ashby v. State, 604 S.W.2d 897 (Tex.Cr.App.1980).

14. Mitchum v. State, 45 Ala. 29 (1871).

15. Commonwealth v. Stratton, 114 Mass. 303 (1873). And a wife who consented to marital intercourse did not consent to the communication of a loathsome disease with which her husband was infected without her knowledge. State v. Lankford, 29 Del. 594, 102 A. 63 (1917).

have included some entirely different article if it had been substituted by sleight of hand undetected by her.

Consent even to prolonged kissing and hugging is not consent to sexual intercourse. And if a man forces sex upon an unwilling female, it is no defense to rape that she did not object to his lesser advances.[16]

B. LEGALLY–RECOGNIZED CONSENT

The phrase "legally-recognized consent" is employed with two different meanings. In one sense it is used when the question is whether or not the law will give force and effect to the consent as in the phrase, "there is no legally-recognized consent to sexual intercourse by a girl under the statutory age." The other usage is in situations in which the person could have given a legally-effective consent and the question is whether what was said or done amounts to consent as a matter of law,—which is the meaning adopted for the present discussion.

1. DURESS

It has been said: "A compelled consent is in law no consent at all," [17] and this is beyond question if the compulsion is sufficient. This, it should be emphasized, does not require the extremity needed for the common-law rule of duress—a threat of imminent death or great bodily injury. One who hands over property under a threat of any serious injury to his person has "submitted," but has done so without consent and the threatener is guilty of robbery.[18]

Enlightening are certain statutory additions to the crime of extortion that provide a punishment for the obtaining of property from another "with his consent, induced by a wrongful use of force or fear." [19] The ways in which consent may be so induced may specifically include a threat to accuse him of crime, to impute to him any deformity or disgrace, or to expose a secret affecting him.[20] If the threat generates a well-grounded fear that the property must be handed over to avoid serious personal injury, the submission thereto is not consent and obtaining property by this means is robbery. If the property is handed over without any compulsion, it is a gift. Only between these extremes is the property obtained "with his consent by a wrongful use of force or fear."

---

16. State v. Myers, 606 P.2d 250 (Utah 1980).

17. Shehany v. Lowry, 170 Ga. 70, 72, 152 S.E. 114, 115 (1929).

Consent was no defense to the intentional and unnecessary infliction of pain under the guise of "fraternity hazing." People v. Lenti, 46 Misc.2d 682, 260 N.Y.S.2d 284 (1965).

Compare: " 'Consent' to a confinement means not mere acquiescence but a voluntary assent, as, for example, occurs when an individual is threatened with arrest and volunteers to accompany the police to the station in order to straighten matters out." Rosario v. Amalgamated Ladies Garment, Etc., 605 F.2d 1228, 1249 (2d Cir. 1979).

18. 4 Bl.Comm. *242; State v. Stephens, 66 Ariz. 219, 186 P.2d 346 (1947). The Model Penal Code is worded in terms of "serious bodily injury." Section 222.1(1).

19. West's Ann.Cal.Pen.Code § 518 (1970).

A Utah statute provided a punishment for the obtaining of property from another "with his consent, induced by a wrongful use of force or fear." Utah Code Ann. 1953 § 76–19–1.

20. Id. at § 519.

It is common to include, among the list of extorsive threats, one "to do an unlawful injury to his person." [21] This suggests that ordinary robbery would be extortion. Sometimes the section on robbery will be worded in terms of a threat of "serious injury," while the section on extortion speaks of a threat of "physical injury." [22] Since "serious injury" is used to mean "serious physical injury," the same suggestion is encountered. The proper solution is to interpret the extortion statute to mean conduct not amounting to robbery, so that where the threat was of serious injury the crime committed was not extortion, but robbery, although a conviction of extortion might be affirmed as a lesser included offense.

Illustrations may help to avoid confusion at this point. A obtained three watches unlawfully under the following circumstances: (1) He was unarmed when he encountered B, but by superior strength he threw B down, twisted his arm behind his back and tore the watch off B's wrist despite the latter's utmost resistance; (2) while no stronger than C, A was armed on this occasion and ordered C to hand over his watch at gunpoint under threat of instant death, whereupon C in fear for his life removed the watch from his wrist and handed it to A; (3) when A saw D they were in a restaurant filled with people where A did not dare resort either to violence or the show of a deadly weapon, but he told D that he would file a complaint charging D with embezzlement unless D handed over his watch, and although D was innocent of such an offense he thought the accusation would be damaging and reluctantly delivered his watch to A. B, the victim of *vis absoluta*, had no choice and his watch was acquired by A without the help of any act by B—whose only act in this regard was the futile effort to prevent what happened. C had a choice either to obey A's order or to refuse in the hope A was bluffing. He was no doubt wise to hand over his watch rather than to risk his life, but he was the victim of *vis compulsiva* and his handing over of the watch was an act on his part. But in legal theory while he "yielded" or "surrendered" the watch C did not "consent" to the transfer of the property to A, and since robbery is defined in terms of "force or fear" A is guilty of robbery from both B and C. As to D, however, the rule is different and the law recognizes not only that D had a choice as a result of which he elected to hand over his watch and did so, but also that he consented to have the property pass to A, although he gave this consent reluctantly and under undue influence. Conceivably the rule of law as to C and D might have been the same but the actual development was otherwise due, no doubt, to a realization of the fact that it is common experience for consent to be given reluctantly under some sort of "pressure." It is only when the will is overwhelmed by extreme compulsion that the act of compliance is without legally-recognized consent.

The three situations, it should be emphasized, are all different. A acquired the watch from B without B's consent and without any act of B contributing to the result; A obtained the watch from C with the aid of C's act in handing it over but without any legally-recognized consent by C; whereas D was induced both to act and to consent. A's guilt of robbery from both B and C should not obscure the difference between the two cases because in corresponding situations involving some other problem the legal result itself may be different, as pointed out in the discussion of compulsion and necessity. The difference in the result as to C and D, it may be added, is not limited

21. Ibid.   22. Iowa Criminal Code § 711.1 and §
                                         711.4 (1978).

to the criminal law. Any of the victims would be entitled to require **A** to return the watch because of the unlawful manner of its acquisition, but if **A** should sell the watches to a bona-fide purchaser, for value and without notice, the picture would change. Not even such a purchaser would be able to withhold his acquisition from **B** or **C** because **A** had no title to either of those watches; but **D** would lose out because he had transferred title to **A** and **A's** sale to the innocent purchaser cut off **D's** equity to have the property returned to him.

2. FRAUD

Any discussion of the relation of fraud to the presence or absence of consent should be prefaced by an explanation of the two different kinds of fraud. The general rule is that if deception causes a misunderstanding as to the fact itself (fraud in the *factum*) there is no legally-recognized consent because what happened is not that for which consent was given; whereas consent induced by fraud is as effective as any other consent, so far as direct and immediate legal consequences are concerned, if the deception relates not to the thing done but merely to some collateral matter (fraud in the inducement). Suppose, for example, **D** has a certificate of stock in a company no longer in existence but which **D** falsely and fraudulently represents to be a going and prosperous concern. Misled by this fraud, **X** writes out and signs a promissory note for $1,000 which he hands to **D** in payment for this stock. This is fraud in the inducement since **X** knew he was signing and delivering a note and intended to do so. It is in fact and in law his note and the direct and immediate consequences are the same as if no fraud had been perpetrated. Because of **D's** fraud **X** can repudiate the note and refuse to pay it if it has not reached the hands of a holder in due course, but it is his note with the usual consequences until and unless he successfully disaffirms it.

On the other hand suppose **D**, having no worthless certificate, resorts to other means. Having prepared (1) a receipt for a package and (2) a note for $1,000 in such form that they have the same general shape and appearance, he delivers a fake package to **X** and shows him the receipt with a request for his signature. After **X** has read the receipt and is ready to sign **D** distracts his attention and substitutes the note by sleight of hand, so that **X** signs the note thinking it is a receipt for a package. This is fraud in the *factum*. **X** did not consent to sign a note, had no intention of signing a note, and although the paper with the wording of a note has his signature at the bottom, it is not as a matter of law his note, and he has a defense available against anyone, even a holder in due course.[23]

The most striking illustration of the criminal-law distinction between the two types of fraud is found in prosecutions for rape. In several cases a doctor or pretended doctor has had sexual intercourse with a female patient under the fraudulent pretense of medical treatment. In some of these cases the doctor has not hesitated to make it clear that he intended to have sexual intercourse with the patient, his fraud being in the deceitful suggestion that this was necessary to cure some malady, which was fraud in the inducement

---

23. United States v. Klatt, 135 F.Supp. 648 (D.C.Cal.1955); Gate City National Bank v. Bunton, 316 Mo. 1338, 296 S.W. 375 (1927). If **X** was negligent in letting his name appear at the foot of such a writing he will be liable to a holder in due course, but the theory is that he is estopped and not that it is really his note. Ibid.

since the patient knew exactly what was to be done and was deceived only in regard to a collateral matter,—the reason why it was to be done. And here as usual the direct and immediate consequence of consent obtained by fraud in the inducement is the same as consent given in the absence of fraud, and since the patient consented to the intercourse it was not rape[24] so long as she was over the statutory age. It is quite obvious by way of analogy, that obtaining sexual intercourse with a prostitute by giving her counterfeit money does not constitute the crime of rape.[25] In certain other cases a doctor has obtained sexual intercourse with a patient by means of fraud in the *factum*. In these cases the woman did not realize what was happening but supposed it was merely a vaginal examination or surgical operation. "The evidence in this case, if the prosecuting witness is to be believed, is to the effect that she supposed the doctor was examining her physically with his fingers."[26] In another case the patient had believed "that what was taking place was a surgical operation and nothing else," believing "that penetration was being effected with the hand or with an instrument."[27] Again: "The evidence wholly fails to show that Rebecca ever consented to, or even had knowledge of, the act of sexual intercourse, until after it was fully accomplished."[28] In such cases the unlawful intercourse is rape[29] for the very sufficient reason that it was without the woman's consent. "She consented to one thing, he did another materially different, ..."[30]

Another fraudulent scheme of obtaining intercourse has been perpetrated at times by a man getting into bed in the dark with another man's wife who submitted in the belief the person was her husband. As pointed out in the discussion of the crime of rape[31] the courts are not in accord as to whether or not this crime was committed under such facts, but the disagreement is not in regard to the underlying principle but only as to its application. Some courts have taken the position that such a misdeed is fraud in the inducement on the theory that the woman consents to exactly what is done (sexual intercourse) and hence there is no rape;[32] other courts, with better reason it would seem, hold such a misdeed to be rape on the theory that it involves

---

24. Don Moran v. People, 25 Mich. 356 (1872). In reversing a conviction of rape because of an instruction that: "If the woman ultimately consented to such intercourse, such consent . . . being obtained through . . . fraud . . . then the offence is rape," the court said: "We are satisfied that it is never proper or safe to instruct the jury in any case that the crime of rape may be committed with the consent of the woman, however obtained, ..." Whittaker v. State, 50 Wis. 518, 524, 7 N.W. 431, 433 (1880). And see the *dictum* by Kelly, C.B. that, "where a man by fraud induces a woman to submit to sexual connection, it is not rape." The Queen v. Flattery, 2 Q.B.D. 410, 413 (1887).

A woman consented to sex in return for being permitted to participate in a card game for money. The fact that the game was fraudulently "rigged" so she could not win had no bearing on a rape trial. It was not sex without her con-

sent. People v. Harris, 93 Cal.App.3d 103, 155 Cal.Rptr. 472 (1979).

25. Compare Restatement, Second, Torts § 57, Illustration 1 (1965). The offense is uttering counterfeit coin. The Queen v. _____, 1 Cox C.C. 250 (1845).

26. State v. Ely, 114 Wash. 185, 192, 194 N.W. 988, 991 (1921).

27. The Queen v. Flattery, 2 Q.B.D. 410, 413 (1877).

28. Pomeroy v. State, 94 Ind. 96, 100 (1883).

29. Ely; Flattery; Pomeroy.

30. Per Mellor, J., in Flattery at 414.

31. See supra, chapter 2, section 5, D, 5, b.

32. Defendant led the victim to believe that signing certain cards at the Registry Office was a marriage ceremony and that they were married. They subsequently lived together for four days

fraud in the *factum* since the woman's consent is to an innocent act of marital intercourse while what is actually perpetrated upon her is an act of adultery. Her innocence seems never to have been questioned in such a case and the reason she is not guilty of adultery is because she did not consent to adulterous intercourse. Statutory changes in the law of rape have received attention earlier [33] and need not be repeated here.

The offense of operating a motor vehicle "without the consent of the owner" [34] obviously belongs in this same category. Such a statute is directed against one who takes possession of the vehicle without the consent of the owner. It does not apply to one who takes the car with the consent of the owner, even if that consent was induced by fraud—as where the owner was misled as to the extent of the trip to be taken by the borrower.[35]

It should be noted that some of the very recent "joyriding" statutes, or perhaps it should be said statutes substituted for or added to the original "joyriding" statutes, are differently worded and apply to a use beyond that granted by the owner.[36]

The intermediate category, embracing offenses which do not require the absence of consent by definition, on the one hand, and yet cannot be committed as readily with consent as without, on the other, requires special consideration, because the presence or absence of consent will be the determining factor under some circumstances but not under others, as pointed out above. The typical testing ground is battery, with the addition of assault under the criminal-law theory that every battery includes an assault.

Under the early law of torts one had an action of trespass for battery if he had suffered a harmful contact as the result of an intentional act of another to which the one had not consented and which was not otherwise privi-

before the defendant disappeared during which time they had sexual relations.

". . . Rape is carnal knowledge of a woman without her consent; carnal knowledge is the physical fact of penetration; it is the consent to that which is in question; such a consent demands a perception as to what is about to take place, as to the identity of the man and the character of what he is doing. But once the consent is comprehending and actual, the inducing causes cannot destroy its reality and leave the man guilty of rape." Papadimitropoulos v. Queen, (Aust.H.C. 1957), 98 C.L.R. 249.

33. Id. at c.

34. See e.g., West's Ann.Cal.Veh. Code § 10851 (1970).

35. State v. Boggs, 181 Iowa 358, 164 N.W. 759 (1917); State v. Mularky, 195 Wis. 549, 218 N.W. 809 (1928); People v. Cook, 228 Cal.App.2d 716, 39 Cal.Rptr. 802 (1964). *Cook* was reaffirmed in People v. Donell, 32 Cal.App.3d 613, 108 Cal. Rptr. 232 (1973).

Where there was nothing in the evidence to support a finding that the wrongful taking and driving away of a truck was with intent to use it temporarily, it was not error to refuse an instruction on joyriding. State v. Pulliam, 101 Idaho 482, 616 P.2d 261 (1980). In a trial for grand larceny the court did not find it necessary to determine whether joyriding was a lesser included offense.

Under the Ohio statute joyriding is a lesser included offense of auto theft. Brown v. Ohio, 432 U.S. 161, 97 S.Ct. 2221 (1977).

The statute providing a penalty for the possession of a stolen vehicle means a vehicle obtained by theft and does not include one used in violation of the joyriding statute. State v. Roberts, 16 Or.App. 397, 519 P.2d 380 (1974).

36. The Oregon statute on unauthorized use of a vehicle expressly applies to the borrower who "knowingly retains or withholds possession thereof without the consent of the owner for so lengthy a period beyond the specified time as to render such retention of possession a gross deviation from the agreement." State v. Boyd, 28 Or.App. 725, 560 P.2d 689 (1977).

leged. If one had consented to the harmful contact by the other the action of trespass for battery was not available even if the consent had been induced by fraudulent misrepresentations by the other, but this did not mean no redress was available since trespass on the case could be brought to recover for the tortious means by which the consent had been procured. Where the harmful contact was with consent induced by fraud the early tort cases did not speak of it as "battery" because the action was "case" but since a civil remedy is available whether the contact was without consent, or with consent induced by fraud, the ancient distinction is of no importance today except in jurisdictions still using strict common-law pleading.[37]

In criminal procedure there has never been an indictment or information comparable to the civil action known as "trespass on the case" and from earliest times any unlawful application of force to the person of another has been prosecuted under a charge of battery (or assault, or assault and battery) unless the harm amounted to felony such as murder, mayhem, rape or robbery. And since the definition of criminal battery is not an application of force to the person of another *without his consent*, but an *unlawful* application of force to the person of another,[38] it follows that the decisive question is not whether the harmful contact was with or without consent, but whether it was lawful or unlawful. And just as a harmful contact with consent not induced by fraud may be unlawful in a particular case for one reason, so a harmful contact with consent induced by fraud may be unlawful in another case for a different reason. In other words, consent procured by fraud in the inducement presents an entirely different problem in a prosecution for battery (or assault) than it does in a prosecution for an offense in which *lack of consent* is *per se* essential to guilt.

The leading cases are *Bartell* [39] and *Gregory*.[40] In *Bartell* one pretending to be a magnetic healer treated a young girl afflicted with some nervous disorder by causing her to disrobe completely while he gave her a massage treatment. Since the evidence made it clear that the disrobing was quite unnecessary for purposes of the treatment and was directed merely for defendant's lewd personal gratification, a conviction of assault and battery was affirmed. This was a case of fraud in the inducement and the girl consented to exactly what was done, being deceived only as to a collateral matter, but such consent did not make this indecent contact lawful. In another case a young girl permitted a man to take indecent liberties with her person because he was a police officer in uniform and she was worried about what he might do if she refused. There was no evidence of such duress as would disprove consent but consent so obtained did not make the indecent contact lawful and the conviction was affirmed.[41] This was not a case of fraud and is mentioned only to emphasize that consent which otherwise would make the contact lawful does not necessarily have that effect if the consent was improperly obtained.

37. Restatement, Torts § 13, comments g and h (1934). See now Restatement, Second, Torts § 18, comment f (1965).

38. Supra, chapter 2, section 2, A.

39. Bartell v. State, 106 Wis. 342, 82 N.W. 142 (1900).

40. Commonwealth v. Gregory, 132 Pa.Super. 507, 1 A.2d 501 (1938).

41. Commonwealth v. Carpenter, 172 Pa.Super. 271, 94 A.2d 74 (1953).

In *Gregory*, a doctor of theology, fraudulently representing himself to be a doctor of medicine particularly interested in the proper functioning of artificial limbs, convinced a young woman with such a handicap that it would aid him in his professional work if she would permit him to make an intimate examination of her body and the functioning of her prosthesis. She consented and he, having pulled down her stepins below her hips, made an intimate examination not only of the attachment but of the stub both before and after the artificial limb had been removed. In affirming a conviction the court said, "any consent claimed to have been given was obtained by fraud, and was vitiated by such fraud and is not a defense to the charge of assault and battery or indecent assault." [42] A simpler explanation would be that a fraudulently-induced consent will not make such an indecent contact lawful.[43]

In those prosecutions for rape in which sexual intercourse with a female patient was procured under the fraudulent pretense of medical treatment, but in which the offense of rape is not established because it was fraud in the inducement and consent to the intercourse was given, it seems clear from such cases as *Bartell* and *Gregory* that defendant is guilty of assault and battery, and it has been so held.[44]

The other chief example of an offense in the intermediate category is larceny. Obviously it cannot be said that consent or lack of consent is unimportant, but on the other hand the definition is not in terms of a taking without consent. The requirement is a *trespassory* taking.[45] And while the absence or presence of consent will usually determine whether the taking was or was not trespassory, this is not true in all situations.

Pear [46] is one of the most helpful cases on this point. In a larceny trial the evidence showed that **D** had borrowed a mare to take a short trip, as he said, but sold the animal the same day, having given the lender a false address. The jury found that the journey was a mere pretense and that **D** obtained possession of the mare with the intention of selling her. In affirming the conviction the judges said the "fraud supplied the place of force" and added that such a taking "was in the construction of law such a taking as would have made the prisoner liable to an action of trespass at the suit of the owner." [47] In other words, property obtained by fraudulently-induced consent is obtained by trespass and hence larceny if the other elements of the crime are present.

---

42. Gregory at 515–6, 1 A.2d at 505.

43. The court recognized that an indecent assault is a species of assault and battery (pp. 504, 513). See 18 P.S. § 4708 (1963) (Repealed 1980).

44. Regina v. Case, 4 Cox C.C. 220 (1850). In this case it was not clear whether the girl's consent to "medical treatment" was consent to intercourse fraudulently represented to be necessary for therapeutic reasons or was consent to something else. Platt, B., concluded that she did not consent to the intercourse.

Id. at 223–4. But the prosecution was for assault and the judges held that defendant was clearly guilty of assault whether rape had been committed or not.

For a comparable holding see Regina v. Saunders, 8 C. & P. 265, 173 Eng.Rep. 488 (1838).

45. See supra, chapter 4, section 1.

46. Pear's Case, 2 East P.C. 685 (1779).

47. Id. at 688.

As in the assault and battery cases mentioned, the courts dealing with larceny by trick [48] do not say there was "no consent" to the taking but that "fraud vitiates the transaction."[49]

The general provision of the Model Penal Code seems to be in line with existing law as to consent.[50] One special provision is:

"A male who has sexual intercourse with a female not his wife commits a felony of the third degree if: . . .

(c) he knows she is unaware that a sexual act is being committed upon her or that she submits because she falsely supposes that he is her husband."[51]

The Model Penal Code makes no mention of the distinction between fraud in the inducement and fraud in the *factum*, no doubt because no consent is involved in the latter.

In sum, the distinction between fraud in the *factum* and fraud in the inducement is controlling in the prosecution of offenses in which absence of consent is an element of the crime, but unimportant in the prosecution of other offenses.

SECTION 4. GUILT OF OTHER PARTY

Guilt of the injured party will be a complete defense as to acts which would otherwise be criminal if such acts were committed in self-defense or otherwise to prevent crime and did not exceed the privilege recognized by law for this purpose. In such a case the person has no wrongful intent in mind but is merely seeking to frustrate another who is attempting to commit crime. On the other hand it is an established principle of law that one crime is no excuse for another, and that the doctrine of particeps criminis, which bars one party to an unlawful deed from recovering in a civil action against another party thereto, "has no place in the administration of the criminal law."[1]

"One crime can not be permitted to become a shield against the punishment of another crime. One who has committed a crime ought not to escape punishment by showing that another person ought also to be punished for the same or another crime. Public policy requires that both be punished, and not that both be permitted to escape because of their mutual relations."[2]

The fact that the person killed was himself a murderer is no defense to a charge of murder, and it is just as much larceny to steal from a thief as to steal from anyone else,[3]—although needless to say the recapture of stolen property from the thief, by or for the lawful owner, is not larceny. It is also

48. See supra, chapter 4, D, 1.

49. English v. State, 80 Fla. 70, 71, 85 So. 150, 151 (1920).

50. Section 2.11.

51. 213.1(2)(c). See also Section 213.2(2)(c).

1. State v. Mellenberger, 163 Or. 233, 256, 95 P.2d 709, 718 (1939).

2. Gilmore v. People, 87 Ill.App. 128, 140–1 (1899).

". . . the doctrine of particeps criminis has no place in the administration of the criminal law." State v. Mellenberger, 163 Or. 233, 95 P.2d 709, 718 (1939).

3. Ward v. People, 3 Hill 395 (N.Y.1842). Horton v. State, 85 Ohio St. 13, 96 N.E. 797 (1911). Defendants, who paid prostitutes for their services and, after the agreement had been completed, forcibly took back the money paid to the women, were guilty of larceny from the

larceny to steal "contraband" from one who is violating the law by possessing it,[4] and malicious mischief wilfully to destroy such property so held by another;[5] the fact that a city acquired money illegally is no defense to a charge of embezzling that money from the city,[6] and the fact that counterfeit coin was paid to a prostitute for unlawful intercourse is no defense to a charge of uttering counterfeit coin.[7]

The one point at which this basic principle of the criminal law has been seriously questioned is found in prosecutions for false pretenses, and the leading case for the minority view is *McCord*,[8] in which the defendant obtained a gold watch and a diamond ring as a "bribe" by falsely pretending to be an officer with a warrant for the victim's arrest. In reversing a conviction for false pretenses the New York court said that neither law nor public policy designs the protection of rogues in their dealing with one another. The reason given includes a correct statement which, however, is improperly applied to this particular situation, as pointed out in the dissenting opinion of Judge Peckham.[9] If two willingly engage in an unlawful fist fight in which one suffers more injury than the other the law does not protect the loser by giving him a remedy in the form of a civil action against the winner, and the rule of the criminal law under which both may be convicted of assault and battery (or affray), cannot be said to give any protection to either. The policy of punishing both rather than excusing both is as applicable to the crime of false pretenses as to any other. In fact the *McCord* rule was particularly unfortunate because confidence men were able to obtain complete immunity by proposing an illegal scheme to their victims, and fortunately the prevailing view is that *particeps criminis* has no more application to false pretenses than to any other crime.[10]

The New York court felt bound to follow *McCord* but suggested to the legislature in 1906[11] that it would be wise to change the rule by enactment, and this was accomplished by statute the following year.[12] Very little now remains of the minority view[13] and convictions of false pretenses have been upheld where money was fraudulently obtained by (1) falsely altering a number punched from an illegal punch board,[14] (2) falsely pretending to have an unlawful plan to tap wires coming from horse races,[15] and (3) a confidence game in which the victim was induced to place a bet under the belief that a trick had been played whereby he was to cheat the other party.[16] It is no

person. People v. Newsom, 25 Mich.App. 371, 181 N.W.2d 551 (1970).

4. State v. Donovan, 108 Wash. 276, 183 P. 127 (1919).

5. State v. Stark, 63 Kan. 529, 66 P. 243 (1901).

6. State v. Patterson, 66 Kan. 447, 77 P. 860 (1903).

7. The Queen v. _____, 1 Cox C.C. 250 (1845).

8. McCord v. People, 46 N.Y. 470 (1871). The Wisconsin court reached a similar result under other facts. State v. Crowley, 41 Wis. 271 (1870).

9. McCord at 473.

10. Horton v. State, 85 Ohio St. 13, 96 N.E. 797 (1911). And see the cases therein cited.

11. People v. Thompkins, 186 N.Y. 413, 417, 79 N.E. 326, 327 (1906).

12. N.Y.Laws 1907, c. 581, § 1.

13. The rule was changed by statute in Wisconsin much more recently. Wis. Stats.1975, § 939.14. "It is no defense to a prosecution for crime that the victim also was guilty of a crime. . . ."

14. State v. Mellenberger, 163 Or. 233, 95 P.2d 709 (1939).

15. Gilmore v. People, 87 Ill.App. 128 (1899).

16. Regina v. Hudson, 8 Cox C.C. 305 (1860).

defense to a prosecution for false pretenses that the victim thought he was buying stolen property,[17] or that each party in an exchange of goods was equally guilty of false and fraudulent representations with reference to the property offered by him.[18]

A question is sometimes raised in regard to the latter case in some such form as this: Suppose **D** has a watch, for which he paid $50, which he fraudulently says cost him $100, while **X** fraudulently represents that he paid $100 for a ring the price of which was actually $50. If each deceives the other and the articles are exchanged how has any fraud been perpetrated? The answer becomes apparent if the fraud is limited to one side. Suppose **X** admits frankly that he paid $50 for the ring while **D** fraudulently represents that he paid $100 for the watch, and **X** being deceived makes the trade. **X** has clearly been defrauded because while willing to make the exchange for a $100 watch he might much prefer to keep his ring than trade it for a $50 watch, and he is entitled to know the facts when parting with his property. As said by a federal court: [19]

"A man is none the less cheated out of his property, when he is induced to part with it by fraud, because he gets a quid pro quo of equal value. It may be impossible to measure his loss by the gross scales available to a court, but he has suffered a wrong; he has lost his chance to bargain with the facts before him."

The Model Penal Code does not deal with guilt of the other party as a defense. The notion that one may escape punishment for his criminal conduct because someone else was equally guilty, which once had a trace of support in connection with certain offenses, is now too completely repudiated to require inclusion in a code.

SECTION 5. CONDUCT OF THE INJURED PARTY

The rules of law concerning negligence as a defense in civil actions for personal injuries have no application to criminal prosecutions.[1] "It is enough to say that contributory negligence, if shown, is never a defense or excuse for crime, nor can it in any degree serve to purge an act otherwise constituting a public offense of its criminal character." [2]

There is no legal recognition of the claim that a dishonest man cannot be defrauded. Barbee v. United States, 392 F.2d 532 (5th Cir. 1968).

Victim's intent to obtain usurious interest did not mitigate defendant's conduct in connection with fraud and embezzlement schemes. State v. Schifani, 92 N.M. 127, 584 P.2d 174 (App.1978).

17. Frazier v. Commonwealth, 291 Ky. 467, 165 S.W.2d 33 (1942).

18. Commonwealth v. Morrill, 62 Mass. 571 (1851).

19. United States v. Rowe, 56 F.2d 747, 749 (2d Cir. 1932).

Defendant is guilty of theft by deception in the sale of an automobile where the odometer was turned back from 73,000 to 33,000 miles. State v. Forshee, 588 P.2d 181 (Utah 1978).

1. Bowen v. State, 100 Ark. 232, 140 S.W. 28 (1911); People v. McKee, 80 Cal. App. 200, 251 P. 675 (1926); State v. Campbell, 82 Conn. 671, 74 A. 927 (1910); State v. Medlin, 355 Mo. 564, 197 S.W.2d 626 (1946); Click v. State, 144 Tex.Cr.R. 468, 164 S.W.2d 664 (1942); State v. Ramser, 17 Wn.2d 581, 136 P.2d 1013 (1943); State v. Lunz, 86 Wis.2d 695, 273 N.W.2d 767 (1979); United States v. Kreimer, 609 F.2d 126 (5th Cir. 1980).

2. State v. Moore, 129 Iowa 514, 519, 106 N.W. 16, 17 (1906). Accord, Penix v. Commonwealth, 313 Ky. 587, 233 S.W.2d 89 (1950).

". . . comparative negligence, like contributory negligence, is not a defense

In one case a man threw a handful of blasting powder into an open fireplace causing an explosion and resulting fire in which a woman and her nineteen-year-old son were burned to death. Several others, some younger and less able to take care of themselves than those who were killed, managed to get out of the burning building without harm, but this did not entitle the wrongdoer to an instruction that he was excused if the deceased had failed to use due care in the effort to reach safety.[3] In another case defendants, having been charged with manslaughter for running over and killing a pedestrian while they were driving a horse and carriage at an excessive rate and were somewhat intoxicated, thought they should be excused because deceased, who was deaf, had the habit of walking in the middle of the road at various times of the day and night, and was doing so at the time of the fatal accident,—but the court held otherwise.[4]

The fact that the negligence of some third person contributed to the death, or other harm, is also not available as an excuse to the defendant.[5] In one case the victim of a criminally-negligent traffic accident was moved from the hospital by his mother, contrary to the doctor's orders, and while it was not shown that death was actually hastened by the moving, the court considered it unimportant whether such was the fact or not.[6] Even the victim's obstinate refusal to submit to an operation which might have saved his life is no defense to the one whose malicious blow resulted in the death.[7]

It does not follow, however, that the conduct of the injured party must be ignored because it may have a bearing on whether or not the one who caused the injury was culpably negligent,[8] or it may be found that the negligence of the injured person was the *sole* cause of his injury.[9] "If the decedents were negligent," said the Washington court, "and such negligence was the sole cause of their death, then the appellant would not be guilty of manslaughter."[10]

to a criminal charge." Overton v. State, 606 P.2d 586, 587 (Okl.Cr.App.1979).

3. Embry v. Commonwealth, 236 Ky. 204, 32 S.W.2d 979 (1930).

4. Regina v. Longbottom, 3 Cox C.C. 439 (1849). See also Regina v. Kew, 12 Cox C.C. 355 (1872).

5. Graives v. State, 127 Fla. 182, 172 So. 716 (1936); State v. Sauter, 120 Ariz. 222, 585 P.2d 242 (1978).

6. People v. Clark, 106 Cal.App.2d 271, 235 P.2d 56 (1951). For the rule under the Texas statute see Noble v. State, 54 Tex.Cr.R. 436, 113 S.W. 281 (1908).

7. Regina v. Holland, 2 Moody & R. 351, 174 Eng.Rep. 313 (1841).

8. Held v. Commonwealth, 183 Ky. 209, 208 S.W. 772 (1919); People v. Campbell, 237 Mich. 424, 212 N.W. 97 (1927).

9. Cain v. State, 55 Ga.App. 376, 190 S.E. 371 (1937). And see State v. Diamond, 16 N.J.Super. 26, 83 A.2d 799 (1951).

"Where, however, a wound is not dangerous or calculated to produce death, and the victim dies solely as a result of improper or negligent treatment, this will be an intervening cause of death and the defendant will not be liable for homicide." Wright v. State, 374 A.2d 824, 829 (Del.1977).

10. State v. Ramser, 17 Wn.2d 581, 590, 136 P.2d 1013, 1017 (1943). And see Commonwealth v. Aurick, 138 Pa.Super. 180, 10 A.2d 22 (1939).

While contributory negligence is not a defense in a criminal case, D is not guilty of negligent homicide if the death of the decedent was the proximate result of his own negligence, and not that of D. Williams v. State, 554 P.2d 842 (Okl.Cr.App. 1976).

In some instances the decedent's negligence may have intervened between the conduct of D and the fatal result so as to have been the sole proximate cause of the death. State v. Gordon, 219 Kan. 643, 549 P.2d 886 (1976).

In a manslaughter case the evidence disclosed that defendants manufactured and stored large quantities of torpedoes in a small wooden shanty in a thickly populated part of the city, which was in violation of law and would seem to have been sufficient for criminal negligence apart from the ordinance. After a small explosion had started a fire, members of the fire department went into the shanty after being warned not to do so because the place was "full of dynamite," and were killed by a series of explosions. In reversing a judgment adverse to the defendants the court said: "There can be no conviction where it appears that the person injured was apprised of the danger, and unnecessarily, and over the protest of the defendant, exposed himself thereto." [11] In another case an officer, who knew he had a serious heart condition which made violent exercise extremely dangerous and had avoided anything of that nature on previous occasions, undertook to assist in subduing a drunken prisoner who was resisting an effort to take him to jail. As a result of this effort and excitement the officer suffered a fatal heart attack and the prisoner was indicted for manslaughter, but his misconduct was held to have been too remote to be a legally-recognized cause of the death.[12]

This section deals with certain problems of causation which are considered here for the sake of emphasis. They are not dealt with separately in the Model Penal Code.

SECTION 6. CONDONATION BY INJURED PARTY

Consideration of this much-misunderstood subject should be prefaced by a word of caution starting with reference to an ancient offense. *Theft bote*, says Blackstone, "is where the party robbed not only knows the felon, but also takes his goods again, or other amends, upon agreement not to prosecute. This is frequently called compounding of felony, and formerly was held to make a man an accessory; but it is now punished only with fine and imprisonment. . . . By statute 25 Geo. II, c. 36, even to advertise a reward for the return of things stolen, with no questions asked, or words to the same purport, subjects the advertiser and the printer to a forfeiture of 50*l*. each."[1]

The owner's reacquisition of a chattel previously stolen from him is not of itself sufficient to taint him with criminal guilt;[2] it is his act of obtaining it under an agreement or understanding to abstain from prosecution or to withhold evidence of the larceny that is illegal, and this it may be added is merely a particular instance of a general crime. For anyone to obtain anything of value, or a promise thereof, upon such an agreement or understanding in regard to any felony is a common-law offense known as compounding a felony, as pointed out in an earlier chapter.[3] The ancient classification of such an offender as an accessory to the crime after the fact suggests that it was

---

11. Carbo v. State, 4 Ga.App. 583, 62 S.E. 140, 141 (1908). The court says defendants were not criminally negligent toward the deceased but the theory is that they took pains to keep them out of danger after the fire started—not that keeping great quantities of high explosives in such a place was not criminal negligence. The statement of the firemen that they had a duty to investigate,

ignored by the court, would seem entitled to attention although perhaps it is not sufficient to change the result.

12. Hubbard v. Commonwealth, 304 Ky. 818, 202 S.W.2d 634 (1947).

1. 4 Bl.Comm. *133–4.

2. 1 Hale P.C. *619.

3. See supra, chapter 5, section 3, J.

originally limited to cases of felony, but that limitation has tended to disappear, and it has been said that to take a reward to forbear or stifle a criminal prosecution for a misdemeanor is also indictable at common law, except for offenses largely of the nature of private injuries or of low grade,[4] the chief exception being outside the boundaries of true crime and in the category of the so-called "civil offense." [5] It has not been uncommon for statutes to forbid the compounding of any criminal offense.[6]

Discussions of the subject often suggest that an attempt by the offender and the offended to settle the offense outside the criminal courtroom is usually a crime and always quite ineffective, but this is far from the true picture.[7] To begin with, a multitude of offenses, including a substantial number of serious crimes, are not prosecuted because they are settled between the two persons involved and never reach the attention of the prosecuting authorities, which of course is merely a factual matter and does not dispute the statement as to the law. The law itself, however, has taken definite strides in this direction, the most extensive being an enactment expressly authorizing the compromise of a misdemeanor for which the injured person has a civil action (except where there are special circumstances of aggravation).[8] The court may have discretion to permit the prosecution to proceed notwithstanding such a compromise,[9] but it will be exercised rarely and only under unusual circumstances.

There are also certain specific provisions to be considered, one of the most common being the enactment that intermarriage of the parties shall bar a prosecution for seduction,[10] although important differences in statutes on this subject are to be noted.[11] A provision whereby intermarriage of the parties will bar a prosecution for rape, while it has not been unknown,[12] is

---

4. State v. Carver, 69 N.H. 216, 39 A. 973 (1897).

5. Holsey v. State, 4 Ga.App. 453, 61 S.E. 836 (1908).

6. Ill.Crim. Law & Proc., § 32–1 (1977). Murphy v. Rochford, 55 Ill.App. 3d 695, 13 Ill.Dec. 543, 371 N.E.2d 260 (1977).

7. For an elaborate consideration of the field see Miller, The Compromise of Criminal Cases, 1 So.Cal.L.Rev. 1 (1927).

8. West's Ann.Cal.Pen.Code §§ 1377–9 (1970).

ORS 135.705 provides: "When a defendant is charged with a crime punishable as a misdemeanor for which the person injured by the act constituting the crime has a remedy by a civil action, the crime may be compromised, as provided in ORS 135.705 . . ." ORS 135.705 provides: "If the party injured at any time before trial . . . acknowledges in writing that he has received satisfaction for the injury, the court may, in its discretion, . . . order the accusatory instrument to be dismissed; . . ."

It was held improper for the judge to attempt to direct the terms of the com-

promise, or to dismiss the case because he thought the injured party was seeking too much. State v. Martindale, 30 Or. App. 1127, 569 P.2d 659 (1977). See also Hoines v. Barney's Club, Inc., 28 Cal.3d 603, 170 Cal.Rptr. 42, 620 P.2d 628 (1980).

9. Id. at § 1378.

10. Id. at § 269.

11. In Michigan it was held that marriage after arrest and during a recess in the preliminary examination, although followed by desertion, barred a conviction. People v. Gould, 70 Mich. 240, 38 N.W. 232 (1888).

12. Ill.Rev.Stats.1955, c. 38, § 490 repealed 1961, but see: Ill.Crim.Code of 1961, Ch. 38, § 11–4 Committee Comments (Ill.Ann.Stats. Ch. 38, Crim.Law & Pro. § 11–4, p. 211).

"Marriage of the accused and the victim is not specified as a bar to prosecution under the provisions of this code as it was under the former . . . This is deliberate because the committee felt that marriage should not be coerced by the criminal law, nor substituted for punishment otherwise provided for a criminal offense."

relatively rare although anciently under different type of procedure "an appeal of rape was not unfrequently the prelude to a marriage."[13] Where such marriage does not bar a prosecution for rape it may make conviction impossible in certain cases under a different provision which makes the wife incompetent to be a witness against her husband.[14]

Some statutes invite a settlement by the parties such as a worthless check act providing a penalty for the issuance of such an instrument unless it is paid within five days after written notice,[15] or an enactment making the refusal of an officer, clerk, agent or other, to hand over on demand money or property in his care, prima-facie evidence of embezzlement.[16] Any provision such as these, or those mentioned above, gives to the person harmed by a crime more or less power to determine whether criminal proceedings shall be instituted but none is more significant in this regard than the enactment found in some states providing that no prosecution for adultery shall be brought except upon complaint of the aggrieved spouse.[17]

These exceptions have been mentioned because of their outstanding importance, but they are definitely exceptions since a criminal offense is a public wrong. The act which constitutes a crime may be also a private wrong such as larceny or battery, or may be a public wrong only, such as joining enemy forces in time of war or making fraudulent misstatements in an income tax return.

Insofar as an act constitutes a private wrong the injured individual is free to make a settlement with the wrongdoer, or to forgive him entirely without any reparation, so long as there is no agreement or understanding tending in any way to stifle or handicap a prosecution brought, or to be brought, on behalf of the public. But the general rule is that a private individual has no power to ratify, settle or condone a public wrong even if it was a wrong which injured his person or harmed his property; and if he is able to do so

---

13. 2 Pollock & Maitland, History of English Law 491 (2d ed. 1899). This seems to have disappeared after the second Statute of Westminster (1285). Ibid. From the time of the Conquest rape was not regarded as a felony unless prosecuted by the woman by way of appeal, but the appeal could be compromised and sometimes was compromised on the basis of a marriage. 3 Holdsworth, History of English Law 316 (5th ed. 1942).

14. State v. McKay, 122 Iowa 658, 98 N.W. 510 (1904). This would not be important if there was sufficient evidence of the rape without the testimony of the victim, but such is seldom the fact.

By marrying the witness before trial, and invoking the marital privilege, defendant could effectively preclude the state from calling her as a witness or using her testimony given at the preliminary hearing. State v. Jaques, 256 N.W.2d 559 (S.D.1977).

15. Tenn.Code Ann. § 39–1960 (1975). Under some of the statutes payment on written notice does not bar the prosecution but merely negatives the presumption of fraudulent intent. Cook v. Commonwealth, 178 Va. 251, 16 S.E.2d 635 (1941). See also 10 U.S.C.A. § 923a. Prima facie evidence of intent to defraud if payment is made within five days.

16. Tenn.Code Ann. § 39–4233 (1978).

17. Whether or not consent given by filing the complaint can be withdrawn later, so as to stop the prosecution, is discussed in State v. Allison, 175 Minn. 218, 220 N.W. 563 (1928). If only one of the guilty parties is married, prosecution may be brought against either or both by the injured spouse. Remarriage of husband and wife after divorce, even if the husband then has knowledge of the wife's adultery during the prior marriage, does not bar a complaint by the husband charging the unmarried paramour with adultery. State v. Smith, 108 Iowa 440, 79 N.W. 115 (1899).

it is only because of some exception to the general rule and in the exact manner provided.[18]

One who sells or removes a mortgaged chattel without consent and with intent to defraud the mortgagee may be convicted even if the latter has since ratified the act,[19] and the fact that an insurance company, to maintain good will, later issued policies with no charge for the initial premium, did not prevent conviction of one who had obtained money by fraudulently representing himself to be an agent of that company.[20] In the absence of any exception such as mentioned above the victim of rape cannot excuse the ravisher by ratifying or forgiving the act[21] or even by marrying him;[22] the owner of money or property, even after complete restitution has been made, cannot forgive the crime of larceny,[23] embezzlement,[24] or false pretenses;[25] and it is even beyond the power of a mother's love to wipe out the criminal guilt of an erring son who has forged her name to a note,[26] or maliciously burned her barn.[27] As said in *Breaker*:[28] "A father would naturally not be inclined to prosecute his own son. Any man might not be inclined to prosecute some neighbor or acquaintance who had stolen property, but it would be none the less a crime, and the state's obligation would be none the less to prosecute."

---

18. Commonwealth v. Heckman, 113 Pa.Super. 70, 172 A. 28 (1934).

The "misdemeanor compromise statute" A.R.S. § 13–3981 (1978) does not apply. The damage to another vehicle was only incidental to the crime of leaving the scene of an accident. Hence the fact that defendant reached a settlement with the driver of the other vehicle does not bar a prosecution for leaving the scene of an accident. State ex rel. Baumert v. Municipal Court, 125 Ariz. 429, 610 P.2d 63 (1980).

"A.R.S. § 13–3981 applies only when a misdemeanor offense invariably creates a civil cause of action." As this is not true of indecent exposure, it cannot be compromised. State ex rel. Baumert v. Superior Court, 130 Ariz. 256, 635 P.2d 849, 850 (1981).

19. May v. State, 115 Ala. 14, 22 So. 611 (1896).

20. Mitner (Jones) v. State, 100 Tex. Cr.R. 455, 273 S.W. 565 (1925).

21. Commonwealth v. Slattery, 147 Mass. 423, 18 N.E. 399 (1888).

The fact that the victim of an assault forgave the assailant did not bar a prosecution for the assault. State v. Brown, 74 Wn.2d 799, 447 P.2d 82 (1968).

D could be guilty of assault with intent to commit rape if the woman's consent was after the assault but before penetration. Such consent does not undo the previous wrongdoing. Copeland v. State, 55 Ala.App. 99, 313 So.2d 219 (1975), writ denied 294 Ala. 755, 313 So.2d 223.

22. State v. Newcomer, 59 Kan. 668, 54 P. 685 (1898); Huckaby v. State, 94 Okl.Cr. 29, 229 P.2d 235 (1951).

23. Breaker v. State, 103 Ohio St. 670, 134 N.E. 479 (1921); State v. Odom, 86 N.M. 761, 527 P.2d 802 (App.1974); Glassey v. Ramada Inn, 5 Kan.App.2d 121, 612 P.2d 1261 (1980).

If the victim's threat to call the police if the stolen property was not returned could be construed as a promise not to prosecute if it was returned, it was merely a personal representation and not binding on the state. State v. Keller, 114 Ariz. 572, 562 P.2d 1070 (1977).

24. Fleener v. State, 58 Ark. 98, 23 S.W. 1 (1893). The fact that an embezzler later offered to hand over the amount appropriated is no defense. People v. DeLay, 80 Cal. 52, 22 P. 90 (1889).

25. Donohoe v. State, 59 Ark. 375, 27 S.W. 226 (1894); Bruce v. State, 223 Ark. 357, 265 S.W.2d 956 (1954); Donald v. State, 453 S.W.2d 825 (Tex.Cr.App.1969).

26. State v. Tull, 119 Mo. 421, 24 S.W. 1010 (1893). "Ratification" by one whose name was forged is no defense. Countee v. State, 33 S.W. 127 (Tex.App.1895). State v. May, 93 Idaho 343, 461 P.2d 126 (1969).

"Second, the general rule is that subsequent ratification constitutes no defense to crime." People v. Lucero, __ Colo. App. __, 623 P.2d 424, 427 (1980).

27. State v. Craig, 124 Kan. 340, 259 P. 802 (1927).

28. Breaker v. State, 103 Ohio St. 670, 671–2, 134 N.E. 479, 480 (1921).

In a recent case it was emphasized that taking a 13-year-old child out of the state to conceal her from her parents was a crime against the state which neither the child nor the parents had power to forgive.[29]

The Model Penal Code does not deal with condonation by the injured party, probably because when legal and effective it is usually in the form of a compromise of the offense which is rather a matter of criminal procedure than of the substantive law.[30]

29. State v. Jackson, 72 Wn.2d 50, 431 P.2d 615 (1967). The fact that the taking was not for an immoral purpose was held not to establish innocence.

30. In misdemeanor cases, upon motion of the prosecutor, the court may dismiss the case if it is compromised by the defendant and the injured party. The injured party shall first acknowledge the compromise before the court or in writing. The reasons for the order shall be set forth therein and entered in the minutes. The order shall be a bar to another prosecution for the same offense; provided however, that dismissal by compromise shall not be granted when the misdemeanor is committed by or upon a peace officer while in the performance of his duties, or riotously, or with an intent to commit a felony. Utah Code Ann. 77–35–26(e), 1953 as amended.

Chapter 10

SPECIAL DEFENSES

SECTION 1. PUBLIC AUTHORITY

Nothing done under valid public authority is a crime if such authority is in no way exceeded or abused.

Deeds which otherwise would be criminal, such as taking or destroying property, taking hold of a person by force and against his will, placing him in confinement, or even taking his life, are not crimes if done with proper public authority. The typical instances in which even the extreme act of taking human life is done by public authority are (1) the killing of an enemy as an act of war and within the rules of war, and (2) the execution of a sentence of death pronounced by a competent tribunal.

Any unauthorized departure from the authority given destroys the privilege which otherwise would be present. Even in time of war an alien enemy may not be killed needlessly after he has been disarmed and securely imprisoned,[1] and no one other than the proper officer or his duly appointed deputy may lawfully execute the sentence of death,—"even though it be the judge himself." [2] If for example in a state in which the electric chair is used for capital punishment, and this method has been directed in the judgment, the officer in charge should discover that no electric current was available at the time set for execution and should shoot or hang the prisoner, he would be guilty of criminal homicide.[3]

"And, further, if judgment of death be given by a judge not authorized by lawful commission, and execution is done accordingly, the judge is guilty of murder. And upon this account Sir Matthew Hale himself, though he accepted the place of a judge of the common pleas under Cromwell's government (since it is necessary to decide the disputes of civil property in the worst of times,) yet declined to sit on the crown side at the assizes and try prisoners, having very strong objections to the legality of the usurper's commission; a distinction perhaps rather too refined, since the punishment of crimes is at least as necessary to society as maintaining the boundaries of property." [4]

1. "That it is legal to kill an alien enemy in the heat and exercise of war, is undeniable; but to kill such an enemy after he has laid down his arms, and especially when he is confined in prison, is murder." State v. Gut, 13 Minn. (Gil. ed.) 315, 330 (1868).

". . . an order to kill unresisting Vietnamese would be an illegal order, and that if Calley knew the order was illegal or should have known it was illegal,

obedience to an order was not a valid defense." Calley v. Callaway, 519 F.2d 184, 193 (5th Cir. 1975), cert. denied 425 U.S. 911, 96 S.Ct. 1505.

2. 4 Bl.Comm. *179.

3. "If an officer beheads one who is adjudged to be hanged, or *vice versa*, it is murder." Ibid.

4. Id. at 178.

Wilful abuse of authority will also destroy the privilege. Thus an obviously excessive flogging of a disobedient convict, by a guard, constituted criminal assault and battery.[5]

The exercise of public authority most commonly resulting in an application of force to the person of another is the making of an arrest, or the prevention of an escape by one already in lawful custody. A peace officer, or even a private person, may have authority to arrest a certain individual, and this authority is sometimes by virtue of a warrant and at other times without a warrant. At common law either officer or private person is privileged to arrest without a warrant for treason, felony or breach of the peace committed in his presence, except that arrest for a nonfelonious breach of the peace is not privileged without a warrant unless affected while the breach is being committed or on immediate and continuous pursuit thereafter.[6] At common law, moreover, either officer or private person is privileged, without a warrant, to arrest one who is reasonably believed to be guilty of felony with this important distinction: The officer is protected if he believes upon reasonable grounds (1) that a felony has been committed, and (2) that the arrestee is the guilty person; whereas for the protection of a private person it is necessary (1) that a felony has in fact been committed and (2) that he has reasonable grounds for believing the arrestee guilty of committing it.[7]

---

5. State v. Mincher, 172 N.C. 895, 90 S.E. 429 (1916).

6. United States v. Watson, 423 U.S. 411, 96 S.Ct. 820 (1976). See the scholarly analysis by Professor Wilgus in Arrest Without a Warrant, 22 Mich.L.Rev. 673 (1924). Compare Restatement, Second, Torts. §§ 119, 121 (1965).

A crime is committed within the presence of an officer, so as to authorize a warrantless arrest, when the facts and circumstances occurring within his observation, in connection with what under the circumstances may be considered common knowledge, give him probable cause to believe, or reasonable grounds to suspect that such is the case. City of Roswell v. Mayer, 78 N.M. 533, 433 P.2d 757 (1967).

Any of the police officers' sensory perceptions may provide probable cause to believe offense committed in his presence. People v. Alonzo, 87 Cal.App.3d 707, 151 Cal.Rptr. 192 (1979).

7. Ibid.; A.L.I. Code of Criminal Procedure, 236–40 (official draft with commentaries, 1931). Professor Hall has taken the position that the common law prior to the Revolution required an actual felony, plus reasonable cause to believe the arrestee guilty thereof, to authorize an arrest without a warrant by either an officer or a private person. Hall, Legal and Social Aspects of Arrest Without a Warrant, 49 Harv.L.Rev. 566 (1936).

Without doubt the generalizations of the early writers lend support to this theory, but Hall was unable to produce any early case in which an officer, having made an arrest on reasonable grounds for believing the arrestee guilty of felony, was held to have acted unlawfully because no felony had in fact been committed. In fact he cites an early case holding the arrest lawful without actual proof of the felony said to have been committed. Ward's Case, Clayt. 44 pl. 76 (N.P.1636), id. at 571, note 23. Probably the most that can be said is that some of the early writers were thinking of this requirement, but that when the point was actually raised in the cases it was held that a peace officer is not required to act at his peril on the question whether a felony has in fact been committed or not.

The New York Law, effective September 1, 1971, authorized a police officer to arrest for felony *or misdemeanor* if he had reasonable cause to believe **D** had committed it, even if not in his presence. McKinney's Consol.L.N.Y. § 140.-10 (1971).

"At common law, when a felony has actually been committed, a private citizen, acting in good faith, may lawfully arrest a person whom he reasonably believes to have committed the felony." United States v. Brown, 551 F.2d 639, 645 (5th Cir. 1977).

Under the general rule at common law a private person may arrest for a misdemeanor only if it constitutes a breach of the peace and is committed in his presence. Some states, however, have statutes that permit the owner or employee of a mercantile establishment to arrest for shoplifting committed in his presence.[8] And some states, without such statutes, have recognized such arrests at common law, as an exception to the general rule.[9] Thus in upholding such an arrest by a department store security officer, it was said: "The owner of a mercantile establishment or his employee may make a warrantless arrest of a thief who he has observed shoplifting, even though no breach of the peace has occurred." [10]

Under the English common law an officer arresting for felony who apprehended an innocent person was not justified unless he had probable ground to believe him guilty, but proof that the arrestee was in fact guilty of the felony charged was justification in itself.[11] This has sometimes been codified as in a statute providing that a peace officer "may, without a warrant, arrest a person; . . . (2) When a person arrested has committed a felony, although not in his presence. (3) Whenever he has reasonable cause to believe that the person to be arrested has committed a felony, whether or not a felony has in fact been committed." [12] At the present time, however, "An arrest is not justified by what the subsequent search discloses." [13] And the case law is such as to cast doubt upon the validity of a statute purporting to authorize an arrest without either a warrant or probable cause to believe the arrestee guilty.

Today the authority to arrest without a warrant is governed almost entirely by statute. The several different patterns resulting from the various

A peace officer, while outside his bailiwick, may make any arrest that a private person would be authorized to make. United States v. Brown, 551 F.2d 639 (5th Cir. 1977).

"Today's decision is the first square holding that the Fourth Amendment permits a duly authorized law enforcement officer to make a warrantless arrest in a public place even though he had adequate opportunity to procure a warrant after developing probable cause for arrest." United States v. Watson, 423 U.S. 411, 96 S.Ct. 820, 829 (1976). The quotation is from the concurring opinion of Mr. Justice Powell who emphasizes that this differs from a warrantless search which is authorized only in "exigent circumstances."

With reference to the statutory requirements before breaking in to make an arrest, it was said: "The announcement requirements of Penal Code section 844 are excused when there are reasonable grounds to believe that compliance would endanger the officers or frustrate arrest." People v. Amos, 70 Cal.App.3d 562, 139 Cal.Rptr. 30, 34 (1977).

8. People v. Zelinski, 24 Cal.3d 357, 155 Cal.Rptr. 575, 594 P.2d 1000 (1979);

State v. McDaniel, 44 Ohio App.2d 163, 337 N.E.2d 173 (1975).

9. Boquist v. Montgomery Ward & Co., Inc., 516 S.W.2d 769 (Mo.App.1974); State v. De Santi, 8 Ariz.App. 77, 443 P.2d 439 (1968).

10. State v. Gonzales, 24 Wn.App. 437, 604 P.2d 168, 169 (1979).

11. 2 Hale, P.C. *85. Even a private person was justified if the arrestee was in fact the felon. Id. at *78. And see State v. Williams, 14 S.W.2d 434, 435–36 (Mo.1929). And see Restatement, Second, Torts § 119, comment g (1965).

12. West's Ann.Cal.Pen.Code § 836 (1970).

13. Henry v. United States, 361 U.S. 98, 104, 80 S.Ct. 168 (1959).

"A valid arrest [without a warrant] must be based upon probable cause. Probable cause is a reasonable ground of suspicion, supported by circumstances sufficiently strong to warrant a cautious man to believe that an offense has been or is being committed by the person arrested." Scott v. People, 166 Colo. 432, 444 P.2d 388, 394 (1968).

PUBLIC AUTHORITY

Ch. 10

enactments have been summarized elsewhere[14] and here it must suffice to
say that the trend has been in the direction of enlarging this authority although at particular points it has been narrowed, apparently by inadvertence. In most states an officer is now authorized to arrest without a warrant for any offense, felony or misdemeanor, committed in his presence, and
in nearly half the states the same authority has been extended to a private
person.[15]

The place of arrest is of importance to a peace officer. The common law
authorized a peace officer to go beyond the boundaries of his bailiwick [16] in
fresh pursuit of one fleeing to avoid arrest,[17] and statutes sometimes authorize an officer to execute a warrant anywhere in the state, but apart from
some such exception, an officer has authority, as such, to make an arrest
only within his bailiwick. But when beyond such authority he has whatever
authority a private person would have. This was recently expressed by the
Colorado court.

> We conclude that the Denver police did not have authority, as peace
> officers, to arrest the defendant in Adams County because they were not
> in fresh pursuit and they did not have a warrant for the defendant's ar-
> rest.

> Nonetheless, a peace officer acting outside the territorial limits of his
> authority does not have less authority to arrest than a person who is a
> private citizen.[18]

And this, under Colorado law, includes authority to arrest for any offense
committed in his presence.[19] It should be emphasized in this connection that
if an officer makes an arrest in the capacity of a private person,[20] he is subject to whatever limitations and restrictions are placed upon such a person in
making an arrest.

In addition to the authority to make the arrest it is necessary to consider
the degree of force privileged for this purpose. Unless the arrester has authority to make the particular arrest any force to effect the apprehension is
unprivileged,[21] hence it is necessary to distinguish between the authority to

14. A.L.I. Code of Criminal Procedure
231–42 (official draft with commentaries,
1930).

15. Ibid.

16. In the early days a village was
called a "wick." Each village had a bailiff who was its peace officer. His authority was limited to the territory of the
wick. A bailiff was popularly referred to
as a "bailie," and before long a bailie's
wick was expressed as his "bailiwick."
And in time this word came to be used to
indicate the special territory over which a
peace officer exercises his authority as
such. Although it may be changed by
statute, the normal situation is that the
bailiwick of a policeman is his city, the
bailiwick of a sheriff is his county and
the bailiwick of a state officer, such as a
member of the Highway Patrol, is the
state.

17. The state cannot authorize its officer to go into another state to make an
arrest. If any officer has such authority
it must be found in the law of the state
into which he enters. The widely adopted Uniform Fresh Pursuit Law authorizes the officer of another state, in the
effort to arrest for felony on fresh pursuit, to enter the state and make the arrest. If this is done the officer must
turn the arrestee over to a local magistrate to await extradition proceedings.
See e.g. The Iowa Code of Criminal Procedure, ch. 806 (1978).

18. People v. Wolf, ___ Colo. ___, 635
P.2d 213, 216 (1981).

19. Ibid.

20. Stevenson v. State, 287 Md. 504,
413 A.2d 1340 (1980).

21. Even touching to effect an unlawful arrest is a battery so far as the law of

arrest and the authority to use force in accomplishing the arrest. The general rule is that an arrester is privileged to use reasonable force to make an authorized arrest, and this applies whether the arrester is an officer or a private person. It assumes lawful authority for the arrest itself and states in substance that in making or attempting such an arrest the arrester is privileged to make use of reasonable force and is not privileged to use any greater degree of force, except that for practical reasons the question is not whether the force used in a particular arrest exceeded the actual necessity of the case in some slight way but whether it was grossly excessive.[22]

When no flight or resistance is encountered or reasonably expected the arrester is not privileged to seize and collar his prisoner rudely and with violence.[23] In one case, for example, officers with a posse rushed upon an arrestee while he was quietly dining at a public hotel and violently threw him to the floor. As he was neither a desperate character nor reasonably supposed to be such, and there was no reason for such extreme measures in this case, the method of arrest was held to be clearly unlawful.[24] On the other hand even such measures would be privileged if they were reasonably necessary to accomplish the arrest of a dangerous offender without undue risk to the officers. Even striking a prisoner with a "billy" is justifiable when it is needed to subdue his persistent violence,[25] although this measure should be reserved for extreme situations and should be exercised with discretion;[26] and an arrester is never privileged to strike an unnecessary blow prompted merely by anger or annoyance.[27]

Of chief concern in this regard is the privilege of using deadly force in making or attempting an arrest, and for the moment there will be an exclusion of all cases in which the arrestee resists by the use of force because the problem there is self-defense, to be considered later. Another point requiring attention is that of accidental homicide. If an officer, having authority to arrest a misdemeanant, causes his death quite unexpectedly by tripping him, or by some other means neither intended nor likely to cause death or serious harm, the officer is completely absolved [28] because this is an uninten-

torts is concerned. Restatement, Second, Torts § 118, comment b (1965).

22. See State v. Fuller, 96 Mo. 165, 168, 9 S.W. 583, 584 (1888); Colorado v. Hutchinson, 9 F.2d 275, 276 (8th Cir. 1925); State v. Dunning, 177 N.C. 559, 562, 98 S.E. 530, 531 (1919).

"An officer of the law has the right to use such force as he may reasonably believe necessary in the proper discharge of his duties to effect an arrest. (citations omitted). Within reasonable limits the officer is properly left with the discretion to determine the amount of force required under the circumstances as they appeared to him at the time of the arrest." State v. Anderson, 40 N.C.App. 318, 253 S.E.2d 48, 50 (1979); Restatement of Torts 2d, §§ 132–135.

23. See State v. Mahon, 3 Del. 568, 569 (1839). If there is no resistance and no attempt to escape it is an assault for an officer to strike his prisoner and the

prisoner may use reasonable force to defend himself. State v. Belk, 70 N.C. 10 (1877).

24. Beaverts v. State, 4 Tex.App. 175 (1878).

25. State v. Phillips, 119 Iowa 652, 94 N.W. 229 (1903); State v. Pugh, 101 N.C. 737, 7 S.E. 757 (1888); State v. Yingling, 44 N.E.2d 361 (Ohio App.1942).

26. Striking with a billy with such force as to break a leg was held to be excessive. Kulczyk v. Board of Fire & Police Commissioners, 344 Ill.App. 555, 101 N.E.2d 626 (1951). See also State v. Foster, 60 Ohio Misc. 46, 396 N.E.2d 246, 14 O.O.3d 144 (1979).

27. Churn v. State, 184 Tenn. 646, 202 S.W.2d 345 (1947).

28. The King v. Smith, 17 Man.L.Rep. 282, 13 Can.Cr. 326, 330 (1907); cf. State v. Phillips, 119 Iowa 652, 94 N.W. 229 (1903).

tional killing without he use of deadly force. On the other hand shooting at another with intent to wound him is using deadly force even if there is no actual intent to cause his death.[29]

Under the common law the use of deadly force is never permitted for the sole purpose of stopping one fleeing from arrest on a misdemeanor charge,[30] and this applies whether the flight is to avoid an original apprehension,[31] or to effect an escape afterwards;[32] whether the arrest is in obedience to a warrant[33] or under general authority to arrest without a warrant;[34] and whether the arrestee is guilty[35] or innocent[36] of the misdemeanor for which the arrest is being made or attempted.

As explained by one court: "It is considered better to allow one guilty only of a misdemeanor to escape altogether than to take his life."[37] If, for example, an officer is unable to take alive one wanted for a violation of the speed law he is bound to let him go rather than kill him.[38] Deliberately to take the life of such a misdemeanant is murder,[39] and to shoot at the car with intent to stop the flight by disabling the vehicle has been held to be such criminal negligence as to support a conviction of manslaughter if death results.[40] The use of deadly force to stop the flight of one wanted only for a misdemeanor has been held not to be permitted even under a statute so worded as *seemingly* to authorize an officer acting under the command of a warrant to use whatever force may be needed to accomplish the arrest.[41]

29. "If a man fires at another only intending to wound, but actually causes death, he is guilty of manslaughter at least" unless justified in shooting. Smith, at 331, State v. Gray, 189 Kan. 398, 369 P.2d 330 (1962).

30. Johnson v. State, 173 Tenn. 134, 114 S.W.2d 819 (1938); Harding v. State, 26 Ariz. 334, 225 P. 482 (1924). Palmer v. Hall, 380 F.Supp. 120 (D.C.M.D.Ga. 1974) aff'd in part and rev'd in part on other grounds, 517 F.2d 705 (5th Cir. 1975) reh. denied 521 F.2d 815. And see other cases cited in the Tennessee Law of Arrest, 2 Vand.L.Rev. 509, 597, note 541 (1949).

31. Handley v. State, 96 Ala. 48, 11 So. 322 (1892); Fults v. Pearsall, 408 F.Supp. 1164 (D.C.Tenn.1975).

32. Thomas v. Kinkead, 55 Ark. 502, 18 S.W. 854 (1892). See Restatement, Torts 2d, §§ 134, 135.

33. Ibid. Owen v. State, 58 Tex.Cr.R. 261, 125 S.W. 405 (1911).

34. Klinkel v. Saddler, 211 Iowa 368, 233 N.W. 538 (1930).

35. State v. O'Neil, Houst.Cr. 468 (Del.Oyer & Ter. 1875); Garner v. State, ex rel. Askins, 37 Tenn.App. 510, 266 S.W.2d 358 (1953).

36. State v. Boggs, 87 W.Va. 738, 106 S.E. 47 (1921).

37. Reneau v. State, 70 Tenn. 720, 721 (1879).

38. People v. Klein, 305 Ill. 141, 137 N.E. 145 (1922).

39. Hill v. Commonwealth, 239 Ky. 646, 40 S.W.2d 261 (1931).

40. Klein, note 38.

41. Durham v. State, 199 Ind. 567, 159 N.E. 145 (1927); Johnson v. State, 173 Tenn. 134, 114 S.W.2d 819 (1938). A comparison of statutes is illuminating. For example: "When the arrest is being made by an officer under the authority of a warrant, after information of the intention to make the arrest, if the person to be arrested either flees or forcibly resists, the officer may use all necessary means to effect the arrest." West's Ann.Cal.Pen.Code § 843 (1970). "Homicide is justifiable when committed by public officers and those acting by their command in their aid and assistance, either— . . . When necessarily committed . . . in arresting persons charged with *felony*, and who are fleeing from justice. . . ." Id. at § 196. Emphasis added. See Long Beach Police Officers Association v. City of Long Beach, 61 Cal.App.3d 364, 132 Cal.Rptr. 348 (1976) rev'd 24 Cal.3d 238, 155 Cal.Rptr. 360, 594 P.2d 447 (1979). See Pearson, The Right to Kill in Making Arrests, 28 Mich.L.Rev. 957 (1930).

Quite different is the law with reference to arrests for felony. Firmly established in the common law of England was the privilege to kill a fleeing felon if he could not otherwise be taken,[42] a privilege extended to the private person as well as to the officer,[43] and not dependent upon the existence of a warrant for the felon's apprehension.[44]

No exception was recognized because the felon had forfeited his life under the original common law[45] and the "extirpation was but a premature execution of the inevitable judgment." [46] This reason would not apply to a person fleeing from a charge of felony of which he was in fact innocent, and the rule was not quite the same in such a case. If the arrest was being made by virtue of a warrant charging the commission of a felony and the person named therein fled so that he could not otherwise be overtaken the use of deadly force was privileged by either an officer or a private person.[47] If the arrest was on reasonable suspicion of felony thought to have been committed by the arrestee, who was in fact innocent, the officer was privileged to use deadly force if necessary to overtake the arrestee,[48] but a private person was not.[49] Arrest by a private person on reasonable suspicion of felony was unlawful even without the use of deadly force if in fact no felony had been committed, no matter how misleading the appearances may have been, and no force will be lawful if used to effect an unlawful arrest. If a felony had been committed in fact, but the arrestee was not guilty thereof, a private person was privileged to arrest him if he believed him guilty and had reasonable grounds for this belief, but deadly force by him was not permitted.[50] In other words according to the English common law a *private person* was nev-

---

42. "If a felony be committed and the felon fly from justice, . . . it is the duty of every man to use his best endeavours for preventing an escape; and if in the pursuit the felon be killed, where he cannot otherwise be overtaken, the homicide is justifiable." 1 East P.C. 298 (1803). Bircham v. Commonwealth, 239 S.W.2d 111 (Ky.1951).

In holding that a policeman was justified in shooting a suspect at the scene of a breaking and entering, when the suspect appeared to be about to attack him "or to flee from a lawful arrest into the night" it was said: "Under such facts, it is unnecessary to decide whether the elements of self-defense were present because the defendant was justified in shooting even in the absence of those elements." People v. Doss, 78 Mich.App. 541, 260 N.W.2d 880, 888 (1977).

Outlawry. The North Carolina statute on outlawry authorized the Judge to outlaw any person charged by affidavit with a felony if the accused evaded arrest. The law further authorized any person to kill the outlaw if he ran after being called upon to stop. This law (an echo of ancient law) was held to be unconstitutional. Autry v. Mitchell, 420 F.Supp. 967 (E.D.N.C.1976).

43. Ibid.; 2 Hale P.C. *118; 1 Hawk. P.C. c. 28, § 11 (6th ed. 1788).

44. 4 Bl.Comm. *292–3.

45. See Petrie v. Cartwright, 114 Ky. 103, 109, 70 S.W. 297, 299 (1902).

46. Note, 15 Va.L.Rev. 582, 583 (1929).

47. "And therefore the Sherife, bailife, or any other, that hath a warrant to arrest a man endicted of Felonie, may justify the killing of him, if otherwise they cannot take him." Lambard, Eirenarcha *238. Hale makes a similar statement without mention of indictment. 2 Hale P.C. *118.

48. 2 Hale P.C. *85–6, 93. If the one killed is not a felon "there must be these cautions. 1. He must be a lawful officer, or there must be a *hue* and *cry*, or there must be a lawful warrant." Id. at *118.

49. Id. at *78, 82–3.

"We find . . . that the law no longer allows a private person to use deadly force to arrest for every felony. . . . the felony must be one which reasonably creates a fear of great bodily injury." State v. Barr, 115 Ariz. 346, 565 P.2d 526 (App.1977).

50. Ibid.

er privileged to use deadly force merely to stop the flight of one he was seeking to arrest without a warrant, if that one was in fact innocent.[51]

It seems that this statement with reference to a private person is equally applicable in this country[52] and here, it should be added, the statutes usually require a warrant of arrest to be executed by a peace officer. While the authority of a private person to make an arrest without a warrant is very broad it is seldom exercised, and is not to be encouraged except in extreme situations. Furthermore, when a private person takes the enforcement of the law into his own hands it seems wise to let him understand that any use of deadly force by him for this purpose will be at his peril.

The Model Penal Code wisely would restrict the use of deadly force in making an arrest to one "authorized to act as a peace officer or . . . assisting a person whom he believes to be authorized to act as a peace officer." [53]

It is quite otherwise in the case of an officer who has the duty of enforcing the law imposed upon him for, while it is quite proper to require him to exercise reasonable care, it is most improper to require that in performing his duty he must "act at his peril." Unfortunately some courts in this country have held that an officer arresting on suspicion of felony does act at his peril in this regard,[54] but under the prevailing view, if the arrest itself is lawful and is for felony, the officer is privileged to use deadly force if this reasonably seems to be the only means by which the arrest can be accomplished.[55] As said by the Missouri court: [56]

51. "Arrest without a warrant" is used in the text to mean without any *special* authority to arrest. One who joined in the hue and cry for example had special authority and was privileged to use deadly force if this was necessary to stop the flight of the arrestee. "Hue and *cry* is the old common law process after felons. . . ." Id. at *98.

When a private person uses deadly force to prevent escape he must know that the other has committed a dangerous felony, or assisted in its commission. He acts at his peril if he acts on suspicion. Commonwealth v. Chermansky, 430 Pa. 170, 242 A.2d 237 (1968).

52. See State v. Rutherford, 8 N.C. 457, 458–9 (1821). For a summary of the statutes see A.L.I. Code of Criminal Procedure 188–9 (official draft with commentaries (1931).

Private person may not use deadly force to arrest felon unless arrestee is actually guilty. People v. Whitty, 96 Mich. App. 403, 292 N.W.2d 214 (1980).

Private person's authority, in making arrest for felony, to shoot or kill alleged felon, see generally 32 A.L.R.3d 1078 (1970).

53. Section 3.07(2)(b)(ii). See also State v. Ghiloni, 35 Conn.Sup. 570, 398 A.2d 1204 (1978).

54. Petrie v. Cartwright, 114 Ky. 103, 70 S.W. 297 (1902); Commonwealth v.

Duerr, 158 Pa.Super. 484, 45 A.2d 235 (1946). "The defendant Amis therefore had no right to shoot the plaintiff while he was in flight, unless the plaintiff had in fact committed a felony." Young v. Amis, 220 Ky. 484, 487, 295 S.W. 431, 432 (1927).

55. Vaccaro v. Collier, 38 F.2d 862 (D.C.Md.1930); Union Indemnity Co. v. Webster, 218 Ala. 468, 118 So. 794 (1928). The American Law Institute does not include guilt of the arrestee as a requisite for the use of deadly force in any case in which the arrest itself is lawfully authorized. Restatement, Torts § 131 and illus. 4 (1934). The Texas statute which tells the officer in substance that he must not shoot in making any arrest unless harm is threatened by the arrestee, while questionable as a measure of law enforcement is definitely preferable to a requirement that the officer act at his peril. Tex.Pen.Code art. 1212 (1925); Caldwell v. State, 41 Tex. 86 (1874).

The Tennessee statute, as construed, permits an officer to use deadly force to prevent the escape of one he is attempting to arrest if "(1) he reasonably believes that the person has committed a felony and (2) he notifies the person that intends to arrest him and (3) he reasona-

56. See note 56 on page 1101.

"If a sheriff or other peace officer arrest a person without a warrant, he will be justified in doing so although no felony be actually committed; it is sufficient if he have reasonable cause either on his own knowledge of facts, or on facts communicated to him by others, to suspect the one apprehended. And in thus arresting such suspected felon, or conveying him to the place of confinement, if the person arrested, or attempted to be arrested, in his endeavor to escape, kill the officer, the crime will be murder; but if the officer necessarily kill him when he resists, or endeavors to escape, the homicide will be altogether justifiable."

Elimination of most felonies from the category of capital crimes, coupled with the inclusion in the felony list of many misdeeds never punishable by death, has caused some to doubt the propriety of continuing the ancient rule which permitted any fleeing felon to be killed if he could not otherwise be overtaken.[57] Limitation of such force for this purpose to arrests for capital crimes would be too restrictive and has seldom been suggested; [58] the question has been whether it should be limited to the so-called "dangerous felonies" such as murder, manslaughter, arson, rape, robbery, burglary, mayhem, kidnapping and various types of felonious assault.

In the original Restatement of Torts the privilege of using deadly force to stop the flight of one whose arrest was being attempted was stated in terms of an arrest for "treason or for a felony which normally threatens death or serious bodily harm, or which involves the breaking and entry of a dwelling place. . . ." [59] However desirable such a position may be it is so obviously not a restatement of existing law that in the revision it is worded in terms of an arrest for "treason or a felony." [60]

References to a change of the original rule sometimes suggest a limitation to cases of dangerous felonies by legislative enactment,[61] and sometimes take the position that this limitation has already been accomplished by the gradual evolution of the common law itself. Cases venturing the latter suggestion have usually involved arrest by private persons,[62] and such a limita-

---

bly believes that no means less than such force will prevent the escape. The parties agree that, as so construed, the statute merely states the common law." Wiley v. Memphis Police Department, 548 F.2d 1247, 1251 (6th Cir. 1977).

56. State v. Evans, 161 Mo. 95, 110–111, 61 S.W. 590, 594 (1901).

57. Regina v. Murphy, 1 Cr. & Dix 20 (Ireland, 1839); State v. Bryant, 65 N.C. 327 (1871); Reneau v. State, 70 Tenn. 720 (1879).

58. Dean Mikell made this suggestion in regard to a proposed draft of a statute but had practically no support. 9 A.L.I. Proceedings 181 (1931).

59. Restatements, Torts § 131 (1934).

60. Restatement, Second, Torts § 131 (1965).

Mattis v. Schnarr, 547 F.2d 1007 (8th Cir. 1976), held the Missouri statutes on arrest, which codified the common law at this point, were unconstitutional. This opinion was vacated by the Supreme Court. Ashcroft v. Mattis, 431 U.S. 171, 97 S.Ct. 1739 (1977). Other federal courts have been unwilling to follow the Eighth Circuit's lead. Wiley v. Memphis Police Department, 548 F.2d 1247 (6th Cir. 1977) cert. denied 434 U.S. 822, 98 S.Ct. 65; Jones v. Marshall, 528 F.2d 132 (2d Cir. 1975).

61. See Reneau v. State, 70 Tenn. 720, 721–2 (1879); Officer's Right to Use Deadly Force to Arrest Fleeing Arrestee, 24 Iowa L.Rev. 154 (1938); Justifiable Use of Deadly Force by the Police: A Statutory Survey, 12 William & Mary L.Rev. 67 (1970); Day, Shooting the Fleeing Felon: State of the Law, 14 Crim.L. Bull. 285 (1978).

62. State v. Bryant, 65 N.C. 327 (1871); Regina v. Murphy, 1 Cr. & Dix 20 (Ireland, 1839); Commonwealth v. Klein, 372 Mass. 823, 363 N.E.2d 1313 (1977); Commonwealth v. Allen, 443 Pa. 15, 276 A.2d 539 (1971).

tion on the privilege of a private person acting merely "on his own authority" seems free from question. The law does not permit the use of deadly force for the mere purpose of *preventing* a nondangerous felony,[63] and a private person cannot defeat this restriction merely by saying his purpose is arrest rather than prevention.

As mentioned, the American Law Institute originally took the position that no one, officer or private person, with or without a warrant, is privileged to use deadly force merely to stop the flight of one whose arrest is sought for a nondangerous felony,[64] but it did so admittedly without the support of actual decisions[65] which seem to point the other way. Time and again the privilege of an officer to use deadly force if necessary to stop a fleeing felon has been announced with no mention of any limitation based upon the grade of the felony involved,[66] and often it has been in a case in which the apprehension was for a felony of the nondangerous grade, such as a violation of military discipline,[67] a violation of the prohibition law,[68] or larceny.[69] Since this position was first suggested by the Institute some cases have expressly repudiated the notion that the common law places any such limitation upon the privilege of an officer in making an arrest.[70]

63. One is not permitted to kill merely to prevent a thief from taking away his horse, even if the offense is a felony. Storey v. State, 71 Ala. 329 (1882).

The court assumes that the common-law rule authorizes a private person to kill to prevent the escape of a felon but announces that for the future the use of deadly force by a private person in order to prevent the escape of a felon is limited to felonies of "treason, murder, voluntary manslaughter, mayhem, arson, robbery, common-law rape, common-law burglary, kidnapping, assault with intent to murder, rape or rob, or a felony which normally causes or threatens death or great bodily harm." Commonwealth v. Chermansky, 430 Pa. 170, 242 A.2d 237 (1968).

64. Restatement, Torts § 131, and Illustration 1 (1934).

65. This position was taken in reliance upon *dicta* and upon the analogy drawn from the limitations placed upon the privilege to kill to prevent a felony. Bohlen & Shulman, Arrest With and Without a Warrant, 75 U. of Pa.L.Rev. 485, 494–504 (1927).

66. People v. Adams, 85 Cal. 231, 24 P. 629 (1890); Dilger v. Commonwealth, 88 Ky. 550, 560, 11 S.W. 651, 653 (1889); Life & Casualty Co. v. Hargraves, 169 Tenn. 388, 88 S.W.2d 451 (1935); Hendricks v. Commonwealth, 163 Va. 1102, 178 S.E. 8 (1935).

"[A]t common law an officer may use deadly force where necessary to apprehend the fleeing perpetrator of any felo-

ny." Clark v. Ziedonis, 513 F.2d 79, 82–83 (7th Cir. 1975).

67. United States v. Clark, 31 F. 710 (D.C.Mich.1887).

68. Ex parte Warner, 21 F.2d 542 (D.C.Okl.1927).

69. Johnson v. Chesapeake & Ohio Railway Co., 259 Ky. 789, 33 S.W.2d 521 (1935); Jackson v. State, 66 Miss. 89, 5 So. 690 (1888).

70. Stinnett v. Virginia, 55 F.2d 644, 646–7 (4th Cir. 1932); Thompson v. Norfolk & W. Ry., 116 W.Va. 705, 182 S.E. 880 (1935). Stinnett was decided prior to the adoption of the Torts Restatement, but the Institute had made a similar suggestion in another connection, and this was expressly referred to and held not to represent the common law. Thompson did not mention the Institute but held that such a position "is not the common law rule." Id. at 711, 182 S.E. at 883. See also Jones v. Marshall, 383 F.Supp. 358 (D.C.Conn.1974); Schumann v. McGinn, 307 Minn. 446, 240 N.W.2d 525 (1976).

"With respect to the principle of justification involved in the present case, the common law allowed the use of deadly force when necessary to secure the arrest of any felon, with no distinction made between those felonies which did or did not pose a threat of violence. In contrast, there was no right to use deadly force, even though necessary, to arrest a misdemeanant." State v. Sundberg, 611 P.2d 44, 48 (Alaska 1980).

When nothing is involved other than the effort to stop one in flight, it would seem wise to limit the use of deadly force, but this should be a matter of legislative action[71] and should not be adopted by a court in a decision which holds an officer guilty of crime for doing what was his legal duty at the time of performance.

One assisting an officer in making an arrest, at the officer's request, is not acting as a private person but in the capacity of a posse[72] because, despite the frequent use of the term to indicate a considerable group of persons called upon by an officer to aid him in the enforcement of law, the legal position is not dependent upon the number and an officer may summon a one-person posse.[73] One acting in such a capacity has the same protection as that accorded to the officer himself and may resort to the same measures,[74] and since one so called upon by an officer for assistance is guilty of a misdemeanor if he improperly refuses,[75] and is not entitled to delay while he conducts an inquiry into the officer's actual authority in the particular case,[76] he is protected even if the latter is actually exceeding his authority[77] so long as the assister does not know or have reason to know of the lack of authority.[78]

"A subordinate stands as regards the application of these principles, in a different position from the superior whom he obeys, and may be absolved from liability for executing an order which it was criminal to give. The question is, as we have seen, had the accused reasonable cause for believing in the necessity of the act which is impugned, and in determining this point a soldier or member of the posse comitatus may obviously take the orders of the person in command into view as proceeding from one who is better able to judge and well informed; and if the circumstances are such that the command may be justifiable, he should not be held guilty for declining to decide that it is wrong with the responsibility incident to disobedience, unless the case is so plain as not to admit of a reasonable doubt. A soldier, consequently, runs little risk in obeying any order which a man of common sense so placed would regard as warranted by the circumstances." [79]

The privilege of using deadly force had its common-law development primarily in the areas of law enforcement and crime prevention, and the extent of the development is not surprising since all felonies were punishable by death in those early days. As the felon had forfeited his life by the perpetration of his crime, it was quite logical to authorize the use of deadly force if this reasonably seemed necessary to bring him to justice. And as he would forfeit his life if the felony was accomplished it was equally logical to au-

71. Alaska Stats. 11.81.370 (1980); Del.Code tit. 11 § 467(c) (1974); Haw. Rev.Stat. tit. 37, § 703–307(3) (1976); Ky. Rev.Stat. § 503.090(2) (1975); Me.Rev. Stat. tit. 17A, § 107–2(B) (1975); Nev. Rev.Stat. § 28–839(3) (1975); Tex.Penal Code Ann. tit. 2, § 9.51(c) (1974); N.C. Gen.Stat. § 15A–401(d)(2)(b) (1975).

72. Robinson v. State, 93 Ga. 77, 83, 18 S.E. 1018, 1019 (1893).

73. Ibid.

74. See Commonwealth v. Fields, 120 Pa.Super. 397, 401, 183 A. 78, 80 (1936); Byrd v. Commonwealth, 158 Va. 897, 164 S.E. 400 (1932).

75. 1 Hale P.C. *588; 1 Bl.Comm. *343.

76. See Firestone v. Rice, 71 Mich. 377, 380, 38 N.W. 885, 886 (1888); McMahan v. Green, 34 Vt. 69 (1861).

77. Watson v. State, 83 Ala. 60, 3 So. 441 (1888); Dehm v. Hinman, 56 Conn. 320, 15 A. 741 (1887); Restatement, Second, Torts § 139(2), and Comment d (1965).

78. Ibid.

79. Commonwealth ex rel. Wadsworth v. Shortall, 206 Pa. 165, 175, 55 A. 952, 956 (1903).

thorize the use of deadly force if this reasonably seemed necessary to prevent its consummation. An appreciation of this background will aid in understanding the present state of existing law as well as the urgent need for modification.

The Model Penal Code would limit the use of deadly force to effect an arrest to a situation in which the arrest is for a felony, by an officer or one assisting an officer and in which

"the actor believes that the force employed creates no substantial risk of injury to innocent persons; and

the actor believes that

(1) the crime for which the arrest is made involved conduct including the use or threatened use of deadly force; or

(2) there is a substantial risk that the person to be arrested will cause death or serious bodily harm if his apprehension is delayed." [80]

Desirable as it is to limit the use of deadly force in making an arrest, the Code seems to go too far. For example, when an officer has to make a split-second decision in arresting for burglary or robbery he should not be required to stop to consider whether the felon had used or threatened to use deadly force or would cause death or serious bodily harm if the apprehension is delayed. Perhaps the limitation should be to an arrest for certain named felonies or for a felony perpetrated or attempted by the use or threatened use of deadly force.[81]

Worthy of note is the fact that shortly after the adoption of the Revised Penal Law of New York, which was patterned somewhat after the Model Penal Code in this respect, it was said:

"Legislative efforts are presently under way to modify several of its provisions, and passions are running high. The outcome of this legislative battle is bound to have a major impact on the law in many other states." [82]

---

80. Section 3.07(2)(b).

With reference to Model Penal Code § 3.07(2)(b) dealing with the use of deadly force in making an arrest, it was said: "As of 1978, seven states had enacted some version of the Code's approach, and a version of the Model Penal Code has been enacted in Alaska's new criminal code, which became effective January 1, 1980." State v. Sundberg, 611 P.2d 44, 49 (Alaska 1980). The court cited statutes from Delaware, Hawaii, Kentucky, Maine, Nevada, North Carolina and Texas.

The Detroit Free Press conducted a poll to determine whether or not the public favored some such plan. The result published June 30, 1980, was that over 82 percent were opposed to such a plan. This was not a scientific test and would have no significance had it been close, but with over four-fifths opposed it tends to indicate the opinion in that area.

81. For an argument against the limitations of the Code, see Model Penal Code pp. 60–63 (Tent. Draft No. 8, 1958).

82. 4 Criminal Law Bulletin 3 (1968). And see Trial 5 (Apr.-May 1968).

Much of the legal literature favors a more limited use of deadly force to effect an arrest or apprehend a fleeing law violator. The contention is made that the common standard is unconstitutional. See, e.g., Sherman, Execution Without Trial: Police Homicide and the Constitution, 33 Vand.L.Rev. 71 (1980); Mogin, The Policeman's Privilege to Shoot a Fleeing Suspect: Constitutional Limits on the Use of Deadly Force, 18 Am.Crim. L.Rev. 533 (1981); Use of Deadly Force in the Arrest Process, 31 La.L.Rev. 131 (1970); Deadly Force to Arrest: Triggering Constitutional Review, 11 Harv.Civil Lib.L.Rev. 361 (1976).

THE NEW PENAL CODES

Those of the new codes which have made specific provision for the use of deadly force by an officer, or one assisting an officer, in making or attempting an arrest, have differed widely. A few have provisions much like that of the Model Penal Code.[83] Some grant such authority if the arrest is for felony,[84] or for a forcible felony[85] or for a felony involving physical injury or violence.[86] And at least one has specifically defined "forcible felony" to include, among others, arson, robbery and burglary.[87] Some have a special provision for the guard or officer in charge of a jail, or other facility for the detention of prisoners convicted of, or charged with the commission of crime. He is authorized to use deadly force if it reasonably seems necessary to prevent the escape of such a prisoner.[88]

SECTION 2. DOMESTIC AUTHORITY

References may be found to an ancient authority of a husband to chastise his wife[1] with a "whip or rattan no bigger than my thumb, in order to inforce the salutary restraints of domestic discipline."[2] This was doubted in Blackstone's time[3] and is definitely not recognized in the modern common law.

Hence a husband who strikes his wife, even to enforce obedience to his just commands, is guilty of battery,[4] although he may use moderate force to *restrain* her from committing crimes or torts.[5] Wife-beating has sometimes been made punishable by express statutory provision, this being at times merely to emphasize the fact that it is unlawful, whereas in other codes it is to provide a special penalty for this type of battery. Most jurisdictions have dropped any special reference to a wife and punish the corporal abuse of any

83. E.g., Alabama, Colorado, Iowa, Kentucky and Maine.

84. E.g., Arkansas, Connecticut, Indiana, Minnesota, New Hampshire and Oregon

85. E.g., Illinois, Pennsylvania and Utah.

86. E.g., Delaware and North Dakota.

87. Utah.

88. E.g., Delaware, Florida, Illinois, Kentucky, Montana, North Dakota, Pennsylvania and Utah. A few limit this to the escape of a prisoner convicted of, or charged with, felony. E.g., Colorado and Minnesota.

1. "They refused to bind him to keep the peace at her suit unless her life be in danger, because by the law he hath the power of castigation; . . ." Bradley v. His Wife, 1 Keb. 637, 83 Eng.Rep. 1157 (1663).

2. Bradley v. State, Walker, 156, 157 (Miss.1824).

3. 1 Bl.Comm. *444–5.

4. Fulgham v. State, 46 Ala. 143 (1871). D slapped his wife who was drunk and insolent causing her to lose her balance and fall against a chair, receiving injuries from which she died. In affirming a conviction of manslaughter the court held there was no error in the judge's *refusal* to instruct that a husband has a right to administer due and proper chastisement to his wife. Commonwealth v. McAfee, 108 Mass. 458 (1871). "We may assume that the old doctrine that a husband had a right to whip his wife, provided he used a switch no larger than his thumb, is not law in North Carolina. Indeed, the courts have advanced from that barbarism until they have reached the position that the husband has no right to chastise his wife under any circumstances." State v. Oliver, 70 N.C. 60 (1874). And see Johnson v. Johnson, 201 Ala. 41, 44, 77 So. 335, 338 (1917); Bailey v. People, 54 Colo. 337, 130 P. 832 (1913).

5. See People v. Winters, 2 Park.Cr.R. 10 (N.Y.1823).

person by his or her spouse[6] and several states have enacted statutes for the prevention of domestic violence and protections of the victims.[7]

Firmly recognized in the law, however, is the right of the parent to discipline his minor child by means of moderate chastisement.[8] The right to correct an adopted child is the same as the right of a natural parent in this regard,[9] and this authority has been extended even to one who has taken a child into his home to be brought up as a member of the family without formal adoption.[10] Similarly a guardian may lawfully administer moderate chastisement for the correction of his ward.[11]

The common law authorized a master to punish his apprentice in the same manner,[12] but true apprenticeship was a special relation, and an employer has no authority to administer corporal punishment to an ordinary servant merely because the particular employee happens to be a minor.[13] The parent's authority to punish a minor child may be delegated to an employer, but the employer has no such privilege unless he has received permission from the parent.[14]

"By law as well as immemorial usage, a schoolmaster is regarded as standing in loco parentis, and, like the parent, has the authority to moderately chastise pupils under his care." [15] A statute, ordinance, or school-board regulation may restrict the privilege of the teacher in this regard, or may forbid the teacher to resort to corporal punishment in any form, but in the absence of such restriction the ordinary whipping of a pupil, for wilful disobedience of lawful rules, is not an assault and battery by the teacher, if administered for discipline and not in anger or with undue severity.[16]

An apparent diversity in the cases concerns the source of the teacher's authority to chastise the pupil. The English cases spoke of this as an authority which was delegated to the teacher by the parent,[17] and this was no doubt true in the private schools with which the cases were dealing. But this is definitely not the theory which applies to the public schools in this country.[18] In such schools the authority of the teacher is a quasi-public authority granted to him to enable him to maintain proper discipline in the school, and to give proper training to his pupils; hence it cannot be withdrawn by the parent, and in some cases may be broader than the authority of

---

6. West's Ann.Cal.Pen.Code § 273.5 (1977).

7. E.g. Mass.Gen.Laws C 208 § 34c (1978).

8. Richardson v. State Board, 98 N.J.L. 690, 121 A. 457 (1923). See discussion State v. Fischer, 245 Iowa 170, 60 N.W.2d 105 (1953); Restatement, Second, Torts § 147 (1) (1965).

9. State v. Koonse, 123 Mo.App. 655, 101 S.W. 139 (1907).

10. See the instruction in State v. Gillett, 56 Iowa 459, 9 N.W. 362 (1881).

11. Stanfield v. State, 43 Tex. 167 (1875).

12. 1 Bl.Comm. *428.

13. Tinkle v. Dunivant, 84 Tenn. 503 (1886). "The rule obtaining in this state is that a master has no authority to chastise his servant, no matter how flagrant his violation of duty may be." Cook v. Cook, 232 Mo.App. 994, 996, 124 S.W.2d 675, 676 (1939).

14. Cooper v. State, 67 Tenn. 324 (1874).

15. Roberson v. State, 22 Ala.App. 413, 414, 116 So. 317, 318 (1928). See discussion Ingraham v. Wright, 430 U.S. 651, 664, 97 S.Ct. 1401 (1977).

16. Danenhoffer v. State, 69 Ind. 295 (1879).

17. Per Collins, J., in Cleary v. Booth, [1893] 1 Q.B. 465.

18. State v. Mizner, 45 Iowa 248 (1876).

the parent himself.[19]　The authority of the teacher to enforce obedience to lawful rules, it has been held, is not limited strictly to violations occurring within the building or on school premises, but extends also to those committed by pupils going to or from school.[20]

The authority of a parent or teacher to punish a child will not justify immoderate punishment, and any excess of this nature will constitute an assault and battery;[21] but the test of unreasonableness in this regard should be found, not in some slight error of judgment as to the force to be used, but in the substitution of a malicious desire to inflict pain in place of a genuine effort to correct the child by proper means.[22]

Those in charge of trains, boats, theaters, stadia and similar places, while without authority to punish members of the public for misbehavior, may use reasonable and moderate force to expel a person who refuses to pay his fare or admission,[23] or is guilty of serious misconduct even after he had paid. But one with authority to remove such a person will be guilty of assault and battery if he does so improperly as by ejecting a passenger from a moving train.[24]

The Model Penal Code would authorize moderate chastisement of a minor by parent, guardian or teacher,[25] but with this difference: it limits the teacher to force he believes is necessary for the purpose of discipline, and so forth, whereas it permits the parent to use force which in his judgment is an appropriate corrective measure, without the requirement that it be deemed necessary.　The difference between a belief that corporal punishment is *necessary* for the maintenance of discipline and a use for the purpose of discipline, without a requirement of a belief in its necessity, may be more theoretical than actual in the matter of enforcement.

High-school students, who claimed to have been severely paddled for misconduct in school, brought a civil-rights action alleging a violation of their constitutional rights.　The Supreme Court held that the cruel-and-unusual-punishments clause of the Eighth Amendment applies only to punishments for violation of the criminal law and hence is inapplicable to school discipline. The wording of the Amendment was emphasized: "Excessive bail shall not be required, nor excessive fines imposed, nor cruel and unusual punishments inflicted."　It was recognized that due process is involved, but held that the traditional common-law remedies are fully adequate to afford due process. In other words, if a teacher or other school authority exceeds the bounds of reasonable discipline, he is subject to a civil action for damages and, if malice is shown, to criminal prosecution.　It was further held that due process does not require notice and hearing prior to the imposition of corporal punishment

---

19.　Ibid.　The court pointed out that under Iowa law girls become of age at eighteen but are permitted to attend public school until twenty-one, and while the father's privilege to inflict corporal punishment ends when the girl is eighteen, the teacher's authority to maintain discipline in the school is not so limited.　Baker v. Owen, 395 F.Supp. 294 (D.C.N.C. 1975), aff'd 423 U.S. 907, 96 S.Ct. 210.

20.　Cleary v. Booth, [1893] 1 Q.B. 465.

21.　State v. Mizner, 50 Iowa 145 (1878); Clasen v. Pruhs, 69 Neb. 278, 95 N.W. 640 (1903).

22.　See Boyd v. State, 88 Ala. 169, 172, 7 So. 268, 269 (1890).

23.　Carpenter v. Washington & G. R. Co., 121 U.S. 474, 7 S.Ct. 1002 (1887); Griego v. Wilson, 91 N.M. 74, 570 P.2d 612 (App.1977).

24.　State v. Kinney, 34 Minn. 311, 25 N.W. 705 (1885).

25.　Section 3.08.

in public schools.[26] The Court had previously held that a student must be given an informal opportunity to be heard before he is finally suspended from a public school.[27]

SECTION 3. PREVENTION OF CRIME

Important privileges overlap. They are the privilege (1) to intervene for the purpose of preventing the perpetration of crime and (2) to defend person or property. To the extent of the overlap both privileges are available to the one thus benefited. "It is not necessary that he should intervene solely for the purpose of protecting the public order or of protecting the private interests imperiled. His act, though a single one, may well be done for both purposes. If so, either privilege is available to him." [1]

As a matter of logic the chief emphasis of the criminal law in this regard should be upon intervention for the purpose of preventing crime, and any act done, or claimed to be done, within the protection of such a privilege should be discussed here. The fact that this would leave relatively little to such topics as self-defense, defense of others and defense of property, would not be an important consideration in and of itself, but since the major emphasis in this country has been upon these topics it seems advisable to follow the beaten path in this discussion. Hence the privilege to intervene for the prevention of crime will be barely introduced at this point with the understanding that it will be encountered again in the consideration of self-defense and related topics.

Perhaps it should be said that any unoffending person may intervene for the purpose of preventing the commission or consummation of any crime if he does so without resorting to measures which are excessive under all the facts of the particular case. No such statement has been found because, perhaps, the measures permissible for the prevention of minor misdemeanors are so mild as scarcely to require a privilege for their support.

In the absence of legislative authority, the privilege to intervene for the purpose of preventing the commission or consummation of a crime does not authorize the use of force in case of a misdemeanor which is not a breach of the peace.[2] In considering statutory enlargements of this field it is important to bear in mind that the "privilege to use force to prevent the commission of crime is usually coextensive with the privilege to make an arrest therefor without a warrant." [3] It is not uncommon for modern statutes to authorize either a peace officer[4] or a private person[5] to arrest without a war-

---

26. Ingraham v. Wright, 430 U.S. 651, 97 S.Ct. 1401 (1977). Four Justices joined in a dissent. They insisted that the Constitution forbids cruel and unusual punishment not only for crime but for any purpose whatever. They emphasized, however, that they would not hold spanking for misbehavior in public school to be unconstitutional if it was reasonable. They also disagreed with the holding that the due-process clause does not require notice and hearing prior to the imposition of corporal punishment in school. They said it does not require an "elaborate hearing" before a neutral party, but simply an "informal give-and-take between student and disciplinarian" which gives the student "an opportunity to explain his version of the facts." 430 U.S. at 693, 97 S.Ct. at 1423.

27. Goss v. Lopez, 419 U.S. 565, 95 S.Ct. 729 (1975).

1. Restatement, Second, Torts, Scope Note to c. 5, Topic 2 (1965).

2. Id. at § 140.

3. Id. at § 140, Comment a.

4. For example, West's Ann.Cal.Pen. Code § 836 (1970).

5. Id. at § 837.

rant for any public offense committed or attempted in his presence, and such an enactment *may* be held to make a corresponding enlargement in the field of crime prevention. No legislative authority is needed for the privilege other than that indicated above.

The common law recognizes the privilege to use force to prevent the commission or consummation, not only of a felony, but also of a misdemeanor amounting to a breach of the peace, such as assault and battery.[6] As to all such offenses the question is not whether force may be used but only under what circumstances and to what extent.

The use of deadly force for crime prevention is limited. Restricting attention for the moment to force neither intended nor likely to cause death or serious bodily harm, and to offenses within the general scope of the preventive privilege (whether by common law or by statutory enlargement), the following generalization may be offered: Any amount of such force is privileged to prevent the commission or consummation of such an offense if reasonably believed to be necessary for this purpose,[7] and if the reasonable use of such force should unexpectedly result in accidental death it does not constitute criminal homicide.[8] On the other hand the use of force, although not intended or likely to cause death or serious bodily harm, constitutes a battery if it is obviously in excess of that reasonably believed necessary for prevention.[9]

This leads to the more difficult part of the field which deals with the use of force intended or likely to cause death or great bodily injury. One privilege available to anyone, officer or private person, provided it has not been forfeited by misconduct, is that of using any force that reasonably seems necessary to prevent the perpetration or consummation of a dangerous felony.[10] Statements can be found to the effect that deadly force is privileged, if necessary, to "oppose another who is attempting to perpetrate *any felony*," [11] but as pointed out by the Alabama Court: [12]

"After a careful consideration of the subject we are fully persuaded that the rule, as thus stated, is neither sound in principle, nor is it supported by

---

6. Ward v. De Martini, 108 Cal.App. 745, 292 P. 192 (1930); Spicer v. People, 11 Ill.App. 294 (1882). As so used a "breach of the peace" means a public offense done by violence or one causing or likely to cause an immediate disturbance of public order. Restatement, Second, Torts § 116 and § 140, comment a (1965).

7. Restatement, Second, Torts §§ 141–143 (1965).

8. Morgan v. Durfee, 69 Mo. 469 (1897); Hinchcliffe's Case, 1 Lewin 161, 168 Eng.Rep. 998 (1823).

9. Wild's Case, 2 Lewin 214, 168 Eng. Rep. 1132 (1837).

10. The Institute words the privilege of using deadly force for crime prevention in terms of a felony "of a type threatening death or serious bodily harm

or involving the breaking and entry of a dwelling place." Restatement, Second, Torts § 143(2) (1965).

"A person is justified in the use of force likely to cause death or serious bodily harm only if he reasonably believes that such force is necessary . . . to prevent the commission of a forcible felony." State v. Sunday, ___ Mont. ___, 609 P.2d 1188, 1195 (1980).

11. 1 Bishop, New Criminal Law § 849 (8th ed. 1892). Emphasis added.

12. Storey v. State, 71 Ala. 329, 339 (1882). Emphasis in the text has been added. And see State v. Sorrentino, 31 Wyo. 129, 137–8, 224 P. 420, 422 (1924).

Killing is justified only to prevent a forcible felony. Washington v. State, 245 Ga. 117, 263 S.E.2d 152 (1980).

the weight of modern authority. The safer view is . . . that the rule *does not authorize the killing of persons attempting secret felonies, not accompanied by force,*" but is limited to some *"atrocious crime* attempted to be *committed by force;* such as murder, robbery, house-breaking in the night-time, rape, mayhem, or any other act of felony against the person . . . and such seems to be the general expression of the common law text writers."

The felonies listed in this quotation, it should be emphasized, are illustrative rather than exhaustive; arson is commonly included in such a category,[13] and certain others such as kidnaping should be. The so-called "dangerous" felonies, in other words, are those that either directly involve great personal harm (such as murder, mayhem or rape), or have been shown by human experience to involve an unreasonable risk thereof (such as robbery, burglary or arson). "In all these felonies," it has been said, "from their atrocity and violence, human life is, or is presumed to be in peril. . . ." [14] Included moreover, are all felonies fitting the description whether known to the common law or added by statute.[15]

Blackstone said that the law would not "suffer with impunity any crime to be *prevented* by death, unless the same, if committed, would also be *punished* by death," [16] but he was merely offering his own rationalization of the rule at a time when all felonies were capital. It is clear "that the felony *need not be a capital one* to come within the scope of the rule," [17] and an instruction in terms of such a limitation is reversible error.[18]

On the other hand, except where the law has been modified by statute,[19] deadly force is not permitted for the purpose of preventing a nondangerous

---

13. See United States v. Gilliam, 25 Fed.Cas.No.15,205a, at 1320 (C.C.D.C. 1882); State v. Nyland, 47 Wn.2d 240, 287 P.2d 345 (1955); State v. Marfaudille, 48 Wash. 117, 121, 92 P. 939, 941 (1907).

14. Ibid. Blackstone spoke of the *"prevention* of any forcible and atrocious *crime.* . . ." 4 Bl.Comm. *180.

The statutory authority to use deadly force against one who manifestly intends by violence to commit a felony does not give carte blanche to shoot one who is committing a felony, but only to prevent great bodily injury. State v. McIntyre, 106 Ariz. 439, 477 P.2d 529 (1970).

15. "It seems settled that no distinction can be made between statutory and common law felonies, whatever may be the acknowledged extent of the rule." Storey v. State, 71 Ala. 329, 341 (1882). Accord, Moore v. State, 91 Tex.Cr.R. 118, 237 S.W. 931 (1922).

16. Bl.Comm. *182.

17. Storey v. State, 71 Ala. 329, 338 (1882).

18. State v. Marfaudille, 48 Wash. 117, 92 P. 939 (1907).

19. Ariz.Rev.Stat. § 13–411 (1978). "A person is justified in threatening or using both physical force and deadly physical force against another if and to the extent a reasonable person would believe the physical force or deadly physical force is immediately necessary to prevent the other's commission of arson of an occupied structure under § 13–1704, burglary in the second or first degree under § 13–1507 or 13–1508, kidnapping under § 13–1304, manslaughter under § 13–1103, second or first degree murder under § 13–1104 or 13–1105, sexual assault under § 13–1406, child molestation under § 13–1410, armed robbery under § 13–1904, or aggravated assault under § 13–1204, subsection A, paragraphs 1 and 2."

felony[20] and it is criminal to shoot at a thief, who is not himself threatening any violence, even if the larceny cannot be prevented by any other means.[21]

Although it is possible to find an occasional suggestion indicating otherwise,[22] the reasonable mistake of fact doctrine applies to such cases and the privilege to use force, and the degree of permissible force, are determined not by the actual facts in this regard, but by the reasonable belief of the intervenor as to the crime being committed or attempted and the force needed for its prevention.[23] On the other hand an obviously unnecessary killing will not be excused even if the deceased was attempting to commit an atrocious felony at the time.[24]

For a clear understanding of the privilege next to be considered, it is important to keep in mind that under the English common law one, who was himself free from fault, was authorized to use deadly force if this reasonably seemed necessary to prevent the commission of a dangerous felony such as murder, arson, rape, robbery or burglary; and that this was regarded one of the major privileges so far as the use of deadly force was concerned.

The common law also recognized the right to use deadly force in suppressing a riot or rebellion.[25] Some states and the Model Penal Code have also[26] provided for the use of deadly force in suppressing riots.[27]

The Model Penal Code[28] would authorize the use of reasonable nondeadly force to prevent the commission or consummation of any crime involving or threatening bodily harm, damage to or loss of property or a breach of the peace. This goes a little beyond the authority of the common law[29] but not beyond the statutory trend.[30] On the other hand, except where necessary to suppress a riot or mutiny, the use of deadly force would be limited to situations in which the actor believes there is a substantial risk that the other will

---

20. "In any event . . . the taking of life cannot be justified on the ground that it was necessary to prevent the commission of a mere theft. The crime sought to be prevented must involve the security of the person or home, or contain an element of force or violence." Kinder v. Commonwealth, 263 Ky. 145, 147–8, 92 S.W.2d 8, 9 (1936). And see McNabb v. United States, 123 F.2d 848 (6th Cir. 1941); State v. Powers, 117 Ariz. 220, 571 P.2d 1016 (1977).

21. Ibid.; State v. Storey, 71 Ala. 329 (1882); Commonwealth v. Emmons, 157 Pa.Super. 495, 43 A.2d 568 (1945).

22. See the *dictum* in Mitchell v. State, 22 Ga. 211, 234 (1857). Cf. State v. Beal, 55 N.M. 382, 234 P.2d 331 (1951).

23. Spicer v. People, 11 Ill.App. 294 (1882).

24. Tolbert v. State, 31 Ala.App. 301, 15 So.2d 745 (1943); Cobb v. State, 376 So.2d 230 (Fla.1979).

25. Turner, I Russell on Crime. 12th ed. p. 268 (1964); Clark and Marshall, Crimes, 7th ed. p. 473 (1967). ". . . the intentional infliction of death or bodi-

ly harm is not a crime when it is done either by justices of the peace, peace officers, or private persons, whether such persons are, and whether they act as, soldiers under military discipline or not for the purpose of suppressing a general and dangerous riot which cannot otherwise be suppressed." Stephen, A Digest of the Criminal Law, 5th ed., 157–158 (1894).

26. West's Ann.Cal.Penal Code § 197 (1970); West's Fla.Stat.Ann. § 870.04 (1976).

27. § 3.07(5).

28. Section 3.07(5).

29. For example, if malicious mischief was about to be committed in a manner not involving an actual breach of the peace or personal harm, one having no interest in the property would not be privileged, at common law, to use force to prevent the crime.

30. See the reference in the text, supra, to the effect of statutes authorizing a private person to arrest for any public offense committed in his presence.

cause death or serious harm unless the crime is prevented. If it reasonably seems necessary to save his home from being burned to the ground, the dweller is privileged at common law to shoot the arsonist even if the dweller is on the outside and no personal danger is being threatened to him. He would not have this privilege under the Code. At common law, but not under the Code, a bank messenger carrying $25,000 in a briefcase would be privileged to shoot if necessary to prevent being robbed, even if the robbers, by superior strength and numbers, would be able to take the money without causing any serious injury to him and assured him that they would not hurt him in any way.[31]

Undoubtedly the privilege of using deadly force in crime prevention is too broad under prevailing law, but the Code seems to go too far in restricting it.

THE NEW PENAL CODES

The effort of those who drafted the Model Penal Code to de-emphasize crime prevention as a source of privilege to use force upon the person of another, has been very effective. The new codes tend to deal with the prevention of murder, manslaughter and other offenses against the person, under the headings of self-defense and defense of another. This is desirable legislation although, as mentioned above, under the common law of England the privilege of using force in crime prevention was one of the major privileges, particularly as to the use of deadly force; and as will be emphasized presently, self-defense was a secondary privilege developed to give some protection to a person who was too much at fault to be entitled to exercise the privilege of crime prevention. And the privilege of defending another (as distinguished from the privilege of crime prevention) was very limited indeed at common law. The new penal codes have very properly followed the lead of the Model Penal Code to this extent. But most of them seem to have been drafted on the theory that the Model Penal Code is unduly restrictive in the authority to use deadly force in crime prevention. A very few are patterned closely after the Model Penal Code on crime prevention,[32] but most of them have found it important to authorize the use of deadly force in certain other situations, such as where it reasonably seems necessary to prevent arson,[33] burglary,[34] kidnaping,[35] rape,[36] robbery,[37] or a forcible felony.[38] And at least one has taken pains to insure that the term "forcible felony" will receive its common-law interpretation by expressly providing that as used in these statutes it "also includes arson, robbery and burglary." [39]

31. Section 3.04. Use of Force in Self-Protection, has a similar limitation on the use of deadly force.

In explaining the effect of sections 3.04 and 3.07 it was said: "Thus deadly force may be employed if necessary to prevent a robbery provided that the victim is in danger of death or serious harm." Model Penal Code 67 (Tent.Draft No. 8, 1958).

32. E.g., Hawaii and Pennsylvania. A threat to use deadly force, intended only as a bluff, is not deadly force. State v. Realina, 1 Haw.App. 167, 616 P.2d 229 (1980).

33. E.g., Alabama, Arkansas, Colorado, Connecticut, Kentucky, New Hampshire, Oregon and Texas.

34. E.g., Arkansas, Connecticut, Georgia, Illinois, Indiana, Kentucky, Minnesota and New York. Texas includes theft at night.

35. E.g., Colorado and Texas.

36. E.g., Colorado, Kentucky and Texas.

37. E.g., Colorado, Maine and Texas.

38. E.g., Arkansas, Florida, Georgia, Illinois, Indiana, Montana and Utah.

39. Utah.

SECTION 4.　SELF–DEFENSE*

In considering the law of self-defense it is particularly important to keep in mind the distinction between deadly force (force intended or likely to cause death or great bodily harm) [1] and nondeadly force (force neither intended nor likely to do so). It is also important to distinguish force which is reasonable from that which is unreasonable. Deadly force and reasonable force are neither mutually exclusive nor collectively exhaustive. Deadly force is unreasonable if nondeadly force is obviously sufficient to avert the threatened harm,[1.5] but may be entirely reasonable under other circumstances. And even nondeadly force is unreasonable if it is obviously and substantially in excess of what is needed for the particular defense.[2]

There are some indications of an original requirement of actual necessity,[3] but they seem to be false conclusions drawn from incomplete generalizations. They clearly do not represent the modern common law of self-defense.[4] At the other extreme is an occasional holding to the effect that if the other requirements are satisfied, the defender will be excused if he acted from an honest belief in the greatness and imminence of his peril.[5] This was too broad a position and hence the limitation was added that this belief must be based upon reasonable grounds.[6] The reasonable belief of the defender

* Whether the claim is defense of self or others or of property, it is always necessary to distinguish defensive force from punitive force. The latter is never justified. Commonwealth v. Monico, 373 Mass. 298, 366 N.E.2d 1241 (1977).

1. "We define deadly force as force likely to cause death or great bodily harm." State v. Clay, 297 N.C. 555, 256 S.E.2d 176, 182 (1979). Hitting another with a baseball bat with sufficient force to break his arm, is the use of deadly force. State v. Napoleon, ___ Haw.App. ___, 633 P.2d 547 (1981).

1.5 Etter v. State, 185 Tenn. 218, 205 S.W.2d 1 (1947).

2. People v. Moody, 62 Cal.App.2d 18, 143 P.2d 978 (1943); Restatement, Second, Torts § 70 (1965). A kick is not a justifiable method of turning a trespasser out of the house. Wild's Case, 2 Lewin C.C. 214, 168 Eng.Rep. 1132 (1837). Force may be unreasonable although no weapon is used. State v. Wilson, 196 Wash. 534, 83 P.2d 749 (1938). Use of excessive force constitutes battery. Coleman v. State, 320 A.2d 740 (Del.1974).

3. Scott v. State, 203 Miss. 349, 34 So. 2d 718 (1948); Regina v. Smith, 8 Car. & P. 160, 173 Eng.Rep. 441 (1837); Regina v. Bull, 9 Car. & P. 22, 173 Eng.Rep. 723 (1839).

4. Pond v. People, 8 Mich. 150 (1860); Logue v. Commonwealth, 38 Pa. 265 (1861).

The requirement is reasonable belief. State v. Realina, 1 Haw.App. 167, 616 P.2d 229 (1980).

5. Granger v. State, 13 Tenn. 459 (1830).

6. People v. Syed Shah, 91 Cal.App.2d 722, 205 P.2d 1077 (1949); Morgan v. State, 35 Tenn. 475 (1856). The question is not the actuality of imminent danger but the reasonable apprehension thereof. Harris v. State, 96 Ala. 24, 11 So. 255 (1891); State v. McGreevey, 17 Idaho 453, 105 P. 1047 (1909); State v. Howard, 14 Kan. 173 (1875); People v. Kennedy, 159 N.Y. 346, 54 N.E. 51 (1899); State v. Daw, 99 Mont. 232, 43 P.2d 240 (1935); Haines v. State, 275 P.2d 347 (Okl.Cr. 1954).

If the slayer honestly but unreasonably believes his life to be in danger and kills in what he assumes to be necessary self-defense, he is guilty of manslaughter rather than murder. Allison v. State, 74 Ark. 444, 86 S.W. 409 (1904); Popps v. State, 120 Fla. 387, 162 So. 701 (1935). This seems to be much more sound than the assumption that in such situations there is no midway ground between guilt of murder and innocence.

There is a trace of authority to the contrary. See State v. Cope, 78 Ohio App. 429, 67 N.E.2d 912 (1946); Teal v. State, 22 Ga. 75, 84 (1857). This was no doubt due to a failure to recognize the possibility of criminal liability less than murder in such a case.

under the circumstances as they appear at the moment is both necessary and sufficient for this aspect of the privilege of self-defense.[7] The question is not whether the jury believes the force used was necessary in self-defense, but whether the defendant, acting as a reasonable person had this belief.[8] One who invokes the privilege of self-defense is neither limited by, nor entitled to the benefit of, unknown factors. One who has knocked down another, in the reasonable belief that this was necessary to prevent being stabbed, is not guilty of battery because it is later learned that the other intended no harm but was merely playing too realistic a joke with a rubber dagger.[9] On the other hand, proof that a fatal shot actually saved the life of the slayer is no defense if he fired in cold blood while utterly unaware of the impending danger.[10] Two cautions should be added: (1) A bona-fide belief which is correct will not be held to be unreasonable merely because the defender is unable to paint a word-picture explaining exactly how he knew what the real facts were.[11] (2) The danger must be, or appear to be, pressing and urgent. A fear of danger at some future time is not sufficient.[12]

A person is not entitled to use all the force which he believes to be necessary to repel an attack if his belief is unreasonable. State v. Bius, 23 Wn.App. 807, 599 P.2d 16 (1979). State v. Sunday, ___ Mont. ___, 609 P.2d 1188 (1980).

7. People v. Anderson, 44 Cal. 65 (1872); People v. Toledo, 85 Cal.App.2d 577, 193 P.2d 953 (1948); Territory v. Yadas, 35 Hawaii 198 (1939); Weston v. State, 17 Ind. 324, 78 N.E. 1014 (1906); State v. Anderson, 230 N.C. 54, 51 S.E.2d 895 (1949); United States v. Ah Chong, 15 Philippine 488 (1910). One whose life has been threatened by another, and who sees that other apparently reaching for a weapon, may shoot in self-defense although the other does not have a weapon in hand or in sight at the moment. Lomax v. State, 205 Miss. 635, 39 So.2d 267 (1949). As to the rule under the Texas statute see Brown v. State, 152 Tex.Cr.R. 440, 214 S.W.2d 792 (1948).

"Fear alone is not enough to justify one person to take the life of another. Such fear must have been induced by some overt act, gesture, or word spoken by the deceased at the time the homicide occurred which would form a reasonable ground for the belief of the accused that he is about to suffer death or great bodily harm." West v. State, 617 P.2d 1362, 1365–66 (Okl.Cr.App.1980).

8. People v. Miller, 403 Ill. 561, 87 N.E.2d 649 (1949); Wireman v. Commonwealth, 290 Ky. 704, 162 S.W.2d 557 (1942).

"In determining whether the defendant acted in necessary self-defense or what appeared to her necessary self-defense, it is your duty to look at the transaction from what you believe from the evidence was the standpoint of the defendant as a reasonable person at the time, and consider the same in the light of the facts and circumstances as you believe they appeared to the defendant as a reasonable person at the time. . . ." This was a proper instruction. State v. Anderson, 102 Ariz. 295, 428 P.2d 672, 674 (1967).

The belief is measured by an objective test. State v. Eddington, 95 Ariz. 10, 386 P.2d 20 (1963).

It was held "that the provisions of the new criminal code were not intended to abrogate common law self-defense requirements. . . . Therefore, the court's instruction can stand only if it included the essential element that the person using the force need only reasonably believe, in the light of all the facts and circumstances known to him, that he or another person is in danger." State v. Fischer, 23 Wn.App. 756, 598 P.2d 742, 744 (1979).

9. Restatement, Second, Torts, § 63, illus. 5 (1965). People v. White, 87 Ill. App.3d 321, 42 Ill.Dec. 578, 409 N.E.2d 73 (1980).

10. Trogdon v. State, 133 Ind. 1, 32 N.E. 725 (1892); Josey v. United States, 77 App.D.C. 321, 135 F.2d 809 (1943); Restatement, Second, Torts, § 63, comment f (1965).

11. The American Law Institute has stated this result in other words: ". . . correctly or reasonably believes. . . ." Restatement, Second, Torts §§ 63(1)(a), 70(1) (1965).

12. People v. Lombard, 17 Cal. 316 (1861); State v. Schroeder, 103 Kan. 770, 176 P. 659 (1918).

For convenience of expression the word "threaten" is used herein in its broadest sense. It is to be understood to include not only a declaration of intention to do harm but also an ominous indication of harm by gestures or other appearances.

With this introduction the following generalization may be offered: One who is himself free from fault [13] is privileged to use force in the effort to defend himself against personal harm threatened by the unlawful act of another if the force he uses for this purpose is not unreasonable under all the circumstances. This does not cover the entire field of self-defense. And it requires elaboration. The test, let us repeat, is not the actuality of impending harm nor the actual amount of force needed to prevent it. The reasonable belief of the defender is controlling in both respects. What harm did he reasonably believe was impending and what amount of force did he reasonably believe necessary to overcome it? [14] And in the excitement of the moment he is not required to judge these matters with precise calculations. [15]

Although at common law the unnecessary use of force, believed to be necessary in self-defense, is not excusable if the belief was unreasonable, this is not always a complete explanation of the situation. For example, if deadly force had been used in such a belief, with fatal consequences, the slayer is not guilty of murder, because there was no malice aforethought, but as the killing is not excusable it is manslaughter. [16] "A self-defense and a voluntary manslaughter instruction should be given when any evidence is given showing the defendant's subjective belief that the use of force was

13. One whose unlawful act has created the necessity of acting in self-defense has no legally recognized privilege to do so. State v. Gregory, 79 Wn.2d 637, 488 P.2d 757 (1971). A robber who shot and killed his intended victim has no claim of self-defense even though the victim, in defense, had fired first. Daniel v. State, 187 Ga. 411, 1 S.E.2d 6 (1939). "The law of self-defense is designed to afford protection to one who is beset by an aggressor and confronted by a necessity not of his own making." Loesche v. State, 620 P.2d 646, 651 (Alaska 1980).

14. Acers v. United States, 164 U.S. 388, 17 S.Ct. 91 (1896); People v. Holt, 25 Cal.2d 59, 153 P.2d 21 (1944); Cook v. State, 194 Miss. 647, 12 So.2d 137 (1943); Shorter v. People, 2 N.Y. 193 (1849); Restatement, Second, Torts § 63, comments i and j (1965). This is subject to the previous explanation in the text in reference to a correct belief.

15. Sikes v. Commonwealth, 304 Ky. 429, 200 S.W.2d 956 (1947). "In the heat of blood he could hardly be expected to . . . . measure or count his blows or shots very carefully." Taylor v. Clendening, 4 Kan. 524, 535 (1868). Most famous of all such statements is that of Mr. Justice Holmes: "Detached reflection cannot be demanded in the presence of an uplifted knife." Brown v. United States,

256 U.S. 335, 343, 41 S.Ct. 501, 502 (1921).

"When one is threatened by a person who carried out his threats on a previous occasion, he does not have much time to reason out his response or judge precisely how much force is necessary to repel the threatened attack. While it is true he cannot take the law into his own hands, we must bear in mind that a person placed in such a position is not in a contest governed by established rules enforced by an on-the-scene umpire. Consequently, the law does not charge a person, when he has reasonable grounds to believe himself in apparent danger of losing his life or suffering great bodily injury, to use inerrable judgment. It would be unreasonable to require such an exacting decision to be made in the space of a few seconds while one is fearful and under great stress.

"The question in a case such as this is whether on the basis of quickly unfolding events the defendant's response was reasonable under the exigencies that existed at the moment." People v. White, 87 Ill. App.3d 321, 42 Ill.Dec. 578, 580, 509 N.E. 2d 73, 75 (1980). See also, Commonwealth v. Fisher, 491 Pa. 231, 420 A.2d 427 (1980).

16. People v. Flannel, 25 Cal.3d 668, 160 Cal.Rptr. 84, 603 P.2d 1 (1979).

necessary. If the subjective belief is reasonable, the result is justifiable use of force; if the subjective belief is unreasonable, the result is voluntary manslaughter."[17] For the provision of the Model Penal Code, adopted in some of the new penal codes, see supra chapter 2, section 1, C, a, (B).

In applying the broad generalization to a particular case it is important to determine the type of force against which the defender was attempting to guard himself, and also the type of force he employed in the effort. And for classification purposes the second of these is the logical starting point. An attack with deadly force is likely to require deadly force for defense, but this is not necessarily so. And if the defender is able to save himself from harm by the use of nondeadly force, the case is dealt with in that category whether the threatened harm was deadly or nondeadly.

The law of self-defense makes use of (1) rules, and (2) the reasonable-person standard. The court determines what the rules are, but it is for the jury to determine whether the standard has been met by the evidence in the particular case. It is a rule of law that deadly force may not be used to defend against nondeadly force, but that nondeadly force may be used to defend against any unlawful force endangering the person, provided the force so used is not unreasonable under all the circumstances. In such a case, if the only threat was with obviously nondeadly force and the jury finds that defendant used deadly force to defend against it, the inquiry should go no farther. The instruction will be that the defendant is guilty upon such a finding. If the jury finds that the defendant used only nondeadly force in his defense, a further finding is necessary; namely, whether the force thus used was reasonable under the circumstances. And if the finding is that defendant used no more force than a reasonable person would have used in a similar situation, the verdict should be not guilty.

A. NONDEADLY FORCE

One who is himself free from fault[18] is privileged to use nondeadly force in self-defense whenever three conditions are satisfied. The first is that he reasonably believes the other intends to commit a battery upon him, or unlawfully to imprison him, and this belief has been induced by the other's conduct. The second is that the defensive force used is not unreasonable in view of the harm which it is intended to prevent. And the third is that the defender reasonably believes he cannot avoid the threatened harm without either using defensive force or giving up some right or privilege.[19]

17. People v. Lockett, 82 Ill.2d 546, 45 Ill.Dec. 900, 903, 413 N.E.2d 378, 381 (1980).

18. It must not be assumed that fault in any degree will always rule out all possibility of self-defense. "Where, however, the officer uses unreasonable force to arrest a person who is offering no resistance, that person is entitled to defend himself." State v. Castle, 48 Or.App. 15, 616 P.2d 510, 512 (1980).

19. Restatement, Second, Torts, § 63 (1965). The language of an occasional case might suggest that the privilege of using force in self-defense is limited to cases in which this reasonably seems necessary to prevent death or great bodily harm. But these are cases in which the defensive force was of a deadly nature, as by shooting. Cooke v. State, 18 Ala. App. 416, 93 So. 86 (1921). Where the issue has been clearly presented the privilege of using reasonable nondeadly force in defense against nondeadly force has been recognized. State v. Woodard, 58 Idaho 385, 74 P.2d 92 (1937); State v. Evenson, 122 Iowa 88, 97 N.W. 979

Whatever the rule may be as to the use of deadly force, it is clear that an innocent person in the position stated is under no obligation to retreat rather than use nondeadly force in his defense.[20] He may stand his ground and defend himself where he is. He may do this moreover, without "yielding ground" in the broader sense. He may do so without giving up any other right or privilege and without complying with any unauthorized order or command.[21]

One may also use nondeadly force to defend himself against bodily harm which he reasonably believes to be immediately threatened by the negligent conduct of another, but he should yield ground rather than use force to avoid harm which he realizes is unintentional.[22]

It is to be noted that reasonableness is determined by a standard—a reasonable person under like circumstances—and the determination is made by the jury. But there are certain rules with regard to the use of deadly force. One such rule is that deadly force is not permitted in defense against nondeadly force. The court does not ask the jury to determine whether such use of deadly force was reasonable under all the circumstances. The instruction will be that if the jury finds as a fact that defendant used deadly force to defend against force which he realized was nondeadly, he is not excused.[23]

(1904); State v. Sherman, 16 R.I. 631, 18 A. 1040 (1889).

"However, it is well settled that a person cannot use greater force than is reasonably necessary to resist the attack . . . ." State v. Marks, 226 Kan. 704, 602 P.2d 1344, 1351 (1979).

"The right reasonably to use nondeadly force, such as one's fists, in self defense, arises at a somewhat lower level of danger (a reasonable concern for one's personal safety) than the right to use a deadly weapon." Commonwealth v. Bastarache, ___ Mass. ___, 414 N.E.2d 984, 996 (1980).

"Therefore, an instruction which limits the right of self defense to only those circumstances in which the accused apprehends great bodily harm is erroneous." Degenias v. State, ___ Ind.App. ___, 386 N.E.2d 1230, 1231 (1979).

20. State v. Gough, 187 Iowa 363, 174 N.W. 279 (1919); State v. Evenson, 122 Iowa 88, 97 N.W. 979 (1904); People v. Katz, 263 App.Div. 883, 32 N.Y.S.2d 157 (1942); State v. Sherman, 16 R.I. 631, 18 A. 1040 (1889). Retreat, if available, is required where the attack is with nondeadly force or where the attack occurs at the place of employment of the one attacked. Commonwealth v. DeCaro, 359 Mass. 388, 269 N.E.2d 673 (1971). This case stands almost alone in holding that the innocent victim of an attack must retreat rather than use nondeadly force in his defense.

21. Restatement, Second, Torts § 63(2)(a) and (b) (1965).

"The taking and retention of a gun (from an assailant) until it is safe to return it, however, is permissible where self-defense is justified. State v. Campbell, 214 N.W.2d 195 (Iowa 1974)." State v. Antwine, 4 Kan.App.2d 389, 607 P.2d 519, 528–29 (1980).

22. Id. at § 64.

23. Sikes v. Commonwealth, 304 Ky. 429, 200 S.W.2d 956 (1947); State v. Doherty, 52 Or. 591, 98 P. 152 (1908); Restatement, Second, Torts § 65 (1965). Compare State v. Bartlett, 170 Mo. 658, 71 S.W. 148 (1902). As to the rule under a particular statute see Prater v. State, 142 Tex.Cr.R. 626, 155 S.W.2d 934 (1941).

In a prosecution for an assault it is error to charge that self-defense is privileged only if defendant "did not use any more force than was reasonably necessary" and "actually believed he was in danger at the time he fired." This would be proper in a trial for homicide but not in a trial for assault. People v. Di Cupillo, 271 App.Div. 1032, 69 N.Y.S.2d 182 (2d Dept.1947).

But if the defendant shot with intent to kill in alleged self-defense the rule with reference to the privilege should be the same whether his shot was fatal or not.

For example, one must submit to a box on the ear and seek redress in the courts if he is unable to prevent it by means other than resort to deadly force.[24] It would be a criminal assault for him to shoot or stab his assailant under these circumstances.[25] And if homicide should result it would not be less than manslaughter.[26] Where there is great disparity of strength between the two, death or great bodily harm is possible without any weapon, and circumstances may justify deadly force to repel such an attack.[27] Unintentional homicide, resulting from force neither intended nor likely to cause death or great bodily harm, must be distinguished. If the blow itself was privileged, death unexpectedly and unintentionally resulting therefrom is excusable.[28]

At common law any unlawful arrest was a trespass which could be resisted by whatever nondeadly force reasonably seemed necessary to retain or regain the liberty of the arrestee.[29] It seems, however, that when an arrest is being made by a known peace officer, any disagreement as to the authority to make the arrest should be settled in court rather than by violence on the street. Hence the modern trend is in the direction of some such statutory provision as this: "If a person has knowledge, or by the exercise of reasonable care, should have knowledge, that he is being arrested by a peace

State v. Daw, 99 Mont. 232, 43 P.2d 240 (1935).

We "hold that a defendant may employ deadly force in self-defense *only* if it reasonably appears to be necessary to protect against death or great bodily harm." State v. Clay, 297 N.C. 555, 256 S.E.2d 176, 182 (1979).

The use of fists does not justify the use of a deadly weapon in self-defense. People v. Enriquez, 19 Cal.3d 221, 137 Cal.Rptr. 171, 561 P.2d 261 (1977).

"You are instructed that the use of a deadly weapon by a private party to eject a *non-violent trespasser* is not a justifiable use of force." Held a "correct statement of the law." State v. Theroff, 25 Wn.App. 590, 608 P.2d 1254, 1257 (1980).

24. Restatement, Second, Torts § 65, Illustration 1 (1965).

25. Floyd v. State, 36 Ga. 91 (1867); State v. Jayson, 94 N.J.L. 467, 111 A. 7 (1920); Regina v. Hewlett, 1 Fost. and F. 91, 175 Eng.Rep. 640 (1858).

26. State v. Thompson, 9 Iowa 188 (1859); Shorter v. People, 2 N.Y. 193 (1849); State v. Rader, 94 Or. 432, 186 P. 79 (1919).

27. Cook v. State, 194 Miss. 467, 12 So.2d 137 (1943); Easterling v. State, 267 P.2d 185 (Okl.Cr.1954); State v. Gray, 43 Or. 446, 74 P. 927 (1904); Kress v. State, 176 Tenn. 478, 144 S.W.2d 735 (1940). To avoid being choked to death, one may stab a stronger opponent. State v. Rash, 359 Mo. 215, 221 S.W.2d 124 (1949). But

one must not use deadly force to defend against an attack with naked hands unless he reasonably believes that he is in imminent danger of death or great bodily harm. State v. Spear, 178 Wash. 57, 33 P.2d 905 (1934).

A partially disabled man assaulted by a larger younger man who was a karate expert was justified in using deadly force. Bacom v. State, 317 So.2d 148 (Fla.App.1975).

28. Hinchcliffe's Case, 1 Lewin 161, 168 Eng.Rep. 998 (1823); State v. Phillips, 37 Del. 544, 187 A. 108 (1936); Weston v. State, 167 Ind. 324, 78 N.E. 1014 (1906); Sikes v. Commonwealth, 304 Ky. 429, 200 S.W.2d 956 (1947). If a shot properly fired in privileged self-defense should kill an innocent third person by accident the defender will be excused. Gaines v. State, 67 Tex.Cr.R. 325, 148 S.W. 717 (1912). Such a defender would not be excused if he shot with criminal negligence. Henwood v. People, 54 Colo. 188, 129 P. 1010 (1913). If the killing or injuring of the person intended to be hit would have been excusable or justifiable, the unintended shooting and injuring of a bystander by a shot properly fired in the exercise of that privilege is also excusable. Pittman v. State, 272 P.2d 458 (Okl. Cr.1954).

29. State v. Belk, 76 N.C. 10 (1877). No right existed at common law to resist arrest by unreasonable force. State v. Mather, 28 Wn.App. 700, 626 P.2d 44 (1981).

officer, it is the duty of such person to refrain from using force or any weapon to resist such arrest." [30]   In any event if the unlawful arrest is attempted under circumstances which obviously threaten no more than a very temporary deprivation of liberty, the use of deadly force in resistance is not privileged; [31] but if the unlawful manner of the arrest reasonably leads the arrestee to believe he is the victim of a murderous assault, or of kidnapers, [32] homicide committed by him will not be criminal if he uses no more force than reasonably appears to be necessary under the circumstances.

B. DEADLY FORCE

It is in regard to the use of deadly force that most of the difficulties have arisen in the self-defense cases. Before turning to other problems a reference to burden of proof may be injected. The Supreme Court has held that a state may validly place upon the defendant the burden of proof of a defense that does not involve any element of the offense charged, but merely establishes a separate basis for exculpation. [33]   But with reference to any element of the offense charged, while the state may require defendant to introduce enough evidence to place the matter in issue, it may not shift the burden of proof to him because the due process clause of the Fourteenth Amendment requires the prosecution to prove beyond a reasonable doubt every fact necessary to constitute the crime of which the defendant is charged. [34]   This invites inquiry as to whether self-defense negates an element of the offense charged or establishes an independent basis for exculpation. This may depend upon the wording of pertinent statutes. In holding that its new crimi-

---

30. West's Ann.Cal.Pen.Code § 834a (1970). This was adopted from section 5 of the Uniform Arrest Act. It is in substance the provision of the Model Penal Code. Section 3.04(2)(a)(i).

31. Palmquist v. United States, 149 F.2d 352 (5th Cir. 1945), cert. denied 326 U.S. 727, 66 S.Ct. 33 (1945); Green v. State, 238 Ala. 143, 189 So. 763 (1939); Lawrence v. State, 29 Ariz. 247, 240 P. 863 (1925); Mims v. Commonwealth, 236 Ky. 186, 32 S.W.2d 986 (1930); State v. Long, 88 W.Va. 669, 108 S.E. 279 (1921); State v. Gonzales, 24 Wn.App. 437, 604 P.2d 168 (1979).

32. Sanders v. State, 181 Ala. 35, 61 So. 336 (1913); Howard v. Commonwealth, 246 Ky. 738, 56 S.W.2d 362 (1933); State v. Phillips, 118 Iowa 660, 92 N.W. 876 (1902).

". . . where excessive force is used in making what otherwise is a technically lawful arrest, the arrest becomes unlawful and a defendant may not be convicted of an offense which requires the officer

to be engaged in the performance of his duties. . . ."

". . . when excessive force by the officer in making his arrest is used as the excuse for resistance by the defendant, the court is under a sua sponte duty to instruct on self-defense." People v. White, 101 Cal.App.3d 161, 161 Cal.Rptr. 541, 543 (1980).

"The policy reasons for prohibiting suspects from determining on the streets whether an arrest complies with due process do not justify the abrogation of the right of self-defense against bodily harm from the use of excessive force by a policeman, even during an arrest." State v. Martinez, 122 Ariz. 596, 596 P.2d 734, 736 (App.1979).

33. Patterson v. New York, 432 U.S. 197, 97 S.Ct. 2319 (1977).

34. In re Winship, 397 U.S. 358, 90 S.Ct. 1068 (1970); Mullaney v. Wilbur, 421 U.S. 684, 95 S.Ct. 1881 (1975); Sandstrom v. Montana, 442 U.S. 510, 99 S.Ct. 2450 (1979).

nal code has not shifted the burden of proof of self-defense to the defendant, the Washington court said: [35]

> Since recklessness is expressly made an element of the crime of first-degree manslaughter, the prosecution must prove it beyond a reasonable doubt. . . . A person acting in self-defense cannot be acting recklessly as that term is defined in RCW 9A.08.010(1)(c). There can be no recklessness without disregard of risk of a wrongful act, and self-defense, as defined, is not "wrongful." Since self-defense negates the element of recklessness in first-degree manslaughter, requiring an accused to prove self-defense places on him or her the burden of proving the absence of recklessness. Such a result is proscribed by *Winship* and *Mullaney*.

Turning to the substantive law, we find the fragmentary references available at this day[36] fail to give a clear picture of the law as it stood prior to the year 1532. It was not clear then. The recognized ambiguity was sufficient to call forth the clarifying enactment of 24 Henry VIII.[37] This statute, said by Hale to be "declarative" of the common law,[38] may have removed all doubt at the moment but not for all time. The first analytical treatment of the subject was by Sir Michael Foster in 1762.[39] Under his analysis a sharp distinction is to be made between the defensive killing of one who started out with the intent to murder, and a defensive killing which may become necessary during the progress of a "chance-medley." [40] The first he classified as

---

35. State v. Hanton, 94 Wn.2d 129, 614 P.2d 1280 (1980). The trial judge had a correct understanding of the law and intended to give a proper instruction to the jury. He told them that "the burden is upon the defendant only to produce some evidence tending to prove that the homicide was done in self defense. It is not necessary for the defendant to prove this to you beyond a reasonable doubt, nor by a preponderance of the evidence. The defendant sustains this burden of proof, if from a consideration of the evidence you have a reasonable doubt as to whether or not the killing was done in self-defense." This is a correct statement of the Washington law. But for some reason the judge refused to give the added instruction requested: "It is the duty of the State to prove beyond a reasonable doubt the lack of self-defense." The court held that this added instruction would not have been necessary if the judge had given an adequate instruction on the elements of recklessness. But without either it was held that the effect was to place upon the defendant the burden of proving self-defense, and the conviction was reversed.

36. For example—The Case of Robert of Herthale, 1 Selden Society Select Pleas of the Crown 31 (1203); The Case of Leonin and Jacob, 1 id. at 85 (1221); The Case of the Carter, 1 id. at 94 (1221); Anonymous, Fitzherbert, Grand Abridgment, C. and P.C. No. 284 (1328); Note,

id. at No. 361 (1328); Note, Y.B.Hil. 21 Edw.III, f. 17, pl. 23 (1346); Note, Fitzherbert, Grand Abridgment, C. and P.C. No. 261 (1347); Anonymous, Lib. Ass.Ann. 26, f. 123, pl. 23 (1352); Note, Lib.Ass. 43 f. 274, pl. 31 (1369); Memorandum, Y.B.Hil. 4 Hy. VII, f. 2, pl. 3 (Chancery, 1489).

37. 24 Henry VIII, c. 5 (1532). (Because of uncertainty in this regard, be it enacted:) "That if any person or persons, at any time hereafter, be indicted or appealed of or for the death of any such evil disposed person or persons attempting to murder, rob, or burglarily to break mansion-houses, as is above said, that the person or persons so indicted or appealed thereof, and of the same by verdict so found and tried, shall not forfeit or lose any lands, tenements, goods or chattels, for the death of any such evil disposed person in such manner slain, but shall be thereof, and for the same fully acquitted and discharged, in like manner as the same person or persons should be if he or they were lawfully acquitted of the death of said evil disposed person or persons."

38. 1 Hale P.C. *487. The statute "was made in affirmance of the common law. . . ." A killing to prevent the burning of one's house is on the same footing although not mentioned in the enactment. 1 East P.C. 272 (1803).

39. Foster, Crown Law (1762).

40. Id. at 273–8.

"perfectly innocent and justifiable," whereas the second was said to be "in some measure blameable and barely excusable."

Foster's analysis, plus other clear statements of the common law upon another point,[41] suggest that the use of deadly force in self-defense must be considered in the light of three different positions of the parties.

(1) One, entirely free from fault, is the victim of an assault which was murderous from the beginning. He is under no obligation to retreat (under Foster's analysis) but may stand his ground, and if he reasonably believes it necessary to use deadly force to save himself from death or great bodily harm, he is privileged to do so.[42]

(2) One who was the aggressor in a chance-medley (an ordinary fist fight, or other nondeadly encounter), or who culpably entered into such an engagement, finds that his adversary has suddenly and unexpectedly changed the nature of the contest and is resorting to deadly force. This (under Foster's analysis) is the only type of situation which requires "retreat to the wall." Such a defender, not being entirely free from fault, must not resort to deadly force if there is any other reasonable method of saving himself. Hence if a reasonable avenue of escape is available to him he must take it[43] unless he is in his "castle" at the time.[44] And if he kills as a last resort after no further retreat (or no retreat) is reasonably safe, the homicide is not justifiable but only excusable.[45]

(3) One who starts an encounter with a murderous assault upon another, or who willingly engages in mutual combat with malice aforethought (as in case of a duel) has forfeited all right of self-defense during that contest. If he kills the other before that fight is over he is guilty of murder regardless of any extremity to which he may have been driven.[46]

---

41. If **A** strike **B** in malice and **B** draweth at **A** and **A** flees to the wall and then kills **B**,—this is murder. Anonymous, J. Kelyng 58, 84 Eng.Rep. 1081.

42. Ibid.; Foster, Crown Law 273 (1762); 1 Bishop, New Criminal Law § 850 (9th ed. 1923).

"Where an attack is made with murderous intent, the person attacked is under no obligation to fly; he may stand his ground, and, if necessary, kill his adversary." People v. Ye Park, 62 Cal. 204, 208 (1882) (quoted from Bishop).

43. Foster, Crown Law 276 (1762); 1 Bishop, New Criminal Law § 850 (9th ed. 1923); People v. Hecker, 109 Cal. 451, 42 P. 307 (1895); Hash v. Commonwealth, 88 Va. 172, 13 S.E. 398 (1891).

44. Lambard, Eirenarcha 250 (4th ed. 1599).

45. ". . . it is pointed out that our law nowhere imposes the duty of retreat upon one who without fault himself is exposed to a sudden felonious attack, and that the duty of withdrawal or retreat is imposed upon him alone who is the first aggressor, or who has joined in a mutual combat. . . . The right to stand one's

ground should form an element of the instructions upon the necessity of killing and the law of self-defense." People v. Lewis, 117 Cal. 186, 191–2, 48 P. 1088, 1089 (1897); accord, Ragland v. State, 111 Ga. 211, 36 S.E. 682 (1900); Page v. State, 141 Ind. 236, 40 N.E. 745 (1894); State v. Hatch, 57 Kan. 420, 46 P. 708 (1896); State v. Bryant, 213 N.C. 752, 197 S.E. 530 (1938); Erwin v. State, 29 Ohio St. 186 (1876).

"It is only the faultless, who are exempt from the necessity of retreating while acting in self-defense. Cain's Case, supra. Those in fault must retreat, if able to do so; if from the fierceness of the attack or for other reasons they are unable to retreat, they will be excused by the law for not doing so." State v. Greer, 22 W.Va. 800, 819 (1883). State v. Kennamore, 604 S.W.2d 856 (Tenn.1980).

46. Lambard, Eirenarcha 234 (4th ed. 1599); 4 Bl.Comm. *185.

"However, it is well settled . . . that self-defense is not available to a person who is committing or attempting to commit a forcible felony." State v.

Until the turn of the century the foregoing outline could have been offered with firm assurance, so far as the law of England is concerned. But three years later Professor Joseph H. Beale disputed Foster's analysis of self-defense.[47] While Foster did not cite Coke he undoubtedly relied in part upon this passage: "Some without any giving back to a wall, . . . As if a thiefe offer to rob or murder **B** either abroad, or in his house, and thereupon assault him, and **B** defend himselfe without any giving back, and in his defence killeth the thief, this is no felony; for a man shall never give way to a thief, &c. Neither shall he forfeit any thing."[48] Foster interpreted this to cover either of two kinds of assault: (1) an assault to rob, or (2) an assault to murder. No, said Beale in substance, it covers one assault only—the demand for **B**'s money or his life.[49] Starting with this analysis Beale insisted that the innocent victim of a murderous assault is always required to take advantage of an obviously safe retreat, rather than resort to deadly force, if it is not an attempted robbery and the victim is not in his "castle" at the time, and is not lawfully attempting to arrest his assailant.[50] If the victim retreats from a robber, said Beale, he may by that act facilitate the robbery.[51] If one retreats from his "castle" he abandons his place of refuge.[52] If one attempting arrest retreats from the arrestee he thereby abandons his original undertaking.[53] But one who retreats from a would-be murderer merely frustrates his assailant.[54] Any idea that retreat is humiliating, he continues, is based on the same ground as the code of "honor" which supports dueling, and should give way to the desire to spare human life if possible.[55]

The position of so great a legal scholar is entitled to the highest regard. But at this point it seems impossible to support Beale's view. To begin with, if we had no guide other than the words used by Coke himself we should feel certain that the word "thiefe" was employed in this sentence in a broad sense as a synonym of scoundrel. Had he intended the specific meaning inferred by Beale he would unquestionably have said "robber" which indicates one who steals by force or intimidation rather than "thiefe" which suggests larceny by stealth.

We have, however, guides other than Coke's words to aid in the determination of his meaning. He relies upon, and cites, the statute of 24 Henry VIII.[56] And this enactment uses, not the word "thief," but the phrase "evil disposed person." And it refers to the purpose of such person, not with the couplet "to rob or murder," but in inverse order plus an addition—"to murder, rob, or burglarily to break mansion-houses."[57]

An effort to determine the law of that time, quite apart from the statement of Coke, should not ignore the familiar phrase "retreat to the wall." For generations the employment of this phrase in self-defense cases has been metaphorical. One under such a duty is not privileged to use deadly

Marks, 226 Kan. 704, 602 P.2d 1344, 1351 (1979).

47. Beale, Retreat from a Murderous Assault, 16 Harv.L.Rev. 567 (1903).

48. 3 Co.Inst. *56.

49. Beale, supra n. 47, at 572.

50. Id. at 574.

51. Ibid.

52. Id. at 574–5.

53. Id. at 574.

54. Ibid.

55. Id. at 577, 581–2.

56. 3 Co.Inst. *56.

57. 24 Henry VIII, C. 5 (1532).

force in his defense if an obviously safe retreat is available to him. But when he has retreated as far as he can in safety, or if there was no obviously safe retreat available to begin with, his "back is at the wall" figuratively speaking.[58] It was no figure of speech, however, in the ancient case[59] from which the phrase has been formulated. The defendant in that case had been driven "to a certain wall situated between two houses beyond which he was not able in any way to pass." Only there did the defendant stand and kill the other in his own defense. This finding by the jury did not entitle the defendant to an acquittal. He was kept in prison to await the king's pardon. But the jury's finding makes clear that the starting point was not a murderous attack by the deceased upon the defendant. The two were on the way to a tavern when a "quarrel and contest against each other" arose. During this quarrel the deceased resorted to deadly force and the defendant, having fled to the wall, did likewise with fatal consequences. In other words this was a typical example of what judges and writers for generations referred to as a killing in *"self-defence upon chance-medley."* [60] Had the defendant killed the other without any effort to retreat under these circumstances he would have been guilty of manslaughter.[61] Since he retreated to the wall before resort to fatal force he is entitled to a pardon. In the words of Foster, he was not "perfectly innocent and justifiable" but "in some measure blameable and barely excusable." [62]

This invites exploration into the distinction between justifiable homicide and excusable homicide. Despite the difficulty in drawing the exact boundary line between the two no student of homicide questions the existence of this distinction in the early law. And the importance of this distinction was obvious at that time. He who was found to have committed justifiable homicide was acquitted. He lost nothing. He was discharged as fully as if the finding had been that he did not do the killing.[63] But it was not so with the person found to have committed excusable homicide. He was not entitled to an acquittal. Although he was not a felon[64] and might hope for a pardon, he had forfeited his life and his goods, according to the legal theory of that day. Whether such a defendant ever actually lost his life by failure to secure a pardon is a matter of conjecture at the present time.[65] If so it must have been quite unusual and very early. As years went by the king issued pardons in these cases with such regularity that eventually they were issued by the chancellor as a matter of course, without bothering the king with this

---

58. State v. Borwick, 193 Iowa 639, 187 N.W. 460 (1922); State v. Partlow, 90 Mo. 608, 4 S.W. 14 (1886).

59. Anonymous, Fitzherbert, Grand Abridgment, C. & P.C. No. 284 (1328).

60. Foster, Crown Law 276 (3d ed. 1809); 1 East P.C. 279 (1803) ("homicide upon *chance-medley* in self-defence").

61. 3 Co.Inst. *55; 1 Hale P.C. *479; 4 Bl.Comm. *184; 1 East P.C. 279 (1803); 1 Bishop, New Criminal Law § 870 (8th ed. 1892).

62. Foster, Crown Law 273 (3rd ed. 1809).

63. Homicide "which amounts not to felony is either justifiable, and causes no forfeiture at all, or excusable, and causes the forfeiture of the party's goods." 1 Hawk.P.C. c. 28 (6th ed. by Leach, 1788). Accord: 4 Bl.Comm. *177–8; 1 East P.C. 219–20 (1803); 2 Bishop, New Criminal Law § 617 (8th ed. 1892).

64. 3 Co.Inst. *55; 1 Hawk.P.C. c. 28 (6th ed. by Leach, 1788).

65. "And . . . at the common law he should have suffered death:" 3 Co. Inst. *55. Stephen, referring to a similar statement in the Year Book, Hil. 21 Edw. III f. 17, pl. 23 (1346), said it was "remarkable" that the reporter should have had such a belief. 3 Stephen, History of the Criminal Law of England 42 (1883).

detail.[66] Such homicides were pardonable—excusable. But while this pardon saved the defendant's life it did not save his goods and chattels. These remained forfeited to the king until this practice gradually fell into disuse and was ultimately abolished by statute.[67] During the generations prior to this change justifiable homicide resulted in an acquittal and full discharge with no forfeiture, whereas excusable homicide resulted in some forfeiture and the retention of the defendant, at first in custody and later under bail,[68] until the pardon was received.

In those days it was a matter of importance to determine whether a homicide which was not felonious was justifiable or excusable. Homicide was not justifiable unless it was commanded or authorized by law. The typical instances of homicide commanded by law were (1) the execution of a sentence of death pronounced by a competent tribunal, and (2) the killing of an enemy on the field of battle as an act of war and within the rules of war. The typical instances of killings which were authorized by law, although not actually commanded, were homicides which became necessary in (1) arresting a felon, preventing his escape or recapturing him after escape,[69] and (2) preventing the commission of a felony perpetrated by violence or surprise.[70] Typical instances of excusable homicide were killings by misadventure, by a madman, and certain kinds of homicides committed in self-defense.[71]

Hale emphasizes early in his discussion of the field that: "Homicide *se defendendo* is of two kinds. (1) Such, as tho it excuseth from death, yet it excuseth not the forfeiture of goods, . . . (2) Such as wholly acquits from all kinds of forfeiture." [72] The other early writers seem to have reserved the phrase *"se defendendo"* to indicate only the first kind mentioned by Hale. For example, Hawkins says: "it seems also to be confirmed by the general tenor of our law-books, which speaking of homicide *se defendendo*, suppose it to be done in some quarrel or affray; from whence it seems reasonable to conclude, that where the law judges a man guilty of homicide *se defendendo*, there must be some precedent quarrel in which both parties always are, or at least may justly be supposed to have been, in some fault.

---

66. Fitzherbert, Grand Abridgment, C. & P.C. No. 361 (1328); 1 Hawk.P.C. c. 29, § 25 (6th ed. by Leach, 1788).

67. Such a slayer "shall then loose his goodes, and seeke his pardon." Lambard, Eirenarcha 249 (4th ed. 1599). Though his life is saved "yet he shall forfeit all his goods and chattels." 3 Co. Inst. *55. The formal change of the law by statute came late. 9 Geo. IV, c. 31, § 10 (1828). Long before that only a vestige of the original rule remained. In Blackstone's time the defendant was entitled, not only to a pardon, but also to a "writ of restitution of his goods as a matter of course and right, only paying for suing out the same." 4 Bl.Comm. *188. He indicated that this had long been the practice at that time.

68. 2 Hale P.C. *129; Note, Fitzherbert, Grand Abridgment, C. & P.C. No. 361 (1328).

69. 3 Co.Inst. *56; 4 Bl.Comm. *179.

70. 1 East P.C. 271 (1803). "In the next place, such homicide as is committed for the *prevention* of any forcible and atrocious *crime* is justifiable. . . ." 4 Bl.Comm. *180.

71. "On the patent rolls of Henry VIII, pardons for those who have committed homicide by misadventure, in self-defence, or while of unsound mind, are common." 2 Pollock and Maitland, History of English Law 480 (2d ed. 1899).

To support an instruction on excusable homicide "there must be evidence tending to show that at the time of the homicide the defendant was doing a lawful act by lawful means with usual and ordinary caution and without any unlawful intention." Reynolds v. State, 617 P.2d 1357, 1360 (Okl.Cr.App.1980). See also Kaye, The Making Of English Criminal Law, [1977] Crim.L.Rev.(Eng.) 4.

72. 1 Hale P.C. *478.

. . ." [73] Most, if not all, of the confusion and misunderstanding at this point stems from this use of the phrase.

It is inconceivable that the law should have held homicide justifiable if committed for the prevention of the murder of anyone else, but only excusable if for the prevention of the murder of oneself. Conceivably the judges might have taken the position that anyone must elect an obviously safe retreat in preference to the use of deadly force in self-defense and that homicide by one whose "back is at the wall" is justifiable if he is the innocent victim of a murderous assault but only excusable if by one who had provoked, or willingly engaged in, an encounter which he expected would not assume deadly proportions. But while this is conceivable it is not the position taken by the English judges. He who was under a duty to "retreat to the wall" was only excused—not justified—if he was forced to kill after he had done so. [74]

Foster's statement that the duty to retreat to the wall applied, not to the innocent victim of a murderous assault, but only to the culpable participant of a chance-medley, merely clarified the stand previously taken by Lambard, Coke and Hale. [75] It was later summed up by East [76] in these words: "A man may repel force by force in defence of his person, habitation, or property, against one who manifestly intends or endeavors, *by violence or surprize*, to commit a *known felony*, such as murder, rape, robbery, arson, burglary, and the like, upon either. In these cases he is not obliged to retreat, but may pursue his adversary until he has secured himself from all danger; and if he kill him in so doing, it is called justifiable self-defence: . . . It has been shown, that where death ensues from a combat on a sudden quarrel, without prepense malice, such act amounts but to manslaughter; being attributed to heat of blood arising from human infirmity. Now in order to reduce such offence from manslaughter to self-defence upon chance-medley, it is encumbent on the defendant to prove two things: 1st, that before a mortal stroke given he had declined any further combat, and had retreated as far as he could with safety; 2dly, that he then killed his adversary through mere necessity, in order to avoid immediate death."

Professor Beale's explanation for requiring the innocent victim of a murderous assault to retreat if he can, although the innocent victim of attempted robbery is not required to do so, is quite unconvincing. True, a successful retreat from a would-be murderer defeats his purpose. But so also does such a retreat from a would-be robber who wants money or other valuables which are in the intended victim's pockets. And this is the common case. Moreover, under his reasoning, the intended victim would be required to retreat from a would-be robber if he could do so safely without loss of his property. But there was no such requirement in the common law. [77]

One of Beale's arguments actually begs the question. He starts with the limitation of deadly force in self-defense to situations in which this drastic step reasonably seems to be necessary. This limitation, he says, requires

---

73. 1 Hawk.P.C. c. 28, § 24 (6th ed. by Leach, 1788).

74. 3 Co.Inst. *55–6; 1 East P.C. 271, 279 (1803).

75. Lambard, Eirenarcha 248–9 (4th ed. 1599); 3 Co.Inst. *55–6; 1 Hale P.C. *478, 481.

76. 1 East P.C. 271–2, 279–80 (1803).

77. 3 Co.Inst. *56; 1 Hale P.C. *481; 1 East P.C. 271 (1803); State v. Bonofiglio, 67 N.J.L. 239, 52 A. 712 (1901). And see Storey v. State, 71 Ala. 329, 336–7 (1882); Ragland v. State, 111 Ga. 211, 216–7, 36 S.E. 682, 684 (1900).

resort to an obviously safe retreat, because it cannot reasonably appear to be necessary to kill if such a retreat is available.[78] But the basic issue is whether the requirement of apparent necessity means (1) at that place, or (2) there or elsewhere. The innocent victim of a murderous assault, who is in his own home at the time, is not privileged to kill as a matter of choice.[79] There must be the reasonable appearance of necessity, but this means there—without retreat.[80] This could be repeated with reference to the attack upon one lawfully attempting an arrest, or the victim of attempted robbery.

It is not out of place to mention the position of another legal scholar. Bishop concluded that the innocent victim of a murderous assault has no duty to retreat from his assailant. He went far beyond that. Not only is there no duty to retreat, there is a duty on his part not to retreat and thereby leave a potential murderer at large. His suggestion is that an innocent victim who could defend himself where he is, but runs away from the would-be murderer, is really guilty of misprision although he will not be convicted.[81]

At the present time it seems natural to assume that self-defense is the starting point so far as the privilege of using deadly force is concerned—and perhaps it should be. But this very definitely was not the starting point under the English common law. Anyone who was himself free from fault was privileged to use deadly force if this reasonably seemed necessary to prevent the murder of an innocent victim. Hence the innocent victim who used deadly force to prevent being murdered was exercising the privilege of crime prevention which was one of the major privileges of the common law and did not require him to surrender any right—such as the right to remain where he was at the time.

Self-defense was a secondary and imperfect privilege developed by the judges to give some protection to the person who was too much at fault to be entitled to the privilege of crime prevention. The typical illustration is the case of one who had provoked, or willingly entered into, an unlawful, nondeadly scuffle with an adversary who suddenly and unexpectedly seized a weapon with intent to kill. The one first mentioned had forfeited his privilege of crime prevention, which would have permitted him to stand his ground and use whatever force reasonably seemed necessary to prevent the threatened felony. But his fault was so far exceeded by the greater fault of the other that the secondary privilege was recognized for his protection—the privilege of self-defense. This required him to retreat, if a safe retreat was available, and if he killed the other as a last resort, when his back was "at the wall," this homicide was not justifiable but only excusable. He was not entitled to an acquittal but was recommended for a pardon.

78. Beale, Retreat from a Murderous Assault, 16 Harv.L.Rev. 567, 574 (1903).

79. Restatement, Second, Torts § 65 (1965).

80. Id. at comment i. The Iowa court reversed a conviction of second degree murder because the instruction did not clearly state the distinction between the necessity of using deadly force where the defendant was—without retreat, and such necessity elsewhere. State v. Baratta, 242 Iowa 1308, 49 N.W.2d 866 (1951).

"It is true that all authorities agree that the taking of life in defense of one's person can not be either justified or excused, except on the ground of *necessity;* . . . but a true man, who is without fault, is not obliged to fly from an assailant, who, by violence or surprise, maliciously seeks to take his life, or do him enormous bodily harm." Erwin v. State, 29 Ohio St. 186, 199–200 (1876).

81. 1 Bishop, New Criminal Law § 851 (9th ed. 1923).

In this country, while a majority of the courts followed the position which had been taken in the mother country, a substantial minority misunderstood the English cases on self-defense and thought they applied to the innocent victim of a murderous attack. The result has been a divergence with reference to the matter of retreat. While there is no requirement of retreat where the defensive force to be used is nondeadly in its nature,[82] there is a split of authority where the defense must be by deadly force. The two views are loosely referred to as the "retreat rule" and the "no-retreat rule." These labels are not precise because no jurisdiction either requires retreat, or permits a standing of ground, under all circumstances. The basic question is this:

Is the innocent victim of a murderous assault who is himself free from fault, and reasonably believes he must use deadly force to save himself from death or great bodily harm, if he does not retreat, privileged to stand his ground and resort to deadly force *there* merely because he is where he has a right to be,—or must he take advantage of an obviously safe retreat if one is available?

The counterpart of the rule, that deadly force is not authorized in defense against nondeadly force, is that deadly force is authorized to defend against deadly force if this reasonably seems necessary to avoid death or great bodily injury. Whether it reasonably seems necessary is determined by the reasonable-person standard, but whether or not it means that he can thus defend himself where he is depends upon rules, and these rules are far from uniform. At one point all agree. A trespasser does not forfeit his life by trespassing upon the property of another, and hence does not forfeit his privilege of self-defense by doing so. But he is not privileged to use any force, particularly deadly force, to defend himself, if he can safely avoid the harm by terminating his trespass—by retreating from the other's premises. At the other extreme, also, almost all agree.[83] If an innocent dweller is murderously attacked in his dwelling, by an intruder, the dweller can use deadly force if this reasonably seems necessary to defend himself where he is. Even if he could safely avoid his assailant by running out of the house, he is not required to do so. Between these extremes the rules differ widely.

1. THE "NO–RETREAT RULE"

He may stand his ground and use deadly force if this reasonably seems necessary to save himself there, according to the majority view.[84]

82. State v. Evenson, 122 Iowa 88, 97 N.W. 979 (1904); People v. Katz, 263 App.Div. 883, 32 N.Y.S.2d 157 (1942); State v. Sherman, 16 R.I. 631, 18 A. 1040 (1889).

83. It has never been the law of Massachusetts that one assaulted in his own home has no duty to retreat before resorting to the use of deadly force. The right to use deadly force by way of self-defense is not available to one threatened until he has availed himself of all reasonable and proper means in the circumstances to avoid combat. This has equal application to one assaulted in his own home. The fact that the accused was attacked in his own home is one factor to be considered by the jury, but there is no rule in this state that one attacked in his own home has no duty to retreat. Commonwealth v. Shaffer, 367 Mass. 508, 326 N.E.2d 880 (1975).

84. "American jurisdictions have divided on the question, no less in crime

One suggestion has been that liberty itself is threatened if a law-abiding citizen can be forced from a place where he has a right to be.[85] This extreme privilege is not granted to an "aggressor."[86] One who started the encounter with an unlawful attack, or who culpably engaged in an unlawful exchange of blows, enjoys no such position.[87] He is in no sense blameless. But if he started, or joined in, the contest with no thought of causing death or great bodily harm, his fault in doing so is entirely overshadowed if the other wilfully changes it to a deadly encounter.[88] Hence he has not entirely forfeited his privilege of self-defense. If he kills without availing himself of an obviously safe retreat he is guilty of manslaughter.[89] If he retreats as

than tort, with the preponderant position favoring the right to stand one's ground." Model Penal Code 24 (Tent. Draft No. 8, 1958). Accord, People v. Collins, 189 Cal.App.2d 575, 11 Cal.Rptr. 504 (1961).

"The law in Oklahoma is clear: There is no duty to retreat if one is threatened with bodily harm." Neal v. State, 597 P.2d 334, 337 (Okl.Cr.App.1979).

It was not error to include in the charge that if the defendant had a reasonable belief that he was about to be killed or suffer great bodily harm, he had no duty to retreat but could stand his ground and shoot his assailant in self-defense. State v. Ward, 26 N.C.App. 159, 215 S.E.2d 394 (1975).

One is entitled to stand his ground and use such force as is reasonably necessary to save himself from death or serious bodily harm "only if he believes on reasonable grounds that such danger is imminent." United States v. Deon, 656 F.2d 354, 356 (8th Cir. 1981).

Because California's no-retreat rule is "controversial," counsel must be permitted to include this in questioning the jury panel. People v. Williams, 29 Cal.3d 392, 174 Cal.Rptr. 317, 628 P.2d 869 (1981).

"Upon retrial, we suggest that the law is, and should be, that there is no invariable duty to retire to a place of safety on the part of a victim of an aggressor, but the reasonableness of retreat or standing one's ground and the fact of aggression by one party against the other are circumstances which the jury can consider in deciding whether the right of self-defense exists."

"Similarly, instructions, like court's instructions no. 27 and 31, which state the general law of self-defense adequately cover Montana's 'no retreat' rule." State v. Sunday, ___ Mont. ___, 609 P.2d 1188, 1195 (1980).

85. State v. Bartlett, 170 Mo. 658, 668, 71 S.W. 148, 151 (1902).

86. The aggressor must retreat rather than use deadly force in his defense. State v. Robison, 54 Nev. 56, 6 P.2d 433 (1931).

An aggressor has a duty to retreat even in his own home. Commonwealth v. Dinkins, 272 Pa.Super. 387, 416 A.2d 94 (1979).

Although there is no duty to retreat, "once having retreated from a place of danger, an act of voluntarily returning which is deliberately calculated to lead to further conflict deprives the defendant of his claim of self-defense." State v. Britson, 130 Ariz. 380, 636 P.2d 628, 634 (1981).

87. State v. Schroeder, 103 Kan. 770, 176 P. 659 (1918).

"In other words, when a defendant seeks or induces the quarrel which leads to the necessity for killing his adversary, the right to stand his ground is not immediately available to him, but, instead, he must first decline to carry on the affray and must honestly endeavor to escape from it. Only when he has done so will the law justify him in thereafter standing his ground and killing his antagonist." People v. Holt, 25 Cal.2d 59, 66, 153 P.2d 21, 25 (1944). Cited with approval in People v. McDonnel, 94 Cal.App.2d 885, 211 P.2d 910 (1949). In a mutual combat the duty to retreat applies to both. Danford v. State, 53 Fla. 4, 43 So. 593 (1907). The one who provoked the difficulty cannot justify a killing in self-defense unless he retreated as far as he could in safety. See State v. Flory, 40 Wyo. 184, 276 P. 458 (1929); Howard v. State, 122 Ark. 422, 183 S.W. 743 (1916); State v. Morgan, 296 N.W.2d 397 (Minn.1980).

88. See State v. Hill, 20 N.C. 629, 634 (1839).

89. 1 Hale P.C. *483; Foster, Crown Law 277 (3d ed. 1809); 4 Bl.Comm. *184; 1 East P.C. 279 (1803); People v. Pursley, 302 Ill. 62, 134 N.E. 128 (1922); State v. Hill, 20 N.C. 629 (1839). See State v.

far as he can in reasonable safety, he may use deadly force if this reasonably seems necessary to save himself from death or great bodily harm.[90] And if by reason of the suddenness and fierceness of the change in the nature of the contest there is no reasonable opportunity to retreat, he may resort to deadly force where he is.[91] Where both parties are in the wrong, neither is privileged to use deadly force without retreating.[92]

One who starts, or willingly engages in, an encounter with malice afore-thought is in a still worse position. Not even "retreat to the wall" is availa-ble to him. Though he retreats as far as he can and then kills the other as the only possible means of saving his own life he is guilty of murder.[93] But even the murderous assailant has not necessarily forfeited his privilege of self-defense forever.[94] He has forfeited it for the moment. He cannot reac-

Vaughan, 141 Mo. 514, 522, 42 S.W. 1080, 1081 (1897).

90. People v. Hecker, 109 Cal. 451, 42 P. 307 (1895); People v. Miceli, 101 Cal. App.2d 643, 226 P.2d 14 (1951); Kinney v. People, 108 Ill. 519 (1884); Adams v. Peo-ple, 47 Ill. 376 (1868); Story v. State, 99 Ind. 413 (1885); State v. Whitnah, 129 Io-wa 211, 105 N.W. 432 (1905); State v. Hatch, 57 Kan. 420, 46 P. 708 (1896); Pond v. People, 8 Mich. 150 (1860); Cot-ton v. State, 31 Miss. 504 (1856); State v. Taylor, 602 S.W.2d 820 (Mo.App.1980); State v. Hill, 20 N.C. 629 (1839); Foutch v. State, 95 Tenn. 711, 34 S.W. 423 (1895); Crowder v. State, 76 Tenn. 669 (1881); Hash v. Commonwealth, 88 Va. 172, 13 S.E. 398 (1891); State v. Cook, 94 W.Va. 166, 117 S.E. 777 (1923); State v. Banks, 55 W.Va. 388, 47 S.E. 142 (1904). "If, up-on consideration of all the evidence, the jury came to the conclusion that the first assault of the prisoner was not of malice prepense, then the subsequent occur-rences demanded their careful considera-tion, because upon these the prisoner's guilt might be extenuated into man-slaughter or excused as a homicide in self-defense." State v. Hill, 20 N.C. 629, 633 (1839).

Defendant had no duty to leave the area when victim invited him to go outside and fight since such retreat may have been interpreted as an affirmative response. Justified in using deadly force when victim then came at him. Bacom v. State, 317 So.2d 148 (Fla.App.1975).

91. People v. Hecker, 109 Cal. 451, 42 P. 307 (1895); Pond v. People, 8 Mich. 150 (1860); Crowder v. State, 76 Tenn. 669 (1881).

"[T]he accused already has his back 'to the wall,' if the assault is of such sudden and vengeful character that he cannot re-tire without increasing his danger or ex-posure to death or serious injury.

. . . ." State v. Borwick, 193 Iowa 639, 647, 187 N.W. 460, 463 (1922). And see State v. Partlow, 90 Mo. 608, 628, 4 S.W. 14, 23 (1886), quoting Wharton. See also Commonwealth v. Fisher, 491 Pa. 231, 420 A.2d 427 (1980).

92. See Story v. State, 99 Ind. 413, 415 (1885). "Cases of mutual combat are those in which this duty of 'retreating to the wall' oftenest appears. Two men be-ing in the wrong, neither can right him-self except by 'retreating to the wall'" (quoting Bishop). Jackson v. Common-wealth, 98 Va. 845, 850, 36 S.E. 487, 489 (1900).

93. Wallace v. United States, 162 U.S. 466, 16 S.Ct. 859 (1895); People v. Hin-shaw, 194 Cal. 1, 227 P. 156 (1924); El-schilde v. Commonwealth, 280 Ky. 690, 134 S.W.2d 600 (1939); State v. Smith, 10 Nev. 106 (1875); State v. Hill, 20 N.C. 629 (1839); Dodson v. State, 284 P.2d 437 (Okl.Cr.1955); Smith v. State, 128 Tex.Cr. R. 34, 78 S.W.2d 621 (1935).

"If the defendant in any way chal-lenged the fight, and went to it armed, he cannot afterward maintain that in taking his assailant's life he acted in self de-fense." People v. Hamilton, 257 Cal. App.2d 296, 64 Cal.Rptr. 578 (1967), quot-ing from previous cases. See also People v. Otwell, 61 Cal.Rptr. 427 (Cal.App. 1967).

94. State v. Goode, 271 Mo. 43, 195 S.W. 1006 (1917). A murderous assailant who had abandoned his purpose, with-drawn from the conflict, and fled into his house had regained the privilege of self-defense and could use deadly force when the other broke into the house to kill him. Stoffer v. State, 15 Ohio St. 47 (1864). It is an assault for the victim of an attack to hunt up his assailant and strike him after he has withdrawn completely. Wendler v. State, 128 Fla. 618, 175 So. 255 (1937).

quire it by "retreat to the wall." Nothing short of "withdrawal" will restore this privilege to such a one.[95] This means that he must bring his attack to an end. And if he is unable to get entirely away from the other, he must in some manner convey to him the information that the fight is over.[96] If the circumstances do not permit him to do so, this is his own misfortune for bringing such a predicament upon himself.[97] In the excitement of deadly combat, it may be added, one who has in his hand and continues to hold a deadly weapon, available for instant use, may frequently find it impossible to convey this information to his adversary. Even a plain statement in words may reasonably be interpreted by the other to be merely a ruse, intended for no purpose other than to gain an advantage in the fight. And a murderous assailant has not met this rigid requirement if he has failed "to remove any just apprehension from his adversary." [98] Unless withdrawal has been manifested and communicated to the original victim such that apprehension of further danger would not be reasonable a claim of self-defense is not valid.[99]

Without meeting the requirements of "retreat" or "withdrawal" (whichever may be applicable to the particular case), no one can shelter himself under the privilege of self-defense when he himself brought about the difficulty.[1] As in other problems of causation, however, this does not include the entire factual area. It includes only one who is legally recognized as having

---

95. People v. Button, 106 Cal. 628, 39 P. 1073 (1895); State v. Broadhurst, 184 Or. 178, 196 P.2d 407 (1948), cert. denied 337 U.S. 906, 69 S.Ct. 1046.

"It is a well-established rule of law that an aggressor forfeits the right to claim self-defense except in two situations: (1) where an aggressor using nondeadly force . . . is met with deadly force, the initial aggressor may justifiably defend himself against the deadly attack; (2) when an aggressor withdraws from the altercation that he has started, he may then defend himself from further attack. This, however, requires actual notice of his intent to withdraw or at least that he take reasonable steps to give such notice." Castillo v. State, 614 P.2d 756, 766 (Alaska 1980).

96. Ibid.; State v. Smith, 10 Nev. 106 (1875).

"One who is the aggressor, or provokes an altercation (of a deadly nature) in which he kills another, cannot successfully invoke the right of self-defense to justify or excuse the killing unless he has withdrawn from the fray at a time and in a manner to clearly advise his adversary that he, in good faith, is desisting or intending to desist from further aggression." State v. Jelle, 21 Wn.App. 872, 587 P.2d 595, 597 (1978).

97. Ibid.; People v. Filippelli, 173 N.Y. 509, 66 N.E. 402 (1903). This is true no matter how hard he was pressed or how great was his danger. Freeman

v. State, 97 Okl.Cr. 275, 262 P.2d 713 (1953).

98. Stoffer v. State, 15 Ohio St. 47, 53 (1864). Quoted with approval, State v. Medlin, 126 N.C. 1127, 1133, 36 S.E. 344, 346 (1900).

"Under Ill.Rev.Stat.1973, ch. 38, par. 7–4, entitled Use of Force by Aggressor, only a completed withdrawal followed by a new encounter, initiated by the victim, . . . would allow defendant to avail himself of the theory of self-defense." People v. Carmack, 50 Ill.App.3d 983, 8 Ill.Dec. 941, 944, 366 N.E.2d 103, 106 (1977).

99. Pressley v. State, 395 So.2d 1175 (Fla.App.1981); People v. Peoples, 75 Mich.App. 616, 255 N.W.2d 707 (1977); State v. Ramey, 4 N.C.App. 469, 166 S.E.2d 868 (1969).

1. Mackin v. People, 214 Ill. 232, 73 N.E. 344 (1905); Johnson v. Commonwealth, 285 Ky. 374, 147 S.W.2d 1048 (1941).

"You are instructed that any *unlawful act* of a person which is reasonably calculated to lead to an affray or deadly conflict, and which provokes the difficulty, is an act of aggression or provocation which deprives him of the right of self-defense, although he does not strike the first blow." Held to be accurate. State v. Theroff, 25 Wn.App. 590, 608 P.2d 1254, 1257 (1980).

brought about the difficulty (unless he culpably participated in an unlawful contest of force). One does not become an "aggressor" by the mere use of reasonable efforts to restrain a trespasser and this is true even if he took the precaution of having a weapon with which to defend himself if necessary.[2] If the encounter arose out of a dispute as to the legal rights of the parties the privilege of self-defense is not dependent upon whose contention is correct. Such disputes are to be settled by due process of law rather than by physical violence. And he who resorts to violence in such a situation is a wrongdoer irrespective of the merits of the underlying claims.[3]

The fact that one who has been threatened arms himself for defense does not deprive him of the normal privilege, or of his right to go about his business as usual.[4] Where it seems a wise precaution, such a person may arm himself and go about his lawful business despite the fact that this will take him into the vicinity of the other[5] and thereby probably cause an attempt upon his life.[6] But one forfeits the privilege if he goes into the vicinity of the other on a mere pretext, knowing and intending that his mere presence will cause the attack.[7] It is not available to one who finds trouble by going out of his way to look for it.[8]

Not every unlawful act is of such a nature as to make one an "aggressor" in this sense. The fact that the difficulty arose out of an unlawful gambling game does not deprive the victim of a murderous assault of the privi-

2. Ayers v. State, 60 Miss. 709 (1883).

3. "If it be assumed that at the time of the killing deceased was at the opening in the fence for the purpose of preventing the defendant at all hazards from going through, and if it also be assumed that defendant was there intending to pass through at all hazards, still the question of self-defense is presented to the jury, regardless of the respective rights of the parties to the road. Under such circumstances, the man who began the deadly affray—that is, who by some overt act caused the other, as a reasonable man, to believe he was in great danger of loss of life or limb—placed himself without the protection of the law, and must take the consequences, whether those consequences be his death upon the ground, or the penalty imposed after trial by judge and jury." (Conviction reversed.) People v. Conkling, 111 Cal. 616, 621–2, 44 P. 314, 316 (1896).

4. "For one may know that if he travels along a certain highway he will be attacked by another with a deadly weapon, and be compelled in self-defense to kill his assailant, and yet he has the right to travel that highway, and is not compelled to turn out of his way to avoid the expected unlawful attack." People v. Gonzales, 71 Cal. 569, 578, 12 P. 783, 787 (1887).

One who has reason to fear an attack endangering his life has the right to arm himself in order to be prepared for defense. State v. Cochran, 78 N.M. 292, 430 P.2d 863 (1967).

5. State v. Evans, 124 Mo. 397, 28 S.W. 8 (1894). One who has been threatened with death may take suitable precautions for his defense. People v. Moore, 43 Cal.2d 517, 275 P.2d 485 (1954).

"One is entitled to go where he has a right to be without losing his right to assert self-defense in a murder prosecution." State v. Starks, 627 P.2d 88, 91 (Utah 1981).

6. People v. Batchelder, 27 Cal. 69 (1864).

7. State v. Neely, 20 Iowa 108 (1865); State v. Hawkins, 18 Or. 476, 23 P. 475 (1890).

". . . appellant had no legitimate claim to the defense of self-defense, since he had voluntarily placed himself in a position which he could reasonably expect would result in violence. Self-defense 'is not available to one who finds trouble by going out of his way looking for it.'" Nowlin v. United States, 382 A.2d 9, 14 (D.C.App.1978).

8. "The right of self-defense does not justify an act of retaliation or revenge. The self-defense concept is to protect person, not pride." People v. Woods, 81 Ill. 2d 537, 43 Ill.Dec. 733, 736, 410 N.E.2d 866, 869 (1980).

lege of self-defense.[9] Carrying a weapon in violation of law has its own penalty but does not deprive the person of the privilege of using it if necessary to defend himself against an attack threatening death or great bodily injury.[10] A trespasser, however, is not privileged to kill in self-defense if a safe retreat is available.[11] But even a trespasser may use deadly force in necessary self-defense if he has availed himself of every reasonable means of retreat.[12]

The use of words so vile that they are calculated to result in combat, and do so result, makes one an aggressor and deprives him of the privilege of self-defense, at least if they were spoken with this intent.[13] And there are indications that the mere use of such words will produce this result if they cause an encounter.[14] On the other hand, the use of words neither intended nor likely to result in physical violence does not impair the privilege of self-defense, even if they unexpectedly have this consequence.[15] Needless to say, conduct other than violence, menaces or words, may be so calculated to stir up strife as to constitute one an aggressor if a conflict does ensue: such conduct, for example, as dating another's wife after being ordered not to do so under threat of death.[16]

As one who has uttered words neither intended nor calculated to stir up strife is sometimes not entirely free from fault in regard to an ensuing encounter, it follows that no such perfection is required by the "no-retreat rule." Foster, in his distinction between the two types of homicide in self-defense, characterized the first as "perfectly innocent" and the second as "in some measure blameable." [17] And the rule has frequently been couched in terms of one "without fault." [18] Such a one clearly comes within the rule, when the other requisites are present. It need only be emphasized that a literal compliance with this phrase is not required. One may be recognized as "without fault" for the purpose of this rule if he is not the legally-recog-

9. State v. Leaks, 114 S.C. 257, 103 S.E. 549 (1919).

10. State v. Doris, 51 Or. 136, 94 P. 44 (1908); People v. King, 22 Cal.3d 12, 148 Cal.Rptr. 409, 582 P.2d 1000 (1978).

11. Macias v. State, 36 Ariz. 140, 283 P. 711 (1929).

The following instruction was approved: "A person who was a trespasser is not entitled to the defense of self-defense if he failed to use a reasonable safe [opportunity] to retreat from the imminent danger of death or great bodily harm." Walston v. State, 597 P.2d 768, 770 (Okl.Cr.App.1979).

12. Womack v. State, 36 Okl.Cr. 44, 253 P. 1027 (1927).

13. State v. Robinson, 213 N.C. 273, 195 S.E. 824 (1938).

"A person can become an aggressor if he or she purposely or knowingly provokes the other verbally." State v. Sorenson, ___ Mont. ___, 619 P.2d 1185, 1193 (1980).

14. Howard v. State, 122 Ark. 422, 183 S.W. 743 (1916); State v. Crisp, 170 N.C. 785, 87 S.E. 511 (1916); State v. Hunter, 82 S.C. 153, 63 S.E. 685 (1909); State v. Woodham, 162 S.C. 492, 160 S.E. 885 (1931); Scott v. Commonwealth, 143 Va. 510, 129 S.E. 360 (1925); State v. Bougneit, 97 Wis.2d 687, 294 N.W.2d 675 (App.1980).

"The right of self-defense is not available to a person who seeks a quarrel with the intent to create a real or apparent necessity of exercising self-defense." People v. Martin, 101 Cal.App.3d 1000, 162 Cal.Rptr. 133, 139 (1980).

15. Butler v. State, 92 Ga. 601, 19 S.E. 51 (1893); State v. Doris, 51 Or. 136, 94 P. 44 (1908).

16. Gillen v. State, 185 Tenn. 193, 204 S.W.2d 820 (1931).

17. Foster, Crown Law 273 (3d ed. 1809).

18. See, for example, People v. Holt, 25 Cal.2d 59, 63, 153 P.2d 21, 24 (1944).

nized cause of the encounter, did not culpably participate therein, and was at the time where he had a lawful right to be.

2. THE "RETREAT RULE"

A substantial minority of jurisdictions has adopted the so-called "retreat rule." [19] While the application has been considerably whittled away by exceptions, the underlying position can be stated in a summary of the stand taken by Beale.[20]

Even the innocent victim of a murderous assault must elect an obviously safe retreat, if available, rather than resort to deadly force unless (1) he is in his "castle" at the time,[21] or his assailant is (2) one he is lawfully attempting to arrest [22] or (3) a robber.[23]

The American Law Institute, adopting this position in general with a clear understanding of its status as a minority view,[24] did not include the third exception.[25] If the innocent victim is obliged to retreat, if he can with rea-

---

19. King v. State, 233 Ala. 198, 171 So. 254 (1936); State v. Lee, 36 Del. 11, 171 A. 195 (1933); Scoll v. State, 94 Fla. 1138, 115 So. 43 (1927); State v. Emery, 236 Iowa 60, 17 N.W.2d 854 (1945); State v. Cox, 138 Me. 151, 23 A.2d 634 (1941); State v. Rheams, 34 Minn. 18, 24 N.W. 302 (1885); State v. Di Maria, 88 N.J.L. 416, 97 A. 248 (1916), aff'd 90 N.J.L. 341, 100 A. 1071; Commonwealth v. Kwayne, 221 Pa. 449, 70 A. 809 (1908); State v. George, 119 S.C. 120, 111 S.E. 880 (1921); State v. Roberts, 63 Vt. 139, 21 A. 424 (1890).

"The law of excusable homicide requires that the defendant must have employed all means reasonably in his power, consistent with his own safety, to avoid danger and avert the necessity of taking another's life. This requirement includes the duty to retreat, if, and, to the extent, that it can be done in safety." State v. Kennamore, 604 S.W.2d 856, 859–60 (Tenn.1980).

Because the evidence indicated that defendant could have safely retreated he was not entitled to a judgment of acquittal on the basis of self-defense. State v. Watts, 29 Or.App. 397, 563 P.2d 770 (1977).

A police officer is under no obligation to retreat before using deadly force to protect himself against threatened deadly force. United States v. Thomas, 11 MJ 315 (CMA 1981). 2 Wharton's Criminal Law (14th ed. Torcia) § 126 (1979).

Under the Hawaii statute the use of deadly force in defense is not justifiable if: "The actor knows that he can avoid the necessity of using such force with complete safety by retreating." State v.

Napoleon, ___ Hawaii App. ___, 633 P.2d 547, 549 (1981).

20. Beale, Retreat from a Murderous Assault, 16 Harv.L.Rev. 567 (1903).

21. State v. Robinson, 42 Del. 419, 36 A.2d 27 (1944); Commonwealth v. Fraser, 369 Pa. 273, 85 A.2d 126 (1952); State v. Preece, 116 W.Va. 176, 179 S.E. 524 (1935).

22. Boykin v. People, 22 Colo. 496, 45 P. 419 (1896).

23. Sovereign Camp, W. O. W. v. Gunn, 229 Ala. 508, 158 So. 192 (1935); State v. Bonofiglio, 67 N.J.L. 239, 52 A. 712 (1901); Commonwealth v. Foster, 364 Pa. 288, 72 A.2d 279 (1950).

24. In regard to this provision Professor Bohlen made this explanation at the annual meeting: "The Reporter, with the approval of the Council, has taken a position which, on investigation seems to be supported by a minority of American jurisdictions." 4 Proceedings A.L.I., Appendix 230 (1926).

25. The innocent victim of a murderous assault is privileged to stand his ground and use deadly force, if this reasonably seems necessary for his own defense there, although he "reasonably believes that he can safely avoid the necessity of so defending himself,

(a) by retreating, if, but only if, he is attacked within his dwelling place which is not also the dwelling place of the other, or

(b) by permitting the other to intrude upon or dispossess him of his dwelling place, or

sonable safety, rather than use deadly force in defense against one who comes to murder him, it seems logical to conclude that he should have the same duty in regard to one who comes to rob him. But this provision of the Restatement seems to be the one and only indication of such a common-law requirement in case of attempted robbery while countless statements and holdings have been made to the contrary.[26]

The contention that the "retreat rule" tends to enhance the risk of the innocent is without foundation. The proper application of this rule never requires the innocent victim to increase his own peril for the safety of a murderous assailant.[27] "The doctrine of 'retreat to the wall' had its origin before the general introduction of guns," said the Minnesota court.[28] "Justice demands that its application have due regard to the present general use and to the type of firearms. It would be good sense for the law to require, in many cases, an attempt to escape from a hand to hand encounter with fists, clubs, and even knives, as a condition of justification for killing in self-defense; while it would be rank folly to so require when experienced men, armed with repeating rifles, face each other in an open space, removed from shelter, with intent to kill or to do great bodily harm. What might be a reasonable chance for escape in the one situation might in the other be certain death. Self-defense has not, by statute nor by judicial opinion, been distorted, by an unreasonable requirement of the duty to retreat, into self-destruction." No relaxation of the "retreat rule" concept was intended. This was offered merely as an interpretation of the requirement.

Real exceptions to the original concept have appeared in the form of additional places from which no retreat is required. They create an "enlarged castle," so to speak. No enlargement was involved in the holding in regard to a roomer. His room is his dwelling place and hence he is under no obligation to retreat if attacked in his room,[29] although if attacked in another part of the house he must (under the "retreat rule") retreat to his room, if he can in safety, before using deadly force,—at least if the assailant is the owner or another occupant of the building.[30]

Probably no enlargement has been involved in the curtilage cases[31] although this is not entirely beyond question. In its origin the "castle doc-

(c) by abandoning an attempt to effect a lawful arrest." Restatement, Second, Torts § 65(2)(c) (1965).

26. Lambard, Eirenarcha 248 (4th ed. 1599); 3 Co.Inst. *56; 1 Hale P.C. *481; Foster, Crown Law 274 (3d ed. 1809); 1 East P.C. 271 (1803); Sovereign Camp W. O. W. v. Gunn, 229 Ala. 508, 158 So. 192 (1934); State v. Bonofiglio, 67 N.J.L. 239, 52 A. 712 (1901); Commonwealth v. Foster, 364 Pa. 288, 72 A.2d 279 (1950).

27. State v. Borwick, 193 Iowa 639, 187 N.W. 460 (1922).

Under the retreat rule the innocent victim of a murderous attack is not deprived of the right to use deadly force in his defense by reason of an avenue of escape which he did not know existed. Commonwealth v. Palmer, 467 Pa. 476, 359 A.2d 375 (1976).

28. State v. Gardner, 96 Minn. 318, 327, 104 N.W. 971, 975 (1905).

29. Thomas v. State, 255 Ala. 632, 53 So.2d 340 (1951); Harris v. State, 96 Ala. 24, 11 So. 255 (1891); State v. Sorrentino, 31 Wyo. 129, 224 P. 420 (1924); State v. Browning, 28 N.C.App. 376, 221 S.E.2d 375 (1976).

30. State v. Dyer, 147 Iowa 217, 124 N.W. 629 (1910).

Since both deceased and appellant were residents of the house, appellant had a duty to retreat in event of assault from deceased. Commonwealth v. Walker, 447 Pa. 146, 288 A.2d 741 (1972).

31. People v. Godsey, 54 Mich.App. 316, 220 N.W.2d 801 (1974).

Area of backyard between garage and backdoor of kitchen was within curtilage

trine" was thought of, not in connection with the innocent victim of a murderous assault, but as a place from which not even the participant in a "chance-medley" was obliged to retreat.[32] And the scope of this special privilege granted to one so far at fault might have been limited to the actual building. This is mere speculation. But cases are available in regard to the innocent victim of a murderous assault. Even in "retreat rule" jurisdictions such a one may stand his ground if he is within the curtilage of his dwelling at the time.[33]

Without question, however, there has been a tendency to enlarge the "castle" concept if this word is used figuratively to mean all places from which the innocent victim of a murderous assault is not required to retreat, before resorting to deadly force, in a "retreat rule" jurisdiction. There has been a definite trend in the direction of holding that one is no more obliged to retreat from his place of business[34] than from his dwelling. And this has been extended to include the private driveway leading to the place of business of a garage owner,[35] and even to the open field if that is where one

of home so as to occasion rule that one attacked on his own premises is entitled to stand his ground. State v. Browning, 28 N.C.App. 376, 221 S.E.2d 375 (1976). But see State v. Bonano, 59 N.J. 515, 284 A.2d 345 (1971).

32. Lambard, Eirenarcha 250 (3d ed. 1599).

33. Bowen v. State, 217 Ala. 574, 117 So. 204 (1928); Naugher v. State, 105 Ala. 26, 17 So. 24 (1894); Hart v. State, 161 Ark. 649, 257 S.W. 354 (1924); State v. Bennett, 128 Iowa 713, 105 N.W. 324 (1905); People v. Kuehn, 93 Mich. 619, 53 N.W. 721 (1892); Fortune v. Commonwealth, 133 Va. 669, 112 S.E. 861 (1922); State v. Cushing, 14 Wash. 527, 45 P. 145 (1896).

Washington seems to have gone over to the "no retreat rule" position. State v. Hiatt, 187 Wash. 226, 60 P.2d 71 (1936). But it had not definitely taken such a stand at the time of the Cushing case, supra. But see Collier v. State, 49 Ala.App. 685, 275 So.2d 364 (1973).

Where **D**, who used a gun to kill **X**, could easily have gone back into **D**'s house and closed the door, thus preventing the approach of **X** who was coming with a knife, there was no error in refusing to instruct the jury that **D** was under no duty to retreat from his assailant. "A human life, even that of an aggressor, is regarded as more valuable than the fetish of the close." State v. Bonano, 113 N.J.Super. 210, 273 A.2d 392 (1971), rev'd on finding that at the time **X** approached **D** was in his doorway and had no duty to retreat. 59 N.J. 515, 284 A.2d 345 (1971).

Under new Texas penal code (V.T.C.A. Penal Code § 9.32(2)) (1974), a person is required to retreat if a reasonable person in his position would have done so. The fact that defendant was inside her home at the time she shot the deceased is only a factor to be considered by the jury in determining whether she satisfied the retreat obligation imposed by statute. Valentine v. State, 587 S.W.2d 399 (Tex.Cr. App.1979).

34. Askew v. State, 94 Ala. 4, 10 So. 657 (1891); State v. Baratta, 242 Iowa 1308, 49 N.W.2d 866 (1951); Willis v. State, 43 Neb. 102, 61 N.W. 254 (1894); State v. Griggs, 218 S.C. 86, 61 S.E.2d 653 (1950); State v. Turner, 95 Utah 129, 79 P.2d 46 (1938).

And see Bryant v. State, 252 Ala. 153, 39 So.2d 657 (1949). Contra: Wilson v. State, 69 Ga. 224 (1882).

And see Hail v. Commonwealth, 94 Ky. 322, 22 S.W. 333 (1893) (not a deadly attack).

There is no duty to retreat imposed upon one attacked at his place of business. State v. Smith, 376 So.2d 261 (Fla.App. 1979). See also People v. Johnson, 75 Mich.App. 337, 254 N.W.2d 667 (1977) (private security guard on employer's premises).

The right to stand his ground applies to one while in his dwelling house, office or place of business, or within the curtilage thereof. Bryant v. State, 252 Ala. 153, 39 So.2d 657 (1949).

35. State v. Sipes, 202 Iowa 173, 209 N.W. 458 (1926).

works.[36] Some courts have held that the privilege is available whenever the innocent victim is on his own premises at the time.[37] Missouri added also the public highway,[38] but there is so little difference between this and the "no retreat rule" that the court moved on to the latter position.[39]

What seems to be the greatest enlargement of the "castle" in a "retreat rule" jurisdiction is found in South Carolina. One is in his "castle" there not only if he is in his home or place of business, including an employee while working at his place of employment,[40] but also if "on property owned or lawfully occupied by him."[41] This is true also when he is at his club. "A man is no more bound to allow himself to be run out of his rest room than his workshop."[42] It is not true, however, merely because he is on a public highway.[43] Nor does it apply to an employee who is at his place of employment at other than regular hours and not for any purpose connected with his employment.[44]

The "castle" of the host becomes that also of his guest while the latter is present in that capacity. Hence the guest is under no more obligation to retreat than his host if attacked by an intruder.[45] If the assailant should be another guest the legal view is that one occupant has attacked another occupant of the same "castle." On this point the "retreat rule" jurisdictions are not in accord. A number of cases have held that there is no greater duty to retreat from another occupant than from an outsider,[46] but other cases have denied the special privilege in such a situation.[47]

36. State v. Gordon, 128 S.C. 422, 122 S.E. 501 (1924).

37. Foster v. Territory, 6 Ariz. 240, 56 P. 738 (1899); State v. Hewitt, 205 S.C. 207, 31 S.E.2d 257 (1944). Contra: Lee v. State, 92 Ala. 15, 9 So. 407 (1890).

It seems that in *Hewitt* the defendant was within the curtilage at the time. This fact was not relied upon in the opinion and in a later case the court made it clear that the rule was not limited to the curtilage. State v. Davis, 214 S.C. 34, 37, 51 S.W.2d 86, 87 (1948).

38. State v. Hudspeth, 150 Mo. 12, 51 S.W. 483 (1899).

39. State v. Bartlett, 170 Mo. 658, 71 S.W. 148 (1902).

40. State v. Gordon, 128 S.C. 422, 122 S.E. 501 (1924).

41. State v. Davis, 214 S.C. 34, 37, 51 S.E.2d 86, 87 (1948).

Appellant had no duty to retreat because he was on his "own land" at the time of the confrontation. The land in question was not appellant's home but lakefront property which he owned. The dissent points out that "the final meeting between the two men occurred by chance on a portion of Mr. Hendrix's property next to a road." State v. Hendrix, 270 S.C. 653, 244 S.E.2d 503, 507 (1978).

42. State v. Marlowe, 120 S.C. 205, 207, 112 S.E. 921, 922 (1922).

43. State v. McGee, 185 S.C. 184, 193 S.C. 303 (1937).

44. State v. Davis, 214 S.C. 34, 51 S.E.2d 86 (1948).

45. Kelley v. State, 226 Ala. 80, 145 So. 816 (1933); State v. Osborne, 200 S.C. 504, 21 S.E.2d 178 (1942).

A guest has no duty to retreat. Barton v. State, 46 Md.App. 616, 420 A.2d 1009 (1980).

46. Bryant v. State, 252 Ala. 153, 39 So.2d 657 (1949); State v. Phillips, 38 Del. 24, 187 A. 721 (1936); State v. Leeper, 199 Iowa 432, 200 N.W. 732 (1925); People v. Tomlins, 213 N.Y. 240, 107 N.E. 496 (1914); State v. Gordon, 128 S.C. 422, 122 S.E. 501 (1924).

Tomlins was decided while New York was still following the "retreat rule."

The Model Penal Code provides that the innocent victim of an attack is not required to retreat from his dwelling, nor from his place of work unless the attack is by one known to be a co-worker there. Section 3.04(2)(b)(ii)(1).

47. Baker v. Commonwealth, 305 Ky. 88, 202 S.W.2d 1010 (1947); State v. Grierson, 96 N.H. 36, 69 A.2d 851 (1950);

A statement by Cardozo has been frequently quoted.

It is not now and never has been the law that a man assailed in his own dwelling is bound to retreat. If assailed there, he may stand his ground and resist the attack. He is under no duty to take to the fields and the highways, a fugitive from his own home. . . . The rule is the same whether the attack proceeds from some other occupant or from an intruder.[48]

Despite the stand taken by the Institute the trend has been rather in the direction of enlarging, than of narrowing, the defensive privilege against murderous attack. Courts which adopted the "no-retreat rule," frequently under the false impression that this required departure from the English common law,[49] have shown little tendency to alter this stand. The other courts, as pointed out, have shown an inclination to enlarge the "castle" concept, sometimes to the point of going over entirely to the other position.

The most abrupt and striking change occurred in New York a few years ago. In *Ligouri*,[50] in 1940, the New York court, long regarded as one of the leading proponents of "retreat," switched suddenly over to "no retreat" in one bold stroke. In doing so it did not purport to overrule its previous decisions.[51] The holding was grounded upon an interpretation of the statute.[52] The requirement of retreat, it was said, is when the privilege is based upon the subdivision authorizing the use of force in self-defense; but there is no such requirement under the subdivision authorizing force in actual resistance of an attempted felony upon the person. Neither subdivision mentioned either retreat or standing ground. But if they were intended to codify the English common law the interpretation was unquestionably sound. In the familiar terminology of the early courts and writers, the innocent victim who was using force against one attempting to murder him, was doing so for the prevention of a violent felony rather than *se defendendo*.

3. "PERFECT" AND "IMPERFECT" SELF-DEFENSE

In the classification of nonfelonious homicide in self-defense as either justifiable or excusable, Lambard, Coke, Hale, Hawkins, Foster, Blackstone and East all [53] had in mind the distinction between a privilege which is perfect and one that is imperfect, although they did not use those words. The one did not require retreat as a condition of its exercise, and if death resulted there was an acquittal with no forfeiture whatever. The other required "retreat to the wall," and if the defender used fatal force as a last extremity

Commonwealth v. Johnson, 213 Pa. 432, 62 A. 1064 (1906).

48. People v. Tomlins, 213 N.Y. 240, 107 N.E. 496, 497-98 (1914).

49. See, e.g., Enyart v. People, 67 Colo. 434, 438, 180 P. 722, 723 (1919); Runyan v. State, 57 Ind. 80, 84 (1877); State v. Bartlett, 170 Mo. 658, 668, 71 S.W. 148, 151 (1902).

50. People v. Ligouri, 284 N.Y. 309, 31 N.E.2d 37 (1940).

51. E.g., People v. Kennedy, 159 N.Y. 346, 54 N.E. 51 (1899); People v. Constantino, 153 N.Y. 24, 47 N.E. 37 (1897).

52. McKinney's N.Y.Penal Law § 1055 (1909). The present statute requires a different interpretation and is a return to the retreat rule. McKinney's N.Y.Rev.Pen.Law § 35.15 (1980).

53. Lambard, Eirenarcha 248 (4th ed. 1599); 3 Co.Inst. *55; 1 Hale P.C. *481; 1 Hawk.P.C. c. 28, §§ 21, 24 (6th ed. by Leach 1788); Foster, Crown Law 273 (3d ed. 1809); Bl.Comm. 180, 183-4; 1 East P.C. 271-2, 279 (1803).

after the "wall" was reached he was, for generations, not entitled to an acquittal but subjected to some forfeiture.

Bishop employed these labels to express a different distinction. His emphasis was upon the degree of permissible force.[54] He would apply the label "perfect defence" if the law, under the circumstances, placed no limit upon the use of force other than what reasonably seems necessary to ward off the threatened harm; whereas, if deadly force is not permitted, even if the harm cannot be prevented without it, his label would be "imperfect defence." [55] Thus he would speak of the privilege of defense against a nonfelonious attack as "imperfect" since one must submit to an ordinary battery and have his remedy in court rather than endanger the life of his assailant.[56] In other words, while one privilege permits more to be done, if necessary, than the other, the exercise of either leaves the user entirely free from criminal guilt.

A few courts have used these terms to express results different from either of these. They apply the label "perfect" if the defense, having resulted in homicide, entitles the defender to an acquittal; and "imperfect" if it merely reduces the grade of his offense to manslaughter.[57] This position seems to have crept into the cases as a result of accident or oversight. A Texas case, *Reed*,[58] is generally considered the cornerstone of an "imperfect right of self-defence" [59] the fatal exercise of which does not entitle the user to an acquittal but reduces the grade of the homicide to manslaughter. The court in that case was not dealing with an ordinary battery or fisticuffs which unexpectedly led to mortal combat. No such problem was involved. A paramour had killed the outraged husband who had caught him in adultery. His explanation was that the husband had attacked him and he was forced to kill to save his own life. An important element of the case was the unusual provision of the Texas statute[60] by which the husband would have been justified had he killed the paramour under those circumstances. That is, defendant had intentionally killed an innocent man,—one not guilty of any violation of law. This is quite different from the so-called killing in "chance-medley," where the circumstances are such that the deceased could have been convicted of assault had he survived. Reed's conviction of murder was reversed because of a holding that it was error to omit an instruction on manslaughter.[61] It is quite understandable why the court did not suggest an acquittal under those circumstances. But certain generalizations in the opinion, quite beyond anything needed for the decision, have received undue attention in some of the later cases.[62]

---

54. 1 Bishop, New Criminal Law §§ 836–877 (8th ed. 1892).

55. Id. at § 840.

56. Id. at § 867.

57. State v. Painter, 329 Mo. 314, 44 S.W.2d 79 (1931); State v. Davidson, 95 Mo. 155, 8 S.W. 413 (1888); Carver v. State, 67 Tex.Cr.R. 116, 148 S.W. 746 (1912); People v. Flannel, 25 Cal.3d 668, 160 Cal.Rptr. 84, 603 P.2d 1 (1979).

58. Reed v. State, 11 Tex.App. 509 (1882).

59. Id. at 513.

60. "Homicide is justifiable when committed by the husband upon one tak-

en in the act of adultery with the wife, provided the killing take place before the parties to the act of adultery have separated." Article 567 of the then Penal Code. Id. at 516.

61. If an adulterer, caught in the act, kills the husband to ward off an attack by him, this is not necessarily manslaughter, it was pointed out in a later case. The rule is merely that the jury may find the circumstances "mitigate his offense" so that it is less than murder. Davis v. State, 81 Tex.Cr.R. 450, 451, 196 S.W. 520, 522 (1917).

62. E.g., Carver v. State, 67 Tex.Cr.R. 116, 148 S.W. 746 (1912).

Few courts have had more occasion to refer to the concept of "imperfect self-defense" than is to be found in the Missouri decisions. And the whole development there seems traceable to the unfortunate use of a single word in a leading case.

In *Partlow*[63] the court was seeking to emphasize the distinction between one who is at fault in bringing on a quarrel with malice aforethought, and one who provokes an encounter with no intent to kill or injure. It intended to announce the very sound position that one who starts out with the malicious intention of using deadly force is guilty of murder if he slays the other in that encounter no matter what danger to himself may be involved. And also that he who brings on an encounter intending no more than an ordinary battery is guilty of manslaughter if he kills in self-defense without retreating, but excused if forced to use deadly force to save himself after he has "retreated to the wall." It is clear that the court had in mind the common-law duty of retreat by one engaged in a "chance-medley" because it discusses "retreating to the wall," mentions the theory that the "wall" is reached when further retreat is dangerous, adding: "And retreat need not be attempted when the attack is so fierce that the assailed, by retreating, will apparently expose himself to death." [64]

The court was not thinking in terms of "withdrawal" in the sense of one who succeeds in actually removing himself from the combat or effectively communicating an intent to abandon it. Had that been the concept the court would not have denied the privilege even to one who had made a murderous attack upon the other. Moreover the court reversed the conviction because the judge had instructed the jury that if they believed the defendant provoked or sought the difficulty they would not be authorized to *acquit* him no matter "how hard he was pressed, or how imminent his peril may have become during said difficulty." [65] In discussing these problems the court speaks in terms of "the right of perfect and the right of imperfect self-defence." [66] As it quotes Bishop, and relies upon him for the position taken, it was no doubt employing these terms with the meanings assigned to them by that author. Unfortunately, however, in speaking of the law of "retreat to the wall" the court made use of the word "withdraw." [67]

The following year, in a case in which there was no effort on the part of the defendant to retreat, the court took the sound position that if he started the difficulty with no intent to cause death or great bodily harm, and killed the other in a sudden heat of passion engendered by the conflict, he was guilty of manslaughter,[68] which was repeated some years later.[69] In another

---

63. State v. Partlow, 90 Mo. 608, 4 S.W. 14 (1886).

64. Id. at 628, 4 S.W. 23 (quoting Wharton).

65. Id. at 613, 4 S.W. 16. The defendant requested the judge to qualify this instruction so that defendant's plea of self-defense would not be denied unless he provoked the difficulty with felonious intent. Refusal of this request was part of the ground for reversal.

66. Id. at 620, 4 S.W. 19.

67. Id. at 627, 4 S.W. 22. This is further evidence of the court's reliance upon

Bishop because that author uses this word as a synonym of "retreat" and not in the sense of getting entirely away from the other or effectively giving notice that the fight is over. 1 Bishop, New Criminal Law §§ 870, 871 (8th ed. 1892).

68. State v. Hicks, 92 Mo. 431, 4 S.W. 742 (1887).

69. State v. Goddard, 146 Mo. 177, 180, 48 S.W. 82, 83 (1898). In reversing a conviction of murder because the judge's instruction ignored the intention with which defendant started the encounter,

case,[70] after pointing out that *Partlow* held that whether self-defense was "perfect" or "imperfect" depended upon the intent with which defendant brought on the quarrel, or willingly entered therein, the court said: "or if, having entered into a fight without felonious intent, he seeks in good faith to abandon it and withdraws as far as he can, and his adversary still pursues him, then if necessary to save his own life he slay his opponent, he will be justified." The court had combined both points in an earlier case.[71] In reversing a conviction of murder because of an improper instruction with reference to one who entered the contest with no intent to kill or injure, the court said: "notwithstanding defendant may have been the aggressor, he may withdraw in good faith from the combat, and if pressed to the wall may kill his adversary to save his own life and be justifiable; or without withdrawing, if he kills his adversary *under such circumstances*, he will be guilty only of manslaughter and not of murder."

In these cases the court seems to have had clearly in mind the common-law distinction between a killing in the sudden heat of passion, and a killing after "retreat to the wall," by one who has provoked or willingly engaged in an encounter in which he intended no more than an ordinary battery. It was not true, however, in certain other cases. In these, "imperfect self-defense" was thought of as something which does not exonerate but merely reduces the grade of the offense to manslaughter.[72] And when the court came to distinguish between "retreat" and "withdrawal" it regarded the latter as a bona fide effort to get away, but the former as merely a combat maneuver or fighting technique.[73] In this analysis the concept of "retreat to the wall" was lost sight of entirely because of the requirement, clearly recognized by the court, that "withdrawal" (to be effective) must be made known to the other party. After "withdrawal" in this sense (which is the usual meaning

the court says that if he did so with intent to kill he has no right of self-defense, but if he had no felonious purpose "and in the heat of passion slays his adversary" he is guilty of manslaughter only.

70. State v. Gordon, 191 Mo. 114, 125, 89 S.W. 1025, 1028 (1905). This was quoted with approval in State v. Sebastian, 215 Mo. 58, 85, 114 S.W. 522, 529–30 (1908). And see State v. Herrell, 97 Mo. 105, 110, 10 S.W. 387, 389 (1889).

71. State v. Vaughan, 141 Mo. 514, 522, 42 S.W. 1080, 1081 (1897).

The requirement of "withdrawal" in the law of self-defense is not satisfied by a retreat as far as safety permits. Hence the court's statement that one in defendant's position is privileged to kill "if pressed to the wall," shows that it was referring to the concept of "retreat" although the word used is "withdraw."

72. State v. Davidson, 95 Mo. 155, 8 S.W. 413 (1888). And see State v. Pennington, 146 Mo. 27, 36, 47 S.W. 799, 801

(1898). The idea is found in certain cases in which the point was not involved because a conviction of murder was affirmed. State v. Gilmore, 95 Mo. 554, 8 S.W. 359, 912 (1888); State v. Parker, 106 Mo. 217, 17 S.W. 180 (1891); State v. Painter, 329 Mo. 314, 44 S.W.2d 79 (1931). In one case in which a conviction of murder was reversed because of a failure to give an instruction which might have reduced the verdict to manslaughter the defendant had shot another who was approaching with an ax on the other side of a fence. State v. Roberts, 280 Mo. 669, 217 S.W. 988 (1920). In one case this was the very instruction requested by the defendant. State v. Darling, 202 Mo. 150, 100 S.W. 631 (1906). See also People v. Flannel, 25 Cal.3d 668, 160 Cal.Rptr. 84, 603 P.2d 1 (1979).

73. State v. Heath, 237 Mo. 255, 267, 141 S.W. 26, 29 (1911); State v. Gadwood, 342 Mo. 466, 492, 116 S.W.2d 42, 57 (1938).

of the term in the law of self-defense) the normal privilege of self-defense is restored whether the original assault was felonious or not felonious.[74]

The difference in the various uses of the terms can be emphasized to best advantage by assuming a situation in which one, who provoked an encounter with no thought of more than an ordinary battery, suddenly and unexpectedly finds himself confronted with deadly force. Had the early English judges or writers been asked for a classification of such a situation in these terms they would have labeled this "imperfect self-defense." Their reason would have been that such a person was not entitled to stand his ground. And if he killed as a last resort after "retreating to the wall" the homicide would not have been justifiable but only excusable. Bishop would have said that if any such right was available in this case it would be "perfect self-defense." His explanation would have been that this participant in a "chance-medley" would not be authorized to use any force until he had "retreated to the wall." But when his back was at the "wall" (no safe retreat available) the only limit upon the force he might use was what reasonably seemed necessary to save himself from death or great bodily harm. Courts employing these terms in the third sense would apply the label "imperfect self-defense." And they would do so because they hold that under these circumstances even a necessary killing as the only means of avoiding death or great bodily harm is not excusable but only sufficient to reduce the grade of the homicide to manslaughter.

4. CONCLUSION

It is quite unsound to speak of a privilege or "right" the exercise of which subjects to criminal liability. To explain that this is because it is "imperfect" is unacceptable. If it has such a consequence it is not a privilege or right at all but an unlawful act. And if homicide resulting from an unlawful act, with intent to kill, is reduced to manslaughter it is because of mitigating circumstances.[75] Moreover, if a guilty participant in what started out as a nondeadly scuffle has killed his adversary, there should be a difference between one who did so as a last resort in self-defense when his back was at the "wall" and another who did so, not defensively, but in the sudden heat of passion engendered by the fight. Those who take the position that homicide resulting from the "imperfect right of self-defense" is manslaughter, do so upon the ground that the slayer is not entitled to go free because of his wrong in starting, or culpably participating in, the encounter. The premise is sound but the conclusion faulty. One who has struck an ordinary blow without justification or excuse is not entitled to go free, of course. He should be convicted of assault and battery which is his real offense. But he should not be held criminally responsible for a homicide which was forced upon him by the greater wrong of the other party. While statistics are not available it is a safe estimate that not once in a thousand times does the ordinary angry slap or fisticuffs result in the use of deadly force on either side. On the rare occasion when this does happen, only he who unexpectedly

---

74. State v. Mayberry, 360 Mo. 35, 226 S.W.2d 725 (1950); State v. Williams, 337 Mo. 884, 894, 87 S.W.2d 175, 180 (1935); State v. Patterson, 159 Mo. 560, 562, 60 S.W. 1047, 1048 (1901).

75. "Mitigate his offense." Davis v. State, 81 Tex.Cr.R. 450, 451, 196 S.W. 520, 522 (1917).

changed the ordinary encounter into a life and death struggle should be regarded as having brought about the mortal combat.[76]

The term has recently been applied to a different situation. California held, as a rule of common law, that an honest but unreasonable belief in the necessity of using deadly force in self-defense, while not excusable, is sufficiently mitigating to reduce what would otherwise be murder to manslaughter.[77] And this was referred to as "imperfect self-defense." [78] It was mentioned earlier that it is unacceptable to use the term "imperfect" in speaking of a claim of privilege or right, the exercise of which subjects to criminal liability. It should be added that no impropriety is involved in referring to self-defense that is inexcusable, but exercised under circumstances amounting to mitigation, as "imperfect self-defense."

The Texas court found still a different use for the term "imperfect self-defense." Evans was convicted of murder and the punishment assessed at death. It had been shown that he entered a jewelry store to commit robbery. He pointed a pistol at the manager who then fired at him. Evans then shot and killed the manager. Because he entered the store with intent to commit robbery, Evans had no right of self-defense, and he was not entitled to have a self-defense issue submitted to the jury in the "guilt-or-innocence" phase of the trial. But he was entitled to have his "imperfect self-defense claim" submitted at the penalty phase of the trial, as a mitigating circumstance. Shooting after being fired upon is less culpable than shooting without such provocation.[79]

This also seems to be an acceptable use of the term. In other words, if self-defense is exercised under circumstances sufficient to justify the killing, the defense is "perfect." If it is under circumstances not sufficient to justify the killing, but sufficient to establish some lesser position of advantage to the slayer, it is "imperfect." But there is no *right* of self-defense unless the use of force for this purpose would be fully justified. Imperfect self-defense may be spoken of as a "claim" or a "benefit."

Other considerations may require attention in a particular case. Taking the precaution of being armed is such a consideration. Arming oneself to be ready to defend against an expected murderous attack is one thing. Taking along a weapon to be used if an unlawful blow should be countered with deadly force is quite another. He who has killed his adversary in an encounter entered into under these circumstances, is guilty of manslaughter,[80] if not murder. Under other circumstances the development of the contest into

---

76. "But when an assault is returned with a violence manifestly disproportionate to that of the assault, the character of the combat is essentially changed, and the assaulted becomes in his turn the assailant." State v. Hill, 20 N.C. 629, 634 (1839).

77. People v. Flannel, 25 Cal.3d 668, 160 Cal.Rptr. 84, 603 P.2d 1 (1979). A Kansas court has apparently concluded the mistaken use of excessive deadly force could reduce a killing to the offense of involuntary manslaughter under the Kansas statute. State v. Warren, 5 Kan. App.2d 754, 624 P.2d 476, 479 (1981).

78. People v. Gott, 117 Cal.App.3d 125, 173 Cal.Rptr. 469, 472 (1981).

79. Evans v. State, 601 S.W.2d 943 (Tex.Cr.App.1980).

80. Macias v. State, 39 Ariz. 303, 6 P.2d 423 (1931); State v. McCaskill, 160 Iowa 554, 142 N.W. 445 (1913); State v. Schroeder, 103 Kan. 770, 176 P. 659 (1918). In these cases the court did not emphasize the fact that defendant had armed himself in advance but this was the factual situation back of the decision. Compare these cases with State v. Whitnah, 129 Iowa 211, 105 N.W. 432

deadly proportions may have been so clearly probable that this is one of the most important factors in the case. But one who has struck an unlawful blow with no intention or expectation of inflicting more than an ordinary battery should not be held criminally accountable for a homicide he is forced to commit to save his own life, no reasonable retreat being available, unless from the start this necessity was plainly foreseeable as a likely consequence.

The controversy over "retreat" or "no retreat" is also entitled to a parting word. While it seems impossible to support Beale's position, as a statement of the common law of England, it is very difficult to give a successful answer to his argument that the "no-retreat" rule tends to perpetuate a rough frontier philosophy which places a false notion of "honor" above life itself. The claim that the "retreat rule" tends to breed a race of cowards is quite spurious.[81] There is seldom an obviously safe retreat where both parties have firearms.[82] The usual situation is where the defender is so armed while the assailant is approaching with some other weapon which is deadly but does not have so long a reach.[83] Under such circumstances it does not require much bravery to shoot the other while he is still beyond the effective range of his own weapon. But this is an argument which should be addressed to the legislative body rather than to the court. In a jurisdiction in which the "no-retreat" rule has prevailed in the past, the change to the other rule must not be made by a judicial decision which has the effect of convicting a man of crime for doing what was privileged at the time it was done.

MODEL PENAL CODE

Whereas the English common law, with reference to the privilege of using deadly force, placed the major emphasis upon law enforcement and crime prevention, the Code places it upon self-defense and the defense of others. At common law an innocent victim is privileged to use deadly force if this reasonably seems necessary to prevent being robbed. In doing so he is exercising the privilege of crime prevention. He is preventing the commission of a violent felony. The different approach of the Code is emphasized by the following explanation of its provisions: "The victim of a robbery may then refuse to yield his property and, if his refusal should precipitate a threat of deadly force, use equal force—not to prevent the robbery—but to defend himself." [84]

(1905); State v. Hatch, 57 Kan. 420, 46 P. 708 (1896).

81. It is "formed in the ethics of the duelist, the German officer, and the buccaneer." Beale, Retreat from a Murderous Assault, 16 Harv.L.Rev. 567, 577 (1903).

The law does not consider the wounded pride which may result from declining to fight. Springfield v. State, 96 Ala. 81, 85, 11 So. 250, 252 (1892).

The law recognizes the right of a man to stand in all proper places; but when it comes to the question whether one man shall flee or another shall live, the law

decides that the former shall flee rather than that the latter shall die. Commonwealth v. Drum, 58 Pa. 9, 22 (1868).

82. State v. Gardner, 96 Minn. 318, 104 N.W. 971 (1905).

83. In one case, for example, the defendant shot the deceased who was angrily approaching with a pitchfork. But the deceased was so old and decrepit that defendant could have avoided him by simply walking away. State v. Donnelly, 69 Iowa 705, 27 N.W. 369 (1886).

84. Model Penal Code 26 (Tent.Draft No. 8, 1958).

For the most part the Code follows the prevailing law with reference to the use of nondeadly force in self-defense, and the "retreat rule" position in the use of deadly force.[85]

THE NEW PENAL CODES

The effort of those who drafted the Model Penal Code to substitute the word "protection" for the time-honored "defense" in dealing with this topic has had little effect upon legislation. A very few of the new codes speak in terms of "protection" [86] but the vast majority are worded in terms of "defense." [87] With reference to the dispute whether the innocent victim of a murderous attack must take advantage of a safe method of retreat, if available, or is privileged to stand his ground and use deadly force if that seems reasonably necessary to defend his life at the point of attack, the new codes seem to make little change. A substantial number do not mention retreat,[88] while almost an equal number require the safe retreat[89] unless the defender is attacked in his dwelling[90] or his place of work,[91] or is an officer in the lawful performance of his duties, or a private person assisting such officer.[92] Some of the codes requiring such retreat also deny the use of deadly force if it can be avoided by surrendering possession of a thing to a person asserting a claim of right thereto,[93] or by complying with a demand to abstain from action which is not required by any duty.[94]

SECTION 5. DEFENSE OF ANOTHER

The privilege of using force in defense of others, as a separate privilege, developed partly by accident. It had its roots in the law of property.[1] The privilege of one to protect what was "his" was extended to include the pro-

---

85. Section 3.04. Use of Force in Self-Protection.

86. E.g., Hawaii, Indiana, Kentucky, Pennsylvania and Washington.

A Nebraska statute, Neb.Rev.Stat. Supp. § 29–114 (1969) which allowed the actor to use any kind of force for protecting himself or his family was declared unconstitutional. State v. Goodseal, 186 Neb. 359, 183 N.W.2d 258 (1971).

87. E.g., Alabama, Arkansas, Colorado, Connecticut, Delaware, Florida, Georgia, Illinois, Iowa, Kansas, Maine, Montana, New Hampshire, New York, North Dakota, Oregon, Texas, Utah and Wisconsin.

88. E.g., Colorado, Florida, Georgia, Illinois, Indiana, Kansas, Kentucky, Minnesota, Montana, Oregon, Utah, Washington and Wisconsin. This would leave the law in each such state as it had been developed by the cases. For example the Iowa code does not mention retreat except that it is not required from the dwelling or place of business or employment. Compare, "if a reasonable person in the actor's situation would not have retreated; . . . ." Texas.

89. E.g., Alabama, Arkansas, Connecticut, Delaware, Hawaii, Maine, New Hampshire, New York, North Dakota and Pennsylvania.

90. E.g., Arkansas, Maine, New Hampshire and New York.

91. E.g., (Dwelling or place of work.) Alabama, Connecticut, Delaware, Hawaii, Iowa, North Dakota and Pennsylvania. Some of the codes which do not require retreat from the place of work, limit this to cases in which the assailant is not known to have the same place of work. E.g., Hawaii, North Dakota and Pennsylvania.

92. E.g., Alabama, Arkansas, Connecticut, Delaware, Hawaii, New Hampshire, New York, North Dakota and Pennsylvania.

93. E.g., Alabama, Arkansas, Connecticut, Delaware, Hawaii, Maine, New Hampshire and Pennsylvania.

94. E.g., Alabama, Connecticut, Delaware, Hawaii, Maine, New Hampshire and Pennsylvania.

1. Restatement, Second, Torts § 76, comment e (1965).

tection of his wife, his children and his servants. In the course of time this privilege outgrew the property analogy and came to be regarded as a "mutual and reciprocal defence." [2] The household was regarded as a group, any member of which had a privilege to defend any other member. "A man may defend his family, his servants or his master, whenever he may defend himself." [3] Even this concept of the privilege was outgrown and it came to include the members of one's immediate family or household and any other "whom he is under a legal or socially recognized duty to protect." [4] Thus a conductor was privileged to defend his passenger, and a man privileged to defend a lady friend whom he was escorting at the moment.[5] The present position, which represents a merging of the privilege of crime prevention with the privilege of defending others, is that one may go to the defense of a stranger if that person is the innocent victim of an unlawful attack.[6]

Since the common-law privilege of using force for crime prevention authorized anyone who was himself free from fault to use whatever force reasonably seemed necessary to save the innocent victim of a felonious attack, no special privilege was needed for this purpose. One was authorized to take the life of a felonious assailant if this reasonably seemed necessary to save an innocent spouse, parent,[7] child,[8] brother,[9] or other member of the family[10] from murder—but an utter stranger could have intervened for the protection of the victim in exactly the same way.[11]

In the early days, however, the privilege of using force for crime prevention did not include authority to intervene to protect third persons from invasions of their person which involved no danger of death or serious bodily harm.[12] The special privilege of using force for the defense of others was developed to provide such authority—narrowly limited at first. It has now been extended to include even the protection of a stranger; and the privilege of using force for crime prevention has been extended to include nonfelonious personal attacks.

"It may safely be assumed that at the present day . . . every man has the right of defending any man by reasonable force against unlawful force." [13]

It has been said that the privilege of using force in the defense of another person does not supersede the privilege of using force for the prevention of crime, but is in addition thereto,[14] and one may be in a position to claim both.

2. 3 Bl.Comm. *3.

3. Pond v. People, 8 Mich. 150, 176 (1860).

4. Restatement, Torts, § 76(b) (1934).

5. Id. at Illus. 4 and 5.

6. Restatement, Second, Torts § 76, Illus. 4 (1965); Model Penal Code § 3.05 (1962).

7. Crowder v. State, 76 Tenn. 669 (1881).

8. Ibid.

9. Warnack v. State, 3 Ga.App. 590, 60 S.E. 288 (1908).

10. Lacy v. State, 38 Ariz. 60, 297 P. 872 (1931). And see note, 45 L.R.A., N.S., 145 (1913).

11. State v. Hennessey, 29 Nev. 320, 90 P. 221 (1907). "In all cases where a felonious attack is made, a servant *or any other person present* may lawfully interpose to prevent the mischief intended; and if death ensue, the party so interposing will be justified." 1 East P.C. 289 (1803). Emphasis added.

12. Restatement, Second, Torts § 76, comment e (1965).

13. Salmond, Torts 375 (11th ed. 1953). See McKinney's Consol.L.N.Y. § 35.15 (1975).

14. In a case in which the relation between the parties was not emphasized the court said: "The law makes it the duty of everyone, who sees a felony at-

"As to the defendant," it was said in *Robinson*,[15] "the court failed to charge the law with respect to both (a) his right to fight in the necessary defense of his step-father, and (b) his right and duty as a private citizen to interfere to prevent a felonious assault. Each right is recognized in the decisions of this court."

The availability of two privileges, however, would seem to be no better than one if neither gave any greater authority than the other, which was the common law position so far as these two were concerned (except that the privilege of crime prevention did not originally extend to the prevention of nonfelonious attacks but did extend to felonies not threatening personal harm). But a statute, as interpreted, may make a difference in this regard and if so the question whether one who has used force in the effort to save another from harm is, or is not, justified in having done so may depend upon which of the two privileges is available to him, if both are not.[16]

If two are engaged unlawfully in a mutual fight (deadly or nondeadly) the law does not authorize anyone (close relative or stranger) to take sides in the contest and aid one in the effort to overcome his adversary, but the problem is quite different if the fight is not mutual. If one is using only privileged force in the effort to defend himself against an unlawful attack anyone is authorized to go to his defense and use force (subject to the familiar limitations) in the effort to save him from the threatened crime; whereas obviously the law does not authorize anyone to join forces with the offender and aid him in harming the innocent victim.[17] Because of this it has been common but quite unfortunate to say that the defender "stands in the shoes" [18] of the one defended with exactly the same privilege or lack of privilege as possessed by the latter. This is entirely true if all the facts are known and clearly understood,[19] but the statement should always include this qualification because some courts have assumed that it rules out the normal and salutary mistake-of-fact doctrine and may leave the defender guilty of the most

---

tempted by violence, to prevent it, if possible, and allows him to use the necessary means to make his resistance effectual. One may kill in defense of another under the same circumstances that he would have the right to kill in defense of himself." State v. Hennessey, 29 Nev. 320, 344, 90 P. 221, 227 (1907).

15. State v. Robinson, 213 N.C. 273, 281, 195 S.E. 824, 829–30 (1938).

16. Mitchell v. State, 43 Fla. 188, 30 So. 803 (1901). The statute spoke in terms of reasonable ground to apprehend in the subdivision dealing with defense of spouse or child or servant, but in terms of necessity in the subdivision dealing with the prevention of a dangerous felony. Perhaps the construction of the statute may be supported but the court was in error in assuming that the reasonable-mistake-of-fact doctrine did not apply to the privilege to use force to prevent crime at common law.

17. People v. Travis, 56 Cal. 251 (1880); State v. Turner, 246 Mo. 598, 152

S.W. 313 (1912); Steele v. State, 389 So. 2d 591 (Ala.Cr.App.1980).

18. Wood v. State, 128 Ala. 27, 30, 29 So. 557, 558 (1900).

"A person who intervenes to defend another acts in the stead of the other, so that force by the intervenor is justified to the same extent force by the party defended would have been justified." State v. Grier, 609 S.W.2d 201, 204 (Mo.App. 1980).

19. " . . . provided always that the father knew that his son had sought or brought on the difficulty." State v. Linney, 52 Mo. 40, 41 (1873). One who has seen the entire encounter is not entitled to intervene in behalf of the aggressor. People v. Travis, 56 Cal. 251 (1880); State v. Turner, 246 Mo. 598, 152 S.W. 313 (1912).

Where the facts are known one is not justified in doing more in defense of another than the other could do for himself. State v. Gibson, 36 Or.App. 111, 583 P.2d 584 (1978).

serious crime although he acted entirely without mens rea, and perhaps even from the highest sense of duty.[20] The position of one court, obviously untenable and inconsistent, is that a defender may be protected by a reasonable mistake of fact as to the necessity of using force and the degree of force needed for this purpose but acts at his peril on the question whether the one defended is an innocent victim or an unlawful participant.[21] The fault of any such position is that it deals with such a defender as the willing participant in a brawl, whereas from his standpoint (with the facts as they reasonably appear to him) he may be seeking to defend an innocent victim from a felonious assault.[22]

Fortunately other courts have made a much more sound analysis, holding that while the *known* circumstances place both in the same position in this regard, each must be considered separately with reference to what he knew or did not know or have any reasonable opportunity to ascertain.[23] The New York Court held that it is prejudicial error even to admit in evidence against the defender the acts and declarations of the one defended, showing him to be the aggressor or guilty participant, if such acts and declarations were in the absence of the defender and under such circumstances that he had no opportunity to know about them.[24]

Subject to the familiar limitations as to the degree of force permitted, one who is himself free from fault may intervene and use force to protect an innocent victim of intended crime. And under the sound view he is protected by the usual mistake-of-fact doctrine and may act upon the situation as it reasonably seems to be.[25]

20. Wood v. State, 128 Ala. 27, 29 So. 557 (1900); Stanley v. Commonwealth, 86 Ky. 440, 6 S.W. 155 (1887); Murphy v. State, 188 Tenn. 583, 221 S.W.2d 812 (1949). One who killed in defense of his son was not entitled to rely upon a reasonable belief that his son was free from fault; nothing short of this actual fact would justify his act. Lovejoy v. State, 33 Ala.App. 414, 34 So.2d 692 (1948); cert. denied 250 Ala. 409, 34 So.2d 700.

"A person who intervenes in a struggle and has no duty to do so, acts at his own peril if the person assisted was in the wrong." State v. Wenger, 58 Ohio St.2d 336, 390 N.E.2d 801, 803 (1979).

21. Stanley v. Commonwealth, 86 Ky. 440, 6 S.W. 155 (1887).

22. See the dissenting opinion of Gary, A. J., in State v. Cook, 78 S.C. 253, 264, 59 S.E. 862, 864 (1907).

23. Hathaway v. State, 32 Fla. 56, 13 So. 592 (1893); Williams v. State, 70 Ga. App. 10, 27 S.E.2d 109 (1943); State v. Minella, 177 Iowa 283, 158 N.W. 645 (1916); State v. Mounkes, 88 Kan. 193, 127 P. 637 (1912); Carrol v. Commonwealth, 26 Ky.L.Rep. 1083, 83 S.W. 552 (1904); Pond v. People, 8 Mich. 150 (1860); Staten v. State, 30 Miss. 619 (1856); State v. Harper, 149 Mo. 514, 51

S.W. 89 (1899); Parnell v. State, 50 Tex. Cr.R. 419, 98 S.W. 269 (1906). And see Reeves v. State, 153 Tex.Cr.R. 32, 217 S.W.2d 19 (1949). State v. Penn, 89 Wn. 2d 63, 568 P.2d 797, 799 (1977).

"An individual who acts in defense of another person, reasonably believing him to be the innocent party and in danger, is justified in using force necessary to protect that person even if, in fact, the party he is defending was the aggressor." State v. Bernardy, 25 Wn.App. 146, 605 P.2d 791, 792 (1980).

24. People v. Maine, 166 N.Y. 50, 59 N.E. 696 (1901).

After the New York court had taken this very sound position in regard to a homicide case it reached the astounding conclusion that in case of assault one who goes to the aid of an apparent victim does so "at his peril" and is not protected if the one he aids was in the wrong however misleading the appearances may be. People v. Young, 11 N.Y.2d 274, 229 N.Y.S.2d 1, 183 N.E.2d 319 (1962).

A different result would seem to be required now. See McKinney's N.Y.Rev. Pen.Law § 35.15 (1975).

25. State v. Chiarello, 69 N.J.Super. 479, 174 A.2d 506 (1961).

MODEL PENAL CODE

The Code places considerable stress upon the privilege of using force for the protection of other persons.[26] This is in line with its general policy of downgrading the use of force in law enforcement and crime prevention and placing the emphasis upon the protection of life and personal safety.

THE NEW PENAL CODES

The new codes tend for the most part to treat the privilege of using force in defense of another as comparable to the privilege of self-defense. In fact a number are worded in terms of authority to use force to defend "himself or a third person," [27] or "himself or another." [28] Most of the codes that deal separately with the defense of another[29] seem to leave no trace of the view that one who goes to the aid of another acts "at his peril" with reference to the right of that person to receive such aid, but there is at least one exception.[30]

SECTION 6.   DEFENSE OF THE HABITATION

The concept of one's habitation as his "castle," [1] however humble it may be, runs throughout the law and the privilege to defend the habitation must not be confused with the privilege to defend property which stands on a much lower level.[2] In fact, as is true in case of offenses against the habita-

The court was careful to "distinguish the cases involving the ignorant defender, such as State v. Fair, 45 N.J. 77, 211 A.2d 359 (1965)." Leeper v. State, 589 P.2d 379, 383 (Wyo.1979).

The test of whether a person may use force in defense of another, is not what the facts actually were, but whether circumstances as they appeared to the defendant made it reasonably necessary for him to protect the other. State v. Penn, 89 Wn.2d 63, 568 P.2d 797 (1977).

26. Section 3.05.

27. E.g., Alabama, Arkansas, Colorado, Connecticut, Georgia, Indiana, Iowa, Maine, New Hampshire, New York, Oregon and Utah.

28. E.g., Florida, Illinois and Kansas. The Minnesota code is worded differently. It speaks of "him or another," Minn. St.Ann. § 609.065 (1964).

29. E.g., Delaware, Hawaii, Kentucky, North Dakota, Pennsylvania and Wisconsin.

30. E.g., Ky.Rev.Stat. 503.070 (1980) is worded: "The use of deadly physical force by a defendant upon another person is justifiable when:

(a) The defendant believes that such force is necessary to protect a third person against imminent death, serious physical injury, kidnapping or sexual intercourse compelled by force or threat; and

(b) Under the circumstances as they actually exist, the person whom he seeks to protect would have himself been justified . . . in using such protection."

1. " . . . the house of everyone is to him as his castle and fortress, as well for his defence against injury and violence, as for his repose; . . ." Semayne's Case, 5 Co.Rep. 91a, 91b, 77 Eng.Rep. 194, 195 (1620). "As a matter of history, the defense of habitation has been the most favored branch of self-defense from earliest times. Lord Coke in his Commentaries, says: 'A man's house is his castle—for where shall a man be safe if it be not in his house?' (3 Institute, 162). And in the Pandects, long before Coke, it is stated 'One's house is the safest refuge for everyone.'" People v. Eatman, 405 Ill. 491, 498, 91 N.E.2d 387, 390 (1950).

2. "The same rule limiting the amount of force which may be used in defense of other property does not apply in defense of habitation." State v. Couch, 52 N.M. 127, 137, 193 P.2d 405, 411 (1948).

"The right of a person to defend his home from attack is a substantive right. . . . He may kill when necessary in

tion, the determinant is not title but occupancy,[3] the house is the "castle" of the dweller whether he is owner or tenant and he is privileged to use deadly force if this reasonably seems necessary to repel the landlord who has opened the door with his key and attempts to force an entry with felonious intent.[4]

Bishop says,[5] "it may now be deemed reasonably clear that, to prevent an unlawful entrance into a dwelling-house, the occupant may make defence to the taking of life, without being liable even for manslaughter," but this seems not to be the accepted view where the defender has no reason to fear that the trespasser intends to commit a felony or to inflict personal harm upon him or some other person within the house.[6] The difference between this and Bishop's view is not so wide as might appear at first glance, because when an intruder insists upon an unlawful entrance into the dwelling with such violence that only deadly force can stop him, the defender will usually have good reasons to fear for his safety or the safety of members of his household,—but this is not always the fact. A householder who is on the outside, for example, and too far away at the moment to make use of nondeadly force would not be privileged to shoot to prevent the entrance of one he knew did not intend to commit a felony or to inflict any personal harm,[7] but it has been held that he may shoot if this is necessary, or reasonably seems to be necessary, to prevent burglary or the consummation of the burglarious intent even if the burglar is reaching in from the outside to steal, and hence is not endangering those within.[8] This was the original position which was still the prevailing view in 1935. It would be considered an extreme position today. Years later the same court had a different opinion and went to the opposite extreme. It said the statute which provides that a homicide is justifiable when committed by a person "in defense of habitation or property, against one who manifestly intends and endeavors, by violence or surprise, to commit a felony," does not give carte blanche to shoot another simply because that other person is committing an act which might be considered a felony. "Rather, it is necessary that the act 'reasonably creates a

defense of himself, his family, or his home, and he has the same right when not actually necessary, if he believes it to be so, and has a reasonable ground for the belief." State v. McCombs, 38 N.C. App. 214, 247 S.E.2d 660, 662 (1978).

"The facts of the case *sub judice* require a holding that defendant is entitled to a charge on defense of habitation. '. . . one of the most compelling justifications for the rules governing defense of habitation is the desire to afford protection to the occupants of a home under circumstances which might not allow them an opportunity to see their assailant or ascertain his purpose, other than to speculate from his attempt to gain entry by force that he poses a grave danger to them.'" State v. Hedgepeth, 46 N.C. App. 569, 265 S.E.2d 413, 416 (1980).

3. People v. Stombaugh, 52 Ill.2d 130, 284 N.E.2d 640 (1972); State v. Mitcheson, 560 P.2d 1120 (Utah 1977).

4. People v. Eatman, 405 Ill. 491, 91 N.E.2d 387 (1950).

5. 2 Bishop, New Criminal Law § 707 (9th ed. 1923).

6. Carroll v. State, 23 Ala. 28 (1853); Miller v. Commonwealth, 188 Ky. 435, 222 S.W. 96 (1920); State v. Taylor, 143 Mo. 150, 44 S.W. 785 (1898); Wooten v. State, 171 Tenn. 362, 365, 103 S.W.2d 324, 325 (1937); State v. Patterson, 45 Vt. 308 (1873). "He can kill intentionally only in defense of his life or person, or to prevent a felony." People v. Hubbard, 64 Cal.App. 27, 35, 220 P. 315, 319 (1923).

7. See Restatement, Second, Torts § 79, Illustration 1 (1965).

8. Viliborghi v. State, 45 Ariz. 275, 43 P.2d 210 (1935). And see Restatement, Second, Torts § 79, Illustration 3 (1965).

fear of great bodily injury.' " [9] Today most jurisdictions take a position falling somewhere between those extremes.

Defense of the dwelling may be for the purpose of saving the house itself from damage or destruction, or it may be to preserve its character as a place of refuge and repose by preventing the unlawful intrusion of outsiders. The dweller is privileged to use reasonable nondeadly force to prevent any unlawful harm or injury to his place of abode and if a malicious attack is made for the purpose of destroying it by fire, explosion or in some other manner, he is privileged to use deadly force if this reasonably seems necessary to defend his "castle" against such threatened harm. [10]

If the defense is for the purpose of preventing an unlawful intrusion it becomes necessary to inquire into the nature or apparent nature of the threatened invasion. There is a strong social interest in preventing any unlawful entry of the dwelling and the dweller is privileged to use reasonable nondeadly force in the effort to prevent such an entry regardless of its nature or purpose, [11] but the social interest in human life is too great to permit the use of deadly force for the prevention of a mere civil trespass even in the dwelling itself, as mentioned above. [12] On the other hand deadly force is privileged if it is necessary or reasonably seems to be necessary to prevent an unlawful entry attempted for the purpose of committing burglary, or of killing or inflicting great bodily injury upon the dweller or some member of his household. [13]

The point of difficulty has been in regard to an unlawful entry attempted for the purpose of a personal attack of a *nonfelonious* nature upon the dweller or some member of his household. The rule mentioned above in the discussion of self-defense, which prohibits the use of deadly force in defending against an obviously nondeadly attack, has induced some courts to make a similar limitation to the privilege of defending the habitation against an unlawful entry. Such courts hold that the privilege to use deadly force to prevent an unlawful entry of the dwelling is limited to cases of entry with intent to commit a felony [14] and does not apply to an entry attempted for the mere purpose of making a personal assault which is neither intended nor

---

9. State v. McIntyre, 106 Ariz. 439, 445, 477 P.2d 529, 535 (1970).

10. Anonymous, Lib.Ass.Ann. 26, f. 123, pl. 23 (1352); 1 Hale P.C. *487; State v. Couch, 52 N.M. 127, 193 P.2d 405 (1948).

Where the evidence was that D acted in defense of his home, an instruction on his right to act in self-defense without an instruction also on his right to act in defense of his home, was prejudicial error. State v. Edwards, 28 N.C.App. 196, 220 S.E.2d 158 (1975).

11. 1 Hale P.C. *485; State v. Taylor, 143 Mo. 150, 44 S.W. 785 (1897).

12. Ibid.; Horton v. State, 110 Ga. 739, 35 S.E. 659 (1900); People v. Horton, 4 Mich. 67 (1855); Commonwealth v. McLaughlin, 163 Pa. 651, 30 A. 216 (1894). One who uses unreasonably excessive force in ejecting a trespasser and thereby

causes his death is guilty of manslaughter. State v. Hibler, 79 S.C. 170, 60 S.E. 438 (1907).

Merely because the intruder enters the home of another, without permission, does not justify the use of deadly force. People v. Sizemore, 69 Mich.App. 672, 245 N.W.2d 159 (1976).

13. 1 Hale P.C. *487; Thomas v. State, 255 Ala. 632, 53 So.2d 340 (1951); Brown v. People, 39 Ill. 407 (1866); Sparks v. Commonwealth, 89 Ky. 644, 20 S.W. 167 (1885); State v. Peacock, 40 Ohio St. 333 (1883).

14. The dweller has no right to kill unless this is necessary or reasonably appears to be necessary to prevent a felonious destruction of his property, or to defend against loss of life or the infliction of great bodily injury. Carroll v. State, 23 Ala. 28 (1853).

likely to kill or to inflict great bodily injury.[15] On the other hand there are strong reasons for recognizing the dwelling as a place of refuge in which the dweller may expect to be free from personal attack even of a nondangerous character, and the trend has been in the direction of holding that an unlawful entry of the dwelling for the purpose of an assault upon some person therein may be resisted by deadly force if this reasonably seems necessary for the purpose "although the circumstances may not be such as to justify a belief that there was actual peril of life or great bodily harm." [16]

"We think it may be safely laid down to be the law of this State," said the Illinois court,[17] "that a man's habitation is one place where he may rest secure in the knowledge that he will not be disturbed by persons coming within, without proper invitation or warrant, and that he may use all of the force apparently necessary to repel any invasion of his home."

Strictly speaking the habitation is the place where one dwells rather than where he works, if the two represent different places, but there has been a tendency to extend the rule of defense of habitation to include also the defense of one's store,[18] office[19] or other place of business,[20] which is said to be *pro hac vice* his dwelling.[21] This view has not been entirely free from question.[22]

Whenever the dweller is privileged to defend his habitation a member of the household, including a servant or guest, is entitled to make the same

15. Ibid.; State v. Countryman, 57 Kan. 815, 48 P. 137 (1897); State v. Taylor, 143 Mo. 150, 165 (1898).

16. People v. Eatman, 405 Ill. 491, 498, 91 N.E. 387, 390 (1950). The statute says so in substance but this statute is "but a restatement of the ancient law of England." Ibid. Accord: Smith v. State, 106 Ga. 673, 32 S.E. 851 (1899); Leverette v. State, 104 Ga.App. 743, 122 S.E.2d 745 (1961); Hayner v. People, 213 Ill. 142, 72 N.E. 792 (1904); Armstrong v. State, 11 Okl.Cr. 159, 143 P. 870 (1914). And see State v. Holder, 237 Iowa 72, 79, 20 N.W. 909, 913 (1945); State v. Bradley, 126 S.C. 528, 533, 120 S.E. 240, 242 (1923).

The Utah statute authorizes one to use deadly force if this reasonably appears to be necessary to prevent an unlawful entry into the dwelling, and the entry is attempted in a violent manner and is reasonably believed to be for the purpose of offering personal violence to anyone dwelling or being therein. State v. Mitcheson, 560 P.2d 1120 (Utah 1977).

17. Eatman, supra.

One is justified in the use of force against another to the extent he reasonably believes it necessary to prevent or *terminate* the other's unlawful entry into one's dwelling. State v. Farley, 225 Kan. 127, 587 P.2d 337 (1978).

18. Sparks v. Commonwealth, 89 Ky. 644, 20 S.W. 167 (1885).

19. Morgan v. Durfee, 69 Mo. 469 (1879).

20. "While one's house formerly meant his home, his dwelling, the rule has also been extended to one's place of business or his place of refuge, consequently a man's place of business must be regarded pro hac vice his dwelling. He has the same right to defend it against intrusion, and he is under no more necessity of retreating from the one than from the other; his duty to defend one is the same as the other. Jones v. State, 76 Ala. 8; Cary v. State, 76 Ala. 78; Lee v. State, 92 Ala. 15, 9 So. 407, 25 Am.St.Rep. 17." Snell v. Derricott, 161 Ala. 259, 273, 49 So. 895, 901 (1909).

21. Ibid.

The law with reference to the defense of habitation includes not only a person's actual residence, but also whatever place he may be occupying peacefully as a substitute home, such as a hotel, motel, or even when he is a guest in the home of another. State v. Mitcheson, 560 P.2d 1120, 1122 (Utah 1977).

22. State v. Smith, 100 Iowa 1, 69 N.W. 269 (1896).

defense,[23] but the privilege to repel a violent intruder does not apply when both are members of the same household.[24]

The statutory authority to use force to prevent *or terminate* an unlawful entry, has no application to a lawful entry, even if the entrant later engaged in unlawful conduct.[25]

Illustrations

(1) **X** advances upon the dwelling of **D** with a bomb, for the purpose of blowing up the house. **D** is justified in shooting **X** if there seems to be no other reasonable way of stopping him.[26]

(2) **X** attempts to break and enter **D**'s dwelling with burglarious intent. The original view that still prevails in a few jurisdictions is that, without any additional showing, deadly force is privileged if it reasonably seems necessary to prevent this entry. At the other extreme is the view that deadly force is privileged to prevent the entry only if the circumstances have created a reasonable apprehension of death or great bodily injury if this is not done. Most jurisdictions take a position somewhere between these extremes. They are not all in accord but require something more than technical burglary, such as an entry likely to result in physical injury (not necessarily great bodily injury), or an intent to commit a felony therein.[27]

(3) **X** attempts to force his way into **D**'s dwelling for the purpose of a personal assault upon **D** but without intent to cause death or great bodily harm. While the courts are not in accord it would appear that **D** should be privileged to use deadly force if there seemed to be no other reasonable way of preventing this entry.[28]

(4) **A** comes to **B**'s premises during a severe storm and asks permission to take shelter in **B**'s dwelling house. **B** refuses to permit him to do so, although he knows that **A** neither intends nor is likely to harm any person or thing in the house. **A**, much larger than **B**, attempts to overcome **B**'s resistance by physical force which **B** is unable to resist except by shooting **A**. **B** is not privileged to do so to prevent **A** from entering his dwelling place.[29]

MODEL PENAL CODE

The Code does not deal with the privilege of using force in defense of the habitation except in the section dealing with the protection of property.[30]

23. Cooper's Case, Cro.Car. 544, 79 Eng.Rep. 1069 (1639); Hendrickson v. Commonwealth, 232 Ky. 691, 24 S.W.2d 564 (1930); Davis v. Commonwealth, 252 S.W.2d 9 (Ky.1952).

"So if any do attempt . . . feloniously to breake into his dwelling house in the night time; and in this attempt the partie or his servants then with him, do kill any of the misdoers, he or they shall forfeit nothing thereby. . . ." Lambard Eirenarcha 239 (1581).

24. Commonwealth v. Johnson, 213 Pa. 432, 62 A. 1064 (1906); People v. Chapman, 49 Ill.App.3d 553, 7 Ill.Dec. 416, 364 N.E.2d 577 (1977).

25. State v. Sorenson, ___ Mont. ___, 619 P.2d 1185 (1980).

26. Anonymous, Lib.Ass.Ann. 26, f. 123, pl. 23 (1352); 1 Hale P.C. *487.

27. This means a felony other than the burglary itself. It would not include, for example, an entry with intent to commit petty larceny.

28. People v. Eatman, 405 Ill. 491, 91 N.E.2d 387 (1950).

29. Quoted from Restatement, Second, Torts § 79, Illustration 1 (1965).

30. Section 3.06(3)(d). "The use of deadly force is not justifiable under this Section unless the actor believes that:

The social interest in the protection of the habitation, as such, would seem to entitle it to special attention and to a greater privilege than is provided in the Code. Those in charge of drafting the Code were in error when they assumed that defense of the habitation "is a purely property concept." [31]

THE NEW PENAL CODES

The law of the defense of the habitation seems to be essentially the same under the new penal codes as before, although it may have been changed in some individual state. Some codes, by silence, have left this to the common law—meaning the common law as it had been developed in that particular state. Some have codified the original common-law rule by providing that a person may use deadly force "when he reasonably believes such to be necessary to prevent or terminate the commission or attempted commission of such burglary;" [32] or "if he reasonably believes that the force is necessary to prevent or terminate the other person's unlawful entry of or attack on his dwelling or curtilage;" [33] or some equivalent. [34] Some have reached the same result by providing that deadly force may be used if reasonably believed necessary to prevent the "commission of a forcible felony." [35] Burglary has regularly been classified as a forcible felony, and at least one state has emphasized this by statutory definition. [36]

At least two of the states have gone to the other extreme by limiting the use of deadly force in defense of the dwelling to a situation in which deadly force by the intruder is employed, threatened or expected, by providing that it is authorized only against one who: "Had employed or threatened deadly force against or in the presence of the defendant; or The use of force other than deadly force to prevent the commission of the crime would expose the defendant or another person in his presence to substantial danger of serious physical injury." [37]

Most place this defense somewhere between these extremes. This may be by authorizing the use of deadly force if necessary to prevent the commission of certain offenses, including burglary, with the qualification that "the use of force other than deadly force for such purposes would expose anyone to substantial danger of serious bodily injury." [38] Or the use of deadly force may be justifiable: "When committed against a person whom one reasonably believes to be likely to use any unlawful force against a person present in a

(1) the person against whom the force is used is attempting to dispossess him of his dwelling otherwise than under a claim of right to the possession; . . ."

The following subdivision authorizes the use of deadly force against one who is attempting to commit arson or burglary, but only if the offender "has employed or threatened deadly force against or in the presence of the actor;" or the failure to use deadly force "would expose the actor or another in his presence to substantial danger of serious bodily harm."

31. Model Penal Code 39 (Tent.Draft No. 8, 1958). The statement there is: "This is a purely property concept and

permits the use of deadly force to protect a property right."

"Alternatively, homicide is justifiable when made in the actual resistance of an attempt to commit a felony upon the slayer or his dwelling." State v. Griffith, 91 Wn.2d 572, 589 P.2d 799, 802 (1979).

32. E.g. New York.

33. E.g. Indiana.

34. E.g. Arkansas, Kansas and Texas.

35. E.g. Florida and Utah.

36. E.g. Utah.

37. E.g. Delaware. The Hawaii statute is in substance the same.

38. E.g. North Dakota.

dwelling while committing burglary of such dwelling." [39] The qualification may be in terms of limiting the use of deadly force to one reasonably believed to be "committing or likely to commit some other crime within the dwelling place." [40] Some statutes use "felony" in such a clause.[41]

The fact that defense of the habitation is quite different from the defense of property is emphasized by some such reference as to "property other than a habitation." [42]

SECTION 7. DEFENSE OF PROPERTY

Criminal cases in which defense of property has been relied upon as an exculpating circumstance have seldom been entirely divorced from some other privilege such as crime prevention, self-defense or defense of habitation,[1] and the fact that the exercise of such other privilege may result incidentally in the protection of property does not in any way narrow its scope; hence property protection is usually overshadowed by some other defense. In fact, the chief importance of the privilege of protecting property is frequently that its proper exercise does not make one an "aggressor," or in any way at fault, and thus leaves all other privileges unimpaired.[2]

It is often stated with variations as to the exact wording that one may oppose force with force, even to the taking of life if necessary, in defense of his person, family or property against one who manifestly endeavors by violence to commit a felony such as murder, robbery, rape, arson or burglary, as in such felonies, because of their atrocity and violence human life is, or is presumed to be, in danger.[3] The true analysis of such a situation, however, is that the actual privilege being exercised is that of preventing a dangerous felony which may, as an incidental result in certain cases, prevent the loss of personal property. Thus the innocent victim of attempted robbery may resort to deadly force if this reasonably seems necessary to frustrate the robber.[4] If the effort is successful the robber gets nothing, but the privilege to use deadly force is to prevent the dangerous felony rather than to defend property, and the same is true where the saving of property is the incidental result of preventing a burglary.[5]

With this in mind, and also the fact that the defense of habitation is placed on quite a different basis than the defense of property, it may be said:

---

39. E.g. Louisiana. Compare the Codes in Georgia, Illinois and Montana.

40. E.g. Maine.

41. E.g. Minnesota and Pennsylvania.

42. E.g. Georgia, Indiana and Kansas.

1. For example, State v. Pollard, 139 Mo. 220, 40 S.W. 949 (1897).

2. Ayers v. State, 60 Miss. 709 (1883).

3. State v. Nyland, 47 Wn.2d 240, 287 P.2d 345 (1955). See also section 3, supra. At times the courts refer to the privilege to use deadly force if necessary to prevent a "felony attempted by force or surprise." See Commonwealth v. Emmons, 157 Pa.Super. 495, 498, 43 A.2d 568, 569 (1945). As so used the word "surprise" adds nothing because it is employed in the sense of an unexpected attack—which includes force and violence. See also People v. Ceballos, 12 Cal.3d 470, 116 Cal.Rptr. 233, 526 P.2d 241 (1974).

4. Sovereign Camp, W. O. W. v. Gunn, 229 Ala. 508, 158 So. 192 (1934); State v. Bonofiglio, 67 N.J.L. 239, 52 A. 712 (1901).

5. Viliborghi v. State, 45 Ariz. 275, 43 P.2d 210 (1935). See discussion State v. Barr, 115 Ariz. 346, 565 P.2d 526 (App. 1977).

In the absence of statutory authority[6] the use of force intended or likely to cause death or great bodily injury is never authorized for the defense of property (as such).[7]

"He cannot justifiably kill a man merely in defense of his property." [8] Or in the words of an Irish judge: "I cannot allow it to go abroad that it is lawful to fire upon a person committing trespass or larceny. . . ." [9]

"The preservation of human life, and of limb and member from grievous harm, is of more importance to society than the protection of property. . . . It is an inflexible principle of the criminal law of this State, and we believe of all the States, as it is of the common law, that for the prevention of a bare trespass, not the dwelling-house, human life may not be taken, nor grievous bodily harm inflicted. If in the defence of property, not the dwelling-house, life is taken with a deadly weapon, it is murder, though the killing may be actually necessary to prevent the trespass." [10]

And in the absence of some other privilege, as mentioned above, or of special statutory authority, one may not shoot to prevent larceny of his property,[11] even if the larceny amounts to a felony,[12] nor may he use deadly force to prevent the destruction or removal of a fence even if it cannot otherwise be prevented,[13] or to regain money wrongfully taken from him.[14]

6. "(1) A person in lawful possession or control of premises is justified in using physical force upon another person when and to the extent that he reasonably believes it necessary to prevent or terminate what he reasonably believes to be the commission or attempted commission of a criminal trespass by the other person in or upon the premises.

"(2) A person may use deadly physical force under the circumstances set forth in subsection (1) of this section only:

"(a) In defense of a person as provided in ORS 161.219; or

"(b) When he reasonably believes it necessary to prevent the commission of arson or a felony by force and violence by the trespasser." Or.Rev.Stats. § 161.225.

And see V.A.T.C. Penal Code § 9.42 (1974). Johnson v. State, 86 Tex.Cr.R. 566, 218 S.W. 496 (1920); Eckerman v. State, 129 Tex.Cr.R. 563, 89 S.W.2d 999 (1936).

On the other hand some statutes codify the common-rule. E.g., "It is not reasonable to intentionally use force intended or likely to cause death or great bodily harm for the sole purpose of defense of one's property." Wis.Stats. § 939.49 (1958).

7. McNabb v. United States, 123 F.2d 848 (6th Cir. 1941); Dunn v. State, 23 Ala.App. 321, 124 So. 744 (1929); Davidson v. People, 90 Ill. 221 (1878); Utterbach v. Commonwealth, 105 Ky. 723,

49 S.W. 479 (1899); Carmouche v. Bouis, 6 La.Ann. 95, 97 (1851); McDaniel v. State, 8 Smedes & M. 401 (Miss.1847); State v. Matthews, 148 Mo. 185, 49 S.W. 1085 (1899); Jones v. State, 59 Okl.Cr. 53, 56 P.2d 423 (1936).

"Under common law, one is privileged to use reasonable physical force in defending or recapturing property . . . ." Hatfield v. Gracen, 279 Or. 303, 567 P.2d 546, 549 (1977).

"Generally, there is no privilege to use *deadly* force simply for the purpose of defending or recapturing property." Id. at p. 550, note 5.

8. State v. Clark, 51 W.Va. 547, 564, 41 S.E. 204, 207 (1902).

9. Per Doherty, C. J., in Regina v. Murphy, 1 Craw. & D. 20 (1839). See also State v. Marfaudille, 48 Wash. 117, 121, 92 P. 939, 941 (1907).

10. Simpson v. State, 59 Ala. 1, 14 (1877).

11. Grigsley v. Commonwealth, 151 Ky. 496, 152 S.W. 580 (1913); State v. Plumlee, 177 La. 687, 149 So. 425 (1933).

12. Storey v. State, 71 Ala. 329 (1882); Carmouche v. Bouis, 6 La.Ann. 95, 97 (1851); Commonwealth v. Emmons, 157 Pa.Super. 495, 43 A.2d 568 (1945).

13. State v. Ciaccio, 163 La. 563, 112 So. 486 (1927).

14. Oldacre v. State, 196 Ala. 690, 72 So. 303 (1916).

One in lawful possession of real or personal property is privileged to use reasonable nondeadly force if this is necessary or is reasonably believed to be necessary to prevent or terminate an unprivileged intrusion upon his right of possession,[15] from which it necessarily follows that one is privileged to use such force under the same limitations to prevent the larceny of his chattel.[16] Even nondeadly force is unreasonable and hence unprivileged if it is obviously in excess of what is needed for the purpose.

In the case of an ordinary trespasser Hale said[17] the owner "may not beat him, but may gently lay his hands upon him to put him out," but at the present time no force is privileged if a mere request will suffice,[18] and hence even mild force should not be used until a request has first been made and disregarded unless there is reason to believe that a request would be either useless, dangerous or not in time to prevent substantial harm.[19] If a blind person is about to tread upon valuable flowers, for example, the owner may seize him gently if a warning would be too late.[20]

If milder measures are ineffective the one in lawful possession of land or chattels may defend his property by any nondeadly force "made necessary by the circumstances," [21] and if death should unexpectedly result from the privileged use of nondeadly force the homicide is excusable.[22] Should the use of privileged force in defense of property result in an attack by the wrongdoer the problem becomes one of self-defense.[23] If the wrongdoer does not attack but persists in his wrongdoing the law will not undertake to measure with precision the exact amount of nondeadly force permissible in the effort to prevent or terminate his trespass[24] but any force clearly out of proportion to the apparent necessity will constitute an assault and battery[25]

---

15. 1 Hale P.C. *485–6; Hinchcliffe's Case, 1 Lewin 161, 168 Eng.Rep. 998 (1823); People v. Payne, 8 Cal. 341 (1857); People v. Dann, 53 Mich. 490, 19 N.W. 159 (1884); Ayres v. State, 60 Miss. 709 (1883); Restatement, Second, Torts § 77 (1965).

16. "In brief,—a man may defend his property by any force made necessary by the circumstances, such as assault and battery, short of taking the aggressor's life." 1 Bishop, New Criminal Law § 875 (8th ed. 1892). And see 2 id. § 706; McNabb v. United States, 123 F.2d 848, 854 (6th Cir. 1941).

Reasonable force may be used to protect property lawfully in one's possession. State v. Antwine, 4 Kan.App.2d 389, 607 P.2d 519, 528 (1980).

17. 1 Hale P.C. * 485.

18. Restatement, Second, Torts § 77, Illustration 15 (1965).

19. Id. at § 77(c). See Government of Virgin Islands v. Stull, 280 F.Supp. 460 (D.C.Virgin Islands 1968).

20. Id. at Illustration 17.

21. 1 Bishop, New Criminal Law § 875 (8th ed. 1892).

22. Morgan v. Durfee, 69 Mo. 469 (1897); Hinchcliffe's Case, 1 Lewin 161, 168 Eng.Rep. 998 (1823).

23. See supra, section 4.

24. Cf. Sikes v. Commonwealth, 304 Ky. 429, 200 S.W.2d 956 (1947).

The proprietor of a poolroom asked a noisy trouble-maker to leave and when this produced no result he "grabbed him by the arm and led him to the door." In reversing a conviction of assault and directing the entrance of a verdict of not guilty, the court said: "Had Stull kicked Matthew . . . this would be a different case, but the taking of Matthew by the arm and pushing, pulling, or leading him to the door was, in the Court's opinion, entirely reasonable and in fact the minimal amount of force employable under the circumstances." Government of Virgin Islands v. Stull, 280 F.Supp. 460 (D.C.Virgin Islands 1968).

25. Chapell v. Schmidt, 104 Cal. 511, 58 P. 892 (1894). A trespasser picking flowers was attacked with a cane without even a request that he desist. This was a civil case but a prosecution for criminal assault and battery should have reached the same result.

and if death should result from such obviously excessive force the homicide will not be less than manslaughter.[26] Needless to add there is no justification or excuse for a blow which is struck, not to defend property, but in revenge after the harm has been done.[27]

Wisely or unwisely the law tolerates a bluff which it would not permit to be carried out,[28] and in a case in which **D** drew a knife which he threatened to use, but did not use, in defense of his property a conviction of assault was reversed on the ground that a threat to use a weapon may be privileged when its actual use would not be.[29]

The same degree of nondeadly force, and subject to the same limitations, which is permissible in defense of property may be used to recapture property tortiously taken by another[30] if the recaption takes place at once or upon fresh pursuit.[31]

As pointed out above[32] the common law does not authorize a "warrantless arrest" [33] for a misdemeanor not amounting to a breach of the peace. The trend of modern legislation has been to authorize either an officer or a private person to arrest for any public offense committed in his presence[34] which would include petty larceny. Where this change has been made the owner of property being stolen in his presence is privileged to (a) arrest the thief and (b) protect his property by preventing the theft or immediately retaking the property. Where such a change in the law of arrest has not been made the owner of the property would have no authority to arrest the thief if the larceny was a misdemeanor, but even so would be privileged to protect his property. One court overlooking this fact came up with the following solution:

26. A kick is not a justifiable mode of putting a mere trespasser out of the house and death resulting from such unreasonable force is criminal homicide. Wild's Case, 2 Lewin 214, 168 Eng.Rep. 1132 (1837).

27. State v. Allen, 131 W.Va. 667, 49 S.E.2d 847 (1948).

28. Restatement, Second, Torts §§ 70(2), 81(2) (1965).

"In instructing the jury, the military judge failed to sufficiently differentiate between the drawing of the weapon versus the use of deadly force; that is the firing of the weapon. . . . This instruction is misleading because a policeman is often justified in drawing his weapon on an assailant, although he may not be justified in intentionally killing him." United States v. Thomas, 11 M.J. 315, 317 (CMA1981). See also State v. Realina, 1 Haw.App. 167, 616 P.2d 229 (1980).

29. State v. Yancey, 74 N.C. 244 (1876).

D was charged with obstructing administration of internal revenue laws by appearing in his driveway armed with a shotgun and threatening two revenue agents who were backing his truck out of his driveway. His conviction was reversed because there was no evidence to indicate that he knew they were officers, and if they had been thieves he had a right to make the threat. United States v. Rybicki, 403 F.2d 599 (6th Cir. 1968).

30. Commonwealth v. Donahue, 148 Mass. 529, 20 N.E. 171 (1889); Restatement, Torts §§ 100–108 (1934). "Force may be used by the owner to retake property from a person who has obtained possession of it by force or fraud and is overtaken while carrying it away." Riffel v. Letts, 31 Cal.App. 426, 428, 160 P. 845, 846 (1916).

31. If "he acts promptly after his dispossession or after his timely discovery of it." Restatement, Second, Torts § 103 (1965).

32. See supra, Section 1.

33. The phrase quoted is commonly used today to indicate an arrest without a warrant—which under many circumstances is entirely valid. A "warranted arrest" is one with a warrant.

34. See supra, Section 1.

Although the statute says a private person may make an arrest "when the person to be arrested has in his presence committed a misdemeanor amounting to a breach of the peace, or a felony," the owner of the property stolen has a right to arrest the thief for petty larceny. Otherwise the owner would be helpless to prevent the theft of property worth less than $100. "Private person" in this section means one other than the owner of the property stolen.[35]

The common-law solution would be that, although the owner would have no authority to arrest the person attempting to commit a misdemeanor not amounting to a breach of the peace, he would be privileged to use whatever nondeadly force seemed to be necessary to prevent the theft of his property.

MODEL PENAL CODE

The Code provides for the use of reasonable nondeadly force for the protection of one's property.[36] Under the section on this subject there are limited provisions for the use of deadly force but these relate to what are in fact problems of defense of the habitation and crime prevention.[37]

The Code goes quite beyond the common law in authorizing one to use force for the protection of property in the possession of another (any other) to the same extent as if it were in his own possession.[38]

THE NEW PENAL CODES

The new codes do not authorize the use of deadly force in defense of property (as distinguished from defense of the habitation, self-defense and use of force in crime prevention). Some authorize the use of nondeadly force in defense of the property of a third person.[39]

SECTION 8.   SPRING GUNS AND BOOBY TRAPS

There is no special privilege to use spring guns or other mechanical devices in the effort to frustrate wrongdoers, but as more than one privilege may be involved in such cases it is convenient to give the topic separate consideration.

The only sound advice either to give or to follow is that except in time of war and as an act of war no mechanical device should ever be set which is intended or likely to cause death or great bodily injury,—not because death or injury so caused will necessarily be criminal but because it may be,—due to circumstances which the one who sets it is unable to determine in advance or to avoid at the time.

---

35. State v. DeSanti, 8 Ariz.App. 77, 443 P.2d 439 (1968).

36. Section 3.06.

37. See footnote 30 to Section 6.

38. It "permits the actor to use force for the protection of property in the possession of another to the same extent as if it were in his own possession." Model Penal Code 37 (Tent.Draft No. 8, 1958).

39. E.g., Delaware, Hawaii, Iowa, Kentucky, Texas, Washington and Wisconsin. Many of the new codes are silent on the subject, thereby seemingly withholding such authority. Some expressly limit the use of force to protect the actor's own property or property "he has a legal duty to protect." E.g., Georgia, Illinois, Indiana, Montana, Utah.

If a spring gun, set in a dwelling to protect it against burglars while the dweller is away, should cause the death of one attempting to burglarize the house, the homicide could be justifiable if the deadly force was privileged and necessary to prevent a dangerous felony and there seems to have been no other reasonable way in which this particular crime could have been prevented;[1] but if no would-be burglar approached the place and the life taken was that of a little child,[2] a member of the fire department entering to extinguish a blaze therein, a police officer making a proper check of the building for security purposes,[3] or a trespasser entering wrongfully but with no burglarious intent[4] there is no justification or excuse for the homicide.

Since the use of deadly force is not permitted for the defense of property (as distinguished from the prevention of burglary) the setting of deadly spring guns in open fields or in outhouses not within the curtilage is not protected by any privilege and death resulting therefrom is without justification or excuse.[5] Some statutes have wisely forbidden the use of mechanical devices intended or likely to cause death or great bodily injury.[6]

---

1. United States v. Gilliam, 25 Fed. Cas. 1319, No. 15,205a (C.C.D.C.1882); State v. Moore, 31 Conn. 479 (1863). But see State v. Barr, 11 Wash. 481, 489, 39 P. 1080, 1082 (1895). This case has a dictum indicating the absence of a privilege to kill a burglar with a spring gun when there is no one in the house, on the theory that such a burglar is not actually endangering any person; but the deceased was not a burglar but merely a weary traveler seeking shelter from the rain; and the case was expressly disapproved in a later decision which quoted State v. Moore with approval. State v. Marfaudille, 48 Wash. 117, 120–1, 92 P. 939, 940–1 (1907). "Tested by these principles, one might set a spring gun in his own home, and if its discharge prevented the ingress of a burglar, he might be justified because if he had been present he could have fired the shot." State v. Childers, 133 Ohio St. 508, 515, 14 N.E.2d 767, 770 (1938). In taking the position that a spring gun could not lawfully be set to protect property, the court said: "If in defence of property, *not the dwelling house*, life is taken with a deadly weapon, it is murder. . . ." Simpson v. State, 59 Ala. 1, 14 (1877). Emphasis added.

"The user of a device likely to cause death or serious bodily harm . . . is relieved from liability only if the intruder is, in fact, one whose intrusion involves danger of life and limb of the occupants of the dwelling place or is for the purpose of committing certain serious crimes, as to which see §§ 142(2) and 143(2)." Restatement, Second, Torts § 85, comment d (1965). Section 143(2) expressly includes a crime "involving the breaking and entry of a dwelling place."

"However, in view of the wide scope of burglary under Penal Code section 459, as compared with the common law definition of that offense in our opinion it cannot be said that in all circumstances burglary under section 459 constitutes a forcible and atrocious crime. Where the character and manner of the burglary do not reasonably create a fear of great bodily harm, there is no cause for exaction of human life." People v. Ceballos, 12 Cal.3d 470, 116 Cal.Rptr. 233, 526 P.2d 241, 246 (1974). See also Falco v. State, 407 So.2d 203 (Fla.1981).

2. Commonwealth v. Keith, 46 Berks 137 (Pa.Co.1954).

3. Pierce v. Commonwealth, 135 Va. 635, 115 S.E. 686 (1923). A conviction of second-degree murder was reversed for other reasons but the court said a conviction would be affirmed if reached in a trial free from error.

4. State v. Green, 118 S.C. 279, 110 S.E. 145 (1921). And see Restatement, Second, Torts § 85, comment d (1965).

5. Simpson v. State, 59 Ala. 1 (1877); State v. Plumlee, 177 La. 687, 149 So. 425 (1933). And see United States v. Gilliam, 25 Fed.Cas. 1319, No. 15,205a (C.C.D.C. 1882).

6. O.R.S. (Or.) § 166.320 (1979); Schmidt v. State, 159 Wis. 15, 149 N.W. 388 (1914).

It seems that no criminal liability results from the fact that a trespasser was alarmed or received slight chastisement from a nondeadly devise set for the protection of property.[7]

MODEL PENAL CODE

The Code would authorize the use of a mechanical device to protect property only if it "is not designed to cause or known to create a substantial risk of causing death or serious bodily harm; . . ."[8]

THE NEW PENAL CODES

Most of the new codes leave the law as it has been developed by the cases so far as it relates to the use of spring guns or traps set for the defense of the habitation or other property. The few giving attention to this problem have imposed special restrictions such as permitting the use of such a device only if it "is not designed to cause or known to create a substantial risk of causing death or serious physical injury;"[9] or by prohibiting the use of any unattended spring gun or trap set for the defense of property.[10]

SECTION 9.   CHOICE OF EVILS

One of the innovations of the Model Penal Code is a section on Choice of Evils,[1] which provides in substance that a violation of the letter of the law is justifiable if believed to be necessary to avoid harm to the actor, or another, provided that the harm avoided is greater than the harm caused. The actor's belief applies only to the need to take action and not to the relative degree of the two harms.

Oregon has a statute on choice of evils[2] that has been construed to provide defendant with a defense if there is evidence that "(1) . . . his conduct was necessary to avoid a threatened injury; (2) . . . the threatened injury was imminent; and (3) . . . it was reasonable for defendant to believe that the need to avoid that injury was greater than the need to avoid the injury which the [other statute] seeks to prevent."[3] In a case in which defendant was convicted of carrying a concealed weapon, she had claimed that she put her companion's gun in her purse because she was afraid that in his then state of mind he might use it. The failure to submit the choice-of-evils defense to the trier of fact was held to be reversible error.[4]

Under a proper showing such a defense would be recognized under the common law rule of duress.[5]

7. See Simpson v. State, 59 Ala. 1 (1877). As to tort liability see Restatement, Second, Torts § 84 (1965).

8. Section 3.06(5).

9. E.g., 11 Del.Code § 466 (1979); Haw.Rev.Stat. § 703–306 (1976).

10. E.g., Iowa Code § 704.4 (1978).

1. Section 3.02.

2. ORS § 161.200 (1979).

3. State v. Matthews, 30 Or.App. 1133, 1136, 569 P.2d 662, 663 (1977).

4. State v. Lawson, 37 Or.App. 739, 588 P.2d 110 (1978).

5. Use of a concealable firearm in defense of self or others in an emergency situation does not violate the statute making it an offense for a felon or drug addict to have such a firearm in his possession. People v. King, 22 Cal.3d 12, 148 Cal.Rptr. 409, 582 P.2d 1000 (1978).

SECTION 10.   ENTRAPMENT (AGENT PROVOCATEUR)

Entrapment, so-called, is a relatively simple and very desirable concept which was unfortunately misnamed, with some resulting confusion. It is socially desirable for criminals to be apprehended and brought to justice. And there is nothing whatever wrong or out of place in setting traps for those bent on crime, provided the traps are not so arranged as likely to result in offenses by persons other than those who are ready to commit them. What the State cannot tolerate is having crime instigated by its officers who are charged with the duty of enforcing the law.

Obviously "entrapment" is not the appropriate word to express the idea of official instigation of crime, but it is so firmly entrenched that it seems wiser to accept it with due explanation than attempt to supplant it, although one court has said bluntly: "It is not the entrapment of a criminal upon which the law frowns, but the seduction of innocent people into a criminal career by its officers is what is condemned and will not be tolerated," [1] and another has distinguished between "factual entrapment" and such entrapment as is "illegal." [2]

It is well to permit attention to extend beyond the technical concept of entrapment because when officers have gone too far in their zeal to secure convictions,—so far as to defeat their own purpose, this may have been for some entirely different reason, as in those cases in which the plan to trap an offender has been laid in such a manner as to leave out some element essential to guilt. The classic example is *Martin*[3] in which officers planning to catch the person who had been aiding prisoners of war to escape obtained the aid of one prisoner willing to cooperate who was directed exactly what to do. The defendant took this prisoner in her vehicle beyond the ordinary prison limits to a point where she was arrested under the prearranged plan, but her conviction of aiding a prisoner of war to escape was held to be improper because there had been no escape,—since the prisoner had gone only where he was directed to go by those in charge. Furthermore a detective who

---

1. People v. Braddock, 41 Cal.2d 794, 802, 264 P.2d 521, 525 (1953).

The defense of entrapment has not been recognized in Great Britain, Regina v. Sang [1979] 2 All E.R. 1222, [1980] A.C. 402.

"The fact that the counselor and procurer is a policeman or a police informer, although it may be of relevance in mitigation of penalty for the offense, cannot affect the guilt of the principal offender; both the physical element (actus reus) and the mental element (mens rea) of the offense with which he is charged are present in his case." L. Diplock, id. [1979] 2 All E.R. at 1226. "My Lords, it is now well settled that the defense called entrapment does not exist in English law." Id. L. Salmon, 1235.

The Canadian position as to the availability of the entrapment defense is not precisely clear. Although there are decisions stating no such defense is available, see Regina v. Kirzner, 32 CCC2d 76, 74 D.L.R.3d 351, 14 OR2d 665 (1976), decisions and opinions from the Canadian Supreme Court have suggested the defense might be proper in appropriate cases, Lemieux v. Queen, [1961] SCR 492, 63 D.L.R.2d 75; Regina v. Kirzner, 38 CCC2d 131, 81 D.L.R.3d 229 (SCC1977); and this seems to be the position accepted by other authorities, Regina v. Ridge, 51 CCC2d 261 (B.C.1979). See Mewett and Manning, Criminal Law 368–375 (1978).

2. Trice v. United States, 211 F.2d 513, 518 (9th Cir. 1954).

3. Rex v. Martin, Russ. & R. 196, 168 Eng.Rep. 757 (1811).

seemingly joins a criminal venture, not to promote its success but to secure evidence of the crime, is not a real conspirator[4] and his acts cannot be imputed to the others;[5] and if the detective himself unlocks and opens the door through which the others enter there can be no conviction of common-law burglary.[6] Since his intent is to prevent consummation of the criminal design he is not a guilty party and his act cannot be imputed to the others, hence an essential element of common-law burglary (the breaking) is lacking.[7] In a case involving a similar type of defect a detective placed an obstruction on a railroad track, with authority from the company and with the intent to remove it before any harm was done, which he did, with the intention of convicting another on the theory that he was present aiding and abetting the commission of a crime, but a conviction under these facts could not be upheld.[8] If officers have reason to believe a thief is committing larcenies to supply some unknown "fence" they may, after detecting him in a particular theft, direct him to dispose of the goods as usual without barring a possible conviction of the guilty receiver; but they must take pains to see that the goods do not come under the control of the owner or the police in the meantime, because if this happens they will lose their contraband character and what the receiver takes will not be "stolen goods."[9]

Midway, in a sense, between the type of case in which it is claimed that an element essential to guilt is lacking and that in which it is urged that conviction is barred because of entrapment (although it did not fall within either) was the case in which money was stolen from a constable who feigned drunkenness with the intention of making an arrest if his money should be taken. The claim that no larceny had been committed was properly rejected because merely providing an opportunity for this crime if a thief should come that way was not consent by the constable that his money

---

4. One who merely pretends to aid another in order to get evidence is not guilty of burglary and an entry by him alone cannot be imputed to the other. People v. Collins, 53 Cal. 185 (1878).

5. State v. Neely, 90 Mont. 199, 300 P. 561 (1931). "The defendant is not to be charged with what was done by the detective, as the two were not acting together with a common purpose." State v. Currie, 13 N.D. 655, 661, 102 N.W. 875, 877 (1905).

In a prosecution for the sale of narcotics, one who procures the narcotics at the request of a government agent cannot be convicted of sale to the agent since he acts as the procuring agent of the buyer. Such person may be convicted of a possession offense. Commonwealth v. Harvard, 356 Mass. 452, 253 N.E.2d 346 (1969).

6. Statutory burglary in some jurisdictions has eliminated the element of breaking. West's Ann.Cal.Pen.Code § 459 (1981 Supp.). Under such a provision the opening of the door by the detective would not bar a conviction of the others but such a conviction would be barred if only the detective entered. See Collins, supra.

7. Love v. People, 160 Ill. 501, 43 N.E. 710 (1896).

8. State v. Douglass, 44 Kan. 618, 26 P. 476 (1890).

In one case it was held that where D initiated the plan to smuggle marijuana into the United States, the fact that a government agent actually carried the drug across the boundary line did not prevent a conviction. Haynes v. United States, 319 F.2d 620 (5th Cir. 1963). This seems questionable. Certainly the agent should be instructed not to go so far.

9. People v. Jaffe, 185 N.Y. 497, 78 N.E. 169 (1906); People v. Rojas, 55 Cal. 2d 252, 10 Cal.Rptr. 465, 358 P.2d 921 (1961); Booth v. State, 398 P.2d 863 (Okl. Cr.1964); State v. Durham, 196 N.W.2d 428 (Iowa 1972). These cases are not in accord on the question whether an attempt to receive stolen goods has been committed (see supra, chapter 6, section 3(5)) but agree that the substantive offense has not.

should be taken; [10] and while this case was prior to the wide acceptance of the concept of entrapment, it could not be maintained that the mere sight of an apparently unconscious man would implant the idea of larceny in an innocent mind.[11]

As pointed out above, when technical entrapment is alleged the distinction is between detection and instigation; traps may be laid or "decoys" employed to secure the conviction of those bent on crime,[12] but the zeal for enforcement must not induce officers to implant criminal ideas in innocent minds.[13] An officer who has reasonable ground for suspicion that the law is being violated, may place himself in a position to apprehend the offenders and may set traps for this purpose, but when the officer has no ground for suspicion and induces another to commit an offense simply for the purpose of making an arrest, such conduct constitutes entrapment.[14] Most courts have held that a defendant must admit the commission of the offense charged before he can raise the defense of entrapment,[15] however, recently

10.   People v. Hanselman, 76 Cal. 460, 18 P. 425 (1888).

For a recent case in which one was convicted for having taken money from the pocket of an officer who pretended to be in a drunken stupor, see People v. Walker, ____ Colo.App. ____, 615 P.2d 57 (1980).

11.   The mere fact that officers in disguise afforded D an opportunity to commit a crime which he was ready and willing to accept does not constitute entrapment. Kivette v. United States, 230 F.2d 749 (5th Cir. 1956). "The defense of entrapment is not available to one standing ready to commit an offense given an opportunity." Block v. United States, 226 F.2d 185, 188 (9th Cir. 1955).

12.   United States v. Sosa, 379 F.2d 525 (7th Cir. 1967).

"Artifice and stratagem may be employed to catch those engaged in criminal enterprises. . . ." Sorrells v. United States, 287 U.S. 435, 441, 53 S.Ct. 210, 212 (1932).

"In the instant case it is clear the jury was justified in finding from the evidence that the criminal intent originated in the mind of the defendant and therefore the mere fact that he was solicited by a decoy to commit the crime raises no inference of an unlawful entrapment." People v. Nunn, 46 Cal.2d 460, 471, 296 P.2d 813, 820 (1956).

"If the crime originates in the mind of the accused, an officer may, when acting in good faith, make use of deception." City of Seattle v. Muldrew, 71 Wn.2d 903, 431 P.2d 589 (1967). State v. Smith, 229 Kan. 533, 625 P.2d 1139 (1981).

"This is one of those cases in which a question of fact was presented as to entrapment for determination by the jury. The evidence did not, however, demand a finding that defendant Royal was entrapped into the commission of a crime." State v. Royal, 247 Ga. 309, 275 S.E.2d 646, 648–49 (1981).

13.   "Decoys are permissible to entrap criminals, but not to create them; . . ." United States v. Healy, 202 F. 349 (D.C.Mont.1913). "Entrapment is the conception and planning of an offense by an officer and his procurement of its commission by one who would not have perpetrated it except for the trickery, persuasion, or fraud of the officer." People v. Lindsey, 91 Cal.App.2d 914, 916, 205 P.2d 1114, 1115 (1949).

14.   State v. Griffith, 13 Ohio Supp. 53 (1944).

"People v. Cross (1979) . . . held that the presence or absence of a predisposition on the part of the defendant was relevant in determining whether entrapment had been established." People v. Pates, 84 Ill.2d 82, 48 Ill.Dec. 886, 888, 417 N.E.2d 618, 620 (1981).

15.   "This defense (entrapment) requires admission of guilt of the crime charged and all of its elements, including the required mental state." United States v. Hill, 655 F.2d 512, 514 (3d Cir. 1981).

"The general rule of this Circuit is that a defendant cannot both plead entrapment and deny committing the acts on which the prosecution is predicated." United States v. Sedigh, 658 F.2d 1010, 1014 (5th Cir. 1981); United States v. Smith, 629 F.2d 650 (10th Cir. 1980); People v. Bradley, 73 Ill.App.3d 347, 29 Ill. Dec. 395, 391 N.E.2d 1078 (1979); State

other courts have rejected such position[16] and some statutes[17] also allow a defendant to deny the commission of the offense and claim entrapment.

The mere fact that officers have given the defendant an opportunity to furnish a specific instance of an habitual course of criminal conduct is no defense,[18] and they may provide this opportunity by sending decoy letters or by making purchases.[19] Thus one may be convicted of using the United States mails to give information telling where obscene matter may be obtained although his letter was in response to a request written by a post office inspector under an assumed name,[20] and evidence of contraband purchased by officers may be used to convict the seller of having made a sale in violation of law.[21]

v. Amodei, 222 Kan. 140, 563 P.2d 440 (1977); Norman v. State, 588 S.W.2d 340 (Tex.Cr.App.1979); Annotation, Availability in State Court of Defense of Entrapment Where Accused Denies Committing Acts Which Constitute Offense Charged, 5 A.L.R. 4th 1128 (1981); Annotation, Availability in Federal Court of Defense of Entrapment Where Accused Denies Committing Acts Which Constitute Offense Charged, 54 A.L.R.Fed. 644 (1981).

One court took the position that defendant may not insist both that (1) he did not do the prohibited act, and (2) he was entrapped into doing it, because the two are inconsistent. But that a defendant may claim entrapment even if he does not testify, because refusal to testify does not admit anything, expressly or impliedly, except a desire not to testify. United States v. Annese, 631 F.2d 1041 (1st Cir. 1980). See also United States v. Valencia, 645 F.2d 1158 (2d Cir. 1980). Note, Denial of The Crime and The Availability of The Entrapment Defense in The Federal Courts, 22 Bost.Col.L.Rev. 911 (1981).

"Therefore, we hold that the defendant is precluded from raising the entrapment issue after a plea of guilty has properly been entered." People v. Bonner, 102 Mich.App. 514, 302 N.W.2d 253, 254 (1981).

16. United States v. Demma, 523 F.2d 981 (9th Cir. en banc 1975). A defendant may assert entrapment without being required to concede that he committed the crime charged or any of its elements.

"We decline to follow those cases that hold the entrapment defense unavailable unless defendant first admits the criminal act charged." State v. McBride, 287 Or. 315, 599 P.2d 449, 452 (1979). People v. Barraza, 23 Cal.3d 675, 153 Cal.Rptr. 459, 591 P.2d 947 (1979).

17. The Utah statute on Entrapment states: "The defense provided by this section is available even though the actor denies commission of the conduct charged to constitute the offense." State v. Stone, 629 P.2d 442, 447 (Utah 1981).

18. People v. Lindsey, 91 Cal.App.2d 914, 205 P.2d 1114 (1949).

"Whenever the state induces a person to pursue a course of conduct upon which he would not otherwise have embarked and he commits a criminal act which he would not have committed but for the action of the state's agent, conviction for such a crime is against public policy. However, where the criminal intent originates in the mind of the accused and the offense is completed, the mere fact that the accused is furnished an opportunity to commit a crime or was aided in the commission thereof by an agent of the state should constitute no defense." Hill v. State, 95 Nev. 327, 594 P.2d 699 (1979).

19. Mitchell v. United States, 143 F.2d 953 (10th Cir. 1944). Accord, State v. Parr, 129 Mont. 175, 283 P.2d 1086 (1955). Marked money may be used to obtain a conviction. State v. Thomas, 177 Kan. 230, 277 P.2d 577 (1954).

20. Grimm v. United States, 156 U.S. 604, 15 S.Ct. 470 (1895).

21. Moss v. State, 4 Okl.Cr. 247, 111 P. 950 (1910). It has been suggested that whenever the officers solicit the act (sale of heroin here) there is a problem of entrapment for the jury to consider. United States v. Moses, 220 F.2d 166 (3d Cir. 1955). On the other hand entrapment has been held to be an affirmative defense with the burden on defendant to show that he was induced to commit the offense. People v. Terry, 44 Cal.2d 371, 282 P.2d 19 (1955).

Two of the significant cases on entrapment are *Sorrells*[22] and *Baymouth*.[23] In *Sorrells* M, a prohibition agent in the days of the "noble experiment," went to S's house to purchase liquor posing as a tourist. His first request was without success but learning that both had served in the same Division in World War I, he engaged S in extensive reminiscences of their war experiences, and after at least two rejections of his proposal he pleaded with S a third time for aid to a thirsty tourist; whereupon S left the house, procured half a gallon of liquor and sold it to M for five dollars. Since there was no evidence of any prior violation by S his conviction was reversed by the Supreme Court on the ground of entrapment. In *Baymouth* after B had telephoned Mrs. H time and again making indecent suggestions and proposals, she reported this fact to an officer and was advised that on the next call she should agree to meet the man and notify the police, which she did, resulting in the arrest of B whose identity was discovered when he appeared for the agreed meeting. B was convicted of enticing a woman to commit an act of lewdness and sought to have the conviction reversed on the claim of entrapment, but since the criminal idea had originated in his mind the trap set to discover his identity was held not to be a defense.

Although the entrapment defense has been recognized and enforced in the federal courts, at least since 1915,[24] it was first considered by the Supreme Court in *Sorrells*, supra, a 1932 case. The evidence of entrapment was so extreme and uncontradicted that the members of the Court were unanimous in voting for a reversal of the conviction, but they were sharply divided (five to four) as to the proper explanation. They disagreed on three major points: (1) the theory of entrapment, (2) the proper fact-finder of entrapment, and (3) the test of entrapment.

The Theory of Entrapment. In the opinion of the majority of the Court, one who has been entrapped by a federal officer or his agent is entitled to an acquittal because he has not committed the offense charged, on the theory that "it cannot be supposed that the Congress intended that the letter of the enactment should be used to support such a gross perversion of its purpose."[25] In other words, by judicial "interpretation" an exception is added to the statute to the effect that such a sale is an offense unless the seller was entrapped by a federal officer or his agent. These Justices did not suggest that Congress actually had such an intent, but only that they would have so intended if they had thought of it. Fortunately the judicial amendment of a statute on the theory that it is what the legislative body would have done if it had been thought of, has not had wide acceptance.

The notion that the nonpunishability of an entrapped defendant is grounded upon innocence is difficult to support, even apart from its far-fetched foundation. Although no misdeed is punishable in the federal courts unless so provided in the federal code,[26] there have been convictions of common-law offenses in some state cases where no statute was involved.[27] Even

22. Sorrells v. United States, 287 U.S. 435, 53 S.Ct. 210 (1932).

23. Baymouth v. State, 294 P.2d 856 (Okl.Cr.1956).

24. Woo Wai v. United States, 223 F. 412 (9th Cir. 1915).

25. Sorrells v. United States, 287 U.S. 435, 452, 53 S.Ct. 210, 216 (1932).

26. United States v. Hudson & Goodwin, 11 U.S. (7 Cranch) 32 (1812); United States v. Coolidge, 14 U.S. (1 Wheat.) 415 (1916).

27. E.g., State v. Cawood, 2 Stew. 360 (Ala.1830); Johnson v. State, 18 Ala.App. 70, 88 So. 348 (1921); Commonwealth v. Szliakys, 254 Mass. 424, 150 N.E. 190 (1926).

the most extreme case of entrapment could not be supported on the theory of "legislative intent" where no statute was involved, but there can be no doubt that the defense would be recognized. On the other hand, if an officer by the most extreme inducement and persuasion has caused the taking of human life with malice aforethought, we may be sure that no defense of entrapment would be permitted.

The concurring minority denied that there was any such intent of Congress, claiming in effect that one who has been entrapped is guilty of the offense, but that the government is estopped because of the misconduct of its officer.[28] They added in a later case (Sherman) in which there was the same division of opinion: "it is surely fiction to suggest that a conviction cannot be had when a defendant has been entrapped by government officers or informers because 'Congress could not have intended that its statutes were to be enforced by tempting innocent persons into violations.' "[29] And in a still more recent case this explanation was given: "In their concept, the defense is not grounded on some unexpressed intent of Congress to exclude from punishment under its statutes those otherwise innocent persons tempted into crime by the Government, but rather in the belief that 'the methods employed on behalf of the Government to bring about conviction cannot be countenaced.' "[30]

An advantage of the estoppel theory is that, being grounded upon public policy, it can be applied as readily to common-law crimes as to statutory crimes, and can easily be rejected in cases involving the intentional and unlawful taking of human life or the infliction of bodily injury.

The dispute as to the rationale of entrapment is not even mentioned in most cases, but in some it is decisive. For example, under the California statutes,[31] if the defendant asserts an affirmative defense (other than insanity), and presents enough evidence to raise the issue, this places upon the state the burden of proof because it must establish his guilt beyond a reasonable doubt, which includes disproving the claimed defense. This, the court holds however, does not apply to the entrapment defense, because this "is not based on the defendant's innocence." Hence the defendant has the burden of proving entrapment by a preponderance of the evidence.[32]

"In Pennsylvania, the crime of bribery is indictable at common law, . . . and an indictment which defectively charges a statutory offense can be held valid as charging common law bribery." United States v. Forsythe, 560 F.2d 1127, 1138, n. 24 (3d Cir. 1977).

28. The opinion did not use the word "estopped" but it expressed what is in effect an estoppel doctrine. In another case it was said: "The act of the officer estops the government from a conviction." United States v. Healy, 202 F. 349 (D.C.Mont.1913).

29. Sherman v. United States, 356 U.S. 369, 372, 78 S.Ct. 819, 821 (1958).

30. United States v. Russell, 411 U.S. 423, 93 S.Ct. 1673 (1973).

31. West's California Evidence Code, sec. 501 (1966); West's California Penal Code, sec. 1096 (1970).

32. People v. Moran, 1 Cal.3d 755, 83 Cal.Rptr. 411, 463 P.2d 763 (1970); In re Foss, 10 Cal.3d 910, 112 Cal.Rptr. 649, 519 P.2d 1073 (1974). This seems to be the general view. "The burden of entrapment is now on the defendant, he must prove this issue by a preponderance of the evidence." State v. Kelsey, 58 Hawaii 234, 566 P.2d 1370, 1373 (1977). But federal cases have held that the government must prove defendant's "predisposition" beyond a reasonable doubt. United States v. Martinez-Carcano, 557 F.2d 966, 970 (2d Cir. 1977). "Two stages of inquiry are involved. First, the defendant must prove by a preponderance of the evidence that the crime charged was initiated or induced by a government agent.

The Proper Fact-Finder of Entrapment. In both *Sorrells* and *Sherman*, the evidence of entrapment was undisputed, so it was possible for the Court to rule that it was entrapment as a matter of law.[33] But in any case of dispute, the majority insisted that the issue must be decided by the jury; whereas the concurring minority insisted that it must be decided by the judge and not by the jury. The position of the majority, that proof of entrapment establishes innocence of the crime charged, required the second position, that the issue must be decided by the jury, because no issue bearing on guilt or innocence can be taken from the jury in a criminal trial. The estoppel theory of the minority permitted their position that the issue should be decided by the judge—but did not require it. It would be consistent with the estoppel theory that the issue should be decided by the jury under proper instructions from the judge. Most of the cases leave this issue to the jury,[34] but some hold that it must be decided by the judge.[35]

The Test of Entrapment. The position of the majority in *Sorrells* and *Sherman* stems from the premise that entrapment is the official instigation of crime. It is the act of an officer causing a crime by implanting the criminal idea in an otherwise innocent mind. As said by Mr. Chief Justice Warren in *Sherman*: "To determine whether entrapment has been established, a line must be drawn between the trap for the unwary innocent and the trap for the unwary criminal." [36] And as said earlier in *Sorrells*, entrapment occurs only when the criminal conduct was "the product of the creative activity" of law-enforcement officials.[37] This standard uses the "origin of intent" as the determinant. Did the criminal intent start in the mind of the officers, or was the defendant "predisposed" to commit the offense when the officer first appeared on the scene?[38] It is the subjective test of entrapment.

The Supreme Court has made its stand on "predisposition" very clear. Russell was convicted of having unlawfully manufactured and sold "speed."

. . . Thereupon the burden shifts to the government to prove beyond a reasonable doubt that the defendant was predisposed to commit the offense." United States v. Steinberg, 551 F.2d 510, 513–14 (2d Cir. 1977). See also State v. Pappas, 588 P.2d 175 (Utah 1978).

33. "If the evidence presents no genuine dispute as to whether the defendant was entrapped, there is no factual issue for the jury, and then the judge has a duty to rule on the defense as a matter of law." United States v. Glaeser, 550 F.2d 483, 487 (9th Cir. 1977).

34. United States v. Martinez-Carcano, 557 F.2d 996 (2d Cir. 1977); United States v. Martin, 533 F.2d 268 (5th Cir. 1976); State v. Kelsey, 58 Hawaii 234, 566 P.2d 1370 (1977); State v. Amodei, 222 Kan. 140, 563 P.2d 440 (1977).

35. The issue of entrapment must be decided by the trial judge. People v. Van Riper, 65 Mich.App. 230, 237 N.W.2d 262 (1976).

"We conclude . . . that under the objective test . . . the issue of en-

trapment is best decided by the trial court outside the presence of the jury." People v. D'Angelo, 401 Mich. 167, 257 N.W.2d 655, 660 (1977).

Because Michigan rejects the subjective test of entrapment and adopts the objective test, it was reversible error to submit the issue of entrapment to the jury. People v. Van Riper, 65 Mich.App. 230, 237 N.W.2d 262 (1976).

36. Sherman v. United States, 356 U.S. 369, 372, 78 S.Ct. 819, 821 (1958).

37. Sorrells v. United States, 287 U.S. 435, 451, 53 S.Ct. 210, 216 (1932).

38. "The defendant's lack of predisposition is the crux of the entrapment defense. Hampton v. United States, 425 U.S. 484, 96 S.Ct. 1646, 48 L.Ed.2d 113 (1976); . . . ." United States v. Glaeser, 550 F.2d 483, 487 (9th Cir. 1977). Thus, the standard for determining the validity of the entrapment defense remains the predisposition of the defendant." United States v. Benavidez, 558 F.2d 308, 310 (5th Cir. 1977).

The evidence had disclosed that an undercover agent had asked Russell to produce the drug for him, offering to supply one essential element in its manufacture. And that the agent had in fact supplied some of this element, which was difficult although not impossible to obtain, and was not unlawful to possess. Even though Russell admitted that he was predisposed to commit the offense, the United States Court of Appeals for the Ninth Circuit reversed the conviction on the ground that "a defense to a criminal charge may be founded upon an intolerable degree of governmental participation in the criminal enterprise." This, however, was reversed by the Supreme Court on the ground that since Russell admitted that he was predisposed to commit the offense, the defense of entrapment was not available to him.[39] Later, in a subsequent case, the Court held that entrapment was not available as a defense to trafficking in contraband, even if the government agent supplied the contraband itself, to one who was predisposed to traffic therein.[40] Two of the Justices who joined three others in affirming the conviction, refused to join in the statement that entrapment could never be based upon governmental misconduct, no matter what the circumstances, where predisposition is established. They would leave that to the future since in the case at bench there was no need to go so far. If the activity of government agents was so extreme as to be outrageous or "grossly shocking" this would no doubt be held to be a bar to conviction, but probably the Court would hold that the defense was not entrapment, but a violation of due process, which does not involve "predisposition." [41]

---

39. United States v. Russell, 411 U.S. 423, 93 S.Ct. 1637 (1973).

40. Hampton v. United States, 425 U.S. 484, 96 S.Ct. 1646 (1976).

Although not involved in the case the court includes this dictum: "On the other end of the spectrum, however, the government may not instigate the criminal activity, provide the place, equipment, supplies and know-how, and run the entire operation with only meager assistance from the defendants without violating fundamental fairness." United States v. Tobias, 662 F.2d 381, 386 (5th Cir. 1981).

41. It was so indicated in United States v. Smith, 538 F.2d 1359, 1361 (9th Cir. 1976). A defendant who was predisposed to commit the offense has no entrapment defense, but due process may bar a conviction where the government's involvement in a criminal enterprise has become sufficiently outrageous and shocking to the universal sense of justice. United States v. Russell, 411 U.S. 423, 431–32, 93 S.Ct. 1637, 1642–43 (1973). In Hampton v. United States, 425 U.S. 484, 96 S.Ct. 1646 (1976), the plurality opinion did not completely reject the argument that due process could sometimes, in especially outrageous cases of governmental misconduct, require a conviction of an otherwise willing defendant

to be set aside, the opinion is ambiguous, but it did suggest prosecution of the offending government officer was the proper approach. The concurring and dissenting opinions accepted the possibility that due process standards might in a proper case require stopping a prosecution. These opinions make up a majority of the justices of the court.

"The rule that is left by *Hampton* is that although proof of predisposition to commit the crime will bar application of the entrapment defense, fundamental fairness will not permit any defendant to be convicted of a crime in which police conduct was 'outrageous.' " . . . "[W]e have no trouble in concluding that the governmental involvement in the criminal activities of this case has reached 'a demonstrable level of outrageousness.' At the behest of the Drug Enforcement Agency, Kubica, a convicted felon striving to reduce the severity of his sentence, communicated with Neville and suggested the establishment of a speed laboratory. The Government gratuitously supplied about 20 percent of the glassware and the indispensable ingredient, phenyl-2-propanone. It is unclear whether the parties had the means or the money to obtain the chemical on their own. The DEA made arrangements with chemical supply houses to facilitate the

The minority of the Justices in *Sorrells* and *Sherman* urged what has come to be known as the objective test of entrapment. In their view the purpose of the defense is to control the conduct of law-enforcement officers—to prohibit unlawful governmental activity in instigating crime. The entrapped defendant must not be convicted because the methods employed by officers to bring about the perpetration cannot be tolerated. Under this test the only question is whether the nature of police activity involved was so improper that it was likely to induce one to commit a crime that he had not previously intended. As pointed out by the Iowa court, under the objective test of entrapment the predisposition of the defendant is irrelevant.[42] And as expressed by Mr. Chief Justice Traynor, dissenting in a California case: "Because the purpose of the defense is to control impermissible police conduct, 'it is wholly irrelevant to ask if the "intention" to commit the crime originated with the defendant or governmental officers, or if the criminal conduct was the product of "the creative activity" of law enforcement officials.' "[43]

Whether the test of entrapment should be objective or subjective, depends upon the purpose underlying the entrapment defense. If the purpose is to discipline officers who have overstepped the line, the "predisposition" of the defendant is unimportant. If the purpose is to save from conviction one who would not have violated the law had it not been for official incitement, without excusing those who were quite ready and willing to commit the

purchase of the rest of the materials. Kubica, operating under the business name 'Chem Kleen' supplied by the DEA, actually purchased all of the supplies with the exception of a separatory funnel. (The funnel was secured by Twigg at the direction of Kubica who was engaged in operating the laboratory.) When problems were encountered in locating an adequate production site, the Government found the solution by providing an isolated farmhouse well-suited for the location of an illegally operated laboratory. Again, there was no cost to the defendants. At all times during the production process, Kubica was completely in charge and furnished all of the laboratory expertise. Neither defendant had the know-how with which to actually manufacture methamphetamine. The assistance they provided was minimal and then at the specific direction of Kubica." The Court found a violation of fundamental fairness. United States v. Twigg, 588 F.2d 373, 378–381 (3d Cir. 1978).

The New York Court of Appeals found a due process violation in People v. Isaacson, 44 N.Y.2d 511, 406 N.Y.S.2d 714, 378 N.E.2d 78 (1978).

"The question of the outrageous involvement of government agents is a question of law for the court." United States v. Wylie, 625 F.2d 1371, 1378 (9th Cir. 1980). "Oscar testified that the in-

formant, Henry, initiated the drug transaction and in fact provided him with the drugs which he then sought to deliver to Featherly. This claimed version of the facts falls short of the outrageous conduct which would violate the defendant's due process rights." United States v. Nunez-Rios, 622 F.2d 1093, 1097 (2d Cir. 1980).

Most courts have failed to find the circumstances before them sufficient to make out a due process violation. The effect of the due process standard is to adopt an objective standard to work in tandem with the subjective approach. Note, The Need For a Dual Approach to Entrapment, 59 Wash.U.L.Q. 199 (1981).

42. State v. Mullen, 216 N.W.2d 375 (Iowa 1974). "It is sufficient for the accused to claim entrapment and to show the law enforcement agent used persuasion or other means likely to cause normally law-abiding persons to commit the offense." State v. Powell, 256 N.W.2d 235, 239 (Iowa 1977).

43. People v. Moran, 1 Cal.3d 755, 83 Cal.Rptr. 411, 463 P.2d 763 (1970). The *Moran* case is no longer the standard in California. Justice Traynor's position has prevailed. People v. Barraza, 23 Cal. 3d 675, 153 Cal.Rptr. 459, 591 P.2d 947 (1979).

crime, the predisposition of the defendant is a matter of primary importance. The prevailing view seems to favor the subjective test,[44] but the objective test has substantial support.[45] One state purports to make use of both tests. Thus if the defendant had a strong predisposition for committing the offense charged, a greater degree of governmental participation will be condoned. But if the degree of governmental participation is so great that there is serious question whether a crime would have been committed without it, the extent of defendant's criminal predisposition will be given little consideration.[46] "Tennessee is the only jurisdiction in the United States that does not recognize the defense of entrapment. . . . From this day forward entrapment is a defense to a Tennessee criminal prosecution." [47]

If two are indicted for crime, it is no defense that one was induced to join in the venture by the other, because the entrapment defense does not extend to an act of inducement by private citizens who are neither public officers nor acting as agents for public officers.[48]

---

44. United States v. Glaeser, 550 F.2d 483 (9th Cir. 1977); United States v. Harper, 505 F.2d 924 (5th Cir. 1974); United States v. Martin, 533 F.2d 268 (5th Cir. 1976); United States v. Robinson, 539 F.2d 1181 (8th Cir. 1976); State v. Smith, 229 Kan. 533, 625 P.2d 1139 (1981); Crosbie v. State, 330 P.2d 602 (Okl.Cr.1958); State v. Swain, 10 Wn. App. 885, 520 P.2d 950 (1974).

"In order to defeat an entrapment defense, the Government must prove beyond a reasonable doubt that it did not initiate the crime or that the defendant was predisposed to commit it. The key inquiry is a subjective one; did the intent to commit the crime originate with the defendant or with the Government?" United States v. Bocra, 623 F.2d 281, 288 (3d Cir. 1980).

"Since the defense of entrapment focuses on an appellant's predisposition to commit the crime as charged, evidence that he previously supplied marijuana was relevant in establishing his state of mind while supplying marijuana to the undercover agent." Hill v. State, 95 Nev. 327, 594 P.2d 699, 701 (1979).

45. State v. Provard, ___ Hawaii ___, 631 P.2d 181 (1981); State v. Mullen, 216 N.W.2d 375 (Iowa 1974); People v. Barraza, 23 Cal.3d 675, 153 Cal.Rptr. 459, 591 P.2d 947 (1979); State v. Pfister, 264 N.W.2d 694 (N.D.1978); People v. Turner, 390 Mich. 7, 210 N.W.2d 336 (1973).

In reversing a conviction in a case in which the evidence of entrapment was extreme, the court pointed out that the statute had adopted the objective test of entrapment. The court said: "No matter what the defendant's past record and present inclinations to criminality, or the

depths to which he has sunk in the estimation of society, certain police conduct to ensnare him into further crime is not to be tolerated by an advanced society. . . . "In assessing police conduct under the objective standard, the test to determine an unlawful entrapment is whether a law enforcement official or agent, in order to obtain evidence of the commission of an offense, induced the defendant to commit an offense by persuasion or inducement which would be effective to persuade an average person, other than one who was merely given the opportunity to commit the offense.

"Extreme pleas of desperate illness or appeals based primarily on sympathy, pity, or close personal friendship, or offers of inordinate sums of money, are examples, depending upon an evaluation of the circumstances in each case, of what might constitute prohibited police conduct." State v. Taylor, 599 P.2d 496, 502, 503 (Utah 1979).

46. State v. Jackson, 88 N.M. 98, 537 P.2d 706 (App.1975).

47. State v. Jones, 598 S.W.2d 209, 212 (Tenn.1980).

48. State v. Farris, 218 Kan. 136, 542 P.2d 725 (1975).

On the other hand while the alleged entrapment may have been by an officer, such as the "undercover agent" in United States v. Russell, 411 U.S. 423, 93 S.Ct. 1637 (1973); it is frequently the case that it was by one who was merely cooperating with officers, such as the "police informant" in People v. Moran, 1 Cal.3d 755, 83 Cal.Rptr. 411, 463 P.2d 763 (1970).

"Manipulation of a third party by law enforcement officers to procure the com-

In any case in which the defendant is not punishable because of the inducement of a public officer, it is clear that the officer himself is guilty of the offense so far as the letter of the law is concerned, but the opinion seems to have been that it would be unwise to convict him in the ordinary case. Since the entrapment defense is grounded upon public policy rather than upon legal technicality, there is no reason why public policy may not be applied in the case of the officer as well as in that of the other. And since the claim of entrapment is frequently false it might be wise not to turn this into an additional weapon in the hands of the offender and against the officer. This, however, has reference to the normal situation. In one case game wardens, in order to get credit for a conviction, sought to induce two boys, not then so engaged, to go into the business of trapping beaver unlawfully. There was no unlawful trapping, and hence no basis for such a charge, but the conduct of the officers was so outrageous that the court did not hesitate to affirm their conviction of conspiracy to commit such an offense.[49] And it is clear from the opinion that a conviction of unlawful trapping would have been upheld if this offense had resulted from the officer's inducement.

The Model Penal Code, since it is proposed legislation, could have provided that the entrapped defendant is not guilty of the offense charged, but it does not do so. Section 2.13 gives a clear-cut answer to two of the points on which the Supreme Court was divided in *Sorrells* and *Sherman*, adopting as to each the position of the minority. "The issue of entrapment shall be tried by the Court in the absence of the jury." This answers one point directly, and the other by necessary implication. No issue determinative of guilt or innocence can be taken from the jury in a criminal trial; hence leaving this to the court means that the Code recognizes what we have called the estoppel theory of entrapment. The defendant is guilty but the government is estopped from procuring a conviction because of the misconduct of its officers.[50] This is the sound theory. It may be added that the Code would require the defendant to prove entrapment by a preponderance of the evidence.

The position of the Code on the third point also adopts the position of the minority of the Court. It would have entrapment depend entirely upon the activity of the police and their helpers, and not on the predisposition of the defendant. The wording is "employing methods of persuasion or inducement which create a substantial risk that such an offense will be committed by persons other than those who are ready to commit it."[51] This is the objective test of entrapment.

mission of a criminal offense by another renders the third party a government agent for purposes of the entrapment defense, even though the third party remains unaware of the law enforcement objective." People v. McIntire, 23 Cal.3d 742, 153 Cal.Rptr. 237, 240, 591 P.2d 527 (1979).

49. Reigan v. People, 120 Colo. 472, 210 P.2d 991 (1949).

50. "The applicable principle is that the courts must be closed to the trial of a crime instigated by the government's own agents." Per Roberts, J., concurring in Sorrells v. United States, 287 U.S. 435, 459, 53 S.Ct. 210, 219 (1932).

51. This is subsection 2.13(1)(b). The wording in the first draft of this section, then number 2.10, was in terms of "solicits, encourages or otherwise induces another person to engage in conduct constituting such an offense when he is not then otherwise disposed to do so." This, which would have incorporated the subjective test of entrapment, was rejected in the final draft.

The Code also provides that an officer "perpetrates an entrapment if for the purpose of obtaining evidence of the commission of an offense he induces or encourages another person to engage in conduct which constitutes such an offense by . . . making knowingly false representations designed to induce the belief that such conduct is not prohibited; . . ."

That an offense was committed under such official misguidance should be a defense at common law, whether it was knowingly or unknowingly made by the officer, under the "authorized reliance" exception to the rule that mistake of law is no defense.[52] If this is to be included in an entrapment statute it should be so worded as to provide a defense where the prohibited conduct was the result of reliance upon the advice of the government's own agent, even if the erroneous statement was the result of the agent's own misunderstanding of the law.

THE NEW PENAL CODES

Some of the new codes leave the law of entrapment as it has been developed by cases, either by having no statute on the subject or one in too general terms to do otherwise. Some have language sufficiently like that of the Model Penal Code to indicate insistence upon the objective theory of entrapment.[53] Others have clearly adopted the subjective theory.[54] A few are so worded that an entrapped defendant has committed no crime.[55]

CONCLUSION

The first point of the threefold diversity, resulting from differences of opinion in the Supreme Court, is seldom even mentioned in the cases any more. No doubt it will eventually be forgotten, and estoppel of the prosecution from obtaining a conviction because of the impermissible conduct of its officers or their agents will be taken for granted as the reason for the result in such cases.

With reference to the second point, when the evidence in a case raises the issue of entrapment, this is usually left to the jury, more frequently on the assumption that this is the proper procedure than with an explanation to this effect. An occasional case, however, holds that this issue is for the determination of the court.

It is the third point that has presented a real battle ground. At one time the subjective theory seemed to be clearly the prevailing view, but the objective theory has been gaining ground. The ultimate solution may be something like this: The test of entrapment is subjective—one was not entrapped to do what he was predisposed to do—with the qualification that if the methods employed by officers or their agents were so extreme as to constitute a deprivation of due process, the prosecution is estopped from convicting on

52. The government should be estopped where its own official has told the defendant that it would not be unlawful to do what was innocently done in reliance on this advice. See People v. Ferguson, 134 Cal.App. 41, 24 P.2d 965 (1933).

53. E.g., Alabama, Arkansas, Colorado, Hawaii, New Hampshire, New York, North Dakota and Pennsylvania.

54. E.g., Connecticut, Delaware, Georgia, Indiana, Kentucky and Washington.

55. E.g., Alabama, Colorado, Illinois, Kansas, Montana and Oregon. It should be noted that while there was no proper basis for such a position at common law, it is clearly within the legislative power. Even so the "estoppel theory" seems preferable.

this ground without reference to predisposition; plus the interpretation that law-enforcement methods are thus extreme if clearly calculated to induce one, not so predisposed, to yield to temptation and commit a prohibited act.

*

TABLE OF CASES

References are to Pages

A

E

INDEX

†